THE GREAT GEOGRAPHICAL ATLAS

THE GREAT GEOGRAPHICAL ATLAS

RAND McNALLY

CHICAGO • NEW YORK • SAN FRANCISCO

CONTENTS

Our Planet Earth Section

Part 1

THE EARTH AND THE UNIVERSE

Part 2

MAKING AND SHAPING THE EARTH

Part 3

THE EMERGENCE OF LIFE

Part 4

THE DIVERSITY OF LIFE

Part 5

UNDERSTANDING MAPS

THE GREAT GEOGRAPHICAL ATLAS

Copyright © 1991
Rand McNally & Company

Pages 1 through 240 and A·16 through A·144
Copyright © 1982
Istituto Geografico De Agostini
Revised, 1991

Pages 241 through 304
Copyright © 1983
Rand McNally & Company
Revised, 1991

All rights reserved.

No part of this work may be reproduced or utilized in any form by any means, electronic or mechanical, including photocopying, recording or by any information storage or retrieval system, without the prior written permission of the publisher.

ISBN: 528-83384-7

Library of Congress
Catalog Card Number: 89-40418

Printed in the United States of America by
Rand McNally & Company

Jacket photo by David Muench
Title page photo by Ric Ergenbright

International Map Section

PAGE		MAP NUMBER
114–115	Legend	
116–117	Index maps	
118–125	World Maps	1–4
126–155	Europe	5–20
156–173	Asia	21–29
174–189	Africa	30–37
190–213	North America	38–51
214–223	South America	52–56
224–237	Australia and Oceania	57–65
238–240	Antarctic and Arctic	66–67

Maps of the United States and Canada

PAGE	
241	Legend
242–243	United States
244	Alabama
245	Alaska
246	Arizona
247	Arkansas
248	California
249	Colorado
250	Connecticut
251	Delaware
252	Florida
253	Georgia
254	Hawaii
255	Idaho
256	Illinois
257	Indiana
258	Iowa
259	Kansas
260	Kentucky
261	Louisiana
262	Maine
263	Maryland
264	Massachusetts
265	Michigan
266	Minnesota
267	Mississippi
268	Missouri
269	Montana
270	Nebraska
271	Nevada
272	New Hampshire
273	New Jersey
274	New Mexico
275	New York
276	North Carolina
277	North Dakota
278	Ohio
279	Oklahoma
280	Oregon
281	Pennsylvania
282	Rhode Island
283	South Carolina
284	South Dakota
285	Tennessee
286	Texas
287	Utah
288	Vermont
289	Virginia
290	Washington
291	West Virginia
292	Wisconsin
293	Wyoming
294–295	Canada
296	Alberta
297	British Columbia
298	Manitoba
299	Maritime Provinces
300	Newfoundland
301	Ontario
302	Quebec
303	Saskatchewan
304	United States and Canada Information Table

Geographical Information & International Map Index

A·1–A·24	Geographical Information
A·25–A·144	International Map Index

Maps

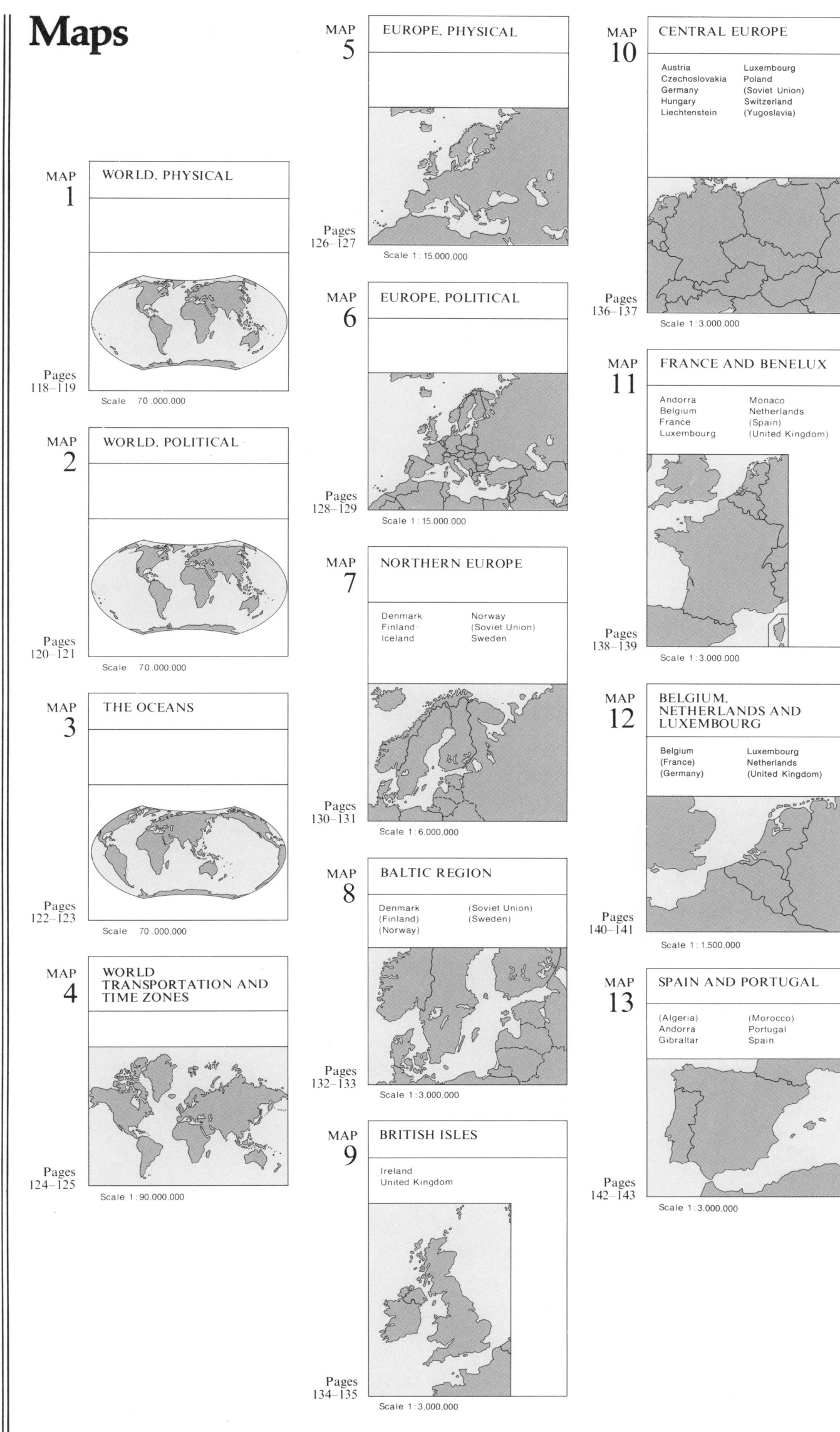

MAP 1 — WORLD, PHYSICAL

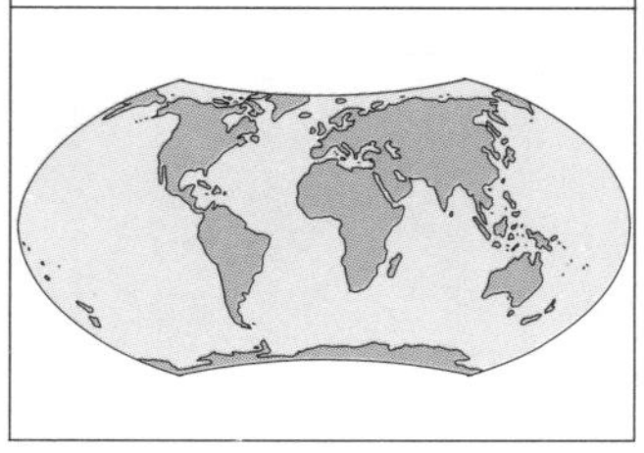

Pages 118–119

Scale 70.000.000

MAP 2 — WORLD, POLITICAL

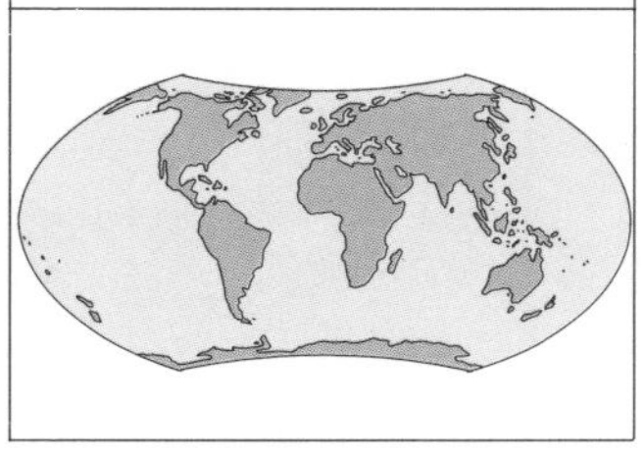

Pages 120–121

Scale 70.000.000

MAP 3 — THE OCEANS

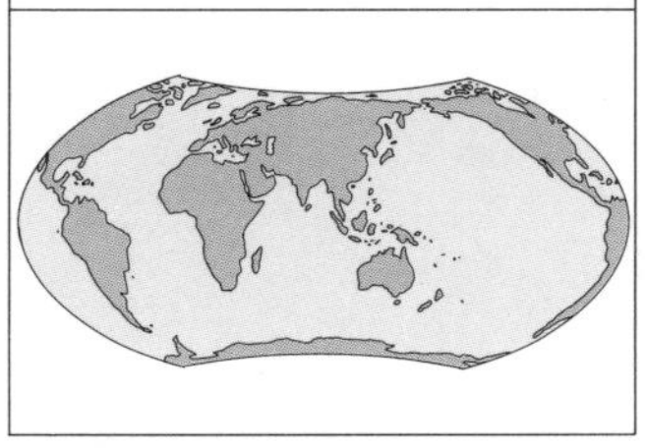

Pages 122–123

Scale 70.000.000

MAP 4 — WORLD TRANSPORTATION AND TIME ZONES

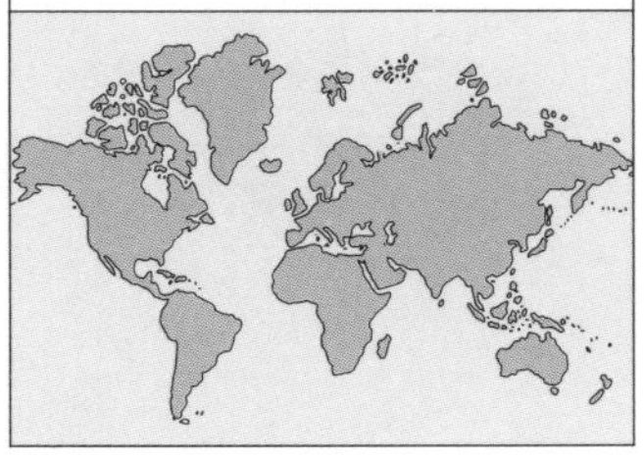

Pages 124–125

Scale 1:90.000.000

MAP 5 — EUROPE, PHYSICAL

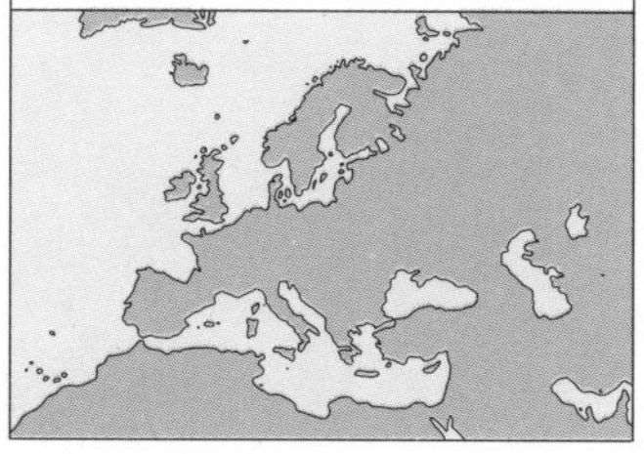

Pages 126–127

Scale 1:15.000.000

MAP 6 — EUROPE, POLITICAL

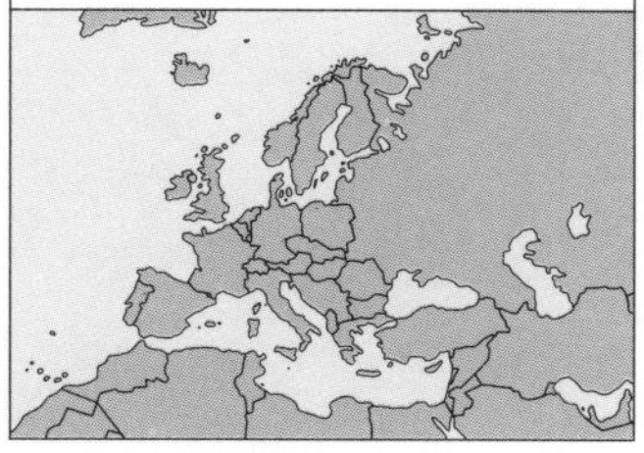

Pages 128–129

Scale 1:15.000.000

MAP 7 — NORTHERN EUROPE

Denmark, Finland, Iceland, Norway, (Soviet Union), Sweden

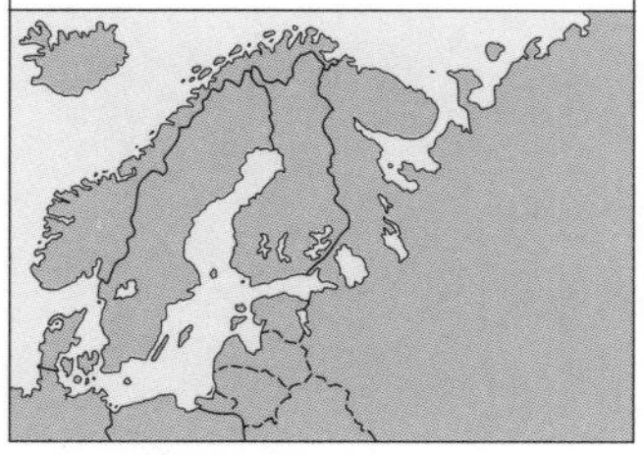

Pages 130–131

Scale 1:6.000.000

MAP 8 — BALTIC REGION

Denmark, (Finland), (Norway), (Soviet Union), (Sweden)

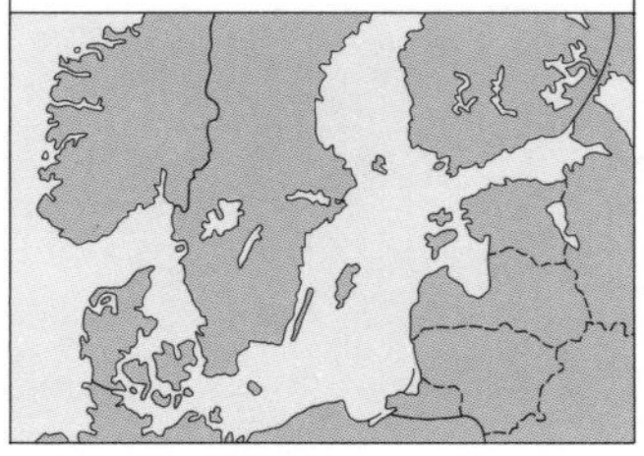

Pages 132–133

Scale 1:3.000.000

MAP 9 — BRITISH ISLES

Ireland, United Kingdom

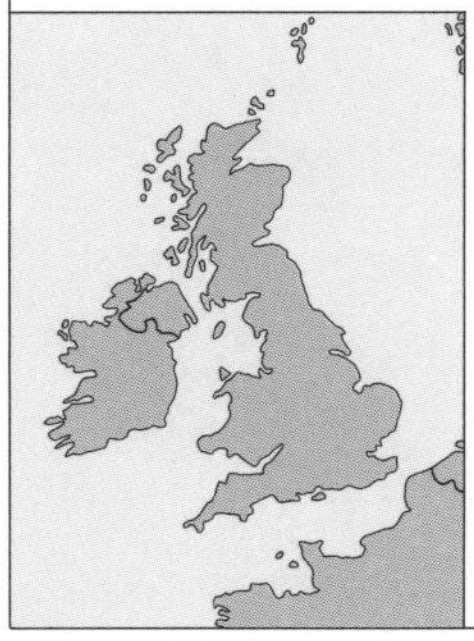

Pages 134–135

Scale 1:3.000.000

MAP 10 — CENTRAL EUROPE

Austria, Czechoslovakia, Germany, Hungary, Liechtenstein, Luxembourg, Poland, (Soviet Union), Switzerland, (Yugoslavia)

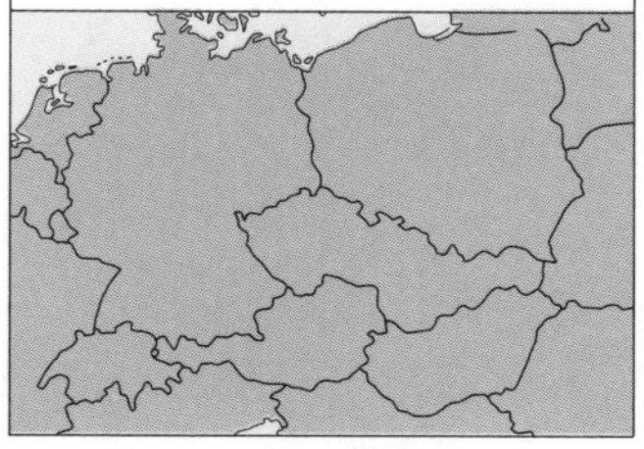

Pages 136–137

Scale 1:3.000.000

MAP 11 — FRANCE AND BENELUX

Andorra, Belgium, France, Luxembourg, Monaco, Netherlands, (Spain), (United Kingdom)

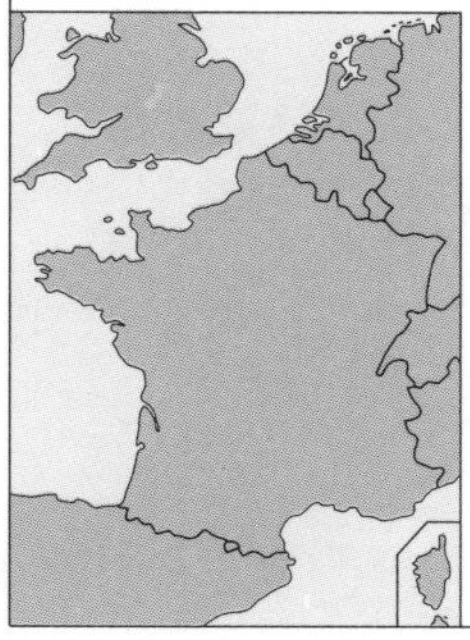

Pages 138–139

Scale 1:3.000.000

MAP 12 — BELGIUM, NETHERLANDS AND LUXEMBOURG

Belgium, (France), (Germany), Luxembourg, Netherlands, (United Kingdom)

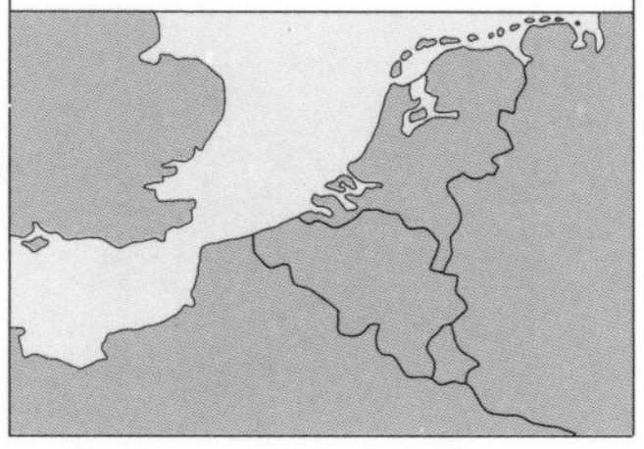

Pages 140–141

Scale 1:1.500.000

MAP 13 — SPAIN AND PORTUGAL

(Algeria), Andorra, Gibraltar, (Morocco), Portugal, Spain

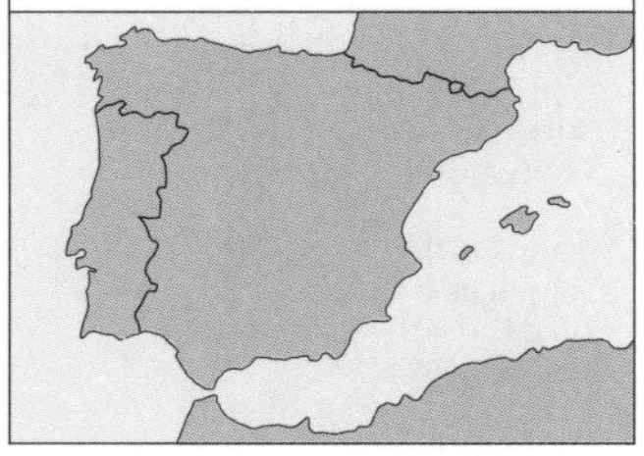

Pages 142–143

Scale 1:3.000.000

MAP 14
ITALY, AUSTRIA AND SWITZERLAND

(Algeria), Austria, Italy, Liechtenstein, Malta, Monaco, San Marino, Switzerland, (Tunisia), Vatican City, Yugoslavia

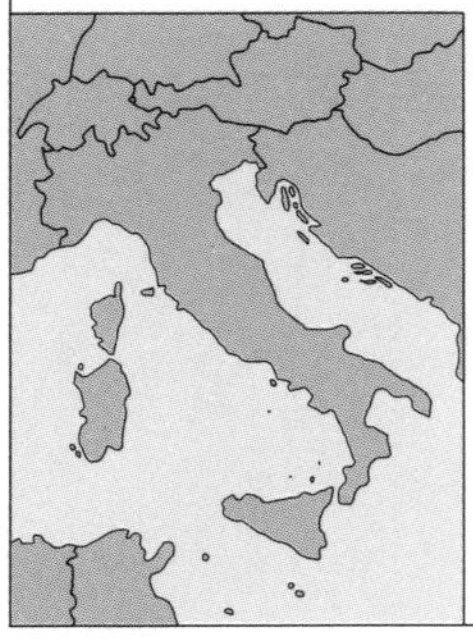

Pages 144–145
Scale 1 : 3.000.000

MAP 15
SOUTHEASTERN EUROPE

Albania, Bulgaria, Greece, (Hungary), Romania, (Soviet Union), Turkey, (Yugoslavia)

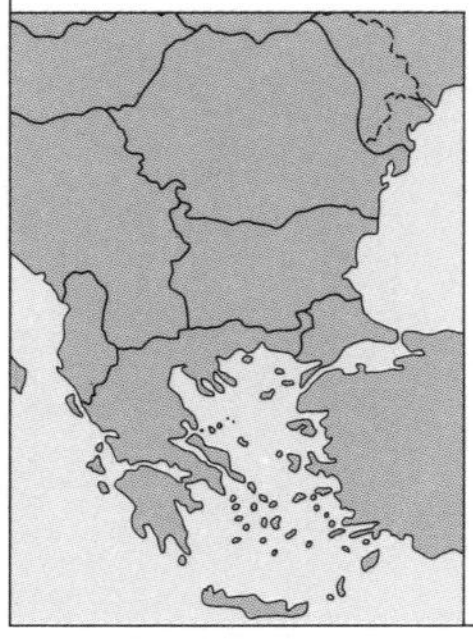

Pages 146–147
Scale 1 : 3.000.000

MAP 16
SOUTHWESTERN SOVIET UNION

(Soviet Union), (Turkey)

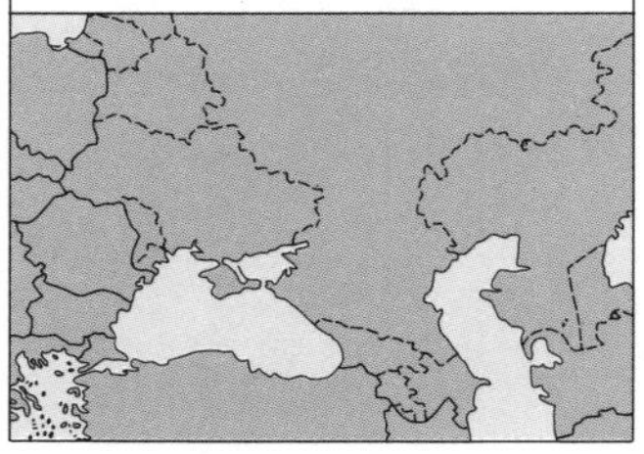

Pages 148–149
Scale 1 : 6.000.000

MAP 17
THE URALS

(Soviet Union)

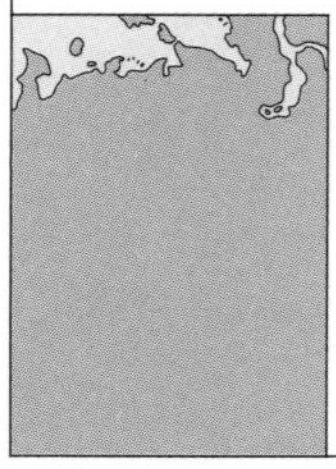

Page 150
Scale 1 : 6.000.000

MAP 18
SOUTH-CENTRAL SOVIET UNION

(Afghanistan), (China), (India), (Iran), (Pakistan), (Soviet Union)

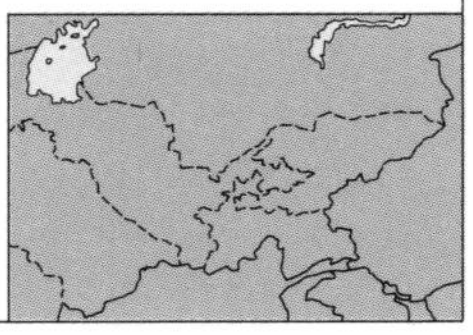

Page 151
Scale 1 : 6.000.000

MAP 19
WESTERN SOVIET UNION

(China), Finland, (Mongolia), Norway, (Soviet Union), Sweden, Turkey

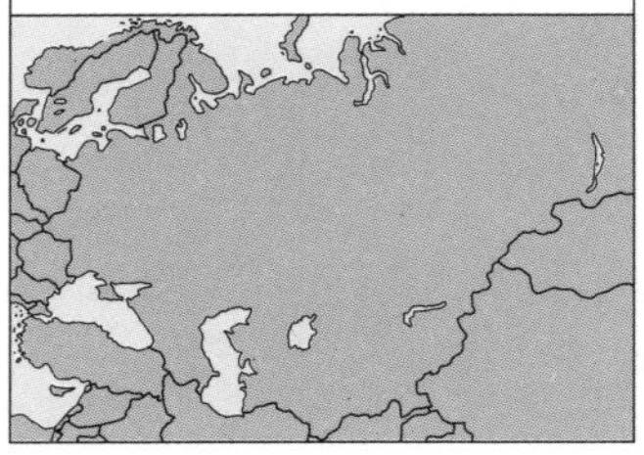

Pages 152–153
Scale 1 : 12.000.000

MAP 20
EASTERN SOVIET UNION

(China), Mongolia, (Soviet Union)

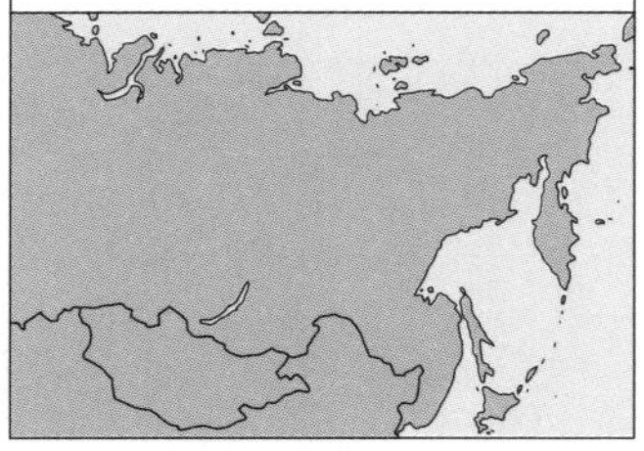

Pages 154–155
Scale 1 : 12.000.000

MAP 21
ASIA, PHYSICAL

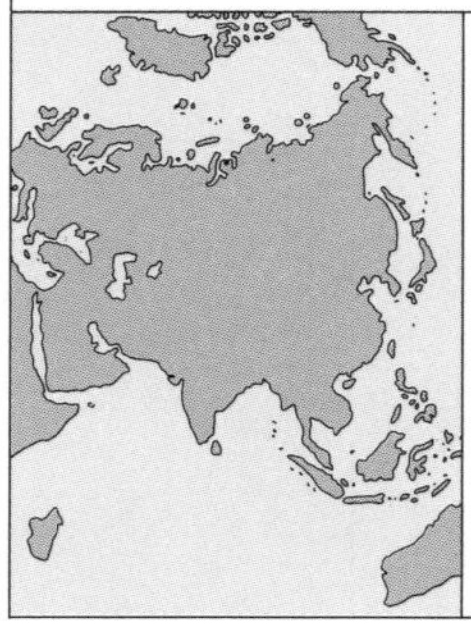

Pages 156–157
Scale 1 : 30.000.000

MAP 22
ASIA, POLITICAL

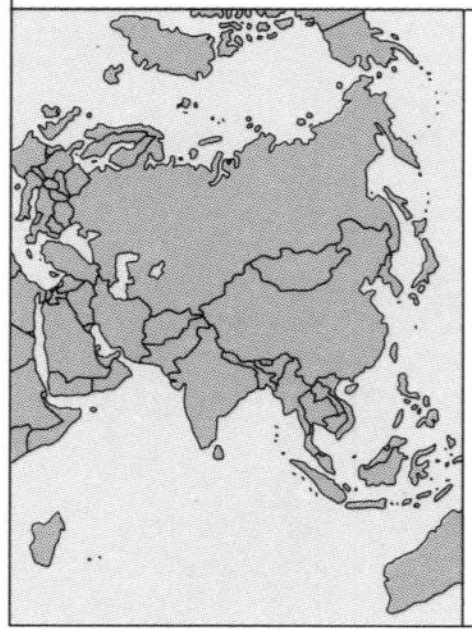

Pages 158–159
Scale 1 : 30.000.000

MAP 23
SOUTHWESTERN ASIA

Afghanistan, Bahrain, Cyprus, Djibouti, Egypt, Greece, (India), Iran, Iraq, Israel, Jordan, Kuwait, Lebanon, Oman, Pakistan, Qatar, Saudi Arabia, (Soviet Union), (Sudan), Syria, Turkey, United Arab Emirates, Yemen

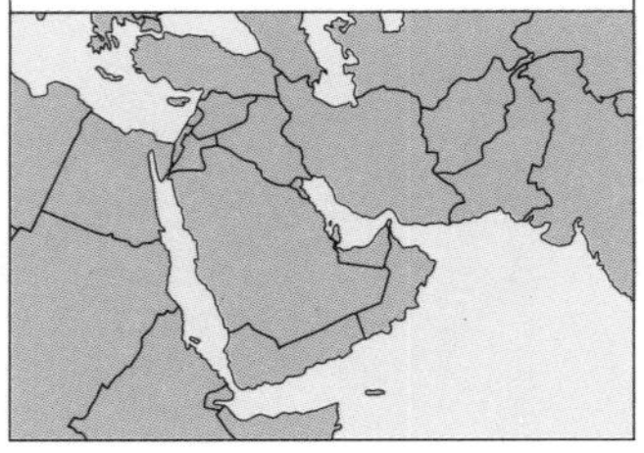

Pages 160–161
Scale 1 : 12.000.000

MAP 24
MIDDLE EAST

Bahrain, Cyprus, (Egypt), (Iran), Iraq, Israel, Jordan, Kuwait, Lebanon, (Oman), Qatar, (Saudi Arabia), (Soviet Union), Syria, Turkey, (United Arab Emirates)

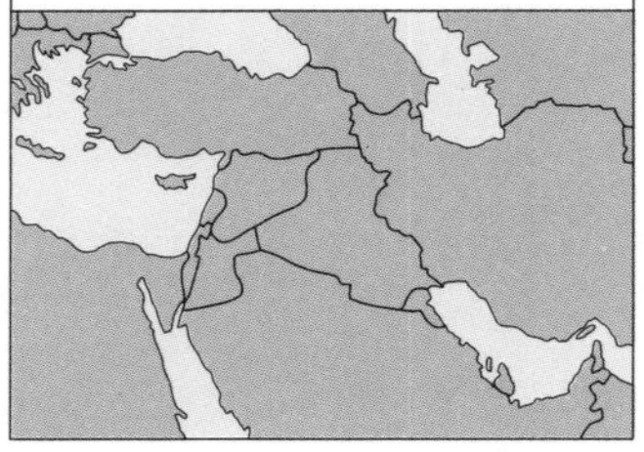

Pages 162–163
Scale 1 : 6.000.000

MAP 25
SOUTH-CENTRAL ASIA

Afghanistan, Bangladesh, Bhutan, Burma, Cambodia, (China), India, Laos, Maldives, Nepal, Pakistan, Sri Lanka, Thailand, Vietnam

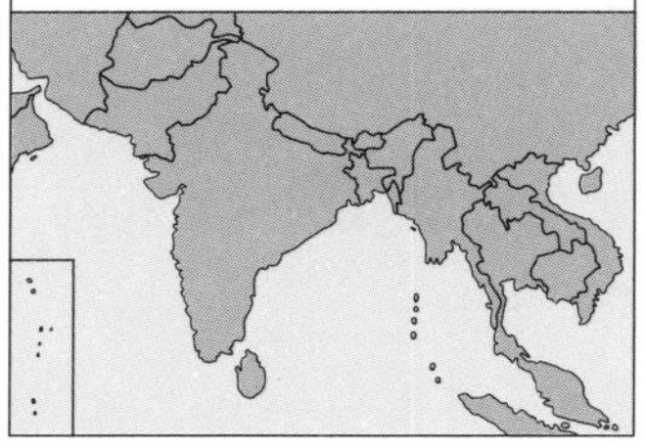

Pages 164–165
Scale 1 : 12.000.000

MAP 26
SOUTHEAST ASIA

Brunei, (Burma), Cambodia, Hong Kong, Indonesia, Laos, Macau, Malaysia, (Papua New Guinea), Philippines, Taiwan, Thailand, (Trust Territory of the Pacific Islands), Vietnam

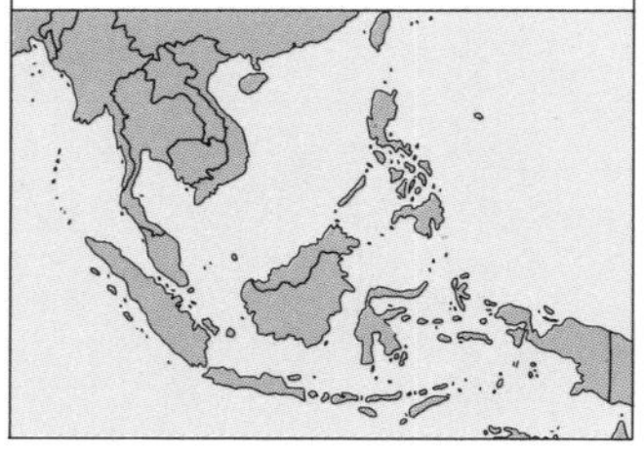

Pages 166–167
Scale 1 : 12.000.000

MAP 27
CHINA AND MONGOLIA

Bangladesh, Bhutan, (Burma), China, Hong Kong, (India), Japan, Korea, North, Korea, South, Macau, Mongolia, Nepal, (Soviet Union), Taiwan

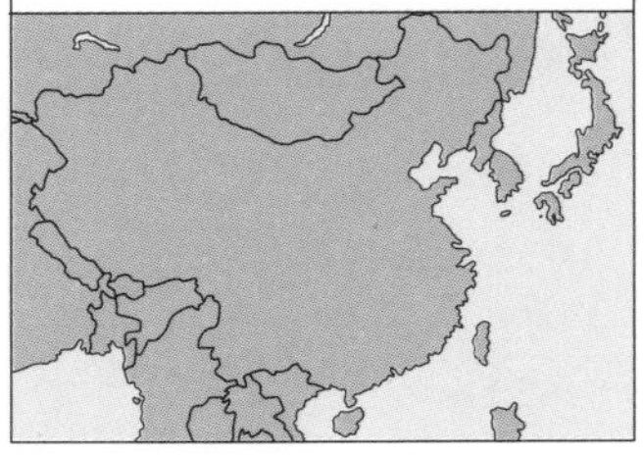

Pages 168–169
Scale 1 : 12.000.000

MAP 28
NORTHEASTERN CHINA, KOREA AND JAPAN

(China), Japan, Korea, North, Korea, South, (Mongolia), (Soviet Union)

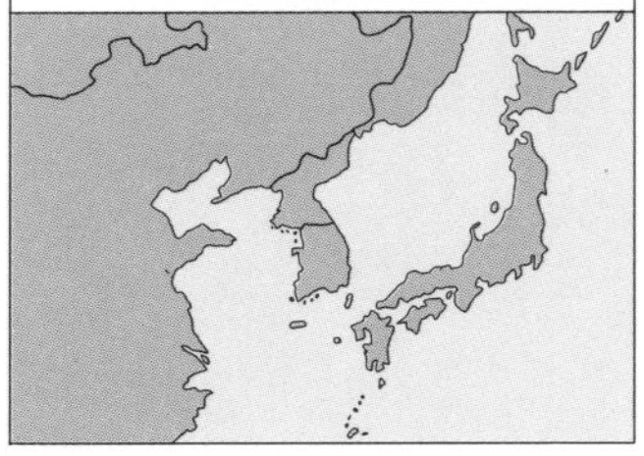

Pages 170–171
Scale 1 : 6.000.000

MAP 29
JAPAN

Japan, (Korea, South), (Soviet Union)

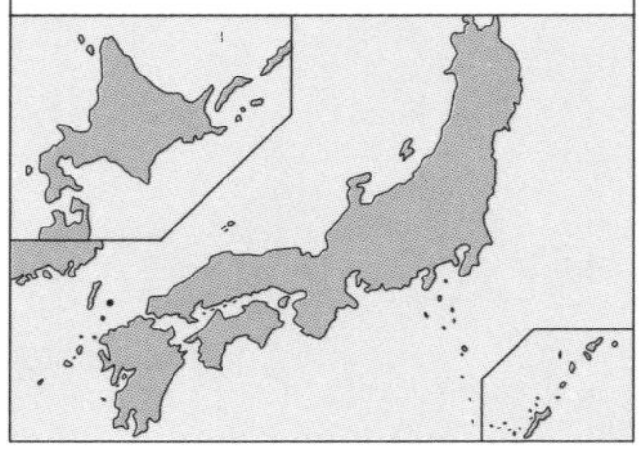

Pages 172–173
Scale 1 : 3,000,000

MAP 30
AFRICA, PHYSICAL

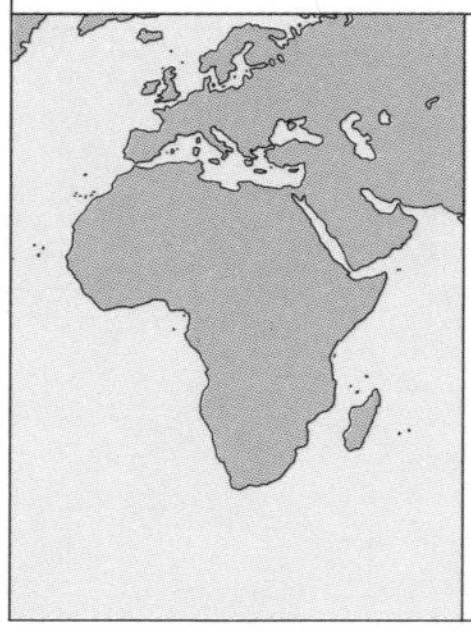

Pages 174–175
Scale 1 : 30,000,000

MAP 31
AFRICA, POLITICAL

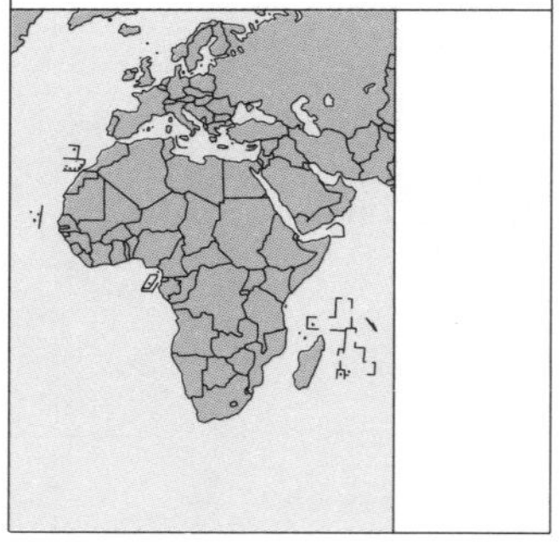

Pages 176–177
Scale 1 : 30,000,000

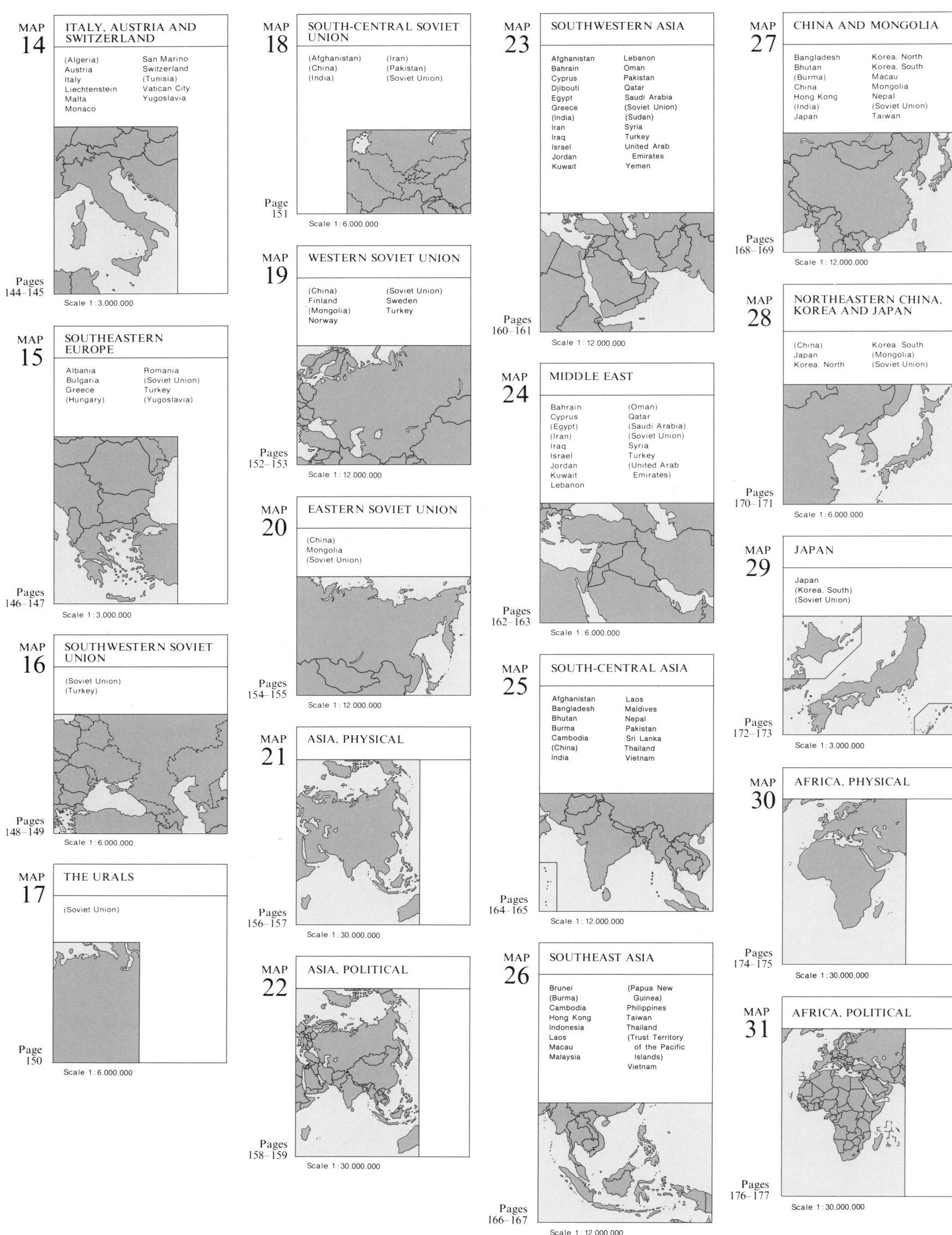

MAP 32
NORTHWESTERN AFRICA

Algeria
Canary Islands
Cape Verde
(Libya)
(Mali)
Morocco
(Niger)
Tunisia
Western Sahara

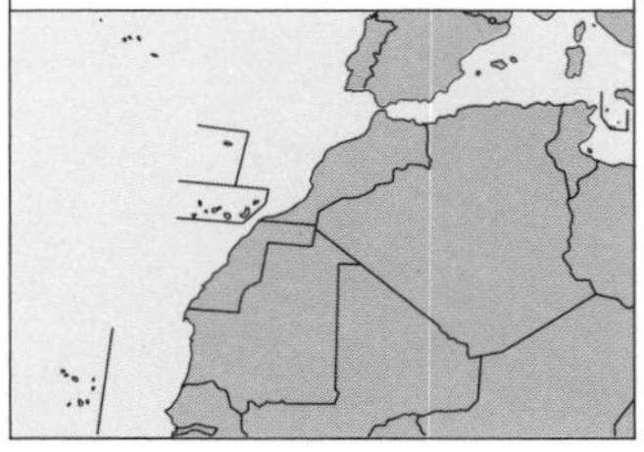

Pages 178–179

Scale 1:9,000,000

MAP 33
NORTHEASTERN AFRICA

(Algeria)
(Chad)
Egypt
Libya
(Niger)
(Sudan)
Tunisia

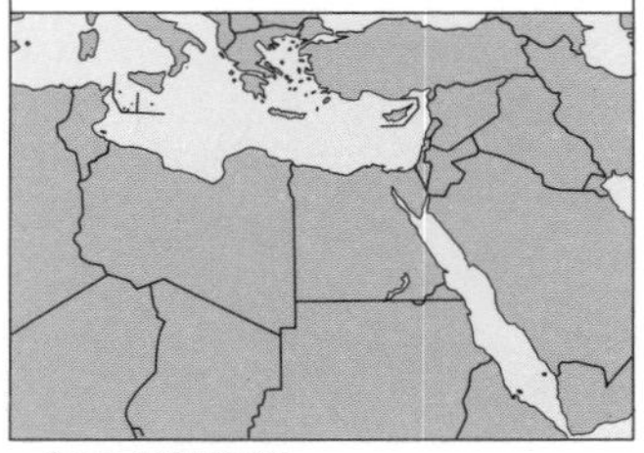

Pages 180–181

Scale 1:9,000,000

MAP 34
WEST-CENTRAL AFRICA

(Algeria)
Benin
Burkina Faso
Cameroon
(Central African Republic)
(Chad)
(Congo)
Equatorial Guinea
(Gabon)
Gambia
Ghana
Guinea
Ivory Coast
Liberia
Mali
(Mauritania)
Niger
Nigeria
Senegal
Sierra Leone
Togo
(Western Sahara)

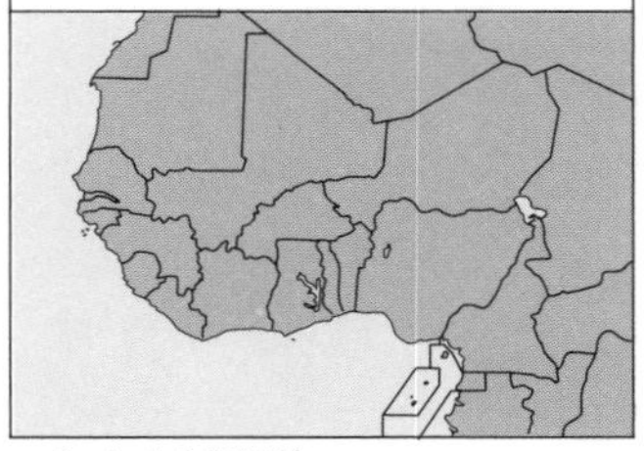

Pages 182–183

Scale 1:9,000,000

MAP 35
EAST-CENTRAL AFRICA

(Cameroon)
Central African Republic
Chad
(Congo)
Djibouti
(Egypt)
Ethiopia
(Kenya)
(Libya)
(Niger)
(Rwanda)
Somalia
Sudan
Uganda
(Zaire)

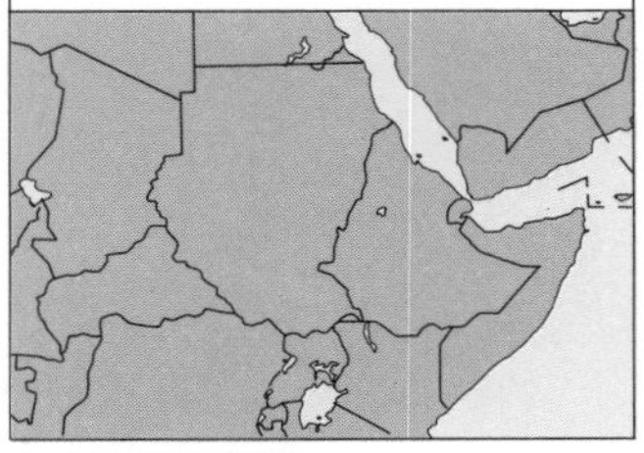

Pages 184–185

Scale 1:9,000,000

MAP 36
EQUATORIAL AFRICA

Angola
Burundi
(Cameroon)
(Central African Republic)
Congo
Equatorial Guinea
Gabon
Kenya
Malawi
(Mozambique)
Rwanda
(Somalia)
Tanzania
Uganda
Zaire
Zambia
(Zimbabwe)

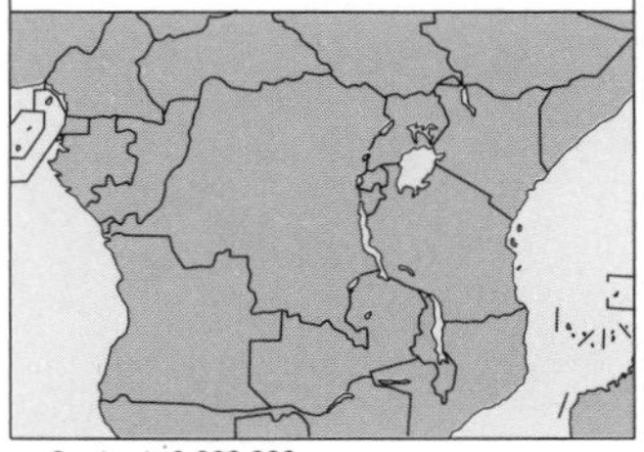

Pages 186–187

Scale 1:9,000,000

MAP 37
SOUTHERN AFRICA

(Angola)
Botswana
Comoros
Lesotho
Madagascar
(Malawi)
Mauritius
Mayotte
Mozambique
Namibia
Seychelles
South Africa
Swaziland
(Zambia)
Zimbabwe

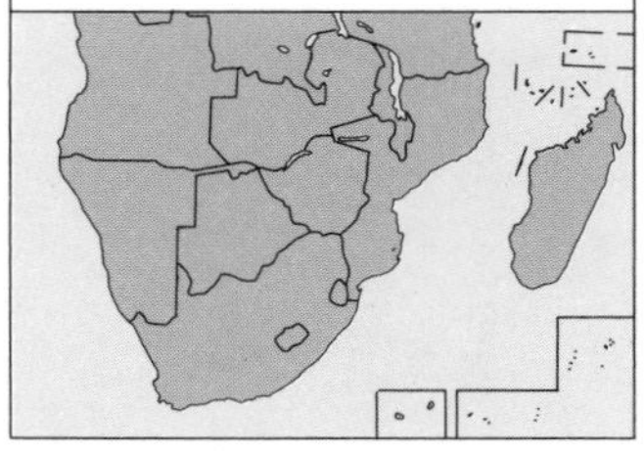

Pages 188–189

Scale 1:9,000,000

MAP 38
NORTH AMERICA, PHYSICAL

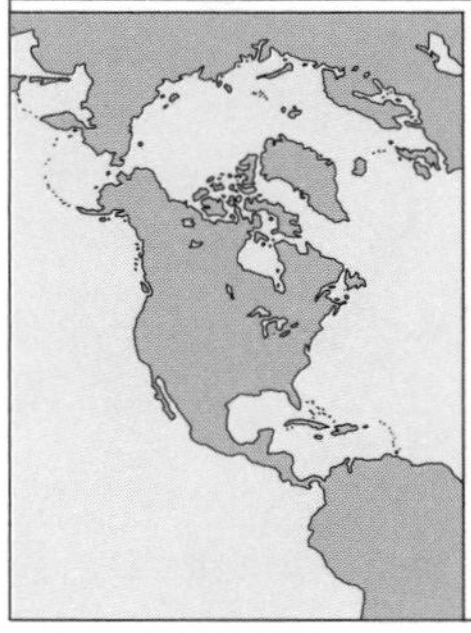

Pages 190–191

Scale 1:30,000,000

MAP 39
NORTH AMERICA, POLITICAL

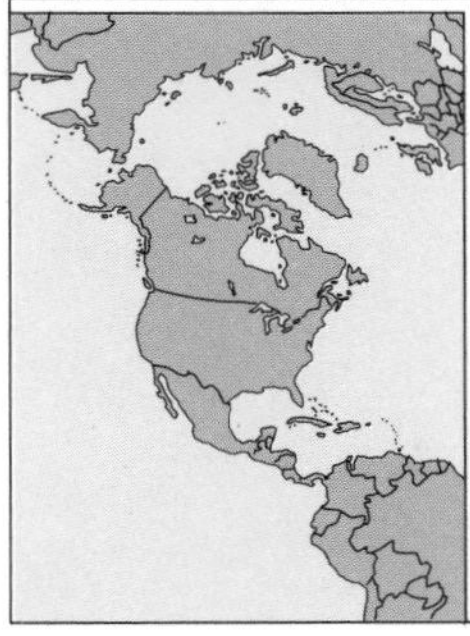

Pages 192–193

Scale 1:30,000,000

MAP 40
ALASKA

(Canada)
(Soviet Union)
(United States)

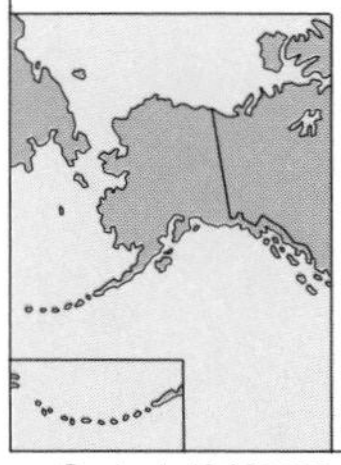

Page 194

Scale 1:12,000,000

MAP 41
GREENLAND

(Canada)
Greenland
Iceland
Svalbard

Page 195

Scale 1:12,000,000

MAP 42
CANADA

(Canada)
Saint Pierre and Miquelon
(United States)

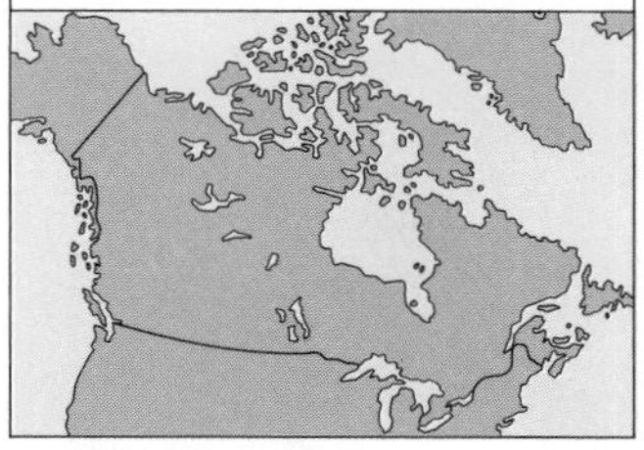

Pages 196–197

Scale 1:12,000,000

MAP 43
UNITED STATES

Bahamas
Bermuda
(Canada)
Cuba
Dominican Republic
Haiti
Jamaica
(Mexico)
(United States)

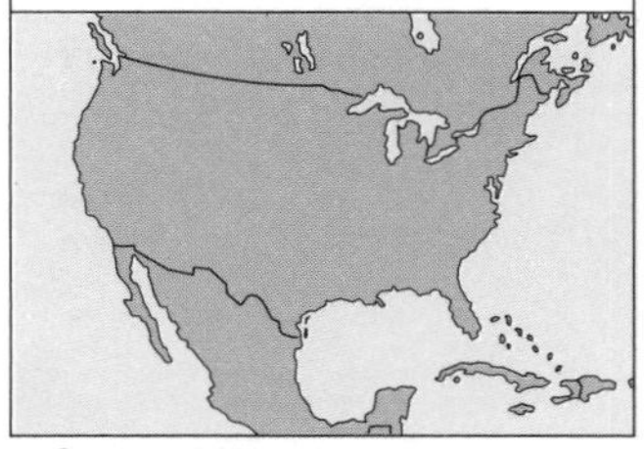

Pages 198–199

Scale 1:12,000,000

MAP 44
EASTERN UNITED STATES

(Bahamas)
(Canada)
(United States)

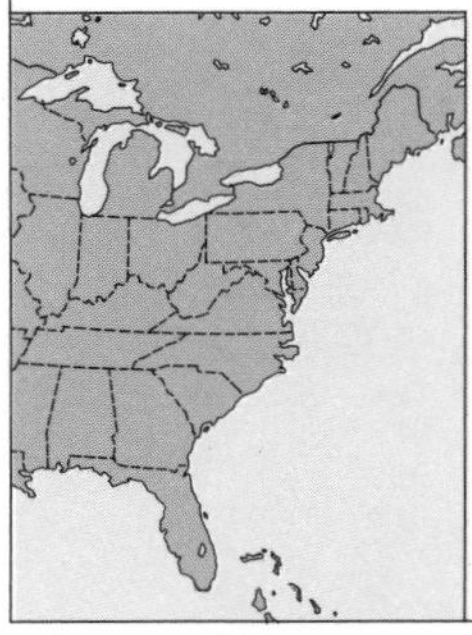

Pages 200–201

Scale 1:6,000,000

MAP 45
CENTRAL UNITED STATES

(Canada)
(Mexico)
(United States)

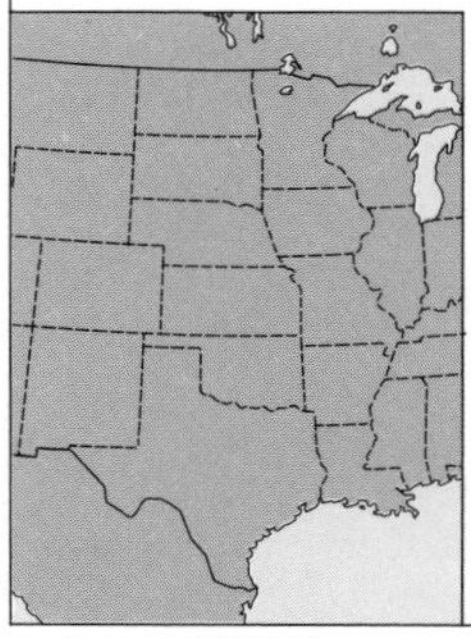

Pages 202–203

Scale 1:6,000,000

MAP 46
WESTERN UNITED STATES

(Canada)
(Mexico)
(United States)

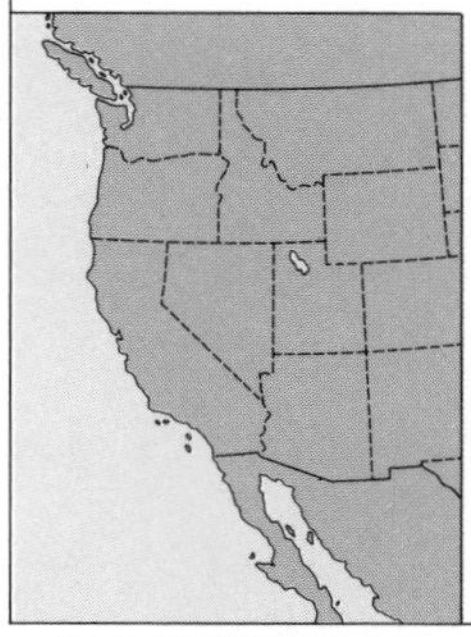

Pages 204–205

Scale 1:6,000,000

MAP 47
MIDDLE AMERICA

Bahamas
Belize
Bermuda
(Colombia)
Costa Rica
Cuba
Dominican Republic
El Salvador
Guatemala
Haiti
Honduras
Jamaica
Mexico
Nicaragua
Panama
Puerto Rico
Trinidad and Tobago
(United States)
(Venezuela)

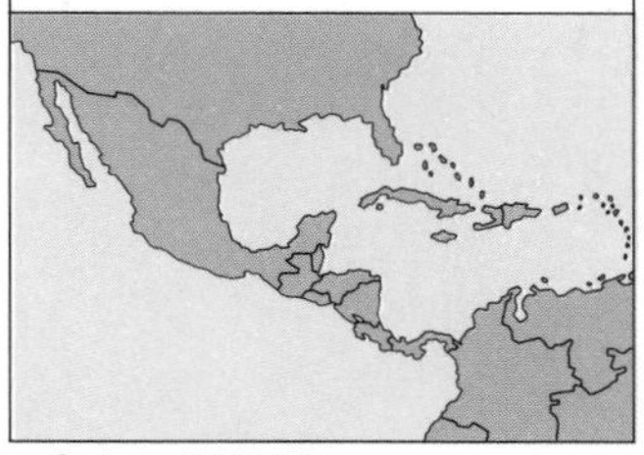

Pages 206–207

Scale 1:12,000,000

MAP 48
MEXICO

Belize
Guatemala
Mexico
(United States)

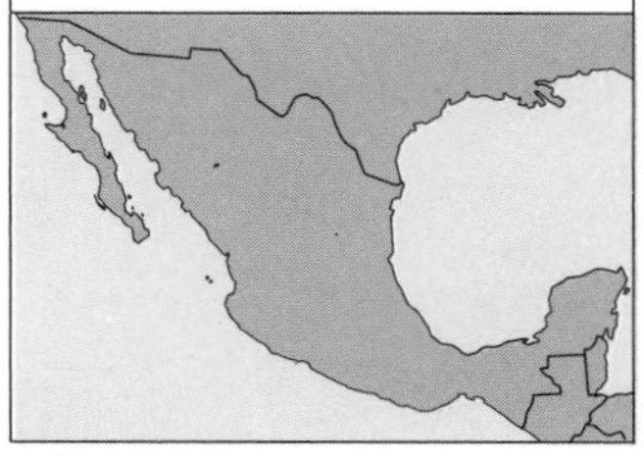

Pages 208–209

Scale 1:6,000,000

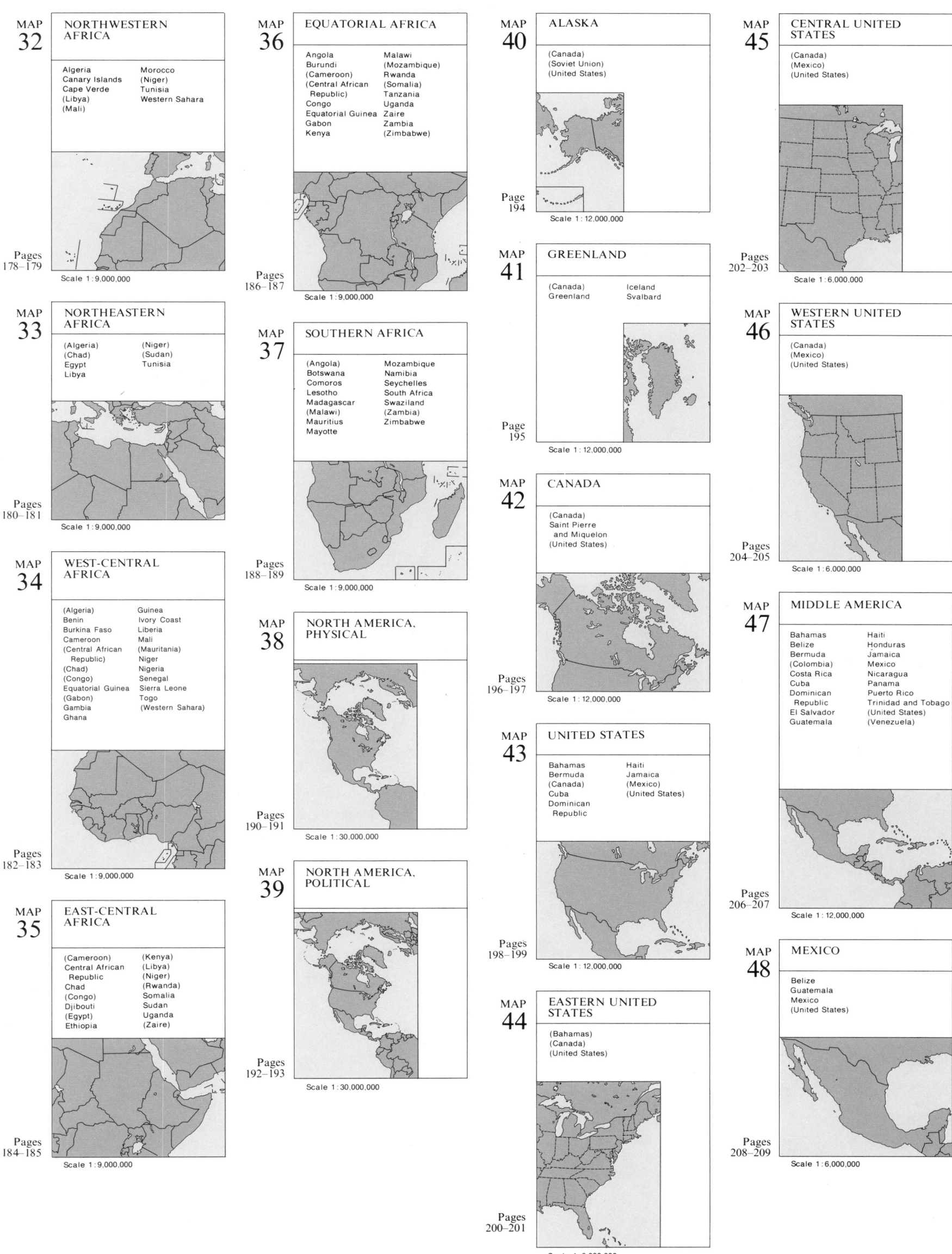

MAP 49

CENTRAL AMERICA AND WESTERN CARIBBEAN

(Bahamas), Belize, Cayman Islands, (Colombia), Costa Rica, Cuba, Dominican Republic, El Salvador, Guatemala, Haiti, Honduras, Jamaica, Nicaragua, Panama, Puerto Rico, Turks and Caicos Islands, (Venezuela)

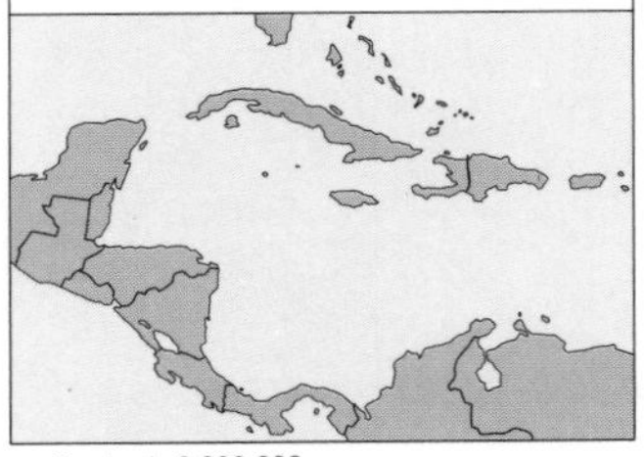

Pages 210–211

Scale 1 : 6,000,000

MAP 50

EASTERN CARIBBEAN

Anguilla, Antigua, Barbados, (Colombia), Dominica, Dominican Republic, Grenada, Guadeloupe, (Guyana), Martinique, Montserrat, Netherlands Antilles, Puerto Rico, Saint Kitts-Nevis, Saint Lucia, Saint Vincent, Trinidad and Tobago, (Venezuela), Virgin Islands

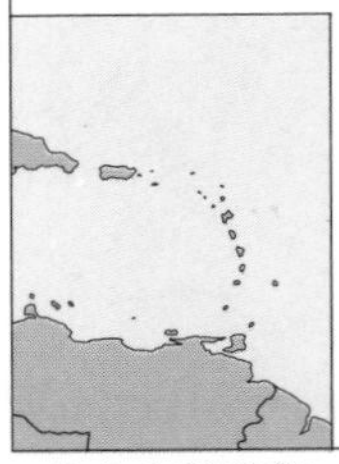

Page 212

Scale 1 : 6,000,000

MAP 51

CARIBBEAN ISLANDS

Anguilla, Antigua, Barbados, Dominica, Grenada, Guadeloupe, Martinique, Montserrat, (Netherlands Antilles), Puerto Rico, Saint Kitts-Nevis, Saint Lucia, Saint Vincent, Virgin Islands, British, Virgin Islands of the United States

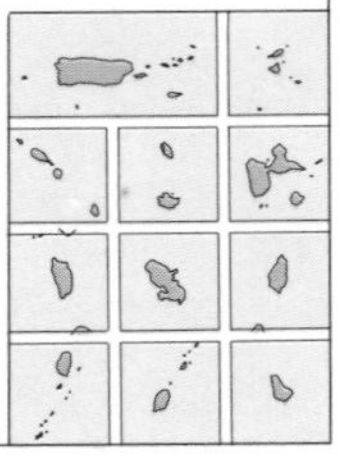

Page 213

Various scales

MAP 52

SOUTH AMERICA, PHYSICAL

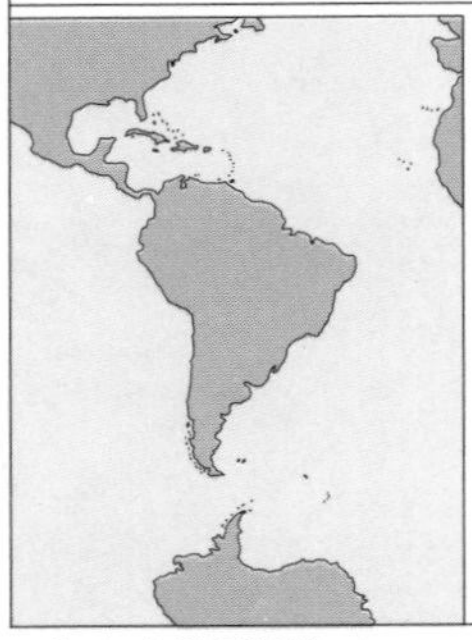

Pages 214–215

Scale 1 : 30,000,000

MAP 53

SOUTH AMERICA, POLITICAL

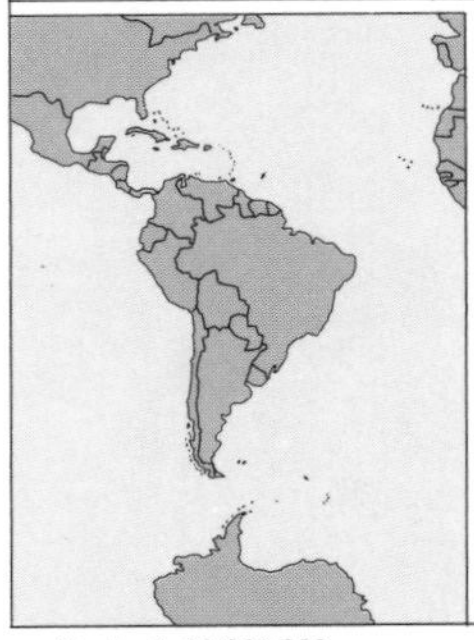

Pages 216–217

Scale 1 : 30,000,000

MAP 54

NORTHERN SOUTH AMERICA

Bolivia, (Brazil), Colombia, Costa Rica, Ecuador, French Guiana, Guyana, Panama, Peru, Suriname, Venezuela

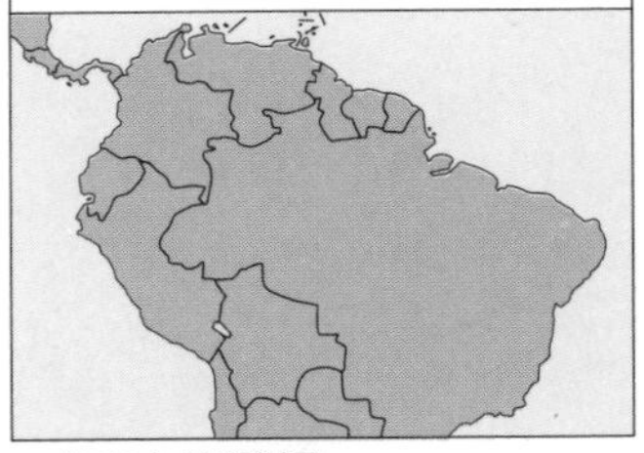

Pages 218–219

Scale 1 : 12,000,000

MAP 55

EAST-CENTRAL SOUTH AMERICA,

(Argentina), (Bolivia), (Brazil), Paraguay, Uruguay

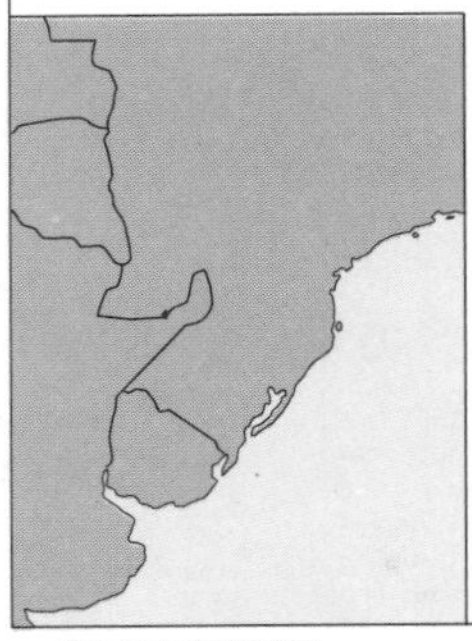

Pages 220–221

Scale 1 : 6,000,000

MAP 56

SOUTHERN SOUTH AMERICA

Argentina, (Bolivia), (Brazil), Chile, Falkland Islands, Paraguay, Uruguay

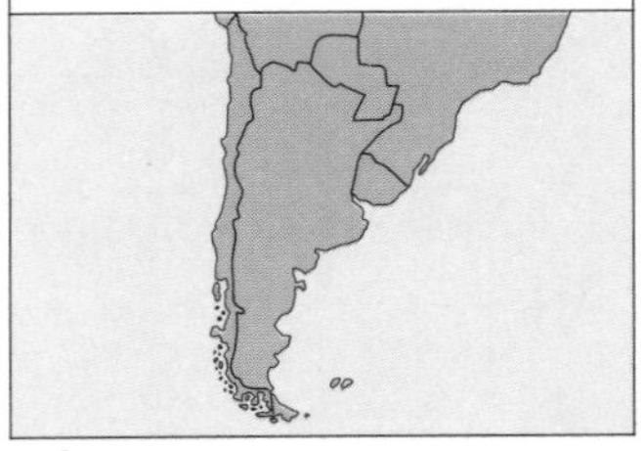

Pages 222–223

Scale 1 : 12,000,000

MAP 57

AUSTRALIA AND OCEANIA, PHYSICAL

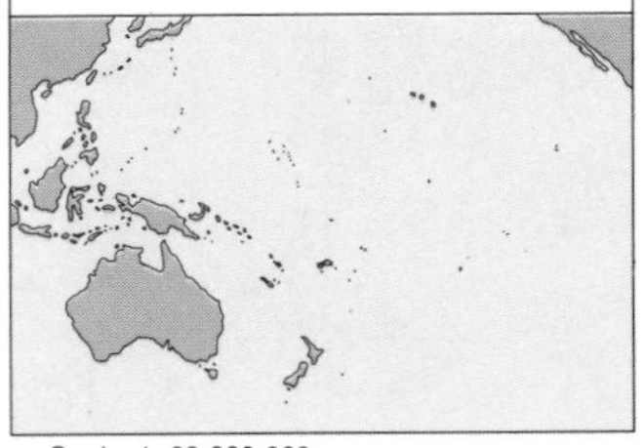

Pages 224–225

Scale 1 : 30,000,000

MAP 58

AUSTRALIA AND OCEANIA, POLITICAL

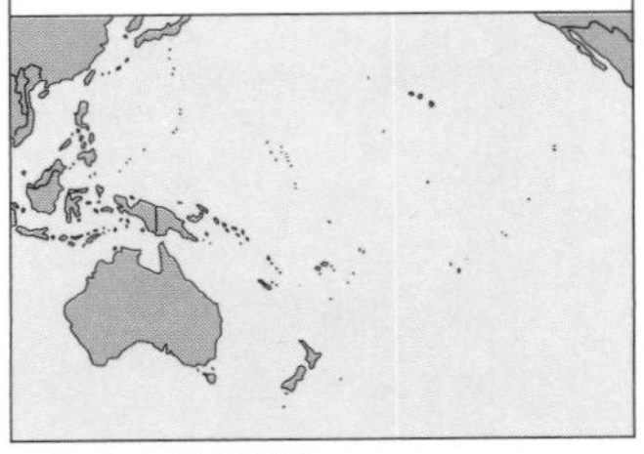

Pages 226–227

Scale 1 : 30,000,000

MAP 59

AUSTRALIA

Australia, Coral Sea Islands Territory, (New Caledonia), (Papua New Guinea), (Solomon Islands)

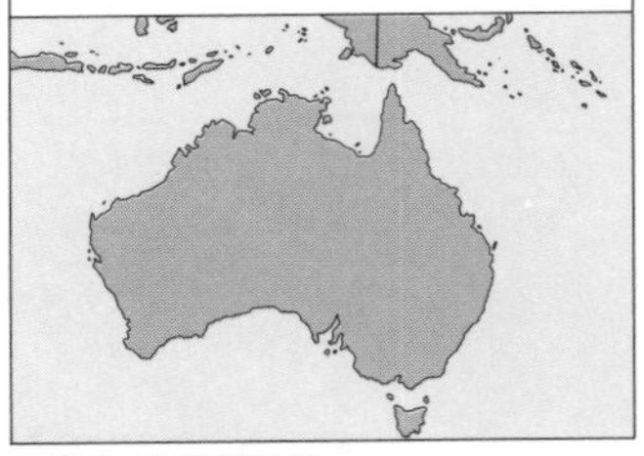

Pages 228–229

Scale 1 : 12,000,000

MAP 60

THE NORTH PACIFIC

American Samoa, (Fiji), Guam, Hawaii, (Indonesia), (Kiribati), Midway Islands, Nauru, Papua New Guinea, Solomon Islands, Trust Territory of the Pacific Islands, (Tuvalu), Wake Island

Pages 230–231

Scale 1 : 15,000,000

MAP 61

THE SOUTH PACIFIC

Cook Islands, French Polynesia, (Kiribati), New Caledonia, New Zealand, Niue, Norfolk Island, Pitcairn, Tokelau, Tonga, Vanuatu, Wallis and Futuna, Western Samoa

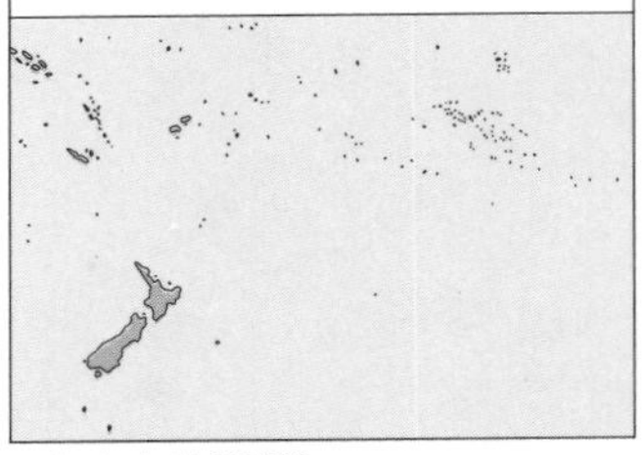

Pages 232–233

Scale 1 : 15,000,000

MAP 62

NEW ZEALAND

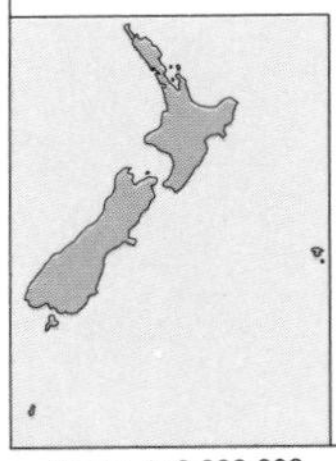

Page 234

Scale 1 : 6,000,000

MAP 63

ISLANDS OF MELANESIA

Fiji, New Caledonia, (Papua New Guinea), Solomon Islands, Vanuatu

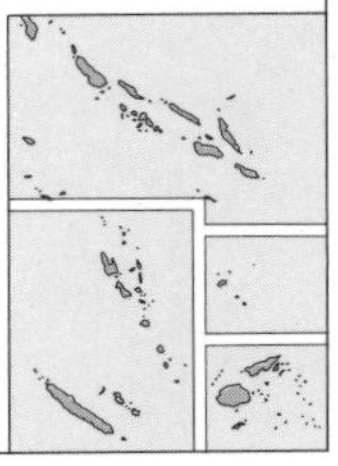

Page 235

Various scales

MAP 64

ISLANDS OF MICRONESIA-POLYNESIA

(Cook Islands), (Federated States of Micronesia), Guam, (Kiribati), Nauru, Niue, (Northern Mariana Islands), (Palau), (Pitcairn), (Wallis and Futuna)

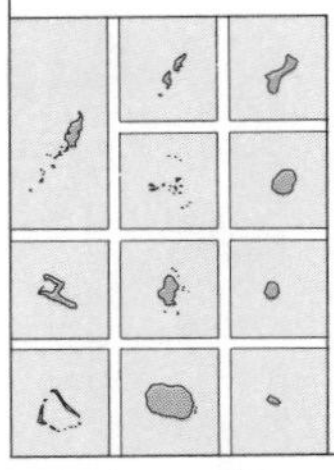

Page 236

Various scales

MAP 65

ISLANDS OF POLYNESIA

American Samoa, Pascua, (French Polynesia), (Hawaii), Tonga, Western Samoa

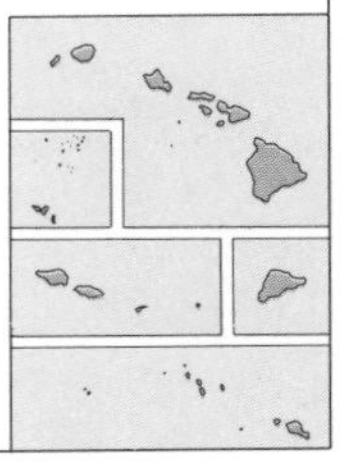

Page 237

Various scales

MAP 66

ANTARCTIC REGION

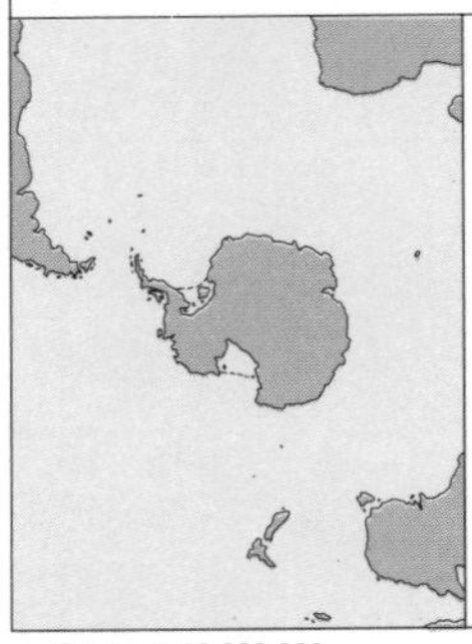

Pages 238–239

Scale 1 : 30,000,000

MAP 67

ARCTIC REGION

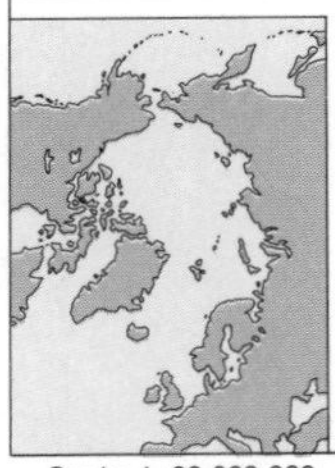

Page 240

Scale 1 : 30,000,000

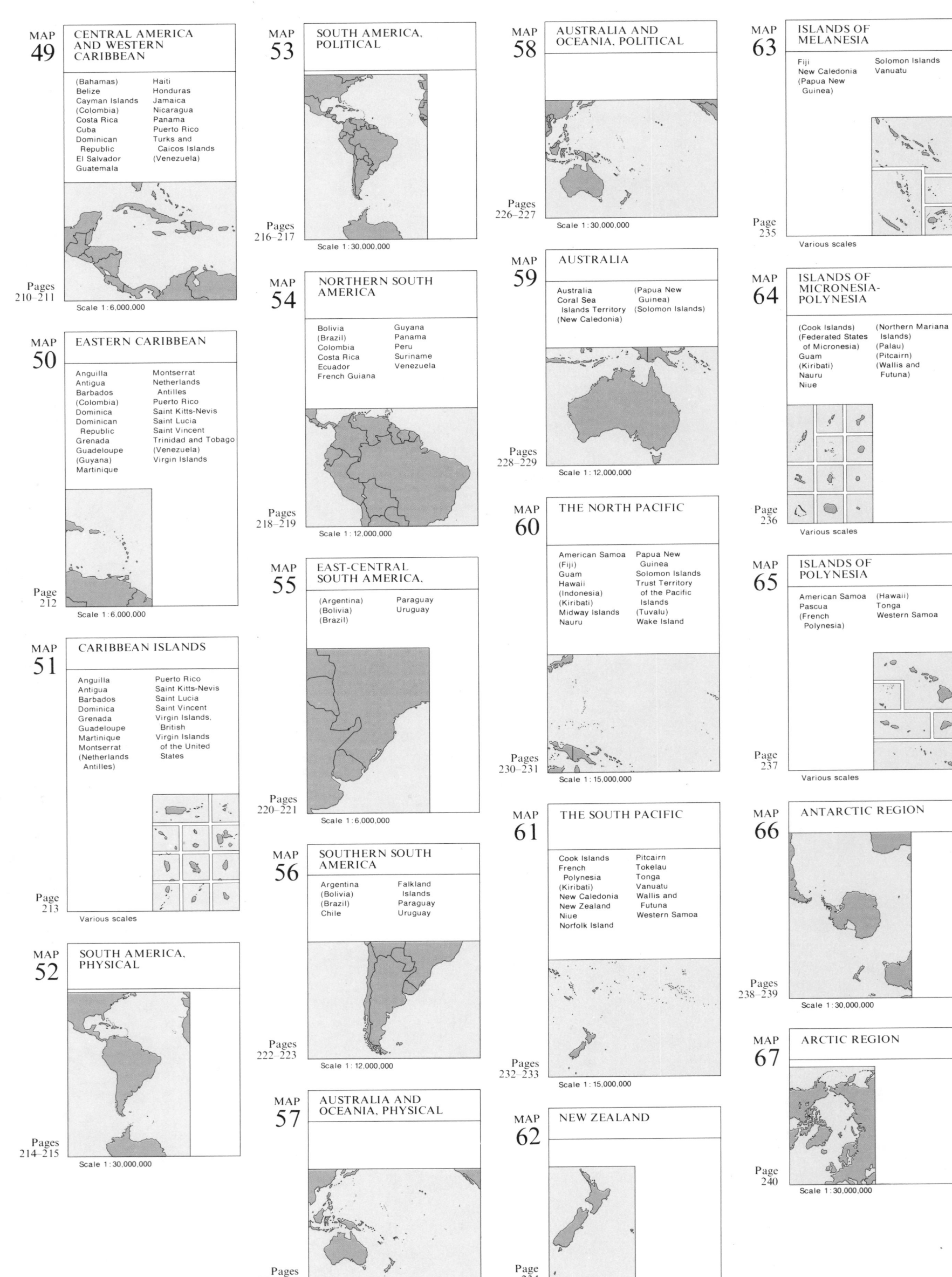

Our Planet Earth Section

Part 1

THE EARTH AND THE UNIVERSE

How the universe began · Earth's place in the Solar System
How the Earth became fit for life
Man looks at Earth from outer space

CREATION AND DESTRUCTION

Violent activity pervades our universe and has done so ever since the primordial fireball of creation. Evidence of violence comes from radio telescopes scanning the farthest reaches: entire galaxies may be exploding, torn apart by gravitational forces of unimaginable power. Some very large stars may burst apart in supernovas, spraying interstellar space with cosmic debris. From this violence new stars and new planets are constantly being formed throughout the universe.

The Big Bang theory (left) of the origin of the universe envisages all matter originating from one point in time and space—a point of infinite density. In the intensely hot Big Bang all the material that goes to make up the planets, stars and galaxies that we see now began to expand outward in all directions. This expansion has been likened to someone blowing up a balloon on which spots have been painted. As the air fills and expands the balloon, the spots get farther away from each other. Likewise, clusters of galaxies that formed from the original superdense matter began, and continue, to move away from neighboring clusters. The Big Bang generated enormous temperatures and the remnants of the event still linger throughout space. A leftover, background radiation provides a uniform and measurable temperature of 3°C. It is generally believed that the universe will continue to expand into complete nothingness.

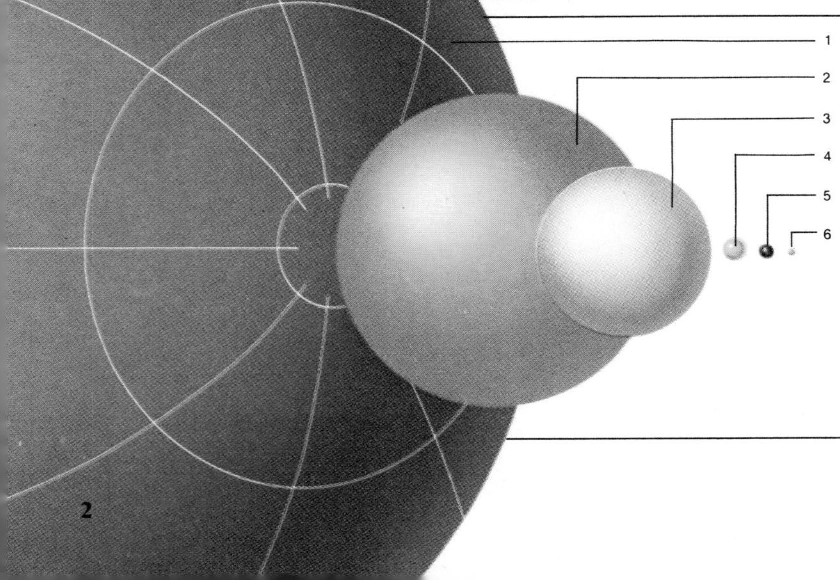

Stars vary enormously in size, temperature and luminosity. The largest, so-called red giants like Antares (1)—the biggest yet known—or Aldebaran (2), are nearing the end of their lives: diminishing nuclear "fuel" causes their thinning envelopes to expand. Rigel (3) is many times brighter than our Sun (4)—a middle-aged star—but both are so-called main-sequence stars. Epsilon Eridani (5) is rather like the Sun. Wolf 359 (6) is a red dwarf.

Our Solar System was formed from a collapsing cloud of gas and dust (A). Collapse made the center hotter and denser (B) until nuclear reactions started. Heat blew matter from the heart of the now flattened, spinning disc (C). Heavier materials condensed closest to the young Sun, now a hot star, eventually forming the inner ring of planets; the lighter ones accumulated farther out, making up the atmosphere and composition of the giant outer planets (D).

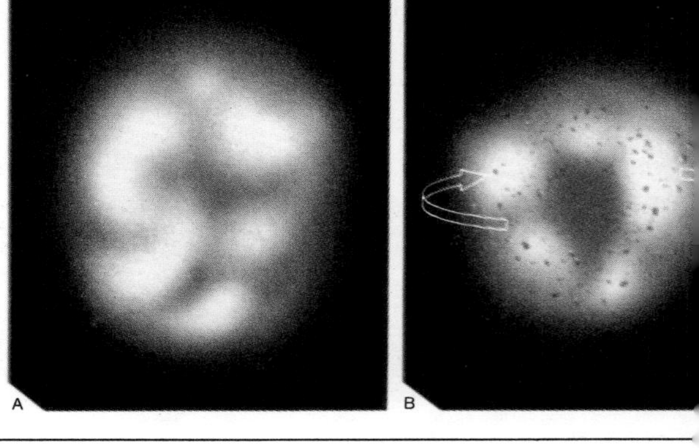

The Making of the Universe

Most astronomers believe that the universe began in a great explosion of matter and energy – the "Big Bang" – about 15,000 million years ago. This event was implied by Einstein's theory of general relativity, as well as by more recent astronomical observations and calculations. But the clinching evidence came in 1965, when two American radio astronomers discovered a faint, uniform, background radiation which permeated all space. This they identified as the remnants of the primordial Big Bang.

Billions of galaxies exist outside our own Milky Way, each thousands of light-years across and filled with millions of stars. Found in clusters, they are either elliptical or spiral in form. The clusters recede from each other following the space-time geometry, as established by Hubble in 1929, proving that the universe is expanding.

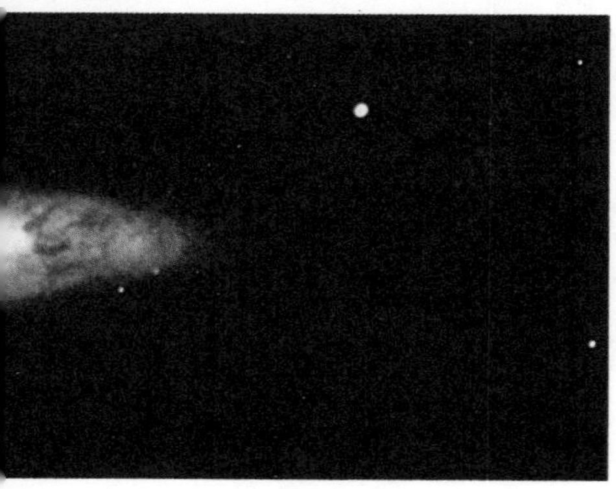

The "exploding" galaxy M82 may be an example of the violence of our universe. Clouds of hydrogen gas, equivalent in mass to 5,000,000 suns, have been ejected from the nucleus at 160 km (100 miles) per second. Black holes may cause the explosions, when gravity sucks in all matter, so that even light cannot escape.

Our own cluster of galaxies (below), the Local Group (A), consists of about 30 members, weakly linked by the force of gravity. Earth lies in the second-largest galaxy, the Milky Way (B)—here shown edge-on and at an angle—which is a spiral galaxy of about 100,000 million stars. Its rotating "arms" are great masses of clouds, dust and stars that sweep around a dense nucleus. In the course of this new stars are regularly created from dust and gas. Our Sun (S) lies 33,000 light-years from the nucleus and takes 225 million years to complete an orbit. The Andromeda Galaxy (C), known to astronomers as M31, is the largest of our Local Group. It too is a spiral, and lies about two million light-years away. Roughly 130,000 light-years in diameter, it appears as a flattened disc, and indicates how our galaxy would look if viewed from outside. Two smaller elliptical galaxies, M32 and NGC 205, can also be seen.

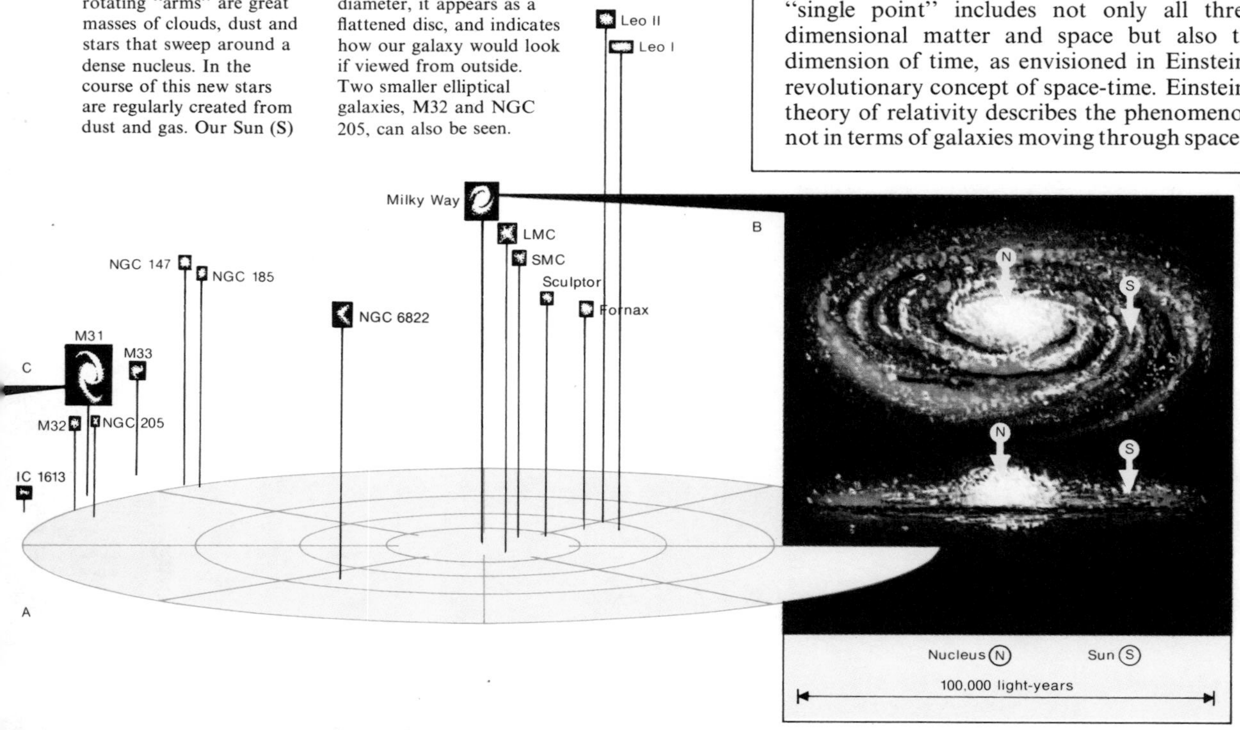

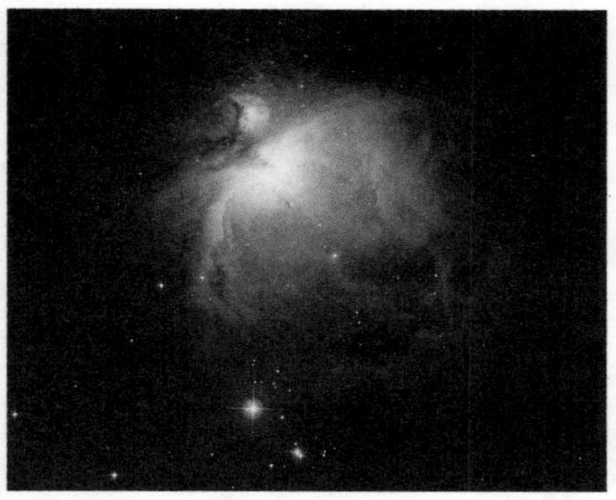

Stars are being born (left) in the Great Nebula of Orion, visible from Earth. The brilliant light comes from a cluster of very hot young stars, the Trapezium, surrounded by a glowing aura of hydrogen gas. Behind the visible nebula there is known to be a dense cloud where radio astronomers have detected emissions from interstellar molecules, and have identified high-density globules. These probably indicate that stars are starting to form.

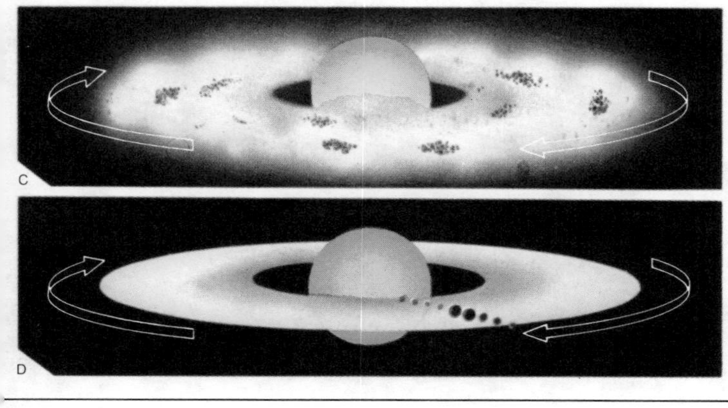

The generally accepted explanation for the so-called "cosmic microwave" background, detected by American astronomers Arno Penzias and Robert Wilson, is indeed that it is the echo of the Big Bang itself, the radio noise left over from the fireball of creation. In recognition of their discovery, Penzias and Wilson shared a Nobel Prize in 1978.

The Big Bang has also been identified by astronomers in other ways. All the evidence shows that the universe is expanding, and its constituent parts—clusters of galaxies, each containing thousands of millions of stars like our Sun—are moving away from each other at great speeds. From this and other evidence scientists deduce that long ago the galaxies must have been closer together, in a superdense phase, and that at some time in the remote past all the material in the universe must have started spreading out from a single point. But this "single point" includes not only all three-dimensional matter and space but also the dimension of time, as envisioned in Einstein's revolutionary concept of space-time. Einstein's theory of relativity describes the phenomenon, not in terms of galaxies moving through space in the expansion, but as being carried apart by the expansion of space-time itself. Space-time may be imagined as a rubber sheet speckled with paint blobs (galaxies), which move apart as the rubber sheet expands.

Galaxies consist of star systems, dust clouds and gases formed from the hot material exploding outward from the original cosmic fireball. Our own Milky Way system, the band of light that stretches across the night sky, is typical of many galaxies, containing millions of stars slowly rotating around a central nucleus.

Exploding space

The original material of the universe was hydrogen, the simplest of all elements. Nuclear reactions that occurred during the superdense phase of the Big Bang converted about 20 percent of the original hydrogen into helium, the next simplest element. So the first stars were formed from a mixture of about 80 percent hydrogen and 20 percent helium. All other matter in the universe, including the atoms of heavier elements such as carbon and oxygen—which help to make up the human body or the pages of this book—has been processed in further nuclear reactions. The explosion of a star—a relatively rare event called a supernova—scatters material across space, briefly radiating more energy than a trillion suns and ejecting matter into the cosmic reservoir of interstellar space. This is then reused to form new stars and planets.

Thus, from the debris of such explosions new stars can form to repeat the creative cycle, and at each stage more of the heavy elements are produced. Today's heavenly bodies are very much the products of stellar violence in the universe, and indeed the universe itself is now seen to be an area of violent activity. During the past two decades the old idea of the universe as a place of quiet stability has been increasingly superseded by evidence of intense activity on all scales. Astronomers have identified what appear to be vast explosions involving whole galaxies, as well as those of individual stars.

Black holes

The evidence of just why these huge explosions occur is often hard to obtain, because the exploding galaxies may be so far away that light from them takes millions of years to reach telescopes on Earth. But it is becoming increasingly accepted by astronomers that such violent events may be associated with the presence of black holes at the centers of some galaxies.

These black holes are regions in which matter has become so concentrated that the force of gravity makes it impossible for anything—even light itself—to escape. As stars are pulled into super-massive black holes they are torn apart by gravitational forces, and their material forms into a swirling maelstrom from which huge explosions can occur. Collapse into black holes, accompanied by violent outbursts from the maelstrom, may be the ultimate fate of all matter in the universe. For our own Solar System, however, such a fate is far in the future: the Sun in its present form is believed to have enough "fuel" to keep it going for at least another 5,000 million years.

A star is born

The origins of the Earth and the Solar System are intimately connected with the structure of our own galaxy, the Milky Way. There are two main types of galaxies: flattened, disc-shaped spiral galaxies (like the Milky Way), and the more rounded elliptical galaxies, which range in form from near spheres to cigar shapes. The most important feature of a spiral galaxy is that it is rotating, a great mass of stars sweeping around a common center. In our galaxy the Sun, located some way out from the galaxy's center, takes about 225 million years to complete one circuit, called a cosmic year.

New stars are born out of the twisting arms of a spiral galaxy, with each arm marking a region of debris left over from previous stellar explosions. These arms are in fact clouds of dust and gas, including nitrogen and oxygen. As the spiral galaxy rotates over a period of millions of years, the twisting arms are squeezed by a high-density pressure wave as they pass through the cycle of the cosmic year. With two main spiral arms twining around a galaxy such as our own, large, diffuse clouds get squeezed twice during each orbit around the center of the galaxy.

Even if one orbit takes as long as hundreds of millions of years, a score or more squeezes have probably occurred since the Milky Way was first formed thousands of millions of years ago. At a critical point, such repeated squeezing increases the density of a gas cloud so much that it begins to collapse rapidly under the inward pull of its own gravity. A typical cloud of this kind contains enough material to make many stars. As it breaks up it collapses into smaller clouds—which are also collapsing—and these become stars in their own right.

Our own Solar System may have been formed in this way from such a collapsing gas cloud, which went on to evolve into the system of planets that we know today.

Earth in the Solar System

The Sun is an ordinary, medium-sized star located some two-thirds of the way from the center of our galaxy, the Milky Way. Yet it comprises more than 99 percent of the Solar System's total mass and provides all the light and heat that make life possible on Earth. This energy comes from nuclear reactions that take place in the Sun's hot, dense interior. The reactions convert hydrogen into helium, with the release of vast amounts of energy – the energy that keeps the Sun shining.

Nuclear reactions in the Sun's core maintain a temperature of some 15,000,000°C and this heat prevents the star from shrinking. The surface temperature is comparatively much lower—a mere 6,000°C. Thermonuclear energy-generating processes cause the Sun to "lose" mass from the center at the rate of four million tonnes of hydrogen every second. This mass is turned into energy (heat), and each gram of matter "burnt" produces the heat equivalent of 100 trillion electric fires. The Sun's total mass is so great, however, that it contains enough matter to continue radiating at its present rate for several thousand million years before it runs out of "fuel."

The Sun's retinue

The Solar System emerged from a collapsing gas cloud. In addition to the Sun there are at least nine planets, their satellites, thousands of minor planets (asteroids), comets and meteors. Most stars occur in pairs, triplets or in even more complicated systems, and the Sun is among a minority of stars in being alone except for its planetary companions. It does seem, however, that a single star with a planetary system offers the greatest potential for the development of life. When there are two or more stars in the same system, any planets are likely to have unstable orbits and to suffer from wide extremes of temperature.

The Solar System's structure is thought to be typical of a star that formed in isolation. As the hot young Sun threw material outward, inner planets (Mercury, Venus, Earth and Mars) were left as small rocky bodies, whereas outer planets (Jupiter, Saturn, Uranus and Neptune) kept their lighter gases and became huge "gas giants." Jupiter has two and a half times the mass of all the other planets put together. Pluto, a small object with a strange orbit, which sometimes carries it within the orbit of Neptune, is usually regarded as a ninth planet, but some astronomers consider it to be an escaped moon of Neptune or a large asteroid.

Planetary relations

Several planets are accompanied by smaller bodies called moons or satellites. Jupiter and Saturn have at least 17 and 22 respectively, whereas Earth has its solitary Moon. Sizes vary enormously, from Ganymede, one of Jupiter's large, so-called Galilean satellites, which has a diameter of 5,000 km (3,100 miles), to Mars' tiny Deimos, which is only 8 km (5 miles) across.

The Earth's Moon is at an average distance of 384,000 km (239,000 miles) and has a diameter of 3,476 km (2,160 miles). Its mass is $\frac{1}{81}$ of the Earth's. Although it is referred to as the Earth's satellite, the Moon is large for a secondary body. Some astronomers have suggested that the Earth/Moon system is a double planet. Certain theories of the origins of the Moon propose that it was formed from the solar nebula in the same way as the Earth was and very close to it. The Moon takes 27.3 days to orbit the Earth—exactly the same time that it takes to rotate once on its axis. As a result, it presents the same face to the Earth all the time.

Our planet's orbit around the Sun is not a perfect circle but an ellipse and so its distance from the Sun varies slightly. More importantly, the Earth is tilted, so that at different times of the year one pole or another "leans" toward the Sun. Without this tilt there would be no seasons. The angle of tilt is not constant: over tens of thousands of years the axis of the Earth "wobbles" like a slowly spinning top, so that the pattern of the seasons varies over the ages. These changes have been linked to recent ice ages, which seem to occur when the northern hemisphere has relatively cool summers.

Patterns of time

The Earth's movements on its axis and around the Sun give us our basic measurements of time—the day and the year—as well as setting the rhythm of the seasons and the ice ages. One rotation of the Earth on its axis—the time from one sunrise to the next—originally defined the day, and the time taken for one complete orbit around the Sun defined the year. Today, however, scientists define both the day and the year in terms of time units "counted" by precision instruments called atomic clocks.

A third basic rhythm is set not by the Sun but by the Moon, which runs through a cycle of phases $29\frac{1}{2}$ days long. This is the basis of the calendar month. But just as the modern calendar cannot cope with months $29\frac{1}{2}$ days long, so too it would have trouble with the precise year, which is, inconveniently, just less than $365\frac{1}{4}$ days long. This is the reason for leap years, by means of which an extra day is added to the month of February every fourth year.

Even this system does not keep the calendar exactly in step with the Sun. Accordingly, the leap year is left out in the years which complete centuries, such as 1900, but retained when they divide exactly by 400. The year 2000 will, therefore, be a leap year. With all these corrections, the average length of the calendar year is within 26 seconds of the year defined by the Earth's movements around the Sun. Thus the calendar will be one day out of step with the heavens in the year 4906.

Cosmic rubble

The other planets are too small and too far away to produce noticeable effects on the Earth, but the smallest members of the Sun's family, the asteroids, can affect us directly. Some of them have orbits that cross the orbit of the Earth around the Sun. From time to time they penetrate the Earth's atmosphere: small fragments burn up high in the atmosphere as meteors, whereas larger pieces may survive to strike the ground as meteorites. These in fact provide an echo of times gone by. All the planets, as the battered face of the Moon shows, suffered collisions from many smaller bodies in the course of their evolution from the collapsing pre-solar gas cloud.

Eclipses occur because the Moon, smaller than the Sun, is closer to Earth and looks just as big. This means that when all three are lined up the Moon can blot out the Sun, causing a solar eclipse. When the Earth passes through the main shadow cone, or umbra, the eclipse is total; in the area of partial shadow, or penumbra, a partial eclipse is seen. A similar effect is produced when Earth passes between the Moon and the Sun, causing a lunar eclipse. At most full moons, eclipses do not occur; the Moon passes either above or below the Earth's shadow, because the Moon's orbit is inclined at an angle of 5° to the orbit of the Earth.

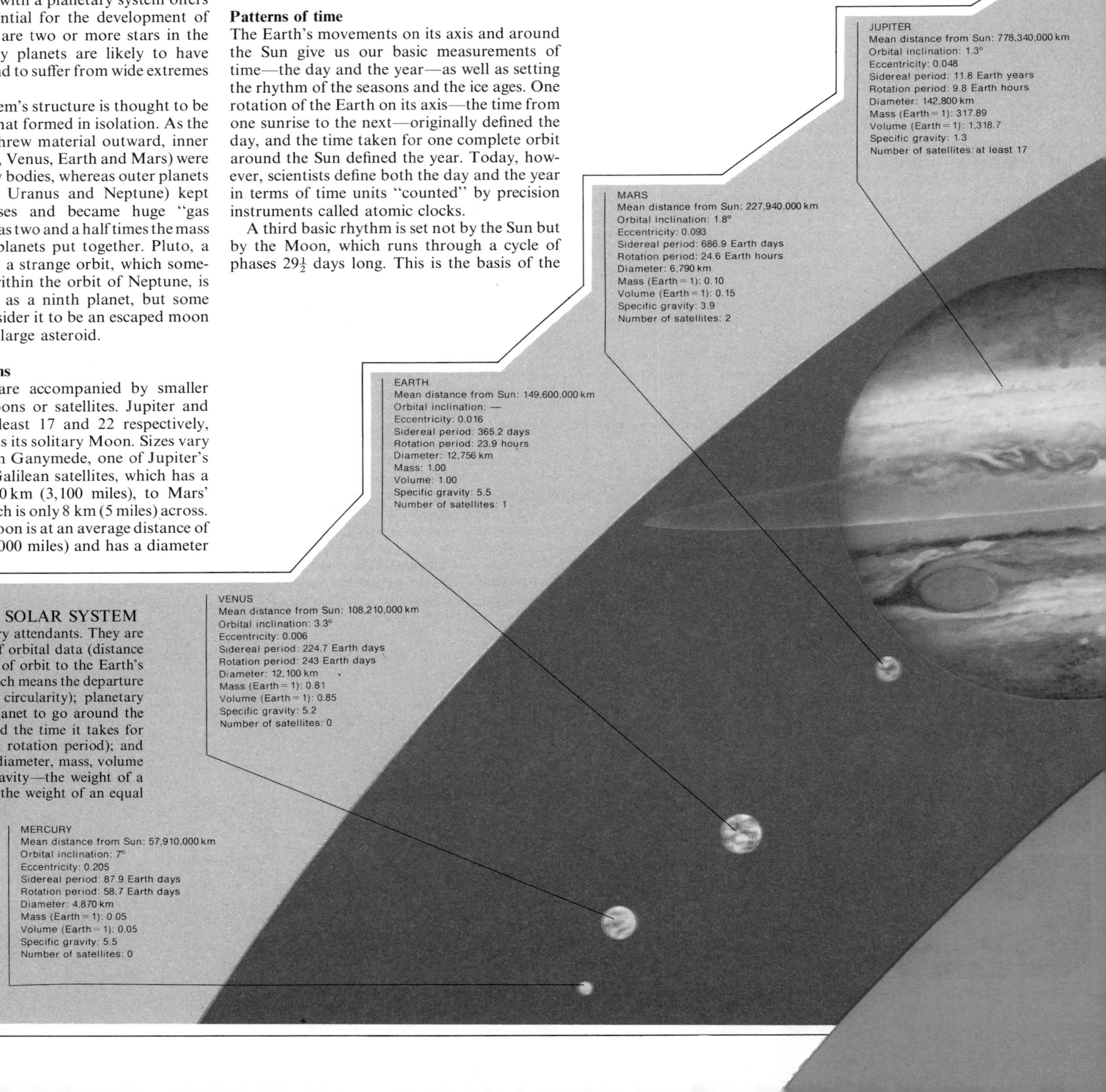
JUPITER
Mean distance from Sun: 778,340,000 km
Orbital inclination: 1.3°
Eccentricity: 0.048
Sidereal period: 11.8 Earth years
Rotation period: 9.8 Earth hours
Diameter: 142,800 km
Mass (Earth = 1): 317.89
Volume (Earth = 1): 1,318.7
Specific gravity: 1.3
Number of satellites: at least 17
MARS
Mean distance from Sun: 227,940,000 km
Orbital inclination: 1.8°
Eccentricity: 0.093
Sidereal period: 686.9 Earth days
Rotation period: 24.6 Earth hours
Diameter: 6,790 km
Mass (Earth = 1): 0.10
Volume (Earth = 1): 0.15
Specific gravity: 3.9
Number of satellites: 2
EARTH
Mean distance from Sun: 149,600,000 km
Orbital inclination: —
Eccentricity: 0.016
Sidereal period: 365.2 days
Rotation period: 23.9 hours
Diameter: 12,756 km
Mass: 1.00
Volume: 1.00
Specific gravity: 5.5
Number of satellites: 1
VENUS
Mean distance from Sun: 108,210,000 km
Orbital inclination: 3.3°
Eccentricity: 0.006
Sidereal period: 224.7 Earth days
Rotation period: 243 Earth days
Diameter: 12,100 km
Mass (Earth = 1): 0.81
Volume (Earth = 1): 0.85
Specific gravity: 5.2
Number of satellites: 0
MERCURY
Mean distance from Sun: 57,910,000 km
Orbital inclination: 7°
Eccentricity: 0.205
Sidereal period: 87.9 Earth days
Rotation period: 58.7 Earth days
Diameter: 4,870 km
Mass (Earth = 1): 0.05
Volume (Earth = 1): 0.05
Specific gravity: 5.5
Number of satellites: 0

MEMBERS OF THE SOLAR SYSTEM

The Sun has nine planetary attendants. They are best compared in terms of orbital data (distance from the Sun, inclination of orbit to the Earth's orbit, and eccentricity, which means the departure of a planet's orbit from circularity); planetary periods (the time for a planet to go around the Sun—sidereal periods, and the time it takes for one axial revolution—the rotation period); and physical data (equatorial diameter, mass, volume and density or specific gravity—the weight of a substance compared with the weight of an equal volume of water).

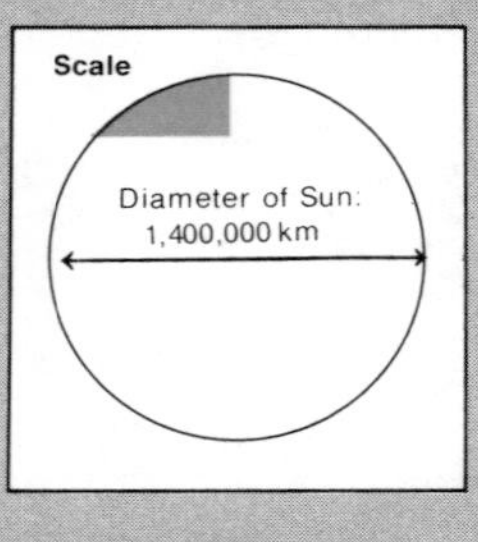
Scale
Diameter of Sun:
1,400,000 km

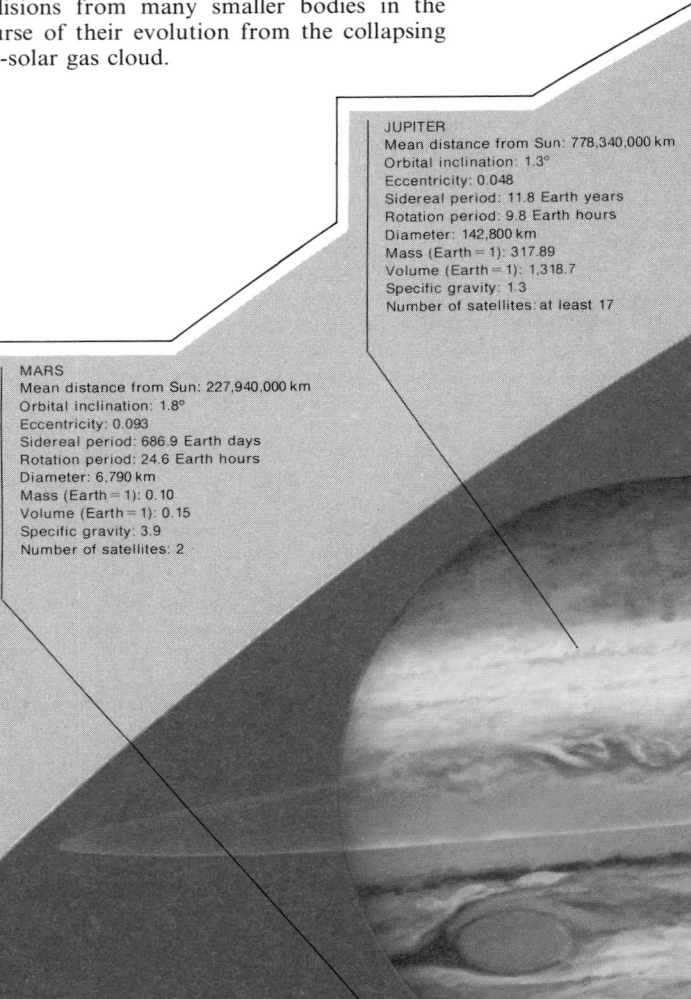

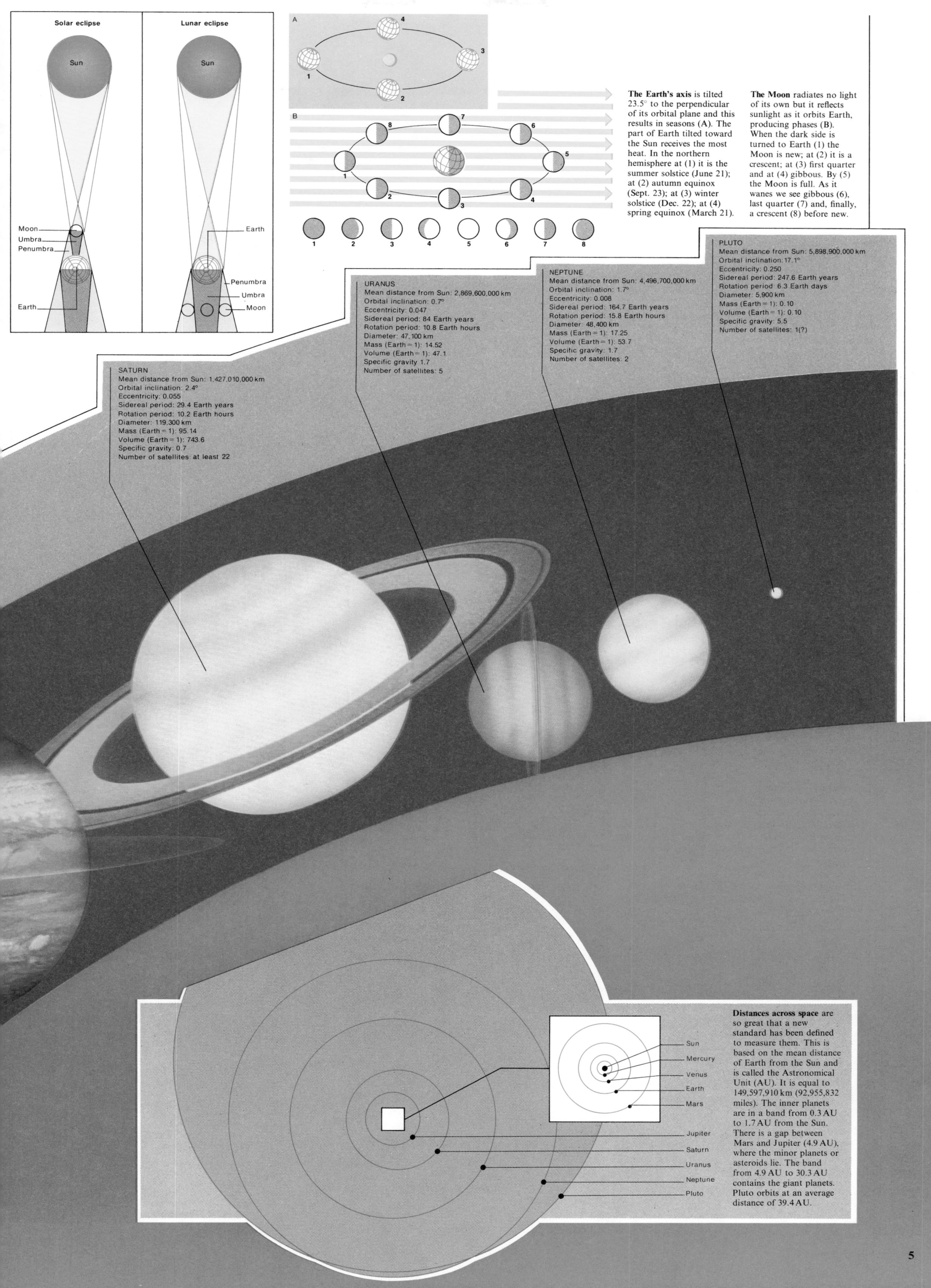

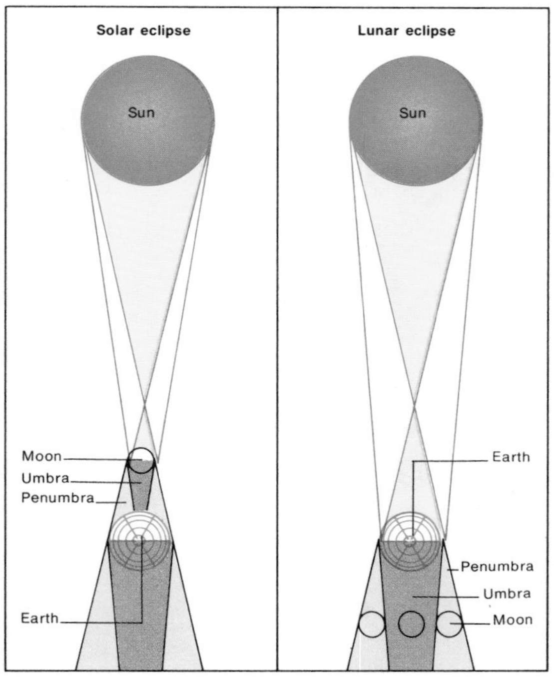
Solar eclipse
Sun
Moon
Umbra
Penumbra
Earth
Lunar eclipse
Sun
Earth
Penumbra
Umbra
Moon

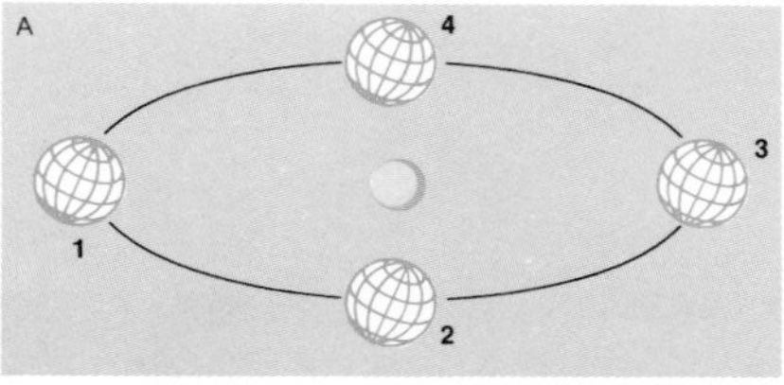
A
1
2
3
4

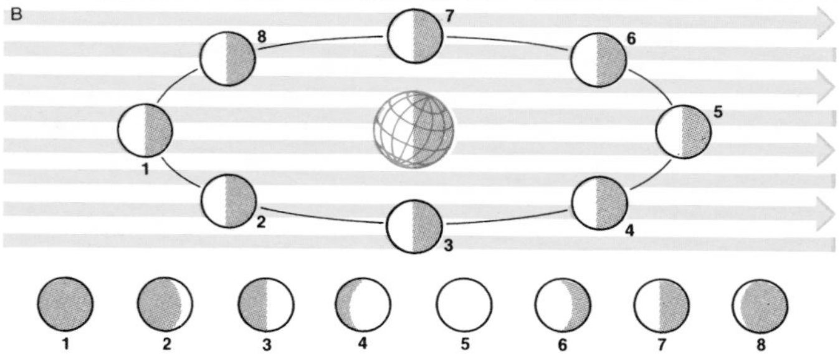
B
1
2
3
4
5
6
7
8
1
2
3
4
5
6
7
8

The Earth's axis is tilted 23.5° to the perpendicular of its orbital plane and this results in seasons (A). The part of Earth tilted toward the Sun receives the most heat. In the northern hemisphere at (1) it is the summer solstice (June 21); at (2) autumn equinox (Sept. 23); at (3) winter solstice (Dec. 22); at (4) spring equinox (March 21).

The Moon radiates no light of its own but it reflects sunlight as it orbits Earth, producing phases (B). When the dark side is turned to Earth (1) the Moon is new; at (2) it is a crescent; at (3) first quarter and at (4) gibbous. By (5) the Moon is full. As it wanes we see gibbous (6), last quarter (7) and, finally, a crescent (8) before new.

SATURN
Mean distance from Sun: 1,427,010,000 km
Orbital inclination: 2.4°
Eccentricity: 0.055
Sidereal period: 29.4 Earth years
Rotation period: 10.2 Earth hours
Diameter: 119,300 km
Mass (Earth = 1): 95.14
Volume (Earth = 1): 743.6
Specific gravity: 0.7
Number of satellites: at least 22

URANUS
Mean distance from Sun: 2,869,600,000 km
Orbital inclination: 0.7°
Eccentricity: 0.047
Sidereal period: 84 Earth years
Rotation period: 10.8 Earth hours
Diameter: 47,100 km
Mass (Earth = 1): 14.52
Volume (Earth = 1): 47.1
Specific gravity 1.7
Number of satellites: 5

NEPTUNE
Mean distance from Sun: 4,496,700,000 km
Orbital inclination: 1.7°
Eccentricity: 0.008
Sidereal period: 164.7 Earth years
Rotation period: 15.8 Earth hours
Diameter: 48,400 km
Mass (Earth = 1): 17.25
Volume (Earth = 1): 53.7
Specific gravity: 1.7
Number of satellites: 2

PLUTO
Mean distance from Sun: 5,898,900,000 km
Orbital inclination: 17.1°
Eccentricity: 0.250
Sidereal period: 247.6 Earth years
Rotation period: 6.3 Earth days
Diameter: 5,900 km
Mass (Earth = 1): 0.10
Volume (Earth = 1): 0.10
Specific gravity: 5.5
Number of satellites: 1(?)

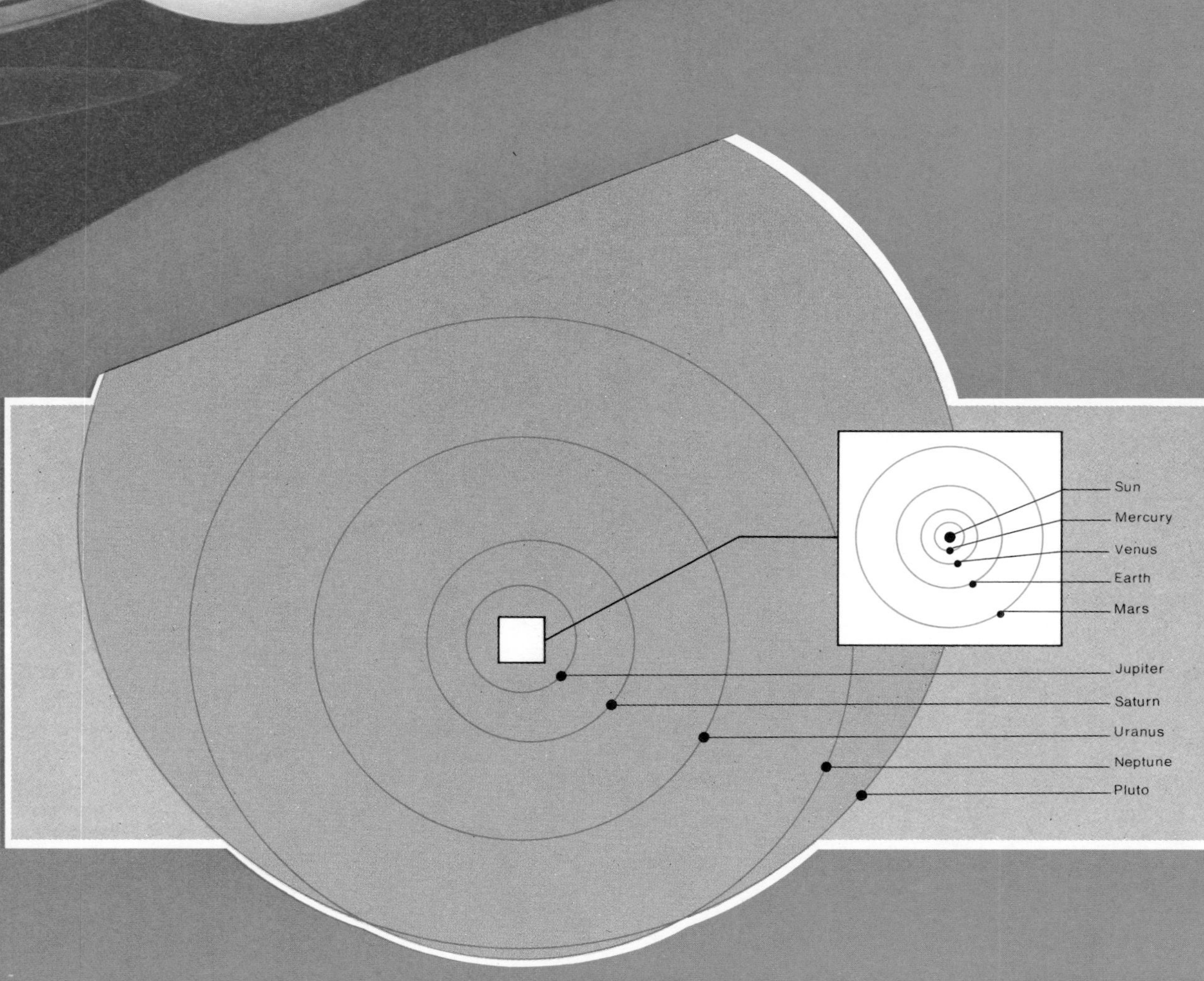
Sun
Mercury
Venus
Earth
Mars
Jupiter
Saturn
Uranus
Neptune
Pluto

Distances across space are so great that a new standard has been defined to measure them. This is based on the mean distance of Earth from the Sun and is called the Astronomical Unit (AU). It is equal to 149,597,910 km (92,955,832 miles). The inner planets are in a band from 0.3 AU to 1.7 AU from the Sun. There is a gap between Mars and Jupiter (4.9 AU), where the minor planets or asteroids lie. The band from 4.9 AU to 30.3 AU contains the giant planets. Pluto orbits at an average distance of 39.4 AU.

Earth as a Planet

Viewed from space, the Earth appears to be an ordinary member of the group of inner planets orbiting the Sun. But the Earth is unique in the Solar System because it has an atmosphere that contains oxygen. It is the nature of this surrounding blanket of air that has allowed higher life forms to evolve on Earth and provides their life-support system. At the same time the atmosphere acts as a shield to protect living things from the damaging effects of radiation from the Sun.

Any traces of gas that may have clung to the newly formed Earth were soon swept away into space by the heat of the Sun before it attained a stable state powered by nuclear fusion. Farther out in the Solar System, the Sun's heat was never strong enough to blow these gases away into space, so that even today the giant planets retain atmospheres composed of these primordial gases—mostly methane and ammonia.

The evolution of air

Until the Sun "settled down," Earth was a hot, airless ball of rock. The atmosphere and oceans—like the atmospheres of Venus and Mars—were produced by the "outgassing" of material from the hot interior of the planet as the crust cooled. Volcanoes erupted constantly and produced millions of tonnes of ash and lava. They also probably yielded, as they do today, great quantities of gas, chiefly carbon dioxide, and water vapor. A little nitrogen and various sulphur compounds were also released. Other things being equal, we would expect rocky planets, like the young Earth, to have atmospheres rich in carbon dioxide and water vapor. Venus and Mars do indeed have carbon dioxide atmospheres today, but the Earth now has a nitrogen/oxygen atmosphere. This results from the fact that life evolved on Earth, converting the carbon dioxide to oxygen and storing carbon in organic remains such as coal. Some carbon dioxide was also dissolved in the oceans. The Earth's oxygen atmosphere is a clear sign of life; the carbon dioxide atmospheres of Venus and Mars suggest the absence of life. Why did the Earth begin to evolve in a different way from the other inner planets?

When the Sun stabilized, Earth, Venus and Mars started off down the same evolutionary road, and carbon dioxide and water vapor were the chief constituents of the original atmospheres. On Venus the temperature was hot enough for the water to remain in a gaseous form, and both the water vapor and carbon dioxide in the Venusian atmosphere trapped heat by means of the so-called "greenhouse effect." In this process, radiant energy from the Sun passes through the atmospheric gases and warms the ground. The warmed ground reradiates heat energy, but at infrared wavelengths, with the result that carbon dioxide and water molecules absorb it and stop it escaping from the planet. Instead of acting like a window, the atmosphere acts like a mirror for outgoing energy. As a result, the surface of Venus became hotter still. Today the surface temperature has stabilized at more than 500°C.

Mars, farther out from the Sun than Earth, was never hot enough for the greenhouse effect to dominate. The red planet once had a much thicker atmosphere than it does today, but, being smaller than the Earth, its gravity is too weak to retain a thick atmosphere. As a result, the planet cooled into a frozen desert as atmospheric gases escaped into space. Mars then, in fact, suffered a climatic change. At one time—hundreds of millions of years ago—there must have been running water because traces of old riverbeds still scar the Martian surface. Today, however, Mars has a thin atmosphere of carbon dioxide and surface temperatures below zero.

Earth—the ideal home

On Earth conditions were just right. Water stayed as a liquid and formed the oceans, while some carbon dioxide from outgassing went into the atmosphere, and some dissolved in the oceans. The resulting modest greenhouse effect

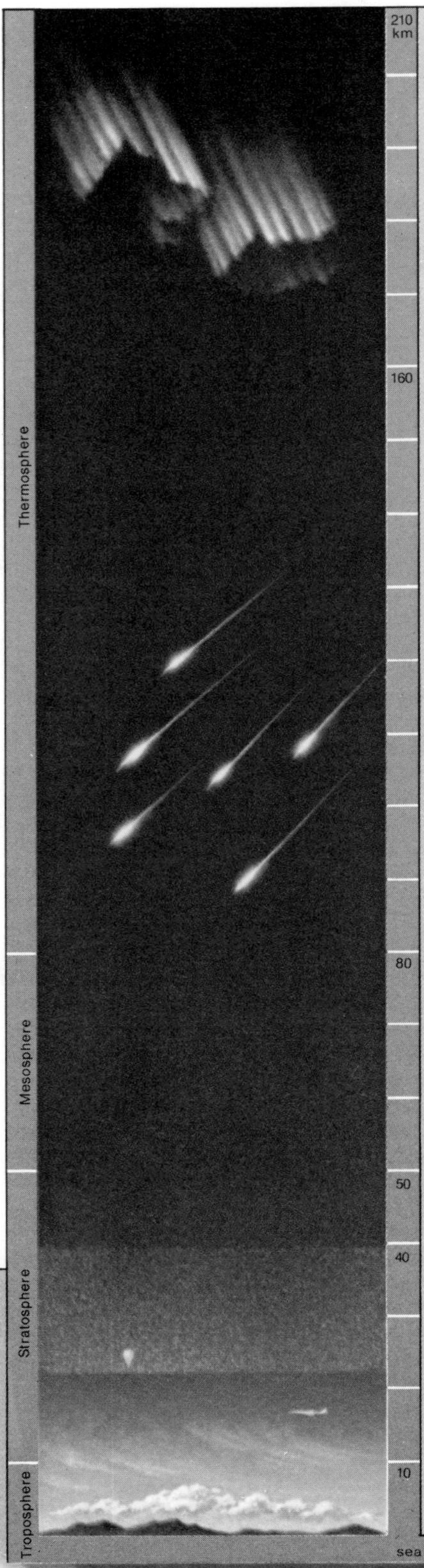

The thermosphere extends from 80 km (50 miles) up to 400 km (250 miles). Within this zone temperatures rise steadily with height to as much as 1,650°C (3,000°F), but the air is so thin that temperature is not a meaningful concept. At this height the air is mostly composed of nitrogen molecules to a height of 200 km (125 miles), when oxygen molecules become the dominant constituent.

The mesosphere is between 50 and 80 km (30 and 50 miles) above ground level. The stratopause is its lower limit and the mesopause its upper. This zone of the atmosphere is mainly distinguished by its ever decreasing temperatures and, unlike the stratosphere, it does not absorb solar energy.

The stratosphere is the level above the troposphere and extends as far as 50 km (30 miles). The chemical composition of the air up to this height is nearly constant and, in terms of volume, it is composed of nitrogen (78%) and oxygen (20%). The rest is mostly argon and other trace elements. The percentage of carbon dioxide (0.003) is small but crucial because this gas absorbs heat. There is virtually no water vapor or dust in this region of the atmosphere, but it does include the ozone layer, which is strongest between 20 km (12 miles) and 40 km (24 miles) high.

The troposphere extends from ground level to a height of between 10 and 15 km (6 and 9 miles). This height varies with latitude and season of the year: it is greater at the Equator than at the poles. Most weather phenomena occur in this zone. Mixed with the gases of the troposphere is water vapor and millions of tiny dust particles, around which vapor condenses to form clouds. The upper limit of this zone is called the tropopause.

EARTH'S OUTER SKIN

The Earth's atmosphere is wafer thin when compared with the size of the planet. Half of the atmosphere's mass lies in the 5.5 km ($3\frac{1}{2}$ miles) nearest the ground and more than 99 percent of it lies within 40 km (24 miles) of the Earth.

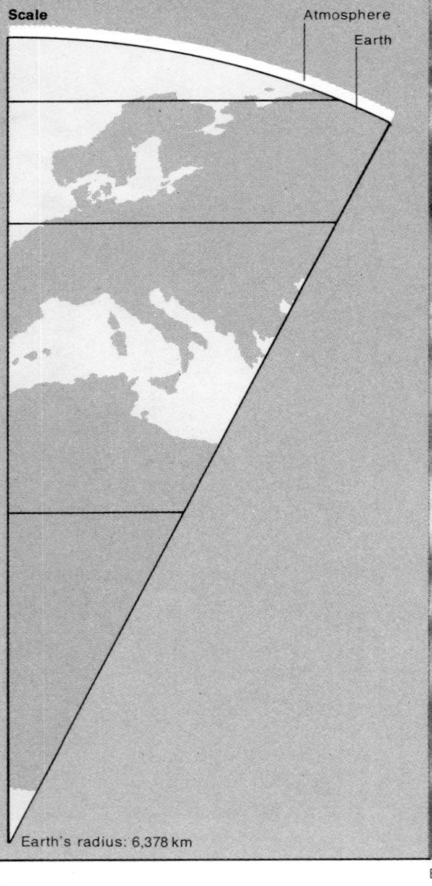

Earth reduced by 90% in proportion to this scale

1
3
3
3
3
1

was compensated for by the formation of shiny white clouds of water droplets which reflected some of the Sun's radiation back into space. Our planet stabilized with an average temperature of 15°C. This proved ideal for the emergence of life, which evolved first in the seas and then moved onto land, converting carbon dioxide into oxygen as it did so.

In any view from space, planet Earth is dominated by water—in blue oceans and white clouds—and water is the key to life as we know it. Animal life—oxygen-breathing life—could only evolve after earlier forms of life had converted the atmosphere to an oxygen-rich state. The nature of the air today is a product of life as well as being vital to its existence.

An atmospheric layer cake

Starting at ground level, the first zone of the atmosphere is the troposphere, kept warm near the ground by the greenhouse effect but cooling to a chilly −60°C at an altitude of 15 km (9 miles). Above the troposphere is a warming layer, the stratosphere, in which energy from the Sun is absorbed and temperatures increase to reach 0°C at an altitude of 50 km (30 miles). The energy—in the form of ultraviolet radiation—is absorbed by molecules of ozone, a form of oxygen. Without the ozone layer in the atmosphere, ultraviolet rays would penetrate the ground and sterilize the land surface: without life, there would be no oxygen from which an ozone layer could form.

The Earth's magnetic field behaves as if there were a huge bar magnet placed inside the globe, with its magnetic axis tilted at a slight angle to the geographical north–south axis. The speed of rotation of the liquid core differs from that of the mantle, producing an effect like a dynamo (below). The region in which the magnetic field extends beyond the Earth is the magnetosphere (1). Streams of charged particles (2) from the Sun distort its shape into that of a teardrop. Zones of the magnetosphere include the Van Allen Belts (3), which are regions of intense radioactivity where magnetic particles are "trapped."

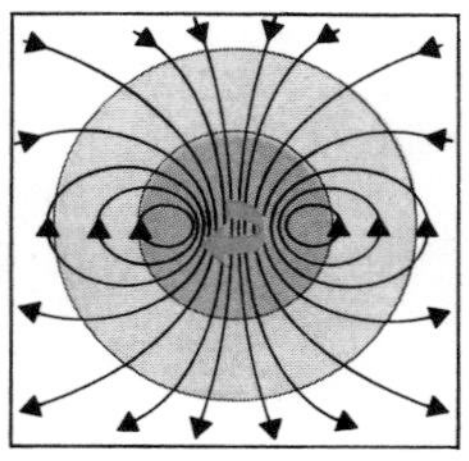

Above the stratosphere, another cooling layer, the mesosphere, extends up to 80 km (50 miles), at which point the temperature has fallen to about −100°C. Above this level the gases of the atmosphere are so thin that the standard concept of temperature is no real guide to their behavior, and from the mesosphere outwards the atmosphere is best described in terms of its electrical properties.

In the outer layers of the atmosphere, the Sun's energy is absorbed by individual atoms in such a way that it strips electrons off them, leaving behind positively charged ions, which give the region its name—the ionosphere. A few hundred kilometers above the Earth's surface, gravity is so feeble that electromagnetic forces begin to determine the behavior of the charged particles, which are shepherded along the lines of force in the Earth's magnetic field. Above 500 km (300 miles), the magnetic field is so dominant that yet another region, the magnetosphere, is distinguished. This is the true boundary between Earth and interplanetary space.

The magnetosphere has been likened to the hull of "spaceship Earth." Charged particles (the solar wind) streaming out from the Sun are deflected around Earth by the magnetosphere like water around a moving ship, while the region of the Earth's magnetic influence in space trails "downstream" away from the Sun like the wake of a ship. The Van Allen Belts, at altitudes of 3,000 and 15,000 km (1,850 and 9,300 miles) are regions of space high above the Equator where particles are trapped by the magnetic field. Particles spilling out of the belts spiral towards the polar regions of Earth, producing the spectacle of the auroras—the northern and southern lights. The Earth and Mercury are the only inner planets with magnetospheres such as this. The cause of the Earth's magnetism is almost certainly the planet's heavy molten core, which is composed of magnetic materials.

The Earth's atmosphere exhibits a great variety of characteristics on a vertical scale. As well as variations of temperature and the electrical properties of the air, there are differences in chemical composition—in the mixture of gases and water vapor—according to altitude. The Earth's gravitational pull means that air density and pressure decrease with altitude. Pressure of about 1,000 millibars at sea level falls to virtually nothing (10^{-42} millibars) by a height of 700 km (435 miles) above the Earth. All these factors, and their interrelationships, help to maintain the Earth's atmosphere as a protective outer covering or radiation shield and an essential life-support system.

The ionosphere is another name for the atmospheric layer beyond 80 km (50 miles). The region is best described in terms of the electrical properties of its constituents rather than by temperature. It is here that ionization occurs. Gamma and X-rays from the Sun are absorbed by atoms and molecules of nitrogen and oxygen and, as a result, each molecule or atom gives up one or more of its electrons, thus becoming a positively charged ion. These ions reflect radio waves and are used to bounce back radio waves transmitted from the surface of the Earth.

The exosphere is the layer above the thermosphere and it extends from 400 km (250 miles) up to about 700 km (435 miles), the point at which, it may be said, space begins. It is almost a complete vacuum because most of its atoms and molecules of oxygen escape the Earth's gravity.

The magnetosphere includes the exosphere, but it extends far beyond the atmosphere—to a distance of between 64,000 and 130,000 km (40,000 and 80,000 miles) above the Earth. It represents the Earth's external magnetic field and its outer limit is called the magnetopause.

The atmosphere protects the Earth from harmful solar radiation and also from bombardment by small particles from space. Most meteors (particles orbiting the Sun) burn up in the atmosphere, but meteorites (debris of minor planets) reach the ground. Of all incoming solar radiation, only visible light, radio waves and infrared rays reach the surface of Earth. X-rays are removed in the ionosphere, and ultraviolet and some infrared radiations are filtered out in the stratosphere. Studies of such radiations have, therefore, to be made from observatories in space.

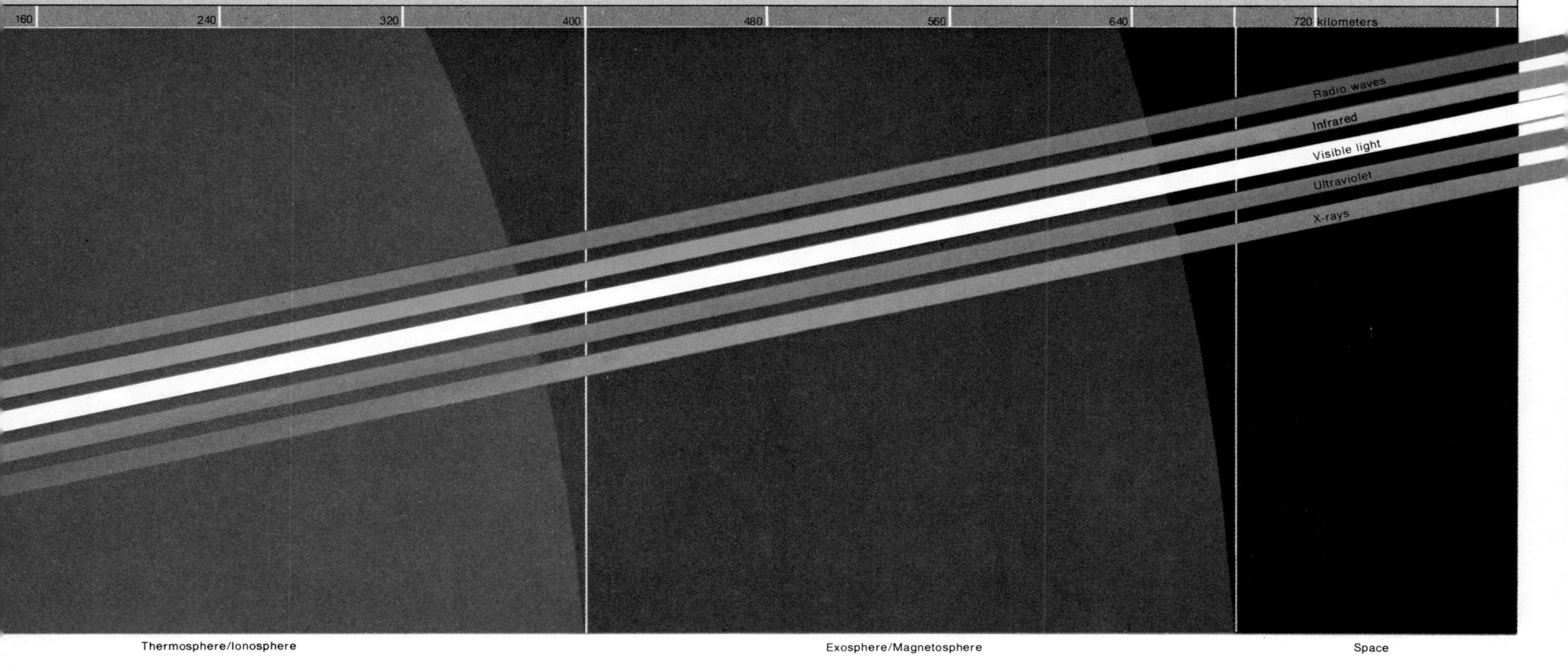

160
240
320
400
480
560
640
720 kilometers
Radio waves
Infrared
Visible light
Ultraviolet
X-rays
Thermosphere/Ionosphere
Exosphere/Magnetosphere
Space

Man Looks at the Earth

Orbiting satellites keep a detailed watch on the Earth's land surface, oceans and atmosphere, feeding streams of data to meteorologists, geologists, oceanographers, farmers, fishermen and many others. Some information would be unobtainable by any other means. Surveys from orbit are quicker and less expensive than from aircraft, for example, because a satellite can scan a much larger area. And, surprisingly enough, certain features on the ground are easier to see from space.

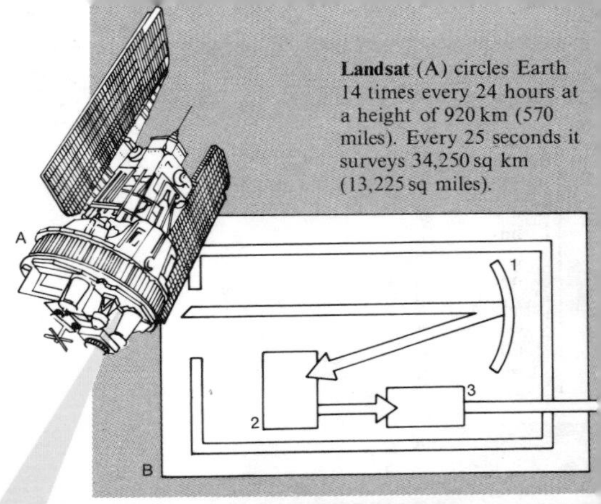

Landsat (A) circles Earth 14 times every 24 hours at a height of 920 km (570 miles). Every 25 seconds it surveys 34,250 sq km (13,225 sq miles).

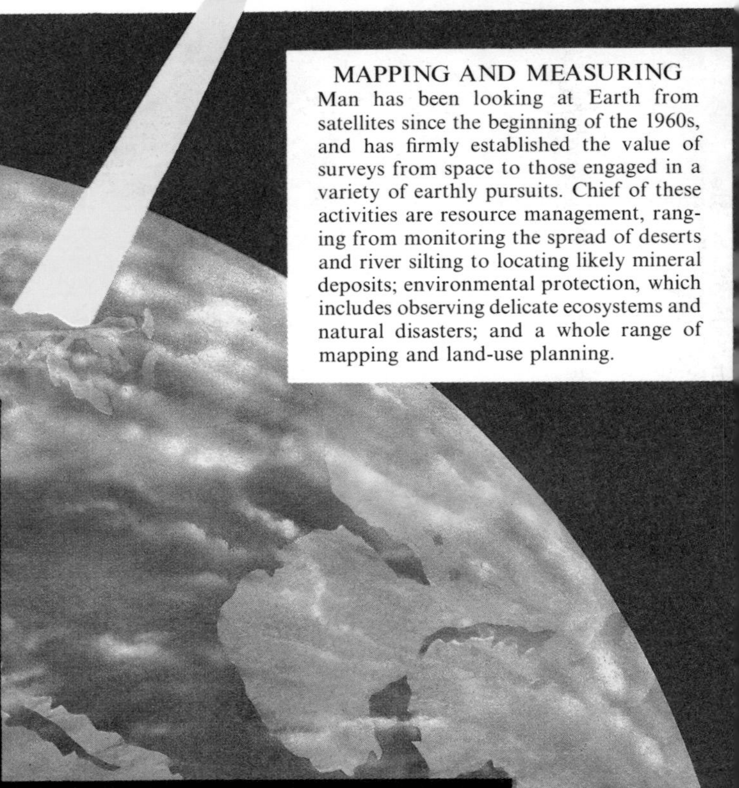

MAPPING AND MEASURING

Man has been looking at Earth from satellites since the beginning of the 1960s, and has firmly established the value of surveys from space to those engaged in a variety of earthly pursuits. Chief of these activities are resource management, ranging from monitoring the spread of deserts and river silting to locating likely mineral deposits; environmental protection, which includes observing delicate ecosystems and natural disasters; and a whole range of mapping and land-use planning.

1

2

3

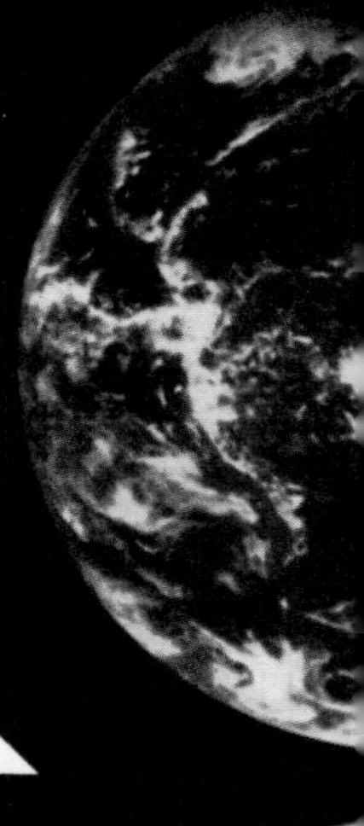

4

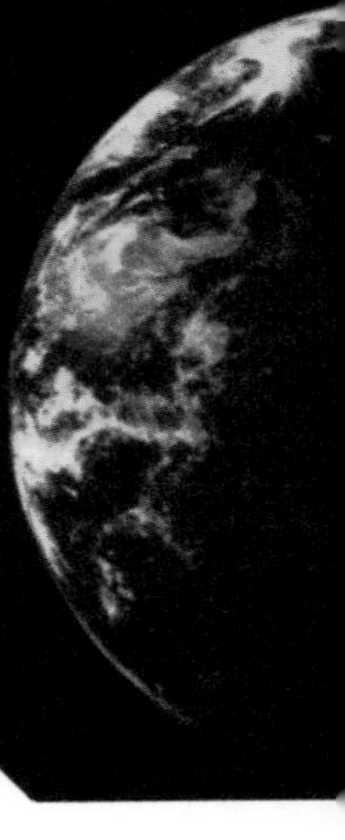

5

Satellites give us a greater overview of numerous aspects of life on Earth than any earth-bound eye could see.

Of all the information gleaned from satellites, accurate weather forecasts are of particular social and economic value. The first weather satellite was Tiros 1 (Television and Infrared Observation Satellite), launched by the United States in 1960. By the time Tiros 10 ceased operations in 1967, the series had sent back more than half a million photographs, firmly establishing the value of satellite imagery.

Tiros was superseded by the ESSA (Environmental Science Services Administration) and the NOAA (National Oceanic and Atmospheric Administration) satellites. These orbited the Earth from pole to pole, and they covered the entire globe during the course of a day. Other weather satellites, such as the European Meteosat, are placed in geostationary orbit over the Equator, which means they stay in one place and continually monitor a single large region.

Watching the weather

In addition to photographing clouds, weather satellites monitor the extent of snow and ice cover, and they measure the temperature of the oceans and the composition of the atmosphere. Information about the overall heat balance of our planet gives clues to long-term climatic change, and includes the effects on climate of human activities such as the burning of fossil fuels and deforestation.

Infrared sensors allow pictures to be taken at night as well as during the day. The temperature of cloud tops, measured by infrared devices, is a guide to the height of the clouds. In a typical infrared image, high clouds appear white because they are the coldest, lower clouds and land areas appear gray, and oceans and lakes are black. Information on humidity in the atmosphere is provided by sensors tuned to wavelengths between 5.5 and 7 micrometers, at which water vapor strongly absorbs the radiation.

To "see" inside clouds, where infrared and visible light cannot penetrate, satellites use sensors tuned to short-wavelength radio waves (microwaves) around the 1.5 centimeter wavelength. These sensors can reveal whether or not clouds will give rise to heavy rainfall, snow or hail. Microwave sensors are also useful for locating ice floes in polar regions, making use of the different microwave reflections from land ice, sea ice and open water.

Satellites that send out such pictures are in relatively low orbits, at a height of about 1,000 km (620 miles), and they pass over each part of the Earth once every 12 hours. But to build up a global model of the Earth's weather and climate, meteorologists need continual information on wind speed and direction at various levels in the atmosphere, together with temperature and humidity profiles. This data is provided by geostationary satellites. Cloud photographs taken every half-hour give information on winds, and computers combine this with temperature and humidity soundings to give as complete a model as is possible of the Earth's atmosphere.

Increasing attention is also being paid to the Earth's surface, notably by means of a series of satellites called Landsat (originally ERTS or Earth Resource Technology Satellites), the first of which was launched by the United States in 1972. The third and current Landsat is in a similar pole-to-pole orbit as the weather satellites, but its cameras are more powerful and they make more detailed surveys of the Earth. Landsat rephotographs each part of the Earth's surface every 18 days.

How to map resources

The satellite has two sensor systems: a television camera, which takes pictures of the Earth using visible light; and a device called a multispectral scanner, which scans the Earth at several distinct wavelengths, including visible light and infrared. Data from the various channels of the multispectral scanner can be combined to produce so-called false-color images, in which each wavelength band is assigned a color (not necessarily its real one) to emphasize features of interest.

An important use of Landsat photographs is for making maps, particularly of large countries with remote areas that have never been adequately surveyed from the ground. Several countries, including Brazil, Canada and China, have set up ground stations to receive Landsat data directly. Features previously unknown or incorrectly mapped, including rivers, lakes and glaciers, show up readily on Landsat images. Urban mapping and hence planning are aided by satellite pictures that can distinguish areas of industry, housing and open parkland.

Landsat photographs have also proved invaluable for agricultural land-use planning. They are used for estimates of soil types and for determining land-use patterns. Areas of crop disease or dying vegetation are detectable by their different colors. Yields of certain crops such as wheat can now be accurately predicted from satellite imagery, so that at last it is becoming possible to keep track of the worldwide production of vital food crops. Fresh water, too, is one of our most valuable resources, and knowing its sources and seasonal variation is vital to irrigation projects.

Finally, the geologist and mineral prospector have benefited from remote sensing. Features such as fault lines and different types of sediments and rocks show up clearly on Landsat pictures. This allows geologists to select promising areas in which the prospector can look for mineral deposits.

Another way to study the Earth is by bouncing radar beams off it. Radar sensing indicates the nature of soil or rock on land and movement of water at sea, for example. This was not done by Landsat, but by equipment aboard the United States' Skylab and by a short-lived American satellite called Seasat. The Soviet Union has included Earth surveying in its Salyut program, and resource mapping is also a feature of the spacelab aboard the American space shuttle. All these activities help man to manage the limited resources on our planet and to preserve the environment.

C

41 22 33 24 32 22 19 12 9 13 69 5 3

ral scanner (B) ating mirror ses visible and l radiation on (2). This intensity of into a electronics unit voltage a series of nbers that can computer.

D

The numbers (C) are then transmitted back to a receiving station (D) as a radio frequency at the rate of 15 million units a second. The numbers are translated back into the digital voltage pattern and converted by computer (E) into the equivalent binary numbers, each of which represents a color.

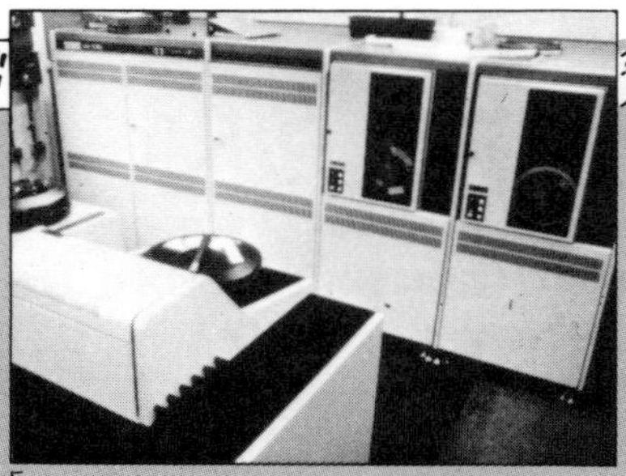

E

F

G

H

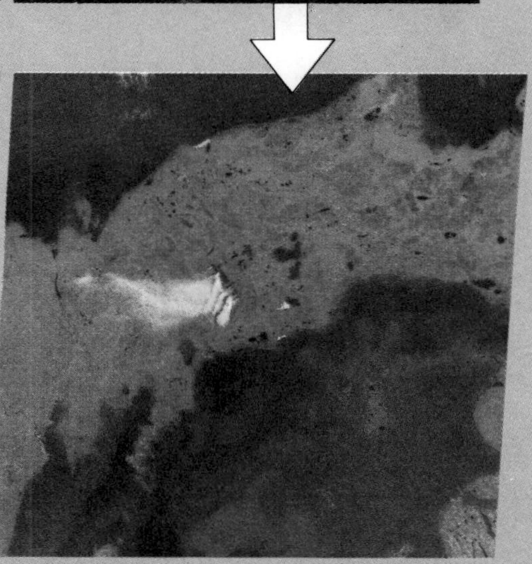

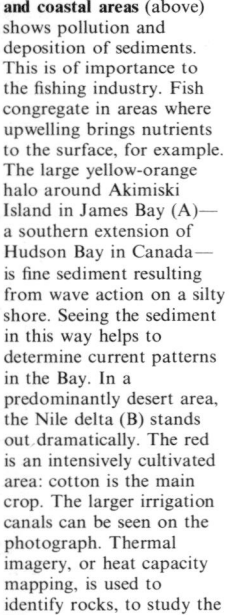

A Landsat image is made up of very many points, each of which is obtained by means of the procedure described above. Each number in the image (F) represents the radiation from a small area of land, or pixel, 0.44 hectares (1.1 acres) in size. A computer then translates the numbers into different colors, or different shades of one color, which are projected on to a TV screen (G) and the image is seen for the first time. Finally, photographs of this false-color image are produced (H). This picture, showing a forest fire in the Upper Peninsula, Michigan, is of use to those engaged in forest management. Other satellite data of use in forestry include types of trees, patterns of growth and the spread of disease.

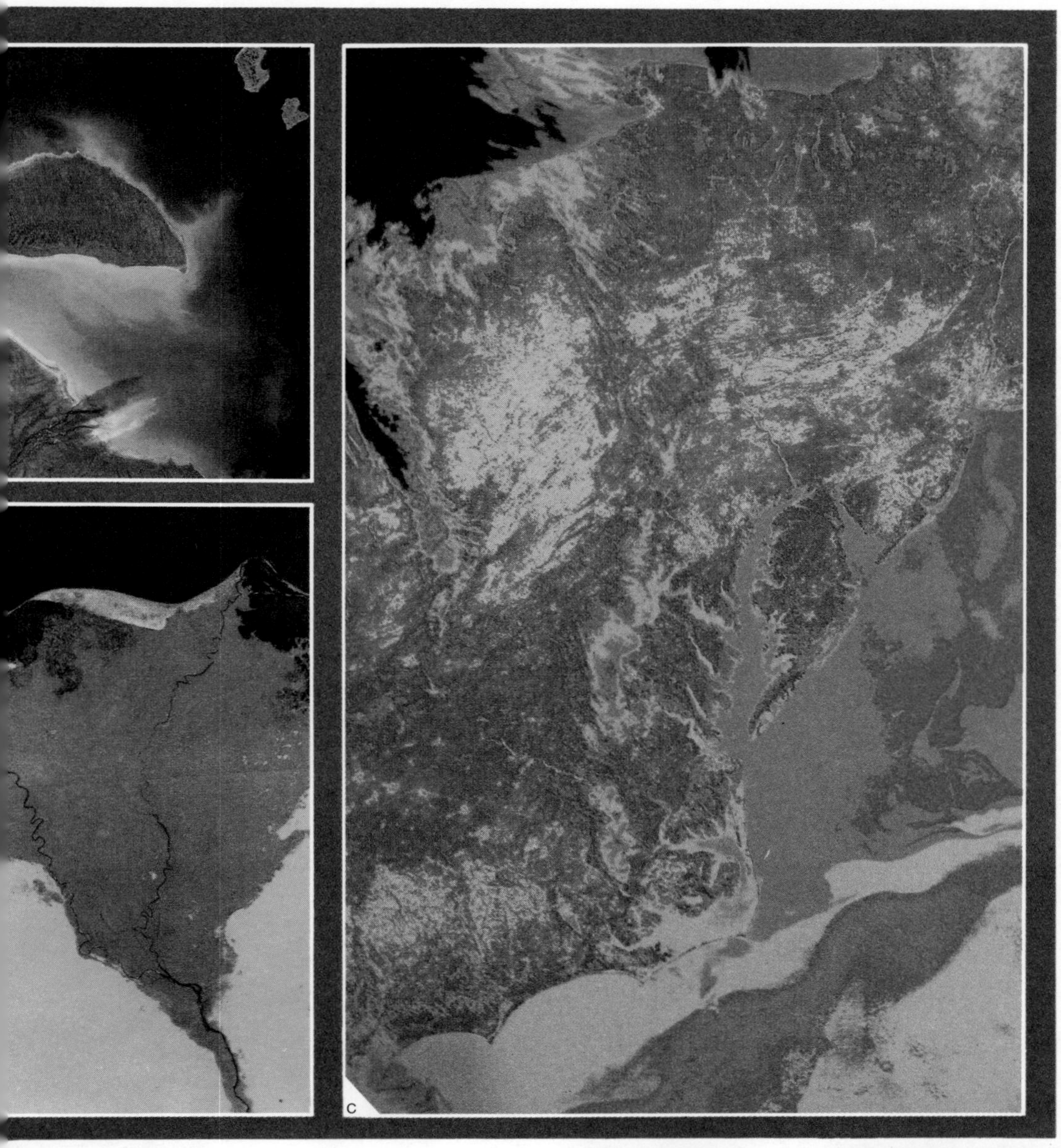

C

Observation of waterways and coastal areas (above) shows pollution and deposition of sediments. This is of importance to the fishing industry. Fish congregate in areas where upwelling brings nutrients to the surface, for example. The large yellow-orange halo around Akimiski Island in James Bay (A)—a southern extension of Hudson Bay in Canada—is fine sediment resulting from wave action on a silty shore. Seeing the sediment in this way helps to determine current patterns in the Bay. In a predominantly desert area, the Nile delta (B) stands out dramatically. The red is an intensively cultivated area: cotton is the main crop. The larger irrigation canals can be seen on the photograph. Thermal imagery, or heat capacity mapping, is used to identify rocks, to study the effects of urban "heat islands," to estimate soil moisture and snow melt, and to map shallow ground water. In this photograph of the northeast coast of North America (C) purple represents the coldest temperatures—in Lakes Erie and Ontario. The coldest parts of the Atlantic Ocean are deep blue, whereas warmer waters near the coast are light blue. Green is the warmer land, but also the Gulf Stream in the lower right part of the image. Brown, yellow and orange represent successively warmer land surface areas. Red is hot regions around cities and coal-mining regions found in eastern Pennsylvania (to the upper left of center in the picture); and, finally, gray and white are the very hottest areas—the urban heat islands of Baltimore, Philadelphia and New York City. Black areas in the upper left are cold clouds. The temperature range of the image is about 30°C (55°F).

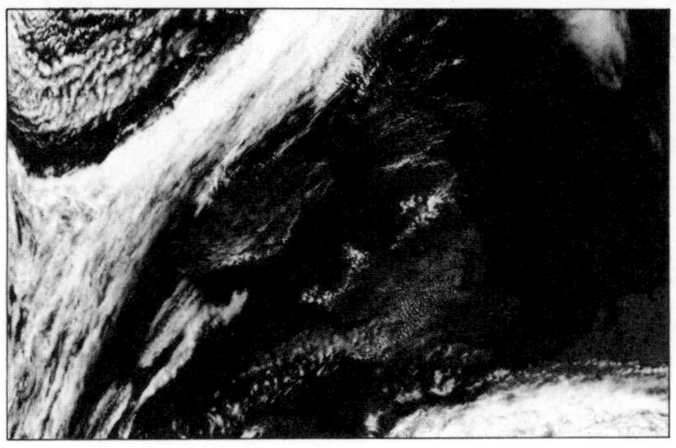

Weather satellite imagery can save lives and property by giving advance warning of bad weather conditions, as well as providing day-to-day forecasts. This Tiros image (left) shows a cold front moving west of Ireland with low-level wave clouds over southern and central England. There are low-pressure systems over northern France and to the northwest of Ireland.

The Earth seen from space shows phases just like the Moon, Mercury and Venus do to us. These dramatic photographs were taken from a satellite moving at 35,885 km (22,300 miles) above South America at 7.30 am (1), 10.30 am (2), noon (3), 3.30 pm (4) and at 10.30 pm (5), and clearly show the Earth in phase.

LANDSAT AND THE FARMER

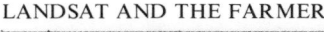

sown
grows
dormant
grows
ripe
harvest
Sep
Oct
Nov
Dec
Jan
Feb
Mar
Apr
May
Jun
Jul
Aug

Agriculturists benefit from "multitemporal analysis" by satellites (left). This is the comparison of data from the same field recorded on two or more dates. It is also able to differentiate crops, which may have an identical appearance, or signature, on one day, but on another occasion exhibit different rates of growth. The pattern of growth is different for small grains than most other crops. A "biowindow" is the period of time in which vegetation is observed. These three biowindows (right) show the emergence and ripening (light blue to red to dark blue) of wheat in May, July and August.

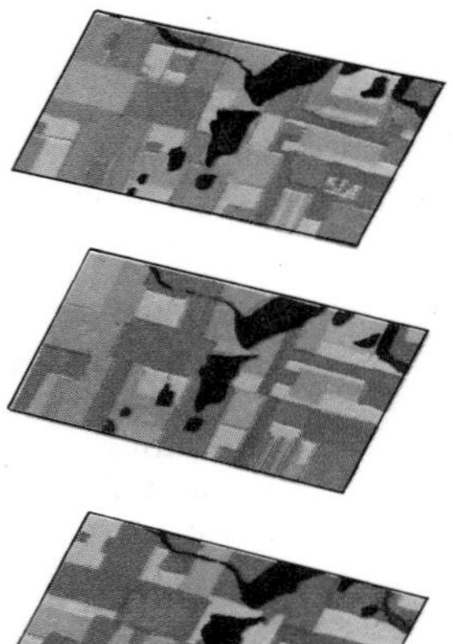

Part 2

MAKING AND SHAPING THE EARTH

The structure and substance of the Earth
Forces that move continents · Forces that fashion Earth's landscapes
How man has changed the face of the Earth

A NEW GEOLOGY

A revolution in geological thinking during the first half of this century transformed man's ideas about the structure of the planet Earth. The science of palaeomagnetism, which studies the magnetic properties of rocks and the history of the Earth's magnetic field, and later the new science of marine geology, contributed greatly to the refinement of theories such as continental drift. Man has even looked beyond the Earth for knowledge of this planet's innermost depths.

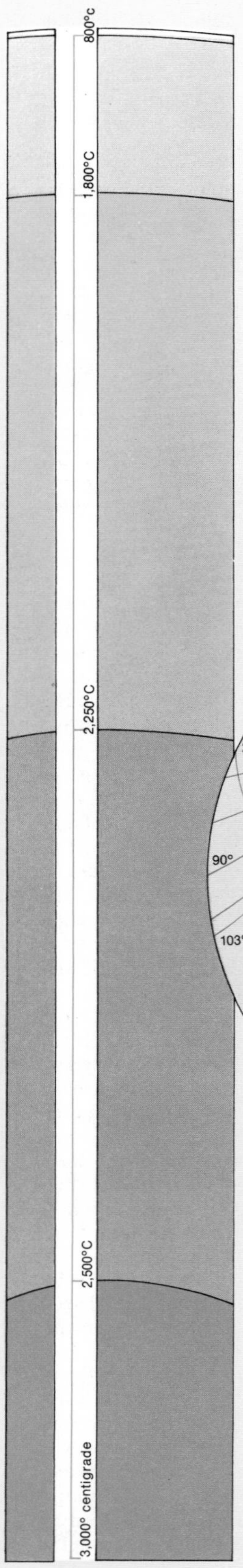

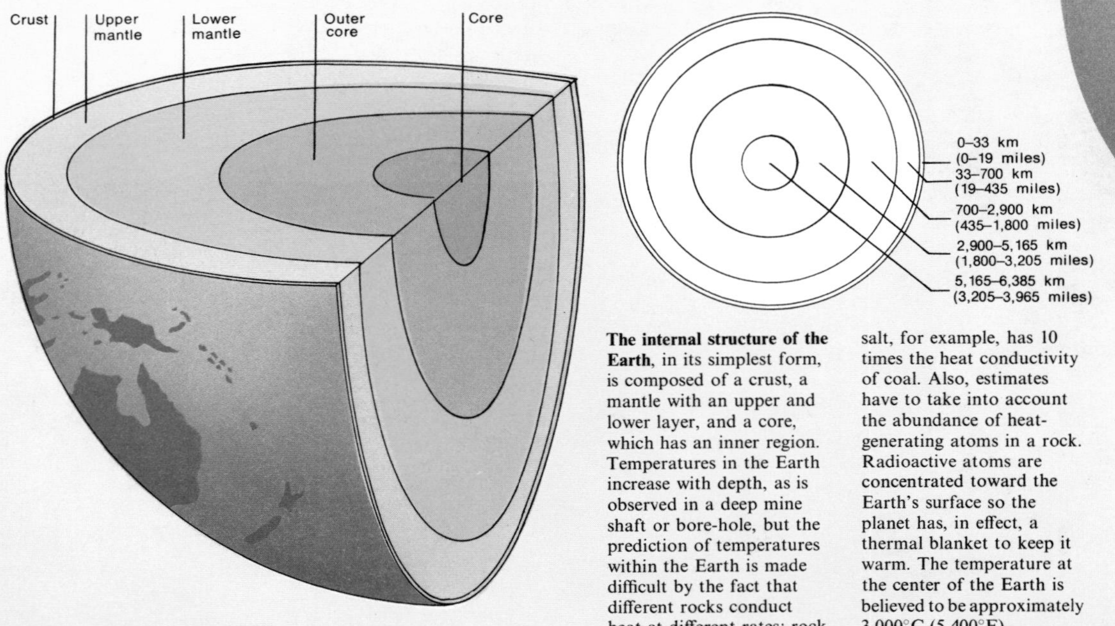

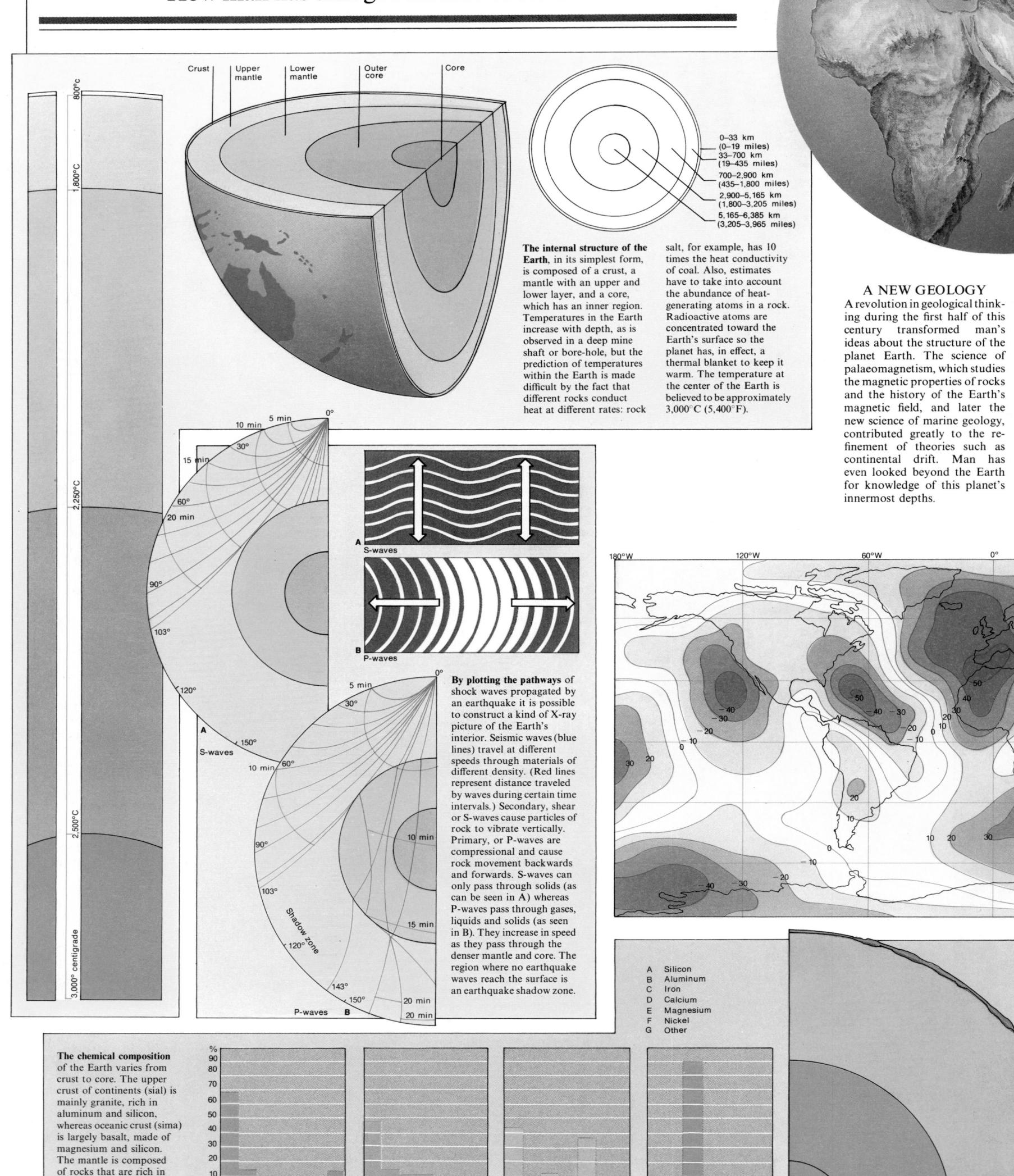

The internal structure of the Earth, in its simplest form, is composed of a crust, a mantle with an upper and lower layer, and a core, which has an inner region. Temperatures in the Earth increase with depth, as is observed in a deep mine shaft or bore-hole, but the prediction of temperatures within the Earth is made difficult by the fact that different rocks conduct heat at different rates: rock salt, for example, has 10 times the heat conductivity of coal. Also, estimates have to take into account the abundance of heat-generating atoms in a rock. Radioactive atoms are concentrated toward the Earth's surface so the planet has, in effect, a thermal blanket to keep it warm. The temperature at the center of the Earth is believed to be approximately 3,000°C (5,400°F).

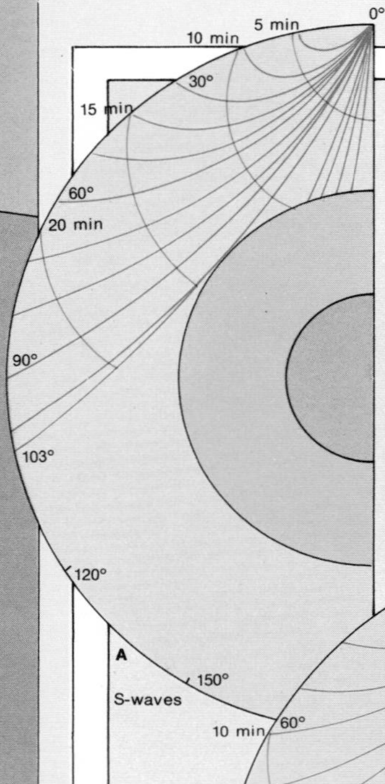

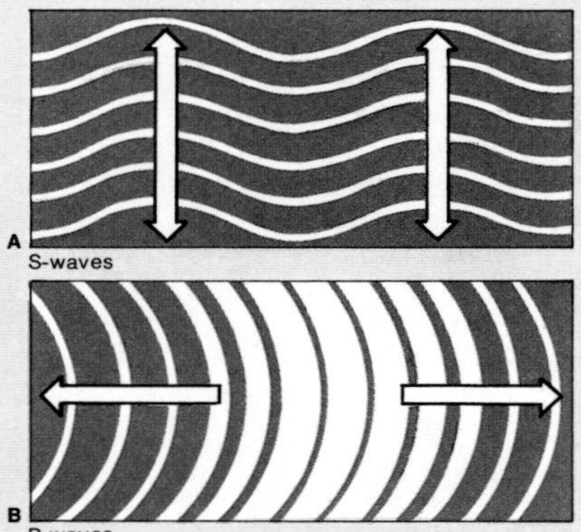

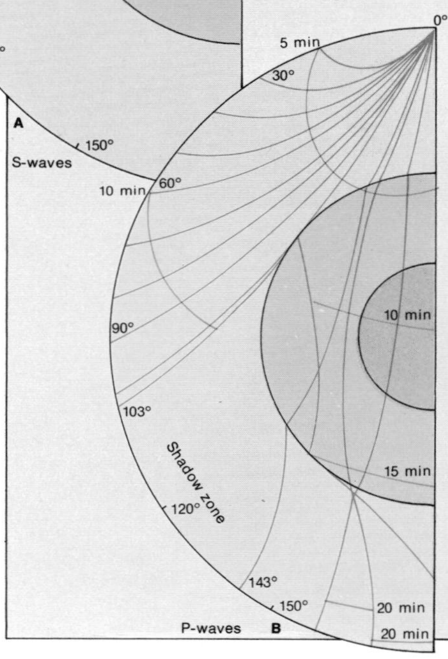

By plotting the pathways of shock waves propagated by an earthquake it is possible to construct a kind of X-ray picture of the Earth's interior. Seismic waves (blue lines) travel at different speeds through materials of different density. (Red lines represent distance traveled by waves during certain time intervals.) Secondary, shear or S-waves cause particles of rock to vibrate vertically. Primary, or P-waves are compressional and cause rock movement backwards and forwards. S-waves can only pass through solids (as can be seen in A) whereas P-waves pass through gases, liquids and solids (as seen in B). They increase in speed as they pass through the denser mantle and core. The region where no earthquake waves reach the surface is an earthquake shadow zone.

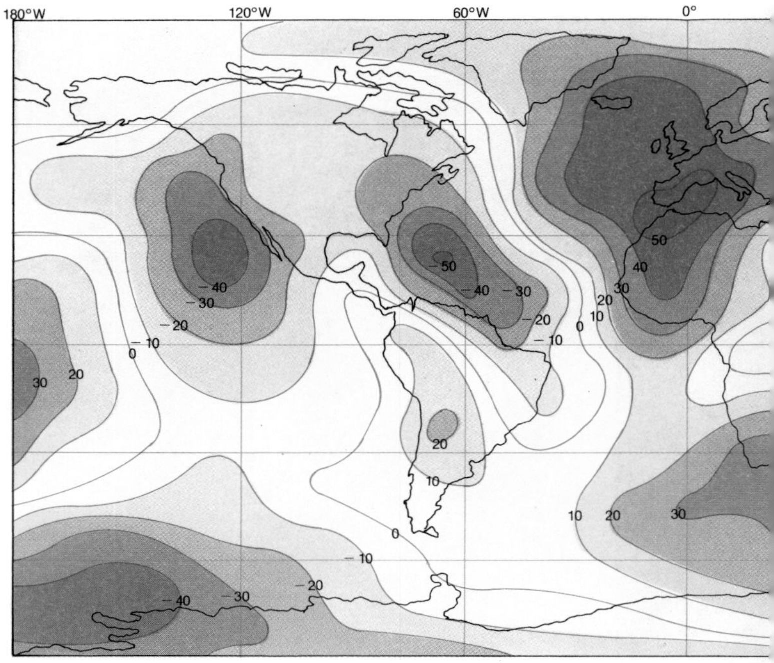

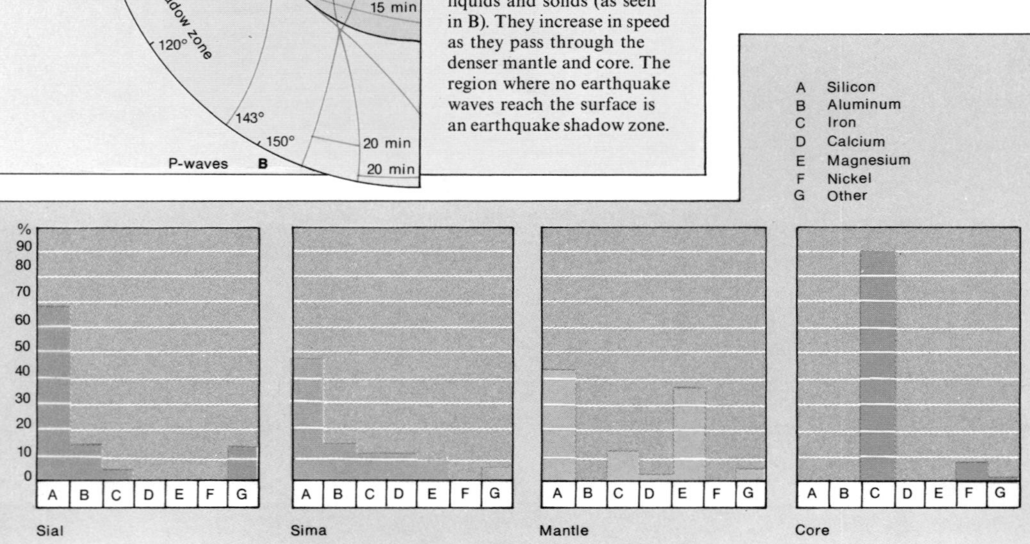

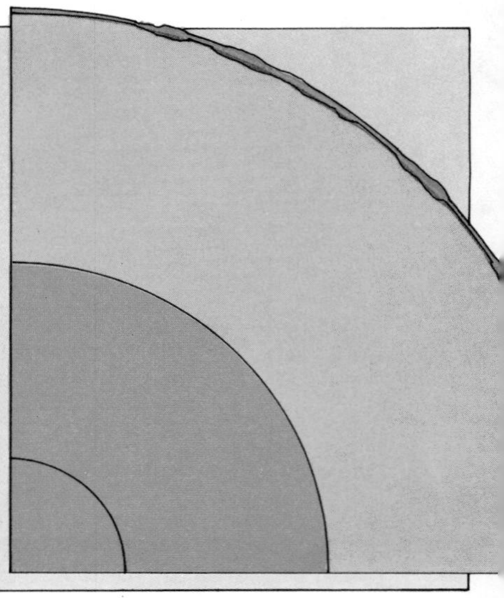

The chemical composition of the Earth varies from crust to core. The upper crust of continents (sial) is mainly granite, rich in aluminum and silicon, whereas oceanic crust (sima) is largely basalt, made of magnesium and silicon. The mantle is composed of rocks that are rich in magnesium and iron silicates, whereas the core, it is believed, is made of iron and nickel oxides.

Earth's Structure

The Earth is made up of concentric shells of different kinds of material. Immediately beneath us is the crust; below that is the mantle; and at the center of the globe is the core. Knowledge of the internal structure of Earth is the key to an understanding of the substances of Earth and an appreciation of the forces at work, not only deep in the center of the planet but also affecting the formation of surface features and large-scale landscapes. The workings of all these elements are inextricably linked.

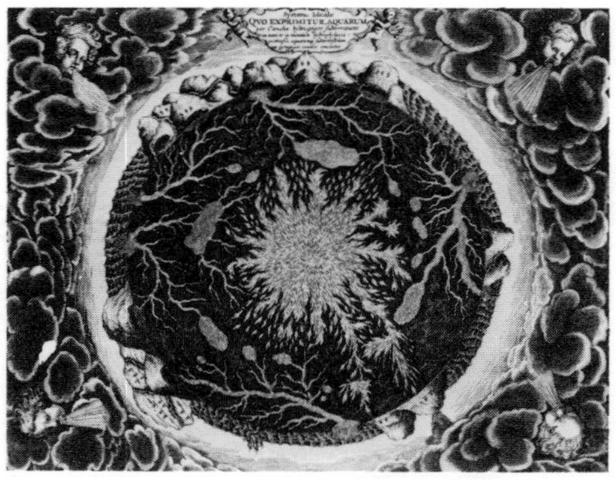

A 17th-century diagram of the Earth shows an internal structure of fire and subterranean rivers.

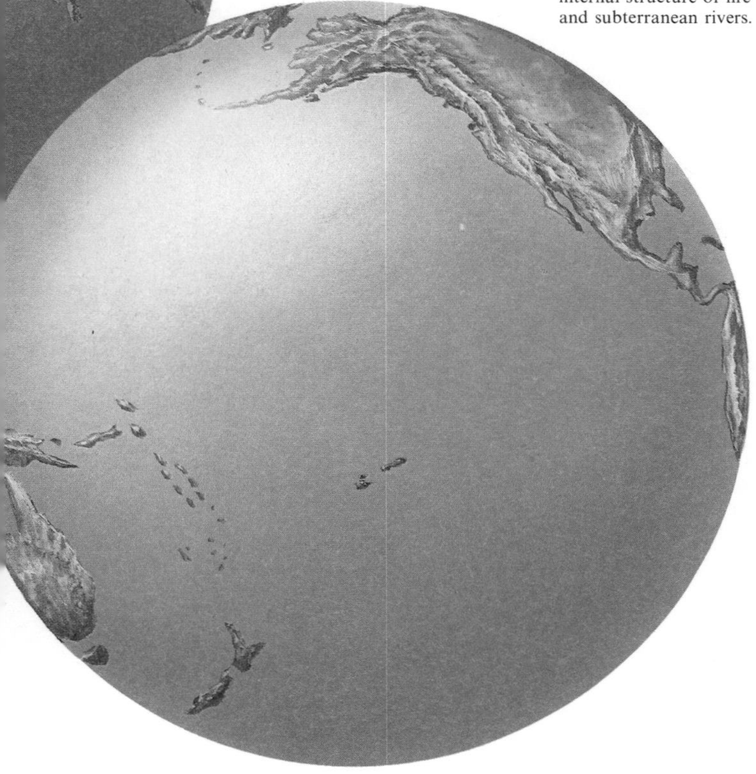

Our knowledge of the Earth is largely restricted to the outer crust. The deepest hole that man has drilled reaches only 10 km (6 miles)—less than 1/600th of the planet's radius—and so our knowledge about the rest of the Earth has had to come via indirect means: by the study of earthquake waves, and a comparison between rocks on Earth and those that make up meteorites—small fragments of asteroids and other minor planetary bodies that originated from similar materials to the Earth.

The Earth's crust

The outermost layer of the Earth is called the crust. The crust beneath the oceans is different from the material that makes up continental crust. Ocean crust is formed at mid-ocean ridges where melted rocks (magma) from the mantle rise up in great quantities and solidify to form a layer a few kilometers thick over the mantle. As this ocean crust spreads out from the ridge it becomes covered with deep-ocean sediments. The ocean crust was initially called "sima," a word made up from the first two letters of the characteristic elements—silicon and magnesium. Sima has a density of 2.9 gm/cc (1 gm/cc is the density of water).

Continental crust was named "sial"—from silicon and aluminum, the most abundant elements. Sial is lighter than sima with a density of 2.7 gm/cc. The continental crust is like a series of giant rafts, 17 to 70 km (9–43 miles) thick. As a result of numerous collisions and breakages, these continental rafts have been bulldozed into their present shape, but they have been forming for at least 4,000 million years. The oldest known rocks, in Greenland, are 3,750 million years old, which is only about 800 million years younger than the Earth itself. The complex history of the continents' evolution over this vast time span makes construction of an ideal cross section difficult, but the rocks of the lower two-thirds of the crust appear to be denser (2.9 gm/cc) than the upper levels.

The Moho, or Mohorovičić discontinuity, discovered in 1909, marks the base of the crust and the beginning of the mantle rocks, where the density increases from 2.9 to 3.3 gm/cc. The Moho is at an average depth of 10 km (6 miles) under the sea and 35 km (20 miles) below land.

The mantle

Our knowledge of the mantle comes from mantle rocks that are sometimes brought to the surface. These are even more enriched in magnesium oxides than the sima, with lesser amounts of iron and calcium oxides. The uppermost mantle to a depth of between 60 and 100 km (40–60 miles), together with the overlying crust, forms the rigid lithosphere, which is divided into plates. Below this is a pasty layer, or asthenosphere, extending to a depth of 700 km (435 miles). The upper mantle is separated from the lower mantle by another discontinuity where the density of the rock increases from 3.3 to 4.3 gm/cc.

Scientists now believe that the mantle is the planetary motor force behind the movements of the continents. By studying in detail the chemistry of the volcanic rocks that have come directly from the mantle, they have gathered much information about this mantle motor. The rocks that come up along oceanic ridges and form new oceanic crust reveal by their chemical composition that they have formed from mantle that has undergone previous melting. By contrast, islands such as Hawaii and Iceland have formed from mantle material that, for the most part, has never been melted before. One explanation for these chemical observations is that, while the top 700 km (435 miles) of the mantle region is moving in accordance with movement of the plates, the mantle beneath it is moving independently and sending occasional rivers of unaltered material through the surface to form islands like volcanic Hawaii.

The core

Structurally, the most important boundary in the Earth lies at a depth of 2,900 km (1,800 miles) below the surface, where the rock density almost doubles from about 5.5 to 9.9 gm/cc. This is known as the Gutenberg discontinuity and was discovered in 1914. Below this level the material must have the properties of a liquid since certain earthquake waves cannot penetrate it. Scientists infer from the composition of meteorites, some of which are composed of iron and nickel, that this deep core material is composed largely of iron, with some nickel and perhaps lighter elements such as silicon. The processes involved in the formation of a planet have been compared to the separation of the metals (the core) from the slag (the mantle and crust) in a blast furnace.

The core has a radius of 3,485 km (2,165 miles) and makes up only one-sixth of the Earth's volume, yet it has one-third of its mass. In the middle of the liquid outer core there is an even denser ball with a radius of 1,220 km (760 miles)—two-thirds the size of the Moon—where, under intense pressure, the metals have solidified. The inner core is believed to be solid iron and nickel and is 20 percent denser (12–13 gm/cc) than the surrounding liquid.

Electric currents in the core are the only possible source of the Earth's magnetic field. This drifts and alters in a way which could arise only from some deeply buried fluid movement. At the top of the core, the pattern of the field moves about 100 m (330 ft) west each day. Every million years or so during the Earth's history, the north–south magnetic poles have switched so that compasses pointed south, not north.

The dynamo that generates magnetism and its strange variations is still not fully understood. Motion in the core may be powered by giant slabs of metal that crystallize out from the liquid and sink to join the inner core. Our knowledge of the Earth's structure has increased greatly over the last 50 years, but many intriguing questions remain to be answered.

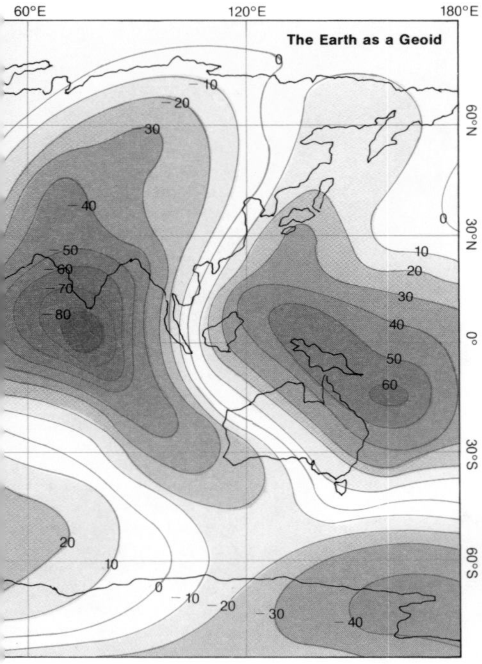
60°E
120°E
180°E
The Earth as a Geoid
60°N
30°N
0°
30°S
60°S

The Earth is not a sphere but an ellipsoid (below) that is flattened at the poles, where the radius is 6,378 km (3,960 miles), and bulging at the Equator, where the radius is 6,536 km (4,060 miles). This results from the Earth's rapid rotation. But, rather than a perfect ellipsoid, the true shape is a "geoid"—the actual shape of sea level—which is lumpy, with variations away from ellipsoid of up to 80 m (260 ft) (left). This reflects major variations in density in Earth's outer layers.

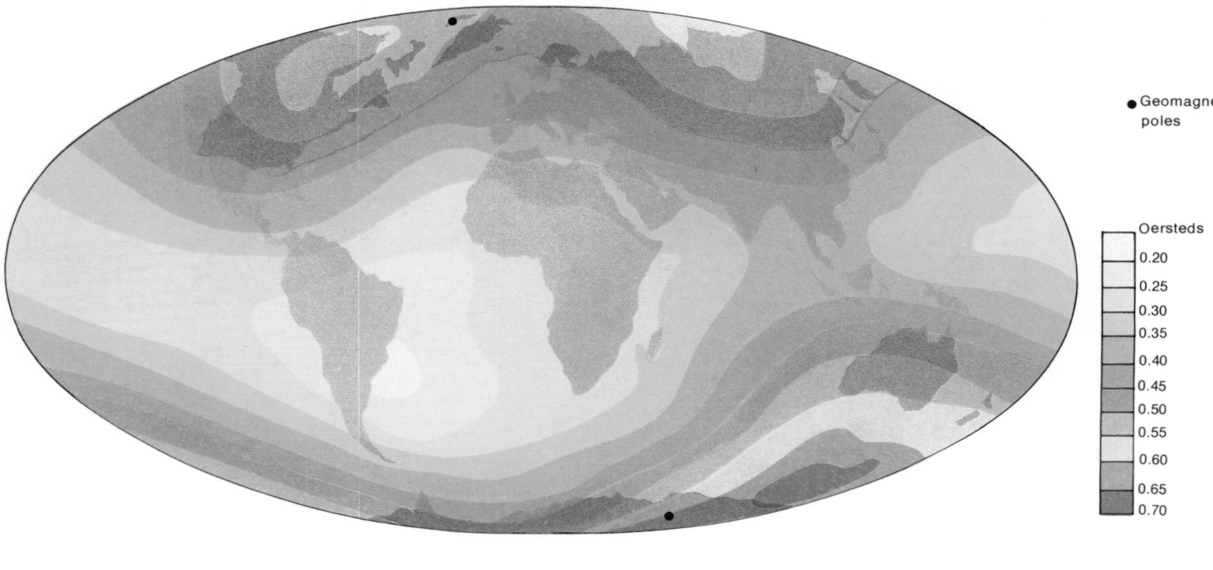
Geomagnetic poles
Oersteds
0.20
0.25
0.30
0.35
0.40
0.45
0.50
0.55
0.60
0.65
0.70

The Earth's magnetic field is strongest at the poles and weakest in equatorial regions. If the field were simply like a bar magnet inside the globe, lines of intensity would mirror lines of latitude; but the field is inclined at an angle of 11° to the Earth's axis. The geomagnetic poles are similarly inclined and they do not coincide with the geographic poles. In reality, the field is much more complex than that of a bar magnet. In addition, over long periods of time, the magnetic poles and the north–south orientation of the field change slowly. The strength of the Earth's magnetic field is measured in units called oersteds.

Earth's Moving Crust

The top layer of the Earth is known as the lithosphere and is composed of the crust and the uppermost mantle. It is divided into six major rigid plates and several smaller platelets that move relative to each other, driven by movements that lie deep in the Earth's liquid mantle. The plate boundaries correspond to the zones of earthquakes and the sites of active volcanoes. The concept of plate tectonics – that the Earth's crust is mobile despite being rigid – emerged in the 1960s and helped to confirm the early twentieth-century theory of continental drift proposed by Alfred Wegener.

THE DYNAMIC EARTH

As early as the 17th century, the English philosopher Francis Bacon noted that the coasts on either side of the Atlantic were similar and could be fitted together like pieces of a jigsaw puzzle. Three hundred years later Alfred Wegener proposed the theory of continental drift, but no one would believe the Earth's rigid crust could move. Today, geological evidence has provided the basis for the theory of plate tectonics, which demonstrates that the Earth's crust is slowly but continually moving.

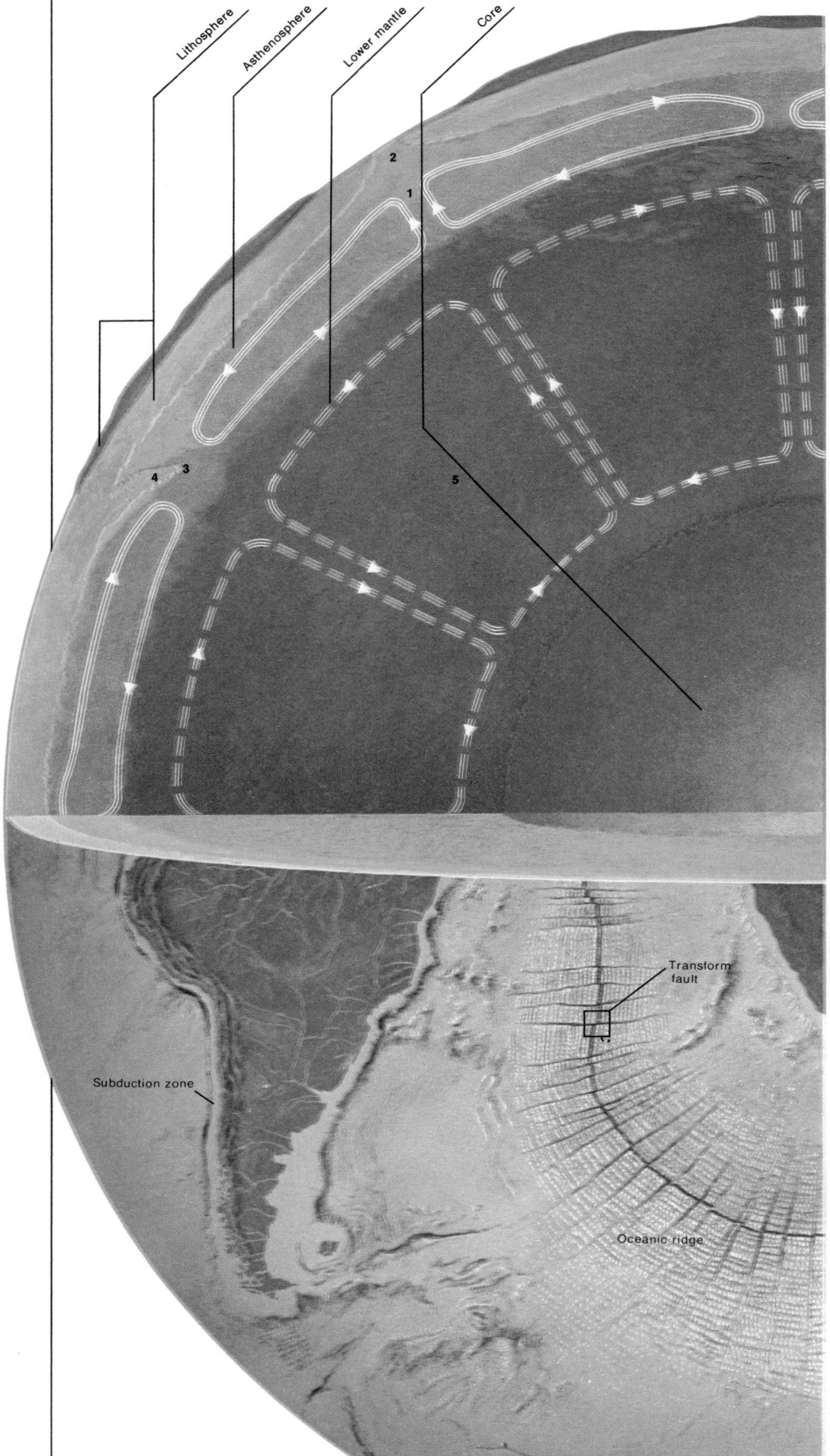

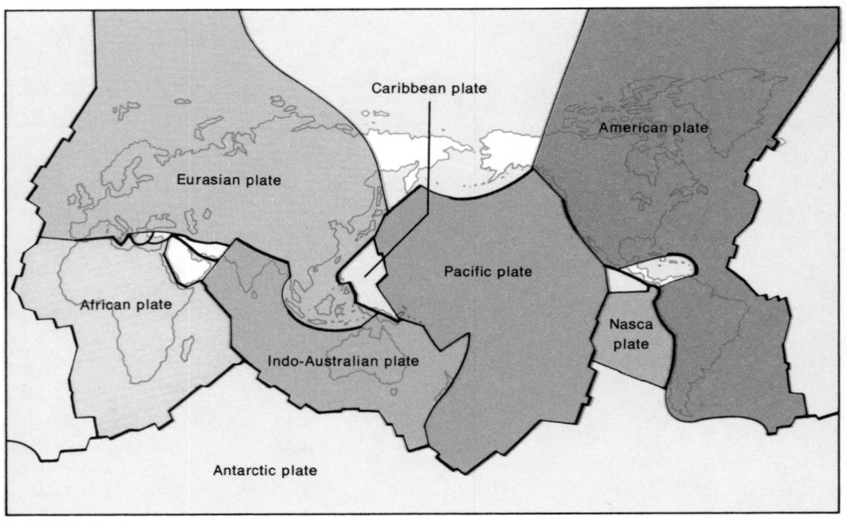

Earth's lithosphere—the rocky shell, or crust—is made up of six major plates and several smaller platelets, each separated from each other by ridges, subduction zones or transcurrent faults. The plates grow bigger by accretion along the mid-ocean ridges, are destroyed at subduction zones beneath the trenches, and slide beside each other along the transcurrent faults. The African and Antarctic plates have no trenches along their borders to destroy any of their crust, so they are growing bigger. This growth is compensated by the subduction zone that is developing to the north of the Tonga Islands and subduction zones in the Pacific. Conversely, the Pacific and Indo-Australian plates are shrinking. Along the plate boundaries magma wells up from the mantle to form volcanoes. Here, too, are the origins of earthquakes as the plates collide or slide slowly past each other.

Subduction zones are the sites of destruction of the ocean crust. As one plate passes beneath another down into the mantle, the ocean floor is pulled downward and a deep ocean trench is formed. The movement taking place along the length of the subduction zone causes earthquakes, while melting of the rock at depth produces magma that rises to create the volcanoes that form island arcs.

An oceanic ridge is formed when two plates move away from each other. As they move, molten magma from the mantle forces its way to the surface. This magma cools and is in turn injected with new magma. Thus the oceanic ridge is gradually forming the newest part of Earth's crust.

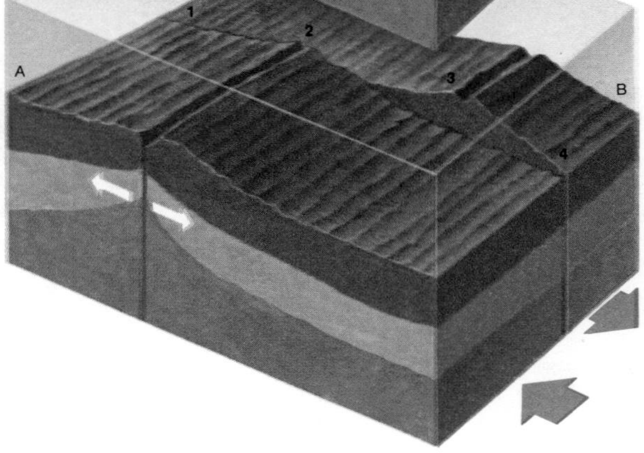

Transform, or transcurrent, faults are found where two plates slide past each other. They may, for example, link two parts of a ridge (A, B). A study of the magnetic properties of the seabed may suggest a motion shown by the white arrows, but the true movements of the plates are shown by the red arrows. The transform fault is active only between points (2) and (3). Between points (1) and (2) and between (3) and (4) the scar of the fault is healed and the line of the fault is no longer a plate boundary.

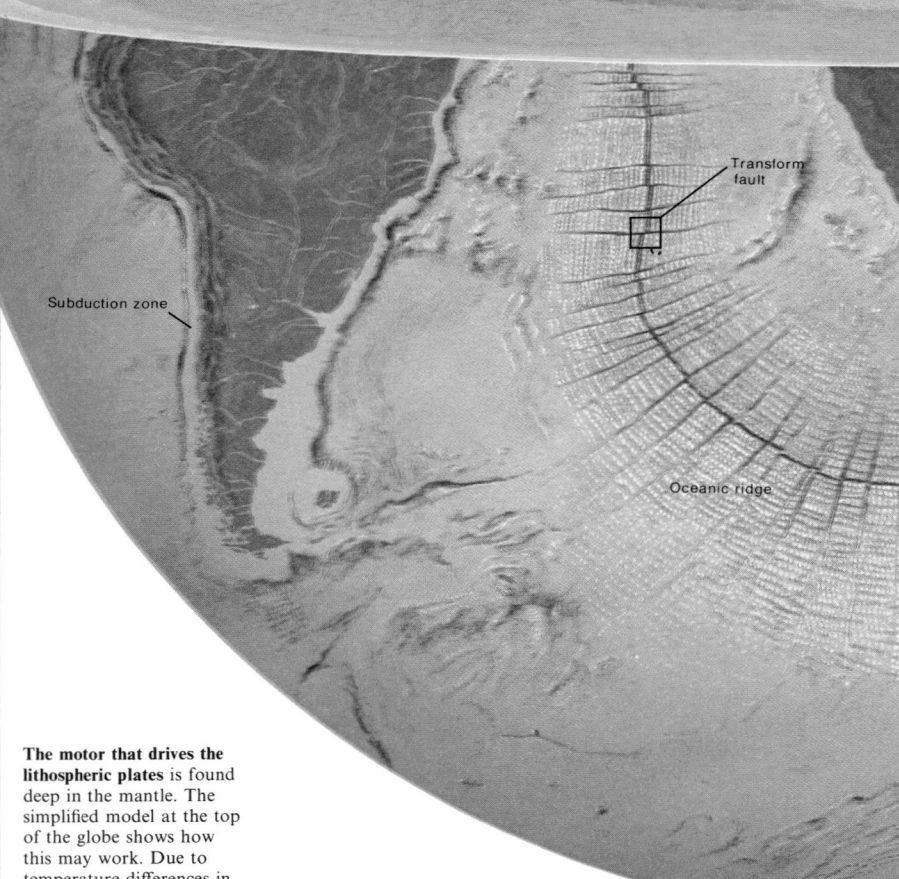

The motor that drives the lithospheric plates is found deep in the mantle. The simplified model at the top of the globe shows how this may work. Due to temperature differences in the mantle, slow convection currents circulate. Where two current cycles move upwards together and separate (1), the plates bulge and move apart along mid-ocean ridges (2). Where there is a downward moving current (3), the plates move together and sometimes one slips under the other to form a subduction zone (4). Another model proposes that the convection currents are found deep in the mantle (5). Only time and more research, however, will reveal the true mechanism of plate movement.

The early evidence for continental drift was gathered by Alfred Wegener, a German meteorologist. He noticed that the coastlines on each side of the Atlantic Ocean could be made to fit together, and that much of the geological history of the flanking continents—shown by fossils, structures and past climates—also seemed to match. Wegener compared the two sides of the Atlantic with a sheet of torn newspaper and reasoned that if not just one line of print but 10 lines match then there is a good case for arguing that the two sides were once joined. Yet for 50 years continental drift was generally considered to be a fanciful dream.

Seafloor spreading

In the 1950s the first geological surveys of the oceans began, and a 60,000 km (37,200 mile) long chain of mountains was discovered running down the center of the Atlantic Ocean, all round the Antarctic, up to the Indian Ocean, into the Red Sea and up the Eastern Pacific Ocean into Alaska. Along the axis of this mid-ocean ridge system there was often a narrow, deep rift valley. In places this ridge was offset along sharp fractures in the ocean floor.

The breakthrough in developing the global plate tectonic theory came with the first large-scale survey of the ocean floor. Magnetometers, which were developed during World War II for tracking submarines, showed the ocean floor to be magnetically striped. The ocean floor reveals magnetic characteristics because the ocean crust basalts are full of tiny crystals of the magnetic mineral magnetite. As the basalt cooled, the magnetic field of these crystals aligned itself with the Earth's magnetic field. This would be insignificant if it were not for the fact that the magnetic pole of the Earth has switched from north to south at different times in the past. Half the magnetite compasses of the ocean floor point south rather than north.

In the middle 1960s, two Cambridge geophysicists, Drummond Matthews and Fred Vine, noticed that the pattern of stripes was symmetrical around the mid-ocean ridge. Such an extraordinary and unlikely symmetry could mean only one thing—any two matching stripes must originally have been formed together at the mid-ocean ridge and then moved away from each other as newer crust formed between them to create new stripes. It was soon calculated that the North Atlantic Ocean was growing wider by about 2 cm ($\frac{3}{4}$ in) a year. At last, drifting continents was accepted.

Consumption of the seafloor

Seafloor spreading soon became included in an even more sensational model—plate tectonics. If the oceans are growing wider, then either the whole planet is expanding or the spreading ocean floor is consumed elsewhere. In the late 1950s a global network of seismic stations had been set up to monitor nuclear explosions and earthquakes. For the first time the positions of all earthquakes could be accurately defined.

It was found that the zones of earthquake activity were predominantly narrow, following the mid-ocean ridges and extending along the rim of the Pacific, beneath the island arcs of the West Pacific and beneath the continental margins in the East Pacific as well as underlying the Alpine-Himalayan Mountain Belt. The seismic zones around the Pacific dipped away from the ocean and continued to depths as great as 700 km (430 miles). They intercepted the surface at the curious arc-shaped deep-ocean trenches. It had been known for 20 years that the pull of gravity over these trenches is strangely reduced, so to survive they must continually be dragged downwards. Here was the site of ocean-floor consumption—now known as a subduction zone. Subduction zones must be efficient at consuming ocean crust because no known ocean crust is older than 200 million years—less than five percent of Earth's lifetime.

The oceanic lithosphere (the Earth's rocky crust) is extraordinarily rigid. Even where the oceanic lithosphere becomes consumed within subduction zones it still maintains its rigidity. As it bends down into the Earth it tends to corrugate, forming very long folds. These corrugations give rise to the pattern of chains of deep-ocean trenches and chains of volcanic islands formed above the subduction zone.

As oceanic lithosphere grows older it cools, contracts and sinks. From the depth of the ocean floor it is possible to make an accurate estimate of the age of the crust beneath. Even the steepness of the subduction zone is a function of the age, and therefore the density, of the lithosphere. The oldest crust provides the strongest downward pull and hence the steepest angle of dip of the subduction zone.

As well as the spreading ridges (constructive margins) and the subduction zones (destructive margins) there is another kind of plate boundary (conservative margins), where the plates slip past one another along a major fault such as the San Andreas Fault of California.

The past positions of the continents

Continental drift is thus the result of the creation and destruction of oceanic lithosphere, but only the continents can record the oceanic plate motions taking place more than 200 million years ago. The discovery of ancient lines of subduction zone volcanoes can testify to the destruction of long-gone oceans. One particularly important technique for finding the positions of the continents is to study the magnetism of certain rocks, particularly lavas, that record the position of the north–south magnetic poles at the time when the rock cooled. If the rock "compass" points, for example, west, then the continent must have rotated by 90°. The vertical dip of the rock compass can reveal the approximate latitude of the rock at its formation (the dip increases from horizontal at the Equator to vertical at the magnetic poles).

As longitude is entirely arbitrary (defined on the position of Greenwich) one can only hope to gain the relative positions of the continents with regard to one another. The best additional information is provided by studies of fossils—if the remains of shallow-water marine organisms are very different they must have been separated by an ocean. The full impact of continental drift on the development of land animals and plants is only beginning to be realized.

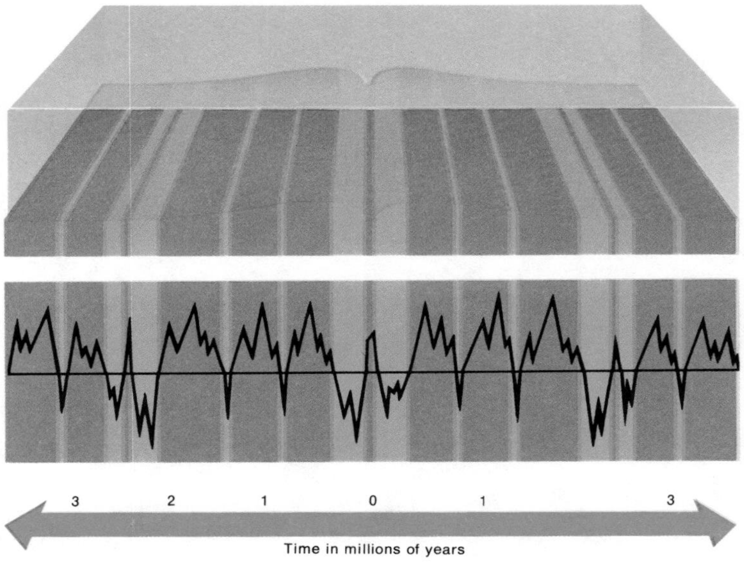

Magnetic surveys of the seabed helped build the plate tectonics theory. Research vessels equipped with magnetometers sailed back and forth over a mid-ocean ridge and recorded the varying magnetism of the seabed. The Earth's magnetic pole has switched from north to south at different times in the past, and this mapping revealed a striped magnetic pattern on the seabed. It was noticed that the stripes on either side of the ridge were symmetrical. The explanation was that the matching stripes must have formed together and moved apart as more crust was injected between them—a notion that was subsequently supported by dating of the seafloor.

THE DRIFTING CONTINENTS

It is now accepted that the continents have changed their positions during the past millions of years, and by studying the magnetism preserved in the rocks the configuration of the continents has been plotted for various geological times. The sequence of continental drifting, illustrated below, begins with one single landmass—the so-called supercontinent Pangaea—and the ancestral Pacific Ocean, called the Panthalassa Ocean. Pangaea first split into a northern landmass called Laurasia and a southern block called Gondwanaland, and subsequently into the continents we see today. The maps illustrate the positions of the continents in the past, where they are now and their predicted positions in 50 million years' time.

225 million years ago one large landmass, the supercontinent Pangaea, exists and Panthalassa forms the ancestral Pacific Ocean. The Tethys Sea separates Eurasia and Africa and forms an ancestor of the Mediterranean Sea.

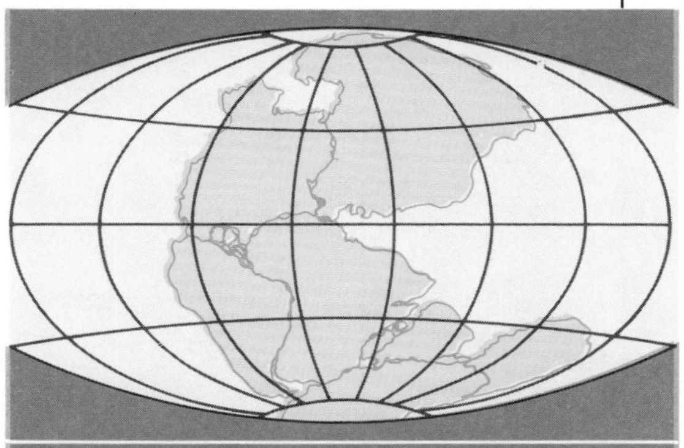

180 million years ago Pangaea splits up, the northern block of continents, Laurasia, drifts northwards and the southern block, Gondwanaland, begins to break up. India separates and the South American–African block divides from Australia–Antarctica. New ocean floor is created between the continents.

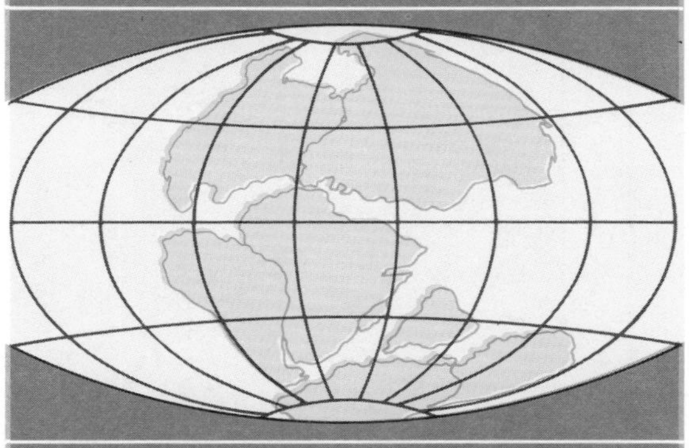

135 million years ago the Indian plate continues its northward drift and Eurasia rotates to begin to close the eastern end of the Tethys Sea. The North Atlantic and the Indian Ocean have opened up and the South Atlantic is just beginning to form.

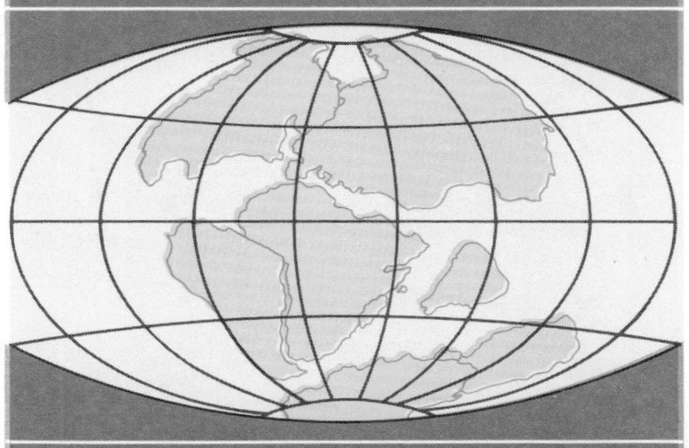

65 million years ago Madagascar has split from Africa and the Tethys Sea has closed, with the Mediterranean Sea opening behind it. The South Atlantic Ocean has opened up considerably, but Australia is still joined to the Antarctic and India is about to collide with Asia.

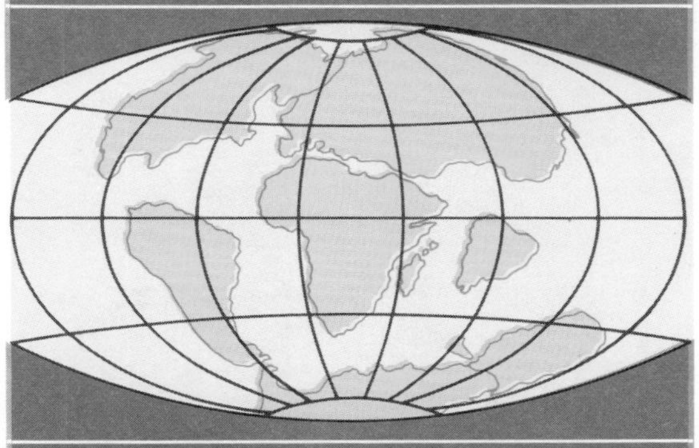

The present day: India has completed its northward migration and collided with Asia, Australia has set itself free from Antarctica, and North America has freed itself from Eurasia to leave Greenland between them. During the past 65 million years (a relatively short geological span of time) nearly half of the present-day ocean floor has been created.

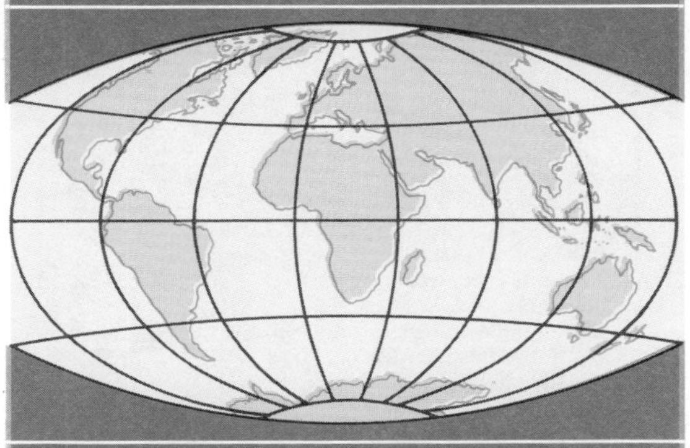

50 million years in the future, Australia may continue its northward drift, part of East Africa will separate from the mainland, and California west of the San Andreas Fault will separate from North America and move northwards. The Pacific Ocean will become smaller, compensating for the increase in size of both the Atlantic and Indian oceans. The Mediterranean Sea will disappear as Africa moves to the north.

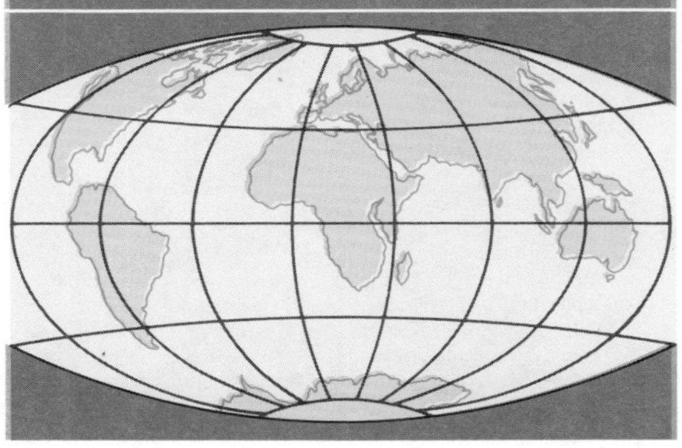

Folds, Faults and Mountain Chains

The continents are great rafts of lighter rock that float in the mantle of the Earth. When drifting continents collide, great mountain chains are thrown up as the continental crust is forced to thicken to absorb the impact of the collision. The highest mountains are formed out of thick piles of sediment that are built up from the debris of erosion constantly washed off the land and deposited on the continental margins. Through the massive deformations of rock faults and folds these remains of old mountains become recycled, thus building new mountains from the remains of old ones.

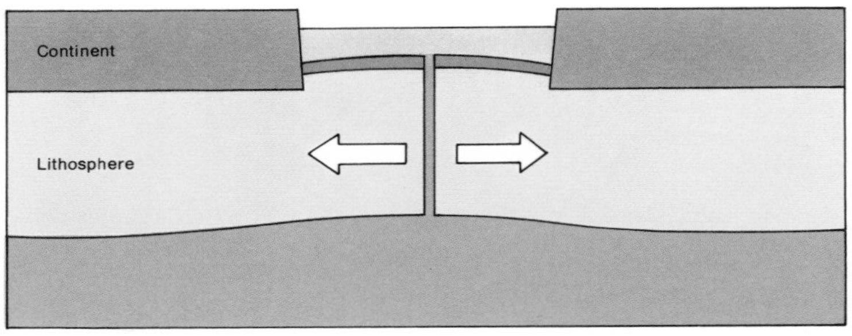

For the formation of mountain ranges such as the Appalachians or the Himalayas, or the Caledonian mountain chain of Norway, Scotland and Newfoundland, the pattern of development is very much the same. First, a widening ocean with passive margins is located between two continents.

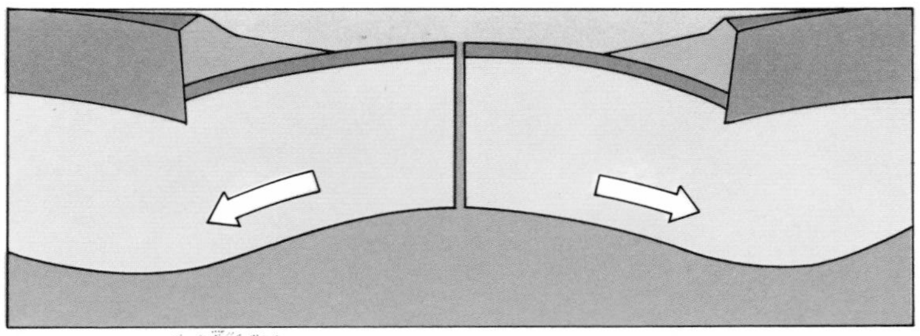

As more ocean floor is created the continents move farther apart, and at the edge of each continent sediment accumulates from the debris of erosion. These piles of thick sediment are known as sedimentary basins.

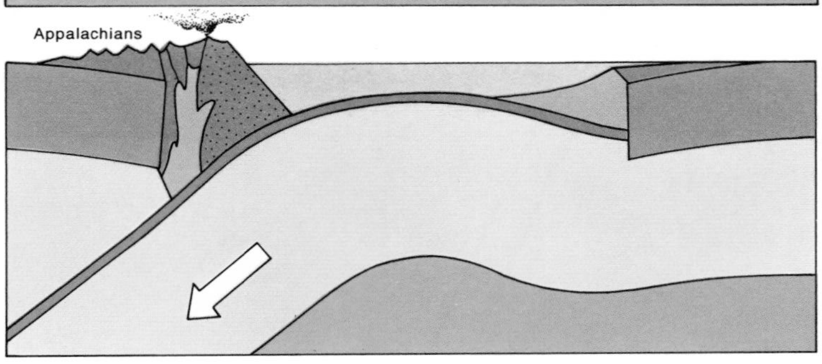

For the formation of the Appalachians, the ancestral Atlantic Ocean began to close, a subduction zone was formed at the ocean–continent boundary, and the oceanic lithosphere began to be absorbed into the mantle. Magma intruded to form granite "plutons" and volcanoes, and much of the sedimentary basin was metamorphosed.

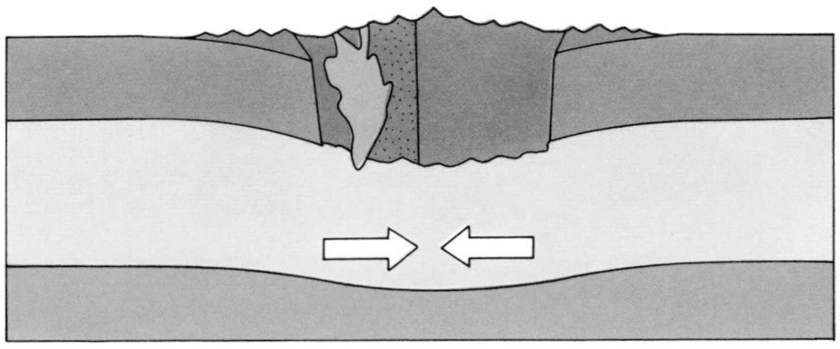

The ocean continued to close until North America and Africa were joined together, further compressing the sediments in the sedimentary basin at the passive ocean margin. The two continents were joined like this between 350 and 225 million years ago.

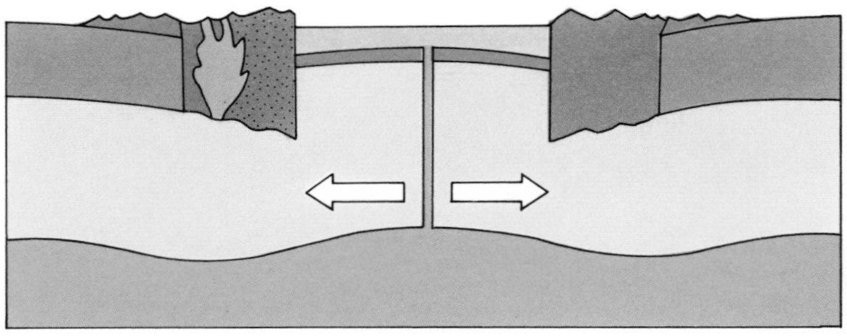

About 180 million years ago, after the original Appalachians had been worn down in size, the present Atlantic Ocean opened along a new break in the continental crust, offset from the line of the original mountains. As the continents split, so the crust became stretched along great curved faults.

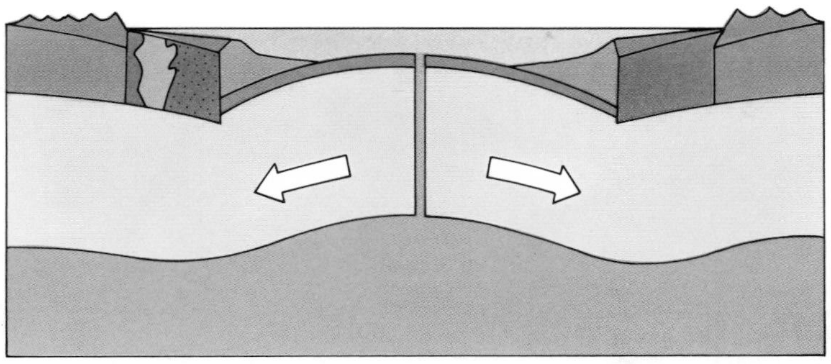

Parts of the ancient Appalachian mountains have been eroded to sea level, leaving the Appalachians, that formed on the edge of the old continent, inland.

Continental shelf
Granite
Metamorphic rock
Sediment
Ocean crust

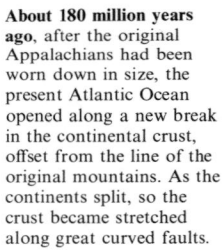

BIRTH AND DEATH OF A MOUNTAIN

Mountains are thrust upward by the pressure exerted by the moving plates of the Earth's crust, and are formed out of the sediments that have been eroded from the continental masses. Young mountains are lofty and much folded, but the agents of erosion and weathering soon begin to reduce their height, and over many millions of years the mountain range is eroded to sea level. This eroded material accumulates in the sea at the edge of the continents and becomes the building material for another phase of mountain building.

1

ISOSTASY

The continents float in the Earth's mantle, and because they are only slightly less dense (2.67 g/cc compared to 3.27 g/cc), 85% of their bulk lies below sea level. Thus the higher the mountain the deeper the mountain root. And as the crust can exist only to a maximum depth of about 70 km (43 miles) before it is liquefied in the mantle, mountains can never rise above a maximum of 10 km (6 miles) above sea level.

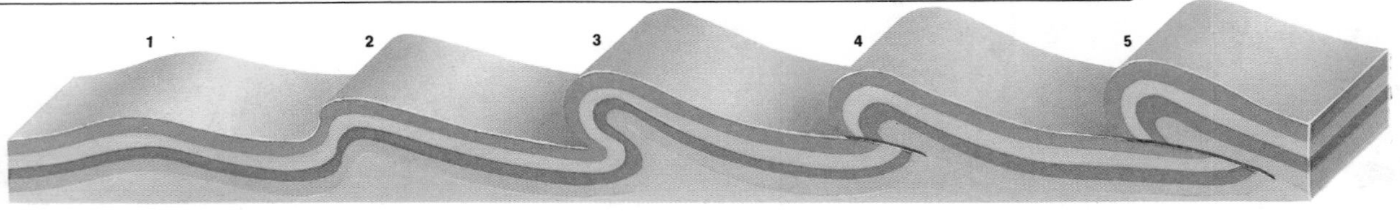

Folds are generally related to underlying faults. The commonest simple folds are monoclines, formed when a single fault exhibits underlying movement. With continued movement a simple symmetrical anticline (1) may fold unevenly to form an asymmetric anticline (2). More movement bends the strata further into a recumbent fold (3) and eventually the strata break to form an overthrust fold (4). Over a long period an overthrust fold may be pushed many kilometers from its original position to form a nappe (5). Faults are generally of three kinds: faults of tension known as normal faults, when one block drops down (6); faults of horizontal shear (7), known as strike-slip faults; and faults of compression (8), known as thrust faults.

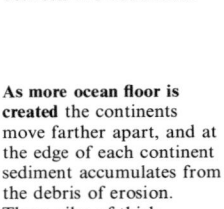

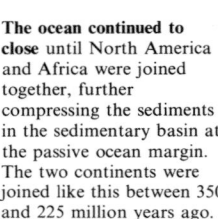

The highest mountains are the product of continental collisions. As the rocks are squeezed, folded and faulted, the original continental crust becomes shortened and thickened. Although the overall extent and height of mountain chains is controlled by mountain building, the whole range can only be viewed from a spacecraft. For the earthbound mountain visitor the familiar shapes of peaks and valleys are those formed by mountain destruction (1). Snow at high altitudes consolidates to form ice that moves slowly downhill in the form of glaciers. To wear away a mountain range at an average of 5 km (3 miles) above sea level requires the removal of more than 20 km (12 miles) of rock, as the thick continental crust that floats in the underlying mantle rises to compensate for the loss of surface mass. Half-eroded mountains (2), such as the Appalachians, pictured above, may linger on for tens of millions of years until, like large regions of the Canadian interior, the mountains are all eroded away and only the hard crystalline surface rocks that were once buried 20 km (12 miles) underground remain (3).

2

3

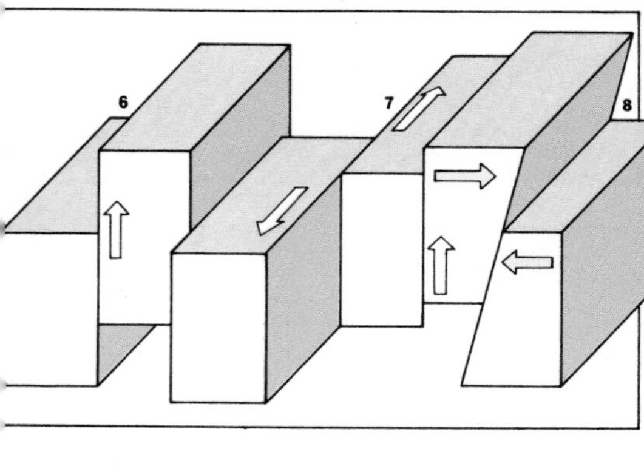

Continents float in the Earth's mantle like icebergs in the sea—more than four-fifths of their bulk lies beneath the surface. The continental crust is 28 km (17 miles) thick at sea level, and where mountains rise above this level there is a corresponding thickening in the crust beneath. The maximum thickness of crust is 70 km (43 miles), so mountains can only ever rise to a maximum height of approximately 10 km (6 miles) above sea level. This relation between upper and underlying crust is known as isostasy, or state of equal pressure.

As mountains become eroded, the process of isostatic rebound allows them to recover about 85 cm (34 in) for every 1 meter (40 in) removed. When, after about 100 million years, a major mountain range has been eroded down to sea level, the rocks exposed at the surface are those that were 15–25 km (9–15 miles) underground when the mountains were at their highest. Such rocks are coarsely crystalline, and make up the fabric of the old, tough continental crust.

Sedimentary basins

As early as the nineteenth century it was noticed that the biggest mountains formed where there had previously been the thickest pile of sediments. According to the principle of isostasy, a thick pile of sediments can form only where the Earth's crust is thin and sinking. The Aegean Sea in the eastern Mediterranean, for example, is at present being pulled apart, and therefore becoming thinner. Over the next few million years, as the Aegean crust sinks, a thick pile of sediments—a sedimentary basin—will accumulate. Most sedimentary basins are at present shallow seas, and form the continental shelves. The depth of water over these shelf seas has been determined by the erosion that accompanied the lowest sea levels of the past 100 million years—about 140 m (460 ft) below the present sea level.

Mountain building

When continents collide, it is the regions of stretched crust that are the first to absorb some of the impact. Such a former sedimentary basin is being turned into the Zagros Mountains of southwestern Iran as Arabia advances northeastward into Asia. The individual blocks of continental crust appear to be sliding back along curved faults, and the sediments that have built up over the thinned crust are now being forced into folds.

Early in the life of such a sedimentary basin sea water may become cut off from the ocean and evaporate to form extensive deposits of salt. Such salt deposits reduce friction and allow the folded pile of sediments overlying the continental blocks to become disconnected and to slide up to 100 km (62 miles) away from the collision zone. In the Zagros Mountains this process has only just begun, but in older mountain ranges, such as the Canadian Rockies or the European Alps, the formation of nappes—disconnected sediment piles forced ahead of the main compression zone—has been widespread.

As mountain ranges often form out of the sedimentary basins along the boundaries between a continent and the ocean, new mountains tend to add on to the fringes of the continents. In North America, for example, the oldest remnants of ranges that make up large tracts of the Canadian shield are found in the center of the continent, while the process of mountain building is continuing in the west. Other continents show a more complex pattern of mountain ranges through subsequent phases of splitting and amalgamation, and the Himalayas and the Urals have formed where smaller continents have come together to make up the continent of Asia.

The boundary between the continent and the ocean along the western coast of the Atlantic Ocean is not a plate boundary and is therefore termed passive, in contrast to active boundaries such as the eastern coast of the Pacific Ocean, where the ocean plate is moving down into the mantle at a subduction zone beneath the Andean mountain chain. The highest Andean mountains are tall volcanoes of andesite (formed from magmas pouring off the underlying subduction zone). The bulk of the mountain range consists of enormous underground batholiths, in which the magma has solidified before being able to erupt, and compressed and uplifted sedimentary basins formed along the continental margin.

The crustal region immediately beyond the volcanoes that form above subduction zones, however, is very often in tension and in the process of being pulled apart. This appears to be caused by mantle material being dragged down with the oceanic lithosphere. Small ocean basins, such as the Sea of Japan, may open up under such conditions.

Folds and faults

When movement of the Earth's crust has taken place along a planar fracture through sedimentary rocks, it can be easily identified by the breaks in the layers, and such planes of movement are known as faults. Folds form where rock layers bend rather than break. Generally, faults form when rocks are brittle, and folds are found when rocks are plastic.

Sediments close to the surface are often so soft that they behave plastically, as do rocks at depths greater than 15–20 km (9–12 miles), where the continental crust is of sufficiently high temperature and pressure for slow rock flow to take place. Thus most continental faults are found between these levels. All major folds found in soft sediments apparently have a fault of some kind beneath them, and it is the failure of the fault to pass right through to the surface that creates the fold.

Folds are often extremely complicated and some geologists have tended to describe them in extraordinary detail, but in fact they are little more than brush strokes in the overall picture. Pre-existing faults beneath the folds tend to determine the folds' orientation. Once a continental fault has formed, it provides a plane of weakness wherever the continental crust is subject to stress. Many faults around the Mediterranean Sea came into existence during a period of tension, and these are now being reactivated and produce the large earthquakes associated with the continuing collision of Africa with Europe.

At the end of all the complications and intricacies of continental collision, the final phase of mountain building—that involving uplift—remains perhaps the least understood. In the last two million years, for example, while man has been increasingly active on Earth, 2,500,000 sq km (almost 1,000,000 sq miles) of Tibet has risen 4,000 m (2 miles). But the origin of such gigantic and rapid movement lies within the Earth's mantle.

Rock Formation and History

All the rocks on Earth are interrelated through the rock cycle – a never-ending chain of processes that forms and modifies rocks and minerals on the Earth's surface, in its crust and in the mantle. These events are powered both by energy from the Sun and the heat of the Earth itself, and the processes include the forces of nature – from wind and water to the movements of the continents. This geological cycle of creation and destruction is one of the most distinctive features of our planet. Each feature of geological activity, each agent of landscape-making is but a stage of the continuing rock cycle.

CONSTANT CHANGE

The processes of formation and destruction of the three basic rock types—igneous, sedimentary and metamorphic—are linked in an interminable cycle of change. Igneous rocks are thrown up from inside the Earth, are eroded and eventually laid down as sediments. As accumulated sediments sink into the Earth, they are changed by heat and pressure—metamorphosed—before surfacing again in the processes of mountain building.

Extrusive igneous rock

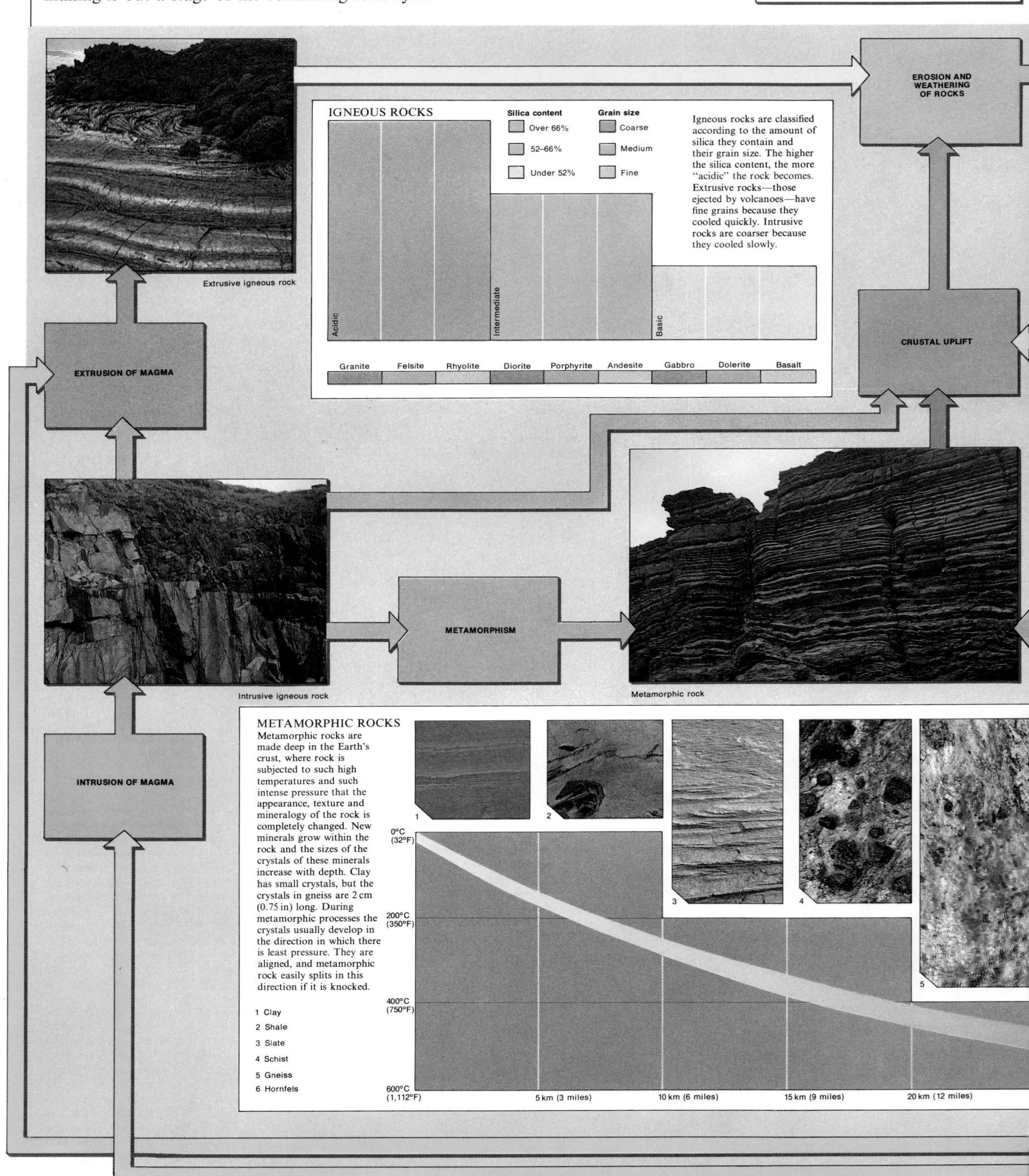

EROSION AND WEATHERING OF ROCKS

IGNEOUS ROCKS

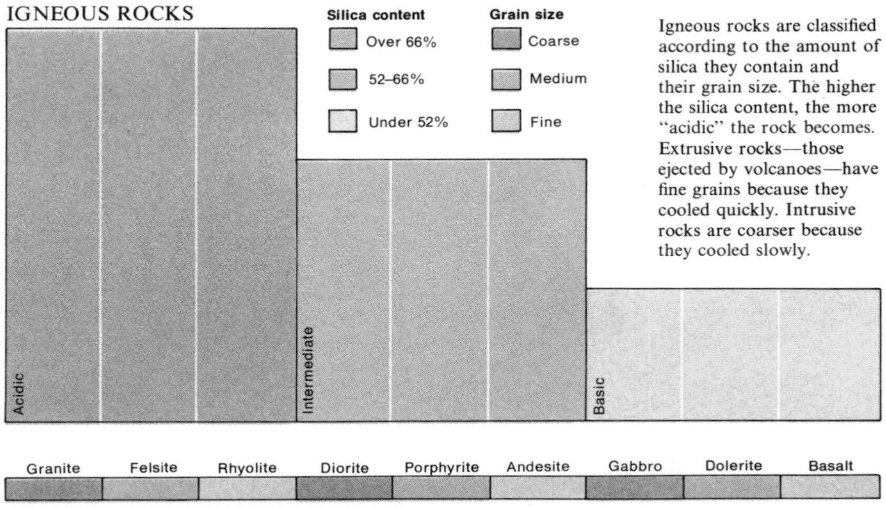
Silica content
Over 66%
52–66%
Under 52%
Grain size
Coarse
Medium
Fine
Acidic
Intermediate
Basic
Granite
Felsite
Rhyolite
Diorite
Porphyrite
Andesite
Gabbro
Dolerite
Basalt

Igneous rocks are classified according to the amount of silica they contain and their grain size. The higher the silica content, the more "acidic" the rock becomes. Extrusive rocks—those ejected by volcanoes—have fine grains because they cooled quickly. Intrusive rocks are coarser because they cooled slowly.

EXTRUSION OF MAGMA

CRUSTAL UPLIFT

Intrusive igneous rock

METAMORPHISM

Metamorphic rock

INTRUSION OF MAGMA

METAMORPHIC ROCKS

Metamorphic rocks are made deep in the Earth's crust, where rock is subjected to such high temperatures and such intense pressure that the appearance, texture and mineralogy of the rock is completely changed. New minerals grow within the rock and the sizes of the crystals of these minerals increase with depth. Clay has small crystals, but the crystals in gneiss are 2 cm (0.75 in) long. During metamorphic processes the crystals usually develop in the direction in which there is least pressure. They are aligned, and metamorphic rock easily splits in this direction if it is knocked.

1 Clay
2 Shale
3 Slate
4 Schist
5 Gneiss
6 Hornfels

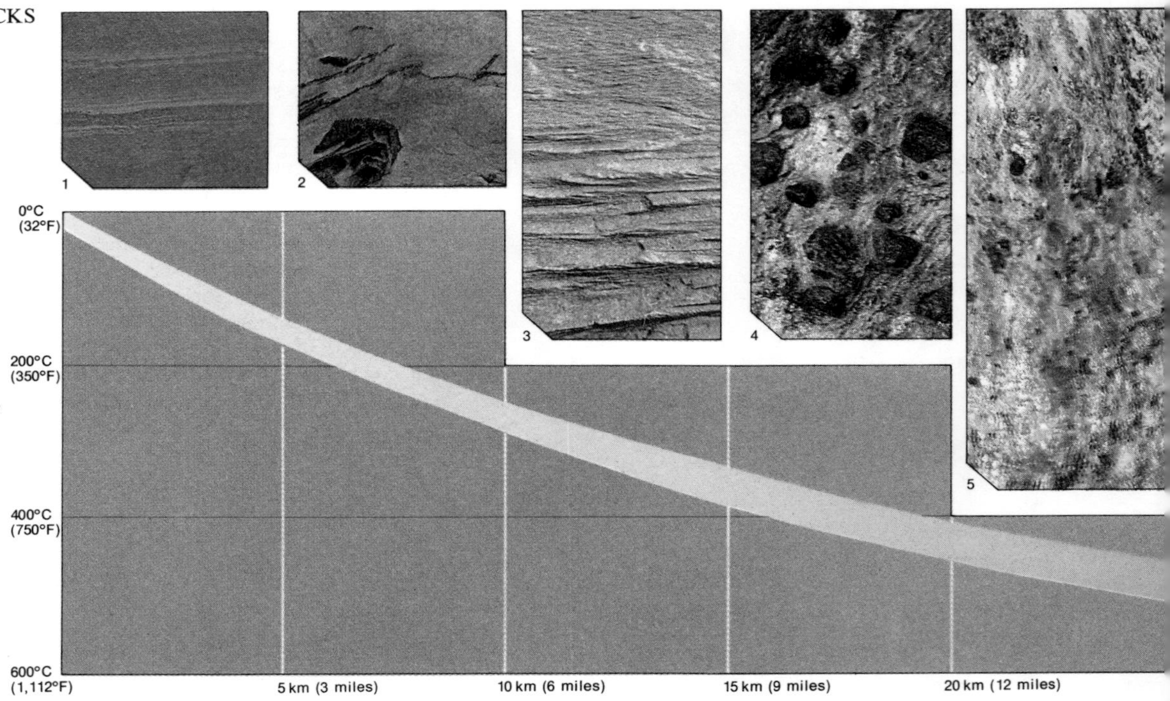
1
2
3
4
5
0°C (32°F)
200°C (350°F)
400°C (750°F)
600°C (1,112°F)
5 km (3 miles)
10 km (6 miles)
15 km (9 miles)
20 km (12 miles)

SEDIMENTARY ROCKS

1
2
3

Sediments can be turned into rock by means of three main processes. Cementation is the term used when water percolates between grains of sand. As it does so, any iron oxide, silica or calcium carbonate that were in solution are deposited in thin layers around the grains, thus cementing them into a hard sandstone (1). As more sediment is laid down, the increasing weight of the sediments on top exerts pressure on the underlying layers. Water is squeezed out and a dense rock is formed (2) by the process of compaction. This is the way clay becomes mudstone. Finally, during mountain-building processes forces are exerted on rock minerals that cause them to recrystallize into a solid mass of rock (3) that has no spaces between its mineral constituents.

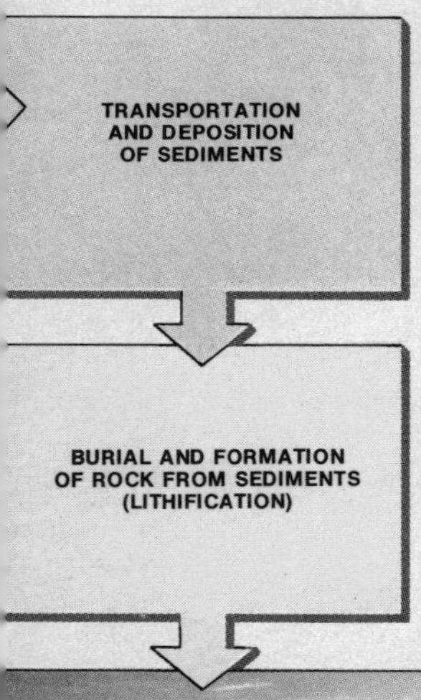

TRANSPORTATION AND DEPOSITION OF SEDIMENTS
BURIAL AND FORMATION OF ROCK FROM SEDIMENTS (LITHIFICATION)

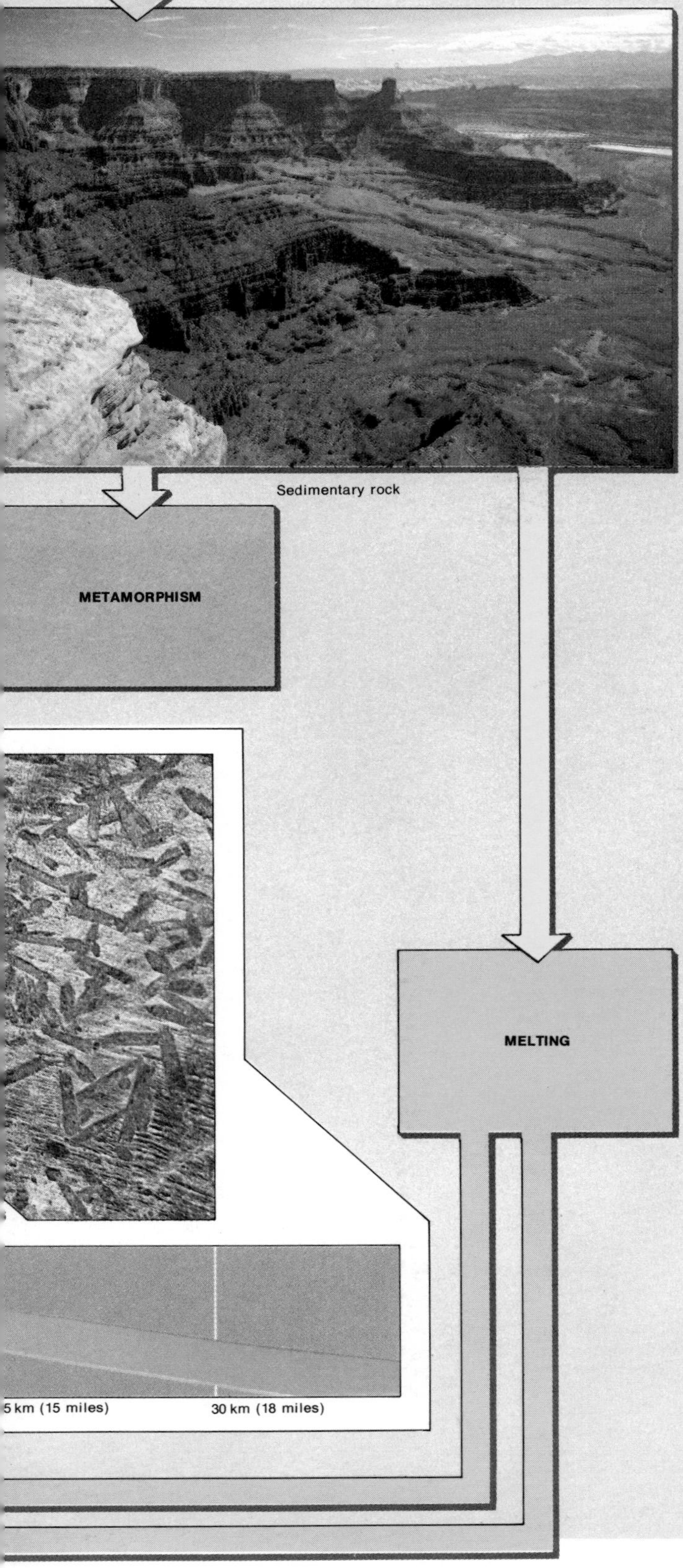

Sedimentary rock
METAMORPHISM
MELTING
30 km (18 miles)

All the rocks on Earth are formed at one stage or another in what is known as the rock cycle. All high ground on the continents suffers erosion; the eroded material is transported and deposited on lower ground; in time, these sediments may be elevated by mountain-building processes and so, in turn, become eroded. If, between their formation and destruction, sediments pass deep into the Earth's crust, they may be transformed by heat or pressure into metamorphic rock; or, at even greater depths, they may melt to form yet another kind of rock—igneous rock.

Materials at the bottom of a thick pile of sediments may be heated enough to melt. If this material then cools and solidifies underground, it is called plutonic rock. Sometimes, however, it escapes to the surface by means of a short cut—a volcano—to become part of the rock cycle. On the other hand, some sediments are lost off the edge of the continents on to the deep ocean floor, and they disappear into the mantle of the Earth by means of the downward movements of the oceanic crust. A measure of the difference between the input and the output of the continental rock cycle is a measure of how fast the continental crust is increasing or decreasing. Scientists believe it is increasing—at a rate of between 0.1 and 1.0 cu km a year.

Types of rock

The range of rock types found on the continents has been classified under three headings: sedimentary, igneous and metamorphic. Sedimentary rocks include all those formed at low temperatures on the Earth's surface; igneous rocks have all solidified from molten rock, or magma; and metamorphic rocks are sedimentary or igneous rocks that have changed their nature under conditions of high temperature and pressure.

There is a certain amount of difficulty in defining the boundaries between the different types. Ash formed from solidified magma falling out of the air after a volcanic eruption is igneous, but what if it should move downhill in a mudslide? If a metamorphic rock is deeply buried it may start to melt and form a "migmatite," which is part liquid and part solid. Is this igneous? And where does the boundary lie between a deeply buried sediment and a metamorphic rock? Coal seams that have been thoroughly metamorphosed from their original peat deposits are found as layers in unaltered sandstones. This classification does, however, provide a useful preliminary guide to understanding the nature of different types of rock.

Rock types are defined by studying their texture, the way they were formed, and their composition. There are interesting textural similarities between evaporites—salt deposits formed as an inland sea dries up—and some plutonic igneous rocks. Both have crystallized directly from a liquid. There are similarities between sandstones and plutonic "cumulates," which form at the base of enormous magma reservoirs where strong magma currents deposit thick layers of crystals. So rock types must be defined in terms of more than just texture.

Rock formation

The simplest sedimentary rocks are those made up of whole fragments of eroded material. "Scree" deposits that accumulate at the base of a cliff or a steep valley side from angular rock fragments that have broken off the rock face above can make a sedimentary "breccia." A rock made from rounded stream pebbles is a "conglomerate." Further erosion reduces the rock into three components: dissolved ions (atoms with an electrical charge) such as those of calcium or magnesium; mineral grains (sand) that cannot be broken down chemically, such as quartz; and a variety of minerals containing sheet-like layers of silicate and alumina (silicon and aluminum oxides)—the minerals that are often the main constituents of clays.

A river carrying these minerals first deposits the sand, and then the clay, while the dissolved ions pass out into the sea, where some are absorbed by living organisms and used to construct protective shells and rigid skeletons. When the creatures die, the shells and bones again become part of the rock cycle, building up great thicknesses of limestone.

Igneous rocks are chemically far more complex than are sedimentary rocks, but are texturally simpler. The slower the magma cools, the larger are the crystals that form within it. If it cools too quickly it may not crystallize at all, forming instead a super-cooled liquid, or glass. A plutonic igneous rock—one cooled deep underground—is coarse grained; a volcanic rock is fine grained. A rock can, however, have both large and small crystals, testifying to a more complex history.

The most striking feature of Earth magmas is their uniformity. With few exceptions, they are all rich in silica. The greater the silica content, the higher their viscosity (resistance to flowing). Those rich in silica tend to solidify underground. The complex chemistry of magmas comes from the melting of the variety of minerals making up the mantle.

The chemistry of metamorphic rocks is like that of their igneous or sedimentary starting materials. As these become more deeply buried and heated, the constituent minerals grow larger. A mudstone metamorphoses to a slate, then to a schist and finally a gneiss. The "slatiness" or "schistosity" of these rocks is provided by micas and other sheet-shaped mineral grains. Such minerals require abundant alumina to form. If this is not present in the starting rock, it will be metamorphosed into more granular material.

A record in the rocks

Rocks contain an unwritten history of the Earth. Sedimentary rocks hold information about climates of the past and fossil relics of organisms that lived when the sediments were laid down. Igneous rocks record periods of crustal activity that relate to the movements of the continents; and metamorphic rocks indicate periods of uplift that exposed previously buried rock. From such information it is possible to construct a geological time scale. Although fossils are a useful means of correlating one pile of sediment with another, good fossils go back only 600 million years. Earlier organisms are believed to have been soft bodied and were not easily fossilized.

The only complete time scale comes from the radioactive "clocks" in many igneous and metamorphic rocks. Certain forms of natural elements, or isotopes, are unstable and emit energy. By measuring the amount of "daughter" atoms that have been formed by the radioactive decay of a larger "parent" atom, it is possible to determine the age of a rock and events in the history of its formation. The dating of rocks from radioactive decay has thus enabled a true time scale for the history of the Earth to be constructed.

Earth's Minerals

Minerals are the basic ingredients of the Earth, from crust to core. They make up not only the ores on which man has based much of his technology, and the gemstones which he values for their beauty or rarity, but also the components of rocks, pebbles and sands. Two million years ago minerals – in the form of stones – provided early man with his first tools. Today, man's use of minerals, such as uranium for nuclear power or silicon for microcomputers, is revolutionizing our lives.

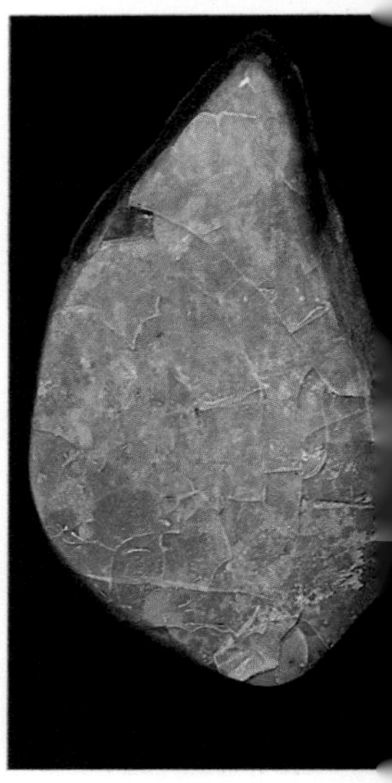

SUBSTANCES OF THE EARTH
Minerals are made up of chemical elements, arranged according to various crystal structures. Man's chief interest in minerals has been as precious stones and, increasingly, as a resource in the form of useful metal ores. But of the 2,500 minerals so far identified, the majority are rock-forming substances—the material components of the Earth. Relatively infrequent geological processes over vast time spans are responsible for concentrating minerals dispersed through rocks into richer deposits, and it is these economically important ores that have provided man with his supply of workable mineral resources through the ages.

Minerals, and the metals derived from them, have always had an inherent fascination for man, as well as providing the basis for his technology. Gold in particular, which was worked in Egypt as early as 5000 BC, still retains its mysterious attraction. Because of its chemical inactivity it is imperishable, immutable and nontarnishing, and has served as the basis of world trade for almost 2,000 years. Copper has been smelted since the early part of the third millennium BC, to be replaced eventually by harder alloys. Arsenical bronze, for instance, bridged the gap between the Copper and Bronze ages (bronze is an alloy of copper and tin). More complex technology was needed for the working of iron, which began *c.*1100 BC, whereas brass (an alloy of copper and zinc) did not appear until Roman times.

Although the steel-making process had its roots in antiquity, it was not until the nineteenth century that new techniques changed man's attitude to minerals. Before the modern age of plastics, the capacity to produce steel was the hallmark of industrial development, and together with coal it formed the linchpin of western industrial progress. Today minerals have come to assume their greatest importance as exploitable—but nonrenewable—resources.

Components of the Earth

The terms "mineral," "rock" and "stone" are often used interchangeably, but in fact all rocks are made up of minerals, which are natural and usually inorganic substances with a particular chemical makeup and crystal structure.

Certain stones have properties that satisfy basic human needs for beauty and color. Some possess a flashing sparkle, others have special optical characteristics such as refraction and dispersion ("fire"), or contain inclusions that give rise to phenomena like the "asterism" found in opals and sapphires. About 100 such minerals are classified as gemstones and valued for their beauty, durability or rarity.

Most minerals occur as either pure (ore) deposits or mixed with other minerals in rocks—an economically important difference. Their exploitation has been vastly extended in recent decades through our greater understanding of the mineral-forming processes that take place in the Earth's crust. All mineral ores result from a separation process in which a mineral-rich solution separates into its various components according to the temperature, pressure and composition of the original mixture. Precipitation is the simplest kind of separation, as when calcium salts separate from circulating groundwater to yield stalactites and stalagmites in caves, in the form of calcite crystals.

Mineral formation

Most deposits of metallic ores originate in the intense physicochemical activity that takes place at the boundaries between the Earth's huge crustal plates. Very high concentrations of minerals occur in association with warm solutions coming from springs in the seabed, notably along the spreading zones in the southeastern Pacific Ocean, the Red Sea, the African Rift Valley and the Gulf of Aden. This process also occurs in shallow-water volcanic areas, as near the Mediterranean island of Thira and the submarine volcano of Bahu Wuhu, Indonesia. Cold seawater penetrates the crust and leaches out minerals from the basalts of these "hot spots," returning to the surface of the seabed as hot springs. The minerals then precipitate in the cold, oxygen-rich seawater.

Mineral separation may also occur when part of the deep-seated magma forces its way into the upper layers of the Earth's crust and begins to cool. The great plugs of magma that form the rock kimberlite, in which diamonds are found, must have come from a depth of at least 100 km (62 miles). If the magma reaches the surface through fissures as extrusive rocks, the pattern of minerals in the surrounding rocks is also changed by a process called contact metamorphism, with various bands or zones of minerals occurring at various distances from the contact boundary.

As rocks become weathered, mineral concentrations that resist weathering may be left. Alternatively, all the weathered materials may be transported by running water, becoming concentrated as they are sorted out according to their different densities. Gold is the best-known example of this alluvial type of mineral deposit—known as a placer deposit. If the minerals are washed into the sea, they may be distributed over deltas or over the seafloor, but when this happens the concentrations of minerals are usually very low.

Mineral energy

Fossil fuels such as coal and petroleum are major mineral sources of energy. But with the twentieth-century discovery of nuclear fission, uranium also became an important energy resource. The richest deposits occur, as with other minerals, as veins deposited in fractures by hot-water movements. These deposits, consisting of a uranium oxide called pitchblende, were the first to be mined, for example at Joachimstal (Czechoslovakia), Great Bear Lake (Canada) and Katanga (Zaire). Weathered products of such rocks, redeposited as sandstones, also contain uranium, as in Wyoming (USA) and in the Niger basin. In many respects uranium is similar to silver: both occur with similar geological abundance, their ores are enriched about 2,000 times during processing, and the metals are recovered by using chemicals to dissolve the metal selectively and then by "stripping" the metal from the solution.

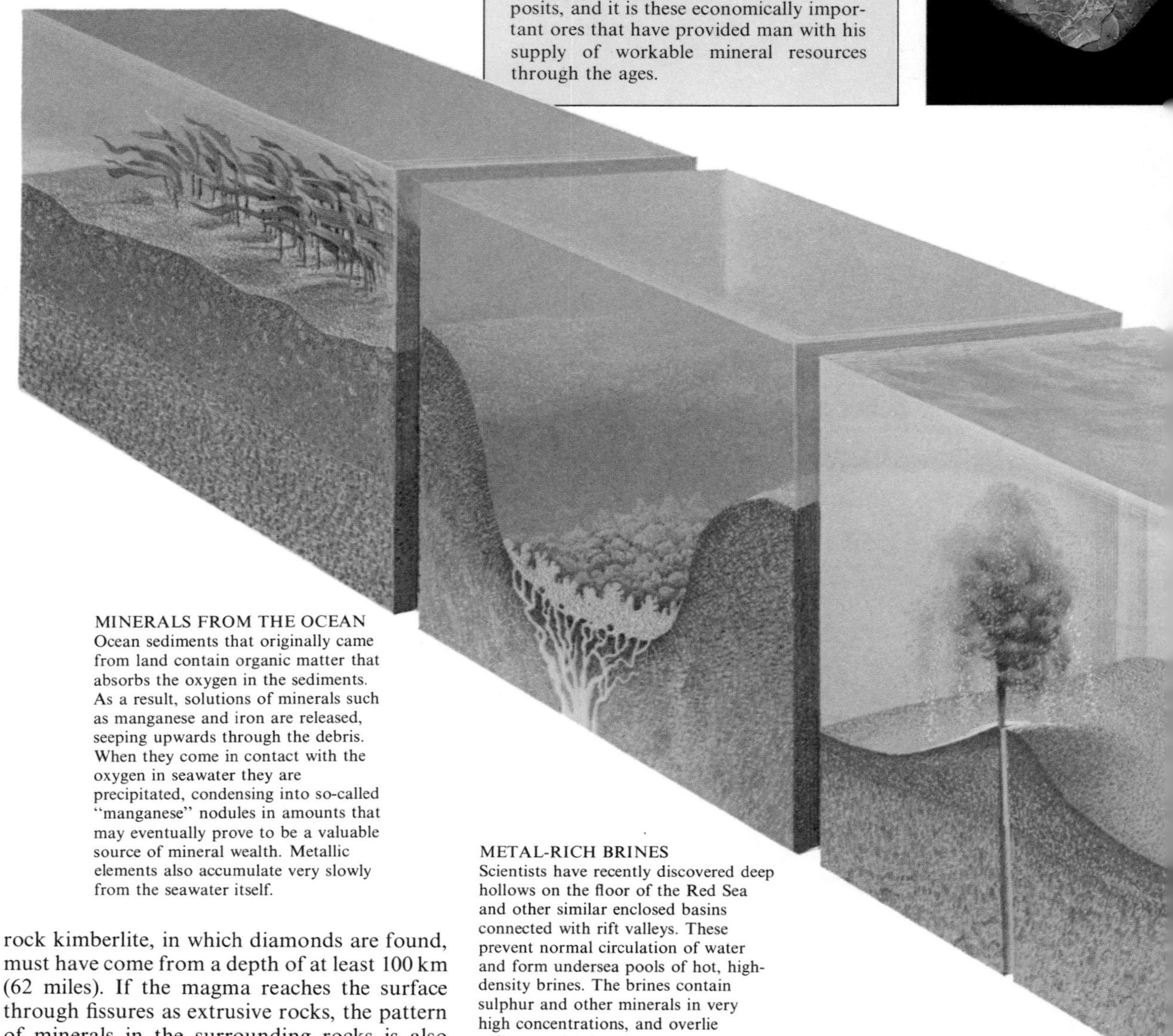

MINERALS FROM THE OCEAN
Ocean sediments that originally came from land contain organic matter that absorbs the oxygen in the sediments. As a result, solutions of minerals such as manganese and iron are released, seeping upwards through the debris. When they come in contact with the oxygen in seawater they are precipitated, condensing into so-called "manganese" nodules in amounts that may eventually prove to be a valuable source of mineral wealth. Metallic elements also accumulate very slowly from the seawater itself.

METAL-RICH BRINES
Scientists have recently discovered deep hollows on the floor of the Red Sea and other similar enclosed basins connected with rift valleys. These prevent normal circulation of water and form undersea pools of hot, high-density brines. The brines contain sulphur and other minerals in very high concentrations, and overlie sediments rich in metals such as zinc, copper, lead, silver and gold. Hot springs in fissures below the pools escape into them, carrying up solutions of the metallic minerals which combine with sulphur to create a concentrated broth rich in metals.

METALS FROM THE INTERIOR
Rift zones on the bed of the Pacific Ocean, where the Earth's crustal plates are slowly separating, provide sensational visual evidence of metallic ores in the actual process of creation. Seawater percolates through the fractured surface to the molten rock below, where it leaches out the soluble metallic components, erupting in superheated hydrothermal springs to form geysers of mineral-rich water. Oxygen in the cold water of the seafloor causes the minerals to condense out, precipitating in plumes of dark powder. Continental drift, collision and sedimentation over millions of years will eventually incorporate these deposits into the landmasses.

Uranium, chromium and many other minerals are widely distributed through the Earth's crust, but they are valuable as a resource only if the technology exists to extract them economically. In mineral development, the high-grade ores are worked out first, followed by the poorer deposits if demand remains or increases. With uranium, the low-grade deposits contain far more of the total quantity of the mineral, but these are worth exploiting because of uranium's importance and because the technology exists. Chromium, on the other hand, is currently extracted only from high-grade ores. Large deposits of low-grade ores do exist, but technology for exploiting them economically has not yet been developed.

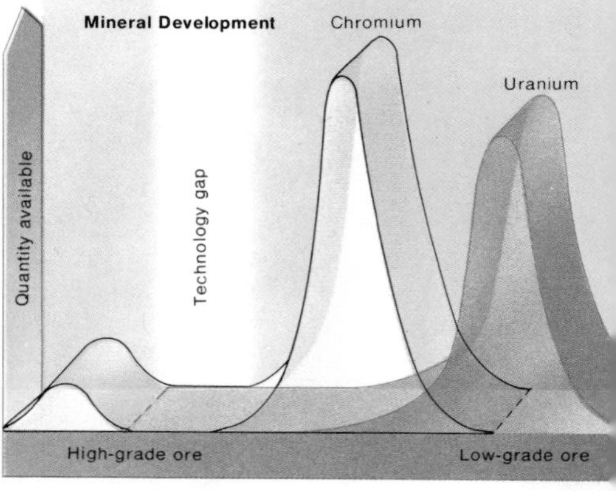

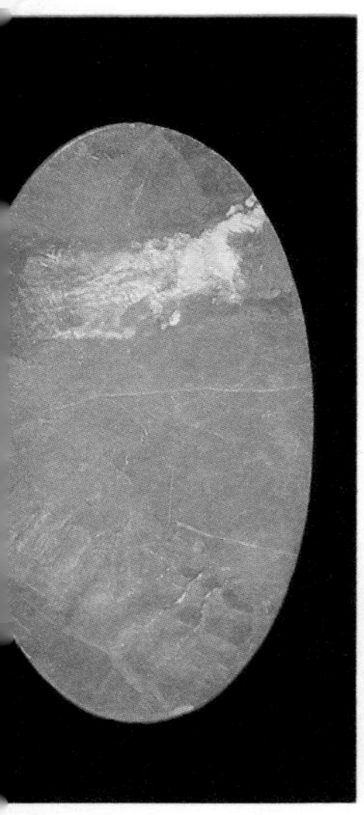

Opal (above), a silica mineral, often contains impurities which give it a range of colors. These flash and change according to the angle of vision, a result of the interference of light along minute internal cracks in the stone.

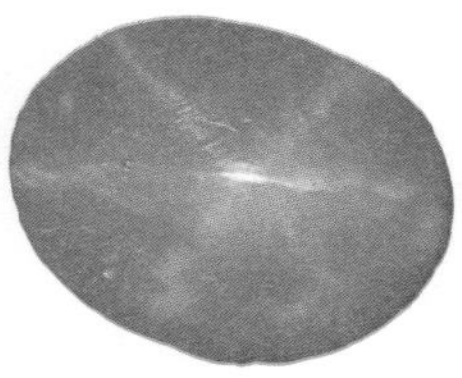

Sapphire gemstone (left), a form of the dull gray mineral carborundum (below), owes its color to inclusions of titanium and iron. If cut with a rounded top it gives a starry effect known as asterism.

MINERALS IN THE SERVICE OF MAN

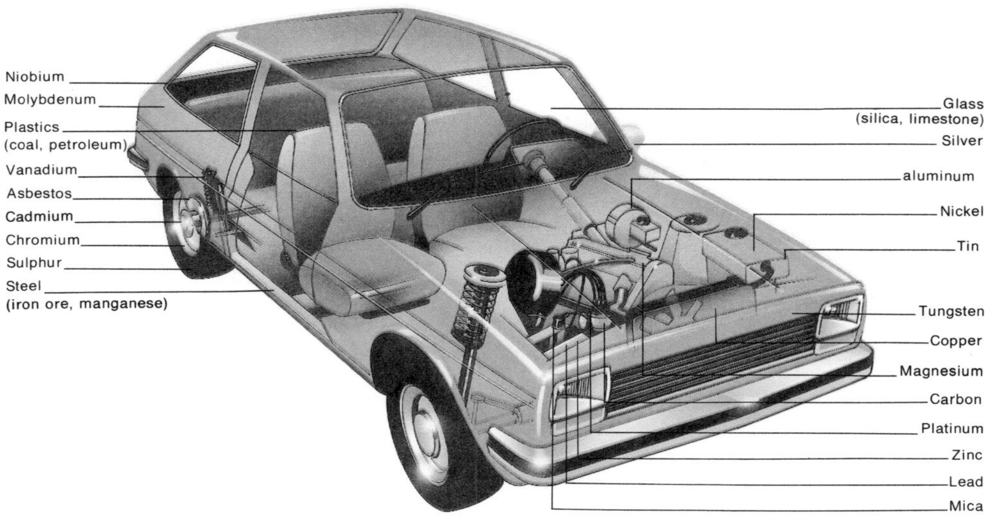

Niobium
Molybdenum
Plastics (coal, petroleum)
Vanadium
Asbestos
Cadmium
Chromium
Sulphur
Steel (iron ore, manganese)
Glass (silica, limestone)
Silver
aluminum
Nickel
Tin
Tungsten
Copper
Magnesium
Carbon
Platinum
Zinc
Lead
Mica

The modern automobile makes use of a whole alphabet of minerals in its composition, from aluminum to zinc. The importance of plastics, made from petroleum and coal, is constantly increasing, but the need for specialist metals is as great as ever. Cadmium, for example, is used in electroplating; carbon goes into making electrodes and graphite seals; transistors and electric contact points require platinum; sulphur is present in vulcanizing rubber and lubricants; lamp filaments contain tungsten. Of basic metals, iron and steel still account for almost three-quarters of the total quantity of the metals used; lead for 1.19 percent and copper for only 0.94 percent. But the amount of useful metal is often a small fraction of the rock that has to be mined and processed. A copper ore, for instance, only yields about 0.7 percent of metal, so to equip a single car's radiator with copper well over one and a half tonnes of rock will have to be excavated, of which 99.3 percent will simply be discarded.

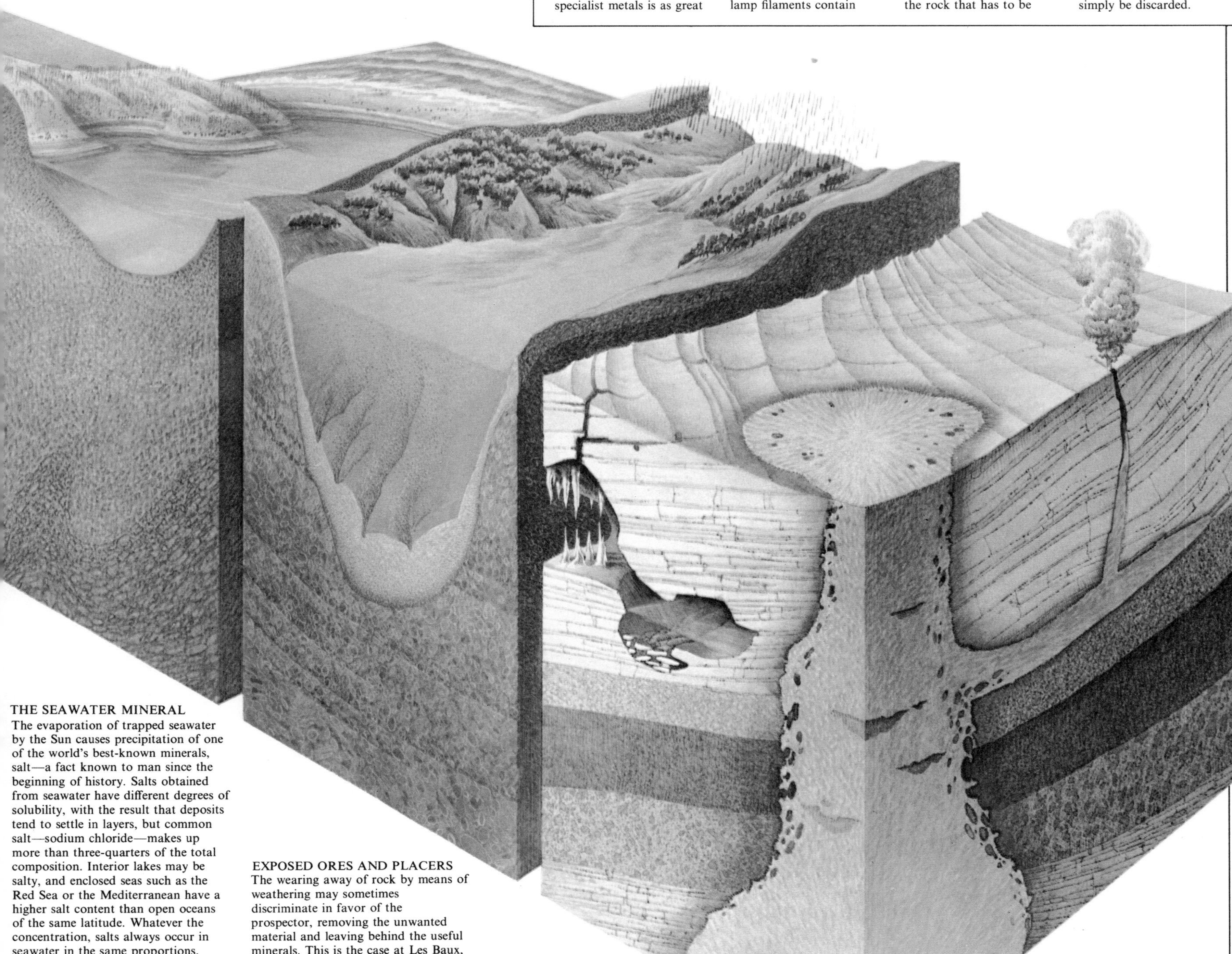

THE SEAWATER MINERAL

The evaporation of trapped seawater by the Sun causes precipitation of one of the world's best-known minerals, salt—a fact known to man since the beginning of history. Salts obtained from seawater have different degrees of solubility, with the result that deposits tend to settle in layers, but common salt—sodium chloride—makes up more than three-quarters of the total composition. Interior lakes may be salty, and enclosed seas such as the Red Sea or the Mediterranean have a higher salt content than open oceans of the same latitude. Whatever the concentration, salts always occur in seawater in the same proportions, ranging from sodium chloride to sulphur, magnesium, calcium, potassium, boron and strontium.

EXPOSED ORES AND PLACERS

The wearing away of rock by means of weathering may sometimes discriminate in favor of the prospector, removing the unwanted material and leaving behind the useful minerals. This is the case at Les Baux, France (from which the word bauxite comes). At other times the weathering removes the valuable materials along with the rest, so that all the eroded rock is carried down by the movement of water until it eventually reaches the sea. So-called "placer" deposits occur where the heavier particles of minerals have become separated, accumulating as deposits of mineral sand and concentrating in riverbeds or estuaries. Gold is the best-known example of this alluvial type of deposit, but tin and other minerals are also found as placers in many parts of the world.

UNDERGROUND PROCESSES

Limestone rock, formed from calcium carbonate, is dissolved by seeping water containing carbon dioxide from the air and the soil. The subsurface water may create vast networks of underground caverns in the limestone, and as the water slowly evaporates it leaves deposits of calcium carbonate, forming stalactites and stalagmites.

VOLCANOES AND MINERALS

Volcanic magma penetrating the Earth's crust may form important mineral deposits. On cooling, the heavy or "basic" minerals are the first to crystallize and sink to the bottom. The minerals may also separate out chemically. The intense heat affects surrounding rocks, causing mineral changes in banded zones.

Earthquakes and Volcanoes

Earthquakes and volcanic eruptions challenge man's faith in the stability of the world, but these violent releases of energy testify to our planet's ever-dynamic activity. Earthquakes are caused when the rigid crust is driven past or over itself by underlying movements that extend deep into the Earth's mantle. Stress builds up until it exceeds the strength of the rocks, when there follows a sudden movement. Volcanoes occur where molten rock, or magma, from the mantle forces its way to the surface through lines of weakness in the crust, often at the lithospheric plate boundaries.

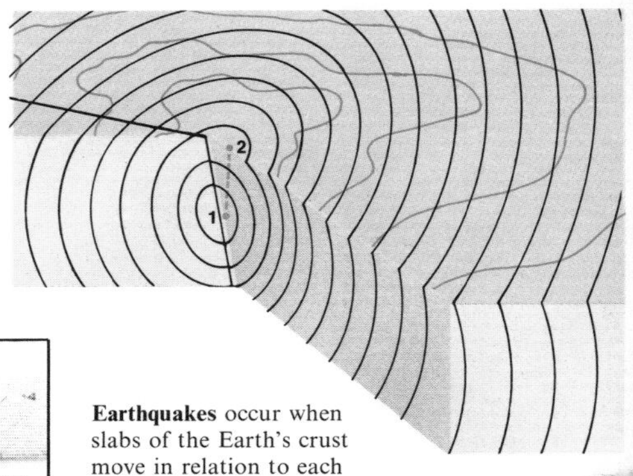

Earthquakes occur when slabs of the Earth's crust move in relation to each other. The focus of the earthquake is the point where movement occurs (1), and the epicenter is the point on the surface directly above it (2). Blue lines represent zones of surface damage as measured on the Modified Mercalli scale.

MODIFIED MERCALLI SCALE

I Earthquake not felt, except by a few.

II Felt on upper floors by few at rest. Swinging of suspended objects.

III Quite noticeable indoors, especially on upper floors. Standing cars may sway.

IV Felt indoors. Dishes and windows rattle, standing cars rock. Like a heavy truck hitting a building.

V Felt by nearly all, many wakened. Fragile objects broken, plaster cracked, trees and poles disturbed.

VI Felt by all, many run outdoors. Slight damage, heavy furniture moved, some fallen plaster.

VII People run outdoors. Average homes slightly damaged, substandard ones badly damaged. Noticed by car drivers.

VIII Well-built structures slightly damaged, others badly damaged. Chimneys and monuments collapse. Car drivers disturbed.

IX Well-designed buildings badly damaged, substantial ones greatly damaged, shifted off foundations. Conspicuous ground cracks open up.

X Well-built wood-structures destroyed, masonry structures destroyed. Rails bent, ground cracked, landslides. Rivers overflow.

XI Few masonry structures left standing. Bridges and underground pipes destroyed. Broad cracks in ground. Earth slumps.

XII Damage total. Ground waves seem like sea waves. Line of sight disturbed, objects thrown into the air.

The Earth's crust generally breaks along pre-existing planes of weakness, or faults. Such breakages give rise to an "explosive" release of stress that is familiar to surface dwellers as the vibrations of an earthquake.

Not all earthquakes, however, take place along pre-existing faults, otherwise no new faults would be generated. Many recent large earthquakes have been located immediately north of the Tonga Islands because a giant rent is developing through previously unbroken ocean crust. The crust to the south is being swallowed down into the mantle and that to the north continues at the surface to be subducted farther to the west. Once a fault has formed, however, it remains a plane of weakness even though the two sides tend to become partly resealed, so that when movement does occur there is a considerable release of energy.

The aftermath of an earthquake that struck the village of Tomici, near Titograd, Yugoslavia, in 1979: the epicenter of the earthquake was recorded 55 km (35 miles) away in the Adriatic Sea.

Measuring earthquakes

Earthquakes are quantified in two ways. The actual energy release (magnitude) at the source of the earthquake (the focus) is measured on the Richter scale, a log scale where every unit of increase represents approximately 24 times the energy release. A magnitude 7 earthquake is roughly equivalent to the explosion of a one megaton nuclear bomb (one million tonnes of TNT). The strongest earthquake recorded this century was a magnitude 8.5 event in Alaska in 1964. Earthquakes as they are perceived are measured on the Modified Mercalli scale by their impact in terms of the amount of surface destruction. A medium-size earthquake under a town, such as that beneath Tangshan, China, in 1976 which killed more than a quarter of a million people, might record higher on the Mercalli scale than the Alaska event, which affected a large but sparsely populated region.

The magnitude of the earthquake depends on the frictional resistance that has to be overcome before movement can take place. This total frictional resistance, therefore, increases with the area of the fault plane. So the bigger the fault plane that moves, the bigger the earthquake. The largest earthquakes occur on wide fault planes that dip at a very shallow angle and can pass through a great deal of relatively shallow crust that will not deform plastically.

Earthquakes are unlikely to occur where rocks are plastic and can flow to accommodate the buildup of stress. Some faults, such as the San Andreas Fault in the western United States, pass from brittle rocks into a plastic zone at depths of only a few kilometers. Therefore, the next San Francisco earthquake cannot be as great as the 1964 Alaskan one, although this may be of little comfort to the potential victims. Along some sections of the San Andreas Fault the plastic zone comes directly to the surface, and motion occurs without large earthquakes.

Earthquake prediction is still in its infancy, although it is recognized that a number of phenomena may occur before a major earthquake—the ground may swell, the electrical conductivity of groundwater may change, and the water height of wells may rapidly alter.

How volcanoes are formed

Volcanoes, although spectacular, are safer than earthquakes. While an average of 20,000 people are killed each year in earthquakes, only about 400 are killed by volcanoes; and many of the victims die from starvation due to crop failure after heavy ash falls.

Volcanoes are formed when molten rock (magma) escapes through the Earth's crust to the Earth's surface. Most of this magma forms within the upper mantle between 30 and 100 km (20–60 miles) underground. The temperature increases with depth between 20° and 50°C per km (35°–90°F per 3,250 ft) from the crust to the mantle, but even so the rocks are normally not hot enough to melt.

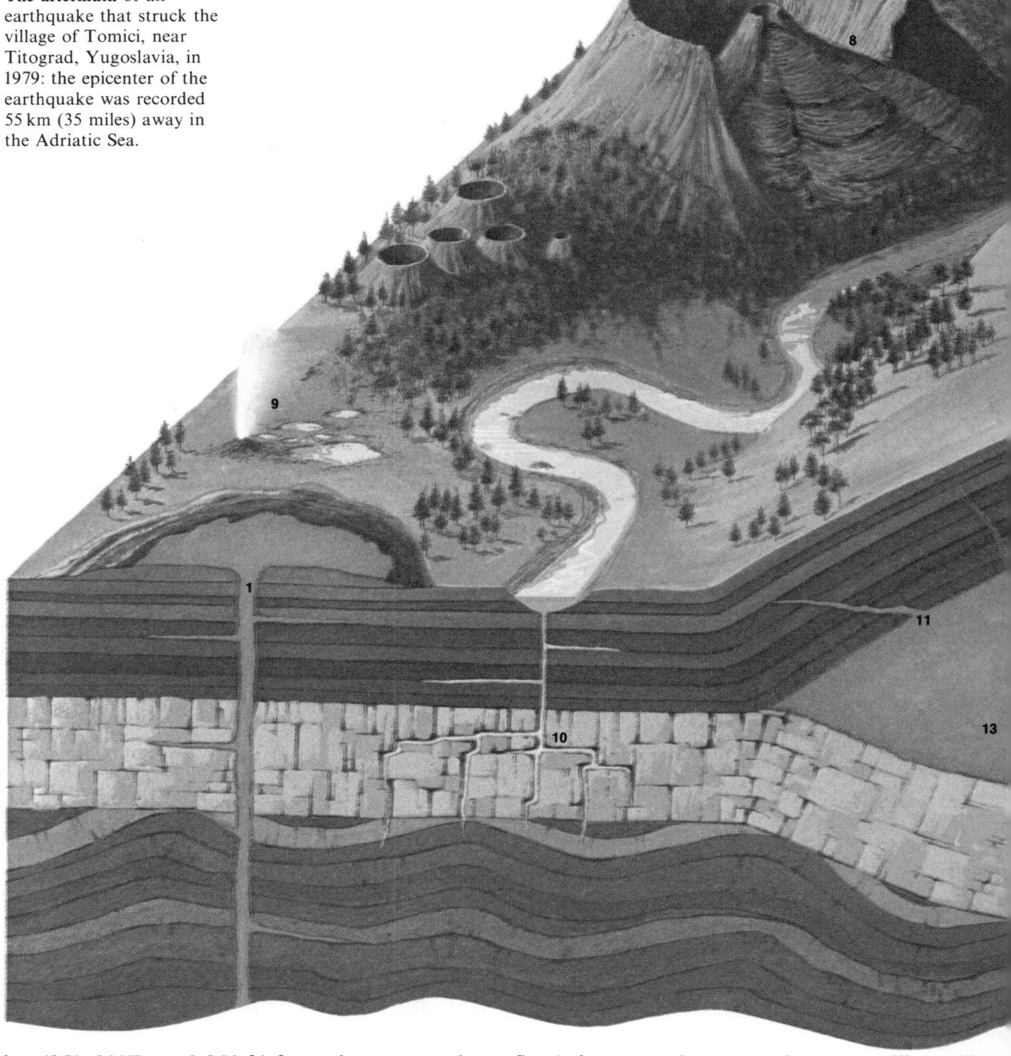

Basaltic magmas, found along mid-ocean spreading ridges and oceanic islands, are formed when hot, deep mantle rises and, on reduction of pressure, begins to melt. Such "basic" magmas generally have low silica and water content, a high temperature and flow easily—often, as in Hawaii, "quietly erupting" to form volcanoes with very gentle gradients known as shield volcanoes. Silica-rich magma forms under continental crust. Ocean crust sucks up water after it has formed at the oceanic spreading ridges and much of this water later becomes taken with the crust down a subduction zone, where it helps to lower the melting point of both mantle and ocean-crust rocks.

By the time these magmas reach the surface they are cooler and have a higher water content than basalts. These "intermediate" or andesite magmas are also more viscous (less willing to flow) because they contain more silica. The eruptions are more explosive as the water and other gases dissolve out of the magma as it approaches the surface, and the lava remains close to the volcanic vent, building up the archetypal steep-sided conical stratified volcano, such as Mount Fujiyama in Japan. Sometimes the conical form may be destroyed in catastrophic eruptions, as has happened at Mount St Helens in the United States.

The most violent of all eruptions are found where magmas from the mantle have penetrated and melted a great thickness of continental rocks, so as to create highly viscous silica- and water-rich "acid" magmas. As such magmas approach the surface they may turn into a red-hot froth that blasts out from fissures to cover enormous areas in a volcanic material known as ignimbrite. The most extensive eruption known to have occurred in the past 2,000 years was probably on Mount Taupo, on North Island, New Zealand. In AD 150 it discharged some

THE VIOLENT EARTH

Large, destructive earthquakes occur somewhere in the world approximately every two weeks, but fortunately most take place under the sea, where they cause little harm. Most of the millions of small earthquakes that occur on Earth pass unnoticed. Volcanoes are the most impressive display of the Earth's dynamic activity and are also responsible for forming the starting materials of the Earth's crust.

ASH FALLOUT

Some volcanic eruptions are so violent that ash is thrown high into the atmosphere to be carried away on the prevailing winds. Krakatoa in 1883 distributed ash around the world. The map shows the limits of airborne ash deposited by the eruption of Quizapu in Chile in 1932, the bulk of which fell within 10 km (6 miles).

Volcanoes are fed by magma, or molten rock, that wells up from deep in the Earth's mantle. The magma can either rise directly to the surface through fissures in the Earth's crust (1) and pour forth gently and continuously to form a shield volcano, or lava plateau, or be stored in a magma chamber (2) that swells up before erupting to the surface. To form the traditional cone-shaped stratified volcano, magma reaches the surface through a vent (3) and spews forth as gases, ash and lava (4, 5). Eventually the conical shape is made up of alternate layers of ash consolidated by lava. As rock and other debris build up around the main vent, and pressure increases, flank vents (6) open up other pathways to the surface, thereby creating parasitic cones (7).

When a volcano erupts violently the surrounding countryside can be devastated. The power of the blast flattens trees, poisonous gases kill all forms of wildlife, ash falls damage property and crops and can create mudflows and avalanches, and lava pouring from the vent can dam rivers to create floods.

Other special features of a volcanic landscape include extinct craters, which sometimes fill with water to form lakes, and calderas (8). Calderas are created either by vast explosions or when the magma chamber and vent are emptied of magma and the volcano collapses in on itself. Magma may later force itself through the collapsed debris so as to form new active cones on the floor of the caldera.

In volcanic regions there are other forms of volcanic activity. Water may seep down to be heated by the hot magma and reach the surface some distance away as a geyser (9) or hot spring, or be mixed with soil and ejected as a mud volcano. Some vents emit gases and steam, and these are called fumaroles. Geysers are created when water is heated in underground passageways or caverns (10). Water is periodically converted to superheated steam, which builds up pressure until it is able to rush up a vent and throw steam and water great distances into the air.

Not all magma reaches the surface: some cools and solidifies underground to form volcanic intrusions. Dykes (11) are sheets of cooled magma that have cut through strata of overlying rock, sills (12) are magma sheets injected between strata, and laccoliths (13) are large lens-shaped pools of solidified magma. Years later, when weathering and erosion have removed the overlying rock, these intrusions become features of the landscape.

10 cu km ($2\frac{1}{2}$ cu miles) of ignimbrite in about 15 minutes—spreading across the landscape at more than 100 m (330 ft) per second.

Other more explosive eruptions, such as that of Krakatoa in 1883, or Santorini more than 3,000 years ago, can result in the collapse of the volcano into the underlying magma chamber after it has become partly emptied during an eruption to create a caldera. Many of the largest explosions are caused by the mixing of water with magma—at Krakatoa the cataclysm probably resulted from seawater breaking into the magma and flashing straight to steam, thereby allowing more seawater to enter until the chain reaction could set off more energy than the most powerful nuclear bomb.

Predicting at least the approximate time of an eruption is relatively easy. Small earthquakes indicate that a new batch of magma is rising toward the surface. Many volcanoes also swell prior to an eruption and release gases that indicate the arrival of new magma.

The Oceans

Earth is the water planet. Of all the planets of the solar system only the Earth has abundant liquid water, and 97 percent of this surface water is found in the seas and oceans. The water of the oceans appears to be passive and unchanging, whereas the rain and rivers seem active, but this is far from true. In reality the oceans are a turmoil of giant sluggish rivers – far larger than any of the land rivers – and of circulating surface currents that are driven by the prevailing winds.

No topographic map of the Earth can be drawn unless there is some kind of base line from which to measure depths and heights. This base line has always been taken as the level of the sea, yet the sea is perpetually changing level. One can choose some kind of average to call "sea level," but even today different countries have defined that base line in different ways. The currents found within the sea itself can also give the water surface a slope—the calm Sargasso Sea off the northern coast of South America is, for example, about 1.5 m (5 ft) higher than the water to the west adjacent to the Gulf Stream.

Waves

The changes in the level of the sea, at its surface, provide the most familiar image of motion within the waters. Various changes take place over many different time periods, but the most rapid are those that we call waves.

Waves are produced by the wind moving over the water and catching on the surface. They can move at between 15 and 100 km/hr (10–60 mph) and wave crests may be separated by up to 300 m (1,000 ft) in the open ocean. In general, the greater the wavelength, the faster the wave's speed and the farther the distance traveled by the wave. Waves that have traveled a long way from the winds that created them are known as swell. Without the wind continually pushing them they become symmetrical and smooth. Wind waves produce spilling breakers more like the rapids of a mountain torrent, whereas swell produces giant plunging breakers.

A combination of strong winds and low atmospheric pressure associated with storms can cause yet another kind of wave, known as a storm surge. A storm surge is formed by the water being driven ahead of the wind, and rising as the atmospheric pressure weighing down on the water decreases. Where storms drive water into funnel-shaped coasts, the water can rise more than 10 m (33 ft) above normal sea level, flooding large areas of low-lying land at the head of the bay. Venice, the Netherlands and Bangladesh have been particularly subject to destructive storm surges. Other catastrophic changes in sea level have their origins in the seabed. These are tsunamis (Japanese for "high-water in the harbor") and are generally triggered by underwater earthquakes that suddenly raise or lower large areas of the seafloor.

Tides

As the Earth orbits around the Sun the water in the oceans experiences a changing pull of gravity from both the Moon and the Sun. The Sun is overhead once a day, and because the Moon is itself orbiting the Earth, it is overhead once every 24 hours 50 minutes. The pull of gravity from the Sun is less than half that from the Moon, and so it is the Moon that sets the rhythm of the water movements we call tides. The variation in gravitational pull from the Moon is extremely small, however, and even if the whole of the Earth were covered with deep water a tide of only about 30 cm (12 in) would be produced, rushing around the world keeping pace with the circling Moon. Yet the tides in shallow coastal regions are often very much higher than this—for example, up to 18 m (60 ft) in the Bay of Fundy, Canada. The seas and bays with the highest tides are located where the whole mass of water is resonating—rebounding backwards and forwards like water in a bath, as the smaller tides in the outlying oceans push it twice each day.

The Bay of Fundy experiences a particularly high tidal range because it happens to have a resonant frequency—a range of movement—very close to the $12\frac{1}{2}$-hour frequency between tides. Large enclosed seas such as the Mediterranean have very small tides because there is no outside push from an ocean to set them resonating. In contrast, where water movement associated with the tides passes through a narrow channel it can produce tidal currents of up to 30 km/hr (19 mph), such as the famous maelstrom of northern Norway.

After these relatively short-lived disturbances the sea returns to its normal, or at least to its average, level again. When the total volume of free water at the Earth's surface alters, or when the shapes of the ocean basins vary, the sea level itself may start to wander.

How does the volume of water vary? It can be buried in rocks—but the steam clouds above volcanoes return such water so it is normally recycled rather than lost. Some vapor can be broken down through radiation in the upper atmosphere and the hydrogen lost to outer space, but this is relatively insignificant. Or it can be frozen and stacked up on land in the form of ice—this is significant as we are still living in an ice age. The lowest ice-age sea levels produced beaches at about 130 m (430 ft) below present sea level, and the low-lying coastal regions of that period have now become flooded to form the continental shelves.

The salt content of the oceans

Average ocean water contains about 35 parts per 1,000 of salts which include 14 elements in concentrations greater than 1 part per million—the most abundant being sodium and chlorine. Where there is considerable surface evaporation, for example in enclosed seas such as the Dead Sea, the salt concentration builds up and the water becomes denser. Where the sea-surface is turning to ice the salt also becomes concentrated in the water.

The coldest, saltiest ocean water comes from the Antarctic. As it is also the densest it hugs the ocean bottom as it flows northwards, reaching as far as the latitudes of Spain. A similar current from the Arctic is slightly lighter and therefore rides above it—but traveling southwards, as far as the southern Atlantic. A second slightly lighter body of Antarctic water rides above the Arctic water—again traveling northwards. Where these water movements meet each other they rise up, bringing to the surface oxygenated water that can support a profusion of life in oceans that have been compared to a desert because of their lack of biological activity. Unlikely as it seems, it is the icy, stormy, polar waters that provide the lungs of the oceans.

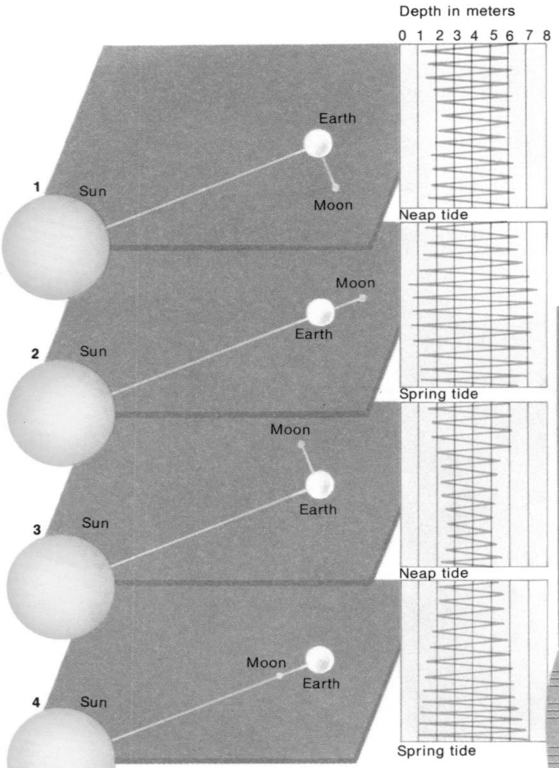

Both the Sun and the Moon exert gravitational pull on the water in the oceans, but the pull of the Sun is less than half that of the Moon. It is the Moon, therefore, that sets the rhythm of the tides. Because the Moon orbits the Earth every 24 hours and 50 minutes, the time of high or low tide advances approximately an hour each day. When the Moon is in its first and last quarters (1, 3) it forms a right angle with the Earth and the Sun and the gravitational fields are opposed, thus causing only a small difference between high and low tide. These are called neap tides. When the Sun, Moon and Earth lie in a straight line (2, 4), at the full and the new Moon, then the high tides become higher and the low tides lower. These are the spring tides. The graph illustrates tidal range over a period of a month.

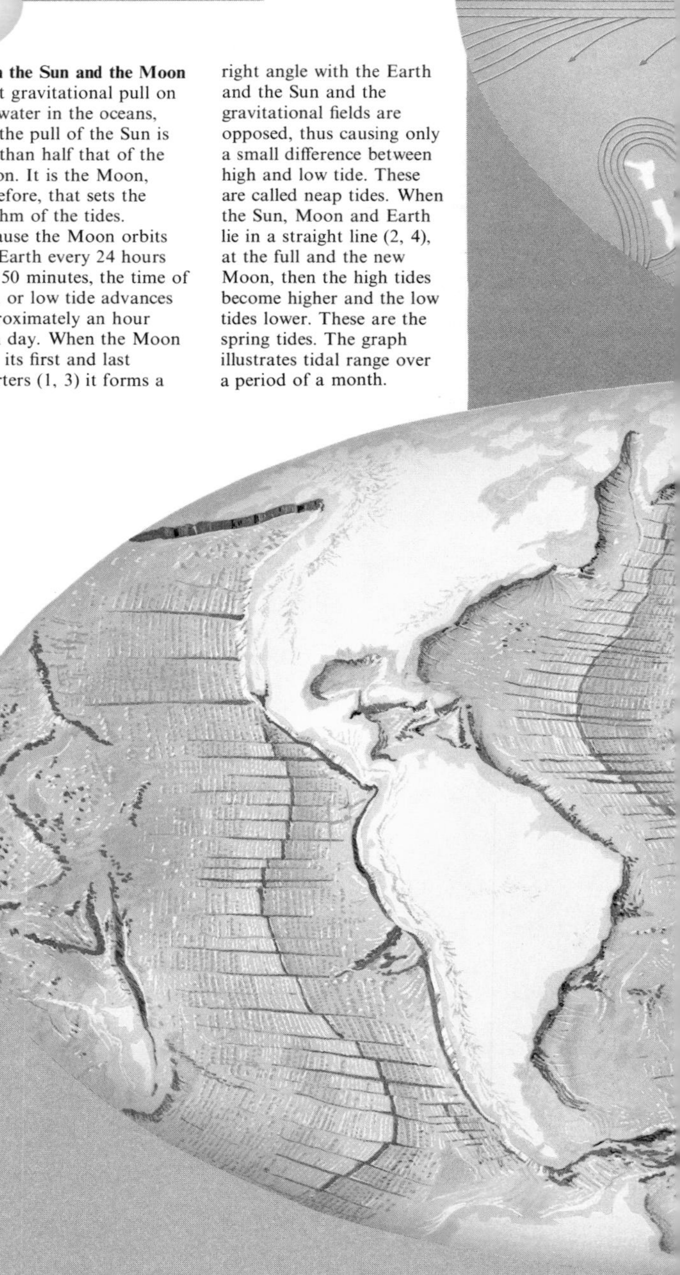

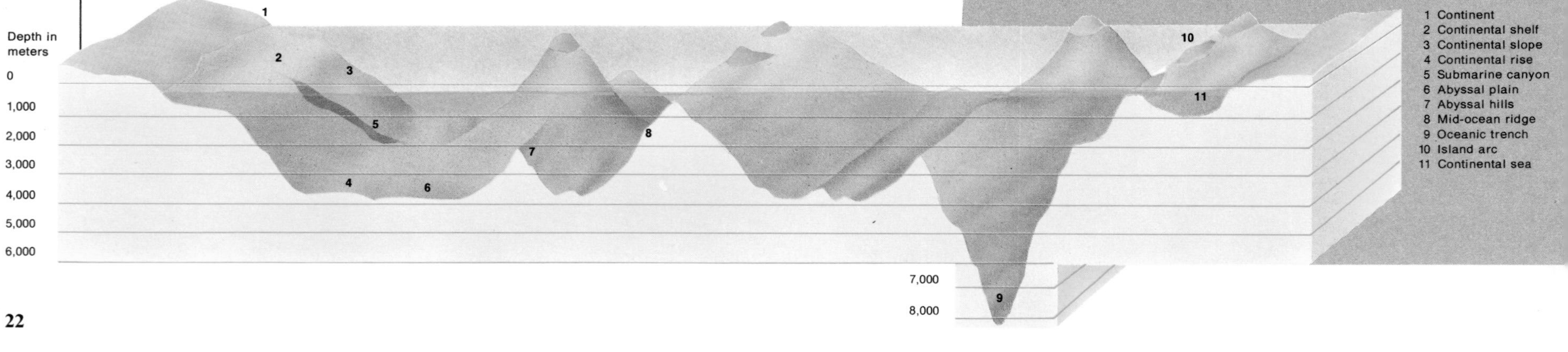

THE CHANGING OCEANS

Nearly two-thirds of the Earth's surface is covered by the seas and oceans and this great expanse of water is continually in movement. The most familiar movements are waves formed by the wind and the rising and falling tides that respond to the position of the Moon. But even greater movements take place. Currents driven by prevailing winds form whirlpools an ocean in width, and below the surface flow great rivers of colder water. Sea level is also rising as ice melts from the polar caps.

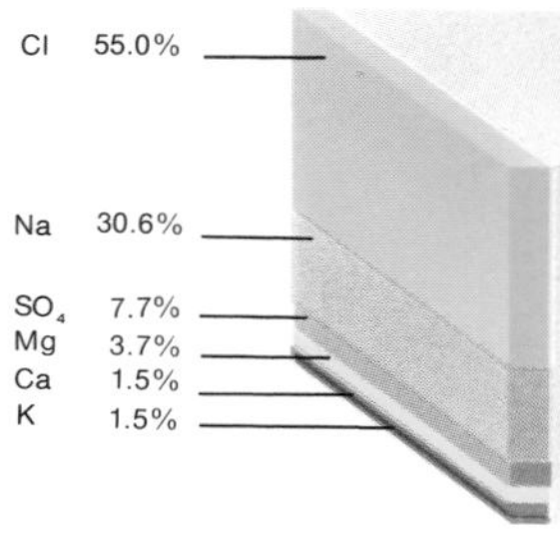

Seawater is about 96% pure water and the rest is made up of dissolved salts. Many elements are present in minute quantities, but only chlorine (Cl), sodium (Na), sulphate (SO_4), magnesium (Mg), calcium (Ca) and potassium (K) appear in concentrations of more than 1% of the total dissolved salts.

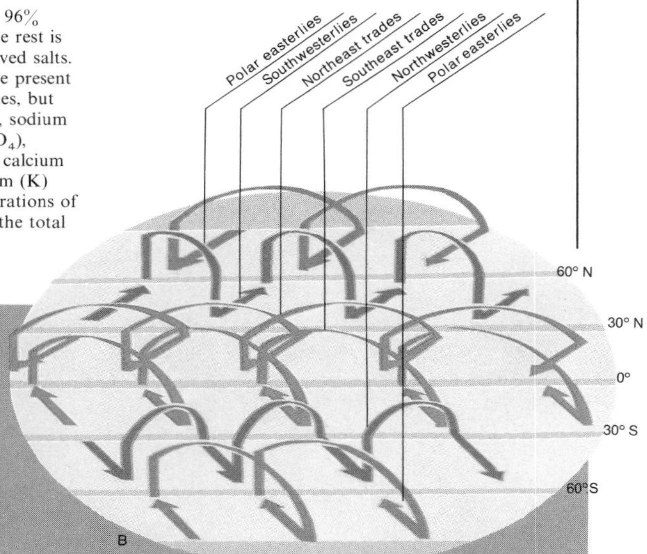

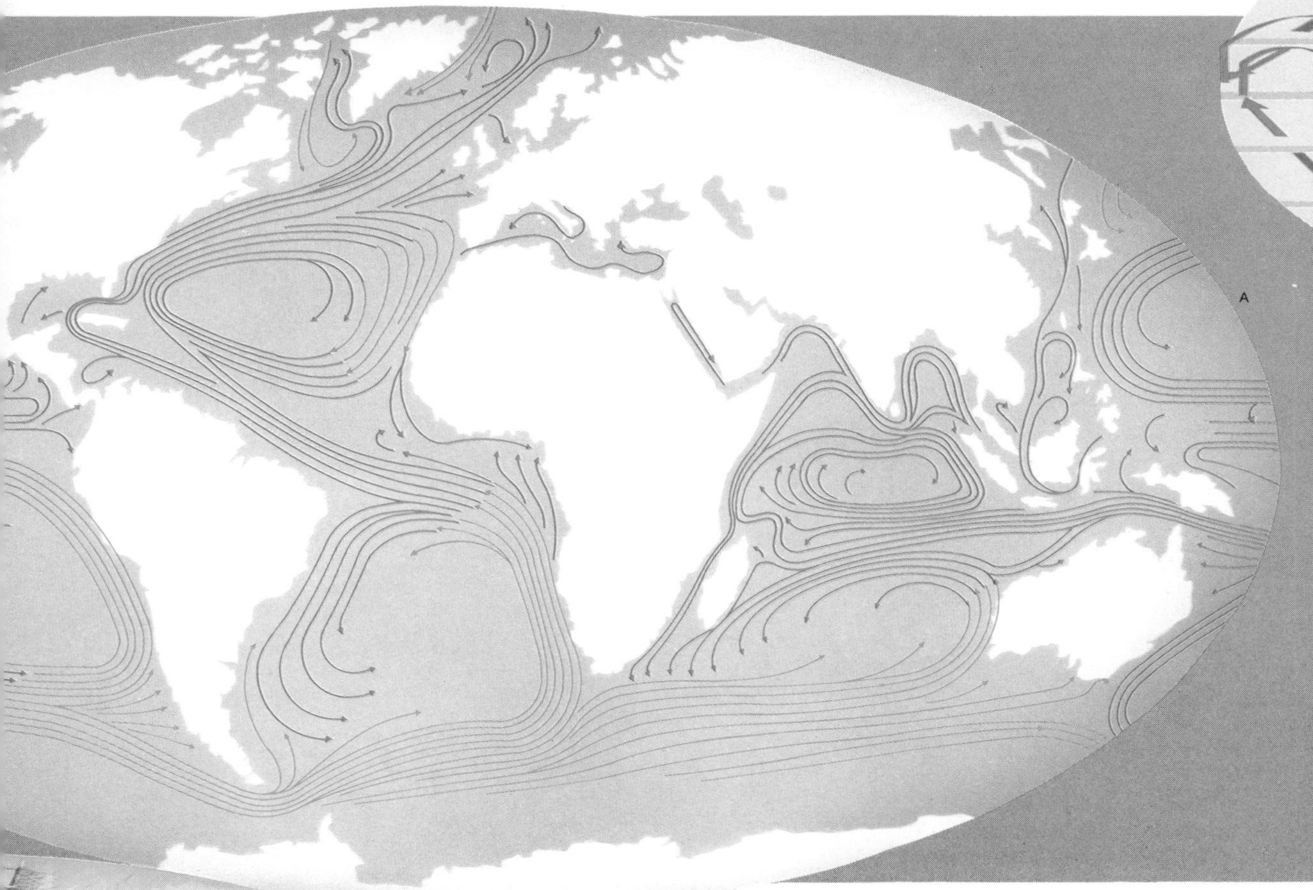

The surface currents of the world's oceans (A) are driven by the prevailing winds (B). The winds and the spinning motion of the Earth drive the currents into gyres—massive whirlpools the width of an ocean. These gyres draw warm water away from the Equator and pull cold polar waters towards it. The centers of gyres are characterized by areas of high pressure, around which winds circulate. Because the Earth is spinning, gyres formed in the northern hemisphere rotate in a clockwise direction, whereas those of the southern hemisphere turn anticlockwise. In all, there are five major gyres, made up of the 38 major named currents. The formation of warm (red) and cold (blue) surface currents is not difficult to understand, given the regions from which they flow. However, even in temperate and subtropical regions, the warm waters of the oceans' surfaces have a permanent layer of cold water beneath them. This cold layer has been formed in the polar regions, where, as the ocean waters have been chilled, they have sunk and then spread out into all the other major ocean basins of the world. The warm subtropical and temperate waters float like an oil slick, from 10 m to 550 m (33–1,900 ft) thick, on top of this cold layer. There is very little mixing between the two layers because the warm water is lighter than the cold water.

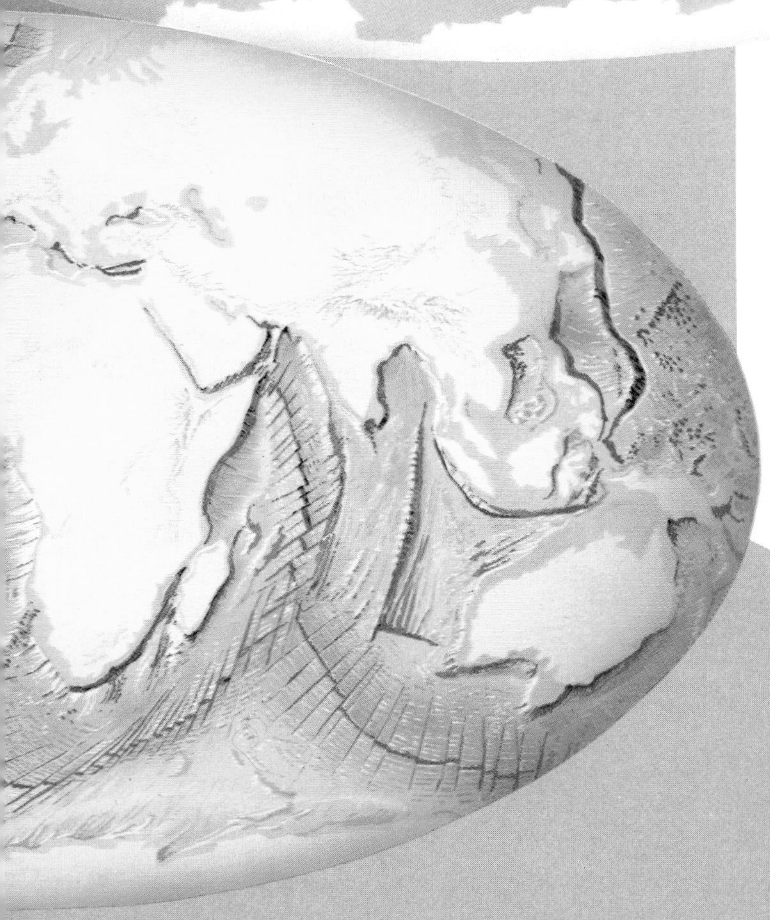

Much of the Earth's water is locked up as ice and stacked on the land. As the ice melts the sea level rises. Only 20,000 years ago the sea level was a full 100 m (330 ft) lower than it is today, and the continental shelves were dry land. About 10,000 years ago the sea level was rising as fast as 3 cm (1 in) each year. Today the melting ice is causing the sea level to rise about 1 mm (0.04 in) each year: only a small increment, but if all the ice melted, the sea level would rise by about 60 m (197 ft) and would flood many of the world's major cities.

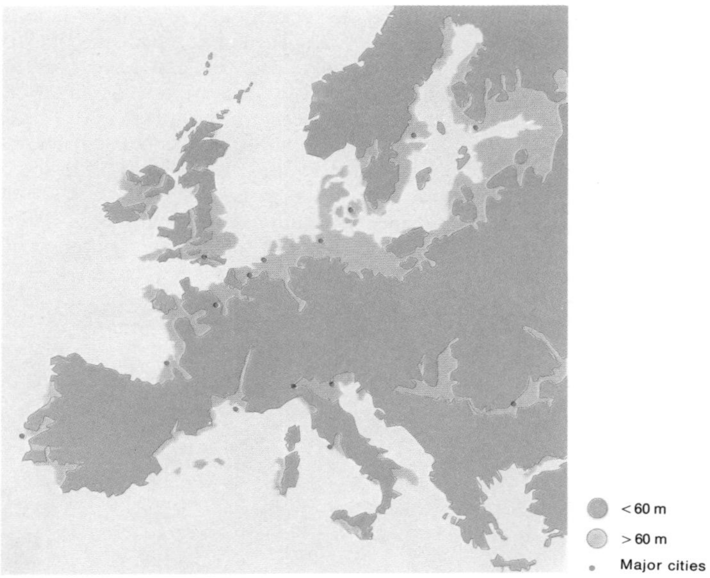

The seabed, more uniform than the land surface, also contains a landscape of underwater features that resemble the plains, valleys and mountains of the continents. Off the edge of continents lie the flat, shallow continental shelves, which are bounded by the steeper incline of the continental slope, which meets the true ocean floor at the continental rise. Here deep submarine canyons may be found. These seem to be in a process of continual erosion from turbidity currents. River water pouring into major estuaries and carrying sediment can also scour out the slope—especially during periods of low sea level. The abyssal plain is rarely interrupted by volcanic hills and mountains. The largest chains are at the mid-ocean ridge, where two crustal plates are moving apart and new ocean floor is being created. At some ocean margins deep trough-shaped valleys or trenches are the sites of ocean floor consumption at a subduction zone. The volcanic island arcs that form behind it sometimes isolate a continental sea.

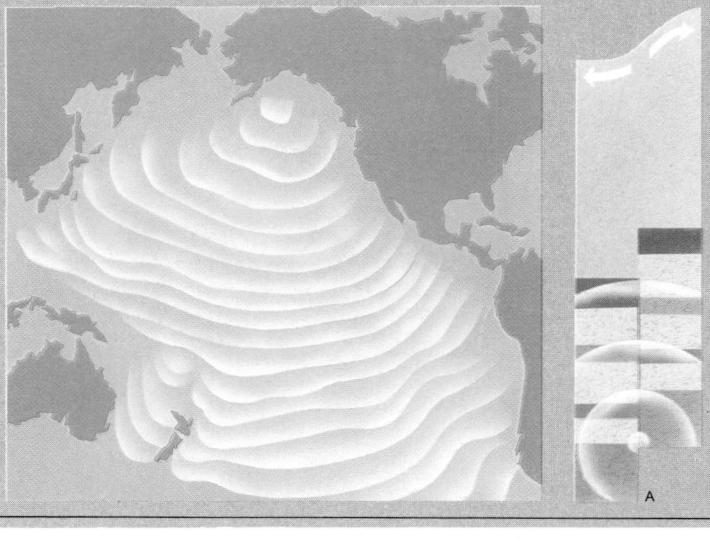

TSUNAMIS

Tsunamis are generated by massive underwater earthquakes (A) and are common around the Pacific. They can travel at more than 700 km/hr (435 mph) and individual waves may occur at intervals of 15 minutes, or 200 km (125 miles). Low-lying atolls of the Pacific have extremely steep sides underwater, and are generally unharmed, but the gently shelving islands such as Hawaii slow down the tsunami and build it into a giant wave 30 m (100 ft) or more in height. This map plots the hourly position of a tsunami that originated south of Alaska.

Landscape-makers: Water

Of all the natural agents of erosion at work on the Earth's surface, water is probably the most powerful. Many of the finer details of the landscape, from the contouring of hills and valleys to the broad spread of plains, are the work of water. In recent years we have come to understand more fully the subtle factors at work in a river, for example, as it deepens mountain gorges or builds up sedimentary layers in its approach to the sea. The full force of a waterfall, the instability of a meandering stream, the multiple layering of river terraces – all are features of this most versatile landscape-maker.

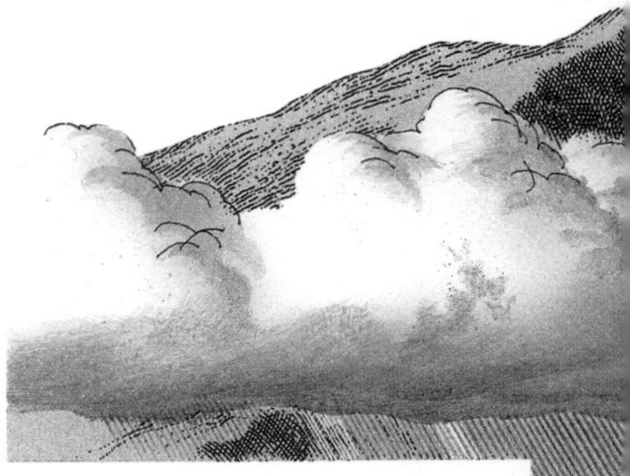

Ninety-seven percent of the world's water is in the oceans, another two percent is locked up in the ice caps of Greenland and Antarctica, which leaves one percent only on the surface of Earth, under the ground and in the air. The importance of this one percent is, however, inestimable: most life forms could not exist without it, and yet at the same time many are threatened by it, in the form of flood and storm.

The Sun's energy "powers" the evaporation of water from the oceans. Water vapor then circulates in the atmosphere and is precipitated as rain or snow over land, from which it eventually drains back to the oceans. This is the vast, never-ending water cycle. Water in the air that falls as, for example, rain is replaced on average every 12 days. The total water supply remains constant and is believed to be exactly the same as it was 3,000 million years ago.

From raindrops to rivers

Rain falling on to the surface of the land has a great deal of energy: large drops may hit the ground with a terminal velocity of about 35 km/hr (20 mph). If the rain falls on bare soil, it splashes upwards, breaking off and transporting tiny fragments of soil, which come to rest downhill. Vegetation-covered soil breaks the impact and some of the rain may evaporate without ever reaching the ground.

Soil is rather like a sponge. If the holes or pores are very small, rain finds it difficult to penetrate and water runs over the surface of the soil. If the pores are large, rain infiltrates, filling up the pore spaces. Soils that are thin, have low infiltration rates, or already have a lot of water in them, are very susceptible to overland flow. The water may then concentrate into a channel called a gully, and this can have a dramatic effect upon the landscape. The creation of gullies, together with the splash effect, leads to soil erosion. The problem is particularly severe in semiarid regions, where rainfall is sporadic but intense, vegetation is sparse and overgrazing is common. In extreme cases, badlands are formed and by this time recuperation of the land is impossible or is prohibitively expensive.

Where the infiltration rate is high, water percolates through the soil and eventually into the bedrock. There are two well-defined regions, the saturated and the unsaturated. The upper limit of the saturated zone is the water table. Beneath this, water moves at a rate of a few meters a day, but in rocks such as limestone it can move much more quickly along cracks and joints. In most rock types there are some soluble components which are removed as water continually flows through. In limestone regions, the dissolution of calcium salts results in spectacular cave formations.

Groundwater often provides a vital source for domestic consumption. In porous materials, especially chalk, water is stored in large quantities. Such strata are called aquifers and in some areas, notably North Africa, it is believed that water being pumped up now resulted from rainfall when the climate was wetter tens of thousands of years ago.

Water from a number of sources—from overland flow, soil seepage and springs draining aquifers—produces the flow in rivers. Groundwater appears days or even weeks after a heavy rainfall, but overland flow reaches the channel in hours, producing the sudden peak in flow that may cause flooding and occasionally great damage farther downstream. Flood waves usually rise quickly in mountain areas and the wave moves downstream as the river collects more and more water from its tributaries. Eventually, although the volume continues to increase downstream, the flood wave becomes broader and flatter, so it moves more slowly and causes less damage. The most serious floods occur after intense rainfall on already saturated soils where upland rivers issue on to plains.

Rivers at work

The work of a river from its source to its mouth involves three processes, the first of which is erosion. This includes corrasion, or abrasion—the grinding of rocks and stones against the river's banks and bed—which produces both

A RIVER SYSTEM

Rivers form by the accumulation of runoff water, groundwater and from springs and small streams. Few rivers reach the sea without gaining tributaries, thus forming a river system. Highland regions at source are called catchment areas and the total area drained by a river system is the drainage basin.

The course of a river from source to mouth includes distinctive stages and land forms. All rivers flow from high ground to lower ground. Many rise in an upland area where precipitation is heavy. The upper course is where vertical erosion is dominant and the resulting valley is narrow, deep and V-shaped. A gorge is formed if this downcutting is particularly rapid. If the river has a winding course, the valley walls project to produce interlocking spurs. In the middle course erosion is lateral rather than vertical and the valley takes a more open V-shape. The river may start to meander and bluffs are formed as interlocking spurs are eroded. In the lower course the river deposits much material as it meanders across an almost flat flood plain. The bed is sometimes higher than the plain and the river has raised banks, or levées, formed from material deposited when the river is in flood. Ox-bow lakes are common, as is a delta where the slow-flowing river enters the sea.

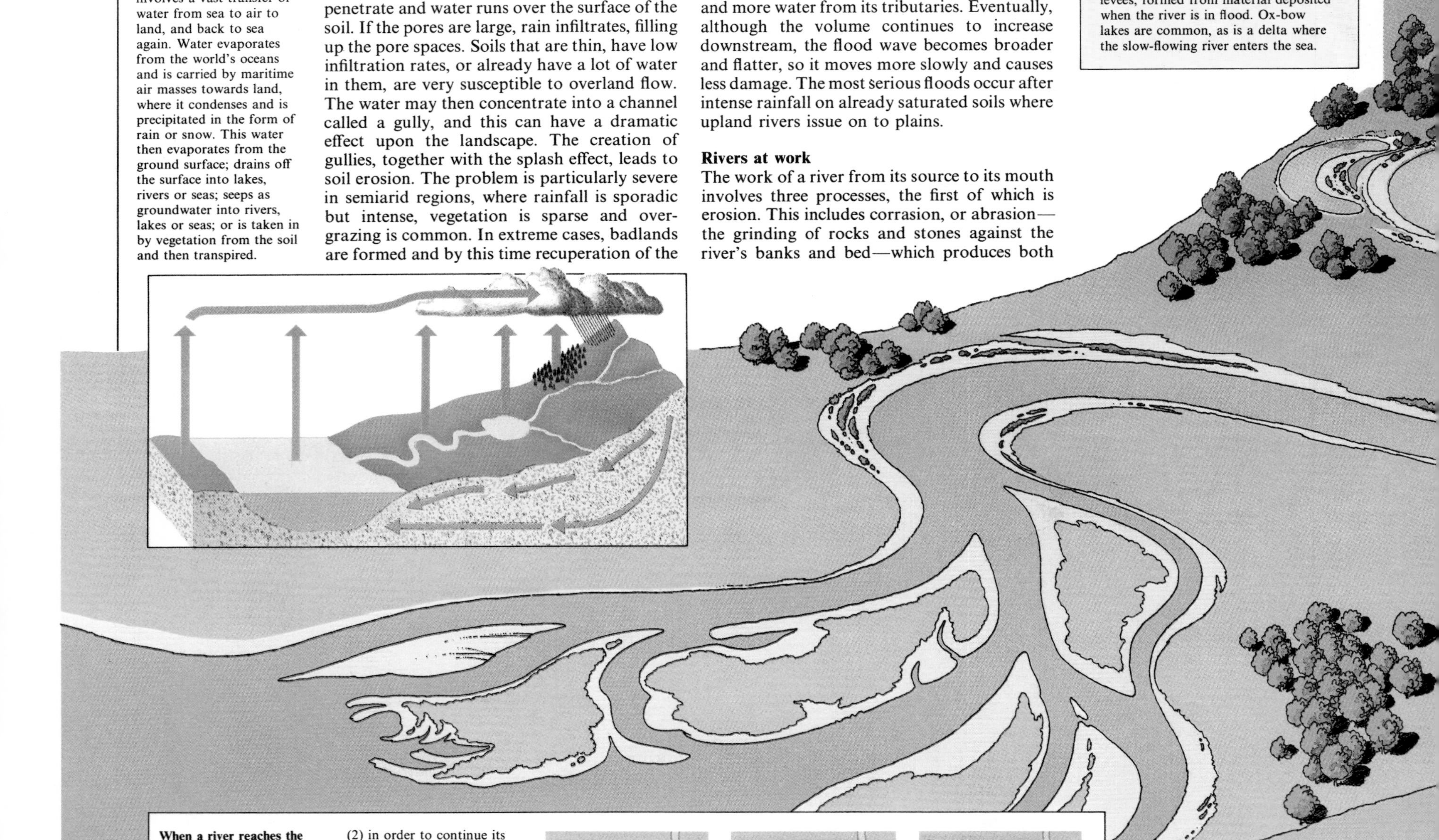

The hydrological cycle involves a vast transfer of water from sea to air to land, and back to sea again. Water evaporates from the world's oceans and is carried by maritime air masses towards land, where it condenses and is precipitated in the form of rain or snow. This water then evaporates from the ground surface; drains off the surface into lakes, rivers or seas; seeps as groundwater into rivers, lakes or seas; or is taken in by vegetation from the soil and then transpired.

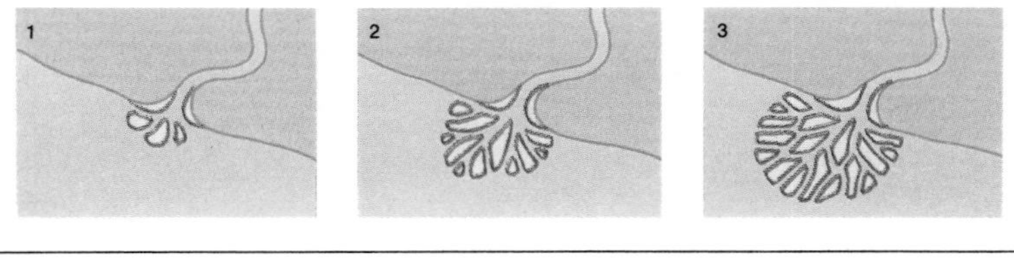

When a river reaches the sea, providing the coast is sheltered and the sea is shallow with no strong currents, its speed is checked and material is deposited (1). The river then forms distributaries (2) in order to continue its flow to the sea. A delta forms its characteristic fan shape (3) as it grows sideways and seawards. A river needs active erosion in its upper course in order to form a delta.

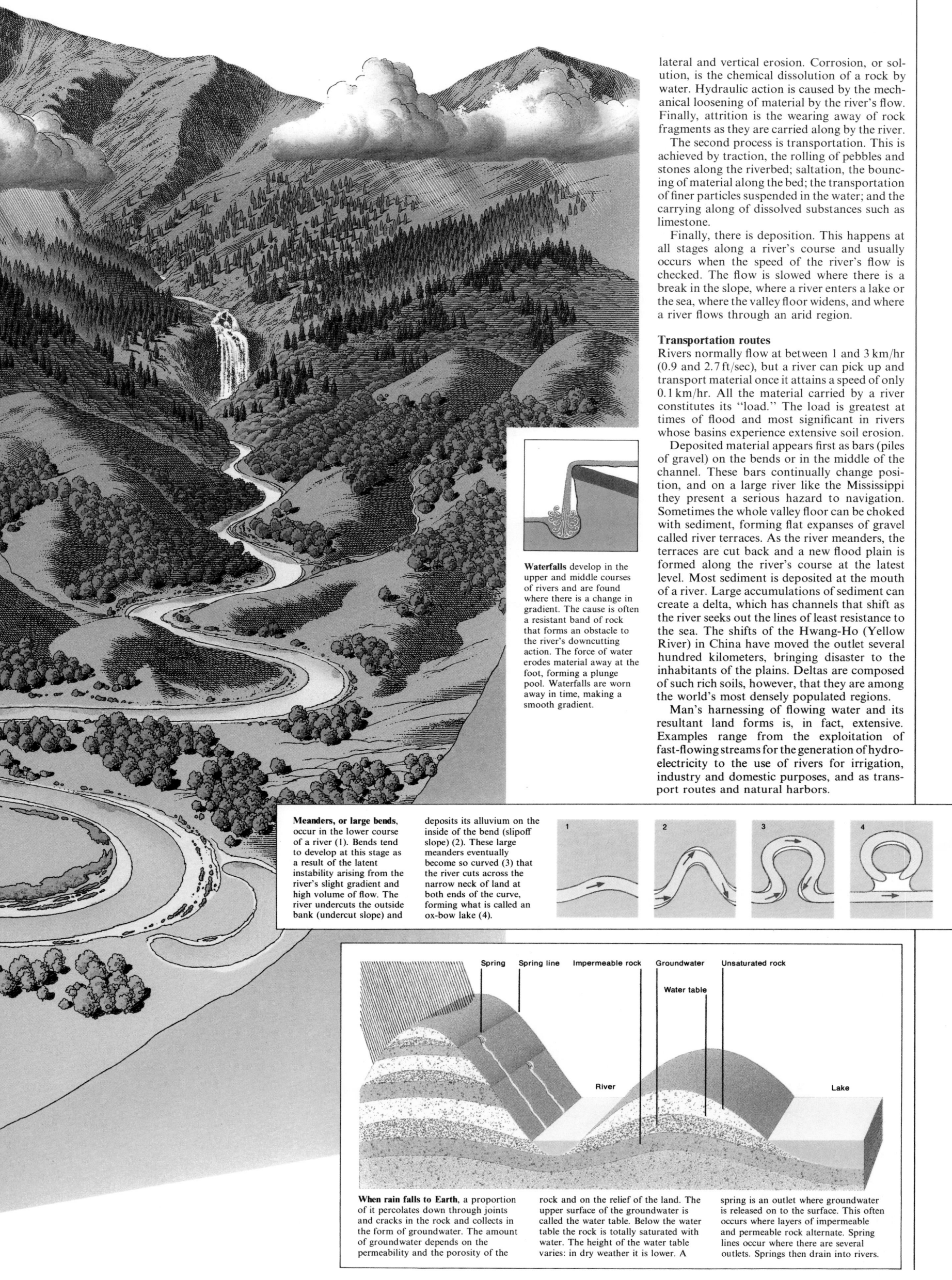

lateral and vertical erosion. Corrosion, or solution, is the chemical dissolution of a rock by water. Hydraulic action is caused by the mechanical loosening of material by the river's flow. Finally, attrition is the wearing away of rock fragments as they are carried along by the river.

The second process is transportation. This is achieved by traction, the rolling of pebbles and stones along the riverbed; saltation, the bouncing of material along the bed; the transportation of finer particles suspended in the water; and the carrying along of dissolved substances such as limestone.

Finally, there is deposition. This happens at all stages along a river's course and usually occurs when the speed of the river's flow is checked. The flow is slowed where there is a break in the slope, where a river enters a lake or the sea, where the valley floor widens, and where a river flows through an arid region.

Transportation routes

Rivers normally flow at between 1 and 3 km/hr (0.9 and 2.7 ft/sec), but a river can pick up and transport material once it attains a speed of only 0.1 km/hr. All the material carried by a river constitutes its "load." The load is greatest at times of flood and most significant in rivers whose basins experience extensive soil erosion.

Deposited material appears first as bars (piles of gravel) on the bends or in the middle of the channel. These bars continually change position, and on a large river like the Mississippi they present a serious hazard to navigation. Sometimes the whole valley floor can be choked with sediment, forming flat expanses of gravel called river terraces. As the river meanders, the terraces are cut back and a new flood plain is formed along the river's course at the latest level. Most sediment is deposited at the mouth of a river. Large accumulations of sediment can create a delta, which has channels that shift as the river seeks out the lines of least resistance to the sea. The shifts of the Hwang-Ho (Yellow River) in China have moved the outlet several hundred kilometers, bringing disaster to the inhabitants of the plains. Deltas are composed of such rich soils, however, that they are among the world's most densely populated regions.

Man's harnessing of flowing water and its resultant land forms is, in fact, extensive. Examples range from the exploitation of fast-flowing streams for the generation of hydroelectricity to the use of rivers for irrigation, industry and domestic purposes, and as transport routes and natural harbors.

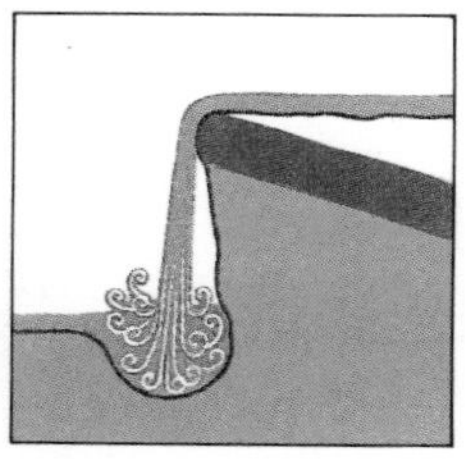

Waterfalls develop in the upper and middle courses of rivers and are found where there is a change in gradient. The cause is often a resistant band of rock that forms an obstacle to the river's downcutting action. The force of water erodes material away at the foot, forming a plunge pool. Waterfalls are worn away in time, making a smooth gradient.

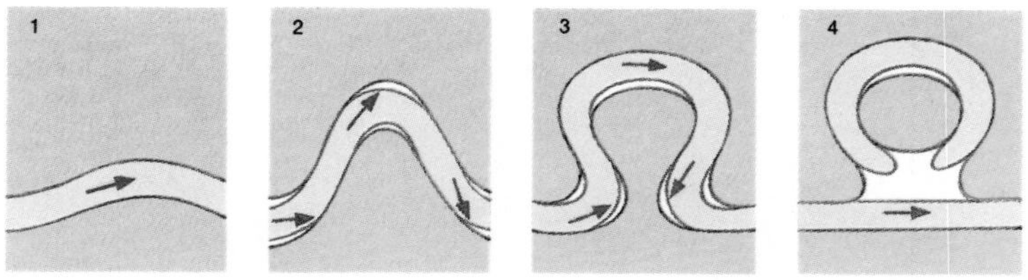

Meanders, or large bends, occur in the lower course of a river (1). Bends tend to develop at this stage as a result of the latent instability arising from the river's slight gradient and high volume of flow. The river undercuts the outside bank (undercut slope) and deposits its alluvium on the inside of the bend (slipoff slope) (2). These large meanders eventually become so curved (3) that the river cuts across the narrow neck of land at both ends of the curve, forming what is called an ox-bow lake (4).

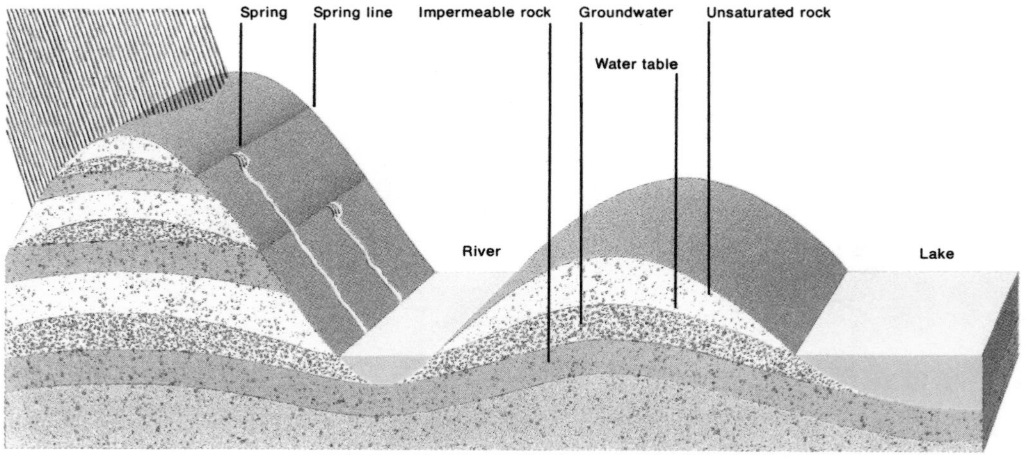

When rain falls to Earth, a proportion of it percolates down through joints and cracks in the rock and collects in the form of groundwater. The amount of groundwater depends on the permeability and the porosity of the rock and on the relief of the land. The upper surface of the groundwater is called the water table. Below the water table the rock is totally saturated with water. The height of the water table varies: in dry weather it is lower. A spring is an outlet where groundwater is released on to the surface. This often occurs where layers of impermeable and permeable rock alternate. Spring lines occur where there are several outlets. Springs then drain into rivers.

Landscape-makers: Ice and Snow

A series of glacial periods has punctuated the Earth's history for the last two million years. During the last glacial, the ice covered an area nearly three times larger than that covered by ice sheets and glaciers today. Its remnants are still found in the ice caps of the world: most present-day glacial ice is in Antarctica and Greenland in two great ice sheets which together contain about 97 percent of all the Earth's ice. The rest is in glaciers in Iceland, the Alps and other high mountain chains.

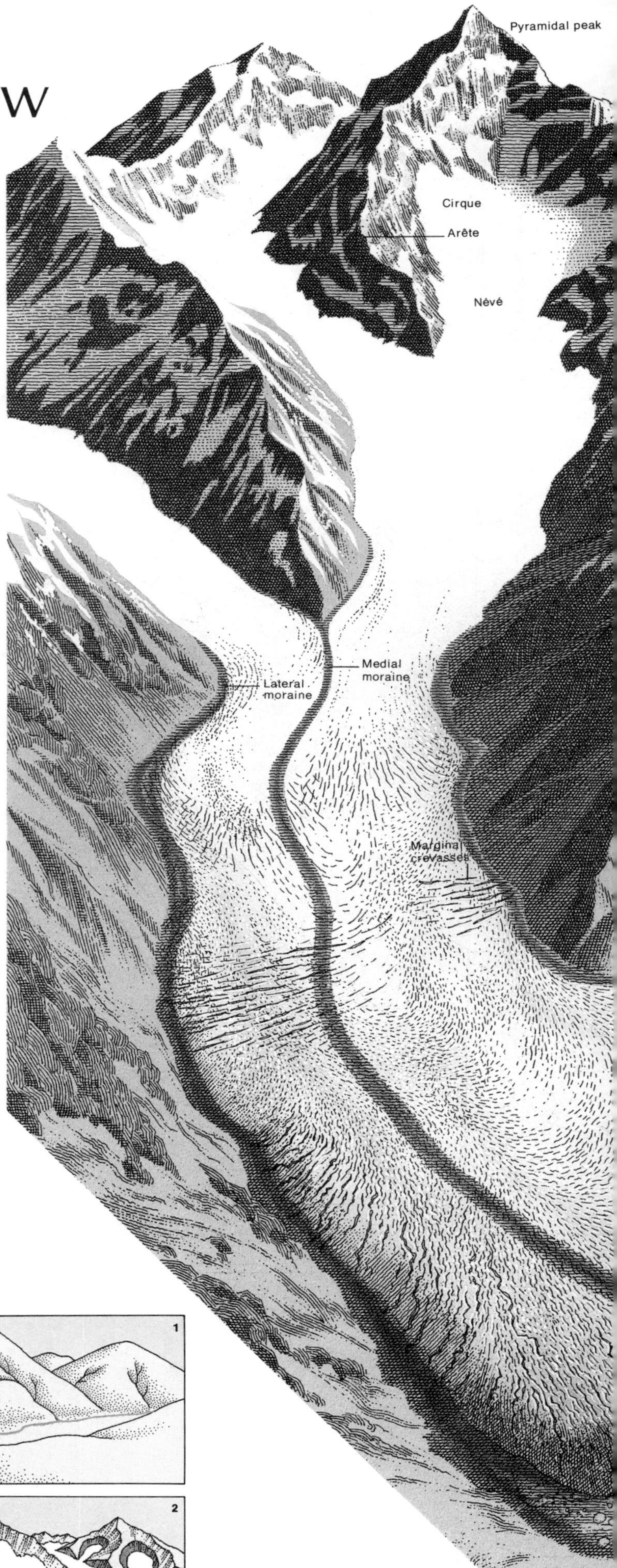

During the Earth's major glacial periods, ice sheets almost as big as that of present-day Antarctica spread over the northern part of North America, reaching as far south as the Ohio River, and over northern Europe as far south as southern England, the Netherlands and southern Poland. Today glacial activity is more restricted, but the mechanisms by which it carves dramatic features of the Earth's landscape remain the same.

Types of glacier

There are six main types of ice mass: cirque glaciers, which occupy basin-shaped depressions in mountain areas; valley glaciers; piedmont glaciers, in which the ice spreads in a lobe over a lowland; floating ice tongues and ice shelves; mountain ice caps; and ice sheets. Climate and relief are responsible for these differences, but glaciers can also be classified according to their internal temperatures.

Cold glaciers are those in which the ice temperature is below freezing point and they are frozen to the rock beneath. This condition, which hinders the movement of glaciers, exists in many parts of Antarctica and Greenland, where air temperatures are low, as well as at high altitudes in some lower-latitude mountain regions. Temperate glaciers, on the other hand, show internal temperatures at or close to the melting point of ice. Unlike cold glaciers, they are not frozen to the rock beneath and can therefore slide over it. Ice melts on the surface of the glacier when the weather is warm, and underneath the glacier as it is warmed by geothermal heat from inside the Earth. Streams collecting meltwater may flow over, through or under the ice and emerge at the ice edge. In other glaciers, cold ice may overlie temperate ice.

Glaciers are formed from snow that, as it accumulates year after year, becomes compacted, turning first into "névé" or "firn" and eventually, after several years or even decades, into glacial ice. This process of accumulation is offset by ablation, through which ice is lost by melting, evaporation or, in glaciers that end in the sea or in lakes, by calving. If accumulation exceeds ablation, the glacier increases in size; conversely, if ablation is higher, the glacier shrinks and eventually disappears.

Glaciers move because of the force of gravity. The fastest-moving glaciers, for example those of coastal Greenland which descend steeply from areas of great accumulation, move at speeds of more than 20 m (65 ft) a day. A few meters a day is more common, however. Some glaciers move exceptionally quickly in surges, which usually last for a few weeks; rates of more than 100 m (330 ft) a day have been recorded. At the other extreme, some glaciers or parts of glaciers—the central zones of ice sheets and ice caps for example—are virtually motionless. When the ice in a glacier is subject to pressure or tension—as it flows down a valley, for example—it behaves rather like a plastic substance and changes its shape to fit the contours of the valley. Part or all of the movement of a glacier is accomplished by means of this internal deformation. In temperate glaciers, or glaciers whose lower layers are temperate, there is also basal sliding. Movement of a glacier produces cracks or crevasses in areas where stress exceeds the strength of the ice.

The work of glaciers

Glaciers and ice sheets can profoundly modify the landscape by both erosion and deposition. Measured rates of erosion of bedrock may be as much as several millimeters a year. Rock surfaces are scratched, or striated, and worn down by the constant grinding action (abrasion) of rock fragments embedded in the base of the ice. The extreme pressure of thick glacial ice on a basal boulder has been known to rupture solid bedrock beneath it.

The products of bedrock erosion range from fine clays and silts produced by abrasion, to large boulders picked up and transported by the ice. Some rocks have been carried hundreds of kilometers, from southern Scandinavia to

A U-shaped valley, such as Langdale (below) in the English Lake District, is a clear indication of a glaciated past. The floor is quite flat and the valley sides rise steeply from it.

A crevasse (below left) is created by stress within a glacier. Internally, the ice is rather like plastic but its surface is rigid and brittle. This causes tension and cracking on the surface.

This erratic (below right) is made of Silurian grit, yet it sits on a limestone perch. Ice left Yorkshire 20,000 years ago, since when the limestone surface has been lowered by solution.

Before the onset of glaciation a mountain region is often sculpted largely by the work of rivers and the processes of weathering. The hills are rounded and the valleys are V-shaped (1). During a period of glacial activity, valleys become filled with snow and eventually glaciers and, after thousands of years, the region shows a typically glaciated landscape (2). When the ice has finally disappeared there remains a glacial trough (3) with hanging valleys, truncated spurs, waterfalls and all the landforms associated with deposition of material.

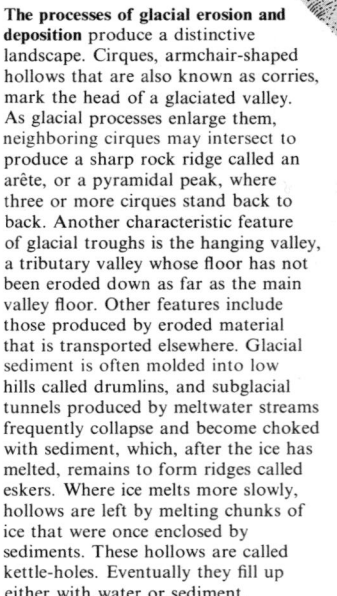

The processes of glacial erosion and deposition produce a distinctive landscape. Cirques, armchair-shaped hollows that are also known as corries, mark the head of a glaciated valley. As glacial processes enlarge them, neighboring cirques may intersect to produce a sharp rock ridge called an arête, or a pyramidal peak, where three or more cirques stand back to back. Another characteristic feature of glacial troughs is the hanging valley, a tributary valley whose floor has not been eroded down as far as the main valley floor. Other features include those produced by eroded material that is transported elsewhere. Glacial sediment is often molded into low hills called drumlins, and subglacial tunnels produced by meltwater streams frequently collapse and become choked with sediment, which, after the ice has melted, remains to form ridges called eskers. Where ice melts more slowly, hollows are left by melting chunks of ice that were once enclosed by sediments. These hollows are called kettle-holes. Eventually they fill up either with water or sediment.

THE SNOW LINE

Glaciation is still evident today in regions that are above the snow line—the lowest limit of perpetual snow cover. The height of the snow line varies with latitude: from about 5,200 m (17,000 ft) at the Equator, to 2,700 m (9,000 ft) in the Alps, to 1,200 m (4,000 ft) in Scandinavia and sea level nearer the north and south polar regions.

A glaciated valley exhibits a distinctive shape and profile. A cross section shows a U-shape, while longitudinally the valley floor is marked by a series of rocky steps and basins. The zone of accumulation is characterized by a cirque, in which snow collects to produce a firn field. A bergschrund is a type of crevasse that opens up near the top of the firn field where the head of the glacier is pulled away from the cirque walls. A rock step is where the gradient becomes much steeper. The speed of the ice flow is accelerated and consequent tension within the ice creates a number of deep crevasses called an ice fall. The zone of ablation has large accumulations of various kinds of rock debris.

Glacial erosion of rock surfaces is typified by a roche moutonnée, a resistant rock hummock that lies in the path of the ice. The upstream side is smooth as a result of abrasion by rock debris that is frozen into the base of the glacier. This debris scratches and scrapes rock, producing striations. The downstream side is rough as a result of ice plucking. Meltwater removes the small blocks of rock.

eastern England, for example, and such far-traveled rocks are termed erratics. The finer sediments, compacted at the base of the glacier by the weight of the overlying ice, form till or boulder clay.

The surface of a glacier is often strewn with rock debris, which either rests on the ice or is within the glacier and revealed as the ice melts. Lateral moraines consist of rock debris that has accumulated along the sides of the glacier as a result of rockfall from, and erosion of, the valley sides. Where two glaciers join, the inner lateral moraines merge to form a medial moraine. In the ablation zone, the surface of the glacier becomes increasingly laden with debris "melting out" so that the ice may become completely buried. At the end of the glacier all rock debris is dumped, forming a terminal moraine.

Meltwater streams pouring out from glaciers or flowing in tunnels beneath them can be powerful agents of erosion and can transport large quantities of sediment. Bedrock surfaces become potholed and carved by channels that are eroded with great speed. As the streams emerge from the edge of the ice, they carry with them and deposit vast quantities of sand and gravel which form flood plains (outwash plains). Alternatively, meltwater streams may deposit sediment between the edge of the glacier and valley side, leaving a "kame terrace" when the ice finally melts. Meltwater streams feeding glacial lakes that are dammed by a glacier or moraine, for example, construct deltas of sand and gravel and lay down finer sediments (varved clays) on the lake floor.

Snow processes

Snow plays a smaller part than glacial ice in landform sculpture. Its most important role is in avalanches, which, in mountain regions, regularly bring down thousands of tonnes of rock debris. The mixture of snow, rock and other debris forms avalanche boulder tongues on the flat ground where the avalanche comes to rest and the snow melts. Gullies (avalanche chutes) on mountain slopes are swept clean of loose debris several times a year and they are gradually enlarged. Snow patches that remain stationary on more gentle slopes or in hollows encourage rock weathering under and around them. Such a process, termed nivation, may lead to deepening and enlargement of hollows and further snow accumulation. This is one way in which new glaciers are formed.

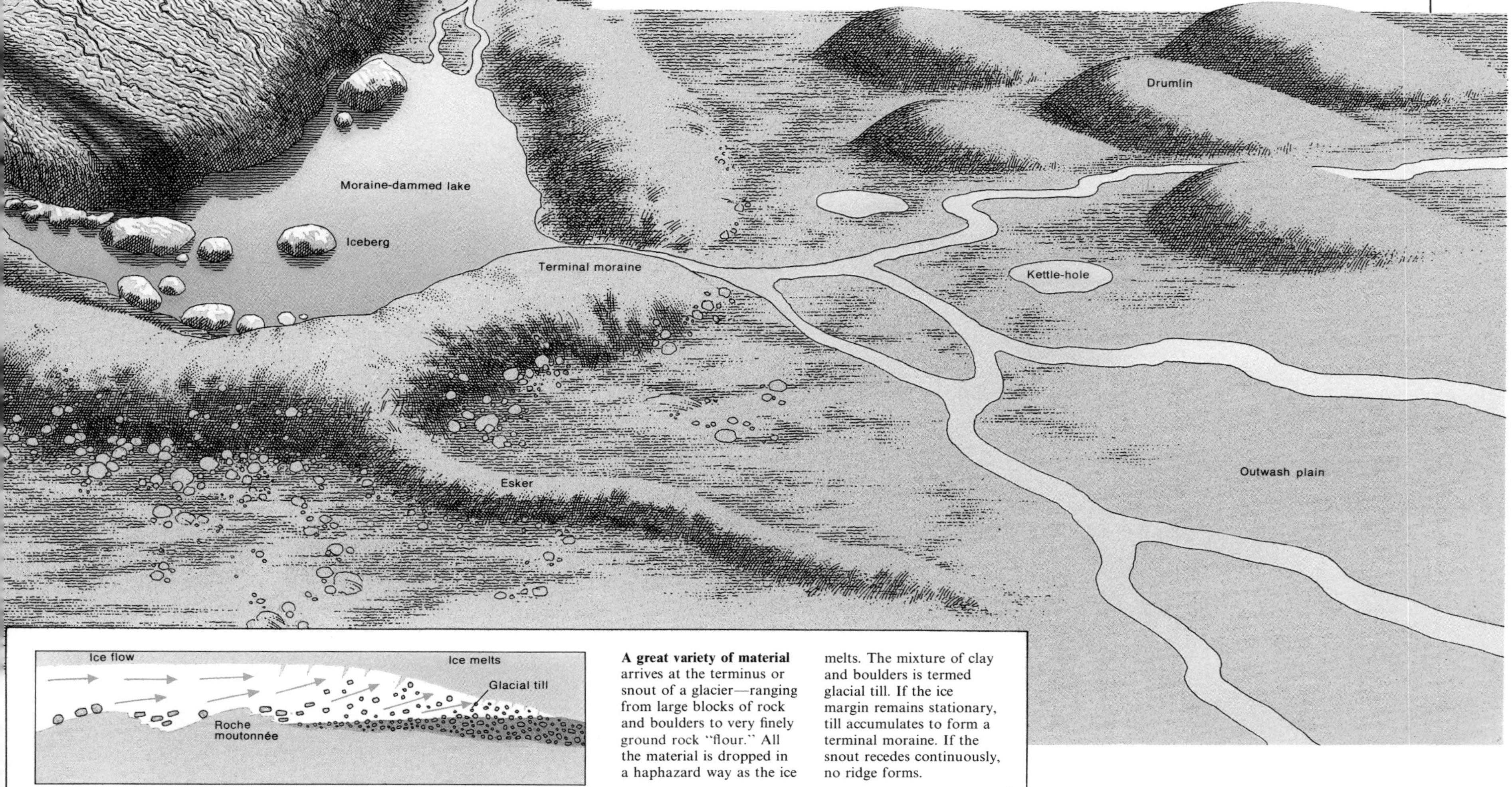

A great variety of material arrives at the terminus or snout of a glacier—ranging from large blocks of rock and boulders to very finely ground rock "flour." All the material is dropped in a haphazard way as the ice melts. The mixture of clay and boulders is termed glacial till. If the ice margin remains stationary, till accumulates to form a terminal moraine. If the snout recedes continuously, no ridge forms.

Landscape-makers: The Seas

The coastline is both the birthplace and the graveyard of the land. Over tens of thousands of years, geological uplift of a continent, or a fall in sea level, may create an emerging fringe of new land, whereas a period of submergence drowns the coasts and floods the adjacent river valleys, destroying land but producing some of the most attractive coastal landscapes. More rapid are the changes brought about by the sea itself. Erosion of coastal rocks or beaches can cut back the coastline at a rate of several meters a year, whereas other coastlines are built up at a comparable rate from marine sediments.

Changing coastlines are apparent on a human time scale. In temperate latitudes, beaches tend to be combed down and narrowed by winter waves, only to be restored during the calmer weather of summer. They may be lost one week and replenished the next, demonstrating an invaluable ability to recover from the wounds of all but the most devastating storms. Cliffs are generally much less dynamic, particularly if composed of resistant rock, but any loss that they suffer is permanent because there is no process that is capable of rebuilding them.

Coasts vary greatly around the world. Tropical areas often have wide beaches made up of fine material which in many cases forms broad mangrove swamps that collect sediment and build up the coast. In more exposed tropical zones coral reefs are common, either fringing the shore or (particularly where the sea level is rising) separated from the shore by a lagoon to give a barrier reef. Continued submergence of a small island surrounded by such a reef may produce an atoll. In contrast, Arctic beaches are narrow and coarse, and may be icebound for up to 10 months each year. Recession of soft rock cliffs results more from melting of ice in the ground than from wave erosion.

Waves at work

Across great expanses of open ocean energy is transferred from the wind to the sea surface to produce waves, thus fueling the machine that ultimately creates the coast. Originating as waves with heights of up to 20 or even 30 m (65–100 ft), they lose part of their energy quite rapidly as they travel, and once they have been reduced in height to the lower but more widely spaced ocean swell, they continue to travel across enormous distances.

The coasts of western Europe receive waves produced almost 10,000 km (6,200 miles) away off Cape Horn, and swell reaching California has sometimes crossed more than 11,000 km

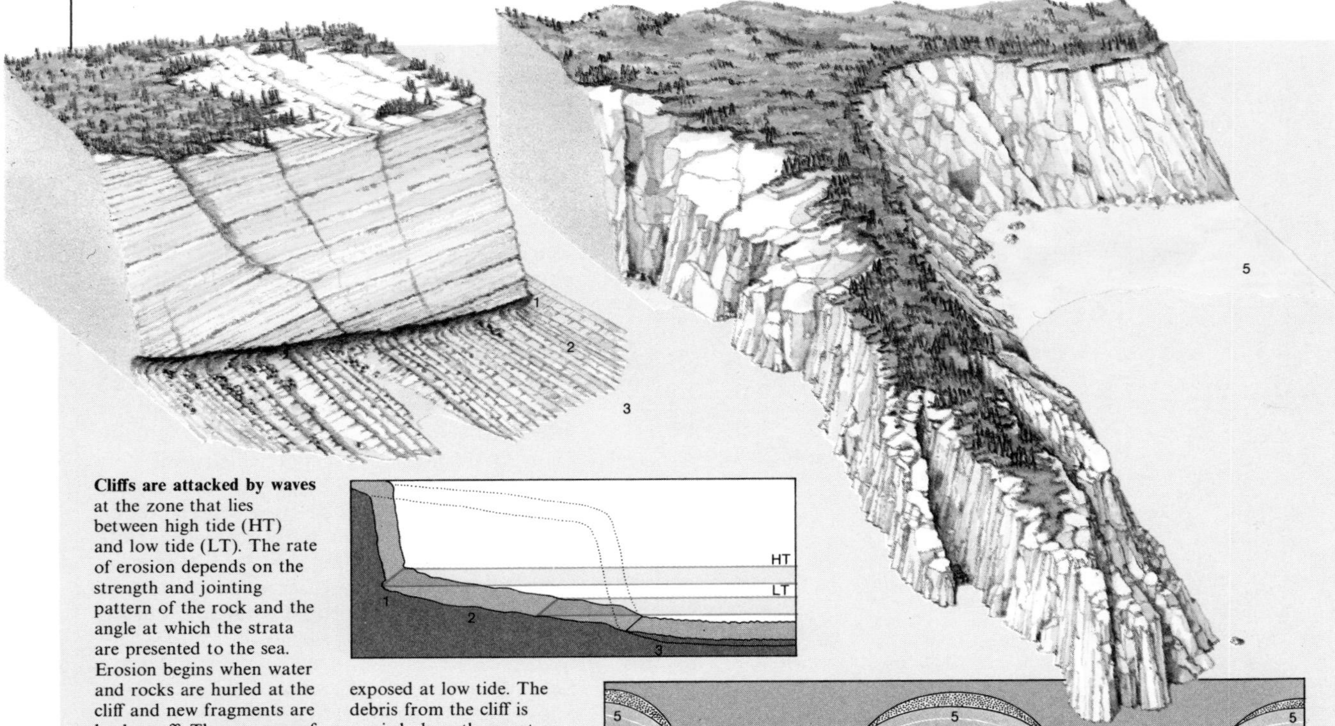

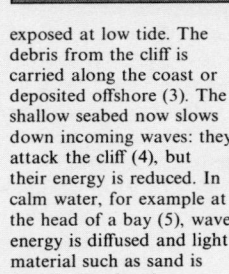

Cliffs are attacked by waves at the zone that lies between high tide (HT) and low tide (LT). The rate of erosion depends on the strength and jointing pattern of the rock and the angle at which the strata are presented to the sea. Erosion begins when water and rocks are hurled at the cliff and new fragments are broken off. The pressure of the water also compresses air in joints and cracks to shatter the rock face. As the base of the cliff is attacked, a notch (1) may be cut, and as this is made deeper the cliff above collapses. Eventually a wave-cut platform (2) is created, the top of which is exposed at low tide. The debris from the cliff is carried along the coast or deposited offshore (3). The shallow seabed now slows down incoming waves: they attack the cliff (4), but their energy is reduced. In calm water, for example at the head of a bay (5), wave energy is diffused and light material such as sand is deposited as beaches.

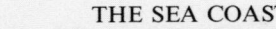

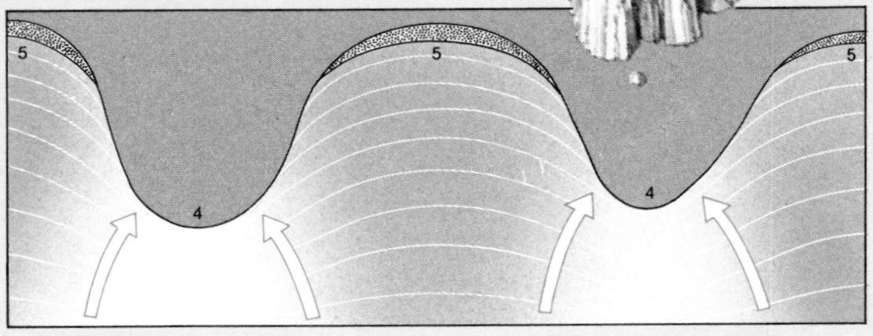

THE SEA COAST

The coastline is continually changing, whether day by day as the tides sift and sort the sand and shingle on the beaches, or over tens of thousands of years as the erosive power of waves carves out headlands and bays. And over millions of years the coastline is subjected to major changes of sea level, whether it is the land uplifting or sinking, or the sea itself rising or receding. Today, interference by man can damage the coast. Dam building and river-channel engineering drastically reduce the amount of sediment reaching the coast; and sea walls built to protect the coast and groynes constructed to retard sand removal both pose a long-term threat to adjacent coasts, which become starved of the sediment that previously supplied their beaches.

When a headland has been created (below), wave erosion continues on both sides and a cave (1) may be formed. After many years of wave action the cave will break through to the other side and an arch (2) may be created.

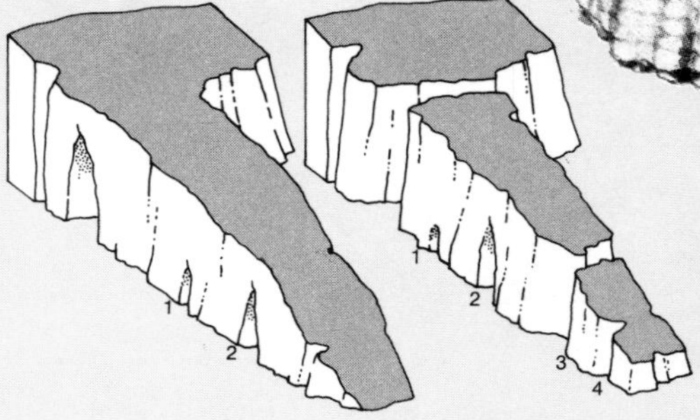

Light material such as mud, sand and shingle is carried by the sea. Waves tend to push the particles obliquely up a beach (right), but the backwash moves the material down again at right-angles to the shore. Thus the materials move in a zigzag fashion along the beach (1). This is known as longshore drift. When the load-carrying capacity of the waves is reduced for any reason, the material is deposited and forms a variety of features. The largest beaches (2) are found in the calmest waters such as in bays or at river mouths, with the finest grains sorted out nearest to the sea and larger pebbles stranded higher up. Spits (3) and bars (4) are sand ridges deposited across a bay or river mouth. When one end of the ridge is attached to the land it is called a spit. Spits are very often shaped like a hook as waves are refracted around the tip of land. Bars are formed where sand is deposited in shallow water offshore across the entrances to bays and run parallel to the coastline. Dunes, pictured above, are formed when sand on the beach is driven inland by onshore winds. Very often they isolate flooded land behind them to form coastal features such as salt marshes and mud flats.

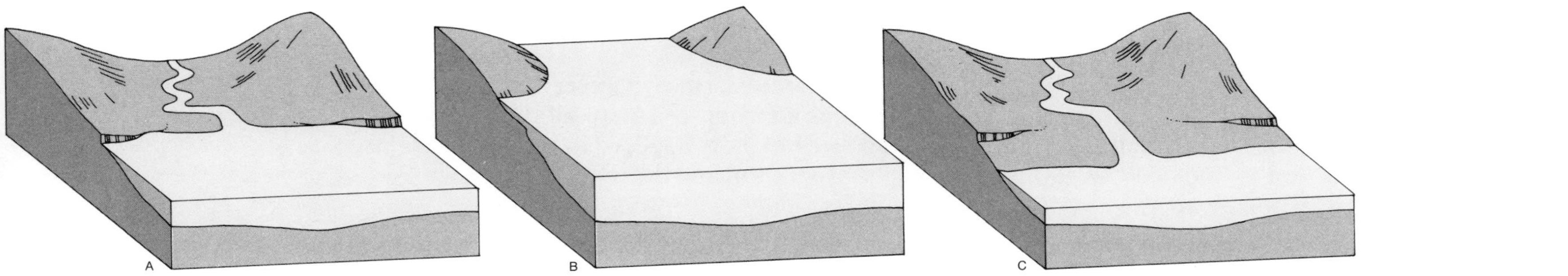

There are two major kinds of coastline—coastlines of submergence and coastlines of emergence. They are created by either a sinking or an uplift of the land, or by a change in sea level. A coastline with wave-cut cliffs and a river valley (A), for example, that experiences a rise in sea level will produce a new coastline (B) with a drowned estuary, coastal uplands isolated as islands, and a submerged coastal plain. The same coastline subjected to a drop in sea level (C) results in an extended river, abandoned cliffs far inland, and a raised beach that forms a new coastal plain.

(6,800 miles) of the Pacific from the storm belt south of New Zealand. The waves thus act as a giant conveyor for the energy that is finally used up in a few seconds of intense activity. Few other natural systems gather their energy so widely and then concentrate it so effectively.

A ball floating on the sea surface shows that, although a passing wave form moves forward, the water (and ball) follow a near-circular path and end up almost where they started. Beneath the surface the water follows similar orbits, but the amount of movement becomes progressively less with depth, until it dies out altogether. The greater the wavelength (the distance between crests) the greater is the depth of disturbance.

Long-swell waves approaching a gentle shore start disturbing the seabed far from the coast and these waves slow up, pack closer together and increase in height until they become unstable, thus producing the spilling white surf that carries much sediment to build up wide sandy beaches. Shorter local storm waves disturb the water to less depth, and thus reach much closer inshore before they interact with the seabed. Such waves do not therefore break until they plunge directly down on to the beach, leading to severe erosion, which results in the production of steep pebble beaches.

Waves slow up in shallow water, and so an undulating seabed causes their crests to bend and change their direction of approach. As a result, waves converge toward headlands (where their erosional attack is concentrated), but they diverge as they enter bays, spreading out their energy and encouraging the deposition of the sediment they carry across the seabed close inshore. The high-energy waves at the headlands remove any rock fragments that become detached and transport them to the beaches that form at the bayheads.

Erosional coasts

Much of the local variability of coastal scenery results from differing rates of erosion on different types of rock. Bays are cut back rapidly into soft rocks such as clay, sand or gravel. Headlands are evidence that the sea takes longer to remove higher areas of harder rock such as granite or limestone. Despite the enormous power of storm waves, erosion of resistant rocks is slow and relies on any weakness that the sea can exploit.

Joints, faults and bedding planes are etched out by the water and by rock fragments hurled against them by breaking waves. Air compressed into such crevices by water pressure widens and deepens them into cracks and then into caves. In this way a solid cliff face can be eroded to form the great variety of features.

Resistant rocks can form steep, simple cliffs of great height—more than 600 m (2,000 ft) in some places—and the sea may have to undercut them to produce collapse and retreat. Cliffs of weaker rocks rarely reach 100 m (330 ft) in height and are more rapidly eroded by atmospheric processes, by running water and by landslips. There the role of the sea is largely confined to removing the rock debris from the foot of the cliff. Soft rock cliffs are gently sloping but complex in form.

Coasts of deposition

Although waves bend as they approach the shore, they rarely become completely parallel to the coastline. Wave crests drive sediment obliquely toward the beach, whereas the troughs carry it back directly offshore down the beach slope. In this way, sand and pebbles are transported in a zigzag motion, called longshore drift, away from the areas where they are produced. One such source of material is cliff erosion, but on average about 95 percent of the material moving on to beaches was originally carried to the coast by rivers.

Beaches are built up wherever longshore drift is impeded (for example, by a headland) or where wave and current energy is reduced (as at the head of a bay). An abundant supply of sediment may build a sandbar across the mouth of a bay or in shallow water offshore. Where the coast changes direction, longshore drift may continue in its original direction and build a spit out from the land. Depositional features may become strengthened by vegetation. Plants may take root and bind together newly deposited sediments, but they constitute relatively delicate coasts that are vulnerable to erosion if for any reason they are not continually supplied with fresh deposits of sediment.

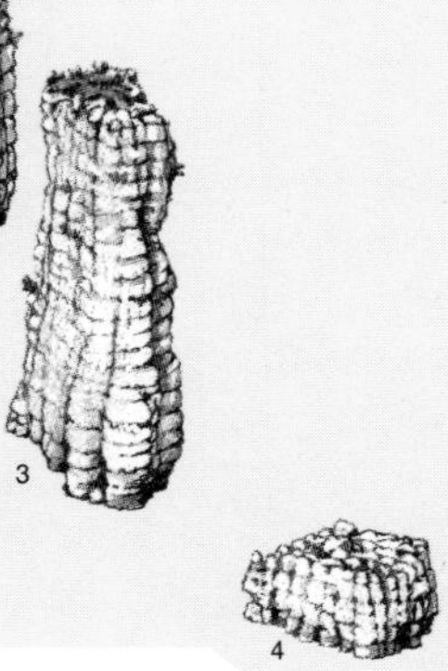

Further wave erosion (above) causes the roof of the arch to collapse, leaving an isolated column of rock called a stack (3). Another cave, and then an arch, may be formed behind the stack, which itself may be eroded to a short stump (4).

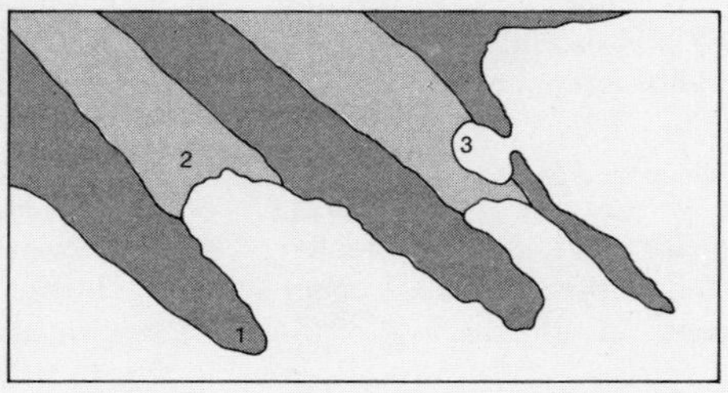

Headlands alternating with bays are found where bands of strong (1) and weak (2) rocks meet the coast at an angle and there is a varied resistance to erosion. The bays are first carved out of the softer rock, leaving the waves to attack the headlands of hard rock. If, in contrast, the strata lie parallel to the coast, then the hard rock has few irregular indentations except where the sea has broken through to the soft rock behind and has scoured out a cove (3).

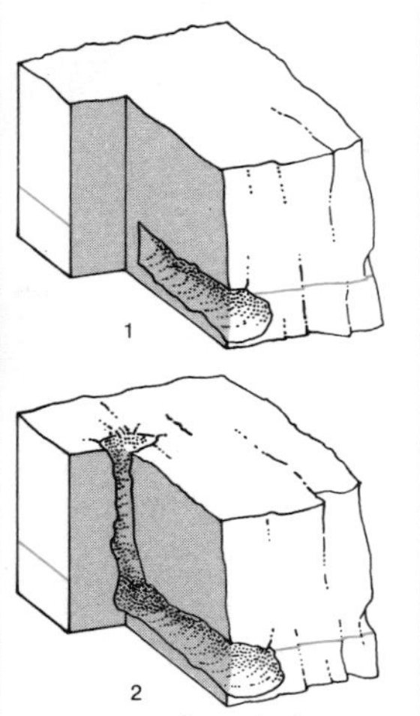

Gloups are formed when waves first erode a cave, then extend it backward as a long shaft running into the cliff (1). If the roof collapses at one point, a blowhole, or gloup (2), is formed. If the whole roof collapses, a deep cleft called a geo is created.

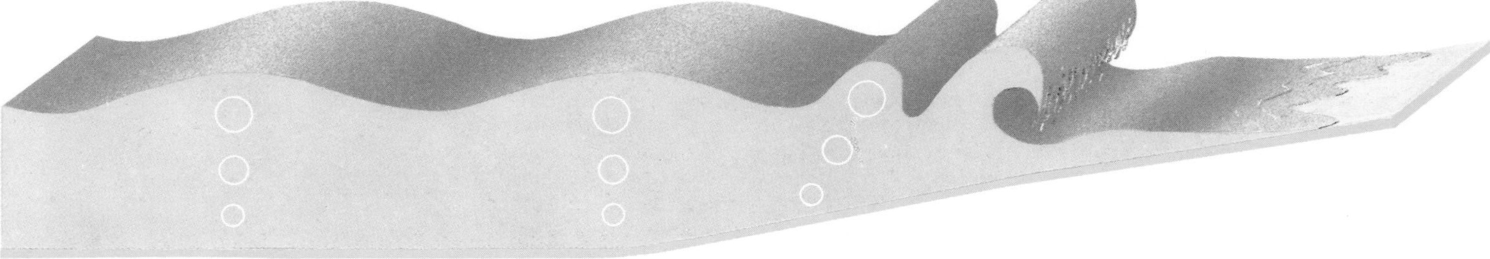

Waves are generated by wind on the surface of the sea. It is the shape of the wave that travels forward—the individual water particles move in near-circular orbits. Disturbance diminishes with depth to about half a wavelength. Waves break when they strike a sloping shore, and the wave height is about the same as the depth of the water.

Landscape-makers: Wind and Weathering

Winds are part of the global circulation of air and they can affect landforms wherever surface material is loose and unprotected by vegetation. The effects of a strong wind are a familiar sight—whether in the dust clouds that rise from a plowed field after a dry spell, or in the sand swept along the beach on a windy day. Weathering is the disintegration and decomposition of rocks through their exposure to the atmosphere. It includes the changes that destroy the original structure of rocks, and few on the Earth's surface have not been weathered at one time or another in the history of our evolving landscape.

Sand dunes cover only 20 percent of the world's deserts, and tend to be concentrated in a small number of sand seas, or ergs, such as the Erg Bourharet in Algeria (above).

Active and fixed dunes in Africa and western Asia

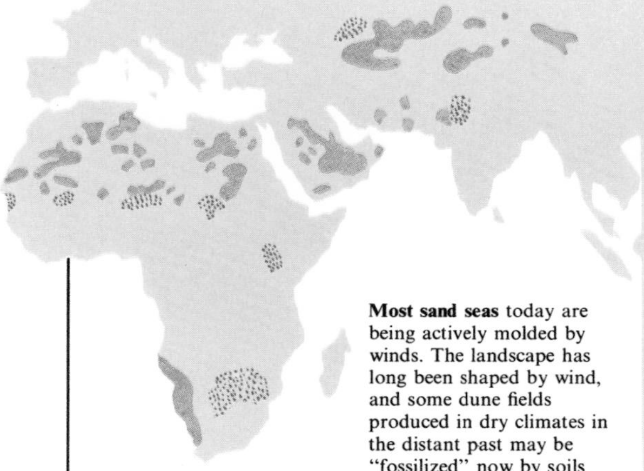

Fixed sand dunes

Active sand dunes

Most sand seas today are being actively molded by winds. The landscape has long been shaped by wind, and some dune fields produced in dry climates in the distant past may be "fossilized" now by soils and vegetation cover. Desertification often occurs where this vegetation is disturbed by man.

Longitudinal, or seif, dunes (below) are long, narrow ridges that lie parallel to the direction of prevailing winds. Surface heating and wind flow produce vertical spiraling motions of air.

Direction of wind

EROSION AND WEATHERING

Winds result from the differential heating of regions of the globe. They act indirectly as agents of erosion through water or waves, but they also directly affect the surface of the Earth, molding landforms either by erosion or deposition. The nature of weathering processes and the rate at which they operate depend upon climate, the properties of the rock and the conditions of the biosphere. Both wind erosion and the various weathering processes are significant landscape-makers.

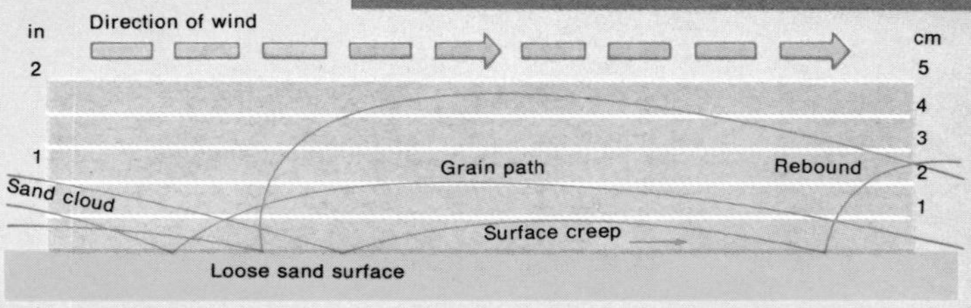
Direction of wind
in
cm
2
5
4
3
1
Grain path
Rebound
2
Sand cloud
1
Surface creep
Loose sand surface

Sand particles move in a series of long jumps—a process called saltation. Particles describe a curved path (above), the height and length of which depends upon the mass of the grain, the wind velocity and the number of other particles moving around. Saltation only occurs in a layer extending up to approximately 1 m (3 ft) above the ground surface. Sand grains moving in this way are also responsible for the abraded base of features such as pedestal rocks (right). These landforms are weathered first—for example by the crystallization of salts—and are then eroded by the sand-laden winds.

Many rocks are formed deep in the Earth, where they are in equilibrium with the forces that created them. If they become exposed at the surface, they are in disequilibrium with atmospheric forces. This brings about the changes—adjustments to atmospheric and organic agents—that we call weathering. Products of weathering are moved by agents of erosion, one of which is the wind. Where the surface is protected, for example by vegetation, the wind has little effect, but where strong winds attack loose surface material that is unprotected, erosion, abrasion and deposition may occur, producing characteristic landforms.

How wind shapes the surface

Strong winds occur in many places, but nowhere are they more effective in forming the surface of the land than in deserts, where their work is largely unhindered by vegetation. There the wind can pick up material and then, charged with sand particles, blast away at the ground, carrying away the debris and depositing it. Many notorious desert winds are associated with sand movement and dust storms—the harmattan of West Africa and the sirocco of the Middle East, for example.

Wind erosion occurs where winds charged with sand attack soils or rock. Dry soils may be broken up and the resulting debris, which includes soil nutrients, is carried away as dust. This poses a serious problem, especially when arid and semiarid lands experience drought. Wind erosion involving the lifting and blowing away of loose material from the ground surface is called deflation.

Erosion by sand and rock fragments carried by winds is called abrasion. In this way winds erode individual surface pebbles into distinctive shapes known as ventifacts. They can also mold larger rock masses into aerodynamic shapes known as yardangs—features that often look rather like upturned rowing boats. Some of these features are so large that they have been identified only since satellite photographs have become available. Finally, winds erode by attrition, which involves the mutual wearing down of particles as they are carried along.

Winds can transport material in three different ways. They can lift loose, sand-sized particles into the air and carry them downwind along trajectories that resemble those of ballistic missiles: the particles rise steeply and descend along gentle flight paths. This produces a bouncing movement known as saltation in a layer extending approximately 1 m (3 ft) above the

Chemical and mechanical weathering occurs in the soil zone. Jointed bedrock assists both processes. The roots of trees help to break up rock, and rainwater gives rise to chemical weathering. Organic acids produced by bacteria in the soil living off decaying organisms also cause decomposition. All these processes contribute toward soil formation.

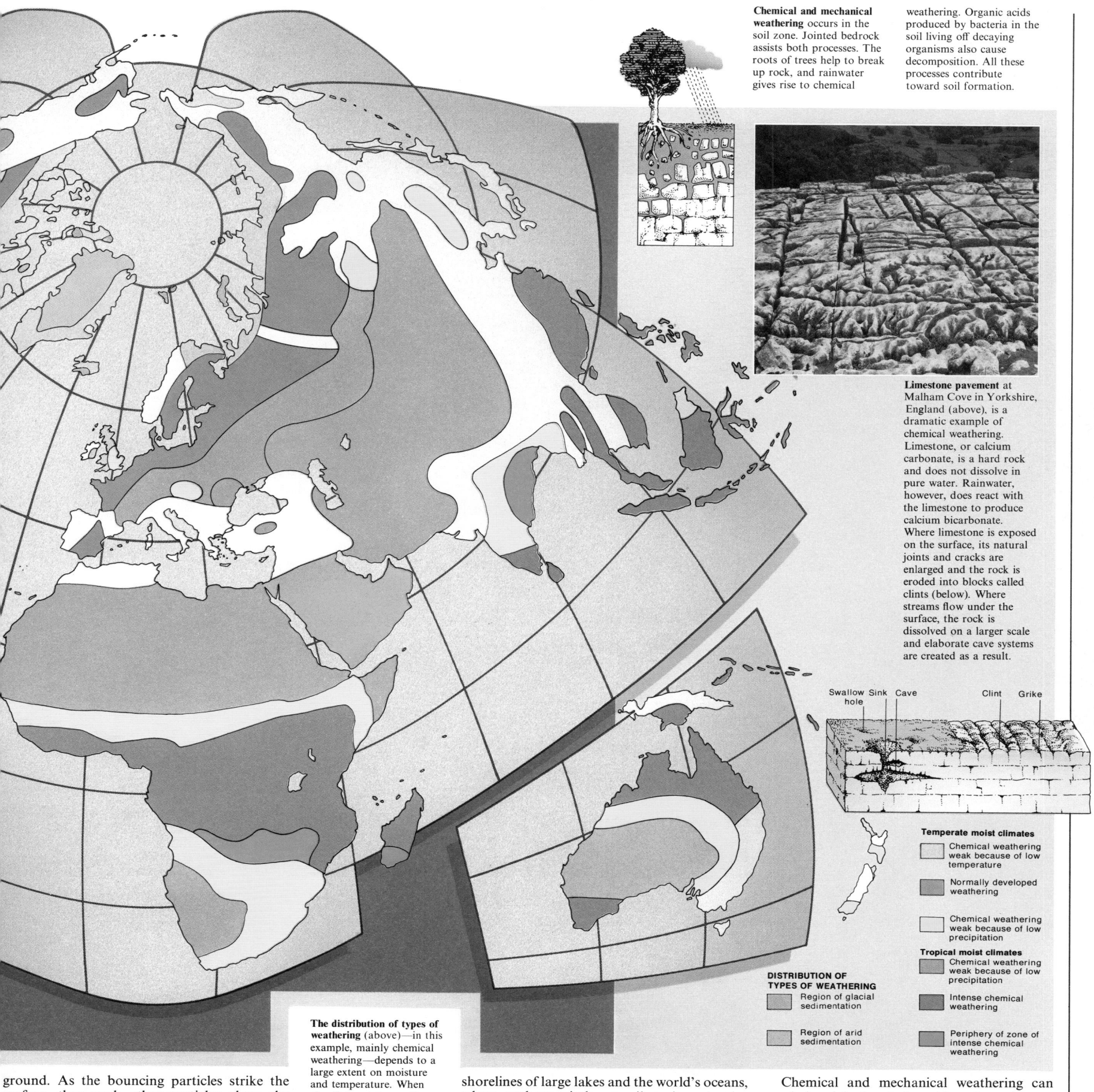

Limestone pavement at Malham Cove in Yorkshire, England (above), is a dramatic example of chemical weathering. Limestone, or calcium carbonate, is a hard rock and does not dissolve in pure water. Rainwater, however, does react with the limestone to produce calcium bicarbonate. Where limestone is exposed on the surface, its natural joints and cracks are enlarged and the rock is eroded into blocks called clints (below). Where streams flow under the surface, the rock is dissolved on a larger scale and elaborate cave systems are created as a result.

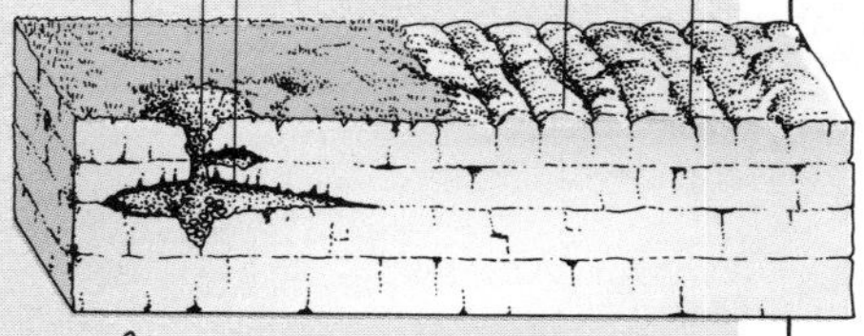
Swallow hole
Sink
Cave
Clint
Grike

DISTRIBUTION OF TYPES OF WEATHERING
Region of glacial sedimentation
Region of arid sedimentation
Temperate moist climates
Chemical weathering weak because of low temperature
Normally developed weathering
Chemical weathering weak because of low precipitation
Tropical moist climates
Chemical weathering weak because of low precipitation
Intense chemical weathering
Periphery of zone of intense chemical weathering

The distribution of types of weathering (above)—in this example, mainly chemical weathering—depends to a large extent on moisture and temperature. When classifying regions with different rates of chemical weathering in terms of climatic zones, many areas of the world can be placed into one of two principal categories: tropical moist climates and temperate moist climates. The white areas on the map are mountain ranges or regions of tectonic activity where there is no appreciable weathering mantle.

ground. As the bouncing particles strike the surface, they push other particles along the ground (creep or drift). Fine particles that are disturbed by saltation rise up into the airflow and are carried away as dust (suspension).

The materials eroded and transported by winds must eventually come to rest in features of deposition, the most extensive of which are sand dunes. Sand seas at first sight appear to be random and complex, rather like a choppy ocean, but their features generally fall into three size groups: small ripples, which have a wavelength of up to 3 m (10 ft) and a height of 20 cm (8 in); dunes, with a wavelength of 20–300 m (65–1,000 ft) and a height of up to 30 m (68 ft); and sand mountains or "draa," which have a wavelength of 1–3 km (0.6–1.5 miles) and rise to a height of up to 200 m (650 ft). Within each size group various forms can be explained in terms of the nature of the sand and the kinds of winds that blow over it. Where winds blow consistently from one direction, long linear dunes form parallel or transverse to the wind direction. Where sand supply is limited, horned "barchan" dunes may form. If winds blow from several directions during a year, then star-shaped dunes and other complex patterns appear. Sand dunes are also common along the shorelines of large lakes and the world's oceans, where onshore winds can pile quite extensive areas of loose drifting sand.

Agents of weathering

Weathering takes two forms: mechanical weathering breaks up rock without altering its mineral constituents, whereas chemical weathering changes in some way the nature of mineral crystals. One agent of mechanical weathering is temperature change. It used to be thought that rocks disintegrated as a result of a huge daily range of temperature (thermal weathering). Despite travelers' tales of rocks splitting in the desert night with cracks like pistol shots, there is little evidence to support this view. In the presence of water, however, alternate heating and cooling of rocks does result in fracture. Frost is also an effective rock breaker. The freezing of water and expansion of ice in the cracks and pores of rocks create disruptive pressures; alternate freezing and thawing eventually causes pieces of rock to break off in angular fragments. Finally, the roots of plants and trees grow into the joints of rock and widen them, thus loosening the structure of the rock. Animals burrowing through the soil can have a similar effect on rocks.

Chemical and mechanical weathering can work hand in hand. In arid regions, for example, the crystallization of salts results in the weathering of rock. As water evaporates from the rock surface, salt crystals grow (from minerals dissolved in the water) in small openings in the rock. In time these crystals bring to bear enough pressure to break off rock fragments from the parent block.

Chemical weathering is most effective in humid tropical climates, however, and it usually involves the decomposition of rocks as a result of their exposure to air and rainwater, which contains dissolved chemicals. Carbon dioxide from the air, for example, becomes dissolved in rainwater, making it into weak carbonic acid. This reacts with minerals such as calcite, which is found in many rocks. Similarly, rocks can be oxidized by oxygen in the air. This happens to rocks that contain iron, for example, if they are exposed on the surface: a reddish iron oxide is produced which causes the rocks to crumble.

Over many thousands, even millions, of years, the processes of mechanical and chemical weathering have affected many of the rocks on the Earth's surface. When rocks are weakened in such a way, they then fall prey to the agents of erosion—water, ice, winds and waves.

Landscape-makers: Man

MAN THE GEOLOGICAL AGENT

In 1864 a conservationist named George Perkins Marsh introduced the thesis that "man in fact made the Earth" rather than the converse. The idea of man as a geological agent was further developed in the 1920s. Man modifies the landscape in many ways; sometimes he transforms the Earth completely—he even creates land where no land was before.

Man has done much to reshape the face of the planet since his first appearance on Earth more than two million years ago. Early man did little to harm the environment but, with the rise of agriculture, the landscape began to change. An increasing population and the growth of urban settlements gradually created greater demands for agricultural land and living space. But industrialization during the last 200 years has had the biggest impact. Man's search for and exploitation of the Earth's resources has to a large extent transformed the natural landscape and at the same time created totally artificial man-made environments.

Man's major impact on the landscape has been through forest clearance. He made the first attack on natural forests about 8,000 years ago in Neolithic times in northern and western Europe, as revealed by the changing composition of tree pollen deposited in bogs. After Roman times, especially in the Mediterranean region, there was another spate of forest clearance, so that by the Middle Ages little original forest survived in the Old World. As population and emigration increased, it was the turn of trees in the New World and Africa to fall before the axe and plow. Man's present voracious appetite for timber and its products could, if unchecked, clear most of the Earth's great forests by the end of this century.

Forest clearance not only changes the appearance of the landscape but can alter the balance of nature within a region. The hydrological cycle may be affected, and soil erosion may be increased, which in turn chokes rivers with sediment and leads to the silting up of harbors and estuaries. The coastal area of Valencia in Spain, for example, has widened by nearly 4 km (2.5 miles) since Roman times, much of which can be accounted for by forest clearance, and subsequent soil erosion and the deposition of the material by rivers as they near the sea. Reafforestation of an area can reduce soil erosion and the threat of flooding. Landscape management can reduce wind speeds: for example, shelter belts in the Russian steppes have been planted over distances of more than 100 km (62 miles).

Water management

The second great impact of man has been on the waterways of the world. The most spectacular changes are caused by the construction of dams to make vast new lakes. Such projects have frequently had effects far beyond those originally anticipated. The Aswan High Dam on the River Nile was completed in 1970, creating Lake Nasser and making possible the irrigation of an additional 550,000 hectares (1,358,000 acres) in upper Egypt. But some would argue that the dam holds back silt from the rivers and stores it in the lake, a fact that has seriously reduced the rate of silting in the Nile delta. This has resulted in increased salinity and some loss of fertility of the soil, as well as changes to the delta's coastline. The storage of silt in Lake Nasser has caused increased erosion of the riverbed downstream and the undermining of the foundations of bridges and barrages.

Other man-made changes to rivers include straightening and canalization, usually for

Massive power plants (left) symbolize man's modifications to the landscape in modern, industrialized society. Demand for energy and mineral resources has led to the creation of huge holes in the ground like this borax mine (below left) in the Mojave desert in California. The open pit is 100 m (330 ft) deep, 1,460 m (4,800 ft) long and 915 m (3,000 ft) wide. In opening up resource areas in Brazil, the Trans-Amazonian highway has disturbed the forest (below).

Hong Kong's bustling waterfront (below) captures the true essence of urban man. If space is in short supply, he expands his world vertically and maximizes his use of every square meter. Central business districts in the world's major cities reflect this concern with space.

flood protection, but also to prevent the channel from shifting. As long ago as the third millennium BC, during the reign of Emperor Yao, a hydraulic engineer was apparently appointed to control the wandering course of the Hwang-Ho (Yellow River), and the system he devised survived for at least 1,500 years. Even so, over the centuries, the river has changed course radically, and today measures are still being taken to control the fine sediment that the river carries and the flooding caused by its deposition. The Missouri River in the United States is estimated to erode material from an area of about 3,680 hectares (9,000 acres) annually over a length of 1,220 km (758 miles). It is little wonder that engineers attempt to control rivers by means of realignment or try to "train" a river's flow by using concrete stays.

New land from old

The continuing pressure of population on food resources and the need to create new agricultural land illustrate still further the impact of man as a landscape shaper. As part of irrigation projects land is often leveled and new waterways are created in the form of canals. Pakistan has one of the most extensive man-made irrigation systems in the world. It controls almost completely the flow of the Indus, Sutlej and Punjab rivers through some 640 km (400 miles) of linking canals.

A huge demand for rice in many parts of southeastern Asia has led to farmers terracing steep slopes on many mountainous islands. In the Netherlands, about one-third of the entire cultivated area of the country is land that has been reclaimed from the sea. In the future more grandiose schemes are likely. Any large-scale expansion of agricultural land in the Soviet Union will be mainly dependent on water supply. There have been plans since the 1930s to divert northward-flowing rivers to irrigated areas in the south and west. This idea, and it is believed that it might become a reality by the turn of the century, could have serious implications for the waters of the Arctic Ocean. If the amount of fresh water flowing into the ocean is reduced, salinity will increase, thus affecting the melting of ice floes and, consequently, sea level.

Man has also made his mark along the coastlines, from small-scale measures, such as the construction of groynes—wooden piles that reduce the amount of sand that is transported along the beach by wave action—to large-scale man-made harbors.

Modern man, the urban dweller of the machine age, has brought great changes to the face of the landscape. The need for materials for the construction of the urban fabric has led to the creation of huge quarries, in which building stone and road-building materials are extracted from the ground. Demand for energy and minerals leads to extensive modification of the landscape, especially where mineral deposits are near the surface and can be extracted by open-cast mining. The largest holes on Earth (excluding ocean basins) are those that result from the extraction of fuel (coal) and minerals.

The side effects of mining can be detrimental to the environment. Land may subside and despoliation of the landscape by slag heaps, for example, is considerable. Escaping coal dust can suffocate vegetation in a mining area, and gases given off during some mining operations can also damage plant and animal life.

Reclamation of spoiled areas is obligatory in many countries. Old open-cast workings are often filled with water to be used for recreational facilities, and slag heaps are treated and planted with vegetation: research has produced certain strains of plants that will grow even in the most acidic soils.

The true impact of man

During the last hundred years or so man has become much more aware of his role as an agent of landscape creation and destruction. The significance of man the landscape-maker, in comparison with slow, natural changes, is the speed with which he effects transformation, the sheer amount of energy which he can apply to a relatively small area, and the selectiveness and determination with which he applies that energy. Man's increased impact has not been a smooth and continuous process: it has occurred at different rates in different places and at different times. While it can be argued that some landscapes have been constructed which themselves conserve and often beautify the natural environment, man's active role has primarily been destructive: he has transformed the Earth's surface, perhaps irreversibly.

THE DUTCH POLDERS

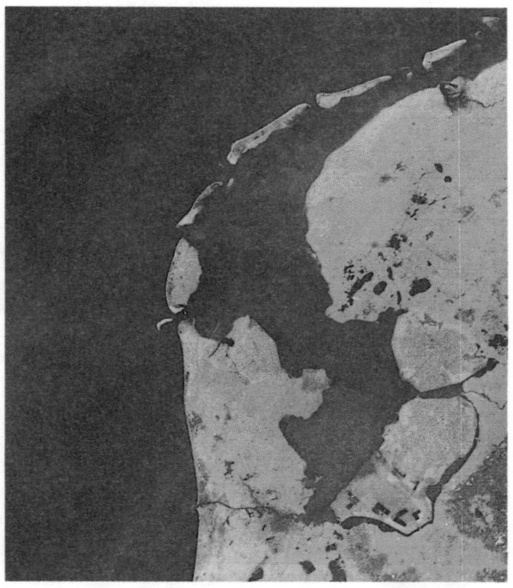

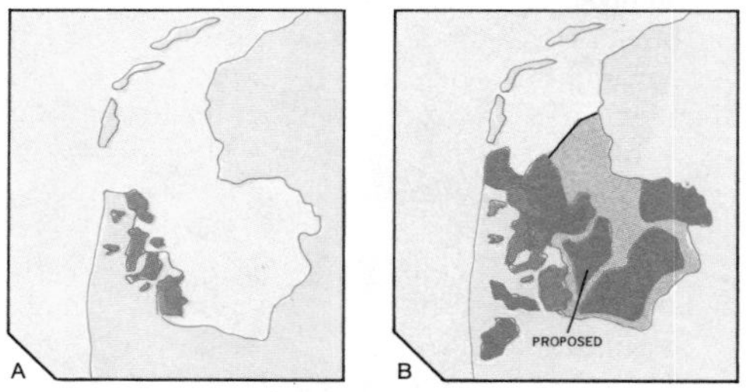

Reclamation of the Dutch polders from the North Sea is an example of man creating land. Many centuries ago a large part of what is now the western Netherlands was beneath the sea. From the 15th to the 17th centuries (A) dykes were constructed to enclose land and protect it against inundation from the sea, and enable it to be farmed. Later, windmills were used to drain away sea water. Further reclamation in the 19th and 20th centuries (B) has brought the total area to 165,000 hectares (408,000 acres). In 1932 a 40 km (25 mile) dam was completed, enclosing the Zuider Zee—which is now a freshwater lake that was renamed the IJsselmeer—and reducing Holland's vulnerable coastline by 320 km (200 miles). To create a polder, a dyke is built and the water pumped out. Reeds are grown to help dry out the soil. After a few years drains are put in to remove water remaining. Newly created polders (light blue) show up well on this satellite image (top).

Man-made environments have become increasingly complex and large scale. Highway construction—this vast interchange (left) is in Chicago—is typical of the extensive use of land for modern transport systems alone. The acreage of land use classified as urban continues to increase. Man's endeavors to make still more land available for his many purposes have extended to cultivating previously inhospitable desert lands (above). More than half the land in Israel is naturally unproductive because of its aridity. By means of elaborate water carriage and storage schemes and scientifically researched irrigation projects, the desert has been totally transformed from a barren wasteland into intensively cultivated fields. Output from agriculture can also be increased by terracing. In densely populated areas, or mountainous regions, as in Luzon in the Philippines (right), man's skillful landscaping has completely reshaped the topography.

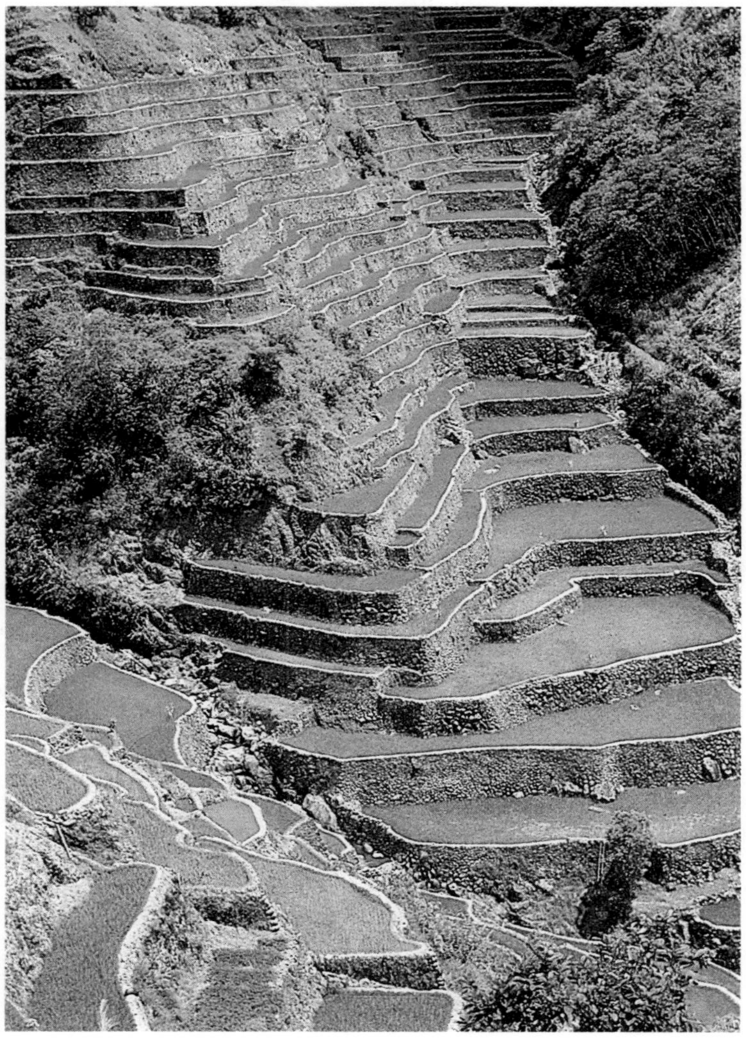

Part 3

THE EMERGENCE OF LIFE

How life on Earth began and developed
How life has evolved and spread over the planet
How man came to inherit the Earth

THE STAGES OF LIFE

Simple organic molecules, the precursors of life, could certainly have evolved in Earth's primitive atmosphere. Energy from the Sun, volcanoes and electric storms had the power to combine the basic chemicals into the amino acids and other molecules that are the constituents of living matter, forming droplets of "pre-life" in pools and on shorelines. Concentrations of droplets collected around some minerals, coagulating in a "soup" of long-chain polymers—proteins and nucleic acids which together form the living cell. Thus far have scientists re-created life's origins, but the combining of proteins and nucleic acids into a living unit remains to be achieved.

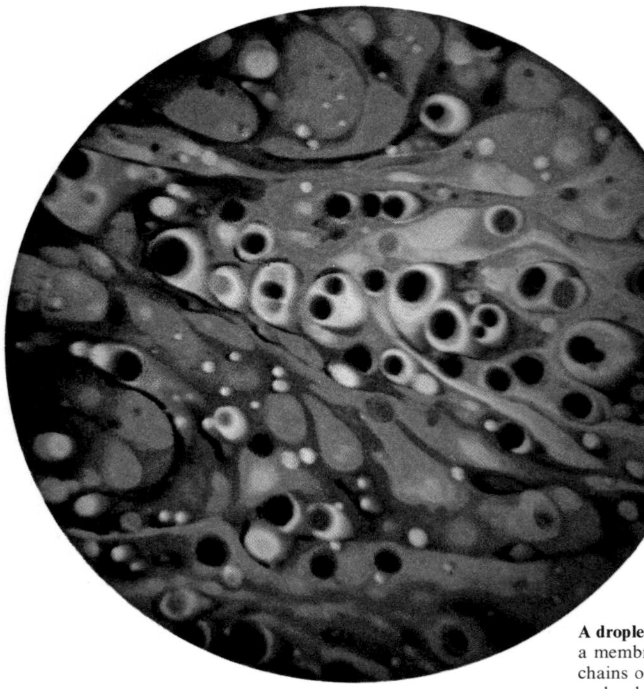

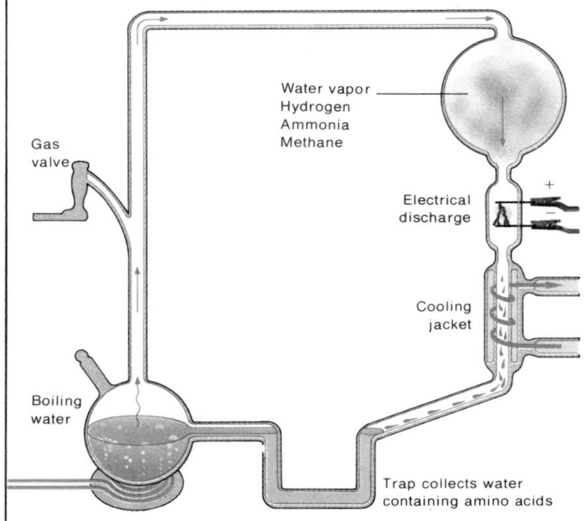
Water vapor
Hydrogen
Ammonia
Methane
Gas valve
Electrical discharge
Cooling jacket
Boiling water
Trap collects water containing amino acids

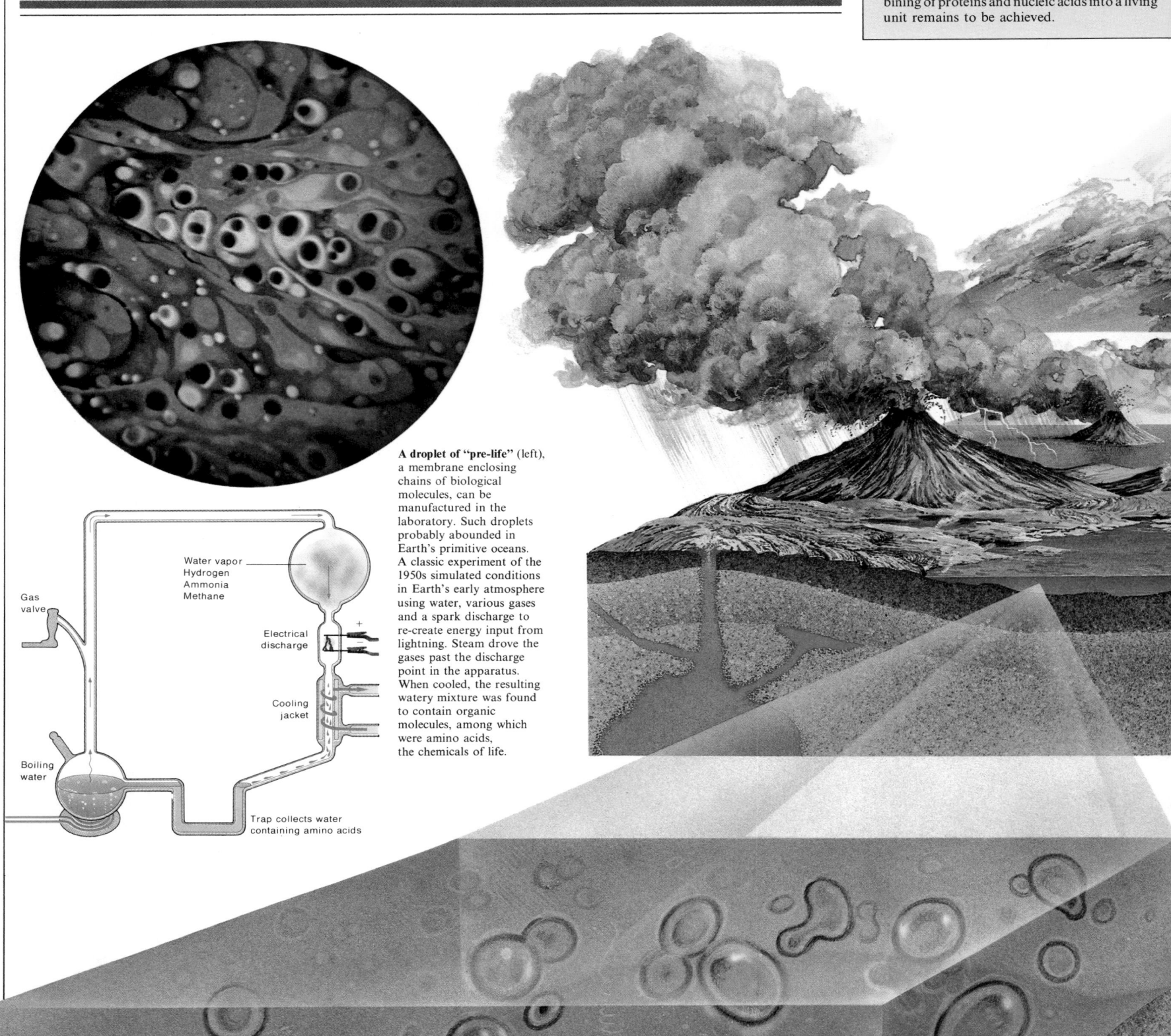

A droplet of "pre-life" (left), a membrane enclosing chains of biological molecules, can be manufactured in the laboratory. Such droplets probably abounded in Earth's primitive oceans. A classic experiment of the 1950s simulated conditions in Earth's early atmosphere using water, various gases and a spark discharge to re-create energy input from lightning. Steam drove the gases past the discharge point in the apparatus. When cooled, the resulting watery mixture was found to contain organic molecules, among which were amino acids, the chemicals of life.

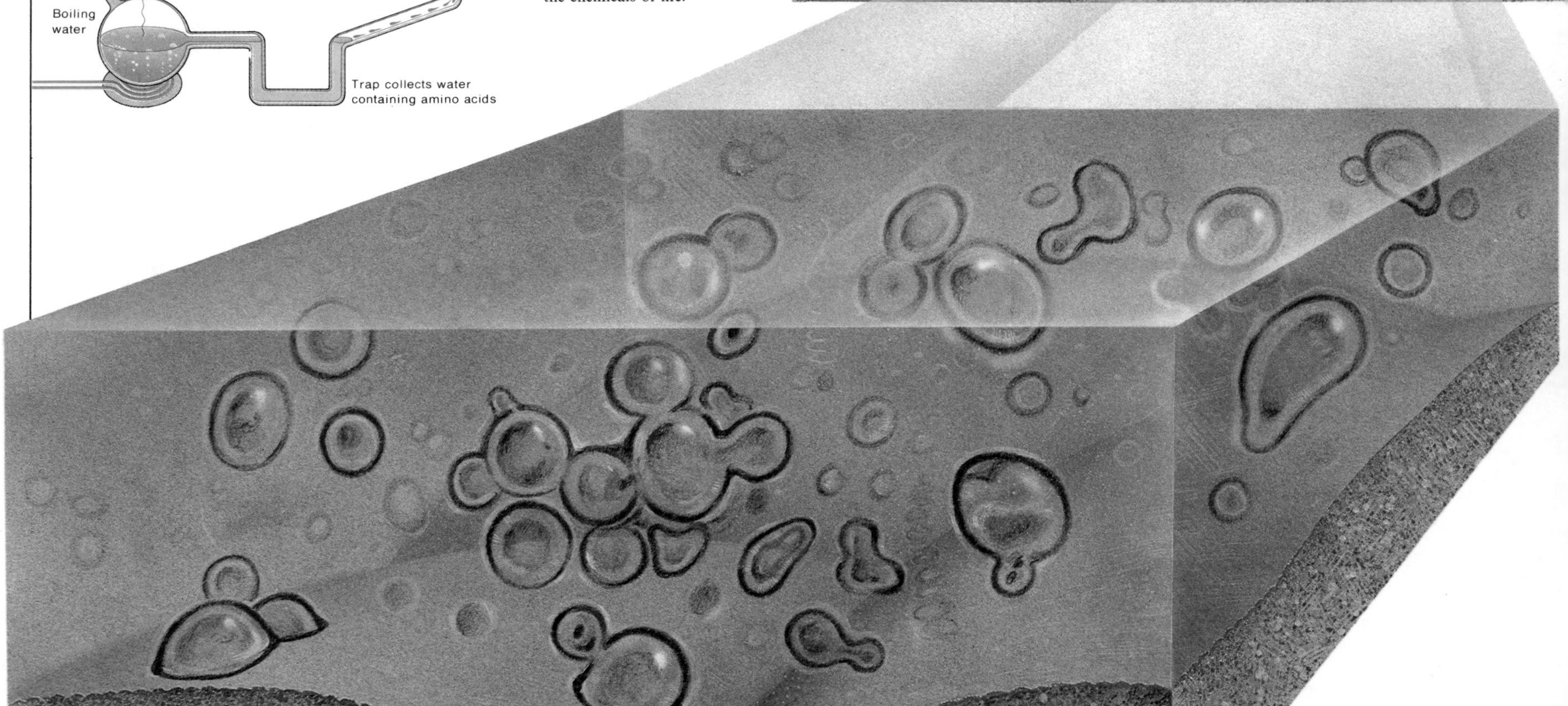

LIFE BEGINS
A "primordial soup" of organic molecules, each separated from the water by a membrane, formed thick concentrations in Earth's shallow pools. From these evolved the long-chain polymers that form proteins and nucleic acids in every living cell.

The Source of Life

Life may have come to Earth from outer space – some meteorites contain life-like organic molecules – but the basic constituents of life, the biochemical structures called proteins and nucleic acids, could just as well have formed on Earth itself. By simulating possible primitive conditions on Earth, and applying a likely energy source, American scientists of the 1950s manufactured, from inorganic substances, the amino acids that form the subunits of all living things.

THE RADIANT SUN
A dense atmosphere of water vapor and various gases—but not oxygen—formed round the cooling planet Earth after its creation 4,600 million years ago. Oxygen in the atmosphere would have prevented the evolution of life from nonliving organic matter by blocking the Sun's ultraviolet radiation (which may have provided energy for the forming of organic compounds), and free oxygen would also have destroyed such compounds as they began to accumulate.

THE PRIMITIVE ATMOSPHERE
Volcanic eruptions drove water vapor and gases into the atmosphere of the young Earth; lightning and other discharges of atmospheric electricity accompanied the torrential rain; dissolved minerals collected in the pools. These were some of the preconditions for life on Earth, whereby mixtures of organic compounds in water may have combined to form more complex units essential for life.

Water played a key part in the creation of life on Earth. At first the temperature of the newly formed planet was far too high for water to exist in a liquid state. Instead, it formed a dense atmosphere of steam, which, as the Earth cooled, condensed into droplets of rain that poured down for perhaps thousands of years. This torrential, thundery rain eroded the land and dissolved the minerals, which collected in pools on the surface.

Earth's original atmosphere was also very different from today's. Most importantly, it contained no free oxygen, the gas which makes air-breathing life possible; the primitive atmosphere was composed of carbon monoxide, carbon dioxide, hydrogen and nitrogen. But the absence of oxygen created two conditions that are essential if life is to evolve. First, without oxygen the atmosphere could have no layer of ozone (an oxygen compound), which now acts as a barrier to most of the Sun's high-energy radiation (mainly ultraviolet light). Second, the absence of free oxygen meant that any complex chemicals that might be formed would not immediately break down again. Thus the molecules of life could form.

The chemistry of life

Life may be distinguished from nonlife in three ways: living organisms are able to increase the complexity of their parts through synthetic, self-building reactions; they obtain and use energy by breaking down chemical compounds; and they can make new copies of themselves.

It is the combined properties of the chemicals of life that make them so special, not just the chemicals themselves. Experiments in the last few decades have given us a very good idea of how life could have arisen from the simple, nonliving chemicals which compose it. In the early 1950s, Harold Urey and Stanley Miller simulated the atmosphere of a primitive world by filling a flask with water, ammonia, methane and hydrogen. They supplied it with energy in the form of heat and an electric spark—to simulate lightning—and the experiment was left to run for a week.

Analyzing the mixture formed, they found it contained many chemicals that are associated with living things, particularly nitrogen compounds called amino acids—the really important chemicals of life. Further experiments brought together other gas mixtures, including the one that is now thought to have covered the young Earth, and these gave similar results, as long as there was no free oxygen present. The resulting mixture of organic compounds in water came to be known as the "primordial soup," and it is from this "soup" that life may have emerged.

THE MAKING OF AN AMINO ACID
The 20 amino acids found in the proteins of all living things are produced by combination, or synthesis, of basic molecules: the latter existed almost from the beginnings of Earth's history. Scientists have shown how molecules such as hydrogen, nitrogen and carbon monoxide can be combined to produce certain intermediate organic units. Further processing of these units involves the removal of water molecules to complete the amino acid.

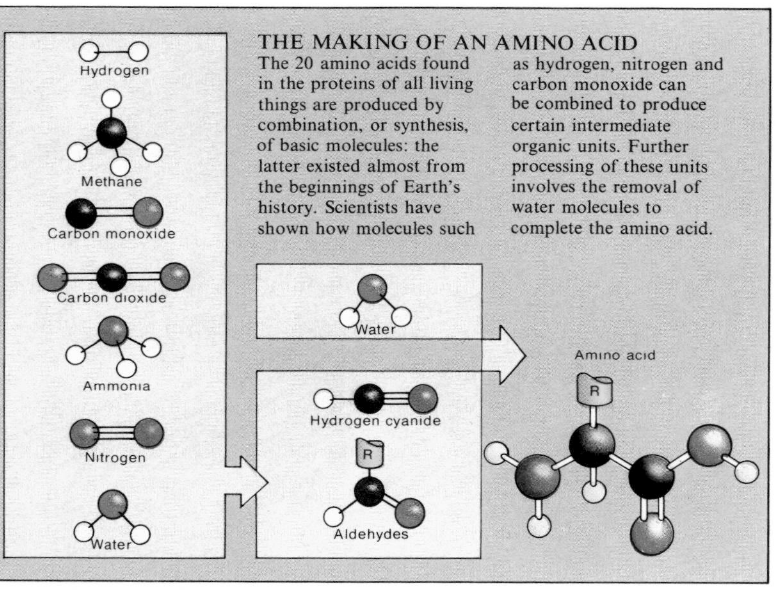
Hydrogen
Methane
Carbon monoxide
Carbon dioxide
Ammonia
Nitrogen
Water
Water
Hydrogen cyanide
R
Aldehydes
Amino acid
R

PROTEIN CHAIN
Two amino acid molecules may combine, through the elimination of a water molecule from their ends. The combination may then form a subunit in the long-chain polymer of a protein basic to life.

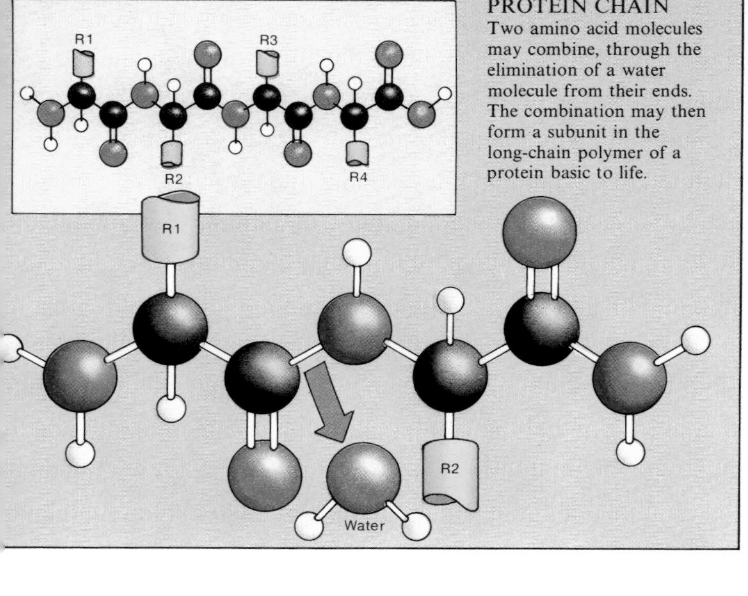
R1
R3
R2
R4
R1
R2
Water

Miller and Urey had shown that the basic substances of life can be derived from a primitive atmosphere. But there are still large gaps in our understanding of how these substances became more organized and self-regulating: in other words, how they became alive. More complex molecular structures somehow developed through the linking up of the basic units to form long, chain-like sequences of larger units, called polymers. But how this happened is still not fully understood.

The two most important classes of biological molecules are proteins and nucleic acids, both of which are polymers. Proteins are the building materials of living matter, the chief components of muscles, skin and hair. They also form enzymes—the chemicals that control biochemical reaction in living cells. Nucleic acids—DNA (deoxyribonucleic acid) and RNA (ribonucleic acid)—are so called because they are found in the central nuclei of cells. They are the cell's genetic material, the raw stuff of heredity. They act as the memories and the messengers of life, storing information in units called genes, and releasing that information to the cells when it is needed. Nucleic acids can reproduce themselves and, without this ability, life would not exist or continue.

The basic units that link together to form proteins are amino acids, and all proteins in living organisms are made up of just 20 different amino acids. In chemical terms, a protein molecule is a polymer consisting of a long chain of amino acid units joined together in a particular sequence, and the code to this sequence is held by DNA.

How living chemicals joined

Experiments with simulated primordial conditions have produced many amino acids other than the 20 commonly found in proteins. All amino acids (and other types of chemicals) tend to "stick" onto the surface of clay, but those 20 found in proteins stick particularly well to clays rich in the metal nickel. This suggests that the first proteins may have been formed in pools or on the fringes of seas, where the primordial soup was in contact with nickel-rich clays. There heat from the Sun or a volcano could have combined the amino acids to form a primitive protein.

The four classes of chemicals that form the basic components of nucleic acids have also, like the amino acids, been "cooked up" in a primordial soup, and they too will stick to clay to form long-chain polymers. And, just as nickel-rich clays are best at absorbing the amino acid constituents of protein, so clays rich in zinc absorb the building blocks of nucleic acids. This suggests that such clays could have been the birthplace of genes, which are the "messengers" of inheritance.

However, the coupling of proteins and nucleic acids, which together form the living cell, has yet to be explained, and it is improbable that proteins or nucleic acids alone could have provided the basis for life.

The Russian biochemist I. A. Oparin has shown that, in water, solutions of polymers (such as proteins) have a tendency to form droplets surrounded by an outer membrane very like that which encloses living cells. As these droplets grow by absorbing more polymers, some split in two when they become too large for stability. If such a droplet had protein enzymes to harness energy and make more polymers, and if it had nucleic acids with instructions for making those proteins, and if each new droplet received a complete copy of the nucleic acid instructions, the droplet would be alive—it would be a living cell.

The Structure of Life

All life forms stem from a single cell, and every cell contains in its nucleus instructions for the re-creation of the organism of which it forms a part. These are encoded in chromosomes, which contain the miraculous molecular substance of DNA, sectioned into units of heredity called genes. The genetic code determines in detail the physical characteristics of an individual creature, so that variations in DNA cause variations in the individual. Scientists believe that it is the interaction of the individual variation with the environment that ultimately leads to the evolution of the similar, interbreeding groups of creatures that are known as species.

THE HIDDEN SECRET

Dramatic discoveries in recent decades have revolutionized biology, the primary life science. Scientists can now trace parts of the genetic blueprint that lays down the pattern for every form of life, linking the large-scale unfolding of species that we know as evolution with the ultramicroscopic activity of the molecules within the nucleus of every cell. This may be the secret behind the rich diversity of life on Earth.

Deoxyribonucleic acid (DNA) consists of a "backbone" of alternating sugar and phosphate molecules, and to each sugar is attached one of four nitrogenous bases (adenine, guanine, thymine and cytostine, or A, G, T, C). A single gene might contain 2,000 of these bases, and in the body cell of a human being the 46 chromosomes (thread-like bodies of DNA and protein) run to 3,000 million bases. The sequence of these bases stores the information for making amino acids into proteins, just as the sequence of letters in this sentence stores the information for making a particular verbal structure. But the DNA alphabet has only four letters (A, G, T, C).

The thread of life

DNA is a double molecule, resembling a twisted ladder, its two main strands twining around each other to form the famous double helix. The strands are linked by pairs of bases—A and T, or G and C—whose shape is such that each pair fits together neatly, like pieces of a jigsaw, to form the rungs of the DNA ladder. As a result, the information on the strands can be duplicated by "unzipping" the double helix and making new strands by using the old ones as templates. DNA stores, duplicates and passes on the information that makes life alive.

Cells multiply by splitting in two, and each newly made cell thus gets instructions for its existence by the mechanism of heredity, the gene. But heredity is a word more often applied to the passing on of DNA from an organism to its offspring. In sexual reproduction the offspring gets some of the DNA (usually half) from one parent, and the rest from the other, ending up with a unique mix all of its own.

The laws of heredity

Man has long known that characteristics can be passed on from one generation to the next, for he has been selectively breeding crops and animals for thousands of years. However, it was not until the mid-nineteenth century that an obscure Austrian monk, Gregor Mendel (1822–84), discovered the laws that govern inheritance, and his work was ignored until the beginning of the twentieth century, when more powerful microscopes made possible the direct observation of the cell.

Mendel experimented with pea plants because they had easily recognizable traits, and because, although normally self-fertilizing, they could be cross-fertilized with pollen from a different plant. Mendel made many crosses between different pure-bred plants and found that in the offspring, or hybrids, some characters always prevailed over others: red flowers over white, tall plants over short, and so on. He called the prevailing characters dominant, and the nonprevailing characters recessive. He then let the first-generation hybrids self-fertilize, and found not only that the recessive traits reappeared in the hybrids' offspring, but also that they reappeared in a constant proportion of three dominant to one recessive; the second generation contained three times as many red-flowered peas as white-flowered peas.

To explain his results, Mendel proposed that each plant had two hereditary "factors"—today called alleles—for each character, and that the dominant factor suppressed the recessive factor. If a plant inherited both a dominant and a recessive factor, the dominant one would prevail. Only if both factors were recessive would the recessive character be apparent. Mendel found many other pairs of traits where one form was dominant and the other recessive. He established that permutations arising from the crossing of the two first-generation hybrids allows the dominant gene to be present in three out of four crosses in the second generation; but in the fourth cross, only the two recessive alleles of the genes are present. So there is always a three-to-one ratio of dominant to recessive.

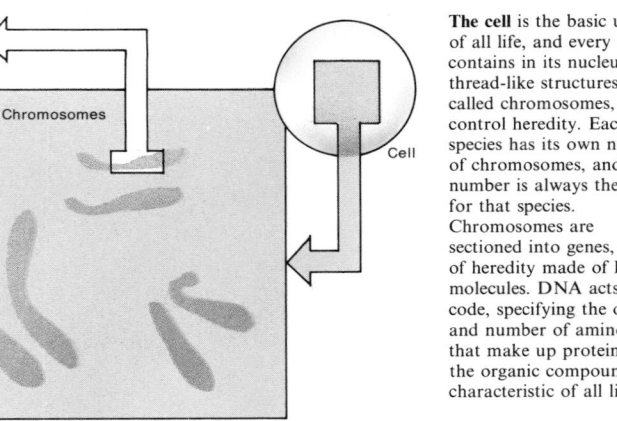

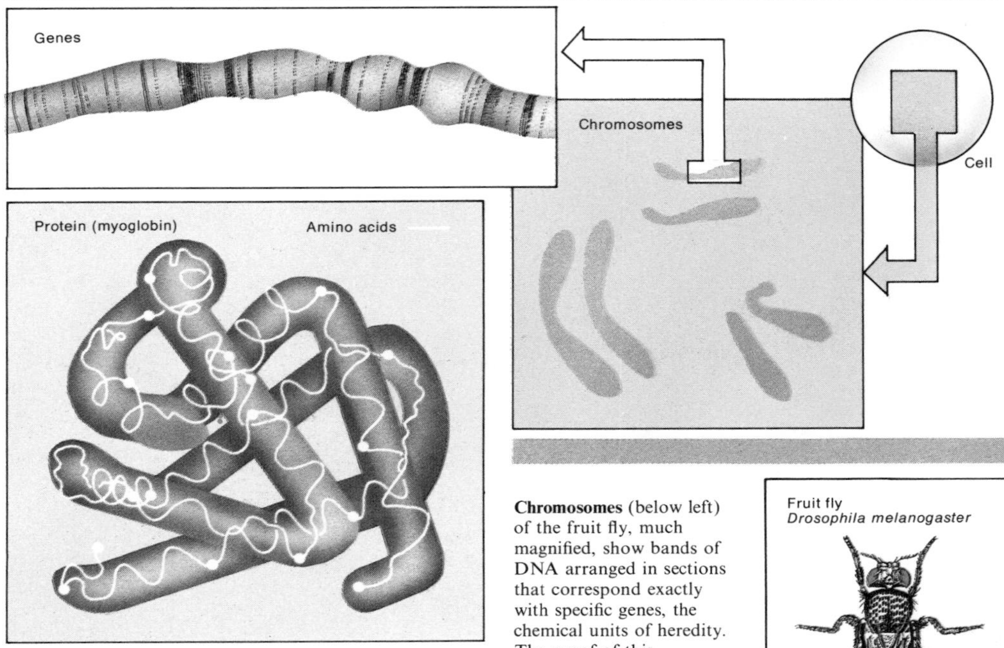
Genes
Chromosomes
Cell
Protein (myoglobin)
Amino acids

The cell is the basic unit of all life, and every cell contains in its nucleus the thread-like structures, called chromosomes, that control heredity. Each species has its own number of chromosomes, and the number is always the same for that species. Chromosomes are sectioned into genes, units of heredity made of DNA molecules. DNA acts like a code, specifying the order and number of amino acids that make up proteins—the organic compounds characteristic of all life.

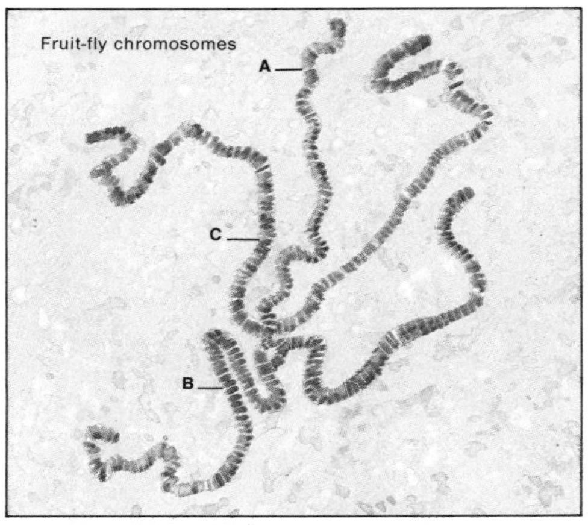
Fruit-fly chromosomes
A
C
B

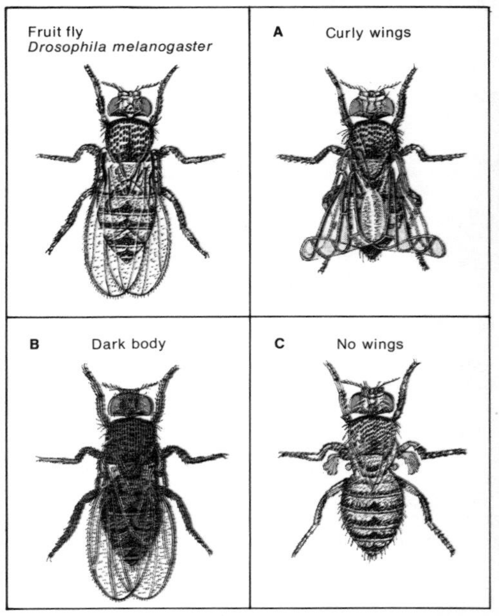
Fruit fly
Drosophila melanogaster
A Curly wings
B Dark body
C No wings

Chromosomes (below left) of the fruit fly, much magnified, show bands of DNA arranged in sections that correspond exactly with specific genes, the chemical units of heredity. The proof of this correspondence came when the American geneticist Hermann Muller introduced the use of ionizing radiation to damage the fruit flies' chromosomes at ultra-microscopic points, causing precise point mutations in offspring of parents whose DNA had been damaged at the places indicated. Random mutations may occur in any organism, and not only as a result of radiation. A gradual accumulation of minor mutations may lead to evolutionary change.

Theories of evolution

Mendel's work was of course unknown to his contemporaries, Charles Darwin and Alfred Russel Wallace, who even then were providing solutions to the major mystery of biology—the way that species evolve, change and develop over time. Evolution was not a new idea in Darwin's day. In 1809 the French naturalist Jean-Baptiste Lamarck had proposed a theory of the inheritance of acquired characteristics, suggesting that new habits learned by an organism in response to environmental change may become physically incorporated in the animal's descendants. For instance, the fact that the ancestral giraffe had to stretch its neck to reach food might give its offspring long necks to enable them to reach food more easily. Less satisfactory than the "natural selection" theory of Darwin and Wallace (who independently reached the same conclusion), Lamarckism founders on the fact that there is no genetic mechanism enabling acquired characters to pass on in this way.

Darwin's theory of natural selection has three key elements: all individuals vary, and some variations are passed on to the next generation; the gap between the potential and the actual number of offspring reproduced by organisms is very wide and implies that not all will survive; organisms best adapted to the environment will survive, their offspring will have been selected, and the favorable variation will spread through the population, perhaps eventually changing it.

Genetic variation, the mainspring of natural selection, is reflected in variations of DNA, the material substance of heredity. Changes in the order of DNA's nitrogenous bases—called mutations—produce changes in the proteins which are usually, but not always, harmful. More important than these is the effect of genes recombining in sexually reproduced offspring.

Sexual reproduction provides the offspring with two sets of DNA, one from each parent. The processes that give rise to a half-set of chromosomes in a sperm or egg shuffle and recombine the genes on each chromosome to provide new combinations. Then, when sperm and egg fuse together at fertilization, the half-sets come together and even more combinations are produced. The world's enormous diversity of life can be explained in terms of a struggle that favors certain genetic combinations.

Iiwi
Vestiaria coccinea

Apapane
Himatione sanguinea
Laysan finch
Psittirostra cantans

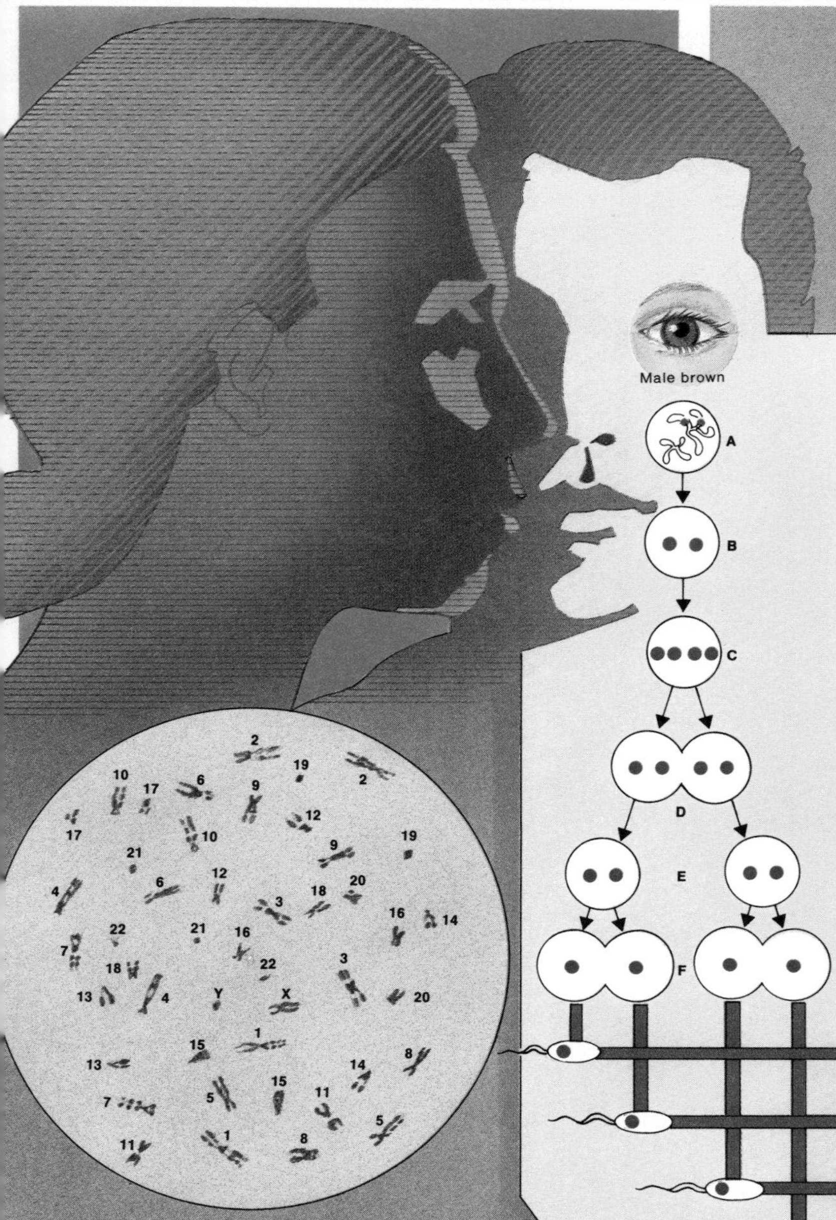

Some human traits, such as eye color, are inherited as single factors (below). In such cases one gene is dominant over the other, recessive, gene, and the gene giving a brown eye color is always dominant over that which gives a blue eye color. The chromosomes carrying eye-color genes (A) pair (B) and duplicate (C, D) before dividing twice (E, F) in the process known as meiosis, or reduction division. This ensures that the offspring gets half the chromosomes from the male and half from the female parent, so each new cell gets both genes when sperm and egg unite. But because brown-eye genes are dominant over blue, all offspring have brown eyes, with the blue-eye gene hidden. But if two brown-eyed parents carry recessive blue-eye genes, half the male sperm cells have blue-eye genes, and the female eggs carry a gene for either blue or brown eyes. So the two recessive genes have a one-in-four chance of being combined to produce a blue-eyed child, no brown-eye genes being present.

Male brown
Female blue
Female brown
Male brown
A
B
C
D
E
F
Brown
Brown
Brown
Brown
Brown
Brown
Brown
Blue

A human body cell (above) contains 46 chromosomes—22 matching pairs and the chromosomes (X, Y) which determine sex. Males have X and Y, females X and X. In sexual reproduction (right) traits carried by the male sperm and the female egg combine in the zygote, the fertilized egg from which new life starts. All growth is the result of repeated cell division, or mitosis, where the nucleus forms paired chromosomes that duplicate themselves; the cell splits, and the chromosomes re-form in the nucleus of the new cells. Sex cells are produced by reduction division, or meiosis, with each cell taking only one from each pair of chromosomes, which exchange corresponding segments in the process called recombination. The genes are thus reshuffled at each generation, so that new combinations of gene traits are available for selection each time meiosis takes place. The result is genetic diversity, with many possibilities for the species to adapt to a changing environment.

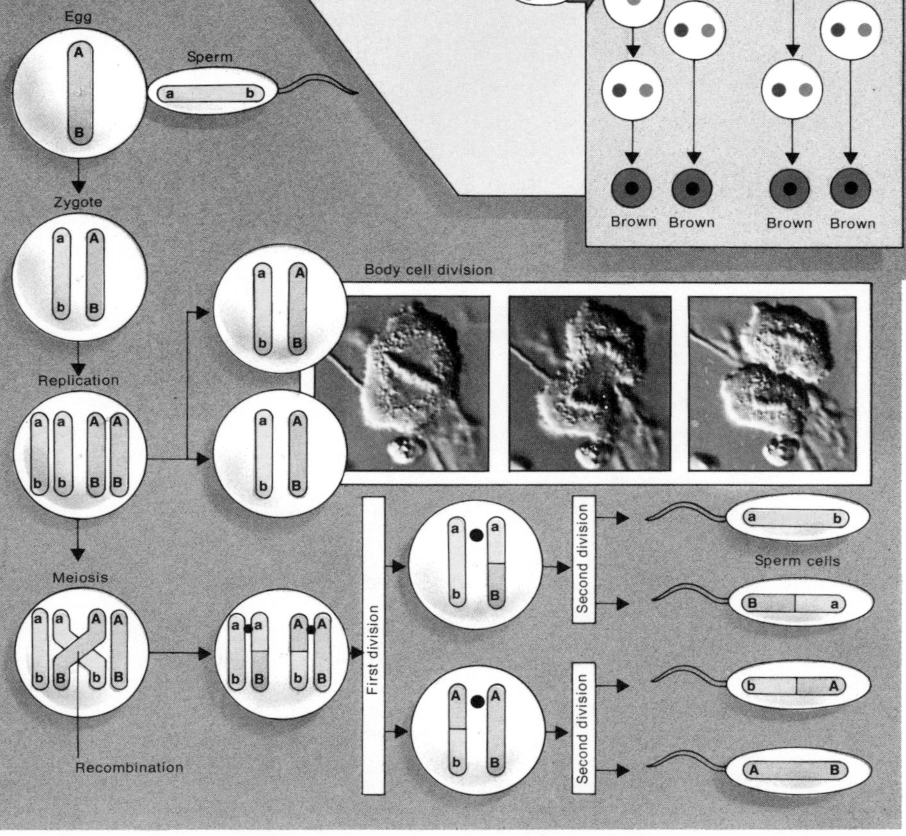

Egg
Sperm
Zygote
Replication
Meiosis
Recombination
Body cell division
First division
Second division
Second division
Sperm cells

VARIANT FORMS

Dark forms of many insects, such as the peppered moth *Biston betularia*, have developed widely in industrial areas of the world since the industrial age. The dark variant, resulting from a single genetic mutation, escapes the eye of predators against the black, lichen-free bark of soot-darkened trees (top), whereas the typical pale form is very conspicuous. In rural, unpolluted areas where tree trunks are light and lichen covered (bottom) the well-concealed pale form is much commoner. *Biston*'s rapid evolutionary response is remarkable: in 1849 only one dark example was recorded at Manchester, England, but by 1900 98% of the moths caught in the area were of the dark type. A similar change occurred in other industrial areas, during the period when the most coal was being burned and the population was most rapidly expanding. But with today's clean-air laws the number of pale moths in these areas is once again on the increase.

A diversity of forms (left) has stemmed from a single ancestor of the Hawaiian honeycreeper, which now numbers 14 species. These have adapted in their mid-Pacific isolation to fill niches usually taken by other birds, ranging from the nectar-feeding iiwi to the Laysan finch with its thick beak for cracking seeds, and the short-billed apapane, which includes insects in its diet. But the honeycreepers' success in divergence may have led to overspecialization, with at least eight species now extinct. The Australian marsupial mouse and the Indian spiny mouse (right) look very similar, due to the fact that they fill similar ecological niches, but they belong to groups evolving separately for almost 100 million years.

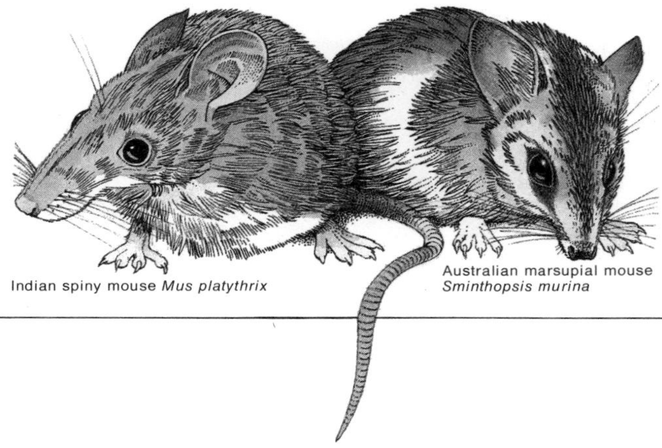

Indian spiny mouse *Mus platythrix*

Australian marsupial mouse *Sminthopsis murina*

Earliest Life Forms

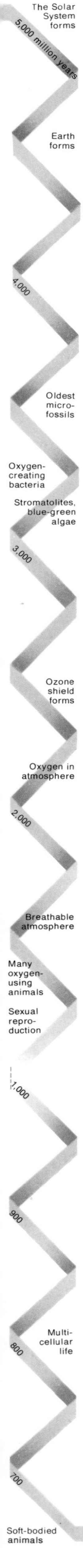

Earth's original atmosphere lacked oxygen, without which there could be no survival for air-breathing creatures. This vital gas was supplied by life itself, in the form of microscopic organisms that flourished in the atmosphere of the time and emitted oxygen as "waste." In this way a breathable atmosphere built up; increasingly complex life forms were able to develop in the seas; early plants and insects gained a foothold on the shores; and, finally, larger animals could survive on land.

A BREATHABLE ATMOSPHERE

Without oxygen, life as we know it could not exist; yet Earth's original atmosphere contained practically none. The oxygenation of the atmosphere was the work of the planet's first life—primeval bacteria and algae. Of these, some released oxygen as waste while consuming carbon dioxide or nitrogen in photosynthesis. Colonies of algae forming stromatolites ("stony carpets") generated even more oxygen, but this was first taken up by ocean rocks, visible today as "banded iron formations." Once all the ocean rocks were oxidized, an oxygen-rich atmosphere could develop, with an ozone layer to filter out harmful radiation from the Sun.

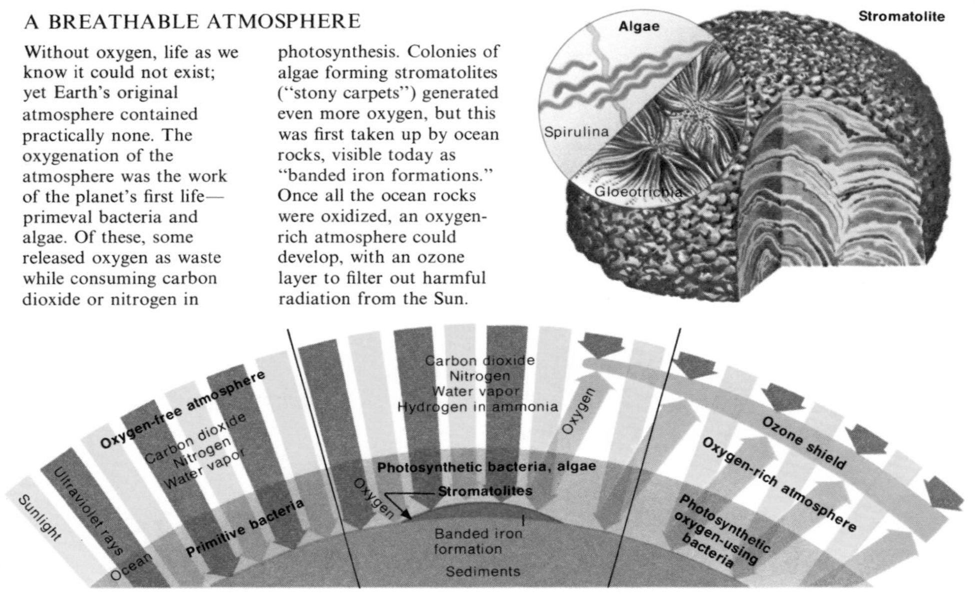

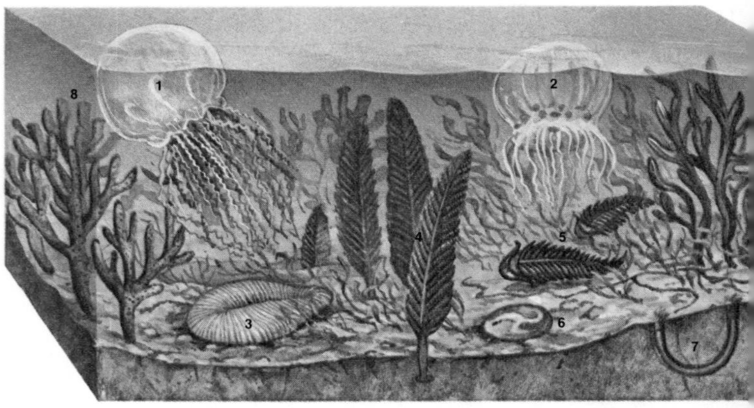

THE FIRST SHELLED CREATURES
These evolved (right) in the seas when conditions allowed soft-bodied life to form protective casings. In the fossil record of 550 million years ago, soft and shelled forms are found. The trilobites (1, 2, 3)—a now extinct order of woodlouse-like animals—dominated the scene, but other early arthropods (4) included a possible insect ancestor (5), and there may even have been an ancestor to fish (6). Sponges (7), crinoids (8), early moluscs (9), bristleworms (10) and lamp-shells (11) were plentiful, but other creatures (12) are bewilderingly strange.

Scientists have identified bacteria-like microfossils in the rocks that were formed more than 3,500 million years ago. Some of these organisms appear to have been capable of photosynthesis—the process of utilizing sunlight, water and carbon dioxide for "food," with release of oxygen as the vitally important by-product. As a result, surplus oxygen very gradually accumulated in the Earth's atmosphere, forming an upper-atmosphere shield of ozone (which kept out damaging ultraviolet radiation from the Sun) and providing an oxygen-rich atmosphere in which breathing life could develop.

At least five types of microfossil have been found in ancient sediments of Western Australia, aged about 3,560 million years, and these provide the earliest evidence of life so far discovered. Other early proof of life comes from the so-called "stromatolites," some of which may date back as far as 3,400 million years. These curious columns, growing in warm, shallow waters, are formed of blue-green algae which have entrapped chalky sediments, bacteria and other microfossils. Their study is made easier by the fact that similar structures have developed at later geological times, and some are even being formed at the present day.

Living below the surface of the water and not initially reliant on oxygen for life, such bacteria and algae were shielded from the Sun's ultraviolet rays as they imperceptibly altered the Earth's atmosphere. For hundreds of millions of years life of this kind persisted, with few obvious developments or changes.

Breathing life

About 1,800 million years ago, the effects of these microscopic photosynthesizers became dramatically apparent in the "rusting" of the ocean sediments, when the red color of the rocks being formed at that time indicates that there was enough free oxygen on Earth to bring about the process known as oxidation. Once the ocean rocks capable of absorbing oxygen had done so, forming the red "banded iron formations" known to geologists, oxygen could enter the atmosphere in ever greater quantities.

It has been estimated that a breathable atmosphere existed on Earth about 1,700 million years ago, and aerobic (oxygen-using) organisms first became abundant not very long afterwards. These organisms were single celled, and it may have been almost 1,000 million years before multicellular animals evolved. The fossilized remains of animals alive 800 million years ago have been found in many parts of the world, but it is not yet known whether multicellular animals had a long history before these earliest known forms, or whether they had developed and radiated rapidly from a creature capable of feeding as well as photosynthesizing.

One of the earliest collections of animals of this type was discovered in the Ediacara Sandstones of the Flinders Range in Australia, where some 650 million years ago the rocks once formed part of an ancient beach. Here a spectacular collection of soft-bodied animals, similar to today's coelenterates (such as jellyfish) and worms, was washed ashore and preserved in silt from the nearby shallow sea. Comparable, mainly floating forms have been found in other parts of the world in rocks dating from between 650 and 580 million years ago.

The first vertebrates

One of the most important changes in animal life seems to have occurred about 580 million years ago. At that date many creatures evolved hard, protective shells, which also acted as areas of muscle attachment and as support for their bodies—in other words, as external skeletons. Hard shells were more easily preserved as fossils than the soft bodies of earlier animals, so rich collections have been recovered from rocks of the Cambrian Period, beginning 580 million years ago, as well as from later strata.

The first fish-like animals—the earliest true vertebrates—are found in rocks of the Ordovician Period, from about 500 million years ago, and these were in many ways very similar to the lampreys and hagfishes of today. But unlike them, these ancient creatures were heavily armored with external bone. They must have been poor swimmers, living mainly on the seabed and filtering edible particles from the sediments, which they sucked into their jawless mouths. From them arose true fishes, with backbones, jaws and teeth, and they came to replace the less efficient earlier forms.

During the Devonian Period, about 400 million years ago, the fishes diversified greatly, adapting to fit all kinds of aquatic environments. Some grew to a huge size, such as *Dunkleosteus*, which achieved a length of up to 9 m (29 ft 7 in), although it belonged to a group of fishes that retained heavy armor. Some of these curious creatures probably used their stilt-like pectoral fins to hitch themselves across the beds of the pools in which they lived.

From water to land

The fishes that teemed in the seas and fresh waters of the Devonian world found their way into difficult environments such as swamps and oasis pools, where there was a danger of drying out in the warmer weather. Many of these fishes had rudimentary lungs, and one group developed powerful jointed fins.

Such marginal habitats were not ideal for fishes, but they were nevertheless rich in species, and it is from them that the first land vertebrates developed. When the water dried up they survived, for their strong fins held them up so that they did not flop over helplessly.

They found themselves in a new, dry world, but one which was already inhabited, at least round the water's edges, with plants related to modern liverworts, mosses and club mosses. There were also numerous invertebrate animals such as millipedes, spiders and wingless insects. These plants and animals provided shelter and food, so that the environment was not wholly hostile to larger animals.

The first steps on land probably took the form of strong flexions of the body—desperate swimming movements which swung the fins forward, pegging the animal's position in the drying mud. But in a very short time geologically, animals had evolved in which the rays of the lobe fins had vanished, leaving stubby legs with which the animals—no longer fishes but amphibians—could haul themselves over land. But they still had to return to water to breed and lay eggs.

A timescale of life on Earth emerges from the record of fossils embedded in rock strata. Major breaks in faunas (animal assemblages) separate eras coinciding roughly with periods of intense mountain-building activity. These eras are broken down into geological periods, which are separated by lesser faunal breaks and which are generally named from the area where rocks of that age were first discovered. The geological eras and periods do not imply particular rock types.

THE FIRST AMPHIBIANS
Amphibians (1) emerged some 345 million years ago (right), inhabiting swampy environments with luxuriant vegetation—club mosses and ferns (2, 3) that made up the early coal forests. Lungfish (4) were well adapted to life in oxygen-poor waters, but the move to land was probably made by related fish with a passage linking nostrils to throat—*Eusthenopteron* (5). Land offered food (6, 7, 8) and suitably damp conditions for a possibly stranded aquatic animal.

THE AGE OF JELLYFISH

Jellyfish (left) and other soft-bodied animals flourished in the pre-Cambrian seas, more than 600 million years ago. The forms of one group, imprinted on sand, have been preserved as fossils in the Australian Ediacara Sandstones. They include varieties similar to modern jellyfish (1, 2); worm-like crawlers (3); sea pens (4) very like modern types; segmented worms (5); "three-legged" creatures like no known animal (6); and sand casts of burrowing worms (7).

LIFE ON SEA AND LAND

For more than half the Earth's existence, its atmosphere has been hostile to air-breathing life. Then, about 1,600 million years ago, the photosynthesizing action of minute organisms built up enough free oxygen in the atmosphere for more complex oxygen-dependent forms to develop. The first multicellular life led to the soft-bodied animals of the pre-Cambrian time—worms, jellyfish and sea pens. About 580 million years ago many animals developed hard parts, including shells. Over 1,200 new marine species date from this period, and the evolutionary explosion came to fill the Earth's seas with fishes. Some of these had powerful jointed fins and rudimentary lungs, and lived in swamps where primitive plants and insects had already made the move to land. As the pools dwindled the stranded animals could survive by breathing air.

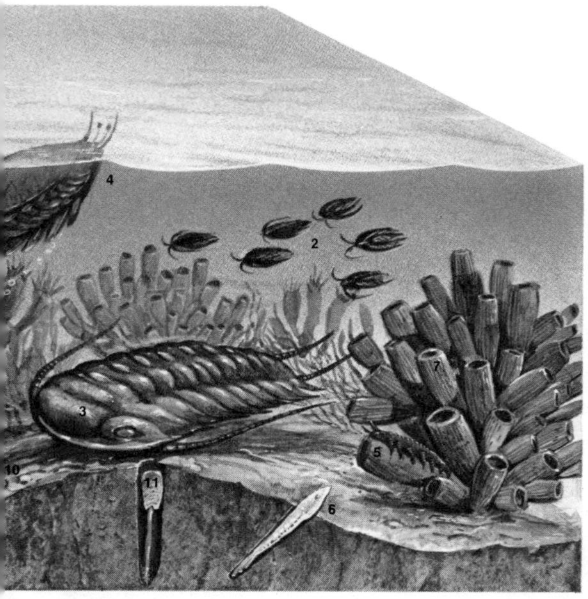

LIVING FOSSILS

Some life forms that emerged 570 million years ago have survived virtually unchanged to the present day. These "living fossils" include *Lingula* (left), today found in warm, brackish coastal waters, poor in oxygen and unsuited to most life, off the Pacific and Indian oceans. *Neopilina* (below), a primitive marine mollusc first found alive in 1952, has features unlike other molluscs but suggesting much closer affinities with the annelids (worms) and arthropods (insects, crabs, etc.).

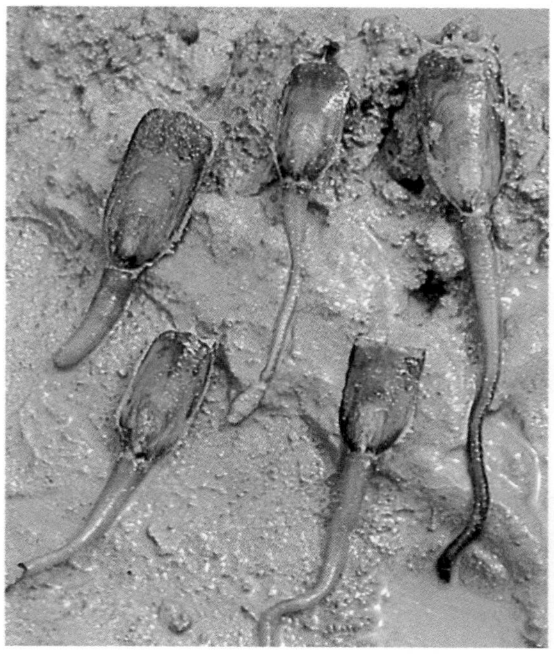

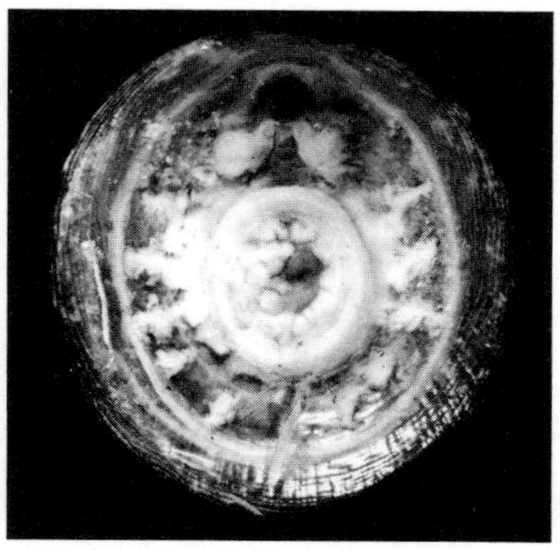

THE AGE OF JELLYFISH
1 Jellyfish (*Ediacaria*)
2 Jellyfish (*Medusina*)
3 Flatworm (*Dickinsonia costata*)
4 Sea pens (*Rangea, Charnia*)
5 Segmented worms (*Spriggina floundersi*)
6 Unknown animal (*Tribrachidium*)
7 Burrowing worm (fossil casts)
8 Sponges and algae (hypothetical)

THE FIRST SHELLED CREATURES
1 Trilobites (*Waptia*)
2 Trilobites (*Marella splendens*)
3 Trilobite (*Olenoides serratus*)
4 Primitive arthropod (*Perspicaris dictynna*)
5 Primitive arthropod (*Aysheaia pedunculata*)
6 Ancestral lancelet fish (*Branchiostoma*)
7 Sponge (*Vauxia*)
8 Crinoids (*Echmatocrinus*)
9 Mollusc (*Wiwaxia*)
10 Bristleworm (*Nereis*)
11 Brachiopod (*Lingulella*)
12 Unknown animal (*Hallucigenia sparsa*)

THE AGE OF FISHES
1 Primitive plant (*Nematophyton*)
2 Psilophite plant (*Asteroxylon*)
3 Psilophite plant (*Rhynia*)
4 Primitive insect (*Rhyniella*)
5 Placoderm fish (*Bothriolepis*)
6 Placoderm fish (*Phyllolepis*)
7 Placoderm fish (*Dunkleosteus*)
8 Early shark (*Cladoselache*)
9 Lungfish (*Dipterus*)
10 Lobe-fin fish (*Osteolepis*)
11 Crustacean (*Montecaris*)

THE FIRST AMPHIBIANS
1 Amphibian (*Ichthyostega*)
2 Club moss (*Cyclostigma*)
3 Fern (*Pseudosporochnus*)
4 Lungfish (*Scaumenacia*)
5 Rhipidistian fish (*Eusthenopteron*)
6 Millipede (*Acantherpestes ornatus*)
7 Early scorpion (*Palaeophonus*)
8 Spider-like creature (*Palaeocharinoides*)
9 Small plant (*Sciadophyton*)

THE AGE OF FISHES

Fishes (left) filled the brackish Devonian waters, about 350 million years ago, while primitive plants and insects had pioneered the land. Giant weeds (1) grew above muddy waters, and vascular plants (2, 3) colonized the shores, sheltering early insects (4). Primitive fishes (5, 6, 7) remained, but ray-finned types (8)—ancestors of modern fish—were dominant. However, it was from the lobe-finned fishes (9, 10) that the first land vertebrates emerged.

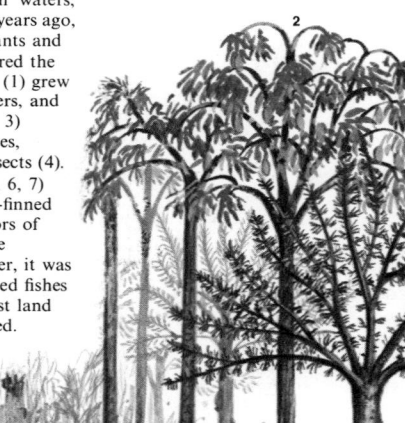

Diversification of fishes | 450 | SILURIAN | First land plants | 400 | DEVONIAN | First insects | First amphibians

The Age of Reptiles

When the Carboniferous Period began, the world was already populated with animals and plants of many kinds. The oceans were full of fishes, invertebrates and aquatic plants. The land, meanwhile, was producing dramatic new species: giant mosses and ferns, spiders and insects and, most important of all, the rapidly evolving amphibians. These creatures were taking the first evolutionary steps on a path that would lead to some of the most remarkable creatures ever to live – the dinosaurs.

The broad, low-lying, swampy plains of the late Carboniferous provided ideal conditions for the world's early plants. They spread and diversified, and some of them grew to enormous size. Giant club mosses, huge horsetails and luxuriant tree ferns took on the proportions of modern-day trees and formed the world's first forests. These new forests were full of animal life: primitive spiders and scorpions hunting their prey, giant dragonflies hovering over the marshy waters and other insects scavenging or hunting on the mossy forest floor or in the branches of the "trees." In the huge coal-forest swamps, the most advanced of all animals, the amphibians, were rapidly evolving. Some of these would ultimately return to life in the water. But others were developing stronger legs and were becoming better able to cope with an existence on dry land.

It was from this second group that the reptiles evolved—the first animals to be equipped with waterproof skins. Unlike their amphibian ancestors, they could stay out of the water indefinitely without losing their body fluids through their skins. They were no longer tied to the water's edge and the pattern of life was revolutionized. The world was soon inhabited by the first wave of land vertebrates—reptiles, which then rapidly diversified.

Included among these first reptiles were creatures known as sailbacks. They had a row of long, bony spines that supported a great fin running down from the back of their heads to the base of their tails. This whole apparatus functioned as a heat-exchange organ: the fin absorbed heat from the atmosphere in the early, cooler parts of the day, when the animal was cold, and blushed off warmth later, when it became overheated. Unlike the cold-blooded reptiles, sailbacked reptiles could, to a certain extent, regulate their body temperatures.

Mammal-like reptiles

It was only about 50 million years later, however, that animals skeletally identical to mammals were found throughout the world. Almost certainly these creatures had a degree of warm-bloodedness. But they were all rather small—the biggest was no larger than a domestic cat—and this may account for their decline. They were destined to be overshadowed for many millions of years by the dinosaurs.

The late Triassic Period, about 200 million years ago, is marked by a sudden decline in the

THE RULING REPTILES
Seymouria and other advanced amphibians evolved to form the first reptiles, such as *Scutosaurus*. From these a multitude of adaptations evolved. Some herbivores, such as *Corythosaurus*, developed 2,000 or more teeth, to help them consume tough, fibrous food plants. Another herbivorous group attained enormous size—*Brachiosaurus* weighed as much as 80 tonnes—and this may have been an adaptation to regulate body temperature (large objects lose and gain heat more slowly than small objects). Another adaptation, but one that developed mainly in the carnivores, was that of offensive weaponry: *Deinonychus* had a huge sickle-shaped claw on each hind foot and the later *Tyrannosaurus* combined a massive body with a jagged mouthful of 60 teeth. Armor plating was a defensive adaptation, produced by herbivores such as *Triceratops*, whereas speed of movement was developed both by some herbivores and by small carnivores such as *Struthiomimus*.

Corythosaurus

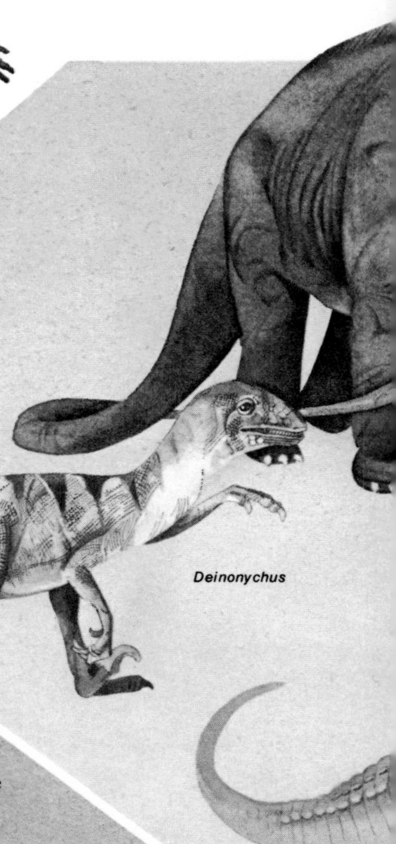

Seymouria

Scutosaurus

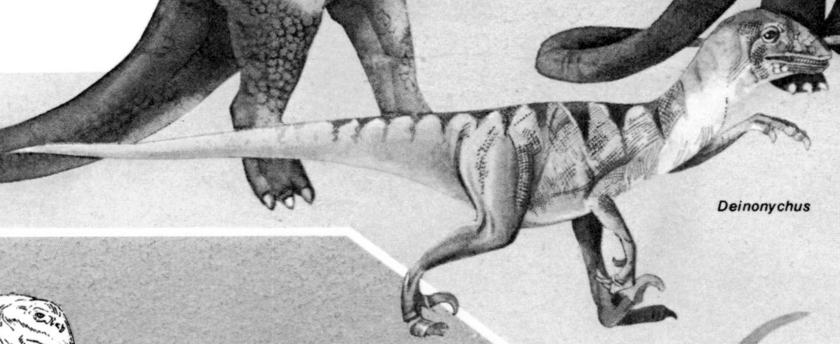

Deinonychus

Lystrosaurus

Dimetrodon

THE MAMMAL LINE
Sailbacks such as *Dimetrodon* mark the beginning of mammal history. These reptiles had developed the first method of regulating body temperature—each was equipped with a large fin on its back which acted as a heat-exchange organ, a living solar panel. From these strange creatures, para-mammals such as *Lystrosaurus* evolved, animals with many mammal-like features. Some of the later members of this group, such as *Thrinaxodon*, probably even had fur on their bodies. Then, about 200 million years ago, the first true warm-blooded mammals, such as *Morganucodon*, developed. But by this time the group as a whole was declining in response to reptilian competition. Mammals would have to wait 140 million years before becoming successful again.

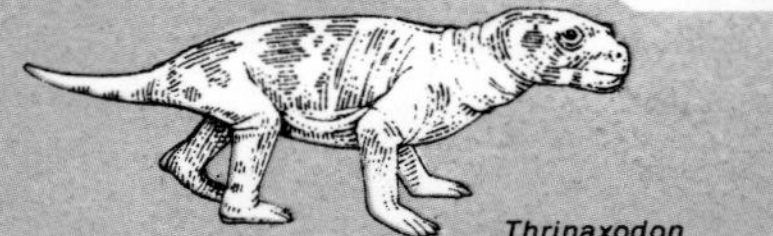

Thrinaxodon

Morganucodon

COAL FORMATION
Coal consists of carbon from plant remains and most of it was formed in the swamp-forests from which reptiles emerged. First, peat formed from rotted vegetation. Sea levels rose, ocean covered the peat bogs and marine sediments were laid down. The resulting pressure converted peat to coal. The cycle recurred and the deepest coal seams were compressed and hardened.

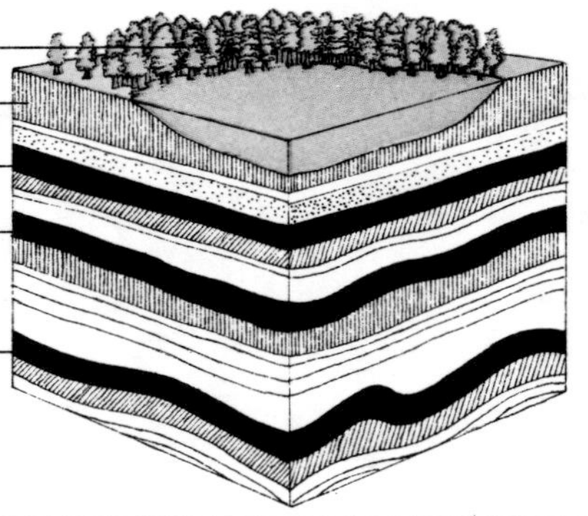
Coal-forming forest swamp
Peat layer
Lignite seam
Bituminous seam
Anthracite seam

Palaeozoic
Mesozoic
Cenozoic
500
400
300
200
100
0
Millions of years ago

Three geological eras mark the evolution of life on Earth. It was the Mesozoic era, beginning 230 million years ago, that spanned the age of reptiles. Until then, throughout the Palaeozoic era, life had been slowly evolving from the primitive organisms that appeared 400 million years earlier.

By the Mesozoic, the earliest reptiles had developed. Among their descendants were dinosaurs and early representatives of the mammalian line. Mammals, however, would have to wait another 165 million years, until the Cenozoic, before they achieved dominance.

Cycadale

Gingko biloba

The plant communities underwent as many developments in the course of the Mesozoic era as did the reptiles. The end of the Palaeozoic saw changes in climate—the Permian Period was much drier than the Carboniferous. Giant horsetails, ferns and club mosses that had formed the world's first forests gave way to other types of plant: early conifers and their relatives (the gymnosperms) came to the fore. These new species, such as the Cycadales, had evolved a new, improved method of reproduction—using seeds not spores. By Jurassic times, the climate had changed again and the moist conditions supported dense forests of ferns and of conifers. The final major Mesozoic development took place in Cretaceous times, when the flowering plants evolved.

CARBONIFEROUS | 300 | Earliest reptiles | PERMIAN | Early conifers | 250 | First radiation of reptiles | TRIASSIC | First mammals

EVOLUTION AND ADAPTATION

Once their amphibian ancestors had crawled from the swamps, reptiles rapidly evolved and developed a remarkable range of adaptations: they took to the air, invaded the seas and held dominion over the land. By early Jurassic times, they had firmly established their claim to the title Ruling Reptiles. Another group of early reptile descendants led to the mammals, and although these were long overshadowed by the dinosaurs, they were destined to rise to dominance.

mammal-like reptiles and by the extraordinary evolutionary radiation of the so-called Archosaurs ("ruling reptiles"). These began to fill every available ecological niche. They evolved into carnivores, herbivores and omnivores. They included the Crocodilians, which adapted to a life in the water; the flying pterosaurs, which were the first vertebrates to fly, and, most important of all, the dinosaurs, whose evolutionary reign over the land was to endure for the next 140 million years.

Dinosaurs adapted well to life on the land. They developed "fully erect" limbs (not unlike those of the later higher mammals) rather than the splayed legs found in most other reptiles. The new position of their limbs, which gave them the necessary mobility on dry land, was also accompanied by a general increase in size. But the dinosaurs were not the only land reptiles of the time; many other forms, including tortoises, snakes and lizards, were also carving their niches during the Mesozoic era.

Similarly, the pterosaurs did not remain the only creatures of the sky. By 170 million years ago, birds in the form of claw-winged *Archaeopteryx* had evolved, and these were to prove a serious challenge to the primitive winged reptiles which had poor flying abilities.

Aquatic reptiles

Just as the land and the air were rapidly inhabited by newly evolving forms, so the water produced many new developments. Several of the Mesozoic reptiles began to adapt to aquatic life in ways often parallel to present-day mammals: the long-necked, fish-eating plesiosaurs led a life much like that of seals; the larger pliosaurs had a streamlined shape similar to that of certain whales; some mollusc-eating placodonts could be likened to the walrus; and the elegant icthyosaurs were in many ways like dolphins. Large invertebrates were also found in the seas. The most dramatic of these were the ammonites—shelled relatives of the octopus—some of which grew to more than 2 m (6 ft) in size. Among fishes a new type emerged, the Teleosts, and these were destined to become the dominant fishes of the modern world.

Wholesale extinction

At the end of the Cretaceous Period, the reptiles were flourishing. Then suddenly, 65 million years ago, a catastrophe occurred. Virtually every species, including all the large animals, were wiped out. Throughout the Mesozoic, a series of dinosaurs and other reptiles had been evolving and slowly becoming extinct, but they were always replaced by other species. This wholesale extinction was unprecedented.

The cause of the catastrophe is unknown, but since the nature of the Earth itself was unchanged, it seems likely that some outside phenomenon was responsible. One theory suggests that a large meteorite collided with the Earth, throwing enough dust into the atmosphere to blot out the sun for several years—long enough to kill almost all the green plants on land and in the sea. If this was the case, only small animals that fed on carrion, decaying vegetation, seeds or nuts could hope to survive. Whatever the cause, the reign of the reptiles was at an end, leaving the small, adaptable mammals and birds to recolonize the virtually empty planet during the Cenozoic era.

Brachiosaurus
Tyrannosaurus rex
Struthiomimus
Triceratops
Rhamphorhynchus
Archaeopteryx
Plesiosaurus
Ichthyornis

Plesiosaurs evolved at the same time as the dinosaurs and were as successful in their marine environment as were the dinosaurs on land. They were most common in Jurassic times.

Pterosaurs such as *Rhamphorhynchus* were the first vertebrates to take to the sky. They were not strong fliers and probably glided on air currents much of the time.

Birds are relatives of the reptiles. The first bird, *Archaeopteryx*, evolving in Jurassic times, had many reptilian features—a long, bony tail, toothed mouth and clawed wings. By Cretaceous times, birds such as *Ichthyornis* had a more familiar form.

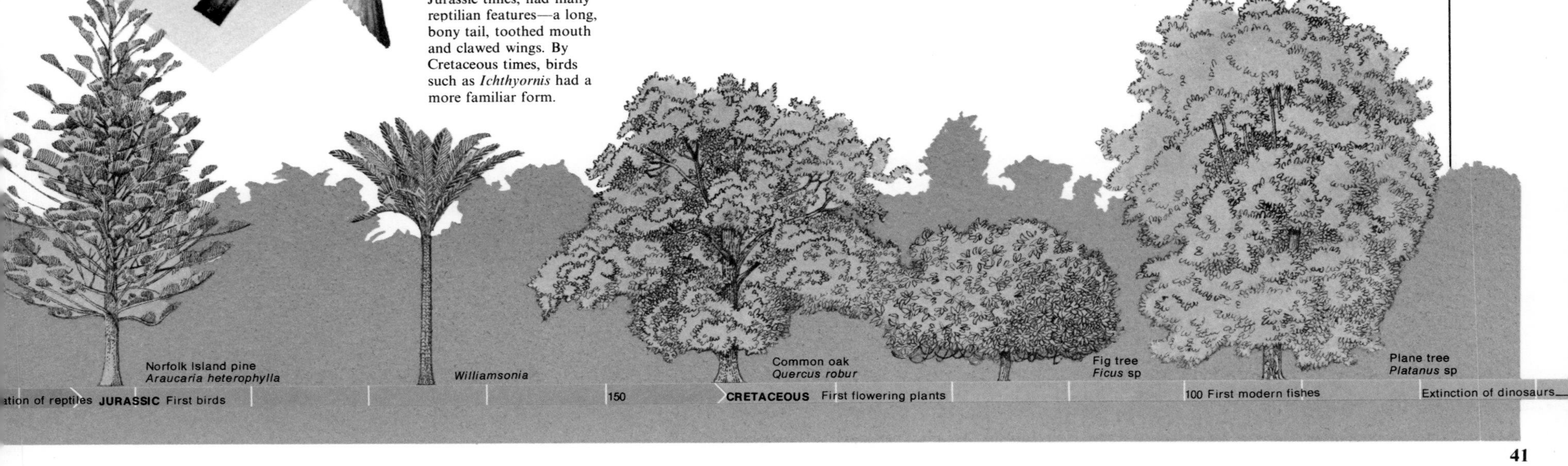

Norfolk Island pine
Araucaria heterophylla
Williamsonia
Common oak
Quercus robur
Fig tree
Ficus sp
Plane tree
Platanus sp
ation of reptiles JURASSIC First birds
150
CRETACEOUS First flowering plants
100 First modern fishes
Extinction of dinosaurs

The Age of Mammals

After the time of the great dying, 65 million years ago, reptiles never regained the importance they had achieved during the Mesozoic era. A new era, the Cenozoic, had begun. On the continental landmasses, mammals and birds, newly released from 160 million years of reptilian domination, began to occupy their niches in the rich, empty habitats. They flourished and diversified, and the cold-blooded reptiles became second-class citizens in a world of warm-blooded animals.

While reptiles still dominated the world, during the late Mesozoic, a new group of mammals had arisen. These were the first creatures on Earth to give birth to fully formed, live young. Until this time, the most advanced of the mammals had been marsupials whose young were still virtually embryos at birth and had to develop in the mother's pouch, or marsupium. The new mammals had evolved a more sophisticated system—the mother retained the fetus safely inside her body until it was fully formed, nourishing it during this time through a special organ, the placenta, developed during pregnancy. These mammals, the placentals, were destined to become the major mammalian group.

Although all the Mesozoic placentals were small, they had already evolved into a number of different forms that existed alongside the dinosaurs. Besides the insectivores, which were the ancestral type, they included early representatives of the Primates (precursors of modern monkeys and apes), the Carnivores, and the now extinct Condylarthrans (primitive hoofed mammals). When suddenly, 65 million years ago, there was no longer competition from the large land reptiles, these early groups rapidly evolved and extravagant forms developed.

But just as the first reptiles had passed through an early evolution, largely to be replaced by a second evolutionary wave, so the first large mammals were, in many cases, superseded by other, more successful lines. In the earliest part of the Cenozoic era, the different groups of placentals, although not closely related, all tended to be heavy limbed and heavy tailed and to walk on the whole length of their feet (as do modern bears) or on thick, stubby toes. These ungainly, thickset mammals soon died out. Some became extinct because their descendants, more efficiently adapted to their environment, overtook and replaced them. Others, such as the powerful taeniodonts and the large rodent-like tillodonts, seem to have been evolutionary blind alleys.

Spectacular developments

It was the Oligocene Period, 36 million years ago, that saw the end of most of these early essays in mammalian gigantism, but, in many parts of the world, they were replaced by others just as spectacular. In South America, the giant sloths and glyptodonts (massive relatives of the armadillos) survived until comparatively recently. The ground sloths, at least, were contemporaries of the first men on the continent.

As each group of early mammals evolved, during the early and middle part of the Cenozoic era, many of their developments closely reflected changes taking place in their environment. The first horse-like creature, for example, was *Hyracotherium*, also called *Eohippus* or "dawn horse." It lived 54 million years ago and was a small, multi-toed creature, well adapted to its densely forested habitat. The teeth of its descendants gradually changed in size and complexity, but it was not until the Miocene Period, nearly 20 million years later, that any radical alterations took place. This was the time when grasses (the Gramineae), until then a rare family of plants, came to the fore. The world's plains suddenly became clothed in a food plant very suitable for the attention of grazing creatures such as the early horses.

Animals of the grasslands

Horses and many other animals moved from the forests to make use of this new and abundant food supply. Once on the plains, different adaptations for survival were required: high-crowned teeth to deal with tough grasses; limbs enabling the animal to run tirelessly without extra, unwanted weight from supporting side toes (which were lost); large eyes capable of seeing for long distances and placed far back on the head for detecting predators approaching from any direction (as a result of which, however, the ability to judge distances ahead had to be sacrificed). Thus, the modern horses are plains-dwelling animals, perfectly adapted to their present way of life.

Mammals reached the climax of diversity during the Pliocene Period, 10 million years ago. But in the following period, the Pleistocene, ice sheets swept down from the polar regions and from the high mountains of the north, bringing massive and sudden changes to the ecology of virtually every region in the world. This dramatic disturbance to the environment brought extinction to an enormous number of species.

The survivors consisted mainly of the smaller species. Unfortunately for many of them, however, they included *Homo sapiens*. Man rose to success at the end of the Pleistocene and has, in the last 10,000 years, taken dominion over virtually every part of the world. During this time, he has proved far more destructive to other animal species than any natural force has ever been. More than 5,000 years ago, the giant sloths may have been a dying species, but there is no doubt that early human hunters hurried on their extinction. Since then, the list of species eliminated by man has grown ever longer. Today the human race is causing the extinction of both animals and plants at a rate comparable to that of 65 million years ago, when some dramatic natural catastrophe swept the dinosaurs from the face of the world. Unless man, the super-efficient species, can curb his numbers and his destructive activities, a new age of dying may soon be upon the world.

Miacis
EARLY STAGES
Andrewsarchus
Hyaenodon

By early Cenozoic times, many forms had evolved from the insectivorous mammals of the Mesozoic Period. *Miacis*, *Hyaenodon* and *Oxyaena* were flesh eaters. Plant-eating mammals, such as Taeniodonts, *Arsinoitherium* and *Phenacodus* (one of the first hoofed mammals), had also evolved, while other early forms, such as *Andrewsarchus*, were omnivorous. The early Primates, however, remained insect eaters for millions of years.

The Carnivores diversified into two major types—the cats and their kin (Aeluroidea), and the dogs and their relatives (Arctoidea). During the Oligocene Period, about 36 million years ago, Aeluroidea gave rise not only to early relatives of modern cats, such as sabre-toothed *Hoplophoneus*, but also to two other families, the civets and the hyenas. At the same time, Arctoidea also diversified and produced the dogs, weasels, bears and racoons. It was a complex group, with many forms that were later to become extinct—the massive bear-dogs, such as *Daphoenus*, for example, which lived during the Miocene Period. Cats and dogs evolved to exploit different habitats. The cats adapted to life in forests, and learned to hide and then stalk and ambush their prey. Dogs evolved as plains animals, and used pack-hunting techniques to catch fleet-footed, grassland animals.

Perissodactyls and Artiodactyls were two important groups that evolved from the primitive hoofed mammals; Perissodactyls had an odd number of toes on each foot, Artiodactyls had an even number. These two groups suffered very different fortunes. Artiodactyls are still at the height of their success; the early stock produced the modern pig, camel, deer, giraffe, hippopotamus, antelope, sheep, goat and cow. Perissodactyls, however, are in decline and the only survivors are the horse, rhinoceros and tapir. But they were once important and many, now-extinct, kinds such as *Moropus* and *Brontotherium* existed alongside more familiar types such as *Hyracotherium*. Few remained after the Pliocene Period, however. This was when the Artiodactyls came to the fore. They, too, had had casualties—the pig-like *Archaeotherium* was by then extinct—but many other Artiodactyls, such as the early giraffe, *Palaeotragus*, were evolving. Most important, however, was small *Archaeomeryx*, for it had developed the key to Artiodactyl success—it was a ruminant and this enabled it to make the best possible use of the world's new grasslands.

Diatryma
Euryapteryx

CENOZOIC BIRDS

Giant flightless birds came to the fore more than once during the Cenozoic era. *Diatryma*, a massive, flesh-eating bird, ruled the North American grasslands in early Cenozoic times, while mammals were still small, fairly primitive and easily dominated. *Euryapteryx* and its relatives (the moas) evolved in New Zealand, where, because there were no mammals, they filled an empty ecological niche.

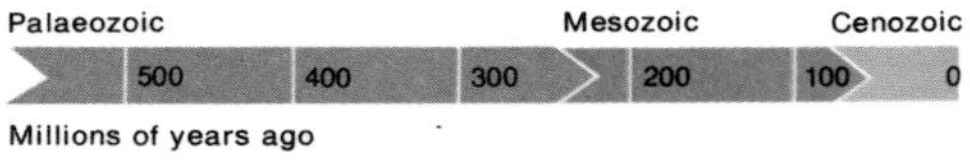
Palaeozoic
Mesozoic
Cenozoic
500
400
300
200
100
0
Millions of years ago

Three geological eras mark the slow evolution of life on Earth. The Palaeozoic era, 570 million years ago, saw the appearance of the first primitive life forms. By the end of the era, 340 million years later, the reptiles had evolved and the following Mesozoic era was the age of reptilian domination. This reign over the land ended 65 million years ago as the Cenozoic era began. Then mammals came to the fore and the age of mammalian dominance of the world had dawned.

EARLY GRASSES

Grasses first appeared in the densely forested lands of 60 million years ago. Probably similar to the sedges (right) found in wet woodland areas today, they offered an attractive meal to many mammals. But it was not until the Miocene Period, when a change in climate reduced forest cover, that grasses became widespread. Then many forest creatures migrated to grassland areas.

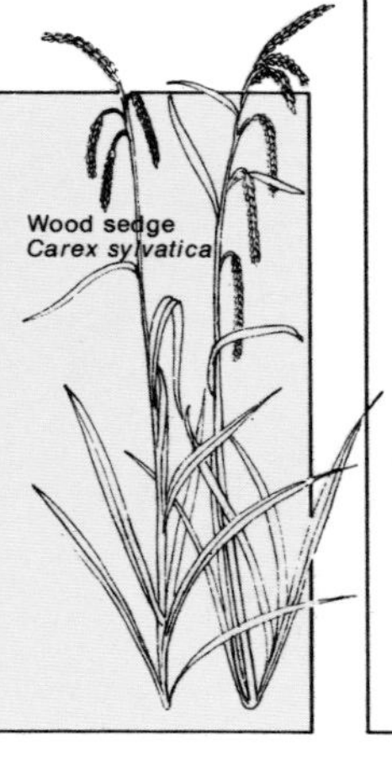
Wood sedge
Carex sylvatica

THE MARSUPIALS

Thylacosmilus and mouse-like *Argyrolagus* were two of the many forms of marsupial mammal that evolved in Cenozoic times in South America. Almost everywhere else, the marsupials, unable to compete with their more efficient placental cousins, met with an early extinction. But in two remote regions—South America (then separate from North America) and Australia—there was no competition from placentals, and there the marsupials flourished.

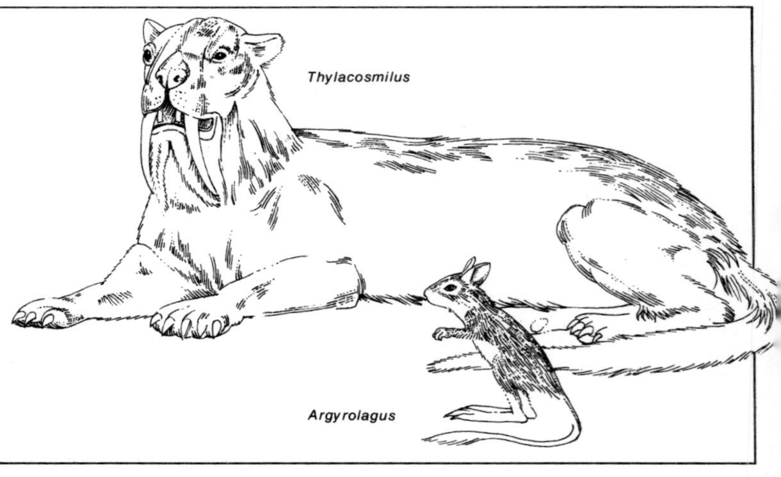
Thylacosmilus
Argyrolagus

TERTIARY | First radiation of mammals and birds | Forest horses | Second radiation of mamma
Palaeocene | 60 | Eocene | 50 | 40 | Oligocene

THE SPREAD OF MAMMALS

Before the death of the dinosaurs, mammals were quietly evolving and diversifying. But as soon as the reign of the reptiles ended, this gentle pace of development changed to a bewilderingly rapid proliferation throughout the world. New species and complete new orders appeared one after another. Old orders rapidly adapted or, overtaken by newer, more efficient groups, died out.

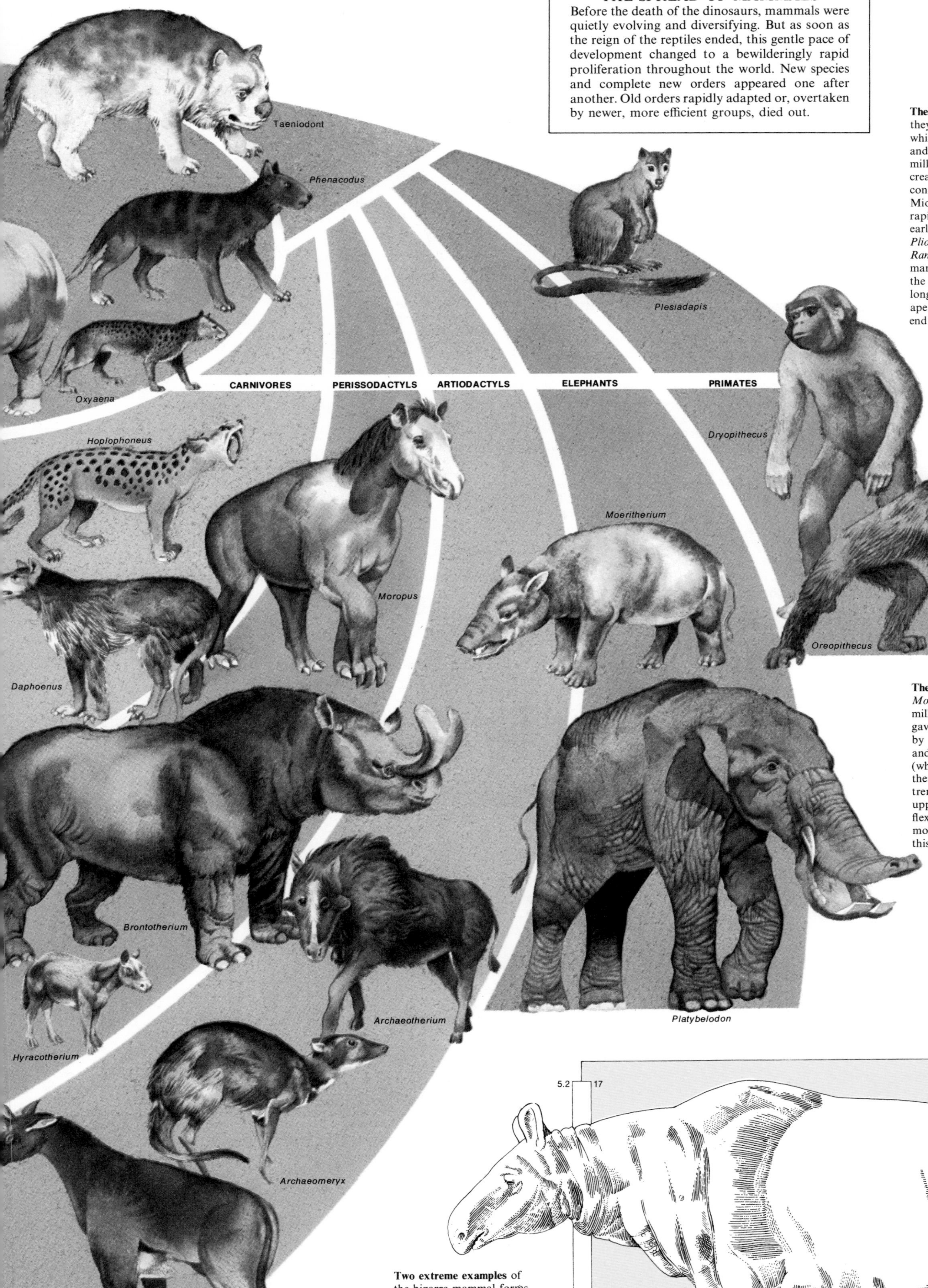

Taeniodont
Phenacodus
Plesiadapis
Oxyaena
CARNIVORES
PERISSODACTYLS
ARTIODACTYLS
ELEPHANTS
PRIMATES
Dryopithecus
Hoplophoneus
Moeritherium
Moropus
Daphoenus
Oreopithecus
Brontotherium
Platybelodon
Archaeotherium
Hyracotherium
Archaeomeryx
Palaeotragus

The Primates are an ancient group—they evolved from ancestral mammals while dinosaurs still walked on Earth, and entered the Palaeocene Period, 65 million years ago, as small squirrel-like creatures such as *Plesiadapis.* They continued to evolve slowly until Miocene times, when new forms rapidly appeared: *Dryopithecus*, the earliest ancestor of modern apes; *Pliopithecus*, the first true gibbon; and *Ramapithecus*, which was possibly man's first direct ancestor. Not all of the Miocene primates survived for long, however—the strangely man-like ape *Oreopithecus* was extinct by the end of the period.

The elephants' first known relative was *Moeritherium*, which lived about 40 million years ago. This pig-like beast gave rise to descendants characterized by their enormous size, huge heads and long legs. To reach the ground (where they found at least some of their food) these creatures developed tremendously long lower jaws and long upper lips and noses, which were flexible enough to pull food into their mouths. The most extreme example of this occurred in *Platybelodon*.

5.2
17
1.8
6
1.2
4
m
ft
Loxodonta falconeri
Paraceratherium

Two extreme examples of the bizarre mammal forms that evolved in response to unusual environments were *Paraceratherium* and *Loxodonta falconeri*. On large landmasses, where food supplies were virtually inexhaustible, species such as *Paraceratherium* grew to enormous size, whereas on small islands, where food was strictly limited, some mammals became extremely small—miniature *Loxodonta falconeri*, a Pleistocene elephant, was no taller than a present-day Great Dane dog.

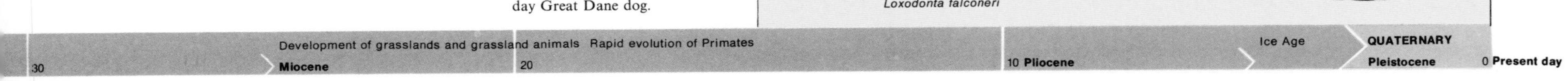

Development of grasslands and grassland animals
Rapid evolution of Primates
Ice Age
QUATERNARY
30
Miocene
20
10 Pliocene
Pleistocene
0 Present day

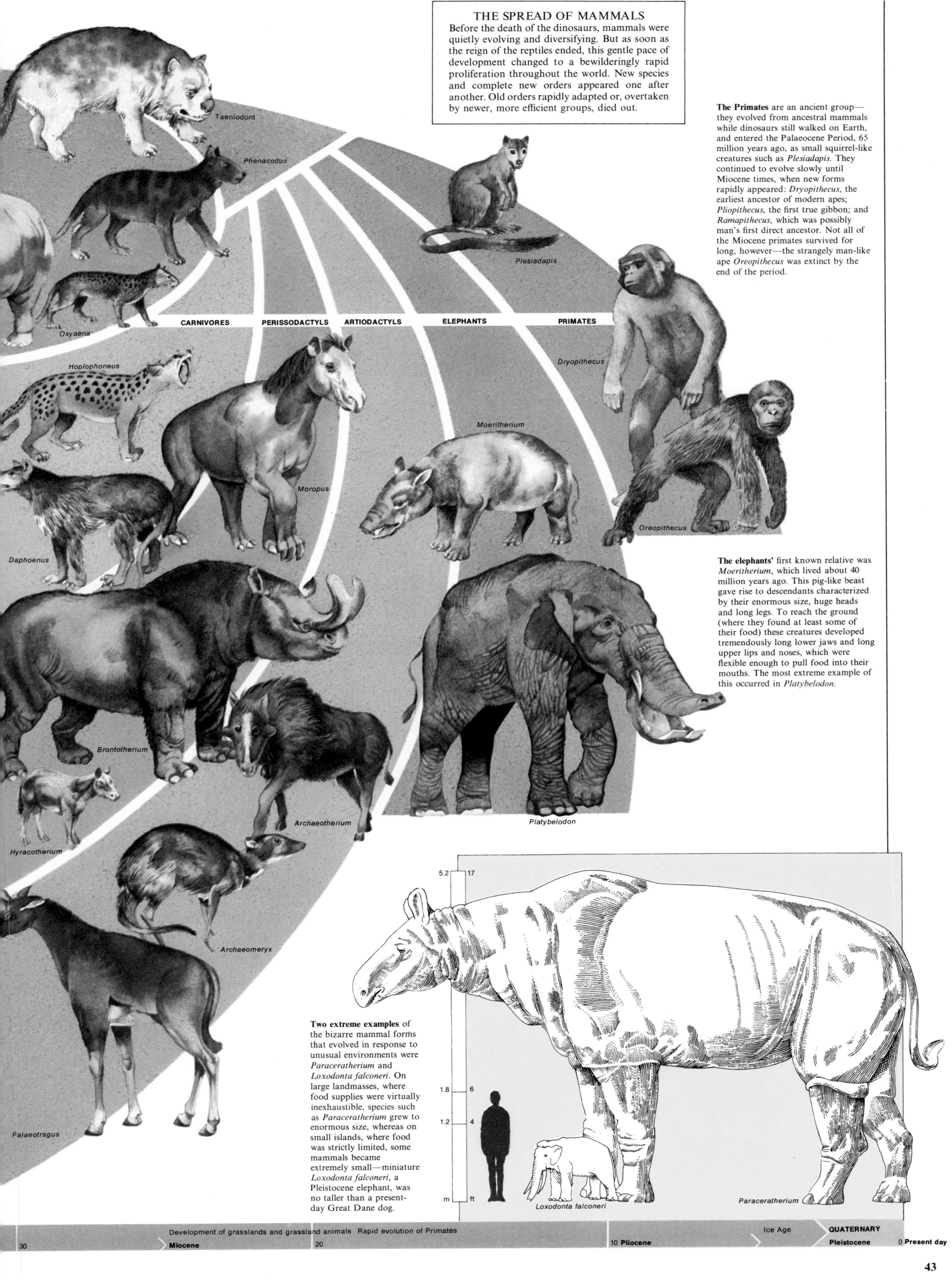

Spread of Life

Different parts of the Earth have their own characteristic groups of animals, and this pattern of distribution caused nineteenth-century zoologists to divide the world into zoogeographical regions. Charles Darwin suggested how these assemblages of animals may have come about by the process of evolution. But we now know that movements of the Earth's land surfaces are also responsible for the present-day distribution of many of the world's animal species and groups.

The evolution of a major group of animals, such as the reptiles or the mammals, tends to follow a set pattern in five stages. First the original ancestral group spreads out, with each subgroup adapting to its environment. This process, called adaptive radiation, results in a variety of different kinds of animals, each suited to life in a particular niche or habitat—determined largely by food supply and environmental conditions. The different kinds then move into all of the areas they can reach in which the environment is right, producing the second stage of widespread distribution.

Competition for food or living space, or changes in climate may then cause some forms to decline and disappear from parts of the range, resulting in a third stage of discontinuous distribution. Any further reduction leads to isolated relict populations—the fourth stage—in which the animal exists only in one or two limited areas. The final stage is extinction.

In all distribution patterns, however, there is not only an ecological element but also a historical one, with past events determining where animals are and where they are not. There are thus two basic types of distribution: continuous, where the area is not interrupted by an insurmountable barrier (such as a mountain range), and discontinuous, where the area of distribution is subdivided and there is no way that members of one group can interchange with members of another.

One of these factors—the earliest and most important—is the (continuing) movement of the Earth's tectonic plates. This caused the supercontinent Pangaea to break up, probably in the Triassic Period (225–180 million years ago), and the continental masses to drift apart to their present positions. New oceans developed, separating the Americas from the Euro-African block and splitting both from Antarctica. Madagascar and Australia became islands, India moved north from Africa to join the Asian block, and mountain ranges such as the Alps, Andes, Rockies and Himalayas were thrown up. As a result, animal types that had already evolved on Pangaea or its fragments before they had significantly separated (i.e. all the major invertebrate groups and most of the earlier vertebrates) can be expected to exist on all the present-day continents.

Bridging the continents

Independently of these activities, ice ages occurred from time to time, resulting in the vast accumulations of ice at the poles and a consequent general lowering of the sea level by as much as 100 m (330 ft). This temporarily exposed the previously submerged continental shelves, providing additional land for colonization, and new corridors that linked existing areas, such as the land bridge that appeared between Alaska and Siberia.

Groups that had evolved after the breakup of Pangaea, e.g. the hare, squirrel and dog families, made use of land bridges as the climate allowed, and came to occupy more than one continent. Flying animals—birds and bats—also made intercontinental crossings and established themselves on both sides of oceans, although a surprising number of these have remained very restricted in distribution. But most animals have to stay where they are because of special dietary or environmental requirements, or because they are "trapped" on islands, such as Madagascar and Australia, and cannot get off. These areas have the most distinctive faunas in the world.

Barriers and corridors

The extent to which an expanding group can spread from its original area depends on whether there are barriers, such as mountain ranges, deserts or seas, or corridors that link major areas in which the animals can live. Different animals have different environmental requirements, and so a topographical feature that is a barrier for one may be a corridor for another.

The dispersal of many animals is achieved by "hopping" from lake to lake across a continent, or from island to island across a sea. Some, such as insects, are good at this, whereas others, such as land mammals, are bad. Thus a considerable range of weevils (Curculionidae) are found on islands from New Caledonia to the Marquesas, some 6,500 km (4,000 miles) across the southern Pacific Ocean, whereas the marsupials of the region are concentrated in Australia, Papua New Guinea and a few adjacent islands, with only one genus reaching the Celebes and none crossing Wallace's Line into Borneo.

An example of colonization by "hopping" is seen on the volcanic island of Krakatoa near Java, which exploded in 1883 destroying all life. Within 25 years there were 263 species of animals on the island. Most were insects, but there were three species of land snails, two species of reptiles and 16 of birds. In another 22 years, 46 species of vertebrates had arrived, including two species of rats.

The effect of man

Animal distribution cannot be considered merely as a natural phenomenon, because it has been greatly and increasingly modified by man's impact on the environment. Agricultural practice has made large sections of the land area unsuitable for many of the animals that originally lived there, notably through the clearing of forests and the draining of marshes.

Man has also introduced animals, either deliberately or accidentally, to regions where they were not endemic. The rabbit in Australia and the deer in New Zealand were both deliberately introduced, but rats, cockroaches and many other animals have been accidentally transported throughout the world on ships and aircraft. The enormous growth in human population has driven many animals from their natural homes and into more remote environments, such as mountains. Indeed, in the past century human interference has altered the pattern of animal distribution more drastically than any topographic or climatic change.

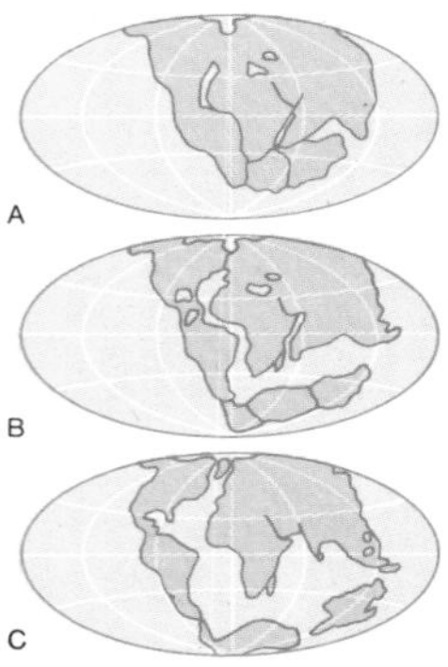
A
B
C

Earth's original single landmass, Pangaea (A), probably began to break up more than 200 million years ago. Species that had already evolved diversified on the Noah's Arks of the drifting supercontinents (B), called Laurasia and Gondwanaland. As the process continued (C), related animals flourished in the separated continents of the southern hemisphere.

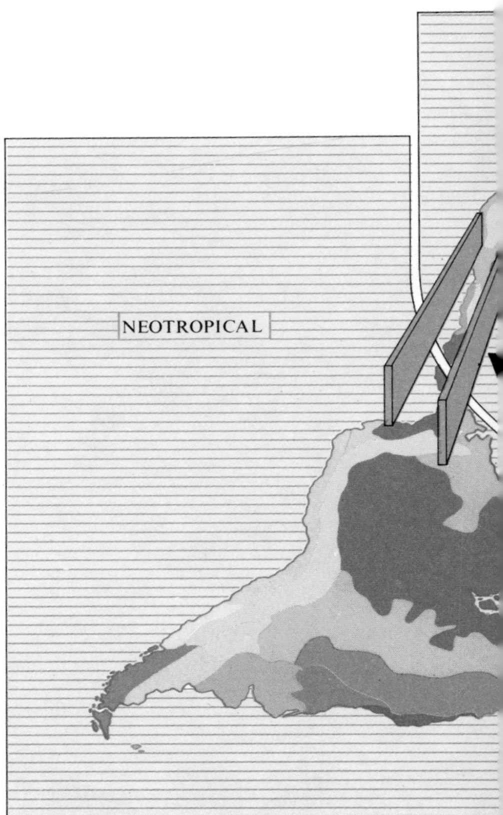
NEOTROPICAL

PATTERNS OF ANIMALS

Over the ages the shape of the Earth has changed. Whole continents have moved; mountains and deserts have grown; land bridges between continents have opened and closed. These events, together with food supply, climate and other animals, account for the present natural pattern of life in the six zoogeographical regions, each containing a unique mix of animals. But man's activities have drastically affected this natural distribution in all parts of the world.

NEARCTIC

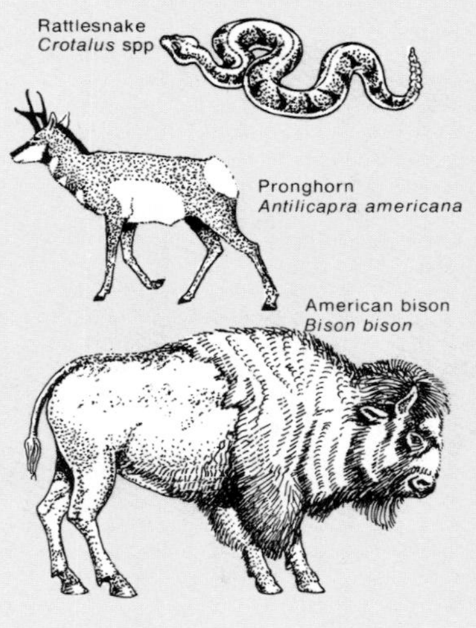
Rattlesnake
Crotalus spp
Pronghorn
Antilicapra americana
American bison
Bison bison

The Nearctic or "New North" region covers all of North America, from the highlands of Mexico in the south to Greenland and the Aleutian Islands in the north. Its climate and vegetation resemble that of the Palearctic region, and many of its mammals crossed over from the Palearctic via the Bering land bridge, which linked Siberia and Alaska when the sea level was lower. Animals unique to the Nearctic group include the pronghorn, an antelope-like mammal that inhabits the grasslands and plains of western and central America, and the bison, another large mammal that inhabits the prairies. Several species of rattlesnake also belong to the Nearctic group, although they are not exclusive to this region.

NEOTROPICAL

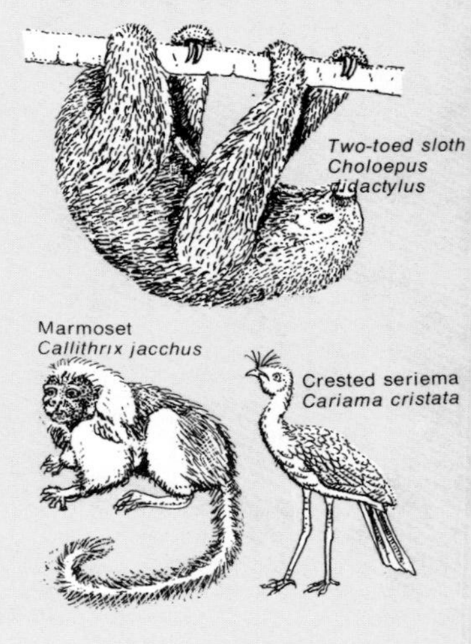
Two-toed sloth
Choloepus didactylus
Marmoset
Callithrix jacchus
Crested seriema
Cariama cristata

The Neotropical or "New Tropical" region consists of South America, the West Indies and most of Mexico. The climate and vegetation are mostly tropical—only the southern tip is in the temperate zone—and it is linked to the Nearctic by the Central American corridor. The Neotropical region has more distinctive families than any other. These include, among mammals, the sloth, which inhabits the tropical forests and has adapted to an upside-down existence. Among birds, the long-legged crested seriema is also unique to the region. Neotropical monkeys, such as the marmoset, have lateral-facing nostrils, which distinguish them from their downward-nosed relatives found in the Old World.

Land routes around the world have altered with the ages, sometimes allowing invaders to penetrate new lands, or closing to form natural sanctuaries for less efficient animals. The Central American isthmus (A) opened South America to placental mammals from the north. The Sahara desert closed most of Africa (B) to Eurasian species. Asia and Australia (C) share "island hoppers" in the transitional zones, but sea barriers have kept the regions separate.

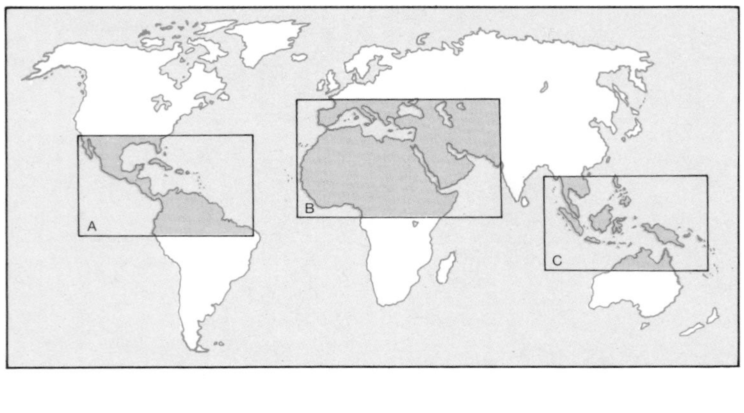
A
B
C

A land bridge between the Americas emerged about three million years ago, breaking the long isolation of the south. The primitive pouched mammals which had developed there were now threatened by more advanced mammals from the north, and many extinctions followed. Northern invaders included peccaries, raccoons and a llama-like camelid. But members of the armadillo and opossum families were successful in making their way to the northern region.

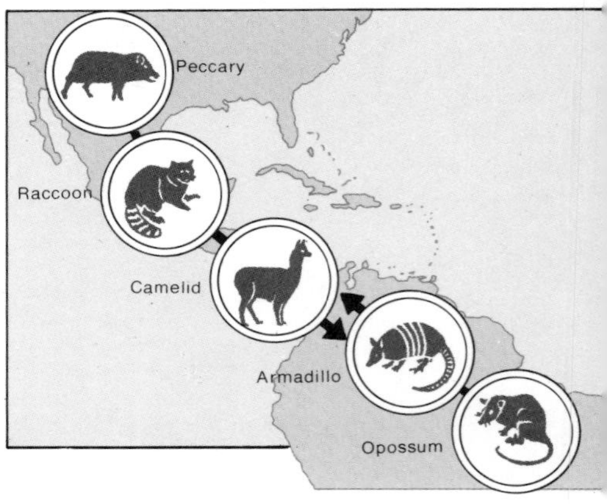
Peccary
Raccoon
Camelid
Armadillo
Opossum

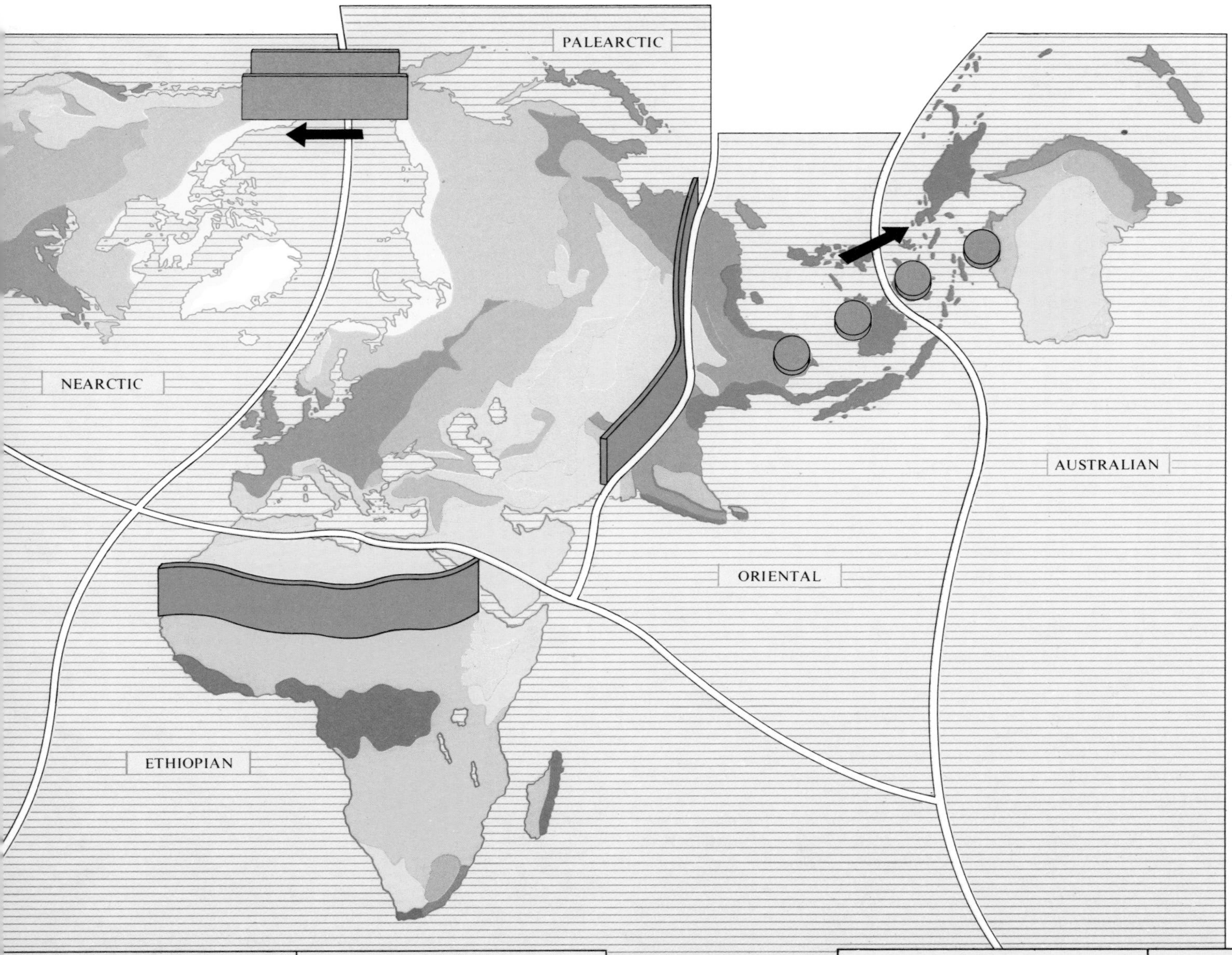

PALEARCTIC
NEARCTIC
AUSTRALIAN
ORIENTAL
ETHIOPIAN

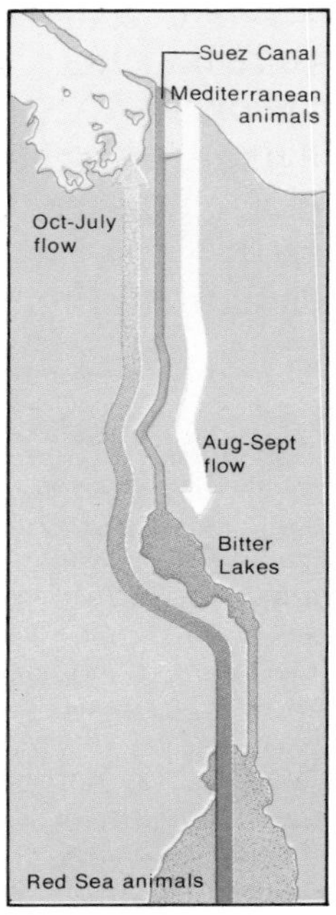

Suez Canal
Mediterranean animals
Oct-July flow
Aug-Sept flow
Bitter Lakes
Red Sea animals

The man-made filter of the Suez Canal, cut in 1869, is an animal corridor between the Mediterranean and Red Sea. But movement is mainly from the latter, for the channel passes through the hot, salty Bitter Lakes, favoring animals adapted to these conditions, and the current flows northwards for 10 months of the year. However, not all the 130 invading species are likely to survive Mediterranean conditions.

PALEARCTIC

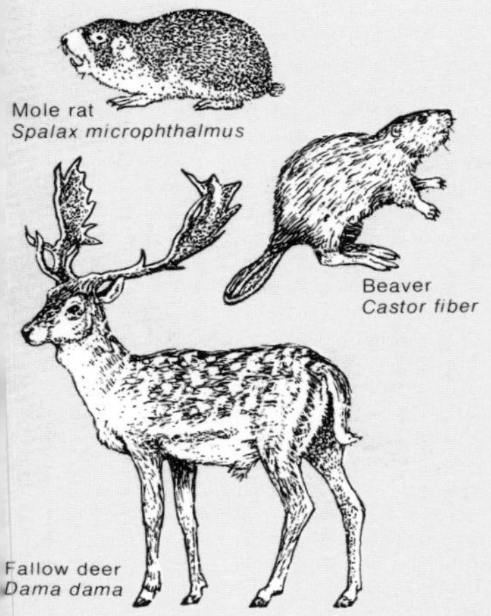

Mole rat
Spalax microphthalmus
Beaver
Castor fiber
Fallow deer
Dama dama

The Palearctic or "Old North" region covers the entire northerly part of the Old World, with seas to the north, east and west. To the south, the Sahara desert and the Himalaya mountains form barriers that separate the Palearctic from the Ethiopian and Oriental regions, although these regions are all part of the same landmass. One of the few species of mammals unique to the Palearctic is the Mediterranean mole rat, a thick-furred rodent. Another Palearctic rodent, the beaver, is shared with the Nearctic region. Fallow deer occur throughout Europe. They have been introduced by man into many other parts of the world, but their origin is almost certainly Mediterranean.

ETHIOPIAN

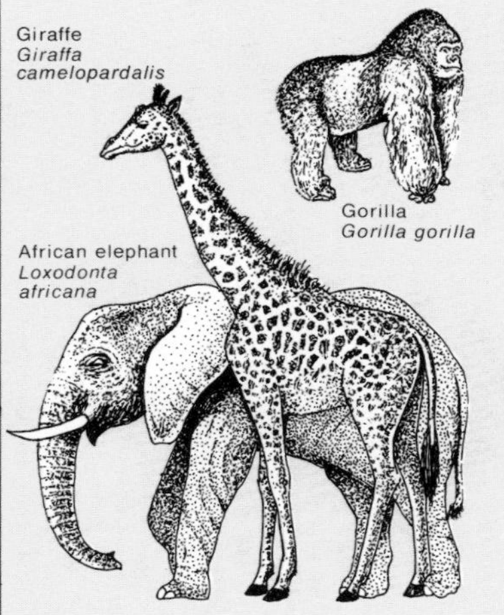

Giraffe
Giraffa camelopardalis
Gorilla
Gorilla gorilla
African elephant
Loxodonta africana

The Ethiopian region includes southern Arabia as well as all Africa south of the Sahara. It resembles in many ways the Neotropical region and is almost as rich in unique families. Its fauna also has much in common with the Oriental region. Unique mammals include the giraffe, at 5.5 m (18 ft) the tallest of living land animals, which inhabits the savanna. The region also supports two of the world's four great apes, the gorilla and the chimpanzee, which are found in the forests of western and central Africa. (The other great apes, the orangutan and the gibbon, are Oriental.) The African elephant is distinguished from its Indian relative by its greater size and by its huge ears and massive tusks.

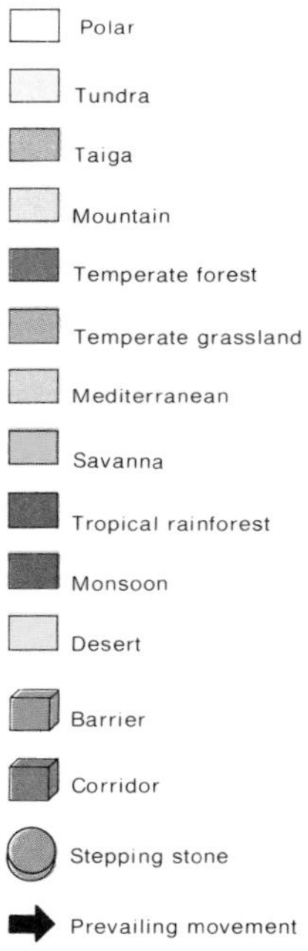

Polar
Tundra
Taiga
Mountain
Temperate forest
Temperate grassland
Mediterranean
Savanna
Tropical rainforest
Monsoon
Desert
Barrier
Corridor
Stepping stone
Prevailing movement

ORIENTAL

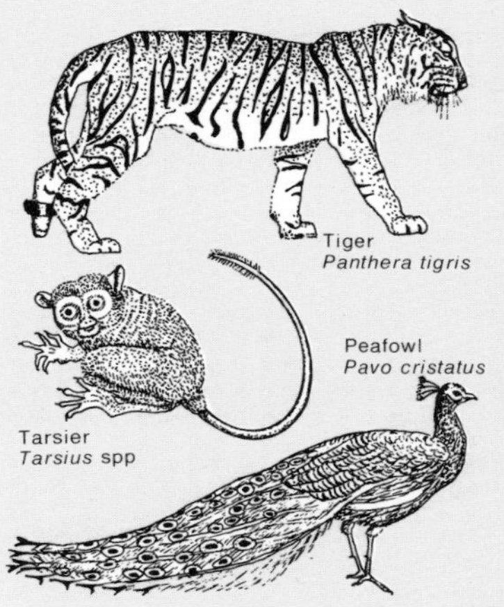

Tiger
Panthera tigris
Tarsier
Tarsius spp
Peafowl
Pavo cristatus

The Oriental region includes India, southern China, southeastern Asia and part of Malaysia. It is bounded to the north by the Himalayas and on either side by ocean, and is separated from the Australian region by a line known as Wallace's Line. It shares a quarter of its mammal families with Africa, but has more primates than any other region. The tarsier, a small relative of the monkey, is unique to southeastern Asia and represents an important early stage of primate evolution. The tiger was once widespread, but its natural habitats are steadily diminishing and the tiger itself is in danger of extinction by man. The peacock is one of the region's many brilliantly colored birds.

AUSTRALIAN

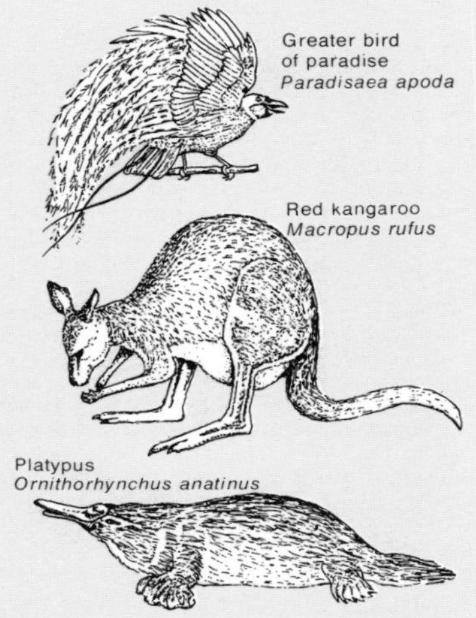

Greater bird of paradise
Paradisaea apoda
Red kangaroo
Macropus rufus
Platypus
Ornithorhynchus anatinus

The Australian region is unique in having no land connection with any other region. Its native fauna has developed in isolation from the rest of the world for at least 50 million years. Most of the mammals are marsupial—animals such as the kangaroo that carry their young in a pouch. Even more of a biological curiosity than the marsupials is the duckbilled platypus, a monotreme or egg-laying mammal. It lives along the banks of streams in Australia and Tasmania, and lays small, leathery eggs like those of snakes and turtles, but it is a true mammal and nurses its young with milk. Some 13 bird families are unique to the region, including the magnificent bird of paradise.

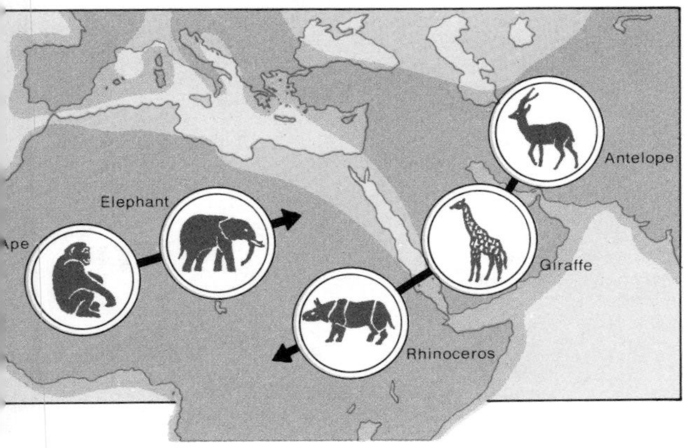

Antelope
Elephant
Giraffe
Rhinoceros

A desert barrier gradually began to form in northern Africa about nine million years ago, replacing the forest corridor between the Ethiopian and Palearctic regions. During the change, many animals typical of the African plains moved in from the north, including ancestors of today's antelopes, giraffes and rhinoceroses. But African animals also moved up north: early elephants and, much later, apes, which may have been precursors of modern man.

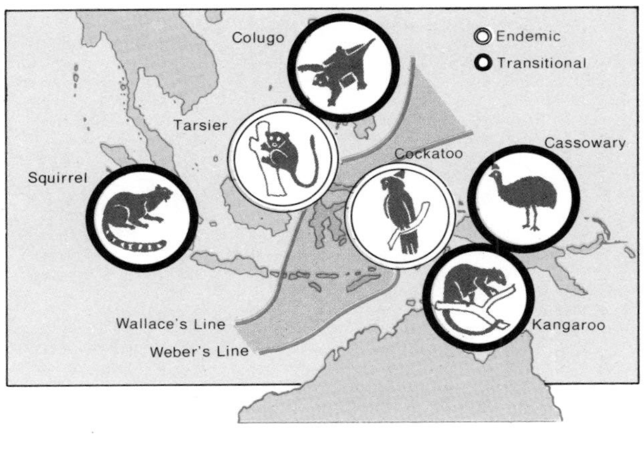

Colugo
Endemic
Transitional
Tarsier
Cockatoo
Cassowary
Squirrel
Wallace's Line
Weber's Line
Kangaroo

The transitional area of "Wallacea" contains animals from both the Oriental and Australian regions, bounded by Wallace's and Weber's Lines, but few have crossed to the other region. Some Oriental mammals, such as tarsiers, are found in Wallacea, but the gliding colugo and varieties of squirrel are not. The Australian cockatoo has reached the transition area, but the flightless cassowary and the tree kangaroo have not.

Spread of Man

Modern Man, *Homo sapiens sapiens*, has proved a highly successful animal since his emergence some 50,000 years ago: today more than 4,000 million members of this subspecies of the *Homo* (Man) group occupy the Earth, living in even the most inhospitable regions. But the fossil record shows that man's lineage goes back millions of years, with different stages of development leading to a greater control of the environment, and with climate itself helping man's ultimate domination of Earth.

Man's lineage may go back at least 14 million years to a small woodland creature known as *Ramapithecus* (Rama's ape). Since the first discoveries of *Ramapithecus* in the Indian subcontinent, its fossils have come to light in many parts of the world, including China, eastern Europe, Turkey and eastern Africa. Fossil remains show that it survived for several million years until, about eight million years ago, there is a tantalizing gap in the fossil record. Then, about four and a half million years later (according to recent discoveries in eastern Africa), we have solid evidence of an upright hominid—a member of man's zoological family. This is "Lucy," a fossil skeleton found in 1973 by Donald Johanson and Tom Gray, and subsequently classified with many other finds as *Australopithecus afarensis*.

This may be man's ancestral "rootstock," but a little later there existed two kinds of "ape-man" (*Australopithecus*), and our own direct ancestor Handy Man (*Homo habilis*). Datable volcanic ash found with the fossils provides a time scale and indicates that, about two million years ago, ape-man and "true" man lived side by side in the lush grassland that then covered the eastern African plains.

One and a half million years ago, according to the fossil evidence, there was again only one hominid species. The varieties of australopithecines had died out, and Handy Man (*Homo habilis*) had apparently evolved into Upright Man (*Homo erectus*). Remains of Upright Man have been found in many regions of the world, from various parts of Africa and Europe to China and Indonesia, although not in the Americas. But there is reason to believe that it was in Africa, well over one million years ago, that he evolved from his ancestor, and began a very gradual expansion out of the continent.

Upright Man had about one million years to spread across the Old World, adapting as he did so to local conditions, just as people of today are adapted in their various ways. He was a nomadic hunter gatherer, socially organized in groups. His skills included the use of fire and cooking, as well as the making of quite large structures out of wood. Recent discoveries suggest that, during the million years of his existence, *Homo erectus* gradually evolved into the next stage of man – *Homo sapiens*.

The next step is revealed most clearly in fossils from more than 100,000 to less than 50,000 years ago. Called Neanderthal Man in Europe, Solo Man in Indonesia, and Rhodesian Man in southern Africa, these types of human being were all descendants of *Homo erectus*.

Variable in brain size, but with prominent eyebrow ridges and receding jaws, they may have been dead ends on the evolutionary road; or some may have led to, or been incorporated in, Modern Man (*Homo sapiens sapiens*).

THE AFRICAN CRADLE
Handy Man (*Homo habilis*), who shared the East African grasslands two million years ago with a related "ape-man" species, was a slender and agile creature with a human way of walking and a capacity for conceptual thought, as evidenced in systematic making of tools. Handy Man collected stones, often from far away, and reshaped them into purpose-made tools, using other stones. Fossil remains suggest that these earliest humans were efficient hunters as well as scavengers of larger predators' kills, and that they brought food to campsites, probably sharing it among the whole group, rather than eating it on the spot. Such specifically human characteristics as the sharing of food may have helped our ancestors to survive their more primitive hominid relations.

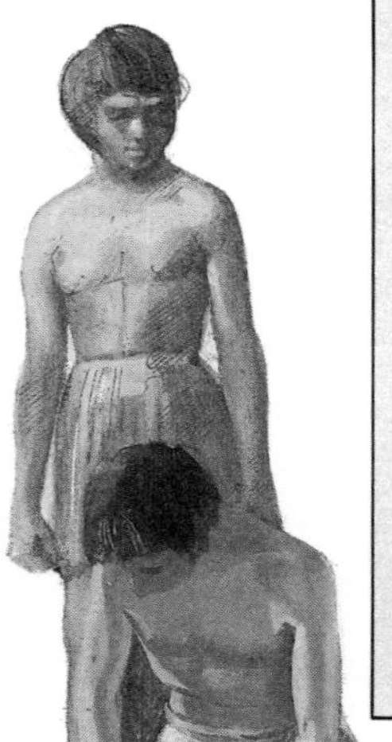

MAN THE FIRE-BRINGER
Upright Man (*Homo erectus*) emerged about 1.5 million years ago, evolving from his predecessor, Handy Man. For one million years these people developed and adapted, spreading over most of the Old World and following a nomadic hunter-gatherer life-style, assisted by a more sophisticated tool technology. The cooler climates of northern Asia and Europe may have encouraged their most impressive innovation—the use of fire for warmth, cooking and hunting game—and also their ability to construct quite elaborate shelters. It seems likely that they possessed language; and traces of ocher lumps at a campsite perhaps 400,000 years old suggest the possibility of ritual adornment or some kind of body painting.

THE HUMANIZING OF MAN
Modern man's predecessor, although called Wise Man (*Homo sapiens*), was long regarded as more brutish than human. But widespread finds have now changed this image, as can be seen in an old and an updated reconstruction of the same Neanderthal skull (right). Many scientists believe that these people showed a human concern for each other, burying their dead with ceremonial reverence, and looking after disabled members of the group. In their Neanderthal form they inhabited Europe and the Middle East from about 100,000 to 40,000 years ago, and were perhaps adapted to ice-age conditions. *Homo sapiens* counterparts of Neanderthal Man also occur in Africa and southeastern Asia.

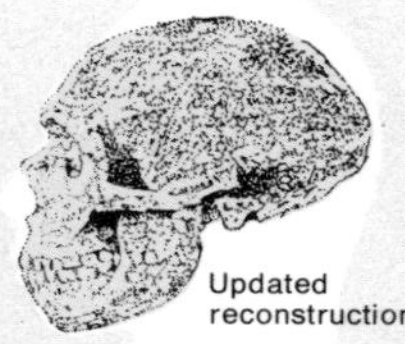

Updated reconstruction

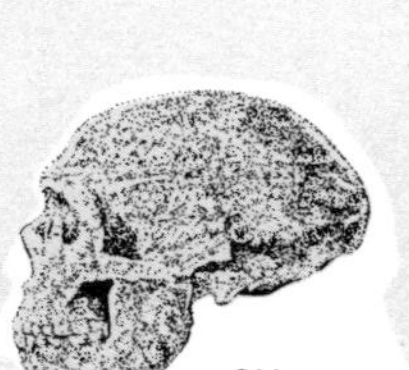

Old reconstruction

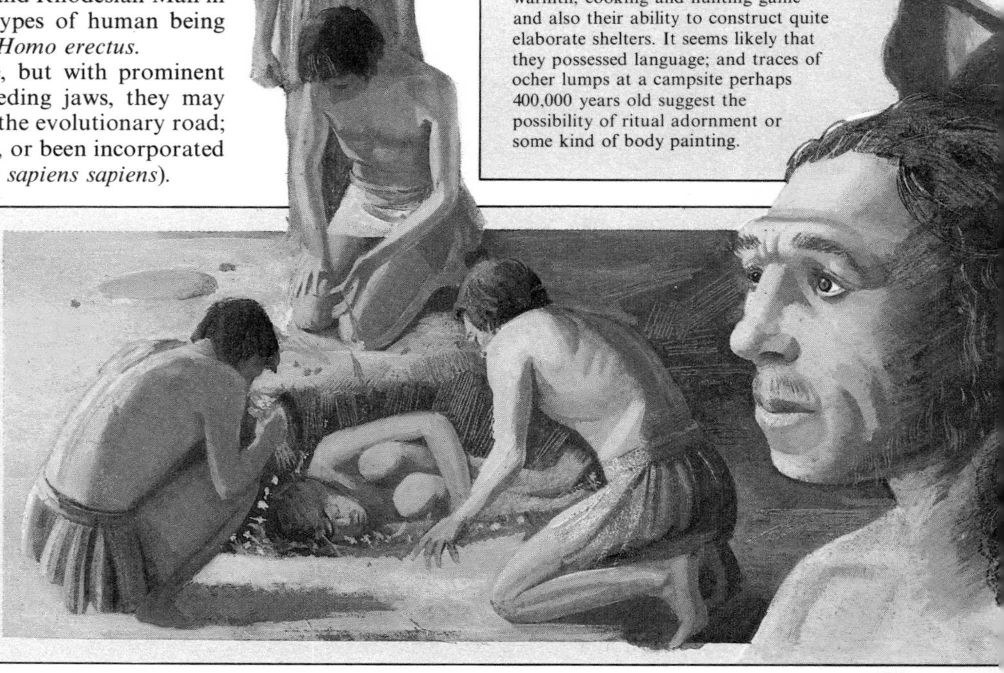

The burial of a Neanderthal man took place 60,000 years ago at Shanidar in the Iraq highlands. Fossil traces suggest that the body was laid on a bed of branches, and that flowers were brought to the grave and placed deliberately around the body. The flowers included many varieties still known locally for their medicinal properties. Ritual burials occur at many Neanderthal sites, from the Pyrenees to Soviet Asia, and indicate a sensitivity that contradicts Neanderthal Man's traditional image.

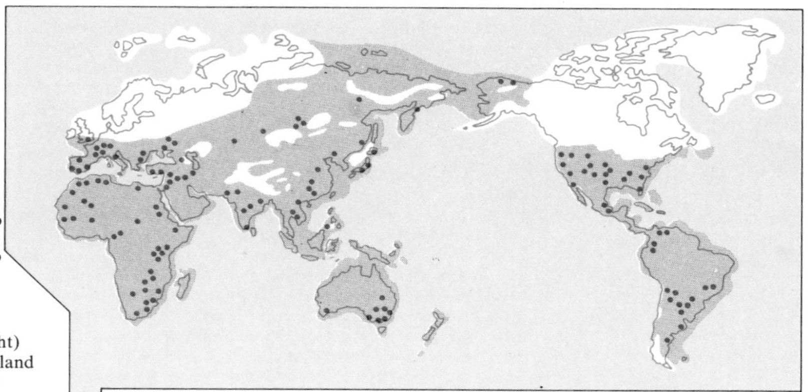

Land areas *c.* 19,000 years ago
Ice sheets *c.* 19,000 years ago
Homo sapiens sapiens remains

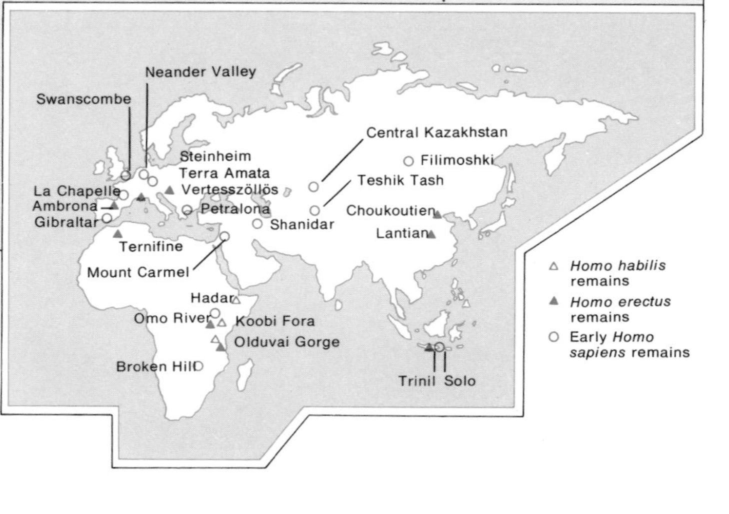

Neander Valley
Swanscombe
Central Kazakhstan
Steinheim
Terra Amata
Filimoshki
La Chapelle
Vertesszöllös
Teshik Tash
Ambrona
Petralona
Chou koutien
Gibraltar
Shanidar
Lantian
Ternifine
Mount Carmel
Hadar
Omo River
Koobi Fora
Olduvai Gorge
Broken Hill
Trinil Solo
Homo habilis remains
Homo erectus remains
Early Homo sapiens remains

The spread of man (right) from the African heartland of Handy Man (*Homo habilis*) probably began about one million years ago. Remains of Upright Man (*Homo erectus*) have been found all over the Old World, and show a gradual physical and cultural evolution toward a later *Homo sapiens* ancestor, beginning about 350,000 years ago. Between 70,000 and 12,000 years ago, glacial periods locked up the sea water as ice (top), lowering sea levels and opening a land bridge to America that was used by later nomadic peoples. But they had to cross open sea to reach Australia.

THE AGE OF ART
Toward the end of the last Ice Age, from about 35,000 years ago, truly modern humans began to depict their world in wonderfully vivid terms. The age of art may have reached its peak at Lascaux, France, some 15,000 years ago, but less well-preserved cave paintings from Africa show that the artistic impulse was equally present elsewhere. Called Cro-Magnon Man in Europe, these people spread to all parts of the world, crossing to the Americas by way of the Bering land bridge (when ice locked up the water of the straits), and even venturing over the seas to Australia. Physically these people were just like present-day humans. They led a nomadic, hunter-gathering life, living in large, organized groups, hunting such animals as mammoths, reindeer, bison and horses, and using a technology, as well as an artistry, far in advance of anything previously developed.

Fossils almost four million years old, found since 1973, may mark the ancestral "rootstock" of humanity, but the earliest form of true man is thought to be *Homo habilis*, who shared his African habitat with "ape-man" relatives some two million years ago. His successor, *Homo erectus*, spread over Asia and Europe, evolving gradually into modern man's predecessors, creatures whose large brow ridges belie many typically human characteristics. These were replaced by Modern Man.

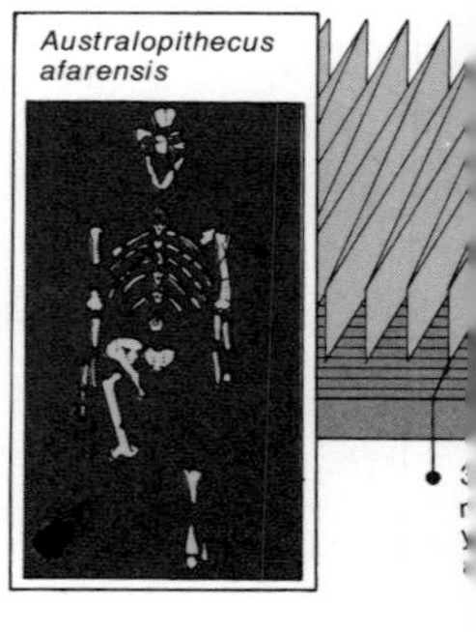

Australopithecus afarensis

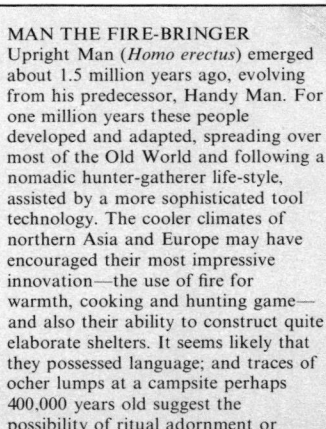

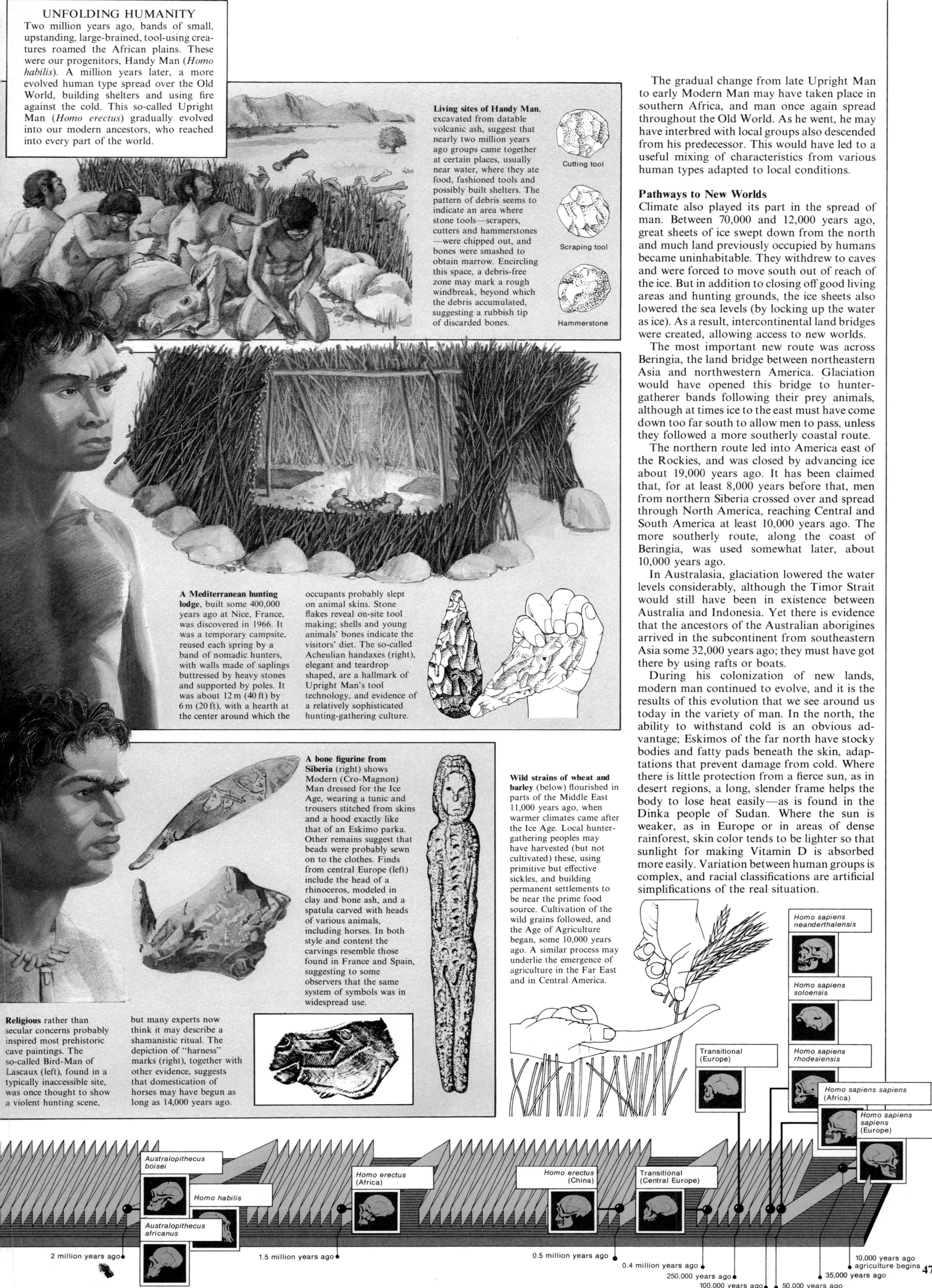

UNFOLDING HUMANITY

Two million years ago, bands of small, upstanding, large-brained, tool-using creatures roamed the African plains. These were our progenitors, Handy Man (*Homo habilis*). A million years later, a more evolved human type spread over the Old World, building shelters and using fire against the cold. This so-called Upright Man (*Homo erectus*) gradually evolved into our modern ancestors, who reached into every part of the world.

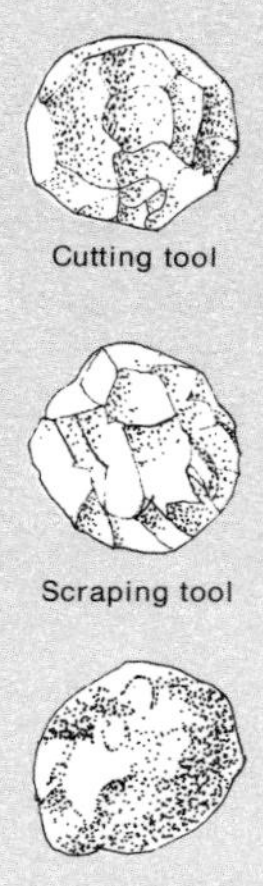

Cutting tool
Scraping tool
Hammerstone

Living sites of Handy Man, excavated from datable volcanic ash, suggest that nearly two million years ago groups came together at certain places, usually near water, where they ate food, fashioned tools and possibly built shelters. The pattern of debris seems to indicate an area where stone tools—scrapers, cutters and hammerstones—were chipped out, and bones were smashed to obtain marrow. Encircling this space, a debris-free zone may mark a rough windbreak, beyond which the debris accumulated, suggesting a rubbish tip of discarded bones.

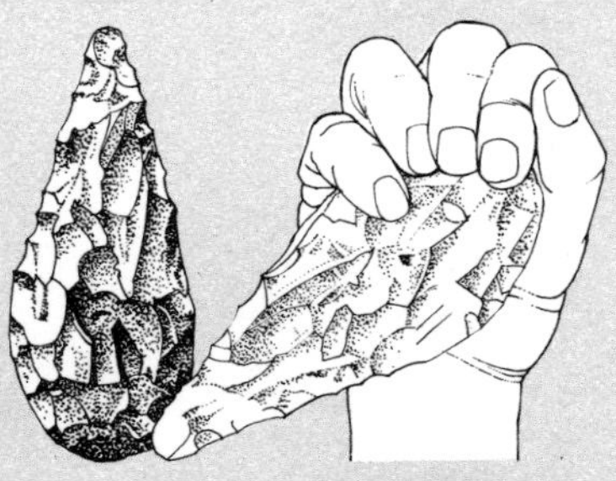

A Mediterranean hunting lodge, built some 400,000 years ago at Nice, France, was discovered in 1966. It was a temporary campsite, reused each spring by a band of nomadic hunters, with walls made of saplings buttressed by heavy stones and supported by poles. It was about 12 m (40 ft) by 6 m (20 ft), with a hearth at the center around which the occupants probably slept on animal skins. Stone flakes reveal on-site tool making; shells and young animals' bones indicate the visitors' diet. The so-called Acheulian handaxes (right), elegant and teardrop shaped, are a hallmark of Upright Man's tool technology, and evidence of a relatively sophisticated hunting-gathering culture.

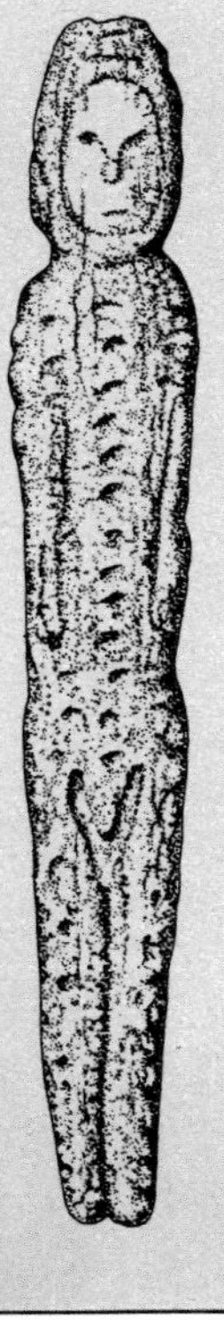

A bone figurine from Siberia (right) shows Modern (Cro-Magnon) Man dressed for the Ice Age, wearing a tunic and trousers stitched from skins and a hood exactly like that of an Eskimo parka. Other remains suggest that beads were probably sewn on to the clothes. Finds from central Europe (left) include the head of a rhinoceros, modeled in clay and bone ash, and a spatula carved with heads of various animals, including horses. In both style and content the carvings resemble those found in France and Spain, suggesting to some observers that the same system of symbols was in widespread use.

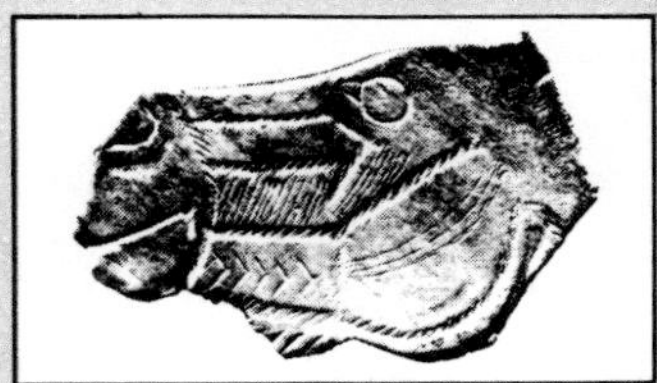

Religious rather than secular concerns probably inspired most prehistoric cave paintings. The so-called Bird-Man of Lascaux (left), found in a typically inaccessible site, was once thought to show a violent hunting scene, but many experts now think it may describe a shamanistic ritual. The depiction of "harness" marks (right), together with other evidence, suggests that domestication of horses may have begun as long as 14,000 years ago.

The gradual change from late Upright Man to early Modern Man may have taken place in southern Africa, and man once again spread throughout the Old World. As he went, he may have interbred with local groups also descended from his predecessor. This would have led to a useful mixing of characteristics from various human types adapted to local conditions.

Pathways to New Worlds

Climate also played its part in the spread of man. Between 70,000 and 12,000 years ago, great sheets of ice swept down from the north and much land previously occupied by humans became uninhabitable. They withdrew to caves and were forced to move south out of reach of the ice. But in addition to closing off good living areas and hunting grounds, the ice sheets also lowered the sea levels (by locking up the water as ice). As a result, intercontinental land bridges were created, allowing access to new worlds.

The most important new route was across Beringia, the land bridge between northeastern Asia and northwestern America. Glaciation would have opened this bridge to hunter-gatherer bands following their prey animals, although at times ice to the east must have come down too far south to allow men to pass, unless they followed a more southerly coastal route.

The northern route led into America east of the Rockies, and was closed by advancing ice about 19,000 years ago. It has been claimed that, for at least 8,000 years before that, men from northern Siberia crossed over and spread through North America, reaching Central and South America at least 10,000 years ago. The more southerly route, along the coast of Beringia, was used somewhat later, about 10,000 years ago.

In Australasia, glaciation lowered the water levels considerably, although the Timor Strait would still have been in existence between Australia and Indonesia. Yet there is evidence that the ancestors of the Australian aborigines arrived in the subcontinent from southeastern Asia some 32,000 years ago; they must have got there by using rafts or boats.

During his colonization of new lands, modern man continued to evolve, and it is the results of this evolution that we see around us today in the variety of man. In the north, the ability to withstand cold is an obvious advantage; Eskimos of the far north have stocky bodies and fatty pads beneath the skin, adaptations that prevent damage from cold. Where there is little protection from a fierce sun, as in desert regions, a long, slender frame helps the body to lose heat easily—as is found in the Dinka people of Sudan. Where the sun is weaker, as in Europe or in areas of dense rainforest, skin color tends to be lighter so that sunlight for making Vitamin D is absorbed more easily. Variation between human groups is complex, and racial classifications are artificial simplifications of the real situation.

Wild strains of wheat and barley (below) flourished in parts of the Middle East 11,000 years ago, when warmer climates came after the Ice Age. Local hunter-gathering peoples may have harvested (but not cultivated) these, using primitive but effective sickles, and building permanent settlements to be near the prime food source. Cultivation of the wild grains followed, and the Age of Agriculture began, some 10,000 years ago. A similar process may underlie the emergence of agriculture in the Far East and in Central America.

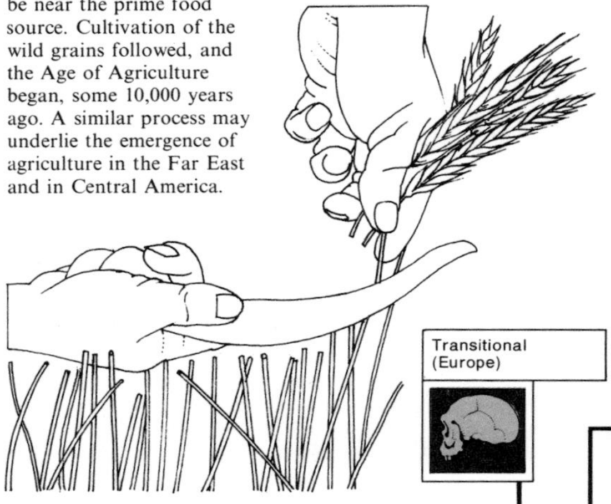

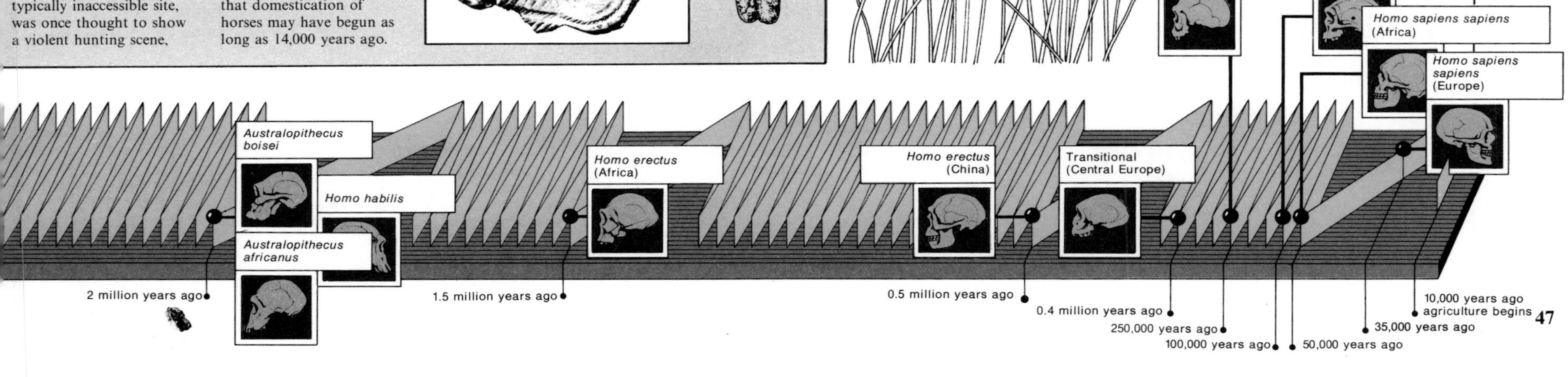

Australopithecus boisei
Homo habilis
Australopithecus africanus
2 million years ago
Homo erectus (Africa)
1.5 million years ago
Homo erectus (China)
0.5 million years ago
Transitional (Central Europe)
0.4 million years ago
Transitional (Europe)
250,000 years ago
Homo sapiens neanderthalensis
Homo sapiens soloensis
Homo sapiens rhodesiensis
100,000 years ago
50,000 years ago
Homo sapiens sapiens (Africa)
35,000 years ago
Homo sapiens sapiens (Europe)
10,000 years ago agriculture begins

Part 4

THE DIVERSITY OF LIFE

Earth's habitats from the Poles to the Equator
Plants and animals of the Earth's natural regions
Man the preserver and man the destroyer

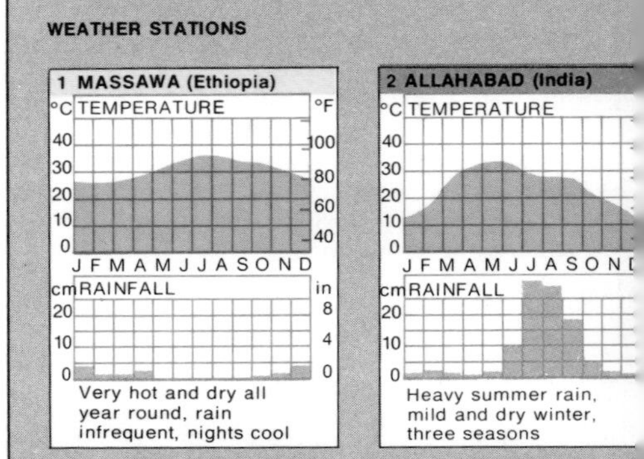

WEATHER STATIONS
1 MASSAWA (Ethiopia)
°C TEMPERATURE °F
J F M A M J J A S O N D
cm RAINFALL in
Very hot and dry all year round, rain infrequent, nights cool
2 ALLAHABAD (India)
°C TEMPERATURE
J F M A M J J A S O N D
cm RAINFALL
Heavy summer rain, mild and dry winter, three seasons

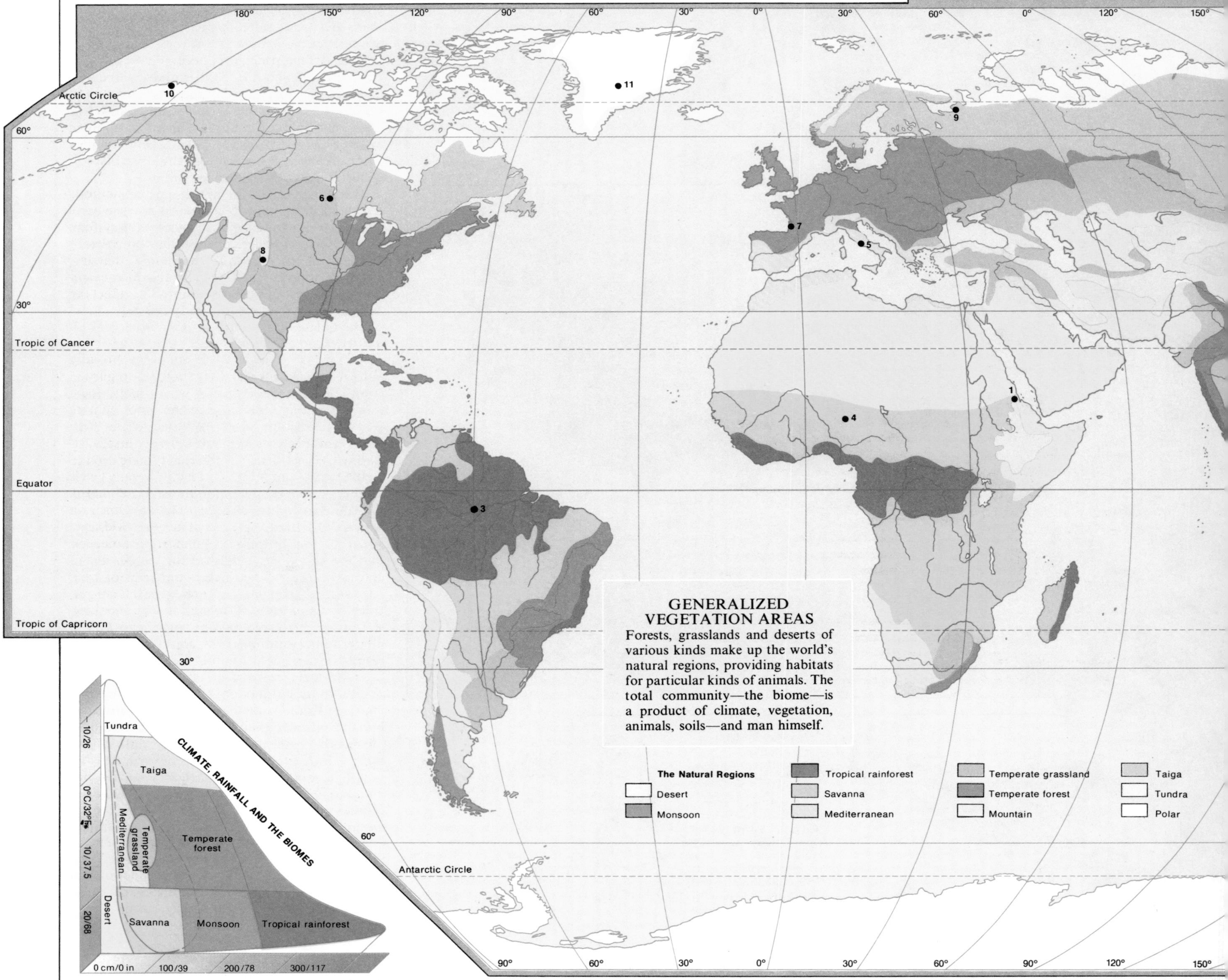

Arctic Circle
Tropic of Cancer
Equator
Tropic of Capricorn
Antarctic Circle
The Natural Regions
Desert
Monsoon
Tropical rainforest
Savanna
Mediterranean
Temperate grassland
Temperate forest
Mountain
Taiga
Tundra
Polar
CLIMATE, RAINFALL AND THE BIOMES
Tundra
Taiga
Temperate grassland
Mediterranean
Temperate forest
Desert
Savanna
Monsoon
Tropical rainforest
-10/26
0°C/32°F
10/37.5
20/68
0 cm/0 in
100/39
200/78
300/117

GENERALIZED VEGETATION AREAS

Forests, grasslands and deserts of various kinds make up the world's natural regions, providing habitats for particular kinds of animals. The total community—the biome—is a product of climate, vegetation, animals, soils—and man himself.

Temperature and rainfall (above) govern the world's zones of plant and animal life. Dryness prevents tree growth both in icy tundra and in hot deserts. Wetter conditions cause savannas and grasslands to yield to forest biomes, tropical or temperate (the dotted line indicates zones within which variations occur).

A broad correlation (below) between soil types, climate and vegetation areas shows the interconnections that define the biomes. The soil of the biome is related to climatic conditions and is also modified by plant and animal activity, but soil types are not necessarily confined to any one particular biome.

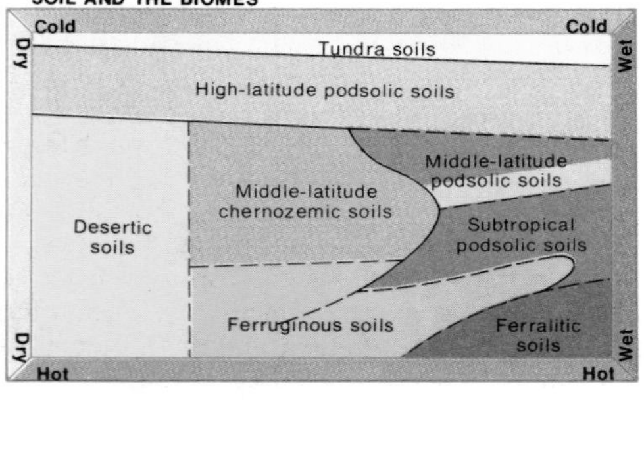

SOIL AND THE BIOMES
Cold
Cold
Dry
Wet
Tundra soils
High-latitude podsolic soils
Middle-latitude chernozemic soils
Middle-latitude podsolic soils
Desertic soils
Subtropical podsolic soils
Ferruginous soils
Ferralitic soils
Dry
Wet
Hot
Hot

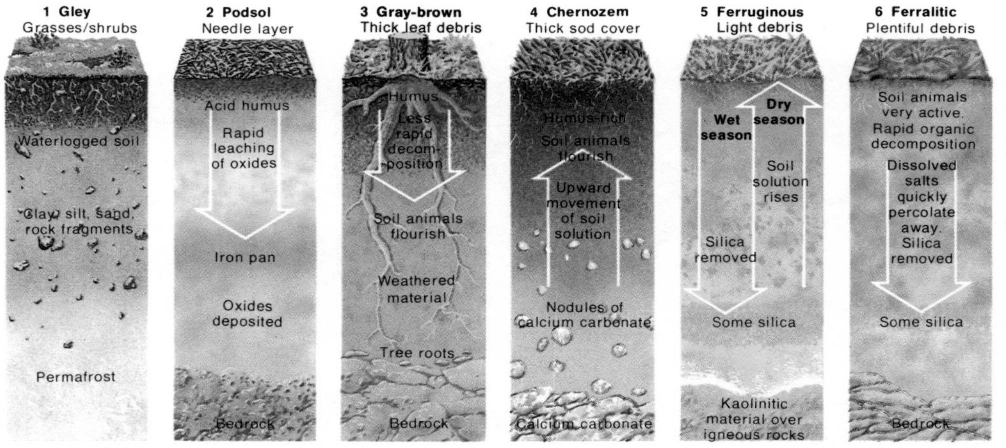

1 Gley
Grasses/shrubs
Waterlogged soil
Clay, silt, sand, rock fragments
Permafrost
2 Podsol
Needle layer
Acid humus
Rapid leaching of oxides
Iron pan
Oxides deposited
Bedrock
3 Gray-brown
Thick leaf debris
Humus
Less rapid decomposition
Soil animals flourish
Weathered material
Tree roots
Bedrock
4 Chernozem
Thick sod cover
Humus-rich
Soil animals flourish
Upward movement of soil solution
Nodules of calcium carbonate
Calcium carbonate
5 Ferruginous
Light debris
Dry season
Wet season
Soil solution rises
Silica removed
Some silica
Kaolinitic material over igneous rocks
6 Ferralitic
Plentiful debris
Soil animals very active
Rapid organic decomposition
Dissolved salts quickly percolate away. Silica removed
Some silica
Bedrock

Soil profiles (above) from surface to bedrock reflect the influence of climate and vegetation on the rock. Depths vary from 1 m in the tundra to 30–40 m at the Equator. Waterlogged gley (1) may form above tundra permafrost. Podsol (2) is typical of taiga forests, where spring snow-melt is heavily leached through a needle layer, sometimes forming an iron "pan." Gray-brown forest soil (3) has rich, organic humus, as has chernozem (4), the typical temperate grassland soil. Ferruginous soils (5) occur in dry-season tropical climates (monsoon, savanna), and ferralitic soils (6) where there is constant rainfall.

ECOSYSTEM DYNAMICS

An ecosystem consists o group of organisms and physical environment. A marshland ecosystem fr North America (right) shows the dynamic interactions between pla and animal communities and their habitats, which include climate, soil and water. The energy and food in the system initia derive from the Sun—th main energy source for living things, notably plants. Plants are food for herbivores, on land and in water; herbivores are food for carnivores; decomposers (bacteria a fungi) nourish plants, breaking down dead bo into compounds.

Earth's Natural Regions

Geographers have long looked for ways of classifying conditions such as climate, soil and vegetation to describe the general similarities and differences from area to area throughout the world. By identifying distinctive patterns of climate and vegetation they have provided a convenient global division into natural regions or biomes. And recent developments in ecology – the study of plants and animals in relation to their environments – have given such divisions a greater depth.

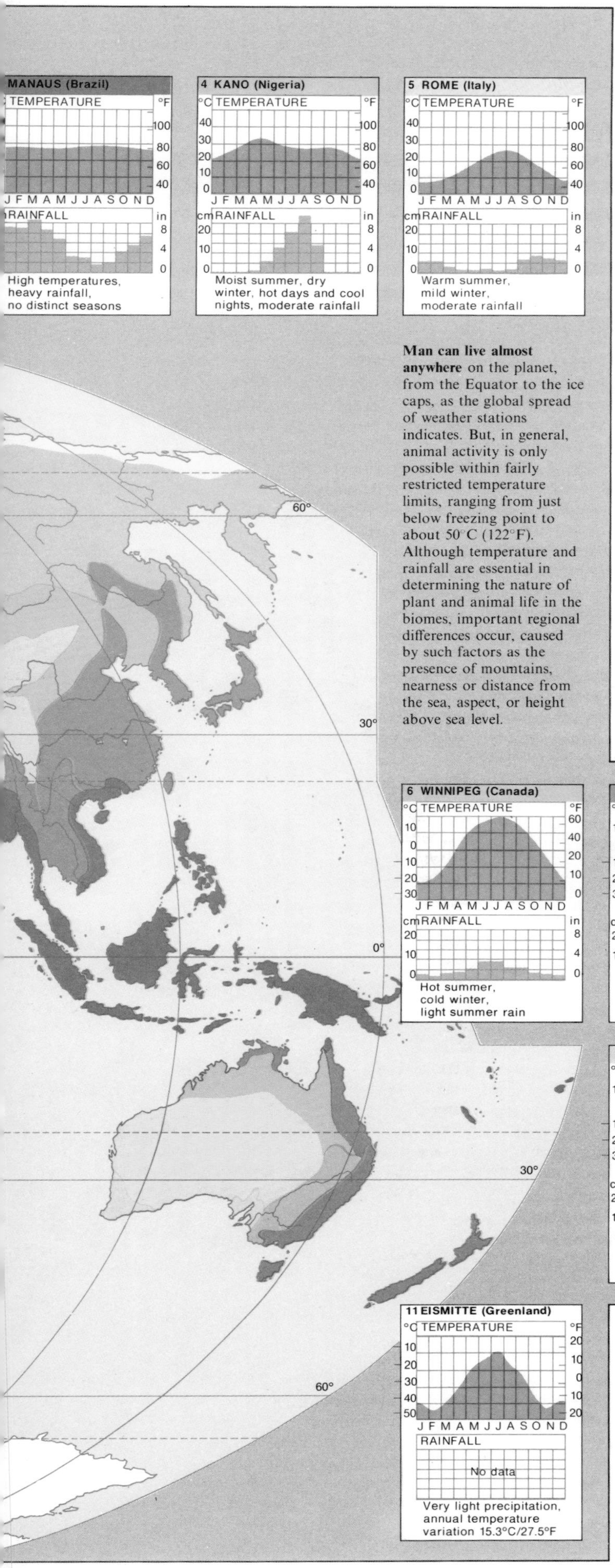
MANAUS (Brazil)
TEMPERATURE
RAINFALL
High temperatures, heavy rainfall, no distinct seasons
4 KANO (Nigeria)
Moist summer, dry winter, hot days and cool nights, moderate rainfall
5 ROME (Italy)
Warm summer, mild winter, moderate rainfall
11 EISMITTE (Greenland)
No data
Very light precipitation, annual temperature variation 15.3°C/27.5°F
60°
30°
0°

Man can live almost anywhere on the planet, from the Equator to the ice caps, as the global spread of weather stations indicates. But, in general, animal activity is only possible within fairly restricted temperature limits, ranging from just below freezing point to about 50°C (122°F). Although temperature and rainfall are essential in determining the nature of plant and animal life in the biomes, important regional differences occur, caused by such factors as the presence of moumtains, nearness or distance from the sea, aspect, or height above sea level.

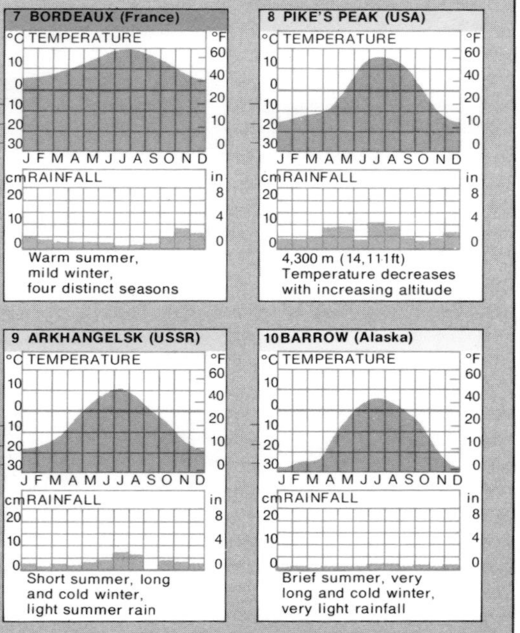
6 WINNIPEG (Canada)
Hot summer, cold winter, light summer rain
7 BORDEAUX (France)
Warm summer, mild winter, four distinct seasons
8 PIKE'S PEAK (USA)
4,300 m (14,111 ft)
Temperature decreases with increasing altitude
9 ARKHANGELSK (USSR)
Short summer, long and cold winter, light summer rain
10 BARROW (Alaska)
Brief summer, very long and cold winter, very light rainfall

Divisions according to climate were first suggested by the Greek philosopher Aristotle, and his ideas were still in use until about 100 years ago. Aristotle posited a number of climatic zones—called torrid, temperate and frigid—defined by latitude. But with time it became increasingly apparent that the complex distribution of atmospheric pressure, winds, rainfall and temperature could not be related to such a simple frame. Nineteenth-century scientists divided the world into 35 climatic provinces. Then in 1900 the German meteorologist Wladimir Köppen produced a more sophisticated climatic classification based on temperature and moisture conditions related to the needs of plants. At about the same time other scientists studied the distribution of vegetation types throughout the world. These studies together provided the basis for much of the later work on climatic regions.

An important step forward was made in 1904 by the British geographer A. J. Herbertson. He argued that subdivision of physical environments should take into account the distribution of the various phenomena as they related to each other. He conceived the idea of *natural regions*, each with "a certain unity of configuration (relief), climate and vegetation." His final classification contained four groups or regions: Polar Types, Cool Temperate Types, Warm Temperate Types and Tropical Hot Lands. Herbertson's scheme, controversial at first, was later much used for teaching geography.

Ecology

Meanwhile the study of environmental problems had been advanced by the idea of *ecology*, the relationship of living things between each other and their surroundings. The term was first used in 1868 by Ernst Haeckel, the German biologist, but it was not until the end of the nineteenth century that scientists really began to study life forms in relation to their habitat. In addition to the central ideas of interdependence between the members of plant and animal communities and between the community and the physical environment, there now came the suggestion that communities develop in a sequence that leads to a "climax"—a final step of equilibrium or balance. Their climax stage depends on conditions of climate or soil.

Later the British botanist A. G. Tansley, a leading exponent of ecological thinking, introduced the term *ecosystem* to describe a group of living organisms and its effective environment. Tansley's definition of 1935 referred to the whole system, including "not only the organism complex, but also the whole complex of physical factors forming what we call the environment of the biome." The idea became very influential and has been used in the social sciences as well as in the natural ones. But it is difficult to apply in practice, partly because of the highly complex and often diverse interactions that take place in different parts of the ecosystem.

Ecologists have developed special methods and have given particular attention to the ways in which energy is transferred within the system. The term *biome* refers to the whole complex of organisms, both animals and plants, that live together naturally as a society. By *environment* is meant all the external conditions that affect the life and development of an organism.

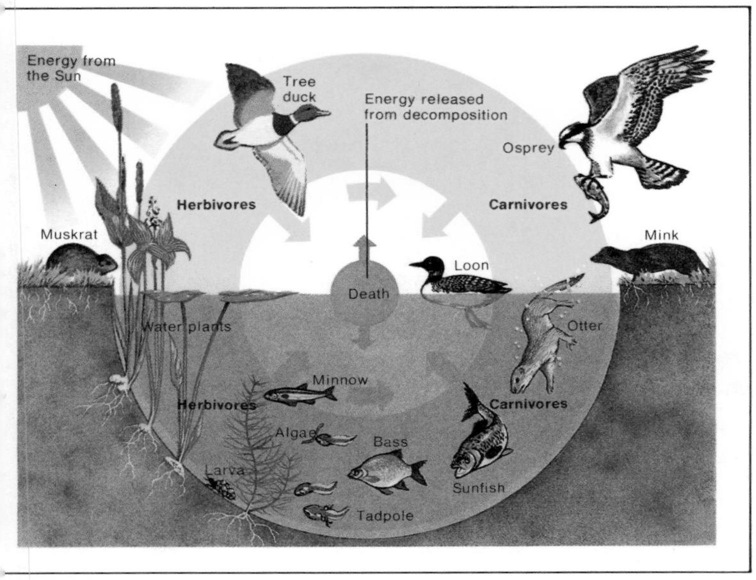
Energy from the Sun
Tree duck
Energy released from decomposition
Osprey
Herbivores
Carnivores
Muskrat
Mink
Loon
Death
Water plants
Otter
Minnow
Herbivores
Carnivores
Algae
Bass
Larva
Sunfish
Tadpole

Biomes

The biomes shown on the map are broadly drawn generalizations. They should be regarded as idealized regions, within which many local variations may exist—for example, of climate or soil conditions. On a larger scale such features as mountain ranges may cause variations at a regional level. Scientists have tried to work out "hierarchies" that include many levels or orders of scale leading to the major climatic-vegetation realms or biomes. These realms give a broad picture that is useful at the world level of scale, and which forms a starting point for further analysis. Any map of the biomes has to have lines to indicate the boundaries of each region, but these too are generalizations. Although climate and vegetation do sometimes change abruptly from place to place, more often there are transitional zones, and the boundaries on the maps give the broad locations of these.

Herbertson's concept of natural regions attempted also to take account of the influence of man as an important factor in the environment. But he was not totally successful in including man in his analysis, no doubt because of the complexity of the problems involved and because of the immense influence that man has had upon the natural vegetation of the world. The cutting of forests, the drainage and reclamation of land, the introduction, use and spread of cultivated plants, the domestication of animals, the development of sophisticated systems of agriculture and many other actions all create, over large areas of the biomes, landscapes that are more man-made than natural.

Resource systems

An idea that clarifies the study of the inter-relations of societies and environments, and the ways in which these change with the passage of time, is that of the *resource system*. This is a model of a population of human beings and their social and economic characteristics, including their technical skills and resources, together with those aspects of the natural environment that affect them and which they influence. The model includes the sequences by which natural materials are obtained, transformed and used. It tries to show how societies are organized according to their natural resources, the effects of that use, and the ways in which natural conditions limit or expand the life and work of the society. But it is easier to apply such a model to societies that have direct relations with natural conditions, through farming, fishing or forestry, than to great urban-industrial complexes.

The sections that follow present a picture of the diversity of habitats from ice caps to equatorial forests, the principal ways man has modified the environment and the problems of maintaining healthy resource systems.

Climate and Weather

The pattern of world climates depends largely on great circulations of air in the atmosphere. These movements of air are driven by energy from the Sun, and they transfer surplus heat from the tropics to the polar regions. Over a long period of time – such as months, seasons or years – they create the climate. Over a short period – day by day, or week by week – they form the weather. Together, climate and weather are among the most significant natural components of the world's diverse environments.

The world's tropical zones receive more heat from the Sun than they re-emit into space, and so their land and sea surfaces become warm. The polar regions, on the other hand, emit more radiation than they receive, and so they become cold. Warm air is less dense than cold air, and this means that atmospheric pressure becomes low at the Equator and high at the poles. As a result, a circulation of air—both vertical and horizontal—is set up. But because of the Earth's rotation and the distribution of land and sea there is not a simple air circulation pattern in each hemisphere; winds are deflected to the right in the northern hemisphere and to the left in the southern hemisphere, a phenomenon known as the Coriolis effect.

A climatic patchwork

When warm air rises it expands and cools and the water vapor it is carrying condenses to form clouds. For this reason heavy, showery rain is frequent in the belt of rising air near the Equator. In the subtropical zones (where the air is sinking), clouds evaporate and the weather is fine. Air moves out of the subtropical high-pressure belts in the lower atmosphere. Some of it flows towards the poles and meets colder air, flowing out of the polar high-pressure region, in a narrow zone called the polar front. This convergence of air is concentrated around low-pressure systems known as depressions.

The pattern of climates does not remain constant throughout the year because of seasonal changes in the amount of radiation from the Sun—the "fuel" of the atmospheric engine. In June, when the northern hemisphere is tilted towards the Sun, the radiation is at a maximum at latitude 23°N and all the climatic belts shift northwards. In December it is summer in the southern hemisphere and all the belts move southwards.

Climate is also affected by the distribution of land and sea across the globe. The temperature of the land changes more quickly than that of

TYPES OF WEATHER

There is a constant flow of air between the world's polar and tropical regions, and this has a prime effect on the weather in other regions. In the high and middle latitudes cold and warm fronts succeed each other, and along coasts sea fogs often form. In temperate and tropical regions thunderstorms are frequent, and the tropics are characterized by the turbulent storms known as hurricanes in the Caribbean area and typhoons in the Pacific.

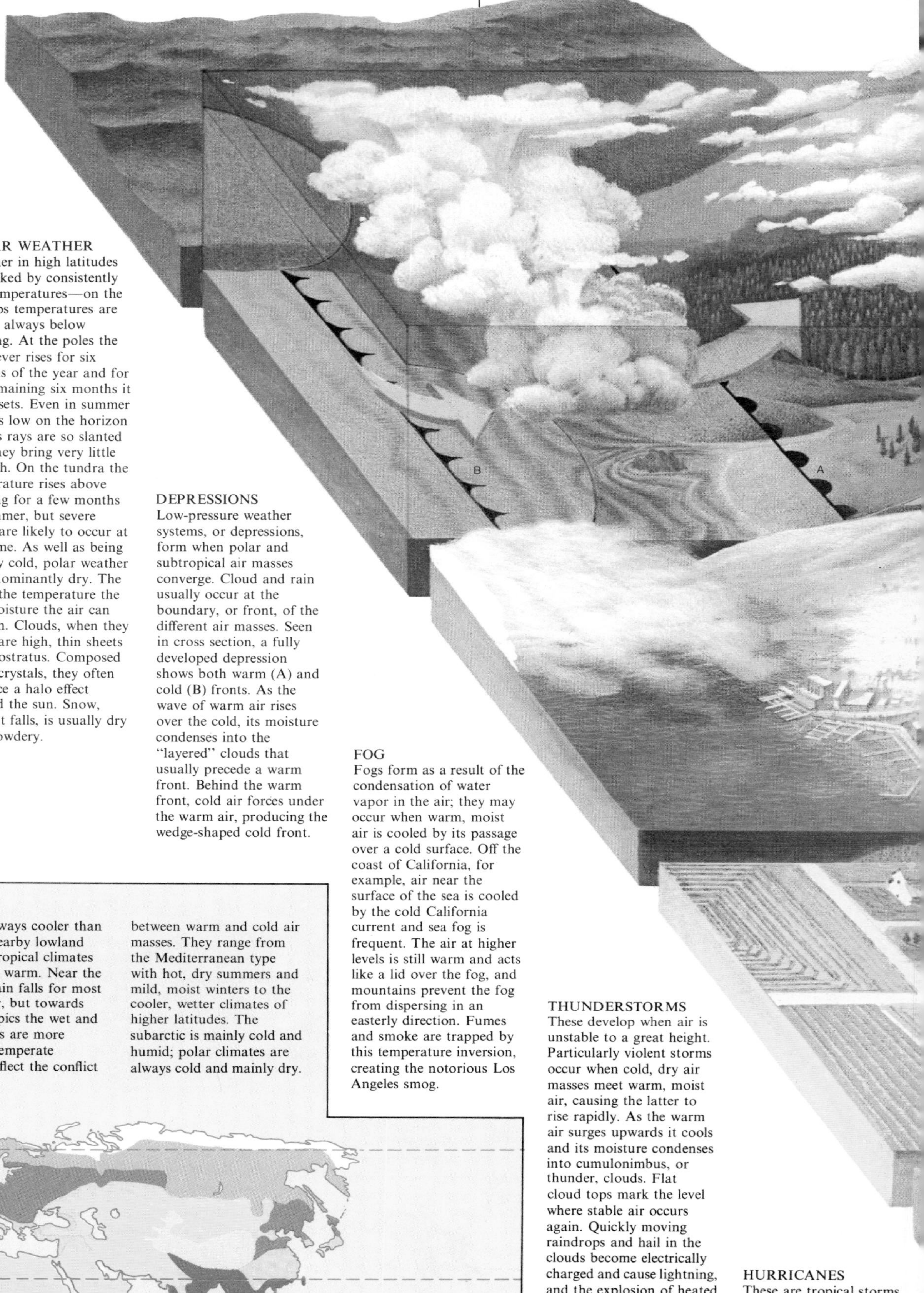
B
A

POLAR WEATHER
Weather in high latitudes is marked by consistently low temperatures—on the ice caps temperatures are nearly always below freezing. At the poles the sun never rises for six months of the year and for the remaining six months it never sets. Even in summer it stays low on the horizon and its rays are so slanted that they bring very little warmth. On the tundra the temperature rises above freezing for a few months in summer, but severe frosts are likely to occur at any time. As well as being bitterly cold, polar weather is predominantly dry. The lower the temperature the less moisture the air can contain. Clouds, when they form, are high, thin sheets of cirrostratus. Composed of ice crystals, they often produce a halo effect around the sun. Snow, when it falls, is usually dry and powdery.

DEPRESSIONS
Low-pressure weather systems, or depressions, form when polar and subtropical air masses converge. Cloud and rain usually occur at the boundary, or front, of the different air masses. Seen in cross section, a fully developed depression shows both warm (A) and cold (B) fronts. As the wave of warm air rises over the cold, its moisture condenses into the "layered" clouds that usually precede a warm front. Behind the warm front, cold air forces under the warm air, producing the wedge-shaped cold front.

FOG
Fogs form as a result of the condensation of water vapor in the air; they may occur when warm, moist air is cooled by its passage over a cold surface. Off the coast of California, for example, air near the surface of the sea is cooled by the cold California current and sea fog is frequent. The air at higher levels is still warm and acts like a lid over the fog, and mountains prevent the fog from dispersing in an easterly direction. Fumes and smoke are trapped by this temperature inversion, creating the notorious Los Angeles smog.

THUNDERSTORMS
These develop when air is unstable to a great height. Particularly violent storms occur when cold, dry air masses meet warm, moist air, causing the latter to rise rapidly. As the warm air surges upwards it cools and its moisture condenses into cumulonimbus, or thunder, clouds. Flat cloud tops mark the level where stable air occurs again. Quickly moving raindrops and hail in the clouds become electrically charged and cause lightning, and the explosion of heated air along the path of the flash creates the sound wave that is heard as thunder.

HURRICANES
These are tropical storms on a vast scale that build up over warm oceans. Their core is an area of low pressure around which large quantities of warm, moist air are carried to the high atmosphere at great speed. The Earth's rotation is responsible for the huge swirling movement: in the northern hemisphere the movement is anticlockwise, in the southern hemisphere it is clockwise. Towering bands of clouds produce torrential rain. The central region, or "eye," of a hurricane, however, has light winds, clear skies and no rainfall.

THE WORLD'S CLIMATIC REGIONS

Climate is the characteristic weather of a region over a long period of time. It is often described in terms of average monthly and yearly temperatures and rainfall. These in turn depend largely on latitude, which determines whether a region is basically hot or cold and whether it has pronounced seasonal changes. Climate is also influenced by prevailing winds, by ocean currents and by geographical features such as the distribution of land and water. Highland climates are influenced by altitude and are always cooler than those of nearby lowland regions. Tropical climates are always warm. Near the Equator rain falls for most of the year, but towards the subtropics the wet and dry seasons are more marked. Temperate climates reflect the conflict between warm and cold air masses. They range from the Mediterranean type with hot, dry summers and mild, moist winters to the cooler, wetter climates of higher latitudes. The subarctic is mainly cold and humid; polar climates are always cold and mainly dry.

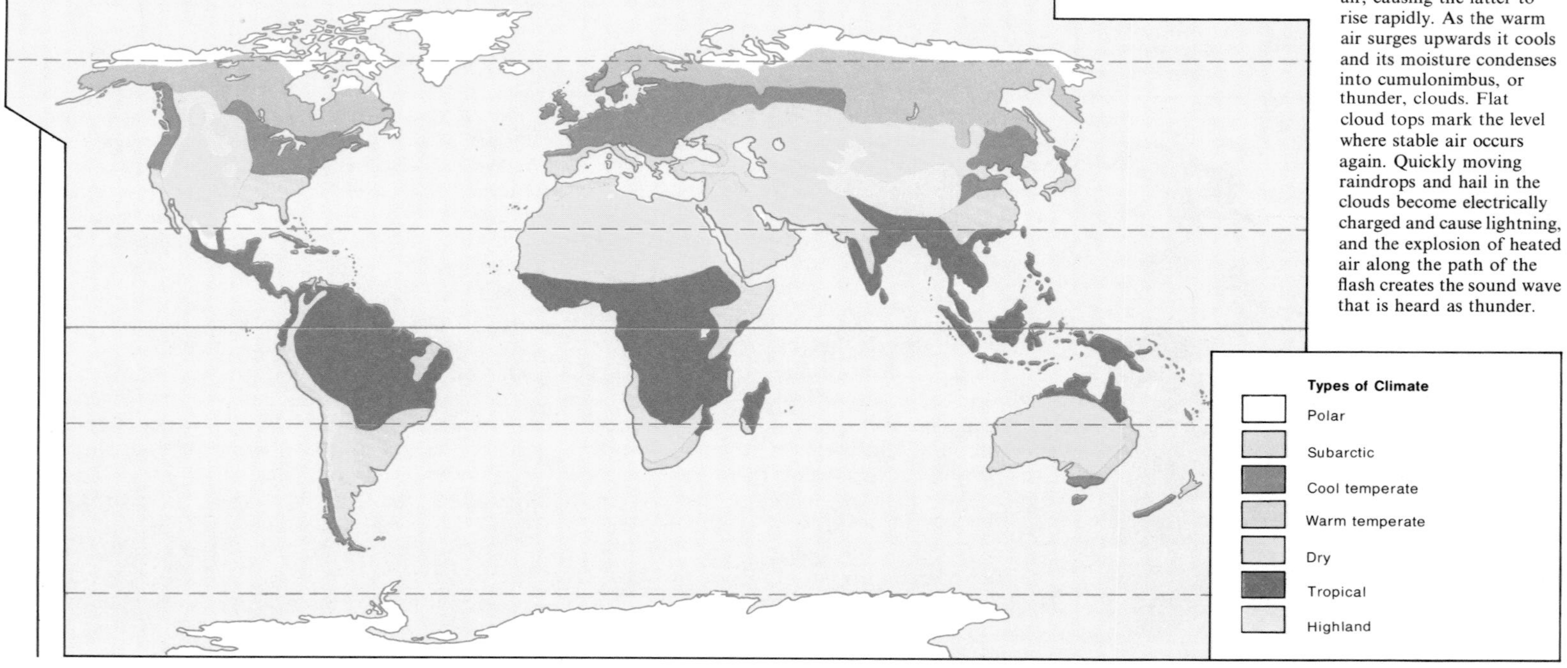
Types of Climate
Polar
Subarctic
Cool temperate
Warm temperate
Dry
Tropical
Highland

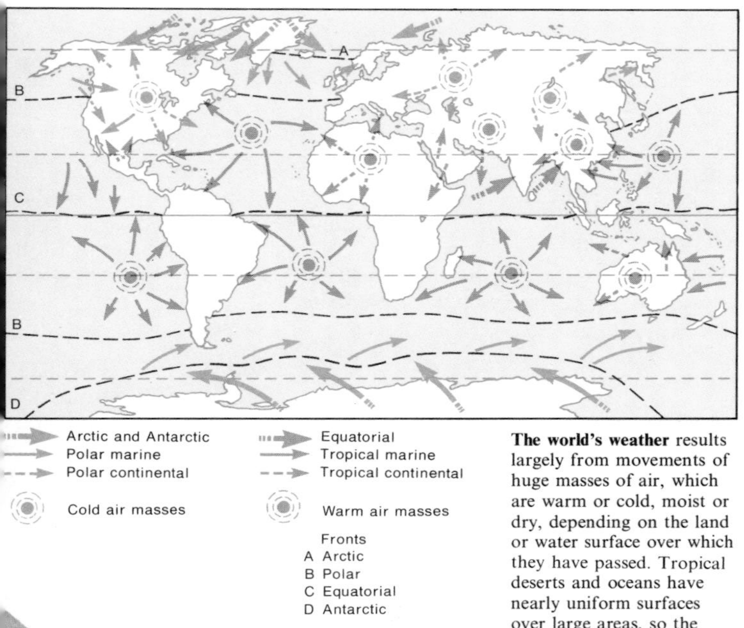

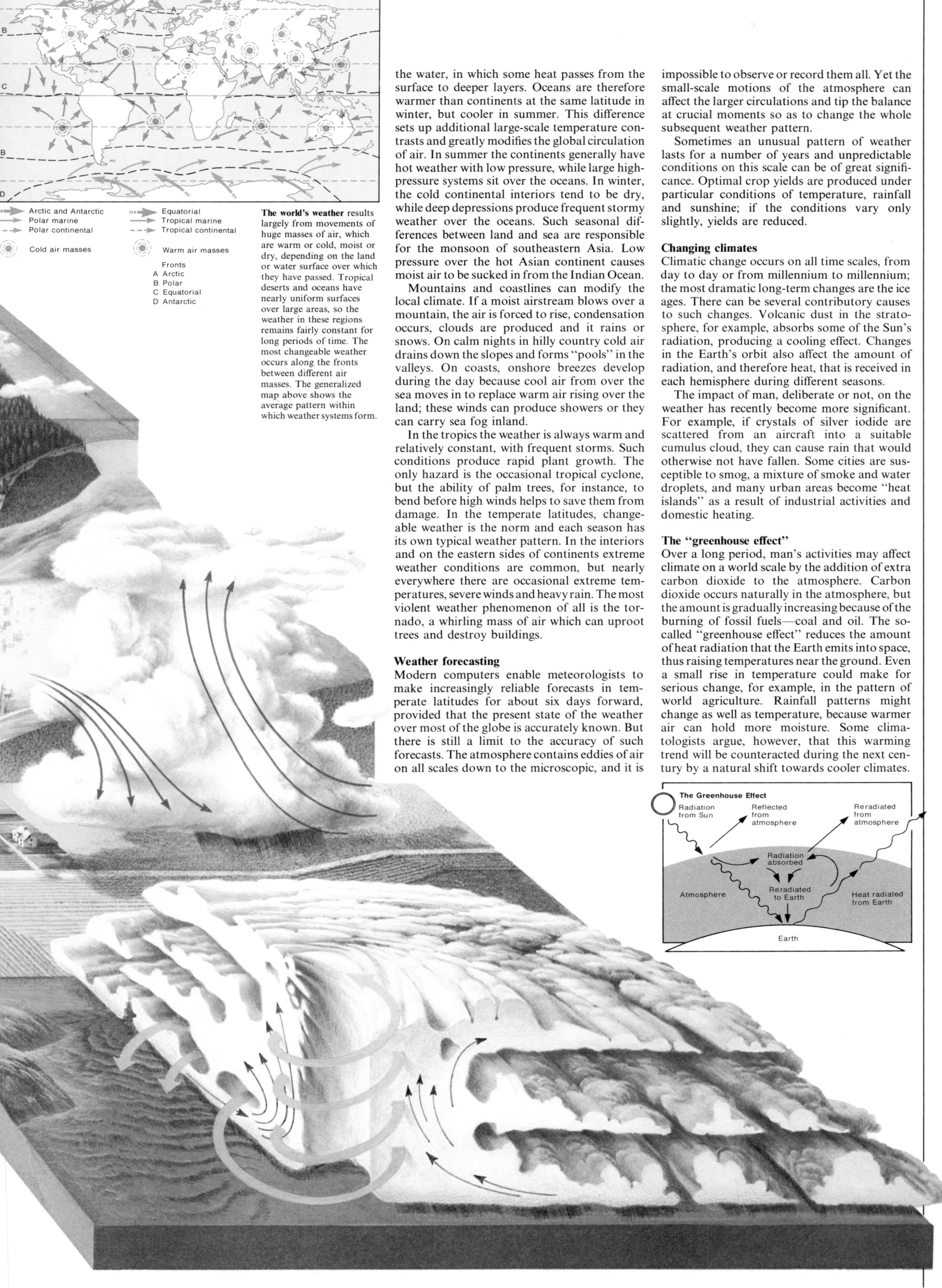

The world's weather results largely from movements of huge masses of air, which are warm or cold, moist or dry, depending on the land or water surface over which they have passed. Tropical deserts and oceans have nearly uniform surfaces over large areas, so the weather in these regions remains fairly constant for long periods of time. The most changeable weather occurs along the fronts between different air masses. The generalized map above shows the average pattern within which weather systems form.

the water, in which some heat passes from the surface to deeper layers. Oceans are therefore warmer than continents at the same latitude in winter, but cooler in summer. This difference sets up additional large-scale temperature contrasts and greatly modifies the global circulation of air. In summer the continents generally have hot weather with low pressure, while large high-pressure systems sit over the oceans. In winter, the cold continental interiors tend to be dry, while deep depressions produce frequent stormy weather over the oceans. Such seasonal differences between land and sea are responsible for the monsoon of southeastern Asia. Low pressure over the hot Asian continent causes moist air to be sucked in from the Indian Ocean.

Mountains and coastlines can modify the local climate. If a moist airstream blows over a mountain, the air is forced to rise, condensation occurs, clouds are produced and it rains or snows. On calm nights in hilly country cold air drains down the slopes and forms "pools" in the valleys. On coasts, onshore breezes develop during the day because cool air from over the sea moves in to replace warm air rising over the land; these winds can produce showers or they can carry sea fog inland.

In the tropics the weather is always warm and relatively constant, with frequent storms. Such conditions produce rapid plant growth. The only hazard is the occasional tropical cyclone, but the ability of palm trees, for instance, to bend before high winds helps to save them from damage. In the temperate latitudes, changeable weather is the norm and each season has its own typical weather pattern. In the interiors and on the eastern sides of continents extreme weather conditions are common, but nearly everywhere there are occasional extreme temperatures, severe winds and heavy rain. The most violent weather phenomenon of all is the tornado, a whirling mass of air which can uproot trees and destroy buildings.

Weather forecasting

Modern computers enable meteorologists to make increasingly reliable forecasts in temperate latitudes for about six days forward, provided that the present state of the weather over most of the globe is accurately known. But there is still a limit to the accuracy of such forecasts. The atmosphere contains eddies of air on all scales down to the microscopic, and it is impossible to observe or record them all. Yet the small-scale motions of the atmosphere can affect the larger circulations and tip the balance at crucial moments so as to change the whole subsequent weather pattern.

Sometimes an unusual pattern of weather lasts for a number of years and unpredictable conditions on this scale can be of great significance. Optimal crop yields are produced under particular conditions of temperature, rainfall and sunshine; if the conditions vary only slightly, yields are reduced.

Changing climates

Climatic change occurs on all time scales, from day to day or from millennium to millennium; the most dramatic long-term changes are the ice ages. There can be several contributory causes to such changes. Volcanic dust in the stratosphere, for example, absorbs some of the Sun's radiation, producing a cooling effect. Changes in the Earth's orbit also affect the amount of radiation, and therefore heat, that is received in each hemisphere during different seasons.

The impact of man, deliberate or not, on the weather has recently become more significant. For example, if crystals of silver iodide are scattered from an aircraft into a suitable cumulus cloud, they can cause rain that would otherwise not have fallen. Some cities are susceptible to smog, a mixture of smoke and water droplets, and many urban areas become "heat islands" as a result of industrial activities and domestic heating.

The "greenhouse effect"

Over a long period, man's activities may affect climate on a world scale by the addition of extra carbon dioxide to the atmosphere. Carbon dioxide occurs naturally in the atmosphere, but the amount is gradually increasing because of the burning of fossil fuels—coal and oil. The so-called "greenhouse effect" reduces the amount of heat radiation that the Earth emits into space, thus raising temperatures near the ground. Even a small rise in temperature could make for serious change, for example, in the pattern of world agriculture. Rainfall patterns might change as well as temperature, because warmer air can hold more moisture. Some climatologists argue, however, that this warming trend will be counteracted during the next century by a natural shift towards cooler climates.

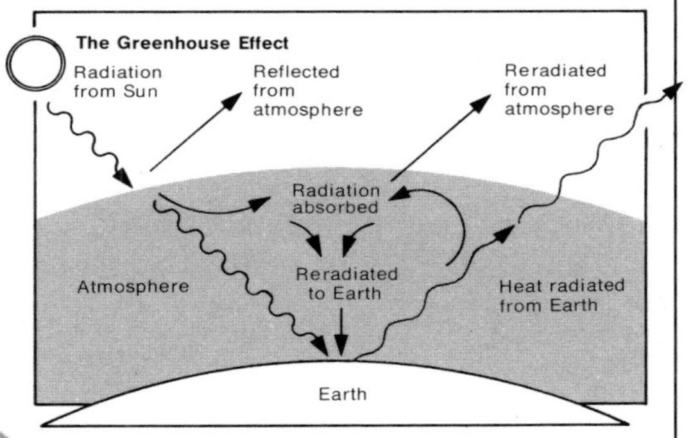

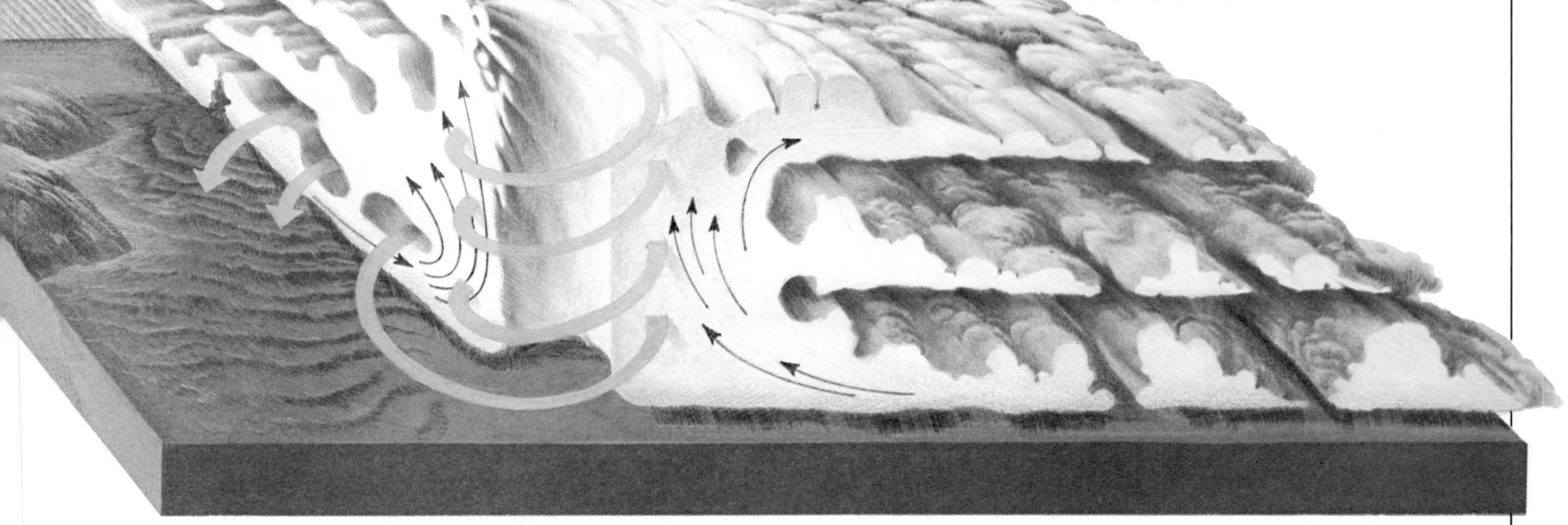

Resources and Energy

Resources, it has been said, comprise mankind's varying needs from generation to generation and are valued because of the uses societies can make of them. They represent human appraisals and are the products of man's ingenuity and experience. While natural resources remain vitally important in themselves, they must always be regarded as the rewards of human skill in locating, extracting and exploiting them. The development of resources depends on many factors, including the existence of a demand, adequate transport facilities, the availability of capital and the accessibility, quality and quantity of the resource itself.

The world's extraction of its resources highlights the inequality of their distribution. Each resource shown on the map is attributed to the three countries with the largest production percentages of that commodity. So, in 1976, the three leading bauxite producers were Australia (26.69%), Jamaica (14.19%) and Rep. of Guinea (13.9%). Usually, the larger and more wealthy a state the greater its monopoly of resources—although the tiny Pacific island of New Caledonia produces more than 14% of the world's nickel. China is reputed to mine 75% of the world's tungsten and to be increasing its oil supply rapidly. Energy consumption figures are for the year 1976, since when there have been some outstanding changes to patterns of availability, perhaps most noticeably in Britain's new-found oil and gas surplus. Bahrain and Tobago, too small to be shown on this map, also have surpluses of energy production.

A dictionary defines the term "resource" as "a means of aid or support," implying anything that lends support to life or activity. Man has always assessed nature with an eye to his own needs, and it is these varying needs that endow resources with their usefulness. Fossil fuels such as oil have lain long in the Earth, but it was not until about 1900 that the large-scale needs fostered by the rising demands of motor vehicles led to the development of new techniques for locating and extracting this raw material. Today oil has also become precious in the manufacture of a wide variety of industrial products, which themselves are resources that are much used by other industries.

The nature of resources

Resources can be most usefully classified in two groups: "renewable" and "nonrenewable." The latter is composed of materials found at or near the Earth's surface, which are sometimes known as "physical" resources. They include such essential minerals as uranium, iron, copper, nickel, bauxite, gold, silver, lead, mercury and tungsten. Oil, coal and natural gas are the principal nonrenewable fuel and energy resources, but after they have been used for producing heat or power their utility is lost and part of the geological capital of 325 million years of history is gone for ever. Some minerals such as iron and its product, steel, can be recycled and renewed, however. "Renewable" resources are basically biological, being the food and other vegetable matter which life needs to sustain human needs. Provided soil quality is maintained, their productivity may even be increased as better strains of plants and breeds of animals are developed.

Work has long been in progress to improve renewable resources, and has moved forward to manufacturing vegetable-flavored protein (VFP) from soybeans as a meat substitute and to viable experiments to extract protein from leaves. In Brazil, many cars have been converted to run successfully on alcohol extracted from sugar. One renewable resource—the tree—can be closely related to other resources: some conservationists are alarmed at the overuse of firewood as a source of fuel and energy in the semiarid areas of Africa. This may be an important factor in increasing the tendency for the deserts to spread in that continent, and in such a situation there is a new realization of the concept of closely managing resources such as soil, timber and fisheries. This is partly because we have a clearer understanding of the ecology of vegetation and the important interdependence of climate, soil, plants and animal life. Much, however, remains to be done.

The politics of nonrenewable resources

Today we are naturally troubled about the availability of natural resources. Oil is a prime cause for concern. Although many believe that production will grow until the mid-2020s and that new oil reserves will be discovered, oil's scarcity, based on a growing rate of demand and increasingly wasteful use, is now widely accepted. Because, like many resources, it is unevenly distributed, those countries with large and accessible supplies—such as the members of OPEC—have used their political power on a number of occasions to raise oil's price, with adverse effects on the economies of most importers. Ironically, these substantial price rises have had the effect of stimulating exploration and development in many new areas; there are already signs of increased production in China.

Other nonrenewable resources are also distributed unevenly, but have not been mined on any scale comparable with their availability; vast reserves of coal in the USSR and China have not been worked on any scale resembling their known extent.

New energy sources

As resources such as oil become less available and more expensive, the renewable resources of power such as water, wind, waves and solar energy, all of which are currently under study or development, will receive new injections of capital. Attention will also have to be paid to more widespread nuclear energy production. Energy has been called "the ultimate resource," and it is imperative that we make wise provisions for its future availability.

Future resources

It has been calculated that within four years of the launch of Sputnik I, more than 3,000 products resulting from space research were put into commercial production. These included new alloys, ceramics, plastics, fabrics and chemical compounds. Satellite developments have meant that land use can now be measured quickly and potential mineral sources closely identified. A satellite capable of converting solar power to electricity and contributing to the Earth's energy deficit has been widely discussed, while the Moon and planets have been mooted as future possible sources of minerals.

Conclusions

Resources are, in the main, the products of man's skill, ingenuity and expertise, and their widespread use, as in the case of timber and iron for shipbuilding, became apparent only as man's needs for them became clear. Our forebears were once concerned about the availability of flint, seaweed, charcoal and natural rubber; countries even went to war over supplies of spices. Today our requirements are slightly different—we no longer depend only on local sites for resources, and improved transport facilities and appropriate technologies have lowered the costs of obtaining materials for manufacture.

Nevertheless, the principles remain the same. A continual search for new resources capable of exploitation and wide application must be maintained, together with a close regard for the value of the renewable resources such as animal and vegetable products required to support man in his search for new resources. Perhaps the most vital consideration is the need for wise policies of conservation relating to the proven reserves of nonrenewable resources still in the ground, and the careful future use of such valuable deposits known or thought to exist.

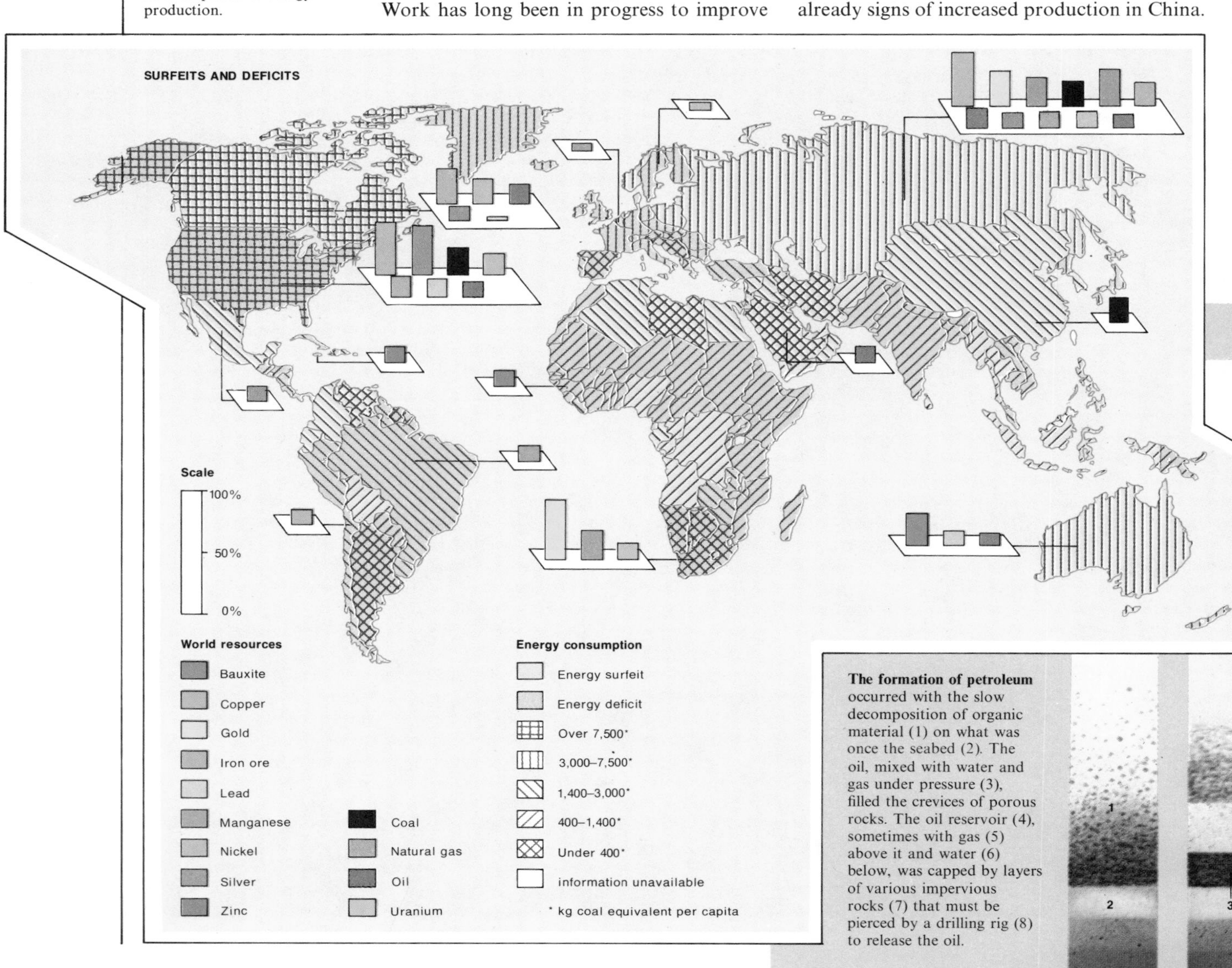
SURFEITS AND DEFICITS
Scale
100%
50%
0%
World resources
Bauxite
Copper
Gold
Iron ore
Lead
Manganese
Nickel
Silver
Zinc
Coal
Natural gas
Oil
Uranium
Energy consumption
Energy surfeit
Energy deficit
Over 7,500*
3,000–7,500*
1,400–3,000*
400–1,400*
Under 400*
information unavailable
* kg coal equivalent per capita

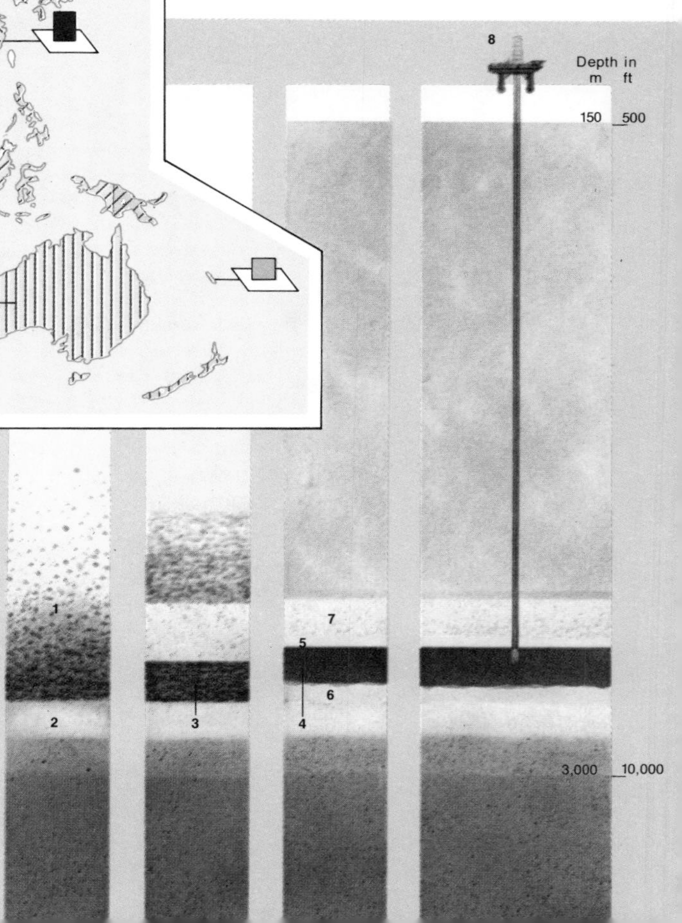
8
Depth in
m ft
150 500
1
2
3
4
5
6
7
3,000 10,000

The formation of petroleum occurred with the slow decomposition of organic material (1) on what was once the seabed (2). The oil, mixed with water and gas under pressure (3), filled the crevices of porous rocks. The oil reservoir (4), sometimes with gas (5) above it and water (6) below, was capped by layers of various impervious rocks (7) that must be pierced by a drilling rig (8) to release the oil.

MAN'S ENDURING INGENUITY

A continuing search for new energy supplies has led man to explore potential oil sources in the offshore waters of the main continental land-masses. A firmly anchored production platform exemplifies the many new sites from which oil is being extracted, in an attempt to reduce reliance on the monopoly of reserves held by powerful organizations such as OPEC.

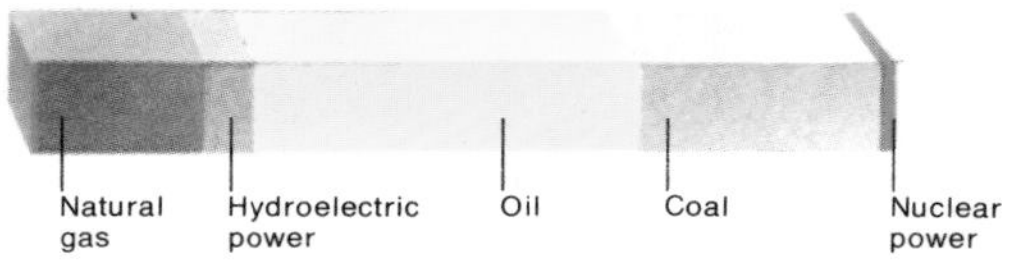

Natural gas
Hydroelectric power
Oil
Coal
Nuclear power

Primary energy consumption (above), globally totalling nearly 7,000 million tonnes of coal equivalent (mtce) in 1979, is dominated by a reliance on the fossil fuels coal and oil (nearly 75%), with little contribution from nuclear energy. However, the use of nuclear fission to generate electricity has increased rapidly in recent years (right). While areas such as North America and Western Europe have kept their early leads, their proportional contributions to consumption are falling as more power stations in Japan and Eastern Europe are brought into use.

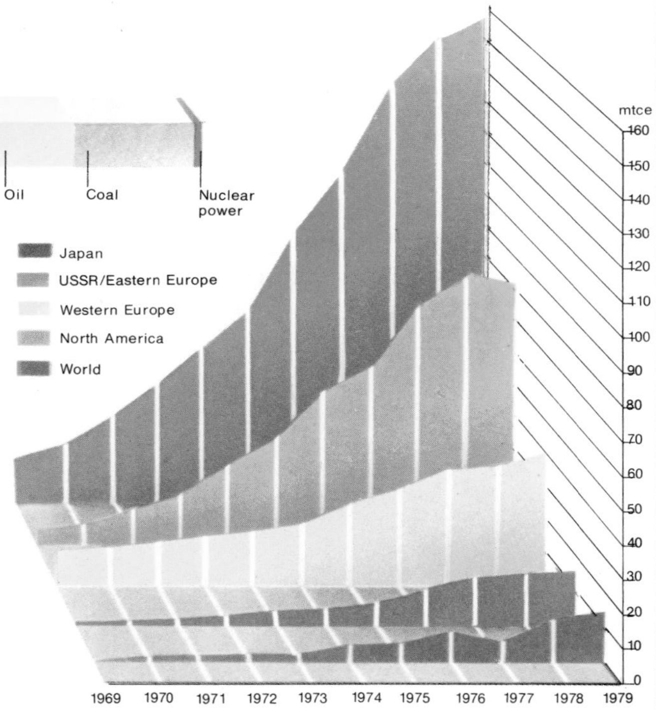

mtce
160
150
140
130
120
110
100
90
80
70
60
50
40
30
20
10
0
Japan
USSR/Eastern Europe
Western Europe
North America
World
1969
1970
1971
1972
1973
1974
1975
1976
1977
1978
1979

The refining of oil into many valuable components (or fractions) is an involved process that makes fullest use of the resource. Crude oil is distilled into a wide range of products including the three main constituents of gasoline, kerosene (for jet fuel) and diesel fuel, of which part is further separated into gas. Other fractions are treated to give fuel oil and lubricating oil, from which wax as paraffin is removed. Chemical feedstock and bitumen are also important by-products.

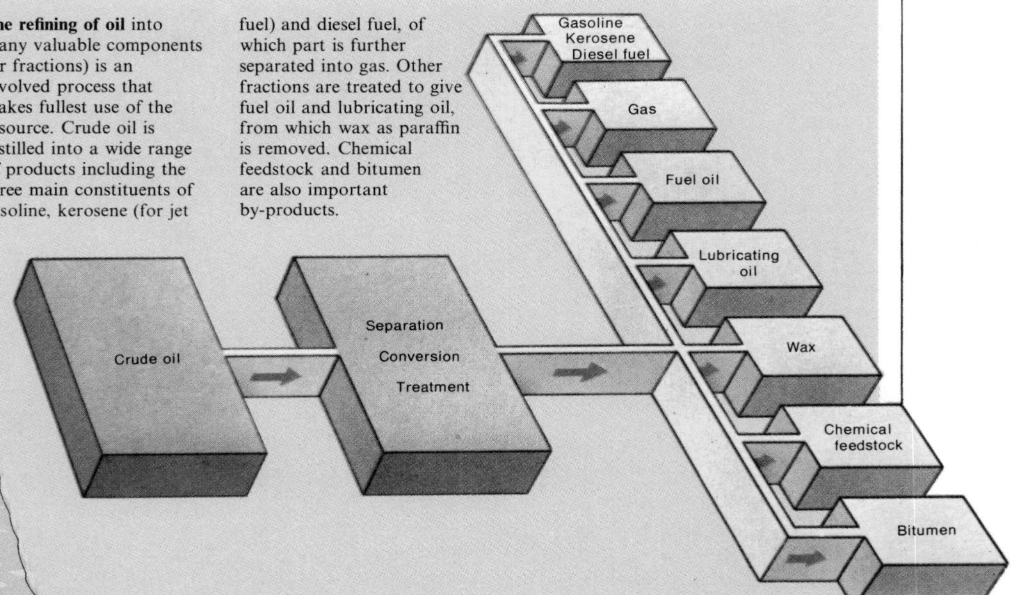

Crude oil
Separation
Conversion
Treatment
Gasoline
Kerosene
Diesel fuel
Gas
Fuel oil
Lubricating oil
Wax
Chemical feedstock
Bitumen

An oil drilling platform is firmly anchored on foundation piles driven 45 m (150 ft) into the sea bed to protect the structure from the 150 m (500 ft) deep waters of the rough North Sea. At its peak rate, a well can produce about 2,000 barrels (320,000 liters) per day and the platform may have an economic life of some 20 years. Such platforms come into use three or four years after oil is struck and annual operating costs can be expected to be in the area of $100 million. Of the world's total oil output, about 20% currently originates beneath the sea.

NEW ENERGY SOURCES

An orbiting collector, shown here, would transform solar radiation to direct-current electric power by the powerful photocells and mirrors positioned on its surface. The electrical energy would be converted into microwaves and beamed to Earth, where they would be converted back to electricity. Because such a geostationary satellite would be independent of clear skies or any seasonal variations, its potential is being quite heavily promoted. A space shuttle would probably be used in its construction. But earnest research continues into many other spheres of energy production, such as Earth-based solar panels, wind power and the extraction of heat from deep in the Earth. Tidal power, hydroelectric power and Ocean Thermal Energy Conversion (OTEC) are receiving much current attention. They are each *renewable* sources, so will relieve the pressure on our reserves of nonrenewable fuels.

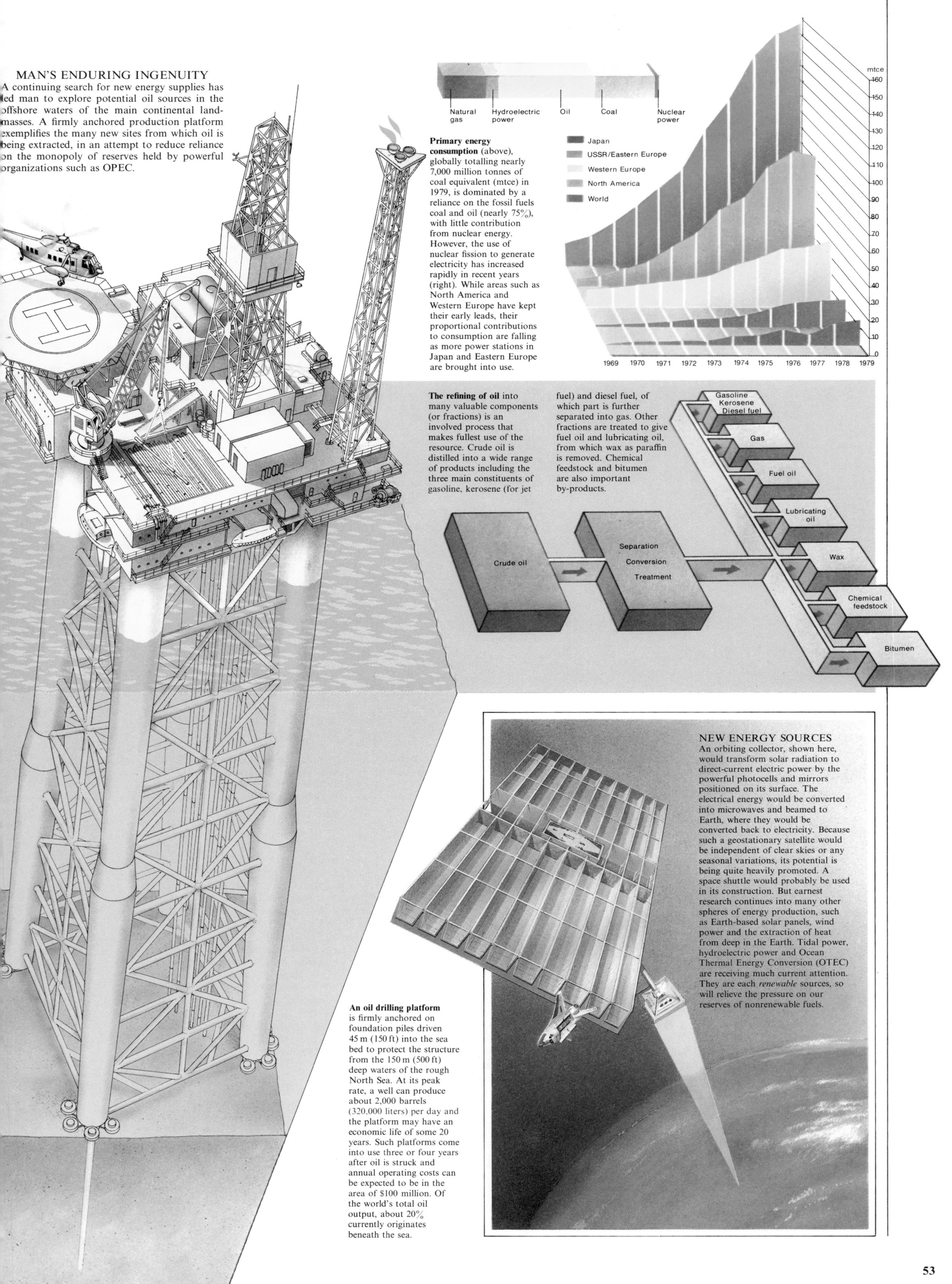

Population Growth

Every minute of every day, more than 250 children are born into the world. The Earth's population now stands at about 4,300 million and is continuing to grow extremely rapidly. The problems associated with such growth are enormous – already, about two-thirds of the world's people are underfed, according to United Nations' recommended standards of nutrition. And an even greater number live in very poor housing conditions, have inadequate access to medical facilities, receive little or no education and, at present, have no hope of improving their lot. As yet, there are no simple or immediate solutions.

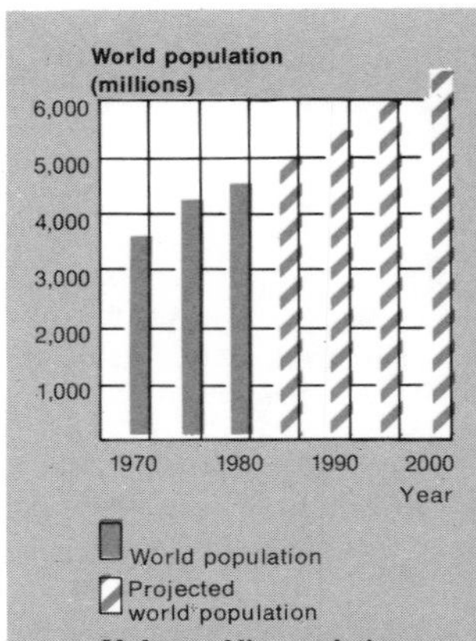

If the world's population continues to grow at its present rate, by the year 2000 there could be more than 6,400 million people on Earth (above). Such growth rates are only a recent phenomenon—for most of mankind's existence on Earth the numbers grew slowly (right). Then in the late 18th century, scientific and industrial developments and the discovery of new food sources (the prairies of the New World) raised living standards. Death rates declined and populations grew rapidly.

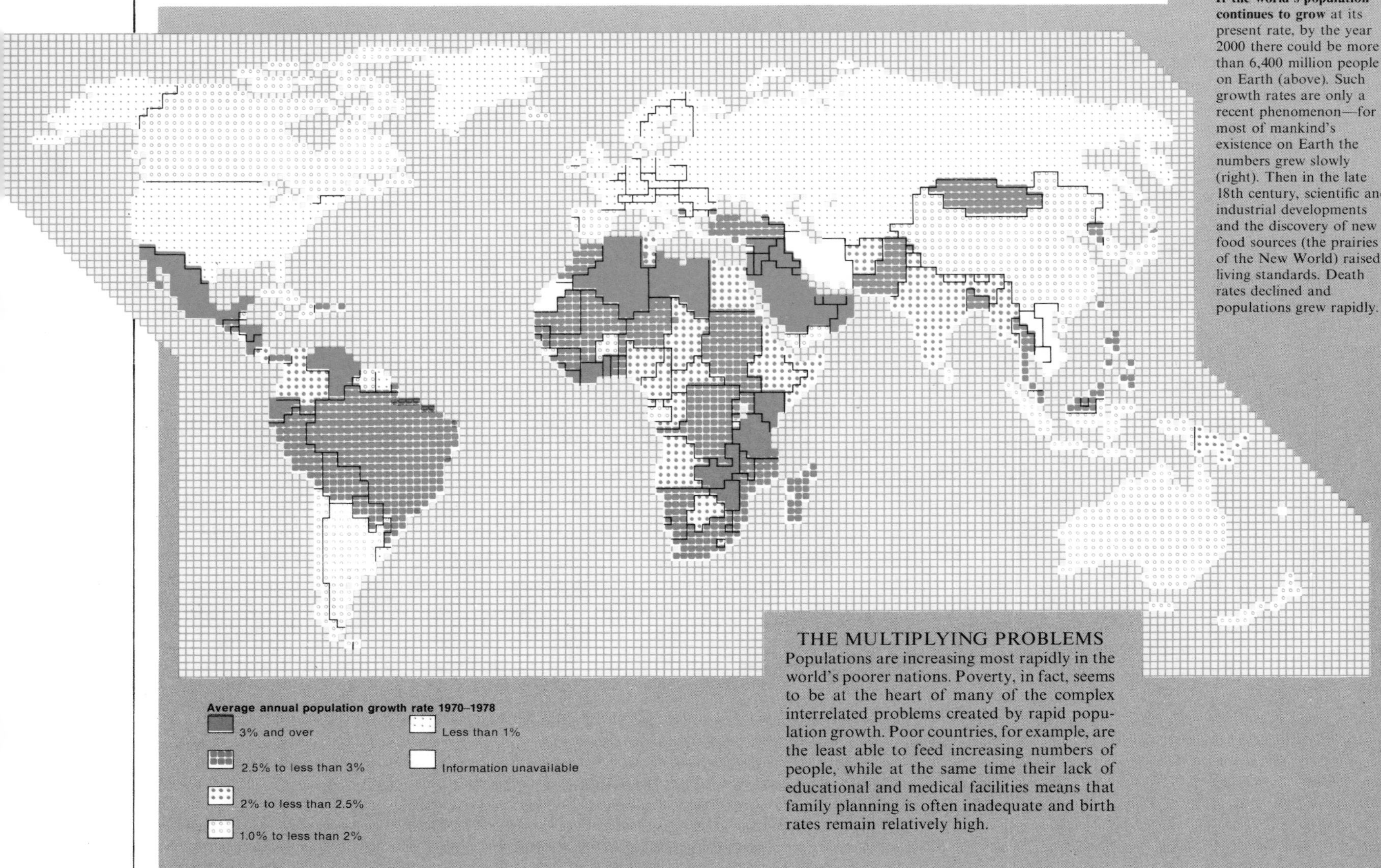

THE MULTIPLYING PROBLEMS

Populations are increasing most rapidly in the world's poorer nations. Poverty, in fact, seems to be at the heart of many of the complex interrelated problems created by rapid population growth. Poor countries, for example, are the least able to feed increasing numbers of people, while at the same time their lack of educational and medical facilities means that family planning is often inadequate and birth rates remain relatively high.

In 1830, there were only about 1,000 million people on Earth. By 1930, this figure had doubled. And by 1975, it had doubled again. If the present rate of increase continues, it will have doubled again by the year 2020.

This may not happen—it is extremely difficult to predict how world population will behave. What is certain is that it will continue to increase and, moreover, that this increase will not be evenly distributed. Since more than 50 percent of the human race lives in Asia, it is inevitable that the largest population increases will take place there. In fact, by the year 2000, the population of Asia may well have grown from about 2,000 million to more than 3,600 million. Substantial increases, of 400 million or more, will probably also occur in Africa, and Latin America is growing equally quickly.

In more prosperous North America and Europe, however, population growth seems to be stabilizing as women have fewer children and families become smaller—several countries, such as West Germany, now record a zero population growth rate. The poorer countries, the so-called Third World, are therefore gaining, and will probably continue to gain, an increasing share of the world's people. In 1930, about 64 percent of the human race lived in the poor countries of Asia, Africa and Latin America. By 1980, this proportion had increased to more than 75 percent. Population growth in these regions is creating enormous problems. It is estimated that there are now more than 800 million people living in absolute poverty in the developing world, and these numbers can but increase as populations swell.

An obvious solution is to reduce birth rates, but this cannot be achieved quickly. In much of Africa and Asia, a very high proportion of the population is made up of young people who are, or soon will be, of childbearing age. Population increases are therefore inevitable. This will probably change as family planning becomes more widespread and women have fewer children, but such relief lies in the future and is likely to affect the poorest countries last. The most pressing problem for the growing numbers of impoverished people today is that of hunger.

Food – the fundamental problem

In theory, no food supply problem should exist—already enough food is produced in the world to feed a population of 5,500 million people. In fact, however, two-thirds of this food is consumed by the rich industrialized nations, and supplies are not reaching many of those in need. The developed nations dominate world food markets because developing nations, and people within those nations, are too poor to buy food, and are themselves unable to produce sufficient quantities to feed their growing populations. The answer to undernutrition and malnutrition lies largely in raising the incomes of poor peoples and improving distribution of supplies of food.

At a local level, food produced or imported by developing countries must reach those in need at a price they can afford. One way of doing this is to encourage the rural poor to produce their own food. Small-scale, intensively farmed plots often prove to be the most efficient form of agriculture in areas where labor is plentiful. At present, many of the rural poor are either without land, or hold plots on extremely unfavorable terms of tenancy. By providing land, appropriate technology (small-scale, inexpensive farming equipment such as windpumps to draw water for irrigation), financial aid and information and education, small farmers could be helped to farm their land as effectively and efficiently as possible.

At a national level, too, developing countries must become more self-sufficient in food. This has already been achieved in some countries. India, although at one time heavily dependent upon imports of one of its staple foodstuffs—rice—has now increased production on such a scale that imports are no longer necessary. Unfortunately, for many developing countries this is not the case. Zaire, for example, was once an exporter of food. Today the country can no longer produce enough to keep pace with the demands of its own expanding population. At a world level, food production must be maintained as well, for unless production is kept high, prices are unstable and at times of bad harvests the poorer nations cannot afford to import essential supplies.

Food alone, however, is not enough to solve

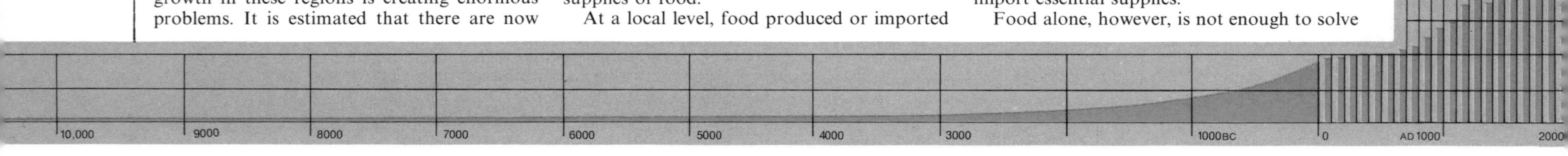

FEEDING THE WORLD

How are the growing numbers of people on Earth to be fed when millions are already undernourished? In the short term, the food problem could be solved by improving distribution of supplies that are already available. But the world can also be made to produce more food. Fertilizers and pest control can make land more productive and genetic engineering could produce higher-yielding and more nutritious crops.

The world will have to produce more food than it does today (below) if future populations are to be fed. At present, large areas of the Earth's land surface cannot be farmed—they are either too cold, dry, marshy, mountainous or forested. Cultivatable areas could be extended, given the necessary investment.

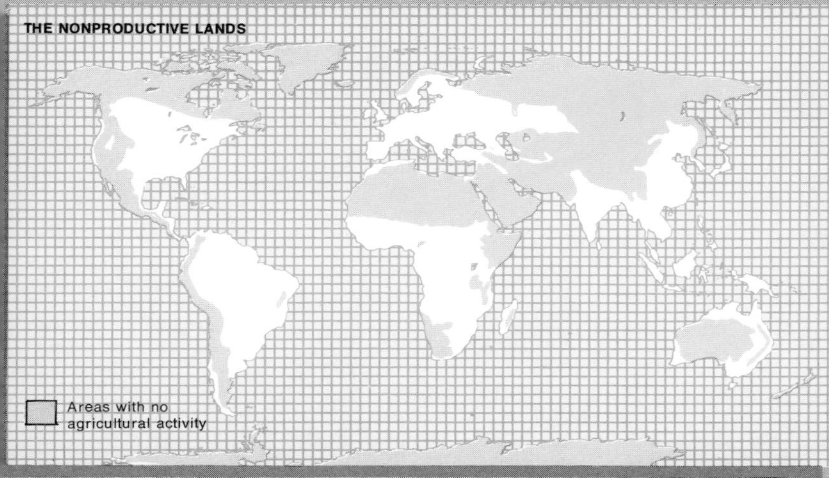

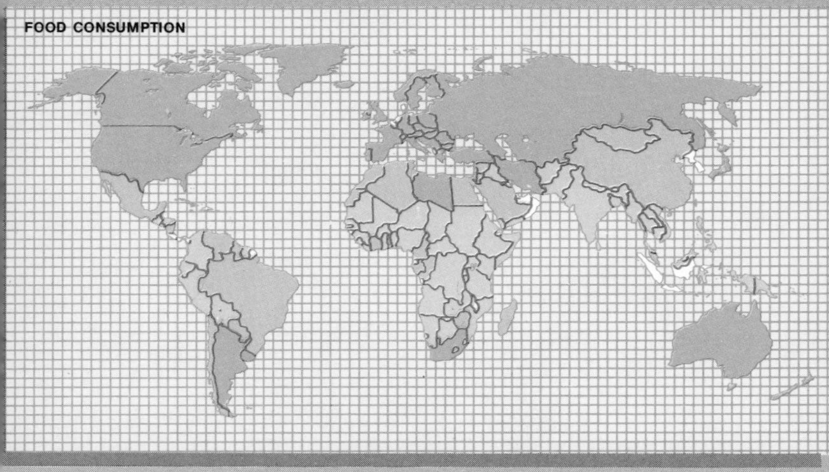

Calories per capita
- Less than 95% of needs
- 95% to 115% of needs
- More than 115% of needs
- Information unavailable

Malnutrition is widespread throughout the developing nations of Africa, Asia and South America. The problem is made worse by the fact that populations in these countries are growing more rapidly than anywhere else in the world.

the problems created by population growth. Broadly based economic development, such as in manufacturing and industry, is essential if developing countries are to have the income and other resources to enable them to cope with their evergrowing numbers of people.

Economic growth

To achieve economic development, certain obstacles must be overcome. First, the Third World needs energy supplies at a price it can afford, for, with the exception of Nigeria and the now-rich Middle East, most developing regions are woefully short of the energy resources needed to fuel growth. Second, for sustained economic development a skilled labor force is required, as are educational facilities to provide the necessary skills from within the nations themselves. Third, investment is required to enable developing nations to exploit the resources they do have—minerals, for example. And this investment must be on terms that are as beneficial to the developing nations as they are to powerful multinational organizations that frequently fund such projects. Finally, and most important, more enlightened social and political outlooks are needed within many countries if their growing populations of impoverished people are to benefit from any economic development and consequent increase in national wealth.

It has been said that wealth is the best method of contraception and, judging by the history of population growth in the rich industrialized nations, this seems to be the case. If it is, economic development of the Third World may well alleviate many of the problems created by population growth.

THE HEALTH OF NATIONS

Many developing nations are severely short of medical and welfare facilities for their growing populations. Yet these are the very countries with high incidences of disease—mainly because of malnutrition, lack of clean water supplies, and inadequate and overcrowded housing. Furthermore, without health services family planning facilities are not widely available, and expanding populations continue to strain existing resources.

Birth and Death Rates
- High birth rate/ High death rate
- High birth rate/ Moderate or low death rate
- Low birth rate/ Low death rate
- Information unavailable

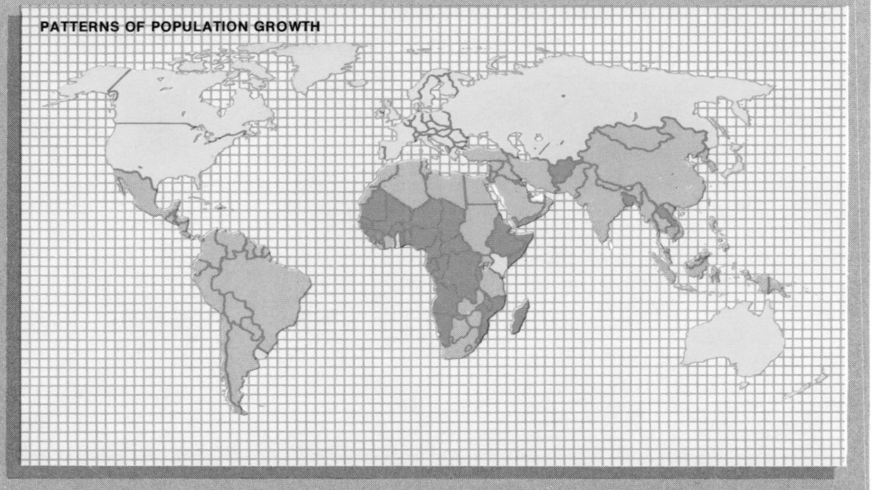

As a country's health facilities improve, its mortality rates decline. Birth rates, however, do not immediately fall (above). Thus, ironically, an improvement in facilities at first exacerbates the problem of rapid growth in population. A country with a declining death rate and a high birth rate gains an increasing percentage of young people who are, or will be, of child-bearing age. Population pyramids (right) plot the percentage balance between age and youth in a nation.

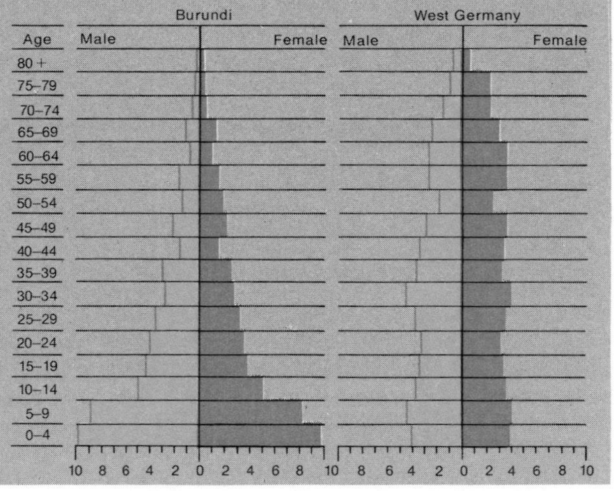

INCOME

When the income level of a population is raised sufficiently, it seems that birth rates ultimately decline. This has been the pattern that has emerged in the Western world. If this is the case, then economic development of the Third World countries could eventually help to stabilize world population growth, as well as provide nations with the means to cope. It could also help provide for their growing numbers.

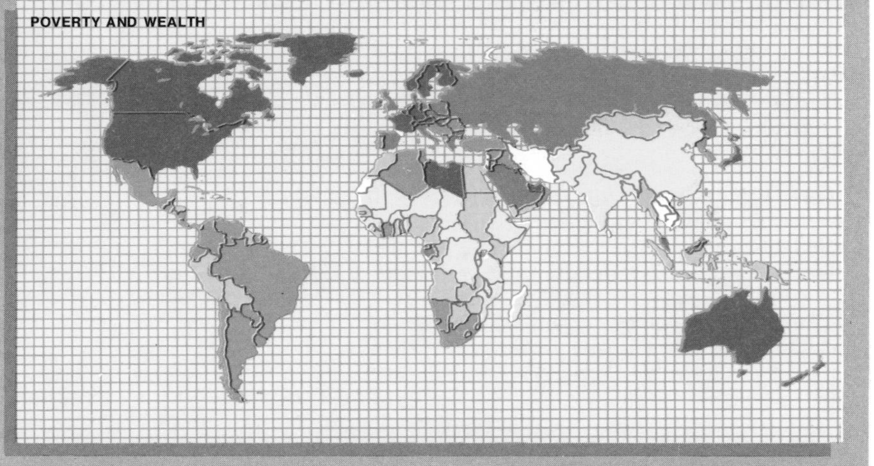

Gross National Product per capita 1978 ($US)
- Less than $300
- $300 to $699
- $700 to $2,999
- $3,000 to $6,999
- $7,000 and over
- Information unavailable

A nation's Gross National Product (GNP), when divided by the number of its population, gives some indication of the relative wealth (or poverty) of its people. But because national wealth is not evenly distributed in many countries (particularly in South America), this figure can conceal the extreme poverty of very large numbers of a nation's people.

EDUCATIONAL RESOURCES

Education is essential if the people of the developing world are to be equipped to improve their lot. Basic education on health and hygiene could dramatically reduce the incidence of disease; education about birth control would help lower birth rates; agricultural advice could help the rural poor to produce more food. Finally, general schooling is required to provide skilled labor.

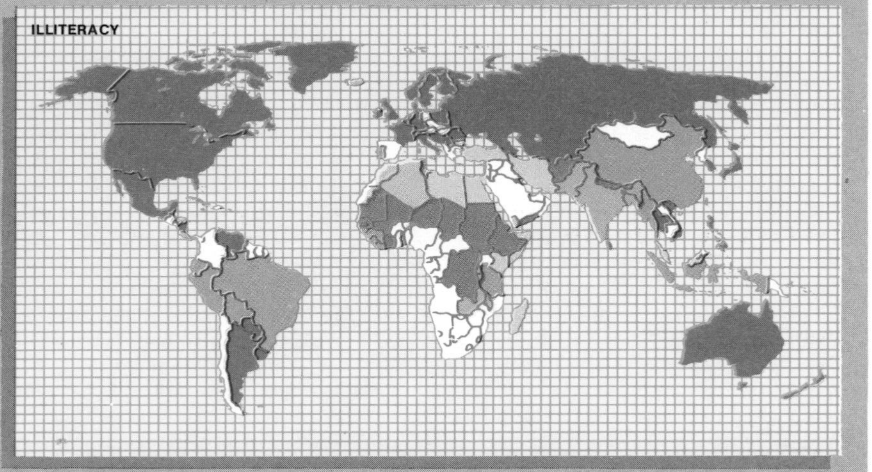

Illiteracy rate
- 80% and over
- 60% to less than 80%
- 40% to less than 60%
- 20% to less than 40%
- Less than 20%
- Information unavailable

Literacy rates are in fact improving in developing countries and national expenditure on schools is growing more quickly than is population. Two major problems are, first, the social traditions that severely restrict the number of girls attending school and, second, the reluctance of many rural poor to send to school children who provide valuable manual labor on the land.

Human Settlement

Man is naturally a gregarious animal. As an agriculturist he first settled in small communities, but it was not long before the emergence of towns and cities. Now nearly half the world's people live in these larger settlements, and by the year 2000, for the first time in history, more people will live in cities than in the countryside. Cities have grown up for various reasons, and are unevenly distributed across the world; but it is in the developing countries that the most rapid rates of urban growth are today taking place.

City life has a long and varied history going back to the early population centers of the Tigris–Euphrates, Indus and Nile valleys. Administrative and political needs led to the development of capital cities. Some, like London and Paris, evolved on conveniently located river crossings; others, such as Canberra, Islamabad and Brasilia, have locations that were deliberately planned.

Types of towns and cities

Market towns were established to exchange produce and, as trade expanded, hierarchies of service centers became established. These ranged from small "central places" that supplied rural areas with simple goods and services from elsewhere, to large cities that provided highly specialized services. Through such centrally placed systems, rural areas became connected with major industrialized areas. Mining towns such as Johannesburg, South Africa, and Broken Hill, Australia, sprang up as man began to exploit the Earth's mineral resources, their locations determined by the presence of rich ore deposits. Fishing ports and settlements dependent on forestry fall into the same group.

Increasing specialization, exemplified by the Black Country, England, and the Ruhr, West Germany, was a feature of European industrial development in the eighteenth and nineteenth centuries, and was based on the availability of capital investment and the presence of sources of fuel and power, especially water and steam power. Such industrialized cities relied on newly developed forms of transport to bring in new materials and to carry away manufactured products. Chicago is a good example of the relationship between the development of rail and water routes and the growth of a city as a market, agricultural processing and manufacturing center. As transport developed, further specialized centers concentrated on locomotive, ship or aircraft construction.

Uneven settlement patterns

Across the world, density and distribution of population are uneven. The land surface of the Earth as a whole has a density of 28 people per sq km (73 per sq mile) although Manhattan, for example, has 26,000 per sq km (63,340 per sq mile) and Australia has only 1.5 per sq km (4 per sq mile). In Brazil, towns and cities are mostly sited in the rich southeast, in contrast to a sparseness of settlement in its interior. Contrasts also occur between Mediterranean North Africa and the deserted Sahara to the south; or Canada of the St. Lawrence and the Canadian Shield to the north. Here the causes are not hard to find: extremes of climate, terrain and vegetation form effective barriers to settlement. Geographers estimate that two-thirds of the world's population lives within 500 km (310 miles) of the sea.

Any true consideration of human settlements must, however, be placed within the context of the economic, political and social systems in which they have evolved. Physical considerations alone cannot fully explain the urban concentrations of Western Europe, Japan or the northeastern USA, or the comparative absence of cities elsewhere. Only 5 percent of Malawi's and 4.7 percent of New Guinea's populations live in towns; in Belgium the percentage is 87, in Australia 86, in the UK 78 and in the USA 73.5. The figure for Norway is only 42 percent. Urbanization is a varied phenomenon and cities grow for many reasons.

The attractions of the city

Cities have always acted as magnets to poor or unemployed rural populations, and migrations from the countryside have assisted high rates of city growth. Very large cities—Tokyo, New York and Los Angeles—are still found in the northern world, but many cities with far faster growth rates are sited in the Third World, especially in Asia. There the total number of inhabitants living in towns and cities is still much lower than in Europe, but centers such as Shanghai, Karachi, Bandung, New Delhi, Seoul, Jakarta and Manila are among the world's most rapidly expanding urban centers. Perhaps as many as a third of these city dwellers in Asia, Africa and Latin America put up with makeshift housing in shanty towns that present enormous problems of health, sanitation, education and unemployment: city growth in the developing world is a daunting prospect.

People on the move

In the past, one solution to population pressure on the land could be found in the migrations which occurred on a large scale from Asia into Europe, from Europe to the Americas and Australasia, and from China into southeastern Asia. But as claims are being made on almost every habitable area of the Earth, mass migrations have largely declined in importance. Many nations restrict movement to or from their countries. Australia has strict immigration quotas; Vietnam and the USSR restrict emigration for largely ideological reasons. Large movements of labor still take place, however, from the poorer regions of the Mediterranean to the industrial cities of France and Germany. Migrant workers from neighboring countries in Africa also play an essential part in the mining economy of South Africa.

New trends in urbanization

In many industrialized countries, a strong process of decentralization is leading to reductions in the populations of cities and corresponding increases in those of the suburbs and beyond. In 1951 the geographer Jean Gottman showed how groups of city regions tend to form chains of functionally linked cities, to which he gave the term "megalopolis." His prime example was Megalopolis, USA, stretching from north of Boston to south of Washington DC. Similar settlements occur in the Tokyo–Yokohama–Osaka area of Japan and the Ruhr megalopolis of northwestern Europe. Ultimately, equally drastic and large-scale patterns are likely to emerge in the already overcrowded human settlements of the Third World.

THE DISTRIBUTION OF POPULATION

Human settlement is highly uneven because it is related to many social and topographical factors. At first, man was tied to the sites of his crops and the grazing land of his cattle; life in nonrural centers only became a typical feature of population development as specialized services came into demand and towns and cities arose to support these needs. But during the 20th century there has been a vast increase in urban populations, particularly in Third World countries.

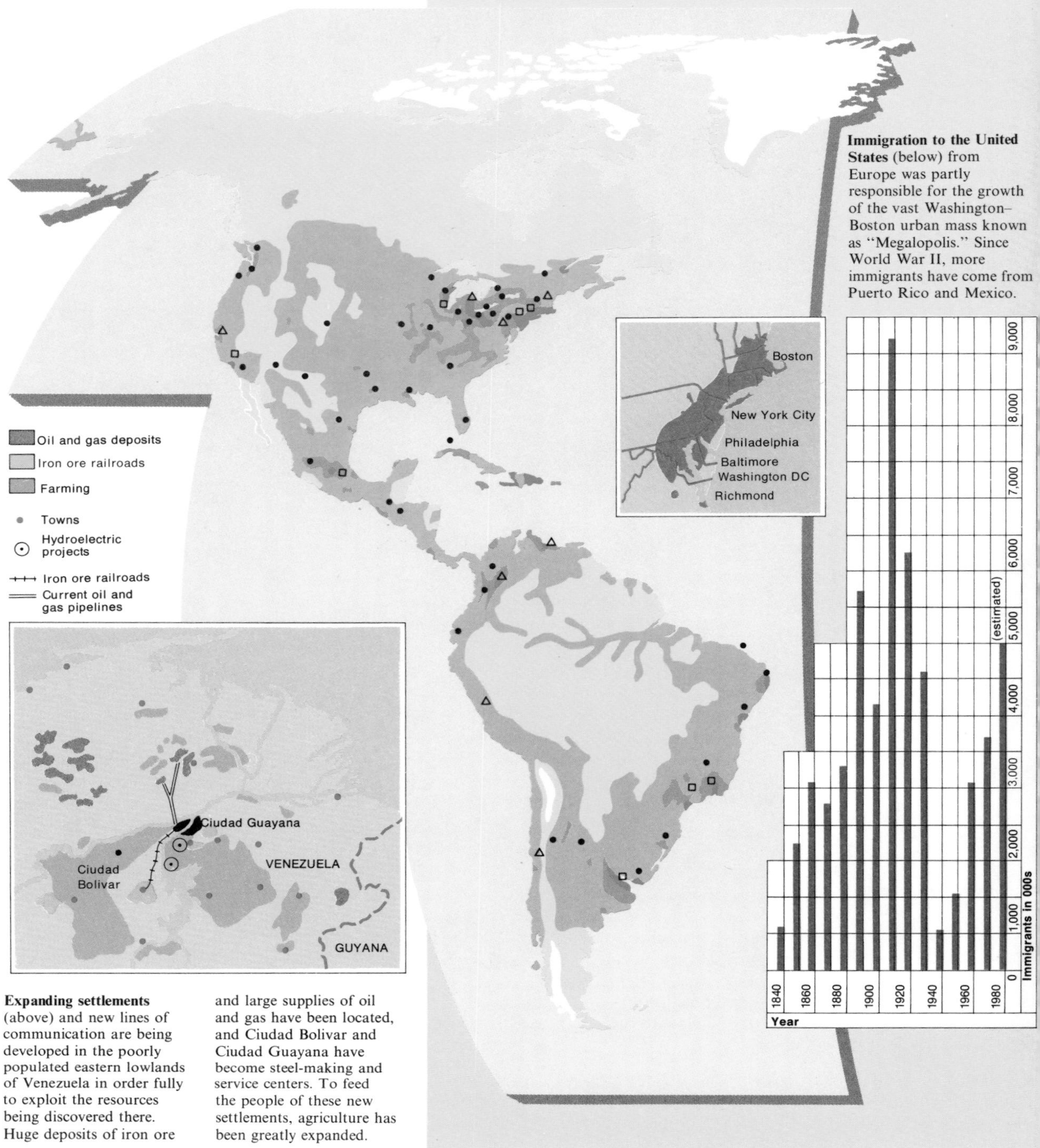

Oil and gas deposits
Iron ore railroads
Farming
Towns
Hydroelectric projects
Iron ore railroads
Current oil and gas pipelines
Ciudad Guayana
Ciudad Bolivar
VENEZUELA
GUYANA
Boston
New York City
Philadelphia
Baltimore
Washington DC
Richmond
Immigrants in 000s
0
1,000
2,000
3,000
4,000
5,000
(estimated)
6,000
7,000
8,000
9,000
Year
1840
1860
1880
1900
1920
1940
1960
1980

Expanding settlements (above) and new lines of communication are being developed in the poorly populated eastern lowlands of Venezuela in order fully to exploit the resources being discovered there. Huge deposits of iron ore and large supplies of oil and gas have been located, and Ciudad Bolivar and Ciudad Guayana have become steel-making and service centers. To feed the people of these new settlements, agriculture has been greatly expanded.

Immigration to the United States (below) from Europe was partly responsible for the growth of the vast Washington–Boston urban mass known as "Megalopolis." Since World War II, more immigrants have come from Puerto Rico and Mexico.

Migrating refugees, the world total of which increases on average by 2,000–3,000 every day, can affect settlement patterns. The Ugandan children (below) fled to the northern province of Karamoja in the wake of the 1979 war with Tanzania and the resultant famine that occurred in much of Uganda.

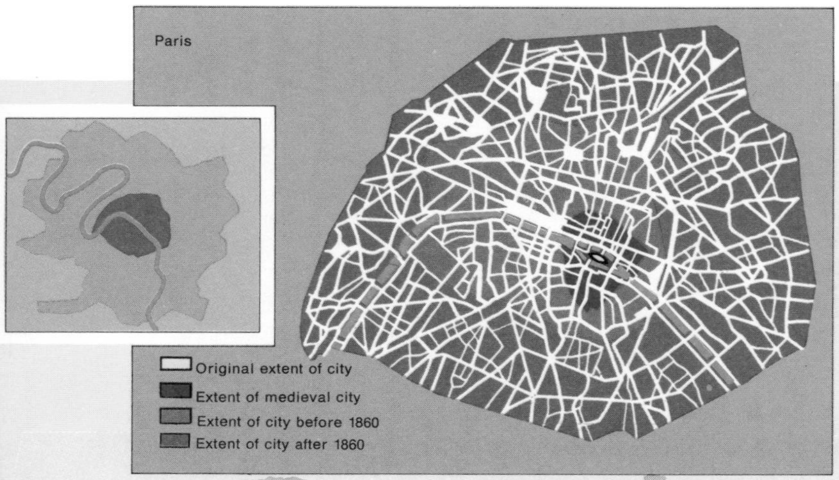
Paris
Original extent of city
Extent of medieval city
Extent of city before 1860
Extent of city after 1860

Paris (left) grew up at a focal crossing point of the river Seine. A strongly defensible island site, it had been fortified by the Romans, and after the election of Hugh Capet in 987 became established as the capital of France. It expanded slowly within a series of stout city walls. In the mid-19th century it covered about 80 sq km (30 sq miles) and its population numbered almost one million. Today Paris and its expanding suburbs cover 12,000 sq km (4,600 sq miles) and accommodate a population of some nine million inhabitants.

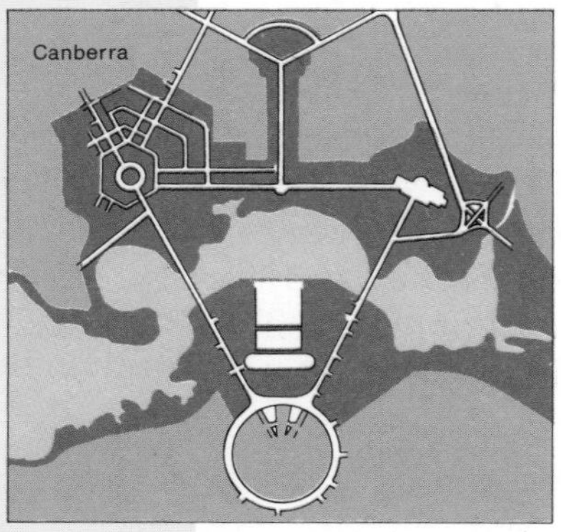
Canberra

Canberra (above), Capital Territory of Australia, has wide, straight streets that form a huge triangle across the shores of Lake Burley Griffin. Its civic center was laid out in 1911 from the winning plan of a worldwide competition, and it includes all the requirements of a capital city. These include Parliament buildings, the National Library, the Australian National University, national embassies and the residences of the Prime Minister and of the Governor-General.

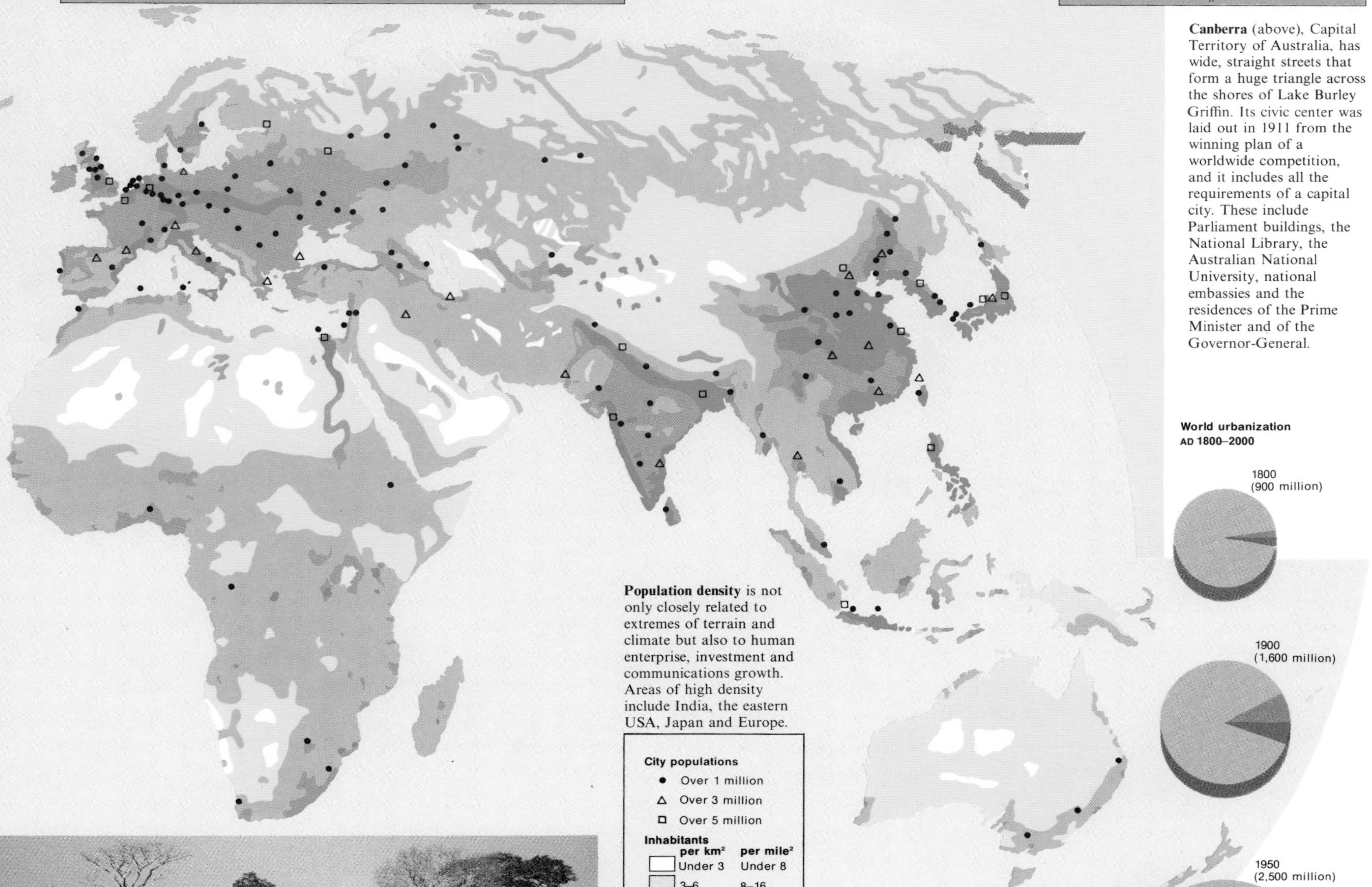
City populations
● Over 1 million
△ Over 3 million
□ Over 5 million
Inhabitants
per km² per mile²
Under 3 Under 8
3–6 8–16
6–25 16–64
25–100 84–256
Over 100 Over 256

Population density is not only closely related to extremes of terrain and climate but also to human enterprise, investment and communications growth. Areas of high density include India, the eastern USA, Japan and Europe.

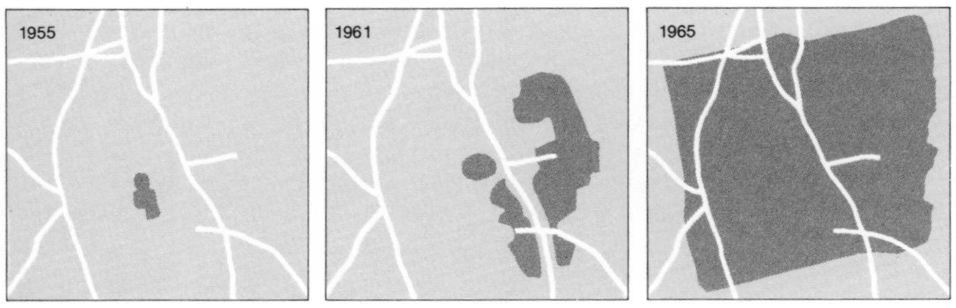
1955
1961
1965

Shanty towns, like that surrounding Lusaka (above left), are a feature of many Third World cities. They represent a makeshift response to the failure of authorities to provide for the thousands of rural poor attracted by city life. The rate of such growth is evident from the maps (left).

Main track

Shanty development

Urbanization (right) is a 20th-century process. Whereas only some 13% of all the world's people lived in towns and cities in 1900, this proportion will have reached 50% for the first time by the year 2000. The largest increases will take place in the urban centers of the Third World as its towns and cities continue to act as magnets to their rural poor. London was the only city with a population of one million in 1900; by 1980, there were more than 200 such cities. By the year 2000, it is certain that many more people will be living in the cities of the developing world, but it is difficult to forecast their proportion in relation to those of the richer cities of the present industrialized world.

Rural population

Urban population of 5,000–100,000 people

Urban population of more than 100,000

World urbanization
AD 1800–2000

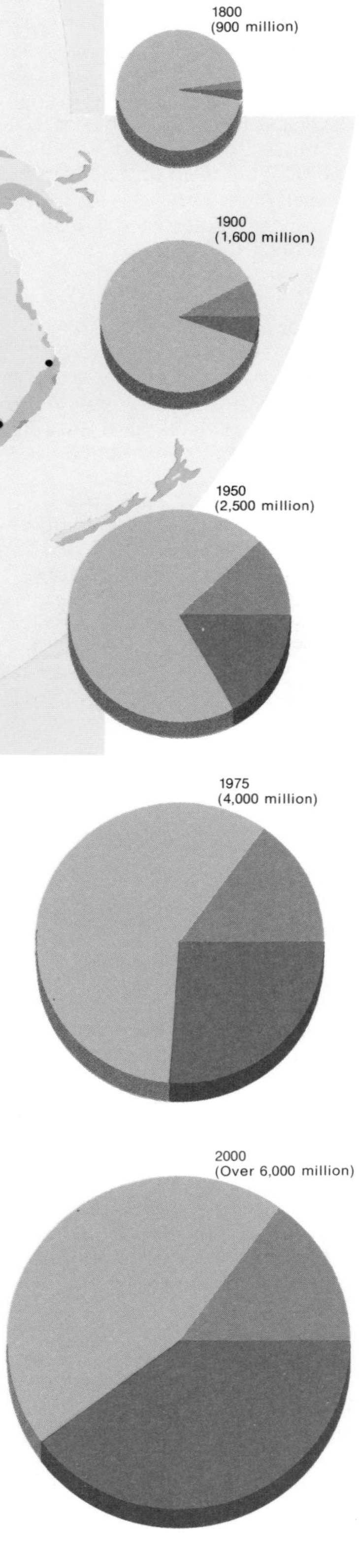
1800
(900 million)
1900
(1,600 million)
1950
(2,500 million)
1975
(4,000 million)
2000
(Over 6,000 million)

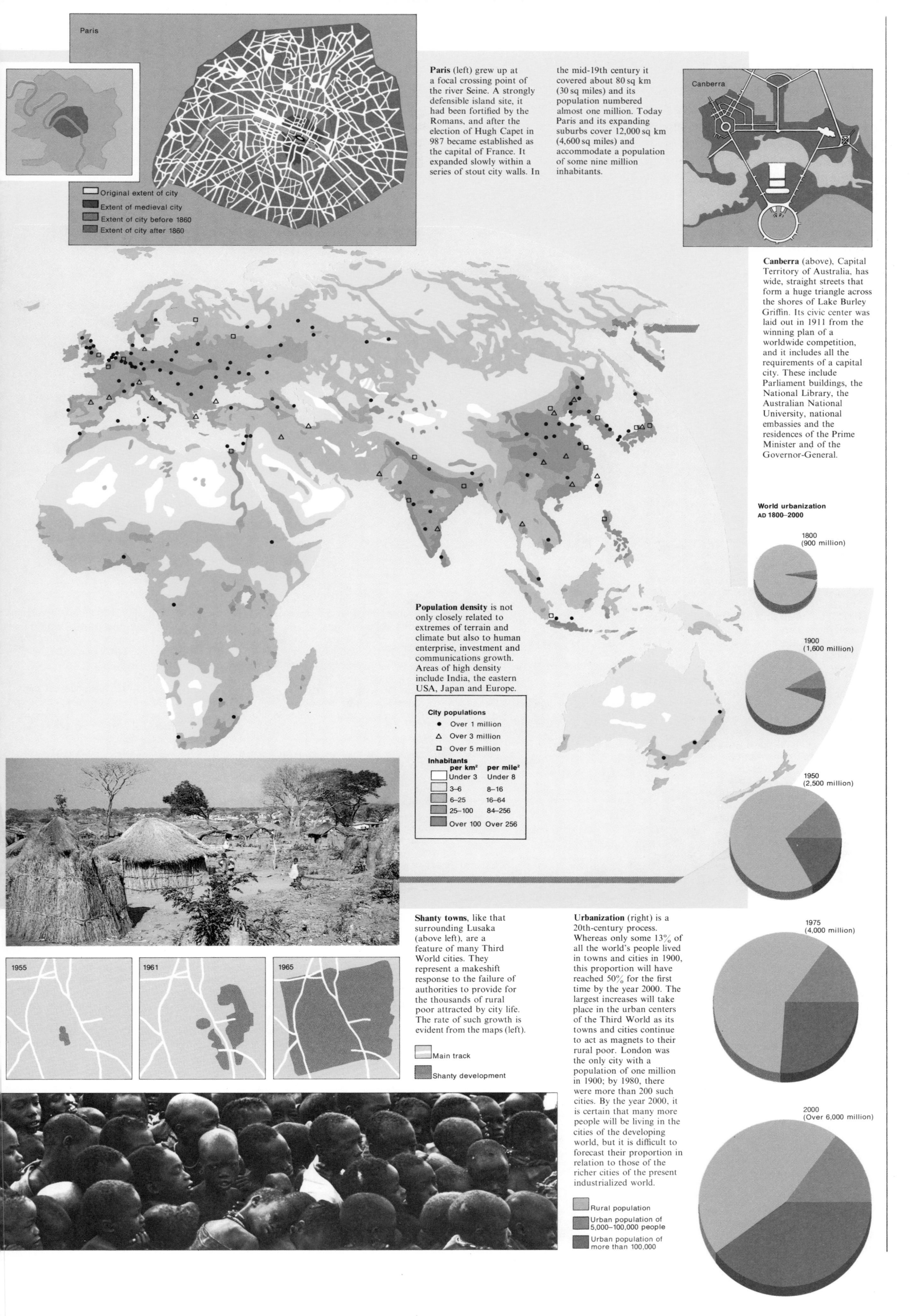

Trade and Transport

It is a commonplace that we live in a "shrinking" world. During the last century the development of communications has been so rapid that man appears almost to have conquered the challenge of distance; but such a concept depends on the kind of area to be covered and the cost of transporting goods in relation to their value, bulk and perishability. People, goods and services become accessible by trade. Transport makes trade possible: trade's demands lead to improvements in transport.

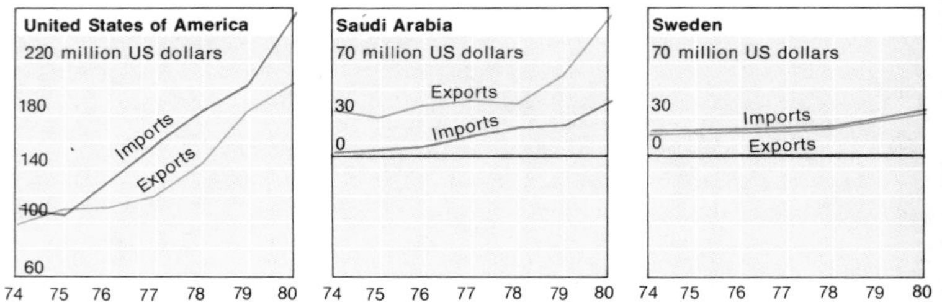
United States of America
220 million US dollars
180
140
100
60
Imports
Exports
Saudi Arabia
70 million US dollars
30
0
Exports
Imports
Sweden
70 million US dollars
30
0
Imports
Exports
74 75 76 77 78 79 80

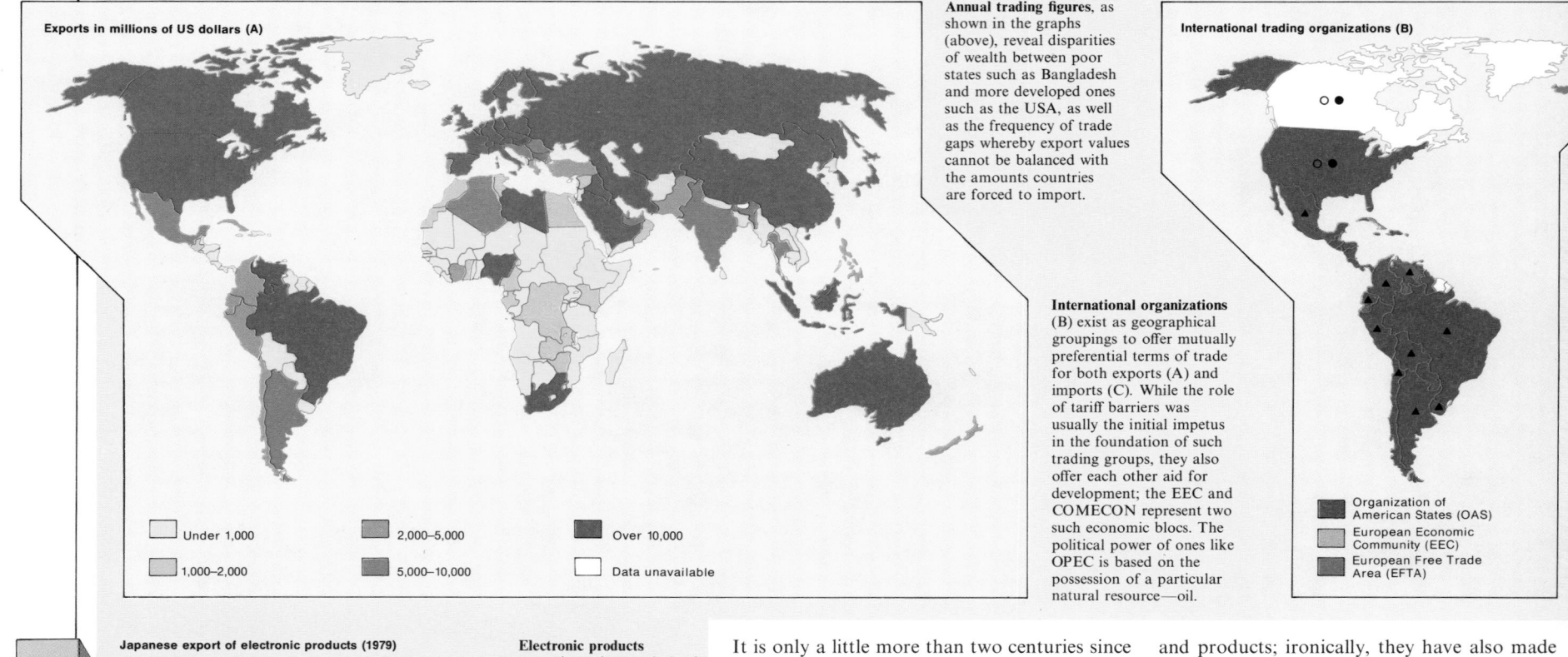

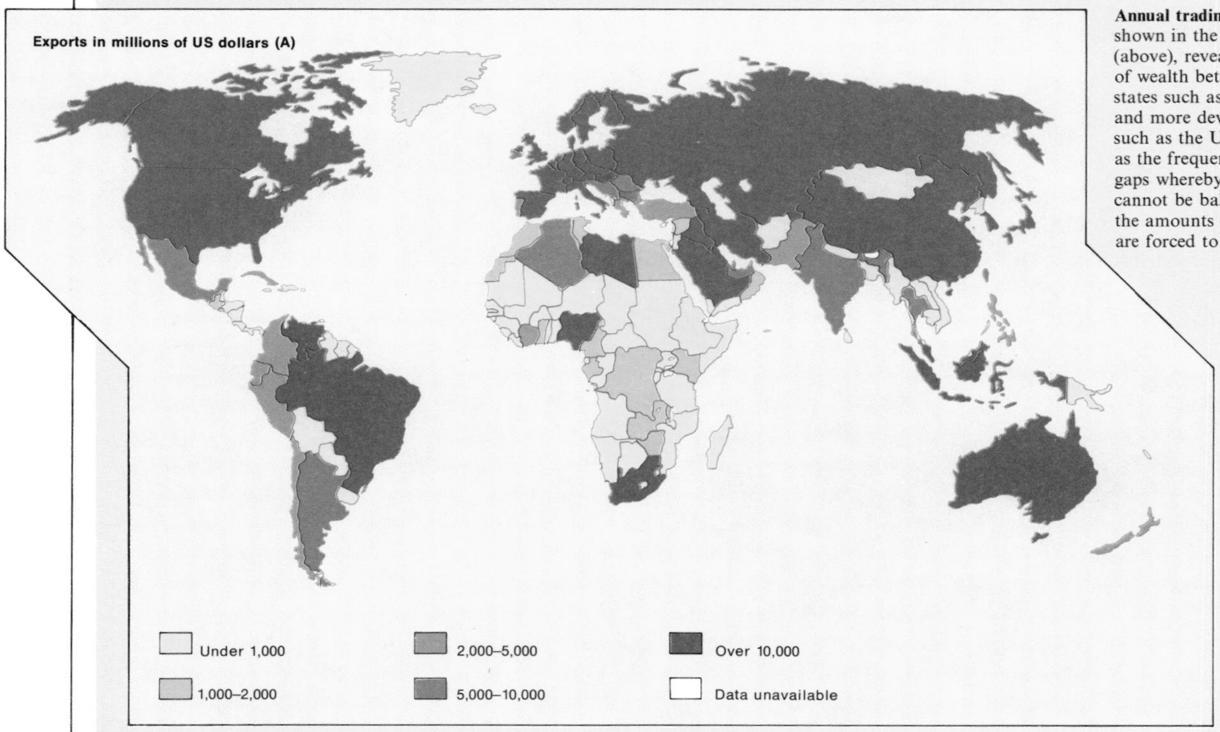
Exports in millions of US dollars (A)
Under 1,000
1,000–2,000
2,000–5,000
5,000–10,000
Over 10,000
Data unavailable

Annual trading figures, as shown in the graphs (above), reveal disparities of wealth between poor states such as Bangladesh and more developed ones such as the USA, as well as the frequency of trade gaps whereby export values cannot be balanced with the amounts countries are forced to import.

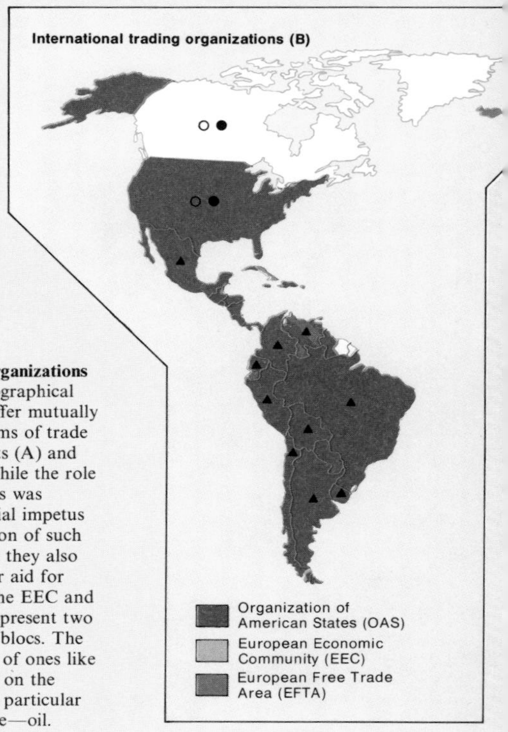
International trading organizations (B)
Organization of American States (OAS)
European Economic Community (EEC)
European Free Trade Area (EFTA)

International organizations (B) exist as geographical groupings to offer mutually preferential terms of trade for both exports (A) and imports (C). While the role of tariff barriers was usually the initial impetus in the foundation of such trading groups, they also offer each other aid for development; the EEC and COMECON represent two such economic blocs. The political power of ones like OPEC is based on the possession of a particular natural resource—oil.

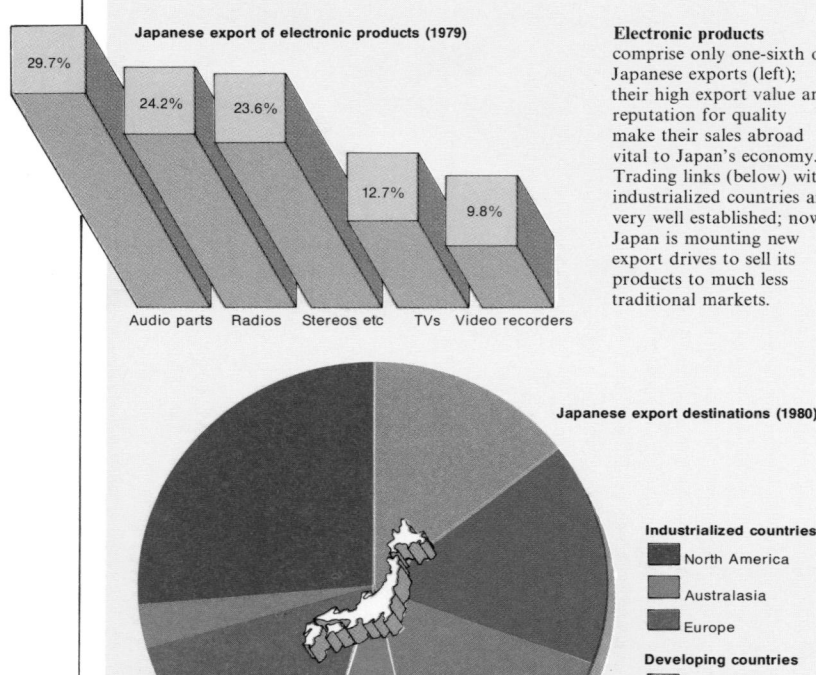

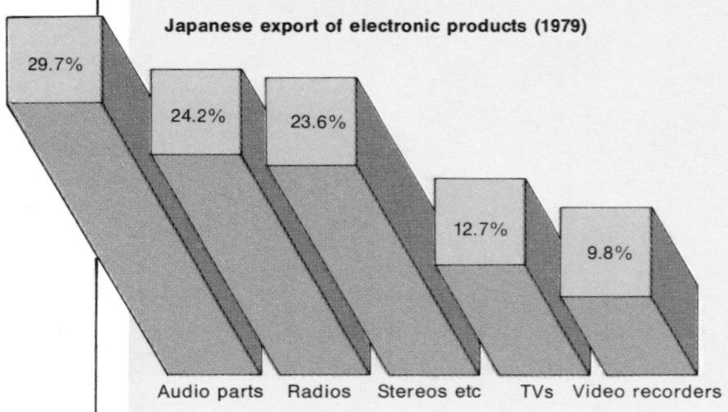
Japanese export of electronic products (1979)
29.7%
24.2%
23.6%
12.7%
9.8%
Audio parts
Radios
Stereos etc
TVs
Video recorders

Electronic products comprise only one-sixth of Japanese exports (left); their high export value and reputation for quality make their sales abroad vital to Japan's economy. Trading links (below) with industrialized countries are very well established; now Japan is mounting new export drives to sell its products to much less traditional markets.

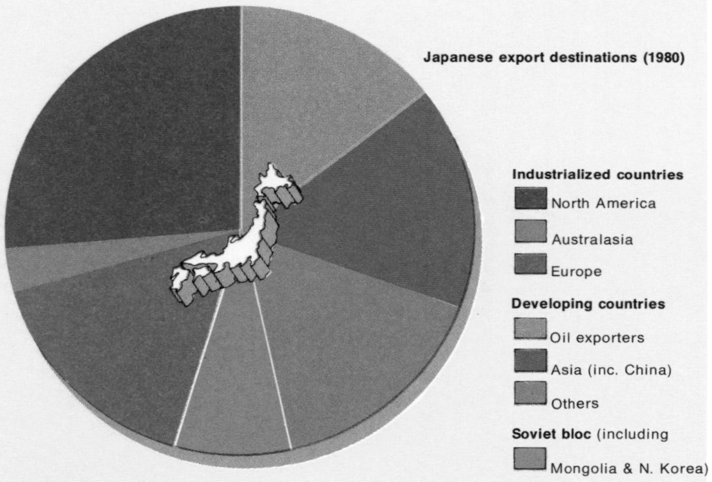
Japanese export destinations (1980)
Industrialized countries
North America
Australasia
Europe
Developing countries
Oil exporters
Asia (inc. China)
Others
Soviet bloc (including
Mongolia & N. Korea)

It is only a little more than two centuries since navigators completed the mapping of the world's major landmasses and much less since the mapping of the continental interiors was completed—even today some gaps still remain. Canals like the Suez (1869) and Panama (1915) reduced the extent of long sea voyages—the Suez Canal shortened the distance from northwestern Europe to India by 15,000 km (9,300 miles)—so that in transport terms, the various parts of the world became more accessible, especially as steamships and motor vessels replaced sailing ships, and time distances were reduced still further by the airplane.

Locational advantages

Inland waterways, roads and railroads opened up new areas for mining or specialized agriculture, and created opportunities for the manufacture of goods and for the distribution of the finished products. The contrast, however, between locations such as London, Tokyo or Chicago (which are accessible to all forms of transport) and parts of South America where modern transport hardly penetrates, has become much more marked over the years. New transport developments tend to connect major centers first of all, and thus increase their already high locational status.

Such developments must nevertheless be seen in the light of the demand for communications and trade between different points, the nature of the goods being carried and the actual cost of transport. Transport improvements have allowed different parts of the world to share ideas and products; ironically, they have also made such places more dissimilar, since each area of the Earth has had the chance to specialize in the services it can provide most efficiently.

Specialization of area

Before the widespread development of canals and railroads, road transport was expensive and towns and villages tended to be more self-sufficient. Railroads played a vital role in reducing transport costs in relation to distance and in providing an opportunity for different areas to specialize. After the emergence of railroad networks in North America, specialized areas of agricultural production quickly developed because they were well adjusted to the climatic conditions needed for growing maize (corn), cotton, fruit and fresh vegetables for the new urban markets. In the southern hemisphere, steamships and the introduction of refrigeration enabled meat, butter and cheese to be kept fresh on their journeys to the north.

This concept of specialization of area is basic to world trading patterns, since regions tend to concentrate on commodities and services that they can exchange for other specialized goods and products from other regional or world markets. Countries and areas do best when they concentrate on products for which they have comparative cost advantages in terms of the presence of natural resources, the availability of the skills to develop them, and a demand for the products. Enterprise in adapting natural conditions for the production of goods at competitive price levels is also important. Settlers in New

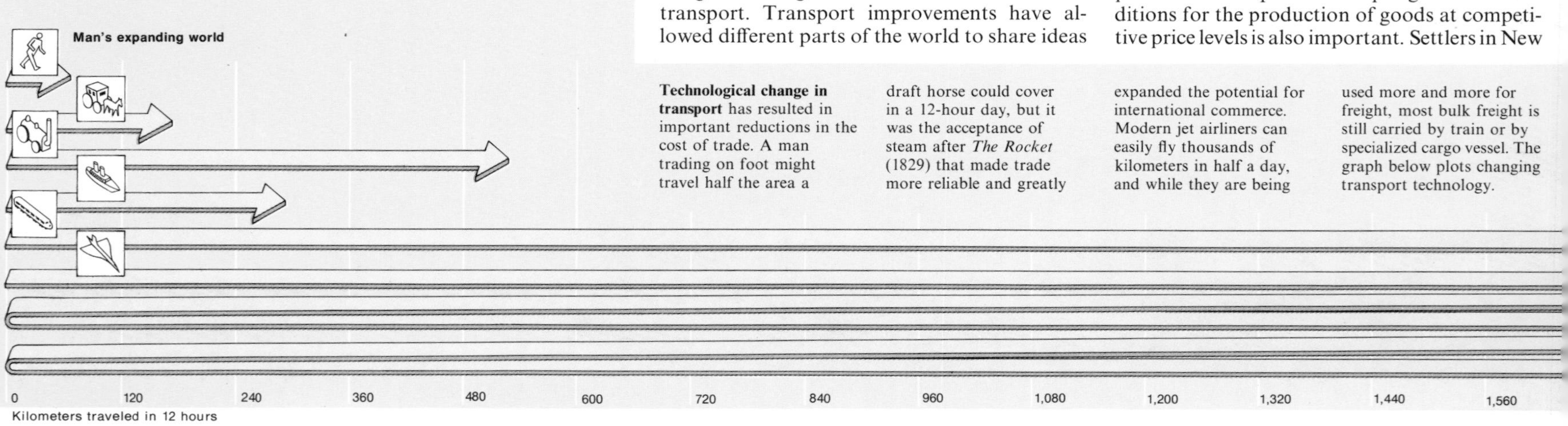
Man's expanding world
0
120
240
360
480
600
720
840
960
1,080
1,200
1,320
1,440
1,560
Kilometers traveled in 12 hours

Technological change in transport has resulted in important reductions in the cost of trade. A man trading on foot might travel half the area a draft horse could cover in a 12-hour day, but it was the acceptance of steam after *The Rocket* (1829) that made trade more reliable and greatly expanded the potential for international commerce. Modern jet airliners can easily fly thousands of kilometers in half a day, and while they are being used more and more for freight, most bulk freight is still carried by train or by specialized cargo vessel. The graph below plots changing transport technology.

THE WEALTH OF NATIONS

Economists measure a country's richness in terms of Gross National Product (GNP), the value of the goods and services available for consumption and for adding to its wealth. The difference in value between its exported and imported goods is often an important aspect of a nation's economy, and effective systems to transport such goods must play a major role in overseas trade. The 1980 Brandt Report highlighted the huge gap between the income of the rich world and the poverty of many developing states, but solutions to such problems of inequality will be difficult to obtain.

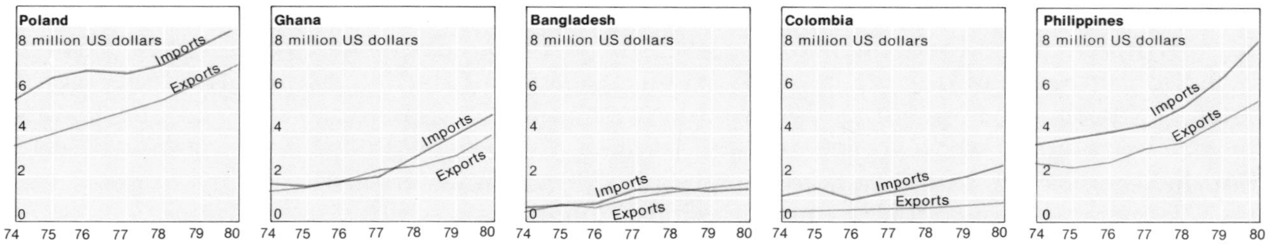

Poland
8 million US dollars
Imports
Exports
Ghana
8 million US dollars
Imports
Exports
Bangladesh
8 million US dollars
Imports
Exports
Colombia
8 million US dollars
Imports
Exports
Philippines
8 million US dollars
Imports
Exports
0 2 4 6
74 75 76 77 78 79 80

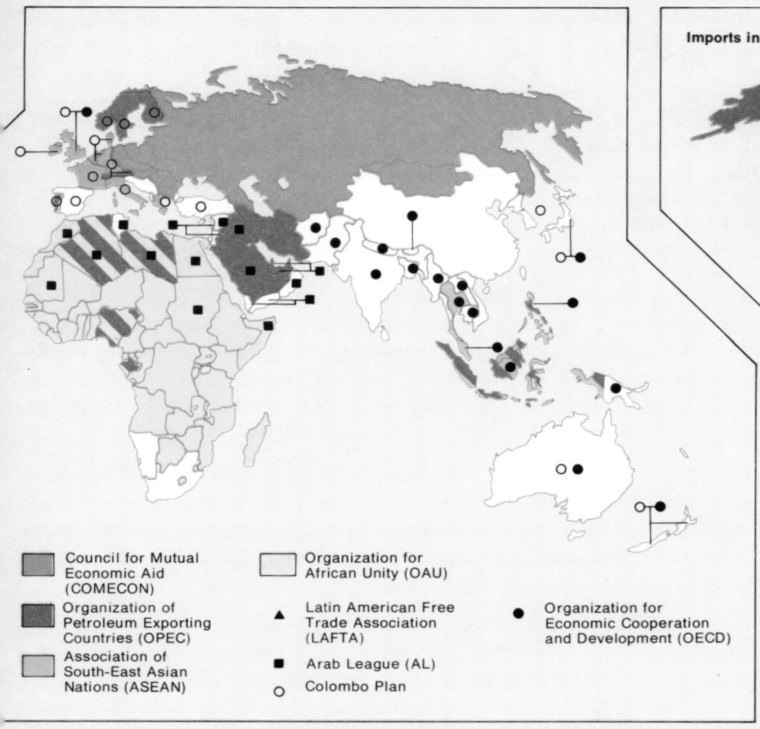

Council for Mutual Economic Aid (COMECON)
Organization of Petroleum Exporting Countries (OPEC)
Association of South-East Asian Nations (ASEAN)
Organization for African Unity (OAU)
Latin American Free Trade Association (LAFTA)
Arab League (AL)
Colombo Plan
Organization for Economic Cooperation and Development (OECD)

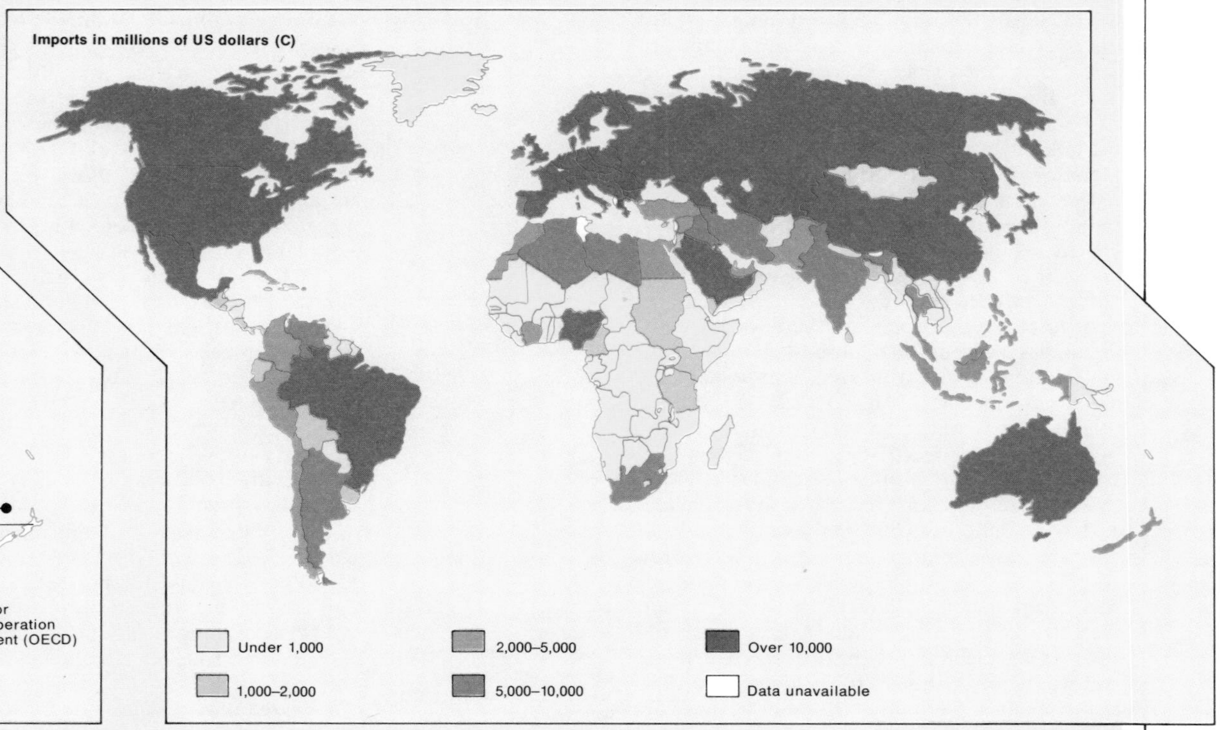

Imports in millions of US dollars (C)
Under 1,000
1,000–2,000
2,000–5,000
5,000–10,000
Over 10,000
Data unavailable

Zealand, for example, had little hesitation in clearing the prevailing tussock grass to create a new pastoral environment for their large-scale production of sheep and dairy products.

In the real world, however, there are many impediments to the operation of a free market system, and it is unwise for states like New Zealand to assume that they will always dominate Commonwealth dairy trade.

Impediments to free markets

Countries erect protectionist tariff barriers to assist their home industries and/or to obtain extra revenue. Import or export quotas may be imposed, and trade agreements with other countries give special preference to certain commodities. Problems arise from the exchange of currencies and their fluctuations in value. Tariff barriers may be erected for political, welfare or defense reasons. Sometimes special measures may be adopted to encourage the internal production of certain goods rather than obtaining them more cheaply from abroad, and such methods may be economically important to a new country that has always relied on the export of raw materials for its income but now wishes domestically to manufacture previously imported goods.

Political ties are vital to the groupings of certain countries. For reasons of international politics, countries such as those of the Soviet bloc trade with each other rather than with the outside world; and historical links, as between the UK and the Commonwealth, France and her ex-colonies, and Spain and Portugal with Latin America, are also influential. The European Economic Community (EEC) is composed of countries that have formed a strong bloc among the developed countries.

Rich man, poor man

The developed countries of "the North" have more than 80 percent of the world's manufacturing income but only a quarter of its population, whereas the poorer peoples of "the South" number 3,000 million and receive only a fifth of world income. Attempts have been made to obtain a better economic balance. The 1948 General Agreement on Tariffs and Trade (GATT) and the United Nations Conference on Trade and Development (UNCTAD) provided mechanisms for multinational trade negotiations, and the World Bank and the International Monetary Fund (IMF) together with the 1960 International Development Association (IDA) have all provided easier loans for less developed states.

The widening gap between rich and poor countries has led to understandable demands for a new international order calling for basic changes in the structure of world production, aid and trade, and the transfer of resources. The 1980 Independent Commission on International Development Issues (The Brandt Commission) advocated just such a transfer to the Third World. But during a major world recession there seems little sign of any international political will strong enough to take action on the scale needed to solve the problems that contrasts in wealth and poverty involve.

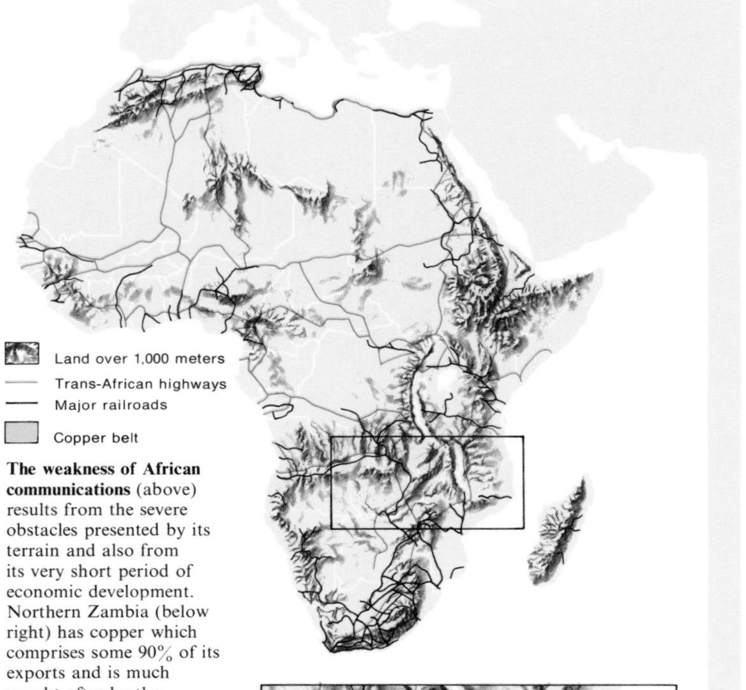

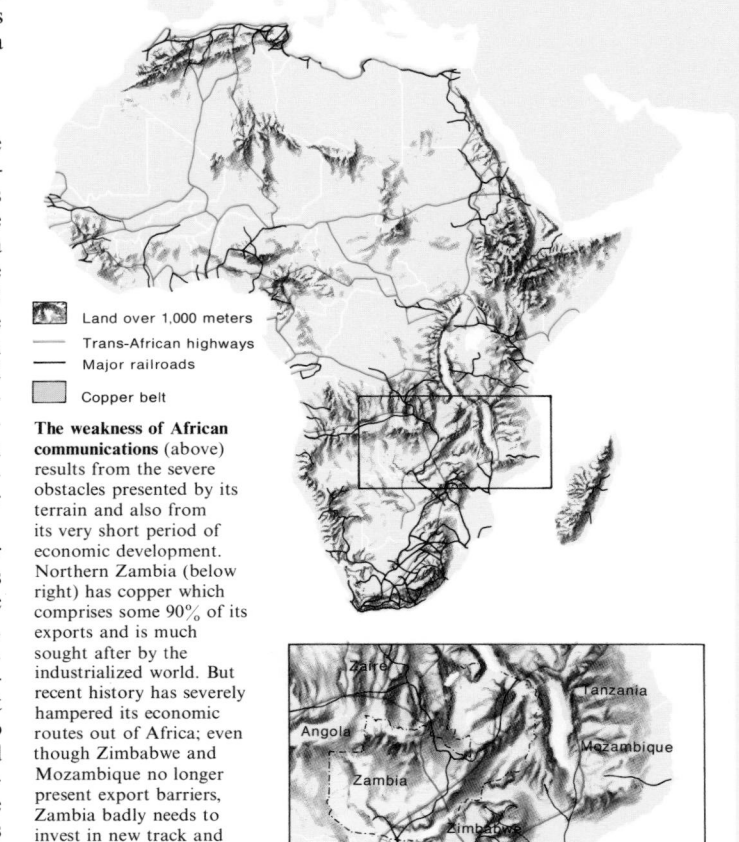

Land over 1,000 meters
Trans-African highways
Major railroads
Copper belt

The weakness of African communications (above) results from the severe obstacles presented by its terrain and also from its very short period of economic development. Northern Zambia (below right) has copper which comprises some 90% of its exports and is much sought after by the industrialized world. But recent history has severely hampered its economic routes out of Africa; even though Zimbabwe and Mozambique no longer present export barriers, Zambia badly needs to invest in new track and rolling stock.

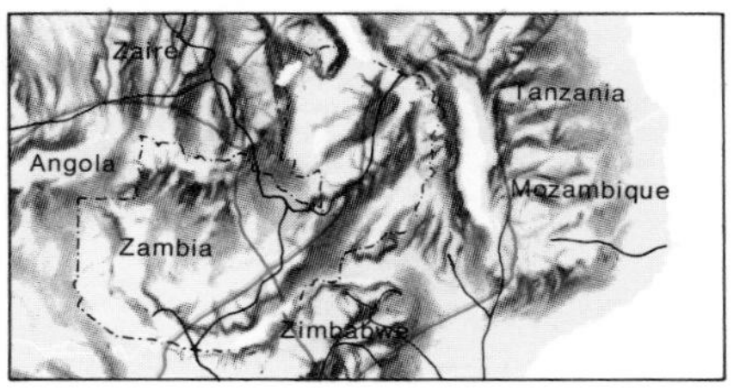

Zaire
Tanzania
Angola
Mozambique
Zambia
Zimbabwe

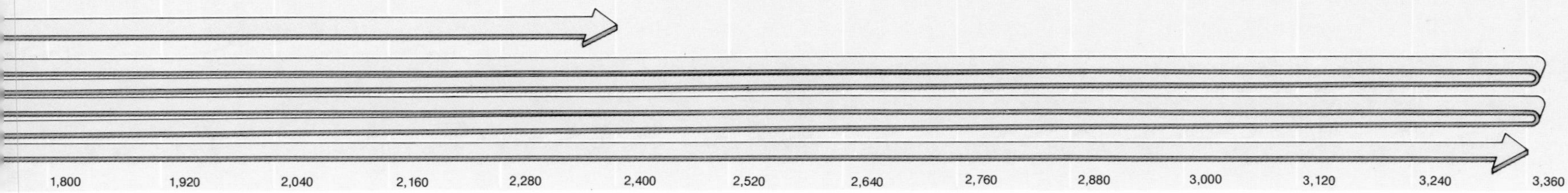

1,800
1,920
2,040
2,160
2,280
2,400
2,520
2,640
2,760
2,880
3,000
3,120
3,240
3,360

Polar Regions

Sunless in winter, and capped with permanent land ice and shifting sea ice, the world's polar regions present an image of intense and everlasting cold. But permanent ice caps have been the exception rather than the rule in the 4,600 million years of Earth's history. The most recent intensification of the present ice age (which began at least two million years ago) reached its maximum about 20,000 years ago and still continues to fluctuate. Polar conditions preclude all but the toughest life forms on land, but the plankton-rich waters attract many animals, and man is beginning to exploit the polar regions' potential.

There have been about a dozen ice ages since the world began. During the intervening periods there was still a zonal pattern of world temperatures, with hot equatorial regions and cooler poles. But the ice caps, which are both chilling and self-sustaining, were absent altogether—the poles being cold temperate rather than icebound. The shiny ice surfaces of today's poles reflect more than 90 percent of the solar radiation which reaches them from the low-angled summer sun, while in winter the sun never rises at all. Thus the regions are now permanently ice capped.

Antarctica, the great southern polar continent, lies under an ice mantle 14 million sq km (5.4 million sq miles) in area, and sometimes more than 4,000 m (13,000 ft) thick. Many of its neighboring islands also carry permanent ice. In the Arctic, the three islands of Greenland lie under a pall of ice of subcontinental size, more than 1.8 million sq km (700,000 sq miles) in area and up to 3,000 m (9,800 ft) thick.

The ice cover of polar seas varies. The central core of the Arctic Ocean carries a mass of permanent pack ice, slowly circulating within the polar basin, which is added to each winter by a belt of ice forming over the open sea. Currents and winds break this up to form pack ice that also circulates, gradually melting in summer or drifting south. Antarctica too is surrounded by fast ice, which breaks up in spring to form a broad belt of persistent pack ice. Circulating slowly about the continent, the pack ice forms huge gyres spreading far to the north, dotted with tabular bergs that have broken away from the continental ice sheet.

The frozen land

In the present glacial phase, the ice caps reached their farthest spread about 20,000 years ago, and then began the retreat which brought them, some 10,000 to 12,000 years ago, to their current position and size. Since then the climate of the polar regions has been both warmer and colder than it is at the present time.

The fluctuating nature of the polar climates creates very difficult conditions for plants and animals. Very little will grow on the terrestrial ice caps, but water scarcity rather than cold is the most important factor inhibiting plant growth: the small patches of lichens, algae and mosses that occur on rock faces and nunataks (points of rock jutting above the land ice) are usually in the path of a snowmelt runnel. Vegetation patches sometimes contain tiny populations of insects and mites, which may be active for only a few days each year when the sun warms them from a state of dormancy.

However, these tiny scattered plant communities appear all over Antarctica wherever rock surfaces break through the ice cap, and have been seen less than 300 km (190 miles) from the South Pole, and on peaks 2,000 m (6,600 ft) above sea level. Insects and mites occur within 600 km (380 miles) of the Pole itself. In specially favored positions on the Antarctic Peninsula and the offshore islands, carpets of moss and grasses may be seen. Conditions around the northern terrestrial ice cap are similar, with aridity, strong winds and cold discouraging all but the hardiest plants and the smallest, toughest animal colonies.

The frozen seas

The marine ice caps, by contrast, are relatively lively places, especially during summer, when days are long and the sea ice is patchy. Waterlanes between floes are often rich in microscopic algae and the minute zooplanktonic animals that feed on them. These animals in turn attract fish, sea birds and seals in their thousands, as well as whales—including the largest baleen species. Some of the richest patches of sea are close to islands where strong currents stir the water and bring nutrients to the surface, and these attract semipermanent populations of seals and birds. The birds breed on the island cliffs and feed in the sheltered waters among the ice; the seals may breed on the ice itself, producing their pups on a floating nursery where food is close at hand.

Different species of seals are found on inshore and offshore ice environments. In the Arctic, bearded and ringed seals, which produce their young in spring as the inshore ice begins to break up, are often preyed upon by floe-riding polar bears; Eskimos too prize both species for their meat, blubber and skins. Farther out on the offshore pack ice live hooded and harp seals, where their pups are safe from all but the shipborne commercial hunters. In the Antarctic, Weddell seals are the inshore species, whereas crabeater and Ross seals prefer the distant pack ice. Crabeaters, which feed largely on planktonic krill (once thought to be crab larvae), are probably the most numerous of all seal species, with a population estimated at 10 to 15 million.

Sea ice in the north provides a precarious platform on which coastal human populations of the Arctic, such as Eskimos, can extend their winter hunting range. When the land is snowbound and animals are scarce, the sea may still provide food for hunters skilled in fishing, and in stalking seals to their breathing holes.

Nonindigenous inhabitants of the ice caps have greatly increased in recent years, following the discovery and exploitation of oil in the north, as well as other valuable minerals in both the regions. Scientists and technicians today occupy bases and weather stations which in some cases, such as the Amundsen-Scott at the South Pole, are several decades old and have to be maintained by means of aircraft.

The coldness of the poles is caused by the tilt of the Earth's axis, which prevents sunlight from reaching them at all in the winter. Even in summer, little heat is received from the sun because of the low angle at which its rays reach the surface; much even of this is reflected away by the ice.

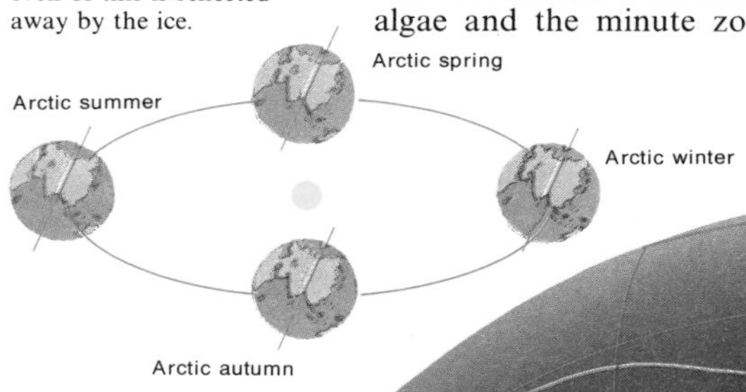
Arctic spring
Arctic summer
Arctic winter
Arctic autumn

EARTH'S FROZEN LIMITS

The permanent ice around Earth's poles covers whole oceans, as well as landmasses of immense size. These ice sheets fluctuate, and on land may be thousands of meters thick, sometimes covering all but the highest mountains, and allowing hardly any life. In the circumpolar seas, however, conditions encourage a very rich growth of plankton, and this supports a plentiful and varied range of wildlife. Man, too, is active in the Arctic, where there are indigenous populations. But in the far south the presence of man is confined to scientists and their support groups. The Antarctic Treaty of 1959 has reserved the continent for nonpolitical scientific use.

THE FAR SOUTH

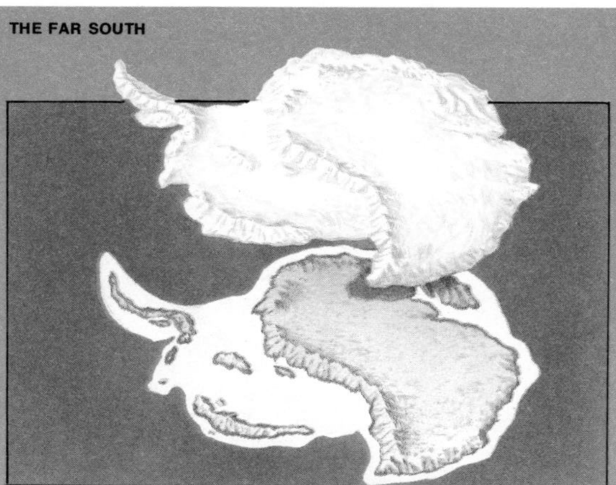

A crushing weight of ice (above) permanently covers the continent and seas of Antarctica, forcing much of the land below sea level. The Antarctic convergence (right), the line at which northern and southern water masses meet, marks a sharp change in temperature and marine life. Especially in areas of upwelling, nutrients make these waters rich in plankton. This feeds a multitude of shrimp-like krill that provide food for a huge number of other animals—fish, penguins, flying birds, seals and whales. The Antarctic landmass allows little natural life, but since the 1959 Antarctic Treaty it has proved to be an area of international scientific cooperation.

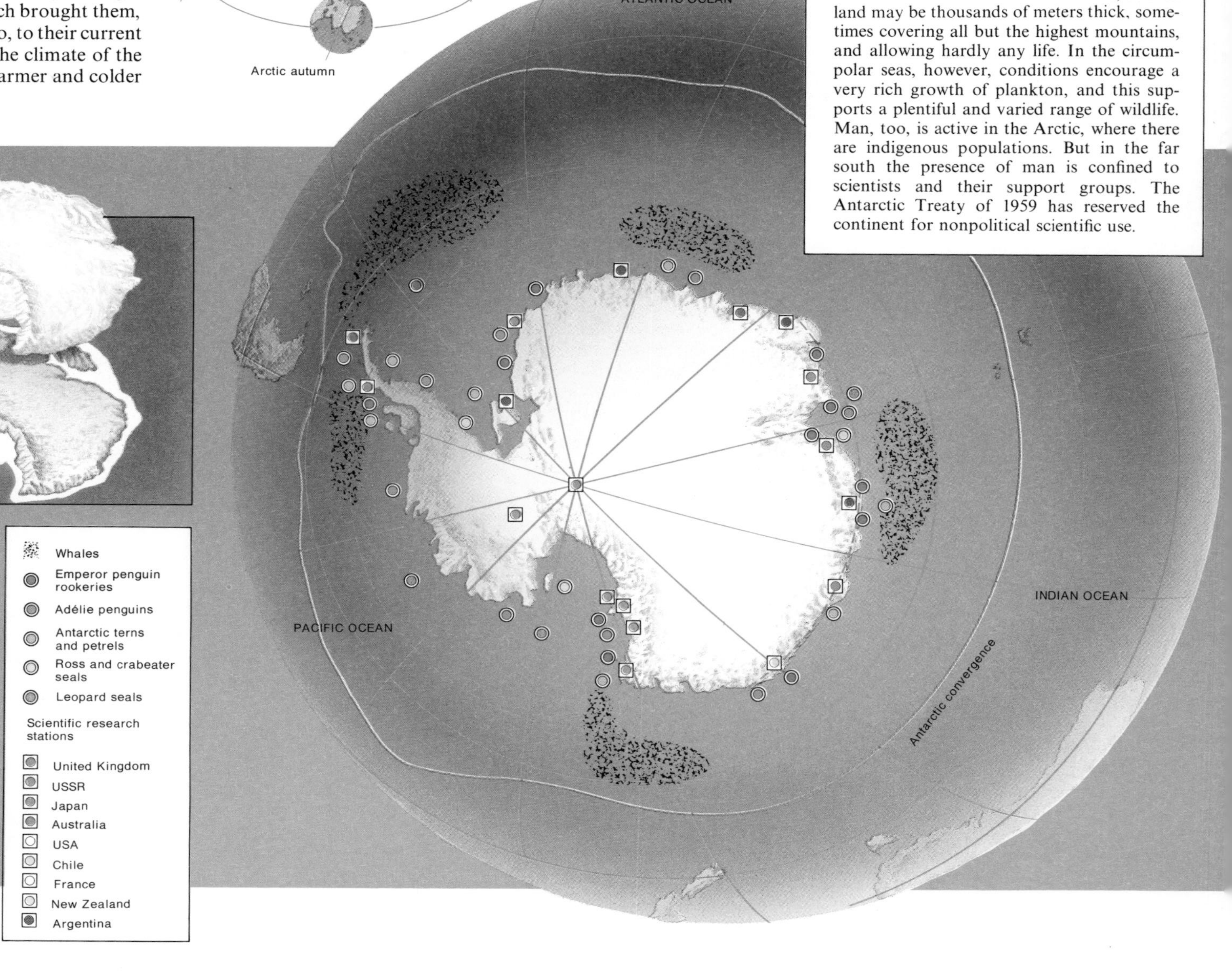
Whales
Emperor penguin rookeries
Adélie penguins
Antarctic terns and petrels
Ross and crabeater seals
Leopard seals
Scientific research stations
United Kingdom
USSR
Japan
Australia
USA
Chile
France
New Zealand
Argentina
ATLANTIC OCEAN
PACIFIC OCEAN
INDIAN OCEAN
Antarctic convergence

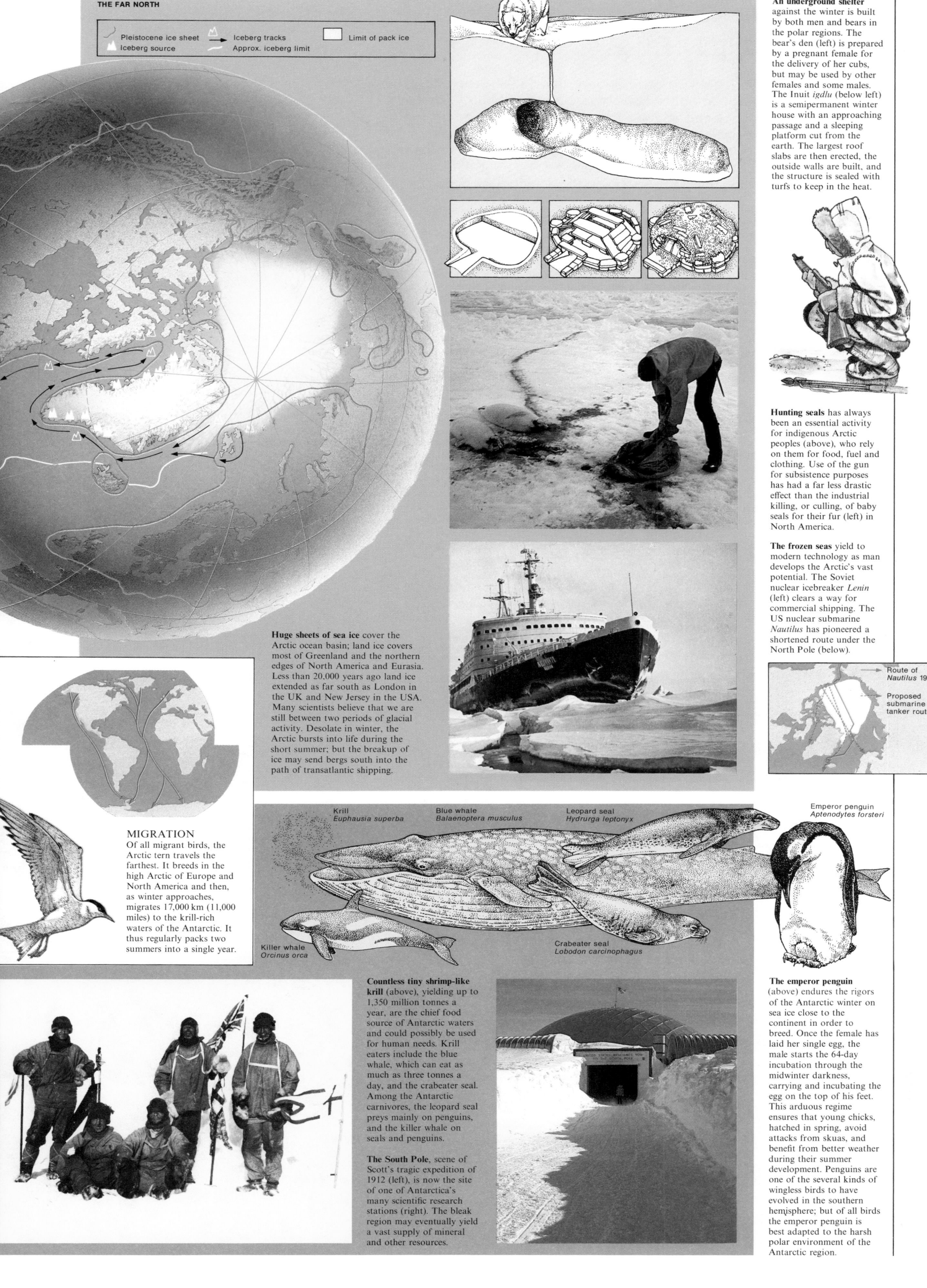

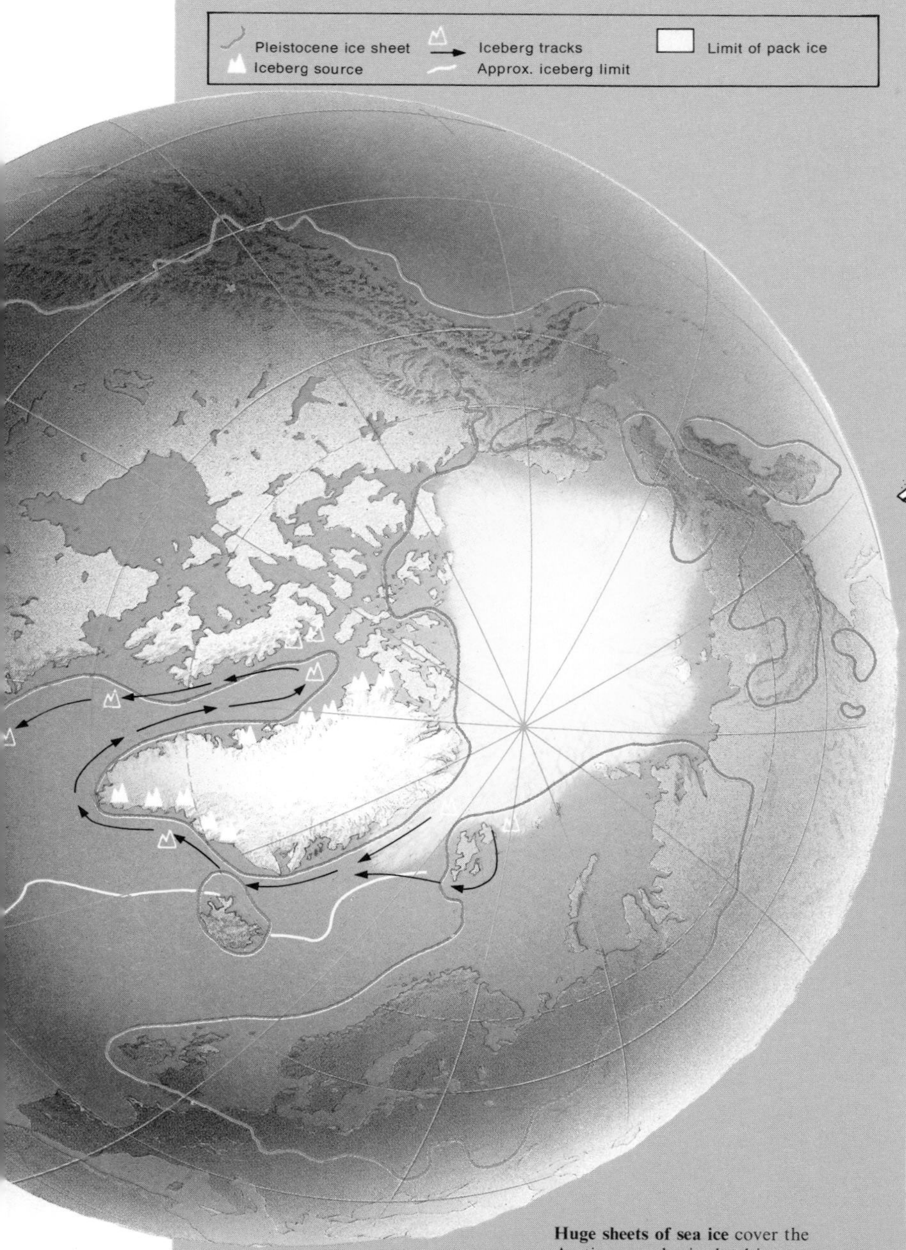
Pleistocene ice sheet
Iceberg source
Iceberg tracks
Approx. iceberg limit
Limit of pack ice

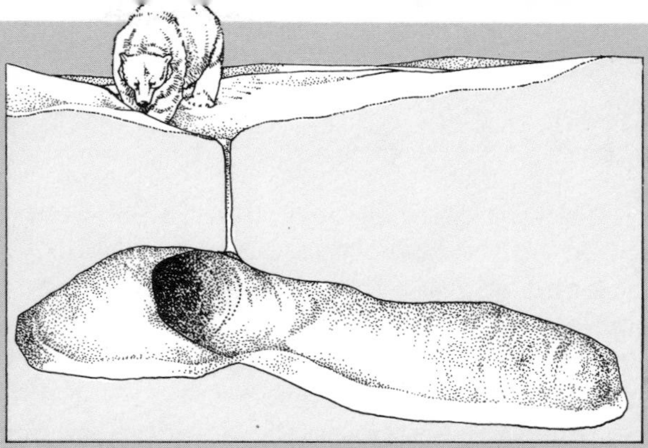

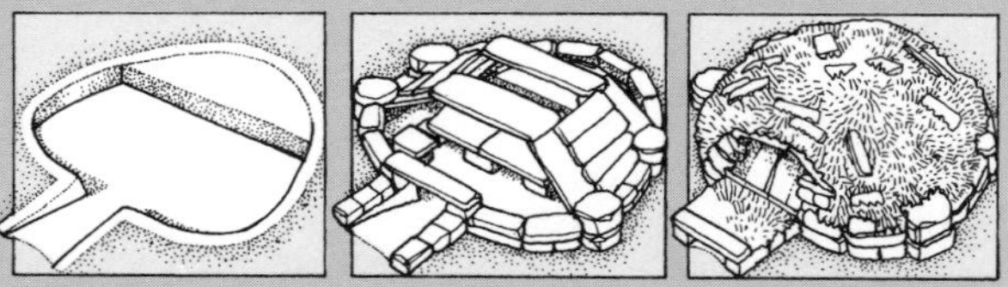

An underground shelter against the winter is built by both men and bears in the polar regions. The bear's den (left) is prepared by a pregnant female for the delivery of her cubs, but may be used by other females and some males. The Inuit *igdlu* (below left) is a semipermanent winter house with an approaching passage and a sleeping platform cut from the earth. The largest roof slabs are then erected, the outside walls are built, and the structure is sealed with turfs to keep in the heat.

Hunting seals has always been an essential activity for indigenous Arctic peoples (above), who rely on them for food, fuel and clothing. Use of the gun for subsistence purposes has had a far less drastic effect than the industrial killing, or culling, of baby seals for their fur (left) in North America.

The frozen seas yield to modern technology as man develops the Arctic's vast potential. The Soviet nuclear icebreaker *Lenin* (left) clears a way for commercial shipping. The US nuclear submarine *Nautilus* has pioneered a shortened route under the North Pole (below).

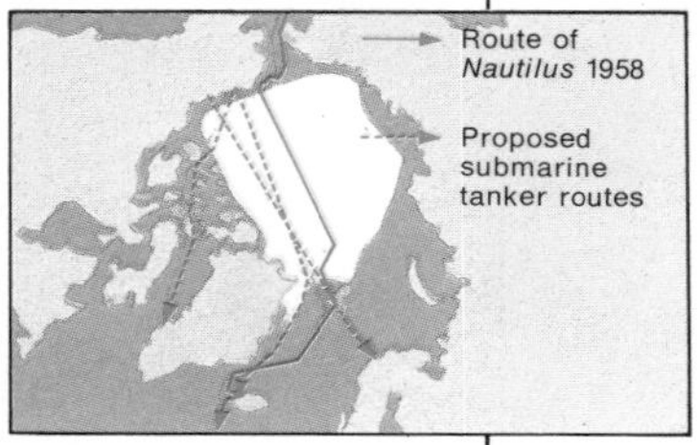
Route of
Nautilus 1958
Proposed
submarine
tanker routes

Huge sheets of sea ice cover the Arctic ocean basin; land ice covers most of Greenland and the northern edges of North America and Eurasia. Less than 20,000 years ago land ice extended as far south as London in the UK and New Jersey in the USA. Many scientists believe that we are still between two periods of glacial activity. Desolate in winter, the Arctic bursts into life during the short summer; but the breakup of ice may send bergs south into the path of transatlantic shipping.

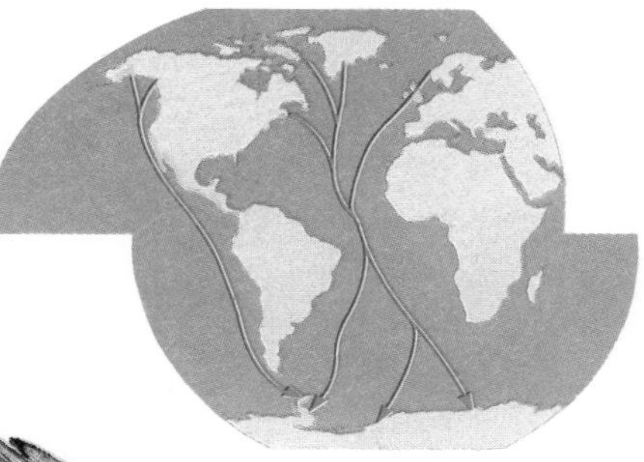

MIGRATION

Of all migrant birds, the Arctic tern travels the farthest. It breeds in the high Arctic of Europe and North America and then, as winter approaches, migrates 17,000 km (11,000 miles) to the krill-rich waters of the Antarctic. It thus regularly packs two summers into a single year.

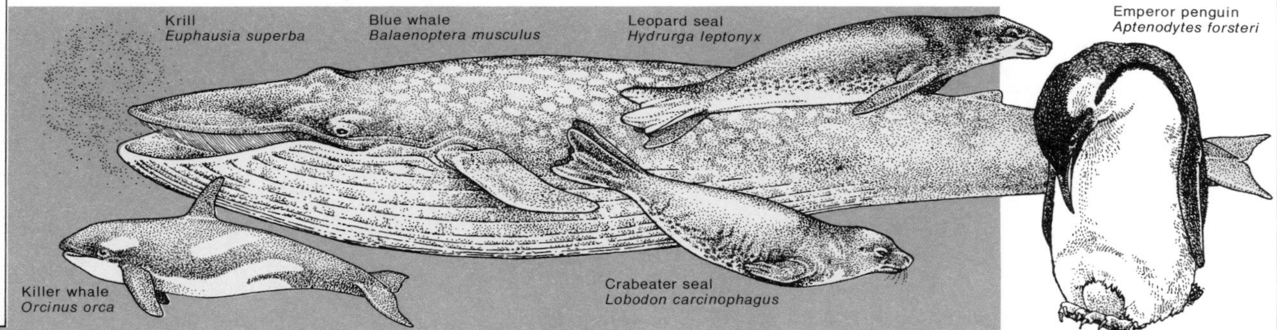
Krill
Euphausia superba
Blue whale
Balaenoptera musculus
Leopard seal
Hydrurga leptonyx
Emperor penguin
Aptenodytes forsteri
Killer whale
Orcinus orca
Crabeater seal
Lobodon carcinophagus

The emperor penguin (above) endures the rigors of the Antarctic winter on sea ice close to the continent in order to breed. Once the female has laid her single egg, the male starts the 64-day incubation through the midwinter darkness, carrying and incubating the egg on the top of his feet. This arduous regime ensures that young chicks, hatched in spring, avoid attacks from skuas, and benefit from better weather during their summer development. Penguins are one of the several kinds of wingless birds to have evolved in the southern hemisphere; but of all birds the emperor penguin is best adapted to the harsh polar environment of the Antarctic region.

Countless tiny shrimp-like krill (above), yielding up to 1,350 million tonnes a year, are the chief food source of Antarctic waters and could possibly be used for human needs. Krill eaters include the blue whale, which can eat as much as three tonnes a day, and the crabeater seal. Among the Antarctic carnivores, the leopard seal preys mainly on penguins, and the killer whale on seals and penguins.

The South Pole, scene of Scott's tragic expedition of 1912 (left), is now the site of one of Antarctica's many scientific research stations (right). The bleak region may eventually yield a vast supply of mineral and other resources.

Tundra and Taiga

Tundra is land that has been exposed for only about 8,000 years, since the retreat of the ice caps, and only relatively recently occupied by plants. In consequence, few plants and animals have yet had time to adapt to the virtually soilless and treeless environment. The less rigorous conditions of neighboring taiga forest allow a longer growing season and a somewhat wider range of species. The delicately balanced ecology of both areas is being increasingly threatened, however, by the activities of man.

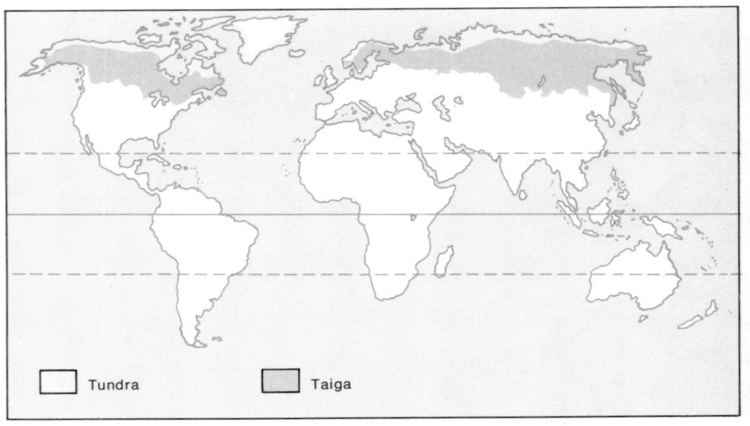
Tundra
Taiga

The circumpolar north that surrounds the permanently frozen ice cap is dominated by tundra—open plain that remains snowfree for only several months in the summer—and taiga, the vast coniferous forest stretching right round the northern hemisphere. The Siberian taiga, for example, is one-third larger than the entire United States.

"Tundra," from a Lapp word meaning "rolling, treeless plain," defines the narrow band of open, low ground that surrounds the Arctic Ocean. It lies north of the line beyond which the temperature of the warmest month usually fails to reach 10°C (50°F). North of this trees do not generally grow well, so the line forms a natural frontier between tundra and the broad band of coniferous forest that circles the northern hemisphere to its south between about 60°N and 48°N. This forest, forming the world's largest and most uninterrupted area of vegetation, is usually referred to by its Russian name of "taiga."

Cheerless landscapes

The tundra presents a desolate and restrictive environment for most of the year: in winter there are several months of semidarkness. While there is considerable variation in the climates of places at the same latitude, temperatures average only −5°C (23°F) and are well below freezing for many months of the year. Frost-free days are restricted to a few weeks in midsummer and even then, although days are warmer, the sun is never high in the sky. Nearly all tundra has been free from ice for only a few thousand years. As a result, it either has no soil at all or has developed only a thin covering of sandy, muddy or peaty soil, successfully colonized by only a few types of plants.

Trimmed by such grazing animals as hares, musk oxen and reindeer or caribou, and by strong winds carrying abrasive rock dust and ice particles, typical tundra vegetation forms a low, patchy mat a few centimeters deep. Much of it grows on permafrost — ground that thaws superficially in summer but remains perennially frozen beneath the surface. Here drainage is poor, shallow ponds are frequent and the scanty soils tend to be waterlogged and acidic. Nevertheless, a small number of grasses, sedges, mosses and marsh plants may grow well and the summer tundra in flower can be an impressive sight. Knee-high forests of dwarf birch, willow and alder grow in valleys sheltered from the strong and biting wind.

The taiga also is a dark and monotonous habitat. Again, while there is a good deal of variation in climatic conditions, on average the region has somewhat milder summers than the tundra with mean average temperatures of 2–6°C (34–42°F), less wind and a slightly longer growing season. The taiga is mostly older than the tundra, and its soils have had longer to mature. They support a small number of tree species, with coniferous spruce, pine, fir and larch predominating. Short-season broadleaves such as willows, alders, birches and poplars tend to occur on the better soils of river valleys and the edges of forest lakes.

Animals of the far north

The number of animal species supported throughout the year by tundra and taiga is also comparatively small, with interdependent populations that may fluctuate wildly from season to season. In winter both tundra and taiga are silent, although far from deserted. Mice, voles and lemmings remain active, living in tunnels under the snow, which keeps them well insulated from the wind and subzero temperatures. Above the snow Arctic hares forage; they tend to gather in snow-free areas where food can still be found. Arctic foxes are mainly tundra animals and the musk oxen, too, winter on high, exposed tundra where their dense, shaggy coats protect them from the worst

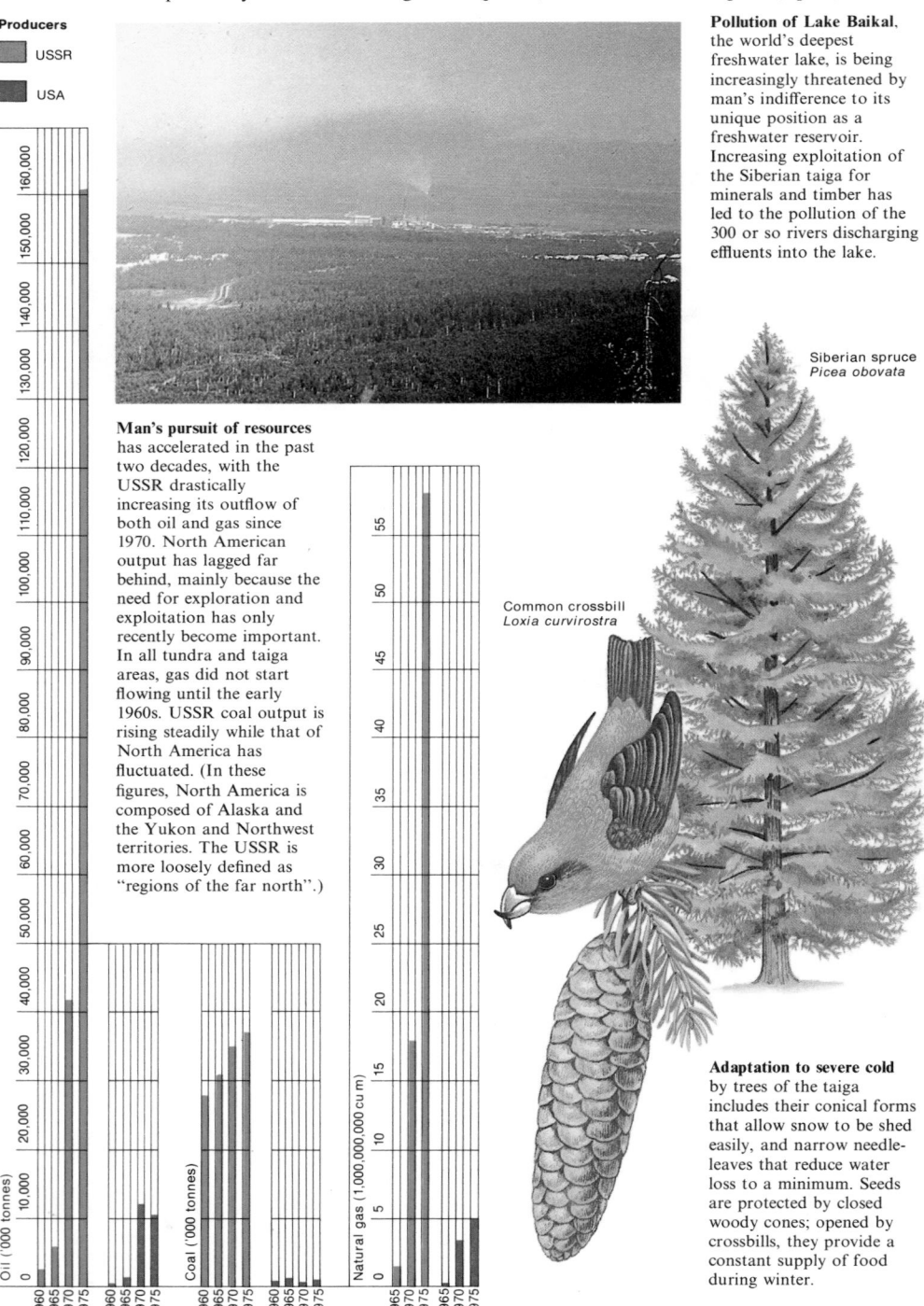

Pollution of Lake Baikal, the world's deepest freshwater lake, is being increasingly threatened by man's indifference to its unique position as a freshwater reservoir. Increasing exploitation of the Siberian taiga for minerals and timber has led to the pollution of the 300 or so rivers discharging effluents into the lake.

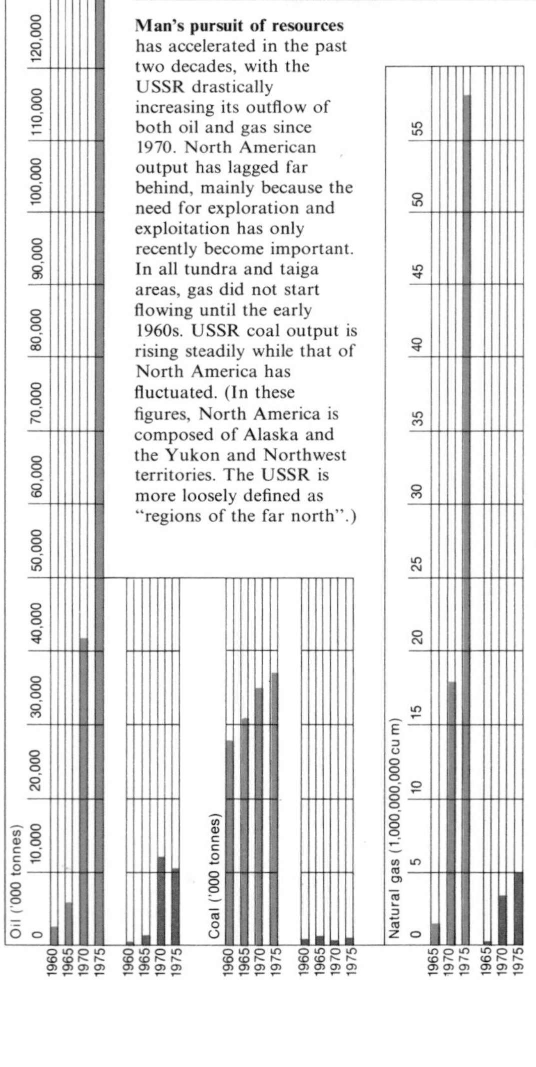
Producers
USSR
USA
Oil ('000 tonnes)
Coal ('000 tonnes)
Natural gas (1,000,000,000 cu m)
1960
1965
1970
1975

Man's pursuit of resources has accelerated in the past two decades, with the USSR drastically increasing its outflow of both oil and gas since 1970. North American output has lagged far behind, mainly because the need for exploration and exploitation has only recently become important. In all tundra and taiga areas, gas did not start flowing until the early 1960s. USSR coal output is rising steadily while that of North America has fluctuated. (In these figures, North America is composed of Alaska and the Yukon and Northwest territories. The USSR is more loosely defined as "regions of the far north".)

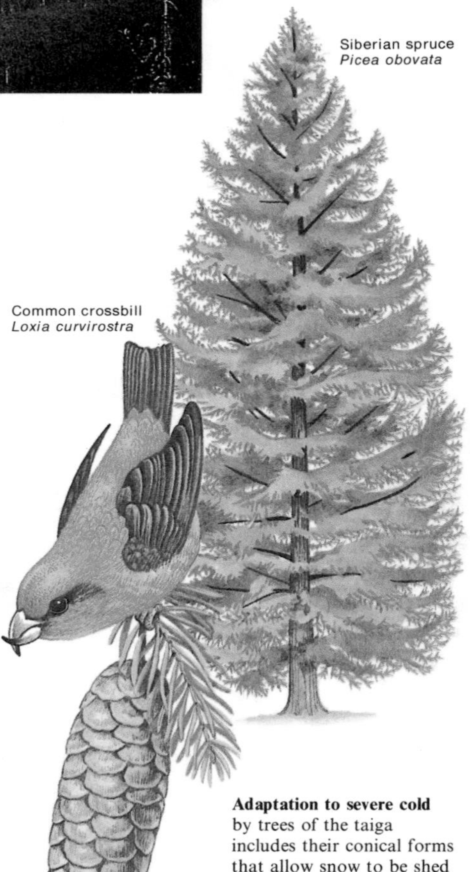
Siberian spruce
Picea obovata
Common crossbill
Loxia curvirostra

Adaptation to severe cold by trees of the taiga includes their conical forms that allow snow to be shed easily, and narrow needle-leaves that reduce water loss to a minimum. Seeds are protected by closed woody cones; opened by crossbills, they provide a constant supply of food during winter.

Reindeer or caribou
Rangifer tarandus
Raven
Corvus corax
Arctic fox
Alopex lagopus
Capercaillie
Tetrao urogallus
Snowy owl
Nyctea scandiaca
Brown lemming
Lemmus lemmus
Arctic skua
Stercorarius parasiticus
January
February
March
April
May
June

Movement in these regions takes many directions. The capercaillie spends all winter in the taiga, where it thrives on the abundant conifer needles, buds and shoots. Some move southward into deciduous woods during the summer months. The Arctic skua breeds on the tundra but moves to the warmer oceans in winter, while the tundra movements of the all-scavenging raven and the snowy owl are governed by those of their prey. The raven picks clean the carcasses left by other predators; the snowy owl feeds on small rodents such as mice and lemmings, as does the Arctic fox. Lemmings remain static and inconspicuous in normal years but some populations expand rapidly every third or fourth year, leading to mass local migration in every direction, possibly caused by an abundance of vegetation that encourages more frequent breeding.

The rough boundary between the tundra and taiga—the tree line—approximates to the 10°C July isotherm, the climatic point north of which trees fail to grow successfully. Seasonal caribou migration in the Canadian barren grounds (boxed) is shown in the main diagram (below). Such migration is also undertaken by reindeer in northern Eurasia.

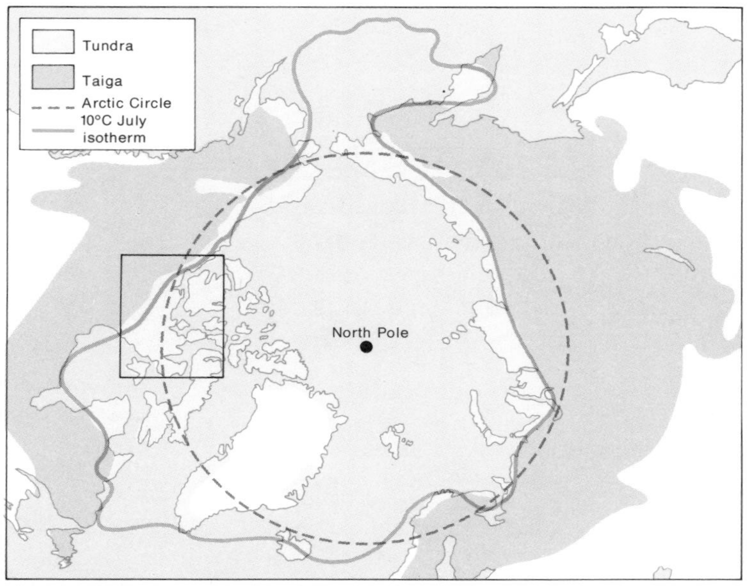

Tundra
Taiga
Arctic Circle
10°C July isotherm
North Pole

The summer tundra—seen here in Swedish Lapland—provides a wide cover of low plants including "reindeer mosses" and other lichens. Grazing reindeer return minerals to the soil. Shallow ponds form as the frozen ground above the permafrost thaws for a few months in summer. Mountains stay partly snow covered in the warmest weather and are a prominent physical feature of the tundra.

weather. Bears, badgers, beavers and squirrels are common taiga mammals. Elk and reindeer (in North America, moose and caribou) winter in the shelter of the taiga; wolves are mostly woodland animals in winter, following their prey to the open tundra in spring. Red foxes, coyotes, mink and wolverines also move to the tundra in summer.

Snow buntings, ptarmigans and snowy owls live on the tundra throughout the coldest months and are fully adapted to life there. Crossbills and capercaillies are among taiga residents, equipped to live on its abundant conifer buds, seeds and needles. Enormous populations of migrant birds, especially water birds and waders, fly north to both tundra and taiga with the spring thaw. Waxwings, bramblings, siskins and redpolls leave their temperate latitudes to feed on the lush and fast-growing vegetation and the profusion of insects that appear as soon as the snows begin to melt.

Man in the northlands

These circumpolar regions act as a strategic buffer between the USA and the USSR. Situated between the world's greatest centers of population, they are now crisscrossed with air routes. A total population of about nine million people currently inhabits the tundra and taiga. Numbers have been increased by the immigration of technicians and administrators during the last few decades; oil prospecting and mining, forest exploitation and other activities of these newcomers is altering the seminomadic lives of the million or so aboriginal peoples such as the Khanty (Ostyaks) and Nentsy (Samoyeds) of the USSR, the Samer (Lapps) of Scandinavia and the Soviet Union, and the Inuit (formerly Eskimos) of North America. New roads, exploitation of minerals and forests, and pipeline construction have disrupted the migration of their reindeer (caribou) and their land has been appropriated for hydroelectric schemes.

In the taiga, the Soviets are constructing railroads and towns and extracting huge amounts of timber; they have prospected widely and successfully for gold, nickel, iron, tin, mica, diamonds and tungsten, and have discovered vast reserves of oil and natural gas in western Siberia. Alaskan oil, discovered in 1968, now flows across the state at 54–62°C (130–145°F), and to protect the permafrost from this heat the pipeline has had to be elevated for half its 1,300 km (800 mile) length. The pipe's route to the ice-free port of Valdez has interfered with the migration of caribou; hunting and other pressures have led to a drop in their population from three million to some 200,000 in about 30 years. Only official protection has saved the musk ox from a similar fate. These bleak areas are so vast and inhospitable that living space there will never be threatened. However, if only on a local scale, their ecologies are under increasing pressure from man.

Many Norwegian Lapps (or Samer) derive their income from reindeer, which they domesticated many centuries ago to provide meat, milk and skins. Now they follow them through the seasons along well-worn and familiar routes. Such nomadic life styles are becoming rarer as Samer settle down.

MOVEMENT THROUGH THE SEASONS

Life on tundra and taiga is dominated by the mark of the seasons. In this diagrammatic representation of the north–south migration of the American caribou, each block represents the same area of terrain through the 12 months of the year. From February to April, the caribou move north in a steady file from the forest, emerging to eat the newly exposed lichen and moving to grounds where calving takes place in late May and early June. In the summer months they disperse freely before returning south in smaller groups on a broader front in late July and August. Rutting and mating take place in October/early November before the caribou regain the shelter of the taiga.

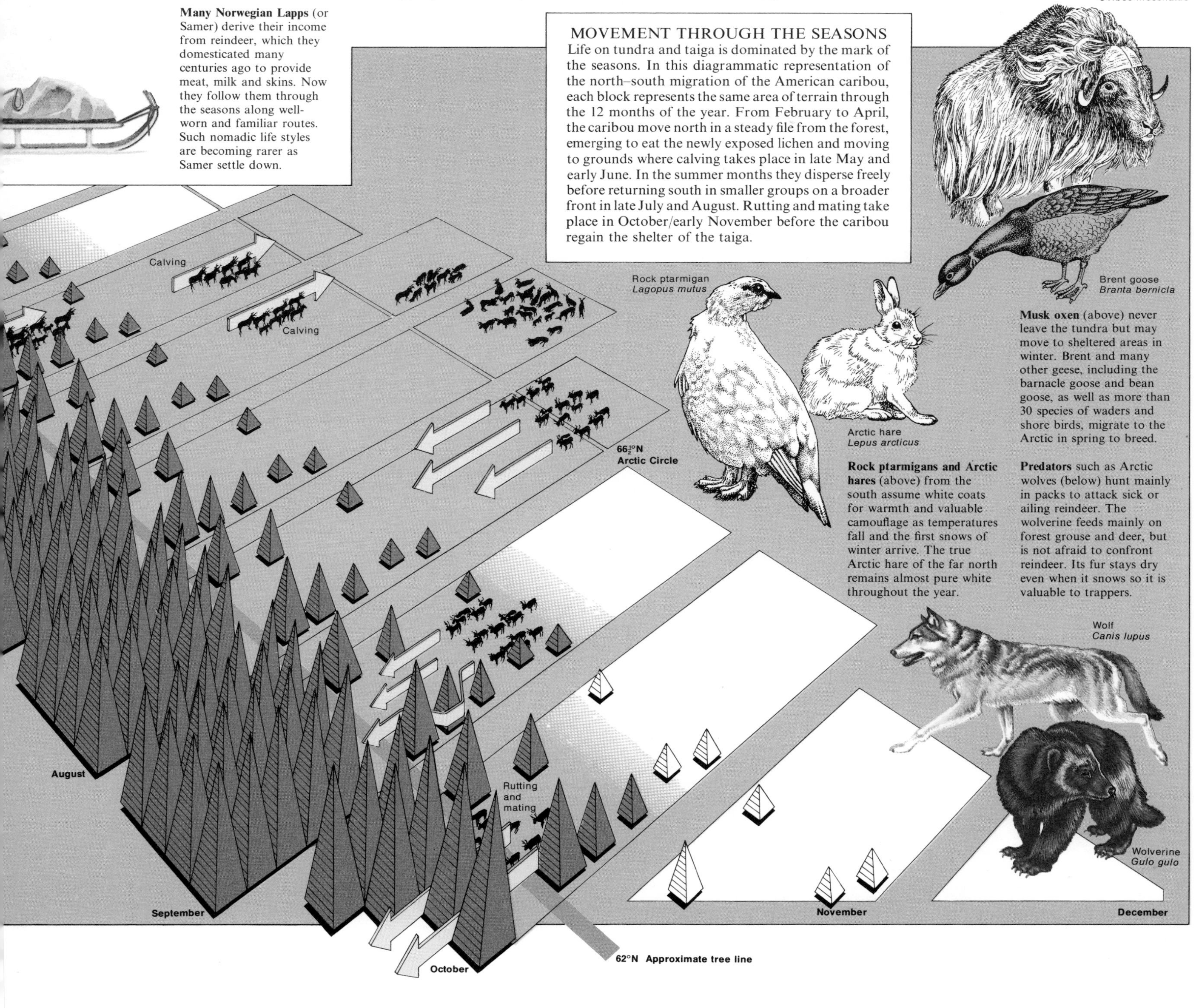

Musk ox
Ovibos moschatus
Brent goose
Branta bernicla
Rock ptarmigan
Lagopus mutus
Arctic hare
Lepus arcticus
Wolf
Canis lupus
Wolverine
Gulo gulo
Calving
Calving
66½°N
Arctic Circle
August
September
October
November
December
Rutting and mating
62°N Approximate tree line

Musk oxen (above) never leave the tundra but may move to sheltered areas in winter. Brent and many other geese, including the barnacle goose and bean goose, as well as more than 30 species of waders and shore birds, migrate to the Arctic in spring to breed.

Rock ptarmigans and Arctic hares (above) from the south assume white coats for warmth and valuable camouflage as temperatures fall and the first snows of winter arrive. The true Arctic hare of the far north remains almost pure white throughout the year.

Predators such as Arctic wolves (below) hunt mainly in packs to attack sick or ailing reindeer. The wolverine feeds mainly on forest grouse and deer, but is not afraid to confront reindeer. Its fur stays dry even when it snows so it is valuable to trappers.

Temperate Forests

At one time, dense, primeval forests blanketed large areas of North America, Europe and eastern Asia. Almost all of the trees that flourished in these temperate regions were deciduous – they shed their leaves in autumn, stood bare branched through winter and produced new foliage every spring. Little of this forest now exists. The few remaining pockets, however, still provide habitats for a large range of shade-loving plants: lichens and fungi, tree-hugging mosses, scrambling creepers and shrubs. And this vegetation in turn provides sanctuary for a surprisingly wide variety of forest creatures.

Common oak
Quercus robur

Silver beech
Nothofagus menziesii

Deciduous trees such as the oak (top) make up the temperate forests in cooler temperate regions. In milder, wetter climates, where the seasons are less distinct, evergreens such as southern beech (above) are typical temperate species.

The greater part of the temperate forest zone lies in the northern hemisphere, where winter soil temperatures reduce the ability of plants to absorb water. Hence the trees tend to shed their leaves, which use up moisture through evaporation. In the southern hemisphere, however, the temperate latitudes encourage a type of rainforest in such areas as southern Chile, Tasmania, New Zealand and parts of southeastern Australia. Here the climate is maritime, often with high rainfall and frequent fogs, and evergreen rather than deciduous types of trees grow. Temperate rainforests also occur in the northern hemisphere, in China and in northwestern and northeastern North America.

Deciduous forest consists of a mixture of trees, sometimes with one variety predominant. In central Europe, beech is the leading—and sometimes the only—tree species, whereas oaks mixed with other species made up the forest farther west and east. In North America, beech and maple were once extensive.

The climate in temperate forest zones varies sharply according to seasons—summers tend to be warm, winters moderately cold, and rainfall fairly regular. In fact, the seasonal rhythm is a central feature of temperate forests, and it affects the entire ecosystem—the whole community of plants and animals found there. Soils are generally of the fertile "brown earth" type: the leaf litter of deciduous forests in particular breaks down easily, and is quickly worked into the soil by burrowing animals such as earthworms. In wetter or rockier regions, the soil is more "podsolic"—bleached, sandy and less fertile than the true brown earths.

After the ice

Two million years ago, a series of ice sheets began to extend into the temperate latitudes. In Europe, species moving south before the advancing cold were cut off from the warmer climates by the east–west run of mountains. As a result, many varieties of plants and animals were killed off. Species were reduced still further in islands such as Britain, where the newly formed barriers of the English Channel, Irish Sea and North Sea made recolonization even more difficult after the ice had retreated.

Eastern Asia was one of the few areas in the world that escaped the extreme climatic changes of the ice ages and therefore its temperate forests, unlike those of Europe, still contain an enormous variety of tree species. North America also fared better than Europe, for although glaciers at one time extended deep into the continent, the north–south direction of the mountain ranges allowed relatively easy migration of trees southwards as the climate worsened. Hence most species survived and were able to reoccupy their former territories when the ice retreated. As a result, some 40 species of deciduous trees occur in the North American forests, and contribute to the spectacular display of color during the autumn, notably in the eastern USA. But a combination of climatic change and, more recently and importantly, of intense human activity, has meant that the remnants of temperate forest seen today differ greatly from the original forest in both composition and form. Only in remote regions such as the southern Appalachian Mountains do substantial areas of the original forest survive. Elsewhere, regrowth has occurred, but much of this is essentially scrub woodland.

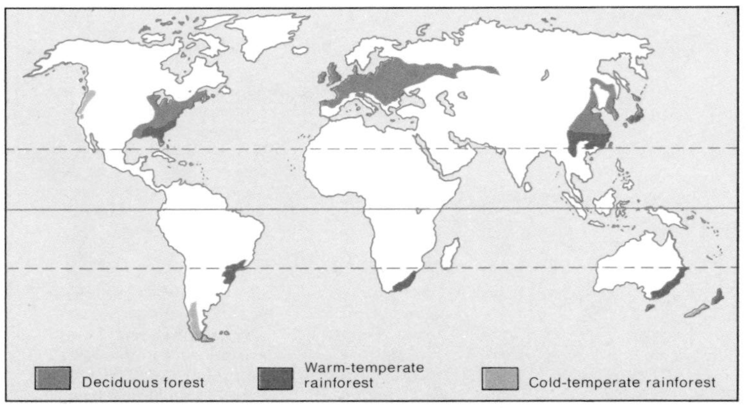

Natural distribution: in the northern hemisphere's temperate zone deciduous forests occur in the cooler areas—in eastern USA, northeastern China, Korea, the northern parts of Japan's Honshu island and western Europe. These forests only give way to evergreens in the warmer and wetter parts of the zone. In the southern hemisphere, the climate is generally rather milder throughout the temperate zone and so there are virtually no deciduous forests. Evergreen forests, however, can be found in southeastern South Africa, Chile, New Zealand, Australia and Tasmania.

The forest structure

Mature temperate deciduous forest is made up of distinct horizontal layers, particularly where the dominant tree is the oak, which allows enough light for a rich shrub layer to grow beneath it. The largest trees, such as oak, maple or ash, may be 25–50 m (80–160 ft) tall, and beneath them grows a prominent layer of smaller trees such as hazel, hornbeam or yew. Lower down again, a varied ground cover of perennial herbs, ferns, lichens and mosses flourishes in the comparative dampness of the forest floor. Because the trees are bare of leaves in winter, many of the plants growing on the forest floor take advantage of the warmth and light of spring to flower early in the year before the main trees come into full leaf and prevent the sun from reaching them. Various woody climbers, such as ivy and honeysuckle, are also present, growing over the trees and shrubs.

Much of the food supply in temperate forests is locked up in the trees themselves, but the annual fall of leaves in the deciduous forests produces a soil rich in nourishment. This supports a vast quantity of life, ranging in size from earthworms and insects to microscopic bacteria of the soil. The death of individual trees and branches also releases the food supply back to the earth. In shady, damp locations, insects, fungi, bacteria and other decomposing agents break down the leaves and other plant and animal debris more quickly, returning them to the soil as food for new plants.

Creatures of the forest

Temperate forests once contained many varieties of animal life, including several species of large animals. Herbivores such as wild oxen, wood bison, elk and moose ate grass and leaves; scavengers such as wild pigs rooted in the forest floor; predators such as wolves preyed on the other animals. Most of these have now been hunted to extinction by man or are extremely rare. Smaller animals still survive in comparatively large numbers, and include squirrels, chipmunks and raccoons, hedgehogs, wood mice, badgers and foxes.

The bird life of temperate forests is very diverse. Some species are insect eaters, exploring the bark and crevices for insects and grubs. Others, such as the wood pigeon, concentrate on seeds. Yet others, like the tawny owl, are predators. Complex interactions between predators and prey have developed at all levels of the forest, from the high canopy to the rotting ground litter, with each group evolving more efficient techniques of capture or escape in a kind of evolutionary race for survival.

The invertebrate insect life is also extremely varied and numerous, and forms a key component of the ecosystem. Oaks are particularly rich in insect life, and more than 100 species of moths feed on their leaves.

The plant and animal life of the temperate forest is remarkably rich and plentiful. And yet it is only a fraction of what once existed. Ever since man has occupied these regions he has found them so suited to his needs that he has long since cleared most of the original tree cover, replaced it with "civilization" and, in the process, destroyed innumerable species of forest wildlife.

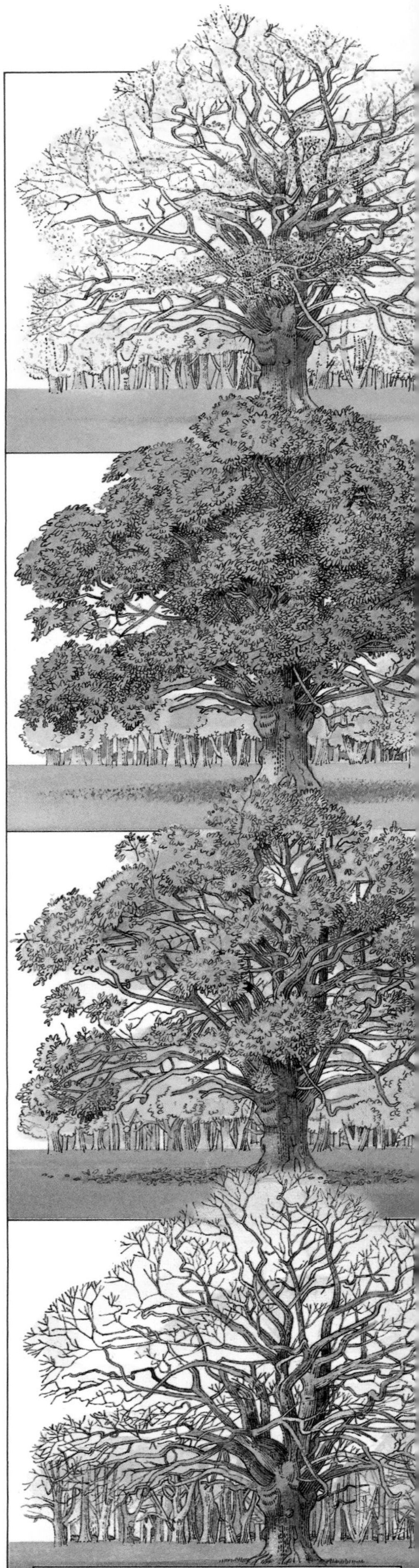

THE SEASONAL CYCLE

It is the cycle of the four seasons that gives the temperate deciduous forest its distinctive character. All animals and plants have adapted their ways of life to cope with the seasonal changes in heat, light, moisture and food. The yearly shedding and regrowth of the forest's leaves is one of the most striking and important of adaptations to the seasonal cycle and one that affects all other life in the forest. In summer the leafy canopy of the trees blocks out the sunlight from the forest floor and creates unsuitable conditions for many other plants to flourish. When the leaves fall they form a layer over the soil and provide winter protection for the plant roots and hibernating animals beneath the ground. Finally, once the dead leaves have been broken down, they give fertility to the soil and provide food for future generations of plants.

SPRING

Between February and April, the low spring sun climbs steadily higher in the sky and, streaming through the still leafless branches of the trees, falls more directly on the forest floor, warming the soil and melting the last frosts. As soon as the days become warmer the sluggish sap in the trees begins to flow more quickly, carrying nutrients to the branches, where leaf buds start to form.

Bluebell *Endymion non-scriptus*

Small plants of the forest floor, such as European bluebells and hepaticas taking advantage of the warm soil and plentiful light, flower in spring.

Hepatica *Hepatica nobilis*

European blackbird *Turdus merula*

Small emperor moth *Saturnia pavonia*

Forest insects emerge in spring, some, such as the emperor moth, from their winter cocoons, some from hibernation and some newly hatched from eggs.

Birds building nests in early spring make use of the forest's winter litter—broken twigs, dead leaves and dried grasses all serve as construction materials.

White-tailed deer *Odocoileus virginianus*

Woodchuck *Marmota monax*

Western European hedgehog *Erinaceus europaeus*

New plant growth and the increase in insects provide food for such animals as the North American woodchuck and the European hedgehog that wake thin and hungry from months of hibernation. Deer and other non-hibernating animals are also weak and thin—indeed many may have died during the harsh weather. The spring birth of young, however, soon restores their numbers.

SUMMER

By early summer the leaves of the trees are fully grown. They form a dense canopy, blocking out the sun and cooling the soil of the forest floor. Most of the small ground plants have long since finished flowering, but their leaves remain green and they continue actively storing food in their roots ready for their rapid spring growth.

Cranberry *Vaccinium oxycoccus*

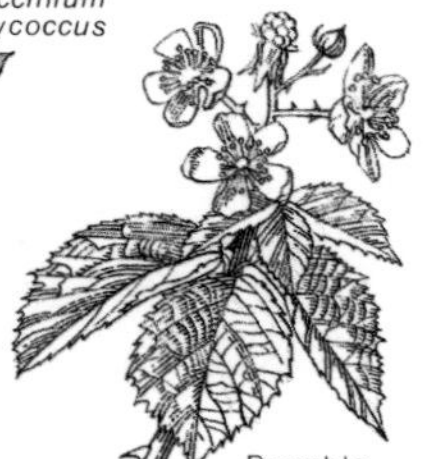

Bramble *Rubus* spp

Shrubs and bushes, such as bramble and cranberry, form tangled flowering masses wherever sunlight manages to filter through the forest's gloomy canopy.

Hordes of insects inhabit the forest in summer, living off the vast supply of food plants. The European stag beetle feeds on the sap of chestnut and oak trees.

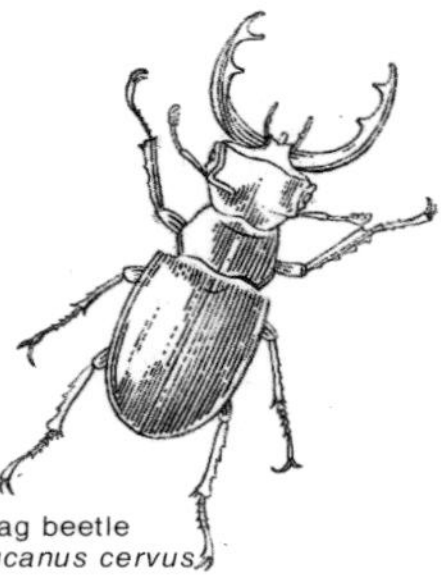

Stag beetle *Lucanus cervus*

Willow warbler *Phylloscopus trochilus*

The North American pewee and the willow warbler are two of the forest's many summer visitors that feed on the insect population. Some seed-eating birds, finches for example, also take advantage of this summer food supply.

Eastern wood pewee *Contopus virens*

Hazel mouse *Muscardinus avellanarius*

The hazel mouse protects its young by raising them in a summer nest, which it builds in a tree: almost every creature in the forest is viewed as a source of food by some other animal and the young litters are particularly at risk.

AUTUMN

As the autumn days grow shorter and cooler the forest foliage begins to turn color; the trees are responding to the drop in temperature and are cutting off the food supply to their leaves, which lose their green color and fall to the ground, forming a thick carpet on the forest's floor. Rain, frost, insects, earthworms and fungi then break down the leaves, making them part of the fertile forest soil.

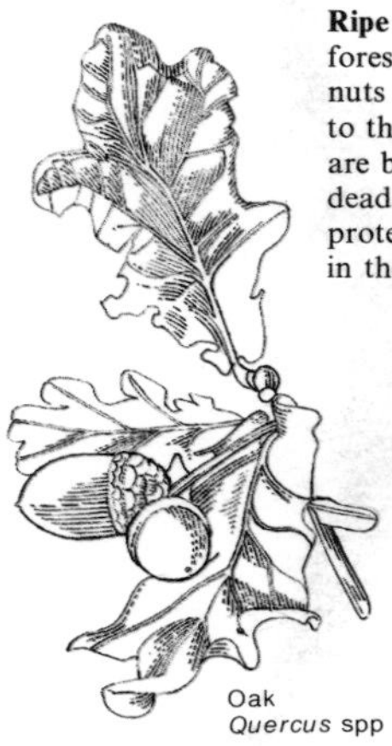

Oak *Quercus* spp

Ripe fruits and seeds of the forest trees—acorns, beech nuts and hazel nuts—drop to the ground, where a few are buried in the layers of dead leaves and remain protected until they sprout in the early spring.

Common hazel *Corylus avellana*

Acorn woodpecker *Melanerpes formicivorus*

Preparing for winter, the acorn woodpecker stores seeds in holes that it drills in tree trunks. Chipmunks hide supplies of nuts in their winter nests.

Eastern chipmunk *Tamias striatus*

American black bear *Ursus americanus*

The black bear of North America, like other winter hibernators, consumes vast quantities of food during autumn to build up its winter stores of food in the form of body fat.

WINTER

By winter, only evergreen shrubs and a few small hardy plants remain green. Many of the plants of the forest floor lose their green leaves during the first deep frost. The leaves of the trees still lie rotting on the bare ground, but within the soil, beneath the protective layers of leaf litter, plants are growing and spring flowers are developing buds.

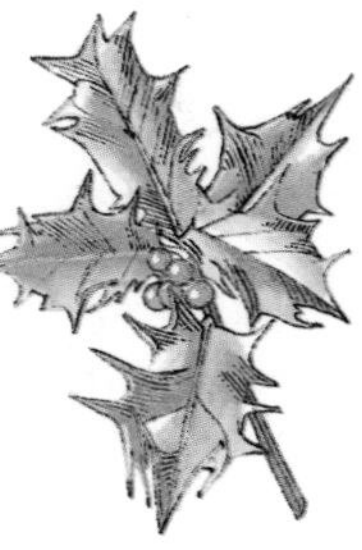

Holly *Ilex* spp

Late-fruiting plants, such as holly, mistletoe and dog rose, provide food for winter residents of the temperate forest such as the European hawfinch.

Hawfinch *Coccothraustes coccothraustes*

North American screech owl *Otus asio*

European woodcock *Scolopax rusticola*

Woodcocks are insect-eaters. They can survive winter by prizing insects from the soil with their long beaks, providing that the ground is not too deeply frozen.

Owls and foxes remain fairly active in winter, regularly leaving their nests or lairs to catch small animals or birds that are also in search of food.

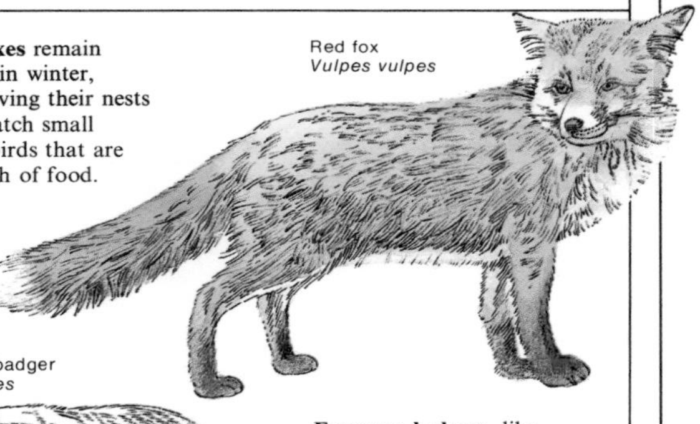

Red fox *Vulpes vulpes*

European badger *Meles meles*

European badgers, like racoons, opossums, bears and skunks, are "shallow" hibernators. On mild winter days they wake and go to search for food.

THE EVERGREEN TEMPERATE RAINFORESTS

There are two main kinds of temperate rainforest, the warm temperate, such as can still be found on North Island, New Zealand (left), and the cold temperate, such as that of the Chilean coast. Both of these kinds of forest have one major feature in common: they have enough water for even the most moisture-greedy plants, such as mosses and ferns, to grow throughout the year. The animal life of the forest is also affected by the abundance of rain, so that snails, slugs, frogs and other water-loving creatures flourish. Most temperate rainforest is of the warm-temperate kind, normally found on the edges of subtropical regions, and the vegetation, with palms, lianas, bamboos, as well as ferns and mosses, is similar to, although less rich than, the tropical rainforest's vegetation. The cold-temperate rainforests grow in cooler regions but their coastal position means that the climate is milder and wetter than inland (where deciduous trees dominate). Their vegetation is less lush and less varied than the warm-temperate forests, but mosses and ferns grow in abundance. Broad-leaved evergreens, such as New Zealand's southern beech, are the most common trees of these forests, although on the northwestern coast of North America Douglas firs and other conifers outnumber the broad-leaved evergreen species.

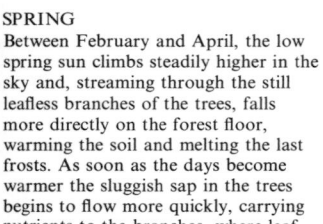

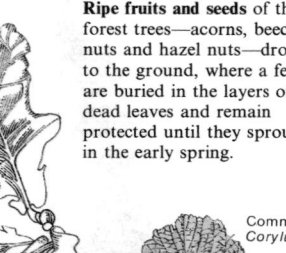

Man and the Temperate Forests

Temperate forests have suffered enormously at the hands of man. For the great civilizations of China, Europe and, later, North America the forests not only yielded cropland for expanding populations but also contributed materials and fuel for early technologies. More recently the demands of industry have reduced the forests still further. But today, scientists believe that this depleted resource could again play an important role in providing energy, food and materials for future generations.

PERMANENT SETTLEMENT
The Bronze Age and, later, the Iron Age laid the foundations of Chinese and Western civilizations. The forest shrank as permanent settlements grew (3) and, with the use of metals and improved technology, agricultural land was extended (4). But the forest was recognized as an important resource and areas were protected. Management techniques were introduced that, especially in medieval Europe, changed dense forest to coppice woods (5).

EARLY INDUSTRIAL TIMES
Sources of cropland and timber had been discovered in the New World, but in the Far East and Europe forests were drastically reduced. Virtually no Chinese forest remained, and in Europe nations began importing timber to serve growing industrial needs (6). To help solve shortages, plantations were established on country estates (7), which were often landscaped into parkland and planted with introduced species of trees (8).

PREHISTORIC FORESTS
Hunter gatherers made clearings in the forest when they cut brushwood for building shelters and for fuel (1): human impact on the temperate forest was small. But 7,000 years ago in Europe, 6,000 years ago in eastern Asia and 1,000 years ago in eastern North America, the first farming communities of the temperate forest (2) began to clear larger pockets of forest to provide land for crops and timber for houses and tools.

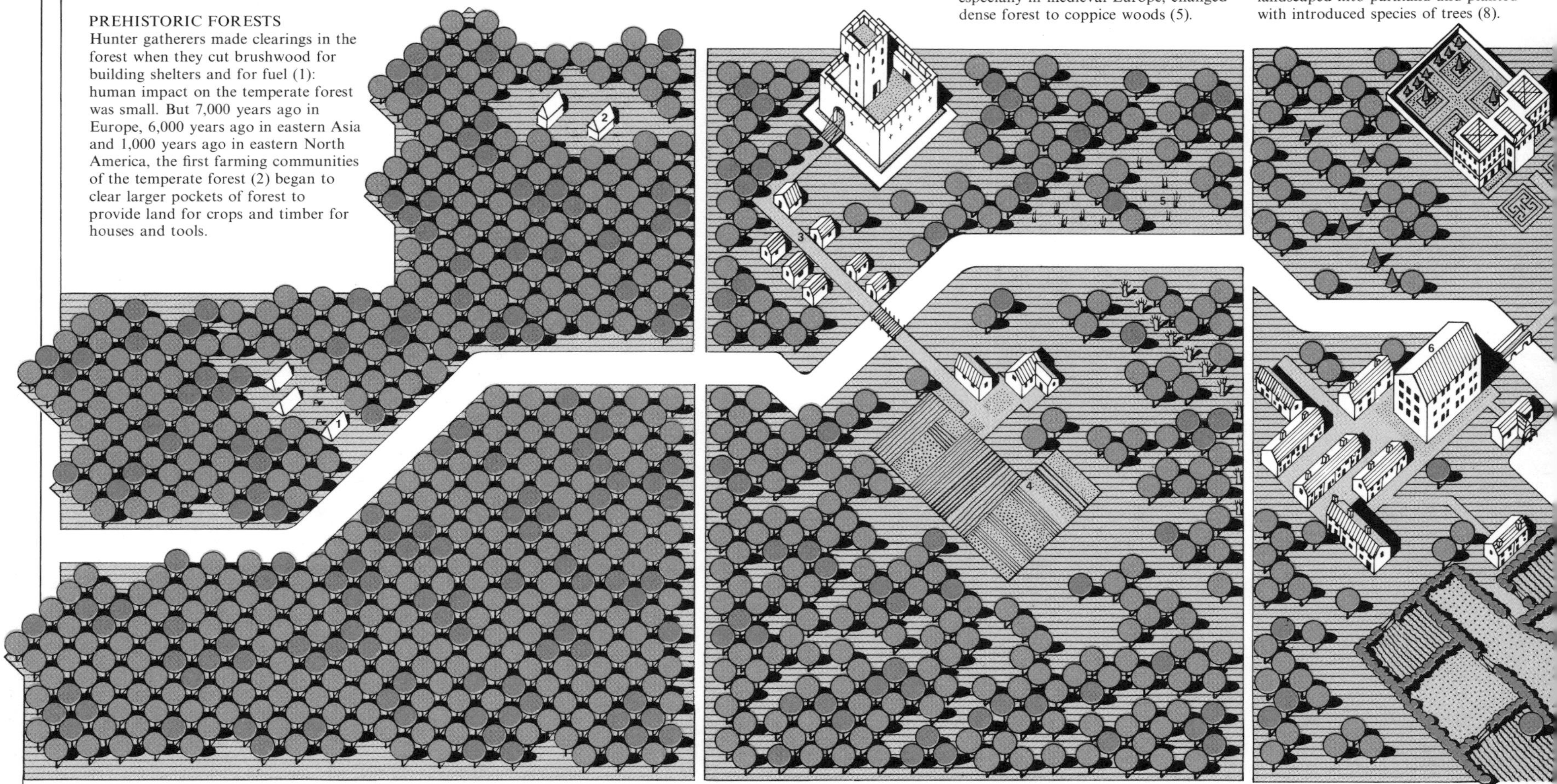

The aurochs, or wild ox, was one of the many forest animals that provided food for early hunter gatherers. Once man began to farm the land, he domesticated some of these animals—the wild boar, the aurochs and the wild turkey.

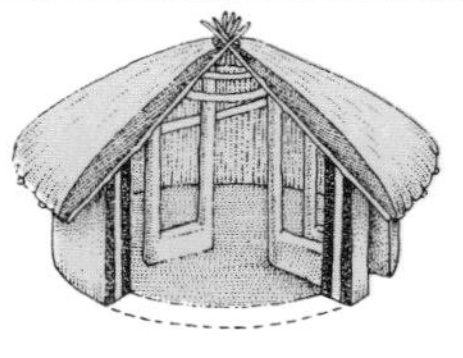

The dwellings of the late Neolithic Chinese were relatively sophisticated, reflecting an increasingly settled way of life that was soon to alter the landscape as forests were felled to provide building materials and land to plant crops.

The fortified villages and the farms of the Eastern Woodland Indians were set in semipermanent clearings cut in the North American forest. Before European settlement, however, human populations were small and deforestation was negligible.

Grain harvesting is depicted in a Chinese tomb image. By the 1st century AD, China contained nearly 60 million people, and agriculture, along with stock raising and metal mining, was drastically depleting the tree cover.

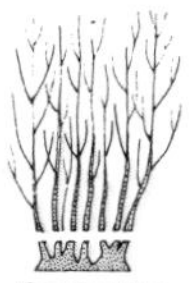

Coppicing

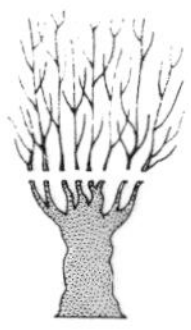

Pollarding

Coppicing and pollarding allowed continual cropping of forests. Branches were cut from trees, the bases of which were left to regrow shoots. This technique reduced the density of tree cover, encouraging a richer growth of ground plants.

Production of charcoal (below), which was a basic raw material for smelting in early industrial times, was responsible for much deforestation of the land.

Human interference with the forests goes back deep into prehistory. There is evidence that fire was used to stampede hunted animals in southern Europe as long as 400,000 years ago. Human populations, while they remained small, had only a slight effect on the vast stretches of primeval forest. Even so, hunting practices and the use of fire to clear land reduced some of the forests of Europe and Asia even before the invention of agriculture. In the New World, too, Eastern Woodland Indians had already affected the North American forests, and early Maori hunters had burned much of the tree cover of New Zealand by the time Europeans arrived.

Nevertheless it was the development of agriculture in Neolithic (New Stone Age) times that had the first really destructive effect on the temperate forests. Clearings were made for crops and the felled trees provided fuel and building material for the new communities. Large forest animals suffered as well, some (such as deer) being hunted for food and others (such as wolves) because they threatened grazing animals. But it was the population increase resulting from the new, settled way of life that caused the extension of man-made cropland deep into former forests.

With man's development of metals, more forests were destroyed: wood and charcoal were used for smelting and the new iron tools made tree clearance easier and more thorough. Firing of forests was also a familiar military ploy, used by such warriors as the Romans.

Medieval woodlands

By medieval times, large tracts of forest had been cleared in Europe and in the Far East, although in the former area there remained extensive royal hunting forest reserves. Local woodlands were carefully managed to serve the needs of the community; the techniques used included pollarding and coppicing.

Pollarding involved the cropping of main branches at a certain height above ground. In coppicing, the "coppice with standards" method was used to harvest the smaller species, such as hazel and hornbeam, whereas the standards (such as oaks) were cut on a longer rotation of 100 years or so. Alternatively, the oak itself could be part of the coppice crop, its stems being cut near ground level so that shoots arose from the stump, to be cut 10 to 20 years later. For local communities, industries and cities, forests provided a variety of materials for building, tanning and fencing, as well as dyestuffs, charcoal and domestic fuel.

The growth of the iron and shipbuilding industries in the sixteenth century devastated so much woodland and forest that in many regions good timber became scarce and had to be imported from considerable distances. The pressure on woodland continued until the production of coke and cheap coal brought some relaxation, but by the early twentieth century the coppice system had broken down and management of Europe's woodlands had largely been abandoned. In Europe the poor state of the deciduous forests was further worsened by two world wars. Many countries have since set up organizations with the specific task of building reserves of timber. Economic pressures, however, have led to the planting mainly of quick-growing conifers, rather than typical trees of the temperate deciduous forest.

New World forests

The migrants who settled in the New World were the descendants of the people who had largely destroyed the forests of Europe. Confronted by the temperate deciduous forests of eastern North America, they virtually continued where they had left off. Tracts were cleared to create arable and range land and to provide the massive amounts of timber needed for the colonization, industrialization and urbanization of North America. With the opening of the prairie lands for agriculture, however,

Disturbance to the natural vegetation has occurred throughout the temperate forest zone. Exploitation of this biome's greatest resource, its agricultural potential, has been one of the major causes of deforestation. The only forests that have escaped major disturbance are in remote areas, too rocky or too steep for cultivation. Today, intensive farming is still a major economic activity of the temperate forest regions. But farmland is not the only important resource to have disturbed the forests. Mining for key minerals such as copper, iron and coal, all of which made possible the development of Western and Chinese civilization, has also contributed to destruction of the forest cover. For centuries the forests provided man with food, fuel and materials, but, ironically, it has been the removal of the forest that has enabled man to exploit the most important of these regions' resources.

THE CHANGING LANDSCAPE

Mankind has been occupying the temperate forest regions for many thousands of years, at first with little effect on the natural forest ecology. But during the last 2,000 years human activity has destroyed the original tree cover at an accelerating pace. As populations increased and economies developed—at different rates in the three major regions—forests disappeared to be replaced by farms, cities, industries and communications networks. Today, scarcely any of the original forest cover remains.

THE 19TH CENTURY
The Industrial Revolution developed in Europe and the New World, large towns and cities sprang up (9), pushing back the woodlands and forests still farther. This process was aided by the spreading network of railroads (10). Coke, iron and other minerals were replacing timber products as raw materials for growing industries (11), but demands were still made on the forests to provide, for example, railway sleepers and mine pit props.

FORESTS TODAY
The 20th century has seen an increasing trend towards urbanization in areas that were once temperate forest. Housing complexes (12) and new factory sites (13) cover large areas, while roadbuilding (14), industrial agriculture (15) and open-cast mining (16) destroy remaining woodland. Leisure areas (17) and nature reserves protect some woods, but plantations of exotic conifers (18) do not always provide suitable wildlife habitats.

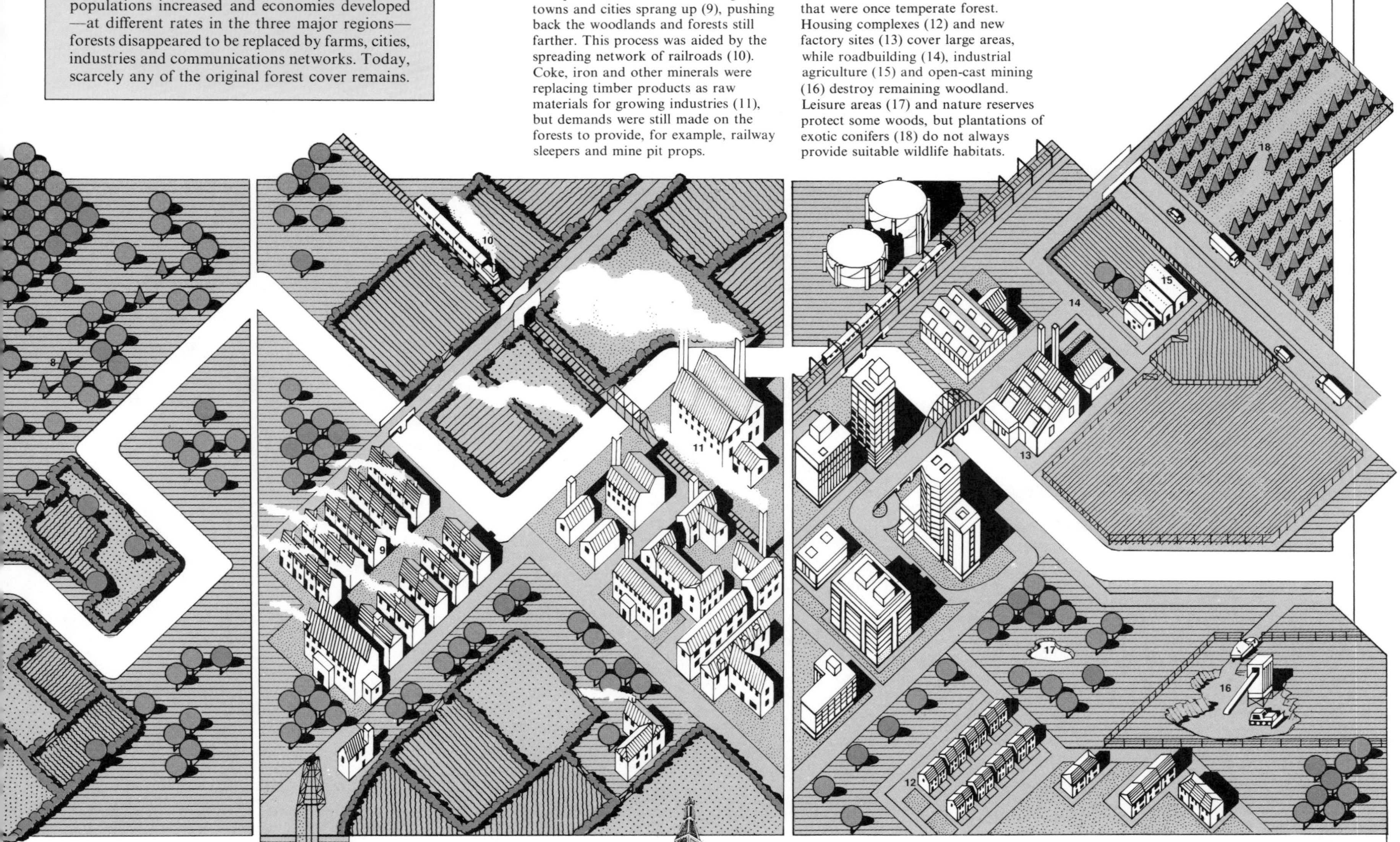

Early pioneers in the USA (below) transformed forestland as they moved west. By 1830 most of the eastern forests had been felled for settlement.

Mining in the 19th century (below) made available coal, which, for the first time, was being converted to coke and iron makers no longer needed charcoal.

Large department stores appeared in 19th-century Chicago, a town that, within 100 years, had been transformed from a remote fort to a city. This rapid growth reflected the huge population increase in many 19th-century towns.

A reafforestation scheme (below) was set up in China in 1950 to replant areas that lost their original forest cover many centuries ago. Similar projects are under way in many other temperate forest regions.

The European wood bison has escaped extinction because one herd of the animals has lived, for centuries, in a royal hunting reserve. Today, wildlife parks throughout temperate regions protect endangered forest species.

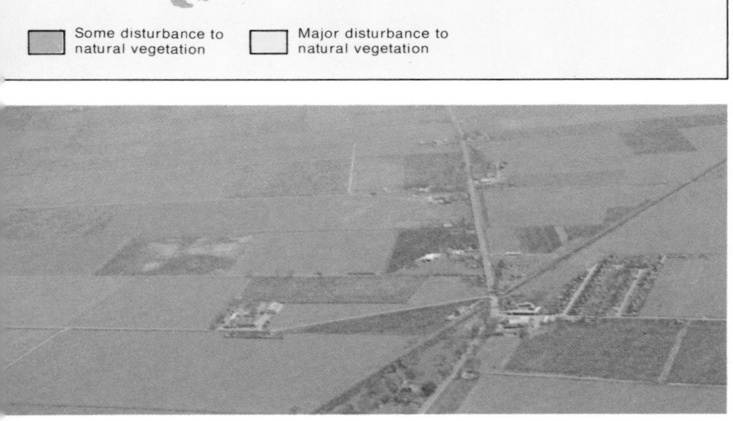

the pressures shifted, some of the east coast deciduous forest grew up again, and it is possible that parts of the eastern USA may have nearly as much forest cover now as when the settlers first arrived. Nevertheless, other areas of forestland have been destroyed in recent decades by strip mining and the creation of a vast road and rail network. In the southern hemisphere, especially in the last 200 years, the temperate rainforests of Australia and New Zealand have been subjected to much the same pattern of events, although on a smaller and somewhat less devastating scale.

Conservation

Today the general need to preserve and extend the woodlands is clearly recognized, but great uncertainty exists about their future. The demand for hardwoods for veneers, quality papermaking and furniture still exceeds supply. Oak is still the preferred material for some types of boat building and, especially in Europe, for joinery work. But one of the major difficulties with forestry as a land use is forecasting future trends within the industry, largely as a result of the long-term nature of the crop—hardwood trees planted today will not yield their timber until well into the next century. Government tax policies can be all important in deciding whether the majority of woodlands are, or will continue to be, sound economic investments.

Temperate forests and woodlands still exist in sizeable quantities in central Europe and the USA, but many of today's plots, particularly in western Europe, are far too small for efficient conservation of plant and animal life, and are isolated from other woods. As a result, successful breeding and exchange of genetic material is very difficult, especially when modern agriculture is rapidly destroying the linking corridors of hedgerows. The use of woodlands for recreation is also presenting considerable problems. Controlling agencies have been formed to cope with leisure demands, and a start has been made in the multiple use of forests for recreation, conservation and timber felling, but progress still needs to be made in harmonizing these potentially conflicting interests. Meanwhile, natural expanses of woodland and forest are still being lost to agricultural and urban expansion and to plantations of nonnative conifers.

Temperate forests are a biologically efficient form of land use. In terms of biomass—the amount of living material (animal and plant) in any one area—they could still play an important role in the provision of food, materials and even renewable energy. Thus on scientific, economic and aesthetic grounds a strong case can be made for immediate conservation measures.

Mediterranean Regions

Forests of evergreen trees once covered much of the Mediterranean regions. They flourished in spite of the hot, rainless summer months – as the original plant life, they had evolved to survive such harsh conditions. Man, however, has proved to be a greater threat than the climate. He introduced domestic animals and cleared the land to grow crops; the natural vegetation was burned, browsed and plowed into nonexistence. Man's activities left behind tracts of impoverished soil which rapidly became scrubland. Today, scrub is the most typical vegetation in all the Mediterranean climate zones throughout the world.

CONVERGENCE
Isolated from each other by enormous areas of land and ocean, regions with a Mediterranean type of climate rarely have any plant species in common. But, by a process known as "convergent evolution," the plant communities in each of these areas have produced remarkably similar responses to their similar environments. This can be seen in the conifer communities, the broad-leaved evergreen trees, and in the various hardy shrubs and ground plants typical of each of the regions.

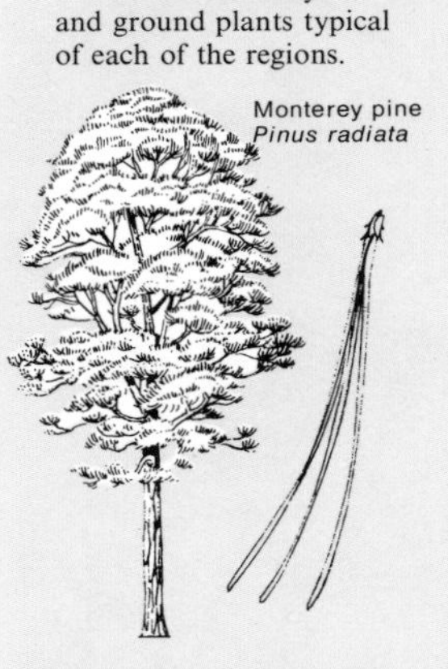
Monterey pine
Pinus radiata

California's Monterey pine and other Mediterranean conifers—South African podocarps and Chile pines, for example—have needle-shaped leaves that prevent rapid loss of water from such trees during drought.

Bailey's mimosa
Acacia baileyana

Nonconiferous evergreens such as Australia's acacias and eucalypts, Chile's *quillajas* and California's evergreen oaks are typical Mediterranean trees. Their leathery leaves limit summer moisture loss.

Giant protea
Protea cynaroides

Shrubs and ground plants show various adaptations to drought. South African proteas and Europe's laurel have thick evergreen leaves. Narrow leaves and water-storing roots are other common adaptations.

Long, hot, dry summers and warm, moist winters form the seasonal rhythm of the "Mediterranean" year. This climatic pattern can be found in small areas of nearly every continent in the world, typically on the western side of landmasses and in the mild, temperate latitudes. North America's "Mediterranean" is in California, South America's occurs in Chile and Africa's lies at the southern tip of Cape Province. Australia has two small "Mediterranean" areas, one on the southern coast and one on the western. Europe's Mediterranean region, which has given its name to this climate, covers much of the southern part of the continent and extends into northern Africa.

Wherever Mediterranean conditions prevail, the native plant life has adapted to survive the scanty annual rainfall and the long summer droughts. Some species have developed deep root systems that can tap low summer water tables, and many of the ground plants—such as bulbs and aromatic herbs—grow vigorously only in early summer while rain still moistens the soil. But it is the broad-leaved evergreens with their drought-resistant leaves that are the most typical of the Mediterranean areas.

This natural pattern of vegetation has been drastically altered by man. In southern Europe in particular, almost all the original evergreen forests have long since been destroyed and thickets of fast-growing, tough scrub plants have grown up in their place. This scrub, which once probably covered only small areas, is now so widespread that it is considered the most typically Mediterranean of all kinds of vegetation. It is the *maquis* of France, the *macchia* of Italy and the *mattoral* of Spain. A similar type of vegetation (although containing different species) can also be found in South Africa's fynbos, in California's chapparal, and in Australia's tracts of natural mallee scrub.

Classical land use

Southern Europe, with its long history of human settlement, farming and pastoralism, is the most altered of all the Mediterranean regions. Over the centuries vast tracts of original vegetation have been removed, either by farmers (for crop growing) or by grazing animals. And, particularly on the steep slopes and rocky outcrops, this has resulted in extensive deterioration and erosion of the soil. Agriculture generally has less serious effects upon the vegetation than has animal grazing. Mankind has learned, over many hundreds of years, which are the most suitable crops for the various soils, terrain and climatic conditions of the region. The Mediterranean "triad" of wheat on the lowlands and olives and vines on the hills has been a successful combination since Classical times.

Pastoral plundering of the land, however, has more serious consequences. The virtually omnivorous goat is particularly damaging and can strip a whole forest of its foliage, bark, shrubs, ground plants and grass. After such an assault the vegetation rarely returns to its former condition; normally, a scrubby growth of kermes oak and shrubs springs up to form a typical maquis-type vegetation.

The rise and fall of each great Mediterranean civilization has seen forests destroyed in one area after another. The Greek colonization of southern Italy was provoked by deforestation and soil erosion in Attica. The Romans extended clearance north to the Po valley and into eastern Tunisia. From the seventh century onwards, Muslims made great inroads into the forests of North Africa as well as southern and eastern Spain; and in the north of Spain and southern France, medieval monks cleared forested valleys. During the seventeenth and eighteenth centuries large areas of Provence and Italy were cleared to plant vines and this process continued in the 1800s, when the great wine-producing areas of Languedoc and Algeria were established. During this time the iron industries of Spain and northern Italy, with their growing need for charcoal, were adding to the destruction. Recent reafforestation efforts have been puny compared to past degradation.

Protected species

But throughout this history of forest removal some tree species have been protected. These have been the natural tree crops that have, at times, supported complete peasant economies. The chestnut forests of Corsica, for example, sustained a large rural population until this century; the chestnuts provided flour for bread and fodder for pigs. In Portugal and Sardinia the cork-oak forests are still important today.

It is the olive, however, symbol of peace and of New Testament landscapes, that is the Mediterranean's most characteristic tree crop. Of all the Mediterranean plants, it is the most perfectly adapted to its environment, with its deep roots to search out scarce water and its hard, shiny leaves to conserve what it finds. In fact, the summer drought is essential to olive growers for it encourages the build-up of oil in the fruit. Paradoxically, however, the olive—like the vine, the fig and many other "Mediterranean" crops—did not originate in the Mediterranean but was introduced from Asia Minor.

In spite of massive destruction of the natural landscape, mankind has learned many valuable lessons during his occupation of this region. Ideas that were to become important in laying the foundations of sound land management policy were developed in the Mediterranean area. Hillside terracing, irrigation, crop rotation and manuring were all, from necessity, practiced from early times. The flourishing agricultural industries of the world's other Mediterranean regions—the wine industry of California, the vast soft-fruit plantations of Australia and the citrus industry of South Africa—all owe a considerable debt to the generations of farmers who learned to exploit the red soils of the Mediterranean basin.

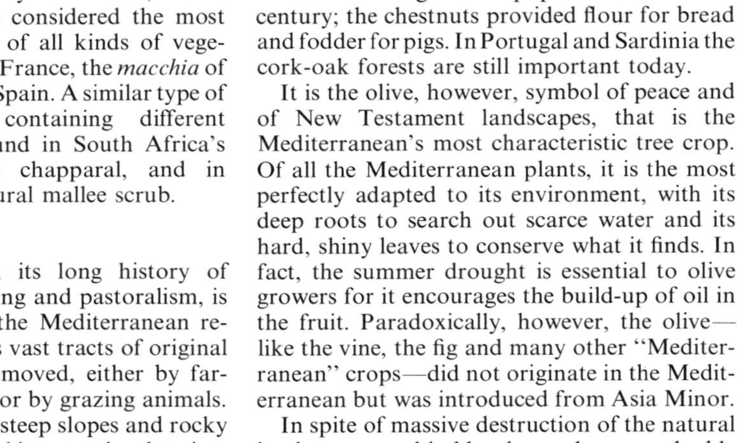
Mediterranean climate regions

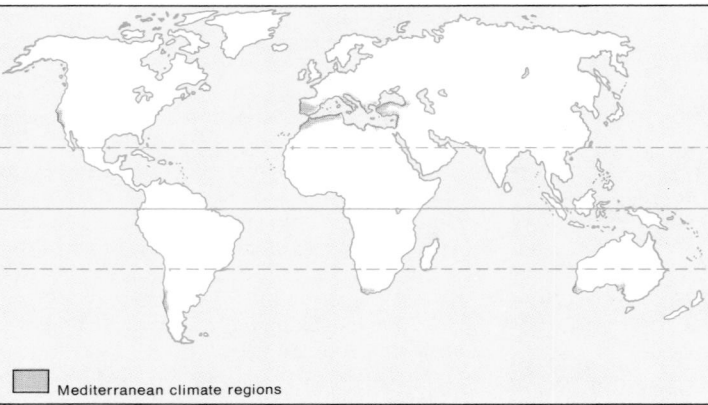

The Mediterranean regions occur between the latitudes 30° and 40°, on the western and southwestern sides of the continents. These areas are affected in summer by the high-pressure systems of nearby desert regions, and in winter by wet, low-pressure systems brought in from the oceans and over the land by the prevailing Westerlies. This distinct seasonal shifting of major influences on the climate produces the hot, waterless summers and warm, moist, sometimes stormy winters typical of the Mediterranean climate.

MAN AND THE MEDITERRANEAN
Even by Classical times, the once-forested lands fringing the Mediterranean Sea were suffering from massive deforestation and soil erosion. In the 5th century BC, Plato described the bare, dry hills of Attica, recently stripped of their woodlands. "What now remains," he wrote, "is like the skeleton of a sick man, all the fat and soft earth having been wasted away." By the end of the Classical period, irreparable damage had been done. At the same time, however, mankind was gradually learning through the mistakes he had already made. Suitable patterns of land use, better farming practices and improved land management techniques were slowly being adopted and were enabling man to make better use of the much-altered Mediterranean landscape.

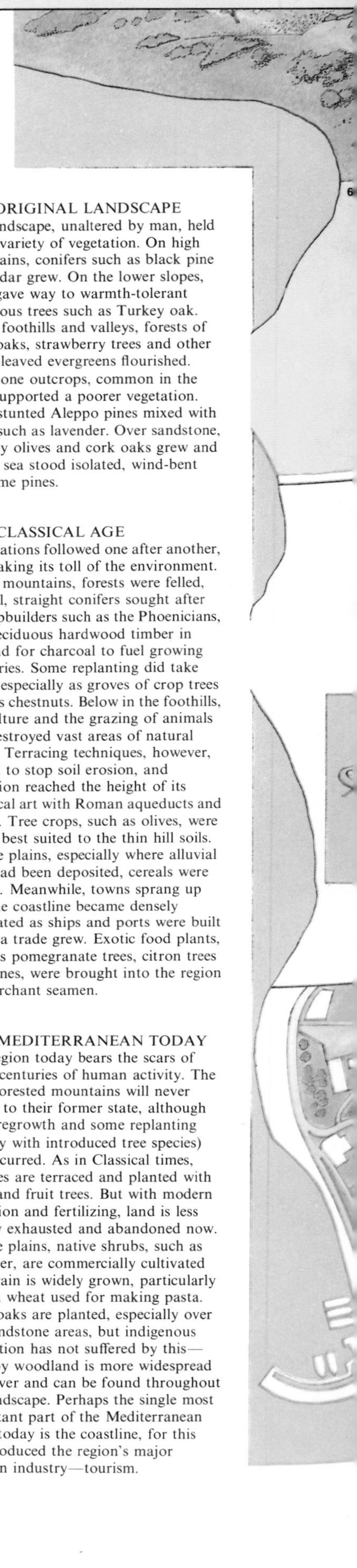

THE ORIGINAL LANDSCAPE
The landscape, unaltered by man, held a rich variety of vegetation. On high mountains, conifers such as black pine and cedar grew. On the lower slopes, these gave way to warmth-tolerant deciduous trees such as Turkey oak. In the foothills and valleys, forests of holm oaks, strawberry trees and other broad-leaved evergreens flourished. Limestone outcrops, common in the area, supported a poorer vegetation. Here, stunted Aleppo pines mixed with herbs such as lavender. Over sandstone, scrubby olives and cork oaks grew and by the sea stood isolated, wind-bent maritime pines.

THE CLASSICAL AGE
Civilizations followed one after another, each taking its toll of the environment. In the mountains, forests were felled, the tall, straight conifers sought after by shipbuilders such as the Phoenicians, and deciduous hardwood timber in demand for charcoal to fuel growing industries. Some replanting did take place, especially as groves of crop trees such as chestnuts. Below in the foothills, agriculture and the grazing of animals had destroyed vast areas of natural forest. Terracing techniques, however, helped to stop soil erosion, and irrigation reached the height of its Classical art with Roman aqueducts and canals. Tree crops, such as olives, were found best suited to the thin hill soils. On the plains, especially where alluvial soils had been deposited, cereals were grown. Meanwhile, towns sprang up and the coastline became densely populated as ships and ports were built and sea trade grew. Exotic food plants, such as pomegranate trees, citron trees and vines, were brought into the region by merchant seamen.

THE MEDITERRANEAN TODAY
The region today bears the scars of many centuries of human activity. The once-forested mountains will never return to their former state, although some regrowth and some replanting (mostly with introduced tree species) has occurred. As in Classical times, hillsides are terraced and planted with vines and fruit trees. But with modern irrigation and fertilizing, land is less readily exhausted and abandoned now. On the plains, native shrubs, such as lavender, are commercially cultivated and grain is widely grown, particularly durum wheat used for making pasta. Cork oaks are planted, especially over dry sandstone areas, but indigenous vegetation has not suffered by this—scrubby woodland is more widespread than ever and can be found throughout the landscape. Perhaps the single most important part of the Mediterranean basin today is the coastline, for this has produced the region's major modern industry—tourism.

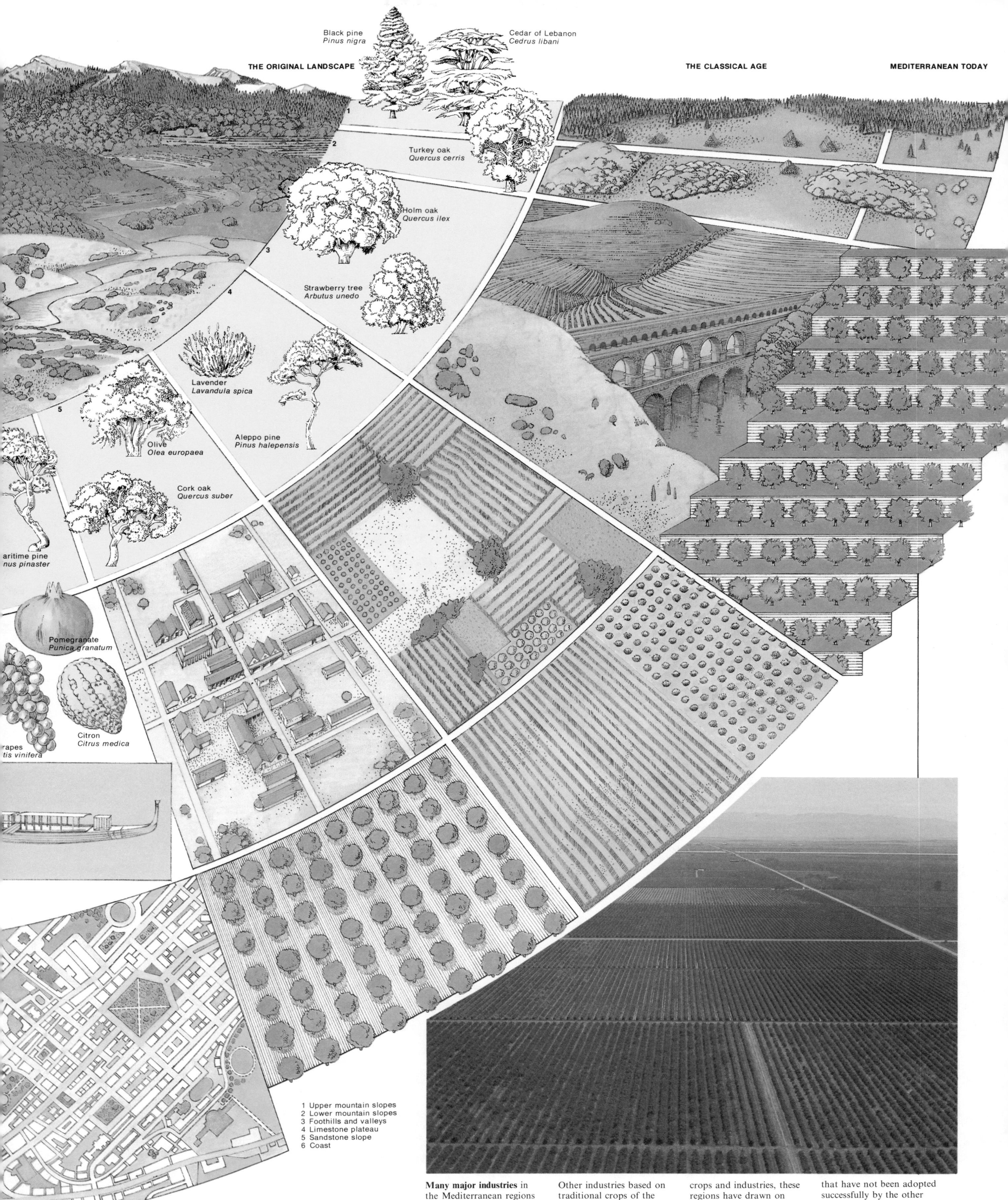

Black pine
Pinus nigra
Cedar of Lebanon
Cedrus libani
THE ORIGINAL LANDSCAPE
THE CLASSICAL AGE
MEDITERRANEAN TODAY
1
2
Turkey oak
Quercus cerris
Holm oak
Quercus ilex
3
Strawberry tree
Arbutus unedo
4
Lavender
Lavandula spica
Aleppo pine
Pinus halepensis
5
Olive
Olea europaea
Cork oak
Quercus suber
aritime pine
nus pinaster
Pomegranate
Punica granatum
Citron
Citrus medica
rapes
tis vinifera
1 Upper mountain slopes
2 Lower mountain slopes
3 Foothills and valleys
4 Limestone plateau
5 Sandstone slope
6 Coast

Many major industries in the Mediterranean regions are based on processing and packaging of traditional Mediterranean crops—the vineyards of California (above) support a vast wine industry, for example. Other Mediterranean areas in Australia, in South Africa and even in Chile also now produce wines. Other industries based on traditional crops of the Mediterranean basin include the preserving, canning and drying of soft fruits, such as peaches and apricots, and citrus fruits. Today, all of these are grown and processed on a large scale in Australia, North America and South Africa. When first establishing their crops and industries, these regions have drawn on southern Europe's long experience and well-tested practices, although, particularly in California, mechanization has been widely introduced and the scale of production has increased phenomenally. There are only two major southern European crops that have not been adopted successfully by the other Mediterranean regions—olives and cork. Today, the Mediterranean basin is still the source of 90 percent of the world's olive oil and, despite repeated attempts to introduce cork oaks into other regions, this area is still the world's only producer of cork.

Temperate Grasslands

Compared with other flowering plants, grasses are newcomers to the Earth. They appeared only 60 million years ago, but since then they have proved to be an extremely successful family of plants. Today, the grasses dominate large areas of the world's natural vegetation and play a vital part in the intricate balance of plant and animal life in these regions. In spite of the inroads made by man, vast stretches of original grassland still cover the interiors of the North American and Eurasian landmasses.

The prairies of North America and the steppes of Eurasia extend far into the interiors of the northern continents. These are the best known and the most extensive of the world's temperate grasslands. The southern hemisphere, however, has examples in the veld of South Africa and the pampas of South America. Extensive grasslands also occur in southern Australia, although these are sometimes described as semiarid scrub because of the high average temperatures and the prolonged droughts in the region.

Temperate grasslands probably developed wherever the rainfall was too low to support forest and too high to result in semiarid regions, conditions found typically in the interiors of large continents. Continental interiors tend to be somewhat drier than coastal regions, but they are also characterized by extreme changes in temperature from one season to the next. In the North American grasslands, for example, winter temperatures may fall well below freezing whereas summer temperatures of 38°C (100°F) are not unusual. And these sharp fluctuations in seasonal temperature greatly influence how much of the rainfall is made available to plants. In summer particularly, when most of the rain falls, high temperatures, strong winds and lack of protective tree cover cause much of the moisture to evaporate before it can be absorbed into the soil.

Climatic conditions are not the only factor responsible for the distribution and form of the temperate grasslands. There are many pointers that indicate the importance of fire in determining their continuing existence and their extent. Natural fires, caused by lightning and fueled by the dry summer grasses, have always been a feature of these regions, but more recently, man-made fires have been crucial in fixing the boundary between forest and grassland.

Trees and shrubs frequently invade the margins of grasslands, but whenever there is a fire few of them survive. Grasses, however, have certain characteristics that enable them to withstand the potentially destructive impact of fire. The growing point of grasses is at the base of the leaves, close to the ground, and so destruction of the leaves above this point does not interrupt growth—in fact it may stimulate it. These same characteristics also serve to protect grasses from destruction by grazing animals. The large animals of these lands, such as the North American bison and the Eurasian horse, are able to crop the grasses without permanently damaging their food supply.

Grazers and predators

Large migrating herbivores with a strong herd instinct characterize one of the major types of temperate grassland animal. In the North American grasslands the bison (which may have numbered 60 million before being virtually exterminated by settlers) and the antelope-like pronghorn were the major examples of large herbivores. In Eurasia large herds of saiga antelopes, wild horses and asses at one time roamed the steppes, although they too have suffered from human activities, as has South America's largest grassland herd animal, the pampas deer. As these herds of grazing animals have been reduced, so have the carnivorous animals of the grasslands that preyed upon them. At one time, however, these predators played an important part in protecting the grasslands by continually keeping the numbers of grazing herd animals in check.

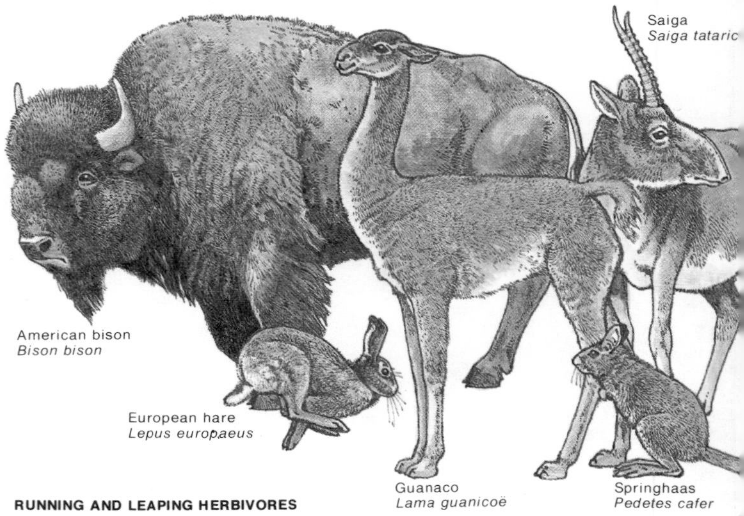
Saiga
Saiga tataric
American bison
Bison bison
European hare
Lepus europaeus
Guanaco
Lama guanicoë
Springhaas
Pedetes cafer
RUNNING AND LEAPING HERBIVORES

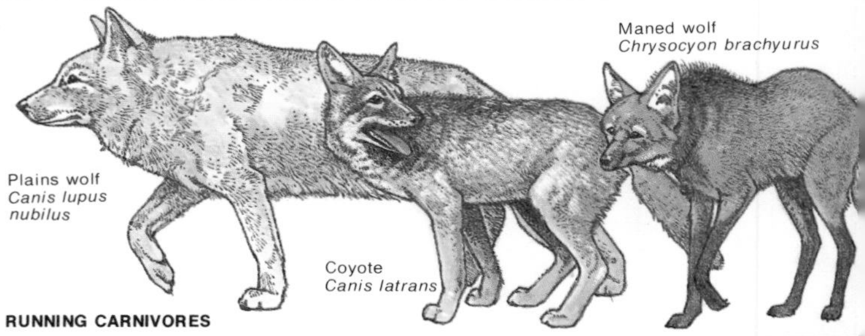
Maned wolf
Chrysocyon brachyurus
Plains wolf
Canis lupus nubilus
Coyote
Canis latrans
RUNNING CARNIVORES

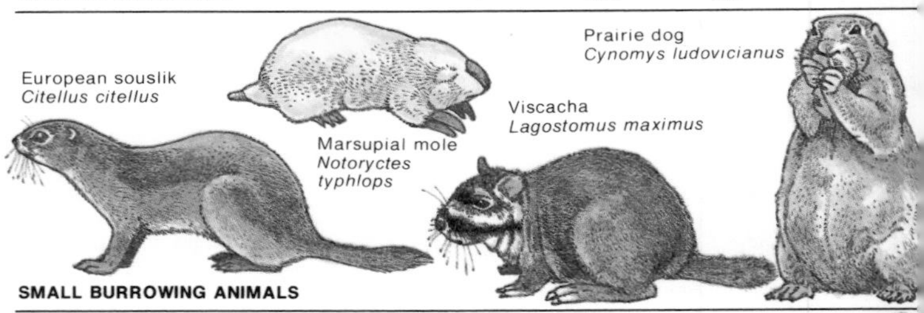
Prairie dog
Cynomys ludovicianus
European souslik
Citellus citellus
Viscacha
Lagostomus maximus
Marsupial mole
Notoryctes typhlops
SMALL BURROWING ANIMALS

Pampas cat
Lynchailurus pajeros
Black-footed ferret
Mustela nigripes
Marbled polecat
Vormela peregusna
Gopher snake
Pituophis melanoleucus
SMALL CARNIVORES

Russian tarragon
Artemisia dracunculoides

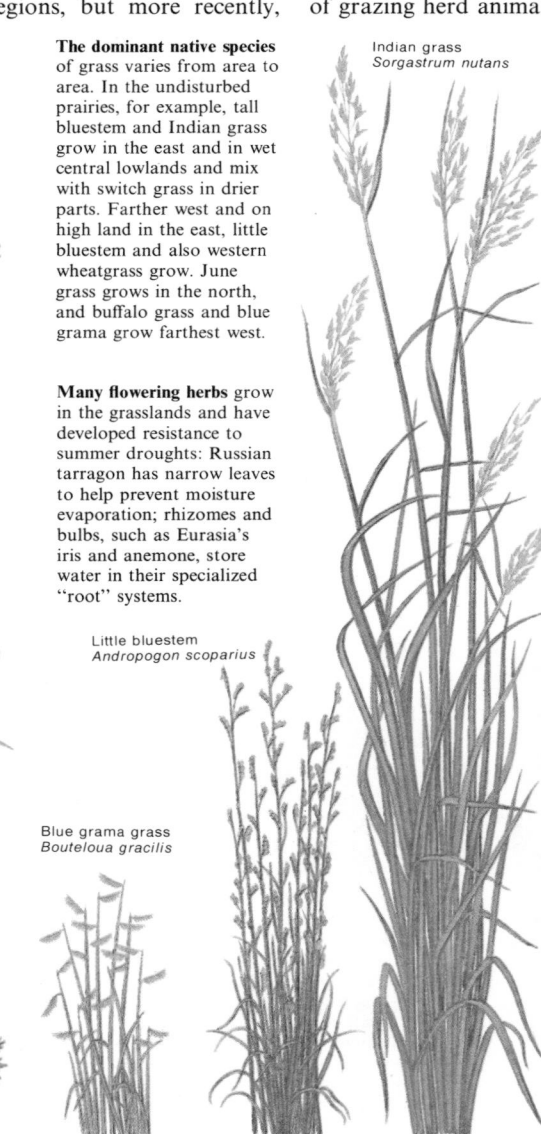

The dominant native species of grass varies from area to area. In the undisturbed prairies, for example, tall bluestem and Indian grass grow in the east and in wet central lowlands and mix with switch grass in drier parts. Farther west and on high land in the east, little bluestem and also western wheatgrass grow. June grass grows in the north, and buffalo grass and blue grama grow farthest west.

Many flowering herbs grow in the grasslands and have developed resistance to summer droughts: Russian tarragon has narrow leaves to help prevent moisture evaporation; rhizomes and bulbs, such as Eurasia's iris and anemone, store water in their specialized "root" systems.

Iris
Iris sibirica

Anemone
Anemone patens

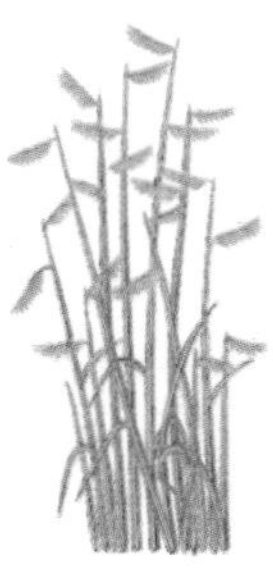
Blue grama grass
Bouteloua gracilis

Little bluestem
Andropogon scoparius

Indian grass
Sorgastrum nutans

The natural distribution of the temperate grasslands is dictated mainly by rainfall: most occur in continental interiors where there is too little rain for forest but enough to prevent desert from forming. Between these limits the large range in rainfall allows three main types of grassland: tall grass in wetter areas, mid-grass, and short grass in drier parts. The largest grasslands exist in North America, Eurasia, South America, in Australia's Murray–Darling river basin and on the South African plateau.

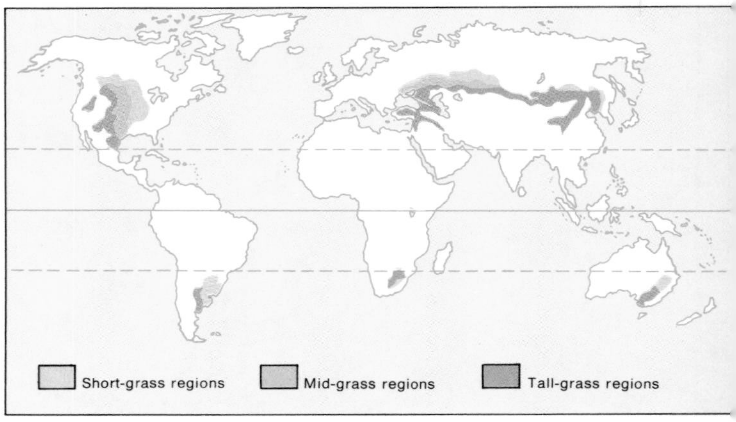
Short-grass regions
Mid-grass regions
Tall-grass regions

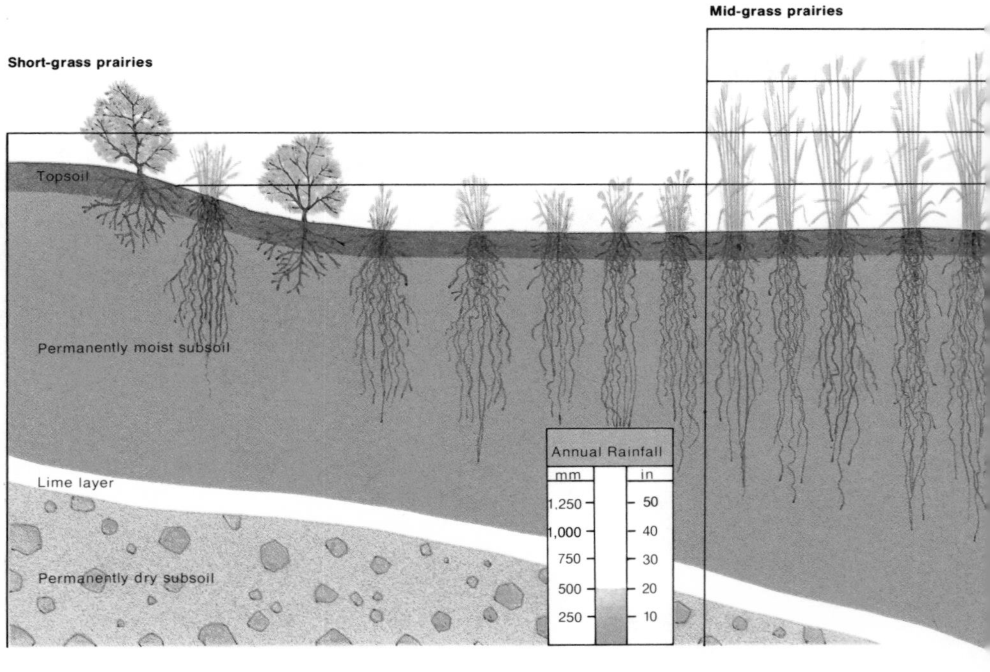
Short-grass prairies
Mid-grass prairies
Topsoil
Permanently moist subsoil
Lime layer
Permanently dry subsoil
Annual Rainfall
mm
in
1,250
1,000
750
500
250
50
40
30
20
10

GRASSLAND ADAPTATION

Animals of these regions have had to adapt to a difficult environment: vast, treeless expanses of grass offer little protection from harsh weather or predators. Different animals have found various answers to the problem and a clearly defined pattern of these adaptations can be traced throughout the grasslands.

Running and leaping herbivores survive because of their ability to move faster than a pursuer. The larger animals such as the Eurasian saiga, North America's bison and pronghorn and the guanaco of South America are runners. The leaping herbivores are usually smaller creatures that escape danger by bounding away to boltholes. They include the European hare and the African springhaas.

Running carnivores follow, and prey on, running and leaping herbivores. These animals, such as the coyote and the now extinct plains wolf of North America, and South America's maned wolf, also depend on speed—to enable them to catch their prey.

Small burrowing animals hide from predators by digging under the ground. Some, such as Australia's marsupial mole, spend most of their lives below ground. Others, such as the European souslik, South America's viscacha and North America's prairie dog, live and sleep under the ground but come to the surface to find food.

Small carnivores concentrate on the burrowers as their main source of food. They either, like the pampas cat, rely on surprise attack of their prey, or, like Eurasia's marbled polecat and the grasslands' many kinds of snake, depend on their long, lithe shape to follow creatures into their burrows.

Two distinctive types of grassland bird can be distinguished: the sky birds, which spend long periods of time on the wing, and the ground birds.

Birds of the sky include songbirds such as the skylark which, having no perch from which to proclaim its territory, sings in the sky, and birds of prey such as Eurasia's tawny eagle and North America's red-tailed hawk and prairie falcon, which ride the thermals scanning the ground for their prey.

Ground birds rarely take to the wing, although none has actually lost the ability to fly when necessary. They include birds such as the New World sage grouse and burrowing owl (which lives below ground in abandoned prairie dog burrows), the black grouse of Eurasia and songbirds such as North America's meadowlark.

Insects and other invertebrates have developed many different survival techniques. Some use camouflage: the praying mantis resembles a leaf bud and the tumble bug is the color of the dark grassland soil. Grasshoppers are miniature leaping herbivores and earthworms are small-scale versions of the grassland burrowers.

Skylark
Alauda arvensis
Red-tailed hawk
Buteo jamaicensis
Tawny eagle
Aquila rapax
Prairie falcon
Falco mexicanus
BIRDS OF THE SKY
Western meadowlark
Sturnella neglecta
Burrowing owl
Speotyto cunicularia
Sage grouse
Centrocercus urophasianus
Black grouse
Lyurus tetrix
GROUND BIRDS
Lubber grasshopper
Romalea microptera
Tumble bug
Canthonlaevis drury
Common earthworm
Lumbricus terrestris
Praying mantis
Mantis religiosa
INSECTS AND OTHER INVERTEBRATES

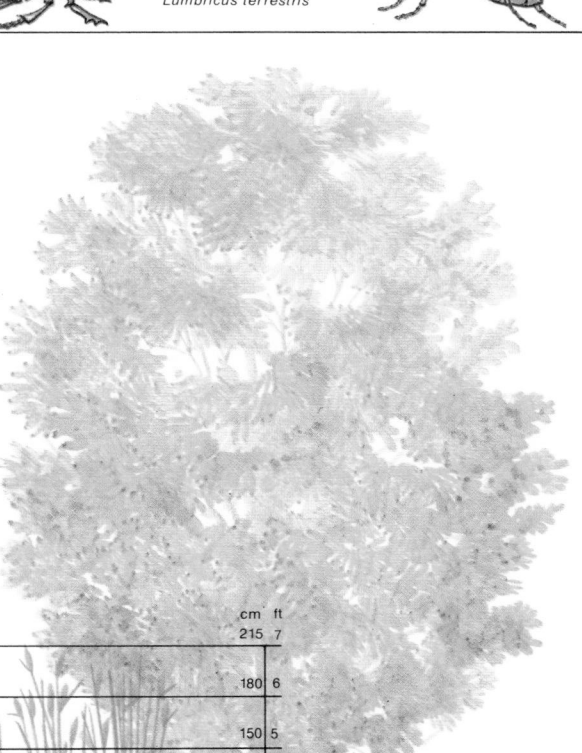

A typical cross section, based on the North American prairies, shows temperate grasslands in relation to rainfall. Annual rainfall determines the depth of the permanently moist subsoil, which in turn dictates the length to which grass roots can grow. Tall grasses have deep root systems and need a considerable depth of moist subsoil. As the rainfall decreases, they gradually give way to shorter grass species. Short grasses require less water and their shallower roots are well suited to drier regions. On dry margins, desert plants start to dominate, and on the wet margins, trees appear.

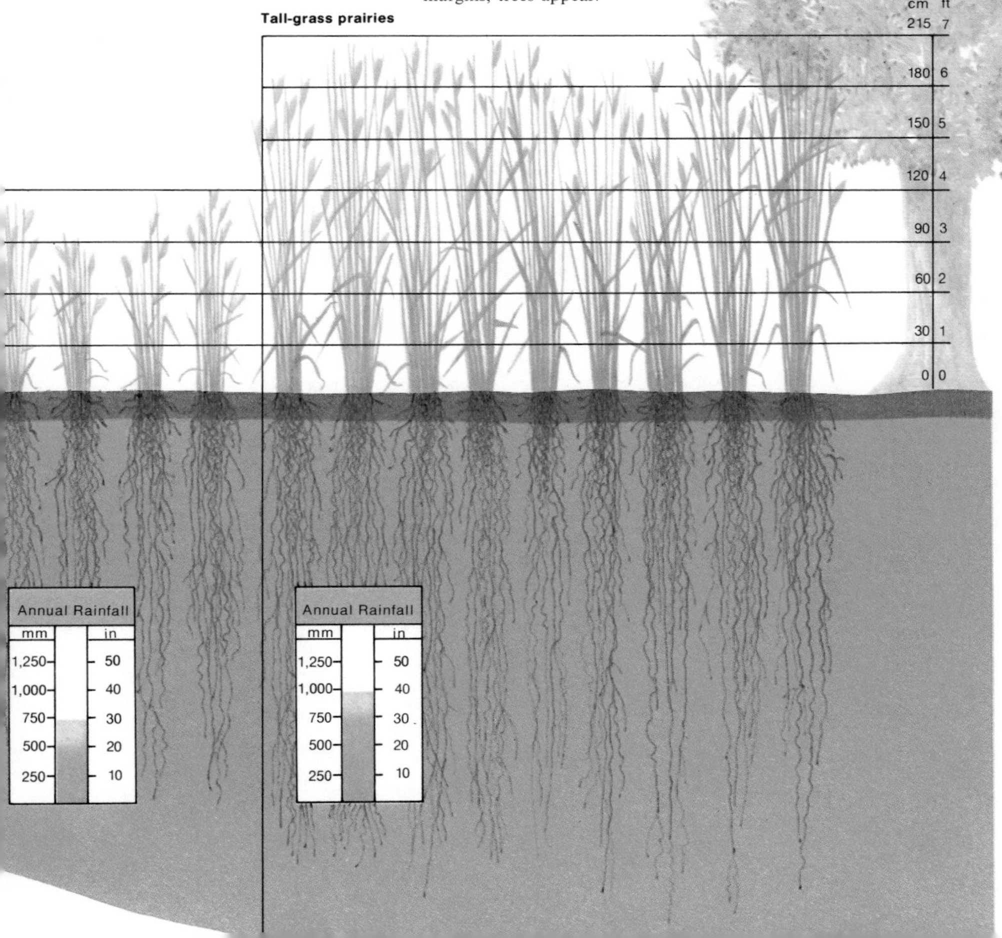

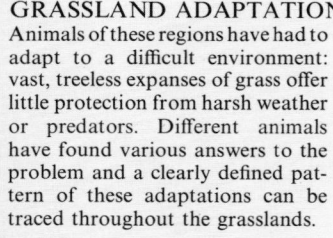

Tall-grass prairies
cm ft
215 7
180 6
150 5
120 4
90 3
60 2
30 1
0 0
Annual Rainfall
mm in
1,250 50
1,000 40
750 30
500 20
250 10
Annual Rainfall
mm in
1,250 50
1,000 40
750 30
500 20
250 10

Another major type of animal found in the temperate grasslands, and one that is better adapted to survive man's activities, is the small, burrowing animal, for example the prairie dog and the gopher of North America, the viscacha of South America and the little ground squirrel known as the souslik in Eurasia.

Unlike the large herd animals, these creatures tend not to migrate. Many of them live together in complex, permanent, underground communities. The colonial "townships" of the prairie dog, for example, may house more than one million individuals, which each year excavate vast quantities of the grassland soil. This has considerable effect upon the structure of the soil. By bringing up earth from lower layers to the surface, these animals are responsible for changing the mineral content of certain areas of topsoil. This then encourages isolated pockets of different plant species to flourish.

A third group of grassland animals, consisting of insects and other invertebrates such as earthworms, has an even more important effect upon the soil. They live in or on the soil and play a vital role in maintaining grassland fertility. These creatures may be herbivores, carnivores or primary (first stage) decomposers (which break down such material as dead grass and animal remains). These three types of activity allow a complete range of organic matter to be processed and incorporated into the earth, where it is further broken down by the second-stage decomposers, the countless millions of soil bacteria. In this way nutrients continuously flow back to the earth and restore its fertility.

Fertile black earths

The topsoil of temperate grassland regions, therefore, contains large amounts of organic material, which is produced every year and is quickly incorporated into the soil. The low and intermittent rainfall and the protective cover of grasses mean that the topsoil undergoes little chemical leaching, a process in which minerals are removed and carried down to lower layers by rainfall percolating through the earth. The soils are thus dark in color, generally fertile and of the "black earth" type ("chernozem" in Russian) which is, at least at first, capable of producing high yields of crops.

The most suitable and most widely grown crops are, predictably, the cultivated grasses, and it is these grasses that provide more food for mankind (either directly as grain or indirectly as animal fodder) than any other source. The temperate grassland biome is therefore an important agricultural resource. Undisturbed natural grasslands, however, are also valuable resources. They need to be preserved both for the information that they can provide about how complex communities of wildlife function efficiently, and because, as a rich source of genetic material, they hold many of the answers to the major agricultural problems that probably lie ahead for the human race.

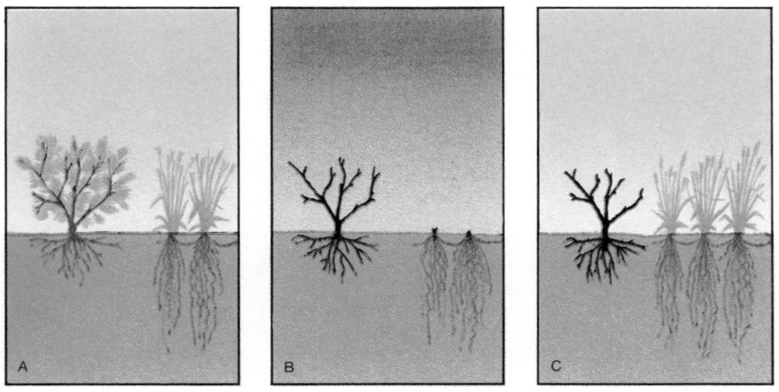

A
B
C

Fire plays a major part in fixing and maintaining the natural boundaries of the temperate grasslands, where tree saplings and shrubs are continually attempting to invade (A). Man-made fires are recent phenomena, natural fires have always occurred. In summer, low-pressure systems build up in continental interiors, causing violent electrical storms. The dry sward of summer grass is easily ignited by lightning and fire is quickly spread by wind. Shrubs and saplings are killed or badly damaged by fire, but grasses, with their growing points close to the soil, remain unharmed (B). They may even benefit from this "pruning" and grow more quickly. Some species grow new buds from their underground shoots. Removal of the main shoot may encourage growth of "tillers" (shoots growing out sideways), which then increase the spread of the grasses as they begin to invade the area left vacant by the dead, or slowly recuperating, shrubs (C).

Man and the Temperate Grasslands

The vast areas of temperate grassland lay virtually empty until the end of the eighteenth century. Over the next 125 years they were occupied by millions of people, most of them migrants from overcrowded Europe. By 1914, the grasslands had become the granaries and the stockyards of the world. Today, they are still the most important food-producing regions on Earth and their riches, properly distributed, are the world's first reserve against the possibility of a hungry future for the human race.

The great nineteenth-century migration to the grasslands proved of immense significance to the human race. It meant that, within a single century, the area of productive land available was suddenly enlarged by thousands of millions of hectares. In all of mankind's history, such a thing had never happened before.

But before the grasslands could be occupied a number of major problems had to be solved. First, in order to reach these regions it was almost always necessary to travel deep into the continental interiors, and there were few navigable rivers and no mechanized forms of transportation for early pioneers. Second, with virtually no indigenous population, newcomers had to learn by their mistakes how best to exploit the new and unfamiliar environment. Third, even if settlers succeeded in using the land, they still had to find markets for their produce.

A number of technological developments, however, that took place in the nineteenth century provided the right combination of circumstances for the opening up of the grasslands. The Industrial Revolution in Europe produced the steamship and the railway locomotive, which created both a means of travel to and from these distant parts and an internal transport system for moving produce to ports and markets. It also produced the kind of machinery needed to plow and farm the great new open spaces; it made it possible for one family to cultivate an area 50 times as large as that which most farmers had known in Europe. Industrialization also threw thousands of Europeans out of work, and therefore provided a large supply of eager migrants. And it crowded further thousands into cities, thus creating vast markets for the settlers' produce.

It was the coming together of these various circumstances that acted as the catalyst and converted, for example, the Russian penetration of the Eurasian steppes in the late eighteenth

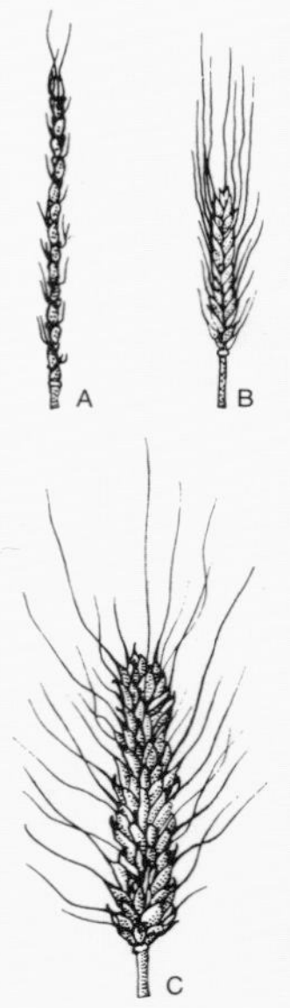

THE CRADLE OF AGRICULTURE

Stands of wild einkorn (A), emmer wheat (B) and wild barleys can be seen today in the grassy foothills that flank the Taurus and the Zagros mountains, and the uplands of northern Israel. It was in this region 10,000 years ago that the world's earliest farmers gathered seeds from these species and sowed the first crops. Wild einkorn is probably the oldest of all wheats and the parent of every modern variety—including the most important and most widely grown kind of grain in the world today, common bread wheat (C).

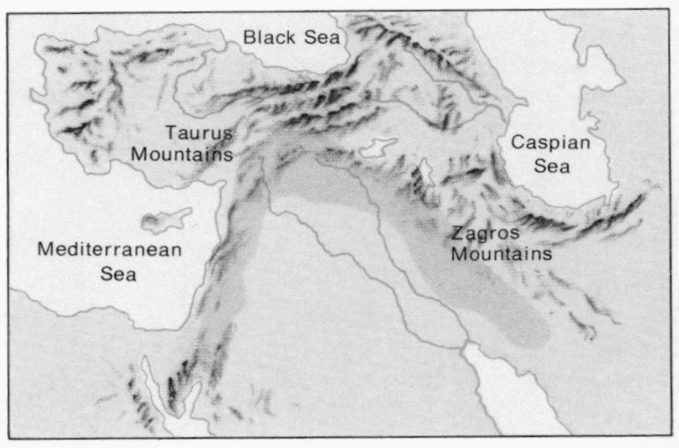

GRASSLAND EXPLOITATION

Today, temperate grasslands provide mankind with a superabundance of food. But the vast potential of these regions was not exploited until the mid-19th century, when mass migration by Europeans, combined with new technology, allowed full-scale development and settlement.

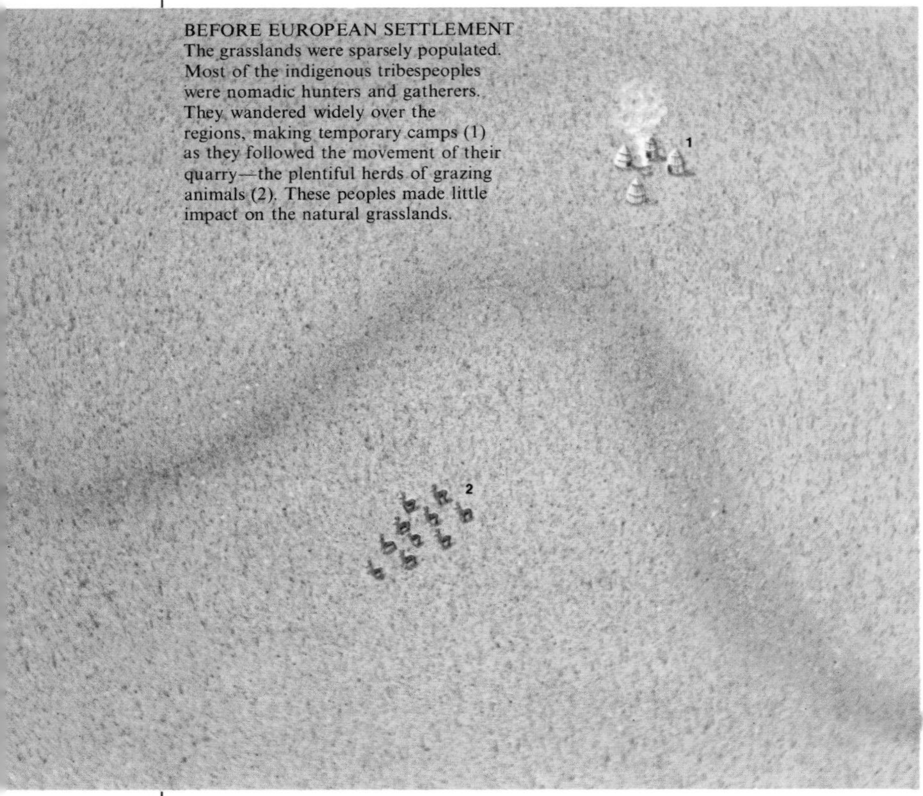

BEFORE EUROPEAN SETTLEMENT
The grasslands were sparsely populated. Most of the indigenous tribespeoples were nomadic hunters and gatherers. They wandered widely over the regions, making temporary camps (1) as they followed the movement of their quarry—the plentiful herds of grazing animals (2). These peoples made little impact on the natural grasslands.

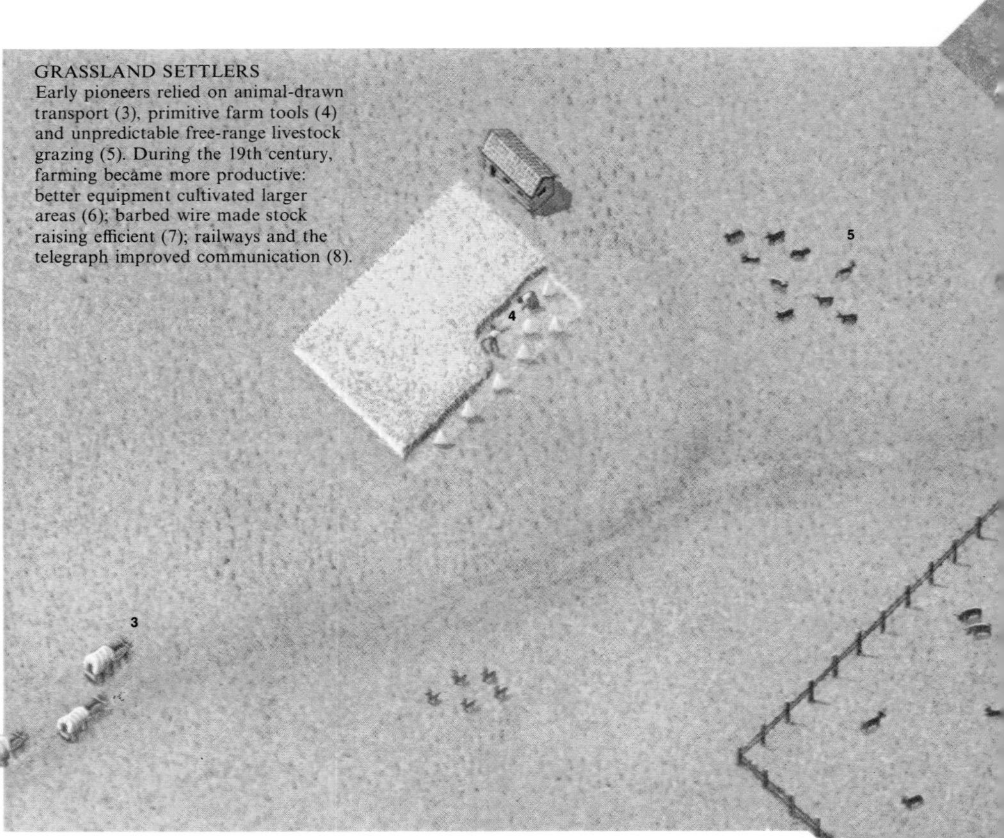

GRASSLAND SETTLERS
Early pioneers relied on animal-drawn transport (3), primitive farm tools (4) and unpredictable free-range livestock grazing (5). During the 19th century, farming became more productive: better equipment cultivated larger areas (6); barbed wire made stock raising efficient (7); railways and the telegraph improved communication (8).

Tehuelche Indians (above) adopted horses for hunting from early Spanish settlers to the pampas. In South Africa and North America, too, the introduced horse became a valued asset for grassland hunters. For people of the Eurasian steppes, for example the Mongols (right), native horses have always been culturally important.

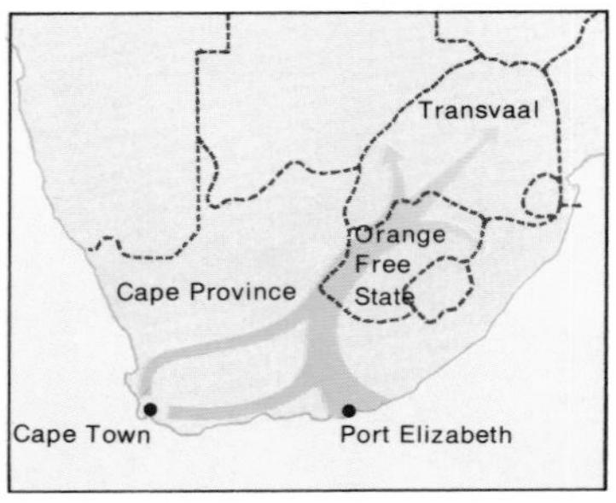

The South African veld was first settled by Europeans after 1836 (left). Dutch farmers (Boers), rejecting British rule of the Cape Colony, trekked north in search of new land. Moving into the Transvaal they discovered rich grassland, recently emptied of its original inhabitants, who had fled to escape the aggressive attentions of neighboring Zulus.

Vaqueros were the original cowboys (left). Tending herds of cattle for the missionaries in 18th-century California, they developed techniques and traditions that served hundreds of later cowboys working the prairie ranges. In other grassland regions, as free-range stock raising became important, similar "cowboy" professions evolved—the Australian stockman and the gaucho of South America.

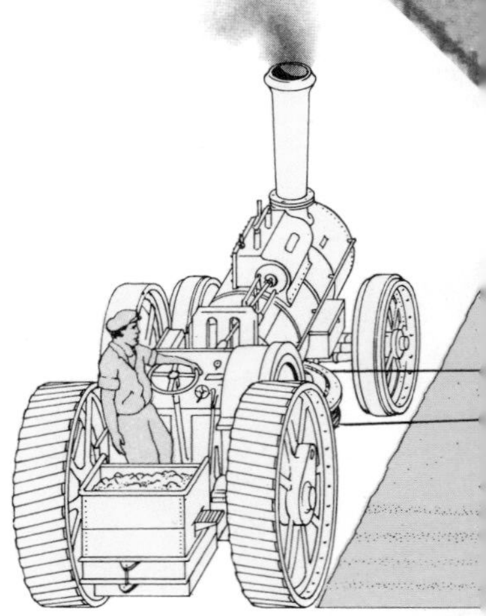

century into the explosive movement of hundreds of thousands of settlers a few years later. In the USA, too, by the year 1850, settlement had reached and then rapidly crossed the Mississippi. In the Argentine, genuine colonization of the pampas had begun, in South Africa, the Boers had reached the high veld, and in Australia pioneer settlers were moving outwards from the various areas of coastal settlement into the scrub grasslands of the interior.

Farmers or ranchers?

The fundamental question posed for these settlers was whether their newly found land should be used for crops or for livestock. Most grasslands have a dry edge and a wet edge, and it was therefore sensible to use the drier parts for stock raising and the wetter parts for cultivation. But the question was complicated by the fact that most of the newcomers were cultivators, and also that the line dividing dry from wet was vague—worse, it shifted from year to year.

Early attempts to define the dividing line tended to be ignored by the settlers themselves, and they pushed the limit of cultivation into areas where plowing the soil led to its destruction. Several generations of farmers had to learn this bitter lesson, and they learned only slowly: the worst disasters on the American grasslands occurred in the 1930s and created the infamous Dust Bowl region in the dry grasslands of the Midwest. Similarly, the Soviet Virgin Lands Program for growing cereal crops on the dry steppes was established in 1954 and is still experiencing difficulties.

Special methods are required both for farming and for ranching the grasslands successfully. Farming has to take account of the open, treeless surface, the scanty and variable rainfall and the comparatively shallow topsoil. To minimize the risk of soil erosion, farmers plant windbreaks, plow fields along the contour, and protect the soil with a covering of the previous year's stubble and by planting cover crops in rotation with cereals. Ranchers, too, have learned to live with variable rainfall. They build stock ponds, irrigate areas of fodder crops to be used as a reserve in dry years and avoid overstocking and consequent overgrazing, which destroys the quality of the grass.

Food for the world

Today, the world's principal trading supplies of cereals and meat flow from these lands, over the networks of railway which link the grasslands to mill towns, slaughter yards and ports of shipment such as Adelaide in Australia, Buenos Aires in Argentina and Montreal in Canada. Without these links to large towns, the grasslands would be of little value, for even today their populations are sparse and the local markets are relatively insignificant.

Throughout most of the world, however, the human population continues to soar and it remains to be seen whether the grasslands can continue to supply these growing numbers with food. Undoubtedly, the output of cereals and meat can be increased, although at considerable cost in fertilizers, new crop strains, more irrigation and more machines. On the other hand, the problem at present is not mainly one of production, nor will it be in the near future. The land can produce more, but there is no point in doing so unless the yields can be made available where they are most needed.

The world's hungry people live in other regions, many of them in countries that are unable to afford imported food supplies, particularly during those years when prices are high. The major importers of temperate grassland produce are the rich industrialized nations, such as those of western Europe. Furthermore, much of the grain imported by these countries is not consumed by humans but used to feed stalled, beef-producing cattle—a highly inefficient way of using these supplies. Consequently, unless producer nations and wealthy importing nations can create a system for produce to reach those in need of it, extra output from the grasslands will be irrelevant.

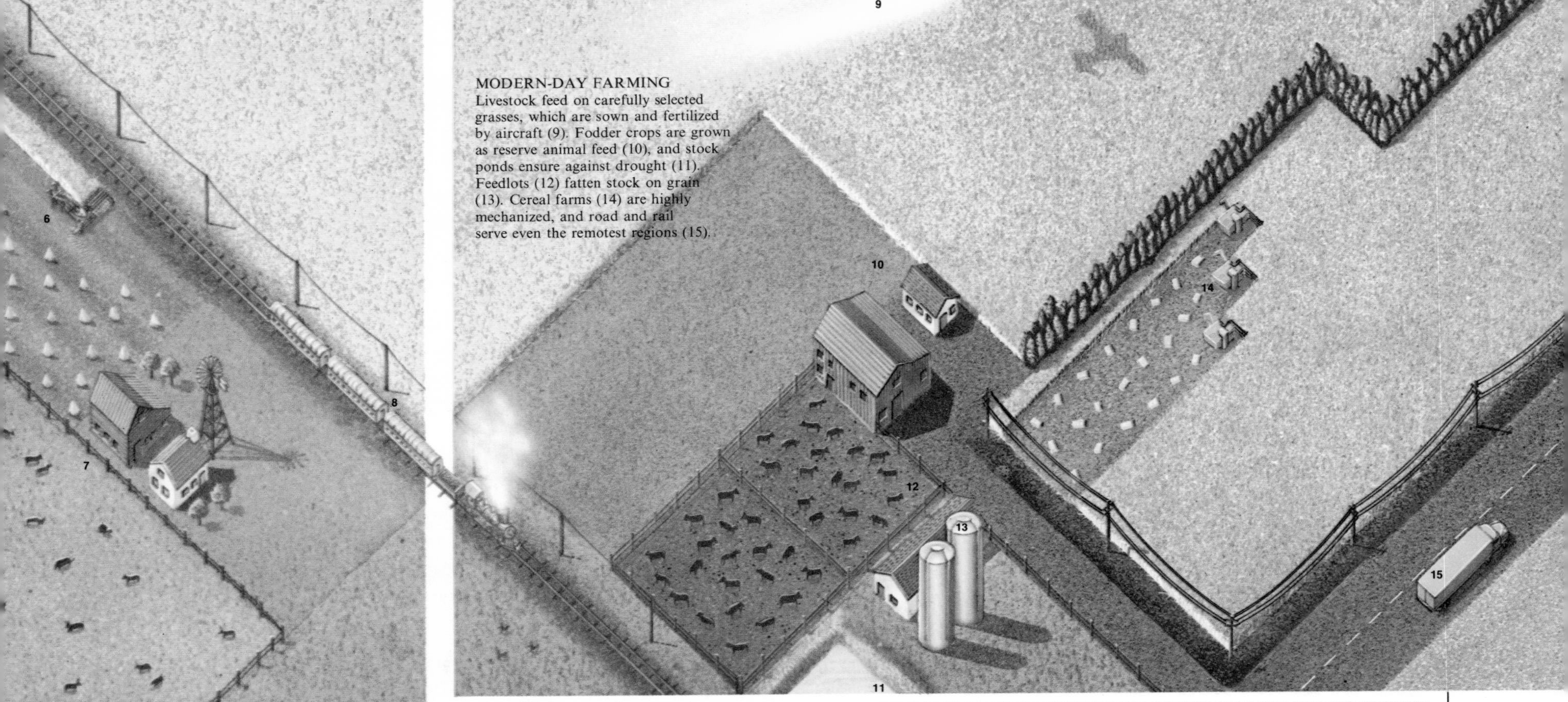

9
6
10
14
8
7
12
13
15
11

MODERN-DAY FARMING
Livestock feed on carefully selected grasses, which are sown and fertilized by aircraft (9). Fodder crops are grown as reserve animal feed (10), and stock ponds ensure against drought (11). Feedlots (12) fatten stock on grain (13). Cereal farms (14) are highly mechanized, and road and rail serve even the remotest regions (15).

Sand-smothered farms in the heart of the Dust Bowl were rapidly abandoned during the 1930s and 40s (above). This was one costly lesson that man had to learn in the process of developing the grasslands. Traditionally grazing land, the western part of the prairies was first plowed this century. Years of drought arrived, crops died and the desert encroached.

The steam-driven plow (below) went through many developments to reduce its unwieldiness and heaviness. The version produced in 1858 used a traction engine and pulley wheel system. The plow was drawn back and forth between these by a power-driven cable. This design was, however, superseded by the steam tractor, which, although unsuited to small European fields, was ideal for drawing multifurrow plows across the grasslands.

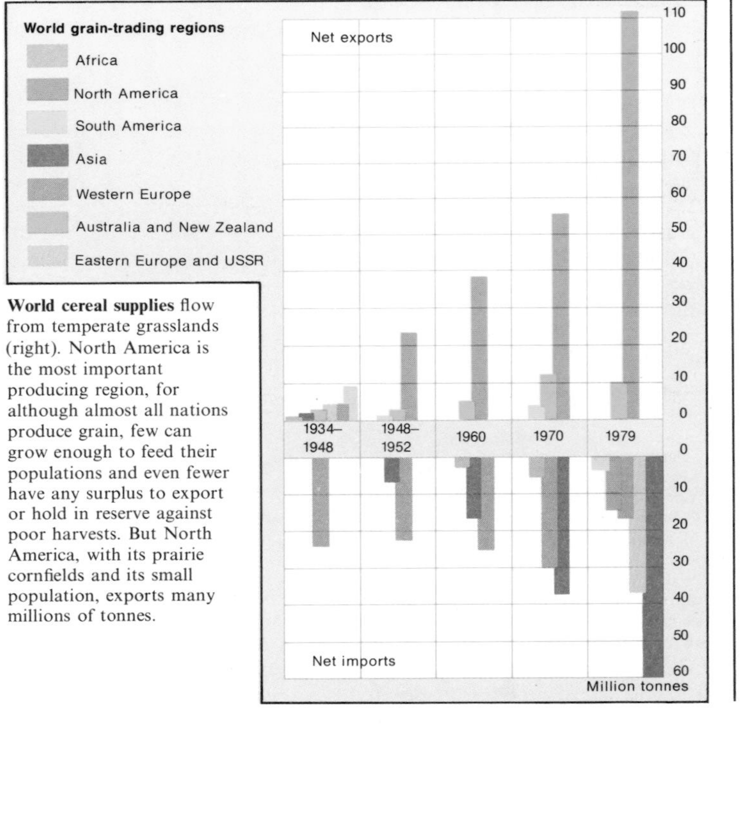

World grain-trading regions
Africa
North America
South America
Asia
Western Europe
Australia and New Zealand
Eastern Europe and USSR
Net exports
Net imports
1934–1948
1948–1952
1960
1970
1979
110
100
90
80
70
60
50
40
30
20
10
0
0
10
20
30
40
50
60
Million tonnes

World cereal supplies flow from temperate grasslands (right). North America is the most important producing region, for although almost all nations produce grain, few can grow enough to feed their populations and even fewer have any surplus to export or hold in reserve against poor harvests. But North America, with its prairie cornfields and its small population, exports many millions of tonnes.

Deserts

Much of the Earth's land surface is so short of water that it is defined as desert. Not all deserts are hot, sandy wastelands; some are cold, some are rocky, but all lack moisture for most of the year. Even so, a surprising variety of plants and animals have adapted to these hostile environments. Plants have developed ingenious ways of surviving long periods of drought, and many desert animals shelter during the intense heat of the day, emerging only at night to feed.

LIFE IN THE DESERT

The overriding need to obtain and conserve water dictates the pattern of desert life. Many plants close their pores during the day and most daytime creatures limit their activity to early morning and late afternoon. At night the temperature drops sharply and dew provides welcome moisture. Some plants bloom at night, and the desert is alive with insects, night-hunting birds, reptiles and small mammals.

DESERTS BY DAY

Many birds are at home in the desert. The lanner falcon of Africa and Asia gets all the moisture it needs from its diet of small birds and rodents. Sandgrouse live in the open deserts of Eurasia and North Africa; mainly seed eaters, they must make long flights each day to find water. Roadrunners, in American deserts, hunt insects, lizards and small rattlesnakes.

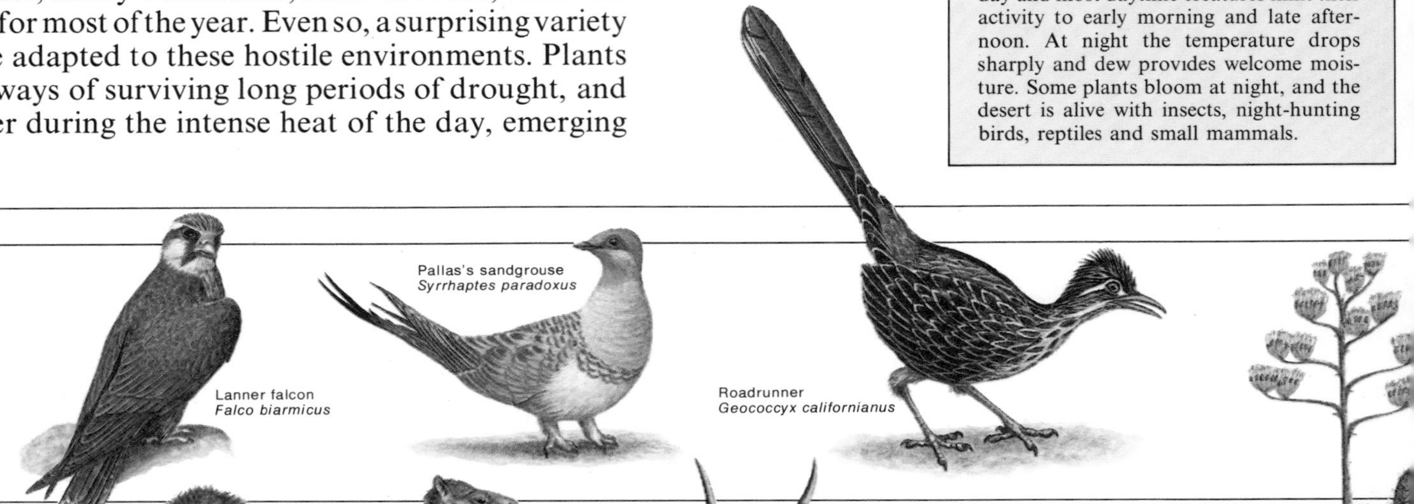
Pallas's sandgrouse *Syrrhaptes paradoxus*
Lanner falcon *Falco biarmicus*
Roadrunner *Geococcyx californianus*

Large mammals are nomadic and obtain most of the moisture they need from plants. Camels can go for long periods without food or water because their humped back stores fat which can be drawn on when food is scarce, and water stored in their body tissues prevents dehydration. Addax antelopes survive entirely on plants. They roam remote parts of the Sahara, their broad hooves enabling them to travel easily over soft sand. Gazelles rely on speed. Small and fleet footed, they are able to disperse quickly over great distances to find food and water.

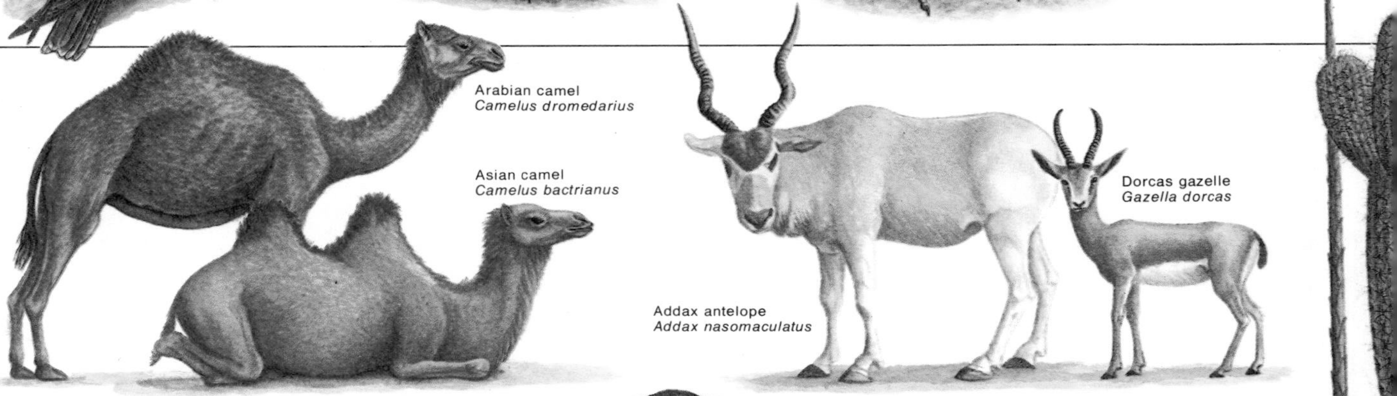
Arabian camel *Camelus dromedarius*
Asian camel *Camelus bactrianus*
Dorcas gazelle *Gazella dorcas*
Addax antelope *Addax nasomaculatus*

Insects and reptiles are well adapted to desert life. Desert locusts, when overpopulation threatens their food supply, change from a solitary to a swarming migratory form. Harvester ants store seeds against times of drought; desert tortoises withstand drought by becoming torpid. Lizards are cold blooded and need the sun to warm them, but must shelter from the intense heat of midday. The thorny devil, a small Australian ant-eating lizard, is protected from potential predators by its prickly scales.

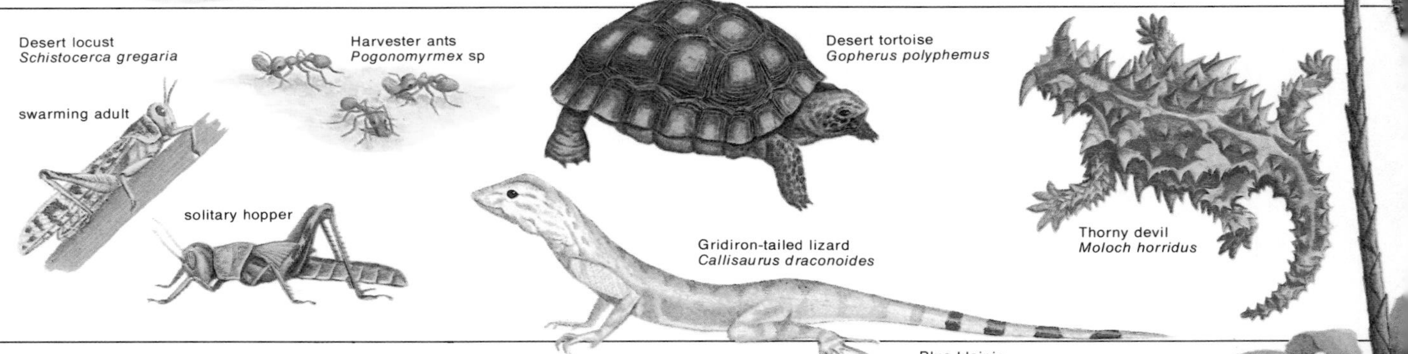
Desert locust *Schistocerca gregaria*
Harvester ants *Pogonomyrmex sp*
Desert tortoise *Gopherus polyphemus*
swarming adult
solitary hopper
Gridiron-tailed lizard *Callisaurus draconoides*
Thorny devil *Moloch horridus*

Desert plants have evolved various ways of coping successfully with drought. The ocotillo of southwestern America sheds its leaves, reducing its need for water. Euphorbias, and cacti such as the prickly pear, store water in their stems. Blue kleinia, a South African succulent, has a waxy coating that limits water loss. Agaves mature very slowly, building up reserves of food and water in their leaves before they flower. Esparto, a needlegrass, is typical of many desert grasses.

Blue kleinia *Senecio articulatus*
Prickly pear *Opuntia ficus-indica*
Euphorbia *Euphorbia obesa*
Ocotillo *Fouquieria splendens*
Agave *Agave americana*

Esparto grass *Stipa tenacissima*

Deserts occur where rainfall is low and infrequent and where any moisture quickly evaporates or disappears instantly into the parched ground. In the driest deserts, rainfall rarely exceeds 100 mm (4 in) a year, and is so unreliable that some places may have no rain for 10 years or more. These are deserts in the truest sense of the word: harsh wildernesses that are almost totally without life. Regions with less than 255 mm (10 in) of rain a year are generally classified as arid and those with less than 380 mm (15 in) as semiarid.

Hot deserts have very high daytime temperatures in summer, although they drop sharply at night, and the winters are relatively mild. In the so-called cold deserts the summers are hot but the winters are so cold that temperatures may fall as low as −30°C (−22°F).

Desert climates and landscapes

In the subtropical latitudes, swept by hot, drying winds, high-pressure weather systems prevent rain clouds from forming. In these regions, rain comes only from local storms or follows low-pressure weather systems (often seasonal) when they move in across the desert. Large areas of central Asia have become desert because they are so far from the sea that clouds have shed all their rain before they reach them. Other deserts occur because mountains cut them off from moisture-bearing winds. The Andes, for example, shelter the drylands of Argentina, and a high sierra stops rain from reaching the Mojave and Great Basin deserts of North America. Rain is also rare on the western sides of continents where cold ocean currents flow from the polar regions towards the Equator.

Desert climates vary not only from place to place but also with time. Over short periods rainfall is much less predictable than it is in temperate regions and droughts are frequent. Some droughts, such as those that occur along the southern fringe of the Sahara, are so severe that it may seem that the climate has changed permanently. But most droughts are short-lived and are followed by years of normal (although sparse) rainfall. Over longer periods of time, however, desert climates do change. Prehistoric cave drawings in the Saharan highlands, for example, show that elephants, rhinoceroses and even hippopotamuses—animals that are at home in wetter climates—lived in these now dry, barren uplands in a more moist period between 7,000 and 4,000 years ago.

Desert landscapes also vary enormously. They are as contrasted as the Colorado canyon country of the United States and the sandy wastes of the Middle East, but most include one or more of several basic features: steep, rocky mountain slopes, broad plains, basin floors dominated by dry lake beds or sand seas, and canyon-like valleys. In low-lying areas, evaporation sometimes leaves a glistening residue of salt. Where there is soil, it is often sandy or consists of little more than fragmented rock, and because plant life is usually sparse there is little or no humus to enrich the ground.

Where water is life

Plant growth depends on water, and desert plants are usually widely spaced to reduce competition for what little moisture is available. Many plants rely on short, sharp rainstorms; others make use of dew and grow in locations, such as crevices in rocks, where water can accumulate. Some complete their life cycle in a single wet season, producing seeds that lie dormant during the following drought and germinate only when enough moisture is available for them to grow. These are the ephemerals that carpet the desert with a brief but brilliant display of flowers shortly after rain has fallen.

Most desert plants, however, are able to tolerate or resist drought. These are the xerophytes ("dry plants") and phreatophytes ("deep-water plants"). Xerophytic trees and shrubs have a wide-spreading network of shallow roots that take in water from a large area of ground. Many xerophytes also limit the amount of water

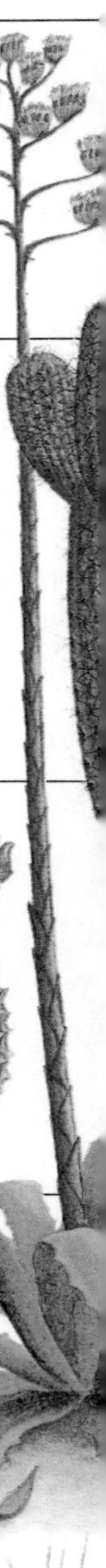

Adaptations to desert life: kangaroo rats, jerboas and gerbils (A) make prodigious leaps with their long back legs to escape predators, and some desert lizards (B) run at high speed on their hind legs when pursued, using their tail for balance. Spadefoot toads have scoop-like hind feet with which they dig burrows to avoid the intense heat of day. Skinks use flattened toes fringed with scales to "swim" through the sand. Fan-toed geckos have toes that spread into fans at the tips, enabling them to walk easily on sand dunes, and the Namib palmate gecko has webbed feet that support it on loose sand.

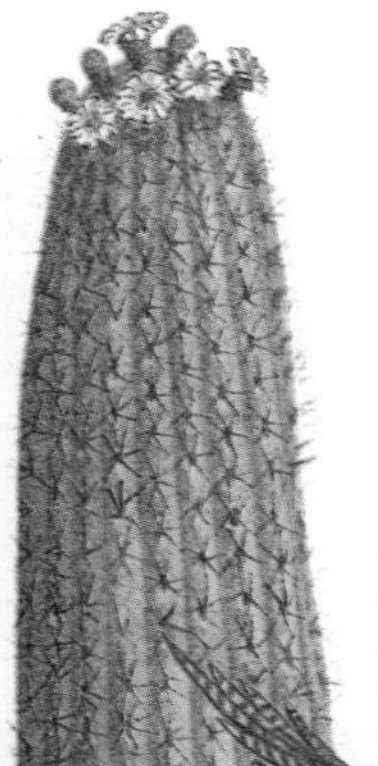

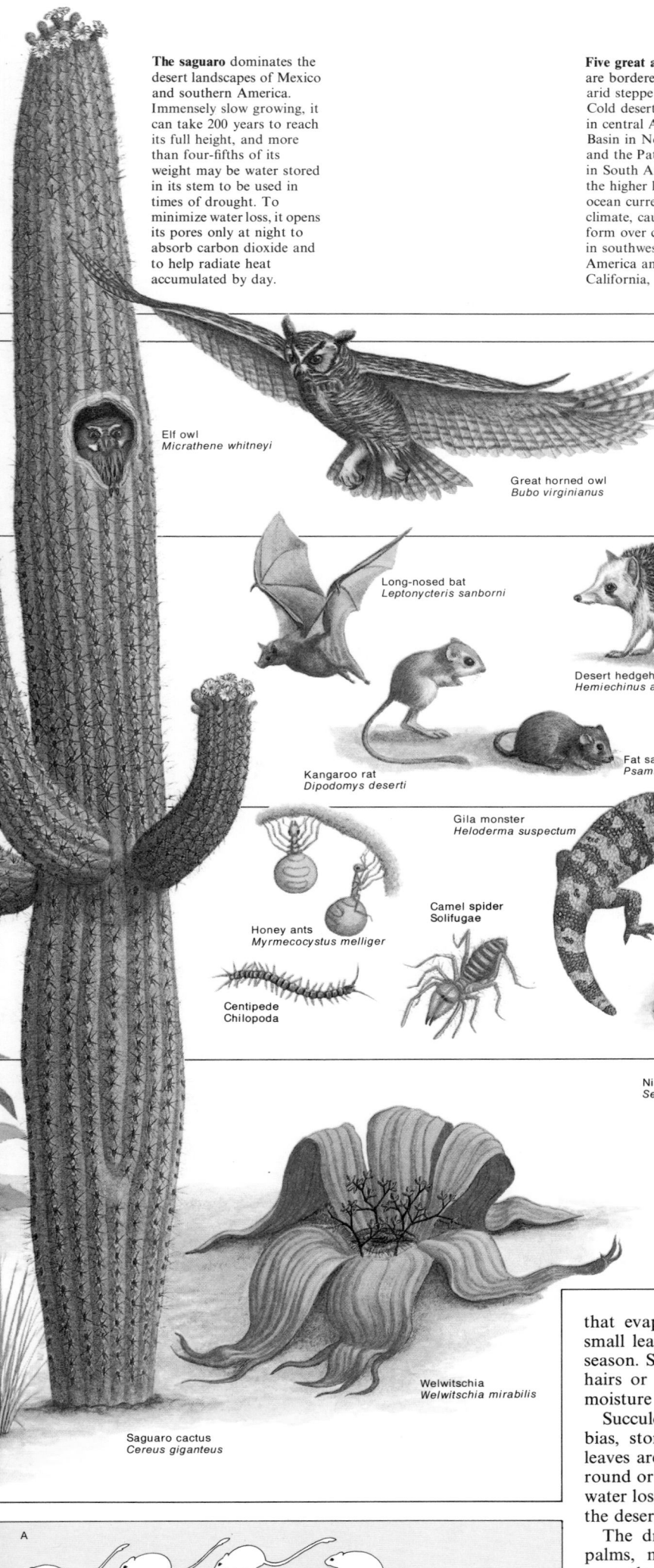

The saguaro dominates the desert landscapes of Mexico and southern America. Immensely slow growing, it can take 200 years to reach its full height, and more than four-fifths of its weight may be water stored in its stem to be used in times of drought. To minimize water loss, it opens its pores only at night to absorb carbon dioxide and to help radiate heat accumulated by day.

Five great arid regions are bordered by semi-arid steppe and scrub. Cold deserts—the Gobi in central Asia, the Great Basin in North America and the Patagonian Desert in South America—lie in the higher latitudes. Cold ocean currents also affect climate, causing fogs to form over coastal deserts in southwest Africa, South America and Baja California, Mexico.

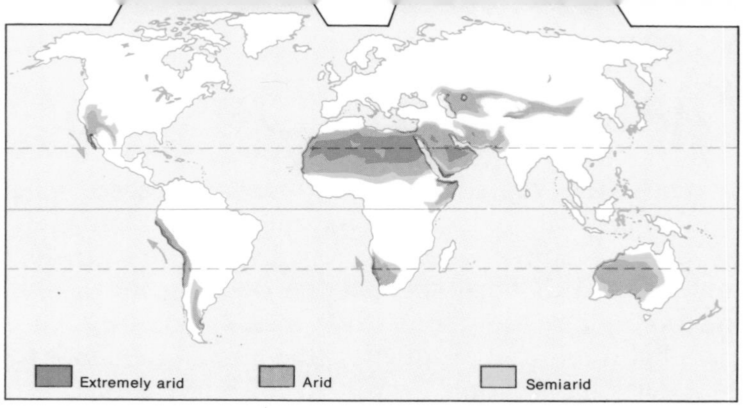

Extremely arid
Arid
Semiarid

DESERTS BY NIGHT

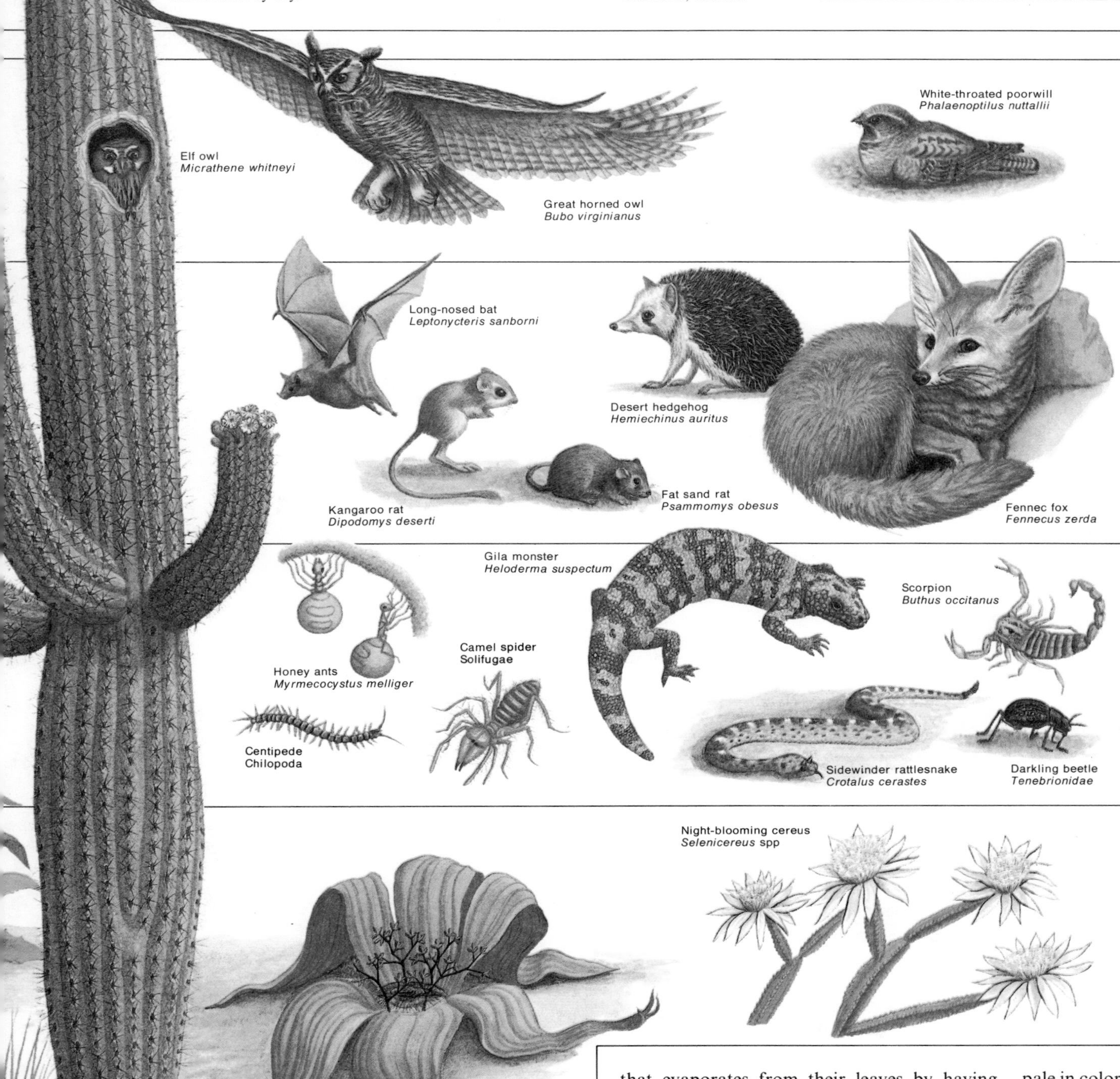

Elf owl
Micrathene whitneyi
Great horned owl
Bubo virginianus
White-throated poorwill
Phalaenoptilus nuttallii
Long-nosed bat
Leptonycteris sanborni
Desert hedgehog
Hemiechinus auritus
Kangaroo rat
Dipodomys deserti
Fat sand rat
Psammomys obesus
Fennec fox
Fennecus zerda
Gila monster
Heloderma suspectum
Scorpion
Buthus occitanus
Honey ants
Myrmecocystus melliger
Camel spider
Solifugae
Centipede
Chilopoda
Sidewinder rattlesnake
Crotalus cerastes
Darkling beetle
Tenebrionidae
Night-blooming cereus
Selenicereus spp

Owls and nightjars hunt under cover of darkness. Elf owls shelter by day, emerging at dusk to catch insects, and great horned owls often come into the desert at night to hunt. The poorwill, a small desert nightjar, is known to American Indians as "the sleeper." An insect eater, it sometimes survives the rigors of winter, when food is scarce, by hibernating.

Most small animals are active at night. Nectar-eating bats visit plants that blossom at night, pollinating the flowers while they feed. American kangaroo rats obtain water from a dry diet of seeds and conserve moisture by producing very concentrated urine. The sand rat of North Africa feeds on salty succulents and excretes great quantities of extremely salty urine. Hedgehogs are mainly insect eaters; the long ears of desert species help to disperse body heat. The Saharan fennec, the smallest type of desert fox, hunts lizards, rodents and locusts.

Among insects and other invertebrates the hunt for food intensifies at night. Honey ants gather nectar; centipedes and camel spiders hunt insects. The gila monster, a poisonous American lizard, eats centipedes, eggs and sometimes other lizards, and uses its tail to store fat. The sidewinder, a small rattlesnake, is active mainly at night, leaving its distinctive parallel tracks in the sand. Scorpions emerge from their burrows to stalk insects and spiders, and darkling beetles feed on dry, decomposing vegetation.

Some desert plants are nocturnal, in the sense that they bloom only at night or make use of the dew that forms when the temperature falls. The welwitschia, unique to the Namib Desert in southwest Africa, has broad, sprawling leaves on which moisture condenses at night. The night-blooming cereus of the American deserts flowers for a single night in summer. Like other nocturnal plants, its flowers are luminously pale and strongly scented to attract pollinating night insects.

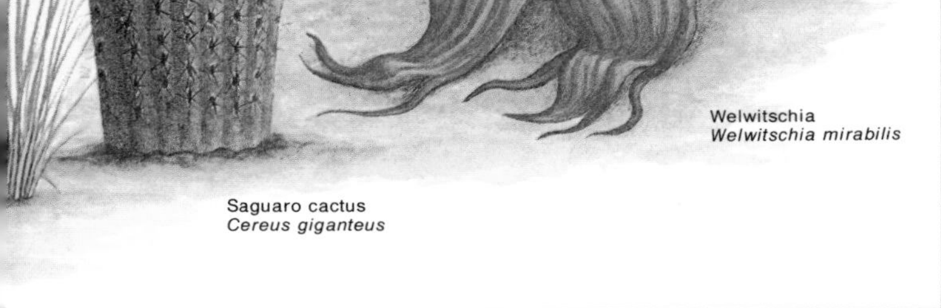

Welwitschia
Welwitschia mirabilis
Saguaro cactus
Cereus giganteus

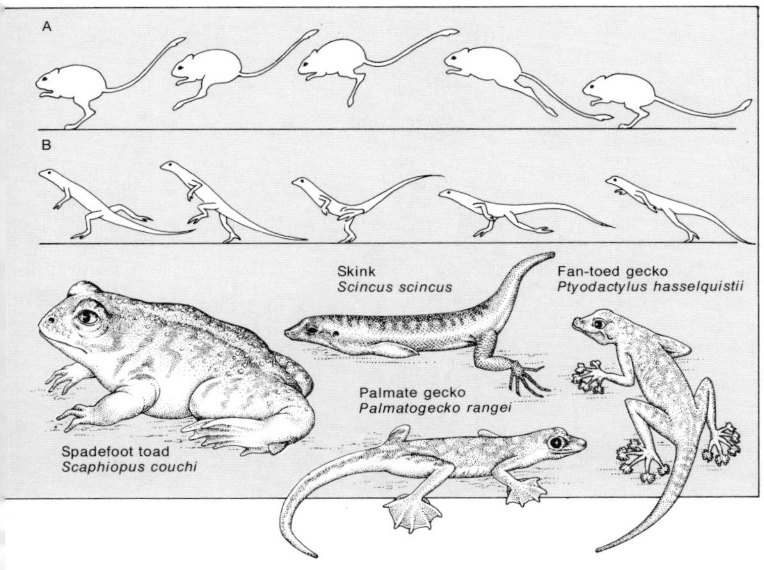

A
B
Skink
Scincus scincus
Fan-toed gecko
Ptyodactylus hasselquistii
Palmate gecko
Palmatogecko rangei
Spadefoot toad
Scaphiopus couchi

that evaporates from their leaves by having small leaves, or by shedding them in the dry season. Some produce a protective covering of hairs or a coating of wax to prevent loss of moisture and to help to withstand heat.

Succulent plants, such as cacti and euphorbias, store water in their thick stems. Their leaves are usually reduced to spines, and their round or cylindrical shape also helps to reduce water loss. Spines have the added advantage in the desert of discouraging foraging animals.

The drought-resisting phreatophytes—date palms, mesquite and cottonwood trees, for example—have a similar variety of adaptations to dry conditions, but their most typical feature is a long tap root that draws water from great depths. Many plants can also tolerate the presence of salt in the soil. These are the halophytes ("salt plants") such as saltbush and other small shrubs that grow in and around salt pans.

The struggle to survive

Animals, too, need to obtain and conserve water at all costs and to be able to adjust to extremes of temperature. Most are small enough to shelter under stones or in burrows during the intense heat of day; others survive adverse conditions by becoming dormant or by migrating. For most desert creatures it is also an advantage to be inconspicuous, and many are pale in color so that they are hard to see against their light background of sand or stones.

Many animals, especially those that are active by day, show adaptations that are strikingly similar to those of desert plants. Frogs and toads are activated by rain, emerging from dormancy to feed and mate in temporary pools and then quickly burying themselves until the next rain falls. Mammals have hairy coats that reduce water loss and also help to keep their body temperature at a tolerable level. Most desert insects have a waxy coating that serves much the same purpose.

Some geckos and other lizards store food, in the form of fat, in their tails, and camels store fat in their humped backs to sustain them when food is scarce. Honey ants force-feed nectar to some members of the colony, creating living "honey pots" for the rest of the community to feed from in times of drought. Many creatures are able to survive on the moisture contained in their food, and rarely need to drink. Most desert dwellers also have extremely efficient kidneys that produce very concentrated urine, so that little or no moisture is lost in the process.

Man enjoys no such advantages. Nevertheless, he still seeks to live in deserts, as he has for thousands of years, and the pressures he exerts on the environment may well have irrevocably changed much of the world's desert landscapes.

Man and the Deserts

Water is the key to man's survival in deserts: where water has been available, great civilizations have flourished, and man's dream of making the desert bloom has become a reality. More recently, discoveries of great mineral wealth have spurred the opening up of some of Earth's most inhospitable regions. But while man's ingenuity has made many deserts both habitable and productive, the human tendency to increase the extent of deserts has become a problem of international proportions.

Given water, much is possible, and not surprisingly man has tended to settle where water is most readily available: along the courses of rivers (such as the Nile) that rise outside the desert, and around oases fed by springs or by wells that tap groundwater supplies. But desert rainfall is so unreliable that often runoff and spring flow are uncertain in quantity and timing. Much groundwater is either also unreliable or it is fossil water that has accumulated in the geological past and is not being replenished by today's rainfall. Thus in areas such as southern Libya and some of the oasis settlements of the Arabian Gulf, and in America's arid west, groundwater is a nonrenewable resource that is being rapidly depleted.

Making water go farther

Man has also used great ingenuity to secure water supplies and to transport them to where they are needed. Runoff from flash floods that follow rare desert storms may be collected in channels and distributed to crops in nearby fields, and terracing slopes to trap runoff is a traditional way of obtaining the maximum benefit from limited rainfall. Reservoirs, ranging from the small night tanks of the southern Atacama desert in Chile to the massive artificial lakes along the Colorado river in the United States, store seasonally or perennially unreliable runoff. Also, surface runoff may be increased by reducing the permeability of runoff surfaces, a solution engineered by the Nabataeans in the Negev desert more than 2,000 years ago and being reemployed by the Israelis today.

The transport of water is a fundamental desert activity. Open canals are typical, usually carrying water to irrigated fields—a practice used throughout the fertile crescent of Mesopotamia more than 8,000 years ago and still widespread today. A striking alternative are the ancient qanats, which limit the evaporation of water while it is in transit. Qanats are still found in the Middle East, although today pipelines are increasingly used.

Ultimately the conversion of salt water to fresh water may ensure plentiful supplies for many desert regions. The process is expensive, but large-scale desalination has already become a reality in some affluent communities such as oil-rich Saudi Arabia and Kuwait. Increasing emphasis is also being placed on more efficient use of existing freshwater supplies: in Egypt and Israel, waste water from towns is being purified and recycled for use in agriculture.

Cultivating the desert

The successful control of water has enabled large areas of otherwise arid and semiarid land to be made productive. The Egyptian civilization along the Nile depended, and still depends, on the management of seasonal floodwaters. In North America, the large-scale, long-distance piping of water has made central

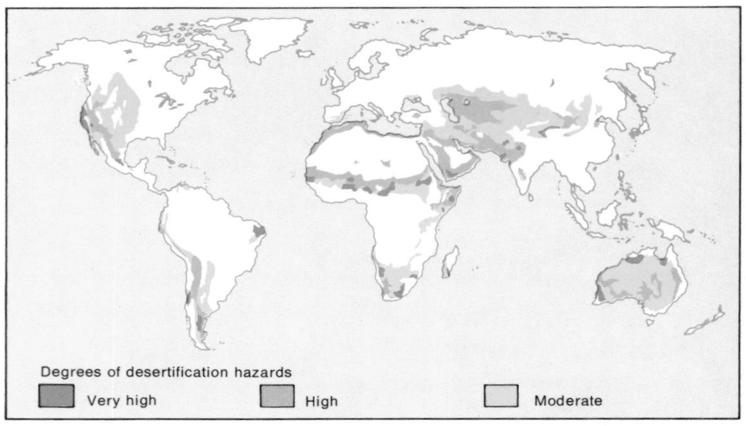
Degrees of desertification hazards
Very high
High
Moderate

Desertification—the advance of desert areas across the Earth—now affects more than 30 million sq km (12 million sq miles) and deserts are continuing to expand at an alarming rate. In recent years, on the southern edge of the Sahara alone, as much as 650,000 sq km (250,900 sq miles) of land that was once productive have been lost, and in places there is little left to show where the Sahara ends and the Sahel–Sudan region begins. Intense and often inappropriate human pressures are major causes, frequently aggravated by drought: overcultivating vulnerable land, chopping down trees for fuelwood and grazing too many livestock, especially on the margins of arid lands.

THE SHIFTING SANDS

Recent decades have seen unprecedented changes in the world's deserts. Increasing pressure on the environment, especially from pastoralists and farmers, has caused extensive damage and a rapid expansion of barren land. In many desert regions, nomadism has long been the only way in which man could survive, except in oases. Today, even these traditional ways of life are changing as the exploitation of oil and other mineral resources, and the introduction of new agricultural techniques, are drawing many of the deserts into a spectacular new age of development.

The traditional pastoral response to limited water supplies and forage in desert regions is nomadic livestock herding, still practiced by the Tuareg of the northern Sahara (right) and by tribal groupings in Mongolia (left). The nomadic way of life has, however, become severely restricted in recent years. Long-distance migrations are often incompatible with the requirements of the modern state, and the poor rewards no longer match the incentives to settle in towns and cities.

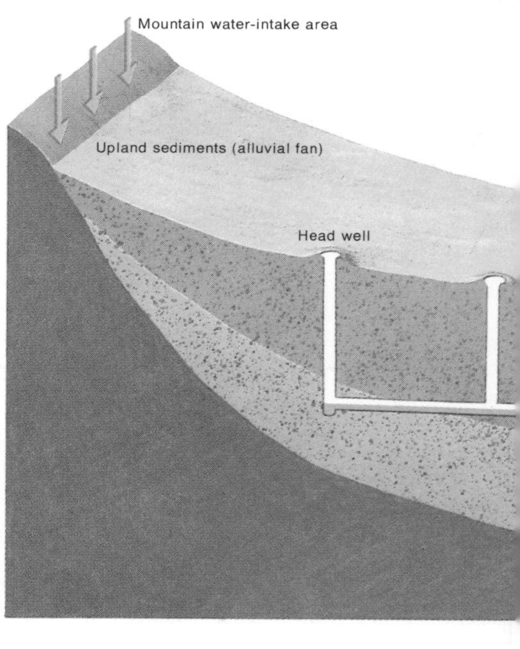
Mountain water-intake area
Upland sediments (alluvial fan)
Head well

Oases have provided welcome refuges in deserts since ancient times. Secure water supplies from wells or springs make settled life possible in the midst of the most arid landscapes. Many oases are intensively cultivated with three tiers of vegetation: tall date palms shade orchards of citrus fruits, apricots, peaches, pomegranates and figs, and both palms and orchard trees shade the ground crops of vegetables and cereals. Irrigation channels distribute water to the desert soils, which are frequently rich in plant foods although they lack humus. Windbreaks help to protect cultivated land from erosion and from migrating dunes, although many oases are losing the battle with encroaching sands and the oasis people are leaving to find work in the oil fields.

California the most productive agricultural region in the world. But while irrigation can bring enormous benefits, it can also create problems. Too much water causes waterlogging of the land, and where water evaporates in the dry desert air, concentrations of dissolved salts build up in the soil.

Farming without irrigation is possible only where rainfall, although meager, is sufficient to sustain crops with a short growing season. Soil moisture is conserved by using dry surface mulches, by fallowing and crop rotation, by planting seeds sparsely and by controlling weeds. Geneticists are also producing new varieties of cereal crops that can survive for weeks without water. Dry farming, however, is precarious. Especially at times of drought it can cause serious problems of soil erosion, chiefly by the action of wind.

Man the desert maker

The extension of dry farming into unsuitable regions, and waterlogging and the accumulation of salts in irrigated areas, are major causes of desertification—the spread of deserts into formerly habitable land. Other major causes are the overgrazing of livestock on land with too little forage and the removal of trees and shrubs for firewood by communities that have no alternative fuel supply. A sequence of drier than normal years does the rest.

Many scientists believe that desertification can be reversed, provided the pressures on the land are reduced sufficiently to allow vegetation to recover. But desertification affects such huge areas, often crossing national frontiers, that broad-scale, international cooperation is needed to coordinate reductions in population and livestock pressures and to improve understanding of drought.

In some countries the battle against desertification has already begun. In China, extensive planting of drought-tolerant trees has created windbreaks to control sand movement and to protect farmland. In Algeria, a broad belt of trees has been planted to keep the Sahara at bay, and in Iran, advancing dunes have been halted by spraying them with petroleum residue: when the spray dries it forms a mulch that retains moisture and allows vegetation to grow, and much desert land has been reclaimed.

The deserts' riches

The exploitation of resources has also led to an "opening up" of many deserts. The rushes for precious metals in Arizona, Australia and South Africa started man's development of these regions in the nineteenth century. Some minerals, such as the evaporite deposits of Searles Basin in California and the nitrates of the Atacama desert in Chile, are actually products of the arid environment.

A resource that deserts also possess in abundance is solar power, and in many hot, dry regions the heat of the sun is used to evaporate mineral-rich solutions of salts, as well as being harnessed as a source of energy. Sunshine and the dry, clear air are also drawing ever-increasing numbers of tourists to the "sun cities" of the western United States and to Saharan oases, which were, until recently, only remote desert outposts.

No resource, however, has created as much attention or wealth as has oil. Oil has transformed the fortunes of several desert nations and provided an economic boom that has led to rapid industrialization and spectacular urban growth. The benefits of such growth in terms of affluence are substantial. The problems—the weakening of traditional desert societies, the submerging of traditional cities in the concrete labyrinths of modern complexes, and the precariousness of prosperity that is based on finite resources—are also clear.

Mineral wealth provides a powerful incentive for man's development of arid lands, and today the flow of oil rather than water is often a measure of a desert nation's prosperity. In some of the world's most desolate regions, flares signal the presence of modern "oases" where fossil fuels are being extracted—products, like the fossil waters that are sometimes trapped in the same sedimentary rocks, of the desert's geological past. Uranium, another mineral "fuel," also often lies beneath desert sands. Arid environments may also provide a rich harvest of other minerals: potash, phosphates and nitrates, valuable sources of commercial fertilizers; gypsum, manganese and salt; and borax, source of the element boron, used in nuclear reactors.

A "plastic" revolution has helped transform much of Israel's desert hinterland into productive farmland. Plastic cloches, plastic mulches and greenhouses trap moisture and reduce evaporation, and water trickled through thin plastic tubes irrigates the plants' roots with a minimum of wastage. Such innovative agricultural techniques enable Israel to produce most of its own food requirements, and fruit and vegetables grown in the relatively mild desert winters are also exported to Europe, where they command high prices.

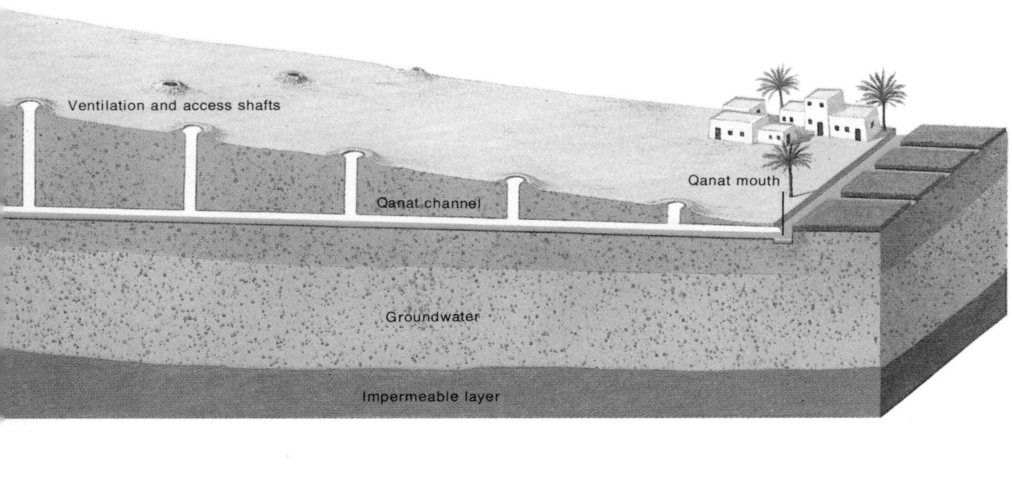
Ventilation and access shafts
Qanat mouth
Qanat channel
Groundwater
Impermeable layer

One of the most ingenious ways man has devised of bringing water to desert regions is by the ancient underground system known as the qanat. Invented by the Persians in the first millennium BC, qanats tap groundwater in upland sediments and carry it by gravity to the surface on lower land. The head well is dug first, sometimes to a depth of 100 m (330 ft), until water is reached. A line of shafts is then sunk to provide ventilation and to give access to the channel being tunneled below. Work begins at the mouth end, and a typical channel is 10–20 km (6–12 miles) long when completed, depending on the depth of the head well and the slope of the land. Its slight gradient ensures that water flows freely but gently down to ground level. Surface canals then divert the water to where it is needed. Thousands of such qanats are still in use, their routes marked by mounds of excavated debris.

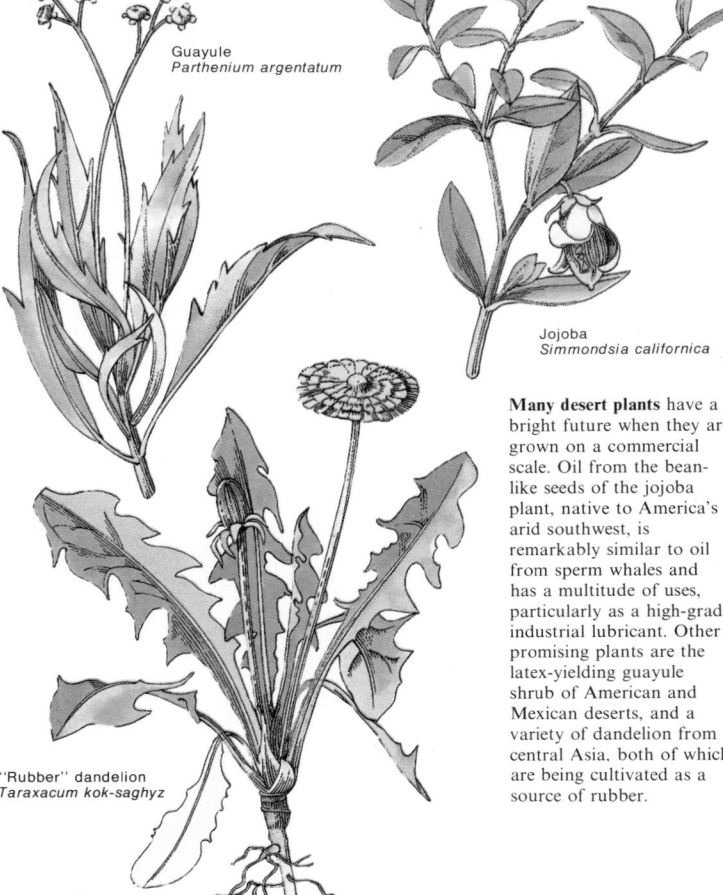

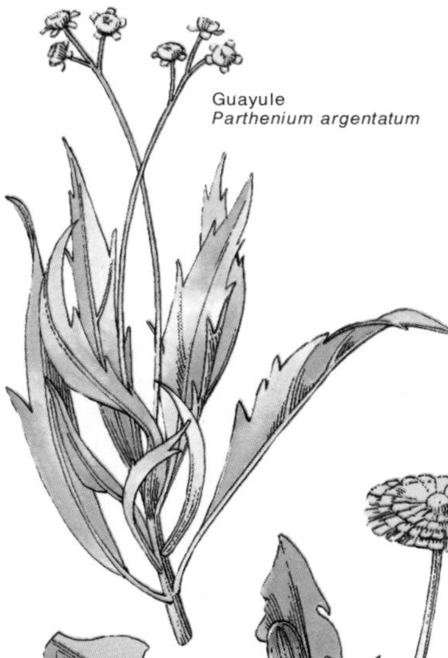
Guayule
Parthenium argentatum

Jojoba
Simmondsia californica

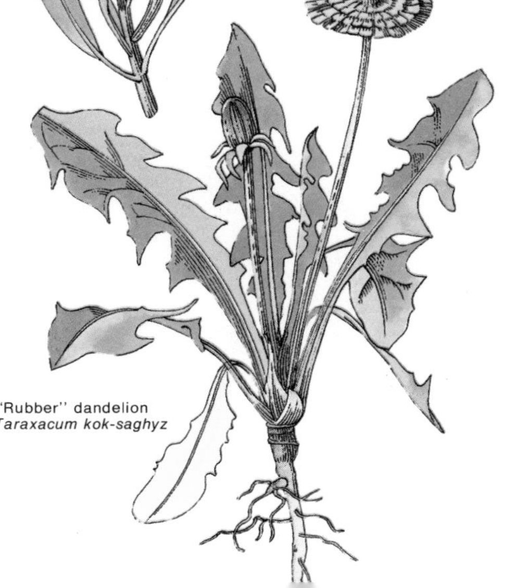
"Rubber" dandelion
Taraxacum kok-saghyz

Many desert plants have a bright future when they are grown on a commercial scale. Oil from the bean-like seeds of the jojoba plant, native to America's arid southwest, is remarkably similar to oil from sperm whales and has a multitude of uses, particularly as a high-grade industrial lubricant. Other promising plants are the latex-yielding guayule shrub of American and Mexican deserts, and a variety of dandelion from central Asia, both of which are being cultivated as a source of rubber.

Savannas

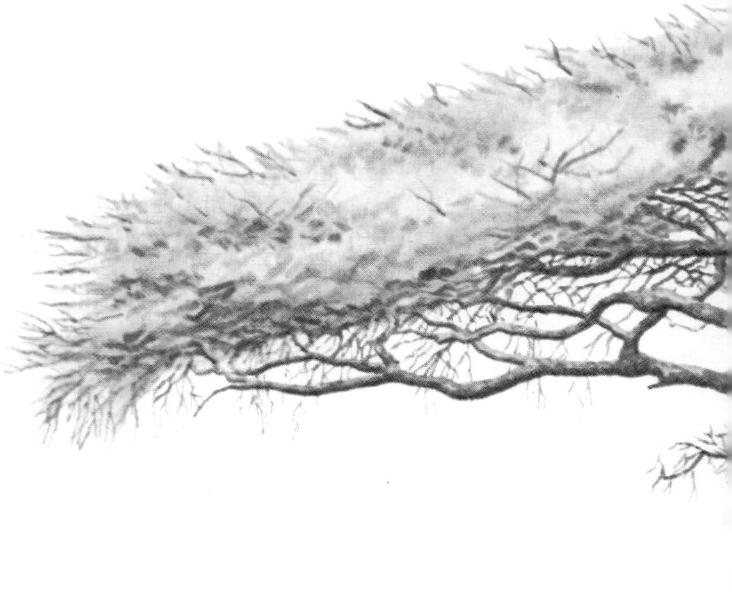

Between the tropical rainforest and desert regions lie large stretches of savanna, which are characterized by seasonal rainfall and long periods of drought. Those nearest to the forests usually take the form of open woodland, whereas those nearest to the deserts consist of widely scattered thorn scrub or tufts of grass. Unlike temperate grasslands, where the summers are hot but the winters are cold, savanna regions are always warm and in the wet season rain falls in heavy tropical downpours.

The most extensive areas of savanna are in Africa, north and south of the rainforest, and in South America, where the two main regions are the *llanos* of Venezuela, north of the Amazon rainforest, and the *campos* of Brazil in the south. Smaller areas of savanna also occur in Australia, India and southeastern Asia.

Savannas range from thickly wooded grasslands to almost treeless plains. Some are the result of man's destruction of the forest, and most are maintained in their present state by the high incidence of fire, both natural and man-made. The grasses tend to be taller and coarser than their temperate counterparts and they grow in tufts rather than as a uniform ground cover. In areas of high rainfall some grasses grow up to 4.5 m (15 ft) tall. Trees and bushes are usually widely spaced so that they do not compete with each other for water in the dry season. Humid, or moist, savannas experience 3 to 5 dry months a year, dry savannas 6 to 7 months, and thornbush savannas 8 to 10 months. Rainfall also varies widely, from more than 1,200 mm (47 in) a year in humid savannas to as little as 200 mm (8 in) where the savanna merges into desert.

Types of savannas

Humid woodland savanna presents an abrupt contrast to the rainforest. Trees tend to be scattered and some are so low growing that they are dwarfed by the tall grass that springs up during the summer rains. In the dry season the grass fuels fierce fires, which destroy all except thick-barked, large-leaved deciduous trees. Consequently, the proportion of fire-resistant trees and shrubs is large, and the grass quickly regenerates with the coming of the next rains.

In Africa this type of savanna is known as Guinea savanna north of the rainforest and as miombo savanna south of the rainforest. In South America it is known as *campo cerrado*, from the Portuguese words meaning field (*campo*) and dense. (*Campos sujos* are *campos* in which stretches of open grassland predominate and *campos limpos* are grasslands from which trees are entirely absent.) The *llanos*, or plains, of northern South America are grasslands interspersed with forests and swamps.

North of the Guinea savanna in Africa lies a belt known as Sudan savanna. The annual rainfall is in the range 500 to 1,000 mm (20–40 in) and the dry season lasts from October to April. This is typical dry savanna. Tall grasses between 1 and 1.5 m (3–5 ft) form an almost continuous ground cover and acacias and other thorny trees dot the landscape, together with branching dôm palms and massive water-storing baobab trees. Because of the interrupted tree cover the old name given to many savannas of this type was orchard steppe, and this description gives a good idea of the countryside. Like the humid woodland savannas it is maintained by regular burning of the grass in the dry season, and there is a delicate balance and interaction between climate, soil, vegetation, animals and fire. On the desert margins the grasses grow in short tufts and the scattered acacias are seldom more than 3 m (10 ft) tall. The scrub and grasses are too widely dispersed for fires to spread, and this type of savanna is modified not by fire but by aridity and blistering heat.

Thorn-scrub and thorn-forest savannas frequently form transitional zones between tropical forests and grasslands. The *caatinga*, or "light forest," of northeastern Brazil is a typical thorn-forest savanna. Long, hot, dry seasons alternate with erratic downpours of rain, and the rate of evaporation is high. Drought-resisting trees and thorny shrubs mix with bromeliads, cacti and palm trees.

Abundance of life

No other environment supports animals so spectacular in size and so immense in numbers as do the African savannas. In spite of the concentration of animal life, however, competition for food is not severe. Each species has its own preferences and feeds from different levels of the vegetation. Giraffes and elephants can easily reach the upper branches of trees, antelopes feed on bushes at different heights from the ground, zebras and impalas eat the grasses and warthogs root for the underground parts of plants. With the onset of the dry season, massed herds assemble for the great migrations that are a major part of savanna life, moving to areas where rain has recently fallen and new grass is plentiful.

Following the grazing animals are the large predators: the lions, leopards and cheetahs. Wild dogs hunt in packs, and the scavengers—jackals, hyenas and vultures—move in to dispose of the remains of the kill.

The savannas of South America and Australia are much poorer in animal species. The only mammal of any size on the South American savanna is the elusive, nocturnal maned wolf, which eats almost anything from small animals to wild fruit. On the Australian savanna the largest inhabitant is the kangaroo, and the prime predator—apart from man—is the dingo, or native dog.

Many of the resident savanna birds are ground-living species such as the ostrich in Africa and its counterparts, the rhea in South America and the emu in Australia. The warm African climate attracts large numbers of visiting birds, which migrate each year across the Sahara to escape from the severe winter of the northern hemisphere.

For many thousands of years man has lived in harmony with the savanna. Within the last century, however, and in recent decades in particular, the savanna has come under increasing pressure. Inevitably, there is competition between the needs of the environment and those of the human population, and the future of the savanna is very much in the balance.

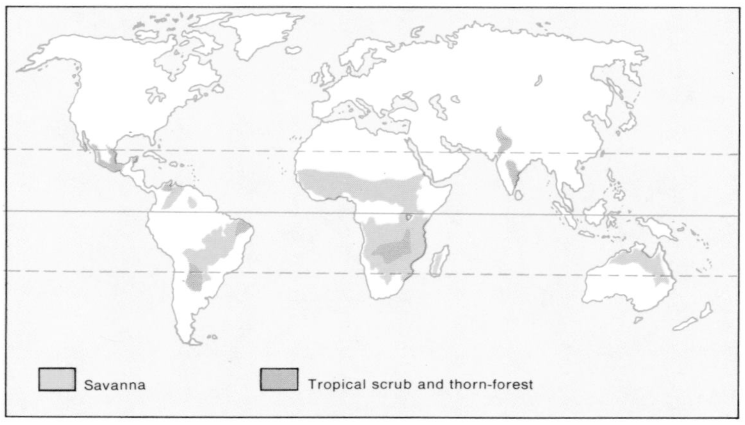

Savanna
Tropical scrub and thorn-forest

On each side of the Equator are broad tracts of tropical grassland known as savannas. In these regions there are distinct wet and dry seasons and temperatures are high all the year round, seldom falling below 21°C (70°F). Rain falls mainly in the hottest months, whereas the cooler months are generally dry. Thorn-scrub and thorn-forest savannas occur where the rainfall is more erratic; they have relatively little grass cover, and trees and bushes can tolerate long periods of drought.

THE AFRICAN SAVANNA

More than a third of Africa is savanna, the vast parklike plains and gently rolling foothills providing the setting for a supreme wildlife spectacle. Vegetation is the basis of the immense wealth of animal life. It supports the large herds of grazing animals, and they return nutrients to the grassland in their droppings. The plant eaters, in turn, provide food for the hunters and for the scavengers that play an indispensable role by keeping the savanna free from carrion. Most of the plant-eating animals are agile and swift-footed, which enables them to escape from their enemies, and live in herds, which also provides some protection in the open habitat. Many of the animals, both predators and prey, are camouflaged: stripes or spots, at a distance, help to break up their outline; dappled markings merge with the pattern of sunlight and shade in the undergrowth; and tawny colors make them difficult to see against a background of dry grass.

Giraffe
Giraffa camelopardalis

THE PLANT EATERS
Most plant eaters have adapted to feeding at a particular level of the vegetation. Giraffes browse on acacia tips that other animals cannot reach and elephants use their trunks to tear down succulent branches and leaves, although both feed on low-growing vegetation when it is easily available. Elephants will also uproot trees to gather leaves that are otherwise out of reach. The black rhinoceros plucks low-growing twigs and leaves by grasping them with its upper lip (the white rhinoceros has a broad, square mouth for grazing on grass). Eland often use their horns to collect twigs by twisting and breaking them. Zebra, wildebeest, topi and gazelle all graze on the same grasses, but at different stages of the plants' growth.

Lion
Panthera leo

HUNTERS OF THE PLAINS
The plant eaters provide rich hunting for the carnivores. Lions kill the largest prey and hunt in family groups; the lioness usually makes the kill but the male is the first to eat. The leopard is a solitary hunter. It lies in ambush or stalks its prey, mainly at night, in brush country where it has ground cover. Cheetahs are the swiftest of all the hunters. They usually hunt in pairs in open grassland, stalking their prey and then charging in a lightning-fast sprint. Hunting dogs travel in well-organized packs. They exhaust their quarry by chasing it to a standstill and attacking as a team. Whereas lions, leopards and cheetahs usually kill by leaping for the neck or throat, packs of hunting dogs characteristically attack from the rear.

Jackal
Canis aureus

THE SCAVENGERS
When the hunters have eaten, the scavengers move in. Jackals, small and quick, make darting runs to snatch titbits while packs of hyenas use their powerful bone-crushing jaws to demolish the bulk of the carcass. Hyenas are the most voracious of the carnivores, often driving the primary predator from its kill. Vultures are frequently the first to see a kill as they circle high in the sky, but must await their turn to feed on the skin and scraps because their descent attracts the more aggressive scavengers. Carrion beetles, carrion flies and the larvae of the horn-boring moth dispose of what is left. Most of the large scavengers, particularly the hyenas, also do their own hunting, singling out prey that is small, weak or sickly.

Acacia
Acacia sp
Red oat grass
Themeda triandra

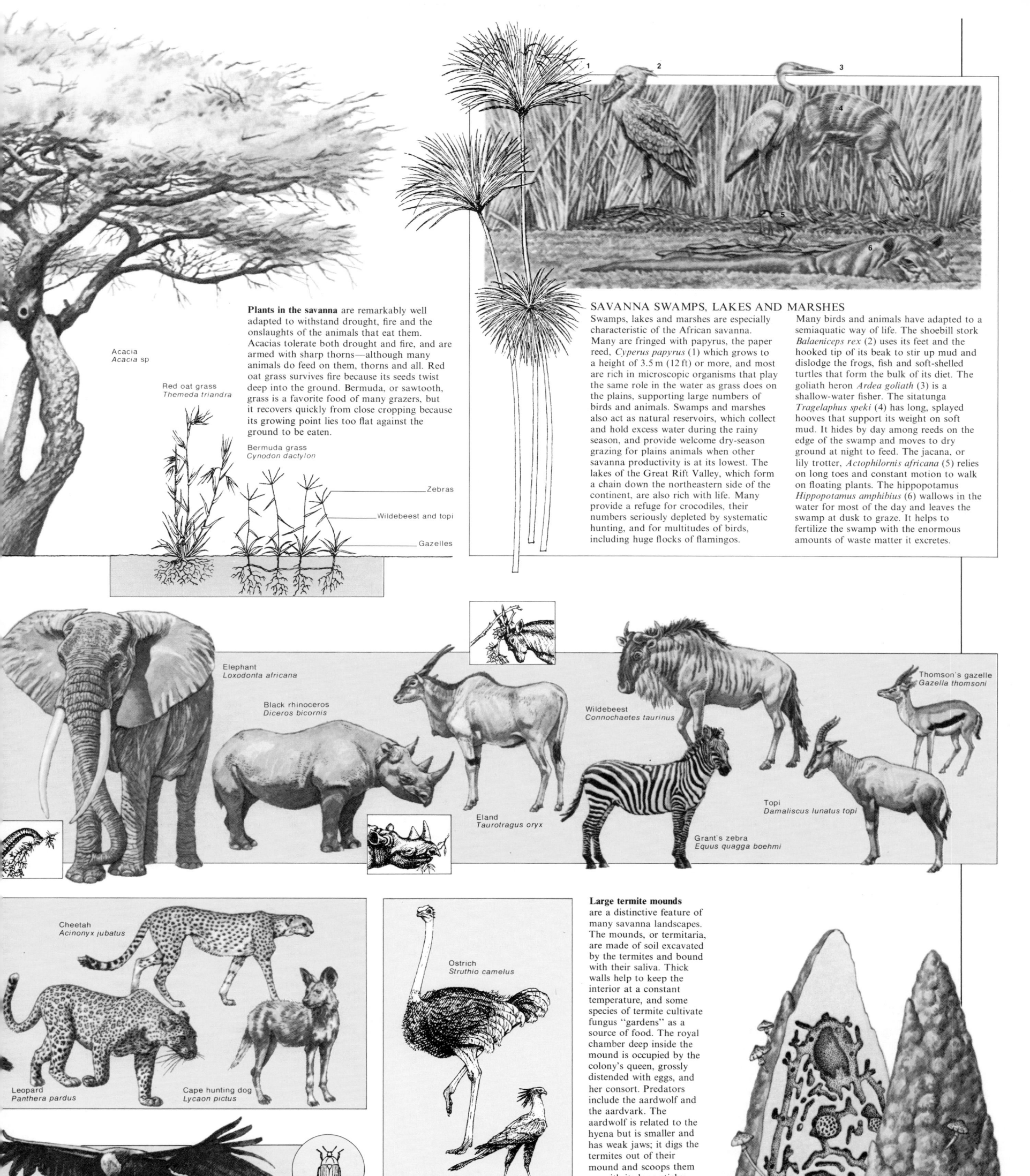

Plants in the savanna are remarkably well adapted to withstand drought, fire and the onslaughts of the animals that eat them. Acacias tolerate both drought and fire, and are armed with sharp thorns—although many animals do feed on them, thorns and all. Red oat grass survives fire because its seeds twist deep into the ground. Bermuda, or sawtooth, grass is a favorite food of many grazers, but it recovers quickly from close cropping because its growing point lies too flat against the ground to be eaten.

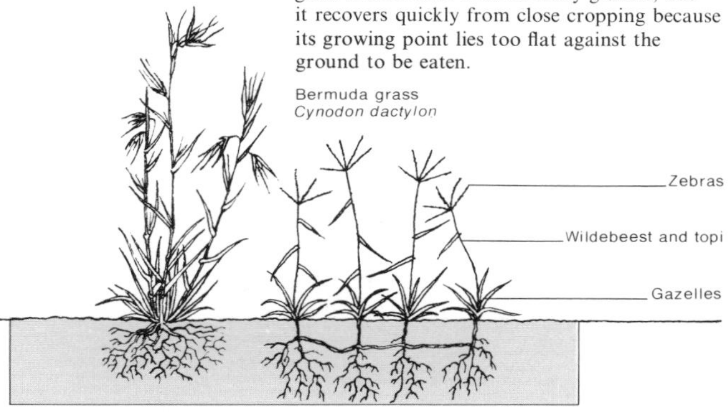

Bermuda grass
Cynodon dactylon
Zebras
Wildebeest and topi
Gazelles

1
2
3
4
5
6

SAVANNA SWAMPS, LAKES AND MARSHES

Swamps, lakes and marshes are especially characteristic of the African savanna. Many are fringed with papyrus, the paper reed, *Cyperus papyrus* (1) which grows to a height of 3.5 m (12 ft) or more, and most are rich in microscopic organisms that play the same role in the water as grass does on the plains, supporting large numbers of birds and animals. Swamps and marshes also act as natural reservoirs, which collect and hold excess water during the rainy season, and provide welcome dry-season grazing for plains animals when other savanna productivity is at its lowest. The lakes of the Great Rift Valley, which form a chain down the northeastern side of the continent, are also rich with life. Many provide a refuge for crocodiles, their numbers seriously depleted by systematic hunting, and for multitudes of birds, including huge flocks of flamingos.

Many birds and animals have adapted to a semiaquatic way of life. The shoebill stork *Balaeniceps rex* (2) uses its feet and the hooked tip of its beak to stir up mud and dislodge the frogs, fish and soft-shelled turtles that form the bulk of its diet. The goliath heron *Ardea goliath* (3) is a shallow-water fisher. The sitatunga *Tragelaphus speki* (4) has long, splayed hooves that support its weight on soft mud. It hides by day among reeds on the edge of the swamp and moves to dry ground at night to feed. The jacana, or lily trotter, *Actophilornis africana* (5) relies on long toes and constant motion to walk on floating plants. The hippopotamus *Hippopotamus amphibius* (6) wallows in the water for most of the day and leaves the swamp at dusk to graze. It helps to fertilize the swamp with the enormous amounts of waste matter it excretes.

Elephant
Loxodonta africana
Black rhinoceros
Diceros bicornis
Eland
Taurotragus oryx
Wildebeest
Connochaetes taurinus
Grant's zebra
Equus quagga boehmi
Topi
Damaliscus lunatus topi
Thomson's gazelle
Gazella thomsoni

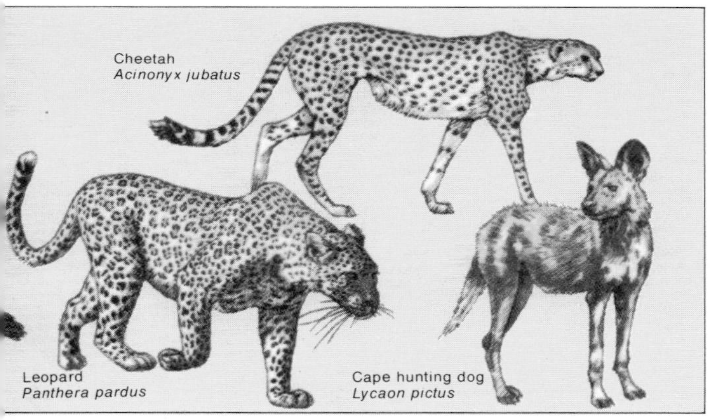

Cheetah
Acinonyx jubatus
Leopard
Panthera pardus
Cape hunting dog
Lycaon pictus

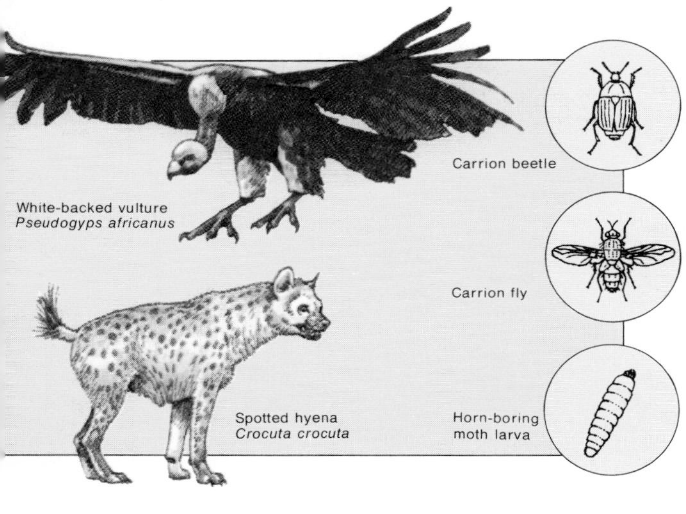

White-backed vulture
Pseudogyps africanus
Carrion beetle
Carrion fly
Spotted hyena
Crocuta crocuta
Horn-boring
moth larva

Ostrich
Struthio camelus
Secretary bird
Sagittarius serpentarius

LONG-LEGGED BIRDS

The ostrich, up to 2.4 m (8 ft) tall, can see for great distances across the plains and can outrun most of its enemies. Its territory is often shared with grazing animals, such as wildebeest, which take advantage of the ostrich's keen sight to alert them to danger. The secretary bird (so-called because of its quill-like crest) strides through the grass hunting small mammals, insects and snakes; it kills snakes by battering them with its powerful, long-clawed feet.

Large termite mounds are a distinctive feature of many savanna landscapes. The mounds, or termitaria, are made of soil excavated by the termites and bound with their saliva. Thick walls help to keep the interior at a constant temperature, and some species of termite cultivate fungus "gardens" as a source of food. The royal chamber deep inside the mound is occupied by the colony's queen, grossly distended with eggs, and her consort. Predators include the aardwolf and the aardvark. The aardwolf is related to the hyena but is smaller and has weak jaws; it digs the termites out of their mound and scoops them up with its long sticky tongue. The aardvark, distantly related to the elephant, uses its powerful hoof-like claws to break into termite nests.

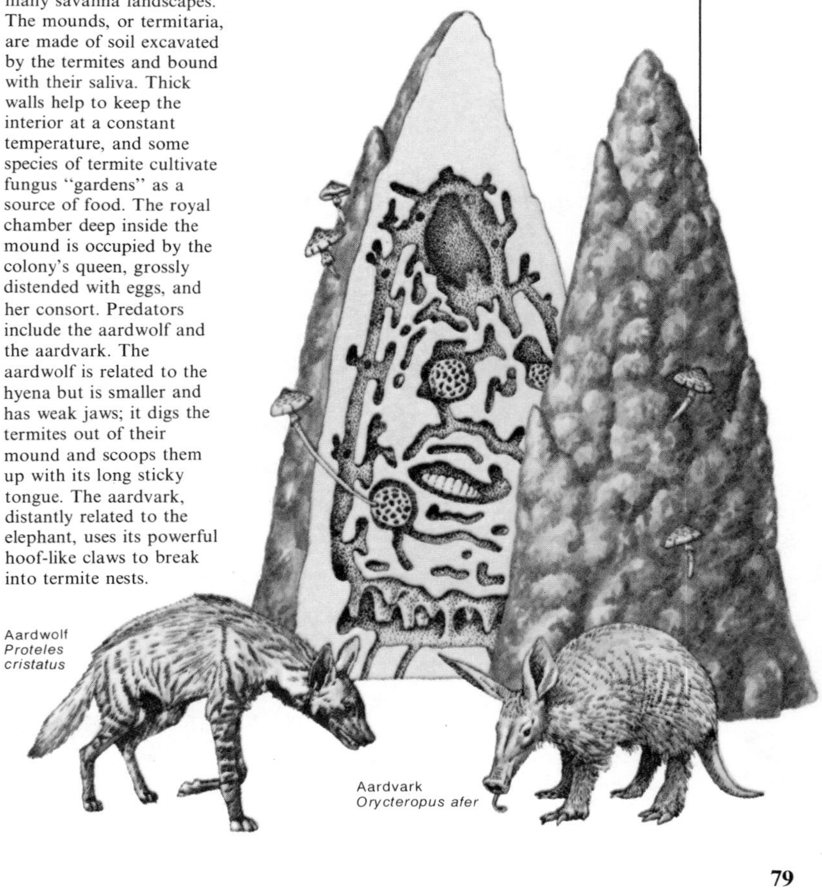

Aardwolf
Proteles
cristatus
Aardvark
Orycteropus afer

Man and the Savannas

In their natural state, savannas are among the most strikingly productive of all Earth's regions. Before the coming of man they supported a wealth of animal life that has seldom been surpassed. As yet they are relatively undeveloped, but many of them lie in areas where the pressures of population growth are becoming increasingly acute. Wisely used, they offer great hope for the future, both as cattle lands and for the cultivation of food crops. But without proper management savannas can rapidly turn into wasteland, and man will be the poorer for the loss of such a great natural resource.

Throughout much of the savannas the climate is semiarid and the soils tend to be poor: stripped of their plant cover, they bake hard and crack during the long months of hot sunshine, and during the wet season they often become waterlogged or are washed away by the rains. Man's indiscriminate use of fire, unwise agricultural methods and the unrestricted grazing of domestic animals have already led to much soil loss, and erosion is widespread in tropical Africa, Asia, South America and Australia.

Systematic burning has long been practiced by the people of the savannas. Large areas are burned each year to clear land for agriculture or to remove dead grass and encourage a fresh growth to feed livestock. The resulting ash provides much-needed nutrients for crops, and the grasses rapidly produce new green shoots that provide a rich pasture for domestic herds. But although the short-term effects may be beneficial, repeated burning is harmful to the vegetation, the animals and the soil.

Trees are always more or less damaged by fire. Their trunks become twisted and gnarled, fresh shoots are killed and young trees are prevented from growing. Constant burning can destroy some species altogether, and when they disappear so too does the wildlife that depends on them for food and shelter.

Grasses, on the other hand, may be encouraged by burning, and the lush new growth that springs up when the first rains break the long dry season provides welcome nourishment for domestic herds and game animals alike. But whereas game animals move freely over the range, cropping grasses at various stages of growth, cattle tend to feed on grass only in the neighborhood of wells and other sources of drinking water. They may trample the soil and continue to graze the same area until the grass is completely suppressed.

The hazards of large projects

Cultivation in marginal areas that are unsuited to intensive agriculture also contributes to the impoverishment of the savanna. The Sahel and Sudan savannas on the fringes of the Sahara are particularly vulnerable to large-scale development projects that fail to take account of local climate and soil. Mechanized agriculture in fragile areas bordering the desert may well lead to soil erosion and dustbowl conditions, and large-scale irrigation schemes often result in waterlogging and an accumulation of salts in the soil. Cultivation in the savannas requires understanding and care. Many smaller schemes are safer—and usually more productive—than a few large ones, but not all planners yet realize that agricultural methods that are effective in temperate regions seldom come up to expectations in tropical climates.

Man first inhabited the savannas, as he did many other regions of the world, as a hunter and gatherer. He took from the land only what he needed from day to day, and although he used fire as a hunting tool, his impact was little more than that of any other savanna inhabitant. In East Africa, groups of nomadic Hadza (left) still hunt game and collect roots, fruit and the honey of wild bees, building grass huts as temporary shelters.

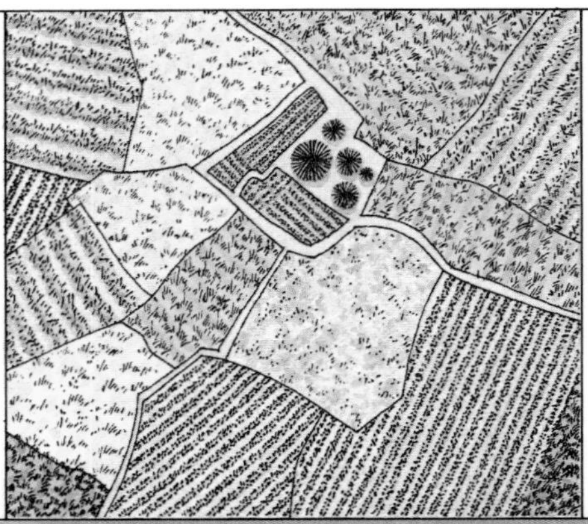

Small farms are scattered over much of the savannas. Plots close to houses are farmed continuously; beyond them lie the main fields, where periods of cultivation are usually followed by periods of fallow. Maize, millet and peanuts are the main food crops, and early and late crops are sometimes sown on the same plot to extend the growing season. Most of the work is done by hand, and any surplus to a family's needs is sold.

THE VULNERABLE WILDERNESS

Nowhere has man's impact on the tropical grasslands been felt more keenly than in Africa, although much of what is happening in Africa is happening also in savannas elsewhere. The majority of the people still live on the land, where the determining factor is the length and severity of the annual dry season. In the moister savannas the people are primarily cultivators, while in savannas that are too dry to sustain agriculture the main occupation is raising livestock. Most of the savannas are as yet sparsely settled, but competition is inevitably growing between man and wildlife, particularly in Africa, for the remaining tracts of relatively untouched wilderness.

The development of mineral resources and industries has led to an increasing movement of people—mainly young adults—from rural areas to towns and mining centers, attracted by opportunities for work—often at the expense of agriculture, since the heavy work of farming is left to the women, old people and children. Mining enterprises such as those in the Zambian Copper Belt (above), may recruit large labor forces from the surrounding countryside. Mining also dramatically alters the landscape, especially where the bedrock containing the ore reaches the surface and is quarried in huge terraces. The need for electricity to power mining and other industries leads, in turn, to the development of hydroelectric schemes, many of which entail resettling people whose villages are flooded by the creation of large artificial lakes.

Large areas of savanna have been set aside in East and Central Africa, and to a lesser extent in South America and Australia, as national parks and reserves where the landscape is kept intact and animals can be studied in their natural habitats. In Africa, observation platforms are frequently built close to waterholes where animals congregate to drink, and wardens use light aircraft to patrol the vast areas involved. Camel units are also used to patrol near-desert regions where much of the wildlife flourishes. Animals, such as elephants, whose numbers can grow out of control in the protected environment of the reserves are culled by licensed hunters to prevent the vegetation being destroyed. Culling maintains the health of the community as a whole and is also an economic source of meat in many countries where the people are short of protein foods.

Similarly, the introduction of European breeds of cattle into the savannas has not been an unqualified success. Not only are these breeds more susceptible to tropical pests and diseases than are the local varieties, but they are also adversely affected by the hot climate and their productivity is greatly reduced. In Africa and Brazil, native breeds are replacing more recent importations, and their productivity is being enhanced by selective breeding. In Australia, where most of the cattle are of British stock, tropical zebu, or humped cattle, are being introduced into the herds.

In the future, much more of the savanna may be developed as ranch lands, because the temperate grasslands will become less able to support enough animals to satisfy the world demand for meat. The *llanos* of Venezuela, the *campos* of Brazil and the tropical grasslands of Argentina and Australia already carry large herds of beef cattle. Throughout the savannas, however, ranching is still hampered by lack of water, poor natural pasture and remoteness from markets. In Africa, where herding is mainly nomadic, the sinking of wells by government organizations is changing the traditional ways of life, and cattle raising on a commercial scale is likely to become increasingly important. In Africa, too, the conservation and controlled cropping of game animals could become one of the most productive—and constructive—forms of land use.

Game as a resource

The value of game animals as a source of food is considerable. Buffaloes, for example, and kangaroos in Australia, can thrive on natural grasses that will not even maintain the weight of domestic stock, and they show greater gains in weight than African and European cattle on most forms of vegetation, while several species of antelopes can survive on a water ration that is wholly inadequate for cattle.

In recent years attention has been directed toward the economics of controlled cropping of wild game, and of ranching animals such as eland, which can be kept as if they were domesticated stock and can convert poor pasture into excellent meat. Game animals are also more resistant than cattle to the tsetse fly, which infests large areas of Africa and transmits the disease trypanosomiasis (known as nagana in cattle and as sleeping sickness in man).

But for the most part game animals are still considered to be a nuisance by man, and it is perhaps fortunate that by denying much of the savanna to domestic animals—and to man—the tsetse fly has preserved these regions from exploitation at the expense of the game. Many countries have also set aside large tracts of savanna as national parks and game reserves, where the natural environment is preserved and the wildlife can thrive.

Safeguarding the savanna

At a time when the pressure of the expanding human population calls for the development of areas hitherto uninhabited or only sparsely populated, it may seem paradoxical to maintain that the development of national parks and nature reserves is essential to the welfare of mankind. The aim of game conservation, however, is not simply to preserve rare or unusual animals for the enjoyment of posterity, or even for their scientific interest. It is to ensure that the land is put to its most economic and efficient use. The next few decades will show whether the savannas of the world will be developed into major sources of food and revenue for the countries that own them, or whether they will be misused and degraded into desert.

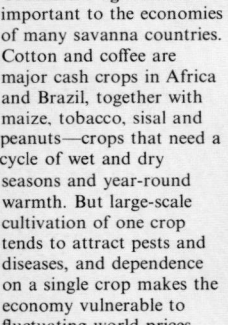

Commercial agriculture is important to the economies of many savanna countries. Cotton and coffee are major cash crops in Africa and Brazil, together with maize, tobacco, sisal and peanuts—crops that need a cycle of wet and dry seasons and year-round warmth. But large-scale cultivation of one crop tends to attract pests and diseases, and dependence on a single crop makes the economy vulnerable to fluctuating world prices.

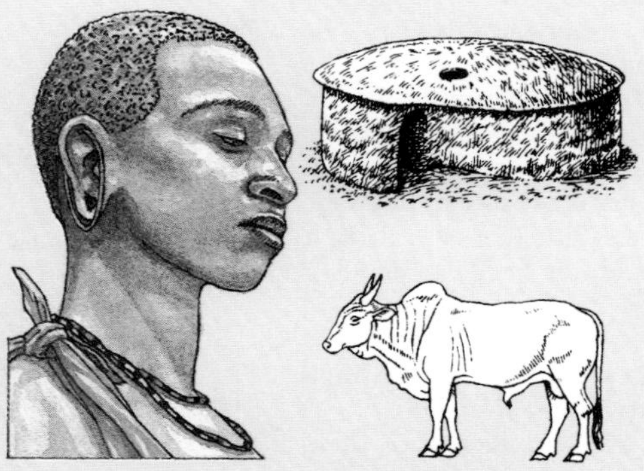

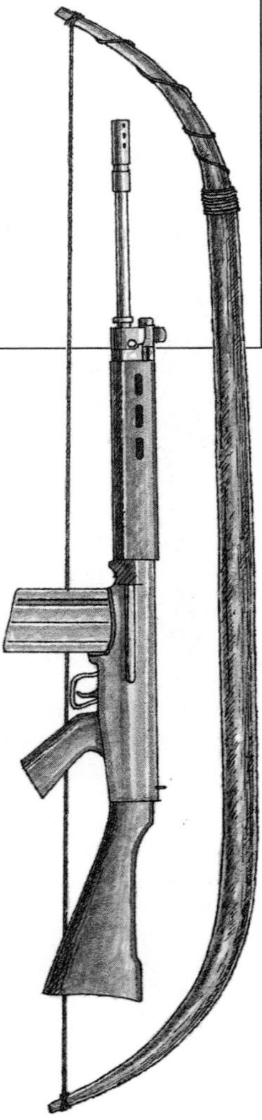

Cattle rearing takes the place of cultivation in areas that are too dry to be cropped successfully. In Africa, people such as the Masai are nomadic herders, moving their cattle long distances in search of pasture. Wealth is counted in terms of the numbers rather than the quality of the cattle they own, but improved management of their herds and better control of animal diseases are now making their cattle much more productive.

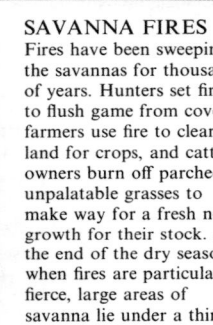

SAVANNA FIRES

Fires have been sweeping the savannas for thousands of years. Hunters set fires to flush game from cover, farmers use fire to clear land for crops, and cattle owners burn off parched, unpalatable grasses to make way for a fresh new growth for their stock. At the end of the dry season, when fires are particularly fierce, large areas of savanna lie under a thin haze of smoke.

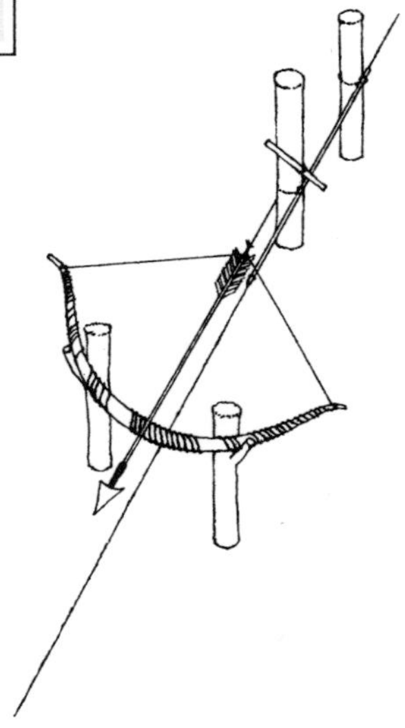

Poaching, together with the takeover of wildlife ranges by farms and livestock, has led many animals to near-extinction in areas where they were once plentiful. Poisoned arrows are capable of killing even the biggest African game: sometimes they are set as traps and are triggered by the animal itself walking into a trip line. More sophisticated poachers use machine-guns and high-powered assault rifles, and airlift their illicit cargos of skins, ivory and rhinoceros horn. Illegal hunting for meat, which is dried and sold, has also become a large, highly organized and very profitable business in many areas.

Game animals also provide the spectacular displays that attract tourists and make tourism an important source of income for many developing nations. Today, most tourists pursue game with cameras instead of guns. The hunting that led to the wholesale slaughter of wildlife in previous years is banned, and so is the traffic in trophies, although even in the sanctuary provided by parks and reserves animals still fall prey to poachers.

Animals are frequently transferred from areas where they are at risk to safer areas such as game parks and reserves. In Kenya, helicopters came to the rescue of a herd of rare antelopes when their range was threatened by a proposed irrigation scheme and moved them to Tsavo National Park. Animals are also moved to introduce new blood to small, isolated herds or to restock areas from which they have been lost.

Tropical Rainforests

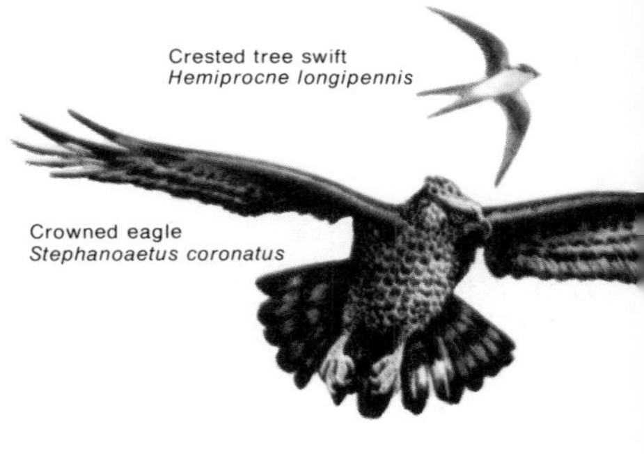
Crested tree swift
Hemiprocne longipennis
Crowned eagle
Stephanoaetus coronatus

Tropical rainforests, extremely rich in both plant and animal life, consist of a series of layered or stratified habitats. These range from the dark and humid forest floor through a layer of shrubs to the emerging tops of the scattered giant trees towering above the dense main canopy of the forest. Each layer of vegetation is a miniature life zone containing a wide selection of animal species. These can be divided into a number of ecological groups according to their various ways of life, and many have evolved special adaptations to enable them to make maximum use of the plentiful food supply surrounding them.

Tropical rainforests occur only in the regions close to the Equator; they have a heavy rainfall and a uniformly hot and moist climate. There are slightly more of these forests in the northern half of the world than in the southern half and they occur at altitudes of up to 1,500 m (5,000 ft). Temperatures are normally between 24°C and 30°C (77°–86°F) and rarely fall below 21°C (70°F) or rise above 32°C (90°F). The skies are often cloudy and the rain falls more or less evenly throughout the year. Rainfall is usually more than 2,000 mm (78 in) a year and is never less than 1,500 mm (59 in). A distinctive feature of this tropical, humid climate is that the average daily temperature range is much greater than the range between the hottest and coolest months.

A stratified habitat

There are usually three to five overlapping layers in the mature tropical rainforest. The tallest trees (called "emergents") rise above a closed, dense canopy formed by the crowns of less tall trees, which nevertheless can reach more than 40 m (130 ft) tall. Below this canopy is a third or middle layer of trees—the understory; their crowns do not meet but they still form a dense layer of growth about 5–20 m (16–65 ft) tall. The fourth layer consists of woody shrubs of varying heights between 1–5 m (3–16 ft). The bottom layer comprises decomposers (fungi) that rarely reach 50 cm (20 in) in height.

Although the trees are so tall, few of them have really thick trunks. Nearly all are evergreens, shedding their dark, leathery leaves and growing new ones continuously. Many of the larger species grow buttresses—thin, triangular slabs of hardwood that spread out from the bases of their trunks. These support the trees, so removing the need for a heavy outlay of energy and resources on deep root systems. Hanging lianas (vines), thin and strong as rope, vanish like cables into the mass of foliage. They are especially abundant on riverbanks, where the canopy of trees is thinner; their leaves and flowers appear only among the treetops.

Epiphytes—plants that grow on other plants but do not take their nourishment from them—festoon the trunks and branches of trees, and up to 80 may grow on a single tree. They include many kinds of orchid and bromeliad. Their aerial roots make use of a humus substitute derived from the remains of other plants, often brought together by ants. The bases of their leaves may be broad and bowl shaped and collect and hold water; they also provide homes for a variety of insects and reptiles.

Rainforest soils are not as fertile as might be supposed by the luxuriance of their vegetation. On the contrary, the silicates and compounds necessary for plant growth are leached away by the rain to leave red or yellow soils of poor quality. This process, known as laterization, is widespread in the humid tropics. Humus is rapidly broken down by bacteria, fungi and termites, while earthworms, which in more temperate regions normally contribute to the mixing of humus with mineral particles, are usually absent.

In rainforests there are often up to 25 different tree species on a single hectare of land (60 species to the acre). Most temperate forests have only a fifth of this number, with nothing like the abundance of plants that grow in the tropics. This incredible variety supports—directly or indirectly—a corresponding variety of animal species which has an abundant food supply because the forest never ceases to be productive. This is why most mammals do not move far; they stay where their food grows.

Life in the canopy

The dense leaves and branches of the canopy provide the most food and so support the greatest number of species. Macaws and toucans (from the American tropics) and parrots and trogons (which live in forests throughout the tropics) eat the fruit growing in the

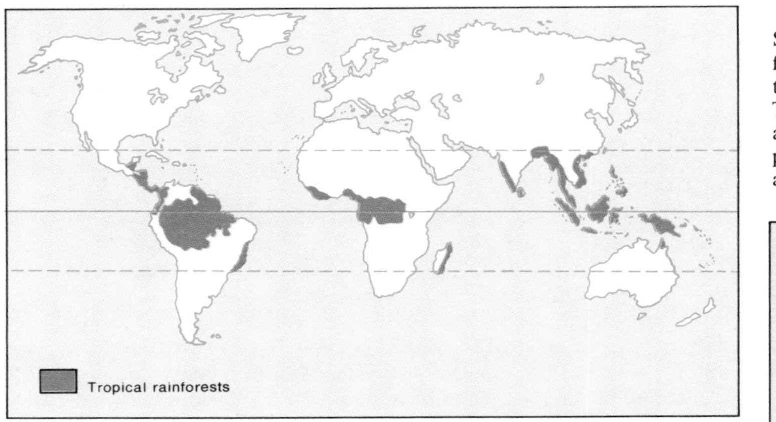
Tropical rainforests

Tropical rainforests are located in the hot and wet equatorial lands of Latin America, West Africa, Madagascar and Asia. These areas have consistently high temperatures throughout the year and receive high rainfall from the moist and unstable winds blowing in from the oceans.

The hummingbird numbers about 300 species, most of which are confined to the forests of South America. It is renowned for its ability to hover while gathering nectar, a feat achieved by the almost 180° rotations of its wings, which beat rapidly more than 80 times per second.

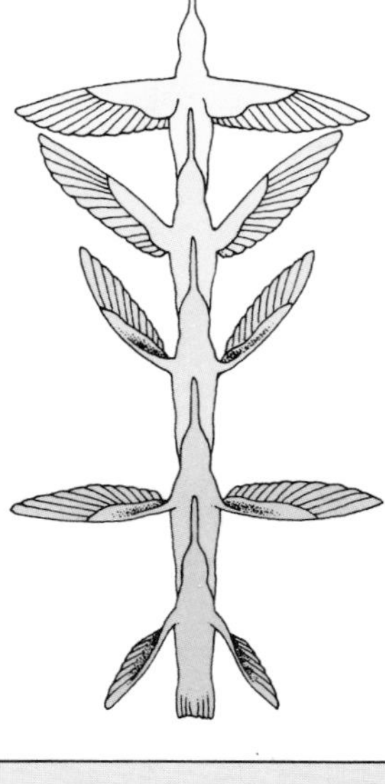

Moth orchid
Phalaenopsis sanderana

Flowering plants of the forest include epiphytes such as bromeliads and orchids like the species of *Phalaenopsis* illustrated here. Epiphytes grow on other plants such as trees where they can receive sunlight and are nourished by humus in the bark. Many epiphytic orchids have swellings in their roots or at the bases of their leaves where water can be stored. Seventy species of *Phalaenopsis* grow in southeast Asian forests and *P. sanderana*, one of the most beautiful, was first discovered in the Philippines in 1882.

THE LAYERS OF THE FOREST

Stratification—the existence of distinct layers o forest vegetation—is especially pronounced in th tropics, where there are usually five main storys These can overlap greatly and may vary in height fron area to area. The large differences between the layer present many varied habitats and ecological niches fo a very wide range of animals.

CANOPY LAYER

This dense story exerts a powerful influence on the levels below since its trees, which grow between 20 m (65 ft) and 40 m (130 ft) tall, form such a thick layer of vegetation that they cut off sunlight from the forest below. The canopy is noted for the diversity of its fauna. Many birds and animals are adapted to running along branches to get the flowers, fruits or nuts that form their diets. The pointed tips of canopy leaves encourage rapid drainage.

Sacred langu
Presbytis ent
Tree shrew
Tupaia glis

MIDDLE LAYER

This understory comprises trees from 5 m (16 ft) to 20 m (65 ft) tall whose long, narrow crowns do not become quite so dense as those of the canopy. There is very often no clear distinction, however, between this level and the canopy. Middle-layer trees are strong enough to bear large animals such as leopards that spend part of their lives on the ground. Epiphytes are plentiful in this layer.

Leopard
Panthera par

Pouched tree frog
Gastrotheca ovifera
Orang-utan
Pongo pygmaeus

SHRUB LAYER

The vegetation of this level is sparse in comparison with that above it and consists of treelets and woody shrubs that rarely reach 5 m (16 ft). These grow up in any available space between the abundant boles of large trees. Life in this story exists equally well at ground level.

Four-striped squirrel
Funisciurus lemniscatus
Oriental civet
Viverra tangalunga
Tree pangolir
Manis tricusp

GROUND LAYER

Shade-tolerant herbs, ferns and tree seedlings represent the only flora at ground level; there is no grass there. Light is less than one percent of full daylight so that many mammals are well camouflaged in the gloom, whereas others have compact bodies to facilitate movement through the undergrowth. Ants and termites are well adapted to the high humidity and darkness of the forest floor. Fungi and a host of invertebrates quickly break down the litter of rotting leaves, fruit and fallen branches to provide vital nutrients for the fast-growing trees of the tropical rainforest.

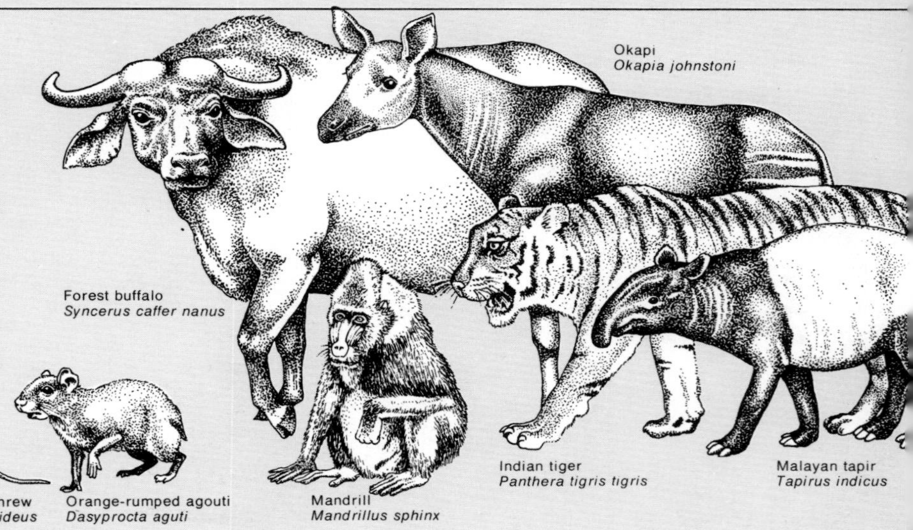
Okapi
Okapia johnstoni
Forest buffalo
Syncerus caffer nanus
Indian tiger
Panthera tigris tigris
Malayan tapir
Tapirus indicus
Mandrill
Mandrillus sphinx

Congo forest mouse
Deomys ferrugineus
Short-eared elephant shrew
Macroscelides proboscideus
Orange-rumped agouti
Dasyprocta aguti

EMERGENT LAYER
Tall, solitary trees that break through the dense canopy below are known as "emergents" and may reach 40 m (130 ft) or more. Life at this level consists largely of birds and insects. Butterflies seldom leave the treetops. Galagos (or bushbabies) are active at night. Hawk eagles and other raptors prey on species from the canopy, while swifts spend all their time in the air at speeds of up to 160 km/hr (100 mph) in pursuit of their insect diet.

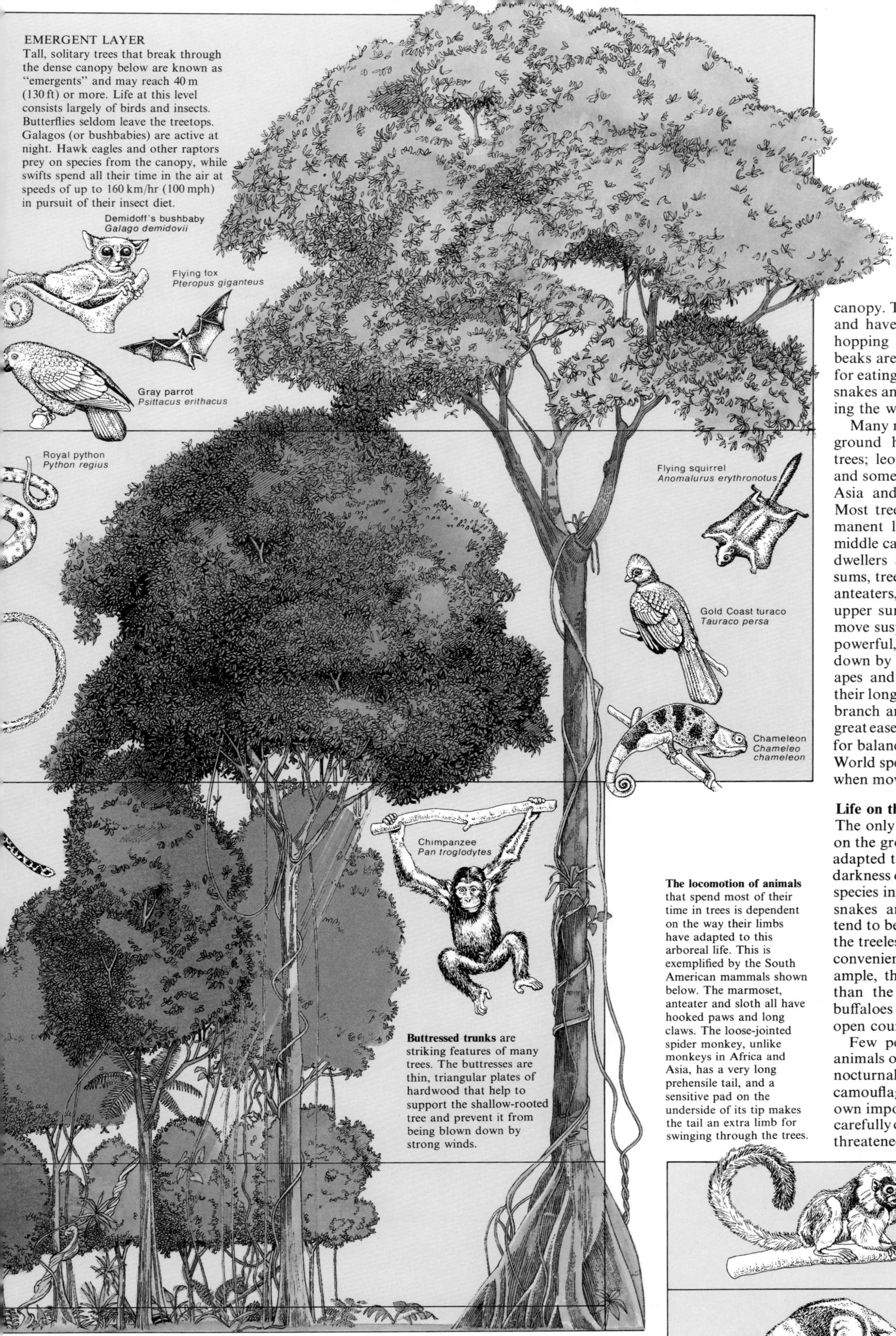
Demidoff's bushbaby
Galago demidovii
Flying fox
Pteropus giganteus
Gray parrot
Psittacus erithacus
Royal python
Python regius
Flying squirrel
Anomalurus erythronotus
Gold Coast turaco
Tauraco persa
Chameleon
Chameleo chameleon
Chimpanzee
Pan troglodytes

Buttressed trunks are striking features of many trees. The buttresses are thin, triangular plates of hardwood that help to support the shallow-rooted tree and prevent it from being blown down by strong winds.

Morpho butterfly
Morpho didius

canopy. They do not need to fly far for this diet and have small wings and legs well suited to hopping or climbing along branches. Their beaks are short and curved—perfectly adapted for eating fruit. Bats, flying squirrels, tree frogs, snakes and geckos are plentiful. Insects, including the world's largest species, also abound.

Many mammals that spend some time on the ground have some adaptation for climbing trees; leopards, jaguars, smaller cats, rodents and some insect eaters such as the pangolins of Asia and Africa can climb reasonably well. Most tree dwellers, however, live almost permanent lives at much greater heights in the middle canopy and above. The majority of tree dwellers are branch runners, including opossums, tree kangaroos, lemurs, squirrels or scaly anteaters, which progress on all fours on the upper surface of branches. In contrast, sloths move suspended beneath the branches by their powerful, incurved claws, and bats hang upside down by their hind limbs when at rest. Certain apes and monkeys are brachiators—they use their long arms to swing rapidly from branch to branch and from tree to tree, holding on with great ease. Many monkeys make use of their tails for balance while resting or eating and, in New World species, as a fifth limb to grasp branches when moving or gathering leaves, fruit or nuts.

Life on the ground

The only animals found in very large numbers on the ground are ants and termites, which are adapted to the high humidity and comparative darkness of the forest floor. Other ground-living species include amphibians and reptiles such as snakes and tortoises. Some forest mammals tend to be smaller than their cousins inhabiting the treeless grasslands, adapting to a size more convenient for life among the trees. For example, the forest elephant of Zaire is smaller than the African bush elephant, and forest buffaloes are smaller than those that inhabit open country.

Few people ever see the large number of animals of the tropical rainforest since most are nocturnal, very shy or are hidden by excellent camouflage. Nonetheless, each species has its own important niche and plays a vital role in a carefully controlled ecosystem, now increasingly threatened by the activities of man.

The locomotion of animals that spend most of their time in trees is dependent on the way their limbs have adapted to this arboreal life. This is exemplified by the South American mammals shown below. The marmoset, anteater and sloth all have hooked paws and long claws. The loose-jointed spider monkey, unlike monkeys in Africa and Asia, has a very long prehensile tail, and a sensitive pad on the underside of its tip makes the tail an extra limb for swinging through the trees.

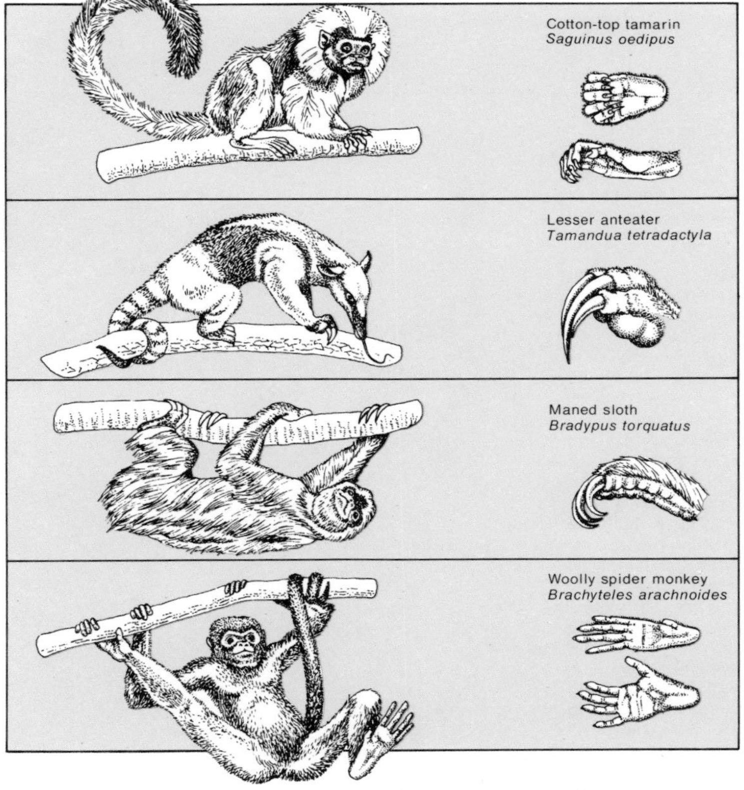
Cotton-top tamarin
Saguinus oedipus
Lesser anteater
Tamandua tetradactyla
Maned sloth
Bradypus torquatus
Woolly spider monkey
Brachyteles arachnoides

Toco toucan
Ramphastos toco
Rhinoceros hornbill
Buceros rhinoceros

The large, decurved beaks of toucans and hornbills allow them to pick fruit and nuts from the outer branches of trees with ease. Despite their similar bills, however, the two groups of birds are unrelated and have different distributions. Toucans live in the forests of Latin America, whereas hornbills inhabit those of Africa and Asia.

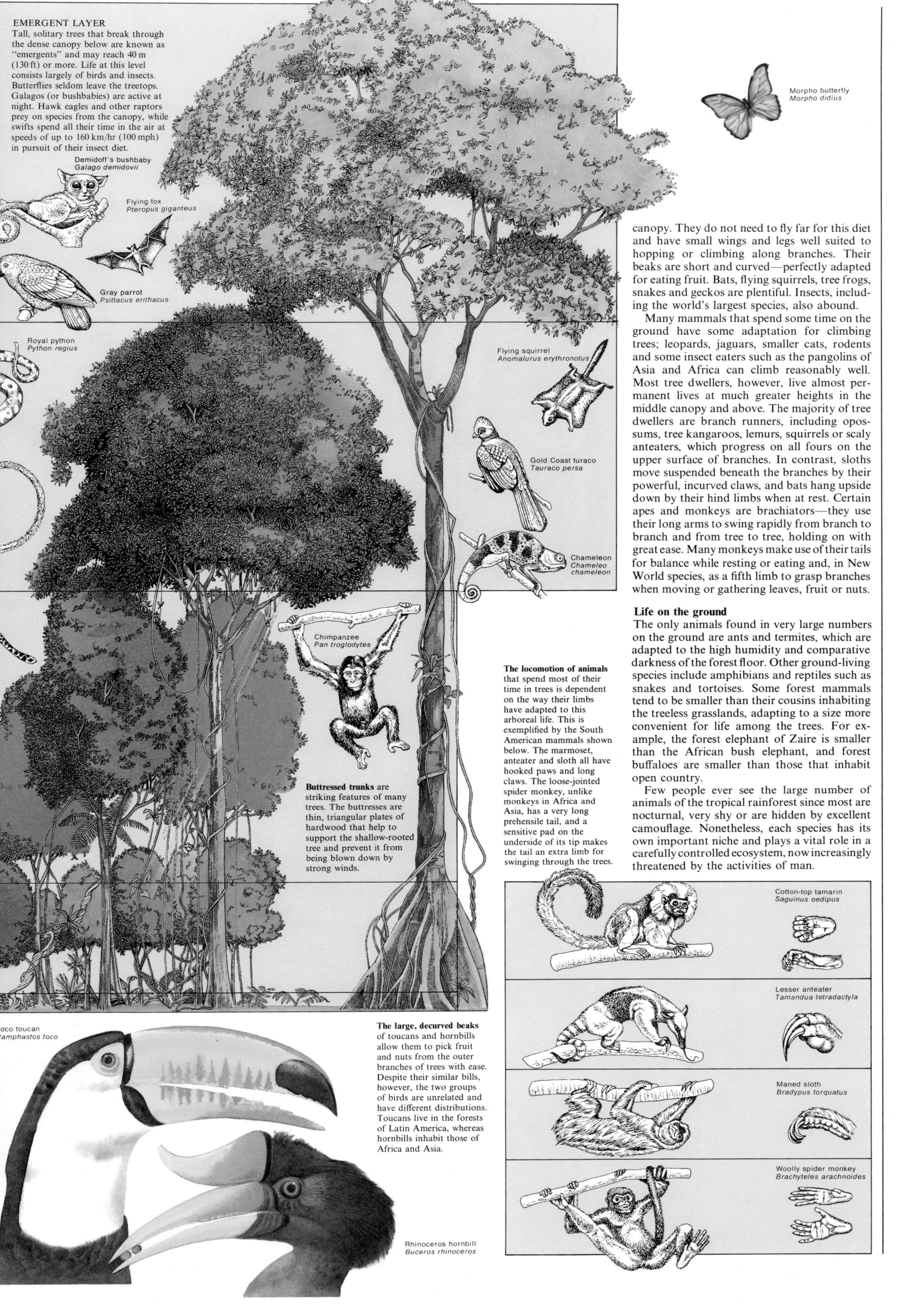

Man and the Tropical Rainforests

Every three seconds a portion of original rainforest the size of a football field disappears as man fells the trees and extends his cultivation. Although tropical conditions allow rapid regrowth of secondary forest, the loss of primary forest is destroying thousands of plant and animal species that will never again be seen on Earth. Even by conservative estimates, it is likely that all the world's primary tropical forest will have disappeared within 85 years unless the trend is reversed.

The activities of man have only recently begun to threaten the tropical rainforest. Since prehistoric times, forests have offered shelter to people who, lacking any knowledge of agriculture, have existed as hunters and gatherers. They used only stone and wooden weapons such as bows and arrows to kill their animal prey, and collected berries, fruit and honey from their surroundings. Their influence on the forest environment was minimal and today a few races such as African pygmies and the Punans of Borneo still live in such a simple state of balance with nature. The Punans, for example, have no permanent homes, but use leaves and branches to construct temporary shelters that are used for only a few weeks before being abandoned. The pygmies build similar homes.

Shifting agriculture

Most forest dwellers, however, live in more permanent settlements and grow most of their food in forest clearings they have made. Such people are expert at chopping down trees in order to set fire to them, and this "slash-and-burn" farming results in small areas littered with charred logs and stumps whose ashes enrich the ground. Crops such as wild tapioca (cassava or manioc) are widely grown, but after a year or two the soil loses the little fertility it once had so that a new tract of forest has to be cleared and burned. Such shifting agriculture provides food for more than 200 million inhabitants of the Third World. As a farming system it has been used throughout the world for more than 2,000 years. When there were few farmers per kilometer the land was allowed to lie fallow for at least 10 years so that the soil could recover. Today, however, population pressures are so great that fallow periods have been drastically reduced and a swift repetition of slash-and-burn degrades and removes nutrients from the soil.

Effects on world climate

Tropical forest floors seldom have deep layers of humus so that, once trees are removed, the shallow topsoil is exposed and soon becomes eroded. In turn, this reduces the capacity of the ground to retain moisture, and without this sponge-like effect runoff can become very erratic and lead to floods, such as those that frequently occur in India and Bangladesh. Estuary sedimentation is often greatly increased

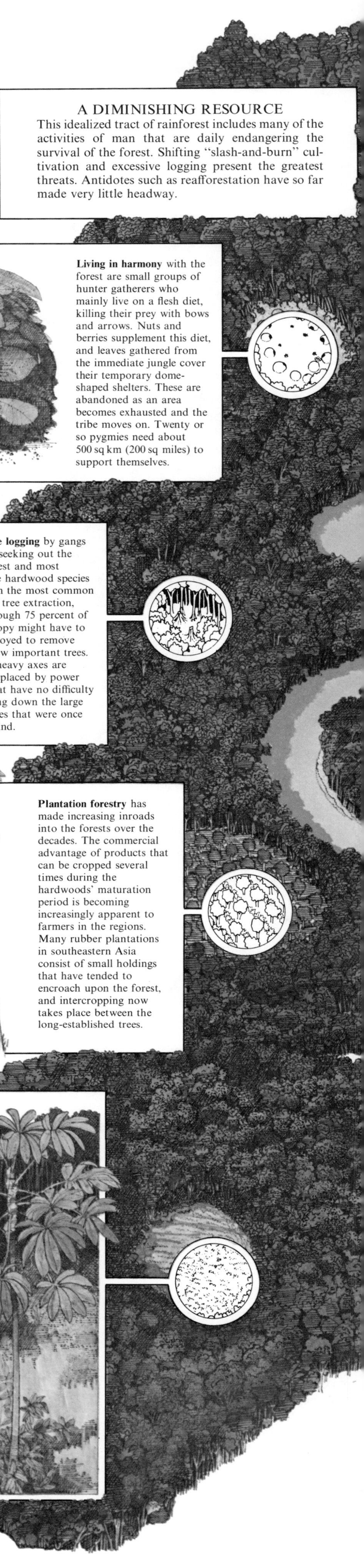

A DIMINISHING RESOURCE

This idealized tract of rainforest includes many of the activities of man that are daily endangering the survival of the forest. Shifting "slash-and-burn" cultivation and excessive logging present the greatest threats. Antidotes such as reafforestation have so far made very little headway.

Living in harmony with the forest are small groups of hunter gatherers who mainly live on a flesh diet, killing their prey with bows and arrows. Nuts and berries supplement this diet, and leaves gathered from the immediate jungle cover their temporary dome-shaped shelters. These are abandoned as an area becomes exhausted and the tribe moves on. Twenty or so pygmies need about 500 sq km (200 sq miles) to support themselves.

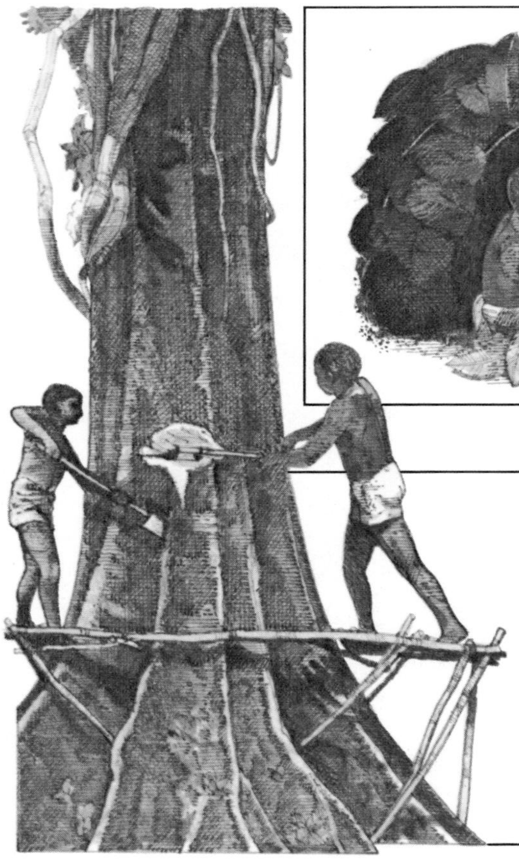

Selective logging by gangs of men seeking out the straightest and most valuable hardwood species has been the most common form of tree extraction, even though 75 percent of the canopy might have to be destroyed to remove just a few important trees. Today heavy axes are being replaced by power saws that have no difficulty in cutting down the large buttresses that were once left behind.

Plantation forestry has made increasing inroads into the forests over the decades. The commercial advantage of products that can be cropped several times during the hardwoods' maturation period is becoming increasingly apparent to farmers in the regions. Many rubber plantations in southeastern Asia consist of small holdings that have tended to encroach upon the forest, and intercropping now takes place between the long-established trees.

Shifting cultivation converts thousands of square kilometers of primary forest to substandard cultivation every year. Forest is cleared by slash-and-burn, the resulting fertile clearing is cropped with staples such as manioc, and then left to degrade to secondary forest once the ash-strewn ground has lost its poor fertility. Inevitably, the ground becomes permanently degraded. One encouraging antidote to the futility of such shifting agriculture is the recent strategy of agroforestry (as used by countries such as Nigeria and Thailand), which encourages the planting of fast-growing trees at the same time as the farmer's normal crops. Such intercropping offers considerable financial incentives to the small itinerant farmer.

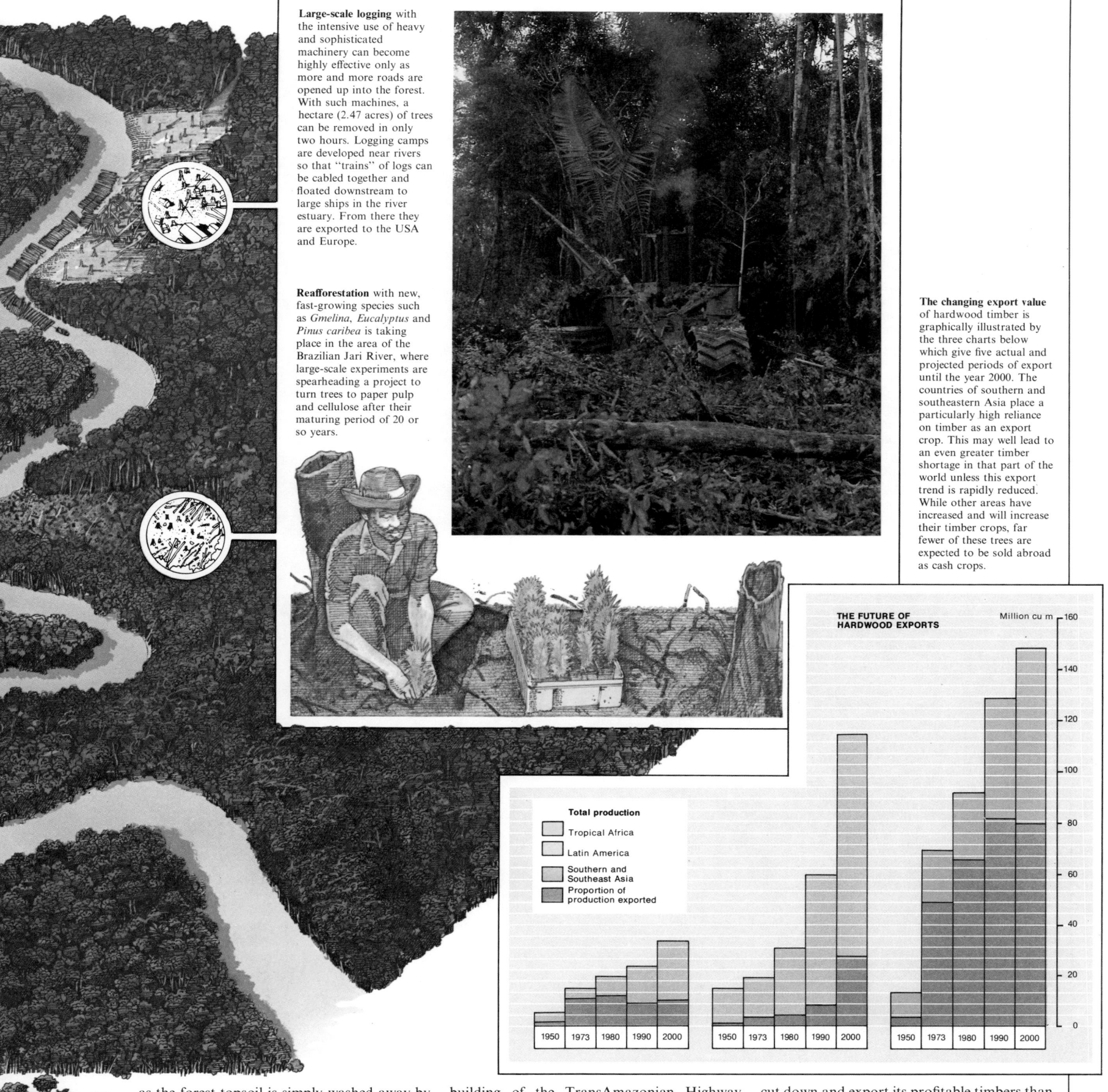

Large-scale logging with the intensive use of heavy and sophisticated machinery can become highly effective only as more and more roads are opened up into the forest. With such machines, a hectare (2.47 acres) of trees can be removed in only two hours. Logging camps are developed near rivers so that "trains" of logs can be cabled together and floated downstream to large ships in the river estuary. From there they are exported to the USA and Europe.

Reafforestation with new, fast-growing species such as *Gmelina*, *Eucalyptus* and *Pinus caribea* is taking place in the area of the Brazilian Jari River, where large-scale experiments are spearheading a project to turn trees to paper pulp and cellulose after their maturing period of 20 or so years.

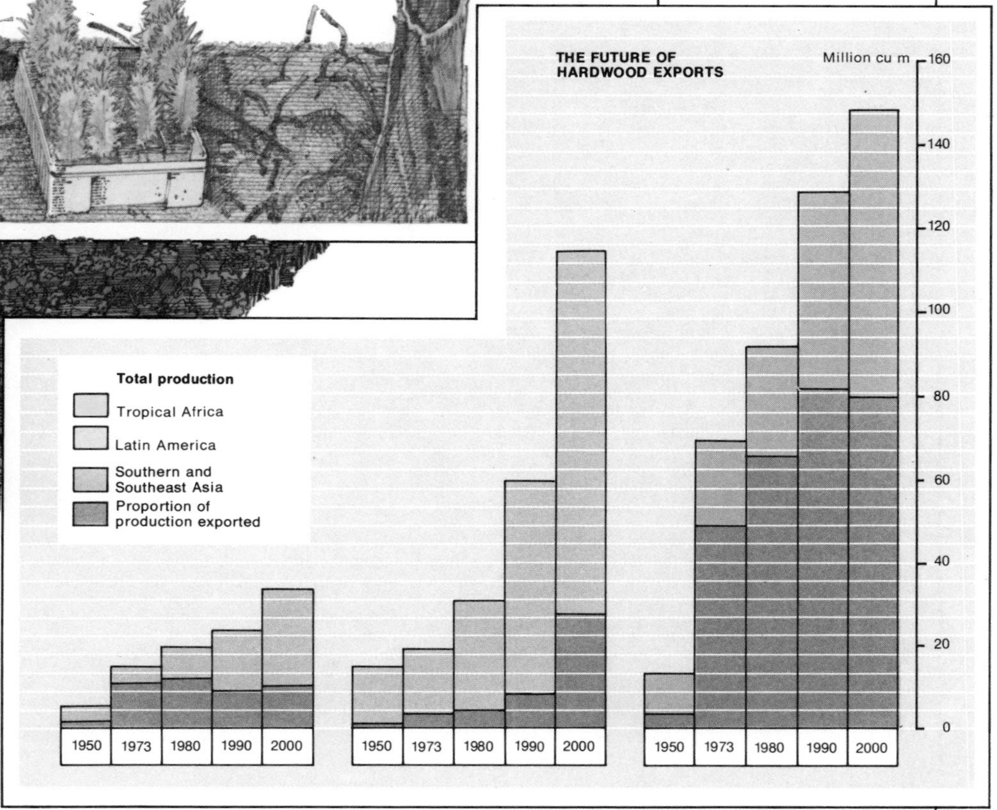
THE FUTURE OF HARDWOOD EXPORTS
Million cu m
160
140
120
100
80
60
40
20
0
Total production
Tropical Africa
Latin America
Southern and Southeast Asia
Proportion of production exported
1950
1973
1980
1990
2000
1950
1973
1980
1990
2000
1950
1973
1980
1990
2000

The changing export value of hardwood timber is graphically illustrated by the three charts below which give five actual and projected periods of export until the year 2000. The countries of southern and southeastern Asia place a particularly high reliance on timber as an export crop. This may well lead to an even greater timber shortage in that part of the world unless this export trend is rapidly reduced. While other areas have increased and will increase their timber crops, far fewer of these trees are expected to be sold abroad as cash crops.

as the forest topsoil is simply washed away by torrential rain. In parts of Asia, deforestation has caused changes in water flow that have interfered with the production of new high-yield rice crops.

Tropical forests contain an enormous store of carbon, and some authorities believe that its release into the air (as carbon dioxide) when the forest is burned down may be as great in volume as that released by the rest of the world's fossil fuels. The higher proportion of carbon dioxide in the atmosphere may lead to an increase in global temperatures, especially at the poles. Trees also release oxygen into the air through photosynthesis, and some scientists have estimated that half of the world's oxygen is derived from this source. Others estimate that half of the rainfall of the Amazon basin is generated by the forest itself, so that any great reduction in tree cover would turn Amazonia into a much drier region.

Threats to Amazonia

Much attention has been paid to the situation of Amazonia, covering as it does some 6.5 million sq km ($2\frac{1}{2}$ million sq miles). In an attempt to give better access to timber and mineral reserves, the Brazilian government's building of the TransAmazonian Highway (3,000 km or 1,860 miles long) has opened the way to deforestation, and settlers have been encouraged to make small holdings on the cleared forest beside the road. Between 1966 and 1978, the government calculated that farmers and big business interests had turned 80,000 sq km (31,000 sq miles) of forest into grazing land for 6 million cattle intended for hamburgers. However, like the wholesale extraction of timber, this has proved to be of doubtful economic value. Because costs rise steeply as less accessible areas are tapped, expenses tend to eliminate logging profits.

Threats in Africa

Even greater threats to tropical forest land have come from less cautious and realistic governments, such as that of Ivory Coast. There neither shifting agriculture nor excessive logging for valuable export sales appear to be under any sort of control. Accordingly, between 1966 and 1974, the area of forest declined from 156,000 sq km (60,000 sq miles) to 54,000 sq km (20,000 sq miles), much of the latter being secondary forest that can never be returned to its original status. Like many other developing countries, Ivory Coast has been more keen to cut down and export its profitable timbers than to think about protecting its invaluable forest environment. Inevitably, forest farmers move into cleared areas and often establish plantation cash crops such as coffee, cocoa and rubber, while the establishment of national parks to curtail depletion has often had very little profitable effect. The Malaysian rainforest is also disappearing rapidly, through widescale logging and open-cast mining for bauxite (aluminum ore).

A large proportion of the world's rainforest occurs in tropical countries faced with severe problems of population control. It is therefore inevitable that the pressures on such forests will be great. Human interference does more than merely destroy the primary forest, to be replaced in time by secondary growth; more importantly, the wholesale removal of trees also drastically reduces the vast genetic reservoir contained in the number of plant and animal species the forests harbor. This in itself is a sound ecological argument for preserving forests and for reversing current trends towards monoculture in the tropics. All the warnings about forest depletion appear to be clear, yet there seems little hope that man will heed them until it is too late.

Monsoon Regions

The word monsoon often conjures up the image of torrential rain and steaming tropical jungles. Yet such a view is misleading, for very great contrasts occur in the regions of the tropical world with a monsoon climate. What distinguishes monsoon regions is not so much the amount of rainfall or the permanently high temperatures, but the dramatic contrast between seasons, with an extended dry season as an essential feature. And in fact the word monsoon derives from the Arabic word for season.

THE SEASON OF RAIN

Life in the monsoon regions balances on the expectation of seasonal heavy rain. In much of India, for instance, 85 percent of the annual rainfall occurs during the limited monsoon periods, and humans as well as plants and animals depend on it wholly. About half the world's people live in these regions, in communities whose rhythm of life necessarily reflects the rains' seasonal nature.

This contrast between wet and dry seasons reflects the reversals of winds over sea and land, which in the northern hemisphere blow from the northeast in the dry winter season, and from the southwest in the wet summer periods.

The monsoon regions occur most widely in southern, southeastern and eastern Asia to the south of latitude 25°N, and in western and central Africa north of the Equator, but there are also smaller regions with a characteristically monsoon climate in eastern Africa, northern Australia and central America. Despite the similar overall climatic pattern, however, the monsoon regions are otherwise very diverse.

Before human settlement the original vegetation of the monsoon regions reflected the dominance of an extended dry season followed by a period of violent rainfall. Typical forest cover was provided by the sal (*Shorea robusta*) deciduous forest, which adjusts to extended periods of moisture deficiency by shedding its leaves. However, within the monsoon region rainfall varies from 200 mm (8 in) a year to more than 20,000 mm (800 in), and the rainy periods may vary between three and nine months.

The range of vegetation found in the monsoon regions reflects this diversity. Where tropical rainforest alters to monsoon forest, as in eastern Java, there is a sharp fall in the total number of plant and animal species, and species adapted to endure seasonal drought begin to be seen. At the other extreme of rainfall the forest thins and shades into semidesert vegetation in India's northwest. But if there is a "type" of monsoon vegetation it is tropical deciduous forest, with sal as the dominant species.

As well as contrasts in climate, the monsoon regions also exhibit pronounced changes in temperature and vegetation as a result of variations in altitude. The Western Ghats of India and the foothills of the Himalayas in Assam both rise to more than 2,500 m (8,200 ft). Temperatures decrease sharply at such altitudes with corresponding changes in vegetation. In southern India on the Nilgiri Hills a wet temperate forest is characteristic, with an intermingling of temperate and tropical species. Magnolias, planes and elms all grow there.

Agriculture in monsoon regions

Despite its extensive area there is no part of the monsoon world that is untouched by man and by man's activities. In southern Asia, agricultural activity can be traced back at least 5,000 years, and there have been agricultural settlements throughout the monsoon regions for at least 1,500 years. Man's activity and the grazing of domesticated animals have interfered with, and progressively modified, the natural vegetation. The range of species indicates that, in the whole of the monsoon biome, there is now virtually no primary forest left. The pace of man's interference has speeded up considerably over the last 100 years. As a result, less than 10 percent of the land in southern Asia is now forested, and other parts of the monsoon regions are similarly losing their forest cover.

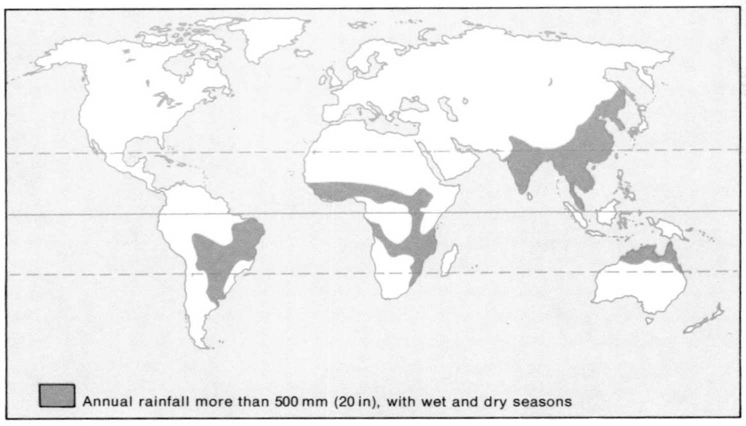
Annual rainfall more than 500 mm (20 in), with wet and dry seasons

Many parts of the world experience "monsoon" winds, blowing from sea to land in summer, and from land to sea in winter; but typical monsoon vegetation is most clearly seen in the regions of southeastern Asia and the Indian subcontinent. In climatic terms, however, the monsoon circulation of seasonal wind reversals, with wetter summers and dry winters, also affects considerable areas of Africa, South America and northern Australia.

Many of today's farming methods incorporate traditional cultivation practices, but there have also been very significant changes in recent decades. Traditional agriculture in the monsoon regions has been developed to take into account the seasonal nature of its rainfall pattern and the total rainfall received. The fundamental role of water throughout the region and the absence of low temperatures have placed great importance on either cultivating crops that can tolerate the seasonal rainfall pattern, or on providing irrigation.

Through most of southern Asia, overwhelmingly the most populous of the monsoon regions, the most important single crop is rice, which covers about one-third of the total cultivated area. Rice needs a great deal of water and for this reason is grown mainly in areas of high irrigation, such as the delta lands of the southern and eastern coasts of India, and in areas where rainfall is more than 1,500 mm (59 in) a year. Its cultivation creates a very distinctive landscape as a result of the fact that rice must spend much of its growing period with a few centimeters of water over the soil.

Rice cultivation gives the monsoon regions their characteristic pattern of paddy fields, but other cereal crops such as wheat, the millets and sorghum are also very important. These can tolerate far drier conditions than can rice and occur in areas such as central India or upland Thailand, where uncertain and less abundant rainfall puts a premium on drought tolerance.

Even with traditional crops, man has often interfered extensively with the environment in order to increase yields and attempt to guarantee successful cropping. Traditional irrigation schemes range from diverting rivers at times of flood, in order to lead water to dry land, to digging wells and building small reservoirs. But recent technological developments have brought a new dimension to agricultural activity in the monsoon regions. Large-scale dam and irrigation canal schemes have become important in Africa as well as in monsoon Asia. The introduction and speed of electric or diesel "pumpsets" have transformed well irrigation in regions with extensive groundwater. The reliable water supply that irrigation can give has brought in its train the opportunity for farmers to adopt a wide range of new farming practices. Chemical fertilizers and new strains of seed have made possible great increases in the productivity of the land in many parts of the monsoon regions, but their use is generally restricted to areas of reliable water supply.

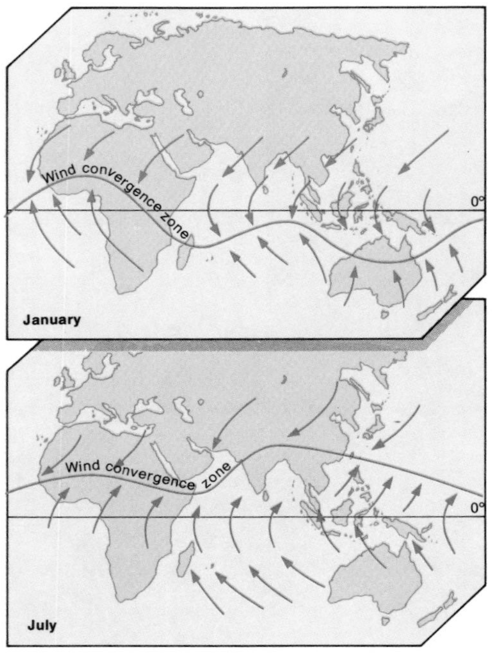
Wind convergence zone
0°
January
Wind convergence zone
0°
July

Heat differences in the atmosphere cause the seasonal wind reversals (left) characteristic of monsoon circulation. In January the northern hemisphere is tilted away from the sun, and cold, dry winds blow from the central Asian landmass toward the Equator. Here they change direction (an effect of the Earth's rotation), converge with other winds, and drop their rain. In July the situation is reversed when the heated Asian landmass attracts a flow of cooler air from the equatorial oceans, which moves northward with the sun. The moist air condenses on reaching land, and the monsoon rains descend.

Subsistence cultivation over thousands of years has been by far the most important element in the transformation of the landscape and vegetation of the monsoon world, but the introduction of plantation cultivation during the last centuries has also had a major effect. Tea plantations, for instance, have led to the almost total replacement of natural vegetation in the hills of southern India and Sri Lanka.

Populations in all the countries of the monsoon regions are rapidly increasing, and demands for economic development are constantly growing, placing increasing pressures on the environment, pressures which to date have seemed almost irresistible.

DISAPPEARING ANIMALS

The dwindling wildlife of southeastern Asia includes species that may be regarded locally as pests—a fact that makes their protection difficult outside game reserves. Animals such as the tiger and the wild pig are doubly threatened as human cultivation spreads into the natural habitat: their hunting and foraging grounds are reduced, and their destruction of crops or livestock provides villagers with an obvious incentive for killing them in order to protect their own livelihoods.

Tiger
Panthera tigris
Wild pig
Sus scrofa

SELF-SUFFICIENCY IN CHINA

Local materials are turned into saleable products at a ratan factory in southern China. This factory is not owned by the state but by the village-sized brigade responsible for the manufacturing. The brigade functions as a smaller economic unit within the Ting Chow people's commune of 20 to 30 villages, but is encouraged to act independently, owning what it creates. The commune takes care of such matters as waterways—it contains 82 km (51 miles) of canals.

Tea
Thea sinensis

UPLAND AREAS

Year-round warmth, seasonal rain, and population pressure have led to the development of even comparatively inaccessible upland areas of the monsoon règions. Terracing, an age-old practice, provides subsistence for local populations and crops for local markets; irrigation dams and tea plantations reflect development on an industrial scale. Tea grows on well-drained hillsides where the climate allows the plant to survive frequent leaf removal. The younger the leaf the better the tea, in general, but local variation is wide.

Bamboo scaffolding

FERTILE FORESTLANDS

Human demands for agricultural land, fuel and building materials have virtually destroyed all the natural monsoon forest cover. But although clearance has left some areas bare, the climate allows luxuriant regrowth elsewhere. Teak, sal and bamboo all provide useful materials, both locally and for export. The extraction and transport of the timber to riverbanks is often carried out more effectively by elephants, responding sensitively to the *mahout*'s directions, than by machines. Bamboo, most widely used today for paper making, may even be erected as scaffolding for skyscrapers.

THE CROWDED COASTS

Rice is such a staple diet of monsoon peoples, from eastern India to middle China, that in many Asian languages it is synonymous with the word for food. Originally a swamp grass, it grows best in lower river and delta regions with a large and dependable water supply, where young shoots can be transplanted to flooded fields for maximum growth. The climate may allow three crops to be grown in one year, with plowing, transplanting and reaping all taking place at the same time. Groves of coconuts often merge with rice fields, and both contribute to the agricultural village economy that still characterizes most of the region. On the coastline of southeastern Asia, mangroves trap the thick silt of the rivers in their tangled roots, reclaiming land from the sea. Industries such as tin mining bring in valuable foreign exchange, but the drift from villages to towns and the rapidly growing populations often raise more problems than they solve.

Common mangrove
Rhizophora mangle

Mountain Regions

A quarter of Earth's land surface lies at heights of 1,000 m (3,300 ft) or more above sea level. But the highland regions are thinly populated by man, who is, generally speaking, a lowland dweller (most major population centers are less than 100 m (330 ft) above sea level). Some formerly lowland animals have fled from man to the harsh refuge of the mountains, joining with specially adapted plants and wildlife, but today man himself is finding the highland regions increasingly useful and desirable.

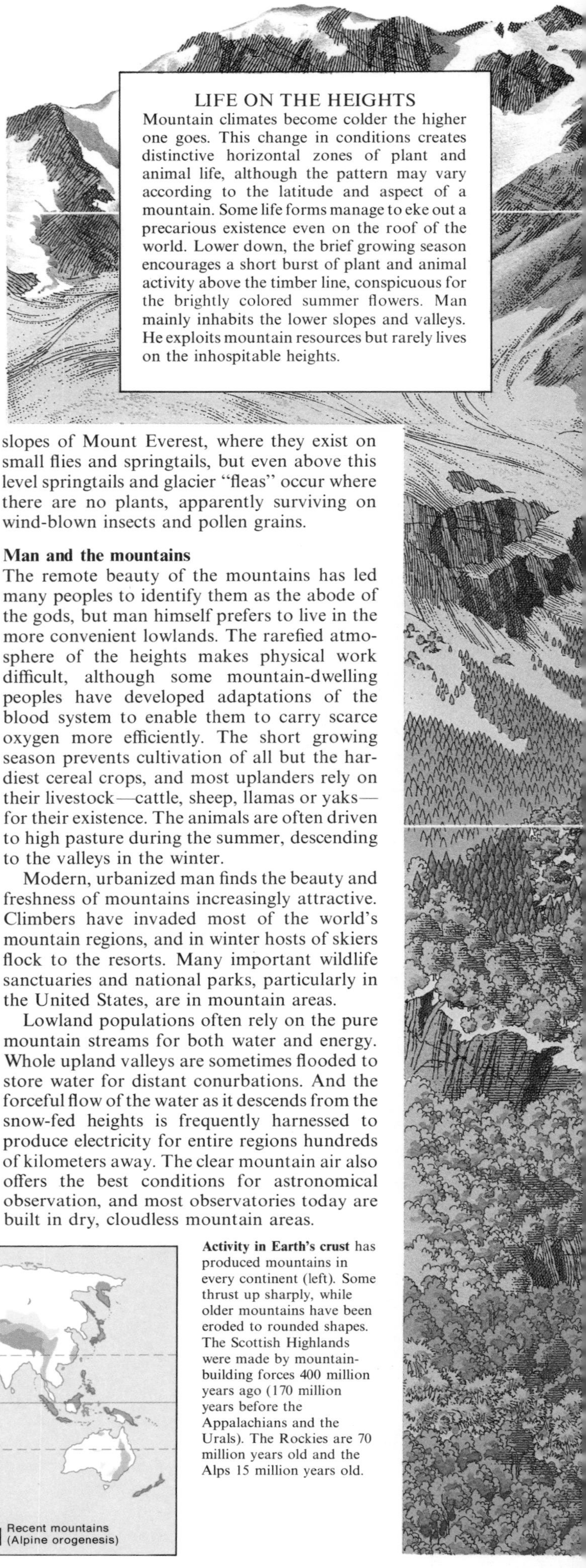

LIFE ON THE HEIGHTS
Mountain climates become colder the higher one goes. This change in conditions creates distinctive horizontal zones of plant and animal life, although the pattern may vary according to the latitude and aspect of a mountain. Some life forms manage to eke out a precarious existence even on the roof of the world. Lower down, the brief growing season encourages a short burst of plant and animal activity above the timber line, conspicuous for the brightly colored summer flowers. Man mainly inhabits the lower slopes and valleys. He exploits mountain resources but rarely lives on the inhospitable heights.

The world's highest mountain peaks rise to almost 9.6 km (6 miles) above sea level, but these heights are small compared to the total diameter of the Earth. The rough surface of an orange would have mountains higher than the Himalayas if scaled up to world size. But mountain environments, although they vary enormously from system to system, all tend to demand remarkable endurance and adaptability from the plants and animals that inhabit them.

Altitude rather than geological variation determines conditions of life on mountains. The temperature falls by 2°C with every 300 m (3.4°F every 1,000 ft)—hence the snowcapped beauty of the heights—and life forms must be adapted to increasingly harsh conditions as height increases. As a result, zones of different life occur at different levels, from tropical forests (at the base of low-latitude mountains) to arctic-type life in the zone of ice and snow at the summit. The latitude of the mountain affects the heights to which these zones extend: trees occur at 2,300 m (7,500 ft) in the southern Alps, whereas farther north, in central Sweden, trees cannot survive above 1,000 m (3,300 ft).

Life at the top

The specially adapted plant and animal life of the mountains occurs above the tree line, for here the variations in living conditions reach their greatest extremes. A plant that has found a foothold on a bare rock face may have to endure intense heat, even where the average temperature is low, when the summer sun blazing through the clear air warms the slabs to tropical temperatures. But when that part of the mountain falls into shadow, the temperature decreases very rapidly, often assisted by the high winds that blow almost constantly throughout the year in many mountain areas.

Soil necessary for plant life develops with the breakdown of the rock through the agency of water, frost and ice. Lichens, whose acids may aid in this destruction, can survive at very high levels, and as they die may add some humus to the newly forming soil. This may first accumulate in sheltered places where plants requiring high humidity, such as mosses and filmy ferns, are found. Flowering plants follow where a greater depth of soil has formed, although some grow in cracks between rocks.

Flowering plants of the mountains all tend to be small (to avoid harsh, drying winds), deep rooted (to anchor the plant firmly), and abundantly flowering (to benefit from the short growing season). Many unrelated species have independently developed a similar cushion form. This enables them to shed excess rainwater easily and to retain heat better in a tight tangle of stems and leaves, where the temperature may be more than 10°C (18°F) higher than that of the outside air. Insects sheltering there are well placed to perform the vital task of pollination. But pollinating insects are relatively rare at high altitudes, and some mountain plants are wind pollinated. The brilliant color of many others may be to increase their attractiveness for the insects. Nearly all upland plants are very slow-growing perennials, and many are evergreen, with leaves that exploit all available light.

Some large animals, such as the ibex or the Rocky Mountain goat, are adapted to spend their lives among the rocks and slopes. These stocky creatures, with hooves that act rather like suction cups, produce their summer young in the security of the heights, although in winter they descend to the shelter of the upper forests. Among smaller mammals, most of which are rodents, some dig burrows in which they hibernate through the winter. Others have very thick insulating coats, and may stay awake through the coldest weather in burrows under the snow.

Refugees from the lowlands

Some mountain animals, particularly carnivorous mammals and birds, have been driven by human persecution into remote mountain fastnesses. Many birds of prey, which could otherwise survive well in lowland areas, have their last strongholds among the mountains. They survive by feeding on small rodents, many of which are extremely wary. Some upland birds feed on insects or on seeds, but their number is comparatively small. The Alpine chough is one of the most interesting of mountain birds, for it has learned to find food among the scraps provided by climbers and skiers, whom it often follows to very high altitudes.

Insects and other small invertebrates, like their Arctic counterparts, may take several years to mature. Some are wingless, and many tend to fly low in order not to be blown away from their home range. Jumping spiders have been seen at heights of 6,700 m (22,000 ft) on the slopes of Mount Everest, where they exist on small flies and springtails, but even above this level springtails and glacier "fleas" occur where there are no plants, apparently surviving on wind-blown insects and pollen grains.

Man and the mountains

The remote beauty of the mountains has led many peoples to identify them as the abode of the gods, but man himself prefers to live in the more convenient lowlands. The rarefied atmosphere of the heights makes physical work difficult, although some mountain-dwelling peoples have developed adaptations of the blood system to enable them to carry scarce oxygen more efficiently. The short growing season prevents cultivation of all but the hardiest cereal crops, and most uplanders rely on their livestock—cattle, sheep, llamas or yaks—for their existence. The animals are often driven to high pasture during the summer, descending to the valleys in the winter.

Modern, urbanized man finds the beauty and freshness of mountains increasingly attractive. Climbers have invaded most of the world's mountain regions, and in winter hosts of skiers flock to the resorts. Many important wildlife sanctuaries and national parks, particularly in the United States, are in mountain areas.

Lowland populations often rely on the pure mountain streams for both water and energy. Whole upland valleys are sometimes flooded to store water for distant conurbations. And the forceful flow of the water as it descends from the snow-fed heights is frequently harnessed to produce electricity for entire regions hundreds of kilometers away. The clear mountain air also offers the best conditions for astronomical observation, and most observatories today are built in dry, cloudless mountain areas.

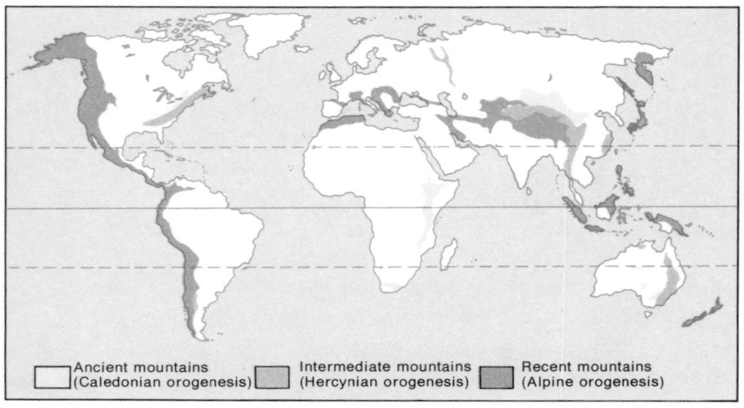

Ancient mountains (Caledonian orogenesis)
Intermediate mountains (Hercynian orogenesis)
Recent mountains (Alpine orogenesis)

Activity in Earth's crust has produced mountains in every continent (left). Some thrust up sharply, while older mountains have been eroded to rounded shapes. The Scottish Highlands were made by mountain-building forces 400 million years ago (170 million years before the Appalachians and the Urals). The Rockies are 70 million years old and the Alps 15 million years old.

Many peoples have believed that the gods have their abodes in the high places of the world. Tibet (above), one of the highest and most mountainous of all countries, has a large number of religious sites. Modern man also finds the clear, dry air suitable for the study of heavenly bodies: most modern observatories, such as Kitt Peak, USA (right), are built on mountain sites far from cities.

MOUNTAIN ADAPTATIONS

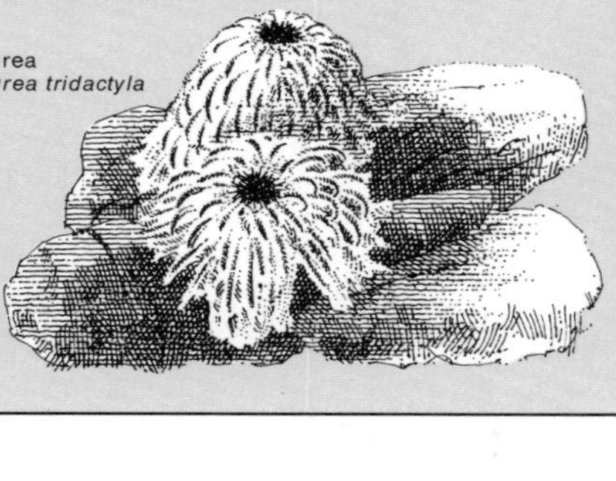

Saussurea
Saussurea tridactyla

Ingenious adaptations to harsh mountain conditions have been evolved by many plants, most of which have tiny cells with thick sap that does not freeze easily. Saussurea masks itself with white hair to reduce evaporation from the leaf surface. Alpine soldanellas are active even under snow, pushing up their flowers before the thaw.

Alpine soldanella
Soldanella alpina

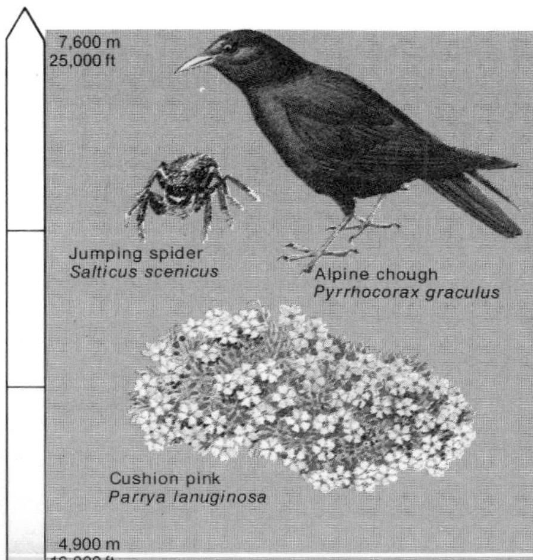
7,600 m
25,000 ft
Jumping spider
Salticus scenicus
Alpine chough
Pyrrhocorax graculus
Cushion pink
Parrya lanuginosa
4,900 m
16,000 ft

SNOWBOUND PEAKS
Perpetual snow, violent winds and atmospheric dryness impose harsh conditions on life in the high Himalayas. But wind-blown organic debris from the plains does support some life forms—springtails, flies and jumping spiders—where the air is too dry to allow even lichens to survive. Lower down, a cushion plant may take root in a rock-base niche, but there is little other vegetation. Among birds, the Alpine chough is a scavenger that has followed Everest expeditions to heights of 7,900 m (26,000 ft).

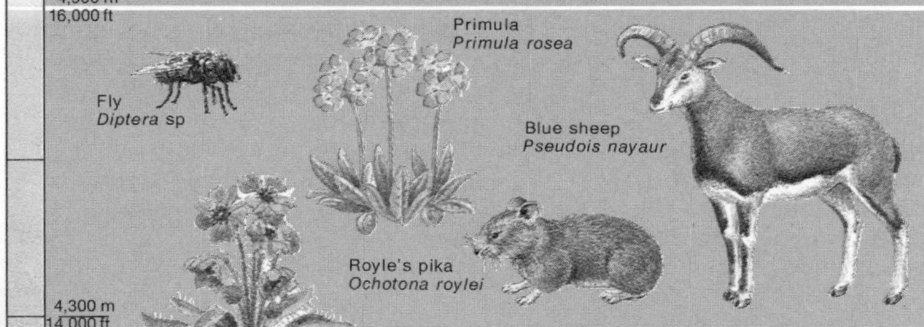
Fly
Diptera sp
Primula
Primula rosea
Blue sheep
Pseudois nayaur
Royle's pika
Ochotona roylei

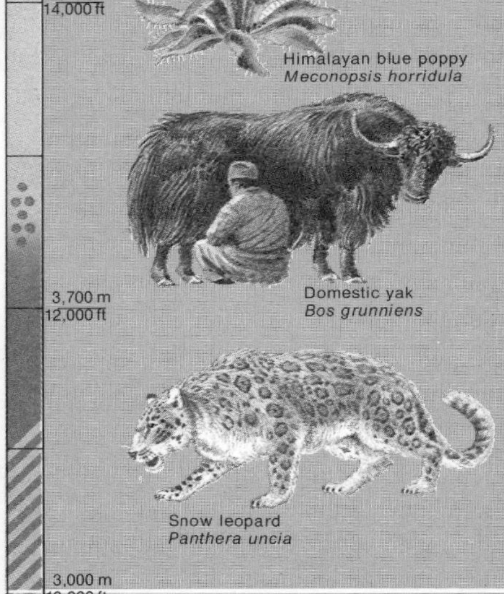
4,300 m
14,000 ft
Himalayan blue poppy
Meconopsis horridula
Domestic yak
Bos grunniens
3,700 m
12,000 ft
Snow leopard
Panthera uncia
3,000 m
10,000 ft

MOUNTAIN MEADOWS
Between the snow line and the zone of coniferous trees, the Himalayan slopes exhibit a glorious variety of flowering plants during summer. Small and slow growing, these often have bright flowers which attract pollinating insects such as fly-like *Diptera*. The pika and other small, thick-furred rodents are the most common animals, although larger creatures, such as blue (bharal) sheep and yaks, also find summer pasturage at these heights. Snow leopards tend to inhabit the coniferous forests, but they travel up to higher parts to prey on the grazing herds. Few people live within the zone, but some Sherpas take their yak herds as high as 4,600 m (15,000 ft) for summer grazing, and even grow crops of potatoes at this height. Their permanent villages, however, are on the lower alpine slopes.

Rhododendron
Rhododendron sp
2,400 m
8,000 ft
Asiatic black bear
Selenarctos thibetanus
1,800 m
6,000 ft

FORESTED SLOPES
Isolated birches mark the tree line—the transition from meadow to coniferous and rhododendron forest. In the upper parts of the forest, trees are dwarfed by cold and lack of moisture, and are twisted and bent from the wind. These low and tangled masses provide shelter for animals such as the Asian black bear and the red panda. Below the conifers lies a zone of broad-leaved evergreens, and in the foothills these in turn give way to tropical monsoon forests of sal trees (*Shorea robusta*) and thickets of bamboo. The raucous flocks of hill mynahs represent just one of the many kinds of birds found in this zone, which has the widest range of wildlife of all the kinds of mountain vegetation. Unfortunately, many species are in danger of extinction, for here man has settled, cut down forests and terraced hillsides to grow crops.

Red panda
Ailurus fulgens
Hill mynah bird
Gracula religiosa
1,200 m
4,000 ft
Permanent snow
Alpine meadows
Isolated birches
Coniferous forest
Rhododendron groves
Broadleaved evergreen forest
Bamboo
Tropical monsoon forest

Rocky Mountain goat
Oreamnos americanus

Animals and humans adapt to mountain conditions in many ways. The Rocky Mountain goat (left) has evolved a fleecy undercoat and hooves with concave pads to grip on any surface. Comparison of the blood counts (right) of a lowlander (A) and an Andean (B) shows how the latter has a higher total content and more red cells.

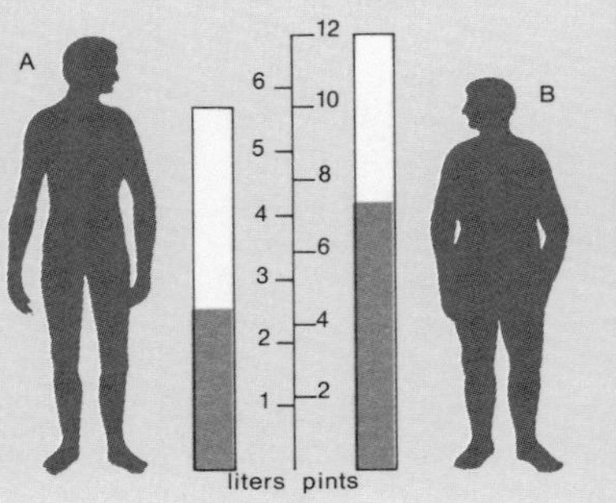
A
B
1
2
3
4
5
6
2
4
6
8
10
12
liters
pints

The golden eagle *Aquila chrysaetos* (left) epitomizes the grandeur of the heights. Although it lives and nests in remote regions, it could equally well find its food in the lowlands were it not for human competition. An eagle's territory may cover 130 sq km (50 sq miles): it preys on small mammals and even (it is believed) on young deer and lambs. It mates for life and returns each year to the same nest.

Freshwater Environments

Broad, muddy rivers, fast-running streams, miniature ponds and deep, ancient lakes all provide their own distinctive environments for populations of animals and colonies of aquatic plants. And in spite of the fact that these, the world's freshwater systems, contain only a minute proportion of the Earth's total supplies of water, the remarkable variety and richness of the wildlife they support make them among the most valuable and significant of all the world's natural habitats.

Fresh water is never really pure for, like sea water, and indeed like all other natural waters, it contains various dissolved minerals. Fresh water differs from seawater only in the relatively low concentrations of the minerals it contains. But these mineral traces are extremely important; they provide essential nutrients without which freshwater plants could not exist. And without plant life, there would be virtually no animal life either.

Not all parts of every freshwater system are rich in both plants and animals. Large, deep lakes are very similar to oceans—no light can penetrate their gloomy depths, and few plants can live in these conditions. The surface waters, on the other hand, where light is plentiful, teem with microscopic floating plants, mainly single-celled algae such as desmids and diatoms. The edges of lakes provide a different set of conditions again, for here the water is shallow and light can penetrate right through it. Plants can take root in the silt on the bottom, grow up through the water and thrust their leaves out into the light and air. Edges of lakes and, for the same reasons, the waters of small ponds are usually full of such plant life, which in turn supports many freshwater animals.

Running waters

Just as the still waters of lakes and ponds offer a variety of habitats, so the running waters of rivers support many different forms of life, each adapted to the particular conditions of its environment. In the upper reaches, where rivers are scarcely more than upland streams, water is fast flowing and clear of silt. Few plants, except close-clinging mosses, can gain a hold on the bare stony bottom and most of the fish are well muscled and strong bodied to enable them to withstand the constant tug of the current. As a river swells to form a mature lowland water course, however, it becomes slower moving and the water is warmer and richer in nutrients. Plants grow readily in these lower reaches and provide a supply of food for aquatic animals.

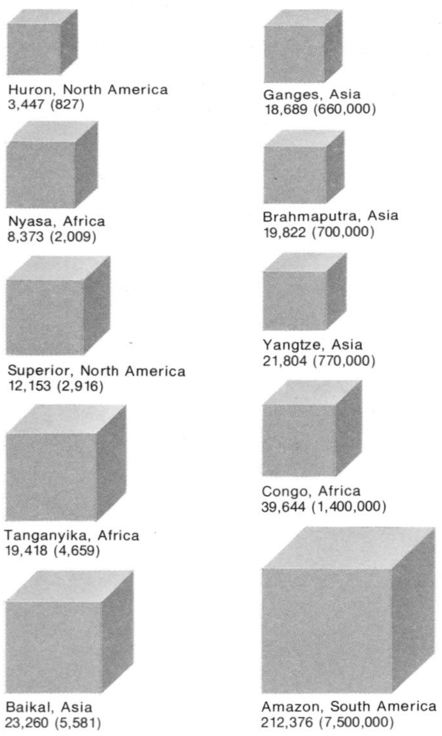
Volume of Lakes
in cu km (cu miles)
Discharge of Rivers
in cu m (cu ft) per second
Huron, North America
3,447 (827)
Nyasa, Africa
8,373 (2,009)
Superior, North America
12,153 (2,916)
Tanganyika, Africa
19,418 (4,659)
Baikal, Asia
23,260 (5,581)
Ganges, Asia
18,689 (660,000)
Brahmaputra, Asia
19,822 (700,000)
Yangtze, Asia
21,804 (770,000)
Congo, Africa
39,644 (1,400,000)
Amazon, South America
212,376 (7,500,000)

The five largest lakes in the world hold more than 53% of all fresh water that flows over the land. The rest of the world's lakes account for another 45%.

The world's largest river, the Amazon, discharges more than one-fifth of all fresh water that flows from the mouths of the world's rivers into the oceans.

With such a wide range of conditions, freshwater environments support an enormous variety of animal life—insects, fishes, amphibians, reptiles, mammals and birds. In some ways insects are the most important of all these creatures: freshwater systems contain more insects and other invertebrates, representing a greater variety of species, than any other kind of animal. Furthermore, these, the smallest representatives of the freshwater animal world, provide one of the most important links in the complex freshwater food chain.

Insects may be the most numerous, but fishes are probably the most familiar of all freshwater creatures, and they certainly show some of the greatest varieties of adaptations to the many different habitats. Their sizes vary from the tiny, 14 mm ($\frac{1}{2}$ in) of the virtually transparent dwarf goby fish found in small streams and lakes in the Philippines to the 4 m (14 ft) of the arapaima found in deep rivers in tropical South America. Their feeding habits vary from those of the ferocious carnivorous piranha of South America to those of the North American paddle fish which, although more than three times the size of the largest piranha, feed solely on microscopic organisms which they filter from the water with their specially adapted throats.

The breeding habits of freshwater fish also vary widely, from the carefully maternal instincts of the African mouthbreeding cichlids—these retain the developing eggs safely in their mouths until the offspring hatch—to the rather more common ejection of eggs into the water, where their fertilization and survival is simply left to chance. Other adaptations include the ability to breathe air (as does the African lungfish), to leap waterfalls (a common practice among migrating salmon) and to emit an electric shock of up to 600 volts (an adaptation of the South American electric eel).

Creatures of the water's edge

Of all the other major groups of animals, amphibians (such as frogs and toads) are probably the most reliant on freshwater systems. Because their skins must not dry out and they have to lay their eggs in water, few amphibians can venture far from the water's edge. And because they cannot tolerate the salt in seawater (it causes them to lose their body fluids through their skins) they are totally dependent upon fresh water for their existence. Reptiles, rather less typical of freshwater environments, range in size from miniature North American terrapins to the giant crocodiles that live along the banks of the Nile. Freshwater mammals, on the other hand, with the considerable exception of the hippopotamus, all tend to be rather small creatures such as otters, beavers, coypus, aquatic moles and water shrews.

Birds are another important group of freshwater creatures. Although few birds are truly aquatic an enormous number of species live in or near freshwater systems and take advantage of the various food supplies: the plants and fish within the waters; the bankside vegetation and small animal life; and the many forms of freshwater insects. Marshes and swamps, for example, provide some of the richest bird habitats in the world.

Also numbered among the species dependent on Earth's freshwater systems is man. And although strictly a nonaquatic, land-living animal, man uses more fresh water than any other creature. His needs seem to be inexhaustible as he harnesses, channels, diverts and often pollutes freshwater systems throughout the world. Unfortunately, the vast requirements of the human race are not always compatible with the rather more humble needs of all other species that depend upon fresh water.

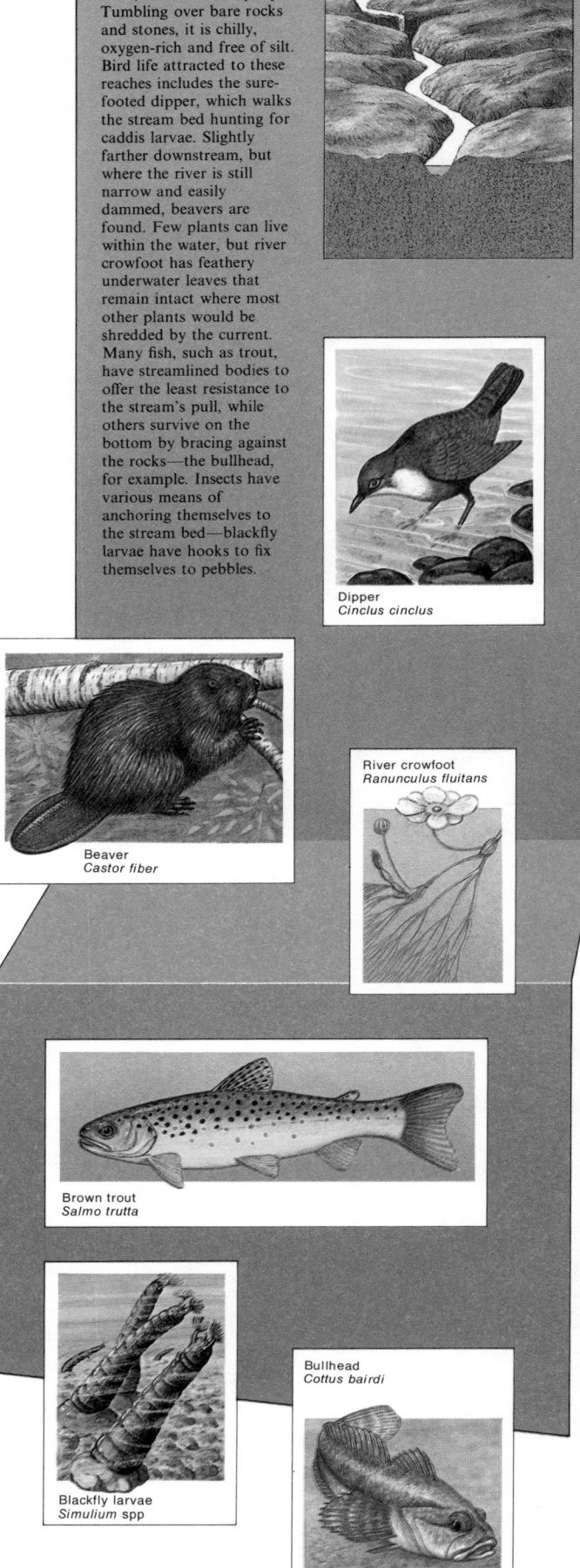

THE UPPER REACHES
Here, water flows rapidly. Tumbling over bare rocks and stones, it is chilly, oxygen-rich and free of silt. Bird life attracted to these reaches includes the sure-footed dipper, which walks the stream bed hunting for caddis larvae. Slightly farther downstream, but where the river is still narrow and easily dammed, beavers are found. Few plants can live within the water, but river crowfoot has feathery underwater leaves that remain intact where most other plants would be shredded by the current. Many fish, such as trout, have streamlined bodies to offer the least resistance to the stream's pull, while others survive on the bottom by bracing against the rocks—the bullhead, for example. Insects have various means of anchoring themselves to the stream bed—blackfly larvae have hooks to fix themselves to pebbles.

Dipper
Cinclus cinclus

Beaver
Castor fiber

River crowfoot
Ranunculus fluitans

Brown trout
Salmo trutta

Blackfly larvae
Simulium spp

Bullhead
Cottus bairdi

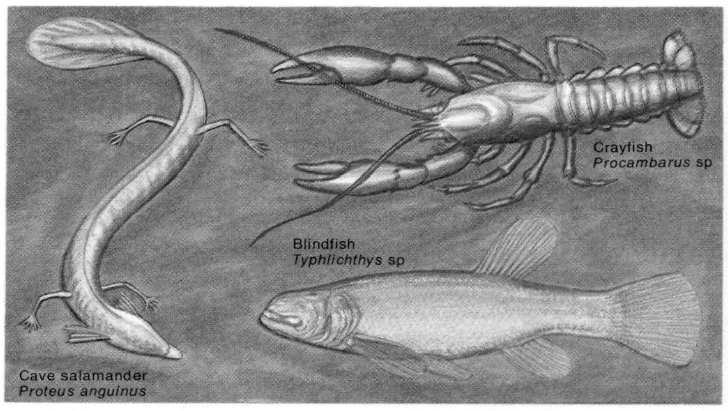

Crayfish
Procambarus sp

Blindfish
Typhlichthys sp

Cave salamander
Proteus anguinus

THE LIFE OF A RIVER

As a river makes its way from its upland source to the sea, it gradually changes its character. And at every stage in its progress, the animals and plants that inhabit the riverbanks and the waters reflect these changes by their adaptations to their environments. Most distinctive and dramatic are those adaptations produced in the wildlife of the upper and lower river reaches.

THE LOWER REACHES

The slowly flowing river and its muddy banks are rich in animals and plants. Many birds live along the water's edge; spoonbills wade in the shallows, filtering food from the water with their beaks. The banks, fringed with reedmaces and other plants, provide habitats for many reptiles, such as the American painted turtle, and mammals, such as the platypus. Plants also grow on the water—they range from large waterlilies to tiny algae that are food for river fishes: Africa's upside-down-feeding catfish, for example. In these waters, mammals as well as fish are to be found—Amazonian manatees live entirely aquatic lives. The plentiful river plants, such as curled pondweed, provide food for water snails and other herbivores, and cover for predators such as pike. Crustacea and insects living in the silt of the river-bed are food for bottom-feeding fish such as the strange-looking North American paddle fish.

African spoonbill
Platalea alba

Southern painted turtle
Chrysemys picta dorsalis

LAKES: CHANGE AND EVOLUTION

No two lakes are alike: each is virtually a self-contained world for its population of aquatic animals and plants. Furthermore, no individual lake remains the same for long: in every lake, slow, inexorable changes in conditions are gradually but constantly changing the balance of species inhabiting the lake bed, the bankside and the water.

Changing conditions may be caused by one of several processes. Accumulating sediments, one of the most common of these processes, may eliminate a lake altogether. The water becomes shallower as sediments thicken (1) and these sediments are then added to and consolidated by water plants taking root. Ultimately, land plants (2) invade the area.

Lakes develop their own peculiar species when the aquatic wildlife that evolves within them has no means of migrating to other freshwater systems to interbreed. The world's only existing species of freshwater seal, for example, is found in just one lake—isolated Lake Baikal in Asia.

Baikal seal
Phoca sibirica

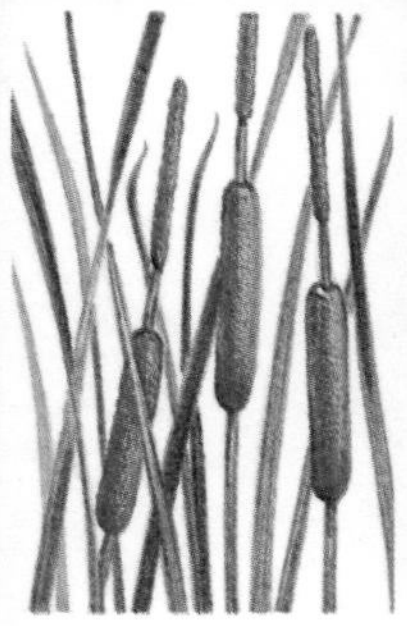

Reedmace
Typha sp

Platypus
Ornithorhynchus anatinus

Waterlily
Nymphaea sp

African catfish
Synodontis batensoda

Amazonian manatee
Trichechus inunguis

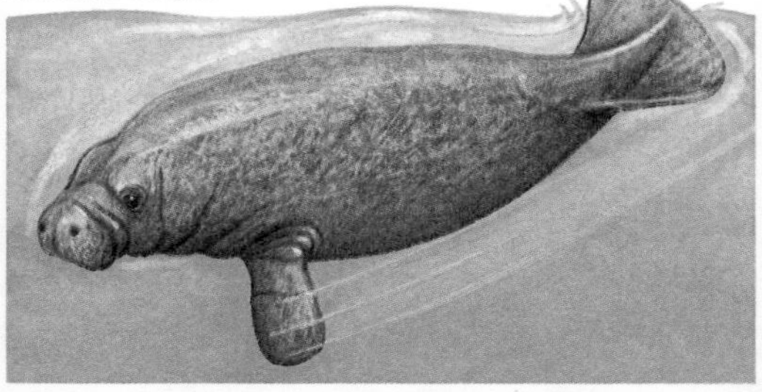

Curled pondweed
Potamogeton crispus

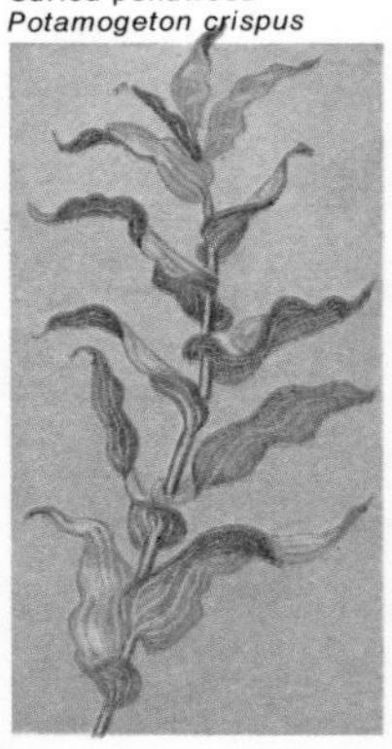

White ramshorn snail
Planorbis albus

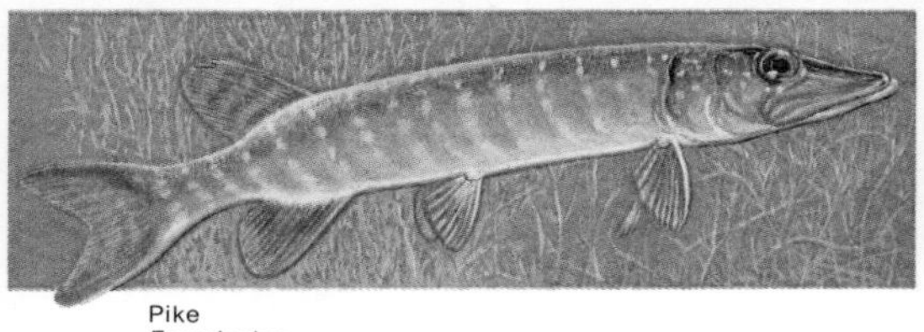

Pike
Esox lucius

DARK WATERS

Underground rivers that flow through many of the world's cave systems support surprising numbers of creatures that have adapted to the permanent darkness. Many of these, such as the American cave crayfish, have lost the coloration of their surface-living kin. Some, such as Kentucky blind fishes, no longer possess eyes. Some salamanders are sighted and black when born, but become blind and colorless by adulthood.

Paddle fish
Polydon spathula

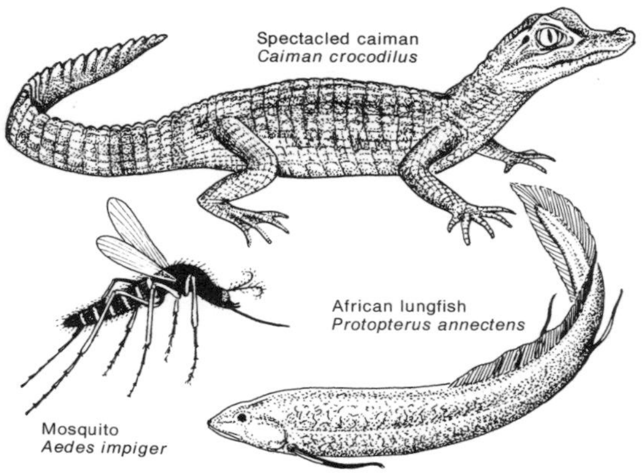

Spectacled caiman
Caiman crocodilus

African lungfish
Protopterus annectens

Mosquito
Aedes impiger

WETLANDS

Marshes and swamps are the richest of freshwater habitats. Wading birds, such as Asia's painted stork *Ibis leucocephalus* (above), are particularly common. Reptiles include caimans, which lay their eggs in swamps' warm, rotting vegetation. Of the many insects, mosquitoes are probably the most numerous, and of the many fishes, African lungfish are perhaps best adapted to life in wetlands. They survive drought, when marshes dry up, by their ability to breathe air.

Man and the Freshwater Environments

From earliest times, man has been finding new uses for and making new demands upon the world's freshwater resources. Today, the whole of modern society depends upon a vast supply to serve its agricultural, industrial, domestic and other needs. To meet the ever-growing demand for water, man has performed remarkable engineering feats: altering the courses of rivers, creating and destroying lakes, drowning valleys and tapping water sources that lie deep within the Earth.

Water is essential to human life. Simply to remain alive, an active adult living in a temperate climate needs a liquid intake of about two liters ($3\frac{1}{2}$ pints) every day. In warmer climates, the body's fluid requirements are even greater. Consequently, man has always been tied to reliable sources of drinking water—rivers, springs, lakes and ponds—and the availability of these, until very recently, has dictated the routes of all his wanderings and determined the sites of all his settlements.

From the time of the earliest human settlements, however, man has looked upon freshwater systems not simply as a source of drinking water but also as an increasingly useful resource for a multitude of other purposes. Today, water enters into virtually every aspect of modern life, and enormous quantities are used in agriculture, in industry, in the home, in the production of energy, for transport and for recreation.

The farmer's resource

Of all the major activities that rely on fresh water, agriculture is by far the world's largest consumer. In much of Europe and North America, rainfall is usually plentiful and lack of sufficient water for crops is rarely a problem. But in other parts of the world the climate simply does not produce enough rainfall and water shortages are a perennial problem. There, irrigation is not just a sophisticated technique to improve the yields and increase the varieties of crops grown; it is, and always has been, an essential element of agriculture.

Methods of irrigation range from small-scale devices—such as miniature windpumps—used in many developing countries simply to lift water from rivers for bankside crops, to vast dams, reservoirs and canal systems such as the Indus River project in Pakistan, which irrigates 10 million hectares (25 million acres) of land.

Traditional irrigation techniques usually involve using open channels or furrows for conducting water to fields. But one of the major problems with these, particularly in hot climates, is that much of the water evaporates and is lost before it can be used. Several new techniques, such as sprinklers and drip-feed systems, have recently been developed, however, to help make more efficient use of available supplies.

Although the most severe water deficiencies are experienced in the dry subtropical and tropical regions of the world, the temperate regions of North America and Europe, in spite of their relatively wet climates, do suffer shortages. Large towns and cities rarely have enough locally available rainfall or river flow to satisfy both domestic demand and the insatiable needs of industry. In the developed nations, industry consumes more water than any other activity.

Industrial demands

Fresh water is not only an integral part of almost every manufacturing process, it has other important industrial uses. As a source of power, it has been used since the early days of civilization—water wheels were one of man's first industrial inventions. Today, these simple devices are rarely seen in industrial societies, but water power is more important than ever before. Giant dams allow enormous volumes of water to be controlled and the power harnessed to drive turbines and generate electricity.

Freshwater systems have also, for centuries, provided industry with an important means of transporting its goods, and canal systems are still an essential part of industrial infrastructure in many countries of the world: the Europa Canal, when completed, will link three of Europe's major rivers, the Rhine, Main and Danube, and so form a continuous waterway running east–west across the breadth of Europe. Already, the finished sections of the canal are carrying oil, chemicals, fertilizers, coal, coke and building materials to and from some of Europe's major industrial regions.

Many of Europe's waterways date back to the great canal-building days of the Industrial Revolution. Although a few of these are still used for commerce, many are today considered too narrow to transport economical quantities of goods. Some, however, are now finding a role to play in one of the world's fastest-growing new industries—the leisure market. Today, canals provide a wide range of aquatic activities for holiday makers, tourists and sportsmen.

Recreation and sport

Freshwater systems throughout the world, in fact, are rapidly being recognized and developed as major recreational resources. Lakes and reservoirs are stocked with fish for anglers, silted waterways are dredged to provide sailing and swimming facilities, and old quarries and open-cast workings are landscaped and flooded to provide entirely new freshwater systems purely for leisure pursuits. The projects not only help to rejuvenate previously misused land, they also provide significant incomes to otherwise underdeveloped areas, especially highland regions that are too remote to attract other industries, and are unsuitable for farming.

Unfortunately, however, few of the world's freshwater systems can continue indefinitely to absorb the ever-growing demands that are being made upon them. Overuse of water resources is already a problem and has led to the pollution and destruction of many water systems—in some places overtapping has lowered water tables so drastically that rivers and lakes have been permanently destroyed. Although steps have been taken to protect certain waterways, legislation to guard against misuse and overuse is costly, time consuming and, inevitably, comes up against vested interests. Nevertheless, stringent conservation measures are becoming increasingly necessary if society is to maintain one of its most precious resources.

THE VERSATILE RESOURCE

Every day, more than seven trillion liters (12 trillion pints) of water are removed from the world's freshwater systems. Almost all of this water is then directed to one of four destinations—some is destined for industry, a certain amount is piped to towns and cities for use in public services and in homes, some is fed to agricultural regions, and the rest is stored in reservoirs for future use.

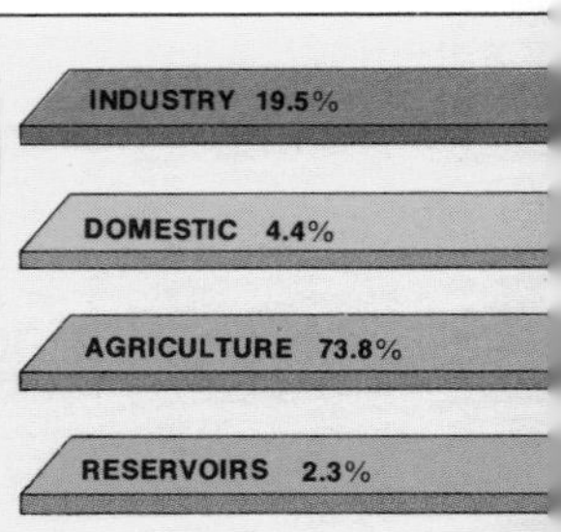

Man obtains fresh water by trapping it as it passes through one of the stages in the hydrological cycle—the never-ending circulation of Earth's waters from the ocean, to the atmosphere, to land. This cycle can be traced from the point at which water evaporates from the sea. The water vapor is blown across the land and falls as rain, hail or snow. Some then evaporates, but the rest completes the cycle by flowing over the land or through the soil or rocks back to the sea. It is at this point in its journey that man obtains his water supplies—from lakes (1), boreholes and wells (2) and dammed rivers (3). These supplies are then either used locally, or are transported by pipe or canal (4) to reservoirs (5) where they are stored ready for distribution.

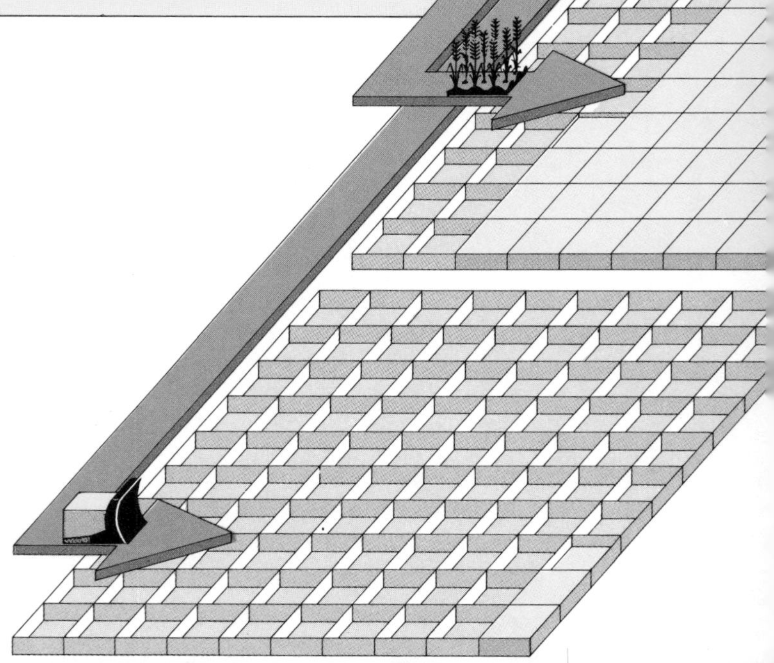

RESERVOIRS

About 70 trillion liters (15 trillion gallons) of fresh water are held in storage during any one year. Reservoirs ensure a continuous supply of water in spite of the inevitable seasonal fluctuations in demand and in the natural supply from rivers and rainfall. And where reservoirs are formed by damming rivers, there are additional benefits—the vast quantities of water held can be controlled and the power used to generate electricity. The Kariba Dam in Zimbabwe (right) has the potential for producing 8,500 million kilowatt hours of electrical power every year.

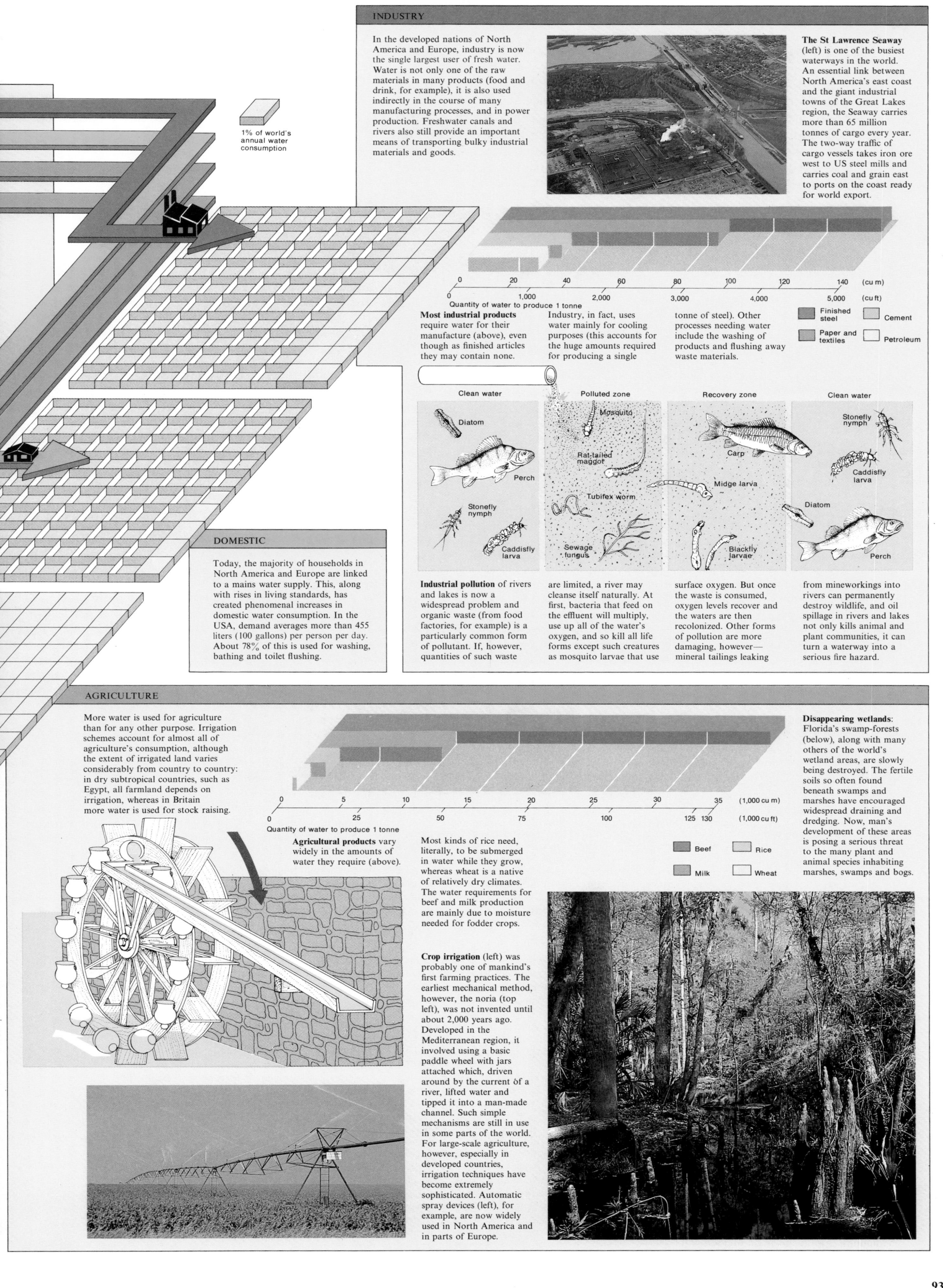

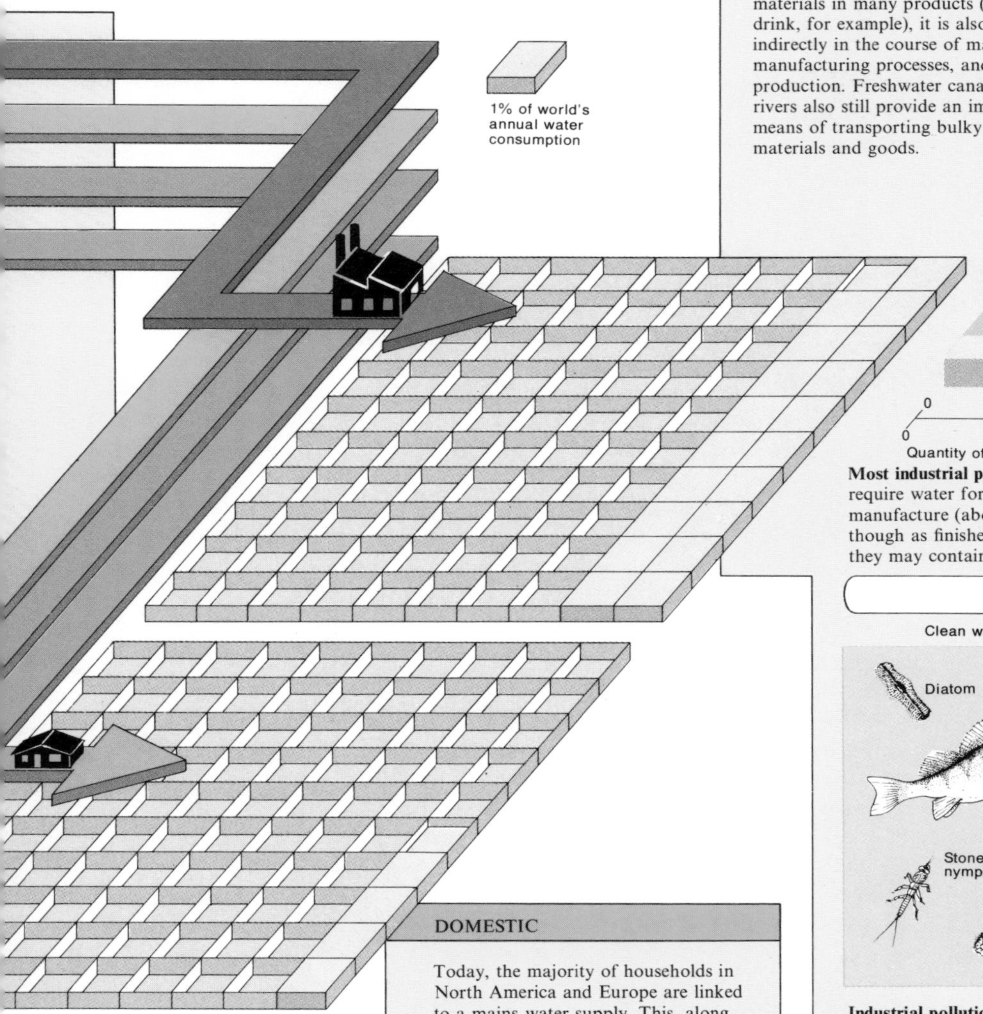
1% of world's
annual water
consumption

INDUSTRY

In the developed nations of North America and Europe, industry is now the single largest user of fresh water. Water is not only one of the raw materials in many products (food and drink, for example), it is also used indirectly in the course of many manufacturing processes, and in power production. Freshwater canals and rivers also still provide an important means of transporting bulky industrial materials and goods.

The St Lawrence Seaway (left) is one of the busiest waterways in the world. An essential link between North America's east coast and the giant industrial towns of the Great Lakes region, the Seaway carries more than 65 million tonnes of cargo every year. The two-way traffic of cargo vessels takes iron ore west to US steel mills and carries coal and grain east to ports on the coast ready for world export.

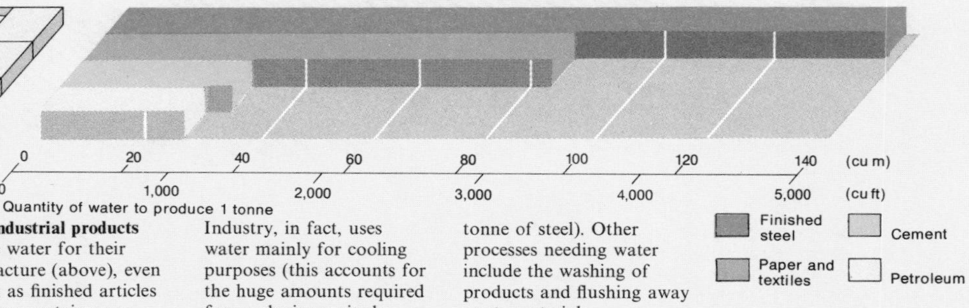
0
20
40
60
80
100
120
140
(cu m)
0
1,000
2,000
3,000
4,000
5,000
(cu ft)
Quantity of water to produce 1 tonne
Finished steel
Cement
Paper and textiles
Petroleum

Most industrial products require water for their manufacture (above), even though as finished articles they may contain none. Industry, in fact, uses water mainly for cooling purposes (this accounts for the huge amounts required for producing a single tonne of steel). Other processes needing water include the washing of products and flushing away waste materials.

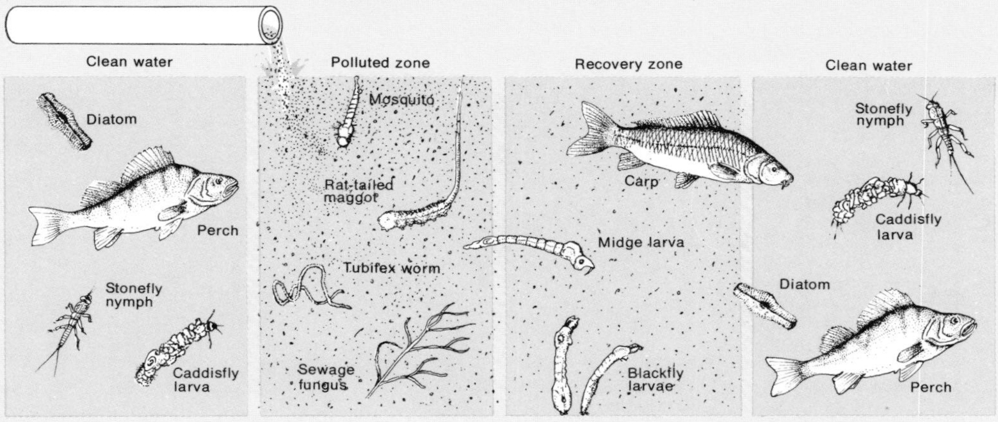
Clean water
Polluted zone
Recovery zone
Clean water
Diatom
Perch
Stonefly nymph
Caddisfly larva
Mosquito
Rat-tailed maggot
Tubifex worm
Sewage fungus
Carp
Midge larva
Blackfly larvae
Stonefly nymph
Caddisfly larva
Diatom
Perch

Industrial pollution of rivers and lakes is now a widespread problem and organic waste (from food factories, for example) is a particularly common form of pollutant. If, however, quantities of such waste are limited, a river may cleanse itself naturally. At first, bacteria that feed on the effluent will multiply, use up all of the water's oxygen, and so kill all life forms except such creatures as mosquito larvae that use surface oxygen. But once the waste is consumed, oxygen levels recover and the waters are then recolonized. Other forms of pollution are more damaging, however—mineral tailings leaking from mineworkings into rivers can permanently destroy wildlife, and oil spillage in rivers and lakes not only kills animal and plant communities, it can turn a waterway into a serious fire hazard.

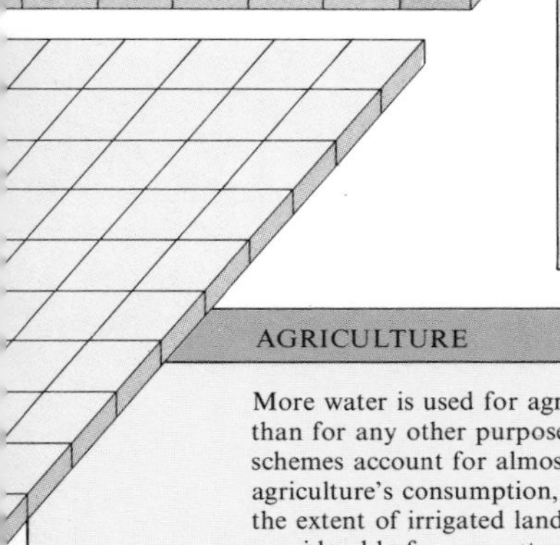

DOMESTIC

Today, the majority of households in North America and Europe are linked to a mains water supply. This, along with rises in living standards, has created phenomenal increases in domestic water consumption. In the USA, demand averages more than 455 liters (100 gallons) per person per day. About 78% of this is used for washing, bathing and toilet flushing.

AGRICULTURE

More water is used for agriculture than for any other purpose. Irrigation schemes account for almost all of agriculture's consumption, although the extent of irrigated land varies considerably from country to country: in dry subtropical countries, such as Egypt, all farmland depends on irrigation, whereas in Britain more water is used for stock raising.

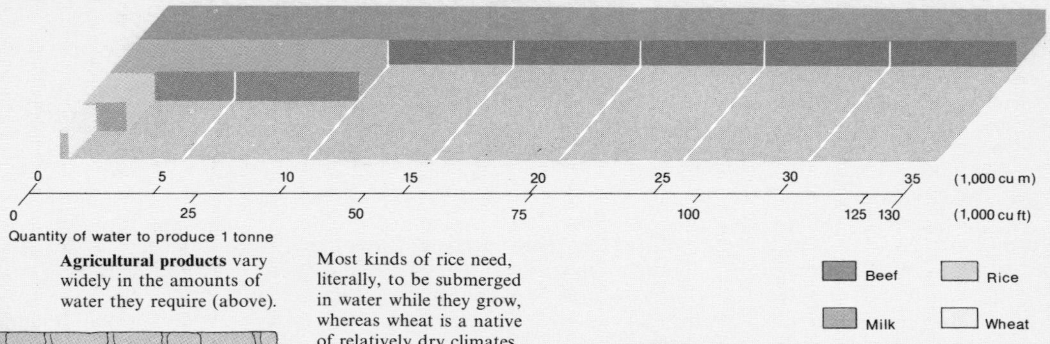
0
5
10
15
20
25
30
35
(1,000 cu m)
0
25
50
75
100
125
130
(1,000 cu ft)
Quantity of water to produce 1 tonne
Beef
Rice
Milk
Wheat

Agricultural products vary widely in the amounts of water they require (above).

Most kinds of rice need, literally, to be submerged in water while they grow, whereas wheat is a native of relatively dry climates. The water requirements for beef and milk production are mainly due to moisture needed for fodder crops.

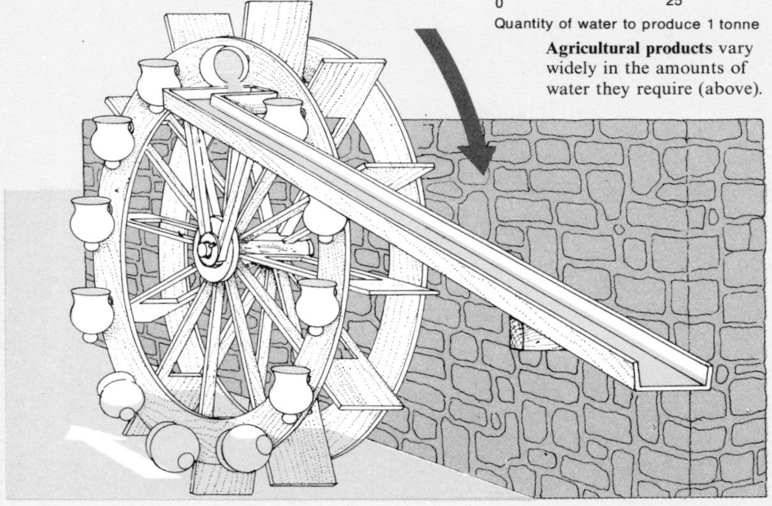

Crop irrigation (left) was probably one of mankind's first farming practices. The earliest mechanical method, however, the noria (top left), was not invented until about 2,000 years ago. Developed in the Mediterranean region, it involved using a basic paddle wheel with jars attached which, driven around by the current of a river, lifted water and tipped it into a man-made channel. Such simple mechanisms are still in use in some parts of the world. For large-scale agriculture, however, especially in developed countries, irrigation techniques have become extremely sophisticated. Automatic spray devices (left), for example, are now widely used in North America and in parts of Europe.

Disappearing wetlands: Florida's swamp-forests (below), along with many others of the world's wetland areas, are slowly being destroyed. The fertile soils so often found beneath swamps and marshes have encouraged widespread draining and dredging. Now, man's development of these areas is posing a serious threat to the many plant and animal species inhabiting marshes, swamps and bogs.

Seawater Environments

The oceans form by far the largest of the world's habitable environments, covering almost three-quarters of the Earth's surface at an average depth of more than 3,500 m (11,500 ft). Little more than a century ago, scientists believed that the deep sea's low temperatures, perpetual darkness and immense pressures made life in these regions completely untenable. But we now know that animals live at all depths in the ocean, even at the bottom of trenches more than 11,000 m (36,000 ft) deep.

THE PATTERN OF MARINE LIFE
The distribution of life in the seas is like an inverted pyramid whose broad base is formed by billions of minute single-celled plants—the phytoplankton. Plants need sunlight and nutrient salts, so phytoplankton occurs only in the upper, sunlit layers and where salts are present. Elsewhere, the distribution of marine life thins out rapidly.

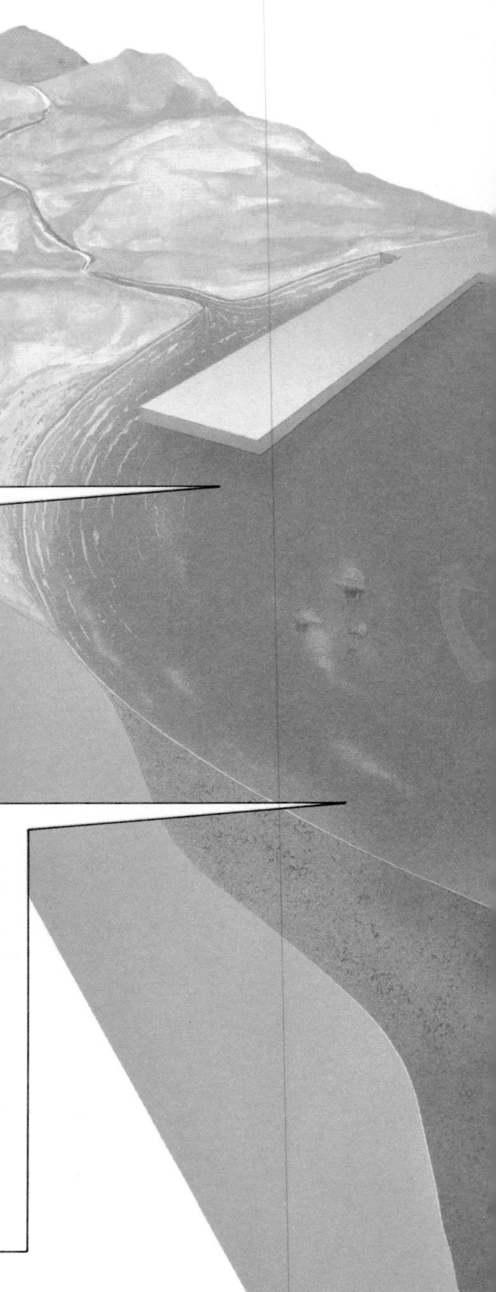

Shore life belongs to both land and sea, and thus has to cope with a wide range of conditions. Seaweeds get all their food from the sea and are quite unlike land plants. Many animals take refuge below the surface: tellin shell molluscs sift food particles through special "lips"; lugworms swallow sand, digesting any organic matter; cockles take in food and eject waste through two siphons. Some birds have bills adapted for opening bivalve molluscs.

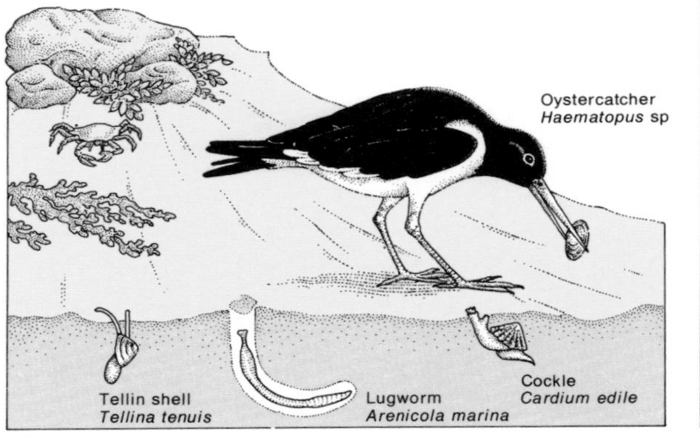
Oystercatcher
Haematopus sp
Tellin shell
Tellina tenuis
Lugworm
Arenicola marina
Cockle
Cardium edile

Marine plant life consists largely of diatoms—minute single-celled specks, each enclosed in a lidded box of silicon. Dinoflagellates, classed as plants but able to swim, dominate warmer waters. Both are food for copepods, the flea-sized grazers whose total weight, in the North Sea alone, is some seven million tonnes.

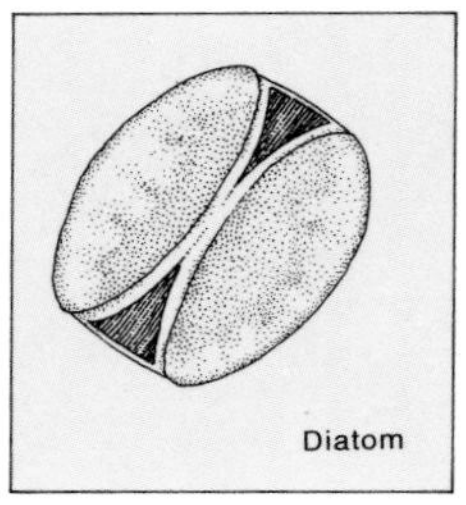
Diatom

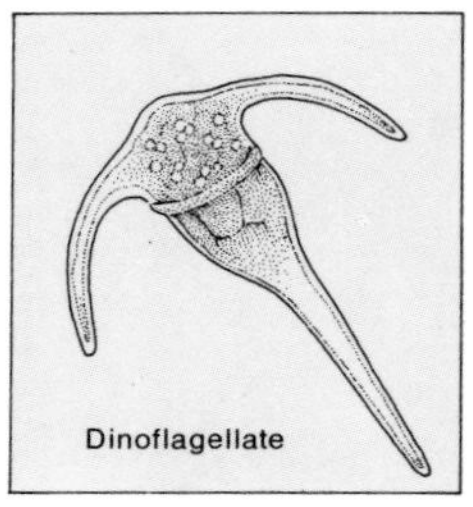
Dinoflagellate

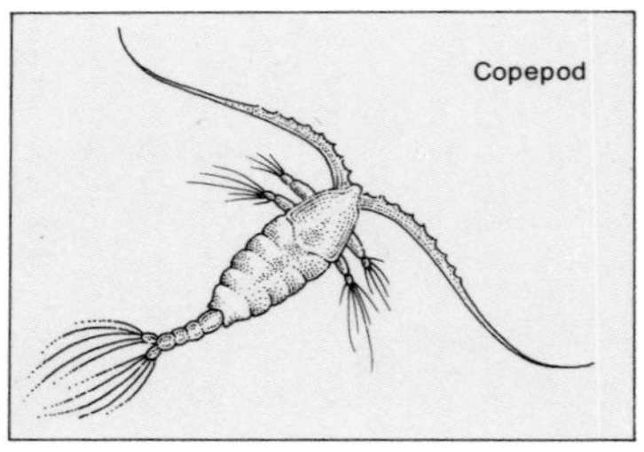
Copepod

A coral atoll, forming in warm shallow water round an extinct volcano, makes up a living aquarium for thousands of tropical marine life forms. Countless billions of tiny polyps, each secreting a hard, calcareous skeleton, form the first layer of the reef, but die as the volcano gradually sinks. Their skeletons provide a base for further layers of corals, which enclose the sinking island to create a shallow, salt water lagoon. Different coral species in the same reef provide homes for a great variety of life.

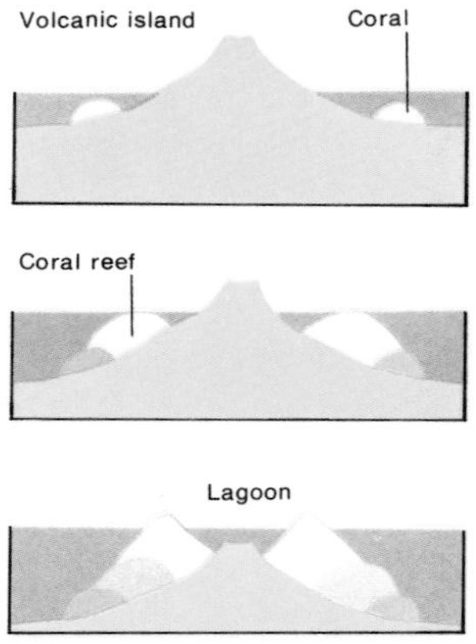
Volcanic island
Coral
Coral reef
Lagoon

Life is by no means evenly distributed throughout the oceans, either vertically or horizontally. The great majority of marine creatures are concentrated in the upper few hundred meters, for the biological organization of life in the seas, as on land, depends on photosynthesis (the process by which plants use the Sun's energy to combine carbon dioxide and water to produce more complex compounds). This near-surface layer is the euphotic ("well-lighted") zone.

Some of the Sun's rays are reflected from the surface of the sea, and those that penetrate are scattered and absorbed as they pass through the water, so that even in the clearest oceanic water there is insufficient light to support photosynthesis at depths greater than about 100 m (330 ft). In turbid inshore regions, where the water is less clear, this near-surface layer may be reduced to a very few meters. So the large seaweeds that anchor themselves to the seabed are restricted to the small areas of the sea where the water is sufficiently shallow to allow them to photosynthesize. Of much greater importance over most of the oceans are the tiny floating plants of the phytoplankton, which live suspended in the sunlit surface layers.

Pastures of the sea

Phytoplankton, like all plant life, requires not only sunlight for survival but also adequate supplies of nutrient salts and chemical trace elements. River waters carry down considerable quantities of dissolved mineral salts and other matter, so that high levels of phytoplankton production may occur locally around major estuaries. But a far more important source of nutrient supply to the euphotic zone is the recycling of salts that have sunk into the deeper layers, locked up in the bodies of plants and animals or in their fecal pellets.

In those areas of the oceans that overlie the continental shelves (about six percent of the total), the depth is nowhere more than about 200 m (650 ft), and the nutrient-rich bottom water is fairly readily brought back to the surface by currents and the stirring effect of storms. This stirring can reach much greater depths in near-polar latitudes, where the "water column" is not layered by temperature but remains more or less uniformly cold from top to bottom. In the Antarctic, cold (and therefore heavy) surface water sinks and is replaced by nutrient-rich water that may surface from depths of 1,000 m (3,300 ft).

In subtropical and tropical regions of the open ocean, where the warm surface layer is only a few tens of meters deep, the temperature falls rapidly with depth. There is little exchange between deep and shallow layers, and the euphotic zone receives an adequate supply of nutrient salts only in certain areas. These occur between westward-flowing and eastward-flowing currents in each of the major oceans. The Earth's rotation causes these currents to diverge so as to create an upwelling of nutrient-rich water along their common boundaries. Finally, in restricted coastal regions of the tropics and subtropics the local climatic conditions cause an offshore movement of surface water, which is again replaced by upwelling nutrient-rich deep water. The central oceanic regions, including the deep blue subtropical waters, are in effect the deserts of the sea.

Sea grazers and carnivores

The abundance of animals in the oceans closely follows that of the plants. But very few of the larger marine animals can feed directly on the phytoplankton because the individual plants are so small—often only a fraction of a millimeter across. Instead, the phytoplankton supports an amazingly diverse community of planktonic animals, which also spend their lives in mid-water and are swept along by the ocean currents. This community, the zooplankton, includes many different protozoans (single-celled animals), crustaceans, worms and molluscs, and also the juvenile stages of fishes and of many invertebrate animals that live as adults on the seabed. Most members of the zooplankton are very small and many of them graze on the phytoplankton. But some planktonic animals, particularly among the jellyfish and salps, may be a meter or more across and are voracious carnivores feeding on their planktonic neighbors. In turn, the zooplankton provides food for many of the active swimmers such as the fishes and baleen whales, while at the top of the food chain are larger carnivores including

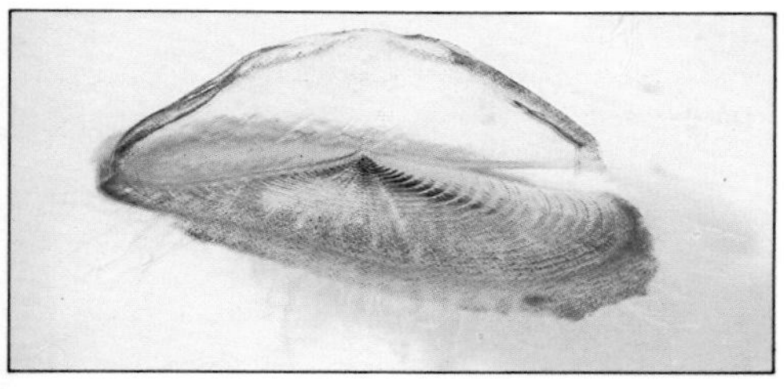

The by-the-wind sailor, *Velella*, is a so-called colonial animal, consisting of a whole collection of animals that function as a single individual. The gas-filled float of its body carries a vertical sail to catch the wind, and below dangle a group of modified polyps specialized for particular roles such as deterrence, reproduction, feeding and digesting.

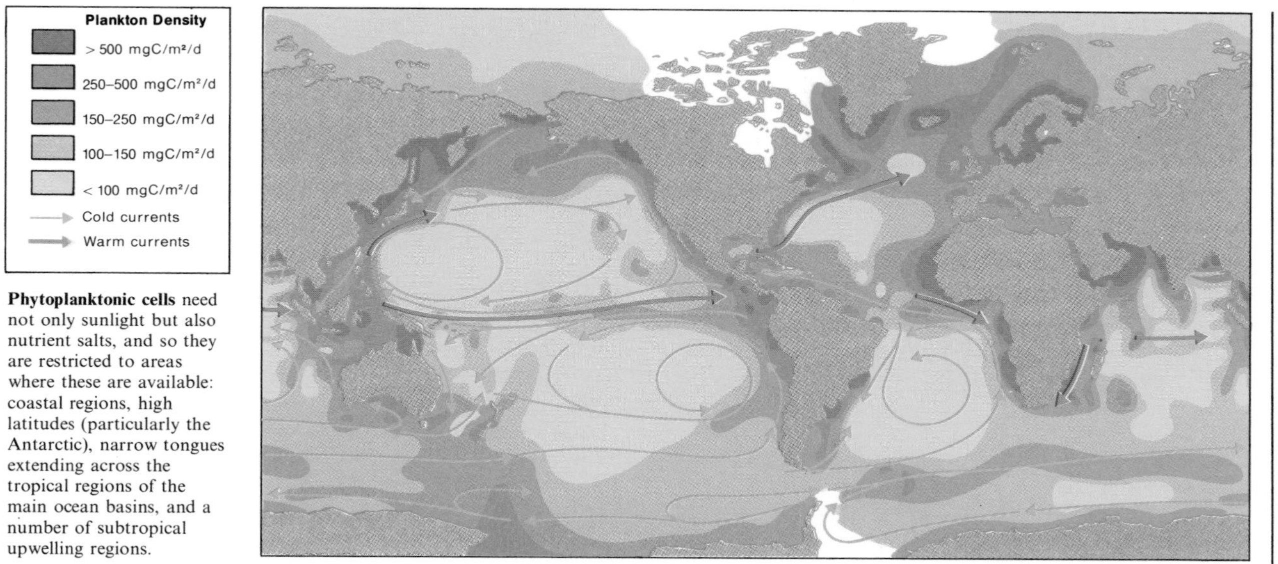
Plankton Density
> 500 mgC/m²/d
250–500 mgC/m²/d
150–250 mgC/m²/d
100–150 mgC/m²/d
< 100 mgC/m²/d
Cold currents
Warm currents

Phytoplanktonic cells need not only sunlight but also nutrient salts, and so they are restricted to areas where these are available: coastal regions, high latitudes (particularly the Antarctic), narrow tongues extending across the tropical regions of the main ocean basins, and a number of subtropical upwelling regions.

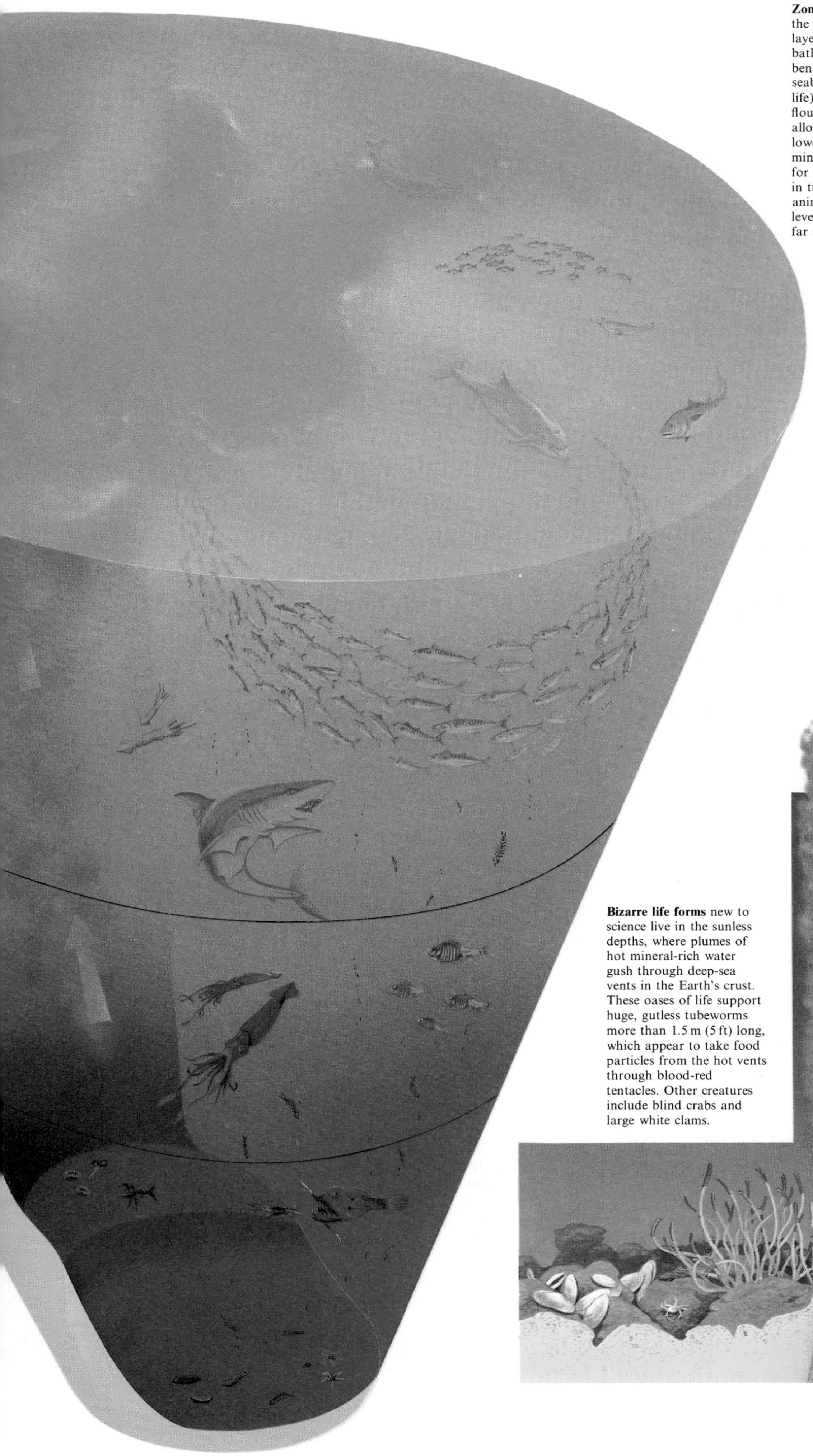

Zones of life (below) extend from the teeming euphotic ("well-lighted") layer to the sparsely populated bathypelagic ("deep-sea") depths, while benthic ("bottom") life occurs at all seabed levels. Phytoplankton (plant life) (1) dictates the pattern of the rest, flourishing where surface conditions allow nutrient salts to well up from lower depths. Herbivores such as minute zooplankton (2) provide food for a host of surface-layer life, which in turn feeds larger predators. Dead animals and fecal pellets fall to lower levels, where they sustain life, but in far smaller quantity.

1 Phytoplankton
2 Zooplankton
3 Blue whale *Balaenoptera musculus*
4 Herring *Clupea harengus*
5 Gray seal *Halichoerus grypus*
6 Bluefin tuna *Thunnus thynnus*
7 Bottlenosed dolphin *Tursiops truncatus*
8 Mackerel *Scomber scomber*
9 Common squid *Loligo* spp
10 White shark *Carcharadon carcharias*
11 Hatchet fish *Argyropelecus hemigymnus*
12 Giant squid *Architeuthis* spp
13 Sea anemone *Cerianthus orientalis*
14 Tripod fish *Benthosaurus grallator*
15 Scarlet shrimp *Notostomus longirostris*
16 Angler fish *Linophryne bicornis*
17 Brittle star *Ophiothrix fragilis*
18 Sea cucumber class Holothuroidea

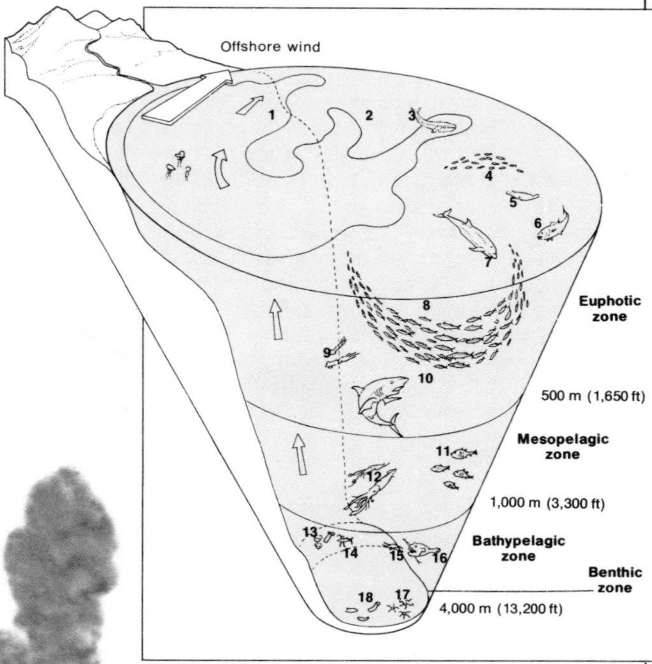
Offshore wind
1
2
3
4
5
6
7
8
9
10
11
12
13
14
15
16
17
18
Euphotic zone
500 m (1,650 ft)
Mesopelagic zone
1,000 m (3,300 ft)
Bathypelagic zone
Benthic zone
4,000 m (13,200 ft)

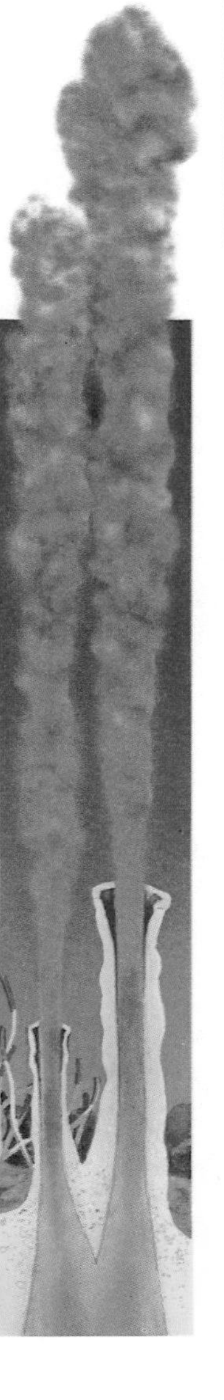

Bizarre life forms new to science live in the sunless depths, where plumes of hot mineral-rich water gush through deep-sea vents in the Earth's crust. These oases of life support huge, gutless tubeworms more than 1.5 m (5 ft) long, which appear to take food particles from the hot vents through blood-red tentacles. Other creatures include blind crabs and large white clams.

sharks, tuna-like fishes and toothed whales.

Beneath the euphotic zone, of course, there can be no herbivores at all, although some animals that spend the daylight hours in the deeper layers move upwards at night to feed in the plankton-rich surface waters. All of the permanent members of the deep-living communities are dependent for food upon material that sinks or is carried downwards from the euphotic zone. Many of them feed on dead animal remains and fecal material as it sinks through the water column or after it reaches the seabed. These detritus eaters in turn support the predatory carnivores that feed upon the detritivores or upon each other.

In shallow areas the food material that reaches the bottom supports complex communities, notably the rich and varied groups of invertebrates and fishes associated with coral reefs. In the deep sea, however, where the euphotic zone is separated from the seabed by several kilometers of water, much of the sinking material is recycled within the water column and relatively little reaches the bottom. Life on the deep-sea floor therefore becomes more and more sparse with increasing depth, but in recent years scientists have discovered that this community includes a surprising number of fishes, some many meters in length. So far man's knowledge of these deep-sea communities is relatively meager, but with our increasing use of the deep oceans we may need to know much more about the life in this environment.

Man and the Seawater Environments

For thousands of years man has used the oceans as a source of food and other materials, and as a repository for wastes. But only in the last 100 years have technological advances and fast-growing human populations had a significant effect, to a point where overfishing and pollution are becoming a cause for concern. Harvesting of krill and seaweeds may ease the pressure on traditional seafoods, but legal restrictions on dumping of wastes or on overfishing are notoriously hard to enforce.

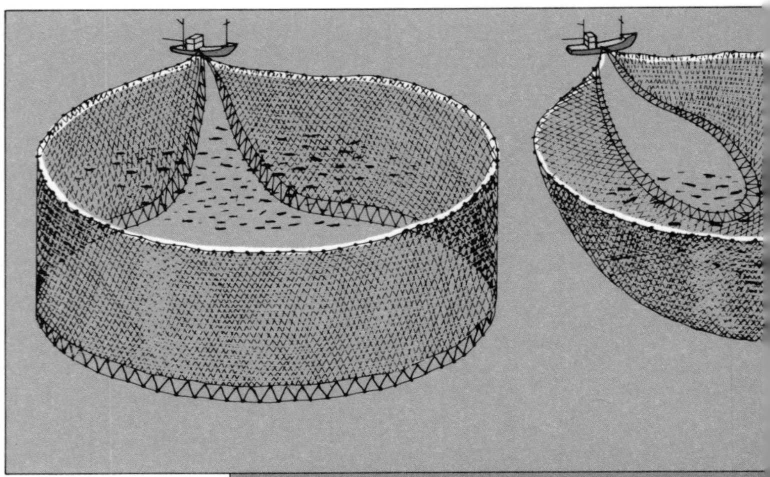

Until about the middle of the nineteenth century the seas had always seemed to be a boundless source of food and of income for fishermen who were brave enough to face the elements with their relatively small sailing ships and primitive gear. But once fishing vessels began to be fitted with steam engines in the 1880s they became relatively independent of the weather, while improvements in the fishing gear itself, such as steam-powered winches in trawling and harpoon guns in whaling, made the whole business of fishing much more efficient.

At first these advances resulted in enormous increases in catches, but in many fisheries this was rapidly followed by a distressing fall in the catch per unit of effort—that is, it was becoming more and more difficult in successive years to catch the same amount of fish as before. In most fisheries the initial response to this situation was to increase the size and number of fishing vessels and to search for new fishing grounds. But as the fishing pressure on the stocks increased, with smaller fish being captured, often before they were able to reproduce, the catch per unit of effort frequently continued to fall.

In many cases attempts were made to counter the effects of overfishing by introducing regulations to control the mesh size of the nets, so allowing the small fish to escape; by establishing closed seasons or quotas of fish which might legitimately be taken from a particular fishing ground in any one year; or even, as in the case of the British herring fishery in the late 1970s, by imposing a complete ban on fishing. Moral questions also sometimes intervene, as in whaling operations, which, many conservationists believe, have driven some species close to extinction despite attempts to rationalize the fisheries.

Fisheries in decline

The North Sea trawl fishery, the first to be affected by the new technology in the nineteenth century, has been declining in terms of catch per unit of effort since the early decades of this century. Dramatic but short-lived improvements after the "closed seasons" of the two world wars proved that fishing pressure had a serious effect on stocks, but by the 1970s many North Sea fishing ports had become almost deserted. This decline put pressure on more distant fishing grounds used by European fishermen, and recent decades have been marked by a series of fishing disputes, with nations fighting for the continued existence of their fisheries despite clear evidence that there are not enough catchable fish to satisfy everyone.

A similar story of declining catches during the present century could be told of many of the old-established fisheries around the world, but at the same time the demand for fish in a protein-hungry world has increased. To satisfy this demand the total annual world catch increased by about seven percent from the end of World War II until the early 1970s, by this time reaching a figure of around 60–70 million tonnes. But this increase was achieved only by exploiting previously unfished stocks or new geographical areas. Such an increase cannot go on indefinitely, for we are rapidly running out of "new" areas and some of the new fisheries have already shown the same symptoms of overfishing as the older ones—and sometimes even more dramatically.

New foods from the sea

The indications are that the present total catch is close to the maximum that can be obtained from relatively conventional fisheries even with careful management, and that, to increase the total, or even to sustain it, we must look to completely new sources such as krill, the shrimp-like food of the whalebone whales. Estimates of the sustainable annual catch of krill in the Antarctic range from about 50 to 500 million tonnes, that is up to about seven times as much as the current total from all other fisheries put together. Of course, the use of such an enormous quantity of small crustaceans would present considerable problems. Part of it might be converted into a protein-rich paste for human consumption, but much would be used indirectly as a feed for farm animals.

Many larger seaweeds are already cropped in several parts of the world, particularly in Japan, and are used not only for human food but also for animal food and in many industrial processes. About one million tonnes of seaweed are taken each year, but because seaweeds grow naturally only in relatively shallow areas of the oceans this figure could probably not be significantly increased using natural populations. However, seaweeds can be grown artificially on frames floating over deep water. Experiments suggest that, by enriching the surface layers through artificial upwelling of nutrient-rich deep water, each square kilometer of such a floating seaweed farm could produce enough food to feed 1,000–2,000 people, and enough energy and other products to satisfy the needs of a further 1,000. With an estimated 260 million sq km (100 million sq miles) of "arable" surface, the seas might thus support up to 10 times the present world population.

Polluted waters

Of course, the present century has seen an increase not only in what man takes out of the sea but also in the harmful substances that he throws into it. Not only oil but many other substances are dumped into the seas accidentally or intentionally, usually either in the discharged effluent from industrial plant or as a result of agricultural chemicals being leached into rivers and thence into the ocean. In many cases the amounts are very small compared with the amounts present in the oceans as a whole; the problem is that they are usually released, and accumulate, in restricted inshore areas near which we live and from which we obtain most of our sea-caught food.

Since the 1930s there have been both national and international attempts to control pollution by legislation, and since 1958 a series of United Nations conferences has sought agreement on many aspects of international maritime law, including pollution. Despite many prophecies of imminent doom, it does not seem that marine pollution yet poses any general threat to humanity. Nevertheless, with ever-increasing industrialization and the production of more and more toxic materials, including radioactive wastes, it is essential that we monitor the effects of man's activities on the ocean.

The ocean is home to the Bajau (above), the "sea gypsies" of southeastern Asia, who inhabit a tract of sea and islands stretching more than 6,500 km (4,000 miles). Each group has its own clan pattern, blazoned on the sails of their *praus*. The Bajau may live on the open sea in clusters of boats, or in stilt-house villages built over estuaries.

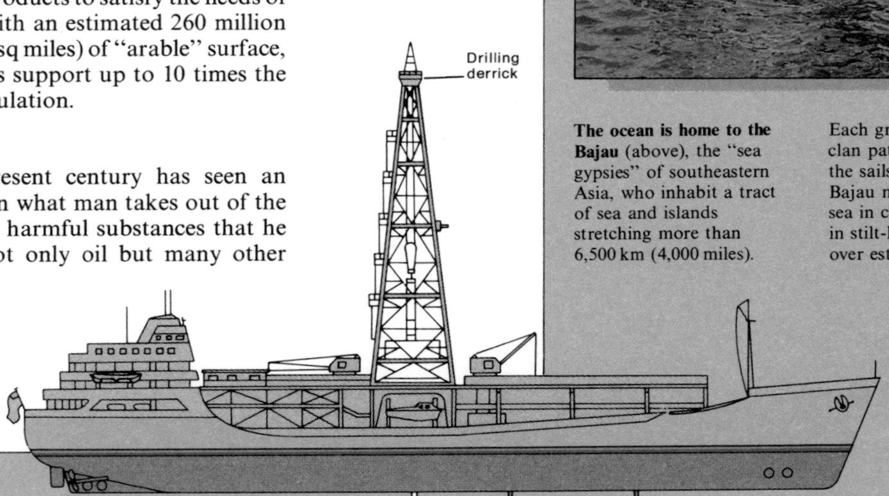
Drilling derrick
Hydrophones
Sonar beacons
Core sample tube
Drilling head

THE MARINE RESOURCES

Modern technology has enabled man to expand his age-old exploitation of the seas to the limit in some areas, and a need for the careful management of our marine resource is imperative. But in some fields, such as energy and the extraction of fresh water, the seas may yield inexhaustible riches.

The deep-sea drilling ship *Glomar Challenger* (above) plays an important role in surveying and prospecting the oceans. It can drill in water depths of 7,000 m (23,000 ft) and obtain core samples 1,200 m (4,000 ft) below the ocean bed. The ship is positioned over the drill hole through signals from a sonar beacon to hydrophones in the hull.

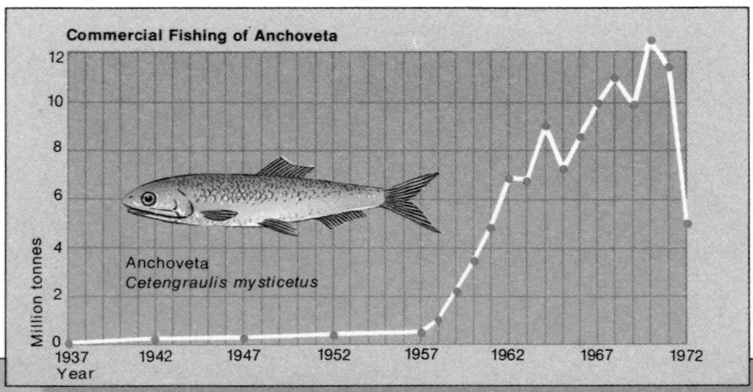

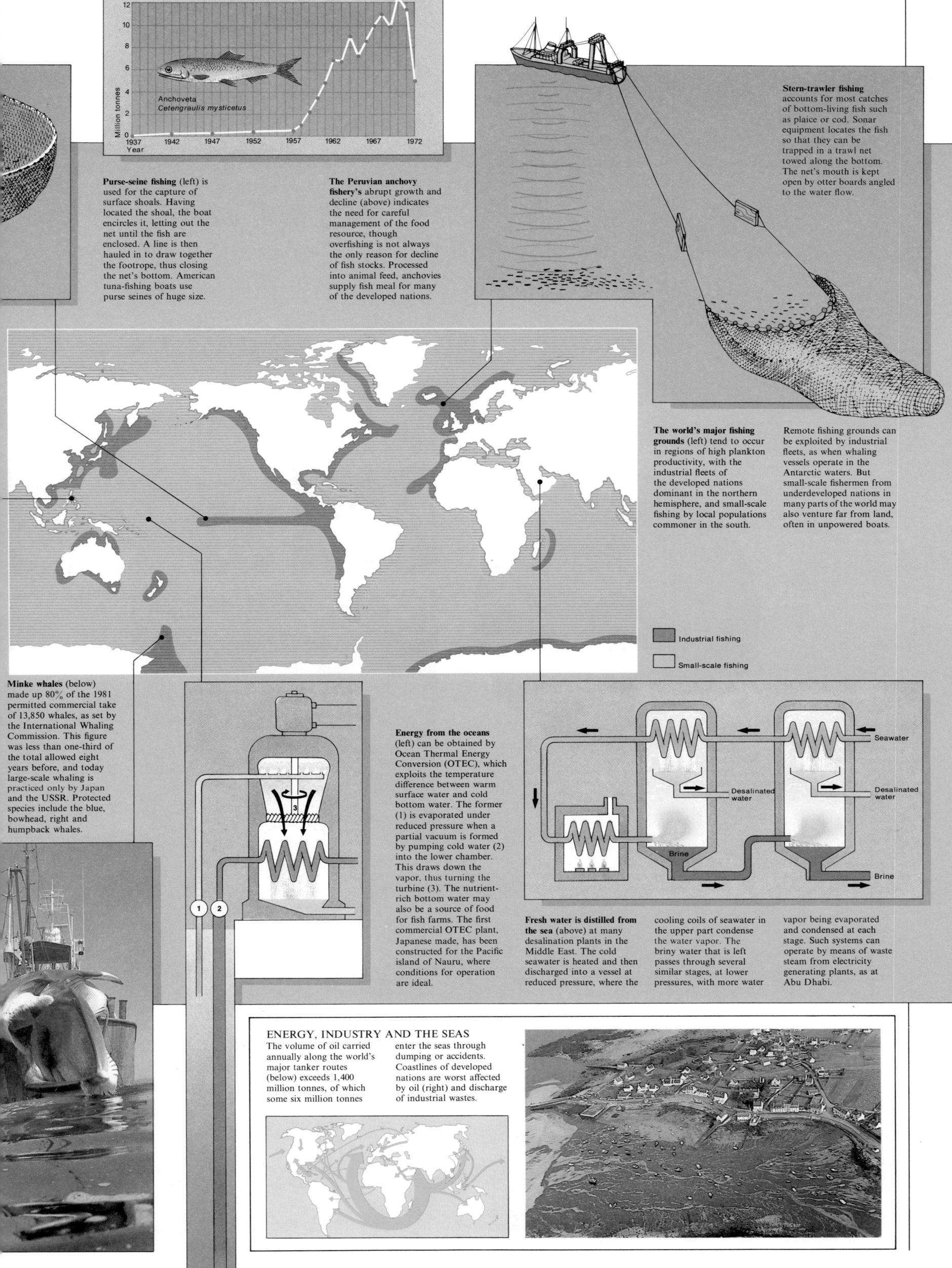

Commercial Fishing of Anchoveta
Anchoveta
Cetengraulis mysticetus
Million tonnes
12
10
8
6
4
2
0
1937
1942
1947
1952
1957
1962
1967
1972
Year

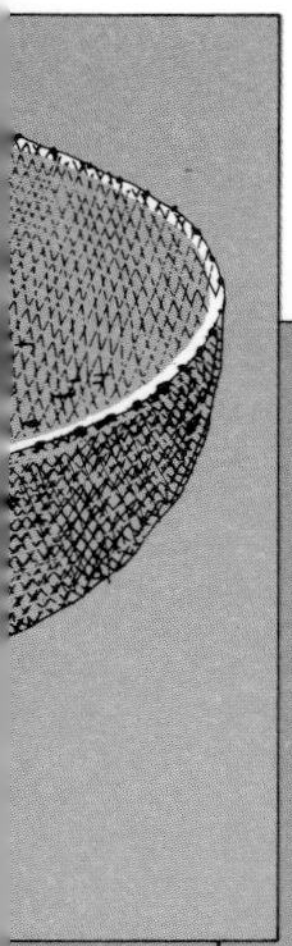

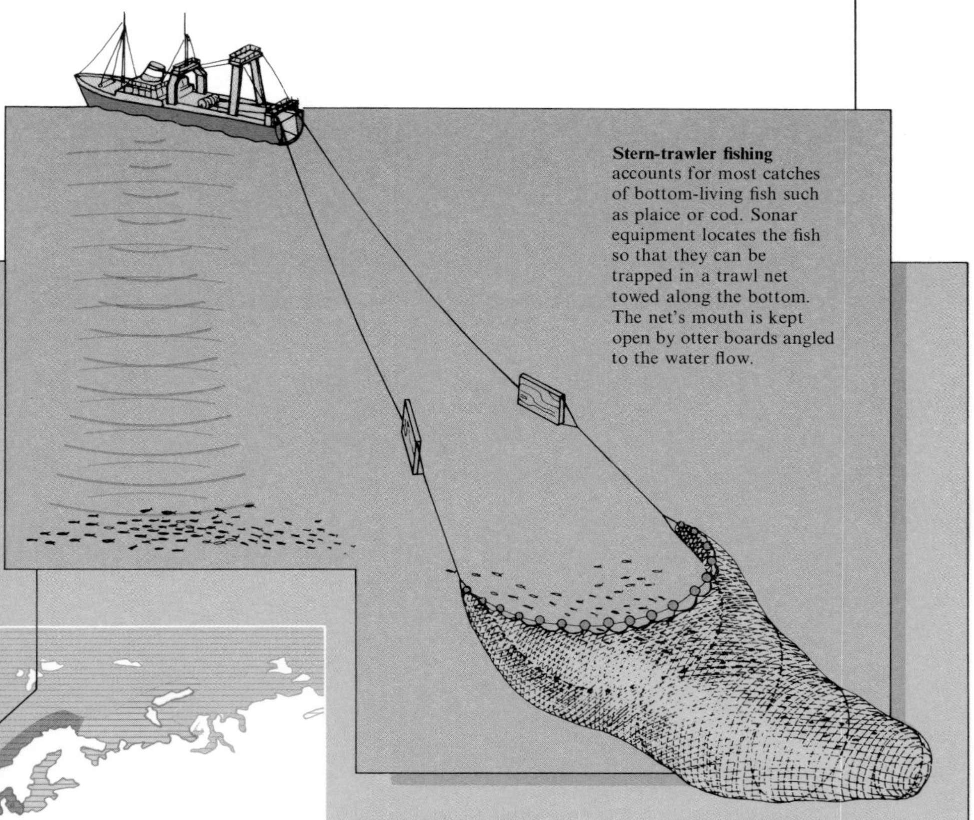

Stern-trawler fishing accounts for most catches of bottom-living fish such as plaice or cod. Sonar equipment locates the fish so that they can be trapped in a trawl net towed along the bottom. The net's mouth is kept open by otter boards angled to the water flow.

Purse-seine fishing (left) is used for the capture of surface shoals. Having located the shoal, the boat encircles it, letting out the net until the fish are enclosed. A line is then hauled in to draw together the footrope, thus closing the net's bottom. American tuna-fishing boats use purse seines of huge size.

The Peruvian anchovy fishery's abrupt growth and decline (above) indicates the need for careful management of the food resource, though overfishing is not always the only reason for decline of fish stocks. Processed into animal feed, anchovies supply fish meal for many of the developed nations.

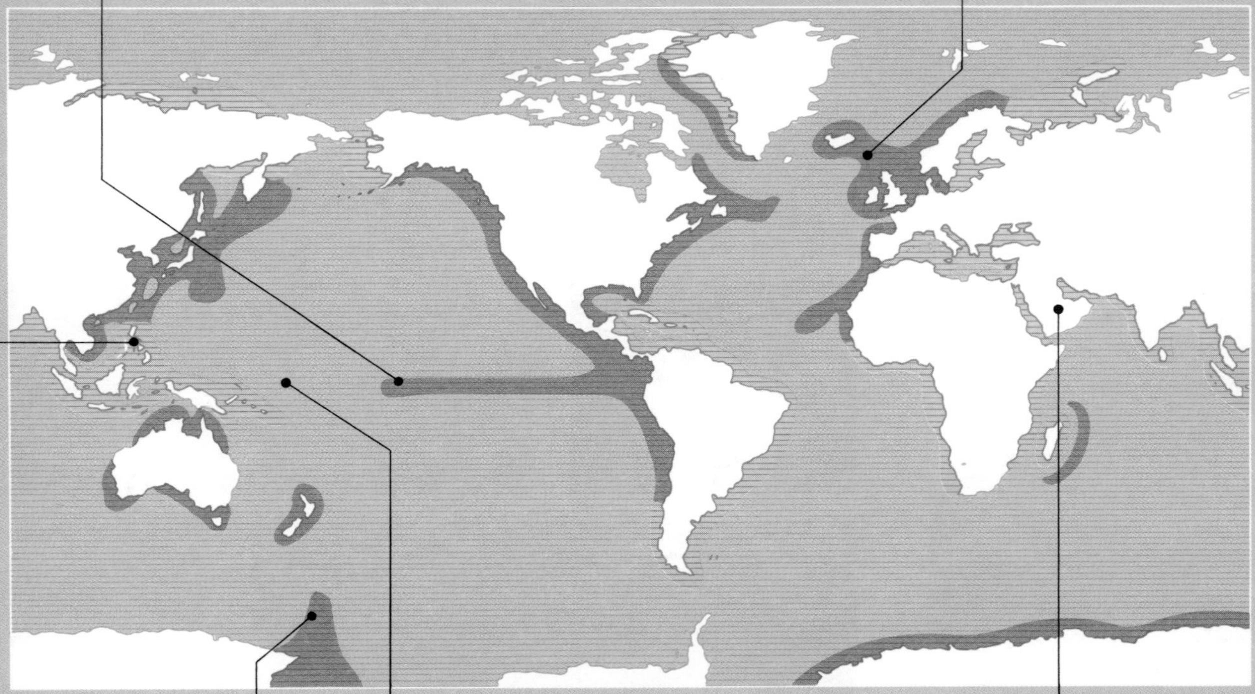

Industrial fishing
Small-scale fishing

The world's major fishing grounds (left) tend to occur in regions of high plankton productivity, with the industrial fleets of the developed nations dominant in the northern hemisphere, and small-scale fishing by local populations commoner in the south.

Remote fishing grounds can be exploited by industrial fleets, as when whaling vessels operate in the Antarctic waters. But small-scale fishermen from underdeveloped nations in many parts of the world may also venture far from land, often in unpowered boats.

Minke whales (below) made up 80% of the 1981 permitted commercial take of 13,850 whales, as set by the International Whaling Commission. This figure was less than one-third of the total allowed eight years before, and today large-scale whaling is practiced only by Japan and the USSR. Protected species include the blue, bowhead, right and humpback whales.

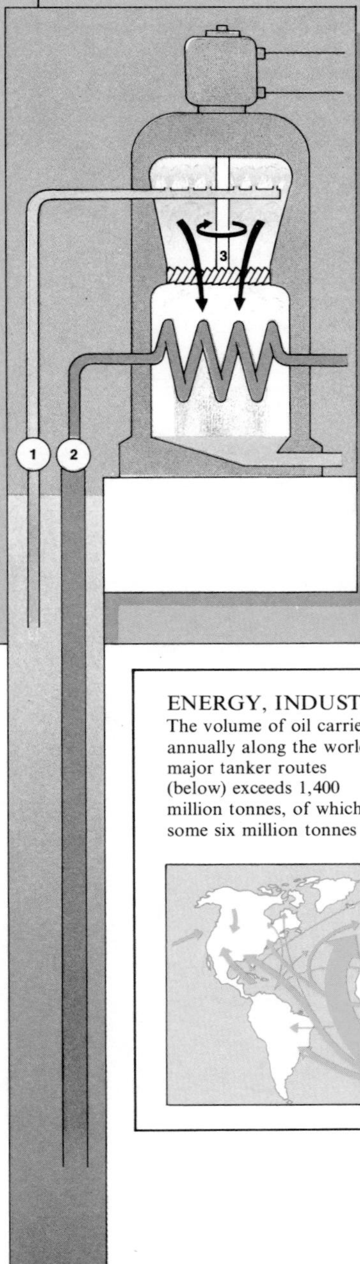

3
1
2

Energy from the oceans (left) can be obtained by Ocean Thermal Energy Conversion (OTEC), which exploits the temperature difference between warm surface water and cold bottom water. The former (1) is evaporated under reduced pressure when a partial vacuum is formed by pumping cold water (2) into the lower chamber. This draws down the vapor, thus turning the turbine (3). The nutrient-rich bottom water may also be a source of food for fish farms. The first commercial OTEC plant, Japanese made, has been constructed for the Pacific island of Nauru, where conditions for operation are ideal.

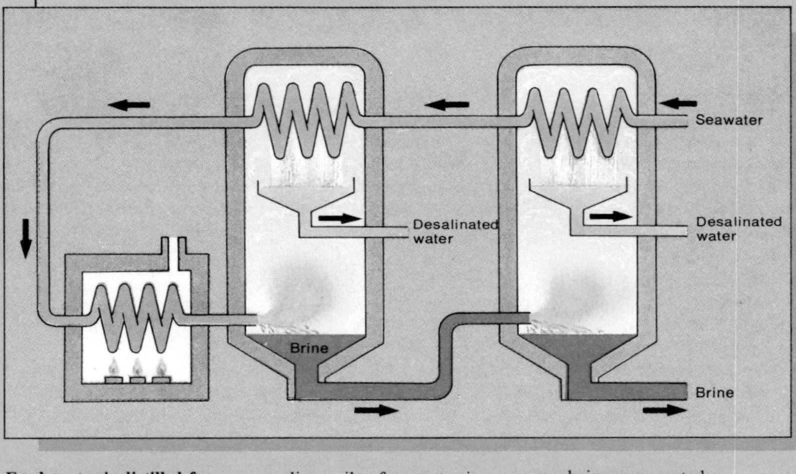

Seawater
Desalinated water
Desalinated water
Brine
Brine

Fresh water is distilled from the sea (above) at many desalination plants in the Middle East. The cold seawater is heated and then discharged into a vessel at reduced pressure, where the cooling coils of seawater in the upper part condense the water vapor. The briny water that is left passes through several similar stages, at lower pressures, with more water vapor being evaporated and condensed at each stage. Such systems can operate by means of waste steam from electricity generating plants, as at Abu Dhabi.

ENERGY, INDUSTRY AND THE SEAS

The volume of oil carried annually along the world's major tanker routes (below) exceeds 1,400 million tonnes, of which some six million tonnes enter the seas through dumping or accidents. Coastlines of developed nations are worst affected by oil (right) and discharge of industrial wastes.

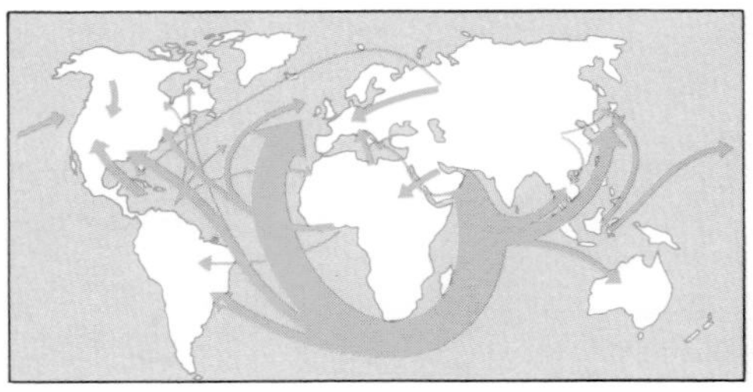

Part 5

UNDERSTANDING MAPS

What maps are and how they are made
New horizons and latest developments in maps and mapmaking
How to read the language of maps

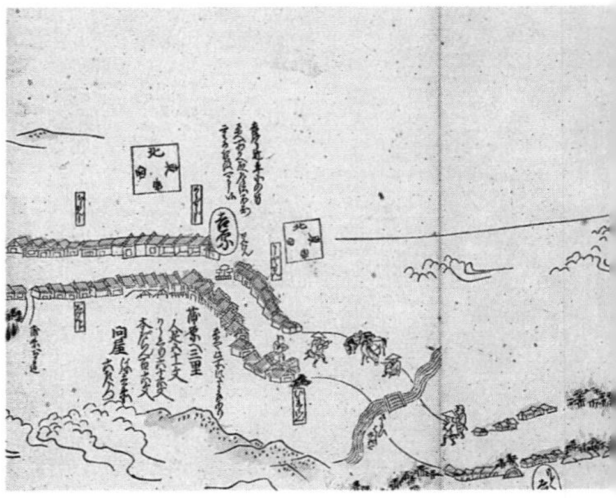

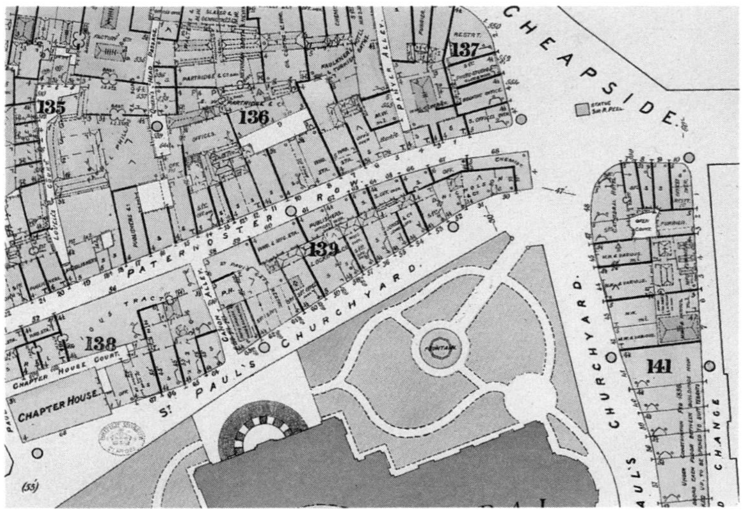

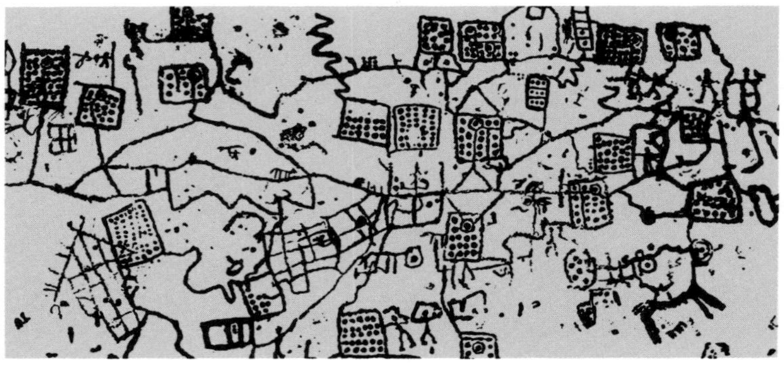

Maps defining territory and ownership are almost as old as the human territorial instinct itself. The rock-carving maps of the Val Camonica, Italy (above), dating from the second and first millennia BC, show stippled square fields, paths, river lines, houses, and even humans and animals. It is uncertain whether their purpose was legal, but the need to establish ownership is a basic function of many maps, as seen in a detail from Goad's 19th-century insurance map of London (left), where every occupation is recorded.

Elegant road maps with pictorial and geographical features have been produced by many different cultures. The woodcut map of the Tōkaidō (detail above), the great Japanese highway, 555 km (345 miles) long, between Edo (Tokyo) and Kyoto, was drawn as a panorama by the famous artist Moronobu in 1690. Its pictorial details do not prevent it being an accurate representation of the road's track. A Mexican map of the Tepetlaoztoc valley (right) drawn in 1583 marks roads with footprints between parallel lines, and hill ranges with wavy lines. Symbols in panels represent place-names.

America first appears as a separate continent (below) in an inset to Martin Waldseemüller's world map of 1507, with the two hemispheres facing each other. Presiding over the Old World is Claudius Ptolemy, the 2nd-century geographer whose remarkably scientific maps, copied and recopied over a thousand years, were revised and emended by Waldseemüller to show some of the results of Portuguese exploration. His New World counterpart is the Italian Amerigo Vespucci, one of the early explorers of the continent, after whom it was named. This is the first map to show the Pacific (not yet named) as an ocean between America and Asia. The west coast of South America, still to be explored by Europeans, seems to be inspired guesswork. The island between the landmasses is Cipango (Japan) known from Marco Polo.

The earliest surviving Chinese globe (above) was made in 1623 by two Jesuit missionaries, probably for the emperor of China. The long legend in Chinese expresses terms and ideas derived from early Chinese cosmology. It describes the Earth as "floating in the Heavens like the yolk of an egg . . . with all objects having mass tending toward its center"—one of the first known references to gravity.

1

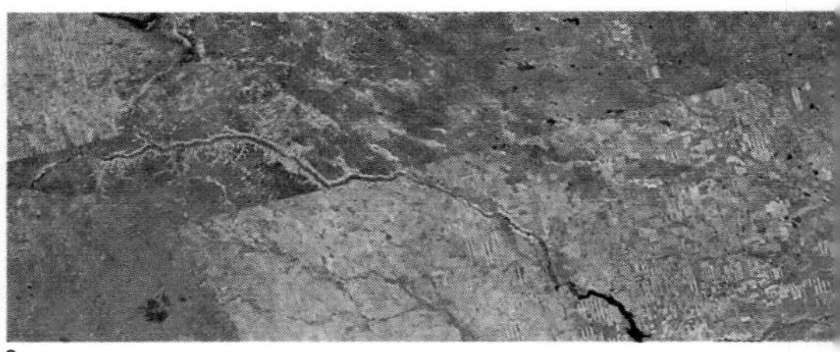

2

High-altitude photography (left) allows accurate updating of topographic maps (right), while data gathering by satellites (above) expands the range. Landsat satellites carry electronic remote-sensing equipment that detects the energy emitted by surface materials and translates it into images. Healthy plants may show as bright red, sparse vegetation as pink, barren lands as light gray, and urban areas as green or dark gray. The folded shape of the Appalachians (1) is clearly seen; the Canada–US border (2) is revealed by land-use patterns; silt from the Mississippi (3) builds up the delta. Sudan irrigation (4) shows up as brilliant red.

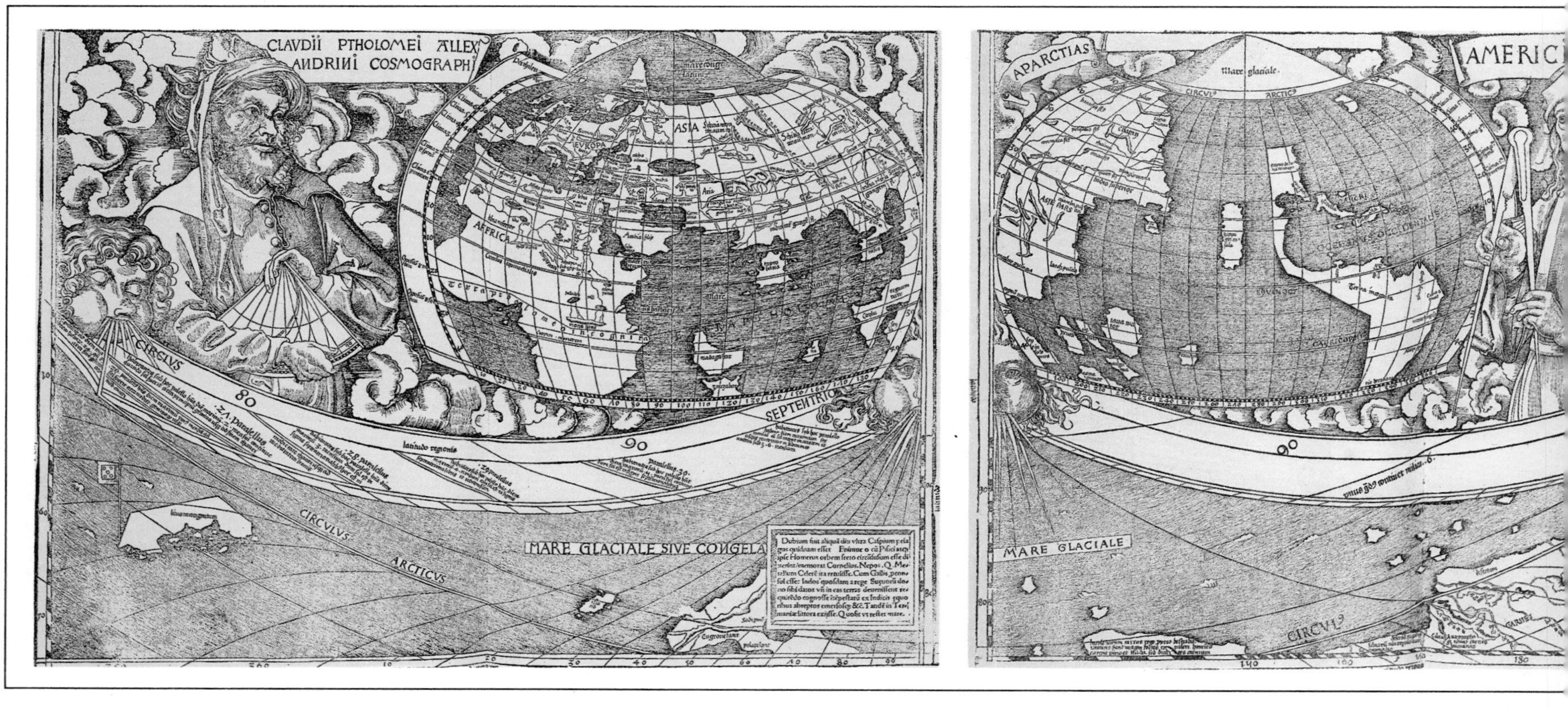

Mapping, Old and New

Mapmaking must have its origins in the earliest ages of human history, since people of preliterate as well as literate cultures possess an innate skill in map drawing. This innate capacity is further indicated by the ease with which almost anyone can sketch in the sand or on paper simple directions for showing the way. But maps may also define territory and express man's idea of the world in graphic representation. Today, modern technology has vastly extended the scope of cartography.

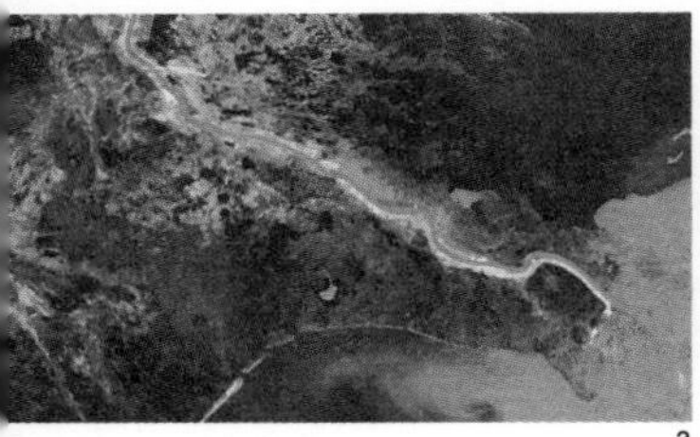

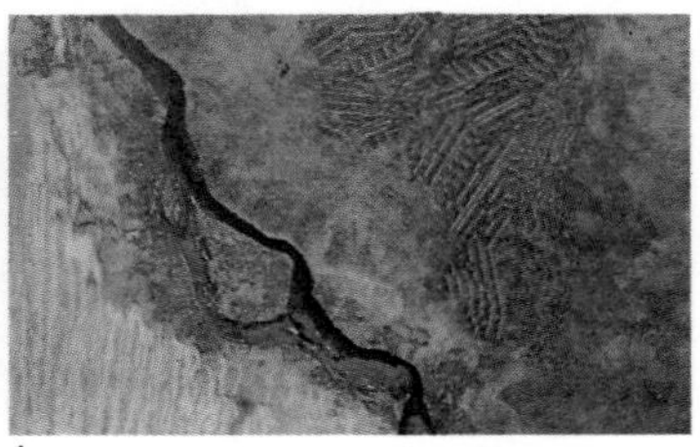

3 4

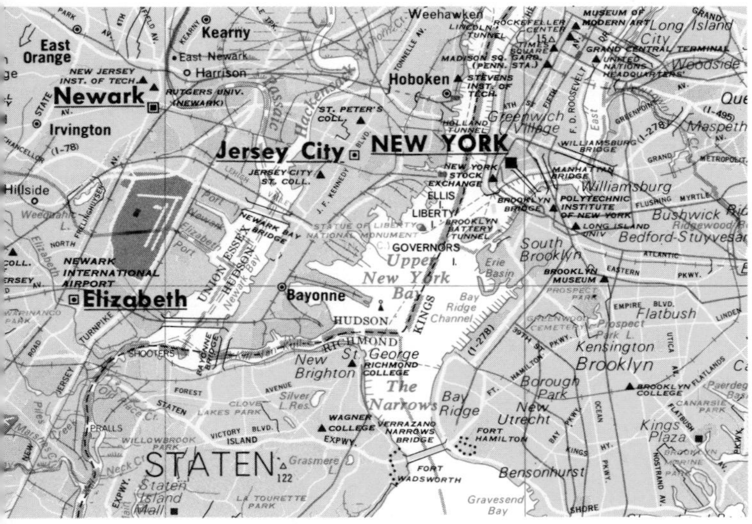

Space technology helps cartographers to map even interior details of the planet: its geology and mineral wealth. A photo (below) taken from Gemini 12 at an altitude of 272 km (168 miles) forms the basis of a geologic sketch map of SW Asia (below right), showing the oil-rich area around the region between the Persian Gulf and the Gulf of Oman. The symbol S on the map indicates salt plugs; diamonds show fold trends; double-headed arrows anticlines.

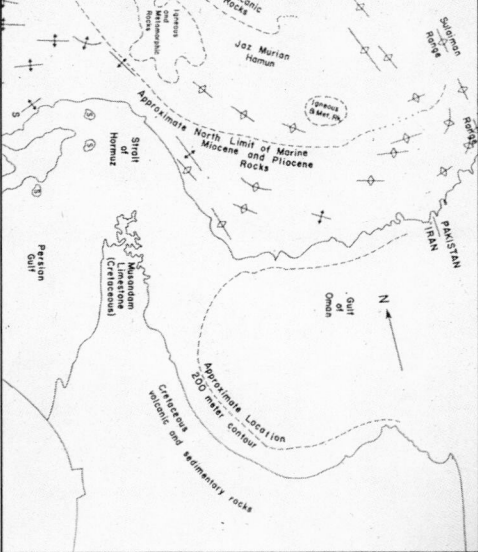

Many non-European cultures developed ingenious route-map techniques: the North American Indians, for example, made sketch maps of routes on birch bark. These were diagrammatic maps in which directions and distances were not accurate but relationships were true, as in New York Subway or London Underground maps. The people of the Marshall Islands in the western Pacific made route maps over the seas, depicting the direction of the main seasonal wave swells in relation to the islands.

Although maps of routes are the simplest type of map in concept, they developed complex forms as cartography progressed. A road map of the whole Roman Empire, drawn about AD 280, survives today in a thirteenth-century copy known as the Peutinger Table. Hernando Cortes, the Spanish conqueror, made his way across Mexico in the 1520s with the help of pre-conquest Mexican maps painted on cloth. These showed roads with double lines or colored bands marked with footprints. Another type of map is the strip map depicting a single road along its entire length. Pictorial maps of the Tōkaidō highway from Edo to Kyoto in Japan, made from a survey of 1651, were popular in the Edo period of Japanese history.

Nautical charts evolved as a special type of direction-finding map to meet the needs of seamen. Those of the late Middle Ages came to be known as "portolan" charts, from the word "portolani," or sailing directions. They showed the sea and adjacent coasts superimposed on a network of radiating compass lines.

Territorial maps

Another basic type of map derives from man's sense of territorial possession. The earliest example of a "cadastral" plan (a map showing land parcels and property boundaries) appears to be that preserved as rock carvings at Bedolina in Val Camonica in northern Italy. However, in the ancient civilizations of Mesopotamia and Egypt, land surveying had become an established profession by 2000 BC. An idea of what Egyptian surveyors' plans of 1000 BC were like can be seen from the "Fields of the Dead" representing the Egyptians' idea of life after death. These show plots of land surrounded by water and intersected by canals. The Romans used cadastral surveys to determine land ownership and assess tax liability.

Another form of map showing territorial demarcations is the map of administrative units. The Chinese in the thirteenth century AD were making official district maps to help in the organization of grain supplies and the collection of taxes. Many of their gazetteers (*fang chih*), written in the form of local geographies and

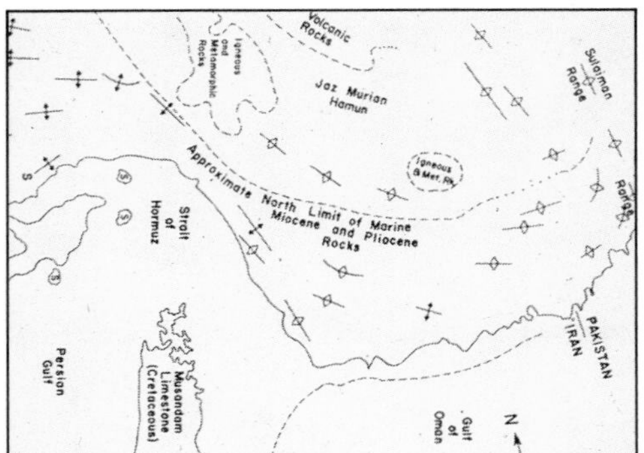

histories from the eleventh century onward, were illustrated with maps. Political maps showing the boundaries of states were increasingly significant in European cartography from the sixteenth century onward.

A third major class of map is the general or topographical map expressing man's perception of the world, its regions and its place in the universe. A Babylonian world map of the seventh century BC is drawn on a clay tablet and shows the Earth as a circular disc surrounded by the Earthly Ocean. With the ancient Greeks, geography developed on scientific principles. The treatise on mapmaking by Claudius Ptolemy (AD 87–150), later known as the *Geographia*, was the most famous cartographic text of the period. It influenced the Arabic geographers of the Middle Ages, notably Muhammad Ibn Muhammad, Al-Idrisi (1099–1164), and with the revival of Ptolemy in fifteenth-century Europe became one of the major works of the Renaissance. Published, with engraved maps, at Bologna in 1477, the *Geographia* ranks as the first printed atlas in the western world. The invention of techniques of engraving in wood and copper facilitated a wide diffusion of geographical knowledge through the map-publishing trade. The first atlas made up of modern maps to a uniform design was Abraham Ortelius's *Theatrum Orbis Terrarum* published at Antwerp in 1570. From 1492, when Martin Behaim made his "Erdapfel" at Nürnberg, globes also became popular, and globemakers vied with each other to make larger and more elaborate ones to keep pace with the growth of knowledge about the world.

Over the last two hundred years cartography has made rapid and remarkable advances. Observatories built in Paris in 1671 and at Greenwich in 1675 enabled the location of places to be established more exactly with the use of astronomical tables. Improvements in surveying instruments facilitated more accurate and rapid land survey. France was the pioneer in establishing (from 1679 onward) a national survey on a geometrical basis of triangulation. By the end of the eighteenth century national surveys on small and medium scales had been begun by most European countries. In the United States the Geological Survey was set up in 1879 to undertake the topographical and geological mapping of the country.

Mapping today

Since World War II cartographic techniques have undergone a revolution. The use of air survey and photogrammetry has made it possible to map most of the Earth's surface. Electronic distance measurement by laser or light beams in surveying, and digital computers in mapping, are among the most recent advances in methods. Mosaics or air photography are used to produce orthophoto maps which can supplement or substitute for the conventional topographic map. Artificial satellites and manned space craft make it possible to provide a world-wide framework of geodetic networks.

Earth Resource Technology Satellites (ERTS) imagery has made it possible to map mountain ranges in Africa and features on the surface of Antarctica that were hitherto unknown. The imagery is made available by means of remote-sensing instruments, carried by the satellites, that are sensitive to invisible portions of the electromagnetic spectrum—longer and shorter wavelengths than can be sensed by the human eye. Remote-sensing instruments usually work in the infrared bands. They can also pick up the energy emitted by all types of surface material—rocks, soils, vegetation, water and man-made structures—and produce photographs or images from it.

The Language of Maps

Mapmakers for more than 4,000 years have tried to find the best way to represent the shape and features of the three-dimensional Earth on two-dimensional paper, parchment and cloth. The measurement of distance and direction is a basic requirement for accurate surveys, but until about 1800 theoretical understanding of the method was well in advance of the technical equipment available. Today the use of lasers and light beams sometimes takes the place of direct measurement on the ground.

A reference system must be used to show distance and direction correctly in the construction of maps. The simplest type is the rectangular or square grid. The Chinese mapmaker Pei Xin made a map with a grid in about AD 270, and this system remained in continuous use in China until modern times. The Roman system of centuriation, a form of division of public lands on a square or rectangular basis, was also a "coordinate" system starting from a point of origin at the intersection of two perpendicular axes. Roman surveyors' maps, dating from the first century AD, are the earliest known European maps based on a grid system.

Latitude and longitude

Makers of small-scale regional maps and of world maps in early times also had to take account of the fact that the Earth is a sphere. The Greeks derived from the Babylonians the idea of dividing a circle into 360 degrees. In the second century BC the Greek geographer Eratosthenes (*c.* 276–194 BC) was the first to calculate the circumference of the globe and was reported to have made a world map based on the concept of the Earth's sphericity. From this the Greeks went on to develop the system of spherical coordinates which remains in use today. The poles at each end of the Earth's axis provide reference points for the Earth in its rotation in relation to the celestial sphere. Parallel circles around the Earth are degrees of latitude and express the idea of distance north or south of the Equator. Lines of longitude running north and south through the poles express east–west distances. One meridian is chosen as the meridian of origin, known as the prime meridian.

Whereas latitude from early times could be observed from the height of the Sun or (in the northern hemisphere) from the position of the Pole Star at night, accurate observations of longitude were not possible until the middle of the eighteenth century, when the chronometer was invented and more accurate astronomical tables were provided. In 1884 most countries agreed, at an international conference in Washington DC, to adopt the prime meridian through the Royal Greenwich Observatory in England and to calculate longitude to 180 degrees east and west of Greenwich.

Projection and distortion

The mathematical system by which the spherical surface of the Earth is transferred to the plane surface of a map is called a map projection. The Greek geographer Ptolemy gave instructions in his geographical treatise of AD 150 for the construction of two projections. When the *Geographia* was revised in Europe in the fifteenth century, and navigators began sailing across the oceans, mapmakers devised new projections more appropriate to the expanding geographical knowledge of the world. The Dutch geographer Gerard Mercator invented the projection named after him, applying it to his world chart of 1569. This cylindrical projection, in which all points are at true compass courses from each other, was of great benefit to navigators and is still one of the most commonly used projections. Another advance was made when Johann Heinrich Lambert of Alsace (1728–1777) invented the azimuthal equal-area projection, in which the sizes of all areas are represented on the projection in correct proportion to one another, and the conformal projection, in which at any point on the map the scale is constant in all directions.

Since all projections involve deformation of the geometry of the globe, the cartographer has to choose the one that best suits the purpose of his map. "Conformal" or "orthomorphic" projections, in which angular relations (or shape) are preserved, are widely used for the construction of topographical maps. "Equivalent" or "equal-area" projections retain relative sizes and are particularly useful for general reference maps displaying economic, historical, political and other geographical phenomena.

Since the mid-fifteenth century, European mapmakers have generally arranged their maps with north at the top of the sheet. Earlier maps, however, were not standardized in this way. The circular world maps of the Middle Ages were orientated with east at the top, because this was where the terrestrial paradise was traditionally sited. Indeed, the word "orientation" originally meant the arrangement of something so as to face east.

Map scale

Scale is another basic property of a map. The scale of a map is the ratio of the distance on the map to the actual distance represented. Whereas the Babylonians, Egyptians, Greeks and Romans drew surveys to scale, in medieval Europe mapmakers used customary methods of estimating. The earliest known local map since Roman times which is drawn to scale (it displays a scale bar) is a plan of Vienna, 1422.

Projection, grid, orientation and scale form the framework of a map. The language of maps in concept and content is much more complex. To represent the surface of the Earth on a map, the cartographer must select and generalize from a vast quantity of material, using symbols and conventional signs as codes.

MAP PROJECTIONS

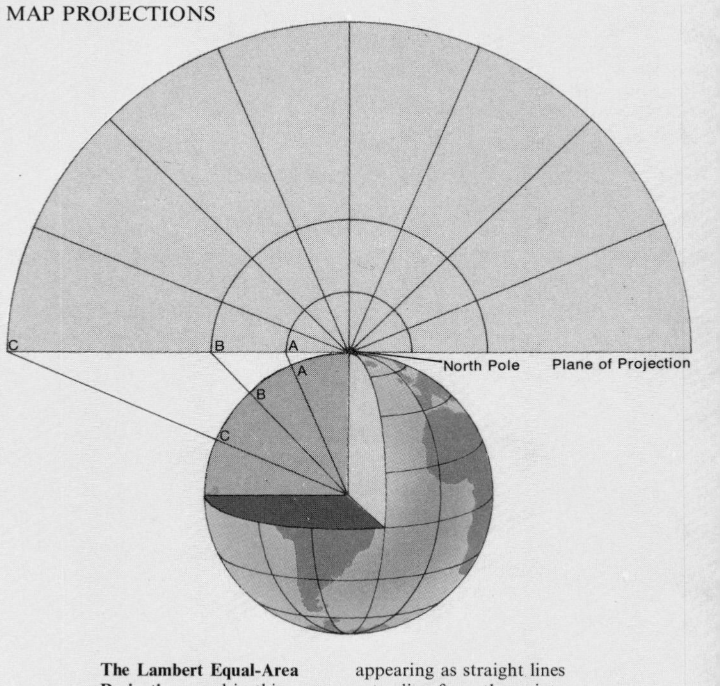
C
B
A
A
B
C
North Pole
Plane of Projection

The Lambert Equal-Area Projection, used in this atlas, may be visualized as a flat plane placed at a tangent to the globe, with the lines of longitude appearing as straight lines extending from the point of tangency, the North Pole (above). Deformation increases away from this point (below).

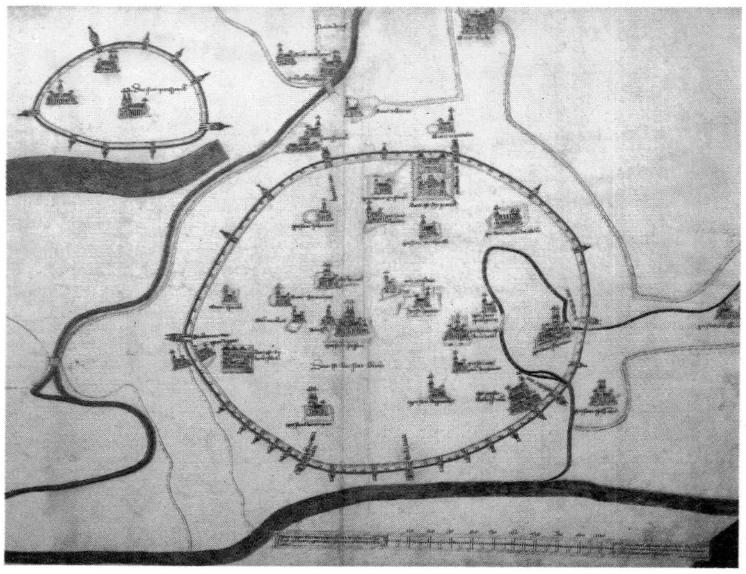

Map scales express the relationship between a distance measured on the map and the true distance on the ground. A plan of Vienna (left), originally made in 1422, is drawn in the bird's-eye-view style typical of early medieval town plans. But the scale bar at its foot shows that it has been explicitly drawn to scale, indicating that the concept of a uniform scale had been grasped in medieval Europe.

Direction and distance are concepts used in the relative location of two or more points (below). These concepts are organized according to a general frame of reference, with direction following the grid system of coordinates. Thus places shown in (A) can be precisely located in terms of longitude and of latitude (B), with the degrees further subdivided into one-sixtieths of minutes.

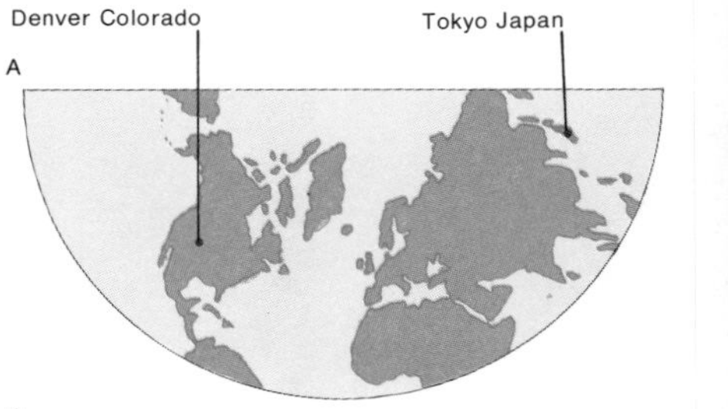
Denver Colorado
Tokyo Japan
A

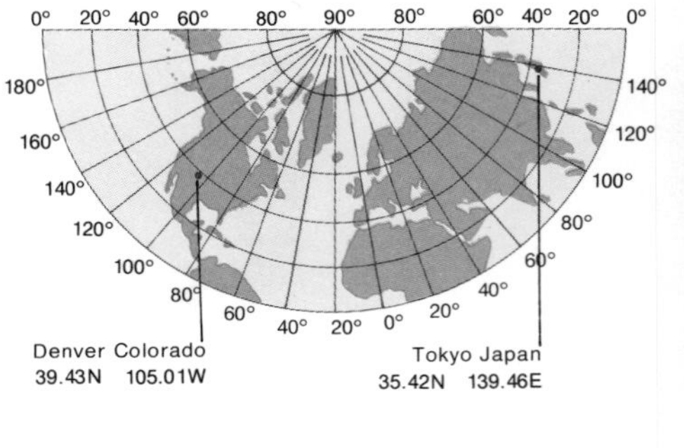
B
0° 20° 40° 60° 80° 90° 80° 60° 40° 20° 0°
180° 160° 140° 120° 100° 80° 60° 40° 20° 0° 20° 40° 60° 80° 100° 120° 140°
Denver Colorado
39.43N 105.01W
Tokyo Japan
35.42N 139.46E

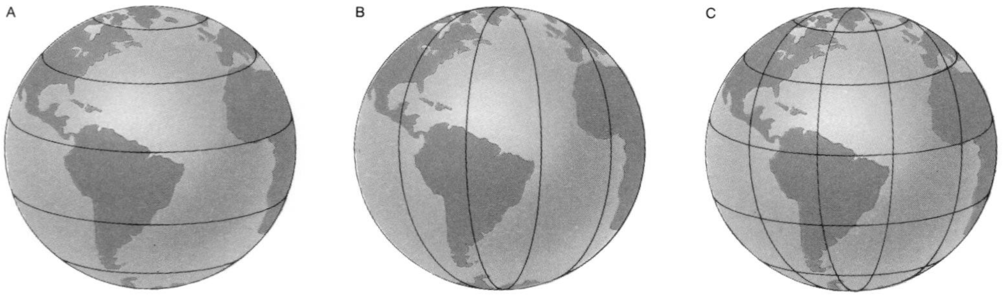
A
B
C

Superimposed on the globe (left), lines of latitude (A) and longitude (B) allow every place to be exactly located in terms of a coordinate system (C). The parallels of latitude measure distance from 0° to 90° north and south of the Equator. The meridians of longitude measure distance from 0° to 180° east and west of a "prime meridian" at Greenwich.

The Hammer Projection (far right), developed from the Lambert Projection of one hemisphere (right), is designed to show the whole world in a single view, and is used in this atlas in a version modified by Wagner and known as the Hammer-Wagner Projection. The Earth appears as an ellipse because the lines of longitude are plotted at twice their horizontal distance from the center line, and numbered at twice their previous values. The central meridian is half the length of the Equator.

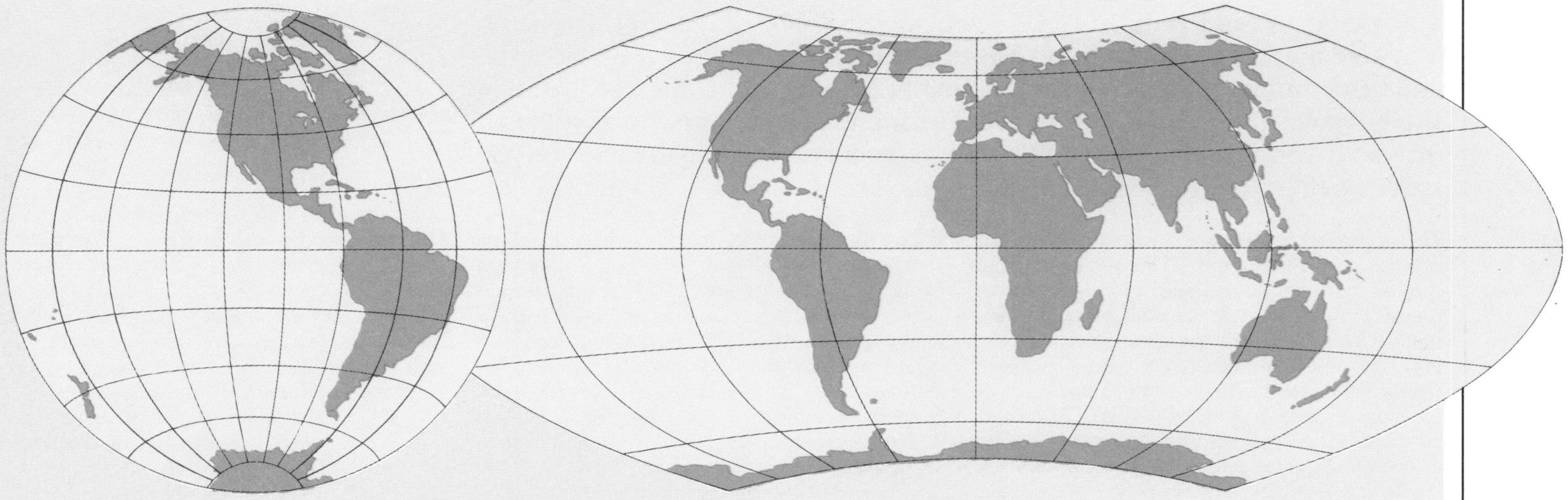

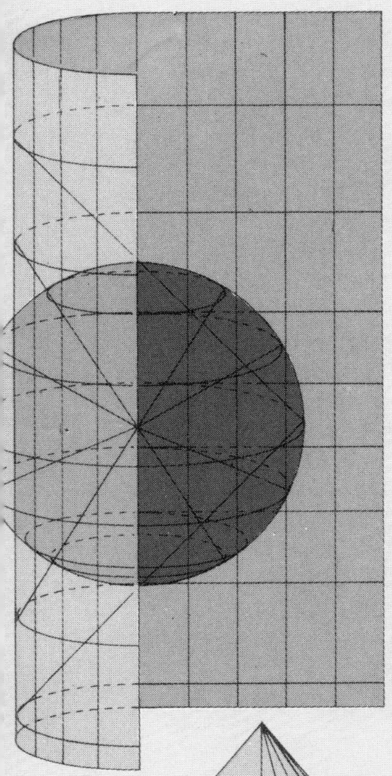

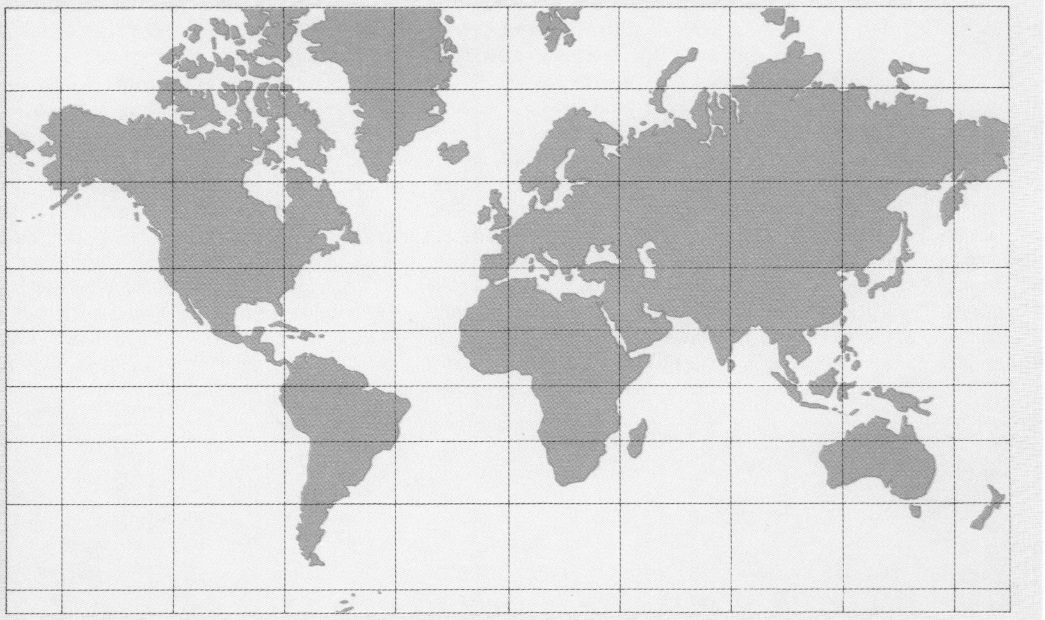

In a cylindrical projection like Gall's (above left), the sphere is "unwrapped" on to a cylinder, making a complete transformation to a flat surface. Mercator's Projection (above), devised in 1569, is a cylindrical projection that aids navigation by showing all compass directions as straight lines. A projection (below), based on Peters', distorts shape to show land surface area ratios, emphasizing the Third World.

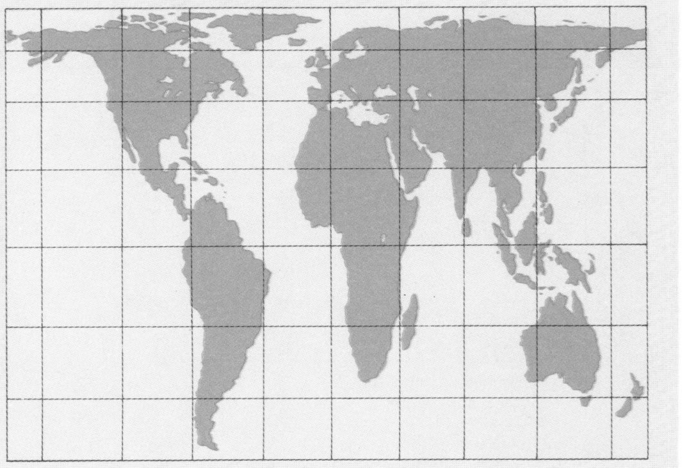

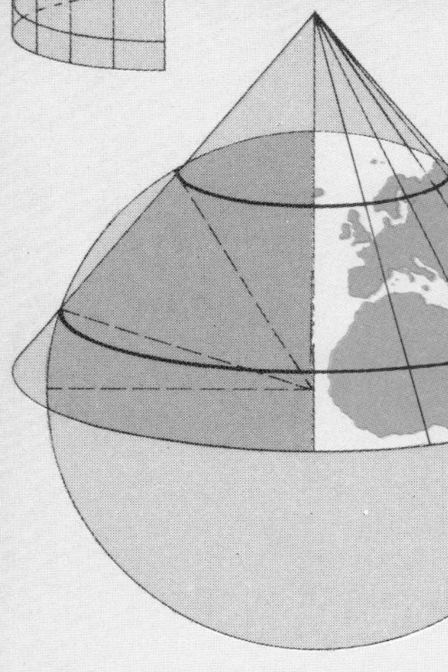

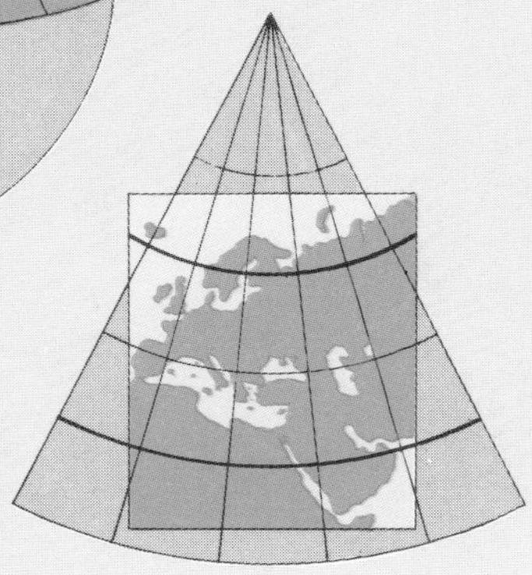

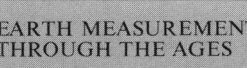

Delisle's Conic Projection (right), used in this atlas, intersects the globe at two points (above). Distortion is least at the parallels where the cone "touches" the globe, increasing with distance from them. Thus it is good for mid-latitudes.

Photogrammetric plotting instruments (above) are now used in the preparation of large-scale accurate topographic maps. These are sophisticated machines that provide very precise measurements, plotting the map data in orthogonal projection.

The theodolite (above), a basic surveying instrument dating back to the 16th century, can measure angles and directions horizontally and vertically. A swivel telescope with cross-hairs inside it permits accurate alignment, and it may be used in the field.

EARTH MEASUREMENT THROUGH THE AGES

Surveying—the technique of making accurate measurements of the Earth's surface—is as old as civilization and has been an essential element in mankind's development of his environment. The need to establish land boundaries arose at least 3,500 years ago in the fertile valleys of the Nile, Tigris and Euphrates rivers. Man's urge to explore and to describe the world also led to the development of instruments determining position, distance and direction. The astrolabe, sometimes called the world's oldest scientific instrument, may date to the 3rd century BC. Today's techniques make increasing use of computers.

An Egyptian wall painting (left) from the middle of the second millennium BC shows what appears to be the measurement of a grain field by means of a rope with knots at regular intervals on its length.

The astrolabe (right), used in classical times to observe the positions of celestial bodies, became a navigational instrument in the Middle Ages, when it was developed to permit establishment of latitude.

How to Use Maps

Today maps play a role more important than ever before in increasing our knowledge of the Earth, its regions and peoples. How maps communicate knowledge is now a subject of scientific study. The process comprises the collection and mapping of the data and the reading of the map. In this final stage the map user is all important. Through him the map is transformed into an image in the mind, and the effectiveness of the map depends on the reader being able to understand it.

The cartographer's map has to convey an objective picture of reality. To compile the map the cartographer selects and generalizes information, taking into account the purpose of his map. If he is making a topographical reference map, he has to reduce the three-dimensional landforms of the Earth on to the flat surface of the map. He adds cultural detail such as towns, roads and railroads, and features not apparent to the eye, such as administrative boundaries. On the topographical base map he adds appropriate place-names, using typefaces which reflect their class and significance. All this requires the classification of phenomena, with emphasis to direct the reader's attention.

Themes and symbolization

The cartographer who seeks not merely to represent visible features but to convey geographical ideas about specific phenomena uses the techniques of thematic cartography, where the emphasis is on one or two elements, or themes. Maps today provide one of the most effective means of communicating many kinds of data and ideas relating to the world and its peoples. Their extensive use makes them an important force in education, planning, recreation and in many other human affairs.

The map is designed in code, with symbols to represent features, and a legend, or key, to explain them. There are three types of symbol: point, line and area. Point symbols usually denote places, which may be distinguished into classes by the shape, color and size of the symbol. Line symbols express connections, such as roads or traffic flow, and they may also define and distinguish areas. Area symbols in which variations of color are often combined with patterns of lines or dots are used to depict spatial phenomena, such as types of soil, vegetation and density of population.

How much detail can be shown on a map will depend on its scale, which controls the process of generalization. Scale expresses the relationship of the distance on the map to the distance on the Earth, with the distance on the map always given as the unit 1. It is denoted in various ways: as a representative fraction such as 1:1,000,000; as a written statement; or by means of a graph or bar. Some map scales have become widely used and are generally familiar to map users. The scale 1:25,000 is ideal for walkers and relief can be shown in detail. That of 1:50,000 is a typical medium scale for national surveys. The publication of an international map of the world on a scale of one to one million (1:1,000,000) has been in progress since 1909. On this scale 1 mm represents 1 km on the ground. The regional maps of countries in this atlas are drawn on scales of 1:6,000,000, 1:3,000,000 and 1:1,500,000; those of the continents are at 1:30,000,000 and 1:15,000,000. The Map Section index maps show the arrangement.

Terrain depiction

Since the early days of map making in ancient Chinese and classical Greek and Roman civilizations, map makers have been concerned to show the configuration of the land. For many centuries they symbolized mountains and hills by pictorial features often looking like caterpillars or sugar loaves. As topographical mapping developed in Europe from the seventeenth century onward, new techniques were devised to improve the visual impression of the features and to depict them accurately in terms of height and location. The system of hachuring (shading with fine parallel or crossed lines), first used in 1674, gives a good idea of relief but not of height. The use of contours, which became general from the nineteenth century onward, is more exact in representing actual elevation, but for many regions, especially those of irregular relief, the appearance of the land is lost.

The addition of hypsometric tints (tints between contours which show elevation) helps clarify the elevation. Applying shadows to the form of the land through the process called hill shading or relief shading creates a visual impression of the configuration of the land surface. Hypsometric tints combined with hill shading gives both elevation information and surface form of the area being depicted, leading to an almost three-dimensional effect.

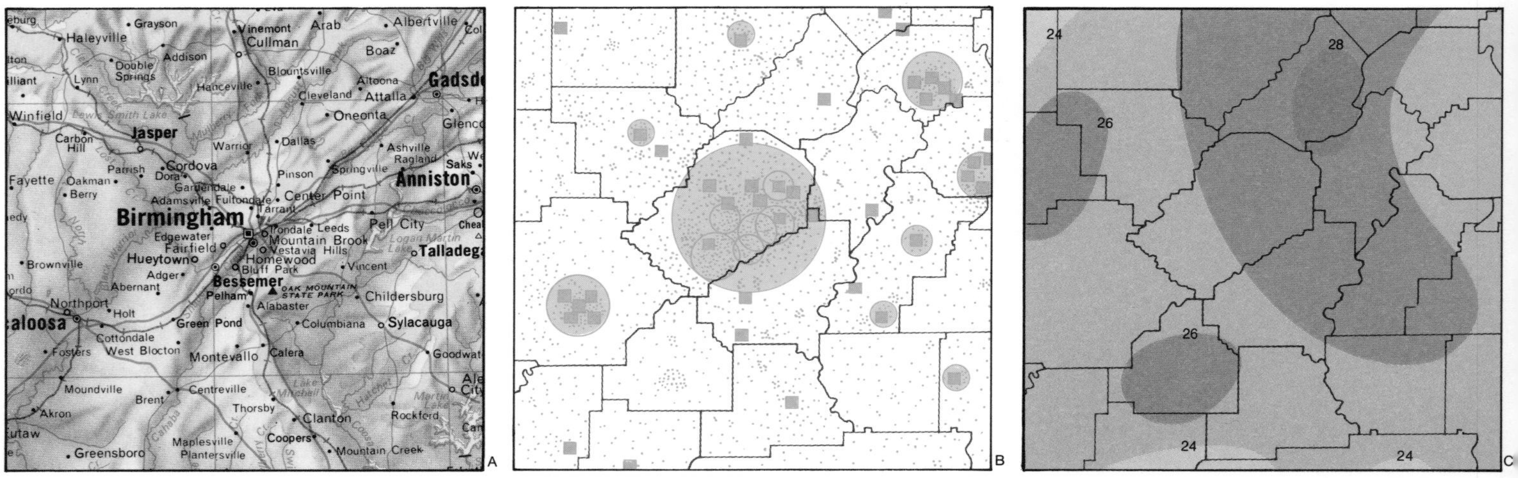

Maps are classed (right) as either general (A) or thematic (B,C). The purpose of a general reference map is to provide locational information, showing how the positions of various geographical phenomena relate to each other. Thematic maps concentrate on a particular type of information, or theme, such as the distribution of people (B) or rainfall (C), and are generally based on statistical data.

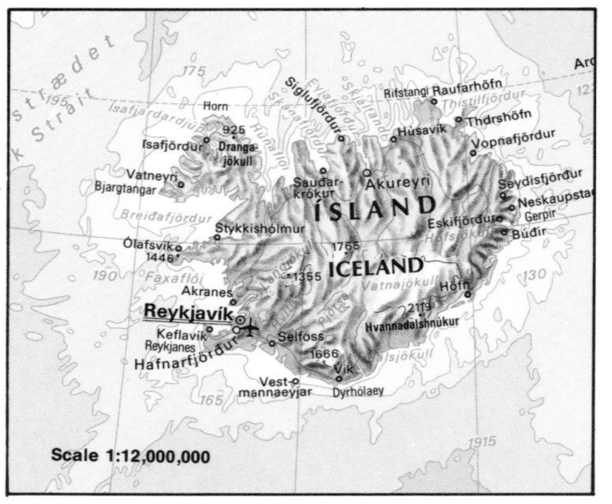

The ratio between a map's dimensions and those of the physical world is defined by the map scale (left and below), with the map distance always given as the unit 1. The larger the reduction, the smaller the scale, so that a scale of 1:6,000,000—1 mm (.04 in) to 6 km (3.74 miles)—is twice that of 1:12,000,000 (.04 in to 7.5 miles). The size of the scale reflects the amount of detail that needs to be shown. The projections are the Lambert Azimuthal Equal-Area (left) and Delisle Conic Equidistant (below).

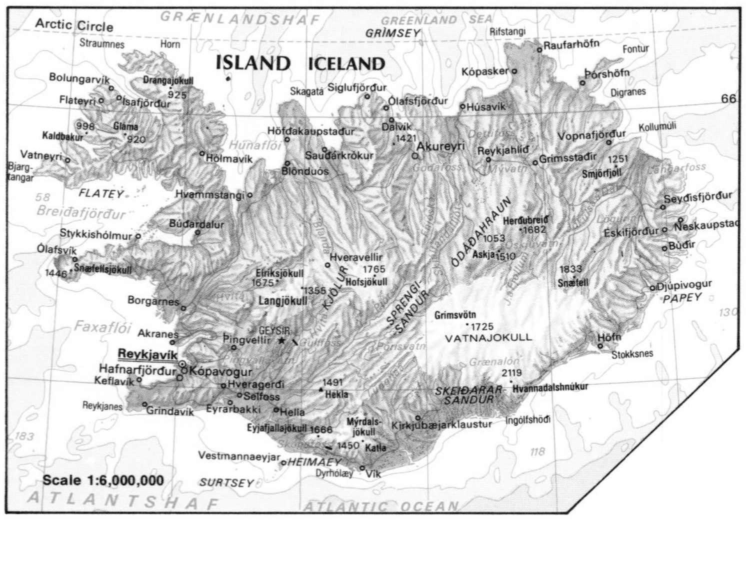

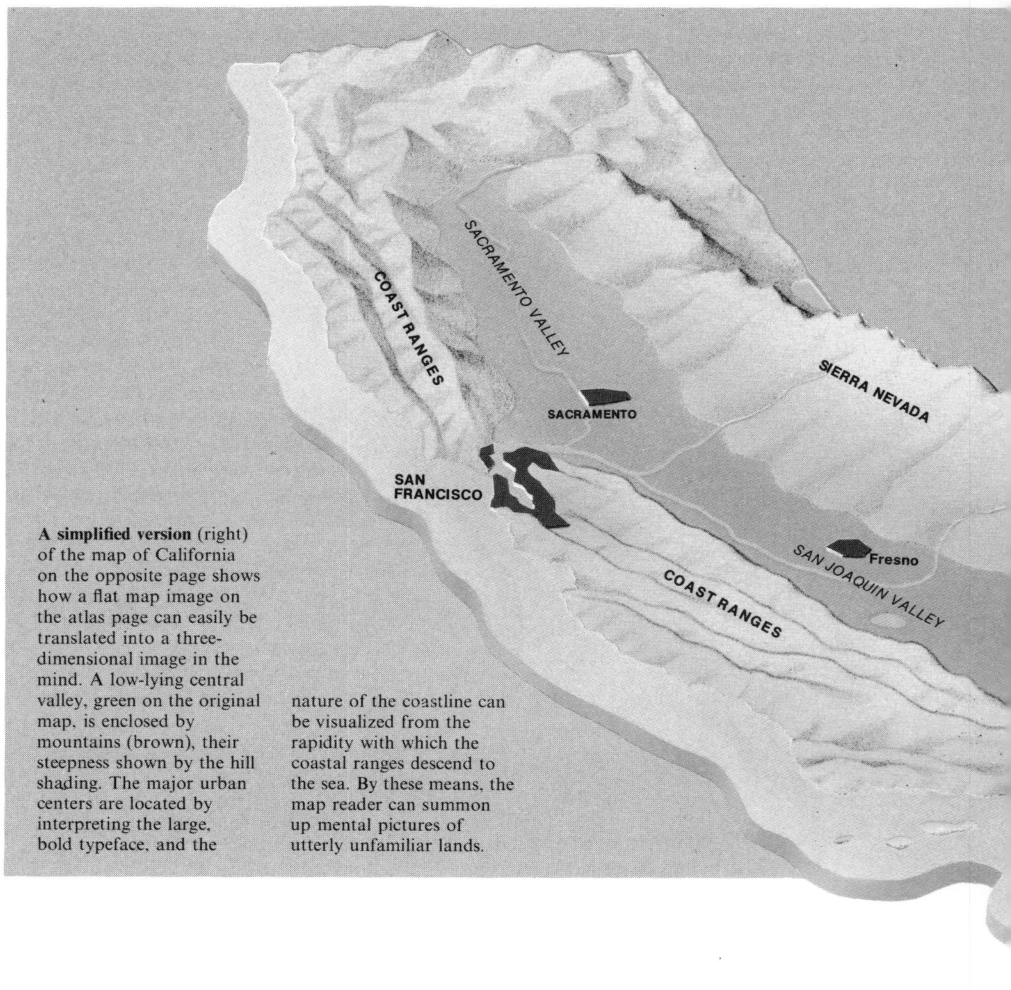

A simplified version (right) of the map of California on the opposite page shows how a flat map image on the atlas page can easily be translated into a three-dimensional image in the mind. A low-lying central valley, green on the original map, is enclosed by mountains (brown), their steepness shown by the hill shading. The major urban centers are located by interpreting the large, bold typeface, and the nature of the coastline can be visualized from the rapidity with which the coastal ranges descend to the sea. By these means, the map reader can summon up mental pictures of utterly unfamiliar lands.

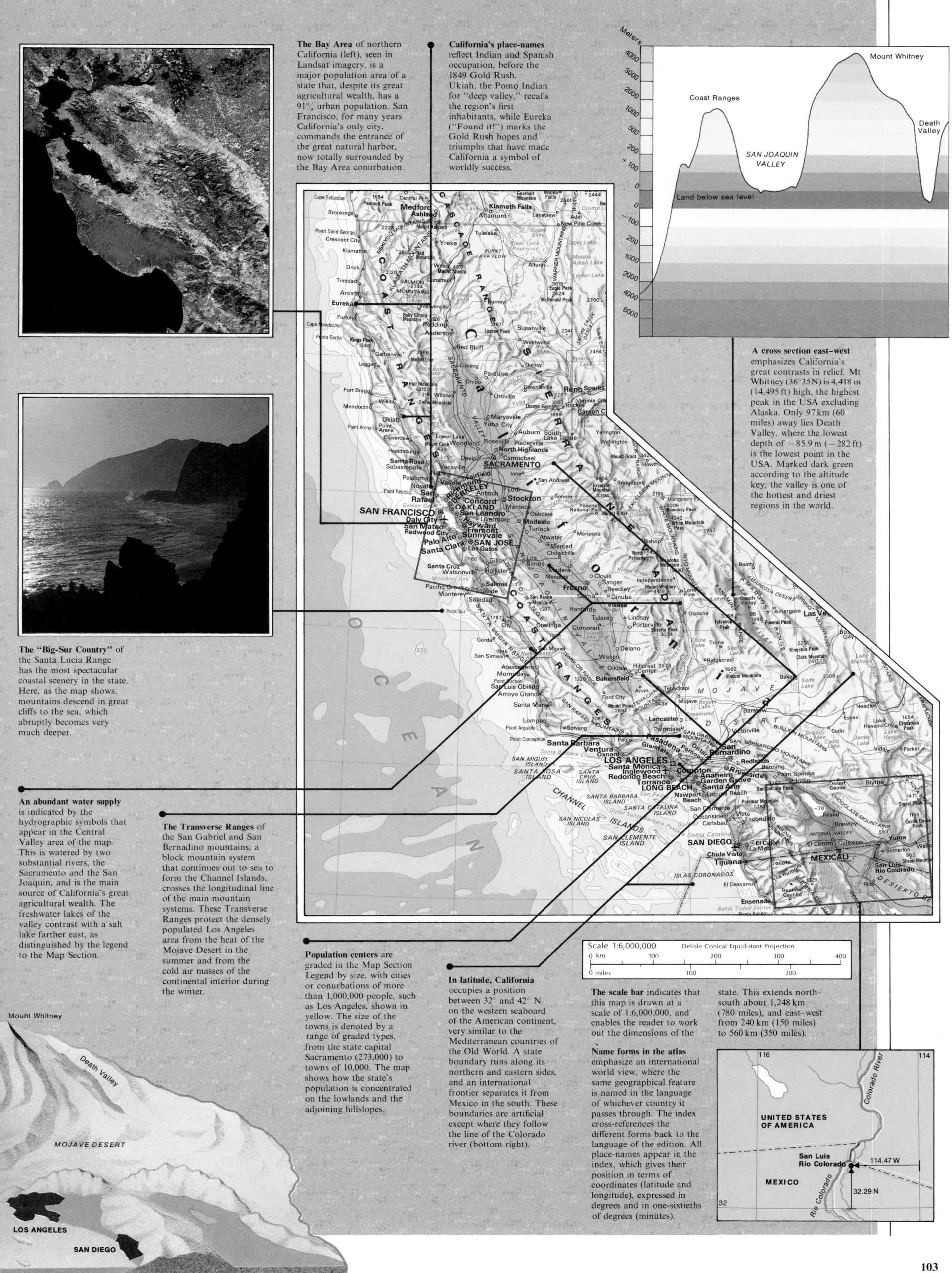

The Bay Area of northern California (left), seen in Landsat imagery, is a major population area of a state that, despite its great agricultural wealth, has a 91% urban population. San Francisco, for many years California's only city, commands the entrance of the great natural harbor, now totally surrounded by the Bay Area conurbation.

California's place-names reflect Indian and Spanish occupation, before the 1849 Gold Rush. Ukiah, the Pomo Indian for "deep valley," recalls the region's first inhabitants, while Eureka ("Found it!") marks the Gold Rush hopes and triumphs that have made California a symbol of worldly success.

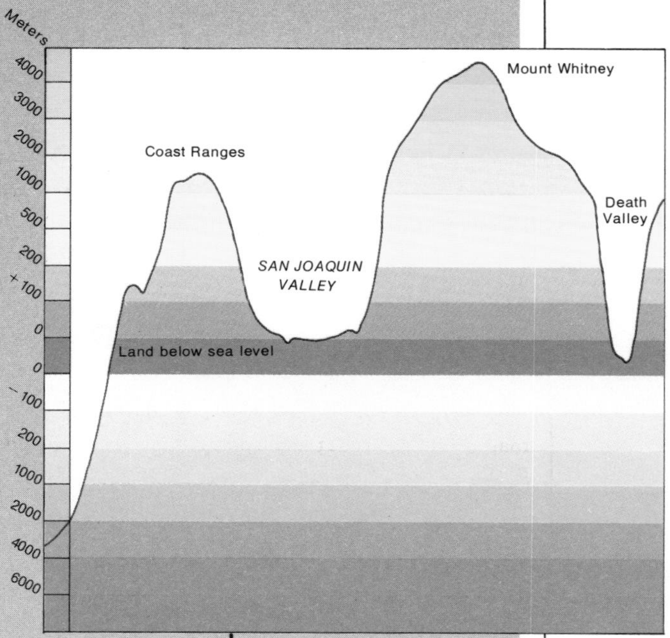

A cross section east–west emphasizes California's great contrasts in relief. Mt Whitney (36°35N) is 4,418 m (14,495 ft) high, the highest peak in the USA excluding Alaska. Only 97 km (60 miles) away lies Death Valley, where the lowest depth of −85.9 m (−282 ft) is the lowest point in the USA. Marked dark green according to the altitude key, the valley is one of the hottest and driest regions in the world.

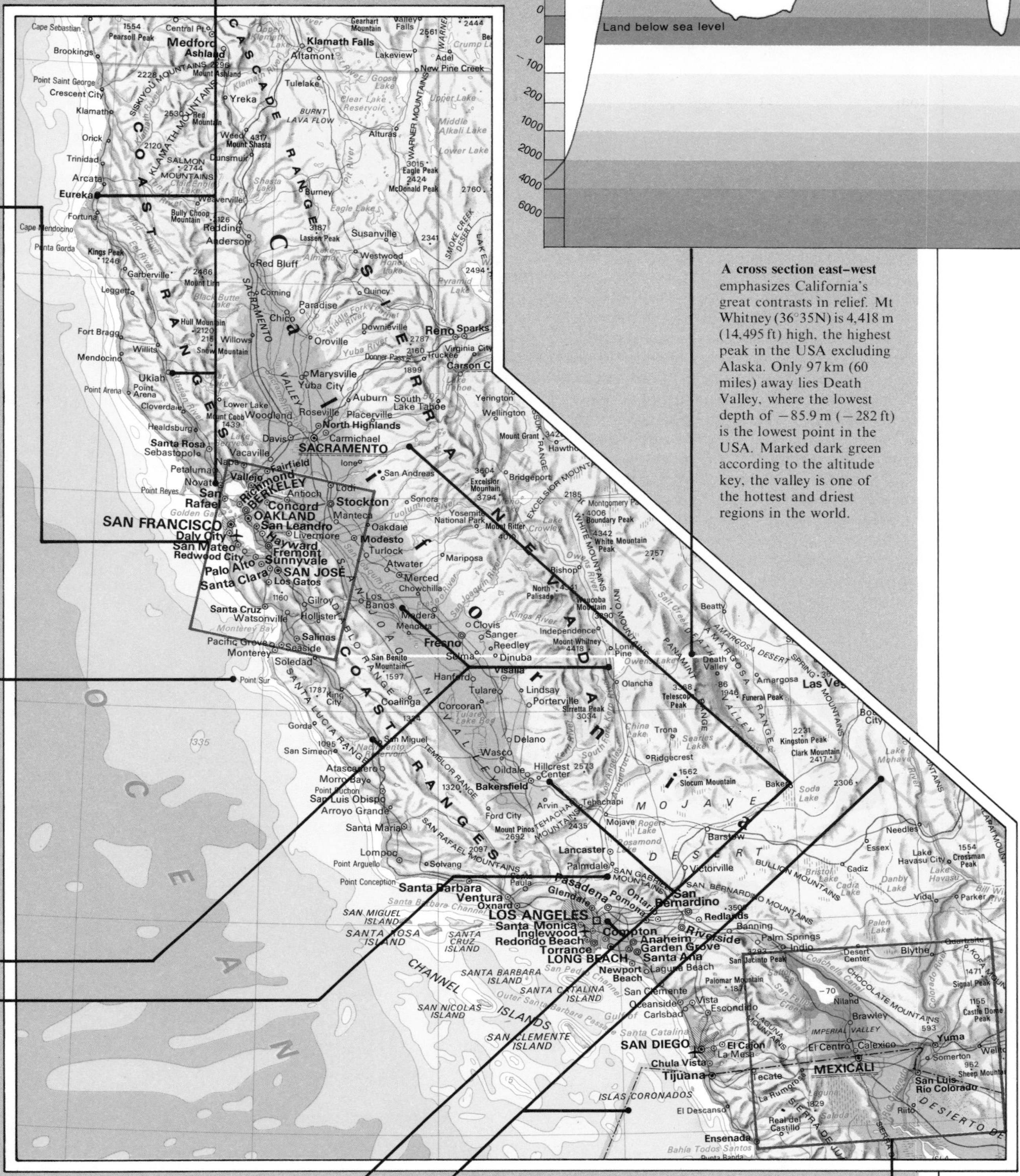

Scale 1:6,000,000 Delisle Conical Equidistant Projection
0 km 100 200 300 400
0 miles 100 200

The "Big-Sur Country" of the Santa Lucia Range has the most spectacular coastal scenery in the state. Here, as the map shows, mountains descend in great cliffs to the sea, which abruptly becomes very much deeper.

An abundant water supply is indicated by the hydrographic symbols that appear in the Central Valley area of the map. This is watered by two substantial rivers, the Sacramento and the San Joaquin, and is the main source of California's great agricultural wealth. The freshwater lakes of the valley contrast with a salt lake farther east, as distinguished by the legend to the Map Section.

The Transverse Ranges of the San Gabriel and San Bernardino mountains, a block mountain system that continues out to sea to form the Channel Islands, crosses the longitudinal line of the main mountain systems. These Transverse Ranges protect the densely populated Los Angeles area from the heat of the Mojave Desert in the summer and from the cold air masses of the continental interior during the winter.

Population centers are graded in the Map Section Legend by size, with cities or conurbations of more than 1,000,000 people, such as Los Angeles, shown in yellow. The size of the towns is denoted by a range of graded types, from the state capital Sacramento (273,000) to towns of 10,000. The map shows how the state's population is concentrated on the lowlands and the adjoining hillslopes.

In latitude, California occupies a position between 32° and 42° N on the western seaboard of the American continent, very similar to the Mediterranean countries of the Old World. A state boundary runs along its northern and eastern sides, and an international frontier separates it from Mexico in the south. These boundaries are artificial except where they follow the line of the Colorado river (bottom right).

The scale bar indicates that this map is drawn at a scale of 1:6,000,000, and enables the reader to work out the dimensions of the state. This extends north–south about 1,248 km (780 miles), and east–west from 240 km (150 miles) to 560 km (350 miles).

Name forms in the atlas emphasize an international world view, where the same geographical feature is named in the language of whichever country it passes through. The index cross-references the different forms back to the language of the edition. All place-names appear in the index, which gives their position in terms of coordinates (latitude and longitude), expressed in degrees and in one-sixtieths of degrees (minutes).

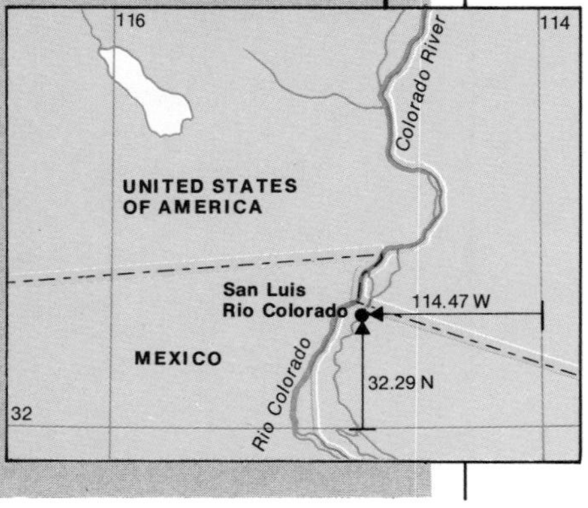

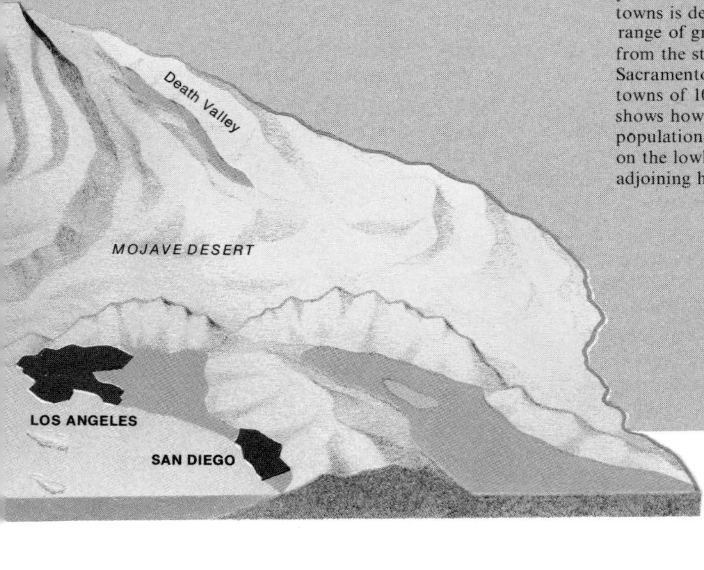

ACKNOWLEDGMENTS

Senior Executive Art Editor
Michael McGuinness

Executive Editor
James Hughes

Coordinating Editor
Dian Taylor

Editors
Lesley Ellis
Judy Garlick
Ken Hewis

Art Editor
Mike Brown

Designers
Sue Rawkins
Lisa Tai

Picture Researcher
Flavia Howard

Researchers
Nicholas Law
Nigel Morrison
Alicia Smith

Editorial Assistant
Barbara Gish

Proofreader
Kathie Gill

Indexers
Hilary and Richard Bird

Production Controller
Barry Baker

Typesetting by Servis Filmsetting Limited, Manchester, England

Reproduction by Gilchrist Brothers Limited, Leeds, England

CONTRIBUTORS AND CONSULTANTS

GENERAL CONSULTANT
Professor Michael Wise, CBE, MC, BA, PhD, D.Univ, Professor of Geography, London School of Economics and Political Science

EDITORIAL CONSULTANT
John Clark

Frances Atkinson, BSc

British Museum (Natural History), Botany Library

Robert W. Bradnock, MA, PhD, Lecturer in Geography with special reference to South Asia at the School of Oriental and African Studies, University of London

Michael J. Bradshaw, MA, Principal Lecturer in Geography, College of St Mark and St John, Plymouth

Dr J. M. Chapman, BSc, ARCS, PhD, MIBiol, Lecturer in Biology, Queen Elizabeth College, University of London

Dr Jeremy Cherfas, Departmental Demonstrator in Zoology, Oxford University

Dr M. J. Clark, Senior Lecturer in Geomorphology, Geography Department, Southampton University

J. L. Cloudsley-Thompson, MA, PhD(Cantab), DSc(Lond), Hon DSc(Khartoum), Professor of Zoology, Birkbeck College, University of London

Professor R. U. Cooke, Department of Geography, University College, London

Professor Clifford Embleton, MA, PhD, Department of Geography, King's College, University of London

Dr John Gribbin, Physics Consultant to *New Scientist* magazine

Dr John M. Hellawell, BSc, PhD, FIBiol, MIWES, Principal, Environmental Aspects, Severn Trent Water Authority, Birmingham

Dr Garry E. Hunt, BSc, PhD, DSc, FRAS, FRMetS, FIMA, MBCS, Head of Atmospheric Physics, Imperial College, London

David K. C. Jones, Lecturer in Geography, London School of Economics and Political Science

Dr Russell King, Department of Geography, University of Leicester

Dr D. McNally, Assistant Director, University of London Observatory

Meteorological Office, Berkshire

Dr Robert Muir Wood, PhD

Dr B. O'Connor, Department of Geography, University of London

J. H. Paterson, MA, Professor of Geography in the University of Leicester

Dr Nigel Pears, Department of Geography, University of Leicester

Joyce Pope, BA

Dr A. L. Rice, Institute of Oceanographic Sciences, Wormley, Surrey

Ian Ridpath, science writer and broadcaster

Royal Geographical Society

Helen Scoging, BSc, Department of Geography, London School of Economics and Political Science

Bernard Stonehouse, DPhil, MA, BSc, Chairman, Post-Graduate School of Environmental Science, University of Bradford

Dr Christopher B. Stringer, PhD, Senior Scientific Officer, Palaeontology Department, British Museum (Natural History)

J. B. Thornes, Professor of Physical Geography and Head of Department, Bedford College, University of London

UN Information Office and Library

Professor J. E. Webb, DSc, *Emeritus*, Department of Zoology, Westfield College, University of London

Peter B. Wright, BSc, MPhil

UNDERSTANDING MAPS
Helen Wallis, MA, DPhil, FSA, The Map Librarian, British Library

A great many other individuals, organizations, and institutions have given invaluable advice and assistance during the preparation of this Our Planet Earth Section and the publishers wish to extend their thanks to them all.

ILLUSTRATION CREDITS

Maps in the Our Planet Earth Section by Creative Cartography Limited unless otherwise specified. Map of the world's climatic regions, page 50, adapted from *An Introduction to Climate* 4th edition by Trewartha/ *Elements of Geography* by G. T. Trewartha, A. H. Robinson and E. H. Hammond © McGraw-Hill Book Co., N.Y., 1967. Used with permission of McGraw-Hill Book Co. Map diagram page 101 (bottom) courtesy Doctor Arno Peters.

2–3 *Exploding universe* Product Support (Graphics); *others* Quill. **4–5** Bob Chapman. **6–7** Bob Chapman. **8–9** Mick Saunders; *Landsat diagrams* Gary Marsh; *biowindows* Chris Forsey. **10–11** Mick Saunders. **12–13** Bob Chapman. **14–15** *Diagrams* Chris Forsey; *mountain sequence* Donald Myall. **16–17** Colin Salmon. **18–19** Peter Morter; *graph* Mick Saunders; *car* Peter Owen. **20–21** Bob Chapman; *diagram* Chris Forsey; *map* Colin Salmon. **22–23** Chris Forsey (*including maps*). **24–25** Brian Delf. **26–27** Brian Delf. **28–29** Dave Etchell/John Ridyard. **30–31** Creative Cartography Ltd. **32–33** Mick Saunders. **34–35** Chris Forsey; *experiment* Gary Hincks; *others* Mick Saunders. **36–37** Chris Forsey; *fruit flies, birds and mice* Donald Myall. **38–39** Chris Forsey; *time scale* Mick Saunders; *stromatolite and diagram* Garry Hincks. **40–41** Donald Myall; *time scale* Mick Saunders. **42–43** Donald Myall; *time scale* Mick Saunders. **44–45** Creative Cartography Ltd. **46–47** Donald Myall; *diagram* Kai Choi; *skulls* Jim Robins. **48–49** Creative Cartography Ltd. **50–51** Peter Morter; *diagram* Marilyn Clark. **52–53** Kai Choi. **54–55** Creative Cartography Ltd. **56–57** Creative Cartography Ltd. **58–59** Creative Cartography Ltd. **60–61** Creative Cartography Ltd; *illustrations* Jim Robins. **62–63** *Migration diagram and graph* Kai Choi; *illustrations* Coral Mula. **64–65** Donald Myall. **66–67** *Landscape diagram* Bill le Fever; *illustrations* Russell Barnett. **68–69** Donald Myall. **70–71** Jim Robins; *plants, bottom left* Andrew Macdonald. **72–73** Rory Kee; *bottom left* Russell Barnett; *plow* Kai Choi; *grains and graph* Creative Cartography Ltd. **74–75** Bob Bampton/The Garden Studio; *animal adaptations* Russell Barnett. **76–77** Donald Myall; *qanat* Bob Chapman. **78–79** David Ashby. **80–81** David Ashby. **82–83** Coral Mula; *trees, orchid, toucan and hornbill* Donald Myall. **84–85** Jim Robins. **86–87** Creative Cartography Ltd. **88–89** Brian Delf; *blood counts diagram* Colin Salmon. **90–91** Bob Chapman; *animals and plants* Rod Sutterby. **92–93** Kai Choi; *hydrological cycle* Bob Chapman. **94–95** Andy Farmer; *shore and plant life* Russell Barnett; *coral atoll* Colin Salmon. **96–97** Creative Cartography Ltd. **98–99** *Topographic maps* Rand McNally; *sketch map* Space Frontiers Ltd. **100–101** *Diagrams* Creative Cartography Ltd. **102–103** *Maps* Istituto Geografico De Agostini; Rand McNally; *diagrams* Creative Cartography Ltd.

PICTURE CREDITS

Credits read from top to bottom and from left to right on each page. Images that extend over two pages are credited to the left-hand page only.

2 US Naval Observatory; California Institute of Technology and Carnegie Institution of Washington. **3** Both pictures from Royal Observatory, Edinburgh. **8** All pictures from NASA. **9** All pictures from NASA except top and top right, courtesy of Garry Hunt, Laboratory of Planetary Atmospheres, University College, London. **14–15** Maurice and Sally Landre/Colorific! **16–17** All pictures courtesy of Dr Basil Booth, Geoscience Features. **18** Institute of Geological Sciences. **19** Paul Brierley; Institute of Geological Sciences. **20** Camera Press, London. **26** Barnaby's Picture Library; Barnaby's Picture Library; Institute of Geological Sciences. **28** Dr Alan Beaumont. **30** Tom Sheppard/Robert Harding Picture Library; Professor Ronald Cooke. **31** Institute of Geological Sciences. **32** Stuart Windsor; Sefton Photo Library, Manchester; Rio Tinto Zinc; Douglas Botting; Aspect Picture Library. **33** NASA; Mireille Vautier; Explorer/Vision International. **34** Paul Brierley. **37** Paediatric Research Unit, Guy's Hospital Medical School; Dr Laurence Cook, Zoology Department, University of Manchester. **39** Both pictures from British Museum (Natural History). **46** Colophoto Hans Hinz. **47** Dr P. G. Bahn, School of Archaeology and Oriental Studies, University of Liverpool/Musée des Antiquités Nationales, St. Germain-en-Laye. **56** UNICEF (Photo no. 8675 by H. Dalrymple). **57** Dr A. M. O'Connor, Department of Geography, University College, London. **61** International Fund for Animal Welfare; K. Kunov/Novosti Press Agency; Popperfoto; Charles Swithinbank. **62** Alan Robson. **63** Gösta Hakansson/Frank Lane Agency. **65** G. R. Roberts. **67** Anglo-Chinese Educational Trust; Aerofilms. **69** Ted Streshinsky. **72** Engraving from *At Home with the Patagonians*. **73** The Mansell Collection. **76** J. Bitsch/Zefa; Penny Tweedie/Colorific! **77** Alan Hutchison Library; Bill Holden/Zefa. **80** Syndication International; Gerald Cubitt/Bruce Coleman Ltd; Bruce Coleman Ltd. **81** Alan Hutchison Library; R. and M. Borland/Bruce Coleman Ltd; M. P. Kahl/Bruce Coleman Ltd; Jan and Des Bartlett/Bruce Coleman Ltd. **84** J. von Puttkamer/Alan Hutchison Library. **85** Marion Morrison. **86–87** Richard and Sally Greenhill. **88** Alan Hutchison Library; The Association of Universities for Research in Astronomy, Inc. **89** Gunter Ziesler/Bruce Coleman Ltd. **91** Mike Price/Bruce Coleman Ltd. **92** Ian Murphy. **93** Paolo Koch/Vision International; J. Allan Cash; M. Timothy O'Keefe/Bruce Coleman Ltd. **94** Heather Angel. **95** Institute of Oceanographic Sciences. **96** Fritz Prenzel/Bruce Coleman Ltd; Gordon Williamson/Bruce Coleman Ltd. **97** Martin Rogers/Susan Griggs Agency. **98** British Library; British Museum; Centro Camuno di Studi Preistorici; British Library; NASA; NASA; Rand McNally; British Museum; British Museum. **99** British Museum; NASA; NASA; Rand McNally; Space Frontiers Ltd; Paul G. Lowman/NASA Goddard SFC/Space Frontiers Ltd. **100** Historisches Museum, Vienna. **101** Hunting Surveys Ltd; Michael Holford/Science Museum, London; Michael Holford; Michael Holford/Science Museum, London. **103** Space Frontiers Ltd; F. Damm/Zefa.

INDEX

Page numbers in *italic* refer to the illustrations and their captions.

A

B

I

J

K

L

M

INTERNATIONAL MAP SECTION CREDITS AND ACKNOWLEDGMENTS

Cartographic and Geographic Director
Giuseppe Motta

Geographic Research
G. Baselli
M. Colombo

Toponymy and Translation
C. Carpine
M. Colombo
H. R. Fischer
R. Nuñez de las Cuevas
Rand McNally
Cartographic Research Staff
I. Straube

Computerized Data Organization
C. Bardesono
E. Ciano
G. Comoglio
E. Di Costanzo

Index
S. Osnaghi
T. Tomasini

Cartographic Editor
V. Castelli

Cartographic Compilation
G. Albera
L. Cairo
C. Camera
G. Conti
G. Fizzotti
G. Gambaro
M. Mochetti
O. Passarelli
M. Peretti
G. Rassiga
A. Saino
F. Valsecchi

Terrain Illustration
S. Andenna
E. Ferrari

Cartographic Production
F. Tosi
G. Capitini
A. Carnero

Filmsetting
S. Fiorini
P. L. Gatta
E. Geranio
G. Ghezzi
L. Lorena
R. Martelli
E. Morchio
M. Morganti
C. Pezzana
P. Uglietti
D. Varalli

Photographic Processing
G. Fracassina
G. Klaus
L. Mella

Coordination
S. Binda
L. Pasquali
G. Zanetta

The editors wish to thank the many organizations, institutions and individuals who have given their valuable help and advice during the preparation of this International Map Section. Special thanks are extended to the following:

Agenzia Novosti, Rome, Italy
D. Arnold, Acting Chief of Documentation and Terminology Section, United Nations, New York, USA
Australian Bureau of Statistics, Brisbane, Australia
J. Breu, United Nations Group of Experts on Geographical Names, Vienna, Austria
Bureau Hydrographique International, Monaco, Principality of Monaco
Canada Map Office, Ottawa, Canada
Cartactual, Budapest, Hungary
Census and Statistical Department, Tripoli, Libya
Central Bureau of Statistics, Accra, Ghana
Central Bureau of Statistics, Jerusalem, Israel
Central Bureau of Statistics, Ministry of Economic Planning and Development, Nairobi, Kenya
Central Department of Statistics, Riyadh, Saudi Arabia
Central Statistical Board of the USSR, Moscow, USSR
Central Statistical Office, London, UK
Centro de Informaçao e Documentaçao Estadística, Rio de Janeiro, Brazil
Committee for the Reform of Chinese Written Language, Peking, China
Danmark Statistik, Copenhagen, Denmark
Defense Mapping Agency, Distribution Office for Latin America, Miami, USA
Defense Mapping Agency, Washington DC, USA
Department of National Development and Energy, Division of National Mapping, Belconnen ACT, Australia
Department of State Coordinator for Maps and Publications, Washington DC, USA
Department of State Map Division, Sofia, Bulgaria
Department of Statistics, Wellington, New Zealand
Direcçao Nacional de Estadística, Maputo, Mozambique
Dirección de Cartografía Naciónal, Caracas, Venezuela
Dirección de Estadistica y Censo de la Repubblica de Panamá, Panama
Dirección General de Estadística, Mexico City, Mexico
Dirección General de Estadística y Censos, San Salvador, El Salvador
Direcţia Centrala de Statistică, Bucharest, Romania
Directorate of National Mapping, Kuala Lumpur, Malaysia
Directorate of Overseas Surveys, London, UK
Elaborazione Dati e Disegno Automatico, Torino, Italy
Federal Office of Statistics, Lagos, Nigeria
Federal Office of Statistics, Prague, Czechoslovakia
Geographical Research Institute, Hungarian Academy of Sciences, Budapest, Hungary
Geological Map Service, New York, USA
G. Gomez de Silva, Chief Conference Services Section, United Nations Environment Programme, New York, USA
Government of the People's Republic of Bangladesh, Statistics Division, Ministry of Planning, Dacca, Bangladesh
High Commissioner for Trinidad and Tobago, London, UK
L. Iarotski, World Health Organization, Geneva, Switzerland Information Division, Valletta, Malta
Institut für Angewandte Geodäsie, Frankfurt, West Germany
Institut Géographique, Abidjan, Ivory Coast
Institut Géographique du Zaïre, Kinshasa, Zaïre
Institut Géographique National, Brussels, Belgium
Institut Géographique National, Paris, France
Institut Haïtien de Statistique, Port-au-Prince, Haiti
Institut National de Géodésie et Cartographie, Antananarivo, Madagascar
Institut National de la Statistique, Tunis, Tunisia
Institute of Geography, Polish Academy of Sciences, Warsaw, Poland
Instituto Geográfico Militar, Buenos Aires, Argentina
Instituto Nacional de Estadística, La Paz, Bolivia
Instituto Nacional de Estadística, Madrid, Spain
Istituto Centrale di Statistica, Rome, Italy
Istituto Geografico Militare, Florence, Italy
Istituto Idrografico della Marina, Genoa, Italy
Landesverwaltung des Fürstentums, Vaduz, Liechtenstein
Ministère des Affaires Economiques, Brussels, Belgium
Ministère des Ressources Naturelles, des Mines et des Carrières, Kigali, Rwanda
Ministère des Travaux Publics, des Transports et de l'Urbanisme, Ouagadougou, Upper Volta
Ministry of Finance, Department of Statistics and Research, Nicosia, Cyprus
Ministry of Lands, Housing and Urban Development, Surveys and Mapping Division, Dar es Salaam, Tanzania
Ministry of the Interior, Jerusalem, Israel
National Census and Statistics Office, Manila, Philippines
National Central Bureau of Statistics, Stockholm, Sweden
National Geographic Society, Washington DC, USA
National Institute of Polar Research, Tokyo, Japan
National Ocean Survey, Riverdale, Maryland, USA
National Statistical Institute, Lisbon, Portugal
National Statistical Office, Zomba, Malawi
National Statistical Service of Greece, Athens, Greece
J. Novotny, Prague, Czechoslovakia
Office Nationale de la Recherche Scientifique et Technique, Yaoundé, Cameroon
Officina Comercial del Gobierno de Colombia, Rome, Italy
Ordnance Survey of Ireland, Dublin, Ireland
Österreichisches Statistisches Zentralamt, Vienna, Austria
Państwowe Przedsiebiorstwo Wydawnictw Kartograficznych, Warsaw, Poland
Scott Polar Research Institute, University of Cambridge, Cambridge, UK
Secrétariat d'Etat au Plan, Algiers, Algeria
Servicio Geografico Militar, Montevideo, Uruguay
Z. Shiying, Research Institute of Surveying and Mapping, Peking, China
Statistisches Bundesamt, Wiesbaden, West Germany
Statistisk Sentralbyrå, Oslo, Norway
Survey and National Mapping Department, Kuala Lumpur, Malaysia
Ufficio Turismo e Informazioni della Turchia, Rome, Italy
United States Board on Geographic Names, Washington DC, USA
M. C. Wu, Chinese Translation Service, United Nations, New York, USA
Z. Youguang, Committee for the Reform of Chinese Written Language, Peking, China

The editors are also grateful for the assistance provided by the following embassies, consulates and official state representatives:

Angolan Embassy, Rome
Australian Embassy, Rome
Austrian Embassy, Rome
Embassy of Bangladesh, Rome
Embassy of Botswana, Brussels
Brazilian Embassy, Rome
British Embassy, Rome
Burmese Embassy, Rome
Embassy of Cameroon, Rome
Embassy of Cape Verde, Lisbon
Consulate of Chad, Rome
Chilean Embassy, Rome
Embassy of the People's Republic of China in Italy, Rome
Danish Embassy, Rome
Embassy of El Salvador, Rome
Ethiopian Embassy, Rome
Finnish Embassy, Rome
Embassy of the German Democratic Republic, Rome
Greek Embassy, Rome
Honduras Republic Embassy, Rome
Hungarian Embassy, Rome
Consulate General of Iceland, Rome
Embassy of India, Rome
Embassy of the Republic of Indonesia, Rome
Embassy of the Islamic Republic of Iran, Rome
Irish Embassy, Rome
Embassy of Israel, Rome
Japanese Embassy, Rome
Korean Embassy, Rome
Luxembourg Embassy, Rome
Embassy of Malta, Rome
Mexican Embassy, Rome
Moroccan Embassy, Rome
Netherlands Embassy, Rome
Embassy of New Zealand, Rome
Embassy of Niger, Rome
Embassy of Pakistan, Rome
Peruvian Embassy, Rome
Philippine Embassy, Rome
Romanian Embassy, Rome
Somali Embassy, Rome
South African Embassy, Rome
Spanish Embassy, Rome
Consulate General of Switzerland, Milan
Royal Thai Embassy, Rome
Consulate of Upper Volta, Rome
Uruguay Embassy, Rome
Embassy of the Socialist Republic of Vietnam in Italy, Rome
Permanent Mission of Yemen to United Nations Educational, Scientific and Cultural Organization, Paris

International Map Section

Hydrographic and Topographic Features
Symboles hydrographiques et morphologiques
Gewässer- und Geländeformen
Idrografia, Morfologia
Hidrografía y morfología

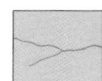

River, Stream
Cours d'eau permanent
Ständig wasserführender Fluß
Corso d'acqua perenne
Corriente de agua de régimen permanente

Intermittent Stream
Cours d'eau intermittent
Zeitweilig wasserführender Fluß
Corso d'acqua periodico
Corriente de agua intermitente

Disappearing Stream
Perte de cours d'eau
Versickernder Fluß
Corso d'acqua che si inabissa
Corriente de agua que desaparece

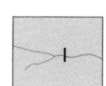

Undefined or Fluctuating River Course
Cours d'eau incertain
Fluß mit veränderlichem Lauf
Fiume dal corso incerto
Corriente de agua incerta

Waterfall, Rapids, Cataract
Chute, Rapide, Cataracte
Wasserfall, Stromschnelle, Katarakt
Cascata, Rapida, Cateratta
Cascada, Rapido, Catarata

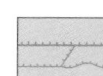

Canal
Canal
Kanal
Canale
Canal

Navigable Canal
Canal navigable
Schiffbarer Kanal
Canale navigabile
Canal navegable

Swamp
Marais
Sumpf
Palude d'acqua dolce
Pantano

Salt Marsh
Marais d'eau salée
Salzsumpf
Palude d'acqua salata
Pantano de agua salada

Salt Pan
Marais salant
Salzpfanne
Salina
Salina

Lake
Lac d'eau douce
Süßwassersee
Lago d'acqua dolce
Lago de agua dulce

Intermittent Lake
Lac d'eau douce temporaire
Zeitweiliger Süßwassersee
Lago d'acqua dolce periodico
Lago de agua dulce intermitente

Salt Lake
Lac d'eau salée
Salzsee
Lago d'acqua salata
Lago de agua salada

Intermittent Salt Lake
Lac d'eau salée temporaire
Zeitweiliger Salzsee
Lago d'acqua salata periodico
Lago de agua salada intermitente

Dry Lake Bed
Lac asséché
Trockener Seeboden
Alveo di lago asciutto
Lecho de lago seco

Lake Surface Elevation
Cote du lac au-dessus du niveau de la mer
Höhe des Seespiegels
Altitudine del lago
Elevación de lago sobre el nivel del mar

315

Lake Depth
Profondeur du lac
Seetiefe
Profondità del lago
Profundidad del lago

80

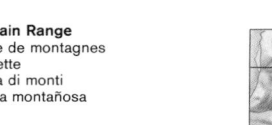

Sand Area
Région de sable, Désert
Sandgebiet, Sandwüste
Area sabbiosa, Deserto
Zona arenosa, desierto

Sandbank, Sandbar
Banc de sable
Sandbank
Bassofondo sabbioso
Banco submarino de arena

Port Facilities
Installations portuaires
Hafenanlagen
Impianti portuali
Instalaciones portuarias

Rocks
Ecueils, Roches
Klippen, Felsriffe
Scogli, Rocce
Escollos, Rocas

Reef, Atoll
Barrière, Atoll
Riff, Atoll
Barriera, Atollo
Barrera de arrecifes

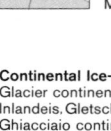

Mangrove
Mangrove
Mangrove
Mangrovie
Manglar

Continental Ice-cap
Glacier continental
Inlandeis, Gletscher
Ghiacciaio continentale
Glaciar continental

Glacial Tongue
Langue glaciaire
Gletscherzunge
Lingua di ghiaccio
Lengua de glaciar

Rocky Areas (Antarctica)
Région de roches (Antarctique)
Eisfreie Gebiete, Gebirge (Antarktika)
Aree rocciose (Antartide)
Area rocosa (Antártida)

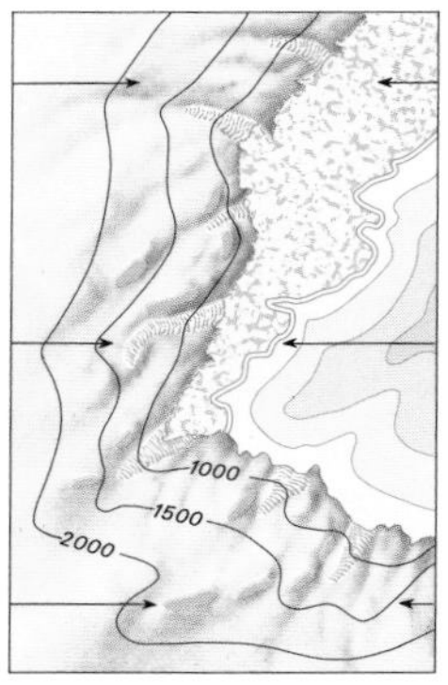
1000
1500
2000

Summer Limit of Pack Ice
Limite du pack en été
Packeisgrenze im Sommer
Limite estivo del pack ghiacciato
Límite estival de banco de hielo

Winter Limit of Pack Ice
Limite du pack en hiver
Packeisgrenze im Winter
Limite invernale del pack ghiacciato
Límite invernal de banco de hielo

Limit of Icebergs
Limite des glaces flottantes
Treibeisgrenze
Limite dei ghiacci alla deriva
Límite de hielo a la deriva

Ice Shelf
Banquise
Schelfeis oder Eisschelf
Banchisa polare (Ice-shelf)
Banquisa

Limit of Ice Shelf
Limite de la banquise
Schelfeisgrenze
Limite della banchisa
Límite de la banquisa

Contour Lines in Continental Ice
Courbes de niveau dans les régions glaciaires
Höhenlinien auf vergletschertem Gebiet
Curve altimetriche nelle aree ghiacciate
Curvas de nivel en aréas heladas

Defined Shoreline
Trait de côte définie
Küsten- oder Uferlinie
Linea di costa definita
Línea de costa definida

Undefined or Fluctuating Shoreline
Trait de côte indéfinie
Unbestimmte oder veränderliche Uferlinie
Linea di costa indefinita
Línea de costa indefinida

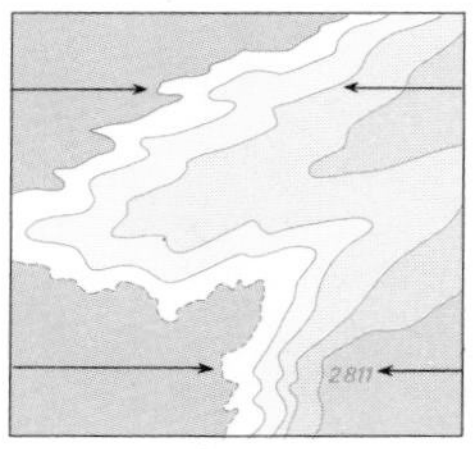
2811

Bathymetric Contour
Courbe bathymétrique
Tiefenlinie
Curva batimetrica
Curva batimétrica

Depth of Water
Valeur de sonde
Tiefenzahl
Quota batimetrica
Cota batimétrica

Mountain Range
Chaîne de montagnes
Bergkette
Catena di monti
Cadena montañosa

Elevation
Cote, Altitude
Höhenzahl
Quota altimetrica
Cota altimétrica

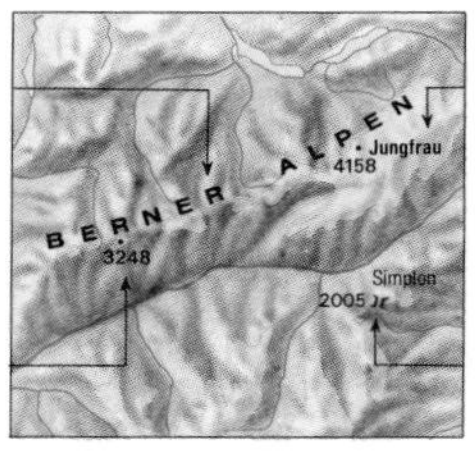
BERNER ALPEN
Jungfrau
4158
3248
Simplon
2005

Mountain
Mont
Berg, Bergmassiv
Monte
Monte

Mountain Pass, Gap
Passage, Col, Port
Paß, Joch, Sattel
Passo, Colle, Valico
Paso, Collado, Puerto de montaña

Key to Elevation and Depth Tints
Hypsométrie, Bathymétrie
Höhenstufen, Tiefenstufen
Altimetria, Batimetria
Altimetría, Batimetría

Scales in Metric and English Measures
Échelle des teintes hypsométriques et bathymétriques
Farbskala der Höhen- und Tiefenstufen
Scala delle tinte Altimetriche e Batimetriche
Escala de tintas hypsométricas y batimétricas

Land Elevation Below Sea Level
Dépression et cote au-dessous du niveau de la mer
Senke mit Tiefenzahl unter dem Meeresspiegel
Depressione e quota sotto il livello del mare
Depresión y elevación bajo el nivel del mar

−155

Map Scale
Échelle
Maßstab
Scala
Escala

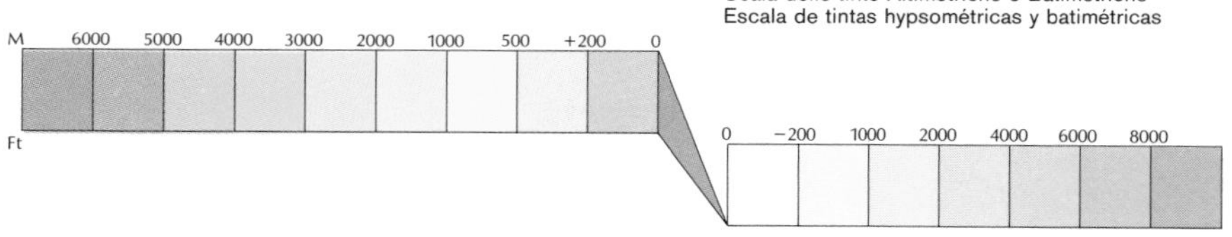
M 6000 5000 4000 3000 2000 1000 500 +200 0
Ft
0 −200 1000 2000 4000 6000 8000

1:30,000,000

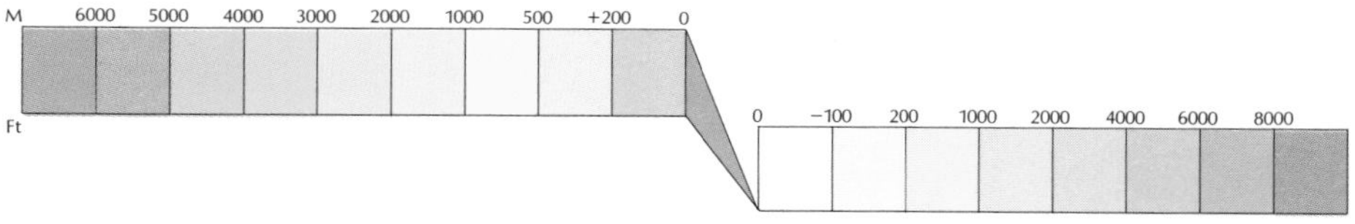
M 6000 5000 4000 3000 2000 1000 500 +200 0
Ft
0 −100 200 1000 2000 4000 6000 8000

1:15,000,000, 1:12,000,000

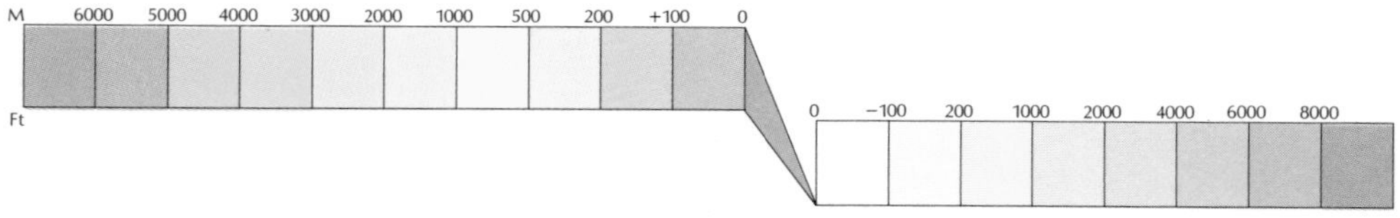
M 6000 5000 4000 3000 2000 1000 500 200 +100 0
Ft
0 −100 200 1000 2000 4000 6000 8000

1:9,000,000, 1:6,000,000

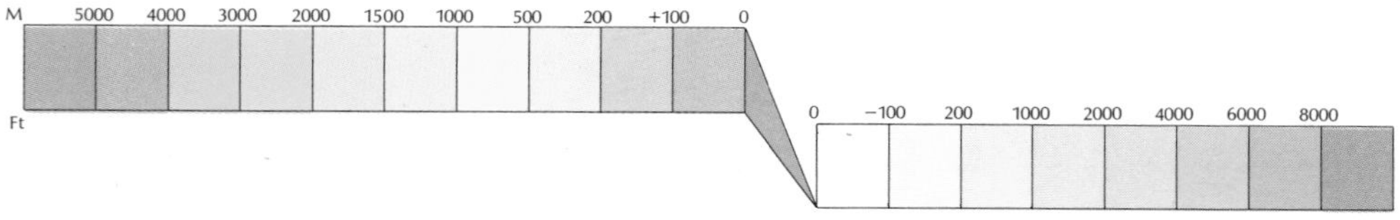
M 5000 4000 3000 2000 1500 1000 500 200 +100 0
Ft
0 −100 200 1000 2000 4000 6000 8000

1:3,000,000, 1:1,500,000
1:600,000, 1:300,000

Map Projections
Projections cartographiques
Kartennetzentwürfe
Proiezioni cartografiche
Proyecciones cartográficas

The projections appearing in this atlas have been plotted by computer

Les réseaux des projections ont été obtenus par élaboration automatique à partir de formules mathématiques

Die Kartennetze aller im Atlas vorkommenden Abbildungen wurden mit Hilfe der Datenverarbeitung (EDV) völlig neu errechnet

I disegni delle proiezioni presenti in quest'opera sono stati realizzati interamente ex-novo con l'uso del computer e del plotter a partire dalle formule matematiche

El reticulado de las proyecciones (redes geográficas) incluidas en esta obra han sido obtenidas por proceso automático a partir de las formulas matemáticas

The meanings of the symbols on the Legend pages are in English, French, German, Italian, and Spanish languages to permit the interpretation of the maps by a broad readership.

Boundaries, Capitals
Frontières, Soulignements — Confini, Sottolineature
Grenzen, Unterstreichungen — Límites, Subrayados

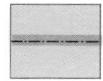

Defined International Boundary
Frontière internationale définie
Staatsgrenze
Confine di Stato definito
Límite de Nación definido

International Boundary (Continent Maps)
Frontière internationale (Continents)
Staatsgrenze (Erdteilkarten)
Confine di Stato (Carte dei Continenti)
Límite de Nación (Continentes)

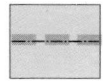

Undefined International Boundary
Frontière internationale indéfinie
Nicht genau festgelegte Staatsgrenze
Confine di Stato indefinito
Límite de Nación indefinido

International Ocean Floor Boundary Defined by Treaty or Bilateral Agreement
Frontière d'état en mer définie par traités et conventions bilatéraux
Durch Verträge festgelegte Staatsgrenze im Meeresgebiet
Confine di Stato nel mare definito da trattati e convenzioni bilaterali
Límite de Nación en el Mar definido por los tratados bilaterales

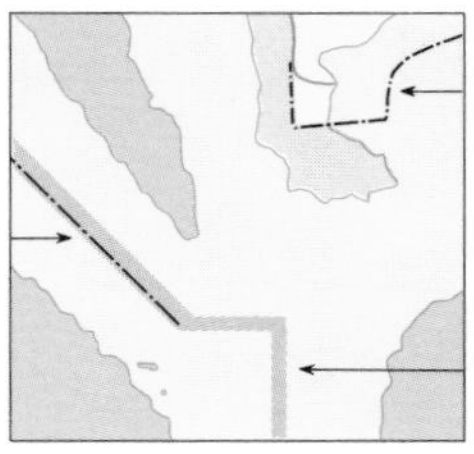

International Ocean Floor Boundary
Frontière d'état en mer
Staatsgrenze im Meeresgebiet
Confine di Stato nel mare
Límite de Nación en el mar

Undefined Ocean Floor Boundary
Frontière indéfinie d'état tracée en meer
Unbestimmte Staatsgrenze im Meeresgebiet
Confine di Stato indefinito nel mare
Límite indefinido de Nación en el mar

Second-order Political Boundary
Frontière d'État fédéré, Région
Bundesstaats-, Regionsgrenze
Confine di Stato federato, Regione
Límite de Estado federado, Región

Third-order Political Boundary
Frontière de Province, Comté, Bezirk
Provinz-, Grafschafts-, Bezirksgrenze
Confine di Provincia, Contea, Bezirk
Límite de Provincia, Condado, Bezirk

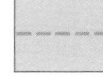

Administrative District Boundary (U.S.S.R.)
Frontière de Circonscription
Kreisgrenze
Confine di Circondario
Límite de Circunscripción administrativa

ROMA — **National Capital**
Capitale d'État
Hauptstadt eines unabhängigen Staates
Capitale di Stato
Capital de Nación

RIGA — **Dependency or Second-order Capital**
Capitale d'État fédéré, Région
Bundesstaats-, Regionshauptstadt
Capitale di Stato federato, Regione
Capital de Estado federado, Región

Kristiansand — **Third - order Capital**
Capitale de Province, Comté, Bezirk
Provinz-, Grafschafts-, Bezirkshauptstadt
Capoluogo di Provincia, Contea, Bezirk
Capital de Provincia, Condado, Bezirk

Anadyr — **Administrative District Capital (U.S.S.R.)**
Capitale de Circonscription
Kreishauptstadt
Capoluogo di Circondario
Capital de Circunscripción administrativa

Other Symbols
Symboles divers — Simboli vari
Sonstige Zeichen — Signos varios

LUTON AIRPORT — **International Airport**
Aéroport international
Internationaler Flughafen
Aeroporto internazionale
Aeropuerto internacional

Lighthouse
Phare
Leuchtturm
Faro
Faro

BUI DAM — **Dam**
Barrage
Staudamm, Staumauer
Diga artificiale, Sbarramento
Presa

L.-GREENWICH, V.-IJmuiden — **Section of a City**
Faubourg
Stadt- oder Ortsteil
Sobborgo urbano
Suburbio

Bidon V — **Uninhabited Locality, Hamlet**
Ville inhabitée, Ferme, Hameau
Unbewohnte Stadt, Gehöft, Weiler
Città disabitata, Fattoria, Nucleo di case
Ciudad despoblada, Granja, Casar

Bi'r Nāhid — **Periodically Inhabited Oasis**
Oasis habitées périodiquement
Zeitweilig bewohnte Oase
Oasi periodicamente abitate
Oasis periodicamente habitados

Casey (Australia) — **Scientific Station**
Base géophysique
Geophysikalische Beobachtungsstation
Base geofisica
Base geofísica

SANTAS CREUS — **Church, Monastery, Abbey**
Monastère, Église, Abbaye
Kloster, Kirche, Abtei
Monastero, Chiesa, Abbazia
Monasterio, Iglesia, Abadía

DAMPIERRE — **Castle**
Château
Burg, Schloß
Castello
Castillo

PAESTUM — **Ruin, Archeological Site**
Ruine, Centre archéologique
Ruine, Archäologisches Zentrum
Rovina, Zona archeologica
Ruina, Zona arqueológica

MOLENS VAN KINDERDIJK — **Monument, Historic Site, etc.**
Monument
Denkmal
Monumento
Monumento

HADRIAN'S WALL — **Wall**
Muraille
Wall, Mauer
Vallo, Muraglia
Muralla

GIANT'S CAUSEWAY — **Point of Interest**
Curiosité
Sehenswürdigkeit
Curiosità
Curiosidad

CUEVAS DE ARTÁ — **Cave**
Grotte, Caverne
Höhle
Grotta, Caverna
Cueva, Gruta

Populated Places
Population — Popolazione
Bevölkerung — Población

Continent Maps
Cartes des Continents — Carte dei Continenti
Erdteilkarten — Mapas de Continentes
< 25 000
25 000-100 000
100 000-250 000
250 000-1 000 000
> 1 000 000

Regional Maps
Cartes à plus grande échelle — Carte di sviluppo
Karten größeren Maßstabs — Mapas a gran escala
< 10 000
10 000-25 000
25 000-100 000
100 000-250 000
250 000-1 000 000
> 1 000 000

Symbols represent population of inhabited localities
Les symboles représentent le nombre d'habitants des localités
Die Signaturen entsprechen der Einwohnerzahl des Ortes
I simboli sono relativi al valore demografico dei centri abitati
Los símbolos son proporcionales a la población del lugar

Town area symbol represents the shape of the urban area
Le petit plan de la ville reproduit la configuration de l'aire urbaine
Die Plansignatur stellt die Gestalt des Stadtgebietes dar
La piantina della città rappresenta la configurazione dell'area urbana
El pequeño plano de la ciudad representa la forma del area urbana

Transportation
Communications — Comunicazioni
Verkehrsnetz — Comunicaciones

Primary Railway
Chemin de fer principal
Hauptbahn
Ferrovia principale
Ferrocarril principal

Secondary Railway
Chemin de fer secondaire
Sonstige Bahn
Ferrovia secondaria
Ferrocarril secundario

Motorway, Expressway
Autoroute
Autobahn
Autostrada
Autopista

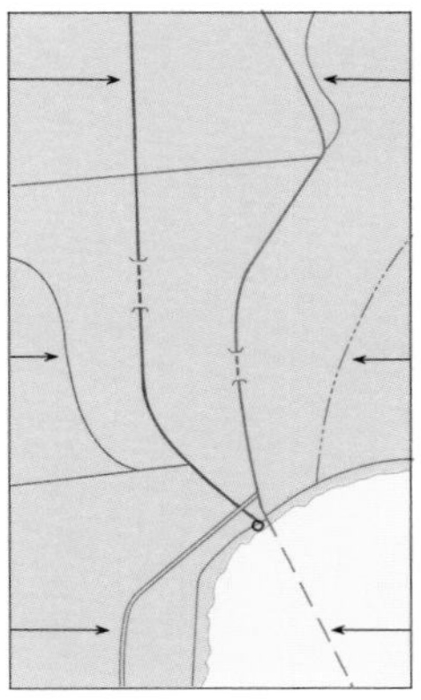

Road
Route de grande communication, Autres Routes
Fernverkehrsstraße, andere Straßen
Strada principale, Altre Strade
Carretera principal, Otras Carreteras

Trail, Caravan Route
Piste, Voie caravanière
Wüstenpiste, Karawanenweg
Pista nel deserto, Carovaniera
Pista en el desierto, Via de Carabanas

Ferry, Shipping Lane
Bac, Ligne maritime
Fähre, Schiffahrtslinie
Traghetto, Linea di navigazione
Transbordador (Ferry), Línea de navegación

Type Styles
Caractères utilisés pour la toponymie — Caratteri usati per la toponomastica
Zur Namenschreibung verwendete Schriftarten — Caracteres utilizados para la toponimia

ITALY / Hessen / RIBE — **Political Units**
Etat, Dépendance, Division administrative
Staat, abhängiges Gebiet, Verwaltungsgliederung
Stato, Dipendenza, Divisione amministrativa
Nación, Dependencia, Division administrativa

SAXONY / *THRACE* / *SUSSEX* — **Historical or Cultural Region**
Région historique ou culturelle
Historische oder Kulturlandschaft
Regione storico - culturale
Región histórica y cultural

PATAGONIA / *BASSIN DE RENNES* / *PENÍNSULA DE YUCATÁN* — **Physical Region (plain, peninsula)**
Région physique (plaine, péninsule)
Landschaft (Ebene, Halbinsel)
Regione fisica (pianura, penisola)
Región natural (llanura, península)

PYRENEES / CUMBRIAN MOUNTAINS / SIERRA DE GÁDOR / LA SILA — **Mountain Range**
Chaîne de montagnes
Bergkette, Gebirge
Catena di monti
Cadena montañosa

Ankaratra / Monte Bianco / Tsiafajavona / Ngorongoro Crater / Nevado del Tolima / Kings Peak — **Small Mountain Range, Mountain, Peak**
Petit massif, Mont, Cime
Bergmassiv, Berg, Gipfel
Piccolo gruppo montuoso, Monte, Vetta
Macizo pequeño, Monte, Cima

Cabo de São Vicente / Land's End / Mizen Head / Point Conception / Col de la Perche / Passo della Cisa — **Cape, Point, Pass**
Cap, Pointe, Passe
Kap, Landspitze, Paß
Capo, Punta, Passo
Cabo, Punta, Paso

MAHÉ / *ALDABRA ISLANDS* / *CORSE* / *CHANNEL ISLANDS* / *SULU ARCHIPELAGO* — **Island, Archipelago**
Ile, Archipel
Insel, Archipel
Isola, Arcipelago
Isla, Archipiélago

Thames / *Po* / *Victoria Falls* / *Lotagipi Swamp* / *Göta kanal* / *Lago Maggiore* — **River, Waterfall, Cataract, Canal, Lake**
Fleuve, Chute d'eau, Cataracte, Canal, Lac
Fluß, Wasserfall, Katarakt, Kanal, See
Fiume, Cascata, Cateratta, Canale, Lago
Rio, Cascada, Catarata, Canal, Lago

LABRADOR SEA / *Gulf of Alaska* / *Hudson Bay* / *Estrecho de Magallanes* — **Sea, Gulf, Bay, Strait**
Mer, Golfe, Baie, Détroit
Meer, Golf, Bucht, Meeresstraße
Mare, Golfo, Baia, Stretto
Mar, Golfo, Bahía, Estrecho

West Mariana Basin / Galapagos Fracture Zone / Mid-Atlantic Ridge — **Undersea Features**
Formes du relief sous-marin
Formen des Meeresbodens
Forme del rilievo sottomarino
Formas del relieve submarino

Tarfaya / Tombouctou / Agadir / Nouakchott / BRAZZAVILLE / CASABLANCA — **Size of type indicates relative importance of inhabited localities**
La dimension des caractères indique l'importance d'une localité
Die Schriftgröße entspricht der Gesamtbedeutung des Ortes
La grandezza del carattere è proporzionale all'importanza della località
La dimensión de los caracteres de imprenta indica la importancia de la localidad

INDEX MAPS

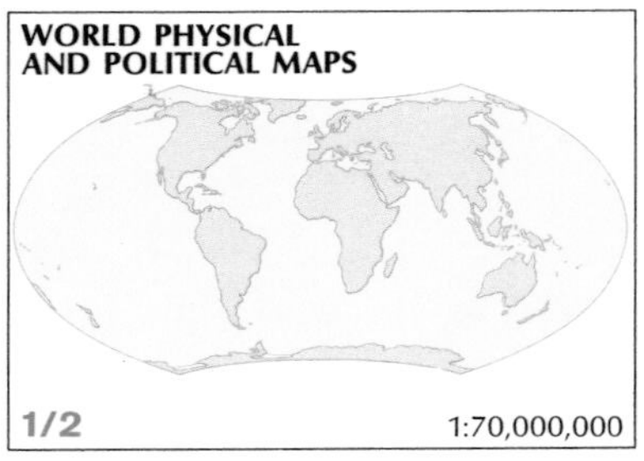
WORLD PHYSICAL
AND POLITICAL MAPS
1/2
1:70,000,000

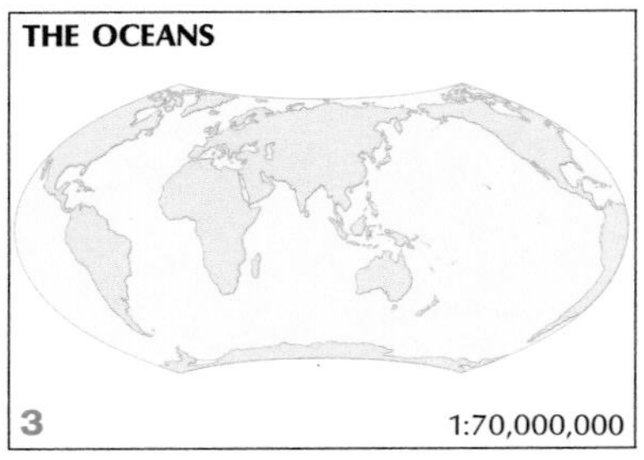
THE OCEANS
3
1:70,000,000

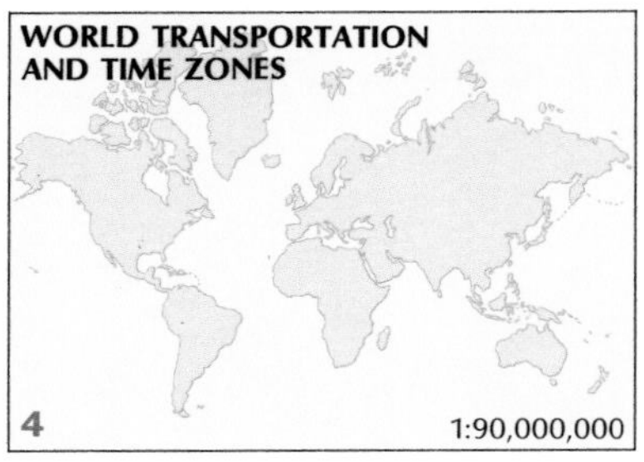
WORLD TRANSPORTATION
AND TIME ZONES
4
1:90,000,000

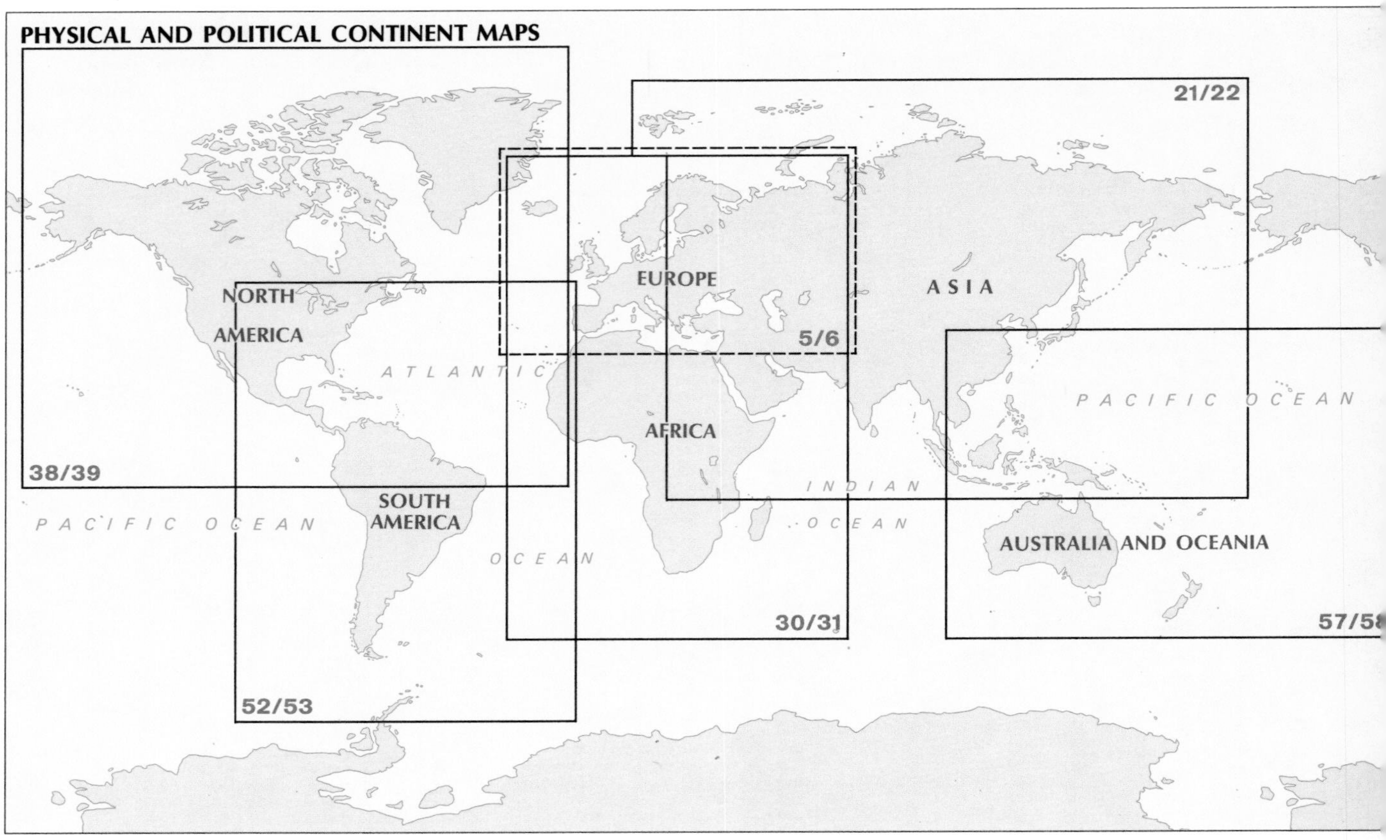
PHYSICAL AND POLITICAL CONTINENT MAPS
21/22
NORTH
AMERICA
EUROPE
ASIA
5/6
ATLANTIC
PACIFIC OCEAN
AFRICA
INDIAN
38/39
SOUTH
AMERICA
PACIFIC OCEAN
OCEAN
OCEAN
AUSTRALIA AND OCEANIA
30/31
57/5
52/53

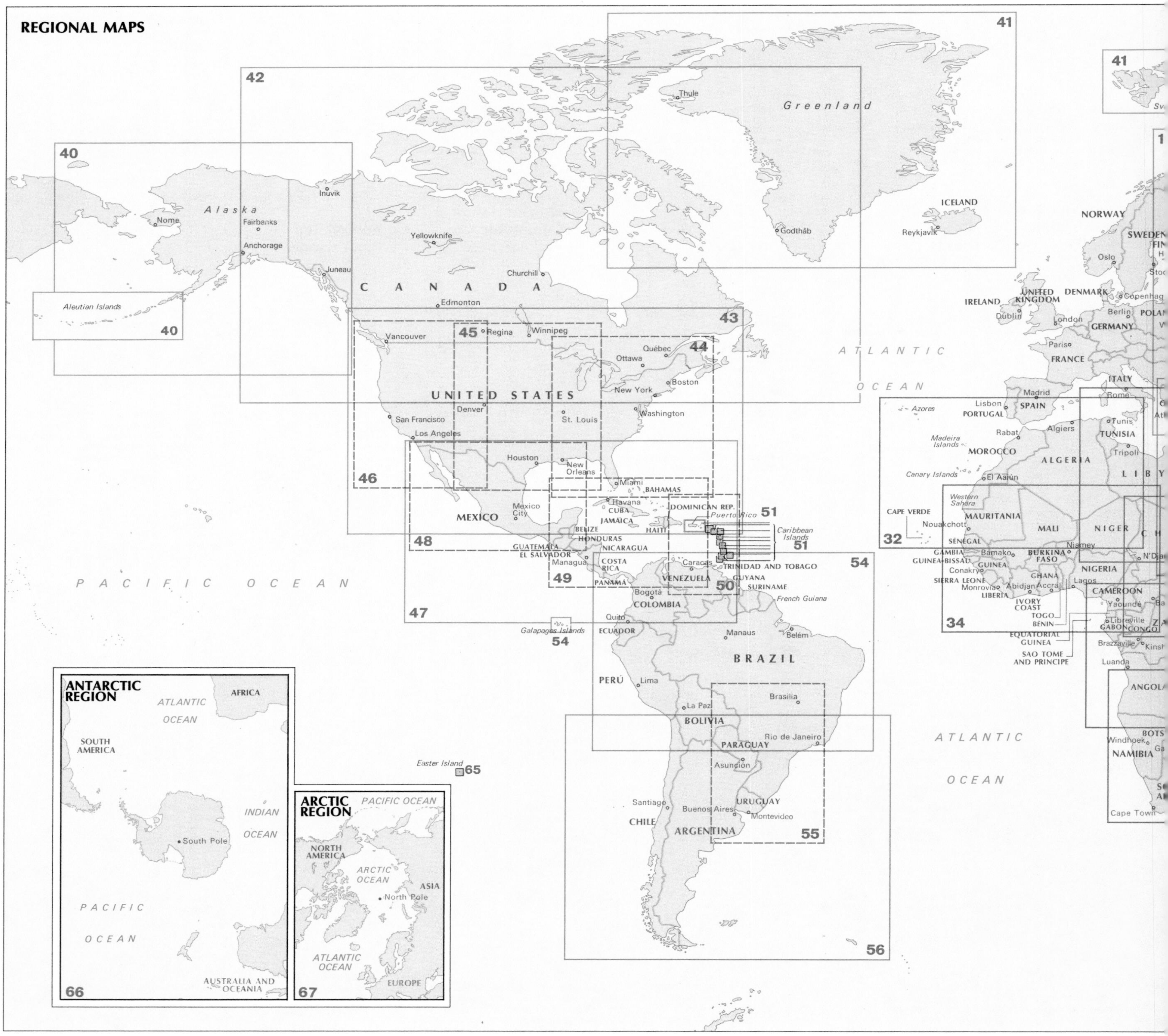
REGIONAL MAPS
41
42
41
Thule
Greenland
40
Alaska
Inuvik
Nome
Fairbanks
Anchorage
Yellowknife
ICELAND
Godthåb
Reykjavik
NORWAY
SWEDEN
Oslo
Juneau
Churchill
CANADA
Edmonton
Aleutian Islands
40
IRELAND
UNITED KINGDOM
DENMARK
Copenhag
Dublin
London
Berlin
GERMANY
POLAN
43
45
Regina
Winnipeg
Vancouver
Québec
44
ATLANTIC
Paris
FRANCE
Ottawa
Boston
UNITED STATES
New York
OCEAN
ITALY
Rome
Denver
Washington
Azores
Lisbon
PORTUGAL
Madrid
SPAIN
San Francisco
St. Louis
Algiers
Tunis
TUNISIA
Los Angeles
Madeira Islands
Rabat
MOROCCO
Tripoli
Houston
New Orleans
ALGERIA
46
Canary Islands
El Aaiún
LIBY
Miami
BAHAMAS
Havana
CUBA
Western Sahara
MEXICO
Mexico City
JAMAICA
DOMINICAN REP.
Puerto Rico
51
CAPE VERDE
MAURITANIA
Nouakchott
HAITI
MALI
NIGER
48
BELIZE
HONDURAS
Caribbean Islands
51
32
SENEGAL
GUATEMALA
EL SALVADOR
NICARAGUA
Niamey
Managua
GAMBIA
GUINEA-BISSAU
Bamako
BURKINA FASO
COSTA RICA
Caracas
TRINIDAD AND TOBAGO
54
GUINEA
Conakry
49
PANAMA
VENEZUELA
GUYANA
SIERRA LEONE
GHANA
NIGERIA
PACIFIC OCEAN
50
SURINAME
Monrovia
Abidjan
Accra
Lagos
Bogotá
French Guiana
LIBERIA
IVORY COAST
CAMEROON
Yaoundé
COLOMBIA
47
Quito
TOGO
BENIN
Libreville
GABON
CONGO
34
Galapagos Islands
54
ECUADOR
Manaus
Belém
EQUATORIAL GUINEA
Brazzaville
Kinsh
SAO TOME AND PRINCIPE
BRAZIL
Luanda
PERU
Lima
ANGOL
ANTARCTIC REGION
ATLANTIC OCEAN
AFRICA
Brasília
La Paz
BOLIVIA
SOUTH AMERICA
Rio de Janeiro
ATLANTIC
PARAGUAY
BOTS
Windhoek
NAMIBIA
Easter Island
65
Asunción
OCEAN
INDIAN
OCEAN
ARCTIC REGION
PACIFIC OCEAN
Santiago
URUGUAY
CHILE
Buenos Aires
Montevideo
Cape Town
South Pole
ARGENTINA
55
NORTH AMERICA
ARCTIC OCEAN
ASIA
North Pole
PACIFIC
OCEAN
ATLANTIC OCEAN
56
AUSTRALIA AND OCEANIA
EUROPE
66
67

EGIONAL MAPS OF EUROPE

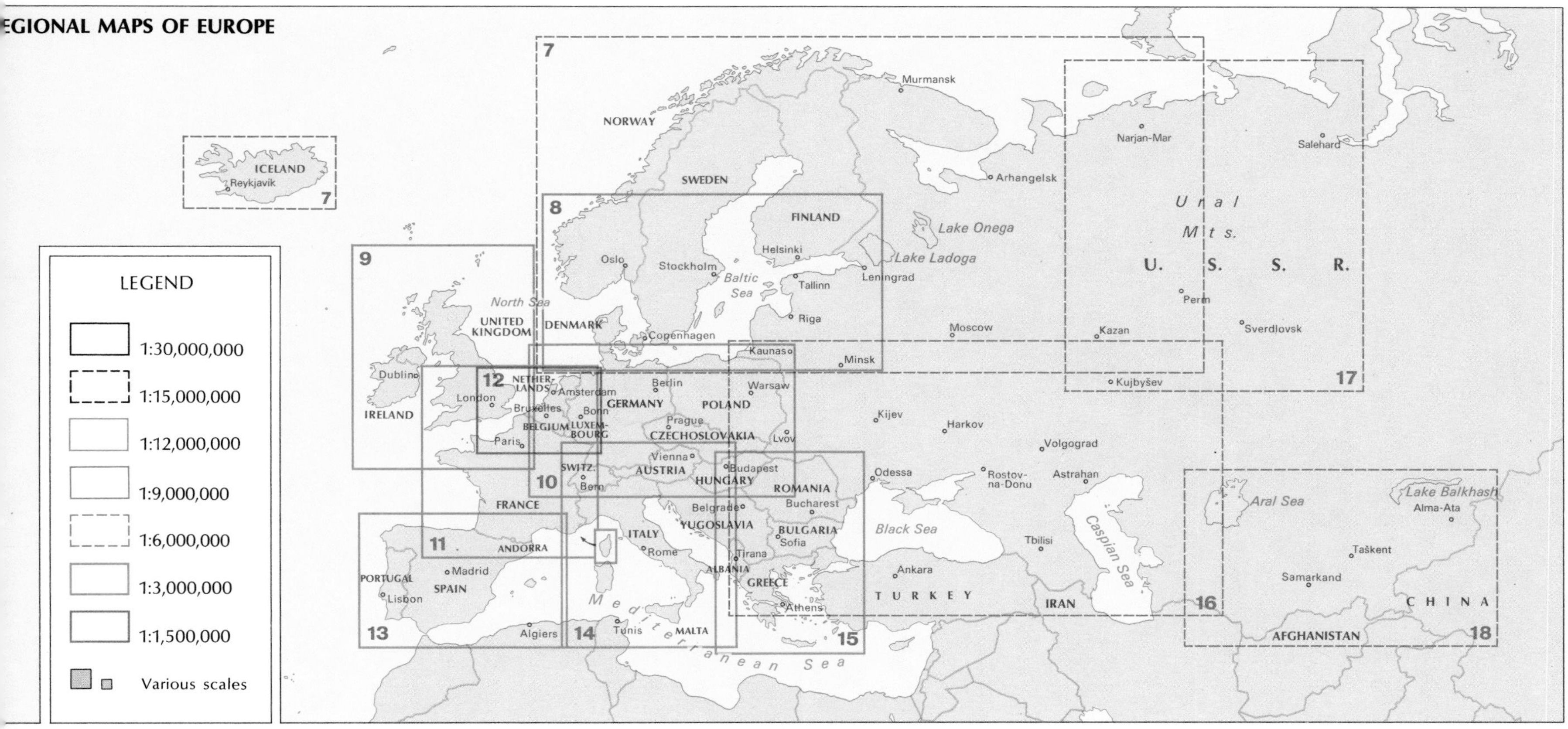

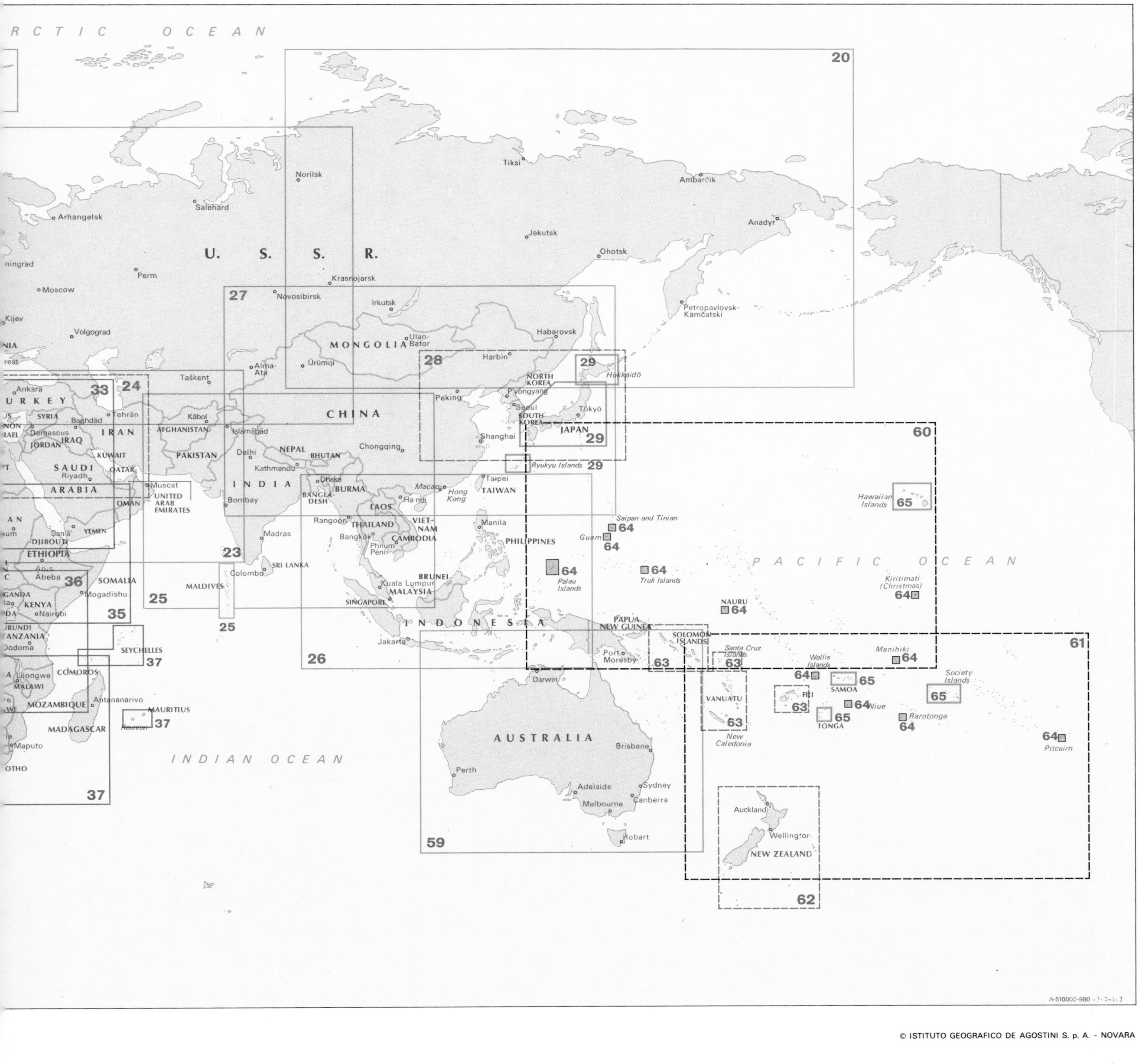

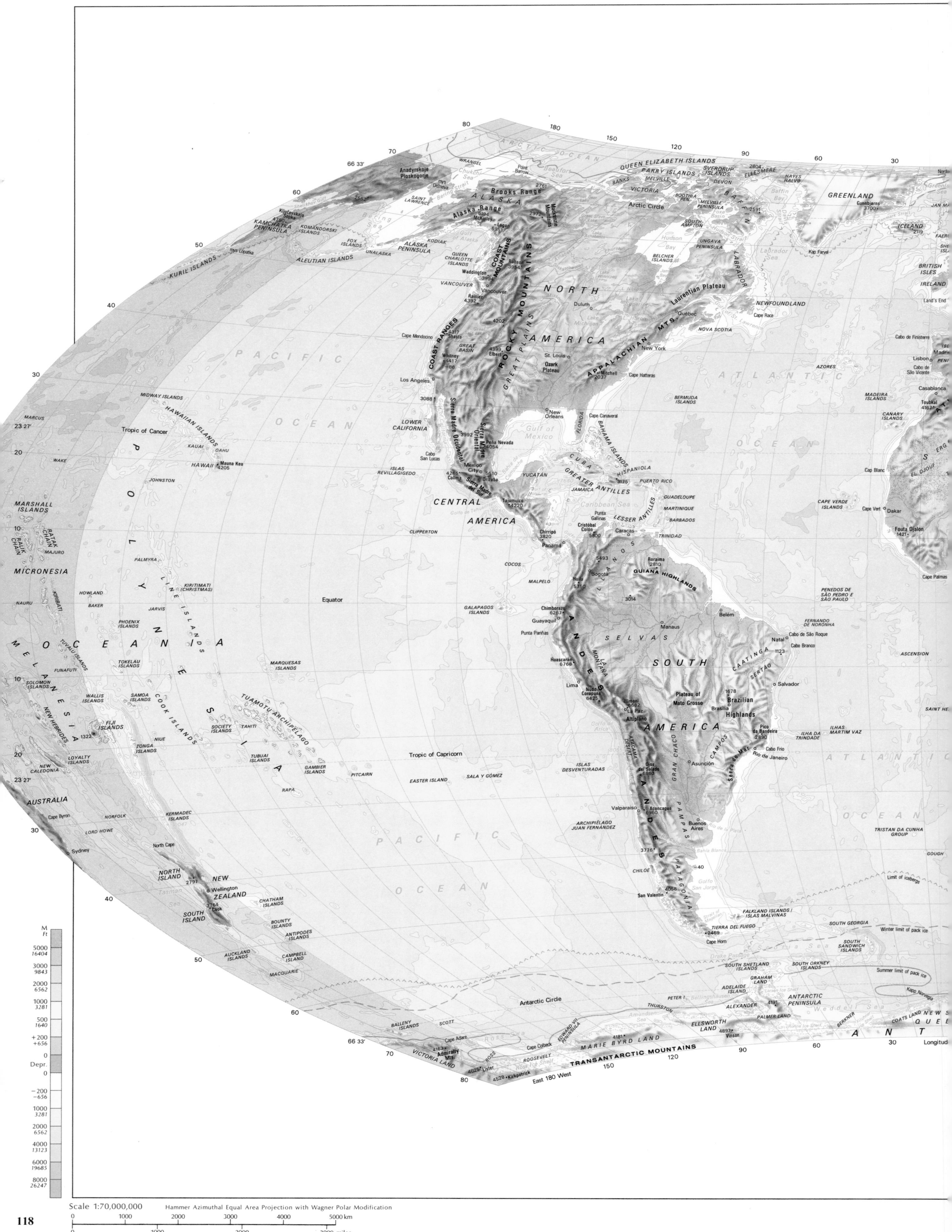

Scale 1:70,000,000 Hammer Azimuthal Equal Area Projection with Wagner Polar Modification

0 1000 2000 3000 4000 5000 km

0 1000 2000 3000 miles

ASIA
EUROPE
AFRICA
AUSTRALIA
OCEANIA
MICRONESIA
MELANESIA
POLYNESIA
PACIFIC OCEAN
INDIAN OCEAN
WESTERN SIBERIAN PLAIN
Central Siberian Uplands
SIBERIA
URAL MOUNTAINS
Verkhoyansk Mountains
Cherski Mts.
Stanovoy Upland
Stanovoy Range
Sayan Mts.
ALTAI
Greater Khingan Range
Sikhote Alin
KAZAKHSTAN
Kazakh Hills
TURKISTAN
TIAN SHAN
DZUNGARIAN BASIN
GOBI DESERT
TAKLA MAKAN
Pamir
Hindu Kush
Karakoram
KUNLUN SHAN
Plateau of Tibet
HIMALAYAS
CHINA
Qin Ling
Nan Ling
HINDUSTAN
DECCAN
Western Ghats
Eastern Ghats
INDOCHINA
ARABIAN PENINSULA
AN NAFŪD
AR RUB' AL KHĀLĪ
Plateau of Iran
ZAGROS MTS.
TAURUS MTS.
ANATOLIA
CAUCASUS
CARPATHIAN MTS.
ALPS
UKRAINE
Tibesti
Ennedi
Darfur
Ethiopian Plateau
Massif des Bongo
CONGO BASIN
Mitumba Range
KALAHARI DESERT
NAMIB DESERT
Drakensberg
MADAGASCAR
GREAT SANDY DESERT
GIBSON DESERT
GREAT VICTORIA DESERT
GREAT ARTESIAN BASIN
GREAT DIVIDING RANGE
Macdonnell Ranges
NEW GUINEA
BORNEO
SUMATRA
JAVA
CELEBES
PHILIPPINE ISLANDS
JAPAN
HONSHŪ
HOKKAIDŌ
SAKHALIN
KAMCHATKA PENINSULA
ALASKA
ALEUTIAN ISLANDS
KURIL ISLANDS
NEW ZEALAND
NORTH ISLAND
SOUTH ISLAND
TASMANIA
HAWAIIAN ISLANDS
MARSHALL ISLANDS
CAROLINE ISLANDS
SOLOMON ISLANDS
NEW HEBRIDES
FIJI ISLANDS
NEW CALEDONIA
Tropic of Cancer
Equator
Tropic of Capricorn
Arctic Circle
Antarctic Circle
WILKES LAND
VICTORIA LAND
TRANSANTARCTIC MTS.
ANTARCTICA
Greenwich
East 180 West
A-510000-780

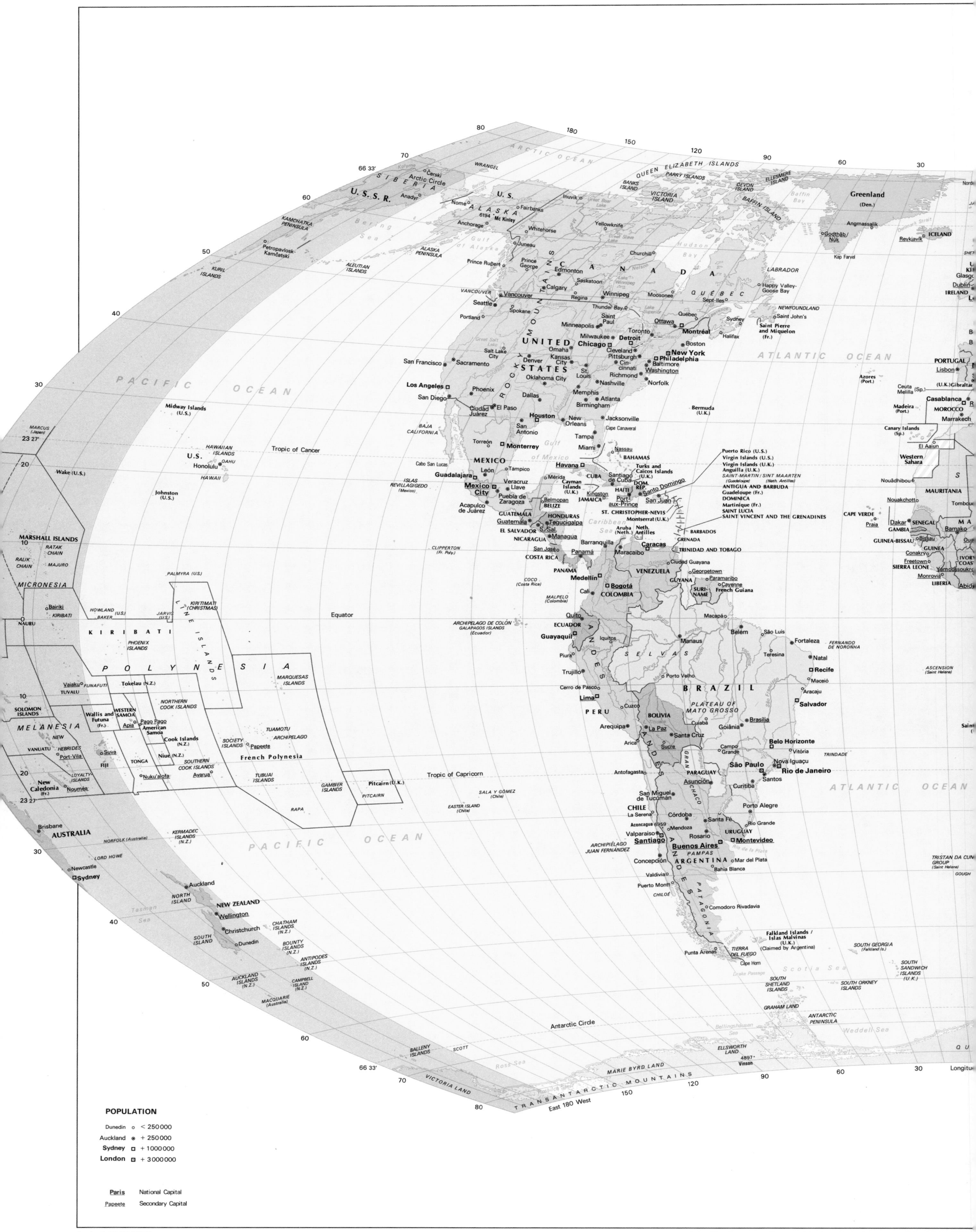

Scale 1:70,000,000 Hammer Azimuthal Equal Area Projection with Wagner Polar Modification

0 1000 2000 3000 4000 5000 km

0 1000 2000 3000 miles

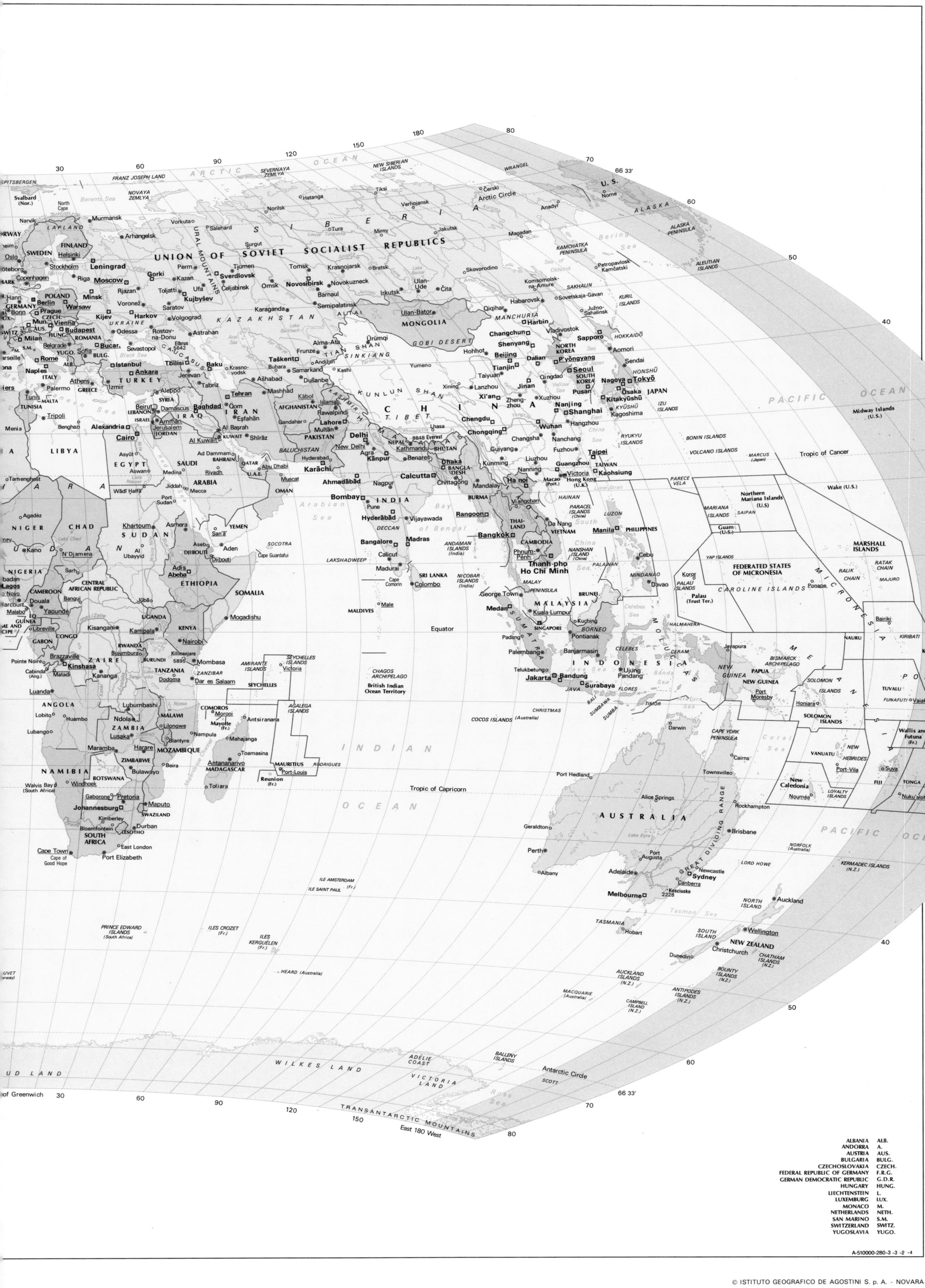

ALBANIA	ALB.
ANDORRA	A.
AUSTRIA	AUS.
BULGARIA	BULG.
CZECHOSLOVAKIA	CZECH.
FEDERAL REPUBLIC OF GERMANY	F.R.G.
GERMAN DEMOCRATIC REPUBLIC	G.D.R.
HUNGARY	HUNG.
LIECHTENSTEIN	L.
LUXEMBURG	LUX.
MONACO	M.
NETHERLANDS	NETH.
SAN MARINO	S.M.
SWITZERLAND	SWITZ.
YUGOSLAVIA	YUGO.

A-510000-280-3 -3 -2 -4

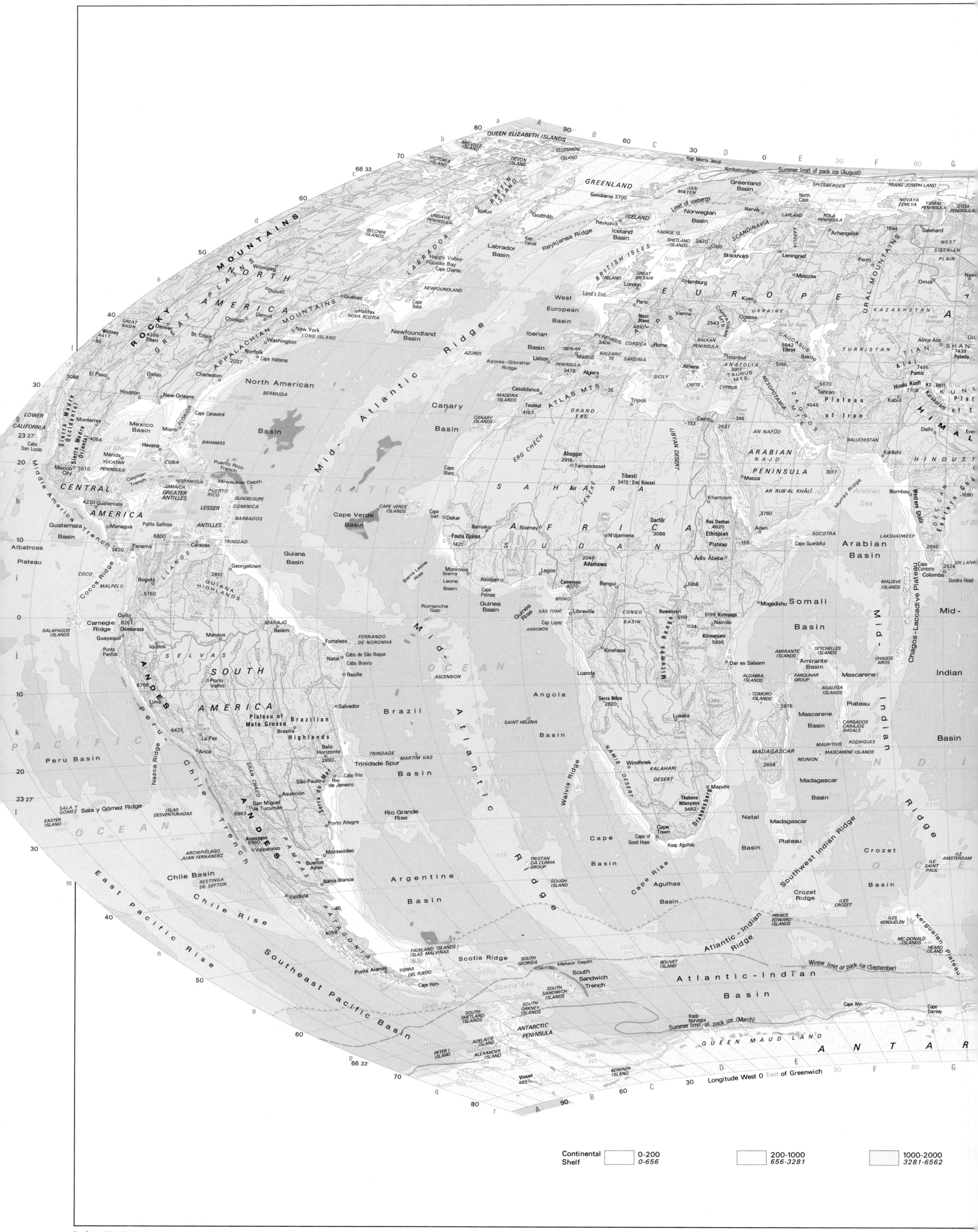

Scale 1:70,000,000 Hammer Azimuthal Equal Area Projection with Wagner Polar Modification

0 1000 2000 3000 4000 5000 km

0 1000 2000 3000 miles

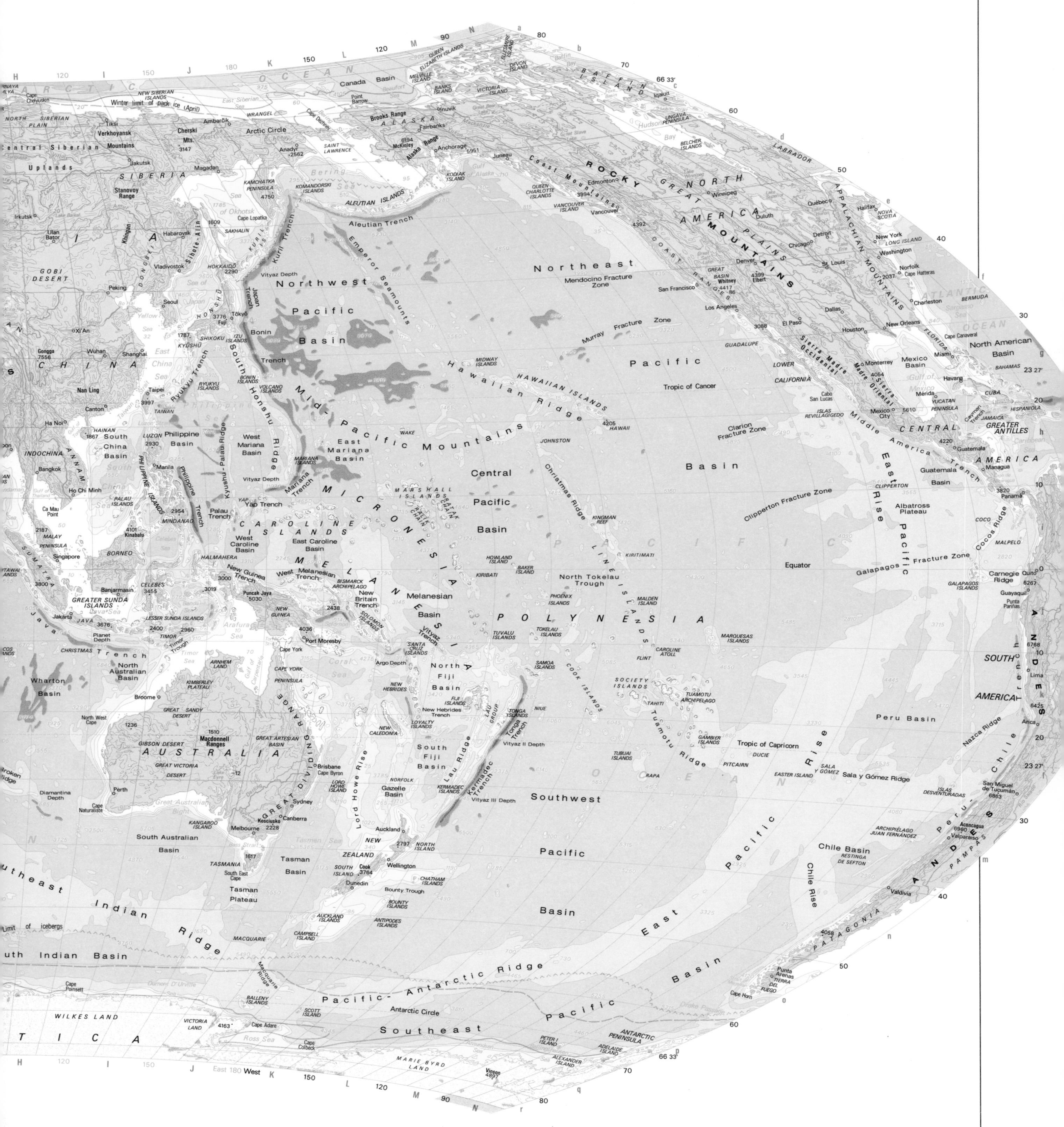

2000–4000	*6562-13123*
4000-6000	*13123-19685*
6000–8000	*19685-26247*
above 8000 M.	*above 26247 Ft.*

A-510000-1C80

Map 4 WORLD TRANSPORTATION AND TIME ZONES

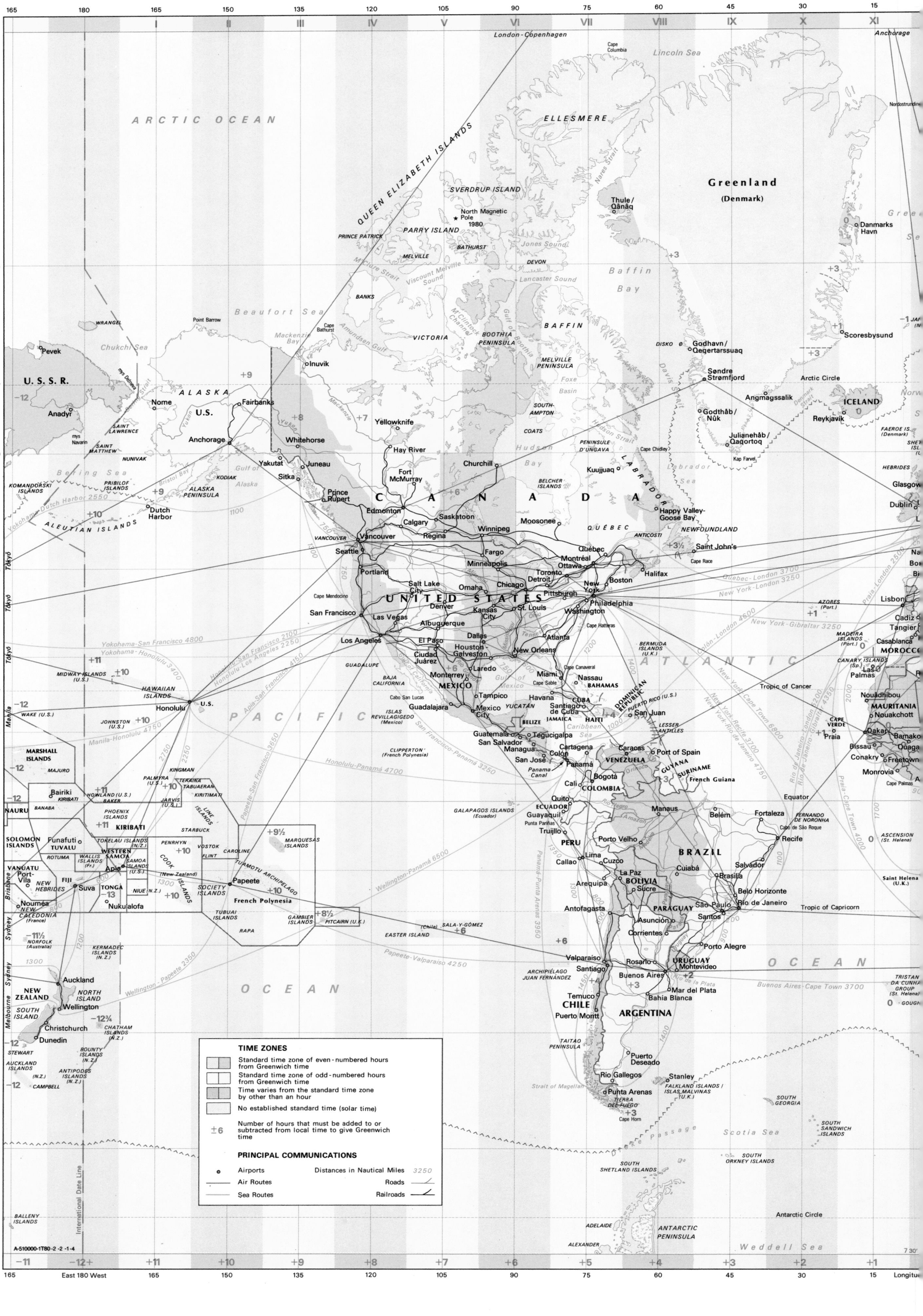

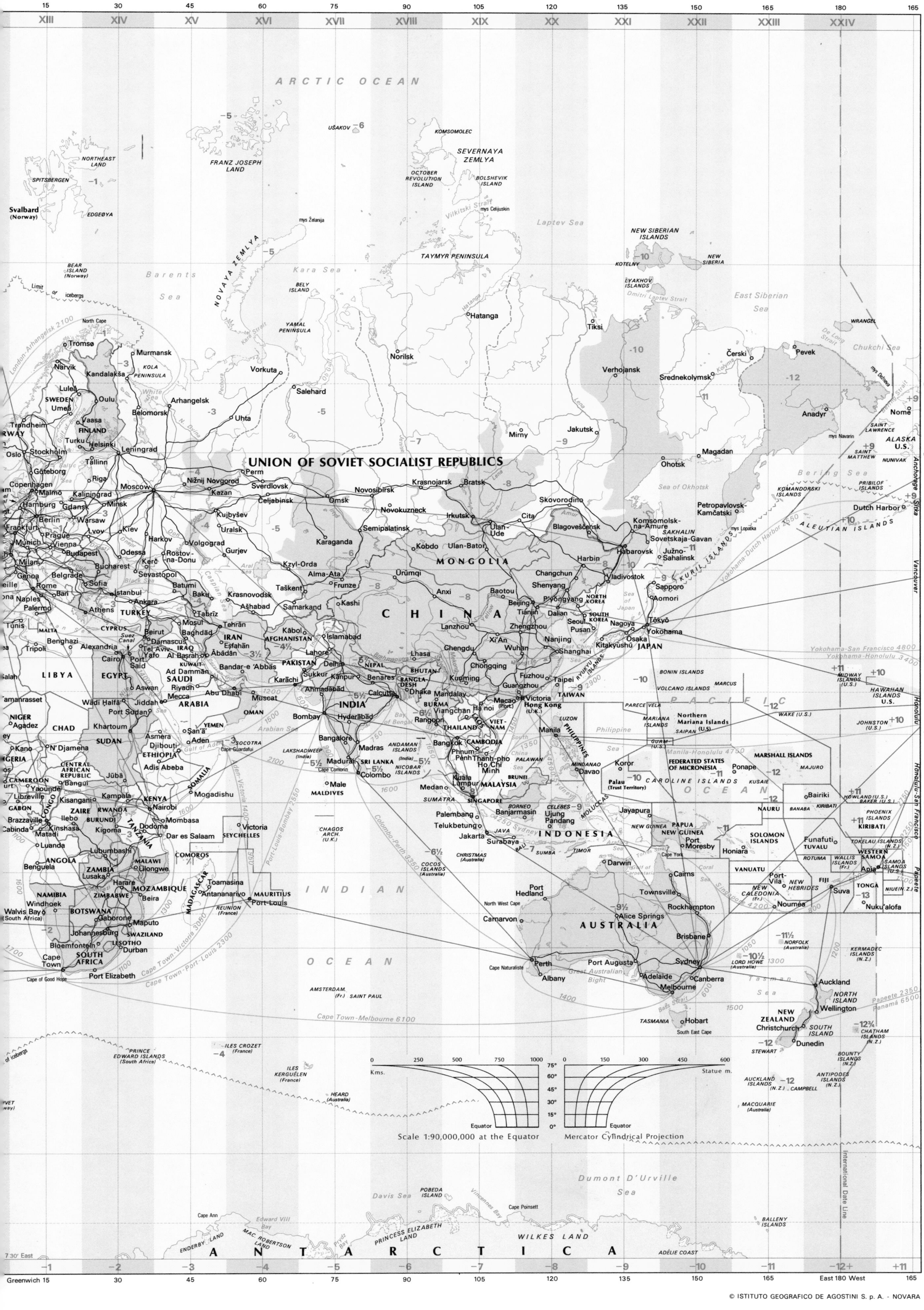

ARCTIC OCEAN
UNION OF SOVIET SOCIALIST REPUBLICS
CHINA
MONGOLIA
INDIA
AUSTRALIA
INDONESIA
JAPAN
PACIFIC OCEAN
INDIAN OCEAN
ANTARCTICA
SEVERNAYA ZEMLYA
FRANZ JOSEPH LAND
NOVAYA ZEMLYA
TAYMYR PENINSULA
NEW SIBERIAN ISLANDS
Barents Sea
Kara Sea
Laptev Sea
East Siberian Sea
Chukchi Sea
Bering Sea
Sea of Okhotsk
Arabian Sea
Moscow
Leningrad
Novosibirsk
Krasnojarsk
Irkutsk
Vladivostok
Beijing
Shanghai
Tōkyō
Hong Kong
Bombay
Calcutta
Singapore
Jakarta
Darwin
Perth
Sydney
Melbourne
Auckland
Wellington
Cape Town
Nairobi
Cairo
Tehrān
Karāchi
Manila
Yokohama-San Francisco 4800
Yokohama-Honolulu 3400
Cape Town-Melbourne 6100
Manila-Honolulu 4750
Colombo-Perth 3350
International Date Line
Dumont D'Urville Sea
Davis Sea
WILKES LAND
ENDERBY LAND
Kms. 0 250 500 750 1000
Statue m. 0 150 300 450 600
Equator
Scale 1:90,000,000 at the Equator
Mercator Cylindrical Projection
Greenwich 15 30 45 60 75 90 105 120 135 150 165 East 180 West 165
XIII XIV XV XVI XVII XVIII XIX XX XXI XXII XXIII XXIV
−1 −2 −3 −4 −5 −6 −7 −8 −9 −10 −11 −12+ +11
7.30' East

Map 5 **EUROPE, PHYSICAL**

Scale 1:15,000,000 Lambert Azimuthal Equal Area Projection

0 200 400 600 800 1000 km

0 250 500 miles

BARENTS SEA
NOVAYA ZEMLYA
KARA SEA
YAMAL PENINSULA
Ob Gulf
OSTROV VAJGAČ
PAJ-HOJ
OSTROV KOLGUJEV
KANIN PENINSULA
KOLA PENINSULA
LAPLAND
WHITE SEA
ONEGA PENINSULA
KARELIA
SUOMENSELKÄ
SALPAUSSELKÄ
Lake Ladoga
Gulf of Finland
ESTONIA
INGERMANLAND
Gulf of Riga
LIVONIA
LITHUANIA
TIMAN RIDGE
SUBPOLAR URALS
POLAR URALS
NORTHERN URALS
CENTRAL URALS
SOUTHERN URALS
URAL MOUNTAINS
NORTHERN UVALS
WEST SIBERIAN PLAIN
ISHIM STEPPE
TURGAI UPLAND
TURGAI GATES
KAZAKHSTAN
KAZAKH HILLS
BETPAK-DALA
MUGODŽARY
KIRGHIZ STEPPE
OBŠČIJ SYRT
VALDAI HILLS
MOSCOW UPLAND
MOSCOW BASIN
SMOLENSK UPLAND
CENTRAL RUSSIAN UPLAND
VOLGA HILLS
PRIPET MARSHES
VOLHYNIA
PODOLIA
UKRAINE
DNEPR UPLAND
DON UPLAND
DONEC RIDGE
JERGENI
CASPIAN DEPRESSION
VOLGA DELTA
BUZACHI PENINSULA
MANGISTAU
USTJURT PLATO
WESTERN TURKISTAN
KYZYLKUM
KARAKUMY
CARPATHIAN MOUNTAINS
TRANSYLVANIAN ALPS
MOLDAVIA
WALACHIA
DOBRUJA
CRIMEA
SEA OF AZOV
CISCAUCASIA
CAUCASUS
TRANSCAUCASIA
LESSER CAUCASUS
APSHERON PENINSULA
KRASNOVODSKIJ PENINSULA
CASPIAN SEA
BLACK SEA
BALKAN MTS.
BALKAN PENINSULA
RHODOPE MTS.
THRACE
ANATOLIA
TAURUS MOUNTAINS
ARMENIA
KURDISTAN
AZERBAIJAN
ELBURZ MOUNTAINS
HREBET KOPETDAG
DASHT-E KAVIR
DASHT-E LŪT
PLATEAU OF IRAN
KHORASAN
ZAGROS MTS.
FARS
LORESTAN
KHUZESTAN
MESOPOTAMIA
AL JAZIRAH
SYRIAN DESERT
AL HAMAD
AL WIDYAN
AN NAFUD
AL HASA
PERSIAN GULF
AEGEAN SEA
PELOPONNESUS
CYCLADES
DODECANESE
CRETE
CYPRUS
SEA
Hellenic Trough
NILE DELTA
SINAI PENINSULA
EL TIH DESERT
MARMARICA
CYRENAICA
QATTARA DEPRESSION
JARABUB OASIS
Moskva Moscow
Leningrad
Kijev
Volgograd
Astrahan
Baku
Tbilisi
Ankara
Istanbul
Tehrān
Baghdād
Dimashq Damascus
Al Qāhirah Cairo
M Ft
5000 16404
4000 13123
3000 9843
2000 6562
1000 3281
500 1640
+200 +656
0 Depr.
0
-100 -328
200 656
1000 3281
2000 6562
4000 13123

Scale 1:15,000,000 Lambert Azimuthal Equal Area Projection

0 200 400 600 800 1000 km

0 250 500 miles

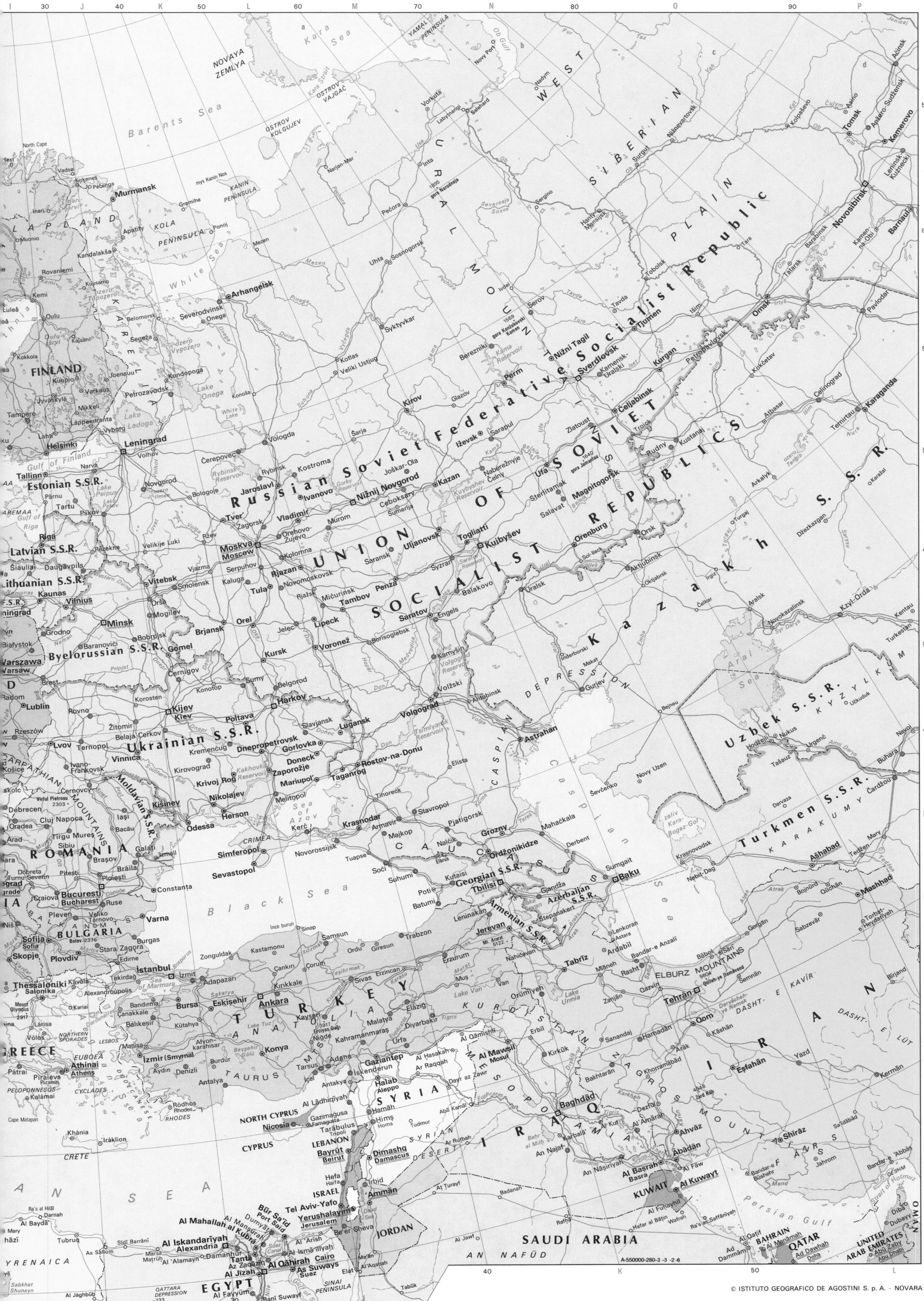
Barents Sea
Kara Sea
NOVAYA ZEMLYA
OSTROV KOLGUJEV
OSTROV VAJGAČ
YAMAL PENINSULA
KANIN PENINSULA
KOLA PENINSULA
LAPLAND
KARELIA
White Sea
FINLAND
Helsinki
Leningrad
Murmansk
Arhangel'sk
Gulf of Finland
Estonian S.S.R.
Tallinn
Latvian S.S.R.
Riga
Lithuanian S.S.R.
Vilnius
Byelorussian S.S.R.
Minsk
Warszawa
Warsaw
Moskva
Moscow
Russian Soviet Federative Socialist Republic
UNION OF SOVIET SOCIALIST REPUBLICS
URAL MOUNTAINS
WEST SIBERIAN PLAIN
Kazakh S.S.R.
Uzbek S.S.R.
Turkmen S.S.R.
Ukrainian S.S.R.
Kijev
Kiev
Moldavian S.S.R.
Kišinev
ROMANIA
Bucureşti
Bucharest
BULGARIA
Sofija
Sofia
CARPATHIAN MOUNTAINS
Black Sea
Sea of Azov
CRIMEA
CAUCASUS
Georgian S.S.R.
Tbilisi
Armenian S.S.R.
Jerevan
Azerbaijan S.S.R.
Baku
Caspian Sea
CASPIAN DEPRESSION
Aral Sea
KYZYLKUM
KARAKUMY
TURKEY
Ankara
İstanbul
ANATOLIA
TAURUS
KURDISTAN
GREECE
Athinai
Athens
CRETE
CYPRUS
NORTH CYPRUS
Nicosia
SYRIA
Dimashq
Damascus
LEBANON
Bayrūt
Beirut
ISRAEL
Yerushalayim
Jerusalem
JORDAN
'Ammān
EGYPT
Al Qāhirah
Cairo
SINAI PENINSULA
IRAQ
Baghdād
MESOPOTAMIA
SYRIAN DESERT
IRAN
Tehrān
ELBURZ MOUNTAINS
ZAGROS MOUNTAINS
DASHT-E KAVĪR
DASHT-E LŪT
KUWAIT
Al Kuwayt
SAUDI ARABIA
AN NAFŪD
Persian Gulf
BAHRAIN
Al Manāmah
QATAR
Ad Dawhah
Doha
UNITED ARAB EMIRATES
Abū Zaby
Abu Dhabi
OMAN
Novosibirsk
Omsk
Tomsk
Sverdlovsk
Čeljabinsk
Perm
Kazan
Kujbyšev
Volgograd
Astrahan
Rostov-na-Donu
Harkov
Odessa
Karaganda
Mashhad
Esfahān
A-550000-280-3 -3 -2-6

ÍSLAND ICELAND
Reykjavík
Arctic Circle
NORGE
NORWAY
SVERIGE
SWEDEN
SUOMI
FINLAND
DANMARK
DENMARK
DEUTSCHLAND
GERMANY
POLSKA
POLAND
Latvian SSR
Lithuanian SSR
Estonian SSR
Belorusskaja
Byelorussian
RSFSR
NORSKE HAVET
NORWEGIAN SEA
NORDSJØEN
NORTH SEA
ATLANTIC OCEAN
OSLO
STOCKHOLM
HELSINKI/HELSINGFORS
COPENHAGEN KØBENHAVN
TALLINN
RĪGA
VILNIUS
MINSK
BERLIN
HAMBURG
GDAŃSK (DANZIG)
KALININGRAD
KAUNAS
Göteborg
Bergen
Trondheim
Malmö
Turku/Åbo
Tampere/Tammerfors
Oulu/Uleåborg
GOTLAND
ÅLAND
BORNHOLM (Denmark)
LAPPI
LAPLAND
FINNMARK
TROMS
NORDLAND
NORRBOTTEN
VÄSTERBOTTEN
JÄMTLAND
LOFOTEN
VESTERÅLEN

Scale 1:6,000,000 Delisle Conic Equidistant Projection

0 100 200 300 400 km

0 100 200 miles

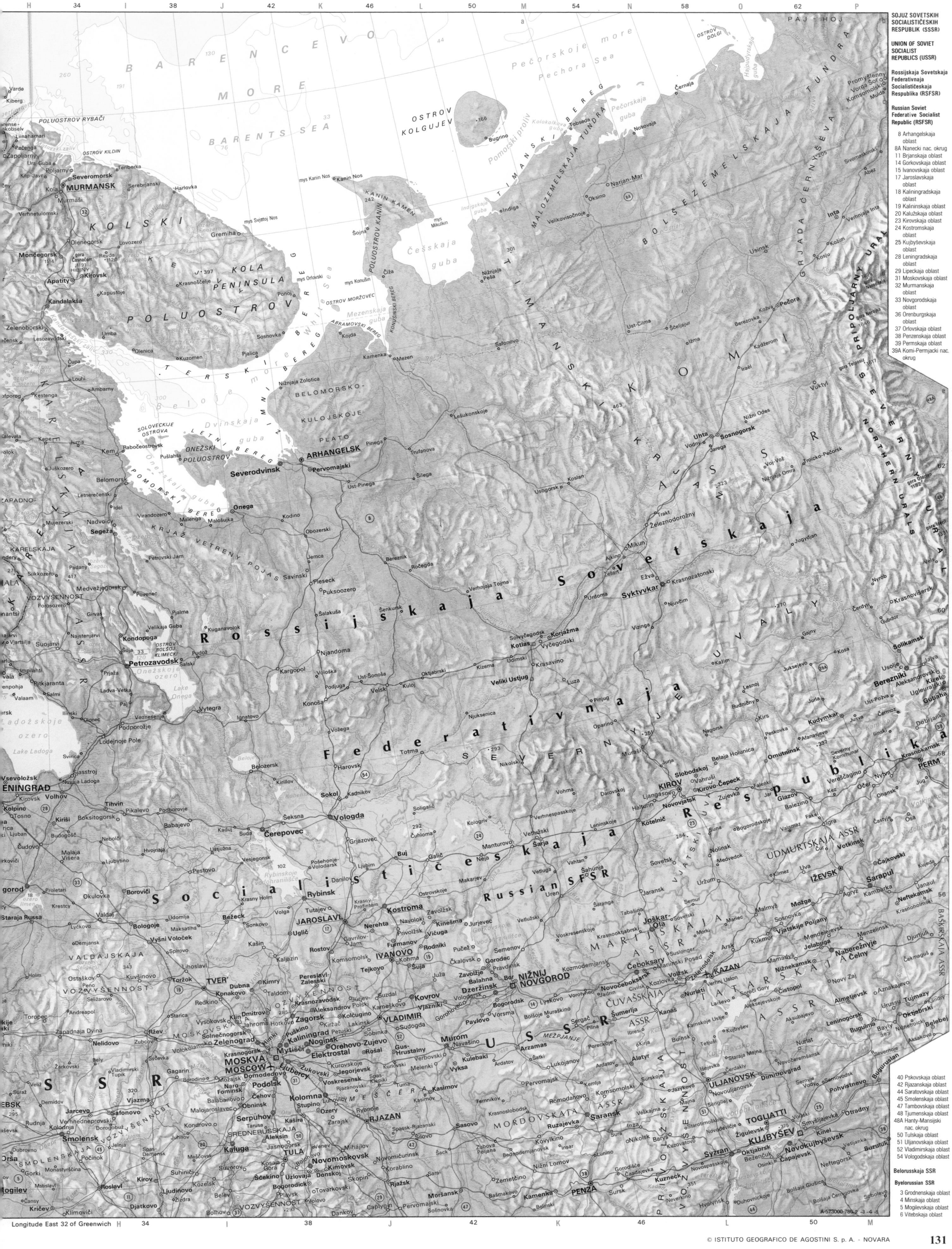
SOJUZ SOVETSKIH SOCIALISTIČESKIH RESPUBLIK (SSSR)
UNION OF SOVIET SOCIALIST REPUBLICS (USSR)
Rossijskaja Sovetskaja Federativnaja Socialističeskaja Respublika (RSFSR)
Russian Soviet Federative Socialist Republic (RSFSR)
8 Arhangelskaja oblast
8A Nanecki nac. okrug
11 Brjanskaja oblast
14 Gorkovskaja oblast
15 Ivanovskaja oblast
17 Jaroslavskaja oblast
18 Kalininskaja oblast
19 Kaliningradskaja oblast
20 Kalužskaja oblast
23 Kirovskaja oblast
24 Kostromskaja oblast
25 Kujbyševskaja oblast
28 Leningradskaja oblast
29 Lipeckaja oblast
31 Moskovskaja oblast
32 Murmanskaja oblast
33 Novgorodskaja oblast
36 Orenburgskaja oblast
37 Orlovskaja oblast
38 Penzenskaja oblast
39 Permskaja oblast
39A Komi-Permjacki nac. okrug
40 Pskovskaja oblast
42 Rjazanskaja oblast
44 Saratovskaja oblast
45 Smolenskaja oblast
47 Tambovskaja oblast
48 Tjumenskaja oblast
48A Hanty-Mansijski nac. okrug
50 Tulskaja oblast
51 Uljanovskaja oblast
52 Vladimirskaja oblast
54 Vologodskaja oblast
Belorusskaja SSR
Byelorussian SSR
3 Grodnenskaja oblast
4 Minskaja oblast
5 Mogilevskaja oblast
6 Vitebskaja oblast
BARENCEVO MORE
BARENTS SEA
Pečorskoje more
Pechora Sea
OSTROV KOLGUJEV
POLUOSTROV RYBAČI
OSTROV KILDIN
KOLSKI POLUOSTROV
KOLA PENINSULA
MURMANSK
ARHANGELSK
Beloje more
White Sea
Dvinskaja guba
Onežskaja guba
Češskaja guba
Mezenskaja guba
POLUOSTROV KANIN
BOLŠEZEMELSKAJA TUNDRA
MALOZEMELSKAJA TUNDRA
TIMANSKI KRJAŽ
Narjan-Mar
Pečora
Uhta
Syktyvkar
Kotlas
Vologda
Čerepovec
Petrozavodsk
Onežskoje ozero
Lake Onega
Ladožskoje ozero
Lake Ladoga
LENINGRAD
Novgorod
KIROV
Perm
IŽEVSK
KAZAN
NIŽNIJ NOVGOROD
JAROSLAVL
Kostroma
IVANOVO
VLADIMIR
MOSKVA
MOSCOW
TVER
Smolensk
Kaluga
TULA
RJAZAN
PENZA
Saransk
ULJANOVSK
TOGLIATTI
KUJBYŠEV
Komi ASSR
UDMURTSKAJA ASSR
MARIJSKAJA ASSR
ČUVAŠSKAJA ASSR
TATARSKAJA ASSR
MORDOVSKAJA ASSR
BAŠKIRSKAJA ASSR
KARELSKAJA ASSR
SEVERNYJE UVALY
SEVERNYJ URAL
NORTHERN URALS
PRIPOLJARNYJ URAL
Rossijskaja Sovetskaja Federativnaja Socialističeskaja Respublika
Russian SFSR
SSSR
Longitude East 32 of Greenwich

NORGE
NORWAY
SVERIGE
SWEDEN
DANMARK
DENMARK
DEUTSCHLAND
GERMANY
Oslo
Bergen
Stavanger
Kristiansand
Trondheim
Ålesund
Göteborg
København
Copenhagen
Malmö
Århus
Aalborg
Odense
Kiel
Lübeck
Rostock
Flensburg
Helsingborg
Karlstad
Örebro
Jönköping
Norwegian Trench
Skagerrak
Kattegat
NORDSJØEN
NORDSØEN
NORTH SEA
NORDSEE
ØSTERSØEN
OSTSEE
BORNHOLM (Denmark)
NORDFRIESISCHE INSELN
NORTH FRISIAN ISLANDS
Jutland Bank
SOGN OG FJORDANE
HORDALAND
ROGALAND
TELEMARK
OPPLAND
HEDMARK
JÄMTLAND
HÄRJEDALEN
VÄRMLAND
DALARNA
VÄSTERGÖTLAND
SMÅLAND
SKÅNE
SJÆLLAND
FYN
JYLLAND
LOLLAND
FALSTER
M Ft
2000 6562
1500 4921
1000 3281
500 1640
200 656
+100 +328
0
Depr. 0
−100 −328
200 656
1000 3281
Scale 1:3,000,000
Delisle Conic Equidistant Projection
0 50 100 150 200 km
0 50 100 miles

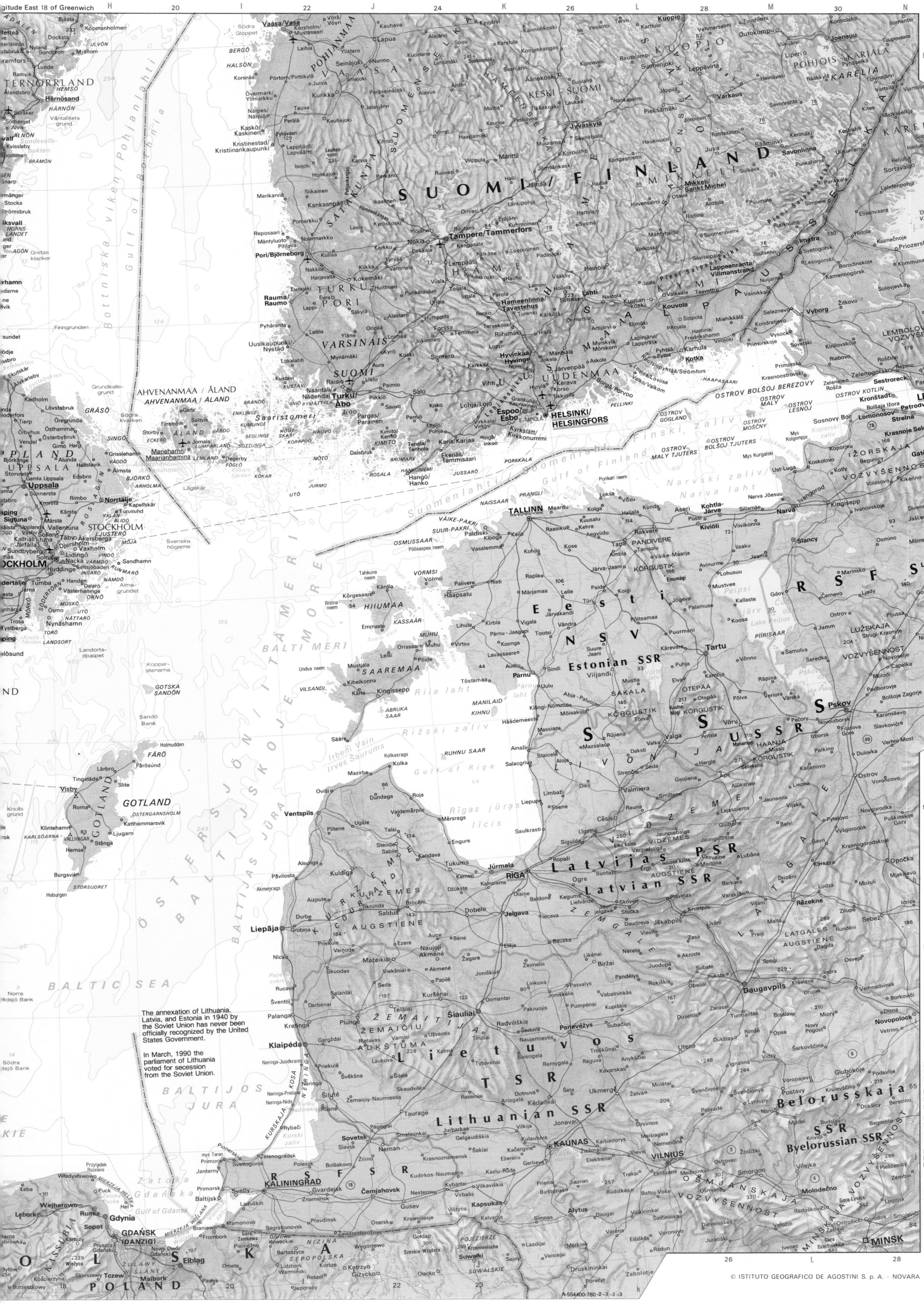

SOJUZ SOVETSKIH SOCIALISTIČESKIH RESPUBLIK (SSSR)
UNION OF SOVIET SOCIALIST REPUBLICS (USSR)
Rossijskaja Sovetskaja Federativnaja Socialističeskaja Respublika (RSFSR)
Russian Soviet Federative Socialist Republic (RSFSR)
18 Kaliningradskaja oblast
28 Leningradskaja oblast
40 Pskovskaja oblast
Belorusskaja SSR
Byelorussian SSR
3 Grodnenskaja oblast
4 Minskaja oblast
6 Vitebskaja oblast

© ISTITUTO GEOGRAFICO DE AGOSTINI S. p. A. - NOVARA

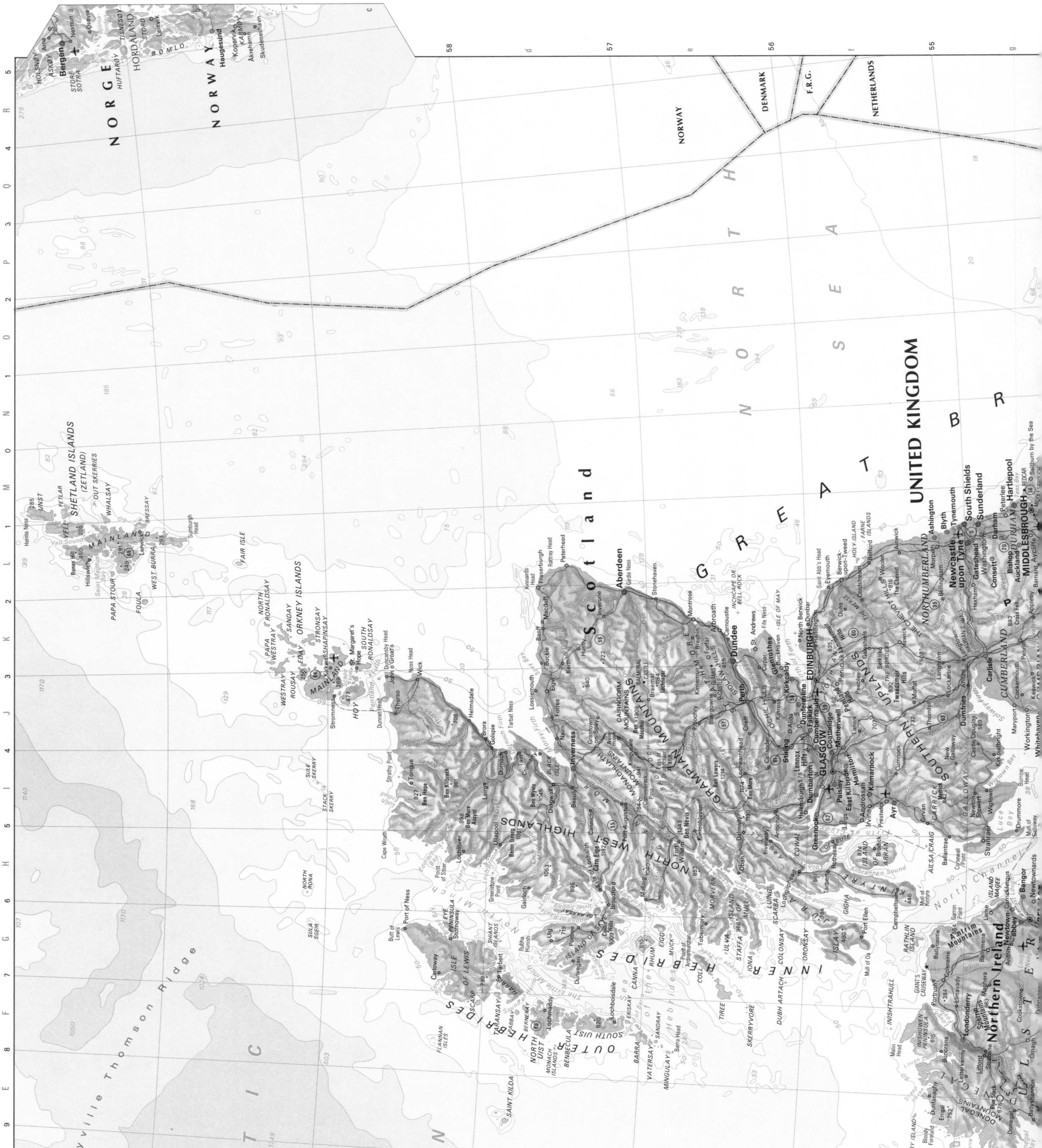
NORGE
NORWAY
Bergen
Haugesund
HORDALAND
NORWAY
DENMARK
F.R.G.
NETHERLANDS
NORTH SEA
GREAT BRITAIN
UNITED KINGDOM
Scotland
SHETLAND ISLANDS
(ZETLAND)
ORKNEY ISLANDS
FAIR ISLE
FOULA
Lerwick
Kirkwall
Stromness
Thurso
Wick
John o' Groat's
Aberdeen
Inverness
Dundee
Perth
EDINBURGH
GLASGOW
Stirling
Paisley
Greenock
Kilmarnock
Ayr
Dumfries
Carlisle
Newcastle upon Tyne
Sunderland
MIDDLESBROUGH
Hartlepool
GRAMPIAN MOUNTAINS
NORTH WEST HIGHLANDS
SOUTHERN UPLANDS
CHEVIOT HILLS
CAIRNGORM MOUNTAINS
Ben Nevis
OUTER HEBRIDES
INNER HEBRIDES
ISLE OF LEWIS
HARRIS
NORTH UIST
SOUTH UIST
BENBECULA
BARRA
SKYE
MULL
ISLAY
JURA
ARRAN
SAINT KILDA
FLANNAN ISLES
NORTH RONA
SULA SGEIR
SULE SKERRY
Cape Wrath
Butt of Lewis
Stornoway
North Channel
Northern Ireland
Londonderry
Belfast
Antrim Mountains
DONEGAL MOUNTAINS
TORY ISLAND
ARAN ISLAND
Malin Head
RATHLIN ISLAND
ATLANTIC OCEAN
Wyville Thomson Ridge
Rosemary Bank
Anton Dohrn Seamount

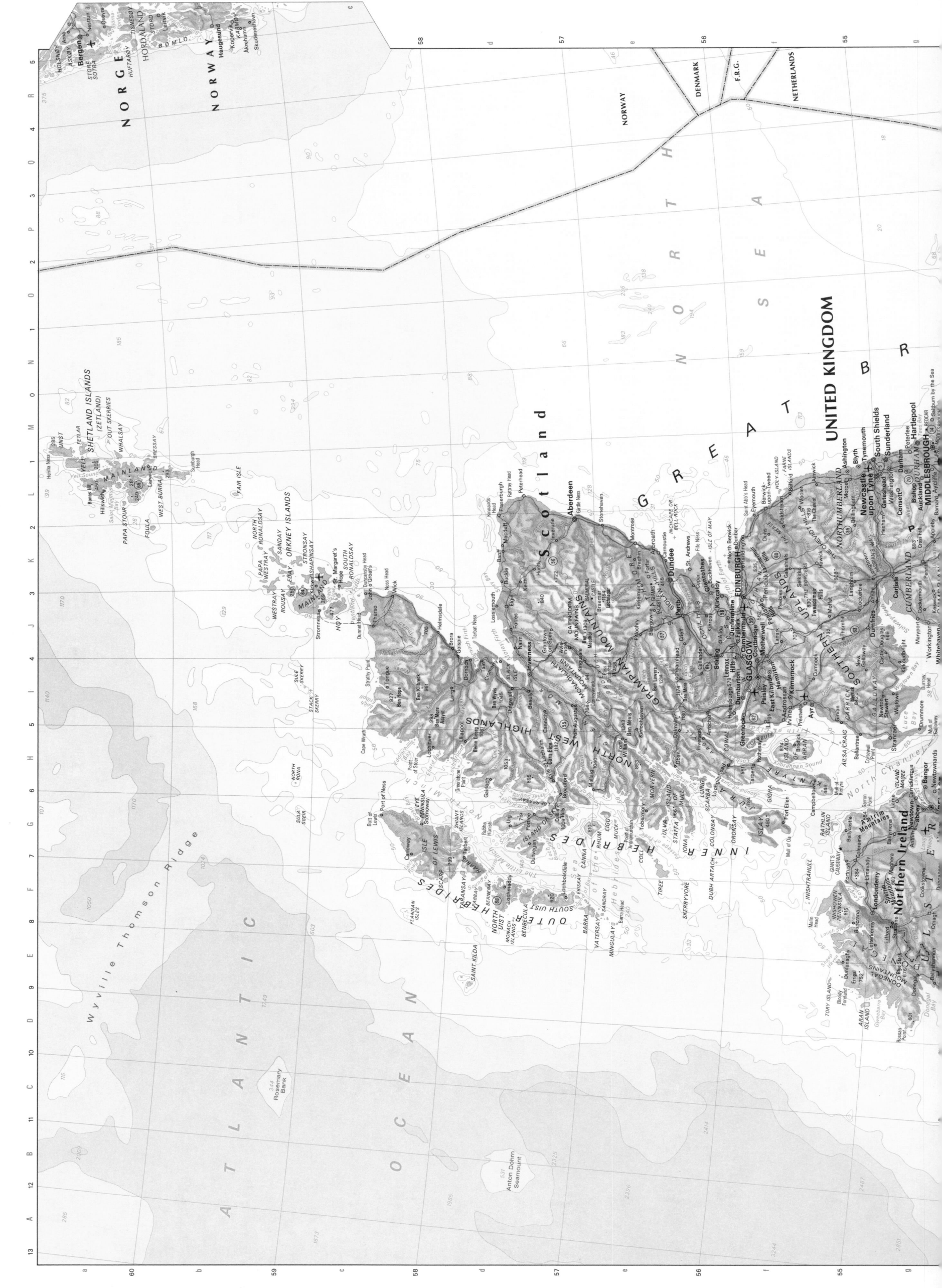

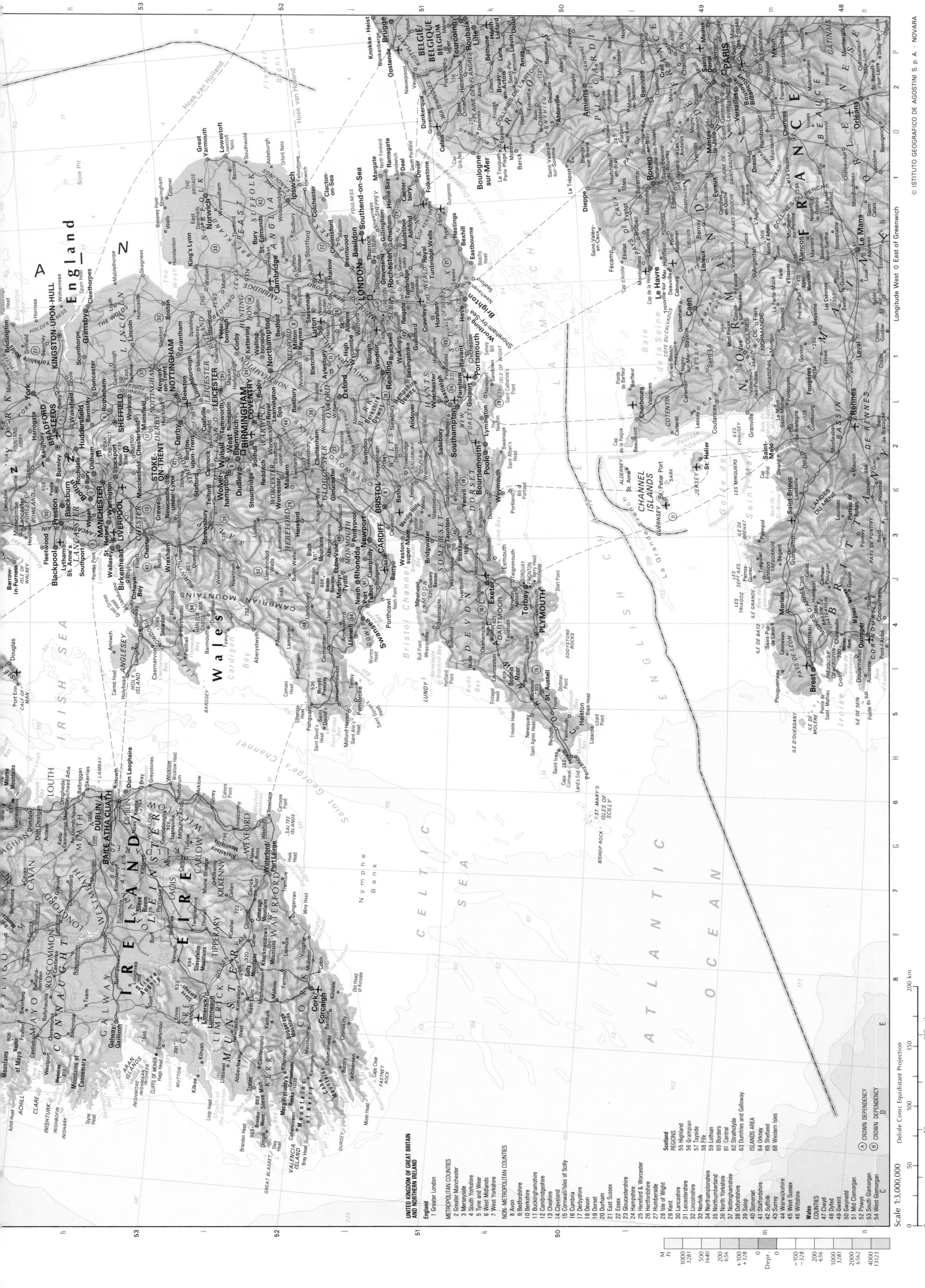
UNITED KINGDOM OF GREAT BRITAIN AND NORTHERN IRELAND
England
1 Greater London
METROPOLITAN COUNTIES
2 Greater Manchester
3 Merseyside
4 South Yorkshire
5 Tyne and Wear
6 West Midlands
7 West Yorkshire
NON-METROPOLITAN COUNTIES
8 Avon
9 Bedfordshire
10 Berkshire
11 Buckinghamshire
12 Cambridgeshire
13 Cheshire
14 Cleveland
15 Cornwall/Isles of Scilly
16 Cumbria
17 Derbyshire
18 Devon
19 Dorset
20 Durham
21 East Sussex
22 Essex
23 Gloucestershire
24 Hampshire
25 Hereford & Worcester
26 Hertfordshire
27 Humberside
28 Isle of Wight
29 Kent
30 Lancashire
31 Leicestershire
32 Lincolnshire
33 Norfolk
34 Northamptonshire
35 Northumberland
36 North Yorkshire
37 Nottinghamshire
38 Oxfordshire
39 Salop
40 Somerset
41 Staffordshire
42 Suffolk
43 Surrey
44 Warwickshire
45 West Sussex
46 Wiltshire
Wales
COUNTIES
47 Clwyd
48 Dyfed
49 Gwent
50 Gwynedd
51 Mid Glamorgan
52 Powys
53 South Glamorgan
54 West Glamorgan
Scotland
REGIONS
55 Highland
56 Grampian
57 Tayside
58 Fife
59 Lothian
60 Borders
61 Central
62 Strathclyde
63 Dumfries and Galloway
ISLANDS AREA
64 Orkney
65 Shetland
66 Western Isles
A CROWN DEPENDENCY
B CROWN DEPENDENCY
Scale 1:3,000,000
Delisle Conic Equidistant Projection
Longitude West 0 East of Greenwich
© ISTITUTO GEOGRAFICO DE AGOSTINI S. p. A. - NOVARA
ATLANTIC OCEAN
CELTIC SEA
ENGLISH CHANNEL
IRISH SEA
England
Wales
IRELAND
EIRE
FRANCE
LONDON
PARIS
M Ft
1000 3281
500 1640
200 656
0
Depr.
200 656
1000 3281
2000 6562
4000 13123

Map 10 CENTRAL EUROPE

Scale 1:3,000,000 Delisle Conic Equidistant Projection

0 50 100 150 200 km

0 50 100 miles

SOJUZ SOVETSKIH SOCIALISTIČESKIH RESPUBLIK (SSSR)

UNION OF SOVIET SOCIALIST REPUBLICS (USSR)

Rossijskaja Sovetskaja Federat'vnaja Socialističeskaja Respublika (RSFSR)

Russian Soviet Federative Socialist Republic (RSFSR)

18 Kaliningradskaja oblast

Ukrainian SSR

9 Ivano-Frankovskaja oblast
13 Lvovskaja oblast
17 Rovenskaja oblast
19 Ternopolskaja oblast
21 Volynskaja oblast
23 Zakarpatskaja oblast

Byelorussian SSR

1 Brestskaja oblast
3 Grodnenskaja oblast

ČESKOSLOVENSKO CZECHOSLOVAKIA

České země
A Hlavní město Praha
1 Středočeský kraj
2 Jihočeský kraj
3 Západočeský kraj
4 Severočeský kraj
5 Východočeský kraj
6 Jihomoravský kraj
7 Severomoravský kraj

Slovensko
B Hlavní město SSR Bratislava
8 Západoslovenský kraj
9 Středoslovenský kraj
10 Východoslovenský kraj

POLSKA POLAND

WOJEWÓDZTWA
1 Biała Podlaska
2 Białystok
3 Bielsko
4 Bydgoszcz
5 Chełm
6 Ciechanów
7 Częstochowa
8 Elbląg
9 Gdańsk
10 Gorzów
11 Jelenia Góra
12 Kalisz
13 Katowice
14 Kielce
15 Konin
16 Koszalin
17 Kraków
18 Krosno
19 Legnica
20 Leszno
21 Łódź
22 Łomża
23 Lublin
24 Nowy Sącz
25 Olsztyn
26 Opole
27 Ostrołęka
28 Piła
29 Piotrków
30 Płock
31 Poznań
32 Przemyśl
33 Radom
34 Rzeszów
35 Siedlce
36 Sieradz
37 Skierniewice
38 Słupsk
39 Suwałki
40 Szczecin
41 Tarnobrzeg
42 Tarnów
43 Toruń
44 Wałbrzych
45 Warszawa
46 Włocławek
47 Wrocław
48 Zamość
49 Zielona Góra

MAGYARORSZÁG HUNGARY

MEGYEI VÁROSOK
A Budapest
B Debrecen
C Győr
D Miskolc
E Pécs
F Szeged

MEGYÉK
1 Bács-Kiskun
2 Baranya
3 Békés
4 Borsod-Abaúj-Zemplén
5 Csongrád
6 Fejér
7 Győr-Sopron
8 Haidú-Bihar
9 Heves
10 Komaróm
11 Nógrád
12 Pest
13 Somogy
14 Szabolcs-Szatmár
15 Szolnok
16 Tolna
17 Vas
18 Veszprém
19 Zala

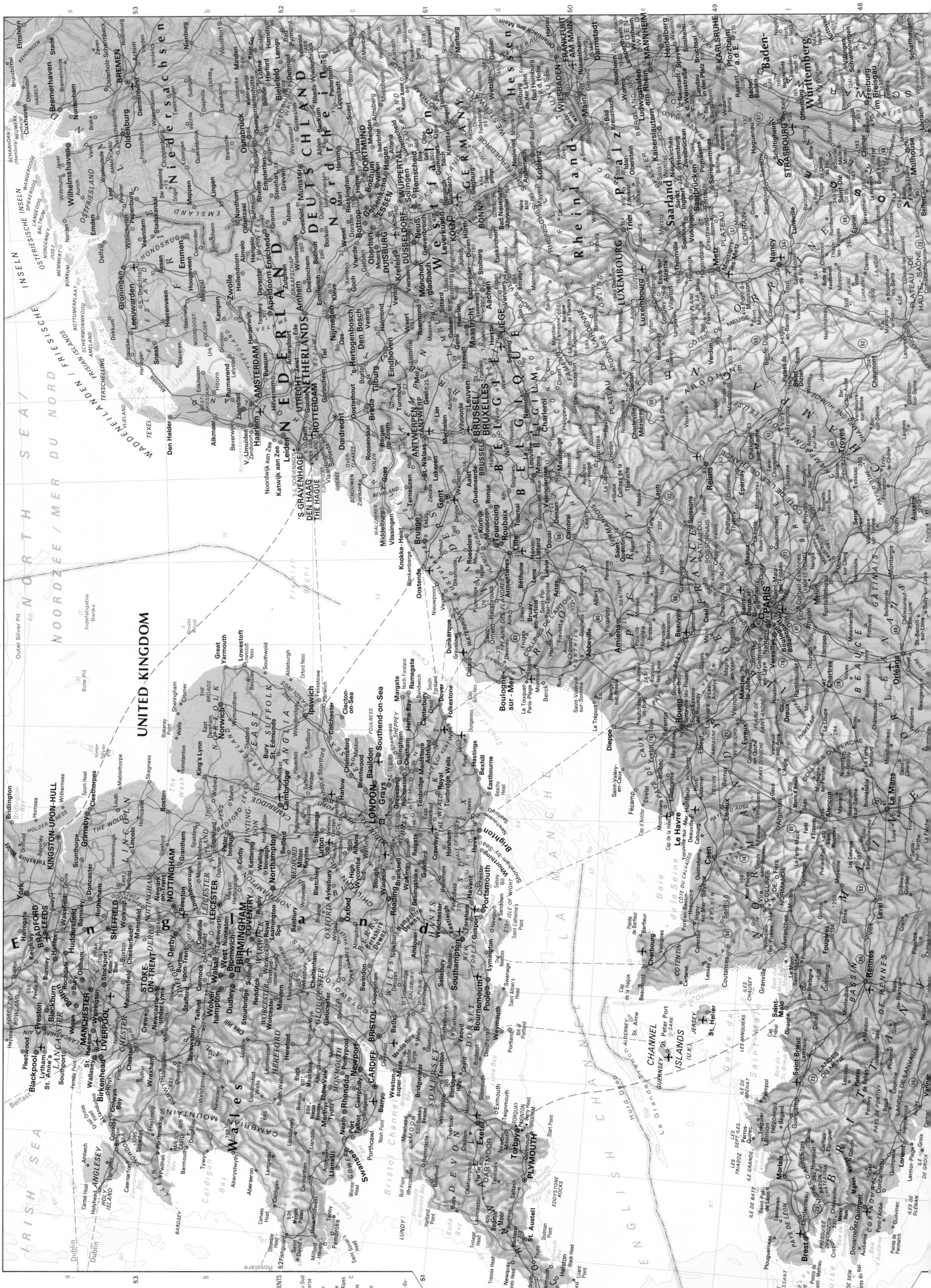

FRANCE
DÉPARTEMENTS
01 Ain
02 Aisne
2A Corse-du-Sud
2B Haute-Corse
03 Allier
04 Alpes-de-Haute-Provence
05 Hautes-Alpes
06 Alpes-Maritimes
07 Ardèche
08 Ardennes
09 Ariège
10 Aube
11 Aude
12 Aveyron
13 Bouches-du-Rhône

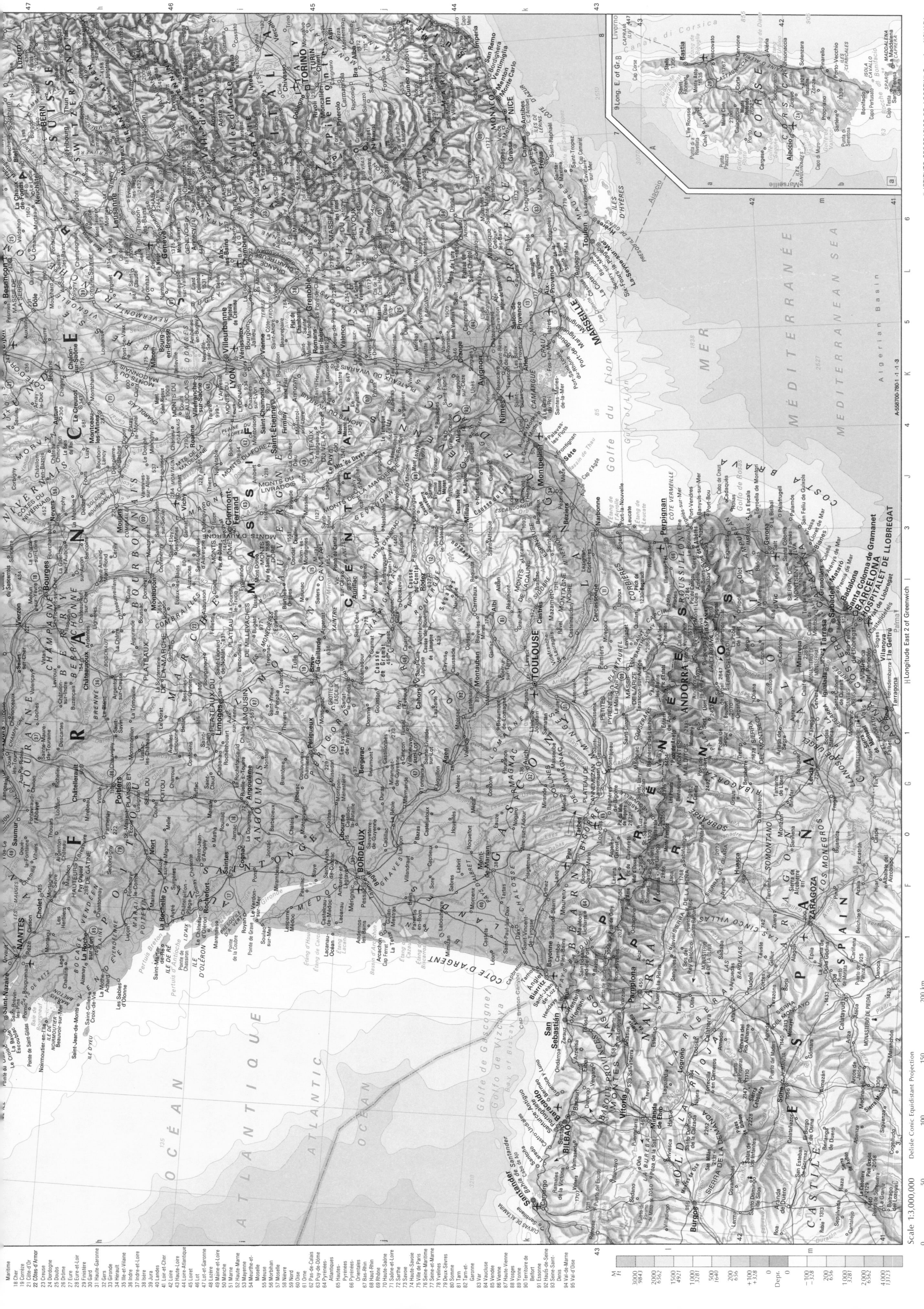
FRANCE
SPAIN
ITALY
SWITZERLAND
CORSE
MASSIF CENTRAL
PROVENCE
GASCOGNE
PYRÉNÉES
ANDORRA
OCÉAN ATLANTIQUE
ATLANTIC OCEAN
Golfe de Gascogne
Bay of Biscay
Golfe du Lion
MER MÉDITERRANÉE
MEDITERRANEAN SEA
Algerian Basin
PARIS
NANTES
BORDEAUX
TOULOUSE
MARSEILLE
NICE
LYON
GRENOBLE
MONTPELLIER
BARCELONA
ZARAGOZA
BILBAO
TORINO
Scale 1:3,000,000
Delisle Conic Equidistant Projection
Longitude East 2 of Greenwich

Scale 1:1,500,000 Delisle Conic Equidistant Projection

0 25 50 75 100 km

0 25 50 miles

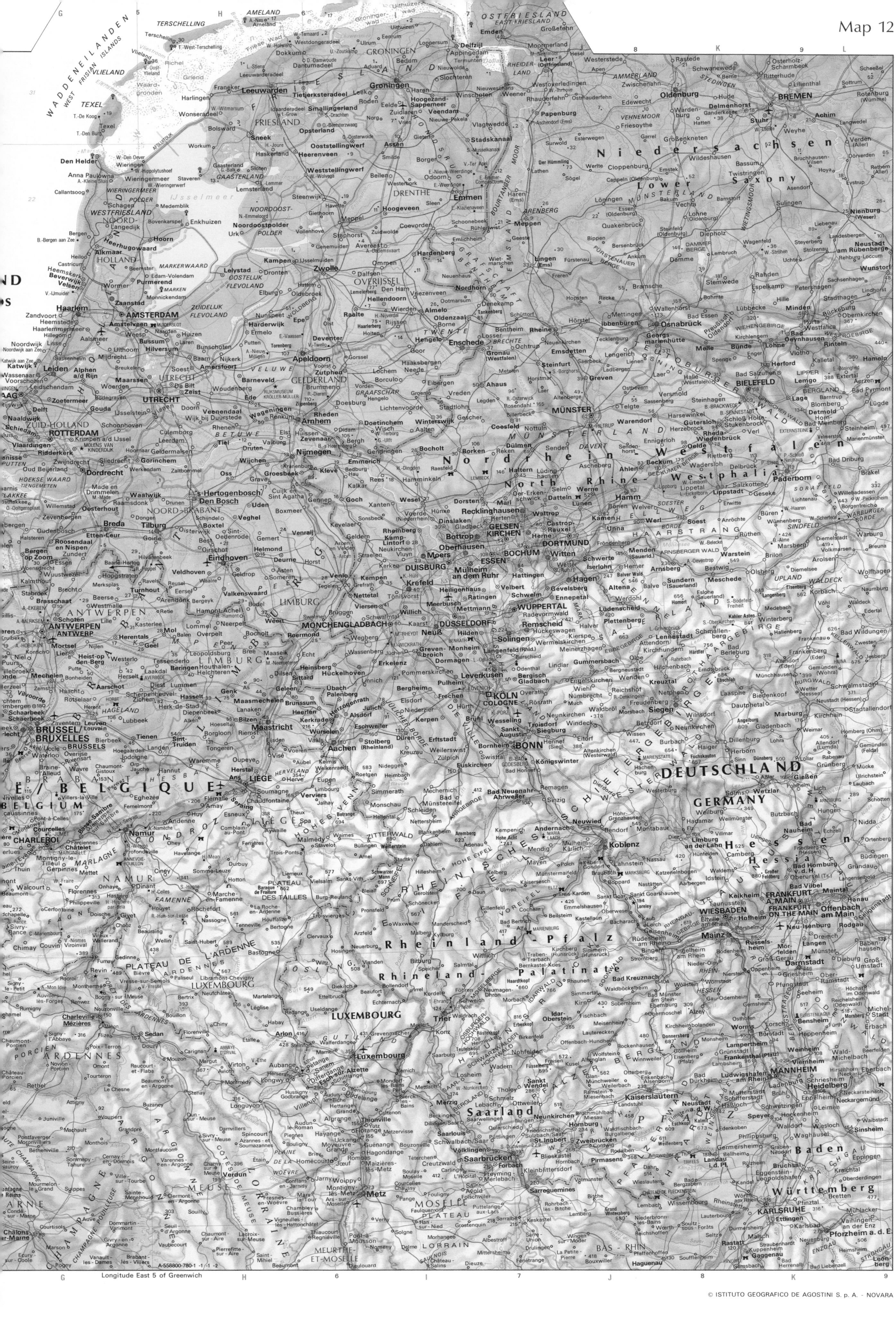
WADDENEILANDEN
WEST FRISIAN ISLANDS
TERSCHELLING
AMELAND
VLIELAND
TEXEL
OSTFRIESLAND
EAST FRIESLAND
GRONINGEN
FRIESLAND
DRENTHE
OVERIJSSEL
GELDERLAND
UTRECHT
NOORD-HOLLAND
ZUID-HOLLAND
NOORD-BRABANT
LIMBURG
IJsselmeer
Niedersachsen
Lower Saxony
Nordrhein-Westfalen
North Rhine-Westphalia
Hessen
Hesse
Rheinland-Pfalz
Rhineland-Palatinate
Saarland
Baden-Württemberg
DEUTSCHLAND
GERMANY
BELGIË / BELGIQUE
BELGIUM
LUXEMBOURG
ARDENNES
LORRAINE
BREMEN
AMSTERDAM
ROTTERDAM
UTRECHT
DÜSSELDORF
KÖLN
COLOGNE
BONN
ESSEN
DORTMUND
FRANKFURT A. MAIN
FRANKFURT ON THE MAIN
WIESBADEN
MANNHEIM
KARLSRUHE
BRUSSEL / BRUXELLES
BRUSSELS
ANTWERPEN
ANTWERP
LIÈGE
Luxembourg
Metz
Saarbrücken
G
H
I
J
K
L
a
b
c
d
e
f
53
52
51
50
49
Longitude East 5 of Greenwich

M
Ft
3000 9843
2000 6562
1500 4921
1000 3281
500 1640
200 656
+100 +328
0
−100 −328
200 656
1000 3281
2000 6562
4000 13123

Scale 1:3,000,000 Delisle Conic Equidistant Projection

0 50 100 150 200 km

0 50 100 miles

FRANCE
LANGUEDOC
PROVENCE
TOULOUSE
MARSEILLE
Montpellier
Nîmes
Avignon
Toulon
Perpignan
Narbonne
Carcassonne
Béziers
Pau
Tarbes
Bayonne
Biarritz
Mont-de-Marsan
Agen
Montauban
Albi
Golfe du Lion
Gulf of Lion
CÔTE VERMEILLE
ANDORRA
PYRÉNÉES
ROUSSILLON
CATALUÑA
ARAGON
NAVARRA
Pamplona
San Sebastián
HUESCA
Huesca
LÉRIDA
Lérida
GERONA
Gerona
BARCELONA
HOSPITALET DE LLOBREGAT
Santa Coloma de Gramanet
Badalona
Sabadell
Tarrasa
Mataró
Manresa
ZARAGOZA
ZARAGOZA SARAGOSSA
TARRAGONA
Tarragona
Reus
COSTA BRAVA
COSTA DORADA
COSTA DEL AZAHAR
COSTA BLANCA
TERUEL
Teruel
CASTELLÓN
Castellón de la Plana
VALENCIA
Sagunto
Gandia
Alcoy
ALICANTE
Alicante
Elche
Benidorm
MURCIA
Cartagena
Lorca
Orihuela
Cuenca
Albacete
ISLAS COLUMBRETES
ISLAS BALEARES
BALEARIC ISLANDS
MALLORCA
MAJORCA
PALMA
MENORCA
MINORCA
Mahón
Ciudadela
IBIZA IVIZA
FORMENTERA
ISLA CABRERA
ISLA DRAGONERA
MEDITERRANEAN SEA
AL BAHR AL MUTAWASSIT
Algerian Basin
ALGERIA
AL JAZĀ'IR
AL JAZA'IR ALGIERS
ORAN
Mostaganem
MOSTAGANEM
MASCARA
Mascara
Sidi Bel Abbes
TLEMCEN
Blida
Médéa
TIZI OUZOU
Béjaïa
Sétif
GRANDE KABYLIE
PETITE KABYLIE
TELL ATLAS
M'SILA
DJELFA
TIARET
Tiaret
Chélif
Miliana
Bou-Saâda
BATNA
Barika

Map 14 ITALY, AUSTRIA AND SWITZERLAND

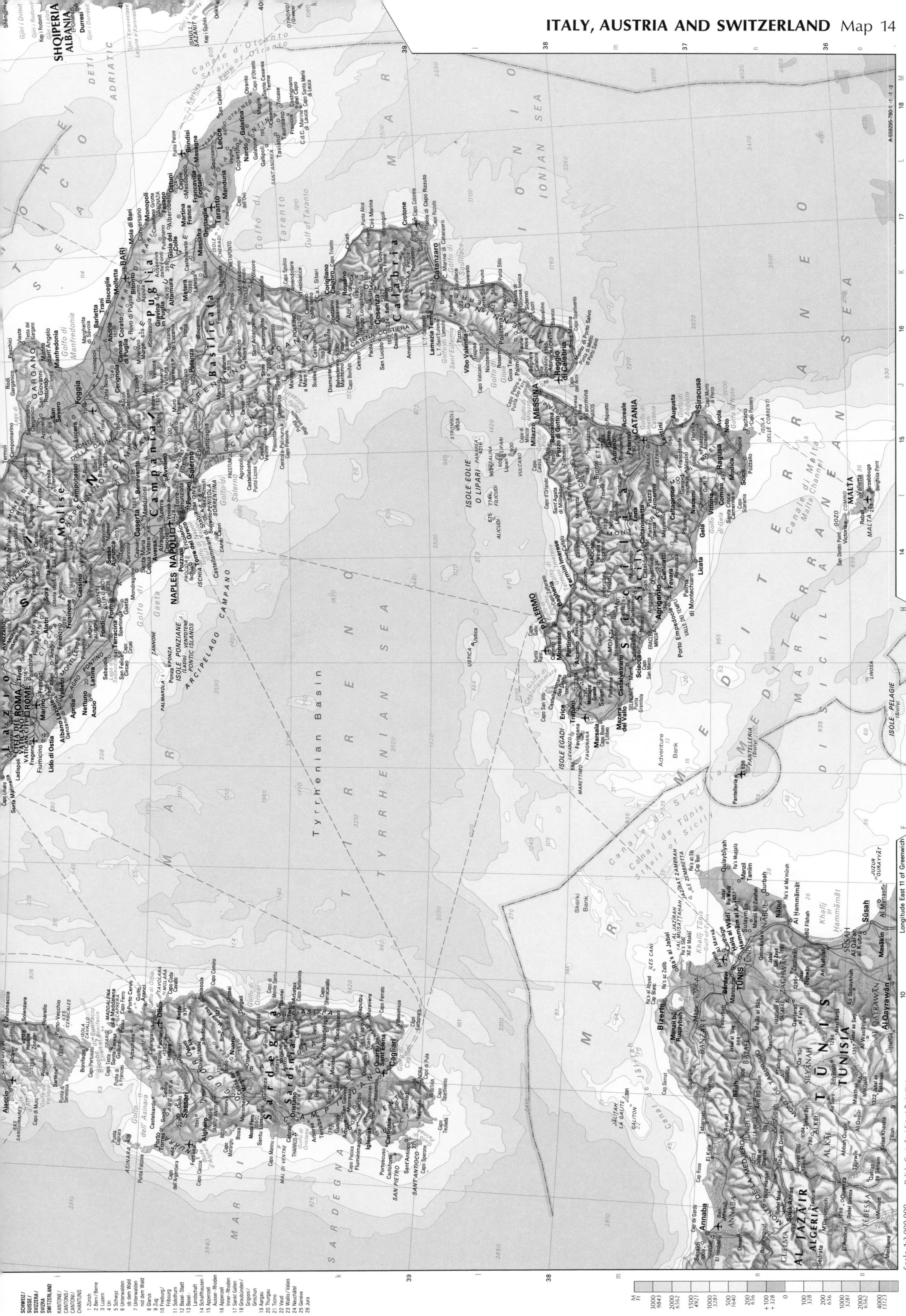

SCHWEIZ / SUISSE / SVIZZERA / SVIZRA
SWITZERLAND
KANTONE / CANTONS / CANTONI / CHANTUNS

1 Zürich
2 Bern / Berne
3 Luzern
4 Uri
5 Schwyz
6 Unterwalden ob dem Wald
7 Unterwalden nid dem Wald
8 Glarus
9 Zug
10 Freiburg / Fribourg
11 Solothurn
12 Basel-Stadt
13 Basel-Landschaft
14 Schaffhausen
15 Appenzell Ausser-Rhoden
16 Appenzell Inner-Rhoden
17 Sankt Gallen
18 Graubünden / Grigioni / Grischun
19 Aargau
20 Thurgau
21 Ticino
22 Vaud
23 Wallis / Valais
24 Neuchâtel
25 Genève
26 Jura

M	Ft
3000	9843
2000	6562
1500	4921
1000	3281
500	1640
200	656
+ 100	+ 328
0	
100	328
200	656
1000	3281
2000	6562
4000	13123

BUCUREŞTI
BUCHAREST
BEOGRAD
BELGRADE
BUDAPEST
SOFIJA
SOFIA
SARAJEVO
SKOPJE
KIŠINEV
Constanţa
Varna
Burgas
Ruse
Craiova
Timişoara
Cluj-Napoca
Szeged
Debrecen
Novi Sad
Plovdiv
Iaşi
Galaţi
Brăila
Niš
Osijek
Pécs
MAGYARORSZÁG
HUNGARY
ROMÂNIA
ROMANIA
BULGARIJA
BULGARIA
JUGOSLAVIJA
Moldavskaja SSR
Ukrainskaja SSR
Ukrainian SSR
Hrvatska
Croatia
Bosna i Hercegovina
Crna Gora
ČERNOJE MORE
BLACK SEA
MAREA NEAGRĂ
JADRANSKO MORE

TÜRKİYE
TURKEY
ELLÁS
GREECE
SHQIPËRIA
ALBANIA
ITALIA
ITALY
ANADOLU
ANATOLIA
Pelopónnisos
Makedhonía
Thessalía
Kríti
Crete
KIKLÁDHES
CYCLADES
Nísoi Aiyaíou
IONIAN SEA
MEDITERRANEAN SEA
ATHÍNAI
ATHENS
İSTANBUL
İZMİR
SMYRNA
BURSA
THESSALONÍKI
SALONIKA
Áyion Óros
Stereá Ellás kai Évvoia
Scale 1:3,000,000
Delisle Conic Equidistant Projection
H Longitude East 25 of Greenwich
© ISTITUTO GEOGRAFICO DE AGOSTINI S. p. A. - NOVARA

Map 16 SOUTHWESTERN SOVIET UNION

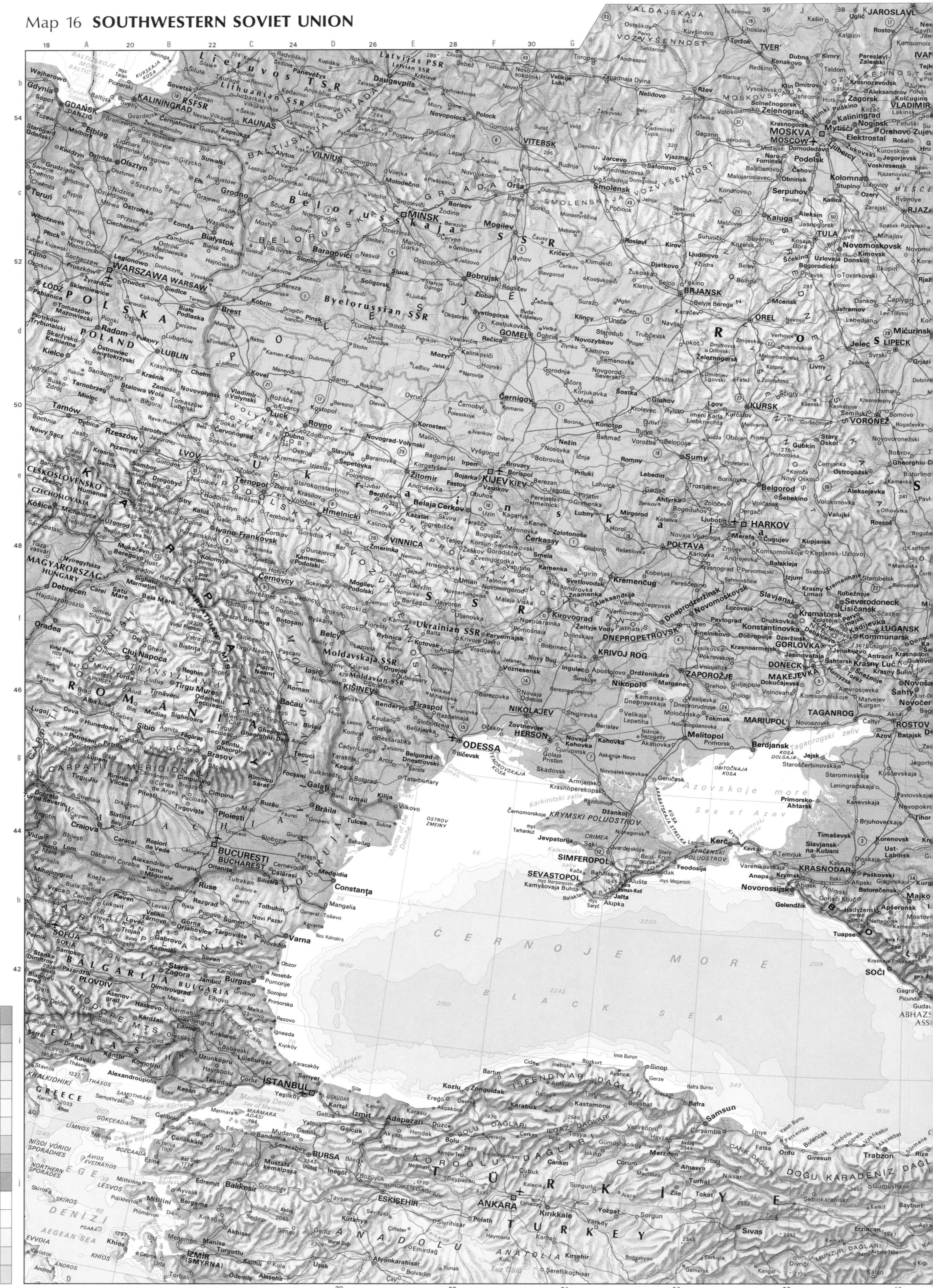

Scale 1:6,000,000 Delisle Conic Equidistant Projection

0 100 200 300 400 km

0 100 200 miles

SOJUZ SOVETSKIH SOCIALISTIČESKIH RESPUBLIK (SSSR)
UNION OF SOVIET SOCIALIST REPUBLICS (USSR)

Rossijskaja Sovetskaja Federativnaja Socialističeskaja Respublika (RSFSR)
Russian Soviet Federative Socialist Republic (RSFSR)

3 Krasnodarski kraj
3A Adygejskaja avtonomnaja oblast
6 Stavropolski kraj
6A Karačajevo-Čerkesskaja avtonomnaja oblast
9 Astrahanskaja oblast
10 Belgorodskaja oblast
11 Brjanskaja oblast
12 Čeljabinskaja oblast
14 Gorkovskaja oblast
15 Ivanovskaja oblast
17 Jaroslavskaja oblast
18 Kaliningradskaja oblast
19 Kalininskaja oblast
20 Kalužskaja oblast
23 Kirovskaja oblast
25 Kostromskaja oblast
25 Kujbyševskaja oblast
26 Kurganskaja oblast
27 Kurskaja oblast
29 Lipeckaja oblast
31 Moskovskaja oblast
33 Novgorodskaja oblast
36 Orenburgskaja oblast
37 Orlovskaja oblast
38 Penzenskaja oblast
40 Pskovskaja oblast
41 Rostovskaja oblast
42 Rjazanskaja oblast
44 Saratovskaja oblast
45 Smolenskaja oblast
47 Tambovskaja oblast
50 Tulskaja oblast
51 Uljanovskaja oblast
52 Vladimirskaja oblast
53 Volgogradskaja oblast
55 Voronežskaja oblast

Ukrainskaja SSR
Ukrainian SSR

1 Čerkasskaja oblast
2 Černigovskaja oblast
3 Černovickaja oblast
4 Dnepropetrovskaja oblast
5 Doneckaja oblast
6 Harkovskaja oblast
7 Hersonskaja oblast
8 Hmelnickaja oblast
9 Ivano-Frankovskaja oblast
10 Kijevskaja oblast
11 Kirovogradskaja oblast
12 Krymskaja oblast
13 Lvovskaja oblast
14 Nikolajevskaja oblast
15 Odesskaja oblast
16 Poltavskaja oblast
17 Rovenskaja oblast
18 Sumskaja oblast
19 Ternopolskaja oblast
20 Vinnickaja oblast
21 Volynskaja oblast
22 Vorošilovgradskaja oblast
23 Zakarpatskaja oblast
24 Zaporožskaja oblast
25 Žitomirskaja oblast

Belorusskaja SSR
Byelorussian SSR

1 Brestskaja oblast
2 Gomelskaja oblast
3 Grodnenskaja oblast
4 Minskaja oblast
5 Mogilevskaja oblast
6 Vitebskaja oblast

Kazahskaja SSR
Kazakh SSR

1 Aktjubinskaja oblast
7 Gurjevskaja oblast
9 Kzyl-Ordinskaja oblast
11 Kustanajskaja oblast
12 Mangyšlakskaja oblast
18 Uralskaja oblast

Gruzinskaja SSR
Georgian SSR

1 Jugo-Osetinskaja avtonomnaja oblast

Azerbajdžanskaja SSR
Azerbaijan SSR

1 Nagorno-Karabahskaja avtonomnaja oblast

Turkmenskaja SSR
Turkmen SSR

1 Ašhabadskaja oblast
3 Krasnovodskaja oblast
5 Tašauzskaja oblast

© ISTITUTO GEOGRAFICO DE AGOSTINI S. p. A. - NOVARA

Map 17 THE URALS

SOJUZ SOVETSKIH SOCIALISTIČESKIH RESPUBLIK (SSSR)

UNION OF SOVIET SOCIALIST REPUBLICS

Rossijskaja Sovetskaja Federativnaja Socialističeskaja Respublika (RSFSR)

Russian Soviet Federated Socialist Republic

- 8 Arhangel'skaja oblast
- 8A Neneckí nac. okrug
- 12 Čeljabinskaja oblast
- 14 Gorkovskaja oblast
- 23 Kirovskaja oblast
- 24 Kostromskaja oblast
- 25 Kujbiševskaja oblast
- 26 Kurganskaja oblast
- 35 Omskaja oblast
- 36 Orenburgskaja oblast
- 39 Permskaja oblast
- 39A Komi-Permjacki nac. okrug
- 44 Saratovskaja oblast
- 46 Sverdlovskaja oblast
- 48 Tjumenskaja oblast
- 48A Hanty-Mansijski nac. okrug
- 48B Jamalo-Nenecki nac. okrug
- 51 Uljanovskaja oblast
- 54 Vologodskaja oblast

Kazahskaja SSR

Kazakh SSR

- 3 Celinogradskaja oblast
- 10 Kokčetavskaja oblast
- 11 Kustanajskaja oblast
- 15 Severo-Kazahstanskaja oblast
- 17 Turgajskaja oblast

Scale 1:6,000,000 Delisle Conic Equidistant Projection

0 100 200 300 400 km

0 100 200 miles

Longitude East 60 of Greenwich

A-570307-280

© ISTITUTO GEOGRAFICO DE AGOSTINI S. p. A. - NOVARA

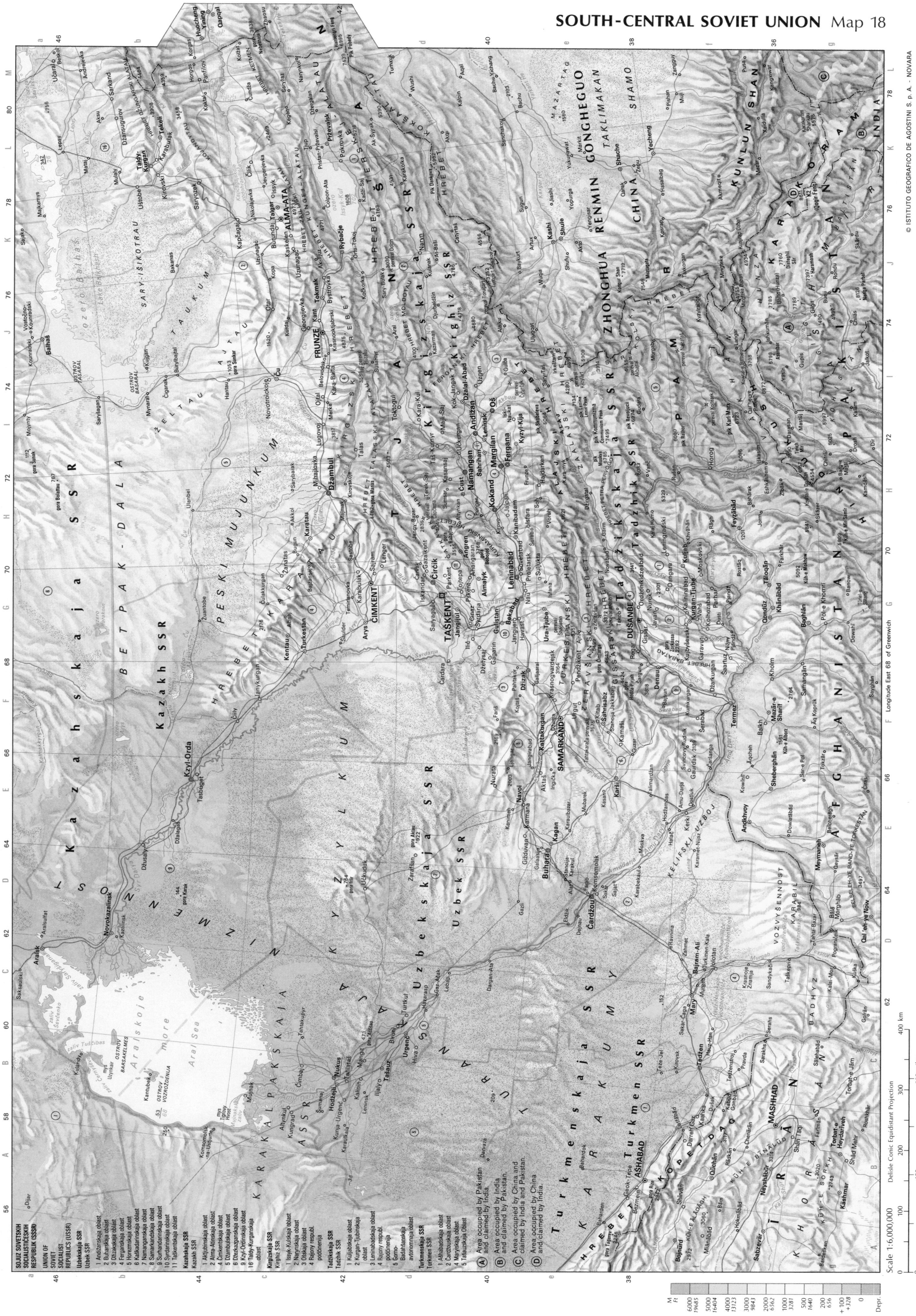
Kazahskaja SSR
Kazakh SSR
Uzbekskaja SSR
Uzbek SSR
Turkmenskaja SSR
Turkmen SSR
Tadžikskaja SSR
Tadzhik SSR
Kirgizskaja SSR
Kirghiz SSR
Aral'skoje more
Aral Sea
KYZYLKUM
KARAKUM
BETPAK-DALA
PESKI MUJUNKUM
ZHONGHUA RENMIN GONGHEGUO
CHINA
TAKLIMAKAN SHAMO
KUNLUN SHAN
KARAKORAM
AFGHANISTAN
IRAN
PAKISTAN
INDIA
ALMA-ATA
FRUNZE
TAŠKENT
DUŠANBE
SAMARKAND
AŠHABAD
MASHHAD
Scale 1:6,000,000
Delisle Conic Equidistant Projection
Longitude East 68 of Greenwich
© ISTITUTO GEOGRAFICO DE AGOSTINI S. p. A. - NOVARA

Map 19

SOJUZ SOVETSKIH SOCIALISTIČESKIH RESPUBLIK (SSSR)

UNION OF SOVIET SOCIALIST REPUBLICS (USSR)

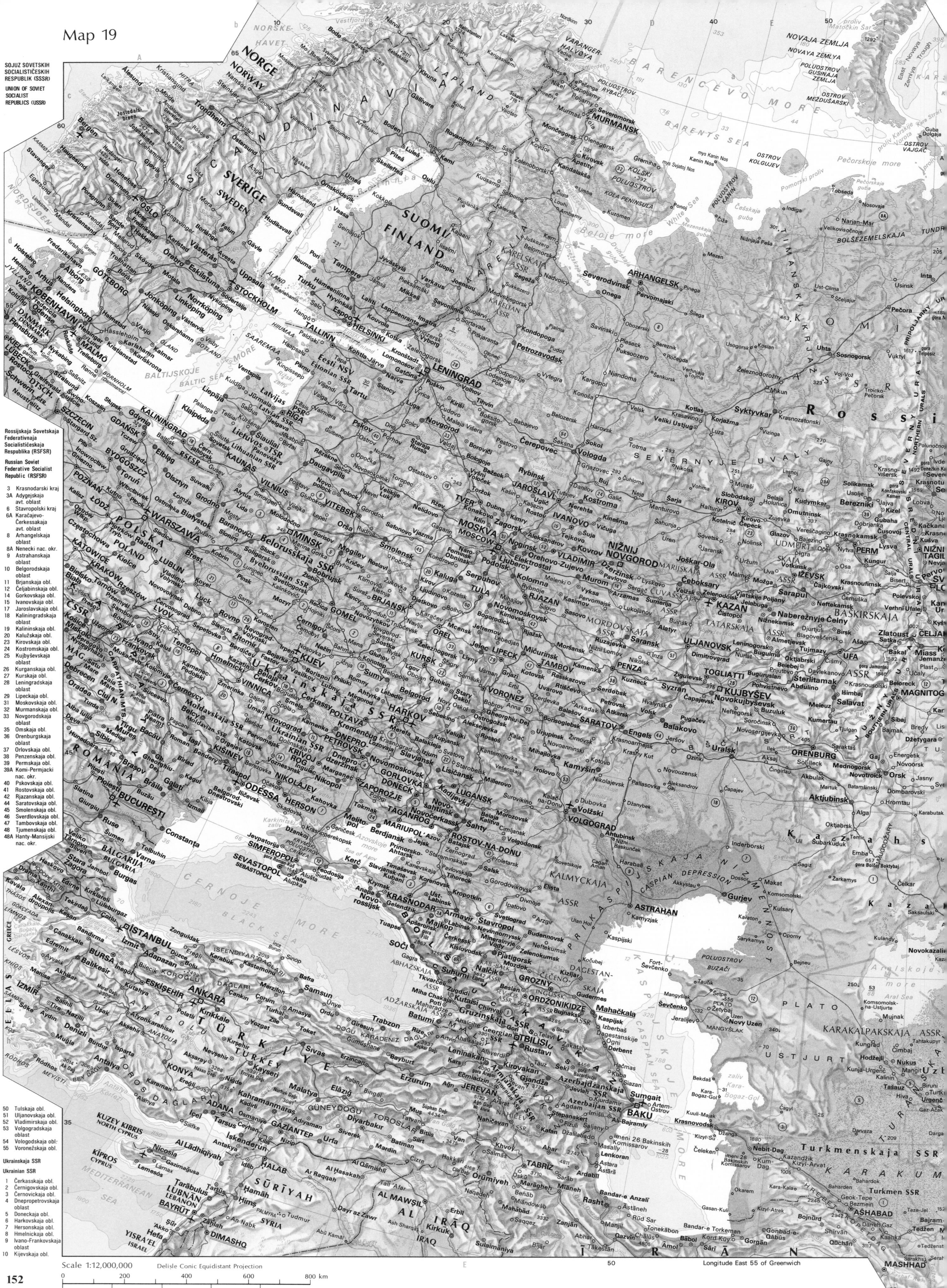

Rossijskaja Sovetskaja Federativnaja Socialističeskaja Respublika (RSFSR)

Russian Soviet Federative Socialist Republic (RSFSR)

3 Krasnodarski kraj
3A Adygejskaja avt. oblast
6 Stavropolski kraj
6A Karačajevo-Čerkesskaja avt. oblast
8 Arhangelskaja oblast
8A Nenecki nac. okr.
9 Astrahanskaja oblast
10 Belgorodskaja oblast
11 Brjanskaja obl.
12 Čeljabinskaja obl.
14 Gorkovskaja obl.
15 Ivanovskaja obl.
17 Jaroslavskaja obl.
18 Kaliningradskaja oblast
19 Kalininskaja obl.
20 Kalužskaja obl.
23 Kirovskaja obl.
24 Kostromskaja obl.
25 Kujbyševskaja oblast
26 Kurganskaja obl.
27 Kurskaja obl.
28 Leningradskaja oblast
29 Lipeckaja obl.
31 Moskovskaja obl.
32 Murmanskaja obl.
33 Novgorodskaja oblast
35 Omskaja oblast
36 Orenburgskaja oblast
37 Orlovskaja obl.
38 Penzenskaja obl.
39 Permskaja obl.
39A Komi-Permjacki nac. okr.
40 Pskovskaja obl.
41 Rostovskaja obl.
42 Rjazanskaja obl.
44 Saratovskaja obl.
45 Smolenskaja obl.
46 Sverdlovskaja obl.
47 Tambovskaja obl.
48 Tjumenskaja obl.
48A Hanty-Mansijski nac. okr.

50 Tulskaja obl.
51 Uljanovskaja obl.
52 Vladimirskaja obl.
53 Volgogradskaja oblast
54 Vologodskaja obl.
55 Voronežskaja obl.

Ukrainskaja SSR

Ukrainian SSR

1 Čerkasskaja obl.
2 Černigovskaja obl.
3 Černovickaja obl.
4 Dnepropetrovskaja obl.
5 Doneckaja obl.
6 Harkovskaja obl.
7 Hersonskaja obl.
8 Hmelnickaja obl.
9 Ivano-Frankovskaja oblast
10 Kijevskaja obl.

Scale 1:12,000,000 Delisle Conic Equidistant Projection

0 200 400 600 800 km

0 200 400 miles

Ukrainskaja SSR
Ukrainian SSR

11 Kirovogradskaja oblast
12 Krymskaja obl.
13 Lvovskaja obl.
14 Nikolajevskaja oblast
15 Odesskaja obl.
16 Poltavskaja obl.
17 Rovenskaja obl.
18 Sumskaja obl.
19 Ternopolskaja obl.
20 Vinnickaja obl.
21 Volynskaja obl.
22 Vorošilovgradskaja oblast
23 Zakarpatskaja obl.
24 Zaporožskaja obl.
25 Žitomirskaja obl.

Belorusskaja SSR
Byelorussian SSR

1 Brestskaja obl.
2 Gomelskaja obl.
3 Grodnenskaja obl.
4 Minskaja obl.
5 Mogilevskaja obl.
6 Vitebskaja obl.

Uzbekskaja SSR
Uzbek SSR

1 Andižanskaja obl.
2 Buharskaja obl.
3 Džizakskaja obl.
4 Ferganskaja obl.
5 Horezmskaja obl.
6 Kaškadarinskaja oblast
7 Namanganskaja oblast
8 Samarkandskaja oblast
9 Surhandarinskaja oblast
10 Syrdarinskaja obl.
11 Taškentskaja obl.

Kazahskaja SSR
Kazakh SSR

1 Aktjubinskaja obl.
2 Alma-Atinskaja oblast
3 Celinogradskaja oblast
4 Čimkentskaja obl.
5 Džambulskaja obl.
6 Džezkazganskaja oblast
7 Gurjevskaja obl.
8 Karagandinskaja oblast
9 Kzyl-Ordinskaja oblast
10 Kokčetavskaja oblast
11 Kustanajskaja obl.
12 Mangyšlakskaja oblast
13 Pavlodarskaja obl.
14 Semipalatinskaja oblast
15 Severo-Kazahstanskaja oblast
16 Taldy-Kurganskaja oblast
17 Turgajskaja obl.
18 Uralskaja obl.
19 Vostočno-Kazahstanskaja obl.

Gruzinskaja SSR
Georgian SSR

1 Jugo-Osetinskaja avt. oblast

Azerbajdžanskaja SSR
Azerbaijan SSR

1 Nagorno-Karabahskaja avt. oblast

Kirgizskaja SSR
Kirghiz SSR

1 Issyk-Kulskaja oblast
2 Narynskaja obl.
3 Ošskaja obl.
4 Rajony respubl. podčinenija

Tadžikskaja SSR
Tajik SSR

1 Kuljabskaja obl.
2 Kurgan-Tjubinskaja oblast
3 Leninabadskaja oblast
4 Rajony respubl. podčinenija
5 Gorno-Badahšanskaja avt. oblast

Turkmenskaja SSR
Turkmen SSR

1 Ašhabadskaja obl.
2 Čardžouskaja obl.
3 Krasnovodskaja oblast
4 Maryjskaja obl.
5 Tašauzskaja obl.

M / Ft
6000 / 19685
5000 / 16404
4000 / 13123
3000 / 9843
2000 / 6562
1000 / 3281
500 / 1640
+200 / +656
0
Depr. / 0
−100 / −328
200 / 656
1000 / 3281
2000 / 6562

Map 20

Scale 1:12,000,000 Delisle Conic Equidistant Projection

0 200 400 600 800 km

0 200 400 miles

SOJUZ SOVETSKIH SOCIALISTIČESKIH RESPUBLIK (SSSR)

UNION OF SOVIET SOCIALIST REPUBLICS (USSR)

Rossijskaja Sovetskaja Federativnaja Socialističeskaja Respublika (RSFSR)

Russian Soviet Federated Socialist Republic (RSFSR)

1 Altajski kraj
1A Gorno-Altajskaja avtonomnaja oblast
2 Habarovski kraj
2A Jevrejskaja avtonomnaja oblast
4 Krasnojarski kraj
4A Hakasskaja avtonomnaja oblast
4B Evenkijski nac. okrug
4C Tajmyrski (Dolgano-Nenecki) nac. okrug
5 Primorski kraj
7 Amurskaja oblast
8A Nenecki nac. okrug
13 Čitinskaja oblast
13A Aginski Burjatski nac. okrug
16 Irkutskaja oblast
16A Ust-Ordynski Burjatski nac. okrug
21 Kamčatskaja oblast
21A Korjakski nac. okrug
22 Kemerovskaja oblast
30 Magadanskaja oblast
30A Čukotski nac. okrug
34 Novosibirskaja oblast
35 Omskaja oblast
43 Sahalinskaja oblast
48 Tjumenskaja oblast
48A Hanty-Mansijski nac. okrug
48B Jamalo-Nenecki nac. okrug
49 Tomskaja oblast

Kazahskaja SSR

Kazakh SSR

13 Pavlodarskaja oblast
14 Semipalatinskaja oblast
19 Vostočno-Kazahstanskaja oblast

PACIFIC
OCEAN
ATLANTIC OCEAN
ALEUTIAN ISLANDS
Aleutian Trench
Kuril Trench
Japan Trench
KURIL ISLANDS
KAMCHATKA PENINSULA
SAKHALIN
SIHOTE-ALIN
HONSHU
HOKKAIDO
SHIKOKU
KYUSHU
KOREAN PEN.
MANCHURIA
GREATER KHINGAN RANGE
LESSER KHINGAN RANGE
STANOVOY RANGE
ALDAN PLATEAU
EASTERN SIBERIA
KOLYMA RANGE
KORJAKSKOJE NAGORJE
CHERSKI MOUNTAINS
VERKHOYANSK MOUNTAINS
LENA MOUNTAINS
CENTRAL SIBERIAN UPLANDS
PLATO SYVERMA
NORTH SIBERIAN PLAIN
TAYMYR PENINSULA
SEVERNAYA ZEMLYA
NEW SIBERIAN ISLANDS
ARCTIC OCEAN
Lomonosov Ridge
Makarov Basin
Eurasia Basin
Canada Basin
Alpha Cordillera
Nansen Cordillera
FRANZ JOSEPH LAND
NOVAYA ZEMLYA
SPITSBERGEN
GREENLAND
ICELAND
QUEEN ELIZABETH ISLANDS
ALASKA
ALASKA RANGE
BROOKS RANGE
ALEUTIAN RANGE
Bering Strait
Chukchi Sea
WEST SIBERIAN PLAIN
URAL MOUNTAINS
KAZAKH HILLS
TIAN SHAN
ALTAI
MONGOLIAN ALTAI
GOBI DESERT
GOBI ALTAI
KHANGAI MTS.
SAYAN
YENISEY RIDGE
Caspian Sea
CASPIAN DEPRESSION
CAUCASUS
ANATOLIA
TAURUS MTS.
Black Sea
Mediterranean Sea
UKRAINE
CENTRAL RUSSIAN UPLAND
VALDAI HILLS
SCANDINAVIA
LAPLAND
KARELIA
BRITISH ISLES
GREAT BRITAIN
IRELAND
North Sea
Norwegian Sea
Baltic Sea
ALPS
APENNINES
CARPATHIAN MTS.
BALKAN PENINSULA
POLAND
Reykjanes Ridge
Mid-Atlantic Ridge
Mohns Ridge
Limit of Icebergs
Summer limit of pack ice (August)
Winter limit of pack ice (April)

INDIAN OCEAN
Bay of Bengal
Arabian Sea
Arabian Basin
Somali Basin
Mascarene Basin
Madagascar Basin
Wharton Basin
Mid-Indian Basin
Ninetyeast Ridge
Mid-Indian Ridge
Southwest Indian Ridge
Broken Ridge
Java Trench
North Australian Basin
South China Sea
Equator
Tropic of Capricorn
Longitude East 80 of Greenwich
Scale 1:30,000,000
Lambert Azimuthal Equal Area Projection
© ISTITUTO GEOGRAFICO DE AGOSTINI S. p. A. - NOVARA

PACIFIC OCEAN
ALEUTIAN ISLANDS
Bering Sea
Sea of Okhotsk
Japan
KURIL ISLANDS
SAKHALIN
KAMCHATKA PENINSULA
Alaska (U.S.)
BROOKS RANGE
ALASKA RANGE
ALASKA PENINSULA
CANADA
VICTORIA
BANKS
MELVILLE
QUEEN ELIZABETH ISLANDS
ELLESMERE
DEVON
BAFFIN
Greenland (Den.)
KNUD RASMUSSEN LAND
ARCTIC OCEAN
North Pole
East Siberian Sea
Laptev Sea
Kara Sea
Barents Sea
Greenland Sea
Norwegian Sea
North Sea
ATLANTIC OCEAN
WRANGEL
NEW SIBERIAN ISLANDS
SEVERNAYA ZEMLYA
FRANZ JOSEPH LAND
NOVAYA ZEMLYA
Svalbard (Norway)
SPITSBERGEN
JAN MAYEN (Norway)
ICELAND
Reykjavík
FAEROE ISLANDS (Den.)
SHETLAND ISLANDS (U.K.)
ORKNEY ISLANDS
HEBRIDES
UNION OF SOVIET SOCIALIST REPUBLICS
VERKHOYANSK MOUNTAINS
CHERSKI MOUNTAINS
STANOVOY RANGE
YABLONOVY RANGE
CENTRAL SIBERIAN UPLANDS
WEST SIBERIAN PLAIN
TAYMYR PENINSULA
SAYAN MOUNTAINS
ALTAI
GOBI
MONGOLIA
Ulan-Bator
KAZAKHSTAN
MANCHURIA
KOREA
Jakutsk
Magadan
Irkutsk
Krasnojarsk
Novosibirsk
Omsk
Sverdlovsk
Murmansk
Arkhangelsk
Leningrad
Moskva (Moscow)
Kijev
Minsk
Vladivostok
Habarovsk
Sapporo
Tokyo
Yokohama
Nagoya
Osaka
Kyoto
Kobe
Beijing
Tianjin
Shenyang
Alma-Ata
Frunze
Taškent
Baku
Tbilisi
Jerevan
Volgograd
Astrahan
Odessa
Sevastopol
Black Sea
Caspian Sea
Mediterranean Sea
NORWAY
SWEDEN
FINLAND
Oslo
Stockholm
Helsinki
København
DENMARK
UNITED KINGDOM
IRELAND
Dublin
London
Edinburgh
Glasgow
FRANCE
Paris
BELGIUM
Bruxelles
NETHERLANDS
GERMANY
Berlin
Hamburg
POLAND
Warszawa
CZECHOSLOVAKIA
Praha
AUSTRIA
Wien
SWITZ.
HUNGARY
Budapest
ROMANIA
Bucureşti
YUGOSLAVIA
Beograd
BULGARIA
Sofija
ALBANIA
GREECE
Athínai
ITALY
Roma
Napoli
Milano
TURKEY
Ankara
İstanbul
SYRIA
Dimashq
LEBANON
Bayrūt
ISRAEL
JORDAN
IRAQ
CYPRUS
EGYPT
Al Qāhirah
Alexandria

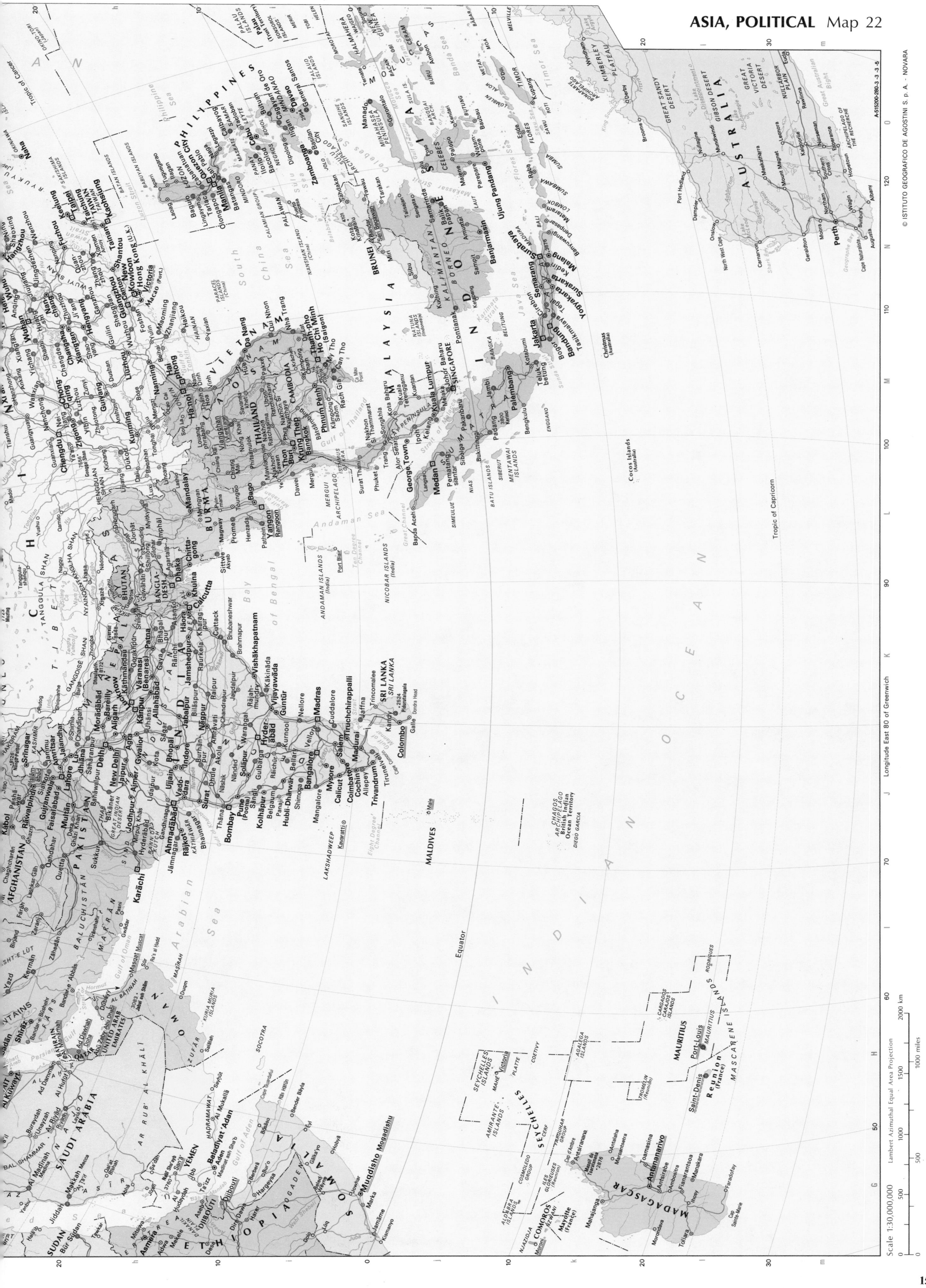
INDIAN OCEAN
INDIA
PAKISTAN
AFGHANISTAN
SAUDI ARABIA
YEMEN
OMAN
UNITED ARAB EMIRATES
QATAR
BAHRAIN
ETHIOPIA
SOMALIA
DJIBOUTI
SUDAN
MADAGASCAR
SEYCHELLES
MAURITIUS
COMOROS
MALDIVES
SRI LANKA
NEPAL
BHUTAN
BANGLADESH
BURMA
THAILAND
CAMBODIA
VIETNAM
LAOS
MALAYSIA
SINGAPORE
BRUNEI
INDONESIA
PHILIPPINES
TAIWAN
CHINA
TIBET
AUSTRALIA
Arabian Sea
Bay of Bengal
South China Sea
Andaman Sea
Java Sea
Timor Sea
Equator
Tropic of Capricorn
Longitude East 80 of Greenwich
Scale 1:30,000,000
Lambert Azimuthal Equal Area Projection
2000 km
1000 miles
A-51520-280-3-3-5

Scale 1:12,000,000 Delisle Conic Equidistant Projection

0 200 400 600 800 km

0 200 400 miles

AFGHANISTAN

VELĀYAT

1 Badakhshan
2 Bādghīsāt
3 Baghlān
4 Balkh
5 Bāmīān
6 Farāh
7 Fāryāb
8 Ghaznī
9 Ghowr
10 Helmand
11 Herāt
12 Jowzjān
13 Kābol
14 Kāpīsā
15 Konarha
16 Laghmān
17 Lowgar
18 Nangarhār
19 Nīmrūz
20 Orūzgān
21 Paktīā
22 Parvān
23 Qandahār
24 Qondūz
25 Samangān
26 Takhār
27 Vardak
28 Zābol

ĪRĀN

OSTĀN

1 Āzarbāijān-e Gharbī
2 Āzarbāijān-e Sharqī
3 Bakhtarān
4 Boyer Ahmadī-e Kohkīlūyeh
5 Būshehr
6 Chahār Mahāl-e Bakhtīārī
7 Esfahān
8 Fārs
9 Gīlān
10 Hamadān
11 Hormozgān
12 Īlām
13 Kermān
14 Khorāsān
15 Khūzestān
16 Kordestān
17 Lorestān
18 Markazī
19 Māzandarān
20 Semnān
21 Sīstān-e Balūchestān
22 Yazd
23 Zanjān

Scale 1:6,000,000 Delisle Conic Equidistant Projection

0 100 200 300 400 km

0 100 200 miles

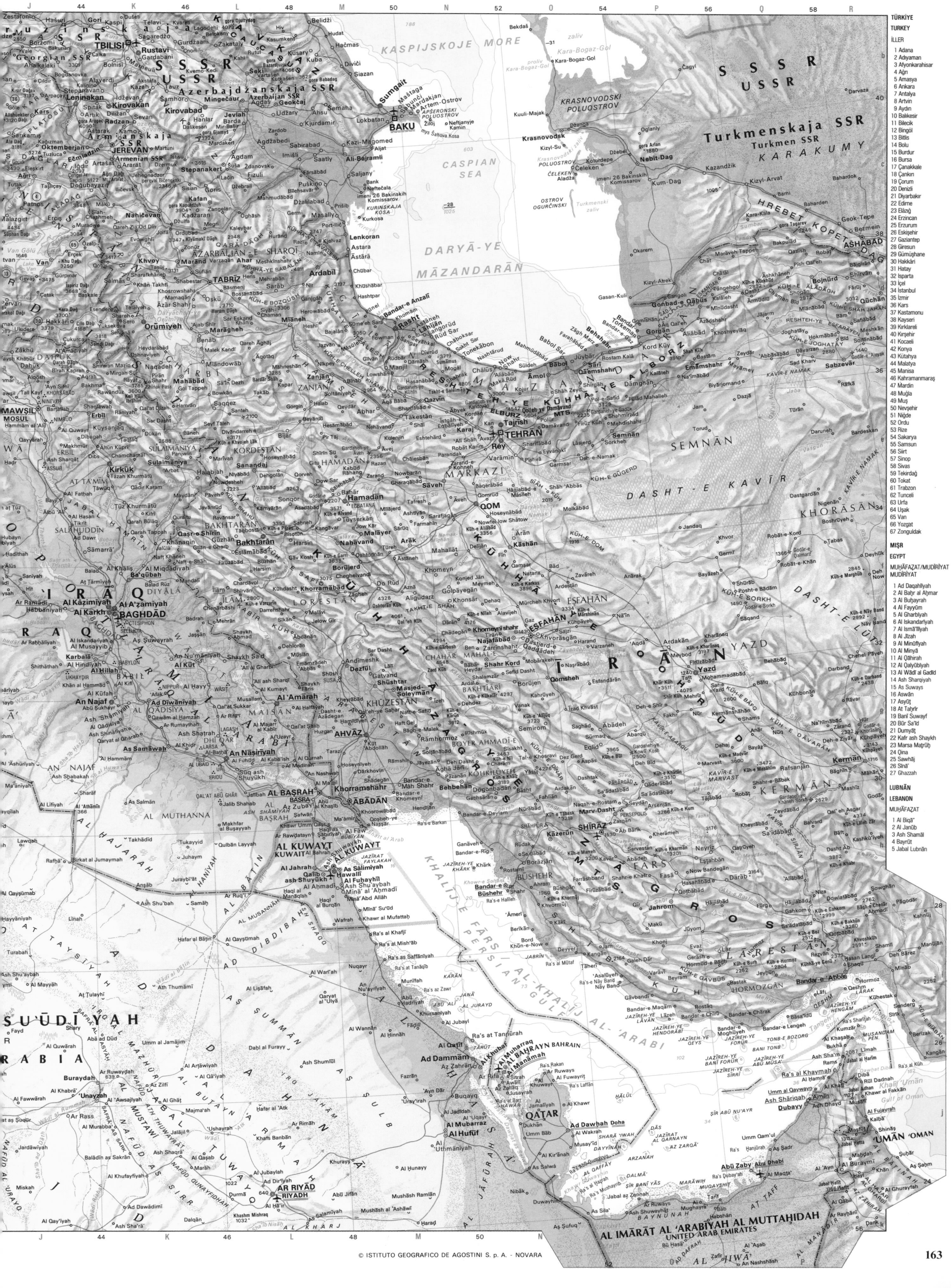
TÜRKİYE
TURKEY
İLLER
1 Adana
2 Adıyaman
3 Afyonkarahisar
4 Ağrı
5 Amasya
6 Ankara
7 Antalya
8 Artvin
9 Aydın
10 Balıkesir
11 Bilecik
12 Bingöl
13 Bitlis
14 Bolu
15 Burdur
16 Bursa
17 Çanakkale
18 Çankırı
19 Çorum
20 Denizli
21 Diyarbakır
22 Edirne
23 Elâzığ
24 Erzincan
25 Erzurum
26 Eskişehir
27 Gaziantep
28 Giresun
29 Gümüşhane
30 Hakkâri
31 Hatay
32 Isparta
33 İçel
34 İstanbul
35 İzmir
36 Kars
37 Kastamonu
38 Kayseri
39 Kırklareli
40 Kırşehir
41 Kocaeli
42 Konya
43 Kütahya
44 Malatya
45 Manisa
46 Kahramanmaraş
47 Mardin
48 Muğla
49 Muş
50 Nevşehir
51 Niğde
52 Ordu
53 Rize
54 Sakarya
55 Samsun
56 Siirt
57 Sinop
58 Sivas
59 Tekirdağ
60 Tokat
61 Trabzon
62 Tunceli
63 Urfa
64 Uşak
65 Van
66 Yozgat
67 Zonguldak
MIŞR
EGYPT
MUḤĀFAẒAT/MUDĪRĪYAT
MUDĪRĪYAT
1 Ad Daqahlīyah
2 Al Baḩr al Aḩmar
3 Al Buḩayrah
4 Al Fayyūm
5 Al Gharbīyah
6 Al Iskandarīyah
7 Al Ismā'īlīyah
8 Al Jīzah
9 Al Minūfīyah
10 Al Minyā
11 Al Qāhirah
12 Al Qalyūbīyah
13 Al Wādī al Gadīd
14 Ash Sharqiyah
15 As Suways
16 Aswān
17 Asyūţ
18 At Taḩrīr
19 Banī Suwayf
20 Būr Sa'īd
21 Dumyāţ
22 Kafr ash Shaykh
23 Marsa Maţrūḩ
24 Qina
25 Sawhāj
26 Sīnā'
27 Ghazzah
LUBNĀN
LEBANON
MUḤĀFAẒAT
1 Al Biqā'
2 Al Janūb
3 Ash Shamāl
4 Bayrūt
5 Jabal Lubnān
SSSR
USSR
Turkmenskaja SSR
Turkmen SSR
KARAKUMY
KASPIJSKOJE MORE
CASPIAN SEA
DARYĀ-YE MĀZANDARĀN
Azerbajdžanskaja SSR
Azerbaijan SSR
Armjanskaja SSR
Armenian SSR
Gruzinskaja SSR
Georgian SSR
BAKU
TBILISI
JEREVAN
IRĀN
TEHRĀN
ESFAHĀN
SHĪRĀZ
DASHT-E KAVĪR
KŪHHĀ-YE ALBORZ
KŪHHĀ-YE ZĀGROS
IRAQ
BAGHDĀD
AL BAŞRAH
AL KUWAYT
KUWAIT
AL BAḨRAYN
BAHRAIN
QAŢAR
AL IMĀRĀT AL 'ARABĪYAH AL MUTTAḨIDAH
UNITED ARAB EMIRATES
AS SU'ŪDĪYAH
ARABIA
AR RIYĀḌ
RIYADH
KHALĪJ-E FĀRS
PERSIAN GULF
AL KHALĪJ AL 'ARABĪ
Gulf of Oman
'UMĀN
OMAN

Map 25

AFGHANISTAN

VELĀYAT

1 Badakhshān
2 Bādghīsāt
3 Baghlān
4 Balkh
5 Bāmīān
6 Farāh
7 Fāryāb
8 Ghaznī
9 Ghowr
10 Helmand
11 Herāt
12 Jowzjān
13 Kābol
14 Kāpīsā
15 Konarha
16 Laghmān
17 Lowgar
18 Nangarhār
19 Nimrūz
20 Orūzgān
21 Paktīā
22 Parvān
23 Qandahār
24 Qonduz
25 Samangān
26 Takhār
27 Vardak
28 Zābol

Scale 1:12,000,000 Delisle Conic Equidistant Projection

0 200 400 600 800 km

0 200 400 miles

ZHONGHUA RENMIN GONGHEGUO
CHINA
GAOYUAN
PLATEAU OF TIBET
Xizang Zizhiqu
Tibet
TANGGULA (DANGLA) SHAN
NYAINQENTANGLHA SHAN
HENGDUAN SHAN
BAYAN HAR SHAN
QAIDAM PENDI
SICHUAN PENDI
YUNGUI GAOYUAN
Guangxi Zhuangzu Zizhiqu
Kwangsi
HIMALAYA
Arunāchal Pradesh
DRUK BHUTAN
BANGLADESH
West Bengal
Assam
Kachin
Shan
Chin
MYANMAR BURMA
ARAKAN
MUANG THAI THAILAND
KAMPUCHEA CAMBODIA
VIET-NAM
LAOS
MALAYSIA
MALAY PENINSULA
SUMATERA SUMATRA
INDONESIA
SINGAPURA SINGAPORE
BAY OF BENGAL
Andaman Basin
ANDAMAN ISLANDS
NICOBAR ISLANDS
ANDAMAN AND NICOBAR (India)
Gulf of Thailand
Ao Thai
Gulf of Tonkin
Vinh Bac Phan
BIEN DONG
SOUTH CHINA SEA
LAUT CINA SELATAN
HAINAN DAO
MEKONG DELTA
Mouths of the Ganges
Mouths of the Ayeyarwady
Gulf of Martaban
MERGUI ARCHIPELAGO
CHENGDU
CHONGQING
KUNMING
GUIYANG
NANNING
WUHAN
CHANGSHA
GUANGZHOU CANTON
LANZHOU
XI'AN
ZHENGZHOU
Lhasa
DHAKA
CALCUTTA
CHITTAGONG
MANDALAY
YANGON RANGOON
KRUNG THEP BANGKOK
Viangchan (Vientiane)
HA NOI
HAI PHONG
DA NANG
PHNUM PENH
THANH-PHO HO CHI MINH (SAIGON)
KUALA LUMPUR
GEORGE TOWN (PINANG)
MEDAN
Johor Baharu
Banda Aceh
Phuket
MACAU
OCEAN
A-569295-780-1 -1 -2 -3

MALAYSIA
Semenanjung Malaysia
WILAYAH PERSEKUTUAN
A Kuala Lumpur
NEGERI
1 Johor
2 Kedah
3 Kelantan
4 Melaka
5 Negeri Sembilan
6 Pahang
7 Perak
8 Perlis
9 Pulau Pinang
10 Selangor
11 Terengganu

M	Ft
5000	16404
4000	13123
3000	9843
2000	6562
1000	3281
500	1640
+ 200	+ 656
0	0
−100	−328
200	656
1000	3281
2000	6562
4000	13123
6000	19685
8000	26247

Scale 1:12,000,000 at the Equator   Mercator Cylindrical Projection

0 200 400 600 800 km
0 200 400 miles

Longitude East 110 of Greenwich

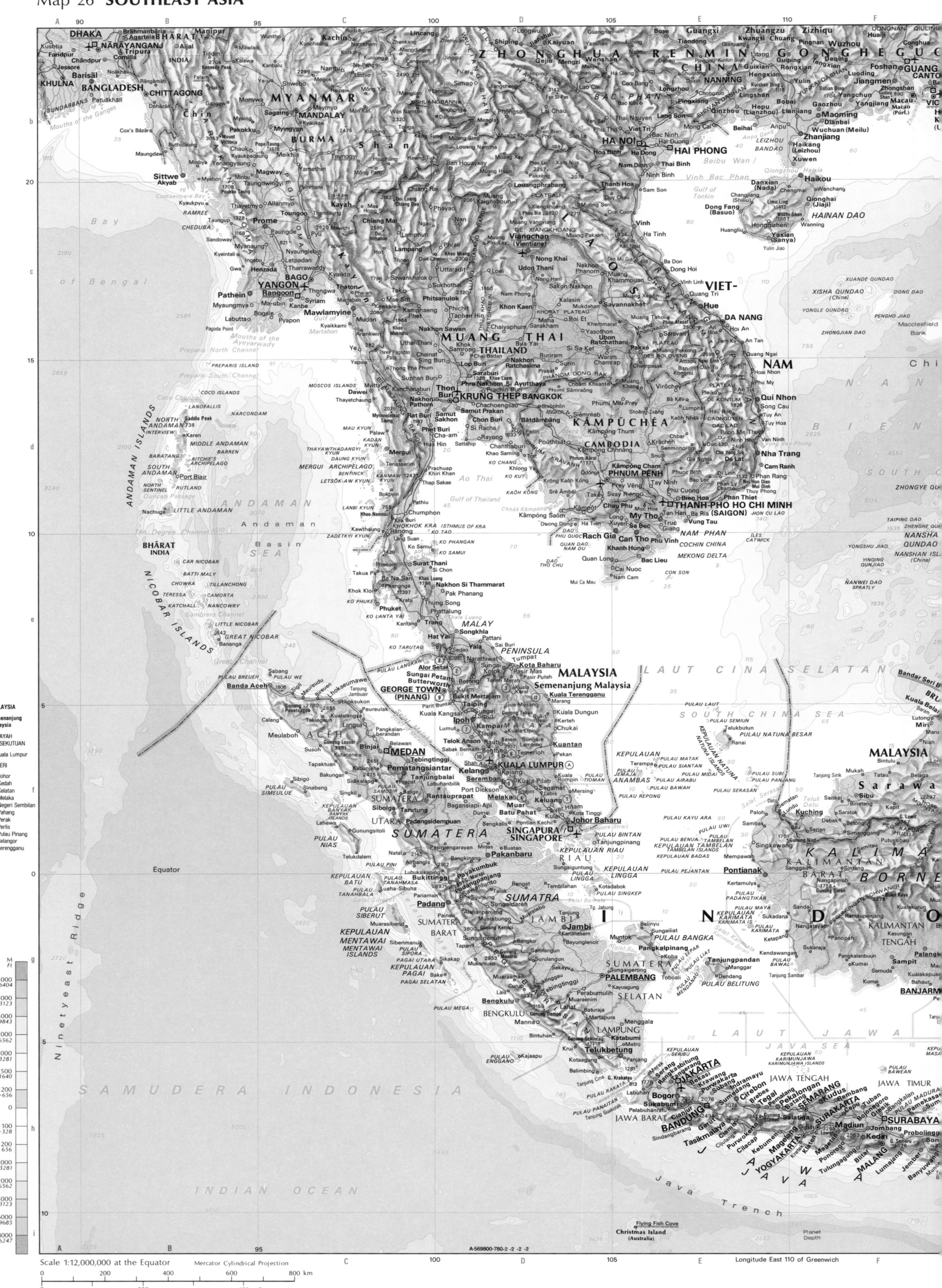

TAIWAN
Taoyuan
KEELUNG
TAIPEI
Hsinchu
TAICHUNG
Changhua
Hualien
CHIAYI
TAINAN
KAOHSIUNG
Pingtung
Xiamen Amoy
Quanzhou
Zhangzhou
SHANTOU
NIPPON JAPAN
Tropic of Cancer
Bashi Channel
Luzon Strait
BATAN ISLANDS
Balintang Channel
BABUYAN ISLANDS
Laoag
Vigan
Tuguegarao
San Fernando
Baguio
LUZON
Dagupan
Tarlac
Cabanatuan
Angeles
Olongapo
MANILA
QUEZON CITY
POLILLO ISLANDS
PILIPINAS
PHILIPPINES
CATANDUANES
San Pablo
Batangas
Lipa
Naga
Legazpi
Sorsogon
MINDORO
Sibuyan Sea
Calbayog
SAMAR
Masbate
MASBATE
PANAY
Roxas
Iloilo
Bacolod
Cadiz
NEGROS
CEBU
San Carlos
Tacloban
LEYTE
Ormoc
BOHOL
Dumaguete
Surigao
Butuan
Cagayan de Oro
Iligan
Dipolog
Ozamiz
Pagadian
Malaybalay
Marawi
Cotabato
DAVAO
MINDANAO
ZAMBOANGA
Basilan City
Isabela
Jolo
General Santos
Cape San Agustin
SULU ARCHIPELAGO
Sulu Basin
SULU SEA
PALAWAN
Puerto Princesa
CALAMIAN GROUP
Sandakan
Sabah
Tawau
Tarakan
LAUT SULAWESI
Celebes Basin
CELEBES SEA
SULAWESI UTARA
Manado
Tondano
Gorontalo
MINAHASSA
Palu
SULAWESI TENGAH
SULAWESI CELEBES
Samarinda
Balikpapan
KALIMANTAN
Palopo
Kendari
SULAWESI TENGGARA
SULAWESI SELATAN
Watampone
UJUNG PANDANG (MAKASAR)
Baubau
Philippine Trench
PHILIPPINE SEA
Philippine Basin
PACIFIC OCEAN
Kyushu-Palau Ridge
OKINO-TORI-SHIMA PARECE VELA (Japan)
West Mariana Basin
FEDERATED STATES OF MICRONESIA
ULITHI ATOLL
YAP ISLANDS
Colonia
NGULU ATOLL
SOROL ATOLL
Yap Trench
KAYANGEL ISLANDS
BABELTHUAP
Koror
PALAU ISLANDS
ANGAUR
PELELIU
CAROLINE ISLANDS
Palau
Belau
(Trust Territory)
West Caroline Basin
SONSOROL ISLANDS
PULO ANNA
MERIR
TOBI
HELEN REEF
KEPULAUAN TALAUD
KEPULAUAN SANGIHE
PULAU MOROTAI
HALMAHERA
Ternate
Tidore
MOLUCCA SEA
MALUKU
KEPULAUAN ASIA
KEPULAUAN MAPIA
PULAU WAIGEO
Sorong
Equator
Manokwari
PULAU BIAK
PULAU YAPEN
New Guinea Trench
Jayapura
IRIAN JAYA
PEGUNUNGAN MAOKE
Puncak Jaya
Wamena
Fakfak
SERAM CERAM
LAUT SERAM
Ambon
PULAU BURU
KEPULAUAN SULA
KEPULAUAN OBI
LAUT BANDA
BANDA SEA
KEPULAUAN KAI
KEPULAUAN ARU
Aru Basin
PULAU IRIAN
Agats
PULAU DOLAK
Merauke
PULAU KOMORAN
KEPULAUAN TANIMBAR
Saumlaki
PULAU WETAR
TIMOR
Kupang
Timor Trough
LAUT TIMOR
TIMOR SEA
LAUT ARAFURA
ARAFURA SEA
FLORES
Ende
PULAU SUMBA
NUSA TENGGARA TIMUR
NUSA TENGGARA BARAT
PULAU SUMBAWA
Mataram
Praya
Bima
SAVU SEA
PULAU SAWU
PULAU ROTI
PAPUA NEW GUINEA
Torres Strait
Darwin
AUSTRALIA
MELVILLE ISLAND
BATHURST ISLAND
Cape Wessel
Nhulunbuy

© ISTITUTO GEOGRAFICO DE AGOSTINI S. p. A. - NOVARA

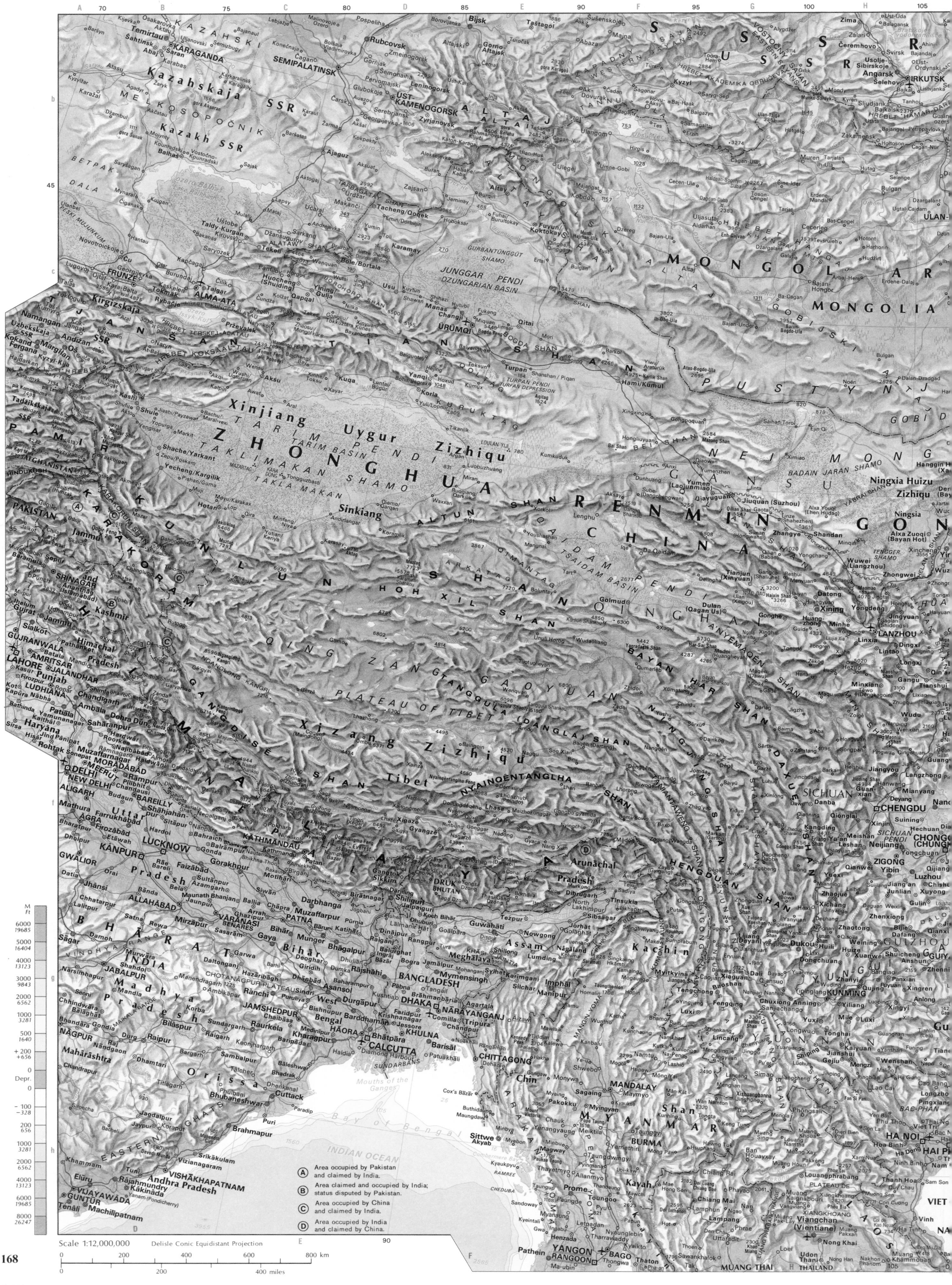
ZHONGHUA RENMIN GONGHEGUO
CHINA
MONGOLIA
MONGOL ARD ULS
Xinjiang Uygur Zizhiqu
Xizang Zizhiqu
Tibet
Sinkiang
Ningxia Huizu Zizhiqu
NEI MONGOL
GANSU
QINGHAI
SICHUAN
GUIZHOU
YUNNAN
Kazahskaja SSR
Kazakh SSR
Kirgizskaja SSR
Uzbekskaja SSR
Tadžikskaja SSR
S S S R
U S S R
AFGHANISTAN
PAKISTAN
Jammu and Kashmir
BHARAT
INDIA
NEPAL
BHUTAN
DRUK
BANGLADESH
MYANMAR
BURMA
LAOS
VIET NAM
MUANG THAI
THAILAND
HIMALAYA
KARAKORAM
KUNLUN SHAN
TIAN SHAN
ALTAJ
MONGOL ALTAJ
GOBI
TARIM PENDI
TARIM BASIN
TAKLIMAKAN SHAMO
TAKLA MAKAN
JUNGGAR PENDI
DZUNGARIAN BASIN
QAIDAM PENDI
TSAIDAM BASIN
QING ZANG GAOYUAN
PLATEAU OF TIBET
TURPAN PENDI
TURPAN DEPRESSION
BADAIN JARAN SHAMO
HENGDUAN SHAN
DAXUE SHAN
BAYAN HAR SHAN
GANGDISE SHAN
NYAINQENTANGLHA SHAN
TANGGULA (DANGLA) SHAN
HOH XIL SHAN
ALTUN SHAN
Bay of Bengal
INDIAN OCEAN
Mouths of the Ganges
BEIJING
ÜRÜMQI
LANZHOU
CHENGDU
KUNMING
Lhasa
KATHMANDU
DHAKA
CALCUTTA
NEW DELHI
DELHI
LAHORE
MANDALAY
YANGON
RANGOON
HA NOI
IRKUTSK
ALMA-ATA
FRUNZE
SEMIPALATINSK
KARAGANDA
UST-KAMENOGORSK
A Area occupied by Pakistan and claimed by India.
B Area claimed and occupied by India; status disputed by Pakistan.
C Area occupied by China and claimed by India.
D Area occupied by India and claimed by China.
Scale 1:12,000,000
Delisle Conic Equidistant Projection
0 200 400 600 800 km
0 200 400 miles
M Ft
6000 19685
5000 16404
4000 13123
3000 9843
2000 6562
1000 3281
500 1640
+200 +656
0
Depr.
0
-100 -328
200 656
1000 3281
2000 6562
4000 13123
6000 19685
8000 26247

ZHONGHUA
RENMIN
GONGHEGUO
CHINA
1 Beijing Shi
2 Shanghai Shi
3 Tianjin Shi
Longitude East 120 of Greenwich
NIPPON
JAPAN
CHOSŎN M.I.K.
NORTH KOREA
TAEHAN-MIN'GUK
SOUTH KOREA
TAIWAN
PHILIPPINES
PILIPINAS
Rossijskaja SFSR
Russian SFSR
Nei Mongol Zizhiqu
Inner Mongolia
BEIJING PEKING
SHANGHAI
TIANJIN
(TIENTSIN)
P'YŎNGYANG
SEOUL SŎUL
TŌKYŌ
VLADIVOSTOK
HARBIN
SHENYANG
DALIAN
QINGDAO
(TSINGTAO)
NANJING (NANKING)
WUHAN
GUANGZHOU
CANTON
NEW KOWLOON
VICTORIA
Hong Kong (U.K.)
MACAU
Macao
(Port.)
Japan Basin
SEA OF JAPAN
HUANG HAI / HWANG-HAE
YELLOW SEA
DONG HAI / HIGASHI-SHINA-KAI
EAST CHINA SEA
NAN HAI
SOUTH CHINA SEA
South China Basin
PHILIPPINE SEA
Philippine Basin
PACIFIC OCEAN
Tropic of Cancer
Shikoku Basin
Nankai Trough
Ryukyu Trench
RYUKYU ISLANDS
NANSEI-SHOTŌ
Kyushu-Palau Ridge
South Honshu Ridge
Bonin Trench
A-569700-780-1 -1 -2 -3

NORTHEASTERN CHINA, KOREA AND JAPAN

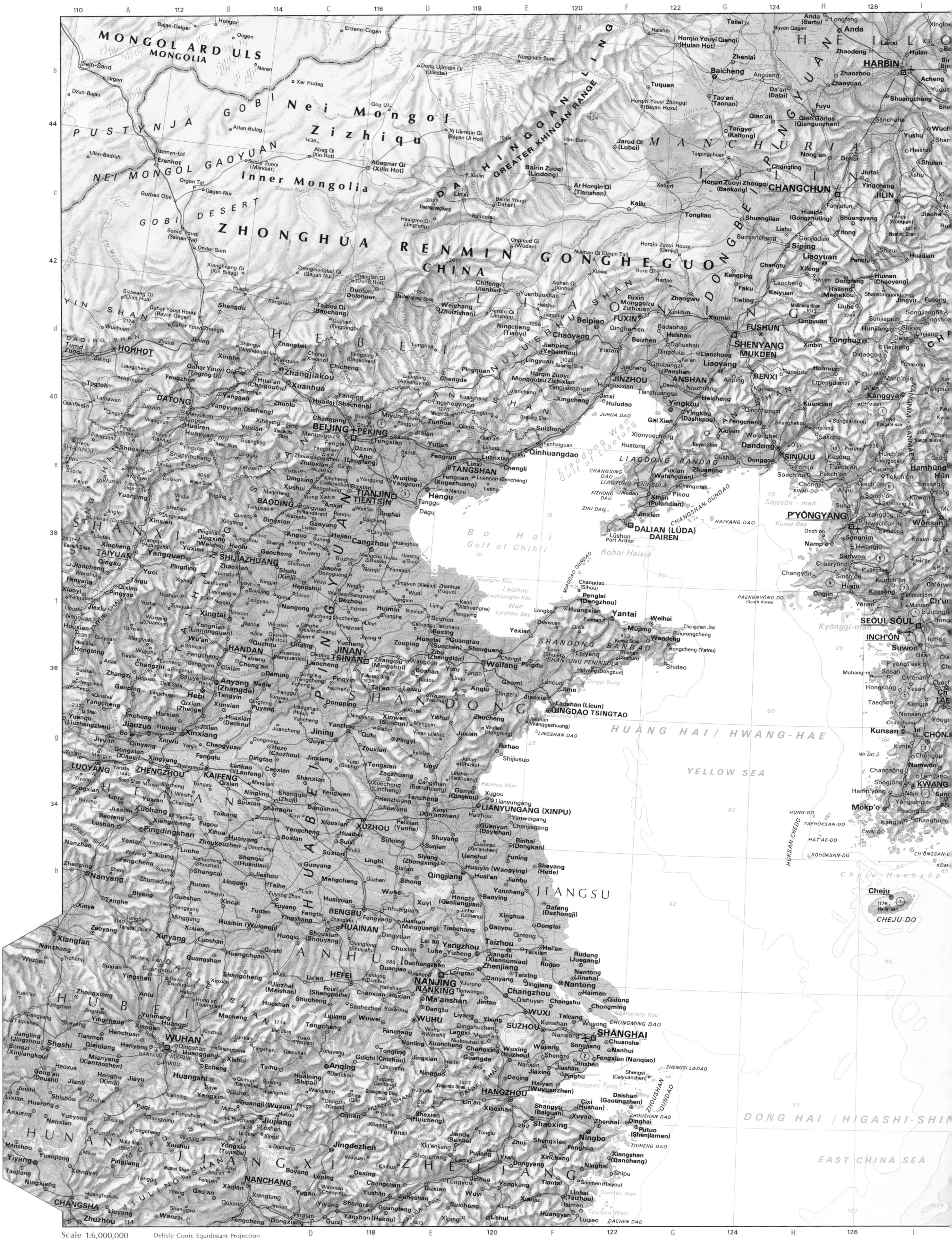

Scale 1:6,000,000 Delisle Conic Equidistant Projection

0 100 200 300 400 km

0 100 200 miles

NIPPON
JAPAN
HONSHŪ
HOKKAIDŌ
SHIKOKU
KYŪSHŪ
CHOSŎN M.I.K.
NORTH KOREA
TAEHAN-MIN'GUK
SOUTH KOREA
USSR
Japan Basin
JAPONSKOJE MORE/
TONG-HAE / NIPPON-KAI
SEA OF JAPAN
Yamato Rise
OHOTSKOJE MORE/
HOK-KAI
SEA OF OKHOTSK
KURILSKIJE OSTROVA/
CHISHIMA-RETTŌ
KURIL ISLANDS
(U.S.S.R.)
OSTROV SAHALIN
SAKHALIN
(U.S.S.R.)
Japan Trench
Bonin Trench
Nankai Trench
Shikoku Basin
South Honshu Ridge
IZU-SHOTŌ
TAIHEIYŌ
PACIFIC OCEAN
TOKYO
YOKOHAMA
KAWASAKI
CHIBA
NAGOYA
KYOTO
ŌSAKA
KŌBE
HIROSHIMA
FUKUOKA
KITAKYŪSHŪ
KAGOSHIMA
NAGASAKI
SAPPORO
HAKODATE
AOMORI
SENDAI
NIIGATA
KANAZAWA
VLADIVOSTOK
CH'ŎNGJIN
PUSAN
ULSAN
Longitude East 130 of Greenwich
NIPPON
JAPAN
1 Hokkaidō Ken
2 Aomori Ken
3 Iwate Ken
4 Miyagi Ken
5 Akita Ken
6 Yamagata Ken
7 Fukushima Ken
8 Ibaraki Ken
9 Tochigi Ken
10 Gunma Ken
11 Saitama Ken
12 Chiba Ken
13 Tokyō To
14 Kanagawa Ken
15 Niigata Ken
16 Toyama Ken
17 Ishikawa Ken
18 Fukui Ken
19 Yamanashi Ken
20 Nagano Ken
21 Gifu Ken
22 Shizuoka Ken
23 Aichi Ken
24 Mie Ken
25 Shiga Ken
26 Kyōto Fu
27 Ōsaka Fu
28 Hyōgo Ken
29 Nara Ken
30 Wakayama Ken
31 Tottori Ken
32 Shimane Ken
33 Okayama Ken
34 Hiroshima Ken
35 Yamaguchi Ken
36 Tokushima Ken
37 Kagawa Ken
38 Ehime Ken
39 Kōchi Ken
40 Fukuoka Ken
41 Saga Ken
42 Nagasaki Ken
43 Kumamoto Ken
44 Ōita Ken
45 Miyazaki Ken
46 Kagoshima Ken
CHOSŎN M.I.K.
NORTH KOREA
1 Chagang-Do
2 Ch'ŏngjin Si
3 Hamgyŏng-Namdo
4 Hamgyŏng-Pukto
5 Hwanghae-Namdo
6 Hwanghae-Pukto
7 Kaesŏng Si
8 Kangwŏn-Do
9 P'yŏngan-Namdo
10 P'yŏngan-Pukto
11 P'yŏngyang Si
12 Yanggang-Do
TAEHAN-MIN'GUK
SOUTH KOREA
1 Cheju-Do
2 Chŏlla-Namdo
3 Chŏlla-Pukto
4 Ch'ungch'ŏng-Namdo
5 Ch'ungch'ŏng-Pukto
6 Kangwŏn-Do
7 Kyŏnggi-Do
8 Kyŏngsang-Namdo
9 Kyŏngsang-Pukto
10 Pusan Si
11 Sŏul Si
ZHONGHUA RENMIN GONGHEGUO
CHINA
1 Beijing Shi
2 Shanghai Shi
3 Tianjin Shi
M Ft
3000 9843
2000 6562
1000 3281
500 1640
200 656
+100 +328
0
−100 −328
200 656
1000 3281
2000 6562
4000 13123
6000 19685
8000 26247
Ⓐ Ostrov Kunašir, ostrov Iturup and Malaja Kurilskaja Grjada, occupied by the U.S.S.R. since 1945, are claimed by Japan pending a final peace treaty.

Longitude East 144 of Greenwich
OHOTSKOJE MORE
HOK-KAI
SEA OF OKHOTSK
NIPPON-KAI
SEA OF JAPAN
Ostrov Kunašir, ostrov Iturup and Malaja Kurilskaja Grjada, occupied by the U.S.S.R. since 1945, are claimed by Japan pending a final peace treaty.
KURILSKIJE OSTROVA/ CHISHIMA-RETTŌ KURIL ISLANDS
OSTROV ITURUP/ ETOROFU-TŌ
OSTROV KUNAŠIR/ KUNASHIRI-TŌ
OSTROV ŠIKOTAN/ SHIKOTAN-TŌ
MALAJA KURILSKAJA GRJADA/ HABOMAI-SHOTŌ
SSSR
USSR
HOKKAIDŌ
Wakkanai
Asahikawa
SAPPORO
Otaru
Muroran
Hakodate
Obihiro
Kushiro
Abashiri
Nemuro
Kitami
KITA-TAIHEIYŌ
PACIFIC OCEAN
HONSHŪ
AOMORI
Oki Ridge
Oki Trench
OKI-SHOTŌ
TAEHAN-MIN'GUK SOUTH KOREA
PUSAN
TSUSHIMA
Korea Strait
FUKUOKA
KITAKYŪSHŪ
SHIMONOSEKI
NAGASAKI
KUMAMOTO
KAGOSHIMA
Miyazaki
KYŪSHŪ
HIROSHIMA
OKAYAMA
MATSUYAMA
TAKAMATSU
KŌCHI
SHIKOKU
KYŌTO
KŌBE
ŌSAKA
WAKAYAMA
HIMEJI
Tottori
Matsue
CHŪGOKU-SANCHI
SHIKOKU-SANCHI
HIGASHI-SHINA KAI
EAST CHINA SEA
Nankai Trough
Scale 1:3,000,000
Delisle Conic Equidistant Projection
0 50 100 150 200 km
0 50 100 miles

NIPPON
JAPAN
1 Hokkaidō Ken
2 Aomori Ken
3 Iwate Ken
4 Miyagi Ken
5 Akita Ken
6 Yamagata Ken
7 Fukushima Ken
8 Ibaraki Ken
9 Tochigi Ken
10 Gunma Ken
11 Saitama Ken
12 Chiba Ken
13 Tōkyō To
14 Kanagawa Ken
15 Niigata Ken
16 Toyama Ken
17 Ishikawa Ken
18 Fukui Ken
19 Yamanashi Ken
20 Nagano Ken
21 Gifu Ken
22 Shizuoka Ken
23 Aichi Ken
24 Mie Ken
25 Shiga Ken
26 Kyōto Fu
27 Ōsaka Fu
28 Hyōgo Ken
29 Nara Ken
30 Wakayama Ken
31 Tottori Ken
32 Shimane Ken
33 Okayama Ken
34 Hiroshima Ken
35 Yamaguchi Ken
36 Tokushima Ken
37 Kagawa Ken
38 Ehime Ken
39 Kōchi Ken
40 Fukuoka Ken
41 Saga Ken
42 Nagasaki Ken
43 Kumamoto Ken
44 Ōita Ken
45 Miyazaki Ken
46 Kagoshima Ken
47 Okinawa Ken

URAL MOUNTAINS
CAUCASUS
Caspian Sea
Black Sea
CARPATHIAN MTS.
PYRENEES
IBERIAN PENINSULA
BRITISH ISLES
GREAT BRITAIN
IRELAND
ICELAND
LIBYAN DESERT
AHAGGAR
TIBESTI
ETHIOPIAN PLATEAU
CANARY ISLANDS
MADEIRA ISLANDS
AZORES
CAPE VERDE ISLANDS
Tropic of Cancer
Arctic Circle

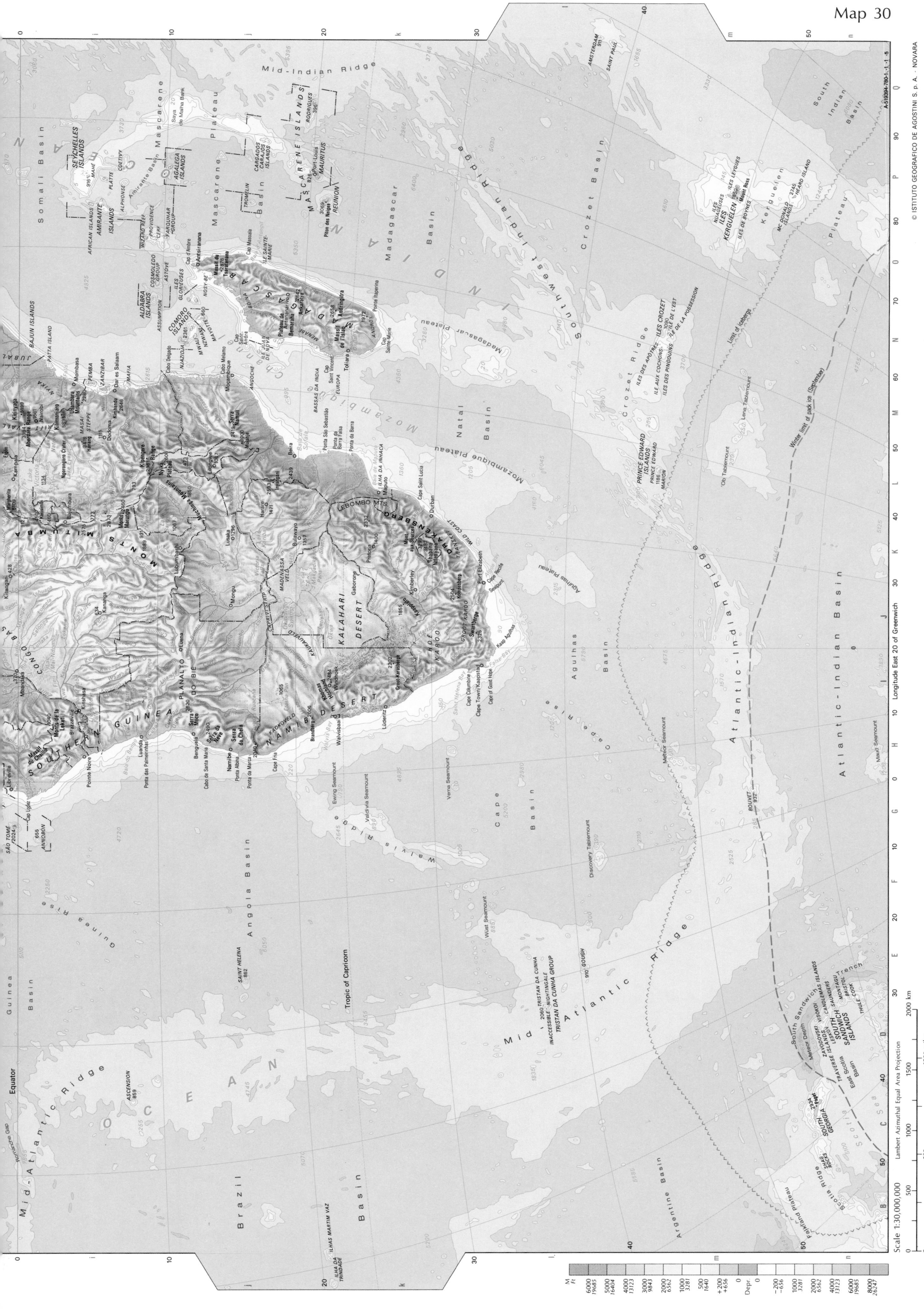
Mid-Atlantic Ridge
Equator
Guinea Basin
Guinea Rise
Angola Basin
Brazil Basin
Cape Basin
Agulhas Basin
Agulhas Plateau
Walvis Ridge
Cape Rise
Mid Atlantic Ridge
Atlantic-Indian Ridge
Atlantic-Indian Basin
Argentine Basin
Scotia Ridge
Scotia Sea
East Scotia Basin
South Sandwich Trench
Falkland Plateau
Tropic of Capricorn
OCEAN
ASCENSION
SAINT HELENA
TRISTAN DA CUNHA GROUP
GOUGH
BOUVET
SOUTH GEORGIA
SOUTH SANDWICH ISLANDS
ILHAS MARTIN VAZ
ILHA DA TRINDADE
SÃO TOMÉ
ANNOBON
Discovery Tablemount
Meteor Seamount
Wüst Seamount
Valdivia Seamount
Ewing Seamount
Vema Seamount
SOUTHERN GUINEA
PLANALTO DO BIÉ
KALAHARI DESERT
NAMIB DESERT
KAROO
DRAKENSBERG
LEBOMBO MTS.
MONTS MITUMBA
Kinshasa
Luanda
Lusaka
Harare
Pretoria
Maputo
Durban
Cape Town/Kaapstad
Cape of Good Hope
Kaap Agulhas
Port Elizabeth
Gaborone
Windhoek
Walvisbaai
Lüderitz
Beira
Nairobi
Dar es Salaam
Mombasa
Kilimanjaro
Kampala
Dodoma
Mozambique Channel
Mozambique Plateau
Natal Basin
Madagascar Basin
Madagascar Plateau
MADAGASCAR
Antananarivo
Toliara
Mascarene Basin
Mascarene Plateau
MASCARENE ISLANDS
MAURITIUS
RÉUNION
RODRIGUES
COMORO ISLANDS
SEYCHELLES ISLANDS
AMIRANTE ISLANDS
Somali Basin
Mid-Indian Ridge
Southwest Indian Ridge
INDIAN OCEAN
Crozet Basin
Crozet Ridge
ÎLES CROZET
PRINCE EDWARD ISLANDS
ÎLES KERGUELEN
Kerguelen Plateau
HEARD ISLAND
MC DONALD ISLANDS
South Indian Basin
AMSTERDAM
SAINT PAUL
Limit of icebergs
Winter limit of pack ice (September)
Longitude East 20 of Greenwich
Scale 1:30,000,000
Lambert Azimuthal Equal Area Projection
0 500 1000 1500 2000 km
0 500 1000 miles
M Ft
6000 19685
5000 16404
4000 13123
3000 9843
2000 6562
1000 3281
500 1640
+200 +656
0 Depr.
0
−200 −656
1000 3281
2000 6562
4000 13123
6000 19685
8000 26247
© ISTITUTO GEOGRAFICO DE AGOSTINI S. p. A. · NOVARA

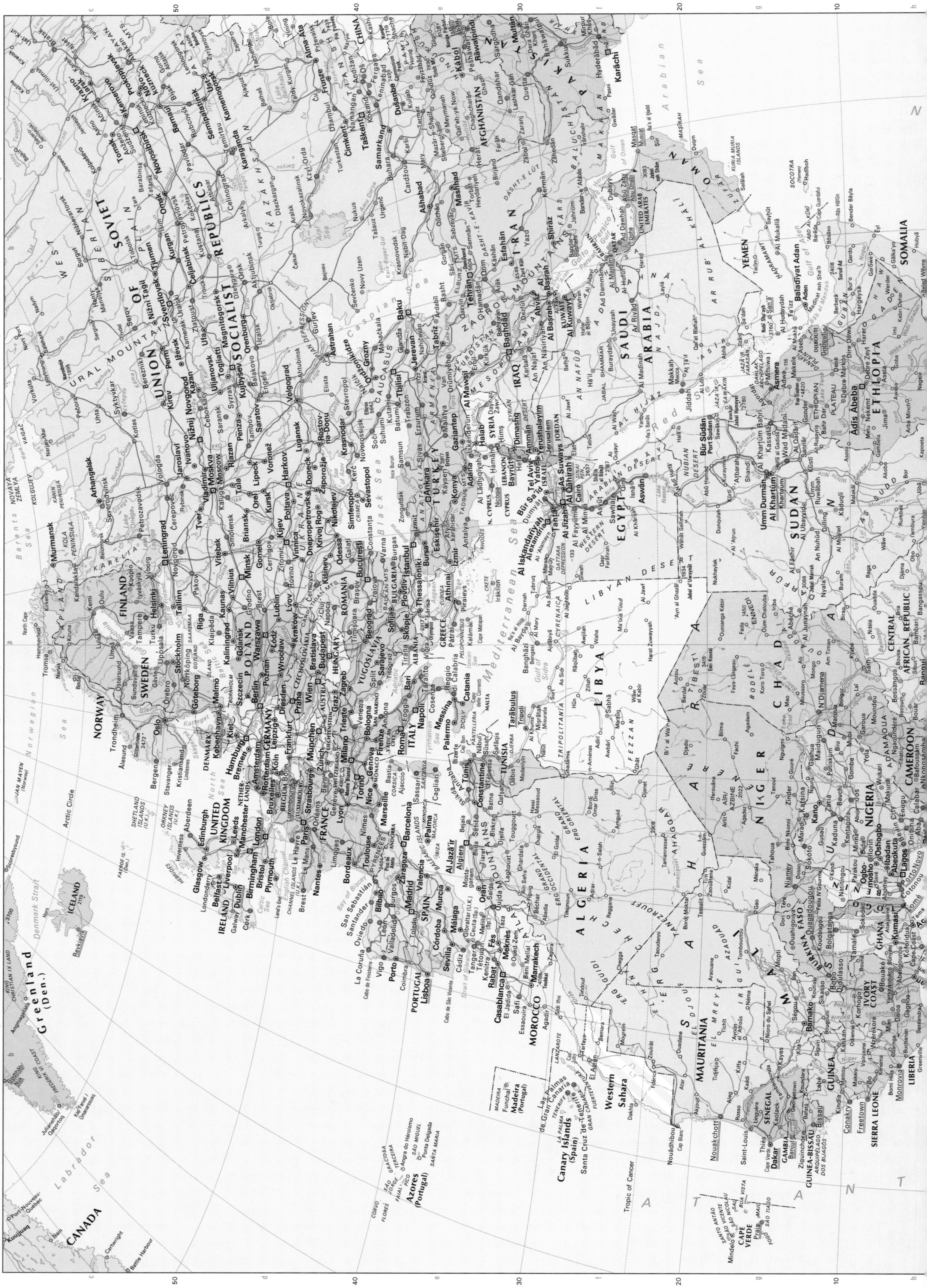
UNION OF SOVIET SOCIALIST REPUBLICS
WEST SIBERIAN PLAIN
URAL MOUNTAINS
KAZAKHSTAN
FINLAND
SWEDEN
NORWAY
DENMARK
UNITED KINGDOM
IRELAND
NETHERLANDS
BELGIUM
GERMANY
POLAND
CZECHOSLOVAKIA
AUSTRIA
HUNGARY
ROMANIA
BULGARIA
YUGOSLAVIA
ALBANIA
GREECE
TURKEY
ITALY
FRANCE
SPAIN
PORTUGAL
CYPRUS
SYRIA
LEBANON
ISRAEL
JORDAN
IRAQ
IRAN
KUWAIT
QATAR
BAHRAIN
UNITED ARAB EMIRATES
OMAN
YEMEN
SAUDI ARABIA
AFGHANISTAN
PAKISTAN
CHINA
EGYPT
LIBYA
TUNISIA
ALGERIA
MOROCCO
Western Sahara
MAURITANIA
MALI
NIGER
CHAD
SUDAN
ETHIOPIA
SOMALIA
DJIBOUTI
SENEGAL
GAMBIA
GUINEA-BISSAU
GUINEA
SIERRA LEONE
LIBERIA
IVORY COAST
BURKINA FASO
GHANA
TOGO
BENIN
NIGERIA
CAMEROON
CENTRAL AFRICAN REPUBLIC
CAPE VERDE
Canary Islands (Spain)
Madeira (Portugal)
Azores (Portugal)
ICELAND
Greenland (Den.)
CANADA
Mediterranean Sea
Black Sea
Caspian Sea
Red Sea
Arabian Sea
Norwegian Sea
Barents Sea
Labrador Sea
Arctic Circle
Tropic of Cancer
SAHARA
ATLANTIC

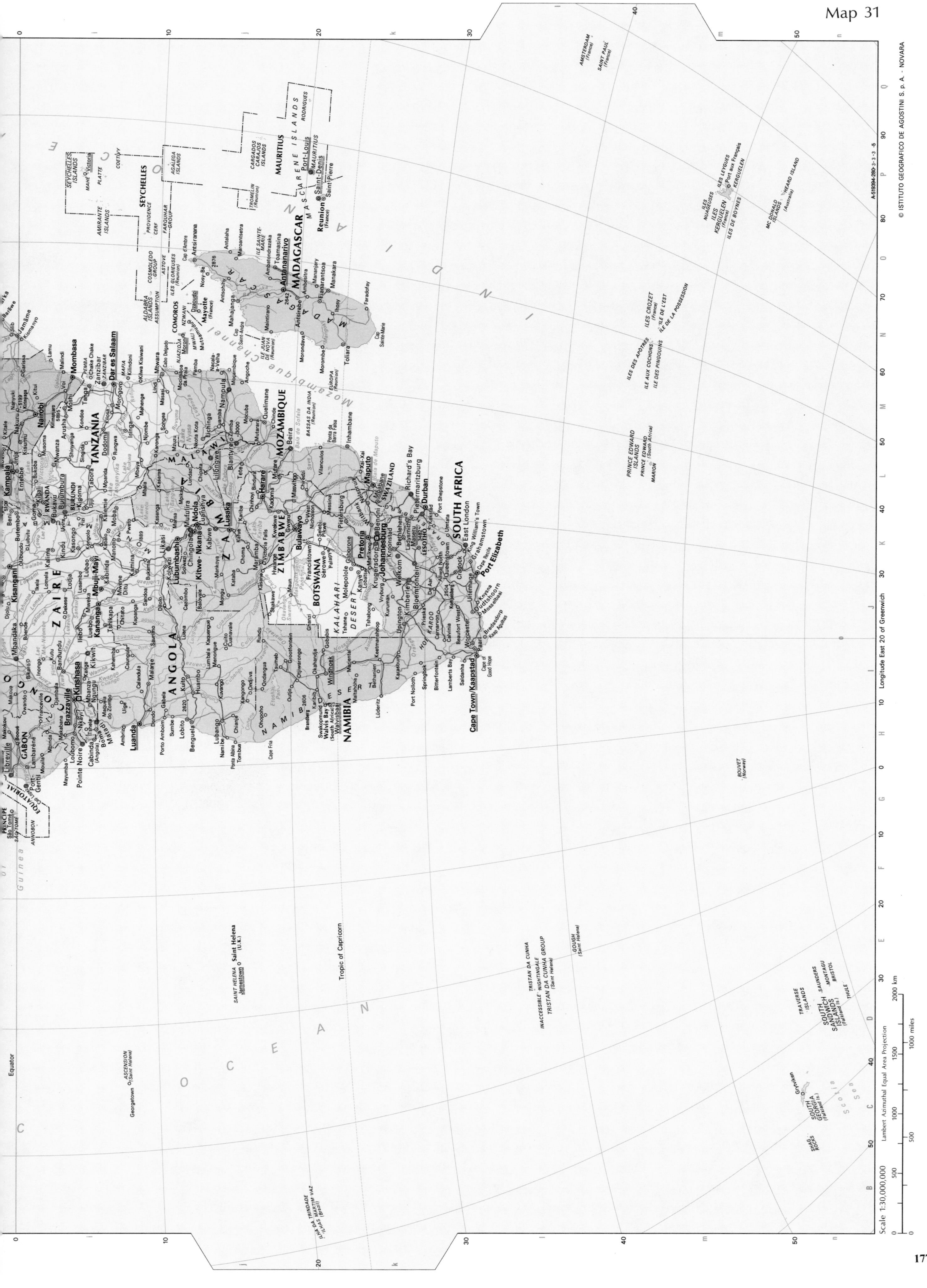
INDIAN OCEAN
ATLANTIC OCEAN
Equator
Tropic of Capricorn
Mozambique Channel
GABON
ZAIRE
ANGOLA
NAMIBIA
BOTSWANA
ZIMBABWE
ZAMBIA
MALAWI
MOZAMBIQUE
TANZANIA
BURUNDI
RWANDA
SOUTH AFRICA
LESOTHO
SWAZILAND
MADAGASCAR
COMOROS
SEYCHELLES
MAURITIUS
KALAHARI DESERT
NAMIB DESERT
KAROO
Libreville
Brazzaville
Kinshasa
Luanda
Lusaka
Harare
Windhoek
Gaborone
Pretoria
Johannesburg
Maputo
Mbabane
Maseru
Durban
Port Elizabeth
Cape Town/Kaapstad
Lilongwe
Dar es Salaam
Nairobi
Mombasa
Kampala
Dodoma
Antananarivo
Port-Louis
Saint-Denis
Reunion (France)
Victoria
Moroni
Saint Helena (U.K.)
Jamestown
ASCENSION (Saint Helena)
Georgetown
TRISTAN DA CUNHA GROUP (Saint Helena)
GOUGH (Saint Helena)
BOUVET (Norway)
SOUTH GEORGIA (Falkland Is.)
SOUTH SANDWICH ISLANDS (Falkland Is.)
PRINCE EDWARD ISLANDS (South Africa)
ILES CROZET (France)
ILES KERGUELEN (France)
HEARD ISLAND (Australia)
MC DONALD ISLANDS
AMSTERDAM (France)
SAINT PAUL (France)
ILHAS MARTIM VAZ (Brazil)
ILHA DA TRINDADE
Scotia Sea
Longitude East 20 of Greenwich
Scale 1:30,000,000
Lambert Azimuthal Equal Area Projection
2000 km
1000 miles

AL JAZĀ'IR
ALGERIA

WILĀYATE
1 Adrar
2 Al Jazā'ir
3 Annaba
4 Batna
5 Béchar
6 Bejaïa
7 Biskra
8 Blida
9 Bouira
10 Cheliff
11 Constantine
12 Djelfa
13 Guelma
14 Jijel
15 Laghouat
16 Mascara
17 Médéa
18 Mostaganem
19 M'Sila
20 Oran
21 Ouargla
22 Oum el Bouaghi
23 Saïda
24 Sétif
25 Sidi Bel Abbes
26 Skikda
27 Tamanrasset
28 Tébessa
29 Tiaret
30 Tizi Ouzou
31 Tlemcen

AL MAGHRIB
MOROCCO

PRÉFECTURES
A Casablanca
B Rabat-Salé

PROVINCES
1 Agadir
2 Al Hoceima
3 Ar Rachidiya
4 Azilal
5 Beni Mellal
6 Boulemane
7 Chechaouene
8 El Jadida
9 El Kelaa des Srarhna
10 Essaouira
11 Fès
12 Figuig
13 Kenitra
14 Khemisset
15 Khenifra
16 Khouribga
17 Marrakech
18 Meknès
19 Nador
20 Ouarzazate
21 Oujda
22 Safi
23 Settat
24 Tanger
25 Tan Tan
26 Taounate
27 Tata
28 Taza
29 Tétouan
30 Tiznit

TŪNIS
TUNISIA

WILĀYATE
1 Al Kāf
2 Al Mahdīyah
3 Al Munastīr
4 Al Qaşrayn
5 Al Qayrawān
6 Bājah
7 Banzart
8 Jundubah
9 Madanīyīn
10 Nābul
11 Qābis
12 Qafşah
13 Qamūdah
14 Şafāqis
15 Silyānah
16 Sūsah
17 Tūnis
18 Zaghwān

M / Ft
4000 / 13123
3000 / 9843
2000 / 6562
1000 / 3281
500 / 1640
200 / 656
+100 / +328
0
Depr.
0
−100 / −328
200 / 656
1000 / 3281
2000 / 6562
4000 / 13123
6000 / 19685

Scale 1:9,000,000 Lambert Azimuthal Equal Area Projection

0 200 400 600 km

0 200 miles

Longitude West 0 East of Greenwich

TŪNIS
TUNISIA

WILĀYATE
1 Al Kāf
2 Al Mahdīyah
3 Al Munastīr
4 Al Qaşrayn
5 Al Qayrawān
6 Bājah
7 Bizerte
8 Jundūbah
9 Madanīyīn
10 Nābul
11 Qābis
12 Qafşah
13 Qamūdah
14 Şafāqis
15 Silyanah
16 Sūsah
17 Tūnis
18 Zaghwān

Scale 1:9,000,000 Lambert Azimuthal Equal Area Projection

0 200 400 600 km

0 200 miles

Longitude East 25 of Greenwich

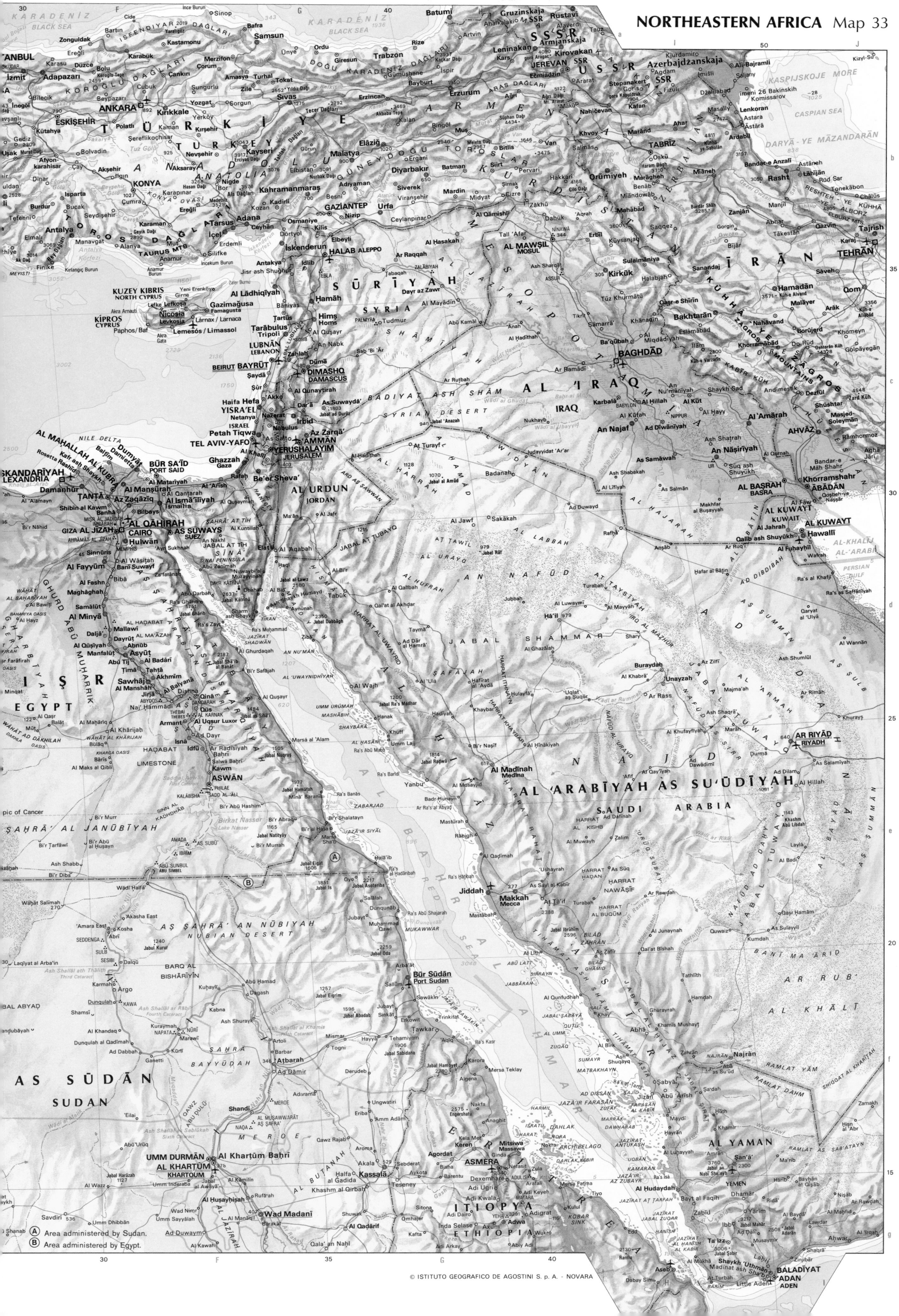
TÜRKIYE
TURKEY
ANATOLIA
ANKARA
KARADENIZ
BLACK SEA
SSSR
USSR
ARMENIA
KURDISTAN
ĪRĀN
TEHRĀN
SŪRĪYAH
SYRIA
LUBNĀN
LEBANON
BAYRŪT
BEIRUT
DIMASHQ
DAMASCUS
YISRA'EL
ISRAEL
YERUSHALAYIM
JERUSALEM
TEL AVIV-YAFO
AL URDUN
JORDAN
AMMĀN
AL 'IRĀQ
IRAQ
BAGHDĀD
MESOPOTAMIA
SYRIAN DESERT
KUZEY KIBRIS
NORTH CYPRUS
KÍPROS
CYPRUS
AL KUWAYT
KUWAIT
AL 'ARABĪYAH AS SU'ŪDĪYAH
SAUDI ARABIA
AR RIYĀD
RIYADH
AN NAFŪD
NAJD
AL HIJĀZ
Makkah
Mecca
Al Madīnah
Medina
Jiddah
AL QĀHIRAH
CAIRO
GIZA AL JĪZAH
NILE DELTA
BŪR SA'ĪD
PORT SAID
AS SUWAYS
SUEZ
SĪNĀ'
SINAI PENINSULA
MIŞR
EGYPT
ASWĀN
AŞ ŞAHRĀ' AN NŪBIYAH
NUBIAN DESERT
AS SŪDĀN
SUDAN
UMM DURMĀN
AL KHARṬŪM
KHARTOUM
Būr Sūdān
Port Sudan
ITIOPYA
ETHIOPIA
ASMERA
AL YAMAN
YEMEN
Ṣan'ā'
BALADĪYAT 'ADAN
ADEN
AR RUB' AL KHĀLĪ
RED SEA
Tropic of Cancer
Ⓐ Area administered by Sudan.
Ⓑ Area administered by Egypt.

© ISTITUTO GEOGRAFICO DE AGOSTINI S. p. A. - NOVARA

LIBERIA

COUNTIES
1 Bong
2 Cape Mount
3 Grand Bassa
4 Grand Gedeh
5 Lofa
6 Maryland
7 Montserrado
8 Nimba
9 Sinoe

CÔTE D'IVOIRE
IVORY COAST

DÉPARTEMENTS
1 Abengourou
2 Abidjan
3 Aboisso
4 Adzopé
5 Agboville
6 Biankouma
7 Bondoukou
8 Bongouanou
9 Bouaflé
10 Bouaké
11 Bouna
12 Boundiali
13 Dabakala
14 Daloa
15 Danané
16 Dimbokro
17 Divo
18 Ferkessédougou
19 Gagnoa
20 Guiglo
21 Issia
22 Katiola
23 Korhogo
24 Lakota
25 Man
26 Mankono
27 Odienné
28 Oumé
29 Sassandra
30 Séguéla
31 Soubré
32 Tengréla
33 Touba
34 Zuenoula

HAUTE-VOLTA
UPPER VOLTA

DÉPARTEMENTS
1 Centre
2 Centre-Est
3 Centre-Nord
4 Centre-Ouest
5 Est
6 Hauts-Bassins
7 Komoé
8 Nord
9 Sahel
10 Sud-Ouest
11 Volta Noire

TOGO

RÉGIONS
1 Centre
2 Kara
3 Maritime
4 Plateaux
5 Savanes

BÉNIN

PROVINCES
1 Atakora
2 Atlantique
3 Borgou
4 Mono
5 Ouémé
6 Zou

Ⓐ Abuja is the future federal capital of Nigeria.
Ⓑ The political subdivisions shown for Guinea represent statistical areas and are not recognized for administrative purposes.

Scale 1:9,000,000 Lambert Azimuthal Equal Area Projection
0 200 400 600 km
0 200 miles

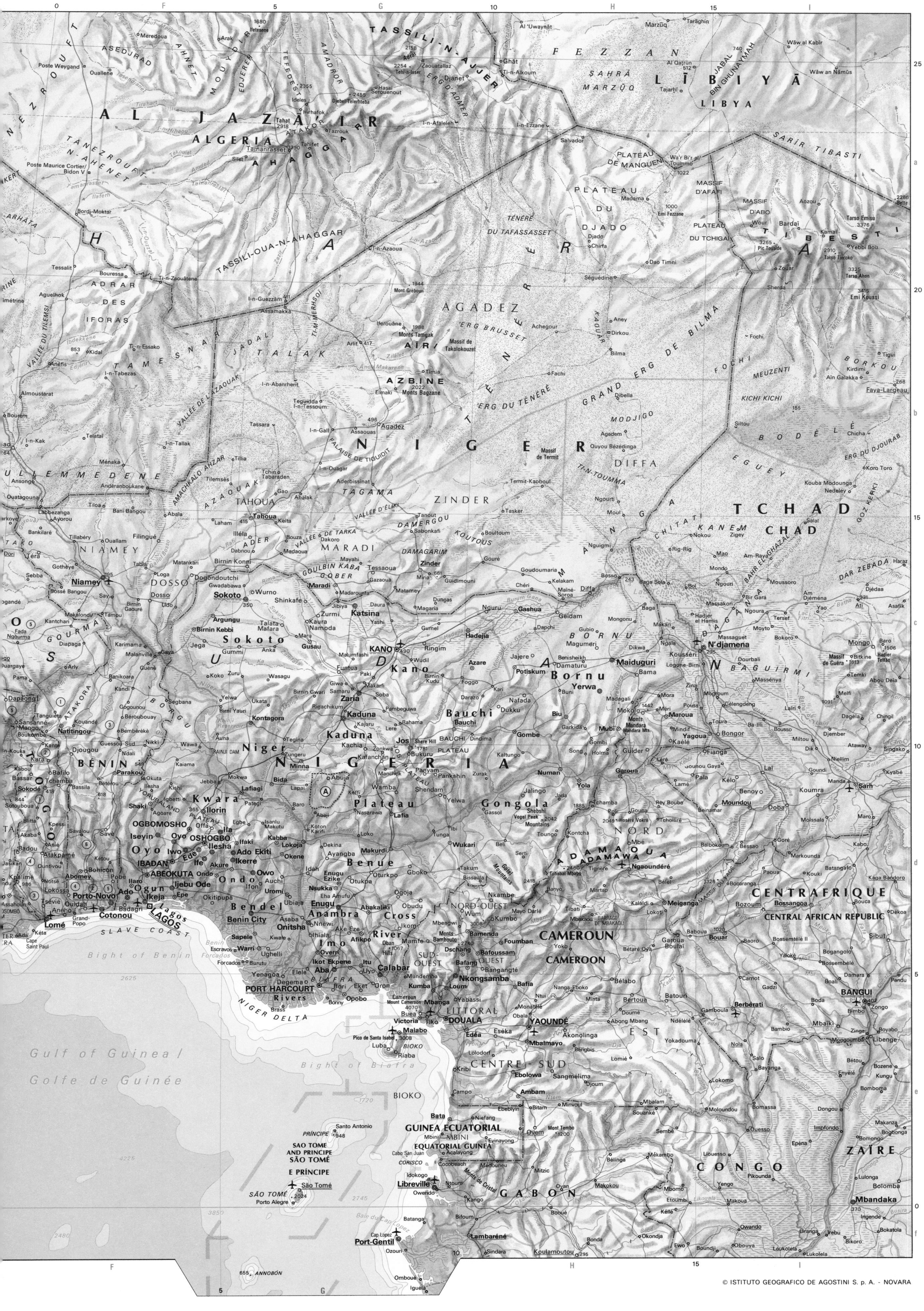
AL JAZĀ'IR
ALGERIA
LĪBIYĀ
LIBYA
FEZZAN
ṢAḤRĀ MARZŪQ
TASSILI-N-AJJER
AHAGGAR
TASSILI-OUA-N-AHAGGAR
TANEZROUFT
ADRAR DES IFORAS
TAMESNA
NIGER
AGADEZ
AÏR
TÉNÉRÉ
GRAND ERG DE BILMA
PLATEAU DU DJADO
TIBESTI
TCHAD
CHAD
BORKOU
BODÉLÉ
KANEM
NIAMEY
Niamey
DOSSO
TAHOUA
MARADI
ZINDER
DIFFA
SARĪR TIBASTI
NIGERIA
Sokoto
Kano
Kaduna
Bauchi
Bornu
Niger
Kwara
Plateau
Gongola
Oyo
Ogun
Ondo
Bendel
Anambra
Benue
Cross River
Imo
Rivers
Lagos
LAGOS
IBADAN
Abuja
Zaria
KANO
Maiduguri
N'djamena
BÉNIN
Cotonou
Porto-Novo
TOGO
Lomé
SLAVE COAST
Bight of Benin
NIGER DELTA
PORT HARCOURT
Calabar
Gulf of Guinea / Golfe de Guinée
Bight of Biafra
CAMEROUN
CAMEROON
DOUALA
YAOUNDÉ
ADAMAOUA
CENTRAFRIQUE
CENTRAL AFRICAN REPUBLIC
BANGUI
GUINEA ECUATORIAL
EQUATORIAL GUINEA
BIOKO
Malabo
SAO TOME AND PRINCIPE
SÃO TOMÉ E PRÍNCIPE
São Tomé
GABON
Libreville
Port-Gentil
CONGO
ZAÏRE
Mbandaka
ANNOBÓN

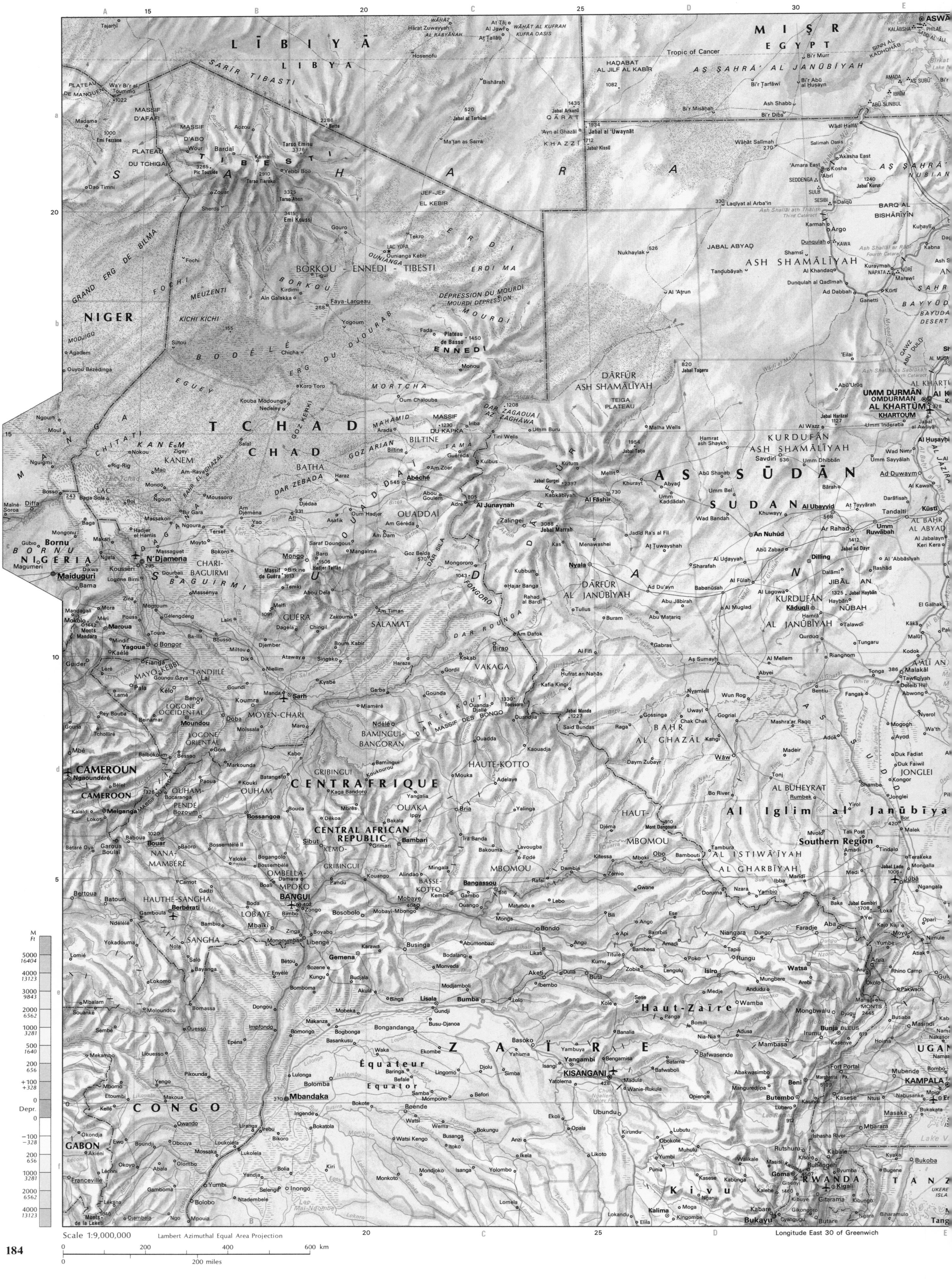
LĪBIYĀ
LIBYA
MIṢR
EGYPT
Tropic of Cancer
AṢ ṢAḤRĀ' AL JANŪBĪYAH
SARĪR TIBASTI
MASSIF D'AFAFI
PLATEAU DU TCHIGAÏ
TIBESTI
Emi Koussi
BORKOU - ENNEDI - TIBESTI
ERDI MA
DÉPRESSION DU MOURDI
GRAND ERG DE BILMA
NIGER
BODÉLÉ
ERG DU DJOURAB
ENNEDI
TCHAD
CHAD
KANEM
BATHA
LAC
N'Djamena
BORNU
NIGERIA
Maiduguri
CHARI-BAGUIRMI
OUADDAÏ
Abéché
GUÉRA
SALAMAT
MOYEN-CHARI
Sarh
LOGONE OCCIDENTAL
LOGONE ORIENTAL
Moundou
TANDJILÉ
MAYO-KÉBBI
CAMEROUN
CAMEROON
Ngaoundéré
OUHAM-PENDÉ
OUHAM
BAMINGUI-BANGORAN
VAKAGA
HAUTE-KOTTO
CENTRAFRIQUE
CENTRAL AFRICAN REPUBLIC
OUAKA
Bambari
KEMO-GRIBINGUI
OMBELLA-MPOKO
BANGUI
BASSE-KOTTO
MBOMOU
HAUT-MBOMOU
NANA-MAMBÉRÉ
HAUTHE-SANGHA
Berbérati
LOBAYE
SANGHA
CONGO
GABON
Mbandaka
Équateur
Equator
ZAÏRE
KISANGANI
Haut-Zaïre
Kivu
Bukavu
Goma
RWANDA
Kigali
UGANDA
KAMPALA
DĀRFŪR ASH SHAMĀLĪYAH
DĀRFŪR AL JANŪBĪYAH
Jabal Marrah
Al Fāshir
Al Junaynah
Nyala
AS SŪDĀN
SUDAN
KURDUFĀN ASH SHAMĀLĪYAH
KURDUFĀN AL JANŪBĪYAH
Al Ubayyid
ASH SHAMĀLĪYAH
UMM DURMĀN
OMDURMAN
AL KHARṬŪM
KHARTOUM
BAHR AL GHAZĀL
Wāw
JONGLEI
AL BUHEYRAT
Al Iglim al Janūbīyah
Southern Region
AL ISTIWĀ'ĪYAH AL GHARBĪYAH
Jūbā
Scale 1:9,000,000
Lambert Azimuthal Equal Area Projection
Longitude East 30 of Greenwich
0 200 400 600 km
0 200 miles
M Ft
5000 16404
4000 13123
3000 9843
2000 6562
1000 3281
500 1640
200 656
+100 +328
0
Depr.
0
−100 −328
200 656
1000 3281
2000 6562
4000 13123

AL 'ARABĪYAH AS SU'ŪDĪYAH
SAUDI ARABIA
AL YAMAN
YEMEN
DJIBOUTI
SOOMAALIYA
SOMALIA
ITIOPYA
ETHIOPIA
ERITREA
KENYA
'UMĀN
OMAN
Gulf of Aden
Badyarada 'Admed
Somali Basin
Jiddah
Makkah
Mecca
Bûr Sûdân
Port Sudan
ASMERA
ADIS ABEBA
(ADDIS ABABA)
Ṣan'ā'
Aden
Djibouti
Hargeysa
MUQDISHO MOGADISHU
NAIROBI
Kismānyo
Al Mukallā
Ta'izz
Al Ḥudaydah
SUQUṬRĀ SOCOTRA
Equator
A-589395-780-2 -2 -1 -2
Ⓐ Area administered by Sudan
Ⓑ Area administered by Egypt

Scale 1:9,000,000   Lambert Azimuthal Equal Area Projection

0   200   400   600 km

0   200 miles

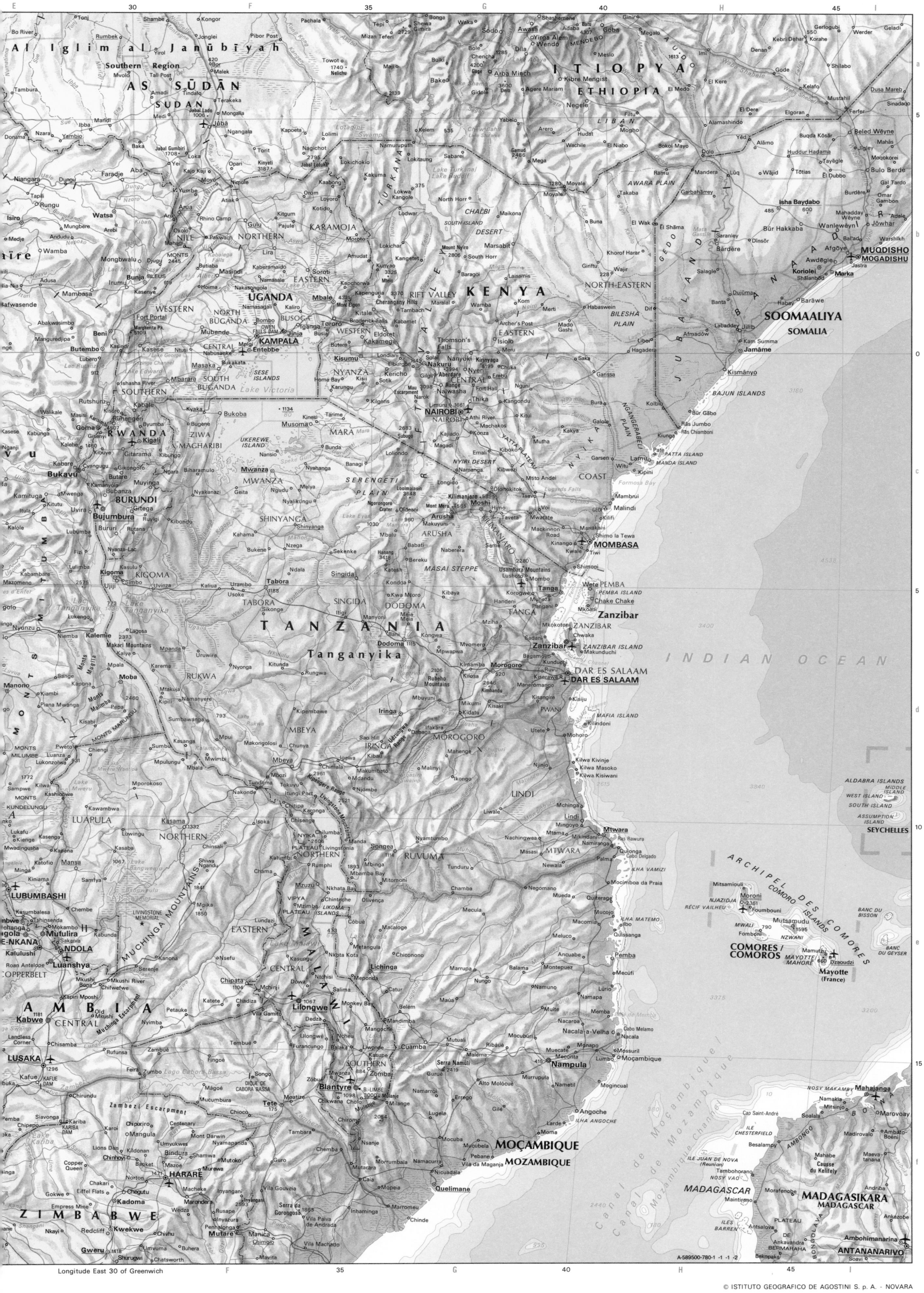
Al Iglim al Janūbīyah
Southern Region
AS SŪDĀN
SUDAN
Jūbā
ITIOPYA
ETHIOPIA
Addis Ababa
KENYA
NAIROBI
Mombasa
UGANDA
KAMPALA
Entebbe
RWANDA
Kigali
BURUNDI
Bujumbura
TANZANIA
Tanganyika
DAR ES SALAAM
Dodoma
Zanzibar
Lake Victoria
Lake Tanganyika
Lake Turkana
Lake Rudolf
SOOMAALIYA
SOMALIA
MUQDISHO
MOGADISHU
Kismānyo
INDIAN OCEAN
COMORES / COMOROS
Moroni
Mayotte (France)
SEYCHELLES
ALDABRA ISLANDS
MADAGASIKARA
MADAGASCAR
ANTANANARIVO
Mahajanga
MOÇAMBIQUE
MOZAMBIQUE
Canal de Moçambique
Mozambique Channel
Nampula
Quelimane
Beira
MALAWI
Lilongwe
Blantyre
ZAMBIA
LUSAKA
LUBUMBASHI
ZIMBABWE
HARARE
Mutare
Longitude East 30 of Greenwich
A-589500-780-1 -1 -1 -2

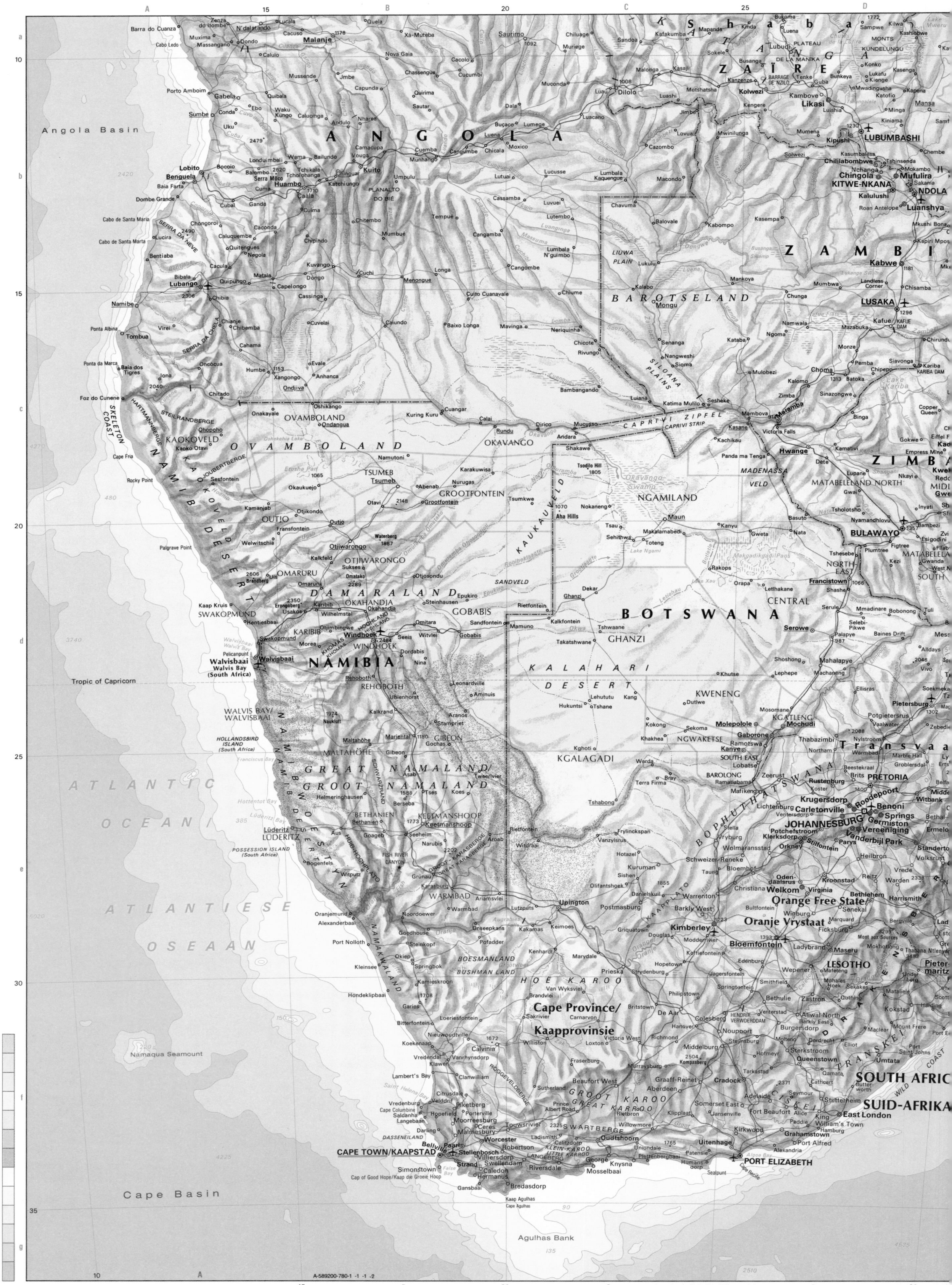

Scale 1:9,000,000 Lambert Azimuthal Equal Area Projection Longitude East 25 of Greenwich

0 200 400 600 km

0 200 miles

MOÇAMBIQUE
MOZAMBIQUE
MADAGASCAR
MADAGASIKARA
MADAGASCAR
COMORES / COMOROS
Mayotte (France)
SEYCHELLES
ALDABRA ISLANDS
ALDABRA GROUP
ARCHIPEL DES COMORES
COMORO ISLANDS
Moroni
Dzaoudzi
ILES GLORIEUSES (Reunion)
BANC DU GEYSER
Canal de Moçambique
Mozambique Channel
ILE JUAN DE NOVA (Reunion)
BASSAS DA INDIA (Reunion)
EUROPA (Reunion)
OCEANO ÍNDICO / OCÉAN INDIEN
INDIAN OCEAN / INDIESE OSEAAN
Natal Basin
Mozambique Plateau
Madagascar Plateau
MALAWI
Lilongwe
Blantyre
Zomba
HARARE
Mutare
Beira
Quelimane
Nampula
Pemba
Mtwara
Lindi
Inhambane
Xai-Xai
MAPUTO
Richard's Bay
Mahajanga
Antsiranana
Toamasina
ANTANANARIVO
Antsirabe
Fianarantsoa
Toliara
Morondava
Manakara
Farafangana
Sambava
Antalaha
NIASSA
CABO DELGADO
NAMPULA
ZAMBÉZIA
SOFALA
MANICA
INHAMBANE
GAZA
MAHAJANGA
ANTANANARIVO
TOAMASINA
FIANARANTSOA
TOLIARA
ANTSIRANANA
SEYCHELLES ISLANDS
Victoria
AMIRANTE ISLANDS
Amirante Basin
Amirante Trench
MAURITIUS
Port-Louis
Saint-Denis
Réunion (France)
ILES MASCAREIGNES/ MASCARENE ISLANDS
Longitude East 50 of Greenwich

GREENLAND
BAFFIN
ELLESMERE
DEVON
VICTORIA
BANKS
QUEEN ELIZABETH ISLANDS
PARRY ISLANDS
Hudson Bay
James Bay
Baffin Bay
Davis Strait
Hudson Strait
Foxe Basin
Labrador Sea
LABRADOR
NEWFOUNDLAND
ICELAND
Denmark Strait
Norwegian Sea
Greenland Sea
Barents Sea
Kara Sea
Laptev Sea
East Siberian Sea
Chukchi Sea
Beaufort Sea
Bering Strait
Bering Sea
Sea of Okhotsk
Sea of Japan
North Sea
Baltic Sea
Black Sea
Gulf of Alaska
Alaska
ALASKA RANGE
BROOKS RANGE
ALEUTIAN ISLANDS
Aleutian Trench
ROCKY
COAST MOUNTAINS
MACKENZIE MOUNTAINS
Franklin Mountains
KODIAK
VANCOUVER ISLAND
QUEEN CHARLOTTE ISLANDS
ALEXANDER ARCHIPELAGO
SEWARD PENINSULA
KENAI PENINSULA
ALASKA PENINSULA
CHUKCHI PENINSULA
KAMCHATKA PENINSULA
SAKHALIN
KURIL ISLANDS
NEW SIBERIAN ISLANDS
WRANGEL
SEVERNAYA ZEMLYA
NOVAYA ZEMLYA
FRANZ JOSEPH LAND
SPITSBERGEN
SCANDINAVIA
LAPLAND
KOLA PENINSULA
KARELIA
BRITISH ISLES
GREAT BRITAIN
IRELAND
SCOTLAND
ENGLAND
WALES
URAL MOUNTAINS
WEST SIBERIAN PLAIN
CENTRAL SIBERIAN UPLANDS
NORTH SIBERIAN PLAIN
TAYMYR PENINSULA
VERKHOYANSK MTS.
CHERSKI MTS.
STANOVOY RANGE
SIKHOTE-ALIN
CAUCASUS
UKRAINE
CARPATHIAN MTS.
North Pole
Arctic Circle
Canada Basin
Makarov Basin
Lomonosov Ridge
Alpha Cordillera
Nansen Cordillera
Eurasia Basin
Fram Basin
Mid-Atlantic Ridge
Reykjanes Ridge
Labrador Basin
Iceland Basin
Newfoundland Basin
Mendocino Fracture
Limit of Icebergs
Summer limit of pack ice (August)
Winter limit of pack ice (April)
North Magnetic Pole 1980

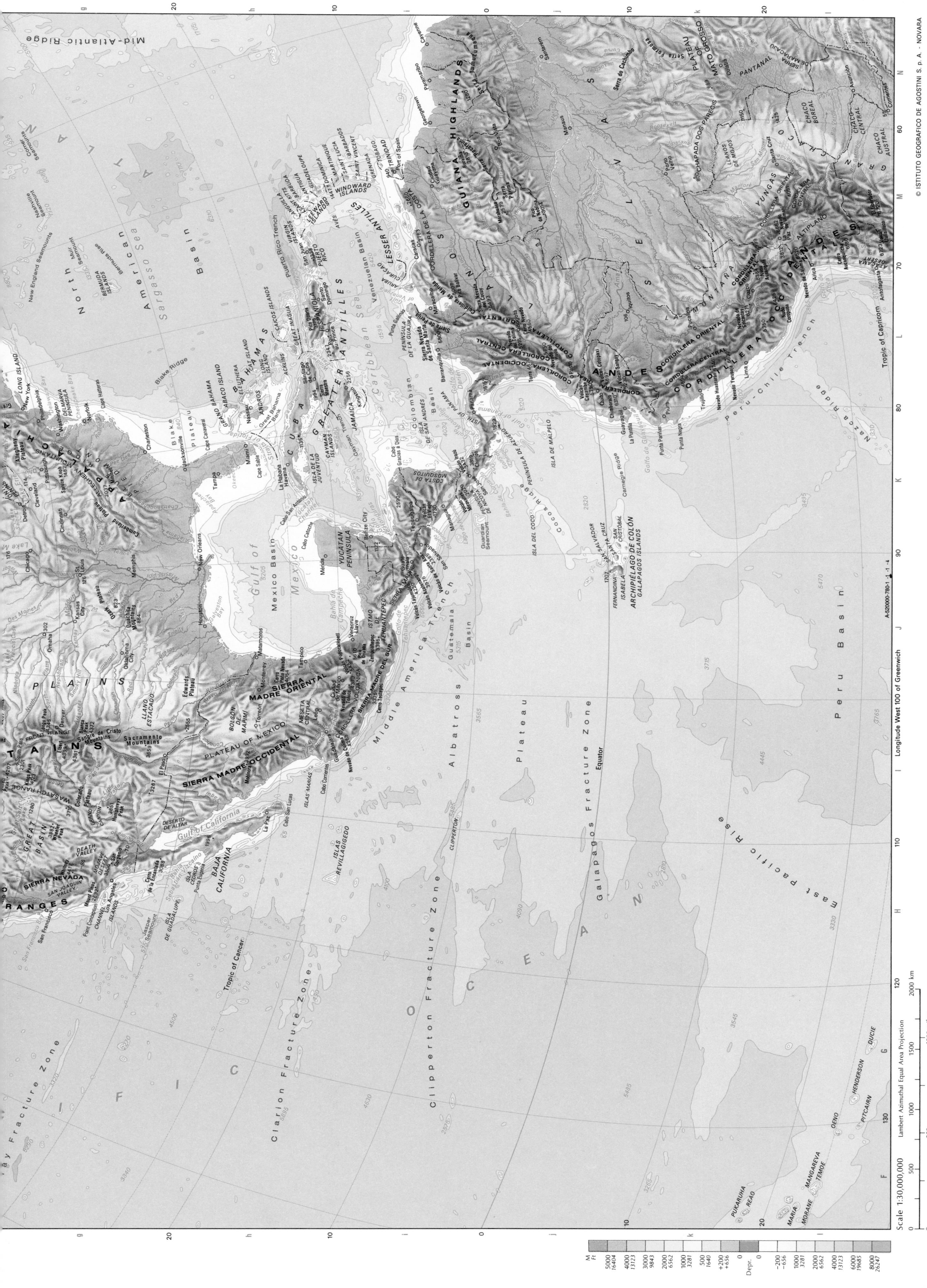
Mid-Atlantic Ridge
North American Basin
Sargasso Sea
BERMUDA ISLANDS
New England Seamounts
Puerto Rico Trench
GREATER ANTILLES
LESSER ANTILLES
Caribbean Sea
Venezuelan Basin
Colombian Basin
Gulf of Mexico
Mexico Basin
YUCATAN PENINSULA
SIERRA MADRE ORIENTAL
SIERRA MADRE OCCIDENTAL
SIERRA MADRE DEL SUR
PLATEAU OF MEXICO
BAJA CALIFORNIA
Gulf of California
SIERRA NEVADA
GREAT BASIN
Middle America Trench
Guatemala Basin
Albatross Plateau
Galapagos Fracture Zone
Clipperton Fracture Zone
Clarion Fracture Zone
Tropic of Cancer
Equator
ARCHIPIÉLAGO DE COLÓN
GALAPAGOS ISLANDS
Cocos Ridge
Carnegie Ridge
Peru Basin
Peru-Chile Trench
Nazca Ridge
East Pacific Rise
Tropic of Capricorn
GUIANA HIGHLANDS
PLATEAU OF MATO GROSSO
ANDES
CORDILLERA OCCIDENTAL
CORDILLERA ORIENTAL
ALTIPLANO
GRAN CHACO
Longitude West 100 of Greenwich
Lambert Azimuthal Equal Area Projection
Scale 1:30,000,000
© ISTITUTO GEOGRAFICO DE AGOSTINI S. p. A. - NOVARA

UNION OF SOVIET SOCIALIST REPUBLICS
WEST SIBERIAN PLAIN
CENTRAL SIBERIAN UPLANDS
URAL MOUNTAINS
VERKHOYANSK MTS.
CHERSKI MTS.
STANOVOY RANGE
S I B E R I A
KAMCHATKA PENINSULA
CHUKCHI PENINSULA
Sea of Okhotsk
Bering Sea
ALEUTIAN ISLANDS
KURIL ISLANDS
SAKHALIN
JAPAN
NORTH KOREA
C H I N A
Harbin
Vladivostok
Magadan
Moskva
Moscow
Leningrad
Kiev
Minsk
Arhangelsk
Murmansk
KOLA PENINSULA
KARELIA
FINLAND
SWEDEN
NORWAY
LAPLAND
Helsinki
Stockholm
Oslo
København
Warszawa
POLAND
GERMANY
Berlin
Praha
Wien
Budapest
ROMANIA
TURKEY
Black Sea
UNITED KINGDOM
London
IRELAND
Dublin
FRANCE
Paris
ICELAND
Reykjavík
SHETLAND ISLANDS (U.K.)
FAEROE ISLANDS
JAN MAYEN (Norway)
Norwegian Sea
Greenland Sea
Barents Sea
Kara Sea
Laptev Sea
East Siberian Sea
Chukchi Sea
Beaufort Sea
Svalbard (Norway)
SPITSBERGEN
NORDAUSTLANDET
FRANZ JOSEPH LAND
NOVAJA ZEMLJA
NOVAYA ZEMLYA
SEVERNAJA ZEMLJA
SEVERNAYA ZEMLYA
NEW SIBERIAN ISLANDS
WRANGEL
A R C T I C O C E A N
North Pole
Greenland (Den.)
KING FREDERIK VIII LAND
KING CHRISTIAN X LAND
KING CHRISTIAN IX LAND
KING FREDERIK VI LAND
KNUD RASMUSSEN LAND
Denmark Strait
Davis Strait
Baffin Bay
QUEEN ELIZABETH ISLANDS
ELLESMERE
AXEL HEIBERG
DEVON
BATHURST
MELVILLE
PRINCE PATRICK
BANKS
VICTORIA
SOMERSET
PRINCE OF WALES
BOOTHIA PENINSULA
B A F F I N
SOUTHAMPTON
Hudson Bay
Hudson Strait
UNGAVA PENINSULA
NEWFOUNDLAND
Saint Pierre and Miquelon (France)
CAPE BRETON ISLAND
ANTICOSTI
Q U E B E C
C A N A D A
Ottawa
Québec
Winnipeg
Edmonton
Calgary
Saskatoon
Regina
Vancouver
Seattle
Portland
MACKENZIE MOUNTAINS
ROCKY MOUNTAINS
COAST MOUNTAINS
Whitehorse
Juneau
Alaska (U.S.)
BROOKS RANGE
ALASKA RANGE
Mount McKinley 6194
Anchorage
Fairbanks
Nome
Point Barrow
Gulf of Alaska
KODIAK
ALASKA PENINSULA
Bristol Bay
SAINT LAWRENCE
NUNIVAK
PRIBILOF ISLANDS
FOX ISLANDS
UNIMAK
ALEXANDER ARCHIPELAGO
QUEEN CHARLOTTE ISLANDS
VANCOUVER ISLAND
A T L A N T I C O C E A N
Azores (Port.)

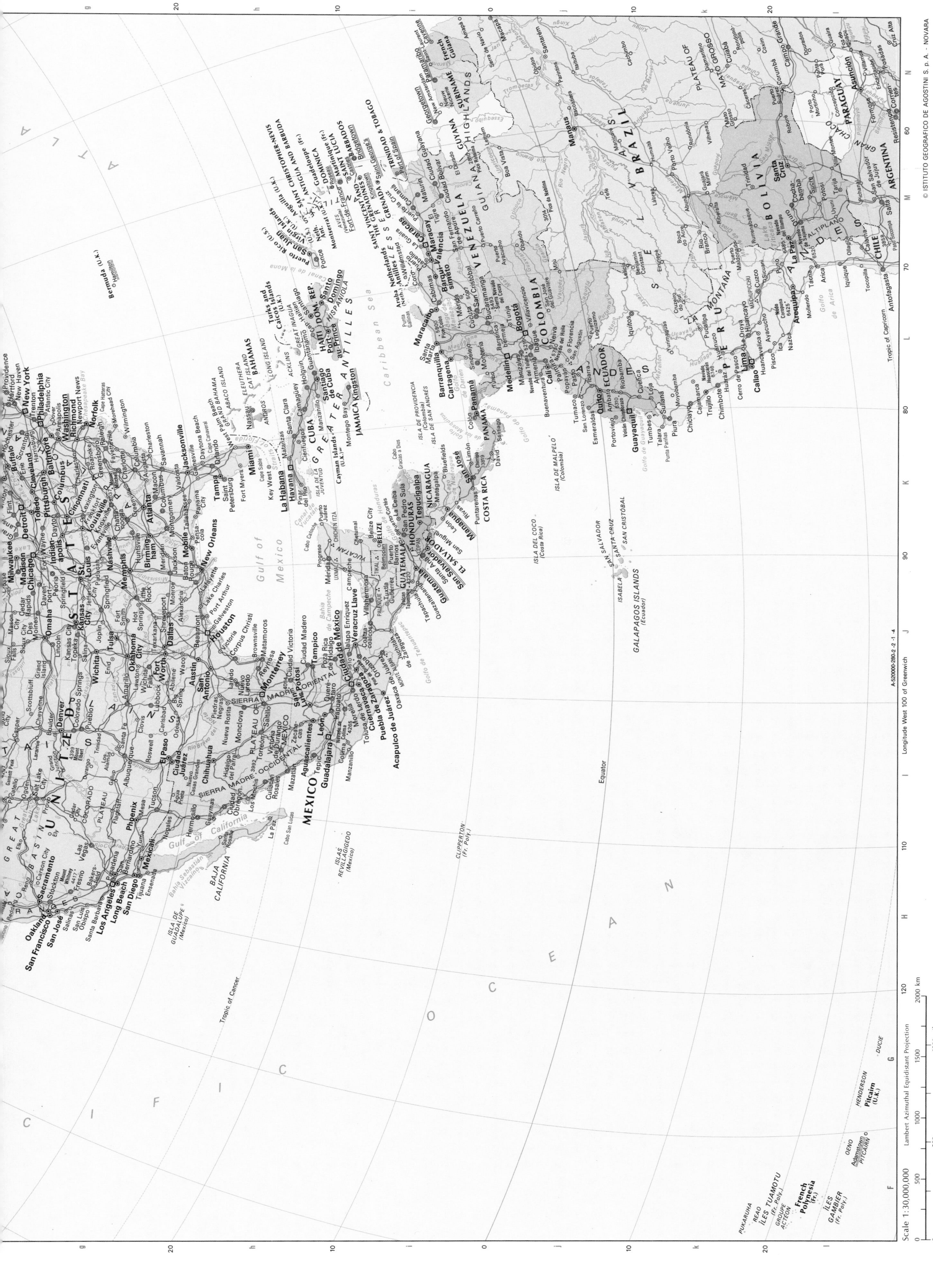
UNITED STATES
MEXICO
CUBA
HAITI
DOM. REP.
JAMAICA
BAHAMAS
BELIZE
GUATEMALA
HONDURAS
EL SALVADOR
NICARAGUA
COSTA RICA
PANAMA
COLOMBIA
VENEZUELA
GUYANA
SURINAME
French Guiana
ECUADOR
PERU
BOLIVIA
BRAZIL
PARAGUAY
CHILE
ARGENTINA
Gulf of Mexico
Caribbean Sea
GREATER ANTILLES
LESSER ANTILLES
PACIFIC OCEAN
Tropic of Cancer
Equator
Tropic of Capricorn
GALAPAGOS ISLANDS (Ecuador)
Bermuda (U.K.)
Pitcairn (U.K.)
French Polynesia (Fr.)
Longitude West 100 of Greenwich
Lambert Azimuthal Equidistant Projection
Scale 1:30,000,000

© ISTITUTO GEOGRAFICO DE AGOSTINI S. p. A. - NOVARA

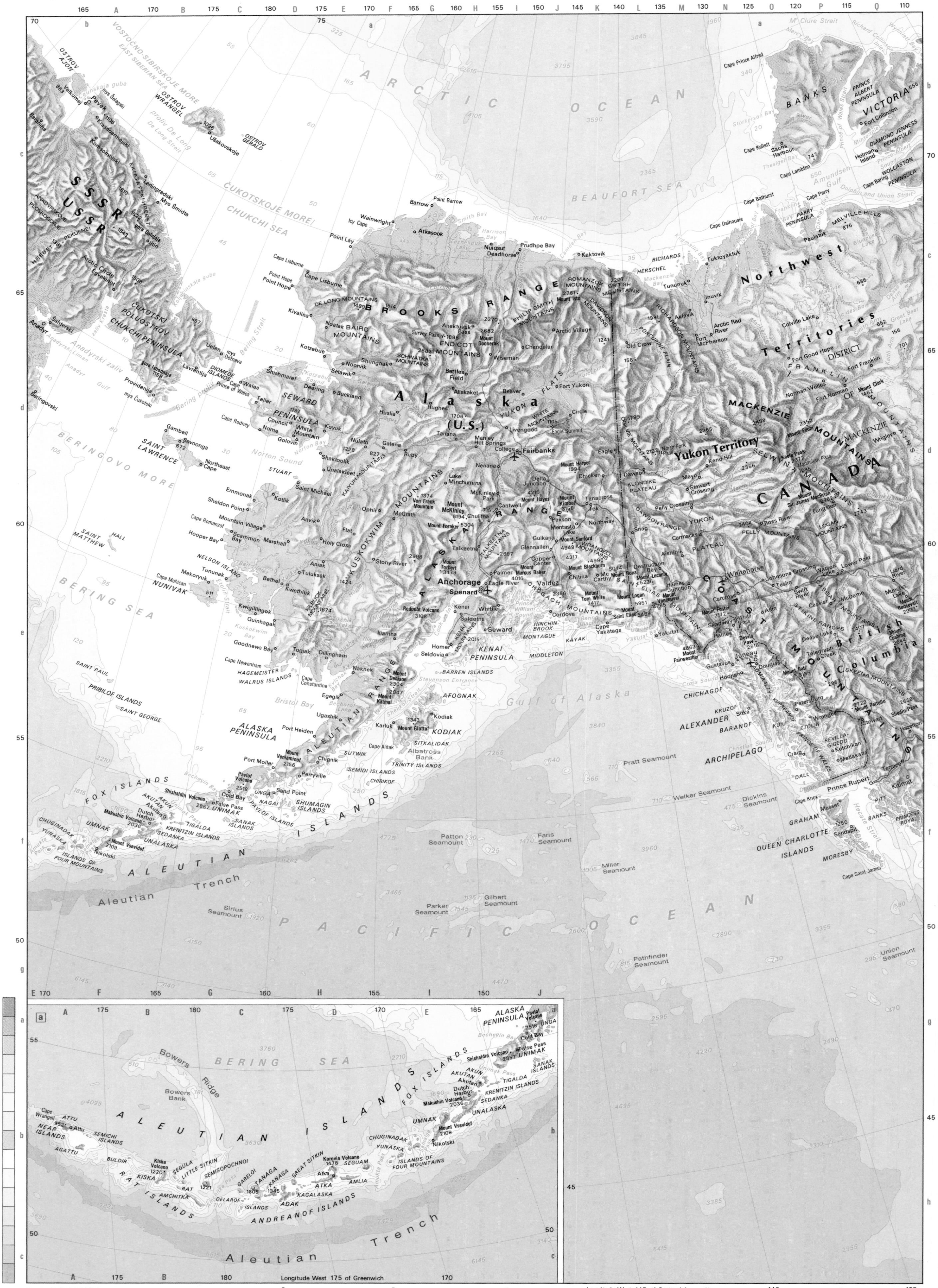
ARCTIC OCEAN
BEAUFORT SEA
ČUKOTSKOJE MORE
CHUKCHI SEA
VOSTOČNO-SIBIRSKOJE MORE
EAST SIBERIAN SEA
OSTROV WRANGEL
SSSR
USSR
ČUKOTSKIJ POLUOSTROV
CHUKCHI PENINSULA
Bering Strait
BERINGOVO MORE
BERING SEA
SAINT LAWRENCE
NUNIVAK
SAINT MATTHEW
PRIBILOF ISLANDS
SAINT PAUL
SAINT GEORGE
SEWARD PENINSULA
Norton Sound
BROOKS RANGE
Alaska
(U.S.)
Point Barrow
Barrow
Prudhoe Bay
Kaktovik
Point Hope
Cape Lisburne
Kotzebue
Nome
Fairbanks
Anchorage
Spenard
Valdez
Seward
Kenai
Homer
Kodiak
KODIAK
KENAI PENINSULA
ALASKA RANGE
Mount McKinley
6194
KUSKOKWIM MOUNTAINS
YUKON FLATS
Bethel
Dillingham
Bristol Bay
ALASKA PENINSULA
ALEUTIAN RANGE
AFOGNAK
SHUMAGIN ISLANDS
FOX ISLANDS
UNIMAK
UNALASKA
UMNAK
ALEUTIAN ISLANDS
Aleutian Trench
Gulf of Alaska
PACIFIC OCEAN
Patton Seamount
Pratt Seamount
Welker Seamount
Dickins Seamount
Parker Seamount
Gilbert Seamount
Sirius Seamount
Miller Seamount
Pathfinder Seamount
Union Seamount
Faris Seamount
CHUGACH MOUNTAINS
WRANGELL MOUNTAINS
SAINT ELIAS MOUNTAINS
Mount Logan
5951
Yukon Territory
Whitehorse
Dawson
Juneau
Sitka
Ketchikan
Prince Rupert
ALEXANDER ARCHIPELAGO
CHICHAGOF
BARANOF
QUEEN CHARLOTTE ISLANDS
GRAHAM
MORESBY
CANADA
MACKENZIE MOUNTAINS
Northwest Territories
FRANKLIN DISTRICT
British Columbia
COAST MOUNTAINS
BANKS
VICTORIA
Inuvik
Tuktoyaktuk
Aklavik
Old Crow
RICHARDSON MOUNTAINS
a
ALEUTIAN ISLANDS
BERING SEA
Bowers Ridge
Bowers Bank
NEAR ISLANDS
ATTU
RAT ISLANDS
ANDREANOF ISLANDS
ISLANDS OF FOUR MOUNTAINS
Aleutian Trench
Longitude West 175 of Greenwich
Longitude West 145 of Greenwich

Scale 1:12,000,000 Lambert Azimuthal Equal Area Projection

0 200 400 600 800 km

0 200 400 miles

© ISTITUTO GEOGRAFICO DE AGOSTINI S. p. A. - NOVARA

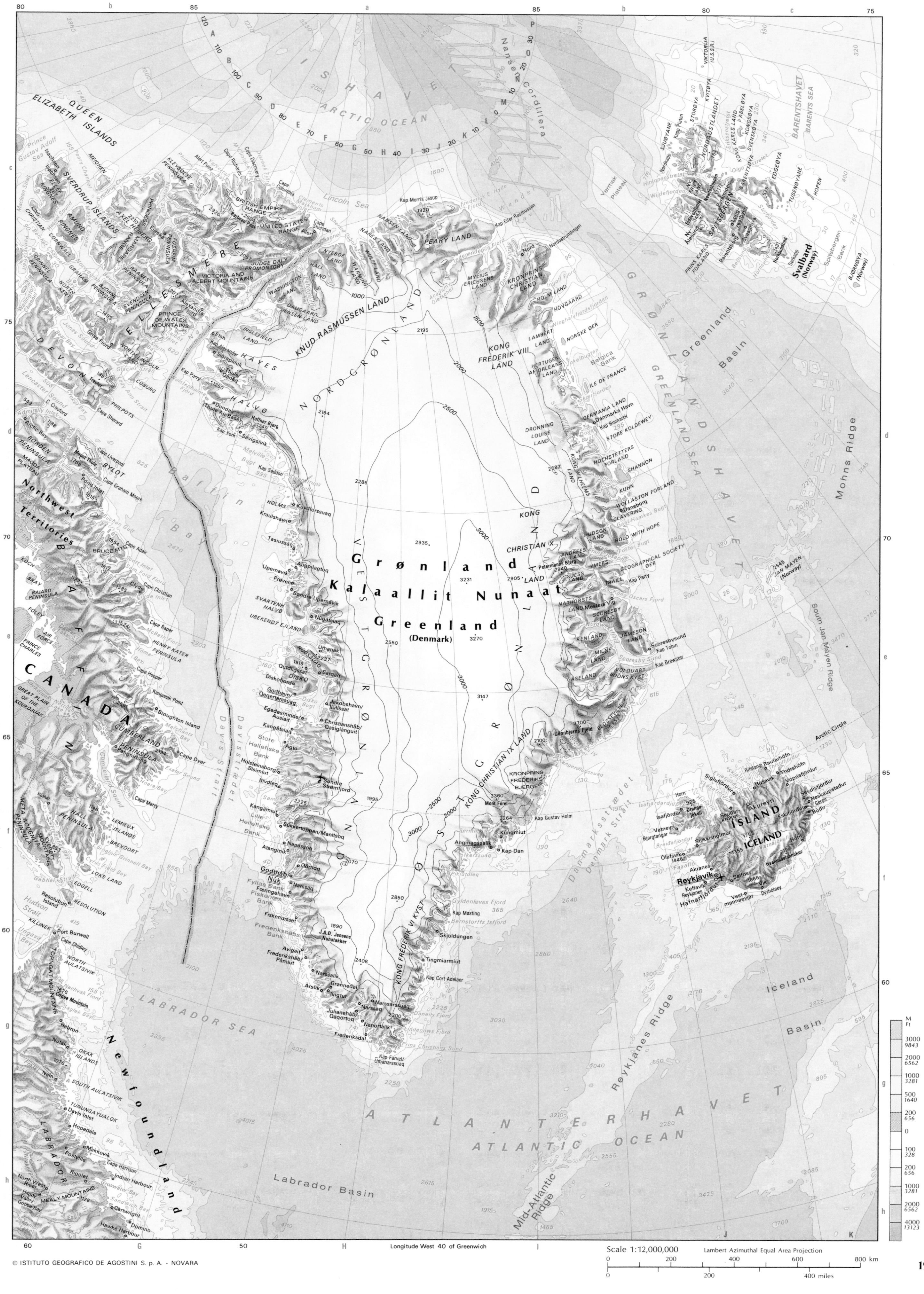

Scale 1:12,000,000 Lambert Azimuthal Equal Area Projection

0 200 400 600 800 km

0 200 400 miles

Scale 1:12,000,000 Lambert Azimuthal Equal Area Projection

0 200 400 600 800 km

0 200 400 miles

Longitude West 100 of Greenwich

Grønland
Kalaallit Nunaat
Greenland
(Denmark)
VESTGRØNLAND
ØSTGRØNLAND
Baffin Bay
Davis Strait
LABRADOR SEA
ATLANTIC OCEAN
Labrador Basin
Newfoundland
Québec
Ontario
CANADA
LABRADOR
BAFFIN
Hudson Bay
Hudson Strait
Foxe Basin
Ungava Bay
James Bay
PÉNINSULE D'UNGAVA
CUMBERLAND PENINSULA
SOUTHAMPTON
DEVON
BYLOT
NORTH LINCOLN LAND
MELVILLE PENINSULA
COAST OF LABRADOR
CLAY BELT
Gulf of Saint Lawrence
ÎLE D'ANTICOSTI
New Brunswick
Nova Scotia
Prince Edward Island
Maine
New York
Pennsylvania
Wisconsin
Michigan
Lake Superior
Saint-Pierre et Miquelon (France)
Grand Banks of Newfoundland
SABLE ISLAND (Nova Scotia)
Georges Bank
Browns Bank
Kelvin Seamount
Thule Air Base
Godthåb/Nûk
Julianehåb/Qaqortoq
Frederikshåb/Paamiut
Iqaluit
Cape Dorset
Pangnirtung
Clyde
Pond Inlet
Arctic Bay
Hall Beach
Igloolik
Repulse Bay
Coral Harbour
Chesterfield Inlet
Rankin Inlet
Whale Cove
Kuujjuaq
Kuujjuarapik
Nain
Hopedale
Cartwright
Labrador City
Churchill Falls
Schefferville
Sept-Îles
Baie-Comeau
Saint John's
Corner Brook
Gander
Sydney
Halifax
Dartmouth
Truro
Moncton
Fredericton
Saint John
Charlottetown
QUÉBEC
MONTRÉAL
OTTAWA
TORONTO
HAMILTON
Kingston
Sudbury
Sault Sainte Marie
Thunder Bay
Timmins
Chicoutimi
Trois-Rivières
Sherbrooke
Moosonee
Fort Severn
Winisk
Attawapiskat
BOSTON
Providence
Worcester
Hartford
Albany
Syracuse
Rochester
BUFFALO
Erie
CLEVELAND
TOLEDO
DETROIT
Lansing
Flint
Grand Rapids
CHICAGO
MILWAUKEE
Madison
SAINT PAUL
Duluth
NEWARK
NEW YORK
JERSEY CITY
Trenton
Harrisburg
AKRON
Youngstown
Scranton
Portland
Bangor
Augusta

Scale 1:12,000,000 Lambert Azimuthal Equidistant Projection Longitude West 100 of Greenwich

0 200 400 600 800 km

0 200 400 miles

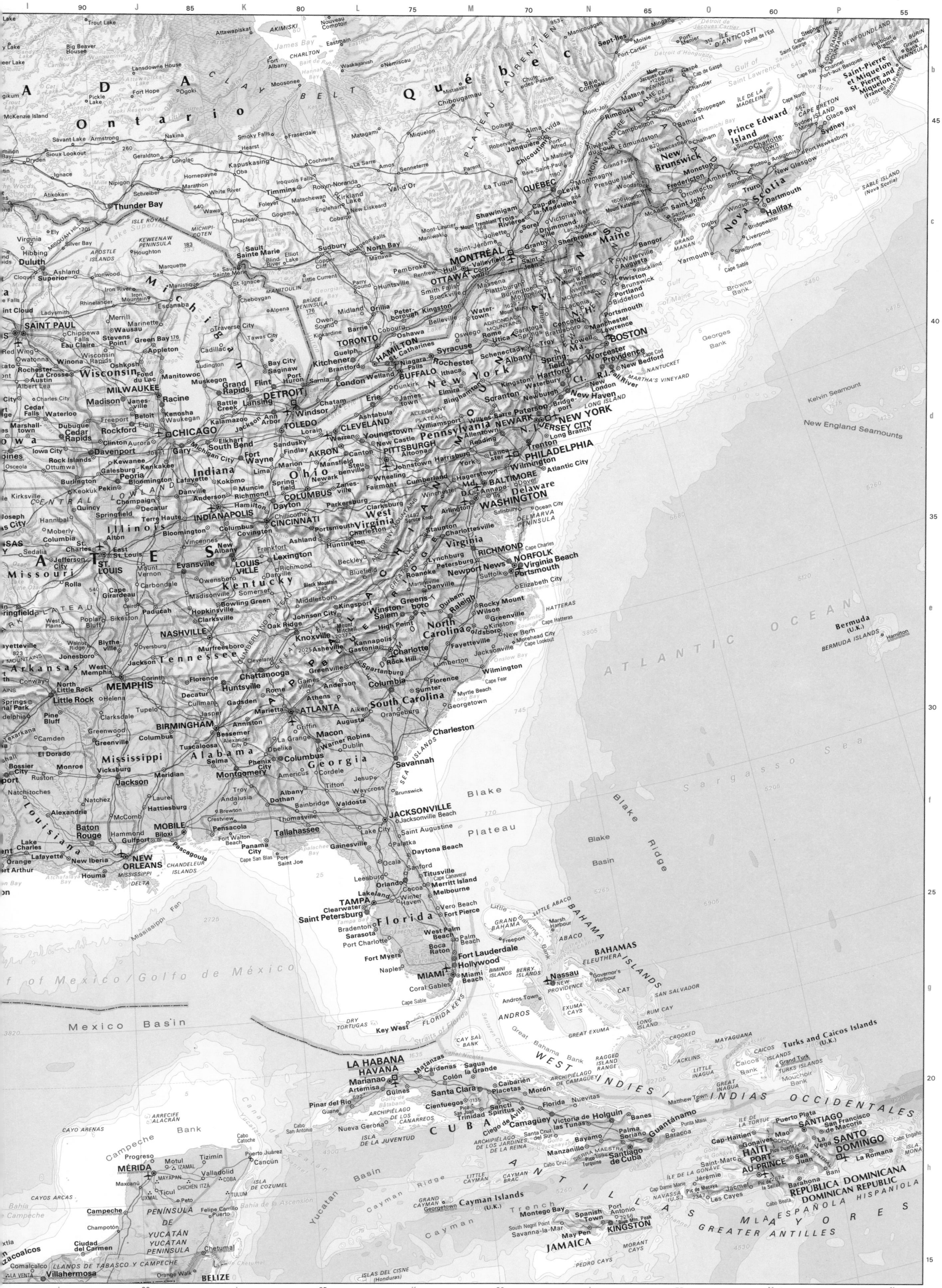
Ontario
Québec
Michigan
Wisconsin
Minnesota
Iowa
Illinois
Indiana
Ohio
Pennsylvania
New York
Maine
Kentucky
Tennessee
Missouri
Arkansas
Mississippi
Alabama
Georgia
South Carolina
North Carolina
Virginia
West Virginia
Florida
Louisiana
New Brunswick
Nova Scotia
Prince Edward Island
ATLANTIC OCEAN
Sargasso Sea
Blake Plateau
Blake Basin
Blake Ridge
New England Seamounts
Kelvin Seamount
Mexico Basin
Golfo de México
BAHAMA ISLANDS
WEST INDIES / INDIAS OCCIDENTALES
CUBA
JAMAICA
Cayman Islands (U.K.)
Turks and Caicos Islands (U.K.)
HAITI
REPÚBLICA DOMINICANA
DOMINICAN REPUBLIC
GREATER ANTILLES
Yucatan Basin
Cayman Trench
PENÍNSULA DE YUCATÁN
Bermuda (U.K.)
MONTRÉAL
OTTAWA
TORONTO
QUÉBEC
BOSTON
NEW YORK
PHILADELPHIA
BALTIMORE
WASHINGTON
DETROIT
CHICAGO
CLEVELAND
PITTSBURGH
BUFFALO
MILWAUKEE
SAINT PAUL
INDIANAPOLIS
CINCINNATI
COLUMBUS
LOUISVILLE
ST. LOUIS
NASHVILLE
MEMPHIS
ATLANTA
BIRMINGHAM
NEW ORLEANS
MOBILE
JACKSONVILLE
MIAMI
TAMPA
NORFOLK
RICHMOND
LA HABANA
HAVANA
KINGSTON
SANTO DOMINGO
PORT-AU-PRINCE
MÉRIDA
BELIZE

Georges Bank
Hudson Canyon
New Brunswick
Nova Scotia
Maine
New Hampshire
Massachusetts
Connecticut
Rhode Island
New York
New Jersey
Delaware
Maryland
Pennsylvania
Ohio
West Virginia
Virginia
Michigan
Indiana
Illinois
Wisconsin
Minnesota
Iowa
Kentucky
Québec
Ontario
CANADA
BOSTON
NEW YORK
PHILADELPHIA
BALTIMORE
WASHINGTON
PITTSBURGH
CLEVELAND
DETROIT
CHICAGO
MILWAUKEE
TORONTO
MONTRÉAL
OTTAWA
BUFFALO
CINCINNATI
COLUMBUS
INDIANAPOLIS
LOUISVILLE
ST. LOUIS

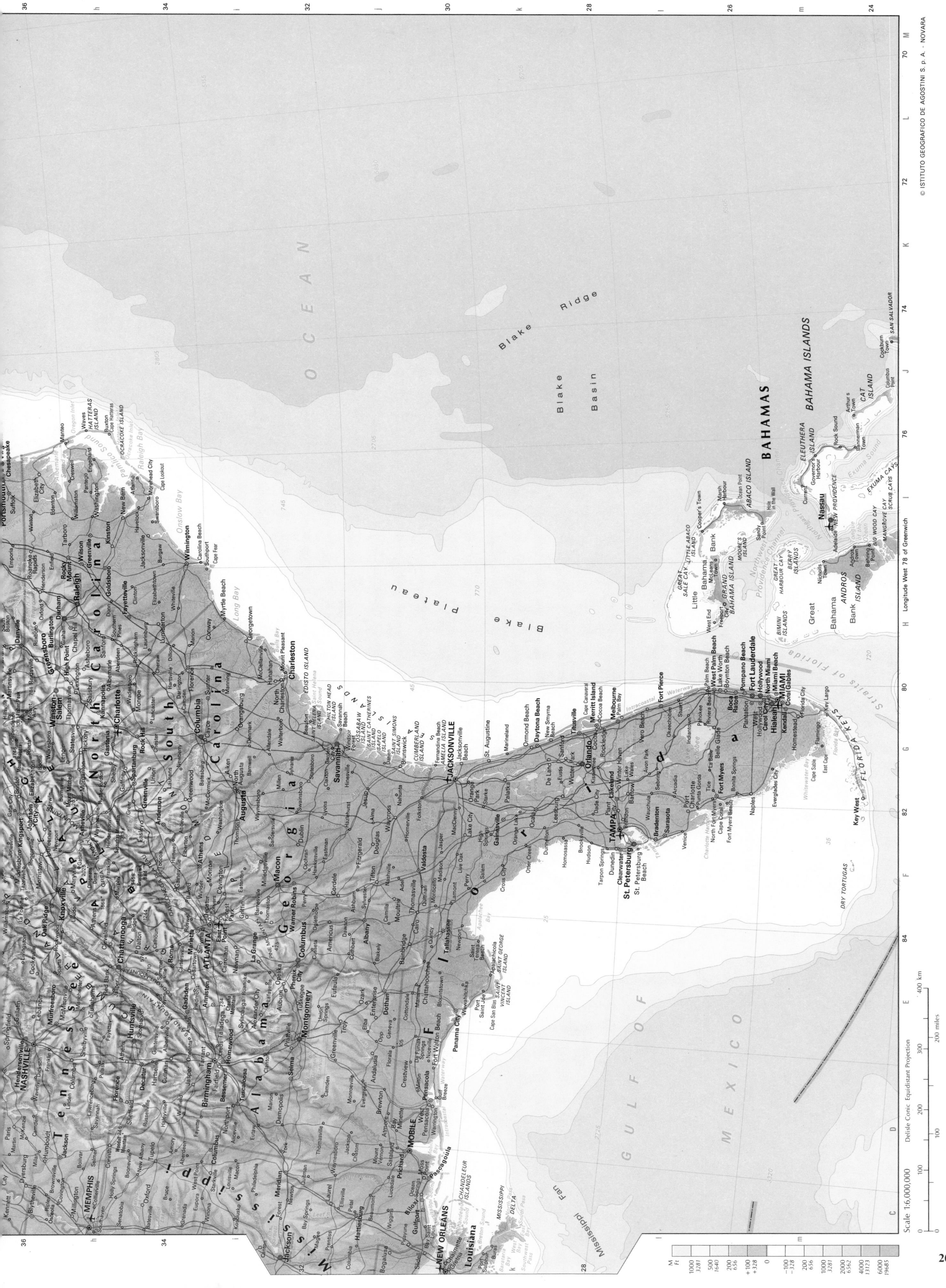
ATLANTIC OCEAN
Blake Ridge
Blake Basin
Blake Plateau
BAHAMAS
BAHAMA ISLANDS
GULF OF MEXICO
Straits of Florida
FLORIDA KEYS
Tennessee
Alabama
Georgia
South Carolina
North Carolina
Florida
Mississippi
Louisiana
JACKSONVILLE
ATLANTA
MIAMI
TAMPA
NEW ORLEANS
MEMPHIS
NASHVILLE
Nassau
Scale 1:16,000,000
Delisle Conic Equidistant Projection
Longitude West 78 of Greenwich

CANADA
Alberta
Saskatchewan
Manitoba
Ontario
Montana
North Dakota
South Dakota
Minnesota
Wisconsin
Michigan
Iowa
Illinois
Indiana
Nebraska
Missouri
Kansas
Colorado
Wyoming
Utah
WINNIPEG
MINNEAPOLIS
SAINT PAUL
MILWAUKEE
CHICAGO
OMAHA
KANSAS CITY
DENVER
INDIANAPOLIS
ST. LOUIS

GULF OF MEXICO
Texas
Oklahoma
Arkansas
Louisiana
Mississippi
Alabama
Tennessee
Kentucky
New Mexico
Arizona
Chihuahua
Coahuila
Nuevo León
Tamaulipas
Durango
Sinaloa
Sonora
MEXICO
HOUSTON
DALLAS
FORT WORTH
SAN ANTONIO
AUSTIN
NEW ORLEANS
MEMPHIS
OKLAHOMA CITY
TULSA
MONTERREY
CIUDAD JUÁREZ
EL PASO
Scale 1:6,000,000
Delisle Conic Equidistant Projection
Longitude West 98 of Greenwich
© ISTITUTO GEOGRAFICO DE AGOSTINI S. p. A. - NOVARA

CANADA
Alberta
Saskatchewan
British Columbia
North Dakota
South Dakota
Nebraska
Montana
Wyoming
Idaho
Washington
Oregon
Nevada
Utah
Colorado
California
PACIFIC
COLUMBIA MOUNTAINS
COAST MOUNTAINS
CASCADE RANGE
COAST RANGES
BITTERROOT RANGE
BIGHORN MOUNTAINS
WIND RIVER RANGE
LARAMIE MOUNTAINS
UINTA MOUNTAINS
COLUMBIA PLATEAU
GREAT BASIN
GREAT SALT LAKE DESERT
VANCOUVER ISLAND
CALGARY
SPOKANE
SEATTLE
PORTLAND
SALT LAKE CITY
DENVER
VANCOUVER
Regina
Saskatoon
Medicine Hat
Lethbridge
Billings
Great Falls
Helena
Butte
Missoula
Bozeman
Boise
Pocatello
Idaho Falls
Ogden
Provo
Casper
Cheyenne
Fort Collins
Boulder
Tacoma
Olympia
Yakima
Eugene
Salem
Medford
Klamath Falls
Bend
Pendleton
Walla Walla
Lewiston
Victoria
Nanaimo
Kamloops
Kelowna
Penticton
Red Deer
Eureka
Redding
Reno
Elko
Winnemucca

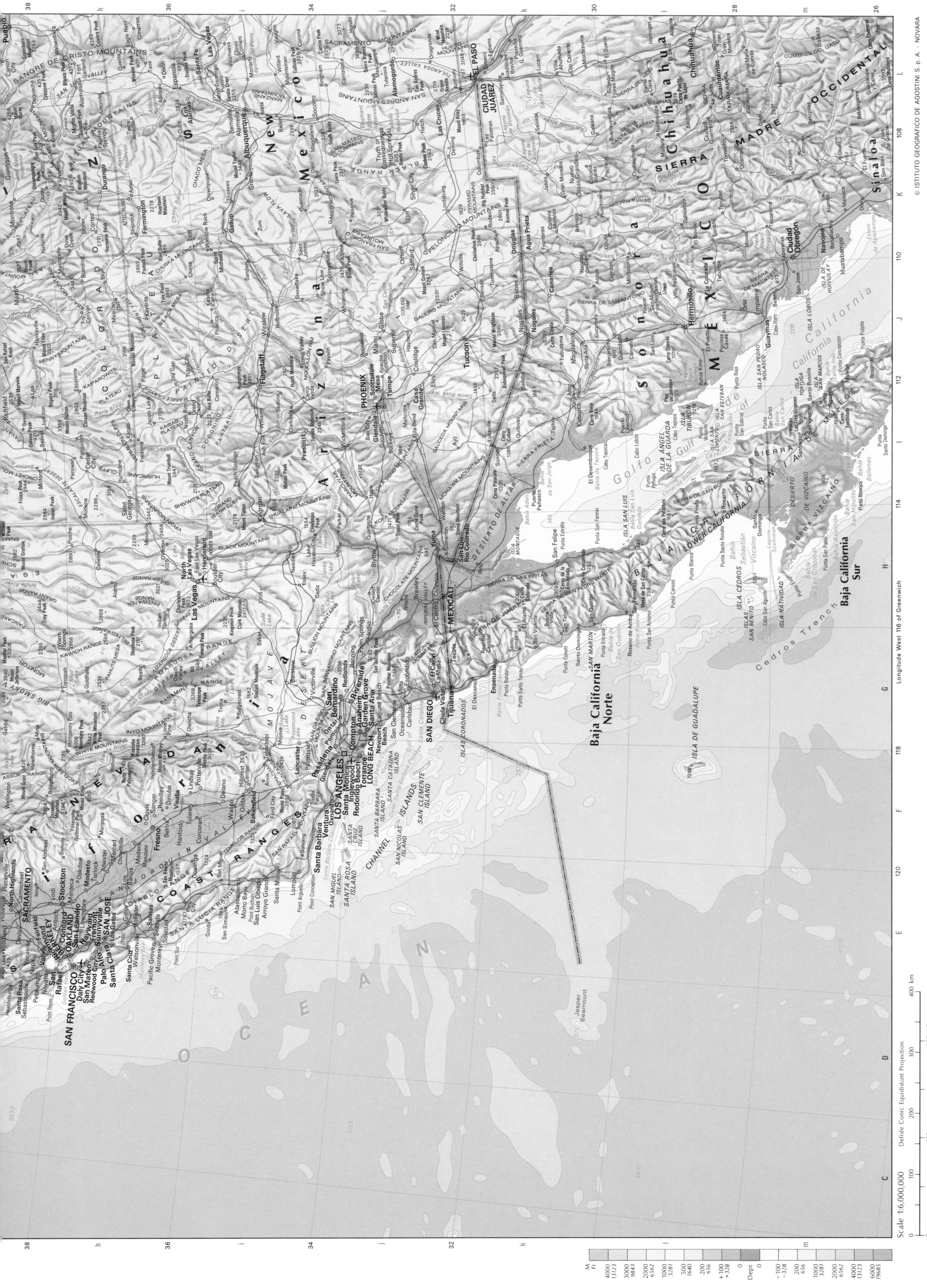
Arizona
New Mexico
Chihuahua
Sonora
Sinaloa
MEXICO
SIERRA MADRE OCCIDENTAL
Baja California Norte
Baja California Sur
Golfo de California
PACIFIC OCEAN
Longitude West 116 of Greenwich
Scale 1:6,000,000
Delisle Conic Equidistant Projection
© ISTITUTO GEOGRAFICO DE AGOSTINI S. p. A. - NOVARA

UNITED STATES
California
Arizona
New Mexico
Texas
Oklahoma
Kansas
Missouri
Arkansas
Louisiana
Mississippi
MÉXICO
GUATEMALA
LOS ANGELES
SAN DIEGO
Tijuana
MEXICALI
PHOENIX
Tucson
Albuquerque
EL PASO
CIUDAD JUÁREZ
Amarillo
Lubbock
OKLAHOMA CITY
TULSA
DALLAS
FORT WORTH
AUSTIN
SAN ANTONIO
HOUSTON
MEMPHIS
NEW ORLEANS
CHIHUAHUA
Hermosillo
Ciudad Obregón
Culiacán Rosales
Mazatlán
Victoria de Durango
Torreón
Saltillo
MONTERREY
Nuevo Laredo
Reynosa
Matamoros
Ciudad Victoria
SAN LUIS POTOSÍ
TAMPICO
Ciudad Madero
Aguascalientes
Zacatecas
GUADALAJARA
LEÓN
Querétaro
Morelia
CIUDAD DE MÉXICO
MEXICO CITY
PUEBLA DE ZARAGOZA
VERACRUZ LLAVE
Acapulco de Juárez
Oaxaca de Juárez
MÉRIDA
Campeche
Villahermosa
GUATEMALA
SAN SALVADOR
La Paz
SIERRA MADRE OCCIDENTAL
SIERRA MADRE ORIENTAL
SIERRA MADRE DEL SUR
BAJA CALIFORNIA
Gulf of Mexico / Golfo de México
Mexico Basin
Middle America Trench
Albatross Plateau
Guatemala Basin
Tehuantepec Ridge
Mathematicians Seamounts
OCÉANO PACÍFICO
PACIFIC OCEAN
Equator
ISLAS REVILLAGIGEDO (Mexico)
ÎLE CLIPPERTON (Fr. Poly.)
Longitude West 90 of Greenwich

MÉXICO

ESTADOS

- D.F. Distrito Federal
- 1 Aguascalientes
- 2 Baja California Norte
- 3 Baja California Sur
- 4 Campeche
- 5 Coahuila
- 6 Colima
- 7 Chiapas
- 8 Chihuahua
- 9 Durango
- 10 Guanajuato
- 11 Guerrero
- 12 Hidalgo
- 13 Jalisco
- 14 México
- 15 Michoacán
- 16 Morelos
- 17 Nayarit
- 18 Nuevo León
- 19 Oaxaca
- 20 Puebla
- 21 Querétaro
- 22 Quintana Roo
- 23 San Luis Potosí
- 24 Sinaloa
- 25 Sonora
- 26 Tabasco
- 27 Tamaulipas
- 28 Tlaxcala
- 29 Veracruz
- 30 Yucatán
- 31 Zacatecas

M	Ft
5000	16404
4000	13123
3000	9843
2000	6562
1000	3281
500	1640
+200	+656
0	
Depr.	
0	
−100	−328
200	656
1000	3281
2000	6562
4000	13123
6000	19685
8000	26247

Scale 1:12,000,000 Lambert Azimuthal Equal Area Projection

0 200 400 600 800 km

0 200 400 miles

ATLANTIC OCEAN
Sargasso Sea
Bermuda Rise
Bermuda (U.K.)
BERMUDA ISLANDS
Hamilton
Muir Seamount
Tropic of Cancer
Blake Plateau
Blake Ridge
Blake Basin
North Carolina
South Carolina
Georgia
Florida
Kentucky
APPALACHIAN MOUNTAINS
BLUE RIDGE
NORFOLK
Virginia Beach
Raleigh
Charlotte
Columbia
ATLANTA
Charleston
Savannah
JACKSONVILLE
Tallahassee
Gainesville
Orlando
TAMPA
Saint Petersburg
Fort Lauderdale
Hollywood
MIAMI
Key West
FLORIDA KEYS
BAHAMAS
BAHAMA ISLANDS
Nassau
ANDROS
GREAT EXUMA
LONG ISLAND
Great Bahama Bank
Turks and Caicos Islands (U.K.)
WEST INDIES
INDIAS OCCIDENTALES
LA HABANA
HAVANA
CUBA
Santa Clara
Camagüey
Holguín
Guantánamo
Santiago de Cuba
ISLA DE LA JUVENTUD
Cayman Islands (U.K.)
Georgetown
Cayman Trench
Cayman Ridge
Yucatan Basin
JAMAICA
KINGSTON
Montego Bay
Spanish Town
HAITI
PORT-AU-PRINCE
Cap-Haïtien
REPÚBLICA DOMINICANA
SANTO DOMINGO
SANTIAGO
LA ESPAÑOLA
Puerto Rico Trench
SAN JUAN
Puerto Rico (U.S.)
Mayagüez
Ponce
ANTILLAS MAYORES
GREATER ANTILLES
VIRGIN ISLANDS
Anguilla (U.K.)
ANTIGUA
Saint John's
Basseterre
Guadeloupe (Fr.)
DOMINICA
Roseau
Martinique (Fr.)
Fort-de-France
SAINT LUCIA
Castries
SAINT VINCENT
Kingstown
BARBADOS
Bridgetown
GRENADA
Saint George's
TRINIDAD AND TOBAGO
Port of Spain
LEEWARD ISLANDS
WINDWARD ISLANDS
ISLAS DE BARLOVENTO
ANTILLAS MENORES
LESSER ANTILLES
ISLAS DE SOTAVENTO
Aruba (Neth.)
Nederlandse Antillen
Netherlands Antilles
Oranjestad
Willemstad
Venezuelan Basin
Aves Ridge
MAR CARIBE
MAR DE LAS ANTILLAS
CARIBBEAN SEA
Colombian Basin
Beata Ridge
NICARAGUA
Managua
COSTA RICA
SAN JOSÉ
PANAMÁ
Colón
Golfo de Panamá
Puerto Cabezas
Bluefields
Limón
David
ISLA DE MALPELO (Colombia)
COLOMBIA
BOGOTÁ
MEDELLÍN
CALI
BARRANQUILLA
CARTAGENA
Santa Marta
Bucaramanga
Cúcuta
Ibagué
Pasto
Manizales
Pereira
Armenia
Buenaventura
CORDILLERA OCCIDENTAL
CORDILLERA CENTRAL
CORDILLERA ORIENTAL
VENEZUELA
CARACAS
MARACAIBO
VALENCIA
MARACAY
BARQUISIMETO
San Cristóbal
Mérida
Barinas
Maturín
Cumaná
Ciudad Bolívar
Ciudad Guayana
LLANOS
MACIZO DE LA GUAYANA
GUIANA HIGHLANDS
ECUADOR
BRASIL
BRAZIL
GUYANA

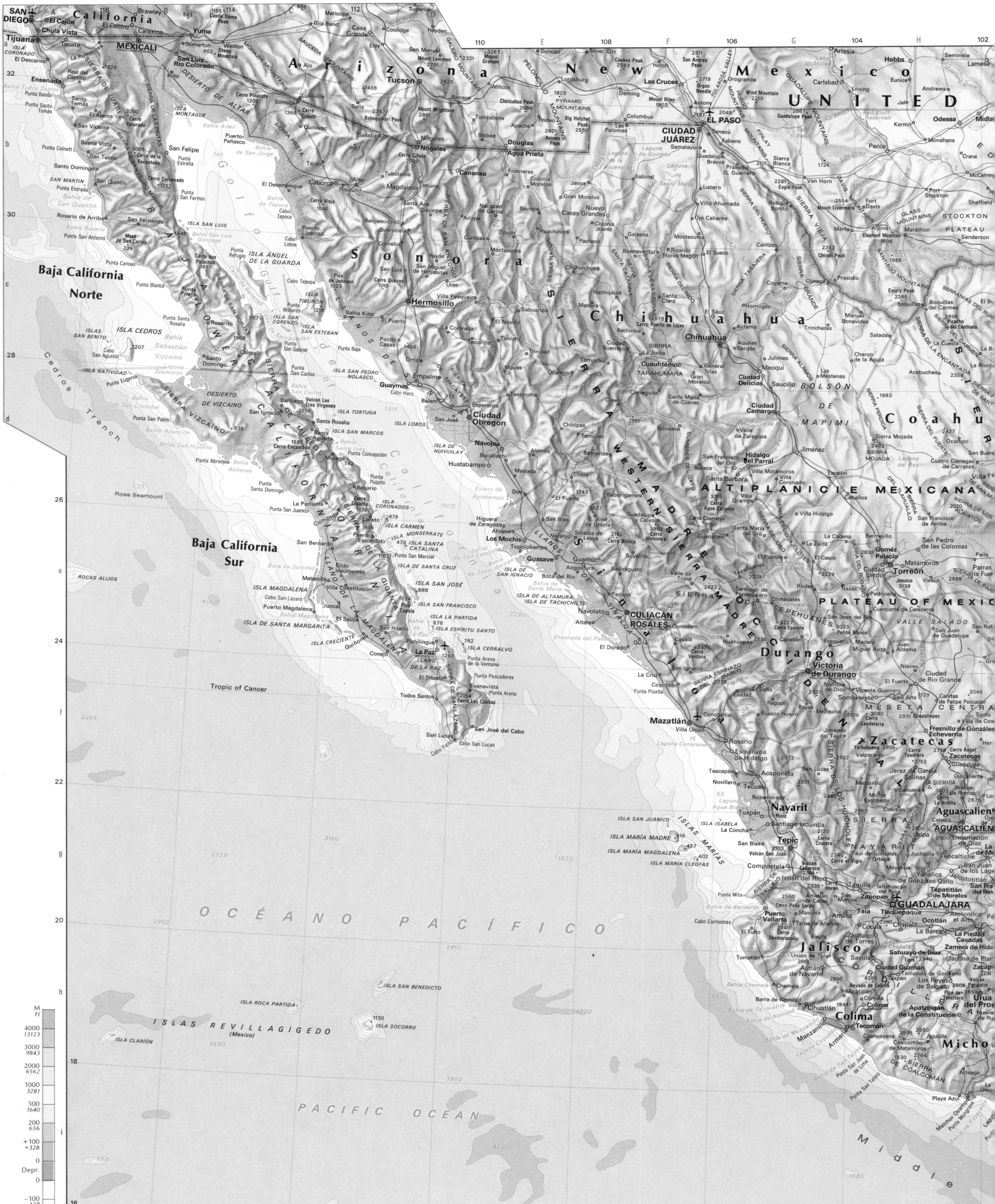

Scale 1:6,000,000 Delisle Conic Equidistant Projection

Longitude West 104 of Greenwich

0 100 200 300 400 km

0 100 200 miles

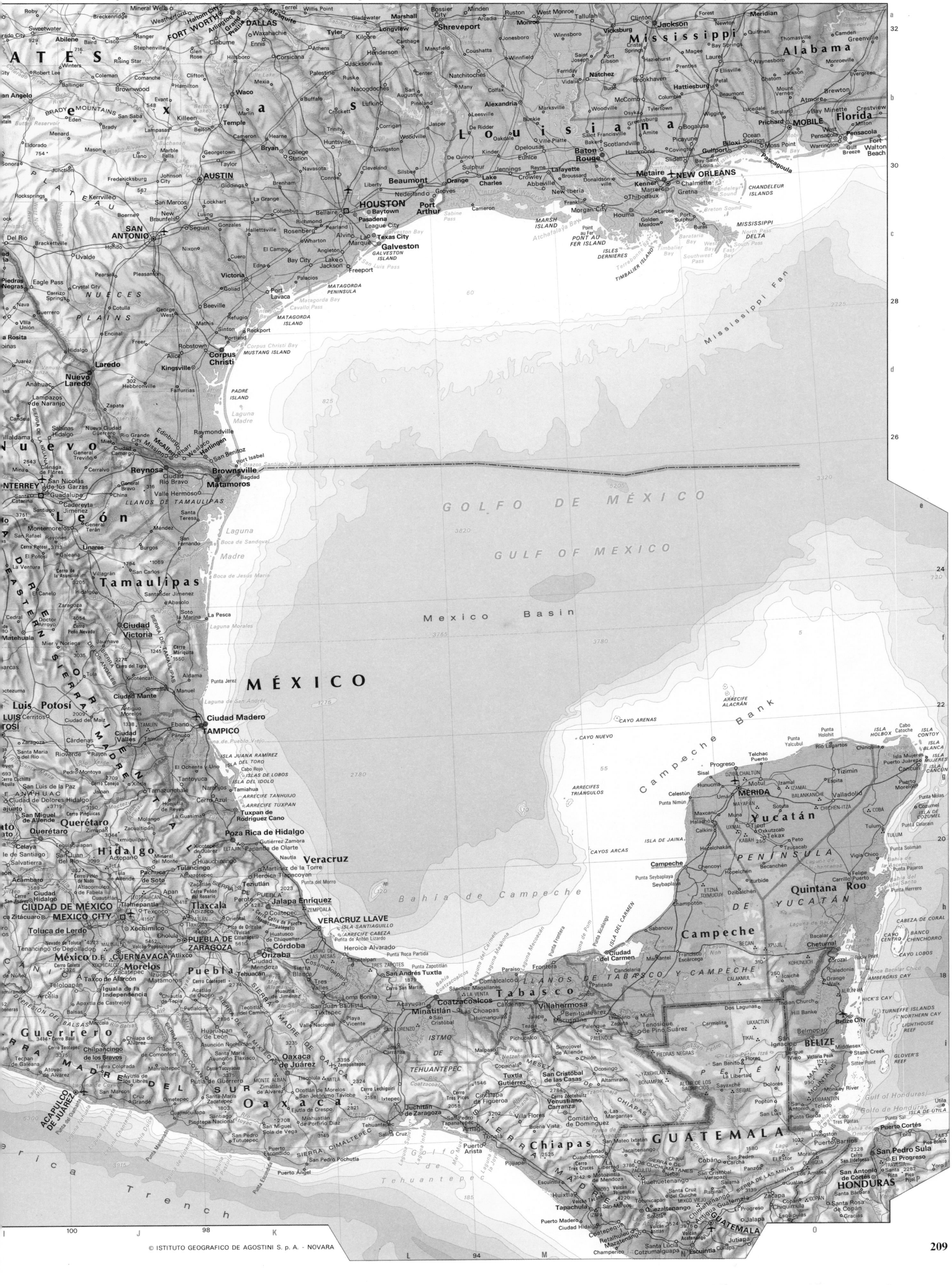
GOLFO DE MÉXICO
GULF OF MEXICO
Mexico Basin
MÉXICO
Mississippi Fan
Campeche Bank
Bahía de Campeche
Golfo de Tehuantepec
Texas
Louisiana
Mississippi
Alabama
Florida
Nuevo León
Tamaulipas
Veracruz
Yucatán
Quintana Roo
Campeche
Tabasco
Chiapas
Oaxaca
Guerrero
Puebla
Tlaxcala
Hidalgo
Querétaro
GUATEMALA
BELIZE
HONDURAS
PENÍNSULA DE YUCATÁN
ISTMO DE TEHUANTEPEC
SIERRA MADRE DEL SUR
SIERRA MADRE ORIENTAL
HOUSTON
AUSTIN
SAN ANTONIO
FORT WORTH
DALLAS
NEW ORLEANS
MOBILE
Jackson
Shreveport
Baton Rouge
Galveston
Corpus Christi
Brownsville
Matamoros
Laredo
Nuevo Laredo
Reynosa
MONTERREY
Ciudad Victoria
TAMPICO
Ciudad Madero
Poza Rica de Hidalgo
Jalapa Enríquez
VERACRUZ LLAVE
CIUDAD DE MÉXICO
MEXICO CITY
PUEBLA DE ZARAGOZA
Toluca de Lerdo
CUERNAVACA
Oaxaca de Juárez
ACAPULCO DE JUÁREZ
Coatzacoalcos
Minatitlán
Villahermosa
Ciudad del Carmen
Campeche
MÉRIDA
Progreso
Cancún
Chetumal
Belize City
GUATEMALA
Tapachula
Tuxtla Gutiérrez
San Cristóbal de las Casas
San Pedro Sula
ARRECIFE ALACRÁN
CAYO ARENAS
Middle America Trench
100
98
96
94
92
90
88
32
30
28
26
24
22
20
18

GOLFO DE MÉXICO
GULF OF MEXICO
UNITED STATES
Florida
MIAMI
Fort Lauderdale
Key West
FLORIDA KEYS
LA HABANA
HAVANA
CUBA
Yucatán
PENÍNSULA DE YUCATÁN
Quintana Roo
MÉXICO
Campeche
Tabasco
Chiapas
BELIZE
Belize City
Belmopan
GUATEMALA
EL SALVADOR
SAN SALVADOR
HONDURAS
TEGUCIGALPA
NICARAGUA
MANAGUA
COSTA RICA
SAN JOSÉ
PANAMÁ
Yucatan Basin
Cayman Ridge
Cayman Trench
Cayman Islands (U.K.)
Explorer Tablemount
Rosalind Bank
SAN ANDRÉS Y PROVIDENCIA (Colombia)
Middle America Trench
OCÉANO PACÍFICO
PACIFIC OCEAN
Guardian Seamount
Scale 1:6,000,000
Delisle Conic Equidistant Projection
0 100 200 300 400 km
0 100 200 miles

CUBA
PROVINCIAS
1 Camagüey
2 Ciego de Ávila
3 Cienfuegos
4 Ciudad de la Habana
5 Granma
6 Guantánamo
7 Holguín
8 La Habana
9 Las Tunas
10 Matanzas
11 Pinar del Río
12 Sancti Spíritus
13 Santiago de Cuba
14 Villaclara

BELIZE
DISTRICTS
1 Belize
2 Cayo
3 Corozal
4 Orange Walk
5 Stann Creek
6 Toledo

GUATEMALA
DEPARTAMENTOS
1 Alta Verapaz
2 Baja Verapaz
3 Chimaltenango
4 Chiquimula
5 El Progreso
6 Escuintla
7 Guatemala
8 Huehuetenango
9 Izabal
10 Jalapa
11 Jutiapa
12 Petén
13 Quezaltenango
14 Quiché
15 Retalhuleu
16 Sacatepéquez
17 San Marcos
18 Santa Rosa
19 Sololá
20 Suchitepéquez
21 Totonicapán
22 Zacapa

HONDURAS
DEPARTAMENTOS
1 Atlántida
2 Choluteca
3 Colón
4 Comayagua
5 Copán
6 Cortés
7 El Paraíso
8 Francisco Morazán
9 Gracias a Dios
10 Intibucá
11 Islas de la Bahía
12 La Paz
13 Lempira
14 Ocotepeque
15 Olancho
16 Santa Bárbara
17 Valle
18 Yoro

NICARAGUA
DEPARTAMENTOS
1 Boaco
2 Carazo
3 Chinandega
4 Chontales
5 Estelí
6 Granada
7 Jinotega
8 León
9 Madriz
10 Managua
11 Masaya
12 Matagalpa
13 Nueva Segovia
14 Río San Juan
15 Rivas
16 Zelaya

COSTA RICA
PROVINCIAS
1 Alajuela
2 Cartago
3 Guanacaste
4 Heredia
5 Limón
6 Puntarenas
7 San José

PANAMÁ
PROVINCIAS
1 Bocas del Toro
2 Chiriquí
3 Coclé
4 Colón
5 Darién
6 Herrera
7 Los Santos
8 Panamá
9 San Blas
10 Veraguas

© ISTITUTO GEOGRAFICO DE AGOSTINI S. p. A. - NOVARA

Scale 1:6,000,000 Delisle Conic Equidistant Projection

Longitude West 64 of Greenwich

© ISTITUTO GEOGRAFICO DE AGOSTINI S. p. A. - NOVARA

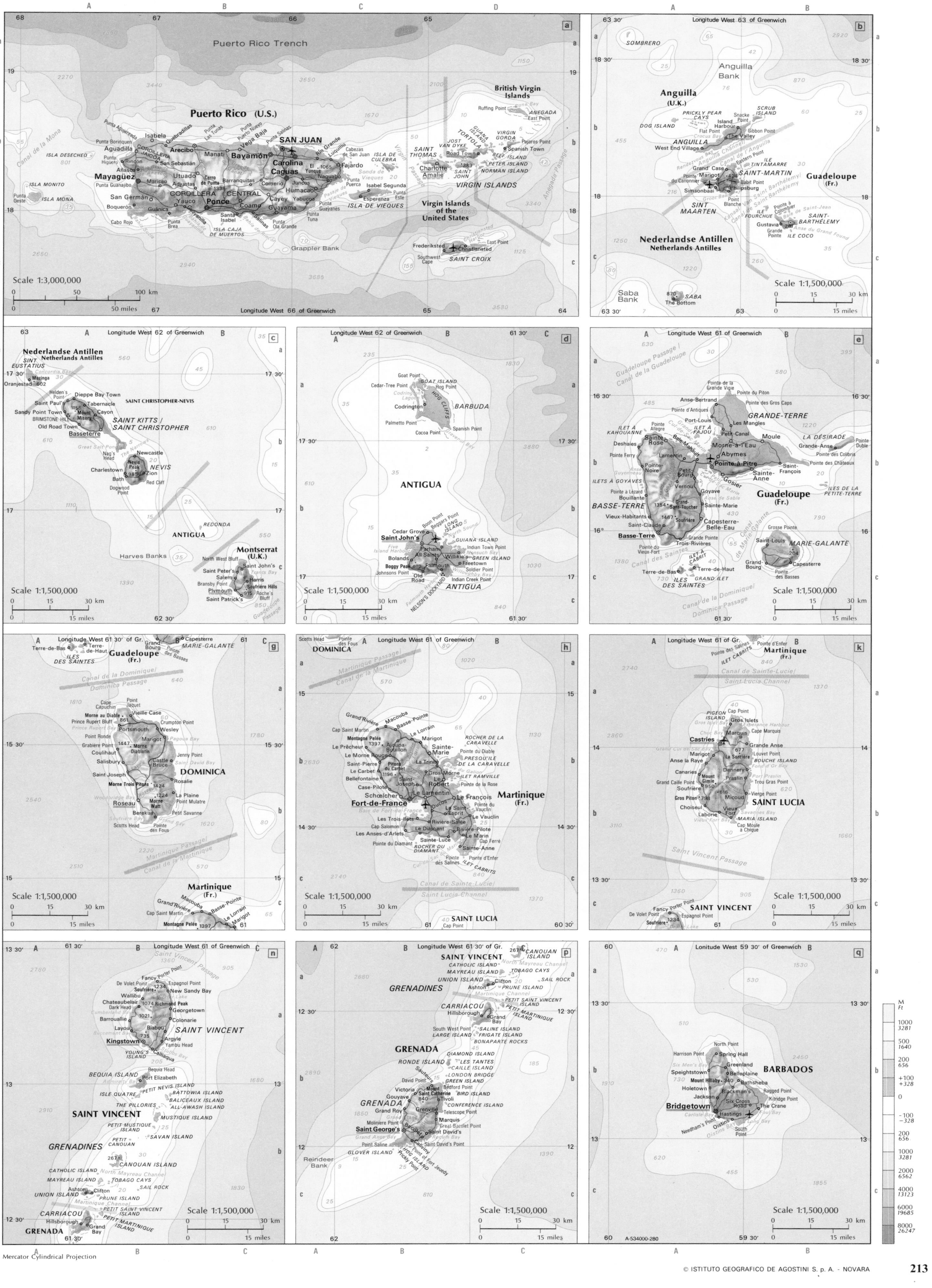

Mercator Cylindrical Projection

© ISTITUTO GEOGRAFICO DE AGOSTINI S. p. A. - NOVARA

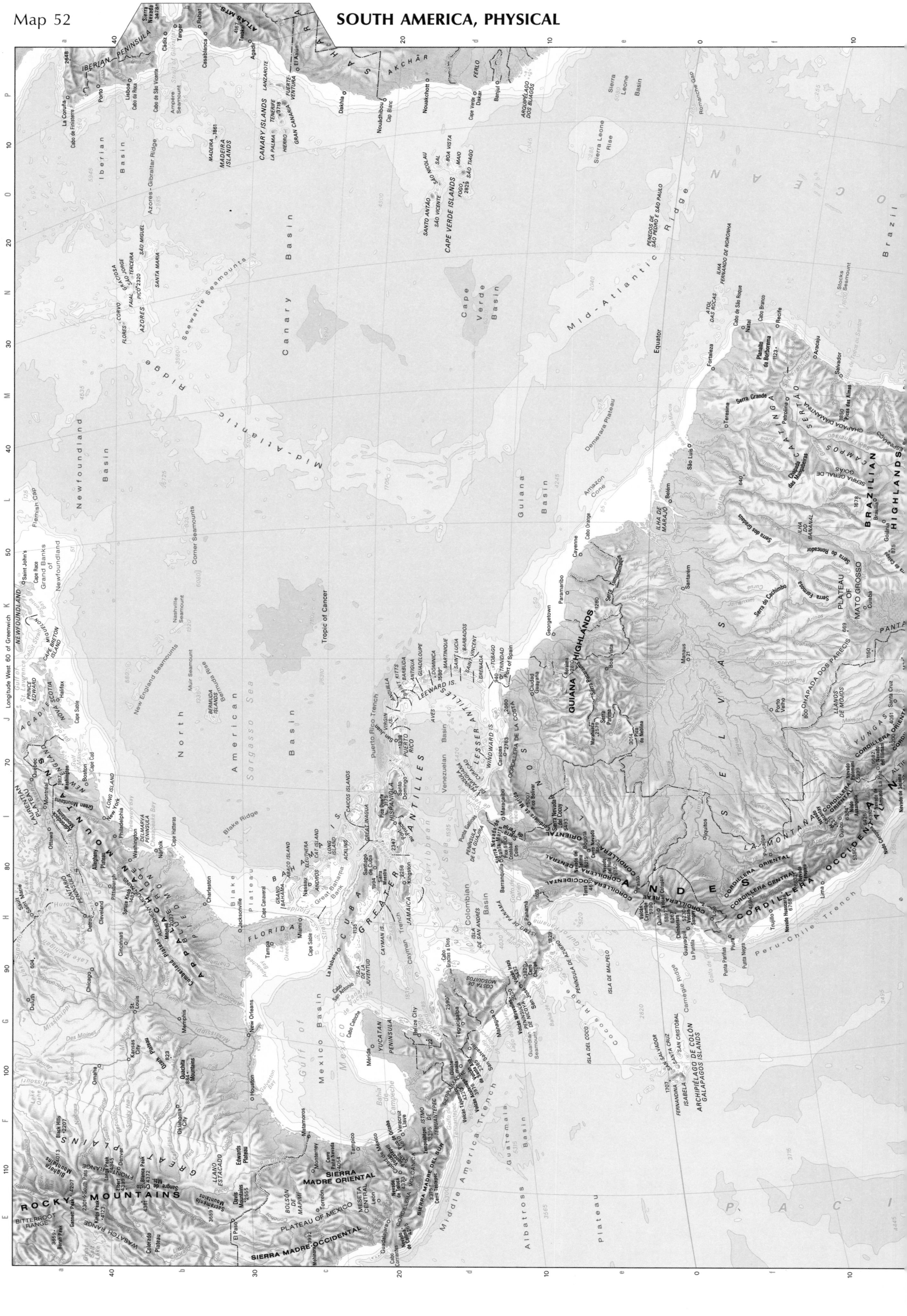
ROCKY MOUNTAINS
APPALACHIAN MOUNTAINS
SIERRA MADRE ORIENTAL
SIERRA MADRE OCCIDENTAL
PLATEAU OF MEXICO
ANDES
GUIANA HIGHLANDS
BRAZILIAN HIGHLANDS
Newfoundland Basin
North American Basin
Sargasso Sea
Canary Basin
Cape Verde Basin
Guiana Basin
Mid-Atlantic Ridge
Gulf of Mexico
Caribbean Sea
Tropic of Cancer
Equator
GREATER ANTILLES
LESSER ANTILLES
CANARY ISLANDS
CAPE VERDE ISLANDS
AZORES
IBERIAN PENINSULA
ATLAS MTS.

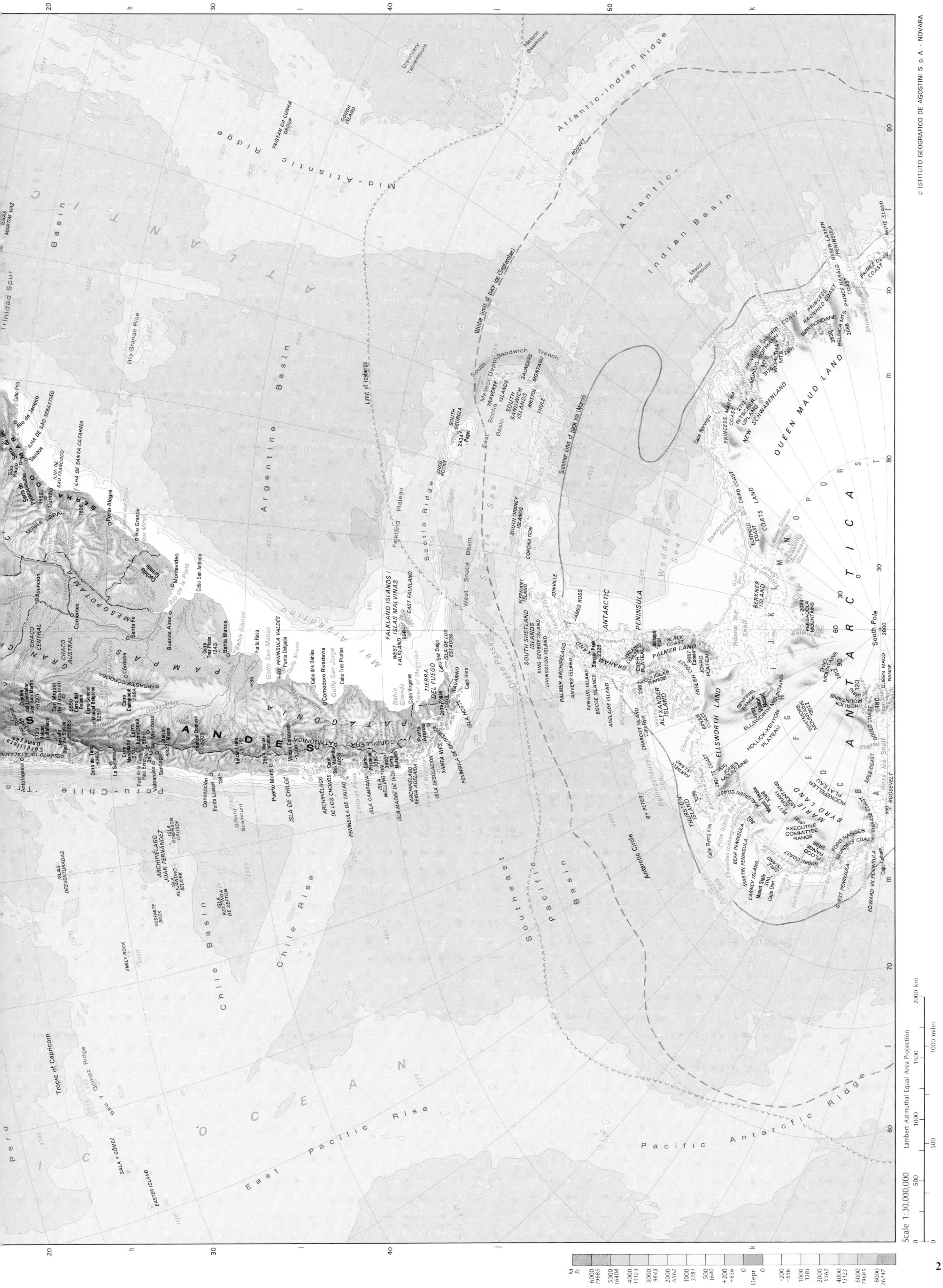

Atlantic-Indian Ridge
Mid-Atlantic Ridge
TRISTAN DA CUNHA GROUP
GOUGH ISLAND
Discovery Tablemount
Meteor Seamount
BOUVET
Atlantic-Indian Basin
Maud Seamount
Winter limit of pack ice (September)
Summer limit of pack ice (March)
Limit of icebergs
Argentine Basin
Rio Grande Rise
Trinidad Spur
South Sandwich Trench
SOUTH SANDWICH ISLANDS
SOUTH GEORGIA
SHAG ROCKS
Scotia Ridge
Scotia Sea
East Scotia Basin
West Scotia Basin
Falkland Plateau
FALKLAND ISLANDS / ISLAS MALVINAS
EAST FALKLAND
WEST FALKLAND
SOUTH ORKNEY ISLANDS
CORONATION
ELEPHANT ISLAND
SOUTH SHETLAND ISLANDS
KING GEORGE ISLAND
LIVINGSTON ISLAND
Drake Passage
TIERRA DEL FUEGO
ISLA DE LOS ESTADOS
Cape Horn
Strait of Magellan
PATAGONIA
ANDES
PAMPAS
MESOPOTAMIA
GRAN CHACO
CHACO CENTRAL
CHACO AUSTRAL
SERRA GERAL
Rio de Janeiro
Santos
Pôrto Alegre
Montevideo
Buenos Aires
Bahía Blanca
Mar Argentino
Golfo San Jorge
Golfo San Matías
PENÍNSULA VALDÉS
Asunción
Córdoba
Mendoza
Santiago
Valparaíso
Concepción
Puerto Montt
ISLA DE CHILOÉ
ARCHIPIÉLAGO DE LOS CHONOS
PENÍNSULA DE TAITAO
Antofagasta
Cerro Aconcagua 6960
Chile Basin
Chile Rise
Southeast Pacific Basin
East Pacific Rise
Pacific-Antarctic Ridge
Sala y Gómez Ridge
EASTER ISLAND
SALA Y GÓMEZ
ISLAS DESVENTURADAS
ARCHIPIÉLAGO JUAN FERNÁNDEZ
PACIFIC OCEAN
ATLANTIC OCEAN
Tropic of Capricorn
Antarctic Circle
ANTARCTICA
ANTARCTIC PENINSULA
GRAHAM LAND
PALMER LAND
ALEXANDER ISLAND
ELLSWORTH LAND
ELLSWORTH MOUNTAINS
HOLLICK-KENYON PLATEAU
MARIE BYRD LAND
ROCKEFELLER PLATEAU
EXECUTIVE COMMITTEE RANGE
THURSTON ISLAND
PETER I
Bellingshausen Sea
Amundsen Sea
Weddell Sea
Ronne Ice Shelf
BERKNER ISLAND
COATS LAND
QUEEN MAUD LAND
NEW SCHWABENLAND
PRINCESS MARTHA COAST
PRINCESS ASTRID COAST
PRINCESS RAGNHILD COAST
PRINCE HARALD COAST
PRINCE OLAV COAST
SØR RONDANE
BELGICA MTS.
PENSACOLA MOUNTAINS
THIEL MOUNTAINS
HORLICK MOUNTAINS
QUEEN MAUD RANGE
South Pole 2800
ROOSEVELT
Ross Ice Shelf
EDWARD VII PENINSULA
Scale 1:30,000,000
Lambert Azimuthal Equal Area Projection
0 500 1000 1500 2000 km
0 500 1000 miles
M Ft
6000 19685
5000 16404
4000 13123
3000 9843
2000 6562
1000 3281
500 1640
+200 +656
0 0
Depr.
0
-200 -656
1000 3281
2000 6562
4000 13123
6000 19685
8000 26247

© ISTITUTO GEOGRAFICO DE AGOSTINI S. p. A. - NOVARA

SOUTH AMERICA, POLITICAL

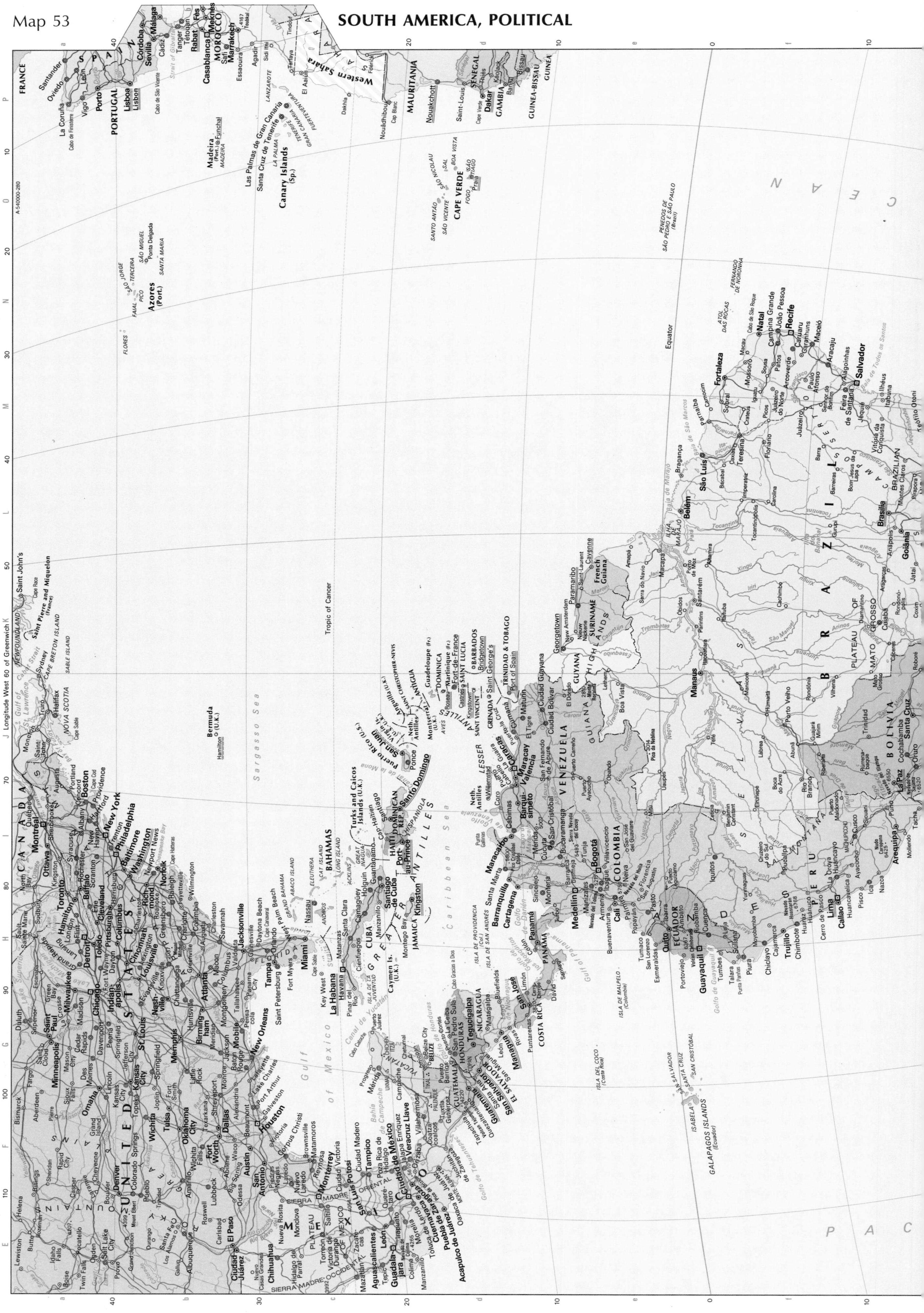

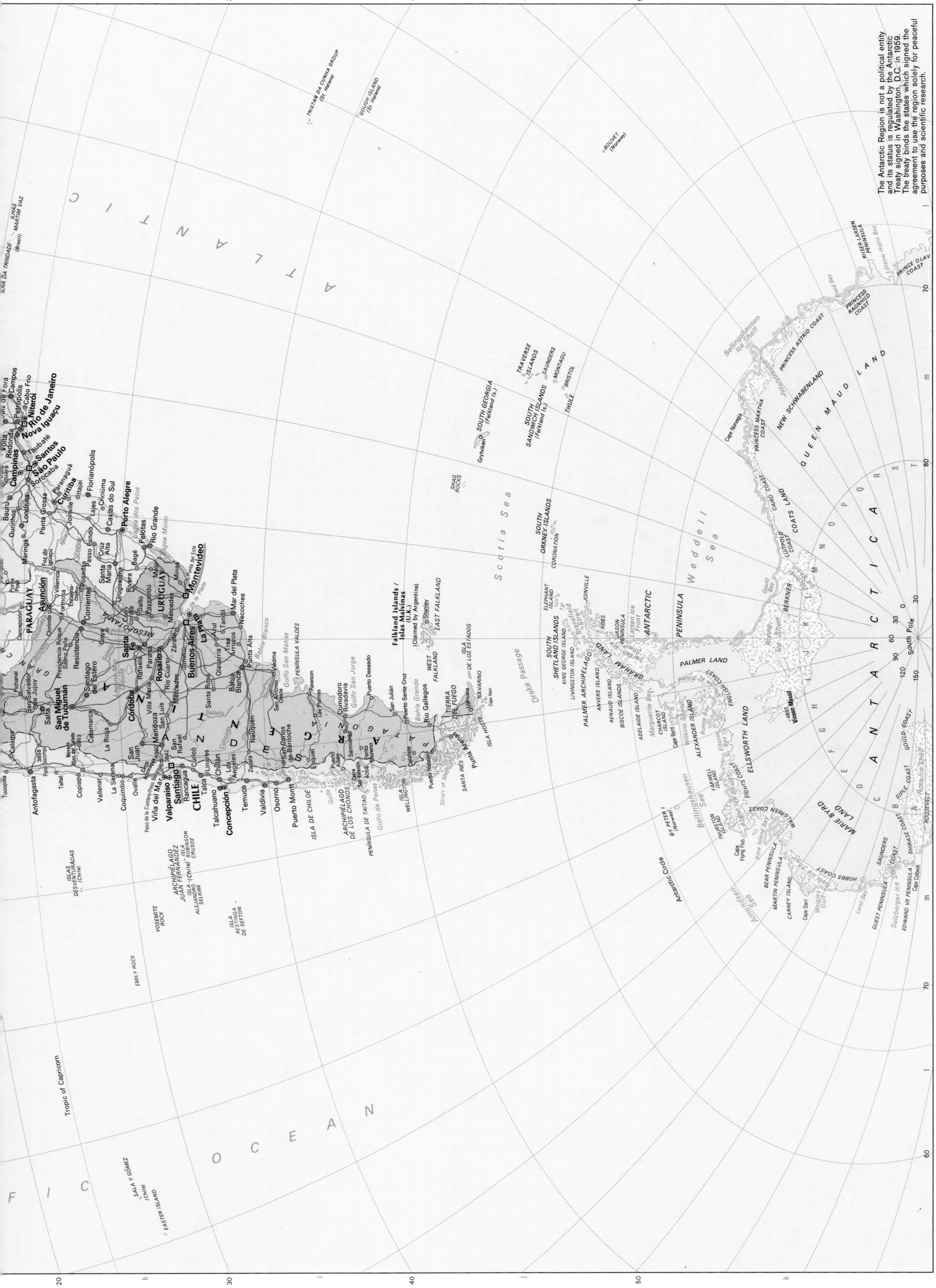

The Antarctic Region is not a political entity and its status is regulated by the Antarctic Treaty signed in Washington, D.C. in 1959. The treaty binds the states which signed the agreement to use the region solely for peaceful purposes and scientific research.
ATLANTIC
PACIFIC OCEAN
Tropic of Capricorn
Antarctic Circle
South Pole
ANTARCTICA
Scotia Sea
Weddell Sea
Drake Passage
Bellingshausen Sea
Amundsen Sea
PARAGUAY
URUGUAY
CHILE
ARGENTINA
PATAGONIA
Asunción
Montevideo
Buenos Aires
Santiago
Rio de Janeiro
São Paulo
Porto Alegre
Curitiba
Florianópolis
Córdoba
Rosario
Santa Fe
La Plata
Mar del Plata
Bahía Blanca
Mendoza
San Miguel de Tucumán
Salta
Valparaíso
Concepción
Temuco
Valdivia
Osorno
Puerto Montt
Antofagasta
Comodoro Rivadavia
Río Gallegos
Ushuaia
Punta Arenas
Falkland Islands / Islas Malvinas (U.K.) (Claimed by Argentina)
Stanley
EAST FALKLAND
WEST FALKLAND
TIERRA DEL FUEGO
ISLA DE LOS ESTADOS
SOUTH GEORGIA (Falkland Is.)
Grytviken
SHAG ROCKS
SOUTH SANDWICH ISLANDS (Falkland Is.)
TRAVERSE ISLANDS
SAUNDERS
MONTAGU
BRISTOL
THULE
SOUTH ORKNEY ISLANDS
CORONATION
SOUTH SHETLAND ISLANDS
KING GEORGE ISLAND
LIVINGSTON ISLAND
ELEPHANT ISLAND
JOINVILLE
PALMER ARCHIPELAGO
ANVERS ISLAND
RENAUD ISLAND
BISCOE ISLANDS
ADELAIDE ISLAND
ALEXANDER ISLAND
CHARCOT ISLAND
ANTARCTIC PENINSULA
GRAHAM LAND
PALMER LAND
ELLSWORTH LAND
Vinson Massif
BERKNER
COATS LAND
QUEEN MAUD LAND
NEW SCHWABENLAND
PRINCESS MARTHA COAST
PRINCESS ASTRID COAST
PRINCESS RAGNHILD COAST
PRINCE OLAV COAST
RISER-LARSEN PENINSULA
CAIRD COAST
LUITPOLD COAST
MARIE BYRD LAND
HOBBS COAST
WALGREEN COAST
EIGHTS COAST
SIPLE COAST
GOULD COAST
Ross Ice Shelf
ROOSEVELT
EDWARD VII PENINSULA
THURSTON ISLAND
CARNEY ISLAND
MARTIN PENINSULA
BEAR PENINSULA
PETER I (Norway)
BOUVET (Norway)
GOUGH ISLAND (St. Helena)
TRISTAN DA CUNHA GROUP (St. Helena)
ILHA DA TRINDADE (Brazil)
ILHAS MARTIM VAZ
ISLAS DESVENTURADAS (Chile)
ARCHIPIÉLAGO JUAN FERNÁNDEZ
ISLA ROBINSON CRUSOE
ISLA ALEJANDRO SELKIRK
SALA Y GÓMEZ (Chile)
EASTER ISLAND
EMILY ROCK
YOSEMITE ROCK
ISLA RESTINGA DE SEFTON
ISLA DE CHILOÉ
ARCHIPIÉLAGO DE LOS CHONOS
PENÍNSULA DE TAITAO
ISLA WELLINGTON
PENÍNSULA VALDÉS
Scale 1:30,000,000
Lambert Azimuthal Equal Area Projection

© ISTITUTO GEOGRAFICO DE AGOSTINI S. p. A. - NOVARA

Map 54 NORTHERN SOUTH AMERICA

COLOMBIA

DISTRITO ESPECIAL

A Bogotá

DEPARTAMENTOS

1 Antioquia
2 Atlántico
3 Bolívar
4 Boyacá
5 Caldas
5A Caquetá
6 Cauca
7 Cesar
8 Chocó
9 Córdoba
10 Cundinamarca
11 Huila
12 La Guajira
13 Magdalena
14 Meta
15 Nariño
16 Norte de Santander
17 Quindío
18 Risaralda
19 Santander
20 Sucre
21 Tolima
22 Valle

INTENDENCIAS

23 Arauca
25 Casanare
26 Putumayo
27 San Andrés y Providencia

COMISARÍAS

28 Amazonas
29 Guainía
30 Guaviare
31 Vaupés
32 Vichada

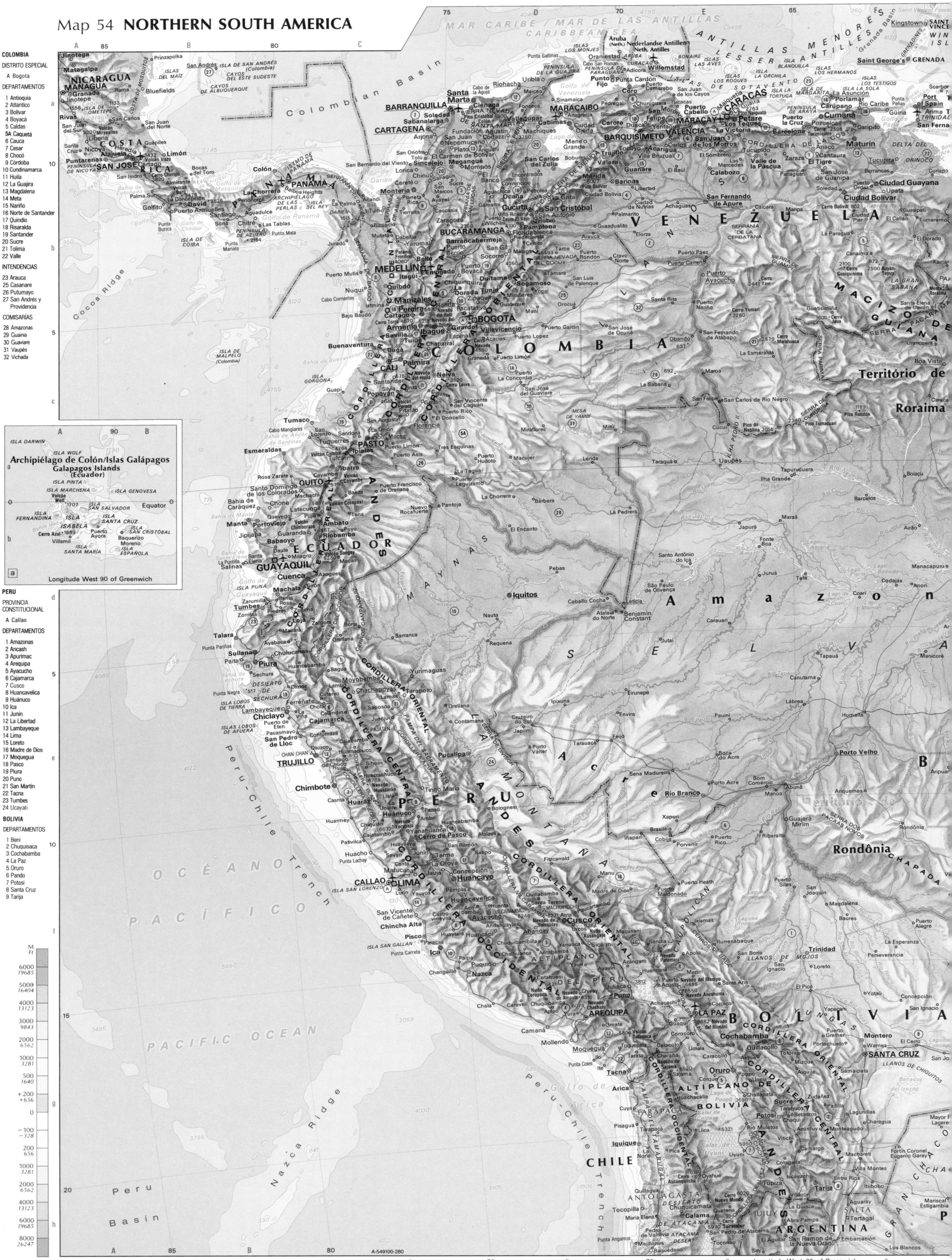

PERU

PROVINCIA CONSTITUCIONAL

A Callao

DEPARTAMENTOS

1 Amazonas
2 Ancash
3 Apurímac
4 Arequipa
5 Ayacucho
6 Cajamarca
7 Cusco
8 Huancavelica
9 Huánuco
10 Ica
11 Junín
12 La Libertad
13 Lambayeque
14 Lima
15 Loreto
16 Madre de Dios
17 Moquegua
18 Pasco
19 Piura
20 Puno
21 San Martín
22 Tacna
23 Tumbes
24 Ucayali

BOLIVIA

DEPARTAMENTOS

1 Beni
2 Chuquisaca
3 Cochabamba
4 La Paz
5 Oruro
6 Pando
7 Potosí
8 Santa Cruz
9 Tarija

M	Ft
6000	19685
5000	16404
4000	13123
3000	9843
2000	6562
1000	3281
500	1640
+200	+656
0	
−100	−328
200	656
1000	3281
2000	6562
4000	13123
6000	19685
8000	26247

Scale 1:12,000,000 Lambert Azimuthal Equal Area Projection

0 200 400 600 800 km

0 200 400 miles

VENEZUELA
DISTRITO FEDERAL
A Caracas
ESTADOS
1 Anzoátegui
2 Apure
3 Aragua
4 Barinas
5 Bolívar
6 Carabobo
7 Cojedes
8 Falcón
9 Guárico
10 Lara
11 Mérida
12 Miranda
13 Monagas
14 Nueva Esparta
15 Portuguesa
16 Sucre
17 Táchira
18 Trujillo
19 Yaracuy
20 Zulia
TERRITORIOS FEDERALES
21 Amazonas
22 Delta Amacuro
23 DEPENDENCIAS FEDERALES
Islas Los Monjes
Isla La Tortuga
Islas Los Frailes
Isla La Sola
Islas Los Testigos
Islas Las Aves
Islas Los Roques
Isla La Orchila
Isla Blanquilla
Islas Los Hermanos
Isla de Patos
Isla de Aves
Mid-Atlantic Ridge
Guiana Basin
OCEANO ATLÂNTICO
ATLANTIC OCEAN
Equator
Tropic of Capricorn
SURINAME
Guyane Française
French Guiana
GUAYANA HIGHLANDS
Georgetown
Paramaribo
Cayenne
Território do Amapá
Macapá
ILHA DE MARAJÓ
BELÉM
São Luís
FORTALEZA
NATAL
João Pessoa
RECIFE
Olinda
Maceió
Aracaju
SALVADOR
Pará
Maranhão
Piauí
Ceará
Rio Grande do Norte
Paraíba
Pernambuco
Alagoas
Sergipe
Bahia
Goiás
Mato Grosso
Mato Grosso do Sul
Minas Gerais
Espírito Santo
São Paulo
Paraná
BRAZIL
BRASÍLIA
Distrito Federal
GOIÂNIA
BELO HORIZONTE
Vitória
RIO DE JANEIRO
SÃO PAULO
SANTOS
CAMPINAS
Campo Grande
Cuiabá
Corumbá
Teresina
Território de Fernando de Noronha
ATOL DAS ROCAS
PLANALTO DO MATO GROSSO
MATO GROSSO PLATEAU
PLANALTO DO BRASIL
BRAZILIAN HIGHLANDS
SERRA DO CACHIMBO
SERRA DO RONCADOR
SERRA DOS CARAJÁS
CHAPADA DIAMANTINA
SERRA DO ESPINHAÇO
SERRA DA MANTIQUEIRA
SERRA DE MARACAJU
ESPIGÃO MESTRE
PARAGUAY
Stocks Seamount
Gröll Seamount
Hotspur Seamount
Columbia Seamount
Trinidade Spur
ARQUIPÉLAGO DOS ABROLHOS

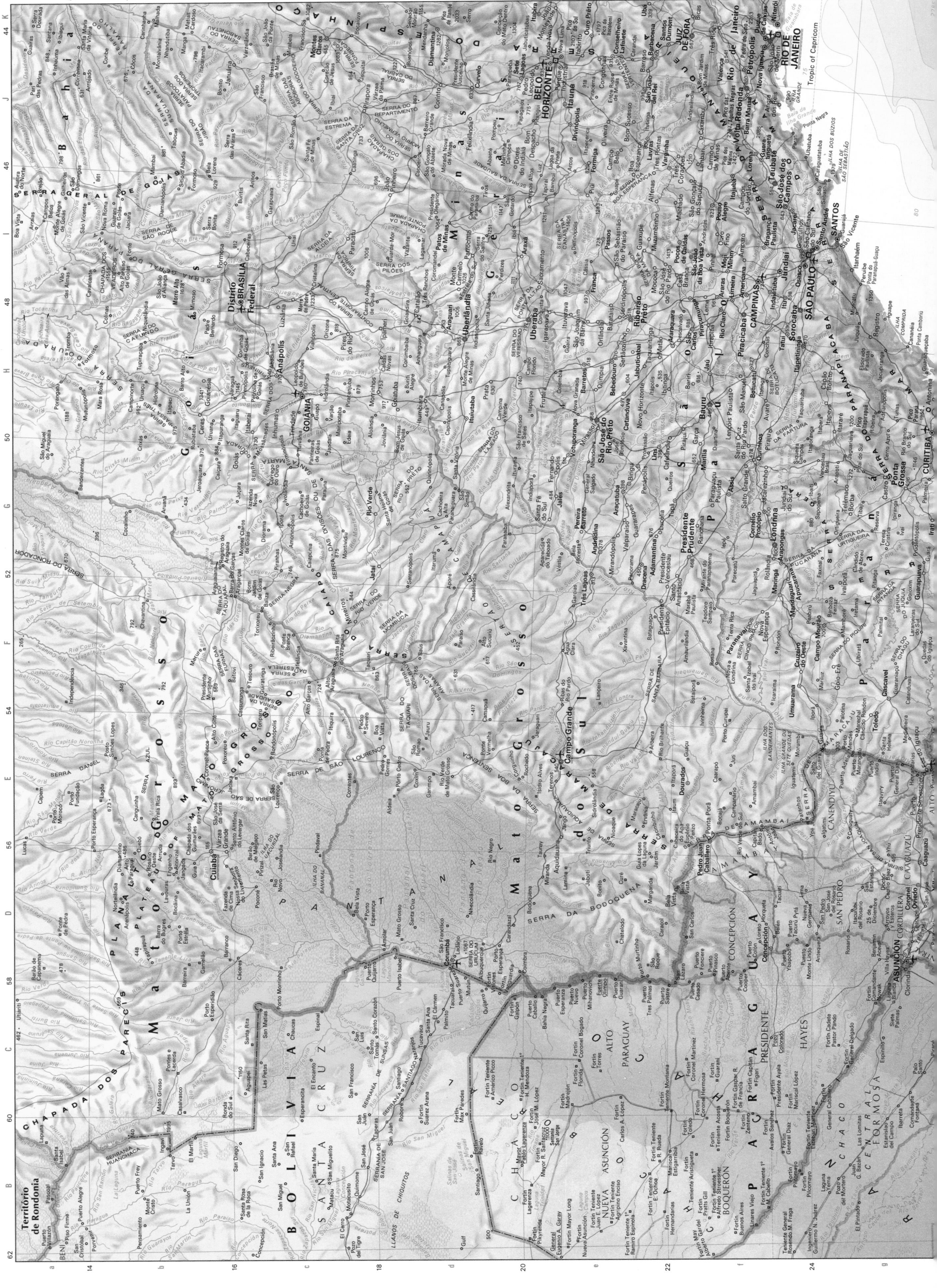
RIO DE JANEIRO
SÃO PAULO
BELO HORIZONTE
BRASÍLIA
Distrito Federal
GOIÂNIA
CURITIBA
ASUNCIÓN
SANTOS
CAMPINAS
Juiz de Fora
Uberlândia
Campo Grande
Cuiabá
Corumbá
Londrina
Tropic of Capricorn
Território de Rondonia
BOLIVIA
PARAGUAY
Mato Grosso
Mato Grosso do Sul
Goiás
Minas Gerais
São Paulo
Paraná
Bahia

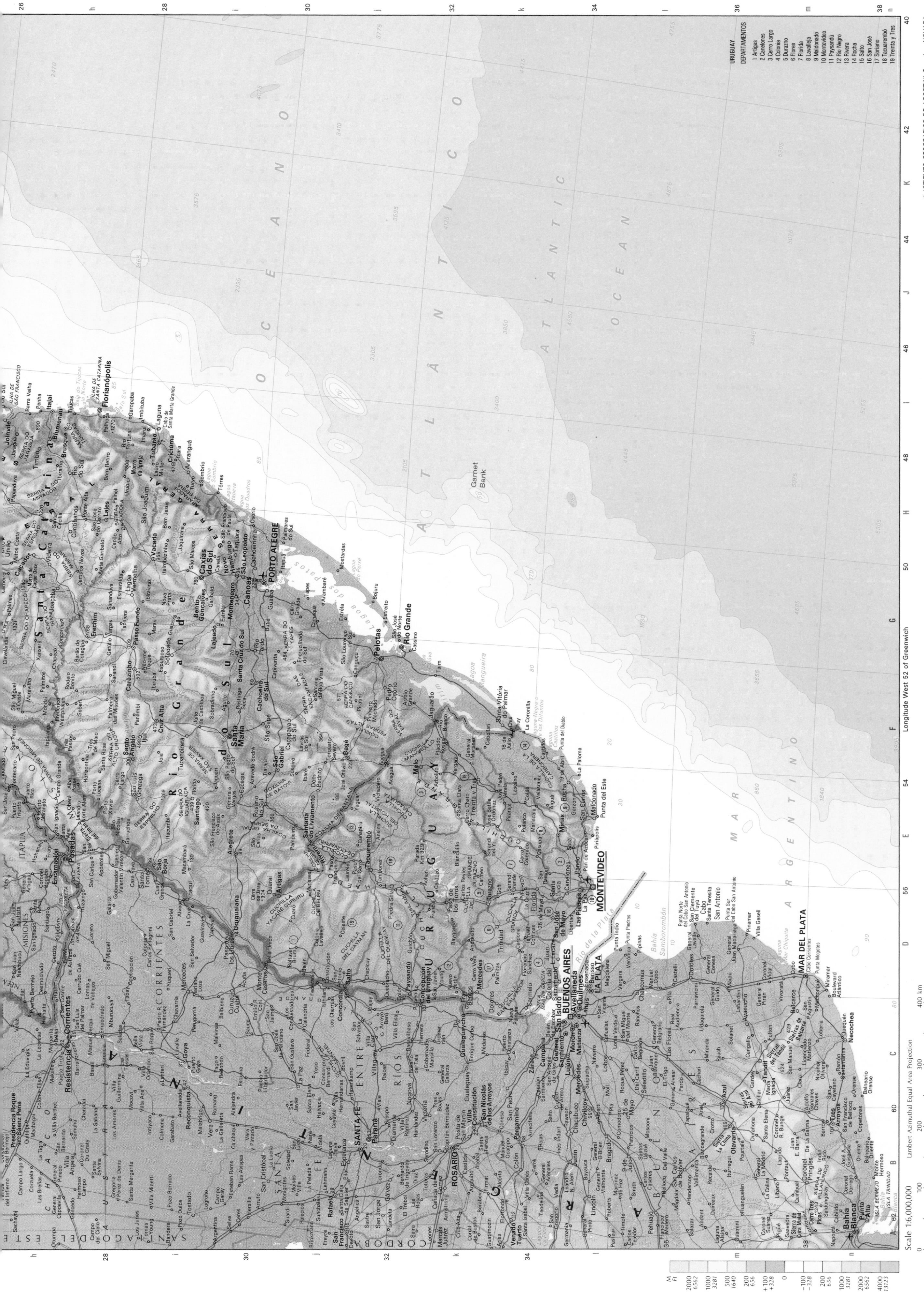
ATLANTIC OCEAN
OCEANO ATLÂNTICO
MAR ARGENTINO
URUGUAY DEPARTAMENTOS
1 Artigas
2 Canelones
3 Cerro Largo
4 Colonia
5 Durazno
6 Flores
7 Florida
8 Lavalleja
9 Maldonado
10 Montevideo
11 Paysandú
12 Río Negro
13 Rivera
14 Rocha
15 Salto
16 San José
17 Soriano
18 Tacuarembó
19 Treinta y Tres
Garnet Bank
Florianópolis
PORTO ALEGRE
Pelotas
Rio Grande
MONTEVIDEO
BUENOS AIRES
LA PLATA
MAR DEL PLATA
ROSARIO
SANTA FE
Paraná
Corrientes
Resistencia
Posadas
Encarnación
Bahía Blanca
Necochea
Río de la Plata
Lagoa dos Patos
Longitude West 52 of Greenwich
Scale 1:6,000,000
Lambert Azimuthal Equal Area Projection
© ISTITUTO GEOGRAFICO DE AGOSTINI S. p. A. - NOVARA

CHILE
REGIÓN METROPOLITANA
A Santiago
REGIONES
1 Tarapacá
2 Antofagasta
3 Atacama
4 Coquimbo
5 Aconcagua
6 Libertador General Bernardo O'Higgins
7 Maule
8 Bío Bío
9 Araucanía
10 Los Lagos
11 Aisén del General Carlos Ibáñez del Campo
12 Magallanes y Antártica Chilena

ARGENTINA
A CAPITAL FEDERAL
PROVINCIAS
1 Buenos Aires
2 Catamarca
3 Chaco
4 Chubut
5 Córdoba
6 Corrientes
7 Entre Ríos
8 Formosa
9 Jujuy
10 La Pampa
11 La Rioja
12 Mendoza
13 Misiones
14 Neuquén
15 Río Negro
16 Salta
17 San Juan
18 San Luis
19 Santa Cruz
20 Santa Fe
21 Santiago del Estero
22 Tierra del Fuego
23 Tucumán

M / Ft
6000 / 19685
5000 / 16404
4000 / 13123
3000 / 9843
2000 / 6562
1000 / 3281
500 / 1640
+200 / +656
0
Depr.
0
– 100 / –328
200 / 656
1000 / 3281
2000 / 6562
4000 / 13123
6000 / 19685
8000 / 26247

Scale 1:12,000,000 Lambert Azimuthal Equal Area Projection
0 200 400 600 800 km
0 200 400 miles

OCÉANO ATLÁNTICO
ATLANTIC OCEAN
Argentine Basin
Rio Grande Rise
Falkland Plateau
Scotia Ridge
West Scotia Basin
Trinidade Spur
Hotspur Seamount
Columbia Seamount
BRASIL
BRAZIL
URUGUAY
Mato Grosso do Sul
Minas Gerais
São Paulo
Paraná
Santa Catarina
Rio Grande do Sul
Espírito Santo
Malvinas
SÃO PAULO
RIO DE JANEIRO
BELO HORIZONTE
CURITIBA
PORTO ALEGRE
MONTEVIDEO
BUENOS AIRES
LA PLATA
ASUNCIÓN
SANTOS
CAMPINAS
Campo Grande
Florianópolis
Vitória
Rio Grande
Mar del Plata
Pelotas
Corrientes
Posadas
Londrina
Uberlândia
Uberaba
Ribeirão Prêto
Joinvile
Blumenau
Caxias do Sul
Juiz de Fora
Campos
Governador Valadares
Colatina
Paysandú
Salto
Rivera
Melo
Minas
Punta del Este
Maldonado
SHAG ROCKS
BLACK ROCK
SOUTH GEORGIA/ ISLAS GEORGIAS DEL SUR (Falkland Is.)
Grytviken
Cape Disappointment
Stanley/ Puerto Stanley
EAST FALKLAND/ ISLA SOLEDAD
Rhine Bank
Longitude West 50 of Greenwich

CHINA
QIN LING
NAN LING
WUYI SHAN
Shanghai
Nanjing
Wuhan
Chongqing
Chengdu
Guangzhou Canton
Fuzhou
Xiamen Amoy
Victoria
HAINAN
TONKIN
INDOCHINA
Phnum Pénh
Ho Chi Minh Saigon
MEKONG DELTA
PARACEL ISLANDS
South China Basin
South China Sea
East China Sea
Yellow Sea
Sea of Japan
HONSHU
SHIKOKU
KYUSHU
Tōkyō
Osaka
Nagasaki
Pusan
RYUKYU ISLANDS
TAIWAN FORMOSA
Taipei
PHILIPPINE ISLANDS
LUZON
Manila
MINDORO
PALAWAN
SAMAR
LEYTE
PANAY
NEGROS
CEBU
BOHOL
MINDANAO
Davao
Philippine Sea
Philippine Basin
Philippine Trench
Ryukyu Trench
Kyushu-Palau Ridge
West Mariana Basin
South Honshu Ridge
Bonin Trench
IZU ISLANDS
BONIN ISLANDS
VOLCANO ISLANDS
MARIANA ISLANDS
GUAM
SAIPAN
TINIAN
Mariana Trench
East Mariana Basin
Northwest Pacific Basin
MARCUS ISLAND
WAKE
Mid-Pacific Mountains
MARSHALL ISLANDS
MICRONESIA
CAROLINE ISLANDS
West Caroline Basin
East Caroline Basin
PALAU ISLANDS
YAP ISLANDS
TRUK ISLANDS
KIRIBATI
NAURU
BORNEO
KALIMANTAN
Kinabalu
CELEBES
Celebes Sea
MOLUCCAS
HALMAHERA
CERAM
BURU
GREATER SUNDA ISLANDS
Java Sea
JAVA
Jakarta
Surabaya
SUMATRA
LESSER SUNDA ISLANDS
BALI
LOMBOK
SUMBAWA
FLORES
SUMBA
TIMOR
Banda Sea
TANIMBAR ISLANDS
ARU ISLANDS
NEW GUINEA
Jayapura
Puncak Jaya
Port Moresby
Gulf of Papua
BISMARCK ARCHIPELAGO
NEW BRITAIN
NEW IRELAND
ADMIRALTY ISLANDS
MELANESIA
SOLOMON ISLANDS
BOUGAINVILLE
GUADALCANAL
Solomon Sea
Coral Sea
Coral Sea Basin
NEW HEBRIDES
NEW CALEDONIA
LOYALTY IS.
FIJI ISLANDS
TUVALU (ELLICE) ISLANDS
North Fiji Basin
South Fiji Basin
Melanesian Basin
Arafura Sea
Timor Sea
Java Trench
North Australian Basin
Gulf of Carpentaria
CAPE YORK PENINSULA
ARNHEM LAND
Darwin
KIMBERLEY PLATEAU
Broome
GREAT BARRIER REEF
GREAT DIVIDING RANGE
AUSTRALIA
GREAT SANDY DESERT
TANAMI DESERT
BARKLY TABLELAND
MACDONNELL RANGES
Alice Springs
GIBSON DESERT
SIMPSON DESERT
GREAT ARTESIAN BASIN
MUSGRAVE RANGES
GREAT VICTORIA DESERT
NULLARBOR PLAIN
Lake Eyre
Lake Torrens
Lake Frome
Brisbane
Sydney
Canberra
Melbourne
Perth
Albany
Great Australian Bight
KANGAROO
Bass Strait
TASMANIA
Hobart
Mount Kosciusko
Tasman Sea
Tasman Basin
Lord Howe Rise
NORFOLK
LORD HOWE
NEW ZEALAND
NORTH ISLAND
SOUTH ISLAND
Auckland
Wellington
Christchurch
Dunedin
Mount Cook
South Australian Basin
INDIAN OCEAN
Tasman Plateau
Campbell Plateau
AUCKLAND ISLANDS
M Ft
6000 19685
5000 16404
4000 13123
3000 9843
2000 6562
1000 3281
500 1640
+200 +656
0
Depr.
0
−200 −656
1000 3281
2000 6562
4000 13123
6000 19685
8000 26247
A-590000-780
Longitude East 170 of Greenwich

Scale 1:30,000,000 Lambert Azimuthal Equal Area Projection

0 500 1000 1500 2000 km

0 500 1000 miles

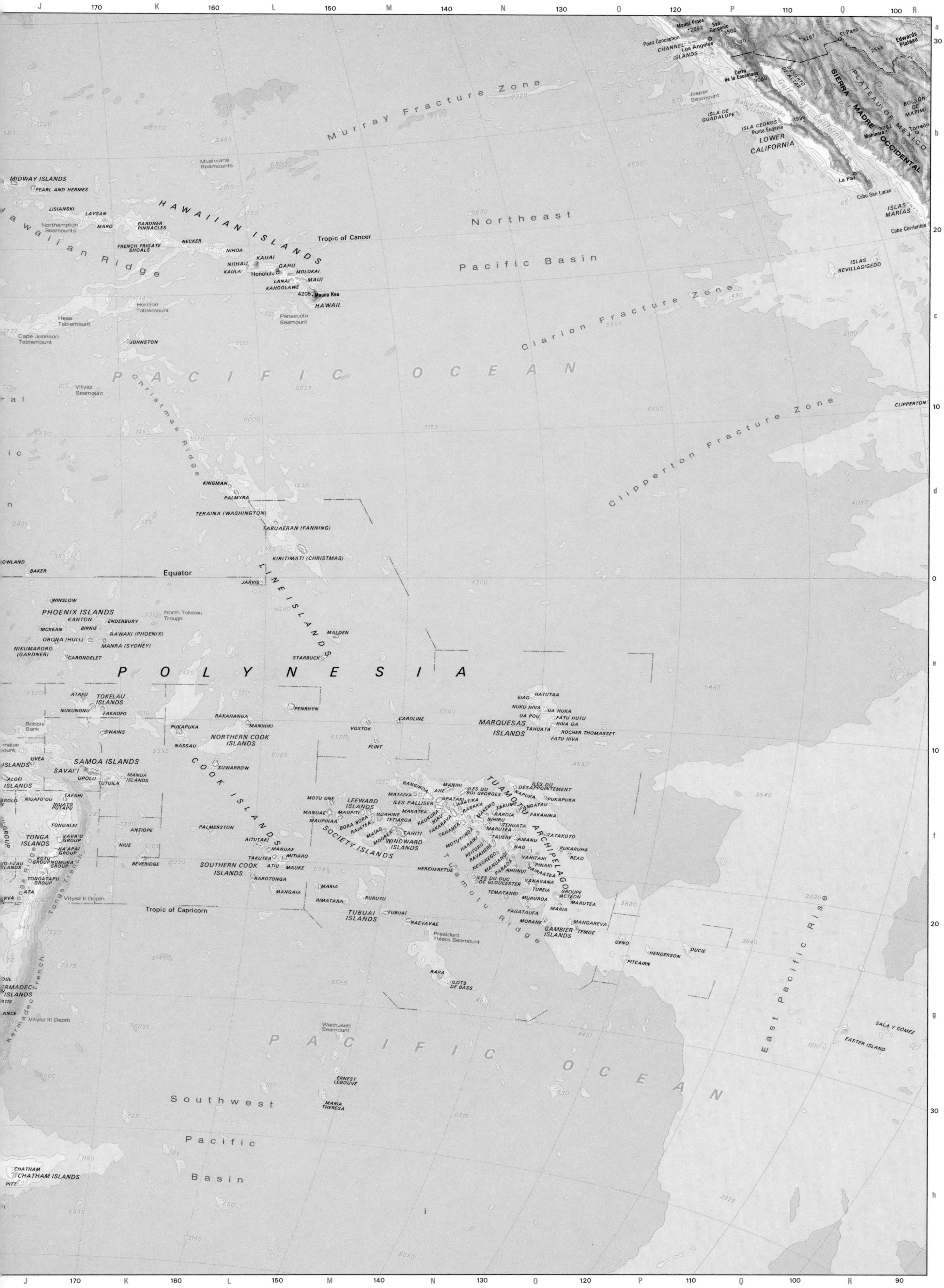
PACIFIC OCEAN
POLYNESIA
HAWAIIAN ISLANDS
Hawaiian Ridge
MIDWAY ISLANDS
PEARL AND HERMES
LISIANSKI
LAYSAN
MARO
Northampton Seamounts
GARDNER PINNACLES
FRENCH FRIGATE SHOALS
NECKER
NIHOA
KAUAI
NIIHAU
KAULA
OAHU
Honolulu
MOLOKAI
LANAI
MAUI
KAHOOLAWE
Mauna Kea
HAWAII
Tropic of Cancer
Murray Fracture Zone
Northeast Pacific Basin
Clarion Fracture Zone
Clipperton Fracture Zone
CLIPPERTON
Musicians Seamounts
Horizon Tablemount
Hess Tablemount
Cape Johnson Tablemount
JOHNSTON
Pensacola Seamount
Vityaz Seamount
Christmas Ridge
KINGMAN
PALMYRA
TERAINA (WASHINGTON)
TABUAERAN (FANNING)
KIRITIMATI (CHRISTMAS)
LINE ISLANDS
JARVIS
BAKER
Equator
WINSLOW
PHOENIX ISLANDS
KANTON
ENDERBURY
MCKEAN
BIRNIE
ORONA (HULL)
RAWAKI (PHOENIX)
MANRA (SYDNEY)
NIKUMARORO (GARDNER)
CARONDELET
North Tokelau Trough
MALDEN
STARBUCK
TOKELAU ISLANDS
ATAFU
NUKUNONU
FAKAOFO
SWAINS
PENRHYN
RAKAHANGA
MANIHIKI
PUKAPUKA
NASSAU
NORTHERN COOK ISLANDS
SUWARROW
COOK ISLANDS
SAMOA ISLANDS
SAVAI'I
UPOLU
TUTUILA
MANUA ISLANDS
UVEA
TAFAHI
NIUATOPUTAPU
FONUALEI
TONGA ISLANDS
VAVA'U GROUP
HA'APAI GROUP
NOMUKA GROUP
TONGATAPU GROUP
ATA
Tonga Trench
Vityaz II Depth
Tropic of Capricorn
NIUE
BEVERIDGE
ANTIOPE
PALMERSTON
AITUTAKI
MANUAE
TAKUTEA
MITIARO
ATIU
MAUKE
SOUTHERN COOK ISLANDS
RAROTONGA
MANGAIA
MARIA
RIMATARA
RURUTU
TUBUAI
TUBUAI ISLANDS
RAEVAVAE
RAPA
ILOTS DE BASS
President Thiers Seamount
CAROLINE
VOSTOK
FLINT
MARQUESAS ISLANDS
EIAO
HATUTAA
NUKU HIVA
UA HUKA
UA POU
FATU HUTU
HIVA OA
TAHUATA
ROCHER THOMASSET
FATU HIVA
TUAMOTU ARCHIPELAGO
SOCIETY ISLANDS
LEEWARD ISLANDS
WINDWARD ISLANDS
MOTU ONE
MANUAE
MAUPITI
MAUPIHAA
BORA BORA
RAIATEA
HUAHINE
TETIAROA
MAIAO
MOOREA
TAHITI
MATAIVA
RANGIROA
ILES PALLISER
MAKATEA
KAUKURA
NIAU
APATAKI
ARATIKA
FAKARAVA
MANIHI
AHE
ILES DU ROI GEORGES
TAKAROA
NAPUKA
PUKAPUKA
ILES DU DESAPPOINTEMENT
TAKUME
FANGATAU
FAKAHINA
RAROIA
NIHIRU
MAKEMO
TEHUATA
TATAKOTO
MARUTEA
TAUERE
AMANU
HAO
PUKARUHA
REAO
MOTUTUNGA
TAHANEA
HARAIKI
REITORU
RAVAHERE
NENGONENGO
MANUHANGI
PARAOA
AHUNUI
VAHITAHI
PINAKI
VAIRAATEA
NUKUTAVAKE
VANAVANA
ILES DU DUC DE GLOUCESTER
HEREHERETUE
TEMATANGI
TUREIA
MURUROA
GROUPE ACTÉON
MARUTEA
MARIA
FAGATAUFA
MANGAREVA
MORANE
GAMBIER ISLANDS
TEMOE
Tuamotu Ridge
OENO
HENDERSON
DUCIE
PITCAIRN
East Pacific Rise
SALA Y GOMEZ
EASTER ISLAND
Wachusett Seamount
ERNEST LEGOUVE
MARIA THERESA
Southwest Pacific Basin
KERMADEC ISLANDS
Kermadec Trench
Vityaz III Depth
CHATHAM ISLANDS
CHATHAM
PITT
Robbie Bank
Mount Pinos
San Gorgonio
Point Conception
CHANNEL ISLANDS
Los Angeles
Cerro de la Encantada
DESIERTO DE ALTAR
Gulf of California
Jasper Seamount
ISLA DE GUADALUPE
Bahía Sebastián Vizcaíno
ISLA CEDROS
Punta Eugenia
LOWER CALIFORNIA
La Paz
Cabo San Lucas
ISLAS MARÍAS
Cabo Corrientes
ISLAS REVILLAGIGEDO
SIERRA MADRE OCCIDENTAL
PLATEAU OF MEXICO
El Paso
Edwards Plateau
BOLSÓN DE MAPIMÍ
Torreón
Mohinora

CHINA
JAPAN
SOUTH KOREA
TAIWAN
LAOS
THAILAND
CAMBODIA
VIET-NAM
PHILIPPINES
BRUNEI
MALAYSIA
INDONESIA
PAPUA NEW GUINEA
SOLOMON ISLANDS
AUSTRALIA
NEW ZEALAND
VANUATU
TUVALU
New Caledonia (France)
NAURU / NAOERO
Northern Mariana Islands (U.S.)
Guam (U.S.)
FEDERATED STATES OF MICRONESIA
Palau Belau (Trust Territory)
MARSHALL ISLANDS
Wake (U.S.)
Norfolk (Australia)
MICRONESIA
MELANESIA
CAROLINE ISLANDS
MARIANA ISLANDS
East China Sea
South China Sea
Philippine Sea
Celebes Sea
Sulu Sea
Banda Sea
Java Sea
Flores Sea
Timor Sea
Arafura Sea
Coral Sea
Solomon Sea
Tasman Sea
Great Australian Bight
Gulf of Carpentaria
INDIAN OCEAN
GREAT SANDY DESERT
GIBSON DESERT
GREAT VICTORIA DESERT
SIMPSON DESERT
NULLARBOR PLAIN
GREAT DIVIDING RANGE
TASMANIA
NORTH ISLAND
SOUTH ISLAND
NEW GUINEA
KALIMANTAN/BORNEO
CELEBES
SUMATRA
JAVA
LUZON
MINDANAO
Shanghai
Tōkyō
Hong Kong
Manila
Quezon City
Jakarta
Surabaya
Ho Chi Minh (Saigon)
Ha noi
Port Moresby
Darwin
Brisbane
Sydney
Canberra
Melbourne
Adelaide
Perth
Hobart
Auckland
Christchurch
Honiara
Port-Vila
Nouméa
Scale 1:30,000,000
Lambert Azimuthal Equal Area Projection
Longitude East 170 of Greenwich
0 500 1000 1500 2000 km
0 500 1000 miles

UNITED STATES
Los Angeles
Long Beach
San Diego
Phoenix
Tucson
El Paso
Ciudad Juárez
Mexicali
Tijuana
Ensenada
Hermosillo
Chihuahua
Guaymas
Ciudad Obregón
Los Mochis
Culiacán Rosales
La Paz
Mazatlán
Torreón
Monclova
MEXICO
BAJA CALIFORNIA
ISLA DE GUADALUPE (Mexico)
Cabo San Lucas
Tropic of Cancer
ISLAS REVILLAGIGEDO (Mexico)
Midway Islands (U.S.)
PEARL AND HERMES
LISIANSKI
LAYSAN
MARO
GARDNER PINNACLES
FRENCH FRIGATE SHOALS
NECKER
NIHOA
KAUAI
NIHAU
OAHU
MOLOKAI
KAULA
LANAI
MAUI
KAHOOLAWE
Honolulu
Hilo
HAWAII
Hawaii (U.S.)
HAWAIIAN ISLANDS
Johnston (U.S.)
PACIFIC OCEAN
CLIPPERTON (French Polynesia)
KINGMAN (U.S.)
PALMYRA (U.S.)
TERAINA (WASHINGTON)
TABUAERAN (FANNING)
KIRITIMATI (CHRISTMAS)
HOWLAND (U.S.)
BAKER (U.S.)
JARVIS (U.S.)
LINE ISLANDS
Equator
WINSLOW
PHOENIX ISLANDS
KANTON
ENDERBURY
MCKEAN
BIRNIE
RAWAKI (PHOENIX)
ORONA (HULL)
MANRA (SYDNEY)
NIKUMARORO (GARDNER)
CARONDELET
KIRIBATI
MALDEN
STARBUCK
POLYNESIA
Tokelau (New Zealand)
TOKELAU ISLANDS
ATAFU
NUKUNONU
FAKAOFO
PENRHYN
SWAINS
WESTERN SAMOA
SAMOA ISLANDS
SAVAI'I
Apia
UPOLU
Pago Pago
TUTUILA
MANUA ISLANDS
American Samoa (U.S.)
Mata-Utu
WALLIS
UVEA
FUTUNA
ALOFI
NIUAFO'OU
TAFAHI
NIUATO PUTAPU
TONGA
FONUALEI
VAVA'U GROUP
HA'APAI GROUP
TONGA ISLANDS
KOTU GROUP
NOMUKA GROUP
Nuku'alofa
TONGATAPU GROUP
ATA
ANTIOPE
Niue (New Zealand)
Alofi
BEVERIDGE
RAKAHANGA
MANIHIKI
PUKAPUKA
NASSAU
NORTHERN COOK ISLANDS
SUWARROW
Cook Islands (New Zealand)
PALMERSTON
AITUTAKI
MANUAE
TAKUTEA
MITIARO
ATIU
MAUKE
SOUTHERN COOK ISLANDS
RAROTONGA
Avarua
MANGAIA
VOSTOK
CAROLINE
FLINT
EIAO
NUKU HIVA
UA HUKA
MARQUESAS ISLANDS
UA POU
HIVA OA
TAHUATA
FATU HIVA
TUAMOTU ARCHIPELAGO
RANGIROA
MANIHI
ILES DU ROI GEORGES
ILES DU DÉSAPPOINTEMENT
PUKAPUKA
MATAIVA
ILES PALLISER
APATAKI
ARATIKA
TAKUME
FANGATAU
KAUKURA
FAKARAVA
MAKEMO
FAKAHINA
MOTU ONE
LEEWARD ISLANDS
MANUAE
MAUPITI
MAUPIHAA
BORA-BORA
HUAHINE
RAIATEA
TETIAROA
MOOREA
Papeete
TAHITI
TAHANEA
MOTUTUNGA
MARUTEA
TATAKOTO
AMANU
SOCIETY ISLANDS
WINDWARD ISLANDS
RAVAHERE
HAO
PUKARUHA
VAHITAHI
REAO
MANUANGI
HEREHERETUE
AHUNUI
ILES DU DUC DE GLOUCESTER
TUREIA
GROUPE ACTEON
French Polynesia
TEMATANGI
MURUROA
MARUTEA
MARIA
FAGATAUFA
MORANE
MANGAREVA
GAMBIER ISLANDS
TEMOE
MARIA
RIMATARA
RURUTU
TUBUAI
TUBUAI ISLANDS
RAEVAVAE
RAPA
ILOTS DE BASS
OENO
HENDERSON
DUCIE
PITCAIRN
Adamstown
Pitcairn (U.K.)
Tropic of Capricorn
RAOUL
KERMADEC ISLANDS (New Zealand)
ESPERANCE ROCK
SALA Y GÓMEZ (Chile)
EASTER ISLAND (Chile)
ERNEST LEGOUVE
MARIA THERESA
CHATHAM ISLANDS (New Zealand)
PITT
A-590000-280-2 -2 -2 -3

INDONESIA
LAUT JAWA
JAVA SEA
JAWA
SURABAYA
SEMARANG
SURAKARTA
YOGYAKARTA
MALANG
PULAU MADURA
PULAU BALI
Denpasar
PULAU LOMBOK
PULAU SUMBAWA
PULAU SUMBA
PULAU FLORES
LAUT SAWU
PULAU TIMOR
Kupang
Dili
KEPULAUAN TANIMBAR
ARAFURA
TIMOR SEA
Timor Trough
Java Trench
North Australian Basin
INDIAN OCEAN
Cuvier Basin
Exmouth Plateau
Tropic of Capricorn
Darwin
BATHURST ISLAND
MELVILLE ISLAND
Katherine
Joseph Bonaparte Gulf
KIMBERLEY PLATEAU
Wyndham
Kununurra
Derby
Broome
DAMPIER LAND
Halls Creek
Northern Territory
TANAMI DESERT
CANNING BASIN
EIGHTY MILE BEACH
GREAT SANDY DESERT
Port Hedland
Dampier
HAMERSLEY RANGE
Newman
Onslow
Exmouth
Carnarvon
AUSTRALIA
GIBSON DESERT
Western Australia
MACDONNELL RANGES
Alice Springs
GREAT VICTORIA DESERT
South Australia
NULLARBOR PLAIN
Kalgoorlie
Coolgardie
Geraldton
PERTH
Fremantle
Bunbury
Albany
Esperance
ARCHIPELAGO OF THE RECHERCHE
Great Australian Bight
South Australian Basin
Diamantina Deep
Diamantina Trench
INDIAN OCEAN
M Ft
4000 13123
3000 9843
2000 6562
1000 3281
500 1640
200 656
0
Depr.
100 328
200 656
1000 3281
2000 6562
4000 13123
6000 19685
8000 26247
Longitude

Scale 1:12,000,000 Delisle Conic Equidistant Projection

0 200 400 600 800 km

0 200 400 miles

PAPUA NEW GUINEA
PULAU IRIAN
NEW GUINEA
BISMARCK ARCHIPELAGO
NEW BRITAIN
NEW IRELAND ISLAND
BOUGAINVILLE ISLAND
Solomon Basin
SOLOMON ISLANDS
SOLOMON SEA
Port Moresby
Lae
Gulf of Papua
Torres Strait
Gulf of Carpentaria
CAPE YORK PENINSULA
CORAL SEA
Coral Sea Basin
Coral Sea Islands Territory
GREAT BARRIER REEF
GREAT DIVIDING RANGE
Queensland
New South Wales
Victoria
Tasmania
Australian Capital Territory
GREAT ARTESIAN BASIN
SIMPSON DESERT
STURT DESERT
RIVERINA
Cairns
Townsville
Mackay
Rockhampton
Bundaberg
BRISBANE
Gold Coast
Toowoomba
Newcastle
SYDNEY
Wollongong
Canberra
MELBOURNE
Geelong
ADELAIDE
Hobart
Launceston
Broken Hill
Mount Isa
Nouvelle-Calédonie
New Caledonia
(France)
Tropic of Capricorn
PACIFIC OCEAN
TASMAN SEA
Tasman Basin
Bass Strait
LORD HOWE ISLAND
(Australia)

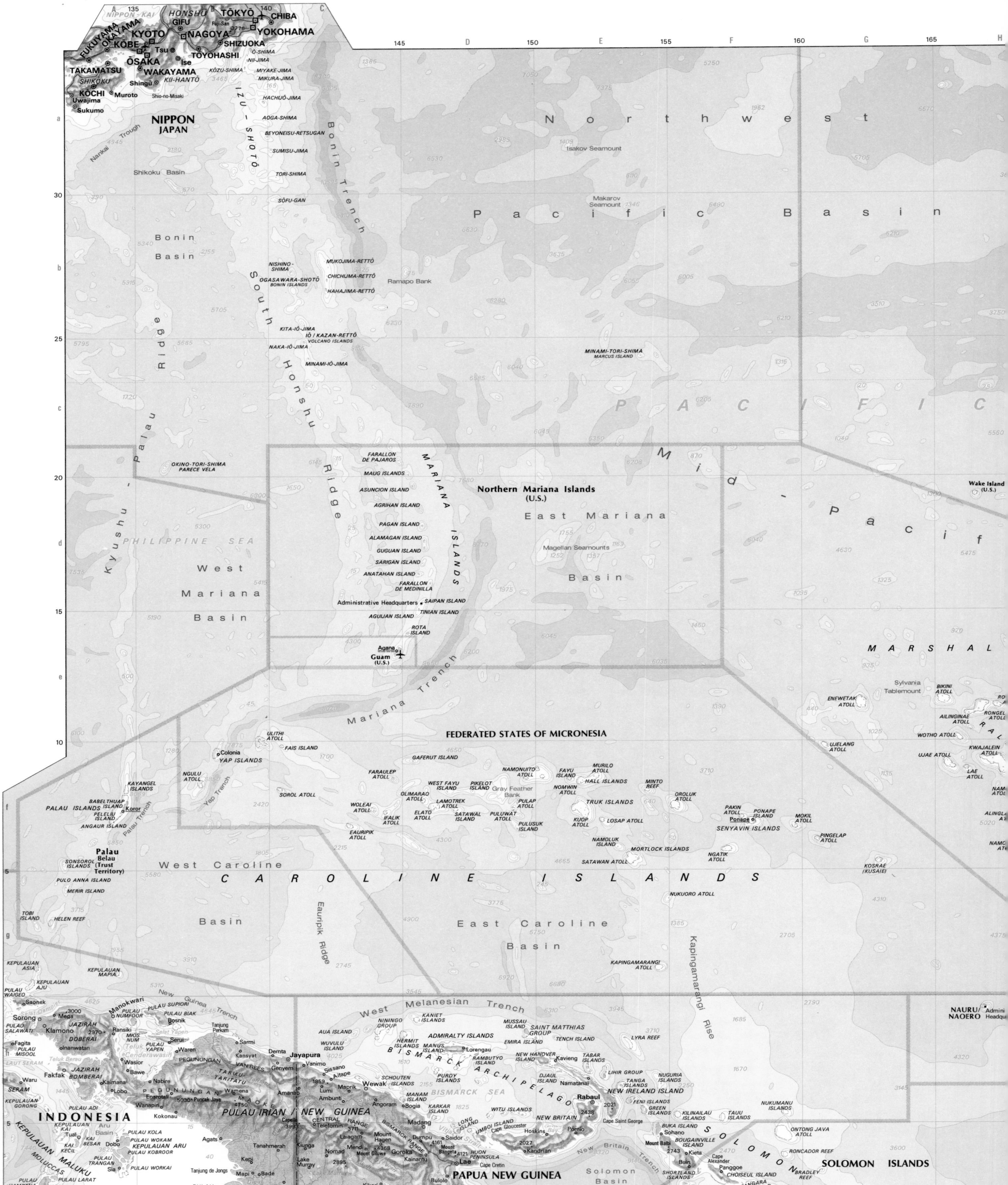

Scale 1:15,000,000 at 25°   Mercator Cylindrical Projection

0 200 400 600 800 1000 km

0 250 500 miles

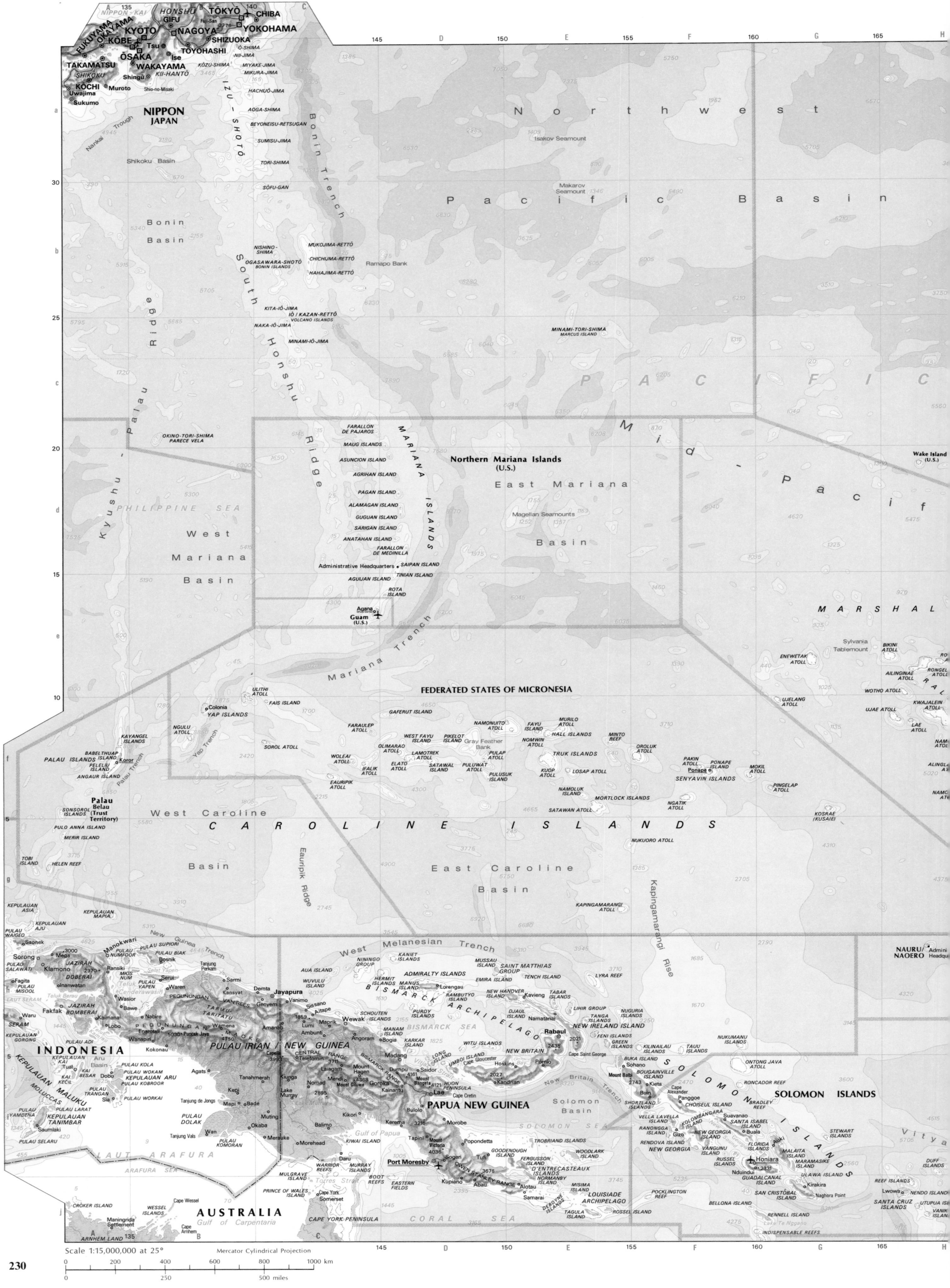

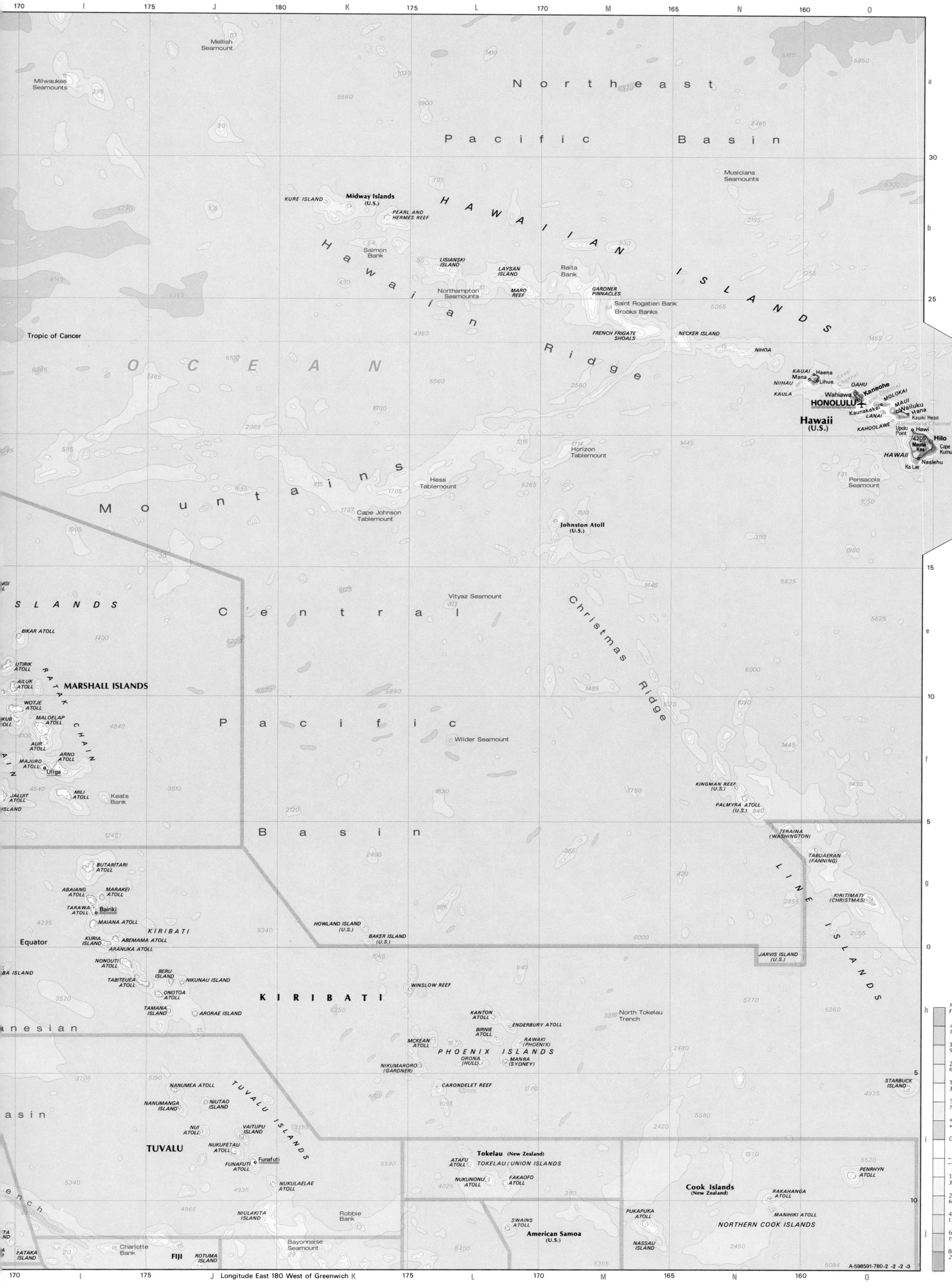
North east Pacific Basin
Mellish Seamount
Milwaukee Seamounts
Musicians Seamounts
Midway Islands (U.S.)
KURE ISLAND
PEARL AND HERMES REEF
HAWAIIAN ISLANDS
Hawaiian Ridge
Salmon Bank
LISIANSKI ISLAND
LAYSAN ISLAND
Raita Bank
Northampton Seamounts
MARO REEF
GARDNER PINNACLES
Saint Rogatien Bank
Brooks Banks
FRENCH FRIGATE SHOALS
NECKER ISLAND
NIHOA
Tropic of Cancer
OCEAN
KAUAI
Haena
Mana
Lihue
NIIHAU
KAULA
OAHU
Wahiawa
Kaneohe
HONOLULU
MOLOKAI
Kaunakakai
LANAI
MAUI
Wailuku
Hana
Kauiki Head
KAHOOLAWE
Hawaii (U.S.)
Upolu Point
Hawi
Hilo
Mauna Kea
Cape Kumukahi
HAWAII
Naalehu
Ka Lae
Horizon Tablemount
Hess Tablemount
Cape Johnson Tablemount
Pensacola Seamount
Mountains
Johnston Atoll (U.S.)
Vityaz Seamount
Central Pacific Basin
Christmas Ridge
Wilder Seamount
ISLANDS
BIKAR ATOLL
UTIRIK ATOLL
AILUK ATOLL
MARSHALL ISLANDS
RATAK CHAIN
WOTJE ATOLL
MALOELAP ATOLL
AUR ATOLL
ARNO ATOLL
MAJURO ATOLL
Uliga
JALUIT ATOLL
MILI ATOLL
Keats Bank
KINGMAN REEF (U.S.)
PALMYRA ATOLL (U.S.)
TERAINA (WASHINGTON)
TABUAERAN (FANNING)
LINE ISLANDS
KIRITIMATI (CHRISTMAS)
BUTARITARI ATOLL
ABAIANG ATOLL
MARAKEI ATOLL
TARAWA ATOLL
Bairiki
MAIANA ATOLL
KIRIBATI
Equator
KURIA ISLAND
ABEMAMA ATOLL
ARANUKA ATOLL
HOWLAND ISLAND (U.S.)
BAKER ISLAND (U.S.)
JARVIS ISLAND (U.S.)
NONOUTI ATOLL
BERU ISLAND
TABITEUEA ATOLL
NIKUNAU ISLAND
ONOTOA ATOLL
TAMANA ISLAND
ARORAE ISLAND
WINSLOW REEF
KANTON ATOLL
ENDERBURY ATOLL
BIRNIE ATOLL
RAWAKI (PHOENIX)
MCKEAN ATOLL
PHOENIX ISLANDS
ORONA (HULL)
MANRA (SYDNEY)
NIKUMARORO (GARDNER)
North Tokelau Trench
CARONDELET REEF
STARBUCK ISLAND
NANUMEA ATOLL
TUVALU ISLANDS
NANUMANGA ISLAND
NIUTAO ISLAND
NUI ATOLL
VAITUPU ISLAND
NUKUFETAU ATOLL
TUVALU
FUNAFUTI ATOLL
Funafuti
NUKULAELAE ATOLL
Tokelau (New Zealand)
ATAFU ATOLL
TOKELAU/UNION ISLANDS
NUKUNONU ATOLL
FAKAOFO ATOLL
Cook Islands (New Zealand)
PENRHYN ATOLL
RAKAHANGA ATOLL
MANIHIKI ATOLL
NORTHERN COOK ISLANDS
PUKAPUKA ATOLL
NASSAU ISLAND
SWAINS ATOLL
American Samoa (U.S.)
NIULAKITA ISLAND
Robbie Bank
Bayonnaise Seamount
Charlotte Bank
FIJI
ROTUMA ISLAND
FATAKA ISLAND
Longitude East 180 West of Greenwich
M Ft
4000 13123
3000 9843
2000 6562
1000 3281
500 1640
+200 +656
0
−200 −656
1000 3281
2000 6562
4000 13123
6000 19685
8000 26247
A-598591-780-2 -2 -2 -3

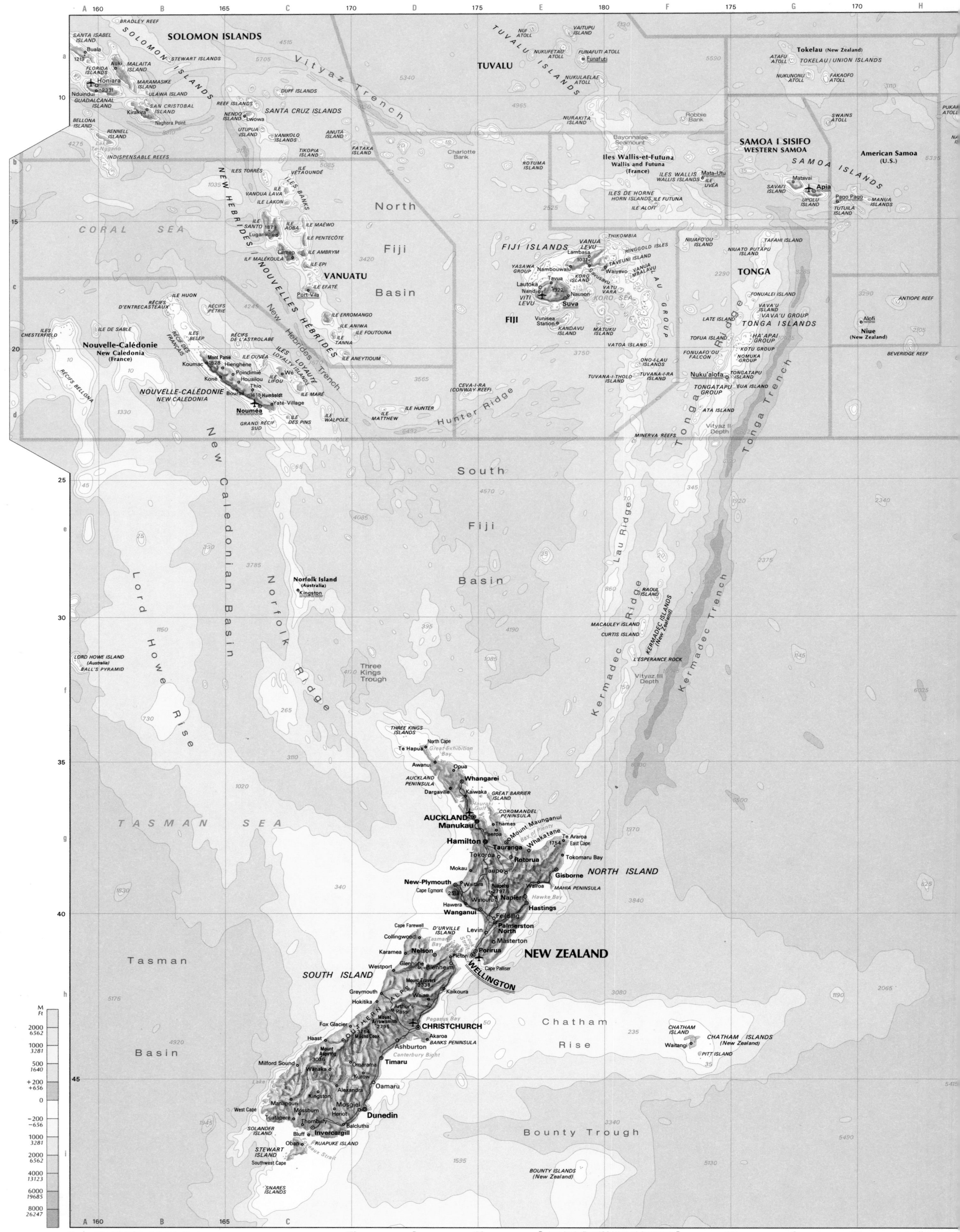

Scale 1:15,000,000 at 25° latitude Mercator Cylindrical Projection

Longitude East 180 West of Greenwich

0 200 400 600 800 1000 km

0 250 500 miles

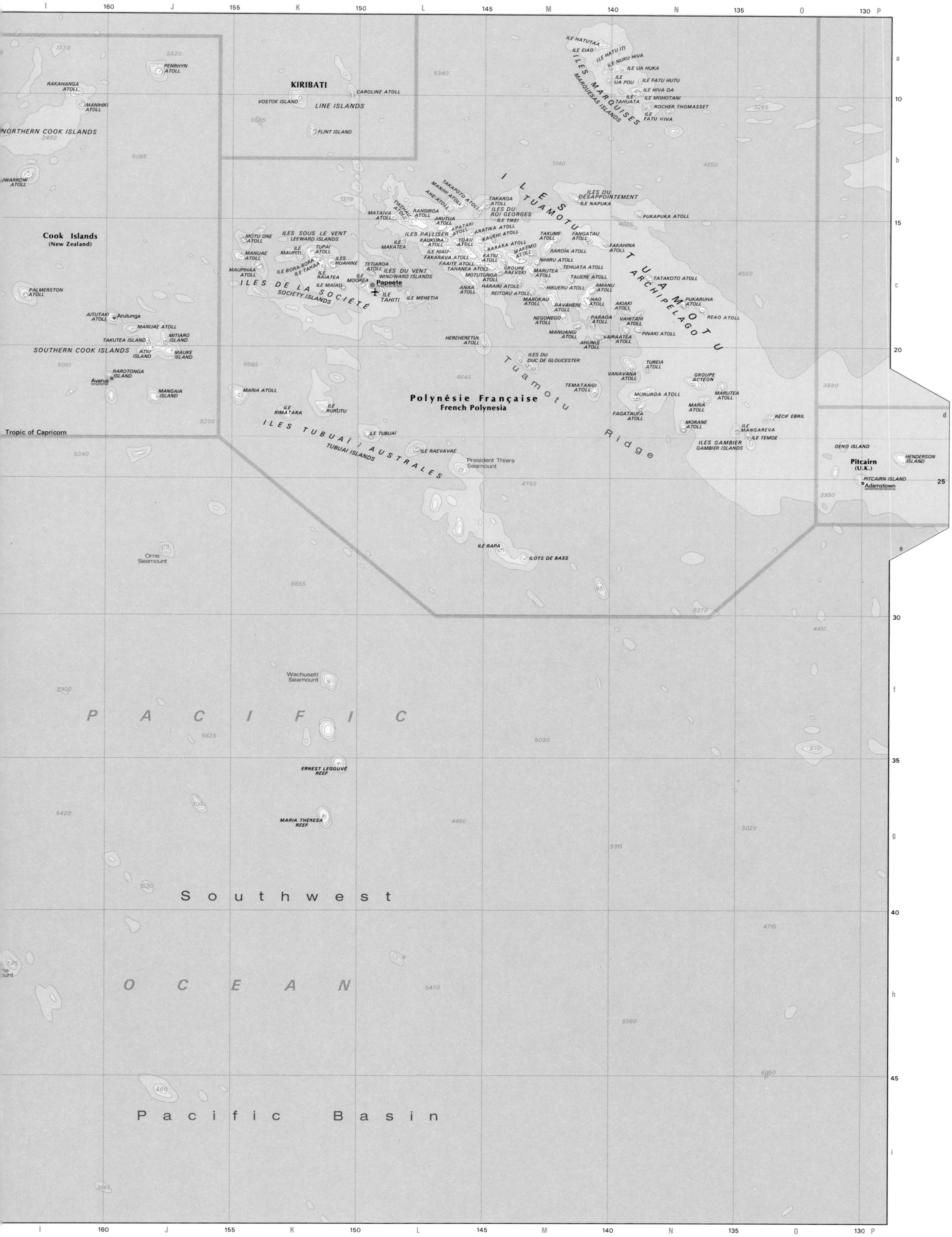
KIRIBATI
LINE ISLANDS
VOSTOK ISLAND
CAROLINE ATOLL
FLINT ISLAND
PENRHYN ATOLL
RAKAHANGA ATOLL
MANIHIKI ATOLL
NORTHERN COOK ISLANDS
Cook Islands
(New Zealand)
PALMERSTON ATOLL
AITUTAKI ATOLL
Arutunga
MANUAE ATOLL
TAKUTEA ISLAND
MITIARO ISLAND
SOUTHERN COOK ISLANDS
ATIU ISLAND
MAUKE ISLAND
RAROTONGA ISLAND
Avarua
MANGAIA ISLAND
Tropic of Capricorn
ILES MARQUISES
MARQUESAS ISLANDS
ILE HATUTAA
ILE EIAO
ILE HATU ITI
ILE NUKU HIVA
ILE UA HUKA
ILE UA POU
ILE FATU HUTU
ILE HIVA OA
ILE MOHOTANI
ILE TAHUATA
ROCHER THOMASSET
ILE FATU HIVA
ILES TUAMOTU
TUAMOTU ARCHIPELAGO
ILES DU DÉSAPPOINTEMENT
ILE NAPUKA
PUKAPUKA ATOLL
TAKAPOTO ATOLL
MANIHI ATOLL
AHE ATOLL
TAKAROA ATOLL
ILES DU ROI GEORGES
ILE TIKEI
TIKEHAU ATOLL
RANGIROA ATOLL
MATAIVA ATOLL
ARUTUA ATOLL
APATAKI ATOLL
ARATIKA ATOLL
KAUEHI ATOLL
ILES PALLISER
KAUKURA ATOLL
TOAU ATOLL
ILE MAKATEA
ILE NIAU
FAKARAVA ATOLL
RARAKA ATOLL
MAKEMO ATOLL
TAKUME ATOLL
FANGATAU ATOLL
FAKAHINA ATOLL
RAROIA ATOLL
KATIU ATOLL
NIHIRU ATOLL
FAAITE ATOLL
TAHANEA ATOLL
GROUPE RAEVSKI
MARUTEA ATOLL
TEHUATA ATOLL
MOTUTUNGA ATOLL
TAUERE ATOLL
TATAKOTO ATOLL
ANAA ATOLL
HARAIKI ATOLL
REITORU ATOLL
HIKUERU ATOLL
AMANU ATOLL
MAROKAU ATOLL
RAVAHERE ATOLL
HAO ATOLL
AKIAKI ATOLL
PUKARUHA ATOLL
REAO ATOLL
NEGONEGO ATOLL
PARAOA ATOLL
VAHITAHI ATOLL
MANUANGI ATOLL
AHUNUI ATOLL
VAIRAATEA ATOLL
PINAKI ATOLL
HEREHERETUE ATOLL
ILES DU DUC DE GLOUCESTER
TUREIA ATOLL
VANAVANA ATOLL
TEMATANGI ATOLL
MURUROA ATOLL
GROUPE ACTÉON
MARUTEA ATOLL
MARIA ATOLL
FAGATAUFA ATOLL
RÉCIF EBRIL
MORANE ATOLL
ILE MANGAREVA
ILE TEMOE
ILES GAMBIER
GAMBIER ISLANDS
Tuamotu Ridge
MOTU ONE ATOLL
ILES SOUS LE VENT
LEEWARD ISLANDS
MANUAE ATOLL
ILE MAUPITI
TUPAI ATOLL
MAUPIHAA ATOLL
ILE BORA-BORA
ILE TAHAA
ILES HUAHINE
ILE RAIATEA
TETIAROA ATOLL
ILES DU VENT
WINDWARD ISLANDS
ILE MOOREA
Papeete
ILE MAIAO
ILE TAHITI
ILE MEHETIA
ILES DE LA SOCIÉTÉ
SOCIETY ISLANDS
Polynésie Française
French Polynesia
MARIA ATOLL
ILE RIMATARA
ILE RURUTU
ILE TUBUAI
ILE RAEVAVAE
ILES TUBUAÏ / AUSTRALES
TUBUAI ISLANDS
President Thiers Seamount
ILE RAPA
ILOTS DE BASS
OENO ISLAND
HENDERSON ISLAND
Pitcairn
(U.K.)
PITCAIRN ISLAND
Adamstown
Orne Seamount
Wachusett Seamount
ERNEST LEGOUVÉ REEF
MARIA THERESA REEF
PACIFIC OCEAN
Southwest Pacific Basin

© ISTITUTO GEOGRAFICO DE AGOSTINI S. p. A. - NOVARA

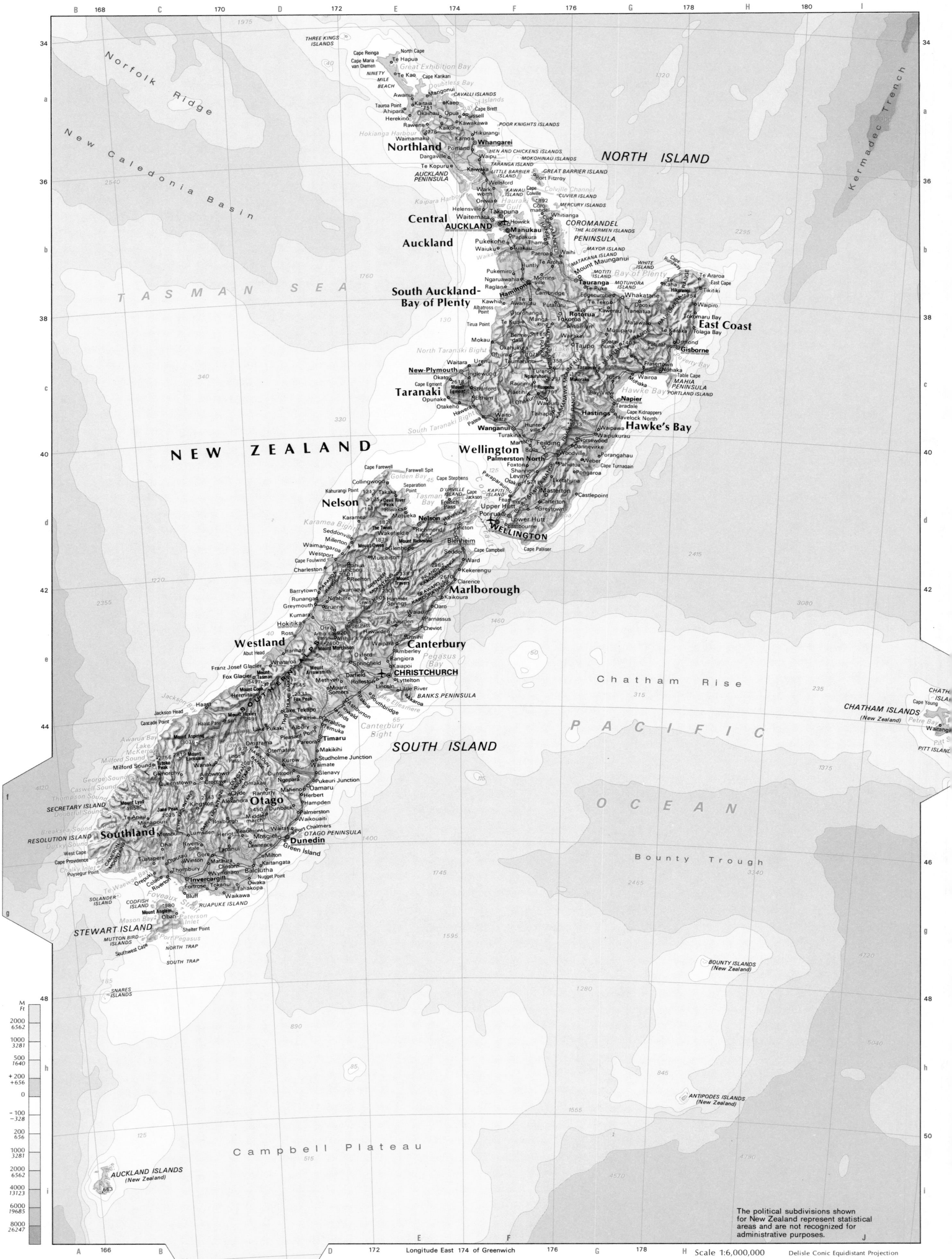
NORTH ISLAND
SOUTH ISLAND
NEW ZEALAND
TASMAN SEA
PACIFIC OCEAN
Norfolk Ridge
New Caledonia Basin
Kermadec Trench
Chatham Rise
Bounty Trough
Campbell Plateau
Northland
Central Auckland
South Auckland-Bay of Plenty
East Coast
Taranaki
Hawke's Bay
Wellington
Nelson
Marlborough
Westland
Canterbury
Otago
Southland
AUCKLAND
WELLINGTON
CHRISTCHURCH
Dunedin
Hamilton
Whangarei
Tauranga
Rotorua
Gisborne
Napier
Hastings
Wanganui
Palmerston North
New-Plymouth
Blenheim
Invercargill
Timaru
Hokitika
STEWART ISLAND
CHATHAM ISLANDS (New Zealand)
BOUNTY ISLANDS (New Zealand)
ANTIPODES ISLANDS (New Zealand)
AUCKLAND ISLANDS (New Zealand)
CAMPBELL ISLAND (New Zealand)
SNARES ISLANDS
THREE KINGS ISLANDS
COROMANDEL PENINSULA
BANKS PENINSULA
OTAGO PENINSULA
Foveaux Strait
Cook Strait
The political subdivisions shown for New Zealand represent statistical areas and are not recognized for administrative purposes.
Longitude East 174 of Greenwich
Scale 1:6,000,000
Delisle Conic Equidistant Projection
0 100 200 300 km
0 100 miles

©ISTITUTO GEOGRAFICO DE AGOSTINI S. p. A. NOVARA

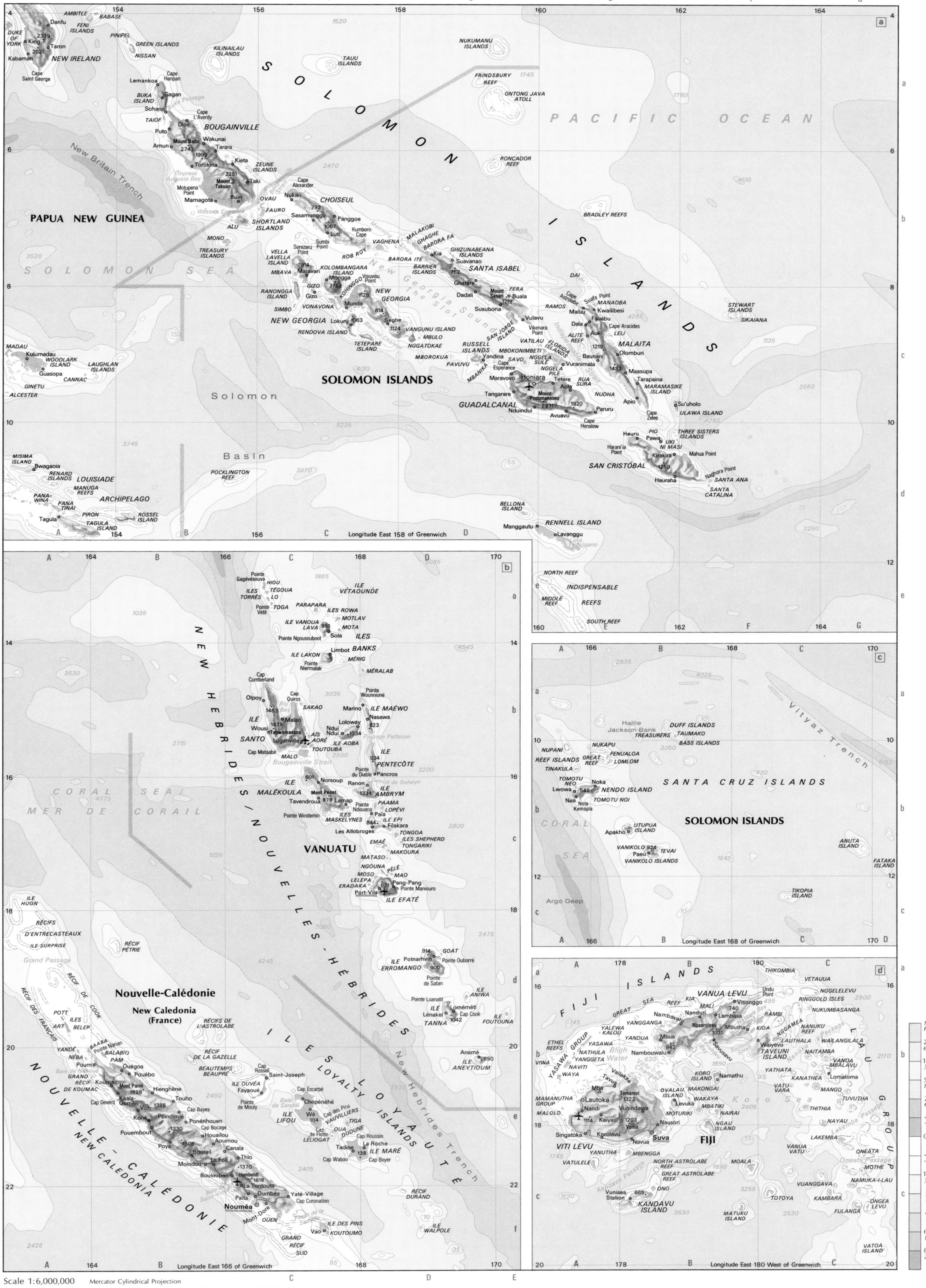

Scale 1:6,000,000 Mercator Cylindrical Projection

0 100 200 300 400 km

0 100 200 miles

© ISTITUTO GEOGRAFICO DE AGOSTINI S. p. A. - NOVARA

Map 64 **ISLANDS OF MICRONESIA-POLYNESIA**

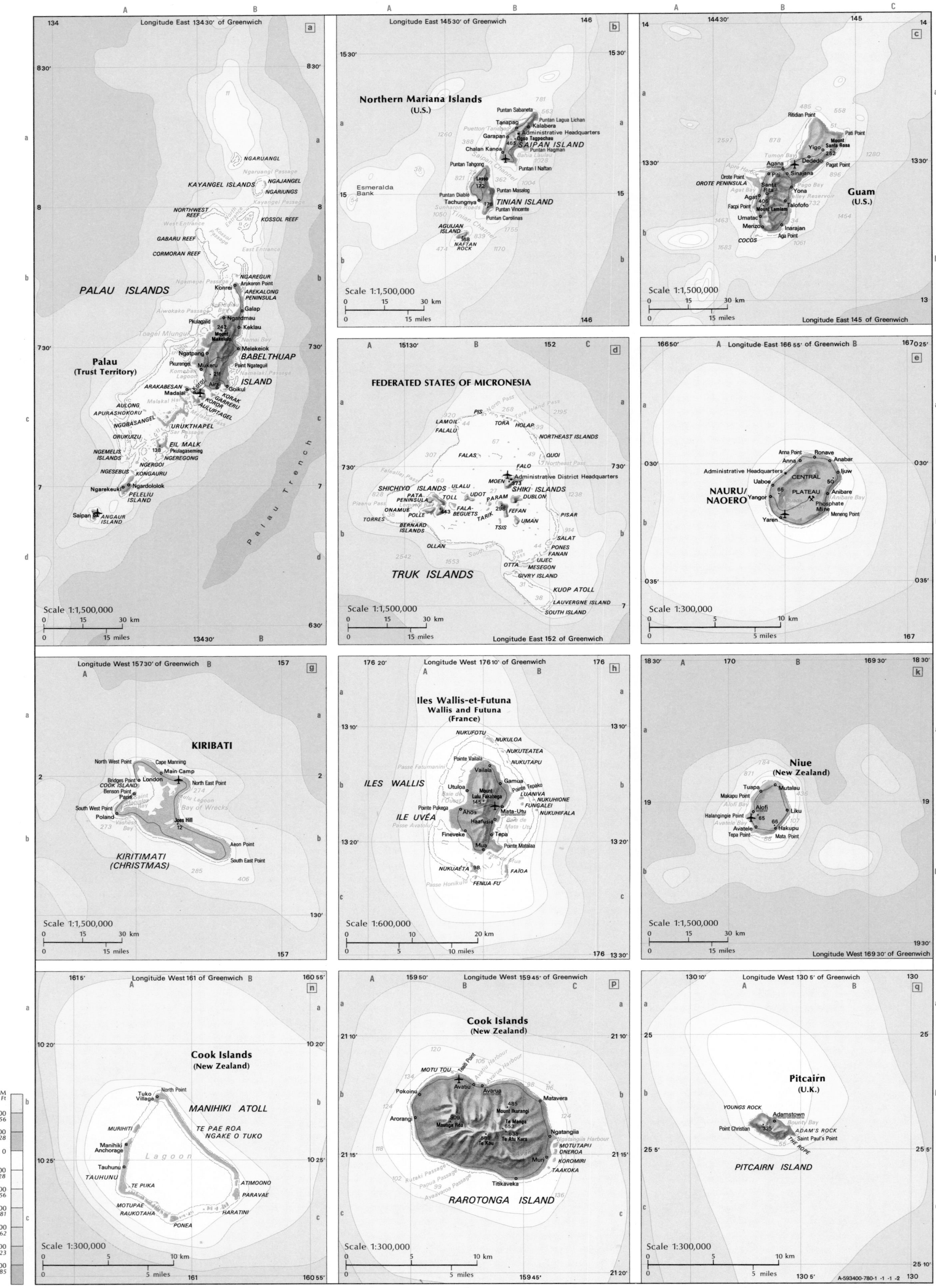

Mercator Cylindrical Projection

© ISTITUTO GEOGRAFICO DE AGOSTINI S. p. A. - NOVARA

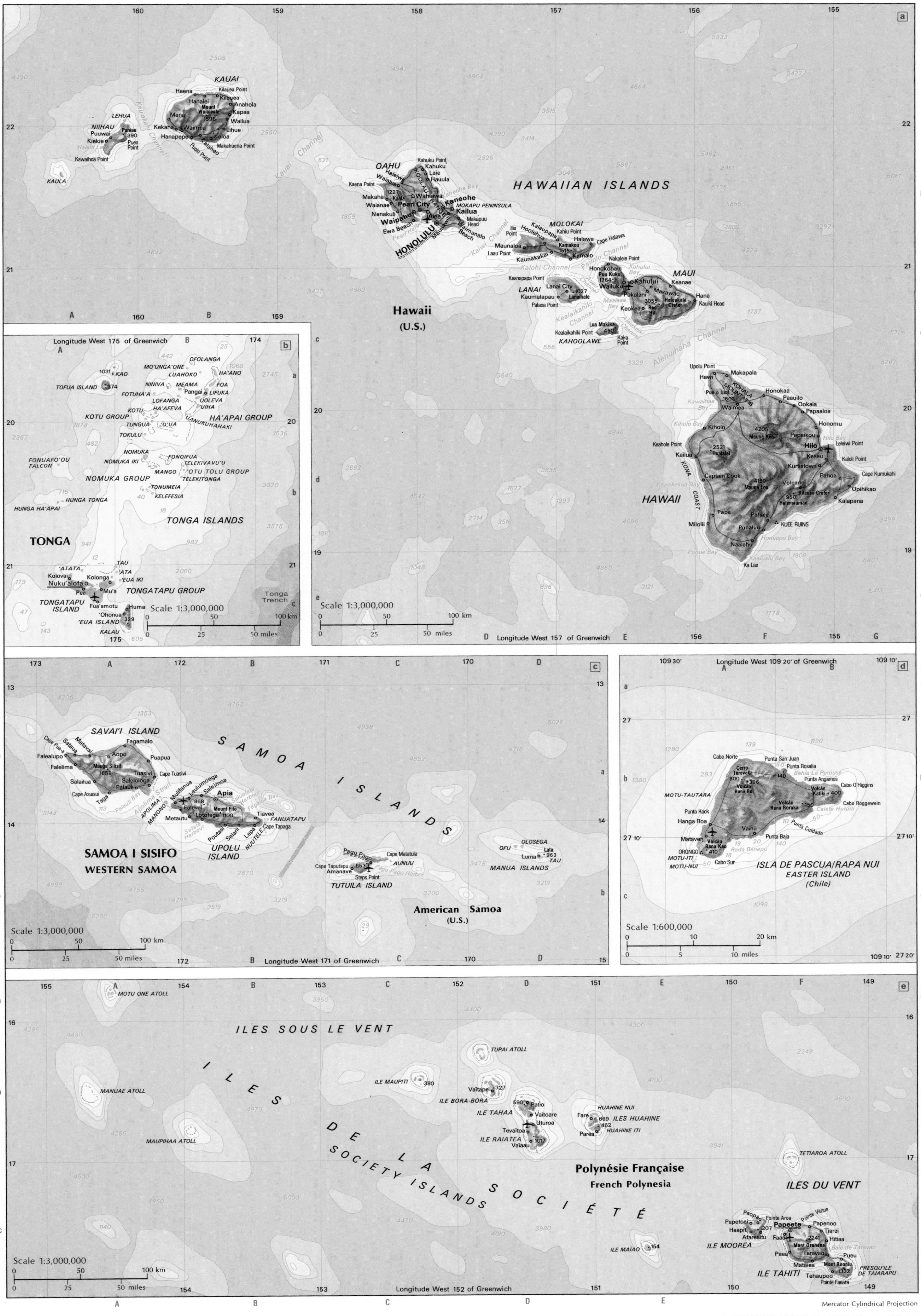
HAWAIIAN ISLANDS
KAUAI
NIIHAU
LEHUA
KAULA
OAHU
HONOLULU
Pearl City
Kaneohe
Kailua
MOLOKAI
LANAI
MAUI
KAHOOLAWE
HAWAII
Hilo
Kailua
Mauna Kea
Mauna Loa
Kauai Channel
Kaiwi Channel
Kalohi Channel
Pailolo Channel
Alenuihaha Channel
Hawaii
(U.S.)
Scale 1:3,000,000
Longitude West 157 of Greenwich
TONGA
TONGA ISLANDS
HA'APAI GROUP
NOMUKA GROUP
TONGATAPU GROUP
TONGATAPU ISLAND
Nuku'alofa
'EUA ISLAND
Tonga Trench
Scale 1:3,000,000
Longitude West 175 of Greenwich
SAMOA ISLANDS
SAVAI'I ISLAND
UPOLU ISLAND
Apia
SAMOA I SISIFO
WESTERN SAMOA
TUTUILA ISLAND
Pago Pago
MANUA ISLANDS
American Samoa
(U.S.)
Scale 1:3,000,000
Longitude West 171 of Greenwich
ISLA DE PASCUA/RAPA NUI
EASTER ISLAND
(Chile)
Hanga Roa
MOTU-TAUTARA
Scale 1:600,000
Longitude West 109 20' of Greenwich
ILES SOUS LE VENT
ILES DE LA SOCIÉTÉ
SOCIETY ISLANDS
ILES DU VENT
Polynésie Française
French Polynesia
ILE BORA-BORA
ILE TAHAA
ILE RAIATEA
ILE MAUPITI
ILES HUAHINE
TUPAI ATOLL
MANUAE ATOLL
MAUPIHAA ATOLL
MOTU ONE ATOLL
TETIAROA ATOLL
ILE MAÏAO
ILE MOOREA
ILE TAHITI
Papeete
PRESQU'ILE DE TAIARAPU
Scale 1:3,000,000
Longitude West 152 of Greenwich

Mercator Cylindrical Projection

© ISTITUTO GEOGRAFICO DE AGOSTINI S. p. A. - NOVARA

Longitude West 0 East of Greenwich
ANGOLA
TANZANIA
ZAIRE
ZAMBIA
MALAWI
MOZAMBIQUE
ZIMBABWE
BOTSWANA
Namibia
SOUTH AFRICA
LESOTHO
SWAZILAND
MADAGASCAR
Cape Town
Johannesburg
Pretoria
Durban
Maputo
Harare
Lusaka
Tropic of Capricorn
Angola Basin
Walvis Ridge
Cape Basin
Agulhas Basin
Agulhas Plateau
Mozambique Plateau
Natal Basin
Madagascar Basin
Southwest Indian Ridge
Crozet Basin
Atlantic-Indian Ridge
Atlantic-Indian Basin
Mid-Atlantic Ridge
ATLANTIC OCEAN
INDIAN
PRINCE EDWARD ISLANDS (South Africa)
ILES CROZET (France)
ILES KERGUELEN
BOUVET (Norway)
TRISTAN DA CUNHA GROUP (St. Helena)
GOUGH ISLAND
Limit of icebergs
Winter limit of pack ice (September)
Summer limit of pack ice (March)
Antarctic Circle
South Sandwich Trench
SOUTH SANDWICH ISLANDS
SOUTH GEORGIA
East Scotia Basin
Scotia Sea
SOUTH ORKNEY ISLANDS
SOUTH SHETLAND ISLANDS
Falkland Islands / Islas Malvinas (U.K.) (Claimed by Argentina)
Falkland Plateau
Argentine Basin
Brazil Basin
Rio Grande Rise
Weddell Sea
ANTARCTIC PENINSULA
QUEEN MAUD LAND
COATS LAND
ENDERBY LAND
MAC ROBERTSON LAND
Pole of Inaccessibility
ANTARCTICA
BRAZIL
URUGUAY
ARGENTINA
CHILE
PATAGONIA
Rio de Janeiro
São Paulo
Montevideo
Buenos Aires
Porto Alegre
Salvador
Recife

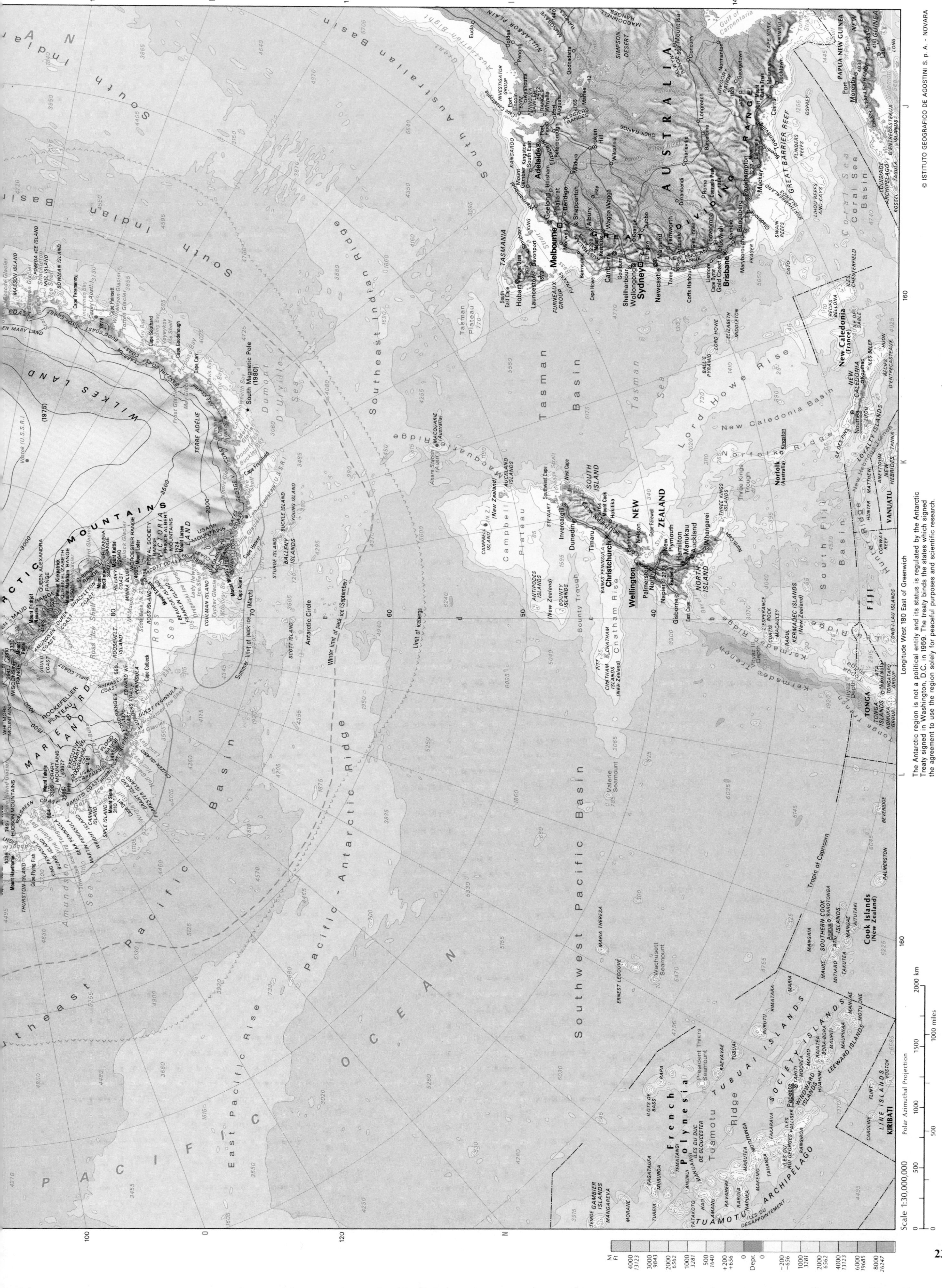
AUSTRALIA
NEW ZEALAND
TASMANIA
NEW CALEDONIA
FIJI
TONGA
VANUATU
Cook Islands (New Zealand)
French Polynesia
KIRIBATI
PAPUA NEW GUINEA
WILKES LAND
TERRE ADÉLIE
VICTORIA LAND
MARIE BYRD LAND
ANTARCTIC MOUNTAINS
Ross Sea
Ross Ice Shelf
Tasman Sea
Coral Sea
Tasman Basin
Southwest Pacific Basin
South Indian Basin
Southeast Indian Ridge
Pacific - Antarctic Ridge
East Pacific Rise
South Australian Basin
PACIFIC OCEAN
South Magnetic Pole (1980)
Antarctic Circle
Tropic of Capricorn
Winter limit of pack ice (September)
Summer limit of pack ice (March)
Limit of icebergs
Longitude West 180 East of Greenwich
The Antarctic region is not a political entity and its status is regulated by the Antarctic Treaty signed in Washington, D.C. in 1959. The treaty binds the states which signed the agreement to use the region solely for peaceful purposes and scientific research.
Polar Azimuthal Projection
Scale 1:30,000,000
0 500 1000 1500 2000 km
0 500 1000 miles
M 4000 3000 2000 1000 500 200 0 Depr. 0 −200 1000 2000 4000 6000 8000
Ft 13123 9843 6562 3281 1640 +656 0 −656 3281 6562 13123 19685 26247

© ISTITUTO GEOGRAFICO DE AGOSTINI S. p. A. · NOVARA

Scale 1:30,000,000 Polar Azimuthal Projection

Longitude West 0 East of Greenwich

0 500 1000 1500 2000 km

0 500 1000 miles

© ISTITUTO GEOGRAFICO DE AGOSTINI S. p. A. - NOVARA

UNITED STATES AND CANADA MAP SECTION

MAP LEGEND

CULTURAL FEATURES

Political Boundaries

International

Secondary (State)

County

Populated Places

Cities, towns, and villages

Symbol size represents population of the place

Chicago
Gary
Racine
Glenview
Edgewood

Type size represents relative importance of the place

Major Urban Areas
Area of continuous commercial, industrial, and residential development in and around a major city

Community within a city

Capital of major political unit

Capital of U.S. state

County Seat

Military Installation

Transportation

Major Highway

Railroad

Tunnel

Miscellaneous

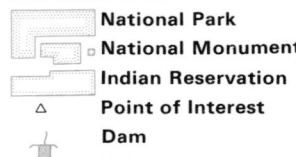

National Park

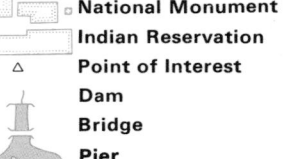

National Monument

Indian Reservation

Point of Interest

Dam

Bridge

Pier

LAND FEATURES

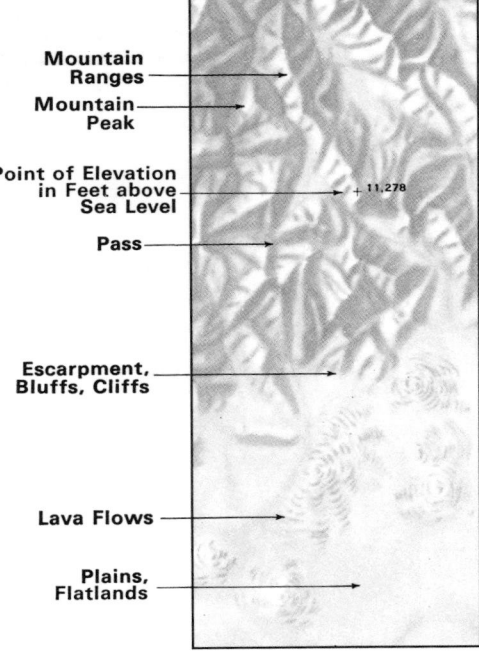

Mountain Ranges

Mountain Peak

Point of Elevation in Feet above Sea Level

Pass

Escarpment, Bluffs, Cliffs

Lava Flows

Plains, Flatlands

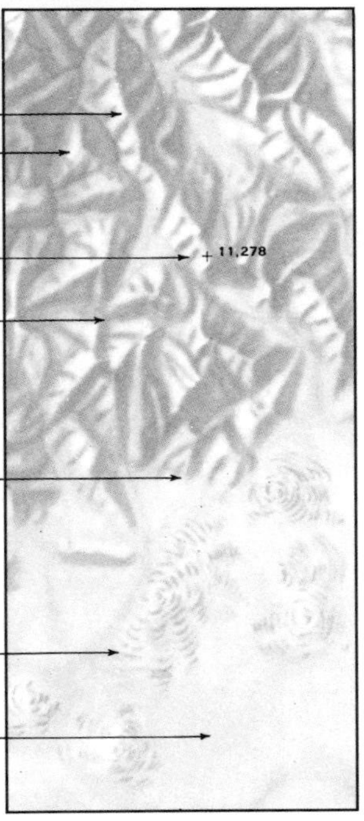

WATER FEATURES

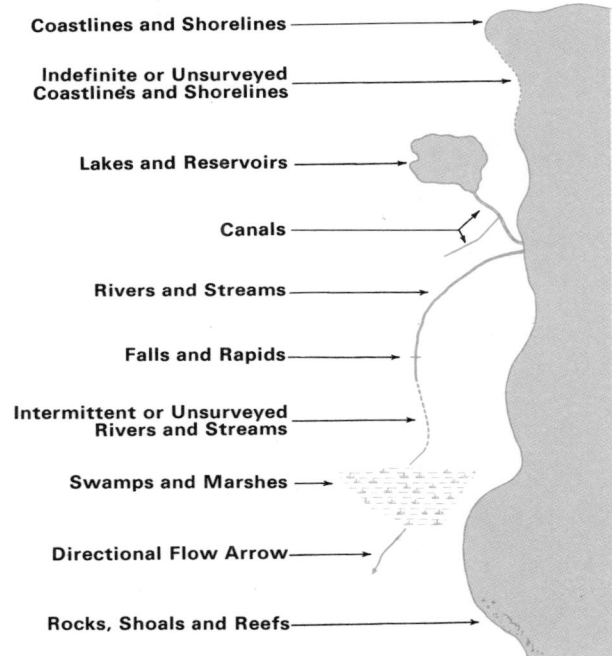

Coastlines and Shorelines

Indefinite or Unsurveyed Coastlines and Shorelines

Lakes and Reservoirs

Canals

Rivers and Streams

Falls and Rapids

Intermittent or Unsurveyed Rivers and Streams

Swamps and Marshes

Directional Flow Arrow

Rocks, Shoals and Reefs

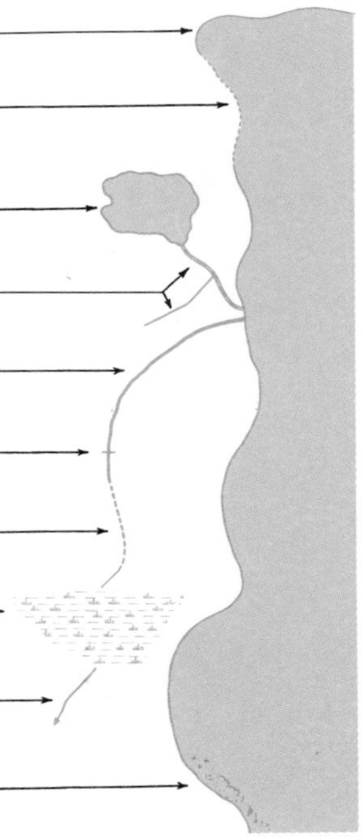

TYPE STYLES USED TO NAME FEATURES

Note: Size of type varies according to importance and available space. Letters for names of major features are spread across the extent of the feature.

CANADA	Country, State, or Province	UINTA DESERT	Major Terrain Features	NUNIVAK	Island or Coastal Feature
Naval Air Station	Military Installation	MT. MORIAH	Individual Mountain	Ocean Lake River Canal	Hydrographic Features
CROCKETT	County	MESA VERDE SAN XAVIER	National Park or Monument, Indian Res.		

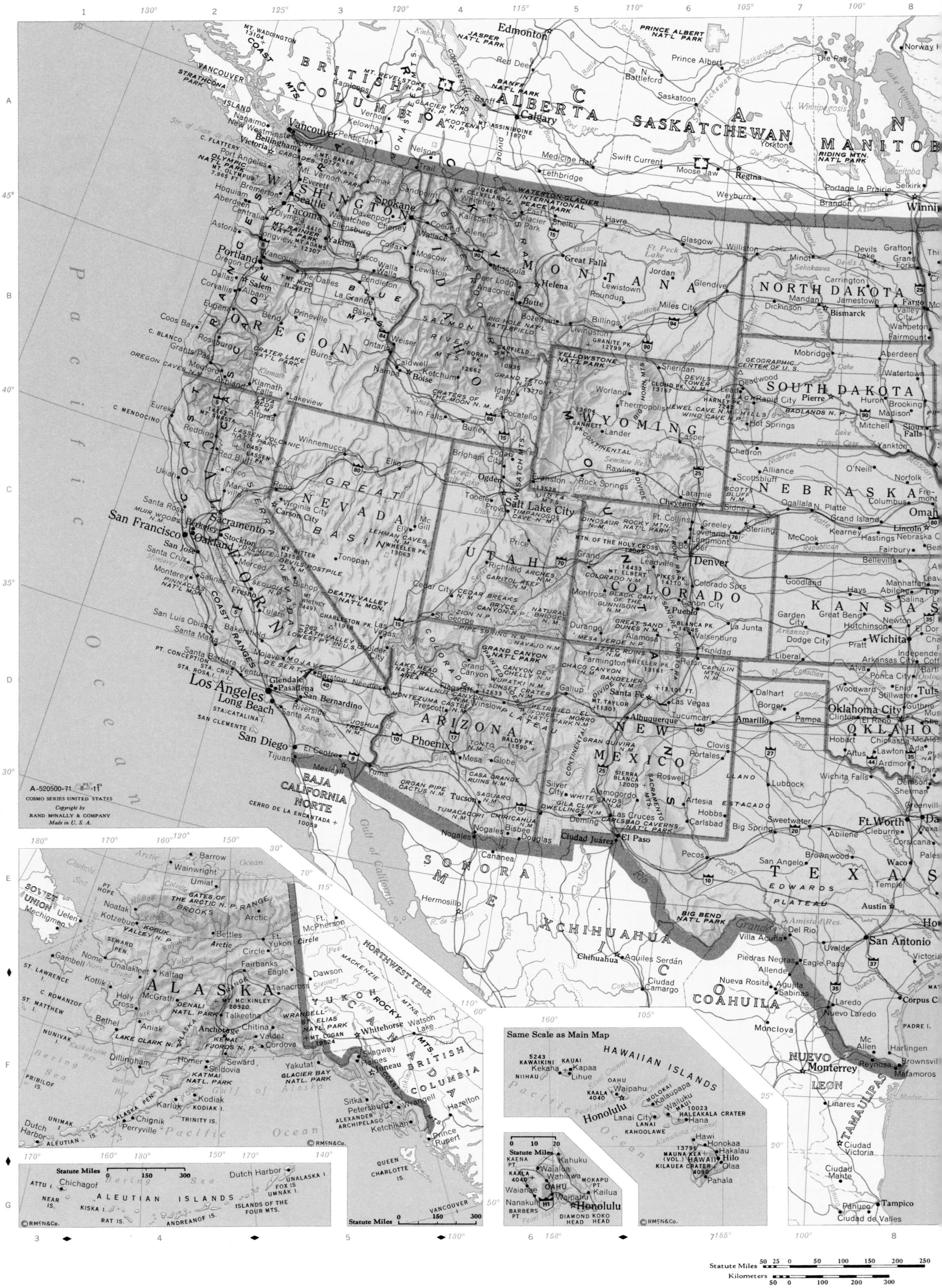

Pacific Ocean
BRITISH COLUMBIA
ALBERTA
SASKATCHEWAN
MANITOBA
CANADA
WASHINGTON
OREGON
CALIFORNIA
NEVADA
IDAHO
MONTANA
WYOMING
UTAH
COLORADO
ARIZONA
NEW MEXICO
NORTH DAKOTA
SOUTH DAKOTA
NEBRASKA
KANSAS
OKLAHOMA
TEXAS
MEXICO
BAJA CALIFORNIA NORTE
SONORA
CHIHUAHUA
COAHUILA
NUEVO LEON
TAMAULIPAS
Seattle
Portland
San Francisco
Los Angeles
San Diego
Sacramento
Salt Lake City
Denver
Phoenix
El Paso
San Antonio
Oklahoma City
Edmonton
Calgary
Vancouver
Regina
GREAT BASIN
Gulf of California
A-520500-71
COSMO SERIES UNITED STATES
Copyright by RAND McNALLY & COMPANY
Made in U. S. A.
ALASKA
Arctic Ocean
Bering Sea
Gulf of Alaska
SOVIET UNION
YUKON
NORTHWEST TERR.
Anchorage
Fairbanks
Juneau
Same Scale as Main Map
HAWAIIAN ISLANDS
Honolulu
OAHU
HAWAII
ALEUTIAN ISLANDS
Statute Miles
Kilometers

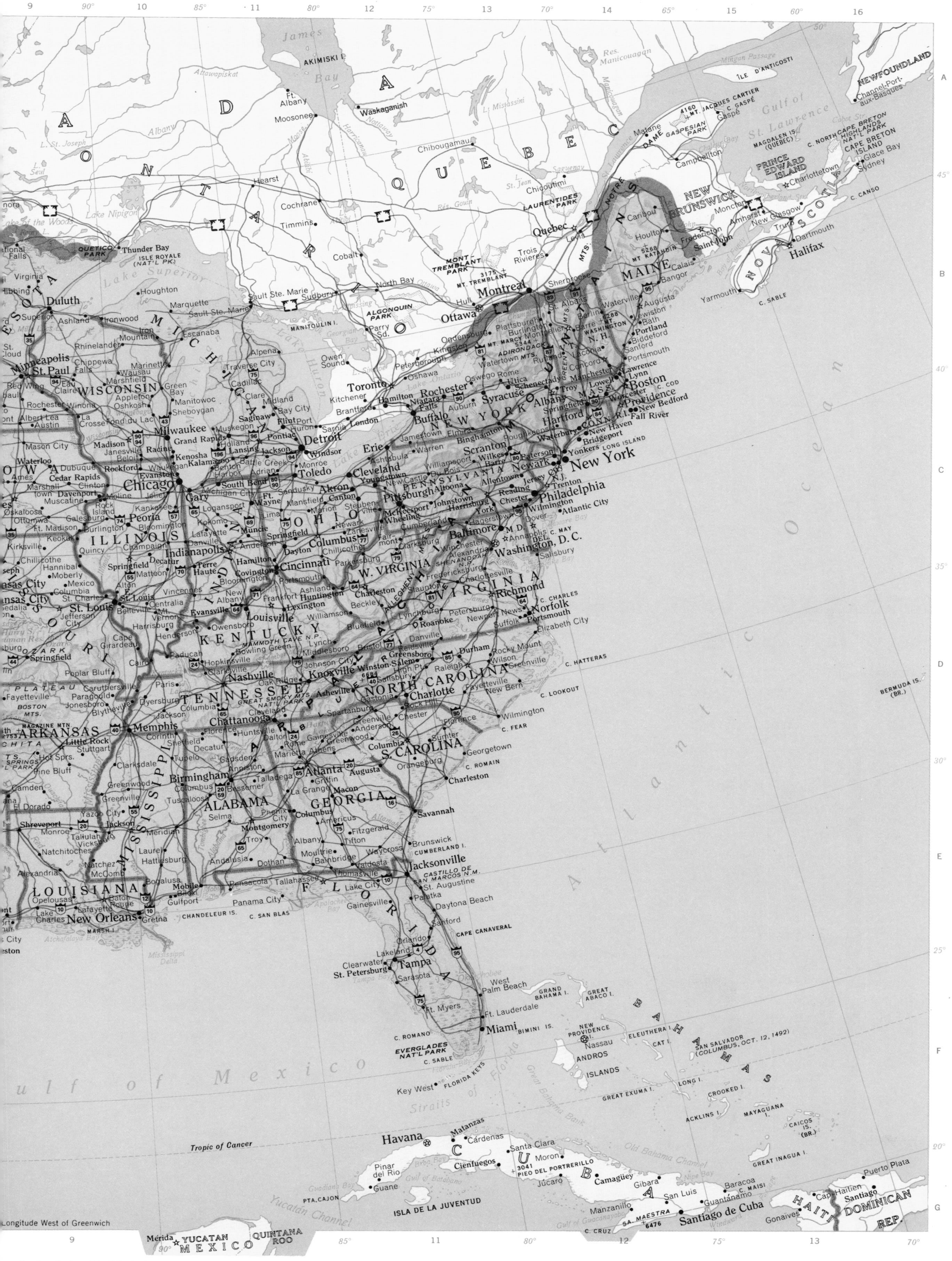

Lambert Conformal Conic Projection
SCALE 1:12,000,000 1 Inch = 189 Statute Miles

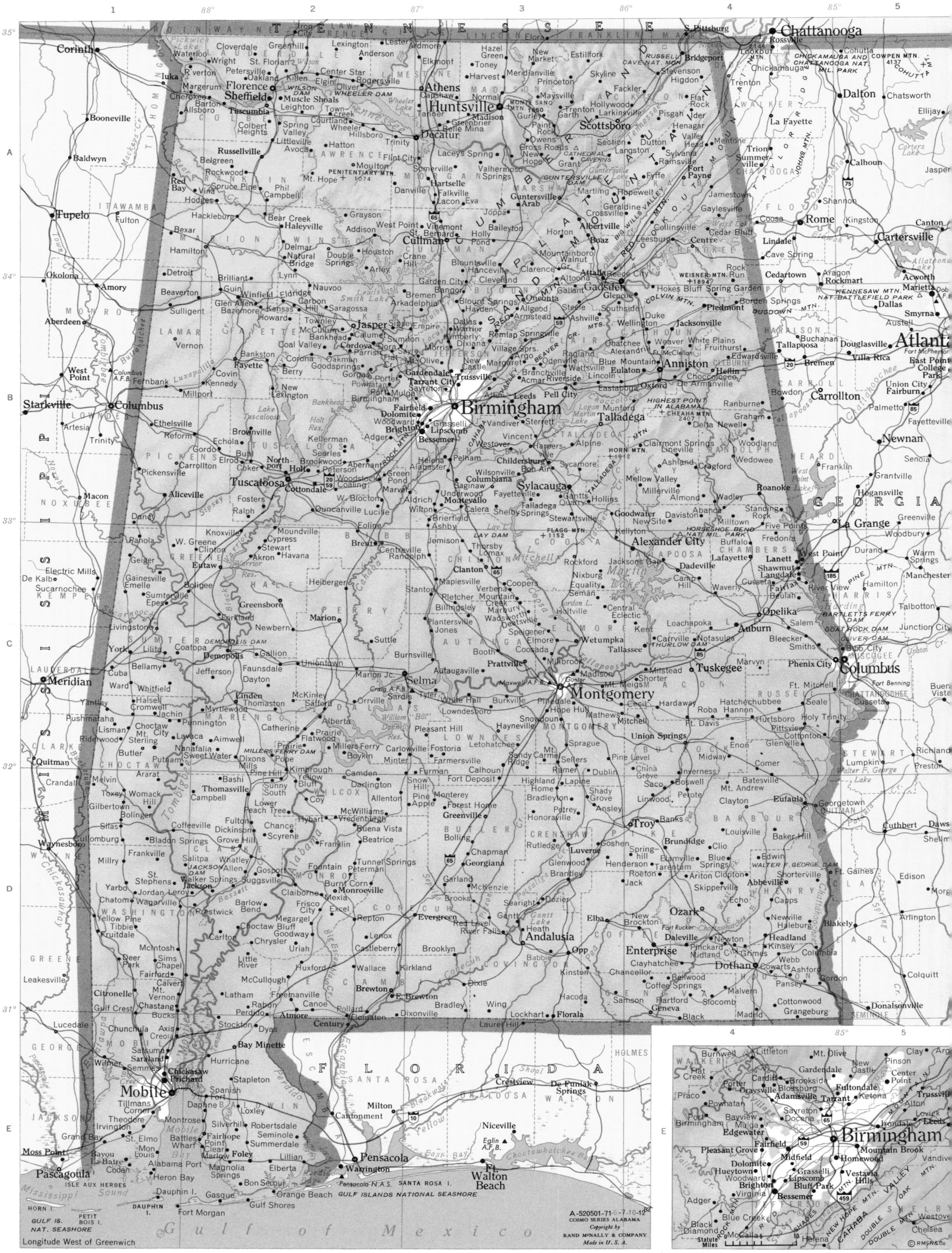

Cities and Towns

Albertville 12,039 **A3**
Alexander City 13,807 **C4**
Andalusia 10,415 **D3**
Anniston 29,523 **B4**
Arab 5,967 **A3**
Athens 14,558 **A3**
Atmore 8,789 **D2**
Auburn 28,471 **C4**
Bay Minette 7,455 **E2**
Bessemer 31,729 **B3**
Birmingham 286,799 **B3**
Bluff Park 12,000 **g7**
Boaz 7,151 **A3**
Brewton 6,680 **D2**
Center Point 23,317 **f7**
Childersburg 5,084 **B3**
Clanton 5,832 **C3**
Cullman 13,084 **A3**
Decatur 42,002 **A3**
Demopolis 7,678 **C2**
Dothan 48,750 **D4**
Enterprise 18,033 **D4**
Eufaula 12,097 **D4**
Fairfield 13,242 **B3**
Fayette 5,287 **B2**
Florence 37,029 **A2**
Fort Payne 11,485 **A4**
Gadsden 47,565 **A3**
Geneva 4,866 **D4**
Greenville 7,807 **D3**
Guntersville 7,041 **A3**
Haleyville 5,306 **A2**
Hamilton 5,093 **A2**
Hartselle 8,858 **A3**
Homewood 21,412 **g7**
Hueytown 13,478 **g6**
Huntsville 142,513 **A3**
Jackson 6,073 **D2**
Jacksonville 9,735 **B4**
Jasper 11,894 **B2**
Lanett 6,897 **C4**
Leeds 8,638 **B3**
Mobile 200,452 **E1**
Monroeville 5,674 **D2**
Montgomery 177,857 **C3**
Moundville 1,310 **C2**
Mountain Brook 19,718 **g7**
Muscle Shoals 8,911 **A2**
Northport 14,291 **B2**
Opelika 21,896 **C4**
Opp 7,204 **D3**
Ozark 13,188 **D4**
Pell City 6,616 **B3**
Phenix City 26,928 **C4**
Piedmont 5,544 **B4**
Prattville 18,647 **C3**
Prichard 39,541 **E1**
Roanoke 5,896 **B4**
Russellville 8,195 **A2**
Saraland 9,833 **E1**
Scottsboro 14,758 **A3**
Selma 26,684 **C2**
Sheffield 11,903 **A2**
Spanish Fort 3,415 **E2**
Sylacauga 12,708 **B3**
Talladega 19,128 **B3**
Tallassee 4,763 **C4**
Troy 12,945 **D4**
Tuscaloosa 75,211 **B2**
Tuscumbia 9,137 **A2**
Tuskegee 13,327 **C4**
Vestavia Hills 15,722 **g7**
Warrior 3,260 **B3**
Wetumpka 4,341 **C3**

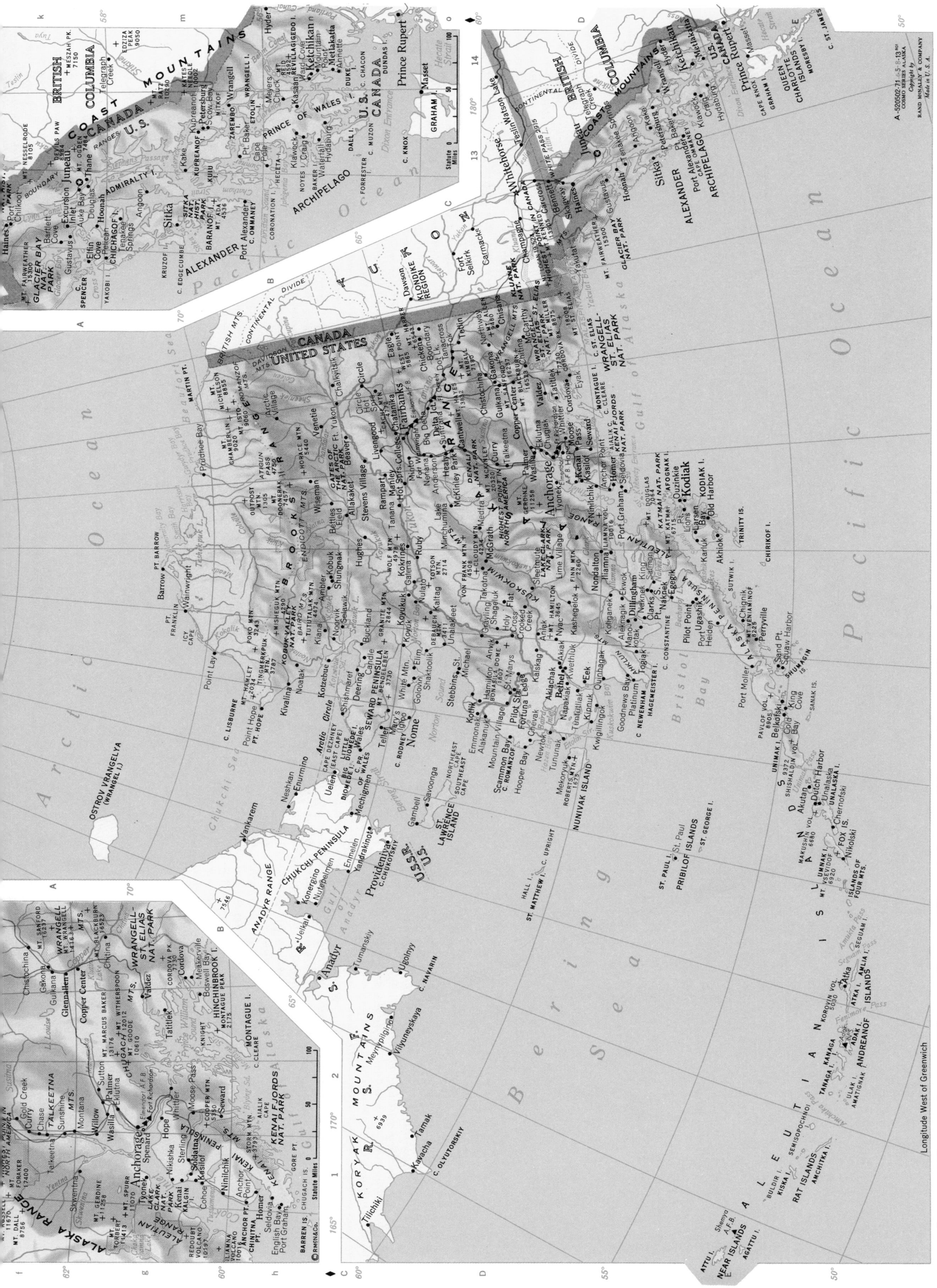

Statute Miles 50 25 0 50 100 150 200 250
Kilometers 50 0 100 200 300

Polyconic Projection
SCALE 1:12,000,000 1 Inch = 189 Statute Miles

Cities and Towns

Akiachak *438* **C7**
Alakanuk *522* **C7**
Anchorage *174,431* **C10**
Anderson *517* **C10**
Angoon *465* **D13**
Aniak *341* **C8**
Barrow *2,207* **A8**
Bethel *3,576* **C7**
Chevak *466* **C6**
Circle *81* **B11**
College *800* **B10**
Cordova *1,879* **C10**
Craig *527* **D13**
Delta Junction *945* **C10**
Dillingham *1,563* **D8**
Emmonak *567* **C7**
Fairbanks *22,645* **C10**
Fort Yukon *619* **B10**
Galena *765* **C8**
Gambell *445* **C5**
Glennallen *511* **f19**
Haines *993* **D12**
Homer *2,209* **D9**
Hoonah *680* **D12**
Hooper Bay *627* **C6**
Juneau *19,528* **D13**
Kake *555* **D13**
Kenai *4,324* **C9**
Ketchikan *7,198* **D13**
King Cove *460* **E7**
King Salmon *545* **D8**
Kipnuk *371* **C7**
Kodiak *4,756* **D9**
Kotzebue *2,054* **B7**
Kwethluk *454* **C7**
McGrath *355* **C8**
Metlakatla *1,056* **D13**
Mountain Point *396* **n24**
Mountain Village *583* **C7**
Naknek *600* **D8**
Nenana *470* **C10**
Nikishka *1,109* **g16**
Nome *2,301* **C6**
Noorvik *492* **B7**
Nulato *350* **C8**
Old Harbor *340* **D9**
Palmer *2,141* **C10**
Petersburg *2,821* **D13**
Pilot Station *325* **C7**
Point Hope *464* **B6**
Prudhoe Bay *50* **A10**
Quinhagak *412* **D7**
St. Marys *382* **C7**
St. Paul *551* **D5**
Sand Point *625* **D7**
Savoonga *491* **C5**
Selawik *361* **B7**
Seldovia *479* **D9**
Seward *1,843* **C10**
Shishmaref *394* **B6**
Sitka *7,803* **D12**
Skagway *768* **D12**
Soldotna *2,320* **g16**
Sterling *919* **g16**
Tanana *388* **B9**
Togiak *470* **D7**
Tok *589* **C11**
Unalakleet *623* **C7**
Unalaska *1,322* **E6**
Valdez *3,079* **C10**
Wainwright *405* **A8**
Wasilla *1,559* **C10**
Wrangell *2,184* **D13**
Yakutat *3,478* **D12**

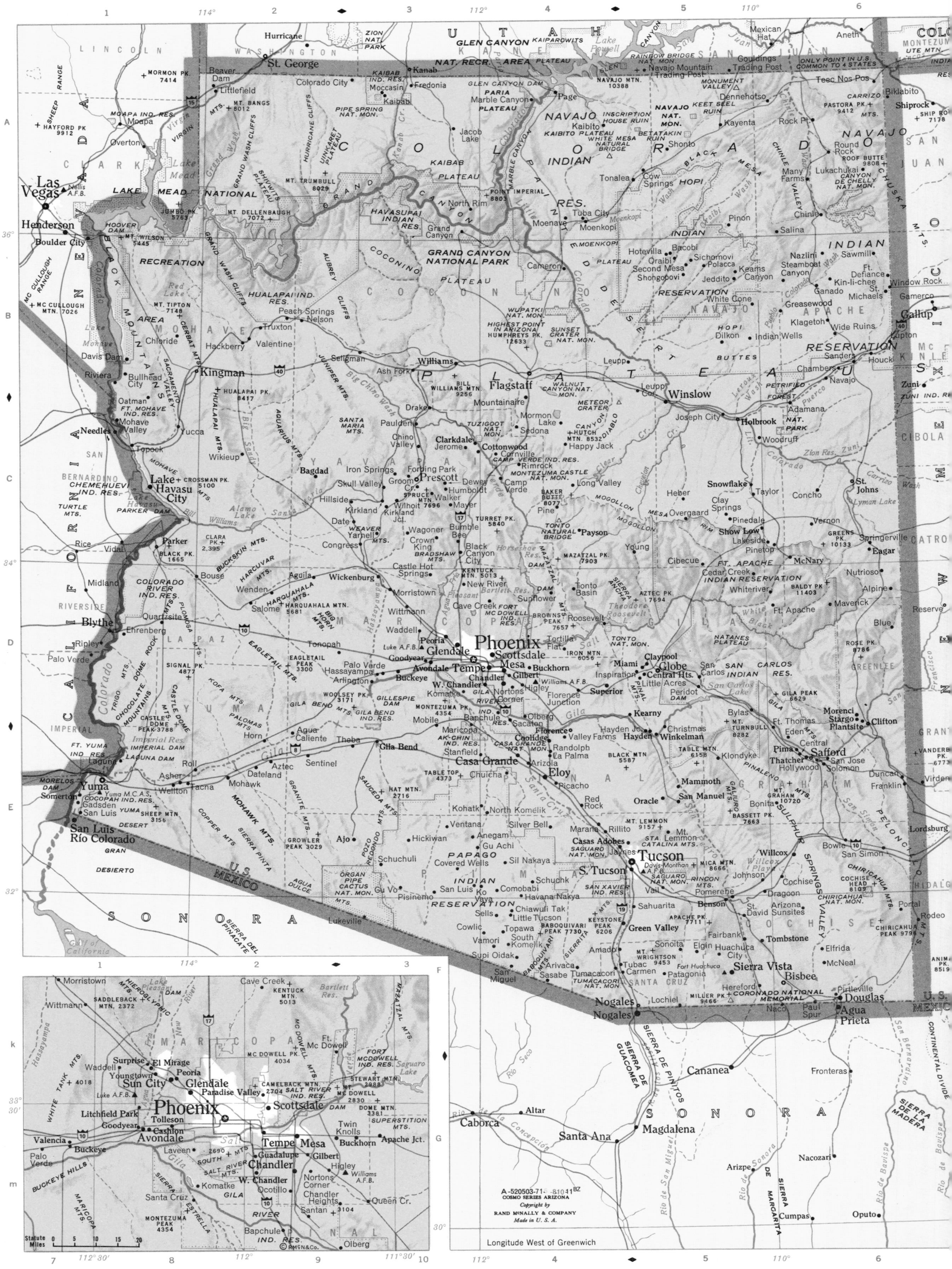

Statute Miles 10 0 10 20 30 40 50 60 70 80 90

Kilometers 10 0 10 20 40 60 80 100 120

Lambert Conformal Conic Projection

SCALE 1:2,725,000 1 Inch = 43 Statute Miles

Cities and Towns

Ajo *5,189* **E3**
Apache Junction *9,935* **m9**
Avondale *8,168* **D3**
Bagdad *2,331* **C2**
Benson *4,190* **F5**
Bisbee *7,154* **F6**
Buckeye *3,434* **D3**
Bullhead City *5,000* **B1**
Casa Grande *14,971* **E4**
Casas Adobes *5,300* **E5**
Chandler *29,673* **D4**
Chinle *2,815* **A6**
Chino Valley *2,858* **C3**
Claypool *2,362* **D5**
Clifton *4,245* **D6**
Coolidge *6,851* **E4**
Cottonwood *4,550* **C3**
Douglas *13,058* **F6**
Eagar *2,791* **C6**
Eloy *6,240* **E4**
Flagstaff *34,743* **B4**
Florence *3,391* **D4**
Fort Defiance *3,431* **B6**
Gila Bend *1,585* **E3**
Gilbert *5,717* **D4**
Glendale *97,172* **D3**
Globe *6,886* **D5**
Green Valley *7,999* **F5**
Holbrook *5,785* **C5**
Kayenta *3,343* **A5**
Kearny *2,646* **D5**
Kingman *9,257* **B1**
Lake Havasu City *15,909* **C1**
Mammoth *1,906* **E5**
Mesa *152,453* **D4**
Miami *2,716* **D5**
Nogales *15,683* **F5**
Oracle *2,484* **E5**
Page *4,907* **A4**
Paradise Valley *11,085* **k9**
Parker *2,542* **C1**
Payson *5,068* **C4**
Peoria *12,307* **D3**
Phoenix *789,704* **D3**
Prescott *20,055* **C3**
Riviera *4,500* **B1**
Sacaton *1,951* **D4**
Safford *7,010* **E6**
St. Johns *3,368* **C6**
San Carlos *2,668* **D5**
San Luis *1,946* **E1**
San Manuel *5,443* **E5**
Scottsdale *88,622* **D4**
Sedona *5,368* **C4**
Sells *1,864* **F4**
Show Low *4,298* **C5**
Sierra Vista *24,937* **F5**
Snowflake *3,510* **C5**
Somerton *5,761* **E1**
South Tucson *6,554* **E5**
Sun City *40,505* **k8**
Superior *4,600* **D4**
Taylor *1,915* **C5**
Tempe *106,743* **D4**
Thatcher *3,374* **E6**
Tombstone *1,632* **F5**
Tuba City *5,041* **A4**
Tucson *330,537* **E5**
Wickenburg *3,535* **D3**
Willcox *3,243* **E6**
Williams *2,266* **B3**
Window Rock *2,230* **B6**
Winslow *7,921* **C5**
Yuma *42,481* **E1**

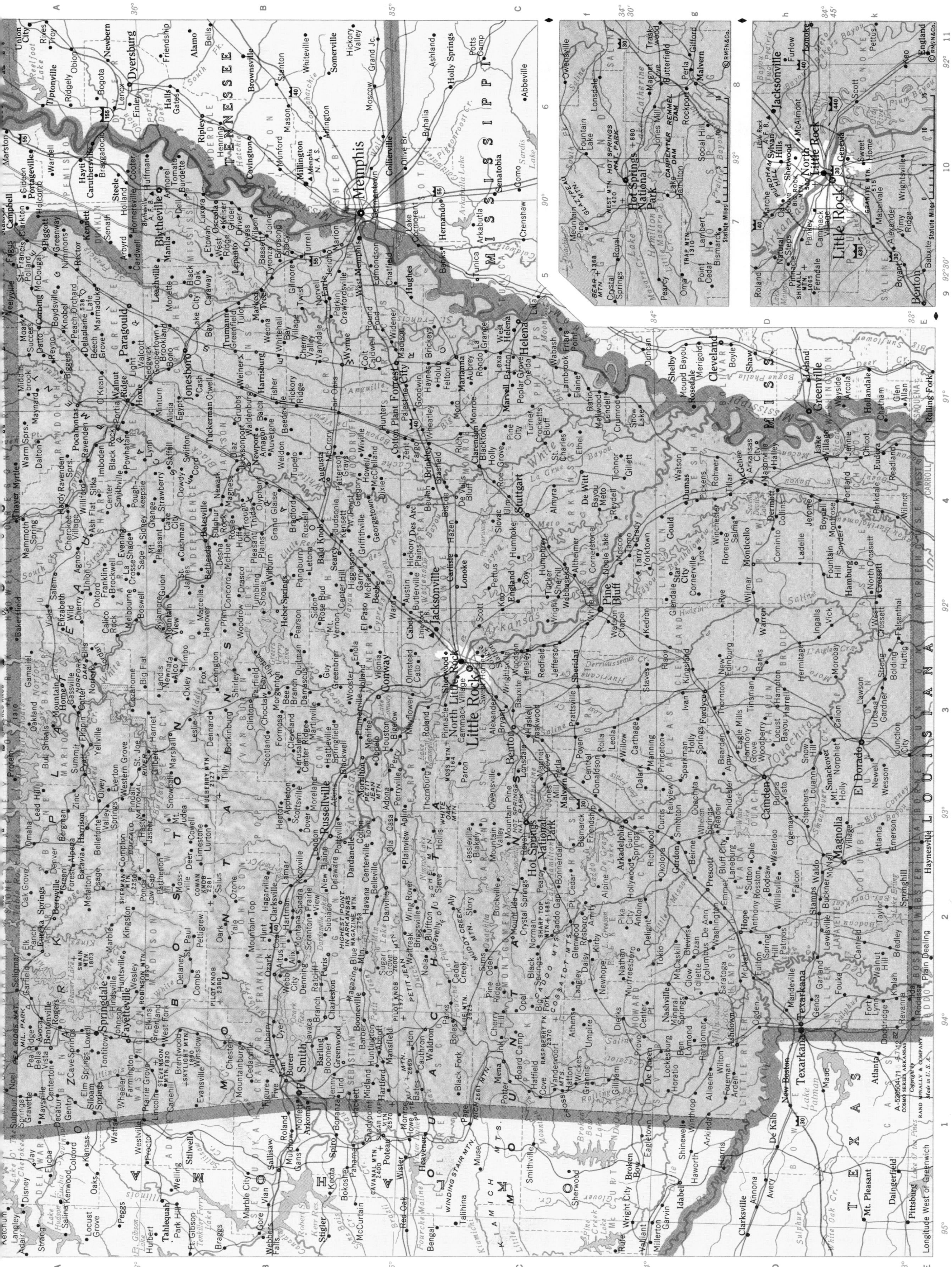

Statute Miles 5 0 5 10 20 30 40
Kilometers 5 0 5 15 25 35 45 55

Lambert Conformal Conic Projection
SCALE 1:1,832,000 1 Inch = 29 Statute Miles

Cities and Towns

Arkadelphia *10,005* **C2**
Ashdown *4,218* **D1**
Barling *3,761* **B1**
Batesville *8,263* **B4**
Beebe *3,599* **B4**
Benton *17,717* **C3**
Bentonville *8,756* **A1**
Berryville *2,966* **A2**
Blytheville *23,844* **B6**
Booneville *3,718* **B2**
Brinkley *4,909* **C4**
Cabot *4,806* **C3**
Camden *15,356* **D3**
Clarksville *5,237* **B2**
Conway *20,375* **B3**
Corning *3,650* **A5**
Crossett *6,706* **D4**
Dardanelle *3,621* **B2**
De Queen *4,594* **C1**
Dermott *4,731* **D4**
De Witt *3,928* **C4**
Dumas *6,091* **D4**
El Dorado *25,270* **D3**
Eudora *3,840* **D4**
Eureka Springs *1,989* **A2**
Fayetteville *36,608* **A1**
Fordyce *5,175* **D3**
Forrest City *13,803* **B5**
Fort Smith *71,636* **B1**
Harrison *9,567* **A2**
Heber Springs *4,589* **B3**
Helena *9,598* **C5**
Hope *10,290* **D2**
Hot Springs National Park *35,781* **C2**
Jacksonville *27,589* **C3**
Jonesboro *31,530* **B5**
Little Rock *158,461* **C3**
Lonoke *4,128* **C4**
McGehee *5,671* **D4**
Magnolia *11,909* **D2**
Malvern *10,163* **C3**
Marianna *6,220* **C5**
Mena *5,154* **C1**
Monticello *8,259* **D4**
Morrilton *7,355* **B3**
Mountain Home *8,066* **A3**
Mountain View *2,147* **B3**
Nashville *4,554* **D2**
Newport *8,339* **B4**
North Little Rock *64,288* **C3**
Osceola *8,881* **B6**
Ozark *3,597* **B2**
Paragould *15,248* **A5**
Paris *3,991* **B2**
Piggott *3,762* **A5**
Pine Bluff *56,636* **C3**
Pocahontas *5,995* **A5**
Prescott *4,103* **D2**
Rogers *17,429* **A1**
Russellville *14,031* **B2**
Searcy *13,612* **B4**
Sherwood *10,406* **C3**
Siloam Springs *7,940* **A1**
Springdale *23,458* **A1**
Stuttgart *10,941* **C4**
Texarkana *21,459* **D1**
Tontitown *615* **A1**
Trumann *6,405* **B5**
Van Buren *12,020* **B1**
Walnut Ridge *4,152* **A5**
Warren *7,646* **D3**
West Helena *11,367* **C5**
West Memphis *28,138* **B5**
Wynne *7,805* **B5**

Cities and Towns

Anaheim *219,494* **F5**
Antioch *42,683* **h9**
Bakersfield *105,735* **E4**
Berkeley *103,328* **D2**
Beverly Hills *32,367* **m12**
Burbank *84,625* **E4**
Calexico *14,412* **F6**
Chico *26,603* **C3**
Chula Vista *83,927* **F5**
Concord *103,255* **h8**
Costa Mesa *82,562* **n13**
Davis *36,640* **C3**
East Los Angeles *110,017* **m12**
El Cajon *73,892* **F5**
El Centro *23,996* **F6**
Escondido *64,355* **F5**
Eureka *24,153* **B1**
Fairfield *58,099* **C2**
Fremont *131,945* **D2**
Fresno *217,289* **D4**
Fullerton *102,034* **n13**
Garden Grove *123,307* **n13**
Glendale *139,060* **m12**
Hayward *94,342* **h8**
Huntington Beach *170,505* **F4**
Indio *21,611* **F5**
Lancaster *48,027* **E4**
Lompoc *26,267* **E3**
Long Beach *361,334* **F4**
Los Angeles *2,966,850* **E4**
Marysville *9,898* **C3**
Menlo Park *26,369* **k8**
Merced *36,499* **D3**
Modesto *106,602* **D3**
Monterey *27,558* **D3**
Napa *50,879* **C2**
Newport Beach *62,556* **n13**
Oakland *339,337* **D2**
Oceanside *76,698* **F5**
Ontario *88,820* **E5**
Oxnard *108,195* **E4**
Palm Springs *32,366* **F5**
Palo Alto *55,225* **D2**
Pasadena *118,072* **E4**
Pomona *92,742* **E5**
Redding *41,995* **B2**
Redwood City *54,951* **D2**
Richmond *74,676* **D2**
Riverside *170,591* **F5**
Sacramento *275,741* **C3**
Salinas *80,479* **D3**
San Bernardino *118,794* **E5**
San Clemente *27,325* **F5**
San Diego *875,538* **F5**
San Francisco *678,974* **D2**
San Jose *629,546* **D3**
San Juan Capistrano *18,959* **F5**
San Luis Obispo *34,252* **E3**
Santa Ana *204,023* **F5**
Santa Barbara *74,414* **E4**
Santa Cruz *41,483* **D2**
Santa Maria *39,685* **E3**
Santa Monica *88,314* **m12**
Santa Rosa *83,320* **C2**
South Lake Tahoe *20,681* **C4**
Stockton *149,779* **D3**
Sunnyvale *106,618* **k8**
Torrance *129,881* **n12**
Tulare *22,526* **D4**
Turlock *26,287* **D3**
Vallejo *80,303* **C2**
Ventura *74,393* **E4**
Visalia *49,729* **D4**
Yuba City *18,736* **C3**

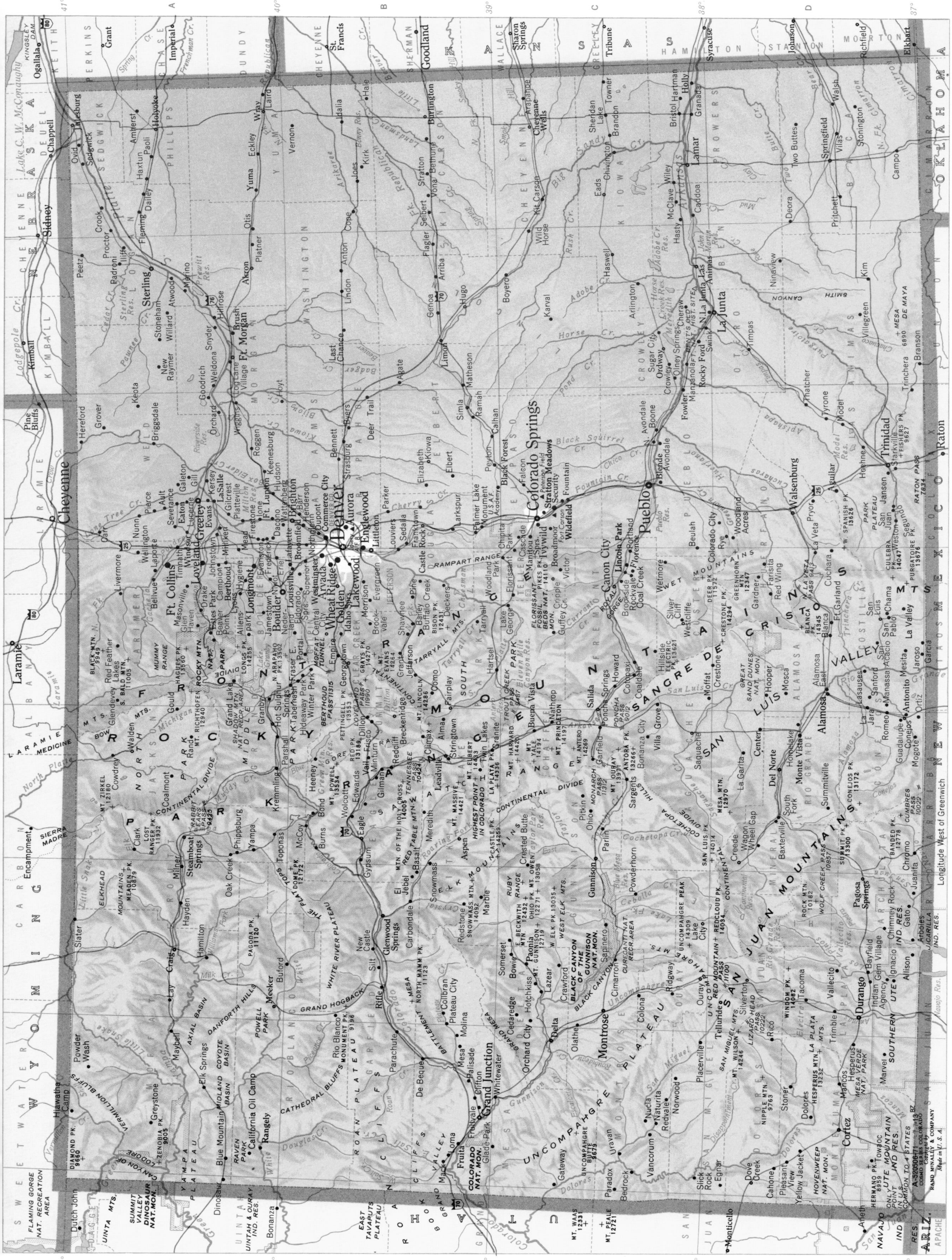

Statute Miles 5 0 5 10 20 30 40 50

Kilometers 5 0 5 15 25 35 45 55 65 75

Lambert Conformal Conic Projection

SCALE 1:2.186.000 1 Inch = 34.5 Statute Miles

Cities and Towns

Alamosa *6,830* **D5**
Arvada *84,576* **B5**
Aspen *3,678* **B4**
Aurora *158,588* **B6**
Black Forest *3,372* **C6**
Boulder *76,685* **A5**
Breckenridge *818* **B4**
Brighton *12,773* **B6**
Broomfield *20,730* **B5**
Burlington *3,107* **B8**
Canon City *13,037* **C5**
Castle Rock *3,921* **B6**
Central City *329* **B5**
Clifton *5,223* **B2**
Colorado Springs *214,821* **C6**
Commerce City *16,234* **B6**
Cortez *7,095* **D2**
Craig *8,133* **A3**
Delta *3,931* **C2**
Denver *492,365* **B6**
Durango *11,649* **D3**
Englewood *30,021* **B6**
Estes Park *2,703* **A5**
Evans *5,063* **A6**
Evergreen *6,376* **B5**
Fort Collins *65,092* **A5**
Fort Lupton *4,251* **A6**
Fort Morgan *8,768* **A7**
Fountain *8,324* **C6**
Glenwood Springs *4,637* **B3**
Golden *12,237* **B5**
Grand Junction *27,956* **B2**
Greeley *53,006* **A6**
Gunnison *5,785* **C4**
Holyoke *2,092* **A8**
Julesburg *1,528* **A8**
Lafayette *8,985* **B5**
La Junta *8,338* **D7**
Lakewood *113,808* **B5**
Lamar *7,713* **C8**
Las Animas *2,818* **C7**
Leadville *3,879* **B4**
Limon *1,805* **B7**
Littleton *28,631* **B6**
Longmont *42,942* **A5**
Louisville *5,593* **B5**
Loveland *30,244* **A5**
Meeker *2,356* **A3**
Monte Vista *3,902* **D4**
Montrose *8,722* **C3**
Northglenn *29,847* **B6**
Ouray *684* **C3**
Pagosa Springs *1,331* **D3**
Pueblo *101,686* **C6**
Rangely *2,113* **A2**
Rifle *3,215* **B3**
Rocky Ford *4,804* **C7**
Salida *4,870* **C5**
Security *11,000* **C6**
Springfield *1,657* **D8**
Steamboat Springs *5,098* **A4**
Sterling *11,385* **A7**
Stratton Meadows *6,223* **C6**
Telluride *1,047* **D3**
Trinidad *9,663* **D6**
USAF Academy *8,000* **C6**
Vail *2,261* **B4**
Walsenburg *3,945* **D6**
Westminster *50,211* **B5**
Wheat Ridge *30,293* **B5**
Widefield *7,500* **C6**
Windsor *4,277* **A6**
Wray *2,131* **A8**
Yuma *2,824* **A8**

CONNECTICUT

Cities and Towns*

Ansonia *19,039* **D3**
Bethel *8,755* **D2**
Bloomfield *7,400* **B5**
Blue Hills *6,600* **B5**
Branford *5,438* **D4**
Bridgeport *142,546* **E3**
Bristol *57,370* **C4**
Cheshire *5,722* **D4**
Clinton *11,195* **D5**
Cromwell *10,100* **C5**
Danbury *60,470* **D2**
Darien *18,892* **E2**
Derby *12,346* **D3**
East Hartford *52,563* **B5**
East Haven *25,028* **D4**
Enfield *8,151* **B5**
Fairfield *54,849* **E2**
Glastonbury *7,049* **C5**
Greenwich *59,578* **E1**
Groton *10,086* **D7**
Hamden *51,071* **D4**
Hartford *136,392* **B5**
Hazardville *5,436* **B5**
Kensington *7,502* **C4**
Manchester *49,761* **B5**
Meriden *57,118* **C4**
Middletown *39,040* **C5**
Milford *49,101* **E3**
Monroe Center *6,950* **D3**
Mystic *2,333* **D8**
Naugatuck *26,456* **D3**
Nautilus Park *6,500* **D7**
New Britain *73,840* **C4**
New Canaan *17,931* **E2**
New Haven *126,109* **D4**
Newington *28,841* **C5**
New London *28,842* **D7**
North Haven *22,080* **D4**
Norwalk *77,767* **E2**
Norwich *38,074* **C7**
Oakville *8,737* **C3**
Orange *13,237* **D3**
Plainville *16,401* **C4**
Plantsville *5,700* **C4**
Portland *8,383* **C5**
Putnam *6,855* **B8**
Ridgefield *6,066* **D2**
Seymour *13,434* **D3**
Shelton *31,314* **D3**
Sherwood Manor *6,303* **A5**
Simsbury *5,488* **B4**
Southington *17,400* **C4**
South Windsor *10,200* **B5**
Southwood Acres *9,779* **B5**
Stamford *102,453* **E1**
Storrs *11,394* **B7**
Stratford *50,541* **E3**
Terryville *5,234* **C3**
Torrington *30,987* **B3**
Trumbull *32,989* **E3**
Vernon *27,974* **B6**
Wallingford *37,274* **D4**
Waterbury *103,266* **C3**
Watertown *6,000* **C3**
West Hartford *61,306* **B4**
West Haven *53,184* **D4**
Wethersfield *26,013* **C5**
Willimantic *14,652* **C7**
Wilton *6,500* **E2**
Windsor *17,517* **B5**
Windsor Locks *12,190* **B5**
Winsted *8,092* **B3**
Wolcott *5,500* **C4**
Woodbridge *7,600* **D3**

Statute Miles 5 0 5 10 15

Kilometers 5 0 5 10 15 20

Lambert Conformal Conic Projection
SCALE 1:545,000 1 Inch = 8.6 Statute Miles

*Populations are for localities, not incorporated towns.

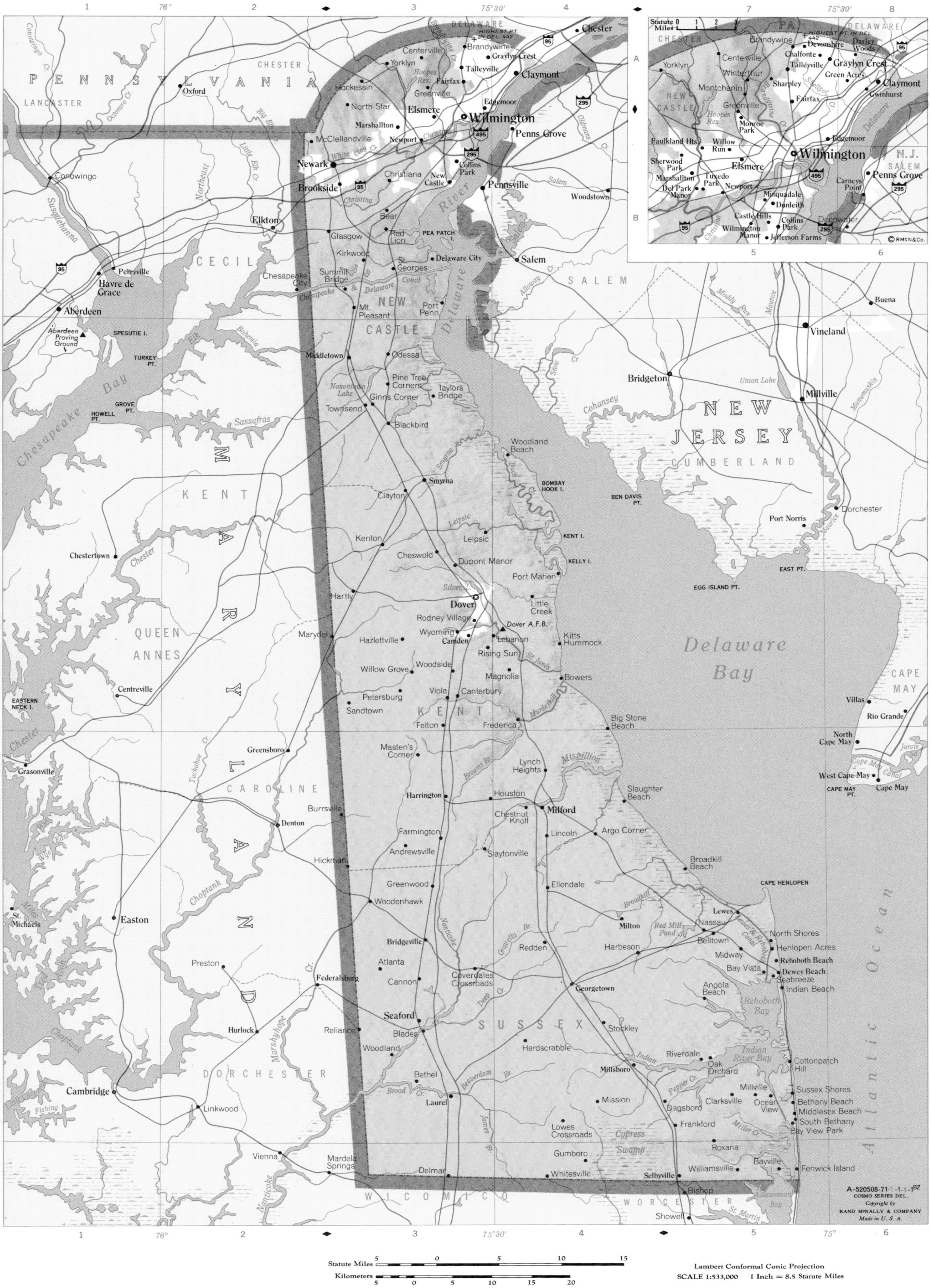

Cities and Towns

- Bear 950 **B3**
- Bethany Beach 330 **F5**
- Blades 664 **F3**
- Bridgeville 1,238 **F3**
- Broadkill Beach 200 **E5**
- Brookside 15,255 **B3**
- Camden 1,757 **D3**
- Canterbury 500 **D3**
- Castle Hills 1,950 **I7**
- Chalfonte 2,200 **h7**
- Cheswold 269 **D3**
- Christiana 500 **B3**
- Clarksville 450 **F5**
- Claymont 10,022 **A4**
- Clayton 1,216 **C3**
- Collins Park 2,850 **B3**
- Dagsboro 344 **F5**
- Delaware City 1,858 **B3**
- Delmar 948 **G3**
- Dewey Beach 1,500 **F5**
- Dover 23,507 **D3**
- Dunleith 2,700 **I7**
- Dupont Manor 1,059 **D3**
- Edgemoor 7,397 **A3**
- Ellendale 361 **E4**
- Elsmere 6,493 **B3**
- Fairfax 2,850 **A3**
- Felton 547 **D3**
- Frankford 828 **F5**
- Frederica 864 **D4**
- Georgetown 1,710 **F4**
- Graylyn Crest 5,000 **A3**
- Greenwood 578 **E3**
- Gumboro 200 **G4**
- Gwinhurst 1,400 **h8**
- Harbeson 250 **F4**
- Harrington 2,405 **E3**
- Hockessin 950 **A3**
- Houston 357 **E3**
- Jefferson Farms 2,400 **I7**
- Kenton 243 **D3**
- Kirkwood 400 **B3**
- Laurel 3,052 **F3**
- Leipsic 228 **D3**
- Lewes 2,197 **E5**
- Lincoln 500 **E4**
- Little Creek 230 **D4**
- Marshallton 3,950 **B3**
- Middletown 2,946 **C3**
- Midway 500 **F5**
- Milford 5,366 **E4**
- Millsboro 1,233 **F4**
- Milton 1,359 **E4**
- Minquadale 1,700 **I7**
- Newark 25,247 **B2**
- New Castle 4,907 **B3**
- Newport 1,167 **B3**
- Oak Orchard 250 **F5**
- Ocean View 495 **F5**
- Odessa 384 **C3**
- Port Penn 300 **B3**
- Rehoboth Beach 1,730 **F5**
- Rodney Village 1,100 **D3**
- St. Georges 500 **B3**
- Seaford 5,256 **F3**
- Selbyville 1,251 **G5**
- Smyrna 4,750 **C3**
- Talleyville 6,880 **A3**
- Townsend 386 **C3**
- Willow Run 1,950 **I7**
- Wilmington 70,195 **B3**
- Wilmington Manor 2,000 **I7**
- Wyoming 960 **D3**
- Yorklyn 600 **A3**

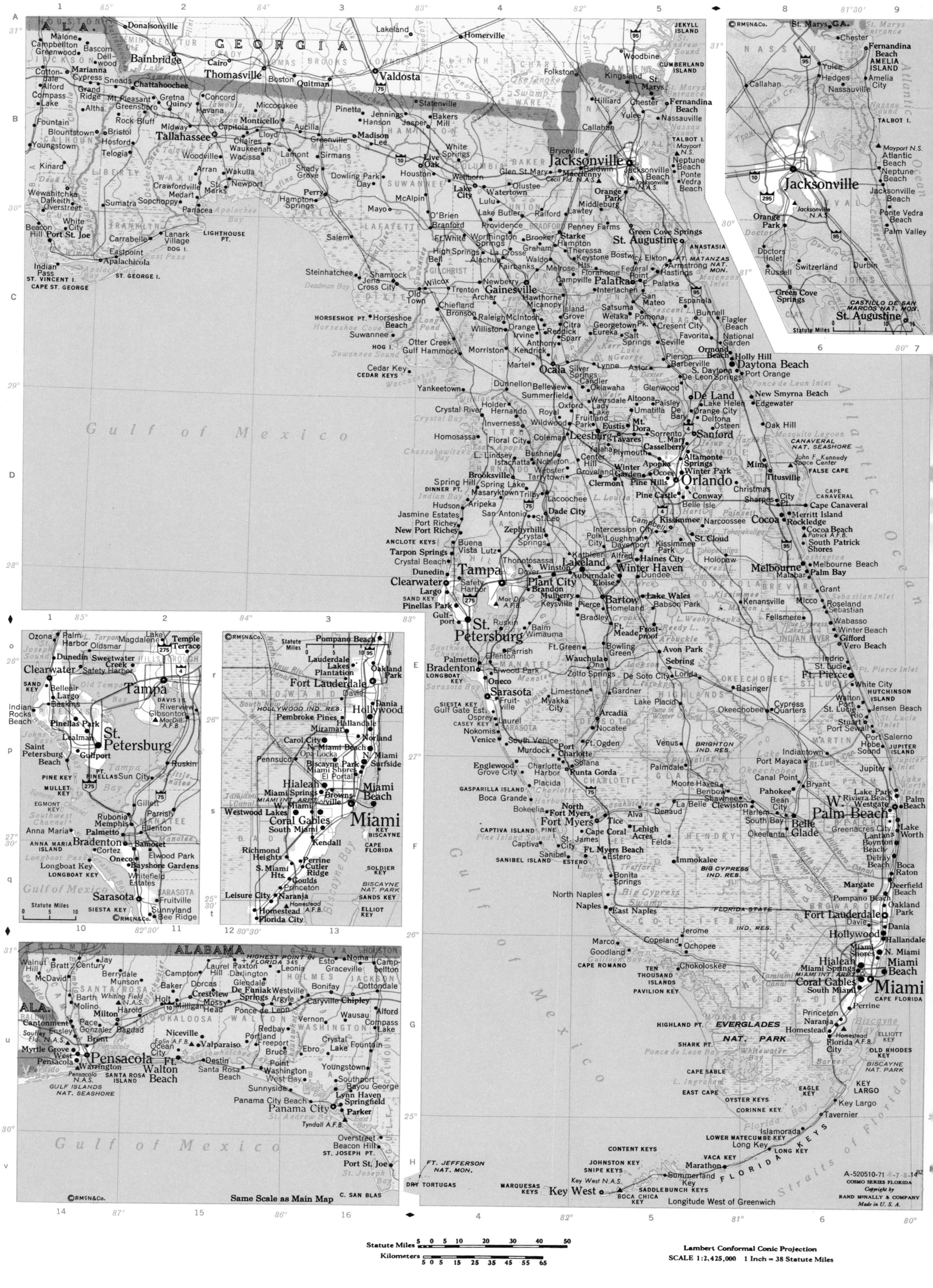

Cities and Towns

Bartow *14,780* **E5**
Belle Glade *16,535* **F6**
Boca Raton *49,505* **F6**
Boynton Beach *35,624* **F6**
Bradenton *30,170* **E4**
Brandon *29,100* **E4**
Cape Canaveral *5,733* **D6**
Cape Coral *32,103* **F5**
Carol City *47,349* **s13**
Clearwater *85,528* **E4**
Cocoa *16,096* **D6**
Coral Gables *43,241* **G6**
Daytona Beach *54,176* **C5**
Deerfield Beach *39,193* **F6**
De Land *15,354* **C5**
Delray Beach *34,325* **F6**
Dunedin *30,203* **D4**
Fort Lauderdale *153,279* **F6**
Fort Myers *36,638* **F5**
Fort Pierce *33,802* **E6**
Fort Walton Beach *20,829* **u15**
Gainesville *81,371* **C4**
Hallandale *36,517* **G6**
Hialeah *145,254* **G6**
Hollywood *121,323* **F6**
Homestead *20,668* **G6**
Immokalee *11,038* **F5**
Jacksonville *540,920* **B5**
Kendall *51,000* **s13**
Key Largo *7,447* **G6**
Key West *24,382* **H5**
Kissimmee *15,487* **D5**
Lake City *9,257* **B4**
Lakeland *47,406* **D5**
Lake Worth *27,048* **F6**
Largo *58,977* **E4**
Leesburg *13,191* **D5**
Marathon *7,508* **H5**
Margate *35,900* **F6**
Melbourne *46,536* **D6**
Merritt Island *30,708* **D6**
Miami *346,865* **G6**
Miami Beach *96,298* **G6**
Miramar *32,813* **s13**
Naples *17,581* **F5**
New Smyrna Beach *13,557* **C6**
North Miami *36,553* **G6**
North Miami Beach *36,481* **s13**
Ocala *37,170* **C4**
Orlando *128,291* **D5**
Panama City *33,346* **u16**
Pembroke Pines *35,776* **r13**
Pensacola *57,619* **u14**
Pinellas Park *32,811* **E4**
Plantation *48,653* **r13**
Plant City *17,064* **D4**
Pompano Beach *52,618* **F6**
Port Charlotte *25,770* **F4**
Riviera Beach *26,489* **F6**
St. Augustine *11,985* **C5**
St. Petersburg *238,647* **E4**
Sanford *23,176* **D5**
Sarasota *48,868* **E4**
Sebring *8,736* **E5**
Tallahassee *81,548* **B2**
Tampa *271,523* **E4**
Tarpon Springs *13,251* **D4**
Titusville *31,910* **D6**
Venice *12,153* **E4**
Vero Beach *16,176* **E6**
West Palm Beach *63,305* **F6**
West Pensacola *24,571* **u14**
Winter Haven *21,119* **D5**

Statute Miles 5 0 5 10 20 30 40

Kilometers 5 0 5 15 25 35 45 55

Lambert Conformal Conic Projection

SCALE 1:1,962,000 1 Inch = 31 Statute Miles

Cities and Towns

Adel *5,592* **E3**
Albany *74,550* **E2**
Americus *16,120* **D2**
Athens *42,549* **C3**
Atlanta *425,022* **C2**
Augusta *47,532* **C5**
Bainbridge *10,553* **F2**
Blakely *5,880* **E2**
Brunswick *17,605* **E5**
Buford *6,578* **B2**
Cairo *8,777* **F2**
Calhoun *5,563* **B2**
Camilla *5,414* **E2**
Carrollton *14,078* **C1**
Cartersville *9,247* **B2**
Cedartown *8,619* **B1**
Cochran *5,121* **D3**
College Park *24,632* **C2**
Columbus *169,441* **D2**
Cordele *11,184* **E3**
Covington *10,586* **C3**
Dalton *20,939* **B2**
Dawson *5,699* **E2**
Decatur *18,404* **C2**
Douglas *10,980* **E4**
Douglasville *7,641* **C2**
Dublin *16,083* **D4**
Eastman *5,330* **D3**
East Point *37,486* **C2**
Elberton *5,686* **B4**
Fitzgerald *10,187* **E3**
Forest Park *18,782* **h8**
Fort Oglethorpe *5,443* **B1**
Fort Valley *9,000* **D3**
Gainesville *15,280* **B3**
Griffin *20,728* **C2**
Hinesville *11,309* **E5**
Kennesaw *5,095* **B2**
La Fayette *6,517* **B1**
La Grange *24,204* **C1**
Lawrenceville *8,928* **C3**
Mableton *20,200* **h7**
Macon *116,896* **D3**
Marietta *30,829* **C2**
Martinez *16,472* **C4**
Milledgeville *12,176* **C3**
Monroe *8,854* **C3**
Moultrie *15,708* **E3**
Newnan *11,449* **C2**
North Atlanta *22,800* **h8**
Perry *9,453* **D3**
Quitman *5,188* **F3**
Rome *29,654* **B1**
Roswell *23,337* **B2**
St. Simons Island *6,566* **E5**
Sandersville *6,137* **D4**
Sandy Springs *20,300* **h8**
Savannah *141,390* **D5**
Smyrna *20,312* **C2**
Statesboro *14,866* **D5**
Stone Mountain *4,867* **C2**
Swainsboro *7,602* **D4**
Sylvester *5,860* **E3**
Thomaston *9,682* **D2**
Thomasville *18,463* **F3**
Thomson *7,001* **C4**
Tifton *13,749* **E3**
Toccoa *9,104* **B3**
Tucker *18,200* **h8**
Valdosta *37,596* **F3**
Vidalia *10,393* **D4**
Warner Robins *39,893* **D3**
Waycross *19,371* **E4**
Waynesboro *5,760* **C4**

HAWAII

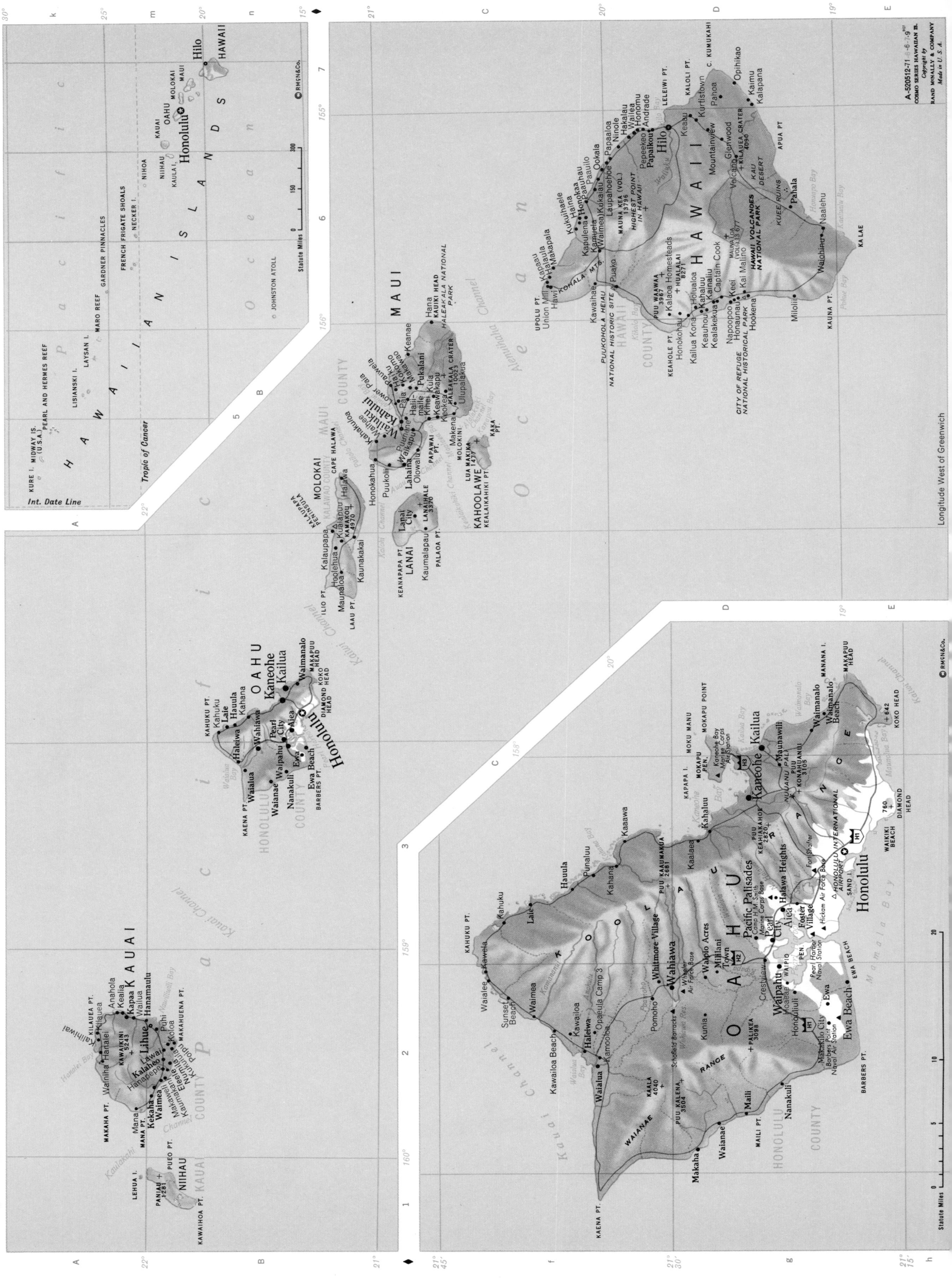

Statute Miles 5 0 5 10 20 30 40 50
Kilometers 5 0 5 10 20 30 40 50 60

Lambert Conformal Conic Projection
SCALE 1:2,000,000 1 Inch = 32 Statute Miles

Cities and Towns

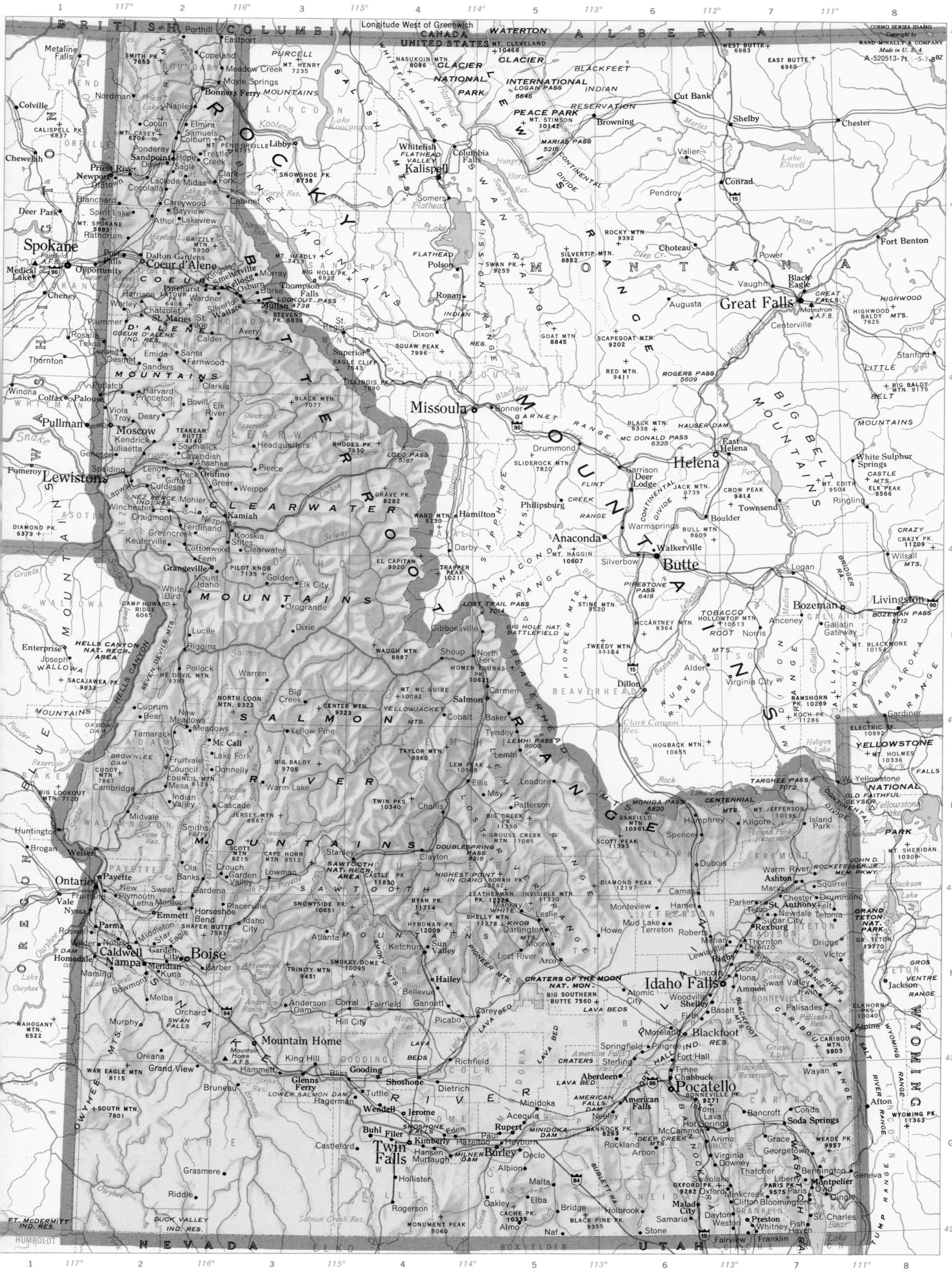

Statute Miles 5 0 5 10 20 30 40 50 60

Kilometers 5 0 5 15 25 35 45 55 65 75

Lambert Conformal Conic Projection

SCALE 1:2,633,000 1 Inch = 41.5 Statute Miles

Cities and Towns

- Aberdeen 1,528 G6
- American Falls 3,626 G6
- Ammon 4,669 F7
- Arco 1,241 F5
- Ashton 1,219 E7
- Blackfoot 10,065 F6
- Boise 102,160 F2
- Bonners Ferry 1,906 A2
- Buhl 3,629 G4
- Burley 8,761 G5
- Caldwell 17,699 F2
- Cascade 945 E2
- Chubbuck 7,052 G6
- Coeur d'Alene 20,054 B2
- Dalton Gardens 1,795 B2
- Eagle 2,620 F2
- Emmett 4,605 F2
- Filer 1,645 G4
- Fort Hall 900 F6
- Fruitland 2,559 F2
- Garden City 4,571 F2
- Glenns Ferry 1,374 G3
- Gooding 2,949 G4
- Grace 1,216 G7
- Grangeville 3,666 D2
- Hailey 2,109 F4
- Heyburn 2,889 G5
- Homedale 2,078 F2
- Idaho Falls 39,590 F6
- Jerome 6,891 G4
- Kamiah 1,478 C2
- Kellogg 3,417 B2
- Ketchum 2,200 F4
- Kimberly 2,307 G4
- Kuna 1,767 F2
- Lewiston 27,986 C1
- McCall 2,188 E2
- Malad City 1,915 G6
- Meridian 6,658 F2
- Middleton 1,901 F2
- Montpelier 3,107 G7
- Moscow 16,513 C2
- Mountain Home 7,540 F3
- Mullan 1,269 B3
- Nampa 25,112 F2
- New Plymouth 1,186 F2
- Nezperce 517 C2
- Orofino 3,711 C2
- Osburn 2,220 B3
- Parma 1,820 F2
- Payette 5,448 E2
- Pierce 1,060 C3
- Pocatello 46,340 G6
- Post Falls 5,736 B2
- Preston 3,759 G7
- Priest River 1,639 A2
- Rathdrum 1,369 B2
- Rexburg 11,559 F7
- Rigby 2,624 F7
- Rupert 5,476 G5
- St. Anthony 3,212 F7
- St. Maries 2,794 B2
- Salmon 3,308 D5
- Sandpoint 4,460 A2
- Shelley 3,300 F6
- Shoshone 1,242 G4
- Soda Springs 4,051 G7
- Sugar City 1,022 F7
- Sun Valley 545 F4
- Twin Falls 26,209 G4
- Wallace 1,736 B3
- Weiser 4,771 E2
- Wendell 1,974 G4
- Wilder 1,260 F2

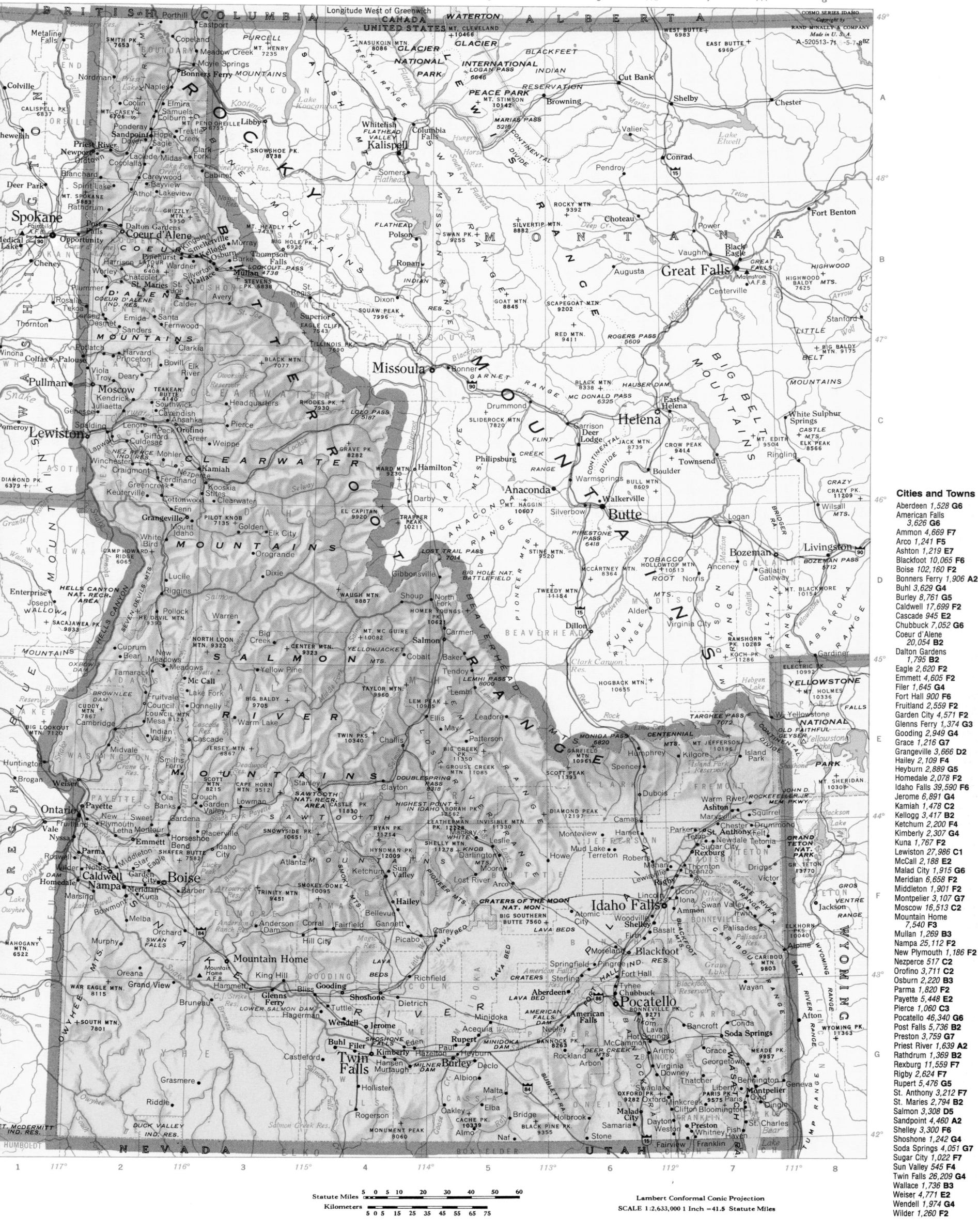

Cities and Towns

Alton *34,171* **E3**
Arlington Heights *66,116* **A5**
Aurora *81,293* **B5**
Belleville *41,580* **E4**
Berwyn *46,849* **k9**
Bloomington *44,189* **C4**
Bourbonnais *13,280* **B6**
Brookfield *19,395* **k9**
Cahokia *18,904* **E3**
Cairo *5,931* **F4**
Calumet City *39,697* **B6**
Canton *14,626* **C3**
Carbondale *26,414* **F4**
Centralia *15,126* **E4**
Champaign *58,133* **C5**
Charleston *19,355* **D5**
Chicago *3,005,072* **B6**
Cicero *61,232* **B6**
Danville *38,985* **C6**
Decatur *94,081* **D5**
De Kalb *33,099* **B5**
Des Plaines *53,568* **A6**
Dixon *15,701* **B4**
Downers Grove *42,572* **B5**
East St. Louis *55,200* **E3**
Elgin *63,981* **A5**
Elmhurst *44,276* **B6**
Evanston *73,706* **A6**
Freeport *26,266* **A4**
Galena *3,876* **A3**
Galesburg *35,305* **C3**
Granite City *36,815* **E3**
Gurnee *7,179* **h9**
Highland Park *30,611* **A6**
Jacksonville *20,284* **D3**
Joliet *77,956* **B5**
Kankakee *30,141* **B6**
Kewanee *14,508* **B4**
Lake Forest *15,245* **A6**
La Salle *10,347* **B4**
Lincoln *16,327* **C4**
Lombard *36,897* **k8**
Macomb *19,863* **C3**
Marion *14,031* **F5**
Mattoon *19,055* **D5**
Moline *46,278* **B3**
Monmouth *10,706* **C3**
Mount Prospect *52,634* **A6**
Mount Vernon *17,193* **E5**
Nauvoo *1,133* **C2**
Normal *35,672* **C5**
North Chicago *38,774* **A6**
Oak Lawn *60,590* **B6**
Oak Park *54,887* **B6**
Ottawa *18,166* **B5**
Pekin *33,967* **C4**
Peoria *124,160* **C4**
Peru *10,886* **B4**
Pontiac *11,227* **C5**
Quincy *42,554* **D2**
Rockford *139,712* **A4**
Rock Island *46,928* **B3**
Salem *7,813* **E5**
Schaumburg *53,305* **h8**
Skokie *60,278* **A6**
Springfield *100,054* **D4**
Sterling *16,281* **B4**
Streator *14,795* **B5**
Taylorville *11,386* **D4**
Urbana *35,978* **C5**
Vandalia *5,338* **E4**
Waukegan *67,653* **A6**
Wheaton *43,043* **B5**
Zion *17,861* **A6**

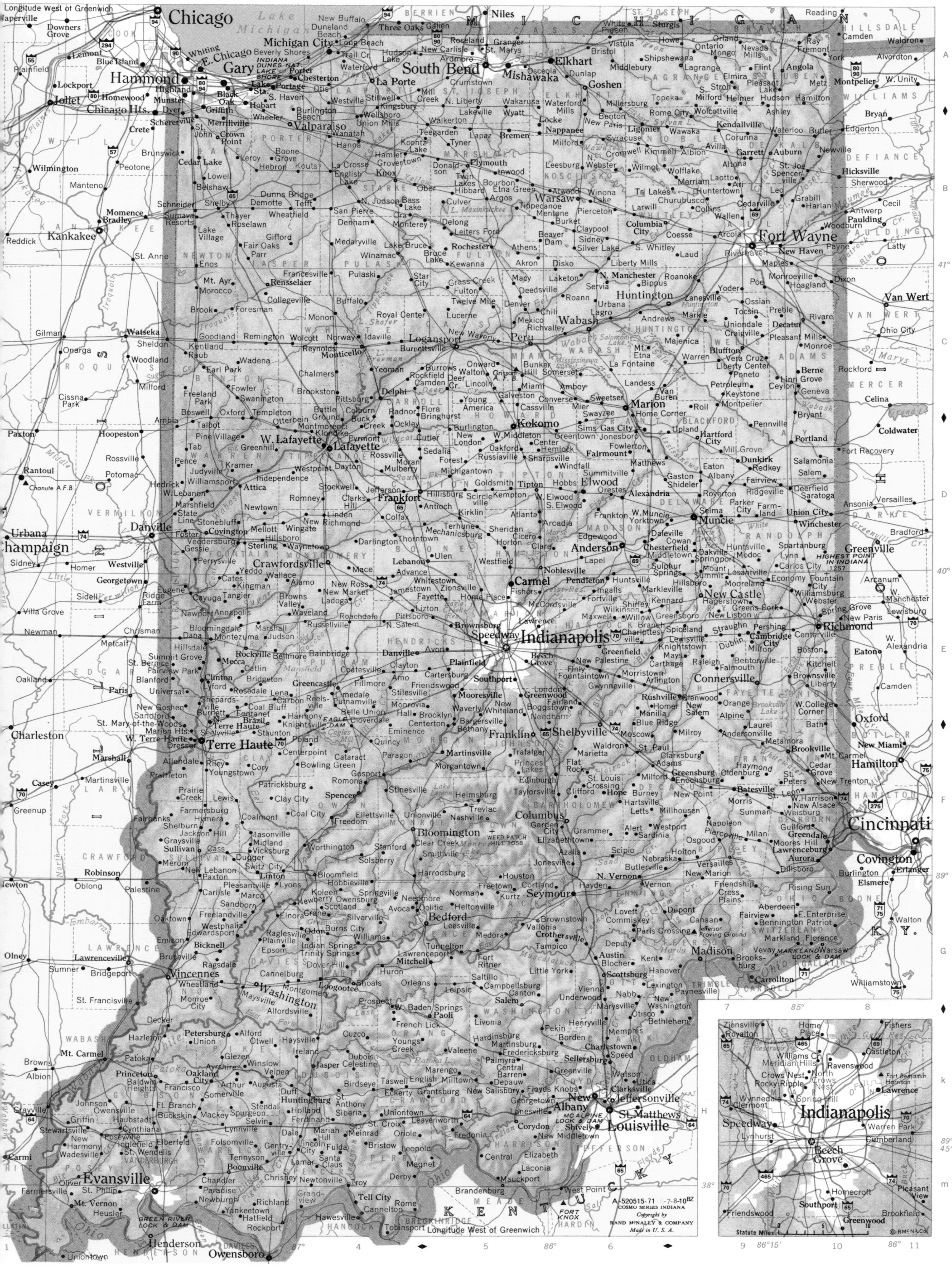

Statute Miles 5 0 5 10 15 20 25 30

Kilometers 5 0 5 15 25 35

Lambert Conformal Conic Projection

SCALE 1:1,465,000 1 Inch=23 Statute Miles

Cities and Towns

Anderson 64,695 D6
Auburn 8,122 B7
Bedford 14,410 G5
Beech Grove 13,196 E5
Bloomington 52,044 F4
Bluffton 8,705 C7
Brazil 7,852 E3
Carmel 18,272 E5
Clarksville 15,164 H6
Columbus 30,614 F6
Connersville 17,023 E7
Corydon 2,724 H5
Crawfordsville 13,325 D4
Crown Point 16,455 B3
Decatur 8,649 C8
East Chicago 39,786 A3
Elkhart 41,305 A6
Elwood 10,867 D6
Evansville 130,496 I2
Fort Wayne 172,028 B7
Frankfort 15,168 D4
Franklin 11,563 F5
French Lick 2,265 G4
Gary 151,953 A3
Goshen 19,665 A6
Greencastle 8,403 E4
Greensburg 9,254 F7
Greenwood 19,327 E5
Griffith 17,026 A3
Hammond 93,714 A2
Highland 25,935 A3
Hobart 22,987 A3
Huntington 16,202 C7
Indianapolis 700,807 E5
Jasper 9,097 H4
Jeffersonville 21,220 H6
Kokomo 47,808 D5
Lafayette 43,011 D4
Lake Station 14,294 A3
La Porte 21,796 A4
Lawrence 25,591 E5
Lebanon 11,456 D5
Logansport 17,731 C5
Madison 12,472 G7
Marion 35,874 C6
Martinsville 11,311 F5
Merrillville 27,677 B3
Michigan City 36,850 A4
Mishawaka 40,201 A5
Mount Vernon 7,656 I2
Muncie 77,216 D7
Munster 20,671 A2
New Albany 37,103 H6
New Castle 20,056 E7
Noblesville 12,056 D6
Peru 13,764 C5
Plymouth 7,693 B5
Portage 27,409 A3
Princeton 8,976 H2
Richmond 41,349 E8
Rockville 2,785 E3
Schererville 13,209 B3
Seymour 15,050 G6
Shelbyville 14,989 F6
South Bend 109,727 A5
Speedway 12,641 E5
Tell City 8,704 I4
Terre Haute 61,125 F3
Valparaiso 22,247 B3
Vincennes 20,857 G2
Wabash 12,985 C6
Warsaw 10,647 B6
Washington 11,325 G3
West Lafayette 21,247 D4

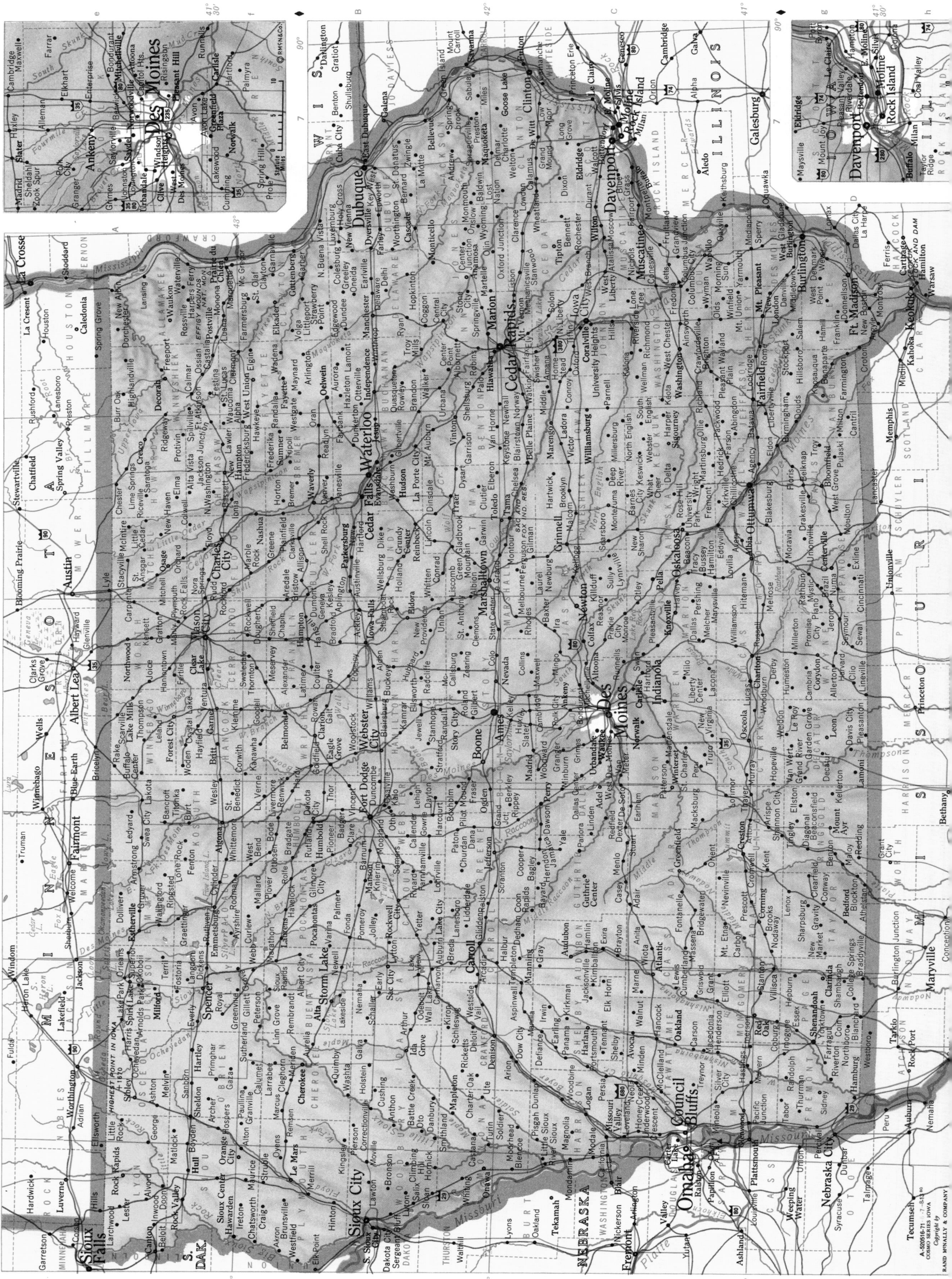

Statute Miles 5 0 5 10 20 30 40

Kilometers 5 0 5 15 25 35 45 55

Lambert Conformal Conic Projection
SCALE 1:1,834,000 1 Inch = 29 Statute Miles

Cities and Towns

Algona *6,289* **A3**
Amana *600* **C6**
Ames *45,775* **B4**
Anamosa *4,958* **B6**
Ankeny *15,429* **C4**
Atlantic *7,789* **C2**
Bettendorf *27,381* **C7**
Boone *12,602* **B4**
Burlington *29,529* **D6**
Carroll *9,705* **B3**
Cedar Falls *36,322* **B5**
Cedar Rapids *110,243* **C6**
Centerville *6,558* **D5**
Chariton *4,987* **C4**
Charles City *8,778* **A5**
Cherokee *7,004* **B2**
Clarinda *5,458* **D2**
Clinton *32,828* **C7**
Council Bluffs *56,449* **C2**
Creston *8,429* **C3**
Davenport *103,264* **C7**
Decorah *7,991* **A6**
Denison *6,675* **B2**
Des Moines *191,003* **C4**
De Witt *4,512* **C7**
Dubuque *62,321* **B7**
Emmetsburg *4,621* **A3**
Estherville *7,518* **A3**
Fairfield *9,428* **C6**
Fort Dodge *29,423* **B3**
Fort Madison *13,520* **D6**
Glenwood *5,280* **C2**
Grinnell *8,868* **C5**
Guttenberg *2,428* **B6**
Hampton *4,630* **B4**
Harlan *5,357* **C2**
Humboldt *4,794* **B3**
Independence *6,392* **B6**
Indianola *10,843* **C4**
Iowa City *50,508* **C6**
Iowa Falls *6,174* **B4**
Jefferson *4,854* **B3**
Keokuk *13,536* **D6**
Knoxville *8,143* **C4**
Le Mars *8,276* **B1**
Manchester *4,942* **B6**
Maquoketa *6,313* **B7**
Marion *19,474* **B6**
Marshalltown *26,938* **B5**
Mason City *30,144* **A4**
Mount Pleasant *7,322* **D6**
Muscatine *23,467* **C6**
Newton *15,292* **C4**
Oelwein *7,564* **B6**
Orange City *4,588* **B1**
Oskaloosa *10,989* **C5**
Ottumwa *27,381* **C5**
Pella *8,349* **C5**
Perry *7,053* **C3**
Red Oak *6,810* **D2**
Sheldon *5,003* **A2**
Shenandoah *6,274* **D2**
Sioux Center *4,588* **A1**
Sioux City *82,003* **B1**
Spencer *11,726* **A2**
Storm Lake *8,814* **B2**
Urbandale *17,869* **C4**
Vinton *5,040* **B5**
Washington *6,584* **C6**
Waterloo *75,985* **B5**
Waverly *8,444* **B5**
Webster City *8,572* **B4**
West Branch *1,867* **C6**
West Des Moines *21,894* **C4**

See main index for complete listing.

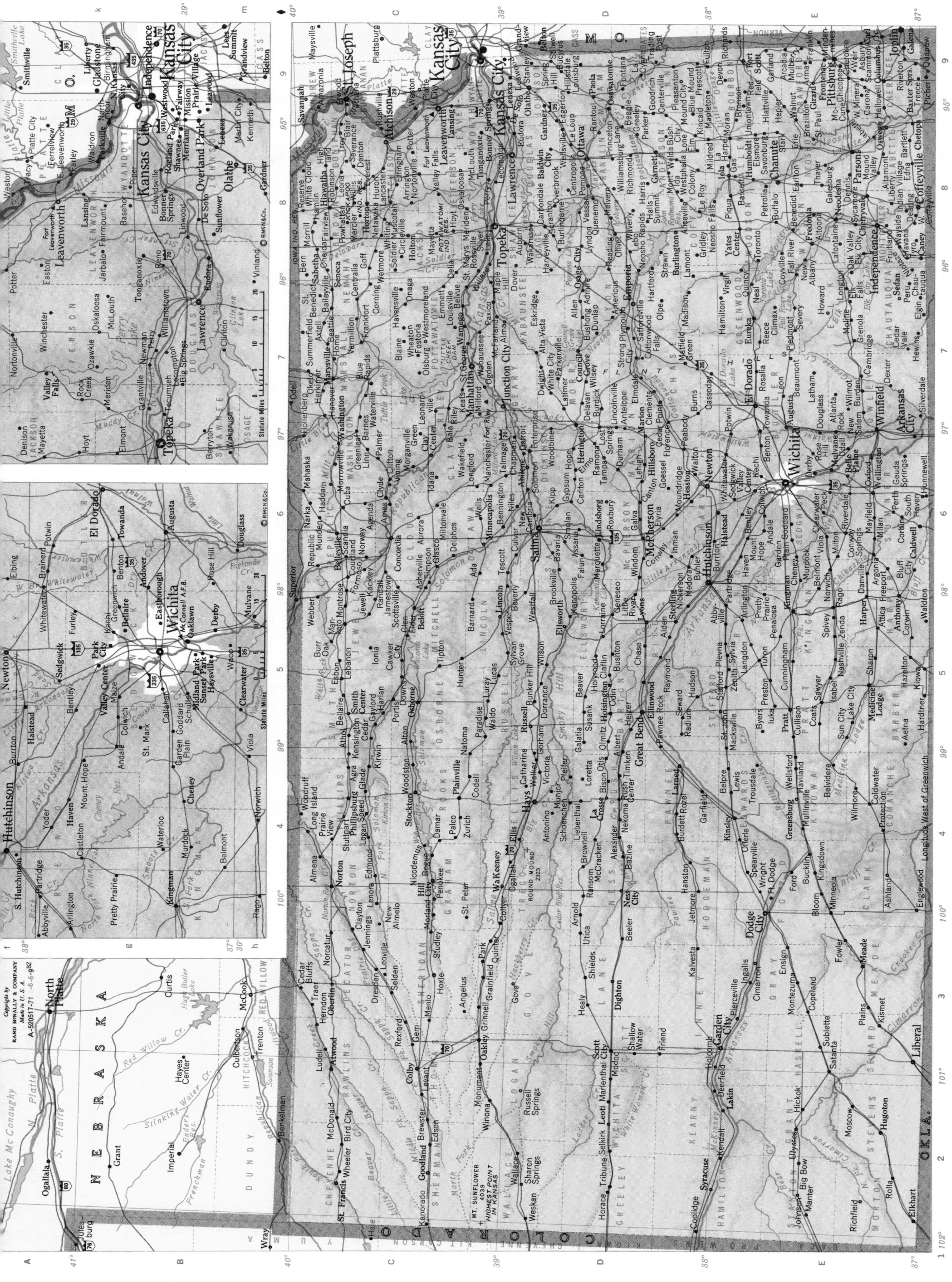

Statute Miles 5 0 5 15 25 35 45
Kilometers 5 0 5 15 25 35 45 55 65

Lambert Conformal Conic Projection
SCALE 1:2,208,000 1 Inch = 35 Statute Miles

Cities and Towns

Abilene *6,572* **D6**
Arkansas City *13,201* **E6**
Atchison *11,407* **C8**
Augusta *6,968* **E7**
Baxter Springs *4,730* **E9**
Beloit *4,367* **C5**
Bonner Springs *6,266* **C9**
Chanute *10,506* **E8**
Clay Center *4,948* **C6**
Coffeyville *15,185* **E8**
Colby *5,544* **C2**
Columbus *3,426* **E9**
Concordia *6,847* **C6**
Derby *9,786* **E6**
Dodge City *18,001* **E3**
El Dorado *10,510* **E7**
Emporia *25,287* **D7**
Eureka *3,425* **E7**
Fort Scott *8,893* **E9**
Garden City *18,256* **E3**
Garnett *3,310* **D8**
Goodland *5,708* **C2**
Great Bend *16,608* **D5**
Hays *16,301* **D4**
Haysville *8,006* **G12**
Hesston *3,013* **D6**
Hiawatha *3,702* **C8**
Hoisington *3,678* **D5**
Holton *3,132* **C8**
Hugoton *3,165* **E2**
Hutchinson *40,284* **D6**
Independence *10,598* **E8**
Iola *6,938* **E8**
Junction City *19,305* **C7**
Kansas City *161,148* **C9**
Kingman *3,563* **E5**
Lansing *5,307* **C9**
Larned *4,811* **D4**
Lawrence *52,738* **D8**
Leavenworth *33,656* **C9**
Leawood *13,360* **D9**
Lenexa *18,639* **D9**
Liberal *14,911* **E3**
Lindsborg *3,155* **D6**
Lyons *4,134* **D5**
McPherson *11,753* **D6**
Manhattan *32,644* **C7**
Marysville *3,670* **C7**
Merriam *10,794* **k16**
Mission *8,643* **m16**
Neodesha *3,414* **E8**
Newton *16,332* **D6**
Norton *3,400* **C4**
Olathe *37,258* **D9**
Osawatomie *4,459* **D9**
Ottawa *11,016* **D8**
Overland Park *81,784* **m16**
Paola *4,557* **D9**
Parsons *12,898* **E8**
Phillipsburg *3,229* **C4**
Pittsburg *18,770* **E9**
Prairie Village *24,657* **m16**
Pratt *6,885* **E5**
Roeland Park *7,962* **k16**
Russell *5,427* **D5**
Salina *41,843* **D6**
Scott City *4,154* **D3**
Shawnee *29,653* **k16**
Topeka *115,266* **C8**
Ulysses *4,653* **E2**
Wamego *3,159* **C7**
Wellington *8,212* **E6**
Wichita *279,835* **E6**
Winfield *10,736* **E7**

KENTUCKY

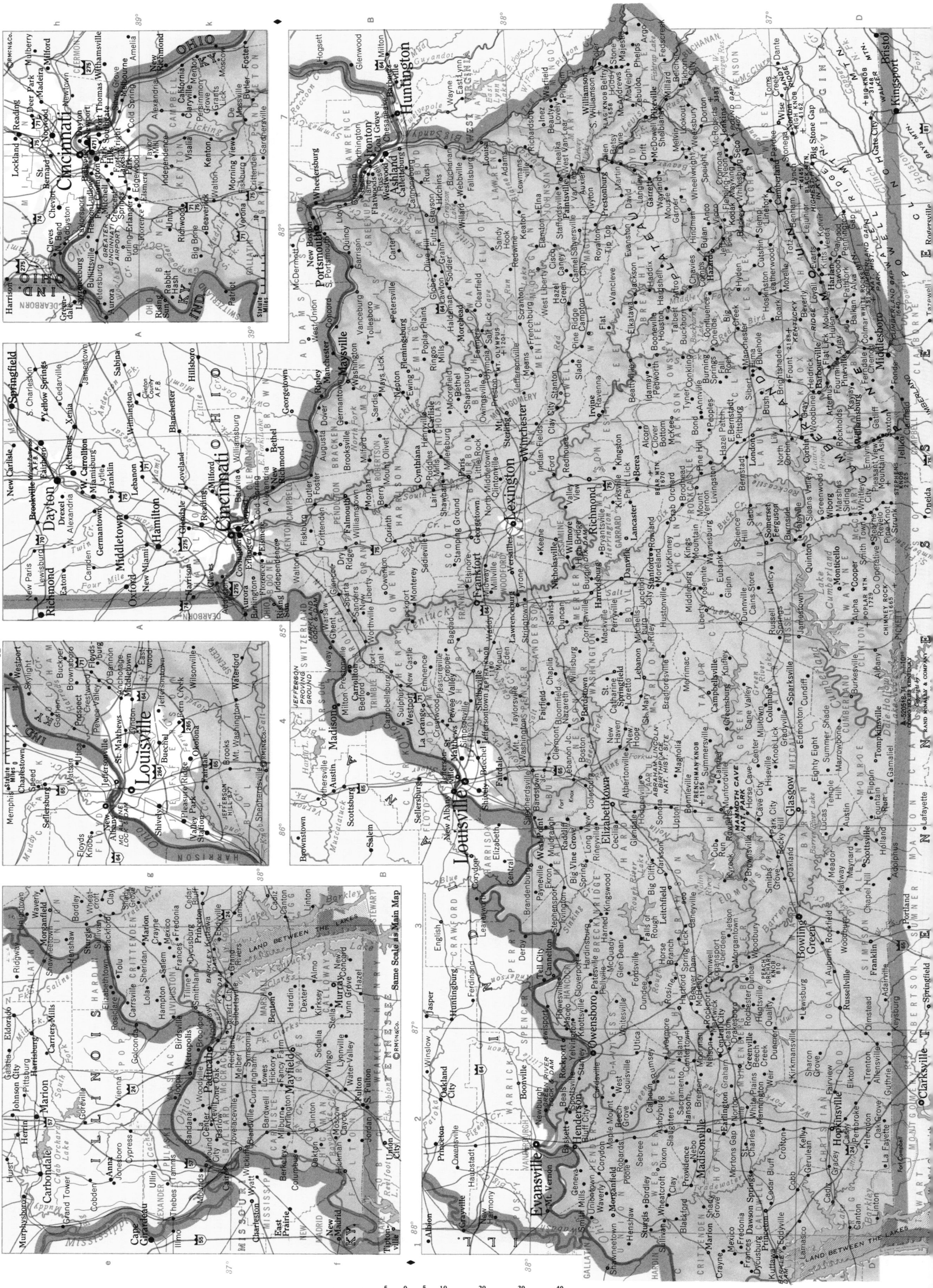

Statute Miles 5 0 5 10 20 30 40

Kilometers 5 0 5 10 20 30 40 50 60

Lambert Conformal Conic Projection

SCALE 1:1,738,000 1 Inch = 27 Statute Miles

Cities and Towns

Alexandria *4,735* **B5**
Ashland *27,064* **B7**
Barbourville *3,333* **D6**
Bardstown *6,155* **C4**
Berea *8,226* **C5**
Bowling Green *40,450* **D3**
Campbellsville *8,715* **C4**
Carrollton *3,967* **B4**
Cave City *2,098* **C4**
Central City *5,214* **C2**
Corbin *8,075* **D5**
Covington *49,563* **A5**
Cynthiana *5,881* **B5**
Danville *12,942* **C5**
Edgewood *7,230* **h13**
Elizabethtown *15,380* **C4**
Elsmere *7,203* **B5**
Erlanger *14,433* **A5**
Fairdale *7,315* **B4**
Fern Creek *16,866* **g11**
Flatwoods *8,354* **B7**
Florence *15,586* **A5**
Fort Mitchell *7,297* **h13**
Fort Thomas *16,012* **h14**
Frankfort *25,973* **B5**
Franklin *7,738* **D3**
Georgetown *10,972* **B5**
Glasgow *12,958* **C4**
Greenville *4,631* **C2**
Harrodsburg *7,265* **C5**
Hazard *5,371* **C6**
Henderson *24,834* **C2**
Hopkinsville *27,318* **D2**
Independence *7,998* **B5**
Jeffersontown *15,795* **B4**
Lawrenceburg *5,167* **B5**
Lebanon *6,590* **C4**
Leitchfield *4,533* **C3**
Lexington *204,165* **B5**
London *4,002* **C5**
Louisville *298,840* **B4**
Madisonville *16,979* **C2**
Mayfield *10,705* **f9**
Maysville *7,983* **B6**
Middlesboro *12,251* **D6**
Monticello *5,677* **D5**
Morehead *7,789* **B6**
Mount Sterling *5,820* **B6**
Murray *14,248* **f9**
Newport *21,587* **A5**
Nicholasville *10,319* **C5**
Okolona *20,039* **g11**
Owensboro *54,450* **C2**
Paducah *29,315* **e9**
Paris *7,935* **B5**
Pikeville *4,756* **C7**
Pleasure Ridge Park *27,332* **g11**
Prestonsburg *4,011* **C7**
Providence *4,434* **C2**
Radcliff *14,519* **C4**
Richmond *21,705* **C5**
Russellville *7,520* **D3**
St. Matthews *13,519* **B4**
Scottsville *4,278* **D3**
Shelbyville *5,329* **B4**
Shepherdsville *4,454* **C4**
Shively *16,819* **B4**
Somerset *10,649* **C5**
Tompkinsville *4,366* **D4**
Valley Station *20,000* **g11**
Versailles *6,427* **B5**
Westwood *5,973* **B7**
Williamsburg *5,560* **D5**
Winchester *15,216* **C5**

See main index for complete listing.

Statute Miles 5 0 5 10 20 30 40

Kilometers 5 0 5 15 25 35 45 55

Lambert Conformal Conic Projection

SCALE 1:2,083,000 1 Inch = 33 Statute Miles

Cities and Towns

Abbeville *12,391* **E3**
Alexandria *51,565* **C3**
Arabi *10,248* **k11**
Baker *12,865* **D4**
Bastrop *15,527* **B4**
Baton Rouge *219,419* **D4**
Bogalusa *16,976* **D6**
Bossier City *50,817* **B2**
Breaux Bridge *5,922* **D4**
Bunkie *5,364* **D4**
Chalmette *33,847* **E6**
Covington *7,892* **D5**
Crowley *16,036* **D3**
Denham Springs *8,563* **D5**
De Ridder *11,057* **D2**
Donaldsonville *7,901* **D4**
Eunice *12,479* **D3**
Franklin *9,584* **E4**
Galliano *5,159* **E5**
Gonzales *7,287* **D5**
Grambling *4,226* **B3**
Gretna *20,615* **E5**
Hammond *15,043* **D5**
Harahan *11,384* **k11**
Harvey *15,000* **E5**
Houma *32,602* **E5**
Jeanerette *6,511* **E4**
Jefferson *15,550* **k11**
Jena *4,375* **C3**
Jennings *12,401* **D3**
Jonesboro *5,061* **B3**
Kaplan *5,016* **D3**
Kenner *66,382* **E5**
Lacombe *5,146* **D6**
Lafayette *81,961* **D3**
Lake Charles *75,226* **D2**
Lake Providence *6,361* **B4**
La Place *16,112* **h11**
Leesville *9,054* **C2**
Mandeville *6,076* **D5**
Mansfield *6,485* **B2**
Marrero *36,548* **E5**
Metairie *164,160* **k11**
Minden *15,084* **B2**
Monroe *57,597* **B3**
Morgan City *16,114* **E4**
Moss Bluff *7,004* **D2**
Natchitoches *16,664* **C2**
New Iberia *32,766* **D4**
New Orleans *557,927* **E5**
Oakdale *7,155* **D3**
Opelousas *18,903* **D3**
Pineville *12,034* **C3**
Plaquemine *7,521* **D4**
Raceland *6,302* **E5**
Rayne *9,066* **D3**
Reserve *7,288* **h10**
River Ridge *17,146* **k11**
Ruston *20,585* **B3**
St. Martinville *7,965* **D4**
Scotlandville *15,113* **D4**
Shreveport *205,820* **B2**
Slidell *26,718* **D6**
Springhill *6,516* **A2**
Sulphur *19,709* **D2**
Tallulah *11,634* **B4**
Thibodaux *15,810* **E5**
Vidalia *5,936* **C4**
Ville Platte *9,201* **D3**
West Monroe *14,993* **B3**
Westwego *12,663* **k11**
Winnfield *7,311* **C3**
Winnsboro *5,921* **B4**
Zachary *7,297* **D4**

MAINE

Statute Miles 5 0 5 10 20 30

Kilometers 5 0 5 10 20 30 40

Lambert Conformal Conic Projection

SCALE 1:1,581,000 1 Inch = 25 Statute Miles

Cities and Towns*

Auburn *23,128* **D2**
Augusta *21,819* **D3**
Bangor *31,643* **D4**
Bar Harbor *2,685* **D4**
Bath *10,246* **E3**
Belfast *6,243* **D3**
Berwick *2,378* **E2**
Biddeford *19,638* **E2**
Boothbay Harbor *2,207* **E3**
Brewer *9,017* **D4**
Brunswick *10,990* **E3**
Bucksport *2,853* **D4**
Calais *4,262* **C5**
Camden *3,743* **D3**
Cape Elizabeth *7,838* **E2**
Caribou *9,916* **B5**
Cumberland Center *2,015* **g7**
Dexter *3,118* **C3**
Dover-Foxcroft *2,974* **C3**
East Millinocket *2,361* **C4**
Eastport *1,982* **D6**
Eliot *2,450* **E2**
Ellsworth *5,179* **D4**
Fairfield *3,169* **D3**
Falmouth *6,853* **E2**
Farmingdale *2,014* **D3**
Farmington *3,583* **D2**
Fort Fairfield *2,282* **B5**
Fort Kent *2,375* **A4**
Freeport *1,906* **E2**
Gardiner *6,485* **D3**
Gorham *4,052* **E2**
Hallowell *2,502* **D3**
Hampden *2,300* **D4**
Houlton *5,730* **B5**
Kennebunk *3,294* **E2**
Kittery *5,465* **E2**
Lewiston *40,481* **D2**
Lincoln *3,524* **C4**
Lisbon Falls *4,370* **E2**
Livermore Falls *2,441* **D2**
Madawaska *4,165* **A4**
Madison *2,788* **D3**
Mechanic Falls *2,616* **D2**
Mexico *3,207* **D2**
Millinocket *7,567* **C4**
Milo *2,255* **C4**
North Windham *5,492* **E2**
Norway *2,653* **D2**
Oakland *3,387* **D3**
Old Orchard Beach *6,291* **E2**
Orono *10,578* **D4**
Pittsfield *3,117* **D3**
Portland *61,572* **E2**
Presque Isle *11,172* **B5**
Rockland *7,919* **D3**
Rumford *6,256* **D2**
Saco *12,921* **E2**
Sanford *10,268* **E2**
Scarborough *2,280* **E2**
Skowhegan *6,517* **D3**
South Berwick *2,120* **E2**
South Paris *2,128* **D2**
South Portland *22,712* **E2**
Thomaston *2,348* **D3**
Topsham *4,657* **E3**
Van Buren *3,282* **A5**
Waterville *17,779* **D3**
Westbrook *14,976* **E2**
Wilton *2,262* **D2**
Winslow *5,903* **D3**
Winthrop *3,264* **D3**
Yarmouth *2,421* **E2**
York *3,130* **E2**

***Populations are for localities, not incorporated towns.**

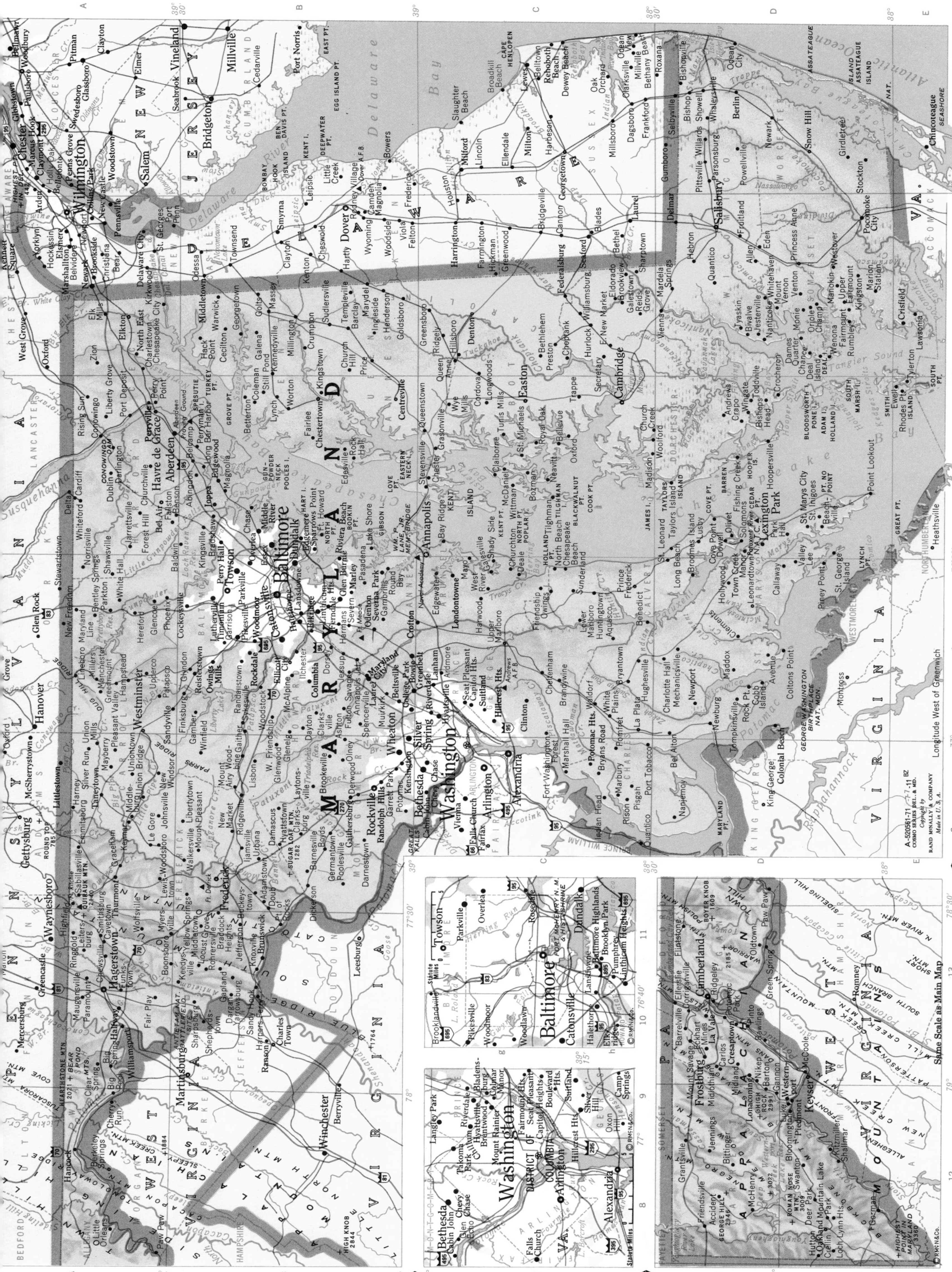

Statute Miles 5 0 5 10 15 20
Kilometers 5 0 5 10 15 20 25 30

Lambert Conformal Conic Projection
SCALE 1:985,000 1 Inch = 15.5 Statute Miles

Cities and Towns

Aberdeen *11,533* **A5**
Annapolis *31,740* **C5**
Baltimore *786,775* **B4**
Bel Air *7,814* **A5**
Beltsville *12,760* **B4**
Bethesda *63,022* **C3**
Bladensburg *7,691* **f9**
Bowie *33,695* **B4**
Brunswick *4,572* **B2**
Cambridge *11,703* **C5**
Catonsville *33,208* **B4**
Chevy Chase *12,232* **C3**
Clinton *16,438* **C4**
Cockeysville *17,013* **B4**
College Park *23,614* **C4**
Columbia *52,518* **B4**
Crofton *12,009* **B4**
Cumberland *25,933* **k13**
Dundalk *71,293* **B4**
Easton *7,536* **C5**
Edgewood *19,455* **B5**
Elkton *6,468* **A6**
Essex *39,614* **B5**
Frederick *28,086* **B3**
Frostburg *7,715* **k13**
Gaithersburg *26,424* **B3**
Germantown *9,721* **B3**
Glen Burnie *30,000* **B4**
Greenbelt *17,332* **C4**
Hagerstown *34,132* **A2**
Halethorpe *20,163* **B4**
Halfway *8,659* **A2**
Havre de Grace *8,763* **A5**
Hillcrest Heights *17,021* **C4**
Hyattsville *12,709* **C4**
Joppa *11,348* **B5**
Langley Park *11,100* **f9**
Lansdowne *10,000* **B4**
Laurel *12,103* **B4**
Lexington Park *10,361* **D5**
Lutherville-Timonium *17,854* **B4**
Middle River *26,756* **B5**
Oakland *1,994* **m12**
Ocean City *4,946* **D7**
Olney *10,000* **B3**
Overlea *12,965* **B4**
Owings Mills *9,526* **B4**
Oxon Hill *11,800* **f9**
Parkville *35,159* **B4**
Perry Hall *13,455* **B5**
Pikesville *20,000* **B4**
Pocomoke City *3,558* **D6**
Potomac *22,800* **B3**
Randallstown *20,500* **B4**
Reisterstown *19,385* **B4**
Rockville *43,811* **B3**
Rosedale *19,956* **g11**
Salisbury *16,429* **D6**
Severn *20,147* **B4**
Severna Park *21,253* **B4**
Sharpsburg *721* **B2**
Silver Spring *64,100* **C3**
Snow Hill *2,192* **D7**
Suitland *24,800* **C4**
Takoma Park *16,231* **f8**
Towson *51,083* **B4**
Waldorf *9,782* **C4**
Westminster *8,808* **A4**
Wheaton *48,600* **B3**
White Plains *5,167* **C4**
Woodlawn *8,000* **g10**
Washington D.C. *638,432* **C3**

MASSACHUSETTS

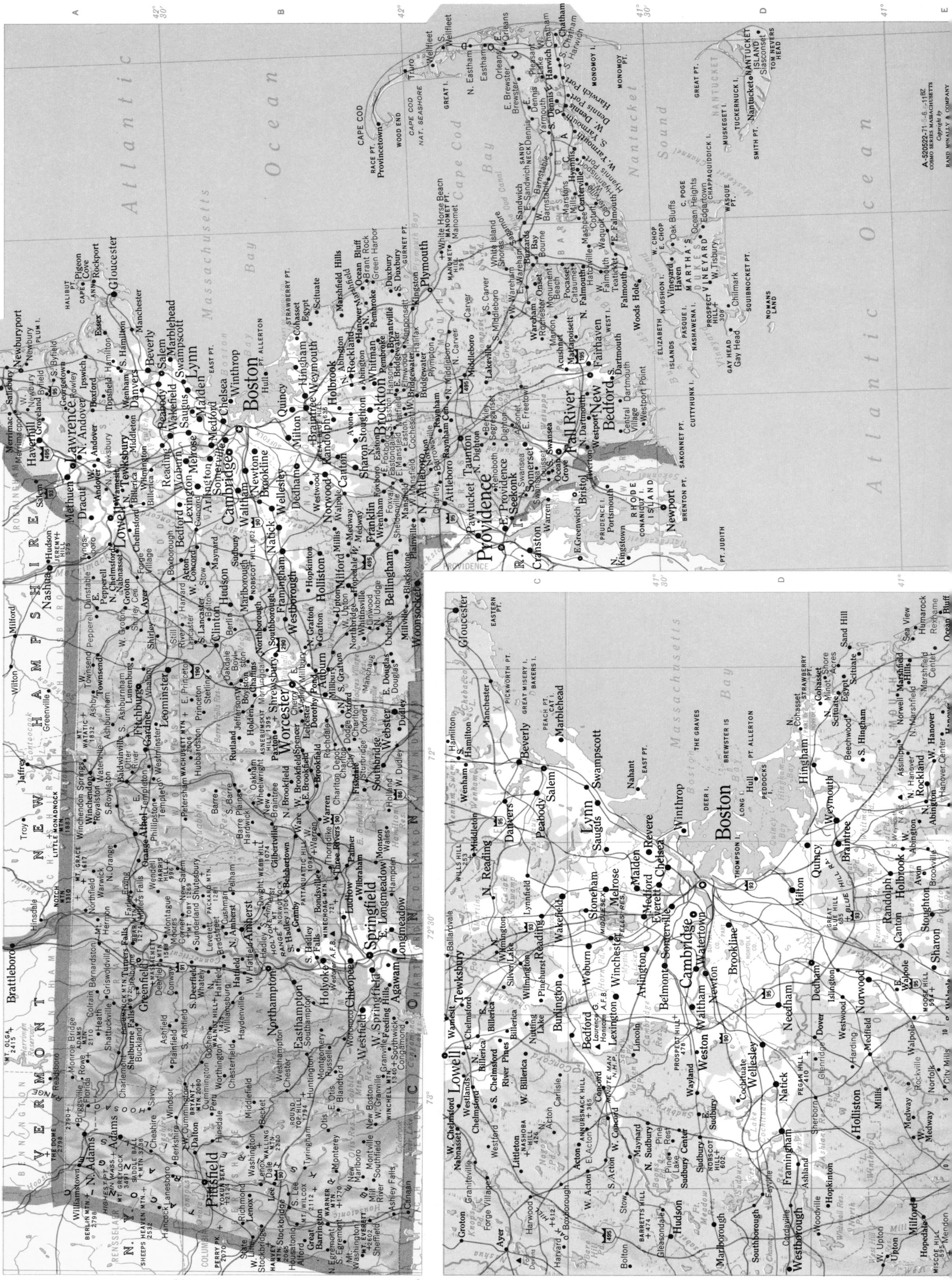

Statute Miles 5 0 5 10 15 20

Kilometers 5 0 5 10 15 20 25

Lambert Conformal Conic Projection
SCALE 1:978,000 1 Inch = 15.5 Statute Miles

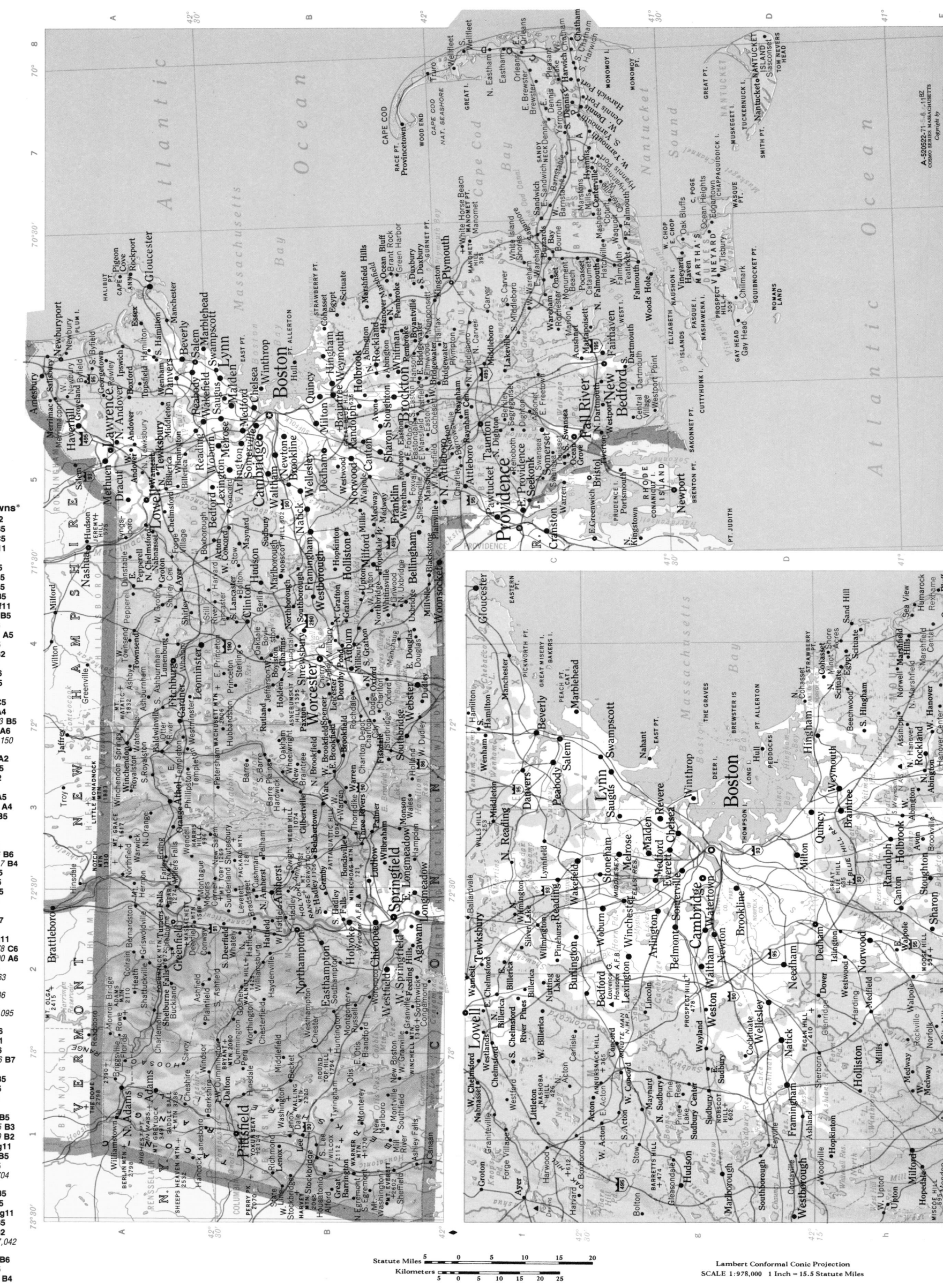

Cities and Towns*

Amherst *26,300* **B2**
Arlington *48,219* **B5**
Attleboro *34,196* **C5**
Belmont *26,100* **g11**
Beverly *37,655* **A6**
Boston *562,994* **B5**
Braintree *36,337* **B5**
Brockton *95,172* **B5**
Brookline *55,062* **B5**
Burlington *23,486* **f11**
Cambridge *95,322* **B5**
Chatham *1,922* **C8**
Chelmsford *31,174* **A5**
Chelsea *25,431* **B5**
Chicopee *55,112* **B2**
Concord *6,400* **B5**
Danvers *24,100* **A6**
Dedham *25,298* **B5**
Dracut *21,249* **A5**
Fall River *92,574* **C5**
Fitchburg *39,580* **A4**
Framingham *65,113* **B5**
Gloucester *27,768* **A6**
Great Barrington *3,150* **B1**
Greenfield *14,198* **A2**
Haverhill *46,865* **A5**
Holyoke *44,678* **B2**
Hyannis *8,000* **C7**
Lawrence *63,175* **A5**
Leominster *34,508* **A4**
Lexington *29,479* **B5**
Lowell *92,418* **A5**
Lynn *78,471* **B6**
Malden *53,386* **B5**
Marblehead *20,126* **B6**
Marlborough *30,617* **B4**
Medford *58,076* **B5**
Melrose *30,055* **B5**
Methuen *36,701* **A5**
Milford *23,390* **B4**
Milton *25,860* **B5**
Nantucket *3,229* **D7**
Natick *29,461* **B5**
Needham *27,901* **g11**
New Bedford *98,478* **C6**
Newburyport *15,900* **A6**
Newton *83,622* **B5**
North Adams *18,063* **A1**
Northampton *29,286* **B2**
North Attleboro *21,095* **C5**
Peabody *45,976* **A6**
Pittsfield *51,974* **B1**
Plymouth *7,232* **C6**
Provincetown *3,536* **B7**
Quincy *84,743* **B5**
Randolph *22,218* **B5**
Reading *22,678* **A5**
Revere *42,423* **g11**
Salem *38,220* **A6**
Somerville *77,372* **B5**
Southbridge *16,665* **B3**
Springfield *152,319* **B2**
Stoneham *21,424* **g11**
Stoughton *26,710* **B5**
Taunton *45,001* **C5**
Vineyard Haven *1,704* **D6**
Wakefield *24,895* **B5**
Waltham *58,200* **B5**
Watertown *34,384* **g11**
Wellesley *27,209* **B5**
Westfield *36,465* **B2**
West Springfield *27,042* **B2**
Weymouth *55,601* **B6**
Woburn *36,626* **B5**
Worcester *161,799* **B4**

*Populations are for localities, not incorporated towns.

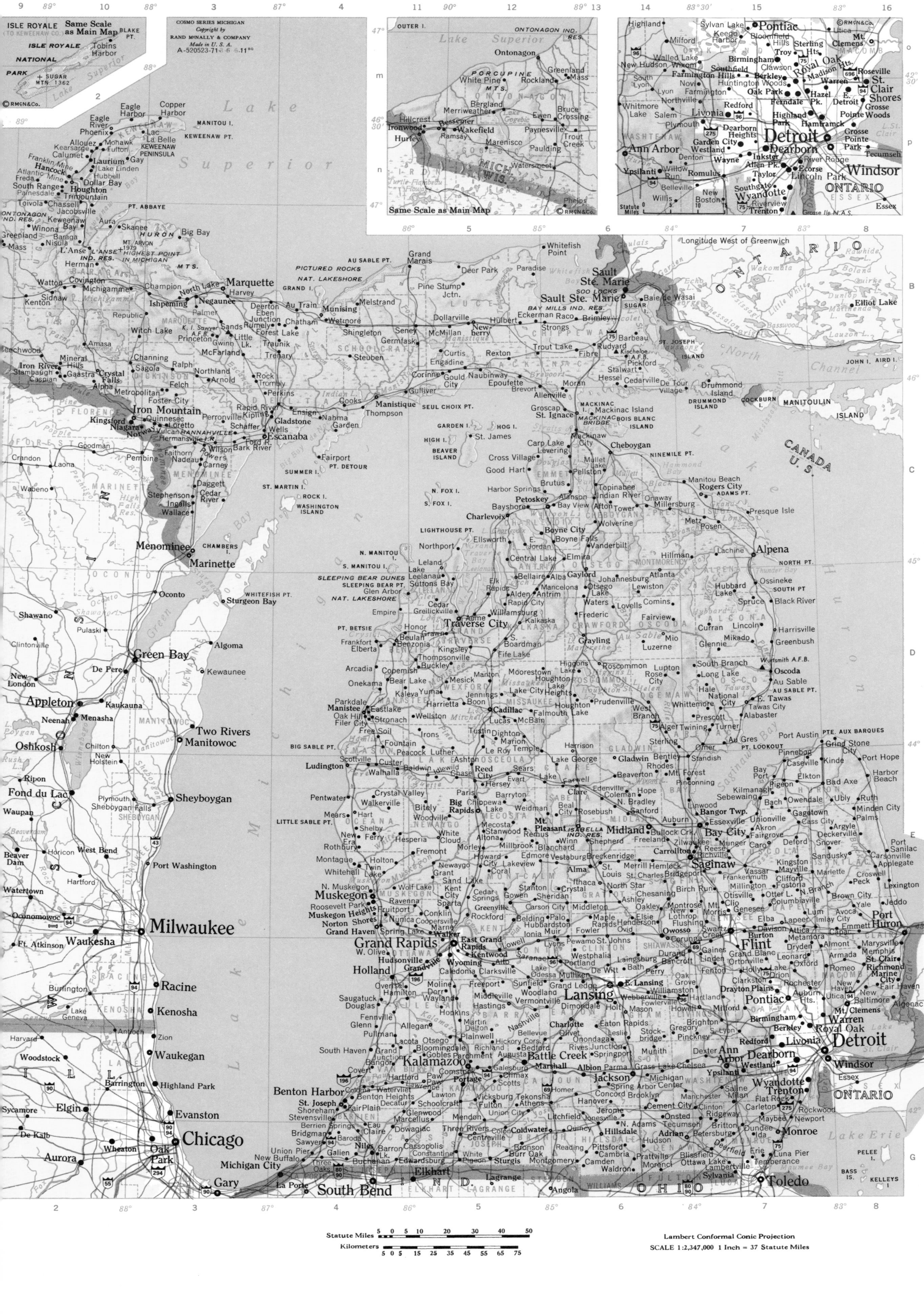

Cities and Towns

Adrian *21,186* **G6**
Albion *11,059* **F6**
Alpena *12,214* **C7**
Ann Arbor *107,966* **F7**
Battle Creek *35,724* **F5**
Bay City *41,593* **E7**
Benton Harbor *14,707* **F4**
Big Rapids *14,361* **E5**
Birmingham *21,689* **F7**
Burton *29,976* **F7**
Cadillac *10,199* **D5**
Cheboygan *5,106* **C6**
Coldwater *9,461* **G5**
Dearborn *90,660* **F7**
Dearborn Heights *67,706* **p15**
Detroit *1,203,339* **F7**
East Detroit *38,280* **p16**
East Lansing *51,392* **F6**
Escanaba *14,355* **C3**
Farmington Hills *58,056* **o15**
Flint *159,611* **E7**
Garden City *35,640* **p15**
Grand Haven *11,763* **E4**
Grand Rapids *181,843* **F5**
Grosse Pointe Woods *18,886* **p16**
Hamtramck *12,300* **p15**
Highland Park *27,909* **p15**
Holland *26,281* **F4**
Houghton *7,512* **A2**
Iron Mountain *8,341* **C2**
Ironwood *7,741* **n11**
Jackson *39,739* **F6**
Kalamazoo *79,722* **F5**
Kentwood *30,438* **F5**
Lansing *130,414* **F6**
Lincoln Park *45,105* **p15**
Livonia *104,814* **F7**
Ludington *8,937* **E4**
Mackinaw City *820* **C6**
Madison Heights *35,375* **o15**
Manistee *7,566* **D4**
Marquette *23,288* **B3**
Menominee *10,099* **C3**
Midland *37,250* **E6**
Monroe *23,531* **G7**
Mount Pleasant *23,746* **E6**
Muskegon *40,823* **E4**
Niles *13,115* **G4**
Norton Shores *22,025* **E4**
Novi *22,525* **p15**
Oak Park *31,537* **p15**
Owosso *16,455* **E6**
Petoskey *6,097* **C6**
Pontiac *76,715* **F7**
Portage *38,157* **F5**
Port Huron *33,981* **F8**
Romulus *24,857* **p15**
Roseville *54,311* **o16**
Royal Oak *70,893* **F7**
Saginaw *77,508* **E7**
St. Clair Shores *76,210* **p16**
Sault Ste. Marie *14,448* **B6**
Southfield *75,568* **o15**
Southgate *32,058* **p15**
Sterling Heights *108,999* **o15**
Sturgis *9,468* **G5**
Taylor *77,568* **p15**
Traverse City *15,516* **D5**
Trenton *22,762* **F7**
Troy *67,102* **o15**
Warren *161,134* **F7**
Westland *84,603* **F7**
Wyandotte *34,006* **F7**
Wyoming *59,616* **F5**
Ypsilanti *24,031* **F7**

MINNESOTA

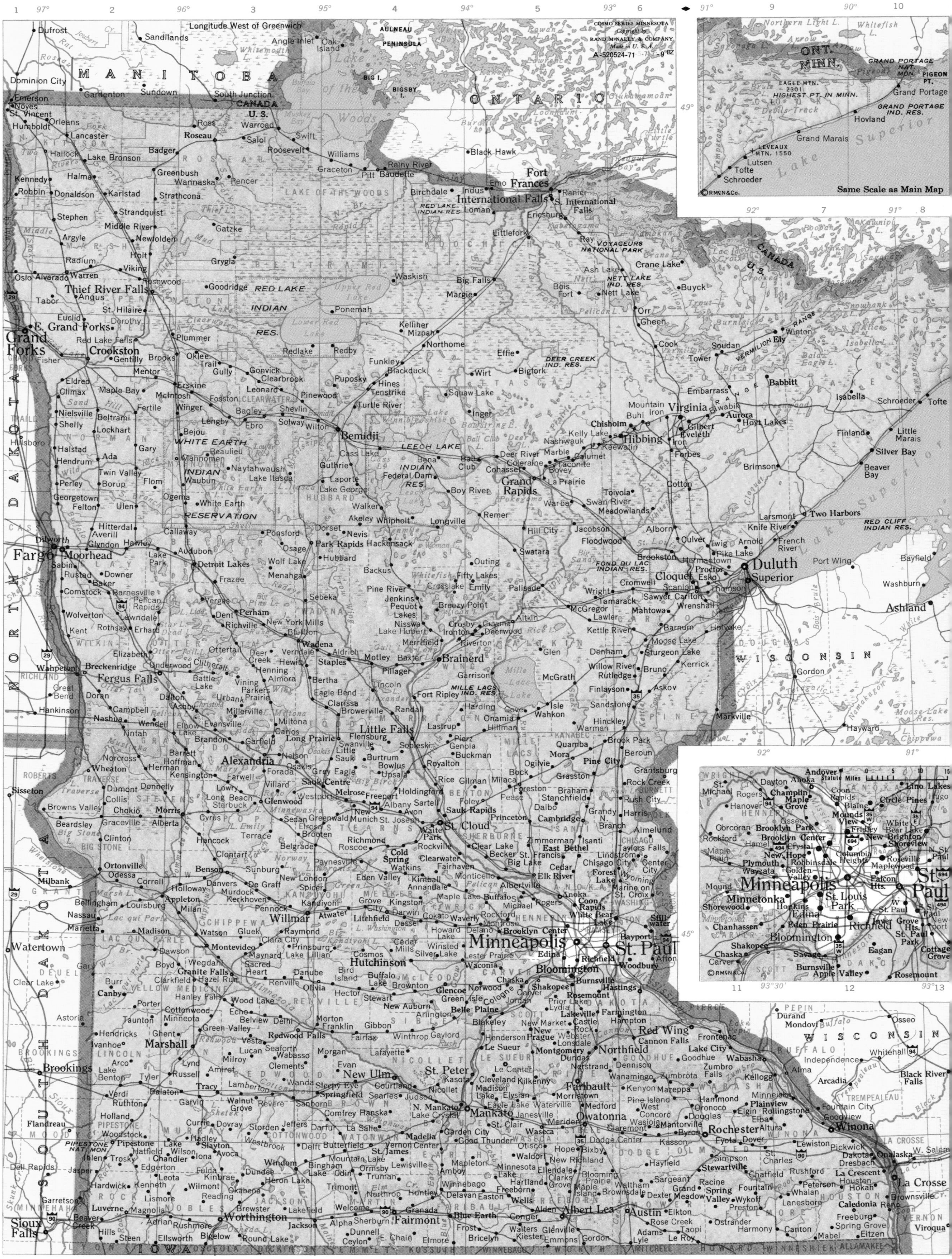

Statute Miles 5 0 5 10 20 30 40 50

Kilometers 5 0 5 15 25 35 45 55 65

Lambert Conformal Conic Projection

SCALE 1:2,179,000 1 Inch = 34 Statute Miles

Cities and Towns

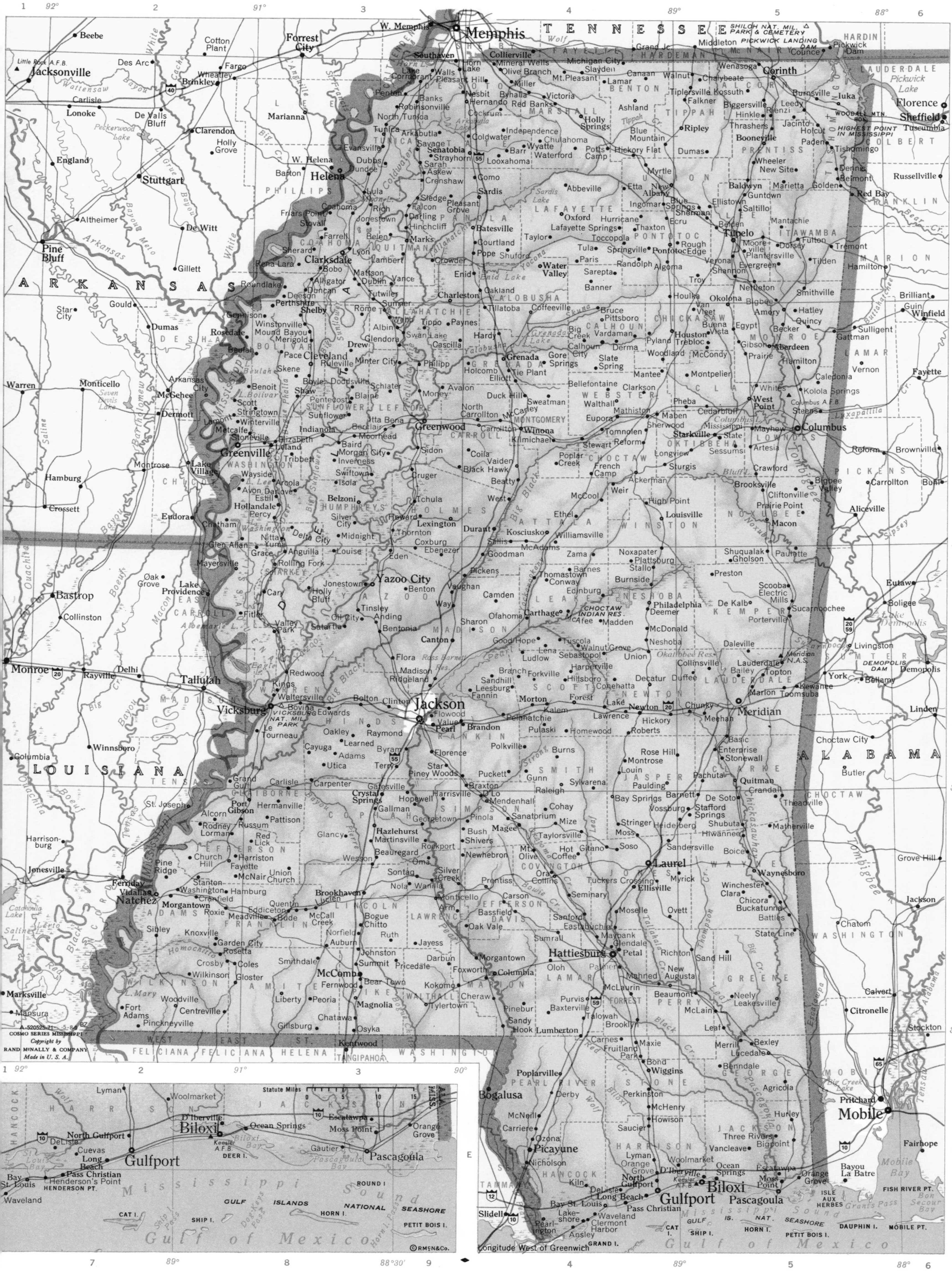

Statute Miles 5 0 5 10 20 30 40

Kilometers 5 0 5 15 25 35 45 55

Lambert Conformal Conic Projection

SCALE 1:1,837,000 1 Inch = 29 Statute Miles

Cities and Towns

Aberdeen *7,184* **B5**
Amory *7,307* **B5**
Baldwyn *3,427* **A5**
Batesville *4,692* **A4**
Bay Saint Louis *7,891* **E4**
Belzoni *2,982* **B3**
Biloxi *49,311* **E5**
Booneville *6,199* **A5**
Brandon *9,626* **C4**
Brookhaven *10,800* **D3**
Canton *11,116* **C3**
Carthage *3,453* **C4**
Clarksdale *21,137* **A3**
Cleveland *14,524* **B3**
Clinton *14,660* **C3**
Columbia *7,733* **D4**
Columbus *27,383* **B5**
Corinth *13,839* **A5**
Crystal Springs *4,902* **D3**
D'Iberville *9,000* **E5**
Ellisville *4,652* **D4**
Forest *5,229* **C4**
Fulton *3,238* **A5**
Gautier *8,917* **f8**
Greenville *40,613* **B2**
Greenwood *20,115* **B3**
Grenada *12,641* **B4**
Gulfport *39,676* **E4**
Hattiesburg *40,829* **D4**
Hazlehurst *4,437* **D3**
Hollandale *4,336* **B3**
Holly Springs *7,285* **A4**
Horn Lake *4,326* **A3**
Houston *3,747* **B4**
Indianola *8,221* **B3**
Jackson *202,895* **C3**
Kosciusko *7,415* **B4**
Laurel *21,897* **D4**
Leland *6,667* **B3**
Long Beach *7,967* **g7**
Louisville *7,323* **B4**
McComb *12,331* **D3**
Magee *3,497* **D4**
Meridian *46,577* **C5**
Morgantown *3,445* **D2**
Morton *3,303* **C4**
Moss Point *18,998* **E5**
Natchez *22,015* **D2**
New Albany *7,072* **A4**
Newton *3,708* **C4**
Ocean Springs *14,504* **E5**
Okolona *3,409* **B5**
Oxford *9,882* **A4**
Pascagoula *29,318* **E5**
Pass Christian *5,014* **E4**
Pearl *18,580* **C3**
Petal *8,476* **D4**
Philadelphia *6,434* **C4**
Picayune *10,361* **E4**
Pontotoc *4,723* **A4**
Ripley *4,271* **A5**
Ruleville *3,332* **B3**
Senotobia *5,013* **A4**
Southaven *16,071* **A3**
Starkville *15,169* **B5**
Tupelo *23,905* **A5**
Vicksburg *25,434* **C3**
Water Valley *4,147* **A4**
Waveland *4,186* **E4**
Waynesboro *5,349* **D5**
West Point *8,811* **B5**
Wiggins *3,205* **E4**
Winona *6,177* **B4**
Yazoo City *12,092* **C3**

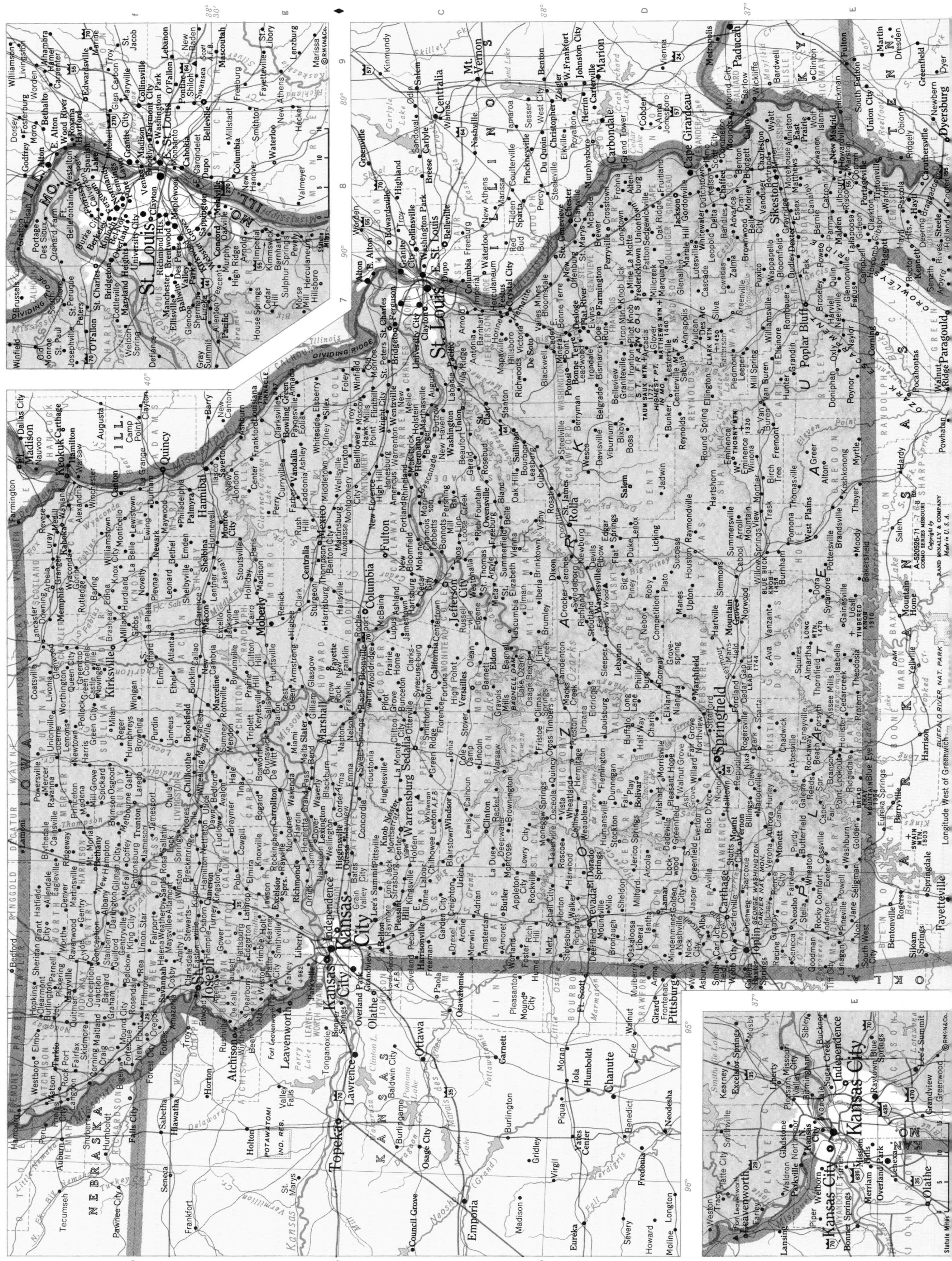

Statute Miles 5 0 5 15 25 35 45

Kilometers 5 0 5 15 25 35 45 55 65

Lambert Conformal Conic Projection

SCALE 1:2,283,000 1 Inch = 36 Statute Miles

Cities and Towns

Arnold 19,141 **C7**
Aurora 6,437 **E4**
Ballwin 12,656 **f12**
Belton 12,708 **C3**
Berkeley 15,922 **f13**
Blue Springs 25,927 **h11**
Bolivar 5,919 **D4**
Boonville 6,959 **C5**
Branson 2,550 **E4**
Bridgeton 18,445 **C7**
Cape Girardeau 34,361 **D8**
Carthage 11,104 **D3**
Caruthersville 7,958 **E8**
Charleston 5,230 **E8**
Chillicothe 9,089 **B4**
Clayton 14,273 **f13**
Clinton 8,366 **C4**
Columbia 62,061 **C5**
Concord 20,896 **f13**
De Soto 5,993 **C7**
Dexter 7,043 **E8**
Eureka 3,862 **f12**
Excelsior Springs 10,424 **B3**
Farmington 8,270 **D7**
Ferguson 24,740 **C7**
Festus 7,574 **C7**
Florissant 55,372 **f13**
Fulton 11,046 **C6**
Gladstone 24,990 **h10**
Grandview 24,502 **C3**
Hannibal 18,811 **B6**
Independence 111,806 **B3**
Jackson 7,827 **D8**
Jefferson City 33,619 **C5**
Jennings 17,026 **f13**
Joplin 39,023 **D3**
Kansas City 448,159 **B3**
Kennett 10,145 **E7**
Kirksville 17,167 **A5**
Kirkwood 27,987 **f13**
Lebanon 9,507 **D5**
Lees Summit 28,741 **C3**
Liberty 16,251 **B3**
Malden 6,096 **E8**
Marshall 12,781 **B4**
Maryville 9,558 **A3**
Mehlville 22,900 **f13**
Mexico 12,276 **B6**
Moberly 13,418 **B5**
Monett 6,148 **E4**
Neosho 9,493 **E3**
Nevada 9,044 **D3**
Overland 19,620 **f13**
Perryville 7,343 **D8**
Poplar Bluff 17,139 **E7**
Raytown 31,759 **h11**
Richmond Heights 11,516 **f13**
Rolla 13,303 **D6**
St. Charles 37,379 **C7**
Ste. Genevieve 4,481 **D7**
St. Joseph 76,691 **B3**
St. Louis 453,085 **C7**
St. Peters 14,700 **C7**
Sappington 11,388 **f13**
Sedalia 20,927 **C4**
Sikeston 17,431 **E8**
Spanish Lake 20,632 **f13**
Springfield 133,116 **D4**
Sullivan 5,461 **C6**
Trenton 6,811 **A4**
University City 42,738 **C7**
Warrensburg 13,807 **C4**
Washington 9,251 **C6**
Webster Groves 23,097 **f13**
West Plains 7,741 **E6**

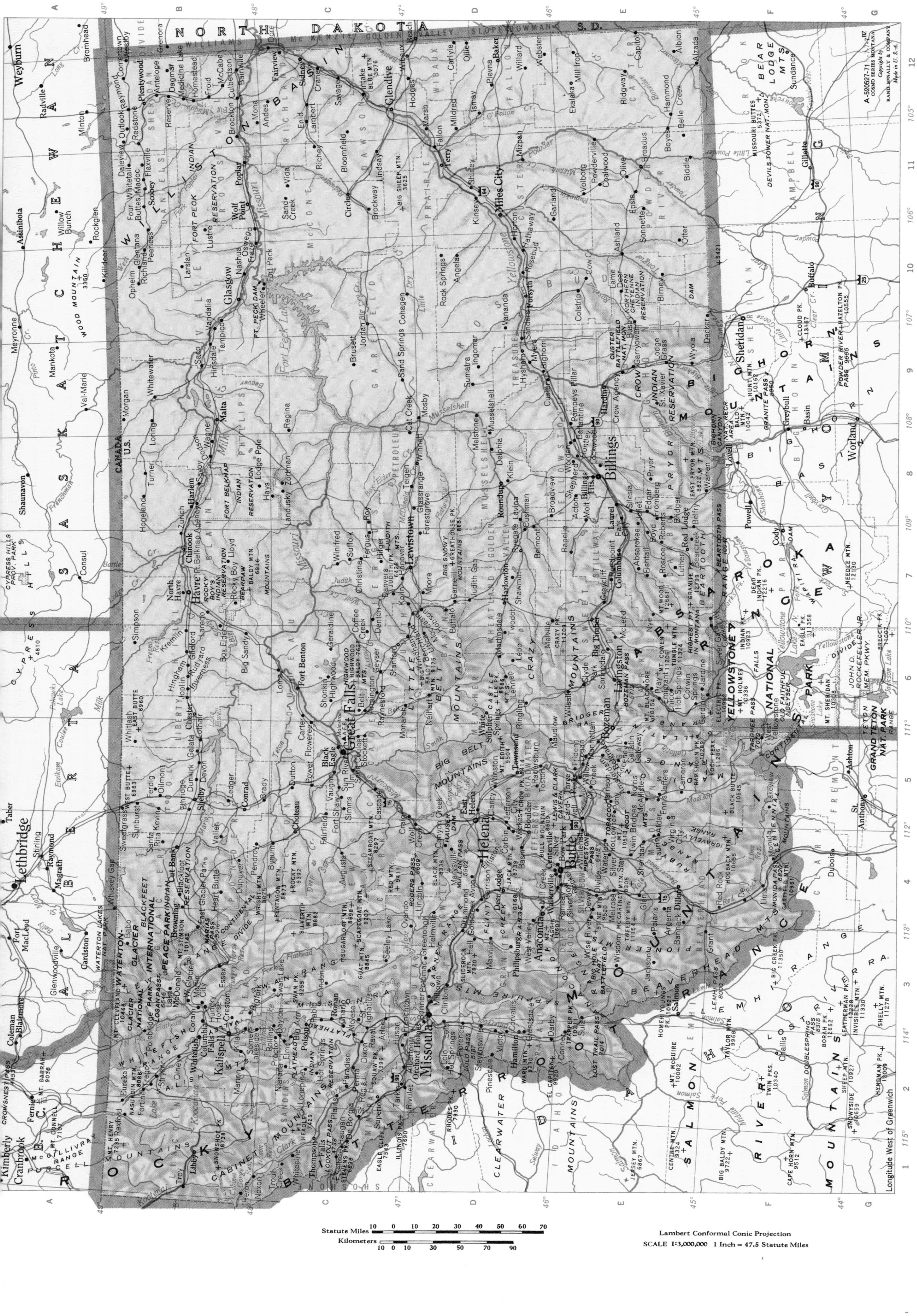

Cities and Towns

Anaconda *12,518* **D4**
Baker *2,354* **D12**
Belgrade *2,336* **E5**
Bigfork *1,080* **B2**
Big Timber *1,690* **E7**
Billings *66,842* **E8**
Billings Heights *8,480* **E8**
Black Eagle *1,100* **C5**
Boulder *1,441* **D4**
Bozeman *21,645* **E5**
Browning *1,226* **B3**
Butte *37,205* **E4**
Chester *963* **B6**
Chinook *1,660* **B7**
Choteau *1,798* **C4**
Circle *931* **C11**
Colstrip *1,476* **E10**
Columbia Falls *3,112* **B2**
Columbus *1,439* **E7**
Conrad *3,074* **B5**
Crow Agency *750* **E9**
Cut Bank *3,688* **B4**
Deer Lodge *4,023* **D4**
Dillon *3,976* **E4**
East Glacier Park *500* **B3**
East Helena *1,647* **D5**
Eureka *1,119* **B1**
Fairview *1,366* **C12**
Forsyth *2,553* **D10**
Fort Benton *1,693* **C6**
Glasgow *4,455* **B10**
Glendive *5,978* **C12**
Great Falls *56,725* **C5**
Hamilton *2,661* **D2**
Hardin *3,300* **E9**
Harlem *1,023* **B8**
Harlowton *1,181* **D7**
Havre *10,891* **B7**
Helena *23,938* **D4**
Hungry Horse *900* **B2**
Kalispell *10,648* **B2**
Laurel *5,481* **E8**
Lewistown *7,104* **C7**
Libby *2,748* **B1**
Livingston *6,994* **E6**
Lockwood *1,600* **E8**
Lolo *2,418* **D2**
Malta *2,367* **B9**
Manhattan *988* **E5**
Miles City *9,602* **D11**
Missoula *33,388* **D2**
Orchard Homes *4,000* **D2**
Philipsburg *1,138* **D3**
Plains *1,116* **C2**
Plentywood *2,476* **B12**
Polson *2,798* **C2**
Poplar *995* **B11**
Red Lodge *1,896* **E7**
Ronan *1,530* **C2**
Roundup *2,119* **D8**
St. Ignatius *877* **C2**
Scobey *1,382* **B11**
Shelby *3,142* **B5**
Sidney *5,726* **C12**
Superior *1,054* **C2**
Terry *929* **D11**
Thompson Falls *1,478* **C1**
Three Forks *1,247* **E5**
Townsend *1,587* **D5**
Troy *1,088* **B1**
Vaughn *2,270* **C5**
Whitefish *3,703* **B2**
Whitehall *1,030* **E4**
White Sulphur Springs *1,302* **D6**
Wolf Point *3,074* **B11**

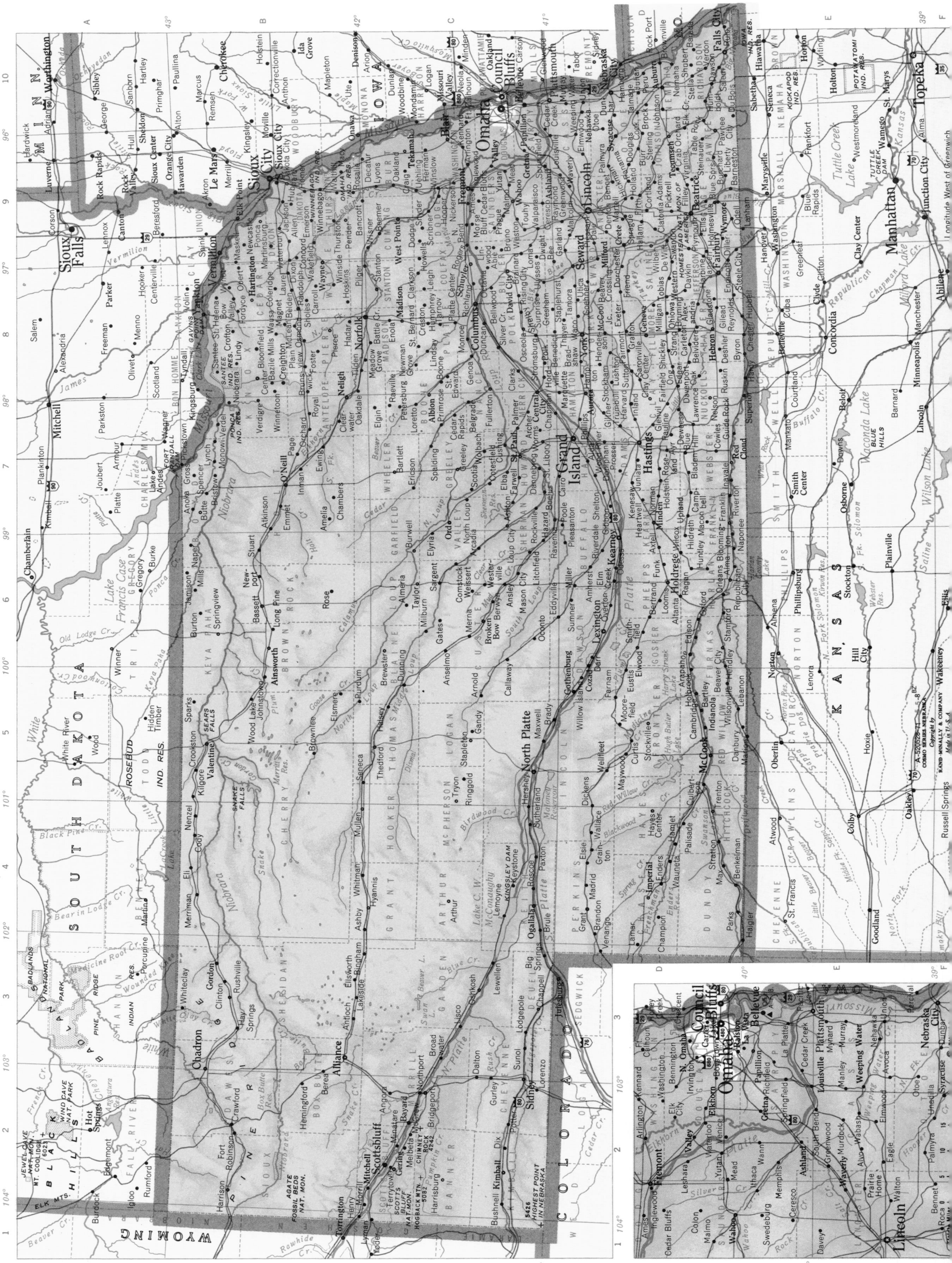

Cities and Towns
Ainsworth 2,256 **B6**
Albion 1,997 **C7**
Alliance 9,920 **B3**
Ashland 2,274 **C9**
Atkinson 1,521 **B7**
Auburn 3,482 **D10**
Aurora 3,717 **D7**
Beatrice 12,891 **D9**
Bellevue 21,813 **C10**
Blair 6,418 **C9**
Bridgeport 1,668 **C2**
Broken Bow 3,979 **C6**
Central City 3,083 **C7**
Chadron 5,933 **B3**
Columbus 17,328 **C8**
Cozad 4,453 **D6**
Crete 4,872 **D9**
David City 2,514 **C8**
Fairbury 4,885 **D8**
Falls City 5,374 **D10**
Fremont 23,979 **C9**
Fullerton 1,506 **C8**
Geneva 2,400 **D8**
Gering 7,760 **C2**
Gibbon 1,531 **D7**
Gordon 2,167 **B3**
Gothenburg 3,479 **D5**
Grand Island 33,180 **D7**
Gretna 1,609 **C9**
Hartington 1,730 **B8**
Hastings 23,045 **D7**
Hebron 1,906 **D8**
Holdrege 5,624 **D6**
Imperial 1,941 **D4**
Kearney 21,158 **D6**
Kimball 3,120 **C2**
La Vista 9,588 **g12**
Lexington 7,040 **D6**
Lincoln 171,932 **D9**
McCook 8,404 **D5**
Madison 1,950 **C8**
Milford 2,108 **D8**
Minden 2,939 **D7**
Mitchell 1,956 **C2**
Nebraska City 7,127 **D10**
Neligh 1,893 **B7**
Norfolk 19,449 **B8**
North Platte 24,509 **C5**
Ogallala 5,638 **C4**
Omaha 313,911 **C10**
O'Neill 4,049 **B7**
Ord 2,658 **C7**
Papillion 6,399 **C9**
Pierce 1,535 **B8**
Plattsmouth 6,295 **D10**
Ralston 5,143 **g12**
St. Paul 2,094 **C7**
Schuyler 4,151 **C8**
Scottsbluff 14,156 **C2**
Seward 5,713 **D8**
Sidney 6,010 **C3**
South Sioux City 9,339 **B9**
Stanton 1,603 **C8**
Superior 2,502 **D7**
Syracuse 1,638 **D9**
Tecumseh 1,926 **D9**
Tekamah 1,886 **C9**
Valentine 2,829 **B5**
Valley 1,716 **C9**
Wahoo 3,555 **C9**
Waverly 1,726 **D9**
Wayne 5,240 **B8**
West Point 3,609 **C9**
Wilber 1,624 **D9**
Wymore 1,841 **D9**
York 7,723 **D8**

Statute Miles 5 0 5 10 20 30 40 50 60
Kilometers 5 0 5 15 35 55 75 95

Lambert Conformal Conic Projection
SCALE 1:2,460,000 1 Inch = 39 Statute Miles

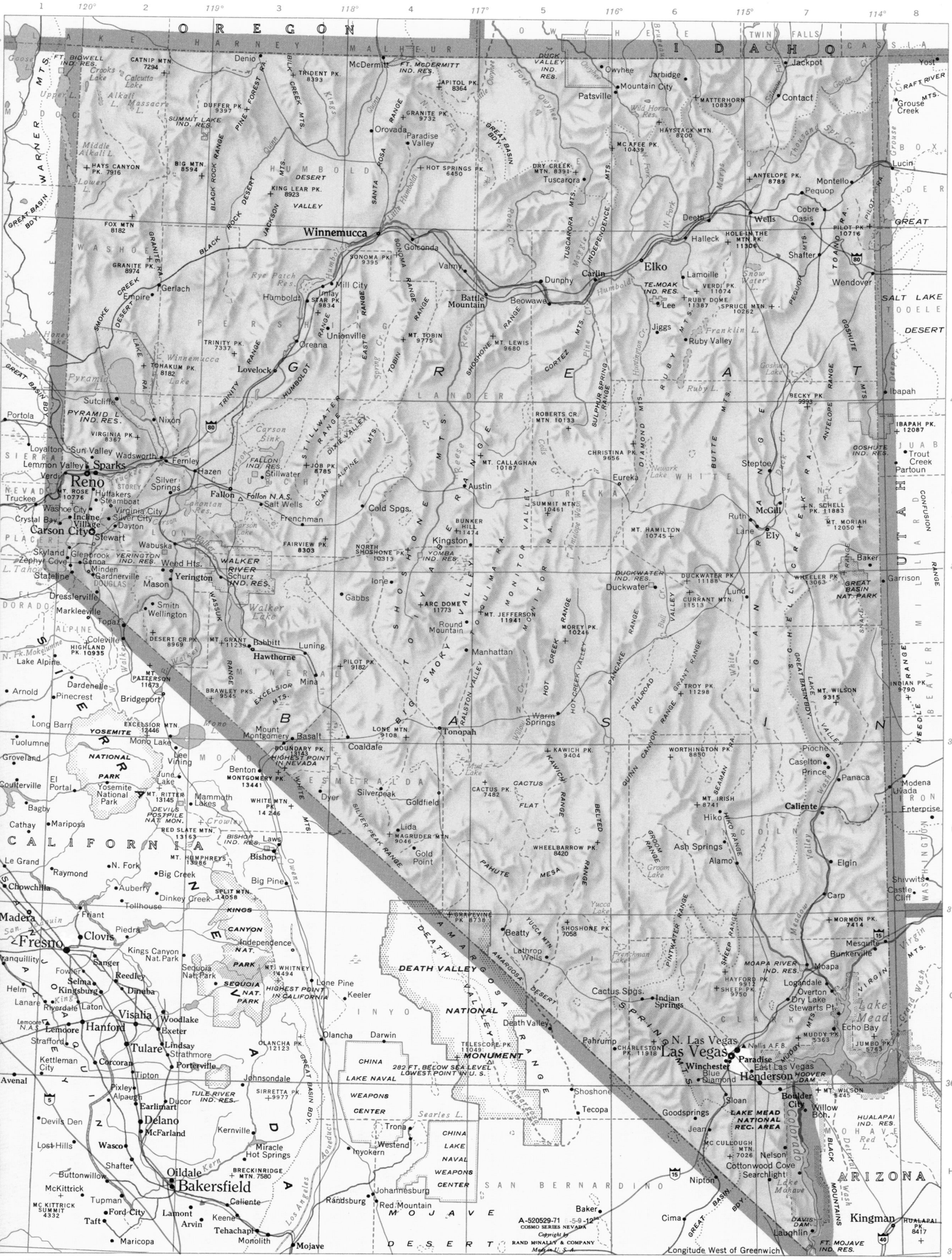

Statute Miles 5 0 5 10 20 30 40 50 60 70 80
Kilometers 5 0 10 20 40 60 80 100 120

Lambert Conformal Conic Projection
SCALE 1:2,630,000 1 Inch = 41.5 Statute Miles

Cities and Towns

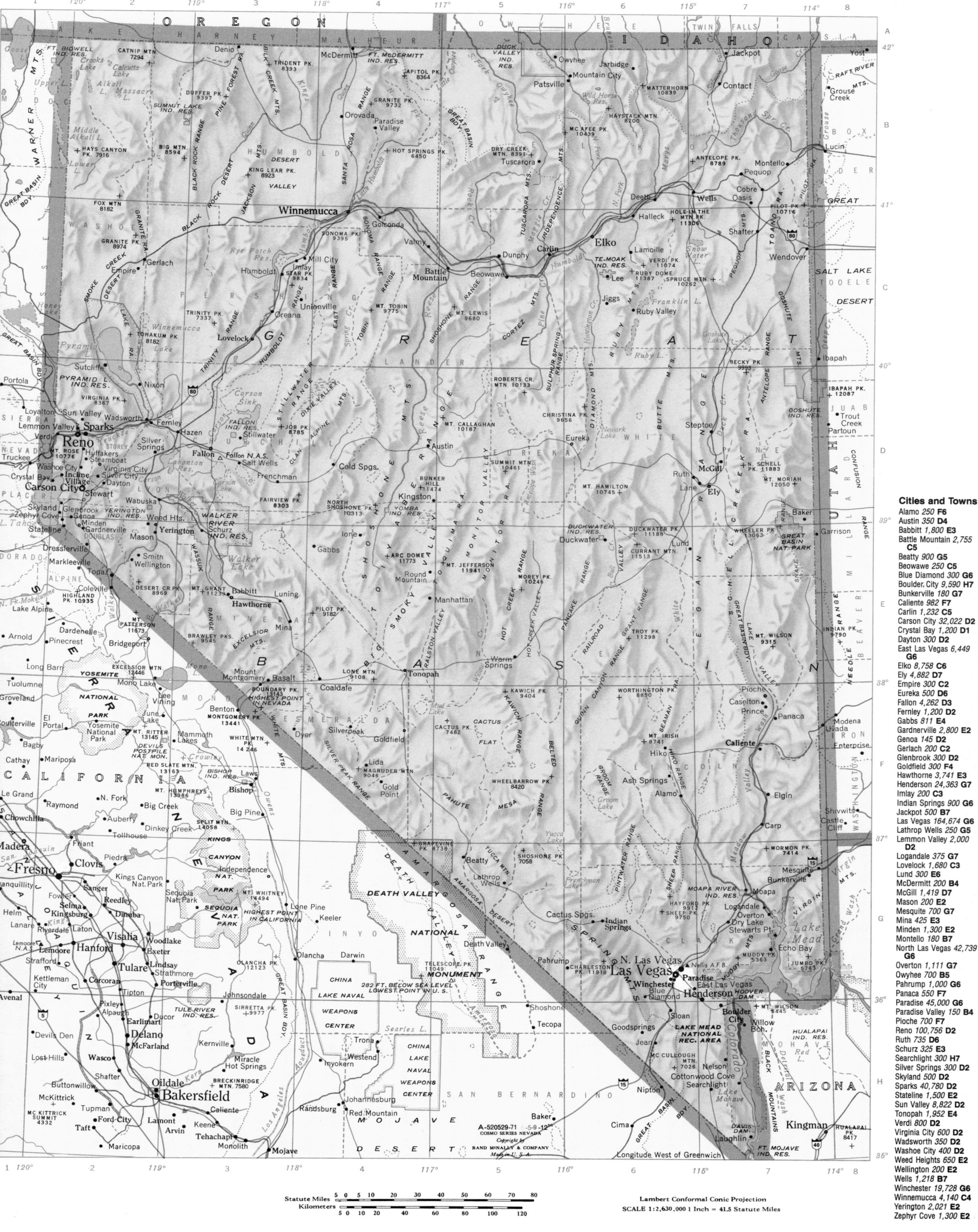

Cities and Towns*

Antrim *1,142* **D3**
Ashland *1,479* **C3**
Bedford *1,300* **E3**
Berlin *13,084* **B4**
Bristol *1,258* **C3**
Charlestown *1,294* **D2**
Claremont *14,557* **D2**
Colebrook *1,131* **g7**
Concord *30,400* **D3**
Contoocook *1,499* **D3**
Conway *1,781* **C4**
Derry *12,248* **E4**
Dover *22,377* **D5**
Durham *8,448* **D5**
Enfield *1,581* **C2**
Epping *1,384* **D4**
Exeter *8,947* **E5**
Farmington *3,284* **D4**
Franconia *600* **B3**
Franklin *7,901* **D3**
Goffstown *2,500* **D3**
Gorham *2,180* **B4**
Greenville *1,447* **E3**
Groveton *1,389* **A3**
Hampton *6,779* **E5**
Hanover *6,861* **C2**
Henniker *1,538* **D3**
Hillsboro *1,797* **D3**
Hinsdale *1,546* **E2**
Hooksett *1,868* **D4**
Hudson *6,248* **E4**
Jaffrey *2,684* **E2**
Keene *21,449* **E2**
Laconia *15,575* **C4**
Lancaster *2,134* **B3**
Lebanon *11,134* **C2**
Lincoln *950* **B3**
Lisbon *1,151* **B3**
Littleton *4,480* **B3**
Manchester *90,936* **E4**
Marlborough *1,231* **E2**
Meredith *1,202* **C3**
Merrimack *1,200* **E4**
Milford *6,289* **E3**
Milton *1,000* **D5**
Nashua *67,865* **E4**
New Castle *975* **D5**
New London *1,335* **D3**
Newmarket *3,749* **D5**
Newport *4,388* **D2**
North Conway *2,184* **B4**
Northfield *1,340* **D3**
North Hampton *1,000* **E5**
North Walpole *950* **D2**
Peterborough *2,100* **E3**
Pinardville *4,500* **E3**
Pittsfield *1,584* **D4**
Plaistow *1,800* **E4**
Plymouth *3,628* **C3**
Portsmouth *26,254* **D5**
Raymond *1,192* **D4**
Rochester *21,560* **D5**
Salem *11,500* **E4**
Somersworth *10,350* **D5**
South Hooksett *1,200* **D4**
Suncook *4,698* **D4**
Tilton *1,230* **D3**
Troy *1,318* **E2**
West Swanzey *1,022* **E2**
Whitefield *1,005* **B3**
Wilton *1,310* **E3**
Winchester *1,732* **E2**
Wolfeboro *2,000* **C4**
Woodsville *1,195* **B2**

*Populations are for localities, not incorporated towns.

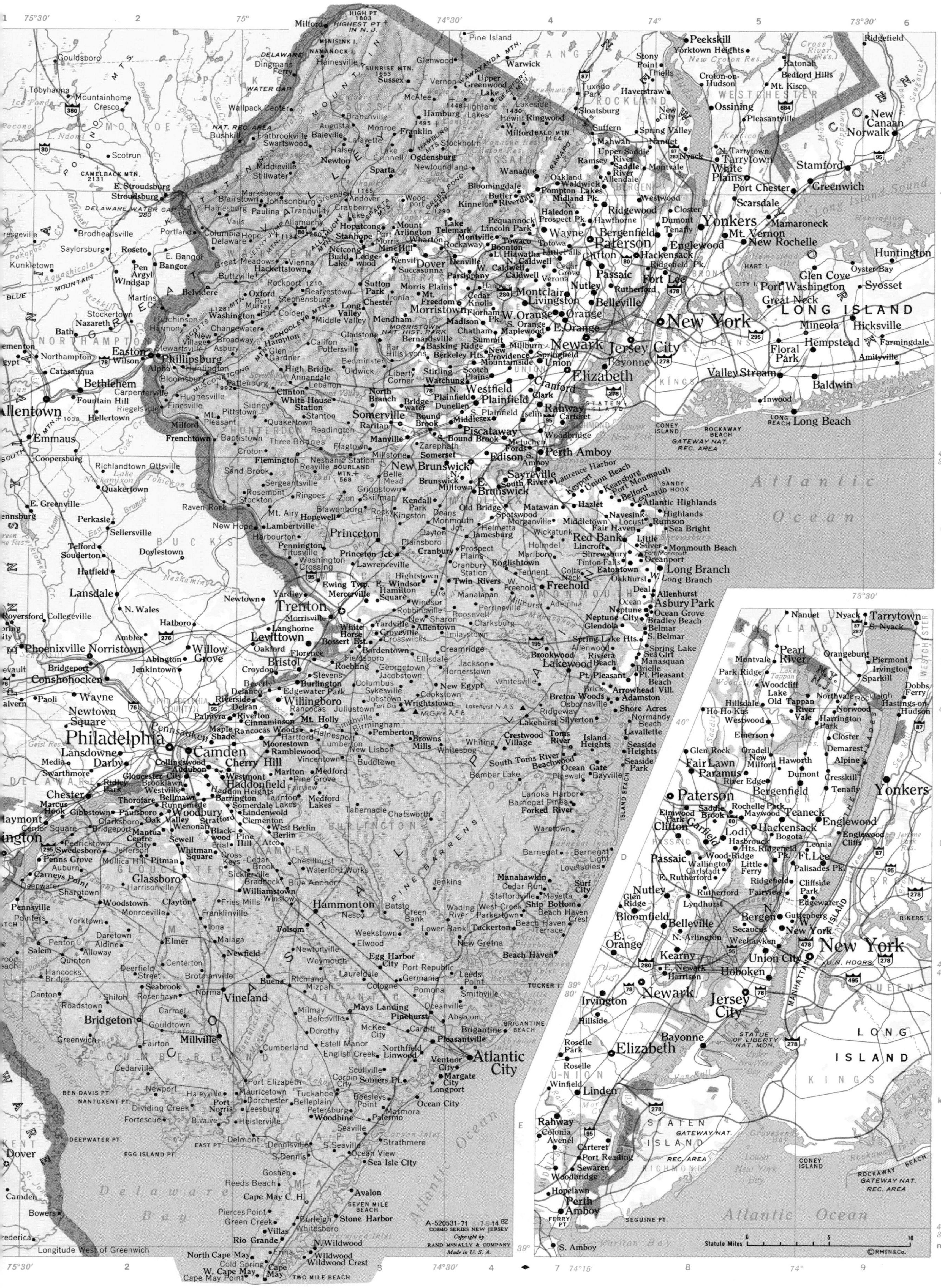

Cities and Towns

Asbury Park 17,015 C4
Atlantic City 40,199 E4
Bayonne 65,047 B4
Belleville 35,367 B4
Bergenfield 25,568 B4
Bloomfield 47,792 h8
Bridgeton 18,795 E2
Camden 84,910 D2
Cape May 4,853 F3
Carteret 20,598 B4
Cherry Hill 68,785 D2
Clifton 74,388 B4
Cranford 24,573 B4
Dover 14,681 B3
East Brunswick 37,711 C4
East Orange 77,690 B4
Edison 70,193 B4
Elizabeth 106,201 B4
Fair Lawn 32,229 h8
Fort Lee 32,449 B5
Freehold 10,020 C4
Garfield 26,803 h8
Glassboro 14,574 D2
Hackensack 36,039 B4
Hackettstown 8,850 B3
Hammonton 12,298 D3
Hazlet 28,013 C4
Hoboken 42,460 k8
Irvington 61,493 k8
Jersey City 223,532 B4
Kearny 35,735 h8
Lakewood 22,863 C4
Linden 37,836 k8
Livingston 28,040 B4
Lodi 23,956 h8
Long Branch 29,819 C5
Maplewood 22,950 B4
Middletown 61,615 C4
Millville 24,815 E2
Montclair 38,321 B4
Morristown 16,614 B4
Newark 329,248 B4
New Brunswick 41,442 C4
North Bergen 47,019 h8
Nutley 28,998 B4
Paramus 26,474 h8
Passaic 52,463 B4
Paterson 137,970 B4
Pennsauken 33,775 D2
Pennsville 12,467 D1
Perth Amboy 38,951 B4
Phillipsburg 16,647 B2
Piscataway 42,223 B4
Plainfield 45,555 B4
Princeton 12,035 C3
Rahway 26,723 B4
Red Bank 12,031 C4
Ridgewood 25,208 B4
Sayreville 29,969 C4
Somerset 21,731 B3
Somerville 11,973 B3
Summit 21,071 B4
Sussex 2,418 A3
Teaneck 39,007 h8
Trenton 92,124 C3
Union 50,181 B4
Union City 55,593 h8
Vineland 53,753 E2
Wayne 46,474 B4
Westfield 30,447 B4
West New York 39,194 h8
West Orange 39,400 B4
Willingboro 39,912 C3
Woodbine 2,809 E3

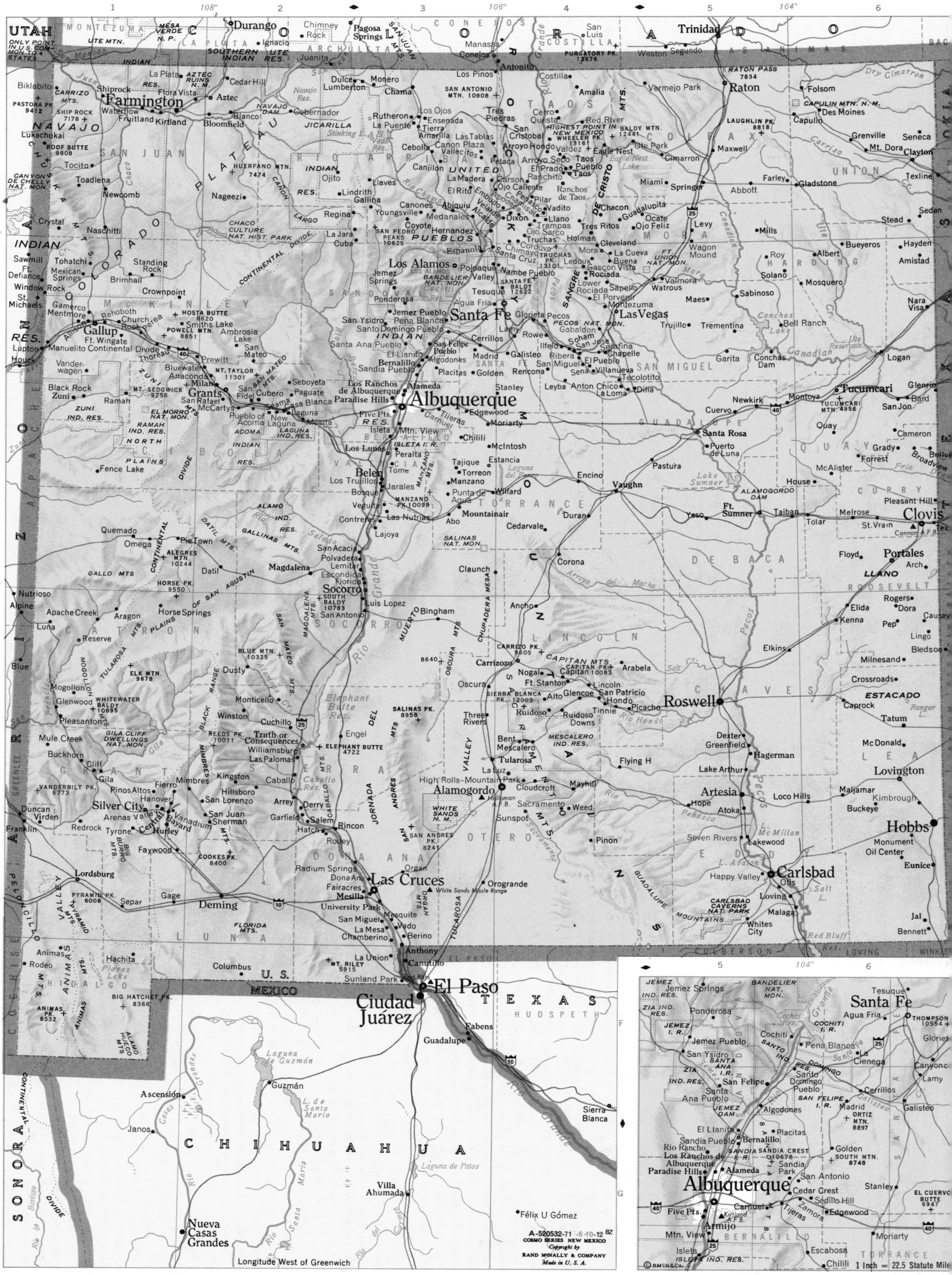

Statute Miles 10 0 10 20 30 40 50 60 70 80 90

Kilometers 10 0 10 20 40 60 80 100 120

Lambert Conformal Conic Projection

SCALE 1:2,600,000 1 Inch = 41 Statute Miles

Cities and Towns

Alameda *7,800* **B3**
Alamagordo *24,024* **E4**
Albuquerque *331,767* **B3**
Anthony *3,285* **F3**
Armijo *18,900* **k7**
Artesia *10,385* **E5**
Aztec *5,512* **A2**
Bayard *3,036* **E1**
Belen *5,617* **C3**
Bernalillo *3,012* **B3**
Bloomfield *4,881* **A2**
Carlsbad *25,496* **E5**
Carizozo *1,222* **D4**
Central *1,968* **E1**
Chama *1,090* **A3**
Chimayo *1,993* **A4**
Clayton *2,968* **A6**
Clovis *31,194* **C6**
Crownpoint *1,134* **B1**
Deming *9,964* **E2**
Dulce *1,648* **A2**
Espanola *6,803* **B3**
Eunice *2,970* **E6**
Farmington *31,222* **A1**
Five Points *5,500* **B3**
Fort Sumner *1,421* **C5**
Gallup *18,167* **B1**
Grants *11,439* **B2**
Hatch *1,028* **E2**
Hobbs *29,153* **E6**
Hurley *1,616* **E1**
Isleta *1,246* **C3**
Jal *2,675* **E6**
Jemez Pueblo *1,503* **B3**
Kirtland *2,358* **A1**
La Luz *1,194* **D4**
Las Cruces *45,086* **E3**
Las Vegas *14,322* **B4**
Lordsburg *3,195* **E1**
Los Alamos *11,039* **B3**
Los Lunas *3,525* **C3**
Los Ranchos de Albuquerque *2,702* **B3**
Loving *1,355* **E5**
Lovington *9,727* **E6**
Magdalena *1,022* **C2**
Mescalero *1,259* **D4**
Mesilla *2,029* **E3**
Milan *3,747* **B2**
Moriarty *1,276* **C3**
Mountain View *1,900* **C3**
Paradise Hills *5,096* **B3**
Portales *9,940* **C6**
Questa *1,202* **A4**
Ranches of Taos *1,411* **A4**
Raton *8,225* **A5**
Roswell *39,676* **D5**
Ruidoso *4,260* **D4**
Ruidoso Downs *949* **D4**
Santa Fe *48,953* **B4**
Santa Rosa *2,469* **C5**
Santo Domingo Pueblo *2,082* **B3**
Shiprock *7,237* **A1**
Silver City *9,887* **E1**
Socorro *7,173* **C3**
Springer *1,657* **A5**
Sunland Park *3,377* **F3**
Taos *3,369* **A4**
Tesuque *1,014* **B4**
Thoreau *1,099* **B1**
Truth or Consequences *5,219* **D2**
Tucumcari *6,765* **B6**
Tularosa *2,536* **D3**
University Park *4,383* **E3**
Zuni *5,551* **B1**

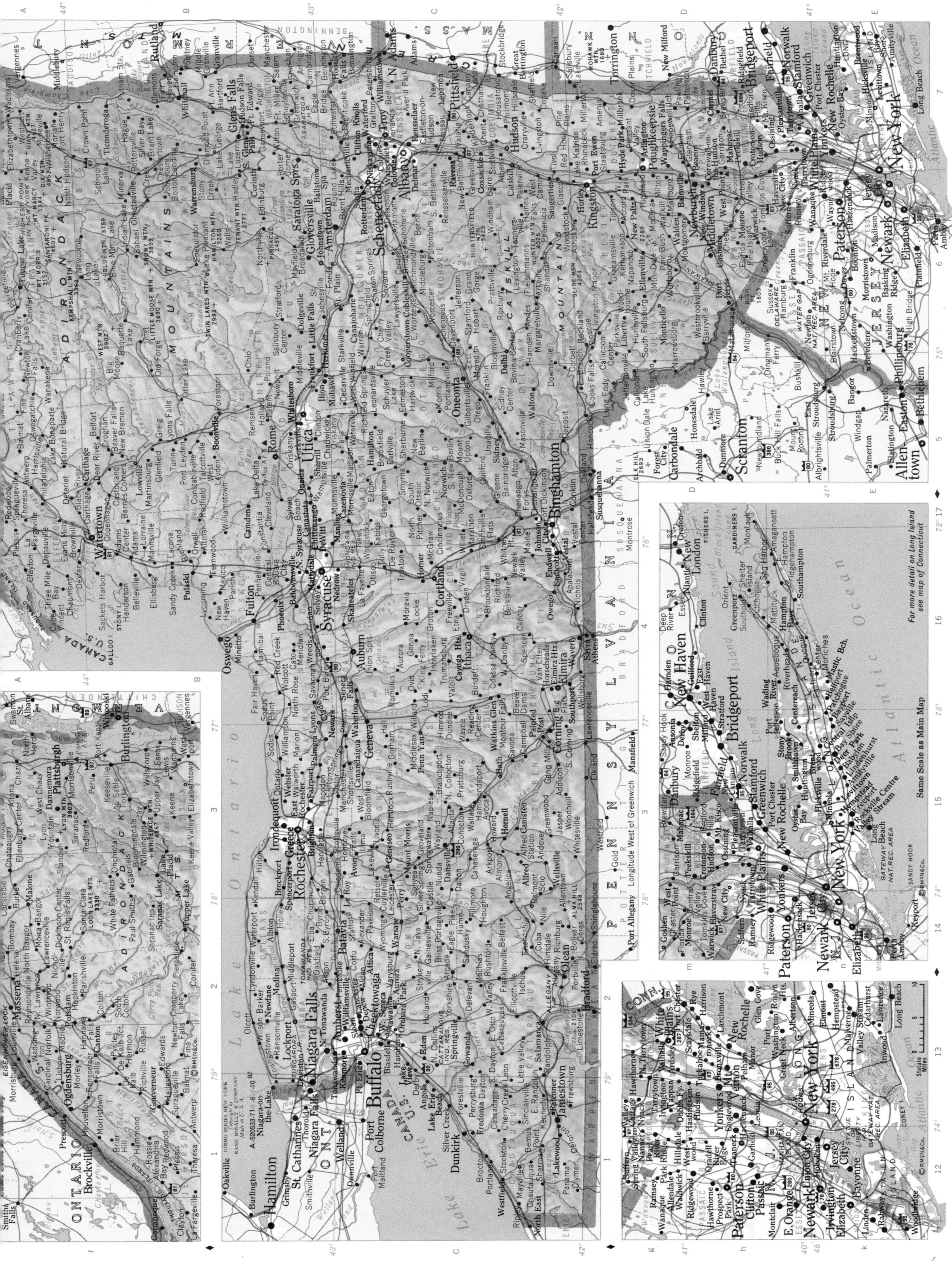

Statute Miles 5 0 5 10 20 30 40

Kilometers 5 0 5 15 25 35 45 55

Lambert Conformal Conic Projection

SCALE 1:1,862,000 1 Inch = 29 Statute Miles

Cities and Towns

Albany *101,727* **C7**
Amherst *66,100* **C2**
Amityville *9,076* **E7**
Amsterdam *21,872* **C6**
Auburn *32,548* **C4**
Batavia *16,703* **C2**
Binghamton *55,860* **C5**
Brentwood *48,800* **E7**
Brighton *35,776* **B3**
Buffalo *357,870* **C2**
Centereach *34,600* **n15**
Central Islip *26,000* **n15**
Cheektowaga *100,400* **C2**
Cooperstown *2,342* **C6**
Corning *12,953* **C3**
Cortland *20,138* **C4**
Deer Park *33,400* **n15**
Dunkirk *15,310* **C1**
Elmira *35,327* **C4**
Elmont *30,000* **k13**
Freeport *38,272* **n15**
Fulton *13,312* **B4**
Geneseo *6,746* **C3**
Geneva *15,133* **C4**
Glens Falls *15,897* **B7**
Gloversville *17,836* **B6**
Greece *63,700* **B3**
Hempstead *40,404* **n15**
Hicksville *50,000* **E7**
Hornell *10,234* **C3**
Hudson *7,986* **C7**
Hyde Park *2,805* **D7**
Irondequoit *57,648* **B3**
Ithaca *28,732* **C4**
Jamestown *35,775* **C1**
Kingston *24,481* **D6**
Lackawanna *22,701* **C2**
Lake Placid *2,490* **A7**
Levittown *65,400* **E7**
Lockport *24,844* **B2**
Long Beach *34,073* **E7**
Massena *12,851* **f10**
Middletown *21,454* **D6**
Mount Vernon *66,713* **h13**
Newburgh *23,438* **D6**
New City *30,800* **D6**
New Rochelle *70,794* **E7**
New York *7,071,639* **E7**
Niagara Falls *71,384* **B1**
North Tonawanda *35,760* **B2**
Ogdensburg *12,375* **f9**
Olean *18,207* **C2**
Oneonta *14,933* **C5**
Ossining *20,196* **D7**
Oswego *19,793* **B4**
Palmyra *3,729* **B3**
Plattsburgh *21,057* **f11**
Port Chester *23,565* **E7**
Poughkeepsie *29,757* **D7**
Rochester *241,741* **B3**
Rome *43,826* **B5**
Rotterdam *24,800* **C6**
Saratoga Springs *23,906* **B7**
Schenectady *67,972* **C7**
Syracuse *170,105* **B4**
Ticonderoga *2,938* **B7**
Troy *56,638* **C7**
Utica *75,632* **B5**
Valley Stream *35,769* **n15**
Watertown *27,861* **B5**
West Point *8,000* **D7**
West Seneca *51,210* **C2**
White Plains *46,999* **D7**
Yonkers *195,351* **E7**

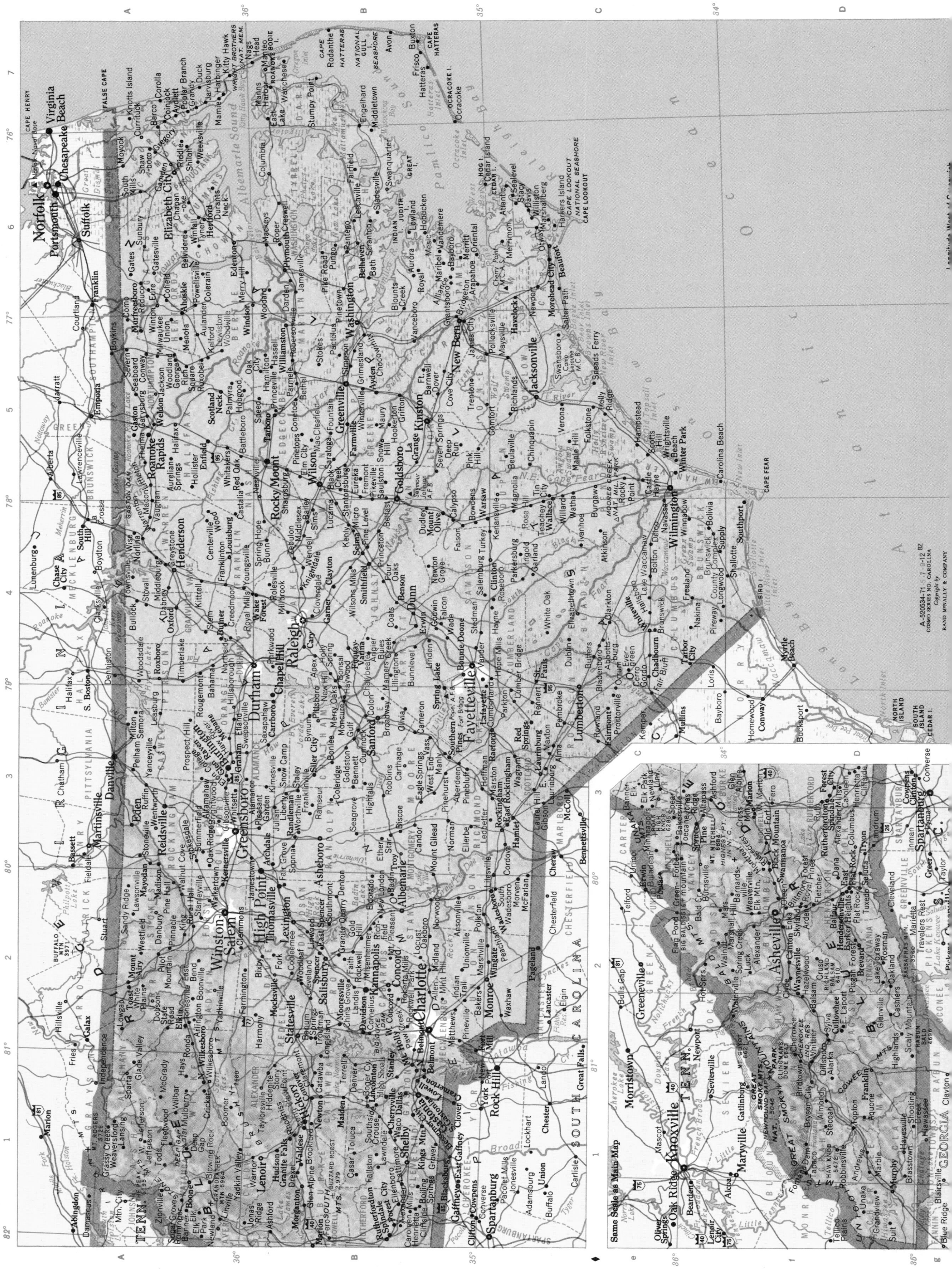

Cities and Towns

Albemarle 15,110 **B2**
Archdale 5,326 **B3**
Asheboro 15,252 **B3**
Asheville 53,583 **f10**
Boone 10,191 **A1**
Brevard 5,323 **f10**
Burlington 37,266 **A3**
Carrboro 7,336 **B3**
Chapel Hill 32,421 **B3**
Charlotte 314,447 **B2**
Clemmons 7,401 **A2**
Clinton 7,552 **C4**
Concord 16,942 **B2**
Dunn 8,962 **B4**
Durham 100,538 **B4**
Eden 15,672 **A3**
Edenton 5,357 **A6**
Elizabeth City 13,784 **A6**
Fayetteville 59,507 **B4**
Forest City 7,688 **B1**
Garner 10,073 **B4**
Gastonia 47,333 **B1**
Goldsboro 31,871 **B5**
Graham 8,674 **A3**
Greensboro 155,642 **A3**
Greenville 35,740 **B5**
Havelock 17,718 **C6**
Henderson 13,522 **A4**
Hendersonville 6,862 **f10**
Hickory 20,757 **B1**
High Point 63,808 **B2**
Jacksonville 18,237 **C5**
Kannapolis 34,564 **B2**
Kernersville 6,802 **A2**
Kings Mountain 9,080 **B1**
Kinston 25,234 **B5**
Laurinburg 11,480 **C3**
Lenoir 13,748 **B1**
Lexington 15,711 **B2**
Lincolnton 4,879 **B1**
Lumberton 18,241 **C3**
Monroe 12,639 **C2**
Mooresville 8,575 **B2**
Morehead City 4,359 **C6**
Morganton 13,763 **B1**
Mount Airy 6,862 **A2**
Mount Olive 4,876 **B4**
Nags Head 1,020 **B7**
New Bern 14,557 **B5**
Newton 7,624 **B1**
Oxford 7,603 **A4**
Plymouth 4,571 **B6**
Raleigh 150,255 **B4**
Reidsville 12,492 **A3**
Roanoke Rapids 14,702 **A5**
Rockingham 8,300 **C3**
Rocky Mount 41,283 **B5**
Roxboro 7,532 **A4**
Salisbury 22,677 **B2**
Sanford 14,773 **B3**
Selma 4,762 **B4**
Shelby 15,310 **B1**
Smithfield 7,288 **B4**
Southern Pines 8,620 **B3**
Statesville 18,622 **B2**
Swannanoa 5,586 **f10**
Tarboro 8,634 **B5**
Thomasville 14,144 **B2**
Washington 8,418 **B5**
Whiteville 5,565 **C4**
Williamston 6,159 **B5**
Wilmington 44,000 **C5**
Wilson 34,424 **B5**
Winston-Salem 131,885 **A2**

Statute Miles 5 0 5 10 20 30 40
Kilometers 5 0 5 15 25 35 45 55

Lambert Conformal Conic Projection
SCALE 1:1,950,000 1 Inch = 31 Statute Miles

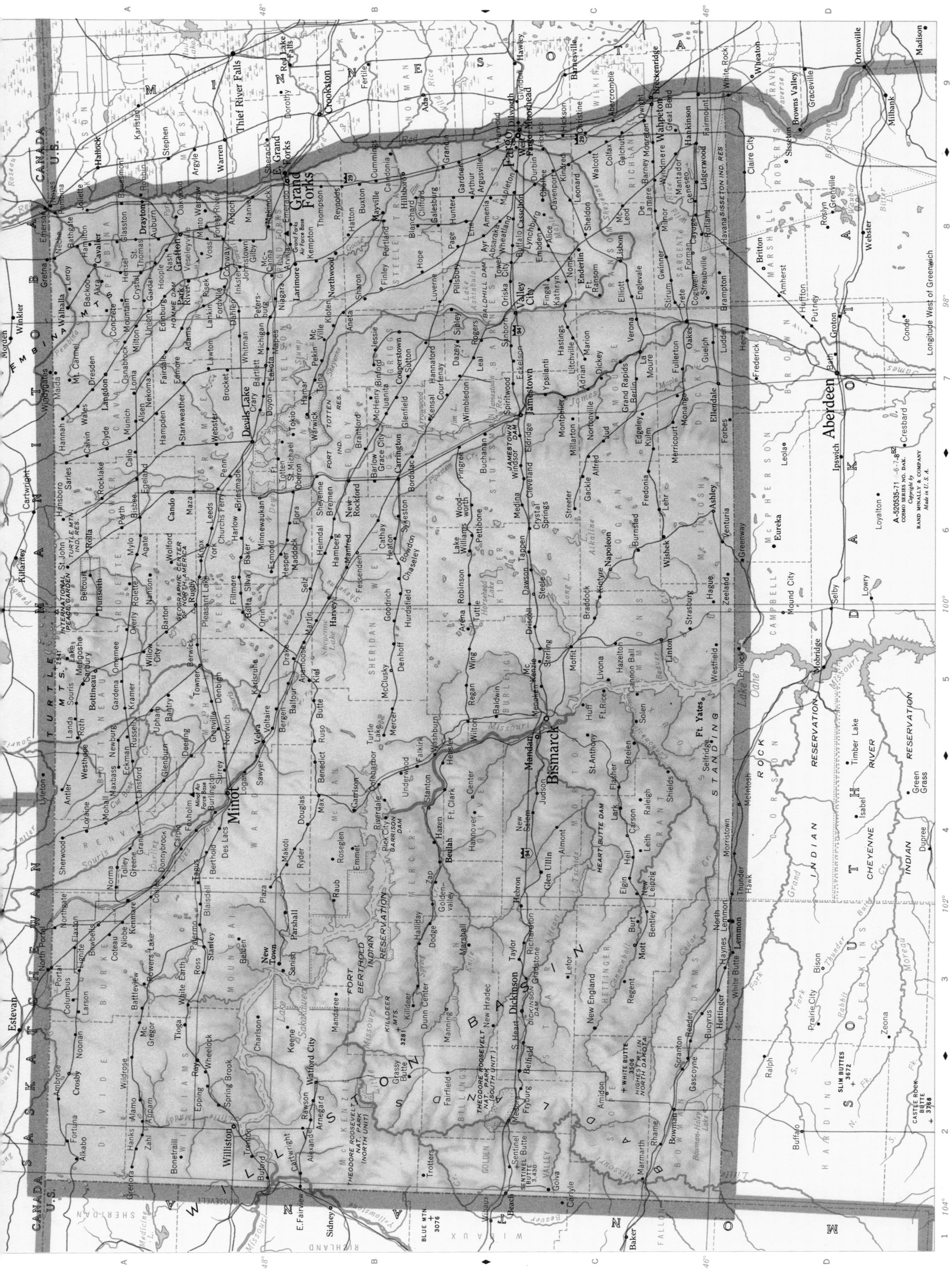

Statute Miles 5 0 5 10 20 30 40 50 60
Kilometers 5 0 5 15 25 35 45 55 65 75

Lambert Conformal Conic Projection
SCALE 1:2,091,000 1 Inch = 33 Statute Miles

Cities and Towns

Ashley *1,192* **C6**
Beach *1,381* **C1**
Belcourt *1,803* **A6**
Belfield *1,274* **C2**
Beulah *2,908* **B4**
Bismarck *44,485* **C5**
Bottineau *2,829* **A5**
Bowman *2,071* **C2**
Cando *1,496* **A6**
Carrington *2,641* **B6**
Casselton *1,661* **C8**
Cavalier *1,505* **A8**
Center *900* **B4**
Cooperstown *1,308* **B7**
Crosby *1,469* **A2**
Devils Lake *7,442* **A7**
Dickinson *15,924* **C3**
Drayton *1,082* **A8**
Edgeley *843* **C7**
Elgin *930* **C4**
Ellendale *1,967* **C7**
Enderlin *1,151* **C8**
Fargo *61,383* **C9**
Garrison *1,830* **B4**
Glen Ullin *1,125* **C4**
Grafton *5,293* **A8**
Grand Forks *43,765* **B8**
Hankinson *1,158* **C9**
Harvey *2,527* **B6**
Hazen *2,365* **B4**
Hebron *1,078* **C3**
Hettinger *1,739* **D3**
Hillsboro *1,600* **B8**
Jamestown *16,280* **C7**
Kenmare *1,456* **A3**
Lakota *963* **A7**
La Moure *1,077* **C7**
Langdon *2,335* **A7**
Larimore *1,524* **B8**
Lidgerwood *971* **C8**
Linton *1,561* **C5**
Lisbon *2,283* **C8**
Mandan *15,513* **C5**
Mayville *2,255* **B8**
Minot *32,843* **A4**
Mohall *1,049* **A4**
Mott *1,315* **C3**
Napoleon *1,103* **C6**
New Rockford *1,791* **B6**
New Salem *1,081* **C4**
New Town *1,335* **B3**
Northwood *1,240* **B8**
Oakes *2,112* **C7**
Park River *1,844* **A8**
Parshall *1,059* **B3**
Rolla *1,538* **A6**
Rugby *3,335* **A6**
Stanley *1,631* **A3**
Steele *796* **C6**
Surrey *999* **A4**
Tioga *1,597* **A3**
Towner *867* **A5**
Turtle Lake *802* **B5**
Underwood *1,329* **B4**
Valley City *7,774* **C8**
Velva *1,101* **A5**
Wahpeton *9,064* **C9**
Walhalla *1,429* **A8**
Washburn *1,767* **B5**
Watford City *2,119* **B2**
West Fargo *10,099* **C9**
Williston *13,336* **A2**
Wilton *950* **B5**
Wishek *1,345* **C6**

Cities and Towns

Akron *237,177* **A4**
Alliance *24,315* **B4**
Ashland *20,326* **B3**
Ashtabula *23,449* **A5**
Athens *19,743* **C3**
Barberton *29,751* **A4**
Bellefontaine *11,888* **B2**
Boardman *39,161* **A5**
Bowling Green *25,728* **A2**
Brunswick *28,104* **A4**
Bucyrus *13,433* **B3**
Cambridge *13,573* **B4**
Canton *93,077* **B4**
Chillicothe *23,420* **C3**
Cincinnati *385,457* **C1**
Circleville *11,700* **C3**
Cleveland *573,822* **A4**
Cleveland Heights *56,438* **A4**
Columbus *565,032* **C2**
Conneaut *13,835* **A5**
Coshocton *13,405* **B4**
Cuyahoga Falls *43,890* **A4**
Dayton *193,444* **C1**
Defiance *16,810* **A1**
Delaware *18,780* **B2**
East Cleveland *36,957* **g9**
East Liverpool *16,687* **B5**
Elyria *57,538* **A3**
Euclid *59,999* **A4**
Findlay *35,594* **A2**
Fostoria *15,743* **A2**
Fremont *17,834* **A2**
Greenville *12,999* **B1**
Hamilton *63,189* **C1**
Ironton *14,290* **D3**
Kettering *61,186* **C1**
Lakewood *61,963* **A4**
Lancaster *34,953* **C3**
Lima *47,381* **B1**
Lorain *75,416* **A3**
Mansfield *53,927* **B3**
Marietta *16,467* **C4**
Marion *37,040* **B2**
Massillon *30,557* **B4**
Medina *15,268* **A4**
Mentor *42,065* **A4**
Middletown *43,719* **C1**
Mount Vernon *14,323* **B3**
Newark *41,200* **B3**
New Philadelphia *16,883* **B4**
North Olmsted *36,486* **h9**
Norwalk *14,358* **A3**
Oxford *17,655* **C1**
Parma *92,548* **A4**
Piqua *20,480* **B1**
Portsmouth *25,943* **D3**
Salem *12,869* **B5**
Sandusky *31,360* **A3**
Shaker Heights *32,487* **A4**
Springfield *72,563* **C2**
Steubenville *26,400* **B5**
Strongsville *28,577* **A4**
Tiffin *19,549* **A2**
Toledo *354,635* **A2**
Upper Arlington *35,648* **B2**
Urbana *10,762* **B2**
Van Wert *11,035* **B1**
Warren *56,629* **A5**
Washington Court House *12,682* **C2**
Westerville *23,414* **B3**
Wooster *29,289* **B4**
Xenia *24,653* **C2**
Youngstown *115,436* **A5**
Zanesville *28,655* **C4**

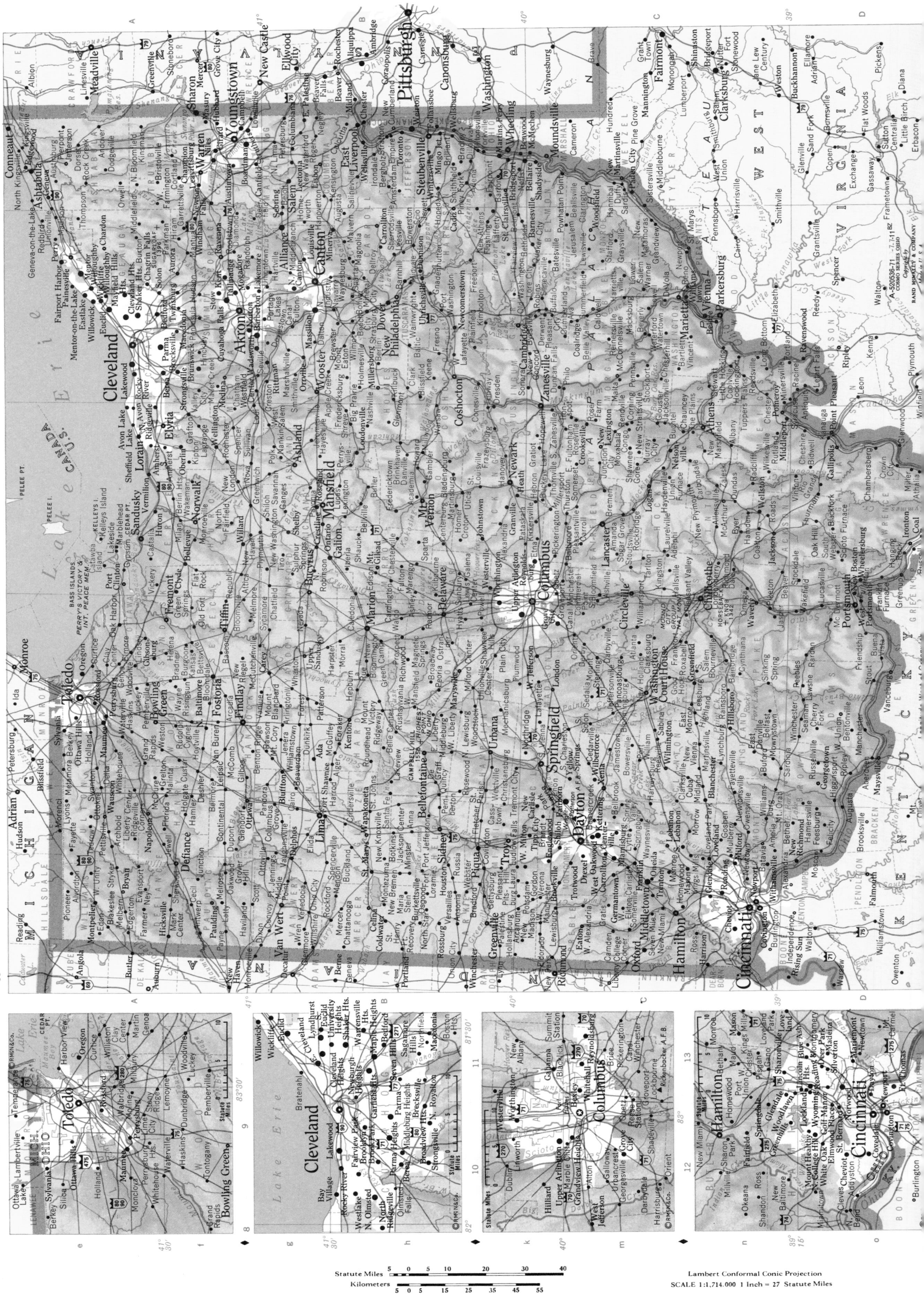

Statute Miles 5 0 5 10 20 30 40
Kilometers 5 0 5 15 25 35 45 55

Lambert Conformal Conic Projection
SCALE 1:1,714,000 1 Inch = 27 Statute Miles

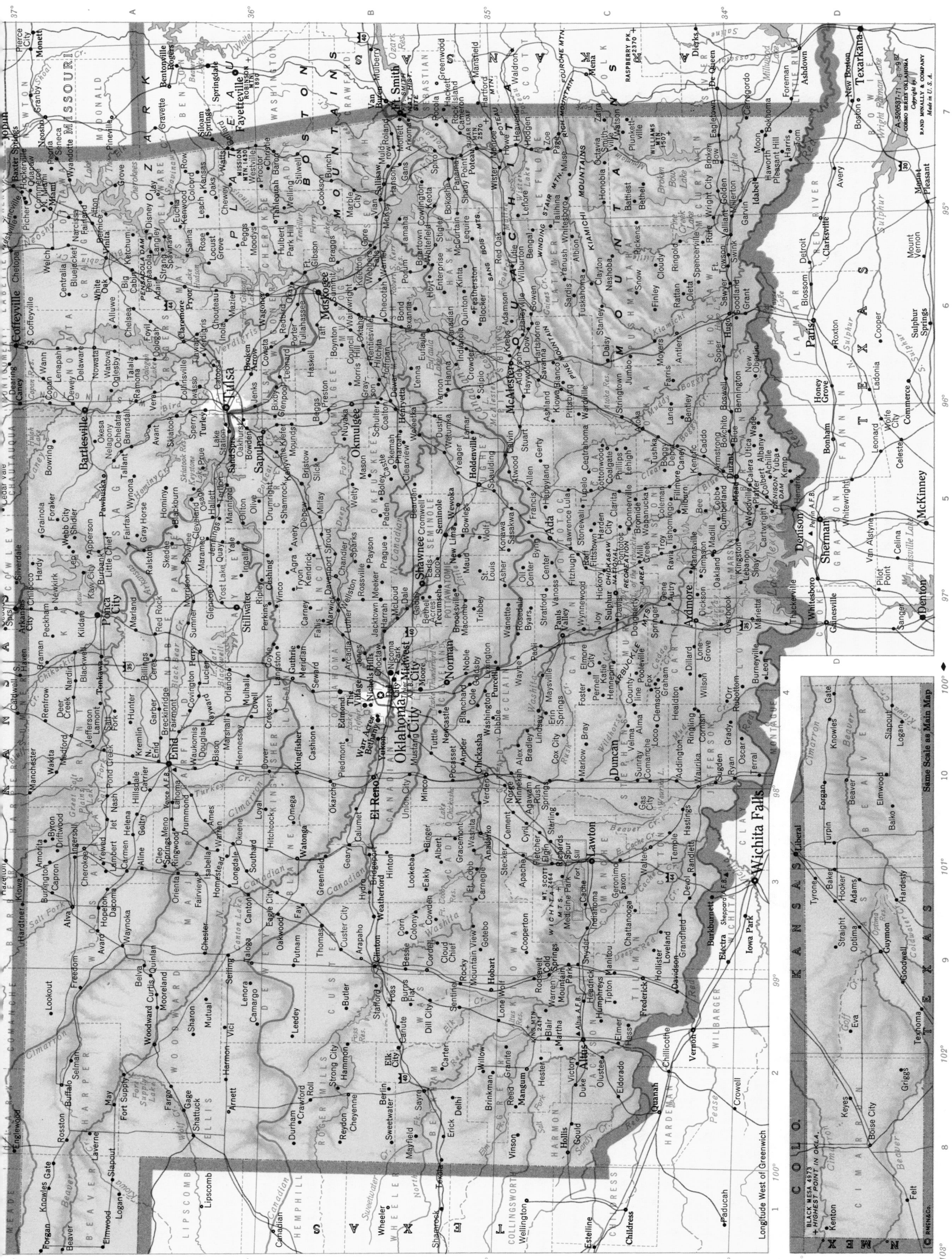

Cities and Towns

Ada *15,902* **C5**
Altus *23,101* **C2**
Alva *6,416* **A3**
Anadarko *6,378* **B3**
Ardmore *23,689* **C4**
Bartlesville *34,568* **A6**
Bethany *22,130* **B4**
Bixby *6,969* **B6**
Blackwell *8,400* **A4**
Bristow *4,702* **B5**
Broken Arrow *35,761* **A6**
Broken Bow *3,965* **C7**
Chickasha *15,828* **B4**
Choctaw *7,520* **B4**
Claremore *12,085* **A6**
Clinton *8,796* **B3**
Coweta *4,554* **B6**
Cushing *7,720* **B5**
Del City *28,523* **B4**
Duncan *22,517* **C4**
Durant *11,972* **D5**
Edmond *34,637* **B4**
Elk City *9,579* **B2**
El Reno *15,486* **B4**
Enid *50,363* **A4**
Frederick *6,153* **C2**
Guthrie *10,312* **B4**
Guymon *8,492* **e9**
Henryetta *6,432* **B6**
Hobart *4,735* **B2**
Holdenville *5,469* **B5**
Hugo *7,172* **C6**
Idabel *7,622* **D7**
Kingfisher *4,245* **B4**
Lawton *80,054* **C3**
McAlester *17,255* **C6**
Madill *3,173* **C5**
Marlow *5,017* **C4**
Miami *14,237* **A7**
Midwest City *49,559* **B4**
Moore *35,063* **B4**
Muskogee *40,011* **B6**
Mustang *7,496* **B4**
Norman *68,020* **B4**
Nowata *4,270* **A6**
Oklahoma City *403,136* **B4**
Okmulgee *16,263* **B6**
Owasso *6,149* **A6**
Pauls Valley *5,664* **C4**
Pawhuska *4,771* **A5**
Perry *5,796* **A4**
Ponca City *26,238* **A4**
Poteau *7,089* **B7**
Pryor *8,483* **A6**
Purcell *4,638* **B4**
Sallisaw *6,403* **B7**
Sand Springs *13,121* **A5**
Sapulpa *15,853* **B5**
Seminole *8,590* **B5**
Shawnee *26,506* **B5**
Stillwater *38,268* **A4**
Sulphur *5,516* **C5**
Tahlequah *9,708* **B7**
Tecumseh *5,123* **B5**
The Village *11,049* **B4**
Tulsa *360,919* **A6**
Vinita *6,740* **A6**
Wagoner *6,191* **B6**
Warr Acres *9,940* **B4**
Watonga *4,139* **B3**
Weatherford *9,640* **B3**
Wewoka *5,480* **B5**
Woodward *13,610* **A2**
Yukon *17,112* **B4**

OREGON

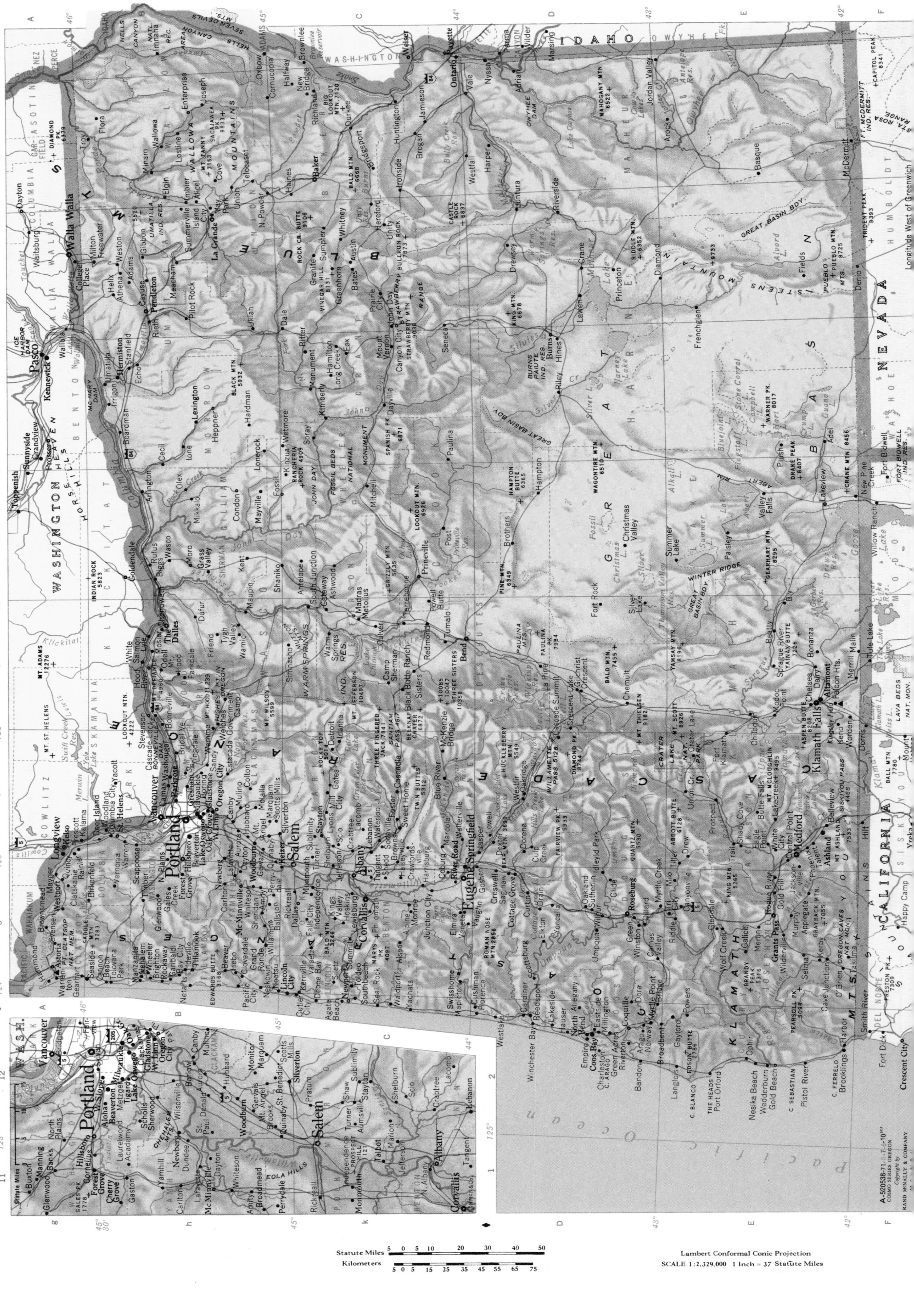

Statute Miles 5 0 5 10 20 30 40 50

Kilometers 5 0 5 15 25 35 45 55 65 75

Lambert Conformal Conic Projection

SCALE 1:2,329,000 1 Inch = 37 Statute Miles

Cities and Towns

Albany *26,678* **C3**
Aloha *10,000* **h12**
Altamont *19,805* **E5**
Ashland *14,943* **E4**
Astoria *9,998* **A3**
Baker *9,471* **C9**
Beaverton *30,582* **B4**
Bend *17,263* **C5**
Burns *3,579* **D7**
Canby *7,659* **B4**
Central Point *6,357* **E4**
Coos Bay *14,424* **D2**
Coquille *4,481* **D2**
Corvallis *40,960* **C3**
Cottage Grove *7,148* **D3**
Crater Lake *25* **E4**
Dallas *8,530* **C3**
Eugene *105,624* **C3**
Florence *4,411* **D2**
Forest Grove *11,499* **B3**
Gladstone *9,500* **B4**
Grants Pass *15,032* **E3**
Gresham *33,005* **B4**
Hermiston *9,408* **B7**
Hillsboro *27,664* **B4**
Hood River *4,329* **B5**
Independence *4,024* **C3**
John Day *2,012* **C8**
Keizer *18,592* **C3**
Klamath Falls *16,661* **E5**
La Grande *11,354* **B8**
Lake Oswego *22,527* **B4**
Lakeview *2,770* **E6**
Lebanon *10,413* **C4**
Lincoln City *5,469* **C3**
McMinnville *14,080* **B3**
Medford *39,603* **E4**
Metzger *5,544* **h12**
Milton-Freewater *5,086* **B8**
Milwaukie *17,931* **B4**
Monmouth *5,594* **C3**
Myrtle Creek *3,365* **D2**
Newberg *10,394* **B4**
Newport *7,519* **C2**
North Bend *9,779* **D2**
Oak Grove *11,640* **B4**
Ontario *8,814* **C10**
Oregon City *14,673* **B4**
Parkrose *21,103* **B4**
Pendleton *14,521* **B8**
Portland *366,383* **B4**
Prineville *5,276* **C6**
Redmond *6,452* **C5**
Reedsport *4,984* **D2**
River Road *10,370* **C3**
Roseburg *16,644* **D3**
St. Helens *7,064* **B4**
Salem *89,233* **C4**
Scappoose *3,213* **B4**
Seaside *5,193* **B3**
Silverton *5,168* **C4**
Springfield *41,621* **C4**
Stayton *4,396* **C4**
Sutherlin *4,560* **D3**
Sweet Home *6,921* **C4**
The Dalles *10,820* **B5**
Tigard *14,286* **h12**
Tillamook *3,981* **B3**
Tri City *3,439* **E3**
Umatilla *3,199* **B7**
West Linn *12,956* **B4**
West Slope *5,364* **g12**
White City *5,445* **E4**
Woodburn *11,196* **B4**

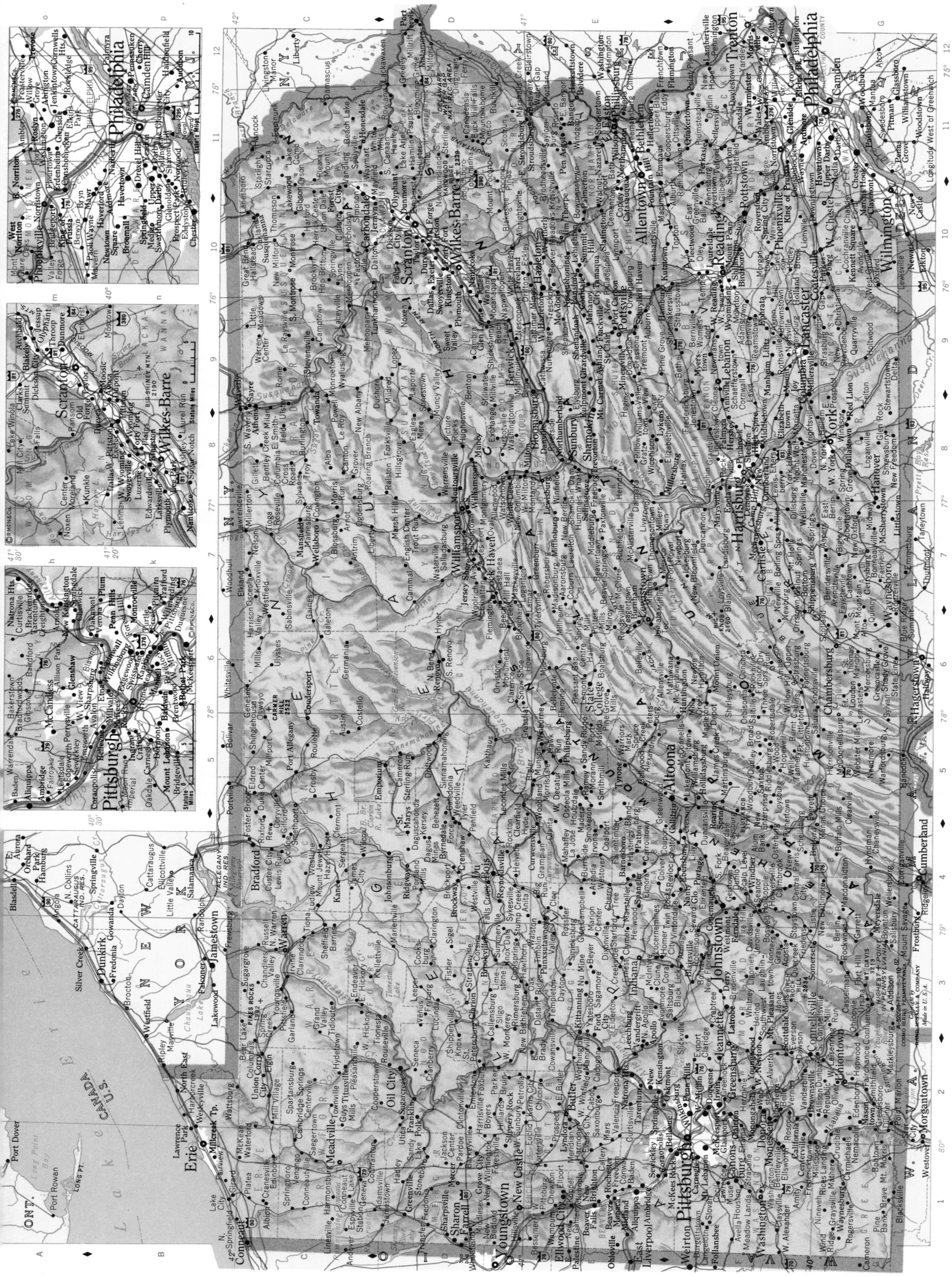

Statute Miles 5 0 5 10 20 30

Kilometers 5 0 5 15 25 35 45

Lambert Conformal Conic Projection

SCALE 1:1,593,000 1 Inch = 25 Statute Miles

Cities and Towns

Aliquippa *17,094* **E1**
Allentown *103,758* **E11**
Altoona *57,078* **E5**
Beaver Falls *12,525* **E1**
Berwick *11,850* **D9**
Bethel Park *34,755* **k14**
Bethlehem *70,419* **E11**
Bloomsburg *11,717* **E9**
Bradford *11,211* **C4**
Broomall *23,642* **p20**
Butler *17,026* **E2**
Carbondale *11,255* **C10**
Carlisle *18,314* **F7**
Chambersburg *16,174* **G6**
Chester *45,794* **G11**
Coatesville *10,698* **G10**
Connellsville *10,319* **F2**
Du Bois *9,290* **D4**
Easton *26,027* **E11**
Ephrata *11,095* **F9**
Erie *119,123* **B1**
Gettysburg *7,194* **G7**
Greensburg *17,558* **F2**
Hanover *14,890* **G8**
Harrisburg *53,264* **F8**
Havertown *36,000* **G11**
Hazleton *27,318* **E10**
Hershey *9,000* **F8**
Indiana *16,051* **E3**
Jeannette *13,106* **F2**
Johnstown *35,496* **F4**
King of Prussia *18,200* **F11**
Lancaster *54,725* **F9**
Lansdale *16,526* **F11**
Latrobe *10,799* **F3**
Lebanon *25,711* **F9**
Levittown *78,600* **F12**
Lewistown *9,830* **E6**
Lock Haven *9,617* **D7**
McKeesport *31,012* **F2**
Meadville *15,544* **C1**
Middletown *10,122* **F8**
Millcreek Township *44,303* **B1**
Monroeville *30,977* **k14**
Mount Lebanon *34,414* **F1**
New Castle *33,621* **D1**
Norristown *34,684* **F11**
Oil City *13,881* **D2**
Penn Hills *57,632* **F2**
Philadelphia *1,688,210* **G11**
Pittsburgh *423,959* **F1**
Plum *25,390* **k14**
Pottstown *22,729* **F10**
Pottsville *18,195* **E9**
Punxsutawney *7,479* **E4**
Reading *78,686* **F10**
Scranton *88,117* **D10**
Shamokin *10,357* **E8**
Sharon *19,057* **D1**
Springfield *25,326* **p20**
State College *36,130* **E6**
Sunbury *12,292* **E8**
Uniontown *14,510* **G2**
Upper Darby *50,200* **G11**
Warminster *35,543* **F11**
Warren *12,146* **C3**
Washington *18,363* **F1**
Waynesboro *9,726* **G6**
West Chester *17,435* **G10**
West Mifflin *26,552* **F2**
Wilkes-Barre *51,551* **D10**
Wilkinsburg *23,669* **F2**
Williamsport *33,401* **D7**
Willow Grove *21,300* **F11**
York *44,619* **G8**

RHODE ISLAND

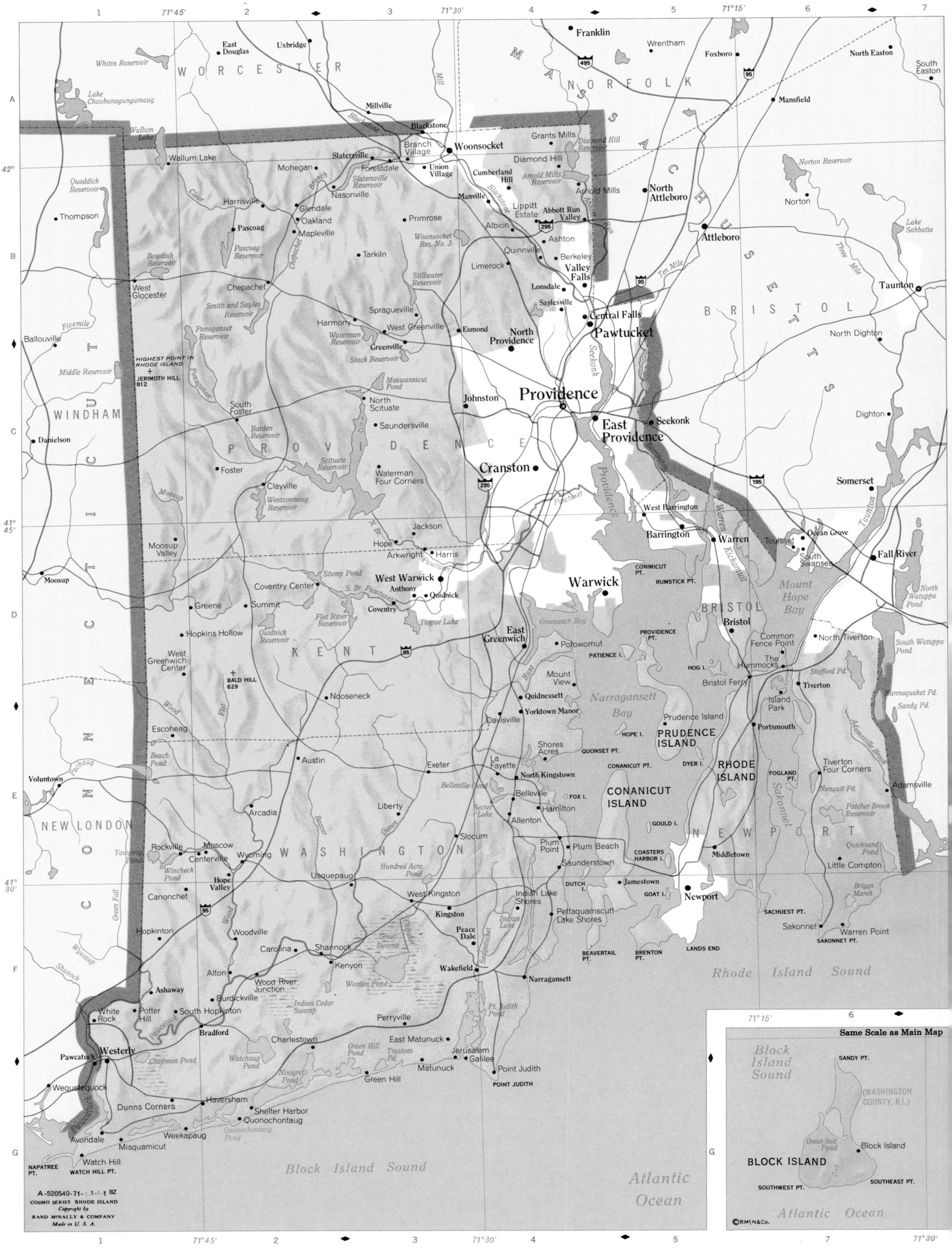

Statute Miles 1 0 1 2 3 4 5 6 7 8 9 10

Kilometers 1 0 1 2 3 4 5 6 7 8 9 10 11 12 13 14 15

Lambert Conformal Conic Projection
SCALE 1:304,000 1 Inch = 4.9 Statute Miles

Cities and Towns*

Albion *1,200* **B4**
Allenton *600* **E4**
Anthony *4,500* **D3**
Arnold Mills *600* **B4**
Ashaway *1,747* **F1**
Ashton *875* **B4**
Barrington *16,174* **D5**
Berkeley *930* **B4**
Block Island *620* **h7**
Bradford *1,354* **F1**
Bristol *20,128* **D5**
Carolina *500* **F2**
Central Falls *16,995* **B4**
Charlestown *1,200* **F2**
Chepachet *900* **B2**
Coventry *8,000* **D3**
Cranston *71,992* **C4**
Cumberland Hill *5,421* **B4**
Davisville *550* **E4**
Diamond Hill *1,150* **B4**
East Greenwich *10,211* **D4**
East Providence *50,980* **C4**
Esmond *3,500* **B4**
Forestdale *450* **B3**
Glendale *600* **B2**
Greenville *7,576* **C3**
Harmony *800* **B3**
Harris *1,000* **D3**
Harrisville *1,224* **B2**
Hope *490* **D3**
Hope Valley *1,414* **E2**
Island Park *1,000* **E6**
Jamestown *4,040* **F5**
Johnston *24,907* **C4**
Kingston *5,419* **F3**
La Fayette *680* **E4**
Little Compton *300* **E6**
Lonsdale *4,100* **B4**
Manville *3,100* **B4**
Mapleville *900* **B2**
Middletown *3,350* **E5**
Mount View *560* **D4**
Narragansett *3,342* **F4**
Newport *29,259* **F5**
North Kingstown *3,100* **E4**
North Providence *29,188* **C4**
North Scituate *325* **C3**
Oakland *500* **B2**
Pascoag *3,807* **B2**
Pawtucket *71,204* **C4**
Peace Dale *3,100* **F3**
Portsmouth *4,300* **E6**
Providence *156,804* **C4**
Quidnessett *3,300* **D4**
Quidnick *2,300* **D3**
Saylesville *3,200* **B4**
Shannock *600* **D2**
Slatersville *2,000* **A3**
South Hopkinton *500* **F1**
Spragueville *430* **B3**
Tiverton *7,653* **D6**
Union Village *2,400* **B3**
Valley Falls *10,892* **B4**
Wakefield *3,400* **F3**
Warren *10,640* **D5**
Warwick *87,123* **D4**
Watch Hill *500* **G1**
West Barrington *3,700* **C5**
Westerly *14,093* **F1**
West Kingston *700* **F3**
West Warwick *27,026* **D3**
Woonsocket *45,914* **A3**
Wyoming *600* **E2**
Yorktown Manor *2,500* **E4**

*Populations are for localities, not incorporated towns.

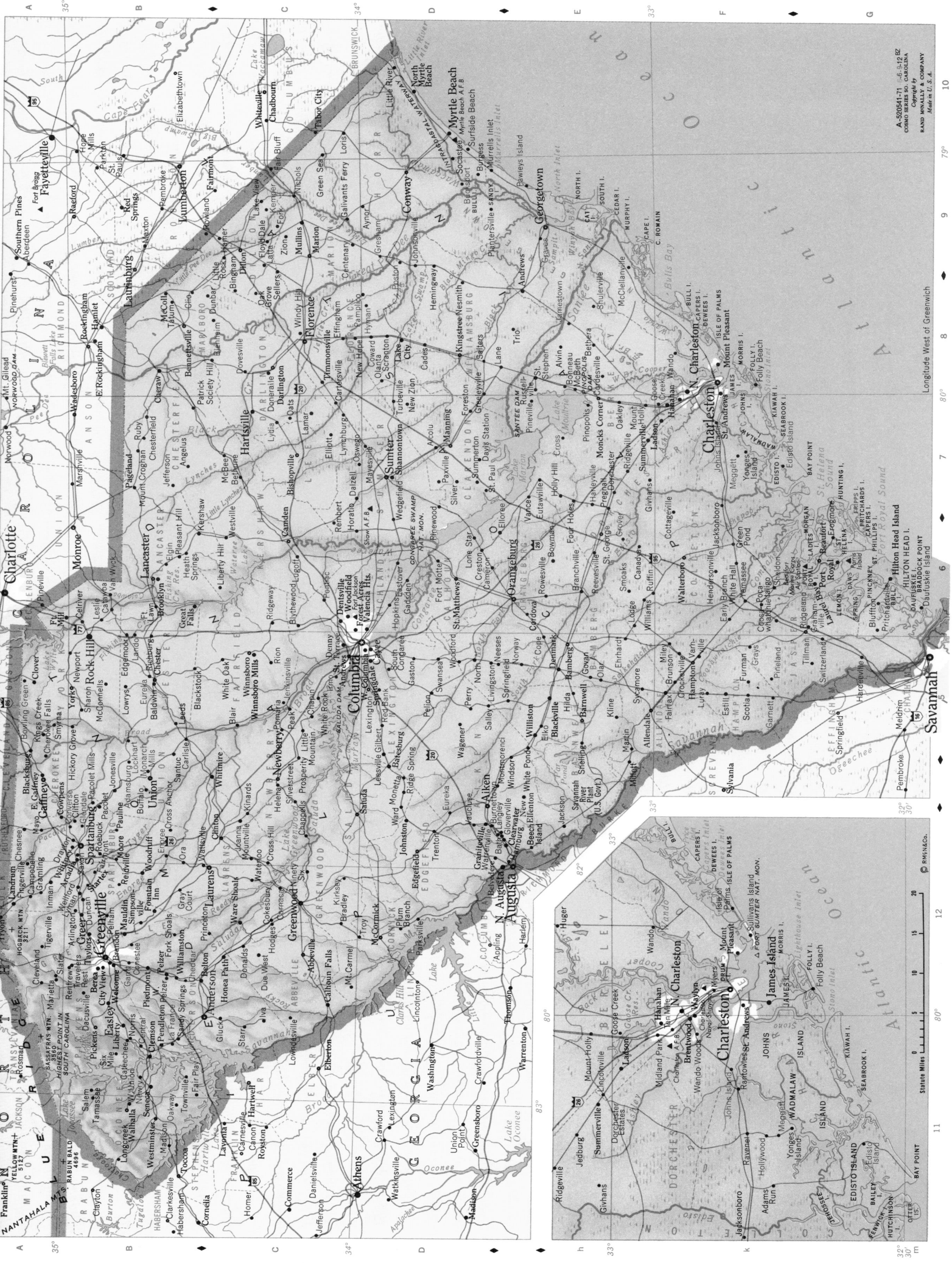

Statute Miles 5 0 5 10 20 30
Kilometers 5 0 5 15 25 35 45

Lambert Conformal Conic Projection
SCALE 1:1,566,000 1 Inch = 25 Statute Miles

Cities and Towns

Abbeville *5,833* **C3**
Aiken *14,978* **D4**
Allendale *4,400* **E5**
Anderson *27,965* **B2**
Barnwell *5,572* **E5**
Batesburg *4,023* **D4**
Beaufort *8,634* **G6**
Belton *5,312* **B3**
Belvedere *6,859* **D4**
Bennettsville *8,774* **B8**
Berea *7,500* **B3**
Bishopville *3,429* **C7**
Camden *7,462* **C6**
Cayce *11,701* **D5**
Charleston *69,510* **F8**
Cheraw *5,654* **B8**
Chester *6,820* **B5**
Clemson *8,118* **B2**
Clinton *8,596* **C4**
Columbia *100,385* **C5**
Conway *10,240* **D9**
Cowpens *2,023* **A4**
Darlington *7,989* **C8**
Denmark *4,434* **E5**
Dillon *7,060* **C9**
Easley *14,264* **B2**
Florence *29,176* **C8**
Fort Mill *4,162* **A6**
Fountain Inn *4,226* **B3**
Gaffney *13,453* **A4**
Georgetown *10,144* **E9**
Goose Creek *17,811* **F7**
Greenville *58,242* **B3**
Greenwood *21,613* **C3**
Greer *10,525* **B3**
Hanahan *13,224* **F7**
Hartsville *7,631* **C7**
Hilton Head Island *11,344* **G6**
Honea Path *4,114* **C3**
James Island *24,124* **k12**
Kingstree *4,147* **D8**
Ladson *13,246* **F7**
Lake City *6,731* **D8**
Lancaster *9,703* **B6**
Laurel Bay *5,238* **G6**
Laurens *10,587* **C3**
Manning *4,746* **D7**
Marion *7,700* **C9**
Mauldin *8,143* **B3**
Moncks Corner *3,699* **E7**
Mount Pleasant *14,209* **F8**
Mullins *6,068* **C9**
Myrtle Beach *18,446* **D10**
Newberry *9,866* **C4**
North Augusta *13,593* **D4**
North Charleston *62,534* **F8**
North Myrtle Beach *3,960* **D10**
Orangeburg *14,933* **E6**
Rock Hill *35,344* **B5**
St. Andrews *9,908* **F7**
St. Andrews *20,245* **C5**
Seneca *7,436* **B2**
Shannontown *7,900* **D7**
Simpsonville *9,037* **B3**
Spartanburg *43,826* **B4**
Summerville *6,706* **E7**
Sumter *24,890* **D7**
Taylors *12,100* **B3**
Union *10,523* **B4**
Walhalla *3,977* **B1**
West Columbia *10,409* **D5**
Williamston *4,310* **B3**
Woodruff *5,171* **B3**
York *6,412* **B5**

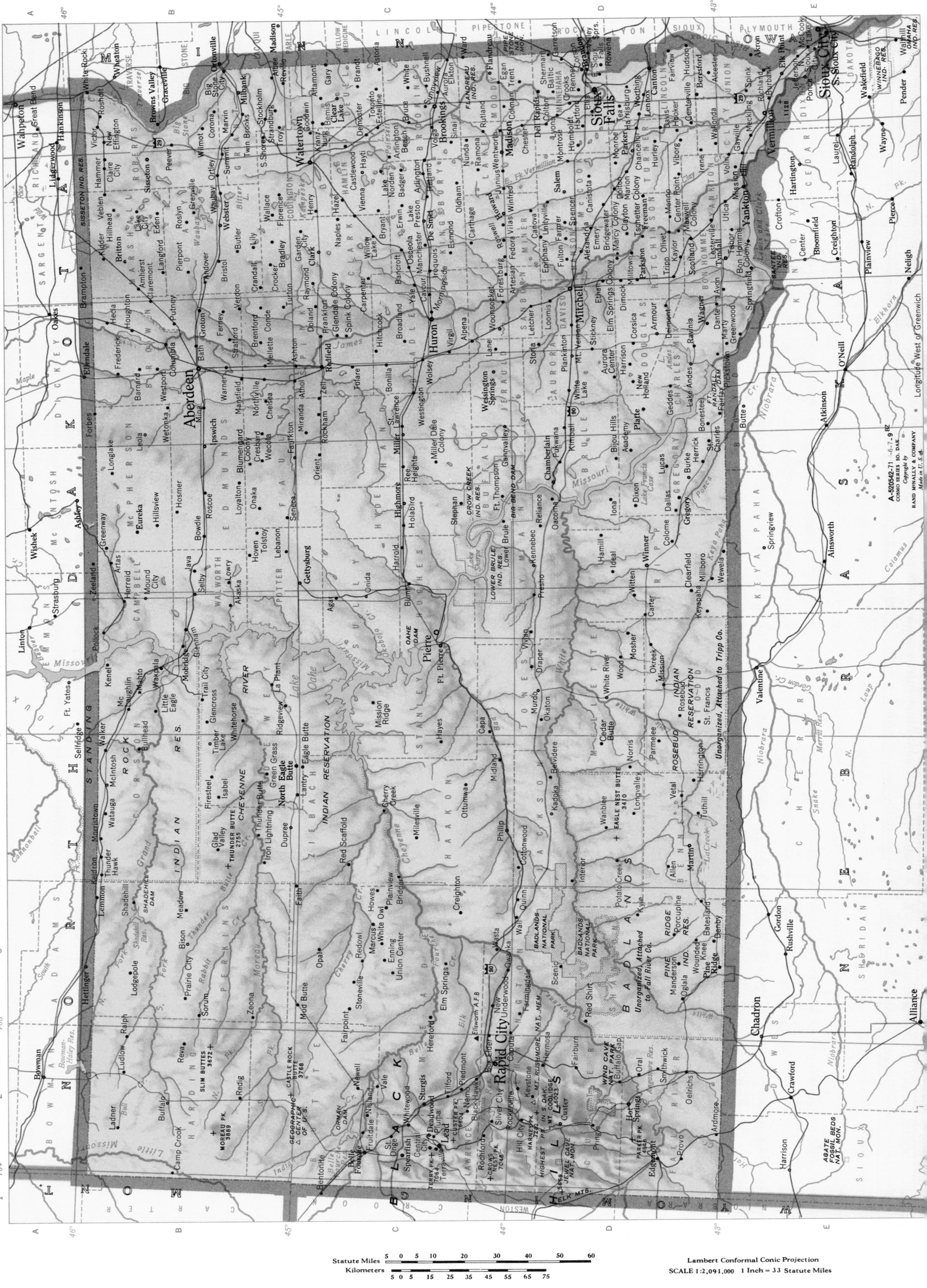

Cities and Towns

Aberdeen *25,851* **B7**
Alcester *885* **D9**
Arlington *991* **C8**
Armour *819* **D7**
Belle Fourche *4,692* **C2**
Beresford *1,865* **D9**
Black Hawk *1,608* **C2**
Box Elder *3,186* **C2**
Brandon *2,589* **D9**
Britton *1,590* **B8**
Brookings *14,951* **C9**
Burke *859* **D6**
Canton *2,886* **D9**
Centerville *892* **D9**
Chamberlain *2,258* **D6**
Clark *1,351* **C8**
Clear Lake *1,310* **C9**
Custer *1,830* **D2**
Deadwood *2,035* **C2**
De Smet *1,237* **C8**
Edgemont *1,468* **D2**
Elk Point *1,661* **E9**
Eureka *1,360* **B6**
Faulkton *981* **B6**
Flandreau *2,114* **C9**
Fort Pierre *1,789* **C5**
Freeman *1,462* **D8**
Garretson *963* **D9**
Gettysburg *1,623* **C6**
Gregory *1,503* **D6**
Groton *1,230* **B7**
Hartford *1,207* **D9**
Highmore *1,055* **C6**
Hot Springs *4,742* **D2**
Howard *1,169* **C8**
Huron *13,000* **C7**
Ipswich *1,153* **B6**
Lake Andes *1,029* **D7**
Lead *4,330* **C2**
Lemmon *1,871* **B3**
Lennox *1,827* **D9**
Martin *1,018* **D4**
Milbank *4,120* **B9**
Miller *1,931* **C7**
Mitchell *13,916* **D7**
Mobridge *4,174* **B5**
North Eagle Butte *1,354* **B4**
North Sioux City *1,992* **E9**
Parker *999* **D8**
Parkston *1,545* **D8**
Philip *1,088* **C4**
Pierre *11,973* **C5**
Pine Ridge *3,059* **D3**
Platte *1,334* **D7**
Rapid City *46,492* **C2**
Redfield *3,027* **C7**
Salem *1,486* **D8**
Scotland *1,022* **D8**
Selby *884* **B5**
Sioux Falls *81,343* **D9**
Sisseton *2,789* **B8**
Spearfish *5,251* **C2**
Springfield *1,377* **E8**
Sturgis *5,184* **C2**
Tyndall *1,253* **E8**
Vermillion *10,136* **E9**
Volga *1,221* **C9**
Wagner *1,453* **D7**
Wall *770* **D3**
Watertown *15,649* **C8**
Webster *2,417* **B8**
Wessington Springs *1,203* **C7**
Winner *3,472* **D6**
Yankton *12,011* **E8**

Statute Miles 5 0 5 10 20 30 40 50 60
Kilometers 5 0 5 15 25 35 45 55 65 75

Lambert Conformal Conic Projection
SCALE 1:2,091,000 1 Inch = 33 Statute Miles

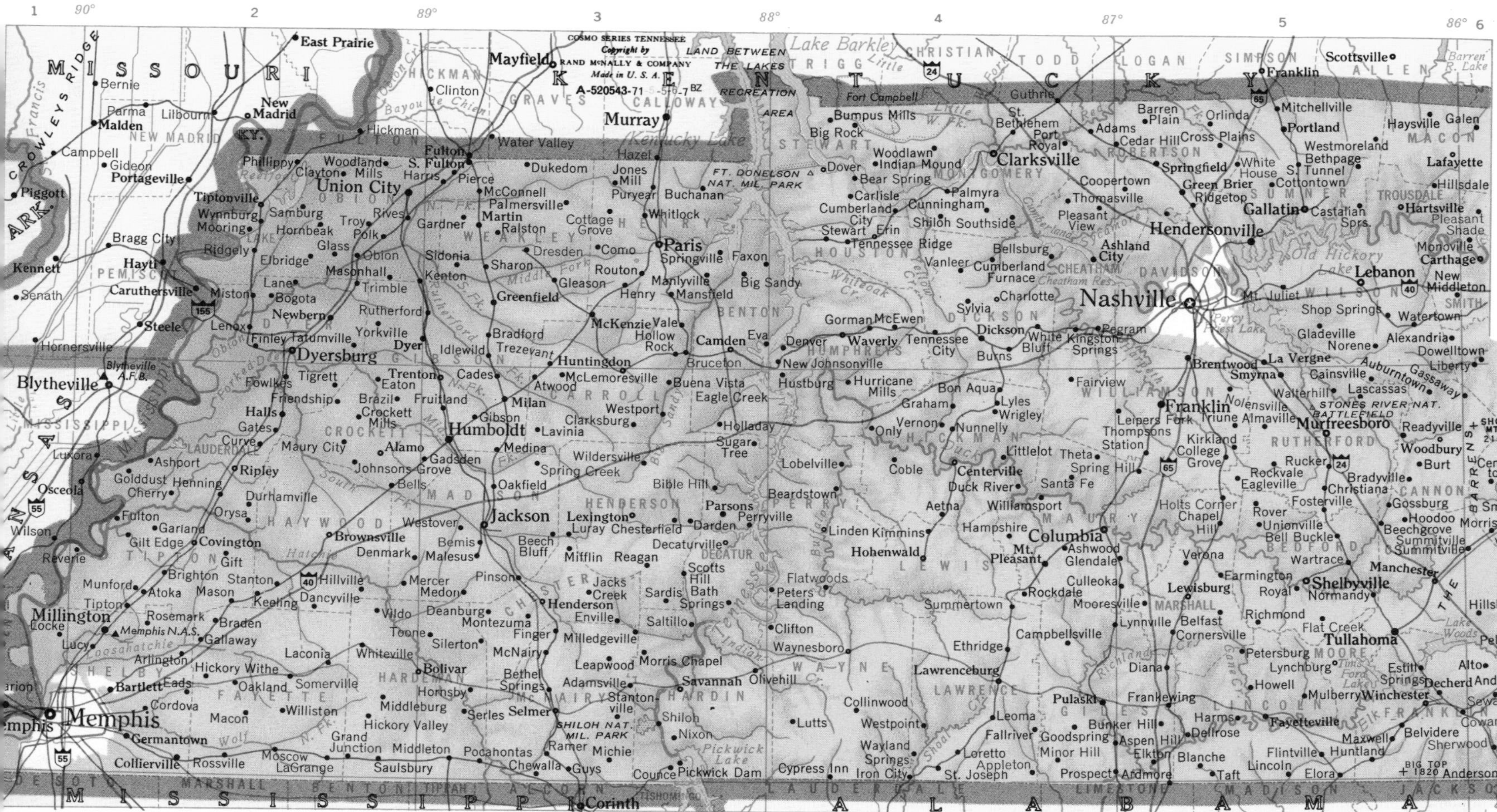

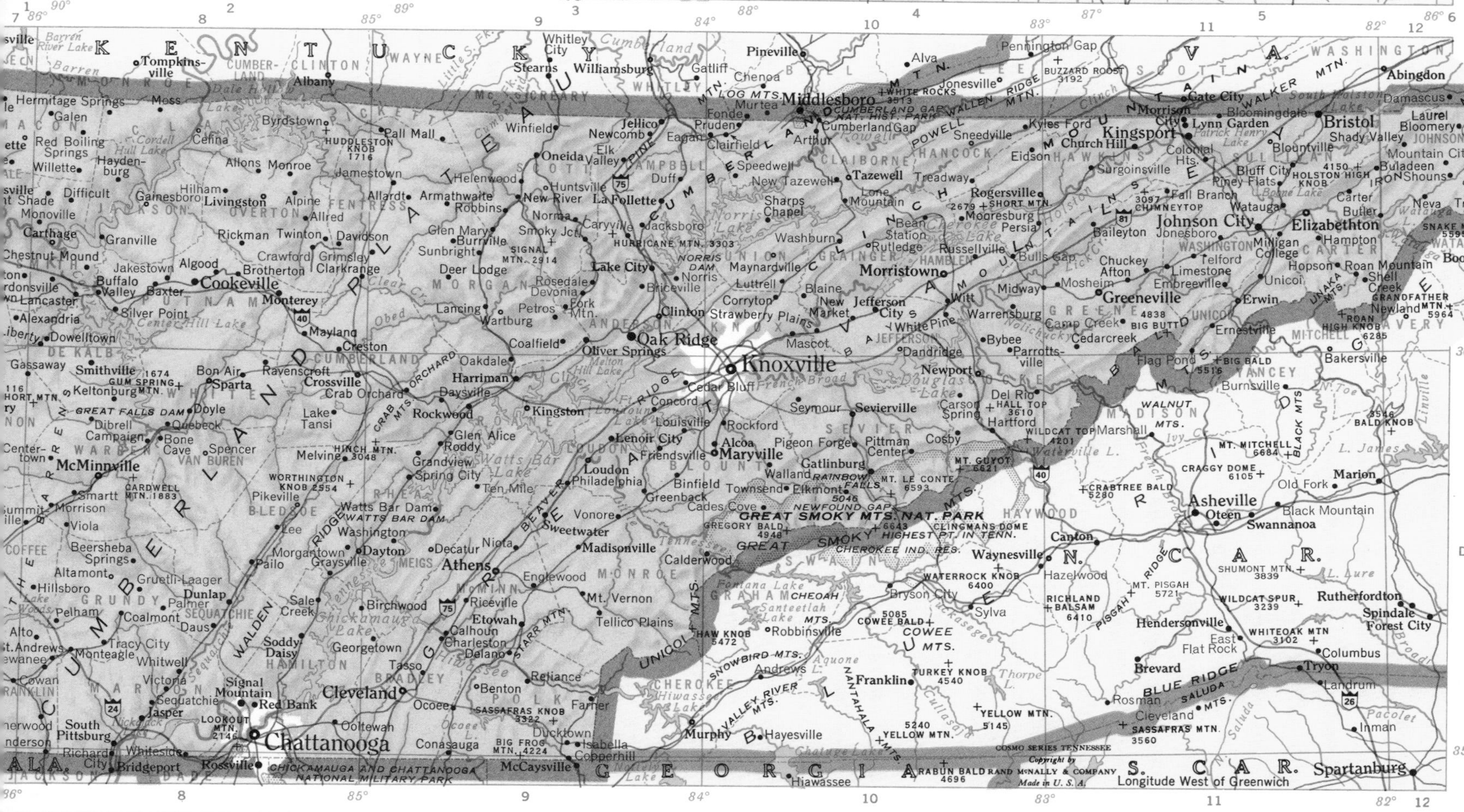

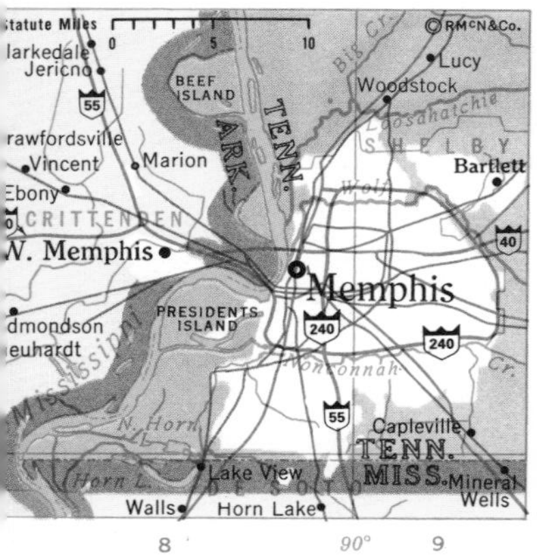

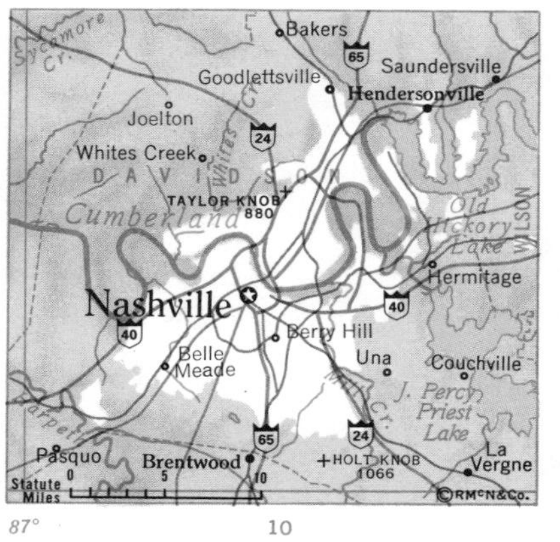

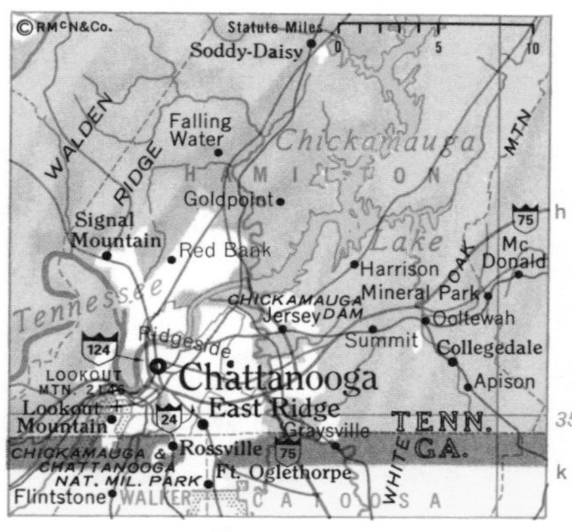

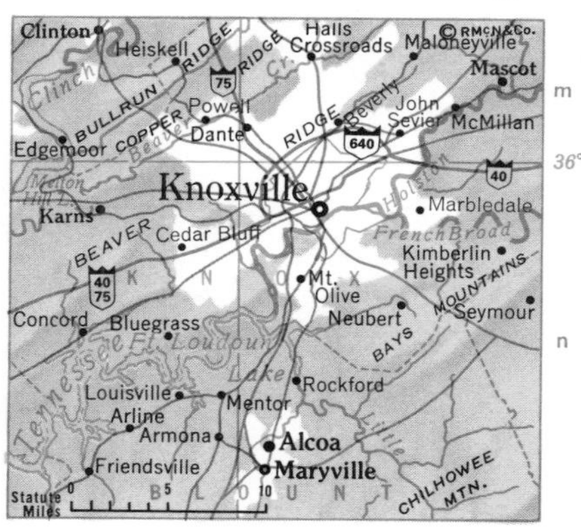

Statute Miles 5 0 5 10 20 30 40
Kilometers 5 0 5 15 25 35 45 55

Lambert Conformal Conic Projection
SCALE 1:1,713,000 1 Inch = 27 Statute Miles

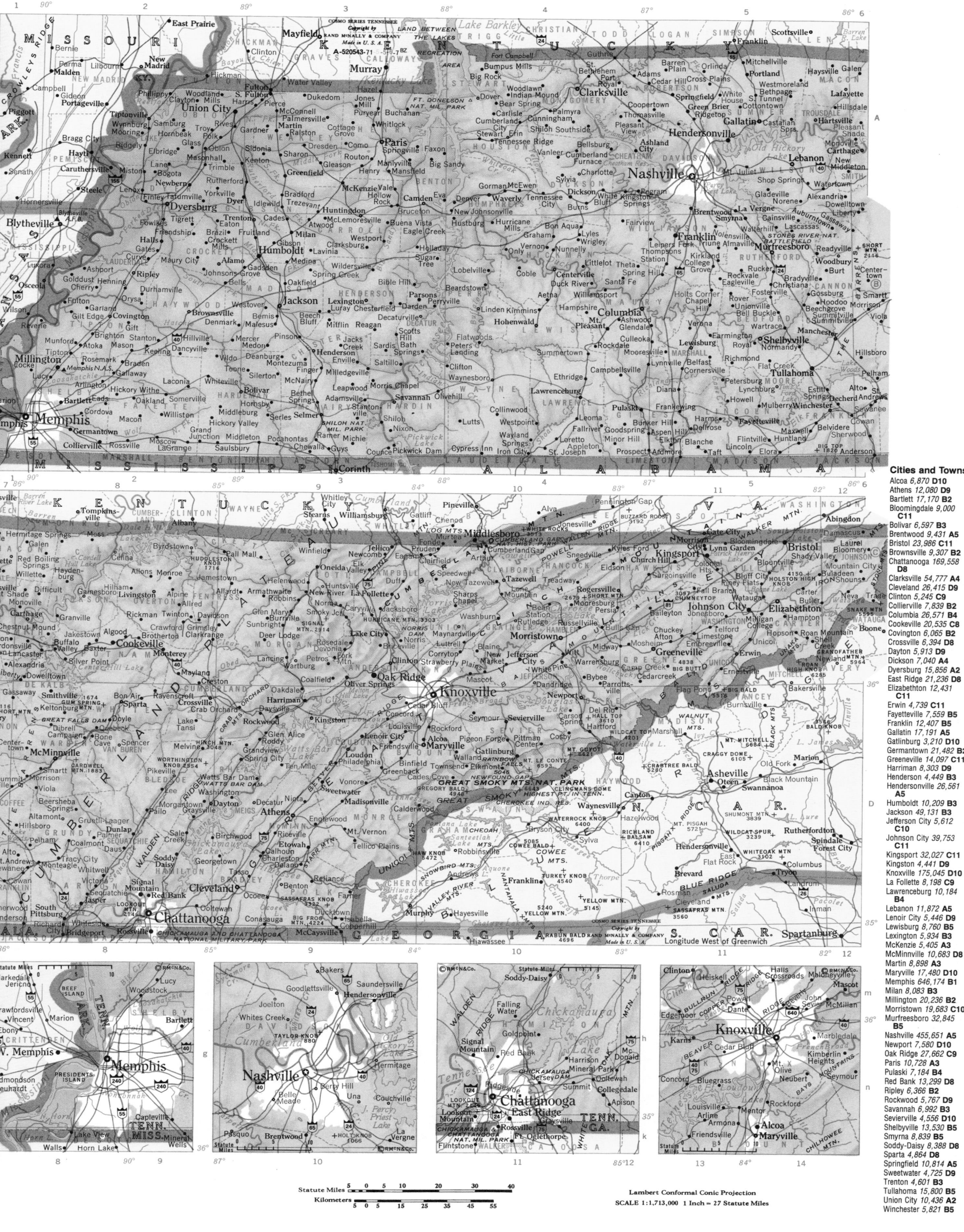

Cities and Towns

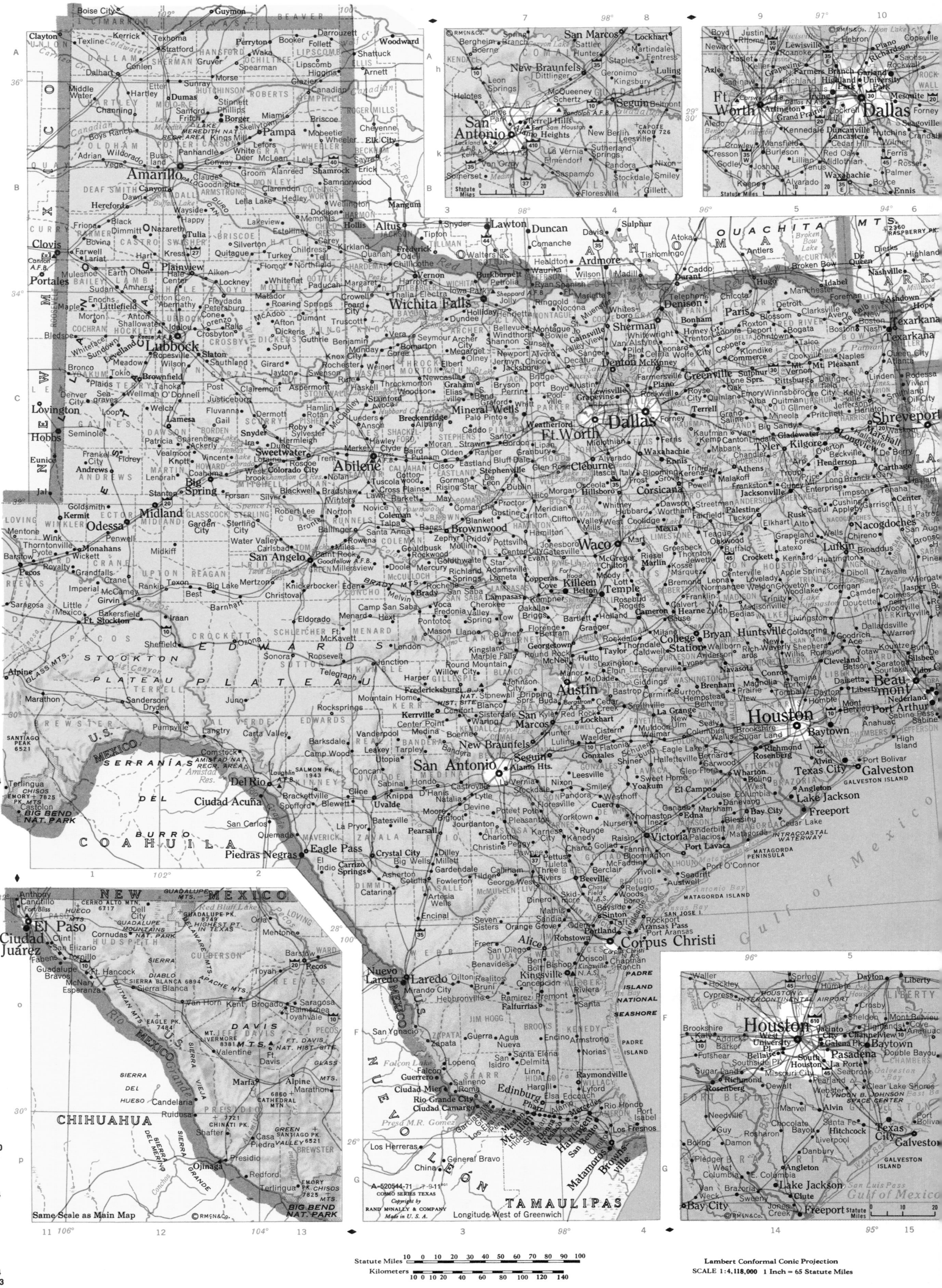

Cities and Towns

Abilene 98,315 C3
Alice 20,961 F3
Amarillo 149,230 B2
Arlington 160,113 n9
Austin 345,496 D4
Bay City 17,837 E5
Baytown 56,923 E5
Beaumont 118,102 D5
Beeville 14,574 E4
Big Spring 24,804 C2
Borger 15,837 B2
Brownsville 84,997 G4
Brownwood 19,396 D3
Bryan 44,337 D4
Cleburne 19,218 C4
College Station 37,272 D4
Conroe 18,034 D5
Copperas Cove 19,469 D4
Corpus Christi 231,999 F4
Corsicana 21,712 C4
Dallas 904,078 C4
Del Rio 30,034 E2
Denison 23,884 C4
Denton 48,063 C4
Eagle Pass 21,407 E2
Edinburg 24,075 F3
El Paso 425,259 o11
Fort Worth 385,164 C4
Galveston 61,902 E5
Garland 138,857 n10
Grand Prairie 71,462 n10
Greenville 22,161 C4
Harlingen 43,543 F4
Hereford 15,853 B1
Houston 1,595,138 E5
Huntsville 23,936 D5
Irving 109,943 n10
Kerrville 15,276 D3
Killeen 46,296 D4
Kingsville 28,808 F4
Lake Jackson 19,102 E5
Laredo 91,449 F3
Longview 62,762 C5
Lubbock 173,979 C2
Lufkin 28,562 D5
McAllen 66,281 F3
Marshall 24,921 C5
Mesquite 67,053 n10
Midland 70,525 D1
Mineral Wells 14,468 C3
Nacogdoches 27,149 D5
New Braunfels 22,402 E3
Odessa 90,027 D1
Orange 23,628 D6
Palestine 15,948 D5
Pampa 21,396 B2
Paris 25,498 C5
Pasadena 112,560 r14
Pecos 12,855 D1
Plainview 22,187 B2
Port Arthur 61,251 E6
Richardson 72,496 n10
San Angelo 73,240 D2
San Antonio 786,023 E3
San Benito 17,988 F4
San Marcos 23,420 E4
Sherman 30,413 C4
Temple 42,354 D4
Texarkana 31,271 C5
Texas City 41,403 E5
Uvalde 14,178 E3
Victoria 50,695 E4
Waco 101,261 D4
Waxahachie 14,264 C4
Wichita Falls 94,201 C3

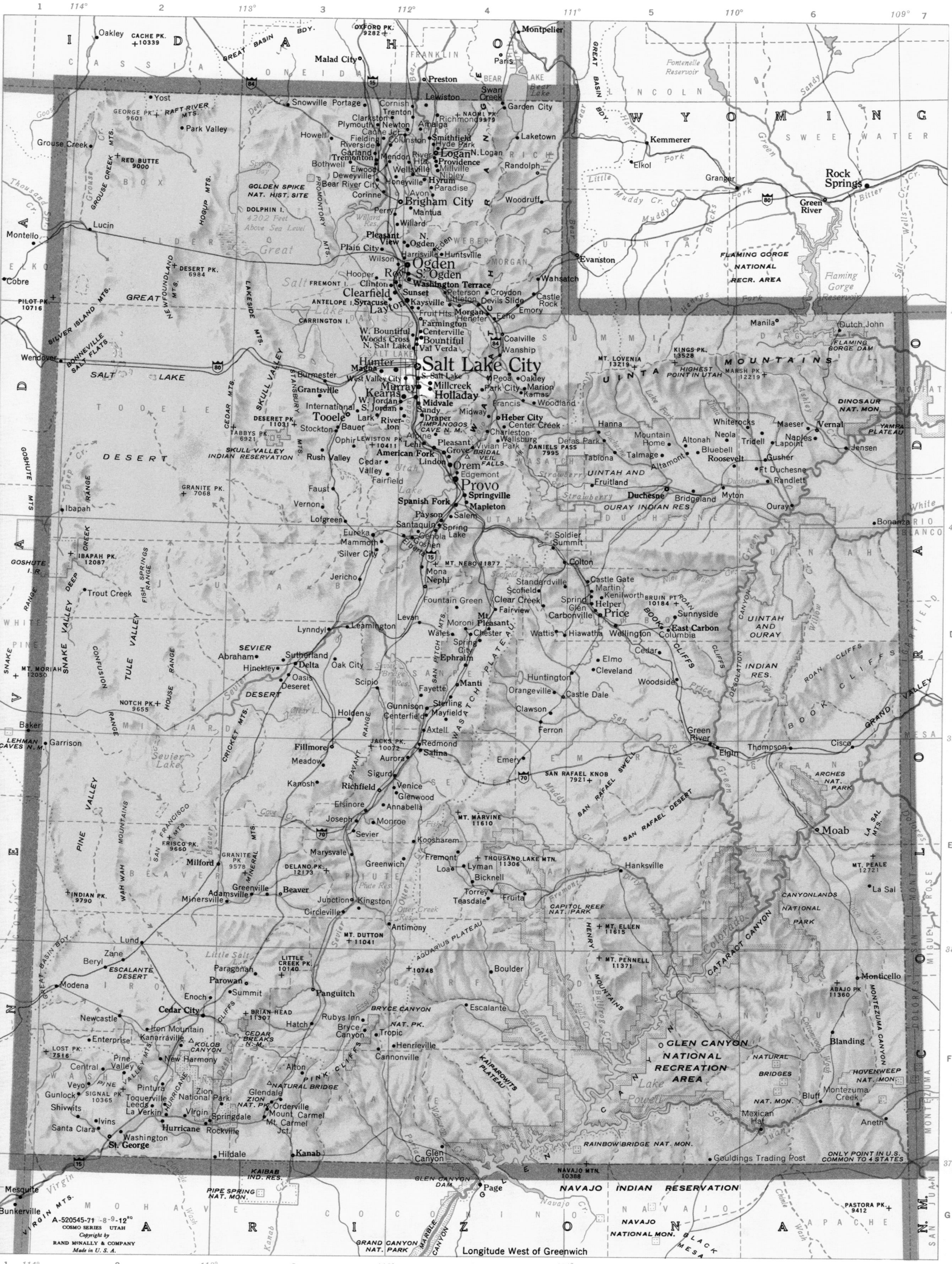

Statute Miles 5 0 5 10 20 30 40 50 60
Kilometers 5 0 5 20 30 40 50 60 70 80

Lambert Conformal Conic Projection
SCALE 1:2,100,000 1 Inch = 33 Statute Miles

Cities and Towns

American Fork *12,693* **C4**
Beaver *1,792* **E3**
Blanding *3,118* **F6**
Bountiful *32,877* **C4**
Brigham City *15,596* **B3**
Cedar City *10,972* **F2**
Centerville *8,069* **C4**
Clearfield *17,982* **B3**
Clinton *5,777* **B3**
Delta *1,930* **D3**
Draper *5,521* **C4**
Ephraim *2,810* **D4**
Farmington *4,691* **C4**
Fillmore *2,083* **E3**
Fruit Heights *2,728* **B4**
Grantsville *4,419* **C3**
Heber City *4,362* **C4**
Helper *2,724* **D5**
Holladay *28,700* **C4**
Huntington *2,316* **D5**
Hurricane *2,361* **F2**
Hyrum *3,952* **B4**
Kanab *2,148* **F3**
Kaysville *9,811* **B4**
Kearns *17,000* **C4**
Layton *26,393* **B4**
Lehi *6,848* **C4**
Logan *26,844* **B4**
Magna *8,600* **C3**
Manti *2,080* **D4**
Midvale *10,146* **C4**
Moab *5,333* **E6**
Monticello *1,929* **F6**
Mount Pleasant *2,049* **D4**
Murray *25,750* **C4**
Nephi *3,285* **D4**
North Ogden *9,309* **B4**
North Salt Lake *5,548* **C4**
Ogden *64,407* **B4**
Orem *52,399* **C4**
Panguitch *1,343* **F3**
Payson *8,246* **C4**
Pleasant Grove *10,833* **C4**
Price *9,086* **D5**
Providence *2,675* **B4**
Provo *74,108* **C4**
Richfield *5,482* **E3**
Riverton *7,293* **C4**
Roosevelt *3,842* **C5**
Roy *19,694* **B3**
St. George *11,350* **F2**
Salem *2,233* **C4**
Salina *1,992* **E4**
Salt Lake City *163,697* **C4**
Sandy *52,210* **C4**
Santaquin *2,175* **D4**
Smithfield *4,993* **B4**
South Jordan *7,492* **C3**
South Ogden *11,366* **B4**
Spanish Fork *9,825* **C4**
Springville *12,101* **C4**
Sunset *5,733* **B3**
Syracuse *3,702* **B3**
Tooele *14,335* **C3**
Tremonton *3,464* **B3**
Val Verda *6,500* **C4**
Vernal *6,600* **C6**
Washington *3,092* **F2**
Washington Terrace *8,212* **B4**
Wendover *1,099* **C1**
West Bountiful *3,556* **C4**
West Jordan *27,192* **C4**
West Valley City *72,511* **C4**
Woods Cross *4,263* **C4**

Cities and Towns*

Arlington *800* **E2**
Barre *9,824* **C4**
Barton *1,062* **B4**
Bellows Falls *3,456* **E4**
Bennington *8,600* **F2**
Bethel *900* **D3**
Bradford *831* **D4**
Brandon *1,720* **D2**
Brattleboro *11,886* **F3**
Bristol *1,793* **C2**
Burlington *37,712* **C2**
Castleton *600* **D2**
Derby *598* **B4**
Dorset *550* **E2**
East Arlington *600* **E2**
East Barre *900* **C4**
East Middlebury *550* **D2**
East Montpelier *600* **C4**
Enosburg Falls *1,207* **B3**
Essex *800* **B2**
Essex Junction *7,033* **C2**
Fair Haven *2,819* **D2**
Gilman *550* **C5**
Graniteville *600* **C4**
Hardwick *1,476* **B4**
Hartford *600* **D4**
Jericho *1,340* **B3**
Johnson *1,393* **B3**
Ludlow *1,352* **E3**
Lyndonville *1,401* **B4**
Manchester *563* **E2**
Manchester Center *1,060* **E2**
Middlebury *4,000* **C2**
Milton *1,411* **B2**
Montpelier *8,241* **C3**
Morrisville *2,074* **B3**
Newport *4,756* **B4**
North Bennington *1,635* **F2**
Northfield *2,033* **C3**
Northfield Falls *600* **C3**
North Springfield *750* **E3**
North Troy *717* **B4**
Norwich *1,000* **D4**
Orleans *983* **B4**
Pittsford *666* **D2**
Plainfield *599* **C4**
Poultney *1,554* **D2**
Proctor *1,998* **D2**
Putney *1,100* **F3**
Randolph *2,217* **D3**
Richford *1,471* **B3**
Richmond *865* **C3**
Rutland *18,436* **D3**
St. Albans *7,308* **B2**
St. Johnsbury *6,400* **C4**
Saxtons River *593* **E3**
Shaftsbury *700* **E2**
South Barre *900* **C3**
South Burlington *10,679* **C2**
South Royalton *700* **D3**
Springfield *5,632* **E4**
Stowe *531* **C3**
Swanton *2,520* **B2**
Vergennes *2,273* **C2**
Wallingford *800* **E3**
Waterbury *1,892* **C3**
Websterville *600* **C4**
West Rutland *2,351* **D2**
White River Junction *2,379* **D4**
Wilder *1,328* **D4**
Williamstown *650* **C3**
Wilmington *545* **F3**
Winooski *6,318* **C2**
Woodstock *1,178* **D3**

*Populations are for localities, not incorporated towns.

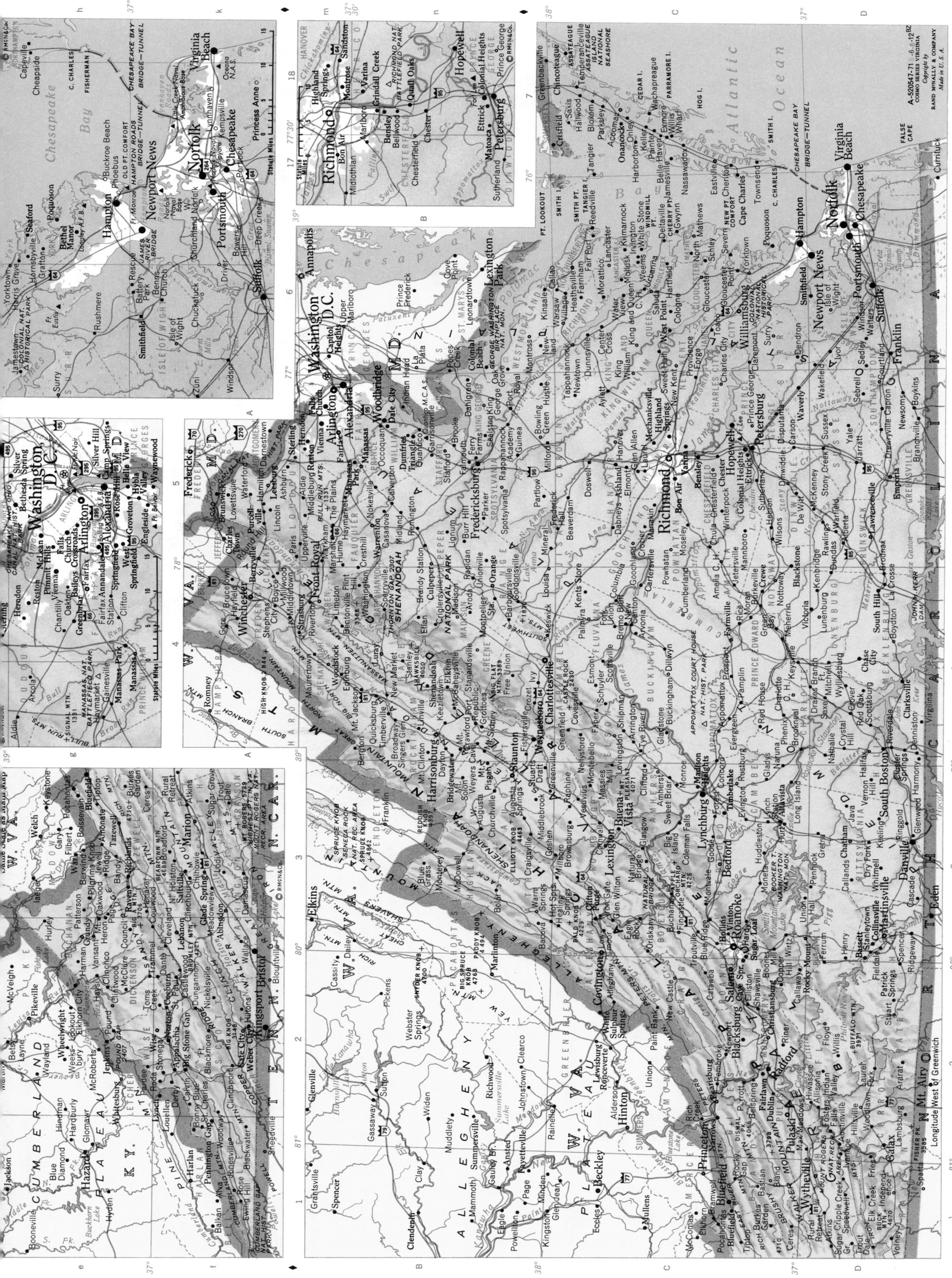

Statute Miles 5 0 5 10 20 30 40
Kilometers 5 0 5 15 25 35 45 55

Lambert Conformal Conic Projection
SCALE 1:1,822,000 1 Inch = 29 Statute Miles

Cities and Towns

Alexandria *103,217* **B5**
Annandale *35,300* **g12**
Appomattox *1,345* **C4**
Arlington *152,700* **B5**
Bedford *5,991* **C3**
Big Stone Gap *4,748* **f9**
Blacksburg *30,638* **C2**
Bluefield *5,946* **C1**
Bon Air *13,000* **C5**
Bristol *19,042* **f9**
Buena Vista *6,717* **C3**
Charlottesville *39,916* **B4**
Chesapeake *114,486* **D6**
Chester *7,000* **C5**
Chincoteague *1,607* **C7**
Christiansburg *10,345* **C2**
Clifton Forge *5,046* **C3**
Collinsville *7,400* **D3**
Colonial Heights *16,509* **C5**
Covington *9,063* **C3**
Culpepper *6,621* **B5**
Dale City *23,000* **B5**
Danville *45,642* **D3**
Emporia *4,840* **D5**
Engleside *21,400* **g12**
Fairfax *19,390* **B5**
Farmville *6,067* **C4**
Franklin *7,308* **D6**
Fredericksburg *15,322* **B5**
Front Royal *11,126* **B4**
Galax *6,524* **D2**
Hampton *122,617* **C6**
Harrisonburg *19,671* **B4**
Herndon *11,449* **B5**
Highland Springs *7,500* **C5**
Hollins *11,000* **C3**
Hopewell *23,397* **C5**
Leesburg *8,357* **A5**
Lexington *7,292* **C3**
Lynchburg *66,743* **C3**
McLean *22,000* **g12**
Manassas *15,438* **B5**
Manassas Park *6,524* **B5**
Marion *7,029* **f10**
Martinsville *18,149* **D3**
Mechanicsville *9,000* **C5**
Newport News *144,903* **D6**
Norfolk *266,979* **D6**
Norton *4,757* **f9**
Petersburg *41,055* **C5**
Poquoson *8,726* **C6**
Portsmouth *104,577* **D6**
Pulaski *10,106* **C2**
Radford *13,225* **C2**
Reston *32,000* **B5**
Richlands *5,796* **e10**
Richmond *219,214* **C5**
Roanoke *100,220* **C3**
Salem *23,958* **C2**
Shenandoah *1,861* **B4**
South Boston *7,093* **D4**
Springfield *12,500* **g12**
Staunton *21,857* **B3**
Sterling *12,000* **A5**
Suffolk *47,621* **D6**
Tazewell *4,468* **e10**
Vienna *15,469* **B5**
Vinton *8,027* **C3**
Virginia Beach *262,199* **D7**
Waynesboro *15,329* **B4**
West Springfield *16,000* **g12**
Williamsburg *9,870* **C6**
Winchester *20,217* **A4**
Woodbridge *35,000* **B5**
Wytheville *7,135* **D1**
Yorktown *390* **C6**

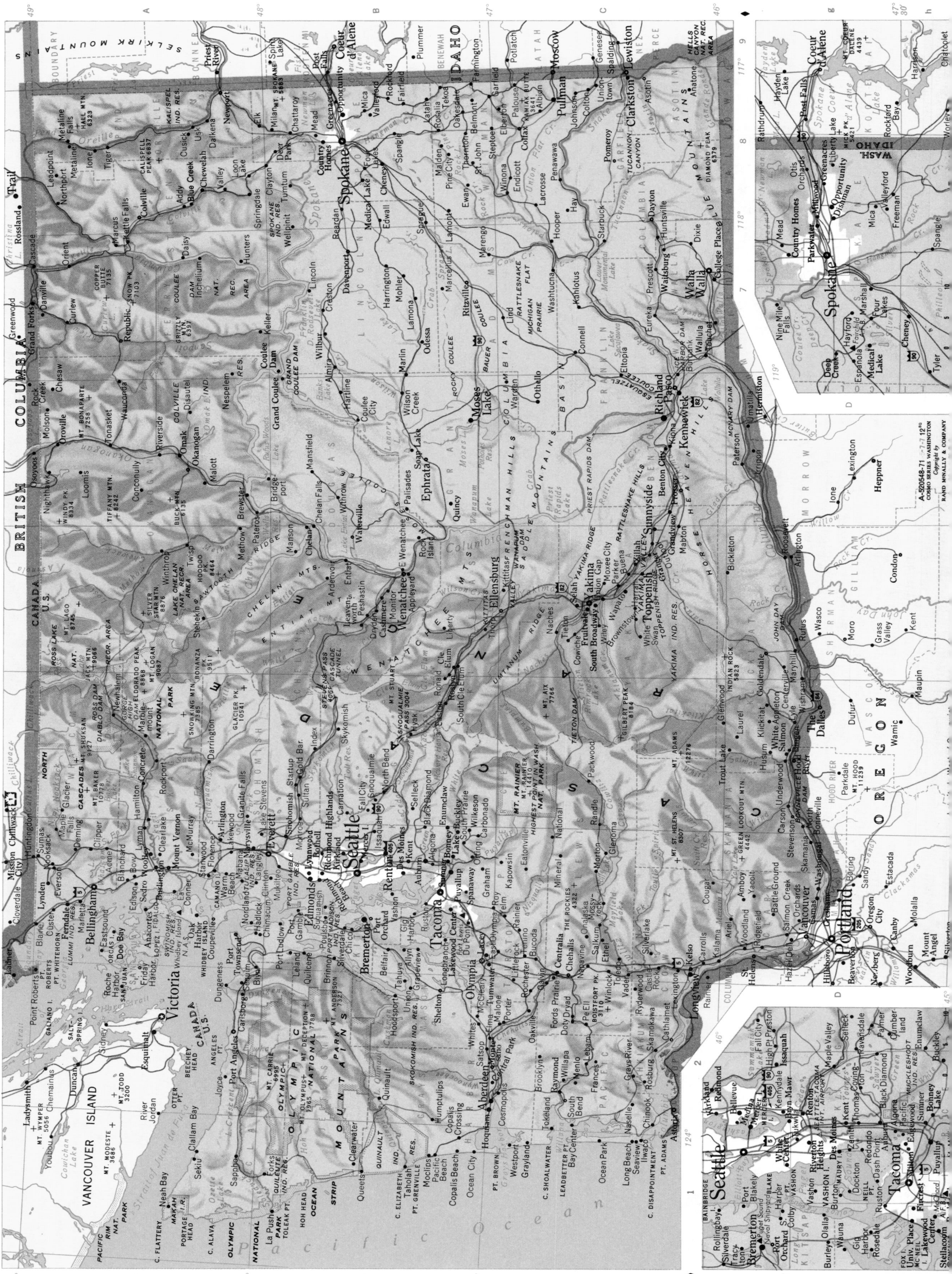
BRITISH COLUMBIA
CANADA
U.S.
IDAHO
OREGON
VANCOUVER ISLAND
Pacific Ocean
Seattle
Spokane
Tacoma
Portland
A-520548-71 -7-7-12
COSMO SERIES WASHINGTON
Copyright by RAND McNALLY & COMPANY

Cities and Towns

Aberdeen 18,739 **C2**
Anacortes 9,013 **A3**
Bellevue 73,903 **e11**
Bellingham 45,794 **A3**
Bonney Lake 5,328 **B3**
Bothell 7,943 **B3**
Bremerton 36,208 **B3**
Camas 5,681 **D3**
Centralia 11,555 **C3**
Chehalis 6,100 **C3**
Chelan 2,802 **B5**
Cheney 7,630 **B8**
Clarkston 6,903 **C8**
Colville 4,510 **A8**
Coulee Dam 1,412 **B7**
Des Moines 7,378 **B3**
Dishman 9,900 **g14**
Edmonds 27,679 **B3**
Ellensburg 11,752 **C5**
Enumclaw 5,427 **B4**
Ephrata 5,359 **B6**
Everett 54,413 **B3**
Ferndale 3,855 **A3**
Forks 3,060 **B1**
Goldendale 3,575 **D5**
Grandview 5,615 **C6**
Hoquiam 9,719 **C2**
Kelso 11,129 **C3**
Kennewick 34,397 **C6**
Kent 23,152 **B3**
Kirkland 18,779 **B3**
Lacey 13,940 **B3**
Lakewood Center 51,300 **B3**
Longview 31,052 **C3**
Lynden 4,022 **A3**
Lynnwood 22,641 **B3**
Medical Lake 3,600 **B8**
Mercer Island 21,522 **B3**
Montesano 3,247 **C2**
Moses Lake 10,629 **B6**
Mount Vernon 13,009 **A3**
Oak Harbor 12,271 **A3**
Okanogan 2,302 **A6**
Olympia 27,447 **B3**
Omak 4,007 **A6**
Opportunity 17,600 **B8**
Othello 4,454 **C6**
Parkland 22,300 **f11**
Pasco 18,425 **C6**
Port Angeles 17,311 **A2**
Port Townsend 6,067 **A3**
Prosser 3,896 **C6**
Pullman 23,579 **C8**
Puyallup 18,251 **B3**
Quincy 3,525 **B6**
Redmond 23,318 **e11**
Renton 30,612 **B3**
Richland 33,578 **C6**
Richmond Highlands 20,300 **B3**
Riverton Heights 33,500 **f11**
Seattle 493,846 **B3**
Sedro Woolley 6,110 **A3**
Shelton 7,629 **B2**
Snohomish 5,294 **B3**
Spokane 171,300 **B8**
Sunnyside 9,225 **C5**
Tacoma 158,501 **B3**
Toppenish 6,517 **C5**
Tumwater 6,705 **B3**
University Place 13,620 **f10**
Vancouver 42,834 **D3**
Walla Walla 25,618 **C7**
Wenatchee 17,257 **B5**
White Center 19,700 **e11**
Yakima 49,826 **C5**

Statute Miles 5 0 5 10 20 30 40 50
Kilometers 5 0 5 15 25 35 45 55 65

Lambert Conformal Conic Projection
SCALE 1:2,091,000 1 Inch = 33 Statute Miles

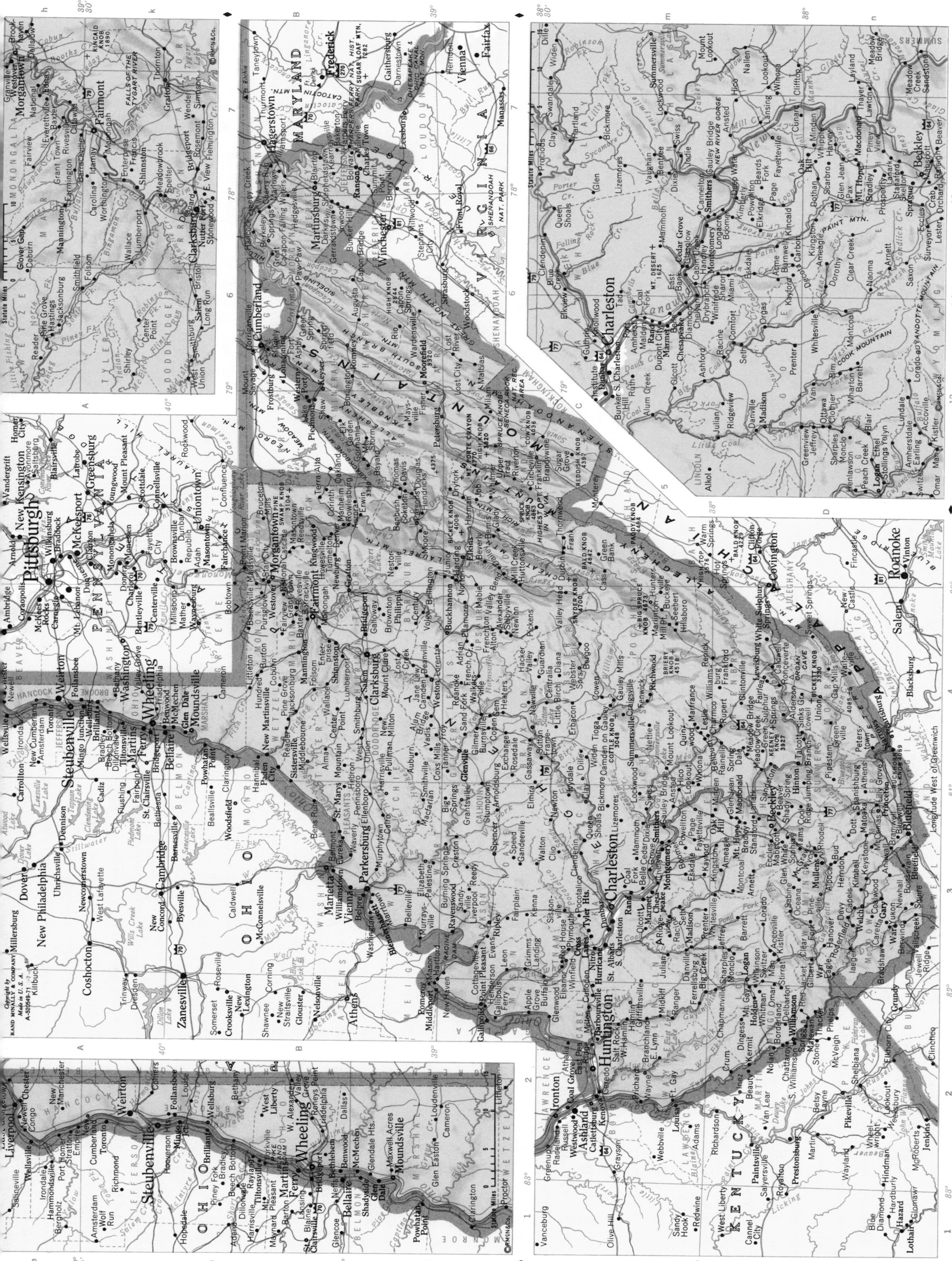

Statute Miles 5 0 5 10 20 30 40

Kilometers 5 0 5 15 25 35 45 55

Lambert Conformal Conic Projection

SCALE 1:1,704,000 1 Inch = 27 Statute Miles

Cities and Towns

Barboursville *2,871* **C2**
Beckley *20,492* **D3**
Bluefield *16,060* **D3**
Bridgeport *6,604* **B4**
Buckhannon *6,820* **C4**
Charleston *63,968* **C3**
Charles Town *2,857* **B7**
Chesapeake *2,364* **C3**
Chester *3,297* **A4**
Clarksburg *22,371* **B4**
Cross Lanes *3,500* **C3**
Dunbar *9,285* **m12**
Elkins *8,536* **C5**
Fairmont *23,863* **B4**
Fayetteville *2,366* **C3**
Follansbee *3,994* **A4**
Gary *2,233* **D3**
Grafton *6,845* **B4**
Harpers Ferry *361* **B7**
Hinton *4,622* **D4**
Huntington *63,684* **C2**
Hurricane *3,751* **C2**
Kenova *4,454* **C2**
Keyser *6,569* **B6**
Kingwood *2,877* **B5**
Lewisburg *3,065* **D4**
Logan *3,029* **D3**
McMechen *2,402* **B4**
Madison *3,228* **C3**
Mannington *3,036* **B4**
Martinsburg *13,063* **B7**
Montgomery *3,104* **C3**
Moorefield *2,257* **B6**
Morgantown *27,605* **B5**
Moundsville *12,419* **B4**
Mullens *2,919* **D3**
New Martinsville *7,109* **B4**
Nitro *8,074* **C3**
Oak Hill *7,120* **D3**
Oceana *2,143* **D3**
Paden City *3,671* **B4**
Parkersburg *39,967* **B3**
Petersburg *2,084* **C5**
Philippi *3,194* **B4**
Point Pleasant *5,682* **C2**
Princeton *7,493* **D3**
Rand *2,500* **C3**
Ranson *2,471* **B7**
Ravenswood *4,126* **C3**
Richwood *3,568* **C4**
Ripley *3,464* **C3**
Romney *2,094* **B6**
Ronceverte *2,312* **D4**
St. Albans *12,402* **C3**
St. Marys *2,219* **B3**
Salem *2,706* **B4**
Shinnston *3,059* **B4**
Sistersville *2,367* **B4**
South Charleston *15,968* **C3**
Spencer *2,799* **C3**
Stonewood *2,058* **k10**
Summersville *2,972* **C4**
Tyler Heights *3,200* **C3**
Vienna *11,618* **B3**
War *2,158* **D3**
Weirton *25,371* **A4**
Welch *3,885* **D3**
Wellsburg *3,963* **A4**
Weston *6,250* **B4**
Westover *4,884* **B5**
Wheeling *43,070* **A4**
White Sulphur Springs *3,371* **D4**
Williamson *5,219* **D2**
Williamstown *3,095* **B3**

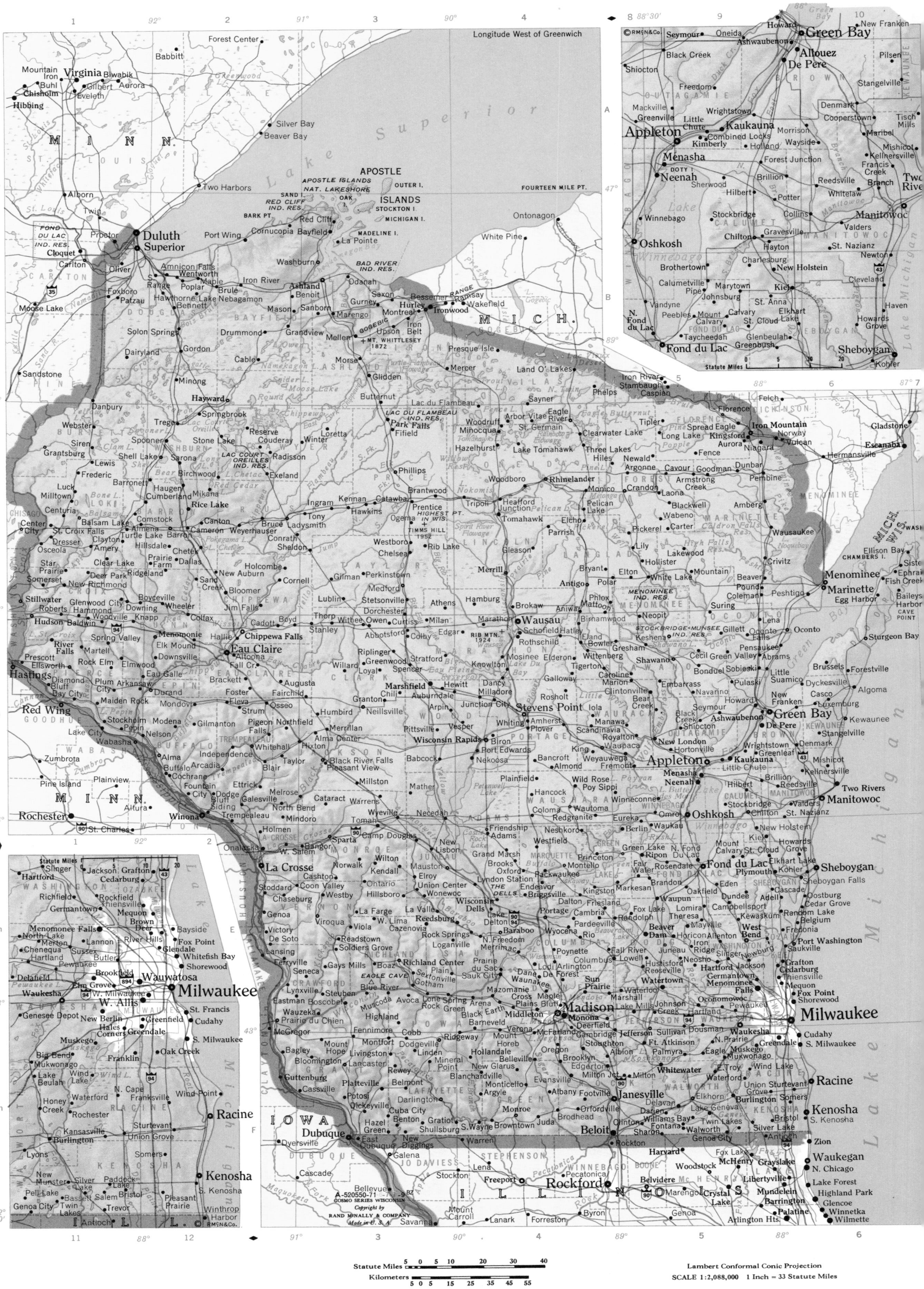

Cities and Towns

Antigo *8,653* **C4**
Appleton *58,913* **D5**
Ashland *9,115* **B3**
Baraboo *8,081* **E4**
Beaver Dam *14,149* **E5**
Beloit *35,207* **F4**
Brookfield *34,035* **m11**
Burlington *8,385* **F5**
Chippewa Falls *12,270* **D2**
Cudahy *19,547* **F6**
De Pere *14,892* **D5**
Eau Claire *51,509* **D2**
Fond du Lac *35,863* **E5**
Fort Atkinson *9,785* **F5**
Franklin *16,871* **n11**
Green Bay *87,899* **D6**
Greendale *16,928* **F5**
Greenfield *31,467* **n11**
Hayward *1,698* **B2**
Hudson *5,434* **D1**
Janesville *51,071* **F4**
Kaukauna *11,310* **D5**
Kenosha *77,685* **F6**
La Crosse *48,347* **E2**
Lake Geneva *5,612* **F5**
Madison *170,616* **E4**
Manitowoc *32,547* **D6**
Marinette *11,965* **C6**
Marshfield *18,290* **D3**
Menasha *14,728* **D5**
Menomonee Falls *27,845* **E5**
Menomonie *12,769* **D2**
Mequon *16,193* **E6**
Merrill *9,578* **C4**
Milwaukee *636,236* **E6**
Monroe *10,027* **F4**
Muskego *15,277* **F5**
Neenah *22,432* **D5**
New Berlin *30,529* **n11**
New London *6,210* **D5**
Oak Creek *16,932* **n12**
Oconomowoc *9,909* **E5**
Oconto *4,505* **D6**
Oshkosh *49,620* **D5**
Park Falls *3,192* **C3**
Platteville *9,580* **F3**
Portage *7,896* **E4**
Port Washington *8,612* **E6**
Prairie du Chien *5,859* **E2**
Racine *85,725* **F6**
Reedsburg *5,038* **E3**
Rhinelander *7,873* **C4**
Rice Lake *7,691* **C2**
River Falls *9,019* **D1**
Shawano *7,013* **D5**
Sheboygan *48,085* **E6**
South Milwaukee *21,069* **F6**
Stevens Point *22,970* **D4**
Stoughton *7,589* **F4**
Sturgeon Bay *8,847* **D6**
Sun Prairie *12,931* **E4**
Superior *29,571* **B1**
Tomah *7,204* **E3**
Two Rivers *13,354* **D6**
Watertown *18,113* **E5**
Waukesha *50,365* **E5**
Waupun *8,132* **E5**
Wausau *32,426* **D4**
Wauwatosa *51,308* **m11**
West Allis *63,982* **m11**
West Bend *21,484* **E5**
Whitefish Bay *14,930* **m12**
Whitewater *11,520* **F5**
Wisconsin Dells *2,521* **E4**
Wisconsin Rapids *17,995* **D4**

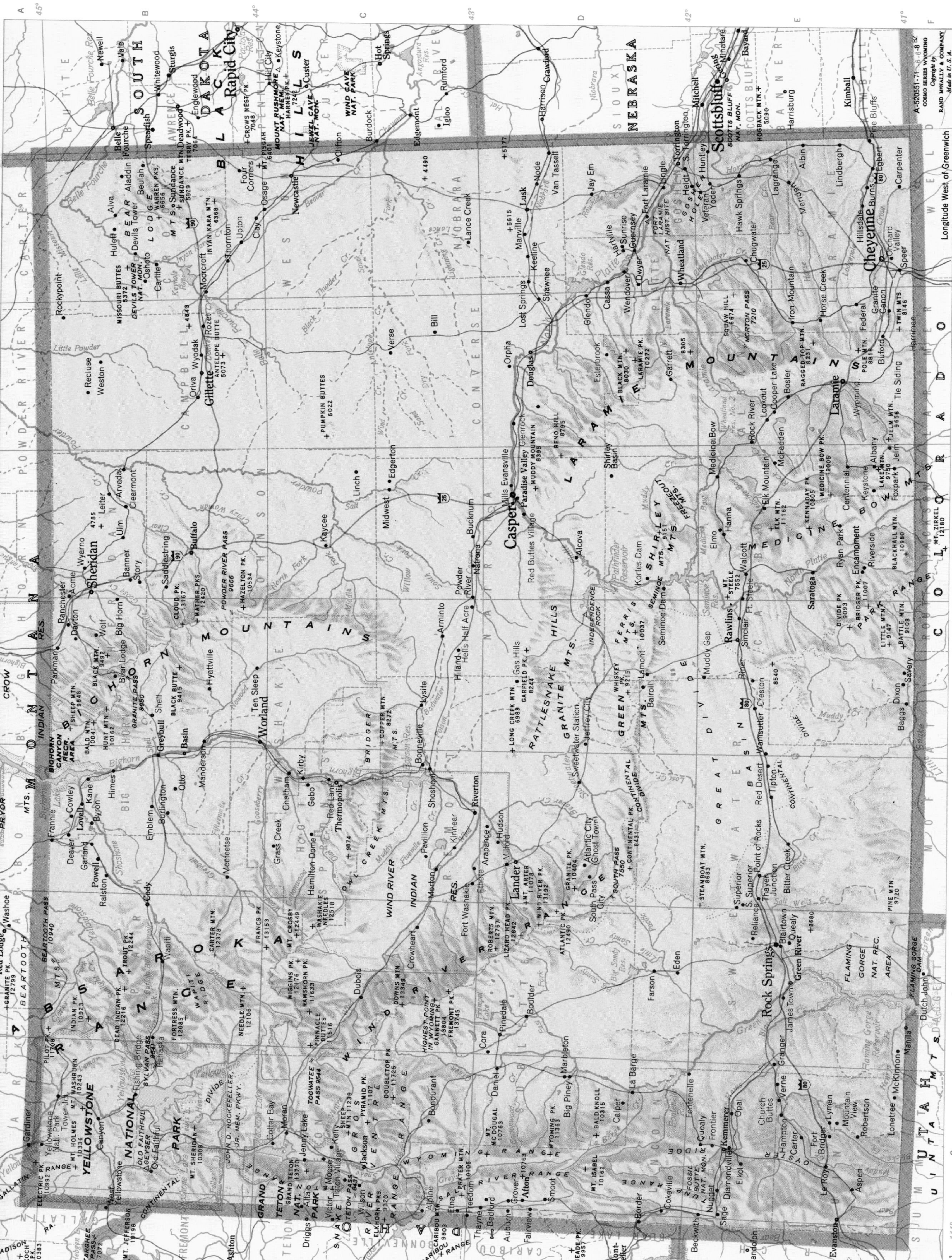

Statute Miles 5 0 5 10 20 30 40 50

Kilometers 5 0 5 15 25 35 45 55 65 75

Lambert Conformal Conic Projection

SCALE 1:2,186,000 1 Inch = 34.5 Statute Miles

Cities and Towns

Afton *1,481* **D2**
Baggs *433* **E5**
Basin *1,349* **B4**
Big Piney *530* **D2**
Buffalo *3,799* **B6**
Byron *633* **B4**
Casper *51,016* **D6**
Cheyenne *47,283* **E8**
Cody *6,790* **B3**
Cokeville *515* **D2**
Cowley *455* **B4**
Dayton *701* **B5**
Devils Tower *40* **B8**
Diamondville *1,000* **E2**
Douglas *6,030* **D7**
Dubois *1,067* **C3**
Edgerton *510* **C6**
Encampment *611* **E6**
Etna *400* **C1**
Evanston *6,421* **E2**
Evansville *2,335* **D6**
Fort Laramie *356* **D8**
Gillette *12,134* **B7**
Glenrock *2,736* **D7**
Green River *12,807* **E3**
Greybull *2,277* **B4**
Guernsey *1,512* **D8**
Hanna *2,288* **E6**
Hudson *514* **D4**
Jackson *4,511* **C2**
Jeffrey City *400* **D5**
Kemmerer *3,273* **E2**
Lander *7,867* **D4**
Laramie *24,410* **E7**
Lingle *475* **D8**
Lovell *2,447* **B4**
Lusk *1,650* **D8**
Lyman *2,284* **E2**
Marbleton *537* **D2**
Medicine Bow *953* **E6**
Meeteetse *512* **B4**
Midwest *638* **C6**
Mills *2,139* **D6**
Moorcroft *1,014* **B8**
Mountain View *628* **E2**
Newcastle *3,596* **C8**
Orchard Valley *800* **E8**
Paradise Valley *2,300* **D6**
Pine Bluffs *1,077* **E8**
Pinedale *1,066* **D3**
Powell *5,310* **B4**
Ranchester *655* **B5**
Rawlins *11,547* **E5**
Reliance *500* **E3**
Riverton *9,247* **C4**
Rock River *415* **E7**
Rock Springs *19,458* **E3**
Saratoga *2,410* **E6**
Sheridan *15,146* **B6**
Shirley Basin *450* **D6**
Shoshoni *879* **C4**
Sinclair *586* **E5**
South Superior *586* **E4**
Story *700* **B6**
Sundance *1,087* **B8**
Ten Sleep *407* **B5**
Teton Village *200* **C2**
Thermopolis *3,852* **C4**
Torrington *5,441* **D8**
Upton *1,193* **B8**
Wamsutter *681* **E5**
West Laramie *2,000* **E7**
Wheatland *5,816* **D8**
Worland *6,391* **B5**
Yellowstone National Park *350* **B2**

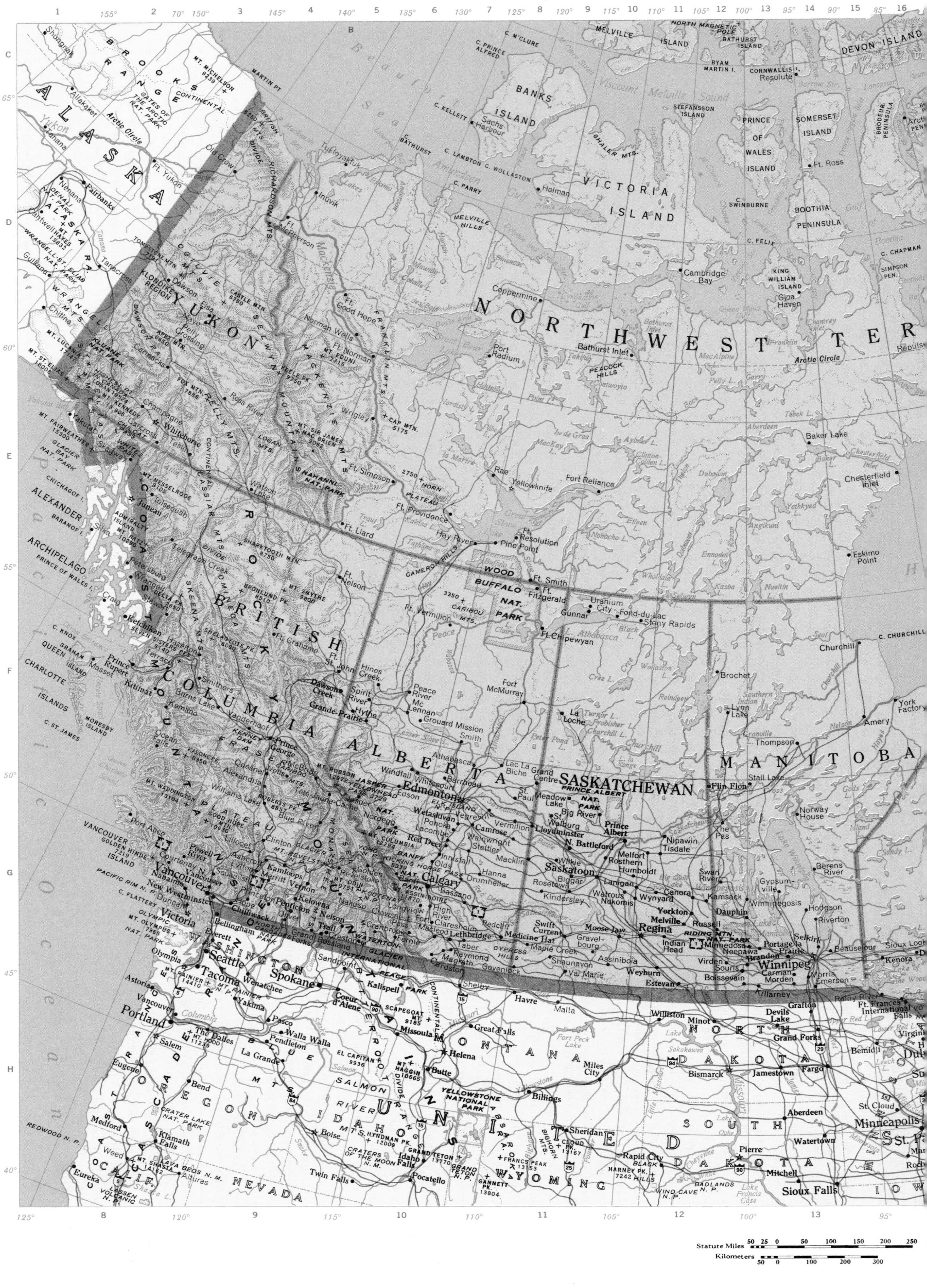
ALASKA
YUKON
NORTHWEST TER
BRITISH COLUMBIA
ALBERTA
SASKATCHEWAN
MANITOBA
VICTORIA ISLAND
BANKS ISLAND
PRINCE OF WALES ISLAND
SOMERSET ISLAND
DEVON ISLAND
MELVILLE ISLAND
BOOTHIA PENINSULA
KING WILLIAM ISLAND
QUEEN CHARLOTTE ISLANDS
ALEXANDER ARCHIPELAGO
VANCOUVER ISLAND
WASHINGTON
OREGON
IDAHO
MONTANA
WYOMING
NORTH DAKOTA
SOUTH DAKOTA
NEVADA
CALIF.
Beaufort Sea
Pacific Ocean
Arctic Circle
Fairbanks
Whitehorse
Dawson
Juneau
Inuvik
Yellowknife
Coppermine
Cambridge Bay
Baker Lake
Churchill
Prince Rupert
Prince George
Edmonton
Calgary
Vancouver
Victoria
Seattle
Spokane
Portland
Saskatoon
Regina
Winnipeg
Minneapolis
Helena
Boise
Bismarck
Sioux Falls
Statute Miles 50 25 0 50 100 150 200 250
Kilometers 50 0 100 200 300

Lambert Conformal Conic Projection
SCALE 1:12,000,000 1 Inch = 189 Statute Miles

Northwest Territories

Cities and Towns
Alert **k9**
Arctic Bay *375* **B16**
Baker Lake *954* **D13**
Bathurst Inlet *20* **C11**
Cambridge Bay *815* **C12**
Chesterfield Inlet *249* **D14**
Coppermine *352* **C15**
Eskimo Point *1,022* **D14**
Eureka **m34**
Ft. Franklin *521* **C8**
Ft. Good Hope *463* **C7**
Ft. Laird *405* **D8**
Ft. McPherson *632* **C6**
Ft. Norman *286* **D7**
Ft. Providence *605* **D9**
Ft. Resolution *480* **D10**
Ft. Simpson *980* **D8**
Ft. Smith *2,298* **D10**
Gjoa Haven *523* **C13**
Hay River *2,863* **D9**
Inuvik *3,147* **C6**
Norman Wells *420* **C7**
Pine Point *1,861* **D10**
Rae *1,378* **D9**
Rankin Inlet *1,109* **D14**
Repulse Bay *352* **C15**
Snowdrift *253* **D10**
Spence Bay *431* **C14**
Yellowknife *9,483* **D10**

Yukon

Cities and Towns
Carmacks *256* **D5**
Carcross *216* **D6**
Dawson *697* **D5**
Destruction Bay *45* **D5**
Elas *336* **D5**
Faro *1,652* **D6**
Haines Junction *366* **D5**
Mayo *398* **D5**
Old Crow *243* **C5**
Pelly Crossing *182* **D5**
Ross River *294* **D6**
Teslin *310* **D6**
Watson Lake *748* **D7**
Whitehorse *14,814* **D6**

ALBERTA

Alberta

Cities and Towns

Airdrie *8,414* **D3**
Athabasca *1,731* **B4**
Banff *4,208* **D3**
Barrhead *3,736* **B3**
Bonnyville *4,454* **B5**
Bow Island *1,491* **E5**
Brooks *9,421* **D5**
Calgary *592,743* **D3**
Camrose *12,570* **C4**
Canmore *3,484* **D3**
Cardston *3,267* **E4**
Coaldale *4,579* **E4**
Cochrane *3,544* **D3**
Cold Lake *2,110* **B5**
Coronation *1,309* **C5**
Crowsnest Pass *7,306* **E3**
Devon *3,885* **C4**
Didsbury *3,095* **D3**
Drayton Valley *5,042* **C3**
Drumheller *6,508* **D4**
Edmonton *532,246* **C4**
Edson *5,835* **C2**
Fairview *2,869* **A1**
Fort Chipewyan *944* **f8**
Fort Macleod *3,139* **E4**
Fort McMurray *31,000* **A5**
Fort Saskatchewan *12,169* **C4**
Gibbons *2,276* **C4**
Grand Centre *3,146* **B5**
Grande Cache *4,523* **C1**
Grande Prairie *24,263* **B1**
Grimshaw *2,316* **A2**
Hanna *2,806* **D5**
High Prairie *2,506* **B2**
High River *4,792* **D4**
Hinton *8,342* **C2**
Innisfail *5,247* **C4**
Jasper *3,269* **C1**
Lac La Biche *2,007* **B5**
La Crete *479* **f7**
Lake Louise *355* **D2**
Leduc *12,471* **C4**
Lethbridge *54,072* **E4**
Lloydminster *15,031* **C5**
Magrath *1,576* **E4**
Medicine Hat *40,380* **D5**
Morinville *4,657* **C4**
Nordegg *63* **C2**
Okotoks *3,847* **D4**
Olds *4,813* **D3**
Peace River *5,907* **A2**
Pincher Creek *3,757* **E4**
Ponoka *5,221* **C4**
Raymond *2,837* **E4**
Redcliff *3,876* **D5**
Red Deer *46,393* **C4**
Rocky Mountain House *4,698* **C3**
St. Albert *31,996* **C4**
St. Paul *4,884* **B5**
Sherwood Park *29,285* **C4**
Slave Lake *4,506* **B3**
Smith *216* **B3**
Spruce Grove *10,326* **C4**
Stettler *5,136* **C4**
Stony Plain *4,839* **C3**
Strathmore *2,986* **D4**
Swan Hills *2,497* **B3**
Sylvan Lake *3,779* **C3**
Taber *5,988* **E4**
Valleyview *2,061* **B2**
Vegreville *5,251* **C4**
Vermilion *3,766* **C5**
Vulcan *1,489* **D4**
Wainwright *4,266* **C5**
Westlock *4,424* **B4**
Wetaskiwin *9,597* **C4**
Whitecourt *5,585* **B3**

British Columbia

Cities and Towns

Abbotsford *12,745* **f13**
Armstrong *2,683* **D8**
Burnaby *136,494* **f13**
Burns Lake *1,777* **B5**
Campbell River *15,832* **D5**
Castlegar *6,902* **E9**
Chase *1,777* **D8**
Chetwynd *2,553* **B7**
Chilliwack *40,642* **f14**
Comax *6,607* **E5**
Courtenay *8,992* **E5**
Cranbrook *15,915* **E10**
Creston *4,190* **E9**
Cumberland *1,947* **E5**
Dawson Creek *11,373* **B7**
Duncan *4,228* **g12**
Enderby *1,816* **D8**
Esquimalt *15,870* **h12**
Fernie *5,444* **E10**
Fort Langley *2,326* **f13**
Fort Nelson *3,724* **m18**
Fort St. James *2,284* **B5**
Fort St. John *13,891* **A7**
Fraser Lake *1,543* **B5**
Fruitvale *1,904* **E9**
Gibsons *2,594* **E6**
Golden *3,476* **D9**
Grand Forks *3,486* **E8**
Houston *1,714* **B4**
Invermere *1,969* **D9**
Kamloops *64,048* **D7**
Kelowna *59,196* **E8**
Kimberley *7,375* **E9**
Kitimat *12,814* **B3**
Ladysmith *4,558* **g12**
Lake Cowichan *2,391* **g11**
Langley *15,124* **f13**
Lillooet *1,725* **D7**
Masset *1,569* **C1**
Merritt *6,110* **D7**
Mission *9,948* **f13**
Nanaimo *47,069* **f12**
Nelson *9,143* **E9**
New Westminster *38,550* **f13**
North Vancouver *33,952* **E6**
Oak Bay *16,990* **h12**
100 Mile House *1,925* **D7**
Osoyoos *2,738* **E8**
Parksville *5,216* **E5**
Penticton *23,181* **E8**
Port Alberni *19,892* **E5**
Port Alice *1,668* **D4**
Port Coquitlam *27,535* **f13**
Port Hardy *3,778* **D4**
Powell River *13,423* **E5**
Prince George *67,559* **C6**
Prince Rupert *16,197* **B2**
Qualicum Beach *2,844* **E5**
Quesnel *8,240* **C6**
Revelstoke *5,544* **D8**
Richmond *96,154* **f12**
Salmon Arm *1,946* **D8**
Sidney *7,946* **g12**
Smithers *4,570* **B4**
Squamish *1,590* **E6**
Summerland *7,473* **E8**
Terrace *10,914* **B3**
Trail *9,599* **E9**
Ucluelet *1,593* **E5**
Vancouver *414,281* **f12**
Vanderhoof *2,323* **C5**
Vernon *19,987* **D8**
Victoria *64,379* **h12**
Warfield *1,969* **E9**
White Rock *13,550* **f13**
Williams Lake *8,362* **C6**

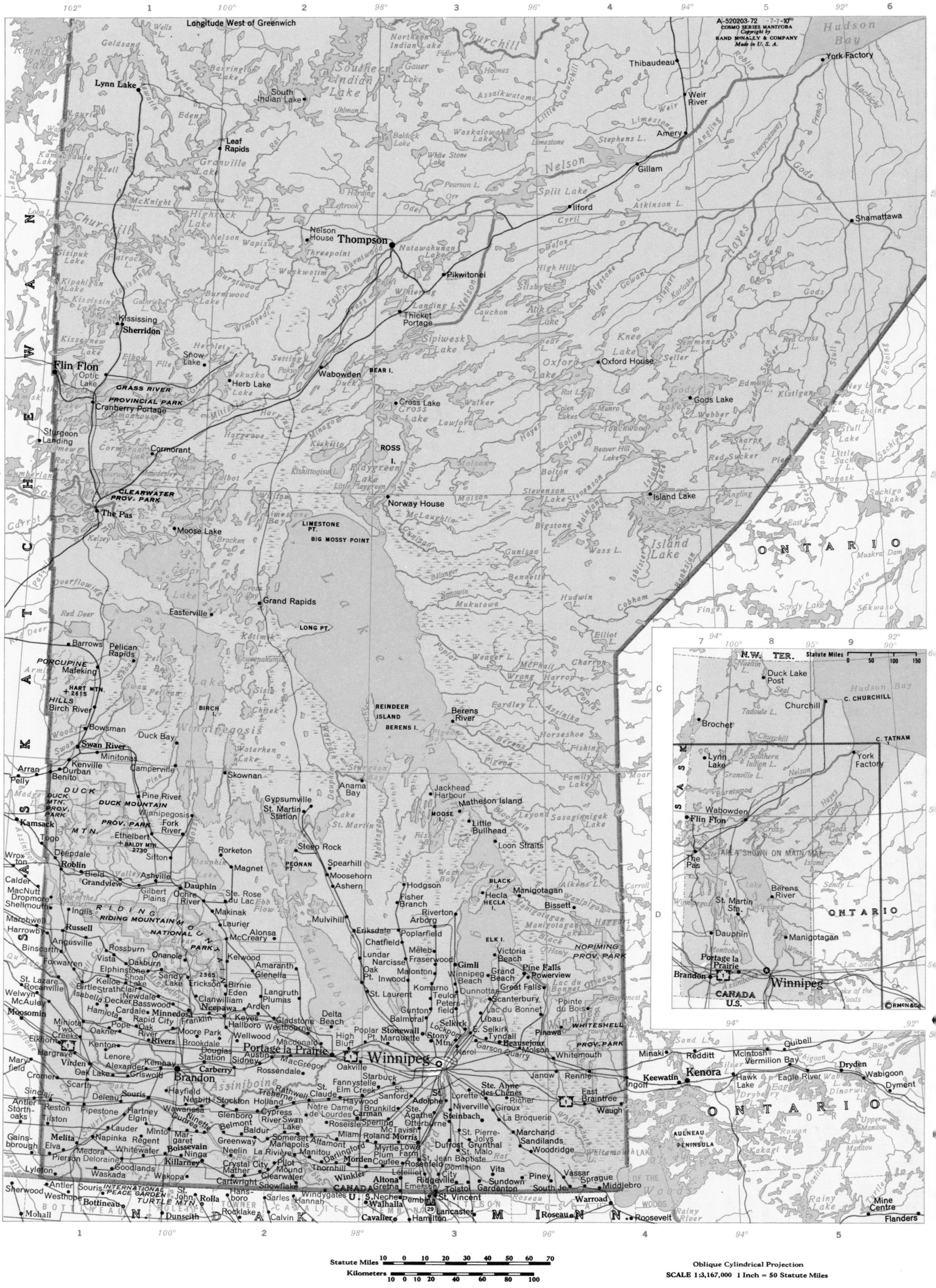

Manitoba

Cities and Towns

Altona *2,757* **E3**
Arborg *974* **D3**
Ashern *570* **D2**
Beausejour *2,462* **D3**
Berens River *238* **C3**
Birch River *597* **C1**
Birtle *887* **D1**
Boissevain *1,660* **E1**
Brandon *36,242* **E2**
Camperville *586* **D1**
Carberry *1,510* **E2**
Carman *2,408* **E2**
Churchill *1,304* **I9**
Cormorant *445* **B1**
Cranberry Portage *948* **B1**
Cross Lake *510* **B3**
Dauphin *8,971* **D1**
Deloraine *1,136* **E1**
Duck Bay *594* **C1**
Easterville *589* **C2**
Emerson *762* **E3**
Flin Flon *8,261* **B1**
Gilbert Plains *812* **D1**
Gillam *1,427* **A4**
Gladstone *964* **D2**
Glenboro *741* **E2**
Grand Rapids *567* **C2**
Grandview *1,013* **D1**
Hamiota *728* **D1**
Ilford *149* **A4**
Killarney *2,342* **E2**
Lac-du-Bonnet *985* **D3**
Lorette *1,092* **E3**
Lynn Lake *2,087* **A1**
MacGregor *795* **E2**
Manigotagan *216* **D3**
Manitou *861* **E2**
Melita *1,156* **E1**
Minnedosa *2,637* **D2**
Moose Lake *557* **C1**
Morden *4,579* **E2**
Morris *1,570* **E3**
Neepawa *3,425* **D2**
Niverville *1,329* **E3**
Norway House *441* **C3**
Pilot Mound *838* **E2**
Pine Falls *885* **D3**
Plum Coulee *592* **E3**
Portage-la-Prairie *13,086* **E2**
Rivers *1,107* **D1**
Roblin *1,953* **D1**
Rossburn *696* **D1**
Russell *1,660* **D1**
Ste. Anne-des-Chênes *1,338* **E3**
St. Laurent *1,114* **D3**
St. Pierre-Jolys *919* **E3**
Ste. Rose-du-Lac *1,090* **D2**
Selkirk *10,037* **D3**
Sherridon *138* **B1**
Shoal Lake *835* **D1**
Snow Lake *1,853* **B1**
Souris *1,731* **E1**
South Indian Lake *770* **A2**
Steinbach *6,676* **E3**
Stonewall *2,210* **D3**
Stony Mountain *1,313* **D3**
Swan River *3,782* **C1**
The Pas *6,390* **C1**
Thompson *14,288* **B3**
Virden *2,940* **E1**
Wabowden *655* **B2**
Winkler *5,046* **E3**
Winnipeg *564,473* **E3**
Winnipegosis *855* **D2**
York Factory **A5**

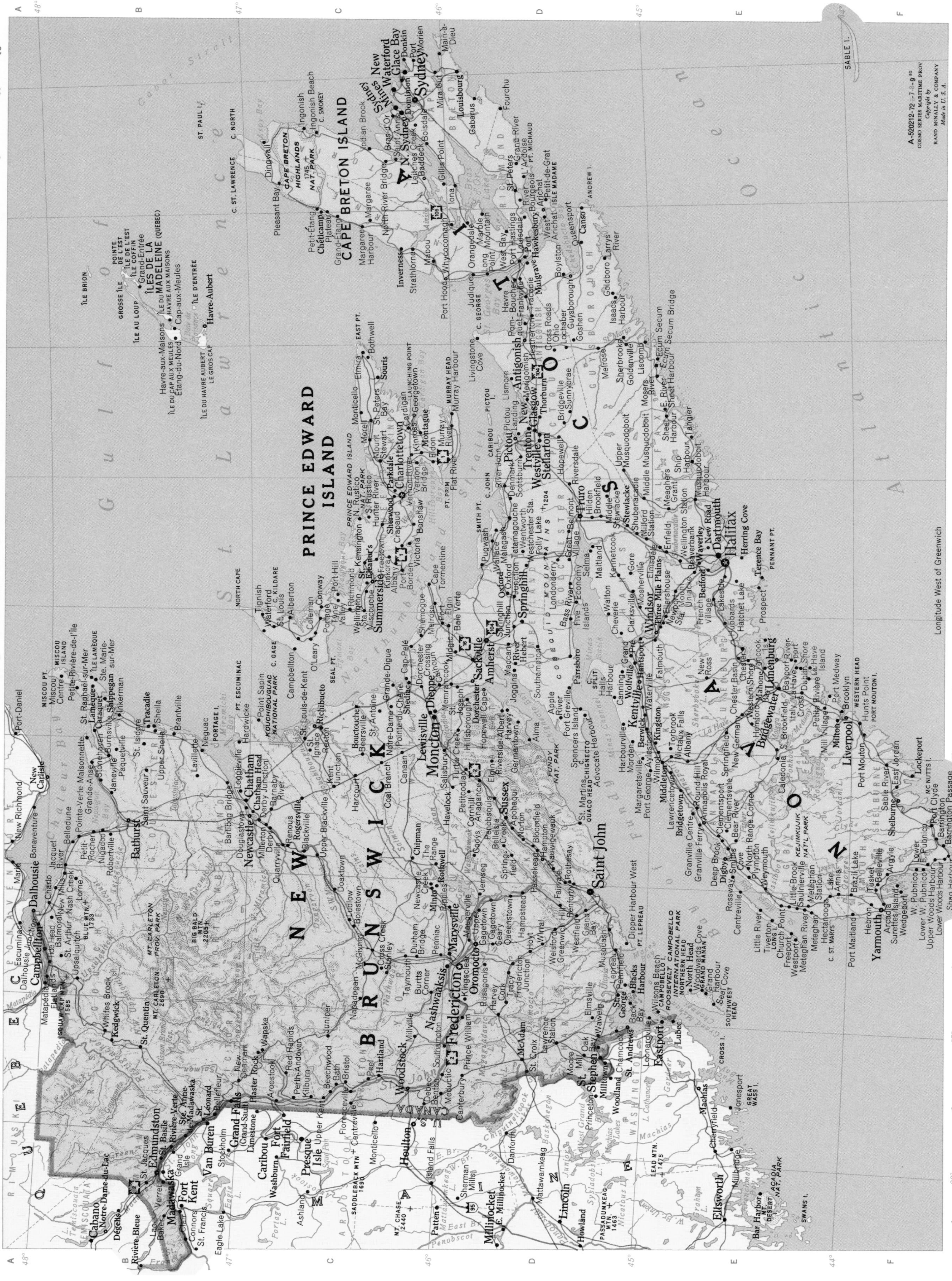

Oblique Cylindrical Projection
SCALE 1:2,312,000 1 Inch = 36.5 Statute Miles

Statute Miles 5 0 5 10 20 30 40 50
Kilometers 5 0 5 15 25 35 45 55 65 75

Nova Scotia

Cities and Towns

Amherst *9,684* **D5**
Antigonish *5,205* **D8**
Bridgewater *6,669* **E5**
Canso *1,255* **D8**
Cheticamp *1,022* **C8**
Dartmouth *62,277* **E6**
Dingwall *311* **C9**
Dominion *2,856* **C9**
Glace Bay *21,466* **C10**
Halifax *114,594* **E6**
Inverness *2,013* **C8**
Kentville *4,974* **D5**
Liverpool *3,304* **E5**
Lunenburg *3,014* **E5**
New Glasgow *10,464* **D7**
New Waterford *8,808* **C9**
Pictou *4,628* **D7**
Port Hawkesbury *3,850* **D8**
Shelburne *2,303* **F4**
Springhill *4,896* **D5**
Stellarton *5,435* **D7**
Sydney *29,444* **C9**
Sydney Mines *8,501* **C9**
Trenton *3,154* **D7**
Truro *12,552* **D6**
Westville *4,522* **D7**
Windsor *3,646* **E5**
Wolfville *3,235* **D5**
Yarmouth *7,475* **F3**

Prince Edward Island

Cities and Towns

Charlottetown *15,282* **C6**
Elmira *140* **C7**
Murray Harbour *443* **D7**
Parkdale *2,018* **C6**
St. Eleanor's *2,716* **C6**
Sherwood *5,681* **C6**
Souris *1,413* **C7**
Summerside *7,828* **C6**
Tignish *982* **C5**

New Brunswick

Cities and Towns

Bathurst *15,705* **B4**
Blacks Harbour *1,356* **D3**
Buctouche *2,476* **C5**
Campbellton *9,818* **A3**
Caraquet *4,315* **B5**
Chatham *6,779* **B4**
Dalhousie *4,958* **A3**
Dieppe *8,511* **C5**
Edmundston *12,044* **B1**
Fairvale *3,960* **D4**
Fredericton *43,723* **D3**
Grand Bay *3,173* **D3**
Grand Falls *6,203* **B2**
Hampton *3,141* **D4**
Minto *3,399* **C3**
Moncton *54,743* **C5**
Newcastle *6,284* **C4**
Oromocto *9,064* **D3**
Sackville *5,654* **D5**
Saint John *80,521* **D3**
St. Stephen *5,120* **D2**
Shediac *4,285* **C5**
Shippegan *2,471* **B5**
Sussex *3,972* **D4**
Tracadie *2,452* **B5**
Woodstock *4,649* **C2**

NEWFOUNDLAND

Statute Miles 5 0 5 10 20 30 40 50 60
Kilometers 5 0 5 10 20 30 40 50 60 70 80

Lambert Conformal Conic Projection
SCALE 1 : 3,000,000 1 Inch = 47 Statute Miles

Newfoundland

Cities and Towns

Badger *1,090* **D3**
Baie Verte *2,491* **D3**
Bay Bulls *1,081* **E5**
Bay Roberts *4,512* **E5**
Bishop's Falls *4,395* **D4**
Bonavista *4,460* **D5**
Botwood *4,074* **D4**
Buchans *1,655* **D3**
Burgeo *2,504* **E3**
Burin *2,904* **E4**
Carbonear *5,335* **E5**
Cartwright *658* **D4**
Catalina *1,162* **D5**
Channel-Port-aux-Basques *5,988* **E2**
Clarenville *2,878* **D4**
Corner Brook *24,339* **D3**
Deer Lake *4,348* **D3**
Dunville *1,817* **E5**
Durrell *1,145* **D4**
Fogo *1,105* **D4**
Fortune *2,473* **E4**
Gambo *2,932* **D4**
Gander *10,404* **D4**
Glenwood *1,129* **D4**
Glovertown *2,165* **D4**
Grand Bank *3,901* **E4**
Grand Falls *8,765* **D4**
Happy Valley-Goose Bay *7,103* **B1**
Harbour Breton *2,464* **E4**
Harbour Grace *2,988* **E5**
Hare Bay *1,520* **D4**
Isle-aux-Morts *1,238* **E2**
Joe Batt's Arm *1,155* **D4**
Labrador City *11,538* **h8**
La Scie *1,422* **D4**
Lewisporte *3,963* **D4**
Marystown *6,299* **E4**
Middle Brook *1,083* **D4**
Milltown *1,376* **E4**
Musgrave Harbour *1,554* **D5**
Nain *938* **g9**
Norris Arm *1,216* **D4**
Norris Point *1,033* **D3**
Pasadena *2,685* **D3**
Placentia *2,204* **E5**
Pouch Cove *1,522* **E5**
Ramea *1,386* **E3**
Red Bay *316* **C3**
Rigolet *271* **A2**
Robert's Arm *1,005* **D4**
Rocky Harbour *1,273* **D3**
Roddickton *1,142* **C3**
St. Alban's *1,968* **E4**
St. Anthony *3,107* **C4**
St. George's *1,756* **D2**
St. John's *83,770* **E5**
St. Lawrence *2,012* **E4**
Spaniard's Bay *2,125* **E5**
Springdale *3,501* **D3**
Stephenville *8,876* **D2**
Stephenville Crossing *2,172* **D2**
Summerford *1,198* **D4**
Torbay *3,394* **E5**
Trepassey *1,473* **E5**
Twillingate *1,506* **D4**
Upper Island Cove *2,025* **E5**
Victoria *1,870* **E5**
Wabana (Bell Island) *4,254* **E5**
Wabush *3,155* **h8**
Wesleyville *1,225* **D5**
Windsor *5,747* **D4**

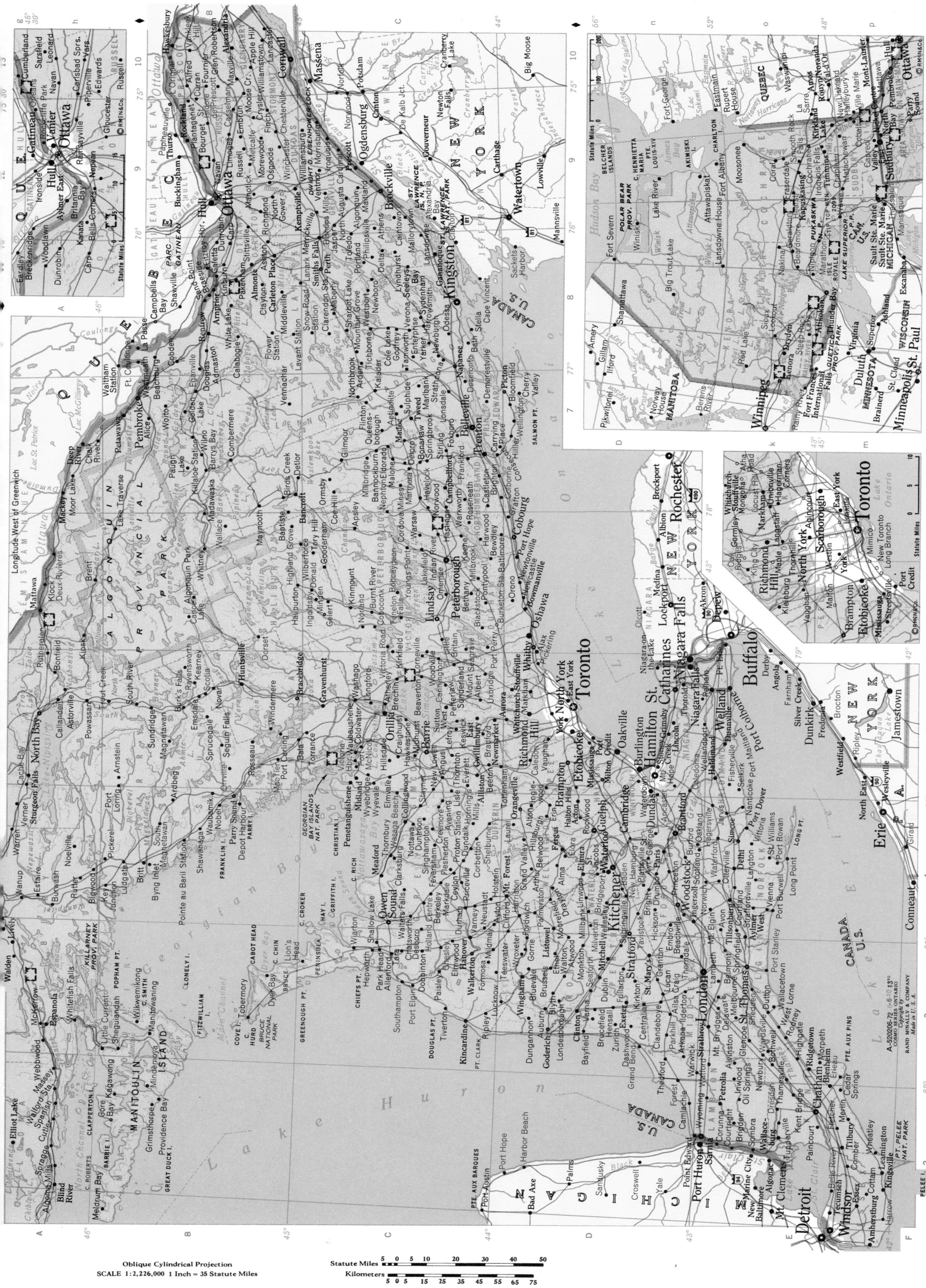

Oblique Cylindrical Projection
SCALE 1:2,226,000 1 Inch = 35 Statute Miles

Statute Miles 5 0 5 10 20 30 40 50
Kilometers 5 0 5 15 25 35 45 55 65 75

Ontario

Cities and Towns

Ajax *25,475* **D6**
Atikokan *4,389* **o17**
Barrie *38,423* **C5**
Belleville *34,881* **C7**
Brampton *149,030* **D5**
Brantford *74,315* **D4**
Brockville *19,896* **C9**
Burlington *114,853* **D5**
Cambridge *77,183* **D4**
Chatham *40,952* **E2**
Cobourg *11,385* **D6**
Cornwall *46,144* **B10**
Dryden *6,640* **o16**
Dundas *19,586* **D5**
Etobicoke *298,713* **D5**
Fergus *6,064* **D4**
Fort Erie *24,096* **E6**
Gloucester *72,859* **h12**
Guelph *71,207* **D4**
Haileybury *4,925* **p20**
Hamilton *306,434* **D5**
Hawkesbury *9,877* **B10**
Kapuskasing *12,014* **o19**
Kenora *9,817* **o16**
Kingston *52,616* **C8**
Kirkland Lake *12,219* **o19**
Kitchener *139,734* **D4**
Lansdowne House *161* **n18**
Leamington *12,528* **E2**
Lindsay *13,596* **C6**
London *254,280* **E3**
Markham *77,037* **k15**
Midland *12,132* **C5**
Milton *28,067* **D5**
Mississauga *315,056* **D5**
Moosonee *1,433* **o19**
Nakina *936* **o18**
Nanticoke *19,816* **E4**
Newcastle *32,229* **D6**
Newmarket *29,753* **C5**
Niagara Falls *70,960* **D5**
Nipigon *2,377* **o17**
North Bay *51,268* **A5**
Oakville *75,773* **D5**
Orillia *23,955* **C5**
Oshawa *117,519* **D6**
Ottawa *295,163* **h12**
Owen Sound *19,883* **C4**
Pembroke *14,026* **B7**
Petawawa *5,520* **B7**
Peterborough *60,620* **C6**
Port Colborne *19,225* **E5**
Red Lake *2,065* **o16**
Richmond Hill *37,778* **k15**
St. Catharines *124,018* **D5**
Sarnia *50,892* **E2**
Sault Ste. Marie *82,697* **p18**
Scarborough *443,353* **m15**
Sioux Lookout *3,074* **o17**
Smiths Falls *8,831* **C8**
Stratford *26,262* **D3**
Sturgeon Falls *6,045* **A5**
Sudbury *91,829* **A4**
Tecumseh *6,364* **E2**
Thunder Bay *112,486* **o17**
Timmins *46,114* **o19**
Toronto *599,217* **m15**
Trenton *15,085* **C7**
Vanier (Eastview) *18,792* **h12**
Vaughan *29,674* **k14**
Welland *45,448* **E5**
Whitby *36,698* **D6**
Windsor *192,083* **E1**
Woodstock *26,603* **D4**
York *134,617* **m15**

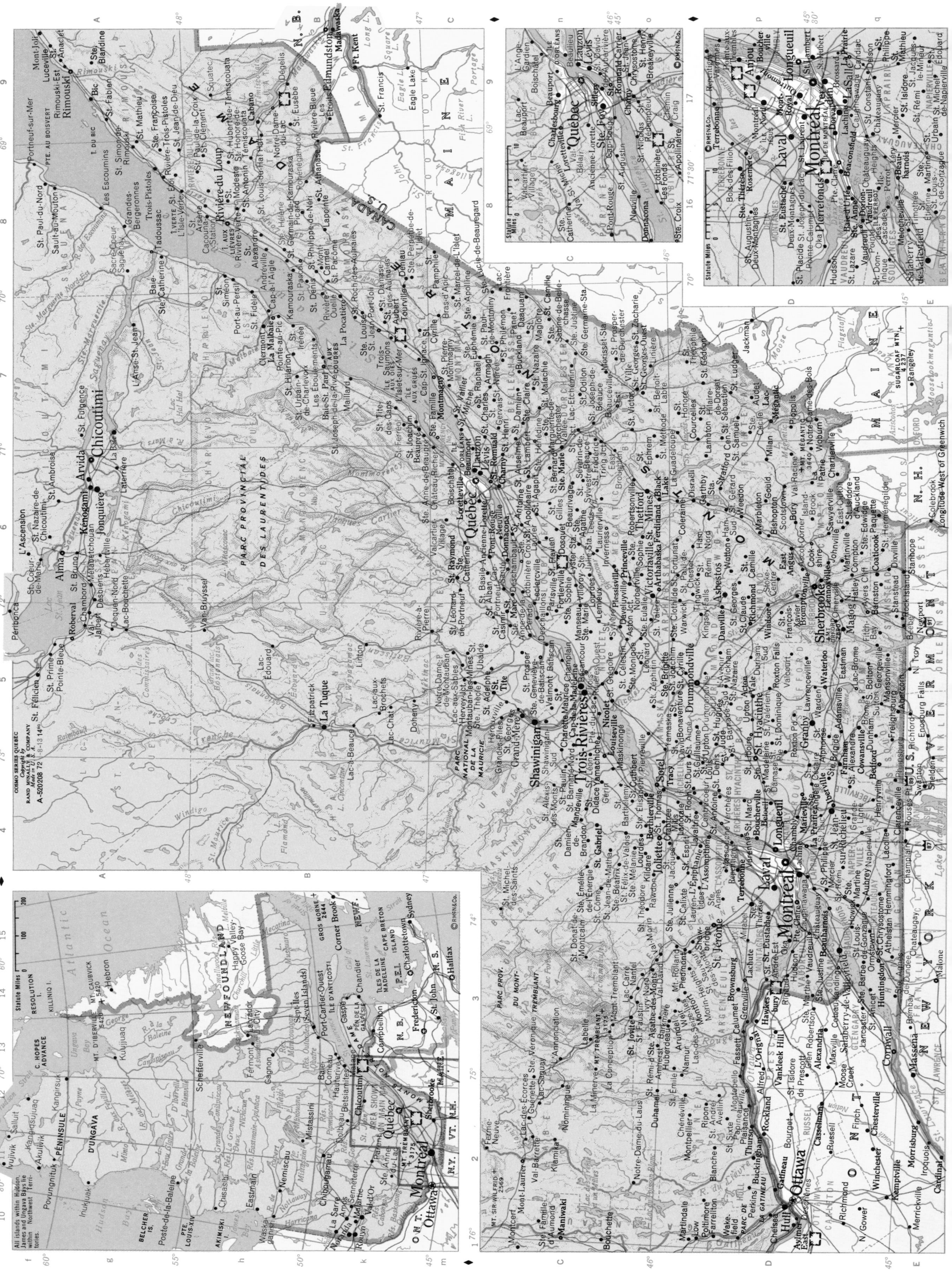

Statute Miles 5 0 5 10 20 30 40

Kilometers 5 0 5 15 25 35 45 55

Oblique Cylindrical Projection
SCALE 1:1,929,000 1 Inch = 30.5 Statute Miles

Quebec

Cities and Towns

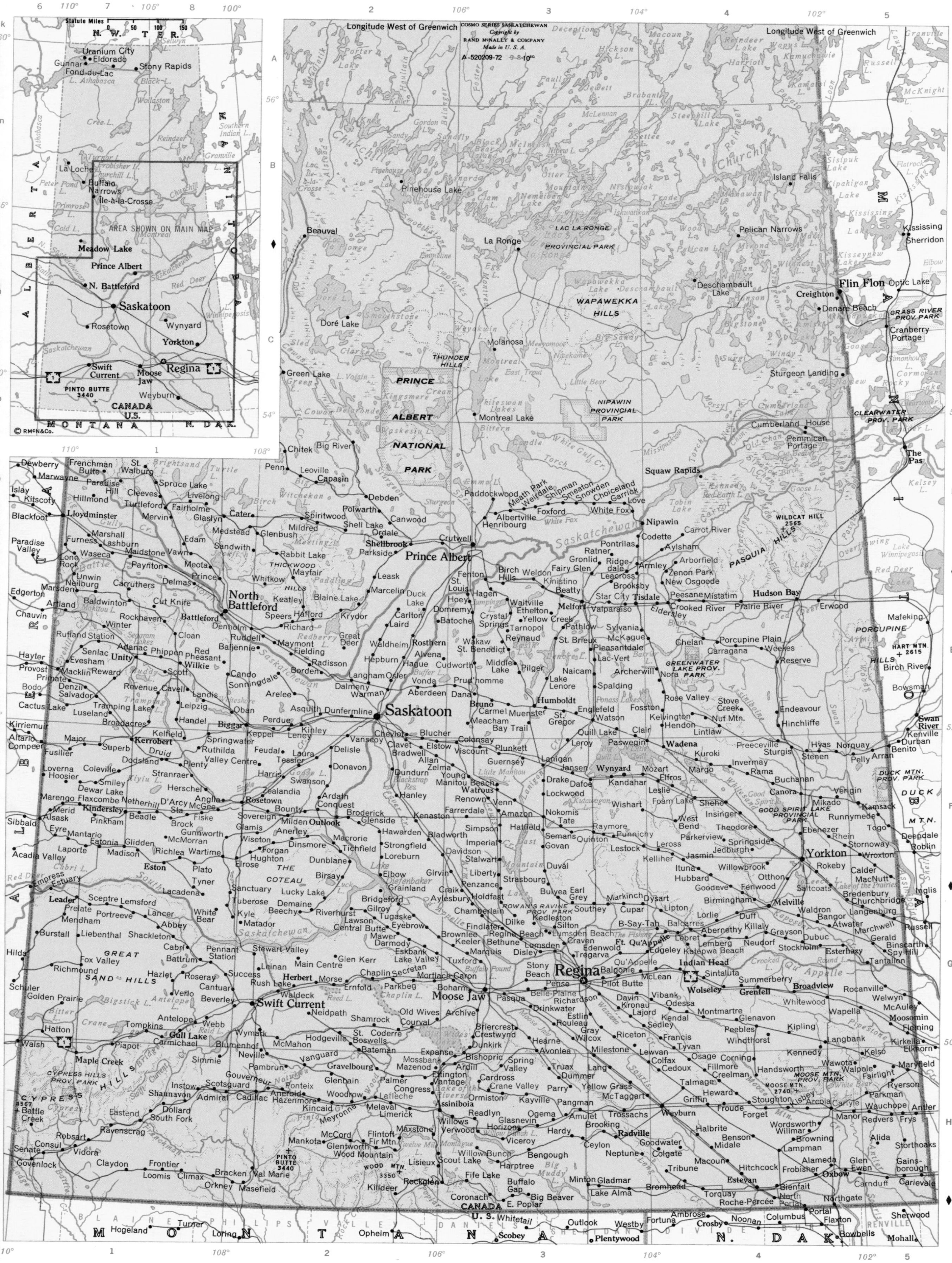

Oblique Cylindrical Projection
SCALE 1:2,827,000 1 Inch = 44 Statute Miles

Statute Miles 10 0 10 20 30 40 50 60
Kilometers 10 0 10 20 40 60 80

Cities and Towns

Assiniboia *2,924* **H2**
Battleford *3,565* **E1**
Biggar *2,561* **E1**
Buffalo Narrows *1,088* **m7**
Canora *2,667* **F4**
Carlyle *1,074* **H4**
Carnduff *1,043* **H5**
Carrot River *1,169* **D4**
Coronach *1,032* **H3**
Creighton *1,636* **C5**
Dalmeny *1,064* **E2**
Davidson *1,166* **F3**
Eldorado *229* **m7**
Esterhazy *3,065* **G4**
Estevan *9,174* **H4**
Eston *1,413* **F1**
Foam Lake *1,452* **F4**
Fort Qu'Appelle *1,827* **G4**
Gravelbourg *1,338* **H2**
Grenfell *1,307* **G4**
Gull Lake *1,095* **G1**
Herbert *1,019* **G2**
Hudson Bay *2,361* **E4**
Humboldt *4,705* **E3**
Île-à-la-Crosse *1,035* **m7**
Indian Head *1,889* **G4**
Kamsack *2,688* **F5**
Kelvington *1,054* **E4**
Kerrobert *1,141* **F1**
Kindersley *3,969* **F1**
Kipling *1,016* **G4**
La Loche *1,635* **m7**
Langenburg *1,324* **G5**
Langham *1,151* **E2**
Lanigan *1,732* **F3**
La Ronge *2,579* **B3**
Leader *1,108* **G1**
Lloydminster *15,031* **D1**
Lumsden *1,303* **G3**
Maidstone *1,001* **D1**
Maple Creek *2,470* **H1**
Meadow Lake *3,857* **n7**
Melfort *6,010* **E3**
Melville *5,092* **G4**
Moose Jaw *33,941* **G3**
Moosomin *2,579* **G5**
Nipawin *4,376* **D3**
North Battleford *14,030* **E1**
Outlook *1,976* **F2**
Oxbow *1,191* **H4**
Pilot Butte *1,255* **G3**
Preeceville *1,243* **F4**
Prince Albert *31,380* **D3**
Radville *1,012* **H3**
Regina *162,613* **G3**
Rosetown *2,664* **F1**
Rosthern *1,609* **E2**
Saskatoon *154,210* **E2**
Shaunavon *2,112* **H1**
Shellbrook *1,228* **D2**
Swift Current *14,747* **G2**
Tisdale *3,107* **E3**
Unity *2,408* **E1**
Uranium City *2,507* **m7**
Wadena *1,495* **F4**
Wakaw *1,030* **E3**
Warman *2,076* **E2**
Watrous *1,830* **F3**
Weyburn *9,523* **H4**
Whitewood *1,003* **G4**
Wilkie *1,501* **E1**
Wolseley *904* **G4**
Wynyard *2,147* **F3**
Yorkton *15,339* **F4**

United States and Canada Information Table

United States

STATE	CAPITAL	LARGEST CITY	ENTERED UNION AS STATE: Date of Entry	ENTERED UNION AS STATE: Rank of Entry	GREATEST MEASUREMENT: N-S km	GREATEST MEASUREMENT: N-S mi	GREATEST MEASUREMENT: E-W km	GREATEST MEASUREMENT: E-W mi	HIGHEST POINT: Location	HIGHEST POINT: Altitude m	HIGHEST POINT: Altitude ft	OFFICIAL FLOWER
Alabama	Montgomery	Birmingham	Dec. 14, 1819	22	531	*330*	322	*200*	Cheaha Mtn.	734	*2,407*	Camellia
Alaska	Juneau	Anchorage	Jan. 3, 1959	49	2,144	*1,332*	3,621	*2,250*	McKinley, Mt.	6,194	*20,320*	Forget-me-not
Arizona	Phoenix	Phoenix	Feb. 14, 1912	48	628	*390*	539	*335*	Humphreys Pk.	3,851	*12,633*	Saguaro Cactus Blossom
Arkansas	Little Rock	Little Rock	June 15, 1836	25	386	*240*	443	*275*	Magazine Mtn.	839	*2,753*	Apple Blossom
California	Sacramento	Los Angeles	Sept. 9, 1850	31	1,287	*800*	604	*375*	Whitney, Mt.	4,417	*14,491*	Golden Poppy
Colorado	Denver	Denver	Aug. 1, 1876	38	435	*270*	612	*380*	Elbert, Mt.	4,399	*14,433*	Rocky Mountain Columbine
Connecticut	Hartford	Bridgeport	Jan. 9, 1788	5	121	*75*	145	*90*	Frissell, Mt.	725	*2,380*	Mountain Laurel
Delaware	Dover	Wilmington	Dec. 7, 1787	1	153	*95*	56	*35*	In New Castle County	137	*448*	Peach Blossom
District of Columbia	Washington	Washington	January, 1791	. . .	24	*15*	24	*15*	Unnamed	125	*410*	American Beauty Rose
Florida	Tallahassee	Jacksonville	March 3, 1845	27	740	*460*	644	*400*	In Walton County	105	*345*	Orange Blossom
Georgia	Atlanta	Atlanta	Jan. 2, 1788	4	507	*315*	402	*250*	Brasstown Bald	1,458	*4,784*	Cherokee Rose
Hawaii	Honolulu	Honolulu	Aug. 21, 1959	50	1,070	*665*	2,575	*1,600*	Mauna Kea	4,205	*13,796*	Hibiscus
Idaho	Boise	Boise	July 3, 1890	43	772	*480*	491	*305*	Borah Pk.	3,859	*12,662*	Syringa
Illinois	Springfield	Chicago	Dec. 3, 1818	21	612	*380*	330	*205*	Charles Mound	376	*1,235*	Native Violet
Indiana	Indianapolis	Indianapolis	Dec. 11, 1816	19	426	*265*	257	*160*	In Wayne County	383	*1,257*	Peony
Iowa	Des Moines	Des Moines	Dec. 28, 1846	29	330	*205*	499	*310*	In Osceola County	509	*1,670*	Wild Rose
Kansas	Topeka	Wichita	Jan. 29, 1861	34	330	*205*	660	*410*	Sunflower, Mt.	1,231	*4,039*	Native Sunflower
Kentucky	Frankfort	Louisville	June 1, 1792	15	282	*175*	563	*350*	Black Mtn.	1,263	*4,145*	Goldenrod
Louisiana	Baton Rouge	New Orleans	April 30, 1812	18	443	*275*	483	*300*	Driskill Mtn.	163	*535*	Magnolia
Maine	Augusta	Portland	March 15, 1820	23	499	*310*	338	*210*	Katahdin, Mt.	1,606	*5,268*	White Pine Cone and Tassel
Maryland	Annapolis	Baltimore	April 28, 1788	7	193	*120*	322	*200*	Backbone Mtn.	1,024	*3,360*	Black-eyed Susan
Massachusetts	Boston	Boston	Feb. 6, 1788	6	177	*110*	306	*190*	Greylock, Mt	1,064	*3,491*	Mayflower
Michigan	Lansing	Detroit	Jan. 26, 1837	26	644	*400*	499	*310*	Arvon, Mt.	603	*1,979*	Apple Blossom
Minnesota	St. Paul	Minneapolis	May 11, 1858	32	644	*400*	563	*350*	Eagle Mtn.	701	*2,301*	Pink and White Lady's-slipper
Mississippi	Jackson	Jackson	Dec. 10, 1817	20	547	*340*	290	*180*	Woodall Mtn.	246	*806*	Magnolia
Missouri	Jefferson City	Kansas City	Aug. 10, 1821	24	451	*280*	483	*300*	Taum Sauk Mtn.	540	*1,772*	Hawthorn
Montana	Helena	Billings	Nov. 8, 1889	41	507	*315*	917	*570*	Granite Pk.	3,901	*12,799*	Bitterroot
Nebraska	Lincoln	Omaha	March 1, 1867	37	338	*210*	668	*415*	In Kimball County	1,654	*5,426*	Goldenrod
Nevada	Carson City	Las Vegas	Oct. 31, 1864	36	781	*485*	507	*315*	Boundary Pk.	4,005	*13,140*	Sagebrush
New Hampshire	Concord	Manchester	June 21, 1788	9	298	*185*	145	*90*	Washington, Mt.	1,917	*6,288*	Purple Lilac
New Jersey	Trenton	Newark	Dec. 18, 1787	3	267	*166*	113	*70*	High Point	550	*1,803*	Purple Violet
New Mexico	Santa Fe	Albuquerque	Jan. 6, 1912	47	628	*390*	563	*350*	Wheeler Pk.	4,011	*13,161*	Yucca
New York	Albany	New York	July 26, 1788	11	499	*310*	531	*330*	Marcy, Mt.	1,629	*5,344*	Rose
North Carolina	Raleigh	Charlotte	Nov. 21, 1789	12	322	*200*	837	*520*	Mitchell, Mt.	2,037	*6,684*	Dogwood
North Dakota	Bismarck	Fargo	Nov. 2, 1889	39	338	*210*	579	*360*	White Butte	1,069	*3,506*	Wild Prairie Rose
Ohio	Columbus	Columbus	March 1, 1803	17	370	*230*	330	*205*	Campbell Hill	472	*1,550*	Scarlet Carnation
Oklahoma	Oklahoma City	Oklahoma City	Nov. 16, 1907	46	338	*210*	740	*460*	Black Mesa	1,516	*4,973*	Mistletoe
Oregon	Salem	Portland	Feb. 14, 1859	33	467	*290*	604	*375*	Hood, Mt.	3,426	*11,239*	Oregon Grape
Pennsylvania	Harrisburg	Philadelphia	Dec. 12, 1787	2	290	*180*	499	*310*	Davis, Mt.	979	*3,213*	Mountain Laurel
Rhode Island	Providence	Providence	May 29, 1790	13	80	*50*	56	*35*	Jerimoth Hill	247	*812*	Violet
South Carolina	Columbia	Columbia	May 23, 1788	8	346	*215*	459	*285*	Sassafras Mtn.	1,085	*3,560*	Carolina Jessamine
South Dakota	Pierre	Sioux Falls	Nov. 2, 1889	40	386	*240*	579	*360*	Harney Pk.	2,207	*7,242*	Pasque Flower
Tennessee	Nashville	Memphis	June 1, 1796	16	193	*120*	692	*430*	Clingmans Dome	2,025	*6,643*	Iris
Texas	Austin	Houston	Dec. 29, 1845	28	1,143	*710*	1,223	*760*	Guadalupe Pk.	2,667	*8,749*	Bluebonnet
Utah	Salt Lake City	Salt Lake City	Jan. 4, 1896	45	555	*345*	443	*275*	Kings Pk.	4,123	*13,528*	Sego Lily
Vermont	Montpelier	Burlington	March 4, 1791	14	249	*155*	145	*90*	Mansfield, Mt.	1,339	*4,393*	Red Clover
Virginia	Richmond	Virginia Beach	June 25, 1788	10	330	*205*	684	*425*	Rogers, Mt.	1,746	*5,729*	Dogwood
Washington	Olympia	Seattle	Nov. 11, 1889	42	370	*230*	547	*340*	Rainier, Mt.	4,392	*14,410*	Western Rhododendron
West Virginia	Charleston	Charleston	June 20, 1863	35	322	*200*	362	*225*	Spruce Knob	1,482	*4,862*	Big Rhododendron
Wisconsin	Madison	Milwaukee	May 29, 1848	30	483	*300*	467	*290*	Timms Hill	595	*1,951*	Wood Violet
Wyoming	Cheyenne	Cheyenne	July 10, 1890	44	443	*275*	587	*365*	Gannett Pk.	4,207	*13,804*	Indian Paintbrush
UNITED STATES	Washington, D.C.	New York	. . .	. . .	. . .	. . .	. . .	. . .	McKinley, Mt.	6,194	*20,320*	. . .

Canada

PROVINCE	CAPITAL	LARGEST CITY	ENTERED CONFEDERATION: Date of Entry	ENTERED CONFEDERATION: Rank of Entry	GREATEST MEASUREMENT: N-S km	GREATEST MEASUREMENT: N-S mi	GREATEST MEASUREMENT: E-W km	GREATEST MEASUREMENT: E-W mi	HIGHEST POINT: Location	HIGHEST POINT: Altitude m	HIGHEST POINT: Altitude ft	FLORAL EMBLEM
Alberta	Edmonton	Edmonton	Sept. 1, 1905	8	1,207	*750*	644	*400*	Columbia, Mt.	3,747	*12,293*	Wild Rose
British Columbia	Victoria	Vancouver	July 20, 1871	6	1,263	*785*	1,022	*635*	Fairweather, Mt.	4,663	*15,300*	Dogwood
Manitoba	Winnipeg	Winnipeg	July 15, 1870	5	1,207	*750*	740	*460*	Baldy Mtn.	832	*2,730*	Pasque Flower
New Brunswick	Fredericton	St. John	July 1, 1867	1	378	*235*	314	*195*	Carleton, Mt.	820	*2,690*	Purple Violet
Newfoundland	St. John's	St. John's	March 31, 1949	10	1,545	*960*	1,022	*635*	Caubvick, Mt. (Mont d'Iberville)	1,652	*5,420*	Pitcher Plant
Northwest Territories	Yellowknife	Yellowknife	. . .	. . .	2,414	*1,500*	3,219	*2,000*	Unnamed	2,773	*9,098*	Mountain Avens
Nova Scotia	Halifax	Halifax	July 1, 1867	1	177	*110*	314	*195*	White Hill	532	*1,745*	Trailing Arbutus
Ontario	Toronto	Toronto	July 1, 1867	1	1,489	*925*	1,682	*1,045*	Ishpatina Ridge	693	*2,274*	White Trillium
Prince Edward Island	Charlottetown	Charlottetown	July 1, 1873	7	80	*50*	177	*110*	Unnamed	142	*466*	Lady's-slipper
Quebéc	Quebéc	Montréal	July 1, 1867	1	1,915	*1,190*	1,545	*960*	d'Iberville, Mont (Mt. Caubvick)	1,652	*5,420*	White Garden Lily
Saskatchewan	Regina	Saskatoon	Sep. 1, 1905	8	1,207	*750*	636	*395*	Unnamed	1,392	*4,567*	Prairie Lily
Yukon Territory	Whitehorse	Whitehorse	. . .	. . .	1,054	*655*	909	*565*	Logan, Mt.	5,951	*19,524*	Fireweed
CANADA	Ottawa	Toronto	. . .	. . .	. . .	. . .	. . .	. . .	Logan, Mt.	5,951	*19,524*	. . .

Geographical Information and International Map Index

World Nations

This table gives the area, population, population density, form of government, capital and location of every country in the world.

Area figures include inland water.

The populations are estimates made by Rand McNally on the basis of official data, United Nations estimates and other available information.

Besides specifying the form of government for all political areas, the table classifies them into five groups according to their political status. Units labeled *A* are independent sovereign nations. Units labeled *B* are independent as regards internal affairs, but for purposes of foreign affairs they are under the protection of another country. Units labeled *C* are colonies, overseas territories, dependencies, etc. of other countries. Units labeled *D* are states, provinces or other major administrative subdivisions of important countries. Units in the table with no letter designations are regions, islands or other areas that do not constitute separate political units by themselves.

Map Plate numbers refer to the International Map section of the atlas.

Country, Division, or Region English (Conventional)	Local Name	Area km²	Area sq mi	Population 1/1/89	Population Density per km²	Population Density per sq mi	Form of Government and Political Status	Capital	Continent	Map Plate
Afars and Issas, *see* Djibouti	...	...	...	...	...	...	...	...	...	...
† AFGHANISTAN	Afghānestān	652,225	*251,826*	14,655,000	22	*58*	Republic	*A* Kābol	Asia	23
Africa	...	30,300,000	*11,700,000*	642,100,000	21	*55*	...	...	Africa	30-31
Alabama	Alabama	133,913	*51,704*	4,125,000	31	*80*	State (U.S.)	*D* Montgomery	N. Amer	44
Alaska	Alaska	1,530,693	*591,004*	558,000	0.4	*0.9*	State (U.S.)	*D* Juneau	N. Amer	40
† ALBANIA	Shqiperia	28,748	*11,100*	3,181,000	111	*287*	Socialist republic	*A* Tirana	Europe	15
Alberta	Alberta	661,190	*255,287*	2,450,000	3.7	*9.6*	Province (Canada)	*D* Edmonton	N. Amer	42
† ALGERIA	Al Jazā'ir	2,381,741	*919,595*	24,215,000	10	*26*	Socialist republic	*A* Al Jazā'ir (Algiers)	Africa	32
American Samoa	American Samoa (English) / Amerika Samoa (Samoan)	199	*77*	40,000	201	*519*	Unincorporated territory (U.S.)	*C* Pago Pago	Oceania	65
Andaman and Nicobar Islands	Andaman and Nicobar Islands	8,293	*3,202*	... (1)	...	...	Territory (India)	*D* Port Blair	Asia	25
ANDORRA	Andorra	453	*175*	51,000	113	*291*	Coprincipality (Spanish and French protection)	*B* Andorra la Vella	Europe	13
† ANGOLA	Angola	1,246,700	*481,354*	8,385,000	6.7	*17*	Socialist republic	*A* Luanda	Africa	36
ANGUILLA	Anguilla	91	*35*	7,000	77	*200*	Dependent territory (U.K. protection)	*B* The Valley	N. Amer	51
Anhui	Anhui	140,000	*54,054*	53,970,000	386	*998*	Province (China)	*D* Hefei	Asia	28
Antarctica	...	14,000,000	*5,400,000*	... (1)	...	...	...	...	Antarctica	66
† ANTIGUA AND BARBUDA	Antigua	443	*171*	84,000	190	*491*	Parliamentary state	*A* St. John's	N. Amer	51
Arabian Peninsula	...	3,010,000	*1,112,000*	34,630,000	12	*31*	...	...	Asia	23
† ARGENTINA	Argentina	2,780,092	*1,073,400*	32,205,000	12	*30*	Republic	*A* Buenos Aires	S. Amer	56
Arizona	Arizona	295,264	*114,002*	3,558,000	12	*31*	State (U.S.)	*D* Phoenix	N. Amer	46
Arkansas	Arkansas	137,764	*53,191*	2,410,000	17	*45*	State (U.S.)	*D* Little Rock	N. Amer	45
Armenian S.S.R.	Armjanskaja S.S.R.	29,800	*11,506*	3,505,000	118	*305*	Soviet socialist republic (U.S.S.R.)	*D* Jerevan	Asia	16
ARUBA	Aruba	193	*75*	66,000	342	*880*	Self-governing territory (Netherlands protection)	*B* Oranjestad	N. Amer	49
Ascension	Ascension	88	*34*	1,800	20	*53*	Dependency (St. Helena)	*C* Georgetown	Africa	30-31
Asia	...	45,000,000	*17,400,000*	3,130,600,000	70	*180*	...	...	Asia	21-22
† AUSTRALIA	Australia	7,682,300	*2,966,155*	16,955,000	2.2	*5.7*	Federal parliamentary state	*A* Canberra	Oceania	59
Australian Capital Territory	Australian Capital Territory	2,400	*927*	281,000	117	*303*	Territory (Australia)	*D* Canberra	Oceania	59
† AUSTRIA	Österreich	83,855	*32,377*	7,584,000	90	*234*	Federal republic	*A* Wien (Vienna)	Europe	14
Azerbaijan S.S.R.	Azerbajdžanskaja S.S.R.	86,600	*33,436*	7,020,000	81	*210*	Soviet socialist republic (U.S.S.R.)	*D* Baku	Asia	16
Azores	Açores	2,247	*868*	260,000	116	*300*	Autonomous region (Portugal)	*D* Ponta Delgada	Europe	32
Baden-Wurttemberg	Baden-Württemberg	35,751	*13,804*	9,445,000	264	*684*	State (Fed. Rep. of Germany)	*D* Stuttgart	Europe	10
† BAHAMAS	Bahamas	13,939	*5,382*	243,000	17	*45*	Parliamentary state	*A* Nassau	N. Amer	47
† BAHRAIN	Al Baḩrayn	662	*256*	458,000	692	*1,789*	Monarchy	*A* Al Manāmah (Manama)	Asia	24
Balearic Islands	Islas Baleares	5,014	*1,936*	771,000	154	*398*	Province (Spain)	*D* Palma	Europe	13
Baltic Republics	...	174,000	*67,182*	7,995,000	46	*119*	...	...	Europe	...
† BANGLADESH	Bangladesh	143,998	*55,598*	111,390,000	774	*2,003*	Republic	*A* Dhaka	Asia	25
† BARBADOS	Barbados	430	*166*	255,000	593	*1,536*	Parliamentary state	*A* Bridgetown	N. Amer	51
Bavaria	Bayern	70,553	*27,241*	11,135,000	158	*409*	State (Fed. Rep. of Germany)	*D* München (Munich)	Europe	10
† BELGIUM	Belgique (French) / België (Flemish)	30,518	*11,783*	9,862,000	323	*837*	Constitutional monarchy	*A* Bruxelles (Brussels)	Europe	12
† BELIZE	Belize	22,963	*8,866*	184,000	8.0	*21*	Parliamentary state	*A* Belmopan	N. Amer	49
Benelux	...	74,889	*28,914*	25,045,000	334	*866*	...	...	Europe	12
† BENIN	Bénin	112,622	*43,484*	4,725,000	42	*109*	Socialist republic	*A* Porto-Novo and Cotonou	Africa	34
Berlin (West)	Berlin (West)	480	*185*	1,925,000	4,010	*10,405*	State (Fed. Rep. of Germany)	*D* Berlin (West)	Europe	10
Bermuda	Bermuda	54	*21*	56,000	1,037	*2,667*	Dependent territory (U.K.)	*C* Hamilton	N. Amer	47
† BHUTAN	Druk	46,500	*17,954*	1,519,000	33	*85*	Monarchy (Indian protection)	*B* Thimphu	Asia	25
Bioko	Bioko	2,034	*785*	83,000	41	*106*	Province of Equatorial Guinea	*D* Malabo	Africa	34
† BOLIVIA	Bolivia	1,098,581	*424,165*	7,184,000	6.5	*17*	Republic	*A* La Paz and Sucre	S. Amer	54
BOPHUTHATSWANA (2)	Bophuthatswana	40,509	*15,641*	2,202,000	54	*141*	National state (South African protection)	*B* Mmabatho	Africa	37
Borneo, Indonesian	Kalimantan	539,460	*208,287*	8,480,000	16	*41*	Part of Indonesia (4 provinces)	...	Asia	26
† BOTSWANA	Botswana	582,000	*224,711*	1,230,000	2.1	*5.5*	Republic	*A* Gaborone	Africa	37
† BRAZIL	Brasil	8,511,965	*3,286,488*	145,930,000	17	*44*	Federal republic	*A* Brasília	S. Amer	54-56
Bremen	Bremen	404	*156*	645,000	1,597	*4,135*	State (Fed. Rep. of Germany)	*D* Bremen	Europe	10
British Columbia	British Columbia (English) / Columbie-Britannique (French)	947,800	*365,948*	2,965,000	3.1	*8.1*	Province (Canada)	*D* Victoria	N. Amer	42
British Indian Ocean Territory	British Indian Ocean Territory	60	*23*	... (1)	...	...	Dependent territory (U.K.)	*C* ...	Africa	22
† BRUNEI	Brunei	5,765	*2,226*	247,000	43	*111*	Monarchy	*A* Bandar Seri Begawan	Asia	26
† BULGARIA	Balgarija	110,912	*42,823*	8,997,000	81	*210*	Socialist republic	*A* Sofija (Sofia)	Europe	15
† BURKINA FASO	Burkina Faso	274,200	*105,869*	8,596,000	31	*81*	Provisional military government	*A* Ouagadougou	Africa	34
† BURMA	Myanmar	676,577	*261,228*	41,860,000	62	*160*	Socialist republic	*A* Yangon (Rangoon)	Asia	25
† BURUNDI	Burundi	27,830	*10,745*	5,200,000	187	*484*	Provisional military government	*A* Bujumbura	Africa	36
† Byelorussian S.S.R.	Belorusskaja S.S.R.	207,600	*80,155*	10,215,000	49	*127*	Soviet socialist republic (U.S.S.R.)	*D* Minsk	Europe	16
California	California	411,041	*158,704*	28,630,000	70	*180*	State (U.S.)	*D* Sacramento	N. Amer	46
† CAMBODIA	Kâmpŭchéa	181,035	*69,898*	6,760,000	37	*97*	Socialist republic	*A* Phnum Pénh (Phnom Penh)	Asia	26
† CAMEROON	Cameroon (English) / Cameroun (French)	475,442	*183,569*	11,495,000	24	*63*	Republic	*A* Yaoundé	Africa	34
† CANADA	Canada	9,970,610	*3,849,674*	25,895,000	2.6	*6.7*	Federal parliamentary state	*A* Ottawa	N. Amer	42
Canary Islands	Islas Canarias	7,273	*2,808*	1,535,000	211	*547*	Part of Spain (2 provinces)	...	Africa	32
† CAPE VERDE	Cabo Verde	4,033	*1,557*	359,000	89	*231*	Republic	*A* Praia	Africa	32
Cayman Islands	Cayman Islands	259	*100*	25,000	97	*250*	Dependent territory (U.K.)	*C* Georgetown	N. Amer	49
Celebes	Sulawesi	189,216	*73,057*	12,405,000	66	*170*	Part of Indonesia (4 provinces)	...	Asia	26
† CENTRAL AFRICAN REPUBLIC	Centrafrique	622,984	*240,535*	3,089,000	5.0	*13*	Republic	*A* Bangui	Africa	35
Central America	...	520,000	*200,000*	28,195,000	54	*141*	...	...	N. Amer	49
Central Asia, Soviet	...	1,277,100	*493,090*	33,145,000	26	*67*	...	...	Asia	19
Ceylon, *see* Sri Lanka	...	...	...	...	...	...	...	...	...	...
† CHAD	Tchad	1,284,000	*495,755*	4,845,000	3.8	*9.8*	Republic	*A* N'Djamena	Africa	35

Country, Division, or Region English (Conventional)	Local Name	Area km²	Area sq mi	Population 1/1/89	Population Density per km²	Population Density per sq mi	Form of Government and Political Status	Capital	Continent and Map Plate
Channel Islands	. . .	194	75	137,000	706	1,827	. . .	. . .	Europe . . . 9
† CHILE	Chile	756,626	292,135	12,925,000	17	44	Provisional military government	A Santiago	S. Amer . . . 56
† CHINA (excl. Taiwan)	Zhongguo Renmin Gongheguo	9,631,600	3,718,782	1,094,700,000	114	294	Socialist republic	A Beijing (Peking)	Asia . . . 27
China (Nationalist), *see* Taiwan	. . .	. . .	. . .	. . .	. . .	. . .	. . .	. . .	. . .
Christmas Island	Christmas Island	135	52	2,000	15	38	External territory (Australia)	C Flying Fish Cove	Oceania . . . 26
CISKEI (2)	Ciskei	7,790	3,008	1,006,000	129	334	National state (South African protection)	B Bisho	Africa . . . 37
Cocos (Keeling) Islands	Cocos (Keeling) Islands	14	5.4	600	43	111	Part of Australia	. . .	Oceania . . . 22
† COLOMBIA	Colombia	1,141,748	440,831	30,465,000	27	69	Republic	A Bogotá	S. Amer . . . 54
Colorado	Colorado	269,602	104,094	3,392,000	13	33	State (U.S.)	D Denver	N. Amer . . . 45
† COMOROS (excl. Mayotte)	Al-Qumur (Arabic) / Comores (French)	2,171	838	436,000	201	520	Federal islamic republic	A Moroni	Africa . . . 37
† CONGO	Congo	342,000	132,047	2,191,000	6.4	17	Socialist republic	A Brazzaville	Africa . . . 36
Connecticut	Connecticut	12,999	5,019	3,233,000	249	644	State (U.S)	D Hartford	N. Amer . . . 44
COOK ISLANDS	Cook Islands	236	91	17,000	72	187	Self-governing territory (New Zealand protection)	B Avarua	Oceania . . . 61
Coral Sea Islands Territory	Coral Sea Islands Territory	2.6	1.0	(1)	. . .	. . .	External territory (Australia)	C . . .	Oceania . . . 59
Corsica	Corse	8,681	3,352	253,000	29	75	Part of France (2 departments)	D . . .	Europe . . . 11
† COSTA RICA	Costa Rica	51,100	19,730	2,990,000	59	152	Republic	A San José	N. Amer . . . 49
† CUBA	Cuba	110,861	42,804	10,440,000	94	244	Socialist republic	A La Habana (Havana)	N. Amer . . . 49
Curacao	Curaçao	444	171	167,000	376	977	Division of Netherlands Antilles (Neth.)	D Willemstad	N. Amer . . . 49
† CYPRUS	Kípros (Greek) / Kıbrıs (Turkish)	5,896	2,276	573,000	97	252	Republic	A Nicosia (Levkosía)	Asia . . . 24
CYPRUS, NORTH	Kuzey Kıbrıs	3,355	1,295	172,000	51	133	Republic	A Nicosia (Lefkoşa)	Asia . . . 24
† CZECHOSLOVAKIA	Československo	127,905	49,384	15,605,000	122	316	Federal socialist republic	A Praha (Prague)	Europe . . . 10
Delaware	Delaware	5,297	2,045	655,000	124	320	State (U.S.)	D Dover	N. Amer . . . 44
† DENMARK	Danmark	43,092	16,638	5,135,000	119	309	Constitutional monarchy	A København (Copenhagen)	Europe . . . 8
Denmark and Possessions	. . .	2,220,091	857,182	5,238,000	2.4	6.1	. . .	. . .	. . .
District of Columbia	District of Columbia	179	69	619,000	3,458	8,971	Federal district (U.S.)	D Washington	N. Amer . . . 44
† DJIBOUTI	Djibouti	23,200	8,958	324,000	14	36	Republic	A Djibouti	Africa . . . 35
† DOMINICA	Dominica	752	290	100,000	133	345	Republic	A Roseau	N. Amer . . . 51
† DOMINICAN REPUBLIC	República Dominicana	48,442	18,704	7,069,000	146	378	Republic	A Santo Domingo	N. Amer . . . 49
† ECUADOR	Ecuador	283,561	109,484	10,345,000	36	94	Republic	A Quito	S. Amer . . . 54
† EGYPT	Mişr	1,001,450	386,662	52,490,000	52	136	Socialist republic	A Al Qāhirah (Cairo)	Africa . . . 33
Ellis Islands, *see* Tuvalu	. . .	. . .	. . .	. . .	. . .	. . .	. . .	. . .	. . .
† EL SALVADOR	El Salvador	21,041	8,124	5,122,000	243	630	Republic	A San Salvador	N. Amer . . . 49
England	England	130,439	50,363	47,510,000	364	943	Administrative division (U.K.)	D London	Europe . . . 9
† EQUATORIAL GUINEA	Guinea Ecuatorial	28,051	10,831	438,000	16	40	Republic	A Malabo	Africa . . . 36
Estonian S.S.R.	Eesti N.S.V.	45,100	17,413	1,585,000	35	91	Soviet socialist republic (U.S.S.R.)	D Tallinn	Europe . . . 8
† ETHIOPIA	Itiopya	1,251,282	483,123	48,470,000	39	100	Socialist republic	A Ādīs Ābeba (Addis Ababa)	Africa . . . 35
Eurasia	. . .	54,900,000	21,200,000	3,816,000,000	70	180	. . .	. . .	. . .
Europe	. . .	9,900,000	3,800,000	685,400,000	69	180	. . .	. . .	Europe . . . 5-6
FAEROE ISLANDS	Føroyar	1,399	540	48,000	34	89	Self-governing territory (Danish protection)	B Thorshavn	Europe . . . 6
Falkland Islands (3)	Falkland Islands (English) / Islas Malvinas (Spanish)	12,173	4,700	2,000	0.2	0.4	Dependent territory (U.K.)	C Stanley	S. Amer . . . 56
† FIJI	Fiji (French) / Viti (Fijian)	18,333	7,078	749,000	41	106	Republic	A Suva	Oceania . . . 63
† FINLAND	Suomi (Finnish) / Finland (Swedish)	338,145	130,559	4,949,000	15	38	Republic	A Helsinki (Helsingfors)	Europe . . . 7
Florida	Florida	151,949	58,668	12,605,000	83	215	State (U.S.)	D Tallahassee	N. Amer . . . 44
† FRANCE (excl. Overseas Departments)	France	547,026	211,208	55,970,000	102	265	Republic	A Paris	Europe . . . 11
France and Possessions	. . .	667,359	257,667	57,780,000	87	224	. . .	. . . Paris	. . .
French Guiana	Guyane Française	91,000	35,135	93,000	1.0	2.6	Overseas department (France)	C Cayenne	S. Amer . . . 54
French Polynesia	Polynésie Française	4,000	1,544	194,000	49	126	Overseas territory (France)	C Papeete	Oceania . . . 61
French West Indies	. . .	2,880	1,112	678,000	235	610	. . .	. . .	N. Amer . . . 50
Fujian	Fujian	123,000	47,491	28,355,000	231	597	Province (China)	D Fuzhou	Asia . . . 27
† GABON	Gabon	267,667	103,347	1,056,000	3.9	10	Republic	A Libreville	Africa . . . 36
Galapagos Islands	Archipiélago de Colón (Islas Galápagos)	7,964	3,075	10,000	1.3	3.3	Province (Ecuador)	D Baquerizo Moreno	S. Amer . . . 54
† GAMBIA	Gambia	11,295	4,361	789,000	70	181	Republic	A Banjul	Africa . . . 34
Gansu	Gansu	390,000	150,580	21,345,000	55	142	Province (China)	D Lanzhou	Asia . . . 27
Georgia	Georgia	152,587	58,914	6,401,000	42	109	State (U.S.)	D Atlanta	N. Amer . . . 44
Georgian S.S.R.	Gruzinskaja S.S.R.	69,700	26,911	5,330,000	76	198	Soviet socialist republic (U.S.S.R.)	D Tbilisi	Asia . . . 16
† GERMAN DEMOCRATIC REPUBLIC (EAST GERMANY)	Deutsche Demokratische Republik	108,333	41,828	16,582,000	153	396	Socialist republic	A Berlin (Ost-) (East Berlin)	Europe . . . 10
† GERMANY, FEDERAL REPUBLIC OF (WEST GERMANY)	Bundesrepublik Deutschland	248,707	96,027	61,380,000	247	639	Federal republic	A Bonn	Europe . . . 10
Germany (entire)	. . .	357,040	137,855	77,960,000	218	566	. . .	. . .	Europe . . . 10
† GHANA	Ghana	238,533	92,098	14,575,000	61	158	Provisional military government	A Accra	Africa . . . 34
Gibraltar	Gibraltar	6.0	2	31,000	5,167	13,478	Dependent territory (U.K.)	C Gibraltar	Europe . . . 13
Gilbert Islands, *see* Tuvalu	. . .	. . .	. . .	. . .	. . .	. . .	. . .	. . .	. . .
Great Britain, *see* United Kingdom	. . .	. . .	. . .	. . .	. . .	. . .	. . .	. . .	. . .
† GREECE	Ellas	131,944	50,944	10,030,000	76	197	Republic	A Athínai (Athens)	Europe . . . 15
GREENLAND	Kalaallit Nunaat (Inuit) / Grønland (Danish)	2,175,600	840,004	55,000	0.1	0.1	Self-governing territory (Danish protection)	B Godthåb (Nûk)	N. Amer . . . 41
† GRENADA	Grenada	344	133	95,000	276	714	Parliamentary state	A St. George's	N. Amer . . . 51
Guadeloupe (incl. Dependencies)	Guadeloupe	1,780	687	340,000	191	495	Overseas department (France)	C Basse-Terre	N. Amer . . . 51
Guam	Guam	541	209	137,000	253	656	Unincorporated territory (U.S.)	C Agana	Oceania . . . 64
Guangdong	Guangdong	197,000	76,062	58,730,000	298	772	Province (China)	D Guangzhou (Canton)	Asia . . . 27
† GUATEMALA	Guatemala	108,889	42,042	8,818,000	81	210	Republic	A Guatemala	N. Amer . . . 49
Guernsey (incl. Dependencies)	Guernsey	78	30	56,000	718	1,867	Bailiwick (Channel Islands)	C St. Peter Port	Europe . . . 9
† GUINEA	Guinée	245,857	94,926	6,999,000	28	74	Provisional military government	A Conakry	Africa . . . 34
† GUINEA-BISSAU	Guiné-Bissau	36,125	13,948	962,000	27	69	Republic	A Bissau	Africa . . . 34
Guizhou	Guizhou	174,000	67,182	30,980,000	178	461	Province (China)	D Guiyang	Asia . . . 27
† GUYANA	Guyana	214,969	83,000	765,000	3.6	9.2	Republic	A Georgetown	S. Amer . . . 54
Hainan	Hainan	34,000	13,127	6,520,000	192	497	Province (China)	D Haikou	Asia . . . 27
† HAITI	Haïti	27,750	10,714	6,346,000	229	592	Provisional military government	A Port-au-Prince	N. Amer . . . 49
Hamburg	Hamburg	755	292	1,555,000	2,060	5,325	State (Fed. Rep. of Germany)	D Hamburg	Europe . . . 10
Hawaii	Hawaii	16,765	6,473	1,110,000	66	171	State (U.S.)	D Honolulu	N. Amer . . . 60
Hebei	Hebei	203,000	78,379	58,020,000	286	740	Province (China)	D Shijiazhuang	Asia . . . 28
Heilongjiang	Heilongjiang	460,000	177,607	34,810,000	76	196	Province (China)	D Harbin	Asia . . . 27
Henan	Henan	167,000	64,479	80,900,000	484	1,255	Province (China)	D Zhengzhou	Asia . . . 27
Hesse	Hessen	21,114	8,152	5,575,000	264	684	State (Fed. Rep. of Germany)	D Wiesbaden	Europe . . . 10

Country, Division, or Region: English (Conventional)	Local Name	Area km²	Area sq mi	Population 1/1/89	Population Density per km²	Population Density per sq mi	Form of Government and Political Status	Capital	Continent and Map Plate
Hispaniola	La Española	76,192	*29,418*	13,415,000	176	*456*	. . .	. . .	N. Amer . . . 49
Holland, *see* Netherlands	. . .	. . .	. . .	. . .	. . .	. . .	. . .	. . .	. . .
† HONDURAS	Honduras	112,088	*43,277*	5,047,000	45	*117*	Republic	*A* Tegucigalpa	N. Amer . . . 49
Hong Kong	Hong Kong (English) / Xianggang (Chinese)	1,068	*412*	5,731,000	5,366	*13,910*	Dependent territory (U.K.)	*C* Victoria (Hong Kong)	Asia . . . 27
Hubei	Hubei	188,000	*72,587*	51,560,000	274	*710*	Province (China)	*D* Wuhan	Asia . . . 27
Hunan	Hunan	211,000	*81,468*	58,790,000	279	*722*	Province (China)	*D* Changsha	Asia . . . 27
† HUNGARY	Magyarország	93,033	*35,920*	10,580,000	114	*295*	Socialist republic	*A* Budapest	Europe . . . 10
† ICELAND	Ísland	103,000	*39,769*	248,000	2.4	*6.2*	Republic	*A* Reykjavík	Europe . . . 7
Idaho	Idaho	216,435	*83,566*	1,010,000	4.7	*12*	State (U.S.)	*D* Boise	N. Amer . . . 46
Illinois	Illinois	149,888	*57,872*	11,615,000	77	*201*	State (U.S.)	*D* Springfield	N. Amer . . . 45
† INDIA (incl. part of Jammu and Kashmir)	India (English) / Bhārat (Hindi)	3,203,975	*1,237,062*	825,000,000	257	*667*	Federal republic	*A* New Delhi	Asia . . . 25
Indiana	Indiana	94,320	*36,417*	5,539,000	59	*152*	State (U.S.)	*D* Indianapolis	N. Amer . . . 44
† INDONESIA	Indonesia	1,919,443	*741,101*	185,860,000	97	*251*	Republic	*A* Jakarta	Asia . . . 26
Inner Mongolia	Nei Mongol Gaoyuan	1,200,000	*463,323*	20,020,000	17	*43*	Autonomous region (China)	*D* Hohhot	Asia . . . 27
Iowa	Iowa	145,752	*56,275*	2,818,000	19	*50*	State (U.S.)	*D* Des Moines	N. Amer . . . 45
† IRAN	Īrān	1,648,000	*636,296*	52,760,000	32	*83*	Islamic republic	*A* Tehrān	Asia . . . 23
† IRAQ	Al ʿIrāq	438,317	*169,235*	17,900,000	41	*106*	Republic	*A* Baghdād	Asia . . . 24
† IRELAND	Ireland (English) / Éire (Gaelic)	70,283	*27,136*	3,524,000	50	*130*	Republic	*A* Dublin (Baile Átha Cliath)	Europe . . . 9
ISLE OF MAN	Isle of Man	572	*221*	62,000	108	*281*	Self-governing territory (U.K. protection)	*B* Douglas	Europe . . . 9
† ISRAEL (excl. Occupied Areas)	Yisra'el (Hebrew) / Isrāʾīl (Arabic)	20,770	*8,019*	4,374,000	211	*545*	Republic	*A* Yerushalayim (Jerusalem)	Asia . . . 24
Israeli Occupied Areas [4]	. . .	7,632	*2,947*	1,728,000	226	*586*	. . .	. . .	Asia . . . 24
† ITALY	Italia	301,268	*116,320*	57,500,000	191	*494*	Republic	*A* Roma (Rome)	Europe . . . 14
† IVORY COAST	Côte d'Ivoire	320,763	*123,847*	11,400,000	36	*92*	Republic	*A* Abidjan and Yamoussoukro [5]	Africa . . . 34
† JAMAICA	Jamaica	10,991	*4,244*	2,470,000	225	*582*	Parliamentary state	*A* Kingston	N. Amer . . . 49
† JAPAN	Nippon	377,801	*145,870*	123,010,000	326	*843*	Constitutional monarchy	*A* Tōkyō	Asia . . . 29
Java	Jawa	132,187	*51,038*	106,140,000	803	*2,080*	Part of Indonesia (5 provinces)	. . .	Asia . . . 26
Jersey	Jersey	116	*45*	81,000	698	*1,800*	Bailiwick (Channel Islands)	*C* St. Helier	Europe . . . 9
Jiangsu	Jiangsu	102,000	*39,382*	65,240,000	640	*1,657*	Province (China)	*D* Nanjing (Nanking)	Asia . . . 28
Jiangxi	Jiangxi	165,000	*63,707*	36,235,000	220	*569*	Province (China)	*D* Nanchang	Asia . . . 27
Jilin	Jilin	187,000	*72,201*	24,195,000	129	*335*	Province (China)	*D* Changchun	Asia . . . 27
Johnston Atoll	Johnston Atoll	1.3	*0.5*	300	231	*600*	Unincorporated territory (U.S.)	*C* . . .	Oceania . . . 60
† JORDAN (excl. West Bank)	Al Urdun	91,000	*35,135*	2,904,000	32	*83*	Constitutional monarchy	*A* ʿAmmān	Asia . . . 24
Kansas	Kansas	213,109	*82,282*	2,500,000	12	*30*	State (U.S.)	*D* Topeka	N. Amer . . . 45
Kashmir, Jammu and	Jammu and Kashmir	222,801	*86,024*	8,960,000	40	*104*	Disputed territory (India and Pakistan)	*D* . . .	Asia . . . 25
Kazakh S.S.R.	Kazahskaja S.S.R.	2,717,300	*1,049,156*	16,680,000	6.1	*16*	Soviet socialist republic (U.S.S.R.)	*D* Alma-Ata	Asia . . . 19
Kentucky	Kentucky	104,672	*40,414*	3,741,000	36	*93*	State (U.S.)	*D* Frankfort	N. Amer . . . 44
† KENYA	Kenya	582,646	*224,961*	25,825,000	44	*115*	Republic	*A* Nairobi	Africa . . . 36
Kerguelen Islands	Iles Kerguélen	6,993	*2,700*	100	. . .	. . .	Part of French Southern and Antarctic Territories	*C* . . .	S. Amer . . . 30-31
Kirghiz S.S.R.	Kirgizskaja S.S.R.	198,500	*76,641*	4,330,000	22	*56*	Soviet socialist republic (U.S.S.R.)	*D* Frunze	Asia . . . 18
KIRIBATI	Kiribati	726	*280*	69,000	95	*246*	Republic	*A* Bairiki	Oceania . . . 60
KOREA, NORTH	Chosŏn Minjujuŭi Inmin Konghwaguk	120,538	*46,540*	22,250,000	185	*478*	Socialist republic	*A* P'yŏngyang	Asia . . . 28
KOREA, SOUTH	Taehan-min'guk	98,484	*38,025*	42,840,000	435	*1,127*	Republic	*A* Sŏul (Seoul)	Asia . . . 28
Korea (entire)	. . .	219,022	*84,565*	65,090,000	297	*770*	. . .	. . .	Asia . . . 28
† KUWAIT	Al Kuwayt	17,818	*6,880*	2,002,000	112	*291*	Constitutional monarchy	*A* Al Kuwayt (Kuwait)	Asia . . . 24
Kwangsi	Guangxi Zhuangzu Zizhiqu	237,000	*91,506*	40,285,000	170	*440*	Autonomous region (China)	*D* Nanning	Asia . . . 27
Labrador	Labrador	292,218	*112,826*	31,000	0.1	*0.3*	Part of Newfoundland province (Canada)	. . .	N. Amer . . . 42
† LAOS	Lao	236,800	*91,429*	3,892,000	16	*43*	Socialist republic	*A* Viangchan (Vientiane)	Asia . . . 26
Latin America	. . .	20,500,000	*8,000,000*	372,800,000	18	*47*	. . .	. . .	N.A., S.A. 52-53
Latvian S.S.R.	Latvijas P.S.R.	63,700	*24,595*	2,695,000	42	*110*	Soviet socialist republic (U.S.S.R.)	*D* Rīga	Europe . . . 8
† LEBANON	Lubnān	10,400	*4,015*	3,351,000	322	*835*	Republic	*A* Bayrūt (Beirut)	Asia . . . 24
† LESOTHO	Lesotho	30,355	*11,720*	1,689,000	56	*144*	Constitutional monarchy	*A* Maseru	Africa . . . 37
Liaoning	Liaoning	151,000	*58,301*	38,645,000	256	*663*	Province (China)	*D* Shenyang (Mukden)	Asia . . . 28
† LIBERIA	Liberia	99,067	*38,250*	2,553,000	26	*67*	Republic	*A* Monrovia	Africa . . . 34
† LIBYA	Lībiyā	1,759,540	*679,362*	4,019,000	2.3	*5.9*	Socialist republic	*A* Ṭarābulus (Tripoli)	Africa . . . 33
LIECHTENSTEIN	Liechtenstein	160	*62*	29,000	181	*468*	Constitutional monarchy	*A* Vaduz	Europe . . . 14
Lithuanian S.S.R. [6]	Lietuvos T.S.R.	65,200	*25,174*	3,715,000	57	*148*	Soviet socialist republic (U.S.S.R.)	*D* Vilnius	Europe . . . 8
Louisiana	Louisiana	123,672	*47,750*	4,517,000	37	*95*	State (U.S.)	*D* Baton Rouge	N. Amer . . . 45
Lower Saxony	Niedersachsen	47,438	*18,316*	7,195,000	152	*393*	State (Fed. Rep. of Germany)	*D* Hannover	Europe . . . 10
† LUXEMBOURG	Luxembourg (French) / Lezebuurg (Luxembourgish)	2,586	*998*	368,000	142	*369*	Constitutional monarchy	*A* Luxembourg	Europe . . . 12
Macao	Macau	17	*6.6*	432,000	25,412	*65,455*	Chinese territory under Portuguese administration	*C* Macau	Asia . . . 27
† MADAGASCAR	Madagasikara	587,041	*226,658*	11,250,000	19	*50*	Republic	*A* Antananarivo	Africa . . . 37
Madeira	Madeira	794	*307*	277,000	349	*902*	Autonomous region (Portugal)	*D* Funchal	Europe . . . 32
Maine	Maine	86,156	*33,265*	1,205,000	14	*36*	State (U.S.)	*D* Augusta	N. Amer . . . 44
† MALAWI	Malaŵi	118,484	*45,747*	8,440,000	71	*184*	Republic	*A* Lilongwe	Africa . . . 36
Malaya	Semenanjung Malaysia	131,312	*50,700*	14,240,000	108	*281*	Part of Malaysia (11 states)	*D* . . .	Asia . . . 26
† MALAYSIA	Malaysia	330,228	*127,502*	17,255,000	52	*135*	Federal constitutional monarchy	*A* Kuala Lumpur	Asia . . . 26
† MALDIVES	Maldives	298	*115*	209,000	701	*1,817*	Republic	*A* Male	Asia . . . 25
† MALI	Mali	1,240,000	*478,767*	9,039,000	7.3	*19*	Republic	*A* Bamako	Africa . . . 34
† MALTA	Malta	316	*122*	370,000	1,171	*3,033*	Republic	*A* Valletta	Europe . . . 14
Manitoba	Manitoba	649,950	*250,947*	1,095,000	1.7	*4.4*	Province (Canada)	*D* Winnipeg	N. Amer . . . 42
Maritime Provinces	. . .	134,590	*51,965*	1,734,000	13	*33*	. . .	. . .	N. Amer . . . 42
MARSHALL ISLANDS	Marshall Islands	181	*70*	40,000	221	*571*	Republic (U.S. protection)	*B* Uliga	Oceania . . . 60
Martinique	Martinique	1,100	*425*	338,000	307	*795*	Overseas department (France)	*C* Fort-de-France	N. Amer . . . 51
Maryland	Maryland	27,094	*10,461*	4,605,000	170	*440*	State (U.S.)	*D* Annapolis	N. Amer . . . 44
Massachusetts	Massachusetts	21,461	*8,286*	5,880,000	274	*710*	State (U.S.)	*D* Boston	N. Amer . . . 44
† MAURITANIA	Mūrītāniyā (Arabic) / Mauritanie (French)	1,030,700	*397,956*	1,948,000	1.9	*4.9*	Provisional military government	*A* Nouakchott	Africa . . . 32
† MAURITIUS (incl. Dependencies)	Mauritius	2,040	*788*	1,057,000	518	*1,341*	Parliamentary state	*A* Port-Louis	Africa . . . 37
Mayotte [7]	Mayotte	373	*144*	79,000	212	*549*	Territorial collectivity (France)	*C* Dzaoudzi and Mamoudzou [5]	Africa . . . 37
† MEXICO	México	1,972,547	*761,605*	85,300,000	43	*112*	Federal republic	*A* Ciudad de México (Mexico City)	N. Amer . . . 48

Country, Division, or Region: English (Conventional)	Local Name	Area km²	Area sq mi	Population 1/1/89	Population Density per km²	Population Density per sq mi	Form of Government and Political Status	Capital	Continent and Map Plate	
Michigan	Michigan	251,506	*97,107*	9,186,000	37	*95*	State (U.S.)	*D* Lansing	N. Amer	44
MICRONESIA, FEDERATED STATES OF	Federated States of Micronesia	702	*271*	108,000	154	*399*	Republic (U.S. protection)	*B* Ponape	Oceania	60
Middle America	. . .	2,730,000	*1,050,000*	85,300,000	31	*81*	. . .	. . .	N. Amer	47
Midway Islands	Midway Islands	5.2	*2.0*	500	96	*250*	Unincorporated territory (U.S.)	*C* . . .	Oceania	60
Minnesota	Minnesota	224,329	*86,614*	4,283,000	19	*49*	State (U.S.)	*D* St. Paul	N. Amer	45
Mississippi	Mississippi	123,519	*47,691*	2,647,000	21	*56*	State (U.S.)	*D* Jackson	N. Amer	45
Missouri	Missouri	180,514	*69,697*	5,145,000	29	*74*	State (U.S.)	*D* Jefferson City	N. Amer	45
Moldavian S.S.R.	Moldavskaja S.S.R.	33,700	*13,012*	4,260,000	126	*327*	Soviet socialist republic (U.S.S.R.)	*D* Kišinev (Kishinev)	Europe	16
MONACO	Monaco	1.9	*0.7*	29,000	15,263	*41,429*	Constitutional monarchy	*A* Monaco	Europe	11
†MONGOLIA	Mongol Ard Uls	1,565,000	*604,250*	2,097,000	1.3	*3.5*	Socialist republic	*A* Ulan-Bator (Ulaanbaatar)	Asia	27
Montana	Montana	380,845	*147,045*	814,000	2.1	*5.5*	State (U.S.)	*D* Helena	N. Amer	46
Montserrat	Montserrat	103	*40*	12,000	117	*300*	Dependent territory (U.K.)	*C* Plymouth	N. Amer	51
†MOROCCO (excl. Western Sahara)	Al Maghrib	446,550	*172,414*	25,600,000	57	*148*	Consitutional monarchy	*A* Rabat	Africa	32
†MOZAMBIQUE	Moçambique	799,379	*308,642*	17,660,000	22	*57*	Socialist republic	*A* Maputo	Africa	37
NAMIBIA (excl. Walvis Bay)	Namibia	823,144	*317,818*	1,337,000	1.6	*4.2*	Republic	*A* Windhoek	Africa	37
NAURU	Nauru (English) / Naoero (Nauruan)	21	*8.1*	9,000	429	*1,111*	Republic	*A* Domaneab	Oceania	64
Navassa Island	Navassa Island	4.9	*1.9*	. . . (1)	. . .	. . .	Unincorporated territory (U.S.)	*C* . . .	N. Amer	49
Nebraska	Nebraska	200,336	*77,350*	1,599,000	8.0	*21*	State (U.S.)	*D* Lincoln	N. Amer	45
†NEPAL	Nepāl	147,181	*56,827*	18,415,000	125	*324*	Constitutional monarchy	*A* Kāṭhmāṇḍāũ	Asia	25
†NETHERLANDS	Nederland	41,785	*16,133*	14,815,000	355	*918*	Constitutional monarchy	*A* Amsterdam and 's-Gravenhage (The Hague)	Europe	12
NETHERLANDS ANTILLES	Nederlandse Antillen	800	*309*	194,000	243	*628*	Self-governing territory (Netherlands protection)	*B* Willemstad	N. Amer	50
Nevada	Nevada	286,354	*110,562*	1,061,000	3.7	*9.6*	State (U.S.)	*D* Carson City	N. Amer	46
New Brunswick	New Brunswick (English) / Nouveau-Brusnwick (French)	73,440	*28,355*	718,000	9.8	*25*	Province (Canada)	*D* Fredericton	N. Amer	42
New Caledonia	Nouvelle-Calédonie	19,079	*7,366*	161,000	8.4	*22*	Overseas territory (France)	*C* Nouméa	Oceania	63
New England	New England	172,685	*66,674*	12,955,000	75	*194*	Part of U.S. (6 states)	. . .	N. Amer	43
Newfoundland	Newfoundland (English) / Terre-Neuve (French)	405,720	*156,649*	571,000	1.4	*3.6*	Province (Canada)	*D* St. John's	N. Amer	42
Newfoundland (island)	Newfoundland (English) / Terre-Neuve (French)	108,860	*42,031*	540,000	5.0	*13*	Part of Newfoundland province (Canada)	. . .	N. Amer	42
New Hampshire	New Hampshire	24,030	*9,278*	1,089,000	45	*117*	State (U.S.)	*D* Concord	N. Amer	44
New Hebrides, *see* Vanuatu	. . .	. . .	. . .	. . .	. . .	. . .	. . .	. . .	. . .	. . .
New Jersey	New Jersey	20,168	*7,787*	7,739,000	384	*994*	State (U.S.)	*D* Trenton	N. Amer	44
New Mexico	New Mexico	314,927	*121,594*	1,547,000	4.9	*13*	State (U.S.)	*D* Santa Fe	N. Amer	45
New South Wales	New South Wales	801,600	*309,500*	5,820,000	7.3	*19*	State (Australia)	*D* Sydney	Oceania	59
New York	New York	136,588	*52,737*	17,880,000	131	*339*	State (U.S.)	*D* Albany	N. Amer	44
†NEW ZEALAND	New Zealand	268,112	*103,519*	3,391,000	13	*33*	Parliamentary state	*A* Wellington	Oceania	62
†NICARAGUA	Nicaragua	130,000	*50,193*	3,689,000	28	*73*	Republic	*A* Managua	N. Amer	49
†NIGER	Niger	1,267,000	*489,191*	7,329,000	5.8	*15*	Provisional military government	*A* Niamey	Africa	34
†NIGERIA	Nigeria	923,768	*356,669*	113,580,000	123	*318*	Provisional military government	*A* Lagos and Abuja (5)	Africa	34
Ningsia	Ningxia Huizu Zizhiqu	66,000	*25,483*	4,270,000	65	*168*	Autonomous region (China)	*D* Yinchuan	Asia	27
NIUE	Niue	263	*102*	2,400	9.1	*24*	Self-governing territory (New Zealand protection)	*B* Alofi	Oceania	64
Norfolk Island	Norfolk Island	36	*14*	2,000	56	*143*	External territory (Australia)	*C* Kingston	Oceania	61
North America	. . .	24,400,000	*9,400,000*	420,100,000	17	*45*	. . .	. . .	N. Amer	38-39
North Borneo, *see* Sabah	. . .	. . .	. . .	. . .	. . .	. . .	. . .	. . .	. . .	. . .
North Carolina	North Carolina	136,412	*52,669*	6,532,000	48	*124*	State (U.S.)	*D* Raleigh	N. Amer	44
North Dakota	North Dakota	183,117	*70,702*	676,000	3.7	*9.6*	State (U.S.)	*D* Bismarck	N. Amer	45
Northern Ireland	Northern Ireland	14,122	*5,453*	1,575,000	112	*289*	Administrative division (U.K.)	*D* Belfast	Europe	9
NORTHERN MARIANA ISLANDS	Northern Mariana Islands	477	*184*	22,000	46	*120*	Commonwealth (U.S. protection)	*B* Saipan (island)	Oceania	60
Northern Territory	Northern Territory	1,346,200	*519,771*	168,000	0.1	*0.3*	Territory (Australia)	*D* Darwin	Oceania	59
North Rhine-Westphalia	Nordrhein-Westfalen	34,068	*13,154*	16,685,000	490	*1,268*	State (Fed. Rep. of Germany)	*D* Düsseldorf	Europe	10
Northwest Territories	Northwest Territories (English) / Territoires du Nord-Ouest (French)	3,426,320	*1,322,910*	56,000	. . .	. . .	Territory (Canada)	*D* Yellowknife	N. Amer	42
†NORWAY (incl. Svalbard and Jan Mayen)	Norge	386,975	*149,412*	4,221,000	11	*28*	Constitutional monarchy	*A* Oslo	Europe	7
Nova Scotia	Nova Scotia (English) / Nouvelle-Écosse (French)	55,490	*21,425*	886,000	16	*41*	Province (Canada)	*D* Halifax	N. Amer	42
Oceania (incl. Australia)	. . .	8,500,000	*3,300,000*	26,300,000	3.1	*8.0*	. . .	. . .	Oceania	57-58
Ohio	Ohio	115,995	*44,786*	10,780,000	93	*241*	State (U.S.)	*D* Columbus	N. Amer	44
Oklahoma	Oklahoma	181,188	*69,957*	3,327,000	18	*48*	State (U.S.)	*D* Oklahoma City	N. Amer	45
†OMAN	'Umān	212,457	*82,030*	1,284,000	6.0	*16*	Monarchy	*A* Masqaṭ (Muscat)	Asia	23
Ontario	Ontario	1,068,580	*412,581*	9,375,000	8.8	*23*	Province (Canada)	*D* Toronto	N. Amer	42
Oregon	Oregon	251,426	*97,076*	2,743,000	11	*28*	State (U.S.)	*D* Salem	N. Amer	46
Orkney Islands	Orkney Islands	976	*377*	19,000	19	*50*	Part of Scotland (U.K.)	*D* Kirkwall	Europe	9
PACIFIC ISLANDS, TRUST TERRITORY OF THE	Trust Territory of the Pacific Islands	508	*196*	15,000	30	*77*	United Nations trusteeship (U.S. administration)	*B* Saipan (island)	Oceania	60
†PAKISTAN (incl. part of Jammu and Kashmir)	Pākistān	879,902	*339,732*	108,990,000	124	*321*	Federal Islamic republic	*A* Islāmābād	Asia	25
PALAU	Palau (English) / Belau (Palauan)	508	*196*	15,000	30	*77*	Part of Trust Territory of the Pacific Islands	*B* Koror	Oceania	60
†PANAMA	Panamá	77,082	*29,762*	2,346,000	30	*79*	Republic	*A* Panamá	N. Amer	49
†PAPUA NEW GUINEA	Papua New Guinea	462,840	*178,704*	3,639,000	7.9	*20*	Parliamentary state	*A* Port Moresby	Oceania	60
†PARAGUAY	Paraguay	406,752	*157,048*	4,210,000	10	*27*	Republic	*A* Asunción	S. Amer	56
Peking	Beijing	16,800	*6,487*	10,070,000	599	*1,552*	Autonomous city (China)	*D* Beijing (Peking)	Asia	28
Pennsylvania	Pennsylvania	119,261	*46,047*	11,950,000	100	*260*	State (U.S.)	*D* Harrisburg	N. Amer	44
†PERU	Perú	1,285,216	*496,225*	21,535,000	17	*43*	Republic	*A* Lima	S. Amer	54
†PHILIPPINES	Pilipinas (Tagalog) / Philippines (English)	300,000	*115,831*	60,110,000	200	*519*	Republic	*A* Manila	Asia	26
Pitcairn (incl. Dependencies)	Pitcairn	49	*19*	70	1.4	*3.7*	Dependent territory (U.K.)	*C* Adamstown	Oceania	61
†POLAND	Polska	312,683	*120,728*	37,955,000	121	*314*	Socialist republic	*A* Warszawa (Warsaw)	Europe	10
†PORTUGAL	Portugal	91,985	*35,516*	10,445,000	114	*294*	Republic	*A* Lisboa (Lisbon)	Europe	13
Prairie Provinces	Prairie Provinces	1,963,470	*758,100*	4,575,000	2.3	*6.0*	Part of Canada (3 provinces)	. . .	N. Amer	42
Prince Edward Island	Prince Edward Island / Île-du Prince-Édouard (French)	5,660	*2,185*	130,000	23	*59*	Province (Canada)	*D* Charlottetown	N. Amer	42

Country, Division, or Region English (Conventional)	Local Name	Area km²	Area sq mi	Population 1/1/89	Population Density per km²	Population Density per sq mi	Form of Government and Political Status	Capital	Continent and Map Plate	
PUERTO RICO	Puerto Rico	9,104	*3,515*	3,301,000	363	*939*	Commonwealth (U.S. protection)	*B* San Juan	N. Amer	51
†QATAR	Qaṭar	11,437	*4,416*	400,000	35	*91*	Monarchy	*A* Ad Dawḥah (Doha)	Asia	24
Qinghai	Qinghai	721,000	*278,380*	4,270,000	5.9	*15*	Province (China)	*D* Xining	Asia	27
Quebec	Québec	1,540,680	*594,860*	6,595,000	4.3	*11*	Province (Canada)	*D* Québec	N. Amer	42
Queensland	Queensland	1,727,200	*666,876*	2,849,000	1.6	*4.3*	State (Australia)	*D* Brisbane	Oceania	59
Reunion	Réunion	2,504	*967*	580,000	232	*600*	Overseas department (France)	*C* Saint-Denis	Africa	37
Rhineland-Palatinate	Rheinland-Pfalz	19,848	*7,663*	3,605,000	182	*470*	State (Fed. Rep. of Germany)	*D* Mainz	Europe	10
Rhode Island	Rhode Island	3,139	*1,212*	994,000	317	*820*	State (U.S.)	*D* Providence	N. Amer	44
Rhodesia, *see* Zimbabwe	...	...	...	...	...	...	...	...	...	...
Rodrigues	Rodrigues	104	*40*	35,000	337	*875*	Part of Mauritius	...	Africa	30-31
†ROMANIA	România	237,500	*91,699*	23,085,000	97	*252*	Socialist republic	*A* Bucureşti (Bucharest)	Europe	15
Russian Soviet Federative Socialist Republic	Rossijskaja Sovetskaja Federativnaja Socialističeskaja Respublika	17,075,400	*6,592,849*	147,780,000	8.7	*22*	Soviet socialist republic (U.S.S.R.)	*D* Moskva (Moscow)	Eur.-Asia	19-20
Russian S.F.S.R. in Europe	Rossijskaja S.F.S.R.	3,955,818	*1,527,350*	107,940,000	27	*71*	...	...	Europe	19
†RWANDA	Rwanda	26,338	*10,169*	7,192,000	273	*707*	Republic	*A* Kigali	Africa	36
Saarland	Saar	2,569	*992*	1,035,000	403	*1,043*	State (Fed. Rep. of Germany)	*D* Saarbrücken	Europe	10
Sabah	Sabah	73,711	*28,460*	1,405,000	19	*49*	State (Malaysia)	*D* Kota Kinabalu	Asia	26
†ST. CHRISTOPHER-NEVIS	St. Christopher-Nevis	269	*104*	47,000	175	*452*	Parliamentary state	*A* Basseterre	N. Amer	51
St. Helena (incl. Dependencies)	St. Helena	419	*162*	7,800	19	*48*	Dependent territory (U.K.)	*C* Jamestown	Africa	31
†ST. LUCIA	St. Lucia	616	*238*	148,000	240	*622*	Parliamentary state	*A* Castries	N. Amer	51
St. Pierre and Miquelon	St.-Pierre et Miquelon	242	*93*	6,500	27	*70*	Overseas department (France)	*C* Saint-Pierre	N. Amer	42
†ST. VINCENT AND THE GRENADINES	St. Vincent	388	*150*	125,000	322	*833*	Parliamentary state	*A* Kingstown	N. Amer	51
SAN MARINO	San Marino	61	*24*	24,000	393	*1,000*	Republic	*A* San Marino	Europe	14
†SAO TOME AND PRINCIPE	São Tomé e Príncipe	964	*372*	119,000	123	*320*	Republic	*A* São Tomé	Africa	34
Sarawak	Sarawak	125,205	*48,342*	1,610,000	13	*33*	State (Malaysia)	*D* Kuching	Asia	26
Sardinia	Sardegna	24,090	*9,301*	1,665,000	69	*179*	Autonomous region (Italy)	*D* Cagliari	Europe	14
Saskatchewan	Saskatchewan	652,330	*251,866*	1,030,000	1.6	*4.1*	Province (Canada)	*D* Regina	N. Amer	42
†SAUDI ARABIA	Al 'Arabīyah as Su'ūdīyah	2,240,000	*864,869*	15,775,000	7.0	*18*	Monarchy	*A* Ar Riyāḍ (Riyadh)	Asia	23
Scandinavia	...	1,320,000	*510,000*	23,045,000	17	*45*	...	...	Europe	7
Schleswig-Holstein	Schleswig-Holstein	15,727	*6,072*	2,580,000	164	*425*	State (Fed. Rep. of Germany)	*D* Kiel	Europe	10
Scotland	Scotland	77,167	*29,794*	5,150,000	67	*173*	Administrative division (U.K.)	*D* Edinburgh	Europe	9
†SENEGAL	Sénégal	196,722	*75,955*	7,394,000	38	*97*	Republic	*A* Dakar	Africa	34
†SEYCHELLES	Seychelles	453	*175*	70,000	155	*400*	Republic	*A* Victoria	Africa	37
Shaanxi	Shaanxi	196,000	*75,676*	31,420,000	160	*415*	Province (China)	*D* Xi'an (Sian)	Asia	27
Shandong	Shandong	153,000	*59,074*	80,790,000	528	*1,368*	Province (China)	*D* Jinan	Asia	27
Shanghai	Shanghai	5,800	*2,239*	12,700,000	2,190	*5,672*	Autonomous city (China)	*D* Shanghai	Asia	28
Shanxi	Shanxi	157,000	*60,618*	27,475,000	175	*453*	Province (China)	*D* Taiyuan	Asia	27
Shetland Islands	Shetland Islands	1,433	*553*	24,000	17	*43*	Part of Scotland (U.K.)	*D* Lerwick	Europe	9
Sichuan	Sichuan	569,000	*219,692*	106,950,000	188	*487*	Province (China)	*D* Chengdu	Asia	27
Sicily	Sicilia	25,708	*9,926*	5,195,000	202	*523*	Autonomous region (Italy)	*D* Palermo	Europe	14
†SIERRA LEONE	Sierra Leone	72,325	*27,925*	4,015,000	56	*144*	Republic	*A* Freetown	Africa	34
†SINGAPORE	Singapore (English) / Singapura (Malay)	636	*236*	2,663,000	4,187	*11,284*	Republic	*A* Singapore	Asia	26
Sinkiang	Xingiang Uygur Zizhiqu	1,647,000	*635,910*	14,230,000	8.6	*22*	Autonomous region (China)	*D* Ürümqi	Asia	27
†SOLOMON ISLANDS	Solomon Islands	28,369	*10,953*	295,000	10	*27*	Parliamentary state	*A* Honiara	Oceania	63
†SOMALIA	Soomaaliya	637,657	*246,201*	8,118,000	13	*33*	Socialist republic	*A* Muqdisho (Mogadishu)	Africa	35
†SOUTH AFRICA (incl. Walvis Bay)	South Africa (English) / Suid-Afrika (Afrikaans)	1,123,226	*433,680*	35,480,000	32	*82*	Republic	*A* Pretoria, Cape Town, and Bloemfontein	Africa	37
South America	...	17,800,000	*6,900,000*	287,500,000	16	*42*	...	...	S. Amer	52-53
South Australia	South Australia	984,000	*379,925*	1,435,000	1.5	*3.8*	State (Australia)	*D* Adelaide	Oceania	59
South Carolina	South Carolina	80,590	*31,116*	3,494,000	43	*112*	State (U.S.)	*D* Columbia	N. Amer	44
South Dakota	South Dakota	199,740	*77,120*	713,000	3.6	*9.2*	State (U.S.)	*D* Pierre	N. Amer	45
South Georgia (incl. Dependencies)	South Georgia	3,755	*1,450*	... (1)	...	...	Dependent territory (U.K.)	*C* ...	S. Amer	56
South West Africa, *see* Namibia	...	...	...	...	...	...	...	...	...	...
Soviet Union, *see* Union of Soviet Socialist Republics	...	...	...	...	...	...	...	...	...	...
†SPAIN	España	504,750	*194,885*	39,330,000	78	*202*	Constitutional monarchy	*A* Madrid	Europe	13
Spanish North Africa (8)	Plazas de Soberanía en el Norte de África	32	*12*	100,000	3,125	*8,333*	Five possessions (Spain)	*C* ...	Africa	13
Spanish Sahara, *see* Western Sahara	...	...	...	...	...	...	...	...	...	...
†SRI LANKA	Sri Lanka	64,652	*24,962*	16,730,000	259	*670*	Socialist republic	*A* Colombo and Sri Jayawardenapura	Asia	25
†SUDAN	As Sūdān	2,505,813	*967,500*	24,255,000	9.7	*25*	Republic	*A* Al Kharṭūm (Khartoum)	Africa	35
Sumatra	Sumatera	473,606	*182,860*	36,140,000	76	*198*	Part of Indonesia (7 provinces)	...	Asia	26
†SURINAME	Suriname	163,820	*63,251*	398,000	2.4	*6.3*	Provisional military government	*A* Paramaribo	S. Amer	54
†SWAZILAND	Swaziland	17,364	*6,704*	727,000	42	*108*	Monarchy	*A* Mbabane and Lobamba (5)	Africa	37
†SWEDEN	Sverige	449,964	*173,732*	8,444,000	19	*49*	Constitutional monarchy	*A* Stockholm	Europe	7
SWITZERLAND	Schweiz (German) / Suisse (French) / Svizzera (Italian)	41,293	*15,943*	6,590,000	160	*413*	Federal republic	*A* Bern (Berne)	Europe	14
†SYRIA	Sūrīyah	185,180	*71,498*	11,530,000	62	*161*	Socialist republic	*A* Dimashq (Damascus)	Asia	24
TAIWAN	Taiwan	36,002	*13,900*	20,125,000	559	*1,448*	Republic	*A* Taipei	Asia	27
Tajik S.S.R.	Tadžikskaja S.S.R.	143,100	*55,251*	5,135,000	36	*93*	Soviet socialist republic (U.S.S.R.)	*D* Dušanbe (Dushanbe)	Asia	18
†TANZANIA	Tanzania	945,087	*364,900*	24,055,000	25	*66*	Republic	*A* Dar es Salaam and Dodoma (5)	Africa	36
Tasmania	Tasmania	67,800	*26,178*	452,000	6.7	*17*	State (Austl.)	*D* Hobart	Oceania	59
Tennessee	Tennessee	109,150	*42,143*	4,913,000	45	*117*	State (U.S.)	*D* Nashville	N. Amer	44
Texas	Texas	691,022	*266,805*	17,415,000	25	*65*	State (U.S.)	*D* Austin	N. Amer	45
†THAILAND	Muang Thai	513,115	*198,115*	55,375,000	108	*280*	Constitutional monarchy	*A* Krung Thep (Bangkok)	Asia	26
Tibet	Xizang Zizhiqu	1,222,000	*471,817*	2,080,000	1.7	*4.4*	Autonomous region (China)	*D* Lhasa	Asia	27
Tientsin	Tianjin	11,000	*4,247*	8,430,000	766	*1,985*	Autonomous city (China)	*D* Tianjin (Tientsin)	Asia	28
†TOGO	Togo	56,785	*21,925*	3,393,000	60	*155*	Republic	*A* Lomé	Africa	34
Tokelau	Tokelau	12	*4.6*	1,700	142	*370*	Island territory (New Zealand)	*C* ...	Oceania	61
TONGA	Tonga	699	*270*	100,000	143	*370*	Constitutional monarchy	*A* Nuku'alofa	Oceania	61
Transcaucasia	...	186,100	*71,853*	15,855,000	85	*221*	...	...	Asia	16
TRANSKEI (2)	Transkei	42,000	*16,216*	3,900,000	93	*241*	National state (South African protection)	*B* Umtata	Africa	37
†TRINIDAD AND TOBAGO	Trinidad and Tobago	5,128	*1,980*	1,295,000	253	*654*	Republic	*A* Port of Spain	N. Amer	50
Tristan da Cunha	Tristan da Cunha	104	*40*	300	2.9	*7.5*	Dependency (St. Helena)	*C* Edinburgh	Africa	30-31

Country, Division, or Region English (Conventional)	Local Name	Area km²	Area sq mi	Population 1/1/89	Population Density per km²	Population Density per sq mi	Form of Government and Political Status	Capital	Continent	Map Plate
† TUNISIA	Tunisie (French) / Tūnis (Arabic)	163,610	63,170	7,876,000	48	125	Republic	*A* Tūnis	Africa	32
† TURKEY	Türkiye	779,452	300,948	51,970,000	67	173	Republic	*A* Ankara	Eur.-Asia	24
Turkey in Europe	. . .	23,764	9,175	5,025,000	211	548	. . .	. . .	Europe	24
Turkmen S.S.R.	Turkmenskaja S.S.R.	488,100	188,456	3,545,000	7.3	19	Soviet socialist republic (U.S.S.R.)	*D* Ašhabad	Asia	19
Turks and Caicos Islands	Turks and Caicos Islands	430	166	10,000	23	60	Dependent territory (U.K.)	*C* Grand Turk	N. Amer	49
TUVALU	Tuvalu	26	10	8,700	335	870	Parliamentary state	*A* Funafuti	Oceania	60
† UGANDA	Uganda	241,139	93,104	16,725,000	69	180	Republic	*A* Kampala	Africa	36
† Ukrainian S.S.R.	Ukrainskaja S.S.R.	603,700	233,090	51,620,000	86	221	Soviet socialist republic (U.S.S.R.)	*D* Kijev (Kiev)	Europe	16
† UNION OF SOVIET SOCIALIST REPUBLICS	Sojuz Sovetskich Socialističeskich Respublik	22,274,900	8,600,387	287,550,000	13	33	Federal socialist republic	*A* Moskva (Moscow)	Eur.-Asia	19-20
U.S.S.R. in Europe	. . .	4,974,818	1,920,789	182,030,000	37	95	. . .	. . .	Europe	. . .
† UNITED ARAB EMIRATES	Al Imārāt al 'Arabīyah al Muttaḥidah	83,600	32,278	2,047,000	24	63	Federation of monarchs	*A* Abū Ẓaby (Abu Dhabi)	Asia	23
† UNITED KINGDOM	United Kingdom	242,496	93,629	57,090,000	235	610	Constitutional monarchy	*A* London	Europe	9
United Kingdom and Possessions	. . .	258,127	99,664	63,180,000	245	634	. . .	. . .	. . .	. . .
† UNITED STATES	United States	9,529,202	3,679,245	247,410,000	26	67	Federal republic	*A* Washington	N. Amer	43
United States and Possessions	. . .	9,541,271	3,683,905	251,180,000	26	68	. . .	. . .	. . .	. . .
Upper Volta, *see* Burkina Faso	. . .	. . .	. . .	. . .	. . .	. . .	. . .	. . .	. . .	. . .
† URUGUAY	Uruguay	175,016	67,574	3,184,000	18	47	Republic	*A* Montevideo	S. Amer	55
Utah	Utah	219,895	84,902	1,732,000	7.9	20	State (U.S.)	*D* Salt Lake City	N. Amer	46
Uzbek S.S.R.	Uzbekskaja S.S.R.	447,400	172,742	20,135,000	45	117	Soviet socialist republic (U.S.S.R.)	*D* Taškent (Tashkent)	Asia	19
† VANUATU	Vanuatu	12,189	4,706	155,000	13	33	Republic	*A* Port-Vila	Oceania	63
VATICAN CITY	Città del Vaticano	0.4	0.2	800	2,000	4,000	Ecclesiastical city-state	*A* Vatican City	Europe	14
VENDA (2)	Venda	6,875	2,654	556,000	81	209	National state (South African protection)	*B* Thohoyandou	Africa	37
† VENEZUELA	Venezuela	912,050	352,145	19,010,000	21	54	Federal republic	*A* Caracas	S. Amer	54
Vermont	Vermont	24,900	9,614	556,000	22	58	State (U.S.)	*D* Montpelier	N. Amer	44
Victoria	Victoria	227,600	87,877	4,325,000	19	49	State (Australia)	*D* Melbourne	Oceania	59
† VIETNAM	Viet Nam	329,556	127,242	66,030,000	200	519	Socialist republic	*A* Ha Noi	Asia	26
Virginia	Virginia	105,576	40,763	6,031,000	57	148	State (U.S.)	*D* Richmond	N. Amer	44
Virgin Islands of the United States	Virgin Islands of the United States	344	133	106,000	308	797	Unincorporated territory (U.S.)	*C* Charlotte Amalie	N. Amer	51
Virgin Islands, British	British Virgin Islands	153	59	13,000	85	220	Dependent territory (U.K.)	*C* Road Town	N. Amer	51
Wake Island	Wake Island	7.8	3.0	300	38	100	Unincorporated territory (U.S.)	*C* . . .	Oceania	60
Wales	Wales	20,768	8,019	2,855,000	137	356	Administrative Division (U.K.)	*D* Cardiff	Europe	9
Wallis and Futuna	Îles Wallis et Futuna	255	98	15,000	59	153	Overseas territory (France)	*C* Mata-Utu	Oceania	61
Washington	Washington	176,479	68,139	4,630,000	26	68	State (U.S.)	*D* Olympia	N. Amer	46
Western Australia	Western Australia	2,525,500	975,101	1,625,000	0.6	1.7	State (Australia)	*D* Perth	Oceania	59
Western Sahara	. . .	266,000	102,703	97,000	0.4	0.9	Occupied by Morocco	*C* El Aaiún	Africa	32
† WESTERN SAMOA	Western Samoa (English) / Samoa i Sisifo (Samoan)	2,842	1,097	180,000	63	164	Constitutional monarchy	*A* Apia	Oceania	65
West Indies	West Indies (English) / Indias Occidentales (Spanish)	235,000	91,000	33,130,000	141	364	. . .	. . .	N. Amer	47
West Virginia	West Virginia	62,771	24,236	1,886,000	30	78	State (U.S.)	*D* Charleston	N. Amer	44
Wisconsin	Wisconsin	171,491	66,213	4,828,000	28	73	State (U.S.)	*D* Madison	N. Amer	45
Wyoming	Wyoming	253,322	97,808	494,000	2.0	5.1	State (U.S.)	*D* Cheyenne	N. Amer	46
† YEMEN	Al Yaman	531,869	205,356	12,661,000	24	62	Islamic republic	*A* Ṣan'ā'	Asia	23
† YUGOSLAVIA	Jugoslavija	255,804	98,766	23,970,000	94	243	Federal socialist republic	*A* Beograd (Belgrade)	Europe	14-15
Yukon Territory	Yukon Territory	483,450	186,661	24,000	0.1	0.1	Territory (Canada)	*D* Whitehorse	N. Amer	42
Yunnan	Yunnan	436,000	168,341	35,580,000	82	211	Province (China)	*D* Kunming	Asia	27
† ZAIRE	Zaïre	2,345,409	905,568	33,795,000	14	37	Republic	*A* Kinshasa	Africa	36
† ZAMBIA	Zambia	752,614	290,586	7,682,000	10	26	Republic	*A* Lusaka	Africa	36
Zanzibar	Zanzibar	1,660	641	634,000	382	989	Part of Tanzania	. . . Zanzibar	Africa	36
Zhejiang	Zhejiang	102,000	39,382	42,255,000	414	1,073	Province (China)	*D* Hangzhou	Asia	27
† ZIMBABWE	Zimbabwe	390,759	150,873	9,003,000	23	60	Republic	*A* Harare	Africa	37
WORLD	. . .	149,900,000	57,900,000	5,192,000,000	35	90	. . .	. . .	. . .	1-2

† Member of the United Nations (1988).
. . . None, or not applicable.
(1) No permanent population.
(2) Bophuthatswana, Ciskei, Transkei, and Venda are not recognized by the United Nations.
(3) Claimed by Argentina.
(4) Includes West Bank, Golan Heights, and Gaza Strip.
(5) Future capital.
(6) On March 11, 1990 Lithuania unilaterally declared its independence from the Soviet Union.
(7) Claimed by Comoros.
(8) Comprises Ceuta, Melilla, and several small islands.

World Geographical Tables

The Earth: Land and Water

	Total Area km²	Total Area *sq mi*	Area of Land km²	Area of Land *sq mi*	%	Area of Oceans and Seas km²	Area of Oceans and Seas *sq mi*	%
Earth	510,100,000	*197,000,000*	149,900,000	*57,900,000*	29.4	360,200,000	*139,100,000*	70.6
N. Hemisphere	255,050,000	*98,500,000*	106,429,000	*41,109,000*	41.6	148,762,600	*57,448,300*	58.4
S. Hemisphere	255,050,000	*98,500,000*	43,471,000	*16,791,000*	17.0	211,437,400	*81,651,700*	83.0

The Continents

Continent	Area km² *sq mi*	Population Estimate (1/1/89)	Population per km² *sq mi*	Mean Elevation m *ft*	Highest Elevation m/*ft*	Lowest Elevation m/*ft* (below sea level)	Highest Recorded Temperature °C/°F	Lowest Recorded Temperature °C/°F
Europe	9,900,000 *3,800,000*	685,400,000	69 *180*	300 *980*	gora Elbrus, U.S.S.R. 5,642/*18,510*	Caspian Sea, U.S.S.R.-Iran -28/*-92*	Sevilla, Spain 50°/*122°*	Ust-Ščugor, U.S.S.R. -55°/*-67°*
Asia	45,000,000 *17,400,000*	3,130,600,000	70 *180*	910 *3,000*	Everest, China-Nepal 8,848/*29,028*	Dead Sea, Israel-Jordan -403/*-1,322*	Tirat Zevi, Israel 54°/*129°*	Ojmjakon and Verkhoyansk, U.S.S.R. -68°/*-90°*
Africa	30,300,000 *11,700,000*	642,100,000	21 *55*	580 *1,900*	Kilimanjaro, Tanzania 5,895/*19,340*	Lac Assal, Djibouti -155/*-509*	Al 'Azīzīyah, Libya 58°/*136°*	Ifrane, Morocco -24°/*-11°*
North America	24,400,000 *9,400,000*	420,100,000	17 *45*	610 *2,000*	Mt. McKinley, U.S. 6,194/*20,320*	Death Valley, U.S. -86/*-282*	Death Valley, U.S. 57°/*134°*	Northice, Greenland -66°/*-87°*
South America	17,800,000 *6,900,000*	287,500,000	16 *42*	550 *1,800*	Cerro Aconcagua, Argentina 6,960/*22,835*	Salinas Chicas -42/*-138*	Rivadavia, Argentina 49°/*120°*	Sarmiento, Argentina -33°/*-27°*
Oceania, incl. Australia	8,500,000 *3,300,000*	26,300,000	3 *8*	....	Mt. Wilhelm, Papua New Guinea 4,509/*14,793*	Lake Eyre, Australia -12/*-39*	Cloncurry, Australia 53°/*128°*	Charlotte Pass, Australia -22°/*-8°*
Australia	7,682,300 *2,966,155*	16,955,000	2 *6*	300 *1,000*	Mt. Kosciusko, Australia 2,228/*7,310*	Lake Eyre, Austraila -12/*-39*	Cloncurry, Australia 53°/*128°*	Charlotte Pass, Australia -22°/*-8°*
Antarctica	14,000,000 *5,400,000*	....	... ...	1,830 *6,000*	Vinson Massif 4,897/*116,06*	sea level	Vanda Station 15°/*59°*	Vostok -89°/*-129°*
World	149,900,000 *57,900,000*	5,192,000,000	35 *90*	....	Everest, China-Nepal 8,848/*29,028*	Dead Sea, Israel-Jordan -403/*-1,322*	Al 'Azīzīyah, Libya 58°/*136°*	Vostok -89°/*-129°*

Principal Mountains

Mountain	Country	Height M	Height *Ft*
Europe			
Elbrus, gora	U.S.S.R.	5,642	*18,510*
Dyhtau, gora	U.S.S.R.	5,204	*17,073*
Blanc, Mont	△France-△Italy	4,807	*15,771*
Rosa, Monte	Italy-△Switzerland	4,634	*15,203*
Matterhorn	Italy-Switzerland	4,478	*14,692*
Grossglockner	△Austria	3,797	*12,457*
Teide, Pico de	△Spain (Canary Is.)	3,718	*12,198*
Aneto, Pico de	Spain	3,404	*11,168*
Etna	Italy	3,323	*10,902*
Zugspitze	Austria-△Germany, Fed. Rep. of	2,963	*9,721*
Ólimbos, Óros	△Greece	2,917	*9,570*
Corno Grande	Italy	2,912	*9,554*
Gerlachovský štít	△Czechoslovakia	2,663	*8,737*
Glittertind	△Norway	2,472	*8,110*
Kebnekaise	△Sweden	2,111	*6,926*
Narodnaja, gora	U.S.S.R.	1,895	*6,217*
Nevis, Ben	△United Kingdom	1,343	*4,406*
Asia			
Everest	△China-△Nepal	8,848	*29,028*
K2 (Qogir Feng)	China-△Pakistan	8,611	*28,250*
Kānchenjunga	△India-Nepal	8,598	*28,208*
Makālu	China-Nepal	8,481	*27,825*
Dhaulāgiri	Nepal	8,172	*26,810*
Annapurna	Nepal	8,078	*26,504*
Muztag	China	7,723	*25,338*
Tirich Mīr	Pakistan	7,690	*25,230*
Kommunizma, pik (Communism Peak)	△U.S.S.R.	7,495	*24,590*
Pobedy, pik	China-U.S.S.R.	7,439	*24,406*
Damāvand, Qolleh-ye	△Iran	5,604	*18,386*
Ağrı Dağı, Büyük (Mt. Ararat)	△Turkey	5,122	*16,804*
Jaya, Puncak	△Indonesia	5,030	*16,503*
Ključevskaja Sopka, vulkan	U.S.S.R.	4,750	*15,584*
Kinabalu, Gunong	△Malaysia	4,101	*13,455*
Yushan	△Taiwan	3,997	*13,114*
Fuji-San	△Japan	3,776	*12,388*
Nabī Shu'ayb, Jabal an	△Yemen	3,760	*12,336*
Apo, Mt.	△Philippines	2,954	*9,692*
Shaykh, Jabal ash- (Mt. Hermon)	Lebanon-△Syria	2,814	*9,232*
Mayon, Mt.	Philippines	2,462	*8,077*
Chili-san	△South Korea	1,915	*6,283*
Meron, Hare	△Israel	1,208	*3,963*
Africa			
Kilimanjaro	△Tanzania	5,895	*19,340*
Kirinyaga (Mt. Kenya)	△Kenya	5,199	*17,058*
Margherita	△Uganda-△Zaire	5,109	*16,762*
Ras Dashan Terara	△Ethiopia	4,620	*15,158*
Toubkal, Jebel	△Morocco	4,165	*13,665*
Cameroon, Mt.	△Cameroon	4,100	*13,451*
North America			
McKinley, Mt.	△United States	6,194	*20,320*
Logan, Mt.	△Canada	5,951	*19,524*
Orizaba, Pico de	△Mexico	5,610	*18,406*
Popocatépetl, Volcán	Mexico	5,452	*17,887*
Whitney, Mt.	United States	4,417	*14,491*
Elbert, Mt.	United States	4,399	*14,433*
Rainier, Mt.	United States	4,392	*14,410*
Shasta, Mt.	United States	4,317	*14,162*
Pikes Pk.	United States	4,301	*14,110*
Tajumulco, Volcán	△Guatemala	4,220	*13,845*
Mauna Kea	United States	4,205	*13,796*
Grand Teton	United States	4,197	*13,770*
Waddington, Mt.	Canada	3,994	*13,104*
Robson, Mt.	Canada	3,954	*12,972*
Chirripó, Cerro	△Costa Rica	3,819	*12,530*
Gunnbjørns Fjeld	△Greenland	3,700	*12,139*
Duarte, Pico	△Dominican Rep.	3,175	*10,417*
Mitchell, Mt.	United States	2,037	*6,684*
Marcy, Mt.	United States	1,629	*5,344*
South America			
Aconcagua, Cerro	△Argentina	6,960	*22,835*
Ojos del Salado, Nevado	Argentina-△Chile	6,863	*22,516*
Huascarán, Nevado	△Peru	6,746	*22,133*
Illimani, Nevado del	△Bolivia	6,682	*21,923*
Chimborazo, Volcán	△Ecuador	6,310	*20,702*
Cristóbal Colón, Pico	△Colombia	5,800	*19,029*
Neblina, Pico da	△Brazil-Venezuela	3,014	*9,888*
Oceania			
Wilhelm, Mt.	△Papua New Guinea	4,509	*14,793*
Cook, Mt.	△New Zealand	3,764	*12,349*
Kosciusko, Mt.	△Australia	2,228	*7,310*
Antarctica			
Vinson Massif	△Antarctica	4,897	*16,066*
Kirkpatrick, Mt.	Antarctica	4,528	*14,856*

△ Highest mountain in country.

Oceans, Seas, and Gulfs

Name	Area km²	Area sq mi	Greatest Depth m	Greatest Depth ft
Pacific Ocean	165,200,000	*63,800,000*	11,020	*36,155*
Atlantic Ocean	82,400,000	*31,800,000*	9,220	*30,249*
Indian Ocean	74,900,000	*28,900,000*	7,450	*24,442*
Arctic Ocean	14,000,000	*5,400,000*	5,450	*17,881*
Arabian Sea	3,864,000	*1,492,000*	5,800	*19,029*
South China Sea	3,447,000	*1,331,000*	5,560	*18,241*
Caribbean Sea	2,753,000	*1,063,000*	7,680	*25,197*
Mediterranean Sea	2,505,000	*967,000*	5,020	*16,470*
Bering Sea	2,269,000	*876,000*	4,096	*13,438*
Bengal, Bay of	2,173,000	*839,000*	5,258	*17,251*
Okhotsk, Sea of	1,603,000	*619,000*	3,372	*11,063*
Norwegian Sea	1,546,000	*597,000*	4,020	*13,189*
Mexico, Gulf of	1,544,000	*596,000*	4,380	*14,370*
East China Sea	1,248,000	*482,000*	4,424	*14,514*
Hudson Bay	1,230,000	*475,000*	259	*850*

Waterfalls

Waterfall	Country	River	Height m	Height ft
Angel	Venezuela	Churún	972	*3,189*
Tugela	South Africa	Tugela	948	*3,110*
Yosemite	United States	Yosemite Creek	739	*2,425*
Sutherland	New Zealand	Arthur	579	*1,900*
Gavarnie	France	Gave de Pau	421	*1,381*
Lofoi	Zaire	Lofoi	384	*1,260*
Krimml	Austria	Krimml	381	*1,250*
Takakkaw	Canada	Yoho	380	*1,248*
Staubbach	Switzerland	Staubbach	305	*1,001*
Mardalsfoss	Norway	. . .	297	*974*
Gersoppa	India	Sharavati	253	*830*
Kaieteur	Guyana	Potaro	247	*810*

Principal Rivers

River	Continent	Length km	Length mi
Nile	Africa	6,671	*4,145*
Amazon-Ucayali	South America	6,400	*4,000*
Yangtze (Chang Jiang)	Asia	6,300	*3,900*
Yellow (Huang He)	Asia	5,464	*3,395*
Ob-Irtyš	Asia	5,410	*3,362*
Río de la Plata-Paraná	South America	4,876	*3,030*
Congo (Zaïre)	Africa	4,700	*2,900*
Paraná	South America	4,500	*2,800*
Amur (Heilong Jiang)	Asia	4,416	*2,744*
Lena	Asia	4,400	*2,700*
Mekong	Asia	4,200	*2,600*
Niger	Africa	4,200	*2,600*
Jenisej	Asia	4,092	*2,543*
Mississippi	North America	3,779	*2,348*
Missouri	North America	3,726	*2,315*
Volga	Europe	3,531	*2,194*
São Francisco	South America	3,199	*1,988*
Rio Grande	North America	3,034	*1,885*
Indus	Asia	2,900	*1,800*
Danube	Europe	2,858	*1,776*
Yukon	North America	2,849	*1,770*
Brahmaputra	Asia	2,849	*1,770*
Salween (Thanlwin)	Asia	2,816	*1,750*
Zambezi	Africa	2,700	*1,700*
Tocantins	South America	2,639	*1,640*
Orinoco	South America	2,600	*1,600*
Paraguay	South America	2,591	*1,610*
Amudarja	Asia	2,540	*1,578*
Murray	Australia	2,520	*1,566*
Ganges	Asia	2,511	*1,560*
Euphrates	Asia	2,430	*1,510*
Ural	Asia	2,428	*1,509*
Arkansas	North America	2,348	*1,459*
Colorado	North America (U.S.-Mex.)	2,334	*1,450*
Syrdarja	Asia	2,205	*1,370*
Tarim	Asia	2,137	*1,328*
Orange	Africa	2,100	*1,300*
Negro	South America	2,100	*1,300*
Irrawaddy (Ayeyarwady)	Asia	2,100	*1,300*
Red	North America	2,044	*1,270*
Columbia	North America	2,000	*1,200*
Xingu	South America	1,979	*1,230*
Ucayali	South America	1,963	*1,220*
Saskatchewan-Bow	North America	1,939	*1,205*
Peace	North America	1,923	*1,195*
Tigris	Asia	1,899	*1,180*
Sungari	Asia	1,835	*1,140*
Pechora	Europe	1,809	*1,124*
Limpopo	Africa	1,800	*1,100*
Snake	North America	1,670	*1,038*

Principal Islands

Island	Area km²	Area sq mi	Name	Highest Point m	Highest Point ft
Grønland (Greenland)	2,175,600	*840,000*	Gunnbjørns Fjeld	3,700	*12,139*
New Guinea	800,000	*309,000*	Puncak Jaya	5,030	*16,503*
Borneo	744,100	*287,300*	Gunong Kinabalu	4,101	*13,455*
Madagascar	587,000	*227,000*	Maromokotro	2,876	*9,436*
Baffin Island	507,451	*195,928*	Unnamed	2,591	*8,501*
Sumatera (Sumatra)	473,606	*182,860*	Gunung Kerinci	3,800	*12,467*
Honshū	230,966	*89,176*	Fuji-San	3,776	*12,388*
Great Britain	229,978	*88,795*	Ben Nevis	1,343	*4,406*
Victoria Island	217,291	*83,897*	Mt. Bumpus	655	*2,149*
Ellesmere Island	196,236	*75,767*	Barbeau Peak	2,604	*8,543*
Sulawesi (Celebes)	189,216	*73,057*	Bulu Rantekombola	3,455	*11,335*
South Island	149,883	*57,870*	Mt. Cook	3,764	*12,349*
Jawa (Java)	132,187	*51,038*	Gunung Semeru	3,676	*12,060*
Seram (Ceram)	118,625	*45,801*	Gunung Binaiya	3,019	*9,905*
North Island	114,669	*44,274*	Mt. Ruapehu	2,797	*9,177*
Cuba	110,800	*42,800*	Pico Turquino	1,994	*6,542*
Newfoundland	108,860	*42,031*	Unnamed	814	*2,670*
Luzon	104,688	*40,420*	Mt. Pulog	2,930	*9,613*
Ísland (Iceland)	103,000	*39,800*	Hvannadalshnúkur	2,119	*6,952*
Mindanao	94,630	*36,537*	Mt. Apo	2,954	*9,692*
Ireland	84,400	*32,600*	Carrauntoohil	1,038	*3,406*
Hokkaidō	83,515	*32,245*	Taisetsu-Zan	2,290	*7,513*
Novaja Zemlja (Novaya Zemlya)	82,600	*31,900*	Unnamed	1,547	*5,075*
Sahalin, ostrov (Sakhalin)	76,400	*29,500*	gora Lopatina	1,609	*5,279*
Hispaniola	76,000	*29,300*	Pico Duarte	3,175	*10,417*
Banks Island	70,028	*27,038*	Unnamed	747	*2,451*
Tasmania	67,800	*26,200*	Mt. Ossa	1,617	*5,305*
Sri Lanka	64,600	*24,900*	Pidurutalagala	2,524	*8,281*
Devon Island	55,247	*21,331*	Unnamed	1,887	*6,191*
Tierra del Fuego, Isla Grande de	48,200	*18,600*	Cerro Yogan	2,469	*8,100*

Major Lakes

Lake	Location	Area km²	Area sq mi	Depth m	Depth ft
Caspian Sea	Iran-U.S.S.R.	370,990	*143,240*	1,025	*3,363*
Superior, L.	Canada-U.S.	82,100	*31,700*	406	*1,332*
Victoria, L.	Africa	69,463	*26,820*	85	*279*
Aral'skoje more (Aral Sea)	U.S.S.R.	64,100	*24,700*	68	*223*
Huron, L.	Canada-U.S.	60,000	*23,000*	229	*750*
Michigan, L.	U.S.	57,800	*22,300*	282	*924*
Tanganyika. L.	Africa	31,986	*12,350*	1,463	*4,800*
Bajkal, ozero (L. Baikal)	U.S.S.R.	31,500	*12,200*	1,620	*5,315*
Great Bear Lake	Canada	31,326	*12,095*	413	*1,356*
Nyasa, L.	Africa	28,878	*11,150*	695	*2,280*
Great Slave Lake	Canada	28,568	*11,030*	614	*2,015*
Erie, L.	Canada-U.S.	25,667	*9,910*	62	*204*
Winnipeg, L.	Canada	24,387	*9,416*	28	*92*
Ontario, L.	Canada-U.S.	19,529	*7,540*	243	*798*
Balhaš, ozero (L. Balkhash)	U.S.S.R.	18,300	*7,100*	26	*85*
Chad, L.	Africa	16,300	*6,300*	7	*24*
Onežskoje ozero (L. Onega)	U.S.S.R.	9,720	*3,753*	127	*417*
Eyre, L.	Australia	9,500	*3,700*	1	*4*
Titicaca, Lago	Bolivia-Peru	8,300	*3,200*	302	*990*
Nicaragua, Lago de	Nicaragua	8,158	*3,150*	70	*230*
Mai-Ndombe, Lac	Zaire	8,000	*3,100*	11	*36*
Athabasca, L.	Canada	7,935	*3,064*	124	*407*
Reindeer Lake	Canada	6,650	*2,568*	219	*720*
Tônlé Sab, Bœng	Cambodia	6,500	*2,500*	12	*39*
Rudolf, L.	Ethiopia-Kenya	6,405	*2,473*	219	*720*
Torrens, L.	Australia	5,900	*2,300*	*	*
Albert, L.	Uganda-Zaire	5,594	*2,160*	51	*168*
Vänern	Sweden	5,584	*2,156*	99	*325*

* Intermittently dry lake

Drainage Basins

Name	Continent	Area km²	Area sq mi
Amazon	South America	6,151,000	*2,375,000*
Congo (Zaïre)	Africa	3,823,000	*1,476,000*
Mississippi-Missouri	North America	3,230,000	*1,247,000*
Río de la Plata-Paraná	South America	3,100,000	*1,197,000*
Ob'-Irtyš	Asia	2,989,000	*1,154,000*
Nile	Africa	2,802,000	*1,082,000*
Lena	Asia	2,489,000	*961,000*
Amur-Argun	Asia	2,051,000	*792,000*
Niger	Africa	1,891,000	*730,000*
Yangtze (Chang Jiang)	Asia	1,826,000	*705,000*
Mackenzie	North America	1,572,000	*607,000*
Volga	Europe	1,360,000	*525,000*
Zambezi	Africa	1,331,000	*514,000*
St. Lawrence	North America	1,303,000	*503,000*

World Geographical Tables

Historical Population of the World

AREA	1650	1750	1800	1850	1900	1914	1920	1939	1950	1989
Europe	*100,000,000*	*140,000,000*	*190,000,000*	265,000,000	400,000,000	470,000,000	453,000,000	526,000,000	530,000,000	685,400,000
Asia	*335,000,000*	*476,000,000*	*593,000,000*	*754,000,000*	*932,000,000*	*1,006,000,000*	*1,000,000,000*	*1,247,000,000*	*1,418,000,000*	3,130,600,000
Africa	*100,000,000*	*95,000,000*	*90,000,000*	*95,000,000*	*118,000,000*	*130,000,000*	*140,000,000*	170,000,000	199,000,000	642,100,000
North America	*5,000,000*	*5,000,000*	*13,000,000*	*39,000,000*	106,000,000	141,000,000	147,000,000	186,000,000	219,000,000	420,100,000
South America	*8,000,000*	*7,000,000*	*12,000,000*	*20,000,000*	38,000,000	55,000,000	61,000,000	90,000,000	111,000,000	287,500,000
Oceania, incl. Australia	*2,000,000*	*2,000,000*	*2,000,000*	*2,000,000*	6,000,000	8,000,000	9,000,000	11,000,000	13,000,000	26,300,000
Australia					4,000,000	5,000,000	6,000,000	7,000,000	8,000,000	16,955,000
World	*550,000,000*	*725,000,000*	*900,000,000*	*1,175,000,000*	*1,600,000,000*	*1,810,000,000*	*1,810,000,000*	*2,230,000,000*	*2,490,000,000*	5,192,000,000

Figures in italics represent very rough estimates.

Largest Countries: Population

Country	Population 1/1/89
1. China	1,094,700,000
2. India	825,000,000
3. U.S.S.R.	287,550,000
4. United States	247,410,000
5. Indonesia	185,860,000
6. Brazil	145,930,000
7. Japan	123,010,000
8. Nigeria	113,580,000
9. Bangladesh	111,390,000
10. Pakistan	108,990,000
11. Mexico	85,300,000
12. Vietnam	66,030,000
13. Germany, Fed. Rep.	61,380,000
14. Philippines	60,110,000
15. Italy	57,500,000
16. United Kingdom	57,090,000
17. France	55,970,000
18. Thailand	55,375,000
19. Iran	52,760,000
20. Egypt	52,490,000
21. Turkey	51,970,000
22. Ethiopia	48,470,000
23. South Korea	42,840,000
24. Burma	41,860,000
25. Spain	39,330,000
26. Poland	37,955,000
27. South Africa	35,480,000
28. Zaire	33,795,000
29. Argentina	32,205,000
30. Colombia	30,465,000
31. Canada	25,895,000
32. Kenya	25,825,000
33. Morocco	25,600,000
34. Sudan	24,255,000
35. Algeria	24,215,000
36. Tanzania	24,055,000
37. Yugoslavia	23,970,000
38. Romania	23,085,000
39. North Korea	22,250,000
40. Peru	21,535,000
41. Taiwan	20,125,000
42. Venezuela	19,010,000
43. Nepal	18,415,000
44. Iraq	17,900,000
45. Mozambique	17,660,000

Largest Countries: Area

Country	Area km²	Area *sq mi*
1. U.S.S.R.	22,274,900	*8,600,387*
2. Canada	9,970,610	*3,849,674*
3. China	9,631,600	*3,718,782*
4. United States	9,529,202	*3,679,245*
5. Brazil	8,511,965	*3,286,488*
6. Australia	7,682,300	*2,966,155*
7. India	3,203,975	*1,237,062*
8. Argentina	2,780,092	*1,073,400*
9. Sudan	2,505,813	*967,500*
10. Algeria	2,381,741	*919,595*
11. Zaire	2,345,409	*905,568*
12. Saudi Arabia	2,240,000	*864,869*
13. Greenland	2,175,600	*840,004*
14. Mexico	1,972,547	*761,605*
15. Indonesia	1,919,443	*741,101*
16. Libya	1,759,540	*679,362*
17. Iran	1,648,000	*636,296*
18. Mongolia	1,565,000	*604,250*
19. Peru	1,285,216	*496,225*
20. Chad	1,284,000	*495,755*
21. Niger	1,267,000	*489,191*
22. Ethiopia	1,251,282	*483,123*
23. Angola	1,246,700	*481,354*
24. Mali	1,240,000	*478,767*
25. Colombia	1,141,748	*440,831*
26. South Africa	1,123,226	*433,680*
27. Bolivia	1,098,581	*424,165*
28. Mauritania	1,030,700	*397,956*
29. Egypt	1,001,450	*386,662*
30. Tanzania	945,087	*364,900*
31. Nigeria	923,768	*356,669*
32. Venezuela	912,050	*352,145*
33. Pakistan	879,902	*339,732*
34. Mozambique	799,379	*308,642*
35. Turkey	779,452	*300,948*
36. Chile	756,626	*292,135*
37. Zambia	752,614	*290,586*
38. Burma	676,577	*261,228*
39. Afghanistan	652,225	*251,826*
40. Somalia	637,657	*246,201*
41. Central African Republic	622,984	*240,535*
42. Madagascar	587,041	*226,658*
43. Kenya	582,646	*224,961*
44. Botswana	582,000	*224,711*
45. France	547,026	*211,208*

Smallest Countries: Population

Country	Population 1/1/89
1. Vatican City	800
2. Niue	2,400
3. Anguilla	7,000
4. Tuvalu	8,700
5. Nauru	9,000
6. Palau	15,000
7. Cook Islands	17,000
8. Northern Mariana Is.	22,000
9. San Marino	24,000
10. Liechtenstein	29,000
Monaco	29,000
11. Marshall Islands	40,000
12. St. Christopher-Nevis	47,000
13. Faeroe Islands	48,000
14. Andorra	51,000
15. Greenland	55,000
16. Isle of Man	62,000
17. Aruba	66,000
18. Kiribati	69,000
19. Seychelles	70,000
20. Antigua	84,000
21. Grenada	95,000
22. Dominica	100,000
Tonga	100,000
23. Micronesia, Federated States of	108,000
24. Sao Tome and Principe	119,000
25. St. Vincent	125,000
26. St. Lucia	148,000
27. Vanuatu	155,000
28. Cyprus, North	172,000
29. Western Samoa	180,000
30. Belize	184,000
31. Netherlands Antilles	194,000
32. Maldives	209,000
33. Bahamas	243,000
34. Brunei	247,000
35. Iceland	248,000
36. Barbados	255,000
37. Solomon Islands	295,000
38. Djibouti	324,000
39. Cape Verde	359,000
40. Luxembourg	368,000
41. Malta	370,000
42. Suriname	398,000

Smallest Countries: Area

Country	Area km²	Area *sq mi*
1. Vatican City	0.4	*0.2*
2. Monaco	1.9	*0.7*
3. Nauru	21	*8.1*
4. Tuvalu	26	*10*
5. San Marino	61	*24*
6. Anguilla	91	*35*
7. Liechtenstein	160	*62*
8. Marshall Islands	181	*70*
9. Aruba	193	*75*
10. Cook Islands	236	*91*
11. Niue	263	*102*
12. St. Christopher-Nevis	269	*104*
13. Maldives	298	*115*
14. Malta	316	*122*
15. Grenada	344	*133*
16. St. Vincent	388	*150*
17. Barbados	430	*166*
18. Antigua	443	*171*
Andorra	453	*175*
19. Seychelles	453	*175*
20. Northern Mariana Is.	477	*184*
21. Palau	508	*196*
22. Isle of Man	572	*221*
23. St. Lucia	616	*238*
24. Singapore	636	*236*
25. Bahrain	662	*256*
26. Tonga	699	*270*
27. Micronesia, Federated States of	702	*271*
28. Kiribati	726	*280*
29. Dominica	752	*290*
30. Netherlands Antilles	800	*309*
31. Sao Tome and Principe	964	*372*
32. Faeroe Islands	1,399	*540*
33. Mauritius	2,040	*788*
34. Comoros	2,171	*838*
35. Luxembourg	2,586	*998*
36. Western Samoa	2,842	*1,097*
37. Cyprus, North	3,355	*1,295*
38. Cape Verde	4,033	*1,557*
39. Trinidad and Tobago	5,128	*1,980*
40. Brunei	5,765	*2,226*
41. Cyprus	5,896	*2,276*
42. Venda	6,875	*2,654*
43. Ciskei	7,790	*3,008*

Highest Population Densities

Country	Density per km²	Density per *sq mi*
1. Monaco	15,263	*41,429*
2. Singapore	4,187	*11,284*
3. Vatican City	2,000	*4,000*
4. Malta	1,171	*3,033*
5. Bangladesh	774	*2,003*
6. Maldives	701	*1,817*
7. Bahrain	692	*1,789*
8. Barbados	593	*1,536*
9. Taiwan	559	*1,448*
10. Mauritius	518	*1,341*
11. South Korea	435	*1,127*
12. Nauru	429	*1,111*
13. San Marino	393	*1,000*
14. Puerto Rico	363	*939*
15. Netherlands	355	*918*
16. Aruba	342	*880*
17. Tuvalu	335	*870*
18. Japan	326	*843*
19. Belgium	323	*837*
20. Lebanon	322	*835*
21. St. Vincent	322	*833*
22. Grenada	276	*714*
23. Rwanda	273	*707*
24. Sri Lanka	259	*670*
25. India	257	*667*
26. Trinidad and Tobago	253	*654*
27. Germany, Fed. Rep. of	247	*639*
28. El Salvador	243	*630*
29. Netherlands Antilles	243	*628*
30. St. Lucia	240	*622*

Lowest Population Densities

Country	Density per km²	Density per *sq mi*
1. Greenland	...	*0.1*
2. Mongolia	1.3	*3.5*
3. Mauritania	1.9	*4.9*
4. Botswana	2.1	*5.5*
5. Australia	2.2	*5.7*
6. Libya	2.3	*5.9*
7. Iceland	2.4	*6.2*
8. Suriname	2.4	*6.3*
9. Canada	2.6	*6.7*
10. Guyana	3.6	*9.2*
11. Chad	3.8	*9.8*
12. Gabon	3.9	*10*
13. Central African Republic	5.0	*13*
14. Niger	5.8	*15*
15. Oman	6.0	*16*
16. Congo	6.4	*17*
Bolivia	6.5	*17*
Angola	6.7	*17*
17. Saudi Arabia	7.0	*18*
18. Mali	7.3	*19*
19. Papua New Guinea	7.9	*20*
20. Belize	8.0	*21*
21. Niue	9.1	*24*
22. Sudan	9.7	*25*
23. Algeria	10	*26*
Zambia	10	*26*
24. Paraguay	10	*27*
Solomon Islands	10	*27*
25. Norway	11	*28*

... Less than 0.1

Major Metropolitan Areas of the World

This table lists the major metropolitan areas of the world according to their estimated population on January l, 1989. For convenience in reference, the areas are grouped by major region with the total for each region given. The number of areas by population classification is given in parentheses with each size group.

For ease of comparison, each metropolitan area has been defined by Rand McNally according to consistent rules. A metropolitan area includes a central city, neighboring communities linked to it by continuous built-up areas, and more distant communities if the bulk of their population is supported by commuters to the central city. Some metropolitan areas have more than one central city; in such cases each central city is listed.

SIZE	ANGLO-AMERICA	LATIN AMERICA	EUROPE	U.S.S.R.	WEST ASIA	EAST ASIA	AFRICA-OCEANIA
Over 15,000,000 (6)	New York	Ciudad de México (Mexico City) São Paulo				Ōsaka-Kōbe-Kyōto Sŏul (Seoul) Tōkyō-Yokohama	
10,000,000-15,000,000 (9)	Los Angeles	Buenos Aires Rio de Janeiro	London Paris	Moskva (Moscow)	Bombay Calcutta		Al Qāhirah (Cairo)
5,000,000-10,000,000 (18)	Chicago Philadelphia-Trenton-Wilmington San Francisco-Oakland-San Jose	Lima		Leningrad	Delhi-New Delhi İstanbul Karāchi Madras Tehrān	Beijing (Peking) Jakarta Krung Thep (Bangkok) Manila Shanghai Taipei Tianjin (Tientsin) Victoria (Hong Kong)	
3,000,000-5,000,000 (38)	Boston Dallas-Fort Worth Detroit-Windsor Houston Miami-Fort Lauderdale Toronto Washington	Belo Horizonte Bogotá Caracas Guadalajara Santiago	Athínai (Athens) Barcelona Berlin Essen-Dortmund-Duisburg (Ruhr Area) Madrid Milano (Milan) Roma (Rome)		Baghdād Bangalore Dhaka (Dacca) Hyderābād, India Lahore	Guangzhou (Canton) Nagoya Pusan Yangon (Rangoon) Shenyang (Mukden) Singapore Ho Chi Minh (Saigon) Wuhan	Al Iskandarīyah (Alexandria) Johannesburg Kinshasa Lagos Melbourne Sydney
2,000,000-3,000,000 (49)	Atlanta Baltimore Cleveland Minneapolis-St. Paul Montréal Phoenix Pittsburgh St. Louis San Diego-Tijuana Seattle-Tacoma	Fortaleza La Habana (Havana) Medellín Monterrey Porto Alegre Recife Salvador	Birmingham Bruxelles (Brussels) București (Bucharest) Budapest Hamburg Katowice-Bytom-Gliwice Lisboa (Lisbon) Manchester Napoli (Naples) Warszawa (Warsaw)	Baku Doneck-Makejevka Gorki Kijev (Kiev) Taškent	Ahmadābād Ankara Colombo Kānpur Pune (Poona)	Bandung Chongqing (Chungking) Harbin Kuala Lumpur Nanjing (Nanking) Sapporo-Otaru Surabaya Taegu Xi'an (Sian)	Cape Town Casablanca Al Jazā'ir (Algiers)
1,500,000-2,000,000 (57)	Cincinnati Denver	Brasília Cali Curitiba Guayaquil Montevideo San Juan Santo Domingo	Amsterdam Beograd (Belgrade) Frankfurt am Main Glasgow København (Copenhagen) Köln (Cologne) Leeds-Bradford Liverpool München (Munich) Stuttgart Torino (Turin) Wien (Vienna)	Char'kov (Kharkov) Dnepropetrovsk Kujbyšev (Kuybyshev) Minsk Novosibirsk Sverdlovsk	Al Kuwayt (Kuwait) 'Amman Ar Riyāḑ (Riyadh) Bayrūt (Beirut) Chittagong Dimashq (Damascus) İzmir Jīddah Mashhad Nāgpur Tel Aviv-Yafo	Changchun (Hsinking) Chengdu (Chengtu) Dalian (Lüda) Fukuoka Ha Noi Hiroshima-Kure Jinan (Tsinan) Kaohsiung Kitakyūshū-Shimonoseki Medan P'yŏngyang Semarang Taiyuan	Abidjan Adis Abeba Al Kharṭūm-Umm Durmān (Khartoum-Omdurman) Dakar Dar es Salaam Durban
1,000,000-1,500,000 (105)	Buffalo-Niagara Falls-St. Catharines Columbus El Paso-Ciudad Juárez Hartford-New Britain Indianapolis Kansas City Milwaukee New Orleans Portland Riverside-San Bernardino Sacramento St. Petersburg-Clearwater San Antonio Vancouver	Barranquilla Belém Campinas Córdoba Goiânia Guatemala La Paz Maracaibo Puebla Quito Rosario Santos	Antwerpen (Antwerp) Dublin (Baile Átha Cliath) Düsseldorf Hannover Lille-Roubaix Łódź Lyon Mannheim Marseille Newcastle-Sunderland Nürnberg Porto Praha (Prague) Rotterdam Sofija (Sofia) Stockholm Valencia	Alma-Ata Čeljabinsk (Chelyabinsk) Jerevan Kazan Odessa Omsk Perm Rīga Rostov-na-Donu Saratov Tbilisi Ufa Volgograd	Asansol Coimbatore Eşfahān Faisalabad Halab (Aleppo) Indore Jaipur Kābol Lucknow Madurai Patna Rāwalpindi-Islāmābād Surat Tabrīz Vārānasi (Benares)	Anshan Baotou Changsha Fushun Guiyang (Kweiyang) Hangzhou (Hangchow) Jilin (Kirin) Kunming Kwangju Lanzhou (Lanchow) Nanchang Palembang Qingdao (Tsingtao) Qiqihar (Tsitsihar) Sendai Shijiazhuang Tangshan Ujung Pandang (Makasar) Ürümqi Zhengzhou (Chengchow)	Accra Adelaide Brisbane Douala Harare Ibadan Luanda Maputo Nairobi Perth Pretoria Rabat-Salé Ṭarābulus (Tripoli) Tūnis
Total by region (282)	38	36	48	26	43	61	30

Populations of Major Cities

The largest and most important of the world's major cities are listed in the following table. Also included are some smaller cities because of their regional significance.

Local official name forms have been used throughout the table. When a commonly used "conventional" name form exists, it has been featured within parentheses, following the official name. Each city name is followed by the English name of its country. Names in the United States, the United Kingdom, and Canada are further distinguished by the name of the state, region, or province in which they are located.

Many cities have population figures within parentheses following the country name. These are metropolitan populations, comprising the central city and its suburbs. When a city is within the metropolitan area of another city the name of the metropolitan central city is specified in parentheses preceded by a *. The symbol † identifies a political district population which includes some rural population. For these cities the estimated city population has been based upon the district figure.

The population of each city has been dated for ease of comparison. The date is followed by a letter designating: Census (C) or Official Estimate (E).

City and Country	Population	Date
Aachen, Fed. Rep. of Ger. (535,000)	239,170	87E
Ābādān, Iran	296,081	76C
Abidjan, Ivory Coast	1,500,000	83E
Abū Ẓaby (Abu Dhabi), United Arab Emirates	242,975	80C
Acapulco [de Juárez], Mexico	301,900	80C
Accra, Ghana (1,250,000)	859,640	84C
Adana, Turkey	777,550	85C
Ad Dawḩah (Doha), Qatar (310,000)	217,294	86E
Addis Ababa, see Ādīs Ābeba		
Adelaide, Australia (977,721)	14,157	86C
Aden, see Baladiyad ʻAdan		
Ādīs Ābeba (Addis Ababa), Ethiopia (1,500,000)	1,412,575	84C
Agana, Guam (44,000)	896	80C
Āgra, India (747,318)	694,190	81C
Aguascalientes, Mexico	293,152	80C
Ahmadābād, India (2,400,000)	2,059,725	81C
Ahvāz, Iran	471,000	82E
Akita, Japan	296,400	85C
Akron, Oh., U.S. (614,100)	237,177	80C
Albany, N.Y., U.S. (729,100)	101,727	80C
Al Başrah, Iraq	616,700	85E
Albuquerque, N.M., U.S. (453,200)	332,336	80C
Aleppo, see Halab		
Alexandria, see Al Iskandarīyah		
Algiers, see Al Jazā'ir		
Al Iskandarīyah (Alexandria), Egypt (3,350,000)	2,821,000	85E
Al Jazā'ir (Algiers), Algeria (2,300,000)	1,721,607	83E
Al Jīzah (Giza), Egypt (*Al Qāhirah)	1,608,400	85E
Al Kharţūm (Khartoum), Sudan (1,450,000)	476,218	83C
Al Kuwayt (Kuwait), Kuwait (1,375,000)	44,335	85C
Allahābād, India (650,070)	616,050	81C
Alma-Ata, U.S.S.R. (1,170,000)	1,108,000	87E
Al Madīnah (Medina), Saudi Arabia	290,000	80E
Al Maḩallah al Kubrā, Egypt (375,000)	328,700	85E
Al Manāmah (Manama), Bahrain (224,643)	108,684	81C
Al Manşūrah, Egypt (375,000)	328,700	85E
Al Mawşil (Mosul), Iraq	570,920	85E
Al Qāhirah (Cairo), Egypt (9,300,000)	6,205,000	85E
Amagasaki, Japan (*Ōsaka)	509,110	85C
ʻAmmān, Jordan (1,250,000)	833,500	86E
Amritsar, India	594,840	81C
Amsterdam, Netherlands (1,860,000)	679,140	86E
Anchorage, Ak., U.S. (184,300)	174,431	80C
Andorra la Vella, Andorra	14,928	82C
Ankara, Turkey (2,400,000)	2,235,035	85C
Annaba (Bône), Algeria (†348,322)	302,700	83E
Anshan, China	1,300,000	87E
Antananarivo, Madagascar	663,000	85E
Antwerpen (Antwerp), Belgium (1,100,000)	490,524	83E
Apia, Western Samoa	33,170	81C
Arequipa, Peru (446,942)	108,020	81C
Arhangelsk, U.S.S.R.	416,000	87E
Arnhem, Netherlands (294,085)	127,960	86E
Ar Riyāḑ (Riyadh), Saudi Arabia	1,250,000	80E
Asansol, India (1,050,000)	183,370	81C

City and Country	Population	Date
As Suways (Suez), Egypt	254,000	85E
Astrahan, U.S.S.R.	509,000	87E
Asunción, Paraguay (700,000)	455,517	82C
Athínai (Athens), Greece (3,027,331)	885,737	81C
Atlanta, Ga., U.S. (1,962,500)	425,022	80C
Auckland, New Zealand (850,000)	149,046	86C
Augsburg, Fed. Rep. of Ger. (405,000)	245,960	87E
Austin, Tx., U.S. (430,200)	345,890	80C
Baghdād, Iraq (4,000,000)	2,200,000	85E
Bakhtarān, Iran	532,000	82E
Baku, U.S.S.R. (2,005,000)	1,115,000	87E
Baladiyat ʻAdan (Aden), Yemen (318,000)	176,100	84E
Balikpapan, Indonesia (†279,852)	208,040	80C
Baltimore, Md., U.S. (1,960,400)	786,741	80C
Bamako, Mali	600,000	80E
Bandar Seri Begawan, Brunei	63,868	81C
Bandung, Indonesia (1,800,000)	1,461,407	80C
Bangalore, India (2,950,000)	2,476,355	81C
Banghāzī (Benghazi), Libya	367,600	81E
Bangkok, see Krung Thep		
Bangui, Cen. Afr. Rep.	473,800	84E
Banjul, Gambia (95,000)	44,536	83C
Barcelona, Spain (4,040,000)	1,694,064	86E
Barnaul, U.S.S.R. (655,000)	596,000	87E
Barquisimeto, Venezuela	497,630	81C
Barranquilla, Colombia	1,140,000	85C
Basel, Switzerland (575,000)	173,160	87E
Basse-Terre, Guadeloupe (26,000)	13,656	82C
Basseterre, St. Chris.-Nevis	14,725	80C
Baton Rouge, La., U.S. (434,400)	238,876	80C
Bayrūt (Beirut), Lebanon (1,675,000)	509,000	82
Beijing (Peking), China (6,450,000)	5,970,000	87E
Beirut, see Bayrūt		
Belém, Brazil (1,200,000)	1,116,578	85E
Belfast, N. Ire., U.K. (685,000)	318,600	84E
Belgrade, see Beograd		
Belize City, Belize	39,041	80C
Belmopan, Belize	2,907	80C
Belo Horizonte, Brazil (2,950,000)	2,114,429	85E
Benares, see Vārānasi		
Bengbu, China (†612,600)	403,900	86E
Benxi, China	840,000	87E
Beograd (Belgrade), Yugoslavia (1,400,000)	936,200	81C
Bergamo, Italy (340,000)	121,840	81C
Berlin, Ost- (East), Ger. Dem. Rep. (*Berlin, West)	1,236,248	87E
Berlin, West, Fed. Rep. of Ger. (3,825,000)	1,879,225	87E
Bern (Berne), Switzerland (298,800)	137,134	87E
Bhopāl, India	671,010	81C
Bielefeld, Fed. Rep. of Ger. (515,000)	299,360	87E
Bilbao, Spain (985,000)	378,221	86E
Billings, Mt., U.S. (96,100)	66,842	80C
Birmingham, Eng., U.K. (2,675,000)	1,013,995	81C
Birmingham, Al., U.S. (747,400)	286,799	80C
Bissau, Guinea-Bissau	109,486	79C
Blackpool, Eng., U.K. (280,000)	146,290	81C
Bloemfontein, South Africa (235,000)	104,380	85C
Bogor, India (560,000)	246,940	80C
Bogotá, Colombia (4,550,000)	4,260,000	85C

City and Country	Population	Date
Boise, Id., U.S. (164,200)	102,160	80C
Bologna, Italy (530,000)	455,850	81C
Bombay, India (9,950,000)	8,243,405	81C
Bonn, Fed. Rep. of Ger. (570,000)	291,439	87E
Bordeaux, France (640,012)	208,150	82C
Boston, Ma., U.S. (3,971,700)	562,994	80C
Brasília, Brazil	1,567,709	85E
Bratislava, Czechoslovakia	417,100	86E
Braunschweig, Fed. Rep. of Ger. (330,000)	247,830	87E
Brazzaville, Congo	595,102	84C
Bremen, Fed. Rep. of Ger. (800,000)	521,976	87E
Brest, France (201,145)	156,060	82C
Bridgetown, Barbados (115,000)	7,466	80C
Brighton, Eng., U.K. (420,000)	134,580	81C
Brisbane, Australia (1,149,401)	705,755	86C
Bristol, Eng., U.K. (1,630,000)	413,860	8IC
Bruxelles / Brussel (Brussels), Belgium (2,395,000)	137,738	83E
Bucaramanga, Colombia	550,000	85C
Bucureşti (Bucharest), Romania (2,250,000)	1,989,823	86E
Budapest, Hungary (2,565,000)	2,104,700	88E
Buenos Aires, Argentina (10,750,000)	2,922,829	80C
Buffalo, N.Y., U.S. (1,483,000)	357,870	80C
Bujumbura, Burundi	229,980	83E
Bulawayo, Zimbabwe	413,810	82C
Burlington, Vt., U.S. (115,300)	37,712	80C
Bursa, Turkey	612,510	85C
Būr Sa'īd (Port Said), Egypt	374,000	85E
Cádiz, Spain (240,000)	160,839	84E
Cagliari, Italy (300,000)	232,780	81C
Cairo, see Al Qāhirah		
Calcutta, India (11,100,000)	3,305,006	81C
Calgary, Alta., Can. (671,326)	636,100	86C
Cali, Colombia (1,400,000)	1,350,565	85C
Calicut (Kozhikode), India (546,058)	394,440	81C
Callao, Peru (*Lima)	264,133	81C
Campinas, Brazil (1,125,000)	841,010	85E
Canberra, Australia (271,362)	247,194	86C
Cannes, France (295,525)	72,250	82C
Canton, see Guangzhou		
Cape Town, South Africa (1,790,000)	776,617	85C
Caracas, Venezuela (3,600,000)	3,041,000	81E
Cardiff, Wales, U.K. (625,000)	262,310	81C
Cartagena, Colombia	531,420	85C
Casablanca, Morocco (2,475,000)	2,139,204	82C
Castries, St. Lucia	50,798	84E
Catania, Italy (515,000)	378,520	81C
Cayenne, French Guiana	38,093	82C
Cebu, Philippines (600,000)	490,280	80C
Čeljabinsk (Chelyabinsk), U.S.S.R. (1,300,000)	1,119,000	87E
Chandīgarh, India (422,841)	373,780	81C
Changchun, China (†1,910,000)	1,740,000	87E
Changshu, China (†998,000)	281,300	86E
Changzhou, China	522,700	86E
Chao'an, China (†1,214,500)	265,400	86E
Charleston, W.V., U.S. (236,300)	63,968	80C
Charlotte, N.C., U.S. (479,200)	315,473	80C
Chattanooga, Tn., U.S. (359,200)	169,728	80C
Chengdu, China (†2,640,000)	1,810,000	87E
Chiba, Japan (*Tōkyō)	788,930	85C
Chicago, Il., U.S. (7,717,100)	3,005,072	80C
Chiclayo, Peru (279,527)	213,090	81C
Chihuahua, Mexico	385,600	80C

City and Country	Population	Date
Chittagong, Bangladesh (1,391,877)	980,000	81C
Ch'ŏngjin, N. Korea	490,000	81E
Chongqing (Chungking), China (†2,830,000)	2,450,000	87E
Chŏnju, S. Korea	426,470	85C
Christchurch, New Zealand (320,000)	168,200	86C
Chungking, see Chongqing		
Cincinnati, Oh., U.S. (1,480,100)	385,457	80C
Ciudad de México, Mexico (14,100,000)	8,831,079	80C
Ciudad Juárez, Mexico (*El Paso)	544,490	80C
Clermont-Ferrand, France (256,189)	147,360	82C
Cleveland, Oh., U.S. (2,218,400)	573,822	80C
Cochin, India (685,836)	513,240	81C
Coimbatore, India (965,000)	704,510	81C
Cologne, see Köln		
Colombo, Sri Lanka (2,050,000)	623,000	83E
Columbia, S.C., U.S. (375,900)	101,229	80C
Columbus, Oh., U.S. (963,600)	565,032	80C
Conakry, Guinea	705,280	83C
Concepción, Chile (535,000)	267,890	82C
Constanța, Romania	327,670	86E
Constantine, Algeria	448,570	83E
Córdoba, Argentina (1,070,000)	993,050	80C
Córdoba, Spain	291,370	84E
Cotonou, Benin	215,000	80E
Coventry, Eng., U.K. (645,000)	318,710	81C
Cúcuta, Colombia (440,000)	445,000	85C
Cuernavaca, Mexico	192,770	80C
Curitiba, Brazil (1,700,000)	1,279,205	85E
Cusco, Peru (184,550)	89,563	81C
Dakar, Senegal	1,428,084	85E
Dalian (Lüda), China	1,680,000	87E
Dallas, Tx., U.S. (2,727,300)	904,078	80C
Dandong, China	579,800	86E
Danzig, see Gdańsk		
Daqing, China (†850,000)	620,000	87E
Dar es Salaam, Tanzania	757,346	78C
Darmstadt, Fed. Rep. of Ger. (305,000)	133,570	87E
Datong, China (†1,020,000)	790,000	87E
Davao, Philippines (†610,375)	408,770	80C
Dayton, Oh., U.S. (768,200)	193,536	80C
Delhi, India (7,200,000)	4,884,234	81C
Denver, Co., U.S. (1,405,300)	492,365	80C
Des Moines, Ia., U.S. (320,400)	191,003	80C
Detroit, Mi., U.S. (4,691,900)	1,202,463	80C
Dhaka, Bangladesh (3,430,312)	2,365,695	81C
Dhānbād, India (825,000)	120,220	81C
Dimashq (Damascus), Syria (1,850,000)	1,259,000	86E
Djibouti, Djibouti	120,000	76E
Dnepropetrovsk, U.S.S.R. (1,600,000)	1,182,000	87E
Doneck, U.S.S.R. (2,220,000)	1,090,000	87E
Dongguan, China (†1,208,500)	254,900	86E
Dortmund, Fed. Rep. of Ger. (*Essen)	568,160	87E
Douala, Cameroon	853,000	85E
Dresden, Ger. Dem. Rep. (670,000)	519,810	87E
Dublin (Baile Átha Cliath), Ireland (1,140,000)	502,749	86C
Duisburg, Fed. Rep. of Ger. (*Essen)	514,620	87E
Durban, South Africa (1,550,000)	634,301	85C
Dušanbe, U.S.S.R.	582,000	87E
Düsseldorf, Fed. Rep. of Ger. (1,190,000)	560,572	87E
Ecatepec de Morelos, Mexico (*Ciudad de México)	741,820	80C
Edinburgh, Scot., U.K. (630,000)	408,822	81C
Edmonton, Alta., Can. (785,465)	573,980	86C
El Paso, Tx., U.S. (1,037,700)	425,259	80C
Enschede, Netherlands (288,000)	144,040	86E
Erbīl, Iraq	333,900	85E
Eșfahān (Isfahan), Iran	927,000	82E
Essen, Fed. Rep. of Ger. (4,950,000)	615,421	87E
Faisalabad, Pakistan	1,104,209	81C
Fargo, N.D., U.S (108,800)	61,383	80C
Fès, Morocco (535,000)	448,820	82C
Firenze (Florence), Italy (650,000)	453,293	81C
Florianópolis, Brazil (365,000)	178,400	85E
Fortaleza, Brazil (1,825,000)	1,582,414	85E
Fort-de-France, Martinique (116,017)	99,844	82C
Fort Worth, Tx., U.S. (*Dallas)	385,164	80C
Frankfurt am Main, Fed. Rep. of Ger. (1,855,000)	592,411	87E
Freetown, Sierra Leone (315,000)	276,600	74C
Frunze, U.S.S.R.	632,000	87E
Fukuoka, Japan (1,750,000)	1,160,440	85C
Funabashi, Japan (*Tōkyō)	506,960	85C
Funafuti, Tuvalu	2,191	79C
Fushun, China	1,270,000	87E
Fuxian, China (†960,700)	246,200	86E
Fuxin, China	690,000	87E
Fuzhou, China (†1,210,000)	890,000	87E
Gaborone, Botswana	95,163	86E
Gdańsk (Danzig), Poland (909,000)	468,400	87E
General Sarmiento, Argentina (*Buenos Aires)	502,920	80C
Genève (Geneva), Switzerland (460,000)	160,645	87E
Genova (Genoa), Italy (830,000)	760,300	81C
Gent (Ghent), Belgium (465,000)	236,540	83E
Georgetown, Cayman Islands	11,500	87E
Georgetown, Guyana (188,000)	78,500	83E
George Town (Pinang), Malaysia (495,000)	248,240	80C
Gifu, Japan	411,740	85C
Giza, see Al Jīzah		
Glasgow, Scot., U.K. (1,800,000)	754,586	81C
Godthåb (Nûk), Greenland	10,972	86E
Goiânia, Brazil (990,000)	923,330	85E
Gorki, U.S.S.R. (2,005,000)	1,425,000	87E
Göteborg, Sweden (710,894)	429,330	87E
Granada, Spain	280,590	86E
Graz, Austria (325,000)	243,160	81C
Grenoble, France (392,021)	156,640	82C
Guadalajara, Mexico (2,325,000)	1,626,152	80C
Guadalupe, Mexico (*Monterrey)	370,520	80C
Guangzhou (Canton), China (†3,360,000)	3,050,000	87E
Guarulhos, Brazil (*São Paulo)	571,700	86E
Guatemala, Guatemala (1,100,000)	754,243	81C
Guayaquil, Ecuador (1,255,000)	1,204,532	82C
Guilin, China (†457,500)	342,200	86E
Guiyang, China (†1,400,000)	1,010,000	87E
Gujranwala, Pakistan (658,753)	600,990	81C
Gwalior, India (555,862)	539,010	81C
Haicheng, China (†984,800)	210,700	86E
Haikou, China (†289,600)	209,200	86E
Hai Phong, Vietnam (†1,279,067)	385,210	79C
Halab (Aleppo), Syria (1,115,000)	1,060,002	83E
Halifax, N.S., Can. (295,990)	113,570	86C
Hamamatsu, Japan	514,110	85C
Hamburg, Fed. Rep. of Ger. (2,225,000)	1,571,267	87E
Hamilton, Bermuda (15,000)	1,676	85E
Hamilton, Ont., Can. (557,029)	306,720	86C
Handan, China (†1,010,000)	850,000	87E
Hannover, Fed. Rep. of Ger. (1,000,000)	505,718	87E
Ha Noi (Hanoi), Vietnam (1,500,000)	897,500	79C
Hāora (Howrah), India (*Calcutta)	744,420	81C
Harare, Zimbabwe (890,000)	656,011	82C
Harbin, China	2,670,000	87E
Harkov, U.S.S.R. (1,905,000)	1,587,000	87E
Hartford, Ct., U.S. (1,013,600)	136,392	80C
Havana, see La Habana		
Ḥefa (Haifa), Israel (435,000)	223,400	87E
Hefei, China (†900,000)	720,000	87E
Hegang, China	588,300	86E
Helsinki, Finland (900,000)	484,263	84E
Hibli, India	527,100	81C
Ḥims (Homs), Syria	346,870	81C
Hiroshima, Japan (1,575,000)	1,044,118	85C
Hohhot, China (†810,000)	650,000	87E
Hong Kong, see Victoria		
Honiara, Solomon Is.	30,499	86C
Honolulu, Ha., U.S. (762,600)	365,048	80C
Houston, Tx., U.S. (2,755,100)	1,595,138	80C
Huainan, China (†1,090,000)	690,000	87E
Hyderābād, India (2,750,000)	2,187,262	81C
Ibadan, Nigeria	1,144,000	87E
Ilorin, Nigeria	380,000	87E
Inch'ŏn, S. Korea (*Seoul)	1,386,991	85C
Indianapolis, In., U.S. (1,072,500)	700,807	80C
Indore, India (850,000)	829,320	81C
Irkutsk, U.S.S.R.	609,000	87E
Isfahan, see Eșfahān		
Islāmābād, Pakistan (*Rāwalpindi)	204,364	81C
İstanbul, Turkey (5,750,000)	5,475,982	85C
Iževsk, U.S.S.R.	631,000	87E
İzmir, Turkey (1,550,000)	1,489,772	85C
Jabalpur, India (757,303)	614,160	81C
Jackson, Ms., U.S. (306,900)	202,895	80C
Jacksonville, Fl., U.S. (635,900)	540,920	80C
Jaipur, India (1,025,000)	977,160	81C
Jakarta, Indonesia (8,600,000)	6,503,449	80C
Jamshedpur, India (669,580)	438,380	81C
Jaroslavl, U.S.S.R.	634,000	87E
Jerevan, U.S.S.R. (1,280,000)	1,168,000	87E
Jiaozuo, China (†509,900)	335,400	86E
Jiddah, Saudi Arabia	1,300,000	80E
Jinan, China	1,460,000	87E
Jinzhou, China (†790,000)	690,000	87E
Jixi, China (†820,000)	700,000	87E
João Pessoa, Brazil (550,000)	348,500	85E
Jodhpur, India	506,340	81C
Johannesburg, South Africa (3,650,000)	632,369	85C
Kābol, Afghanistan	972,836	81E
Kagoshima, Japan	530,500	80C
Kaifeng, China (†629,100)	458,800	86E
Kalinin, U.S.S.R.	447,000	87E
Kaliningrad, U.S.S.R.	394,000	87E
Kampala, Uganda	460,000	82E
Kano, Nigeria	538,300	87E
Kānpur, India (1,875,000)	1,481,789	81C
Kansas City, Mo., U.S. (1,272,400)	448,033	80C
Kaohsiung, Taiwan (1,785,000)	1,302,849	85E
Karāchi, Pakistan (5,300,000)	4,901,627	81C
Karaganda, U.S.S.R.	633,000	87E
Karl-Marx-Stadt, Ger. Dem. Rep. (450,000)	313,790	87E
Kāṭhmāṇḍau, Nepal (320,000)	235,160	81C
Katowice, Poland (2,778,000)	367,300	87E
Kawasaki, Japan (*Tōkyō)	1,088,624	85C
Kayseri, Turkey	373,930	85C
Kazan, U.S.S.R. (1,120,000)	1,068,000	87E
Keelung (Chilung), Taiwan	351,520	85E
Kemerovo, U.S.S.R.	520,000	87E
Khartoum, see Al Kharṭūm		
Khulna, Bangladesh	648,350	81C
Kiel, Fed. Rep. of Ger. (335,000)	245,682	86E
Kigali, Rwanda	181,600	83E
Kijev (Kiev), U.S.S.R. (2,850,000)	2,544,000	87E
Kingston, Jamaica (770,000)	586,930	82C
Kingston-upon-Hull, Eng., U.K. (350,000)	322,140	81C
Kingstown, St. Vin. and the Gren. (27,948)	18,378	84E
Kinshasa, Zaire	3,000,000	86E
Kisangani (Stanleyville), Zaire	282,650	84C
Kišinev, U.S.S.R.	663,000	87E
Kitakyūshū, Japan (1,525,000)	1,056,402	85C
Kitchener, Ont., Can. (311,195)	150,600	86C
Kitwe-Nkana, Zambia (283,962)	207,500	80C
Knoxville, Tn., U.S. (490,000)	175,045	80C
Kōbe, Japan (*Ōsaka)	1,410,834	85C
København (Copenhagen), Denmark (1,685,000)	473,000	86E
Köln (Cologne), Fed. Rep. of Ger. (1,760,000)	914,336	87E
Kowloon, Hong Kong (*Victoria)	799,123	81C
Kraków, Poland (828,000)	744,000	87E
Krasnodar, U.S.S.R.	623,000	87E
Krasnojarsk, U.S.S.R.	899,000	87E
Krivoj Rog, U.S.S.R.	698,000	87E
Krung Thep (Bangkok), Thailand (6,450,000)	5,446,708	86E
Kuala Lumpur, Malaysia (1,475,000)	919,610	80C
Kujbyšev, U.S.S.R. (1,510,000)	1,280,000	87E
Kumamoto, Japan	555,710	85C
Kumasi, Ghana (600,000)	348,880	84C
Kunming, China (†1,520,000)	1,280,000	87E
Kuwait, see Al Kuwayt		
Kwangju, S. Korea (975,000)	905,890	85C
Kyōto, Japan (*Ōsaka)	1,479,218	85C
Lagos, Nigeria (3,800,000)	1,213,000	87E

Metropolitan area populations are shown in parentheses.
* City is located within the metropolitan area of another city; for example, Kyōto, Japan is located in the Ōsaka metropolitan area.
† Population of entire municipality or district, including rural area.

C Census
E Official estimate

City and Country	Population	Date
La Habana (Havana), Cuba (1,975,000)	1,914,466	81C
Lahore, Pakistan (3,025,000)	2,707,215	81C
Lansing, Mi., U.S. (352,600)	130,414	80C
Lanzhou, China (†1,390,000)	1,270,000	87E
La Paz, Bolivia	992,592	85E
La Plata, Argentina (*Buenos Aires)	477,170	80C
Las Palmas de Gran Canaria, Spain	372,270	86E
Las Vegas, Nv., U.S. (453,800)	164,674	80C
Lausanne, Switzerland (259,900)	124,200	87E
Leeds, Eng., U.K. (1,540,000)	445,242	81C
Le Havre, France (254,595)	199,380	82C
Leicester, Eng., U.K. (495,000)	324,390	81C
Leipzig, Ger. Dem. Rep. (700,000)	550,641	87E
Leningrad, U.S.S.R. (5,750,000)	4,393,000	87E
León, Mexico	593,000	80C
Leshan, China (†972,300)	307,300	86E
Lexington, Ky., U.S. (255,600)	204,165	80C
Libreville, Gabon	235,700	85E
Liège, Belgium (755,000)	207,496	83E
Lille, France (1,020,000)	168,424	82C
Lilongwe, Malawi	175,000	85E
Lima, Peru (4,608,010)	371,122	81C
Linyi, China (†1,365,000)	190,000	86E
Linz, Austria (355,000)	199,910	81C
Lisboa (Lisbon), Portugal (2,250,000)	807,167	81C
Little Rock, Ar., U.S. (382,000)	167,744	80C
Liuzhou, China	660,000	87E
Liverpool, Eng., U.K. (1,525,000)	538,809	81C
Ljubljana, Yugoslavia (†305,211)	205,600	81C
Łódź, Poland (1,061,000)	847,400	87E
Lomas de Zamora, Argentina (*Buenos Aires)	510,130	80C
Lomé, Togo	369,926	81C
London, Ont., Can. (342,302)	269,140	86C
London, Eng., U.K. (11,100,000)	6,851,400	81C
Los Angeles, Ca., U.S. (9,763,600)	2,968,579	80C
Louisville, Ky., U.S. (891,400)	298,694	80C
Luanda, Angola	1,200,000	82E
Lubumbashi, Zaire	543,260	84C
Lucknow, India (1,060,000)	895,721	81C
Ludhiāna, India	607,050	81C
Luoyang, China (1,060,000)	740,000	87E
Lusaka, Zambia	535,830	80C
Luxembourg, Luxembourg (133,000)	78,924	81C
Lvov, U.S.S.R.	767,000	87E
Lyon, France (1,275,000)	413,095	82C
Madison, Wi., U.S. (294,300)	170,616	80C
Madras, India (4,475,000)	3,276,622	81C
Madrid, Spain (4,650,000)	3,123,713	86E
Madurai, India (960,000)	820,890	81C
Magdeburg, Ger. Dem. Rep. (400,000)	288,970	87E
Magnitogorsk, U.S.S.R.	430,000	87E
Makkah (Mecca), Saudi Arabia	550,000	80E
Malabo, Equatorial Guinea	30,710	83C
Málaga, Spain	595,260	86E
Malang, Indonesia	511,780	80C
Male, Maldives	46,334	85E
Malmö, Sweden (445,000)	230,050	87E
Managua, Nicaragua	644,588	81E
Manama, see Al Manāmah		
Manaus, Brazil	809,910	85E
Manchester, Eng., U.K. (2,775,000)	437,612	81C
Manchester, N.H., U.S. (129,300)	90,936	80C
Mandalay, Burma	532,890	83C
Manila, Philippines (6,800,000)	1,630,485	80C
Manizales, Colombia	330,000	85C
Mannheim, Fed. Rep. of Ger. (1,400,000)	294,648	87E
Maputo, Mozambique	755,300	80C
Maracaibo, Venezuela	929,000	81E
Mar del Plata, Argentina	414,690	80C
Mariupol', U.S.S.R.	529,000	87E
Marrakech, Morocco (535,000)	439,720	82C
Marseille, France (1,225,000)	874,436	82C
Maseru, Lesotho	14,686	76C
Masqaṭ (Muscat), Oman	50,000	81E
Mbabane, Swaziland	53,000	84E
Mbuji-Mayi, Zaire	423,360	84C
Medan, Indonesia	1,208,678	80C
Medellín, Colombia	2,095,000	85C
Medina, see Al Madīndah		
Meknès, Morocco (375,000)	319,780	82C
Melbourne, Australia (2,832,893)	60,828	86C
Memphis, Tn., U.S. (852,900)	646,174	80C
Mendoza, Argentina (650,000)	119,080	80C
Mexicali, Mexico (365,000)	341,550	80C
Mexico City, see Ciudad de México		
Miami, Fl., U.S. (2,827,300)	346,865	80C
Middlesbrough (Teesside), Eng., U.K. (580,000)	158,510	81C
Milano (Milan), Italy (3,775,000)	1,634,638	81C
Milwaukee, Wi., U.S. (1,374,700)	636,297	80C
Minneapolis, Mn., U.S. (2,012,400)	370,951	80C
Minsk, U.S.S.R. (1,600,000)	1,543,000	87E
Mobile, Al., U.S. (361,900)	200,452	80C
Mombasa, Kenya	425,600	84E
Mönchengladbach, Fed. Rep. of Ger. (410,000)	255,080	87E
Monrovia, Liberia	425,000	84E
Monterrey, Mexico (2,015,000)	1,090,009	80C
Montevideo, Uruguay (1,550,000)	1,246,500	85C
Montgomery, Al., U.S. (225,000)	177,857	80C
Montréal, Que., Can. (2,921,357)	1,015,420	86C
Morón, Argentina (*Buenos Aires)	598,420	80C
Moroni, Comoros	20,112	80C
Moskva (Moscow), U.S.S.R. (12,900,000)	8,614,000	87E
Mudanjiang, China	630,000	87E
Multān, Pakistan (732,070)	696,310	81C
München (Munich), Fed. Rep. of Ger. (1,955,000)	1,274,716	87E
Münster, Fed. Rep. of Ger.	267,620	87E
Muqdisho (Mogadishu), Somalia	600,000	83E
Murcia, Spain (†305,221)	200,300	84E
Murmansk, U.S.S.R.	432,000	87E
Mysore, India (479,081)	441,750	81C
Naberežnyje Čelny (Brežnev), U.S.S.R.	480,000	87E
Nagasaki, Japan	449,380	85C
Nagoya, Japan (4,800,000)	2,116,381	85C
Nāgpur, India (1,302,066)	1,219,461	81C
Nairobi, Kenya	1,103,600	84E
Nanchang, China (†1,190,000)	1,030,000	87E
Nancy, France (306,982)	96,310	82C
Nanjing (Nanking), China	2,290,000	87E
Nanning, China (†960,000)	690,000	87E
Nantes, France (464,857)	240,530	82C
Napoli (Naples), Italy (2,765,000)	1,210,503	81C
Nashville, Tn., U.S. (633,900)	455,651	80C
Nassau, Bahamas	135,000	82E
Natal, Brazil	510,100	85E
N'Djamena, Chad	303,000	79E
Netzahualcóyotl, Mexico (*Ciudad de México)	1,341,230	80C
Newark, N.J., U.S. (*New York)	329,248	80C
Newcastle, Australia (405,089)	129,490	86C
Newcastle upon Tyne, Eng., U.K. (1,300,000)	199,064	81C
New Delhi, India (*Delhi)	273,036	81C
New Kowloon, Hong Kong (*Victoria)	1,651,064	81C
New Orleans, La., U.S. (1,185,000)	557,927	80C
Newport, Wales, U.K. (310,000)	115,890	81C
New York, N.Y., U.S. (16,800,900)	7,071,639	80C
Niamey, Niger	399,100	83C
Nice, France (449,496)	337,080	82C
Nicosia, Cyprus (185,000)	48,221	82E
Nikolajev, U.S.S.R.	501,000	87E
Ningbo, China (†1,030,000)	560,000	87E
Niterói, Brazil (*Rio de Janeiro)	441,680	85E
Norfolk, Va., U.S. (795,600)	266,979	80C
North York, Ont., Can. (*Toronto)	556,290	86C
Nottingham, Eng., U.K. (655,000)	273,300	81C
Nouakchott, Mauritania	285,000	87E
Nouméa, New Caledonia (83,000)	60,112	83C
Nova Iguaçu, Brazil (*Rio de Janeiro)	592,800	85E
Novokuzneck, U.S.S.R.	589,000	87E
Novosibirsk, U.S.S.R. (1,580,000)	1,423,000	87E
Nuku'alofa, Tonga	21,265	86C
Nürnberg, Fed. Rep. of Ger. (1,030,000)	467,392	87E
Odessa, U.S.S.R. (1,210,000)	1,141,000	87E
Ogbomosho, Nigeria	582,900	87E
Okayama, Japan	572,470	85C
Oklahoma City, Ok., U.S. (742,000)	403,484	80C
Omaha, Nb., U.S. (538,600)	322,133	80C
Omdurman, see Umm Durmān		
Omsk, U.S.S.R. (1,160,000)	1,134,000	87E
Oran, Algeria	663,500	83E
Orenburg, U.S.S.R.	537,000	87E
Orlando, Fl., U.S. (619,300)	128,291	80C
Orūmīyeh, Iran	263,000	82E
Ōsaka, Japan (16,450,000)	263,624	85C
Osasco, Brazil (*São Paulo)	591,560	85E
Oshogbo, Nigeria	380,800	87E
Oslo, Norway (720,000)	448,747	83E
Ostrava, Czechoslovakia (755,000)	327,790	86E
Ottawa, Ont., Can. (819,263)	300,763	86C
Ouagadougou, Burkina Faso	442,223	85C
Palembang, Indonesia	786,600	80C
Palermo, Italy	699,690	81C
Palma, Spain	311,197	84E
Panamá, Panama (625,000)	413,992	82E
Papeete, French Polynesia (80,000)	23,496	83C
Paramaribo, Suriname (192,810)	67,905	80C
Paris, France (9,775,000)	2,127,100	86E
Patna, India (1,025,000)	776,370	81C
Peking, see Beijing		
Penza, U.S.S.R.	540,000	87E
Perm, U.S.S.R. (1,145,000)	1,075,000	87E
Perth, Australia (994,472)	79,409	86C
Peshāwar, Pakistan (566,248)	506,890	81C
Philadelphia, Pa., U.S. (5,208,600)	1,688,210	80C
Phnum Pénh, Cambodia	700,000	86E
Phoenix, Az., U.S. (1,482,400)	790,044	80C
Pingxiang, China (†1,286,700)	368,700	86E
Pittsburgh, Pa., U.S. (2,218,800)	423,959	80C
Ploiești, Romania (300,000)	234,880	86E
Plovdiv, Bulgaria	349,140	86E
Pointe-à-Pitre, Guadeloupe (83,000)	25,310	82C
Port-au-Prince, Haiti (760,000)	684,284	82C
Port Elizabeth, South Africa (690,000)	272,840	85C
Port Harcourt, Nigeria	327,300	87E
Portland, Me., U.S. (193,800)	61,572	80C
Portland, Or., U.S. (1,227,200)	368,139	80C
Port-Louis, Mauritius (415,000)	138,272	86E
Port Moresby, Papua New Guinea	123,624	80C
Porto (Oporto), Portugal (1,225,000)	327,368	81C
Porto Alegre, Brazil (2,600,000)	1,272,121	85E
Port of Spain, Trinidad and Tobago (370,000)	55,800	80C
Porto-Novo, Benin	123,000	80E
Port Said, see Būr Sa'īd		
Portsmouth, Eng., U.K. (485,000)	174,210	81C
Port-Vila, Vanuatu (18,000)	13,067	86E
Poznań, Poland (672,000)	578,100	87E
Praha (Prague), Czechoslovakia (1,310,000)	1,193,513	86E
Praia, Cape Verde	37,480	80C
Pretoria, South Africa (960,000)	443,059	85C
Providence, R.I., U.S. (921,800)	156,804	80C
Puebla [de Zaragoza], Mexico (1,055,000)	835,750	80C
Pune, India (1,775,000)	1,203,351	81C
Pusan, S. Korea (3,550,000)	3,514,798	85C
P'yŏngyang, N. Korea (1,600,000)	1,283,000	80E
Qingdao, China	1,270,000	87E
Qiqihar, China (†1,300,000)	1,150,000	87E
Qom, Iran	424,000	82E
Québec, Que., Can. (603,267)	164,580	86C
Quetta, Pakistan (285,791)	244,840	81C
Quezon City, Philippines (*Manila)	1,165,865	80C
Quilmes, Argentina (*Buenos Aires)	446,580	80C
Quito, Ecuador (1,050,000)	890,355	82C
Rabat, Morocco (980,000)	518,616	82C
Rājkot, India	445,070	81C
Raleigh, N.C., U.S. (282,800)	150,255	80C
Rānchī, India (502,771)	489,620	81C
Rangoon, see Yangon		
Rāwalpindi, Pakistan (1,040,000)	457,091	81C
Recife, Brazil (2,625,000)	1,287,623	85E
Reno, Nv., U.S. (176,200)	100,756	80C
Reykjavík, Iceland (130,722)	88,745	84E
Ribeirão Prêto, Brazil	383,120	85E
Richmond, Va., U.S. (690,600)	219,214	80C
Rīga, U.S.S.R. (990,000)	900,000	87E

City and Country	Population	Date
Rio de Janeiro, Brazil (10,150,000)	5,603,388	85E
Riverside, Ca., U.S. (768,300)	170,591	80C
Riyadh, see Ar Riyāḍ		
Rjazan, U.S.S.R.	508,000	87E
Rochester, N.Y., U.S. (816,200)	241,741	80C
Roma (Rome), Italy (3,115,000)	2,830,569	81C
Rosario, Argentina (1,045,000)	938,120	80C
Rostov-na-Donu, U.S.S.R. (1,145,000)	1,004,000	87E
Rotterdam, Netherlands (1,110,000)	571,372	86E
Rouen, France (379,879)	101,945	82C
Rouseau, Dominica	9,348	84E
Sacramento, Ca., U.S. (866,400)	275,741	80C
Safāqis, Tunisia (310,000)	231,910	84C
Saigon, see Ho Chi Minh		
St. Catharines, Ont., Can. (343,258)	123,450	86C
St.-Étienne, France (317,228)	204,950	82C
St. George's, Grenada (25,000)	4,788	81C
St. John's, Antigua and Barbuda	24,359	77E
St. Louis, Mo., U.S. (2,203,000)	452,801	80C
St. Paul, Mn., U.S. (*Minneapolis)	270,230	80C
St. Petersburg, Fl., U.S. (852,300)	238,647	80C
Sakai, Japan (*Ōsaka)	818,270	85C
Salem, India (518,615)	361,390	81C
Salt Lake City, Ut., U.S. (682,400)	163,034	80C
Salvador, Brazil (2,050,000)	1,804,438	85E
Samarkand, U.S.S.R.	388,000	87E
Ṣan'ā', Yemen	277,818	81C
San Antonio, Tx., U.S. (968,200)	786,023	80C
San Diego, Ca., U.S. (2,098,500)	875,538	80C
San Francisco, Ca., U.S. (4,683,200)	678,974	80C
San José, Costa Rica (670,000)	241,464	84C
San Jose, Ca., U.S. (*San Francisco)	629,400	80C
San Juan, Puerto Rico (1,775,260)	424,600	80C
San Luis Potosí, Mexico (470,000)	362,370	80C
San Miguel de Tucumán, Argentina (525,000)	392,880	80C
San Salvador, El Salvador (920,000)	459,902	85E
San Sebastián, Spain (285,000)	180,040	86E
Santiago, Chile (4,025,000)	425,924	82C
Santo André, Brazil (São Paulo)	635,120	85E
Santo Domingo, Dominican Rep.	1,313,172	81C
Santos, Brazil (1,065,000)	460,100	85E
São Bernardo do Campo, Brazil (*São Paulo)	562,480	85E
São Luís, Brazil (600,000)	227,900	85E
São Paulo, Brazil (15,175,000)	10,063,110	85E
São Tomé, Sao Tome and Prin.	17,380	70C
Sapporo, Japan (1,900,000)	1,542,979	85C
Sarajevo, Yugoslavia (†448,500)	374,500	81C
Saratov, U.S.S.R. (1,170,000)	918,000	87E
Sargodha, Pakistan (291,362)	231,890	81C
Savannah, Ga., U.S. (212,800)	141,651	80C
Scarborough, Ont., Can. (*Toronto)	484,670	86C
Seattle, Wa., U.S. (2,077,100)	493,846	80C
Semarang, Indonesia	820,140	80C
Semipalatinsk, U.S.S.R.	330,000	87E
Sendai, Japan (1,175,000)	700,250	85C
Seoul, see Sŏul		
Sevilla (Seville), Spain (945,000)	668,350	86E
's-Gravenhage (The Hague), Netherlands (770,000)	443,961	86E
Shanghai, China (9,300,000)	7,100,000	87E
Shantou, China (†770,000)	550,000	87E
Sheffield, Eng., U.K. (710,000)	470,680	81C
Shenyang (Mukden), China (†4,290,000)	3,840,000	87E
Shīrāz, Iran	800,000	82E
Shubrā al Khaymah, Egypt (*Al Qāhirah)	515,500	85E
Sialkot, Pakistan (302,009)	258,140	81C
Singapore, Singapore (3,000,000)	2,631,000	88E
Sioux Falls, S.D., U.S. (92,200)	81,343	80C
Sofija (Sofia), Bulgaria (1,205,000)	1,119,152	86E
Solāpur, India (514,860)	511,100	81C
Sŏul (Seoul), S. Korea (14,100,000)	9,639,110	85C
Southampton, Eng., U.K. (415,000)	211,320	81C
Soweto, South Africa (*Johannesburg)	521,940	85C
Springfield, Il., U.S. (154,200)	100,054	80C
Springfield, Ma., U.S. (485,900)	152,319	80C
Srīnagar, India (606,002)	594,770	81C
Stalingrad, see Volgograd		
Stockholm, Sweden (1,449,972)	663,217	87E
Stoke-on-Trent, Eng., U.K. (440,000)	272,440	81C
Strasbourg, France (400,000)	248,710	82C
Stuttgart, Fed. Rep. of Ger. (1,925,000)	565,486	87E
Suez, see As Suways		
Suichang, China (†2,216,500)	363,500	86E
Suixian, China (†1,281,600)	187,700	86E
Surabaya, Indonesia	2,027,913	80C
Surakarta, Indonesia (575,000)	469,530	80C
Surat, India (913,806)	776,580	81C
Suva, Fiji (141,273)	69,665	86C
Suzhou, China	720,000	87E
Sverdlovsk, U.S.S.R. (1,575,000)	1,331,000	87E
Swansea, Wales, U.K. (275,000)	172,430	81C
Sydney, Australia (3,364,858)	86,311	86C
Syracuse, N.Y., U.S. (518,600)	170,105	80C
Szczecin, Poland (449,000)	395,000	87E
Tabrīz, Iran	852,000	82E
Tacoma, Wa., U.S. (*Seattle)	158,501	80C
Taegu, S. Korea	2,029,853	85C
Taejŏn, S. Korea	866,140	85C
Tai'an, China (†1,325,400)	215,900	86E
Taichung, Taiwan	674,930	85E
Tainan, Taiwan	639,880	85E
Taipei, Taiwan (5,725,000)	2,507,620	85E
Taiyuan, China (†1,930,000)	1,660,000	87E
Tallinn, U.S.S.R.	478,000	87E
Tampa, Fl., U.S. (594,500)	271,598	80C
Tampico, Mexico (435,000)	267,950	80C
Tanger (Tangier), Morocco (370,000)	266,340	82C
Tangshan, China (†1,410,000)	1,060,000	87E
Ṭanṭā, Egypt	364,700	85E
Ṭarābulus (Tripoli), Libya	858,500	81E
Taškent (Tashkent), U.S.S.R. (2,370,000)	2,124,000	87E
Tbilisi, U.S.S.R. (1,380,000)	1,194,000	87E
Tegucigalpa, Honduras	597,500	85E
Tehrān, Iran (6,400,000)	5,734,199	82C
Tel Aviv-Yafo, Israel (1,670,000)	320,300	87E
Teresina, Brazil (525,000)	425,300	85E
Thanh Pho Ho Chi Minh (Saigon), Vietnam (3,100,000)	2,700,849	79C
The Hague, see 's-Gravenhage		
Thessaloníki, Greece (706,180)	406,410	81C
Thimphu, Bhutan	12,000	82E
Thunder Bay, Ont., Can. (122,217)	112,272	86C
Tianjin (Tientsin), China (†5,460,000)	4,880,000	87E
Tianshui, China (†953,200)	209,500	86E
Tijuana, Mexico (*San Diego)	429,500	80C
Tirana, Albania	210,800	84E
Tiruchchirāppalli, India (609,548)	362,040	81C
Tlalnepantla, Mexico (*Ciudad de México)	778,170	80C
Togliatti (Stavropol), U.S.S.R.	627,000	87E
Tōkyō, Japan (27,700,000)	8,354,615	85C
Tomsk, U.S.S.R.	489,000	87E
Torino (Turin), Italy (1,600,000)	1,103,520	81C
Toronto, Ont., Can. (3,427,168)	612,289	86C
Torreón, Mexico (575,000)	328,080	80C
Toulon, France (410,393)	179,420	82C
Toulouse, France (541,271)	347,990	82C
Tours, France (262,786)	132,209	82C
Tripoli, see Ṭarābulus		
Trivandrum, India (520,125)	483,080	81C
Trujillo, Peru (354,301)	202,460	81C
Tsun Wan, Hong Kong (*Victoria)	599,010	81C
Tucson, Az., U.S. (495,600)	336,503	80C
Tula, U.S.S.R. (635,000)	538,000	87E
Tulsa, Ok., U.S. (742,000)	360,919	80C
Tūnis, Tunisia (1,225,000)	596,654	84C
Ufa, U.S.S.R. (1,110,000)	1,092,000	87E
Ujung Pandang (Makasar), Indonesia	708,460	80C
Ulan-Bator, Mongolia	488,200	85E
Ulsan, S. Korea	551,010	85C
Umm Durmān (Omdurman), Sudan (*Khartoum)	526,280	83C
Utrecht, Netherlands (511,195)	229,930	86E
Vadodara (Baroda), India (744,881)	734,470	81C
Vaduz, Liechtenstein	4,920	87E
Valencia, Spain (1,270,000)	738,575	86E
Valletta, Malta (215,000)	9,263	87E
Valparaíso, Chile (700,000)	265,350	82C
Vancouver, B.C., Can. (1,380,729)	431,147	86C
Vārānasi (Benares), India (925,000)	708,640	81C
Venezia (Venice), Italy (415,000)	332,770	81C
Veracruz [Llave], Mexico (385,000)	284,820	80C
Vereeniging, South Africa (525,000)	60,580	85C
Verona, Italy	261,208	81C
Viangchan (Vientiane), Laos	377,000	85C
Victoria, B.C., Can. (255,547)	66,300	86C
Victoria, Hong Kong (4,515,000)	1,183,621	81C
Victoria, Seychelles	23,000	74C
Vienna, see Wien		
Vientiane, see Viangchan		
Vilnius, U.S.S.R.	566,000	87E
Vishākhapatnam, India (603,530)	565,320	81C
Vitória, Brazil (735,000)	201,500	85E
Vladivostok, U.S.S.R.	615,000	87E
Volgograd (Stalingrad), U.S.S.R. (1,335,000)	988,000	87E
Volta Redonda, Brazil (375,000)	219,260	85E
Voronež, U.S.S.R.	872,000	87E
Vorošilovgrad, U.S.S.R.	509,000	87E
Warszawa (Warsaw), Poland (2,323,000)	1,664,700	87E
Washington, D.C., U.S. (3,221,400)	638,432	80C
Weifang, China (†1,042,200)	312,500	86E
Wellington, New Zealand (350,000)	137,495	86C
Wichita, Ks., U.S. (372,200)	279,835	80C
Wien (Vienna), Austria (1,875,000)	1,489,153	85E
Wiesbaden, Fed. Rep. of Ger. (795,000)	266,540	87E
Willemstad, Netherlands Antilles (130,000)	31,883	81C
Wilmington, De., U.S. (*Philadelphia)	70,195	80C
Windhoek, Namibia	120,000	84E
Windsor, Ont., Can. (253,988)	193,110	86C
Winnipeg, Man., Can. (625,304)	594,550	86C
Wrocław, Poland	640,000	87E
Wuhan, China	3,490,000	87E
Wuppertal, Fed. Rep. of Ger. (830,000)	374,217	87E
Wuxi, China	860,000	87E
Wuxing (Huzhou), China (†964,400)	208,500	86E
Xiamen, China (†546,400)	343,700	86E
Xi'an, China (†2,390,000)	2,050,000	87E
Xiaogan, China (†1,204,400)	125,500	86E
Xining, China	610,000	87E
Xuzhou, China	840,000	87E
Yancheng, China (†1,251,400)	258,400	86E
Yangon (Rangoon), Burma (2,800,000)	2,458,712	83C
Yaoundé, Cameroon	583,000	85E
Yerushalayim (Jerusalem), Israel (490,000)	468,900	87E
Yichun, China	830,000	87E
Yokohama, Japan (*Tōkyō)	2,992,926	85C
Yulin, China (†1,228,800)	115,600	86E
Zagreb, Yugoslavia	768,700	81C
Zanzibar, Tanzania	110,669	78C
Zaozhuang, China (†1,592,000)	292,200	86E
Zaporožje, U.S.S.R.	875,000	87E
Zaragoza (Saragossa), Spain	596,080	86E
Zhangjiakou, China (†626,500)	492,800	86E
Zhengzhou, China (†1,610,000)	1,170,000	87E
Zhongshan, China (†1,059,700)	238,700	86E
Zibo, China (†2,330,000)	830,000	87E
Zurich, Switzerland (860,000)	349,549	87E

Metropolitan area populations are shown in parentheses.
* City is located within the metropolitan area of another city; for example, Kyōto, Japan is located in the Ōsaka metropolitan area.
† Population of entire municipality or district, including rural area.

C Census
E Official estimate

Transliteration Systems

Toponymy: Criteria Used for the Writing of Names on the Maps

The language of geography is a language which defines geographic features in universally recognized terms. In creating this language, toponymy experts and cartographers have confronted complex problems in finding terms which are universally acceptable. So that the reader can fully understand the maps in this atlas, here is a brief explanation of how the toponyms (place-names for geographic features) have been written, particularly those relating to regions or countries where the Roman alphabet is not used. Among these are the Slavic-speaking nations such as the Soviet Union, Yugoslavia and Bulgaria; and China and Japan, which use ideographic characters. Of the European countries, Greece has its own alphabet, which is totally different from the Roman alphabet. Many of the Islamic countries use Arabic, with variations derived from local dialects.

There are two basic systems for Romanizing writing. The first is by phonetic transcription, using combinations of different alphabetical signs for each language when the phonetic sound in other languages should be maintained. For example, the Italian sound "sc" (which must be followed by an "e" or "i" to remain soft) in French is "ch," in English is "sh," and in German is "sch."

The second system is transliteration, in which the words, letters or characters of one language are represented or spelled in the letters or characters of another language.

Chinese, Japanese and Arabic Languages

Various Asian and African countries use non-Roman forms in their writing. For example, the Chinese and Japanese languages use ideographic characters instead of an alphabet, and these ideographic characters are transformed into the Roman alphabet through phonetic transcription. Until recently, one of the methods used for transforming Chinese was the Wade-Giles system, named for its English authors. Used in this atlas is the Pinyin system, which was approved by the Chinese government in 1958 and has been incorporated into the official maps of the People's Republic of China. The Pinyin system also has been adopted by the United States Board on Geographic Names and is used in official United Nations documents. The Pinyin names, however, often are accompanied by the Wade-Giles form, as the latter was widely known.

In Japan, ideographic characters are used, although the Roman alphabet is used in many Japanese scientific works. Japan uses two principal systems for standardizing names. They are the Kunreisiki, used by the government in official publications, and the Hepburn method. Adopted for this atlas is the Hepburn method, the system used in international English-language publications and by the United States Board on Geographic Names.

Romanization of the Arabic alphabet, which is used in many Islamic countries, is by transliteration. Since English and French are still used as an international language in many Arab countries, the name forms proposed by the major English and French sources have been taken into consideration. Generally, the systems proposed by the United States Board on Geographic Names and the Permanent Committee on Geographical Names have been used for most Asian countries and Arab-speaking countries.

Greek, Russian and Other Slavic Languages

Practically all written languages in Europe use the Roman alphabet. The differences in phonetics and grammar are shown by the use of diacritical marks and by groupings of consonants, vocals and syllables which give meaning to the various tones in the language. According to a centuries-old tradition, each written language maintains its formal characters, using the translated form rather than the phonetic transcription when a geographical term must be given in another language. This system, therefore, makes it more a translation than a transliteration.

In the Aegean area, Greek and the Greek alphabet are particularly significant because of historical links to the beginning of European civilization. The 1962 United States Board on Geographic Names and the Permanent Committee on Geographical Names systems, based on modern Greek pronunciation, have been used in transcribing toponyms from official sources for these maps. (The table that follows has an example indicating essential norms for Romanizing the modern Greek alphabet.)

A different situation arises in countries using the Cyrillic alphabet. Six principal Slavic languages using this alphabet are Russian, Byelorussian, Ukrainian, Bulgarian, Serbian, and Macedonian. The Cyrillic alphabet also is used by the non-Slavic people of the central Soviet Union. The nomenclature of these regions has been transliterated in accordance with the system proposed by the International Organization for Standardization, taking into consideration sounds and letters and uses of the diacritical marks normal in Slavic languages. The International Organization for Standardization method is accepted and used in bibliographical works and international documents. (The table which follows gives the relationship between the letters of the Cyrillic and Roman alphabets for the above six languages.) An exception to this transliteration is made by the Soviet Balkan republics of Estonia, Latvia and Lithuania. Here the name forms deriving from the national languages have been adopted, using the Roman alphabet.

Special Cases: Conventional Forms and Multilinguals

Cartographic nomenclature generally derives from the official nomenclature of the sovereign and nonsovereign countries, although a number of cases need an explanation.

In numerous situations, English conventional forms are used along with the local or conventional name in referring to a geographical entity used outside the official language area. For example, Vienna, Prague, Copenhagen and Moscow are English forms for Wien, Praha, København and Moskva, respectively. There have been cases, however, where the conventional or historical form commonly used in English cartography has been applied with the same meaning. Thus, Peking and Nanking are the English conventional forms for Beijing and Nanjing, while Tsinan, Tientsin and Mukden are the former conventional spellings or names for Jinan, Tianjin and Shenyang, respectively. Other examples are Saigon, the former name for Ho Chi Minh, Vietnam; and Bangkok, the name for Krung Thep, which is used in Thailand.

The lack of reliable data for countries, especially ex-colonies without a firm national cartographic tradition, has made it necessary to utilize mapping skills of former colonist nations such as France, the United Kingdom and Belgium. A lack of data has led to the adoption of French and British forms in many areas, as these two languages are widely used for official purposes.

Another special case is that of the multilingual areas. Many countries and areas officially recognize two or more written and spoken languages; therefore, all of the principal written forms appear on the maps. This is true, for example, of Belgium where the official languages are French and Dutch (e.g. Bruxelles/Brussel) and of Italian regions such as Valle d'Aosta and Alto Adige, where French, German and Italian are used (e.g. Aosta/Aoste) (Bolzano/Bozen).

In preparing this atlas, each of these special cases has been taken into full consideration within the limits of the scale, space and readability of the maps.

Transliteration of the Cyrillic Alphabet
(International System—ISO)

Cyrillic Letter		Roman Letter	
А	а	a	
Б	б	b	
В	в	v	
Г	г	g	
Д	д	d	
Е	е	e	initially, after a vowel or after the mute sign "Ъ", becomes "je"
Ё	ё	ë	
Ж	ж	ž	
З	з	z	
И	и	i	
Й	й	j	not written if preceded by "И" or "Ы"
К	к	k	
Л	л	l	
М	м	m	
Н	н	n	

Cyrillic Letter		Roman Letter	
О	о	o	
П	п	p	
Р	р	r	
С	с	s	
Т	т	t	
У	у	u	
Ф	ф	f	
Х	х	h	
Ц	ц	c	
Ч	ч	č	
Ш	ш	š	
Щ	щ	šč	
Ъ	ъ	—	not written
Ы	ы	y	
Ь	ь	—	not written
Э	э	e	
Ю	ю	ju	
Я	я	ja	

Transcription of Modern Greek
(U.S. B. G. N./P.C.G.N.)

Greek Letter (or combination)		Roman Letter (or combination)	
Α	α	a	
	αι	ai	
	αυ	av	
Β	β	v	
Γ	γ	g	
	γγ	ng	
	γκ	g	beginning a word
		ng	within a word
Δ	δ	d	
Ε	ε	e	
	ει	i	
	ευ	ev	
Ζ	ζ	z	
Η	η	i	
	ηυ	iv	
Θ	θ	th	
Ι	ι	i	
Κ	κ	k	
Λ	λ	l	
Μ	μ	m	

Greek Letter (or combination)		Roman Letter (or combination)	
	μπ	b	beginning a word
		mb	within a word
Ν	ν	n	
	ντ	d	beginning a word
		nd	within a word
Ξ	ξ	x	
Ο	ο	o	
	οι	oi	
	ου	ou	
Π	π	p	
Ρ	ρ	r	
Σ	σ	s	
	ς	s	ending a word
Τ	τ	t	
	τζ	tz	
Υ	υ	i	
	υι	i	
Φ	φ	f	
Χ	χ	kh	
Ψ	ψ	ps	
Ω	ω	o	

The "Geographical Glossary" lists the principal geographical terms used on the maps. All of these terms, including abbreviations, prefixes and suffixes, appear in the cartographic table as they appear on the maps. Terms are listed in accordance with the English alphabet, without consideration of diacritical marks on letters or of particular groups of letters.
Prefixes and suffixes relating to principal names or forming part of geographical toponyms are followed or preceded by a dash and the language to which they refer: e.g. Chi-/*Dan.* (Chi, a Danish prefix, means large); -bor/*Slvn.* (-bor, a Slovakian suffix, means city). Suffixes can also appear as words in themselves. In this case, the suffix and primary word are coupled together: e.g. Berg, -berg (Berg, which means mountain, can be used alone or as part of another word, such as Hapsberg).
Certain terms are followed or preceded by their abbreviation used on the maps. Both instances are listed: e.g. Fjord, Fj. and Fj., Fjord.
All geographical terms are identified by the language or languages to which each belongs. The language or languages in italics follows the term: e.g. Abbey/*Eng.*; -bad/*Nor., Dut., Swed., Germ.* Each term is translated into a corresponding English term or terms.
Below is a table identifying the abbreviations of various language names used on the maps. Note that certain abbreviations represent a group of languages, instead of one language: e.g. Ural. is the abbreviation for Uralic, a group word for Udmurt, Komi, and Nenets.
Alt. = Altaic (Turkmen, Tatar, Bashkir, Kazakh, Karalpak, Nogai, Kirghiz, Uzbek, Uigur, Altaic, Ýakut, Khakass)
Ban. = Bantu (KiSwahili, ChiLuba, Lingala, KiKongo)
Cauc. = Caucasian (Chechen, Ingush, Kalmuck, Georgian)
Iran. = Iranian (Baluchi, Tagus)
Mel. = Melanesian (Fijian, New Caledonian, Micronesian, Nauruan)
Mong. = Mongolian (Buryat, Khalka Mongol)
Poly. = Polynesian (Maori, Samoan, Tongan, Tahitian, Hawaiian)
Sah. = Saharan (Kanuri, Tubu)
Som. = Somalian (Somali, Galla)
Sud. = Sudanese (Peul, Ehoué, Mossi, Yoruba, Ibo)
Ural. = Uralic (Udmurt, Komi, Nenets).
Because of their technical application to geography, some geographical terms may not fully correspond with the meaning given for them in some dictionaries.

Abbreviations of Language Names

Abbreviations in English	English
Afr.	Afrikaans
A.I.	American Indian
Alb.	Albanian
Alt.	Altaic
Amh.	Amharic
Ar.	Arabic
Arm.	Armenian
Az.	Azerbaidzhani
Ban.	Bantu
Bas.	Basque
Beng.	Bengali
Ber.	Berber
Br.	Breton
Bulg.	Bulgarian
Burm.	Burmese
Cat.	Catalan
Cauc.	Caucasian
Chin.	Chinese
Cz.	Czech
Dan.	Danish
Dut.	Dutch
Eng.	English
Esk.	Eskimo
Est.	Estonian
Far.	Faroese
Finn.	Finnish
Fle.	Flemish
Fr.	French
Gae.	Gaelic
Georg.	Georgian
Germ.	German
Gr.	Greek
Hebr.	Hebrew
Hin.	Hindi
Hung.	Hungarian
Icel.	Icelandic
Indon.	Indonesian
Ir.	Irish
Iran.	Iranian
It.	Italian
Jap.	Japanese
Khm.	Khmer
Kor.	Korean
K.S.	Khoi-San
Laot.	Laotian
Lapp.	Lappish
Latv.	Latvian
Lith.	Lithuanian
Mal.	Malay
Malag.	Malagasy
Mel.	Melanesian
Mong.	Mongolian
Nep.	Nepalese
Nor.	Norwegian
Pash.	Pashto
Pers.	Persian
Pol.	Polish
Poly.	Polynesian
Port.	Portuguese
Prov.	Provençal
Rmsh.	Romansh
Rom.	Romanian
Rus.	Russian
Sah.	Saharan
S.C.	Serbo-Croatian
Sin.	Sinhalese
Slvk.	Slovak
Slvn.	Slovene
Som.	Somalian
Sp.	Spanish
Sud.	Sudanese
Swa.	Swahili
Swed.	Swedish
Tam.	Tamil
Thai	Thai
Tib.	Tibetan
Tur.	Turkish
Ural.	Uralic
Urdu	Urdu
Viet.	Vietnamese
Wall.	Walloon
Wel.	Welsh

Glossary of Geographical Terms

A

Local Form	English
A- / *Ban.*	people
A' / *Icel.*	river
Å / *Dan.; Nor.; Swed.*	stream
a., an / *Germ.*	on
Aa / *Germ.*	stream
Aache / *Germ.*	stream
Aaiún / *Ar.*	springs
Aan / *Dut.; Fle.*	on
Āb / *Pers.*	stream
Ābād / *Pers.*	city, town
Abad, -abad / *Pers.*	city, town
Ābār / *Ar.*	spring
Abbadia / *It.*	abbey
Abbaye / *Fr.*	abbey
Abbazia / *It.*	abbey
Abbi / *Amh.*	great
Abd / *Ar.*	servant
Abeba / *Amh.*	flower
Aber / *Br.; Wel.*	estuary
Abhang / *Germ.*	slope
Abū / *Ar.*	father, master
Abyad / *Ar.*	white
Abyaḍ / *Ar.*	white
Abyār / *Ar.*	well
Abyss / *Eng.*	ocean depth, deep
Ach / *Germ.*	stream
Achaïf / *Ar.*	dunes
Ache / *Germ.*	stream
Achter / *Afr.; Dut.; Fle.*	back
Acqua / *It.*	water
Açu / *A.I.*	great
Açude / *Port.*	reservoir, dam
Ada / *Tur.*	island
Adalar / *Tur.*	archipelago
Adasr / *Tur.*	island
Addis / *Amh.*	new
Adi / *Amh.*	village
Adrar / *Ber.*	mount, mountains
Aéroport / *Fr.*	airport
Aeroporto / *It.; Port.*	airport
Aeropuerto / *Sp.*	airport
Af / *Som.*	mouth, gorge
Afsluitdijk / *Dut.*	dam
Agadir / *Ber.*	castle
Ağiz / *Tur.*	mouth
Agro / *Sp.; It.*	plain
Agua / *Sp.*	water
Aguja / *Sp.*	needle
Agulha / *Port.*	needle, promontory
Ahal / *Georg.*	new
Aḥmar / *Ar.*	red
Ahrāmāt / *Ar.*	pyramids
Ahzar / *Ber.*	wadi
Aigialós / *Gr.*	coast
Aigue / *Prov.*	water
Aiguille / *Fr.*	needle
Ain / *Ar.*	spring
Ait / *Ar.; Ber.*	sons
Aivi, -aivi / *Lapp.*	mountain
Ak / *Tur.*	white
'Aklé / *Ar.*	dunes
Akmeņs / *Latv.*	stone
Ákra / *Gr.*	point
Aktí / *Gr.*	coast
Ala / *Malag.*	forest
Ala / *Finn.*	low, lower
Alan / *Tur.*	field
Alb / *Rom.*	white
Albo / *Sp.*	white
Albufera / *Sp.*	lagoon
Alcalá / *Sp.*	castle
Alcázar / *Sp.*	castle
Aldea / *Sp.*	village
Alföld / *Hung.*	lowland
Ali / *Amh.*	mountain
Alia / *Poly.*	stream
Alin / *Mong.*	range
Alm / *Germ.*	mountain pasture
Alor / *Mal.*	river
Alp / *Germ.*	mountain pasture
Alpe / *Germ.; Fr.; It.*	mountain pasture
Alps / *Eng.*	mountains
Alsó / *Hung.*	low, lower
Alt / *Germ.*	old
Altin / *Tur.*	lower
Altiplano / *Sp.*	plateau
Alto / *Sp.; It.; Port.*	high
Altopiano / *It.*	plateau
Älv / *Swed.*	river
Am / *Kor.*	mountain, peak
Amane / *Ber.*	water
Amba / *Amh.*	mountain
Ambato / *Malag.*	rock
An / *Gae.*	of
An, a. / *Germ.*	on
Ana / *Poly.*	grotto
Anatolikós / *Gr.*	eastern
Äng / *Swed.*	meadow
Angra / *Port.*	bay, anchorage
Ani- / *Malag.*	center
Áno / *Gr.*	upper
Ânou / *Ber.*	well
Anse / *Fr.*	inlet
Ant- / *Malag.*	center
Ao / *Chin.; Khm.; Thai*	gulf
'Âouâna / *Ar.*	well
Apă / *Rom.*	water
'Aqabat / *Ar.*	pass
Aqueduc / *Fr.*	aqueduct
Ar / *Mong.*	north
Ar / *Sin.; Tam.*	river
'Arâguîb / *Ar.*	hills
Arba / *Amh.*	mount
Arbore / *Rom.*	tree
Archipiélago / *Sp.*	archipelago
Arcipelago / *It.*	archipelago
Arḍ / *Ar.*	region
Ard- / *Gae.*	high
Areg / *Ar.*	dune
Areia / *Port.*	beach
Arena / *Sp.*	beach
Argent / *Fr.*	silver
Arhipelag / *Rus.*	archipelago
Arkhaíos / *Gr.*	old, antique
Arm / *Eng.; Germ.*	branch
Arquipélago / *Port.*	archipelago
Arr., Arroyo / *Sp.*	stream
Arrecife / *Sp.*	reef
Arroio / *Port.*	stream
Art / *Tur.*	pass, watershed
Aru / *Sin.; Tam.*	river
Ås / *Dan.; Nor.; Swed.*	hills
Asfar / *Ar.*	yellow
Asif / *Ber.*	river
Asky / *Alt.*	lower
Áspros / *Gr.*	white
Assa / *Ber.*	wadi
Atalaya / *Sp.*	frontier
Áth / *Gae.*	ford
Átha / *Gae.*	ford
Atol / *Port.*	atoll
Au / *Germ.*	meadow
Aue / *Germ.*	irrigated field
Aust / *Nor.*	east
Austur / *Icel.*	east
Ava / *Poly.*	canal
Aven / *Fr.*	doline, sink
Awa / *Poly.*	bay
Àyios / *Gr.*	saint
'Ayn / *Ar.*	spring, well
'Ayoún / *Ar.*	springs, wells
'Ayoûn / *Ar.*	spring
Aza / *Ber.*	wadi
Azraq / *Ar.*	light blue
Azul / *Port.; Sp.*	light blue
Azur / *Fr.*	light blue

B

Local Form	English
B., Bay / *Eng.*	bay
b., bei / *Germ.*	by
B., Bucht / *Germ.*	bay
Ba / *Sud.*	river
Ba- / *Ban.*	people
Ba / *Mel.*	hill, mountain
Baai / *Afr.*	bay
Bab / *Ar.*	gate
Bac / *Viet.*	north
Bach / *Germ.*	brook, torrent
Bacino / *It.*	reservoir
Back / *Eng.*	ridge
Back / *Swed.*	brook
Bäck / *Swed.*	brook
Backe / *Swed.*	hill
Bad, -bad / *Dan.; Germ.; Nor.; Swed.*	thermal springs
Baden, -baden / *Germ.*	thermal springs
Bādiyat / *Ar.*	desert
Badwēynta / *Som.*	ocean
Badyarada / *Som.*	gulf
Baeg / *Kor.*	white
Bæk / *Dan.*	brook
Bælt / *Dan.*	strait
Bagni / *It.*	thermal springs
Baharu / *Mal.*	new
Bahia / *Port.*	bay
Bahía / *Sp.*	bay
Bahir / *Ar.*	river, lake, sea
Bahnhof / *Germ.*	railway station
Bahr / *Ar.*	wadi
Baḩr / *Ar.*	river, lake, sea
Baḩrat / *Ar.*	lake
Bahri / *Ar.*	north, northern
Baḩrī / *Ar.*	north
Bahrīyah / *Ar.*	northern
Bai / *Chin.*	white
Băi / *Rom.*	thermal springs
Baia / *Port.*	bay
Baie / *Fr.*	bay
Baigne / *Fr.*	seaside resort
Baile / *Gae.*	city, town
Bain / *Fr.*	thermal springs
Bains / *Fr.*	thermal springs
Baixo / *Port.*	low, lower
Bajan / *Mong.*	rich
Bajo / *Sp.*	low
Bajrak / *Alb.*	tribe
Bakhtīyārī / *Pers.*	western
Bakki / *Icel.*	hill
Bālā / *Pers.*	high
Bald / *Eng.*	peak
Balka / *Rus.*	gorge
Balkan / *Bulg.; Tur.*	mountain range
Ballin / *Gae.*	mouth
Ballon / *Fr.*	dome
Bally / *Gae.*	city, town
Balta / *Rom.*	marsh
Báltos / *Gr.*	marsh
Ban / *Laot.*	village
Bana / *Jap.*	promontory
Baňa / *Slvk.*	mine
Bañados / *Sp.*	marsh
Banc / *Fr.*	bank
Banco / *It.; Sp.*	bank
Band / *Pers.*	dam, mountain range
Bandao / *Chin.*	peninsula
Bandar / *Ar.; Mal.; Pers.*	port, market
Bang / *Indon.; Mal.*	stream
Bangoù / *Sah.*	well
Banhado / *Port.*	marsh
Bani / *Ar.*	sons
Banja / *Bulg.; S.C.; Slvn.*	thermal springs
Banjaran / *Mal.*	mountain range
Banka / *Rus.*	sandbank
Banke / *Dan.*	bank
Baño / *Sp.*	thermal springs
Banský / *Cz.*	upper
Bánya / *Hung.*	mine
Bar / *Gae.*	peak
Bar / *Eng.*	sandbar

Local Form	English
Bar / Hin.	great
Bāra / Hin.	great
Bara / S.C.	pond
Barā / Urdu	great
Barajı / Tur.	dam
Barat / Indon.; Mal.	west, western
Barkas / Lith.	castle, city, town
Barlovento / Sp.	windward
Barq / Ar.	hill
Barra / Port.; Sp.	bar, bank
Barrage / Fr.	dam
Barragem / Port.	reservoir
Barranca / Sp.	gorge
Barranco / Port.; Sp.	gorge
Barre / Fr.	bar
Barun / Mong.	western
Bas / Fr.	low
-bas / Rus.	reservoir
Bassa / Port.	flat
Bassejn / Rus.	reservoir
Bassin / Fr.	basin
Bassure / Fr.	flat
Bassurelle / Fr.	flat
Bašta / S.C.	garden
Bataille / Fr.	battle
Batalha / Port.	battle
Batang / Indon.; Mal.	river
Batha / Sah.	stream
Baṭin / Ar.	depression
Bāṭlāq / Pers.	marsh
Batu / Mal.	rock
Bayan / Mong.	rich
Bayır / Tur.	mountain, slope
Bayou / Fr.	branch, stream
Bayt / Ar.	house
Bazar / Pers.	market
Be / Malag.	great
Beau / Fr.	beautiful
Becken / Germ.	basin
Bed / Eng.	river bed
Beek / Dut.	creek
Be'er / Hebr.	spring
Bei / Chin.	north
Bei, b. / Germ.	by
Beida / Ar.	white
Beinn / Gae.	mount
Bel / Ar.	son
Bel / Bulg.	white
Bel / Tur.	pass
Beled / Ar.	village
Belen / Tur.	mount
Belet / Ar.	village
Beli / S.C.; Slvn.	white
Beli / Tur.	pass
Bellah / Sah.	well
Belogorje / Rus.	mountains
Belt / Dan.; Germ.	strait
Bely / Rus.	white
Bělý / Cz.	white
Ben / Ar.	son
Ben / Gae.	mount
Bender / Pers.	port, market
Bendi / Tur.	dam
Beni / Ar.	son
Beo / S.C.	white
Bereg / Rus.	bank
Berg, -berg / Afr.; Dut.; Fle.; Germ.; Nor.; Swed.	mount
Berge / Afr.	mountain
Bergen / Dut.; Fle.	dunes
Bergland / Germ.	upland
Bermejo / Sp.	red
Besar / Mal.	great
Betsu / Jap.	river
Betta / Tam.	mountain
Bhani / Hin.	community
Bharu / Mal.	new
Bheag / Gae.	little
Bīābān / Pers.	desert
Biały / Pol.	white
Bianco / It.	white
Bien / Viet.	lake
Bight / Eng.	bay
Bijeli / S.C.	white
Bill / Eng.	promontory
Bilo / S.C.	range
Bílý / Cz.	white
Binnen / Dut.; Fle.; Germ.	inner
Biqā' / Ar.	valley
Bir / Ar.	well
Bi'r / Ar.	well
Birkat / Ar.	pond
Bistrica / Bulg.; S.C.; Slvn.	stream
Bjarg / Icel.	rock
Bjerg / Dan.	mount
Bjeshkët / Alb.	mountain pasture
Blaauw / Afr.	blue
Blanc / Fr.	white
Blanco / Sp.	white
Blau / Germ.	blue
Bleu / Fr.	blue
Bluff / Eng.	cliff
Bo- / Ban.	people
Bo / Chin.	white
Bo / Swed.	habitation
Boca / Sp.	gap, mouth
Bôca / Port.	gap, mouth
Bocage / Fr.	forest
Bocca / It.	gap, pass
Bocchetta / It.	gap, pass
Bodden / Germ.	bay, lagoon
Boden / Germ.	soil
Bœng / Khm.	lake, marsh
Bog / Eng.	marsh
Bogaz / Alt.; Az.; Tur.	strait
Boğazi / Tur.	strait
Bogdo / Mong.	high
Bogen / Nor.	bay
Bois / Fr.	forest
Boka / S.C.	channel
Boloto / Rus.	marsh
Bolšoj / Rus.	great
Bolsón / Sp.	basin
Bom / Port.	good
Bong / Kor.	peak
Bongo / Malag.	upland
Bor / Cz.; Rus.	coniferous forest
Bór / Pol.	forest
-bor / Slvn.	city, town
Bóras / Gr.	north
Börde / Germ.	fertile plain
Bordj / Ar.	fort
Bóreios / Gr.	northern
Borg, -borg / Dan.; Nor.; Swed.	castle
Borgo / It.	village
Born / Germ.	spring
Bory / Pol.	forest
Bosch / Dut.; Fle.	forest
Bosco / It.	wood
Bosque / Sp.	forest
Bosse / Fr.	hill
Botn / Nor.	bay
Bou / Ar.	father, master
Bouche / Fr.	mouth
Boula / Sud.	well
Bourg / Fr.	city, town
Bourne, - bourne / Eng.	frontier
Boven / Afr.	upper
Boz / Tur.	grey
Bozorg / Pers.	great
Brána / Cz.	gate
Braña / Sp.	mountain pasture
Branche / Fr.	branch
Branco / Port.	white
Braṭul / Rom.	branch
Bravo / Sp.	wild
Brazo / Sp.	branch
Brdo / Cz.; S.C.	hill
Bre / Nor.	glacier
Bredning / Dan.	bay
Breg / Alb.; Bulg.; S.C.	hill, coast
Brjag / Bulg.	bank
Bro / Dan.; Nor.; Swed.	bridge
Brod / Bulg.; Cz.; Rus.; S.C.; Slvk.; Slvn.	ford
Bród / Pol.	ford
Bron / Afr.	spring
Bronn / Germ.	spring
Bru / Nor.	bridge
Bruch / Germ.	peat-bog
Bruchzone / Germ.	fracture zone
Bruck, -bruck / Germ.	bridge
Brücke / Germ.	bridge
Brug / Dut.; Fle.	bridge
Brugge / Dut.; Fle.	bridge
Bruk / Nor.	factory
Brunn / Swed.	spring
-brunn / Germ.	spring
Brunnen / Germ.	spring
Brygg / Swed.	bridge
Brzeg / Pol.	coast
Bū / Ar.	father, master
Bucht, B. / Germ.	bay
Bugt / Dan.	bay
Buḥayrat / Ar.	lake, lagoon
Bühel / Germ.	hill
Bühl / Germ.	hill
Buhta / Rus.	bay
Bukit / Mal.	mountain, peak
Bukt / Nor.; Swed.	bay
Buku / Indon.	hill, mountain
Bulag / Mong.; Tur.	spring
Bulak / Mong.; Tur.	spring
Būlāq / Tur.	spring
Bult / Afr.	hill
Bulu / Indon.	mountain
Bur / Som.	mount
Būr / Ar.	port
Burg, - burg / Afr.; Ar.; Dut.; Eng.; Germ.	castle
Burgh / Eng.	city, town
Burgo / Sp.	village
Burha / Hin.	old
Buri / Thai	city, town
Burj / Ar.	village
Burn / Eng.	stream
Burnu / Tur.	promontory
Burqat / Ar.	mount, marsh
Burun / Tur.	cape
Busen / Germ.	bay
Busu / Ban.	land
Būṭat / Ar.	lake, pond
Butte / Eng.; Fr.	flat-topped hill
Büyük / Tur.	great
By / Eng.	near
By, -by / Dan.; Nor.; Swed.	city, town
Bystrica / Cz.; Slvk.	stream
Bystrzyca / Pol.	stream

C

Local Form	English
C., Cap / Cat.; Fr.; Rom.	cape
C., Cape / Eng.	cape
C., Colle / It.	pass
Caatinga / A.I.	forest
Cabeça / Port.	peak
Cabeço / Port.	peak
Cabeza / Sp.	peak
Cabezo / Sp.	peak, mountain
Cabo / Port.; Sp.	cape
Cachoeira / Port.	waterfall, rapids
Cachopo / Port.	reef
Cadena / Sp.	range
Caer / Wel.	castle
Cagan / Cauc.; Mong.	white
Cairn / Gae.	hill
Čaj / Az.; Tur.	river
Cajdam / Mong.	salt marsh
Caka / Chin.	lake
Cala / Sp.; It.	inlet
Calar / Sp.	plateau
Caldas / Sp.; Port.	thermal springs
Caleta / Sp.	inlet
Camp / Cat.; Fr.; Eng.	field
Campagna / It.	plain
Campagne / Fr.	plain
Campo / Sp.; It.; Port.	field
Cañada / Sp.	gorge, ravine
Canale / It.	canal, channel
Caño / Sp.	branch
Cañón / Sp.	gorge
Canyon / Eng.	gorge
Cao / Viet.	mountain
Cap, C. / Cat.; Fr.; Rom.	cape
Car / Gae.	castle
Càrn / Gae.	peak
Carrera / Sp.	road
Carrick / Gae.	rock
Casale / It.	hamlet
Cascada / Sp.	waterfall
Cascata / It.	waterfall
Castel / It.	castle
Castell / Cat.	castle
Castello / It.	castle
Castelo / Port.	castle
Castillo / Sp.	castle
Castro / Sp.; It.	village
Catarata / Sp.	cataract
Catena / It.	mountain range
Catinga / Port.	degraded forest
Cauce / Sp.	river bed
Causse / Fr.	highland
Cava / It.	stone quarry
Çay / Tur.	river
Cay / Eng.	islet, island
Caye / Fr.	island
Cayo / Sp.	islet, island
Ceann / Gae.	promontory
Centralny / Rus.	middle
Čeren / Alb.	black
Černi / Bulg.	black
Černý / Cz.	black
Čërny / Rus.	black
Cerrillo / Sp.	hill
Cerrito / Sp.	hill
Cerro / Sp.; Port.	hill, mountain
Cêrro / Port.	hill, mountain
Červen / Bulg.	red
Červony / Rus.	red
Cetate / Rom.	city, town
Chaco / Sp.	scrubland
Chāh / Pers.	well
Chaïf / Ar.	dunes
Chaîne / Fr.	mountain range
Champ / Fr.	field
Chang / Chin.	highland
Chapada / Port.	highland
Chapadão / Port.	highland
Château / Fr.	castle
Châtel / Fr.	castle
Chāy / Tur.	river
Chedo / Kor.	archipelago
Chenal / Fr.	canal
Cheng / Chin.	city, town, wall
Cheon / Kor.	city, river
Chergui / Ar.	eastern
Cherry, -cherry / Hin.; Tam.	city, town
Chew / Amh.	salt mine, salt
Chhâk / Khm.	bay
Chhotla / Hin.	little
Chi- / Ban.	great
Chi / Chin.	marsh, lake
Chi / Kor.	lake, pond
Chi- / Swa.	land
Chiang / Thai	city, town
Chico / Sp.	little
Chine / Eng.	ridge
Ch'on / Kor.	station
Ch'ŏn / Kor.	river
Chŏsuji / Kor.	reservoir
Chott / Ar.	salt marsh
Chu / Chin.; Viet.	mountain, hill
Chuŏr phnum / Khm.	mountain range
Chute / Fr.	waterfall
Chutes / Fr.	waterfalls
Cidade / Port.	city, town
Ciems / Latv.	village
Čierny / Slvk.	black
Cime / Fr.	peak
Cîmp / Rom.	field
Cîmpie / Rom.	plain
Cinco / Sp.; Port.	five
Citeli / Georg.	red
Città / It.	city, town
Ciudad / Sp.	city, town
Ckali / Georg.	water
Ckaro / Georg.	spring
Co / Chin.	lake
Col / Cat.; Fr.	pass
Colina / Port.; Sp.	hill
Coll / Cat.	hill
Collado / Sp.	pass
Colle, C. / It.	pass
Collina / It.	hill
Colline / Fr.	hill
Colonia / Sp.; It.	colony
Coma / Sp.	hill country
Comb / Eng.	basin
Comba / Sp.	basin
Combe / Fr.	basin
Comté / Fr.	county, shire
Con / Viet.	island
Conca / It.	depression
Condado / Sp.	county, shire
Cone / Eng.	volcanic cone
Cône / Fr.	volcanic cone
Contraforte / Port.	front range
Cordal / Sp.	crest
Cordilheira / Port.	mountain range
Cordillera / Sp.	mountain range
Coring / Chin.	lake
Corixa / A.I.	stream
Corno / It.	peak
Cornone / It.	peak
Corrente / It.; Port.	stream
Corriente / Sp.	stream
Costa / Sp.; It.; Port.	coast
Côte / Fr.	coast
Coteau / Fr.	height, slope
Coxilha / Port.	ridge
Craig / Gae.	rock
Cratère / Fr.	crater
Cresta / Sp.; It.	crest
Crêt / Fr.	crest
Crête / Fr.	crest
Crkva / S.C.	church
Crni / S.C.; Slvn.	black
Crven / S.C.	red
Csatorna / Hung.	canal
Cuchilla / Sp.	ridge
Cuenca / Sp.	basin
Cuesta / Sp.	escarpment
Cueva / Sp.	cave
Čuka / Bulg.; S.C.	peak
Çukur / Tur.	well
Cu Lao / Viet.	island
Cumbre / Sp.	peak
Cun / Chin.	village
Cura / A.I.	stone
Curr / Alb.	rock
Cy., City / Eng.	city, town
Czarny / Pol.	black

D

Local Form	English
Da / Chin.	great
Da / Viet.	mountain, peak
Daal / Dut.; Fle.	valley
Daba / Mong.	pass
Daba / Som.	hill
Daban / Chin.; Mong.	pass
Dae / Kor.	great
Dağ / Tur.	mountain
Dağ., Daği / Tur.	mountain
Dāgh / Pers.; Tur.	mountain
Dağı, Dağ. / Tur.	mountain
Dağları / Tur.	mountain range
Dahar / Ar.	hill
Dahr / Ar.	plateau, escarpment
Dai / Chin.; Jap.	great
Daiet / Ar.	marsh
Dak / Viet.	stream
Dake / Jap.	mountain
Dakhla / Ar.	depression
Dakhlet / Ar.	depression, bay
Dal, -dal / Afr.; Dan.; Dut.; Fle.; Nor.; Swed.	valley
Dala / Alt.	steppe, plain
Dalaj / Mong.	lake, sea
Dalan / Mong.	wall
Dallol / Sud.	valley, torrent
Dalur / Icel.	valley
Damm / Germ.	dam
Dan / Kor.	point

Local Form	English
Danau / *Indon.*	lake
Danda / *Nep.*	mountains
Dao / *Chin.*	island, peninsula
Dao / *Viet.*	island
Dar / *Ar.*	house, region
Dar / *Swa.*	port
Dara / *Tur.*	torrent, valley
Darb / *Ar.*	track
Darja / *Alt.*	river, sea
Darya, Daryā / *Pers.*	river, sea
Daryācheh / *Pers.*	lake, sea
Daš / *Alt.; Az.*	rock
Dasht / *Pers.*	desert, plain
Dawḩat / *Ar.*	bay
Dayr / *Ar.*	convent
De / *Sp.; Fr.*	of
Deal / *Rom.*	hill
Dearg / *Gae.*	red
Debre / *Amh.*	hill, monastery
Dega / *Som.*	stone
Deh / *Pers.*	village
Dēḥ / *Som.*	stream
Deich / *Germ.*	dike
Dél / *Hung.*	south
Delft / *Dut.; Fle.*	deep
Delger / *Mong.*	wide, market
-den / *Eng.*	city, town
Deniz / *Tur.*	sea
Denizi / *Tur.*	sea
Dent / *Fr.*	peak
Deo / *Laot.; Viet.*	pass
Dépression / *Fr.*	depression
Depressione / *It.*	depression
Der / *Som.*	high
Dera / *Hin.; Urdu*	temple
Derbent / *Tur.*	gorge, pass
Dere / *Tur.*	river, valley
Désert / *Fr.*	desert
Desfiladero / *Sp.*	pass
Desh / *Hin.*	land, country
Desierto / *Sp.*	desert
Det / *Alb.*	sea
Détroit / *Fr.*	strait
Deux / *Fr.*	two
Dezh / *Pers.*	castle
Dhar / *Ar.*	heights, hills
Dhār / *Hin.; Urdu*	mountain
Dhitikós / *Gr.*	western
Dien / *Khm.; Viet.*	rice-field
Diep / *Dut.; Fle.*	deep, strait
Dijk, -dijk / *Dut.; Fle.*	dam
Ding / *Chin.*	mountain, peak
Dique / *Sp.*	dam
Di Sopra / *It.*	upper
Di Sotto / *It.*	lower
Distrito / *Sp.; Port.*	district
Diu / *Hin.*	island
Diz / *Pers.*	castle
Djebel / *Ar.*	mountain
Dji / *Ban.*	water
Djup / *Swed.*	deep
Do / *Kor.*	Island
Do / *S.C.*	valley
Dō / *Jap.*	island, administrative division
Dōho / *Som.*	valley
Doi / *Thai*	mountain, peak
Dol / *Bulg.; Cz.; Rus.; S.C.*	valley
Doł / *Pol.*	valley
Dolen / *Bulg.*	low
Dolgi / *Rus.*	long
Dolina / *Bulg.; Cz.; Pol.; Rus.; S.C.; Slvn.*	valley
Dolni / *Bulg.*	low
Dolni / *Pol.*	lower
Dolny / *Pol.*	lower
Domb / *Hung.*	hill
Dôme / *Fr.*	dome
Dong / *Chin.; Viet.*	east
Dong / *Kor.*	city, town
Dong / *Thai*	mountain
Dong / *Viet.*	marsh, plain
Donji / *S.C.*	low, lower
Dorf, -dorf / *Germ.*	village
Doroga / *Rus.*	road
Dorp, -dorp / *Afr.; Dut.; Fle.*	village
Dos / *Rom.*	ridge
Dos / *Sp.*	two
Douarn / *Br.*	land
Dougou / *Sud.*	settlement
Doukou / *Sud.*	settlement
Down / *Eng.*	hill
Drâa / *Ar.*	dunes, hills
Dracht / *Germ.*	sandbank
Draw / *Eng.*	ravine, valley
Drif / *Afr.*	ford
Drift / *Afr.*	ford
Droichead / *Gae.*	bridge
Droûs / *Ar.*	crest
Dry / *Pash.*	river
Dubh / *Gae.*	black
Dugi / *S.C.*	long
Dugu / *Sud.*	settlement
Dun / *Gae.*	castle
Duna / *Sp.; It.*	dune
Düne / *Germ.*	dune
Dungar / *Hin.*	mountain
Dūngar / *Hin.*	mountain
Duong / *Viet.*	stream
Durchbruch / *Germ.*	gorge
Ḍurg / *Hin.*	castle
-durga / *Hin.*	castle
Duży / *Pol.*	great
Dvor / *Cz.*	court
Dvorec / *Rus.*	castle
Dvůr / *Cz.*	castle
Dwór / *Pol.*	court
Džebel / *Bulg.*	mountain
Dzong / *Tib.*	fort, monastery

E

Local Form	English
Ea / *Thai*	river
Eau / *Fr.*	water
Ebe / *Ban.*	forest
Ebene / *Germ.*	plain
Eck / *Germ.*	point
Eclusa / *Sp.*	lock
Écluse / *Fr.*	lock
Écueil / *Fr.*	cliff
Edeien / *Ber.*	sand desert
Edjérir / *Ber.*	wadi
Egg / *Germ.; Nor.*	crest, point
Eglab / *Ar.*	hills
Ehi / *Sah.*	mountain
Eid / *Nor.*	isthmus
Eiland / *Afr.*	island
Eisen / *Germ.*	iron
Eisenerz / *Germ.*	iron ore
El / *Amh.*	well
Elv, -elv / *Nor.*	river
Embalse / *Sp.*	reservoir
Embouchure / *Fr.*	mouth
Emi / *Sah.*	mountain
En / *Fr.*	in
Ende / *Germ.*	end
Enneri / *Sah.*	stream
Ennis / *Gae.*	island
Enseada / *Port.*	Bay, inlet
Ensenada / *Sp.*	bay, inlet
Ér / *Hung.*	stream
Erdő / *Hung.*	forest
Erg / *Ar.*	sand desert
Erz / *Germ.*	ore
Espigão / *Port.*	plateau
Ēstān / *Pers.*	land
Este / *Sp.*	east
Estero / *Sp.*	estuary, marsh
Estrecho / *Sp.*	strait
Estreito / *Port.*	strait
Estuaire / *Fr.*	estuary
Estuário / *Port.*	estuary
Estuario / *Sp.; It.*	estuary
Észak / *Hung.*	north
Étang / *Fr.*	pond
Ewaso / *Ban.*	river
Ey / *Icel.*	island
Eyja / *Icel.*	island
Eyjar / *Icel.*	islands
Eylandt / *Dut.*	island
Ežeras / *Lith.*	lake
Ezers / *Latv.*	lake

F

Local Form	English
Fa / *Mel.*	stream
Falaise / *Fr.*	cliff
Fall, -fall / *Germ.; Eng.; Swed.*	waterfall
Falls / *Eng.*	waterfall
Falu / *Hung.*	village
-falva / *Hung.*	village
Fan / *Sah.*	village
Faraglione / *It.*	cliff
Farallón / *Sp.*	cliff
Faro / *Sp.; It.*	lighthouse
Farvand / *Dan.*	strait
Fehér / *Hung.*	white
Fehn / *Germ.*	peat fen, peat-bog
Fekete / *Hung.*	black
Feld / *Dan.; Germ.*	field
Fell / *Eng.*	upland moor
Fell / *Icel.*	mountain
Fels / *Germ.*	rock
Fen / *Eng.*	marsh, peat-bog
Feng / *Chin.*	mountain, peak
Feste / *Germ.*	fort
Festung / *Germ.*	fort
Fier / *Rom.*	iron
Firn / *Germ.*	snow-field
Firth / *Eng.*	estuary, fjord
Fiume / *It.*	river
Fjäll / *Swed.*	mountain
Fjärd / *Swed.*	fjord
Fjell / *Nor.*	mountain
Fjöll / *Icel.*	mountain
Fjord, Fj. / *Dan.; Nor.; Swed.*	fjord
Fjörður / *Icel.*	fjord, bay
Fleuve / *Fr.*	river
Fließ / *Germ.*	torrent
Fljót / *Icel.*	river
Flói / *Icel.*	bay, gulf
Floresta / *Sp.; Port.*	forest
Flow / *Eng.*	strait
Flughafen / *Germ.*	airport
Fluß / *Germ.*	river
Fo / *Mel.*	stream
Foa / *Mel.*	stream
Foa / *Poly.*	cove
Foce / *It.*	mouth
Föld / *Hung.*	plain
Fonn / *Nor.*	glacier
Fontaine / *Fr.*	fountain
Fonte / *It.; Port.*	spring
Fontein / *Afr.; Dut.*	spring
Foort / *Afr.; Dut.*	ford
Forca / *It.*	pass
Forcella / *It.*	defile
Ford / *Rus.*	fjord
Förde / *Germ.*	fjord, gulf
Foreland / *Eng.*	promontory
Foresta / *It.*	forest
Forêt / *Fr.*	forest
Fors / *Swed.*	rapids, waterfall
Forst / *Germ.; Dut.*	forest
Forte / *It.; Port.*	fort
Fortin / *Sp.*	fort
Fosa / *Sp.*	trench
Foss / *Icel.; Nor.*	rapids, waterfall
Fossé / *Fr.*	trench
Foum / *Ar.*	pass
Fourche / *Fr.*	pass
Foz / *Sp.; Port.*	mouth
Frei / *Germ.*	free
Fronteira / *Port.*	frontier
Frontera / *Sp.*	frontier
Frontón / *Sp.*	promontory
Fuente / *Sp.*	spring
Fuerte / *Sp.*	fort
Fuji / *Jap.*	mountain
Fülat / *Ar.*	marsh
Furt / *Germ.*	ford
Fushë / *Alb.*	plain

G

Local Form	English
G., Gora / *Bulg.; Rus.; S.C.*	mountain, hill
G., Gunung / *Indon.*	mountain
Ga / *Jap.*	bay
Ga / *Mel.*	mountain, peak
Gabel / *Germ.*	pass
Gaissa / *Lapp.*	mountain
Gala / *Sin.; Tam.*	mountain
Gam / *Hin.; Urdu*	village
Gamle / *Nor.; Swed.*	old
Gana / *Sud.*	little
Gang / *Germ.*	passage
Gang / *Chin.*	port, bay
Gang / *Kor.*	stream, bay
Gang / *Tib.*	glacier
Ganga / *Hin.*	river
Ganj / *Hin.; Urdu*	market
-gaon / *Hin.*	city, town
Gaoyuan / *Chin.*	plateau
Gap / *Kor.*	point
Gar / *Hin.*	house
Gara / *Bulg.*	station
Gara / *Ar.*	hills, range
Gară / *Rom.*	station
Garaet / *Ar.*	marsh, intermittent lake
Garam / *Beng.; Hin.; Urdu*	village
-gard / *Pol.*	city, town
Gård, -gård / *Dan.; Nor.; Swed.*	farmhouse
Gardaneh / *Pers.*	pass
Gare / *Fr.*	railway station
Garet / *Ar.*	hill
Garh, -garh / *Hin.; Urdu*	castle
Garhi / *Hin.; Nep.; Urdu*	fort
Garten / *Germ.*	garden
Gat / *Dan.; Fle.; Dut.*	strait
Gata / *Jap.*	bay, lake
Gau, -gau / *Germ.*	district
Gäu, -gäu / *Germ.*	district
Gavan / *Rus.*	port
Gave / *Bas.*	torrent
Gawa / *Jap.*	river
Geb., Gebirge / *Germ.*	mountain range
Gebergte / *Afr.; Dut.*	mountain range
Gebirge, Geb. / *Germ.*	mountain range
Geç., Geçit / *Tur.*	pass
Geçidi / *Tur.*	pass
Geçit, Geç. / *Tur.*	pass
Geysir / *Icel.*	geyser
Ghar / *Hin.; Urdu*	house
Ghar / *Pash.*	mountain, mountain range
Gharbīyah / *Ar.*	western
Ghat / *Hin.; Nep.; Urdu*	pass
Ghubbat / *Ar.*	bay
Ghurd / *Ar.*	dune
Gi / *Kor.*	peninsula
Giang / *Viet.*	stream
Giri / *Hin.; Urdu*	mountain, hill
Girlo / *Rus.*	branch
Gjebel / *Ar.*	mountain
Gji / *Alb.*	bay
Glace / *Fr.*	ice
Glaciar / *Sp.*	glacier
Glacier / *Eng.; Fr.*	glacier
Glen / *Gae.*	valley
Gletscher / *Germ.*	glacier
Gobi / *Mong.*	desert
Godār / *Pers.*	ford
Gok / *Kor.*	river
Gök / *Tur.*	blue
Gol / *Cauc.; Mong.*	river
Göl / *Tur.*	lake
Gola / *It.*	gorge
Gold / *Germ.; Eng.*	gold
Golet / *S.C.*	mountain
Golf / *Germ.*	gulf
Golfe / *Fr.*	gulf
Golfete / *Sp.*	inlet
Golfo / *Sp.; It.; Port.*	gulf
Goljam / *Bulg.*	great
Gölü / *Tur.*	lake
Gong / *Tib.*	high
Gonggar / *Tib.*	mountain
Gongo / *Ban.*	mountain
Góra / *Pol.*	mountain
Gora, G. / *Bulg.; Rus.; S.C.*	mountain, hill
Gorica / *S.C.; Slvn.*	hill
Gorje / *S.C.*	mountain range
Gorlo / *Rus.*	gorge
Gorm / *Gae.*	blue
Gorni / *Bulg.; S.C.; Slvn.*	upper
Gornji / *S.C.; Slvn.*	upper
Górny / *Pol.*	high
Gorod / *Rus.*	city, town
Gorodok / *Rus.*	village
Gorski / *Bulg.*	upper
Gory / *Rus.*	mountains
-gou / *Chin.*	river
Goulbi / *Sud.*	river, lake
Goulbin / *Sud.*	wadi
Goulet / *Fr.*	gap
Gour / *Ar.*	hills, range
Gourou / *Sud.*	wadi
Goz / *Sah.*	dune
Graafschap / *Dut.*	county, shire
Graben / *Germ.*	ditch, canal
Gracht / *Dut.*	canal
Grad, -grad / *Bulg.; Rus.; S.C.; Slvn.*	city, town, castle
Gradac / *S.C.*	castle
Gradec / *Bulg.*	village
Gradec / *Slvn.*	castle
Græn / *Icel.*	green
Gran / *Sp.; It.*	great
Grande / *Sp.; It.; Port.*	great
Grao / *Cat.; Sp.*	gap
Grat / *Germ.*	crest
Grève / *Fr.*	beach
Grind / *Germ.*	peak
Grjada / *Rus.*	range
Gród, -gród / *Pol.*	castle, city, town
Grön / *Icel.*	green
Grond / *Afr.*	soil
Gronden / *Dut.; Fle.*	flat
Groot / *Afr.; Dut.; Fle.*	great
Groß / *Germ.*	great
Grotta / *It.*	grotto
Grotte / *Fr.; Germ.*	grotto
Grube / *Germ.*	mine
Grün / *Germ.*	green
Grunn / *Nor.*	ground
Gruppe / *Germ.*	mountain system
Gruppo / *It.*	mountain system
Gua / *Mal.*	cave
Guaçu / *A.I.*	great
Guan / *Chin.*	pass
Guazú / *A.I.*	great
Guba / *Rus.*	bay
Guchi / *Jap.*	strait
Guelb / *Ar.*	hill, mountain
Guelta / *Ar.*	well
Guic / *Br.*	village
Güney / *Tur.*	south, southern
Gunong / *Mal.*	mountain
Guntō / *Jap.*	archipelago
Gunung, G. / *Indon.*	mountain
Guo / *Chin.*	state, land
Gur / *Rom.*	mountain
Guri / *Jap.*	cliff
Gurud / *Ar.*	hills, dunes
Gyár / *Hung.*	factory

H

Local Form	English
Haag / *Dut.; Fle.*	hedge
-håb / *Dan.*	port
Haḑabat / *Ar.*	highland
Hadd / *Ar.*	point
Hadjer / *Ar.*	hill, mountain
Hae / *Kor.*	bay, sea
Haehyeop / *Kor.*	strait

Geographical Glossary

Local Form	English
Haf / *Icel.*	sea
Ḩafar / *Ar.*	well
Hafen / *Germ.*	port
Haff / *Germ.*	lagoon
Hafir / *Ar.*	spring, ditch
Hafnar / *Icel.*	port
Hāfūn / *Som.*	bay
Hage / *Dan.*	point
Hage / *Dut.; Fle.*	hedge
Hågna / *Swed.*	peak
Hai / *Chin.*	sea, lake, bay
Hain / *Germ.*	forest
Haixia / *Chin.*	strait
Ḩajar / *Ar.*	hill, mountain
Hajar / *Ar.*	hill country
Halbinsel / *Germ.*	peninsula
Halma / *Hung.*	hill
Halom / *Hung.*	hill
Halq / *Ar.*	gap
Hals / *Nor.*	peninsula
Halvø / *Dan.*	peninsula
Halvøy / *Nor.*	peninsula
Hama / *Jap.*	beach
Hamāda / *Ar.*	rocky desert
Ḩamādah / *Ar.*	plateau
Ḩamādat / *Ar.*	plateau
Hammam / *Ar.*	thermal springs
Ḩammām / *Ar.*	well
Hamn / *Nor.; Swed.*	port
Hamrā' / *Ar.*	red
Hāmūn / *Jap.*	salt lake
Hana / *Jap.*	cape
Hana / *Poly.*	bay
Hane / *Tur.*	house
Hang / *Kor.*	port
Hank / *Ar.*	escarpment, plateau
Hantō / *Jap.*	peninsula
Har / *Hebr.*	mountain
Hara / *Mong.*	black
Harar / *Swa.*	well
Ḩarrah / *Ar.*	lava field
Ḩarrat / *Ar.*	lava field
Hasi / *Ar.*	well
Ḩasi / *Ar.*	well
Hassi / *Ar.*	well
Ḩasy / *Ar.*	well
Haug / *Nor.*	hill
Haupt- / *Germ.*	principal
Haure / *Lapp.*	lake
Haus / *Germ.*	house
Hausen / *Germ.*	village
Haut / *Fr.*	high
Hauteur / *Fr.*	hill
Hauts Plateaux / *Fr.*	highlands
Hauz / *Pers.*	reservoir
Hav / *Dan.; Nor.; Swed.*	sea, gulf
Haven / *Eng.; Fle.; Dut.*	port
Havn / *Dan.; Nor.*	port
Havre / *Fr.*	port
Hawr / *Ar.*	lake, marsh
Ház / *Hung.*	house
-háza / *Hung.*	house
Hazm / *Ar.*	height, mountain range
He / *Chin.*	river
Head / *Eng.*	headland
Hed / *Dan.; Swed.*	heath
Hegy / *Hung.*	mountain
Hegység / *Hung.*	mountain
Hei / *Nor.*	heath
Heide / *Germ.*	heath
Heijde / *Dut.; Fle.*	heath
Heilig / *Germ.*	saint
Heim, -heim / *Germ.; Nor.*	house
Heiya / *Jap.*	plain
-hely / *Hung.*	locality
Hem / *Swed.*	home
Hen / *Br.*	old
Higashi / *Jap.*	east, eastern
Hima / *Hin.*	ice
Himal / *Nep.*	peak
Hisar / *Tur.*	castle
Ho / *Chin.*	reservoir, river
Ho / *Kor.*	river, reservoir
Hō / *Jap.*	mountain
Hoch / *Germ.*	high, upper
Hochland / *Germ.*	highland
Hochplato / *Afr.*	highland
Hodna / *Ar.*	highland
Hoek / *Dut.; Fle.*	cape
Hof / *Dut.; Germ.*	court
Höfn / *Icel.*	port
Høg / *Nor.*	peak
Hög / *Swed.*	mountain
Hogna / *Nor.*	peak
Höhe / *Germ.*	peak
Høj / *Dan.*	hill
Hoj / *Ural.*	mountain range
Hok / *Jap.*	north
Hoku / *Jap.*	north, northern
Holm / *Dan.; Nor.; Swed.*	island
Holz / *Germ.*	forest
Hon / *Viet.*	island, point
Hong / *Chin.; Viet.*	red
Hono / *Poly.*	bay, anchorage
Hoog / *Afr.; Dut.; Fle.*	high
Hook / *Eng.*	point
Hoorn / *Afr.; Dut.; Fle.*	cape, point

Local Form	English
Hora / *Cz.; Slvk.*	point
Horn / *Eng.; Germ.; Icel.; Nor.; Swed.*	point
Horni / *Cz.*	high
Horný / *Slvk.*	upper
Horst / *Germ.*	mountain
Horvot / *Hebr.*	ruins
Hory / *Cz.; Slvk.*	mountain range
Hout / *Dut.; Fle.*	forest
Hovd, -hovd / *Dan.; Nor.*	cape
Ḩowz / *Pers.*	basin
Hrad / *Cz.; Slvk.*	castle, city, town
Hradiště / *Cz.*	citadel
Hřeben / *Cz.*	crest
Hrebet / *Rus.*	mountain range
Hu / *Rmsh.*	lake
Huang / *Chin.*	yellow
Hude / *Germ.*	pasture
Huerta / *Sp.*	market garden
Hügel / *Germ.*	hill
Hügelland / *Germ.*	hill country
Huis, -huis / *Afr.; Dut.; Fle.*	house
Huisie / *Afr.*	house
Huizen, -huizen / *Dut.*	houses
Huk / *Afr.; Dan.; Swed.*	cape
Hum / *S.C.*	hill
Hurst / *Eng.*	grove
Hus / *Dut.; Nor.; Swed.*	house
Huta / *Pol.; Slvk.*	hut
Hütte / *Germ.*	hut
Hver / *Icel.*	crater
Hvit / *Icel.*	white
Hvost / *Rus.*	spit

I

Local Form	English
I., Island / *Eng.*	island
Ierós / *Gr.*	holy
Igarapé / *A.I.*	river
Ighazer / *Ber.*	torrent
Ighil / *Ber.*	hill
Iguidi / *Ber.*	dunes
Ih / *Mong.*	great
Ike / *Jap.*	pond
Ile / *Fr.*	island
Ilha / *Port.*	island
Iller / *Tur.*	administrative division
Ilot / *Fr.*	islet
Imi / *Ar.*	spring
I-n / *Ber.*	well
Inch / *Gae.*	island
Inder / *Dan.; Nor.*	inner
Indre / *Nor.*	inner
Inferiore / *It.*	lower
Inish / *Gae.*	island
Insel / *Germ.*	island
Insulă / *Rom.*	island
Inver / *Gae.*	mouth
Irhazér / *Ber.*	wadi
Irmak / *Tur.*	river
'Irq / *Ar.*	dunes
Is / *Nor.*	glacier
Ís / *Icel.*	ice
Isblink / *Dan.*	glacier
Ishi / *Jap.*	rock
Iske / *Alt.*	old
Isla / *Sp.*	island
Iso / *Finn.*	great
Iso / *Jap.*	cliff
Isola / *It.*	island
Isthmós / *Gr.*	isthmus
Istmo / *Sp.; It.*	isthmus
Ita / *A.I.*	stone
Itä / *Finn.*	east
Itivdleq / *Esk.*	isthmus
Iwa / *Jap.*	rock, cliff
Iztočni / *Bulg.*	eastern
Izvor / *Bulg.; Rom.; S.C.; Slvn.*	spring

J

Local Form	English
J., Jazīrat / *Ar.*	island
J., Jiang / *Chin.*	river
Jabal / *Ar.*	mountain
Jaha / *Ural.*	river
Jam / *Ural.*	lake, river
Jama / *Rus.*	cave
Jan / *Alt.*	great
Janga / *Tur.*	north
Jangi / *Alt.; Iran.*	new
Janūbīyah / *Ar.*	southern
Jar / *Rus.*	bank
Järv / *Est.*	lake
Järve / *Finn.*	lake
Järvi / *Finn.*	lake
Jasirēd / *Som.*	island
Jaun / *Latv.*	new
Jaur / *Lapp.*	lake
Jaure / *Lapp.*	lake
Javr / *Lapp.*	lake
Javrre / *Lapp.*	lake
Jazā'ir / *Ar.*	islands
Jazīrat, J. / *Ar.*	island
Jazovir / *Bulg.*	reservoir
Jbel / *Ar.*	mountain
Jebel / *Ar.*	mountain
Jedid / *Ar.*	new
Jedo / *Kor.*	archipelago
Jezero / *S.C.; Slvn.*	lake
Jezioro / *Pol.*	lake
Jhil / *Hin.; Urdu*	lake
Jian / *Chin.*	mountain
Jiang, J. / *Chin.*	river
Jiao / *Chin.*	cape, cliff
Jibāl / *Ar.*	mountain
Jih / *Cz.*	south
Jima / *Jap.*	island
Jin / *Kor.*	cove
Jing / *Chin.*	spring
Jisr / *Ar.*	bridge
Joch / *Germ.*	pass
Jõgi / *Est.*	river
Jøkel / *Nor.*	glacier
Joki / *Finn.*	river
Jokka / *Lapp.*	river
Jökull / *Icel.*	glacier
Jord, -jord / *Nor.*	earth
Ju / *Ural.*	river
Judeţ / *Rom.*	district
Jugan / *Ural.*	river
Jura / *Lith.*	sea
Jūra / *Latv.*	sea
Jūras Līcis / *Latv.*	bay
Jūrmala / *Latv.*	beach
Jurt / *Cauc.*	village
Južni / *Bulg.; S.C.; Slvn.*	southern
Južny / *Rus.*	southern
Juzur / *Ar.*	islands

K

Local Form	English
Ka / *Poly.*	lake
Kaap / *Afr.*	cape
Kabīr / *Ar.*	great
Kae / *Kor.*	inlet
Kāf / *Ar.*	peak, mountain
Kafr / *Ar.*	village
Kaga / *Ban.*	hills, mountain range
Kahal / *Ar.*	plateau, escarpment
Kai / *Jap.*	sea
Kaikyō / *Jap.*	strait
Kaise / *Lapp.*	mountain
Kal / *Pers.*	stream
Kala / *Az.; Kor.*	fort
Kala / *Finn.*	river
Kala / *Hin.*	black
Kala / *Tur.*	castle
Kalaa / *Ar.*	castle
Kalaki / *Georg.*	city, town
Kale / *Tur.*	castle
Kali / *Hin.*	black
Kali / *Indon.; Mal.*	bay, river
Kallio / *Finn.*	rock
Kaln / *Latv.*	mountain
Kalós / *Gr.*	beautiful, good
Kamen / *Bulg.; Rus.; S.C.; Slvn.*	mountain, peak
Kámen / *Cz.*	rock
Kameň / *Slvk.*	rock
Kami / *Jap.*	upper
Kamień / *Pol.*	rock
Kamm / *Germ.*	crest
Kamp / *Germ.*	field
Kâmpóng / *Khm.*	village
Kámpos / *Gr.*	field
Kampung / *Indon.; Mal.*	village
Kan., Kanal / *Alb.; Dan.; Germ.; Nor.; Rus.; S.C.; Slvn.; Swed.; Tur.*	canal, channel
Kanaal / *Dut.; Fle.*	canal
Kanał / *Pol.*	canal
Kanal, Kan. / *Alb.; Dan.; Germ.; Nor.; Rus.; S.C.; Slvn.; Swed.; Tur.*	canal, channel
Kand, -kand / *Pers.; Tur.*	city, town
Kang / *Chin.; Kor.*	bay, river
Kangas / *Fle.*	heath
Kange / *Esk.*	east
Kangri / *Tib.*	snow-capped mountain
Kantara / *Ar.*	bridge
Kaōh / *Khm.*	island
Kap / *Dan.; Germ.*	cape
Kapija / *S.C.*	gate, gorge
Kapp / *Nor.*	cape
Kar / *Tib.*	white
Kar / *Ural.*	city, town
Kara / *Tur.*	black
Karang / *Indon.; Mal.*	sandbank, cliff
Kari / *Finn.*	cliff
Kariba / *Ban.*	gorge
Kariet / *Ar.*	village
Karki / *Finn.*	peninsula
Kastel / *Germ.*	castle
Kástron / *Gr.*	fort, city, town
Káto / *Gr.*	lower
Kaupstadur / *Icel.*	city, town
Kaupunki / *Finn.*	city, town
Kavīr / *Pers.*	salt desert
Kawa / *Jap.*	river
Kawm / *Ar.*	hill
Kebir / *Ar.*	great
Kedi / *Georg.*	mountain range
Kédia / *Ar.*	mountain, plateau
Kedim / *Ar.*	old
Kef / *Ar.*	mountain
Kefála / *Gr.*	mountain, peak
Kefar / *Hebr.*	village
Kei / *Jap.*	river
Kelet / *Hung.*	east
Ken / *Gae.*	cape
Kent / *Alt.; Iran.; Tur.*	city, town
Kenya / *Swa.*	fog
Kep / *Alb.*	cape
Kep., Kepulauan / *Mal.*	archipelago
Kepulauan, Kep. / *Mal.*	archipelago
Kereszt / *Hung.*	cross
Kerk / *Dut.; Fle.*	church
Keski / *Finn.*	middle
Kette / *Germ.*	mountain range
Keur / *Sud.*	village
Key / *Eng.*	coral island
Kha / *Tib.*	valley
Khal / *Hin.*	canal
Khalīj / *Ar.*	gulf
Khand / *Hin.*	district
Khao / *Thai*	hill, mountain
Kharābeh / *Pers.*	ruins
Khashm / *Ar.*	promontory
Khatt / *Ar.*	wadi
Khawr / *Ar.*	mouth, bay
Khazzān / *Ar.*	dam
Khemis / *Ar.*	fifth
Khersónisos / *Gr.*	peninsula
Khirbat / *Ar.*	ruins
Khlong / *Thai*	stream, mouth
Khokhok / *Thai*	isthmus
Khor / *Ar.*	mouth, bay
Khóra / *Gr.*	land
Khorion / *Gr.*	village
Khowr / *Pers.*	bay
Khrisós / *Gr.*	gold
Ki- / *Ban.*	little
Kibali / *Sud.*	river
Kil / *Gae.*	church
Kilde / *Dan.*	spring
Kilima / *Swa.*	mountain
Kill / *Gae.*	strait
Kilwa / *Ban.*	lake
Kin / *Gae.*	cape
Kinn / *Nor.*	cape, point
Kirche / *Germ.*	church
Kirk / *Eng.*	church
Kis / *Hung.*	little
Kisiwa / *Swa.*	island
Kita / *Jap.*	north, northern
Kızıl / *Tur.*	red
Klein / *Afr.; Dut.; Germ.*	little
Kliff / *Germ.*	cliff
Klint / *Dan.*	reef
Klip / *Afr.; Dut.*	rock, cliff
Klit / *Dan.*	dune
Kloof / *Afr.; Dut.*	gorge
Kloster / *Dan.; Germ.; Nor.; Swed.*	convent
Knob / *Eng.*	mountain
Knock / *Gae.*	mountain, hill
Ko / *Jap.*	bay, lake, little
Ko / *Sud.*	stream
Ko / *Thai*	island, point
Købing / *Dan.*	town
Kogel / *Germ.*	dome
Kōgen / *Jap.*	plateau
Koh / *Hin.; Pers.*	mountain, mountain range
Kol / *Alt.*	river, valley
Kol / *Alt.; Tur.*	lake
Koll / *Nor.*	peak
Kólpos / *Gr.*	gulf
Kong / *Dan.; Nor.; Swed.*	king
Kong / *Indon.; Mal.*	mountain
Kong / *Viet.*	mountain, hill
Konge / *Ban.*	river
König / *Germ.*	king
Koog / *Germ.*	polder
Kop / *Afr.*	hill
Kopec / *Cz.; Slvk.*	hill
Kopf / *Germ.*	peak
Köping / *Swed.*	town
Köprü / *Tur.*	bridge
Körfezi / *Tur.*	gulf
Korfi / *Gr.*	rock
Koro / *Mel.*	mountain, island
Koro / *Sud.*	old
Koru / *Tur.*	forest
Kosa / *Rus.*	spit
Koška / *Rus.*	cliff
Koski / *Finn.*	rapids
Kosui / *Jap.*	lake
Kot / *Urdu*	castle
Kota / *Mal.*	city, town
Kotal / *Pash.; Pers.*	pass
Kotar / *S.C.*	cultivated area
Kotlina / *Pol.*	basin

Local Form	English
Kotlovina / *Rus.*	basin, plain
Kou / *Chin.*	mouth, pass
Kourou / *Sud.*	well
Kowr / *Pers.*	river
Kowtal / *Pers.*	pass
Koy / *Tur.*	bay
Köy / *Tur.*	village
Kraal / *Afr.*	village
Kraina / *Pol.*	land
Kraj / *Rus.; S.C.*	land
Kraj / *Rus.*	administrative division
Krajina / *S.C.*	land
Krak / *Ar.*	hill, castle
Krans / *Afr.*	mountain
Kras / *S.C.; Slvn.*	karst landscape
Krasny / *Rus.*	red
Kreb / *Ar.*	hills, mountain range
Kriaž / *Ar.*	mountain range
Krš / *S.C.*	karst area, limestone area
Krung / *Thai*	city, town
Ksar / *Ar.*	castle
Ksour / *Ar.*	fortified village
Ku- / *Ban.*	river branch
Kuala / *Mal.*	river, mouth
Kubra / *Ar.*	bridge
Küçük / *Tur.*	little
Kuduk / *Tur.*	spring
Kūh / *Pers.*	mountain
Kūhhā / *Pers.*	mountain range
Kul / *Alt.; Iran.; Tur.*	lake
Kulam, -kulam / *Hin.; Tam.*	pond
Kulle / *Swed.*	hill
Kulm / *Germ.*	peak
Kultuk / *Rus.*	bay
Kum / *Tur.*	dunes, sand desert
Kuppe / *Germ.*	dome, seamount
Kurayb / *Ar.*	hill
Kurgan / *Alt.*	hill
Kurgan / *Tur.*	fort
Kuro / *Jap.*	black
Kurort / *Bulg.; Germ.; Rus.*	spa
Kust / *Dut.; Fle.*	coast
Kust- / *Swed.*	coast
Küste / *Germ.*	coast
Kút / *Hung.*	spring
Kuyu / *Tur.*	spring
Kvemo / *Georg.*	low, lower
Kwa / *Ban.*	village
Kylä / *Finn.*	village
Kyle / *Gae.*	strait, channel
Kyō / *Jap.*	strait
Kyrka / *Swed.*	church
Kyst / *Dan.; Nor.*	coast
Kyun / *Burm.*	island
Kyūryō / *Jap.*	hills, mountains
Kyzyl / *Tur.*	red
Kzyl / *Tur.*	red

L

Local Form	English
L., Lake, Lago / *Eng.; It.; Port.; Sp.*	lake
La / *Tib.*	pass
Laagte / *Afr.*	stream, valley
Labuan / *Indon.; Mal.*	bay, port
Lac / *Fr.*	lake
Lach / *Som.*	stream, wadi
Lacul / *Rom.*	lake
Lae / *Poly.*	cape, point
Laem / *Thai*	bay, port
Låg / *Nor.; Swed.*	low, lower
Lag / *Swed.*	stream, wadi
Läge / *Swed.*	beach
Lagh / *Som.*	stream, wadi
Lago, L. / *It.; Port.; Sp.*	lake
Lagoa / *Port.*	lagoon
Laguna / *Alb.; It.; Rus.; Sp.*	lagoon, lake
Lagune / *Fr.*	lagoon
Laht / *Est.*	bay
Lahti / *Finn.*	bay, gulf
Laks / *Finn.*	bay
Lalla / *Ar.*	saint
Lampi / *Finn.*	pond
Lande / *Fr.*	heath
Lang / *Afr.; Dut.; Germ.*	long
Lang / *Viet.*	village
Lao / *Chin.*	old
Lapa / *Poly.*	mountain range, peak
Largo / *Port.; Sp.*	basin
Las / *Pol.*	forest
Las, Lās / *Som.*	well
Laut / *Mal.*	sea
Law / *Gae.*	hill, mountain
Lázně / *Cz.*	thermal springs
Lednik / *Rus.*	glacier
Leite / *Germ.*	coast
Lekh / *Nep.*	mountain range
Les / *Bulg.; Cz.; Rus.; Slvk.*	forest
Leso / *Rus.*	forested
Levante / *It.; Sp.*	eastern
Levkós / *Gr.*	white
Levy / *Rus.*	left
Lha / *Tib.*	temple
Lhari / *Hin.; Nep.*	mountain
Lho / *Tib.*	south
Lido / *It.*	sandbar
Liedao / *Chin.*	archipelago
Liehtao / *Chin.*	archipelago
Liels / *Latv.*	great
Lilla / *Swed.*	little
Lille / *Dan.; Nor.*	little
Liman / *Alb.; Rus.; Tur.*	lagoon, bay
Liman / *Tur.*	bay, port
Limin / *Gr.*	port
Limni / *Gr.*	lake
Ling / *Chin.*	mountain range, peak
Linna / *Finn.*	castle
Liqen / *Alb.*	lake
Lithos / *Gr.*	stone
Litoral / *Port.; Sp.*	littoral
Litorale / *It.*	littoral
Llan / *Wel.*	church
Llano / *Sp.*	plain
Llanura / *Sp.*	plain
Lo- / *Ban.*	river
Loch / *Gae.*	lake, inlet
Loch / *Germ.*	grotto
Loka / *Slvn.*	forest
Loma / *Sp.*	hill
Long / *Indon.*	stream
Loo / *Dut.; Fle.*	clearing
Lough / *Gae.*	lake
Loutrá / *Gr.*	thermal springs
Ložbina / *Rus.*	depression
Lu- / *Ban.*	river
Lua / *Ban.*	river
Lua / *Mel.*	island, reef
Lua / *Poly.*	crater
Luang / *Thai*	yellow
Luch / *Germ.*	peat-bog
Lücke / *Germ.*	pass
Lug / *Rus.*	meadow
Luka / *S.C.; Slvn.*	port
Lule / *Lapp.*	east, eastern
Lum / *Alb.*	river
Lund / *Dan.; Swed.*	forest
Lung / *Rom.*	long
Lung / *Tib.*	valley
Luoto / *Finn.*	shoal
Lurg / *Pers.*	salt flat
Lut / *Pers.*	desert

M

Local Form	English
M., Monte / *It.; Port.; Sp.*	mountain
Ma / *Ar.*	water
Ma- / *Ban.*	people
Maa / *Est.; Finn.*	island, land
Ma'arrat / *Ar.*	height
Machi / *Jap.*	district
Macizo / *Sp.*	massif
Madhya / *Hin.*	central
Madīnah / *Ar.*	city, town
Madīq / *Ar.*	strait
Mado / *Swa.*	well
Madu / *Tam.*	pond
Mae / *Thai*	stream
Mae nam / *Thai*	stream, mouth
Magh / *Gae.*	plain
Mägi / *Est.*	mountain
Măgura / *Rom.*	height
Mahā / *Hin.*	great
Mahal / *Hin.; Urdu*	palace
Mai / *Amh.; Ban.*	stream
Majdan / *S.C.*	quarry
Mäki / *Finn.*	mountain, hill
Makrós / *Gr.*	long
Mala / *Hin.; Tam.*	mountain
Malai / *Hin.; Tam.*	mountain
Malal / *A.I.*	fence
Malhão / *Port.*	dome
Mali / *Alb.*	mountain
Mali / *S.C.; Slvn.*	little
Malki / *Bulg.*	little
Malla / *Tam.*	mountain
Maly / *Rus.*	little
Malý / *Cz.; Slvk.*	little
Mały / *Pol.*	little
Man / *Kor.*	bay
Manastir / *Bulg.; S.C.*	monastery
Manche / *Fr.*	channel
Mar / *It.; Port.; Sp.*	sea
Mar / *Tib.*	red
Mar / *Ural.*	city, town
Marais / *Fr.*	marsh
Marché / *Fr.*	market
Mare / *Fr.*	pond
Mare / *It.; Rom.*	sea
Mare / *Rom.*	great
Marea / *Rom.*	sea
Marécage / *Fr.*	marsh
Marios / *Lith.*	reservoir
Marisma / *Sp.*	marsh
Mark / *Dan.; Nor.; Swed.*	land
Markt / *Germ.*	market
Marsa / *Ar.*	anchorage, bay
Marsch / *Germ.*	marsh
Maru / *Jap.*	mountain
Mas / *Prov.*	farmhouse
Maşabb / *Ar.*	mouth
Mashra' / *Ar.*	landing, pier
Masivul / *Rom.*	massif
Massiv / *Germ.; Rus.*	massif
Mata / *Poly.*	point
Mata / *Port.; Sp.*	forest
Mata / *Som.*	waterfall
Mato / *Port.; Sp.*	forest
Matsu / *Jap.*	point
Mauna / *Poly.*	mountain
Mávros / *Gr.*	black
Mayo / *Sud.*	river
Maza / *Lith.*	little
Mazar / *Pers.; Tur.*	sanctuary
Mazs / *Latv.*	little
Me / *Khm.*	river
Me / *Mel.*	hill, mountain
Me / *Thai*	great
Medina / *Ar.*	city, town
Medjez / *Ar.*	ford
Meer / *Dut.; Fle.*	lake
Meer / *Germ.*	lake, sea
Megálos / *Gr.*	great
Mégas / *Gr.*	great
Megye / *Hung.*	district
Mélas / *Gr.*	black
Melkosopočnik / *Rus.*	hill country
Mellan / *Swed.*	central
Men / *Chin.*	gate, channel
Ménez / *Br.*	mountain
Menzel / *Ar.*	bivouac
Meos / *Indon.*	island
Mer / *Fr.*	sea
Mercato / *It.*	market
Merdja / *Ar.*	lagoon, marsh
Meri / *Est.; Finn.*	sea
Meridional / *Rom.; Sp.*	southern
Merin / *A.I.*	little
Merja / *Ar.*	lagoon, marsh
Mers / *Ar.*	port
Mersa / *Ar.*	port
Mesa / *Sp.*	mesa, tableland
Meseta / *Sp.*	plateau
Mésos / *Gr.*	central
Mesto / *Bulg.; S.C.; Slvk.; Slvn.*	city, town
Město / *Cz.*	city, town
Mestre / *Port.*	principal
Meydan / *Tur.*	square
Meẓad / *Hebr.*	castle
Mező / *Hung.*	field
Mgne., Montagne / *Fr.*	mountain
Mgnes., Montagnes / *Fr.*	mountains
Miao / *Chin.*	temple
Miasto / *Pol.*	city, town
Mic / *Rom.*	little
Middel / *Afr.; Dut.; Fle.*	middle
Midi / *Fr.*	noon, south
Między / *Pol.*	central
Miedzyrzecze / *Pol.*	interfluve
Mierzeja / *Pol.*	sand spit
Mifraz / *Hebr.*	bay, gulf
Miftah / *Ar.*	gorge
Mikrós / *Gr.*	little
Mina / *Port.; Sp.*	mine
Mīnā' / *Ar.*	port
Minami / *Jap.*	south, southern
Minamoto / *Jap.*	spring
Minato / *Jap.*	port
Mine / *Jap.*	peak
Mirim / *A.I.*	little
Misaki / *Jap.*	cape
Mittel- / *Germ.*	middle
Mo / *Chin.*	sand desert
Mo / *Nor.; Swed.*	heath
Moana / *Poly.*	lake
Mogila / *Bulg.; Rus.*	hill
Moku / *Poly.*	island
Mølle / *Dan.*	mill
Monasterio / *Sp.*	monastery
Mond / *Afr.; Dut.; Fle.*	mouth
Mong / *Burm.; Thai; Viet.*	city, town
Moni / *Gr.*	monastery
Mont / *Cat.; Fr.*	mountain
Montagna / *It.*	mountain
Montagne, Mgne. / *Fr.*	mountain
Montagnes, Mgnes. / *Fr.*	mountains
Montaña / *Sp.*	mountain
Monte, M. / *It.; Port.; Sp.*	mountain
Monts, Mts. / *Fr.*	mountains
Moos / *Germ.*	moor
Mór / *Gae.*	great
More / *Bulg.; Rus.; S.C.*	sea
More / *Gae.*	great
Mori / *Jap.*	mountain, forest
Morne / *Fr.*	mountain
Moron / *Mong.*	river
Morro / *Port.; Germ.*	hill, peak
Morrón / *Sp.*	mountain
Morze / *Pol.*	sea
Most / *Bulg.; Cz.; Pol.; Rus.; S.C.; Slvn.*	bridge
Moto / *Jap.*	spring
Motte / *Fr.*	hill
Motu / *Mel.; Poly.*	island, rock
Moutier / *Fr.*	monastery
Movilă / *Rom.*	hill
Moyen / *Fr.*	central
Mta / *Georg.*	mountain
Mts., Monts, Mountains / *Eng.; Fr.*	mountains
Muang / *Laot.; Thai*	city, town, land
Muara / *Indon.; Mal.*	mouth
Muela / *Sp.*	mountain
Mühle / *Germ.*	mill
Mui / *Mel.*	point
Mui / *Viet.*	point, cape
Muiden / *Dut.; Fle.*	mouth
Muir / *Gae.*	sea
Mukh / *Hin.*	mouth
Mull / *Gae.*	promontory
Münde / *Germ.*	mouth
Mündung / *Germ.*	mouth
Municipiul / *Rom.*	commune
Munkhafaḍ / *Ar.*	depression
Münster / *Germ.*	monastery
Munte / *Rom.*	mountain
Muntele / *Rom.*	mountain
Munţii / *Rom.*	mountain range
Muren / *Mong.*	river
Mushāsh / *Ar.*	spring
Muz / *Tur.*	ice
Muztagh / *Tur.*	snow-capped mountain
Mwambo / *Ban.*	rock, cliff
Myit / *Burm.*	stream
Mynydd / *Wel.*	mountain
Myo / *Burm.*	city, town
Mýri / *Icel.*	marsh
Mys / *Rus.*	cape

N

Local Form	English
Na / *Cz.; Pol.; Rus.; S.C.; Slvn.*	on
Nab / *Ar.*	spring
Nad / *Cz.; Pol.; Rus.*	on
Nada / *Jap.*	bay, sea
Nadi, -nadi / *Hin.; Urdu*	river
Næs / *Dan.*	point
Nafūd / *Ar.*	dunes
Nag / *Tib.*	black
Nagar, -nagar / *Hin.; Tib.*	city, town
Nagaram / *Hin.; Tam.*	city, town
Nagorje / *Rus.*	plateau, mountains
Nagy / *Hung.*	great
Nahr / *Ar.*	river
Naikai / *Jap.*	sea
Naka / *Jap.*	central
Nakhon / *Thai*	city, town
Nam / *Burm.; Laot.; Thai*	river
Nam / *Kor.*	south
Namakzar / *Pers.*	salt desert
Nan / *Chin.*	south
Narrows / *Eng.*	strait
Narssaq / *Esk.*	plain, valley
Näs / *Swed.*	cape
Nationalpark / *Swed.; Germ.*	national park
Nau / *Lith.*	new
Nauja / *Lith.*	new
Navolok / *Rus.*	cape, promontory
Ne / *Jap.*	cliff
Neder / *Fle.; Dut.*	low
Neem / *Est.*	cape
Negro / *Port.; Sp.*	black
Negru / *Rom.*	black
Nehir / *Tur.*	river
Nei / *Chin.*	inner
Nene, -nene / *Ban.*	great
Néos / *Gr.*	new
Nero / *It.*	black
Nes / *Icel.; Nor.*	cape
Ness / *Gae.*	promontory
Neu / *Germ.*	new
Neuf / *Fr.*	new
Nevado / *Sp.*	snow-capped mountain
Nez / *Fr.*	cape
Ngok / *Viet.*	mountain, peak
Ngolo / *Ber.*	great
Ni / *Kor.*	village
Niecka / *Pol.*	basin
Niemi / *Finn.*	peninsula
Nieuw / *Fle.; Dut.*	new
Nij / *Dut.*	new
Nīl / *Hin.*	blue
Nishi / *Jap.*	west
Niski / *Pol.*	lower
Nisko / *S.C.*	low
Nisoi / *Gr.*	islands
Nisos / *Gr.*	island
Nizina / *Pol.*	lowland
Nižina / *Cz.*	depression
Nízký / *Cz.*	low, lower

Local Form	English
Nizmennost / *Rus.*	lowland, depression
Nižni / *Rus.*	low, lower
Nižný / *Slvk.*	low, lower
No / *Mel.*	stream
Nock / *Gae.*	ridge
Noir / *Fr.*	black
Non / *Thai*	hill
Nong / *Thai*	lake, marsh
Noord / *Afr.; Fle.; Dut.*	north
Noordoost / *Afr.; Fle.; Dut.*	northeast
Nor / *Arm.*	new
Nord / *Fr.; It.; Germ.*	north
Nördlich / *Germ.*	northern
Nørdre / *Dan.; Nor.*	northern
Norra / *Swed.*	northern
Nørre / *Dan.*	northern
Norte / *Sp.*	north
Nos / *Bulg.; Rus.; S.C.; Slvn.*	cape
Nosy / *Malag.*	island
Nótios / *Gr.*	southern
Nou / *Rom.*	new
Novi / *Bulg.; S.C.; Slvn.*	new
Novo / *Port.*	new
Novy / *Rus.*	new
Nový / *Cz.; Slvk.*	new
Now / *Pers.*	new
Nowy / *Pol.*	new
Nudo / *Sp.*	mountain
Nuevo / *Sp.*	new
Nui / *Viet.*	mountain
Numa / *Jap.*	marsh, lake
Nummi / *Finn.*	heath
Nunatak / *Esk.*	peak
Nuovo / *It.*	new
Nur / *Chin.*	lake
Nusa / *Mal.*	island
Nut, -nut / *Nor.*	peak
Nuwara / *Sin.; Tam.*	city, town
Nuwe / *Afr.*	new
Nyanza / *Ban.*	water, river, lake
Nyasa / *Ban.*	lake
Nyeong / *Kor.*	pass
Nyika / *Ban.*	upland
Nyŏng / *Kor.*	mount, pass
Nyugat / *Hung.*	west

O

Local Form	English
Ō / *Jap.*	great
Ó / *Hung.*	old
Ö / *Swed.*	island
Ø, -ø / *Dan.; Nor.*	island
Öar / *Swed.*	islands
Ober / *Germ.*	upper
Oblast / *Rus.*	province
Obo / *Mong.*	mountain, hill
Occidental / *Fr.; Rom.; Sp.*	western
Océan / *Fr.*	ocean
Océano / *Sp.*	ocean
Oceano / *It.; Port.*	ocean
Ocnă / *Rom.*	salt mine
Odde / *Dan.; Nor.*	promontory
Oeste / *Port.; Sp.*	west
Oever / *Fle.; Dut.*	bank
Oewer / *Afr.*	bank
Oie / *Germ.*	islet
Ojos / *Sp.*	spring
Oka / *Jap.*	coast
Oke / *Sud.*	height
Okean / *Rus.*	ocean
Oki / *Jap.*	bay
Okrug / *Rus.*	district
Ola / *Alt.*	city, town
Omuramba / *K.S.*	stream
Onder / *Afr.*	under
Oni / *Malag.*	river
Oos / *Afr.*	east
Oost / *Fle.; Dut.*	east
Oostelijk / *Dut.*	eastern
Opatija / *Slvn.*	abbey
Or / *Fr.*	gold
Oraş / *Rom.*	city, town
Óri / *Gr.*	mountains
Oriental / *Fr.; Port.; Rom.; Sp.*	eastern
Orientale / *It.*	eastern
Orilla / *Sp.*	bank
Órmos / *Gr.*	bay
Óros / *Gr.*	mountain
Ország / *Hung.*	land
Ort / *Germ.*	cape
Orta / *Tur.*	central
Orto / *Alt.*	central
Oseaan / *Afr.*	ocean
Ōshima / *Jap.*	large island
Ost / *Dan.; Germ.*	east
Öst / *Swed.*	east
Ostān, -ostān / *Pers.*	province
Øster / *Dan.; Nor.*	east, eastern
Öster / *Swed.*	east, eastern
Östlich / *Germ.*	eastern
Ostrog / *Rus.*	castle
Ostrov / *Rus.*	island
Ostrovul / *Rom.*	island
Ostrów / *Pol.*	island
Ostrvo / *S.C.*	island
Otok / *S.C.; Slvn.*	island
Otrog / *Rus.*	front range (mountains)
Oua / *Mel.*	stream
Ouar / *Ar.*	rocky desert
Oud / *Fle.; Dut.*	old
Oued / *Ar.*	wadi
Ouest / *Fr.*	west
Ouled / *Ar.*	son
Oum / *Ar.*	mother
Ouro / *Port.*	gold
Outu / *Poly.*	cape
Ova / *Ban.*	people
Ova / *Tur.*	plain
Ovasi / *Tur.*	plain
Øver / *Nor.*	over
Över / *Swed.*	over
Övre / *Swed.*	over
Øy / *Dan.; Nor.*	island
oz., Ozero / *Rus.*	lake
Ozek / *Alt.*	hollow
Ozera / *Rus.*	lakes
Ozero, oz. / *Rus.*	lake

P

Local Form	English
P., Pulau / *Mal.; Indon.*	island
Pää / *Finn.*	principal
Pad / *Rus.*	valley
Padang / *Indon.*	plain
Padiş / *Rom.*	upland
Padół / *Pol.*	valley
Pădure / *Rom.*	forest
Pahorek / *Cz.*	hill
Pahorkatina / *Cz.*	plateau, hills
País / *Port.; Sp.*	land, country
Pak / *Thai*	mouth
Pala / *It.*	peak
Palaiós / *Gr.*	old
Palanka / *S.C.*	village
Pali / *Poly.*	cliff
-palli / *Hin.*	village
Pampa / *Sp.*	plain, prairie
Panda / *Swa.*	junction
Panev / *Cz.*	basin
Pantanal / *Sp.*	swamp
Pantano / *Sp.*	swamp, lake
Pao / *Mel.*	hill
Pará / *A.I.*	river
Paramera / *Sp.*	desert highland
Páramo / *Sp.*	moor
Paraná / *A.I.*	river
Parbat / *Hin.; Urdu*	mountain
Parc / *Fr.*	park
Parco / *It.*	park
Parco Nazionale / *It.*	national park
Pardo / *Port.*	grey
Parque / *Sp.*	park
Parque Nacional / *Sp.; Port.*	national park
Pas / *Fr.; Rom.*	pass, strait
Pasaje / *Sp.*	passage
Pasir / *Mal.*	sand, beach
Paso / *Sp.*	pass
Passagem / *Port.*	passage
Passe / *Fr.*	pass
Passo / *It.; Port.*	pass
Pasul / *Rom.*	pass
Patak / *Hung.*	stream
Patam, -patam / *Hin.*	city, town
Patnā / *Hin.*	city, town
Patnam, -patnam / *Hin.*	city, town
Pattinam, -pattinam / *Hin.*	city, town
Pays / *Fr.*	land, country
Pazar / *Tur.*	market
Pea / *Est.*	cape
Pech / *Cat.*	hill
Pedhiás / *Gr.*	plain
Pedra / *Port.*	rock, mountain
Peg., Pegunungan / *Mal.; Indon.*	mountain range
Pegunungan, Peg. / *Mal.; Indon.*	mountain range
Pélagos / *Gr.*	sea
Pele / *Poly.*	peak, hill
Pen / *Br.*	principal
Pen / *Br.; Gae.*	cape, mountain
Peña / *Sp.*	peak
Pendi / *Chin.*	basin
Pendiente / *Sp.*	slope
Penha / *Port.*	peak
Peninsula / *Port.; Sp.*	peninsula
Péninsule / *Fr.*	peninsula
Penisola / *It.*	peninsula
Peñon / *Sp.*	rock, island
Pente / *Fr.*	slope
Perekop / *Rus.*	channel
Pereval / *Rus.*	pass
Perevoz / *Rus.*	ford
Pertuis / *Fr.*	strait
Peščara / *S.C.*	sandy soil
Peski / *Rus.*	sand desert
Petit / *Fr.*	little
Pétra / *Gr.*	rock
Phanom / *Thai; Khm.*	mountain range, mountain
Phau / *Laot.*	mountain
Phnum / *Khm.*	hill, mountain
Phu / *Viet.*	mountain, hill
Phum / *Thai*	forest
Phumĭ / *Khm.*	village
Pi / *Chin.*	cape
Piana, Pianura / *It.*	plain
Piano / *It.*	plain
Piatră / *Rom.*	stone
Pic / *Cat.; Fr.*	peak
Picacho / *Sp.*	peak
Piccolo / *It.*	little
Pico / *Port.; Sp.*	peak
Piedra / *Sp.*	rock, cliff
Pietra / *It.*	stone
Pieve / *It.*	parish
Pik / *Rus.*	peak
Pils / *Latv.*	city, town
Pinar / *Sp.*	pine forest
Pingyuan / *Chin.*	plain
Pioda / *It.*	crest
Pirgos / *Gr.*	tower, peak
Pīsh / *Pers.*	anterior, before
Pitkä / *Finn.*	great
Piton / *Fr.*	mountain, peak
Piz / *Rmsh.*	peak
Pizzo / *It.*	peak
Pjasăci / *Bulg.*	beach
Plaat / *Fle.; Dut.*	sandbank
Plage / *Fr.*	beach
Plaine / *Fr.*	plain
Plan / *Fr.*	plain
Planalto / *Port.*	plateau
Planina / *Bulg.*	mountain
Plano / *Sp.*	plain
Plas / *Dut.; Fle.*	lake, marsh
Plato / *Bulg.; Rus.*	plateau
Platosu / *Tur.*	plateau
Platte / *Germ.*	plain, plateau
Plav / *S.C.*	blue
Plavnja / *Rus.*	marsh
Playa / *Sp.*	beach
Ploskogorje / *Rus.*	plateau
Plou / *Br.*	church
Po / *Kor.*	port
Po / *Chin.*	lake, white
P'o / *Kor.*	bay, lake
Poa / *Mel.*	hill
Poarta / *Rom.*	pass
Poartă / *Rom.*	gate
Pobla / *Cat.*	village
Pobrzeże / *Pol.*	littoral, coast
Poço / *Port.*	well
Poço / *Port.*	point
Pod / *Cz.; Pol.; Rus.; S.C.; Slvn.*	bridge
Podkamenny / *Rus.*	stony
Poggio / *It.*	hill
Pohja / *Finn.*	north, northern
Pohjois- / *Finn.*	north
Pojezierze / *Pol.*	lake region
Pol / *Pers.*	bridge
Pol, -pol / *Rus.*	city, town
Pola / *Port.; Sp.*	village
Polder / *Fle.; Dut.*	reclaimed land
Pole / *Pol.*	field
Pólis / *Gr.*	city, town
Poljana / *Bulg.; Rus.; S.C.; Slvn.*	field, terrace
Poljarny / *Rus.*	polar
Polje / *S.C.; Slvn.*	valley, field, basin
Poluostrov / *Rus.*	peninsula
Pomorije / *Bulg.*	littoral
Pomorze / *Pol.*	littoral
Ponente / *It.*	western
Pont / *Cat.; Fr.*	bridge
Ponta / *Port.*	point
Ponte / *It.; Port.*	bridge
Póntos / *Gr.*	sea
Poort / *Afr.; Fle.; Dut.*	pass
Pore, -pore / *Hin.; Urdu*	city, town
Porog / *Rus.*	rapids
Porte / *Fr.*	gate
Portile / *Rom.*	gorge
Portillo / *Sp.*	pass
Portiţa / *Rom.*	small gate
Porto / *It.*	port
Pôrto / *Port.*	port
Posht / *Pers.*	back, posterior
Potjo / *Indon.*	peak
Potok / *Bulg.; Cz.; Pol.; Rus.; S.C.; Slvn.*	stream
Póvoa / *Port.*	village
Pozo / *Sp.*	well
Pozzo / *It.*	well
Pradesh / *Hin.*	region, state
Prado / *Sp.*	meadow
Praia / *Port.*	beach
Prato / *It.*	meadow
Pré / *Fr.*	meadow
Prealpi / *It.*	prealps
Presa / *Sp.*	reservoir
Presqu'île / *Fr.*	peninsula
Prêto / *Port.*	black
Priehradní nádrž / *Cz.*	reservoir
Pripoljarny / *Rus.*	subpolar
Pristan / *Rus.*	port
Prohod / *Bulg.*	pass
Proliv / *Rus.*	strait
Promontoire / *Fr.*	promontory
Průchod / *Cz.*	pass
Przedgorze / *Pol.*	front range (mountains)
Przełęcz / *Pol.*	pass
Przemysł / *Pol.*	industry
Przylądek / *Pol.*	cape
Pua / *Mel.*	hill
Puebla / *Sp.*	village
Puente / *Sp.*	bridge
Puerto / *Sp.*	port, pass
Puig / *Cat.*	peak
Puits / *Fr.*	well
Pul / *Pash.*	bridge
Pulau, P. / *Mal.; Indon.*	island
Pulau Pulau / *Mal.*	islands
Pulo / *Mal.; Indon.*	island
Puna / *A.I.*	upland
Puncak / *Indon.*	mountain
Punjung / *Mal.; Indon.*	mountain
Punt / *Afr.*	point
Punta / *It.; Sp.*	point
Pur, -pur / *Hin.; Urdu*	city, town
-pura / *Hin.; Urdu*	city, town
Pura / *Indon.*	city, town, temple
Puri, -puri / *Hin.; Urdu*	city, town
Pus / *Alb.*	spring
Pušča / *Rus.*	forest
Pustynja / *Rus.*	desert
Puszcza / *Pol.*	heath
Puszta / *Hung.*	lowland
Put / *Afr.*	well
Put / *Rus.; S.C.*	road
Putra, -putra / *Hin.*	son
Puu / *Poly.*	mountain, volcano
Puy / *Fr.*	peak
Pwell / *Wel.*	pond
Pyeong / *Kor.*	plain
Pyhä / *Finn.*	saint

Q

Local Form	English
Qagan / *Mong.*	white
Qala / *Pash.*	fortified town
Qal'at / *Ar.*	castle
Qalb / *Ar.*	hill
Qalīb / *Ar.*	spring
Qalīq / *Ar.*	spring
Qanāt / *Ar.*	canal
Qantara / *Ar.*	bridge
Qaqortoq / *Esk.*	white
Qar / *Som.*	mountain
Qara / *Pers.*	black
Qarah / *Tur.*	black
Qārat / *Ar.*	height, mountain
Qāret / *Ar.*	village, hill
Qaryah / *Ar.*	village
Qaryat / *Ar.*	village
Qaşr / *Ar.*	castle
Qawz / *Ar.*	dunes
Qeqertarssuaq / *Esk.*	peninsula
Qezel / *Tur.*	red
Qi / *Chin.*	river
Qing / *Chin.*	blue, green
Qiryat / *Hebr.*	city, town
Qolleh / *Pers.*	mountain, peak
Qu / *Chin.*	river, canal
Quan dao / *Viet.*	islands
Quebracho / *Sp.*	stream
Quebrada / *Sp.*	gorge, stream
Quedas / *Port.*	waterfalls
Qulbān / *Ar.*	well
Qundao / *Chin.*	archipelago
Qūr / *Ar.*	height, hill
Qytet / *Alb.*	city, town
Qyteti / *Alb.*	city, town

R

Local Form	English
R., Rio, River / *Eng.; Sp.*	river
Rada / *It.; Sp.*	anchorage
Rade / *Fr.*	anchorage
Rags / *Latv.*	cape
Rahad / *Ar.*	lake, pond
Rajon / *Rus.*	district
Rak / *Fle.; Dut.*	strait
Rakai / *Poly.*	reef
Ramla / *Ar.*	sand
Rancho / *Port.; Sp.*	farm, ranch
Rand / *Afr.; Germ.*	escarpment
Range / *Eng.*	mountain range
Rann / *Urdu*	marsh
Rano / *Malag.*	water
Ranta / *Finn.*	bank, beach
Rapide / *Fr.*	rapids
Ras / *Amh.*	peak
Rās / *Ar.*	point, cape

Local Form	English
Ras, Râs / *Ar.*	promontory, peak
Rāsiga / *Som.*	promontory
Rass / *Ar.*	promontory, peak
Rassa / *Lapp.*	mountain
Ráth / *Gae.*	castle
Raunina / *Bulg.; Rus.*	plain
Raz / *Fr.*	strait
Razliv / *Rus.*	flood plain
Récif / *Fr.*	reef
Recife / *Port.*	reef
Reede / *Germ.; Dut.; Slvn.*	anchorage
Reek / *Afr.; Gae.*	mountain range
Reg / *Pash.*	dunes
Région / *Fr.*	region
Rei / *Port.*	king
Reka / *Bulg.; Rus.; S.C.; Slvn.*	river
Řeka / *Cz.*	river
Réma / *Gr.*	torrent
Renne / *Dan.; Nor.*	deep
Reprêsa / *Port.*	dam, reservoir
Represa / *Sp.*	dam, reservoir
República / *Port.; Sp.*	republic
République / *Fr.*	republic
Rés., Réservoir / *Fr.*	reservoir
Res., Reservoir / *Eng.*	reservoir
Réservoir, Rés. / *Fr.*	reservoir
Reshteh / *Pers.*	mountain range
Respublika / *Rus.*	republic
Restinga / *Port.*	cliff, sandbank
Retsugan / *Jap.*	reef
Rettō / *Jap.*	archipelago
Rev / *Dan.; Nor.; Swed.*	reef
Rey / *Sp.*	king
Ri / *Tib.*	mountain
Ria / *Sp.*	estuary
Riacho / *Port.*	stream
Rialto / *It.*	plateau
Rialto / *It.*	rise
Riba / *Port.*	bank
Ribeira / *Port.*	river
Ribeirão / *Port.*	stream
Ribeiro / *Port.*	stream
Ribera / *Sp.*	coast
Ribnik / *Slvn.*	pond
Rid / *Bulg.*	mountain range
Rif / *Icel.*	cliff
Riff / *Germ.*	reef
Rīg / *Pash.*	dunes
Rijeka / *S.C.*	river
Rimāl / *Ar.*	sand desert
Rincón / *Sp.*	peninsula between two rivers
Ring / *Tib.*	long
Rinne / *Germ.*	trench
Rio / *Port.*	river
Río, R. / *Sp.*	river
Riu / *Rom.*	river
Riva / *It.*	bank
Rive / *Fr.*	bank
Rivera / *Sp.*	brook, stream
Rivier, -rivier / *Afr.; Dut.; Fle.*	river
Riviera / *It.*	coast
Rivière / *Fr.*	river
Roads / *Eng.*	anchorage
Roc / *Fr.*	rock
Roca / *Port.; Sp.*	rock
Rocca / *It.*	castle
Roche / *Fr.*	rock
Rocher / *Fr.*	rock
Rock / *Eng.*	rock
Rod / *Pash.*	river
Rode / *Germ.*	tilled soil
Rodnik / *Rus.*	spring
Rog / *Rus.; S.C.; Slvn.*	peak
Roi / *Fr.*	king
Rojo / *Sp.*	red
Roque / *Sp.*	rock
Rot / *Germ.*	red
Roto / *Poly.*	lake
Rouge / *Fr.*	red
Równina / *Pol.*	plain
Rt / *S.C.; Slvn.*	cape
Ru / *Tib.*	mountain
Ruck / *Germ.*	ridge
Rücken / *Germ.*	ridge
Rud / *Pers.*	river
Ruda / *Cz.; Slvk.*	mine
Ruda / *Pol.*	ore
Rūdbār / *Pers.*	river
Rudha / *Gae.*	point
Rudnik / *Rus.; S.C.; Slvn.*	mine
Rug / *Fle.; Dut.*	ridge
Ruggen / *Afr.*	ridge
Ruina / *Sp.*	ruins
Ruine / *Fr.; Dut.; Germ.*	ruins
Rujm / *Ar.*	hill
Run / *Eng.*	stream

S

Local Form	English
S., See / *Germ.*	lake, sea
Saar / *Est.*	island
Saari / *Finn.*	island
Sabbia / *It.*	sand
Sabkhat / *Ar.*	salt flat, salt marsh
Sable / *Fr.; Eng.*	beach
Sacca / *It.*	anchorage
Saco / *Port.*	bay
Sad / *Cz.; Slvk.*	park
Sad / *Pers.*	wall
Sadd / *Ar.; Pers.*	cataract, dam
Safīd / *Pash.; Urdu; Hin.*	white
Şafrā' / *Ar.*	desert
Sāgar / *Hin.*	reservoir
Saguia / *Ar.*	irrigation canal
Sahara / *Ar.*	desert
Sahel / *Ar.*	plain, coast
Sahr / *Iran.*	city, town
Şaḩrā' / *Ar.*	desert
Said / *Ar.*	sweet
Saj / *Alt.*	stream, valley
Saki / *Jap.*	point
Sala / *Latv.; Lith.*	island
Saladillo / *Sp.*	salt desert
Salar / *Sp.*	salt lake
Sale / *Ural.*	village
Salina / *It.; Sp.*	salt flat, salt marsh
Saline / *Dut.; Fr.; Germ.*	salt flat, salt marsh
Salmi / *Finn.*	strait
Salseleh-ye Kūh / *Pers.*	mountain range
Salto / *Port.; Sp.*	waterfall, rapids
Salz / *Germ.*	salt
Samudera / *Indon.*	ocean
Samudra / *Hin.*	lake
Samut / *Thai*	sea
San / *Jap.; Kor.*	mountain
San / *It.; Sp.*	saint
Sanchi / *Jap.*	mountain range
Sand / *Dan.; Eng.; Nor.; Swed.; Germ.*	beach
Šand / *Mong.*	spring
Sandur / *Icel.*	sand
Sank / *Pers.*	rock
Sankt, St. / *Germ.; Swed.*	saint
Sanmaeg / *Kor.*	mountain range
Sanmyaku / *Jap.*	mountain range
Sansanné / *Sud.*	campsite
Santo / *It.; Port.; Sp.*	saint
Santuario / *It.*	sanctuary
São / *Port.*	saint
Sar / *Pers.*	cape; peak
Šar / *Rus.; Tur.*	strait
Saraf / *Ar.*	well
Sari / *Finn.*	island
Sari / *Tur.*	yellow
Sarīr / *Ar.*	rocky desert
Sary / *Tur.*	yellow
Sasso / *It.*	stone
Sat / *Rom.*	village
Sattel / *Germ.*	pass
Saurum / *Latv.*	strait
Schleuse / *Germ.*	lock
Schloß / *Germ.*	castle
Schlucht / *Germ.*	gorge
Schnee / *Germ.*	snow
Schwarz / *Germ.*	black
Scoglio / *It.*	cliff
Se / *Jap.*	bank, shoal
Sebkha / *Ar.*	salt flat
Sebkhet / *Ar.*	salt flat
Sed / *Ar.*	dam
Seda / *Ural.*	mountain
See, S. / *Germ.*	lake, sea
Sefra / *Ar.*	yellow
Segara / *Indon.*	lagoon
Şehir / *Tur.*	city, town
Seki / *Jap.*	dam
Selat / *Mal.; Indon.*	strait
Selatan / *Indon.*	southern
Selkä / *Finn.*	ridge, lake
Sella / *It.*	pass
Selo / *Bulg.; Rus.; S.C.; Slvn.*	village
Selsela Kohe / *Pers.*	mountain range
Selva / *It.; Sp.*	forest
Semenanjung / *Mal.*	peninsula
Sen / *Jap.*	mountain
Seong / *Kor.*	castle
Sep / *Alt.*	canal
Serīr / *Ar.*	rocky desert
Serra / *Cat.; Port.*	mountain range
Serra / *It.*	mountain
Serranía / *Sp.*	mountain range
Sertão / *Port.*	steppe
Seto / *Jap.*	strait
Sett., Settentrionale / *It.*	northern
Settentrionale, Sett. / *It.*	northern
Seuil / *Fr.*	sill
Sev / *Arm.*	black
Sever / *Rus.*	north
Severny / *Rus.*	northern
Sfînt / *Rom.*	saint
Sfîntu / *Rom.*	saint
Sgeir / *Gae.*	cliff
Sha'b / *Ar.*	cliff
Shahr / *Pers.; Hin.*	city, town
Sha'īb / *Ar.*	stream
Shallāl / *Ar.*	cataract
Shām / *Ar.*	north; northern
Shamo / *Chin.*	sand desert
Shan / *Chin.*	mountain, mountain range
Shan / *Gae.*	old
Shand / *Mong.*	spring
Shankou / *Chin.*	pass
Shaqq / *Ar.*	wadi
Sharm / *Ar.*	bay
Sharqī / *Ar.*	east, eastern
Sharqīyah / *Ar.*	eastern
Shatt / *Ar.*	river, salt lake
Shatt / *Tur.*	stream
Shën / *Alb.*	saint
Sheng / *Chin.*	province
Shi / *Chin.*	city, town
Shibīn / *Ar.*	village
Shih / *Chin.*	rock
Shima / *Jap.*	island
Shimo / *Jap.*	lower
Shin / *Jap.*	new
Shō / *Jap.*	island
Shotō / *Jap.*	archipelago
Shū / *Jap.*	administrative division
Shui / *Chin.*	river
Shuiku / *Chin.*	reservoir
Shur / *Pers.*	salt
Sidhiros / *Gr.*	iron
Sidi / *Ar.*	master
Sieben / *Germ.*	seven
Sierra / *Sp.*	mountain range
Sikt / *Ural.*	village
Sillon / *Fr.*	furrow
Šine / *Mong.*	new
Sink / *Eng.*	depression
Sinn / *Ar.*	point
Sint / *Dut.; Fle.*	saint
Sirt / *Tur.*	mountain range
Sirtlar / *Tur.*	mountain range
Sistema / *It.; Sp.*	mountain system
Sīyāh / *Pers.*	black
Sjø / *Nor.*	lake
Sjö / *Swed.*	lake, sea
Skag / *Icel.*	peninsula
Skala / *Bulg.; Rus.*	rock
Skála / *Slvk.*	rock
Skar / *Nor.*	pass
Skär / *Swed.*	cliff
Skeir / *Gae.*	cliff
Skerry / *Gae.*	cliff
Skog / *Nor.; Swed.*	forest
Skóg / *Icel.*	forest
Skov / *Dan.; Nor.*	forest
Slatina / *S.C.; Slvn.*	mineral water
Slätt / *Swed.*	plain
Slieve / *Gae.*	mountain
Slot / *Dut.; Fle.*	castle
Slott / *Nor.; Swed.*	castle
Slough / *Eng.*	creek, pond, marsh
Sluis / *Dut.; Fle.*	sluice
Små / *Swed.*	little
Sne / *Nor.*	snow
Sneeuw / *Afr.; Dut.*	snow
Snežny / *Rus.*	snowy
Snø / *Nor.*	snow
So / *Kor.*	little
Sø / *Dan.; Nor.*	lake; sea
So / *Ural.*	passage
Söder / *Swed.*	south
Södra / *Swed.*	southern
Solončak / *Rus.*	salt flat
Sommet / *Fr.*	peak
Son / *Viet.*	mountain
Sønder / *Dan.; Nor.*	southern
Søndre / *Dan.*	southern
Sone / *Jap.*	bank
Song / *Viet.*	river
Sopka / *Rus.*	volcano
Sopočnik / *Rus.*	mountain system
Soprana / *It.*	upper
Šor, Sor / *Alt.*	salt marsh
Sos / *Sp.*	upon
Sotavento / *Sp.*	leeward
Sotoviento / *Sp.*	leeward
Sottana / *It.*	lower
Souk / *Ar.*	market
Souq / *Ar.*	market
Sour / *Ar.*	rampart
Source / *Eng.; Fr.*	spring
Souto / *Port.*	forest
Spitze / *Germ.*	peak
Spruit / *Afr.*	current
Sreden / *Bulg.*	central
Sredni / *Rus.*	central
Średni / *Pol.*	central
Srednji / *S.C.; Slvn.*	central
St., Saint, Sankt / *Eng.; Fr.; Germ.; Swed.*	saint
Stadhur / *Icel.*	city, town
Stadt, -stadt / *Germ.*	city, town
Stag / *Eng.*	city, town
Stagno / *It.*	pond
-stan / *Hin.; Pers.; Urdu*	land
Star / *Bulg.*	old
Stari / *S.C.; Slvn.*	old
Stary / *Pol.; Rus.*	old
Starý / *Cz.; Slvk.*	old
Stat / *Afr.; Dan.; Fle.; Nor.; Dut.; Swed.*	city, town
Stathmós / *Gr.*	railway station
Stausee / *Germ.*	reservoir
Stavrós / *Gr.*	cross
Sted / *Dan.; Nor.*	place
Stedt / *Germ.*	place
Stein, -stein / *Nor.; Germ.*	stone
Sten / *Nor.; Swed.*	stone
Stena / *S.C.; Slvn.*	rock
Stěna / *Cz.*	mountain range
Stenón / *Gr.*	strait, pass
Step / *Rus.*	steppe
-sthān / *Hin.; Pers.; Urdu*	land
Stift / *Germ.*	foundation
Štít / *Cz.; Slvk.*	peak
Stock / *Germ.*	massif
Stok / *Pol.*	slope
Stor / *Dan.; Nor.; Swed.*	great
Store / *Dan.*	great
Stræde / *Dan.*	strait
Strana / *Rus.*	land
Strand / *Germ.; Nor.; Swed.; Afr.; Dan.*	beach
Straße / *Germ.*	street, road
Strath / *Gae.*	valley
Straum / *Nor.; Swed.*	stream
Střední / *Cz.*	central
Stredný / *Slvk.*	central
Strelka / *Rus.*	spit
Stret / *Nor.*	strait
Stretto / *It.*	strait
Strom / *Germ.*	stream
Strøm / *Nor.*	stream
Ström / *Swed.*	stream
Stroom / *Dut.*	stream
Su / *Jap.*	sandbank
Su / *Tur.*	river
Suando / *Finn.*	pond
Suid / *Afr.*	south
Suidō / *Jap.*	strait
Sul / *Port.*	south
Sund / *Dan.; Nor.; Swed.; Germ.*	strait
Sungai / *Mal.*	river
Sunn / *Nor.*	south
Sūq / *Ar.*	market
Sur / *Fr.*	on
Sur / *Sp.*	south
Surkh / *Pers.*	red
Suu / *Finn.*	mouth, river mouth
Suur / *Cat.*	great
Svart / *Nor.; Swed.*	black
Sveti / *S.C.; Slvn.*	saint
Swa / *Ban.*	great
Swart / *Afr.*	black
Święty / *Pol.*	saint
Syrt / *Alt.*	ridge
Szállás / *Hung.*	village
Szczyt / *Pol.*	peak
Szeg / *Hung.*	bend
Székes / *Hung.*	residence
Szent / *Hung.*	saint
Sziget / *Hung.*	river island

T

Local Form	English
Tadi / *Ban.*	rock, cliff
Tae / *Kor.*	great
Tafua / *Poly.*	mountain
Tag / *Alt.; Tur.*	mountain
Tahta / *Ar.*	lower
Tahti / *Ar.*	lower
Tai / *Chin.; Jap.*	great
Taipale / *Finn.*	isthmus
Tajga / *Rus.*	forest
Take / *Jap.*	mountain
Tal / *Germ.*	valley
Tala / *Mong.*	plain, steppe
Tala / *Ber.*	spring
Tall / *Ar.*	hill
Talsperre / *Germ.*	dam
Tam / *Viet.*	stream
Tamgout / *Ber.*	peak
Tan / *Chin.; Kor.*	sandbank
Tana / *Malag.*	city, town
Tanana / *Malag.*	city, town
Tandjung / *Mal.*	cape, point
Tanezrouft / *Ber.*	desert
Tang / *Tib.*	upland
Tangeh / *Pers.*	strait
Tanjong / *Mal.*	cape, point
Tanjung, Tg. / *Indon.*	cape, point
Tanout / *Ber.*	well
Tao / *Chin.*	island
Taourirt / *Ber.*	peak
Targ / *Pol.*	market
Tărg / *Bulg.*	market
Tarn / *Eng.*	glacial lake
Tarso / *Sah.*	crater
Taš / *Alt.*	stone

Local Form	English
Tassili / *Ber.*	upland
Tau / *Tur.*	mountain
Taung / *Burm.*	mountain
Ṭawīl / *Ar.*	hill
Tégi / *Sah.*	hill
Teguidda / *Ber.*	well
Tehi / *Ber.*	pass, mountain
Teich / *Germ.*	pond
Tell / *Tur.*	hill
Telok / *Mal.*	bay, port
Teluk / *Mal.*	bay, port
Tempio / *It.*	temple
Ténéré / *Ber.*	rocky desert
Tengah / *Indon.; Mal.*	central
Tepe / *Tur.*	hill
Tepesi / *Tur.*	hill
Termas / *Sp.*	thermal springs
Terme / *It.*	thermal springs
Terra / *It.; Dut.*	land, earth
Terrazzo / *It.*	guyot, tablemount
Terre / *Fr.*	land, earth
Teso / *Cat.*	hill
Téssa / *Ber.*	wadi, depression
Testa / *It.*	point
Tête / *Fr.*	peak
Tetri / *Georg.*	white
Teu / *Poly.*	reef
Teze / *Alt.*	new
Tg., Tanjung / *Indon.*	cape, point
Thaba / *Ban.*	mountain
Thabana / *Ban.*	mountain
Thal / *Germ.*	valley
Thálassa / *Gr.*	sea
Thale / *Thai*	lagoon
Thamad / *Ar.*	well
Theós / *Gr.*	god
Thermes / *Fr.*	thermal springs
Thog / *Tib.*	high, upper
Tian / *Chin.*	field
Tiefe / *Germ.*	deep
Tierra / *Sp.*	land, earth
Timur / *Indon.; Mal.*	eastern
Tind / *Nor.*	mountain
Tinto / *Sp.*	black
Tirg / *Rom.*	market
Tis / *Amh.*	new
Tizgui / *Ber.*	forest
Tizi / *Ber.*	pass
Tjåkko / *Lapp.*	mountain
Tjärn / *Swed.*	tarn, glacial lake
Tji / *Mal.*	stream
To / *Kor.*	island
To / *Mel.*	stream
Tō / *Jap.*	island
Tó / *Hung.*	lake
To / *Ural.*	lake
Tobe / *Tur.*	hill
Tofua / *Poly.*	mountain
Tog / *Som.*	valley
Tōge / *Jap.*	pass
Tokoj / *Alt.*	forest
Tônle / *Khm.*	stream, lake
Tope / *Dut.*	peak
Toplice / *S.C.; Slvn.*	thermal springs
Topp / *Nor.*	peak
Tor / *Gae.*	rock
Tor / *Germ.*	gate
Torbat / *Pers.*	tomb
Törl / *Germ.*	pass
Torp / *Swed.*	hut
Torre / *Cat.; It.; Sp.; Port.*	tower
Torrente / *It.; Sp.*	torrent, stream
Tossa / *Cat.*	mountain, peak
Tota / *Sin.*	port
Tour / *Fr.*	tower
Traforo / *It.*	tunnel
Träsk / *Swed.*	lake
Trg / *S.C.*	market
Trog / *Germ.*	trough, trench
Trois / *Fr.*	three
Trung / *Viet.*	central
Tse / *Tib.*	peak, point
Tsi / *Chin.*	pond
Tskali / *Georg.*	river
Tsu / *Jap.*	bay
Tulūl / *Ar.*	hills
Tünel / *Pers.*	tunnel
Tunturi / *Lapp.*	mountain, tundra
Tur'ah / *Ar.*	irrigation canal
Turm / *Germ.*	tower
Turn / *Rom.*	tower
Turó / *Cat.*	dome
Tuz / *Tur.*	salt
Týn / *Cz.*	fortress

U

Local Form	English
U., Unter-, Upon / *Eng.; Germ.*	under, lower
Uaimh / *Gae.*	cave
Uchi / *Jap.*	bay
Udde / *Swed.*	cape
Údolní nádrž / *Cz.*	reservoir
Uebi / *Som.*	river
Új- / *Hung.*	new
Ujście / *Pol.*	mouth
Ujung / *Indon.*	point, cape
Ul / *Chin.; Mong.*	mountain, mountain range
Ula / *Mong.*	mountain range
Ulan / *Mong.*	red
Uls / *Mong.*	state
Umi / *Jap.*	bay
Umm / *Ar.*	mother, spring
Umne / *Mong.*	south
Under / *Mong.*	mountain, peak
Ungur / *Alt.*	cave
Unter-, U. / *Germ.*	under, lower
Upar / *Hin.*	river
'Uqlat / *Ar.*	well
Ūr / *Tam.*	city, town
Ura / *Jap.*	bay, coast
Ura / *Alt.*	depression
Urd / *Mong.*	south
Uru / *Tam.*	city, town
Ušće / *S.C.*	mouth
Uske / *Alt.*	upper
Ust / *Rus.*	mouth
Ústí / *Cz.*	mouth
Ustup / *Rus.*	terrace
Utan / *Indon.; Mal.*	forest
Utara / *Indon.*	north, northern
Uusi / *Finn.*	new
Uval / *Rus.*	height
Úval / *Cz.*	mountain
'Uwaynāt / *Ar.*	well
Uzboj / *Alt.*	river bed
Uzun / *Tur.*	long
Užūrekis / *Lith.*	gulf

V

Local Form	English
Va / *Alb.*	ford
Va / *Ural.*	water, river
Vaara / *Finn.*	mountain
Väärti / *Finn.*	bay
Vad / *Rom.*	ford
Vær / *Nor.*	port
Våg / *Nor.*	bay
Vähä / *Finn.*	little
Väike / *Est.*	little
Väin / *Est.*	strait
Val / *Fr.; It.*	valley
Val / *Rom.; Rus.*	wall
Valico / *It.*	pass
Vall / *Cat.*	valley
Vall / *Swed.*	pasture
Valle / *It.; Sp.*	valley
Vallée / *Fr.*	valley
Vallei / *Afr.*	valley
Vallo / *It.*	wall
Valta / *Finn.*	cape
Váltos / *Gr.*	marsh
Valul / *Rom.*	wall
Vann / *Dan.; Nor.*	water, lake
Vanua / *Mel.*	land
Vár / *Hung.*	fort
Vara / *Finn.*	mountain
Varoš / *S.C.*	city, town
Város / *Hung.*	city, town
Varre / *Lapp.*	mountain
Vary / *Cz.*	spring
Vas / *S.C.; Slvn.*	village
Vásár / *Hung.*	market
Väst / *Swed.*	west
Väster / *Swed.*	western
Vatn / *Icel.; Nor.*	lake
Vatten / *Swed.*	water, lake
Vatu / *Mel.; Poly.*	island, reef
Vdhr., Vodohranilišče / *Rus.*	reservoir
Vechiu / *Rom.*	old
Vecs / *Latv.*	old
Veen / *Dut.; Fle.*	moor
Vega / *Sp.*	irrigated crops
Veld / *Afr.; Dut.; Fle.*	field
Veli / *S.C.; Slvn.*	great
Velik / *Bulg.*	great
Veliki / *Rus.; S.C.; Slvn.*	great
Veliký / *Cz.*	great
Velký / *Cz.*	great
Vel'ky / *Slvk.*	great
Vella / *Cat.*	old
Ver / *Ural.*	forest
Verde / *It.; Sp.*	green
Verh / *Rus.*	peak
Verhni / *Rus.*	upper
Verk / *Swed.*	factory
Vermelho / *Port.*	red
Vert / *Fr.*	green
Ves / *Cz.*	village
Vesi / *Finn.*	water, lake
Vest / *Dan.; Nor.*	west
Vester / *Dan.; Nor.*	western
Vestur / *Icel.*	west
Vetta / *It.*	summit
Viaduc / *Fr.*	viaduct
Vidda / *Nor.*	upland
Vidde / *Nor.*	upland
Viejo / *Sp.*	old
Vier / *Germ.*	four
Viertel / *Germ.*	quarter
Vieux / *Fr.*	old
Vig / *Dan.*	bay
Vik / *Icel.; Nor.; Swed.*	gulf, bay
Vila / *Port.*	city, town
Villa / *Sp.*	city, town
Ville, -ville / *Eng.; Fr.*	city, town
Vinh / *Viet.*	bay
Virful / *Rom.*	peak, mountain
Virta / *Finn.*	river
Višni / *Rus.*	high
Visok / *S.C.*	high
Víz / *Hung.*	water
Víztároló / *Hung.*	reservoir
Vlakte / *Dut.; Fle.*	plain
Vlei / *Afr.*	pond
Vliet / *Dut.; Fle.*	river
Vloer / *Afr.*	depression
Voda / *Bulg.; Cz.; Rus.; S.C.; Slvn.*	water
Vodny put / *Rus.*	stream, canal
Vodohranilišče, vdhr. / *Rus.*	reservoir
Vodopad / *Rus.*	waterfall
Volcan / *Fr.*	volcano
Volcán / *Sp.*	volcano
Voll / *Nor.*	meadow
Vórios / *Gr.*	northern
Vorota / *Rus.*	gate
Vorrás / *Gr.*	north
Vostočny / *Rus.*	eastern
Vostok / *Rus.*	east
Vötn / *Icel.*	lake, water
Vož / *Ural.*	mouth
Vozvyšennost / *Rus.*	upland
Vpadina / *Rus.*	depression
Vrah / *Bulg.*	peak
Vrata / *Bulg.; S.C.; Slvn.*	pass
Vrch / *Cz.; Slvk.*	mountain
Vrch / *S.C.; Slvn.*	peak
Vrchni- / *Cz.*	upper
Vrchovina / *Cz.*	upland
Vulcan / *Rom.; Rus.*	volcano
Vulcano / *It.*	volcano
Vulkan / *Germ.; Rus.*	volcano
Vuopio / *Lapp.*	bend
Vuori / *Finn.*	rock
Východný / *Cz.*	eastern
Vyšný / *Slvk.*	upper
Vysoki / *Rus.*	high
Vysoky / *Cz.; Slvk.*	high
Vyšši / *Cz.*	high

W

Local Form	English
W., Wādī / *Ar.*	wadi
Wa / *Ban.*	people
Wabe / *Amh.*	stream
Wad / *Ar.*	wadi
Wad / *Dut.*	tidal flat
Wādī, W. / *Ar.*	wadi
Wāḥāt / *Ar.*	oasis
Wai / *Mel.; Poly.*	stream
Wal / *Afr.*	wall
Wala / *Hin.*	mountain range
Wald / *Germ.*	forest
Wan / *Burm.*	village
Wan / *Chin.; Jap.*	bay
Wand / *Germ.*	bluff
War / *Som.*	pond
Wār / *Ar.*	desert
-waram / *Hin.; Tam.*	village
Wasser / *Germ.*	water
Wat / *Pol.*	wall
Wat / *Thai*	church
Waterval / *Afr.; Dut.*	waterfall
Watt / *Germ.*	tidal flat
Wāw / *Ar.*	oasis
Weald / *Eng.*	wooded country
Webi / *Som.*	stream
Weg / *Germ.*	way, road
Wei / *Chin.*	cape, point
Weide / *Germ.*	pasture
Weiler / *Germ.*	village
Weiß / *Germ.*	white
Weon / *Kor.*	field
Wer / *Som.*	pond
Werder / *Germ.*	river island
Werk / *Germ.*	factory
Wes / *Afr.*	west
Westlich / *Germ.*	western
Westr- / *Sca.*	western
Wēyn / *Som.*	great
Wēyne / *Som.*	great
Wick / *Eng.*	village
Wiek / *Germ.*	bay
Wielki / *Pol.*	great
Wieś / *Pol.*	village
Wijk / *Dut.; Fle.*	quarter, district
-willer / *Germ.*	village
Woda / *Pol.*	water
Woestyn / *Afr.*	desert
Wold / *Dut.; Fle.; Eng.*	forest
Wörth / *Germ.*	river island
Woud / *Dut.; Fle.*	forest
Wschodni / *Pol.*	eastern
Wysoczyzna / *Pol.*	upland
Wysoki / *Pol.*	upper
Wyspa / *Pol.*	island
Wyżyna / *Pol.*	highland
Wzgórze / *Pol.*	hill

X

Local Form	English
Xi / *Chin.*	west
Xia / *Chin.*	gorge, strait
Xian / *Chin.*	county, shire
Xiang / *Chin.*	village
Xiao / *Chin.*	little
Xin / *Chin.*	new
Xu / *Chin.*	island

Y

Local Form	English
Yam / *Hebr.*	lake, sea
Yama / *Jap.*	mountain
Yan / *Chin.*	mountain
Yang / *Chin.*	strait, ocean
Yani / *Tur.*	new
Yar / *Tur.*	gorge
Yarimada / *Tur.*	peninsula
Yazı / *Tur.*	plain
Yegge / *Sah.*	well
Yeni / *Tur.*	new
Yeon / *Kor.*	sea
Yeong / *Kor.*	mountain
Yeşil / *Tur.*	green
Ylä / *Finn.*	upper
Yli- / *Finn.*	upper
Yō / *Jap.*	ocean
Yobe / *Sud.*	great
Yŏm / *Kor.*	island
Yoma / *Burm.*	mountain range
Yŏn / *Kor.*	lake, pond
Yŏng / *Kor.*	mountain, peak
Ytter / *Nor.; Swed.*	outer
Yttre / *Swed.*	outer
Yu / *Chin.*	old
Yu / *Chin.*	island
Yu / *Jap.*	thermal spring
Yüan / *Chin.*	spring, river
Yunhe / *Chin.*	canal

Z

Local Form	English
Zāb / *Ar.*	river
Zachodni / *Pol.*	western
Zaki / *Jap.*	cape
Zalew / *Pol.*	gulf
Zaliv / *Bulg.; Rus.; S.C.; Slvn.*	gulf
Zaljev / *Slvn.*	bay
Zámek / *Cz.*	castle
Zan / *Jap.*	mountain
Zand / *Dut.; Fle.*	sand
Zandt / *Dut.; Fle.*	sand
Zangbo / *Chin.*	river
Zapad / *Rus.*	west
Zapaden / *Bulg.*	western
Zapadni / *S.C.; Slvn.*	western
Západní / *Cz.*	western
Zapadny / *Rus.*	western
Zapovednik / *Rus.*	reserve
Zatoka / *Pol.*	gulf
Zavod / *Rus.*	roadstead
Zāwiyat / *Ar.*	monastery
Zdrój / *Pol.*	thermal springs
Ze / *Jap.*	islet
Zee / *Dut.; Fle.*	sea
Zelëny / *Rus.*	green
Žem / *Lith.*	land, country
Zemé / *Cz.; Slvk.*	land, country
Zemlja / *Rus.*	land
Zen / *Jap.*	mountain
Zhan / *Chin.*	mountain
Zhen / *Chin.*	market
Zhong / *Chin.*	central
Zhou / *Chin.*	quarter, district
Zhuang / *Chin.*	village
Ziemia / *Pol.*	land
Zigos / *Gr.*	pass
Zipfel / *Germ.*	tip, point
Ziwa / *Swa.*	marsh
Zizhiqu / *Chin.*	autonomous region
Zlato / *Bulg.*	gold
Zuid / *Dut.; Fle.*	south
Zuidelijk / *Dut.*	southern
Żuława / *Pol.*	marsh
Zun / *Mong.*	east
Zwart / *Dut.*	black
Zwei / *Germ.*	two

International Map Index

All of the toponyms (place-names) which appear on the maps are listed in the International Map Index. Each entry includes the following: Place-name and, where applicable, other forms by which it is written or known; a symbol, where applicable, indicating what kind of feature it is; the number of the map on which it appears; and the map-reference letters and geographical coordinates indicating its location on the map.

Toponyms

Each toponym, or place-name, is written in full, with accents and diacritical marks. Since many countries have more than one official language, many of these forms are included on the maps. For example, many Belgian place-names are listed as follows: Bruxelles/Brussel; Antwerpen/Anvers, and vice versa, Brussel/Bruxelles; Anvers/Antwerpen. In Italy, certain regions have a special status—they are largely autonomous and officially bilingual. As a result, Index listings appear as follows: Aosta/Aoste; Alto Adige/Sud Tirol, and vice versa. One name, however, may be the only name on the map.

In China, the written forms of commonly used regional languages have been taken into account. These forms are enclosed in parenthesis following the official name: e.g. Xiangshan (Dancheng). However, when the regional is listed first, it is linked to the official name with an→: e.g. Dancheng→Xiangshan. The same style is used for former or historical name forms: e.g. Rhodesia→Zimbabwe and Zimbabwe (Rhodesia).

Place-names for major features (countries, major cities, and large physical features), where applicable, include the English conventional form identified by (EN) and linked in the local name or names with an = sign: e.g. Italia=Italy (EN), and vice versa, Italy (EN)=Italia. Former English names are linked in the Index to the conventional form by an→.

Symbols

The last component with the place-name is a symbol, where applicable, specifying the broad category of the feature named. A table preceding the Index lists all of the symbols used and their meanings; this information also appears as a footnote on each page of the Index. Place-names without symbols are cities and towns.

Alphabetization

Place-names are listed in English alphabetical order—26 letters, from A to Z—because of its international usage. Names including two or more words are listed alphabetically according to the first letter of the word: e.g. De Ruyter is listed under D; Le Havre is listed under L. Names with the prefix Mc are listed as if spelled Mac. The generic portion of a name (lake, sierra, mountain, etc.) is placed after the name: e.g. Lake Erie is listed as Erie, Lake; Sierra Morena is listed as Morena, Sierra. In Spanish, "ch" and "ll" groups and the letter "n" are included respectively under C, L, and N, without any distinction.

The same place-name sometimes is listed in the Index several times. It may because of the various translations of a name, or it may be that several places have the same name.

Various translations of a name appear as follows:

Danube (EN)=Dunav   Danube (EN)=Donau
Danube (EN)=Dunărea   Danube (EN)=Dunaj

Several places with the same name appear as follows; however, only in these cases is the location—abbreviated and enclosed in brackets—included. A table of these abbreviations precedes the Index.

Abbeville [U.S.]   Aberdeen [Scot.-U.K.]
Abbeville [Fr.]   Aberdeen [N.C.-U.S.]
Aberdeen [S. Afr.]

Map Number

Each map in the atlas is identified by a number. Where multiple maps are on one page, each map is additionally identified by a boxed letter in the upper-right-hand corner of the map. In the Index listing following the place-name and its variations in language and spelling, where applicable, is the number of the map on which it appears. If the map is one of several on a page, the Index listing includes the map number and letter.

Although a place-name may appear on one or more maps, it is indexed to only one map. Most places are indexed to the regional maps. However, if a place-name appears on either the physical or political continental maps, it is indexed to one of the two types of map. For example, a river or mountain would be indexed to a physical continental map; a city or state would be indexed to a political continental map.

Map-Reference Letters and Geographical Coordinates

The next elements in the Index listing are the map-reference letters and the geographical coordinates, respectively, locating the place on the map.

Map-reference letters consist of a capital and a lowercase letter. Capital letters are across the top and bottom of the maps; lowercase letters are down the sides. The map-reference letters assigned to each place-name refer to the location of the name within the area formed by grid lines connecting the geographical coordinates on either sides of the letters.

Geographical coordinates are the latitude (N for North, S for South) and longitude (E for East, W for West) expressed in degrees and minutes and based on the prime meridian, Greenwich.

Map-reference letters and coordinates for extensive geographical features, such as mountain ranges and countries, are given for the approximate central point of the area. Those for waterways, such as canals and rivers, are given for the mouth of the river, the point where it enters another river or where the feature reaches the map margin. On this page are sample maps showing points to which features are indexed according to map-reference letters and coordinates.

On most maps there is not enough space to place all of the names of administrative subdivisions. In these cases the location of the place is shown on the map by a circled letter or number and the place-name and circled letter or number are listed in the map margin. The map-reference numbers and coordinates for these places refer to the location of the circled letter or number on the map.

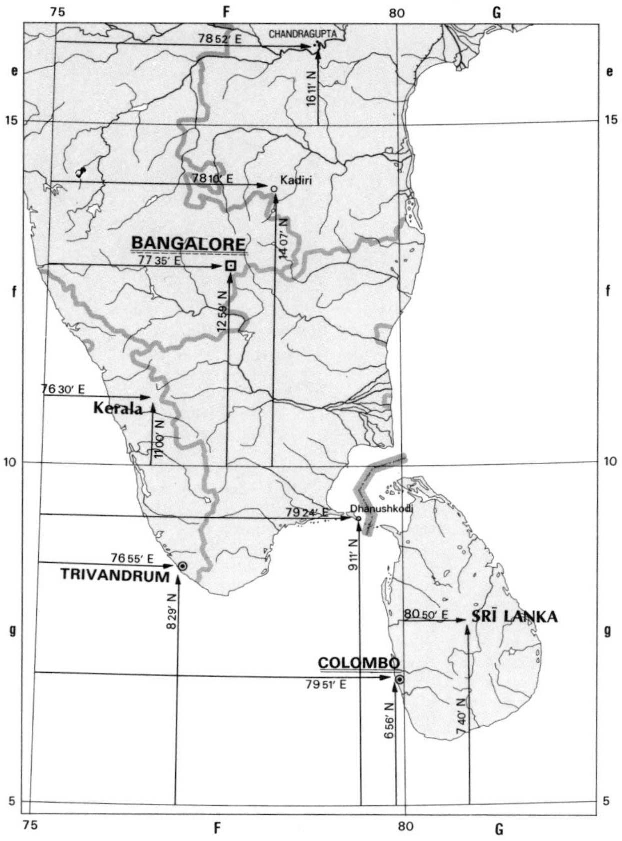

Bangalore	25	Ff	12°59'N	77°35'E
Chandragupta	35	Fe	16°11'N	78°52'E
Colombo	25	Fg	6°56'N	79°51'E
Dhanushkodi	25	Fg	9°11'N	79°24'E
Kadiri	25	Ff	14°07'N	78°10'E
Kerala	25	Ff	11°00'N	76°30'E
Srī Lanka	25	Gg	7°40'N	80°50'E
Trivandrum	25	Fg	8°29'N	76°55'E

Alaska	38	Dc	65°00'N	153°00'W
Alaska, Gulf of-	38	Ed	58°00'N	146°00'W
Alexander Archipelago	38	Fd	56°30'N	134°00'W
Barrow, Point-	38	Db	71°23'N	156°30'W
Bering Strait	38	Cc	65°30'N	169°00'W
Coast Mountains	38	Gd	55°00'N	129°00'W
Kodiak	38	Dd	57°30'N	153°30'W
Yukon	38	Cc	62°33'N	163°59'W

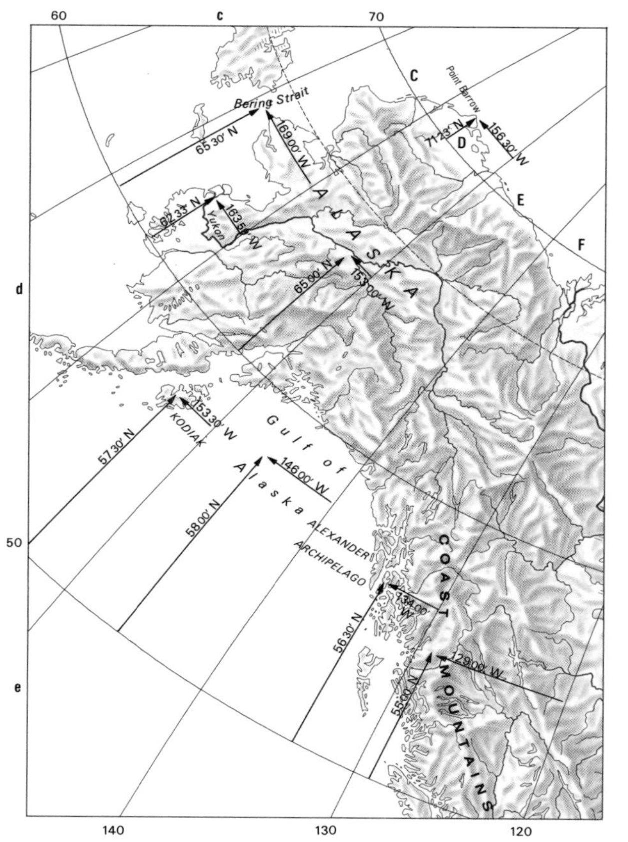

List of Abbreviations

Abz.-U.S.S.R. Azerbaijan S.S.R., U.S.S.R.
Afg. Afghanistan
Afr. Africa
Agl. Anguilla
Ak.-U.S. Alaska, U.S.
Al.-U.S. Alabama, U.S.
Alb. Albania
Alg. Algeria
Alta.-Can. Alberta, Canada
Am. Sam. American Samoa
And. Andorra
Ang. Angola
Ant. Antarctica
Ar.-U.S. Arkansas, U.S.
Arg. Argentina
Arm.-U.S.S.R. Armenian S.S.R., U.S.S.R.
Asia Asia
Atg. Antigua and Barbuda
Aus. Austria
Austl. Australia
Az.-U.S. Arizona, U.S.
Azr. Azores
Bah. Bahamas
Bar. Barbados
B.A.T. British Antarctic Territory
B.C.-Can. British Columbia, Canada
Bel. Belgium
Ben. Benin
Ber. Bermuda
Bhr. Bahrain
Bhu. Bhutan
Blz. Belize
Bnd. Burundi
Bngl. Bangladesh
Bol. Bolivia
Bots. Botswana
Braz. Brazil
Bru. Brunei
Bul. Bulgaria
Bur. Burma
Burkina Burkina Faso
B.V.I. British Virgin Islands
Bye.-U.S.S.R. Byelorussian S.S.R., U.S.S.R.
Ca.-U.S. California, U.S.
Cam. Cameroon
C. Amer. Central America
Can. Canada
Can. Is. Canary Islands
C.A.R. Central African Republic
Cay. Is Cayman Islands
Chad Chad
Chan. Is. Channel Islands
Chile Chile
China China
Co.-U.S. Colorado, U.S.
Cocos Is. Cocos Islands
Col. Colombia
Con. Congo
Cook Cook Islands
Cor. Sea Is. Coral Sea Islands
C.R. Costa Rica
Ct.-U.S. Connecticut, U.S.
Cuba Cuba
C.V. Cape Verde
Cyp. Cyprus
Czech. Czechoslovakia
D.C.-U.S. District of Columbia, U.S.
De.-U.S. Delaware, U.S.
Den. Denmark
Dji. Djibouti
Dom. Dominica
Dom. Rep. Dominican Republic
Ec. Ecuador
Eg. Egypt
El Sal. El Salvador
Eng.-U.K. England, U.K.
Eq. Gui. Equatorial Guinea
Est.-U.S.S.R. Estonian S.S.R., U.S.S.R.
Eth. Ethiopia
Eur. Europe
Falk. Is. Falkland Islands
Far. Is. Faeroe Islands
Fiji Fiji
Fin. Finland
Fl.-U.S. Florida, U.S.
Fr. France
Fr. Gui. French Guiana
Fr. Poly. French Polynesia
F.S.M. Federated States of Micronesia
Ga.-U.S. Georgia, U.S.
Gabon Gabon
Gam. Gambia
Geo.-U.S.S.R. Georgian S.S.R., U.S.S.R.
Ger. Germany
Ghana Ghana
Gib. Gibraltar
Grc. Greece
Gren. Grenada
Grld. Greenland
Guad. Guadeloupe
Guam Guam
Guat. Guatemala
Gui. Guinea
Gui. Bis. Guinea Bissau
Guy. Guyana
Haiti Haiti
Hi.-U.S. Hawaii, U.S.
H.K. Hong Kong
Hond. Honduras
Hun. Hungary
Ia.-U.S. Iowa, U.S.
I.C. Ivory Coast
Ice. Iceland
Id.-U.S. Idaho, U.S.
Il.-U.S. Illinois, U.S.
In.-U.S. Indiana, U.S.
India India
Indon. Indonesia
I. of M. Isle of Man
Iran Iran
Iraq Iraq
Ire. Ireland
Isr. Israel
It. Italy
Jam. Jamaica
Jap. Japan
Jor. Jordan
Kam. Cambodia
Kaz.-U.S.S.R. Kazakh S.S.R., U.S.S.R.
Kenya Kenya
Ker. Is. Kermadec Islands
Kir. Kiribati
Kirg.-U.S.S.R. Kirghiz S.S.R., U.S.S.R.
Ks.-U.S. Kansas, U.S.
Kuw. Kuwait
Ky.-U.S. Kentucky, U.S.
La.-U.S. Louisiana, U.S.
Laos Laos
Lat.-U.S.S.R. Latvian S.S.R., U.S.S.R.
Lbr. Liberia
Leb. Lebanon
Les. Lesotho
Lib. Libya
Liech. Liechtenstein
Lith.-U.S.S.R. Lithuanian S.S.R., U.S.S.R.
Lux. Luxembourg
Ma.-U.S. Massachusetts, U.S.
Mac. Macao
Mad. Madagascar
Mala. Malaysia
Mald. Maldives
Mali Mali
Malta Malta
Man.-Can. Manitoba, Canada
Mar. Is. Marshall Islands
Mart. Martinique
Maur. Mauritius
May. Mayotte
Mco. Monaco
Md.-U.S. Maryland, U.S.
Me.-U.S. Maine, U.S.
Mex. Mexico
Mi.-U.S. Michigan, U.S.
Mid. Is. Midway Islands
Mn.-U.S. Minnesota, U.S.
Mo.-U.S. Missouri, U.S.
Mold.-U.S.S.R. Moldavian S.S.R., U.S.S.R.
Mong. Mongolia
Mont. Montserrat
Mor. Morocco
Moz. Mozambique
Ms.-U.S. Mississippi, U.S.
Mt.-U.S. Montana, U.S.
Mtna. Mauritania
Mwi. Malawi
Nam. Namibia
N. Amer. North America
Nauru Nauru
N.B.-Can. New Brunswick, Canada
Nb.-U.S. Nebraska, U.S.
N.C.-U.S. North Carolina, U.S.
N. Cal. New Caledonia
N.D.-U.S. North Dakota, U.S.
Nep. Nepal
Neth. Netherlands
Neth. Ant. Netherlands Antilles
Newf.-Can. Newfoundland, Canada
N.H.-U.S. New Hampshire, U.S.
Nic. Nicaragua
Nig. Nigeria
Niger Niger
N. Ire.-U.K. Northern Ireland, U.K.
N.J.-U.S. New Jersey, U.S.
N. Kor. North Korea
N.M.-U.S. New Mexico, U.S.
N. M. Is. Northern Mariana Islands
Nor. Norway
Nor. I. Norfolk Island
N.S.-Canada Nova Scotia, Canada
Nv.-U.S. Nevada, U.S.
N.W.T.-Can. Northwest Territories, Canada
N.Y.-U.S. New York, U.S.
N.Z. New Zealand
Ocn. Oceania
Oh.-U.S. Ohio, U.S.
Ok.-U.S. Oklahoma, U.S.
Oman Oman
Ont.-Ont. Ontario, Canada
Or.-U.S. Oregon, U.S.
Pa.-U.S. Pennsylvania, U.S.
Pak. Pakistan
Pal. Palau
Pan. Panama
Pap. N. Gui. Papua New Guinea
Par. Paraguay
Pas. Pascua
P.E.I.-Can. Prince Edward Island, Canada
Peru Peru
Phil. Philippines
Pit. Pitcairn
Pol. Poland
Port. Portugal
P.R. Puerto Rico
Qatar Qatar
Que.-Can. Quebec, Canada
Reu. Reunion
R.I.-U.S. Rhode Island, U.S.
Rom. Romania
R.S.F.S.R.-U.S.S.R. Russian Soviet Federative Socialist Republic, U.S.S.R.
Rwn. Rwanda
S. Afr. South Africa
S. Amer. South America
Sao T.P. Sao Tome and Principe
Sask.-Can. Saskatchewan, Canada
Sau. Ar. Saudi Arabia
S.C.-U.S. South Carolina, U.S.
Scot.-U.K. Scotland, U.K.
S.D.-U.S. South Dakota, U.S.
Sen. Senegal
Sey. Seychelles
Sing. Singapore
S. Kor. South Korea
S.L. Sierra Leone
S. Lan. Sri Lanka
S.M. San Marino
S.N.A. Spanish North Africa
Sol. Is. Solomon Islands
Som. Somalia
Sp. Spain
St. C.N. Saint Christopher-Nevis
St. Hel. Saint Helena
St. Luc. Saint Lucia
St. P.M. Saint Pierre and Miquelon
St. Vin. Saint Vincent and the Grenadines
Sud. Sudan
Sur. Suriname
Sval. Svalbard
Swe. Sweden
Switz. Switzerland
Syr. Syria
Tad.-U.S.S.R. Tajik S.S.R., U.S.S.R.
Tai. Taiwan
Tan. Tanzania
T.C. Is. Turks and Caicos Islands
Thai. Thailand
Tn.-U.S. Tennessee, U.S.
Togo Togo
Ton. Tonga
Trin. Trinidad and Tobago
T.T.P.I. Trust Territory of the Pacific Islands
Tun. Tunisia
Tur. Turkey
Tur.-U.S.S.R. Turkmen S.S.R., U.S.S.R.
Tuv. Tuvalu
Tx.-U.S. Texas, U.S.
U.A.E. United Arab Emirates
Ug. Uganda
U.K. United Kingdom
Ukr.-U.S.S.R. Ukrainian S.S.R., U.S.S.R.
Ur. Uruguay
U.S. United States
U.S.S.R. Union of Soviet Socialist Republics
Ut.-U.S. Utah, U.S.
Uzb.-U.S.S.R. Uzbek S.S.R., U.S.S.R.
Va.-U.S. Virginia, U.S.
Van. Vanuatu
V.C. Vatican City
Ven. Venezuela
Viet. Vietnam
V.I.U.S. Virgin Islands of the U.S.
Vt.-U.S. Vermont, U.S.
Wa.-U.S. Washington, U.S.
Wake Wake Island
Wales-U.K. Wales, U.K.
W.F. Wallis and Futuna
Wi.-U.S. Wisconsin, U.S.
W. Sah. Western Sahara
W. Sam. Western Samoa
W.V.-U.S. West Virginia, U.S.
Wy.-U.S. Wyoming, U.S.
Yem. Yemen
Yugo. Yugoslavia
Yuk.-Can. Yukon, Canada
Zaire Zaire
Zam. Zambia
Zimb. Zimbabwe

List of Symbols

Plains and Associated Features
Plain, Basin, Lowland
Delta
Salt Flat

Valleys and Depressions
Valley, Gorge, Ravine, Canyon
Cave, Crater, Quarry
Karst Features
Depression
Polder, Reclaimed Marsh

Vegetational Features
Desert, Dunes
Forest, Woods
Heath, Steppe, Tundra, Moor
Oasis

Political/Administrative Units
1 Independent Nation
2 State, Canton, Region
3 Province, Department, County, Territory, District
4 Municipality
5 Colony, Dependency, Administered Territory

Geographical Regions
Continent
Physical Region
Historical or Cultural Region

Mountain Features
Mount, Mountain, Peak
Volcano
Hill
Mountains, Mountain Range
Hills, Escarpment
Plateau, Highland, Upland
Pass, Gap

Coastal Features
Cape, Point
Coast, Beach
Cliff
Peninsula, Promontory
Isthmus
Sandbank, Tombolo, Sandbar

Islands Rocks, Reefs
Island
Atoll
Rock, Reef
Islands, Archipelago
Rocks, Reefs
Coral Reef

Hydrographic Features
Well, Spring
Geyser, Fumarole
River, Stream, Brook
Waterfall, Rapids, Cataract
River Mouth, Estuary
Lake
Salt Lake
Intermittent Lake, Dry Lake Bed
Reservoir, Artificial Lake
Swamp, Marsh, Pond
Irrigation Canal, Navigable Canal, Ditch, Aqueduct

Ice Features
Glacier, Snowfield
Ice Shelf, Pack Ice

Marine Features
Ocean
Sea
Gulf, Bay
Strait, Fjord, Sea Channel
Lagoon, Anchorage

Submarine Features
Bank, Shoal
Seamount
Rise, Plateau, Tablemount
Seamount Chain, Ridge
Platform, Shelf
Basin, Depression
Escarpment, Slope, Sea Scarp
Fracture
Trench, Abyss, Valley, Canyon

Other Features
National Park, Nature Reserve
Scenic Area, Point of Interest
Recreation Site, Sports Arena
Cave, Cavern
Historic Site, Memorial, Mausoleum, Museum
Ruins
Wall, Walls, Tower, Castle, Fortress
Church, Abbey, Cathedral, Sanctuary
Temple, Synagogue, Mosque
Research or Scientific Station
Airport, Heliport
Port, Dock
Lighthouse
Mine
Tunnel
Dam, Bridge

A

Name	Map	Grid	Lat.	Long.
Å	7	Cc	67.53N	12.59 E
Aa [Eur.]	12	Ic	51.50N	6.25 E
Aa [Fr.]	11	Ic	51.01N	2.06 E
Aa [Fr.]	12	Dd	50.44N	2.18 E
Aa [Ger.]	12	Kb	52.07N	8.41 E
Aa [Ger.]	12	Jb	52.15N	7.18 E
Aachen	10	Cf	50.46N	6.06 E
Aalen	10	Gh	48.50N	10.06 E
A'ālī an Nīl [3]	35	Ed	9.15N	33.00 E
Aalsmeer	12	Gb	52.15N	1.45 E
Aalst/Alost	11	Kd	50.56N	4.02 E
Aalten	12	Ic	51.55N	6.35 E
Aalter	12	Fc	51.05N	3.27 E
Äänekoski	7	Fe	62.36N	25.44 E
Aa of Weerijs	12	Gc	51.35N	4.46 E
Aar	12	Kd	50.23N	8.00 E
Aarau	14	Cc	47.25N	8.02 E
Aarbergen	12	Kd	50.13N	8.03 E
Aare	14	Cc	47.37N	8.13 E
Aargau [2]	14	Cc	47.30N	8.10 E
Aarlen/Arlon	11	Le	49.41N	5.49 E
Aarschot	11	Kd	50.59N	4.50 E
Aat/Ath	11	Jd	50.38N	3.47 E
Aazanèn	13	Ii	35.06N	3.02W
Āb	24	Md	36.00N	48.05 E
Aba [Nig.]	31	Hh	5.07N	7.22 E
Aba [Zaire]	31	Hk	3.52N	30.14 E
Aba/Ngawa	27	He	32.55N	101.45 E
Abā ad Dūd	24	Ki	27.02N	44.04 E
Abā as Su'ūd	23	Ff	17.28N	44.06 E
Abacaxis, Rio-	54	Gd	3.54S	58.50W
Abaco Island	38	Lg	26.25N	77.10W
Abacou, Pointe l'-	49	Kd	18.03N	73.47W
Abadab. Jabal-	35	Fb	18.53N	35.59 E
Ābādān	22	Gf	30.10N	48.50 E
Ābādeh [Iran]	23	Hc	31.10N	52.37 E
Ābādeh [Iran]	24	Oh	29.08N	52.52 E
Abadiânia	55	Hc	16.06S	48.48W
Abadla	31	Ge	31.01N	2.43W
Abaeté	55	Jd	19.09S	45.27W
Abaeté, Rio-	55	Jd	18.02S	45.12W
Abaetetuba	54	Id	1.42S	48.54W
Abagnar Qi (Xilin Hot)	22	Ne	43.58N	116.08 E
Abag Qi (Xin Hot)	27	Jc	44.01N	114.59 E
Abai	55	Eh	26.01S	55.57W
Abaiang Atoll	57	Id	1.51N	172.58 E
Abaj	19	Hf	49.38N	72.50 E
Abaji	34	Gd	8.28N	6.57 E
Abajo Mountains	46	Kh	37.50N	109.25W
Abakaliki	34	Gd	6.20N	8.03 E
Abakan	20	Ef	53.43N	91.30 E
Abakan	22	Ld	53.43N	91.26 E
Abakwasimbo	36	Eb	0.36N	28.43 E
Abala [Con.]	36	Cc	1.21S	15.30 E
Abala [Niger]	34	Fc	14.56N	3.26 E
Abalak	34	Gb	15.27N	6.17 E
Aban	20	Ee	56.40N	96.10 E
Abancay	54	Df	13.35S	72.55W
Abancourt	12	De	49.42N	1.46 E
Abanga	36	Bb	0.13N	10.28 E
Abano Terme	14	Fe	45.21N	11.47 E
Ābār al Jidd	24	Hf	32.50N	39.50 E
Abarqū	23	Hc	31.08N	53.17 E
Abarqu, Kavīr-e-	24	Og	31.00N	53.50 E
Abashiri	27	Pc	44.01N	144.17 E
Abashiri-Gawa	29a	Db	43.56N	144.09 E
Abashiri-Ko	29a	Da	44.00N	144.10 E
Abashiri-Wan	29a	Da	44.00N	144.35 E
Abasolo	48	Je	24.04N	98.22W
Abatski	19	Hd	56.18N	70.28 E
Abau	60	Dj	10.11S	148.42 E
Abava	7	Eh	57.06N	21.54 E
Abay=Blue Nile (EN)	30	Kg	15.38N	32.31 E
Abaya, Lake-	30	Kh	6.20N	37.55 E
Abaza	20	Ef	52.39N	90.06 E
Abbadia San Salvatore	14	Fh	42.53N	11.41 E
Abbah Quşūr	14	Co	35.57N	8.50 E
Āb Bārīk	24	Oh	29.45N	52.37 E
'Abbāsābād	24	Qd	36.20N	56.25 E
Abbekås	8	Ei	55.24N	13.36 E
Abberton Reservoir	12	Cc	51.50N	0.55 E
Abbeville [Fr.]	11	Hd	50.06N	1.50 E
Abbeville [La.-U.S.]	45	Jl	29.58N	92.08W
Abbeville [S.C.-U.S.]	44	Fh	34.10N	82.23W
Abbey	46	Ka	50.43N	108.45W
Abbeyfeale/Mainistir na Féile	9	Di	52.24N	9.18W
Abbiategrasso	14	Ce	45.24N	8.54 E
Abbot, Mount-	59	Jd	20.03S	147.45 E
Abbot Ice Shelf	66	Pf	72.45S	96.00W
'Abd Al 'Azīz, Jabal-	24	Id	36.25N	40.20 E
'Abd al Kurī	21	Hh	12.12N	52.13 E
Ābdānān	24	Lf	32.57N	47.26 E
Abdul Ghadir	35	Gc	10.42N	42.59 E
Abdulino	19	Fe	53.42N	53.38 E
Abe, Lake-	35	Gc	11.10N	41.45 E
Abéché	31	Jg	13.49N	20.49 E
Abeek	12	Hc	51.15N	6.00 E
Abe-Gawa	29	Fd	34.55N	138.22 E
Abeløya	41	Pc	79.00N	30.15 E
Abelvær	7	Cd	64.44N	11.11 E
Abemama Atoll	57	Id	0.21N	173.51 E
Abenab	37	Bc	19.12S	18.06 E
Abengourou [3]	34	Ed	6.35N	3.25W
Abengourou	31	Gh	6.44N	3.29W
Åbenrå	7	Bi	55.02N	9.26 E
Åbenrå Fjord	8	Ci	55.05N	9.35 E
Abeokuta	31	Hh	7.09N	3.21 E
Āb-e-Pany	23	If	37.06N	68.20 E
Aberayron	9	Ii	52.15N	4.15W
Aberdare Range	30	Ki	0.25S	36.38 E
Aberdeen [Id.-U.S.]	46	Ie	42.57N	112.50W
Aberdeen [Md.-U.S.]	44	If	39.30N	76.14W
Aberdeen [Ms.-U.S.]	45	Lj	33.49N	88.33W
Aberdeen [N.C.-U.S.]	44	Hh	35.08N	79.26W
Aberdeen [S.Afr.]	37	Cf	32.29S	24.03 E
Aberdeen [Scot.-U.K.]	6	Fd	57.10N	2.04W
Aberdeen [S.D.-U.S.]	39	Je	45.28N	98.29W
Aberdeen [Wa.-U.S.]	43	Cb	46.59N	123.50W
Aberdeen Lake	42	Hd	64.28N	99.00W
Abergavenny	9	Kj	51.50N	3.00W
Aberystwyth	9	Ii	52.25N	4.05W
Abetone	14	Ef	44.08N	10.40 E
Abez	19	Gb	66.32N	61.46 E
Abhā	22	Gh	18.13N	42.30 E
Abhainn an Chláir/Clare	9	Dh	53.20N	9.03W
Abhainn an Lagáin/Lagan	9	Hg	54.37N	5.53W
Abhainn na Bandan/Bandon	9	Ej	51.40N	8.30W
Abhainn na Deirge/Derg	9	Fg	54.40N	7.25W
Abhar	24	Md	36.02N	49.45 E
Abhar	23	Gb	36.09N	49.13 E
Abhazskaja ASSR [3]	19	Eg	43.00N	41.10 E
Abibe, Serrania de-	54	Cb	8.00N	76.30W
Abidjan	31	Gh	5.19N	4.02W
Abidjan [3]	34	Ed	5.30N	4.30W
Abilene [Ks.-U.S.]	45	Hg	38.55N	97.13W
Abilene [Tx.-U.S.]	39	Jf	32.27N	99.44W
Abingdon	9	Lj	51.41N	1.17W
Abinsk	16	Kg	44.52N	38.10 E
Abiquiu	45	Ch	36.12N	106.19W
Abiquiu Reservoir	45	Ch	36.18N	106.32W
Abisko	7	Eb	68.20N	18.51 E
Abitibi	42	Jf	51.04N	80.55W
Abitibi, Lake-	38	Le	48.42N	79.45W
Abiy Adi	35	Fc	13.37N	39.01 E
Abiyata, Lake-	35	Fd	7.38N	38.36 E
Abja-Paluoja	8	Kf	58.02N	25.14 E
Abnūb	33	Fd	27.16N	31.09 E
Åbo/Turku	6	Ic	60.27N	22.17 E
Abo, Massif d'-	35	Ba	21.41N	16.08 E
Abóboras, Serra das-	55	Jc	16.12S	44.35W
Abodo	35	Ed	7.50N	34.25 E
Aboisso [3]	34	Ed	5.28N	3.02W
Aboisso	34	Ed	5.28N	3.12W
Abomey	31	Hh	7.11N	1.59 E
Abong Mbang	34	He	3.59N	13.11 E
Abony	10	Pi	47.11N	20.00 E
Aborigen, Pik-	20	Jd	62.05N	149.10 E
Aborlar	26	Ge	9.26N	118.33 E
Aborrebierg	8	Ej	54.59N	12.32 E
Abou Deïa	35	Bc	11.27N	19.17 E
Abou Goulem	35	Cc	13.37N	21.38 E
Abovjan	16	Ni	40.14N	44.37 E
Abrād, Wādī-	23	Gf	15.51N	46.05 E
Abraham's Bay	49	Kb	22.21N	72.55W
Abramovski Bereg	7	Kc	66.25N	43.05 E
Abrántes	13	De	39.28N	8.12W
Abra Pampa	56	Gb	22.43S	65.42W
Abrego	49	Ki	8.04N	73.14W
Abreojos, Punta-	47	Bc	26.42N	113.35W
'Abrī	35	Ea	20.48N	30.20 E
Abrolhos, Arquipélago dos-	54	Kg	18.00S	38.40W
Abrud	15	Gc	46.16N	23.04 E
Abruka, Ostrov-/Abruka Saar	8	Jf	58.08N	22.25 E
Abruka Saar/Abruka, Ostrov-	8	Jf	58.08N	22.25 E
Abruzzi [2]	14	Hh	42.20N	13.45 E
Absaroka Range	43	Fc	44.45N	109.50W
Abtenau	14	Hc	47.33N	13.21 E
Abū, Ḩād, Wādī-	24	Ei	27.46N	33.30 E
Abū ad Duhūr	24	Ge	35.44N	37.02 E
Abū 'Alī	24	Mi	27.20N	49.33 E
Abū al Khaşīb	24	Lg	30.27N	47.59 E
Abū an Na'am	24	Hj	25.14N	38.49 E
Abū 'Arīsh	23	Ff	16.58N	42.50 E
Abū Ballaş	33	Ee	24.26N	27.39 E
Abū Daghmah	24	Hd	36.25N	38.15 E
Abū Darbah	33	Fd	28.29N	33.20 E
Abu Dhabi (EN)=Abū Ẓaby	22	Hg	24.28N	54.22 E
Abū Ḩadrīyah	24	Mi	27.20N	48.58 E
Abū Ḩamad	31	Kg	19.32N	33.19 E
Abū Ḩammād	24	Dg	30.32N	31.40 E
Abū Ḩarbah, Jabal-	24	Ei	27.17N	33.13 E
Abū Ḩashā'ifah, Khalīj-	24	Bg	31.16N	27.25 E
Abuja	31	Hh	9.10N	7.11 E
Abu Jābirah	35	Dc	11.04N	26.51 E
Abū Jifān	24	Lj	24.31N	47.43 E
Abū Kabīr	24	Dg	30.44N	31.40 E
Abū Kamāl	23	Fc	34.27N	40.55 E
Abukuma-Gawa	29	Gb	38.06N	140.52 E
Abukuma-Sanchi	29	Gc	37.20N	140.45 E
Abū Latt	33	Hf	19.58N	40.08 E
Abū Libdah, Khashm-	33	Ie	22.58N	46.13 E
Abū Maţāriq	35	Dc	10.58N	26.17 E
Abu Mendi	35	Fc	11.47N	35.42 E
Abumônbazi	36	Db	3.42N	22.10 E
Abū Muḩarrik, Ghurd-	33	Ed	27.00N	30.00 E
Abū Musā, Jazīreh-ye-	23	Id	25.52N	55.03 E
Abunã	53	Jf	9.42S	65.23W
Abuná, Río-	52	Jf	9.41S	65.23W
Abune Yosef	35	Fc	12.09N	39.12 E
Abū Qīr	24	Dg	31.19N	30.04 E
Abū Qīr, Khalīj-	24	Dg	31.20N	30.15 E
Abū Qumayyis, Ra's-	24	Nj	24.34N	51.30 E
Abu Road	25	Ed	24.29N	72.47 E
Abū Sawmah, Ra's-	24	Ei	26.51N	33.59 E
Abū Shanab	35	Dc	13.57N	27.47 E
Abu Simbel (EN)=Abū Sumbul	33	Fe	22.22N	31.38 E
Abū Şukhayr	24	Kg	31.52N	44.27 E
Abū Sumbul=Abu Simbel (EN)	33	Fe	22.22N	31.38 E
Abuta	28	Pc	42.31N	140.46 E
Abut Head	62	De	43.06S	170.15 E
Abū Tij	33	Fd	27.02N	31.19 E
Abū Ţurţūr, Jabal-	24	Cj	25.20N	30.00 E
Abū'Urūq	35	Eb	15.54N	30.27 E
Abuyemeda	35	Fc	10.38N	39.43 E
Abū Zabad	35	Dc	12.21N	29.15 E
Abū Ẓaby=Abu Dhabi (EN)	22	Hg	24.28N	54.22 E
Abū Zanīmah	33	Fd	29.03N	33.06 E
Abwong	35	Ed	9.07N	32.12 E
Åby	8	Gf	58.40N	16.11 E
Abyaḑ	35	Dc	13.46N	26.28 E
Abyaḑ, Al Baḩr al-=White Nile (EN)	30	Kg	15.38N	32.31 E
Abyaḑ, Al Baḩr al-=White Nile (EN) [3]	35	Ec	12.40N	32.30 E
Abyaḑ, Ar Ra's al-	23	Ee	23.32N	38.32 E
Abyaḑ, Jabal-	35	Db	18.55N	28.40 E
Abyaḑ, Ra's al-=Blanc, Cape- (EN)	30	He	37.20N	9.50 E
Abyār Alī	24	Hj	24.25N	39.33 E
Abyār ash Shuwayrif	33	Bd	29.59N	14.16 E
Åbybro	7	Bh	57.09N	9.45 E
Abydos	33	Fd	26.11N	31.55 E
Abyei	35	Dd	9.36N	28.26 E
Ābyek	24	Nd	36.02N	50.31 E
Abymes	51e	Ab	16.16N	61.31W
Acacías	54	Dc	3.59N	73.47W
Academy Gletscher	41	Ib	81.45N	33.35W
Acadie	38	Me	46.00N	65.00W
Acaill/Achill	9	Dh	54.00N	10.00W
Acajutla	49	Cg	13.36N	89.50W
Acalayong	34	Ge	1.05N	9.40 E
Acámbaro	47	Dd	20.02N	100.44W
Acandí	54	Cb	8.31N	77.17W
Acaponeta	47	Cd	22.30N	105.22W
Acaponeta, Río-	48	Gf	22.20N	105.37W
Acapulco de Juárez	39	Jh	16.51N	99.55W
Acará	54	Id	1.57S	48.11W
Acarai, Serra-	54	Gc	1.50N	57.40W
Acaraú	54	Jd	2.53S	40.07W
Acaray, Río-	55	Eg	25.29S	54.42W
Acari, Rio- [Braz.]	54	Ge	5.18S	59.42W
Acari, Rio- [Braz.]	55	Jb	16.00S	45.03W
Acarigua	54	Eb	9.33N	69.12W
Acatenango, Volcán-	38	Jh	14.30N	91.40W
Acatlán de Osorio	48	Jh	18.12N	98.03W
Acayucan	47	Fe	17.57N	94.55W
Accéglio	14	Af	44.28N	7.00 E
Aččitau, Gora-	18	Cc	42.07N	60.31 E
Accomac	44	Jg	37.43N	75.40W
Accra	31	Gh	5.33N	0.13W
Acebal	55	Bk	33.14S	60.50W
Acebuches	48	Hc	28.15N	102.43W
Aceguá [Braz.]	55	Ej	31.52S	54.09W
Aceguá [Ur.]	55	Ej	31.52S	54.12W
Aceh [3]	26	Cf	4.10N	96.50 E
Acerenza	14	Jj	40.48N	15.56 E
Acerra	14	Ij	40.57N	14.22 E
Achacachi	54	Eg	16.03S	68.43W
Achaguas	54	Eb	7.46N	68.14W
Achaïf, 'Erg-	34	Ea	20.49N	4.34W
Achao	56	Ff	42.28S	73.30W
Achegour	34	Hb	19.03N	11.53 E
Acheng	27	Mb	45.32N	126.56 E
Acheux-en-Amiénois	12	Ed	50.04N	2.32 E
Achiet-le-Grand	12	Ed	50.08N	2.47 E
Achill/Acaill	9	Dh	54.00N	10.00W
Achílleion	15	Cj	39.34N	19.55 E
Achill Head/Ceann Acla	9	Ch	53.59N	10.13W
Achim	10	Fc	53.02N	9.01 E
Achim	35	Bb	15.53N	19.31 E
Achterwasser	10	Jb	54.00N	13.57 E
Acı Gölü	24	Cd	37.50N	29.54 E
Ačinsk	22	Ld	56.17N	90.30 E
Acıpayam	24	Cd	37.25N	29.22 E
Acireale	14	Jm	37.37N	15.10 E
Acîş	15	Fb	47.32N	22.47 E
Ačisaj	18	Gc	43.33N	68.53 E
Ačit	17	Hh	56.48N	57.54 E
Ačit-Nur	27	Fb	49.30N	90.30 E
Acklins	38	Lg	22.25N	74.00W
Acklins, The Bight of-	49	Jb	22.30N	74.15W
Acle	12	Db	52.38N	1.33 E
Acobamba	54	Df	12.48S	74.34W
Acolin	11	Jh	46.49N	3.23 E
Aconcagua [2]	56	Fd	32.15S	70.50W
Aconcagua, Cerro-	52	Ji	32.39S	70.00W
Açor, Serra de-	13	Ed	40.13N	7.48W
Açores=Azores (EN) [5]	31	Ee	38.30N	28.00W
Açores, Arquipélago dos-=Azores (EN)	30	Ee	38.30N	28.00W
Acorizal	55	Db	15.12S	56.22W
Acoyapa	49	Eh	11.58N	85.10W
Acquapendente	14	Fh	42.44N	11.52 E
Acquasanta Terme	14	Hh	42.46N	13.24 E
Acquasparta	14	Gh	42.41N	12.33 E
Acquaviva delle Fonti	14	Kj	40.54N	16.50 E
Acqui Terme	14	Cf	44.41N	8.28 E
Acraman, Lake-	59	Hf	32.05S	135.25 E
Acre [2]	54	Ee	9.00S	70.00W
Acre, Rio-	52	Jf	8.45S	67.22W
Acri	14	Kk	39.29N	16.23 E
Actéon, Groupe-	57	Ng	21.20S	136.30W
Actopan	48	Jg	20.16N	98.56W
Açu	54	Ke	5.34S	36.54W
Acuña	55	Di	29.55S	57.58W
Ada [Ghana]	34	Fd	5.47N	0.38 E
Ada [Ok.-U.S.]	43	He	34.46N	96.41W
Ada [Yugo.]	15	Dd	45.48N	20.08 E
Adaba	35	Fd	7.03N	39.31 E
'Adād	35	Hb	8.23N	46.48 E
'Adādle	35	Gd	9.45N	44.41 E
Adair, Bahia-	48	Cb	31.30N	113.50W
Adair, Cape -	42	Kb	71.31N	71.24W
Adaja	13	Hc	41.32N	4.52W
Adak	40a	Cb	51.45N	176.40W
Adalar	15	Mi	40.52N	29.07 E
'Adale	35	He	2.46N	46.20 E
Ådalen	8	Ga	63.20N	17.30 E
Adalselv	8	Dd	60.04N	10.11 E
Adam, Mount-	56	Hh	51.34S	60.04W
Adamantina	55	Ge	21.42S	51.04W
Adamaoua=Adamawa (EN)	30	Ih	7.00N	15.00 E
Adamawa (EN)=Adamaoua	30	Ih	7.00N	15.00 E
Adamello	14	Ed	46.09N	10.30 E
Adamovka	16	Ud	51.32N	59.59 E
Adams	45	Le	43.58N	89.49W
Adams, Mount-	43	Cb	46.12N	121.28W
Adams Lake	46	Fa	51.13N	119.33W
Adams River	42	Ff	50.54N	119.33W
Adam's Rock	64q	Ab	25.04S	130.05W
Adamstown	58	Ng	25.04S	130.05W
Adamuz	13	Hf	38.02N	4.31W
Adana	22	Ff	37.01N	35.18 E
Adapazarı	24	Db	40.46N	30.24 E
Adarama	35	Eb	17.05N	34.54 E
Adarān, Jabal-	33	Ig	13.46N	45.08 E
Adare, Cape-	66	Kf	71.17S	170.14 E
Adavale	59	Ie	25.55S	144.36 E
Adda [It.]	5	Gf	45.08N	9.53 E
Adda [Sud.]	35	Cd	9.51N	24.50 E
Aḑ Ḑab'ah	33	Ec	31.02N	28.26 E
Ad Dabbah	35	Eb	18.03N	30.57 E
Ad Dafīnah	33	He	23.18N	41.58 E
Aḑ Ḑafrah	24	Ok	23.25N	53.25 E
Ad Dahnā'	21	Gg	24.30N	48.10 E
Addala-Šuhgelmeer, Gora-	16	Oh	42.20N	46.15 E
Aḑ Ḑālī'	33	Hg	13.42N	44.44 E
Ad Damazin	35	Ec	11.49N	34.23 E
Ad 'Dāmir	35	Eb	17.35N	33.58 E
Ad Dammām	22	Hg	26.26N	50.07 E
Ad Dār al Ḩamrā'	23	Ed	27.19N	37.44 E
Ad Dawādimī	23	Fe	24.28N	44.18 E
Ad Dawḩah=Doha (EN)	22	Hg	25.17N	51.32 E
Ad Dawr	24	Je	34.27N	43.47 E
Ad Dayr	33	Fd	25.20N	32.35 E
Ad Dibdibah	24	Lh	28.00N	46.30 E
Aḑ Ḑiffah	33	Ec	30.30N	25.30 E
Ad Dikākah	35	Ib	19.25N	51.30 E
Ad Dılam	23	Ge	23.59N	47.10 E
Ad Dindar	35	Ec	13.20N	34.05 E
Ad Dir'īyah	24	Lj	24.48N	46.32 E
Ad Dissān	33	Hf	16.56N	41.41 E
Addis Zemen	35	Fc	12.05N	37.44 E
Ad Dīwānīya	23	Fc	31.59N	44.56 E
Addu Atoll	21	Jj	0.25S	73.10 E
Ad Du'ayn	35	Dc	11.26N	26.09 E
Ad Duwayd	24	Jg	30.13N	42.18 E
Ad Duwaym	35	Ec	14.00N	32.19 E
Adel [Ga.-U.S.]	44	Fj	31.18N	83.25W
Adel [Or.-U.S.]	46	Fe	42.11N	119.54W
Adelaide [Austl.]	58	Eh	34.56S	138.36 E
Adelaide [Bah.]	44	Im	25.00N	77.31W
Adelaide [S.Afr.]	37	Df	32.42S	26.20 E
Adelaide Island	66	Qe	67.15S	68.30W
Adelaide Peninsula	42	Hc	68.05N	97.50W
Adelaide River	58	Ef	13.15S	131.06 E
Adelaye	35	Cd	7.07N	22.49 E
Adelboden	14	Bd	46.30N	7.33 E
Adèle Island	59	Ec	15.30S	123.10 E
Adélie, Terre-	66	Ie	67.00S	139.00 E
Ademuz	13	Kd	40.04N	1.17W
Aden (EN)=Baladiyat 'Adan	22	Gh	12.46N	45.01 E
Aden, Gulf of-	30	Lg	12.00N	48.00 E
Aden, Gulf of- (EN)='Admēd, Badyarada-	30	Lg	12.00N	48.00 E
Adenau	12	Id	50.23N	6.56 E
Ader	30	Hg	14.10N	5.05 E
Aderbissinat	34	Gb	15.37N	7.52 E
Adhan, Jabal-	24	Qj	25.27N	56.13 E
Adh Dhahībāt	32	Jc	32.01N	10.42 E
Adh Dhayd	24	Pj	25.17N	55.53 E
Adhélfi	15	Gj	39.08N	23.59 E
Adhelfoí	15	Jm	36.25N	26.37 E
'Adhırīyāt, Jıbāl- al-	24	Gg	30.25N	36.48 E
Adi, Pulau-	26	Jg	4.18S	133.26 E
Adiaké	34	Ed	5.16N	3.17W
Adi Arkay	35	Fc	13.31N	38.00 E
Adícora	54	Ea	11.57N	69.48W
Adi Dairo	35	Fc	14.21N	38.12 E
Adigala	35	Gc	10.24N	42.18 E
Adige/Etsch	5	Hf	45.10N	12.20 E
Adigrat	35	Fc	14.16N	39.28 E
Adi Keyeh	35	Fc	14.48N	39.23 E
Adi Kwala	35	Fc	14.37N	38.51 E
Ādilābād	25	Fe	19.40N	78.32 E
Adīrī	31	If	27.30N	13.16 E
Adirondack Mountains	38	Le	44.00N	74.00W
Adis Abeba	31	Kh	9.01N	38.46 E
Adis Alem	35	Fd	9.03N	38.24 E
Adi Ugri	35	Fc	14.53N	38.49 E
Adiyaman	23	Eb	37.46N	38.17 E
Adjud	15	Kc	46.06N	27.10 E
Adjuntas	51a	Bb	18.09N	66.43W
'Admēd, Badyarada-=Aden, Gulf of- (EN)	30	Lg	12.00N	48.00 E
Admer, Erg d'-	32	Ie	24.12N	9.10 E
Admiralty	40	Me	57.50N	134.30W
Admiralty Bay	51n	Ba	13.00N	61.16W
Admiralty Gulf	59	Fb	14.20S	125.50 E
Admiralty Inlet	42	Ib	72.30N	86.00W
Admiralty Islands	57	Fe	2.10S	147.00 E
Admiralty Mountains	66	Kf	71.45S	168.30 E
Admont	14	Ic	47.34N	14.27 E
Ado	34	Fd	6.36N	2.56 E
Ado Ekiti	34	Gd	7.38N	5.13 E
Adok	35	Ed	8.11N	30.19 E
Adolfo Gonzales Chaves	55	Bn	38.02S	60.06W
Adolfo López Mateos, Presa-	48	Fe	25.05N	107.20W
Adonara, Pulau-	26	Hh	8.20S	123.10 E
Ādoni	25	Fe	15.38N	77.17 E
Adra	13	Ih	36.44N	3.01W
Adrano	14	Im	37.40N	14.50 E
Adrar	30	Ff	20.30N	13.30W
Adrar	31	Gf	27.54N	0.17W
Adrar	30	Hf	25.12N	8.10 E
Adrar [Alg.] [3]	32	Gd	27.00N	1.00W
Adrar [Mtna.] [3]	32	Ee	21.00N	11.00W
Adré	35	Cc	13.28N	22.12 E
Adria	14	Ge	45.03N	12.03 E
Adrian	44	Ee	41.54N	84.02W
Adrianópolis	55	Hg	24.41S	48.50W
Adriatic, Deti-=Adriatic Sea (EN)	5	Hg	43.00N	16.00 E
Adriatico, Mar-=Adriatic Sea (EN)	5	Hg	43.00N	16.00 E
Adriatic Sea (EN)=Adriatic, Deti-	5	Hg	43.00N	16.00 E
Adriatic Sea (EN)=Adriatico, Mar-	5	Hg	43.00N	16.00 E
Adriatic Sea (EN)=Jadransko More	5	Hg	43.00N	16.00 E
Aduard	12	Ia	53.15N	6.25 E
Adula	14	Dd	46.30N	9.05 E
Adulis	35	Fb	15.15N	39.37 E
Adur	12	Bd	50.49N	0.16W
Adusa	36	Eb	1.23N	28.01 E
Adventure Bank (EN)	14	Gm	37.20N	12.10 E
Adwa	31	Kg	14.10N	38.55 E
Adyča	21	Pc	68.13N	135.03 E
Adygalah	20	Jd	62.57N	146.25 E
Adygejskaja Avt. Oblast [3]	19	Eg	44.30N	40.05 E
Adžarskaja ASSR [3]	19	Eg	41.40N	42.10 E
Adzopé [3]	34	Ed	6.15N	3.45W
Adzopé	34	Ed	6.06N	3.52W
Adzva	17	Ic	66.36N	59.28 E
Aegean Sea (EN)=Aiyaíon Pélagos	5	Ih	39.00N	25.00 E
Aegean Sea (EN)=Ege Denizi	5	Ih	39.00N	25.00 E
Aegina (EN) = Aiyina	15	Gl	37.40N	23.30 E
Aegviidu	8	Ke	59.17N	25.37 E
Aeon Point	64g	Bb	1.46N	157.11W
Aerfort na Sionainne/Shannon	9	Ei	52.42N	8.57W
Ærø	8	Dj	54.55N	10.20 E
Ærøskøbing	8	Dj	54.53N	10.25 E
Aerzen	12	Lb	52.02N	9.16 E
Afafi, Massif d'-	34	Ha	22.15N	15.00 E
'Afak	24	Kf	32.04N	45.15 E
Afanasjevo	7	Mg	58.54N	53.16 E
Afareaitu	65e	Fc	17.33S	149.47W
Afars and Issas→Djibouti [1]	31	Lg	11.30N	43.00 E
Aff	11	Dg	47.43N	2.07W
Affollé	30	Fg	16.55N	10.25W
Affrica, Scoglio d'-	14	Eh	42.20N	10.05 E
Afghanistan [1]	22	If	33.00N	65.00 E
Afgōye	35	He	2.09N	45.07 E
'Afīf	23	Fe	23.55N	42.56 E
Afikpo	34	Gd	5.53N	7.55 E
Afipski	16	Kg	44.52N	38.50 E
Aflou	32	Hc	34.07N	2.06 E
Afmadōw	35	Ge	0.29N	42.06 E
Afognak	40	Ie	58.15N	152.30W
Afonso Cláudio	54	Jh	20.05S	41.08W
Afon Teifi	9	Ii	52.06N	4.43W
Afon Tywi	9	Ij	51.40N	4.15W
Afragola	14	Ij	40.55N	14.18 E
Afrērā, Lake-	35	Gc	13.20N	41.03 E
Africa	30	Jh	10.00N	22.00 E
African Islands	30	Mi	4.53S	43.24 E
Afşin	24	Gc	38.36N	36.55 E
Afsluitdijk	11	La	53.00N	5.15 E
Afton	46	Je	42.44N	110.56W
Afuá	54	Hd	0.10S	50.23W
'Afula	24	Ff	32.36N	35.17 E
Afyonkarahisar	22	Ff	38.45N	30.40 E
Agadem	31	Ig	16.50N	13.17 E
Agadez	31	Hg	16.58N	7.59 E
Agadez [2]	34	Hb	19.45N	10.15 E
Agadir	31	Ge	30.25N	9.37W
Agadir [3]	32	Fc	30.00N	9.00W
Agadyr	19	Hf	48.17N	72.53 E
Agalega Islands	30	Mj	10.24S	56.30 E
Agalta, Sierra de-	47	Ge	15.00N	85.53W
Agan	19	Hc	61.23N	74.35 E
Agana	58	Fc	13.28N	144.45 E
Agano-Gawa	28	Of	37.57N	139.07 E
Aga Point	64c	Bb	13.14N	144.43 E
Agapovka	17	Ij	53.18N	59.10 E
Agaro	35	Fd	7.53N	36.36 E
Agartala	22	Lg	23.49N	91.16 E
Agassiz Pool	45	Ib	48.20N	95.58W
Agat	64c	Bb	13.23N	144.39 E
Agat Bay	64c	Bb	13.24N	144.39 E
Agats	58	Ee	5.33S	138.08 E
Agattu	40a	Ab	52.25N	173.35 E
Agawa Bay	44	Eb	47.22N	84.33W
Agawa Bay	44	Eb	47.20N	84.42W
Agboville	34	Ed	5.56N	4.13W
Agboville [3]	34	Ed	6.00N	4.15W
Agdam	19	Eh	39.58N	46.57 E
Agdaš	16	Oi	40.38N	47.29 E
Agde	11	Jk	43.19N	3.28 E
Agde, Cap d'-	11	Jk	43.16N	3.30 E
Agder	8	Cf	58.25N	8.15 E
Agdz	32	Fc	30.27N	7.56W
Agdžabedi	16	Oi	40.03N	47.28 E
Agematsu	29	Ed	35.47N	137.41 E
Agen	11	Gj	44.12N	0.38 E
Ageo	29	Fd	35.58N	139.35 E
Agepsta, Gora-	16	Lh	43.32N	40.30 E
Ager	14	Hb	48.05N	13.51 E
Agere Mariam	35	Fd	5.39N	38.15 E
Agersø	8	Di	55.10N	11.10 E
Agger	12	Jd	50.48N	7.11 E
Āghā Jārī	23	Gc	30.42N	49.50 E
Aghireşu	15	Gc	46.53N	23.15 E
Agiabampo, Estero de-	48	Ed	26.15N	109.15W
Ağın	24	Hc	38.57N	38.43 E

Index Symbols

- [1] Independent Nation
- [2] State, Region
- [3] District, County
- [4] Municipality
- [5] Colony, Dependency
- Continent
- Physical Region
- Historical or Cultural Region
- Mount, Mountain
- Volcano
- Hill
- Mountains, Mountain Range
- Hills, Escarpment
- Plateau, Upland
- Pass, Gap
- Plain, Lowland
- Delta
- Salt Flat
- Valley, Canyon
- Crater, Cave
- Karst Features
- Depression
- Polder
- Desert, Dunes
- Forest, Woods
- Heath, Steppe
- Oasis
- Cape, Point
- Coast, Beach
- Cliff
- Peninsula
- Isthmus
- Sandbank
- Island
- Atoll
- Rock, Reef
- Islands, Archipelago
- Rocks, Reefs
- Coral Reef
- Well, Spring
- Geyser
- River, Stream
- Waterfall Rapids
- River Mouth, Estuary
- Lake
- Salt Lake
- Intermittent Lake
- Reservoir
- Swamp, Pond
- Canal
- Glacier
- Ice Shelf, Pack Ice
- Ocean
- Sea
- Gulf, Bay
- Strait, Fjord
- Lagoon
- Bank
- Seamount
- Tablemount
- Ridge
- Shelf
- Basin
- Escarpment, Sea Scarp
- Fracture
- Trench, Abyss
- National Park, Reserve
- Point of Interest
- Recreation Site
- Cave, Cavern
- Historic Site
- Ruins
- Wall, Walls
- Church, Abbey
- Temple
- Scientific Station
- Airport
- Port
- Lighthouse
- Mine
- Tunnel
- Dam, Bridge

Aginski Burjatski Nacionalnyj Okrug [3] 20 Gf 51.00N 114.30 E
Aginskoje 20 Gf 51.03N 114.33 E
Agnew 59 Ee 28.01S 120.30 E
Agnibilékrou 34 Ed 7.08N 3.12W
Agnita 15 Hd 45.58N 24.37 E
Agno 14 Fe 45.32N 11.21 E
Agnone 14 Ii 41.48N 14.22 E
Ago 29 Ed 34.19N 136.50 E
Agoare 34 Fd 8.30N 3.25 E
Agogna 14 Ce 45.04N 8.54 E
Agön 8 Ge 61.35N 17.25 E
Agordat 31 Kg 15.32N 37.53 E
Agordo 14 Gd 46.17N 12.02 E
Agout 11 Hk 43.47N 1.41 E
Āgra 22 Jg 27.11N 78.01 E
Agrahanski Poluostrov 16 Oh 43.45N 47.35 E
Agramunt 13 Nc 41.47N 1.06 E
Agreda 13 Kc 41.51N 1.56W
Ağrı 23 Fb 39.44N 43.03 E
Ağrı Dağı = Mount Ararat (EN) 21 Gf 39.40N 44.24 E
Agričaj 16 Oi 41.17N 46.43 E
Agrigento 6 Hh 37.19N 13.34 E
Agrihan Island 57 Fc 18.46N 145.40 E
Agrij 15 Gb 47.15N 23.16 E
Agrinion 15 Ek 38.38N 21.25 E
Agropoli 14 Ij 40.21N 14.59 E
Agro Pontino 14 Gi 41.25N 12.55 E
Agryz 7 Mh 56.31N 53.01 E
Agto 41 Ge 67.37N 53.49W
Agua Brava, Laguna- 48 Gf 22.10N 105.32W
Agua Caliente, Cerro- 47 Cc 26.27N 106.12W
Aguachica 54 Db 8.18N 73.38W
Agua Clara 55 Fe 20.27S 52.52W
Aguada de Pasajeros 49 Gb 22.23N 80.51W
Aguadez, Irhazer Oua-n- 34 Gb 17.28N 6.26 E
Aguadilla 49 Nd 18.26N 67.09W
Aguadulce 49 Gi 8.15N 80.33W
Agua Fria River 46 Ij 33.23N 112.21W
Agua Limpa, Rio- 55 Gb 14.58S 51.20W
Aguán, Rio- 49 Ef 15.57N 85.44W
Aguanaval, Rio- 48 Hf 25.28N 102.53W
Aguapei 55 Cc 16.12S 59.43W
Aguapei, Rio- 56 Jb 21.03S 51.47W
Aguapei, Rio- 55 Cb 15.53S 58.25W
Agua Prieta 39 If 31.18N 109.34W
Aguaray 56 Hb 22.16S 63.44W
Aguaray Guazú, Rio- [Par.] 55 Dg 24.05S 56.40W
Aguaray Guazú, Rio- [Par.] 55 Dg 24.47S 57.19W
Aguasay 50 Eh 9.25N 63.44W
Aguascalientes 39 Ig 21.53N 102.18W
Aguascalientes [2] 47 Dd 22.00N 102.30W
Aguasvivas 13 Lc 41.20N 0.25W
Água Verde, Rio- 55 Da 13.42S 56.43W
Agua Vermelha, Reprêsa- 56 Ja 19.53S 50.17W
Agudo [Braz.] 55 Fi 29.38S 53.15W
Agudo [Sp.] 13 Hf 38.59N 4.52W
Agueda 13 Fc 41.02N 6.56W
Águeda 13 Dd 40.34N 8.27W
Aguelhok 34 Fb 19.28N 0.51 E
Agüenit 32 Ee 22.11N 13.08W
Aguerguer 30 Ff 23.09N 16.01W
Aguijan Island 57 Fc 14.51N 145.34 E
Aguilar de Campóo 13 Hb 42.48N 4.16W
Aguilar de la Frontera 13 Hg 37.31N 4.39W
Aguilas 13 Kg 37.24N 1.35W
Aguililla 48 Hh 18.44N 102.44W
Aguirre, Rio- 50 Fh 8.28N 61.02W
Aguja, Cabo de la- 54 Da 11.21N 73.59W
Agujereada, Punta- 51a Ab 18.31N 67.08W
Agul 20 Ee 55.40N 95.45 E
Agulhas, Cape-(EN) = Agulhas, Kaap- 30 Jl 34.50S 20.00 E
Agulhas, Kaap- = Agulhas, Cape-(EN) 30 Jl 34.50S 20.00 E
Agulhas Negras, Pico das- 52 Lh 22.23S 44.38W
Agulhas Plateau (EN) 30 Jm 40.00S 26.00 E
Agung, Gunung- 26 Gh 8.21S 115.30 E
Aguni-Shima 27 Mf 26.35N 127.15 E
Agupey, Rio- 55 Di 29.07S 56.36W
Agustin Codazzi 54 Da 10.02N 73.15W
Ağva 24 Cb 41.05N 29.50 E
Ahaggar 30 Hf 23.10N 5.50 E
Ahaggar, Tassili-oua-n- 30 Hf 20.30N 5.00 E
Aha Hills 37 Cc 19.45S 21.10 E
Ahalcihe 19 Eg 41.38N 42.59 E
Ahalkalaki 19 Eg 41.25N 43.29 E
Ahangaran 18 Gd 40.57N 69.37 E
Ahar 23 Gb 38.28N 47.04 E
Ahat 15 Mk 38.39N 29.47 E
Ahaus 10 Cd 52.04N 7.00 E
Ahe Atoll 57 Mf 14.30S 146.18W
Ahenet, Tanezrouft-n- 32 He 22.00N 1.00 E
Ahini 20 Ff 53.18N 105.01 E
Ahipara 62 Ea 35.10S 173.09 E
Ahja Jõgi 8 Lf 58.19N 27.15 E
Ahlat 24 Jc 38.45N 42.29 E
Ahlen 10 De 51.45N 7.55 E
Ahmadābād 22 Jg 23.02N 72.37 E
Aḩmadī 24 Qi 27.56N 56.42 E
Ahmadnagar 25 Ee 19.05N 74.44 E
Ahmadpur East 25 Ec 29.09N 71.16 E
Ahmar 30 Lh 9.23N 41.13 E
Aḩmar, Al Baḩr al- = Red Sea (EN) 30 Kf 25.00N 38.00 E
Ahmeta 16 Nh 42.02N 45.11 E
Ahmetli 15 Kk 38.31N 27.57 E
Ahnet 32 He 24.35N 3.15 E
Ahoa 64h Ab 13.17S 176.12W
Ahome 48 Ee 25.55N 109.11W
Ahon, Tarso- 35 Ba 20.23N 18.18 E
Ahr 10 Df 50.33N 7.17 E
Ahram 24 Nh 28.52N 51.16 E
Ahrāmāt al Jīzah 33 Fd 29.55N 31.05 E
Ahrensburg 10 Gc 53.41N 10.15 E
Ahrgebirge 12 Id 50.31N 6.54 E
Ahse 12 Jc 51.42N 7.51 E
Ahsu 16 Pi 40.35N 48.26 E
Ähtäri 7 Ee 62.02N 21.20 E
Ähtärinjarvi 8 Kb 62.40N 24.05 E
Ähtävänjoki 7 Fe 63.38N 22.48 E
Ahtopol 15 Kg 42.06N 27.57 E
Ahtuba 5 Kf 46.42N 48.00 E
Ahtubinsk 6 Kf 48.14N 46.14 E
Ahtyrka 19 De 50.19N 34.55 E
Ahuacapán 49 Cg 13.55N 89.51W
Ahuazotepec 48 Jg 20.03N 98.09W
Ahunui Atoll 57 Mf 19.35S 140.28W
Åhus 7 Di 55.55N 14.17 E
Ahvāz 22 Gf 31.19N 48.42 E
Ahvenanmaa/Åland [2] 7 Ef 60.15N 20.00 E
Ahvenanmaa/Åland = Aland Islands (EN) 5 Hc 60.15N 20.00 E
Ahvenanmeri 8 Hd 60.00N 19.30 E
Aḩwar 23 Gg 13.31N 46.42 E
Aibag Gol 28 Ad 41.42N 110.24 E
Aibetsu 29a Cb 43.55N 142.33 E
Aichach 10 Hh 48.28N 11.08 E
Aichi Ken [2] 28 Ng 35.00N 137.07 E
Aiea 65a Db 21.23N 157.56W
Aigle 14 Ad 46.20N 6.59 E
Aigoual, Mont- 11 Jj 44.07N 3.35 E
Aiguá 55 El 34.12S 54.45W
Aigues 11 Kj 44.07N 4.43 E
Aigues-Mortes 11 Kk 43.34N 4.11 E
Aiguilles 11 Mj 44.47N 6.52 E
Aiguillon 11 Gj 44.18N 0.21 E
Aigurande 11 Hh 46.26N 1.50 E
Ai He 28 Hd 40.13N 124.30 E
Aihui (Heihe) 22 Od 50.13N 127.26 E
Aikawa 29 Fb 38.02N 138.14 E
Aiken 43 Ke 33.34N 81.44W
Ailao Shan 27 Hg 23.15N 102.20 E
Ailette 12 Fe 49.35N 3.10 E
Ailinginae Atoll 57 Hc 11.08N 166.24 E
Aillte an Mhothair/Moher, Cliffs of- 9 Di 52.58N 9.27W
Ailly-le-Haut-Clocher 12 Dd 50.05N 1.59 E
Ailly-sur-Noye 12 Ee 49.45N 2.22 E
Ailsa Craig 9 Hf 55.16N 5.07W
Ailuk Atoll 57 Hc 10.20N 169.56 E
Aim 20 Ie 58.48N 134.12 E
Aimogasta 56 Gc 28.33S 66.49W
Aimorés 54 Jg 19.30S 41.04W
Ain [3] 11 Lh 46.10N 5.20 E
Ain 11 Li 45.48N 5.10 E
Ainazi/Ajnazi 7 Fh 57.52N 24.25 E
Aïn Beïda 32 Ib 35.48N 7.24 E
Aïn Beni Mathar 32 Gc 34.01N 2.01W
Aïn Bessem 13 Ph 36.18N 3.40 E
Aïn Boucif 13 Pi 35.53N 3.09 E
Aïn Defla 13 Nh 36.16N 1.58 E
Aïn el Berd 13 Li 35.21N 0.31W
Aïn el Hammam 13 Qh 36.34N 4.19 E
Aïn el Turck 13 Li 35.44N 0.46W
Aïn Galakka 35 Bb 18.05N 18.31 E
Ainos Óros 15 Dk 38.07N 20.40 E
Aïn Oulmene 13 Ri 35.55N 5.18 E
Aïn Oussera 13 Oi 35.27N 2.54 E
Aïn Sefra 31 Ge 32.45N 0.35W
Ainsworth 45 Ge 42.33N 99.52W
Aïn Taghrout 13 Rh 36.08N 5.05 E
Aïn Tedeles 13 Mh 36.00N 0.18 E
Aïn Témouchent 32 Gb 35.18N 1.08W
Aïn Tolba 13 Ki 35.15N 1.15W
Aioi 29 Dd 34.49N 134.28 E
Aiquile 54 Eg 18.10S 65.10W
Aïr/Azbine 30 Hg 18.00N 8.30 E
Airabu, Pulau- 26 Ef 2.46N 106.14 E
Airai 64a Bc 7.21N 134.34 E
Airaines 12 De 49.58N 1.57 E
Airão 54 Fd 1.56S 61.22W
Airbangis 26 Cf 0.12N 99.23 E
Airdrie 46 Ha 51.18N 114.02W
Aire 11 Id 50.38N 2.24 E
Aire [Eng.-U.K.] 9 Mh 53.44N 0.54W
Aire [Fr.] 11 Ke 49.19N 4.49 E
Aire, Canal d'- 11 Id 50.38N 2.25 E
Aire, Isla del- 13 Qe 39.47N 4.16 E
Aire-sur-l'Adour 11 Fk 43.42N 0.16W
Air Force 42 Kc 67.55N 74.05W
Airolo 14 Cd 46.33N 8.35 E
Aïs 63b Cb 15.26S 167.15 E
Aisch 10 Hg 49.46N 11.01 E
Aisén del General Carlos Ibáñez del Campo [2] 56 Fg 46.00S 73.00W
Aishihik 42 Dd 61.34N 137.30W
Ai-Shima 29 Bd 34.30N 131.18 E
Aisne [3] 11 Je 49.30N 3.30 E
Aisne 11 Ie 49.26N 2.50 E
Aisne à la Marne, Canal de l'- 11 Je 49.24N 3.55 E
Aissa, Djebel- 32 Gc 32.51N 0.30W
Aitana, Pico- 13 Lf 38.39N 0.16W
Aitape 60 Ch 3.08S 142.21 E
Aitolikón 15 Ek 38.26N 21.21 E
Aitutaki Atoll 57 Lf 18.52S 159.45W
Ait Youssef ou Ali 13 Ii 35.09N 3.55W
Aiud 15 Gc 46.18N 23.43 E
Aiviekste 7 Fh 56.36N 25.44 E
Aiviekste/Ajviekste 7 Fh 56.36N 25.44 E
Aiwokako Passage 64a Bb 7.39N 134.33 E
Aix, Ile d'- 11 Eh 46.01N 1.10W
Aix-en-Provence 11 Lk 43.32N 5.26 E
Aixe-sur-Vienne 11 Hi 45.48N 1.08 E
Aix-les-Bains 11 Li 45.42N 5.55 E
Aiyaion Pélagos = Aegean Sea (EN) 5 Ih 39.00N 25.00 E
Aiyina 15 Gl 37.45N 23.26 E
Aiyina = Aegina (EN) 15 Gl 37.40N 23.30 E
Aiyinion 15 Fi 40.30N 22.33 E
Aiyion 15 Fk 38.15N 22.05 E
Aizawl 25 Id 23.44N 92.43 E
Aizenay 11 Eh 46.44N 1.37W
Aizpute/Ajzpute 7 Eh 56.45N 21.39 E
Aizubange 29 Fc 37.34N 139.49 E
Aizutakada 29 Fc 37.29N 139.48 E
Aizuwakamatsu 28 Of 37.30N 139.56 E
Ajā', Jabal- 24 Ii 27.30N 41.30 E
'Ajab Shīr 24 Kd 37.28N 45.54 E
Ajaccio 6 Gg 41.55N 8.44 E
Ajaccio, Golfe d'- 11a Ab 41.50N 8.41 E
Ajaguz 22 Ke 47.58N 80.27 E
Ajakli 20 Eb 70.13N 95.55 E
Ajan [R.S.F.S.R.] 20 Fe 59.38N 106.45 E
Ajan [R.S.F.S.R.] 20 Ie 56.27N 138.10 E
Ajanka 20 Ld 63.40N 167.30 E
Ajanta Range 25 Fd 20.30N 76.00 E
Ajat 17 Kj 52.54N 62.50 E
Ajax Peak 46 Id 45.20N 113.40W
Ajdābiyā 31 Je 30.46N 20.14 E
Ajdabul 19 Ge 52.42N 69.01 E
Ajdar 16 Ke 48.42N 39.13 E
Ajdar, Solončak- 18 Fd 40.50N 66.50 E
Ajdovščina 14 He 45.53N 13.53 E
Ajdyrlinski 17 Ij 52.03N 59.50 E
Ajhal 20 Gc 66.00N 111.32 E
Ajigasawa 29 Pd 40.47N 140.12 E
Aji-Shima 29 Gb 38.15N 141.30 E
Ajjer, Tassili-n- 30 Hf 25.30N 9.00 E
Ajka 10 Ni 47.06N 17.34 E
Ajke, Ozero- 16 Vd 50.55N 61.35 E
Ajkino 17 De 62.15N 49.56 E
'Ajlūn 24 Ff 32.20N 35.45 E
'Ajmah, Jabal al- 24 Fh 29.12N 34.02 E
'Ajmān 23 Id 25.25N 55.27 E
Ajmer 22 Jg 26.27N 74.38 E
Ajnaži/Ainaži 7 Fh 57.52N 24.25 E
Ajni 18 Ge 39.23N 68.36 E
Ajo 43 Ee 32.22N 112.52W
Ajo, Cabo de- 13 Ia 43.31N 3.35W
Ajon, Ostrov- 21 Sc 69.50N 168.40 E
Ajoupa-Bouillon 51h Ab 14.50N 61.08W
Ajsary 19 He 53.05N 71.00 E
Ajtos 15 Kg 42.42N 27.15 E
Aju, Kepulauan- 26 Jf 0.28N 131.03 E
'Ajūz, Jabal al- 24 Dj 25.49N 30.43 E
Ajviekste 7 Fh 56.36N 25.44 E
Ajviekste/Aiviekste 7 Fh 56.36N 25.44 E
Ajzpute/Aizpute 7 Eh 56.45N 21.39 E
Akaba 34 Fd 7.57N 1.03 E
Akabira 28 Qc 43.30N 142.04 E
Akabli 32 Hd 26.42N 1.22 E
Akademika Obručeva, Hrebet- 20 Ef 51.30N 96.45 E
Akadomari 29 Fc 37.54N 138.24 E
Aka-Gawa 29 Fb 38.54N 139.50 E
Akagi-San 29 Fc 36.33N 139.11 E
Akaishi-Dake 29 Fd 35.27N 138.09 E
Akaishi-Sanmyaku 29 Fd 35.25N 138.10 E
Akajaure 7 Dc 67.42N 17.30 E
Aka-Jima 29b Ab 26.14N 127.17 E
Akaki 35 Fd 8.51N 38.48 E
Akala 35 Fb 15.38N 36.12 E
Akan 29a Db 43.08N 144.07 E
Akan-Gawa 29a Db 43.00N 144.16 E
Akar 24 Dc 38.38N 31.06 E
Akarnaniká Óri 15 Dk 38.45N 21.00 E
Akaroa 61 Dh 43.48S 172.59 E
Akasaki 29 Cd 35.31N 133.38 E
'Akasha East 35 Ea 21.05N 30.43 E
Akashi 28 Mg 34.38N 134.59 E
Akbaba Tepe 24 Hc 39.32N 39.33 E
Akbajtal, Pereval- 19 Hh 38.31N 73.41 E
Akbou 13 Qh 36.28N 4.32 E
Akbulak 19 Fe 51.03N 55.37 E
Akbura 18 Id 40.34N 72.45 E
Akçaabat 24 Hb 40.59N 39.34 E
Akçadağ 24 Gc 38.21N 37.59 E
Akçakale 24 Hd 36.41N 38.56 E
Akçakara Dağı 24 Ic 38.40N 40.52 E
Akçakoca 24 Db 41.05N 31.09 E
Akçaova [Tur.] 15 Mh 41.03N 29.57 E
Akçaova [Tur.] 15 Ll 37.30N 28.02 E
Akčatau 19 Hf 47.59N 74.02 E
Akçay 15 Ll 37.50N 28.15 E
Akçay 15 Mm 36.36N 29.45 E
Akchār 30 Ff 20.20N 14.28W
Ak Dağ [Tur.] 24 Ib 40.35N 41.46 E
Ak Dağ [Tur.] 23 Cb 36.32N 29.34 E
Akdağ [Tur.] 24 Gd 37.53N 37.56 E
Akdağ [Tur.] 24 Fb 40.57N 35.55 E
Akdağ [Tur.] 24 Cc 39.15N 28.49 E
Akdağ [Tur.] 15 Ll 37.42N 28.56 E
Akdağ [Tur.] 15 Mk 38.18N 29.58 E
Akdağ [Tur.] 15 Jk 38.33N 26.30 E
Ak Dağlar 24 Gc 39.30N 36.00 E
Ak Dağları 24 Ic 38.40N 40.12 E
Akdağmadeni 24 Fc 39.40N 35.54 E
Akdeniz = Mediterranean Sea (EN) 5 Hh 35.00N 20.00 E
Ak-Dovurak 20 Ef 51.10N 90.40 E
Akechi 29 Ed 35.18N 137.22 E
Ake Eze 34 Gd 5.55N 7.40 E
Akera 16 Oj 39.09N 46.48 E
Åkersberga 8 He 59.29N 18.18 E
Akershus [2] 7 Cf 60.00N 11.10 E
Aketi 31 Jh 2.44N 23.46 E
Akharnai 15 Gk 38.05N 23.44 E
Akhdar, al Jabal al- 21 Hg 23.30N 57.00 E
Akhḑar, Al Jabal al- 30 Je 32.30N 21.30 E
Akhḑar, Wādī al- 24 Gh 28.35N 36.35 E
Akhelöos 15 Ej 38.18N 21.10 E
Akhisar 23 Cb 38.55N 27.51 E
Akhmīm 33 Fd 26.34N 31.44 E
Akhtarīn 24 Gd 36.31N 37.20 E
Aki 29 Ce 33.30N 133.53 E
Akiaki Atoll 61 Nc 18.30S 139.12W
Akiéni 36 Bc 1.11S 13.53 E
Akimiski 38 Kd 53.00N 81.20W
Akimovka 16 If 46.42N 35.09 E
Aki-Nada 29 Cd 34.05N 132.40 E
Åkirkeby 8 Fi 55.04N 14.56 E
Akita 22 Qf 39.43N 140.07 E
Akita Ken [2] 28 Pe 39.45N 140.20 E
Akjoujt 31 Fg 19.44N 14.22W
Akka 32 Fd 29.25N 8.15W
Akkanburluk 17 Mj 52.46N 66.35 E
'Akko 23 Ec 32.55N 35.05 E
Akkol 18 Hc 43.25N 70.47 E
Akköy 24 Bd 37.29N 27.15 E
Akkystau 19 Ff 47.17N 51.03 E
Aklavik 42 Dc 68.14N 135.02W
Aklé Mseiguilé 34 Eb 16.20N 4.45W
Akmenė/Akmene 8 Jh 56.14N 22.43 E
Akmene/Akmenė 8 Jh 56.14N 22.43 E
Akmenrags/Akmeņrags 8 Ih 56.54N 20.55 E
Akmeņrags/Akmenrags 8 Ih 56.54N 20.55 E
Akmeqit 27 Cd 37.05N 76.55 E
Akniste 8 Kh 56.10N 25.54 E
Akō 29 Dd 34.45N 134.23 E
Akobo 30 Kh 7.48N 33.03 E
Akobo 31 Kh 7.47N 33.01 E
Akola 22 Jg 20.44N 77.00 E
Akonolinga 34 He 3.46N 12.15 E
Akosombo Dam 34 Fd 6.16N 0.03 E
Akpatok 42 Kd 60.24N 68.05W
Akqi 27 Cc 40.50N 78.01 E
Ákra Ámbelos 15 Gj 39.56N 23.56 E
Ákra Kambanós 15 Hl 37.59N 24.45 E
Akranes 7a Ab 64.19N 22.06W
Ákra Spathi 15 Gl 37.27N 23.31 E
Åkrehamn 7 Ag 59.16N 5.11 E
Akritas; Ákra- = Akritas, Cape- (EN) 15 Em 36.43N 21.53 E
Akritas Cape- (EN) = Akritas, Ákra- 15 Em 36.43N 21.53 E
Akron [Co.-U.S.] 45 Ef 40.10N 103.13W
Akron [Oh.-U.S.] 43 Kc 41.04N 81.31W
Akrotiri 24 Ee 34.36N 32.57 E
Akša 20 Gf 50.17N 113.17 E
Aksaj 16 Oh 43.32N 46.55 E
Aksaj [Kaz.-U.S.S.R.] 19 Fe 51.13N 53.01 E
Aksaj [R.S.F.S.R.] 16 Kf 47.15N 39.52 E
Aksakal 15 Li 40.09N 28.07 E
Aksakovo 17 Gi 54.02N 54.09 E
Aksaray 23 Db 38.23N 34.03 E
Aksay 27 Fd 39.28N 94.15 E
Akşehir 23 Db 38.21N 31.25 E
Akşehir Gölü 24 Dc 38.30N 31.28 E
Akseki 24 Dd 37.02N 31.48 E
Aksenovo-Zilovskoje 20 Gf 53.00N 117.35 E
'Aks-e Rostam 24 Ph 28.23N 54.52 E
Aksoran, Gora 19 Hf 48.25N 75.30 E
Akstafa 16 Ni 41.13N 45.27 E
Akstafa 16 Ni 41.06N 45.28 E
Aksu [China] 22 Ke 41.09N 80.15 E
Aksu [Kaz.-U.S.S.R.] 19 He 52.28N 71.59 E
Aksu [Kaz.-U.S.S.R.] 18 Lb 45.34N 79.30 E
Aksu [Kaz.-U.S.S.R.] 18 Hf 46.20N 78.15 E
Aksu [Tur.] 15 Ll 37.56N 28.56 E
Aksu [Tur.] 24 Dd 36.51N 30.54 E
Aksuat 19 If 47.48N 82.50 E
Aksubajevo 7 Mi 54.52N 50.50 E
Aksu He 21 Ke 40.28N 80.52 E
Aksum 35 Fc 14.07N 38.44 E
Ak-Šyjrak 18 Ld 41.49N 78.44 E
Aktag 27 Dd 36.45N 84.40 E
Aktaš [R.S.F.S.R.] 20 Df 50.18N 87.44 E
Aktaš [Uzb.-U.S.S.R.] 19 Gh 39.55N 65.53 E
Aktau 19 He 50.16N 73.07 E
Aktau, Gora- 19 Gg 41.45N 64.30 E
Aktjubinsk 6 Le 50.17N 57.10 E
Aktjubinskaja Oblast [3] 19 Ff 48.00N 58.00 E
Ak-Tjuz 18 Kc 42.50N 76.07 E
Akto 27 Cd 39.05N 76.02 E
Aktogaj 19 Hf 47.01N 79.40 E
Akula 36 Db 2.22N 20.11 E
Akun 40a Eb 54.12N 165.35W
Akune 28 Kh 32.01N 130.11 E
Akure 34 Gd 7.15N 5.12 E
Akureyri 6 Eb 65.40N 18.06W
Akuseki-Jima 28 Jj 29.28N 129.33 E
Akutan 40a Eb 54.10N 165.55W
Akutan 40a Eb 54.08N 165.46W
Akyab → Sittwe 22 Lg 20.09N 92.54 E
Akyazı 24 Db 40.41N 30.37 E
Akžajkyn, Ozero- 18 Fb 44.55N 67.45 E
Akzāl 19 If 49.13N 81.30 E
Ål 8 Cd 60.38N 8.34 E
Alà, Monti di- 14 Dj 40.35N 9.16 E
Alabama 38 Kf 31.08N 87.57W
Alabama [2] 43 Je 32.50N 87.30W
Al'Abbāsīyah 35 Ec 12.10N 31.18 E
Alaca 24 Fb 40.10N 34.51 E
Alaçam Dağlari 15 Lj 39.20N 28.32 E
Alaçan 24 Fb 41.37N 35.37 E
Alaçati 15 Jk 38.16N 26.23 E
Aladağ 24 Jc 43.35N 39.20 E
Ala Dağ [Tur.] 24 Jb 40.11N 42.49 E
Ala Dağ [Tur.] 24 Ed 37.58N 32.04 E
Alādāgh, Kūh-e- 24 Qd 37.13N 57.30 E
Ala Dağları 24 Fd 37.55N 35.13 E
Aladža 16 Rj 39.21N 53.12 E
Aladža Manastir 15 Lf 43.17N 28.01 E
Alagir 16 Nh 43.01N 44.12 E
Alagna Valsesia 14 Be 45.51N 7.56 E
Alagnon 11 Ji 45.27N 3.19 E
Alagoas [2] 54 Ke 9.30S 36.30W
Alagoinhas 53 Mg 12.07S 38.26W
Alagón 13 Kc 41.46N 1.07W
Alagón 13 Fe 39.44N 6.53W
Ala Gou 27 Ec 42.42N 89.12 E
Alahanpanjang 26 Dg 1.05S 100.47 E
Alahärmä 7 Fe 63.14N 22.51 E
Al Aḩmadī 24 Mh 29.05N 48.04 E
Alaid, Vulkan 20 Kf 50.50N 155.33 E
Alajärvi 7 Fe 63.00N 23.49 E
Alajku 19 Hg 40.18N 74.29 E
Alajski Hrebet 21 Jf 39.45N 72.30 E
Alajuela [3] 49 Eh 10.30N 84.30W
Alajuela 47 Hf 10.01N 84.13W
Alajuela, Lago- 49 Hi 9.05N 79.24W
Alakol, Ozero- 21 Ke 46.05N 81.50 E
Alakurtti 7 Hc 66.59N 30.20 E
Alalakeiki Channel 65a Ec 20.35N 156.30W
Al 'Alamayn 31 Je 30.49N 28.57 E
Alalau, Rio- 54 Fd 0.30S 61.10W
Al Amādīyah 24 Jd 37.06N 43.29 E
Alamagan Island 57 Fc 17.36N 145.50 E
Al 'Amārah 23 Gc 31.50N 47.09 E
'Alam ar Rūm, Ra's- 24 Bg 31.22N 27.21 E
Alāmarvdasht 24 Oi 27.52N 52.34 E
Alamashindo 35 Ge 4.51N 42.04 E
Alamata 35 Fc 12.25N 39.37 E
Alameda 45 Ci 35.11N 106.37W
Alaminos 26 Gc 16.10N 119.59 E
Al 'Āmirīyah 24 Cg 31.01N 29.48 E
Alamito Creek 45 Dl 29.31N 104.17W
Alamitos, Sierra de los- 48 Hd 26.20N 102.15W
'Alāmo 35 Ge 4.23N 43.09 E
Alamo 46 Hh 37.22N 115.10W
Alamogordo 43 Fe 32.54N 105.57W
Alamos 47 Cc 27.01N 108.56W
Alamos, Sierra- 48 Gc 28.25N 105.00W
Alamosa 43 Fd 37.28N 105.52W
Al Anbār [3] 24 If 34.00N 42.00 E
Åland/Ahvenanmaa [2] 7 Ef 60.15N 20.00 E
Åland/Ahvenanmaa = Aland Islands (EN) 5 Hc 60.15N 20.00 E
Aland Islands (EN) = Ahvenanmaa/Åland 5 Hc 60.15N 20.00 E
Aland Islands (EN) = Åland/Ahvenanmaa 5 Hc 60.15N 20.00 E
Ålandsbro 8 Gb 62.40N 17.50 E
Ålandshav 8 Hd 60.00N 19.30 E
Alange 13 Ff 38.47N 6.15W
Alanje 49 Fi 8.24N 82.33W
Alanya 23 Db 36.33N 32.01 E
Alaotra, Lac- 37 Hc 17.30S 48.30 E
Alapaha River 44 Fj 30.26N 83.06W
Alapajevsk 19 Gd 57.52N 61.42 E
Alaplı 24 Db 41.08N 31.25 E
Al 'Aqabah = Aqaba (EN) 23 Dd 29.31N 35.00 E
Al 'Aqabah aş Şaghīrah 24 Ej 24.14N 32.53 E
Al 'Arabīyah As-Su'ūdīyah = Saudi Arabia (EN) [1] 22 Gg 25.00N 45.00 E
Alarcón, Embalse de- 13 Je 39.45N 2.20W
Al 'Arish 33 Fc 31.08N 33.48 E
Al 'Armah 24 Lj 25.30N 46.30 E
Al Arṭāwīyah 24 Ki 26.30N 45.20 E
Alas, Selat- 26 Gh 8.40S 116.40 E
Al 'Aşab 24 Pk 23.20N 54.10 E
Alaşehir 24 Cc 38.21N 28.32 E
Al Ashkharah 23 Ie 21.47N 59.30 E
Al 'Āshūrīyah 24 Jg 31.02N 43.05 E
Alaska [2] 40 Ic 65.00N 153.00W
Alaska 38 Dc 65.00N 153.00W
Alaska, Gulf of- 38 Ed 58.00N 146.00W
Alaska Peninsula 38 Dd 57.00N 158.00W
Alaska Range 38 Ec 62.30N 150.00W
Alassio 14 Cf 44.00N 8.10 E
Alastaro 8 Jd 60.57N 22.51 E
Alat 18 De 39.26N 63.48 E
Alatau Shan 27 Cb 45.00N 80.00 E
Alatau Shankou = Dzungarian Gate (EN) 21 Ke 45.25N 82.25 E
Al 'Athāmīn 24 Jg 30.35N 43.40 E
Alatri 14 Hi 41.43N 13.21 E
Al Aṭrun 31 Jg 18.11N 26.36 E
Alatyr 7 Li 54.52N 46.36 E
Alatyr 19 Ee 54.50N 46.35 E
Álava [3] 13 Jb 42.50N 2.45W
Alava, Cape- 46 Cb 48.10N 124.43W
Alaverdi 19 Eg 41.08N 44.37 E
Alavijeh 24 Nf 33.03N 51.05 E
Alavo/Alavus 7 Fe 62.35N 23.37 E
Alavus/Alavo 7 Fe 62.35N 23.37 E
Al 'Awāliq 23 Gg 14.15N 46.30 E
Al 'Awāriq 35 Ha 20.25N 48.40 E
Al 'Awsajīyah 24 Ki 26.04N 44.08 E
'Ālayh 24 Ff 33.48N 35.36 E
Al 'Ayn [Sau.Ar.] 24 Hj 25.04N 38.06 E
Al 'Ayn [U.A.E.] 24 Pj 24.13N 55.45 E
Alayor 13 Qe 39.56N 4.08 E
Al 'Ayyūṭ 24 Dh 29.37N 31.15 E
Al A'zamīyah 24 Kf 33.23N 44.22 E
Alazani 16 Oi 41.03N 46.40 E
Alazeja 20 Kb 70.55N 153.40 E
Al'Azīzīyah 33 Bc 32.32N 13.01 E
Alazores, Puerto de los- 13 Hg 37.05N 4.15W
Alb [Ger.] 12 Ke 49.04N 8.20 E
Alb [Ger.] 10 Ei 47.35N 8.08 E
Alba 15 Gc 46.08N 23.30 E
Alba 14 Cf 44.42N 8.02 E
Alba Adriatica 14 Hh 42.50N 13.56 E
Al Bāb 24 Gd 36.22N 37.31 E
Albac 15 Fc 46.27N 22.58 E
Albacete 6 Fh 38.59N 1.51W
Albacete [3] 13 Kf 38.50N 2.00W
Al Badārī 33 Fd 26.59N 31.25 E
Alba de Tormes 13 Gd 40.49N 5.31W
Al Badi 33 Ie 22.02N 46.34 E
Al Bādi 24 Ie 35.56N 41.32 E
Ålbæk 8 Dg 57.36N 10.25 E
Ålbæk Bugt 8 Dg 57.35N 10.30 E
Al Bahrah 24 Lh 29.40N 47.52 E
Al Baḩr al Aḩmar [3] 35 Fb 19.50N 35.30 E
Al Baḩrayn 21 Hg 26.00N 50.30 E

Index Symbols

[1] Independent Nation
[2] State, Region
[3] District, County
[4] Municipality
[5] Colony, Dependency
Continent
Physical Region
Historical or Cultural Region
Mount, Mountain
Volcano
Hill
Mountains, Mountain Range
Hills, Escarpment
Plateau, Upland
Pass, Gap
Plain, Lowland
Delta
Salt Flat
Valley, Canyon
Crater, Cave
Karst Features
Depression
Polder
Desert, Dunes
Forest, Woods
Heath, Steppe
Oasis
Cape, Point
Coast, Beach
Cliff
Peninsula
Isthmus
Sandbank
Island
Atoll
Rock, Reef
Islands, Archipelago
Rocks, Reefs
Coral Reef
Well, Spring
Geyser
River, Stream
Waterfall Rapids
River Mouth, Estuary
Lake
Salt Lake
Intermittent Lake
Reservoir
Swamp, Pond
Canal
Glacier
Ice Shelf, Pack Ice
Ocean
Sea
Gulf, Bay
Strait, Fjord
Lagoon
Bank
Seamount
Tablemount
Ridge
Shelf
Basin
Escarpment, Sea Scarp
Fracture
Trench, Abyss
National Park, Reserve
Point of Interest
Recreation Site
Cave, Cavern
Historic Site
Ruins
Wall, Walls
Church, Abbey
Temple
Scientific Station
Airport
Port
Lighthouse
Mine
Tunnel
Dam, Bridge

Al Baḩrayn=Bahrain (EN) [1] 22 Hg 26.00N 50.29 E
Albaida 13 Lf 38.51N 0.31W
Alba Iulia 15 Gc 46.04N 23.35 E
Albalate del Arzobispo 13 Lc 41.07N 0.31W
Al Balyanā 33 Fd 26.14N 32.00 E
Alban 11 Ik 43.54N 2.28 E
Albanel, Lac- 42 Kf 51.05N 73.05W
Albani, Colli- 14 Gi 41.45N 12.45 E
Albania (EN)=Shqiperia [1] 6 Hg 41.00N 20.00 E
Albano, Lago- 14 Gi 41.45N 12.40 E
Albano Laziale 14 Gi 41.44N 12.39 E
Albany 38 Kd 52.17N 81.31W
Albany [Austl.] 58 Ch 35.02S 117.53 E
Albany [Ga.-U.S.] 43 Ke 31.35N 84.10W
Albany [Ky.-U.S.] 44 Eg 36.42N 85.08W
Albany [N.Y.-U.S.] 39 Le 42.39N 73.45W
Albany [Or.-U.S.] 43 Cc 44.38N 123.06W
Alba Posse 55 Eh 27.33S 54.42W
Albarche 13 He 39.58N 4.46W
Albardón 56 Gd 31.26S 68.32W
Albarracín 13 Kd 40.25N 1.26W
Albarracín, Sierra de- 13 Kd 40.30N 1.30W
Al Başalīyah Qiblī 24 Ej 25.06N 32.47 E
Al Başrah [3] 24 Lg 30.30N 47.27 E
Al Başrah=Basra (EN) 22 Gf 30.30N 47.47 E
Al Baţḩā' 24 Kg 31.07N 45.54 E
Al Bāţin 24 Lh 29.00N 46.35 E
Al Bāţinah 21 Hg 23.45N 57.20 E
Albatross Bank (EN) 40 Ie 56.10N 152.20W
Albatross Bay 59 Ib 12.45S 141.43 E
Albatross Plateau (EN) 3 Mi 10.00N 103.00W
Albatross Point 62 Fc 38.07S 174.40 E
Al Batrūn 24 Fe 34.15N 35.39 E
Al Bawīţī 33 Ed 28.21N 28.52 E
Al Bayāḑ 21 Gg 22.00N 47.00 E
Al Bayḑā' [3] 33 Dc 32.00N 21.30 E
Al Bayḑā' 33 Cd 28.21N 18.58 E
Al Bayḑā' 31 Je 32.46N 21.43 E
Al Bayḑā' 33 Ig 13.58N 45.35 E
Albegna 14 Fh 42.30N 11.11 E
Albemarle 44 Gh 35.21N 80.12W
Albemarle Sound 43 Ld 36.03N 76.12W
Albenga 14 Cf 44.03N 8.13 E
Alberdi 56 Ic 26.10S 58.09W
Albères, Chaîne des- 11 Il 42.28N 2.56 E
Albères, Montes-/Les Alberes 11 Il 42.28N 2.56 E
Albergaria-a-Velha 13 Dd 40.42N 8.29W
Alberique 13 Le 39.07N 0.31W
Alberobello 14 Lj 40.47N 17.16 E
Albert 11 Id 50.00N 2.39 E
Albert, Canal-/Albert Kanaal =Albert Canal (EN) 11 Ld 50.39N 5.37 E
Albert, Lake- [Afr.] 30 Kh 1.40N 31.00 E
Albert, Lake- [Or.-U.S.] 46 Ee 42.38N 120.13W
Albert, Lake- (EN)=Mobuto Sese Seko, Lac- 30 Kh 1.40N 31.00 E
Alberta [3] 42 Gf 55.00N 115.00W
Albert Canal (EN)=Albert, Canal-/Albert Kanaal 11 Ld 50.39N 5.37 E
Albert Canal (EN)=Albert Kanaal/Albert, Canal- 11 Ld 50.39N 5.37 E
Albert Edward, Mount- 59 Ja 8.23S 147.27 E
Albert Edward Bay 42 Hc 69.35N 103.10W
Alberti 56 He 35.02S 60.16W
Albertirsa 10 Pi 47.15N 19.37 E
Albert Kanaal/Albert, Canal- =Albert Canal (EN) 11 Ld 50.39N 5.37 E
Albert Lea 43 Ic 43.39N 93.22W
Albert Nile 30 Kh 3.36N 32.02 E
Albertville [Al.-U.S.] 44 Dh 34.16N 86.12W
Albertville [Fr.] 11 Mi 45.41N 6.23 E
Albestroff 12 If 48.56N 6.51 E
Albi 11 Ik 43.56N 2.09 E
Albia 45 Jf 41.02N 92.48W
Al Bid' 24 Fh 28.28N 35.01 E
Albina 54 Hb 5.30N 54.03W
Albina, Ponta- 30 Ij 15.51S 11.44 E
Albino 14 De 45.46N 9.47 E
Albion [Mi.-U.S.] 44 Ed 42.15N 84.45W
Albion [Nb.-U.S.] 45 Hf 41.42N 98.00W
Albion [N.Y.-U.S.] 44 Hd 43.15N 78.12W
Al Biqā' 24 Ge 34.10N 36.10 E
Al Bi'r 23 Ed 28.51N 36.15 E
Al Bi'r al Jadīd 23 Ed 26.01N 38.29 E
Al Birk 23 Ff 18.13N 41.33 E
Albis 14 Cc 47.20N 8.30 E
Albo, Monte- 14 Dj 40.32N 9.35 E
Albocácer/Albocasser 13 Md 40.21N 0.02 E
Albocasser/Albocácer 13 Md 40.21N 0.02 E
Alborán, Isla de- 5 Fh 35.58N 3.02W
Alboran Basin (EN) 13 Ii 36.00N 4.00W
Ålborg 6 Gd 57.03N 9.56 E
Ålborg Bugt 7 Ch 56.45N 10.30 E
Alborz, Reshteh-ye Kūhhā-ye-=Elburz Mountains (EN) 21 Hf 36.00N 53.00 E
Albox 13 Jg 37.23N 2.08W
Albret, Pays d'- 11 Fj 44.10N 0.20W
Ālbū 'Alī 24 Je 34.49N 43.35 E
Albufeira 13 Dg 37.05N 8.15W
Albū Gharz, Sabkhat- 24 Ie 34.45N 41.15 E
Al Buheyrat [3] 35 Dd 7.00N 29.30 E
Al Bumbah 33 Dc 32.13N 23.00 E
Albuñol 13 Ih 36.47N 3.12W
Albuquerque [Braz.] 55 Dd 19.23S 57.26W
Albuquerque [N.M.-U.S.] 39 If 35.05N 106.40W
Albuquerque, Cayos de- 47 Hf 12.10N 81.50W
Al Burayj 24 Ge 34.15N 36.46 E
Al Buraymī 23 Ie 24.15N 55.45 E
Al Burnah 32 Ic 31.45N 9.02 E
Alburquerque 13 Fe 39.13N 7.00W
Albury [Austl.] 58 Fh 36.05S 146.55 E
Albury [N.Z.] 62 Df 44.14S 170.53 E
Al Buţanah 30 Kg 15.00N 35.00 E
Al Buţayn 24 Kj 25.52N 45.50 E
Alby 8 Fb 62.30N 15.28 E
Alcácer do Sal 13 Df 38.22N 8.30W
Alcáçovar 13 Df 38.25N 8.13W
Alcalá de Chivert 13 Md 40.18N 0.14 E
Alcalá de Guadaira 13 Gg 37.20N 5.50W
Alcalá de Henares 13 Id 40.29N 3.22W
Alcalá del Júcar 13 Ke 39.12N 1.26W
Alcalá de los Gazules 13 Gh 36.28N 5.44W
Alcalá del Río 13 Gg 37.31N 5.59W
Alcalá la Real 13 Ig 37.28N 3.56W
Alcamo 14 Gm 37.59N 12.58 E
Alcanandre 13 Mc 41.37N 0.12 E
Alcanices 13 Fc 41.42N 6.21W
Alcañiz 13 Lc 41.03N 0.08W
Alcántara 13 Fe 39.43N 6.53W
Alcântara 54 Jd 2.24S 44.24W
Alcantara 14 Jm 37.49N 15.16 E
Alcántara, Embalse de- 13 Fe 39.45N 6.48W
Alcantarilla 13 Kg 37.58N 1.13W
Alcaraz 13 Jf 38.40N 2.29W
Alcaraz, Sierra de- 13 Jf 38.35N 2.25W
Alcaudete 13 Hg 37.36N 4.05W
Alcázar de San Juan 13 Ie 39.24N 3.12W
Alcester 63a Ac 9.33S 152.25 E
Alcira/Alzira 13 Le 39.09N 0.26W
Alcobaça [Braz.] 54 Kg 17.30S 39.13W
Alcobaça [Port.] 13 De 39.33N 8.59W
Alcobendas 13 Id 40.32N 3.38W
Alcoi/Alcoy 13 Lf 38.42N 0.28W
Alcolea del Pinar 13 Jc 41.02N 2.28W
Alcorta 55 Bk 33.32S 61.07W
Alcoutim 13 Eg 37.28N 7.28W
Alcova 46 Le 42.37N 106.36W
Alcoy/Alcoi 13 Lf 38.42N 0.28W
Alcubierre, Sierra de- 13 Lc 41.44N 0.29W
Alcudia 13 Pe 39.52N 3.07 E
Alcúdia, Badia d'-/Alcudia, Bahia de- 13 Pe 39.48N 3.13 E
Alcudia, Bahia de-/Alcúdia, Badia d'- 13 Pe 39.48N 3.13 E
Alcudia, Sierra de- 13 Hf 38.35N 4.35W
Aldabra Group 37b Ab 9.25S 46.22 E
Aldabra Islands 30 Li 9.25S 46.22 E
Aldama [Mex.] 48 Jf 22.55N 98.04W
Aldama [Mex.] 47 Cc 28.51N 105.54W
Aldan 22 Od 58.37N 125.24 E
Aldan [R.S.F.S.R.] 20 Hd 63.20N 129.25 E
Aldan [U.S.S.R.] 21 Oc 63.28N 129.35 E
Aldan Plateau (EN)=Aldanskoje Nagorje 21 Od 57.30N 127.30 E
Aldanskoje Nagorje=Aldan Plateau (EN) 21 Od 57.30N 127.30 E
Aldarhan 27 Gb 47.42N 96.36 E
Alde 12 Db 52.10N 1.32 E
Aldeburgh 9 Oi 52.09N 1.35 E
Aldeia 55 Ed 18.12S 55.10W
Aldeia, Serra da- 55 Ic 17.00S 46.50W
Alderney 9 Kl 49.43N 2.12W
Aldershot 12 Bc 51.15N 0.46W
Alderson 46 Ja 50.18N 111.26W
Aledo 45 Kf 41.12N 90.45W
Aleg 31 Fg 17.03N 13.53W
Alegranza 32 Ed 29.23N 13.30W
Alegre 54 Jh 20.46S 41.32W
Alegre, Rio- 55 Cb 15.14S 59.58W
Alegrete 56 Ic 29.46S 55.46W
Alej 20 Df 52.50N 83.35 E
Alejandra 55 Ci 29.54S 59.50W
Alejandro Selkirk, Isla- 52 Hi 33.45S 80.46W
Alejsk 20 Df 52.28N 82.45 E
Aleksandrija 16 He 48.40N 33.07 E
Aleksandrov 19 Dd 56.25N 38.42 E
Aleksandrov Gaj 19 Ee 50.08N 48.32 E
Aleksandrovka 16 He 48.59N 32.13 E
Aleksandrovsk 17 Hg 59.10N 57.35 E
Aleksandrovskoje 16 Mg 44.39N 43.00 E
Aleksandrovsk-Sahalinsk 22 Qd 50.54N 142.10 E
Aleksandrów Kujawski 10 Od 52.52N 18.42 E
Aleksandrów Łódzki 10 Pe 51.49N 19.19 E
Aleksandry, Zemlja- 21 Ga 80.45N 46.00 E
Alekseyevka [Kaz.-U.S.S.R.] 19 If 48.26N 85.40 E
Alekseyevka [Kaz.-U.S.S.R.] 19 He 51.58N 70.59 E
Alekseyevka [Kaz.-U.S.S.R.] 19 Nj 53.31N 69.28 E
Alekseyevka [R.S.F.S.R.] 19 De 50.39N 38.42 E
Alekseyevsk 20 Fe 57.50N 108.23 E
Alekseyevskoje 7 Mi 55.19N 50.03 E
Aleksin 16 Jb 54.31N 37.07 E
Aleksinac 15 Ef 43.32N 21.43 E
Alem 56 Ic 27.31S 55.15W
Ålem 7 Dh 56.57N 16.23 E
Alem Maya 35 Gd 9.27N 41.58 E
Ålen 8 Db 62.51N 11.17 E
Alençon 11 Gf 48.26N 0.05 E
Alenquer 54 Hd 1.56S 54.46W
Alenuihaha Channel 60 Oc 20.26N 156.00W
Alépé 34 Ed 5.30N 3.39W
Aleppo (EN)=Ḩalab 22 Ff 36.12N 37.10 E
Aléria 11a Ba 42.06N 9.31 E
Aléria, Plaine d'- 11a Ba 42.05N 9.30 E
Alert 39 Ma 82.30N 62.00W
Alert Bay 46 Ba 50.35N 126.55W
Alès 11 Kj 44.08N 4.05 E
Aleşd 15 Fb 47.04N 22.25 E
Alessandria 14 Cf 44.54N 8.37 E
Ålestrup 8 Ch 56.42N 9.30 E
Ålesund 6 Gc 62.28N 6.09 E
Aleutian Basin (EN) 38 Ad 57.00N 177.00 E
Aleutian Islands 38 Bd 52.00N 176.00W
Aleutian Range 38 Dd 59.00N 155.00W
Aleutian Trench (EN) 3 Je 51.00N 179.00 E
Alexander, Cape- 60 Fi 6.35S 156.30 E
Alexander, Kap- 41 Ec 78.10N 72.45W
Alexander Archipelago 38 Fd 56.30N 134.00W
Alexanderbaai 37 Be 28.40S 16.30 E
Alexander City 43 Je 32.56N 85.57W
Alexander Island 66 Qe 71.00S 70.00W
Alexandra 61 Ci 45.15S 169.24 E
Alexandra Fiord 42 Ka 79.17N 75.00W
Alexandretta (EN)=İskenderun 22 Ff 36.37N 36.07 E
Alexandretta, Gulf of- (EN) =İskenderun Körfezi 23 Eb 36.30N 35.40 E
Alexándria 15 Fi 40.38N 22.27 E
Alexandria [Austl.] 59 Hc 19.05S 136.40 E
Alexandria [La.-U.S.] 39 Jf 31.18N 92.27W
Alexandria [Mn.-U.S.] 43 Hb 45.53N 95.22W
Alexandria [Rom.] 15 If 43.59N 25.20 E
Alexandria [S.Afr.] 37 Df 33.39S 26.24 E
Alexandria [Va.-U.S.] 44 If 38.49N 77.06W
Alexandria (EN)=Al Iskandarīyah [Eg.] 31 Je 31.12N 29.54 E
Alexandria Bay 44 Jc 44.20N 75.55W
Alexandrina, Lake- 59 Hg 35.25S 139.10 E
Alexandrita 54 Hg 19.42S 50.27W
Alexandroúpolis 6 Ig 40.51N 25.52 E
'Aleyak, Godār-e- 24 Qd 36.30N 57.45 E
Alf 10 Df 50.03N 7.07 E
Alfabia, Sierra de- 13 Oe 39.45N 2.48 E
Alfambra 13 Kd 40.21N 1.07W
Al Fardah 35 Hc 14.51N 48.26 E
Alfaro 13 Kb 42.11N 1.45W
Al Fāshir 31 Jg 13.38N 25.21 E
Al Fashn 33 Fd 28.49N 30.54 E
Alfatar 15 Kf 43.57N 27.17 E
Al Fathah 24 Je 35.04N 43.34 E
Al Fāw 23 Gd 29.58N 48.29 E
Al Fawwārah 24 Ji 26.03N 43.05 E
Al Fayyūm 31 Kf 29.19N 30.58 E
Alfbach 12 Jd 50.03N 7.08 E
Alfeld 10 Fe 51.59N 9.50 E
Alfenas 54 Ih 21.26S 45.57W
Al Fifi 35 Dc 10.03N 25.01 E
Alfiós 15 El 37.37N 21.27 E
Alföld 5 If 47.15N 20.25 E
Alfonsine 14 Gf 44.30N 12.03 E
Alford 12 Ca 53.15N 0.11 E
Ålfotbreen 8 Ac 61.45N 5.40 E
Alfreton 12 Aa 53.06N 1.23W
Alfta 7 Df 61.21N 16.05 E
Al Fuḩayḩīl 23 Gd 29.05N 48.08 E
Al Fuhūd 24 Lg 30.58N 46.43 E
Al Fujayrah 23 Id 25.06N 56.21 E
Al Fūlah 35 Dc 11.48N 28.24 E
Al Fuqahā' 33 Cd 27.50N 16.21 E
Al Furāt=Euphrates (EN) 21 Gf 31.00N 47.25 E
Al Fuwayriţ 24 Ni 26.02N 51.22 E
Alga 19 Ff 49.55N 57.20 E
Algador 13 Ie 39.55N 3.53W
Al Gārah 24 Ih 29.52N 40.15 E
Algarås 8 Ff 58.48N 14.14 E
Ålgård 8 Af 58.46N 5.51 E
Algarrobo 49 Jh 10.12N 74.04W
Algarve 13 Dg 37.10N 8.15W
Algarve 5 Fh 37.10N 8.15W
Algeciras 6 Fh 36.08N 5.30W
Algeciras, Bahía de- 13 Gh 36.09N 5.25W
Algena 35 Fb 17.20N 38.34 E
Algeria (EN)=Al Jazā'ir [1] 31 Hf 28.00N 3.00 E
Algerian Basin (EN) 5 Gh 39.00N 5.00 E
Al Gharaq as Sulţānī 24 Dh 29.08N 30.42 E
Al Gharbī 32 Jc 34.40N 11.13 E
Al Ghāţ 24 Ki 26.00N 45.03 E
Al Ghaydah 23 Hf 16.12N 52.15 E
Alghero 14 Cj 40.33N 8.19 E
Alghero, Rada d'- 14 Cj 40.35N 8.20 E
Älghult 8 Fg 57.01N 15.34 E
Al Ghurāb 24 Dj 25.20N 30.20 E
Al Ghurayfah 24 Qk 23.59N 56.29 E
Al Ghurdaqah 24 Fd 27.14N 33.50 E
Algiers (EN)=Al Jazā'ir 31 He 36.47N 3.03 E
Algiers (EN)=Al Jazā'ir [3] 32 Hb 36.35N 3.00 E
Algoa Bay 30 Jl 33.50S 25.50 E
Algodoeiro, Serra do- 55 Jc 16.30S 44.45W
Algoma 45 Md 44.36N 87.27W
Algoma Uplands 44 Fb 47.00N 83.35W
Algona 45 Ie 43.04N 94.14W
Algonquin Park 44 Hc 45.27N 78.26W
Algrange 12 Ie 49.21N 6.03 E
Al Ḩabakah 24 Jh 29.51N 42.16 E
Al Ḩadd 23 Ie 22.29N 59.58 E
Al Ḩadīdah 35 Ia 21.31N 50.28 E
Al Ḩadīthah 23 Fc 34.07N 42.23 E
Al Ḩadīthah 24 Gg 31.28N 37.08 E
Al Ḩaḑr 24 Je 35.35N 42.44 E
Al Haffah 24 Ge 35.35N 36.02 E
Al Ḩahjarah 23 Fc 30.25N 44.30 E
Al Ḩā'ir 24 Lj 24.23N 46.50 E
Al Ḩajar 35 Hb 16.08N 47.50 E
Al Hajar 23 Ie 23.15N 57.30 E
Al Halfāyah 24 Lg 31.49N 47.26 E
Alhama 13 Kb 42.11N 1.45W
Al Ḩamād 21 Ff 32.00N 39.30 E
Alhama de Granada 13 Ih 37.00N 3.59W
Alhama de Murcia 13 Kg 37.51N 1.25W
Alhamilla, Sierra- 13 Jh 36.58N 2.20W
Al Ḩammāh 32 Ic 33.54N 9.48 E
Al Ḩammām [Eg.] 24 Cg 30.50N 29.23 E
Al Ḩammām [Iraq] 24 Kg 31.08N 44.04 E
Al Ḩamrā 24 Pj 25.42N 55.47 E
Al Ḩanīyah 24 Kh 29.10N 45.50 E
Al Ḩarrah 24 Ch 28.20N 29.07 E
Al Ḩarrah 24 Hg 31.00N 38.40 E
Al Harūj al Aswad 30 If 27.00N 17.10 E
Al Ḩasā 24 Fg 30.49N 35.59 E
Al Ḩasā' 21 Gg 26.35N 48.10 E
Al Ḩasakah 23 Fb 36.29N 40.45 E
Al Ḩasan 24 Je 34.39N 43.43 E
Al Ḩasānī 24 Gj 24.58N 37.05 E
Alhaurín el Grande 13 Hh 36.38N 4.41W
Al Ḩawāmidīyah 24 Dh 29.54N 31.15 E
Al Ḩawātah 35 Ec 13.25N 34.38 E
Al Ḩawjā' 24 Hh 28.59N 38.34 E
Al Ḩawrah 35 Hc 13.49N 47.35 E
Al Ḩayy 23 Gc 32.10N 46.03 E
Al Ḩayz 33 Ed 28.02N 28.39 E
Al Hibāk 23 He 20.20N 53.10 E
Al Ḩijāz 21 Fg 24.30N 38.30 E
Al Ḩillah 33 Ie 23.50N 46.51 E
Al Ḩillah 23 Fc 32.29N 44.25 E
Al Ḩinākīyah 23 Fe 24.51N 40.31 E
Al Hindīyah 24 Kf 32.32N 44.13 E
Al Ḩinnāh 24 Mi 26.56N 48.45 E
Al Hirmil 24 Ge 34.23N 36.23 E
Al Hoceima 32 Gb 35.15N 3.55W
Al Hoceima [3] 32 Gb 35.00N 4.15W
Alhucemas, Peñón de- 13 Ii 35.13N 3.53W
Al Ḩudaydah 22 Gh 14.48N 42.57 E
Al Ḩufrah 33 Cd 29.30N 17.55 E
Al Hufrah 23 Ed 28.49N 38.15 E
Al Hufūf 22 Gg 25.22N 49.34 E
Al Hūj 24 Hh 29.00N 38.25 E
Al Ḩunayy 24 Mj 24.48N 48.45 E
Al Ḩuşayḩişah 35 Ec 14.44N 33.18 E
Al Ḩuwaimī 23 Fg 13.58N 47.40 E
Al Ḩuwayyiţ 24 Ij 25.36N 40.23 E
Al Ḩyyānīyah 24 Jh 28.42N 42.18 E
'Alīābād [Iran] 23 Id 28.37N 55.51 E
'Alīābād [Iran] 24 Le 35.04N 46.58 E
'Alīābād [Iran] 24 Nd 36.37N 51.33 E
Alīābād 24 Pd 36.56N 54.50 E
'Alīābād, Kūh-e- 23 Hc 34.13N 50.46 E
Aliaga 13 Ld 40.40N 0.42W
Aliağa 24 Bc 38.48N 26.59 E
Aliákmon 15 Fi 40.30N 22.40 E
'Alī al Gharbī 24 Lf 32.27N 46.41 E
'Alī ash Sharqī 24 Lf 32.07N 46.44 E
Ali-Bajramly 19 Eh 39.55N 48.57 E
Alibej, Ozero- 15 Nd 45.50N 30.00 E
Alibey Adasi 15 Jj 39.20N 26.38 E
Alibo 35 Fd 9.53N 37.05 E
Alibori 34 Fc 11.56N 3.17 E
Alibunar 15 Dd 45.04N 20.58 E
Alicante 6 Fh 38.21N 0.29W
Alicante [3] 13 Lf 38.30N 0.30W
Alicante, Golfo de- 13 Lf 38.20N 0.15W
Alice [S.Afr.] 37 Df 32.47S 26.50 E
Alice [Tx.-U.S.] 43 Hf 27.45N 98.04W
Alice, Punta- 14 Lk 39.12N 17.09 E
Alice Springs 58 Eg 23.42S 133.53 E
Aliceville 44 Ci 33.08N 88.09W
Alicudi 14 Il 38.30N 14.20 E
Alīgarh 22 Jg 28.02N 78.17 E
Alīgūdarz 24 Mf 33.24N 49.41 E
Alihe → Oroqen Zizhiqi 27 La 50.35N 123.42 E
Alijó 13 Ec 41.16N 7.28W
Alijos, Rocas- 47 Ad 24.57N 115.44W
'Alī Jūq, Kūh-e- 24 Ng 31.30N 51.45 E
Al Ikhwan 21 Hh 12.08N 53.10 E
Al Ikhwān 24 Fi 26.19N 34.52 E
Alima 30 Ii 1.36S 16.36 E
Al Imārāt al 'Arabīyah al Muttaḩidah=United Arab Emirates (EN) [1] 22 Hg 24.00N 54.00 E
Alimiá 15 Km 36.16N 27.43 E
Alindao 35 Cd 5.02N 21.13 E
Alinglapalap Atoll 57 Hd 7.08N 168.16 E
Alingsås 7 Ch 57.56N 12.31 E
Aliquippa 44 Ge 40.38N 80.16W
Al 'Irāq=Iraq (EN) [1] 22 Gf 33.00N 44.00 E
Al'Irq 33 Dd 29.01N 21.31 E
Al 'Irqah 23 Gg 13.40N 47.18 E
Ali-Sabjeh 35 Gc 11.08N 42.43 E
'Alī Shāh 'Avaz 24 Ne 35.39N 51.04 E
Al Iskandarīyah [Eg.] = Alexandria (EN) 31 Je 31.12N 29.54 E
Al Iskandarīyah [Iraq] 24 Kf 32.53N 44.21 E
Aliskerovo 20 Lc 67.52N 167.40 E
Al Ismā'īlīyah=Ismailia (EN) 33 Fc 30.35N 32.16 E
Al Istiwā'īyah al Gharbīyah [3] 35 Dd 5.20N 28.30 E
Al Istiwā'īyah al Sharkīyah [3] 35 Ed 5.20N 33.50 E
Alistráti 15 Gh 41.04N 23.58 E
Alitak, Cape- 40 Ie 56.51N 154.21W
Alite Reef 63a Ec 8.53S 160.38 E
Alitus/Alytus 19 Ce 54.25N 24.08 E
Alivérion 15 Hk 38.25N 24.02 E
Aliwal North 31 Jl 30.44S 26.40 E
Al Jabalayn 35 Ec 12.36N 32.48 E
Al Jadīdah [Eg.] 24 Cj 25.34N 28.51 E
Al Jadīdah [Sau.Ar.] 24 Mj 25.39N 49.32 E
Al Jafr 24 Gg 30.18N 36.13 E
Al Jāfūrah 35 Ia 23.25N 50.17 E
Al Jāfūrah 24 Nj 25.00N 50.15 E
Al Jaghbūb 31 Jf 29.45N 24.31 E
Al Jahrah 23 Gc 29.20N 47.40 E
Al Jalāmīd 24 Ig 31.17N 40.06 E
Al Jamalīyah 24 Nj 25.37N 51.05 E
Al Jamm 32 Jb 35.18N 10.43 E
Al Janā'in 32 Jc 31.44N 10.09 E
Aljat 16 Pj 39.58N 49.27 E
Al Jawf [Lib.] 31 Jf 24.12N 23.18 E
Al Jawf [Sau.Ar.] 22 Fg 29.50N 39.52 E
Al Jazā'ir=Algeria (EN) [1] 31 Hf 28.00N 3.00 E
Al Jazā'ir=Algiers (EN) [3] 32 Hb 36.35N 3.00 E
Al Jazā'ir=Algiers (EN) 31 He 36.47N 3.03 E
Al Jazā'ir-El Harrach 13 Ph 36.43N 3.08 E
Al Jazīrah [3] 35 Ec 14.40N 33.30 E
Al Jazīrah [Asia] 21 Gf 35.10N 42.00 E
Al Jazīrah [Sud.] 30 Kg 14.25N 33.00 E
Aljezur 13 Dg 37.19N 8.48W
Aljibe 13 Gh 36.31N 5.37W
Al Jifārah 30 Ie 32.30N 11.45 E
Al Jiwā' 23 He 23.00N 54.00 E
Al Jīzah=Giza (EN) 31 Ke 30.01N 31.13 E
Al Jubayl 23 Gd 27.01N 49.40 E
Al Jubaylah 24 Lj 24.54N 46.27 E
Al Junaynah [Sau.Ar.] 33 He 20.17N 42.48 E
Al Junaynah [Sud.] 31 Jg 13.27N 22.27 E
Al Juraid 24 Mi 27.11N 49.52 E
Aljustrel 13 Dg 37.52N 8.10W
Alka 40a Db 52.15N 174.30W
Al Kaba'ish 24 Lg 30.58N 47.00 E
Al Kāf [3] 32 Ib 36.00N 9.00 E
Al Kāf 32 Ib 36.11N 8.43 E
Alkali Lake 46 Ff 41.42N 119.50W
Al Kamāsin 23 Fe 20.25N 44.48 E
Al Kāmilīn 35 Eb 15.05N 33.11 E
Al Karak 24 Fg 31.11N 35.42 E
Al Karkh 24 Kf 33.20N 44.20 E
Al Karnak 33 Fd 25.43N 32.39 E
Al Kawah 35 Ec 13.44N 32.30 E
Al Kāẓimīyah 24 Kf 33.22N 44.20 E
Alken 12 Hd 50.52N 5.18 E
Al Khabrā' 23 Fd 26.04N 43.33 E
Al Khābūra 23 Ie 23.50N 57.18 E
Al-Khalīj al- 'Arabi=Persian Gulf (EN) 21 Hg 27.00N 51.00 E
Al Khalīl 24 Fg 31.32N 35.06 E
Al Khālis 24 Kf 33.51N 44.32 E
Al Khandaq 35 Eb 18.36N 30.34 E
Al Khārijah 31 Kf 25.26N 30.33 E
Al Kharj 24 Lj 24.10N 47.30 E
Al Kharţūm=Khartoum (EN) [3] 35 Eb 15.50N 33.00 E
Al Kharţūm=Khartoum (EN) 31 Kg 15.36N 32.32 E
Al Kharţūm Baḩrī=Khartoum North (EN) 31 Kg 15.38N 32.33 E
Al Khaşab 24 Qi 26.12N 56.15 E
Al Khaţţ 24 Qk 25.37N 56.01 E
Al Khawr 23 Hd 25.40N 51.30 E
Al Khidr 24 Kg 31.12N 45.33 E
Al Khubar 23 Hd 26.17N 50.12 E
Al Khufayfīyah 23 Fe 24.55N 44.42 E
Al Khums [3] 33 Bc 31.20N 14.10 E
Al Khums 31 Ie 32.39N 14.16 E
Al Khunn 33 Ha 23.18N 49.15 E
Al Khuwayr 24 Ni 26.04N 51.05 E
Al Kidn 35 Ia 22.30N 54.00 E
Al Kilḩ Sharq 24 Ej 25.03N 32.52 E
Alkionídhon, Kólpos- 15 Fk 38.05N 23.00 E
Al Kir'ānah 24 Nj 25.00N 51.03 E
Alkmaar 11 Kb 52.37N 4.44 E
Al Kūfah 24 Kf 32.02N 44.24 E
Al Kumayt 24 Lf 32.02N 46.52 E
Al Kuntillah 33 Fc 30.00N 34.41 E
Al Kushḩ 24 Ei 26.14N 32.05 E
Al Kut 23 Gc 32.30N 45.49 E
Al Kuwayt=Kuwait (EN) [1] 22 Gg 29.30N 47.45 E
Al Kuwayt=Kuwait (EN) 22 Gg 29.20N 47.59 E
Al Labbah 24 Ih 29.20N 41.30 E
Al Lādhiqīyah=Latakia (EN) 22 Ff 35.31N 35.07 E
Allagash River 44 Mb 47.05N 69.20W
Al Lagowa 35 Dc 11.24N 29.08 E
Allahābād 22 Kg 25.27N 81.51 E
Allah-Jun 20 Id 60.27N 134.57 E
Allah-Jun 20 Id 61.08N 137.59 E
Allahüekber DaGı 24 Jb 40.35N 42.32 E
Allakaket 40 Ic 66.34N 152.41W
Allanmyo 25 Je 19.22N 95.13 E
Allariz 13 Eb 42.11N 7.48W
All-Awash Island 51n Bb 12.55N 61.10W
Alldays 37 Dd 22.41S 29.06 E
Ålleberg 8 Ef 58.08N 13.36 E
Allegan 44 Ed 42.32N 85.51W
Allegheny Mountains 38 Lf 38.30N 80.00W
Allegheny Plateau 38 Le 41.30N 78.00W
Allegheny Reservoir 44 He 42.00N 78.56W
Allegheny River 44 Ge 40.27N 80.00W
Allègre, Pointe- 51e Ab 16.22N 61.45W
Allen 26 Hd 12.30N 124.17 E
Allen, Bog of- 9 Gh 53.20N 7.00W
Allen, Lough-/Loch Aillionn 9 Eg 54.08N 8.08W
Allendale 44 Gi 33.01N 81.19W
Allende 47 Dc 28.20N 100.51W
Allendorf (Eder) 12 Kc 51.02N 8.40 E
Allendorf (Lumda) 12 Kd 50.41N 8.50 E
Allentown 43 Lc 40.37N 75.30W
Alleppey 22 Ji 9.29N 76.19 E
Aller 10 Fd 52.57N 9.11 E
Allevard 11 Mi 45.24N 6.04 E
Allgäuer Alpen 10 Gi 47.20N 10.25 E
Alliance [Nb.-U.S.] 43 Gc 42.06N 102.52W
Alliance [Oh.-U.S.] 44 Ge 40.56N 81.06W
Allier [3] 11 Ih 46.30N 3.00 E
Allier 5 Gf 46.57N 3.05 E
Al Lifīyah 23 Fc 30.35N 43.09 E
Al Lişāfah 24 Li 27.37N 46.52 E
Alliston 44 Hc 44.09N 79.52W
Al Līth 23 Fe 20.09N 40.16 E
Alloa 9 Je 56.07N 3.49W
Allonnes 11 Gg 47.58N 0.09 E
Allos 11 Mj 44.14N 6.38 E
All Saints 51d Bb 17.03N 61.48W
Al Luḩayyah 23 Ff 15.43N 42.42 E
Al Luwaymī 23 Fd 27.54N 42.22 E
Alm 14 Hb 48.05N 13.55 E
Alma [Ga.-U.S.] 44 Fj 31.33N 82.28W
Alma [Mi.-U.S.] 44 Ed 43.23N 84.39W
Alma [Nb.-U.S.] 45 Gf 40.06N 99.22W
Alma [Que.-Can.] 42 Kg 48.32N 71.40W
Alma-Ata 22 Je 43.15N 76.57 E
Alma-Atinskaja Oblast [3] 19 Hg 44.00N 77.00 E
Almada 13 Cf 38.41N 9.09W
Almadén 13 Hf 38.46N 4.50W
Al Madīnah [Iraq] 24 Lg 30.57N 47.16 E
Al Madīnah [Sau.Ar.] = Medina (EN) 22 Fg 24.28N 39.36 E
Al Madīnah al Fikrīyah 24 Di 27.56N 30.49 E
'Al Madōw 35 Hc 10.59N 48.42 E
Al Mafraq 24 Gf 32.21N 36.12 E
Al Maghrib=Morocco (EN) [1] 31 Ge 32.00N 5.50W
Almagro 13 If 38.53N 3.43W
Almagrundet 8 He 59.06N 19.00 E

Index Symbols

[1] Independent Nation
[2] State, Region
[3] District, County
[4] Municipality
[5] Colony, Dependency
Continent
Physical Region
Historical or Cultural Region
Mount, Mountain
Volcano
Hill
Mountains, Mountain Range
Hills, Escarpment
Plateau, Upland
Pass, Gap
Plain, Lowland
Delta
Salt Flat
Valley, Canyon
Crater, Cave
Karst Features
Depression
Polder
Desert, Dunes
Forest, Woods
Heath, Steppe
Oasis
Cape, Point
Coast, Beach
Cliff
Peninsula
Isthmus
Sandbank
Island
Atoll
Rock, Reef
Islands, Archipelago
Rocks, Reefs
Coral Reef
Well, Spring
Geyser
River, Stream
Waterfall Rapids
River Mouth, Estuary
Lake
Salt Lake
Intermittent Lake
Reservoir
Swamp, Pond
Canal
Glacier
Ice Shelf, Pack Ice
Ocean
Sea
Gulf, Bay
Strait, Fjord
Lagoon
Bank
Seamount
Tablemount
Ridge
Shelf
Basin
Escarpment, Sea Scarp
Fracture
Trench, Abyss
National Park, Reserve
Point of Interest
Recreation Site
Cave, Cavern
Historic Site
Ruins
Wall, Walls
Church, Abbey
Temple
Scientific Station
Airport
Port
Lighthouse
Mine
Tunnel
Dam, Bridge

Al Maḥallah al Kubrá 33 Fc 30.58N 31.10 E
Al Maḥāriq 33 Fd 25.37N 30.39 E
Al Mahdīyah 32 Jb 35.30N 11.04 E
Al Mahdīyah [3] 32 Jb 35.35N 11.00 E
Al Maḥfid 33 Ig 14.03N 46.55 E
Al Mahrah 23 Hf 16.56N 52.15 E
Al Maḥras 32 Jc 34.32N 10.30 E
Al Majarr al Kabīr 24 Lg 31.34N 47.10 E
Almajului, Munţii- 15 Fe 44.43N 22.12 E
Al Maks al Qiblī 33 Fe 24.35N 30.38 E
Almalyk 19 Gg 40.49N 69.38 E
Al Manādir 24 Pk 23.10N 55.10 E
Al Manāmah=Manama (EN) 22 Hg 26.13N 50.35 E
Al Manāqil 35 Ec 14.15N 32.59 E
Almanor, Lake- 46 Ef 40.15N 121.08W
Almansa 13 Kf 38.52N 1.05W
Almansa, Puerto de- 13 Lf 38.49N 0.58W
Al Manshāh 33 Fd 26.28N 31.48 E
Almansor 13 Df 38.56N 8.54W
Al Manṣūrah 33 Fc 31.03N 31.23 E
Al Manzilah 24 Dg 31.09N 31.56 E
Almanzor, Pico de- 13 Gd 40.15N 5.18W
Almanzora 13 Jg 37.21N 2.08W
Al Ma'qil 24 Lg 30.33N 47.48 E
Al Maqnah 24 Fh 28.24N 34.45 E
Al Maqṭa' 24 Pj 24.25N 54.29 E
Almar 13 Gd 40.54N 5.29W
Al Marāghah 24 Di 26.42N 31.36 E
Al Marsá 14 En 36.53N 10.20 E
Al Mary 31 Je 32.30N 20.54 E
Almaş 15 Gb 47.14N 23.19 E
Almas, Picos de- 52 Lg 13.33S 41.56W
Almas, Rio das- 54 If 14.35S 49.02W
'Al Maskād 35 Hc 11.18N 49.41 E
Al Maṭarīyah 33 Fc 31.11N 32.02 E
Al Mawṣil=Mosul (EN) 22 Gf 36.20N 43.08 E
Al Mayādīn 24 Ie 35.01N 40.27 E
Al Mayyāh 24 Ji 27.51N 42.47 E
Almazán 13 Jc 41.29N 2.32W
Al Mazār 24 Eg 31.23N 33.23 E
Almazny 20 Gd 62.19N 114.04 E
Almazora 13 Le 39.57N 0.03W
Al Mazra'ah 24 Fg 31.16N 35.31 E
Alme, Brilon- 12 Kc 51.27N 8.37 E
Almeida 13 Fc 41.16N 6.04W
Almeirim [Braz.] 54 Hd 1.32S 52.34W
Almeirim [Port.] 13 De 39.12N 8.38W
Al Mellem 35 Dd 9.49N 28.45 E
Almelo 11 Mb 52.21N 6.39 E
Almenara, Sierra de la- 13 Kg 37.35N 1.31W
Almendra, Embalse de- 13 Fc 41.13N 6.10W
Almendralejo 13 Ff 38.41N 6.24W
Almeria [3] 13 Jg 37.10N 2.20W
Almeria 6 Fh 36.50N 2.27W
Almería, Golfo de- 13 Jh 36.46N 2.30W
Almetjevsk 19 Fe 54.54N 52.20 E
Al Metlaoui 32 Ic 34.20N 8.24 E
Älmhult 7 Dh 56.33N 14.08 E
Almijara, Sierra de- 13 Ih 36.55N 3.55W
Almina, Punta- 13 Gi 35.54N 5.17W
Al Minyā [Eg.] 24 Dh 29.45N 31.18 E
Al Minyā [Eg.] 31 Kf 28.06N 30.45 E
Al Miqdādīyah 24 Kf 33.59N 44.56 E
Almirante 49 Fi 9.18N 82.24W
Almirante Brown 66 Qe 64.53S 62.53W
Almirós 15 Fj 39.11N 22.46 E
Almiroú, Órmos- 15 Hn 35.23N 24.20 E
Almodôvar 13 Dg 37.31N 8.04W
Almodóvar del Campo 13 Hf 38.43N 4.10W
Almodóvar del Río 13 Gg 37.48N 5.01W
Almonte 13 Fg 37.15N 6.31W
Almonte 13 Fe 39.42N 6.28W
Almora 25 Fc 29.37N 79.40 E
Almoustarat 34 Fb 17.22N 0.07 E
Älmsta 8 He 59.58N 18.48 E
Al Mubarraz 23 Gd 25.25N 49.35 E
Al Mudawwarah 24 Fh 29.19N 35.59 E
Al Mudhari, Rujm- 24 Hf 32.45N 39.08 E
Al Mughayrā' [Sau.Ar.] 24 Gh 29.17N 37.41 E
Al Mughayrā' [U.A.E.] 24 Oj 24.05N 53.32 E
Al Muglad 31 Jg 11.02N 27.44 E
Al Muḥarraq 24 Ni 26.16N 50.37 E
Al Mukallā 22 Gh 14.32N 49.08 E
Al Mukhā 23 Fg 13.19N 43.15 E
Al Munastīr [3] 32 Jb 35.40N 10.50 E
Al Munastīr 32 Jb 35.47N 10.50 E
Almuñécar 13 Ih 36.43N 3.41W
Al Murabba' 24 Kj 25.43N 44.18 E
Almus 24 Gb 40.23N 36.55 E
Al Musannāh 24 Lh 29.02N 47.12 E
Al Muṣawwarāt aṣ Ṣafrā' 35 Eb 16.25N 33.22 E
Al Musayjid 24 Hj 24.05N 39.06 E
Al Musayyib 24 Kf 32.47N 44.18 E
Al Mustawī 24 Kj 25.55N 44.40 E
Al Muthanna [3] 24 Kg 30.50N 45.20 E
Al Muwayh 33 He 22.45N 41.35 E
Al Muwaylih 24 Fi 27.41N 35.28 E
Alnön 8 Gb 62.25N 17.25 E
Alnwick 9 Lf 55.25N 1.42W
Ålö 8 Jd 60.20N 22.15 E
Aloândia 55 Hc 17.43S 49.29W
Alofi 58 Kf 19.03S 169.56W
Alofi, Ile- 57 Jf 14.19S 178.02W
Alofi Bay 64k Bb 19.01S 169.56W
Aloja 7 Fh 57.44N 24.59 E
Along 25 Ic 28.10N 94.46 E
Alónnisos 15 Gj 39.13N 23.55 E
Alonsa 45 Ga 50.47N 99.00W
Alonso, Rio- 55 Gg 24.05S 51.35W
Alor, Kepulauan- 26 Hh 8.15S 124.30 E
Alor, Pulau- 21 Oj 8.15S 124.45 E
Alora 13 Hh 36.48N 4.42W
Alor Setar 22 Mi 6.07N 100.22 E
Alost/Aalst 11 Kd 50.56N 4.02 E
Alotau 60 Ej 10.31S 150.43 E
Aloysius, Mount- 59 Fe 26.00S 128.34 E
Alpen = Alps (EN) 5 Gf 46.25N 10.00 E
Alpena 43 Kb 45.04N 83.26W
Alpera 13 Kf 38.58N 1.13W
Alpes=Alps (EN) 5 Gf 46.25N 10.00 E
Alpes Bernoises/Berner
Alpen=Bernese Alps (EN) 14 Bd 46.25N 7.30 E
Alpes Cottiennes 14 Af 44.45N 7.00 E
Alpes de Haute-Provence [3] 11 Lj 44.10N 6.00 E
Alpes Grées/Alpi Graie 14 Be 45.30N 7.10 E
Alpes Mancelles 11 Ff 48.25N 0.10W
Alpes Maritimes 14 Af 44.15N 7.10 E
Alpes-Maritimes [3] 11 Nk 44.00N 7.10 E
Alpes Pennines/Alpi
Pennine 14 Bd 46.05N 7.50 E
Alpes Valaisannes/Walliser
Alpen 14 Bd 46.10N 7.30 E
Alpha Cordillera (EN) 67 Re 85.30N 125.00W
Alphen aan der Rijn 12 Gb 52.08N 4.42 E
Alphonse Island 30 Mi 7.00S 52.45 E
Alpi=Alps (EN) 5 Gf 46.25N 10.00 E
Alpi Apuane 14 Ef 44.05N 10.20 E
Alpi Aurine 10 Hi 47.00N 11.55 E
Alpi Carniche 14 Gd 46.40N 13.00 E
Alpi Cozie 14 Af 44.45N 7.00 E
Alpi Graie/Alpes Grées 14 Be 45.30N 7.10 E
Alpi Lepontine 14 Cd 46.25N 8.40 E
Alpi Liguri 14 Cf 44.10N 8.05 E
Alpi Marittime 14 Bf 44.15N 7.10 E
Alpine [Az.-U.S.] 46 Kj 33.51N 109.09W
Alpine [Tx.-U.S.] 43 Ge 30.22N 103.40W
Alpine [Wy.-U.S.] 46 Je 43.15N 110.59W
Alpi Orobie 14 Dd 46.00N 10.00 E
Alpi Pennine/Alpes
Pennines 14 Bd 46.05N 7.50 E
Alpi Retiche=Rhaetian Alps
(EN) 14 Dd 46.30N 10.00 E
Alpi Ticinesi 14 Cd 46.20N 8.45 E
Alpi Venoste 10 Gj 46.45N 10.55 E
Alprech, Cap d'- 12 Dd 50.42N 1.34 E
Alps (EN) = Alpen 5 Gf 46.25N 10.00 E
Alps (EN)=Alpes 5 Gf 46.25N 10.00 E
Alps (EN)=Alpi 5 Gf 46.25N 10.00 E
Al qa 'Āmīyāt 35 Hb 18.50N 48.30 E
Al Qābil 24 Pk 23.56N 55.49 E
Al Qaḍārif 31 Kg 14.02N 35.24 E
Al Qaḍīmah 23 Ee 22.21N 39.09 E
Al Qādisīya [3] 24 Kg 31.50N 45.00 E
Al Qādisīya 24 Kg 31.42N 44.28 E
Al Qadmūs 24 Ge 35.05N 36.10 E
Al Qaffāy 24 Nj 24.35N 51.44 E
Al Qāhirah=Cairo (EN) 31 Ke 30.03N 31.15 E
Al Qāhirah-Imbabah 33 Fc 30.05N 31.13 E
Al Qāhirah-Miṣr al Jadīdah 33 Fc 30.06N 31.20 E
Al Qā'īyah 24 Ki 26.27N 45.35 E
Al Qal'ah al Kubrá 14 Eo 35.52N 10.32 E
Al Qalībah 23 Ed 28.24N 37.42 E
Al Qāmishlī 23 Fb 37.02N 41.14 E
Al Qanṭarah 33 Fc 30.52N 32.19 E
Al Qaryah ash Sharqīyah 33 Bc 30.24N 13.36 E
Al Qaryatayn 24 Ge 34.14N 37.14 E
Al Qaṣab 24 Kj 25.18N 45.30 E
Al Qaşabāt 33 Bc 32.35N 14.03 E
Al Qa'şah 24 Ch 28.25N 28.56 E
Al Qash 35 Fb 16.48N 35.51 E
Al Qaşr 33 Ed 25.42N 28.53 E
Al Qaşrayn 32 Ib 35.11N 8.48 E
Al Qaşrayn [3] 32 Ib 35.15N 9.00 E
Al Qaṭif 24 Mi 26.33N 50.00 E
Al Qaṭrānī 24 Gg 31.15N 36.03 E
Al Qaṭrūn 33 Be 24.56N 14.38 E
Al Qay'īyah 23 Fe 24.18N 43.30 E
Al Qayrawān 32 Jb 35.41N 10.07 E
Al Qayrawān [3] 32 Ib 35.30N 10.00 E
Al Qayṣūmah [Sau.Ar.] 24 Jh 29.11N 42.58 E
Al Qayṣūmah [Sau.Ar.] 23 Gd 28.16N 46.03 E
Alqōsh 24 Jd 36.44N 43.06 E
Al Qubayyāt 24 Ge 34.34N 36.17 E
Al Qunayṭirah 23 Ec 33.07N 35.49 E
Al Qunfudhah 23 Ff 19.08N 41.05 E
Al Qurayyah 24 Gh 28.45N 36.12 E
Al Qurnah 24 Lg 31.00N 47.26 E
Al Quşaymah 33 Fc 30.40N 34.22 E
Al Quşayr [Eg.] 31 Kf 26.06N 34.17 E
Al Quşayr [Syr.] 24 Ge 34.31N 36.35 E
Al Qūşīyah 33 Fd 27.26N 30.49 E
Al Quşūr 14 Co 35.54N 8.53 E
Al Quṭayfah 24 Gf 33.44N 36.36 E
Al Quwārah 24 Ji 26.47N 43.28 E
Al Quwayr 24 Jd 36.03N 43.30 E
Al Quzah 35 Hb 15.06N 49.08 E
Als 8 Ci 55.00N 9.55 E
Alsace 11 Nf 48.30N 7.30 E
Alsace, Ballon d'- 11 Mg 47.50N 6.51 E
Alsasua 13 Jb 42.54N 2.10W
Alsdorf 12 Id 50.53N 6.10 E
Alsea River 46 Cd 44.26N 124.05W
Alsenz 12 Je 49.49N 7.51 E
Alsfeld 10 Ff 50.45N 9.16 E
Alsina, Laguna- 55 Am 36.52S 62.07W
Alsten 7 Cd 65.57N 12.36 E
Alsterån 8 Gh 56.55N 16.26 E
Alsunga 8 Ig 57.02N 21.28 E
Alta 7 Fb 69.58N 23.14 E
Altaelva 7 Fb 69.58N 23.23 E
Altafjorden 7 Fa 70.12N 23.06 E
Altagracia 54 Da 10.07N 71.14W
Alta Gracia 56 Hd 31.40S 64.26W
Altagracia de Orituco 50 Ch 9.52N 66.23W
Altai (EN)=
Altay Shan 21 Le 46.30N 93.00 E
Altaj 22 Le 46.20N 96.17 E
Altaj 21 Kd 51.30N 90.00 E
Altajski 20 Df 51.58N 85.30 E
Altajski Kraj [3] 20 Df 52.00N 82.30 E
Altamaha River 43 Ke 31.19N 81.17W
Altamira 53 Kf 3.12S 52.12W
Altamira, Cuevas de- 13 Ha 43.23N 4.05W
Altamira, Sierra de- 13 Ge 39.35N 5.10W
Altamirano 48 Mi 16.53N 92.09W
Altamont 46 Ee 42.12N 121.44W
Altamura 14 Kj 40.49N 16.33 E
Altamura, Isla de- 48 Ee 25.00N 108.10W
Altan Bulag 27 Jc 44.19N 113.28 E
Altan-Emel → Xin Barag
Youqi 27 Kb 48.41N 116.47 E
Altan Xiret→Ejin Horo Qi 27 Id 39.31N 109.45 E
Altar 48 Db 30.43N 111.44W
Altar, Desierto de- 38 Hf 31.50N 114.15W
Altar, Rio- 48 Db 30.39N 111.55W
Altar de los Sacrificios 49 Be 16.28N 90.32W
Altata 47 Cd 24.38N 107.55W
Alta Verapaz [3] 49 Bf 15.40N 90.00W
Altavista 44 Hg 37.07N 79.18W
Altay 22 Ke 47.52N 88.07 E
Altay Shan=Altai
(EN) 21 Le 46.30N 93.00 E
Altdorf 14 Cd 46.53N 8.40 E
Altea 13 Lf 38.36N 0.03W
Altena 10 De 51.18N 7.40 E
Altenberge 12 Jb 52.03N 7.28 E
Altenburg 10 If 50.59N 12.27 E
Altenglan 12 Je 49.33N 7.28 E
Altenkirchen
(Westerwald) 12 Jd 50.42N 7.39 E
Alter do Chão 13 Ee 39.12N 7.40W
Altevatnet 7 Eb 68.32N 19.30 E
Altındağ 24 Ec 39.56N 32.52 E
Altinoluk 15 Jj 39.34N 26.44 E
Altinova 15 Jj 39.13N 26.47 E
Altıntaş 24 Dc 39.04N 30.07 E
Altinyayla 15 Mm 36.59N 29.33 E
Altkirch 11 Ng 47.37N 7.15 E
Altmark 10 Hd 52.40N 11.20 E
Altmühl 10 Hh 48.55N 11.52 E
Alto, Morro- 55 Ib 13.46S 46.50W
Alto, Pico- 54 Kd 4.20S 39.00W
Alto Alentejo 13 Ef 38.50N 7.40W
Alto Araguaia 54 Hg 17.19S 53.12W
Alto Coité 55 Eb 15.47S 54.20W
Alto Garças 55 Fc 16.56S 53.32W
Alto Longá 54 Je 5.15S 42.12W
Alto Molócuè 37 Fc 15.38S 37.42 E
Altomonte 14 Kk 39.42N 16.08 E
Alton [Eng.-U.K.] 12 Bc 51.08N 0.59W
Alton [Il.-U.S.] 43 Id 38.54N 90.10W
Altona, Hamburg- 10 Fc 53.33N 9.57 E
Altoona 43 Lc 40.32N 78.23W
Alto Paraguai 54 Gf 14.30S 56.31W
Alto Paraguay [3] 55 Ce 21.00S 59.00W
Alto Paraíso de Goiás 55 Ib 14.12S 47.38W
Alto Paraná [3] 55 Eg 25.00S 54.50W
Alto Parnaíba 54 Ie 9.06S 45.57W
Alto Purús, Rio- 54 De 9.34S 70.36W
Alto Rio Senguerr 56 Fg 45.02S 70.50W
Altos 54 Jd 5.03S 42.28W
Alto Sucuriú 55 Fd 19.19S 52.47W
Altötting 10 Ih 48.14N 12.41 E
Alto Uruguai, Serra do- 55 Fh 27.35S 53.40W
Altun Ha 49 Ce 17.50N 88.20W
Altın Köprü 24 Ke 35.45N 44.09 E
Altun Shan 21 Kf 38.00N 88.00 E
Alturas 43 Cc 41.29N 120.32W
Alturitas 49 Ki 9.45N 72.25W
Altus 43 He 34.38N 99.20W
Altynkan 18 Hd 41.03N 70.43 E
Altynkul 18 Bc 43.07N 58.55 E
Alu 63a Bb 7.05S 155.47 E
Al 'Ubaylah 35 Ia 21.59N 50.57 E
Al Ubayyiḍ 31 Kg 13.11N 30.13 E
Alucra 24 Hb 40.20N 38.46 E
Al 'Udaysāt 24 Ej 25.35N 32.29 E
Al Uḍayyah 35 Dc 12.03N 28.17 E
Alūksne/Aluksne 7 Gh 57.26N 27.01 E
Alukсne/Alūksne 7 Gh 57.26N 27.01 E
Aluksne Ozero 8 Lg 57.22N 27.10 E
Aluksne Ozero/Alūksnes
Ezers 8 Lg 57.22N 27.10 E
Alūksnes Ezers/Aluksne
Ozero 8 Lg 57.22N 27.10 E
'Alūla 35 Ic 11.58N 50.48 E
Al 'Ulā 23 Ed 26.37N 37.52 E
Al Umm 33 Hf 18.18N 40.45 E
Alunda 8 Hd 60.04N 18.05 E
Alupka 19 Dg 44.24N 34.03 E
Al 'Uqaylah 33 Cc 30.16N 19.12 E
Al 'Uqaylāt 24 Ii 26.43N 41.43 E
Al 'Uqayr 24 Nj 25.39N 50.13 E
Al Uqṣur=Luxor (EN) 33 Fd 25.41N 32.39 E
Al Urayq 24 Hh 29.00N 39.10 E
Al Urdun=Jordan (EN) 22 Ff 31.00N 36.00 E
Al 'Urūq al Mu'Tariḍah 35 Ia 21.00N 54.00 E
Ālūs 24 Ie 34.02N 42.26 E
Alušta 19 Dg 44.42N 34.20 E
Al 'Uthmānīyah 24 Mj 25.15N 49.22 E
Al'Uwaynāt 33 Bd 25.48N 10.33 E
Al 'Uwaynidhīyah 24 Gi 26.38N 36.05 E
Al 'Uwayqīlah 24 Jg 30.21N 42.14 E
Al 'Uyūn 24 Hj 24.33N 39.35 E
Al Uẓayin 24 Ke 34.02N 44.20 E
Al 'Uzayr 24 Lg 31.19N 47.25 E
Alva 43 Hd 36.48N 98.40W
Alva 13 Dd 40.18N 8.15W
Alvand, Kūh-e- 24 Me 34.41N 48.28 E
Älvängen 8 Eg 57.56N 12.09 E
Alvaro Obregón, Presa 48 Ed 28.00N 109.45W
Alvdal 7 Ce 62.07N 10.39 E
Älvdalen 8 Ed 60.30N 13.00 E
Älvdalen 7 Df 61.14N 14.02 E
Alvear 55 Di 29.06S 56.33W
Alvelos, Serra de- 13 De 39.55N 8.01W
Alvesta 7 Dh 56.54N 14.33 E
Alvik 8 Gb 62.25N 17.24 E
Ålvik 7 Bf 60.26N 6.26 E
Alvin 45 Il 29.25N 95.15W
Älvkarleby 7 Df 60.34N 17.27 E
Alvord Valley 46 Fe 42.45N 118.25W
Alvøy 8 Ad 60.35N 4.50 E
Älvros 8 Fb 62.03N 14.39 E
Älvsborg [2] 7 Cg 58.00N 12.30 E
Älvsbyn 7 Ed 65.40N 21.00 E
Al Wāḥidī 23 Gg 14.20N 47.50 E
Al Wajh 22 Fg 26.14N 36.28 E
Al Wakrah 24 Nj 25.10N 51.36 E
Al Wannān 24 Mi 26.55N 48.24 E
Alwar 25 Fc 27.34N 76.36 E
Al Warī'ah 24 Li 27.50N 47.29 E
Al Wāsiṭah 33 Fd 29.20N 31.12 E
Al Waslātīyah 14 Do 35.51N 9.35 E
Al Waṭī'ah 33 Bc 32.28N 11.46 E
Al Wazz 35 Eb 15.01N 30.10 E
Al Widyān 21 Gf 31.10N 40.45 E
Alxa Youqi
(Ehen Hudag) 27 Hd 39.12N 101.40 E
Alxa Zuoqi
(Bayan Hot) 27 Id 38.50N 105.32 E
Al Yaman = Yemen (EN) 22 Gh 15.00N 44.00 E
Al Yaman ad Dīmuqrāṭīyah
→ Yemen (EN) 22 Gh 15.00N 44.00 E
Alyangula 59 Hb 13.50S 136.25 E
Alygdžer 20 Ef 53.38N 98.16 E
Alymka 17 Ng 59.01N 68.40 E
Alytus/Alitus 19 Ce 54.25N 24.08 E
Alz 10 Ih 48.10N 12.48 E
Alzamaj 20 Ee 55.33N 98.39 E
Alzey 10 Eg 49.45N 8.07 E
Alzira/Alcira 13 Le 39.09N 0.26W
Amachkalo Ahzar 34 Fb 15.30N 3.20 E
Amacuro, Rio- 54 Fb 8.32N 60.28W
Amada 33 Fe 22.45N 32.10 E
Amadeus, Lake- 57 Eg 24.50S 130.45 E
Amadi [Sud.] 35 Ed 5.31N 30.20 E
Amadi [Zaire] 36 Eb 3.35N 26.47 E
Amadjuak Lake 42 Kd 64.55N 71.00W
Amadora 13 Cf 38.45N 9.14W
Amadror 32 Ie 24.50N 6.25 E
Amadror 32 Id 26.00N 5.00 E
Amagasaki 29 Dd 34.42N 135.25 E
Amager 8 Ei 55.35N 12.35 E
Amagi [Jap.] 29 Be 33.26N 130.39 E
Amagi [Jap.] 29b Bb 27.47N 128.52 E
Amagi-San 29 Fd 34.51N 139.00 E
Amaha 29 Fd 35.13N 139.51 E
Amahai 26 Ig 3.20S 128.55 E
Amain, Monts d'- 11 Gf 48.39N 0.20 E
Amajac, Rio- 48 Jg 21.15N 98.46W
Amakusa-Nada 28 Jh 32.25N 129.40 E
Amakusa-Shotō 28 Kh 32.22N 130.12 E
Amal 33 Dd 29.25N 21.10 E
Åmal 7 Cg 59.03N 12.42 E
Amalfi 14 Ij 40.38N 14.36 E
Amaliás 15 El 37.48N 21.21 E
Amalner 25 Fd 21.03N 75.04 E
Amambai 54 Gh 23.05S 55.13W
Amambai, Rio- 55 Ff 23.22S 53.56W
Amambai, Serra de- 55 Ef 23.10S 55.30W
Amambay [3] 55 Df 23.00S 56.00W
Amami Islands (EN)=
Amami-Shotō 21 Og 28.16N 129.21 E
Amami-Ō-Shima 27 Mf 28.15N 129.20 E
Amami-Shotō=Amami
Islands (EN) 21 Og 28.16N 129.21 E
Āmān 8 Fc 61.12N 14.45 E
Amanã, Lago- 54 Fd 2.35S 64.40W
Amana, Rio- 50 Eh 9.45N 62.39W
Amanave 65c Cb 14.19S 170.49W
Amangeldy 19 Ge 50.10N 65.13 E
Amankaragaj 17 Lj 52.27N 64.08 E
Amantea 14 Kk 39.07N 16.08 E
Amanu Atoll 57 Mf 17.48S 140.46W
Amanzimtoti 37 Ef 30.05S 30.53 E
Amapá 53 Ke 2.03N 50.48W
Amapá, Territorio do- [2] 54 Hc 1.30N 52.00W
Amapala 49 Dg 13.17N 87.40W
Amara 15 Ke 44.37N 27.19 E
Amara 30 Kg 11.30N 37.45 E
Amaradia 15 Ge 44.22N 23.43 E
'Amara East 35 Ea 20.48N 30.23 E
Amarante [Braz.] 54 Je 6.14S 42.50W
Amarante [Port.] 13 Dc 41.16N 8.05W
Amaranth 45 Ga 50.36N 98.43W
Amargosa 46 Gh 36.18N 116.25W
Amargosa Desert 46 Gh 36.40N 116.30W
Amargosa Range 46 Gh 36.30N 116.45W
Amargosa River 46 Gh 36.13N 116.48W
Amarillo 39 If 35.13N 101.49W
Amárion 15 Hn 35.14N 24.39 E
Amarume 29 Fb 38.50N 139.54 E
Amasra 24 Eb 41.45N 32.34 E
Amasya 23 Ea 40.39N 35.51 E
Amathus 24 Ee 34.42N 33.08 E
Amatique, Bahia de- 49 Cf 15.55N 88.45W
Amatlán de Cañas 48 Gg 20.52N 104.27W
Amatrice 14 Hh 42.38N 13.17 E
Amaurilandia 55 Ff 22.10S 52.38W
Amay 12 Hd 50.33N 5.19 E
Amazar 20 Hf 53.54N 120.57 E
Amazon (EN)=Amazonas,
Rio- (Solimões) 52 Lf 0.10S 49.00W
Amazon, Mouths of the-
(EN) 52 Le 0.10S 49.00W
Amazonas [Braz.] [2] 54 Fd 5.00S 63.00W
Amazonas [Col.] [2] 54 Dd 1.00N 72.00W
Amazonas [Peru] [2] 54 Ce 5.00S 77.00W
Amazonas [Ven.] [2] 54 Ec 3.30N 66.00W
Amazonas, Rio-=Amazon
(EN) 52 Lf 0.10S 49.00W
Amazonas, Rio- (Solimões)
=Amazon (EN) 52 Lf 0.10S 49.00W
Amazon Cone (EN) 52 Ke 4.30N 52.00W
Amba Ferit 35 Fc 10.55N 38.55 E
Ambāla 25 Fb 30.21N 76.50 E
Ambalangoda 25 Gg 6.14N 80.03 E
Ambalavao 37 Hd 21.50S 46.57 E
Ambam 34 He 2.23N 11.17 E
Ambanja 37 Hb 13.39S 48.27 E
Ambarčik 22 Sc 69.39N 162.20 E
Ambarès-et-Lagrave 11 Fj 44.55N 0.29W
Ambargasta, Salinas de- 56 Hc 29.20S 64.30W
Ambarny 19 Db 65.54N 33.41 E
Ambasamudram 25 Fg 8.42N 77.28 E
Ambato 53 If 1.15S 78.37W
Ambato-Boéni 37 Hc 16.28S 46.40 E
Ambatofinandrahana 37 Hd 20.33S 46.47 E
Ambatolampy 37 Hc 19.23S 47.25 E
Ambatondrazaka 31 Lj 17.48S 48.26 E
Ambatosoratra 37 Hc 17.36S 48.32 E
Ambelau, Pulau- 26 Ig 3.51S 127.12 E
Amberg 10 Hg 49.27N 11.52 E
Ambergris Cay 49 Dd 18.03N 87.56W
Ambergris Cays 49 Lc 21.18N 71.37W
Ambérieu-en-Bugey 11 Li 45.57N 5.21 E
Amberley [Eng.-U.K.] 12 Bd 50.55N 0.32W
Amberley [N.Z.] 62 Ee 43.09S 172.45 E
Ambert 11 Ji 45.33N 3.45 E
Ambikāpur 25 Gd 23.07N 83.12 E
Ambila 37 Hd 21.58S 47.59 E
Ambilobe 37 Hb 13.11S 49.03 E
Ambitle 63a Aa 4.05S 153.40 E
Ambjörby 8 Ed 60.30N 13.10 E
Ambla 8 Ke 59.10N 25.44 E
Ambléve 11 Ld 50.28N 5.36 E
Ambléve/Amel 12 Id 50.21N 6.09 E
Ambo 54 Cf 10.07S 76.10W
Amboasary Sud 37 He 25.01S 46.23 E
Ambodifototra 37 Hc 16.58S 49.52 E
Ambohimahasoa 37 Hd 21.08S 47.12 E
Ambohimanarina 37 Hc 18.52S 47.29 E
Ambohitralanana 37 Ic 15.15S 50.28 E
Amboise 11 Gg 47.25N 0.59 E
Ambon 58 De 3.43S 128.12 E
Ambon, Pulau- 26 Ig 3.40S 128.10 E
Ambongo 37 Gc 16.50S 45.00 E
Amboseli, Lake- 36 Gc 2.37S 37.08 E
Ambositra 31 Lk 20.30S 47.14 E
Ambovombe 37 He 25.09S 46.06 E
Ambre, Cap d'-=Ambre,
Cape d'-(EN) 30 Lj 11.57S 49.17 E
Ambre, Cape d'-(EN)=
Ambre, Cap d'- 30 Lj 11.57S 49.17 E
Ambre, Montagne d'- 37 Hb 12.30S 49.10 E
Ambriz 31 Ii 7.50S 13.08 E
Ambrolauri 16 Mh 42.31N 43.05 E
Ambrym, Ile- 57 Hf 16.15S 168.07 E
Ambunti 60 Ch 4.14S 142.50 E
Āmbūr 25 Ff 12.47N 78.42 E
Amchitka 40a Bb 51.30N 179.00 E
Amchitka Pass 40a Cb 51.30N 179.30W
Am Dafok 35 Cc 10.28N 23.17 E
Am Dam 35 Cc 12.46N 20.29 E
Amded 32 He 22.10N 3.15 E
Amderma 19 Gb 69.45N 61.39 E
Am Djéména 35 Bc 13.06N 17.19 E
Amdo 27 Fe 32.29N 91.47 E
Ameca 47 Dd 20.33N 104.02W
Ameca, Rio- 48 Gg 20.41N 105.18W
Amel/Amblève 12 Id 50.21N 6.09 E
Ameland 12 Ha 53.26N 5.48 E
Ameland 11 La 53.25N 5.45 E
Ameland- Nes 12 Ha 53.26N 5.48 E
Amelia Island 44 Gj 30.37N 81.27W
Amélie-les-Bains-Palaloa 11 Il 42.28N 2.40 E
Amendola 14 Hh 42.59N 13.21 E
Amendolara 14 Kk 39.57N 16.35 E
'Āmerī 24 Nh 28.30N 51.05 E
Americana 55 If 22.45S 47.20W
American Falls 46 Ie 42.47N 112.51W
American Falls Reservoir 46 Ie 43.00N 113.00W
American Fork 46 Jf 40.23N 111.48W
American Highland 66 Ff 72.30S 78.00 E
American Samoa [5] 58 Kf 14.50S 170.00W
Americus 43 Ke 32.04N 84.14W
Amersfoort 11 Lb 52.09N 5.24 E
Amery Ice Shelf 66 Fe 69.30S 72.00 E
Ames 43 Ic 42.02N 93.37W
Amfilokhia 15 Ek 38.52N 21.10 E
Ámfissa 15 Fk 38.32N 22.23 E
Amfreville-la-Campagne 12 Ce 49.13N 0.57 E
Amga 20 Id 60.52N 131.50 E
Amga 21 Pc 62.40N 134.59 E
Amgalang→Xin Barag
Zuoqi 27 Kb 48.13N 118.14 E
Am Géréda 35 Cc 12.52N 21.10 E
Amgu 28 Nb 45.51N 137.41 E
Amguema 20 Nc 68.03N 177.55W
Amguid 32 Id 26.30N 5.36 E
Amguid 31 Hf 26.26N 5.22 E
Amgun 21 Pd 52.56N 139.40 E
Amherst 42 Lg 45.49N 64.14W
Amherst, Mount- 59 Fc 18.11S 126.59 E
Amherst Island 44 Ic 44.12N 76.42W
Amiata, Monte- 14 Fh 42.53N 11.37 E
Amiens 6 Gf 49.54N 2.18 E
Āmij, Wādī- 24 If 33.48N 41.46 E
Amik Gölü 24 Gd 36.22N 36.17 E
Amīk Oölü 24 Gd 36.15N 36.12 E
Amili 25 Jc 28.26N 95.52 E
Amīndīvi Islands 25 Ef 11.23N 72.23 E
Aminuis 37 Bd 23.43S 19.21 E
'Āmir, Ra's- 30 Je 32.57N 21.43 E
Amirante Islands 30 Mi 6.00S 53.10 E
Amirante Trench (EN) 37 Bb 6.00S 52.30 E
Amisk Lake 42 Hf 54.35N 102.15W
Amistad, Presa de la- 45 Fl 28.34N 101.15W
Amistad Reservoir 43 Gf 28.34N 101.15W
Amite 45 Kk 30.44N 90.30W
Amlekhganj 25 Gc 27.17N 84.59 E
Amlia 40a Db 52.06N 173.30W
Amlwch 9 Ih 53.25N 4.20W

Index Symbols

[1] Independent Nation
[2] State, Region
[3] District, County
[4] Municipality
[5] Colony, Dependency
Continent
Physical Region
Historical or Cultural Region
Mount, Mountain
Volcano
Hill
Mountains, Mountain Range
Hills, Escarpment
Plateau, Upland
Pass, Gap
Plain, Lowland
Delta
Salt Flat
Valley, Canyon
Crater, Cave
Karst Features
Depression
Polder
Desert, Dunes
Forest, Woods
Heath, Steppe
Oasis
Cape, Point
Coast, Beach
Cliff
Peninsula
Isthmus
Sandbank
Island
Atoll
Rock, Reef
Islands, Archipelago
Rocks, Reefs
Coral Reef
Well, Spring
Geyser
River, Stream
Waterfall Rapids
River Mouth, Estuary
Lake
Salt Lake
Intermittent Lake
Reservoir
Swamp, Pond
Canal
Glacier
Ice Shelf, Pack Ice
Ocean
Sea
Gulf, Bay
Strait, Fjord
Lagoon
Bank
Seamount
Tablemount
Ridge
Shelf
Basin
Escarpment, Sea Scarp
Fracture
Trench, Abyss
National Park, Reserve
Point of Interest
Recreation Site
Cave, Cavern
Historic Site
Ruins
Wall, Walls
Church, Abbey
Temple
Scientific Station
Airport
Port
Lighthouse
Mine
Tunnel
Dam, Bridge

'Amm Adām 35 Fb 16.22N 36.09 E
'Ammān 22 Ff 31.57N 35.56 E
Ammanford 9 Jj 51.48N 3.59W
Ammarnäs 7 Dd 65.58N 16.12 E
Åmmeberg 8 Ff 58.52N 15.00 E
Ammer 10 Hi 47.57N 11.08 E
Ammerån 8 Ga 63.09N 16.13 E
Ammerland 10 Dc 53.15N 8.00 E
Ammersee 10 Hi 48.00N 11.08 E
Ammi-Moussa 13 Ni 35.52N 1.07 E
Ammokhostos → Famagusta (EN) 23 Dc 35.07N 33.57 E
Amnja 17 Me 63.45N 67.07 E
Amnok-kang 27 Ld 39.55N 124.20 E
Āmol 23 Hb 36.23N 52.20 E
Amolar 55 Dd 18.01S 57.30W
Amorgós 15 Im 36.50N 25.53 E
Amorgós 15 Im 36.50N 25.59 E
Amorinópolis 55 Gc 16.36S 51.08W
Amory 45 Lj 33.59N 88.29W
Amos 42 Jg 48.34N 78.07W
Amot [Nor.] 8 Be 59.35N 8.00 E
Amot [Nor.] 7 Bg 59.54N 9.54 E
Amotfors 8 Ee 59.46N 12.22 E
Amoucha 13 Rh 36.23N 5.25 E
Amouliani 15 Gi 40.20N 23.55 E
Amour, Djebel- 32 Hc 33.45N 1.45 E
Amourj 32 Ff 16.10N 7.35W
Ampanihy 37 Gd 24.40S 44.45 E
Amparafaravola 37 Hc 17.36S 48.12 E
Amparo 55 If 22.42S 46.47W
Amper 10 Hh 48.10N 11.50 E
Ampère Seamount (EN) 5 Eh 35.05N 12.13W
Amphitrite Point 46 Cb 48.56N 125.35W
Amposta 13 Md 40.43N 0.35 E
Ampthill 12 Bb 52.02N 0.29W
Ampurdán/L'Empordà 13 Ob 42.12N 2.45 E
Ampurias 13 Pb 42.10N 3.05 E
Amqui 44 Na 48.28N 67.26W
'Amrān 23 Ff 15.41N 43.55 E
Amrāvati 22 Jg 20.56N 77.45 E
Am-Raya 35 Bc 14.05N 16.30 E
Amritsar 22 Jf 31.35N 74.53 E
Amrum 8 Cj 54.40N 8.20 E
Amsaga 32 Ee 20.07N 14.10W
Amsittene, Jebel- 32 Fc 31.11N 9.40W
Amstel 12 Gb 52.22N 4.56 E
Amstelveen 12 Gb 52.18N 4.53 E
Amsterdam 30 Ol 37.57S 77.40 E
Amsterdam [Neth.] 6 Ge 52.22N 4.54 E
Amsterdam [N.Y.-U.S.] 44 Jd 42.56N 74.12W
Amsterdam-Rijnkanaal 12 Hc 51.57N 5.25 E
Amstetten 14 Ib 48.07N 14.52 E
Am Timan 31 Jg 11.02N 20.17 E
Amūd, Jabal al- 23 Ec 30.59N 39.20 E
Āmūdā 24 Id 37.05N 40.54 E
Amu-Darja 18 Ef 37.57N 65.15 E
Amudarja=Amu Darya (EN) 21 He 43.40N 59.01 E
Āmū Daryā=Amu Darya (EN) 21 He 43.40N 59.01 E
Amu Darya (EN)= Amudarja 21 He 43.40N 59.01 E
Amu Darya (EN)=Āmū Daryā 21 He 43.40N 59.01 E
Amudat 36 Fb 1.58N 34.56 E
Amukta Pass 40a Db 52.25N 172.00W
Amun 63a Ba 5.57S 154.45 E
Amund Ringnes 42 Ha 78.15N 97.00W
Amundsen Bay 66 Ee 66.55S 50.00 E
Amundsen Coast 66 Mg 85.30S 159.00W
Amundsen Glacier 66 Mg 85.35S 159.00W
Amundsen Gulf 38 Gb 71.00N 124.00W
Amundsen-Scott Station 66 Bg 90.00S 0.00
Amundsen Sea (EN) 66 Of 72.30S 112.00W
Amungen 8 Fc 61.10N 15.40 E
Amuntai 22 Nj 2.26S 115.15 E
Amur 21 Qd 52.56N 141.10 E
'Amūr, Wādī 35 Eb 18.56N 33.34 E
Amurang 26 Hf 1.11N 124.35 E
Amursk 20 If 50.16N 136.55 E
Amurskaja Oblast [3] 20 Hf 54.00N 128.00 E
Amurzet 20 Ig 47.41N 131.07 E
Amvrakia, Gulf of- (EN) = Amvrakikós Kólpos 15 Dk 39.00N 21.00 E
Amvrakikós Kólpos = Amvrakia, Gulf of- (EN) 15 Dk 39.00N 21.00 E
Amvrosijevka 16 Kf 47.44N 38.31 E
Am Zoer 35 Cc 14.13N 21.23 E
Anaa Atoll 61 Lc 17.25S 145.30W
Anabar 64e Ba 0.29S 166.57 E
Anabar 21 Nb 73.08N 113.36 E
Anabarskoje Ploskogorje 21 Mc 70.00N 108.00 E
An Abhainn Dubh/ Blackwater 9 Gh 53.39N 6.43W
An Abhainn Mhór/ Blackwater [Ire.] 9 Fj 51.51N 7.50W
An Abhainn Mhór/ Blackwater [N.Ire.-U.K.] 9 Gg 54.30N 6.35W
Anabuki 29 Dd 34.02N 134.11 E
Anacasti 56 Gc 28.49S 65.30W
Anaco 54 Fb 9.27N 64.28W
Anaconda 43 Eb 46.08N 112.57W
Anacortes 46 Db 48.30N 122.37W
Anadarko 45 Gi 35.04N 98.15W
Anadolu=Anatolia (EN) 21 Ff 39.00N 35.00 E
Anadyr 21 Tc 64.55N 176.05 E
Anadyr 22 Tc 64.45N 177.29 E
Anadyr Gulf (EN)= Anadyrski Zaliv 21 Uc 64.00N 179.00W
Anadyr Range (EN)= Anadyrskoje Ploskogorje 21 Tc 67.00N 174.00 E
Anadyrski Liman 20 Md 64.30N 178.00 E
Anadyrski Zaliv=Anadyr Gulf (EN) 21 Uc 64.00N 179.00W
Anadyrskoje Ploskogorje= Anadyr Range (EN) 21 Tc 67.00N 174.00 E
Anáfi 15 Im 36.22N 25.47 E
Anaghit 35 Fb 16.20N 38.39 E
Anagni 14 Hi 41.44N 13.09 E
'Ānah 23 Fc 34.28N 41.56 E
Anaheim 46 Gj 33.51N 117.57W
Anahola 65a Ba 22.09N 159.19W
Anáhuac 48 Id 27.14N 100.09W
Anahuac, Meseta de- 47 Dd 21.30N 101.00W
An Aird/Ards Peninsula 9 Hg 54.30N 5.30W
Anaj Mudi 21 Jh 10.10N 77.04 E
Anaktuvuk Pass 40 Ic 68.10N 151.50W
Analalava 37 Hb 14.38S 47.45 E
Analavelona 37 Gd 22.37S 44.10 E
Ana Maria, Golfo de- 49 Hc 21.25N 78.40W
Anambas, Kepulauan-= Anambas Islands (EN) 21 Mi 3.00N 106.00 E
Anambas Islands (EN)= Anambas, Kepulauan- 21 Mi 3.00N 106.00 E
Anambra [2] 34 Gd 6.30N 7.30 E
Anamé 63b De 20.08S 169.49 E
Anamizu 28 Nf 37.14N 136.54 E
Anamur 23 Db 36.06N 32.50 E
Anamur Burun 23 Db 36.03N 32.48 E
Anan [Jap.] 28 Mh 33.55N 134.39 E
Anan [Jap.] 29 Ed 35.19N 137.48 E
Anane, Djebel- 13 Mi 35.12N 0.47 E
Anánes 15 Hm 36.31N 24.08 E
Ananjev 16 Ff 47.43N 29.59 E
Anankwin 25 Je 15.41N 97.59 E
Anantapur 25 Ff 14.41N 77.36 E
Anantnāg (Islāmābād) 25 Fb 33.44N 75.09 E
Anapa 19 Dg 44.53N 37.19 E
Anapo 14 Jm 37.03N 15.16 E
Anápolis 53 Lg 16.20S 48.58W
Anapu, Rio- 54 Hd 2.15S 51.30W
Anār 23 Ic 30.53N 55.18 E
Anārak 23 Hc 33.20N 53.42 E
Anare Station 66 Jd 54.30S 158.55 E
Anaro, Rio- 49 Lj 7.48N 70.12W
Añasco 51a Ab 18.17N 67.10W
Anatahan Island 57 Fc 16.22N 145.40 E
Anatolia (EN)= Anadolu 21 Ff 39.00N 35.00 E
Anatoliki Rodhópi 15 Ih 41.44N 25.31 E
Añatuya 56 Hc 28.28S 62.50W
Anauá, Rio- 54 Fc 0.58N 61.21W
Anazarba 24 Fd 37.15N 35.45 E
An Baile Meánach/ Ballymena 9 Gg 54.52N 6.17W
An Bhanna/Bann 9 Gf 55.10N 6.46W
An Bhearú/Barrow 9 Gi 52.10N 7.00W
An Bhinn Bhui/Benwee Head 9 Dg 54.21N 9.48W
An Bhograch/Boggeragh Mountains 9 Ei 52.05N 9.00W
An Bhóinn/Boyne 9 Gh 53.43N 6.15W
An Bhrosnach/Brosna 9 Fh 53.13N 7.58W
An Blascaod Mór/Great Blasket 9 Ci 52.05N 10.32W
Anbyŏn 28 Ie 39.02N 127.32 E
An Cabhán/Cavan [2] 9 Fh 53.55N 7.30W
An Cabhán/Cavan 9 Fg 54.00N 7.21W
An Caisleán Nua/Newcastle 9 Hg 54.12N 5.54W
An Caisleán Nua/Newcastle West 9 Di 52.27N 9.03W
An Caisleán Riabhach/ Castlerea 9 Eh 53.46N 8.29W
An Caoláire Rua/Killary Harbour 9 Dh 53.38N 9.55W
Ancares, Sierra de- 13 Fb 42.46N 6.54W
Ancash [2] 54 Ce 9.30S 77.45W
Ancenis 11 Eg 47.22N 1.10W
An Chathair/Caher 9 Fi 52.22N 7.55W
An Cheacha/Caha Mountains 9 Dj 51.45N 9.45W
Anchorage 39 Ec 61.13N 149.53W
An Chorr Chriochach/ Cookstown 9 Gg 54.39N 6.45W
Anci (Langfang) 27 Kd 39.29N 116.40 E
An Clár/Clare [2] 9 Ei 52.50N 9.00W
An Cóbh/Cóbh 9 Ej 51.51N 8.17W
Ancohuma, Nevado- 54 Eg 15.51S 68.36W
Ancona 6 Hg 43.38N 13.30 E
Ancón de Sardinas, Bahía de- 54 Cc 1.30N 79.50W
Ancre 11 Ie 49.54N 2.28 E
Ancuabe 37 Fb 12.58S 39.51 E
Ancud 56 Ff 41.52S 73.50W
Ancud, Golfo de- 56 Ff 42.05S 73.00W
Anda 27 Mb 46.24N 125.20 E
Anda (Sartu) 28 Ha 46.35N 125.00 E
Andacollo [Arg.] 56 Fe 37.11S 70.41W
Andacollo [Chile] 56 Fd 30.14S 71.06W
Andahuaylas 54 Df 13.39S 73.23W
An Daingean/Dingle 9 Ci 52.08N 10.15W
Andalgalá 56 Gc 27.36S 66.19W
Åndalsnes 7 Be 62.34N 7.42 E
Andalucia=Andalusia (EN) 13 Hg 37.30N 4.30W
Andalucia=Andalusia (EN) 5 Fh 37.30N 4.30W
Andalusia 43 Je 31.19N 86.29W
Andalusia (EN)= Andalucia 13 Hg 37.30N 4.30W
Andalusia (EN)= Andalucia 5 Fh 37.30N 4.30W
Andaman and Nicobar [3] 25 If 12.30N 92.45 E
Andaman Basin (EN) 21 Lh 10.00N 94.00 E
Andaman Islands 21 Lh 12.30N 92.43 E
Andaman Sea (EN) 21 Lh 10.00N 95.00 E
Andamooka 59 Hf 30.27S 137.12 E
'Andān, Wādī- 23 Ie 21.05N 58.23 E
Andant 55 Am 36.34S 62.07W
Andapa 37 Hb 14.38S 49.33 E
Andara 37 Cc 18.03S 21.27 E
Andelle 12 De 49.19N 1.14 E
Andenes 7 Db 69.19N 16.08 E
Andenne 12 Hd 50.29N 5.06 E
Andenne-Naméche 12 Hd 50.28N 5.00 E
Andéranboukane 34 Fb 15.26N 3.02 E
Anderlecht 12 Gd 50.50N 4.18 E
Anderlues 12 Gd 50.24N 4.16 E
Andermatt 14 Cd 46.38N 8.37 E
Andernach 10 Df 50.26N 7.24 E
Andernos-les-Bains 11 Ej 44.44N 1.06W
Anderson 42 Ec 69.42N 129.01W
Anderson [Ca.-U.S.] 46 Df 40.27N 122.18W
Anderson [In.-U.S.] 43 Jc 40.10N 85.41W
Anderson [S.C.-U.S.] 43 Ke 34.30N 82.39W
Anderstorp 8 Eg 57.17N 13.38 E
Andes (EN) = Andes, Cordillera de los- 52 Jh 20.00S 67.00W
Andes, Cordillera de los- = Andes (EN) 52 Jh 20.00S 67.00W
Andevoranto 37 Hc 18.48S 49.02 E
Andfjorden 7 Db 69.10N 16.20 E
Andhra Pradesh [3] 25 Fe 16.00N 79.00 E
Andia, Sierra de- 13 Kb 42.45N 2.00W
Andikhásia Óri 15 Ej 39.47N 21.55 E
Andikira 15 Fk 38.23N 22.38 E
Andikithira = Andikithira (EN) 15 Gn 35.52N 23.18 E
Andikithira (EN) = Andikithira 15 Gn 35.52N 23.18 E
Andikithiron, Stenón- 15 Gn 35.45N 23.25 E
Andilamena 37 Hc 17.01S 48.32 E
Andilanatoby 37 Hc 17.56S 48.14 E
Andimeshk 24 Mf 32.27N 48.21 E
Andimilos 15 Hm 36.47N 24.14 E
Andiparos 15 Il 37.00N 25.03 E
Andipaxoi 15 Dj 39.08N 20.14 E
Andipsara 15 Ik 38.33N 25.24 E
Andir He 27 Dd 38.00N 83.36 E
Andırın 24 Gd 37.34N 36.20 E
Andirlangar 27 Dd 37.36N 83.50 E
Andirrion 15 Ek 38.20N 21.46 E
Andítilos 15 Km 36.22N 27.28 E
Andižan 22 Je 40.45N 72.22 E
Andižanskaja Oblast [3] 19 Hg 40.45N 72.20 E
Andkhvoy 23 Kb 36.56N 65.08 E
Andong 27 Md 36.36N 128.44 E
Andorra (Valls d'Andorra) [1] 6 Gg 42.30N 1.30 E
Andorra la Vella 6 Gg 42.31N 1.31 E
Andover 9 Lj 51.13N 1.28W
Andøya 7 Db 69.08N 15.54 E
Andradas 55 If 22.05S 46.35W
Andradina 56 Jb 20.54S 51.23W
Andraitx 13 Oe 39.35N 2.25 E
Andreanof Islands 38 Bd 52.00N 176.00W
Andreapol 7 Hh 56.39N 32.16 E
Andrées Land 41 Jd 73.20N 26.30W
Andrejevka [Kaz.-U.S.S.R.] 19 If 45.47N 80.35 E
Andrejevka [Ukr.-U.S.S.R.] 16 Je 49.32N 36.40 E
Andrejevo-Ivanovka 15 Nb 47.31N 30.21 E
Andrejevsk 20 Ge 58.10N 114.15 E
Andrelândia 55 Je 21.44S 44.18W
Andresito 55 Dk 33.08S 57.09W
Andrespol 10 Pe 51.43N 19.40 E
Andrews 45 Ej 32.19N 102.33W
Andria 14 Ki 41.13N 16.17 E
Andriamena 37 Hc 17.28S 47.29 E
Andriba 37 Hc 17.36S 46.53 E
Andrijevica 15 Cg 42.44N 19.48 E
Andringitra 30 Lk 22.20S 46.55 E
Andritsaina 15 El 37.29N 21.54 E
Androka 37 Gd 24.59S 44.04 E
Andropov → Rybinsk 6 Jd 58.03N 38.52 E
Ándros 5 Ih 37.50N 24.50 E
Andros 38 Lg 24.25N 78.00W
Ándros 15 Hl 37.50N 24.56 E
Androscoggin River 44 Md 43.55N 69.55W
Androssan 9 If 55.40N 4.55W
Andros Town 47 Id 24.43N 77.47W
Androth Island 25 Ef 10.50N 73.41 E
Androy 30 Lk 25.00S 45.40 E
Andruševka 16 Fe 49.59N 29.01 E
Andrychów 10 Pg 49.52N 19.21 E
Andselv 7 Eb 69.04N 18.30 E
Andudu 36 Eb 2.29N 28.41 E
Andújar 13 Hf 38.03N 4.04W
Andulo 36 Ce 11.28S 16.43 E
Andu Tan 26 Fe 7.35N 114.15 E
Anduze 11 Jj 44.03N 3.59 E
An Ea agail/Errigal 9 Ef 55.02N 8.07W
Aneby 8 Fg 57.50N 14.48 E
Anéfis 34 Fb 18.03N 0.36 E
Anegada 50 Db 18.45N 64.20W
Anegada, Bahía- 56 Hf 40.15S 62.15W
Anegada Passage 47 Le 18.30N 63.40W
Aného 34 Fd 6.14N 1.36 E
An Eirne/Erne 9 Eg 54.30N 8.15W
An Eithne/Inny 9 Fh 53.35N 7.50W
An Eoghanach/Annalee 9 Fg 54.02N 7.25W
Anet 12 Df 48.51N 1.26 E
Aneto, Pico de- 5 Gg 42.38N 0.40 E
Aney 34 Hb 19.24N 12.56 E
Aneytioum, Ile- 57 Hg 20.12S 169.49 E
An Feabhal 9 Ff 55.04N 7.15W
An Fhéil/Feale 9 Di 52.28N 9.40W
An Fheoir/Nore 9 Gi 52.25N 6.58W
Angamos, Punta- [Chile] 56 Fb 23.01S 70.32W
Angamos, Punta- [Pas.] 65d Bb 27.04S 109.17W
Angara 21 Ld 58.06N 93.00 E
Angarsk 22 Md 52.34N 103.54 E
Angarski, Pereval- 16 Ig 44.47N 34.25 E
Angarski Krjaž 20 Fe 57.30N 103.00 E
Angathonisi 15 Jl 37.28N 27.00 E
Angaur Island 57 Ed 6.54N 134.09 E
Ånge 7 De 62.31N 15.37 E
Ange 8 Fa 63.27N 14.03 E
An Gearran/ Garron Point 9 Hf 55.05N 5.58W
Angel, Cerro- 48 Hf 22.49N 102.34W
Ángel, Salto-=Angel Falls (EN) 52 Je 5.57N 62.30W
Angelburg 12 Kd 50.47N 8.25 E
Angel de la Guarda, Isla- 47 Bc 29.20N 113.25W
Angeles 26 Hc 15.09N 120.35 E
Angeles, Sierra de los- 48 Jf 23.10N 99.20W
Angel Falls (EN)=Ángel, Salto- 52 Je 5.57N 62.30W
Angel Falls (EN)=Churún Merú 52 Je 5.57N 62.30W
Ängelholm 7 Ch 56.15N 12.51 E
Angélica 55 Bj 31.33S 61.33W
Angeln 10 Fb 54.40N 9.45 E
Ängelsberg 8 Ge 59.58N 16.02 E
Anger 35 Fd 9.40N 36.06 E
Angereb 35 Fc 13.44N 36.28 E
Ångermanälven 5 Hc 62.48N 17.56 E
Angermünde 10 Jc 53.02N 14.00 E
Angers 6 Ff 47.28N 0.33W
Angkor 25 Kf 13.26N 103.52 E
Angikuni Lake 42 Hd 62.10N 99.55W
Angistrion 15 Gl 37.40N 23.20 E
Anglem, Mount- 62 Bg 46.44S 167.54 E
Anglés 13 Oc 41.57N 2.39 E
Anglesey 5 Fe 53.18N 4.20W
Anglet 11 Ek 43.29N 1.32W
Angleton 45 Il 29.10N 95.26W
Anglin 11 Gh 46.42N 0.52 E
Anglona 14 Cj 40.45N 8.45 E
Angmagssalik 67 Mc 65.45N 37.30W
Ango 36 Eb 4.02N 25.52 E
Angoche 31 Kj 16.12S 39.54 E
Angoche, Ilha- 30 Kj 16.20S 39.51 E
Angol 56 Fe 37.48S 72.43W
Angola [1] 31 Ij 12.30S 18.30 E
Angola 44 Ee 41.38N 85.00W
Angola Basin (EN) 3 Ek 15.00S 3.00 E
Angoram 60 Ch 4.04S 144.04 E
Angostura 48 Ee 25.22N 108.11W
Angostura, Presa de la- 48 Mi 16.30N 92.30W
Angostura, Salto- 54 Dc 2.43N 70.57W
Angostura Reservoir 45 Ee 43.18N 103.27W
Angoulême 11 Gi 45.39N 0.09 E
Angoumois 11 Fi 45.30N 0.10W
Angra do Heroísmo [3] 32 Bb 38.42N 27.15W
Angra do Heroísmo 31 Ee 38.39N 27.13W
Angra dos Reis 55 Jf 23.00S 44.18W
Angren 19 Hg 41.03N 70.10 E
Angu 36 Db 3.33N 24.28 E
Anguang 28 Gb 45.36N 123.48 E
Anguilla [5] 39 Mh 18.15N 63.05W
Anguilla 38 Mh 18.15N 63.05W
Anguilla, Canal de l'-= Anguilla Channel (EN) 51b Ab 18.09N 63.04W
Anguilla Bank (EN) 51b Ab 18.30N 63.03W
Anguilla Cays 49 Hb 23.31N 78.33W
Anguilla Channel (EN)= Anguilla, Canal de l'- 51b Ab 18.09N 63.04W
Anguli Nur 28 Cd 41.23N 114.30 E
Anguo 28 Ce 38.25N 115.20 E
Anhanca 36 Cf 16.47S 15.33 E
Anhanguera 55 Hd 18.21S 48.17W
An Hoa 25 Le 15.46N 108.03 E
Anholt 7 Ch 56.40N 11.35 E
Anhua (Dongping) 27 Jf 28.27N 111.15 E
Anhui Sheng (An-hui Sheng)=Anhwei (EN) [2] 27 Ke 32.00N 117.00 E
An-hui Sheng→Anhui Sheng=Anhwei (EN) [2] 27 Ke 32.00N 117.00 E
Anhwei (EN)=Anhui Sheng (An-hui Sheng) [2] 27 Ke 32.00N 117.00 E
Anhwei (EN)=An-hui Sheng→Anhui Sheng [2] 27 Ke 32.00N 117.00 E
Ani 29 Gb 39.59N 140.25 E
Aniak 40 Hd 61.34N 159.30W
An Iarmhí/Westmeath [2] 9 Fh 53.30N 7.30W
Anibare 64e Bb 0.32S 166.57 E
Anibare Bay 64e Bb 0.32S 166.57 E
Aniche 12 Fd 50.20N 3.15 E
Ánidros 15 Im 36.37N 25.41 E
Anié 34 Fd 7.45N 1.12 E
Anie, Pic d'- 11 Fl 42.57N 0.43W
Aniene 14 Gi 41.56N 12.30 E
Anijangying → Luanping 28 Dd 40.55N 117.19 E
Anikščiaj/Anykščiai 7 Fi 55.31N 25.08 E
Animas Peak 45 Bk 31.35N 108.47W
Anina 15 Ed 45.05N 21.51 E
Anita Garibaldi 55 Gh 27.37S 51.05W
Anittepe 15 Kh 41.21N 27.42 E
Aniva 20 Jg 46.41N 142.35 E
Aniva, Zaliv- 20 Jg 46.20N 142.40 E
Anivorano Nord 37 Hb 12.43S 49.12 E
Aniwa, Ile- 57 Hf 19.16S 169.35 E
Anizy-le-Château 12 Fe 49.30N 3.27 E
Anjala 7 Gf 60.41N 26.50 E
Anji 28 Ei 30.39N 119.41 E
Anjiang → Qianyang 27 Jf 27.19N 110.13 E
Anjō 29 Ed 34.57N 137.05 E
Anjou 11 Fg 47.20N 0.30W
Anjou, Ostrova-=Anjou Islands (EN) 21 Qb 75.30N 143.00 E
Anjouan → Nzwani 30 Lj 12.15S 44.25 E
Anjou Islands (EN) = Anjou, Ostrova- 21 Qb 75.30N 143.00 E
Anjozorobe 37 Hc 18.24S 47.52 E
Anju 27 Md 39.37N 125.40 E
Anjuj 20 Ig 49.20N 136.20 E
Anjujski Hrebet 20 Lc 67.20N 166.00 E
Anjouu, Val d'- 11 Fg 47.25N 0.15W
Anka 34 Gc 12.07N 5.55 E
Ankang (Xing'an) 22 Mf 32.37N 109.03 E
Ankara 22 Ff 39.56N 32.52 E
Ankaratra 30 Lj 19.25S 47.12 E
Ankarsrum 7 Dh 57.42N 16.19 E
Ankavandra 37 Hc 18.45S 45.18 E
Ankazoabo 37 Gd 22.16S 44.30 E
Ankazobe 37 Hc 18.17S 47.05 E
Ankeny 45 Jf 41.44N 93.36W
Ankhor 35 Hc 10.47N 46.18 E
Anklam 10 Jc 53.52N 13.42 E
Ankober 35 Fd 9.40N 39.44 E
Ankoro 36 Ed 6.45S 26.57 E
Ankum 12 Jb 52.33N 7.53 E
An Laoi/Lee 9 Ej 51.55N 8.30W
Anlong 27 If 25.02N 105.30 E
An Longfort/Longford [2] 9 Fh 53.40N 7.40W
An Longfort/Longfort 9 Fh 53.44N 7.47W
An Lorgain/Lurgan 9 Gg 54.28N 6.20W
Anlu 27 Je 31.12N 113.46 E
An Mhí/Meath [2] 9 Gh 53.35N 6.40W
An Mhuaidh/Moy 9 Dg 54.12N 9.08W
An Mhuir Cheilteach=Celtic Sea (EN) 5 Fe 51.00N 7.00W
An Muileann gCearr/ Mullingar 9 Fh 53.32N 7.20W
An Muirthead/Mullet Peninsula 9 Cg 54.15N 10.04W
Ånn 7 Ce 63.15N 12.35 E
Ånn 8 Ea 63.19N 12.33 E
Ann, Cape- [Ant.] 66 Ee 66.10S 51.22 E
Ann, Cape- [Ma.-U.S.] 44 Ld 42.39N 70.38W
Anna [Il.-U.S.] 45 Lh 37.28N 89.15W
Anna [Nauru] 64e Ba 0.29S 166.56 E
Anna [R.S.F.S.R.] 19 Ee 51.29N 40.26 E
Annaba 31 He 36.54N 7.46 E
Annaba [3] 32 Ib 35.35N 8.00 E
An Nabaţīyah at Taḩtā 24 Gf 33.23N 35.29 E
Annaberg-Buchholz 10 If 50.34N 13.00 E
An Nabi Şāliḩ 24 Eh 28.38N 33.59 E
An Nabk 23 Ec 34.01N 36.44 E
An Nabk Abū Qaşr 24 Hg 30.21N 38.34 E
An Nafīdah 14 En 36.08N 10.23 E
An Nafūd 21 Gg 28.30N 41.00 E
An Najaf 22 Gf 31.59N 44.20 E
An Najaf [3] 24 Kg 31.20N 44.07 E
An Nakhl 33 Fd 29.55N 33.45 E
Annalee/An Eoghanach 9 Fg 54.02N 7.25W
Annam (EN)=Trung Phan 21 Me 15.00N 108.00 E
Annamitique, Chaîne- 25 Le 17.00N 106.00 E
Annan 9 Jg 54.59N 3.16W
Annan 9 Jg 55.00N 3.16W
Anna Paulowna 12 Gb 52.52N 4.52 E
Anna Paulowna-Kleine Sluis 12 Gb 52.52N 4.52 E
Anna Point 64e Ba 0.29S 166.56 E
Annapolis 39 Lf 38.59N 76.30W
Annapolis Royal 44 Oc 44.45N 65.31W
Annapurna 21 Kg 28.34N 83.50 E
Ann Arbor 43 Kc 42.18N 83.45W
Anna Regina 50 Gi 7.16N 58.30W
An Nás/Naas 9 Gh 53.13N 6.39W
An Nashshāsh 24 Pk 23.05N 54.02 E
An Nashwah 24 Lg 30.49N 47.36 E
An Nāşirīyah 23 Gc 31.02N 46.16 E
An Nasser 24 Ej 24.36N 32.58 E
An Nawfalīyah 33 Cc 30.47N 17.50 E
Annecy 11 Mi 45.54N 6.07 E
Annecy, Lac d'- 11 Mi 45.51N 6.11 E
Annemasse 11 Mh 46.12N 6.15 E
Annevoie-Rouillon 12 Gd 50.21N 4.50 E
An Nīl [3] 35 Ea 20.10N 33.00 E
An Nīl al Azraq [3] 35 Ed 12.20N 34.15 E
Anning 27 Hg 24.58N 102.29 E
Anniston 43 Je 33.40N 85.50W
Annobón 30 Hi 1.32S 5.38 E
Annonay 11 Ki 45.14N 4.40 E
Annotto Bay 49 Id 18.16N 76.46W
An Nu'ayrīyah 24 Mi 27.28N 48.27 E
An Nuhūd 31 Jg 12.42N 28.26 E
An Nu' Mān 24 Fi 27.06N 35.46 E
An Nu'mānīyah 24 Kf 32.32N 45.25 E
Annweiler am Trifels 12 Je 49.12N 7.58 E
Anoia/Noya 13 Nc 41.28N 1.56 E
Anoka 45 Jd 45.11N 93.23W
An Ómaigh/Omagh 9 Fg 54.36N 7.18W
Anori 54 Fd 3.47S 61.38W
Anosyennes, Chaînes- 37 Hd 24.20S 47.00 E
Anou Makarene 34 Gb 18.07N 7.35 E
Áno Viánnos 15 In 35.03N 25.25 E
Anóyia 15 Hn 35.15N 24.54 E
Anping [China] 28 Ce 38.13N 115.32 E
Anping [China] 28 Gd 41.10N 123.25 E
An Pointe/Warrenpoint 9 Gg 54.06N 6.15W
Anpu 27 Ig 21.30N 110.00 E
Anpu Gang 27 Ig 21.25N 109.40 E
Anqing 22 Nf 30.32N 116.59 E
Anqiu 28 Ef 36.25N 119.12 E
An Ráth/Ráth Luirc 9 Ei 52.21N 8.41W
An Ribhéar/Kenmare River 9 Dj 51.50N 9.50W
Anröchte 12 Kc 51.34N 8.20 E
Ans 12 Hd 50.39N 5.32 E
Anşāb 23 Fd 29.11N 44.43 E
Ansauvillers 12 Ee 49.34N 2.24 E
Ansbach 10 Gg 49.18N 10.35 E
An Sciobairín/Skibbereen 9 Dj 51.33N 9.15W
An Seancheann/Kinsale, Old Head of- 9 Ej 51.36N 8.32W
Anse-à-Veau 49 Kd 18.30N 73.19W
Anse-Bertrand 51e Ab 16.29N 61.31W
Anse-d'Hainault 49 Jd 18.30N 74.27W
Anse la Raye 51k Ab 13.57N 61.03W
Anshan 22 Oe 41.08N 122.59 E
Anshun 22 Mg 26.15N 105.58 E
Ansina 56 Id 31.54S 55.28W
Ansley 45 Gf 41.18N 99.23W
Anson Bay 59 Gb 13.20S 130.05 E
Ansongo 34 Fb 15.40N 0.31 E
An Srath Bán/Strabane 9 Fg 54.49N 7.27W
Anta 54 Df 13.29S 72.09W

Index Symbols

- [1] Independent Nation
- [2] State, Region
- [3] District, County
- [4] Municipality
- [5] Colony, Dependency
- Continent
- Physical Region
- Historical or Cultural Region
- Mount, Mountain
- Volcano
- Hill
- Mountains, Mountain Range
- Hills, Escarpment
- Plateau, Upland
- Pass, Gap
- Plain, Lowland
- Delta
- Salt Flat
- Valley, Canyon
- Crater, Cave
- Karst Features
- Depression
- Polder
- Desert, Dunes
- Forest, Woods
- Heath, Steppe
- Oasis
- Cape, Point
- Coast, Beach
- Cliff
- Peninsula
- Isthmus
- Sandbank
- Island
- Atoll
- Rock, Reef
- Islands, Archipelago
- Rocks, Reefs
- Coral Reef
- Well, Spring
- Geyser
- River, Stream
- Waterfall Rapids
- River Mouth, Estuary
- Lake
- Salt Lake
- Intermittent Lake
- Reservoir
- Swamp, Pond
- Canal
- Glacier
- Ice Shelf, Pack Ice
- Ocean
- Sea
- Gulf, Bay
- Strait, Fjord
- Lagoon
- Bank
- Seamount
- Tablemount
- Ridge
- Shelf
- Basin
- Escarpment, Sea Scarp
- Fracture
- Trench, Abyss
- National Park, Reserve
- Point of Interest
- Recreation Site
- Cave, Cavern
- Historic Site
- Ruins
- Wall, Walls
- Church, Abbey
- Temple
- Scientific Station
- Airport
- Port
- Lighthouse
- Mine
- Tunnel
- Dam, Bridge

Antabamba 54 Df 14.19S 72.55W
Antakya=Antioch (EN) 23 Eb 36.14N 36.07 E
Antalaha 31 Mj 14.55S 50.15 E
Antalya 22 Ff 36.53N 30.42 E
Antalya, Gulf of- (EN)= Antalya Körfezi 23 Db 36.30N 31.00 E
Antalya Körfezi=Antalya, Gulf of- (EN) 23 Db 36.30N 31.00 E
An Tan 25 Le 15.26N 108.39 E
Antananarivo 31 Lj 18.55S 47.30 E
Antananarivo [3] 37 Hc 19.00S 46.40 E
Antanimora 37 Hd 24.48S 45.39 E
An tAonach/Nenagh 9 Ei 52.52N 8.12W
Antarctica (EN) 66 Bg 90.00S 0.00
Antarctic Peninsula (EN) 66 Qe 69.30S 65.00W
Antas, Cachoeira das- 55 Ha 13.06S 48.09W
Antas, Rio das- 55 Gi 29.04S 51.21W
An Teampall Mór/Templemore 9 Fi 52.48N 7.50W
Antela, Laguna de- 13 Eb 42.07N 7.41W
Antelao 14 Gd 46.27N 12.16 E
Antelope Creek 46 Me 43.29N 105.23W
Anten 8 Ef 58.03N 12.30 E
Antequera [Par.] 55 Dg 24.08S 57.07W
Antequera [Sp.] 13 Hg 37.01N 4.33W
Anthony 45 Cj 32.00N 106.34W
Anti-Atlas 30 Ge 30.00N 8.30W
Antibes 11 Nk 43.35N 7.07 E
Antibes, Cap d'- 11 Nk 43.32N 7.07 E
Antica, Isla- 50 Eg 10.24N 62.43W
Anticosti, Ile d'- 38 Me 49.30N 63.00W
Antigo 45 Ld 45.09N 89.09W
Antigonish 42 Lg 45.37N 61.58W
Antigua 38 Mh 17.03N 61.48W
Antigua and Barbuda 39 Mh 17.03N 61.48W
Antigua Guatemala 47 Ff 14.34N 90.44W
Antiguo Cauce del Río Bermejo 56 Hc 25.39S 60.11W
Antiguo Morelos 48 Jf 22.30N 99.05W
Antilla 49 Jc 20.50N 75.45W
Antillas, Mar de las-/Caribe, Mar-=Caribbean Sea (EN) 38 Lh 15.00N 73.00W
Antillas Mayores=Greater Antilles (EN) 38 Lh 20.00N 74.00W
Antillas Menores=Lesser Antilles (EN) 38 Mh 15.00N 61.00W
Antilles, Mer des-/Caraïbe, Mer-=Caribbean Sea (EN) 38 Lh 15.00N 73.00W
An tInbhear Mór/Arklow 9 Gi 52.48N 6.09W
Antioch 46 Eg 38.00N 121.49W
Antioch (EN)=Antakya 23 Eb 36.14N 36.07 E
Antioche, Pertuis d'- 11 Eh 46.05N 1.20W
Antiope Reef 57 Kf 18.18S 168.40W
Antioquia [2] 54 Cb 7.00N 75.30W
Antipajëta 20 Cc 69.09N 77.00 E
Antipodes Islands 57 Ii 49.40S 178.50 E
Antiques, Pointe d'- 51e Ab 16.26N 61.33W
An t-Iúr/Newry 9 Gg 54.11N 6.20W
Antler River 45 Fb 49.08N 101.00W
Antlers 45 Ii 34.14N 95.37W
Antofagasta [2] 56 Gb 23.30S 69.00W
Antofagasta 53 Ih 23.39S 70.24W
Antofagasta de la Sierra 56 Gc 26.04S 67.25W
Antofalla, Salar de- 56 Gc 25.44S 67.45W
Antofalla, Volcán- 56 Gc 25.34S 67.55W
Antoing 12 Fd 50.34N 3.27 E
Antón 49 Gi 8.24N 80.16W
Anton Dohrn Seamount (EN) 9 Cd 57.30N 11.00W
Antongil, Baie d'- 30 Lj 15.45S 49.50 E
Antonina 56 Kc 25.27S 48.43W
Antônio João 55 Ef 23.15S 55.31W
Antonito 45 Dh 37.05N 106.00W
Antón Lizardo, Punta de- 48 Lh 19.03N 95.58W
Antony 12 Ef 48.45N 2.18 E
Antopol 10 Ud 52.12N 24.53 E
Antracit 16 Ke 48.06N 39.06 E
Antreff 12 Ld 50.52N 9.15 E
Antrim/Aontroim 9 Gg 54.43N 6.13W
Antrim Mountains 9 Gf 55.00N 6.10W
Antrodoco 14 Hh 42.25N 13.05 E
Antsakabary 37 Hc 15.03S 48.56 E
Antsalova 37 Gc 18.42S 44.33 E
Antseranana [3] 37 Hb 13.40S 49.15 E
An tSionainn/Shannon 5 Fe 52.36N 9.41W
Antsirabe 31 Lj 19.51S 47.01 E
Antsiranana 31 Lj 12.17S 49.17 E
An tSiúir/Suir 9 Gi 52.15N 7.00W
Antsla 7 Gh 57.52N 26.33 E
An tSláine/Slaney 9 Gi 52.21N 6.30W
Antsohihy 31 Lj 14.52S 47.58 E
An tSuca/Suck 9 Eh 53.16N 8.03W
Anttola 8 Lc 61.35N 27.39 E
Antu (Songjiang) 28 Jc 42.33N 128.20 E
An Tuc 25 Lf 13.57N 108.39 E
Antufash, Jazīrat- 33 Hf 15.42N 42.25 E
An Tulach/Tullow 9 Gi 52.48N 6.44W
An Tulach Mhór/Tullamore 9 Fh 53.16N 7.30W
Antwerp (EN)=Antwerpen/Anvers 6 Ge 50.38N 5.34 E
Antwerp (EN)=Anvers/Antwerpen 6 Ge 50.38N 5.34 E
Antwerpen [3] 12 Gc 51.10N 4.30 E
Antwerpen/Anvers=Antwerp (EN) 6 Ge 50.38N 5.34 E
Antwerpen-Ekeren 11 Kc 51.17N 4.25 E
Antwerpen-Hoboken 12 Gc 51.10N 4.21 E
Antwerpen-Merksem 12 Gc 51.15N 4.27 E
Antykan 20 If 54.55N 135.13 E
An Uaimh/Navan 9 Gh 53.39N 6.41W
Anuradhapura 25 Gg 8.21N 80.23 E
Anuta Island 57 Hf 11.38S 169.50 E
Anvers/Antwerpen=Antwerp (EN) 6 Ge 50.38N 5.34 E
Anvers Island 66 Qe 64.33S 63.35W
Anvik 40 Gd 62.40N 160.12W
Anxi 22 Le 40.30N 96.00 E
Anxiang 27 Jf 29.26N 112.11 E
Anxin 28 Ce 38.55N 115.56 E
Anxious Bay 59 Gf 33.25S 134.35 E
Anyang (Zhangde) 22 Nf 36.01N 114.25 E
A'nyêmaqen Shan 21 Lf 34.30N 100.00 E
Anyi 28 Cj 28.50N 115.31 E
Anykščiai/Anikščjaj 7 Fi 55.31N 25.08 E
Anyva, Mys- 20 Jg 46.00N 143.25 E
Anza 14 Ce 46.00N 8.17 E
Anze 28 Bf 36.09N 112.14 E
Anzegem 12 Fd 50.50N 3.28 E
Anžero-Sudžensk 22 Kd 56.07N 86.00 E
Anzi 36 Dc 0.52S 23.24 E
Anzio 14 Gi 41.27N 12.37 E
Anzoátegui [2] 54 Fb 9.00N 64.30W
Anzob, Pereval- 18 Ge 39.07N 68.53 E
Aoba, Ile- 61 Cc 15.25S 167.50 E
Ao Ban Don 25 Jg 9.20N 99.25 E
Aoga-Shima 27 Oe 32.30N 139.50 E
Aohan Qi (Xinhui) 28 Ec 42.18N 119.53 E
Aoiz 13 Kb 42.47N 1.22W
Aoji 28 Kc 42.31N 130.24 E
Aola 63a Ec 9.32S 160.29 E
Aomen/Macau=Macao (EN) [5] 22 Ng 22.10N 113.33 E
Aomen/Macau=Macao (EN) 27 Jg 22.12N 113.33 E
Aomori 22 Qe 40.49N 140.45 E
Aomori Ken [2] 28 Pd 40.40N 140.40 E
Aono-Yama 29 Bd 34.27N 131.48 E
Aontroim/Antrim 9 Gg 54.43N 6.13W
Aopo 65c Aa 13.29S 172.30W
Aôral, Phnum- 25 Kf 12.02N 104.10 E
Aoré 63b Cb 15.35S 167.10 E
Aosta / Aoste 14 Be 45.44N 7.20 E
Aosta, Val d'- 14 Be 45.45N 7.20 E
Aoste / Aosta 14 Be 45.44N 7.20 E
Aouk, Bahr- 30 Ih 8.51N 18.53 E
Aoukalé 35 Cd 9.10N 20.30 E
Aoukâr [Afr.] 32 Ge 24.00N 2.30W
Aoukâr [Mtna.] 30 Gg 17.30N 9.30W
Aoulef 32 Hd 26.58N 1.05 E
Aoumou 63b Ce 21.24S 165.49 E
Aourou 34 Cc 14.28N 11.34W
Aoya 29 Cd 35.32N 133.59 E
Aozou 31 If 21.49N 17.25 E
Apa, Rio- 56 Ib 22.06S 58.00W
Apača 20 Kf 52.50N 157.10 E
Apache 46 Kk 31.44N 109.07W
Apache Junction 46 Jj 33.26N 111.32W
Apahida 15 Gc 46.49N 23.45 E
Apakho 63c Bb 11.25S 166.32 E
Apalachee Bay 38 Kg 29.30N 84.00W
Apalachicola 44 Ek 29.44N 84.59W
Apalachicola River 44 Ek 29.44N 84.59W
Apan 48 Jh 19.43N 98.25W
Apaporis, Rio- 52 Jf 1.23S 69.25W
Aparecida do Taboado 54 Hg 20.05S 51.05W
Aparri 22 Oh 18.22N 121.39 E
Apataki Atoll 57 Mf 15.26S 146.20W
Apatin 15 Bd 45.40N 18.59 E
Apatity 6 Jb 67.34N 33.18 E
Apatzingán de la Constitucion 47 De 19.05N 102.21W
Apaxtla de Castrejón 48 Jh 18.09N 99.52W
Ape 7 Gh 57.32N 26.42 E
Apeldoorn 11 Lb 52.13N 5.58 E
Apeldoorn-Nieuw Milligen 12 Hb 52.14N 5.45 E
Apen 12 Ja 53.13N 7.48 E
Apennines (EN) = Appennini 5 Hg 43.00N 13.00 E
Apere, Rio- 54 Ef 13.44S 65.18W
Aphrodisias 24 Cd 37.45N 28.40 E
Api 21 Kf 30.00N 80.57 E
Api 36 Eb 3.40N 25.26 E
Apia 58 Jf 13.50S 171.44W
Apiacás, Serra dos- 54 Gf 10.15S 57.15W
Apio 63a Ec 9.39S 161.23 E
Apipé Grande, Isla- 55 Di 27.30S 56.54W
Apizaco 48 Jh 19.25N 98.09W
Aplao 54 Dc 16.05S 72.31W
Apo, Mount- 21 Oi 6.59N 125.16 E
Apodi 54 Ke 5.39S 37.48W
Apolda 10 He 51.01N 11.30 E
Apolima 65c Aa 13.49S 172.07W
Apolima Strait 65c Aa 13.50S 172.10W
Apollo Bay 59 Ig 38.45S 143.40 E
Apollonia [Alb.] 15 Ci 40.43N 19.27 E
Apollonia [Lib.] 33 Dc 32.54N 21.58 E
Apolo 54 Ef 14.43S 68.31W
Apón, Rio- 49 Kh 10.06N 72.23W
Apopka, Lake- 44 Gk 28.37N 81.38W
Aporé 54 Hg 18.58S 52.01W
Aporé, Rio- 52 Kg 19.27S 50.57W
Apostle Islands 43 Ib 46.50N 90.30W
Apostoles 56 Ic 27.55S 55.46W
Apostolovo 16 Hf 47.39N 33.43 E
Apoteri 54 Gc 4.02N 58.34W
Apôtres, Iles des- 30 Mm 45.40S 50.20 E
Appalachia 44 Fg 36.54N 82.48W
Appalachian Mountains 38 Lc 41.00N 77.00W
Äppelbo 8 Ed 60.30N 14.00 E
Appennini = Apennines (EN) 5 Hg 43.00N 13.00 E
Appennino Abruzzese 14 Hh 42.00N 13.55 E
Appennino Calabro 14 Kl 39.00N 16.30 E
Appennino Campano 14 Ii 40.50N 14.45 E
Appennino Ligure 14 Cf 44.30N 9.00 E
Appennino Lucano 14 Jj 40.30N 16.00 E
Appennino Tosco-Emiliano 14 Fg 44.00N 11.30 E
Appennino Umbro-Marchigiano 14 Gg 43.20N 12.55 E
Appenzell 14 Dc 47.20N 9.25 E
Appenzell Ausser-Rhoden [2] 14 Dc 47.20N 9.20 E
Appenzell Inner-Rhoden [2] 14 Dc 47.15N 9.25 E
Appingedam 12 Ia 53.19N 6.52 E
Appleby 9 Kg 54.36N 2.29W
Appleton 43 Jc 44.16N 88.25W
Appomattox 44 Hg 37.21N 78.51W
Apra Harbor 64c Bb 13.27N 144.38 E
Apricena 14 Ji 41.47N 15.27 E
Aprilia 14 Gi 41.36N 12.39 E
Apšeronsk 19 Dg 44.27N 39.44 E
Apšeronskij Poluostrov=Apsheron Peninsula (EN) 5 Lg 41.00N 50.50 E
Apsheron Peninsula (EN)=Apšeronskij Poluostrov 5 Lg 41.00N 50.50 E
Apt 11 Lk 43.53N 5.24 E
Apucarana 56 Jb 23.33S 51.29W
Apuoarana, Serra da- 55 Gf 23.50S 51.20W
Apuka 20 Ld 60.23N 169.45 E
Apuka 20 Ld 60.25N 169.35 E
Apulia (EN) = Puglia [2] 14 Ki 41.15N 16.15 E
Apurashokoru 64a Ac 7.17N 134.18 E
Apure [2] 54 Eb 7.10N 68.50W
Apure, Rio- 52 Je 7.37N 66.25W
Apurimac [2] 54 Df 14.00S 73.00W
Apurimac, Rio- 52 Ig 12.17S 73.56W
Apurito 50 Bi 7.56N 68.27W
Apuseni, Munţii-=Apuseni Mountains (EN) 5 If 46.30N 22.30 E
Apuseni Mountains (EN)=Apuseni, Munţii- 5 If 46.30N 22.30 E
Āq 24 Kc 38.59N 45.27 E
Āqā 24 Me 35.00N 47.00 E
Aqaba (EN)=Al 'Aqabah 23 Dd 29.31N 35.00 E
Aqaba, Gulf of- (EN)='Aqabah, Khalīj al- 30 Kf 29.00N 34.40 E
Āqā Bāba 24 Md 36.20N 49.46 E
'Aqabah, Khalīj al-=Aqaba, Gulf of- (EN) 30 Kf 29.00N 34.40 E
Āqcheh 23 Kb 36.56N 66.11 E
'Aqdā 24 Of 32.26N 53.37 E
'Aqīq 35 Fb 18.14N 38.12 E
Aqitag 27 Fc 41.49N 90.38 E
Āqotāq 24 Ld 37.10N 47.05 E
Āq Qal'eh 24 Pd 37.01N 54.30 E
Aqqikkol Hu 27 Ed 37.00N 88.20 E
'Aqrah 24 Jd 36.45N 43.54 E
Aqrin, Jabal- 24 Hg 31.32N 38.18 E
Āq Şū 24 Ke 34.35N 44.31 E
Aquidabã, Rio- 55 De 20.58S 57.50W
Aquidabán, Rio- 55 Df 23.11S 57.32W
Aquidauana 54 Gh 20.28S 55.48W
Aquidauana, Rio- 54 Gg 19.44S 56.50W
Aquidauana, Serra de- 55 Ee 20.50S 55.30W
Aquiles Serdán 48 Gc 28.36N 105.53W
Aquin 49 Kd 18.16N 73.24W
Aquitaine, Bassin d'-=Aquitaine Basin (EN) 5 Fg 44.00N 0.10W
Aquitaine Basin (EN)=Aquitaine, Bassin d'- 5 Fg 44.00N 0.10W
Ara 13 Mb 42.25N 0.09 E
'Arab, Baḩr al- 30 Jh 9.02N 29.28 E
'Arab, Khalīj al- 35 Ec 30.55N 29.05 E
'Arab, Shaţţ al- 21 Gf 30.28N 47.59 E
'Arabah, Wādī- 24 Eh 29.07N 32.39 E
'Arabah, Wādī al- 24 Fg 30.58N 32.24 E
Arabatskaja Strelka, Kosa- 16 Ig 45.40N 35.05 E
'Arabestān 24 Mg 30.30N 50.00 E
Arabian Basin (EN) 3 Gh 11.30N 65.00 E
Arabian Desert (EN)=Sharqīyah, Aş Şaḩrā' ash- 30 Kf 28.00N 32.00 E
Arabian Peninsula (EN) 21 Gg 25.00N 45.00 E
Arabian Sea (EN) 21 Ih 15.00N 65.00 E
Araç 24 Eb 41.15N 33.21 E
Aracá, Rio- 54 Fd 0.25S 62.55W
Aracaju 53 Mg 10.55S 37.04W
Aracataca 49 Jh 10.35N 74.13W
Aracati 54 Kd 4.34S 37.46W
Araçatuba 53 Kh 21.12S 50.25W
Aracena 13 Fg 37.53N 6.33W
Aracena, Sierra de- 13 Fg 37.56N 6.50W
Aracides, Cape- 63a Ec 8.39S 161.01 E
Aracruz 54 Jg 19.49S 40.16W
Araçuai 54 Jg 16.52S 42.04W
Arad 6 If 46.11N 21.19 E
'Arad 24 Fg 31.15N 35.13 E
Arad [2] 15 Ec 46.11N 21.25 E
Arada 35 Cb 15.01N 20.40 E
'Arādah 35 Ia 22.59N 53.26 E
Arafali 35 Fb 15.04N 39.45 E
Ara Fana 35 Gd 6.01N 41.11 E
Arafune-Yama 29 Fc 36.12N 138.38 E
Arafura, Laut-=Arafura Sea (EN) 57 Ee 9.00S 133.00 E
Arafura Sea (EN)=Arafura, Laut- 57 Ee 9.00S 133.00 E
Aragac, Gora- 5 Kg 40.31N 44.10 E
Aragarças 53 Kg 15.55S 52.15W
Aragón 13 Kb 42.13N 1.44W
Aragón 5 Fg 41.00N 1.00W
Aragón 13 Lc 41.00N 1.00W
Aragona 14 Hm 37.24N 13.37 E
Aragua [2] 54 Eb 10.00N 67.10W
Araguacema 54 Ie 8.50S 49.34W
Aragua de Barcelona 50 Dh 9.28N 64.49W
Aragua de Maturin 50 Eh 9.58N 63.29W
Araguaia, Rio- 52 Lf 5.21S 48.41W
Araguaiana 55 Gb 16.49S 53.05W
Araguaina 54 Ie 7.12S 48.12W
Araguao, Boca- 54 Fb 9.17N 60.48W
Araguao, Caño- 50 Fh 9.15N 60.50W
Araguapiche, Punta- 50 Fh 9.29N 60.56W
Araguari 54 Ig 18.38S 48.11W
Araguari, Rio- [Braz.] 52 Le 1.15N 49.55W
Araguari, Rio- [Braz.] 55 Hd 18.21S 48.40W
Araguatins 54 Ie 5.38S 48.07W
'Arâguib 32 Ff 18.50N 7.45W
Aragvi 16 Ni 41.50N 44.43 E
Arai 28 Of 37.09N 138.06 E
Árainn/Inishmore 9 Dh 53.07N 9.45W
Árainn Mhór/Aran Island 9 Ef 55.00N 8.30W
Araioses 54 Jd 2.53S 41.55W
Arāk 22 Gf 34.05N 49.41 E
Arak 32 Hd 25.18N 3.45 E
Arakabesan 64a Ac 7.21N 134.27 E
Arakan [2] 25 Ie 19.00N 94.15 E
Arakan Yoma 21 Lh 19.00N 94.40 E
Arakawa 29 Fb 38.09N 139.25 E
Ara-Kawa [Jap.] 29 Fb 38.09N 139.23 E
Ara-Kawa [Jap.] 29 Fc 37.11N 138.15 E
Árakhthos 15 Ej 39.01N 21.03 E
Araks 21 Gf 39.56N 48.20 E
Aral [China] 27 Dc 40.38N 81.24 E
Aral [Kirg.-U.S.S.R.] 19 Hg 41.48N 74.25 E
Aral Sea (EN)=Aralskoje More 21 He 45.00N 60.00 E
Aralsk 22 Ie 46.48N 61.40 E
Aralskoje More=Aral Sea (EN) 21 He 45.00N 60.00 E
Aralsor, Ozero- 16 Pe 49.05N 48.15 E
Aralsulfat 19 Gf 46.50N 61.59 E
Aramac 59 Jd 22.59S 145.14 E
Arambaré 55 Gj 30.55S 51.30W
Ārān 24 Ne 34.03N 51.30 E
Aranda de Duero 13 Ic 41.41N 3.41W
Arandelovac 15 De 44.18N 20.35 E
Arandilla 13 Ic 41.40N 3.41W
Aran Island/Árainn Mhór 9 Dh 53.07N 9.43W
Aran Islands 9 Ef 55.00N 8.30W
Aranjunez 13 Id 40.02N 3.36W
Aranos 37 Bd 24.09S 19.09 E
Arañuelo, Campo- 13 Ge 39.55N 5.30W
Aranuka Atoll 57 Id 0.11N 173.36 E
Arao 29 Be 32.59N 130.27 E
Araouane 31 Gg 18.53N 3.35W
Arapahoe 45 Gf 40.18N 99.54W
Arapey Grande, Rio- 55 Dj 30.55S 57.49W
Arapiraca 54 Ke 9.45S 36.39W
Arápis, Ákra- 15 Gi 40.27N 24.00 E
Arapkir 24 Hc 39.03N 38.30 E
Arapoim, Rio- 55 Kb 15.45S 43.39W
Arapongas 56 Jb 23.23S 51.27W
Arapoti 55 Hg 24.08S 49.50W
'Ar'ar 24 Ig 30.59N 41.02 E
'Ar'ar, Wādī 24 Jg 31.23N 42.26 E
Araranguá 56 Kc 28.56S 49.29W
Araraquara 53 Lh 21.47S 48.10W
Araras 55 If 22.22S 47.23W
Araras, Açude- 54 Jd 4.20S 40.30W
Araras, Serra das- 55 Fd 18.45S 53.30W
Ararat [Arm.-U.S.S.R.] 19 Eh 39.50N 44.43 E
Ararat [Austl.] 59 Ig 37.17S 142.56 E
Ararat, Mount- (EN)=Büyük Ağri Daği 21 Gf 39.40N 44.24 E
Arari 54 Jd 3.28S 44.47W
Arari, Lago- 54 Id 0.37S 49.07W
Aras 21 Gf 39.56N 48.20 E
Aras Dağlari 24 Jc 40.00N 43.00 E
Aratika Atoll 57 Mf 15.32S 145.32W
Aratürük/Yiwu 27 Fc 43.15N 94.35 E
Arauca [2] 54 Db 6.30N 71.00W
Arauca 54 Db 7.03N 70.47W
Arauca, Rio- 52 Je 7.24N 66.35W
Araucania [2] 56 Fe 37.50S 73.15W
Arauco 56 Fe 37.15S 73.19W
Araure 50 Bh 9.38N 69.15W
Aravaca, Madrid- 13 Id 40.27N 3.47W
Aravis 11 Mi 45.53N 6.28 E
Arawalli Range 21 Jg 25.00N 73.30 E
Araxá 54 Ig 19.35S 46.55W
Áraxos, Ákra- 15 Ek 38.10N 21.23 E
Araya 50 Dg 10.34N 64.15W
Araya, Peninsula de- 54 Fa 10.35N 64.00W
Arba 13 Kc 41.52N 1.18W
Arba'āt 35 Fb 19.50N 37.03 E
Arba'in, Darb al- 24 Di 26.40N 30.50 E
Arbaj-Here 27 Hb 46.15N 102.48 E
Arba Minch 31 Kh 5.59N 37.38 E
'Arbat 24 Ke 35.25N 45.35 E
Arbatax 14 Dk 39.56N 9.42 E
Arboga 7 Dg 59.24N 15.50 E
Arbogaån 8 Ge 59.26N 16.04 E
Arbois 11 Lh 46.54N 5.46 E
Arboletes 49 Ii 8.52N 76.25W
Arbolito 55 Ek 32.39S 54.15W
Arbon 14 Dc 47.30N 9.25 E
Arbore 15 Ib 47.44N 25.56 E
Arborea 14 Ck 39.46N 8.35 E
Arborea 14 Ck 39.50N 8.50 E
Arborg 45 Ha 50.55N 97.15W
Arbrå 7 Dc 61.29N 16.23 E
Arbroath 9 Ke 56.34N 2.35W
Arbus 14 Ck 39.32N 8.36 E
Arc [Fr.] 11 Mi 45.34N 6.12 E
Arc [Fr.] 11 Lk 43.31N 5.07 E
Arcachon 11 Ej 44.39N 1.10W
Arcachon, Bassin d'- 11 Ej 44.42N 1.09W
Arcadia [Fl.-U.S.] 44 Gl 27.14N 81.52W
Arcadia [La.-U.S.] 45 Jj 32.33N 92.55W
Arcagly-Ajat 17 Jj 53.00N 61.50 E
Arcas, Cayos- 47 Fd 20.12N 91.58W
Arcata 46 Cf 40.52N 124.05W
Arcelia 48 Ih 18.17N 100.16W
Arcen, Areen en Velden- 12 Ic 51.28N 6.11 E
Arcevia 14 Gg 43.30N 12.56 E
Archangel (EN)=Arhangelsk 6 Kc 64.34N 40.32 E
Archaringa Creek 59 He 28.15S 135.11 E
Archer River 59 Ib 13.28S 141.41 E
Archer's Post 36 Gb 0.39N 37.41 E
Archidona 13 Hg 37.05N 4.23W
Arcidosso 14 Fh 42.52N 11.33 E
Arcipelago Campano 5 Hg 40.30N 13.20 E
Arcipelago Toscano=Tuscan Archipelago (EN) 5 Hg 42.45N 10.20 E
Arcis-sur-Aube 11 Kf 48.32N 4.08 E
Arciz 16 Fg 45.59N 29.27 E
Arco [Id.-U.S.] 46 Ie 43.38N 113.18W
Arco [It.] 14 Ee 45.55N 10.53 E
Arconce 11 Jh 46.27N 4.00 E
Arcos 55 Je 20.17S 45.32W
Arcos de Jalón 13 Jc 41.13N 2.16W
Arcos de la Frontera 13 Gh 36.45N 5.48W
Arcos de Valdevez 13 Dc 41.51N 8.25W
Arcoverde 53 Mf 8.25S 37.04W
Arctic Bay 39 Kb 73.02N 85.11W
Arctic Ocean 67 Be 85.00N 170.00 E
Arctic Ocean (EN)=Ishavet 67 Be 85.00N 170.00 E
Arctic Ocean (EN)=Severny Ledovity Okean 67 Be 85.00N 170.00 E
Arctic Red River 42 Ec 67.27N 133.45W
Arctic Red River 42 Ec 67.22N 133.30W
Arctic Village 40 Jc 68.08N 145.19W
Arda [Eur.] 15 Jh 41.39N 26.29 E
Arda [It.] 14 Ee 45.02N 10.02 E
Ardabīl [Iran] 22 Gf 38.15N 48.18 E
Ardabīl [Iraq] 24 Ie 34.24N 40.59 E
Ardahan 24 Jb 41.07N 42.41 E
Ardakāh 23 Hc 32.19N 53.59 E
Ardakān 24 Og 30.16N 52.01 E
Ardal 24 Ng 31.59N 50.39 E
Ardales 13 Hh 36.52N 4.51W
Ardalsfjorden 8 Bc 61.15N 7.30 E
Årdalstangen 7 Bf 61.14N 7.43 E
Ardanuç 24 Jb 41.08N 42.03 E
Ardatov [R.S.F.S.R.] 7 Ki 55.17N 43.12 E
Ardatov [R.S.F.S.R.] 7 Li 54.53N 46.13 E
'Arde 35 Hd 9.58N 46.04 E
Ardèche 11 Kj 44.16N 4.39 E
Ardèche [3] 11 Kj 44.40N 4.20 E
Ardee/Béal Átha Fhirdhia 9 Gh 53.52N 6.33W
Ardencaple Fjord 41 Jd 75.15N 20.10W
Ardenne, Plateau de l'-/Ardennen, Plateau van der-=Ardennes (EN) 5 Ge 50.10N 5.45 E
Ardennen, Plateau van der-/Ardenne, Plateau de l'-=Ardennes (EN) 5 Ge 50.10N 5.45 E
Ardennes [3] 11 Ke 49.40N 4.40 E
Ardennes (EN)=Ardenne, Plateau de l'-/Ardennen, Plateau van der- 5 Ge 50.10N 5.45 E
Ardennes (EN)=Ardennen, Plateau van der-/Ardenne, Plateau de l'- 5 Ge 50.10N 5.45 E
Ardennes, Canal des- 11 Ke 49.26N 4.02 E
Ardennes, Forêt des- 12 Ge 49.48N 4.50 E
Ardentes 11 Hh 46.45N 1.50 E
Ardeşen 24 Ib 41.12N 41.00 E
Ardestān 24 Of 33.22N 52.23 E
Árdhas 15 Jh 41.39N 26.29 E
Ardila 13 Ef 38.12N 7.28W
Ard Mhacha/Armagh 9 Gg 54.21N 6.39W
Ardmore 43 He 34.10N 97.08W
Ardnamurchan, Point of- 9 Ge 56.45N 6.30W
Ardon 16 Nh 43.07N 44.13 E
Ardooie 12 Fd 50.59N 3.12 E
Ardre 12 Fe 49.18N 3.40 E
Ardres 12 Dd 50.51N 1.59 E
Ards Peninsula/An Aird 9 Hg 54.30N 5.30W
Ar Dub'al Khālī 21 Hg 21.00N 51.00 E
Ardud 15 Fb 47.38N 22.53 E
Arebi 36 Eb 2.50N 29.38 E
Arecibo 47 Ke 18.28N 66.43W
Areen en Valden 12 Ic 51.28N 6.11 E
Areen en Velden-Arcen 12 Ic 51.28N 6.11 E
Arègala/Ariogala 8 Ji 55.13N 23.30 E
Areia, Ribeirão da- 55 Jc 16.07S 45.52W
Areia Branca 54 Kd 4.57S 37.08W
Arekalong Peninsula 64a Bb 7.40N 134.38 E
Aremberg 12 Id 50.25N 6.49 E
Arena 26 He 9.14N 120.46 E
Arena, Point- 43 Cd 38.57N 123.44W
Arena, Punta- 47 Cd 23.30N 109.30W
Arena de la Ventana, Punta- 47 Cd 24.03N 109.52W
Arenápolis 54 Gf 14.26S 56.49W
Arenas, Cayo- 47 Fd 22.08N 91.24W
Arenas, Punta de- 56 Gh 53.09S 68.13W
Arenas de San Pedro 13 Gd 40.12N 5.05W
Arenberg 12 Jb 52.42N 7.20 E
Arendal 7 Bg 58.27N 8.48 E
Arendonk 12 Hc 51.19N 5.05 E
Arénys de Mar/Arenys de Mar 13 Oc 41.35N 2.33 E
Arenys de Mar/Arénys de Mar 13 Oc 41.35N 2.33 E
Areópolis 15 Fm 36.40N 22.23 E
Areq, Sebkha bou- 13 Ji 35.10N 2.45W
Arequipa 53 Ig 16.24S 71.33W
Arequipa [2] 54 Dg 16.00S 72.30W
Arequito 55 Bk 33.09S 61.28W
Arero 35 Fe 4.44N 38.50 E
Ares, Muela de- 13 Ld 40.28N 0.07W
Åreskutan 8 Ea 63.26N 13.06 E
Åreskutan 7 Ce 63.24N 13.06 E
Arévalo 13 Hc 41.04N 4.43W
Arezzo 14 Fg 43.25N 11.53 E
Arga 13 Kb 42.18N 1.47W
Argajas 17 Ji 55.31N 60.55 E
Argamasilla de Alba 13 Ie 39.07N 3.06W
Argan 27 Ec 40.09N 88.22 E
Arganda 13 Id 40.18N 3.26W
Arga-Sala 20 Gc 68.37N 112.05 E
Argelès-Gazost 11 Fk 43.01N 0.06W
Argelès-sur-Mer 11 Jl 42.33N 3.01 E
Argens 11 Mk 43.24N 6.44 E

Index Symbols

[1] Independent Nation
[2] State, Region
[3] District, County
[4] Municipality
[5] Colony, Dependency
Continent
Physical Region
Historical or Cultural Region
Mount, Mountain
Volcano
Hill
Mountains, Mountain Range
Hills, Escarpment
Plateau, Upland
Pass, Gap
Plain, Lowland
Delta
Salt Flat
Valley, Canyon
Crater, Cave
Karst Features
Depression
Polder
Desert, Dunes
Forest, Woods
Heath, Steppe
Oasis
Cape, Point
Coast, Beach
Cliff
Peninsula
Isthmus
Sandbank
Island
Atoll
Rock, Reef
Islands, Archipelago
Rocks, Reefs
Coral Reef
Well, Spring
Geyser
River, Stream
Waterfall Rapids
River Mouth, Estuary
Lake
Salt Lake
Intermittent Lake
Reservoir
Swamp, Pond
Canal
Glacier
Ice Shelf, Pack Ice
Ocean
Sea
Gulf, Bay
Strait, Fjord
Lagoon
Bank
Seamount
Tablemount
Ridge
Shelf
Basin
Escarpment, Sea Scarp
Fracture
Trench, Abyss
National Park, Reserve
Point of Interest
Recreation Site
Cave, Cavern
Historic Site
Ruins
Wall, Walls
Church, Abbey
Temple
Scientific Station
Airport
Port
Lighthouse
Mine
Tunnel
Dam, Bridge

Name	Page	Grid	Lat.	Long.
Argent, Côte d'-	11	Ej	44.00N	1.30W
Argenta	14	Ff	44.37N	11.50 E
Argentan	11	Ff	48.45N	0.01W
Argentario, Monte-	14	Fh	42.24N	11.09 E
Argentat	11	Hi	45.06N	1.56 E
Argentera	14	Bf	44.10N	7.18 E
Argenteuil	11	If	48.57N	2.15 E
Argentiera, Capo dell'-	14	Cj	40.44N	8.08 E
Argentina	55	Ai	29.33S	62.17W
Argentina [1]	53	Ji	34.00S	64.00W
Argentine Basin (EN)	3	Cn	45.00S	45.00W
Argentino, Lago-	52	Ik	50.13S	72.25W
Argentino, Mar-	52	Kj	46.00S	59.40W
Argenton	11	Fg	47.05N	0.13W
Argenton-Château	11	Fh	46.59N	0.27W
Argenton-sur-Creuse	11	Hh	46.35N	1.31 E
Arges	15	Jd	44.04N	26.37 E
Arges [2]	15	Hd	45.00N	24.50 E
Arghandāb	23	Jc	31.27N	64.23 E
Argo	35	Eb	19.31N	30.25 E
Argo Depth (EN)	3	Jk	12.10S	165.40W
Argolikós Kólpos = Argolis, Gulf of- (EN)	15	Fl	37.20N	22.55 E
Argolis, Gulf of- (EN) = Argolikós Kólpos	15	Fl	37.20N	22.55 E
Argonne	12	He	49.30N	5.00 E
Argonne	11	Ke	49.30N	5.00 E
Árgos	15	Fl	37.38N	22.44 E
Árgos Orestikón	15	Ei	40.30N	21.16 E
Argostólion	15	Dk	38.11N	20.29 E
Arguedas	13	Kb	42.10N	1.36W
Argueil-Fry	12	De	49.37N	1.31 E
Arguello, Point-	46	Ei	34.35N	120.39W
Arguenon	11	Df	48.35N	2.13W
Argun	16	Nh	43.16N	45.52 E
Argun	21	Od	53.20N	121.28 E
Argungu	34	Fc	12.45N	4.31 E
Argyle	51n	Bb	13.10N	61.10W
Argyle, Lake-	57	Df	16.15S	128.40 E
Argyll	9	Ie	56.20N	5.00W
Arhangelsk = Archangel (EN)	6	Kc	64.34N	40.32 E
Arhangelskaja Oblast [3]	19	Ec	63.30N	43.00 E
Arhara	20	Ig	49.30N	130.09 E
Arhavi	24	Ib	41.22N	41.16 E
Arholma	8	He	59.50N	19.05 E
Ar Horqin Qi (Tianshan)	27	Lc	43.55N	120.05 E
Århus [2]	8	Dh	56.10N	10.15 E
Århus	6	Hd	56.09N	10.13 E
Århus Bugt	8	Dh	56.10N	10.20 E
Arhust	27	Ib	47.42N	107.50 E
Ariadnoje	20	Ig	45.08N	134.25 E
Ariake-Kai	28	Kh	32.55N	130.27 E
Ariamsvlei	37	Be	28.08S	19.50 E
Ariano Irpino	14	Ji	41.09N	15.05 E
Ariari, Río-	54	Dc	2.35N	72.47W
Arias	56	Hd	33.38S	62.25W
Ari Atoll	25a	Bb	3.30N	72.45 E
Aribinda	34	Ec	14.14N	0.52W
Arica	53	Ig	18.29S	70.20W
Arica, Golfo de-	52	Ig	18.30S	70.30W
Arichuna	50	Ci	7.42N	67.08W
Arid, Cape-	59	Ef	34.00S	123.09 E
Arida	28	Mg	34.05N	135.07 E
Arida-Gawa	29	Dd	34.05N	135.06 E
Aridhaia	15	Fi	40.59N	22.04 E
Ariège	11	Hk	43.31N	1.25 E
Ariège [3]	11	Hk	43.00N	1.30 E
Ariel	55	Cm	36.32S	59.54W
Aries	15	Gc	46.26N	23.59 E
Ariguani	54	Db	9.50N	74.01W
Ariguani, Río-	49	Ki	9.35N	73.46W
Arīḥā [Jor.]	24	Fg	31.52N	35.27 E
Arīḥā [Syr.]	24	Ge	35.48N	36.36 E
Arikaree River	45	Ff	40.01N	101.56W
Arikawa	29	Ae	32.59N	129.07 E
Arilje	15	Df	43.45N	20.06 E
Arima	54	Fa	10.38N	61.17W
Arinos	55	Ib	15.55S	46.04W
Arinos, Rio-	52	Kg	10.25S	58.20W
Arinos Novo, Rio-	55	Db	14.14S	56.01W
Ariogala/Arëgala	8	Ji	55.13N	23.30 E
Aripuanã	54	Fe	9.10S	60.38W
Aripuanã, Rio-	52	Jf	5.07S	60.24W
Ariquemes	54	Fe	9.56S	63.04W
Arisa	35	Gc	11.11N	41.38 E
'Arish, Wādī al-	24	Eg	31.09N	33.49 E
Arismendi	49	Mi	8.29N	68.22W
Arita	29	Ae	33.11N	129.52 E
Aritzo	14	Dk	39.57N	9.12 E
Arixang/Wenquan	27	Dc	44.59N	81.04 E
Ariza	13	Jc	41.19N	2.03W
Arizaro, Salar de-	56	Gb	24.42S	67.45W
Arize, Massif de l'-	11	Hl	42.50N	1.30 E
Arizona [2]	43	Ee	34.00N	112.00W
Arizpe	48	Db	30.20N	110.10W
Årjäng	7	Cg	59.23N	12.08 E
Arjeplog	7	Dc	66.03N	17.54 E
Arjo	35	Fd	8.45N	36.30 E
Arjona	54	Ca	10.15N	75.21W
Arkadak	19	Ee	51.58N	43.28 E
Arkadelphia	43	Ie	34.07N	93.04W
Arkalyk	22	Id	50.13N	66.50 E
Arkansas	38	Jf	33.48N	91.04W
Arkansas [2]	43	Id	34.50N	93.40W
Arkansas City	43	Hd	37.04N	97.02W
Arkanū, Jabal-	33	De	22.15N	24.45 E
Arkatag	21	Kf	36.45N	89.10 E
Arkhángelos	15	Lm	36.12N	28.08 E
Arki	15	Jl	37.22N	26.45 E
Arklow/An tInbhear Mór	9	Gi	52.48N	6.09W
Arkona, Kap-	10	Jb	54.41N	13.26 E
Arkonam	25	Ff	13.06N	79.40 E
Arkösund	8	Gf	58.30N	16.56 E
Arkoúdhion	15	Dk	38.33N	20.43 E
Arktičeskoga Instituta, Ostrova- = Arkticheski Institut Islands (EN)	20	Da	75.20N	81.50 E
Arkticheski Institut Islands (EN) = Arktičeskoga Instituta, Ostrova-	20	Da	75.20N	81.50 E
Arlan, Gora-	16	Sj	39.43N	54.40 E
Arlanza	13	Hb	42.06N	4.09W
Arlanzón	13	Hb	42.03N	4.17W
Arlberg	14	Ec	47.08N	10.12 E
Arles	11	Kk	43.40N	4.38 E
Arlington [Or.-U.S.]	46	Ed	45.46N	120.13W
Arlington [Tx.-U.S.]	45	Hj	32.44N	97.07W
Arlington [Va.-U.S.]	43	Ld	38.52N	77.05W
Arlington Heights	45	Me	42.05N	87.59W
Arlit	31	Hg	19.00N	7.38 E
Arlon/Aarlen	11	Le	49.41N	5.49 E
Arlöv	8	Ei	55.39N	13.05 E
Arly	34	Fc	11.35N	1.28 E
Armagh/Ard Mhacha	9	Gg	54.21N	6.39W
Armagnac	11	Gk	43.45N	0.10 E
Armagnac, Collines de l'-	11	Gk	43.30N	0.30 E
Armah, Wādī-	23	Hf	18.12N	51.02 E
Arman	20	Ke	59.43N	150.12 E
Armançon	11	Jg	47.57N	3.30 E
Armandale, Perth-	59	Df	32.09S	116.00 E
Armant	33	Fd	25.37N	32.32 E
Armáthia	15	Jn	35.26N	26.52 E
Armavir	6	Kf	45.00N	41.08 E
Armenia	53	Ie	4.31N	75.41W
Armenia (EN) = Ermenistan	23	Fb	39.10N	43.00 E
Armenia (EN) = Ermenistan	21	Gf	39.10N	43.00 E
Armenian SSR (EN) = Armjanskaja SSR [2]	19	Eg	40.00N	45.00 E
Armentières	11	Id	50.41N	2.53 E
Armeria	48	Gh	18.56N	103.58W
Armi, Capo dell'-	14	Jm	37.57N	15.41 E
Armidale	58	Gh	30.31S	151.39 E
Armisvesi	8	Lb	62.30N	26.35 E
Armjansk	16	Hf	46.05N	33.41 E
Armjanskaja Sovetskaja Socialističeskaja Respublika [2]	19	Eg	40.00N	45.00 E
Armjanskaja SSR/Haikakan Sovetakan Socialistakan Respublika [2]	19	Eg	40.00N	45.00 E
Armjanskaja SSR = Armenian SSR (EN) [2]	19	Eg	40.00N	45.00 E
Armoricain, Massif- = Armorican Massif (EN)	5	Ff	48.00N	3.00W
Armorican Massif (EN) = Armoricain, Massif-	5	Ff	48.00N	3.00W
Armour	45	Ge	43.19N	98.21W
Arm River	46	Ma	50.46N	105.00W
Armstrong [Arg.]	55	Bk	32.47S	61.36W
Armstrong [B.C.-Can.]	46	Fa	50.27N	119.12W
Armstrong [Ont.-Can.]	42	If	50.18N	89.02W
Ārmūdlü	24	Qd	37.15N	56.05 E
Armutçuk Dağ	15	Ki	40.03N	27.23 E
Armutlu	15	Li	40.31N	28.50 E
Armutova	15	Jj	39.23N	26.50 E
Arnaia	15	Gi	40.29N	23.36 E
Arnaud	42	Kd	60.00N	69.55W
Arnautis, Akrotérion-	24	Ee	35.06N	32.17 E
Arnay-le-Duc	11	Kg	47.08N	4.29 E
Arnedo	13	Jb	42.13N	2.06W
Årnes	7	Cf	60.09N	11.28 E
Arnhem	11	Lc	51.59N	5.55 E
Arnhem, Cape-	57	Ef	12.21S	136.21 E
Arnhem Bay	59	Hb	12.20S	136.10 E
Arnhem Land	57	Ef	13.10S	134.30 E
Arno	5	Hg	43.41N	10.17 E
Arno Atoll	57	Id	7.05N	171.41 E
Arnold	12	Aa	53.00N	1.08W
Arnon	11	Ig	47.13N	2.01 E
Arnøy	7	Ea	70.08N	20.36 E
Arnprior	44	Ic	45.26N	76.21W
Arnsberg	10	Ee	51.23N	8.05 E
Arnsberger Wald	12	Kc	51.26N	8.10 E
Arnsberg-Oeventrop	12	Kc	51.24N	8.08 E
Arnsburg	12	Kd	50.29N	8.48 E
Arnstadt	10	Gf	50.50N	10.57 E
Aro, Río-	50	Di	8.01N	64.11W
Aroa	50	Bg	10.26N	68.54W
Aroa, Pointe-	65e	Fc	17.28S	149.46W
Aroa, Río-	50	Bg	10.41N	68.18W
Aroa, Sierra de-	50	Bg	10.15N	68.55W
Aroab	37	Be	26.47S	19.40 E
Aroánia Óri	15	Fl	37.57N	22.13 E
Aroche	13	Fg	37.57N	6.57W
Aroche, Pico de-	13	Ff	38.01N	6.56W
Aroeira	55	Ee	21.41S	54.25W
Arolsen	10	Ff	51.22N	9.01 E
Aroma	35	Fb	15.49N	36.08 E
Aron	11	Jh	46.50N	3.27 E
Arona	14	Ce	45.46N	8.34 E
Aroostook River	44	Nb	46.48N	67.45W
Arorae Island	57	Ie	2.38S	176.49 E
Arorangi	64p	Bb	21.13S	159.49W
Aros, Río-	48	Ec	29.30N	109.15W
Arosa	14	Dd	46.47N	9.40 E
Arosa, Ría de-	13	Db	42.28N	8.57W
Aros Papigochic, Río-	48	Ec	29.09N	108.35W
Årøsund	8	Ci	55.15N	9.43 E
Arouca	13	Dd	40.56N	8.15W
Arpaçay	24	Jb	40.45N	43.25 E
Arpajon	11	If	48.35N	2.15 E
Arpino	14	Hi	41.39N	13.36 E
Arquata Scrivia	14	Cf	44.41N	8.53 E
Arque	54	Eg	17.48S	66.23W
Arques-la-Bataille	12	De	49.53N	1.08 E
Ar Rachidiya	32	Gc	31.55N	4.40W
Ar Rachidiya [3]	32	Gc	31.00N	4.00W
Ar Radīsīyah Baḥrī	33	Fe	24.57N	32.53 E
Arrah	25	Gc	25.34N	84.40 E
Ar Rahad	35	Ec	12.43N	30.39 E
Ar Rahad	30	Kg	14.28N	33.31 E
Arraias	54	If	12.56S	46.57W
Arraias, Rio- [Braz.]	54	Hf	11.10S	53.35W
Arraias, Rio- [Braz.]	55	Ia	12.28S	47.18W
Arraiolos	13	Ef	38.43N	7.59W
Ar Ramādī	23	Fc	33.25N	43.17 E
Ar Ramlah	24	Fh	29.32N	35.57 E
Ar Ramlī al Kabīr	33	Dd	26.30N	22.10 E
Arran, Island of-	9	Hf	55.35N	5.15W
Ar Rank	35	Ec	11.45N	32.48 E
Ar Raqqah	23	Eb	35.56N	39.01 E
Arras	11	Id	50.17N	2.47 E
Ar Rāshidah	24	Cj	25.35N	28.56 E
Ar Rass	24	Jj	25.52N	43.28 E
Ar Rastān	24	Ge	34.55N	36.44 E
Arrats	11	Gj	44.06N	0.52 E
Ar Rawḍah [Sau.Ar.]	33	He	21.16N	42.50 E
Ar Rawḍatayn	24	Lh	29.53N	47.44 E
Ar Rayḥānī	24	Pk	23.37N	55.58 E
Arrecife	32	Ed	28.57N	13.32W
Arrecife Alacrán	47	Gd	22.24N	89.42W
Arrecifes	56	Hd	34.03S	60.07W
Arrecifes, Río-	55	Ck	33.46S	59.31W
Arrée, Montagnes d'-	11	Cf	48.26N	3.55W
Arresø	8	Ei	55.55N	12.05 E
Arriaga	48	Mi	16.14N	93.54W
Ar Rifā'ī	24	Lg	31.43N	46.07 E
Ar Rihāb	24	Kg	30.52N	45.30 E
Ar Rimāh	24	Lj	25.34N	47.09 E
Ar Rimāl	21	Hg	22.00N	52.50 E
Ar Riyāḍ = Riyadh (EN)	22	Gg	24.38N	46.43 E
Arrochar	9	Ie	56.12N	4.45W
Arroio Grande	55	Fk	32.14S	53.05W
Arrojado	55	Ja	13.29S	44.37W
Arrojado, Rio-	55	Ja	13.24S	44.20W
Arromanches-les-Bains	12	Be	49.20N	0.37W
Arros	11	Gk	43.40N	0.02 E
Arroscia	14	Cg	44.03N	8.11 E
Arroux	11	Jh	46.29N	3.58 E
Arrow, Lough-/Loch Arabhach	9	Eg	54.05N	8.20W
Arrowsmith, Mount-	61	Dh	43.21S	170.59 E
Arrowtown	62	Cf	44.56S	168.50 E
Arroyo Barú	55	Cj	31.52S	58.26W
Arroyo de la Luz	13	Fe	39.29N	6.35W
Arroyo Grande	46	Ei	35.07N	120.34W
Arroyos y Esteros	55	Dg	25.04S	57.06W
Arruda	55	Db	15.02S	56.07W
Arrufó	56	Hd	30.15S	61.45W
Ar Rumaythah	24	Kg	31.32N	45.12 E
Ar Ruq'ī	24	Lh	29.01N	46.33 E
Ar Ruṣāfah	24	He	35.02N	36.17 E
Ar Ruşayriş	35	Ec	11.51N	34.23 E
Ar Ruṭbah	23	Fc	33.02N	40.17 E
Ar Ruwayḍah	24	Ki	26.23N	44.14 E
Ar Ruways [Qatar]	23	Hd	26.08N	51.13 E
Ar Ruways [U.A.E.]	23	He	24.08N	52.45 E
Ar Ruzayqāt	24	Ej	25.35N	32.28 E
Års	8	Ch	56.48N	9.32 E
Arsenjān	24	Oh	29.56N	53.18 E
Arsenjev	20	Ih	44.12N	133.20 E
Arsi [3]	35	Fd	7.10N	40.00 E
Arsk	7	Lh	56.07N	49.52 E
Årskogen	8	Gb	62.05N	17.20 E
Arslanköy	24	Fd	37.01N	34.17 E
Ars-sur-Moselle	12	Ie	49.05N	6.04 E
Arsuk	41	Hf	61.11N	48.30W
Årsunda	8	Gd	60.32N	16.44 E
Art	63b	Ad	19.43S	163.39 E
Artá	13	Pe	39.42N	3.21 E
Arta	35	Gc	11.31N	42.50 E
Árta	15	Dj	39.09N	20.59 E
Artá, Cuevas de-	13	Pe	39.40N	3.24 E
Artašat	16	Nj	39.59N	44.33 E
Arteaga	48	Hh	18.28N	102.25W
Artem	20	Ih	43.23N	132.10 E
Artemisa	47	Hd	22.49N	82.46W
Artemón	15	Hm	36.57N	24.43 E
Artem-Ostrov	19	Fg	40.28N	50.18 E
Artemovsk [R.S.F.S.R.]	20	Ef	54.23N	93.30 E
Artemovsk [Ukr.-U.S.S.R.]	16	Ke	48.33N	38.03 E
Artemovski	17	Jh	57.25N	61.58 E
Artesa de Segre	13	Nc	41.54N	1.03 E
Artesia	43	Ge	32.51N	104.24W
Arthur	45	Ff	41.35N	101.31W
Arthur Creek	59	Hd	23.00S	136.58 E
Arthur River	59	Ih	41.00S	144.55 E
Arthur's Pass	61	Dh	42.57S	171.34 E
Arthur's Pass	62	De	42.54S	171.34 E
Arthur's Town	49	Ja	24.38N	75.32W
Arti	17	Ih	56.26N	58.32 E
Artibonite, Rivière de l'-	49	Kd	19.15N	72.47W
Artigas	56	Id	30.42S	56.28W
Artigas [2]	55	Dj	30.35S	57.00W
Artijarvi/Artsjö	8	Ld	60.45N	26.05 E
Artik	16	Mi	40.36N	43.58 E
Artillery Lake	42	Gd	63.08N	107.45W
Artois	11	Id	50.10N	2.30 E
Artois, Collines de l'-	11	Id	50.30N	2.15 E
Artoli	35	Eb	18.19N	33.54 E
Artsjö/Artijarvi	8	Ld	60.45N	26.05 E
Artux	27	Cd	39.40N	76.10 E
Artvin	23	Fa	41.11N	41.49 E
Artyk	20	Jd	64.12N	145.15 E
Aru	36	Fb	2.52N	30.51 E
Aru, Kepulauan- = Aru Islands (EN)	57	Ee	6.00S	134.30 E
Arua	31	Kh	3.01N	30.55 E
Aruanã	55	Gb	14.54S	51.05W
Aruba	54	Ea	12.30N	70.00W
Aruba	39	Lh	12.30N	71.00W
Aru Islands (EN) = Aru, Kepulauan	57	Ee	6.00S	134.30 E
Arukoron Point	64a	Bb	7.43N	134.38 E
Arun	9	Mk	50.48N	0.33W
Arunāchal Pradesh [3]	25	Ic	27.50N	94.50 E
Arundel	12	Bd	50.51N	0.33W
Arun He	27	Lb	47.36N	124.06 E
Arun Qi	27	Lb	48.09N	123.29 E
Arus, Tanjung-	26	Hf	1.24N	125.06 E
Arusha [3]	36	Gc	3.30S	36.00 E
Arusha	31	Ki	3.22S	36.41 E
Arutua Atoll	61	Lc	15.18S	146.44W
Arutunga	61	Lc	18.52S	159.46W
Aruwimi	30	Jh	1.13N	23.36 E
Arvada [Co.-U.S.]	45	Dg	39.50N	105.05W
Arvada [Wy.-U.S.]	46	Ld	44.40N	106.03W
Arve	11	Mh	46.12N	6.08 E
Arvert, Presqu'île d'-	11	Ei	45.45N	1.05W
Arvida	42	Kg	48.26N	71.11W
Arvidsjaur	7	Ed	65.35N	19.10 E
Arvika	7	Cg	59.39N	12.36 E
Årviksand	7	Ea	70.12N	20.32 E
Arvin	46	Fi	35.12N	118.50W
Aryānah	14	En	36.52N	10.11 E
Arys	18	Gc	42.48N	68.15 E
Arys	19	Gg	42.26N	68.48 E
Arys, Ozero-	18	Fb	45.50N	66.20 E
Arz	11	Dg	47.39N	2.06W
Arzachena	14	Di	41.05N	9.23 E
Arzamas	19	Ed	55.23N	43.50 E
Arzanah	24	Oj	24.47N	52.34 E
Aržano	14	Kg	43.35N	16.59 E
Arzew	32	Gb	35.51N	0.19W
Arzew, Golfe d'-	13	Li	35.50N	0.10W
Arzew, Salines d'-	13	Li	35.42N	0.18W
Arzfeld	12	Id	50.05N	6.16 E
Arzgir	19	Ef	45.22N	44.13 E
Arzúa	13	Db	42.56N	8.09W
As	12	Hc	51.01N	5.35 E
Ås	8	De	59.40N	10.48 E
Aš	10	If	50.13N	12.12 E
Aša	19	Fd	55.02N	57.18 E
Aså	8	Dg	57.09N	10.25 E
Asab	37	Be	25.29S	17.59 E
Asaba	34	Gd	6.11N	6.45 E
Asad, Buḩayrat al-	24	He	35.57N	38.10 E
Asadābād [Afg.]	23	Lc	34.52N	71.09 E
Asadābād [Iran]	24	Me	34.47N	48.07 E
Asafik	35	Bc	13.10N	19.26 E
Asahi [Jap.]	29	Fb	38.15N	139.30 E
Asahi [Jap.]	29a	Ca	44.08N	142.35 E
Asahi [Jap.]	29	Gd	35.43N	140.35 E
Asahi [Jap.]	29	Ec	36.57N	137.34 E
Asahi-Dake	29	Fb	38.16N	139.55 E
Asahi-Gawa	29	Cd	34.36N	133.58 E
Asahikawa	22	Qe	43.46N	142.22 E
Asaka-Drainage	29	Gc	37.30N	140.15 E
Asale, Lake-	35	Gc	14.00N	40.20 E
'Asalūyeh	24	Oi	27.28N	52.37 E
Asama-Yama	28	Of	36.27N	138.30 E
Asan-Man	28	If	36.56N	126.51 E
Asansol	22	Kg	23.41N	86.59 E
Asarna	7	De	62.39N	14.21 E
Asarum	8	Fh	56.12N	14.50 E
'Asayr = Guardafui, Cape- (EN)	30	Mg	11.49N	51.15 E
Asayta	35	Gc	11.33N	41.27 E
Asbest	17	Jh	57.01N	61.31 E
Asbestos	44	Lc	45.46N	71.57W
Asbe Teferi	35	Gd	9.05N	40.51 E
Asbury Park	44	Je	40.14N	74.01W
Ascension	30	Fi	7.57S	14.22W
Ascensión, Bahía de la-	47	Ge	19.40N	87.30W
Ascensión, Bahía de la-	48	Ph	19.40N	87.30W
Ascensión, Laguna de la-	48	Fb	31.05N	107.55W
Aschaffenburg	10	Fg	49.59N	9.09 E
Ascheberg	12	Jc	51.47N	7.37 E
Aschendorf (Ems), Papenburg-	12	Ja	53.04N	7.22 E
Aschersleben	10	He	51.45N	11.28 E
Aščikol, Ozero-	18	Fb	45.05N	67.20 E
Aščiozek	16	Pe	49.12N	48.06 E
Ascoli Piceno	14	Hh	42.51N	13.34 E
Ascoli Satriano	14	Ji	41.12N	15.34 E
Ascot	12	Bc	51.24N	0.40W
Aseb	31	Lg	13.00N	42.44 E
Åseda	7	Dh	57.10N	15.20 E
Asedjrad	30	Hf	24.42N	1.40 E
Asekejevo	16	Rc	53.36N	52.51 E
Asela	31	Kh	7.58N	39.08 E
As Ela	35	Gc	11.06N	42.06 E
Åsele	7	Dd	64.10N	17.20 E
Åsen [Nor.]	7	Ce	63.36N	11.03 E
Åsen [Swe.]	7	Cf	61.17N	13.50 E
Asendabo	35	Fd	9.47N	37.36 E
Asendorf	12	Kb	52.46N	9.00 E
Asenovgrad	15	Hg	42.01N	24.52 E
Åsensbruk	8	Ef	58.48N	12.25 E
Åseral	8	Bf	58.37N	7.25 E
Aseri/Azeri	7	Gg	59.29N	26.51 E
Asfeld	12	Ge	49.28N	4.07 E
Aşfūn al Maṭā'inah	24	Ej	25.23N	32.32 E
Åsgårdstrand	8	De	59.21N	10.28 E
Ašhabad	22	Hf	37.57N	58.23 E
Ašhabadskaja Oblast [3]	19	Fh	38.30N	59.00 E
Ashanti [3]	34	Ed	6.45N	1.30W
Ashburn	44	Fj	31.43N	83.39W
Ashburton	61	Dh	43.54S	171.45 E
Ashburton River	57	Cg	21.40S	114.56 E
Ashdod	24	Fg	31.49N	34.39 E
Ashdown	45	Ij	33.41N	94.08W
Asheboro	44	Hh	35.42N	79.49W
Asheroft	46	Ea	50.43N	121.17W
Asheville	43	Kd	35.34N	82.33W
Ashford	9	Nj	51.09N	0.53 E
Ashford Airport	12	Cc	51.10N	0.59 E
Ash Fork	46	Ii	35.13N	112.29W
Ashibetsu	28	Qc	43.31N	142.11 E
Ashikaga	29	Fc	36.21N	139.27 E
Ashington	9	Lf	55.11N	1.34W
Ashiro	29	Ga	40.06N	141.01 E
Ashiya	29	Be	33.53N	130.40 E
Ashizuri-Misaki	28	Lh	32.44N	133.01 E
Ashkal, Qar'at al-	14	Dm	37.10N	9.40 E
Äshkhāneh	24	Qd	37.28N	57.00 E
Ashland [Ks.-U.S.]	45	Gh	37.11N	99.46W
Ashland [Ky.-U.S.]	43	Kd	38.28N	82.38W
Ashland [Mt.-U.S.]	46	Ld	45.35N	106.16W
Ashland [Oh.-U.S.]	44	Fe	40.52N	82.19W
Ashland [Or.-U.S.]	43	Cc	42.12N	122.42W
Ashland [Wi.-U.S.]	43	Ib	46.35N	90.53W
Ashland, Mount-	46	De	42.05N	122.43W
Ashley	45	Gc	46.02N	99.22W
Ashmore Islands	57	Df	12.15S	123.05 E
Ashmūn	24	Dg	30.18N	30.58 E
Ashoro	29a	Cb	43.14N	143.31 E
Ashqelon	24	Fg	31.40N	34.35 E
Ash Shabakah	24	Jg	30.49N	43.39 E
Ash Shabb	33	Ee	22.19N	29.46 E
Ash Shā'ib	24	Gh	28.59N	37.07 E
Ash Sha'm	23	Id	26.02N	56.05 E
Ash Shamāliyah [3]	35	Db	18.40N	30.00 E
Ash Shāmīyah	24	Kg	31.57N	44.36 E
Ash Shāmīyah	24	Lg	30.15N	46.55 E
Ash Shaqq	24	Lh	28.20N	47.30 E
Ash Shaqrā'	23	Gd	25.15N	45.15 E
Ash Sha'rā'	24	Kj	24.16N	44.11 E
Ash Sharīqah	23	Id	25.22N	55.23 E
Ash Sharqāt	23	Fb	35.27N	43.16 E
Ash Sharqī	32	Jc	34.45N	11.15 E
Ash Sharqī	24	Ge	34.00N	36.30 E
Ash Sharqīyah	23	Ie	22.15N	58.30 E
Ash Shatrah	24	Lg	31.25N	46.10 E
Ash Shawbak	24	Fg	30.32N	35.34 E
Ash Shaykh Ḩumayd	24	Fh	28.07N	34.34 E
Ash Shifā	24	Fh	28.30N	35.30 E
Ash Shiḩr	23	Gg	14.44N	49.35 E
Ash Shināfīyah	24	Kg	31.35N	44.39 E
Ash Shu'aybah [Kuw.]	24	Mh	29.03N	48.08 E
Ash Shu'aybah [Sau.Ar.]	24	Ji	27.53N	42.43 E
Ash Shu'bah	24	Kh	28.54N	44.44 E
Ash Shumlūl	24	Li	26.31N	47.20 E
Ash Shuqayq	23	Ff	17.44N	42.01 E
Ash Shurayk	35	Eb	18.48N	33.34 E
Ash Shuwayhāt	24	Oj	24.05N	52.28 E
Ash Shuwaykh	24	Lh	29.21N	47.55 E
Ashtabula	43	Kc	41.53N	80.47W
Ashtabula, Lake-	45	Hc	47.11N	97.58W
Ashtiyān	24	Me	34.30N	49.55 E
Ashton [Id.-U.S.]	46	Jd	44.04N	111.27W
Ashton [St.Vin.]	51n	Bb	12.36N	61.27W
Ashuanipi	42	Kf	52.55N	66.00W
Ashuanipi Lake	42	Kf	52.45N	66.10W
Asia	21	Ke	40.00N	85.00 E
Asia, Kepulauan-	26	Jf	1.03N	131.18 E
Asiago	14	Fe	45.52N	11.30 E
Asiago, Altopiano di-	14	Fe	45.54N	11.30 E
Asilah	32	Fb	35.28N	6.02W
Asinara	5	Gg	41.04N	8.15 E
Asinara, Golfo dell'-	14	Cj	41.00N	8.35 E
Asino	20	De	56.58N	86.09 E
'Asīr	23	Ff	19.00N	42.00 E
Aşkadar	17	Hi	53.37N	56.01 E
Aşkale	24	Ic	39.55N	40.42 E
Askanija-Nova	16	Hf	46.27N	33.52 E
Asker	8	De	59.50N	10.26 E
Askersund	7	Dg	58.53N	14.54 E
Askī Al Mawşil	24	Jd	36.34N	42.42 E
Askim [Nor.]	8	De	59.35N	11.10 E
Askim [Swe.]	8	Dg	57.38N	11.56 E
Áskion Óros	15	Ei	40.22N	21.34 E
Askiz	20	Ef	53.08N	90.32 E
Askja	5	Eb	65.03N	16.48W
Askola	8	Kd	60.32N	25.36 E
Asköping	8	Ge	59.09N	16.04 E
Askøy	8	Ad	60.30N	5.05 E
Askøy	8	Ad	60.24N	5.11 E
Askrova	8	Ac	61.30N	4.55 E
Askvoll	7	Af	61.21N	5.04 E
Asl	24	Eh	29.30N	32.43 E
Aslanapa	15	Mj	39.13N	29.52 E
Asmara (EN) = Asmera	31	Kg	15.19N	38.57 E
Asmera = Asmara (EN)	31	Kg	15.19N	38.57 E
Åsnen	8	Fh	56.40N	14.40 E
Asni	32	Fc	31.15N	7.59W
Asnières-sur-Seine	12	Ef	48.55N	2.17 E
Aso	14	Hg	43.06N	13.51 E
Aso	29	Be	32.58N	131.02 E
Asola	14	Ee	45.13N	10.24 E
Asosa	31	Kg	10.02N	34.32 E
Aso-San	29	Be	32.53N	131.06 E
Asoteriba, Jabal-	35	Fa	21.51N	36.30 E
Asouf Mellene	32	Hd	25.40N	2.08 E
Asō-Wan	29	Ad	34.20N	129.15 E
Āspās	24	Og	30.40N	52.24 E
Aspe	13	Lf	38.21N	0.46W
Aspen	43	Fd	39.11N	106.49W
Aspermont	45	Fj	33.08N	100.14W
Aspiring, Mount-	61	Ch	44.23S	168.44 E
Aspromonte	14	Jl	38.10N	16.00 E
Assa	32	Fd	28.37N	9.25W
Aş Şadr	23	He	24.40N	54.41 E
Aş Şaff	24	Dh	29.34N	31.17 E
Aş Şāfī	24	Fg	31.02N	35.28 E
As Safīrah	24	Gd	36.04N	37.22 E
Aş Şaḩm	24	Qj	24.10N	56.53 E
Assahoun	34	Fd	6.27N	0.55 E
Aş Şa'īd	30	Kf	26.00N	32.00 E
Assal, Lac-	35	Gc	11.40N	42.22 E
As Salamīyah [Sau.Ar.]	23	Ge	24.12N	47.23 E
As Salamīyah [Syr.]	24	Ge	35.01N	37.03 E
Aş Şālihīyah	24	Ie	34.44N	40.45 E
As Sallūm	31	Je	31.34N	25.09 E
As Salmān	24	Kg	30.26N	44.30 E
As Salt	24	Ff	32.03N	35.44 E
As Salwá	23	He	24.45N	50.49 E

Index Symbols

- [1] Independent Nation
- [2] State, Region
- [3] District, County
- [4] Municipality
- [5] Colony, Dependency
- Continent
- Physical Region
- Historical or Cultural Region
- Mount, Mountain
- Volcano
- Hill
- Mountains, Mountain Range
- Hills, Escarpment
- Plateau, Upland
- Pass, Gap
- Plain, Lowland
- Delta
- Salt Flat
- Valley, Canyon
- Crater, Cave
- Karst Features
- Depression
- Polder
- Desert, Dunes
- Forest, Woods
- Heath, Steppe
- Oasis
- Cape, Point
- Coast, Beach
- Cliff
- Peninsula
- Isthmus
- Sandbank
- Island
- Atoll
- Rock, Reef
- Islands, Archipelago
- Rocks, Reefs
- Coral Reef
- Well, Spring
- Geyser
- River, Stream
- Waterfall Rapids
- River Mouth, Estuary
- Lake
- Salt Lake
- Intermittent Lake
- Reservoir
- Swamp, Pond
- Canal
- Glacier
- Ice Shelf, Pack Ice
- Ocean
- Sea
- Gulf, Bay
- Strait, Fjord
- Lagoon
- Bank
- Seamount
- Tablemount
- Ridge
- Shelf
- Basin
- Escarpment, Sea Scarp
- Fracture
- Trench, Abyss
- National Park, Reserve
- Point of Interest
- Recreation Site
- Cave, Cavern
- Historic Site
- Ruins
- Wall, Walls
- Church, Abbey
- Temple
- Scientific Station
- Airport
- Port
- Lighthouse
- Mine
- Tunnel
- Dam, Bridge

Index Symbols

- Independent Nation
- State, Region
- District, County
- Municipality
- Colony, Dependency
- Continent
- Physical Region
- Historical or Cultural Region
- Mount, Mountain
- Volcano
- Hill
- Mountains, Mountain Range
- Hills, Escarpment
- Plateau, Upland
- Pass, Gap
- Plain, Lowland
- Delta
- Salt Flat
- Valley, Canyon
- Crater, Cave
- Karst Features
- Depression
- Polder
- Desert, Dunes
- Forest, Woods
- Heath, Steppe
- Oasis
- Cape, Point
- Coast, Beach
- Cliff
- Peninsula
- Isthmus
- Sandbank
- Island
- Atoll
- Rock, Reef
- Islands, Archipelago
- Rocks, Reefs
- Coral Reef
- Well, Spring
- Geyser
- River, Stream
- Waterfall Rapids
- River Mouth, Estuary
- Lake
- Salt Lake
- Intermittent Lake
- Reservoir
- Swamp, Pond
- Canal
- Glacier
- Ice Shelf, Pack Ice
- Ocean
- Sea
- Gulf, Bay
- Strait, Fjord
- Lagoon
- Bank
- Seamount
- Tablemount
- Ridge
- Shelf
- Basin
- Escarpment, Sea Scarp
- Fracture
- Trench, Abyss
- National Park, Reserve
- Point of Interest
- Recreation Site
- Cave, Cavern
- Historic Site
- Ruins
- Wall, Walls
- Church, Abbey
- Temple
- Scientific Station
- Airport
- Port
- Lighthouse
- Mine
- Tunnel
- Dam, Bridge

Ayeyarwady	25	Ie	17.00N	95.00 E
Ayeyarwady = Irrawaddy (EN)	21	Lg	15.50N	95.06 E
Ayiá	15	Fj	39.43N	22.46 E
Ayía Marína	15	Jl	37.09N	26.52 E
Ayiásos	15	Jj	39.06N	26.22 E
Áyion Óros = Athos, Mount- (EN) [2]	15	Hi	40.15N	24.15 E
Áyios Evstrátios	15	Hj	39.31N	25.00 E
Áyios Ioánnis, Ákra-	15	In	35.20N	25.46 E
Áyios Kírikos	15	Jl	37.35N	26.14 E
Áyios Minás	15	Jl	37.36N	26.34 E
Áyios Nikólaos	15	In	35.11N	25.43 E
Áyios Yeóryios	15	Gl	37.28N	23.56 E
Aykota	35	Fb	15.10N	37.03 E
Aylesbury	9	Mj	51.50N	0.50W
Ayllón, Sierra de-	13	Ic	41.15N	3.25W
Aylmer Lake	42	Gd	64.05N	108.30W
Aylsham	12	Db	52.47N	1.15 E
Ayna	13	Jf	38.33N	2.05W
'Aynabo	35	Hd	8.57N	46.30 E
'Ayn ad Darāhim	14	Cn	36.47N	8.42 E
'Ayn al Baydā	24	Ge	34.32N	37.55 E
'Ayn al Ghazāl [Eg.]	24	Dj	25.46N	30.38 E
'Ayn al Ghazāl [Lib.]	31	Jf	21.50N	24.55 E
'Ayn al Shigi	24	Ci	27.01N	28.02 E
'Ayn al Wādī	24	Ci	27.23N	28.13 E
'Ayn Bū Sālim	14	Cn	36.37N	8.59 E
'Ayn Dāllah	33	Ed	27.19N	27.20 E
'Ayn Dār	24	Mj	25.58N	49.14 E
'Ayn Dīwār	24	Jd	37.17N	42.11 E
'Ayn Ilwān	24	Dj	25.44N	30.25 E
'Ayn Khalīfah	24	Bi	26.46N	27.47 E
'Ayn Sifnī	24	Jd	36.42N	43.21 E
'Ayn Sukhnah	33	Fd	29.30N	32.10 E
'Aynūnah	23	Ed	28.05N	35.08 E
Ayod	35	Ed	8.08N	31.24 E
Ayora	13	Ke	39.04N	1.03W
Ayorou	34	Fc	14.44N	0.55 E
'Ayoûn el 'Atroûs	31	Gg	16.38N	9.36W
Ayr	9	If	55.29N	4.28W
Ayr [Austl.]	59	Jc	19.35S	147.24 E
Ayr [Scot.-U.K.]	9	If	55.28N	4.38W
Ayre, Point of-	9	Ig	54.26N	4.22W
Ayrolle, Étang de l'-	11	Jk	43.16N	3.30 E
Aysha	35	Gc	10.45N	42.35 E
Aytré	11	Eh	46.08N	1.06W
Ayutla	48	Gg	20.07N	104.22W
Ayutla de los Libres	48	Ji	16.54N	99.13W
Ayvacık	24	Gb	41.00N	36.45 E
Ayvacik	15	Jj	39.36N	26.24 E
Ayvalık	23	Cb	39.18N	26.41 E
Aywaille	12	Hd	50.28N	5.40 E
Āzādshahr	24	Pd	37.05N	55.08 E
'Azahar, Costa del-	13	Me	39.58N	0.01 E
Azaila	13	Lc	41.17N	0.29W
Azambuja	13	De	39.04N	8.52W
Azamgarh	25	Gc	26.04N	83.11 E
Azángaro	54	Df	14.55S	70.13W
Azannes-et-Soumazannes	12	He	49.18N	5.28 E
Azaouâd = Azaouad (EN)	30	Gg	19.00N	3.00W
Azaouad (EN) = Azaouâd	30	Gg	19.00N	3.00W
Azaouak	34	Fb	15.30N	3.18 E
Azaouak	30	Hg	15.20N	4.55 E
Azaouak, Vallée de l'-	30	Hg	17.30N	3.40 E
Azar	34	Fb	16.02N	4.04 E
Āzarbāijān-e Gharbī [3]	23	Fb	37.00N	45.00 E
Āzarbāijān-e Sharqī [3]	23	Gb	37.00N	47.00 E
Azarbaijčan Sovet Socialistik Respublicasy/ Azerbajdžanskaja SSR [2]	19	Eg	40.30N	47.30 E
Azare	34	Hc	11.41N	10.12 E
Āzār Shahr	24	Kd	37.45N	45.59 E
Azay-le-Rideau	11	Gg	47.16N	0.28 E
A 'zāz	24	Gd	36.35N	37.03 E
Azazga	13	Qh	36.44N	4.22 E
Azbine/Aïr	30	Hg	18.00N	8.30 E
Azdaak, Gora-	16	Ni	40.13N	44.59 E
Azdavay	24	Eb	41.39N	33.18 E
Azefal	30	Ff	21.00N	14.45W
Azeffoun	13	Qh	36.53N	4.25 E
Azemmour	32	Fc	33.17N	8.21W
Azerbaijan (EN)	21	Gf	37.00N	46.00 E
Azerbaijan SSR (EN) = Azerbajdžanskaja SSR [2]	19	Eg	40.30N	47.30 E
Azerbajdžanskaja Sovetskaja Socialističeskaja Respublika [2]	19	Eg	40.30N	47.30 E
Azerbajdžanskaja SSR/ Azarbaijčan Sovet Socialistik Respublicasy [2]	19	Eg	40.30N	47.30 E
Azerbajdžanskaja SSR = Azerbaijan SSR (EN)	19	Eg	40.30N	47.30 E
Azeri/Aseri	7	Gg	59.29N	26.51 E
Azevedo Sodré	55	Ej	30.04S	54.36W
Azezo	35	Fc	12.33N	37.25 E
Azilal [3]	32	Fc	32.09N	6.05W
Azilal	32	Fc	31.58N	6.35W
Aznā	24	Mf	33.56N	49.24 E
Aznakajevo	7	Mi	54.56N	53.04 E
Azogues	54	Cd	2.44S	78.48W
Azores (EN) = Açores [5]	31	Ee	38.30N	28.00W
Azores (EN) = Açores, Arquipélago dos-	30	Ee	38.30N	28.00W
Azores-Gibraltar Ridge (EN)	3	Df	37.00N	16.00W
Azoum, Bahr-	30	Jg	10.53N	20.15 E
Azov	19	Df	47.05N	39.25 E
Azov, Sea of- (EN) = Azovskoje More	5	Jf	46.00N	36.00 E
Azovskoje More = Azov, Sea of- (EN)	5	Jf	46.00N	36.00 E
Azpeitia	13	Ja	43.11N	2.16W
Azrak, Bahr-	35	Bc	10.50N	19.50 E
Azraq, Al Baḩr al- = Blue Nile (EN)	30	Kg	15.38N	32.31 E
Azraq ash Shīshān	24	Gg	31.50N	36.49 E
Azrou	32	Fc	33.26N	5.13W
Aztec	45	Ch	36.49N	107.59W
Aztec Ruins	46	Kh	36.51N	108.10W
Azua	49	Ld	18.27N	70.44W
Azuaga	13	Gf	38.16N	5.41W
Azuar	13	Ie	39.08N	3.36W
Azuero, Península de- = Azuero Peninsula (EN)	38	Ki	7.40N	80.30W
Azuero Peninsula (EN) = Azuero, Península de-	38	Ki	7.40N	80.30W
Azul	53	Ki	36.45S	59.50W
Azul, Arroyo del-	55	Cm	36.15S	59.07W
Azul, Cerro-	54a	Ab	0.54S	91.21W
Azul, Cordillera-	54	Ce	8.30S	76.00W
Azul, Río-	48	Oi	17.54N	88.52W
Azul, Serra-	55	Eb	14.50S	54.50W
Azul, Sierras del-	55	Cm	37.02S	59.55W
Azūm	35	Cc	10.53N	20.15 E
Azuma-San	29	Gc	37.44N	140.08 E
Azur, Côte d'-	11	Mk	43.30N	7.00 E
Azurduy	54	Fg	19.59S	64.29W
Azzaba	32	Ib	36.44N	7.06 E
Az Zāb al Kabīr	23	Fb	36.00N	43.21 E
Az Zāb aş Şaghīr	23	Fb	35.12N	43.25 E
Az Zabdānī	24	Gf	33.43N	36.05 E
Az Zabū	24	Ch	28.22N	28.56 E
Aẓ Ẓafīr	23	Ff	19.57N	41.30 E
Az Zaghāwa	35	Cb	15.15N	23.14 E
Aẓ Ẓāhirah	24	Qk	23.30N	56.15 E
Az Zallāq	24	Ni	26.03N	50.29 E
Az Zaqāzīq	33	Fc	30.35N	31.31 E
Az Zarqā'	24	Oj	24.53N	53.04 E
Az Zarqā'	24	Gf	32.05N	36.06 E
Az Zāwiyah [3]	33	Bc	32.40N	12.10 E
Az Zāwiyah	33	Bc	32.45N	12.44 E
Az Zaytūn	33	Ed	29.09N	25.47 E
Azzel Matti, Sebkha-	30	Hf	26.00N	0.55 E
Az Zilfī	24	Ki	26.18N	44.48 E
Az Zubayr	24	Lg	30.23N	47.43 E

B

Baa	26	Hi	10.43S	123.03 E
Baaba	63b	Ae	20.03S	163.58 E
Ba'ādwēyn	35	Hd	7.12N	47.24 E
Bá an Daingin/Dingle Bay	9	Ci	52.05N	10.15W
Baar	10	Ei	48.00N	8.30 E
Baarle-Hertog	12	Gc	51.27N	4.56 E
Baarn	12	Hb	52.14N	5.17 E
Baas, Bassure de-	12	Dd	50.30N	1.15 E
Bāb	24	Ok	23.55N	53.45 E
Baba	35	Bd	6.25N	17.07 E
Baba	15	Ei	40.55N	21.10 E
Baba Burun [Tur.]	24	Db	41.18N	31.26 E
Baba Burun [Tur.]	24	Bc	39.29N	26.04 E
Babadağ	15	Ll	37.48N	28.52 E
Baba Dağ	15	Mm	36.32N	29.10 E
Babadag	15	Le	44.54N	28.43 E
Babadag, Gora-	16	Pi	41.01N	48.29 E
Babaeski	24	Bb	41.26N	27.06 E
Bābā-Ḩeydar	24	Nf	32.20N	50.28 E
Babajevo	19	Dd	59.24N	35.55 E
Babajtag, Gora-	18	Hd	41.13N	70.16 E
Babajurt	16	Oh	43.35N	46.47 E
Bāb al Māndab = Bab el Mandeb (EN)	30	Lg	12.35N	43.25 E
Babanūsah	35	Dc	11.20N	27.48 E
Babao → Qilian	27	Hd	38.14N	100.15 E
Babaoyo	54	Cd	1.50S	79.30W
Babar, Kepulauan-	26	Ih	7.50S	129.45 E
Babar, Pulau-	57	De	7.55S	129.45 E
Babase	63a	Aa	4.01S	153.42 E
Babatag, Hrebet-	18	Ge	38.00N	68.10 E
Babati	36	Gc	4.13S	35.45 E
Babbitt	45	Kc	47.43N	91.57W
B'abdā	24	Ff	33.50N	35.32 E
Bab el Mandeb (EN) = Bāb al Māndab	30	Lg	12.35N	43.25 E
Babelthuap Island	57	Ed	7.30N	134.36 E
Babenhausen [Ger.]	10	Gh	48.09N	10.15 E
Babenhausen [Ger.]	12	Ke	49.58N	8.57 E
Babeni	15	He	44.59N	24.15 E
Baberton	44	Ge	41.02N	81.38W
Bá Bheanntraí/Bantry Bay	9	Dj	51.38N	9.48W
Babian Jiang = Black River (EN)	21	Mg	20.17N	106.34 E
Babil [3]	24	Kf	32.40N	44.50 E
Babine Lake	42	Ef	54.45N	126.00W
Babino Polje	14	Lh	42.43N	17.33 E
Babit Point	51b	Ab	18.03N	63.02W
Babo	26	Jg	2.33S	133.25 E
Bābol	23	Hb	36.34N	52.42 E
Babol Sar	24	Od	36.43N	52.39 E
Baboquivari Peak	46	Jk	31.46N	111.35W
Babor, Djebel-	13	Rh	36.32N	5.28 E
Baborigame	48	Fd	26.27N	107.16W
Baboua	35	Ad	5.48N	14.49 E
Babozero, Ozero-	7	Ic	66.30N	37.25 E
Babu → Hexian	27	Jg	24.28N	111.34 E
Babuna	15	Eh	41.30N	21.40 E
Babuyan	26	Hc	19.32N	121.57 E
Babuyan	26	Gd	10.01N	118.58 E
Babuyan Channel	26	Hc	18.44N	121.40 E
Babuyan Islands	21	Oh	19.15N	121.40 E
Babylon	23	Fc	32.32N	44.25 E
Bač	15	Cd	45.23N	19.14 E
Bacabachi	48	Ed	26.55N	109.24W
Bacabal	53	Lf	4.14S	44.47W
Ba-Cagan	27	Gb	45.40N	99.30 E
Bacajá, Rio-	54	Hd	3.25S	51.50W
Bacalar	48	Oh	18.43N	88.27W
Bacalar, Laguna de-	48	Oh	18.43N	88.22W
Bacalar Chico, Boca-	49	Dd	18.12N	87.53W
Bacan, Kepulauan-	26	Ig	0.35S	127.30 E
Bacan, Pulau-	26	Ig	0.35S	127.30 E
Bacău [2]	15	Jc	46.36N	27.00 E
Bacău	6	If	46.34N	26.54 E
Baccarat	11	Mf	48.27N	6.45 E
Bacchiglione	14	Ge	45.11N	12.14 E
Baceşti	15	Kc	46.51N	27.14 E
Bachaquero	49	Li	9.56N	71.08W
Bacharach	12	Jd	50.04N	7.46 E
Bacheli	25	Ge	18.40N	81.15 E
Bachiniva	48	Fc	28.45N	107.15W
Bachu/Maralwexi	27	Cd	39.46N	78.15 E
Back	38	Jd	67.15N	95.15W
Bačka	15	Cd	45.50N	19.30 E
Bac Kan	25	Ld	22.08N	105.49 E
Bačka Palanka	15	Cd	45.15N	19.22 E
Bačka Topola	15	Cd	45.49N	19.39 E
Bäckefors	8	Ef	58.48N	12.10 E
Bäckhammar	8	Fe	59.10N	14.11 E
Backnang	10	Fh	48.57N	9.26 E
Bačkovski Manastir	15	Hh	41.56N	24.51 E
Bac Lieu	25	Lg	9.17N	105.43 E
Bac Ninh	25	Ld	21.11N	106.03 E
Bacolet	51p	Bb	12.02N	61.41W
Bacolod	22	Oh	10.40N	122.57 E
Bac-Phan = Tonkin (EN)	21	Mg	22.00N	105.00 E
Bacqueville, Lac-	42	Ke	58.00N	74.00W
Bacqueville-en Caux	12	Ce	49.47N	1.00 E
Bácsalmás	10	Pj	46.08N	19.20 E
Bács-Kiskun [2]	10	Pj	46.30N	19.25 E
Bacton	12	Db	52.51N	1.28 E
Bād	23	Hc	33.41N	52.01 E
Badagara	25	Ff	11.36N	75.35 E
Badagri	34	Fd	6.25N	2.53 E
Badain Jaran Shamo	21	Me	40.20N	101.40 E
Badajós, Lago-	54	Fd	3.15S	62.45W
Badajoz	6	Fh	38.53N	6.58W
Badajoz [3]	13	Ff	38.40N	6.10W
Badakhshan [3]	23	Lb	36.45N	72.00 E
Badalona	13	Oc	41.27N	2.15 E
Badanah	23	Fc	30.59N	41.02 E
Badaohao	28	Fd	41.50N	121.59 E
Badas, Kepulauan-	26	Ef	0.35N	107.06 E
Bad Aussee	14	Hc	47.36N	13.47 E
Bad Axe	44	Fd	43.48N	83.00W
Bad Bergzabern	10	Dg	49.06N	8.00 E
Bad Berleburg	12	Kc	51.04N	8.24 E
Bad Bertrich	12	Jd	50.03N	7.02 E
Bad Bramstedt	10	Fc	53.55N	9.53 E
Bad Brückenau	10	Ff	50.18N	9.45 E
Badda	35	Fd	7.55N	39.23 E
Baddo	25	Cc	27.59N	64.21 E
Bad Doberan	10	Hb	54.06N	11.54 E
Bad Driburg	12	Lc	51.44N	9.01 E
Bad Düben	10	Ie	51.36N	12.35 E
Bad Dürkheim	12	Ke	49.28N	8.12 E
Bade	26	Kh	7.10S	139.35 E
Bademli	15	Lk	38.04N	28.04 E
Baden [Aus.]	14	Kb	48.01N	16.14 E
Baden [Switz.]	14	Cc	47.28N	8.18 E
Baden-Baden	10	Eh	48.45N	8.15 E
Badenoch	9	Je	56.50N	4.00W
Baden-Württemberg [2]	10	Eh	48.30N	9.00 E
Bad Essen	12	Kb	52.19N	8.20 E
Bad Freienwalde	10	Kd	52.47N	14.02 E
Badgastein	14	Hc	47.07N	13.08 E
Bādghīsat [3]	23	Jc	35.00N	63.45 E
Bad Gleichenberg	14	Jd	46.52N	15.54 E
Bad Godesberg, Bonn-	10	Df	50.41N	7.09 E
Bad Hall	14	Ib	48.02N	14.12 E
Bad Harzburg	10	Ge	51.53N	10.34 E
Bad Herrenalb	12	Kf	48.48N	8.25 E
Bad Hersfeld	10	Ff	50.52N	9.42 E
Bad Homburg	10	Ef	50.13N	8.37 E
Bad Honnef	12	Jd	50.38N	7.12 E
Bá Dhún na nGall/Donegal Bay	5	Fe	54.30N	8.30W
Badhyz	18	Cg	35.50N	62.00 E
Badiraguato	48	Fe	25.22N	107.31W
Bad Ischl	14	Hc	47.43N	13.37 E
Bad Kissingen	10	Gf	50.12N	10.05 E
Bad Kreuznach	10	Dg	49.50N	7.52 E
Badlands [S.D.-U.S.]	45	Ee	43.30N	102.20W
Badlands [U.S.]	43	Gb	46.45N	103.30W
Bad Langensalza	10	Ge	51.06N	10.39 E
Bad Lautenberg am Harz	10	Ge	51.38N	10.28 E
Bad Liebenwerda	10	Je	51.31N	13.24 E
Bad Liebenzel	12	Kf	48.46N	8.44 E
Bad Mergentheim	10	Fg	49.29N	9.46 E
Bad Mondorf/Mondorf-les-Bains	12	Ie	49.30N	6.17 E
Bad Münster am Stein Ebernburg	12	Je	49.49N	7.51 E
Bad Münstereifel	12	Id	50.34N	6.45 E
Bad Muskau	10	Ke	51.33N	14.43 E
Bad Nauheim	12	Kd	50.22N	8.45 E
Bad Neuenahr-Ahweiler	10	Df	50.33N	7.08 E
Bad Neustadt an der Saale	10	Gf	50.20N	10.13 E
Bad Oeynhausen	12	Kb	52.12N	8.48 E
Bad Oldesloe	10	Gc	53.49N	10.23 E
Ba Don	25	Le	17.45N	106.27 E
Badou [China]	28	Df	36.27N	117.56 E
Badou [Togo]	34	Fd	7.35N	0.36 E
Bad Pyrmont	10	Fe	51.59N	9.15 E
Bad Ragaz	14	Dc	47.00N	9.30 E
Badrah	24	Kf	33.06N	45.58 E
Bad Reichenhall	10	Ii	47.44N	12.53 E
Badr Ḩunayn	23	Ee	23.44N	38.46 E
Bad River	45	Fd	44.22N	100.22W
Bad Salzuflen	12	Kb	52.05N	8.46 E
Bad Salzungen	10	Gf	50.49N	10.14 E
Bad Schwartau	10	Gc	53.55N	10.42 E
Bad Segeberg	10	Gc	53.56N	10.19 E
Bad Tölz	10	Hi	47.46N	11.34 E
Badulla	25	Gg	6.59N	81.03 E
Bad Wildungen	10	Fe	51.07N	9.07 E
Bad Wimpfen	10	Fg	49.14N	9.08 E
Baena	13	Hg	37.37N	4.19W
Baeza [Ec.]	54	Cd	0.28S	77.53W
Baeza [Sp.]	13	Ig	37.59N	3.28W
Baf/Paphos	24	Ee	34.50N	32.35 E
Bafang	34	Hd	5.09N	10.11 E
Bafatà	31	Fg	12.10N	14.40W
Bafélé	34	Cc	10.09N	10.08W
Baffin	38	Mc	68.00N	70.00W
Baffin Bay	38	Mb	73.00N	65.00W
Bafia	34	He	4.45N	11.14 E
Bafilo	34	Fd	9.21N	1.16 E
Bafing [Afr.]	30	Fg	13.49N	10.50W
Bafing [I.C.]	34	Dd	7.52N	7.07W
Bafoulabé	34	Cc	13.48N	10.50W
Bafoussam	31	Ih	5.28N	10.25 E
Bāfq	23	Ic	31.35N	55.24 E
Bāfq, Kūh-e-	24	Pg	31.20N	55.10 E
Bafra	23	Ea	41.34N	35.56 E
Bafra Burnu	24	Fb	41.44N	35.58 E
Bāft	24	Qh	29.14N	56.38 E
Bafwaboli	36	Eb	0.39N	26.10 E
Bafwasende	36	Eb	1.05N	27.16 E
Baga	34	Hc	13.06N	13.50 E
Bagaces	49	Eh	10.31N	85.15W
Bagagem, Rio-	55	Ha	13.58S	48.21W
Bagajevski	16	Lf	47.19N	40.25 E
Bāgalkot	25	Fe	16.11N	75.42 E
Bagamoyo	36	Gd	6.26S	38.54 E
Bagansiapi-Api	26	Df	2.09N	100.49 E
Bağarasi	15	Kl	37.42N	27.33 E
Baga Sola	35	Ac	13.32N	14.19 E
Bagata	36	Cc	3.44S	17.57 E
Bagdad	48	Ke	25.57N	97.09W
Bagdarin	20	Gf	54.30N	113.36 E
Bağdere	24	Ic	38.10N	40.45 E
Bagé	53	Ki	31.20S	54.06W
Bages et de Sigean, Étang de-	11	Jk	43.05N	3.01 E
Baggs	46	Lf	41.02N	107.39W
Bágh Baile na Sgealg/ Ballinskelligs Bay	9	Cj	51.50N	10.15W
Baghdād [3]	24	Kf	33.18N	44.36 E
Baghdād	22	Gf	33.21N	44.23 E
Baghdādī, Ra's-	24	Fj	24.40N	35.06 E
Bāgh-e Chenār	24	Qh	28.11N	56.54 E
Bāgh-e-Malek	24	Mg	31.32N	49.55 E
Bagheria	14	Hl	38.05N	13.30 E
Bāghīn	23	Ic	30.12N	56.48 E
Baghlān [3]	23	Kb	35.45N	69.00 E
Baghlān	23	Kb	36.13N	68.46 E
Bāglung	25	Gc	28.16N	83.36 E
Bagn	8	Cd	60.49N	9.34 E
Bagnara Calabra	14	Jl	38.17N	15.48 E
Bagnères-de-Bigorre	11	Gk	43.04N	0.09 E
Bagnères-de-Luchon	11	Gl	42.47N	0.36 E
Bagni di Lucca	14	Ef	44.01N	10.35 E
Bagno di Romagna	14	Fg	43.50N	11.57 E
Bagnolo Mella	14	Ee	45.26N	10.10 E
Bagnols-sur-Cèze	11	Kj	44.10N	4.37 E
Bago	22	Lh	17.30N	96.30 E
Bagoé	30	Gg	12.36N	6.34W
Bagolino	14	Ee	45.49N	10.28 E
Bagrationovsk	8	Ij	54.23N	20.40 E
Bagrax/Bohu	27	Ec	41.58N	86.29 E
Bagrax Hu/Bosten	21	Ke	42.00N	87.00 E
Bagua	54	Ce	5.40S	78.31W
Baguio	22	Oh	16.25N	120.36 E
Baguirmi	30	Ig	11.40N	16.20 E
Bagzane, Monts-	30	Hg	17.43N	8.45 E
Bahama Islands	38	Lg	24.15N	76.00W
Bahamas [1]	39	Lg	24.15N	76.00W
Bahamas, Canal Viejo de- = Old Bahama Channel (EN)	49	Ib	22.30N	78.05W
Bahār	24	Me	34.54N	48.26 E
Baharampur	25	Hd	24.06N	88.15 E
Baharden	19	Fh	38.28N	57.28 E
Bahardok	19	Fh	38.51N	58.24 E
Baharīyah, Wāḩāt al-	33	Ed	28.10N	29.00 E
Bahariya Oasis (EN) = Baḩarīyah, Wāḩāt al-	33	Ed	28.15N	28.57 E
Bahaur	26	Fg	3.20N	114.00 E
Bahāwalnagar	25	Ec	29.59N	73.16 E
Bahāwalpur	22	Jg	29.24N	71.41 E
Bahčisaraj	16	Hg	44.45N	33.51 E
Bahę	24	Gd	37.14N	36.34 E
Bahi	36	Gd	5.39S	35.19 E
Bahia [2]	54	Jf	12.00S	42.00W
Bahía, Islas de la-	47	Ge	16.20N	86.30W
Bahía Blanca	53	Ji	38.44S	62.16W
Bahía de Caráquez	54	Bd	0.37S	80.25W
Bahía Kino	47	Bc	28.50N	111.55W
Bahía Negra	56	Ib	20.15S	58.12W
Bahías, Cabo dos-	52	Jj	44.55S	65.32W
Bahīj	24	Cg	30.56N	29.35 E
Bahinga	36	Ed	5.57S	27.06 E
Bahi Swamp	36	Gd	6.05S	35.10 E
Bahlui	15	Kb	47.08N	27.44 E
Bahmač	19	De	51.11N	32.50 E
Bahoruco, Sierra de-	49	Ld	18.10N	71.25W
Bahraich	25	Gc	27.35N	81.36 E
Bahrain (EN) = Al Baḩrayn [1]	22	Hg	26.00N	50.29 E
Baḩr al Ghazāl [3]	35	Dd	8.15N	26.50 E
Bahr ar Ramla al Kabīr	33	Ed	27.00N	26.00 E
Baḩrayn, Khalij al-	24	Nj	25.45N	50.40 E
Bahr Dar	31	Kg	11.36N	37.22 E
Bahta	20	Dd	62.20N	89.15 E
Bahusi	15	Jc	46.43N	26.42 E
Baia	15	Le	44.43N	28.40 E
Baia de Aramă	15	Fe	45.00N	22.50 E
Baia de Fier	15	Gd	45.10N	23.46 E
Baía dos Tigres	36	Bf	16.35S	11.43 E
Baia Farta	36	Be	12.37S	13.26 E
Baia Mare	15	Gb	47.40N	23.35 E
Baião	54	Id	2.41S	49.41W
Baia Sprie	15	Gb	47.40N	23.42 E
Baibiene	55	Ci	29.36S	58.10W
Baïbokoum	35	Bd	7.45N	15.41 E
Baicheng	22	Oe	45.34N	122.49 E
Baicheng/Bay	27	Dc	41.46N	81.52 E
Băicoi	15	Id	45.02N	25.51 E
Băiculeşti	15	Hd	45.04N	24.42 E
Baïdou	35	Cd	5.52N	20.41 E
Baie-Comeau	39	Me	49.13N	68.10W
Baie-Mahault	50	Fd	16.16N	61.35W
Baie-Saint-Paul	42	Kg	47.27N	70.30W
Baie-Trinité	44	Na	49.24N	67.19W
Baie Verte	42	Lg	49.55N	56.11W
Baiguan → Shangyu	28	Fi	30.01N	120.53 E
Baihe	27	Je	32.46N	110.06 E
Bai He [China]	28	Bh	32.10N	112.20 E
Bai He [China]	28	Dd	40.43N	116.33 E
Baikal, Lake- (EN) = Bajkal, Ozero-	21	Md	53.00N	107.40 E
Baikal Range (EN) = Bajkalski Hrebet	21	Md	55.00N	108.40 E
Baile an Chaistil/ Ballycastle	118	Gf	55.12N	6.15W
Baile an Róba/Ballinrobe	118	Dh	53.37N	9.13W
Baile Átha Cliath/Dublin [2]	9	Gh	53.20N	6.15W
Baile Átha Cliath/Dublin	6	Fe	53.20N	6.15W
Baile Átha Luain/Athlone	9	Fh	53.25N	7.56W
Baile Átha Troim/Trim	9	Gh	53.34N	6.47W
Băile Borşa	15	Hb	47.41N	24.43 E
Baile Brigín/Balbriggan	9	Gh	53.37N	6.11W
Băile Govora	15	Hd	45.05N	24.11 E
Baile Locha Riach/Loughrea	9	Eh	53.12N	8.34W
Baile Mhistéala/ Mitchelstown	9	Ei	52.16N	8.16W
Bailén	13	If	38.06N	3.46W
Baile na Mainistreach/ Newtownabbey	9	Hg	54.42N	5.54W
Baile Nua na hArda/ Newtownards	9	Hg	54.36N	5.41W
Băile Olăneşti	15	Hd	45.12N	24.14 E
Băileşti	15	Ge	44.01N	23.21 E
Bailleul	12	Ce	49.12N	0.26 E
Bailleul	12	Ed	50.44N	2.44 E
Ba Illi	35	Bc	10.31N	16.29 E
Bailong Jiang	27	Ie	32.42N	105.15 E
Bailundo	36	Ce	12.10S	15.56 E
Baima	27	He	33.05N	100.29 E
Bain	12	Ba	53.04N	0.12W
Bainbridge	43	Ke	30.54N	84.34W
Bain-de-Bretagne	11	Eg	47.50N	1.41W
Baines Drift	37	Dd	22.30S	28.43 E
Baing	26	Hi	10.14S	120.34 E
Baingoin	27	Ee	31.36N	89.48 E
Baiquan	27	Mb	47.38N	126.04 E
Bā'ir	24	Gg	30.46N	36.41 E
Bā'ir, Wādī-	24	Gg	31.12N	37.31 E
Baird	45	Gj	32.24N	99.24W
Baird Inlet	40	Gd	60.45N	164.00W
Baird Mountains	40	Gc	67.35N	161.30W
Baird Peninsula	42	Jc	69.00N	75.15W
Bairiki	58	Id	1.20N	173.01 E
Bairin Youqi (Daban)	27	Kc	43.30N	118.37 E
Bairin Zuoqi (Lindong)	27	Kc	43.59N	119.22 E
Bairnsdale	58	Fh	37.50S	147.38 E
Bais	26	He	9.35N	123.07 E
Bai Shan	27	Fc	40.53N	93.48 E
Baisogala/Bajsogala	8	Ji	55.35N	23.44 E
Baitou Shan	21	Oe	42.00N	128.00 E
Baitoushan Tian Chi	28	Jc	42.00N	128.03 E
Baixiang	28	Cf	37.29N	114.44 E
Baixo Alentejo	13	Dg	37.55N	8.10W
Baixo Guandu	54	Jg	19.31S	41.01W
Baixo Longa	36	Cf	15.42S	18.38 E
Baiyanghe	27	Ec	43.12N	88.28 E
Baiyü	27	Ge	31.13N	98.51 E
Baja	10	Oj	46.11N	18.58 E
Baja, Punta- [Mex.]	48	Dc	28.25N	111.45W
Baja, Punta- [Pas.]	65d	Ab	27.10S	109.22W
Baja California = Lower California (EN)	38	Hg	28.00N	112.00W
Baja California Norte [2]	47	Ac	30.00N	115.00W
Baja California Sur [2]	47	Bd	25.50N	111.50W
Bājah [3]	32	Ib	36.30N	9.30 E
Bājah	32	Ib	36.44N	9.11 E
Bajalān	24	Md	37.18N	48.47 E
Bajan	27	Jb	49.15N	111.58 E
Bajanaul	19	He	50.47N	75.42 E
Bajandaj	20	Ff	53.04N	105.30 E
Bajan-Delger	27	Jb	45.55N	112.15 E
Bajangol	20	Ff	50.40N	103.25 E
Bajan-Hongor	22	Me	46.20N	100.40 E
Bajan-Ula [Mong.]	27	Jb	49.07N	112.45 E
Bajan-Ula [Mong.]	27	Gb	47.05N	95.15 E
Bajan-Under	27	Gc	44.45N	98.45 E
Baja Verapaz [3]	49	Bf	15.05N	90.20W
Bajawa	26	Hh	8.47S	120.59 E
Bajčunas	16	Rf	47.17N	53.03 E
Bajdarackaja Guba	20	Bc	69.00N	67.30 E
Bajdarata	17	Nb	68.12N	68.18 E
Bajdrag Gol	27	Hb	45.10N	100.45 E
Bājgīrān	24	Rd	37.36N	58.24 E
Baj-Haak	20	Ef	51.07N	94.34 E
Bajiazi	28	Jc	42.41N	129.13 E
Bajina Bašta	15	Cf	43.58N	19.34 E
Bajkal	20	Ff	51.53N	104.47 E
Bajkal, Ozero- = Baikal, Lake- (EN)	21	Md	53.00N	107.40 E
Bajkalovo	17	Kh	57.24N	63.40 E
Bajkalsk	20	Ff	51.30N	104.05 E
Bajkalski Hrebet = Baikal Range (EN)	21	Md	55.00N	108.40 E
Bajkit	20	Ed	61.41N	96.25 E
Bajkonur	19	Gf	47.50N	66.07 E
Bajmak	19	Fe	52.36N	58.19 E
Bajmba, Mount-	59	Ke	29.20S	152.05 E
Bajmok	15	Cd	45.58N	19.26 E
Bajo Baudó	54	Cc	4.58N	77.22W

Index Symbols

[1] Independent Nation
[2] State, Region
[3] District, County
[4] Municipality
[5] Colony, Dependency
■ Continent
Physical Region
Historical or Cultural Region
Mount, Mountain
Volcano
Hill
Mountains, Mountain Range
Hills, Escarpment
Plateau, Upland
Pass, Gap
Plain, Lowland
Delta
Salt Flat
Valley, Canyon
Crater, Cave
Karst Features
Depression
Polder
Desert, Dunes
Forest, Woods
Heath, Steppe
Oasis
Cape, Point
Coast, Beach
Cliff
Peninsula
Isthmus
Sandbank
Island
Atoll
Rock, Reef
Islands, Archipelago
Rocks, Reefs
Coral Reef
Well, Spring
Geyser
River, Stream
Waterfall Rapids
River Mouth, Estuary
Lake
Salt Lake
Intermittent Lake
Reservoir
Swamp, Pond
Canal
Glacier
Ice Shelf, Pack Ice
Ocean
Sea
Gulf, Bay
Strait, Fjord
Lagoon
Bank
Seamount
Tablemount
Ridge
Shelf
Basin
Escarpment, Sea Scarp
Fracture
Trench, Abyss
National Park, Reserve
Point of Interest
Recreation Site
Cave, Cavern
Historic Site
Ruins
Wall, Walls
Church, Abbey
Temple
Scientific Station
Airport
Port
Lighthouse
Mine
Tunnel
Dam, Bridge

Index Symbols

1 Independent Nation
2 State, Region
3 District, County
4 Municipality
5 Colony, Dependency
Continent
Physical Region
Historical or Cultural Region
Mount, Mountain
Volcano
Hill
Mountains, Mountain Range
Hills, Escarpment
Plateau, Upland
Pass, Gap
Plain, Lowland
Delta
Salt Flat
Valley, Canyon
Crater, Cave
Karst Features
Depression
Polder
Desert, Dunes
Forest, Woods
Heath, Steppe
Oasis
Cape, Point
Coast, Beach
Cliff
Peninsula
Isthmus
Sandbank
Island
Atoll
Rock, Reef
Islands, Archipelago
Rocks, Reefs
Coral Reef
Well, Spring
Geyser
River, Stream
Waterfall Rapids
River Mouth, Estuary
Lake
Salt Lake
Intermittent Lake
Reservoir
Swamp, Pond
Canal
Glacier
Ice Shelf, Pack Ice
Ocean
Sea
Gulf, Bay
Strait, Fjord
Lagoon
Bank
Seamount
Tablemount
Ridge
Shelf
Basin
Escarpment, Sea Scarp
Fracture
Trench, Abyss
National Park, Reserve
Point of Interest
Recreation Site
Cave, Cavern
Historic Site
Ruins
Wall, Walls
Church, Abbey
Temple
Scientific Station
Airport
Port
Lighthouse
Mine
Tunnel
Dam, Bridge

Index Symbols

[1] Independent Nation
[2] State, Region
[3] District, County
[4] Municipality
[5] Colony, Dependency
Continent
Physical Region
Historical or Cultural Region
Mount, Mountain
Volcano
Hill
Mountains, Mountain Range
Hills, Escarpment
Plateau, Upland
Pass, Gap
Plain, Lowland
Delta
Salt Flat
Valley, Canyon
Crater, Cave
Karst Features
Depression
Polder
Desert, Dunes
Forest, Woods
Heath, Steppe
Oasis
Cape, Point
Coast, Beach
Cliff
Peninsula
Isthmus
Sandbank
Island
Atoll
Rock, Reef
Islands, Archipelago
Rocks, Reefs
Coral Reef
Well, Spring
Geyser
River, Stream
Waterfall Rapids
River Mouth, Estuary
Lake
Salt Lake
Intermittent Lake
Reservoir
Swamp, Pond
Canal
Glacier
Ice Shelf, Pack Ice
Ocean
Sea
Gulf, Bay
Strait, Fjord
Lagoon
Bank
Seamount
Tablemount
Ridge
Shelf
Basin
Escarpment, Sea Scarp
Fracture
Trench, Abyss
National Park, Reserve
Point of Interest
Recreation Site
Cave, Cavern
Historic Site
Ruins
Wall, Walls
Church, Abbey
Temple
Scientific Station
Airport
Port
Lighthouse
Mine
Tunnel
Dam, Bridge

Béal Atha na Muice/Swinford 9 Eh 53.57N 8.57W
Béal Átha na Sluaighe/Ballinasloe 9 Eh 53.20N 8.13W
Béal Átha Seanaidh/Ballyshannon 9 Eg 54.30N 8.11W
Beale, Cape- 46 Cb 48.44N 125.20W
Béal Easa/Foxford 9 Dh 53.59N 9.07W
Béal Feirste/Belfast 6 Fe 54.35N 5.55W
Beal Range 59 Ie 25.30S 141.30 E
Béal Tairbirt/Belturbet 9 Fg 54.06N 7.26W
Beanna Boirche/Mourne Mountains 9 Gg 54.10N 6.04W
Beannchar/Bangor 9 Hg 54.40N 5.40W
Beanntrai/Bantry 9 Dj 51.41N 9.27W
Bear Bay 42 Ia 75.45N 86.30W
Beardmore 45 Mb 49.36N 87.57W
Beardstown 45 Kg 39.59N 90.26W
Bear Island (EN) = Bjørnöya 5 Ha 74.30N 19.00 E
Bear Islands (EN) = Medveži, Ostrova- 21 Sb 70.52N 161.26 E
Bear Lake 43 Ec 42.00N 111.20W
Bear Lodge Mountains 45 Dd 44.35N 104.15W
Béarn 11 Fk 43.20N 0.45W
Bearpaw Mountains 46 Kb 48.15N 109.30W
Bear Peninsula 66 Of 74.36S 110.50W
Bear River 46 If 41.30N 112.08W
Bearskin Lake 42 If 53.57N 90.59W
Beās 25 Eb 31.10N 74.59 E
Beas de Segura 13 Jf 38.15N 2.53W
Beata, Cabo- 47 Je 17.36N 71.25W
Beata, Isla- 49 Le 17.35N 71.31W
Beata Ridge (EN) 47 Je 16.00N 72.30W
Beatrice 43 Hc 40.16N 96.44W
Beatrice, Cape- 59 Hb 14.15S 137.00 E
Beatton 42 Fe 56.06N 120.22W
Beatton River 42 Fe 56.10N 120.25W
Beatty 43 Dd 36.54N 116.46W
Beattyville 44 Ia 48.52N 77.10W
Beatys Butte 46 Fe 42.23N 119.20W
Beau-Bassin 37a Bb 20.13S 57.27 E
Beaucaire 11 Kk 43.48N 4.38 E
Beaucamps-le-Vieux 12 De 49.50N 1.47 E
Beaucanton 44 Ha 49.05N 79.15W
Beauce 11 Hf 48.22N 1.50 E
Beaudesert 59 Ke 27.59S 153.00 E
Beaufort [Mala.] 26 Ge 5.20N 115.45 E
Beaufort [S.C.-U.S.] 44 Gi 32.26N 80.40W
Beaufort/Befort 12 Ie 49.50N 6.18 E
Beaufort, Massif de- 11 Mi 45.50N 6.40 E
Beaufort Island 66 Kf 76.57S 166.56 E
Beaufort Sea 67 Eb 73.00N 140.00W
Beaufort West 31 Jl 32.20S 22.33 E
Beaugency 11 Hg 47.47N 1.38 E
Beaujolais, Monts du- 11 Kh 46.00N 4.22 E
Beauly 9 Id 57.29N 4.29W
Beaumesnil 12 Ce 49.01N 0.43 E
Beaumetz-lès-Loges 12 Ed 50.14N 2.39 E
Beaumont [Bel.] 12 Gd 50.14N 4.14 E
Beaumont [Fr.] 11 Gj 44.46N 0.46 E
Beaumont [Fr.] 11 Ee 49.40N 1.51W
Beaumont [Fr.] 12 Hf 48.51N 5.47 E
Beaumont [Ms.-U.S.] 45 Lk 31.11N 88.55W
Beaumont [N.Z.] 62 Cf 45.49S 169.32 E
Beaumont [Tx.-U.S.] 39 Jf 30.05N 94.06W
Beaumont-de-Lomagne 11 Gk 43.53N 0.59 E
Beaumont-en-Argonne 12 He 49.32N 5.03 E
Beaumont-le-Roger 12 Ce 49.05N 0.47 E
Beaumont-sur-Oise 12 Ee 49.08N 2.17 E
Beaumont-sur-Sarthe 11 Gf 48.13N 0.08 E
Beaune 11 Kg 47.02N 4.50 E
Beaupré 44 Lb 47.03N 70.53W
Beauraing 12 Gd 50.07N 4.48 E
Beaurepaire 11 Li 45.20N 5.03 E
Beausejour 45 Hf 50.04N 96.33W
Beautemps Beaupré 63b Ce 20.25S 166.08 E
Beauvais 11 Ie 49.26N 2.05 E
Beauval 12 Ed 50.06N 2.20 E
Beauvoir-sur-Mer 11 Dh 46.55N 2.03W
Beaver [Ak.-U.S.] 40 Jc 66.22N 147.24W
Beaver [Ok.-U.S.] 45 Fh 36.48N 100.30W
Beaver [Ut.-U.S.] 43 Ed 38.17N 112.38W
Beaver Creek [Co.-U.S.] 45 Ef 40.20N 103.33W
Beaver Creek [U.S.] 45 Ec 47.20N 103.39W
Beaver Creek [U.S.] 45 Gf 40.04N 99.20W
Beaver Creek [U.S.] 45 Ee 43.25N 103.59W
Beaver Dam 45 Le 43.28N 88.50W
Beaver Falls 44 Ge 40.45N 80.21W
Beaverhead Mountains 46 Id 45.00N 113.20W
Beaver Island 44 Ec 45.40N 85.31W
Beaver Lake 45 Jh 36.20N 93.55W
Beaver River [U.S.] 45 Gh 36.10N 98.45W
Beaver River [Ut.-U.S.] 46 Ig 39.10N 112.57W
Beaverton 46 Dd 45.29N 122.48W
Beāwar 25 Ec 26.06N 74.19 E
Bebedouro 56 Kb 20.56S 48.28W
Becan 48 Oh 18.37N 89.35W
Becanchén 48 Oh 19.50N 89.22W
Beccles 9 Oi 52.28N 1.34 E
Bečej 15 Dd 45.37N 20.03 E
Beceni 15 Jd 45.23N 26.47 E
Becerreá 13 Eb 42.51N 7.10W
Becerro, Cayos- 49 Ff 15.57N 83.17W
Béchar 31 Ge 31.37N 2.13W
Béchar 32 Gd 30.00N 2.00W
Becharof Lake 40 He 58.00N 156.30W
Bechet 15 Gf 43.46N 23.57 E
Bechevin Bay 40 Ge 55.00N 163.27W
Bechyně 10 Kg 49.18N 14.28 E
Beckingen 12 Ie 49.24N 6.42 E
Beckley 43 Kd 37.46N 81.12W
Beckum 10 Ee 51.45N 8.02 E
Beckumer Berge 12 Kc 51.43N 8.10 E
Beclean 15 Hb 47.11N 24.11 E
Bédarieux 11 Jk 43.37N 3.09 E
Bedburg-Hau 12 Ic 51.46N 6.11 E
Bedele 35 Fd 8.27N 36.22 E
Bedesa 35 Gd 8.53N 40.46 E
Bedford 9 Mi 52.10N 0.50W
Bedford [Eng.-U.K.] 9 Mi 52.08N 0.29W
Bedford [In.-U.S.] 44 Df 38.52N 86.29W
Bedford [Pa.-U.S.] 44 He 40.00N 78.31W
Bedford [Va.-U.S.] 44 Hg 37.20N 79.31W
Bedford Level 9 Ni 52.30N 0.05 E
Bedford Point 51p Bb 12.13N 61.36W
Bedfordshire 9 Mi 52.05N 0.20W
Bednja 14 Kd 46.18N 16.45 E
Bednodemjanovsk 16 Mc 53.55N 43.12 E
Bedourie 59 Hd 24.21S 139.28 E
Bedum 12 Ia 53.18N 6.39 E
Beech Grove 44 Df 39.43N 86.03W
Beecroft Head 59 Kg 35.01S 150.50 E
Beef Island 51a Db 18.27N 64.31W
Beelitz 10 Id 52.14N 12.58 E
Beemster 12 Gb 52.34N 4.56 E
Beerfelden 12 Ke 49.34N 8.59 E
Beernem 12 Fc 51.09N 3.20 E
Beerse 12 Gc 51.19N 4.52 E
Beersel 12 Gd 50.46N 4.18 E
Beersheba (EN) = Be'er Shevà 23 Dc 31.14N 34.47 E
Be'er Shevà = Beersheba (EN) 23 Dc 31.14N 34.47 E
Beerze 12 Hc 51.36N 5.19 E
Beeskow 10 Kd 52.10N 14.14 E
Beestekraal 37 De 25.23S 27.38 E
Beeston 9 Li 52.56N 1.12W
Beethoven Peninsula 66 Qf 71.40S 73.45W
Beetsterzwaag, Opsterland- 12 Ia 53.03N 6.04 E
Beeville 43 Hf 28.24N 97.45W
Befale 36 Db 0.28N 20.58 E
Befandriana Nord 37 Hc 15.15S 48.32 E
Befandriana Sud 37 Gd 22.06S 43.54 E
Befori 36 Db 0.06N 22.17 E
Befort/Beaufort 12 Ie 49.50N 6.18 E
Bega 15 Dd 45.13N 20.19 E
Bega 58 Fh 36.40S 149.50 E
Bégard 11 Cf 48.38N 3.18W
Begejski kanal 15 Dd 45.27N 20.27 E
Beggars Point 51d Bb 17.10N 61.48W
Bègle 11 Fj 44.48N 0.32W
Begna 7 Bf 60.35N 10.00 E
Begoml 8 Mj 54.46N 28.14 E
Begunicy 8 Me 59.31N 29.30 E
Behābād 24 Pg 31.52N 55.57 E
Behbehān 23 Hc 30.35N 50.14 E
Behring Point 49 Ia 24.27N 77.43W
Behshahr 23 Hb 36.43N 53.34 E
Bei'an 22 Oe 48.16N 126.29 E
Beibu Wan = Tonkin, Gulf of- (EN) 21 Mh 20.00N 108.00 E
Beida He 27 Gc 40.18N 99.01 E
Beihai 22 Mg 21.31N 109.07 E
Bei Hulsan Hu 27 Gd 36.55N 95.55 E
Bei Jiang 27 Jg 23.02N 112.58 E
Beijing = Peking (EN) 22 Nf 39.55N 116.23 E
Beijing Shi (Pei-ching Shih) 27 Kc 40.15N 116.30 E
Beila 32 Df 18.10N 15.53W
Beilen 12 Ib 52.52N 6.32 E
Beiliutang He 28 Eg 34.12N 119.33 E
Beilrstroom 12 Ib 52.41N 6.12 E
Beilstein 12 Jd 50.07N 7.15 E
Beilu He 27 Fe 34.34N 94.00 E
Beinamar 35 Bd 8.40N 15.23 E
Beine-Nauroy 12 Ge 49.15N 4.13 E
Beipiao 27 Lc 41.49N 120.45 E
Beira 31 Kj 19.50S 34.52 E
Beira Alta 13 Ed 40.40N 7.35W
Beira Baixa 13 Ee 39.55N 7.30W
Beira Litoral 13 Dd 40.15N 8.25W
Beiru He 28 Bh 33.40N 113.35 E
Beirut (EN) = Bayrūt 22 Ff 33.53N 35.30 E
Bei Shan 21 Le 41.30N 96.00 E
Beitstad 7 Cd 64.05N 11.22 E
Beiuş 15 Fc 46.40N 22.21 E
Beiwei Tan 27 Kg 21.10N 116.10 E
Beizhen [China] 27 Kd 37.24N 117.59 E
Beizhen [China] 28 Fd 41.36N 121.47 E
Beja 27 Ef 38.01N 7.52W
Beja 13 Eg 37.58N 7.50W
Bejaïa 32 Ib 36.40N 5.10 E
Bejaïa 31 He 36.45N 5.05 E
Bejaïa, Golfe de- 13 Rh 36.45N 5.20 E
Béjar 13 Gd 40.23N 5.46W
Beji 25 Dc 29.47N 67.58 E
Bejneu 19 Ff 45.15N 55.05 E
Bejsug 16 Kf 46.02N 38.35 E
Bejsugski Liman 16 Kf 46.05N 38.25 E
Bekabad 19 Gg 40.13N 69.14 E
Bekasi 26 Eh 6.14S 106.59 E
Bekdaš 19 Fg 41.31N 52.40 E
Békés 10 Rj 46.46N 21.08 E
Békés 10 Qj 46.45N 21.00 E
Békéscsaba 10 Rj 46.41N 21.06 E
Bekilli 15 Mk 38.14N 29.26 E
Bekily 37 Hd 24.12S 45.18 E
Bekkai 29a Db 43.25N 145.07 E
Bekoji 35 Fd 7.32N 39.15 E
Bekopaka 37 Gc 19.08S 44.45 E
Bekovo 16 Mc 52.29N 43.45 E
Bela [India] 25 Gc 25.56N 81.59 E
Bela [Pak.] 25 Dc 26.14N 66.19 E
Bélabo 34 He 4.52N 13.10 E
Bela Crkva 15 Ee 44.54N 21.26 E
Bela Dila 26 Ge 18.40N 80.55 E
Bela Floresta 55 Ge 20.36S 51.16W
Belaga 26 Ff 2.42N 113.47 E
Belaja [R.S.F.S.R.] 20 Mc 65.30N 173.15 E
Belaja [R.S.F.S.R.] 5 Ld 56.00N 54.32 E
Belaja [R.S.F.S.R.] 16 Kg 45.03N 39.25 E
Belaja Cerkov 6 Jf 49.49N 30.07 E
Belaja Gora 20 Jc 68.30N 146.15 E
Belaja Holunica 19 Fd 58.53N 50.50 E
Belaja Kalitva 16 Le 48.09N 40.49 E
Bela Krajina 14 Je 45.35N 15.15 E
Bela Lorena 55 Ib 15.13S 46.01W
Belang 26 Hf 0.57N 124.47 E
Bela Palanka 15 Ff 43.13N 22.19 E
Belarbi 13 Li 35.09N 0.27W
Belaruskaja Sovetskaja Socialističnaja Respublika/Belorusskaja SSR 19 Ce 53.50N 28.00 E
Belasica 15 Fh 41.21N 22.50 E
Belau = Palau (EN) 14 Di 41.11N 9.23 E
Bela Vista [Braz.] 54 Gh 22.06S 56.31W
Bela Vista [Braz.] 55 Dc 17.37S 57.01W
Bela Vista [Moz.] 37 Ee 26.20S 32.40 E
Belawan 26 Cf 3.47N 98.41 E
Běła Woda/Weißwasser 10 Ke 51.31N 14.38 E
Belayan 26 Gg 0.14S 116.36 E
Belbo 14 Cf 44.54N 8.31 E
Bełchatow 10 Pe 51.22N 19.21 E
Belcher Channel 42 Ia 77.20N 94.30W
Belcher Islands 38 Ld 56.20N 79.30W
Belchite 13 Lc 41.18N 0.45W
Belcy 19 Cf 47.46N 27.55 E
Bełżyna 10 Ne 51.25N 17.50 E
Belebej 19 Fe 54.10N 54.07 E
Belecke, Warstein- 12 Kc 51.29N 8.20 E
Beled 10 Ni 47.28N 17.06 E
Beled Wêyne 31 Lh 4.47N 45.12 E
Bélel 34 Hd 7.03N 14.26 E
Belém [Moz.] 37 Fb 14.08S 35.58 E
Belém [Braz.] 53 Lf 1.27S 48.29W
Belem [Mex.] 48 Dd 27.45N 110.28W
Belém de São Francisco 54 Ke 8.46S 38.58W
Belen 43 Fe 34.40N 106.46W
Belén [Arg.] 56 Gc 27.39S 67.02W
Belén [Nic.] 49 Eh 11.30N 85.53W
Belén [Par.] 55 Df 23.30S 57.06W
Belén [Ur.] 55 Dj 30.47S 57.47W
Belén, Cuchilla de- 55 Dj 30.55S 56.30W
Belén de Escobar 55 Cl 34.21S 58.47W
Belene 15 If 43.39N 25.07 E
Bélep, Iles- 57 Hf 19.45S 163.40 E
Beles 35 Fc 10.55N 35.10 E
Belev 16 Jc 53.50N 36.10 E
Beleye 35 Fc 11.24N 36.10 E
Belfast [Me.-U.S.] 44 Mc 44.27N 69.01W
Belfast [S.Afr.] 37 Ee 25.43S 30.03 E
Belfast/Béal Feirste 6 Fe 54.35N 5.55W
Belfast Lough/Loch Lao 9 Hg 54.40N 5.50W
Belfield 45 Ec 46.53N 103.12W
Belford 9 Lf 55.36N 1.49W
Belfort 11 Mg 47.45N 7.00 E
Belgaum 22 Jh 15.52N 74.30 E
Belgica Bank (EN) 67 Ld 78.28N 15.00W
Belgicafjella 66 Df 72.35S 31.10 E
België/Belgique = Belgium (EN) 6 Ge 50.30N 4.30 E
Belgique/België = Belgium (EN) 6 Ge 50.30N 4.30 E
Belgium (EN) = België/Belgique 6 Ge 50.30N 4.30 E
Belgium (EN) = Belgique/België 6 Ge 50.30N 4.30 E
Belgorod 6 Je 50.36N 36.35 E
Belgorod-Dnestrovski 19 Df 46.12N 30.17 E
Belgorodskaja Oblast 19 De 50.45N 37.30 E
Belgrade (EN) = Beograd 6 Ig 44.50N 20.30 E
Bel Hairane 32 Ic 31.17N 6.20 E
Beli 34 Hd 7.52N 10.58 E
Belice 14 Gm 37.35N 12.52 E
Beli Drim 15 Dg 42.05N 20.20 E
Beliđži 16 Pi 41.53N 48.20 E
Beli Lom 15 If 43.41N 26.00 E
Beli Manastir 14 Me 45.46N 18.37 E
Belimbegovo 15 Eh 42.00N 21.35 E
Belin 11 Fj 44.30N 0.47W
Belinga 36 Bb 1.04N 13.12 E
Belinski 16 Mc 52.58N 43.29 E
Belinyu 26 Eg 1.38S 105.46 E
Beliş 15 Gc 46.39N 23.02 E
Beli Timok 15 Ff 43.55N 22.18 E
Belize 39 Kh 17.15N 88.45W
Belize (British Honduras) 49 Ce 17.35N 88.35W
Belize City 39 Kh 17.30N 88.12W
Belize River 49 Ce 17.32N 88.14W
Beljajevka 16 Gf 46.29N 30.14 E
Beljanica 15 Ee 44.07N 21.43 E
Belka 8 Mg 57.40N 29.47 E
Belkovski, Ostrov- 20 Ia 75.30N 136.00 E
Bellac 11 Hh 46.07N 1.03 E
Bella Coola 42 Ef 52.22N 126.46W
Bellagio 14 De 45.59N 9.15 E
Bellaire [Oh.-U.S.] 44 Ge 40.02N 80.46W
Bellaire [Tx.-U.S.] 45 Il 29.43N 95.28W
Bellaria-Igea Marina 14 Gf 44.09N 12.28 E
Bellary 22 Jh 15.09N 76.56 E
Bella Unión 55 Dj 30.15S 57.35W
Bella Vista [Arg.] 56 Ic 28.30S 59.03W
Bella Vista [Par.] 55 Df 22.08S 56.31W
Bellavista, Capo- 14 Dk 39.56N 9.43 E
Bell Bay 42 Jb 71.10N 84.55W
Belle-Anse 49 Kd 18.14N 72.04W
Belledonne 11 Mi 45.18N 6.08 E
Bellefontaine [Mart.] 51h Ab 14.40N 61.10W
Bellefontaine [Oh.-U.S.] 44 Fe 40.22N 83.45W
Belle Fourche 43 Gc 44.40N 103.51W
Belle Fourche River 43 Ed 44.26N 102.19W
Bellegarde 11 If 47.59N 2.26 E
Bellegarde-sur-Valserine 11 Lh 46.06N 5.49 E
Belle Glade 44 Gl 26.41N 80.40W
Belle Ile 5 Ff 47.19N 3.11W
Belle Isle 42 Lf 51.55N 55.20W
Belle Isle, Strait of- 38 Nd 51.35N 56.30W
Bellencombre 12 De 49.42N 1.14 E
Belleplaine 51q Ab 13.15N 59.34W
Belleville [Fr.] 11 Kh 46.06N 4.45 E
Belleville [Il.-U.S.] 45 Lg 38.31N 90.00W
Belleville [Ks.-U.S.] 45 Hg 39.49N 97.38W
Belleville [Ont.-Can.] 42 Jh 44.10N 77.23W
Bellevue [Nb.-U.S.] 45 Ib 15.13S 46.01W
Bellevue [Wa.-U.S.] 46 Dc 47.37N 122.12W
Belley 11 Li 45.46N 5.41 E
Bellheim 12 Ke 49.12N 8.17 E
Bellin → Kangirsuk 39 Lc 60.00N 70.01W
Bellingham [Eng.-U.K.] 9 Kf 55.09N 2.16W
Bellingham [Wa.-U.S.] 39 Ge 48.46N 122.29W
Bellingsfors 8 Ef 58.59N 12.15 E
Bellingshausen 66 Re 62.12S 58.56W
Bellingshausen Ice Shelf 66 Ce 71.00S 89.00W
Bellingshausen Sea (EN) 66 Pf 71.00S 85.00W
Bellinzona 14 Dd 46.11N 9.02 E
Bello 54 Cb 6.19N 75.34W
Bellocq 55 Bl 35.55S 61.32W
Bellona, Récifs- 57 Gg 21.00S 159.00 E
Bellona Island 60 Fj 11.17S 159.47 E
Bellot Strait 42 Ib 72.00N 94.30W
Bellow Falls 44 Kd 43.08N 72.28W
Bell Peninsula 42 Jd 63.45N 81.30W
Bell River 42 Jg 49.49N 77.39W
Bell Rock → Inchcape 9 Ke 56.26N 2.24W
Bellsund 41 Nc 77.39N 14.15 E
Belluno 14 Gd 46.09N 12.13 E
Bell Ville 56 Hd 32.37S 62.42W
Bellville 37 Bf 33.53S 18.36 E
Belmond 45 Je 42.51N 93.37W
Belmont 42 Hd 42.14N 78.02W
Belmonte [Braz.] 54 Kg 15.51S 38.54W
Belmonte [Port.] 13 Ed 40.21N 7.21W
Belmonte [Sp.] 13 Je 39.34N 2.42W
Belmopan 39 Kh 17.15N 88.46W
Beloeil 12 Fd 50.35N 3.43 E
Belogorsk [R.S.F.S.R.] 22 Od 50.57N 128.25 E
Belogorsk [Ukr.-U.S.S.R.] 16 Ig 45.01N 34.33 E
Belogradčik 15 Ff 43.38N 22.41 E
Belogradčiški 15 Ff 43.38N 22.28 E
Belo Horizonte 53 Lg 19.55S 43.56W
Beloit [Ks.-U.S.] 45 Gg 39.28N 98.06W
Beloit [Wi.-U.S.] 43 Jc 42.31N 89.02W
Belojarovo 20 Hf 51.35N 128.55 E
Belojarski 19 Gc 63.40N 66.45 E
Beloje More = White Sea (EN) 5 Kb 66.00N 44.00 E
Beloje Ozero = White Lake (EN) 5 Jc 60.11N 37.35 E
Belokany 16 Oi 41.43N 46.28 E
Belomorsk 6 Jc 64.29N 34.43 E
Belomorsko-Baltijski Kanal = White Sea-Baltic Canal (EN) 5 Jc 63.30N 34.48 E
Belomorsko-Kulojskoje Plato 7 Jd 65.20N 41.50 E
Beloozersk 16 Dc 52.28N 25.13 E
Belopolje 19 De 51.09N 34.18 E
Belorečensk 16 Kg 44.43N 39.52 E
Beloreck 19 Fe 53.58N 58.24 E
Belorusskaja Grjada 16 Ec 53.50N 27.00 E
Belorusskaja Sovetskaja Socialističeskaja Respublika 19 Ce 53.50N 28.00 E
Belorusskaja SSR/Belaruskaja Sovetskaja Socialistyčnaja Respublika 19 Ce 53.50N 28.00 E
Belorusskaja SSR = Byelorussian SSR (EN) 19 Ce 53.50N 28.00 E
Belo-sur-Mer 37 Gd 20.44S 44.00 E
Belo-sur-Tsiribihina 37 Gc 19.39S 44.32 E
Belot, Lac- 42 Ec 66.50N 126.20W
Belovo 20 Df 54.25N 86.18 E
Belovodsk 16 Ke 49.10N 39.33 E
Belovodskoe 18 Jc 42.47N 74.13 E
Belozersk 19 Dd 60.03N 37.48 E
Belper 12 Aa 53.02N 1.28W
Belted Range 46 Gh 37.25N 116.10W
Belton [Mo.-U.S.] 45 Ig 38.49N 94.32W
Belton [Tx.-U.S.] 45 Hk 31.04N 97.28W
Belton Lake 45 Hk 31.08N 97.32W
Belturbet/Béal Tairbirt 9 Fg 54.06N 7.26W
Beluha 21 Ke 49.48N 86.35 E
Belvedere Marittimo 14 Jk 39.37N 15.52 E
Belvidere 45 Le 42.15N 88.50W
Bely 7 Hi 55.50N 32.58 E
Bely, Ostrov- = Bely Island (EN) 21 Jb 73.10N 70.45 E
Belyando River 59 Jd 21.38S 146.50 E
Bely Čeremoš 15 Ia 48.06N 25.04 E
Bely Island (EN) = Bely, Ostrov- 21 Jb 73.10N 70.45 E
Bely Jar 20 De 58.26N 85.03 E
Belyje Berega 16 Ic 53.12N 34.42 E
Belz 16 Dd 50.23N 24.03 E
Bełżec 10 Tf 50.24N 23.26 E
Belzoni 45 Kj 33.11N 90.29W
Bełżyce 10 Se 51.11N 22.18 E
Bemaraha, Plateau de- 30 Lj 19.00S 45.15 E
Bembe 36 Bd 7.02S 14.18 E
Bembéréké 34 Fc 10.13N 2.40 E
Bembézar 13 Gg 37.45N 5.13W
Bembridge 12 Ad 50.41N 1.05W
Bemidji 43 Ib 47.29N 94.53W
Ben 24 Nf 32.32N 50.45 E
Benāb 23 Gb 37.18N 46.05 E
Benabarre/Benavarn 13 Mb 42.07N 0.29 E
Bena Dibele 36 Dc 4.07S 22.50 E
Bénaize 11 Hh 46.34N 1.04 E
Benalla 59 Jg 36.33S 145.59 E
Benares → Vārānasi 22 Kg 25.20N 83.00 E
Benasc/Benasque 13 Mb 42.36N 0.32 E
Benasque/Benasc 13 Mb 42.36N 0.32 E
Benavarn/Benabarre 13 Mb 42.07N 0.29 E
Benavente 13 Gc 42.00N 5.41W
Benbecula 9 Fd 57.27N 7.20W
Bencheng → Luannan 28 Ee 39.30N 118.42 E
Ben-Chicao, Col de- 13 Oh 36.12N 2.51 E
Bend 43 Cc 44.03N 121.19W
Bendaja 34 Cd 7.10N 11.15W
Bendel 34 Gd 6.00N 5.50 E
Bendela 36 Cc 3.18S 17.36 E
Bender Bäyla 31 Mh 9.30N 50.30 E
Bendersiyada 35 Hc 11.14N 48.57 E
Bendery 19 Cf 46.48N 29.22 E
Bendigo 58 Fh 36.46S 144.17 E
Bendorf 12 Jd 50.26N 7.34 E
Bēne/Bene 8 Jh 56.28N 23.01 E
Bene/Bēne 8 Jh 56.28N 23.01 E
Bénéna 34 Ec 13.06N 4.22W
Benepú, Rada- 65d Ac 27.10S 109.25W
Benešov 10 Kg 49.47N 14.40 E
Benevento 14 Ii 41.08N 14.45 E
Bengal 21 Kg 24.00N 90.00 E
Bengal, Bay of- (EN) 21 Kh 15.00N 90.00 E
Bengamisa 36 Eb 0.57N 25.10 E
Bengbis 34 He 3.27N 12.27 E
Bengbu 22 Nf 32.47N 117.23 E
Benghazi (EN) = Banghāzī 31 Je 32.07N 20.04 E
Benghazi (EN) = Banghāzī 33 Dd 27.00N 20.30 E
Benghisa Point 14 Io 35.50N 14.35 E
Bengkalis 26 Df 1.28N 102.08 E
Bengkulu 26 Dg 3.48S 102.16 E
Bengkulu 22 Mj 3.48S 102.16 E
Bengo, Baia do- 30 Ii 8.43S 13.21 E
Bengo He 28 Eg 35.04N 118.22 E
Bengough 46 Mb 49.24N 105.08W
Bengtsfors 7 Cg 59.02N 12.13 E
Benguela 31 Ij 12.35S 13.26 E
Benguela 36 Be 12.00S 15.00 E
Benguerir 32 Fc 32.14N 7.57W
Benguérua, Ilha- 37 Fd 21.53S 35.26 E
Bengue Viejo 49 Ce 17.05N 89.08W
Bengut, Cap- 32 Hb 36.55N 3.54 E
Beni 31 Jh 0.30N 29.28 E
Beni 54 Ef 14.00S 65.30W
Beni, Rio- 52 Jg 10.23S 65.24W
Beni Abbes 32 Gc 30.08N 2.10W
Beni Baufrah 13 Hi 35.05N 4.18W
Benicarló 13 Md 40.25N 0.26 E
Benicasim 13 Md 40.03N 0.04 E
Beni Chougran, Monts des- 13 Mi 35.30N 0.15 E
Benidorm 13 Lf 38.32N 0.08W
Beni Enzar 13 Ji 35.14N 2.57W
Beni Haoua 13 Nh 36.32N 1.34 E
Beni Mellal 32 Fc 32.20N 6.21W
Beni Mellal 32 Fc 32.30N 6.30W
Benin 34 Gd 5.45N 5.04 E
Bénin = Benin (EN) 31 Hh 9.30N 2.15 E
Bénin (Dahomey) 31 Hh 9.30N 2.15 E
Benin (EN) = Bénin 31 Hh 9.30N 2.15 E
Benin, Bight of- 30 Hh 5.30N 4.00 E
Benin City 31 Hh 6.20N 5.38 E
Beni Ounif 32 Gc 32.03N 1.15W
Benisa 13 Mf 38.43N 0.03 E
Beni Saf 13 Ki 35.19N 1.23W
Benisheikh 34 Hc 11.48N 12.29 E
Benito Juárez 48 Ii 17.50N 92.32W
Benito Juárez, Presa- 48 Li 16.27N 95.30W
Benjamen Island 37b Bb 5.27S 53.21 E
Benjamin 45 Gj 33.35N 99.48W
Benjamin Aceval 55 Dg 24.58S 57.34W
Benjamin Constant 54 Df 4.22S 70.02W
Benjamin Hill 48 Db 30.10N 111.10W
Benkei-Misaki 29a Bb 42.50N 140.11 E
Benkelman 45 Ff 40.03N 101.32W
Benkovac 14 Jf 44.02N 15.37 E
Ben Mehidi 14 Bn 36.46N 7.54 E
Bennett, Lake- 59 Gd 23.50S 131.00 E
Bennett, Ostrov- 20 Ja 76.45N 149.00 E
Benneydale 62 Fc 38.31S 175.21 E
Bennichab 32 Df 19.26N 15.21W
Bennington 44 Kd 42.53N 73.12W
Benom 26 Df 3.50N 102.06 E
Benoni 31 Jk 26.19S 28.27 E
Bénoué = Benue (EN) 30 Hh 7.48N 6.46 E
Benoy 35 Bd 8.59N 16.19 E
Benrath 12 Ic 51.10N 6.52 E
Bensekrane 13 Ki 35.04N 1.13W
Bensheim 10 Eg 49.41N 8.37 E
Ben Slimane 32 Fc 33.37N 7.07W
Benson [Az.-U.S.] 46 Jk 31.58N 110.18W
Benson [Mn.-U.S.] 45 Id 45.19N 95.36W
Benson Point 64g Ab 1.56N 157.30W
Bent 23 Id 26.17N 59.31 E
Benteng [Indon.] 26 Hg 0.24S 121.59 E
Benteng [Indon.] 26 Hh 6.08N 120.27 E
Bentheim 10 Dd 52.19N 7.10 E
Bentiaba 36 Be 14.29S 12.50 E
Bentinck 25 Jf 11.45N 98.03 E
Bentinck Island 59 Hc 17.05S 139.30 E
Bentiu 35 Dd 9.14N 29.50 E
Bento Gonçalves 56 Jc 29.10S 51.31W
Bento Gomes, Rio- 55 Dc 16.40S 57.12W
Benton [Ar.-U.S.] 45 Ji 34.34N 92.35W
Benton [Il.-U.S.] 45 Lg 38.01N 88.55W
Bentong 26 Df 3.32N 101.55 E
Benton Harbor 44 Dd 42.07N 86.27W
Bentonville 45 Ih 36.22N 94.13W
Benua, Pulau- 26 Ef 0.56N 107.27 E
Benue 34 Gd 7.15N 8.20 E
Benue 30 Hh 7.48N 6.46 E
Benue (EN) = Bénoué 30 Hh 7.48N 6.46 E
Benwee Head/An Bhinn Bhuí 9 Dg 54.21N 9.48W
Benxi 22 Oe 41.16N 123.48 E
Beo 26 If 4.15N 126.48 E
Beograd = Belgrade (EN) 6 Ig 44.50N 20.30 E
Beograd-Krnjača 15 De 44.52N 20.28 E
Beograd-Zemun 15 De 44.53N 20.25 E
Béoumi 34 Dd 7.40N 5.34W

Index Symbols

Independent Nation	Historical or Cultural Region	Pass, Gap	Depression	Coast, Beach	Rock, Reef	Waterfall Rapids	Canal	Lagoon	Escarpment, Sea Scarp	Historic Site	Port
State, Region	Mount, Mountain	Plain, Lowland	Polder	Cliff	Islands, Archipelago	River Mouth, Estuary	Glacier	Bank	Fracture	Ruins	Lighthouse
District, County	Volcano	Delta	Desert, Dunes	Peninsula	Rocks, Reefs	Lake	Ice Shelf, Pack Ice	Seamount	Trench, Abyss	Wall, Walls	Mine
Municipality	Hill	Salt Flat	Forest, Woods	Isthmus	Coral Reef	Salt Lake	Ocean	Tablemount	National Park, Reserve	Church, Abbey	Tunnel
Colony, Dependency	Mountains, Mountain Range	Valley, Canyon	Heath, Steppe	Sandbank	Well, Spring	Intermittent Lake	Sea	Ridge	Point of Interest	Temple	Dam, Bridge
Continent	Hills, Escarpment	Crater, Cave	Oasis	Island	Geyser	Reservoir	Gulf, Bay	Shelf	Recreation Site	Scientific Station	
Physical Region	Plateau, Upland	Karst Features	Cape, Point	Atoll	River, Stream	Swamp, Pond	Strait, Fjord	Basin	Cave, Cavern	Airport	

Beppu 27 Ne 33.17N 131.30 E
Beppu-Wan 29 Be 33.20N 131.35 E
Bequia Head 51n Ba 13.03N 61.12W
Bequia Island 50 Ff 13.01N 61.13W
Beraketa 37 Hd 24.11S 45.42 E
Berati 15 Ci 40.42N 19.57 E
Beratus, Gunung- 26 Gg 1.02S 116.20 E
Berau, Teluk-=McCluer Gulf (EN) 26 Jg 2.30S 132.30 E
Berberä 31 Lg 10.25N 45.02 E
Berbérati 31 Ih 4.16N 15.47 E
Berberia, Cabo- 13 Nf 38.38N 1.23 E
Berbice River 54 Gb 6.17N 57.32W
Berca 15 Jd 45.17N 26.41 E
Berchères-sur-Vesgre 12 Df 48.51N 1.33 E
Berchtesgaden 10 Ii 47.38N 13.00 E
Berck [Fr.] 12 Dd 50.24N 1.36 E
Berck [Fr.] 11 Hd 50.24N 1.34 E
Berck- Berck Plage 12 Dd 50.24N 1.34 E
Berck-Plage, Berck- 12 Dd 50.24N 1.34 E
Berda 16 Jf 46.47N 36.52 E
Berdäle 35 Hd 7.04N 47.51 E
Berdičev 19 Cf 49.53N 28.36 E
Berdigestjah 20 Hd 62.03N 126.50 E
Berdjansk 19 Df 46.43N 36.48 E
Berdsk 20 Df 54.47N 83.05 E
Beregomet 15 Ia 48.10N 25.24 E
Beregovo 19 Cf 48.13N 22.41 E
Bereku 36 Gc 4.27S 35.44 E
Berekua 50 Fe 15.14N 61.19W
Berekum 34 Ed 7.27N 2.35W
Berens 42 Hf 52.21N 97.01W
Berens River 42 Hf 52.22N 97.02W
Beresford 45 He 43.05N 96.47W
Berestečko 10 Vf 50.16N 25.14 E
Bereşti 15 Kc 46.06N 27.53 E
Berettyó 15 Ec 46.59N 21.07 E
Berettyóújfalu 10 Ri 47.13N 21.33 E
Bereza 19 Ce 52.33N 24.58 E
Berezan 16 Gd 50.19N 31.31 E
Berežany 16 De 49.29N 25.00 E
Berezina [Bye.-U.S.S.R.] 16 Dc 53.48N 25.59 E
Berezina [U.S.S.R.] 5 Je 52.33N 30.14 E
Berezino [Bye.-U.S.S.R.] 16 Fc 53.51N 29.00 E
Berezino [Bye.-U.S.S.R.] 8 Mj 54.55N 28.16 E
Berezino [Ukr.-U.S.S.R.] 15 Mc 46.16N 29.11 E
Bereznegovatoje 16 Hf 47.20N 32.49 E
Bereznik 19 Ec 62.53N 42.42 E
Berezniki 6 Ld 59.24N 56.46 E
Berezno 16 Ed 51.01N 26.45 E
Berezovka [Bye.-U.S.S.R.] 10 Vc 53.40N 25.37 E
Berezovka [R.S.F.S.R.] 17 Hd 64.59N 56.29 E
Berezovka [Ukr.-U.S.S.R.] 19 Df 47.12N 30.56 E
Berezovka Višerka 17 Hf 60.55N 56.50 E
Berezovo 19 Gc 63.58N 65.00 E
Berezovski [R.S.F.S.R.] 17 Jh 56.55N 60.50 E
Berezovski [R.S.F.S.R.] 20 De 55.39N 86.16 E
Berezovy 20 If 51.41N 135.52 E
Berga [Sp.] 13 Nb 42.06N 1.51 E
Berga [Swe.] 8 Gg 57.13N 16.02 E
Bergama 23 Cb 39.07N 27.10 E
Bergamo 14 De 45.41N 9.43 E
Bergantiños 13 Da 43.20N 8.45W
Bergby 7 Df 60.56N 17.02 E
Bergen [Ger.] 10 Jb 54.25N 13.26 E
Bergen [Neth.] 12 Gb 52.40N 4.42 E
Bergen [Nor.] 6 Gc 60.23N 5.20 E
Bergen/Mons 11 Jd 50.27N 3.56 E
Bergen aan Zee, Bergen- 12 Gb 52.40N 4.38 E
Bergen-Bergen aan Zee 12 Gb 52.40N 4.38 E
Bergen op Zoom 11 Kc 51.30N 4.17 E
Bergerac 11 Gj 44.51N 0.29 E
Bergeyk 12 Hc 51.19N 5.22 E
Bergh 12 Ic 51.53N 6.16 E
Bergheim 10 Cf 50.58N 6.39 E
Bergh-s'Heerenberg 12 Ic 51.53N 6.16 E
Bergisches Land 10 De 51.07N 7.10 E
Bergisch Gladbach 10 Df 50.59N 7.08 E
Bergkvara 8 Gh 56.23N 16.05 E
Bergneustadt 12 Jc 51.02N 7.39 E
Bergö 8 Ib 62.55N 21.10 E
Bergsjö 7 Df 61.59N 17.04 E
Bergslagen 8 Fd 60.05N 14.30 E
Bergstraße 12 Ke 49.40N 8.40 E
Bergues 12 Ed 50.58N 2.26 E
Bergum, Tietjerksteradeel- 12 Ha 53.12N 6.00 E
Bergviken 8 Gc 61.10N 16.45 E
Bergville 37 De 28.52S 29.18 E
Berh 27 Jb 47.45N 111.07 E
Berhala, Selat- 26 Dg 0.48S 104.25 E
Berici, Monti- 14 Fe 45.26N 11.31 E
Berīkān 24 Nh 28.17N 51.14 E
Berikulski 20 De 55.32N 88.08 E
Beringa, Ostrov-=Bering Island (EN) 20 Lf 55.00N 166.10 E
Beringen 12 Hc 51.03N 5.13 E
Bering Glacier 40 Kd 60.15N 143.30W
Bering Island (EN)= Beringa, Ostrov- 20 Lf 55.00N 166.10 E
Beringovo More=Bering Sea (EN) 38 Bd 60.00N 175.00W
Beringovski 22 Tc 63.07N 179.19 E
Bering Proliv=Bering Strait (EN) 38 Cc 65.30N 169.00W
Bering Sea 38 Bd 60.00N 175.00W
Bering Sea (EN)=Beringovo More 38 Bd 60.00N 175.00W
Bering Strait 38 Cc 65.30N 169.00W
Bering Strait (EN)=Bering Proliv 38 Cc 65.30N 169.00W
Berislav 16 Hf 46.51N 33.29 E
Berisso 55 Dl 34.52S 57.53W
Berit Dağı 24 Gc 38.01N 36.52 E
Berīzak 24 Qi 26.06N 57.15 E
Berja 13 Jh 36.51N 2.57W
Berkåk 7 Be 62.50N 10.00 E
Berkane 32 Gc 34.56N 2.20W
Berkel 10 Cd 52.09N 6.12 E
Berkeley 43 Cd 37.57N 122.18W
Berkhamsted 12 Bc 51.45N 0.33W
Berkner Island 66 Rf 79.30S 49.30W
Berkovica 15 Gf 43.14N 23.07 E
Berks 9 Lj 51.15N 1.20W
Berkshire 9 Lj 51.30N 1.10W
Berkshire Downs 9 Lj 51.35N 1.25W
Berkshire Hills 44 Kd 42.20N 73.10W
Berlaimont 12 Fd 50.12N 3.49 E
Berlanga de Duero 13 Jc 41.28N 2.51W
Berlengas, Ilhas- 13 Ce 39.25N 9.30W
Berlevåg 7 Ga 70.51N 29.06 E
Berlin [N.H.-U.S.] 43 Mc 44.29N 71.10W
Berlin [Ger.] 6 He 52.31N 13.24 E
Berlin (Ost) = Berlin 6 He 52.31N 13.24 E
Berlin (West) = Berlin 6 He 52.31N 12.24 E
Berlin-Pankow 10 Jd 52.34N 13.24 E
Bermeja, Sierra- 13 Gh 36.30N 5.15W
Bermejillo 47 Dc 25.53N 103.37W
Bermejito, Río- 55 Bg 25.39S 60.11W
Bermejo, Isla- 55 An 39.01S 62.01W
Bermejo, Paso-/Cumbre, Paso de la- 52 Ii 32.50S 70.05W
Bermejo, Río- [Arg.] 52 Ji 31.52S 67.22W
Bermejo, Río- [S.Amer.] 52 Kh 26.52S 58.23W
Bermen, lac- 42 Kf 53.35N 68.55W
Bermeo 13 Ja 43.26N 2.43W
Bermillo de Sayago 13 Fc 41.22N 6.06W
Bermuda 39 Mf 32.20N 64.45W
Bermuda Islands 39 Mf 32.20N 64.45W
Bermuda Rise (EN) 38 Mf 32.30N 65.00W
Bern 14 Bd 46.55N 7.40 E
Bern/Berne 6 Gf 46.55N 7.30 E
Bernalda 14 Kj 40.24N 16.41 E
Bernalillo 45 Ci 35.18N 106.33W
Bernard Islands 64d Bb 7.18N 151.32 E
Bernardo de Irigoyen 55 Bk 32.10S 61.09W
Bernardo do Irigoyen 56 Jc 26.15S 53.39W
Bernasconi 56 He 37.54S 63.43W
Bernau bei Berlin 10 Jd 52.40N 13.35 E
Bernaville 12 Ed 50.08N 2.10 E
Bernay 11 Ge 49.06N 0.36 E
Bernburg 10 He 51.48N 11.44 E
Berndorf 14 Kc 47.57N 16.06 E
Berne [Ger.] 12 Ka 53.11N 8.29 E
Berne [In.-U.S.] 44 Ee 40.39N 84.57W
Berne/Bern 6 Gf 46.55N 7.30 E
Berner Alpen/Alpes Bernoises=Bernese Alps (EN) 14 Bd 46.25N 7.30 E
Berneray 9 Fd 57.43N 7.15W
Bernese Alps (EN)=Alpes Bernoises/Berner Alpen 14 Bd 46.25N 7.30 E
Bernese Alps (EN)=Berner Alpen/Alpes Bernoises 14 Bd 46.25N 7.30 E
Bernesga 13 Gb 42.28N 5.31W
Bernesq 12 Be 49.16N 0.56W
Bernier Bay 42 Ib 71.08N 88.00W
Bernier Island 59 Cd 24.50S 113.10 E
Bernina 14 Ed 46.25N 10.01 E
Bernina 5 Gf 46.22N 9.50 E
Berninapaß 14 Ed 46.25N 10.01 E
Bernissart 12 Fd 50.28N 3.38 E
Bernkastel-Kues 10 Dg 49.55N 7.04 E
Bernstorffs Isfjord 41 Hf 63.10N 40.45W
Berón de Astrada 55 Dh 27.33S 57.32W
Beroroha 37 Hd 21.39S 45.10 E
Béroubouay 34 Fc 10.32N 2.44 E
Beroun 10 Kg 49.58N 14.04 E
Berounka 10 Kg 50.00N 14.24 E
Berovo 15 Fh 41.43N 22.51 E
Berre, Étang de- 11 Lk 43.27N 5.08 E
Berriane 32 Hc 32.50N 3.46 E
Berrouaghia 13 Oh 36.08N 2.55 E
Berry 11 Hh 47.00N 2.00 E
Berry-au-Bac 12 Fe 49.24N 3.54 E
Berryessa, Lake- 46 Dg 38.37N 122.16W
Berry Head 9 Jk 50.24N 3.29W
Berry Islands 47 Ic 25.34N 77.45W
Berry River 46 Ja 50.50N 111.36W
Beršad 19 Cf 48.23N 29.33 E
Berseba 37 Be 26.01S 17.41 E
Bersenbrück 12 Jb 52.33N 7.56 E
Berthierville 44 Kb 46.05N 73.11W
Bertincourt 12 Ed 50.05N 2.59 E
Bertogne 12 Hd 50.05N 5.40 E
Bertolinia 54 Je 7.38S 43.57W
Bertoua 31 Ih 4.35N 13.41 E
Bertraghboy Bay 9 Dh 53.23N 9.50W
Bertrix 12 He 49.51N 5.15 E
Beru Island 57 Ie 1.20S 176.00 E
Berwick-upon-Tweed 9 Lf 55.46N 2.00W
Berwyn 9 Ji 52.53N 3.24W
Besalampy 37 Gc 16.44S 44.24 E
Besançon 6 Gf 47.15N 6.02 E
Besar, Gunung- 26 Gg 1.25S 115.39 E
Besbre 11 Jh 46.33N 3.44 E
Besed 16 Gc 52.38N 31.11 E
Besikama 26 Hh 9.36S 124.57 E
Beskid Mountains (EN) 5 Hf 49.40N 20.00 E
Beskid Niski 10 Rg 49.20N 21.30 E
Beskid Średni 10 Pg 49.45N 19.20 E
Beskid Wysoki 10 Pg 49.32N 20.00 E
Beskidy Wschodnie 10 Sg 49.20N 22.30 E
Beskidy Zachodnie 10 Pg 49.30N 19.30 E
Beskol 18 Ma 46.06N 81.01 E
Beslan 19 Eg 43.10N 44.35 E
Besna Kobila 15 Fg 42.32N 22.14 E
Besni 24 Gd 37.41N 37.52 E
Besparmak Dağ 15 Kl 37.30N 27.35 E
Bessao 35 Bd 7.53N 15.59 E
Bessarabia (EN)= Bessarabija 15 Lb 47.00N 28.30 E
Bessarabija=Bessarabia (EN) 15 Lb 47.00N 28.30 E
Bessarabka 16 Ff 46.20N 28.59 E
Bessèges 11 Kj 44.17N 4.06 E
Bessemer 43 Je 33.25N 86.57W
Bessin 11 Fe 49.10N 1.00W
Bessines-sur-Gartempe 11 Hh 46.06N 1.22 E
Besšoki, Gora- 16 Rh 43.57N 52.30 E
Best 12 Hc 51.30N 5.24 E
Bestjah [R.S.F.S.R.] 20 Hc 66.00N 123.35 E
Bestjah [R.S.F.S.R.] 20 Hd 61.17N 128.50 E
Bestobe 19 He 52.30N 73.05 E
Bestwig 12 Kc 51.22N 8.24 E
Betafo 37 Hc 19.49S 46.50 E
Betanzos [Bol.] 54 Eg 19.34S 65.27W
Betanzos [Sp.] 13 Da 43.17N 8.12W
Betanzos, Ría de- 13 Da 43.23N 8.15W
Bétaré Oya 34 Hd 5.36N 14.05 E
Bétérou 34 Fd 9.12N 2.16 E
Beteta 13 Jd 40.34N 2.04W
Bethal 37 De 26.27S 29.28 E
Bethanien 37 Be 26.30S 17.00 E
Bethanien 31 Ik 26.32S 17.11 E
Bethany [Mo.-U.S.] 45 If 40.16N 94.02W
Bethany [Ok.-U.S.] 45 Hi 35.31N 97.38W
Bethel 39 Cc 60.48N 161.46W
Bétheniville 12 Ge 49.18N 4.22 E
Bethlehem [Pa.-U.S.] 44 Je 40.36N 75.22W
Bethlehem [S.Afr.] 31 Jk 28.15S 28.15 E
Bethlehem (EN)=Bayt Laḩm 24 Fg 31.43N 35.12 E
Bethulie 37 Df 30.32S 25.59 E
Béthune 11 Id 50.32N 2.38 E
Béthune 11 He 49.53N 1.09 E
Betioky 37 Gd 23.42S 44.22 E
Betong 25 Kg 5.45N 101.05 E
Betor 35 Fc 11.37N 39.00 E
Bétou 36 Cb 3.03N 18.31 E
Betpak-Dala 21 Ie 46.00N 70.00 E
Betroka 37 Hd 23.15S 46.05 E
Bet She'an 24 Ff 32.30N 35.30 E
Betsiamites, Rivière- 42 Kg 48.56N 68.38W
Betsiboka 30 Lj 16.03S 46.36 E
Bette 30 If 22.00N 19.12 E
Bettembourg/Bettemburg 12 Ie 49.31N 6.06 E
Bettemburg/Bettembourg 12 Ie 49.31N 6.06 E
Bettendorf 45 Kf 41.32N 90.30W
Bettles Field 40 Ic 66.53N 151.51W
Bettna 8 Gf 58.55N 16.38 E
Bettola 14 Df 44.47N 9.36 E
Betūl 25 Fd 21.55N 77.54 E
Betuwe 11 Lc 51.55N 5.30 E
Betwa 25 Hc 25.55N 80.12 E
Betz 12 Ee 49.09N 2.57 E
Betzdorf 10 Df 50.47N 7.53 E
Beulah 44 Dc 44.38N 86.06W
Beult 12 Cc 51.13N 0.26 E
Bèuvron 11 Hg 47.29N 1.15 E
Beuzeville 12 Ce 49.20N 0.21 E
Beveland 11 Jc 51.30N 3.40 E
Beveren 12 Gc 51.13N 4.15 E
Beveridge Reef 57 Kg 20.00S 168.00W
Beverley [Austl.] 59 Df 32.06S 116.56 E
Beverley [Eng.-U.K.] 9 Mh 53.51N 0.26W
Beverwijk 11 Kb 52.28N 4.40 E
Bewsher, Mount- 66 Ff 70.54S 65.28 E
Bexhill 9 Nk 50.50N 0.29 E
Bexley, London- 12 Cc 51.26N 0.09 E
Beyağaç 15 Ll 37.13N 28.57 E
Beyānlū 24 Ld 36.02N 47.53 E
Bey Dağı 24 Hc 38.15N 38.22 E
Bey Dağlari 23 Db 36.40N 30.15 E
Beykoz 24 Cb 41.08N 29.05 E
Beyla 34 Dd 8.41N 8.38W
Beyoğlu, İstanbul 15 Lh 41.02N 28.59 E
Beyoneisu-Retsugan 27 Oe 31.55N 139.55 E
Beypazari 24 Db 40.10N 31.55 E
Beyra 35 Hd 6.57N 47.19 E
Beyram 24 Oi 27.26N 53.31 E
Beyşehir 24 Dd 37.41N 31.43 E
Beyşehir Gölü 23 Db 37.40N 31.30 E
Bezaha 37 Gd 23.29S 44.30 E
Bežanickaja Vozvyšennost 7 Gh 56.45N 29.30 E
Bežanicy 7 Gh 56.58N 29.57 E
Bezdan 15 Bd 45.51N 18.56 E
Bezděz 10 Kf 50.32N 14.43 E
Bezdež 10 Vd 52.18N 25.20 E
Bežeck 19 Dd 57.50N 36.41 E
Bezenčuk 7 Lj 53.01N 49.24 E
Bezerra, Rio- 55 Ia 13.16S 47.31W
Bezerros 54 Ke 8.14S 35.45W
Beziers 11 Jk 43.21N 3.15 E
Bezmein 19 Fh 38.05N 58.12 E
Bežta 19 Eg 42.08N 46.08 E
Bhadrak 25 Hd 21.04N 86.30 E
Bhadrāvati 25 Ff 13.52N 75.43 E
Bhāgalpur 22 Kg 25.15N 87.00 E
Bhairawa 25 Gc 27.31N 83.24 E
Bhaironghati 25 Fb 31.01N 78.53 E
Bhakkar 25 Eb 31.38N 71.04 E
Bhamo 25 Jd 24.16N 97.14 E
Bhandāra 25 Fd 21.10N 79.39 E
Bhanjan 25 Gc 25.47N 83.36 E
Bhārat Juktarashtra=India (EN) 22 Jh 20.00N 77.00 E
Bharatpur 25 Fc 27.13N 77.29 E
Bharūch 25 Ed 21.46N 72.54 E
Bhatinda → Bathinda 25 Eb 30.12N 74.57 E
Bhātpāra 25 Hd 22.52N 88.24 E
Bhaunagar 22 Jg 21.46N 72.09 E
Bhera 25 Eb 32.29N 72.55 E
Bheri 25 Gc 28.44N 81.16 E
Bhīlwāra 25 Ec 25.21N 74.38 E
Bhīma 21 Jh 16.25N 77.17 E
Bhind 25 Fc 26.34N 78.48 E
Bhiwāni 25 Fc 28.47N 76.08 E
Bhopāl 22 Jg 23.16N 77.24 E
Bhubaneshwar 22 Kg 20.14N 85.50 E
Bhuj 25 Dd 23.16N 69.40 E
Bhusāwal 25 Fd 21.03N 75.46 E
Bhutan (Druk-Yul) 22 Lg 27.30N 90.30 E
Bia 34 Ed 5.21N 3.11W
Bia, Phou- 21 Mh 18.36N 103.01 E
Biá, Rio- 54 Ed 3.28S 67.23W
Bīābān, Kūh-e- 24 Qi 26.30N 57.25 E
Biabou 51n Ba 13.12N 61.09W
Biafra 30 Hh 5.00N 7.30 E
Biafra, Bight of- 30 Hh 3.20N 9.20 E
Biak 26 Kg 1.10S 136.06 E
Biak, Pulau- 57 Ee 1.00S 136.00 E
Biała Piska 10 Sc 53.37N 22.04 E
Biała Podlaska 10 Td 52.00N 23.05 E
Biała Podlaska 10 Td 52.02N 23.06 E
Białobrzegi 10 Qe 51.40N 20.57 E
Białogard 10 Lb 54.01N 16.00 E
Białostocka, Wysoczyzna- 10 Tc 53.23N 23.10 E
Białowieża 10 Td 52.41N 23.50 E
Białystok 6 Ie 53.09N 23.09 E
Białystok 10 Tc 53.10N 23.10 E
Biancavilla 14 Im 37.38N 14.52 E
Bianco 14 Kl 38.05N 16.09 E
Bianco, Monte- 5 Gf 45.50N 6.52 E
Biankouma 34 Dd 7.44N 7.37W
Biankouma 34 Dd 7.43N 7.40W
Bianzhuang → Cangshan 28 Eg 34.51N 118.03 E
Biaro, Pulau- 26 If 2.05N 125.20 E
Biarritz 11 Ek 43.29N 1.34W
Biasca 14 Cd 46.22N 8.57 E
Bibā 33 Fd 28.55N 30.59 E
Bibai 27 Pc 43.19N 141.52 E
Bibala 36 Be 14.50S 13.30 E
Biban, Chaine des- 13 Qh 36.12N 4.25 E
Bibbiena 14 Fg 43.42N 11.49 E
Biberach an der Riß 10 Fh 48.06N 9.48 E
Bibiani 34 Ed 6.28N 2.20W
Bic 44 Ma 48.22N 68.42W
Bicaj 15 Dh 41.59N 20.25 E
Bicas 55 Ke 21.43S 43.04W
Bicaz 15 Jc 46.55N 26.04 E
Bicaz, Pasul- 15 Ic 46.49N 25.52 E
Bičenekski, Pereval- 16 Nj 39.33N 45.48 E
Bicester 9 Lj 51.54N 1.09W
Bichena 35 Fc 10.21N 38.14 E
Bickerton Island 59 Hb 13.45S 136.10 E
Bicske 10 Oi 47.29N 18.38 E
Bičura 20 Ff 50.36N 107.35 E
Bīd 24 Qd 36.33N 57.35 E
Bida 31 Hh 9.05N 6.01 E
Bīdar 25 Fe 17.54N 77.33 E
Bidasoa 13 Ka 43.22N 1.47W
Biddeford 43 Mc 43.30N 70.26W
Bideford 9 Ij 51.01N 4.13W
Bideford Bay→Barnstaple 9 Ij 51.05N 4.20W
Bidon V/Poste Maurice Cortier 32 He 22.18N 1.05 E
Bié 36 Ce 13.00S 17.30 E
Bié, Planalto do- 30 Ij 13.30S 17.02 E
Biebrza 10 Sc 53.13N 22.28 E
Biecz 10 Rg 49.44N 21.14 E
Biedenkopf 10 Ef 50.55N 8.32 E
Biei 29a Cb 43.35N 142.28 E
Biel/Bienne 14 Bc 47.10N 7.15 E
Bielefeld 10 Ed 52.02N 8.32 E
Bielefeld-Brackwede 12 Kc 51.59N 8.31 E
Bielefeld-Sennestadt 12 Kc 51.57N 8.35 E
Biella 14 Ce 45.34N 8.03 E
Bielsk 10 Pd 52.40N 19.49 E
Bielska, Wysoczyzna- 10 Sd 52.35N 23.00 E
Bielsko 10 Og 49.50N 19.00 E
Bielsko-Biała 10 Pg 49.49N 19.02 E
Bielsk Podlaski 10 Td 52.47N 23.12 E
Bien Dong=South China Sea (EN) 21 Ni 10.00N 113.00 E
Bien Hoa 25 Lf 10.57N 106.49 E
Bienne 11 Lh 46.20N -5.38 E
Bienne/Biel 14 Bc 47.10N 7.15 E
Bienvenida 13 Jd 40.30N 2.30W
Bienville, Lac - 42 Ke 55.20N 72.40W
Bierbeek 12 Gd 50.50N 4.46 E
Bieszczady 10 Sg 49.10N 22.35 E
Bièvre 12 He 49.56N 5.01 E
Biferno 14 Ji 41.59N 15.02 E
Bifoum 36 Bc 0.20S 10.23 E
Bifuka 28 Qb 44.29N 142.21 E
Biga 24 Bb 40.13N 27.14 E
Bigadiç 24 Cc 39.23N 28.08 E
Big Bald Mountain 44 Nb 47.37N 66.38W
Big Baldy Mountain 46 Jc 46.58N 110.37W
Big Bay [Mi.-U.S.] 44 Db 46.49N 87.44W
Big Bay [Van.] 63b Cb 15.05S 166.54 E
Big Beaver House 42 If 52.58N 89.57W
Big Belt Mountains 46 Jc 46.40N 111.25W
Big Black River 45 Kj 32.00N 91.05W
Big Blue River 43 Hd 39.11N 96.32W
Big Creek Peak 46 Id 44.28N 113.32W
Big Dry Creek 46 Lc 47.30N 106.19W
Big Falls 45 Jb 48.11N 93.46W
Biggar 42 Gf 52.04N 108.00W
Biggenden 59 Ke 25.30S 152.00 E
Biggleswade 9 Mi 52.05N 0.17W
Big Hatchet Peak 45 Bk 31.37N 108.20W
Big Hole River 46 Id 45.34N 112.20W
Bighorn Basin 43 Fc 44.15N 108.10W
Bighorn Lake 46 Kd 45.08N 108.10W
Bighorn Mountains 38 Ie 44.00N 107.30W
Bighorn River 43 Fb 46.09N 107.28W
Bight, Head of- 59 Gf 31.30S 131.10 E
Big Island 42 Kd 62.43N 70.40W
Big Lake 44 Nc 45.10N 67.40W
Big Lake 45 Fk 31.12N 101.28W
Big Lost River 46 Ie 43.50N 112.44W
Big Muddy Creek 46 Mb 48.08N 104.36W
Big Muddy Lake 46 Mb 49.08N 104.54W
Bignona 34 Bc 12.49N 16.14W
Bigorre 11 Gk 43.06N 0.05 E
Big Porcupine Creek 46 Lc 46.17N 106.47W
Big Quill Lake 42 Hf 51.51N 104.18W
Big Rapids 44 Ed 43.42N 85.29W
Big River 42 Gf 53.50N 107.01W
Big River 42 Fb 72.50N 125.00W
Big Sand Lake 42 He 57.45N 99.45W
Big Sandy 46 Jb 48.11N 110.07W
Big Sandy Creek 45 Eg 38.06N 102.29W
Big Sandy River [Az.-U.S.] 46 Ii 34.19N 113.31W
Big Sandy River [Wy.-U.S.] 46 Kf 41.50N 109.48W
Big Sheep Mountains 46 Mc 47.03N 105.43W
Big Sioux River 43 Hc 42.30N 96.25W
Big Smoky Valley 43 Dd 38.30N 117.15W
Big Snowy Mountains 46 Kc 46.50N 109.30W
Big Spring 39 If 32.15N 101.28W
Big Spruce Knob 44 Gf 38.16N 80.12W
Big Stone Lake 45 Hd 45.25N 96.40W
Big Timber 46 Kd 45.50N 109.57W
Big Trout Lake 42 If 53.45N 90.00W
Biguglia, Étang de- 11a Ba 42.36N 9.29 E
Big Wood Cay 49 Ia 24.21N 77.44W
Big Wood River 46 He 42.52N 114.55W
Bihać 14 Jf 44.49N 15.52 E
Bihār 25 Hd 25.00N 86.00 E
Bihār 25 Hc 25.11N 85.31 E
Biharamulo 36 Fc 2.38S 31.20 E
Bihor 15 Ec 47.00N 22.00 E
Bihoro 27 Pc 43.49N 144.07 E
Bihorului, Munţii- 15 Fc 46.40N 22.45 E
Bija 21 Kd 52.25N 85.05 E
Bijagós, Arquipélago dos-= Bijagos Islands (EN) 30 Fg 11.15N 16.05W
Bijagós Islands (EN)= Bijagós, Arquipélago dos- 30 Fg 11.15N 16.05W
Bijapur 25 Fe 16.50N 75.42 E
Bījār 23 Gb 35.52N 47.36 E
Bijeljina 14 Nf 44.45N 19.13 E
Bijelo Polje 15 Cf 43.02N 19.45 E
Bijiang (Zhiziluo) 27 Gf 26.39N 99.00 E
Bijie 27 If 27.15N 105.16 E
Bijlikol, Ozero- 18 Hc 43.05N 70.40 E
Bijou Creek 45 Ef 40.17N 103.52W
Bijoutier Island 37b Bb 7.04S 52.45 E
Bijsk 22 Kd 52.34N 85.15 E
Bīkāner 22 Jg 28.01N 73.18 E
Bikar Atoll 57 Ic 12.15N 170.06 E
Bikeqi 28 Ad 40.45N 111.17 E
Bikin 20 Ig 46.43N 134.02 E
Bikin 20 Ig 46.51N 134.02 E
Bikini Atoll 57 Hc 11.35N 165.23 E
Bikoro 31 Ii 0.45S 18.07 E
Bilād Ghāmid 33 Hf 19.58N 41.38 E
Bilād Zahrān 33 He 20.15N 41.15 E
Bilāspur 22 Kg 22.03N 82.10 E
Bilate 35 Fd 6.34N 38.01 E
Bilauktaung Range 21 Lh 13.00N 99.00 E
Bilbao 6 Fg 43.15N 2.58W
Bilbays 33 Fc 30.25N 31.34 E
Bileća 14 Mh 42.53N 18.26 E
Bilecik 23 Ca 40.09N 29.59 E
Bīlehsavār 24 Mc 39.28N 48.20 E
Bilé Karpaty=White Carpathians (EN) 10 Nh 48.55N 17.50 E
Bilesha Plain 36 Hb 0.35N 40.45 E
Biłgoraj 10 Sf 50.34N 22.43 E
Bili 36 Db 4.50N 22.29 E
Bili 36 Eb 4.09N 25.10 E
Bilibino 22 Sc 68.03N 166.20 E
Biliran 26 Hd 11.35N 124.28 E
Bilishti 15 Di 40.37N 20.59 E
Biliu He 28 Ge 39.30N 122.36 E
Bill Baileys Bank (EN) 9 Ca 60.40N 10.20W
Billerbeck 12 Jc 51.58N 7.18 E
Billericay 12 Cc 51.37N 0.35 E
Billingen 8 Ef 58.24N 13.45 E
Billings 39 Jf 37.04N 93.33W
Billings, Reprêsa- 55 If 23.45S 46.40W
Billingshurst 12 Bc 51.01N 0.27W
Bill Williams River 46 Hi 34.17N 114.03W
Billy Chinook, Lake- 46 Ed 44.33N 121.20W
Bilma 31 Ig 18.41N 12.56 E
Biloela 59 Kd 24.24S 150.30 E
Bilo Gora 14 Le 45.50N 17.10 E
Biloku 54 Gc 1.46N 58.33W
Biloxi 43 Je 30.24N 88.53W
Bilqās Qism Awwal 24 Dg 31.13N 31.21 E
Bîlteni 15 Ge 44.52N 23.17 E
Biltine 35 Cc 14.32N 20.55 E
Biltine 35 Cc 15.00N 21.00 E
Bilzen 12 Hd 50.51N 5.31 E
Bima 36 Eb 3.23N 25.09 E
Bimbān 24 Ej 24.26N 32.53 E
Bimberi Peak 59 Jg 35.40S 148.47 E
Bimbila 34 Fd 8.51N 0.04 E
Bimbo 35 Be 4.18N 18.33 E
Bimini Islands 47 Ic 25.44N 79.15W
Bināb 24 Md 36.35N 48.41 E
Binačka Morava 15 Eg 42.27N 21.47 E
Binaiya, Gunung- 26 Ig 3.11S 129.26 E
Binatang 26 Ff 2.10N 111.38 E
Bınboga Dağı 24 Gc 38.21N 36.32 E
Binche 12 Gd 50.24N 4.10 E
Binder 27 Jb 48.35N 110.36 E
Bindura 31 Kj 17.17S 31.20 E
Bine el Ouidane 32 Fc 32.08N 6.28W
Binéfar 13 Mc 41.51N 0.18 E
Binem 35 Bb 18.43N 19.40 E
Binga [Zaire] 36 Db 2.23N 20.30 E
Binga [Zimb.] 37 Dc 17.37S 27.20 E

Index Symbols

- Independent Nation
- State, Region
- District, County
- Municipality
- Colony, Dependency
- Continent
- Physical Region
- Historical or Cultural Region
- Mount, Mountain
- Volcano
- Hill
- Mountains, Mountain Range
- Hills, Escarpment
- Plateau, Upland
- Pass, Gap
- Plain, Lowland
- Delta
- Salt Flat
- Valley, Canyon
- Crater, Cave
- Karst Features
- Depression
- Polder
- Desert, Dunes
- Forest, Woods
- Heath, Steppe
- Oasis
- Cape, Point
- Coast, Beach
- Cliff
- Peninsula
- Isthmus
- Sandbank
- Island
- Atoll
- Rock, Reef
- Islands, Archipelago
- Rocks, Reefs
- Coral Reef
- Well, Spring
- Geyser
- River, Stream
- Waterfall Rapids
- River Mouth, Estuary
- Lake
- Salt Lake
- Intermittent Lake
- Reservoir
- Swamp, Pond
- Canal
- Glacier
- Ice Shelf, Pack Ice
- Ocean
- Sea
- Gulf, Bay
- Strait, Fjord
- Lagoon
- Bank
- Seamount
- Tablemount
- Ridge
- Shelf
- Basin
- Escarpment, Sea Scarp
- Fracture
- Trench, Abyss
- National Park, Reserve
- Point of Interest
- Recreation Site
- Cave, Cavern
- Historic Site
- Ruins
- Wall, Walls
- Church, Abbey
- Temple
- Scientific Station
- Airport
- Port
- Lighthouse
- Mine
- Tunnel
- Dam, Bridge

Index Symbols

- [1] Independent Nation
- [2] State, Region
- [3] District, County
- [4] Municipality
- [5] Colony, Dependency
- Continent
- Physical Region
- Historical or Cultural Region
- Mount, Mountain
- Volcano
- Hill
- Mountains, Mountain Range
- Hills, Escarpment
- Plateau, Upland
- Pass, Gap
- Plain, Lowland
- Delta
- Salt Flat
- Valley, Canyon
- Crater, Cave
- Karst Features
- Depression
- Polder
- Desert, Dunes
- Forest, Woods
- Heath, Steppe
- Oasis
- Cape, Point
- Coast, Beach
- Cliff
- Peninsula
- Isthmus
- Sandbank
- Island
- Atoll
- Rock, Reef
- Islands, Archipelago
- Rocks, Reefs
- Coral Reef
- Well, Spring
- Geyser
- River, Stream
- Waterfall Rapids
- River Mouth, Estuary
- Lake
- Salt Lake
- Intermittent Lake
- Reservoir
- Swamp, Pond
- Canal
- Glacier
- Ice Shelf, Pack Ice
- Ocean
- Sea
- Gulf, Bay
- Strait, Fjord
- Lagoon
- Bank
- Seamount
- Tablemount
- Ridge
- Shelf
- Basin
- Escarpment, Sea Scarp
- Fracture
- Trench, Abyss
- National Park, Reserve
- Point of Interest
- Recreation Site
- Cave, Cavern
- Historic Site
- Ruins
- Wall, Walls
- Church, Abbey
- Temple
- Scientific Station
- Airport
- Port
- Lighthouse
- Mine
- Tunnel
- Dam, Bridge

Bogcang Zangbo 27 Ee 31.56N 87.24 E
Bogda Feng 27 Ec 43.45N 88.32 E
Bogdan 15 Hg 42.37N 24.28 E
Bogdanovka 16 Mi 41.15N 43.36 E
Bogda Shan 21 Ke 43.35N 90.00 E
Bogen 7 Db 68.32N 17.00 E
Bogenfels 37 Be 27.23S 15.22 E
Bogense 8 Di 55.34N 10.06 E
Boggeragh Mountains/An Bhograch 9 Ei 52.05N 9.00W
Boggy Peak 51d Bb 17.03N 61.51W
Boghar 13 Oi 35.55N 2.43 E
Boghni 13 Ph 36.32N 3.57 E
Bogia 60 Ch 4.16S 144.58 E
Bognor Regis 12 Bd 50.47N 0.39W
Bogny-sur-Meuse 12 Ge 49.54N 4.43 E
Bogoduhov 16 Id 50.12N 35.31 E
Bogomila 15 Eh 41.36N 21.28 E
Bogor 22 Mj 6.35S 106.47 E
Bogoridick 19 De 53.50N 38.08 E
Bogorodčany 10 Uh 48.45N 24.40 E
Bogorodsk 7 Kh 56.09N 43.32 E
Bogorodskoje [R.S.F.S.R.] 7 Mh 57.51N 50.48 E
Bogorodskoje [R.S.F.S.R.] 20 Jf 52.22N 140.30 E
Bogotá 53 Ie 4.36N 74.05W
Bogotol 20 De 56.17N 89.43 E
Bogøy 7 Dc 67.54N 15.11 E
Bogra 25 Hd 24.51N 89.22 E
Bogučany 20 Ee 58.23N 97.39 E
Bogučar 16 Le 49.57N 40.33 E
Bogué 32 Ef 16.36N 14.15W
Boguševsk 7 Hi 54.50N 30.13 E
Boguslav 19 Df 49.33N 30.54 E
Bo Hai=Chihli, Gulf of- (EN) 21 Nf 38.30N 120.00 E
Bohai Haixia 27 Ld 38.00N 121.30 E
Bohain-en-Vermandois 12 Fe 49.59N 3.27 E
Bohemia (EN)=Čechy 5 Hf 50.00N 14.30 E
Bohemia (EN)=Čechy 10 Kf 50.00N 14.30 E
Bohemian Forest (EN)= Böhmerwald 5 Hf 49.00N 13.30 E
Bohemian Forest (EN)= Český Les 10 Ig 49.50N 12.30 E
Bohemian Forest (EN)= Oberpfälzer Wald 10 Ig 49.50N 12.30 E
Bohemian Forest (EN)= Šumava 5 Hf 49.00N 13.30 E
Bohicon 34 Fd 7.12N 2.04 E
Böhmerwald=Bohemian Forest (EN) 5 Hf 49.00N 13.30 E
Bohmte 12 Kb 52.22N 8.19 E
Bohodoyou 34 Dd 9.46N 9.04W
Bohol 21 Oi 9.50N 124.10 E
Böhönye 10 Nj 46.24N 17.24 E
Bohor 14 Jd 46.04N 15.26 E
Bohu/Bagrax 27 Ec 41.58N 86.29 E
Bohus 8 Eg 57.51N 12.01 E
Bohuslän 8 Df 58.15N 11.50 E
Boiaçu 54 Fd 0.27S 61.46W
Boiano 14 Ii 41.29N 14.29 E
Boina 30 Lj 16.00S 46.30 E
Bois, Lac des- 42 Ec 66.50N 125.15W
Bois, Rio dos- [Braz.] 55 Gd 18.35S 50.02W
Bois, Rio dos- [Braz.] 55 Ha 13.55S 49.51W
Bois Blanc Island 44 Ec 45.45N 84.28W
Boischaut 11 Hh 46.40N 1.45 E
Boise 39 He 43.37N 116.13W
Boise City 45 Eh 36.44N 102.31W
Boise River 46 Ge 43.49N 117.01W
Boissay 12 De 49.31N 1.21 E
Boissevain 42 Hg 49.14N 100.03W
Boizenburg 10 Gc 53.23N 10.43 E
Bojador, Cabo- 30 Ff 26.08N 14.30W
Bojana 15 Ch 41.52N 19.22 E
Bojanowo 10 Me 51.42N 16.44 E
Bojarka 19 De 50.19N 30.20 E
Bojčinovci 15 Gf 43.28N 23.20 E
Bojnūrd 23 Ib 37.28N 57.19 E
Bojonegoro 26 Fh 7.09S 111.52 E
Bojuru 55 Gj 31.38S 51.26W
Bokatola 36 Cc 0.38S 18.46 E
Boké 34 Cc 10.56N 14.13W
Bokhara River 59 Je 29.55S 146.42 E
Bokn 8 Ae 59.15N 5.25 E
Boknafjorden 5 Gd 59.10N 5.35 E
Boko 36 Bc 4.47S 14.38 E
Bokol Mayo 35 Ge 4.31N 41.32 E
Bokoro 35 Bc 12.23N 17.03 E
Bokote 36 Dc 0.05S 20.08 E
Bokpyin 25 Jf 11.16N 98.46 E
Boksitogorsk 19 Dd 59.29N 33.52 E
Bokungu 36 Dc 0.41S 22.19 E
Bol [Chad] 35 Ac 13.30N 14.41 E
Bol [Yugo.] 14 Kg 43.16N 16.40 E
Bola, Bahr- 35 Bd 9.50N 18.59 E
Bolama 34 Bc 11.35N 15.28W
Bolands 51d Bb 17.02N 61.53W
Bolaños, Río- 48 Gg 21.14N 104.08W
Bolattau, Gora- 18 Ha 46.44N 71.54 E
Bolayir 15 Ji 40.31N 26.45 E
Bolbec 11 Ge 49.34N 0.29 E
Bolda 16 Pg 45.58N 48.35 E
Bole [Eth.] 35 Fd 6.37N 37.22 E
Bole [Ghana] 34 Ed 9.02N 2.29W
Bole/Bortala 27 Dc 44.59N 81.57 E
Bolehov 16 Ce 49.03N 23.50 E
Bolesławiec 10 Le 51.16N 15.34 E
Bolgatanga 31 Gg 10.47N 0.51W
Bolgrad 16 Fg 45.40N 28.38 E
Bolhov 19 De 53.30N 36.01 E
Boli 27 Nb 45.46N 130.31 E
Bolia 36 Cc 1.36S 18.23 E
Boliden 7 Ed 64.52N 20.23 E
Bolinao, Cape- 26 Gc 16.22N 119.50 E
Bolintin Vale 15 Ie 44.27N 25.46 E
Bolívar [Col.] [2] 54 Db 9.00N 74.40W
Bolivar [Mo.-U.S.] 45 Jh 37.37N 93.25W
Bolivar [Tn.-U.S.] 44 Ch 35.15N 88.59W
Bolívar [Ven.] [2] 54 Fb 6.20N 63.30W
Bolívar, Cerro- 54 Fb 7.28N 63.25W
Bolívar, Pico- 52 Ie 8.30N 71.02W
Bolivia [1] 53 Jg 17.00S 65.00W
Bolivia, Altiplano de- 52 Jg 18.00S 68.00W
Boljevac 15 Ef 43.50N 21.58 E
Bollendorf 12 Ie 49.51N 6.22 E
Bollène 11 Kj 44.17N 4.45 E
Bollnäs 7 Df 61.21N 16.25 E
Bollon 59 Je 28.02S 147.28 E
Bollstabruk 8 Ga 63.00N 17.41 E
Bollullos par del Condado 13 Fg 37.20N 6.32W
Bolmen 7 Ch 56.55N 13.40 E
Bolnisi 16 Ni 41.28N 44.31 E
Bolobo 36 Cc 2.10S 16.14 E
Bolodek 20 If 53.43N 133.09 E
Bologna 6 Hg 44.29N 11.20 E
Bolognesi 54 Df 10.01S 74.05W
Bologoje 6 Jd 57.54N 34.02 E
Bolohovo 16 Jb 54.05N 37.52 E
Bolomba 36 Cb 0.29N 19.12 E
Bolombo 36 Dc 3.59S 21.22 E
Bolon 20 Ig 49.58N 136.04 E
Bolotnoje 20 De 55.41N 84.33 E
Bolovens, Plateau des- 25 Le 15.20N 106.20 E
Bolšaja Balahnja 20 Fb 73.37N 107.05 E
Bolšaja Berestovica 10 Uc 53.09N 24.02 E
Bolšaja Černigovka 7 Mj 52.08N 50.48 E
Bolšaja Glušica 7 Mj 52.24N 50.29 E
Bolšaja Ižora 8 Me 59.55N 29.40 E
Bolšaja Kinel 7 Mj 53.14N 50.32 E
Bolšaja Koksaga 7 Lh 56.07N 47.48 E
Bolšaja Kuonamka 20 Gc 70.50N 113.20 E
Bolšaja Oju 17 Jb 69.42N 60.42 E
Bolšaja Rogovaja 17 Jc 66.30N 60.40 E
Bolšaja Synja 17 Id 65.58N 58.01 E
Bolšaja Tap 17 Lg 59.55N 65.42 E
Bolšaja Ussurka 20 Ig 46.00N 133.30 E
Bolšaja Vladimirovka 19 He 50.53N 79.30 E
Bolšakovo 8 Ij 54.50N 21.36 E
Bolsena 14 Fh 42.39N 11.59 E
Bolsena, Lago di- 14 Fh 42.35N 11.55 E
Bolšerečje 19 Hd 56.06N 74.38 E
Bolšereck 20 Kf 52.22N 156.24 E
Bolšeustikinskoje 17 Ii 55.57N 58.20 E
Bolševik 20 Jd 62.40N 147.30 E
Bolševik, Ostrov-=Bolshevik Island (EN) 21 Mb 78.40N 102.30 E
Bolšezemelskaja Tundra 19 Fb 67.30N 58.30 E
Bolshevik Island (EN)= Bolševik, Ostrov- 21 Mb 78.40N 102.30 E
Bolšije Uki 19 Hd 56.57N 72.37 E
Bolšoj Anjuj 20 Lc 68.30N 160.50 E
Bolšoj Begičev, Ostrov- 20 Gb 74.20N 112.30 E
Bolšoj Berezovy, Ostrov- 8 Md 60.15N 28.35 E
Bolšoj Boktybaj, Gora- [Kaz.-U.S.S.R.] 19 Ff 48.30N 58.20 E
Bolšoj Boktybaj, Gora- [U.S.S.R.] 16 Ue 48.30N 58.25 E
Bolšoj Bolvanski Nos, Mys- 17 Ia 70.27N 59.05 E
Bolšoj Čeremšan 7 Li 54.12N 49.40 E
Bolšoje Muraškino 7 Ki 55.47N 44.46 E
Bolšoje Vlasjevo 20 Jf 53.25N 140.55 E
Bolšoje Zagorje 8 Mg 57.47N 28.58 E
Bolšoj Gašun 16 Mf 47.22N 42.42 E
Bolšoj Ik 17 Hj 51.47N 56.20 E
Bolšoj Irgiz 19 Ee 52.01N 47.24 E
Bolšoj Jenisej 20 Ef 51.40N 94.26 E
Bolšoj Jugan 19 Hc 60.55N 73.40 E
Bolšoj Kamen 20 Ih 43.08N 132.28 E
Bolšoj Klimecki, Ostrov- 7 Ie 62.00N 35.15 E
Bolšoj Kujalnik 16 Gf 46.46N 30.38 E
Bolšoj Kumak 16 Ud 51.22N 58.55 E
Bolšoj Ljahovski, Ostrov- 20 Jb 73.35N 142.00 E
Bolšoj Murta 20 Ee 56.55N 93.10 E
Bolšoj Nimnyr 20 He 58.08N 125.45 E
Bolšoj Pit 20 Ee 59.02N 91.40 E
Bolšoj Tjuters, Ostrov- 8 Le 59.50N 27.10 E
Bolšoj Uluj 20 Ee 56.45N 90.46 E
Bolšoj Uvat, Ozero- 17 Oh 57.35N 70.30 E
Bolšoj Uzen 5 Kf 48.50N 49.40 E
Bolsón, Cerro del- 52 Jh 27.13S 66.06W
Bolšovcy 10 Ug 49.08N 24.47 E
Bolsward 12 Ha 53.04N 5.30 E
Boltaña 13 Mb 42.27N 0.04 E
Bolton 9 Kh 53.35N 2.26W
Bolu 23 Da 40.44N 31.37 E
Bolu Dağları 24 Eb 41.05N 32.05 E
Bolungarvik 7a Aa 66.09N 23.15W
Boluntay 27 Fd 36.29N 92.18 E
Bolva 16 Ic 53.17N 34.20 E
Bolvadin 24 Dc 38.42N 31.04 E
Bolzano/Bozen 6 Hf 46.31N 11.22 E
Bom, Rio- 55 Gf 23.56S 51.44W
Boma 31 Ii 5.51S 13.03 E
Bomassa 36 Cb 2.12N 16.12 E
Bombala 59 Jg 36.54S 149.14 E
Bombarral 13 Ce 39.16N 9.09W
Bombay 22 Jh 18.58N 72.50 E
Bomberai, Jazirah- 26 Jg 3.00S 133.00 E
Bombo 36 Fb 0.35N 32.32 E
Bomboma 36 Cb 2.26N 18.57 E
Bom Comércio 54 Ee 9.45S 65.54W
Bom Conselho 54 Ke 9.10S 36.41W
Bom Despacho 54 Ig 19.43S 45.15W
Bomdila 25 Ic 27.16N 92.23 E
Bomi/Bowo 27 Ge 30.02N 95.39 E
Bomi Hills 31 Fh 6.52N 10.45W
Bomili 36 Eb 1.40N 27.01 E
Bom Jardim de Goiás 55 Fc 16.17S 52.07W
Bom Jardim de Minas 55 Je 21.57S 44.11W
Bom Jesus 55 Gi 28.42S 50.24W
Bom Jesus da Lapa 53 Lg 13.15S 43.25W
Bom Jesus de Goiás 55 Hd 18.12S 49.37W
Bømlafjorden 8 Ae 59.40N 5.20 E
Bømlo 7 Ag 59.45N 5.10 E
Bomokandi 36 Eb 3.30N 26.08 E
Bomongo 36 Cb 1.22N 18.21 E
Bom Retiro 55 Hh 27.48S 49.31W
Bom Sucesso 55 Je 21.02S 44.46W
Bomu 30 Jh 4.08N 22.26 E
Bomu (EN)=Mbomou 30 Jh 4.08N 22.26 E
Bomu (EN)=Mbomou [3] 35 Cd 5.30N 23.30 E
Bon, Cape- (EN)=Ṭīb, Ra's Aṭ- 30 Ie 37.05N 11.03 E
Bona, Mount- 40 Kd 61.20N 141.50W
Bonaire 54 Ea 12.10N 68.15W
Bonaire Basin (EN) 50 Cg 11.25N 67.30W
Bonampak 48 Ni 16.43N 91.05W
Bonanza 49 Ef 14.01N 84.35W
Bonanza Peak 46 Eb 48.14N 120.52W
Bonao 49 Ld 18.56N 70.25W
Bonaparte, Mount- 46 Fb 48.45N 119.08W
Bonaparte Archipelago 57 Df 14.20S 125.20 E
Bonaparte Lake 46 Ea 51.16N 120.35W
Bonaparte Rocks 51p Cb 12.24N 61.30W
Bonasse 50 Fg 10.05N 61.52W
Bonavista 42 Mg 48.39N 53.07W
Bonavista Bay 42 Mg 49.00N 53.20W
Bon-Cagan-Nur 27 Gb 45.35N 99.15 E
Bondeno 14 Ff 44.53N 11.25 E
Bondo 31 Jh 3.49N 23.40 E
Bondoukou 34 Ed 8.02N 2.48W
Bondoukou [3] 34 Ed 8.20N 2.55W
Bondowoso 26 Fh 7.55S 113.49 E
Bone, Gulf of- (EN)=Bone, Teluk- 21 Oj 4.00S 120.40 E
Bone, Teluk-=Bone, Gulf of- (EN) 21 Oj 4.00S 120.40 E
Bone Bay 51a Db 18.45N 64.22W
Bonelohe 26 Hh 5.48S 120.27 E
Bönen 12 Jc 51.36N 7.46 E
Bone Rate, Kepulauan- 26 Hh 7.00S 121.00 E
Bone Rate, Pulau- 26 Hh 7.22S 121.08 E
Bonete, Cerro- 56 Gc 27.51S 68.47W
Bong 34 Cd 6.49N 10.19W
Bong [3] 34 Dd 7.00N 9.40W
Bonga 35 Fd 7.16N 36.14 E
Bongabong 26 Hd 12.45N 121.29 E
Bongandanga 36 Db 1.30N 21.03 E
Bongo, Massif des- 30 Jh 8.40N 22.25 E
Bongolava 37 Hc 18.35S 45.20 E
Bongor 31 Ig 10.17N 15.22 E
Bongouanou [3] 34 Ed 6.43N 4.12W
Bongouanou 34 Ed 6.39N 4.12W
Bonham 45 Hj 33.35N 96.11W
Bonheiden 12 Gc 51.02N 4.32 E
Bonhomme, Col du- 11 Nf 48.10N 7.06 E
Bonhomme, Pic- 49 Kd 19.05N 72.15W
Bonifacio 11a Bb 41.23N 9.09 E
Bonifacio, Bocche di-=Bonifacio, Strait of- (EN) 5 Gg 41.18N 9.15 E
Bonifacio, Strait of- (EN)= Bonifacio, Bocche di- 5 Gg 41.18N 9.15 E
Bonifati, Capo- 14 Jk 39.33N 15.52 E
Bonin Basin (EN) 60 Bb 29.00N 137.00 E
Bonin Islands (EN)= Ogasawara-Shotō 21 Qg 27.00N 142.10 E
Bonin Trench (EN) 3 If 30.00N 145.00 E
Bonita Springs 44 Gl 26.21N 81.47W
Bonito [Braz.] 55 Jb 15.20S 44.46W
Bonito [Braz.] 55 De 21.08S 56.28W
Bonito, Pico- 47 Ge 15.38N 86.55W
Bonito, Rio- [Braz.] 55 Hb 15.18S 49.36W
Bonito, Rio- [Braz.] 55 Gc 16.31S 51.23W
Bonn 6 Ge 50.44N 7.06 E
Bonn-Bad Godesberg 10 Df 50.41N 7.09 E
Bonnebosq 12 Ce 49.12N 0.05 E
Bonnechère River 44 Ic 45.31N 76.33W
Bonners Ferry 46 Gb 48.41N 116.18W
Bonnet, Lac du- 45 Ia 50.22N 95.55W
Bonnétable 11 Gf 48.11N 0.26 E
Bonnet Plume 42 Ec 65.53N 134.58W
Bonneval 11 Hf 48.11N 1.24 E
Bonneville 11 Mh 46.05N 6.25 E
Bonneville Salt Flats 46 If 40.45N 113.50W
Bonnières-sur-Seine 12 De 49.02N 1.35 E
Bonningues-lès-Ardres 12 Ed 50.47N 2.01 E
Bonny 34 Ge 4.25N 7.10 E
Bono 14 Dj 40.25N 9.02 E
Bō-no-Misaki 29 Bf 31.15N 130.13 E
Bonorva 14 Cj 40.25N 8.46 E
Bontang 26 Gf 0.08N 117.30 E
Bonthain 26 Gh 5.32S 119.56 E
Bonthe 34 Cd 7.32N 12.30W
Bontoc 26 Hc 17.05N 120.58 E
Bonyhád 10 Oj 46.18N 18.32 E
Boo, Kepulauan- 26 Ig 1.12S 129.24 E
Boola 34 Dd 8.22N 8.43W
Booligal 59 If 33.52S 144.53 E
Boone [Ia.-U.S.] 45 Je 42.04N 93.53W
Boone [N.C.-U.S.] 44 Gg 36.13N 81.41W
Booneville [Ar.-U.S.] 45 Ji 35.08N 93.55W
Booneville [Ms.-U.S.] 45 Li 34.39N 88.34W
Boon Point 51d Bb 17.10N 61.50W
Boonville [In.-U.S.] 44 Df 38.03N 87.16W
Boonville [Mo.-U.S.] 45 Jg 38.58N 92.44W
Boos 12 De 49.23N 1.12 E
Boothia, Gulf of- 38 Jb 71.00N 91.00W
Boothia Peninsula 38 Jb 70.30N 95.00W
Boot Reefs 60 Cj 10.00S 144.35 E
Booué 31 Ii 0.06S 11.56 E
Bophuthatswana [1] 37 De 26.00S 25.30 E
Bopolu 34 Cd 7.04N 10.29W
Boppard 12 Jd 50.14N 7.36 E
Boquerón [3] 55 Bf 23.00S 61.00W
Boquerón 51a Ab 18.03N 67.09W
Boquilla, Presa de la- 48 Gd 27.30N 105.30W
Boquillas del Carmen 48 Hc 29.17N 102.53W
Bor [Czech.] 10 Ig 49.43N 12.47 E
Bor [R.S.F.S.R.] 19 Ed 56.23N 44.07 E
Bor [Sud.] 31 Kh 6.12N 31.33 E
Bor [Swe.] 8 Fg 57.07N 14.10 E
Bor [Tur.] 24 Fd 37.54N 34.34 E
Bor [Yugo.] 15 Fe 44.06N 22.06 E
Bora-Bora, Ile- 57 Lf 16.30S 151.45W
Borah Peak 38 He 44.08N 113.14W
Boraldaj 18 Gc 42.30N 69.05 E
Bora Marina 14 Jm 37.56N 15.55 E
Bōramo 35 Gd 9.58N 43.07 E
Borås 7 Ch 57.43N 12.55 E
Borāzjān 24 Nh 29.16N 51.12 E
Borba [Braz.] 54 Gd 4.24S 59.35W
Borba [Port.] 13 Ef 38.48N 7.27W
Borborema, Planalto da- 52 Mf 7.00S 37.00W
Borca 15 Ib 47.11N 25.46 E
Borcea 15 Ke 44.20N 27.45 E
Borcea, Braţul- 15 Ke 44.40N 27.53 E
Borchgrevink Coast 66 Kf 73.00S 171.00 E
Borçka 24 Ib 41.22N 41.40 E
Borculo 12 Ib 52.07N 6.31 E
Borda da Mata, Serra- 55 Ie 21.18S 47.06W
Bordeaux 6 Fg 44.50N 0.34W
Borden 42 Ga 78.30N 110.30W
Borden Peninsula 38 Kb 73.00N 83.00W
Borders [3] 9 Kf 55.35N 3.00W
Bordertown 58 Fh 36.19S 140.47 E
Bordighera 14 Bg 43.46N 7.39 E
Bordj Bou Arreridj 32 Hb 36.04N 4.46 E
Bordj el Emir Abdelkader 13 Oi 35.52N 2.16 E
Bordj Fly Sainte Marie 32 Gd 27.18N 2.59W
Bordj-Menaïel 13 Ph 36.44N 3.43 E
Bordj Messouda 32 Ic 30.12N 9.25 E
Bordj Moktar 31 Hf 21.20N 0.56 E
Bordj Omar Driss 31 Hf 28.09N 6.49 E
Bord Khūn-e Now 24 Nh 28.03N 51.28 E
Bordon Camp 12 Bc 51.07N 0.51W
Boreal, Chaco- 52 Kh 23.00S 60.00W
Boren 8 Ff 58.35N 15.10 E
Borensberg 8 Ff 58.34N 15.17 E
Borgå/Porvoo 7 Ff 60.24N 25.40 E
Borgarnes 7a Bb 64.32N 21.55W
Børgefjell 7 Cd 65.23N 13.50 E
Borgentreich 12 Lc 51.34N 9.15 E
Borger [Neth.] 12 Ib 52.55N 6.48 E
Borger [Tx.-U.S.] 43 Gd 35.39N 101.24W
Borgholm 7 Dh 56.53N 16.39 E
Borghorst, Steinfurt- 12 Jb 52.08N 7.25 E
Borgia 14 Kl 38.49N 16.30 E
Borgloon 12 Hd 50.48N 5.20 E
Borgomanero 14 Ce 45.42N 8.28 E
Borgorose 14 Hh 42.11N 13.15 E
Borgo San Dalmazzo 14 Bf 44.20N 7.30 E
Borgo San Lorenzo 14 Fg 43.57N 11.23 E
Borgosesia 14 Ce 45.43N 8.16 E
Borgou [3] 34 Fc 10.30N 2.50 E
Borgo Val di Taro 14 Df 44.29N 9.46 E
Borgo Valsugana 14 Fd 46.03N 11.27 E
Borgu 30 Hg 10.35N 3.40 E
Borgworm/Waremme 11 Ld 50.42N 5.15 E
Bori 34 Ge 4.42N 7.21 E
Borinquen, Punta- 51a Ab 18.30N 67.10W
Borislav 19 Cf 49.18N 23.27 E
Borisoglebsk 6 Ke 51.23N 42.06 E
Borisov 19 Ce 54.15N 28.30 E
Borisovka 16 Jd 50.36N 36.06 E
Borispol 19 De 50.23N 30.59 E
Bo River 35 Dd 6.48N 27.55 E
Borja 44 Lf 44.31N 16.29 E
Borja [Peru] 54 Cd 4.26S 77.33W
Borja [Sp.] 13 Kc 41.50N 1.32W
Borjas Blancas/Les Borges Blanques 13 Mc 41.31N 0.52 E
Borken 10 Ce 51.51N 6.52 E
Borkou 30 Ig 18.15N 18.50 E
Borkou-Ennedi-Tibesti [3] 35 Bb 18.00N 19.00 E
Borkoviči 8 Mi 55.38N 28.23 E
Borkum 10 Cc 53.35N 6.41 E
Borlänge 7 Df 60.29N 15.25 E
Borlu 24 Cc 38.44N 28.27 E
Bormida 14 Cf 44.56N 8.40 E
Bormio 14 Ed 46.28N 10.22 E
Born 11 Fj 44.30N 1.00W
Borna 10 Ie 51.07N 12.30 E
Borndiep 12 Ha 53.25N 5.35 E
Borne 12 Ib 52.18N 6.45 E
Borneo/Kalimantan 21 Ni 1.00N 114.00 E
Bornheim 12 Id 50.46N 7.00 E
Bornholm 5 Hd 55.10N 15.00 E
Bornholm [2] 8 Fi 55.10N 15.00 E
Bornos 13 Gh 36.48N 5.44W
Bornova, İzmir- 24 Bc 38.27N 27.14 E
Bornu [2] 34 Hc 12.00N 12.40 E
Bornu 30 Ig 12.30N 13.00 E
Boro 30 Jh 8.52N 26.11 E
Borodino [R.S.F.S.R.] 7 Ii 55.32N 35.49 E
Borodino [R.S.F.S.R.] 20 Ee 55.57N 95.03 E
Borodinskoje 8 Md 61.00N 29.29 E
Borogoncy 20 Id 62.39N 131.08 E
Borohoro Shan 21 Ke 42.00N 85.00 E
Boromo 34 Ec 11.45N 2.56W
Borongan 26 Id 11.37N 125.26 E
Borotou 34 Dd 8.44N 7.30W
Borovan 15 Gf 43.26N 23.45 E
Borovec 15 Gg 42.16N 23.35 E
Boroviči 19 Dd 58.24N 33.56 E
Borovici 8 Mg 57.58N 29.47 E
Borovljanka 20 Df 52.38N 84.35 E
Borovo 14 Me 45.24N 18.59 E
Borovski 19 Gd 57.03N 65.44 E
Borovskoj 19 Ge 53.48N 64.17 E
Borrachas, Islas- 50 Dg 10.18N 64.44W
Borrān 35 Hc 10.11N 48.53 E
Borrby 8 Fi 55.27N 14.10 E
Borroloola 58 Ef 16.04S 136.17 E
Borş 15 Eb 47.07N 21.49 E
Borşa 15 Hb 47.39N 24.40 E
Borščovočny Hrebet= Borshchovochny Range (EN) 20 Gf 52.00N 118.30 E
Borsec 15 Ic 46.57N 25.34 E
Borshchovochny Range (EN) =Borščovočny Hrebet 20 Gf 52.00N 118.30 E
Borsod-Abaúj-Zemplén [2] 10 Qh 48.15N 21.00 E
Bortala/Bole 27 Dc 44.59N 81.57 E
Bortala He 27 Dc 44.53N 82.45 E
Bort-les-Orgues 11 Ii 45.24N 2.30 E
Borūjen 24 Ng 31.59N 51.18 E
Borūjerd 23 Gc 33.54N 48.46 E
Borzja 22 Nd 50.24N 116.31 E
Borzna 16 Hd 51.15N 32.29 E
Boržomi 16 Mi 41.50N 43.25 E
Borzsöny 10 Oi 47.55N 19.00 E
Borzyszkowy 10 Nb 54.03N 17.22 E
Bosa 14 Cj 40.18N 8.30 E
Bosanska Dubica 14 Ke 45.11N 16.48 E
Bosanska Gradiška 14 Le 45.09N 17.15 E
Bosanska Krupa 14 Kf 44.53N 16.10 E
Bosanski Brod 14 Me 45.08N 18.01 E
Bosanski Novi 14 Ke 45.03N 16.22 E
Bosanski Petrovac 14 Kf 44.34N 16.21 E
Bosanski Šamac 14 Me 45.04N 18.28 E
Bosansko Grahovo 23 Ff 44.11N 16.22 E
Bōsāso 31 Lg 11.13N 49.08 E
Bosavi, Mount- 59 Ia 6.35S 142.50 E
Bosbeek 12 Hc 51.06N 5.48 E
Bose 22 Mg 24.01N 106.32 E
Boshan 27 Kd 36.30N 117.50 E
Boshrūyeh 24 Qf 33.53N 57.26 E
Bosilegrad 15 Fg 42.30N 22.28 E
Bosingfeld, Extertal- 12 Lb 52.04N 9.07 E
Bosna 14 Me 45.04N 18.28 E
Bosna 15 Kg 42.11N 27.27 E
Bosna=Bosnia (EN) 5 Hg 44.00N 18.00 E
Bosna = Bosnia (EN) 14 Lf 44.00N 18.00 E
Bosna i Hercegovina = Bosnia-Hercegovina (EN) [2] 14 Lf 44.15N 17.50 E
Bosnia (EN) = Bosna 14 Lf 44.00N 18.00 E
Bosnia (EN)=Bosna 5 Hg 44.00N 18.00 E
Bosnia-Hercegovina (EN) = Bosna i Hercegovina [2] 14 Lf 44.15N 17.50 E
Bosnik 26 Kg 1.10S 136.14 E
Bošnjakovo 20 Jg 49.41N 142.10 E
Bosobolo 36 Cb 4.11N 19.54 E
Bōsō-Hantō 28 Pg 35.20N 140.10 E
Bosporus (EN)=İstanbul Boğazi 5 Ig 41.00N 29.00 E
Bosque Bonito 48 Gb 30.42N 105.06W
Bossangoa 31 Ih 6.29N 17.27 E
Bossé Bangou 34 Fc 13.21N 1.18 E
Bossembélé 35 Bd 5.16N 17.39 E
Bossemtélé II 35 Bd 5.41N 16.38 E
Bossier City 43 Ie 32.31N 93.43W
Bosso 34 Hc 13.42N 13.19 E
Bosso, Dallol- 30 Hg 12.25N 2.50 E
Bossut, Cape- 59 Ec 18.43S 121.38 E
Bostān 25 Db 30.26N 67.02 E
Bostānābād 24 Ld 37.50N 46.50 E
Bosten/Bagrax Hu 21 Ke 42.00N 87.00 E
Boston [Eng.-U.K.] 9 Mi 52.59N 0.01W
Boston [Ma.-U.S.] 39 Le 42.21N 71.04W
Boston Bar 46 Eb 49.52N 121.26W
Boston Deeps 12 Ca 53.00N 0.15 E
Boston Mountains 43 Id 35.50N 93.20W
Botan 24 Id 37.44N 41.48 E
Botas, Ribeirão das- 55 Fe 20.26S 53.43W
Botesdale 12 Db 52.20N 1.01 E
Botev 5 Ig 42.43N 24.55 E
Botevgrad 15 Gg 42.54N 23.47 E
Bothnia, Gulf of- (EN)= Bottniska viken 5 Hc 63.00N 20.00 E
Bothnia, Gulf of- (EN)= Pohjanlahti 5 Hc 63.00N 20.00 E
Boticas 13 Ec 41.41N 7.40W
Botletle 37 Cd 21.07S 24.42 E
Botlih 16 Oh 42.41N 46.13 E
Botna 15 Mc 46.48N 29.30 E
Botoşani [2] 15 Jb 47.40N 26.43 E
Botoşani 15 Jb 47.45N 26.40 E
Botrange 11 Md 50.30N 6.08 E
Botswana [1] 31 Jk 22.00S 24.00 E
Botte Donato 14 Kk 39.17N 16.27 E
Bottineau 43 Gb 48.50N 100.27W
Bottniska viken=Bothnia, Gulf of- (EN) 5 Hc 63.00N 20.00 E
Bottrop 10 Ce 51.31N 6.55 E
Botucatu 56 Kb 22.52S 48.26W
Botucatu, Serra de- 55 Hf 23.00S 48.20W
Botwood 42 Lg 49.08N 55.21W
Bouaflé 34 Dd 6.59N 5.45W
Bouaflé [3] 34 Dd 7.03N 5.48W
Bouaké 31 Gh 7.41N 5.02W
Bouaké [3] 34 Dd 7.45N 5.02W
Bou Anane 32 Gc 32.02N 3.03W
Bouar 31 Ih 5.57N 15.36 E
Bou Arfa 32 Gc 32.32N 1.57W
Boubín 10 Jh 48.58N 13.50 E
Bouca 31 Ih 6.30N 18.17 E
Bouchain 12 Fd 50.17N 3.19 E
Bouchegouf 14 Bn 36.28N 7.44 E
Bouche Island 51k Bb 13.57N 60.53W
Bouches-du-Rhône [3] 11 Kk 43.30N 5.00 E
Boudenib 32 Gc 31.57N 3.36W
Boudeuse Cay 37b Bb 6.05S 52.51 E
Boû Djébéha 34 Eb 18.33N 2.45W
Bouenza [3] 36 Bc 3.00S 13.00 E
Boufarik 13 Oh 36.34N 2.55 E
Bougaa 13 Rh 36.20N 5.05 E
Bougainville Island 57 Ge 6.00S 155.00 E
Bougainville Reef 59 Jc 15.30S 147.05 E
Bougainville Strait [Ocn.] 63a Cb 6.40S 156.10 E
Bougainville Strait [Van.] 63b Cb 15.50S 167.10 E
Bougouni 31 Gg 11.25N 7.28W

Index Symbols

[1] Independent Nation
[2] State, Region
[3] District, County
[4] Municipality
[5] Colony, Dependency
Continent
Physical Region
Historical or Cultural Region
Mount, Mountain
Volcano
Hill
Mountains, Mountain Range
Hills, Escarpment
Plateau, Upland
Pass, Gap
Plain, Lowland
Delta
Salt Flat
Valley, Canyon
Crater, Cave
Karst Features
Depression
Polder
Desert, Dunes
Forest, Woods
Heath, Steppe
Oasis
Cape, Point
Coast, Beach
Cliff
Peninsula
Isthmus
Sandbank
Island
Atoll
Rock, Reef
Islands, Archipelago
Rocks, Reefs
Coral Reef
Well, Spring
Geyser
River, Stream
Waterfall Rapids
River Mouth, Estuary
Lake
Salt Lake
Intermittent Lake
Reservoir
Swamp, Pond
Canal
Glacier
Ice Shelf, Pack Ice
Ocean
Sea
Gulf, Bay
Strait, Fjord
Lagoon
Bank
Seamount
Tablemount
Ridge
Shelf
Basin
Escarpment, Sea Scarp
Fracture
Trench, Abyss
National Park, Reserve
Point of Interest
Recreation Site
Cave, Cavern
Historic Site
Ruins
Wall, Walls
Church, Abbey
Temple
Scientific Station
Airport
Port
Lighthouse
Mine
Tunnel
Dam, Bridge

Index Symbols

[1] Independent Nation
[2] State, Region
[3] District, County
[4] Municipality
[5] Colony, Dependency
Continent
Physical Region
Historical or Cultural Region
Mount, Mountain
Volcano
Hill
Mountains, Mountain Range
Hills, Escarpment
Plateau, Upland
Pass, Gap
Plain, Lowland
Delta
Salt Flat
Valley, Canyon
Crater, Cave
Karst Features
Depression
Polder
Desert, Dunes
Forest, Woods
Heath, Steppe
Oasis
Cape, Point
Coast, Beach
Cliff
Peninsula
Isthmus
Sandbank
Island
Atoll
Rock, Reef
Islands, Archipelago
Rocks, Reefs
Coral Reef
Well, Spring
Geyser
River, Stream
Waterfall Rapids
River Mouth, Estuary
Lake
Salt Lake
Intermittent Lake
Reservoir
Swamp, Pond
Canal
Glacier
Ice Shelf, Pack Ice
Ocean
Sea
Gulf, Bay
Strait, Fjord
Lagoon
Bank
Seamount
Tablemount
Ridge
Shelf
Basin
Escarpment, Sea Scarp
Fracture
Trench, Abyss
National Park, Reserve
Point of Interest
Recreation Site
Cave, Cavern
Historic Site
Ruins
Wall, Walls
Church, Abbey
Temple
Scientific Station
Airport
Port
Lighthouse
Mine
Tunnel
Dam, Bridge

Bruchhausen Vilsen	12	Lb	52.50N	9.01 E
Bruchmühlbach Miesau	12	Je	49.23N	7.28 E
Bruchsal	10	Eg	49.08N	8.36 E
Bruck an der Leitha	14	Kb	48.01N	16.46 E
Bruck an der Mur	14	Jc	47.25N	15.17 E
Brue	9	Kj	51.13N	3.00W
Bruges/Brugge	11	Jc	51.13N	3.14 E
Brugg	14	Cc	47.29N	8.12 E
Brugge/Bruges	11	Jc	51.13N	3.14 E
Brugge-Assebroek	12	Fc	51.12N	3.16 E
Brüggen	12	Ic	51.15N	6.11 E
Brugge-Sint-Andries	12	Fc	51.12N	3.10 E
Brühl [Ger.]	12	Ke	49.24N	8.32 E
Brühl [Ger.]	12	Id	50.50N	6.54 E
Bruine Bank = Brown Bank (EN)	12	Fb	52.35N	3.20 E
Bruin Point	43	Ed	39.39N	110.22W
Brule River	44	Cc	45.57N	88.12W
Brumado	54	Jf	14.13S	41.40W
Brummen	12	Ib	52.06N	6.10 E
Brummo	8	Ef	58.50N	13.40 E
Brumunddal	7	Cf	60.53N	10.56 E
Bruna	14	Eh	42.45N	10.53 E
Brune	12	Fe	49.45N	3.47 E
Bruneau	46	He	42.53N	115.48W
Bruneau River	46	He	42.57N	115.58W
Bruneck / Brunico	14	Fd	46.48N	11.56 E
Brunehamel	12	Ge	49.46N	4.11 E
Brunei [5]	22	Ni	4.30N	114.40 E
Brunei, Teluk-	21	Ni	5.05N	115.18 E
Brunette Downs	59	Hc	18.38S	135.57 E
Brunflo	8	Fa	63.05N	14.49 E
Brunico / Bruneck	14	Fd	46.48N	11.56 E
Brunna	8	Ge	59.52N	17.25 E
Brunner	62	De	42.26S	171.19 E
Brunner, Lake-	62	De	42.35S	171.25 E
Brunnsberg	8	Ec	61.17N	13.55 E
Brunsbüttel	10	Fc	53.54N	9.07 E
Brunssum	12	Hd	50.57N	5.57 E
Brunswick [Ga.-U.S.]	43	Ke	31.10N	81.29W
Brunswick [Me.-U.S.]	43	Nc	43.55N	69.58W
Brunswick, Peninsula de-	52	Ik	53.30S	71.25W
Brunswick Lake	44	Fa	49.00N	83.23W
Bruntál	10	Ng	49.59N	17.28 E
Bruny Island	59	Jh	43.30S	147.05 E
Brus	15	Ef	43.23N	21.02 E
Brus, Laguna de-	49	Ef	15.50N	84.35W
Brush	43	Gc	40.15N	103.37W
Brus Laguna	49	Ef	15.47N	84.35W
Brusque	56	Kc	27.06S	48.56W
Brussel/Bruxelles = Brussels (EN)	6	Ge	50.50N	4.20 E
Brussels (EN) = Brussel/Bruxelles	6	Ge	50.50N	4.20 E
Brussels (EN) = Bruxelles/Brussel	6	Ge	50.50N	4.20 E
Brusset, 'Erg-	34	Hb	18.55N	10.30 E
Brusturi	15	Fb	47.09N	22.15 E
Brusy	10	Nc	53.53N	17.45 E
Bruxelles/Brussel = Brussels (EN)	6	Ge	50.50N	4.20 E
Bruzual	50	Bh	8.03N	69.19W
Bryan [Oh.-U.S.]	44	Ee	41.30N	84.34W
Bryan [Tx.-U.S.]	43	He	30.40N	96.22W
Bryan Coast	66	Pf	73.35S	84.00W
Bryne	7	Ag	58.44N	5.39 E
Brza Palanka	15	Fe	44.28N	22.27 E
Brzava kanal	15	Dd	45.16N	20.49 E
Brzeg	10	Nf	50.52N	17.27 E
Brzeg Dolny	10	Me	51.15N	16.40 E
Brzeziny	10	Pe	51.48N	19.46 E
Brzozów	10	Sg	49.42N	22.02 E
Bsharrī	24	Ge	34.15N	36.01 E
Bū	12	Df	48.48N	1.30 E
Bua	8	Eg	57.14N	12.07 E
Buada Lagoon	64e	Ab	0.32S	166.54 E
Buala	58	Ge	8.10S	159.35 E
Bū al Ḥīdān, Wādī-	33	Cd	27.25N	19.22 E
Buapinang	26	Hg	4.46S	121.34 E
Buatan	26	Df	0.44N	101.51 E
Bū aṭ Ṭifl	33	Dd	28.54N	22.30 E
Bua Yai	25	Ke	15.34N	102.24 E
Bu'ayrāt al Ḥasūn	33	Cc	31.24N	15.44 E
Bubanza	36	Ec	3.06S	29.23 E
Bubaque	34	Bc	11.17N	15.50W
Būbiyan	24	Mh	29.45N	48.15 E
Bubu	36	Gd	6.03S	35.19 E
Bubye	37	Ed	22.20S	31.07 E
Buca	15	Kk	38.22N	27.11 E
Bučač	16	De	49.04N	25.23 E
Bucaćača	20	Gf	52.59N	116.55 E
Bucak	24	Dd	37.28N	30.36 E
Bucaramanga	53	Ie	7.08N	73.09W
Bucas Grande	26	Ie	9.40N	125.58 E
Buccament Bay	51n	Ba	13.12N	61.17W
Buccaneer Archipelago	59	Ec	16.17S	123.20 E
Bucecea	15	Jb	47.46N	26.26 E
Buchanan	31	Fh	5.53N	10.03W
Buchanan, Lake- [Austl.]	59	Jd	21.30S	145.50 E
Buchanan, Lake- [Tx.-U.S.]	45	Gk	30.48N	98.25W
Buchanan Bay	42	Ka	78.55N	75.00W
Buchan Gulf	42	Kb	71.48N	74.06W
Buchardo	56	Hd	34.43S	63.31W
Bucharest (EN) = Bucureşti	6	Ig	44.26N	26.06 E
Buchen	10	Fg	49.31N	9.20 E
Buchholz in der Nordheide	10	Fc	53.20N	9.52 E
Buchon, Point-	46	Ei	35.15N	120.54W
Buchs	14	Dc	47.10N	9.30 E
Buchy	12	De	49.35N	1.22 E
Bückeburg	12	Lb	52.16N	9.03 E
Buckeye	46	Ij	33.22N	112.35W
Buckhaven	9	Je	56.11N	3.03W
Buckie	9	Kd	57.40N	2.58W
Buckingham [Eng.-U.K.]	12	Bb	52.00N	0.59W
Buckingham [Que.-Can.]	44	Jc	45.35N	75.25W
Buckingham Bay	59	Hb	12.10S	135.46 E
Buckinghamshire [3]	9	Mj	51.50N	0.55W
Buckland	40	Gc	66.16N	161.20W
Buckle Island	66	Ke	66.47S	163.14 E
Buckley Bay	66	Je	68.16S	148.12 E
Bucks	9	Mj	51.50N	0.55W
Bucksport	44	Mc	44.34N	68.48W
Buco Zau	36	Bc	4.50S	12.33 E
Bu Craa	32	Ed	26.17N	12.46W
Bucureşti [2]	15	Je	44.30N	26.05 E
Bucureşti = Bucharest (EN)	6	Ig	44.26N	26.06 E
Bucy-lès-Pierrepont	12	Fe	49.39N	3.54 E
Bucyrus	44	Fe	40.47N	82.57W
Bud	7	Be	62.55N	6.55 E
Budacu, Vîrful-	15	Ib	47.07N	25.41 E
Buda-Koševelo	16	Gc	52.43N	30.39 E
Budapest [2]	10	Pi	47.30N	19.05 E
Budapest	6	Hf	47.30N	19.05 E
Búdardalur	7a	Bb	65.07N	21.46W
Budaun	25	Fc	28.03N	79.07 E
Budbud	35	He	4.13N	46.31 E
Budd Coast	66	He	66.30S	113.00 E
Buddusò	14	Di	40.35N	9.15 E
Bude [Eng.-U.K.]	9	Ik	50.50N	4.33W
Bude [Ms.-U.S.]	45	Kk	31.28N	90.51W
Bude Bay	9	Ik	50.50N	4.37W
Budel	12	Hc	51.16N	5.30 E
Budennovsk	19	Eg	44.45N	44.08 E
Budeşti	15	Je	44.14N	26.27 E
Budia	13	Jd	40.38N	2.45W
Büdingen	10	Ff	50.18N	9.07 E
Búdir	7a	Cb	64.56N	14.01W
Budjala	36	Cb	2.39N	19.42 E
Budkowiczanka	10	Nf	50.52N	17.33 E
Budogošč	7	Hg	59.19N	32.29 E
Budrio	14	Ff	44.32N	11.32 E
Budslav	8	Lj	54.49N	27.32 E
Budva	15	Bg	42.17N	18.51 E
Budyšin/Bautzen	10	Ke	51.11N	14.26 E
Budžjak	15	Lc	46.15N	28.45 E
Buea	34	Ge	4.09N	9.14 E
Buech	11	Lj	44.12N	5.57 E
Buenaventura [Col.]	53	Ie	3.53N	77.04W
Buenaventura [Mex.]	47	Cc	29.51N	107.29W
Buenaventura, Bahia de-	54	Cc	3.45N	77.15W
Buenavista	48	Ef	23.39N	109.42W
Buena Vista [Co.-U.S.]	45	Cg	38.50N	106.08W
Buena Vista [Mex.]	48	Mi	16.05N	93.00W
Buena Vista [Mex.]	48	Bb	31.10N	115.40W
Buena Vista [Ven.]	50	Eh	9.02N	63.49W
Buenavista, Bahia de-	49	Hb	22.30N	79.08W
Buendia, Embalse de-	13	Jd	40.25N	2.43W
Buenópolis	55	Jc	17.54S	44.11W
Buenos Aires [2]	56	Ie	36.00S	60.00W
Buenos Aires [Arg.]	53	Ki	34.36S	58.27W
Buenos Aires [C.R.]	49	Fi	10.04N	84.26W
Buenos Aires, Lago-	52	Ij	46.30S	72.00W
Buffalo	42	Fe	60.52N	115.03W
Buffalo [N.Y.-U.S.]	39	Le	42.54N	78.53W
Buffalo [Ok.-U.S.]	45	Gh	36.50N	99.38W
Buffalo [S.D.-U.S.]	43	Gb	45.35N	103.33W
Buffalo [Tx.-U.S.]	45	Hk	31.28N	96.04W
Buffalo [Wy.-U.S.]	43	Fc	44.21N	106.42W
Buffalo Bill Reservoir	46	Kd	44.29N	109.13W
Buffalo Lake	42	Fd	60.12N	115.25W
Buffalo Narrows	42	Ge	55.51N	108.30W
Buffalo Pound Lake	46	Ma	50.38N	105.20W
Buffels	37	Be	29.41S	17.04 E
Bū Fishah	14	En	36.18N	10.28 E
Buford	44	Fh	34.07N	84.00W
Buftea	15	Ie	44.34N	25.57 E
Bug	5	Ie	52.31N	21.05 E
Buga	54	Cc	3.55N	76.18W
Bugarach, Pech de-	11	Il	42.52N	2.23 E
Bugeat	11	Hi	45.36N	1.56 E
Bugene	36	Fc	1.35S	31.08 E
Bugey	11	Li	45.48N	5.30 E
Bugojno	23	Ff	44.03N	17.27 E
Bugøynes	7	Gb	69.58N	29.39 E
Bugrino	17	Db	68.48N	49.09 E
Bugsuk	26	Ge	8.15N	117.18 E
Bugt	27	Lb	48.47N	121.55 E
Bugulma	19	Fe	54.33N	52.48 E
Bugun	18	Hc	43.22N	70.10 E
Bugun	18	Gc	42.56N	68.36 E
Bugür/Luntai	27	Dc	41.46N	84.10 E
Buguruslan	19	Fe	53.39N	52.30 E
Buhara	22	If	39.49N	64.25 E
Buharskaja Oblast [3]	19	Gg	41.20N	64.20 E
Bū Ḥaşā'	24	Ok	23.20N	53.20 E
Buhera	37	Ec	19.18S	31.29 E
Buh He	27	Gd	36.58N	99.48 E
Buhl	46	He	42.36N	114.46W
Bühl	10	Eh	48.42N	8.09 E
Bühödle	35	Hd	8.15N	46.20 E
Buhtarminskoje Vodohranilišče	19	If	49.10N	84.00 E
Bui Dam	34	Ed	8.22N	2.10W
Builth Wells	9	Ji	52.09N	3.24W
Buin [Chile]	56	Fd	33.44S	70.44W
Buin [Pap.N.Gui.]	60	Fi	6.50S	155.44 E
Buinsk	19	Ee	54.59N	48.17 E
Buir Nur	27	Kb	47.48N	117.42 E
Buitrago del Lozoya	13	Id	41.00N	3.38W
Buj	17	Gh	56.15N	54.12 E
Buj	18	Ed	58.29N	41.31 E
Bujalance	13	Hg	37.54N	4.22W
Bujanovac	15	Eg	42.28N	21.47 E
Bujaraloz	13	Lc	41.30N	0.09W
Buje	14	Ge	45.24N	13.40 E
Bujnaksk	19	Eg	42.49N	47.07 E
Bujukly	20	Jg	49.33N	142.55 E
Bujumbura	31	Ji	3.23S	29.22 E
Bujunda	20	Kd	62.00N	153.20 E
Buk	10	Md	52.22N	16.31 E
Bük	10	Mi	47.23N	16.45 E
Buk	10	Hb	54.10N	11.42 E
Buka Island	57	Ge	5.15S	154.35 E
Bukakata	36	Fc	0.18S	32.02 E
Bukama	31	Ji	9.12S	25.51 E
Buka Passage	63a	Ba	5.25S	154.41 E
Bukavu	31	Ji	2.30S	28.52 E
Bukene	36	Fc	4.14S	32.53 E
Bukhā	24	Qi	26.10N	56.09 E
Bukit Besi	26	Df	4.46N	103.12 E
Bukit Mertajam	26	De	5.22N	100.28 E
Bukittinggi	22	Mj	0.19S	100.22 E
Bükk	10	Qh	48.05N	20.30 E
Bukoba	31	Ki	1.20S	31.49 E
Bukovina	15	Ia	48.00N	25.30 E
Bukowiec	10	Ld	52.23N	15.20 E
Bukuru	34	Gd	9.48N	8.52 E
Būl, Kūh-e-	23	Hc	30.48N	52.45 E
Bulajevo	19	He	54.53N	70.26 E
Bulan	26	Hd	12.40N	123.52 E
Bulanaš	17	Kh	57.16N	62.02 E
Bulancak	24	Hb	40.57N	38.14 E
Bulanık	24	Jc	39.05N	42.15 E
Būlāq	33	Fd	25.12N	30.32 E
Bulawayo	31	Jk	20.09S	28.34 E
Buldan	24	Cc	38.03N	28.51 E
Buldir	40a	Bb	52.21N	175.54 E
Bulgan [Mong.]	27	Hc	44.05N	103.32 E
Bulgan [Mong.]	27	Hb	48.45N	103.34 E
Bulgan [Mong.]	27	Fb	46.05N	91.34 E
Bulgaria (EN) = Bălgarija [1]	6	Ig	43.00N	25.00 E
Buli	26	If	0.53N	128.18 E
Buli, Teluk-	26	If	0.45N	128.30 E
Buliluyan, Cape-	26	Ge	8.20N	117.11 E
Bulki	35	Fd	6.01N	36.36 E
Bullahār	35	Gc	10.23N	44.27 E
Bullange/Büllingen	12	Id	50.25N	6.16 E
Bullaque	13	Hf	38.59N	4.17W
Bulla Regia	14	Cn	36.33N	8.45 E
Bullas	13	Kf	38.03N	1.40W
Bulle	14	Bd	46.37N	7.04 E
Buller	62	Dd	41.44S	171.35 E
Bullfinch	59	Df	30.59S	119.06 E
Büllingen/Bullange	12	Id	50.25N	6.16 E
Bullion Mountains	46	Hi	34.25N	116.00W
Bulloo River	57	Fg	28.43S	142.30 E
Bull Point [Eng.-U.K.]	9	Ij	51.12N	4.10W
Bull Point [Falk.Is.]	56	Ih	52.19S	59.18W
Bulls	62	Fd	40.10S	175.23 E
Bulls Bay	44	Hi	32.59N	79.33W
Bull Shoals Lake	45	Jh	36.30N	92.50W
Bully Choop Mountain	46	Df	40.35N	122.45W
Bully-les-Mines	12	Ed	50.26N	2.43 E
Bulo Berde	35	He	3.52N	45.40 E
Bulolo	60	Di	7.12S	146.39 E
Bulqiza	15	Dh	41.30N	20.21 E
Bulter	45	Ig	38.16N	94.20W
Bultfontein	37	De	28.20S	26.05 E
Bulukumba	26	Hh	5.33S	120.11 E
Bulungu [Zaire]	36	Cc	4.33S	18.36 E
Bulungu [Zaire]	36	Dd	6.04S	21.54 E
Bumba	31	Jh	2.11N	22.28 E
Bumbah, Khalīj al-	33	Dc	32.25N	23.06 E
Buna	15	Ch	41.52N	19.22 E
Buna	36	Gb	2.47N	39.31 E
Bunbury	58	Ch	33.19S	115.38 E
Buncrana/Bun Cranncha	9	Ff	55.08N	7.27W
Bun Cranncha/Buncrana	9	Ff	55.08N	7.27W
Bunda	36	Fc	2.03S	33.52 E
Bundaberg	58	Gg	24.52S	152.21 E
Bünde	10	Ed	52.12N	8.35 E
Bundesrepublik Deutschland = Germany	6	Ge	51.00N	10.00 E
Bun Dobhráin/Bundoran	9	Eg	54.28N	8.17W
Bundoran/Bun Dobhráin	9	Eg	54.28N	8.17W
Bungay	12	Db	52.27N	1.27 E
Bungku	26	Hg	2.33S	121.58 E
Bungo	36	Cd	7.26S	15.24 E
Bungo Strait (EN) = Bungo-Suidō	28	Lh	32.40N	132.18 E
Bungo-Suidō = Bungo Strait (EN)	28	Lh	32.40N	132.18 E
Bungotakada	29	Be	33.33N	131.27 E
Bungsberg	10	Gb	54.12N	10.43 E
Buni	34	Hc	11.12N	12.02 E
Bunja	31	Kh	1.34N	30.15 E
Bunji	25	Ea	35.40N	74.36 E
Bunker	45	Kh	37.27N	91.13W
Bunker Group	63	Kd	23.50S	152.20 E
Bunkeya	36	Ee	10.24S	26.58 E
Bunkie	45	Jk	30.57N	92.11W
Bunnerfjällen	8	Ea	63.10N	12.34 E
Buñol	13	Le	39.25N	0.47W
Bunschoten	12	Hb	52.14N	5.24 E
Buntingford	12	Bc	51.57N	0.01W
Buntok	26	Fg	1.42S	114.48 E
Bünyan	24	Fc	38.51N	35.52 E
Bunyu, Pulau-	26	Gf	3.30N	117.50 E
Buon Me Thuot	25	Lf	12.40N	108.03 E
Buor-Haja, Guba-	20	Ib	71.00N	131.00 E
Buotama	20	Hd	61.17N	128.55 E
Buqayaq	23	Gd	25.56N	49.40 E
Buqda Kōsār	35	Ge	4.31N	44.49 E
Bur	20	Hb	71.40N	123.40 E
Bura	36	Gc	1.06S	39.57 E
Buram	31	Jg	10.49N	25.10 E
Buran	19	If	48.04N	85.15 E
Burang	27	De	30.18N	81.08 E
Burāq	24	Gf	33.10N	36.29 E
Buras	45	Ll	29.21N	89.32W
Buraydah	22	Gg	26.20N	43.59 E
Burbach	12	Kd	50.43N	8.03 E
Burdab	35	Hd	9.05N	46.30 E
Burdekin River	59	Jc	19.39S	147.30 E
Burdēre	35	He	3.30N	45.37 E
Burdur	23	Db	37.43N	30.17 E
Burdur Gölü	24	Dd	37.44N	30.12 E
Burdwood Bank (EN)	56	Ih	54.15S	59.00W
Bure	12	Db	52.38N	1.45 E
Bure [Eth.]	35	Fd	8.20N	35.08 E
Bure [Eth.]	35	Fc	10.43N	37.03 E
Bureå	7	Ed	64.37N	21.12 E
Bureinski Hrebet = Bureya Range (EN)	21	Pd	50.40N	134.00 E
Bureja	20	Hg	49.43N	129.51 E
Bureja	21	Oe	49.25N	129.35 E
Büren	10	Ee	51.33N	8.34 E
Buren-Cogt	27	Jb	46.45N	111.30 E
Bureya Range (EN) = Bureinski Hrebet	21	Pd	50.40N	134.00 E
Burfjord	7	Fb	69.56N	22.03 E
Bür Gābo	35	Gf	1.10S	41.50 E
Burgas	6	Ig	42.30N	27.28 E
Burgas [2]	15	Kg	42.30N	27.20 E
Burgas, Gulf of- (EN) = Burgaski Zaliv	15	Kg	42.30N	27.33 E
Burgaski Zaliv = Burgas, Gulf of- (EN)	15	Kg	42.30N	27.33 E
Burg auf Fehmarn	10	Hb	54.26N	11.12 E
Burg auf Fehmarn-Puttgarden	10	Hb	54.30N	11.13 E
Burgaw	44	Ih	34.33N	77.56W
Burgaz Daği	15	Mk	38.25N	29.46 E
Burg bei Magdeburg	10	Hd	52.16N	11.51 E
Burgdorf [Ger.]	10	Gd	52.27N	10.01 E
Burgdorf [Switz.]	14	Bc	47.04N	7.37 E
Burgenland [2]	14	Kc	47.30N	16.25 E
Burgersdorp	37	Df	31.00S	26.20 E
Burgess Hill	12	Bd	50.58N	0.08W
Burgfjället	7	Dd	64.56N	15.03 E
Burghausen	10	Ih	48.10N	12.50 E
Burghūth, Sabkhat al-	24	Ie	34.58N	41.06 E
Burglengenfeld	10	Ig	49.12N	12.02 E
Burgos [3]	13	Ib	42.20N	3.40W
Burgos [Mex.]	48	Je	24.57N	98.57W
Burgos [Sp.]	6	Fg	42.21N	3.42W
Burg-Reuland	12	Id	50.12N	6.09 E
Burgsvik	7	Eh	57.03N	18.16 E
Burgundy (EN) = Bourgogne	5	Gf	47.00N	4.30 E
Burgundy (EN) = Bourgogne	11	Kg	47.00N	4.30 E
Burgwald	12	Kd	50.57N	8.48 E
Bür Hakkaba	35	Ge	2.43N	44.10 E
Burhaniye	24	Bc	39.30N	26.58 E
Burhānpur	22	Jg	21.18N	76.14 E
Burias	26	Hd	12.57N	123.08 E
Buribaj	17	Ij	51.57N	58.11 E
Burica, Punta-	47	Hg	8.03N	82.53W
Burien	46	Dc	47.27N	122.21W
Burin Peninsula	42	Lg	47.00N	55.40W
Buriram	25	Kf	14.59N	103.08 E
Buriti, Rio-	55	Ca	12.50S	58.28W
Buriti Alegre	55	Hd	18.09S	49.03W
Buriti Bravo	54	Je	5.50S	43.50W
Buriti dos Lopes	54	Jd	3.10S	41.52W
Buritis	55	Ib	15.37S	46.26W
Burj al Ḥaṭṭābah	32	Ic	30.20N	9.30 E
Burjasot	13	Le	39.31N	0.25W
Burjatskaja ASSR [3]	20	Ff	53.00N	110.00 E
Burj Şāfitā	24	Ge	34.49N	36.07 E
Burkandja	20	Jd	63.27N	147.27 E
Burkburnett	45	Gi	34.06N	98.34W
Burke	45	Ge	43.11N	99.18W
Burke, Mount-	46	Ha	50.18N	114.30W
Burke Island	66	Of	73.08S	105.06W
Burke River	59	Hd	23.12S	139.33 E
Burketown	58	Ef	17.44S	139.22 E
Burkina Faso [1]	31	Gg	13.00N	2.00W
Burley	43	Ec	42.32N	113.48W
Burli	16	Rd	51.28N	52.44 E
Burlingame	45	Ig	38.45N	95.50W
Burlington [Co.-U.S.]	43	Gd	39.18N	102.16W
Burlington [Ia.-U.S.]	43	Ic	40.49N	91.07W
Burlington [Ks.-U.S.]	45	Ig	38.12N	95.45W
Burlington [N.C.-U.S.]	44	Hg	36.06N	79.26W
Burlington [Ont.-Can.]	44	Hd	43.19N	79.43W
Burlington [Vt.-U.S.]	43	Mc	44.28N	73.14W
Burlington [Wi.-U.S.]	45	Le	42.41N	88.17W
Burma [1]	22	Lg	22.00N	98.00 E
Burma [1] (Myanmar-Nainggan-Daw)	22	Lg	22.00N	98.00 E
Burnazului, Cîmpia-	15	Ie	44.10N	25.50 E
Burnett River	59	Kd	24.46S	152.25 E
Burney	46	Ef	40.53N	121.40W
Burnham Market	12	Cb	52.57N	0.44 E
Burnham-on-Crouch	12	Cc	51.37N	0.50 E
Burnie	59	Jh	41.04S	145.54 E
Burnley	9	Kh	53.48N	2.14W
Burns	43	Dc	43.35N	119.03W
Burnside	42	Gc	66.51N	108.04W
Burnside, Lake-	59	Ee	25.20S	123.10 E
Burns Lake	42	Ef	54.14N	125.46W
Burnsville	44	Fh	35.55N	82.18W
Burnt Lava Flow	46	Ef	41.35N	121.35W
Burnt River	44	Hc	44.35N	78.46W
Burntwood	42	He	56.08N	96.33W
Bur'o	31	Lh	9.30N	45.34 E
Burqin	27	Eb	47.43N	86.53 E
Burqin He	27	Eb	47.42N	86.50 E
Burqūm, Ḥarrat al-	33	He	20.54N	42.00 E
Burra	59	Hf	33.40S	138.56 E
Burragorang Lake	59	Kf	34.00S	150.25 E
Burreli	15	Ch	41.37N	20.00 E
Burrendong Reservoir	59	Jf	32.40S	149.10 E
Burriana	13	Le	39.53N	0.05W
Burro, Serranias del	48	Ic	28.50N	101.35W
Burrow Head	9	Ig	54.41N	4.24W
Bursa	22	Ee	40.11N	29.04 E
Bür Sa'īd = Port Said (EN)	31	Ke	31.16N	32.18 E
Burscheid	12	Jc	51.06N	7.07 E
Bürstadt	12	Ke	49.38N	8.27 E
Burštyn	16	De	49.16N	24.37 E
Būr Sūdān = Port Sudan (EN)	31	Kg	19.37N	37.14 E
Burt Lake	44	Ec	45.27N	84.40W
Burtnieku, Ozero-	8	Kg	57.35N	25.10 E
Burtnieku, Ozero-/Burtnieku Ezers	8	Kg	57.35N	25.10 E
Burtnieku Ezers	8	Kg	57.35N	25.10 E
Burtnieku Ezers/Burtnieku, Ozero-	8	Kg	57.35N	25.10 E
Burton	44	Fd	43.02N	83.36W
Burton Latimer	12	Bb	52.21N	0.40W
Burton-upon-Trent	9	Li	52.49N	1.36W
Burträsk	7	Ed	64.31N	20.39 E
Buru, Pulau-	57	De	3.24S	126.40 E
Burullus, Buḥayrat al-	24	Dg	31.30N	30.50 E
Burultokay/Fuhai	27	Eb	47.06N	87.23 E
Burum Gana	34	Hc	13.00N	11.57 E
Burūn, Ra's-	24	Eg	31.14N	33.04 E
Burundaj	19	Hg	43.20N	76.49 E
Burundi [1]	31	Ki	3.15S	30.00 E
Bururi	36	Ec	3.57S	29.37 E
Burutu	34	Gd	5.21N	5.31 E
Bury	9	Kh	53.36N	2.17W
Burylbajtal	18	Ib	44.56N	73.59 E
Buryn	16	Hd	51.13N	33.48 E
Bury Saint Edmunds	9	Ni	52.15N	0.43 E
Burzil Pass	25	Ff	34.54N	75.06 E
Busalla	14	Cf	44.34N	8.57 E
Busanga [Zaire]	36	Ee	10.12S	25.23 E
Busanga [Zaire]	36	Dc	0.51S	22.04 E
Busanga Swamp	36	Ee	14.10S	25.50 E
Buşayrah	24	Ie	35.09N	40.26 E
Būsh	24	Dh	29.09N	31.08 E
Būshehr [3]	23	Hd	28.00N	52.00 E
Būshgān	24	Nh	28.48N	51.42 E
Bushimaie	29	Ji	6.02S	23.45 E
Bushmanland (EN) = Boesmanland	37	Be	29.30S	19.00 E
Busia	36	Fb	0.28N	34.06 E
Busigny	12	Fd	50.02N	3.28 E
Businga	36	Db	3.20N	20.53 E
Busira	30	Ii	0.15S	18.59 E
Busk	16	Dd	50.01N	24.37 E
Buskerud [2]	7	Bf	60.30N	9.10 E
Busko-Zdrój	10	Qf	50.28N	20.44 E
Busoga [3]	36	Fb	0.45N	33.30 E
Buşrá ash Shām	24	Gf	32.31N	36.29 E
Busselton	59	Df	33.39S	115.20 E
Bussum	11	Lb	52.16N	5.10 E
Bustamante, Bahía-	56	Gg	45.07S	66.27W
Buşteni	15	Id	45.24N	25.32 E
Busto Arsizio	14	Ce	45.37N	8.51 E
Buštyna	10	Th	48.03N	23.28 E
Busuanga	26	Hd	12.05N	120.05 E
Busu-Djanoa	36	Db	1.43N	21.23 E
Büsum	10	Eb	54.08N	8.51 E
Buta	31	Jh	2.48N	24.44 E
Butajira	35	Fd	8.08N	38.27 E
Buta Ranquil	56	Ge	37.03S	69.50W
Butare	36	Ec	2.36S	29.44 E
Butaritari Atoll	57	Id	3.03N	172.49 E
Bute, Island of-	9	Hf	55.50N	5.05W
Bute Inlet	46	Ca	50.37N	124.53W
Butembo	31	Jh	0.09N	29.17 E
Butera	14	Im	37.11N	14.11 E
Butere	36	Fb	0.13N	34.30 E
Butha Qi (Zalantum)	27	Lb	48.02N	122.42 E
Buthidaung	25	Id	20.52N	92.32 E
Butiá	56	Jd	30.07S	51.58W
Butiaba	36	Fb	1.49N	31.19 E
Butler	44	He	40.51N	79.55W
Butser Hill	12	Bd	50.57N	0.59W
Butte	39	He	46.00N	112.32W
Butterworth [Mala.]	26	Df	5.25N	100.24 E
Butterworth [S.Afr.]	37	Df	32.23S	28.04 E
Button Bay	42	Ie	58.45N	94.25W
Butuan	22	Oi	8.57N	125.33 E
Butung, Pulau-	21	Oj	5.00S	122.55 E
Buturlinovka	16	Ld	50.48N	40.45 E
Butzbach	12	Kd	50.26N	8.41 E
Bützow	10	Hc	53.50N	11.59 E
Buxtehude	10	Fc	53.27N	9.42 E
Buxton [Eng.-U.K.]	9	Lh	53.15N	1.55W
Buxton [N.C.-U.S.]	44	Jh	35.16N	75.32W
Buyo	34	Dd	6.16N	7.03W
Büyük Ağri Daği = Ararat, Mount- (EN)	21	Gf	39.40N	44.24 E
Büyükanafarta	15	Ji	40.17N	26.22 E
Büyükçekmece	15	Lh	41.01N	28.34 E
Büyükkarıştıran	15	Kh	41.18N	27.32 E
Büyük Kemikli Burun	15	Ji	40.18N	26.14 E
Büyük Mahya	15	Kh	41.47N	27.36 E
Büyük Menderes	23	Cb	37.57N	28.58 E
Büyükorhan	15	Lj	39.45N	28.55 E
Buyun Shan	27	Lc	40.06N	122.42 E
Buzači, Poluostrov-	19	Ff	45.00N	52.00 E
Buzan	16	Pf	46.18N	49.06 E
Buzançais	11	Hh	46.53N	1.25 E
Buzancy	12	Ge	49.25N	4.57 E
Buzău [2]	15	Jd	45.09N	26.50 E
Buzău	15	Jd	45.09N	26.50 E
Buzău	15	Kd	45.26N	27.44 E
Buzaymah	33	De	24.55N	22.02 E
Buzen	29	Be	33.37N	131.08 E
Buzet	14	He	45.24N	13.59 E
Būzhān	24	Le	34.09N	47.05 E
Buzi	37	Ec	19.51S	34.30 E
Búzi	37	Ec	19.52S	34.46 E
Buziaş	15	Ed	45.39N	21.36 E
Búzios, Ilha dos-	55	Jf	23.48S	45.08W
Buzora, Gora-	10	Th	48.24N	23.15 E
Buzuluk	19	Fe	52.46N	52.17 E
Buzuluk [R.S.F.S.R.]	16	Md	50.13N	42.12 E
Buzuluk [R.S.F.S.R.]	16	Rc	52.47N	52.16 E
Buzzards Bay	44	Le	41.33N	70.47W

Index Symbols

- [1] Independent Nation
- [2] State, Region
- [3] District, County
- [4] Municipality
- [5] Colony, Dependency
- Continent
- Physical Region
- Historical or Cultural Region
- Mount, Mountain
- Volcano
- Hill
- Mountains, Mountain Range
- Hills, Escarpment
- Plateau, Upland
- Pass, Gap
- Plain, Lowland
- Delta
- Salt Flat
- Valley, Canyon
- Crater, Cave
- Karst Features
- Depression
- Polder
- Desert, Dunes
- Forest, Woods
- Heath, Steppe
- Oasis
- Cape, Point
- Coast, Beach
- Cliff
- Peninsula
- Isthmus
- Sandbank
- Island
- Atoll
- Rock, Reef
- Islands, Archipelago
- Rocks, Reefs
- Coral Reef
- Well, Spring
- Geyser
- River, Stream
- Waterfall Rapids
- River Mouth, Estuary
- Lake
- Salt Lake
- Intermittent Lake
- Reservoir
- Swamp, Pond
- Canal
- Glacier
- Ice Shelf, Pack Ice
- Ocean
- Sea
- Gulf, Bay
- Strait, Fjord
- Lagoon
- Bank
- Seamount
- Tablemount
- Ridge
- Shelf
- Basin
- Escarpment, Sea Scarp
- Fracture
- Trench, Abyss
- National Park, Reserve
- Point of Interest
- Recreation Site
- Cave, Cavern
- Historic Site
- Ruins
- Wall, Walls
- Church, Abbey
- Temple
- Scientific Station
- Airport
- Port
- Lighthouse
- Mine
- Tunnel
- Dam, Bridge

Index Symbols

[1] Independent Nation
[2] State, Region
[3] District, County
[4] Municipality
[5] Colony, Dependency
Continent
Physical Region
Historical or Cultural Region
Mount, Mountain
Volcano
Hill
Mountains, Mountain Range
Hills, Escarpment
Plateau, Upland
Pass, Gap
Plain, Lowland
Delta
Salt Flat
Valley, Canyon
Crater, Cave
Karst Features
Depression
Polder
Desert, Dunes
Forest, Woods
Heath, Steppe
Oasis
Cape, Point
Coast, Beach
Cliff
Peninsula
Isthmus
Sandbank
Island
Atoll
Rock, Reef
Islands, Archipelago
Rocks, Reefs
Coral Reef
Well, Spring
Geyser
River, Stream
Waterfall Rapids
River Mouth, Estuary
Lake
Salt Lake
Intermittent Lake
Reservoir
Swamp, Pond
Canal
Glacier
Ice Shelf, Pack Ice
Ocean
Sea
Gulf, Bay
Strait, Fjord
Lagoon
Bank
Seamount
Tablemount
Ridge
Shelf
Basin
Escarpment, Sea Scarp
Fracture
Trench, Abyss
National Park, Reserve
Point of Interest
Recreation Site
Cave, Cavern
Historic Site
Ruins
Wall, Walls
Church, Abbey
Temple
Scientific Station
Airport
Port
Lighthouse
Mine
Tunnel
Dam, Bridge

Canakkale Boğazi= Dardanelles (EN) 5 Ig 40.15N 26.25 E
Canala 63b Be 21.32S 165.57 E
Canandaigua 44 Id 42.53N 77.19W
Cananea 47 Bb 30.57N 110.18W
Cananéia 55 Ig 25.01S 47.57W
Canapolis 55 Hd 18.44S 49.13W
Canarias, Islas-=Canary Islands (EN) [5] 31 Ff 28.00N 15.30W
Canarias, Islas-=Canary Islands (EN) 30 Ff 28.00N 15.30W
Canaries 51k Ab 13.55N 61.04W
Canaronero, Laguna- 48 Ff 23.00N 106.15W
Canarreos, Archipiélago de los- 47 Hd 21.50N 82.30W
Canary Basin (EN) 3 Dg 30.00N 25.00W
Canary Islands (EN)= Canarias, Islas- 30 Ff 28.00N 15.30W
Canary Islands (EN)= Canarias, Islas- [5] 31 Ff 28.00N 15.30W
Cañas [C.R.] 49 Eh 10.25N 85.07W
Cañas [Pan.] 49 Gj 7.27N 80.16W
Canastra, Serra da- 55 Ie 20.00S 46.20W
Canatlán 48 Ge 24.31N 104.47W
Cañaveral 13 Fe 39.47N 6.23W
Canaveral, Cape- 38 Kg 28.30N 80.35W
Canavese 14 Be 45.20N 7.40 E
Canavieiras 54 Kg 15.39S 38.57W
Canazei 14 Fd 46.28N 11.46 E
Canberra 58 Fh 35.17S 149.08 E
Canby [Mn.-U.S.] 45 Hd 44.43N 96.16W
Canby [Or.-U.S.] 46 Dd 45.16N 122.42W
Cance 11 Ki 45.12N 4.48 E
Canche 11 Hd 50.31N 1.39 E
Cancon 11 Gj 44.32N 0.37 E
Cancún 47 Gd 21.05N 86.46W
Cancún, Isla- 48 Pg 21.05N 86.46W
Çandarli 15 Jk 38.56N 26.56 E
Çandarli Körfezi 15 Jk 38.52N 26.55 E
Candé 11 Eg 47.34N 1.02W
Candela 48 Id 26.50N 100.40W
Candelaria 48 Nh 18.18N 91.21W
Candelaria, Cerro- 48 Hf 23.25N 103.43W
Candelaria, Rio- [Bol.] 55 Cc 17.17S 58.39W
Candelaria, Rio- [Mex.] 48 Nh 18.38N 91.15W
Candelaro 14 Ji 41.34N 15.53 E
Cândido de Abreu 55 Gg 24.35S 51.20W
Cândido Mendes 54 Id 1.27S 45.43W
Candlemas Islands 66 Ad 57.03S 26.40W
Candói 55 Fg 25.43S 52.11W
Çandyr 16 Jj 38.13N 55.44 E
Canela 56 Jc 29.22S 50.50W
Canelli 14 Cf 44.43N 8.17 E
Canelones [2] 55 El 34.35S 56.00W
Canelones 55 Dl 34.32S 56.17W
Canendiyu [3] 55 Eg 24.20S 55.00W
Cañete [Chile] 56 Fe 37.48S 73.24W
Cañete [Sp.] 13 Kd 40.03N 1.39W
Cangallo 55 Cm 37.13S 58.42W
Cangamba 36 Ce 13.44S 19.53 E
Cangas 13 Db 42.16N 8.47W
Cangas de Narcea 13 Fa 43.11N 6.33W
Cangas de Onis 13 Ga 43.21N 5.07W
Cangola 36 Cd 7.58S 15.53 E
Cangombe 36 Ce 14.24S 19.59 E
Cangshan (Bianzhuang) 28 Eg 34.51N 118.03 E
Canguçu 55 Fj 31.24S 52.41W
Canguçu, Serra do- 55 Fj 31.20S 52.40W
Canguinha 55 Eb 14.42S 55.40W
Cangumbe 36 Ce 12.00S 19.09 E
Cangyuan 27 Gg 23.10N 99.15 E
Cangzhou 27 Kd 38.14N 116.58 E
Cani, Iles- 14 Em 37.21N 10.07 E
Caniapiscau 38 Md 57.40N 69.30W
Caniapiscau, Lac- 42 Kf 54.00N 70.10W
Canicattì 14 Hm 37.21N 13.51 E
Canigou, Pic du- 11 Il 42.31N 2.27 E
Canik Dağlari 24 Gb 40.50N 37.10 E
Canim Lake 46 Ea 51.52N 120.45W
Canindé 54 Kd 4.22S 39.19W
Canindé, Rio- 54 Je 6.15S 42.52W
Cañitas de Felipe Pescador 48 Hf 23.36N 102.43W
Çankaya 24 Ec 39.56N 32.52 E
Çankırı 23 Da 40.36N 33.37 E
Canna 9 Gd 57.03N 6.33W
Cannac 63a Ac 9.15S 153.29 E
Çannakale 23 Ca 40.09N 26.24 E
Cannanore 25 Ff 11.51N 75.22 E
Cannanore Islands 25 Ef 10.05N 72.10 E
Cannes 11 Nk 43.33N 7.01 E
Cannich 9 Id 57.20N 4.45W
Canning Basin 59 Ed 20.10S 123.00 E
Cannobio 14 Cd 46.04N 8.42 E
Cannock 9 Ki 52.42N 2.01W
Cannonball River 45 Fc 46.26N 100.38W
Cann River 59 Jg 37.34S 149.10 E
Caño, Isla del- 49 Fi 8.44N 83.53W
Canoas 56 Jc 29.56S 51.11W
Canoas, Punta- 48 Bc 29.25N 115.10W
Canoas, Rio- 56 Jc 27.36S 51.25W
Canoeiros 54 Ig 18.02S 45.31W
Canoinhas 55 Gh 26.10S 50.24W
Canoinhas, Rio- 55 Gh 26.07S 50.22W
Cañoles 13 Le 39.02N 0.29W
Canon City 43 Fd 38.27N 105.14W
Canon Fiord 42 Ja 80.15N 83.00W
Canonnier, Pointe du- 51b Ab 18.04N 63.10W
Canora 42 Hf 51.37N 102.26W
Canosa di Puglia 14 Ki 41.13N 16.04 E
Canouan Island 50 Ff 12.43N 61.20W
Canourgue 11 Jj 44.25N 3.13 E
Canso, Strait of - 42 Lg 45.35N 61.23W
Canta 54 Cf 11.25S 76.38W
Cantabrian Mountains (EN) =Cantábrica, Cordillera- 5 Fg 43.00N 5.00W
Cantábrica, Cordillera-= Cantabrian Mountains (EN) 5 Fg 43.00N 5.00W
Cantal 5 Gf 45.10N 2.50 E
Cantal [3] 11 Ii 45.05N 2.40 E
Cantalejo 13 Ic 41.15N 3.55W
Cantanhede 13 Dd 40.21N 8.36W
Cantaura 54 Fb 9.19N 64.21W
Cantavieja 13 Ld 40.32N 0.24W
Cantavir 15 Cd 45.55N 19.46 E
Canterbury [2] 62 De 43.30S 171.50 E
Canterbury 9 Oj 51.17N 1.05 E
Canterbury Bight 57 Ii 44.10S 172.00 E
Can Tho 22 Mi 10.02N 105.47 E
Cantiles, Cayo- 49 Fc 21.36N 82.02W
Canto do Buriti 54 Je 8.07S 42.58W
Canton [Il.-U.S.] 45 Kf 40.33N 90.02W
Canton [Mo.-U.S.] 45 Kf 40.08N 91.32W
Canton [Ms.-U.S.] 45 Kj 32.37N 90.02W
Canton [N.Y.-U.S.] 44 Jc 44.37N 75.11W
Canton [Oh.-U.S.] 43 Kc 40.48N 81.23W
Canton [S.D.-U.S.] 45 He 43.18N 96.35W
Canton (EN)=Guangzhou 22 Ng 23.07N 113.18 E
Cantù 14 De 45.44N 9.08 E
Cantwell 40 Jd 63.23N 148.57W
Cañuelas 55 Cl 35.03S 58.44W
Canumã, Rio- 52 Kf 3.55S 59.10W
Canutama 54 Fe 6.32S 64.20W
Canvey 12 Cc 51.31N 0.36 E
Čany 20 Ce 55.19N 76.56 E
Čany, Ozero- 21 Jd 54.50N 77.30 E
Cany-Barville 12 Ce 49.47N 0.38 E
Canyon [Mn.-U.S.] 45 Jc 47.02N 92.29W
Canyon [Tx.-U.S.] 43 Ge 34.59N 101.55W
Canyon [Wy.-U.S.] 46 Jd 44.44N 110.30W
Canyon Lake 45 Gl 29.52N 98.16W
Canzar 36 Dd 7.36S 21.33 E
Cao Bang 25 Ld 22.40N 106.15 E
Caojiahe → Qichun 28 Ci 30.15N 115.26 E
Caojian 27 Gf 25.38N 99.07 E
Caombo 36 Cd 8.42S 16.33 E
Caorle 14 Ge 45.36N 12.53 E
Caoxian 28 Cg 34.49N 115.33 E
Caozhou → Heze 27 Kd 35.14N 115.28 E
Capaccio 14 Jj 40.25N 15.05 E
Čapajev 19 Fe 50.14N 51.08 E
Čapajevsk 19 Ee 53.01N 49.36 E
Capanaparo, Rio- 54 Eb 7.01N 67.07W
Capanema [Braz.] 54 Id 1.12S 47.11W
Capanema [Braz.] 55 Fg 25.40S 53.48W
Capanema, Serra do- 55 Fh 26.05S 53.16W
Capão Alto 55 Gh 27.56S 50.30W
Capão Bonito 55 Hf 24.01S 48.20W
Capão Doce, Morro do- 55 Gh 26.43S 51.25W
Caparo, Rio- 49 Lj 7.46N 70.23W
Capatárida 49 Lh 11.11N 70.37W
Capbreton 11 Ek 43.38N 1.26W
Cap Breton Canyon (EN) 11 Ek 43.40N 1.50W
Čapčama, Pereval- 18 Hd 41.34N 70.50 E
Cap-Chat 44 Na 49.06N 66.42W
Capcir 11 Il 42.45N 2.10 E
Cap-de-la-Madeleine 42 Kg 46.22N 72.32W
Capdenac-Gare 11 Ij 44.34N 2.05 E
Cape Barren Island 59 Jh 40.25S 148.10 E
Cape Basin (EN) 3 Em 37.00S 7.00 E
Cape Breton Island 38 Me 46.00N 60.30W
Cape Charles 44 Jg 37.17N 76.00W
Cape Coast 31 Gh 5.06N 1.15W
Cape Cod Bay 44 Le 41.52N 70.22W
Cape Coral 44 Gl 26.33N 81.58W
Cape Dorset 39 Lc 64.14N 76.32W
Cape Dyer 39 Mc 66.30N 61.18W
Cape Fear River 44 Ii 33.53N 78.00W
Cape Girardeau 43 Jd 37.19N 89.32W
Cape Johnson Tablemount (EN) 57 Jc 17.08N 177.15W
Capel 12 Bc 51.08N 0.19W
Cape Lisburne 40 Fc 68.52N 166.05W
Capelka 8 Mf 58.02N 29.07 E
Capelongo 36 Ce 14.54S 15.05 E
Capem 55 Ea 13.14S 55.14W
Cape May 44 Jf 38.56N 74.54W
Cape Mount [3] 34 Cd 7.05N 10.50W
Cape Province/ Kaapprovinsie [2] 37 Cf 32.00S 22.00 E
Cape Rise (EN) 3 En 42.00S 15.00 E
Cape Smith 42 Jd 60.44N 78.29W
Capesterre 51e Bc 15.54N 61.13W
Capesterre-Belle-Eau 50 Fd 16.03N 61.34W
Cape Town / Kaapstad 31 Il 33.55S 18.22 E
Cape Verde (EN)=Cabo Verde [1] 31 Eg 16.00N 24.00W
Cape Verde (EN)=Cap Vert [3] 34 Bc 14.45N 17.20W
Cape Verde Basin (EN) 3 Ch 15.00N 30.00W
Cape Verde Islands (EN)= Cabo Verde, Ilhas do- 30 Eg 16.00N 24.10W
Cape Yakataga 40 Kd 60.04N 142.26W
Cape York Peninsula 57 Ff 14.00S 142.30 E
Cap-Haïtien 39 Lh 19.45N 72.15W
Capiibary, Arroyo- 55 Dg 24.06S 56.26W
Capiibary, Rio- 55 Eg 25.30S 55.33W
Capim, Rio- 52 Lf 1.40S 47.47W
Capinópolis 55 Hd 18.41S 49.35W
Capira 49 Hi 8.45N 79.53W
Capital Federal [2] 55 Cl 34.36S 58.27W
Capitán Arturo Prat 66 Re 62.29S 59.39W
Capitán Bado 56 Ib 23.16S 55.32W
Capitán Bermúdez 55 Bk 32.49S 60.43W
Capitán Sarmiento 55 Cl 34.10S 59.48W
Capitão Noronha, Rio- 55 Ea 13.19S 54.36W
Capivara, Represa da- 55 Gf 22.40S 50.57W
Capivari, Rio- 55 Dd 19.16S 57.10W
Capivarita 55 Fj 30.18S 52.19W
Cap Lopez, Baie du- 36 Ac 0.40S 9.00 E
Čaplygin 16 Kc 53.17N 39.59 E
Cappeln (Oldenburg) 12 Kb 52.49N 8.07 E
Cap Point 50 Fe 14.07N 60.57W
Capraia 14 Dg 43.05N 9.50 E
Caprara, Punta- 14 Ci 41.07N 8.19 E
Capreol 44 Gb 46.43N 80.56W
Caprera 14 Di 41.10N 9.30 E
Capri 14 Ij 40.35N 14.15 E
Capri 14 Ij 40.33N 14.14 E
Capricorn, Cape- 59 Kd 23.30S 151.15 E
Capricorn Channel 59 Kd 22.15S 151.30 E
Capricorn Group 57 Gg 23.30S 152.00 E
Caprivi Strip (EN)=Caprivi Zipfel 30 Jj 18.00S 23.00 E
Caprivi Zipfel=Caprivi Strip (EN) 30 Jj 18.00S 23.00 E
Captain Cook 65a Fd 19.30N 155.55W
Captains Flat 59 Jg 35.35S 149.27 E
Captieux 11 Fj 44.17N 0.15W
Capua 14 Ii 41.06N 14.12 E
Capuchin, Cape- 51g Ba 15.38N 61.28W
Capunda 36 Ce 10.41S 17.23 E
Cap Vert=Cape Verde (EN) [3] 34 Bc 14.45N 17.20W
Caquetá [2] 54 Dc 1.00N 74.00W
Čara 21 Oc 60.17N 120.40 E
Čara [R.S.F.S.R.] 20 Ge 56.58N 118.17 E
Čara [R.S.F.S.R.] 20 Ge 58.54N 118.12 E
Carabobo [2] 54 Ea 10.10N 68.05W
Caracal 15 He 44.07N 24.21 E
Caracarai 54 Fc 1.50N 61.08W
Caracas 53 Jd 10.30N 66.56W
Carache 49 Li 9.38N 70.14W
Caracol 55 De 21.59S 57.02W
Caracol, Rio- 55 Df 22.13S 57.03W
Caracollo 54 Eg 17.39S 67.10W
Cara Droma Rúisc/Carrick-on-Shannon 9 Eh 53.57N 8.05W
Caraguatá, Cuchilla- 55 Ek 32.05S 54.54W
Caraguatatuba 55 Jf 23.37S 45.25W
Caraïbe, Mer-/Antilles, Mer des-=Caribbean Sea (EN) 38 Lh 15.00N 73.00W
Carajas, Serra dos- 54 He 6.00S 51.20W
Caramoan Peninsula 26 Hd 13.48N 123.40 E
Caramulo, Serra do- 13 Dd 40.34N 8.11W
Caraná, Rio- 55 Ca 13.20S 59.17W
Carandai 55 Ke 20.57S 43.48W
Carandazal 55 Dd 19.50S 57.09W
Caransebeş 15 Fd 45.25N 22.13 E
Carapá, Rio- 55 Eg 24.30S 54.20W
Carapelle 14 Ji 41.30N 15.55 E
Caraş 15 Ee 44.49N 21.20 E
Caraş Severin [2] 15 Ed 45.20N 22.00 E
Caratasca, Cayo- 49 Fe 16.02N 83.20W
Caratasca, Laguna de- 47 He 15.20N 83.50W
Caratinga 54 Jg 19.47S 42.08W
Carauari 54 Ed 4.52S 66.54W
Caraúbas 54 Ke 5.47S 37.34W
Caravaca 13 Kf 38.06N 1.51W
Caravelas 53 Mg 17.45S 39.15W
Caraveli 54 Dg 15.46S 73.22W
Caravelle, Presqu'île de la- 51h Bb 14.45N 60.55W
Caravelle, Rocher de la- 51h Bb 14.48N 60.53W
Carazinho 56 Jc 28.18S 52.48W
Carazo [3] 49 Dh 11.45N 86.15W
Carballino 13 Db 42.26N 8.04W
Carballo 13 Da 43.13N 8.41W
Carberry 45 Gb 49.52N 99.20W
Carbet, Pitons du- 51h Ab 14.42N 61.07W
Carbon, Cap- [Alg.] 13 Rh 36.47N 5.06 E
Carbon, Cap- [Alg.] 13 Li 35.54N 0.20W
Carbonara, Capo- 14 Dk 39.06N 9.31 E
Carbondale [Il.-U.S.] 43 Jd 37.44N 89.13W
Carbondale [Pa.-U.S.] 44 Je 41.35N 75.31W
Carbonera, Cuchilla de la- 55 El 34.10S 54.00W
Carboneras 13 Kh 36.59N 1.54W
Carboneras, Cerro- 48 Ih 18.10N 101.10W
Carbones 13 Gg 37.36N 5.39W
Carbonia 14 Ck 39.10N 8.31 E
Carcans, Étang de- 11 Ei 45.06N 1.07W
Carcar 26 Hd 10.06N 123.38 E
Carcarañá, Rio- 55 Bk 32.27S 60.48W
Carcassonne 11 Ik 43.13N 2.21 E
Carcross 42 Ed 60.10N 134.42W
Çardak [Tur.] 15 Ji 40.22N 26.43 E
Çardak [Tur.] 24 Cd 37.48N 29.40 E
Čardara 19 Gg 41.15N 68.01 E
Čardarinskoje Vodohranilišče 18 Gd 41.05N 68.15 E
Cárdenas [Cuba] 47 Hd 23.02N 81.12W
Cárdenas [Mex.] 47 Ed 22.00N 99.40W
Cárdenas [Mex.] 48 Mi 17.59N 93.22W
Cárdenas, Bahia de- 49 Gb 23.05N 81.10W
Cardener/Cardoner 13 Nc 41.41N 1.51 E
Cardiel, Lago- 56 Fg 48.55S 71.15W
Cardiff 6 Fe 51.30N 3.13W
Cardigan 9 Ii 52.06N 4.40W
Cardigan Bay 6 Fe 52.30N 4.20W
Cardona [Sp.] 13 Nc 41.55N 1.41 E
Cardona [Ur.] 55 Dk 33.54S 57.22W
Cardoner/Cardener 13 Nc 41.41N 1.51 E
Cardozo 55 Dk 32.38S 56.21W
Cardston 42 Gg 49.12N 113.18W
Čardžou 22 If 39.06N 63.34 E
Čardžouskaja Oblast [3] 19 Gh 39.00N 63.00 E
Carei 15 Fb 47.41N 22.28 E
Careiro 54 Gd 3.12S 59.45W
Carentan 11 Ee 49.18N 1.14W
Carey 46 Ie 43.20N 113.58W
Carey, Lake- 57 Dg 29.05S 122.15 E
Cargados Carajos Islands 30 Mj 16.35S 59.40 E
Cargese 11a Aa 42.08N 8.35 E
Carhaix-Plouguer 11 Cf 48.17N 3.35W
Cari 14 Hi 41.23N 13.50 E
Caria 15 Ll 37.30N 29.00 E
Cariacica 54 Jh 20.16S 40.25W
Cariaco 50 Eg 10.29N 63.33W
Cariaco, Golfo de- 50 Eg 10.30N 64.00W
Cariaco Basin (EN) 50 Dg 10.37N 65.10W
Cariati 14 Kk 39.30N 16.57 E
Caribana, Punta- 49 Ii 8.37N 76.52W
Caribbean Sea 38 Lh 15.00N 73.00W
Caribbean Sea (EN)= Antillas, Mar de las-/ Caribe, Mar- 38 Lh 15.00N 73.00W
Caribbean Sea (EN)= Antilles, Mer des-/Caraïbe, Mer- 38 Lh 15.00N 73.00W
Caribbean Sea (EN)= Caribe, Mar-/Antillas, Mar de las- 38 Lh 15.00N 73.00W
Caribe, Mar-/Antillas, Mar de las-=Caribbean Sea (EN) 38 Lh 15.00N 73.00W
Cariboo Mountains 42 Ff 53.00N 121.00W
Caribou 42 Ie 59.20N 94.45W
Caribou 44 Mb 46.52N 68.01W
Caribou Island 44 Eb 47.27N 85.52W
Caribou Lake 45 La 50.25N 89.00W
Caribou Mountains 38 Hd 59.12N 115.40W
Caribou Range 46 Je 43.05N 111.15W
Caričin Grad 15 Eg 42.57N 21.45 E
Carignan 11 Le 49.38N 5.10 E
Carignano 14 Bf 44.55N 7.40 E
Cariñena 13 Kc 41.20N 1.13W
Carinhanha 54 Jf 14.08S 43.47W
Carinhanha, Rio- 55 Kb 14.20S 43.47W
Carini 14 Hl 38.08N 13.11 E
Carinola 14 Hi 41.11N 13.58 E
Carinthia (EN) = Kärnten [2] 14 Hd 46.45N 14.00 E
Carinthia (EN) = Kärnten 14 Hd 46.45N 14.00 E
Caripe 50 Eg 10.21N 63.29W
Caripito 54 Fa 10.08N 63.06W
Caris, Rio- 50 Eh 8.09N 63.46W
Carlet 13 Le 39.14N 0.31W
Carleton Place 44 Ic 45.07N 76.08W
Carletonville 37 De 26.23S 27.22 E
Carlin 46 Gf 40.43N 116.07W
Carling 12 Ie 49.10N 6.43 E
Carlingford Lough/Loch Cairlinn 9 Gg 54.05N 6.14W
Carlinville 45 Lg 39.17N 89.53W
Carlisle [Eng.-U.K.] 6 Fe 54.54N 2.55W
Carlisle [Pa.-U.S.] 44 Ie 40.12N 77.12W
Carlisle Bay 51q Ab 13.05N 59.37W
Carloforte 14 Ck 39.08N 8.18 E
Carlos Beguerie 55 Cl 35.29S 59.06W
Carlos Casares 56 He 35.38S 61.21W
Carlos Chagas 54 Jg 17.43S 40.45W
Carlos Reyles 55 Dk 33.03S 56.29W
Carlos Tejedor 55 Al 35.23S 62.25W
Carlow/Ceatharlach 9 Gi 52.50N 6.55W
Carlow/Ceatharlach [2] 9 Gi 52.50N 7.00W
Carloway 9 Gc 58.17N 6.47W
Carlsbad [Ca.-U.S.] 46 Gj 33.10N 117.21W
Carlsbad [N.M.-U.S.] 39 If 32.25N 104.14W
Carlyle 42 Hg 49.38N 102.16W
Carlyle Lake 45 Lg 38.40N 89.18W
Carmacks 42 Dd 62.05N 136.18W
Carmagnola 14 Bf 44.51N 7.43 E
Carmarthen 9 Ij 51.52N 4.19W
Carmarthen Bay 9 Ij 51.40N 4.30W
Carmaux 11 Ij 44.03N 2.09 E
Carmel Head 9 Ih 53.24N 4.34W
Carmelita 49 Be 17.21N 90.10W
Carmelo 56 Id 34.00S 58.17W
Carmen 55 Dk 33.15S 56.01W
Carmen, Isla- 47 Bc 25.57N 111.12W
Carmen, Isla del- 48 Nh 18.42N 91.40W
Carmen, Laguna del- 48 Mh 18.15N 93.50W
Carmen, Rio del- 48 Fb 30.42N 106.29W
Carmen, Sierra del- 48 Hc 29.00N 102.30W
Carmen de Patagones 56 Hf 40.48S 62.59W
Carmensa 56 Ge 35.08S 67.38W
Carmi 45 Lg 38.07N 88.10W
Carmichael 46 Eg 38.38N 121.19W
Carmo de Minas 55 Jf 22.07S 45.08W
Carmo do Paranaíba 55 Id 18.59S 46.21W
Carmona 13 Gg 37.28N 5.38W
Carnac 11 Cg 47.35N 3.05W
Carnamah 59 De 29.42S 115.53 E
Carnarvon [Austl.] 58 Cg 24.53S 113.40 E
Carnarvon [S.Afr.] 31 Jl 30.56S 22.08 E
Carnarvon Range 59 Ee 25.10S 121.00 E
Carnatic (EN) 21 Jh 10.30N 79.00 E
Carnegie, Lake- 57 Dg 26.10S 122.30 E
Carnegie Ridge (EN) 3 Nj 1.00S 85.00W
Carn Eige 9 Hd 57.30N 5.05W
Carney Island 66 Nf 73.57S 121.00W
Carnia 14 Gd 46.25N 13.00 E
Car Nicobar 25 Ig 9.10N 92.47 E
Carnot 35 Be 4.48N 16.03 E
Carnoustie 9 Ke 56.30N 2.44W
Carnsore Point/Ceann an Chairn 9 Gi 52.10N 6.22W
Carn Ui Néid/Mizen Head 5 Fe 51.27N 9.49W
Caro 44 Fd 43.29N 83.24W
Carol City 44 Gm 25.56N 80.16W
Carolina [Braz.] 53 Lf 7.20S 47.28W
Carolina [P.R.] 51a Cb 18.24N 65.57W
Carolina [S.Afr.] 37 Ee 26.05S 30.06 E
Carolina Beach 44 Ih 34.02N 77.54W
Carolinas, Puntan- 64b Bb 14.54N 145.38 E
Caroline Atoll 57 Le 9.58S 150.13W
Caroline Islands 57 Fd 8.00N 147.00 E
Carondelet Reef 57 Je 5.34S 173.51W
Caroní, Rio- 52 Je 8.21N 62.43W
Caronie→Nebrodi 14 Im 37.55N 14.35 E
Carora 54 Da 10.11N 70.05W
Carpathian Mountains (EN) 5 If 48.00N 24.00 E
Carpathian Mountains (EN) =Carpaţii Occidentali 15 Fc 46.30N 22.10 E
Carpathian Mountains (EN) =Carpaţii Orientali 15 Ib 47.30N 25.30 E
Carpaţii Meridionali= Transylvanian Alps (EN) 5 If 45.30N 22.10 E
Carpaţii Occidentali = Carpathian Mountains (EN) 15 Fc 46.30N 22.10 E
Carpaţii Orientali= Carpathian Mountains (EN) 15 Ib 47.30N 25.30 E
Carpen 15 Ge 44.20N 23.15 E
Carpentaria, Gulf of- 57 Ef 14.00S 139.00 E
Carpentras 11 Lj 44.03N 5.03 E
Carpi 14 Ef 44.47N 10.53 E
Carpina 54 Ke 7.51S 35.15W
Carr, Cape- 66 Ie 66.07S 130.51 E
Carraig Fhearghais/ Carrickfergus 9 Hg 54.43N 5.44W
Carraig na Siúire/Carrick-on-Suir
Carrara 14 Ef 44.05N 10.06 E
Carrauntoohil 5 Fe 52.00N 9.45W
Carreiro, Rio- 55 Gi 29.07S 51.43W
Carreño 13 Ga 43.35N 5.46W
Carreta, Punta- 54 Cf 14.13S 76.18W
Carretero, Puerto- 13 Ig 37.28N 3.40W
Carriacou 50 Ff 12.30N 61.27W
Carrick 9 If 55.15N 4.40W
Carrickfergus/Carraig Fhearghais 9 Hg 54.43N 5.44W
Carrick-on-Shannon/cara Droma Rúisc 9 Eh 53.57N 8.05W
Carrick-on-Suir/Carraig na Siúire 9 Fi 52.21N 7.25W
Carrington 43 Hb 47.27N 99.08W
Carrión 13 Hc 41.53N 4.32W
Carrión de los Condes 13 Hb 42.20N 4.36W
Carrizal 49 Kh 11.58N 72.12W
Carrizo Peak 45 Dj 33.20N 105.38W
Carrizos 48 Gc 29.58N 105.16W
Carrizo Springs 45 Gl 28.31N 99.52W
Carrizo Wash 46 Ki 34.36N 109.26W
Carrizozo 45 Dj 33.38N 105.53W
Carroll 45 Ie 42.04N 94.52W
Carroll Inlet 66 Qf 73.18S 78.30W
Carrollton [Ga.-U.S.] 44 Ei 33.35N 85.05W
Carrollton [Il.-U.S.] 45 Kg 39.18N 90.24W
Carrollton [Ky.-U.S.] 44 Ef 38.41N 85.11W
Carrollton [Mo.-U.S.] 45 Jg 39.22N 93.30W
Carron, Loch- 9 Hd 57.30N 5.40W
Carrot 42 Hf 53.50N 101.18W
Carrowmore Lough 9 Dg 54.12N 9.47W
Çarşamba 24 Gb 41.12N 36.44 E
Çarşamba 24 Ed 37.53N 32.37 E
Čaršanga 19 Gh 37.31N 66.03 E
Čarsk 19 If 49.35N 81.05 E
Carson 46 Ed 45.44N 121.49W
Carson City 39 Hf 39.10N 119.46W
Carson Lake 46 Fg 39.19N 118.43W
Carson Sink 46 Fg 39.45N 118.30W
Cartagena [Col.] 53 Id 10.25N 75.32W
Cartagena [Sp.] 6 Fh 37.36N 0.59W
Cartago [3] 49 Fi 9.50N 83.45W
Cartago [Col.] 54 Cc 4.46N 75.56W
Cartago [C.R.] 47 Hg 9.52N 83.55W
Cartaxo 13 De 39.09N 8.47W
Carter, Mount- 59 Ib 13.05S 143.15 E
Carteret 11 Ee 49.23N 1.47W
Cartersville 44 Eh 34.10N 85.05W
Carterton 62 Fd 41.01S 175.31 E
Carthage [Mo.-U.S.] 45 Ih 37.11N 94.19W
Carthage [Tx.-U.S.] 45 Ij 32.09N 94.20W
Cartier 44 Gb 46.42N 81.32W
Cartier Island 57 Df 12.30S 123.30 E
Caruaru 53 Mf 8.17S 35.58W
Carúpano 54 Fa 10.40N 63.14W
Carutapera 54 Id 1.13S 46.01W
Čarvak 18 Gd 41.38N 69.56 E
Carvin 12 Ed 50.29N 2.58 E
Carvoeiro, Cabo- 13 Ce 39.21N 9.24W
Čaryn 18 Lc 43.50N 79.12 E
Čaryš 20 Df 52.22N 83.45 E
Casablanca [2] 32 Fc 33.37N 7.35W
Casablanca 32 Gc 33.36N 7.37W
Casa Branca 55 Ie 21.46S 47.05W
Casa Grande 43 Ee 32.53N 111.45W
Casalbordino 14 Ih 42.09N 14.35 E
Casale Monferrato 14 Ce 45.08N 8.27 E
Casalmaggiore 14 Ef 44.59N 10.26 E
Casalvasco 55 Cb 15.19S 59.59W
Casal Velino 14 Jj 40.11N 15.06 E
Casamance 34 Bc 12.33N 16.46W
Casamance [3] 34 Bc 12.50N 15.00W
Casanare [2] 54 Db 5.20N 72.00W
Casanare, Rio- 54 Eb 6.02N 69.51W
Casanay 50 Eg 10.30N 63.25W
Casa Nova 54 Je 9.25S 41.08W
Casarano 14 Mj 40.00N 18.10 E
Casas Grandes, Rio- 48 Eb 30.22N 107.31W
Casas-Ibáñez 13 Ke 39.17N 1.28W
Casca, Rio da- 55 Eb 14.52S 55.52W
Cascade 46 Hd 44.31N 115.59W
Cascade Point 62 Cf 44.01S 168.22 E
Cascade Range 38 Ge 45.00N 121.30W
Cascais 13 Cf 38.42N 9.25W
Cascavel 56 Jb 24.57S 53.28W
Cascia 14 Hh 42.43N 13.01 E
Casciana Terme 14 Eg 43.32N 10.38 E
Cascina 14 Eg 43.41N 10.33 E
Casentino 14 Fg 43.40N 11.50 E

Index Symbols

[1] Independent Nation
[2] State, Region
[3] District, County
[4] Municipality
[5] Colony, Dependency
Continent
Physical Region
Historical or Cultural Region
Mount, Mountain
Volcano
Hill
Mountains, Mountain Range
Hills, Escarpment
Plateau, Upland
Pass, Gap
Plain, Lowland
Delta
Salt Flat
Valley, Canyon
Crater, Cave
Karst Features
Depression
Polder
Desert, Dunes
Forest, Woods
Heath, Steppe
Oasis
Cape, Point
Coast, Beach
Cliff
Peninsula
Isthmus
Sandbank
Island
Atoll
Rock, Reef
Islands, Archipelago
Rocks, Reefs
Coral Reef
Well, Spring
Geyser
River, Stream
Waterfall Rapids
River Mouth, Estuary
Lake
Salt Lake
Intermittent Lake
Reservoir
Swamp, Pond
Canal
Glacier
Ice Shelf, Pack Ice
Ocean
Sea
Gulf, Bay
Strait, Fjord
Lagoon
Bank
Seamount
Tablemount
Ridge
Shelf
Basin
Escarpment, Sea Scarp
Fracture
Trench, Abyss
National Park, Reserve
Point of Interest
Recreation Site
Cave, Cavern
Historic Site
Ruins
Wall, Walls
Church, Abbey
Temple
Scientific Station
Airport
Port
Lighthouse
Mine
Tunnel
Dam, Bridge

Index Symbols

[1] Independent Nation
[2] State, Region
[3] District, County
[4] Municipality
[5] Colony, Dependency
Continent
Physical Region
Historical or Cultural Region
Mount, Mountain
Volcano
Hill
Mountains, Mountain Range
Hills, Escarpment
Plateau, Upland
Pass, Gap
Plain, Lowland
Delta
Salt Flat
Valley, Canyon
Crater, Cave
Karst Features
Depression
Polder
Desert, Dunes
Forest, Woods
Heath, Steppe
Oasis
Cape, Point
Coast, Beach
Cliff
Peninsula
Isthmus
Sandbank
Island
Atoll
Rock, Reef
Islands, Archipelago
Rocks, Reefs
Coral Reef
Well, Spring
Geyser
River, Stream
Waterfall Rapids
River Mouth, Estuary
Lake
Salt Lake
Intermittent Lake
Reservoir
Swamp, Pond
Canal
Glacier
Ice Shelf, Pack Ice
Ocean
Sea
Gulf, Bay
Strait, Fjord
Lagoon
Bank
Seamount
Tablemount
Ridge
Shelf
Basin
Escarpment, Sea Scarp
Fracture
Trench, Abyss
National Park, Reserve
Point of Interest
Recreation Site
Cave, Cavern
Historic Site
Ruins
Wall, Walls
Church, Abbey
Temple
Scientific Station
Airport
Port
Lighthouse
Mine
Tunnel
Dam, Bridge

Certaldo	14	Fg	43.33N	11.02 E
Čertkovo	16	Le	49.20N	40.12 E
Červaro	14	Ji	41.30N	15.52 E
Červati	14	Jj	40.17N	15.29 E
Červeh	15	Jf	43.37N	26.02 E
Červen	16	Fc	53.43N	28.29 E
Červen brjag	15	Hf	43.16N	24.06 E
Cervera	13	Nc	41.40N	1.17 E
Cervera del Río Alhama	13	Kb	42.01N	1.57W
Cervera de Pisuerga	13	Hb	42.52N	4.30W
Cerveteri	14	Gh	42.00N	12.06 E
Cervia	14	Gf	44.15N	12.22 E
Cervin/Cervino	14	Be	45.58N	7.39 E
Cervino/Cervin	14	Be	45.58N	7.39 E
Cervione	11a	Ba	42.20N	9.29 E
Červonoarmejsk	10	Vf	50.03N	25.18 E
Červonoarmejskoje	15	Ld	45.50N	28.38 E
Červonograd	19	Ce	50.24N	24.12 E
Cesano	14	Hg	43.45N	13.10 E
Cesar [2]	54	Db	9.50N	73.30W
César, Río-	49	Ki	9.00N	73.58W
Cesena	14	Gf	44.08N	12.15 E
Cesenatico	14	Gf	44.12N	12.24 E
Cēsis/Cesis	19	Cd	57.18N	25.18 E
Cesis/Cēsis	19	Cd	57.18N	25.18 E
Česká Lípa	10	Kf	50.42N	14.32 E
Česká Třebová	10	Mg	49.54N	16.27 E
České Budějovice	10	Kh	48.58N	14.29 E
České středohoří	10	Jf	50.35N	14.00 E
České země [2]	10	Kg	49.45N	15.00 E
Českomoravská Vrchovina= Moravian Upland (EN)	5	Hf	49.20N	15.30 E
Československá Socialistická Republika (ČSSR) [1]	6	Hf	49.30N	17.00 E
Československo= Czechoslovakia (EN) [1]	6	Hf	49.30N	17.00 E
Český Krumlov	10	Kh	48.49N	14.19 E
Český Les=Bohemian Forest (EN)	10	Ig	49.50N	12.30 E
Česma	14	Kf	45.35N	16.29 E
Česma	17	Jj	53.50N	60.40 E
Çeşme	24	Bc	38.18N	26.19 E
Çeşme Yarimadası	15	Jk	38.30N	26.30 E
Češskaja Guba=Chesha Bay (EN)	5	Kb	67.20N	46.30 E
Cessnock	59	Kf	32.50S	151.21 E
Cestos	30	Gh	5.27N	9.35W
Cesvaine/Cesvajne	8	Lh	56.55N	26.20 E
Cesvajne/Cesvaine	8	Lh	56.55N	26.20 E
Cetate	15	Ge	44.06N	23.03 E
Cetina	14	Kg	43.27N	16.42 E
Cetinje	15	Bg	42.24N	18.55 E
Çetinkaya	24	Gc	39.15N	37.38 E
Cetraro	14	Jk	39.31N	15.56 E
Cetynia	10	Sd	52.33N	22.26 E
Ceuta [5]	31	Ge	35.53N	5.19W
Ceva-i-Ra (Conway Reef)	57	Ig	21.45S	174.35 E
Cevedale/Zufallspitze	14	Ed	46.27N	10.37 E
Cévennes	5	Gg	44.40N	4.00 E
Ceyhan	23	Eb	36.45N	35.42 E
Ceyhan	23	Eb	37.04N	35.47 E
Ceylanpınar	24	Id	36.51N	40.02 E
Ceylon→Srī Lanka [1]	22	Ki	7.40N	80.50 E
Cézallier	11	Ii	45.20N	3.00 E
Cèze	11	Kj	44.06N	4.42 E
Chaalis, Abbaye de-	12	Ee	49.10N	2.40 E
Cha-am	25	Jf	12.48N	99.58 E
Chabanais	11	Gi	45.52N	0.43 E
Chabjuwardoo Bay	59	Cd	22.55S	113.50 E
Chablais	11	Mh	46.20N	6.30 E
Chăboksar	24	Nd	36.58N	50.34 E
Chabówka	10	Pg	49.34N	19.58 E
Chacabuco	56	Hd	34.38S	60.29W
Chachan, Nevado-	54	Dg	16.12S	71.33W
Chachapoyas	54	Ce	6.13S	77.51W
Chachoengsao	25	Kf	13.41N	101.03 E
Chaco [2]	56	Hc	26.00S	60.30W
Chaco [3]	55	Bd	20.00S	60.30W
Chaco, Gran-	52	Jh	23.00S	60.00W
Chaco Mesa	45	Ci	35.50N	107.35W
Chaco River	45	Bh	36.46N	108.69W
Chad (EN)=Tchad [1]	31	Ig	15.00N	19.00 E
Chad, Lake- (EN)=Tchad, Lac-	30	Ig	13.20N	14.00 E
Chādegān	24	Nf	32.46N	50.38 E
Chadileuvú, Río-	56	Ee	38.49S	64.57W
Chadiza	36	Fe	14.04S	32.26 E
Chadron	43	Gc	42.50N	103.02W
Chaeryŏng	28	He	38.24N	125.37 E
Chafarinas, Islas-	13	Ji	35.11N	2.26W
Chāgai Hills	21	Ig	29.30N	64.15 E
Chagang-Do [2]	28	Ie	40.50N	126.30 E
Chaghcharān	22	If	34.31N	65.15 E
Chagny	11	Kh	46.55N	4.45 E
Chagos Archipelago	21	Jj	6.00S	72.00 E
Chagos-Laccadive Plateau (EN)	3	Gi	3.00N	73.00 E
Chagu, Serra do-	55	Fg	25.10S	52.40W
Chaguaramas	50	Ch	9.20N	66.16W
Chahār Borjak	23	Jc	30.17N	62.03 E
Chahār Mahāl-e Bakhtīārī [3]	23	Hc	32.00N	50.00 E
Chahbounia	13	Oi	35.33N	2.36 E
Ch'aho	28	Jd	40.12N	128.38 E
Chai Badan	25	Ke	15.05N	101.04 E
Chaibāsa	25	Hd	22.34N	85.49 E
Chaigoubu → Huai'an	28	Cd	40.40N	114.25 E
Chai He	28	Gc	42.20N	123.51 E
Chaillu, Massif du-	30	Ii	2.32S	11.10 E
Chainat	25	Ke	15.10N	100.10 E
Chaitén	56	Ff	42.55S	72.43W
Chaiyaphum	25	Ke	16.09N	102.02 E
Chajul	49	Bf	15.30N	91.02W
Chakari	37	Dc	18.09S	29.52 E
Chak Chak	35	Dd	8.40N	26.54 E
Chake Chake	31	Ki	5.15S	39.46 E
Chakhānsūr	23	Jc	31.10N	62.04 E
Chala	54	Dg	15.52S	74.16W
Chalais	11	Gi	45.17N	0.02 E
Chalaltenango	49	Cf	14.03N	88.56W
Chalan Kanoa	64b	Ba	15.08N	145.43 E
Chālās	22	Gf	37.16N	49.36 E
Chalbi Desert	30	Kh	3.00N	37.20 E
Chalchuapa	49	Cg	13.59N	89.41W
Chalcidice (EN)= Khalkidhikí	5	Ig	40.25N	23.25 E
Chālesbān	24	Ne	35.18N	50.03 E
Chaleur Bay	42	Kg	47.50N	65.30W
Chalhuanca	54	Df	14.17S	73.15W
Chaling	27	Jf	26.47N	113.32 E
Chalky Inlet	62	Bg	46.05S	166.30 E
Challans	11	Eh	46.51N	1.53W
Challapata	54	Eg	18.54S	66.47W
Challis	46	Hd	44.30N	114.14W
Chalmette	45	Ll	29.56N	89.58W
Châlons-sur-Marne	11	Kf	48.57N	4.22 E
Chalon-sur-Saône	11	Kh	46.47N	4.51 E
Chaltubo	16	Mh	42.19N	42.34 E
Chālūs	23	Hb	36.38N	51.26 E
Châlus	11	Gi	45.39N	0.59 E
Cham	10	Ig	49.13N	12.40 E
Chama	36	Fe	11.12S	33.10 E
Chama, Río-	45	Ch	36.03N	106.05W
Chama, Río-	49	Li	9.03N	71.37W
Chaman	25	Db	30.55N	66.27 E
Chaman Bīd	24	Qd	37.25N	56.38 E
Chamba [India]	25	Fb	32.34N	76.08 E
Chamba [Tan.]	36	Ge	11.35S	36.58 E
Chambal	21	Jg	26.29N	79.15 E
Chambaran, Plateau de-	11	Li	45.10N	5.20 E
Chambas	49	Hb	22.12N	78.55W
Chamberlain	45	Ge	43.49N	99.20W
Chamberlain Lake	44	Mb	46.17N	69.20W
Chamberlain River	59	Fc	15.35S	127.51 E
Chambersburg	44	If	39.57N	77.40W
Chambéry	11	Li	45.34N	5.56 E
Chambeshi	30	Jj	11.53S	29.48 E
Chambley-Bussières	12	He	49.03N	5.54 E
Chambly	12	Ee	49.10N	2.15 E
Chambois	12	Cf	48.48N	0.07 E
Chambon, Lac de-	11	Ih	45.35N	2.55 E
Chambord	11	Hg	47.37N	1.31 E
Chamchamal	24	Ke	35.32N	44.50 E
Chame, Punta-	49	Hi	8.39N	79.42W
Chamela	48	Gh	19.32N	105.05W
Chamela, Bahía-	48	Gh	19.30N	105.10W
Chamelecón, Río-	49	Df	15.51N	87.49W
Chamical	56	Gd	30.21S	66.19W
Chamiss Bay	46	Ba	50.07N	127.22W
Chamoli	25	Fb	30.24N	79.21 E
Chamonix-Mont-Blanc	11	Mi	45.55N	6.52 E
Chamouchouane, Rivière-	44	Ka	48.40N	72.20W
Champagne	5	Gf	49.00N	4.30 E
Champagne	11	Kf	49.00N	4.30 E
Champagne Berrichonne	11	Hh	47.00N	2.00 E
Champagne Humide	11	Kf	48.20N	4.30 E
Champagne Pouilleuse	11	Kf	48.40N	4.20 E
Champagnole	11	Lh	46.45N	5.55 E
Champaign	43	Jc	40.07N	88.14W
Champaqui, Cerro-	52	Ji	31.59S	64.56W
Champasak	25	Lf	14.53N	105.52 E
Champaubert	12	Ff	48.53N	3.47 E
Champdoré, Lac-	42	Ke	55.55N	65.45W
Champeigne	11	Gg	47.15N	0.50 E
Champerico	49	Bf	14.18N	91.55W
Champlain, Lake-	43	Mc	44.45N	73.15W
Champlitte-et-le-Prélot	11	Lg	47.37N	5.31 E
Champotón	47	Fe	19.21N	90.43W
Champsaur	11	Mj	44.45N	6.10 E
Chāmrājnagar	25	Ff	11.55N	76.57 E
Chañaral	56	Fc	26.21S	70.37W
Chança	13	Eg	37.33N	7.31W
Chan Chan	54	Ce	8.07S	79.02W
Chanco	56	Fe	35.44S	72.32W
Chandalar	40	Jc	66.36N	145.48W
Chandalar	40	Jc	67.30N	148.30W
Chandausi	25	Fc	28.27N	78.46 E
Chandeleur Islands	43	Jf	29.48N	88.51W
Chandeleur Sound	45	Ll	29.55N	89.10W
Chandīgarh	22	Jf	30.44N	76.55 E
Chandler	42	Lg	48.21N	64.41W
Chandless, Rio	54	Ee	9.08S	69.51W
Chāndpur	25	Id	23.13N	90.39 E
Chandragupta	25	Fe	16.11N	78.52 E
Chandrapur	22	Jh	19.57N	79.18 E
Chang, Ko-	25	Kf	12.00N	102.23 E
Changajn Nuruu→Hangaj, Hrebet-=Khangai Mountains (EN)	21	Le	47.30N	100.00 E
Chang'an → Rong'an	27	If	25.16N	109.23 E
Changane	30	Kk	24.43S	33.32 E
Changbai	28	Jd	41.25N	128.11 E
Changbai Shan	21	Oe	42.00N	128.00 E
Changchun	22	Oe	43.51N	125.20 E
Changdao(Sihou)	28	Ff	37.56N	120.42 E
Changde	22	Ng	29.04N	111.42 E
Ch'angdo	28	Ie	38.30N	127.45 E
Changfeng (Shuijiahu)	28	Dh	32.29N	117.10 E
Changge	28	Bg	34.12N	113.45 E
Changhang	28	If	36.01N	126.42 E
Chang He	28	Ei	31.21N	118.21 E
Changhowŏn	28	If	37.07N	127.38 E
Changhua	27	Lg	24.05N	120.32 E
Changhŭng	28	Ig	34.40N	126.54 E
Changji	27	Ec	44.01N	87.16 E
Chang Jiang	28	Dj	28.59N	116.42 E
Changjiang (Shiliu)	27	Ih	19.20N	109.03 E
Chang Jiang (Yangtze Kiang)	21	Of	31.48N	121.10 E
Changjiang Kou	27	Le	31.24N	121.59 E
Changjin-gang	28	Id	40.30N	127.12 E
Changjin-ho	28	Id	40.30N	127.12 E
Changjin-ŭp	27	Mc	40.23N	127.15 E
Changli	28	Ee	39.43N	119.10 E
Changling	27	Lc	44.15N	123.58 E
Changlung	25	Fb	34.56N	77.29 E
Changping	28	Dd	40.14N	116.13 E
Changsha	22	Ng	28.12N	113.02 E
Changshan	28	Ej	28.55N	118.31 E
Changshan Qundao	28	Ge	39.10N	122.34 E
Changshu	28	Fi	31.38N	120.44 E
Changsŏng	28	Ig	35.19N	126.48 E
Changting	28	Jb	44.27N	128.50 E
Changtu	28	Hc	42.47N	124.08 E
Changuillo	54	Cf	14.40S	75.12W
Changuinola	49	Fi	9.26N	82.31W
Changwu	27	Id	35.17N	107.52 E
Changxing	28	Ei	31.01N	119.55 E
Changxing Dao	28	Fe	39.35N	121.42 E
Changyi	28	Ef	36.52N	119.25 E
Changyŏn	27	Md	38.15N	125.05 E
Changyuan	28	Cg	35.12N	114.40 E
Changzhi	27	Jd	36.07N	113.10 E
Changzhou	28	Ei	31.46N	119.56 E
Channel Islands [5]	9	Kl	49.20N	2.20W
Channel Islands [Chan.Is.]	5	Ff	49.20N	2.20W
Channel Islands [U.S.]	38	Hf	34.00N	120.00W
Channel Port-aux-Basques	39	Ne	47.35N	59.11W
Channel Rock	49	Ib	23.00N	77.55W
Channing	45	Ei	35.41N	102.20W
Chantada	13	Eb	42.37N	7.46W
Chantengo, Laguna-	48	Ji	16.35N	99.10W
Chanthaburi	25	Kf	12.35N	102.06 E
Chantilly	11	Ie	49.12N	2.28 E
Chantonnay	11	Eh	46.41N	1.03W
Chantrey Inlet	38	Jc	67.48N	96.20W
Chanute	45	Ih	37.41N	95.27W
Chanza	13	Eg	37.33N	7.31W
Chao'an (Chaozhou)	27	Kg	23.41N	116.37 E
Chaobai Xinhe	28	De	39.07N	117.41 E
Chao He	28	Dd	40.36N	117.08 E
Chao Hu	28	Di	31.31N	117.33 E
Chao Phraya	21	Mh	13.32N	100.36 E
Chaor He	27	Lb	46.49N	123.45 E
Chaoxian	27	Ke	31.37N	117.49 E
Chaoyang [China]	22	Oe	41.35N	120.26 E
Chaoyang [China]	27	Kg	23.17N	116.37 E
Chaoyang → Huinan	28	Ic	42.41N	126.03 E
Chaoyang → Jiayin	27	Nb	48.52N	130.21 E
Chaoyangchuan	28	Jc	42.53N	129.23 E
Chaoyangcun	27	La	50.01N	124.22 E
Chaozhong	27	La	50.53N	121.23 E
Chaozhou → Chao'an	27	Kg	23.41N	116.37 E
Chapada dos Guimarães	54	Gg	15.26S	55.45W
Chapadinha	54	Jd	3.44S	43.21W
Chapais	44	Ja	49.47N	74.56W
Chapala	48	Hg	20.18N	103.12W
Chapala, Lago de-	38	Ig	20.15N	103.00W
Chaparral	54	Cc	3.43N	75.28W
Chapecó	56	Jc	27.06S	52.36W
Chapecó, Rio-	55	Fh	27.06S	53.01W
Chapecó, Serra do-	55	Gh	26.44S	51.54W
Chapel Hill	44	Hh	35.55N	79.04W
Chapicuy	55	Dj	31.40S	57.55W
Chapleau	42	Jg	47.50N	83.24W
Chaplin	46	La	50.28N	106.40W
Chaplin Lake	46	La	50.18N	106.35W
Chapman, Cape-	42	Ic	69.15N	89.27W
Chappell	45	Ef	41.06N	102.28W
Chăpra	25	Gc	25.46N	84.45 E
Chapultepec	48	Hf	23.27N	103.04W
Chaqui	54	Eg	19.36S	65.32W
Char	32	Ee	21.31N	12.51W
Charadai	55	Ch	27.38S	59.54W
Charagua	54	Fg	19.48S	63.13W
Charām	24	Ng	30.45N	50.44 E
Charaña	54	Eg	17.36S	69.28W
Charcas	48	If	23.08N	101.07W
Charco de la Aguja	48	Gc	28.25N	104.01W
Charcot Island	66	Qe	69.45S	75.15W
Chard [Alta.-Can.]	42	Ge	55.48N	111.10W
Chard [Eng.-U.K.]	9	Kk	50.53N	2.58W
Chardāvol	24	Lf	33.45N	46.38 E
Chardonnières	49	Jd	18.16N	74.10W
Charente [3]	11	Gi	45.40N	0.05 E
Charente	11	Ei	45.57N	1.05W
Charente-Maritime [3]	11	Fi	45.30N	0.45W
Charentonne	12	Ce	49.07N	0.44 E
Chari	30	Ig	12.58N	14.31 E
Chari-Baguirmi [3]	35	Bc	12.00N	17.00 E
Chārikār	23	Kb	35.01N	69.11 E
Charing	12	Cc	51.12N	0.48 E
Chariton	45	Jf	41.00N	93.19W
Chariton River	45	Jg	39.19N	92.57W
Charity	54	Gb	7.24N	58.36W
Charleroi	11	Kd	50.25N	4.26 E
Charleroi-Jumet	11	Kd	50.27N	4.26 E
Charleroi-Marcinelle	12	Gd	50.25N	4.28 E
Charles	42	Kd	62.38N	74.15W
Charles, Cape- [Can.]	38	Nd	52.13N	55.40W
Charles, Cape- [Va.-U.S.]	43	Ld	37.08N	75.58W
Charles, Peak-	59	Ef	32.52S	121.11 E
Charlesbourg	44	Lb	46.52N	71.16W
Charles City	43	Ic	43.04N	92.40W
Charles de Gaulle, Aéroport-=Charles de Gaulle Airport (EN)	12	Ee	49.02N	2.35 E
Charles de Gaulle Airport (EN)=Charles de Gaulle, Aéroport-	12	Ee	49.02N	2.35 E
Charleston [Il.-U.S.]	45	Lg	39.30N	88.10W
Charleston [Mo.-U.S.]	45	Lh	36.55N	89.21W
Charleston [Ms.-U.S.]	45	Ki	34.01N	90.04W
Charleston [N.Z.]	62	Dd	41.54S	171.27 E
Charleston [S.C.-U.S.]	39	Lf	32.48N	79.57W
Charleston [W.V.-U.S.]	39	Kf	38.21N	81.38W
Charleston Peak	43	Dd	36.16N	115.42W
Charles Town	44	If	39.18N	77.52W
Charlestown	50	Ed	17.12N	62.35W
Charleval	12	De	49.22N	1.23 E
Charleville	58	Fg	26.24S	146.15 E
Charleville-Mézières	11	Ke	49.46N	4.43 E
Charleville Mézières-Mohon	12	Ge	49.46N	4.43 E
Charlevoix	44	Ec	45.19N	85.16W
Charlieu	11	Kh	46.09N	4.11 E
Charlotte [Mi.-U.S.]	44	Ed	42.36N	84.50W
Charlotte [N.C.-U.S.]	39	Kf	35.14N	80.50W
Charlotte Amalie	47	Le	18.21N	64.56W
Charlotte Bank (EN)	57	If	11.47S	173.13 E
Charlotte Harbor	44	Fl	26.45N	82.12W
Charlottenberg	8	Ee	59.53N	12.17 E
Charlottesville	43	Ld	38.02N	78.29W
Charlottetown	39	Me	46.14N	63.08W
Charlton	59	Ig	36.16S	143.21 E
Charlton	42	Jf	52.00N	79.26W
Charly	12	Ff	48.58N	3.17 E
Charmes	11	Mf	48.22N	6.17 E
Charnley River	59	Ec	16.20S	124.53 E
Charny-sur-Meuse	12	He	49.12N	5.22 E
Charollais	11	Kh	46.26N	4.16 E
Charouine	32	Gd	29.01N	0.16W
Charroux	11	Gh	46.09N	0.24 E
Chārsadda	25	Eb	34.09N	71.44 E
Charters Towers	58	Fg	20.05S	146.16 E
Chartres	11	Hf	48.27N	1.30 E
Charzykowskie, Jezioro-	10	Nc	53.47N	17.30 E
Chascomus	56	Ie	35.34S	58.01W
Chase	46	Fa	50.49N	119.41W
Chasŏng	28	Id	41.25N	126.35 E
Chassengue	36	Ce	10.26S	18.32 E
Chassezac	11	Kj	44.26N	4.19 E
Chassiron, Pointe de-	11	Eh	46.03N	1.24W
Chat	24	Pd	37.59N	55.16 E
Châtaigneraie	11	Ij	44.45N	2.20 E
Chātāl	24	Pd	37.40N	55.45 E
Château-Arnoux	11	Lj	44.06N	6.00 E
Châteaubelair	51n	Ba	13.17N	61.15W
Châteaubriant	11	Eg	47.43N	1.23W
Château-Chinon	11	Jg	47.04N	3.56 E
Château-du-Loir	11	Gg	47.42N	0.25 E
Châteaudun	11	Hf	48.05N	1.20 E
Château-Gontier	11	Fg	47.50N	0.42W
Châteaulin	11	Bf	48.12N	4.05W
Châteaulin, Bassin de-	11	Cf	48.18N	3.50W
Châteaumeillant	11	Ih	46.34N	2.12 E
Châteauneuf-de-Randon	11	Jj	44.39N	3.04 E
Châteauneuf-sur-Cher	11	Ih	46.51N	2.19 E
Châteauneuf-sur-Loire	11	Ig	47.52N	2.14 E
Château-Porcien	12	Ge	49.32N	4.15 E
Châteaurenard	11	Kk	43.53N	4.51 E
Château-Renault	11	Gg	47.35N	0.54 E
Châteauroux	11	Hh	46.49N	1.42 E
Château-Salins	11	Mf	48.49N	6.30 E
Château-Thierry	11	Je	49.03N	3.24 E
Châteaux, Pointe des-	51e	Bb	16.15N	61.11W
Châtelaillon-Plage	11	Eh	46.04N	1.05W
Châtelet	12	Gd	50.24N	4.31 E
Châtelguyon	11	Ji	45.55N	3.04 E
Châtellerault	11	Gh	46.48N	0.32 E
Chatelodo	55	De	21.19S	57.28W
Chatham [Eng.-U.K.]	9	Nj	51.23N	0.32 E
Chatham [N.B.-Can.]	42	Kg	47.02N	65.26W
Chatham [Ont.-Can.]	42	Jh	42.24N	82.11W
Chatham [Va.-U.S.]	44	Hg	36.49N	79.26W
Chatham Island	57	Ji	44.00S	176.30W
Chatham Islands	57	Ji	44.00S	176.30W
Chatham Rise (EN)	57	Ii	43.30S	180.00
Chatham Strait	40	Me	57.30N	134.45W
Châtillon-en-Bazois	11	Jg	47.03N	3.40 E
Châtillon-sur-Indre	11	Hh	46.59N	1.10 E
Châtillon-sur-Marne	12	Fe	49.06N	3.45 E
Châtillon-sur-Seine	11	Kg	47.51N	4.33 E
Chatom	44	Cj	31.28N	88.16W
Chatsworth	37	Ec	19.38S	30.50 E
Chattahoochee	44	Ej	30.42N	84.51W
Chattahoochee	38	Kf	30.52N	84.57W
Chattanooga	39	Kf	35.03N	85.19W
Chatteris	12	Cb	52.27N	0.03 E
Chaucas	55	Cc	16.46S	58.44W
Chaudfontaine	12	Hd	50.35N	5.38 E
Chaudière, Rivière-	44	Lb	46.43N	71.17W
Chauk	25	Id	20.53N	94.49 E
Chaulnes	12	Ee	49.49N	2.48 E
Chaumont	11	Lf	48.07N	5.08 E
Chaumont-en-Vexin	12	De	49.16N	1.53 E
Chaumont-Gistoux	12	Gd	50.41N	4.44 E
Chaumont-Porcien	12	Ge	49.39N	4.15 E
Chaumont-sur-Aire	12	Hf	48.56N	5.15 E
Chaumont-sur-Loire	11	Hg	47.29N	1.11 E
Chauny	11	Je	49.37N	3.13 E
Chau Phu	25	Lf	10.42N	105.07 E
Chausey, Iles-	11	Ef	48.53N	1.50W
Chauvigny	11	Gh	46.34N	0.39 E
Chavantina	54	Hf	14.40S	52.21W
Chavarria	55	Ci	28.57S	58.35W
Chaves [Braz.]	54	Id	0.10S	49.55W
Chaves [Port.]	13	Ec	41.44N	7.28W
Chavigny, Lac-	42	Je	58.00N	75.05W
Chavuma	36	De	13.05S	22.42 E
Chazelles-sur-Lyon	11	Ki	45.38N	4.23 E
Chbar	25	Lf	12.46N	107.10 E
Cheaha Mountain	44	Ei	33.30N	85.47W
Cheat River	44	Hf	39.45N	79.55W
Cheb	10	If	50.04N	12.23 E
Cheboygan	43	Kb	45.39N	84.29W
Chech, 'Erg-	30	Gf	25.00N	3.00W
Chechaouene [3]	32	Fb	35.00N	5.00W
Chechaouene	32	Fb	35.10N	5.16W
Checheng	27	Lg	22.05N	120.42 E
Che-Chiang Sheng→Zhejiang Sheng [2]	27	Kf	29.00N	120.00 E
Chech'ŏn	28	Jf	37.08N	128.12 E
Chęciny	10	Qf	50.48N	20.28 E
Cheddar Gorge	9	Kj	51.13N	2.47W
Cheduba	25	Ie	18.48N	93.38 E
Chée	12	Gf	48.45N	4.39 E
Cheektowaga	44	Hd	42.57N	78.38W
Chefu	37	Ed	22.27S	32.45 E
Chegga	31	Gf	25.22N	5.49W
Cheghelvandī	24	Mf	33.42N	48.25 E
Chehel Pāyeh	24	Qg	31.54N	57.14 E
Cheju	27	Me	33.31N	126.32 E
Cheju-Do	21	Of	33.25N	126.30 E
Cheju-Do [2]	28	Ih	33.25N	126.30 E
Cheju-Haehyŏp	28	Ih	33.40N	126.28 E
Chela, Serra da-	30	Ij	16.00S	13.10 E
Chelan	46	Ec	47.51N	120.01W
Chelan, Lake-	46	Eb	48.05N	120.30W
Chelforó, Arroyo-	55	Cm	36.55S	58.12W
Cheliff [3]	32	Hb	36.10N	1.45 E
Cheliff	30	He	36.02N	0.08 E
Cheliff	32	Hb	36.10N	1.20 E
Cheliff, Plaine du-	13	Mi	35.57N	0.45 E
Chellalat el Adhaouara	13	Pi	35.56N	3.25 E
Chelleh Khāneh, Kūh-e-	24	Md	36.52N	48.36 E
Chełm [2]	10	Te	51.10N	23.30 E
Chełm	10	Te	51.10N	23.28 E
Chelmer	12	Cc	51.44N	0.42 E
Chełmińskie, Pojezierze-	10	Oc	53.20N	19.00 E
Chełmno	10	Oc	53.22N	18.26 E
Chelmsford	9	Nj	51.44N	0.28 E
Chełmża	10	Oc	53.12N	18.37 E
Cheltenham	9	Kj	51.54N	2.04W
Chelva	13	Le	39.45N	0.59W
Chemainus	46	Db	48.55N	123.43W
Chemāma	32	Ef	16.50N	14.00 E
Chemba	37	Ec	17.09S	34.53 E
Chembe	36	Ee	11.58S	28.45 E
Chemillé	11	Fg	47.13N	0.43W
Chemnitz = Karl-Marx-Stadt	6	He	50.50N	12.55 E
Chemult	46	Ee	43.13N	121.47W
Chenachane	32	Gd	26.00N	4.15W
Chenārbāshi	24	Lf	33.20N	46.20 E
Chen Barag Qi (Bayan Hure)	27	Kb	49.21N	119.25 E
Chencha	35	Fd	6.17N	37.40 E
Chencoyi	48	Nh	19.48N	90.14W
Cheney	46	Gc	47.29N	117.34W
Cheney Reservoir	45	Hh	37.45N	97.50W
Cheng'an	28	Cf	36.27N	114.41 E
Chengde	27	Kc	41.00N	117.57 E
Chengdu	22	Mf	30.45N	104.04 E
Chengkou	27	Ie	31.54N	108.37 E
Chengmai	27	Ih	19.50N	109.59 E
Chengshan Jiao	27	Ld	37.24N	122.42 E
Chengxi Hu	28	Dh	32.22N	116.12 E
Chengzitan	27	Ld	39.31N	122.28 E
Chenisckali	16	Mh	42.06N	42.16 E
Chenjiagang	28	Eg	34.22N	119.48 E
Chenonceaux	11	Hg	47.20N	1.04 E
Chenxi	27	Jf	28.02N	110.15 E
Chenxian	27	Jf	25.49N	113.05 E
Chenying → Wannian	28	Dj	28.42N	117.04 E
Chépénéhé	63b	Ce	20.47S	167.09 E
Chepes	56	Gd	31.21S	66.36W
Chepo	49	Hi	9.10N	79.06W
Cher [3]	11	Ig	47.00N	2.30 E
Cher	5	Gf	47.21N	0.29 E
Cheradi, Isole-	14	Lj	40.25N	17.10 E
Cherangany Hills	36	Gb	1.15N	35.27 E
Cheraw	44	Hh	34.42N	79.53W
Cherbaniani Reef	25	Ef	12.18N	71.53 E
Cherbourg	6	Ff	49.39N	1.39W
Cherchell	32	Hb	36.36N	2.12 E
Chère	11	Eg	47.42N	1.50W
Chergui, Chott Ech-	30	He	34.21N	0.30 E
Chéri	34	Hc	13.26N	11.21 E
Cherlen→Kerulen	21	Ne	48.48N	117.00 E
Cherokee	45	Ie	42.45N	95.33W
Cherokees, Lake O' the-	45	Ih	36.39N	94.49W
Cherski Mountains (EN)= Čerskogo, Hrebet- [R.S.F.S.R.]	21	Qc	65.00N	145.00 E
Chersterfield Inlet	39	Jc	63.21N	90.42W
Chertsey	12	Bc	51.23N	0.30W
Cherwell	9	Lj	51.44N	1.15W
Chesapeake	44	Ig	36.45N	76.15W
Chesapeake Bay	38	Lf	38.40N	76.25W
Chesapeake Bay Bridge-Tunnel	44	Ig	37.00N	76.02W
Chesha Bay (EN)=Češskaja Guba	5	Kb	67.20N	46.30 E
Chesham	12	Bc	51.42N	0.36W
Cheshire [3]	9	Kh	53.15N	2.30W
Cheshire Plain	9	Kh	53.20N	2.40W
Cheshunt	12	Bc	51.42N	0.02W
Chester	9	Kh	53.10N	2.55W
Chester [Eng.-U.K.]	6	Fe	53.12N	2.54W
Chester [Il.-U.S.]	45	Lh	37.55N	89.49W
Chester [Mt.-U.S.]	46	Jb	48.31N	110.58W
Chester [Pa.-U.S.]	44	Jf	39.50N	75.23W
Chester [S.C.-U.S.]	44	Gh	34.40N	81.12W
Chesterfield	9	Lh	53.15N	1.25W
Chesterfield, Ile-	37	Gc	16.20S	43.58 E
Chesterfield, Récifs et Iles-=Chesterfield Reefs and Islands (EN)	57	Gf	20.00S	159.00 E
Chesterfield Inlet	38	Jc	63.25N	90.45W
Chesterfield Reefs and Islands (EN)=Chesterfield, Récifs et Iles-	57	Gf	20.00S	159.00 E
Chesterton Range	59	Je	25.30S	147.30 E
Chestnut Ridge	44	He	40.10N	79.25W
Chesuncook Lake	44	Mb	46.00N	69.20W
Chetaibi	32	Ib	37.04N	7.23 E
Chetumal	39	Kh	18.35N	88.07W
Chetumal, Bahía de	47	Ge	18.20N	88.05W
Cheviot	62	Ee	42.49S	173.16 E
Chew Bahir=Stefanie, Lake- (EN)	30	Kh	4.38N	36.50 E
Chewelah	46	Gb	48.17N	117.43W
Cheyenne [Ok.-U.S.]	45	Gi	35.37N	99.40W

Index Symbols

- [1] Independent Nation
- [2] State, Region
- [3] District, County
- [4] Municipality
- [5] Colony, Dependency
- Continent
- Physical Region
- Historical or Cultural Region
- Mount, Mountain
- Volcano
- Hill
- Mountains, Mountain Range
- Hills, Escarpment
- Plateau, Upland
- Pass, Gap
- Plain, Lowland
- Delta
- Salt Flat
- Valley, Canyon
- Crater, Cave
- Karst Features
- Depression
- Polder
- Desert, Dunes
- Forest, Woods
- Heath, Steppe
- Oasis
- Cape, Point
- Coast, Beach
- Cliff
- Peninsula
- Isthmus
- Sandbank
- Island
- Atoll
- Rock, Reef
- Islands, Archipelago
- Rocks, Reefs
- Coral Reef
- Well, Spring
- Geyser
- River, Stream
- Waterfall Rapids
- River Mouth, Estuary
- Lake
- Salt Lake
- Intermittent Lake
- Reservoir
- Swamp, Pond
- Canal
- Glacier
- Ice Shelf, Pack Ice
- Ocean
- Sea
- Gulf, Bay
- Strait, Fjord
- Lagoon
- Bank
- Seamount
- Tablemount
- Ridge
- Shelf
- Basin
- Escarpment, Sea Scarp
- Fracture
- Trench, Abyss
- National Park, Reserve
- Point of Interest
- Recreation Site
- Cave, Cavern
- Historic Site
- Ruins
- Wall, Walls
- Church, Abbey
- Temple
- Scientific Station
- Airport
- Port
- Lighthouse
- Mine
- Tunnel
- Dam, Bridge

Index Symbols

[1] Independent Nation
[2] State, Region
[3] District, County
[4] Municipality
[5] Colony, Dependency
Continent
Physical Region
Historical or Cultural Region
Mount, Mountain
Volcano
Hill
Mountains, Mountain Range
Hills, Escarpment
Plateau, Upland
Pass, Gap
Plain, Lowland
Delta
Salt Flat
Valley, Canyon
Crater, Cave
Karst Features
Depression
Polder
Desert, Dunes
Forest, Woods
Heath, Steppe
Oasis
Cape, Point
Coast, Beach
Cliff
Peninsula
Isthmus
Sandbank
Island
Atoll
Rock, Reef
Islands, Archipelago
Rocks, Reefs
Coral Reef
Well, Spring
Geyser
River, Stream
Waterfall Rapids
River Mouth, Estuary
Lake
Salt Lake
Intermittent Lake
Reservoir
Swamp, Pond
Canal
Glacier
Ice Shelf, Pack Ice
Ocean
Sea
Gulf, Bay
Strait, Fjord
Lagoon
Bank
Seamount
Tablemount
Ridge
Shelf
Basin
Escarpment, Sea Scarp
Fracture
Trench, Abyss
National Park, Reserve
Point of Interest
Recreation Site
Cave, Cavern
Historic Site
Ruins
Wall, Walls
Church, Abbey
Temple
Scientific Station
Airport
Port
Lighthouse
Mine
Tunnel
Dam, Bridge

Citeli-Ckaro 16 Oi 41.28N 46.06 E
Čitinskaja Oblast [3] 20 Gf 52.30N 117.30 E
Citlaltépetl, Volcán- → Orizaba, Pico de- 38 Jh 19.01N 97.16W
Citrusdale 37 Bf 32.36S 19.00 E
Città del Vaticano = Vatican City (EN) [1] 6 Hg 41.54N 12.27 E
Città di Castello 14 Gg 43.27N 12.14 E
Cittanova 14 Kl 38.21N 16.05 E
Ciucaşu, Virful- 15 Id 45.31N 25.55 E
Ciucea 15 Fd 46.57N 22.49 E
Ciudad 48 Gf 23.44N 105.44W
Ciudad Acuña 47 Dc 29.18N 100.55W
Ciudad Altamirano 48 Ih 18.20N 100.40W
Ciudad Bolívar 53 Je 8.08N 63.33W
Ciudad Bolivia 54 Db 8.21N 70.34W
Ciudad Camargo [Mex.] 47 Ec 26.19N 98.50W
Ciudad Camargo [Mex.] 47 Cc 27.40N 105.10W
Ciudad Cuauhtémoc 48 Mj 15.37N 92.00W
Ciudad Darío 49 Dg 12.43N 86.08W
Ciudad de Areco 55 Cl 34.18S 59.46W
Ciudad de Dolores Hidalgo 48 Ig 21.10N 100.56W
Ciudad de la Habana [3] 49 Fb 23.10N 82.10W
Ciudad del Carmen 47 Fe 18.38N 91.50W
Ciudad del Maíz 48 Jf 22.24N 99.36W
Ciudad de México = Mexico City (EN) 39 Jh 19.24N 99.09W
Ciudad de Nutrias 54 Eb 8.07N 69.19W
Ciudad de Río Grande 47 Dd 23.50N 103.02W
Ciudadela/Ciutadella 13 Pd 40.02N 3.50 E
Ciudad Guayana 53 Je 8.22N 62.40W
Ciudad Guerrero 47 Cc 28.33N 107.30W
Ciudad Guzmán 47 De 19.41N 103.29W
Ciudad Hidalgo [Mex.] 48 Mj 14.41N 92.09W
Ciudad Hidalgo [Mex.] 48 Ih 19.41N 100.34W
Ciudad Juárez 39 If 31.44N 106.29W
Ciudad Lerdo 47 Dc 25.32N 103.32W
Ciudad Madero 39 Jg 22.16N 97.50W
Ciudad Mante 47 Ed 22.44N 98.57W
Ciudad Mendoza 48 Kh 18.48N 97.11W
Ciudad Obregón 39 Ig 27.59N 109.56W
Ciudad Ojeda 54 Da 10.12N 71.19W
Ciudad Piar 54 Fb 7.27N 63.19W
Ciudad Real 13 If 38.59N 3.56W
Ciudad Real [3] 13 If 39.00N 4.00W
Ciudad Rio Bravo 47 Ec 25.59N 98.06W
Ciudad-Rodrigo 13 Fd 40.36N 6.32W
Ciudad Valles 47 Ed 21.59N 99.01W
Ciudad Victoria 39 Jg 23.44N 99.08W
Ciutadella/Ciudadela 13 Pd 40.02N 3.50 E
Civa Burnu 24 Gb 41.22N 36.35 E
Cividale del Friuli 14 Hd 46.06N 13.25 E
Civilsk 7 Li 55.53N 47.29 E
Civita Castellana 14 Gh 42.17N 12.25 E
Civitanova Marche 14 Hg 43.18N 13.44 E
Civitavecchia 14 Fh 42.06N 11.48 E
Civitella del Tronto 14 Hh 42.46N 13.40 E
Çivril 24 Cc 38.56N 35.29 E
Cixerri 14 Ck 39.17N 8.59 E
Cixi (Hushan) 28 Fi 30.10N 121.14 E
Cixian 28 Cf 36.22N 114.22 E
Čiža 19 Eb 67.06N 44.19 E
Cizre 23 Fb 37.20N 42.12 E
Cjurupinsk 16 Hf 46.37N 32.43 E
Čkalovsk 7 Kh 56.47N 43.17 E
Clacton-on-Sea 9 Oj 51.48N 1.09 E
Clain 11 Gh 46.47N 0.33 E
Claire, Côte- 66 Ie 66.30S 133.00 E
Claire, Lake- 42 Ge 58.30N 112.00W
Clair Engle Lake 46 Df 40.52N 122.43W
Claise 11 Gh 46.56N 0.42 E
Clamecy 11 Jg 47.27N 3.31 E
Clan Alpine Mountains 46 Gg 39.40N 117.55W
Clanton 44 Di 32.50N 86.38W
Clanwilliam 37 Bf 32.11S 18.54 E
Claraz 55 Cm 37.54S 59.17W
Clár Chlainne Mhuiris/Claremorris 9 Eh 53.44N 9.00W
Clare [Austl.] 59 Hf 33.50S 138.36 E
Clare [Mi.-U.S.] 44 Ed 43.49N 84.46W
Clare/Abhainn an Chláir 9 Dh 53.20N 9.03W
Clare/An Clár [2] 9 Ei 52.50N 9.00W
Clare/Cliara 9 Dh 53.49N 10.00W
Claremont 44 Kd 43.23N 72.21W
Claremore 45 Ih 36.19N 95.36W
Claremorris/Clár Chlainne Mhuiris 9 Eh 53.44N 9.00W
Clarence 62 Ee 42.10S 173.57 E
Clarence 62 Ee 42.10S 173.56 E
Clarence, Cape- 42 Ib 73.55N 90.12W
Clarence Cannon Reservoir 45 Kg 39.31N 91.45W
Clarence Island 66 Re 61.12S 54.05W
Clarence River 59 Ke 29.25S 153.22 E
Clarence Strait [Ak.-U.S.] 40 Me 55.25N 132.00W
Clarence Strait [Austl.] 59 Gb 12.00S 131.00 E
Clarence Town 49 Jb 23.06N 74.59W
Clarendon 45 Fi 34.56N 100.53W
Clarenville 42 Mg 48.09N 53.58W
Claresholm 42 Gf 50.02N 113.35W
Clarinda 45 If 40.44N 95.02W
Clarines 50 Dh 9.56N 65.10W
Clarion, Isla- 47 Be 18.22N 114.44W
Clarion Fracture Zone (EN) 3 Lh 18.00N 130.00W
Clarion River 44 He 41.07N 79.41W
Clark 45 Hd 44.53N 97.44W
Clark, Lake- 40 Id 60.15N 154.15W
Clark, Mount- 42 Fd 64.25N 124.14W
Clarkdale 46 Ii 34.46N 112.03W
Clarke Range 59 Jd 20.50S 148.35 E
Clark Fork 38 He 48.09N 116.15W
Clark Hill Lake 44 Fi 33.50N 82.20W
Clark Mountain 46 Hi 35.32N 115.35W
Clarksburg 43 Kd 39.17N 80.21W
Clarksdale 43 Ie 34.12N 90.34W
Clarks Fork 46 Kd 45.39N 108.43W
Clark's Harbour 44 Od 43.26N 65.38W
Clarkston 46 Gc 46.30N 117.03W
Clarksville [Ar.-U.S.] 45 Ji 35.28N 93.28W
Clarksville [Tn.-U.S.] 43 Jd 36.32N 87.21W
Clarksville [Tx.-U.S.] 45 Ij 33.37N 95.03W
Claro, Rio- [Braz.] 54 Hg 19.08S 50.40W
Claro, Rio- [Braz.] 54 Hg 15.28S 51.45W
Clary 12 Fd 50.00N 3.24 E
Claude 45 Fi 35.07N 101.22W
Claustra/Klosters 14 Dd 46.52N 9.52 E
Clavering 41 Jd 74.20N 21.10W
Claxton 44 Gi 32.10N 81.55W
Clay Belt 38 Kd 51.50N 82.00W
Clay Center 45 Hg 39.23N 96.08W
Clay Cross 12 Aa 53.09N 1.25W
Claye Souilly 12 Ef 48.57N 2.42 E
Clayton 43 Gd 36.27N 103.11W
Clear, Cape- 9 Dj 51.26N 9.31W
Clear Boggy Creek 45 Ii 34.03N 95.47W
Clear Creek [Az.-U.S.] 46 Ji 34.59N 110.38W
Clear Creek [U.S.] 45 Ld 44.53N 106.04W
Clearfield [Pa.-U.S.] 44 He 41.02N 78.27W
Clearfield [Ut.-U.S.] 46 If 41.07N 112.01W
Clear Fork Brazos 45 Gj 33.01N 98.40W
Clear Lake 43 Cd 39.02N 122.50W
Clear Lake [Ia.-U.S.] 45 Je 43.08N 93.23W
Clear Lake [S.D.-U.S.] 45 Hd 44.45N 96.41W
Clear Lake Reservoir 46 Ef 41.52N 121.08W
Clearwater 42 Ge 56.45N 111.22W
Clearwater 43 Kf 27.58N 82.48W
Clearwater Mountains 43 Db 46.00N 115.30W
Clearwater River [Alta.-Can.] 46 Ha 52.23N 114.50W
Clearwater River [U.S.] 46 Gc 46.25N 117.02W
Cleburne 43 He 32.21N 97.23W
Clécy 12 Bf 48.55N 0.29W
Clee Hills 9 Ki 52.25N 2.35W
Cleethorpes 9 Mh 53.34N 0.02W
Clères 12 De 49.36N 1.07 E
Clerf/Clervaux 12 Id 50.03N 6.02 E
Clermont [Austl.] 59 Jd 22.49S 147.39 E
Clermont [Fr.] 11 Ie 49.23N 2.24 E
Clermont-en-Argonne 12 He 49.06N 5.04 E
Clermont-Ferrand 6 Gf 45.47N 3.05 E
Clermont-l'Hérault 11 Jk 43.37N 3.26 E
Clervaux/Clerf 12 Id 50.03N 6.02 E
Clervé 12 Ie 49.57N 6.01 E
Cles 14 Fd 46.22N 11.02 E
Clevedon 9 Kj 51.27N 2.51W
Cleveland 9 Lg 54.25N 1.05W
Cleveland [3] 9 Mg 54.40N 1.00W
Cleveland [Ms.-U.S.] 45 Kj 33.45N 90.50W
Cleveland [Oh.-U.S.] 39 Ke 41.30N 81.41W
Cleveland [Tn.-U.S.] 43 Kd 35.10N 84.53W
Cleveland [Tx.-U.S.] 45 Ik 30.21N 95.05W
Cleveland, Mount- 43 Eb 48.56N 113.51W
Cleveland Heights 44 Ge 41.30N 81.34W
Clevelândia 55 Fh 26.24S 52.21W
Cleveland Mountain 46 Ic 46.37N 113.47W
Clew Bay/Cuan Mó 9 Dh 53.50N 9.50W
Cliara/Clare 9 Dh 53.49N 10.00W
Cliff 45 Bj 32.59N 108.36W
Clifton [Az.-U.S.] 43 Fe 33.03N 109.18W
Clifton [St.Vin.] 51n Bb 12.36N 61.26W
Clifton [Tx.-U.S.] 45 Hk 31.47N 97.35W
Clinch River 44 Eh 35.53N 84.29W
Cline, Mount- 46 Ga 52.10N 116.40W
Clines Corners 45 Di 35.01N 105.34W
Clingmans Dome 44 Fh 35.35N 83.30W
Clinton [Ar.-U.S.] 45 Ji 35.36N 92.28W
Clinton [B.C.-Can.] 42 Ff 51.05N 121.35W
Clinton [Ia.-U.S.] 43 Ic 41.51N 90.12W
Clinton [Il.-U.S.] 45 Lf 40.09N 88.57W
Clinton [Mo.-U.S.] 45 Jg 38.22N 93.46W
Clinton [Ms.-U.S.] 45 Kj 32.20N 90.20W
Clinton [N.C.-U.S.] 44 Hh 34.59N 78.20W
Clinton [N.Z.] 62 Cg 46.13S 169.23 E
Clinton [Ok.-U.S.] 43 Hd 35.31N 98.59W
Clinton-Colden Lake 42 Gd 63.55N 107.30W
Clintonville 45 Ld 44.37N 88.46W
Clipperton 38 Ih 10.17N 109.13W
Clipperton, Fracture Zone (EN) 3 Mi 10.00N 115.00W
Clisson 11 Eg 47.05N 1.17W
Cloates, Point- 59 Cd 22.45S 113.40 E
Clochán an Aifir/ 9 Gf 55.15N 6.35W
Giant's Causeway 9 Gf 55.15N 6.35W
Clodomira 56 Hc 27.35S 64.08W
Cloich na Coillte/Clonakilty 9 Ej 51.37N 8.54W
Clonakilty/Cloich na Coillte 9 Ej 51.37N 8.54W
Cloncurry 58 Fg 20.42S 140.30 E
Clones/Cluain Eois 9 Fg 54.11N 7.14W
Clonmel/Cluain Meala 9 Fi 52.21N 7.42W
Cloppenburg 10 Ed 52.51N 8.02 E
Cloquet 43 Ib 46.43N 92.28W
Clorinda 53 Kh 25.20S 57.40W
Cloud Peak 43 Fc 44.25N 107.10W
Clouère 11 Gh 46.26N 0.17 E
Cloverdale 46 Dg 38.48N 123.01W
Clovis [Ca.-U.S.] 46 Fh 36.49N 119.42W
Clovis [N.M.-U.S.] 39 If 34.24N 103.12W
Cluain Meala/Clonmel 9 Fi 52.21N 7.42W
Cluan Eois/Clones 9 Fg 54.11N 7.14W
Cluj [2] 15 Gc 46.49N 23.35 E
Cluj Napoca 6 If 46.46N 23.36 E
Cluny 11 Kh 46.26N 4.39 E
Cluses 11 Mh 46.04N 6.36 E
Clusone 14 De 45.53N 9.57 E
Clutha 62 Cg 46.21S 169.48 E
Clwyd 9 Jh 53.20N 3.30W
Clwyd [3] 9 Jh 53.10N 3.15W
Clyde 9 If 55.56N 4.29W
Clyde [N.W.T.-Can.] 39 Mb 70.25N 68.30W
Clyde [N.Z.] 62 Cf 45.11S 169.19 E
Clyde, Firth of- 9 If 55.42N 5.00W
Clyde Inlet 42 Kb 70.20N 68.20W
Cna 5 Ke 54.32N 42.05 E
Cnoc Bréanainn/Brandon Mount 9 Ci 52.14N 10.15W
Cnoc Fola/Bloody Foreland 9 Ef 55.09N 8.17W
Cnoc Mhaoldonn/Knockmealdown Mountains 9 Fi 52.15N 8.00W
Cnori 16 Ni 41.35N 45.59 E
Cnossus (EN) = Knosós 15 In 35.18N 25.10 E
Côa 13 Ec 41.05N 7.06W
Coachella Canal 46 Hj 33.34N 116.00W
Coahuayana 48 Hh 18.44N 103.41W
Coahuila [2] 47 Dc 27.20N 102.00W
Coalcomán, Sierra de- 47 De 18.30N 102.55W
Coalcomán de Matamoros 48 Hh 18.47N 103.09W
Coaldale 46 Ib 49.43N 112.37W
Coalgate 45 Hi 34.32N 96.13W
Coalinga 46 Eh 36.09N 120.21W
Coalville 9 Li 52.44N 1.20W
Coamo 49 Nd 18.05N 66.22W
Coari 54 Fd 4.05S 63.08W
Coari, Lago de- 54 Fd 4.15S 63.25W
Coari, Rio- 52 Jf 4.30S 63.33W
Coast [3] 36 Gc 3.00S 39.30 E
Coast Mountains 38 Gd 55.00N 129.00W
Coast Plain (EN) = Kustvlakte 11 Ic 51.00N 2.30 E
Coast Ranges 38 Ge 41.00N 123.30W
Coatbridge 9 If 55.52N 4.01W
Coatepec 48 Kh 19.27N 96.58W
Coatepel, Cerro- 48 Kh 18.25N 97.35W
Coatepeque 49 Bf 14.42N 91.52W
Coats 38 Kc 62.30N 83.00W
Coats Land (EN) 66 Af 77.00S 28.00W
Coatzacoalcos 39 Jh 18.09N 94.25W
Coatzacoalcos, Bahía- 48 Lh 18.10N 94.27W
Coatzacoalcos, Río- 48 Lh 18.09N 94.24W
Coba 47 Gd 20.36N 87.35W
Cobadin 15 Le 44.05N 28.13 E
Cobalt 42 Jg 47.24N 79.41W
Cobán 47 Fe 15.29N 90.19W
Cobar 59 Jf 31.30S 145.49 E
Cobb, Mount- 46 Dg 38.45N 122.40W
Cobb Seamount (EN) 38 Fe 46.46N 130.43W
Cóbh/An Cóbh 9 Ej 51.51N 8.17W
Cobija 54 Ef 11.02S 68.44W
Cobo 55 Dm 37.48S 57.38W
Cobourg 42 Jh 43.58N 78.10W
Cobourg Peninsula 59 Gb 11.20S 132.15 E
Cóbué 37 Eb 12.07S 34.52 E
Coburg 10 Gf 50.15N 10.58 E
Coburn Mountain 44 Lc 45.28N 70.06W
Coca, Pizzo di- 14 Ed 46.04N 10.01 E
Cocalinho 55 Gb 14.22S 51.00W
Cocentaina 13 Lf 38.45N 0.26W
Cochabamba [2] 54 Eg 17.30S 65.40W
Cochabamba 53 Jg 17.24S 66.09W
Coche, Isla- 50 Eg 10.47N 63.56W
Cochem 10 Df 50.08N 7.09 E
Cochin 22 Ji 9.58N 76.14 E
Cochin China (EN) = Nam Phan 21 Mg 11.00N 107.00 E
Cochinos, Bahía de- = Pigs, Bay of- (EN) 49 Gb 22.07N 81.10W
Cochons, Ile aux- 30 Mm 46.05S 50.08 E
Cochran 44 Fi 32.23N 83.21W
Cochrane 42 He 57.55N 101.32W
Cochrane [Alta.-Can.] 46 Ha 51.11N 114.28W
Cochrane [Ont.-Can.] 39 Ke 49.04N 81.01W
Cockburn, Canal- 56 Fh 54.20S 71.30W
Cockburn, Mount- 59 Gd 22.46S 130.36 E
Cockburn Bank 9 Ei 49.40N 8.50W
Cockburn Island 44 Fc 45.55N 83.22W
Cockburn Town 49 Ja 24.02N 74.31W
Cockermouth 9 Jg 54.40N 3.21W
Coclé [3] 49 Gi 8.30N 80.15W
Coco, Cayo- 49 Hb 22.30N 78.28W
Coco, Ile- 51b Bc 17.52N 62.49W
Coco, Isla del- 38 Ki 5.32N 87.04W
Coco, Rio-o Segovia, Rio- 38 Kh 15.00N 83.08W
Cocoa 43 Kf 28.21N 80.44W
Cocoa Beach 44 Gk 28.19N 80.36W
Cocoa Point 51d Ba 17.33N 61.46W
Cocobeach 36 Ab 0.59N 9.36 E
Coco Channel 25 If 14.00N 93.00 E
Coco Islands 25 If 14.05N 93.18 E
Coconino Plateau 46 Ii 35.50N 112.30W
Cocorocuma, Cayos- 49 Ff 15.45N 83.00W
Cocos 64c Bb 13.14N 144.39 E
Côcos 55 Jb 14.10S 44.33W
Cocos Islands (Keeling Islands) 21 Lk 12.10S 96.55 E
Cocos Islands (Keeling Islands) [5] 22 Lk 12.10S 96.55 E
Cocos Ridge (EN) 3 Ni 5.30N 86.00W
Cocula 48 Hg 20.23N 103.50W
Cocuzzo 14 Kk 39.13N 16.08 E
Cod, Cape- 44 Me 41.50N 70.00W
Cod, Cape- 38 Le 41.42N 70.15W
Coda Cavallo, Capo- 14 Dj 40.51N 9.43 E
Codaeşti 15 Kc 46.52N 27.45 E
Codajás 54 Fd 3.50S 62.05W
Codera, Cabo- 50 Cg 10.35N 66.04W
Codfish Island 62 Bg 46.45S 167.40 E
Codigoro 14 Gf 44.49N 12.08 E
Codlea 15 Id 45.42N 25.27 E
Codó 54 Jd 4.29S 43.53W
Codogno 14 De 45.09N 9.42 E
Codrington 50 Fd 17.38N 61.50W
Codrington Lagoon 51d Ba 17.39N 61.51W
Codrului, Munţii- 15 Fc 46.35N 22.10 E
Cody 43 Fc 44.32N 109.05W
Coen 58 Ff 13.56S 143.12 E
Coesfeld 10 De 51.56N 7.09 E
Coetivy Island 30 Mi 7.08S 56.16 E
Coeur d'Alene 43 Db 47.41N 116.46W
Coevorden 11 Mb 52.40N 6.45 E
Coffeyville 45 Ih 37.02N 95.37W
Coffs Harbour 58 Gh 30.18S 153.08 E
Cofre de Perote, Cerro- (Nauhcampatépetl) 48 Kh 19.29N 97.08W
Cofrentes 13 Ke 39.14N 1.04W
Coggeshall 12 Cc 51.52N 0.41 E
Coghinas 14 Cj 40.56N 8.48 E
Coghinas, Lago del- 14 Dj 40.45N 9.05 E
Coglians 14 Gd 46.37N 12.53 E
Cognac 11 Fi 45.42N 0.20W
Cogne 14 Be 45.37N 7.21 E
Cogolludo 13 Id 40.57N 3.05W
Čograjskoje Vodohranilišče 16 Ng 45.30N 44.30 E
Coiba, Isla de- 47 Hg 7.27N 81.45W
Coig, Río- (Coyle) 56 Gh 50.58S 69.11W
Coihaique 56 Fg 45.34S 72.04W
Coimbatore 22 Jh 11.00N 76.58 E
Coimbra [2] 13 Dd 40.12N 8.25W
Coimbra [Braz.] 55 Dd 19.55S 57.47W
Coimbra [Port.] 6 Fg 40.12N 8.25W
Coin 13 Hh 36.40N 4.45W
Coipasa, Salar de- 54 Eg 19.30S 68.10W
Čojbalsan 22 Ne 48.04N 114.30 E
Cojedes 50 Bh 9.37N 68.55W
Cojedes [2] 54 Eb 9.20N 68.20W
Cojedes, Rio- 50 Bh 8.44N 68.15W
Cojutepeque 49 Cg 13.43N 88.56W
Čoka 15 Dd 45.56N 20.09 E
Cokeville 46 Je 42.05N 110.55W
Cokover River 59 Ed 20.40S 120.45 E
Čokurdah 20 Jb 70.38N 147.55 E
Colac [Austl.] 59 Ig 38.20S 143.35 E
Colac [N.Z.] 62 Bg 46.22S 167.53 E
Colatina 53 Lg 19.32S 40.37W
Colbeck, Cape- 66 Mf 77.06S 157.48W
Colbitz-Letzlinger Heide 10 Hd 52.27N 11.35 E
Colby 45 Fg 39.24N 101.03W
Colchester 9 Nj 51.54N 0.54 E
Cold Bay 40 Ge 55.11N 162.30W
Cold Lake 42 Gf 54.27N 110.10W
Coldstream 9 Kf 55.39N 2.15W
Coldwater [Ks.-U.S.] 45 Gh 37.16N 99.19W
Coldwater [Mi.-U.S.] 44 Ee 41.57N 85.00W
Colebrook 44 Lc 44.53N 71.30W
Coleman 45 Gk 31.50N 99.26W
Coleman River 59 Ic 15.06S 141.38 E
Coleraine/Cúil Raithin 9 Gf 55.08N 6.40W
Coleridge, Lake- 62 De 43.20S 171.30 E
Coles, Punta- 54 Dg 17.42S 71.23W
Colesberg 37 Df 30.45S 25.05 E
Colfax [La.-U.S.] 45 Jk 31.31N 92.42W
Colfax [Wa.-U.S.] 46 Gc 46.53N 117.22W
Colfontaine 12 Fd 50.25N 3.50 E
Colhué Huapi, Lago- 56 Gg 45.30S 68.48W
Colibaşi 15 He 44.56N 24.54 E
Colibris, Pointe des- 51e Bb 16.17N 61.06W
Colima [2] 47 De 19.10N 104.00W
Colima 39 Ih 19.14N 103.43W
Colima, Nevado de- 38 Ih 19.33N 103.38W
Colinas 55 Hb 14.12S 48.03W
Coll 9 Ge 56.40N 6.35W
Collado Bajo 13 Kd 40.14N 1.50W
Collarada 13 Lb 42.43N 0.29W
Colle di Val d'Elsa 14 Fg 43.25N 11.07 E
Colleferro 14 Gi 41.44N 12.59 E
College 40 Jd 64.51N 147.47W
College Place 46 Fc 46.03N 118.23W
College Station 45 Hk 30.37N 96.21W
Collegno 14 Be 45.05N 7.34 E
Collie 59 Df 33.21S 116.09 E
Collier Bay 59 Ec 16.10S 124.15 E
Collierville 44 Ch 35.03N 89.40W
Collingwood [N.Z.] 61 Dh 40.41S 172.41 E
Collingwood [Ont.-Can.] 44 Gc 44.29N 80.13W
Collinson Peninsula 42 Hb 70.00N 101.10W
Collinsville 59 Jd 20.34S 147.51 E
Collmberg 10 Je 51.15N 13.02 E
Colmar 11 Nf 48.05N 7.22 E
Colmena 55 Bi 28.45S 60.06W
Colmenar 13 Hh 36.54N 4.20W
Colmenar Viejo 13 Id 40.40N 3.46W
Colne 12 Cc 51.51N 0.59 E
Colne Point 12 Dc 51.46N 1.03 E
Colnett, Punta- 48 Ab 31.00N 116.20W
Cologne (EN) = Köln 6 Ge 50.56N 6.57 E
Colombia [2] 53 Ie 4.00N 72.00W
Colombia 55 He 20.10S 48.40W
Colombian Basin (EN) 38 Lh 13.00N 76.00W
Colombier, Pointe à- 51b Bc 17.55N 62.53W
Colombo 22 Ji 6.56N 79.51 E
Colón [Arg.] 56 Hd 33.53S 61.07W
Colón [Arg.] 56 Id 32.13S 58.08W
Colón [Cuba] 47 Hd 22.43N 80.54W
Colón [Hond.] [3] 49 Ef 15.20N 84.30W
Colón [Pan.] [3] 49 Hi 9.30N 79.15W
Colón [Pan.] 39 Li 9.22N 79.54W
Colón [Ur.] 55 Ek 33.53S 54.43W
Colon, Archipiélago de-/Galápagos Islands (EN) 52 Gf 0.30S 90.30W
Colón, Montañas de- 49 Ef 14.55N 84.45W
Colona 59 Gf 31.38S 132.05 E
Colonarie 51n Ba 13.14N 61.08W
Colonarie 51n Ba 13.14N 61.08W
Colonel Hill 49 Jb 22.52N 74.15W
Colonia [2] 55 Dl 34.10S 57.30W
Colonia 60 Bf 9.31N 138.08 E
Colonia agricola de Turén 50 Bh 9.15N 69.05W
Colonia Carlos Pellegrini 55 Di 28.32S 57.10W
Colonia del Sacramento 56 Id 34.28S 57.51W
Colonia Elisa 55 Ch 26.56S 59.32W
Colonia Juárez 48 Eb 30.19N 108.05W
Colonia Las Heras 56 Gg 46.33S 68.57W
Colonia Lavalleja 56 Id 31.06S 57.01W
Colonial Heights 44 Ig 37.15N 77.25W
Colonia Morelos 48 Eb 30.50N 109.10W
Colonne, Capo- 14 Lk 39.02N 17.12 E
Colonsay 9 Ge 56.05N 6.10W
Colorado 49 Fh 10.46N 83.35W
Colorado [2] 43 Fd 39.30N 105.30W
Colorado, Cerro- 48 Bb 31.31N 115.31W
Colorado, Rio- [Arg.] 52 Ji 39.50S 62.08W
Colorado, Rio- [N.Amer.] 38 Hf 31.45N 114.40W
Colorado City 45 Fj 32.24N 100.52W
Colorado Plateau 38 Hf 36.30N 118.00W
Colorado River [N.Amer.] 38 Hf 31.45N 114.40W
Colorado River [U.S.] 38 Jg 28.36N 95.58W
Colorados, Archipiélago de los- 49 Eb 22.36N 84.20W
Colorado Springs 39 If 38.50N 104.49W
Colotlán 48 Hf 22.03N 103.16W
Colpon-Ata 18 Kc 42.39N 77.06 E
Coltishall 12 Db 52.44N 1.22 E
Colui 36 Cf 15.10S 16.40 E
Columbia 38 Ge 46.15N 124.05W
Columbia [Ky.-U.S.] 44 Eg 37.06N 85.18W
Columbia [Mo.-U.S.] 43 Id 38.57N 92.20W
Columbia [Ms.-U.S.] 45 Lk 31.15N 89.56W
Columbia [Pa.-U.S.] 44 Ie 40.02N 76.30W
Columbia [S.C.-U.S.] 39 Kf 34.00N 81.03W
Columbia [Tn.-U.S.] 44 Dh 35.37N 87.02W
Columbia, Cape- 38 La 83.08N 70.35W
Columbia, Mount- 38 Hd 57.00N 117.00W
Columbia Basin 43 Db 46.45N 119.05W
Columbia Falls 46 Hb 48.23N 114.11W
Columbia Mountains 38 Hd 52.00N 119.00W
Columbia Plateau 38 He 44.00N 117.30W
Columbia Seamount (EN) 54 Lh 20.40S 31.30W
Columbine, Cape- 30 Il 32.49S 17.51 E
Columbretes, Islas-/Columbrets, Els- 13 Me 39.52N 0.40 E
Columbrets, Els-/Columbretes, Islas- 13 Me 39.52N 0.40 E
Columbus [Ga.-U.S.] 39 Kf 32.29N 84.59W
Columbus [In.-U.S.] 43 Jd 39.13N 85.55W
Columbus [Ks.-U.S.] 45 Ih 37.10N 94.50W
Columbus [Ms.-U.S.] 43 Je 33.30N 88.25W
Columbus [Mt.-U.S.] 46 Kd 45.38N 109.15W
Columbus [Nb.-U.S.] 43 Hc 41.25N 97.22W
Columbus [N.M.-U.S.] 45 Ck 31.50N 107.38W
Columbus [Oh.-U.S.] 39 Kf 39.57N 83.00W
Columbus [Tx.-U.S.] 45 Hl 29.42N 96.33W
Columbus Point 49 Ja 24.08N 75.16W
Colville 38 Dc 70.25N 150.30W
Colville, Cape- 62 Fb 36.28S 175.21 E
Colville Channel 62 Fb 36.25S 175.30 E
Colville Lake 42 Ec 67.10N 126.00W
Colville Lake 42 Ec 67.06N 126.00W
Col Visentin 14 Gd 46.05N 12.20 E
Colwyn Bay 9 Jh 53.18N 3.43W
Coma 35 Fd 8.27N 36.55 E
Comacchio 14 Gf 44.42N 12.11 E
Comacchio, Valli di- 14 Gf 44.40N 12.05 E
Comai (Damxoi) 27 Ff 28.26N 91.32 E
Comala 48 Hh 19.19N 103.45W
Comalcalco 47 Fe 18.16N 93.13W
Coman, Mount- 66 Qf 73.49S 64.18W
Comanche [Mt.-U.S.] 46 Kc 46.02N 108.54W
Comanche [Tx.-U.S.] 45 Gk 31.54N 98.36W
Comandante Fontana 55 Cg 25.20S 59.41W
Comandău 15 Jd 46.26N 26.16 E
Comăneşti 15 Jc 46.25N 26.26 E
Comayagua 47 Gf 14.25N 87.37W
Comayagua [3] 49 Df 14.30N 87.40W
Combarbala 56 Fd 31.11S 71.02W
Combeaufontaine 11 Lg 47.43N 5.53 E
Combermere Bay 25 Ie 19.37N 93.34 E
Comblain-au-Pont 12 Hd 50.28N 5.35 E
Combles 12 Ed 50.01N 2.52 E
Combourg 11 Ef 48.25N 1.45W
Combraille 11 Ih 46.30N 3.10 E
Combrailles 11 Ih 46.15N 2.10 E
Comedero 48 Fe 24.37N 106.46W
Comendador 49 Ld 18.53N 71.42W
Comeragh Mountains/Na Comaraigh 9 Fi 52.13N 7.35W
Comerio 51a Bb 18.13N 66.16W
Comilla 25 Id 23.27N 91.12 E
Comines 12 Fd 50.46N 3.01 E
Comines/Komen 12 Ed 50.46N 2.59 E
Comino 14 In 36.00N 14.20 E
Comino, Capo- 14 Dj 40.32N 9.49 E
Comiso 14 In 36.56N 14.36 E
Comitán de Dominguez 47 Fe 16.15N 92.08W
Commentry 11 Ih 46.17N 2.45 E
Commerce 45 Ij 33.15N 95.54W
Commercy 11 Lf 48.45N 5.35 E
Commiges 11 Gk 43.15N 0.45 E
Committee Bay 38 Kc 68.30N 86.30W
Commonwealth Bay 66 Je 66.54S 142.40 E
Communism Peak (EN) = Kommunizma, Pik- 21 Jf 38.57N 72.08 E
Como [China] 27 Ee 33.26N 85.21 E
Como [It.] 14 De 45.47N 9.05 E
Como, Lago di- 14 Dd 46.00N 9.15 E
Comodoro 55 Bl 35.19S 60.31W
Comodoro Ravadavia 53 Jj 45.50S 67.30W
Comondú 47 Bc 26.03N 111.46W
Comores/Comoros [1] 31 Lj 12.10S 44.10 E
Comores, Archipel des- = Comoro Islands (EN) 30 Lj 12.10S 44.15 E
Comorin, Cape- 21 Ji 8.04N 77.34 E
Comoro Islands (EN) = Comores, Archipel des- 30 Lj 12.10S 44.15 E
Comoros/Comores [1] 31 Lj 12.10S 44.10 E
Comox 46 Cb 49.40N 124.55W
Compiègne 11 Ie 49.25N 2.50 E
Compostela 47 Dd 21.14N 104.55W
Comprida, Ilha- 55 Ig 24.50S 47.42W
Compton 46 Fj 33.54N 118.13W
Comstock 45 Fl 29.41N 101.11W
Comtal, Causse du- 11 Ij 44.26N 2.38 E

Index Symbols

[1] Independent Nation
[2] State, Region
[3] District, County
[4] Municipality
[5] Colony, Dependency
Continent
Physical Region
Historical or Cultural Region
Mount, Mountain
Volcano
Hill
Mountains, Mountain Range
Hills, Escarpment
Plateau, Upland
Pass, Gap
Plain, Lowland
Delta
Salt Flat
Valley, Canyon
Crater, Cave
Karst Features
Depression
Polder
Desert, Dunes
Forest, Woods
Heath, Steppe
Oasis
Cape, Point
Coast, Beach
Cliff
Peninsula
Isthmus
Sandbank
Island
Atoll
Rock, Reef
Islands, Archipelago
Rocks, Reefs
Coral Reef
Well, Spring
Geyser
River, Stream
Waterfall Rapids
River Mouth, Estuary
Lake
Salt Lake
Intermittent Lake
Reservoir
Swamp, Pond
Canal
Glacier
Ice Shelf, Pack Ice
Ocean
Sea
Gulf, Bay
Strait, Fjord
Lagoon
Bank
Seamount
Tablemount
Ridge
Shelf
Basin
Escarpment, Sea Scarp
Fracture
Trench, Abyss
National Park, Reserve
Point of Interest
Recreation Site
Cave, Cavern
Historic Site
Ruins
Wall, Walls
Church, Abbey
Temple
Scientific Station
Airport
Port
Lighthouse
Mine
Tunnel
Dam, Bridge

Čona 21 Mc 62.00N 110.00 E
Cona 27 Ff 28.01N 91.57 E
Co Nag 27 Fe 32.00N 91.25 E
Conakry 31 Fh 9.31N 13.43W
Conara Junction 59 Jh 41.50S 147.26 E
Concarneau 11 Cg 47.52N 3.55W
Conceição da Barra 54 Kg 18.35S 39.45W
Conceição do Araguaia 54 Ie 8.15S 49.17W
Conceição do Mato Dentro 55 Kd 19.01S 43.25W
Concepción [3] 55 Df 23.00S 57.00W
Concepción [Arg.] 56 Gc 27.20S 65.35W
Concepción [Arg.] 55 Di 28.23S 57.53W
Concepción [Bol.] 54 Fg 16.15S 62.04W
Concepción [Chile] 53 Ii 36.50S 73.03W
Concepción [Par.] 53 Kh 23.25S 57.17W
Concepción [Peru] 54 Cf 11.55S 75.17W
Concepción [Ven.] 49 Lh 10.25N 71.41W
Concepción, Bahía- 48 Dd 26.40N 111.48W
Concepción, Laguna- 54 Fg 17.30S 61.25W
Concepción, Punta- 48 Dd 26.50N 111.50W
Concepción, Río- 55 Ab 15.46S 62.10W
Concepción del Bermejo 55 Bh 26.36S 60.57W
Concepción del Oro 47 Dd 24.38N 101.25W
Concepción del Uruguay 56 Id 32.29S 58.14W
Conception, Point- 38 Gf 34.27N 120.27W
Conception Bay 42 Mg 48.00N 52.50W
Conception Island 49 Jb 23.52N 75.03W
Concha 49 Li 9.02N 71.45W
Conchas 55 Hf 23.01S 48.00W
Conchas Dam 45 Di 35.22N 104.11W
Conchas Lake 45 Di 35.25N 104.14W
Conches-en-Ouche 11 Gf 48.58N 0.56 E
Concho River 45 Gk 31.32N 99.43W
Conchos, Río- 38 Ig 29.35N 104.25W
Concoran 46 Fh 36.06N 119.33W
Concord [Ca.-U.S.] 46 Eh 37.59N 122.00W
Concord [N.H.-U.S.] 39 Le 43.12N 71.32W
Concordia [Arg.] 53 Ki 31.24S 58.02W
Concordia [Braz.] 55 Fh 27.14S 52.01W
Concordia [Ks.-U.S.] 45 Hg 39.34N 97.39W
Concordia [Mex.] 48 Ff 23.17N 106.04W
Concordia Baai 51c Aa 17.31N 62.58W
Con Cuong 25 Ke 19.02N 104.54 E
Conda 36 Be 11.06S 14.20 E
Condamine River 59 Je 27.00S 149.50 E
Condat 11 Ii 45.22N 2.46 E
Conde 54 Kf 11.49S 37.37W
Condé-en-Brie 12 Fe 49.01N 3.33 E
Condega 49 Dg 13.21N 86.24W
Condé-sur-l'Escaut 12 Fd 50.27N 3.35 E
Condé-sur-Marne 12 Ge 49.03N 4.11 E
Condé-sur-Noireau 11 Ff 48.51N 0.33W
Condobolin 59 Jf 33.05S 147.09 E
Condom 11 Gk 43.58N 0.22 E
Condon 46 Ed 45.14N 120.11W
Condor, Cordillera del- 54 Cd 4.20S 78.30W
Condroz/Condruzisch Plateau 11 Kd 50.25N 5.00 E
Condruzisch Plateau/Condroz 11 Kd 50.25N 5.00 E
Conecuh River 44 Dj 30.58N 87.14W
Conegliano 14 Ge 45.53N 12.18 E
Conejera, Isla- [Sp.] 13 Nf 38.59N 1.12 E
Conejera, Isla- [Sp.] 13 Oe 39.11N 2.57 E
Conejo 48 De 24.05N 111.00W
Conejo, Cerro- 48 Jg 21.24N 99.06W
Conero 14 Hg 43.33N 13.36 E
Conesa 55 Bk 33.36S 60.21W
Conference Island 51p Bb 12.09N 61.35W
Conflans-en-Jarnisy 12 He 49.10N 5.51 E
Conflans-Sainte-Honorine 12 Ef 48.59N 2.06 E
Confolens 11 Gh 46.01N 0.40 E
Confuso, Río- 55 Dg 25.09S 57.34W
Conghua 27 Jg 23.31N 113.30 E
Congo [1] 31 Ii 1.00S 15.00 E
Congo 30 Ii 6.04S 12.24 E
Congo, Dem. Rep. of the- → Zaïre [1] 31 Ji 1.00S 25.00 E
Congo Basin (EN) 30 Ih 0.00 17.00 E
Congonhas 55 Ke 20.30S 43.52W
Conil de la Frontera 13 Fh 36.16N 6.05W
Coniston 44 Gb 46.29N 80.51W
Conn, Lough-/Loch Con 9 Dg 54.04N 9.20W
Connacht/Connaught 9 Eh 53.30N 9.00W
Connaught/Connacht 9 Eh 53.30N 9.00W
Conneaut 44 Ge 41.58N 80.34W
Connecticut [2] 43 Mc 41.45N 72.45W
Connecticut River 43 Mc 41.17N 72.21W
Connell 46 Fc 46.40N 118.52W
Connellsville 44 He 40.02N 79.38W
Connemara, Mountains of- 9 Dh 53.30N 9.45W
Connersville 44 Ef 39.39N 85.08W
Conn Lake 42 Kb 70.30N 73.30W
Connors Range 59 Jd 21.40S 149.10 E
Conon 9 Id 57.35N 4.30W
Conquista 55 Id 19.56S 47.33W
Conrad 46 Jb 48.10N 111.57W
Conroe 45 Ik 30.19N 95.27W
Conroe Lake 45 Ik 30.25N 95.37W
Conscripto Bernardi 55 Cj 31.03S 59.05W
Conselheiro Lafaiete 54 Jh 20.40S 43.48W
Conselice 14 Ff 44.31N 11.49 E
Consett 9 Lg 54.51N 1.49W
Consolación del Sur 49 Fb 22.30N 83.31W
Con Son 25 Lg 8.43N 106.36 E
Constance, Lake- (EN) = Bodensee 5 Gf 47.35N 9.25 E
Constanța [2] 15 Le 44.30N 28.30 E
Constanța 6 Ig 44.11N 28.39 E
Constantina 13 Gg 37.52N 5.37W
Constantine [3] 32 Ib 36.20N 6.35 E
Constantine 31 He 36.22N 6.37 E
Constantine, Cape- 40 He 58.25N 158.50W
Constitución [Chile] 56 Fe 35.20S 72.25W
Constitución [Ur.] 55 Dj 31.05S 57.50W
Consuegra 13 Ie 39.28N 3.36W
Consuelo Peak 57 Fg 24.58S 148.10 E
Contamana 54 De 7.15S 74.54W
Contas, Rio de- 52 Mg 14.17S 39.01W
Contoy, Isla- 48 Pg 21.30N 86.48W
Contraforte Central, Serra do- 55 Ic 17.15S 47.50W
Contramaestre 49 Ic 20.18N 76.15W
Contraviesa, Sierra- 13 Ih 36.50N 3.10W
Contreras, Embalse de- 13 Ke 39.32N 1.30W
Contreras, Islas- 49 Gj 7.50N 81.47W
Contreras, Puerto de- 13 Ke 39.32N 1.30W
Contres 11 Hg 47.25N 1.26 E
Contumazá 54 Ce 7.22S 78.49W
Contursi 14 Jj 40.39N 15.14 E
Contwig 12 Je 49.15N 7.26 E
Contwoyto Lake 42 Gc 65.40N 110.40W
Conty 12 Ee 49.44N 2.09 E
Convención 54 Db 8.28N 73.20W
Conversano 14 Lj 40.58N 17.07 E
Conway 9 Jh 53.17N 3.50W
Conway [Ar.-U.S.] 43 Id 35.05N 92.26W
Conway [N.H.-U.S.] 44 Ld 43.58N 71.07W
Conway [S.C.-U.S.] 44 Hi 33.51N 79.04W
Conway [Wales-U.K.] 9 Jh 53.17N 3.50W
Conway, Mount- 59 Gd 23.45S 133.25 E
Conway Reef → Ceva-i-Ra 57 Ig 21.45S 174.35 E
Conyers 44 Fi 33.40N 84.00W
Conza, Sella di- 14 Jj 40.50N 15.18 E
Coober Pedy 58 Eg 29.01S 134.43 E
Cooch Behār → Koch Bihār 25 Hc 26.19N 89.26 E
Cook 66 Ad 59.27S 27.10W
Cook 59 Gf 30.37S 130.25 E
Cook, Bahía- 56 Fi 55.10S 70.10W
Cook, Cap- 63b Dd 19.32S 169.30 E
Cook, Cape- 46 Ba 50.08N 127.55W
Cook, Mount- 57 Hi 43.36S 170.09 E
Cook, Récif de- 63b Ad 19.25S 163.50 E
Cooke, Mount- 59 Df 32.25S 116.18 E
Cookes Peak 45 Cj 32.32N 107.44W
Cookeville 44 Eg 36.10N 85.31W
Cook Ice Shelf 66 Je 68.40S 152.30 E
Cook Inlet 38 Dc 60.30N 152.00W
Cook Island 64g Bb 1.57N 157.28W
Cook Islands [5] 58 Lf 20.00S 158.00W
Cookstown/An Chorr Chríochach 9 Gg 54.39N 6.45W
Cook Strait 57 Ii 41.20S 174.25 E
Cooktown 58 Ff 15.28S 145.15 E
Coolgardie 59 Ef 30.57S 121.10 E
Coolidge [Az.-U.S.] 43 Ee 32.59N 111.31W
Coolidge [Ks.-U.S.] 45 Fg 38.03N 101.59W
Coolidge Dam 46 Jj 33.12N 110.32W
Cooma 59 Jg 36.14S 149.08 E
Coonabarabran 59 Jf 31.16S 149.17 E
Coonamble 59 Jf 30.57S 148.23 E
Coonoor 25 Ff 11.21N 76.49 E
Coon Rapids 43 Jd 45.09N 93.18W
Cooper 45 Ij 33.23N 95.35W
Cooper, Mount- 46 Ga 50.13N 117.12W
Cooper Creek 57 Eg 28.29S 137.46 E
Cooper's Town 44 Il 26.51N 77.31W
Cooperstown [N.D.-U.S.] 45 Gc 47.27N 98.07W
Cooperstown [N.Y.-U.S.] 44 Jd 42.43N 74.56W
Coosa River 44 Di 32.30N 86.16W
Coos Bay 43 Cc 43.22N 124.13W
Coos Bay 46 Ce 43.23N 124.16W
Cootamundra 59 Jf 34.39S 148.02 E
Čop 16 Ce 48.26N 22.14 E
Copaiapó, Río- 56 Fc 27.19S 70.56W
Copainalá 48 Mi 17.05N 93.12W
Copán [3] 49 Cf 14.50N 89.00W
Copan 39 Kh 14.50N 89.09W
Copán 49 Cf 14.50N 89.12W
Copenhagen (EN) = København 6 Hi 55.40N 12.35 E
Copertino 14 Mj 40.16N 18.03 E
Copetonas 55 Bn 38.43N 60.27W
Copiapó 53 Ih 27.22S 70.20W
Çöpköy 15 Jh 41.13N 26.49 E
Coporito 50 Fh 8.56N 62.00W
Coporolo 36 Be 12.56S 13.00 E
Copparo 14 Ff 44.54N 11.49 E
Copper 40 Kd 60.30N 144.50W
Copperbelt [3] 36 Ee 13.00S 28.00 E
Copper Center 40 Jd 61.58N 145.19W
Copper Cliff 42 Jg 46.28N 81.04W
Copper Harbor 44 Db 47.27N 87.53W
Coppermine 39 Hc 67.50N 115.05W
Coppermine 38 Hc 67.49N 115.04W
Coppermine Point 44 Eb 46.59N 84.47W
Copper Queen 37 Dc 17.31S 29.20 E
Coqên (Maindong) 27 Ee 31.15N 85.13 E
Coquet 9 Lf 55.22N 1.37W
Coquetá, Río- 52 Jf 3.08S 64.46W
Coquille 46 Ce 43.11N 124.11W
Coquimbo [2] 56 Fd 31.00S 71.00W
Coquimbo 53 Ih 29.58S 71.21W
Corabia 15 Hf 43.47N 24.30 E
Coração de Jesus 55 Jc 16.42S 44.22W
Coradi o Cheradi, Isole- 14 Lj 40.27N 17.09 E
Corail 49 Kd 18.34N 73.53W
Corail, Mer de- = Coral Sea (EN) 57 Gf 20.00S 158.00 E
Coral, Cabeza de- 48 Ph 18.47N 87.19W
Coral Gables 43 Kf 25.45N 80.16W
Coral Harbour 39 Kc 64.08N 83.10W
Coral Sea 57 Gf 20.00S 158.00 E
Coral Sea (EN) = Corail, Mer de- 57 Gf 20.00S 158.00 E
Coral Sea Basin (EN) 57 Gf 14.00S 152.00 E
Coral Sea Islands Territory 59 Lc 18.00S 158.00 E
Coralville 45 Kf 41.40N 91.35W
Coralville Lake 45 Kf 41.47N 91.48W
Corantijn River 52 Ke 5.55N 57.05W
Corato 14 Ki 41.09N 16.25 E
Corbara, Lago di- 14 Gh 42.45N 12.15 E
Corbeil-Essones 11 If 48.36N 2.29 E
Corbie 12 Ee 49.55N 2.30 E
Corbières 11 Il 42.55N 2.38 E
Corbigny 11 Jg 47.15N 3.40 E
Corby 9 Mi 52.29N 0.40W
Corcaigh/Cork [2] 9 Ej 52.00N 8.30W
Corcaigh/Cork 6 Fe 51.54N 8.28W
Corcoran 46 Gi 35.45N 117.23W
Corcovado, Cerro- 48 Bb 30.40N 114.55W
Corcovado, Golfo 56 Ff 43.30S 73.30W
Corcovado, Golfo- 52 Ij 43.30S 73.30W
Corcovado, Volcán- 52 Ij 43.12S 72.48W
Corcubión 13 Cb 42.57N 9.11W
Corcubión, Ría de- 13 Cb 42.54N 9.09W
Cordele 43 Ke 31.58N 83.47W
Cordes 11 Hj 44.04N 1.57 E
Cordevole 14 Gd 46.05N 12.04 E
Cordilheiras, Serra das- 54 Ie 7.30S 48.30W
Cordillera [3] 55 Dg 25.15S 57.00W
Cordillera Central [Phil.] 26 Hc 17.20N 120.57 E
Cordillera Central [S.Amer.] 52 If 8.00S 77.00W
Cordillera Occidental 52 Ig 14.00S 74.00W
Cordillera Oriental 52 If 7.00S 76.00W
Córdoba [3] 13 Hf 38.00N 4.50W
Córdoba [Arg.] [2] 56 Hd 32.00S 64.00W
Córdoba [Arg.] 53 Ji 31.25S 64.10W
Córdoba [Col.] [2] 54 Cb 8.20N 75.40W
Córdoba [Mex.] 47 Ee 18.53N 96.56W
Córdoba [Sp.] 6 Fh 37.53N 4.46W
Córdoba, Sierras de- 52 Ji 31.15S 64.00W
Cordova 39 Ec 60.33N 145.46W
Corfu (EN) = Kérkira 5 Hh 39.40N 19.45 E
Corfu, Strait of- (EN) = Kerkiras, Stenón- 15 Dj 39.35N 20.05 E
Corguinho 55 Ed 19.53S 54.52W
Coria 13 Fe 39.59N 6.32W
Coria del Rio 13 Fg 37.16N 6.03W
Coribe 55 Ja 13.50S 44.28W
Coricudgy, Mount- 59 Kf 32.50S 150.22 E
Corigliano Calabro 14 Kk 39.36N 16.31 E
Coringa Islets 59 Jc 17.00S 150.00 E
Corinne 46 Ma 50.06N 104.32W
Corinth 43 Je 34.56N 88.31W
Corinth (EN) = Kórinthos 15 Fl 37.55N 22.53 E
Corinth, Gulf of- (EN) = Korinthiakós Kólpos 5 Ih 38.12N 22.30 E
Corinth Canal (EN) = Korinthou, Dhiórix- 15 Fl 37.58N 22.58 E
Corinto [Braz.] 54 Jg 18.21S 44.27W
Corinto [Nic.] 49 Dg 12.29N 87.10W
Corisco 34 Ge 0.55N 9.19 E
Cork/Corcaigh 6 Fe 51.54N 8.28W
Cork/Corcaigh [2] 9 Ej 52.00N 8.30W
Cork Harbour 9 Ej 51.45N 8.15W
Corleone 14 Hm 37.49N 13.18 E
Çorlu 23 Ca 41.09N 27.48 E
Çorlu 15 Kh 41.12N 27.28 E
Cormeilles 12 Ce 49.15N 0.23 E
Cormoran Reef 64a Bb 7.50N 134.32 E
Cornelio 48 Dc 29.55N 111.08W
Cornélio Procopio 56 Jb 23.08S 50.39W
Cornelius Grinnel Bay 42 Ld 63.20N 64.50W
Corner Brook 39 Ne 48.57N 57.57W
Corner Seamounts (EN) 38 Nf 35.30N 51.30W
Cornia 14 Eh 42.57N 10.33 E
Corning [Ar.-U.S.] 45 Kh 36.24N 90.35W
Corning [Ca.-U.S.] 46 Dg 39.56N 122.11W
Corning [N.Y.-U.S.] 44 Id 42.10N 77.04W
Corno Grande 14 Hh 42.28N 13.34 E
Cornouaille 11 Cg 48.00N 4.00W
Cornwall [3] 9 Ik 50.30N 4.30W
Cornwall 42 Kg 45.02N 74.44W
Cornwall 42 Ia 73.30N 95.00W
Cornwall 9 Hk 50.20N 5.05W
Cornwall 5 Fe 50.30N 4.40W
Cornwall, Cape- 9 Hk 50.08N 5.43W
Cornwallis 42 Ia 75.15N 95.00W
Coro 53 Jd 11.25N 69.41W
Coro, Golfete de- 49 Mh 11.34N 69.53W
Corocoro 54 Eg 17.12S 68.28W
Corocoro, Isla- 50 Fh 8.31N 60.05W
Corod 15 Kd 45.54N 27.37 E
Çoroh 23 Fa 41.36N 41.35 E
Coroico 54 Eg 16.10S 67.44W
Coromandel [Braz.] 55 Id 18.28S 47.13W
Coromandel [N.Z.] 62 Fb 36.46S 175.30 E
Coromandel Coast 21 Kh 14.00N 80.10 E
Coromandel Peninsula 61 Eg 36.50S 175.35 E
Coromandel Range 62 Fb 37.00S 175.40 E
Coron 26 Hd 12.00N 120.12 E
Corona 45 Di 34.15N 105.36W
Corona Bank (EN) 59 Db 12.20S 118.30 E
Coronado, Bahía de- 38 Ki 9.00N 83.50W
Coronado, Isla- 48 Aa 32.25N 117.15W
Coronados, Isla- 48 Dd 26.07N 111.17W
Coronation 66 Re 60.37S 45.35W
Coronation 46 Ja 52.05N 111.27W
Coronation, Cap- 63b Cf 22.15S 167.02 E
Coronation Gulf 38 Ic 68.25N 110.00W
Coronda 55 Bj 31.58S 60.55W
Coronda, Laguna- 55 Bk 32.06S 60.52W
Coronel 56 Fe 37.01S 73.08W
Coronel Bogado 56 Ic 27.11S 56.18W
Coronel Dorrego 56 He 38.42S 61.17W
Coronel du Graty 55 Bh 27.40S 60.56W
Coronel Fabriciano 54 Jg 19.31S 42.38W
Coronel Oviedo 56 Ic 25.25S 56.27W
Coronel Ponce 55 Eb 15.34S 55.01W
Coronel Pringles 56 He 37.58S 61.22W
Coronel Rodolfo Bunge 55 Bm 37.34S 60.08W
Coronel Suárez 56 He 37.28S 61.55W
Coronel Vidal 55 Dm 37.27S 57.43W
Coronel Vivida 55 Fg 25.58S 52.34W
Coropuna, Nudo- 52 Ig 15.30S 72.41W
Çorovoda 15 Di 40.30N 20.13 E
Corozal [Blz.] 49 Cd 18.24N 88.24W
Corozal [Blz.] 49 Cd 18.15N 88.17W
Corozal [Col.] 49 Ji 9.18N 75.17W
Corpus Christi 39 Jg 27.48N 97.24W
Corpus Christi, Lake- 45 Hl 28.10N 97.53W
Corpus Christi Bay 45 Hm 27.48N 97.20W
Corque 54 Eg 18.21S 67.42W
Corral de Bustos 55 Ak 33.17S 62.12W
Corrèggio 14 Ef 44.46N 10.47 E
Córrego do Ouro 55 Gc 16.18S 50.32W
Corrente 54 If 10.27S 45.10W
Corrente, Rio- [Braz.] 54 Hg 19.19S 50.50W
Corrente, Rio- [Braz.] 55 Ka 13.08S 43.28W
Corrente, Rio- [Braz.] 55 Ib 14.14S 46.58W
Correntes 55 Ec 17.37S 54.59W
Correntes, Rio- 55 Ec 17.38S 55.08W
Correnti, Capo delle- 5 Hh 36.40N 15.05 E
Correntina 54 Jf 13.20S 44.39W
Corrèze 11 Hi 45.10N 1.28 E
Corrèze [3] 11 Hi 45.15N 1.50 E
Corrib, Lough-/Loch Coirib 9 Dh 53.05N 9.10W
Corrientes [2] 56 Ic 29.00S 58.00W
Corrientes 53 Kh 27.30S 58.50W
Corrientes, Cabo- [Arg.] 55 Dn 38.01S 57.32W
Corrientes, Cabo- [Col.] 54 Cb 5.30N 77.34W
Corrientes, Cabo- [Cuba] 49 Ec 21.45N 84.31W
Corrientes, Cabo- [Mex.] 38 Ig 20.25N 105.42W
Corrientes, Ensenada de- 49 Ec 21.45N 84.31W
Corrientes, Río- [Arg.] 55 Cj 30.21S 59.33W
Corrientes, Río- [Peru] 54 Dd 3.43S 74.40W
Corrieyairack Pass 9 Id 57.05N 4.40W
Corrigan 45 Ik 31.00N 94.50W
Corrigin 59 Df 32.21S 117.52 E
Corry 44 He 41.56N 79.39W
Corryong 59 Jg 36.12S 147.54 E
Corse = Corsica (EN) 5 Gg 42.00N 9.00 E
Corse, Cap- 5 Gg 43.00N 9.23 E
Corse-du-Sud [3] 11a Ab 41.50N 9.00 E
Corsewall Point 9 Hf 55.02N 5.05W
Corsica (EN) = Corse 5 Gg 42.00N 9.00 E
Corsica, Canale di- 14 Dh 42.45N 9.45 E
Corsicana 43 He 32.06N 96.28W
Cort Adelaer, Kap- 41 Hf 61.45N 42.00W
Corte 11a Ba 42.18N 9.09 E
Cortegana 13 Fg 37.55N 6.49W
Cortés [3] 49 Cf 15.30N 88.00W
Cortes 13 Kc 41.55N 1.25W
Cortez 43 Fd 37.21N 108.35W
Cortina d'Ampezzo 14 Gd 46.32N 12.08 E
Čortkov 16 De 49.03N 25.50 E
Cortland 44 Id 42.36N 76.10W
Cortona 14 Fg 43.16N 11.59 E
Corubal 34 Bc 11.57N 15.06W
Coruche 13 Df 38.57N 8.31W
Çoruh 23 Fa 41.36N 41.35 E
Çorum 24 Fb 40.29N 35.36 E
Çorum 23 Da 40.33N 34.58 E
Corumbá 53 Kg 19.01S 57.39W
Corumbá, Rio- 54 Ig 18.19S 48.55W
Corumbá de Goiás 55 Hb 15.55S 48.48W
Corumbaíba 55 Hd 18.09S 48.34W
Corumo, Rio- 50 Fi 6.49N 60.52W
Corvallis 43 Cc 44.34N 123.16W
Corvo 30 De 39.42N 31.06W
Corzuela 55 Bh 26.57S 60.58W
Cosalá 48 Fe 24.23N 106.41W
Cosamaloapan 48 Lh 18.22N 95.48W
Cosenza 6 Hh 39.18N 16.15 E
Coshocton 44 Ge 40.16N 81.53W
Cosigüina, Punta- 49 Dg 12.54N 87.41W
Cosmoledo Group 30 Li 9.43S 47.35 E
Cosne-sur-Loire 11 Ig 47.24N 2.55 E
Cosquín 56 Hd 31.15S 64.29W
Cossato 14 Ce 45.34N 8.10 E
Costa, Cordillera de la- 52 Je 9.50N 66.00W
Costa Rica [1] 39 Ki 10.00N 84.00W
Costa Verde 13 Ga 43.40N 5.40W
Costeşti 15 He 44.40N 24.53 E
Costiera, Catena- 14 Kk 39.25N 16.10 E
Coswig 10 Je 51.08N 13.35 E
Cotabato 26 He 7.13N 124.15 E
Cotagaita 54 Eh 20.50S 65.41W
Cotahuasi 54 Dg 15.12S 72.56W
Côte d'Ivoire = Ivory Coast (EN) [1] 31 Gh 8.00N 5.00W
Côte d'Or 11 Kg 47.10N 4.50 E
Côte-d'Or [3] 11 Kg 47.30N 4.50 E
Cotentin 5 Ff 49.30N 1.30W
Côtes-d'Armor 11 Df 48.25N 2.40W
Cotiella 13 Mb 42.31N 0.19 E
Cotmeana 15 He 44.24N 24.45 E
Cotmeana 15 He 44.58N 24.37 E
Cotonou 31 Hh 6.21N 2.26 E
Cotopaxi, Volcán- 52 If 0.40S 78.26W
Cotswold Hills 9 Kj 51.45N 2.10W
Cottage Grove 46 De 43.48N 123.03W
Cottbus/Chośebuz 10 Ke 51.46N 14.20 E
Cottenham 12 Cb 52.17N 0.08 E
Cottondale 44 Ej 30.48N 85.23W
Cottonwood Wash 46 Ji 35.05N 110.22W
Cotui 49 Ld 19.03N 70.09W
Cotulla 45 Gl 28.26N 99.14W
Coubre, Pointe de la- 11 Ei 45.42N 1.14W
Couburg 10 Gf 50.15N 10.58 E
Coucy-le-Château-Auffrique 12 Fe 49.31N 3.19 E
Coudekerque-Branche 12 Ec 51.02N 2.24 E
Coudersport 44 He 41.46N 78.01W
Couedic, Cape du- 59 Hg 36.10S 136.40 E
Couesnon 11 Ef 48.37N 1.31W
Couhé 11 Gh 46.18N 0.11 E
Couilly-Pont-aux-Dames 12 Ef 48.53N 2.52 E
Coulee Dam 46 Fb 48.00N 118.59W
Coulihaut 51g Bb 15.30N 61.29W
Coulman Island 66 Kf 73.28S 169.45 E
Coulogne 12 Dd 50.55N 1.53 E
Coulommiers 11 Jf 48.49N 3.05 E
Coulonge, Rivière- 44 Ic 45.51N 76.45W
Coulounieix-Chamiers 11 Gi 45.10N 0.42 E
Council 46 Gd 44.44N 116.26W
Council Bluffs 43 Hc 41.16N 95.52W
Courcelles 12 Gd 50.28N 4.22 E
Courcelles-Chaussy 12 Ie 49.07N 6.24 E
Courland (EN) = Kurzeme 5 Id 57.00N 20.30 E
Courmayeur 14 Ae 45.47N 6.58 E
Cours 11 Kh 46.06N 4.19 E
Courseulles-sur-Mer 12 Be 49.20N 0.27W
Courtenay 42 Fg 49.41N 125.00W
Courtisols 12 Gf 48.59N 4.31 E
Courtrai/Kortrijk 11 Jd 50.50N 3.16 E
Coushatta 45 Jj 32.00N 93.21W
Cousin 11 Kh 46.58N 4.15 E
Coutances 11 Ee 49.03N 1.26W
Couto de Magalhães, Rio- 55 Fa 13.37S 53.09W
Coutras 11 Fi 45.02N 0.08W
Couture, Lac - 42 Jd 60.05N 75.20W
Couvin 11 Kd 50.03N 4.29 E
Couvin-Mariembourg 12 Gd 50.06N 4.31 E
Covarrubias 13 Ib 42.04N 3.31W
Covasna [2] 15 Id 46.00N 26.00 E
Covasna 15 Jd 45.51N 26.11 E
Coveñas 49 Ji 9.25N 75.42W
Coventry 9 Li 52.25N 1.30W
Covilhã 13 Ed 40.17N 7.30W
Covington [Ga.-U.S.] 44 Fi 33.37N 83.51W
Covington [Ky.-U.S.] 43 Kd 39.05N 84.30W
Covington [La.-U.S.] 45 Kk 30.29N 90.06W
Covington [Tn.-U.S.] 44 Ch 35.34N 89.39W
Covington [Va.-U.S.] 44 Hg 37.48N 79.59W
Cowal 9 He 56.05N 5.10W
Cowan, Lake- 59 Ef 31.50S 121.50 E
Cowan Knob 45 Ji 35.52N 93.29W
Cowell 59 Hf 33.41S 136.55 E
Cowes 12 Ad 50.46N 1.18W
Cowichan Lake 46 Cb 48.54N 124.20W
Cowra 59 Jf 33.50S 148.41 E
Coxim 53 Kg 18.30S 54.45W
Coxim, Rio- 55 Ed 18.34S 54.46W
Cox's Bāzār 25 Id 21.26N 91.59 E
Coyah 34 Cd 9.43N 13.23W
Coyame 48 Gc 29.28N 105.06W
Coyanosa Draw 45 Ek 31.18N 103.06W
Coycoyan, Sierra de- 48 Ji 17.30N 98.20W
Coyle—Coig, Río- 56 Gh 50.58S 69.11W
Coyote, Río- 48 Cb 30.48N 112.35W
Coyotitán 48 Ff 23.47N 106.35W
Coyuca, Laguna de- 48 Ii 16.57N 100.05W
Cozia, Pasul- 15 Hd 45.15N 24.15 E
Cozumel 48 Pg 20.31N 86.55W
Cozumel, Isla de- 47 Gd 20.25N 86.55W
Cradock 31 Jl 32.08S 25.36 E
Craig [Ak.-U.S.] 40 Me 55.29N 133.09W
Craig [Co.-U.S.] 43 Fc 40.31N 107.33W
Craigmont 46 Gc 46.15N 116.28W
Craigs Range 59 Ke 26.40S 151.30 E
Crailsheim 10 Gg 49.09N 10.05 E
Craiova 6 Ig 44.19N 23.48 E
Cranbrook [Austl.] 59 Df 34.18S 117.32 E
Cranbrook [B.C.-Can.] 42 Fg 49.31N 115.46W
Cranbrook [Eng.-U.K.] 12 Cc 51.05N 0.32 E
Crandon 45 Ld 45.34N 88.54W
Crane [Or.-U.S.] 46 Fe 43.25N 118.35W
Crane [Tx.-U.S.] 45 Ek 31.24N 102.21W
Crane Lake 45 Jb 48.16N 92.28W
Crane Lake 46 Ka 50.06N 109.06W
Cranleigh 12 Bc 51.08N 0.29W
Craon 11 Fg 47.51N 0.57W
Craonne 12 Fe 49.26N 3.47 E
Crapaud, Puy- 11 Fh 46.40N 0.40W
Crary Mountains 66 Of 76.48S 117.40W
Crasna 15 Fa 48.09N 22.20 E
Crasna [Rom.] 15 Kc 46.31N 27.51 E
Crasna [Rom.] 15 Fb 47.10N 22.54 E
Crater Lake [Or.-U.S.] 43 Cc 42.56N 122.06W
Crater Lake [St.Vin.] 51n Ba 13.19N 61.11W
Crateús 53 Lf 5.10S 40.40W
Crati 14 Kk 39.43N 16.31 E
Crato [Braz.] 54 Ke 7.14S 39.23W
Crato [Port.] 13 Ee 39.17N 7.39W
Crau 11 Kk 43.36N 4.50 E
Crauford, Cape - 42 Jb 73.44N 84.51W
Cravo Norte 54 Db 6.17N 70.12W
Crawford 45 Ee 42.41N 103.25W
Crawfordsville 44 De 40.02N 86.54W
Crawley 9 Mj 51.07N 0.12W
Crazy Mountains 46 Jc 46.08N 110.20W
Crazy Peak 43 Eb 46.01N 110.16W
Creciente, Isla- 48 De 24.23N 111.37W
Crécy-en-Ponthieu 12 Dd 50.15N 1.53 E
Crécy-la-Chapelle 12 Ef 48.51N 2.55 E
Crécy-sur-Serre 12 Fe 49.42N 3.37 E
Crediton 9 Jk 50.47N 3.39W
Cree [Sask.-Can.] 42 Ge 58.50N 105.40W
Cree [Scot.-U.K.] 9 Ig 54.52N 4.20W
Creede 45 Ch 37.51N 106.56W
Creel 47 Cc 27.45N 107.38W
Cree Lake 42 Ge 57.30N 106.30W
Creglingen 10 Gg 49.28N 10.02 E
Creil 11 Ie 49.16N 2.29 E
Crema 14 De 45.22N 9.41 E
Cremenea, Braţul- 15 Ke 44.57N 27.54 E
Crémieu, Plateau de- 11 Li 45.40N 5.30 E
Cremona 14 Ee 45.07N 10.02 E
Crepaja 15 Dd 45.01N 20.39 E
Crepori, Rio- 54 Ge 5.42S 57.08W
Crépy-en-Valois 11 Ie 49.14N 2.54 E
Cres [Yugo.] 14 If 44.40N 14.25 E
Cres [Yugo.] 14 If 44.58N 14.24 E
Crescent 46 Ee 43.29N 121.41W
Crescent City 43 Cc 41.45N 124.12W
Crescent Lake 44 Gk 29.28N 81.30W
Crespo 55 Bk 32.02S 60.19W

Index Symbols

[1] Independent Nation
[2] State, Region
[3] District, County
[4] Municipality
[5] Colony, Dependency
Continent
Physical Region
Historical or Cultural Region
Mount, Mountain
Volcano
Hill
Mountains, Mountain Range
Hills, Escarpment
Plateau, Upland
Pass, Gap
Plain, Lowland
Delta
Salt Flat
Valley, Canyon
Crater, Cave
Karst Features
Depression
Polder
Desert, Dunes
Forest, Woods
Heath, Steppe
Oasis
Cape, Point
Coast, Beach
Cliff
Peninsula
Isthmus
Sandbank
Island
Atoll
Rock, Reef
Islands, Archipelago
Rocks, Reefs
Coral Reef
Well, Spring
Geyser
River, Stream
Waterfall Rapids
River Mouth, Estuary
Lake
Salt Lake
Intermittent Lake
Reservoir
Swamp, Pond
Canal
Glacier
Ice Shelf, Pack Ice
Ocean
Sea
Gulf, Bay
Strait, Fjord
Lagoon
Bank
Seamount
Tablemount
Ridge
Shelf
Basin
Escarpment, Sea Scarp
Fracture
Trench, Abyss
National Park, Reserve
Point of Interest
Recreation Site
Cave, Cavern
Historic Site
Ruins
Wall, Walls
Church, Abbey
Temple
Scientific Station
Airport
Port
Lighthouse
Mine
Tunnel
Dam, Bridge

Crest 11 Lj 44.44N 5.02 E
Crested Butte 45 Cg 38.52N 106.59W
Creston [B.C.-Can.] 46 Gb 49.06N 116.31W
Creston [Ia.-U.S.] 43 Ic 41.04N 94.22W
Crestone Peak 45 Dh 37.58N 105.36W
Crestview 43 Je 30.46N 86.34W
Creswell 44 Ih 35.52N 76.23W
Creswell Bay 42 Ib 72.40N 93.30W
Creswell Creek 59 Hc 18.10S 135.11 E
Crete 45 Hf 40.38N 96.58W
Crete (EN) = Kriti 5 Ih 35.15N 24.45 E
Crete (EN) = Kriti [2] 15 Hn 35.35N 25.00 E
Crete, Sea of- (EN) = Kritikón Pélagos 15 Hn 36.00N 25.00 E
Créteil 11 If 48.47N 2.28 E
Cretin, Cape- 60 Di 6.40S 147.52 E
Creus, Cabo de-/Creus, Cap de- 5 Gg 42.19N 3.19 E
Creus, Cap de-/Creus, Cabo de- 5 Gg 42.19N 3.19 E
Creuse [3] 11 Hh 46.05N 2.00 E
Creuse 11 Gg 47.00N 0.34 E
Creutzwald 11 Me 49.12N 6.41 E
Crevecoeur-en-Auge 12 Ce 49.07N 0.01 E
Crèvecoeur-le-Grand 12 Ee 49.36N 2.05 E
Crevillente 13 Lf 38.15N 0.48W
Crewe 9 Kh 53.05N 2.27W
Crézancy 12 Fe 49.03N 3.30 E
Criciúma 53 Lh 28.40S 49.23W
Cricket Mountains 46 Ig 38.50N 113.00W
Crieff 9 Je 56.23N 3.52W
Criel-sur-Mer 12 Dd 50.01N 1.19 E
Criel sur Mer-Mesnil Val 12 Dd 50.03N 1.20 E
Crikvenica 14 Ie 45.11N 14.42 E
Crillon 12 De 49.31N 1.56 E
Crimea (EN)=Krymski Poluostrov 5 Jf 45.00N 34.00 E
Crimean Mountains (EN)= Krymskije Gory 5 Jg 44.45N 34.30 E
Crimmitschau 10 If 50.49N 12.23 E
Criquetot-l'Esneval 12 Ce 49.39N 0.16 E
Crissolo 14 Bf 44.42N 7.09 E
Cristal, Monts de- 36 Bb 0.30N 10.30 E
Cristal, Sierra del- 49 Jc 20.33N 75.31W
Cristalândia 54 If 10.36S 49.11W
Cristalina 54 Ig 16.45S 47.36W
Cristalino, Rio- 54 Hf 12.40S 50.40W
Cristallo 14 Gd 46.34N 12.12 E
Cristóbal Colón, Pico 52 Id 10.50N 73.45W
Cristuru Secuiesc 15 Ic 46.35N 25.47 E
Crişu Alb 15 Ec 46.42N 21.16 E
Crişu Negru 15 Ec 46.42N 21.16 E
Crişu Repede 15 Dc 46.55N 20.59 E
Crixás 55 Hb 14.27S 49.58W
Crixás-Açu, Rio- 54 Hf 13.19S 50.36W
Crixás Mirim, Rio- 55 Ga 13.28S 50.36W
Crkvena Planina 15 Fg 42.48N 22.22 E
Crna Gora 15 Eg 42.16N 21.35 E
Crna Gora 15 Ce 44.05N 19.50 E
Crna Gora = Montenegro (EN) [2] 15 Cg 42.30N 19.18 E
Crna Gora=Montenegro (EN) 15 Cg 42.30N 19.18 E
Crna Reka 15 Ef 43.50N 21.55 E
Crna reka 15 Eh 41.33N 21.59 E
Crni Drim 15 Dg 42.05N 20.23 E
Crni Timok 15 Ff 43.55N 22.18 E
Črni Vrh 14 Jd 46.29N 15.14 E
Crni vrh 14 Kf 44.36N 16.30 E
Črnomelj 14 Je 45.34N 15.12 E
Croatia (EN) = Hrvatska [2] 14 Jf 45.00N 15.30 E
Croatia (EN) = Hrvatska 5 Hf 45.00N 15.30 E
Croatia (EN) = Hrvatska 14 Je 45.00N 15.30 E
Crocker, Banjaran- 26 Ge 5.40N 116.20 E
Crockett 45 Ik 31.19N 95.28W
Crocq 11 Ii 45.52N 2.22 E
Crocus Bay 51b Ab 18.13N 63.05W
Croisette, Cap- 11 Lk 43.13N 5.20 E
Croisic, Pointe du- 11 Dg 47.17N 2.33W
Croisilles 12 Ed 50.12N 2.53 E
Croissy-sur-Celle 12 Ee 49.42N 2.11 E
Croix, Lac la- 45 Jb 48.21N 92.05W
Croix-Haute, Col de la- 11 Lj 44.43N 5.40 E
Croker, Cape- 59 Gb 10.58S 132.35 E
Croker Bay 42 Jb 74.38N 83.15W
Croker Island 59 Gb 11.10S 132.30 E
Cromarty 9 Id 57.40N 4.02W
Cromer 9 Oi 52.56N 1.18 E
Cromwell 62 Cf 45.03S 169.14 E
Crooked Island 47 Jd 22.45N 74.13W
Crooked Island Passage 47 Jd 22.55N 74.35W
Crooked River 46 Ed 44.34N 121.16W
Crookston 43 Hb 47.47N 96.37W
Crosby [Mn.-U.S.] 45 Jc 46.28N 93.57W
Crosby [N.D.-U.S.] 45 Eb 48.55N 103.18W
Cross 34 Ge 4.55N 8.15 E
Cross City 44 Fk 29.32N 83.07W
Crossett 45 Kj 33.08N 91.58W
Cross Fell 9 Kg 54.42N 2.29W
Cross Lake 42 Hf 54.47N 97.22W
Crossman Peak 46 Hi 34.32N 114.07W
Cross River [2] 34 Gd 5.40N 8.10 E
Cross Sound 40 Le 58.10N 136.30W
Crotone 14 Lk 39.05N 17.08 E
Crotto 55 Bm 36.35S 60.10W
Crouch 12 Cc 51.37N 0.53 E
Crow Agency 46 Ld 45.36N 107.27W
Crowborough 12 Cc 51.03N 0.09 E
Crow Creek 45 Df 40.23N 104.29W
Crowell 45 Gj 33.59N 99.43W
Crow Lake 45 Jb 49.12N 93.57W
Crowley 45 Jk 30.13N 92.22W
Crowley, Lake- 46 Fh 37.37N 118.44W
Crowley Ridge 45 Ki 35.45N 90.45W
Crownpoint 45 Bi 35.42N 108.07W
Crown Prince Frederik 42 Ic 70.05N 86.40W
Crowsnest Pass 42 Gg 49.00N 114.30W
Crows Nest Peak 45 Ed 44.03N 103.58W
Croydon 59 Ic 18.12S 142.14 E
Croydon, London- 9 Mj 51.23N 0.07W
Crozet, Iles- 30 Mm 46.30S 51.00 E
Crozet Basin (EN) 3 Gm 39.00S 60.00 E
Crozet Ridge (EN) 3 Fn 45.00S 45.00 E
Crozon 11 Bf 48.15N 4.29W
Crozon, Presqu'île de- 11 Bf 48.15N 4.25W
Crucero, Cerro- 48 Gg 21.41N 104.25W
Cruces 49 Gb 22.21N 80.16W
Crump Lake 46 Fe 42.17N 119.50W
Crumpton Point 51g Ba 15.35N 61.19W
Cruz, Cabo- 47 Ie 19.51N 77.44W
Cruz Alta [Arg.] 55 Bk 33.01S 61.49W
Cruz Alta [Braz.] 53 Kh 28.39S 53.36W
Cruz del Eje 56 Hd 30.44S 64.48W
Cruzeiro do Oeste 56 Jb 23.46S 53.04W
Cruzeiro do Sul 53 If 7.38S 72.36W
Cruzen Island 66 Mf 74.47S 140.42W
Cruz Grande 48 Ji 16.44N 99.08W
Crvanj 14 Mg 43.25N 18.11 E
Crvenka 15 Cd 45.39N 19.28 E
Crystal Brook 59 Hf 33.21S 138.13 E
Crystal City [Man.-Can.] 45 Gb 49.08N 98.57W
Crystal City [Tx.-U.S.] 45 Gl 28.41N 99.50W
Crystal Falls 44 Cb 46.06N 88.20W
Crystal Springs 45 Kk 31.59N 90.21W
Csákvár 10 Oi 47.24N 18.27 E
Cserhát 10 Pi 47.55N 19.30 E
Csongrád [2] 10 Qj 46.25N 20.15 E
Csongrád 10 Qj 46.42N 20.09 E
Csorna 10 Ni 47.37N 17.15 E
ČSSR → Československá Socialistická Republika [1] 6 Hf 49.30N 17.00 E
Csurgó 10 Nj 46.16N 17.06 E
Ctesiphon 24 Kf 33.05N 44.35 E
Ču 21 Ie 45.00N 67.44 E
Ču 22 Je 43.33N 73.45 E
Cuajinicuilapa 48 Ji 16.28N 98.25W
Cuale 36 Cd 7.40S 17.01 E
Cuamba 31 Kj 14.49S 36.33 E
Cuan an Fhóid Duibh/ Blacksod Bay 9 Dg 54.08N 10.00W
Cuanavale 36 Cf 15.07S 19.14 E
Cuan Bhaile Átha Cliath/ Dublin Bay 9 Gh 53.20N 6.06W
Cuan Chill Ala/Killala Bay 9 Dg 54.15N 9.10W
Cuan Dhun Dealgan/ Dundalk Bay 9 Gh 53.57N 6.17W
Cuan Dhún Droma/Dundrum Bay 9 Hg 54.13N 5.45W
Cuando 30 Jj 18.27S 23.32 E
Cuando-Cubango [3] 36 Df 16.00S 20.30 E
Cuan Eochaille/Youghal Harbour 9 Fj 51.52N 7.50W
Cuangar 36 Cf 17.36S 18.37 E
Cuango 30 Ii 3.14S 17.22 E
Cuango [Ang.] 36 Cd 9.07S 18.05 E
Cuango [Ang.] 36 Cd 6.17S 16.41 E
Cuan Loch Garman/Wexford Harbour 9 Gi 52.20N 6.25W
Cuan Mó/Clew Bay 9 Dh 53.50N 9.50W
Cuan na Gaillimhe/Galway Bay 5 Fe 53.10N 9.15W
Cuan na gCaorach/Sheep Haven 9 Ff 55.10N 7.52W
Cuan Phort Láirge/ Waterford Harbour 9 Gi 52.10N 6.57W
Cuan Shligigh/Sligo Bay 9 Eg 54.20N 8.40W
Cuanza 30 Ii 9.19S 13.08 E
Cuanza Norte [3] 36 Bd 8.50S 14.30 E
Cuanza Sul [3] 36 Be 10.50S 14.50 E
Cuareim, Arroyo- 55 Dj 30.12S 57.36W
Cuaró 55 Dj 30.37S 56.54W
Cuaró Grande, Arroyo- 55 Dj 30.18S 57.12W
Cuarto, Rio- 56 Hd 33.25S 63.02W
Cuatir 36 Cf 17.01S 18.09 E
Cuatro Ciénegas de Carranza 48 Hd 26.59N 102.05W
Cuauhtémoc 47 Cc 28.25N 106.52W
Cuautitlán 48 Jh 19.40N 99.11W
Cuay Grande 55 Di 28.40S 56.17W
Cuba 38 Lg 21.30N 80.00W
Cuba 39 Lg 21.30N 80.00W
Cuba [Mo.-U.S.] 45 Kg 38.04N 91.24W
Cuba [N.M.-U.S.] 45 Ch 36.01N 107.04W
Cuba [Port.] 13 Ef 38.10N 7.53W
Cubabi, Cerro- 48 Cb 31.42N 112.46W
Cubagua, Isla- 50 Dg 10.49N 64.11W
Cubal 36 Be 13.03S 14.15 E
Cubal [Ang.] 36 Be 11.29S 13.48 E
Cubal [Ang.] 36 Bf 15.22S 12.39 E
Cubango 30 Jj 18.53N 22.24 E
Çubuk 24 Eb 40.59N 32.05 E
Čubukulah, Gora- 20 Kc 66.23N 153.59 E
Cucalón, Sierra de- 13 Kd 40.59N 1.10W
Cuchi 36 Ce 14.40S 16.52 E
Cuchi 30 Ij 15.28S 17.21 E
Cuchibi 36 De 15.00S 20.45 E
Cuchilla Águila, Cerro- 48 Ig 21.27N 101.03W
Cuchivero, Rio- 50 Di 7.40N 65.57W
Cuchumatanes, Sierra de los- 49 Bf 15.35N 91.25W
Cuckfield 12 Bc 51.01N 0.08W
Cuckmere 12 Cd 50.45N 0.09 E
Cucui 54 Ec 1.12N 66.50W
Cucumbi 36 Ce 10.17S 19.03 E
Cucurpe 48 Db 30.20N 110.43W
Cúcuta 53 Ie 7.54N 72.31W
Cudahy 45 Me 42.57N 87.52W
Cudalbi 15 Kd 45.47N 27.42 E
Cuddalore 22 Jh 11.45N 79.45 E
Cuddapah 25 Ff 14.28N 78.49 E
Čudovo 19 Dd 59.08N 31.41 E
Čudskoje Ozero=Peipus, Lake- (EN) 5 Id 58.45N 27.30 E
Cue 59 De 27.25S 117.54 E
Cuebe 36 Cf 15.48S 17.30 E
Cuelei 36 Cf 15.33S 17.21 E
Cuéllar 13 Hc 41.29N 4.19W
Cuemba 36 Ce 12.09S 18.07 E
Cuenca [Ec.] 53 If 2.53S 78.59W
Cuenca [3] 13 Ke 40.00N 2.00W
Cuenca [Sp.] 13 Jd 40.04N 2.08W
Cuenca, Serrania de- 5 Fg 40.10N 1.55W
Cuencamé de Ceniceros 48 He 24.53N 103.42W
Cuera/Chur 14 Dd 46.50N 9.35 E
Cuerda del Pozo, Embalse de la- 13 Jc 41.51N 2.44W
Cuernavaca 39 Jh 18.55N 99.15W
Cuero 45 Hl 29.06N 97.18W
Cuevas del Almanzora 13 Kg 37.18N 1.53W
Cugir 15 Gd 45.50N 23.22 E
Cugo 36 Cd 7.22S 17.06 E
Čugujev 16 Je 49.50N 36.41 E
Čugujevka 28 Mb 44.08N 133.53 E
Čuhloma 19 Ed 58.47N 42.41 E
Cuiabá 53 Kg 15.35S 56.05W
Cuiabá, Rio- 52 Kg 17.05S 56.36W
Cuiabá Mirim, Rio- 55 Ec 16.20S 55.55W
Cuidado, Punta- 65d Bb 27.08S 109.19W
Cuijk, Cuijk en Sint Agatha- 12 Hc 51.44N 5.52 E
Cuijk en Sint Agatha-Cuijk 12 Hc 51.44N 5.52 E
Cuilapa 49 Bf 14.17N 90.18W
Cuillin Hills 9 Gd 57.14N 6.15W
Cuilo 30 Ii 3.22S 17.22 E
Cúil Raithin/Coleraine 9 Gf 55.08N 6.40W
Cuiluan 27 Mb 47.39N 128.34 E
Cuima 36 Ce 13.14S 15.38 E
Cuito 30 Jj 18.01S 20.48 E
Cuito Cuanavale 31 Ij 15.13S 19.08 E
Cuitzeo, Lago de- 48 Ih 19.55N 101.05W
Cuiuni, Rio- 54 Fd 0.45S 63.07W
Cujmir 15 Fe 44.13N 22.56 E
Čukata 15 Ih 41.50N 25.15 E
Čukotski Nacionalny okrug [3] 20 Mc 66.00N 172.30 E
Čukotski Poluostrov= Chukchi Peninsula (EN) 21 Uc 66.00N 175.00W
Čukotskoje More=Chukchi Sea (EN) 67 Bd 69.00N 171.00W
Çukurca 24 Jd 37.15N 43.37 E
Çukurdaği 15 Ll 37.58N 28.44 E
Čulakkurgan 19 Gg 43.48N 69.12 E
Culan 11 Ih 46.33N 2.21 E
Cu Lao, Hon- 25 Lf 10.30N 109.13 E
Culasi 26 Hd 11.26N 122.03 E
Culbertson 46 Mb 48.09N 104.31W
Culebra, Isla de- 49 Od 18.19N 65.17W
Culebra, Sierra de la- 13 Fc 41.55N 6.20W
Culebra Peak 45 Dh 37.06N 105.10W
Culemborg 12 Hc 51.57N 5.14 E
Culiacán, Río de- 48 Fe 24.31N 107.41W
Culiacán Rosales 39 Ig 24.48N 107.24W
Culion 26 Gd 11.50N 119.55 E
Culion 26 Hd 11.53N 120.01 E
Culiseu, Rio- 54 Hf 12.14S 53.17W
Cullera 13 Le 39.10N 0.15W
Cullman 43 Je 34.11N 86.51W
Čulman 22 Od 56.52N 124.52 E
Culpeper 44 Hf 38.28N 78.01W
Culuene, Rio- 52 Kg 12.56S 52.51W
Culukidze 16 Mh 42.18N 42.25 E
Culver, Point- 59 Ef 32.54S 124.43 E
Culverden 62 Ee 42.46S 172.51 E
Čulym 20 De 55.06N 80.58 E
Čulym 21 Kd 57.40N 83.50 E
Čulyšman 20 Df 51.20N 87.45 E
Cuma 36 Ce 12.52S 15.04 E
Cumaná 53 Jd 10.28N 64.10W
Cumanacoa 50 Eg 10.15N 63.55W
Cumaovası 15 Kk 38.15N 27.09 E
Cumbal, Volcán- 54 Cc 0.57N 77.52W
Cumberland 9 Kg 54.40N 2.50W
Cumberland 38 Kf 37.09N 88.25W
Cumberland [B.C.-Can.] 46 Cb 49.37N 125.01W
Cumberland [Md.-U.S.] 43 Ld 39.39N 78.46W
Cumberland [Va.-U.S.] 44 Hg 37.31N 78.16W
Cumberland, Cap- 63b Cb 14.39S 166.37 E
Cumberland, Lake- 44 Eg 36.57N 84.55W
Cumberland Bay 51n Ba 13.16N 61.17W
Cumberland Island 44 Gj 30.51N 81.27W
Cumberland Islands 59 Jd 20.40S 149.10 E
Cumberland Lake 42 Hf 54.00N 102.20W
Cumberland Peninsula 38 Mc 66.50N 64.00W
Cumberland Plateau 38 Kf 36.00N 85.00W
Cumberland Sound 38 Mc 65.10N 65.30W
Cumbernauld 9 Jf 55.58N 3.59W
Cumbre, Paso de la-/ Bermejo, Paso- 52 Ii 32.50S 70.05W
Cumbria [3] 9 Kg 54.35N 2.45W
Cumbrian Mountains 9 Jg 54.30N 3.05W
Čumerna 15 Ig 42.47N 25.58 E
Čumikan 20 If 54.42N 135.19 E
Cummins 59 Hf 34.16S 135.44 E
Cumnock 9 If 55.27N 4.16W
Cumpas 48 Eb 30.02N 109.48W
Çumra 24 Ed 37.34N 32.48 E
Čumyš 20 Df 53.30N 83.10 E
Čuna 21 Ld 57.42N 95.35 E
Cunagua 49 Hb 22.05N 78.20W
Cuñapirú 55 Ej 31.32S 55.35W
Cuñapirú, Arroyo- 55 Ej 31.12S 55.31W
Cuñapirú, Cuchilla de- 55 Ej 31.12S 55.36W
Cunaviche, Rio- 50 Ci 7.19N 67.11W
Cunderdin 59 Df 31.39S 117.15 E
Cundinamarca [2] 54 Db 5.00N 74.00W
Čundža 19 Hg 43.32N 79.28 E
Cunene [3] 36 Cf 16.30S 15.00 E
Cunene=Kunene (EN) 30 Ij 17.20S 11.50 E
Cuneo 14 Bf 44.23N 7.32 E
Čunja 21 Lc 61.30N 96.20 E
Cunnamulla 58 Fg 28.04S 145.41 E
Čunski [R.S.F.S.R.] 20 Ee 56.03N 99.48 E
Čunski [R.S.F.S.R.] 20 Ee 57.23N 97.40 E
Cuorgnè 14 Be 45.23N 7.39 E
Čupa 19 Db 66.17N 33.01 E
Cupar 9 Je 56.19N 3.01W
Cupica, Golfo de- 54 Cb 6.35N 77.30W
Ćuprija 15 Ef 43.56N 21.22 E
Cupula, Pico- 48 De 24.47N 110.50W
Čur 7 Mh 57.11N 53.01 E
Curaçá 54 Ke 8.59S 39.54W
Curacao 52 Jd 12.11N 69.00W
Curacautin 56 Fe 38.26S 71.53W
Cura Malal, Sierra de- 55 Am 37.44S 62.16W
Curanilahue 56 Fe 37.28S 73.21W
Čurapča 20 Id 61.56N 132.18 E
Curaray, Rio- 54 Dd 2.20S 74.05W
Curcúbata, Vîrful- 15 Fc 46.25N 22.35 E
Curdimurka 59 Eg 29.30S 137.10 E
Curé 55 De 21.25S 56.25W
Cure 11 Jg 47.40N 3.41 E
Curepipe 37a Bb 20.19S 57.31 E
Curepto 56 Fe 35.05S 72.01W
Curiapo 54 Fb 8.33N 61.00W
Curicó 53 Ii 34.59S 71.14W
Curicuriari, Rio- 54 Ed 0.14S 66.48W
Curitabanos 56 Jc 27.18S 50.36W
Curitiba 53 Lh 25.25S 49.15W
Curoca 36 Bf 15.43S 11.55 E
Currais Novos 54 Ke 6.15S 36.31W
Curralinho 54 Id 1.48S 49.47W
Curral-Velho 32 Cf 15.59N 22.48W
Current River 45 Kh 36.15N 90.57W
Currie 59 Ig 39.56S 143.52 E
Curtea de Argeş 15 Hd 45.08N 24.41 E
Curtici 15 Ec 46.21N 21.18 E
Curtis 45 Ff 40.38N 100.31W
Curtis Channel 59 Kd 23.55S 152.05 E
Curtis Island 57 Jh 30.35S 178.36W
Curtis Island [Austl.] 59 Kd 23.40S 151.10 E
Curuá, Rio- [Braz.] 55 Ga 13.26S 51.24W
Curuá, Rio- [Braz.] 54 Gd 1.55S 55.07W
Curuá, Rio- [Braz.] 52 Kf 5.23S 54.22W
Curuçá 54 Id 0.43S 47.50W
Curuçá, Rio- 54 Dd 4.27S 71.23W
Curuguaty 56 Ib 24.31S 55.42W
Curuguaty, Arroyo- 55 Dg 24.06S 56.02W
Curup 26 Dg 3.28S 102.32 E
Curupira, Sierra de- 54 Fc 1.25N 64.30W
Cururupu 54 Jd 1.50S 44.52W
Curuzú Cuatiá 56 Ic 29.47S 58.03W
Curvelo 54 Jg 18.45S 44.25W
Cusco 53 Ig 13.31S 71.59W
Cushing 45 Hi 35.59N 96.46W
Cushing, Mount- 42 Ee 57.36N 126.51W
Čusovaja 5 Ld 58.13N 56.30 E
Čusovoj 19 Fd 58.17N 57.50 E
Cusset 11 Jh 46.08N 3.28 E
Cusseta 44 Ei 32.18N 84.47W
Čust 18 Hd 41.00N 71.15 E
Custer 45 Ee 43.46N 103.36W
Cutato 36 Ce 10.33S 16.48 E
Cut Bank 43 Eb 48.38N 112.20W
Cutervo 54 Ce 6.22S 78.51W
Cuthbert 44 Ej 31.46N 84.48W
Cutral Có 56 Ge 38.56S 69.14W
Cutro 14 Kk 39.02N 16.59 E
Cuttack 22 Kg 20.30N 85.50 E
Čuvašskaja ASSR [3] 19 Ed 55.30N 47.10 E
Cuvelai 36 Cf 15.40S 15.47 E
Cuvette [3] 36 Cc 0.10S 15.30 E
Cuvier Basin (EN) 59 Cd 22.00S 111.00 E
Cuvier Island 62 Fb 36.25S 175.45 E
Cuvo ou Queve 30 Ij 10.50S 13.47 E
Cuxhaven 10 Ec 53.53N 8.42 E
Cuya 56 Fa 19.07S 70.08W
Cuyahoga Falls 44 Ge 41.08N 81.55W
Cuyo Islands 26 Hd 11.04N 120.57 E
Cuyubini, Rio- 50 Fh 8.20N 60.20W
Cuyuni, Rio- 52 Kf 6.23N 58.41W
Cuyuni River 52 Kf 6.23N 58.41W
Cuyutlán, Laguna- 48 Gh 19.00N 104.10W
Cuzco [2] 54 Df 12.30S 72.30W
Cuzna 13 Hf 38.04N 4.41W
Cvikov 10 Kf 50.48N 14.40 E
Čvrsnica 14 Lg 43.35N 17.35 E
Cyangugu 36 Ec 2.29S 28.54 E
Cybinka 10 Kd 52.12N 14.48 E
Cyclades (EN) = Kikládhes [3] 5 Ih 37.00N 25.10 E
Čyjyrčyk, Pereval- 18 Id 40.15N 73.20 E
Cypress Hills 38 Ie 49.40N 109.30W
Cypress Lake 46 Kb 49.28N 109.29W
Cyprus (EN)=Kıbrıs/Kypros [1] 22 Ff 35.00N 33.00 E
Cyprus (EN)=Kıbrıs/Kypros 21 Ff 35.00N 33.00 E
Cyprus (EN)=Kypros/Kıbrıs [1] 22 Ff 35.00N 33.00 E
Cyprus (EN)=Kypros/Kıbrıs 21 Ff 35.00N 33.00 E
Cyrenaica (EN)=Barqah 33 Dc 31.00N 22.30 E
Cyrenaica (EN)=Barqah 30 Je 31.00N 23.00 E
Cyrene 33 Dc 32.48N 21.59 E
Cyrus Field Bay 42 Ld 62.50N 65.00W
Cysoing 12 Fd 50.34N 3.13 E
Cythera (EN)=Kíthira 15 Fm 36.09N 23.00 E
Czaplinek 10 Mc 53.34N 16.14 E
Czarna [Pol.] 10 Pe 51.12N 19.53 E
Czarna [Pol.] 10 Rf 50.30N 21.15 E
Czarna Białostocka 10 Tc 53.18N 23.19 E
Czarna Dąbrówka 10 Nb 54.20N 17.32 E
Czarna Hańcza 10 Tc 53.50N 23.47 E
Czarnków 10 Md 52.55N 16.34 E
Czchów 10 Qg 49.50N 20.39 E
Czechoslovakia (EN)= Československo [1] 6 Hf 49.30N 17.00 E
Czechowice-Dziedzice 10 Og 49.54N 19.00 E
Czeremcha 10 Td 52.32N 23.15 E
Czersk 10 Nc 53.48N 18.00 E
Częstochowa 6 He 50.49N 19.06 E
Częstochowa [2] 10 Pf 50.50N 19.05 E
Człopa 10 Mc 53.06N 16.08 E
Człuchów 10 Nc 53.41N 17.21 E

D

Da, Sông-=Black River (EN) 21 Mg 20.17N 106.34 E
Da'an (Dalai) 27 Lb 45.35N 124.16 E
Dabaga 36 Gd 8.07S 35.55 E
Dabakala 34 Ed 8.22N 4.26W
Dabakala [3] 34 Ed 8.27N 4.28W
Daban → Bairin Youqi 27 Kc 43.30N 118.37 E
Dabas 10 Pi 47.11N 19.19 E
Daba Shan 21 Mf 32.15N 109.00 E
Dabat 35 Fc 12.58N 37.45 E
Dabay Sima 35 Gc 12.43N 42.17 E
Dabba/Daocheng 27 Hf 29.01N 100.26 E
Dabbāgh, Jabal- 23 Ed 27.52N 35.45 E
Dabeiba 54 Cb 7.02N 76.16W
Dąbie 10 Od 52.06N 18.49 E
Dabie, Jezioro- 10 Kc 53.29N 14.40 E
Dabie Shan 21 Nf 31.15N 115.00 E
Dabl, Wādī- [Sau.Ar.] 24 Gh 28.35N 39.04 E
Dabl, Wādī- [Sau.Ar.] 24 Gh 29.05N 36.14 E
Dabnou 34 Gc 14.09N 5.22 E
Dabola 34 Cc 10.45N 11.07W
Daborow 35 Hd 6.11N 48.22 E
Dabou 34 Ed 5.19N 4.23W
Dabqig → Uxin Qi 27 Id 38.27N 109.08 E
Dabraš 15 Gh 41.40N 23.50 E
Dabrowa Białostocka 10 Tc 53.40N 23.20 E
Dąbrowa Górnicza 10 Pf 50.20N 19.11 E
Dąbrowa Tarnowska 10 Qf 50.11N 21.00 E
Dabsan Hu 27 Fd 36.58N 95.00 E
Dăbuleni 15 Hf 43.48N 24.05 E
Dabus 35 Fc 10.38N 35.10 E
Dacata 35 Gd 7.16N 42.15 E
Dacca → Dhaka 22 Lg 23.43N 90.25 E
Dachangzhen 28 Eh 32.13N 118.44 E
Dachau 10 Hh 48.16N 11.26 E
Dachen Dao 28 Fj 28.29N 121.53 E
Dachstein 14 Hc 47.30N 13.36 E
Dacia Seamount (EN) 5 Ei 31.10N 13.42W
Dačice 10 Lg 49.05N 15.26 E
Dac Lac, Caonguyen- 25 Lf 12.50N 108.05 E
Đacovica 15 Dg 42.23N 20.26 E
Dadali 63a Dc 8.07S 159.06 E
Dadanawa 54 Gc 2.50N 59.30W
Daday 24 Eb 41.28N 33.28 E
Dade City 44 Fk 28.22N 82.12W
Dadou 11 Hk 43.44N 1.49 E
Dādra and Nagar Haveli [3] 25 Ed 20.20N 72.50 E
Dadu 25 Dc 26.44N 67.47 E
Dadu He 21 Mg 29.32N 103.44 E
Dadukou 28 Di 30.30N 117.03 E
Dăeni 15 Le 44.50N 28.07 E
Daet 26 Hd 14.05N 122.55 E
Dafang 27 If 27.06N 105.32 E
Dafeng (Dazhongji) 28 Fh 33.11N 120.27 E
Dagana 34 Bb 16.31N 15.30W
Dagana 35 Bc 13.05N 16.00 E
Daga Post 35 Ed 9.13N 33.58 E
Dağardi 15 Lj 39.26N 29.00 E
Dagash 35 Eb 19.22N 33.24 E
Dagda 8 Lh 56.04N 27.36 E
Dagdan-Daba 27 Gb 48.20N 96.50 E
Dagéla 35 Bc 10.40N 18.26 E
Dagestanskaja [3] 19 Eg 43.00N 47.00 E
Dagestanskije Ogni 19 Eg 42.06N 48.12 E
Dagezhen → Fengning 28 Dd 41.12N 116.39 E
Dagu 28 De 38.58N 117.40 E
Daguan 27 Hf 27.48N 103.54 E
Dagu He 28 Ff 37.34N 121.17 E
Daguokui Shan 28 Jb 45.19N 129.50 E
Dagupan 26 Hc 16.03N 120.20 E
Dagxoi → Yidun 27 Ge 30.25N 99.28 E
Dagzê 27 Ff 29.41N 91.24 E
Dagzê Co 27 Ee 31.54N 87.29 E
Daheiding Shan 27 Mb 47.58N 129.10 E
Dahei He 28 Ad 40.34N 111.05 E
Da Hinggan Ling=Greater Khingan Range (EN) 21 Oe 49.00N 122.00 E
Dahlak Archipelago 30 Lg 15.40N 40.30 E
Dahlak Kebir 35 Gb 15.38N 40.11 E
Daḩl al Furayy 24 Li 26.45N 47.03 E
Dahlem 12 Id 50.23N 6.33 E
Dahlonega Plateau 44 Fh 34.30N 83.45W
Dahm, Ramlat- 33 If 16.25N 45.45 E
Dahme 10 Je 51.52N 13.26 E
Dahmouni 13 Ni 35.25N 1.29 E
Dahn 12 Je 49.09N 7.47 E
Dahomey → Bénin [1] 31 Hh 9.30N 2.15 E
Dahongliutan 27 Cd 36.00N 79.12 E
Dahra 13 Mh 36.18N 0.55 E
Dahra [Lib.] 33 Cd 29.40N 17.40 E
Dahra [Sen.] 34 Bb 15.21N 15.29W
Dahra, Massif de- 13 Oh 36.30N 2.05 E
Dahūk [3] 24 Jd 36.57N 43.00 E
Dahūk 24 Jd 36.52N 43.00 E
Dahushan 28 Gd 41.37N 122.09 E
Dahy, Nafūd ad- 33 Ie 22.00N 45.25 E
Dai 63a Eb 7.53S 160.37 E
Daia 15 If 44.00N 25.59 E
Daïa, Région des- 32 Hc 33.30N 3.25 E
Daicheng 28 De 38.42N 116.37 E
Daigo 28 Pf 36.46N 140.21 E
Dai Hai 28 Bd 40.31N 112.43 E
Dailekh 25 Gc 28.50N 81.44 E
Daimanji-San 29 Cc 36.15N 133.19 E
Daimiel 13 Ie 39.04N 3.37W

Index Symbols

[1] Independent Nation
[2] State, Region
[3] District, County
[4] Municipality
[5] Colony, Dependency
Continent
Physical Region
Historical or Cultural Region
Mount, Mountain
Volcano
Hill
Mountains, Mountain Range
Hills, Escarpment
Plateau, Upland
Pass, Gap
Plain, Lowland
Delta
Salt Flat
Valley, Canyon
Crater, Cave
Karst Features
Depression
Polder
Desert, Dunes
Forest, Woods
Heath, Steppe
Oasis
Cape, Point
Coast, Beach
Cliff
Peninsula
Isthmus
Sandbank
Island
Atoll
Rock, Reef
Islands, Archipelago
Rocks, Reefs
Coral Reef
Well, Spring
Geyser
River, Stream
Waterfall Rapids
River Mouth, Estuary
Lake
Salt Lake
Intermittent Lake
Reservoir
Swamp, Pond
Canal
Glacier
Ice Shelf, Pack Ice
Ocean
Sea
Gulf, Bay
Strait, Fjord
Lagoon
Bank
Seamount
Tablemount
Ridge
Shelf
Basin
Escarpment, Sea Scarp
Fracture
Trench, Abyss
National Park, Reserve
Point of Interest
Recreation Site
Cave, Cavern
Historic Site
Ruins
Wall, Walls
Church, Abbey
Temple
Scientific Station
Airport
Port
Lighthouse
Mine
Tunnel
Dam, Bridge

Dainanji-San	29	Ec	36.36N	137.42 E
Dainichi-San	29	Ec	36.09N	136.30 E
Dainkog	27	Ge	32.31N	97.59 E
Daiō-Zaki	28	Ng	34.22N	136.53 E
Dairan (EN)=Dalian (Luda)	22	Of	38.55N	121.39 E
Dairan (EN) = Lüda→Dalian	22	Of	38.55N	121.39 E
Dairbhre/Valentia	9	Cj	51.55N	10.20W
Daireaux	55	Bm	36.36S	61.45W
Dai-Sen	29	Cd	35.24N	133.34 E
Daisengen-Dake	29a	Bc	41.35N	140.09 E
Daishan (Gaotingzhen)	28	Gi	30.15N	122.13 E
Daitō [Jap.]	29	Cd	35.19N	132.58 E
Daitō [Jap.]	29	Gb	39.02N	141.22 E
Daito Islands (EN)=Daitō Shotō	21	Pg	25.00N	131.15 E
Daitō Shotō=Daito Islands (EN)	21	Pg	25.00N	131.15 E
Daitō-Zaki	29	Gd	35.18N	140.24 E
Daixian	28	Be	39.03N	112.57 E
Daiyue→Shanyin	28	Be	39.30N	112.48 E
Dajabón	49	Ld	19.33N	71.42W
Dajarra	58	Eg	21.42S	139.31 E
Dajtit, Mali i-	15	Ch	41.22N	19.55 E
Daka	34	Ed	8.19N	0.13W
Dakar	31	Fg	14.40N	17.26W
Dākhilah, Wāḥāt al-=Dakhla Oasis (EN)	30	Jf	25.30N	29.10 E
Dakhla Oasis (EN)=Dākhilah, Wāḥāt al-	30	Jf	25.30N	29.10 E
Dakhlet Nouâdhibou (3)	32	De	20.30N	16.00W
Dakla	31	Ff	23.42N	15.56W
Dakoro	34	Gc	14.30N	6.25 E
Đakovo	14	Me	45.19N	18.25 E
Daksti	8	Kg	57.38N	25.32 E
Dak To	25	Lf	14.42N	107.51 E
Dal	8	Dd	60.15N	11.12 E
Dal, Jökulsá á-	7a	Cb	65.40N	14.20W
Đala	15	Dc	46.09N	20.07 E
Dala [Ang.]	36	De	11.03S	20.17 E
Dala [Sol.Is.]	63a	c	8.36S	160.41 E
Dalaba	34	Cc	10.42N	12.15W
Dalai → Da'an	27	Lb	45.35N	124.16 E
Dalai Nur	27	Kc	43.18N	116.15 E
Dala-Järna	8	Fd	60.33N	14.21 E
Dālaki	24	Nh	29.19N	51.06 E
Dalälven	5	Hc	60.38N	17.27 E
Dalaman	24	Cd	36.40N	28.45 E
Dalaman	15	Lm	36.44N	28.49 E
Dalāmī	35	Ec	11.52N	30.28 E
Dalān	24	Kj	24.15N	45.47 E
Dalan-Dzadgad	22	Me	43.47N	104.29 E
Dalane	8	Bf	58.35N	6.20 E
Dalarna	8	Fd	61.00N	14.05 E
Dalarö	8	He	59.08N	18.24 E
Da Lat	22	Mh	11.56N	108.25 E
Dālbandin	25	Cc	28.53N	64.25 E
Dalbosjön	8	Ef	58.45N	12.50 E
Dalboslätten	8	Ef	58.35N	12.25 E
Dalby	59	Ke	27.11S	151.16 E
Dale [Nor.]	7	Af	60.35N	5.49 E
Dale [Nor.]	7	Af	61.22N	5.25 E
Dale Hollow Lake	44	Eg	36.36N	85.19W
Dalen	7	Bg	59.27N	8.00 E
Dalfsen	12	Ib	52.30N	6.14 E
Dalgaranger, Mount-	59	De	27.51S	117.06 E
Dălgopol	15	Kf	43.03N	27.21 E
Dalhart	43	Gd	36.04N	102.31W
Dalhousie	42	Kg	48.04N	66.23W
Dalhousie, Cape-	42	Eb	70.15N	129.41W
Dali [China]	22	Mg	25.43N	100.07 E
Dali [China]	27	Ie	34.55N	110.00 E
Dalian (Lüda) = Dairan (EN)	22	Of	38.55N	121.39 E
Dalias	13	Jh	36.49N	2.52W
Daling He	28	Fd	40.56N	121.44 E
Dalizi	27	Mc	41.45N	126.50 E
Dalj	14	Me	45.29N	18.59 E
Daljā'	33	Fd	27.39N	30.42 E
Dalkowskie, Wzgórza-	10	Le	51.35N	15.50 E
Dall [Ak.-U.S.]	40	Mf	54.50N	132.55W
Dall [Can.]	2	Ef	55.00N	133.00W
Dallas [Or.-U.S.]	46	Dd	44.55N	123.19W
Dallas [Tx.-U.S.]	39	Jf	32.47N	96.48W
Dalmā'	24	Oj	24.30N	52.20 E
Dalmā', Qārat-	33	Dd	25.32N	23.57 E
Dalmacija	14	Kg	43.00N	17.00 E
Dalmacija = Dalmatia (EN)	5	Hg	43.00N	17.00 E
Dalmaj, Hawr-	24	Kf	32.20N	45.28 E
Dalmally	9	Ie	56.24N	4.58W
Dalmatia (EN) = Dalmacija	5	Hg	43.00N	17.00 E
Dalmatovo	17	Kh	56.16N	63.00 E
Dalnegorsk	22	Pe	44.31N	135.31 E
Dalnerečensk	22	Pe	45.55N	133.45 E
Dalni [R.S.F.S.R.]	20	Kf	53.15N	157.30 E
Dalni [R.S.F.S.R.]	20	Ih	44.57N	135.03 E
Dalnjaja, Gora-	20	Mc	68.08N	179.53 E
Daloa (3)	34	Dd	6.58N	6.23W
Daloa	31	Gh	6.53N	6.27W
Dalou Shan	21	Mg	28.00N	106.40 E
Dalqū	35	Ea	20.07N	30.35 E
Dalrymple, Mount-	57	Fg	21.02S	148.38 E
Dalsbruk	8	Jd	60.02N	22.31 E
Dalsbruk/Taalintendas	8	Jd	60.02N	22.31 E
Dalsfjorden	8	Ac	61.20N	5.05 E
Dalsjöfors	8	Eg	57.43N	13.05 E
Dalsland	8	Ef	58.35N	12.55 E
Dalslands kanal	8	Ef	58.50N	12.25 E
Dals Långed	7	Cg	58.55N	12.18 E
Dalton	44	Eh	34.47N	84.58W
Daltonganj	25	Gd	24.02N	84.04 E
Dalul	35	Gc	14.22N	40.21 E
Daluo	27	Hg	21.38N	100.15 E
Dalupiri	26	Hc	19.05N	121.12 E
Dalvik	7a	Bb	65.58N	18.32W
Dalwallinu	59	Df	30.17S	116.40 E
Dalyan	15	Lm	36.50N	28.39 E
Daly Bay	42	Id	64.00N	89.40W
Daly City	46	Dh	37.42N	122.29W
Daly River	57	Ef	13.20S	130.19 E
Daly Waters	59	Gc	16.15S	133.22 E
Damā, Wādī-	24	Fi	27.09N	35.47 E
Damagarim	34	Gc	13.42N	9.00 E
Damān (3)	25	Ed	20.10N	73.00 E
Damanhūr	33	Fc	31.02N	30.28 E
Damar, Pulau-	26	Ih	7.09S	128.40 E
Damara	35	Be	4.58N	18.42 E
Damaraland	37	Bd	21.00S	17.30 E
Damas Cays	49	Hb	23.58N	79.55W
Damascus (EN)=Dimashq	22	Ff	33.30N	36.15 E
Damāsh	24	Md	36.46N	49.46 E
Damaturu	34	Hc	11.45N	11.58 E
Damāvand	24	He	35.56N	52.08 E
Damāvand, Qolleh-ye-	21	Hf	35.56N	52.08 E
Damba	36	Cd	6.50S	15.07 E
Dambaslar	15	Kh	41.13N	27.14 E
Dame Marie, Cap-	47	Je	18.36N	74.26W
Damerğou	30	Hg	15.00N	9.00 E
Dāmghān	24	Pd	36.09N	54.22 E
Damianópolis	55	Ib	14.33S	46.10W
Damiao	27	He	30.52N	104.38 E
Damietta (EN)=Dumyāṭ	31	Ke	31.25N	31.48 E
Daming	28	Cf	36.17N	115.09 E
Daming Shan	27	Ig	23.23N	108.30 E
Damīr Qābū	24	Id	36.54N	41.47 E
Dammartin en Goële	12	Ee	49.03N	2.41 E
Dammastock	14	Cd	46.38N	8.25 E
Damme [Bel.]	12	Fc	51.15N	3.17 E
Damme [Ger.]	12	Kb	52.31N	8.12 E
Dammer Berge	12	Kb	52.35N	8.17 E
Damoh	25	Fd	23.50N	79.27 E
Damongo	34	Ed	9.05N	1.49W
Damous	13	Nh	36.33N	1.42 E
Dampier	58	Cg	20.39S	116.45 E
Dampier, Selat-=Dampier Strait (EN)	26	Jg	0.40S	130.40 E
Dampier Archipelago	59	Dd	20.35S	116.35 E
Dampier Land	59	Ec	17.30S	122.55 E
Dampierre	12	Df	48.42N	1.59 E
Dampier Strait	59	Ja	5.36S	148.12 E
Dampier Strait (EN)=Dampier, Selat-	26	Jg	0.40S	130.40 E
Damqawt	23	Hf	16.34N	52.50 E
Damqog Kanbab/Maquan He	27	Df	29.36N	84.09 E
Dam Qu	27	Fe	33.56N	92.41 E
Damville	12	Df	48.52N	1.04 E
Damvillers	12	He	49.20N	5.24 E
Damwoude, Dantumadeel-	12	Ha	53.18N	5.59 E
Damxoi → Comai	27	Ff	28.26N	91.32 E
Damxung	27	Fe	30.34N	91.16 E
Danakil=Danakil Plain (EN)	30	Lg	12.25N	40.30 E
Danakil Plain (EN)=Danakil	30	Lg	12.25N	40.30 E
Danané (3)	34	Dd	7.25N	8.10W
Danané	34	Dd	7.16N	8.09W
Da Nang	22	Mh	16.04N	108.13 E
Danba/Rongzhag	27	He	30.48N	101.54 E
Danbury	44	Ke	41.23N	73.27W
Danby Lake	46	Hi	34.14N	115.07W
Dancheng	28	Ch	33.36N	115.14 E
Dancheng→Xiangshan	27	Lf	29.29N	121.52 E
Dandarah	33	Fd	26.10N	32.39 E
Dandeldhura	25	Gc	29.18N	80.35 E
Dandenong, Melbourne-	59	Jg	37.59S	145.12 E
Dandong	22	Oe	40.10N	124.15 E
Daneborg	41	Jd	74.25N	20.10W
Danells Fjord	41	Hf	60.45N	42.45W
Danetj	15	Hf	43.59N	24.03 E
Danfeng (Longjuzhai)	27	Je	33.44N	110.22 E
Danforth Hills	45	Cf	40.15N	108.00W
Danfu	63a	Aa	4.12S	153.04 E
Dangara	19	Gh	38.09N	69.22 E
Dangchengwan → Subei	27	Fd	39.36N	94.58 E
Dang He	27	Fc	40.30N	94.42 E
Dangjin Shankou	21	Lf	39.15N	94.30 E
Dangla	35	Fc	11.16N	36.50 E
Dangla Shan→Tanggula Shan	21	Lf	33.00N	92.00 E
Dangoura, Mount-	35	Dd	6.12N	26.27 E
Dangrek Range (EN)=Dong Rak, Phanom-	21	Mh	14.25N	104.30 E
Dangshan	27	Ke	34.22N	116.21 E
Dangtu	28	Ei	31.33N	118.30 E
Dangu	12	De	49.15N	1.42 E
Dangyang	28	Ai	30.49N	111.47 E
Dan He	28	Bg	35.05N	112.59 E
Daniel	46	Je	42.52N	110.04W
Daniel, Serra-	55	Ea	13.40S	54.55W
Danielskuil	37	Ce	28.11S	23.33 E
Danilov	19	Ed	58.12N	40.13 E
Danilovgrad	15	Cg	42.33N	19.07 E
Danilovka	16	Nd	50.21N	44.06 E
Daning	27	Jd	36.31N	110.45 E
Danjiang → Junxian	27	Je	32.31N	111.32 E
Danjiangkou Shuiku	27	Je	32.37N	111.30 E
Danjo-Guntō	27	Me	32.00N	128.20 E
Ðank	24	Qk	23.33N	56.16 E
Dankov	16	Kc	53.16N	39.07 E
Danli	49	Df	14.00N	86.35W
Danmark=Denmark (EN) (1)	6	Gd	56.00N	10.00 E
Danmark Fjord	67	Me	81.10N	23.20W
Danmarks Havn	67	Ld	76.50N	18.30W
Danmarksstraedet=Denmark Strait (EN)	38	Qc	67.00N	25.00W
Dannenberg	10	Hc	53.06N	11.06 E
Dannevirke	62	Gd	40.12S	176.06 E
Danot	35	Hd	7.33N	45.17 E
Dantumadeel	12	Ha	53.18N	5.59 E
Dantumadeel-Damwoude	12	Ha	53.18N	5.59 E
Danube (EN)=Donau	5	If	45.20N	29.40 E
Danube (EN)=Duna	5	If	45.20N	29.40 E
Danube (EN)=Dunaj	5	If	45.20N	29.40 E
Danube (EN)=Dunărea	5	If	45.20N	29.40 E
Danube (EN)=Dunav	5	If	45.20N	29.40 E
Danube, Mouths of the-(EN) = Dunării, Delta-	5	If	45.30N	29.45 E
Danville [Ar.-U.S.]	45	Ji	35.03N	93.24W
Danville [Il.-U.S.]	43	Jc	40.08N	87.37W
Danville [In.-U.S.]	44	Df	39.46N	86.32W
Danville [Ky.-U.S.]	43	Kd	37.39N	84.46W
Danville [Va.-U.S.]	43	Ld	36.34N	79.25W
Danxian (Nada)	27	Ih	19.38N	109.32 E
Danyang	28	Eh	32.00N	119.33 E
Danzig (EN)=Gdańsk	6	He	54.23N	18.40 E
Dao	26	Hd	10.31N	121.57 E
Dão	13	Dd	40.20N	8.11W
Daocheng/Dabba	27	Hf	29.01N	100.26 E
Daokou → Huaxian	28	Cg	35.33N	114.30 E
Daosa	25	Fc	26.53N	76.20 E
Dao Shui	28	Ci	30.42N	114.40 E
Dao Timni	34	Ha	20.38N	13.39 E
Daoura	32	Gd	29.03N	4.33W
Daoxian	27	Jf	25.37N	111.36 E
Dapaong	34	Fc	10.52N	0.12 E
Dapchi	34	Hc	12.29N	11.29 E
Daqing Shan	28	Ad	41.00N	111.00 E
Daqin Tal→Naiman Qi	27	Lc	42.49N	120.38 E
Daquing Shan	28	Ed	40.30N	119.38 E
Dar'ā	23	Ec	32.37N	36.06 E
Dārāb	24	Ph	28.45N	54.34 E
Darabani	15	Ja	48.11N	26.35 E
Daraçya Yarimadasi	15	Lm	36.40N	28.10 E
Darāfisah	35	Ec	13.23N	31.59 E
Dārān	24	Nf	32.59N	50.24 E
Darasun	20	Gf	51.39N	113.59 E
Đaravica	15	Dg	42.32N	20.08 E
Darāw	24	Ej	24.25N	32.56 E
Darazo	34	Hc	11.00N	10.25 E
Darband	23	Ic	31.38N	57.02 E
Darband, Kūh-e-	24	Qg	31.34N	57.08 E
Darbandī Khān, Sad ad-	24	Ke	35.07N	45.50 E
Darbat Alī, Ra's-	23	Hf	16.43N	53.33 E
Darbėnai/Darbenaj	8	Ih	56.02N	21.08 E
Dar Ben Karriche el Bahri	13	Gi	35.51N	5.21W
Darbhanga	25	Hc	26.10N	85.54 E
Dărboruk	35	Gd	9.44N	44.31 E
Darby	46	Hc	46.01N	114.11W
Darchan→Darhan	22	Me	49.33N	106.21 E
Darda	14	Me	45.38N	18.42 E
Dardanelle Lake	45	Ji	35.25N	93.20W
Dardanelles (EN)=Çanakkale Boğazi	5	Ig	40.15N	26.25 E
Dardo/Kangding	27	He	30.01N	101.58 E
Dar el Kouti	30	Jh	8.50N	21.50 E
Đarende	24	Gc	38.34N	37.30 E
Dar es Salaam (3)	36	Gd	6.50S	39.02 E
Dar es Salaam	31	Ki	6.48S	39.17 E
Darfield	62	Ee	43.29S	172.07 E
Darfo Boario Terme	14	Ee	45.53N	10.11 E
Dārfūr	30	Jg	12.40N	24.20 E
Dārfūr al Janūbīyah (3)	35	Dc	11.30N	25.10 E
Dārfūr ash Shamālīyah (3)	35	Db	16.00N	25.30 E
Dargan-Ata	19	Gg	40.29N	62.12 E
Dargaville	61	Dg	35.56S	173.52 E
Darhan (Darchan)	22	Me	49.33N	106.21 E
Darhan Muminggan Lianheqi	27	Jc	41.45N	110.24 E
Darica [Tur.]	15	Kj	40.00N	27.50 E
Darica [Tur.]	15	Mi	40.45N	29.23 E
Darién	47	Ig	8.30N	77.30W
Darien	44	Gj	31.22N	81.26W
Darién (3)	49	Ii	8.10N	77.45W
Darién, Golfo de-	52	Ie	8.25N	76.53W
Darién, Serrania del-	47	Ig	8.30N	77.30W
Dariense, Cordillera-	49	Eg	12.55N	85.30W
Darja	18	Ee	38.13N	65.46 E
Darjeeling → Dārjiling	25	Hc	27.02N	88.16 E
Dārjiling	25	Hc	27.02N	88.16 E
Dar-Kebdani	13	Ii	35.07N	3.21W
Dark Head	51n	Ba	13.17N	61.17W
Dārkhovin	24	Mg	30.45N	48.25 E
Darlag	27	Ge	33.49N	99.08 E
Darling	37	Bf	33.23S	18.23 E
Darling Downs	59	Ke	27.30S	150.30 E
Darling Range	57	Ch	32.00S	116.30 E
Darling River	57	Fh	34.07S	141.55 E
Darlington [Eng.-U.K.]	9	Lg	54.31N	1.34W
Darlington [S.C.-U.S.]	44	Hh	34.19N	79.53W
Darłowo	10	Mb	54.26N	16.23 E
Darmouth	9	Jk	50.21N	3.35W
Darmstadt	10	Eg	49.52N	8.39 E
Darnah	31	Je	32.46N	22.39 E
Darnah (3)	33	Dc	31.30N	23.40 E
Darnétal	12	De	49.27N	1.09 E
Darney	11	Mf	48.05N	6.03 E
Darnley, Cape-	66	Fe	67.43S	69.30 E
Darnley Bay	42	Fc	69.45N	123.45W
Daroca	13	Kc	41.07N	1.25W
Darou Khoudos	34	Bb	15.06N	16.50W
Darovskoj	7	Lg	58.47N	47.59 E
Darrah, Mount-	46	Hb	49.28N	114.35W
Darregueira	56	He	37.42S	63.10W
Darrehshahr	24	Lf	33.10N	47.18 E
D'Arros Island	37b	Bb	5.24S	53.18 E
Dar Rounga	30	Jg	10.45N	22.20 E
Dar Sila	35	Cc	12.11N	21.21 E
Darss	10	Ib	54.25N	12.31 E
Darßer Ort	10	Ib	54.29N	12.31 E
Dart	9	Jk	50.20N	3.33W
Dart, Cape-	66	Nf	73.06S	126.20W
D'Artagnan Bank (EN)	59	Eb	13.00S	121.00 E
Dartang → Baqên	27	Fe	31.58N	94.00 E
Dartford	12	Cc	51.27N	0.13 E
Dartmoor	9	Jk	50.35N	4.00W
Dartmouth	42	Lh	44.40N	63.34W
Dartuch, Cabo-	13	Pe	39.56N	3.48 E
Daru	60	Ci	9.04S	143.12 E
Daruneh	24	Qe	35.10N	57.18 E
Daruvar	14	Le	45.35N	17.14 E
Darvaza	19	Fg	40.15N	58.24 E
Darvel, Teluk-	26	Gf	4.50N	118.30 E
Darwin	58	Ef	12.28S	130.50 E
Darwin, Bahia-	56	Fg	45.27S	74.40W
Darwin, Isla-	54a	Aa	1.39N	92.00W
Darwin, Port-	59	Gb	12.20S	130.40 E
Dar Zagaoua	35	Cb	15.15N	23.14 E
Dar Zebada	35	Bc	13.45N	18.50 E
Dās	24	Oj	25.09N	52.53 E
Dašava	10	Ug	49.13N	24.05 E
Daš-Balbar	27	Jb	49.31N	114.21 E
Dasha He	28	Ce	38.27N	114.39 E
Dashengtang Shan	28	Dc	42.07N	117.12 E
Dashennongjia	27	Je	31.47N	114.12 E
Dashennongjia	27	Je	31.26N	110.18 E
Dashiqiao → Yingkou	28	Gd	40.39N	122.31 E
Dashitou	28	Jc	43.18N	128.29 E
Dasht	24	Qd	37.17N	56.04 E
Dasht Āb	24	Qh	28.59N	56.32 E
Dashtak	24	Og	30.23N	52.30 E
Dasht-e-Āzādegan	24	Mg	31.32N	48.10 E
Daškesan	16	Oi	40.30N	46.03 E
Dasseneiland	37	Bf	33.26S	18.05 E
Dastgardān	24	Qe	34.19N	56.51 E
Dastjerd-e Qaddādeh	24	Nf	32.44N	51.32 E
Datça	24	Bd	36.45N	27.40 E
Date	28	Pc	42.27N	140.51 E
Dāth, Sha'ib ad-	24	Jj	25.45N	43.10 E
Datia	25	Fc	25.40N	78.28 E
Datian Ding	27	Jg	22.17N	111.13 E
Datil	45	Ci	34.09N	107.47W
Datong [China]	27	Hd	36.56N	101.40 E
Datong [China]	22	Ne	40.09N	113.17 E
Datteln	12	Jc	51.40N	7.23 E
Datteln-Hamm Kanal	12	Jc	51.39N	7.21 E
Datu	21	Mi	2.05N	109.39 E
Datu, Teluk-	21	Ni	2.00N	111.00 E
Datu Plang	26	He	6.58N	124.40 E
Dāūd Khel	25	Eb	32.53N	71.34 E
Daudzeva	8	Kh	56.28N	25.18 E
Daugaard-Jensen Land	41	Fb	80.10N	63.30W
Daugaj/Daugai	8	Kj	54.20N	24.28 E
Daugava=Dvina(EN)	19	Cd	57.04N	24.03 E
Daugavpils	6	Id	55.53N	26.32 E
Daule	54	Cd	1.50S	79.57W
Daun	10	Cf	50.12N	6.50 E
Daung Kyun	25	Jf	12.14N	98.05 E
Daunia, Monti della-	14	Ji	41.25N	15.05 E
Dauphin	42	Hf	51.09N	100.03W
Dauphiné	11	Lj	44.50N	6.00 E
Dauphin Lake	42	Hf	51.15N	99.45W
Daura	34	Gc	13.02N	8.18 E
Dautphetal	12	Kd	50.52N	8.33 E
Dāvangere	25	Ff	14.28N	75.55 E
Davao	22	Oi	7.04N	125.36 E
Davao Gulf	21	Oi	6.40N	125.55 E
Dāvarān, Kūh-e-	24	Qg	30.40N	56.15 E
Dāvar Panāh	23	Jd	27.21N	62.21 E
Dāvarzan	24	Qd	36.23N	56.50 E
Đavat	15	Eh	41.04N	21.06 E
Davenport [Ia.-U.S.]	39	Je	41.32N	90.41W
Davenport [Wa.-U.S.]	46	Fc	47.39N	118.09W
Davenport Range	59	Gd	20.45S	134.50 E
Daventry	12	Ab	52.15N	1.10W
Davert	12	Jc	51.51N	7.36 E
Davey, Port-	59	Jh	43.20S	145.55 E
David	39	Ki	8.25N	82.27W
David City	45	Hf	41.15N	97.08W
David-Gorodok	16	Ec	52.03N	27.13 E
David Point	51p	Bb	12.14N	61.39W
Davidson	46	Ma	51.18N	105.59W
Davidson Mountains	40	Kc	68.45N	142.10W
Davies, Mount-	59	Fe	26.14S	129.16 E
Davis	43	Cd	38.33N	121.44W
Davis	66	Fe	68.35S	77.58 E
Davis, Cape-	66	Ee	66.24S	56.50 E
Davis, Mount-	44	Hf	39.47N	79.10W
Davis Bay	66	Ie	66.08S	134.05 E
Davis Inlet	42	Le	56.00N	61.30W
Davis Mountains	45	Ek	30.35N	104.00W
Davis Sea (EN)	66	Ge	66.00S	92.00 E
Davisstrædet = Davis, Strait (EN)	38	Nc	68.00N	58.00W
Davis Strait	38	Nc	68.00N	58.00W
Davis Strait (EN) = Davisstrædet	38	Nc	68.00N	58.00W
Davlekanovo	19	Fe	54.13N	55.03 E
Davo	34	Dd	5.00N	6.08W
Davos/Tavau	14	Dd	46.47N	9.50 E
Davutlar	15	Kl	37.43N	27.17 E
Dawa	28	Gd	40.58N	122.01 E
Dawanlē	35	Gc	11.06N	42.38 E
Dawāsir, Wādī ad-	21	Gg	20.24N	46.29 E
Dawei	22	Lh	14.05N	98.12 E
Dawen He	28	Dg	35.37N	116.23 E
Dawes Range	59	Kd	24.30S	151.10 E
Dawḩarab	33	Hf	16.17N	41.57 E
Dawson [Ga.-U.S.]	44	Ej	31.47N	84.26W
Dawson [Yuk.-Can.]	39	Fc	64.04N	139.25W
Dawson, Mount-	46	Ga	51.09N	117.25W
Dawson Creek	39	Gd	55.45N	120.07W
Dawson-Lambton Glacier	66	Af	76.15S	27.30W
Dawson Range	42	Dd	65.15N	137.45W
Dawson River	59	Jd	23.38S	149.46 E
Dawu	27	He	30.45N	101.11 E
Dawu (Erlangdian)	28	Ci	31.33N	114.07 E
Dawu→Maqên	27	He	34.29N	100.01 E
Dawukou → Shizuishan	27	Id	39.03N	106.24 E
Dax	11	Ek	43.43N	1.03W
Da Xi	27	Lf	28.10N	120.14 E
Daxian	27	Ie	31.15N	107.28 E
Daxin	27	Ig	22.52N	107.14 E
Daxing	28	De	39.45N	116.19 E
Daxinggou	28	Jc	43.23N	129.39 E
Daxue Shan	21	Mf	30.30N	101.30 E
Dayan→Lijiang	22	Mg	26.56N	100.15 E
Dayang He	28	Ge	39.52N	123.40 E
Dayao	27	Hf	25.49N	101.18 E
Daye	28	Ci	30.05N	114.58 E
Dayishan→Guanyun	28	Eg	34.18N	119.14 E
Daymán, Cuchilla del-	55	Dj	31.38S	57.10W
Daymán, Río-	55	Dj	31.40S	58.02W
Daym Zubayr	35	Dd	7.43N	26.13 E
Dayong	27	Jf	29.09N	110.30 E
Dayr, Jabal ad-	35	Ec	12.27N	30.45 E
Dayr az Zawr	22	Gf	35.20N	40.09 E
Dayr Hāfir	24	Gd	36.09N	37.42 E
Dayr Kātrīnā = Saint Catherine Monastery of- (EN)	33	Fd	28.31N	33.57 E
Dayr Mawās	24	Di	27.38N	30.51 E
Dayrūṭ	33	Fd	27.33N	30.49 E
Dayton [Oh.-U.S.]	39	Kf	39.45N	84.15W
Dayton [Wa.-U.S.]	46	Gc	46.19N	117.59W
Daytona Beach	39	Kg	29.12N	80.59W
Dayu	27	Jf	25.29N	114.22 E
Da Yunhe=Grand Canal (EN)	21	Nf	39.54N	116.44 E
Dayville	44	Fd	44.28N	119.32W
Dayyīnah	24	Oj	24.57N	52.24 E
Dazhongji → Dafeng	28	Fh	33.11N	120.27 E
Dazhu	27	Ie	30.42N	107.12 E
Dazjā	24	Pe	35.50N	55.46 E
Dazkırı	24	Cd	37.54N	29.42 E
De Aar	31	Jl	30.39S	24.00 E
Dead	9	Ei	52.40N	8.30W
Deadhorse	40	Jb	70.11N	148.27W
Deadmans Cay	49	Jb	23.14N	75.14W
Dead Sea (EN)=Mayyit, Al Baḩr al-	21	Ff	31.30N	35.30 E
Deadwood	43	Ed	44.23N	103.44W
Deal	12	Dc	51.13N	1.24 E
Dealu Mare	15	Jb	47.27N	26.40 E
De'an	28	Cj	29.18N	115.45 E
Deán Funes	56	Hd	30.26S	64.21W
Dearborn	44	Fd	42.18N	83.10W
Dearg, Beinn-	9	Id	57.48N	4.57W
Deary	46	Gc	46.52N	116.31W
Dease	42	Ee	59.55N	128.29W
Dease Arm	42	Fc	66.50N	120.00W
Dease Lake	39	Fd	58.35N	130.02W
Dease Strait	42	Gc	69.00N	107.00W
Death Valley	38	Hf	36.30N	117.00W
Death Valley	46	Gh	36.20N	116.50W
Deauville	11	Ge	49.22N	0.04 E
Debak	26	Ff	1.34N	111.25 E
Debalcevo	16	Ke	48.20N	38.29 E
Debao	27	Ig	23.17N	106.21 E
Debar	15	Dh	41.32N	20.32 E
Debark	35	Fc	13.08N	37.53 E
Debdou	32	Gc	33.59N	3.03W
Debed	16	Ni	41.22N	44.58 E
Deben	12	Db	52.01N	1.22 E
De Beque	45	Bg	39.20N	108.13W
Dębica	10	Rf	50.04N	21.24 E
De Bilt	12	Hb	52.06N	5.11 E
Debin	20	Kd	62.18N	150.47 E
Dęblin	10	Re	51.35N	21.50 E
Dębno	10	Kd	52.45N	14.40 E
Débo, Lac-	34	Eb	15.18N	4.09W
Deborah East, Lake-	59	Df	30.45S	119.10 E
Deborah West, Lake-	59	Df	30.45S	119.05 E
Deboyne Islands	57	Gf	10.43S	152.22 E
Debrc	15	Ce	44.37N	19.54 E
Debre Berhan	35	Fd	9.41N	39.33 E
Debrecen	6	If	47.32N	21.38 E
Debrecen (2)	10	Ri	47.31N	21.40 E
Debre Libanos	35	Fd	9.43N	38.52 E
Debre Markos	31	Kg	10.10N	37.36 E
Debre Sina	35	Fd	9.51N	39.46 E
Debre Tabor	35	Fc	11.51N	38.00 E
Debre Zeyt	31	Kh	8.47N	39.00 E
De-Buka, Glacier-	66	Nf	76.00S	131.00W
Decatur [Al.-U.S.]	43	Je	34.36N	86.59W
Decatur [Ga.-U.S.]	44	Ei	33.46N	84.18W
Decatur [Il.-U.S.]	43	Jd	39.51N	89.32W
Decatur [In.-U.S.]	44	Ee	40.50N	84.56W
Decatur [Tx.-U.S.]	45	Hj	33.14N	97.35W
Decazeville	11	Ij	44.33N	2.15 E
Deccan	21	Jh	14.00N	77.00 E
Decelles, Reservoir-	44	Hb	47.40N	78.08W
Deception Bay	59	Ia	7.07S	144.05 E
Dechang	27	Hf	27.22N	102.12 E
Děčín	10	Kf	50.47N	14.13 E
Decize	11	Jh	46.50N	3.28 E
Decorah	45	Ke	43.18N	91.48W
Deda	15	Hc	46.56N	24.54 E
Dededo	64c	Ba	13.31N	144.49 E
Dedegöl Dağı	24	Dd	37.39N	31.17 E
Dedemsvaart, Avereest-	12	Ib	52.37N	6.27 E
Dédougou	34	Ec	12.28N	3.28W
Dedoviči	7	Gh	57.33N	29.58 E
Dedza	36	Fe	14.22S	34.20 E
Dee [Eng.-U.K.]	9	Jh	53.19N	3.11W
Dee [Scot.-U.K.]	9	Kd	57.08N	2.04W
Dee [Scot.-U.K.]	9	Ig	54.50N	4.03W
Deep Creek Range	46	If	40.00N	113.57W
Deering	40	Gc	66.05N	162.43W
Deer Isle	44	Mc	44.13N	68.41W
Deer Lake [Newf.-Can.]	42	Lg	49.10N	57.25W
Deer Lake [Ont.-Can.]	42	If	52.40N	94.30W
Deer Park	46	Gc	47.57N	117.28W
Defiance	44	Ee	41.17N	84.21W
Defla	13	Qi	35.14N	4.26 E
De Funiak Springs	44	Dj	30.43N	86.07W
Dega Ahmedo	35	Gd	7.50N	42.53 E
Dêgê	27	Ge	31.52N	98.36 E
Degebe	13	Ef	38.13N	7.29W
Degeh Bur	35	Gd	8.13N	43.34 E
Degema	34	Ge	4.45N	6.46 E
Degerby	8	Id	60.02N	20.23 E
Degerfors	7	Dg	59.14N	14.26 E
Degerhamn	7	Dh	56.21N	16.24 E
Deggendorf	10	Ih	48.50N	12.58 E

Index Symbols

(1) Independent Nation
(2) State, Region
(3) District, County
(4) Municipality
(5) Colony, Dependency
Continent
Physical Region
Historical or Cultural Region
Mount, Mountain
Volcano
Hill
Mountains, Mountain Range
Hills, Escarpment
Plateau, Upland
Pass, Gap
Plain, Lowland
Delta
Salt Flat
Valley, Canyon
Crater, Cave
Karst Features
Depression
Polder
Desert, Dunes
Forest, Woods
Heath, Steppe
Oasis
Cape, Point
Coast, Beach
Cliff
Peninsula
Isthmus
Sandbank
Island
Atoll
Rock, Reef
Islands, Archipelago
Rocks, Reefs
Coral Reef
Well, Spring
Geyser
River, Stream
Waterfall Rapids
River Mouth, Estuary
Lake
Salt Lake
Intermittent Lake
Reservoir
Swamp, Pond
Canal
Glacier
Ice Shelf, Pack Ice
Ocean
Sea
Gulf, Bay
Strait, Fjord
Lagoon
Bank
Seamount
Tablemount
Ridge
Shelf
Basin
Escarpment, Sea Scarp
Fracture
Trench, Abyss
National Park, Reserve
Point of Interest
Recreation Site
Cave, Cavern
Historic Site
Ruins
Wall, Walls
Church, Abbey
Temple
Scientific Station
Airport
Port
Lighthouse
Mine
Tunnel
Dam, Bridge

- Değirmendere 15 Kk 38.06N 27.09 E
- De Gray Lake 45 Ji 34.15N 93.15W
- De Grey River 59 Dd 20.12S 119.11 E
- Degtarsk 17 Jh 56.42N 60.06 E
- De Haan 12 Fc 51.16N 3.02 E
- Dehaj 24 Pg 30.42N 54.53 E
- Dehaq 24 Nf 32.55N 50.57 E
- Deh Bārez 24 Qi 27.26N 57.12 E
- Deh Bīd 24 Og 30.38N 53.13 E
- Deh Dasht 24 Ng 30.47N 50.34 E
- Dehdez 24 Ng 31.43N 50.17 E
- Deh-e-Namak 24 Oe 35.25N 52.50 E
- Deh-e Shīr 24 Og 31.29N 53.45 E
- Deh-e Ziyār 24 Qg 30.40N 57.00 E
- Dehgolān 24 Le 35.17N 47.25 E
- Dehiwala-Mount Lavinia 25 Fg 6.50N 79.52 E
- Dehlorān 24 Lf 32.41N 47.16 E
- Deh Now 24 Qf 33.01N 57.41 E
- Dehra Dūn 25 Fb 30.19N 78.02 E
- Dehui 27 Mc 44.33N 125.38 E
- Deinze 11 Jd 50.59N 3.32 E
- Dej 15 Gb 47.09N 23.52 E
- Deje 8 Ee 59.36N 13.28 E
- Dejen 35 Fc 10.05N 38.11 E
- Dejës, Mali i- 15 Dh 41.42N 20.10 E
- Dejnau 19 Gh 39.18N 63.11 E
- De Jongs, Tanjung- 26 Kh 6.56S 138.32 E
- De Kalb 45 Lf 41.56N 88.45W
- Dekar 37 Cd 21.30S 21.58 E
- Dekese 31 Ji 3.27S 21.24 E
- Dekina 34 Gd 7.42N 7.01 E
- Dékoa 35 Bd 6.19N 19.04 E
- De Koog, Texel- 12 Ga 53.07N 4.46 E
- De La Garma 55 Bm 37.58S 60.25W
- De Land 43 Kf 29.02N 81.18W
- Delano 43 Dd 35.41N 119.15W
- Delano Peak 43 Ed 38.22N 112.23W
- Delārām 23 Jc 32.11N 63.25 E
- Delarof Islands 40a Cb 51.30N 178.45W
- Delaware 44 Fe 40.18N 83.06W
- Delaware 45 Ek 32.00N 104.00W
- Delaware [2] 43 Ld 39.10N 75.30W
- Delaware Bay 38 Lc 39.05N 75.15W
- Delaware River 43 Ld 39.20N 75.25W
- Delbrück 12 Kc 51.46N 8.34 E
- Del Carril 55 Cl 35.31S 59.30W
- Delčevo 15 Fh 41.58N 22.47 E
- Del City 45 Hi 35.27N 97.27W
- Delegate 59 Jg 37.03S 148.58 E
- Delémont/Delsberg 14 Bc 47.22N 7.21 E
- Delet/Teili 8 Id 60.15N 20.35 E
- Delfinópolis 55 Ie 20.20S 46.51W
- Delft 11 Kb 52.00N 4.21 E
- Delfzijl 11 Ma 53.19N 6.56 E
- Delgada, Punta- 52 Jj 42.46S 63.38W
- Delgado, Cabo-=Delgado, Cape-(EN) 30 Lj 10.40S 40.38 E
- Delgado, Cabo-=Delgado, Cape-(EN) [3] 37 Fb 12.30S 39.00 E
- Delgado, Cape-(EN)= Delgado, Cabo- 30 Lj 10.40S 40.38 E
- Delgado, Cape-(EN)= Delgado, Cabo- [3] 37 Fb 12.30S 39.00 E
- Delger Muren 27 Hb 49.17N 100.40 E
- Delhi [Co.-U.S.] 45 Eh 37.42N 103.58W
- Delhi [India] 25 Jg 28.40N 77.13 E
- Delhi [N.Y.-U.S.] 44 Jd 42.17N 74.57W
- Deliblatska Peščara 15 Dd 45.00N 21.00 E
- Delice 24 Fc 39.58N 34.02 E
- Deliceırmak 24 Fb 40.28N 34.10 E
- Delicias [Cuba] 49 Ic 21.11N 76.34W
- Delicias [Mex.] 47 Cc 28.13N 105.28W
- Delījān 24 Nf 33.59N 50.40 E
- Delingha 27 Gd 37.26N 97.25 E
- Dēliņkalns/Delinkalns, Gora- 8 Lg 57.30N 27.02 E
- Delinkalns, Gora-/Dēliņkalns 8 Lg 57.30N 27.02 E
- Delitzsch 10 Ie 51.32N 12.21 E
- Deljatin 15 Ha 48.29N 24.45 E
- Delle 11 Mg 47.30N 7.00 E
- Dell Rapids 45 He 43.50N 96.43W
- Dellys 32 Hb 36.55N 3.55 E
- Delmarva Peninsula 38 Lf 38.50N 75.30W
- Delme 12 Ka 53.05N 8.40 E
- Delme 12 If 48.53N 6.24 E
- Delmenhorst 10 Ec 53.03N 8.37 E
- Delnice 14 Ie 45.24N 14.48 E
- Delo 35 Fd 5.49N 37.57 E
- De Long Strait (EN)= Longa, Proliv- 21 Tb 70.20N 178.00 E
- De-Longa, Ostrova-=De Long Islands (EN) 21 Rb 76.30N 153.00 E
- De Long Islands (EN)=De-Longa, Ostrova- 21 Rb 76.30N 153.00 E
- De Long Mountains 40 Gc 68.20N 162.00W
- Deloraine 59 Jh 41.31S 146.39 E
- Delorme, Lac- 42 Kf 54.35N 69.55W
- Delphi (EN) = Dhelfoí 15 Fk 38.29N 22.30 E
- Del Rio 43 Gf 29.22N 100.54W
- Delsberg/Delémont 14 Bc 47.22N 7.21 E
- Delsbo 7 Dc 61.48N 16.35 E
- Delta [Co.-U.S.] 43 Fd 38.44N 108.04W
- Delta [Ut.-U.S.] 43 Ed 39.21N 112.35W
- Delta Amacuro [2] 54 Fb 8.30N 61.30W
- Delta Junction 40 Jd 64.02N 145.41W
- Delvāda 25 Ed 20.46N 71.02 E
- Del Valle 55 Bl 35.54S 60.43W
- Delvina 15 Dj 39.57N 20.06 E
- Dēma 17 Gi 54.42N 55.58 E
- Demanda, Sierra de la- 13 Ib 42.15N 3.05W
- Demba 36 Dd 5.30S 22.16 E
- Dembi 35 Fd 8.05N 36.28 E
- Dembia 35 Cd 5.07N 24.25 E
- Dembi Dolo 35 Ed 8.32N 34.49 E
- De Medinilla, Farallon- 57 Fc 16.01N 146.04 E
- Demer 11 Kd 50.58N 4.45 E
- Demerara Plateau (EN) 52 Le 4.30N 44.00W
- Demerara River 50 Gi 6.48N 58.10W
- Demidov 16 Gb 55.15N 31.29 E
- Demidovka 10 Vf 50.20N 25.27 E
- Deming 43 Fe 32.16N 107.45W
- Demini, Rio- 54 Fd 0.46S 62.56W
- Demirci 24 Cc 39.03N 28.40 E
- Demir Kapija 15 Fh 41.25N 22.15 E
- Demirköy 15 Kh 41.49N 27.15 E
- Demirtaş 15 Mi 40.16N 29.06 E
- Demjanka 19 Gd 59.34N 69.20 E
- Demjansk 7 Hh 57.38N 32.29 E
- Demjanskoje 19 Gd 59.36N 69.18 E
- Demmin 10 Jc 53.54N 13.02 E
- Demopolis 44 Di 32.31N 87.50W
- Dempo, Gunung- 21 Mj 4.02S 103.09 E
- Demta 26 Lg 2.20S 140.08 E
- Denain 11 Jd 50.20N 3.23 E
- Denan 35 Gd 6.30N 43.30 E
- Denau 19 Gh 38.18N 67.55 E
- Den Bosch/'s-Hertogenbosch 11 Lc 51.41N 5.19 E
- Den Burg, Texel- 12 Ga 53.03N 4.47 E
- Den Chai 25 Ke 17.59N 100.04 E
- Dendang 26 Eg 3.05S 107.54 E
- Dender/Dendre 11 Kc 51.02N 4.06 E
- Dendermonde/Termonde 12 Gc 51.02N 4.07 E
- Dendre/Dender 11 Kc 51.02N 4.06 E
- Dendtler Island 66 Pf 72.58S 89.57W
- Denekamp 12 Jb 52.23N 7.00 E
- Deneżkin Kamen, Gora- 19 Fc 60.25N 59.31 E
- Dengarh 25 Hd 23.50N 81.42 E
- Dêngkagoin→Têwo 27 He 34.03N 103.21 E
- Dengkou (Bayan Gol) 22 Me 40.25N 106.59 E
- Dêngqên 27 Ge 31.29N 95.32 E
- Dengzhou→Penglai 27 Ld 37.44N 120.45 E
- Den Haag/'s-Gravenhage=The Hague (EN) 6 Ge 52.06N 4.18 E
- Den Ham 12 Ib 52.28N 6.32 E
- Denham→Shak Bay 59 Ce 25.55S 113.32 E
- Denham, Mount- 49 Id 18.13N 77.32W
- Denham Range 59 Jd 21.55S 147.45 E
- Denham Sound 59 Ce 25.40S 113.15 E
- Den Helder 11 Kb 52.54N 4.45 E
- Denia 13 Mf 38.51N 0.07 E
- Deniliquin 59 Ig 35.32S 144.58 E
- Denio 46 Ff 41.59N 118.39W
- Denis Island 37b Ca 3.48S 55.40 E
- Denison [Ia.-U.S.] 43 Hc 42.01N 95.20W
- Denison [Tx.-U.S.] 43 He 33.45N 96.33W
- Denison, Mount- 40 Ie 58.25N 154.27W
- Denizli 23 Cb 37.46N 29.06 E
- Denklingen, Reichshoft- 12 Jd 50.55N 7.39 E
- Denman Glacier 66 Ge 66.45S 99.25 E
- Denmark [Austl.] 59 Df 34.57S 117.21 E
- Denmark [S.C.-U.S.] 44 Gi 33.19N 81.09W
- Denmark (EN)=Danmark [1] 6 Gd 56.00N 10.00 E
- Denmark Strait (EN)= Danmarksstraedet 38 Qc 67.00N 25.00W
- Dennery 51k Bb 13.55N 60.54W
- Den Oever, Wieringen- 12 Hb 52.56N 5.02 E
- Denpasar 22 Nj 8.39S 115.13 E
- Denton 43 He 33.13N 97.08W
- D'Entrecasteaux, Point- 59 Df 34.50S 116.00 E
- D'Entrecasteaux Islands 57 Ge 9.35S 150.40 E
- Denver 39 If 39.43N 105.01W
- Deoghar 25 Hd 24.29N 86.42 E
- Deolāli 25 Ee 19.54N 73.50 E
- De Pajaros, Farallon- 57 Fb 20.32N 144.54 E
- De Panne/La Panne 12 Ec 51.06N 2.35 E
- De Pere 45 Ld 44.27N 88.04W
- Deputatski 20 Ic 69.13N 139.55 E
- Dêqên 27 Gf 28.32N 98.50 E
- Deqing 27 Jg 23.14N 111.42 E
- De Queen 45 Ii 34.02N 94.21W
- De Quincy 45 Jk 30.27N 93.26W
- Dequing 28 Fi 30.34N 120.05 E
- Dera, Lach- 35 Ge 0.15N 42.17 E
- Dera, Lagh- 30 Lh 0.15N 42.17 E
- Dera Bugti 25 Dc 29.02N 69.09 E
- Dera Ghāzi Khan 22 Jf 30.03N 70.38 E
- Dera Ismāil Khan 25 Eb 31.50N 70.54 E
- Derbent [R.S.F.S.R.] 6 Kg 42.00N 48.18 E
- Derbent [Tur.] 15 Lk 38.11N 28.33 E
- Derby 9 Lh 53.05N 1.40W
- Derby [Austl.] 58 Df 17.18S 123.38 E
- Derby [Eng.-U.K.] 9 Li 52.55N 1.30W
- Derby [Ks.-U.S.] 45 Hh 37.33N 97.16W
- Derbyshire [3] 9 Lh 53.10N 1.35W
- Đerdap 15 Fe 44.41N 22.10 E
- Derecske 10 Ri 47.21N 21.34 E
- Dereköy 15 Kh 41.56N 27.21 E
- Dereli 24 Hb 40.45N 38.27 E
- Derg/Abhainn na Deirge 9 Fg 54.40N 7.25W
- Đerg, Lough-/Loch Deirgeirt 9 Ei 53.00N 8.20W
- Dergači [R.S.F.S.R.] 16 Pd 51.13N 48.46 E
- Dergači [Ukr.-U.S.S.R.] 16 Jd 50.09N 36.09 E
- Der Grabow 10 Ib 54.23N 12.50 E
- De Ridder 45 Jk 30.51N 93.17W
- Derik 24 Id 37.22N 40.17 E
- Derkul 16 Qd 51.17N 51.15 E
- Dermott 45 Kj 33.32N 91.26W
- Dernieres, Isles- 45 Kl 29.02N 90.47W
- Derong 27 Gf 28.44N 99.18 E
- De Rose Hill 59 Ge 26.25S 133.15 E
- Déroute, Passage de la- 11 Ee 49.12N 1.51W
- Dersa, Eglab- 32 Gd 26.45N 4.26W
- Dersca 15 Jb 47.59N 26.12 E
- Dersingham 12 Cb 52.51N 0.30 E
- Derudeb 35 Fb 17.32N 36.06 E
- Derventa 14 Lf 44.59N 17.55 E
- Derwent [Eng.-U.K.] 9 Mg 54.10N 0.40W
- Derwent [Eng.-U.K.] 12 Ab 52.53N 1.17W
- Derwent River 59 Jh 43.03S 147.22 E
- Deržavinsk 19 Ge 51.03N 66.19 E
- Desaguadero, Rio- 52 Ji 34.13S 66.47W
- Désappointement, Iles du- 57 Mf 14.10S 141.20W
- Des Arc 45 Ki 34.58N 91.30W
- Desborough 12 Bb 52.26N 0.49W
- Descalvado 55 Ie 21.54S 47.37W
- Descartes 11 Gh 46.58N 0.45 E
- Deschambault Lake 42 Hf 54.50N 103.30W
- Deschutes River 43 Cb 45.38N 120.54W
- Descoberto, Rio- 55 Hc 16.20S 48.19W
- Dese 31 Kg 11.07N 39.38 E
- Deseado, Rio- 52 Jj 47.45S 65.54W
- Desecheo, Isla- 51a Ab 18.25N 67.28W
- Desengaño, Punta- 56 Gg 49.15S 67.37W
- Desenzano del Garda 14 Ee 45.28N 10.32 E
- Desert Center 46 Hj 33.42N 115.26W
- Desert Peak 46 If 40.28N 112.38W
- Deshaies [Guad.] 51e Ab 16.18N 61.48W
- Deshaies [Guad.] 51e Ab 16.18N 61.47W
- Desiderio, Rio- 55 Ja 12.20S 44.50W
- Desmaraisville 44 Ia 49.31N 76.10W
- De Smet 45 Hd 44.23N 97.33W
- Desmochado 55 Ch 27.07S 58.06W
- Des Moines 38 Je 40.22N 91.26W
- Des Moines [Ia.-U.S.] 39 Je 41.35N 93.37W
- Des Moines [N.M.-U.S.] 45 Eh 36.46N 103.50W
- Desmoronado, Cerro- 47 Dd 20.21N 105.01W
- Desna 5 Je 50.33N 30.32 E
- Desnățui 15 Ge 43.53N 23.35 E
- Desolación, Isla- 52 Ik 53.00S 74.10W
- De Soto 45 Kg 38.08N 90.33W
- Despeñaperros, Desfiladero de- 13 If 38.24N 3.30W
- Des Roches, Ile- 37b Bb 5.41S 53.41 E
- Dessau 10 Ie 51.50N 12.15 E
- Destruction Bay 42 Dd 61.20N 139.00W
- Desventuradas, Islas- 52 Ih 26.45S 80.00W
- Desvres 11 Hd 50.40N 1.50 E
- Deta 15 Ed 45.24N 21.14 E
- Dete 37 Dc 18.37S 26.51 E
- Detmold 10 Ee 51.56N 8.53 E
- Detour, Point- 44 Dc 45.36N 86.37W
- Detroit [Mi.-U.S.] 39 Ke 42.20N 83.03W
- Detroit [Or.-U.S.] 46 Dd 44.42N 122.10W
- Detroit Lakes 45 Ic 46.49N 95.51W
- Dettifoss 7a Cb 65.49N 16.24W
- Detva 10 Ph 48.33N 19.25 E
- Deûle 12 Ed 50.44N 2.56 E
- Deurdeur 13 Oh 36.14N 2.16 E
- Deurne 12 Hc 51.28N 5.48 E
- Deutsche Bucht 10 Db 54.30N 7.30 E
- Deutsche Demokratische Republik = Germany 6 Ge 51.00N 10.00 E
- Deutschlandsberg 14 Jd 46.49N 15.13 E
- Deux-Bassins, Col des- 13 Ph 36.27N 3.18 E
- Deux Sèvres [3] 11 Fh 46.30N 0.15W
- Deva 15 Fd 45.53N 22.54 E
- Dévaványa 10 Qi 47.02N 20.58 E
- Deveci Dağları 24 Gb 40.05N 36.00 E
- Devecser 10 Ni 47.06N 17.26 E
- Develi 24 Fc 38.22N 35.06 E
- Deventer 11 Mb 52.15N 6.10 E
- Deverd, Cap- 63b Be 20.46S 164.22 E
- Deveron 9 Kd 57.40N 2.30W
- Devès, Monts du- 11 Jj 44.57N 3.46 E
- Devetak 14 Mg 43.58N 19.00 E
- Devil River Peak 62 Ed 40.58S 172.39 E
- Devil's Hole 9 Ne 56.38N 0.40 E
- Devil's Island (EN)=Diable, Ile du- 54 Hb 5.17N 52.35W
- Devils Lake 43 Hb 48.07N 98.59W
- Devils Lake 45 Gb 48.01N 98.52W
- Devils Paw 40 Me 58.44N 133.50W
- Devils River 45 Fl 29.39N 100.58W
- Devils Tower 46 Md 44.31N 104.57W
- Devin 15 Hh 41.45N 24.24 E
- Devizes 9 Lj 51.22N 1.59W
- Devnja 15 Kf 43.13N 27.33 E
- Devodi Munda 25 Ge 17.37N 82.57 E
- De Volet Point 51n Ba 13.22N 61.13W
- Devolli 15 Ci 40.49N 19.51 E
- Devolli 15 Di 40.30N 20.50 E
- Dévoluy 11 Lj 44.39N 5.53 E
- Devon 9 Jk 50.50N 3.50W
- Devon 9 Jk 50.50N 4.00W
- Devon 38 Kb 75.00N 87.00W
- Devon 12 Ba 53.04N 0.49W
- Devonport 57 Fi 41.11S 146.21 E
- Devoto 55 Aj 31.24S 62.19W
- Devrek 24 Db 41.13N 31.57 E
- Devrez 24 Fb 41.06N 34.25 E
- Dewa 30 Lh 4.11N 42.06 E
- Dewar Lakes 42 Kc 68.00N 73.00W
- Dewās 25 Fd 22.58N 76.04 E
- Dewa-Sanchi 29 Gb 39.30N 140.15 E
- Dewey 45 Ih 36.48N 95.56W
- De Witt 45 Ki 34.18N 91.20W
- Dexemhare 35 Fb 15.04N 39.03 E
- Dexing 28 Dj 28.55N 117.33 E
- Dexter 45 Lh 36.48N 89.57W
- Deyang 27 He 31.07N 104.25 E
- Dey-Dey, Lake- 59 Ge 29.15S 131.05 E
- Deyhūk 24 Qf 33.17N 57.30 E
- Deyyer 23 Hd 27.50N 51.55 E
- Dez 24 Mg 31.39N 48.52 E
- Dezfūl 22 Gf 32.23N 48.24 E
- Dez Gerd 24 Ng 30.45N 51.57 E
- Dezhou 27 Kd 37.28N 116.18 E
- Dháfni 15 Fl 37.46N 22.02 E
- Dhahab 33 Fd 28.29N 34.32 E
- Dhaka 22 Lg 23.43N 90.25 E
- Dhamār 23 Fg 14.37N 44.23 E
- Dhamtari 25 Gd 20.41N 81.34 E
- Dhānbād 25 Hd 23.48N 86.27 E
- Dhanushkodi 25 Fg 9.11N 79.24 E
- Dhaulagiri 21 Kg 28.44N 83.25 E
- Dhekeleia 24 Ee 35.03N 33.40 E
- Dhelfoí = Delphi (EN) 15 Fk 38.29N 22.30 E
- Dhelvinákion 15 Dj 39.56N 20.28 E
- Dhenkanal 25 Hd 20.40N 85.36 E
- Dheskáti 15 Ej 39.55N 21.49 E
- Dhespotikó 15 Hm 36.58N 25.00 E
- Dhiapóndioi Nisoi 15 Cj 39.50N 19.25 E
- Dhībān 24 Fg 31.30N 35.47 E
- Dhidhimótikhon 15 Jh 41.21N 26.30 E
- Dhikti Óros 15 In 35.15N 25.30 E
- Dhilos 15 Il 37.24N 25.16 E
- Dhilos 15 Il 37.24N 25.16 E
- Dhimitsána 15 Fl 37.36N 22.03 E
- Dhionisiádhes, Nísoi- 15 Jn 35.21N 26.10 E
- Dhiórix Potidhaia 15 Gi 40.10N 23.20 E
- Dhī-Qar [3] 24 Lg 31.10N 46.10 E
- Dhī-Qar 24 Kf 32.14N 44.22 E
- Dhirfis Óros 15 Gk 38.38N 23.50 E
- Dhisoron Óros 15 Fh 41.11N 22.57 E
- Dhivounia 15 Jn 35.50N 26.28 E
- Dhodhekánisos = Dodecanese (EN) 15 Jm 36.20N 27.00 E
- Dhodhóni = Dodona (EN) 15 Dj 39.33N 20.46 E
- Dholpur 25 Fc 26.42N 77.54 E
- Dhomokós 15 Fj 39.08N 22.18 E
- Dhone 25 Fe 15.25N 77.53 E
- Dhonoúsa 15 Il 37.10N 25.50 E
- Dhoráji 25 Ed 21.44N 70.27 E
- Dhoxáton 15 Hh 41.06N 24.14 E
- Dhragónisos 15 Il 37.27N 25.29 E
- Dhuburi 25 Hc 26.02N 89.58 E
- Dhule 22 Jg 20.54N 74.47 E
- Dhulián 25 Hd 24.41N 87.58 E
- Dia 15 In 35.27N 25.13 E
- Diable, Ile du-=Devil's Island (EN) 54 Hb 5.17N 52.35W
- Diable, Morne au- 51g Ba 15.37N 61.27W
- Diable, Pointe du- [Mart.] 51h Bb 14.47N 60.54W
- Diable, Pointe du- [Van.] 63b Dc 16.01S 168.12 E
- Diablo, Punta del- 55 Fl 34.22S 53.46W
- Diablo, Puntan- 64b Ba 15.00N 145.34 E
- Diablo Range 46 Eh 36.45N 121.20W
- Diafarabé 34 Ec 14.10N 5.00W
- Dialafara 34 Cc 13.27N 11.23W
- Diamant, Pointe du- 51h Ac 14.27N 61.04W
- Diamant, Rocher du- 51h Ac 14.27N 61.03W
- Diamante [Arg.] 56 Hd 32.04S 60.39W
- Diamante [It.] 14 Jk 39.41N 15.49 E
- Diamante, Punta del- 48 Ji 16.47N 99.52W
- Diamantina 54 Jg 18.15S 43.36W
- Diamantina, Chapada- 52 Lg 11.30S 41.10W
- Diamantina, Rio- 55 Fc 16.42S 52.45W
- Diamantina Depth (EN) 3 Hm 33.30S 102.00 E
- Diamantina Lakes 59 Id 23.46S 141.09 E
- Diamantina River 57 Eg 26.45S 139.10 E
- Diamantina Trench (EN) 3 Hm 36.00S 104.00 E
- Diamantino 53 Kg 14.25S 56.27W
- Diamantino, Rio- 55 Fc 16.08S 52.28W
- Diamond Harbour 25 Hd 22.12N 88.12 E
- Diamond Island 51p Bb 12.20N 61.35W
- Diamond Jenness Peninsula 42 Fb 71.00N 117.00W
- Diamond Peak [Nv.-U.S.] 46 Hg 39.40N 115.48W
- Diamond Peak [Or.-U.S.] 46 De 43.33N 122.09W
- Diamond Peak [U.S.] 46 Id 44.09N 113.05W
- Diamond Peak [U.S.] 46 Gc 46.07N 117.32W
- Diamou 34 Cc 14.05N 11.16W
- Diana, Baie- 42 Kd 61.00N 70.00W
- Dianbai 27 Jg 21.33N 110.58 E
- Dianbu → Feidong 28 Di 31.53N 117.29 E
- Diancang Shan 27 Hf 25.42N 100.02 E
- Dian Chi 27 Hg 24.50N 102.45 E
- Diane, Étang de- 11a Ba 42.07N 9.32 E
- Dianjiang 27 Ie 30.19N 107.25 E
- Diano Marina 14 Cg 43.54N 8.05 E
- Dianópolis 54 If 11.38S 46.50W
- Dianra 34 Dd 8.45N 6.18W
- Diapaga 34 Fc 12.04N 1.47 E
- Diaz 55 Bk 32.22S 61.05W
- Dibā, Dawḥat- 24 Qk 25.38N 56.18 E
- Dībagah 24 Je 35.52N 43.49 E
- Dibang 25 Jc 27.50N 95.32 E
- Dibaya 36 Dd 6.30S 22.57 E
- Dibaya-Lubue 36 Cc 4.09S 19.52 E
- Dibella 34 Hb 17.31N 12.59 E
- Dibrugarh 22 Lg 27.29N 94.54 E
- Dibs 24 Ke 35.40N 44.04 E
- Dibsī Afnān 24 Ee 35.55N 38.16 E
- Dickens 45 Fj 33.37N 100.50W
- Dickinson 43 Gb 46.53N 102.47W
- Dickins Seamount (EN) 40 Lf 54.30N 137.00W
- Dickson 44 Dg 36.05N 87.23W
- Dicle 24 Ic 38.22N 40.04 E
- Dicle=Tigris (EN) 21 Gf 31.00N 47.25 E
- Didam 12 Ic 51.56N 6.09 E
- Didao 28 Kb 45.22N 130.48 E
- Didcot 12 Ac 51.36N 1.15W
- Didesa 35 Fd 9.40N 35.32 E
- Didiéni 34 Dc 13.23N 8.05W
- Didyma 15 Kl 37.21N 27.13 E
- Die 11 Lj 44.45N 5.22 E
- Dieburg 10 Eg 49.54N 8.51 E
- Diecinueve de Abril 55 El 34.22S 54.04W
- Dieciocho de Julio 55 Fk 33.41S 53.33W
- Diefenbaker Lake 42 Gf 51.00N 107.00W
- Diège 11 Ii 45.36N 2.16 E
- Diego Garcia 21 Jj 6.20S 72.20 E
- Diego Ramírez, Islas 56 Gi 56.30S 68.44W
- Diekirch 11 Me 49.53N 6.10 E
- Die Lewitz 10 Hc 53.30N 11.30 E
- Diéma 34 Dc 14.33N 9.11W
- Diemel 10 Fe 51.39N 9.27 E
- Diemelsee 12 Kc 51.19N 8.43 E
- Diemelstadt 12 Lc 51.27N 9.01 E
- Dien Bien Phu 25 Kd 21.23N 103.01 E
- Diepenbeek 12 Hd 50.54N 5.24 E
- Diepholz 10 Ed 52.36N 8.22 E
- Dieppe 11 He 49.56N 1.05 E
- Dieppe Bay Town 51c Ab 17.25N 62.48W
- Dierdorf 12 Jd 50.33N 7.40 E
- Dieren, Rheden- 12 Ib 52.03N 6.08 E
- Di'er Songhua Jiang 27 Lc 45.26N 124.39 E
- Diest 12 Hd 50.59N 5.03 E
- Dieulefit 11 Lj 44.31N 5.04 E
- Dieulouard 12 If 48.51N 6.04 E
- Dieuze 11 Mf 48.49N 6.43 E
- Dieveniškes 8 Kj 54.10N 25.44 E
- Die Ville 12 Id 50.40N 6.55 E
- Diez 12 Kd 50.22N 8.01 E
- Dif 36 Hb 0.59N 40.57 E
- Diffa [2] 34 Hb 16.00N 13.30 E
- Diffa 34 Hc 13.19N 12.37 E
- Differdange/Differdingen 11 Le 49.32N 5.52 E
- Differdingen/Differdange 11 Le 49.32N 5.52 E
- Digby 42 Kh 44.40N 65.50W
- Dighton 45 Fg 38.29N 100.28W
- Digne 11 Mj 44.06N 6.14 E
- Digoin 11 Jh 46.29N 3.59 E
- Digora 16 Nh 43.07N 44.06 E
- Digos 26 Ie 6.45N 125.20 E
- Digranes 7a Ca 66.02N 14.45W
- Digul 26 Kh 7.07S 138.42 E
- Dihang 25 Jc 27.48N 95.30 E
- Dijar 16 Tf 46.33N 56.05 E
- Dijlah=Tigris (EN) 21 Gf 31.00N 47.25 E
- Dijle 12 Kd 50.53N 4.42 E
- Dijon 6 Gf 47.19N 5.01 E
- Dik 35 Bd 9.58N 17.31 E
- Dikanäs 7 Dd 65.14N 16.00 E
- Dikhil 35 Gc 11.06N 42.22 E
- Dikili 24 Bc 39.04N 26.53 E
- Dikli 8 Kg 57.30N 25.00 E
- Diksmuide/Dixmude 11 Ic 51.02N 2.52 E
- Dikson 22 Kb 73.30N 80.35 E
- Dikwa 34 Hc 12.02N 13.55 E
- Dila 35 Fd 6.23N 38.19 E
- Dilbeek 12 Gd 50.51N 4.16 E
- Dili 22 Oj 8.33S 125.34 E
- Di Linh 25 Lf 11.35N 108.04 E
- Diližan 16 Ni 40.46N 44.55 E
- Dilj 14 Me 45.16N 18.01 E
- Dill 12 Kd 50.33N 8.29 E
- Dillenburg 10 Ef 50.44N 8.17 E
- Dillia 30 Ig 14.09N 12.50 E
- Dilling 31 Jg 12.03N 29.39 E
- Dillingen (Saar) 12 Ie 49.21N 6.44 E
- Dillingham 39 Dd 59.02N 158.29W
- Dillon [Mt.-U.S.] 43 Eb 45.13N 112.38W
- Dillon [S.C.-U.S.] 44 Hh 34.25N 79.22W
- Dilly 34 Dc 14.57N 7.43W
- Dilolo 31 Jj 10.42S 22.20 E
- Dilsen 12 Hc 51.02N 5.44 E
- Dimashq=Damascus (EN) 22 Ff 33.30N 36.15 E
- Dimbelenge 36 Dd 5.30S 23.53 E
- Dimbokro [3] 34 Ed 6.50N 4.45W
- Dimbokro 34 Ed 6.39N 4.42W
- Dimboola 59 Ig 36.27S 142.02 E
- Dîmboviţa 15 Je 44.14N 26.27 E
- Dîmboviţa [2] 15 Ie 44.55N 25.30 E
- Dîmbovnic 15 Ie 44.20N 25.40 E
- Dimitrovgrad [Bul.] 15 Ig 42.03N 25.36 E
- Dimitrovgrad [R.S.F.S.R.] 19 Ee 54.14N 49.42 E
- Dimitrovgrad [Yugo.] 15 Fg 43.01N 22.47 E
- Dimmitt 45 Ei 34.33N 102.19W
- Dimona 24 Fg 31.04N 35.02 E
- Dimovo 15 Ff 43.44N 22.44 E
- Dinagat 26 Id 10.12N 125.35 E
- Dinājpur 25 Hc 25.38N 88.38 E
- Dinan 11 Df 48.27N 2.02W
- Dinangourou 34 Ec 14.27N 2.14W
- Dinant 11 Kd 50.16N 4.55 E
- Dinar 24 Dc 38.04N 30.10 E
- Dinar, Kūh-e- 24 Ng 30.50N 51.35 E
- Dinara 14 Kf 44.04N 16.23 E
- Dinara=Dinaric Alps (EN) 5 Hg 43.50N 16.35 E
- Dinard 11 Df 48.38N 2.04W
- Dinaric Alps (EN)= Dinara 5 Hg 43.50N 16.35 E
- Dindar, Nahr ad- 35 Ec 14.06N 33.40 E
- Dinder 35 Ec 14.06N 33.40 E
- Dindigul 25 Ff 10.21N 77.57 E
- Dindima 34 Hc 10.14N 10.09 E
- Dinga 36 Cd 5.19S 16.34 E
- Dingbian 27 Id 37.35N 107.37 E
- Dingden, Hamminkeln- 12 Ic 51.46N 6.37 E
- Dinggyê 27 Ef 28.25N 87.45 E
- Dinghai 27 Le 30.05N 122.07 E
- Dingle 8 Df 58.32N 11.34 E
- Dingle/An Daingean 9 Ci 52.08N 10.15W
- Dingle Bay/Bá an Daingin 9 Ci 52.05N 10.15W
- Dingolfing 10 Ih 48.38N 12.30 E
- Dingshuzhen 28 Ei 31.16N 119.50 E
- Dingtao 28 Cg 35.04N 115.35 E
- Dinguiraye 34 Cc 11.18N 10.43W
- Dingwall 9 Id 57.35N 4.26W
- Dingxi 27 Hd 35.33N 104.32 E
- Dingxian 27 Jd 39.29N 115.00 E
- Dingxiang 28 Be 38.32N 112.59 E
- Dingxing 27 Kd 39.11N 115.48 E
- Dingyuan 28 Dh 32.32N 117.41 E
- Dingzi Gang 28 Ff 36.33N 120.59 E
- Dinh, Mui- 21 Mh 11.22N 109.01 E
- Dinkel 12 Ib 52.30N 6.58 E
- Dinosaur 45 Bf 40.15N 109.01W
- Dinskaja 16 Kg 45.09N 39.12 E
- Dinslaken 12 Ic 51.34N 6.44 E
- Dinsör 35 Ge 2.23N 42.58 E
- Dintel 12 Gc 51.39N 4.24 E
- Dinuba 46 Fh 36.36N 119.27W

Index Symbols

[1] Independent Nation
[2] State, Region
[3] District, County
[4] Municipality
[5] Colony, Dependency
Continent
Physical Region

Historical or Cultural Region
Mount, Mountain
Volcano
Hill
Mountains, Mountain Range
Hills, Escarpment
Plateau, Upland

Pass, Gap
Plain, Lowland
Delta
Salt Flat
Valley, Canyon
Crater, Cave
Karst Features

Depression
Polder
Desert, Dunes
Forest, Woods
Heath, Steppe
Oasis
Cape, Point

Coast, Beach
Cliff
Peninsula
Isthmus
Sandbank
Island
Atoll

Rock, Reef
Islands, Archipelago
Rocks, Reefs
Coral Reef
Well, Spring
Geyser
River, Stream

Waterfall Rapids
River Mouth, Estuary
Lake
Salt Lake
Intermittent Lake
Reservoir
Swamp, Pond

Canal
Glacier
Ice Shelf, Pack Ice
Ocean
Sea
Gulf, Bay
Strait, Fjord

Lagoon
Bank
Seamount
Tablemount
Ridge
Shelf
Basin

Escarpment, Sea Scarp
Fracture
Trench, Abyss
National Park, Reserve
Point of Interest
Recreation Site
Cave, Cavern

Historic Site
Ruins
Wall, Walls
Church, Abbey
Temple
Scientific Station
Airport

Port
Lighthouse
Mine
Tunnel
Dam, Bridge

Index Symbols

[1] Independent Nation	Historical or Cultural Region	Pass, Gap	Depression	Coast, Beach	Rock, Reef	Waterfall Rapids	Canal	Lagoon	Escarpment, Sea Scarp	Historic Site	Port
[2] State, Region	Mount, Mountain	Plain, Lowland	Polder	Cliff	Islands, Archipelago	River Mouth, Estuary	Glacier	Bank	Fracture	Ruins	Lighthouse
[3] District, County	Volcano	Delta	Desert, Dunes	Peninsula	Rocks, Reefs	Lake	Ice Shelf, Pack Ice	Seamount	Trench, Abyss	Wall, Walls	Mine
[4] Municipality	Hill	Salt Flat	Forest, Woods	Isthmus	Coral Reef	Salt Lake	Ocean	Tablemount	National Park, Reserve	Church, Abbey	Tunnel
[5] Colony, Dependency	Mountains, Mountain Range	Valley, Canyon	Heath, Steppe	Sandbank	Well, Spring	Intermittent Lake	Sea	Ridge	Point of Interest	Temple	Dam, Bridge
Continent	Hills, Escarpment	Crater, Cave	Oasis	Island	Geyser	Reservoir	Gulf, Bay	Shelf	Recreation Site	Scientific Station	
Physical Region	Plateau, Upland	Karst Features	Cape, Point	Atoll	River, Stream	Swamp, Pond	Strait, Fjord	Basin	Cave, Cavern	Airport	

Dragon's Mouths/Dragón, Bocas del- 54 Fa 10.45N 61.46W
Dragør 8 Ei 55.36N 12.41 E
Draguignan 11 Mk 43.32N 6.28 E
Drahanska vrchovina 10 Mg 49.30N 16.45 E
Drain 46 De 43.40N 123.19W
Drake 45 Fc 47.55N 100.23W
Drake, Estrecho de-=Drake Passage (EN) 52 Jk 58.00S 70.00W
Drakensberg 30 Jk 29.00S 29.00 E
Drake Passage (EN)=Drake, Estrecho de- 52 Jk 58.00S 70.00W
Dráma 15 Hh 41.09N 24.09 E
Drammen 6 Hd 59.44N 10.15 E
Dramselva 8 De 59.44N 10.14 E
Drangajokull 7a Aa 66.09N 22.15W
Dranse 11 Mh 46.24N 6.30 E
Drau=Drava (EN) 5 Hf 45.33N 18.55 E
Dráva=Drava (EN) 5 Hf 45.33N 18.55 E
Drava (EN)=Drau 5 Hf 45.33N 18.55 E
Drava (EN)=Dráva 5 Hf 45.33N 18.55 E
Dravograd 14 Jd 46.35N 15.01 E
Drawa 10 Ld 52.52N 15.59 E
Drawno 10 Lc 53.13N 15.45 E
Drawsko, Jezioro- 10 Mc 53.33N 16.10 E
Drawsko Pomorskie 10 Lc 53.32N 15.48 E
Drayton Valley 42 Gf 53.13N 115.00W
Drean 14 Bn 36.41N 7.45 E
Dreieich 12 Ke 50.01N 8.43 E
Drenovci 14 Mf 44.55N 18.55 E
Drenthe [3] 12 Ib 52.45N 6.30 E
Dresden 6 He 51.03N 13.45 E
Dreux 11 Hf 48.44N 1.22 E
Drevsjø 7 Cf 61.54N 12.02 E
Drezdenko 10 Ld 52.51N 15.50 E
Dričeni/Driceni 8 Lh 56.39N 27.11 E
Driceni/Dričeni 8 Lh 56.39N 27.11 E
Driffield 9 Mg 54.01N 0.26W
Driggs 46 Je 43.44N 111.14W
Drina 5 Hg 44.53N 19.21 E
Drincea 15 Fe 44.07N 22.59 E
Drin Gulf (EN)=Drinit, Gjiri i- 15 Ch 41.45N 19.28 E
Drini 5 Hg 41.45N 19.34 E
Drini i Zi 15 Dg 42.05N 20.23 E
Drinit, Gjiri i-=Drin Gulf (EN) 15 Ch 41.45N 19.28 E
Drinjača 14 Nf 44.17N 19.10 E
Drinosi 15 Di 40.17N 20.02 E
Drissa 7 Gi 55.47N 27.57 E
Drisvjaty, Ozero-/Drūkšiu Ežeras 8 Lj 55.37N 26.45 E
Driva 8 Cb 62.40N 8.34 E
Drjanovo 15 Ig 42.58N 25.28 E
Drniš 14 Kg 43.52N 16.09 E
Drøbak 7 Cg 59.39N 10.39 E
Drocea, Virful- 15 Fc 46.12N 22.14 E
Drogheda/Droichead Átha 9 Gh 53.43N 6.21W
Drogičin 16 Dc 52.13N 25.10 E
Drogobyč 16 Ce 49.22N 23.33 E
Drohiczyn 10 Sd 52.24N 22.41 E
Droichead Átha/Drogheda 9 Gh 53.43N 6.21W
Droichead na Bandan/Bandon 9 Ej 51.45N 8.45W
Droichead na Banna/Banbridge 9 Gg 54.21N 6.16W
Drokija 16 Ee 48.01N 27.53 E
Drôme 12 Be 49.19N 0.45W
Drôme [3] 11 Lj 44.35N 5.10 E
Drömling 10 Hd 52.29N 11.04 E
Dronero 14 Bf 44.28N 7.22 E
Dronne 11 Fi 45.02N 0.09W
Dronning Fabiola-Fjella 66 Df 71.30S 35.40 E
Dronning Louise Land 41 Jc 76.45N 24.00W
Dronten 11 Lb 52.31N 5.42 E
Dropt 11 Fj 44.35N 0.06W
Drovjanoj 20 Cb 72.25N 72.45 E
Drowning River 45 Na 50.55N 84.35W
Druja 7 Gi 55.47N 27.29 E
Drūkšiu Ežeras/Drisvjaty, Ozero- 8 Lj 55.37N 26.45 E
Druk-Yul→Bhutan [1] 22 Lg 27.30N 90.30 E
Drulingen 12 Jf 48.52N 7.11 E
Drumheller 42 Gf 51.28N 112.42W
Drummond [Mt.-U.S.] 46 Ic 46.40N 113.09W
Drummond [Wi.-U.S.] 45 Kc 46.20N 91.15W
Drummond Island 44 Fb 46.00N 83.40W
Drummond Range 59 Jd 23.30S 147.15 E
Drummondville 42 Kg 45.50N 72.20W
Drummore 9 Ig 54.42N 4.54W
Drumochter, Pass of- 9 Ie 56.50N 4.12W
Drunen 12 Hc 51.41N 5.10 E
Druskininkai/Druskininkaj 7 Fi 54.04N 24.06 E
Druskininkaj/Druskininkai 7 Fi 54.04N 24.06 E
Drut 16 Gc 53.04N 30.35 E
Druten 12 Hc 51.54N 5.38 E
Družba 16 Hc 52.02N 33.59 E
Družba 19 If 45.18N 82.29 E
Družkovka 16 Je 48.36N 37.33 E
Družnaja Gorka 8 Ne 59.11N 30.10 E
Družnino 17 Ih 56.48N 59.29 E
Drużno, Jezioro- 10 Pb 54.08N 19.30 E
Drvar 14 Kf 44.22N 16.23 E
Drvenik 14 Lg 43.09N 17.15 E
Drwęca 10 Oc 53.00N 18.42 E
Dryden 42 Ig 49.47N 92.50W
Dry Fork 46 Me 43.30N 105.24W
Drygalski Ice Tongue 66 Kf 75.24S 163.30 E
Drygalski Island 66 Ge 65.45S 92.30 E
Drysdale River 59 Fb 13.59S 126.51 E
Dry Tortugas 43 Kg 24.38N 82.55W
Drzewica 10 Qe 51.27N 20.28 E
Drzewiczka 10 Qe 51.33N 20.35 E
Dschang 34 Hd 5.27N 10.04 E
Dua 36 Db 3.20N 20.53 E
Duaca 54 Ea 10.18N 69.10W
Duancun→Wuxiang 28 Bf 36.50N 112.51 E
Duarte, Pico- 38 Lh 19.00N 71.00W
Duartina 55 Hf 22.24S 49.25W
Dubawnt 42 Hd 64.30N 100.06W
Dubawnt Lake 38 Ic 63.08N 101.30W
Ḑubay'ah, Ra's- 24 Pj 24.20N 54.09 E
Dubayy 22 Hg 25.18N 55.18 E
Dubbo 58 Fh 32.15S 148.36 E
Dübener Heide 10 Ie 51.40N 12.40 E
Dubenski 16 Td 51.29N 56.38 E
Dubh Artach 9 Ge 56.08N 6.39W
Dubica 14 Ke 45.13N 16.48 E
Dublin 43 Ke 32.32N 82.54W
Dublin/Baile Átha Cliath [2] 9 Gh 53.20N 6.15W
Dublin/Baile Átha Cliath 6 Fe 53.20N 6.15W
Dublin Bay/Cuan Bhaile Átha Cliath 9 Gh 53.20N 6.06W
Dubljany 10 Tg 49.26N 23.16 E
Dublon 64d Bb 7.23N 151.53 E
Dubna 8 Lh 56.20N 26.31 E
Dubna 19 Dd 56.47N 37.10 E
Dubnica nad Váhom 10 Oh 48.58N 18.10 E
Dubno 19 Ce 50.29N 25.46 E
Du Bois 44 He 41.06N 78.46W
Dubois [Id.-U.S.] 46 Id 44.10N 112.14W
Dubois [Wy.-U.S.] 46 Ke 43.33N 109.38W
Dubossary 16 Ff 47.17N 29.10 E
Dubovka 19 Ef 49.03N 44.50 E
Dubovoje 10 Ih 48.08N 23.59 E
Dubreka 34 Cd 9.48N 13.31W
Dubrovica 16 Ed 51.34N 26.34 E
Dubrovnik 6 Hg 42.39N 18.07 E
Dubrovno 7 Hi 54.33N 30.41 E
Dubrovnoje 19 Gd 57.58N 69.25 E
Dubuque 43 Ic 42.30N 90.41W
Dubysa 8 Ji 55.02N 23.27 E
Duc de Gloucester, Iles du-=Duke of Gloucester, Islands (En) 57 Mg 20.38S 143.20W
Duchang 28 Dj 29.16N 116.11 E
Duchesne 46 Jf 40.10N 110.24W
Duchess 59 Hd 21.22S 139.52 E
Ducie Atoll 57 Qg 24.40S 124.47W
Duck River 44 Dg 36.02N 87.52W
Duckwater Peak 46 Hg 38.58N 115.26W
Duclair 12 Ce 49.29N 0.53 E
Duc Lap 25 Lf 12.27N 107.38 E
Ducos 51h Bb 14.34N 60.58W
Dudelange/Düdelingen 12 Ie 49.28N 6.06 E
Duderstadt 10 Ge 51.31N 10.16 E
Dudinka 22 Kc 69.25N 86.15 E
Dudley 9 Ki 52.30N 2.05W
Ðudo 35 Id 9.20N 50.14 E
Dudub 35 Hd 6.55N 46.42 E
Duduné 63b Ce 21.21S 167.44 E
Dudvåh 10 Ni 47.58N 17.50 E
Dudweiler, Saarbrücken- 12 Je 49.17N 7.02 E
Düdwëyn 35 Gd 8.20N 45.03 E
Dudypta 20 Db 70.55N 89.50 E
Duékoué 34 Dd 6.45N 7.21W
Dueodde 8 Fj 54.59N 15.05 E
Duerna 13 Gb 42.19N 5.54W
Duero 5 Fg 41.08N 8.40W
Dufek Coast 66 Lg 84.30S 179.00W
Duffer Peak 46 Ff 41.40N 118.44W
Duff Islands 57 He 9.50S 167.10 E
Dugi Otok 14 Ii 44.00N 15.00 E
Dugo Selo 14 Ke 45.48N 16.15 E
Du Gué, Rivière- 42 Ke 57.20N 70.46W
Duhovnickoje 16 Pc 52.29N 48.15 E
Duijan Yan 27 He 31.01N 103.28 E
Duiru→Wuchuan 27 If 28.28N 107.57 E
Duisburg 10 Ce 51.26N 6.45 E
Duitama 54 Db 5.50N 73.02W
Dujūma 35 Ge 1.14N 42.34 E
Dukagjini 15 Cg 42.18N 19.45 E
Dūkān 24 Ke 35.56N 44.58 E
Dukan, Sad ad- 24 Kd 36.10N 44.56 E
Dukat 15 Fg 42.26N 22.21 E
Duke of Gloucester Islands (EN)=Duc de Gloucester, Iles du- 57 Mg 20.38S 143.20W
Duke of York 63a Aa 4.10S 152.28 E
Duke of York Bay 42 Jc 65.25N 84.50W
Duk Fadiat 35 Ed 7.45N 31.25 E
Duk Faiwil 35 Ed 7.30N 31.29 E
Dukhān 23 Hd 25.25N 50.48 E
Dukielska, Przełecz- 10 Rg 49.25N 21.42 E
Dukku 34 Hc 10.49N 10.46 E
Dukla 10 Rg 49.34N 21.41 E
Dukou 22 Mg 26.31N 101.44 E
Dūkštas/Dukštas 8 Li 55.32N 26.28 E
Dukštas/Dūkštas 8 Li 55.32N 26.28 E
Dulan (Qagan Us) 22 Lf 36.29N 98.29 E
Dulce, Bahía- 48 Ji 16.30N 98.50W
Dulce, Golfo- 47 Hg 8.36N 83.15W
Dulce, Rio- 52 Ji 30.31S 62.32W
Dulce Nombre de Culmí 49 Ef 15.09N 85.37W
Duldurga 20 Gf 50.38N 113.35 E
Dulgalah 20 Ic 67.30N 133.20 E
Dulia 36 Db 2.57N 24.08 E
Dülmen 10 De 51.50N 7.18 E
Dulovka 8 Mg 57.27N 28.29 E
Dulovo 15 Kf 43.49N 27.09 E
Duluth 39 Je 46.47N 92.06W
Dūmā 24 Gf 33.35N 36.24 E
Dumaguete 26 He 9.18N 123.18 E
Dumai 26 Df 1.41N 101.27 E
Dumaran 26 Gd 10.33N 119.51 E
Dumaresq River 59 Ke 28.40S 150.28 E
Dumas [Ar.-U.S.] 45 Kj 33.53N 91.29W
Dumas [Tx.-U.S.] 45 Fi 35.52N 101.58W
Dumayr 24 Gf 33.38N 36.40 E
Dumbarton 9 If 55.57N 4.35W
Dumbéa 63b Cf 22.09S 166.27 E
Dumbrăveni [Rom.] 15 Jb 47.39N 26.25 E
Dumbrăveni [Rom.] 15 Hc 46.14N 24.34 E
Dumfries 9 Jf 55.04N 3.37W
Dumfries and Galloway [3] 9 Jf 55.10N 3.35W
Dumka 25 Hd 24.16N 87.15 E
Dumlupinar 15 Mk 38.52N 30.00 E
Dümmer 10 Ed 52.31N 8.19 E
Dumoine, Lac- 44 Ib 46.52N 77.52W
Dumoine, Rivière- 44 Ib 46.13N 77.50W
Dumont d'Urville 66 Je 66.40S 140.01 E
Dumont D'Urville Sea (EN) 66 Je 63.00S 140.00 E
Dumpu 58 Fe 5.52S 145.46 E
Dümrek 15 Lk 38.40N 28.24 E
Dumuhe 28 La 46.21N 133.33 E
Dumyāt=Damietta (EN) 31 Ke 31.25N 31.48 E
Dumyāţ, Maşabb- 24 Dg 31.27N 31.51 E
Duna=Danube (EN) 5 If 45.20N 29.40 E
Dunaföldvár 10 Oi 46.48N 18.56 E
Dunaharaszti 10 Pi 47.21N 19.05 E
Dunaj 20 Ih 42.57N 132.20 E
Dunaj=Danube (EN) 5 If 45.20N 29.40 E
Dunajec 10 Qf 50.15N 20.44 E
Dunajevcy 16 Ee 48.51N 26.44 E
Dunajská Streda 10 Ni 47.01N 17.38 E
Dunakeszi 10 Pi 47.38N 19.08 E
Dunántúl 10 Nj 47.00N 18.00 E
Dunărea=Danube (EN) 5 If 45.20N 29.40 E
Dunărea Veche 15 Ld 45.17N 28.02 E
Dunării, Delta-=Danube, Mouths of the- (EN) 5 If 45.30N 29.45 E
Duna-Tisza Köze 10 Pj 46.45N 19.30 E
Dunaújváros 10 Oj 46.58N 18.56 E
Dunav=Danube (EN) 5 If 45.20N 29.40 E
Dunavățu de Jos 15 Me 44.59N 29.13 E
Dunav-Tisa-Dunav kanal 15 Dd 45.10N 20.50 E
Dunback 62 Df 45.23S 170.38 E
Dunbar 9 Kf 56.00N 2.31W
Duncan [Az.-U.S.] 46 Kj 32.43N 109.06W
Duncan [B.C.-Can.] 46 Db 48.47N 123.42W
Duncan [Ok.-U.S.] 43 He 34.30N 97.57W
Duncan Passage 25 If 11.00N 92.00 E
Duncansby Head 5 Fd 58.39N 3.01W
Dundaga 8 Jg 57.31N 22.14 E
Dundalk 44 If 39.15N 76.31W
Dundalk/Dún Dealgan 9 Gg 54.01N 6.25W
Dundalk Bay/Cuan Dhun Dealgan 9 Gh 53.57N 6.17W
Dundas [Grld.] 41 Fc 76.30N 69.00W
Dundas [Ont.-Can.] 44 Hd 43.16N 79.58W
Dundas, Lake- 59 Ef 32.35S 121.50 E
Dundas Peninsula 42 Gb 74.40N 113.00W
Dundas Strait 59 Gb 11.20S 131.35 E
Dún Dealgan/Dundalk 9 Gg 54.01N 6.25W
Dundee [S.Afr.] 37 Ee 28.12S 30.16 E
Dundee [Scot.-U.K.] 6 Fd 56.28N 3.00W
Dund Hot→Zhenglan Qi 28 Cc 42.14N 115.59 E
Dundrum Bay/Cuan Dhún Droma 9 Hg 54.13N 5.45W
Dunedin [Fl.-U.S.] 44 Fk 28.02N 82.47W
Dunedin [N.Z.] 58 Ii 45.53S 170.31 E
Dunfanaghy 9 Ff 55.11N 7.59W
Dunfermline 9 Je 56.04N 3.29W
Dungannon/Dún Geanainn 9 Gg 54.31N 6.46W
Dún Garbhán/Dungarvan 9 Fi 52.05N 7.37W
Düngarpur 25 Ed 23.50N 73.43 E
Dungarvan/Dún Garbhán 9 Fi 52.05N 7.37W
Dungas 34 Gc 13.04N 9.20 E
Dungau 10 Ih 48.45N 12.30 E
Dún Geanainn/Dungannon 9 Gg 54.31N 6.46W
Dungeness 9 Nk 50.55N 0.58 E
Dungu 36 Eb 3.42N 28.40 E
Dungu 36 Eb 3.37N 28.34 E
Dunhua 27 Mc 43.22N 128.12 E
Dunhuang 27 Fc 40.10N 94.50 E
Dunkerque 11 Ic 51.03N 2.22 E
Dunkery Beacon 9 Jj 51.11N 3.35W
Dunkirk 43 Lc 42.29N 79.21W
Dunkwa 34 Ed 5.58N 1.47W
Dún Laoghaire 9 Gh 53.17N 6.08W
Dún Mánmhai/Dunmanway 9 Dj 51.43N 9.07W
Dunmanway/Dún Mánmhai 9 Dj 51.43N 9.07W
Dunn 44 Hh 35.19N 78.37W
Dún na nGall/Donegal [2] 9 Fg 54.50N 8.00W
Dún na nGall/Donegal 9 Eg 54.39N 8.06W
Dunnellon 44 Fk 29.03N 82.28W
Dunnet Head 9 Jc 58.39N 3.23W
Dunning 45 Ff 41.50N 100.06W
Dún Pádraig/Downpatrick 9 Hg 54.20N 5.43W
Dunqulah=Dongola (EN) 31 Kg 19.10N 30.29 E
Dunqulah al Qadīmah 35 Eb 18.13N 30.45 E
Dunqunāb 35 Fa 21.06N 37.05 E
Dunqunāb, Khalīj- 35 Fa 21.05N 37.08 E
Dunrankin 44 Fa 48.39N 83.04W
Duns 9 Kf 55.47N 2.20W
Dünsberg 12 Kd 50.39N 8.35 E
Dunsmuir 46 Df 41.13N 122.16W
Dunstable 12 Bc 51.53N 0.31W
Dunstan Mountains 62 Cf 44.55S 169.30 E
Dun-sur-Auron 11 Ih 46.53N 2.34 E
Dun-sur-Meuse 12 He 49.23N 5.11 E
Duntroon 62 Df 44.51S 170.41 E
Dunvegan 9 Gd 57.26N 6.35W
Duobukur 27 La 50.19N 124.57 E
Duolun/Dolonnur 27 Kc 42.10N 116.30 E
Duong Dong 25 Kf 10.13N 103.58 E
Dupree 45 Fd 45.03N 101.36W
Duqm 22 Hf 19.41N 57.32 E
Duque de Bragança, Quedas- 30 Ii 9.05S 16.10 E
Duque de Caxias 54 Jh 22.47S 43.18W
Duque de York, Isla- 56 Eh 50.40S 75.20W
Du Quoin 45 Lg 38.01N 89.14W
Durack Range 59 Fc 17.00S 128.00 E
Durack River 59 Fc 15.33S 127.52 E
Durağan 24 Fb 41.25N 35.04 E
Durance 5 Gg 43.55N 4.44 E
Durand 45 Kd 44.38N 91.58W
Durand, Récif- 63b Df 22.02S 168.39 E
Durango [2] 47 Dd 24.50N 104.50W
Durango [Co.-U.S.] 39 If 37.16N 107.53W
Durango [Sp.] 13 Ja 43.10N 2.37W
Durañona 55 Bm 37.15S 60.31W
Durant 43 He 33.59N 96.23W
Duras 11 Gj 44.40N 0.11 E
Duratón 13 Hc 41.37N 4.07W
Durazno 56 Id 33.22S 56.31W
Durazno [2] 55 Dk 33.05S 56.05W
Durazno, Cuchilla Grande del- 55 Dk 33.15S 56.15W
Durazzo (EN)=Durresi 15 Ch 41.19N 19.26 E
Durban 31 Kk 29.55S 30.56 E
Durbe 8 Ih 56.39N 21.14 E
Durbet-Daba, Pereval- 27 Eb 49.37N 89.25 E
Ðurbo 35 Ic 11.30N 50.18 E
Durbuy 12 Hd 50.21N 5.28 E
Ðurđevac 14 Ld 46.02N 17.04 E
Düren 10 Cf 50.48N 6.29 E
Durg 25 Gd 21.11N 81.17 E
Durgapūr 25 Hd 23.30N 87.15 E
Durgun Nur 27 Fb 47.40N 93.30 E
Durham 9 Lg 54.45N 1.45W
Durham [3] 9 Lg 54.45N 1.40W
Durham [Eng.-U.K.] 9 Lg 54.47N 1.34W
Durham [N.C.-U.S.] 43 Ld 35.59N 78.54W
Durkee 46 Gd 44.36N 117.28W
Durlas/Thurles 9 Fi 52.41N 7.49W
Durmā 23 Ge 24.37N 46.08 E
Durmersheim 12 Kf 48.56N 8.16 E
Durmitor 5 Hg 43.09N 19.02 E
Durnford, Punta- 32 De 23.37N 16.00W
Durresi=Durazzo (EN) 15 Ch 41.19N 19.26 E
Durrësit, Gjiri- 15 Ch 41.16N 19.28 E
Dursey/Oiléan Baoi 9 Cj 51.36N 10.12W
Dursunbey 24 Cc 39.35N 28.38 E
Durtal 11 Fg 47.40N 0.15W
Duru→Wuchuan 27 If 28.28N 107.57 E
Duruksi 35 Hd 8.29N 45.38 E
Durusu Gölü 15 Lh 41.20N 28.38 E
Durūz, Jabal ad- 24 Gf 32.40N 36.44 E
D'Urville Island 61 Dh 40.50S 173.50 E
Dušak 18 Cf 37.15N 60.01 E
Dusa Mareb 35 Hd 5.31N 46.24 E
Dušanbe 22 If 38.35N 68.48 E
Dušeti 16 Nh 42.05N 44.42 E
Dusetos 8 Li 55.42N 26.02 E
Dushan 22 Mg 25.55N 107.36 E
Dushan Hu 28 Dg 35.06N 116.48 E
Dusios Ežeras/Dusja, Ozero- 8 Jj 54.15N 23.45 E
Dusja, Ozero-/Dusios Ežeras 8 Jj 54.15N 23.45 E
Dusky Sound 62 Bf 45.45S 166.30 E
Düsseldorf 6 Ge 51.13N 6.46 E
Dusti 18 Gf 37.22N 68.43 E
Dutch Harbor 40a Eb 53.53N 166.32W
Dutlwe 37 Cd 23.58S 23.54 E
Dutton, Mount- 46 Ig 38.01N 112.13W
Duved 8 Ea 63.24N 12.52 E
Duvergé 49 Ld 18.22N 71.31W
Düvertepe 15 Lj 39.14N 28.27 E
Duvno 14 Lg 43.43N 17.14 E
Duwayhin 23 He 24.16N 51.20 E
Duwayhin, Khawr- 24 Nj 24.20N 51.25 E
Duyfken Point 59 Ib 12.35S 141.40 E
Duyun 27 If 26.12N 107.28 E
Düz 32 Ic 33.28N 9.01 E
Düzce 23 Da 40.50N 31.10 E
Dve Mogili 15 If 43.36N 25.52 E
Dvina (EN)=Daugava 19 Cd 57.04N 24.03 E
Dvina Gulf (EN)=Dvinskaja Guba 5 Jb 65.00N 39.45 E
Dvinskaja Guba=Dvina Gulf (EN) 5 Jb 65.00N 39.45 E
Dvor 14 Ke 45.04N 16.23 E
Dvuh Cirkov, Gora- 20 Lc 67.30N 168.20 E
Dvůr Králové nad Labem 10 Lf 50.26N 15.48 E
Dwārka 25 Dd 22.14N 68.58 E
Dworshak Reservoir 46 Hc 46.45N 116.00W
Dyer, Cape- 38 Mc 66.37N 61.18W
Dyero 34 Dc 12.50N 6.30W
Dyer Plateau 66 Qf 70.45S 65.30W
Dyersburg 43 Jd 36.03N 89.23W
Dyfed [3] 9 Ji 52.05N 4.00W
Dyhtau, Gora- 16 Mh 43.05N 43.12 E
Dyje 10 Mh 48.37N 16.56 E
Dyjsko-Svratecký úval 10 Mh 48.56N 16.25 E
Dyle 12 Gd 50.57N 4.40 E
Dylewska Góra 10 Pc 53.34N 19.57 E
Dynów 10 Sg 49.49N 22.14 E
Dyr, Djebel- 14 Cn 36.13N 8.46 E
Dyrhólæy 5 Ec 63.24N 19.08W
Dysnų Ežeras/Disnaj, Ozero- 7 Gi 55.35N 26.32 E
Dytike Rodhópi 15 Hh 41.45N 24.05 E
Dzabhan 21 Le 48.54N 93.23 E
Džagdy, Hrebet- 20 If 53.40N 131.00 E
Džalagaš 19 Gf 45.05N 64.40 E
Džalal-Abad 18 Id 40.56N 73.05 E
Džalilabad 19 Eh 39.12N 48.31 E
Džalinda 20 Hf 53.31N 123.59 E
Džambejty 16 Rd 50.14N 52.38 E
Džambul [Kaz.-U.S.S.R.] 22 Je 42.54N 71.22 E
Džambul [Kaz.-U.S.S.R.] 19 Hf 47.17N 71.42 E
Džambulskaja Oblast [3] 19 Hg 44.30N 72.30 E
Dzamyn-Ud 27 Jb 43.50N 111.45 E
Džanak 16 Si 40.30N 55.35 E
Džanga 16 Fg 40.01N 53.10 E
Džankoj 19 Df 45.42N 34.22 E
Džansugurov 19 Hf 45.23N 79.29 E
Džanybek 19 Ef 49.24N 46.50 E
Dzaoudzi 31 Lj 12.47S 45.17 E
Džardžan 20 Hc 68.55N 124.05 E
Džargalant 27 Gb 47.20N 99.35 E
Dzargalant 27 Ib 48.35N 105.50 E
Džarkurgan 19 Gh 37.29N 67.25 E
Džava 16 Mh 42.24N 43.53 E
Džebariki-Haja 20 Id 62.23N 135.50 E
Džebel [Bul.] 15 Ih 41.30N 25.18 E
Džebel [Tur.-U.S.S.R.] 16 Sj 39.37N 54.18 E
Džebrail 16 Oj 39.23N 47.01 E
Dzereg 27 Fb 47.08N 92.50 E
Džergalan 18 Lc 42.33N 79.02 E
Dzermuk 16 Nj 39.48N 45.39 E
Dzeržinsk [Bye.-U.S.S.R.] 16 Ec 53.44N 27.08 E
Dzeržinsk [R.S.F.S.R.] 19 Ed 56.16N 43.32 E
Dzeržinsk [Ukr.-U.S.S.R.] 16 Je 48.22N 37.50 E
Dzeržinskaja, Gora- 8 Lk 53.53N 27.10 E
Dzeržinskoje 20 Ee 56.49N 95.18 E
Džetygara 22 Id 52.11N 61.12 E
Džetysaj 18 Gd 40.49N 68.20 E
Džezkazgan [Kaz.-U.S.S.R.] 19 Gf 47.53N 67.27 E
Džezkazgan [Kaz.-U.S.S.R.] 22 Ie 47.47N 67.46 E
Džezkazganskaja Oblast [3] 19 Gf 47.30N 70.00 E
Dzhugdzhur Range (EN)=Džugdžur, Hrebet- 21 Pd 58.00N 136.00 E
Działdówka 10 Qd 52.58N 20.05 E
Działdowo 10 Qc 53.15N 20.10 E
Działoszyce 10 Qf 50.22N 20.21 E
Dzibalchén 48 Oh 19.31N 89.45W
Dzibilchaltún 48 Og 21.05N 89.36W
Dzierzgoń 10 Pc 53.56N 19.21 E
Dzierżoniów 10 Mf 50.44N 16.39 E
Džirgatal 18 He 39.13N 71.12 E
Džizak 19 Gg 40.07N 67.52 E
Džizakskaja Oblast [3] 19 Gg 40.20N 67.40 E
Džugdžur, Hrebet-=Dzhugdzhur Range (EN) 21 Pd 58.00N 136.00 E
Džūkste/Džukste 8 Jh 56.45N 23.10 E
Džukste/Džūkste 8 Jh 56.45N 23.10 E
Džulfa 16 Nj 38.59N 45.35 E
Džuma 18 Fe 39.44N 66.39 E
Dzun-Bajan 27 Jc 44.26N 110.03 E
Dzungarian Basin (EN)=Junggar Pendi 21 Ke 45.00N 88.00 E
Dzungarian Gate (EN)=Alataw Shankou 21 Ke 45.25N 82.25 E
Dzungarian Gate (EN)=Džungarskije Vorota 21 Ke 45.25N 82.25 E
Džungarski Alatau, Hrebet- 21 Ke 45.00N 81.00 E
Džungarskije Vorota=Dzungarian Gate (EN) 21 Ke 45.25N 82.25 E
Dzun-Hara 27 Ib 48.40N 106.40 E
Dzun-Mod 27 Ib 47.50N 106.57 E
Džurak-Sal 16 Mf 47.18N 43.36 E
Džusaly 19 Gf 45.29N 64.05 E
Džvari 16 Mh 42.42N 42.02 E

E

Éadan Doire/Edenderry 9 Fh 53.21N 7.03W
Eads 45 Eg 38.29N 102.47W
Eagle 40 Kd 64.46N 141.16W
Eagle 42 Lf 53.35N 57.25W
Eagle Creek 46 La 52.22N 107.24W
Eagle Lake 44 Mb 47.02N 68.36W
Eagle Lake [Ca.-U.S.] 46 Ef 40.39N 120.44W
Eagle Lake [Me.-U.S.] 44 Mb 46.20N 69.20W
Eagle Lake [Ont.-Can.] 45 Jb 49.42N 93.13W
Eagle Mountain 45 Kc 47.54N 90.33W
Eagle Nest 45 Dh 36.35N 105.14W
Eagle Pass 43 Gf 28.43N 100.30W
Eagle Peak [Ca.-U.S.] 43 Cc 41.17N 120.12W
Eagle Peak [Tx.-U.S.] 45 Dk 30.56N 105.01W
Eagle River [Ak.-U.S.] 40 Jd 61.19N 149.34W
Eagle River [Wi.-U.S.] 45 Ld 45.55N 89.15W
Eagle Summit 40 Jc 65.30N 145.38W
Ealing, London- 12 Bc 51.30N 0.19W
Ear Falls 45 Ja 50.38N 93.13W
Earn 9 Je 56.25N 3.30W
Earn, Loch- 9 Ie 56.28N 4.10W
Earnslaw, Mount- 62 Cf 44.37S 168.25 E
Easley 44 Fh 34.50N 82.36W
East Alligator River 59 Gb 12.08S 132.42 E
East Anglia 9 Ni 52.25N 1.00 E
East Angus 44 Lc 45.29N 71.40W
East Bay [Can.] 42 Jd 64.05N 81.30W
East Bay [U.S.] 45 Ll 29.05N 89.15W
East Berlin = Berlin 6 He 52.31N 13.24 E
Eastbourne [Eng.-U.K.] 9 Nk 50.46N 0.17 E
Eastbourne [N.Z.] 62 Fd 41.17S 174.54 E
East Caicos 49 Lc 21.41N 71.30W
East Cape [Fl.-U.S.] 44 Gm 25.07N 81.05W
East Cape [N.Z.] 57 Ih 37.41S 178.33 E
East Caroline Basin (EN) 3 Ii 4.00N 146.45 E
East Chicago 44 De 41.38N 87.27W
East China Sea (EN)=Dong Hai 21 Og 29.00N 125.00 E
East China Sea (EN)=Higashi-Shina-Kai 21 Og 29.00N 125.00 E
East Coast [2] 62 Gc 38.20S 177.50 E
East Dereham 9 Ni 52.41N 0.56 E
Eastend 46 Kb 49.31N 108.48W
East Entrance 64a Bb 7.50N 134.40 E
Easter Island (EN)=Pascua, Isla de-/Rapa Nui 57 Qg 27.07S 109.22W
Easter Island (EN)=Rapa Nui/Pascua, Isla de- 57 Qg 27.07S 109.22W
Eastern [Ghana] [3] 34 Ed 6.30N 0.30W
Eastern [Kenya] [3] 36 Gb 0.05N 38.00 E
Eastern [S.L.] [3] 34 Cd 8.15N 11.00W
Eastern [Ug.] [3] 36 Fb 1.30N 33.50 E
Eastern [Zam.] [3] 36 Fe 13.00S 32.15 E
Eastern Fields 60 Dj 10.03S 145.22 E

Index Symbols

- [1] Independent Nation
- [2] State, Region
- [3] District, County
- [4] Municipality
- [5] Colony, Dependency
- Continent
- Physical Region
- Historical or Cultural Region
- Mount, Mountain
- Volcano
- Hill
- Mountains, Mountain Range
- Hills, Escarpment
- Plateau, Upland
- Pass, Gap
- Plain, Lowland
- Delta
- Salt Flat
- Valley, Canyon
- Crater, Cave
- Karst Features
- Depression
- Polder
- Desert, Dunes
- Forest, Woods
- Heath, Steppe
- Oasis
- Cape, Point
- Coast, Beach
- Cliff
- Peninsula
- Isthmus
- Sandbank
- Island
- Atoll
- Rock, Reef
- Islands, Archipelago
- Rocks, Reefs
- Coral Reef
- Well, Spring
- Geyser
- River, Stream
- Waterfall Rapids
- River Mouth, Estuary
- Lake
- Salt Lake
- Intermittent Lake
- Reservoir
- Swamp, Pond
- Canal
- Glacier
- Ice Shelf, Pack Ice
- Ocean
- Sea
- Gulf, Bay
- Strait, Fjord
- Lagoon
- Bank
- Seamount
- Tablemount
- Ridge
- Shelf
- Basin
- Escarpment, Sea Scarp
- Fracture
- Trench, Abyss
- National Park, Reserve
- Point of Interest
- Recreation Site
- Cave, Cavern
- Historic Site
- Ruins
- Wall, Walls
- Church, Abbey
- Temple
- Scientific Station
- Airport
- Port
- Lighthouse
- Mine
- Tunnel
- Dam, Bridge

Index Symbols

- [1] Independent Nation
- [2] State, Region
- [3] District, County
- [4] Municipality
- [5] Colony, Dependency
- Continent
- Physical Region
- Historical or Cultural Region
- Mount, Mountain
- Volcano
- Hill
- Mountains, Mountain Range
- Hills, Escarpment
- Plateau, Upland
- Pass, Gap
- Plain, Lowland
- Delta
- Salt Flat
- Valley, Canyon
- Crater, Cave
- Karst Features
- Depression
- Polder
- Desert, Dunes
- Forest, Woods
- Heath, Steppe
- Oasis
- Cape, Point
- Coast, Beach
- Cliff
- Peninsula
- Isthmus
- Sandbank
- Island
- Atoll
- Rock, Reef
- Islands, Archipelago
- Rocks, Reefs
- Coral Reef
- Well, Spring
- Geyser
- River, Stream
- Waterfall Rapids
- River Mouth, Estuary
- Lake
- Salt Lake
- Intermittent Lake
- Reservoir
- Swamp, Pond
- Canal
- Glacier
- Ice Shelf, Pack Ice
- Ocean
- Sea
- Gulf, Bay
- Strait, Fjord
- Lagoon
- Bank
- Seamount
- Tablemount
- Ridge
- Shelf
- Basin
- Escarpment, Sea Scarp
- Fracture
- Trench, Abyss
- National Park, Reserve
- Point of Interest
- Recreation Site
- Cave, Cavern
- Historic Site
- Ruins
- Wall, Walls
- Church, Abbey
- Temple
- Scientific Station
- Airport
- Port
- Lighthouse
- Mine
- Tunnel
- Dam, Bridge

Elm 10 Gd 52.09N 10.53 E
El Macao 49 Md 18.46N 68.33W
Elmadağ 24 Ec 39.55N 33.15 E
Elma Daği 15 Mk 38.46N 29.32 E
El Maestrat/El Maestrazgo 13 Ld 40.30N 0.10W
El Maestrazgo/El Maestrat 13 Ld 40.30N 0.10W
El Mahia 34 Ea 22.30N 2.30W
El Maitén 56 Ff 42.03S 71.10W
Elmaki 34 Gb 17.55N 8.20 E
El Malah 13 Ph 36.18N 3.14 E
Elmalı 24 Ic 39.25N 40.35 E
Elmali 24 Cd 36.44N 29.56 E
El Manteco 50 Ei 7.27N 62.32W
El Marfil 55 Bb 15.35S 60.19W
El Marsa 13 Mh 36.24N 0.55 E
El Medo 35 Gd 5.41N 41.46 E
El Meghaïer 32 Ic 33.57N 5.56 E
Elmhurst 45 Mf 41.53N 87.56W
El Milagro 56 Gd 31.01S 65.59W
Elmira 43 Lc 42.06N 76.50W
El Mrâyer 32 Fe 21.30N 8.10W
El Mreïti 32 Fe 23.29N 7.52W
El Mreyyé 30 Gg 19.30N 7.00W
Elmshorn 10 Fc 53.45N 9.39 E
Elmstein 12 Je 49.22N 7.56 E
Elne 11 Il 42.36N 2.58 E
El Nevado, Cerro- 56 Ge 35.35S 68.30W
El Niabo 35 Fe 4.33N 39.59 E
El Nihuil 56 Gd 34.58S 68.40W
El Novillo 48 Ec 28.40N 109.30W
El Novillo, Presa- 48 Ec 29.05N 109.45W
El Ochenta y Uno 48 Kg 21.35N 97.57W
Elorn 11 Bf 48.27N 4.16W
Elortondo 55 Bk 33.42S 61.37W
Elorza 54 Eb 7.03N 69.31W
Elota, Rio- 48 Ff 23.52N 106.56W
El Oued 32 Ic 33.20N 6.53 E
Eloy 46 Jj 32.45N 111.33W
El Palmar 50 Fh 8.01N 61.53W
El Palmito 48 Ge 25.40N 104.59W
El Panadés/El Penedès 13 Nc 41.25N 1.30 E
El Pao [Ven.] 50 Eh 8.06N 62.33W
El Pao [Ven.] 50 Bh 9.38N 68.08W
El Paraiso [3] 49 Df 14.10N 86.30W
El Paraiso 49 Dg 13.51N 86.34W
El Páramo 13 Gb 42.25N 5.45W
El Pardo, Madrid- 13 Id 40.32N 3.46W
El Paso [Il.-U.S.] 45 Lf 40.44N 89.01W
El Paso [Tx.-U.S.] 39 If 31.45N 106.29W
El Penedès/El Panadés 13 Nc 41.25N 1.30 E
El Perú 50 Fi 7.19N 61.49W
El Pico 54 Fg 15.57S 64.42W
El Pilar 50 Eg 10.32N 63.09W
El Pintado 56 Hb 24.38S 61.27W
El Porvenir [Hond.] 49 Df 14.41N 87.11W
El Porvenir [Pan.] 49 Hi 9.12N 80.08W
El Porvenir [Ven.] 50 Bi 6.55N 68.42W
El Potosí 48 Ie 24.51N 100.19W
El Prat de Llobregat/Prat de Llobregat 13 Oc 41.20N 2.06 E
El Priorat/El Priorato 13 Mc 41.10N 1.00 E
El Priorato/El Priorat 13 Mc 41.10N 1.00 E
El Progreso [3] 49 Cf 14.50N 90.00W
El Progreso [Guat.] 49 Bf 14.51N 90.04W
El Progreso [Hond.] 47 Ge 15.21N 87.49W
El Puente del Arzobispo 13 Ge 39.48N 5.10W
El Puerto 48 Dc 28.45N 111.20W
El Puerto de Santa Maria 13 Fh 36.36N 6.13W
El Rastro 50 Ch 9.03N 67.27W
El Real de Santa Maria 49 Ii 8.08N 77.43W
El Reno 43 Hd 35.32N 97.57W
El Ribeiro 13 Db 42.25N 8.10W
Elrose 46 Ka 51.13N 108.01W
El Saler 13 Le 39.23N 0.20W
El Salto 47 Cd 23.47N 105.23W
El Salvador [1] 39 Kh 13.50N 88.55W
El Samán de Apure 50 Bi 7.55N 68.44W
El Sauce [Mex.] 48 De 24.34N 111.29W
El Sauce [Nic.] 49 Dg 12.53N 86.32W
El Sáuz 48 Fc 29.03N 106.15W
Elsberry 45 Kg 39.10N 90.47W
Elsdorf 12 Id 50.56N 6.34 E
Else 12 Kb 52.12N 8.40 E
El Seibo 49 Md 18.46N 68.52W
Elsen, Paderborn- 12 Kc 51.44N 8.41 E
Elsen Nur 27 Fd 35.08N 92.20 E
'Ēl Shāma 35 Ge 2.46N 41.03 E
El Socorro 50 Dh 8.59N 65.44W
El Sombrero 54 Eb 9.23N 67.03W
Elst 12 Hc 51.55N 5.52 E
Elsterwerda 10 Je 51.27N 13.32 E
El Sueco 47 Cc 29.54N 106.24W
El-Taht 13 Mi 35.27N 0.46 E
El Tajín 47 Ed 20.27N 97.23W
El Tala 56 Gc 26.07S 65.17W
Eltanin Bay 66 Pf 73.40S 82.00W
Eltham 62 Fc 39.26S 174.18 E
El Tigre 53 Je 8.55N 64.15W
El Tigre, Isla- 49 Dg 13.16N 87.38W
El Toboso 13 Je 39.31N 3.00W
El Tocuyo 54 Eb 9.47N 69.48W
Elton 16 Oe 49.08N 46.50 E
Elton, Ozero- 19 Ef 49.10N 46.40 E
El Torcal 13 Hh 36.55N 4.35W
El Trébol 55 Bk 32.12S 61.42W
El Trigo 55 Cl 35.52S 59.24W
El Triunfo [Hond.] 49 Dg 13.06N 87.00W
El Triunfo [Mex.] 48 Df 23.47N 110.08W
El Tuito 48 Gg 20.19N 105.22W
El Turbio 56 Fh 51.41S 72.05W
Eltville am Rhein 12 Kd 50.02N 8.07 E
Eltz 12 Jd 50.12N 7.18 E
Elūru 25 Ge 17.05N 82.15 E
Elva 7 Gg 58.13N 26.25 E
El Valle 49 Gi 8.31N 80.08W
El Valles/Valles 13 Oc 41.35N 2.15 E
Elvas 13 Ef 38.53N 7.10W
El Vejo, Cerro- 54 Db 7.30N 73.05W
El Venado, Isla- 49 Fh 11.57N 83.44W
El Vendrell/Vendrell 13 Nc 41.13N 1.32 E
Elverum 7 Cf 60.53N 11.34 E
El Viejo 49 Dg 12.40N 87.10W
El Viejo, Volcán 38 Kh 12.38N 87.11W
El Vigia 49 Li 8.38N 71.39W
El Vigia, Cerro- 48 Gg 21.25N 104.00W
El Wak 36 Hb 2.49N 40.56 E
Elwell, Lake- 46 Jb 48.22N 111.17W
Elwood 44 Ee 40.17N 85.50W
Ely [Eng.-U.K.] 9 Ni 52.24N 0.16 E
Ely [Mn.-U.S.] 43 Ib 47.54N 91.51W
Ely [Nv.-U.S.] 39 Hf 39.15N 114.53W
Elyria 44 Fe 41.22N 82.06W
El Yunque 51a Cb 18.18N 65.47W
Elz 12 Kd 50.25N 8.02 E
Elzbach 12 Jd 50.12N 7.22 E
Emaé 63b Dc 17.04S 168.22 E
Ema Jõgi/Emajygi 8 Lf 58.20N 27.15 E
Emajygi/Ema Jõgi 8 Lf 58.20N 27.15 E
Emali 36 Gc 2.05S 37.28 E
Emāmshahr [Iran] 23 Ib 36.25N 55.01 E
Emāmshahr [Iran] 22 Hf 36.50N 54.29 E
Emāmzādeh 'Abbās 24 Lf 32.25N 47.55 E
Emån 7 Dh 57.08N 16.30 E
Emba 19 Ff 48.50N 58.10 E
Emba 5 Lf 46.38N 53.04 E
Embaracai, Rio- 55 Ff 23.27S 53.58W
Embarcación 56 Hb 23.13S 64.06W
Embarras Portage 42 Ge 58.25N 111.27W
Embarras River 45 Mg 38.39N 87.37W
Embira, Rio- 54 De 7.19S 70.15W
Embrun 11 Mj 44.34N 6.30 E
Embu 36 Gc 0.32S 37.27 E
Emden 10 Dc 53.22N 7.13 E
Emeldžak 20 He 58.27N 126.57 E
Emerald 58 Fg 23.32S 148.10 E
Emerald 42 Ga 76.50N 114.00W
Emerson 45 Hb 49.00N 97.12W
Emet 24 Cc 39.20N 29.15 E
Emiliano Zapata 48 Ni 17.45N 91.46W
Emilia-Romagna [2] 14 Ef 44.45N 11.00 E
Emilio R. Coni 55 Cj 30.04S 58.16W
Emili Rock 52 Hh 29.40S 87.25W
Emin/Dorbiljin 27 Db 46.32N 83.39 E
Emine, Nos- 15 Kg 42.42N 27.54 E
Emira Island 60 Dh 1.40S 150.00 E
Emirdağ 24 Dc 39.01N 31.10 E
Emisu, Tarso- 30 If 21.13N 18.32 E
Emlichheim 10 Cd 52.37N 6.51 E
Emmaboda 7 Dh 56.38N 15.32 E
Emmaste 7 Fg 58.43N 22.36 E
Emme 14 Bd 47.10N 7.35 E
Emmeloord, Noordoostpolder- 12 Hb 52.42N 5.44 E
Emmelshausen 12 Jd 50.09N 7.34 E
Emmen 11 Mb 52.47N 6.55 E
Emmendingen 10 Dh 48.08N 7.51 E
Emmen-Emmer-Compascuum 12 Jb 52.49N 7.03 E
Emmen-Klazienaveen 12 Jb 52.44N 7.01 E
Emmen-Nieuw Weerdinge 12 Jb 52.52N 7.01 E
Emmental 14 Bd 46.55N 7.45 E
Emmen-Weerdinge 12 Ib 52.49N 6.57 E
Emmer 12 Lb 52.03N 9.23 E
Emmer-Compascuum, Emmen- 12 Jb 52.49N 7.03 E
Emmerich 10 Ce 51.50N 6.15 E
Emmet 59 Id 24.40S 144.28 E
Emmetsburg 45 Ie 43.07N 94.41W
Emmett 46 Ge 43.52N 116.30W
Emmonak 40 Gd 62.46N 164.30W
Emőd 10 Qi 47.56N 20.49 E
Emory 46 Jf 41.05N 111.16W
Emory Peak 43 Gf 29.13N 103.17W
Empalme 47 Bc 27.58N 110.51W
Empangeni 37 Ee 28.50S 31.48 E
Empedrado 56 Ic 27.57S 58.48W
Emperor Seamounts (EN) 3 Je 40.00N 171.00 E
Empoli 14 Eg 43.43N 10.57 E
Emporia [Ks.-U.S.] 43 Hd 38.24N 96.11W
Emporia [Va.-U.S.] 44 Ig 36.42N 77.33W
Emporium 44 He 41.31N 78.14W
Empress Augusta Bay 63a Bb 6.25S 155.05 E
Empress Mine 37 Dc 18.27S 29.27 E
Ems 11 Na 53.19N 7.03 E
Emsbach 12 Kd 50.24N 8.06 E
Emsdetten 10 Dd 52.11N 7.32 E
Ems-Jade-Kanal 10 Dc 53.19N 7.10 E
Emsland 10 Dd 52.50N 7.20 E
Emstek 12 Kb 52.50N 8.09 E
Emumägi/Emumjagi 8 Lf 58.54N 26.23 E
Emumjagi/Emumägi 8 Lf 58.54N 26.23 E
Ena 29 Ed 35.27N 137.24 E
Enånger 7 Df 61.32N 17.00 E
Enaratoli 26 Kg 3.55S 136.21 E
Enard Bay 9 Hc 58.06N 5.20W
Ena-San 29 Ed 35.26N 137.36 E
Enbetsu 28 Pb 44.44N 141.47 E
Encantada, Cerro de la- 38 Hf 31.00N 115.23W
Encantada, Sierra de la- 48 Hc 28.30N 102.20W
Encantadas, Serra das 55 Fj 30.40S 53.00W
Encantado, Cerro- 47 Bc 27.03N 112.30W
Encarnación 53 Kh 27.20S 55.54W
Encarnación de Diaz 48 Hg 21.31N 102.14W
Enchi 34 Ed 5.49N 2.49W
Encinal 45 Gl 28.02N 99.21W
Encinasola 13 Ff 38.08N 6.52W
Encontrados 54 Db 8.46N 72.30W
Encounter Bay 59 Hg 35.35S 138.45 E
Encrucijada 49 Hb 22.37N 79.52W
Encruzilhada do Sul 55 Fj 30.32S 52.31W
Encs 10 Rh 48.20N 21.08 E
Ende 22 Oj 8.50S 121.39 E
Endeavour Strait 59 Ib 10.50S 142.15 E
Endelave 8 Di 55.45N 10.15 E
Enderbury Atoll 57 Je 3.08S 171.05W
Enderby 46 Fa 50.33N 119.08W
Enderby Land 66 Ee 67.30S 53.00 E
Endicott Mountains 40 Ic 67.50N 152.00W
Ené, Rio- 54 Df 11.09S 74.19W
Energetik 19 Fe 51.44N 58.48 E
Enez 24 Bb 40.44N 26.04 E
Enez Körfezi 15 Ii 40.45N 26.00 E
Enfer, Portes d'- 36 Ed 5.05S 27.30 E
Enfield 44 Ig 36.11N 77.47W
Enfield, London- 12 Bc 51.40N 0.04W
Engadin/Engiadin'ota/Engadina 14 Dd 46.35N 10.00 E
Engadina/Engadin/Engiadin'ota 14 Dd 46.35N 10.00 E
Engaño, Cabo- 47 Ke 18.37N 68.20W
Engaru 28 Qb 44.03N 143.31 E
Engelberg 14 Cd 46.50N 8.24 E
Engelhard 44 Jh 35.31N 76.00W
Engels 6 Ke 51.30N 46.07 E
Engelskirchen 12 Jd 50.59N 7.24 E
Engenho 55 Db 15.10S 56.25W
Enger 12 Kb 52.08N 8.34 E
Engeren 8 Ec 61.35N 12.05 E
Engershatu 35 Fb 16.34N 38.15 E
Enggano, Pulau- 21 Mj 5.24S 102.16 E
Enghien/Edingen 12 Gd 50.42N 4.02 E
Engiadin'ota/Engadina/Engadin 14 Dd 46.35N 10.00 E
England 5 Fe 52.30N 1.30W
England [2] 9 Li 52.30N 1.30W
Englehart 42 Jg 47.49N 79.52W
Englewood 45 Dg 39.39N 104.59W
English 44 Df 38.20N 86.28W
English Channel 5 Fe 50.20N 1.00W
English Coast 66 Qf 73.30S 73.00W
English River 45 Ia 50.12N 95.00W
English River 45 Kb 49.13N 90.58W
Engozero, Ozero- 7 Hd 65.45N 33.30 E
Enguera 13 Lf 38.59N 0.41W
Engure/Engures 8 Jg 57.09N 23.06 E
Engures/Engure 8 Jg 57.09N 23.06 E
Engures, Ozero-/Engures Ezers 8 Jg 57.15N 23.10 E
Engures Ezers/Engures, Ozero- 8 Jg 57.15N 23.10 E
Enh-Gajvan 27 Gb 48.05N 97.35 E
Enid 39 Jf 36.19N 97.48W
Enid Lake 45 Li 34.10N 89.50W
Eniwa 28 Pc 42.53N 141.14 E
Eniwa-Dake 29a Bb 42.47N 141.17 E
Eniwetok Atoll 57 Hc 11.30N 162.15 E
Enkenbach Alsenborn 12 Je 49.29N 7.53 E
Enkhuizen 11 Lb 52.42N 5.17 E
Enklinge 8 Id 60.20N 20.45 E
Enköping 7 Dg 59.38N 17.04 E
Enna 14 Im 37.34N 14.16 E
Ennadai 42 Hd 61.10N 101.00W
Ennadai Lake 42 Hd 60.55N 101.20W
Enné 35 Bc 14.24N 18.45 E
Ennedi 30 Jg 17.15N 22.00 E
Ennell, Lough-/Loch Aininn 9 Fh 53.28N 7.24W
Ennepetal 12 Jc 51.18N 7.21 E
Ennigerloh 12 Kc 51.50N 8.01 E
Enning 45 Ed 44.37N 102.31W
Ennis [Mt.-U.S.] 46 Jd 45.21N 111.44W
Ennis [Tx.-U.S.] 45 Hj 32.20N 96.38W
Ennis/Inis 9 Ei 52.50N 8.59W
Enniscorthy/Inis Córthaidh 9 Gi 52.30N 6.34W
Enniskillen/Inis Ceithleann 9 Fg 54.21N 7.38W
Ennistymon/Inis Díomáin 9 Di 52.57N 9.13W
Enns 14 Ib 48.12N 14.28 E
Enns 5 Hf 48.14N 14.30 E
Enstaler Alpen 14 Ic 47.37N 14.35 E
Eno 7 He 62.48N 30.09 E
Enontiekö 7 Fb 68.23N 23.38 E
Enonvesi [Fin.] 8 Mb 62.10N 28.55 E
Enonvesi [Fin.] 8 Lc 61.20N 26.30 E
Enozero, Ozero- 7 Ib 68.10N 38.00 E
Enrekang 26 Gg 3.34S 119.47 E
Enrique Carbó 55 Ck 33.08S 59.14W
Enriquillo 49 Le 17.54N 71.14W
Enriquillo, Lago- 47 Je 18.27N 71.39W
Enschede 11 Mb 52.12N 6.53 E
Ensenada [Arg.] 55 Dl 34.51S 57.55W
Ensenada [Mex.] 39 Hf 31.52N 116.37W
Enshi 27 Ie 30.16N 109.26 E
Enshū-Nada 29 Ed 34.30N 138.00 E
Entebbe 31 Kh 0.04N 32.28 E
Entenbühl 10 Ig 49.46N 12.24 E
Enterprise [Al.-U.S.] 44 Ej 31.19N 85.51W
Enterprise [N.W.T.-Can.] 42 Fd 60.39N 116.08W
Enterprise [Or.-U.S.] 46 Gd 45.25N 117.17W
Entinas, Punta- 13 Jh 36.41N 2.46W
Entrada, Punta- 47 Ab 30.22N 115.59W
Entraygues-sur-Truyère 11 Ij 44.39N 2.34 E
Entrecasteaux, Récifs d'- 57 Hf 18.20S 163.00 E
Entrepeñas, Embalse de- 13 Jd 40.34N 2.42W
Entre Rios [2] 56 Id 32.00S 59.00W
Entre Rios 54 Fh 21.32S 64.12W
Entre Rios de Minas 55 Je 20.41S 44.04W
Entrevaux 11 Mk 43.57N 6.49 E
Entroncamento 13 De 39.28N 8.28W
Enugu 31 Hh 6.26N 7.29 E
Enugu Ezike 34 Gd 6.59N 7.27 E
Envermeu 12 De 49.54N 1.16 E
Envigado 54 Cb 6.08N 75.39W
Envira 54 De 7.18S 70.13W
Enyamba 36 Dc 3.40S 24.58 E
Enyélé 36 Cb 2.49N 18.06 E
Enz 10 Fh 49.00N 9.10 E
Enza 14 Ef 44.54N 10.31 E
Enzan 28 Og 34.52N 138.44 E
Enzgau 12 Kf 48.48N 8.37 E
Eo 13 Ea 43.28N 7.03W
Eochaill/Youghal 9 Fj 51.57N 7.50W
Eolie o Lipari, Isole-=Lipari Islands (EN) 5 Hh 38.35N 14.55 E
Epanomí 15 Fi 40.26N 22.56 E
Epazote, Cerro- 47 Cd 24.35N 105.07W
Epe [Neth.] 12 Hb 52.21N 5.59 E
Epe [Nig.] 34 Fd 6.35N 3.59 E
Epéna 36 Cb 1.22N 17.29 E
Épernay 11 Je 49.03N 3.57 E
Epe-Vaassen 12 Hb 52.17N 5.58 E
Ephesus (EN)=Efes 15 Kl 37.55N 27.20 E
Ephraim 46 Jg 39.22N 111.35W
Ephrata 46 Fc 47.19N 119.33W
Epi, Île- 57 Hf 16.43S 168.15 E
Epidamnus 15 Ch 41.19N 19.26 E
Epidaurus (EN) = Epidhavros 15 Gl 37.38N 23.09 E
Epidhavros = Epidaurus (EN) 15 Gl 37.38N 23.09 E
Epila 13 Kc 41.36N 1.17W
Épinal 11 Mf 48.11N 6.27 E
Epirus (EN)=Ipiros 5 Ih 39.30N 20.40 E
Epirus (EN)=Ipiros 15 Dj 39.30N 20.40 E
Episkopí 24 Ee 34.40N 32.54 E
Epping 12 Cc 51.42N 0.07 E
Eppingen 12 Ke 49.08N 8.54 E
Epsom 9 Mj 51.20N 0.16W
Epte 11 He 49.04N 1.31 E
Epukiro 37 Bd 21.41S 19.08 E
Epukiro 37 Bd 21.28S 19.59 E
Epulu 36 Eb 1.15N 28.21 E
Eqlīd 23 Hc 30.55N 52.39 E
Équateur=Equator (EN) [2] 36 Eb 1.00N 20.00 E
Equator (EN)=Équateur [2] 36 Eb 1.00N 20.00 E
Equatorial Guinea (EN)=Guinea Ecuatorial [1] 1 Hh 2.00N 9.00 E
Equinox Mountain 44 Kd 43.15N 73.10W
Era [It.] 14 Eg 43.40N 10.38 E
Era [Sud.] 35 Dd 5.30N 29.50 E
Eraclea 14 Kj 40.15N 16.40 E
Eraclea Minoa 14 Hm 37.25N 13.18 E
Eradaka 63b Dc 17.39S 168.08 E
Eräjärvi 8 Kc 61.35N 24.34 E
Eratiní 15 Fk 38.22N 22.14 E
Erbaa 24 Gb 40.42N 36.36 E
Erbach 10 Eg 49.39N 9.00 E
Erbeskopf 10 Dg 49.44N 7.05 E
Erbīl [3] 24 Je 36.10N 44.00 E
Erbīl 22 Gf 36.11N 44.01 E
Ercek 24 Jc 38.39N 43.36 E
Erçek Gölü 24 Jc 38.39N 43.32 E
Erciş 24 Jc 39.00N 43.19 E
Erciyas Daği 21 Ff 38.32N 35.28 E
Ercolano 14 Ij 40.48N 14.21 E
Ercsi 10 Oi 47.15N 18.54 E
Érd 10 Oi 47.22N 18.56 E
Erdaobaihe 27 Mc 42.28N 128.05 E
Erdao Jiang 28 Ic 42.35N 127.10 E
Erdek 24 Bb 40.24N 27.48 E
Erdek Körfezi 24 Bb 40.25N 27.45 E
Erdemli 24 Fd 36.37N 34.18 E
Erdene-Cagan 27 Kb 45.55N 115.30 E
Erdene-Dalaj 27 Hb 46.02N 104.55 E
Erdene-Mandal 27 Hb 48.30N 101.21 E
Erdi 30 Jg 19.05N 22.40 E
Erdi Ma 35 Cb 18.35N 23.30 E
Erding 10 Hh 48.18N 11.56 E
Erdinger Moos 10 Hh 48.20N 11.50 E
Erdre 11 Eg 47.13N 1.32W
Erebus, Mount- 66 Kf 77.32S 167.09 E
Erechim 56 Jc 27.38S 52.17W
Ereğli [Tur.] 23 Db 37.31N 34.04 E
Ereğli [Tur.] 23 Da 41.17N 31.25 E
Erei, Monti- 14 Im 37.35N 14.20 E
Ereke 26 Hg 4.45S 123.10 E
Eren 24 Dd 37.25N 30.05 E
Erenhot 22 Ne 43.35N 112.00 E
Erepecu, Lago do- 54 Gd 1.20S 56.35W
Eresma 13 Hc 41.26N 4.45W
Erétria 15 Gk 38.25N 23.48 E
Erfelek 24 Fb 41.55N 34.57 E
Erfengshan 28 Ag 35.50N 111.47 E
Erfoud 32 Gc 31.26N 4.14W
Erft 10 Ce 51.11N 6.44 E
Erftstadt 12 Id 50.48N 6.49 E
Erfurt 6 He 50.59N 11.02 E
Ergani 24 Hc 38.17N 39.46 E
Ergene 24 Bb 41.01N 26.22 E
Erges 13 Ee 39.40N 7.01W
Ergig, Bahr- 35 Bc 11.22N 15.24 E
Ērgļi/Ergli 7 Fh 56.55N 25.41 E
Ergli/Ērgļi 7 Fh 56.55N 25.41 E
Ergun He 21 Od 53.20N 121.28 E
Ergun Youqi (Labudalin) 27 La 50.16N 120.09 E
Ergun Zuoqi (Genhe) 22 Od 50.47N 121.32 E
Er Hai 27 Hf 25.45N 100.10 E
Eria 13 Gb 42.03N 5.44W
Eriba 35 Fb 16.37N 36.04 E
Eriboll, Loch- 9 Ic 58.30N 4.40W
Eric 42 Kf 51.52N 65.45W
Erice 14 Gl 38.02N 12.35 E
Ericeira 13 Cf 38.59N 9.25W
Erichsen Lake 42 Jb 70.38N 80.20W
Ericht, Loch- 9 Ie 56.50N 4.25W
Erick 45 Gi 35.13N 99.52W
Eridu [3] 24 Lg 36.00N 44.00 E
Erie 39 Ke 42.08N 80.04W
Erie, Lake- 38 Ke 42.15N 81.00W
'Erigābo 35 Hc 10.37N 47.24 E
Erigât 30 Gg 19.40N 4.50W
Erikoússa 15 Cj 39.53N 19.35 E
Eriksdale 45 Ga 50.52N 98.06W
Eriksenstretet 41 Oc 79.00N 26.00 E
Erikub Atoll [5] 57 Id 9.08N 170.02 E
Erimanthos Óros 15 El 37.58N 21.48 E
Erimo-Misaki 27 Pc 41.55N 143.15 E
Eriskay 9 Fd 57.04N 7.13W
Eritrea 30 Kg 15.00N 40.00 E
Eritrea [3] 35 Fb 15.00N 39.00 E
Eritrea 35 Fb 15.00N 40.00 E
Erjas 13 Ee 39.40N 7.01W
Erkelenz 12 Ic 51.05N 6.19 E
Erken 8 He 59.50N 18.35 E
Erkowit 35 Fb 18.46N 37.07 E
Erlangdian→Dawu 28 Ci 31.33N 114.07 E
Erlangen 10 Hg 49.36N 11.01 E
Erlang Shan 27 Hf 29.58N 102.20 E
Erlauf 14 Jb 48.12N 15.11 E
Erldunda 59 Ge 25.14S 133.12 E
Erlenbach 12 Ke 49.07N 8.11 E
Erlong Shan 27 Mc 43.30N 128.44 E
Ermelo [Neth.] 12 Hb 52.19N 5.37 E
Ermelo [S.Afr.] 37 De 26.34S 29.58 E
Ermenek 24 Ed 36.38N 32.54 E
Ermenistan=Armenia (EN) 23 Fb 39.10N 43.00 E
Ermenistan=Armenia (EN) 21 Gf 39.10N 43.00 E
Ermenonville 12 Ee 49.08N 2.42 E
Ermesinde 13 Dc 41.13N 8.33W
Ermoúpolis 15 Hl 37.27N 24.56 E
Erndtebrück 12 Kd 50.59N 8.16 E
Erne/An Éirne 9 Eg 54.30N 8.15W
Ernée 11 Ff 48.18N 0.56W
Ernest Legouvé Reef 57 Lh 35.12S 150.35W
Ernici, Monti- 14 Hi 41.50N 13.20 E
Erode 25 Ff 11.21N 77.44 E
Eromanga 59 Ie 26.40S 143.16 E
Erongoberg 37 Bd 21.40S 15.40 E
Erpengdianzi 28 Hd 41.12N 125.29 E
Errego 37 Fc 16.02S 37.10 E
Errigal/An Ea agail 9 Ef 55.02N 8.07W
Erris Head/Ceann Iorrais 5 Fe 54.19N 10.00W
Erromango, Île- 57 Hf 18.48S 169.05 E
Erseka 15 Di 40.20N 20.41 E
Erstein 11 Nf 48.26N 7.40 E
Ertai 27 Fb 46.02N 90.10 E
Ertil 19 Ee 51.50N 40.51 E
Ertix He 21 Ke 47.52N 84.16 E
Erts 37 De 25.08S 29.55 E
Ertvågøy 8 Ca 63.15N 8.25 E
Eruh 24 Jd 37.46N 42.15 E
Ervânia 55 Ee 21.43S 55.32W
Erve 11 Fg 47.50N 0.20W
Ervy-le-Châtel 11 Jf 48.02N 3.55 E
Erwin 44 Fg 36.09N 82.25W
Erwitte 12 Kc 51.37N 8.21 E
Eryuan 27 Gf 26.09N 99.56 E
Erzeni 15 Ch 41.26N 19.27 E
Erzgebirge=Ore Mountains (EN) 5 He 50.30N 13.15 E
Erzin 20 Ef 50.17N 95.10 E
Erzincan 23 Eb 39.44N 39.29 E
Erzurum 22 Gf 39.55N 41.17 E
Esan-Misaki 28 Pd 41.48N 141.12 E
Esashi [Jap.] 28 Pd 41.52N 140.07 E
Esashi [Jap.] 28 Qb 44.56N 142.35 E
Esashi [Jap.] 28 Pe 39.12N 141.09 E
Esbjerg 6 Gd 55.28N 8.27 E
Esbo/Espoo 7 Ff 60.13N 24.40 E
Escalante 46 Jh 37.47N 111.36W
Escalante Desert 46 Ih 37.50N 113.50W
Escalante River 46 Jh 37.17N 110.53W
Escalaplano 14 Dk 39.37N 9.21 E
Escalón 47 Dc 26.45N 104.20W
Escalona 13 Hd 40.10N 4.24W
Escanaba 39 Ke 45.45N 87.04W
Escanaba River 44 Dc 45.47N 87.04W
Escandón, Puerto de- 13 Ld 40.17N 1.00W
Escandorgue 11 Jk 43.46N 3.14 E
Escarpada Point 21 Oh 18.31N 122.13 E
Escarpé, Cap- 63b 20.41S 167.13 E
Escatrón 13 Lc 41.17N 0.19W
Escaut=Schelde (EN) 11 Kc 51.22N 4.15 E
Esch an der Alzette/Esch-sur-Alzette 11 Le 49.30N 5.59 E
Eschkopf 12 Je 49.19N 7.51 E
Esch-sur-Alzette/Esch an der Alzette 11 Le 49.30N 5.59 E
Eschwege 10 Ge 51.11N 10.04 E
Eschweiler 10 Cf 50.49N 6.17 E
Escocesa, Bahía- 49 Md 19.25N 69.45W
Escondida, Punta- 48 Kj 15.49N 97.03W
Escondido 46 Gj 33.07N 117.05W
Escondido, Rio- 49 Fg 12.04N 83.45W
Escravos 34 Gd 5.36N 5.11 E
Escudo, Puerto del- 13 Ia 43.05N 3.50W
Escudo de Veraguas, Isla- 49 Gi 9.06N 81.33W
Escuintla [3] 49 Bf 14.10N 91.00W
Escuintla [Guat.] 47 Ff 14.18N 90.47W
Escuintla [Mex.] 48 Mj 15.20N 92.38W
Escuro, Rio- [Braz.] 55 Ic 17.31S 46.39W
Escuro, Rio- [Braz.] 55 Ha 12.50S 49.28W
Ese 36 Eb 4.04N 26.40 E
Ese-Hajja 20 Ic 67.35N 134.55 E
Eséka 34 He 3.39N 10.46 E
Eşen 24 Cd 36.27N 29.16 E
Esendere 24 Kd 37.46N 44.32 E
Esera 13 Mb 42.06N 0.15 E
Eşfahān [3] 23 Hc 32.50N 51.50 E
Eşfahān=Isfahan (EN) 22 Hf 32.40N 51.38 E
Esfandārān 24 Og 31.52N 52.32 E
Esfarāyen, Reshteh-ye- 24 Qd 36.46N 57.10 E
Esgueva 13 Hc 41.40N 4.43W

Index Symbols

[1] Independent Nation
[2] State, Region
[3] District, County
[4] Municipality
[5] Colony, Dependency
Continent
Physical Region
Historical or Cultural Region
Mount, Mountain
Volcano
Hill
Mountains, Mountain Range
Hills, Escarpment
Plateau, Upland
Pass, Gap
Plain, Lowland
Delta
Salt Flat
Valley, Canyon
Crater, Cave
Karst Features
Depression
Polder
Desert, Dunes
Forest, Woods
Heath, Steppe
Oasis
Cape, Point
Coast, Beach
Cliff
Peninsula
Isthmus
Sandbank
Island
Atoll
Rock, Reef
Islands, Archipelago
Rocks, Reefs
Coral Reef
Well, Spring
Geyser
River, Stream
Waterfall Rapids
River Mouth, Estuary
Lake
Salt Lake
Intermittent Lake
Reservoir
Swamp, Pond
Canal
Glacier
Ice Shelf, Pack Ice
Ocean
Sea
Gulf, Bay
Strait, Fjord
Lagoon
Bank
Seamount
Tablemount
Ridge
Shelf
Basin
Escarpment, Sea Scarp
Fracture
Trench, Abyss
National Park, Reserve
Point of Interest
Recreation Site
Cave, Cavern
Historic Site
Ruins
Wall, Walls
Church, Abbey
Temple
Scientific Station
Airport
Port
Lighthouse
Mine
Tunnel
Dam, Bridge

F

Index Symbols

- [1] Independent Nation
- [2] State, Region
- [3] District, County
- [4] Municipality
- [5] Colony, Dependency
- Continent
- Physical Region
- Historical or Cultural Region
- Mount, Mountain
- Volcano
- Hill
- Mountains, Mountain Range
- Hills, Escarpment
- Plateau, Upland
- Pass, Gap
- Plain, Lowland
- Delta
- Salt Flat
- Valley, Canyon
- Crater, Cave
- Karst Features
- Depression
- Polder
- Desert, Dunes
- Forest, Woods
- Heath, Steppe
- Oasis
- Cape, Point
- Coast, Beach
- Cliff
- Peninsula
- Isthmus
- Sandbank
- Island
- Atoll
- Rock, Reef
- Islands, Archipelago
- Rocks, Reefs
- Coral Reef
- Well, Spring
- Geyser
- River, Stream
- Waterfall Rapids
- River Mouth, Estuary
- Lake
- Salt Lake
- Intermittent Lake
- Reservoir
- Swamp, Pond
- Canal
- Glacier
- Ice Shelf, Pack Ice
- Ocean
- Sea
- Gulf, Bay
- Strait, Fjord
- Lagoon
- Bank
- Seamount
- Tablemount
- Ridge
- Shelf
- Basin
- Escarpment, Sea Scarp
- Fracture
- Trench, Abyss
- National Park, Reserve
- Point of Interest
- Recreation Site
- Cave, Cavern
- Historic Site
- Ruins
- Wall, Walls
- Church, Abbey
- Temple
- Scientific Station
- Airport
- Port
- Lighthouse
- Mine
- Tunnel
- Dam, Bridge

Farīd, Qarāt al- 24 Ch 28.43N 28.21 E
Faridpur 25 Hd 23.36N 89.50 E
Fārila 7 Df 61.48N 15.51 E
Farilhões, Ilhas- 13 Ce 39.28N 9.34W
Farim 34 Bc 12.29N 15.13W
Farini d'Olmo 14 Df 44.43N 9.34 E
Fāris 24 Ej 24.37N 32.54 E
Fariš 18 Fd 40.33N 66.52 E
Fāris 35 Ia 20.11N 50.56 E
Faris Seamount (EN) 40 Jf 54.30N 147.15W
Färjestaden 7 Dh 56.39N 16.27 E
Farkadhón 15 Fj 39.36N 22.04 E
Farmahīn 24 Me 34.30N 49.41 E
Farmakonisi 15 Kl 37.18N 27.08 E
Farmerville 45 Jj 32.47N 92.24W
Farmington [Me.-U.S.] 44 Lc 44.40N 70.09W
Farmington [Mo.-U.S.] 45 Kh 37.47N 90.25W
Farmington [N.M.-U.S.] 43 Fd 36.44N 108.12W
Farmville 44 Hg 37.17N 78.25W
Färnäs 8 Fc 61.00N 14.38 E
Farnborough 12 Bc 51.16N 0.44W
Farne Deep 9 Mf 55.30N 0.50W
Farne Islands 9 Lf 55.38N 1.38W
Farnham [Eng.-U.K.] 12 Bc 51.12N 0.48W
Farnham [Que.-Can.] 44 Kc 45.17N 72.59W
Farnham, Mount- 46 Ga 50.29N 116.30W
Fårö 7 Eh 57.55N 19.10 E
Faro 34 Hd 9.21N 12.55 E
Faro [2] 13 Dg 37.12N 8.10W
Faro 6 Fh 37.01N 7.56W
Faro, Punta- 49 Jh 11.07N 74.51W
Faro, Sierra del- 13 Eb 42.37N 7.55W
Faro de Avión 13 Db 42.18N 8.16W
Faro de Chantada 13 Eb 42.37N 7.55W
Farofa, Serra da- 55 Gh 28.00S 50.10W
Farösund 8 Hg 57.55N 19.05 E
Fårösund 7 Eh 57.52N 19.03 E
Farquhar, Cape- 59 Cd 23.35S 113.35 E
Farquhar Group 30 Mj 10.10S 51.10 E
Farrar 9 Id 57.27N 4.35W
Farrāshband 24 Oh 28.53N 52.06 E
Farris 8 Ce 59.05N 10.00 E
Farruch, Cabo- 13 Pe 39.47N 3.21 E
Farrukhābād 25 Fc 27.24N 79.34 E
Fārs 21 Hg 29.00N 53.00 E
Fārs [3] 23 Hd 29.00N 53.00 E
Fārsābād 24 Mc 39.30N 48.05 E
Fársala 15 Fj 39.18N 22.23 E
Farshūț 24 Ei 26.03N 32.09 E
Farsø 8 Ch 56.47N 9.21 E
Farsund 7 Bg 58.05N 6.48 E
Fartak, Ra's- 23 Hf 15.38N 52.15 E
Fartura, Rio- 55 Gc 16.29S 50.33W
Fartura, Serra da- [Braz.] 55 Hf 23.20S 49.25W
Fartura, Serra da- [Braz.] 55 Fh 26.21S 52.52W
Fārūj 24 Rd 37.14N 58.14 E
Farvel, Kap-/Ūmánarssuaq 67 Nb 59.50N 43.50W
Farwell Island 66 Pf 72.49S 91.10W
Fāryāb [3] 23 Jb 36.00N 65.00 E
Fasā 24 Oh 28.56N 53.42 E
Fasano 14 Lj 40.50N 17.22 E
Fastnet Rock 9 Dj 51.24N 9.35W
Fastov 19 De 50.06N 30.01 E
Fataka Island 57 If 11.55S 170.12 E
Fatala 34 Cc 10.13N 14.00W
Fatehpur 25 Ec 28.01N 74.58 E
Fatež 16 Ic 52.06N 35.52 E
Father Lake 44 Ja 49.24N 75.18W
Fatick 34 Bc 14.20N 16.25W
Fátima 13 De 39.37N 8.39W
Faṭīrah, Wādī- 24 Ei 26.39N 32.58 E
Fatsa 24 Gb 40.59N 37.24 E
Fatu Hiva, Ile- 57 Nf 10.28S 138.38W
Fatu Hutu, Ile- 57 Ne 9.00S 138.50W
Fatumanini, Passe- 64h Ab 13.14S 176.13W
Fatunda 36 Cc 4.08S 17.13 E
Fauabu 63a Ec 8.34S 160.43 E
Faucigny 11 Mh 46.05N 6.35 E
Faucille, Col de la- 11 Mh 46.22N 6.02 E
Faulkton 45 Gd 45.02N 99.08W
Faulquemont 12 Ie 49.03N 6.36 E
Fauquembergues 12 Ed 50.36N 2.05 E
Făurei 15 Kd 45.04N 27.14 E
Fauro 63a Cb 6.55S 156.07 E
Fauske 7 Dc 67.15N 15.24 E
Fauville-en-Caux 12 Ce 49.39N 0.35 E
Faux-Lap 37 He 25.32S 45.30 E
Fåvang 8 Dc 61.26N 10.13 E
Favara 14 Hm 37.19N 13.39 E
Faversham 12 Cc 51.19N 0.54 E
Favignana 14 Gm 37.55N 12.19 E
Favignana 14 Gm 37.56N 12.20 E
Favorite 12 Kf 48.49N 8.16 E
Fawley 12 Ad 50.49N 1.21W
Fawn 42 Ie 55.22N 88.20W
Fa'w Qiblī 24 Ei 26.07N 32.24 E
Faxaflói 5 Dc 64.24N 23.00W
Faxinal 55 Gf 23.59S 51.22W
Faya-Largeau 31 Ig 17.55N 19.07 E
Fayaoué 63b Ce 20.39S 166.32 E
Fayd 24 Ji 27.07N 42.31 E
Fayette [Al.-U.S.] 44 Di 33.42N 87.50W
Fayette [Oh.-U.S.] 44 Ee 41.41N 84.20W
Fayetteville [Ar.-U.S.] 43 Id 36.04N 94.10W
Fayetteville [N.C.-U.S.] 39 Lf 35.03N 78.54W
Fayetteville [Tn.-U.S.] 44 Dh 35.09N 86.35W
Faylakah, Jazīrat- 24 Mh 29.27N 48.20 E
Faysh Khābūr 24 Jd 37.04N 42.23 E
Fayu Island 57 Gd 8.35N 151.22 E
Fazenda de Cima 55 Db 15.56S 56.37W
Fazenda Nova 55 Gc 16.11S 50.48W
Fāzilka 25 Eb 30.24N 74.02 E
Fazrān 24 Mi 26.13N 49.12 E
Fazzān=Fezzan (EN) 33 Bd 25.30N 14.00 E
Fazzān=Fezzan (EN) 30 If 26.00N 14.00 E
Fdérick 31 Ff 22.39N 12.43W
Feale/An Fhéil 9 Di 52.28N 9.40W
Fear, Cape- 43 Le 33.50N 77.58W
Featherston 62 Fd 41.07S 175.19 E
Feathertop, Mount- 59 Jg 36.54S 147.08 E
Fécamp 11 Ge 49.45N 0.22 E
Fecht 11 Nf 48.11N 7.26 E
Federacion 56 Id 31.00S 57.54W
Federal 56 Id 30.55S 58.45W
Federated States of Micronesia [5] 58 Gd 6.30N 152.00 E
Federovka [Kaz.-U.S.S.R.] 19 Ge 53.38N 62.42 E
Federovka [R.S.F.S.R.] 17 Gj 53.10N 55.10 E
Federsee 10 Fh 48.05N 9.38 E
Fedje 7 Af 60.47N 4.42 E
Fedorovka 16 Qd 51.16N 52.00 E
Fefan 64d Bb 7.21N 151.51 E
Fegen 8 Eg 57.11N 13.09 E
Fegen 8 Eg 57.06N 13.02 E
Fehérgyarmat 10 Si 47.59N 22.31 E
Fehmarn 10 Hb 54.30N 11.10 E
Fehmarnbelt 8 Dj 54.35N 11.15 E
Fehrbellin 10 Id 52.48N 12.46 E
Feicheng 28 Df 36.15N 116.46 E
Feidong (Dianbu) 28 Di 31.53N 117.29 E
Fei Huang He 28 Fg 34.15N 120.17 E
Feijó 54 De 8.09S 70.21W
Feilding 61 Eh 40.12S 175.35 E
Feira 36 Ff 15.37S 30.25 E
Feira de Santana 53 Mg 12.15S 38.57W
Feiran Oasis 24 Eh 28.42N 33.38 E
Feistritz 14 Kc 47.01N 16.08 E
Feixi (Shangpaihe) 28 Di 31.42N 117.09 E
Feixian 28 Dg 35.16N 117.59 E
Feixiang 28 Cf 36.32N 114.47 E
Fejão Prêto ou Furtado, Rio- 55 Dc 17.33S 57.23W
Fejér [2] 10 Oi 47.10N 18.35 E
Fejø 8 Dj 54.55N 11.25 E
Feke 24 Fd 37.53N 35.58 E
Fekete-víz 10 Ok 45.47N 18.13 E
Felanitx 13 Pe 39.28N 3.08 E
Feldbach 14 Jd 46.57N 15.53 E
Feldioara 15 Id 45.49N 25.36 E
Feldkirch 14 Dc 47.14N 9.36 E
Feldkirchen 14 Id 46.43N 14.06 E
Feliciano, Arroyo- 55 Cj 31.06S 59.54W
Felidu Atoll 25a Bb 3.30N 73.30 E
Felipe Carrillo Puerto 47 Ge 19.35N 88.03W
Felix, Cape- 42 Hc 69.55N 97.47W
Felixlândia 55 Jd 18.47S 44.55W
Felixstowe 9 Oj 51.58N 1.20 E
Felletin 11 Ii 45.53N 2.11 E
Feltre 14 Fd 46.01N 11.54 E
Femer Bælt 8 Dj 54.35N 11.15 E
Femø 8 Dj 54.55N 11.35 E
Femund 7 Ce 62.15N 11.50 E
Fena Valley Reservoir 64c Bb 13.20N 144.45 E
Fener Burnu 24 Hb 41.07N 39.25 E
Fénérive 37 Hc 17.22S 49.25 E
Fenerwa 35 Fc 13.05N 39.01 E
Fénétrange 12 Jf 48.51N 7.01 E
Fengcheng [China] 27 Lc 40.28N 124.01 E
Fengcheng [China] 28 Cj 28.11N 115.47 E
Fengdu 27 If 29.58N 107.39 E
Fenghua 28 Fj 29.40N 121.24 E
Fengjie 27 He 31.06N 109.30 E
Fenglingdu 27 Je 34.40N 110.19 E
Fengnan (Xugezhuang) 28 Ee 39.34N 118.05 E
Fengning (Dagezhen) 28 Dd 41.12N 116.39 E
Fengqing 27 Gg 24.41N 99.53 E
Fengqiu 28 Cg 35.02N 114.24 E
Fengrun 28 Ee 39.50N 118.09 E
Fengshui Shan 27 La 52.15N 123.30 E
Fengtai [China] 28 Dh 32.43N 116.43 E
Fengtai [China] 28 De 39.51N 116.17 E
Fengweiba → Zhenkang 27 Gg 23.54N 99.00 E
Fengxian 28 Dg 34.42N 116.35 E
Fengxian (Nanqiao) 28 Fi 30.55N 121.27 E
Fengxiang 27 Ie 34.32N 107.34 E
Fengxiang → Luobei 27 Nb 47.36N 130.58 E
Fengxin 28 Cj 28.42N 115.23 E
Fengyang 28 Dh 32.53N 117.33 E
Fengzhen 27 Jc 40.28N 113.09 E
Fen He [China] 27 Jd 35.36N 110.42 E
Fen He [China] 28 Ae 38.06N 111.52 E
Feni Islands 57 Ge 4.05S 153.42 E
Fennimore 45 Ke 42.59N 90.39W
Fensfjorden 8 Ad 60.50N 4.50 E
Fenshui Guan 27 Kf 27.56N 117.50 E
Fenton 44 Fd 42.48N 83.42W
Fenua Fu 64h Ac 13.23S 176.11W
Fenualoa 63c Bb 10.16S 166.15 E
Fenyang 27 Jd 37.17N 111.45 E
Feodosija 19 Df 45.02N 35.23 E
Fer, Cap de- 32 Ib 37.05N 7.10 E
Fer, Point au- 45 Kl 29.20N 91.21W
Feragen 8 Db 62.30N 11.55 E
Férai 15 Jh 40.54N 26.10 E
Ferdows 23 Ic 34.00N 58.09 E
Fère-Champenoise 11 Jf 48.45N 3.59 E
Fère-en-Tardenois 12 Fe 49.12N 3.31 E
Feren 8 Da 63.34N 11.50 E
Ferentino 14 Hi 41.42N 13.15 E
Ferfer [Eth.] 35 Hd 5.06N 45.09 E
Ferfer [Som.] 35 Hd 5.07N 45.07 E
Fergana 22 Je 40.23N 71.46 E
Fergana 21 Je 40.30N 71.00 E
Ferganskaja Oblast [3] 19 Hg 40.30N 71.20 E
Ferganski Hrebet 19 Hg 41.00N 74.00 E
Fergus Falls 43 Hb 46.17N 96.04W
Ferguson Lake 42 Hc 69.00N 105.00W
Fergusson Island 60 Ei 9.30S 150.40 E
Ferkéssédougou [3] 34 Ed 9.20N 4.55W
Ferkéssédougou 34 Dd 9.36N 5.12W
Ferlo 30 Fg 15.00N 14.00W
Ferlo 30 Fg 15.42N 15.30W
Fermo 14 Hg 43.09N 13.43 E
Fermoselle 13 Fc 41.19N 6.23W
Fermoy/Mainistir Fhear Mai 9 Ei 52.08N 8.16W
Fernandina, Isla- 52 Gf 0.25S 91.30W
Fernandina Beach 44 Gj 30.40N 81.27W
Fernando de Noronha, Ilha- 52 Mf 3.51S 32.25W
Fernando de Noronha, Território de- [2] 54 Ld 3.50S 33.00W
Fernandópolis 56 Kb 20.16S 50.00W
Fernán-Núñez 13 Hg 37.40N 4.43W
Fernelmont 12 Hd 50.35N 5.02 E
Fernie 46 Hb 49.30N 115.03W
Ferrandina 14 Kj 40.29N 16.27 E
Ferrara 14 Ff 44.50N 11.35 E
Ferrat, Cap- 13 Li 35.54N 0.23W
Ferrato, Capo- 14 Dk 39.18N 9.38 E
Ferré 55 Bl 34.08S 61.08W
Ferré, Cap- 51h Bc 14.28N 60.49W
Ferreira do Alentejo 13 Df 38.03N 8.07W
Ferreñafe 54 Ce 6.38S 79.48W
Ferret, Cap- 11 Ej 44.37N 1.15W
Ferriday 45 Kk 31.38N 91.33W
Ferrières 12 Hd 50.24N 5.36 E
Ferro, Capo- 14 Di 41.09N 9.31 E
Ferro, Rio- 55 Ea 12.27S 54.31W
Ferru, Monte- 14 Cj 40.08N 8.36 E
Ferry, Pointe- 51e Ab 16.17N 61.49W
Fertilia 14 Cj 40.36N 8.17 E
Fertő → Neusiedler See 10 Mi 47.50N 16.45 E
Fès 31 Ge 34.02N 4.59W
Fès [3] 32 Gc 34.00N 5.00W
Feshi 36 Cd 6.07S 18.10 E
Fessenden 45 Gc 47.39N 99.38W
Festieux 12 Fe 49.31N 3.45 E
Festus 45 Kg 38.13N 90.24W
Fetești 15 Ke 44.23N 27.50 E
Fethiye 23 Cb 36.37N 29.07 E
Fethiye Körfezi 24 Cd 36.40N 29.00 E
Fetlar 9 Ma 60.37N 0.52W
Fetsund 7 Cg 59.56N 11.10 E
Feuchtwangen 10 Gg 49.10N 10.20 E
Feuilles, Baie aux- 42 Ke 58.55N 69.15W
Feuilles, Rivière aux- 42 Ke 58.46N 70.05W
Feurs 11 Ki 45.45N 4.14 E
Fevik 8 Cf 58.23N 8.42 E
Feyzābād 22 Jf 37.06N 70.34 E
Fezzan (EN)=Fazzān 33 Bd 25.30N 14.00 E
Fezzan (EN)=Fazzān 30 If 26.00N 14.00 E
Fezzane, Emi- 34 Ha 21.42N 14.15 E
Ffestiniog 9 Ji 52.58N 3.55W
Fiambalá 56 Gc 27.41S 67.38W
Fianarantsoa 31 Lk 21.28S 47.05 E
Fianarantsoa [3] 37 Hd 21.30S 47.05 E
Fianga 35 Bd 9.55N 15.09 E
Fiche 35 Fd 9.48N 38.44 E
Fichtelgebirge 5 He 50.00N 12.00 E
Ficksburg 37 De 28.57S 27.50 E
Fidenza 14 Ef 44.52N 10.03 E
Fieni 15 Id 45.08N 25.25 E
Fier 11 Li 45.56N 5.50 E
Fieri 15 Ci 40.43N 19.34 E
Fife [3] 9 Je 56.05N 3.15W
Fife Ness 9 Ke 56.17N 2.36W
Fiffa 34 Dc 11.27N 9.52W
Fifth Cataract (EN)=Khāmis, Ash Shallāl al- 30 Kg 18.23N 33.47 E
Figalo, Cap- 13 Ki 35.35N 1.12W
Figeac 11 Ij 44.36N 2.02 E
Figeholm 8 Gg 57.22N 16.33 E
Figtree 37 Dd 20.22S 28.20 E
Figueira, Baia da- 55 Dc 16.33S 57.25W
Figueira da Foz 13 Dd 40.09N 8.52W
Figueira de Castelo Rodrigo 13 Ed 40.54N 6.58W
Figueras 13 Ob 42.16N 2.58 E
Figueras/Figueres 13 Ob 42.16N 2.58 E
Figueres 13 Ob 42.16N 2.58 E
Figueres/Figueras 13 Ob 42.16N 2.58 E
Figuig [3] 32 Gc 33.00N 2.01W
Figuig 31 Ge 32.06N 1.14W
Fiherenana 37 Gd 23.19S 43.37 E
Fijāj, Shaṭṭ al- 32 Ic 33.55N 9.10 E
Fiji [1] 58 If 18.00S 178.00 E
Fiji Islands 57 If 18.00S 178.00 E
Fik 35 Gd 8.08N 42.18 E
Filabres, Sierra de los- 13 Jg 37.15N 2.20W
Filabusi 37 Dd 20.32S 29.16 E
Filadélfia 54 Ie 7.21S 47.30W
Filadelfia [C.R.] 49 Eh 10.26N 85.34W
Filadelfia [It.] 14 Kl 38.47N 16.17 E
Filakara 63b Dc 16.49S 168.24 E
Fiľakovo 10 Ph 48.16N 19.50 E
Filamana 34 Dc 10.30N 7.57W
Filatova Gora 8 Mg 57.39N 28.21 E
Filchner Ice Shelf 66 Af 79.00S 40.00W
Filey 9 Mg 54.12N 0.17W
Filiași 15 Ge 44.33N 23.31 E
Filiátai 15 Dj 39.36N 20.29 E
Filiatrá 15 El 37.09N 21.35 E
Filicudi 14 Il 38.35N 14.35 E
Filingué 34 Fc 14.21N 3.19 E
Filiouri 15 Ii 40.57N 25.20 E
Filippiás 15 Dj 39.12N 20.53 E
Filippoi 15 Hh 41.02N 24.20 E
Filippoi = Philippi (EN) 15 Hh 41.02N 24.18 E
Filipstad 7 Dg 59.43N 14.10 E
Fillefjell 8 Cc 61.09N 8.15 E
Filliévres 12 Ed 50.19N 2.10 E
Fillmore 46 Ig 38.58N 112.20W
Fils 10 Fh 48.35N 9.29 E
Filtu 35 Gd 5.06N 40.40 E
Fimaina 15 Jl 37.35N 26.26 E
Fimi 30 Ii 3.01S 16.58 E
Fin [Iran] 24 Pi 27.38N 55.55 E
Fin [Iran] 24 Nf 33.57N 51.24 E
Finale Emilia 14 Ff 44.50N 11.17 E
Finale Ligure 14 Cf 44.10N 8.20 E
Findhorn 9 Jd 57.41N 3.32W
Fındıklı 24 Ib 41.17N 41.09 E
Findlay 43 Kc 41.02N 83.40W
Findlay, Mount- 46 Ga 50.04N 116.28W
Findlay Group 42 Ha 77.15N 104.00W
Fineveke 64h Ab 13.19S 176.12W
Fingoé 37 Ec 15.10S 31.53 E
Finike 24 Dd 36.18N 30.09 E
Finistère [3] 11 Cf 48.20N 4.00W
Finisterre, Cabo de- 5 Fg 42.53N 9.16W
Finisterre Range 59 Ja 5.50S 146.05 E
Finke 58 Eg 25.34S 134.35 E
Finke, Mount- 59 Gf 30.55S 134.02 E
Finke River 57 Eg 27.00S 136.10 E
Finland/Suomi [1] 6 Ic 64.00N 26.00 E
Finland, Gulf of- (EN)= Finski Zaliv 5 Ic 60.00N 27.00 E
Finland, Gulf of- (EN)= Soomenlaht 5 Ic 60.00N 27.00 E
Finland, Gulf of- (EN)= Suomenlahti 5 Ic 60.00N 27.00 E
Finlay 42 Fe 55.59N 123.50W
Finlay Mountains 45 Dk 31.30N 105.35W
Finne 10 He 51.13N 11.19 E
Finngrunden 8 Hc 61.00N 18.19 E
Finnigan, Mount- 59 Jc 15.50S 145.20 E
Finniss, Cape- 59 Gf 33.38S 134.51 E
Finnmark 8 Fc 61.40N 14.45 E
Finnmark [3] 7 Fb 69.50N 24.10 E
Finnmarksvidda 5 Ib 69.30N 24.20 E
Finnøy 8 Ae 59.10N 5.50 E
Finnskogen 8 Ed 60.40N 12.40 E
Finnsnes 7 Eb 69.14N 18.02 E
Finnveden 8 Eh 56.50N 13.40 E
Finote Selam 35 Fc 10.42N 37.12 E
Finschhafen 59 Ja 6.35S 147.50 E
Finse 8 Bd 60.36N 7.30 E
Finski Zaliv=Finland, Gulf of- (EN) 5 Ic 60.00N 27.00 E
Finspång 7 Dg 58.43N 15.47 E
Finstadåa 8 Dc 61.47N 11.10 E
Finsteraarhorn 14 Cd 46.32N 8.08 E
Finsterwalde 10 Je 51.38N 13.43 E
Finström 8 Hd 60.16N 19.50 E
Fiora 14 Fh 42.20N 11.34 E
Fiorenzuola d'Arda 14 Df 44.56N 9.55 E
Firat=Euphrates (EN) 21 Gf 31.00N 47.25 E
Firenze = Florence (EN) 6 Hg 43.46N 11.15 E
Firenzuola 14 Ff 44.07N 11.23 E
Firmat 55 Bk 33.27S 61.29W
Firminópolis 55 Gc 16.40S 50.19W
Firminy 11 Ki 45.23N 4.18 E
Firozābād 25 Fc 27.09N 78.25 E
Firozpur 25 Eb 30.55N 74.36 E
First Cataract (EN)=Aswān, Sadd al- 30 Kf 24.01N 32.52 E
Fīrūzābād 24 Oh 28.50N 52.36 E
Fīrūzābād 24 Pg 31.59N 54.20 E
Fīrūzābād 24 Le 34.09N 46.25 E
Fīrūz Kūk 24 Oe 35.45N 52.47 E
Fischbach 12 Je 49.44N 7.24 E
Fischbacher Alpen 14 Jc 47.25N 15.30 E
Fischland 10 Ib 54.22N 12.25 E
Fish [Nam.] 30 Ik 17.11S 28.08 E
Fish [S.Afr.] 37 Cf 31.14S 20.15 E
Fisher Glacier 66 Ef 73.15S 66.00 E
Fisher Peak 44 Gg 36.33N 80.50W
Fisher Strait 42 Jd 63.00N 84.00W
Fishguard 6 Fe 51.59N 4.59W
Fish River' Canyon 37 Be 27.35S 17.35 E
Fiskárdhon 15 Dk 38.28N 20.35 E
Fiskenaes Bank (EN) 41 Gf 63.18N 52.10W
Fiskenæsset 41 Gf 63.10N 50.45W
Fismes 11 Je 49.18N 3.41 E
Fišt, Gora- 19 Dg 43.57N 39.55 E
Fitchburg 44 Ld 42.35N 71.48W
Fitjar 7 Ag 59.55N 5.20 E
Fito, Mount- 65c Ba 13.55S 171.44W
Fitri, Lac- 35 Bc 12.50N 17.28 E
Fitzcarrald 54 Df 11.49S 71.48W
Fitzgerald [Alta.-Can.] 42 Ge 59.52N 111.40W
Fitzgerald [Ga.-U.S.] 44 Fj 31.43N 83.15W
Fitzroy Crossing 59 Fc 18.11S 125.35 E
Fitzroy River [Austl.] 59 Kc 23.32S 150.52 E
Fitzroy River [Austl.] 57 Df 17.31S 123.35 E
Fitzwilliam Island 44 Gc 45.30N 81.45W
Fiuggi 14 Hi 41.48N 13.13 E
Fiumicino 14 Gi 41.46N 12.14 E
Five Island Harbour 51d Bb 17.06N 61.54W
Fivizzano 14 Ef 44.14N 10.08 E
Fizi 31 Ji 4.18S 28.57 E
Fizuli 19 Eh 39.35N 47.11 E
Fjærlandsfjorden 8 Bc 61.15N 6.40 E
Fjällbacka 8 Df 58.36N 11.17 E
Fjärås 7 Ch 57.26N 12.09 E
Fjerritslev 8 Cg 57.05N 9.16 E
Fjöllum, Jökulsá á- 7a Ca 66.02N 16.27W
Fjugesta 8 Fe 59.10N 14.52 E
Flacq 37a Bb 20.12S 57.43 E
Flade Isblink 41 Kb 81.25N 16.00W
Fladen 8 Dg 57.07N 11.35 E
Fladen 8 Dg 57.10N 11.45 E
Flagler 45 Eg 39.18N 103.04W
Flagstaff 39 Hf 35.12N 111.39W
Flåm 7 Bf 60.50N 7.07 E
Flamborough Head 9 Mg 54.07N 0.04W
Fläming 10 Ie 52.00N 13.00 E
Flaming Gorge Reservoir 46 Kf 41.15N 109.30W
Flamingo 44 Gm 25.09N 80.56W
Flamingo, Teluk- 26 Kh 5.33S 138.00 E
Flanders (EN)=Flandres/Vlaanderen 5 Ge 51.00N 3.20 E
Flanders (EN)=Flandres/Vlaanderen 11 Jc 51.00N 3.20 E
Flanders (EN)=Vlaanderen/Flandres 5 Ge 51.00N 3.20 E
Flanders (EN)=Vlaanderen/Flandres 11 Jc 51.00N 3.20 E
Flanders Plain (EN)= Flandres, Plaine des- 11 Id 50.40N 2.50 E
Flanders Plain (EN)= Vlamse Vlakte 11 Id 50.40N 2.50 E
Flandreau 45 Hd 44.03N 96.36W
Flandres/Vlaanderen= Flanders (EN) 11 Jc 51.00N 3.20 E
Flandres/Vlaanderen= Flanders (EN) 5 Ge 51.00N 3.20 E
Flandres, Plaine des-= Flanders Plain (EN) 11 Id 50.40N 2.50 E
Flannan Isles 9 Fc 58.20N 7.35W
Flåren 8 Fh 57.00N 14.05 E
Flasher 45 Fc 46.27N 101.14W
Fläsjön 7 Dd 64.06N 15.51 E
Flat 40 Hd 62.27N 158.01W
Flatey 7a Ab 65.22N 22.56W
Flateyri 7a Aa 66.03N 23.31W
Flathead Lake 43 Eb 47.52N 114.08W
Flathead Range 46 Ib 48.05N 113.28W
Flathead River 46 Hc 47.22N 114.47W
Flat Point 51b Ab 18.15N 63.05W
Flat River 45 Kh 37.51N 90.31W
Flattery, Cape- 38 Ge 48.23N 124.43W
Flåvatnet 8 Ce 59.20N 8.50 E
Flaxton 45 Eb 48.54N 102.24W
Flaygreen Lake 42 Hf 53.50N 97.20W
Fleckenstein, Château de- 12 Je 49.05N 7.48 E
Fleet 12 Bc 51.17N 0.50W
Fleetwood 9 Jh 53.56N 3.01W
Flekkefjord 7 Bg 58.17N 6.41 E
Flémalle 12 Hd 50.36N 5.29 E
Flemish Bight [Eur.] 11 Dc 51.44N 2.30W
Flemish Bight [U.K.] 9 Pi 52.10N 2.50 E
Flemish Cap (EN) 38 Oe 47.00N 45.00W
Flemsøya 8 Bb 62.40N 6.20 E
Flen 7 Dg 59.04N 16.35 E
Flensborg Fjord 8 Cj 54.50N 9.45 E
Flensburg 6 Ge 54.47N 9.26 E
Flensburger Förde 8 Cj 54.50N 9.45 E
Flers 11 Ff 48.45N 0.34W
Flesberg 8 Ce 59.51N 9.27 E
Fleurance 11 Gk 43.50N 0.40 E
Fleury-sur-Andelle 12 De 49.22N 1.21 E
Fleuve [3] 34 Cb 16.00N 13.50W
Flevoland 12 Hb 52.25N 5.30 E
Flian 8 Ef 58.27N 13.05 E
Flims 14 Dd 46.50N 9.16 E
Flinders Bay 59 Df 34.25S 115.19 E
Flinders Island 57 Fi 40.00S 148.00 E
Flinders Passage 59 Jc 18.50S 149.00 E
Flinders Ranges 57 Eh 31.25S 138.45 E
Flinders Reefs 57 Ff 17.40S 148.30 E
Flinders River 57 Ff 17.36S 140.36 E
Flin Flon 39 Id 54.46N 101.53W
Flint [Mi.-U.S.] 39 Ke 43.01N 83.41W
Flint [Wales-U.K.] 9 Jh 53.15N 3.07W
Flint Hills 45 Hh 37.20N 96.35W
Flint Island 57 Lf 11.26S 151.48W
Flint River 43 Ke 30.52N 84.38W
Flisa 7 Cf 60.37N 12.04 E
Flisa 8 Ed 60.36N 12.01 E
Flisegga 8 Be 59.50N 7.50 E
Flitwick 12 Bb 52.00N 0.29W
Flix 13 Mc 41.14N 0.33 E
Flixecourt 12 Ed 50.01N 2.05 E
Flize 12 Ge 49.42N 4.46 E
Flobecq/Vloesberg 12 Fd 50.44N 3.44 E
Floby 8 Ef 58.08N 13.20 E
Floda [Swe.] 8 Fd 60.26N 14.49 E
Floda [Swe.] 8 Eg 57.48N 12.22 E
Flood Range 66 Nf 76.03S 134.00W
Flora [Il.-U.S.] 45 Lg 38.40N 88.29W
Flora [Nor.] 7 Af 61.36N 5.00 E
Florac 11 Jj 44.19N 3.36 E
Florala 44 Dj 31.00N 86.20W
Florange 12 Ie 49.20N 6.07 E
Florence [Al.-U.S.] 43 Je 34.49N 87.40W
Florence [Ks.-U.S.] 45 Hg 38.15N 96.56W
Florence [Or.-U.S.] 46 Cd 44.01N 124.07W
Florence [S.C.-U.S.] 43 Le 34.12N 79.44W
Florence (EN) = Firenze 6 Hg 43.46N 11.15 E
Florencia [Arg.] 55 Ci 28.02S 59.15W
Florencia [Col.] 53 Ie 1.36N 75.36W
Florencio Sánchez 55 Dk 33.53S 57.24W
Florennes 12 Gd 50.15N 4.37 E
Florentino Ameghino, Embalse- 56 Gf 43.48S 66.25W
Florenville 11 Le 49.42N 5.18 E
Flores [2] 55 Dk 33.35S 56.50W
Flores 30 De 39.26N 31.13W
Flores [Guat.] 49 Ce 16.56N 89.53W
Flores [Guat.] 47 Ge 16.58N 89.50W
Flores, Arroyo de las- 55 Cl 35.36S 59.01W
Flores, Laut-=Flores Sea (EN) 21 Oj 8.00S 121.00 E
Flores, Pulau- 21 Oj 8.30S 121.00 E
Flores Island 46 Bb 49.20N 126.10W
Flores Sea (EN)=Flores, Laut- 21 Oj 8.00S 121.00 E
Floreşty 16 Ff 47.55N 28.18 E
Floriano 53 Lf 6.47S 43.01W
Florianópolis 53 Lh 27.35S 48.34W
Florida 38 Kg 28.00N 82.00W
Florida [Braz.] 55 Ei 29.15S 54.36W
Florida [Cuba] 47 Id 21.32N 78.14W
Florida [U.S.] [2] 43 Kf 28.00N 82.00W
Florida [Ur.] [2] 55 Ek 33.50S 55.55W
Florida [Ur.] 56 Id 34.06S 56.13W
Florida, Estrecho de-= Florida, Straits of- (EN) 38 Kg 24.00N 81.00W
Florida, Straits of- 38 Kg 24.00N 81.00W
Florida, Straits of- (EN)= Florida, Estrecho de- 38 Kg 24.00N 81.00W
Florida Bay 44 Gm 25.00N 80.45W
Floridablanca 54 Db 7.04N 73.06W

Index Symbols

[1] Independent Nation
[2] State, Region
[3] District, County
[4] Municipality
[5] Colony, Dependency
Continent
Physical Region
Historical or Cultural Region
Mount, Mountain
Volcano
Hill
Mountains, Mountain Range
Hills, Escarpment
Plateau, Upland
Pass, Gap
Plain, Lowland
Delta
Salt Flat
Valley, Canyon
Crater, Cave
Karst Features
Depression
Polder
Desert, Dunes
Forest, Woods
Heath, Steppe
Oasis
Cape, Point
Coast, Beach
Cliff
Peninsula
Isthmus
Sandbank
Island
Atoll
Rock, Reef
Islands, Archipelago
Rocks, Reefs
Coral Reef
Well, Spring
Geyser
River, Stream
Waterfall Rapids
River Mouth, Estuary
Lake
Salt Lake
Intermittent Lake
Reservoir
Swamp, Pond
Canal
Glacier
Ice Shelf, Pack Ice
Ocean
Sea
Gulf, Bay
Strait, Fjord
Lagoon
Bank
Seamount
Tablemount
Ridge
Shelf
Basin
Escarpment, Sea Scarp
Fracture
Trench, Abyss
National Park, Reserve
Point of Interest
Recreation Site
Cave, Cavern
Historic Site
Ruins
Wall, Walls
Church, Abbey
Temple
Scientific Station
Airport
Port
Lighthouse
Mine
Tunnel
Dam, Bridge

Index Symbols

- [1] Independent Nation
- [2] State, Region
- [3] District, County
- [4] Municipality
- [5] Colony, Dependency
- Continent
- Physical Region
- Historical or Cultural Region
- Mount, Mountain
- Volcano
- Hill
- Mountains, Mountain Range
- Hills, Escarpment
- Plateau, Upland
- Pass, Gap
- Plain, Lowland
- Delta
- Salt Flat
- Valley, Canyon
- Crater, Cave
- Karst Features
- Depression
- Polder
- Desert, Dunes
- Forest, Woods
- Heath, Steppe
- Oasis
- Cape, Point
- Coast, Beach
- Cliff
- Peninsula
- Isthmus
- Sandbank
- Island
- Atoll
- Rock, Reef
- Islands, Archipelago
- Rocks, Reefs
- Coral Reef
- Well, Spring
- Geyser
- River, Stream
- Waterfall Rapids
- River Mouth, Estuary
- Lake
- Salt Lake
- Intermittent Lake
- Reservoir
- Swamp, Pond
- Canal
- Glacier
- Ice Shelf, Pack Ice
- Ocean
- Sea
- Gulf, Bay
- Strait, Fjord
- Lagoon
- Bank
- Seamount
- Tablemount
- Ridge
- Shelf
- Basin
- Escarpment, Sea Scarp
- Fracture
- Trench, Abyss
- National Park, Reserve
- Point of Interest
- Recreation Site
- Cave, Cavern
- Historic Site
- Ruins
- Wall, Walls
- Church, Abbey
- Temple
- Scientific Station
- Airport
- Port
- Lighthouse
- Mine
- Tunnel
- Dam, Bridge

Friesoythe 10 Dc 53.01N 7.51 E
Frigate Island 51p Cb 12.25N 61.29W
Friggesund 8 Gc 61.54N 16.32 E
Frignano 14 Ef 44.20N 10.50 E
Frindsbury Reef 63a Da 5.00S 159.07 E
Frinnaryd 8 Fg 57.56N 14.49 E
Frinton-on-Sea 12 Dc 51.50N 1.15 E
Frio, Cabo- 52 Lh 22.53S 42.00W
Frio, Rio- 49 Eh 11.08N 84.46W
Frio Draw 45 Ei 34.50N 102.08W
Friona 45 Ei 34.38N 102.43W
Frio River 45 Gl 28.30N 98.10W
Frisco Peak 46 Ig 38.31N 113.14W
Frisian Islands (EN) 5 Ge 54.00N 7.00 E
Fristad 8 Eg 57.50N 13.01 E
Fritsla 8 Eg 57.33N 12.47 E
Fritzlar 10 Fe 51.08N 9.17 E
Friuli 14 Ge 46.00N 13.00 E
Friuli-Venezia Giulia [2] 14 Gd 46.00N 13.00 E
Frobisher Bay 38 Mc 62.30N 66.00W
Frobisher Lake 42 Ge 56.20N 108.20W
Froidchapelle 12 Gd 50.09N 4.20 E
Froissy 12 Ee 49.34N 2.13 E
Frolovo 19 Ef 49.45N 43.39 E
Fromberg 46 Kd 45.23N 108.54W
Frombork 10 Pb 54.22N 19.41 E
Frome 9 Kj 51.14N 2.20W
Frome, Lake- 57 Eh 30.50S 139.50 E
Frondenberg 12 Jc 51.28N 7.46 E
Fronteira 13 Ee 39.03N 7.39W
Fronteiras 54 Je 7.05S 40.37W
Frontera 48 Mh 18.32N 92.38W
Frontera, Punta- 48 Mh 19.36N 92.42W
Fronteras 48 Eb 30.56N 109.31W
Frontignan 11 Jk 43.27N 3.45 E
Frontino, Paramo- 54 Cb 6.28N 76.04W
Front Range 38 If 39.45N 105.45W
Front Royal 44 Hf 38.56N 78.13W
Frosinone 14 Hi 41.38N 13.19 E
Frösö 8 Fa 63.11N 14.32 E
Frostburg 44 Hf 39.39N 78.56W
Frost Glacier 66 Ie 67.05S 129.00 E
Frövi 8 Fe 59.28N 15.22 E
Frøya 7 Be 63.43N 8.42 E
Frøysjøen 8 Ac 61.50N 5.05 E
Frozen Strait 42 Jc 65.50N 84.30W
Fruges 11 Id 50.31N 2.08 E
Frunze [Kirg.-U.S.S.R.] 18 Hd 40.06N 71.45 E
Frunze [Kirg.-U.S.S.R.] 22 Je 42.54N 74.36 E
Frunzovka 15 Mb 47.20N 29.37 E
Fruška Gora 15 Cd 45.10N 19.35 E
Frutal 54 Ih 20.02S 48.55W
Frutigen 14 Bd 46.35N 7.40 E
Fry Canyon 46 Jh 37.38N 110.08W
Frýdek Mistek 10 Og 49.41N 18.22 E
Frylinckspan 37 Ce 26.46S 22.28 E
Ftéri 15 Ej 39.09N 21.33 E
Fua'amotu 65b Ac 21.15S 175.08W
Fua Mulaku Island 25a Bc 0.15S 73.30 E
Fu'an 27 Kf 27.10N 119.44 E
Fu-chien Sheng → Fujian Sheng = Fukien (EN) [2] 27 Kf 26.00N 118.00 E
Fuchskauten 10 Ef 50.40N 8.05 E
Fuchū [Jap.] 29 Cd 34.34N 133.14 E
Fuchū [Jap.] 29 Fd 35.41N 139.28 E
Fuchun-Jiang 28 Fi 30.15N 120.15 E
Fuchunjiang-Shuiku 28 Ej 29.29N 119.31 E
Fucino, Conca del- 14 Hi 42.01N 13.31 E
Fudai 29 Ga 40.01N 141.52 E
Fuding 27 Lf 27.19N 120.08 E
Fuengirola 13 Hh 36.32N 4.37W
Fuente Alto 56 Fd 33.37S 70.35W
Fuente del Maestre 13 Ff 38.32N 6.27W
Fuente-Obejuna 13 Gf 38.16N 5.25W
Fuentesaúco 13 Gc 41.14N 5.30W
Fuentes de Andalucia 13 Gg 37.28N 5.21W
Fuentes de Cantos 13 Ff 38.15N 6.18W
Fuerte 47 Cc 25.54N 109.22W
Fuerte, Isla- 49 Ii 9.23N 76.11W
Fuerte, Sierra del- 48 Hd 27.30N 102.45W
Fuerte Olimpo 56 Ib 21.02S 57.54W
Fuerteventura 30 Ff 28.20N 14.00W
Fuga 26 Hc 18.52N 121.22 E
Fugong 27 Gf 27.03N 98.57 E
Fugou 28 Cg 34.04N 114.23 E
Fugu 27 Jd 39.02N 111.03 E
Fuguo → Zhanhua 28 Ef 37.42N 118.08 E
Fuhai/Burultokay 27 Eb 47.06N 87.23 E
Fuhayrī, Wādī- 23 Hf 16.04N 52.11 E
Fu He 28 Dj 28.36N 116.04 E
Fuji 28 Og 35.09N 138.38 E
Fujian Sheng (Fu-chien Sheng) = Fukien (EN) [2] 27 Kf 26.00N 118.00 E
Fujieda 29 Fd 34.51N 138.15 E
Fuji-Gawa 29 Fd 35.07N 138.38 E
Fujin 27 Nb 47.15N 132.01 E
Fujinomiya 29 Fd 35.12N 138.38 E
Fujioka 29 Fc 36.15N 139.03 E
Fuji-San 21 Pf 35.26N 138.43 E
Fujisawa 29 Fd 35.21N 139.27 E
Fuji-yoshida 29 Fd 35.29N 138.47 E
Fukagawa 27 Pc 43.43N 142.03 E
Fūkah 24 Bg 31.04N 27.55 E
Fukang 27 Ec 44.10N 87.59 E
Fuka-Shima 29 Be 32.43N 131.56 E
Fukiage 29 Bf 31.30N 130.20 E
Fukien (EN) = Fu-chien Sheng → Fujian Sheng [2] 27 Kf 26.00N 118.00 E
Fukien (EN) = Fujian Sheng (Fu-chien Sheng) [2] 27 Kf 26.00N 118.00 E
Fukuchiyama 28 Mg 35.18N 135.07 E
Fukue 28 Jh 32.41N 128.50 E
Fukueichiao 27 Lf 25.19N 121.34 E
Fukue-Jima 28 Jh 32.41N 128.48 E
Fukui 27 Od 36.04N 136.13 E
Fukui Ken [2] 28 Ng 36.00N 136.20 E
Fukuma 29 Be 33.47N 130.28 E
Fukuoka 22 Pf 33.35N 130.24 E
Fukuoka Ken [2] 28 Kh 33.28N 130.45 E
Fukuroi 29 Ed 34.45N 137.54 E
Fukushima [Jap.] 27 Pd 37.45N 140.28 E
Fukushima [Jap.] 27 Pc 41.29N 140.15 E
Fukushima Ken [2] 28 Pf 37.25N 140.10 E
Fukuyama 27 Ne 34.29N 133.22 E
Fūlādī, Kūh-e- 23 Kc 34.38N 67.32 E
Fūlād Mahalleh 24 Od 36.02N 53.44 E
Fulanga 63d Cc 19.08S 178.34W
Fulda 5 Ge 51.25N 9.39 E
Fulda 10 Ff 50.33N 9.40 E
Fuliji 28 Dh 33.47N 116.59 E
Fulin → Hanyuan 27 Hf 29.25N 102.12 E
Fuling 27 If 29.40N 107.21 E
Fullerton 45 Hf 41.22N 97.58W
Fulton [Arg.] 55 Cm 37.25S 58.48W
Fulton [Il.-U.S.] 45 Kf 41.52N 90.11W
Fulton [Ky.-U.S.] 44 Cg 36.30N 88.53W
Fulton [Mo.-U.S.] 45 Kg 38.52N 91.57W
Fulton [N.Y.-U.S.] 44 Id 43.20N 76.26W
Fulufjället 8 Ec 61.33N 12.43 E
Fumaiolo 14 Gg 43.47N 12.04 E
Fumay 11 Kd 50.00N 4.42 E
Fumel 11 Gj 44.30N 0.58 E
Funabasi 28 Og 35.42N 139.59 E
Funabiki 29 Gc 37.26N 140.35 E
Funafuti 58 Ie 8.01S 178.00 E
Funafuti Atoll 57 Ie 8.31S 179.08 E
Funagata 29 Gb 38.42N 140.18 E
Funagata-Yama 29 Gb 38.27N 140.37 E
Funakoshi-Wan 29 Hb 39.25N 142.00 E
Funan 28 Ch 32.38N 115.35 E
Funäsdalen 7 Ce 62.32N 12.33 E
Funchal 31 Fe 32.38N 16.54W
Fundación 54 Da 10.29N 74.12W
Fundão 13 Ed 40.08N 7.30W
Fundy, Bay of- 38 Me 45.00N 66.00W
Funeral Peak 46 Gh 36.08N 116.37W
Fungalei 64h Bb 13.17S 176.07W
Funhalouro 37 Ed 23.05S 34.24 E
Funing [China] 27 Ig 23.39N 105.33 E
Funing [China] 28 Eh 33.48N 119.47 E
Funing [China] 28 Ee 39.56N 119.15 E
Funiu Shan 27 Je 33.40N 112.10 E
Funtua 34 Gc 11.32N 7.19 E
Fuping 28 Ce 38.49N 114.15 E
Fuqing 27 Kf 25.47N 119.24 E
Furancungo 37 Eb 14.54S 33.37 E
Furano 28 Qc 43.21N 142.23 E
Füren 29a Ca 44.17N 142.25 E
Furenai 29a Cb 42.43N 142.15 E
Füren-Ko 29a Db 43.20N 145.20 E
Fürg 24 Ph 28.18N 55.13 E
Fur Jiang 28 Hc 42.37N 125.33 E
Furmanov 7 Jh 57.16N 41.07 E
Furnas, Represa de- 54 Ih 21.20S 45.50W
Furnas, Serra das- 55 Fb 15.45S 53.20W
Furneaux Group 57 Fi 40.10S 148.05 E
Furnes/Veurne 11 Ic 51.04N 2.40 E
Furqlus 24 Ge 34.36N 37.05 E
Furriyānah 32 Ic 34.57N 8.34 E
Fürstenau 12 Jb 52.31N 7.43 E
Fürstenauer Berge 12 Jb 52.35N 7.45 E
Fürstenfeld 14 Kc 47.03N 16.05 E
Fürstenfeldbruck 10 Hh 48.11N 11.15 E
Fürstenlager 12 Ke 49.42N 8.38 E
Fürstenwalde 10 Kd 52.22N 14.04 E
Fürth [Ger.] 10 Gg 49.28N 11.00 E
Fürth [Ger.] 12 Ke 49.39N 8.47 E
Furth im Wald 10 Ig 49.18N 12.51 E
Furubira 29a Bb 43.16N 140.39 E
Furudal 7 Df 61.10N 15.08 E
Furukawa 27 Pd 38.34N 140.58 E
Furusund 8 He 59.40N 18.55 E
Fury and Hecla Strait 42 Jc 69.55N 84.00W
Fushan [China] 27 Ff 30.30N 121.15 E
Fushan [China] 28 Ag 35.58N 111.51 E
Fushë-Arëzi 15 Dg 42.04N 20.02 E
Fushë-Lura 15 Dh 41.48N 20.13 E
Fu Shui 28 Cj 29.52N 115.26 E
Fushun 22 Oe 41.46N 123.56 E
Fusong 27 Mc 42.20N 127.17 E
Füsselberg 12 Je 49.32N 7.14 E
Füssen 10 Gi 47.34N 10.42 E
Futa, Passo della- 14 Ff 44.05N 11.17 E
Futago-Yama 29 Be 33.35N 131.38 E
Futaoi-Jima 29 Bd 34.06N 130.47 E
Futog 15 Cd 45.15N 19.42 E
Futuna, Ile- 57 Jf 14.17S 178.09W
Fuwah 24 Dg 31.12N 30.33 E
Fuxian (Wafangdian) 27 Ld 39.38N 121.59 E
Fuxian Hu 27 Hg 24.30N 102.55 E
Fuxin 22 Oe 41.59N 121.38 E
Fuxin Monggolzu Zizhixian 28 Fc 42.06N 121.46 E
Fuyang 27 Ke 32.47N 115.46 E
Fuyang He 28 Dg 38.14N 116.05 E
Fuyang Zhan 28 Ch 32.56N 115.53 E
Fuyu [China] 27 Lb 45.10N 124.52 E
Fuyu [China] 27 Lb 47.48N 124.26 E
Fuyuan [China] 27 Lc 42.44N 124.57 E
Fuyuan [China] 27 Nb 48.21N 134.18 E
Fuyuan [China] 27 Hf 25.43N 104.20 E
Fuyun/Koktokay 22 Ke 47.13N 89.39 E
Füzesabony 10 Qi 47.45N 20.25 E
Fuzhou [China] 22 Ng 26.10N 119.20 E
Fuzhou [China] 27 Kf 27.58N 116.20 E
Fuzhou He 28 Fe 39.36N 121.35 E
Fyllas Bank (EN) 41 Gf 64.00N 53.00W
Fyn 5 Hd 55.20N 10.30 E
Fyn [2] 8 Di 55.20N 10.30 E
Fyne, Loch- 9 He 56.10N 5.20W
Fyresdal 7 Bg 59.11N 8.06 E
Fyresvatn 8 Ce 59.05N 8.10 E
Fzāra, Gara'et- 14 Bn 36.47N 7.30 E

G

Gaasbeek 12 Gd 50.48N 4.10 E
Gaasterland 12 Hb 52.54N 5.36 E
Gaasterland 12 Hb 52.53N 5.35 E
Gaasterland-Balk 12 Hb 52.54N 5.36 E
Gabaru Reef 64a Bb 7.53N 134.31 E
Gabas 11 Fk 43.46N 0.42W
Gabba' 35 Id 8.02N 50.08 E
Gabbs 46 Gg 38.52N 117.55W
Gabela 31 Ij 10.52S 14.23 E
Gabès, Gulf of-(EN) = Qābis, Khalīj- 30 Ie 34.00N 10.25 E
Gabon 36 Ab 0.25N 9.20 E
Gabon [1] 31 Ii 1.00S 11.45 E
Gaborone 31 Jk 24.40S 25.55 E
Gabras 35 Dc 10.16N 26.14 E
Gabriel Strait 42 Kd 61.50N 65.40W
Gabriel y Galán, Embalse de- 13 Fd 40.15N 6.15W
Gabrovo 15 Ig 42.52N 25.19 E
Gabrovo [2] 15 Ig 42.52N 25.19 E
Gacé 11 Gf 48.48N 0.18 E
Gachsārān 24 Ng 30.12N 50.47 E
Gackle 45 Gc 46.38N 99.09W
Gacko 14 Mg 43.10N 18.32 E
Gadag 25 Fe 15.25N 75.37 E
Gäddede 7 Dd 64.30N 14.09 E
Gadê 27 Ge 34.13N 99.29 E
Gadjač 16 Id 50.22N 34.01 E
Gádor, Sierra de- 13 Jh 36.55N 2.45W
Gadsden 43 Je 34.02N 86.02W
Gadūk, Gardaneh-ye- 24 Oe 35.55N 52.55 E
Gadzi 35 Be 4.47N 16.42 E
Gael Hamkes Bugt 41 Jd 74.00N 22.00W
Găeşti 15 Ie 44.43N 25.19 E
Gaeta 14 Hi 41.12N 13.35 E
Gaeta, Golfo di- 14 Hi 41.05N 13.30 E
Gaferut Island 57 Fd 9.14N 145.23 E
Gaffney 44 Gh 35.05N 81.39W
Gagan 63a Ba 5.14S 154.37 E
Gagarin [R.S.F.S.R.] 19 Dd 55.35N 35.01 E
Gagarin [Uzb.-U.S.S.R.] 18 Gd 40.40N 68.05 E
Gagévésouva, Pointe- 63b Ca 13.04S 166.32 E
Gaggenau 12 Kf 48.48N 8.20 E
Gagnef 7 Df 60.35N 15.04 E
Gagnoa 31 Gh 6.08N 5.56W
Gagnoa [3] 34 Dd 6.03N 6.00W
Gagnon 42 Kf 51.55N 68.10W
Gagra 19 Eg 43.17N 40.15 E
Gahkom 24 Ph 28.12N 55.50 E
Gahkom, Kūh-e- 24 Ph 28.10N 55.57 E
Gaiba, Laguna- 55 Dc 17.45S 57.43W
Gail 14 Hd 46.36N 13.53 E
Gaillac 11 Hk 43.54N 1.55 E
Gaillefontaine 12 De 49.39N 1.37 E
Gaillimh/Galway 6 Fe 53.16N 9.03W
Gaillimh/Galway [2] 9 Eh 53.20N 9.00W
Gaillon 12 De 49.10N 1.20 E
Gailtaler Alpen 14 Gd 46.40N 13.00 E
Gaiman 56 Gf 43.17S 65.29W
Gaineşti 15 Ib 47.25N 25.55 E
Gainesville [Fl.-U.S.] 39 Kg 29.40N 82.20W
Gainesville [Ga.-U.S.] 43 Ke 34.18N 83.50W
Gainesville [Mo.-U.S.] 45 Jh 36.36N 92.26W
Gainesville [Tx.-U.S.] 43 He 33.37N 97.08W
Gainsborough 9 Mh 53.24N 0.46W
Gairdner, Lake- 57 Eh 31.35S 136.00 E
Gairloch 9 Hd 57.43N 5.40W
Gaizina Kalns/Gajzinkalns 8 Kh 56.50N 25.59 E
Gaj 19 Fe 51.31N 58.30 E
Gajny 19 Fc 60.20N 54.15 E
Gajsin 19 Cf 48.50N 29.27 E
Gajvoron 16 Fe 48.22N 29.52 E
Gajzinkalns/Gaizina Kalns 8 Kh 56.50N 25.59 E
Galaasija 18 Ee 39.52N 64.27 E
Gălăbovo 15 Ig 42.08N 25.51 E
Gala Göllü 15 Ji 40.45N 26.12 E
Galaico, Macizo- 13 Eb 42.30N 7.20W
Galán, Cerro- 56 Gc 25.55S 66.52W
Galana 30 Li 3.09S 40.08 E
Galanta 10 Nh 48.12N 17.44 E
Galap 64a Bb 7.38N 134.39 E
Galápagos, Islas-/Colón, Archipiélago de- = Galapagos Islands (EN) 52 Gf 0.30S 90.30W
Galapagos Fracture Zone (EN) 3 Mi 0.00 100.00W
Galapagos Islands (EN) = Colon, Archipiélago de-/ Galápagos, Islas- 52 Gf 0.30S 90.30W
Galapagos Islands (EN) = Galápagos, Islas-/Colón, Archipiélago de- 52 Gf 0.30S 90.30W
Galarza 55 Di 28.06S 56.41W
Galashiels 9 Kf 55.37N 2.49W
Galaţi [2] 15 Kd 45.33N 27.56 E
Galaţi 6 If 45.27N 28.03 E
Galatina 14 Mj 40.10N 18.10 E
Galatone 14 Mj 40.09N 18.04 E
Galatzó 13 Oe 39.38N 2.29 E
Galdar 32 Dd 28.09N 15.39W
Galdhøpiggen 7 Bf 61.37N 8.17 E
Galeana [Mex.] 48 Fb 30.07N 107.38W
Galeana [Mex.] 48 Ie 24.50N 100.04W
Galeh Dār 24 Oi 27.38N 52.42 E
Galela 26 Id 1.50N 127.50 E
Galena [Ak.-U.S.] 40 Hd 64.44N 156.57W
Galena [Il.-U.S.] 45 Ke 42.25N 90.26W
Galeota Point 50 Fg 10.08N 60.59W
Galera, Punta- 56 Fe 39.59S 73.43W
Galera, Rio- 55 Bb 14.25S 60.07W
Galera Point 50 Fg 10.49N 60.55W
Galesburg 43 Ic 40.57N 90.22W
Galga 10 Pi 47.33N 19.43 E
Gal Gaduud [3] 35 Hd 5.00N 47.00 E
Galheirão, Rio- 55 Ja 12.23S 45.05W
Galheiros 55 Ia 13.18S 46.25W
Gali 16 Lh 42.36N 41.42 E
Galič [R.S.F.S.R.] 19 Ed 58.23N 42.21 E
Galič [Ukr.-U.S.S.R.] 16 De 49.06N 24.43 E
Galicea Mare 15 Ge 44.06N 23.18 E
Galicia 5 Fg 43.00N 8.00W
Galicia 13 Eb 43.00N 8.00W
Galicia (EN) = Galicija 5 If 49.50N 21.00 E
Galicia (EN) = Galicija [Eur.] 10 Qg 49.50N 21.00 E
Galicia (EN) = Galicja 10 Qg 49.50N 21.00 E
Galicia (EN) = Galicja 5 If 49.50N 21.00 E
Galicija [Eur.] = Galicia (EN) 10 Qg 49.50N 21.00 E
Galicija [Ukr.-U.S.S.R.] 10 Jg 49.00N 24.00 E
Galicija = Galicia (EN) 5 If 49.50N 21.00 E
Galicja = Galicia (EN) 5 If 49.50N 21.00 E
Galicja = Galicia (EN) 10 Qg 49.50N 21.00 E
Galilee, Lake- 59 Jd 22.20S 145.55 E
Galimy 20 Kd 62.19N 156.00 E
Galina Point 49 Id 18.24N 76.53W
Galion 44 Fe 40.44N 82.46W
Galion, Baie du- 51h Bb 14.44N 60.57W
Galiton 14 Cm 37.30N 8.52 E
Galiuro Mountains 46 Jj 32.40N 110.20W
Gālka'yo 31 Lh 6.49N 47.23 E
Galkino 17 Ki 55.40N 62.55 E
Gallarate 14 Ce 45.40N 8.47 E
Gallatin 44 Dg 36.24N 86.27W
Gallatin Range 46 Jd 45.15N 111.05W
Gallatin River 46 Jd 45.56N 111.29W
Galle 22 Ki 6.02N 80.13 E
Gállego 13 Lc 41.39N 0.51W
Gallegos, Rio- 52 Jk 51.36S 68.59W
Gallinas, Punta- 52 Id 12.25N 71.40W
Gallinas Peak 45 Di 34.15N 105.45W
Gallipoli 14 Lj 40.03N 17.58 E
Gallipoli Peninsula (EN) = Gelibolu Yarimadası 15 Ji 40.20N 26.30 E
Gallipolis 44 Ff 38.49N 82.14W
Gällivare 6 Ib 67.08N 20.42 E
Galljaaral 18 Fd 40.02N 67.35 E
Gallo 13 Jd 40.48N 2.09W
Gällö 7 De 62.55N 15.14 E
Gallo, Capo- 14 Hl 38.15N 13.19 E
Gallo Mountains 45 Bi 34.00N 108.15W
Galloway 9 If 55.00N 4.25W
Galloway, Mull of- 9 Ig 54.38N 4.50W
Gallup 39 If 35.32N 108.44W
Gallur 13 Kc 41.52N 1.19W
Gallura 14 Dj 41.00N 9.15 E
Galmaarden/Gammerages 12 Fd 50.45N 3.58 E
Galole 36 Hc 1.30S 40.02 E
Galt 44 Gd 43.22N 80.19W
Gal Tardo 35 He 3.37N 45.58 E
Galtasen 8 Eg 57.48N 13.30 E
Galty Mountains/Na Gaibhlte 9 Ei 52.23N 8.11W
Galut 7 Hb 46.43N 100.08 E
Galveston 39 Jg 29.18N 94.48W
Galveston Bay 38 Jg 29.36N 94.57W
Galveston Island 45 Il 29.13N 94.55W
Gálvez 56 Hd 32.02S 61.13W
Galway/Gaillimh [2] 9 Eh 53.20N 9.00W
Galway/Gaillimh 6 Fe 53.16N 9.03W
Galway Bay/Cuan na Gaillimhe 5 Fe 53.10N 9.15W
Gamaches 12 De 49.59N 1.33 E
Gamagōri 29 Ed 34.49N 137.13 E
Gamarra 54 Db 8.19N 73.44W
Gamba [China] 27 Ef 28.17N 88.31 E
Gamba [Gabon] 36 Ac 2.37S 10.00 E
Gambaga 34 Ec 10.32N 0.26W
Gambela 31 Kh 8.15N 34.36 E
Gambell 40 Ed 63.46N 171.46W
Gambia 30 Fg 13.28N 16.34W
Gambia [1] 31 Fg 13.25N 16.00W
Gambie 34 Bc 13.28N 16.34W
Gambier, Iles- = Gambier Islands (EN) 57 Ng 23.09S 134.58W
Gambier Islands (EN) = Gambier, Iles- 57 Ng 23.09S 134.58W
Gambo 35 Ce 4.39N 22.16 E
Gamboma 36 Cc 1.53S 15.51 E
Gamboula 35 Be 4.08N 15.09 E
Gamda → Zamtang 27 He 32.23N 101.05 E
Gamelão 55 Db 15.29S 57.50W
Gamkonora, Gunung- 26 If 1.21N 127.31 E
Gamlakarleby/Kokkola 6 Ic 63.50N 23.07 E
Gamla Uppsala 8 Ge 59.54N 17.38 E
Gamleby 7 Dh 57.54N 16.24 E
Gamo Gofa [3] 35 Fd 5.45N 37.20 E
Gamua 64h Bb 13.15S 176.08W
Gamud 35 Fe 4.05N 38.06 E
Gamvik 7 Ga 71.03N 28.14 E
Ganāne, Webi- = Juba (EN) 30 Lh 0.15S 42.38 E
Gananoque 44 Ic 44.20N 76.10W
Ganāveh 24 Nh 29.32N 50.31 E
Gancedo 55 Bh 27.30S 61.42W
Gancevići 16 Ec 52.45N 26.29 E
Gand/Gent = Ghent (EN) 11 Jc 51.03N 3.43 E
Ganda 36 Be 12.59S 14.40 E
Gandadiwata, Bulu- 26 Gg 2.42S 119.27 E
Gandajika 36 Dd 6.45S 23.57 E
Gandak 25 Hc 25.39N 85.13 E
Gander 39 Ne 48.57N 54.34W
Ganderkesee 12 Ka 53.04N 8.33 E
Gandesa 13 Mc 41.03N 0.26 E
Gāndhinagar 22 Jg 23.21N 72.40 E
Gāndhi Sāgar 25 Fd 24.30N 75.30 E
Gandia 13 Lf 38.58N 0.11W
Gandia-Grao de Gandia 13 Lf 38.59N 0.09W
Gandisê Shan 21 Kf 31.00N 83.00 E
Gandu 54 Kf 13.45S 39.30W
Ganetti 35 Eb 17.58N 31.13 E
Ganga = Ganges (EN) 21 Lg 23.20N 90.30 E
Gangaw 25 Id 22.10N 94.08 E
Gangca (Shaliuhe) 27 Hd 37.30N 100.14 E
Ganges 11 Jk 43.56N 3.42 E
Ganges (EN) = Ganga 21 Lg 23.20N 90.30 E
Ganges, Mouths of the- (EN) 21 Lg 23.20N 90.30 E
Gangi 14 Im 37.48N 14.12 E
Gango 36 Cd 9.48S 15.40 E
Gangtok 22 Kg 27.20N 88.37 E
Gangu 27 Ie 34.45N 105.12 E
Gangziyao 28 Cf 36.17N 114.06 E
Gan He 27 Mb 49.12N 125.14 E
Ganhe 27 La 50.43N 123.00 E
Gani 26 Ig 0.47S 128.13 E
Ganjgah 24 Md 37.42N 48.16 E
Gan Jiang 21 Ng 29.12N 116.00 E
Ganjig → Horqin Zuoyi Houqi 27 Lc 42.57N 122.14 E
Gannan 27 Lb 47.53N 123.26 E
Gannat 11 Jh 46.06N 3.12 E
Gannett Peak 38 Ie 43.10N 109.40W
Gansbaai 37 Bf 34.35S 19.22 E
Gansu Sheng (Kan-su Sheng) = Kansu (EN) [2] 27 Hd 38.00N 102.00 E
Ganta 34 Dd 7.14N 8.59W
Gantang → Taiping 28 Ei 30.18N 118.07 E
Ganyu (Qingkou) 28 Eg 34.50N 119.07 E
Ganzhou 22 Ng 25.49N 114.56 E
Gao [3] 34 Eb 18.15N 1.00W
Gao [Mali] 31 Hg 16.15N 0.01 E
Gao [Niger] 34 Gb 15.25N 5.45 E
Gao'an 27 Kf 28.27N 115.24 E
Gaobeidian → Xincheng 28 Ce 39.20N 115.50 E
Gaocheng 28 Ce 38.02N 114.50 E
Gaolan (Shidongsi) 27 Hd 36.23N 103.55 E
Gaoliangjian → Hongze 27 Ke 33.10N 119.58 E
Gaoligong Shan 27 Gf 25.45N 98.45 E
Gaolou Ling 27 Ig 24.47N 106.48 E
Gaomi 28 Ef 36.23N 119.45 E
Gaoping 27 Jd 35.46N 112.55 E
Gaoqing (Tianzhen) 28 Df 37.10N 117.50 E
Gaotai 27 Gd 39.20N 99.58 E
Gaotingzhen → Daishan 28 Gi 30.15N 122.13 E
Gaoua 34 Ec 10.20N 3.11W
Gaoual 34 Cc 11.45N 13.12W
Gaoyang 28 Ce 38.42N 115.47 E
Gaoyi 28 Cf 37.37N 114.37 E
Gaoyou 28 Eh 32.46N 119.27 E
Gaoyou Hu 27 Ke 32.50N 119.15 E
Gaozhou 27 Jg 21.56N 110.47 E
Gap 11 Mj 44.34N 6.05 E
Gar 27 Ce 32.12N 79.57 E
Gara, Lough-/Loch Ui Ghadra 9 Eh 53.55N 8.30W
Gara'ad 35 Hd 6.54N 49.20 E
Garabato 55 Bi 28.56S 60.09W
Garachiné 49 Hi 8.04N 78.22W
Garachiné, Punta- 49 Hi 8.06N 78.25W
Gara Dragoman 15 Fg 42.55N 22.56 E
Ga'raet el Oubeira 14 Cn 36.50N 8.23 E
Gara Kostenec 15 Gg 42.18N 23.52 E
Garalo 34 Dc 11.00N 7.26W
Gara Muleta 35 Gd 9.05N 41.43 E
Garanhuns 53 Mf 8.54S 36.29W
Garapan 64b Ba 15.12N 145.43 E
Garapuava 55 Ic 16.06S 46.33W
Garavuti 18 Gf 37.36N 68.29 E
Garba 35 Cd 9.12N 20.30 E
Garbahārrey 35 Ge 3.20N 42.17 E
Garberville 46 Df 40.06N 123.48W
Gārbosh, Kūh-e- 24 Nf 32.36N 50.04 E
Garça 55 Hf 22.14S 49.37W
Garças, Rio das- 55 Fb 15.54S 52.16W
Garcias 55 Fe 20.34S 52.13W
Gard [3] 11 Jj 44.00N 4.00 E
Gard 11 Kk 43.51N 4.37 E
Garda 14 Ee 45.34N 10.42 E
Garda, Lago di- = Garda, Lake- (EN) 5 Hf 45.35N 10.35 E
Garda, Lake- (EN) = Garda, Lago di- 5 Hf 45.35N 10.35 E
Gardabani 16 Ni 41.29N 45.05 E
Garde, Cap de- 14 Bn 36.58N 7.47 E
Gardelegen 10 Hd 52.32N 11.22 E
Garden City [Ga.-U.S.] 44 Gi 32.06N 81.09W
Garden City [Ks.-U.S.] 43 Gd 37.58N 100.53W
Garden Grove 46 Gj 33.46N 117.57W
Garden Peninsula 44 Dc 45.40N 86.35W
Gardermoen 8 Dd 60.13N 11.06 E
Gardey 55 Cm 37.17S 59.21W
Gardēz 23 Kc 33.37N 69.07 E
Gardiner 46 Jd 45.02N 110.42W
Gardiner Range 59 Fc 19.15S 128.50 E
Gardner → Nikumaroro Atoll 57 Je 4.40S 174.32W
Gardner Pinnacles 57 Kb 25.00N 167.55W
Gardno, Jezioro- 10 Nb 54.43N 17.05 E
Gardone Riviera 14 Ee 45.37N 10.34 E
Gardždai/Gargždaj 7 Ei 55.43N 21.24 E
Gareloi 40a Cb 51.47N 178.48W
Garessio 14 Cf 44.12N 8.02 E
Garfagnana 14 Ef 44.05N 10.30 E
Gargaliánoi 15 El 37.04N 21.38 E
Gargano 5 Hg 41.50N 16.00 E
Gargano, Testa del- 14 Ki 41.35N 16.12 E
Gargantua, Cape- 44 Eb 47.36N 85.02W
Gargždai/Gargždai 7 Ei 55.43N 21.24 E
Gari 19 Gd 59.28N 62.25 E
Garibaldi 55 Gi 29.15S 51.32W
Garibaldi, Mount- 46 Db 49.51N 123.01W
Garies 37 Bf 30.30S 18.00 E
Garigliano 14 Hi 41.13N 13.45 E
Garimpo 55 Ed 18.41S 54.50W
Garissa 31 Ki 0.28S 39.38 E

Index Symbols

[1] Independent Nation
[2] State, Region
[3] District, County
[4] Municipality
[5] Colony, Dependency
Continent
Physical Region
Historical or Cultural Region
Mount, Mountain
Volcano
Hill
Mountains, Mountain Range
Hills, Escarpment
Plateau, Upland
Pass, Gap
Plain, Lowland
Delta
Salt Flat
Valley, Canyon
Crater, Cave
Karst Features
Depression
Polder
Desert, Dunes
Forest, Woods
Heath, Steppe
Oasis
Cape, Point
Coast, Beach
Cliff
Peninsula
Isthmus
Sandbank
Island
Atoll
Rock, Reef
Islands, Archipelago
Rocks, Reefs
Coral Reef
Well, Spring
Geyser
River, Stream
Waterfall Rapids
River Mouth, Estuary
Lake
Salt Lake
Intermittent Lake
Reservoir
Swamp, Pond
Canal
Glacier
Ice Shelf, Pack Ice
Ocean
Sea
Gulf, Bay
Strait, Fjord
Lagoon
Bank
Seamount
Tablemount
Ridge
Shelf
Basin
Escarpment, Sea Scarp
Fracture
Trench, Abyss
National Park, Reserve
Point of Interest
Recreation Site
Cave, Cavern
Historic Site
Ruins
Wall, Walls
Church, Abbey
Temple
Scientific Station
Airport
Port
Lighthouse
Mine
Tunnel
Dam, Bridge

Name	Map	Grid	Lat.	Long.
Garkida	34	Hc	10.25N	12.34 E
Garland	45	Hj	32.54N	96.39W
Garlasco	14	Ce	45.12N	8.55 E
Garliava/Garljava	8	Jj	54.46N	23.55 E
Garljava/Garliava	8	Jj	54.46N	23.55 E
Garm	18	He	39.02N	70.18 E
Garmisch-Partenkirchen	10	Hi	47.30N	11.06 E
Garmsar	24	Oe	35.20N	52.13 E
Garnet Bank (EN)	55	Hk	33.05S	49.25W
Garnet Range	46	Ic	46.45N	113.15W
Garnett	45	Ig	38.17N	95.14W
Garonne	5	Ff	45.02N	0.36W
Garonne, Canal latéral à la-	11	Fj	44.34N	0.09W
Garopába	55	Hi	28.04S	48.40W
Garoua	31	Ih	9.18N	13.24 E
Garoua Boulaï	35	Ad	5.53N	14.33 E
Garoubi	34	Fc	13.07N	2.18 E
Garôwe	31	Lh	8.25N	48.33 E
Garpenberg	8	Gd	60.19N	16.12 E
Garphyttan	8	Fe	59.19N	14.56 E
Garrel	12	Kb	52.57N	8.01 E
Garreru	64a	Bc	7.20N	134.33 E
Garri, Kūh-e-	24	Mf	33.59N	48.25 E
Garrigues	11	Kj	44.10N	4.30 E
Garrison	45	Fc	47.40N	101.25W
Garron Point/An Gearran	9	Hf	55.05N	5.58W
Garrovillas	13	Fe	39.43N	6.33W
Garruchos	55	Ei	28.11S	55.39W
Garry	9	Je	56.45N	3.45W
Garry Bay	42	Ic	69.00N	85.10W
Garry Lake	38	Jc	66.00N	100.00W
Garsen	36	Hc	2.16S	40.07 E
Gartar/Qianning	27	He	30.27N	101.29 E
Gartempe	11	Gh	46.47N	0.50 E
Gartog → Markam	27	Gf	29.32N	98.33 E
Garut	26	Eh	7.13S	107.54 E
Garuva	55	Hh	26.01S	48.51W
Garvie Mountains	62	Cf	45.30S	168.50 E
Garwa	25	Gd	24.11N	83.49 E
Garwolin	10	Re	51.54N	21.37 E
Gary	43	Jc	41.36N	87.20W
Garyarsa	27	De	31.40N	80.26 E
Garzê	27	Ge	31.42N	99.58 E
Garzón [Col.]	54	Cc	2.13N	75.38W
Garzón [Ur.]	56	Jd	34.36S	54.33W
Gasan-Kuli	19	Fh	37.29N	53.59 E
Gascogne = Gascony (EN)	11	Gk	43.30N	0.10 E
Gasconade River	45	Kg	38.40N	91.33W
Gascony (EN) = Gascogne	11	Gk	43.30N	0.10 E
Gascoyne Junction	59	De	25.03S	115.12 E
Gascoyne River	57	Cg	24.52S	113.37 E
Gasefjord	41	Je	70.00N	27.30W
Gaseland	41	Jd	70.20N	29.00W
Gash	30	Kg	16.48N	35.51 E
Gas Hu	27	Fd	38.08N	90.45 E
Gashua	31	Ig	12.52N	11.03 E
Gaspar Strait (EN)=Kelasa, Selat-	26	Eg	2.40S	107.15 E
Gaspé	39	Me	48.50N	64.29W
Gaspé, Cap de -	42	Lg	48.45N	64.10W
Gaspé, Péninsule de-= Gaspe Peninsula (EN)	38	Me	48.30N	65.00W
Gaspe Peninsula (EN)= Gaspé, Péninsule de-	38	Me	48.30N	65.00W
Gassan	29	Gb	38.34N	140.01 E
Gassol	34	Hd	8.32N	10.28 E
Gaston, Lake-	44	Ig	36.35N	78.00W
Gastonia	43	Kd	35.16N	81.11W
Gastoúni	15	El	37.51N	21.15 E
Gastre	56	Gf	42.17S	69.14W
Gästrikland	8	Gd	60.30N	16.30 E
Gata, Akrōtērion-	24	Ee	34.34N	33.02 E
Gata, Cabo de-	5	Fh	36.43N	2.12W
Gata, Sierra de-	13	Fd	40.15N	6.45W
Gătaia	15	Ed	45.26N	21.26 E
Gatčina	19	Dd	59.34N	30.09 E
Gate	45	Fh	36.51N	100.01W
Gate City	44	Fg	36.38N	82.37W
Gateshead	9	Lg	54.58N	1.37W
Gateshead	42	Hb	70.35N	100.15W
Gathemo	12	Bf	48.46N	0.58W
Gâtinais	11	If	48.00N	2.20 E
Gâtine, Hauteurs de-	11	Fh	46.38N	0.38W
Gatineau, Rivière-	42	Jg	45.27N	75.42W
Gatlinburg	44	Fh	35.43N	83.31W
Gato, Cumbres del-	48	Fd	27.00N	106.35W
Gattinara	14	Ce	45.37N	8.22 E
Gatún	49	Hi	9.16N	79.55W
Gatún, Lago-=Gatun Lake (EN)	47	Ig	9.12N	79.55W
Gatun Lake (EN)=Gatún, Lago-	47	Ig	9.12N	79.55W
Gatvand	24	Mf	32.15N	48.50 E
Gatwick Airport	12	Bc	51.08N	0.12W
Gaucín	13	Gh	36.31N	5.19W
Gauhati → Guwāhāti	22	Lg	26.11N	91.44 E
Gauiena/Gaujiena	8	Lg	57.25N	26.28 E
Gauja	7	Fh	57.10N	24.16 E
Gaujiena/Gauiena	8	Lg	57.25N	26.28 E
Gaula [Nor.]	8	Da	63.21N	10.14 E
Gaula [Nor.]	8	Ac	61.22N	5.41 E
Gauldalen	8	Db	63.00N	11.00 E
Gauley River	44	Gf	38.10N	81.12W
Gau-Odernheim	12	Ke	49.46N	8.12 E
Gaurdak	19	Gh	37.49N	66.01 E
Gausdal	8	Cc	61.20N	9.55 E
Gausta	7	Bg	59.50N	8.39 E
Gāvbandī	24	Oi	27.12N	53.04 E
Gāvbūs, Kūh-e-	24	Oi	27.10N	54.00 E
Gavdhopoúla	15	Go	34.56N	24.00 E
Gávdhos	5	Ii	34.50N	24.05 E
Gāveh	24	Le	35.00N	46.58 E
Gavere	12	Fd	50.56N	3.40 E
Gavkhūnī, Bātlāq-e-	24	Of	32.06N	52.52 E
Gāv Kosh	24	Le	34.00N	48.00 E
Gävle	6	Hc	60.40N	17.10 E
Gävleborg [2]	7	Df	61.30N	16.15 E
Gävlebukten	8	Gd	60.40N	17.20 E
Gavorrano	14	Eh	42.55N	10.54 E
Gavri	8	Lh	56.49N	27.58 E
Gavrilov-Jam	7	Jh	57.19N	39.51 E
Gāw Koshi	23	Id	28.38N	57.12 E
Gawler	59	Hf	34.37S	138.44 E
Gawler Ranges	57	Eh	32.30S	136.00 E
Gaxun Nur	21	Me	42.25N	101.00 E
Gaya [India]	22	Kg	24.47N	85.00 E
Gaya [Niger]	34	Fc	11.53N	3.27 E
Gaya He	28	Jc	42.58N	129.52 E
Gaylord	44	Ec	45.02N	84.40W
Gayndah	59	Ke	25.37S	151.36 E
Gaz	24	Nf	32.48N	51.37 E
Gaza [3]	37	Ed	23.30S	33.00 E
Gaz-Ačak	19	Gg	41.11N	61.27 E
Gazalkent	18	Gd	41.33N	69.46 E
Gazaoua	34	Gc	13.32N	7.55 E
Gazelle, Récif de la-	63b	Be	20.11S	165.27 E
Gaziantep	22	Ff	37.05N	37.22 E
Gaziemir	15	Kk	38.19N	27.10 E
Gazimağusa = Famagusta (EN)	23	Dc	35.07N	33.57 E
Gazipaşa	24	Ed	36.17N	32.20 E
Gazli	19	Gg	40.09N	63.23 E
Gbarnga	31	Gh	7.00N	9.29W
Gboko	34	Gd	7.21N	8.58 E
Gbon	34	Dd	9.50N	6.27W
Gdańsk [2]	10	Ob	54.25N	18.40 E
Gdańsk=Danzig (EN)	6	He	54.23N	18.40 E
Gdansk, Gulf of- (EN)= Gdanska, Zatoka-	5	He	54.40N	19.15 E
Gdov	7	Gg	58.47N	27.54 E
Gdynia	6	He	54.32N	18.33 E
Gearhart Mountain	46	Ee	42.30N	120.53W
Gêba	34	Bc	11.58N	15.00W
Gebe, Pulau-	26	Ig	0.05S	129.20 E
Gebze	24	Cb	40.48N	29.25 E
Gecha	35	Fd	7.29N	35.25 E
Geçitkale	25	Ee	35.15N	33.45 E
Gedi	36	Hc	3.18S	40.01 E
Gedinne	12	Ge	49.59N	4.56 E
Gediz	24	Cc	39.02N	29.25 E
Gedo	35	Ge	2.20N	41.20 E
Gedo [3]	35	Ge	3.00N	42.00 E
Gedo	35	Fd	9.00N	37.29 E
Gedser, Sydfalster-	7	Ci	54.35N	11.57 E
Gedser Odde	8	Dj	54.34N	11.59 E
Geel	11	Kc	51.10N	5.00 E
Geelong	58	Fh	38.08S	144.21 E
Geelvink Channel	59	Ce	28.30S	114.10 E
Geer	12	Hd	50.51N	5.42 E
Geeste	12	Jb	52.36N	7.16 E
Geesthacht	10	Gc	53.26N	10.22 E
Gê'gyai	27	De	32.29N	80.52 E
Ge Hu	28	Ei	31.36N	119.51 E
Geidam	34	Hc	12.53N	11.56 E
Geigar	35	Ec	11.59N	32.46 E
Geihoku	29	Cd	34.44N	132.17 E
Geikie	42	He	57.48N	103.46W
Geilo	7	Bf	60.31N	8.12 E
Geiranger	8	Bb	62.06N	7.12 E
Geisenheim	12	Je	49.59N	7.58 E
Geislingen an der Steige	10	Fh	48.37N	9.51 E
Geita	36	Fc	2.52S	32.10 E
Geithus	7	Bg	59.57N	9.59 E
Geiyo-Shotō	29	Cd	34.15N	132.45 E
Gejiu	22	Mg	23.22N	103.14 E
Gel [Sud.]	30	Jh	7.46N	29.36 E
Gel [Sud.]	35	Ed	6.08N	31.17 E
Gela	14	Im	37.04N	14.15 E
Gela, Golfo di-	14	Im	37.05N	14.10 E
Geladi	35	Hd	6.57N	46.25 E
Geldenaken/Jodoigne	12	Gd	50.43N	4.52 E
Gelderland [3]	12	Hb	52.10N	5.50 E
Geldermalsen	12	Hc	51.53N	5.19 E
Geldern	10	Ce	51.31N	6.20 E
Geldrop	12	Hc	51.25N	5.33 E
Geleen	11	Ld	50.58N	5.52 E
Gelembe	15	Kj	39.10N	27.50 E
Gelemso	35	Gd	8.48N	40.32 E
Gelendžik	19	Dg	44.33N	38.06 E
Gelengdeng	35	Bc	10.56N	15.32 E
Gelgaudiškis	8	Ji	55.02N	22.58 E
Gelibolu	24	Bb	40.24N	26.40 E
Gelibolu Yarimadası = Gallipoli Peninsula (EN)	15	Ji	40.20N	26.30 E
Gélise	11	Gj	44.11N	0.17 E
Gellinsör	35	Hd	6.24N	46.46 E
Gelnhausen	10	Ff	50.12N	9.11 E
Gelsenkirchen	10	De	51.31N	7.06 E
Gemena	31	Ih	3.15N	19.46 E
Gemerek	24	Gc	39.11N	36.05 E
Gemert	12	Hc	51.33N	5.41 E
Gemi, Jabal-	35	Ed	9.01N	34.09 E
Gemlik	24	Cb	40.26N	29.09 E
Gemlik Körfezi	24	Cb	40.25N	28.55 E
Gemona del Friuli	14	Hd	46.16N	13.09 E
Gemünden (Felda)	12	Ld	50.42N	9.03 E
Gemünden (Wohra)	12	Kd	50.58N	8.58 E
Gemünden am Main	10	Ff	50.03N	9.42 E
Genale	30	Lh	0.15S	42.38 E
Genç	24	Ic	38.46N	40.35 E
Gendringen	12	Ic	51.52N	6.23 E
Gendringen-Ulft	12	Ic	51.54N	6.24 E
Genemuiden	12	Ib	52.37N	6.02 E
General Acha	56	He	37.23S	64.36W
General Alvear [Arg.]	56	Gd	34.58S	67.42W
General Alvear [Arg.]	56	He	36.03S	60.01W
General Arenales	55	Bl	34.18S	61.18W
General Artigas	55	Dh	26.53S	56.17W
General Belgrano	56	Ie	35.46S	58.30W
General Belgrano Station	66	Af	77.50S	38.00W
General Bernardo O'Higgins	66	Re	63.19S	57.54W
General Bravo	48	Je	25.48N	99.10W
General Cabrera	56	Hd	32.48S	63.52W
General Capdevila	55	Bh	27.26S	61.28W
General Carneiro	55	Gh	26.28S	51.25W
General Carrera, Lago-	52	Ij	46.30S	72.00W
General Cepeda	48	Ie	25.23N	101.27W
General Conesa [Arg.]	55	Dm	36.30S	57.20W
General Conesa [Arg.]	56	Hf	40.06S	64.26W
General Enrique Martínez	55	Fk	33.12S	53.50W
General Galarza	55	Ck	32.43S	59.24W
General Güemes	56	Hb	24.40S	65.00W
General Guide	56	Ie	36.40S	57.46W
General José de San Martín	55	Ch	26.33S	59.21W
General Juan Madariaga	56	Ie	37.00S	57.09W
General La Madrid	56	He	37.16S	61.17W
General Lavalle	56	Ie	36.24S	56.58W
General Manuel Belgrano, Cerro-	52	Jh	29.01S	67.49W
General O'Brien	55	Bl	34.54S	60.45W
General Pico	56	He	35.40S	63.44W
General Pinedo	56	Hc	27.19S	61.17W
General Pinto	55	Bl	34.46S	61.53W
General Pirán	55	Dm	37.16S	57.45W
General Roca	56	Ge	39.02S	67.35W
General Salgado	55	Ge	20.39S	50.22W
General Santos	22	Oi	6.05N	125.10 E
General Sarmiento	55	Cl	34.33S	58.43W
General Terán	48	Je	25.16N	99.41W
General-Toševo	15	Lf	43.42N	28.02 E
General Treviño	48	Jd	26.14N	99.29W
General Trias	48	Fc	28.21N	106.22W
General Vargas	55	Ei	29.42S	54.40W
General Viamonte	55	Bl	35.01S	61.01W
General Villegas	56	He	35.02S	63.01W
Genesee River	44	Id	43.16N	77.36W
Geneseo	44	Id	42.46N	77.49W
Geneva [Al.-U.S.]	44	Ej	31.02N	85.52W
Geneva [Nb.-U.S.]	45	Hf	40.32N	97.36W
Geneva [N.Y.-U.S.]	44	Id	42.53N	76.59W
Geneva (EN) = Genève	6	Gf	46.10N	6.10 E
Geneva, Lake- (EN) = Léman, Lac-	5	Gf	46.25N	6.30 E
Genève [2]	14	Ad	46.10N	6.15 E
Genève = Geneva (EN)	6	Gf	46.10N	6.10 E
Genevois	11	Mh	46.00N	6.10 E
Genhe → Ergun Zuoqi	22	Od	50.47N	121.32 E
Geni	35	Ed	8.31N	33.10 E
Geničesk	19	Df	46.12N	34.48 E
Genil	13	Gg	37.42N	5.19W
Genk	11	Ld	50.58N	5.30 E
Genkai-Nada	29	Ae	33.45N	130.00 E
Gennargentu	5	Gg	40.00N	9.20 E
Gennep	12	Hc	51.42N	5.59 E
Genoa (EN) = Genova	6	Gg	44.25N	8.57 E
Genoa, Gulf of- (EN) = Genova, Golfo di-	5	Gg	44.10N	8.55 E
Genova = Genoa (EN)	6	Gg	44.25N	8.57 E
Genova, Golfo di- = Genoa, Gulf of- (EN)	5	Gg	44.10N	8.55 E
Genova-Nervi	14	Df	44.23N	9.02 E
Genova-Voltri	14	Cf	44.26N	8.45 E
Genovesa, Isla-	54a	Ba	0.20N	89.58W
Gent/Gand=Ghent (EN)	11	Jc	51.03N	3.43 E
Gentbrugge, Gent-Gentbrugge	12	Fc	51.03N	3.45 E
Gent-Gentbrugge	12	Fc	51.03N	3.45 E
Genthin	10	Id	52.24N	12.10 E
Gent-Sint-Amandsberg	12	Fc	51.04N	3.45 E
Genü, Kūhhā-ye-	23	Id	27.25N	56.09 E
Genyem	26	Lg	2.46S	140.12 E
Genzano di Lucania	14	Kj	40.51N	16.02 E
Genzano di Roma	14	Fi	41.42N	11.41 E
Geographe Bay	57	Ch	33.35S	115.15 E
Geographe Channel	59	Cd	24.40S	113.20 E
Geographical Society Øer	41	Jd	72.40N	22.20W
Geokčaj	16	Oi	40.40N	47.42 E
Geok-Tepe	19	Fh	38.10N	57.58 E
Geomagnetic Pole (1975) (EN)	66	Hf	78.40S	109.33 E
Georga, Zemlja-	21	Ga	80.30N	49.00 E
George	38	Md	58.30N	66.00W
George	37	Cf	33.58S	22.24 E
George, Lake- [Austl.]	59	Jg	35.05S	149.25 E
George, Lake- [Fl.-U.S.]	44	Gk	29.17N	81.36W
George, Lake- [Ug.]	36	Fc	0.00	30.12 E
George, Lake- [U.S.]	44	Kd	43.35N	73.35W
George Gill Range	59	Gd	24.15S	131.35 E
Georges Bank (EN)	43	Nc	41.15N	67.30W
George Sound	62	Bf	44.50S	167.20 E
George Town	58	Fi	41.06S	146.50 E
Georgetown	45	Hk	30.38N	97.41W
George Town	22	Mi	5.25N	100.20 E
Georgetown [Austl.]	58	Ff	18.18S	143.33 E
Georgetown [Bah.]	49	Jb	23.30N	75.46W
Georgetown [Cay.Is.]	47	He	19.18N	81.23W
Georgetown [De.-U.S.]	44	Jf	38.42N	75.23W
Georgetown [Gam.]	31	Fg	13.32N	14.46W
Georgetown [Guy.]	53	Ke	6.48N	58.10W
Georgetown [Ky.-U.S.]	44	Ef	38.13N	84.33W
Georgetown [Oh.-U.S.]	44	Ff	38.52N	83.54W
Georgetown [S.C.-U.S.]	43	Le	33.23N	79.18W
Georgetown [St.Hel.]	31	Fi	7.56S	14.25W
Georgetown [St.Vin.]	50	Ff	13.16N	61.08W
George V Coast	66	Je	68.30S	147.30 E
George VI Sound	66	Qf	71.00S	68.00W
George West	45	Gl	28.20N	98.07W
Georgia [2]	43	Ke	32.50N	83.15W
Georgia (EN)	5	Kg	42.00N	44.00 E
Georgia, Strait of -	42	Fg	49.00N	123.20W
Georgia del Sur, Islas-/South Georgia	66	Ad	54.15S	36.45W
Georgian Bay	38	Ke	45.15N	80.50W
Georgian SSR (EN) = Gruzinskaja SSR [2]	19	Eg	42.00N	44.00 E
Georgijevka [Kaz.-U.S.S.R.]	19	Hg	43.02N	74.43 E
Georgijevka [Kaz.-U.S.S.R.]	19	If	49.19N	81.35 E
Georgijevsk	16	Mg	44.09N	43.28 E
Georgina River	57	Eg	23.30S	139.47 E
Georgsmarienhütte	10	Ed	52.16N	8.02 E
Gera	10	Ge	51.08N	10.56 E
Gera	10	If	50.52N	12.05 E
Geraardsbergen/Grammont	12	Fd	50.46N	3.52 E
Gerais, Chapadão dos-	55	Jc	17.40S	45.35W
Geral, Serra- [Braz.]	55	Gi	29.10S	50.15W
Geral, Serra- [Braz.]	52	Kh	26.30S	50.30W
Geral, Serra- [Braz.]	55	Gf	23.54S	50.46W
Geral da Serra, Coxilha-	55	Ej	30.20S	55.15W
Geral de Goiás, Serra-	52	Lg	13.00S	46.15W
Geraldine	62	Df	44.05S	171.15 E
Geral do Paraná, Serra-	55	Ib	14.45S	47.30W
Geraldton [Austl.]	58	Cg	28.46S	114.36 E
Geraldton [Ont.-Can.]	42	Ig	49.44N	86.57W
Gérardmer	11	Mf	48.04N	6.53 E
Gerāsh	24	Pi	27.40N	54.06 E
Gerbiči, Gora-	20	Fc	66.39N	105.02 E
Gerca	15	Ja	48.10N	26.17 E
Gercüş	24	Id	37.34N	41.23 E
Gerecse	10	Oi	47.41N	18.29 E
Gerede	24	Eb	40.52N	32.39 E
Gerede	24	Eb	40.48N	32.12 E
Gerês, Serra do-	13	Ec	41.48N	8.00W
Gereshk	23	Jc	31.48N	64.34 E
Gérgal	13	Jg	37.07N	2.33W
Gering	45	Ef	41.50N	103.40W
Gerlachovský štít	10	Qg	49.12N	20.09 E
Gerlogubi	35	Hd	6.56N	45.03 E
Gerlos	14	Gc	47.14N	12.02 E
Gerlovo	15	Kf	43.03N	27.35 E
German Democratic Republic = Germany	6	Ge	51.00N	10.00 E
Germania	55	Al	34.34S	62.03W
Germania Land	41	Kc	76.50N	20.00W
Germany, Federal Republic of = Germany	6	Ge	51.00N	10.00 E
Germencik	15	Kl	37.51N	27.37 E
Germersheim	12	Ke	49.13N	8.22 E
Germī	23	Hc	33.32N	54.58 E
Germi	24	Mc	39.01N	48.03 E
Germiston	37	De	26.15S	28.05 E
Gernsbach	12	Kf	48.46N	8.19 E
Gernsheim	12	Ke	49.45N	8.29 E
Gero	28	Ng	35.48N	137.14 E
Gerolstein	12	Id	50.13N	6.40 E
Gerona [3]	13	Ob	42.10N	2.40 E
Gerona/Girona	13	Oc	41.59N	2.49 E
Gerpinnes	12	Gd	50.20N	4.31 E
Gers	11	Gj	44.09N	0.39 E
Gers [3]	11	Gk	43.40N	0.30 E
Gersprenz	12	Le	49.59N	9.04 E
Gêrzê	27	De	32.20N	84.04 E
Gerze	24	Fb	41.48N	35.12 E
Gescher	12	Jc	51.57N	7.00 E
Geseke	12	Kc	51.39N	8.31 E
Geser	26	Jg	3.53S	130.54 E
Gesunda	8	Fd	60.54N	14.32 E
Gesunden	8	Fa	63.10N	15.55 E
Geta	7	Ef	60.23N	19.50 E
Getafe	13	Id	40.18N	3.43W
Gete	11	Ld	50.55N	5.08 E
Getinge	7	Ch	56.49N	12.44 E
Gettysburg	45	Gd	45.01N	99.57W
Gettysburg Seamount (EN)	32	Eb	36.32N	11.37W
Getúlio Vargas	55	Fh	27.50S	52.16W
Getz Ice Shelf	66	Nf	74.15S	125.00W
Geul	12	Hd	50.40N	5.43 E
Gévaudan	11	Jj	44.27N	3.30 E
Gevelsberg	12	Jc	51.19N	7.20 E
Gevgelija	15	Fh	41.08N	22.31 E
Gévora	13	Ff	38.53N	6.57W
Gevsjön	8	Ea	63.25N	12.40 E
Gewane	35	Gc	10.10N	40.39 E
Gex	11	Mh	46.20N	6.04 E
Gexianzhuang → Qinghe	28	Cf	37.03N	115.39 E
Geyersberg	10	Fg	49.50N	9.30 E
Geyik Dağı	24	Ed	36.54N	32.10 E
Geyikli	15	Jj	39.48N	26.12 E
Geyser, Banc du-	37	Hb	12.25S	46.25 E
Geysir	5	Dc	64.19N	20.18W
Geyve	24	Db	40.30N	30.18 E
Ghabārī, Darb al-	24	Cj	25.10N	29.50 E
Ghadāmis	31	He	30.08N	9.30 E
Ghadduwah	33	Bd	26.26N	14.18 E
Ghaghara	21	Kg	24.52N	84.55 E
Ghaghe	63a	Db	7.23S	158.12 E
Ghallah, Wādī al-	30	Jg	10.25N	27.32 E
Ghamrah, Wādī al-	24	Hj	25.47N	38.45 E
Ghana [1]	31	Gh	8.00N	2.00W
Ghanzi	31	Jk	21.42S	21.38 E
Ghanzi [3]	37	Cd	22.00S	23.00 E
Ghār ad Dimā'	14	Cn	36.27N	8.26 E
Gharaqābād	24	Me	35.06N	49.50 E
Gharbī, Al Hajar al-	24	Qj	24.10N	56.15 E
Gharbīyah, Aş Şaḥrā' al-= Western Desert (EN)	30	Jf	27.30N	28.00 E
Ghardaïa	31	He	32.29N	3.40 E
Ghārib, Jabal-	33	Fd	28.07N	32.54 E
Gharrāf, Shaţţ al-	24	Kf	32.30N	45.48 E
Gharsah, Shaţţ al-	32	Ic	34.06N	7.50 E
Gharyān	33	Bc	32.10N	13.01 E
Gharyān [3]	33	Bc	30.35N	12.00 E
Ghāt	31	If	24.58N	10.11 E
Ghatere	63a	Db	7.58S	159.01 E
Ghaţţī	24	Gg	31.16N	37.31 E
Ghazāl, Baḥr al-	35	Ed	9.31N	30.25 E
Ghazal, Bahr el-	30	Ig	13.01N	15.28 E
Ghazal, Bahr el-	35	Bc	14.00N	16.30 E
Ghazaouet	32	Gb	35.06N	1.51W
Ghazipur	25	Gc	25.35N	83.34 E
Ghaznī	22	If	33.33N	68.26 E
Ghaznī [3]	23	Kc	33.00N	68.00 E
Ghent (EN)=Gand/Gent	11	Jc	51.03N	3.43 E
Ghent (EN)=Gent/Gand	11	Jc	51.03N	3.43 E
Gheorghe Gheorghiu-Dej	15	Jc	46.12N	26.46 E
Gheorghieni	15	Ic	46.43N	25.37 E
Gheorghiu-Dej	19	De	51.00N	39.31 E
Gherla	15	Gb	47.02N	23.55 E
Ghidigeni	15	Kc	46.03N	27.30 E
Ghidole (EN)=Gidole	35	Fd	5.37N	37.29 E
Ghilarza	14	Cj	40.07N	8.50 E
Ghimeş, Pasul-	15	Jc	46.33N	26.07 E
Ghisonaccia	11a	Ba	42.00N	9.24 E
Ghizunabeana Islands	63a	Db	7.33S	158.45 E
Ghowr [3]	23	Jc	34.00N	65.00 E
Ghriss	13	Mi	35.15N	0.10 E
Ghubbat al Qamar	21	Hh	16.00N	52.30 E
Ghudāf, Wādī al-	24	Jf	32.56N	43.30 E
Ghurāb, Jabal al-	24	Hf	34.00N	38.42 E
Ghurayrah	33	Hf	18.37N	42.41 E
Ghūrīān	23	Jc	34.21N	61.30 E
Ghurrah, Jabal al-	14	Cn	36.36N	8.23 E
Ghuzayyil, Sabkhat-	33	Dd	29.50N	19.45 E
Giaginskaja	16	Lg	44.47N	40.05 E
Giala, Jabal-	24	Ei	27.20N	32.57 E
Gialo Oasis (EN)=Jālū, Wāḥāt-	30	Jf	29.00N	21.20 E
Gialoúsa	24	Fe	35.35N	34.15 E
Gia Nghia	25	Lf	11.59N	107.42 E
Giannutri	14	Fh	42.15N	11.05 E
Giant's Causeway/Clochán an Aifir	9	Gf	55.15N	6.35W
Giarre	14	Jm	37.43N	15.11 E
Gibara	49	Ic	21.07N	76.08W
Gibbon Point	51b	Bb	18.14N	63.00W
Gibb River	59	Fc	16.25S	126.25 E
Gibbs Islands	66	Re	61.30S	55.31W
Gibellina	14	Gm	37.47N	12.58 E
Gibeon [3]	37	Bd	25.00S	18.30 E
Gibeon	37	Be	25.09S	17.43 E
Gibostad	7	Db	69.21N	18.00 E
Gibraleón	13	Fg	37.23N	6.58W
Gibraltar	6	Fh	36.11N	5.22W
Gibraltar [5]	6	Fh	36.11N	5.22W
Gibraltar, Estrecho de-= Gibraltar, Strait of- (EN)	5	Fh	35.57N	5.36W
Gibraltar, Strait of- (EN)= Djebel Ţāriq, El Bōghāz-	5	Fh	35.57N	5.36W
Gibraltar, Strait of- (EN)= Gibraltar, Estrecho de-	5	Fh	35.57N	5.36W
Gibson Desert	57	Dg	24.30S	126.00 E
Gidami	35	Ed	8.58N	34.40 E
Giddings	45	Hk	30.11N	96.56W
Gidigič	15	Lb	47.04N	28.38 E
Gidole=Ghidole (EN)	35	Fd	5.37N	37.29 E
Gien	11	Ig	47.42N	2.38 E
Giens, Presqu'île de-	11	Mk	43.02N	6.08 E
Gier	11	Ki	45.35N	4.46 E
Gießen	10	Ef	50.35N	8.39 E
Gieten	12	Ia	53.01N	6.48 E
Giethoorn	12	Ib	52.43N	6.07 E
Gifford	42	Jb	70.21N	83.05W
Gifford Seamount (EN)	52	Hi	39.00S	82.00W
Gifhorn	10	Gd	52.29N	10.33 E
Gift Lake	42	Fe	55.49N	115.57W
Gifu	22	Pf	35.25N	136.45 E
Gifu Ken [2]	28	Ng	35.50N	137.00 E
Gigant	16	Lf	46.29N	41.20 E
Giganta, Cerro-	47	Bc	26.07N	111.36W
Giganta, Sierra de la-	47	Bc	26.18N	111.39W
Gigante	54	Cc	2.24N	75.34W
Gigen	15	Hf	43.42N	24.29 E
Gigha	9	Hf	55.41N	5.44W
Giglio	14	Eh	42.20N	10.55 E
Gijón	6	Fg	43.32N	5.40W
Gikongoro	36	Ec	2.30S	29.35 E
Gila Bend	46	Ij	32.57N	112.43W
Gila Bend Mountains	46	Ij	33.10N	113.10W
Gīlān [3]	23	Gb	37.00N	49.50 E
Gīlān-e-Gharb	24	Ke	34.08N	45.55 E
Gila River	43	Ee	32.43N	114.33W
Gilbert, Mount-	46	Ca	50.51N	124.20W
Gilbert River	59	Ic	16.35S	141.15 E
Gilbert Seamount (EN)	40	If	52.50N	150.10W
Gilbués	54	Ie	9.50S	45.21W
Gilé	37	Fc	16.09S	38.19 E
Giles Meteorological Station	59	Fe	25.02S	128.18 E
Gilford Island	46	Ba	50.45N	126.25W
Gilgandra	59	Jf	31.42S	148.39 E
Gilğau	15	Gb	47.17N	23.43 E
Gilgil	36	Gc	0.30S	36.19 E
Gilgit	25	Ea	35.44N	74.38 E
Gilgit	22	Jf	35.55N	74.18 E
Giljuj	20	Hf	54.17N	127.05 E
Gillam	42	Ie	56.21N	94.43W
Gilleleje	8	Eh	56.07N	12.19 E
Gillen, Lake-	59	Ee	26.10S	124.40 E
Gillenfeld	12	Id	50.07N	6.54 E
Gillette	43	Fc	44.18N	105.30W
Gillian, Lake -	42	Jc	69.30N	75.30W
Gillingham	9	Nj	51.24N	0.33 E
Gilo	35	Ed	8.10N	33.15 E
Gilort	15	Ge	44.36N	23.27 E
Gilroy	46	Eh	37.00N	121.34W
Giluwe, Mount-	60	Ci	6.04S	143.53 E
Gilvān	24	Md	37.00N	49.08 E
Gimån	8	Gb	62.28N	16.20 E
Gimbi	35	Fd	9.10N	35.51 E
Gimie, Mount-	50	Ff	13.52N	61.01W
Gimli	42	Hf	50.39N	97.00W
Gimo	8	Hd	60.11N	18.10 E
Gimolskoje, Ozero-	7	He	63.00N	32.15 E
Gimone	11	Hk	44.00N	1.06 E
Ginda	35	Fb	15.27N	39.06 E
Ginetu	63a	Ac	9.30S	152.43 E

Index Symbols

- [1] Independent Nation
- [2] State, Region
- [3] District, County
- [4] Municipality
- [5] Colony, Dependency
- Continent
- Physical Region
- Historical or Cultural Region
- Mount, Mountain
- Volcano
- Hill
- Mountains, Mountain Range
- Hills, Escarpment
- Plateau, Upland
- Pass, Gap
- Plain, Lowland
- Delta
- Salt Flat
- Valley, Canyon
- Crater, Cave
- Karst Features
- Depression
- Polder
- Desert, Dunes
- Forest, Woods
- Heath, Steppe
- Oasis
- Cape, Point
- Coast, Beach
- Cliff
- Peninsula
- Isthmus
- Sandbank
- Island
- Atoll
- Rock, Reef
- Islands, Archipelago
- Rocks, Reefs
- Coral Reef
- Well, Spring
- Geyser
- River, Stream
- Waterfall Rapids
- River Mouth, Estuary
- Lake
- Salt Lake
- Intermittent Lake
- Reservoir
- Swamp, Pond
- Canal
- Glacier
- Ice Shelf, Pack Ice
- Ocean
- Sea
- Gulf, Bay
- Strait, Fjord
- Lagoon
- Bank
- Seamount
- Tablemount
- Ridge
- Shelf
- Basin
- Escarpment, Sea Scarp
- Fracture
- Trench, Abyss
- National Park, Reserve
- Point of Interest
- Recreation Site
- Cave, Cavern
- Historic Site
- Ruins
- Wall, Walls
- Church, Abbey
- Temple
- Scientific Station
- Airport
- Port
- Lighthouse
- Mine
- Tunnel
- Dam, Bridge

Gin Gin	59	Kd	25.00 S	151.58 E
Gingin	59	Df	31.21 S	115.42 E
Gingoog	26	Ie	8.50N	125.07 E
Ginir	35	Gd	7.08N	40.43 E
Ginosa	14	Kj	40.35N	16.45 E
Ginowan	29b	Ab	26.17N	127.45 E
Ginzo de Limia	13	Eb	42.03N	7.43W
Giofra Oasis (EN)=Jufrah, Wāḩāt al-	30	If	29.10N	16.00 E
Gioia, Golfo di-	14	Jl	38.30N	15.45 E
Gioia del Colle	14	Kj	40.48N	16.55 E
Gioia Tauro	14	Jl	38.25N	15.54 E
Gion	35	Fd	8.24N	37.55 E
Gióna Óros	15	Fk	38.35N	22.15 E
Giovi, Passo dei-	14	Cf	44.33N	8.57 E
Giraltovce	10	Rg	49.07N	21.31 E
Girardot	54	Dc	4.18N	74.49W
Girdle Ness	9	Kd	57.08N	2.02W
Giresun	23	Ea	40.55N	38.24 E
Giresun Dağları	24	Hb	40.40N	38.10 E
Giri	36	Cb	0.28N	17.59 E
Giridih	25	Hd	24.11N	86.18 E
Giriftu	36	Gb	2.00N	39.45 E
Girne	24	Ee	35.20N	33.19 E
Girón	54	Cd	3.10S	79.09W
Girona/Gerona	13	Oc	41.59N	2.49 E
Gironde [3]	11	Fj	44.55N	0.30W
Gironde	5	Ff	45.35N	1.03W
Gironella	13	Nb	42.02N	1.53 E
Girou	11	Hk	43.46N	1.23 E
Girvan	9	If	55.15N	4.51W
Girvas	7	He	62.31N	33.44 E
Gisborne	58	Ih	38.39 S	178.01 E
Gisenyi	36	Ec	1.42 S	29.15 E
Gislaved	8	Eg	57.18N	13.32 E
Gisors	11	He	49.17N	1.47 E
Gissar	18	Ge	38.31N	68.36 E
Gissarski Hrebet	18	Ge	39.00N	68.40 E
Gistad	8	Ff	58.27N	15.55 E
Gistel	12	Ec	51.10N	2.57 E
Gistral	13	Ea	43.28N	7.35W
Gitarama	36	Ec	2.05 S	29.16 E
Gitega	36	Ec	3.26 S	29.56 E
Gitu	24	Me	35.20N	48.05 E
Giudicarie, Valli-	14	Ed	46.00N	10.40 E
Giulianova	14	Hh	42.45N	13.57 E
Giumalău, Vîrful-	15	Ib	47.26N	25.29 E
Giurgeni	15	Ke	44.35N	27.48 E
Giurgiu	15	If	43.53N	25.58 E
Give	8	Ci	55.51N	9.15 E
Givors	11	Ki	45.35N	4.46 E
Givry-en-Argonne	12	Gf	48.57N	4.53 E
Givry Island	64d	Bb	7.07N	151.53 E
Giwa	34	Gc	11.18N	7.27 E
Giza (EN)=Al Jīzah	31	Ke	30.01N	31.13 E
Giždvan	19	Gg	40.06N	64.40 E
Gižiga	20	Ld	62.03N	160.30 E
Gižiginskaja Guba	20	Kd	61.10N	158.30 E
Gizo	63a	Cc	8.07 S	156.50 E
Gizo	60	Fi	8.06 S	156.51 E
Giżycko	10	Rb	54.03N	21.47 E
Gjalicës, Mali i-	15	Dg	42.01N	20.28 E
Gjamyš, Gora-	16	Oi	40.20N	46.25 E
Gjandža	6	Kg	40.40N	46.22 E
Gjerstad	8	Cf	58.52N	9.00 E
Gjevilvatn	8	Cb	62.40N	9.25 E
Gjirokastra	15	Di	40.05N	20.10 E
Gjoa Haven	39	Jc	68.38N	95.57W
Gjøvik	6	Hc	60.48N	10.42 E
Gjuhës, Kep i-	15	Ci	40.25N	19.18 E
Glace Bay	42	Lg	46.12N	59.57W
Glacier Bay	40	Le	58.40N	136.00W
Glacier Peak	43	Cb	48.07N	121.07W
Glacier Strait	42	Ja	76.15N	79.00W
Gladbeck	12	Ic	51.34N	6.59 E
Gladenbach	12	Kd	50.46N	8.34 E
Gladewater	45	Ij	32.33N	94.56W
Gladstone [Austl.]	58	Gg	23.51 S	151.16 E
Gladstone [Man.-Can.]	45	Ga	50.15N	98.50W
Gladstone [Mi.-U.S.]	44	Dc	45.51N	87.03W
Gladstone [Mo.-U.S.]	45	Ig	39.13N	94.34W
Glafsfjorden	8	Ee	59.35N	12.35 E
Glåma	5	Hd	59.12N	10.57 E
Gláma	7a	Ab	65.48N	23.00W
Glamis Castle	9	Ke	56.37N	3.00W
Glamoč	23	Ff	44.03N	16.51 E
Glan	7	Dg	58.35N	15.55 E
Glan [Aus.]	14	Id	46.36N	14.25 E
Glan [Ger.]	10	Dg	49.47N	7.43 E
Glan-Münchweiler	12	Je	49.28N	7.26 E
Glarner Alpen	14	Cd	46.55N	9.00 E
Glärnisch	14	Cd	47.00N	9.00 E
Glarus [2]	14	Dd	46.55N	9.05 E
Glarus	14	Dc	47.03N	9.04 E
Glasgow [Ky.-U.S.]	44	Eg	37.00N	85.55W
Glasgow [Mt.-U.S.]	43	Fb	48.12N	106.38W
Glasgow [Scot.-U.K.]	6	Fd	55.53N	4.15W
Glashütte	10	Jf	50.51N	13.47 E
Glass	9	Id	57.25N	4.30W
Glassboro	44	Jf	39.42N	75.07W
Glass Mountains	45	Ek	30.25N	103.15W
Glastonbury	9	Kj	51.09N	2.43W
Glauchau	10	If	50.49N	12.32 E
Glava	8	Ee	59.33N	12.34 E
Glazov	6	Ld	58.09N	52.40 E
Gleann Dá Loch/ Glendalough	9	Gh	53.00N	6.20W
Gledićske Planine	15	Df	43.49N	20.55 E
Gleinalpe	14	Jc	47.10N	15.05 E
Gleisdorf	14	Jc	47.06N	15.43 E
Glen	12	Bb	52.50N	0.07W
Glénan, Iles de-	11	Cg	47.43N	4.00W
Glen Arbor	44	Ec	44.53N	85.58W
Glenavy	62	Df	44.55 S	171.06 E
Glen Canyon	46	Jh	37.05N	111.41W
Glencoe [Mn.-U.S.]	45	Id	44.46N	94.09W
Glencoe [S.Afr.]	37	Ee	28.12 S	30.07 E
Glendale [Az.-U.S.]	43	Ee	33.32N	112.11W
Glendale [Ca.-U.S.]	43	De	34.10N	118.17W
Glendalough/Gleann Dá Loch	9	Gh	53.00N	6.20W
Glendive	43	Gb	47.06N	104.43W
Glendo Reservoir	46	Me	42.31N	104.58W
Glenhope	61	Dh	41.39 S	172.39 E
Glen Innes	58	Gg	29.44 S	151.44 E
Glennallen	40	Jd	62.07N	145.33W
Glenner	14	Dd	46.46N	9.12 E
Glenns Ferry	46	He	42.57N	115.18W
Glenorchy	62	Cf	44.52 S	168.24 E
Glenrock	46	Me	42.52N	105.52W
Glen Rose	45	Hj	32.14N	97.45W
Glenrothes	9	Je	56.12N	3.05W
Glens Falls	44	Kd	43.17N	73.41W
Glenville	44	Gf	38.57N	80.51W
Glenwood [Ia.-U.S.]	45	If	41.03N	95.45W
Glenwood [Mn.-U.S.]	45	Id	45.39N	95.23W
Glenwood Springs	43	Fd	39.32N	107.19W
Glibokaja	15	Ja	48.05N	26.00 E
Glina	14	Ke	45.20N	16.06 E
Glinjany	10	Ug	49.46N	24.33 E
Glittertinden	5	Gc	61.39N	8.33 E
Gliwice	10	Of	50.17N	18.40 E
Globe	43	Ee	33.24 N	110.47 W
Globino	16	He	49.24N	33.18 E
Głogów	10	Me	51.40N	16.05 E
Glomfjord	7	Cc	66.49N	13.58 E
Glommersträsk	7	Ed	65.16N	19.38 E
Glonn	10	Hh	48.11N	11.45 E
Glorieuses, Iles-	30	Lj	11.30 S	47.20 E
Glottof, Mount-	40	Ie	57.30N	153.30W
Gloucester	9	Kj	51.55N	2.15W
Gloucester [Eng.-U.K.]	9	Kj	51.53N	2.14W
Gloucester [Ma.-U.S.]	44	Ld	42.41N	70.39W
Gloucester, Cape-	60	Di	5.27 S	148.25 E
Gloucestershire [3]	9	Lj	51.50N	1.55W
Glover Island	51p	Bb	11.59N	61.47W
Glover's Reef	49	De	16.49N	87.48W
Gloversville	44	Jd	43.03N	74.21W
Głowno	10	Pe	51.58N	19.44 E
Głubczyce	10	Nf	50.13N	17.49 E
Glubokoje [Bye.-U.S.S.R.]	19	Cd	55.08N	27.41 E
Glubokoje [Kaz.-U.S.S.R.]	19	Ie	50.06N	82.19 E
Glubokoje, Ozero-	8	Md	60.30N	29.25 E
Głuchołazy	10	Nf	50.20N	17.22 E
Glücksburg	10	Fb	54.50N	9.33 E
Glückstadt	10	Fc	53.47N	9.25 E
Gluhov	19	De	51.43N	33.57 E
Gluša	16	Fc	53.06N	28.52 E
Glyngøre	8	Ch	56.46N	8.52 E
Gmünd [Aus.]	14	Hd	46.54N	13.32 E
Gmünd [Aus.]	14	Ib	48.46N	14.59 E
Gmunden	14	Hc	47.55N	13.48 E
Gnarp	7	De	62.03N	17.16 E
Gnesta	7	Dg	59.03N	17.18 E
Gniben	8	Dh	56.01N	11.18 E
Gniew	10	Oc	53.51N	18.49 E
Gniewkowo	10	Od	52.54N	18.25 E
Gniezno	10	Nd	52.31N	17.37 E
Gnjilane	15	Eg	42.28N	21.29 E
Gnosjö	7	Ch	57.22N	13.44 E
Gnowangerup	59	Df	33.56 S	117.50 E
Goa, Damān and Diu [3]	25	Ee	15.35N	74.00 E
Goageb	37	Be	26.44 S	17.15 E
Goālpāra	25	Ic	26.10N	90.37 E
Goat	63b	Dd	18.42 S	169.17 E
Goat Island	51d	Ba	17.44N	61.51W
Goat Point	51d	Ba	17.44N	61.51W
Goba	31	Kh	7.01N	39.59 E
Gobabis	31	Ik	22.30 S	18.58 E
Gobabis [3]	37	Bd	22.00 S	19.00 E
Göbel	15	Lj	40.00N	28.09 E
Gober	34	Gc	13.48N	6.51 E
Gobernador Gregores	56	Fg	48.46 S	70.15W
Gobernador Ingeniero Valentín Virasoro	56	Ic	28.03 S	56.02W
Gobernador Mansilla	55	Ck	32.33 S	59.22W
Gobi, Pustynja-=Gobi Desert (EN)	21	Me	43.00N	106.00 E
Gobi Altai (EN)=Gobijski Altaj	21	Me	44.00N	102.00 E
Gobi Desert (EN)=Gobi, Pustynja-	21	Me	43.00N	106.00 E
Gobijski Altaj=Gobi Altai (EN)	21	Me	44.00N	102.00 E
Gobō	28	Mh	33.53N	135.10 E
Göçbeyli	15	Kj	39.13N	27.25 E
Goceano	14	Dj	40.30N	9.15 E
Goceano, Catena del-	14	Cj	40.30N	9.00 E
Goce Delčev	15	Gh	41.33N	23.42 E
Goch	10	Ce	51.40N	6.10 E
Gochas	37	Bd	24.55 S	18.55 E
Goczałkowickie, Jezioro-	10	Og	49.53N	18.50 E
Göd	10	Pi	47.42N	19.08 E
Godafoss	7a	Cb	65.41N	17.33W
Godalming	12	Bc	51.11N	0.36W
Godār	24	Qh	29.45N	57.30 E
Godār-e Shah	24	Me	34.45N	48.10 E
Godāvari	21	Kh	17.00N	81.45 E
Godbout, Rivière-	44	Na	49.21N	67.42W
Gode	35	Gd	5.55N	43.40 E
Godeč	15	Gf	43.01N	23.03 E
Godelbukta Breidvika	66	Df	70.15 S	24.15 E
Goderich	44	Gd	43.45N	81.43W
Goderville	12	Ce	49.39N	0.22 E
Godhavn/Qeqertarssuaq	67	Nc	69.20N	53.35W
Godhra	25	Ed	22.45N	73.38 E
Godinlabe	35	Hd	5.54N	46.40 E
Gödöllő	10	Pi	47.36N	19.22 E
Godoy Cruz	56	Gd	32.55 S	68.50W
Gods Lake	42	If	54.40N	94.09W
Gods Lake	42	If	54.40N	94.20W
Gods Mercy, Bay of -	42	Id	63.30N	86.10W
Gods River	42	Ie	56.22N	92.52W
Godthåb/Nûk	67	Nc	64.15N	51.40W
Godthåbfjord	41	Gf	64.20N	51.30W
Godwin Austen (EN)=K2	21	Jf	35.53N	76.30 E
Godwin Austen (EN)=Qogir Feng	21	Jf	35.53N	76.30 E
Goedereede	12	Fc	51.49N	3.58 E
Goéland, Lac au-	42	Jg	49.45N	76.50W
Goélands, Lac aux-	42	Le	55.30N	64.30W
Goële	12	Ee	49.10N	2.40 E
Goelette Island	37b	Bc	10.13 S	51.08 E
Goeree	11	Jc	51.50N	3.55 E
Goes	11	Jc	51.30N	3.54 E
Gogama	42	Jg	47.40N	81.43W
Gō-Gawa	29	Cd	35.01N	132.13 E
Gogebic Range	44	Cb	46.45N	89.25W
Gogland, Ostrov-	7	Gf	60.05N	27.00 E
Gog Magog Hills	12	Cb	52.09N	0.11 E
Gogounou	34	Fc	10.50N	2.50 E
Gogrial	35	Dd	8.32N	28.07 E
Gogu, Vîrful-	15	Fd	45.12N	22.30 E
Gogui	34	Db	15.39N	9.21W
Goğu Karadeniz Dağları	24	Ib	40.40N	40.00 E
Gohelle	12	Ed	50.28N	2.45 E
Goiandira	54	Ig	18.08 S	48.06W
Goianésia	54	Ig	15.19 S	49.04W
Goiânia	53	Lg	16.40 S	49.16W
Goianinha	54	Ke	6.16 S	35.12W
Goiás [2]	54	If	12.00 S	48.00W
Goiás	54	Hg	15.56 S	50.08W
Goiatuba	54	Ig	18.01 S	49.22W
Goikul	64a	Bc	7.22N	134.36 E
Göinge	8	Eh	56.20N	13.50 E
Goio-Erê	56	Jb	24.12 S	53.01W
Goioxim	55	Gg	25.14 S	52.01W
Goirle	12	Hc	51.34N	5.05 E
Góis	13	Dd	40.09N	8.07W
Goito	14	Ee	45.15N	10.40 E
Gojam [3]	35	Fc	10.33N	37.35 E
Gojō	29	Dd	34.21N	135.42 E
Gojōme	29	Gb	39.56N	140.07 E
Gojra	25	Eb	31.09N	72.41 E
Gojthski, Pereval-	16	Kg	44.15N	39.18 E
Gokase-Gawa	29	Be	32.35N	131.42 E
Gokasho-Wan	29	Ed	34.20N	136.40 E
Gökbel Dağı	15	Kl	37.28N	28.00 E
Gökçay	24	Ed	36.36N	33.23 E
Gökçeada	24	Ac	40.10N	25.50 E
Gökçeören	15	Lk	38.35N	28.32 E
Gökçeyazi	15	Kj	39.38N	27.39 E
Gökdere	24	Ed	36.39N	33.35 E
Gökırmak	24	Fb	41.24N	35.08 E
Göksu [Tur.]	24	Fd	36.20N	34.05 E
Göksu [Tur.]	24	Fd	37.37N	35.35 E
Göksu [Tur.]	15	Mi	40.23N	29.58 E
Göksun	24	Gc	38.03N	36.30 E
Gök Tepe	15	Mm	36.53N	29.17 E
Göktepe	15	Ll	37.16N	28.36 E
Gokwe	37	Dc	18.13 S	28.55 E
Gol	7	Bf	60.42N	8.57 E
Golāghāt	25	Ic	26.31N	93.58 E
Golaja Pristan	16	Hf	46.29N	32.31 E
Gołańcz	10	Nd	52.57N	17.18 E
Golconda [Il.-U.S.]	45	Lh	37.22N	88.29W
Golconda [Nv.-U.S.]	46	Gf	40.57N	117.30W
Gölcük	24	Cb	40.44N	29.44 E
Golčův Jeníkov	10	Lg	49.49N	15.30 E
Gołdap	10	Sb	54.19N	22.19 E
Gold Beach	46	Ce	42.25N	124.25W
Gold Coast	58	Gg	27.58 S	153.25 E
Gold Coast	30	Gh	5.20N	0.45W
Golden [B.C.-Can.]	42	Ff	51.18N	116.58W
Golden [Co.-U.S.]	45	Dg	39.46N	105.13W
Golden Bay	62	Ed	40.50 S	172.50 E
Goldendale	4C	Ed	45.49N	120.50W
Goldene Aue	10	Ge	51.25N	11.00 E
Golden Gate	46	Dh	37.49N	122.29W
Golden Hinde	42	Eg	49.39N	125.45W
Golden Meadow	45	Kl	29.23N	90.16W
Golden Vale/Machaire na Mumhan	9	Fi	52.30N	8.00W
Goldfield	46	Gh	37.42N	117.14W
Gold River	46	Bb	49.41N	126.08W
Goldsboro	43	Ld	35.23N	77.59W
Goldsworthy	59	Dd	20.20 S	119.30 E
Göle	24	Jb	40.48N	42.36 E
Golegã	13	De	39.24N	8.29W
Goleniów	10	Kc	53.36N	14.50 E
Golešnica	15	Eh	41.42N	21.33 E
Goleta, Cerro-	48	Ih	18.38N	100.04W
Golfito	47	Hg	8.38N	83.11W
Golfo Aranci	14	Dj	41.00N	9.37 E
Gölgeli Dağları	15	Ml	37.15N	29.06 E
Gölhisar	15	Ml	37.08N	29.30 E
Goliad	45	Hl	28.40N	97.23W
Golija [Yugo.]	15	Df	43.19N	20.18 E
Golija [Yugo.]	15	Bf	43.02N	18.47 E
Goljak	15	Eg	42.44N	21.31 E
Goljama Kamčija	15	Kf	43.03N	27.29 E
Goljama Sjutkja	15	Hh	41.54N	24.01 E
Goljamo Konare	15	Hg	42.16N	24.33 E
Goljam Perelik	15	Hh	41.36N	24.34 E
Goljam Persenk	15	Hh	41.49N	24.33 E
Gölköy	24	Gb	40.15N	37.26 E
Gölkük	15	Kj	39.19N	27.59 E
Göllheim	12	Ke	49.35N	8.03 E
Gölmarmara	15	Kk	38.42N	27.56 E
Golmud He	27	Gd	36.54N	95.11 E
Golo	11a	Ba	42.31N	9.32 E
Goloby	10	Ve	51.06N	25.06 E
Gologory	10	Ug	49.35N	24.30 E
Gololcha	35	Gd	8.12N	40.05 E
Golovin	40	Gd	64.33N	163.02W
Golovnin Seamount (EN)	20	Kg	46.50N	157.00 E
Golpāyegān	23	Hc	33.27N	50.18 E
Gölpazarı	24	Db	40.17N	30.19 E
Golšanka	10	Kb	54.00N	26.16 E
Golspie	9	Jd	57.58N	3.58W
Gol Tappeh	24	Kd	36.35N	45.45 E
Golubac	15	Ee	44.39N	21.38 E
Golub-Dobrzyń	10	Pc	53.08N	19.02 E
Golungo Alto	36	Bd	9.08 S	14.47 E
Golyšmanovo	19	Gd	56.23N	68.23 E
Goma	31	Ji	1.37 S	29.12 E
Gómara	13	Jc	41.37N	2.13W
Gombe	31	Ig	10.17N	11.10 E
Gombi	34	Hc	10.10N	12.44 E
Gomel	6	Je	52.25N	31.00 E
Gomelskaja Oblast [3]	19	Ce	52.20N	29.40 E
Gomera	30	Ff	28.06N	17.08W
Gómez Farías	48	Ie	24.57N	101.02W
Gómez Palacio	47	Dc	25.34N	103.30W
Gomo Co	27	Ee	33.45N	85.35 E
Goms	14	Cd	46.25N	8.10 E
Gonābād	23	Ic	34.20N	58.42 E
Gonaïves	47	Je	19.27N	72.43W
Gonam	20	Ie	57.18N	131.20 E
Gonâve, Golfe de la-	47	Je	19.00N	73.30W
Gonâve, Ile de la-	47	Je	18.51N	73.03W
Gonbad-e Qābūs	23	Ib	37.15N	55.09 E
Gonda	25	Gc	27.08N	81.56 E
Gonder [3]	35	Fc	12.00N	38.00 E
Gonder	31	Kg	12.38N	37.27 E
Gondia	25	Gd	21.27N	80.12 E
Gondo	30	Gg	14.20N	3.10W
Gondomar	13	Dc	41.09N	8.32W
Gondwana	21	Kg	23.00N	81.00 E
Gönen	24	Bb	40.06N	27.39 E
Gönen	24	Bb	40.06N	27.36 E
Gonfreville-l'Orcher	12	Ce	49.30N	0.14 E
Gong'an (Doushi)	27	Je	30.05N	112.12 E
Gongbo'gyamda	27	Ff	29.59N	93.25 E
Gonggar	27	Ff	29.17N	90.50 E
Gongga Shan	21	Mg	29.34N	101.53 E
Gonghe	27	Hd	36.21N	100.47 E
Gongliu/Tokkuztara	27	Dc	43.30N	82.15 E
Gongola	30	Ih	9.30N	12.04 E
Gongola [2]	34	Hd	8.40N	11.20 E
Gongpoquan	27	Gc	41.50N	97.00 E
Gongshan	27	Gf	27.39N	98.35 E
Gongxian	27	Kf	26.05N	119.32 E
Gongzian (Xiaoyi)	28	Bg	34.46N	112.57 E
Gongzhuling → Huaide	27	Lc	43.30N	124.52 E
Goñi	55	Dk	33.31 S	56.24W
Goniądz	10	Sc	53.30N	22.45 E
Gonīshān	24	Pd	37.04N	54.06 E
Gonjo	27	Ge	30.52N	98.20 E
Gonohe	29	Ga	40.31N	141.19 E
Go-no-ura	29	Ae	33.45N	129.41 E
Gönuk	24	Ic	39.00N	40.41 E
Gonzales	45	Hl	29.30N	97.27W
Gonzáles, Riacho-	55	Df	22.48 S	57.54W
González	48	Jf	22.50N	98.27W
Goodenough, Cape-	66	Ie	66.16 S	126.10 E
Goodenough Bay	59	Ja	9.55 S	150.00 E
Goodenough Island	60	Ei	9.22 S	150.16 E
Good Hope, Cape of-/Groeie Hoop, Kaap die-	30	Il	34.21 S	18.28 E
Goodhouse	37	Be	28.57 S	18.13 E
Gooding	46	He	42.56N	114.43W
Goodland	43	Gd	39.21N	101.43W
Goodnews Bay	40	Ge	59.07N	161.35W
Goodsir, Mount-	46	Ga	51.12N	116.20W
Good Spirit Lake	46	Na	51.34N	102.40W
Goodwin Sands	12	Dc	51.15N	1.35 E
Goodyear	46	Ij	33.26N	112.21W
Goole	9	Mh	53.42N	0.52W
Goomalling	59	Df	31.19 S	116.49 E
Goondiwindi	58	Gg	28.32 S	150.19 E
Goonyella	59	Jd	21.43 S	147.58 E
Goor	12	Ib	52.14N	6.37 E
Goose Lake	43	Cc	41.57N	120.25W
Goose River	45	Hc	47.28N	96.52W
Gopło, Jezioro-	10	Od	52.35N	18.20 E
Göppingen	10	Fh	48.42N	9.40 E
Góra	10	Me	51.40N	16.33 E
Gora	15	Di	40.40N	20.30 E
Góra Kalwaria	10	Re	51.59N	21.12 E
Gorakhpur	22	Kg	26.45N	83.22 E
Goransko	15	Bf	43.07N	18.50 E
Gorata	15	Ih	41.45N	25.55 E
Goražde	14	Mg	43.40N	18.59 E
Gorda	46	Ei	35.55N	121.27W
Gorda, Cayo	49	Ff	15.55N	82.15W
Gorda, Punta- [Ca.-U.S.]	46	Cf	40.16N	124.20W
Gorda, Punta- [Cuba]	49	Fb	22.24N	82.10W
Gorda, Punta- [Nic.]	49	Ff	14.21N	83.12W
Gördes	15	Lk	38.54N	28.18 E
Gördes	15	Kj	38.46N	27.58 E
Gordil	35	Cd	9.44N	21.35 E
Gordior	24	Ec	39.37N	32.00 E
Gordon [Nb.-U.S.]	45	Ee	42.48N	102.12W
Gordon [Wi.-U.S.]	45	Kc	46.15N	91.47W
Gordon, Lake-	59	Jh	43.05 S	146.05 E
Gordon Horne Peak	46	Fa	51.46N	118.50W
Gordonvale	59	Jc	17.05 S	145.47 E
Goré	35	Bd	7.55N	16.38 E
Gore [Eth.]	35	Fd	8.09N	35.34 E
Gore [N.Z.]	62	Cg	46.06 S	168.56 E
Görele	24	Hb	41.02N	39.00 E
Görenez Dağı	15	Lk	39.00N	28.01 E
Gorenjsko	14	Id	46.20N	14.10 E
Gorey/Guaire	9	Gi	52.40N	6.18W
Gorgān	24	Pd	36.59N	54.05 E
Gorgān	24	Jf	33.21N	43.40 E
Gorgān, Khalīj-e-	24	Od	36.40N	53.50 E
Gorgany	10	Jh	48.30N	24.15 E
Gorgin	24	Ld	36.15N	47.55 E
Gorgol [3]	32	Ef	15.45N	13.00W
Gorgol el Abiod	32	Ef	16.14N	12.58W
Gorgona	14	Dg	43.25N	9.55 E
Gorgona, Isla-	54	Cc	2.59N	78.12W
Gorgora	35	Fc	12.14N	37.17 E
Gorham	44	Lc	44.23N	71.11W
Gori	19	Eg	42.00N	44.02 E
Gorinchem	11	Kc	51.50N	5.00 E
Goring	12	Ac	51.31N	1.08W
Goris	16	Oj	39.31N	46.22 E
Gorizia	14	He	45.57N	13.38 E
Gorj [2]	15	Gd	45.00N	23.20 E
Gorjačegorsk	20	De	55.24N	88.55 E
Gorjači Kljuc	16	Kg	44.36N	39.07 E
Gorjanci	14	Je	45.45N	15.20 E
Gorki [Bye.-U.S.S.R.]	16	Gb	54.17N	31.00 E
Gorki [R.S.F.S.R] → Nižnij Novgorod	6	Kd	57.38N	45.05 E
Gorki [R.S.F.S.R.]	20	Bc	65.05N	65.15 E
Gorkovskaja Oblast [3]	19	Ed	56.15N	44.45 E
Gorkovskoje Vodohranilišče =Gorky Reservoir (EN)	5	Kd	57.00N	43.10 E
Gorkum	10	Hf	50.10N	11.08 E
Gorky Reservoir (EN)= Gorkovskoje Vodohr.	5	Kd	57.00N	43.10 E
Gørlev	8	Di	55.32N	11.14 E
Gorlice	10	Rg	49.40N	21.10 E
Görlitz	10	Ke	51.10N	15.00 E
Gorlovka	6	Jf	48.18 N	38.03 E
Gornalunga	14	Jm	37.24N	15.03 E
Gorna Orjahovica	15	If	43.07N	25.41 E
Gornjak [R.S.F.S.R.]	20	Df	51.00N	81.29 E
Gornjak [Ukr.-U.S.S.R.]	10	Uf	50.16N	24.13 E
Gornji Milanovac	15	De	44.02N	20.27 E
Gornji Vakuf	23	Fg	43.56N	17.36 E
Gorno-Altajsk	22	Kd	51.58N	85.58 E
Gorno-Altajskaja Avtonomnaja Oblast [3]	20	Df	51.00N	87.00 E
Gorno-Badahšanskaja Avtonomnaja Oblast [3]	19	Hh	38.15N	73.00 E
Gorno-Čujski	20	Ge	57.40N	111.40 E
Gornozavodsk [R.S.F.S.R.]	20	Jg	46.30N	141.55 E
Gornozavodsk [R.S.F.S.R.]	17	Ig	58.25N	58.20 E
Gorny [R.S.F.S.R.]	20	Ih	44.50N	133.56 E
Gorny [R.S.F.S.R.]	16	Pd	51.45N	48.34 E
Gorny [R.S.F.S.R.]	20	If	50.48N	136.26 E
Gornyje Ključi	28	Lb	45.15N	133.30 E
Gorochan	35	Fd	9.26N	37.05 E
Gorodec [R.S.F.S.R.]	19	Ed	56.40N	43.30 E
Gorodec [R.S.F.S.R.]	8	Mf	58.30N	29.55 E
Gorodenka	16	De	48.42N	25.32 E
Gorodišče [Bye.-U.S.S.R.]	10	Vc	53.16N	26.03 E
Gorodišče [R.S.F.S.R.]	16	Nc	53.16N	45.42 E
Gorodišče [Ukr.-U.S.S.R.]	16	Ge	49.17N	31.27 E
Gorodnica	16	Ed	50.49N	27.22 E
Gorodnja	16	Gd	51.55N	31.31 E
Gorodok [Bye.-U.S.S.R.]	19	Cd	55.26N	29.59 E
Gorodok [Ukr.-U.S.S.R.]	16	Ee	49.10N	26.31 E
Gorodok [Ukr.-U.S.S.R.]	16	Ce	49.47N	23.39 E
Gorodovikovsk	19	Ef	46.05N	41.59 E
Gorohov	10	Uf	50.28N	24.47 E
Gorohovec	7	Kh	56.12N	42.42 E
Goroka	58	Fe	6.02 S	145.22 E
Gorom-Gorom	34	Ec	14.26N	0.14W
Gorong, Kepulauan-	26	Jg	4.05 S	131.20 E
Gorongosa, Serra da-	37	Ec	18.24 S	34.06 E
Gorontalo	22	Oi	0.33N	123.03 E
Goroual	34	Fc	14.42N	0.53 E
Górowo Iławeckie	10	Qb	54.17N	20.30 E
Gorron	11	Ff	48.25N	0.49W
Goršečnoje	16	Kd	51.33N	38.09 E
Gorski Kotar	14	Ie	45.26N	14.40 E
Gorssel	12	Ib	52.12N	6.13 E
Gort	9	Eh	53.04N	8.50W
Goru, Vîrful-	15	Jd	45.48N	26.25 E
Görükle	15	Li	40.14N	28.50 E
Goryn	19	Ce	52.09N	27.17 E
Gorzów [2]	10	Ld	54.25N	15.15 E
Gorzów Wielkopolski	10	Ld	52.44N	15.15 E
Goschen Strait	59	Kb	10.09 S	150.56 E
Gosen	28	Of	37.44N	139.11 E
Gosford	59	Kf	33.26 S	151.21 E
Goshen	44	Ee	41.35N	85.50W
Goshogawara	28	Pd	40.48N	140.27 E
Gosier	51e	Bb	16.12N	61.30W
Goslar	10	Ge	51.54N	10.26 E
Gospić	14	Jf	44.33N	15.23 E
Gosport	9	Lk	50.48N	1.08W
Gossen	8	Bb	62.50N	6.55 E
Gossi	34	Eb	15.47N	1.15W
Gossinga	35	Dd	8.39N	25.59 E
Gostivar	15	Dh	41.48N	20.54 E
Gostyń	10	Me	51.53N	17.00 E
Gostynin	10	Pd	52.26N	19.29 E
Gota älv	5	Hd	57.42N	11.52 E
Göta Kanal	5	Hd	58.50N	13.58 E
Götaland	5	Hd	57.30N	14.30 E
Götaland	7	Dg	57.30N	14.30 E
Göteborg	6	Hd	57.43N	11.58 E
Göteborg och Bohus [2]	7	Cg	58.30N	11.30 E
Gotel Mountains	30	Ih	7.00N	11.40 E
Gotemba	29	Fd	35.18N	138.56 E
Götene	7	Cg	58.32N	13.29 E
Gotha	10	Gf	50.57N	10.43 E
Gothenburg	45	Ff	40.56N	100.09W
Gothèye	34	Fc	13.52N	1.34 E
Gotland [2]	7	Eh	57.30N	18.30 E
Gotland	5	Hd	57.30N	18.30 E
Gotō-Nada	29	Ae	32.45N	129.30 E
Gotō-Rettō	27	Me	32.50N	129.00 E
Gotowasi	26	If	0.38N	128.26 E
Gotska Sandön	7	Eg	58.25N	19.15 E
Gōtsu	28	Lg	35.00N	132.14 E
Göttingen	10	Fe	51.32N	9.56 E
Gottwaldov	10	Ng	49.13N	17.39 E
Goubangzi	28	Fd	41.23N	121.48 E
Gouda	11	Kc	52.01N	4.43 E
Goudiri	34	Cc	14.11N	12.43W
Gouet	11	Df	48.32N	2.45W
Gough Island	30	Gm	40.20 S	10.00W
Gough Lake	46	Ia	52.02N	112.28W
Gouin, Réservoir-	42	Kg	48.35N	74.50W
Goulbin Kaba	34	Gc	13.42N	6.19 E
Goulburn	58	Fh	34.45 S	149.43 E

Index Symbols

[1] Independent Nation
[2] State, Region
[3] District, County
[4] Municipality
[5] Colony, Dependency
Continent
Physical Region

Historical or Cultural Region
Mount, Mountain
Volcano
Hill
Mountains, Mountain Range
Hills, Escarpment
Plateau, Upland

Pass, Gap
Plain, Lowland
Delta
Salt Flat
Valley, Canyon
Crater, Cave
Karst Features

Depression
Polder
Desert, Dunes
Forest, Woods
Heath, Steppe
Oasis
Cape, Point

Coast, Beach
Cliff
Peninsula
Isthmus
Sandbank
Island
Atoll

Rock, Reef
Islands, Archipelago
Rocks, Reefs
Coral Reef
Well, Spring
Geyser
River, Stream

Waterfall Rapids
River Mouth, Estuary
Lake
Salt Lake
Intermittent Lake
Reservoir
Swamp, Pond

Canal
Glacier
Ice Shelf, Pack Ice
Ocean
Sea
Gulf, Bay
Strait, Fjord

Lagoon
Bank
Seamount
Tablemount
Ridge
Shelf
Basin

Escarpment, Sea Scarp
Fracture
Trench, Abyss
National Park, Reserve
Point of Interest
Recreation Site
Cave, Cavern

Historic Site
Ruins
Wall, Walls
Church, Abbey
Temple
Scientific Station
Airport

Port
Lighthouse
Mine
Tunnel
Dam, Bridge

Goulburn Islands	59	Gb	11.50S	133.30 E
Gould Bay	66	Rf	78.10S	44.00W
Gould Coast	66	Mg	84.30S	150.00W
Goulia	34	Dc	10.01N	7.11W
Goulimine	32	Ed	28.59N	10.04W
Gouménissa	15	Fi	40.57N	22.27 E
Gouna	34	Hd	8.32N	13.34 E
Gounda	35	Cd	9.09N	21.15 E
Goundam	34	Eb	16.24N	3.38W
Goundi	35	Bd	9.22N	17.22 E
Goundoumaria	34	Hc	13.42N	11.10 E
Gounou Gaya	35	Bd	9.38N	15.31 E
Gourara	32	Hd	29.30N	0.40 E
Gouraya	13	Nh	36.34N	1.55 E
Gourcy	34	Ec	13.13N	2.21W
Gourdon	11	Hj	44.44N	1.23 E
Gouré	31	Ig	13.58N	10.18 E
Gourin	11	Cf	48.08N	3.36W
Gourma [Mali]	30	Gg	15.45N	2.00W
Gourma [U.V.]	30	Hg	12.20N	1.30 E
Gourma-Rharous	34	Eb	16.52N	1.55W
Gournay-en-Bray	11	He	49.29N	1.44 E
Gourniá	15	In	35.06N	25.48 E
Gouro	35	Bb	19.40N	19.28 E
Gourrama	32	Gc	32.20N	4.05W
Goussainville	12	Ee	49.01N	2.28 E
Gouyave	51p	Bb	12.10N	61.44W
Gouzeaucourt	12	Fd	50.03N	3.07 E
Gouzon	11	Ih	46.11N	2.14 E
Govena, Mys-	20	Le	59.47N	166.02 E
Gove Peninsula	59	Hb	13.02S	136.50 E
Goverla, Gora-	19	Cf	48.10N	24.32 E
Governador Valadares	53	Lg	18.51S	41.56W
Governor's Harbour	47	Ic	25.10N	76.14W
Gowanda	44	Hd	42.28N	78.57W
Gower	9	Ij	51.36N	4.10W
Gowganda	44	Gb	47.38N	80.46W
Goya	53	Kh	29.10S	59.20W
Goyave	51e	Ab	16.08N	61.34W
Goyaves, Ilets 'a-	51e	Ab	16.10N	61.48W
Goyder River	59	Hb	12.38S	135.05 E
Göynücek	24	Fb	40.24N	35.32 E
Göynük	15	Ni	40.20N	30.05 E
Göynük	24	Db	40.24N	30.47 E
Gozaisho-Yama	29	Ed	35.01N	136.24 E
Goz Arian	35	Bc	14.35N	20.00 E
Goz Beïda	35	Cc	12.13N	21.25 E
Gozha Co	27	De	34.59N	81.06 E
Goz Kerki	35	Bb	15.30N	18.50 E
Gözlü Baba Dağı	15	Lk	38.15N	28.28 E
Gozo	5	Hh	36.05N	14.15 E
Graaff-Reinet	37	Cf	32.14S	24.32 E
Graafschap	11	Mb	52.05N	6.30 E
Graben Neudorf	12	Ke	49.10N	8.28 E
Grabia	10	Oe	51.26N	18.56 E
Grabière Point	51g	Bb	15.30N	61.29W
Grabowa	10	Mb	54.26N	16.20 E
Gračac	14	Jf	44.18N	15.51 E
Gračanica	14	Mf	44.42N	18.18 E
Gračanica, Manastir-	15	Eg	42.36N	21.12 E
Gracias	49	Cf	14.35N	88.35W
Gracias a Dios	49	Ef	15.20N	84.20W
Gracias a Dios, Cabo	38	Kh	15.00N	83.08W
Graciosa [Azr.]	30	Ee	39.04N	28.00W
Graciosa [Can.Is.]	32	Ed	29.15N	13.30W
Gradačac	14	Mf	44.53N	18.26 E
Gradaús, Serra dos-	52	Kf	8.00S	50.45W
Grado [It.]	14	He	45.40N	13.23 E
Grado [Sp.]	13	Fa	43.23N	6.04W
Grænalon	7a	Cb	64.10N	17.24W
Grænlandshaf = Greenland Sea (EN)	67	Ld	77.00N	1.00W
Grafenau	10	Jh	48.51N	13.24 E
Grafham Water	12	Bb	52.19N	0.10W
Grafing bei München	10	Hh	48.03N	11.58 E
Grafschaft Bentheim	12	Jb	52.30N	7.05 E
Grafton [Austl.]	59	Ke	29.41S	152.56 E
Grafton [N.D.-U.S.]	43	Hb	48.25N	97.25W
Grafton [W.V.-U.S.]	44	Hf	39.21N	80.00W
Grafton, Mount-	46	Hg	38.40N	114.45W
Graham	42	Ef	53.40N	132.30W
Graham [N.C.-U.S.]	44	Hg	36.05N	79.25W
Graham [Tx.-U.S.]	45	Gj	33.06N	98.35W
Graham, Mount-	43	Fe	32.42N	109.52W
Graham Land (EN)	66	Qe	66.00S	63.30W
Graham Moore, Cape-	42	Jb	72.51N	76.05W
Grahamstown	31	Jl	33.19S	26.31 E
Grain Coast	30	Gh	5.00N	9.00W
Graisivaudan	11	Li	45.15N	5.50 E
Grajaú	54	Ie	5.49S	46.08W
Grajaú, Rio-	54	Jd	3.41S	44.48W
Grajewo	10	Sc	53.39N	22.27 E
Gram	8	Ci	55.17N	9.04 E
Gramalote	49	Kj	7.54N	72.48W
Gramat	11	Hj	44.47N	1.43 E
Gramat, Causse de-	11	Hj	44.40N	1.50 E
Graminha, Represa da-	55	Ie	21.33S	46.38W
Grammerages/Galmaarden	12	Fd	50.45N	3.58 E
Grammichele	14	Im	37.13N	14.38 E
Grammont/Geraardsbergen	12	Fd	50.46N	3.52 E
Grámmos Óros	15	Di	40.20N	20.45 E
Grampian	9	Kd	57.25N	2.35W
Grampian Mountains	5	Fd	56.45N	4.00W
Gramshi	15	Di	40.52N	20.11 E
Gran	8	Dd	60.22N	10.34 E
Granada [Col.]	54	Dc	3.33N	73.44W
Granada [Nic.]	49	Eh	11.50N	86.00W
Granada [Nic.]	47	Gf	11.56N	85.57W
Granada [Sp.]	13	Ig	37.15N	3.15W
Granada [Sp.]	6	Fh	37.13N	3.41W
Granada, Vega de-	13	Ig	37.15N	4.00W
Granard/Granard	9	Fh	53.47N	7.30W
Granard/Gránard	9	Fh	53.47N	7.30W
Granby	42	Kg	45.24N	72.43W
Gran Canaria	30	Ff	28.00N	15.36W
Gran Chaco	52	Jh	23.00S	60.00W
Grand Anse Bay	51p	Bb	12.02N	61.45W
Grand Bahama	38	Lg	26.40N	78.20W
Grand Ballon	11	Ng	47.55N	7.08 E
Grand Bank	42	Lg	47.06N	55.47W
Grand Banks (EN)	38	Oe	45.00N	50.00W
Grand Bassa	34	Dd	6.10N	9.40W
Grand-Bassam	31	Gh	5.12N	3.44W
Grand Bay	51g	Bb	15.14N	61.19W
Grand Bay	51p	Cb	12.29N	61.23W
Grand-Béréby	34	De	4.38N	6.55W
Grand-Bourg	50	Fe	15.53N	61.19W
Grand Cache	42	Ff	53.14N	119.00W
Grand Caille Point	51k	Ab	13.52N	61.05W
Grandcamp-Maisy	12	Ae	49.23N	1.02W
Grand Canal	9	Gh	53.21N	6.14W
Grand Canal (EN) = Da Yunhe	21	Nf	39.54N	116.44 E
Grand Canyon	43	Ed	36.03N	112.09W
Grand Canyon	38	Hc	36.10N	112.45W
Grand' Case	51b	Ab	18.06N	63.03W
Grand Cayman	47	He	19.20N	81.15W
Grand Cess	34	De	4.24N	8.13W
Grand Chartreuse	11	Li	45.22N	5.50 E
Grand Colombier	11	Li	45.54N	5.46 E
Grand Coulee	46	Fc	47.56N	119.00W
Grand-Couronne	12	De	49.21N	1.01 E
Grandcourt	12	De	49.55N	1.30 E
Grand Cul de Sac Bay	51k	Ab	13.59N	61.02W
Grand Cul-de-Sac Marin	51e	Ab	16.20N	61.35W
Grande, Arroyo-	55	Dm	37.32S	57.34W
Grande, Bahía-	52	Jk	50.45S	68.45W
Grande, Boca-	54	Fb	8.45N	60.35W
Grande, Cachoeira-	55	Gb	15.37S	51.48W
Grande, Cerro-	48	If	23.40N	100.40W
Grande, Ciénaga-	49	Ji	9.13N	75.46W
Grande, Corixa-	55	Cc	17.10S	58.20W
Grande, Cuchilla- [Arg.]	55	Cj	31.45S	58.35W
Grande, Cuchilla- [Ur.]	52	Ki	33.15S	55.07W
Grande, Ile-	11	Cf	48.48N	3.35W
Grande, Ilha	54	Jh	23.10S	44.10W
Grande, Rio- [Ven.]	54	Fb	8.39N	60.59W
Grande, Rio- [Braz.]	52	Lg	11.05S	43.09W
Grande, Rio- [N.Amer.]	38	Jg	25.57N	97.09W
Grande, Rio- (EN) = Bravo del Norte, Rio-	38	Jg	25.57N	97.09W
Grande, Rio- o Guapay, Rio-	52	Jg	15.51S	64.39W
Grande, Serra-	52	Lf	6.00S	40.52W
Grande, Sierra-	48	Gc	29.40N	104.55W
Grande-Anse	51e	Bb	16.18N	61.04W
Grande Anse	51k	Ba	14.01N	60.54W
Grande Briere	11	Dg	47.22N	2.15W
Grande Casse	11	Mi	45.24N	6.50 E
Grande Cayemite	49	Kd	18.37N	73.45W
Grande Comore → Njazidja	30	Lj	11.35S	43.20 E
Grande de Santa Marta, Ciénaga-	49	Jh	10.50N	74.25W
Grande de Santiago, Rio-	38	Ig	21.36N	105.26W
Grande do Gurupa, Ilha-	54	Hd	1.00S	51.30W
Grande Inferior, Cuchilla-	55	Dk	33.50S	56.10W
Grande Kabylie	13	Ph	36.45N	4.00 E
Grande ou Sete Quedas, Ilha-	55	Ef	23.45S	54.03W
Grande Pointe [Guad.]	51b	Bc	17.50N	62.50W
Grande Pointe [Guad.]	51e	Ac	15.59N	61.38W
Grande Prairie	39	Hd	55.10N	118.48W
Grand Erg de Bilma	30	Ig	18.30N	13.50 E
Grand Erg Occidental	30	He	30.20N	0.01 E
Grand Erg Oriental	30	He	30.00N	7.00 E
Grande Rio-	52	Kh	20.06S	51.04W
Grande Rivière à Goyaves	51e	Ab	16.18N	61.37W
Grande Rivière de la Baleine	38	Ld	55.15N	77.45W
Grande Rivière du Nord	49	Kd	19.35N	72.11W
Grande Ronde River	46	Gc	46.05N	116.59W
Grandes, Salinas-	52	Ji	30.05S	65.05W
Grande Sebkha d'Oran	13	Li	35.32N	0.48W
Grandes Rousse	11	Mi	45.06N	6.07 E
Grande-Synthe	12	Ec	51.01N	2.17 E
Grand Etang	51p	Bb	12.06N	61.42W
Grande-Terre	50	Fd	16.20N	61.25W
Grande Vigie, Pointe de la-	51e	Ba	16.31N	61.28W
Grand Falls [N.B.-Can.]	42	Kg	47.03N	67.44W
Grand Falls [Newf.-Can.]	39	Ne	48.56N	55.40W
Grand Forks [B.C.-Can.]	46	Fb	49.02N	118.27W
Grand Forks [N.D.-U.S.]	39	Je	47.55N	97.03W
Grand Found, Anse du-	51b	Bc	17.53N	62.49W
Grand Gedeh	34	Dd	5.45N	8.05W
Grand Haven	44	Dd	43.04N	86.10W
Grand Ilet	51e	Ac	15.50N	61.36W
Grand Island	39	Je	40.55N	98.21W
Grand Junction	39	If	39.05N	108.33W
Grand-Lahou	34	Dd	5.08N	5.01W
Grand Lake [La.-U.S.]	45	Kl	29.55N	91.35W
Grand Lake [La.-U.S.]	45	Jl	29.55N	92.47W
Grand Lake [N.B.-Can.]	44	Nc	45.42N	66.05W
Grand Lake [Newf.-Can.]	42	Lg	49.00N	57.20W
Grand Lake [Oh.-U.S.]	44	Ee	40.30N	84.32W
Grand Lake Victoria	44	Ib	47.35N	77.33W
Grand Lieu, Lac de-	11	Eg	47.05N	1.40W
Grand Manan Channel	44	Nc	44.45N	66.52W
Grand Manan Island	42	Kh	44.40N	66.50W
Grand Marais [Mi.-U.S.]	44	Eb	46.40N	85.59W
Grand Marais [Mn.-U.S.]	45	Kc	47.45N	90.20W
Grand-Mère	44	Kb	46.37N	72.41W
Grand Morin	11	If	48.54N	2.50 E
Grândola	13	Df	38.10N	8.34W
Grândola, Serra de-	13	Df	38.06N	8.38W
Grand Passage	63b	Ad	18.45S	163.10 E
Grand-Popo	34	Fd	6.17N	1.50 E
Grand Portage	45	Lc	47.58N	89.41W
Grand Prairie	43	He	32.45N	96.59W
Grandpré	12	Ge	49.20N	4.52 E
Grand Rapids [Man.-Can.]	42	Hf	53.10N	99.17W
Grand Rapids [Mi.-U.S.]	39	Ke	42.58N	85.40W
Grand Rapids [Mn.-U.S.]	43	Ib	47.14N	93.31W
Grand Récif Sud	61	Cd	22.38S	167.00 E
Grand River [Mi.-U.S.]	44	Dd	43.04N	86.15W
Grand River [Mo.-U.S.]	45	Jg	39.23N	93.06W
Grand River [Ont.-Can.]	44	Hd	42.51N	79.34W
Grand River [S.D.-U.S.]	45	Fd	45.40N	100.32W
Grand'Rivière	51h	Ab	14.52N	61.11W
Grand Roy	51p	Bb	12.08N	61.45W
Grand-Sans-Toucher	51e	Ab	16.06N	61.41W
Grand Teton	43	Ec	43.44N	110.48W
Grand Traverse Bay	43	Jb	45.02N	85.30W
Grand Turk	49	Lc	21.30N	71.10W
Grand Turk	47	Jd	21.28N	71.09W
Grand Union Canal	12	Bc	51.30N	0.02W
Grand Valley	45	Bg	39.27N	108.03W
Grandview [Man.-Can.]	45	Fa	51.10N	100.45W
Grandview [Mo.-U.S.]	45	Ig	38.53N	94.32W
Grandvilliers	12	De	49.40N	1.56 E
Grand Wash Cliffs	46	Ii	35.45N	113.45W
Grand Wintersberg	11	Ne	48.59N	7.37 E
Granger	46	Ee	46.21N	120.11W
Grängesberg	8	Fd	60.05N	14.59 E
Grangeville	46	Gd	45.56N	116.07W
Gran Guardia	56	Ic	25.52S	58.53W
Granite City	45	Kg	38.42N	90.09W
Granite Falls	45	Id	44.49N	95.33W
Granite Pass	46	Ld	44.38N	107.30W
Granite Peak [Nv.-U.S.]	43	Dc	41.40N	117.35W
Granite Peak [U.S.]	43	Fb	45.10N	109.48W
Granite Range	46	Ff	41.00N	119.35W
Granitola, Punta-	14	Gm	37.34N	12.41 E
Grankulla/Kauniainen	8	Kd	60.13N	24.45 E
Granma	49	Ic	20.30N	77.00W
Gran Malvina, Isla-/West Falkland	52	Kk	51.40S	60.00W
Gran Morelos [Mex.]	48	Eb	30.40N	108.35W
Gran Morelos [Mex.]	48	Fc	28.15N	106.30W
Gränna	8	Ff	58.01N	14.28 E
Granollers/Granollérs	13	Oc	41.37N	2.18 E
Granollérs/Granollers	13	Oc	41.37N	2.18 E
Gran Paradiso/Gran Paradiso	14	Be	45.32N	7.16 E
Gran Paradiso/Gran Paradis	14	Be	45.32N	7.16 E
Gran Pilastro/Hochfeiler	14	Fd	46.58N	11.44 E
Gran San Bernardo	14	Be	45.50N	7.10 E
Gran Sasso d'Italia	5	Hg	42.25N	13.40 E
Grant	45	Ff	40.50N	101.56W
Grant, Mount-	46	Fg	38.34N	118.48W
Gran Tarajal	32	Ed	28.12N	14.01W
Grantham	9	Mi	52.54N	0.38W
Grant Island	66	Nf	74.24S	131.20W
Grantown-on-Spey	9	Jd	57.20N	3.38W
Grant Range	46	Hg	38.25N	115.30W
Grants	43	Fd	35.09N	107.52W
Grantsburg	45	Jd	45.47N	92.41W
Grants Pass	43	Cc	42.26N	123.19W
Granville	11	Ef	48.50N	1.36W
Granville Lake	42	He	56.00N	100.20W
Granvin	8	Bd	60.33N	6.43 E
Grao de Gandia, Gandia-	13	Lf	38.59N	0.09W
Grao de Sagunto, Sagunto-	13	Le	39.40N	0.16W
Grappa, Monte-	14	Fe	45.52N	11.48 E
Grappler Bank (EN)	51a	Cc	17.48N	65.55W
Graskop	37	Ed	24.58S	30.49 E
Gräsmark	8	Ee	59.57N	12.55 E
Gräsö	7	Ef	60.25N	18.25 E
Grasse	11	Mk	43.40N	6.55 E
Grasset,Lac-	44	Ha	49.58N	78.10W
Grassrange	46	Kc	47.01N	108.48W
Gråsten	7	Bi	54.55N	9.36 E
Grästorp	8	Ef	58.20N	12.40 E
Graubünden	14	Dd	46.35N	9.35 E
Graulhet	11	Hk	43.46N	2.00 E
Graus	13	Mb	42.11N	0.20 E
Grave	12	Hc	51.45N	5.45 E
Grave, Pointe de-	11	Ei	45.34N	1.04W
Gravedona	14	Dd	46.09N	9.18 E
Gravelbourg	42	Gg	49.53N	106.34W
Gravelines	11	Id	50.59N	2.07 E
Gravenhurst	44	Hc	44.55N	79.22W
Gravenor Bay	51d	Ba	17.33N	61.45W
Graves	11	Fj	44.35N	0.30W
Gravesend	9	Nj	51.27N	0.24 E
Gravesend-Tilbury	9	Nj	51.28N	0.23 E
Gravina in Puglia	14	Kj	40.49N	16.25 E
Gravone	11a	Ab	41.55N	8.47 E
Gray	11	Lg	47.27N	5.35 E
Gray Feather Bank (EN)	60	Df	8.00N	148.40 E
Grayling	44	Ec	44.40N	84.43W
Grays Harbor	46	Cc	46.56N	124.05W
Grayson	44	Ff	38.20N	82.57W
Grays Peak	43	Fd	39.37N	105.45W
Graz	6	Hf	47.04N	15.27 E
Grazalema	13	Gh	36.46N	5.22W
Grdelica	15	Fg	42.54N	22.04 E
Greåker	8	De	59.16N	11.02 E
Great	51p	Bb	12.10N	61.38W
Great Artesian Basin	57	Fg	25.00S	143.00 E
Great Astrolabe Reef	63d	Bc	18.52S	178.31 E
Great Australian Bight	57	Eh	35.00S	130.00 E
Great Bacolet Point	51p	Bb	12.05N	61.37W
Great Bahama Bank (EN)	38	Lg	23.15N	78.00W
Great Bardfield	12	Cc	51.56N	0.29 E
Great Barrier Island	57	Ih	36.10S	175.25 E
Great Barrier Reef	57	Ff	19.10S	149.00 E
Great Basin	38	Hf	40.00N	117.00W
Great Bay	44	Jf	39.30N	74.23W
Great Bear	42	Ed	64.54N	125.35W
Great Bear Lake	38	Hc	66.00N	120.00W
Great Belt (EN) = Store Bælt	5	Hd	55.30N	11.00 E
Great Bend	43	Hd	38.22N	98.46W
Great Blasket/An Blascaod Mór	9	Ci	52.05N	10.32W
Great Britain	5	Fd	54.00N	3.00W
Great Central Lake	46	Cb	49.27N	125.12W
Great Channel	21	Li	6.00N	94.00 E
Great Chesterford	12	Cb	52.04N	0.12 E
Great Dismal Swamp	44	Ig	36.30N	76.30W
Great Dividing Range	57	Fg	25.00S	147.00 E
Great Dunmow	12	Cc	51.53N	0.22 E
Greater Accra	34	Fd	5.45N	0.10 E
Greater Antilles (EN) = Antillas Mayores	38	Lh	20.00N	74.00W
Greater Khingan Range (EN) = Da Hinggan Ling	21	Oe	49.00N	122.00 E
Greater London	9	Mj	51.35N	0.05W
Greater Manchester	9	Kh	53.35N	2.10W
Greater Sunda Islands (EN)	21	Nj	3.52S	111.20 E
Great Exhibition Bay	61	Df	34.40S	173.00 E
Great Exuma Island	47	Id	23.32N	75.50W
Great Falls	39	He	47.30N	111.17W
Great Harbour Cay	44	Im	25.45N	77.52W
Great Inagua	38	Lg	21.02N	73.20W
Great Indian Desert/Thar	21	Ig	27.00N	70.00 E
Great Karasberge (EN) = Groot-Karasberge	30	Ik	27.20S	18.45 E
Great Karroo (EN) = Groot Karoo	30	Jl	33.00S	22.00 E
Great Lake	59	Jh	41.52S	146.45 E
Great Namaland/Groot Namaland	37	Be	26.00S	17.00 E
Great Nicobar	21	Li	7.00N	93.50 E
Great North East Channel	59	Ia	9.30S	143.25 E
Great Ormes Head	9	Jh	53.21N	3.52W
Great Ouse	9	Ni	52.44N	0.23 E
Great Plain of the Koukdjuak	42	Kc	66.25N	72.50W
Great Plains	38	Je	42.00N	100.00W
Great Reef	63c	Bb	10.14S	166.02 E
Great Ruaha	30	Ki	7.56S	37.52 E
Great Sacandaga Lake	44	Jd	43.08N	74.10W
Great Sale Cay	44	Hl	27.00N	78.12W
Great Salt Lake	38	He	41.10N	112.30W
Great Salt Lake Desert	43	Ec	40.40N	113.30W
Great Salt Plains Lake	45	Gh	36.44N	98.12W
Great Salt Pond	51c	Ab	17.15N	62.38W
Great Sandy Desert [Austl.]	57	Dg	21.30S	125.00 E
Great Sandy Desert [U.S.]	43	Cc	43.35N	120.15W
Great Sea Reef	63d	Bb	16.15S	178.33 E
Great Shelford	12	Cb	52.07N	0.08 E
Great Sitkin	40a	Cb	52.03N	176.07W
Great Slave Lake	38	Hd	61.30N	114.00W
Great Smoky Mountains	44	Fh	35.30N	83.30W
Great Stour	9	Oj	51.19N	1.15 E
Great Valley [U.S.]	44	Ie	40.15N	76.50W
Great Valley [U.S.]	43	Kd	36.30N	82.00W
Great Victoria Desert	57	Dg	28.30S	127.45 E
Great Yarmouth	9	Oi	52.37N	1.44 E
Grebbestad	7	Cg	58.42N	11.15 E
Grebenka	16	Hd	50.07N	32.25 E
Gréboun, Mont-	34	Gb	20.00N	8.35 E
Greci	15	Ld	45.11N	28.14 E
Gredos, Sierra de-	13	Gd	40.20N	5.05W
Greece (EN) = Ellás	6	Ih	39.00N	22.00 E
Greeley [Co.-U.S.]	43	Gc	40.25N	104.42W
Greeley [Nb.-U.S.]	45	Gf	41.33N	98.32W
Greely Fiord	42	Ja	80.40N	85.00W
Greem-Bell	21	Ia	81.10N	64.00 E
Green	46	De	43.07N	123.28W
Green Bay	43	Jb	45.00N	87.30W
Green Bay	39	Ke	44.30N	88.01W
Greencastle	44	Df	39.38N	86.52W
Green Cay	49	Ia	24.02N	77.11W
Greeneville	44	Fg	36.10N	82.50W
Greenfield [In.-U.S.]	44	Ef	39.47N	85.46W
Greenfield [Ma.-U.S.]	44	Kd	42.36N	72.36W
Greenhorn Mountain	45	Dh	37.57N	105.00W
Green Island	62	Df	45.54S	170.26 E
Green Island [Atg.]	51d	Bb	17.03N	61.40W
Green Island [Gren.]	51p	Bb	12.14N	61.35W
Green Islands	57	Ge	4.30S	154.10 E
Greenland	51q	Ab	13.15N	59.34W
Greenland (EN) = Grønland/Kalaallit Nunaat	38	Pb	70.00N	40.00W
Greenland (EN) = Grønland/Kalaallit Nunaat	39	Pb	70.00N	40.00W
Greenland (EN) = Kalaallit Nunaat/Grønland	38	Pb	70.00N	40.00W
Greenland (EN) = Kalaallit Nunaat/Grønland	39	Pb	70.00N	40.00W
Greenland Basin (EN)	3	Gb	77.00N	0.00
Greenland Sea (EN) = Grænlandshaf	67	Ld	77.00N	1.00W
Greenland Sea (EN) = Grønlandshavet	67	Ld	77.00N	1.00W
Green Lookout Mountain	46	Dd	45.52N	122.08W
Green Mountains	38	Le	43.45N	72.45W
Greenock	9	If	55.57N	4.45W
Greenough River	59	Ce	28.51S	114.38 E
Green Peter Lake	46	Dd	44.28N	122.30W
Green River [U.S.]	44	Dg	37.55N	87.30W
Green River [U.S.]	38	If	38.11N	109.53W
Green River [Ut.-U.S.]	43	Ed	38.59N	110.10W
Green River [Wy.-U.S.]	43	Fc	41.32N	109.28W
Green River Lake	44	Eg	37.15N	85.15W
Greensboro	39	Lf	36.04N	79.47W
Greensburg [In.-U.S.]	44	Ef	39.20N	85.29W
Greensburg [Ks.-U.S.]	45	Gh	37.36N	99.18W
Greensburg [La.-U.S.]	45	Kk	30.51N	90.42W
Greenstone Point	9	Hd	57.55N	5.40W
Greenvale	59	Jc	18.55S	145.05 E
Greenville [Al.-U.S.]	44	Dj	31.50N	86.38W
Greenville [Il.-U.S.]	45	Lg	38.53N	89.25W
Greenville [Lbr.]	31	Gh	4.59N	9.02W
Greenville [Me.-U.S.]	44	Mc	45.28N	69.35W
Greenville [Ms.-U.S.]	43	Ie	33.25N	91.05W
Greenville [N.C.-U.S.]	43	Ld	35.37N	77.23W
Greenville [Oh.-U.S.]	44	Ee	40.06N	84.37W
Greenville [Pa.-U.S.]	44	Ge	41.24N	80.24W
Greenville [S.C.-U.S.]	39	Kf	34.51N	82.23W
Greenville [Tx.-U.S.]	43	He	33.08N	96.07W
Greenwich	44	Fe	41.02N	82.32W
Greenwich, London-	9	Mj	51.30N	0.00
Greenwood [Ms.-U.S.]	43	Ie	33.31N	90.11W
Greenwood [S.C.-U.S.]	44	Fh	34.12N	82.10W
Greenwood, Lake-	44	Gh	34.15N	82.00W
Greer	44	Fh	34.55N	82.14W
Greers Ferry Lake	45	Ji	35.30N	92.10W
Greeson, Lake-	45	Ji	34.10N	93.45W
Grefrath	12	Ic	51.18N	6.19 E
Gregoria Pérez de Denis	55	Bi	28.14S	61.32W
Gregorio, Rio-	54	De	6.50S	70.46W
Gregório, Rio-	55	Ha	13.42S	49.58W
Gregory, Lake-	59	He	28.55S	139.00 E
Gregory Lake	59	Fd	20.10S	127.20 E
Gregory Range	57	Ff	19.00S	143.00 E
Gregory River	59	Hc	17.53S	139.17 E
Greifenburg	14	Hd	46.45N	13.11 E
Greifswald	10	Jb	54.06N	13.23 E
Greifswalder Bodden	10	Jb	54.15N	13.35 E
Greifswalder Oie	10	Jb	54.14N	13.55 E
Grein	14	Ib	48.13N	14.51 E
Greiz	10	If	50.39N	12.12 E
Gréko, Akrotérion-	24	Fe	34.56N	34.05 E
Gremiha	6	Jb	68.03N	39.29 E
Gremjačinsk	17	Hg	58.34N	57.51 E
Grenå	7	Ch	56.25N	10.53 E
Grenada	39	Mh	12.07N	61.40W
Grenada	38	Mh	12.07N	61.40W
Grenada	45	Lj	33.47N	89.55W
Grenada Basin (EN)	47	Lf	13.30N	62.00W
Grenada Lake	45	Lj	33.50N	89.40W
Grenadines	47	Lf	12.40N	61.15W
Grenchen	14	Bc	47.11N	7.25 E
Grenen	5	Hd	57.44N	10.40 E
Grenfell	45	Ea	50.25N	102.56W
Grenoble	6	Gf	45.10N	5.43 E
Grenora	45	Eb	48.37N	103.56W
Grense-Jakobselv	7	Hb	69.47N	30.50 E
Grenville	50	Ff	12.07N	61.37W
Grenville, Cape-	59	Ib	12.00S	143.15 E
Gréoux-les-Bains	11	Lk	43.45N	5.53 E
Gresham	46	Dd	45.30N	122.26W
Gresik	26	Fh	7.09S	112.38 E
Gressoney-la-Trinité	14	Be	45.50N	7.49 E
Gretas Klackar	8	Gc	61.34N	17.50 E
Gretna	45	Kl	29.55N	90.03W
Grevelingen	12	Fc	51.45N	4.00 E
Greven	10	Dd	52.06N	7.37 E
Grevená	15	Ei	40.05N	21.25 E
Grevenbroich	10	Ce	51.05N	6.35 E
Grevenbrück, Lennestadt-	12	Kc	51.08N	8.01 E
Grevenmacher	12	Ie	49.41N	6.27 E
Grevesmühlen	10	Hc	53.52N	11.11 E
Grey	62	De	42.26S	171.12 E
Greybull	46	Kd	44.30N	108.03W
Greybull River	46	Kd	44.28N	108.03W
Grey Islands	42	Lf	50.50N	55.35W
Greymouth	61	Dh	42.27S	171.12 E
Grey Range	57	Fg	27.00S	143.35 E
Greystones/Ná Clocha Liatha	9	Gh	53.09N	6.04W
Greytow	37	Ee	29.07S	30.30 E
Greytown	62	Fd	41.05S	175.28 E
Gribanovski	16	Ld	51.29N	41.58 E
Gribb Bank (EN)	66	Ge	63.00S	90.30 E
Gribës, Mali i-	15	Ci	40.34N	19.34 E
Gribingui	35	Bd	7.00N	19.30 E
Gribingui	35	Bd	8.33N	19.05 E
Griend	12	Ha	53.15N	5.20 E
Griesheim	12	Ke	49.52N	8.33 E
Grieskirchen	14	Hb	48.14N	13.50 E
Griffin	43	Ke	33.15N	84.16W
Griffith	59	Jf	34.17S	146.03 E
Grigoriopol	15	Mb	47.09N	29.13 E
Grijalva	38	Jh	18.36N	92.39W
Grim, Cape-	59	Ih	40.41S	144.41 E
Grimari	35	Cd	5.44N	20.03 E
Grimbergen	12	Gd	50.56N	4.23 E
Grimma	10	Ie	51.14N	12.43 E
Grimmen	10	Jb	54.06N	13.03 E
Grimsby	9	Mh	53.35N	0.05W
Grimsey	7a	Ca	66.33N	18.00W
Grimsstadir	7a	Cb	65.39N	16.07W
Grimstad	7	Bg	58.20N	8.36 E
Grimsvotn	7a	Cb	64.24N	17.22W
Grindavik	7a	Ac	63.50N	22.30W
Grindelwald	14	Cd	46.38N	8.03 E
Grindsted	7	Bi	55.45N	8.56 E
Grinnell	45	Jf	41.45N	92.43W
Grinnel Peninsula	42	Ia	76.40N	95.00W
Grintavec	14	Id	46.22N	14.32 E
Griquatown	37	Ce	28.49S	23.15 E
Grise Fiord	39	Kb	76.10N	83.15W
Gris-Nez, Cap-	11	Hd	50.52N	1.35 E
Grisslehamn	8	Hd	60.06N	18.50 E
Grjazi	19	De	52.29N	39.57 E
Grjazovec	19	Ed	58.53N	40.15 E
Grmeč	14	Kf	44.43N	16.15 E
Grobina/Grobiņa	7	Eh	56.33N	21.11 E
Grobiņa/Grobina	7	Eh	56.33N	21.11 E
Groblersdal	37	De	25.15S	29.25 E
Grocka	15	De	44.41N	20.43 E
Grodk/Spremberg	10	Ke	51.34N	14.22 E
Grodków	10	Nf	50.43N	17.22 E
Grodnenskaja Oblast	19	Ce	53.45N	25.10 E
Grodno	6	Ie	53.41N	23.50 E
Grodzisk Mazowiecki	10	Qd	52.07N	20.37 E
Grodzjanka	16	Fc	53.34N	28.48 E
Groeie Hoop, Kaap die-/Good Hope, Cape of-	30	Il	34.21S	18.28 E

Index Symbols

- 1 Independent Nation
- 2 State, Region
- 3 District, County
- 4 Municipality
- 5 Colony, Dependency
- Continent
- Physical Region
- Historical or Cultural Region
- Mount, Mountain
- Volcano
- Hill
- Mountains, Mountain Range
- Hills, Escarpment
- Plateau, Upland
- Pass, Gap
- Plain, Lowland
- Delta
- Salt Flat
- Valley, Canyon
- Crater, Cave
- Karst Features
- Depression
- Polder
- Desert, Dunes
- Forest, Woods
- Heath, Steppe
- Oasis
- Cape, Point
- Coast, Beach
- Cliff
- Peninsula
- Isthmus
- Sandbank
- Island
- Atoll
- Rock, Reef
- Islands, Archipelago
- Rocks, Reefs
- Coral Reef
- Well, Spring
- Geyser
- River, Stream
- Waterfall Rapids
- River Mouth, Estuary
- Lake
- Salt Lake
- Intermittent Lake
- Reservoir
- Swamp, Pond
- Canal
- Glacier
- Ice Shelf, Pack Ice
- Ocean
- Sea
- Gulf, Bay
- Strait, Fjord
- Lagoon
- Bank
- Seamount
- Tablemount
- Ridge
- Shelf
- Basin
- Escarpment, Sea Scarp
- Fracture
- Trench, Abyss
- National Park, Reserve
- Point of Interest
- Recreation Site
- Cave, Cavern
- Historic Site
- Ruins
- Wall, Walls
- Church, Abbey
- Temple
- Scientific Station
- Airport
- Port
- Lighthouse
- Mine
- Tunnel
- Dam, Bridge

Groenlo	12	Ib	52.04N	6.39 E
Groesbeek	12	Hc	51.47N	5.56 E
Grofa, Gora-	15	Ha	48.34N	24.03 E
Groix	11	Cg	47.38N	3.28W
Groix, Ile de-	11	Cg	47.38N	3.28W
Grójec	10	Qe	51.52N	20.52 E
Gröll Seamount (EN)	54	Lf	14.00S	32.00W
Gromnik	10	Nf	50.42N	17.07 E
Gronau (Westfalen)	10	Dd	52.12N	7.02 E
Grong	7	Cd	64.30N	12.27 E
Groningen [3]	12	Ia	53.13N	6.33 E
Groningen [Neth.]	6	Ge	53.13N	6.33 E
Groningen [Sur.]	54	Gb	5.48N	55.28W
Groninger-wad	12	Ia	53.27N	6.25 E
Groningerwad	12	Ia	53.25N	6.30 E
Grønland/Kalaallit Nunaat= Greenland (EN)	38	Pb	70.00N	40.00W
Grønland/Kalaallit Nunaat= Greenland (EN) [5]	67	Nd	70.00N	40.00W
Grønlandshavet=Greenland Sea (EN)	67	Ld	77.00N	1.00W
Grønnedal	41	Hf	61.20N	47.45W
Grönskara	8	Fg	57.05N	15.44 E
Groot	30	Jl	33.45S	24.58 E
Groot Baai	51b	Ab	18.01N	63.04W
Groote Eylandt	57	Ef	14.00S	136.40 E
Grootfontein	31	Ij	19.32S	18.05 E
Grootfontein [3]	37	Bc	19.00S	19.00 E
Groot-Karasberge=Great Karasberge (EN)	30	Ik	27.20S	18.45 E
Groot Karoo=Great Karroo (EN)	30	Jl	33.00S	22.00 E
Grootlaagte	37	Cd	20.55S	21.27 E
Groot Namaland/Great Namaland	37	Be	26.00S	17.00 E
Grootvloer	37	Ce	30.00S	20.40 E
Gropeni	15	Kd	45.05N	27.54 E
Gros Caps, Pointe des-	51e	Bb	16.28N	61.25W
Gros Islet Bay	51k	Ba	14.05N	60.58W
Gros Islets	51k	Ba	14.05N	60.58W
Gros-Morne	51h	Ab	14.43N	61.01W
Gros-Morne	42	Lg	49.00N	57.22W
Grosne	11	Kh	46.42N	4.56 E
Gros Piton	51k	Ab	13.49N	61.04W
Große Aa	12	Jb	52.25N	7.23 E
Große Aue	12	Kb	52.30N	8.38 E
Großefehn	12	Ja	53.24N	7.33 E
Große Laaber	10	Ih	48.50N	12.30 E
Großenhain	10	Je	51.17N	13.33 E
Großenkneten	12	Kb	52.57N	8.16 E
Grosse Pointe	51e	Bb	16.01N	61.17W
Großer Arber	10	Jg	49.07N	13.07 E
Großer Gleichberg	10	Gf	50.23N	10.35 E
Großer Inselsberg	10	Gf	50.52N	10.28 E
Grosseto	14	Fh	42.46N	11.08 E
Grosseto, Formiche di-	14	Eh	42.40N	10.55 E
Groß-Gerau	10	Eg	49.55N	8.29 E
Großglockner	5	Hf	47.04N	12.42 E
Großräschen	10	Je	51.35N	14.00 E
Groß-Umstadt	12	Ke	49.52N	8.56 E
Großvenediger	14	Gc	47.06N	12.21 E
Grostenquin	12	If	48.59N	6.44 E
Gros Ventre Range	46	Je	43.30N	110.15W
Groswater Bay	38	Nd	54.20N	57.30W
Grøtavær	7	Db	68.58N	16.16 E
Grote Nete	12	Gc	51.07N	4.34 E
Grotli	7	Be	62.01N	7.40 E
Grottaglie	14	Lj	40.32N	17.26 E
Grottammare	14	Hh	42.59N	13.52 E
Groumania	34	Ed	7.55N	4.00W
Groundhog River	44	Ga	49.43N	81.58W
Grouse Creek Montains	46	If	41.55N	113.50W
Grove Mountains	66	Ff	72.53S	74.53 E
Groves	45	Jl	29.57N	93.55W
Grovfjord	7	Db	68.41N	17.09 E
Grow, Idaarderadeel-	12	Ha	53.06N	5.50 E
Grozny	6	Kg	43.20N	45.42 E
Grubišno Polje	14	Le	45.42N	17.10 E
Grudovo	15	Kg	42.21N	27.10 E
Grudziądz	10	Oc	53.29N	18.45 E
Grumento Nova	14	Jj	40.17N	15.53 E
Grumo Appula	14	Ki	41.01N	16.42 E
Grums	8	Ee	59.21N	13.06 E
Grünau	37	Be	27.47S	18.23 E
Grünberg	12	Kd	50.36N	8.57 E
Gründau	12	Ld	50.14N	9.05 E
Grundy	44	Fg	37.17N	82.06W
Gruñidera	48	Ie	24.15N	101.58W
Grünstadt	12	Ke	49.34N	8.10 E
Grunwald	10	Qc	53.30N	20.05 E
Gruppo di Brenta	14	Ed	46.10N	10.55 E
Gruyère	14	Bd	46.40N	7.10 E
Gruža	15	Df	43.54N	20.47 E
Gruzinskaja Sovetskaja Socialističeskaja Respublika [2]	19	Eg	42.00N	44.00 E
Gruzinskaja SSR/ Sakartvelos Sabčata Socialisturi Respublica [2]	19	Eg	42.00N	44.00 E
Gruzinskaja SSR=Georgian SSR (EN) [2]	19	Eg	42.00N	44.00 E
Grybów	10	Qg	49.38N	20.56 E
Grycksbo	8	Fd	60.41N	15.28 E
Gryfice	10	Lc	53.56N	15.12 E
Gryfino	10	Kc	53.15N	14.30 E
Grythyttan	8	Fe	59.42N	14.32 E
Grytviken	66	Ad	54.17S	36.31W
Gstaad	14	Bd	46.28N	7.17 E
Guacanayabo, Golfo de-	47	Id	20.28N	77.30W
Guacara	50	Cg	10.14N	67.53W
Guaçu	55	Ef	22.11S	54.31W
Guadaioz	13	Hg	37.50N	4.51W
Guadaira	13	Fg	37.20N	6.01W
Guadalajara [3]	13	Jd	40.50N	2.30W
Guadalajara [Mex.]	39	Ig	20.40N	103.20W
Guadalajara [Sp.]	13	Id	40.38N	3.10W
Guadalaviar	13	Kd	40.21N	1.08W
Guadalbullón	13	Ig	37.59N	3.47W
Guadalcanal	13	Gf	38.06N	5.49W
Guadalcanal Island	57	He	9.32S	160.12 E
Guadalén	13	If	38.05N	3.32W
Guadalentín o Sangonera	13	Kg	37.59N	1.04W
Guadalete	13	Fh	36.35N	6.13W
Guadalfeo	13	Ih	36.43N	3.35W
Guadalimar	13	Ig	37.59N	3.44W
Guadalmena	13	Jf	38.20N	2.55W
Guadalmez	13	Gf	38.46N	5.04W
Guadalope	13	Lc	41.15N	0.03W
Guadalquivir	5	Fh	36.47N	6.22W
Guadalupe [Mex.]	47	Dc	25.41N	100.15W
Guadalupe [Mex.]	48	Hf	22.45N	102.31W
Guadalupe [Mex.]	48	Id	26.12N	101.23W
Guadalupe [Sp.]	13	Ge	39.27N	5.19W
Guadalupe, Isla de-	38	Hg	29.00N	118.16W
Guadalupe, Sierra de-	13	Ge	39.25N	5.25W
Guadalupe Bravos	48	Fb	31.23N	106.07W
Guadalupe Mountains	45	Dj	32.20N	105.00W
Guadalupe Peak	43	Ge	31.50N	104.52W
Guadalupe River	45	Hl	28.30N	96.53W
Guadalupe Victoria, Presa-	48	Gf	23.50N	104.55W
Guadalupe y Calvo	48	Fd	26.06N	106.58W
Guadarrama	13	He	39.53N	4.10W
Guadarrama, Puerto de-	13	Hd	40.43N	4.10W
Guadarrama, Sierra de-	13	Id	40.55N	4.00W
Guadazaón	13	Ke	39.42N	1.36W
Guadeloupe	38	Mh	16.15N	61.35W
Guadeloupe [5]	39	Mh	16.15N	61.35W
Guadeloupe, Canal de la-= Guadeloupe Passage (EN)	47	Le	16.40N	61.50W
Guadeloupe Passage	50	Fd	16.40N	61.50W
Guadeloupe Passage (EN)= Guadeloupe, Canal de la-	47	Le	16.40N	61.50W
Guadiana	5	Fh	37.14N	7.22W
Guadiana, Canal del-	13	Ie	39.20N	3.20W
Guadiana, Ojos del-	13	Ie	39.08N	3.31W
Guadiana Menor	13	Ig	37.56N	3.15W
Guadiaro	13	Gh	36.17N	5.17W
Guadiela	13	Jd	40.22N	2.49W
Guadix	13	Ig	37.18N	3.08W
Guafo, Boca del-	56	Ff	43.40S	74.15W
Guafo, Isla-	56	Ff	43.36S	74.43W
Guaíba	56	Jd	30.06S	51.19W
Guaíba, Rio-	55	Gj	30.15S	51.12W
Guaimaca	49	Df	14.52N	86.51W
Guaimorato, Laguna de-	49	Ef	15.58N	85.55W
Guainía [2]	54	Ec	2.30N	69.00W
Guainía, Río-	52	Je	2.01N	67.07W
Guaiquinima, Cerro-	54	Fb	5.49N	63.40W
Guaira [3]	55	Dg	25.45S	56.30W
Guaíra [Braz.]	56	Jb	24.04S	54.15W
Guaíra [Braz.]	55	He	20.19S	48.18W
Guaira Falls (EN) = Sete Quedas, Saltos das-	56	Jb	24.02S	54.16W
Guaíras	55	Ja	12.39S	44.16W
Guaire/Gorey	9	Gi	52.40N	6.18W
Guaitecas, Islas-	56	Ff	43.57S	73.50W
Guajaba, Cayo-	49	Ic	21.50N	77.30W
Guajará Mirim	53	Jg	10.48S	65.22W
Guajira, Península de la-	52	Id	12.00N	71.30W
Guajolotes, Sierra del-	48	Ge	26.00N	105.15W
Guakolak, Tanjung-	26	Eh	6.50S	105.14 E
Gualaco	49	Df	15.06N	86.07W
Gualán	49	Cf	15.08N	89.22W
Gualdo Tadino	14	Gg	43.14N	12.47 E
Gualeguay	55	Ck	33.09S	59.20W
Gualeguay, Río-	55	Ck	33.19S	59.39W
Gualeguaychu	56	Id	33.01S	58.31W
Gualeguaychú, Río-	55	Ck	33.05S	58.25W
Gualicho, Salina del-	56	Gf	40.24S	65.15W
Guam [5]	58	Fc	13.28N	144.47 E
Guam	57	Fc	13.28N	144.47 E
Guaminí	56	He	37.02S	62.25W
Guampi, Sierra de-	54	Eb	6.00N	65.35W
Guamuchil	47	Cc	25.22N	108.22W
Gua Musang	26	Df	4.53N	101.58 E
Gu'an	28	De	39.24N	116.10 E
Guanabacoa	49	Fb	23.07N	82.18W
Guanabara, Baía de-	55	Kf	22.50S	43.10W
Guanacaste [3]	49	Eh	10.30N	85.15W
Guanacaste, Cordillera de-	49	Eh	10.45N	85.05W
Guanacevi	48	Ge	25.56N	105.57W
Guanahacabibes, Golfo de-	49	Eb	22.08N	84.35W
Guanahacabibes, Península de-	49	Ec	21.57N	84.35W
Guana Island	51a	Db	18.29N	64.34W
Guanaja	49	Ee	16.27N	85.54W
Guanaja, Isla de-	49	Ee	16.30N	85.55W
Guanajay	49	Fb	22.55N	82.42W
Guanajibo	51a	Ab	18.10N	67.09W
Guanajibo, Punta-	51a	Ab	18.12N	67.10W
Guanajuato	47	Dd	21.01N	101.15W
Guanajuato [2]	47	Dd	21.00N	101.00W
Guanambi	54	Jf	14.13S	42.47W
Guanare	54	Eb	9.03N	69.45W
Guanare, Río-	50	Ch	8.13N	67.46W
Guanare Viejo, Río-	49	Mi	8.19N	68.10W
Guanarito	50	Bh	8.42N	69.12W
Guandacol	56	Gc	29.31S	68.32W
Guandi Shan	27	Jd	38.09N	111.27 E
Guane	47	Hd	22.12N	84.05W
Guangde	27	Ke	30.51N	119.26 E
Guangdong Sheng (Kuang-tung Sheng)= Kwangtung (EN) [2]	27	Jg	23.00N	113.00 E
Guangfeng	28	Ej	28.27N	118.12 E
Guanghua	27	Je	32.18N	111.45 E
Guangji (Wuxue)	27	Kf	29.58N	115.32 E
Guangling	28	Ce	39.46N	114.16 E
Guangmao Shan	27	Hf	26.48N	100.56 E
Guangming Ding	28	Ei	30.09N	118.11 E
Guangnan	27	Ig	24.02N	105.04 E
Guangrao	28	Ef	37.03N	118.25 E
Guangshan	28	Ci	32.02N	114.53 E
Guangshui	28	Ci	31.37N	114.01 E
Guangxi Zhuangzu Zizhiqu (Kuang-hsi-chuang-tsu Tzu-chih-ch'ü)=Kwangsi Chuang (EN) [2]	27	Ig	24.00N	109.00 E
Guangyuan	22	Mf	32.27N	105.55 E
Guangzhou=Canton (EN)	22	Ng	23.07N	113.18 E
Guan He	28	Ch	32.18N	115.44 E
Guánica	51a	Bc	17.59N	66.56W
Guanipa, Río-	50	Eh	9.56N	62.26W
Guannan (Xin'anzhen)	28	Eg	34.04N	119.21 E
Guantánamo [3]	49	Jc	20.10N	75.00W
Guantanamo	39	Lg	20.08N	75.12W
Guantánamo, Bahía de-	49	Jd	20.00N	75.10W
Guantánamo Bay	47	Id	20.00N	75.10W
Guantanamo Bay Naval Station	49	Jd	20.00N	75.08W
Guantao (Nanguantao)	28	Cf	36.33N	115.18 E
Guanting Shuiku	28	Cd	40.13N	115.36 E
Guanxian	22	Mf	31.00N	103.38 E
Guanyun (Dayishan)	28	Eg	34.18N	119.14 E
Guapé	55	Je	20.47S	45.55W
Guapí	54	Cc	2.35N	77.55W
Guápiles	49	Fh	10.13N	83.46W
Guapó	55	Hc	16.51S	49.33W
Guaporé	55	Gi	29.10S	51.54W
Guaporé	56	Jc	28.51S	51.54W
Guaporé, Rio-	52	Jg	11.55S	65.04W
Guaqui	54	Eg	16.35S	68.51W
Guará	55	Gg	25.23S	51.17W
Guara, Sierra de-	13	Lb	42.17N	0.10W
Guarabira	54	Ke	6.51S	35.29W
Guaranda	54	Cd	1.35S	78.59W
Guaraniacu	56	Jc	25.06S	52.52W
Guarani de Goiás	55	Ia	13.57S	46.28W
Guarapiche, Río-	50	Eh	9.57N	62.52W
Guarapuava	56	Jc	25.23S	51.27W
Guaraqueçaba	55	Hg	25.17S	48.21W
Guararapes	55	Ge	21.15S	50.38W
Guaratinguetá	55	Jf	22.49S	45.13W
Guaratuba	55	Hg	25.54S	48.34W
Guarayos, Río-	55	Bb	14.38S	62.11W
Guarda	13	Ed	40.32N	7.16W
Guarda [2]	13	Ed	40.40N	7.10W
Guardafui, Cape-(EN)= 'Asäyr	30	Mg	11.49N	51.15 E
Guardal	13	Jg	37.36N	2.45W
Guarda-Mor	55	Ic	17.47S	47.06W
Guardiagrele	14	Ih	42.11N	14.13 E
Guardian Seamount (EN)	38	Ki	9.32N	87.40W
Guardo	13	Hb	42.47N	4.50W
Guardunha, Serra da-	13	Ed	40.05N	7.31W
Guareí, Rio-	55	Ff	22.40S	53.34W
Guareña	13	Gc	41.29N	5.23W
Guarenas	50	Cg	10.28N	66.37W
Guaribas, Rio-	55	Jc	16.22S	45.03W
Guaribe, Río-	50	Dh	9.53N	65.11W
Guárico [2]	54	Eb	8.40N	66.35W
Guárico, Embalse del-	50	Ch	9.00N	67.20W
Guarico, Río-	54	Eb	7.55N	67.23W
Guariquito, Río-	50	Ci	7.40N	66.18W
Guarita, Rio-	55	Fh	27.11S	53.44W
Guaritico, Caño-	50	Bi	7.52N	68.53W
Guaritire, Rio-	55	Ba	13.43S	60.38W
Guarujá	55	If	24.00S	46.16W
Guarulhos	56	Kb	23.28S	46.32W
Guasave	47	Cc	25.34N	108.27W
Guasdualito	54	Db	7.15N	70.44W
Guasipati	54	Fb	7.28N	61.54W
Guasopa	63a	Ac	9.14S	152.55 E
Guastalla	14	Ef	44.55N	10.39 E
Guatemala	39	Jh	14.38N	90.31W
Guatemala [3]	49	Bf	14.40N	90.30W
Guatemala [1]	39	Jh	14.38N	90.31W
Guatemala Basin (EN)	3	Mh	11.00N	95.00W
Guateque [Col.]	54	Db	5.05N	73.30W
Guateque [Col.]	54	Db	5.00N	73.28W
Guatimozín	55	Ak	33.27S	62.27W
Guatisimiña	54	Fc	4.33N	63.57W
Guatraché	56	He	37.40S	63.32W
Guaviare, Río-	52	Je	4.03N	67.44W
Guaviravi	55	Di	29.22S	56.50W
Guaxupé	55	Ie	21.18S	46.42W
Guayabal [Cuba]	49	Ic	20.42N	77.36W
Guayabal [Ven.]	50	Ci	8.00N	67.24W
Guayabero, Río-	52	Je	4.03N	67.44W
Guayalejo, Río-	48	Kf	22.13N	97.52W
Guayama	49	Ne	17.59N	66.07W
Guayana, Macizo de la- = Guiana Highlands (EN)	52	Ke	5.00N	60.00W
Guayana Basin (EN)	3	Ci	10.00N	52.00W
Guayaneco, Archipiélago-	56	Eg	47.45S	75.10W
Guayanés, Punta-	51a	Cb	18.04N	65.48W
Guayanilla	51a	Bb	18.02N	66.47W
Guayanilla, Bahía de-	51a	Bc	17.58N	66.45W
Guayape, Río-	49	Df	14.26N	86.02W
Guayaquil	53	If	2.10S	79.50W
Guayaquil, Golfo de-	52	Hf	3.00S	80.30W
Guaycurú, Río-	55	Ch	27.19S	58.45W
Guaymas	39	Hg	27.56N	110.54W
Guayquiraró, Río-	55	Cj	30.10S	58.34W
Guba [Eth.]	35	Fc	11.15N	35.20 E
Guba [Zaire]	36	Ee	10.38S	26.25 E
Guba Dolgaja	19	Fa	70.19N	58.45 E
Gubaha	19	Fd	58.52N	57.36 E
Guban	30	Lg	10.15N	44.26 E
Gubbio	14	Gg	43.21N	12.25 E
Gubdor	17	Hf	60.15N	56.35 E
Guber	10	Rb	54.13N	21.02 E
Gubin	10	Ke	51.56N	14.45 E
Gubio	34	Hc	12.30N	12.47 E
Gubkin	19	De	51.17N	37.33 E
Gúdar, Sierra de-	13	Ld	40.27N	0.42W
Gudara	19	Hh	38.23N	72.42 E
Gudauta	16	Lh	43.07N	40.37 E
Gudbrandsdalen	7	Bf	61.30N	10.00 E
Gudenå	8	Dh	56.29N	10.13 E
Gudermes	19	Eg	43.22N	46.08 E
Gudivāda	25	Ge	16.27N	80.59 E
Gudiyāttam	25	Ff	12.57N	78.52 E
Gudou Shan	27	Jg	22.12N	112.57 E
Güdül	24	Eb	40.13N	32.15 E
Gūdūr	25	Ff	14.08N	79.51 E
Gudvangen	8	Bd	60.52N	6.50 E
Guebwiller	11	Ng	47.55N	7.12 E
Guéckédou	34	Cd	8.33N	10.09W
Guelma [3]	32	Ib	36.15N	7.30 E
Guelma	32	Ib	36.28N	7.26 E
Guelph	42	Jh	43.33N	80.15W
Guelta Zemmur	32	Ed	25.08N	12.22W
Guemar	32	Ic	33.29N	6.48 E
Guéméné-Penfao	11	Eg	47.38N	1.50W
Guénange	12	Ie	49.18N	6.11 E
Guéné	34	Fc	11.44N	3.13 E
Guer	11	Dg	47.54N	2.07W
Guéra [3]	35	Bc	11.30N	18.30 E
Güera	32	De	20.52N	17.03W
Guéra, Massif de-	30	Ig	11.55N	18.12 E
Guérande	11	Dg	47.20N	2.26W
Guerara	32	Hc	32.48N	4.30 E
Guercif	32	Gc	34.14N	3.22W
Guerdjoumane, Djebel-	13	Oh	36.25N	2.51 E
Güere, Río-	50	Dh	9.50N	65.08W
Guéréda	35	Cc	14.31N	22.05 E
Guéret	11	Hh	46.10N	1.52 E
Guérin-Kouka	34	Fd	9.41N	0.37 E
Guernica y Luno	13	Ja	43.19N	2.41W
Guernsey	9	Kl	49.27N	2.35W
Guerrero [2]	47	De	17.40N	100.00W
Guerrero	48	Ic	28.20N	100.26W
Guessou-Sud	34	Fc	10.03N	2.38 E
Guest Peninsula	66	Mf	76.18S	148.00W
Guge	35	Fd	6.12N	37.30 E
Gūgerd, Kūh-e-	24	Oe	34.50N	53.00 E
Guglionesi	14	Ii	41.55N	14.55 E
Guguan Island	57	Fc	17.19N	145.51 E
Guia	55	Db	15.22S	56.14W
Guia Lopes da Laguna	55	De	21.26S	56.07W
Guiana Highlands (EN) = Guayana, Macizo de la-	52	Ke	5.00N	60.00W
Guiana Island	51d	Bb	17.06N	61.44W
Guichi (Chizhou)	27	Ke	30.38N	117.30 E
Guichón	55	Dk	32.21S	57.12W
Guide	27	Hd	36.00N	101.30 E
Guider	34	Hd	9.56N	13.57 E
Guidimaka [3]	32	Ef	15.30N	12.00W
Guidimouni	34	Gc	13.42N	9.30 E
Guiding	27	If	26.33N	107.16 E
Guidong	27	Jf	26.11N	113.58 E
Guiers	11	Li	45.37N	5.37 E
Guiglo	34	Dd	6.33N	7.29W
Guiglo [3]	34	Dd	6.30N	7.40W
Guijá	37	Ed	24.29S	33.00 E
Güija, Lago de-	49	Cf	14.13N	89.34W
Gui Jiang	21	Ng	23.28N	111.18 E
Guijk en Sint Agatha	12	Hc	51.44N	5.52 E
Guijuelo	13	Gd	40.33N	5.40W
Guil	11	Mj	44.40N	6.36 E
Guildford	9	Mj	51.14N	0.35W
Guiler Gol	28	Ga	46.03N	122.06 E
Guilin	22	Ng	25.21N	110.15 E
Guillaume Delisle, Lac-	42	Je	56.25N	76.00W
Guillestre	11	Mj	44.40N	6.39 E
Guilvinec	11	Bg	47.47N	4.17W
Guimarães [Braz.]	54	Jd	2.08S	44.36W
Guimarães [Port.]	13	Dc	41.27N	8.18W
Guimaras	26	Hd	10.35N	122.37 E
Guinchos Cay	49	Hb	22.45N	78.06W
Guinea (EN)=Guinée [1]	31	Fg	11.00N	10.00W
Guinea, Gulf of-	30	Hh	2.00N	2.30 E
Guinea, Gulf of- (EN)= Guinée, Golfe de-	30	Hh	2.00N	2.30 E
Guinea Basin (EN)	3	Di	0.00	5.00W
Guinea-Bissau (EN)=Guiné-Bissau [1]	31	Fg	12.00N	15.00W
Guinea Ecuatorial= Equatorial Guinea (EN) [1]	31	Hh	2.00N	9.00 E
Guinea Rise (EN)	3	Dj	4.00S	0.00
Guiné-Bissau=Guinea-Bissau (EN) [1]	31	Fg	12.00N	15.00W
Guinée=Guinea (EN) [1]	31	Fg	11.00N	10.00W
Guinée, Golfe de-=Guinea, Gulf of- (EN)	30	Hh	2.00N	2.30 E
Guinée Forestière [3]	34	Dd	8.40N	9.50W
Guinée Maritime [3]	34	Cc	10.00N	14.00W
Guînes	12	Dd	50.52N	1.52 E
Güines	47	Hd	22.50N	82.02W
Guingamp	11	Cf	48.33N	3.09W
Guinguinéo	34	Bc	14.16N	15.57W
Guiones, Punta-	49	Eh	9.54N	85.41W
Guiping	27	Ig	23.23N	110.00 E
Guipúzcoa [3]	13	Ja	43.10N	2.10W
Guir, Hamada du-	30	Ge	31.00N	3.20W
Güira de Melena	49	Fb	22.48N	82.30W
Guiratinga	54	Hg	16.21S	53.45W
Güiria	54	Fa	10.34N	62.18W
Guiscard	12	Fe	49.39N	3.03 E
Guise	11	Je	49.54N	3.38 E
Guitíriz	13	Ea	43.11N	7.54W
Guiuan	26	Id	11.02N	125.43 E
Guixi	27	Kf	28.18N	117.15 E
Guixian	27	Ig	23.10N	109.35 E
Guiyang	22	Mg	26.38N	106.43 E
Guizhou Sheng (Kuei-chou Sheng)=Kweichow (EN) [2]	27	If	27.00N	107.00 E
Gujan-Mestras	11	Ej	44.38N	1.04W
Gujarāt [3]	25	Ed	22.51N	71.30 E
Gujarāt	21	Jg	22.51N	71.30 E
Gujranwala	22	Jf	32.09N	74.11 E
Gujrāt	25	Eb	32.34N	74.05 E
Gukovo	16	Ke	48.04N	39.58 E
Gulang	27	Hd	37.30N	102.54 E
Gulbarga	22	Jh	17.20N	76.50 E
Gulbene	19	Cd	57.12N	26.49 E
Gulča	19	Hg	40.19N	73.33 E
Gulf	55	Ad	19.08S	62.01W
Gulf Breeze	44	Dj	30.22N	87.07W
Gulf Coastal Plain	38	Jf	31.00N	92.00W
Gulfport	43	Je	30.22N	89.06W
Gulian	27	La	52.58N	122.09 E
Gulin	27	If	28.02N	105.47 E
Gulistan	19	Gg	40.30N	68.45 E
Guliya Shan	27	Lb	49.48N	122.25 E
Gulja	20	Hf	54.43N	121.03 E
Gulja/Yining	27	Dc	43.54N	81.21 E
Guljajpole	16	Jf	47.37N	36.18 E
Gulkana	40	Jd	62.16N	145.23W
Gulkeviči	16	Lg	45.19N	40.44 E
Gull Bay	45	Lb	49.47N	89.02W
Gulleråsen	8	Fc	61.04N	15.11 E
Gullfoss	7a	Bb	64.20N	20.08W
Gullkronafjärd	8	Jd	60.05N	22.15 E
Gull Lake	42	Gf	50.08N	108.27W
Gullringen	8	Fg	57.48N	15.42 E
Gull River	45	Lb	49.50N	89.04W
Gullspång	8	Ff	58.59N	14.06 E
Güllü	15	Mk	38.16N	29.07 E
Güllük	24	Bd	37.14N	27.36 E
Gülpinar	15	Jj	39.32N	26.07 E
Gülşehir	24	Fc	38.45N	34.38 E
Gulstav	8	Dj	54.43N	10.41 E
Gulu	31	Kh	2.47N	32.18 E
Guma /Pishan	27	Cd	37.38N	78.19 E
Gumbiri, Jabal-	35	Ee	4.18N	30.57 E
Gumel	34	Gc	12.38N	9.23 E
Gummersbach	10	De	51.02N	7.33 E
Gummi	34	Gc	12.09N	5.07 E
Gümüşçey	15	Ki	40.17N	27.17 E
Gümüşhacıköy	24	Fb	40.53N	35.14 E
Gümüşhane	23	Ea	40.27N	39.29 E
Gümüşsu	15	Nk	38.14N	30.01 E
Guna	35	Fc	11.44N	38.15 E
Guna	25	Fd	24.19N	77.19 E
Gundagai	59	Jg	35.04S	148.07 E
Gundji	36	Db	2.05N	21.27 E
Gündoğdu	15	Ki	40.15N	27.07 E
Gündoğmuş	24	Ed	36.48N	32.01 E
Güney	15	Mk	38.09N	29.05 E
Güneydoğu Toroslar	21	Gf	38.30N	41.00 E
Gungu	36	Cd	5.44S	19.19 E
Gunma Ken [2]	28	Of	36.20N	139.05 E
Gunnar	42	Ge	59.23N	108.53W
Gunnbjørns Fjeld	67	Mc	68.55N	29.20W
Gunnedah	59	Kf	30.59S	150.15 E
Gunnison	43	Fd	38.33N	106.56W
Gunt	18	Hf	37.30N	71.03 E
Guntakal	25	Fe	15.10N	77.23 E
Guntersville	44	Dh	34.21N	86.18W
Guntersville Lake	44	Dh	34.45N	86.03W
Guntūr	22	Kh	16.18N	80.27 E
Gunungapi, Pulau-	26	Ih	6.38S	126.40 E
Gunungsitoli	26	Cf	1.17N	97.37 E
Günz	10	Gh	48.27N	10.16 E
Günzburg	10	Gh	48.27N	10.16 E
Gunzenhausen	10	Gg	49.06N	10.45 E
Guo He	28	Dh	32.58N	117.13 E
Guojiadian	28	Hc	43.20N	124.37 E
Guoyang	28	Dh	33.31N	116.12 E
Guozhen	28	Bj	29.24N	113.09 E
Gurahonţ	15	Fc	46.16N	22.21 E
Gura Humorului	15	Ib	47.33N	25.54 E
Gurban Obo	27	Jc	43.06N	112.28 E
Gurbantünggüt Shamo	27	Eb	45.30N	87.30 E
Gurdžaani	16	Ni	41.43N	45.48 E
Güre	15	Mk	38.39N	29.10 E
Gurgei, Jabal-	35	Cc	13.50N	24.19 E
Gurghiului, Munţii-	15	Ic	46.41N	25.12 E
Gurgueia, Rio-	52	Lf	6.50S	43.24W
Guri — Raúl Leoni, Represa-	54	Fb	7.30N	63.00W
Gurjev	6	Lf	47.07N	51.56 E
Gurjevsk	20	Df	54.20N	86.00 E
Gurjevskaja Oblast [3]	19	Ff	47.30N	52.00 E
Gurk	14	Id	46.36N	14.31 E
Gurk	14	Id	46.52N	14.18 E
Gurktaler Alpen	14	Hd	46.55N	14.00 E
Guro	37	Ec	17.26S	33.20 E
Gürpınar	24	Jc	38.18N	43.25 E
Gurskoje	20	If	50.20N	138.05 E
Gurskøy	7	Ae	62.15N	5.40 E
Gürsu	15	Mi	40.13N	29.12 E
Gurué	37	Fc	15.28S	36.59 E
Gurumeti	36	Fc	2.05S	33.57 E
Gürün	24	Gc	38.43N	37.17 E
Gurupá	54	Hd	1.25S	51.39W
Gurupi	53	Lg	11.43S	49.04W
Gurupi, Rio-	52	Lf	1.13S	46.06W
Gurupi, Serra do-	54	Id	5.00S	47.30W
Guru Sikhar	25	Ed	24.39N	72.46 E
Gus	7	Ji	55.00N	41.12 E
Gusau	31	Hg	12.10N	6.40 E
Gusev	19	Ce	54.37N	22.12 E
Gushan	28	Ge	39.54N	123.36 E
Gushi	27	Ke	32.02N	115.39 E
Gushikawa	29b	Ab	26.21N	127.52 E
Gūshk	24	Ph	28.13N	55.52 E
Gus-Hrustalny	7	Ji	55.38N	40.40 E
Gusinaja, Guba-	20	Kb	72.00N	150.00 E
Gusinaja Zemlja, Poluostrov-	19	Fa	71.50N	52.00 E
Gusinje	15	Cg	42.34N	19.50 E
Gusinoozersk	20	Ff	51.17N	106.30 E
Guspini	14	Ck	39.32N	8.37 E
Güssing	14	Kc	47.04N	16.20 E
Gustav Holm, Kap-	41	Ie	66.45N	34.00W
Gustavia	51b	Bc	17.54N	62.52W

Index Symbols

[1] Independent Nation
[2] State, Region
[3] District, County
[4] Municipality
[5] Colony, Dependency
Continent
Physical Region
Historical or Cultural Region
Mount, Mountain
Volcano
Hill
Mountains, Mountain Range
Hills, Escarpment
Plateau, Upland
Pass, Gap
Plain, Lowland
Delta
Salt Flat
Valley, Canyon
Crater, Cave
Karst Features
Depression
Polder
Desert, Dunes
Forest, Woods
Heath, Steppe
Oasis
Cape, Point
Coast, Beach
Cliff
Peninsula
Isthmus
Sandbank
Island
Atoll
Rock, Reef
Islands, Archipelago
Rocks, Reefs
Coral Reef
Well, Spring
Geyser
River, Stream
Waterfall Rapids
River Mouth, Estuary
Lake
Salt Lake
Intermittent Lake
Reservoir
Swamp, Pond
Canal
Glacier
Ice Shelf, Pack Ice
Ocean
Sea
Gulf, Bay
Strait, Fjord
Lagoon
Bank
Seamount
Tablemount
Ridge
Shelf
Basin
Escarpment, Sea Scarp
Fracture
Trench, Abyss
National Park, Reserve
Point of Interest
Recreation Site
Cave, Cavern
Historic Site
Ruins
Wall, Walls
Church, Abbey
Temple
Scientific Station
Airport
Port
Lighthouse
Mine
Tunnel
Dam, Bridge

Gustavs/Kustavi	8	Id	60.30N	21.25 E
Gustavs/Kustavi	8	Id	60.33N	21.21 E
Gustavsfors	8	Ee	59.12N	12.06 E
Gustavus	40	Le	58.25N	135.44W
Güstrow	10	Ic	53.48N	12.10 E
Gusum	8	Gf	58.16N	16.29 E
Gütersloh	10	Ee	51.54N	8.23 E
Guthrie [Ok.-U.S.]	45	Hi	35.53N	97.25W
Guthrie [Tx.-U.S.]	45	Fj	33.37N	100.19W
Gutian	27	Kf	26.40N	118.42 E
Gutiérrez Zamora	48	Kg	20.27N	97.05W
Gutii, Vîrful-	15	Gb	47.42N	23.52 E
Guting → Yutai	28	Dg	35.00N	116.40 E
Gutu	37	Ec	19.39S	31.10 E
Guwāhāti	22	Lg	26.11N	91.44 E
Guyana	53	Ke	5.00N	59.00W
Guyane Française = French Guiana (EN) [5]	53	Ke	4.00N	53.00W
Guyang	27	Jc	41.02N	110.04 E
Guyenne	11	Gj	44.35N	1.00 E
Guymon	43	Gd	36.41N	101.29W
Guyonneau, Anse-	51e	Ab	16.14N	61.47W
Guyuan	27	Id	36.01N	106.17 E
Guyuan (Pingdingbu)	28	Cd	41.40N	115.41 E
Guzar	18	Fe	38.37N	66.18 E
Güzelyurt	24	Ee	35.12N	32.59 E
Gūzhān	24	Le	34.20N	46.57 E
Guzhen	28	Dh	33.20N	117.19 E
Guzhou → Rongjiang	27	If	25.58N	108.30 E
Guzmán, Laguna de-	48	Fb	31.20N	107.30W
Gvardejsk	7	Ei	54.40N	21.03 E
Gvardejskoje	16	Hg	45.06N	33.59 E
Gvary	8	Ce	59.23N	9.09 E
Gwa	25	Ie	17.36N	94.35 E
Gwadabawa	34	Gc	13.22N	5.14 E
Gwādar	22	Ig	25.07N	62.19 E
Gwai	30	Jj	17.59S	26.52 E
Gwai	37	Dc	19.17S	27.39 E
Gwalior	22	Jg	26.13N	78.10 E
Gwanda	37	Dd	20.56S	29.00 E
Gwane	36	Eb	4.43N	25.50 E
Gwda	10	Mc	53.04N	16.44 E
Gweebarra Bay/Béal an Bheara	9	Eg	54.52N	8.20W
Gwent	9	Kj	51.45N	2.55W
Gweru	31	Jj	19.27S	29.49 E
Gweta	37	Dd	20.13S	25.14 E
Gwydir River	59	Je	29.27S	149.48 E
Gwynedd [3]	9	Ji	52.50N	3.50W
Gyaca	27	Ff	29.09N	92.38 E
Gya'gya → Saga	27	Ef	29.22N	85.15 E
Gyai Qu	27	Fe	31.30N	94.40 E
Gyaisi/Jiulong	27	Hf	28.58N	101.33 E
Gya La	27	Gf	29.05N	98.41 E
Gyala Shankou	27	Gf	29.05N	98.41 E
Gyangzê	27	Ef	29.00N	89.38 E
Gyaring Co	27	Ee	31.10N	88.15 E
Gyaring Hu	27	Ge	34.55N	98.00 E
Gyda	20	Cb	70.52N	78.30 E
Gydanskaja Guba	20	Cb	71.20N	76.30 E
Gydanski Poluostrov = Gyda Peninsula (EN)	21	Jb	70.50N	79.00 E
Gyda Peninsula (EN) = Gydanski Poluostrov	21	Jb	70.50N	79.00 E
Gyigang → Zayü	27	Gf	28.43N	97.25 E
Gyirong (Zongga)	27	Ef	28.57N	85.12 E
Gyldenløves Fjord	41	Hf	64.10N	40.30W
Gyldenløves Høj	8	Di	55.33N	11.52 E
Gympie	58	Gg	26.11S	152.40 E
Gyoma	10	Qj	46.56N	20.50 E
Gyöngyös	10	Pi	47.47N	19.56 E
Györ	6	Hf	47.41N	17.38 E
Győr [2]	10	Ni	47.40N	17.39 E
Győr-Sopron [2]	10	Ni	47.40N	17.15 E
Gypsumville	42	Hf	51.45N	98.35W
Gysinge	8	Gd	60.17N	16.53 E
Gyttorp	8	Fe	59.31N	14.58 E
Gyula	10	Rj	46.39N	21.17 E

H

Haacht	12	Gd	50.59N	4.38 E
Häädemeeste/Hjademeste	8	Uf	58.00N	24.28 E
Ha'afeva	65b	Ba	19.57S	174.43W
Haafusia	64h	Bb	13.18S	176.09W
Haag, Mount-	66	Qf	77.40S	79.00W
Haaksbergen	12	Ib	52.09N	6.45 E
Haamstede, Westerschouwen-	12	Fc	51.42N	3.45 E
Haanja Körgustik	8	Lg	57.30N	27.30 E
Ha'ano	65b	Ba	19.40S	174.17W
Ha'apai Group	57	Jf	19.47S	174.27W
Haapajärvi	7	Fe	63.45N	25.20 E
Haapamäki	8	Kb	62.15N	24.28 E
Haapasaari	8	Ld	60.15N	27.10 E
Haapaselkä [Fin.]	8	Mc	61.35N	28.15 E
Haapaselkä [Fin.]	8	Mb	62.10N	28.10 E
Haapiti	65e	Fc	17.34S	149.52W
Haapsalu	19	Cd	58.57N	23.32 E
Ha'arava	24	Fg	30.58N	32.24 E
Haardt	10	Dg	49.15N	8.00 E
Haardtkopf	12	Je	49.51N	7.04 E
Haaren, Wünnenberg-	12	Kc	51.34N	8.44 E
Haarlem	11	Kb	52.23N	4.38 E
Haarlemmermeer	12	Gb	52.20N	4.41 E
Haarlerberg	12	Ib	52.20N	6.25 E
Haarstrang	12	Kc	51.30N	8.20 E
Haast	58	Hi	43.52S	169.01 E
Haast Pass	62	Cf	44.06S	169.21 E
Habahe/Kaba	27	Eb	47.53N	86.12 E
Habarovsk	22	Pe	48.27N	135.06 E
Habarovski Kraj [3]	20	If	53.00N	137.00 E
Ḩabarūt	23	Hf	17.22N	52.42 E
Ḩabashīyah, Jabal-	35	Ib	16.45N	50.05 E
Habaswein	36	Gb	1.01N	39.29 E
Habay [Alta.-Can.]	42	Fe	58.52N	118.45W
Habay [Bel.]	12	He	49.45N	5.38 E
Habay [Som.]	35	Ge	1.08N	43.46 E
Ḩabbān	35	Hc	14.21N	47.05 E
Ḩabbānīyah, Hawr al-	24	Jf	33.17N	43.29 E
Habibas, Iles-	13	Ki	35.44N	1.08W
Habichtswald	10	Fe	51.20N	9.25 E
Habo	8	Fg	57.55N	14.04 E
Haboro	27	Pc	44.22N	141.42 E
Ḩabshān	24	Ok	23.50N	53.37 E
Hache	10	Ec	53.05N	8.50 E
Hachenburg	12	Jd	50.39N	7.50 E
Hachijō	29	Fe	35.15N	139.45 E
Hachijō-Fuji	29	Fe	33.08N	139.46 E
Hachijō-Jima	27	Oe	33.05N	139.50 E
Hachiman	29	Ed	35.46N	136.57 E
Hachimori	29	Fa	40.22N	140.00 E
Hachinohe	22	Qe	40.30N	141.29 E
Hachiōji	29	Fd	35.39N	139.18 E
Hachiro-Gata	29	Fa	40.00N	140.00 E
Hacibey De	24	Kd	36.58N	44.18 E
Hackar Daği	24	Ib	40.50N	41.10 E
Hackås	7	De	62.55N	14.31 E
Håckren	8	Ea	63.10N	13.35 E
Hačmas	19	Eg	41.25N	48.52 E
Hadagang	28	Kb	45.24N	131.12 E
Hadamar	12	Kd	50.27N	8.03 E
Ḩaḑan, Ḩarrat-	33	He	21.30N	41.23 E
Hadano	29	Fd	35.22N	139.14 E
Ḩadāribah, Ra's al-	35	Fa	22.04N	36.54 E
Hadd, Ra's al-	21	Hg	22.32N	59.59 E
Haddad	30	Ig	14.40N	18.46 E
Ḩadded	35	Hc	10.10N	48.28 E
Haddington	9	Kf	55.58N	2.47W
Haddummati Atoll	25a	Bb	1.45N	73.30 E
Hadejia	34	Hc	12.27N	10.03 E
Hadejia	34	Hc	12.50N	10.51 E
Hadeland	8	Dd	60.25N	10.35 E
Hadeln	10	Ec	53.45N	8.45 E
Hadera	24	Ff	32.26N	34.55 E
Haderslev	7	Bi	55.15N	9.30 E
Hadībah	23	Hg	12.39N	54.02 E
Hadım	24	Ed	36.59N	32.28 E
Hadimköy	24	Cb	41.09N	28.37 E
Hadīyah	23	Ed	25.34N	38.41 E
Hadjer el Hamis	35	Ac	12.51N	14.50 E
Hadjout	13	Oh	36.31N	2.25 E
Hadleigh	12	Cb	52.03N	0.56 E
Hadley Bay	42	Gb	72.30N	108.30W
Ha Dong	25	Ld	20.58N	105.46 E
Ḩaḑramawt	21	Gh	15.00N	50.00 E
Hadrian's Wall	9	Kg	54.59N	2.26W
Hadsten	8	Dh	56.20N	10.03 E
Hadsund	8	Dh	56.43N	10.07 E
Hadytajaha	17	Nc	66.57N	69.12 E
Hadyžensk	16	Kg	44.25N	39.31 E
Hadzibeiski Liman	15	Nc	46.40N	30.30 E
Haedo, Cuchilla de-	55	Dj	31.40S	56.18W
Haeju	28	He	38.02N	125.42 E
Haena	60	Oc	22.13N	159.34W
Ḩafar al 'Atk	24	Lj	25.56N	46.47 E
Ḩafar al Bātin	23	Gd	28.27N	46.00 E
Haffner Bjerg	41	Fc	76.30N	63.00W
Ḩaffūz	14	Do	35.38N	9.40 E
Hafik	24	Gc	39.52N	37.24 E
Ḩafīrat al 'Aydā	23	Ed	26.26N	39.12 E
Ḩafīt	24	Pk	23.59N	55.49 E
Ḩafīt, Jabal-	24	Pj	24.03N	55.46 E
Hafnarfjördur	7a	Bb	64.04N	21.57W
Haft Gel	24	Mg	31.27N	49.27 E
Hāfūn	35	Ic	10.10N	51.05 E
Hāfūn, Rās- = Hafun, Ras- (EN)	30	Mg	10.27N	51.24 E
Hafun, Ras- (EN) = Hāfūn, Rās-	30	Mg	10.27N	51.24 E
Hāfūn Bay North	35	Ic	10.37N	51.15 E
Hāfūn Bay South	35	Ic	10.15N	51.05 E
Hagadera	36	Hb	0.02N	40.17 E
Hagby	8	Gh	56.33N	16.10 E
Hageland	12	Gd	50.55N	4.45 E
Hagemeister	40	Ge	58.40N	161.00W
Hagen	10	De	51.21N	7.28 E
Hagenow	10	Hc	53.26N	11.12 E
Hagere Hiywet	35	Fd	8.58N	37.53 E
Hagerman	46	He	42.49N	114.54W
Hagerstown	43	Ld	39.39N	77.43W
Hagetmau	11	Fk	43.40N	0.35W
Hagfors	7	Cf	60.02N	13.42 E
Häggenås	8	Fa	63.24N	14.55 E
Hagi	28	Kg	34.24N	131.25 E
Ha Giang	25	Kd	22.50N	104.59 E
Hágios Theódóros	24	Fe	35.20N	34.01 E
Hagman, Puntan-	64b	Ba	15.09N	145.48 E
Hagondange	11	Me	49.15N	6.10 E
Hags Head/Ceanna Caillighe	9	Di	52.57N	9.28W
Hague, Cap de la-	5	Ff	49.43N	1.57W
Haguenau	11	Nf	48.49N	7.47 E
Hagunia	32	Ed	27.26N	12.24W
Hahajima-Rettō	60	Cb	26.37N	142.10 E
Hahns Peak	45	Cf	40.56N	107.01W
Hahót	10	Mj	46.38N	16.56 E
Hai'an	28	Fh	32.33N	120.26 E
Haicheng	27	Lc	40.51N	122.43 E
Haidenaab	10	Ig	49.35N	12.08 E
Hai Duong	25	Ld	20.56N	106.19 E
Haifa (EN) = Hefa	22	Ff	32.50N	35.00 E
Haifeng	27	Kg	22.58N	115.21 E
Haiger	12	Kd	50.45N	8.13 E
Hai He	28	De	38.57N	117.43 E
Haikakan Sovetakan Socialistakan Respublika/Armjanskaja SSR [2]	19	Eg	40.00N	45.00 E
Haikang (Leizhou)	27	Jg	20.56N	110.06 E
Haikou	22	Ng	20.05N	110.20 E
Ḩā'il	22	Gg	27.33N	41.42 E
Hailang He	28	Jb	44.33N	129.33 E
Hailar	22	Ne	49.14N	119.42 E
Hailar He	21	Ne	49.30N	117.50 E
Hailin	27	Mc	44.35N	129.22 E
Hailong (Meihekou)	27	Mc	42.32N	125.37 E
Hailsham	12	Cd	50.52N	0.16 E
Hailun	27	Mb	47.29N	126.55 E
Hailuoto/Karlö	5	Ib	65.02N	24.42 E
Haima Tan	27	Kd	10.52N	116.53 E
Haimen [China]	28	Fi	31.53N	121.10 E
Haimen [China]	28	Fj	28.40N	121.27 E
Haina	12	Kc	51.03N	8.56 E
Hainan Dao	21	Mh	19.00N	109.00 E
Hainaut	11	Jd	50.20N	3.50 E
Hainaut [3]	12	Fd	50.30N	4.00 E
Hainburg an der Donau	14	Kb	48.09N	16.56 E
Haines	39	Fd	59.14N	135.27W
Haines Junction	42	Dd	60.45N	137.30W
Hainich	10	Ge	51.05N	10.27 E
Hainleite	10	Ge	51.20N	10.48 E
Hai Phong	22	Mg	20.52N	106.41 E
Haïti = Haiti (EN) [1]	39	Lh	19.00N	72.25W
Haiti (EN) = Haïti [1]	39	Lh	19.00N	72.25W
Haixing (Suji)	28	De	38.10N	117.29 E
Haixin Shan	27	Hd	37.00N	100.03 E
Haiyan (Sanjiaocheng)	27	Hd	36.58N	100.50 E
Haiyan (Wuyuanzhen)	28	Fi	30.31N	120.56 E
Haiyang (Dongoun)	28	Ff	36.46N	121.09 E
Haiyang Dao	28	Ge	39.03N	123.12 E
Haiyou → Sanmen	27	Lf	29.08N	121.22 E
Haiyuan	27	Id	36.35N	105.40 E
Haizhou	28	Eg	34.34N	119.08 E
Haizhou Wan	21	Nf	35.00N	119.30 E
Ḩajar Banga	35	Cc	11.30N	23.00 E
Hajdarken	19	Hh	39.55N	71.24 E
Hajdú-Bihar [2]	10	Ri	47.25N	21.30 E
Hajdúböszörmény	10	Ri	47.40N	21.31 E
Hajdúhadház	10	Ri	47.41N	21.40 E
Hajdúnánás	10	Ri	47.51N	21.26 E
Hajdúság	10	Ri	47.35N	21.30 E
Hajdúszoboszló	10	Ri	47.27N	21.24 E
Hajihi-Zaki	29	Fb	38.19N	138.31 E
Ḩājjīābād [Iran]	24	Ph	28.19N	55.55 E
Ḩājjīābād [Iran]	24	Ph	28.21N	54.27 E
Ḩājjīabād-e Māsīleh	24	Ne	34.49N	51.13 E
Hajnówka	10	Td	52.45N	23.36 E
Hajós	10	Pj	46.24N	19.07 E
Hajpudyrskaja Guba	17	Ib	68.40N	59.30 E
Hakase-Yama	29	Fc	37.22N	139.43 E
Hakasskaja Avtonomnaja Oblast [3]	20	Df	53.30N	90.00 E
Hakata-Wan	29	Be	33.40N	130.20 E
Hakefjord	8	Dg	57.41N	11.44 E
Hakha	25	Id	22.39N	93.37 E
Hakkâri	23	Fb	37.34N	43.45 E
Hakken-Zan	29	Dd	34.10N	135.54 E
Hakkōda San	29	Ga	40.40N	140.53 E
Hako-Dake	29a	Ca	44.40N	142.25 E
Hakodate	22	Qe	41.45N	140.43 E
Hakone-Yama	29	Fd	35.13N	139.00 E
Hakui	28	Nf	36.53N	136.47 E
Hakupu	64k	Bb	19.06S	169.50W
Haku-San	29	Ec	36.09N	136.45 E
Hal/Halle	11	Kd	50.44N	4.14 E
Halab	24	Md	36.17N	48.03 E
Ḩalab = Aleppo (EN)	22	Ff	36.12N	37.10 E
Ḩalabjah	24	Ke	35.10N	45.59 E
Halač	19	Gh	39.04N	64.53 E
Halachó	48	Ng	20.29N	90.05W
Halahei	28	Ga	46.11N	122.46 E
Ḩalā'ib	31	Kf	22.13N	36.38 E
Halalii Lake	65a	Ab	21.52N	160.11W
Halangingie Point	64k	Bb	19.03S	169.58W
Hålaveden	8	Ff	58.05N	14.45 E
Halawa	65a	Eb	21.10N	156.44W
Halawa, Cape-	65a	Eb	21.10N	156.43W
Ḩalbā	24	Ge	34.33N	36.05 E
Halberstadt	10	He	51.54N	11.03 E
Halcon, Mount-	26	Hd	13.16N	121.00 E
Haldean-Sogotyn-Daba	27	Gb	49.05N	97.55 E
Halden	7	Cg	59.09N	11.23 E
Haldensleben	10	Hd	52.18N	11.25 E
Haldia	25	Hd	22.08N	88.05 E
Haldwani	25	Fc	29.13N	79.31 E
Hale, Mount-	59	De	26.00S	117.10 E
Haleakala Crater	65a	Ec	20.43N	156.12W
Haleiwa	65a	Cb	21.36N	158.06W
Halemaumau	65a	Fd	19.24N	155.17W
Hale River	59	Hd	24.56S	135.53 E
Halesworth	12	Db	52.21N	1.30 E
Haleyville	44	Dh	34.14N	87.37W
Ḩalfā al Gadida	31	Kg	15.19N	35.34 E
Half Assini	34	Ed	5.03N	2.53W
Halfeti	24	Gd	37.15N	37.52 E
Halfway	42	Fe	56.13N	121.26W
Halh-Gol	27	Kb	48.01N	118.10 E
Haliburton	44	Hc	45.03N	78.33W
Halifax	39	Me	44.39N	63.36W
Halifax, Mount-	59	Jc	19.05S	146.20 E
Halifax Bay	59	Jc	18.50S	146.30 E
Hālīl	23	Id	27.28N	58.44 E
Halīleh, Ra's-e-	24	Nh	28.46N	50.56 E
Halilovo	16	Ud	51.27N	58.10 E
Ḩalin	35	Hd	9.08N	48.47 E
Haliut → Urad Zhonghou Lianheqi	27	Ic	41.34N	108.32 E
Haljala	8	Le	59.22N	26.09 E
Haljasavej	20	Cd	63.20N	78.30 E
Hall	40	Ed	60.40N	173.05W
Halladale	9	Jc	58.30N	3.50W
Hallam Peak	46	Fa	52.11N	118.46W
Halland	8	Eh	57.00N	12.45 E
Halland [2]	7	Ch	56.45N	13.00 E
Hallandsås	8	Eh	56.23N	13.00 E
Halla-san	28	Ih	33.22N	126.32 E
Ḩallat 'Ammār	24	Gh	29.08N	36.02 E
Hall Beach	42	Jc	68.10N	81.56W
Halle	10	He	51.30N	12.00 E
Halle/Hal	11	Kd	50.44N	4.14 E
Halle (Westfalen)	12	Kb	52.05N	8.22 E
Halleberg	8	Ef	58.23N	12.25 E
Hällefors	8	Fe	59.47N	14.30 E
Hälleforsnäs	8	Ge	59.10N	16.30 E
Halleim	14	Hc	47.41N	13.06 E
Hällekis	8	Ef	58.38N	13.25 E
Hallen	7	De	63.11N	14.05 E
Hallenberg	12	Kc	51.07N	8.38 E
Hallencourt	12	De	49.59N	1.53 E
Halle-Neustadt	10	He	51.31N	11.53 E
Hallertau	10	Hh	48.35N	11.50 E
Hällestad	8	Ff	58.44N	15.34 E
Hallettsville	45	Hl	29.27N	96.57W
Halley Bay	66	Af	75.31S	26.38W
Halli	8	Kc	61.52N	24.50 E
Hallie-Jackson Bank (EN)	63c	Ba	9.45S	166.10 E
Halligen	10	Eb	54.35N	8.35 E
Hallingdal	7	Bf	60.40N	9.15 E
Hallingdalselva	8	Cd	60.23N	9.35 E
Hallingskarvet	5	Gc	60.37N	7.45 E
Hall Islands	57	Gd	8.37N	152.00 E
Halliste Jõgi	8	Kf	58.23N	24.25 E
Hall Lake	42	Jc	68.40N	82.20W
Hall Land	41	Fb	81.12N	61.10W
Hallock	45	Hb	48.47N	96.57W
Hall Peninsula	38	Mc	63.30N	66.00W
Hallsberg	7	Dg	59.04N	15.07 E
Halls Creek	58	Df	18.13S	127.40 E
Hallstahammar	7	Dg	59.37N	16.13 E
Hallstatt	14	Hb	47.33N	13.39 E
Hallstavik	7	Ef	60.03N	18.36 E
Halluin	12	Fd	50.47N	3.08 E
Halmahera	57	Dd	1.00N	128.00 E
Halmahera, Laut- = Halmahera Sea (EN)	57	De	1.00S	129.00 E
Halmahera Sea (EN) = Halmahera, Laut-	57	De	1.00S	129.00 E
Halmer-Ju	19	Gb	67.58N	64.40 E
Halmeu	15	Gb	47.58N	23.01 E
Halmstad	6	Hd	56.39N	12.50 E
Haloze	14	Jd	46.20N	15.50 E
Ḩalq al Wādī	32	Jb	36.49N	10.18 E
Hals	7	Cg	57.00N	10.19 E
Hälsingland	8	Gc	61.30N	17.00 E
Halsön	8	Ib	62.50N	21.10 E
Halstead	12	Cc	51.57N	0.38 E
Halsteren	12	Gc	51.32N	4.16 E
Haltang He	27	Fd	39.00N	94.40 E
Halten Bank (EN)	7	Bd	64.45N	8.45 E
Haltern	12	Jc	51.44N	7.11 E
Haltiatunturi	7	Eb	69.18N	21.16 E
Haltom City	45	Hj	32.48N	97.16W
Halturin	19	Ed	58.35N	48.55 E
Hālūl	24	Oj	25.40N	52.25 E
Halver	12	Jc	51.12N	7.29 E
Ham	11	Je	49.45N	3.04 E
Ham, Roches de-	12	Ae	49.02N	1.02W
Hamada	29	Cd	34.53N	132.03 E
Hamadān	22	Gf	34.48N	48.30 E
Hamadān [3]	23	Gb	35.00N	48.40 E
Hamadia	13	Ni	35.28N	1.52 E
Hamaguir	32	Gc	30.54N	3.02W
Hamāh	23	Eb	35.08N	36.45 E
Hamakita	29	Ed	34.49N	137.45 E
Hamamasu	29a	Bb	43.36N	141.21 E
Hamamatsu	27	Oe	34.42N	137.44 E
Hamanaka	29a	Db	43.05N	145.05 E
Hamanaka-Wan	29a	Db	43.07N	145.10 E
Hamana-Ko	29	Ed	34.45N	137.34 E
Hamanen, Oued el-	32	Hd	25.52N	1.26 E
Hamaoka	29	Fd	34.39N	138.07 E
Hamar	6	Hc	60.48N	11.06 E
Hamar-Daran, Hrebet-	20	Ff	51.10N	105.00 E
Hamasaka	29	Dd	35.38N	134.27 E
Ḩamāţah, Jabal-	33	Ge	24.12N	35.00 E
Hamatonbetsu	28	Qb	45.07N	142.23 E
Hambantota	25	Gg	6.10N	81.07 E
Hambre, Cayos del-	49	Fb	22.15N	82.47W
Hamburg [2]	10	Fc	53.35N	10.00 E
Hamburg [Ger.]	6	Ge	53.33N	10.00 E
Hamburg [S.Afr.]	37	Df	33.18S	27.28 E
Hamburg-Altona	10	Fc	53.33N	9.57 E
Hamburg-Harburg	10	Fc	53.28N	10.00 E
Hamburgsund	8	Df	58.33N	11.16 E
Ḩamḑah	33	Hf	19.02N	43.36 E
Ḩamḑh, Wādī al-	21	Fg	25.58N	36.42 E
Häme [2]	7	Ff	61.30N	24.30 E
Häme	8	Kc	61.30N	25.30 E
Hämeenkangas	8	Jc	61.45N	22.40 E
Hämeenlinna/Tavastehus	7	Ff	61.00N	24.27 E
Hämeenselkä	8	Kb	62.30N	25.00 E
Hamelin Pool	59	Ce	26.15S	114.05 E
Hameln	10	Fd	52.06N	9.21 E
Hamero Hadad	35	Gd	7.28N	42.13 E
Hamersley Range	59	Dd	21.55S	116.45 E
Hamgyŏng-Namdo [2]	28	Id	40.00N	127.30 E
Hamgyŏng-Pukto [2]	28	Jd	41.45N	129.50 E
Hamgyŏng-Sanmaek	28	Jd	41.00N	128.45 E
Hamhŭng	22	Of	39.54N	127.32 E
Hami/Kumul	22	Le	42.48N	93.27 E
Ḩamīdīyeh	24	Mg	31.29N	48.26 E
Hamilton [Austl.]	59	Ig	37.45S	142.02 E
Hamilton [Ber.]	39	Mf	32.17N	64.46W
Hamilton [Mt.-U.S.]	43	Eb	46.15N	114.09W
Hamilton [N.Z.]	58	Ih	37.47S	175.17 E
Hamilton [Oh.-U.S.]	43	Kd	39.23N	84.33W
Hamilton [Ont.-Can.]	39	Le	43.15N	79.51W
Hamilton [Scot.-U.K.]	9	If	55.47N	4.03W
Hamilton [Tx.-U.S.]	45	Gk	31.42N	98.07W
Hamilton, Lake-	45	Ji	34.30N	93.05W
Hamilton, Mount-	46	Hg	39.14N	115.32W
Hamilton River	59	Hd	23.30S	139.47 E
Ḩamīn, Wādī al-	33	Dc	30.28N	22.00 E
Hamina/Fredrikshamn	7	Gf	60.34N	27.12 E
Hamm	10	De	51.41N	7.48 E
Ḩammām al 'Alīl	24	Jd	36.10N	43.16 E
Ḩammām al Anf	32	Jb	36.44N	10.20 E
Ḩammāmāt	32	Jb	36.24N	10.37 E
Ḩammāmāt, Khalīj-	32	Jb	36.05N	10.40 E
Hammam Bou Hadjar	13	Li	35.23N	0.58W
Hammami	30	Ff	23.03N	11.30W
Hammam Righa	13	Oh	36.23N	2.24 E
Ḩammār, Hawr al-	23	Gc	30.50N	47.10 E
Hammarstrand	8	Ga	63.06N	16.21 E
Hamme	12	Gc	51.06N	4.08 E
Hammelburg	10	Ff	50.07N	9.54 E
Hammerdal	7	De	63.36N	15.21 E
Hammeren	8	Fi	55.18N	14.47 E
Hammerfest	6	Ia	70.40N	23.45 E
Hamminkeln	12	Ic	51.44N	6.35 E
Hamminkeln-Dingden	12	Ic	51.46N	6.37 E
Hammond [In.-U.S.]	44	De	41.36N	87.30W
Hammond [La.-U.S.]	43	Ie	30.30N	90.28W
Hammonton	44	Jf	39.38N	74.48W
Hamont, Hamont-Achel-	12	Hc	51.15N	5.33 E
Hamont-Achel	12	Hc	51.15N	5.33 E
Hamont-Achel-Hamont	12	Hc	51.15N	5.33 E
Hamoyet, Jabal-	30	Kg	17.33N	38.02 E
Hampden	62	Df	45.20S	170.49 E
Hampshire [3]	9	Lk	51.00N	1.10W
Hampshire Downs	9	Lj	51.15N	1.15W
Hampton [Ia.-U.S.]	45	Je	42.45N	93.12W
Hampton [Va.-U.S.]	44	Ig	37.02N	76.23W
Hampton Butte	46	Ee	43.46N	120.17W
Hamp'yong	28	Ig	35.04N	126.31 E
Ḩamrā'	35	Dc	10.54N	29.54 E
Hamra [R.S.F.S.R.]	20	Gd	60.17N	114.10 E
Hamra [Swe.]	8	Fc	61.39N	15.00 E
Ḩamrā', Al Ḩamādah al-	30	If	29.30N	12.00 E
Hamra, Saguia el-	30	Ff	27.24N	13.43W
Hamrān	24	Kd	36.22N	45.44 E
Ḩamrat ash Shaykh	35	Dc	14.35N	27.58 E
Ḩamrīn, Jabal-	24	Ke	34.30N	44.30 E
Hāmūn-e Hirmand, Daryācheh-ye-	23	Jc	31.30N	61.20 E
Han	34	Ec	10.41N	2.27W
Hana	60	Oc	20.45N	155.59W
Hanahan	44	Hi	32.55N	80.00W
Hanaizum	29	Gb	38.51N	141.12 E
Ḩanak	23	Ed	25.33N	36.56 E
Hanalei	65a	Ba	22.13N	159.30W
Hanamaki	28	Pe	39.23N	141.07 E
Hanang	30	Ki	4.26S	35.24 E
Hanaoka	29	Ga	40.21N	140.34 E
Hanapepe	65a	Bb	21.55N	159.35W
Hanau	10	Ef	50.08N	8.55 E
Han-Bogdo	27	Ic	43.12N	107.10 E
Hanceville	42	Ff	51.55N	123.02W
Hancheng	27	Jd	35.30N	110.25 E
Hanchuan	28	Bi	30.39N	113.46 E
Hancock	44	Cb	47.07N	88.35W
Handa	29	Ed	34.53N	136.56 E
Handan	22	Nf	36.35N	114.28 E
Handen	8	He	59.10N	18.08 E
Handeni	36	Gd	5.26S	38.01 E
Handlová	10	Oh	48.44N	18.46 E
Handöl	8	Ea	63.16N	12.26 E
Handyga	22	Pc	62.40N	135.36 E
Ḩānegev = Negev Desert (EN)	24	Fg	30.30N	34.55 E
Hanford	46	Fh	36.20N	119.39W
Hangaj, Hrebet- (Changajn Nuruu) = Khangai Mountains (EN)	21	Le	47.30N	100.00 E
Han-gang	27	Md	37.45N	126.11 E
Hanga Roa	65d	Ab	27.09S	109.26W
Hang'bu He	28	Di	31.33N	117.05 E
Hanggin Houqi (Xamba)	27	Ic	40.59N	107.07 E
Hanggin Qi (Xin Zhen)	27	Id	39.54N	108.55 E
Hangö/Hanko	7	Fg	59.50N	22.57 E
Hangöudde/Hankoniemi	8	Je	59.50N	23.10 E
Hangu	28	De	39.16N	117.50 E
Hangzhou	22	Of	30.18N	120.11 E
Hangzhou Wan	28	Fi	30.25N	121.00 E
Ḩanīsh	33	Hg	13.45N	42.45 E
Ḩanīsh al Kabīr, Jazīrat al-	33	Hg	13.43N	42.45 E
Hanja, Vozvyšennost-	8	Lg	57.30N	27.30 E
Ḩanjūrah, Ra's-	24	Pj	24.44N	54.39 E
Hanka, Ozero- = Khanka Lake (EN)	21	Pe	45.00N	132.24 E
Hankasalmi	8	Lb	62.23N	26.26 E
Hankensbüttel	10	Gd	52.44N	10.36 E
Hanko/Hangö	7	Fg	59.50N	22.57 E
Hankoniemi/Hangöudde	8	Je	59.50N	23.10 E
Hankou, Wuhan-	28	Ci	30.35N	114.16 E
Hanksville	46	Jg	38.25N	110.10W
Hanlar	16	Oi	40.34N	46.20 E
Hanmej, Gora-	17	Lc	67.08N	66.00 E
Hanmer Springs	62	Ee	42.31S	172.50 E
Hann, Mount-	59	Fc	15.50S	125.50 E
Hanna [Alta.-Can.]	42	Gf	51.38N	111.54W
Hanna [Wy.-U.S.]	46	Lf	41.52N	106.34W
Hannah Bay	42	Jf	51.15N	79.50W
Hannibal	43	Id	39.42N	91.22W
Hanningfield Reservoir	12	Cc	51.37N	0.28 E
Hannō	29	Fd	35.53N	139.17 E
Hannover	6	Ge	52.22N	9.43 E
Hann River	59	Fc	17.10S	126.10 E
Hannuit/Hannut	12	Hd	50.40N	5.05 E
Hannut/Hannuit	12	Hd	50.40N	5.05 E
Hano	8	Fi	56.00N	14.50 E
Hanöbukten	8	Fi	55.45N	14.30 E
Ha Noi	22	Mg	21.02N	105.51 E
Hanover [N.H.-U.S.]	44	Kd	43.42N	72.17W
Hanover [Ont.-Can.]	44	Gc	44.09N	81.02W
Hanover [Pa.-U.S.]	44	If	39.47N	76.59W
Hanover [S.Afr.]	37	Cf	31.04S	24.29 E
Hanover, Isla-	56	Fh	51.00S	74.40W
Hanpan, Cape-	59	Ka	5.01S	154.37 E
Han Pijesak	14	Mf	44.05N	18.57 E

Index Symbols

[1] Independent Nation
[2] State, Region
[3] District, County
[4] Municipality
[5] Colony, Dependency
Continent
Physical Region
Historical or Cultural Region
Mount, Mountain
Volcano
Hill
Mountains, Mountain Range
Hills, Escarpment
Plateau, Upland
Pass, Gap
Plain, Lowland
Delta
Salt Flat
Valley, Canyon
Crater, Cave
Karst Features
Depression
Polder
Desert, Dunes
Forest, Woods
Heath, Steppe
Oasis
Cape, Point
Coast, Beach
Cliff
Peninsula
Isthmus
Sandbank
Island
Atoll
Rock, Reef
Islands, Archipelago
Rocks, Reefs
Coral Reef
Well, Spring
Geyser
River, Stream
Waterfall Rapids
River Mouth, Estuary
Lake
Salt Lake
Intermittent Lake
Reservoir
Swamp, Pond
Canal
Glacier
Ice Shelf, Pack Ice
Ocean
Sea
Gulf, Bay
Strait, Fjord
Lagoon
Bank
Seamount
Tablemount
Ridge
Shelf
Basin
Escarpment, Sea Scarp
Fracture
Trench, Abyss
National Park, Reserve
Point of Interest
Recreation Site
Cave, Cavern
Historic Site
Ruins
Wall, Walls
Church, Abbey
Temple
Scientific Station
Airport
Port
Lighthouse
Mine
Tunnel
Dam, Bridge

Hansen Mountains 66 Ee 68.16S 58.47 E
Hanshan 28 Ei 31.43N 118.07 E
Hanshou 28 Aj 28.55N 111.58 E
Han Shui 21 Nf 30.34N 114.17 E
Hanstholm 8 Cg 57.07N 8.38 E
Han Sum 28 Eb 44.33N 119.58 E
Han-sur-Lesse, Rochefort- 12 Hd 50.08N 5.11 E
Han-sur-Nied 12 If 48.59N 6.26 E
Hantajskoje, Ozero- 20 Ec 68.25N 91.00 E
Hantau 19 Hg 44.13N 73.48 E
Hantengri Feng 27 Dc 42.03N 80.11 E
Hants 9 Lj 51.10N 1.10W
Hanty-Mansijsk 22 Ic 61.00N 69.06 E
Hanty-Mansijski Nacionalny Okrug [3] 19 Hc 62.00N 72.30 E
Hantzsch 42 Kc 67.32N 72.26W
Hanušovice 10 Mf 50.05N 16.55 E
Hanwang 27 He 31.25N 104.13 E
Hanyang 28 Ci 30.34N 114.01 E
Hanyang, Wuhan- 28 Ci 30.33N 114.16 E
Hanyū 29 Fc 36.11N 139.32 E
Hanyuan (Fulin) 27 Hf 29.25N 102.12 E
Hanzhong [China] 22 Mf 32.59N 107.11 E
Hanzhong [China] 27 Ie 33.07N 107.00 E
Hanzhuang 28 Dg 34.38N 117.23 E
Hao Atoll 57 Mf 18.15S 140.54W
Hāora 22 Kg 22.35N 88.20 E
Haoud el Hamra 32 Ic 31.58N 5.59 E
Haoxue 28 Bi 30.02N 112.25 E
Haparanda 7 Fd 65.50N 24.10 E
Hapčeranga 20 Gg 49.42N 112.20 E
Happy Valley-Goose Bay 39 Md 53.19N 60.24W
Hapsu 28 Jd 41.13N 128.51 E
Ḩaql 24 Fh 29.18N 34.57 E
Ḩaql al Barqan 24 Lh 28.55N 47.57 E
Ḩaql al Manāqīsh 24 Lh 29.02N 47.32 E
Ḩaql as Şābirīyah 24 Lh 29.48N 47.50 E
Hara, Zaliv-/Hara Laht 8 Ke 59.35N 25.30 E
Hara-Ajrag 27 Ib 45.50N 109.20 E
Harabali 19 Ef 47.25N 47.16 E
Ḩaraḑ 23 Ge 24.14N 49.11 E
Haraiki Atoll 57 Mf 17.28S 143.27W
Hara Laht/Hara, Zaliv- 8 Ke 59.35N 25.30 E
Haramachi 28 Pf 37.38N 140.58 E
Haram Dāgh 23 Gb 37.35N 46.43 E
Harami, Pereval- 16 Oh 42.48N 46.12 E
Harand 24 Of 32.34N 52.26 E
Harani'ia Point 63a Ed 10.21S 161.16 E
Hara Nur 27 Fb 48.05N 93.12 E
Ḩarardēre 35 He 4.32N 47.53 E
Harare 31 Kj 17.50S 31.10 E
Harat 35 Fb 16.05N 39.28 E
Hara-Tas, Krjaž- 20 Fb 72.00N 107.00 E
Haratini 64n Bc 10.28S 160.58W
Ḩarat Zuwayyah 31 Jf 24.14N 21.59 E
Hara-Us-Nur 27 Fb 48.00N 92.10 E
Haraz 35 Bc 13.57N 19.26 E
Harāz 24 Od 36.40N 52.43 E
Harāzah, Jabal- 35 Eb 15.03N 30.27 E
Haraze 35 Cd 9.55N 20.48 E
Harbel 34 Cd 6.16N 10.21W
Harbin 22 Oe 45.45N 126.37 E
Harbor Beach 44 Fd 43.51N 82.39W
Harbour Breton 42 Lg 47.29N 55.50W
Harbour Grace 42 Mg 47.41N 53.15W
Harburg, Hamburg- 10 Fc 53.28N 10.00 E
Harcourt 44 Ob 46.30N 65.15W
Harcuvar Mountains 46 Ii 34.00N 113.30W
Harcyzsk 16 Kf 47.59N 38.11 E
Hardanger 8 Bd 60.20N 6.30 E
Hardangerfjorden 5 Gc 60.10N 6.00 E
Hardangerjøkulen 8 Bd 60.35N 7.25 E
Hardangervidda 7 Bf 60.20N 7.30 E
Hardelot Plage, Neufchâtel Hardelot- 12 Dd 50.38N 1.35 E
Hardenberg 12 Ib 52.34N 6.37 E
Harderwijk 11 Lb 52.21N 5.36 E
Hardin 43 Fb 45.44N 107.37W
Harding 37 Df 30.34S 29.58 E
Hardinsburg 44 Dg 37.47N 86.28W
Härdler 12 Kc 51.06N 8.14 E
Hardoi 25 Gc 27.25N 80.07 E
Hardy, Peninsula- 56 Gi 55.25S 68.30W
Hareid 8 Bb 62.22N 6.02 E
Hareidlandet 7 Ae 62.20N 5.55 E
Hare Indian 42 Ec 66.18N 128.38W
Harelbeke 12 Fd 50.51N 3.18 E
Haren 12 Ia 53.11N 6.38 E
Haren (Ems) 12 Jb 52.47N 7.14 E
Harer 31 Lh 9.18N 42.08 E
Harerge [3] 35 Gd 9.00N 41.30 E
Harēri Mālinwarfā 35 He 4.34N 47.21 E
Harewa 35 Gd 9.54N 41.58 E
Harfleur 12 Ce 49.30N 0.12 E
Harg 8 Hd 60.11N 18.24 E
Hargeysa 31 Lh 9.30N 44.03 E
Harghiţa [2] 15 Ic 46.25N 25.45 E
Harghita, Munţii- 15 Ic 46.31N 25.33 E
Harghita, Vîrful- 15 Ic 46.27N 25.35 E
Hargla 8 Lg 57.31N 26.25 E
Harhorin 27 Hb 47.13N 102.50 E
Har Hu 38.15N 97.40 E
Ḩarīb 23 Gg 14.56N 45.30 E
Haridwār 25 Fc 29.58N 78.10 E
Harihari 62 De 43.09S 170.34 E
Hari Kurk 8 Je 59.00N 22.50 E
Harim 24 Gd 36.12N 36.31 E
Harīm, Jabal al- 24 Qj 25.58N 56.14 E
Harima-Nada 29 Dd 34.30N 134.35 E
Haringey, London- 12 Bc 51.36N 0.06W
Harīrūd 21 If 37.24N 60.38 E
Härjångsfjallet 8 Ea 63.01N 12.35 E
Harjavalta 7 Ff 61.19N 22.08 E
Härjedalen 8 Eb 62.20N 13.05 E
Härjehågna 8 Ec 61.44N 12.08 E
Hårkan 8 Fa 63.20N 14.55 E
Harkov 6 Je 50.00N 36.15 E
Harkovskaja Oblast [3] 19 Df 49.40N 36.30 E
Harlan [Ia.-U.S.] 45 If 41.39N 95.19W
Harlan [Ky.-U.S.] 44 Fg 36.51N 83.19W
Harlan County Lake 45 Gf 40.04N 99.16W
Harlech Castle 9 Ii 52.52N 4.07W
Harlem 46 Kb 48.32N 108.47W
Harleston 12 Db 52.24N 1.18 E
Harlingen [Neth.] 11 La 53.10N 5.24 E
Harlingen [Tx.-U.S.] 43 Hf 26.11N 97.42W
Harlovka 7 Ib 68.47N 37.20 E
Harlovka 7 Ib 68.47N 37.15 E
Harlow 9 Nj 51.47N 0.08 E
Harlowton 46 Kc 46.26N 109.50W
Harlu 7 Hf 61.51N 30.54 E
Hărman 15 Id 45.43N 25.41 E
Harmancık 24 Cc 39.41N 29.10 E
Harmånger 7 Df 61.56N 17.13 E
Harmanli 15 Ih 41.56N 25.54 E
Harmil 35 Gb 16.30N 40.12 E
Harmony 45 Ke 43.33N 91.59W
Harnai 25 Ee 17.48N 73.06 E
Harney Basin 38 Ge 43.15N 120.40W
Harney Lake 43 Dc 43.14N 119.07W
Harney Peak 43 Gc 44.00N 103.30W
Härnön 8 Gb 62.35N 18.00 E
Härnösand 6 Hc 62.38N 17.56 E
Haro 13 Jb 42.35N 2.51W
Harovsk 19 Ed 59.59N 40.11 E
Harøya 8 Bb 62.45N 6.25 E
Harøyfjorden 8 Bb 62.45N 6.35 E
Harpenden 12 Bc 51.48N 0.21W
Harper [Ks.-U.S.] 45 Gh 37.17N 98.01W
Harper [Lbr.] 31 Gh 4.22N 7.43W
Harper, Mount- 40 Kd 64.14N 143.50W
Harper Pass 62 De 42.44S 171.53 E
Harplinge 8 Eh 56.45N 12.43 E
Harqin Qi (Jinshan) 28 Ed 41.57N 118.40 E
Harqin Zuoyi Monggolzu Zizhixian 28 Ed 41.05N 119.40 E
Ḩarrah 23 Hg 14.57N 50.19 E
Ḩarrat al 'Uwayrid 23 Ed 27.00N 37.30 E
Harricana 42 Jf 51.10N 79.47W
Harricana, Rivière- 44 Ha 51.10N 79.45W
Harrington-Harbour 42 Lf 50.26N 59.30W
Harris 9 Gd 57.53N 6.55W
Harris 51c Bc 16.28N 62.10W
Harris, Lake- 44 Gk 28.46N 81.49W
Harris, Sound of- 9 Fd 57.45N 7.08W
Harrisburg 39 Le 40.16N 76.52W
Harrismith 37 De 28.18S 29.03 E
Harrison [Ar.-U.S.] 45 Jh 36.14N 93.07W
Harrison [Mi.-U.S.] 44 Ec 44.01N 84.48W
Harrison [Nb.-U.S.] 45 Ee 42.41N 103.53W
Harrison, Cape - 42 Lf 54.56N 57.55W
Harrison Bay 40 Ib 70.30N 151.30W
Harrisonburg 44 Hf 38.27N 78.54W
Harrison Lake 46 Eb 49.31N 121.59W
Harrison Point 51q Ab 13.18N 59.38W
Harrisonville 45 Ig 38.39N 94.21W
Harrisville [Mi.-U.S.] 44 Fc 44.39N 83.17W
Harrisville [W.V.-U.S.] 44 Gf 39.13N 81.04W
Harrodsburg 44 Eg 37.46N 84.51W
Harrogate 9 Lh 54.00N 1.33W
Harrow, London- 12 Bc 51.36N 0.20W
Harry S. Truman Reservoir 45 Jg 38.00N 93.45W
Har Sai Shan 27 Gd 35.26N 97.41 E
Harsewinkel 12 Kc 51.58N 8.14 E
Harshō 35 Hc 11.17N 47.30 E
Harsim 24 Lf 33.48N 46.50 E
Harsīn 24 Le 34.16N 47.35 E
Harstad 7 Db 68.47N 16.30 E
Harsvik 7 Cd 64.03N 10.02 E
Hart 44 Dd 43.42N 86.22W
Hart 42 Dc 65.51N 136.22W
Hartao 28 Gc 42.30N 122.08 E
Hartbees 30 Jk 28.45S 20.33 E
Hartberg 14 Jc 47.17N 15.58 E
Hårteigen 8 Bd 60.12N 7.04 E
Hartford [Ct.-U.S.] 39 Le 41.46N 72.41W
Hartford [Ky.-U.S.] 44 Dg 37.27N 86.55W
Hartford City 44 Ee 40.29N 85.23W
Hartington 45 He 42.37N 97.16W
Hartland 44 Nb 46.18N 67.32W
Hartland Point 9 Ij 51.02N 4.31W
Hartlepool 9 Lg 54.42N 1.11W
Hartmannberge 37 Ac 17.30S 12.23 E
Hartola 7 Gf 61.35N 26.01 E
Harts 28.24S 24.18 E
Hartselle 44 Dh 34.27N 86.56W
Harts Range 59 Gd 23.05S 134.55 E
Hartsville 44 Gh 34.23N 80.04W
Hartwell 44 Fh 34.21N 82.56W
Hartwell Lake 44 Fh 34.30N 82.55W
Harun, Bukit- 26 Gf 4.06N 115.46 E
Haruno 29 Ce 33.30N 133.30 E
Harves Bank (EN) 51c Ac 16.52N 62.35W
Harvey [Austl.] 59 Df 33.05S 115.54 E
Harvey [N.D.-U.S.] 43 Hb 47.47N 99.56W
Harvey Bay 59 Kd 25.00S 153.00 E
Harwich 9 Oj 51.57N 1.17 E
Haryana [3] 25 Fc 29.30N 76.30 E
Harz 5 He 51.45N 10.30 E
Hasaki 29 Gd 35.44N 140.48 E
Hasama 29 Gb 38.42N 141.13 E
Hasan 20 Ih 42.26N 130.39 E
Ḩasanābād [Iran] 24 Ph 28.47N 54.19 E
Ḩasanābād [Iran] 24 Nd 36.28N 50.17 E
Hasan Dağı 23 Db 38.08N 34.12 E
Ḩasan Langī 24 Qi 27.22N 56.52 E
Hasavjurt 16 Oh 43.16N 46.35 E
Hāsbayyā 24 Ff 33.43N 33.52 E
Hasdo 25 Hd 21.44N 82.44 E
Hase 10 Dd 52.41N 7.18 E
Hasekijata 15 Kg 42.08N 27.30 E
Hasenkamp 55 Cj 31.31S 59.51W
Hashimoto 29 Dd 34.19N 135.37 E
Hashtpar 24 Md 37.48N 48.55 E
Hasi Hausert 32 Ee 22.35N 14.18W
Haskell 43 He 33.10N 99.44W
Haskerland 12 Hb 52.58N 5.47 E
Haskerland-Joure 12 Hb 52.58N 5.47 E
Haskovo 15 Ih 41.56N 25.33 E
Haskovo [2] 15 Ih 41.50N 25.55 E
Hasle 8 Fi 55.11N 14.43 E
Haslemere 9 Mj 51.06N 0.43W
Haslev 8 Di 55.20N 11.58 E
Hăşmaşu Mare, Vîrful- 15 Ic 46.30N 25.50 E
Haspengouws Plateau/Hesbaye 11 Ld 50.35N 5.10 E
Haspres 12 Fd 50.15N 3.25 E
Hassa 24 Gd 36.50N 36.29 E
Hassan 25 Ff 13.00N 76.05 E
Hassberge 10 Gf 50.12N 10.29 E
Hassela 7 De 62.07N 16.42 E
Hassel Sound 42 Ha 78.30N 99.00W
Hasselt 11 Ld 50.56N 5.20 E
Hassi Bel Guebbour 32 Id 28.30N 6.41 E
Hassi el Ghella 13 Ki 35.27N 1.03W
Hassi-Mamèche 13 Mi 35.51N 0.04 E
Hassi Messaoud 31 He 31.43N 6.03 E
Hassi R'mel 32 Hc 32.55N 3.16 E
Hassi Serouenout 32 Ie 24.00N 7.50 E
Hässleholm 7 Ch 56.09N 13.46 E
Hasslö 8 Fh 56.05N 15.25 E
Haßloch 12 Ke 49.23N 8.16 E
Ḩastière 12 Gd 50.13N 4.50 E
Hastière-Hastière par-delà 12 Gd 50.13N 4.50 E
Hastière-par-delà, Hastière- 12 Gd 50.13N 4.50 E
Hastings [Bar.] 51q Ab 13.04N 59.35W
Hastings [Eng.-U.K.] 9 Nk 50.51N 0.36 E
Hastings [Mi.-U.S.] 44 Ed 42.39N 85.17W
Hastings [Mn.-U.S.] 45 Jd 44.44N 92.51W
Hastings [Nb.-U.S.] 43 Hc 40.35N 98.23W
Hastings [N.Z.] 61 Eg 39.38S 176.50 E
Hästveda 8 Eh 56.16N 13.56 E
Hašuri 16 Mi 41.59N 43.33 E
Hasvik 7 Fa 70.29N 22.09 E
Ḩasy al Qaţţār 33 Ec 30.14N 27.11 E
Ḩasy Hague 33 Bd 26.17N 10.31 E
Hat'ae-Do 28 Hg 34.23N 125.17 E
Hatanga 22 Mb 71.58N 102.30 E
Hatanga 21 Mb 72.55N 106.00 E
Hatch 45 Cj 32.40N 107.09W
Hatches Creek 59 Hd 20.56S 135.12 E
Haţeg 15 Fd 45.37N 22.57 E
Hatgal 27 Ha 50.26N 100.09 E
Ḩaţībah, Ra's- 23 Ee 21.59N 38.55 E
Ha Tien 25 Kf 10.23N 104.29 E
Ha Tinh 25 Le 18.20N 105.54 E
Hato Mayor 49 Md 18.46N 69.15W
Ḩattá, Jabal- 24 Qj 24.45N 56.04 E
Hattem 12 Ib 52.28N 6.06 E
Hatten 12 Ka 53.03N 8.23 E
Hatteras, Cape- 38 Lf 35.13N 75.32W
Hatteras Inlet 44 Jh 35.00N 75.40W
Hatteras Island 43 Ld 35.25N 75.30W
Hattfjelldal 7 Cd 65.36N 14.00 E
Hattiesburg 43 Je 31.19N 89.16W
Hattingen 12 Jc 51.24N 7.10 E
Hatu Iti, Ile- 61 Ma 8.42S 140.43W
Hatutaa, Ile- 57 Me 7.30S 140.38W
Hatvan 10 Pi 47.40N 19.41 E
Hat Yai 25 Kg 7.01N 100.27 E
Hatyrka 20 Md 62.03N 175.05 E
Hau Bon 25 Lf 13.24N 108.27 E
Haubourdin 12 Ed 50.36N 2.59 E
Hauge 7 Bg 58.21N 6.17 E
Haugesund 6 Gd 59.25N 5.18 E
Hauho 8 Kc 61.10N 24.33 E
Hauhungaroa Range 62 Fc 38.40S 175.35 E
Haukeligrend 7 Bg 59.51N 7.11 E
Haukipudas 7 Fd 65.15N 25.28 E
Haukivesi 5 Ic 62.05N 28.30 E
Haukivuori 8 Lb 62.01N 27.13 E
Hauraha 63a Ed 10.49S 161.57 E
Hauraki Gulf 61 Eg 36.35S 175.00 E
Hauroko, Lake- 62 Bf 45.55S 167.20 E
Hausa 32 Ed 27.06N 11.01W
Hausruck 14 Hb 48.07N 13.35 E
Haut, Isle au- 44 Mc 44.03N 68.38W
Haut Atlas=High Atlas (EN) 30 Ge 32.00N 6.00W
Haute-Champagne 12 Ge 49.18N 4.15 E
Haute-Corse [3] 11a Aa 42.30N 9.00 E
Haute-Garonne [3] 11 Hk 43.25N 1.30 E
Haute-Guinée [3] 34 Dc 11.30N 10.00W
Haute-Kotto [3] 35 Cd 7.00N 23.00 E
Haute-Loire [3] 11 Ji 45.05N 4.00 E
Haute-Marne [3] 11 Lf 48.05N 5.10 E
Hauterive 44 Ma 49.11N 68.16W
Hautes-Alpes [3] 11 Mj 44.40N 6.30 E
Haute-Sangha [3] 35 Be 4.30N 16.00 E
Haute-Saône [3] 11 Mg 47.40N 6.10 E
Haute-Saône, Plateau de- 11 Lg 47.50N 6.00 E
Haute-Savoie [3] 11 Mi 46.00N 6.20 E
Hautes Fagnes/Hoge Venen 10 Bf 50.30N 6.00 E
Hautes-Pyrénées [3] 11 Gk 43.00N 0.10 E
Haute Vienne [3] 11 Hi 45.50N 1.10 E
Haute Volta→ Burkina Faso 31 Gg 13.00N 2.00W
Haut-Mbomou [3] 35 Dd 6.00N 26.00 E
Hautmont 11 Jd 50.15N 3.56 E
Haut-Ogooué [3] 36 Bc 2.00S 14.00 E
Haut Rhin [3] 11 Ng 48.00N 7.20 E
Hauts-Bassins [3] 34 Ec 12.30N 4.30W
Hauts-de-Seine [3] 11 If 48.50N 2.11 E
Hauts-Plateaux 30 He 34.00N 0.01 E
Haut-Zaïre [2] 36 Eb 2.30N 25.30 E
Hauula 65a 21.36N 157.54W
Hauz-Han 18 Cf 37.16N 61.15 E
Hauz-Hanskoje Vodohr. 18 Cf 37.10N 61.20 E
Havana 45 Kf 40.18N 90.04W
Havana (EN)=La Habana 39 Kg 23.08N 82.22W
Havant 9 Mk 50.51N 0.59W
Havast 18 Gd 40.16N 68.51 E
Havasu, Lake- 46 Hi 34.30N 114.20W
Havel 10 Hd 52.53N 11.58 E
Havelange 12 Hd 50.23N 5.14 E
Havelange-Méan 12 Hd 50.22N 5.20 E
Havelberg 10 Id 52.49N 12.05 E
Havelland 10 Id 52.25N 12.45 E
Havelländisches Luch 10 Id 52.40N 12.40 E
Havelock [N.C.-U.S.] 44 Ih 34.53N 76.54W
Havelock [N.Z.] 62 Ed 41.17S 173.46 E
Havelock North 62 Gc 39.40S 176.53 E
Havelte 12 Ib 52.46N 6.16 E
Haverfordwest 9 Ij 51.49N 4.58W
Haverhill [Eng.-U.K.] 9 Ni 52.05N 0.26 E
Haverhill [Ma.-U.S.] 44 Ld 42.47N 71.05W
Havering, London- 12 Cc 51.36N 0.11 E
Havířov 10 Og 49.48N 18.27 E
Havlíčkův Brod 10 Lg 49.36N 15.34 E
Havøysund 7 Fa 71.03N 24.40 E
Havran 24 Bc 39.33N 27.06 E
Havre 39 Ie 48.33N 109.41W
Havre-Saint-Pierre 39 Md 50.15N 63.36W
Havsa 15 Jh 41.33N 26.49 E
Havza 24 Fb 41.05N 35.45 E
Hawaii [2] 58 Kb 24.00N 167.00W
Hawaiian Islands 57 Kb 24.00N 167.00W
Hawaiian Ridge (EN) 3 Kg 24.00N 165.00W
Hawaii Island 57 Lc 19.30N 155.30W
Ḩawallī 23 Gd 29.19N 48.02 E
Ḩawār 24 Nj 25.40N 50.45 E
Hawarden 62 Ee 42.56S 172.39 E
Ḩawashīyah, Wādī- 24 Eh 28.31N 32.58 E
Hawaymī, Sha'īb al- 24 Kg 30.58N 44.15 E
Hawd 30 Lh 7.40N 47.43 E
Ḩawḑ Al Waqf 24 Ei 26.03N 32.22 E
Hawea, Lake- 62 Cf 44.30S 169.20 E
Hawera 61 Dg 39.35S 174.17 E
Hawi 58 Lb 20.14N 155.50W
Hawick 9 Kf 55.25N 2.47W
Ḩawīzah, Hawr al- 24 Lg 31.35N 47.38 E
Hawkdun Range 62 Cf 44.50S 170.00 E
Hawke Bay 61 Eg 39.25S 177.20 E
Hawke Harbour 42 Lf 53.01N 55.50W
Hawker 59 Hf 31.53S 138.25 E
Hawkes, Mount- 66 Rg 83.55S 56.05W
Hawke's Bay [2] 62 Gc 39.30S 176.40 E
Hawkesbury 44 Jc 45.36N 74.37W
Hawkhurst 12 Cc 51.02N 0.30 E
Hawkinsville 44 Fi 32.17N 83.28W
Hawksbill 44 Hf 38.33N 78.23W
Hawk Springs 46 Mf 41.48N 104.09W
Ḩawmat as Sūq 32 Jc 33.53N 10.51 E
Hawng Tuk 25 Jd 20.28N 99.56 E
Ḩawrā' 35 Hb 15.43N 48.18 E
Hawrān, Wādī al- 23 Fc 33.58N 42.34 E
Ḩawsh 'Isá 24 Dg 30.55N 30.17 E
Hawthorne 43 Dd 38.32N 118.38W
Hawthorne, Mount- 66 Pf 72.10S 98.39W
Haxtun 45 Ef 40.39N 102.38W
Hay 58 Fh 34.30S 144.51 E
Hay 38 Hc 60.51N 115.44W
Hayachine-San 29 Gb 39.34N 141.29 E
Hayakita 29a Bb 42.45N 141.48 E
Hayange 11 Me 49.20N 6.03 E
Hayasui-no-Seto 28 Kh 33.20N 132.00 E
Hayato 29 Bf 31.45N 130.43 E
Haybān 35 Ec 11.13N 30.31 E
Haybān, Jabal- 35 Ec 11.15N 30.31 E
Hayden 46 Jj 33.00N 110.47W
Hayes [Man.-Can.] 42 Ie 57.00N 92.15W
Hayes [N.W.T.-Can.] 42 Hc 67.20N 95.02W
Hayes, Mount- 40 Jd 63.37N 146.43W
Hayes Halvø=Hayes Peninsula (EN) 67 Od 77.40N 64.30W
Hayes Peninsula (EN)= Hayes Halvø 67 Od 77.40N 64.30W
Ḩayl 24 Qj 24.33N 56.06 E
Hayl, Wādī al- 24 He 34.47N 39.18 E
Hayling Island 12 Bd 50.48N 0.58W
Haymana 24 Ec 39.27N 32.30 E
Haymana Platosu 24 Ec 39.25N 32.45 E
Haynin 23 Gf 15.50N 48.18 E
Hayrabolu 24 Bb 41.12N 27.06 E
Ḩayrān 33 Hf 16.02N 42.49 E
Hay River 59 Hd 25.00S 138.00 E
Hay River 39 Hc 60.51N 115.40W
Hayrūt 35 Ib 15.59N 52.09 E
Hays 43 Hd 38.53N 99.20W
Hay Springs 45 Ee 42.41N 102.41W
Haystack Peak 46 Ig 39.50N 113.55W
Hayward [Ca.-U.S.] 46 Dh 37.40N 122.05W
Hayward [Wi.-U.S.] 45 Kc 46.01N 91.29W
Haywards Heath 12 Bc 51.00N 0.06W
Hazar, Wādī- 35 Hb 17.50N 49.07 E
Hazarasp 18 Cd 41.19N 61.08 E
Hazard 44 Fg 37.15N 83 12W
Hazar Gölü 24 Hc 38.30N 39.25 E
Hazāribāgh 25 Hd 23.59N 85.21 E
Hazebrouck 11 Id 50.43N 2.32 E
Hazelton 42 Ee 55.15N 127.40W
Hazen 45 Fc 47.18N 101.38W
Hazen Strait 42 Ga 77.15N 110.00W
Ḩazeva 24 Fg 30.48N 35.15 E
Hazlehurst [Ga.-U.S.] 44 Fj 31.52N 82.36W
Hazlehurst [Ms.-U.S.] 45 Kk 31.52N 90.24W
Hazleton 44 Je 40.58N 76.00W
Hazlett, Lake- 59 Fd 21.30S 128.50 E
Hazrah, Ra's al- 24 Nj 24.22N 51.36 E
Hazro 24 Ic 38.15N 40.47 E
Heacham 12 Cb 52.55N 0.29 E
Headley 12 Bc 51.07N 0.49W
Healdsburg 46 Dg 38.37N 122.52W
Heanor 12 Aa 53.00N 1.18W
Heard Island 30 On 53.00S 73.35 E
Hearne 45 Hk 30.53N 96.36W
Hearst 42 Jg 49.41N 83.40W
Heart River 45 Fc 46.47N 100.51W
Heathrow Airport London 12 Bc 51.28N 0.30W
Hebbronville 45 Gm 27.18N 98.41W
Hebei Sheng (Ho-pei Sheng) =Hopeh (EN) [2] 27 Kd 39.00N 116.00 E
Heber City 46 Jf 40.30N 111.25W
Hebi 27 Jd 35.53N 114.09 E
Hebian 27 Jd 38.35N 113.06 E
Hebiji 28 Cf 36.00N 114.08 E
Hebrides 5 Fd 57.00N 6.30W
Hebrides, Sea of the- 9 Ge 57.00N 7.00W
Hebron [N.D.-U.S.] 45 Ec 46.54N 102.03W
Hebron [Newf.-Can.] 42 Le 58.15N 62.35W
Heby 8 Ge 59.56N 16.53 E
Hecate Strait 42 Ef 53.20N 131.00W
Hecelchakán 48 Ng 20.10N 90.08W
Hechi (Jnchengjiang) 27 Ig 24.44N 108.02 E
Hechingen 10 Eh 48.21N 8.59 E
Hechuan 27 Ie 30.07N 106.15 E
Hecla 45 Gd 45.43N 98.09W
Hecla and Griper Bay 42 Ga 76.00N 111.30W
Hecla Island 45 Ha 51.08N 96.45W
Heddalsvatnet 8 Ce 59.30N 9.15 E
Hede 7 Ce 62.25N 13.30 E
Hede → Sheyang 28 Fh 33.47N 120.15 E
Hedemarken 8 Dd 60.50N 11.20 E
Hedemora 7 Df 60.17N 15.59 E
Hedensted 8 Ci 55.46N 9.42 E
Hedesunda 7 Df 60.25N 17.00 E
Hedesunda fjärdarna 8 Gd 60.20N 17.00 E
Hedmark [2] 7 Cf 61.30N 11.45 E
Hedo-Misaki 29b Bb 26.52N 128.16 E
Heemskerk 12 Gb 52.30N 4.42 E
Heemstede 12 Gb 52.21N 4.37 E
Heerenveen 11 Lb 52.57N 5.55 E
Heerhugowaard 12 Gb 52.40N 4.50 E
Heerlen 11 Ld 50.54N 5.59 E
Hefa=Haifa (EN) 22 Ff 32.50N 35.00 E
Hefei 22 Nf 31.47N 117.15 E
Hefeng 27 Jf 29.49N 110.01 E
Hegang 22 Pe 47.20N 130.12 E
Hegau 10 Ei 47.50N 8.45 E
Hegura Jima 27 Od 37.50N 136.55 E
Heide 10 Fb 54.12N 9.06 E
Heidelberg 10 Eg 49.25N 8.42 E
Heidenheim an der Brenz 10 Gh 48.41N 10.09 E
Heidenreichstein 14 Jb 48.52N 15.07 E
Hei-Gawa 29 Gb 39.38N 141.58 E
Heigun-Tō 29 Ce 33.47N 132.15 E
Hei He 27 Hd 38.15N 100.15 E
Heihe → Aihui 22 Od 50.13N 127.26 E
Heilbron 37 De 27.21S 27.58 E
Heilbronn 10 Fg 49.08N 9.13 E
Heiligenblut 14 Gd 47.02N 12.50 E
Heiligenhafen 10 Gb 54.22N 10.59 E
Heiligenhaus 12 Ic 51.19N 6.58 E
Heiligenstadt 10 Ge 51.23N 10.08 E
Heilinzi 28 Ib 44.33N 126.41 E
Heilong Jiang 21 Qd 52.56N 141.10 E
Heilongjiang Sheng (Hei-lung-chiang Sheng)= Heilungkiang (EN) [2] 27 Mb 48.00N 128.00 E
Heiloo 12 Gb 52.36N 4.43 E
Hei-lung-chiang Sheng → Heilongjiang Sheng=Heilungkiang (EN) [2] 27 Mb 48.00N 128.00 E
Heilungkiang (EN)= Heilongjiang Sheng (Hei-lung-chiang Sheng) [2] 27 Mb 48.00N 128.00 E
Heilungkiang (EN)=Hei-lung-chiang Sheng → Heilongjiang Sheng [2] 27 Mb 48.00N 128.00 E
Heimæy 7a c 63.26N 20.17W
Heimbach 12 Id 50.38N 6.29 E
Heimdal 7 Ce 63.21N 10.22 E
Heimsheim 12 Kf 48.48N 8.51 E
Heinävesi 7 Ge 62.26N 28.36 E
Heinola 7 Gf 61.13N 26.02 E
Heinsberg 12 Ic 51.04N 6.05 E
Heishan 28 Gd 41.42N 122.07 E
Heishan Xia 27 Hd 37.18N 104.39 E
Heishui [China] 28 Ec 42.06N 119.22 E
Heishui [China] 27 He 32.03N 103.05 E
Heist, Knokke- 12 Fc 51.21N 3.15 E
Heist-op-den-Berg 12 Gc 51.05N 4.43 E
Hei-Zaki 29 Hb 39.39N 142.00 E
Hejgijaha 17 Pd 65.27N 72.50 E
Hejian 28 De 38.27N 116.05 E
Hejing 27 Ec 42.18N 86.18 E
Hejjaha 17 Kb 68.18N 62.32 E
Hekimhan 24 Gc 38.49N 37.56 E
Hekinan 29 Ed 34.52N 136.58 E
Hekla 5 Ec 64.00N 19.40W
Hekou 28 Ci 31.20N 114.25 E
Hekou → Yanshan 28 Dj 28.18N 117.41 E
Hel 10 Ob 54.37N 18.48 E
Helagsfjället 7 Ce 62.55N 12.27 E
Helan 27 Id 38.35N 106.16 E
Helan Shan 27 Id 39.00N 106.00 E
Helden's Point 51c Ab 17.24N 62.50W
Helena [Ar.-U.S.] 43 Ie 34.32N 90.35W
Helena [Guy.] 54 Gb 6.41N 57.55W
Helena [Mt.-U.S.] 39 He 46.36N 112.01W
Helen Glacier 66 Ge 66.40S 93.55 E
Helen Reef 57 Ed 2.53N 131.47 E
Helensburgh 9 Ie 56.01N 4.44W
Helensville 62 Fb 36.40S 174.27 E
Helgaå 8 Fi 55.53N 14.08 E
Helgasjön 8 Fh 56.55N 14.45 E
Helgeland 7 Cd 66.15N 13.05 E
Helgoland 10 Db 54.12N 7.53 E

Index Symbols

[1] Independent Nation
[2] State, Region
[3] District, County
[4] Municipality
[5] Colony, Dependency
Continent
Physical Region
Historical or Cultural Region
Mount, Mountain
Volcano
Hill
Mountains, Mountain Range
Hills, Escarpment
Plateau, Upland
Pass, Gap
Plain, Lowland
Delta
Salt Flat
Valley, Canyon
Crater, Cave
Karst Features
Depression
Polder
Desert, Dunes
Forest, Woods
Heath, Steppe
Oasis
Cape, Point
Coast, Beach
Cliff
Peninsula
Isthmus
Sandbank
Island
Atoll
Rock, Reef
Islands, Archipelago
Rocks, Reefs
Coral Reef
Well, Spring
Geyser
River, Stream
Waterfall Rapids
River Mouth, Estuary
Lake
Salt Lake
Intermittent Lake
Reservoir
Swamp, Pond
Canal
Glacier
Ice Shelf, Pack Ice
Ocean
Sea
Gulf, Bay
Strait, Fjord
Lagoon
Bank
Seamount
Tablemount
Ridge
Shelf
Basin
Escarpment, Sea Scarp
Fracture
Trench, Abyss
National Park, Reserve
Point of Interest
Recreation Site
Cave, Cavern
Historic Site
Ruins
Wall, Walls
Church, Abbey
Temple
Scientific Station
Airport
Port
Lighthouse
Mine
Tunnel
Dam, Bridge

International Map Index

Name	Page	Grid	Lat.	Long.
Helgoländer Bucht	10	Eb	54.10N	8.04 E
Helikón Óros	15	Fk	38.20N	22.50 E
Helixi	28	Ei	30.39N	119.01 E
Heljulja	8	Nc	61.37N	30.38 E
Hella	7a	Bc	63.50N	20.24W
Hellberge	10	Hd	52.34N	11.17 E
Hëlleh	24	Nh	29.10N	50.40 E
Hellendoorn	11	Mb	52.24N	6.26 E
Hellendoorn-Nijverdal	12	Ib	52.22N	6.27 E
Hellenic Trough (EN)	5	Ii	35.00N	24.00 E
Hellental	12	Id	50.29N	6.26 E
Hellesylt	7	Be	62.05N	6.54 E
Hellín	13	Kf	38.31N	1.41W
Hells Canyon	43	Db	45.20N	116.45W
Hellweg	12	Kc	51.40N	8.00 E
Helmand	21	If	31.12N	61.34 E
Helmand [3]	23	Jc	31.00N	64.00 E
Helme	10	He	51.20N	11.20 E
Helmeringhausen	37	Be	25.54S	16.57 E
Helmond	11	Lc	51.29N	5.40 E
Helmsdale	9	Jc	58.10N	3.40W
Helmsdale	9	Jc	58.07N	3.40W
Helmstedt	10	Gd	52.14N	11.00 E
Helong	27	Mc	42.32N	129.00 E
Helpe Majeure	12	Fd	50.11N	3.47 E
Helpringham	12	Bb	52.56N	0.18W
Helpter Berge	10	Jc	53.30N	13.36 E
Helsingborg	6	Hd	56.03N	12.42 E
Helsinge	8	Eh	56.01N	12.12 E
Helsingfors/Helsinki	6	Ic	60.10N	24.58 E
Helsingør	7	Ch	56.02N	12.37 E
Helsinki/Helsingfors	6	Ic	60.10N	24.58 E
Helska, Mierzeja-	10	Ob	54.45N	18.39 E
Helston	9	Hk	50.05N	5.16W
Helvecia	55	Bj	31.06S	60.05W
Helwān (EN)=Ḩulwān	33	Fd	29.51N	31.20 E
Ḩemār	24	Qg	31.42N	57.31 E
Hemčik	20	Ef	51.40N	92.10 E
Hemel Hempstead	9	Mj	51.46N	0.28W
Hemer	12	Jc	51.23N	7.46 E
Hemnesberget	7	Cc	66.14N	13.38 E
Hemsby	12	Db	52.41N	1.42 E
Hemse	8	Hg	57.14N	18.22 E
Hemsedal	8	Cd	60.50N	8.40 E
Hemsö	7	Ee	62.45N	18.05 E
Hen	8	Dd	60.13N	10.14 E
Henan	27	He	34.33N	101.55 E
Hen and Chickens Islands	62	Fa	35.55S	174.45 E
Henan Sheng (Ho-nan Sheng)=Honan (EN) [2]	27	Je	34.00N	114.00 E
Henares	13	Id	40.24N	3.30W
Henashi-Zaki	29	Fa	40.37N	139.51 E
Henbury	59	Gd	24.35S	133.15 E
Hendaye	11	Ek	43.22N	1.47W
Hendek	24	Db	40.48N	30.45 E
Henderson [Arg.]	55	Bm	36.18S	61.43W
Henderson [Ky.-U.S.]	44	Dg	37.50N	87.35W
Henderson [N.C.-U.S.]	44	Hg	36.20N	78.25W
Henderson [Nv.-U.S.]	43	Dd	36.02N	115.01W
Henderson [Tx.-U.S.]	45	Ij	32.09N	94.48W
Henderson Island	57	Og	24.22S	128.19W
Henderson Seamount (EN)	43	Df	25.34N	119.33W
Hendersonville [N.C.-U.S.]	44	Fh	35.19N	82.28W
Hendersonville [Tn.-U.S.]	44	Dg	36.18N	86.37W
Hendījān	24	Mg	30.14N	49.43 E
Hendorābī, Jazīreh-ye-	24	Oi	26.40N	53.37 E
Hendrik Verwderddam	30	Km	46.36S	37.55 E
Hengām, Jazīreh-ye-	24	Pi	26.39N	55.53 E
Hengduan Shan	21	Lg	27.30N	99.00 E
Hengelo [Neth.]	11	Mb	52.15N	6.45 E
Hengelo [Neth.]	12	Ib	52.03N	6.20 E
Heng Shan [China]	27	Jd	39.42N	113.45 E
Hengshan [China]	27	Jf	27.16N	112.51 E
Heng Shan [China]	27	Jf	27.18N	112.41 E
Hengshan [China]	27	Id	37.51N	109.20 E
Hengshan [China]	28	Kb	45.24N	131.01 E
Hengshui	27	Kd	37.39N	115.46 E
Hengxian	27	Ig	22.46N	109.15 E
Hengyang	22	Ng	26.56N	112.35 E
Henik Lakes	42	Hd	61.05N	97.20W
Hénin-Liétard	11	Id	50.25N	2.56 E
Henley-on-Thames	12	Bc	51.32N	0.54W
Hennan	8	Fb	62.05N	15.45 E
Hennan	7	De	62.02N	15.54 E
Hennebont	11	Cg	47.48N	3.17W
Hennef (Sieg)	12	Jd	50.47N	7.17 E
Hennigsdorf bei Berlin	10	Jd	52.38N	13.12 E
Henrietta Maria, Cape -	42	Je	55.09N	82.19W
Henrietty, Ostrov-	20	Ka	77.00N	157.00 E
Henry, Mount-	46	Hb	48.53N	115.31W
Henry Bay	66	Ie	66.40S	120.40 E
Henryetta	45	Ii	35.27N	95.59W
Henry Kater Peninsula	42	Kk	69.15N	67.30W
Henry Mountains	46	Jh	37.55N	110.50W
Henrys Fork River	46	Je	43.45N	111.56W
Henslow, Cape-	63a	Ec	9.56S	160.38 E
Hentej	21	Me	48.50N	109.00 E
Hentiesbaai	37	Ad	22.08S	14.18 E
Henzada	22	Lh	17.38N	95.28 E
Heping → Yanhe	27	If	28.31N	108.28 E
Heppenheim (Bergstraße)	12	Ke	49.38N	8.39 E
Heppner	46	Fd	45.21N	119.33W
Hepu (Lianzhou)	27	Ig	21.40N	109.12 E
Hequ	27	Jd	39.22N	111.15 E
Herakol Dağı	24	Id	37.45N	42.35 E
Heralds Cays	59	Jc	16.55S	149.10 E
Herāt [3]	23	Jc	34.30N	62.00 E
Herāt	22	If	34.20N	62.12 E
Hérault [3]	11	Jk	43.40N	3.30 E
Hérault	11	Jk	43.17N	3.26 E
Herbert [N.Z.]	62	Df	45.13S	170.46 E
Herbert [Sask.-Can.]	46	La	50.26N	107.12W
Herberton	59	Jc	17.23S	145.23 E
Herbert River	59	Jc	18.32S	146.17 E
Herborn	10	Ef	50.41N	8.19 E
Herby	10	Of	50.45N	18.40 E
Hercegnovi	15	Bg	42.27N	18.32 E
Hercegovina	14	Lg	43.00N	17.50 E
Hercegovina	5	Hg	43.00N	17.50 E
Herdubreid	7a	Cb	65.11N	16.21W
Heredia [3]	49	Fh	10.30N	84.00W
Heredia	47	Hf	10.00N	84.07W
Hereford	9	Ki	52.15N	2.50W
Hereford [Eng.-U.K.]	9	Ki	52.04N	2.43W
Hereford [Tx.-U.S.]	43	Ge	34.49N	102.24W
Hereford and Worcester [3]	9	Ki	52.10N	2.35W
Hereheretue Atoll	57	Mf	19.54S	144.58W
Hereke	15	Mi	40.48N	29.39 E
Herekino	62	Ea	35.16S	173.13 E
Herent	12	Gd	50.54N	4.40 E
Herentals	12	Gc	51.11N	4.50 E
Herfølge	8	Ei	55.25N	12.10 E
Herford	10	Ed	52.08N	8.41 E
Héricourt	11	Mg	47.35N	6.45 E
Herington	45	Hg	38.40N	96.57W
Heriot	61	Ci	45.51S	169.16 E
Herīs	24	Lc	38.14N	47.07 E
Herisau	14	Dc	47.24N	9.16 E
Herk	12	Hd	50.58N	5.07 E
Herk-de-Stad	12	Hd	50.56N	5.10 E
Herkimer	44	Jd	43.02N	74.59W
Herlen He	27	Kb	48.48N	117.00 E
Hermagor	14	Hd	46.37N	13.22 E
Hermanas	48	Id	27.14N	101.14W
Herma Ness	9	Ma	60.50N	0.54W
Hermano Peak	45	Bh	37.17N	108.48W
Hermansverk	8	Bc	61.11N	6.51 E
Hermanus	37	Bf	34.25S	19.16 E
Hermeskeil	12	Ie	49.39N	6.57 E
Hermiston	46	Fd	45.51N	119.17W
Hermitage	62	De	43.44S	170.05 E
Hermit Islands	57	Fe	1.32S	145.05 E
Hermosa de Santa Rosa, Sierra-	48	Id	28.00N	101.45W
Hermosillo	39	Hg	29.04N	110.58W
Hermoso Campo	55	Bh	27.36S	61.21W
Hérnad	10	Qh	48.00N	20.58 E
Hernandarias	56	Jc	25.22S	54.45W
Hernández [Arg.]	55	Bk	32.21S	60.02W
Hernández [Mex.]	48	Hf	23.02N	102.02W
Hernani	13	Ka	43.16N	1.58W
Herne	10	De	51.33N	7.13 E
Herne Bay	9	Oj	51.23N	1.08 E
Herning	6	Gd	56.08N	8.59 E
Heroica Alvarado	48	Lh	18.46N	95.46W
Heroica Tlapacoyan	48	Kh	19.58N	97.13W
Heroica Zitácuaro	48	Ih	19.24N	100.22W
Herouville-Saint-Clair	12	Be	49.12N	0.19W
Herowābād	24	Md	37.37N	48.32 E
Herradura	55	Ch	26.29S	58.18W
Herre	8	Ce	59.06N	9.34 E
Herrera	55	Ck	32.26S	58.38W
Herrera [3]	49	Gj	7.54N	80.38W
Herrera del Duque	13	Ge	39.10N	5.03W
Herrera de Pisuerga	13	Hb	42.36N	4.20W
Herrero, Punta-	48	Ph	19.10N	87.30W
Herrljunga	8	Ef	58.05N	13.02 E
Hers	11	Hk	43.47N	1.20 E
Herschel	42	Dc	69.35N	139.05W
Herselt	12	Gc	51.03N	4.53 E
Herserange	12	He	49.31N	5.47 E
Hershey	44	Ie	40.17N	76.39W
Hersilia	55	Bj	30.00S	61.51W
Herson	6	Jf	46.38N	32.35 E
Hersonesski, Mys-	16	Hg	44.33N	33.25 E
Hersonskaja Oblast [3]	19	Df	46.40N	33.30 E
Herstal	11	Ld	50.40N	5.38 E
Herten	12	Jc	51.36N	7.08 E
Hertford	9	Mj	51.50N	0.05W
Hertford	9	Mj	51.48N	0.05W
Hertfordshire [3]	9	Mj	51.45N	0.20W
Hertugen Af Orleans Land	41	Jc	78.15N	21.12W
Hervás	13	Gd	40.16N	5.51W
Herve	12	Hd	50.38N	5.48 E
Herve, Plateau van-/Herveland	12	Hd	50.40N	5.50 E
Herveland/Herve, Plateau van-	12	Hd	50.40N	5.50 E
Hervey Bay	59	Ke	25.15S	152.50 E
Herzberg	10	Je	51.41N	13.14 E
Herzberg am Harz	10	Ge	51.39N	10.20 E
Herzebrock	12	Kc	51.53N	8.15 E
Herzele	12	Fd	50.53N	3.53 E
Herzliyya	24	Ff	32.10N	34.51 E
Herzogenrath	12	Id	50.52N	6.06 E
Herzog-Ernst-Bucht (Vahsel Bay)	66	Af	77.48S	34.39W
Hesāmābād	24	Me	35.52N	48.25 E
Hesbaye/Haspengouws Plateau	11	Ld	50.35N	5.10 E
Hesdin	11	Id	50.22N	2.02 E
Hesel	12	Ja	53.18N	7.36 E
Heshī	24	Md	37.30N	48.15 E
Heshun	27	Jd	37.18N	113.32 E
Hesse (EN)=Hessen [2]	10	Ff	50.30N	9.15 E
Hesselberg	10	Gg	49.05N	10.35 E
Hesselø	8	Dh	56.10N	11.45 E
Hessen	12	Ke	49.47N	8.08 E
Hessen=Hesse (EN) [2]	10	Ff	50.30N	9.15 E
Hess Tablemount (EN)	57	Jc	17.50N	174.15W
Heta	21	Mb	71.54N	102.00 E
Heta	20	Eb	71.35N	99.45 E
Hettange-Grande	12	Ie	49.24N	6.09 E
Hettinger	45	Ec	46.00N	102.39W
Heuberg	10	Eh	48.06N	8.55 E
Heuchin	12	Ed	50.28N	2.16 E
Heuru	63a	Ed	10.12S	161.25 E
Hève, Cap de la-	11	Fe	49.31N	0.04W
Heves	10	Qi	47.36N	20.17 E
Heves [2]	10	Qi	47.50N	20.15 E
Hexham	9	Kg	54.58N	2.06W
Hexi	27	Hf	27.44N	102.09 E
Hexian	28	Ei	31.43N	118.22 E
Hexian (Babu)	27	Jg	24.28N	111.34 E
Hexigten Qi (Jingfeng)	27	Kc	43.15N	117.31 E
Heydarābād	24	Kd	37.06N	45.27 E
Heysham	9	Kg	54.02N	2.54W
Heyuan	27	Jg	23.41N	114.43 E
Heywood	59	Ig	38.08S	141.38 E
Heze (Caozhou)	27	Kd	35.14N	115.28 E
Hezuo	27	Hd	35.02N	102.57 E
Hialeah	44	Gm	25.49N	80.17W
Hiawatha	45	Ig	39.51N	95.32W
Hibara-Ko	29	Gc	37.42N	140.03 E
Hibbing	43	Ib	47.25N	92.56W
Hibernia Reef	59	Eb	12.00S	123.25 E
Hibiki-Nada	29	Bd	34.15N	130.40 E
Hibiny	7	Hc	67.40N	33.35 E
Hiburi-Jima	29	Ce	33.10N	132.18 E
Hickman	44	Cg	36.34N	89.11W
Hickory	44	Gh	35.44N	81.21W
Hick's Cay	49	Ce	17.39N	88.08W
Hida-Gawa	29	Ed	35.25N	137.03 E
Hidaka [Jap.]	28	Qc	42.53N	142.28 E
Hidaka [Jap.]	29	Dd	35.28N	134.47 E
Hidaka-Gawa	29	De	33.53N	135.08 E
Hidaka Sanmyaku	28	Qc	42.25N	142.50 E
Hidalgo [2]	47	Ed	20.30N	99.00W
Hidalgo [Mex.]	47	Ed	24.15N	99.26W
Hidalgo [Mex.]	48	Jd	27.47N	99.52W
Hidalgo del Parral	39	Ig	26.56N	105.40W
Hida-Sanchi	29	Ec	36.20N	137.00 E
Hida-Sanmyaku	28	Nf	36.10N	137.30 E
Hiddensee	10	Jb	54.33N	13.07 E
Hidra	8	Bf	58.15N	6.35 E
Hidrolândia	55	Hc	16.58S	49.16W
Hidrolina	55	Hb	14.37S	49.25W
Hieflau	14	Ic	47.36N	14.44 E
Hiei-Zan	29	Dd	35.05N	135.50 E
Hienghène	61	Cd	20.35S	164.56 E
Hierro	30	Ff	27.45N	18.00W
Higashi	29b	b	26.38N	128.08 E
Higashihiroshima	29	Cd	34.25N	132.43 E
Higashi-izu	29	Fd	34.48N	139.02 E
Higashi-matsuyama	29	Fc	36.02N	139.22 E
Higashimuroran	29a	Bb	42.21N	141.02 E
Higashine	28	Pe	38.26N	140.24 E
Higashiōsaka	29	Dd	34.40N	135.37 E
Higashi Rishiri	29a	Ba	45.16N	141.15 E
Higashi-Shina-Kai=East China Sea (EN)	21	Og	29.00N	125.00 E
Higgins	45	Fh	36.07N	100.02W
Higham Ferrers	12	Bb	52.18N	0.35W
High Atlas (EN)=Haut Atlas	30	Ge	32.00N	6.00W
Highland [3]	9	Id	57.30N	5.00W
Highland Park	45	Me	42.11N	87.48W
High Level	42	Fe	58.30N	117.05W
Highmore	45	Gd	44.31N	99.27W
High Plains	38	If	38.30N	103.00W
High Point	43	Ld	35.58N	79.59W
High Prairie	42	Fe	55.27N	116.30W
High River	42	Gf	50.35N	113.52W
Highrock Lake	42	He	55.49N	100.23W
High Springs	44	Fk	29.50N	82.36W
High Tatra (EN)=Vysoké Tatry	10	Pg	49.10N	20.00 E
High Willhays	9	Jk	50.41N	3.59W
Highwood Mountains	46	Jc	47.25N	110.30W
High Wycombe	9	Mj	51.38N	0.46W
Higuera de Zaragoza	48	Ee	25.59N	109.16W
Higüero, Punta-	49	Nd	18.22N	67.16W
Higuerote	50	Cg	10.29N	66.06W
Higüey	49	Md	18.37N	68.43W
Hiidenvesi	8	Kd	60.20N	24.10 E
Hii-Gawa	29	Cd	35.26N	132.52 E
Hiiraan [3]	35	He	4.00N	45.30 E
Hiitola	7	Gf	61.16N	29.42 E
Hiiumaa/Hiuma	5	Id	58.50N	22.40 E
Hijar	13	Lc	41.10N	0.27W
Ḩijāz	23	Ee	24.30N	38.30 E
Hijāz, Jabal al-	33	Hf	19.45N	41.55 E
Hiji	29	Be	33.22N	131.32 E
Hiji-Gawa	29	Ce	33.36N	132.29 E
Hikami	29	Dd	35.11N	135.02 E
Hikari	28	Kh	33.58N	131.56 E
Hiketa	29	Dd	34.13N	134.24 E
Hikiä	8	Kd	60.45N	24.55 E
Hiki-Gawa	29	De	33.35N	135.26 E
Ḩikmah, Ra's al-	24	Bg	31.17N	27.44 E
Hikone	28	Ng	35.15N	136.15 E
Hiko-San	29	Be	33.29N	130.56 E
Hikueru Atoll	61	Mc	17.36S	142.37W
Hikurangi	62	Hb	37.55S	178.04 E
Hikurangi	62	Fa	35.36S	174.17 E
Hila	26	Ih	7.35S	127.24 E
Hilāl, Ra's al-	33	Dc	32.55N	22.11 E
Hiland	46	Le	43.08N	107.18W
Hilchenbach	12	Kc	51.00N	8.06 E
Hildburghausen	10	Gf	50.25N	10.45 E
Hilden	12	Ic	51.10N	6.56 E
Hildesheim	10	Fd	52.09N	9.58 E
Hillaby, Mount-	50	Gf	13.12N	59.35W
Hillared	8	Eg	57.38N	13.09 E
Hillary Coast	6	Kf	79.00S	161.00 E
Hill Bank	49	Ce	17.35N	88.42W
Hill City	45	Gg	39.22N	99.51W
Hillcrest Center	46	Fi	35.23N	118.57W
Hille	12	Kb	52.20N	8.45 E
Hillegom	12	Gb	52.18N	4.35 E
Hillekrog	8	Dj	54.36N	11.30 E
Hillerød	8	Ei	55.56N	12.19 E
Hillerstorp	8	Eg	57.19N	13.52 E
Hillesheim	12	Id	50.19N	6.41 E
Hillingdon, London-	12	Bc	51.31N	0.27W
Hillsboro [Il.-U.S.]	45	Lg	39.09N	89.29W
Hillsboro [N.D.-U.S.]	45	Hc	47.26N	97.03W
Hillsboro [Oh.-U.S.]	44	Ff	39.12N	83.37W
Hillsboro [Or.-U.S.]	46	Dd	45.31N	122.59W
Hillsboro [Tx.-U.S.]	45	Hj	32.01N	97.08W
Hillsborough	51p	Cb	12.29N	61.26W
Hillsdale	44	Ee	41.55N	84.38W
Hillsville	44	Gg	36.46N	80.44W
Hillswich	9	La	60.28N	1.30W
Hilo	58	Lc	19.44N	155.05W
Hilo Bay	65a	Fd	19.44N	155.05W
Hilok	21	Md	51.19N	106.59 E
Hilok	20	Gf	51.22N	110.30 E
Hilton Head Island	44	Gi	32.12N	80.45W
Hiltrup, Münster-	12	Jc	51.54N	7.38 E
Hilvan	24	Hd	37.30N	38.58 E
Hilvarenbeek	12	Hc	51.29N	5.08 E
Hilversum	11	Lb	52.14N	5.10 E
Himāchal Prādesh [3]	25	Fb	31.00N	78.00 E
Himalaya=Himalayas (EN)	21	Kg	29.00N	83.00 E
Himalayas (EN)=Himalaya	21	Kg	29.00N	83.00 E
Himara	15	Ci	40.07N	19.44 E
Himeji	27	Ne	34.49N	134.42 E
Hime-Jima	29	Be	33.43N	131.40 E
Hime-Kawa	29	Ec	37.02N	137.50 E
Hime-Shima	29	Ae	32.49N	128.41 E
Hime-Zaki	29	Fb	38.05N	138.34 E
Himi	28	Nf	36.51N	136.59 E
Himki	7	Ii	55.56N	37.28 E
Himmelbjerget	8	Ch	56.06N	9.42 E
Himmerfjärden	8	Ge	59.00N	17.43 E
Himmerland	8	Ch	56.50N	9.45 E
Himo	36	Gc	3.23S	37.33 E
Ḩimş=Homs (E)	22	Ff	34.44N	36.43 E
Hims, Bahrat-	24	Ge	34.39N	36.34 E
Hinai	29	Ga	40.13N	140.35 E
Hinca Renancó	56	Hd	34.50S	64.23W
Hinche	49	Kd	19.09N	72.01W
Hinchinbrook	40	Jd	60.22N	146.30W
Hinchinbrook Island	59	Jc	18.25S	146.15 E
Hinckley	12	Ab	52.32N	1.22W
Hindås	8	Eg	57.42N	12.27 E
Hindhead	12	Bc	51.06N	0.44W
Ḩindi, Badwēynta-=Indian Ocean (EN)	3	Gl	21.00S	82.00 E
Hindmarsh, Lake-	59	Ig	36.05S	141.55 E
Hinds	62	Df	44.00S	171.34 E
Hindsholm	8	Di	55.33N	10.40 E
Hindukush	21	Jf	35.00N	71.00 E
Hindustan	21	Jg	25.00N	79.00 E
Hinesville	44	Gj	31.51N	81.36W
Hinganghāt	25	Fd	20.34N	78.50 E
Hınıs	24	Ic	39.22N	41.44 E
Hınıs	24	Jc	39.18N	42.12 E
Hinlopenstretet	41	Oc	79.15N	21.00 E
Hinnøya	5	Hb	68.30N	16.00 E
Hino-Gawa	29	Cd	35.27N	133.22 E
Hinojosa del Duque	13	Gf	38.30N	5.09W
Hinokage	29	Be	32.39N	131.24 E
Hi-no-Misaki	29	Cd	35.26N	132.38 E
Hino-Misaki	29	De	33.53N	135.04 E
Hinterrhein	14	Dd	46.49N	9.25 E
Hinton	42	Ff	53.25N	117.34W
Hi-Numa	29	Gc	36.16N	140.30 E
Hınzır Burun	24	Fb	36.22N	35.45 E
Hiou	63b	Ca	13.08S	166.33 E
Hipólito	48	Ie	25.41N	101.26W
Hippolytushoef, Wieringen-	12	Gb	52.54N	4.59 E
Hippone	14	Bn	36.52N	7.44 E
Hirado	28	Jh	33.22N	129.33 E
Hirado-Shima	28	Jh	33.19N	129.32 E
Hiraka	29	Gb	39.16N	140.29 E
Hirakata	29	Dd	34.48N	135.38 E
Hīrākud	25	Gd	21.15N	84.15 E
Hiraman	36	Gc	1.07S	39.55 E
Hiranai	29a	Bc	40.54N	140.57 E
Hirara	27	Mg	24.48N	125.17 E
Hira-Shima	29	Ae	33.01N	129.15 E
Hirata	29	Cd	35.26N	132.49 E
Hiratsuka	29	Fd	35.19N	139.19 E
Hirfanlı barajı Gölü	24	Ec	39.10N	33.32 E
Hirgis	27	Fb	49.32N	93.48 E
Hirgis-Nur	21	Le	49.12N	93.24 E
Hirhafok	32	Ie	23.29N	5.45 E
Hîrlău	15	Jb	47.26N	26.54 E
Hiromi	29	Ce	33.15N	132.38 E
Hiroo	27	Pc	42.17N	143.19 E
Hirosaki	27	Pc	40.35N	140.28 E
Hiroshima	22	Pf	34.24N	132.27 E
Hiroshima Ken [2]	28	Lg	34.35N	132.50 E
Hiroshima-Wan	29	Cd	34.10N	132.20 E
Hirschhorn (Neckar)	12	Ke	49.27N	8.54 E
Hirson	11	Ke	49.55N	4.05 E
Hîrşova	15	Ke	44.41N	27.56 E
Hîrtibaciu	15	Hd	45.44N	24.14 E
Hirtshals	7	Bh	57.35N	9.58 E
Hirvensalmi	8	Lc	61.38N	26.48 E
Ḩīs	35	Hc	10.50N	46.54 E
Hisai	29	Ed	34.40N	136.28 E
Hisaka-Shima	29	Ae	32.48N	128.52 E
Hisar	15	Jg	42.35N	27.00 E
Hisar	25	Fc	29.10N	75.43 E
Hisarcik	15	Mj	39.15N	29.15 E
Hisarja	15	Hg	42.30N	24.42 E
Ḩismā	24	Fh	28.30N	35.50 E
Ḩişn al 'Abr	33	If	16.08N	47.14 E
Ḩişn aş Şaḩābī	33	Dc	30.01N	20.48 E
Hispaniola (EN)=La Española	38	Lh	19.00N	71.00W
Histon	12	Cb	52.15N	0.06 E
Histria	15	Le	44.30N	28.45 E
Hīt	24	Jf	33.38N	42.49 E
Hita	28	Kh	33.19N	130.56 E
Hitachi	28	Pf	36.36N	140.39 E
Hitachi-ōta	29	Gc	36.32N	140.31 E
Hitchin	12	Bc	51.57N	0.16W
Hitiaa	65e	Fc	17.36S	149.18W
Hitotsuse-Gawa	29	Be	32.03N	131.31 E
Hitoyoshi	28	Kh	32.15N	130.45 E
Hitra	5	Gc	63.30N	8.45 E
Hiuchi-ga-Take	29	Fc	36.57N	139.17 E
Hiuchi-Nada	29	Cd	34.05N	133.15 E
Hiuma/Hiiumaa	5	Id	58.50N	22.40 E
Hiv	16	Oi	41.46N	47.57 E
Hiva	19	Gg	41.25N	60.23 E
Hiva Oa, Ile-	57	Ne	9.45S	139.00W
Hiw	24	Ei	26.01N	32.16 E
Hjademeste/Häädemeeste	8	Uf	58.00N	24.28 E
Hjallerup	8	Dg	57.10N	10.09 E
Hjälmare kanal	8	Fe	59.25N	15.55 E
Hjälmaren	5	Hd	59.15N	15.45 E
Hjelm	8	Dh	56.10N	10.50 E
Hjelmelandsvågen	7	Bg	59.15N	6.10 E
Hjelmsøya	7	Fa	71.05N	24.43 E
Hjerkinn	8	Cb	62.13N	9.32 E
Hjo	7	Dg	58.18N	14.17 E
Hjørring	7	Bh	57.28N	9.59 E
Hlatikulu	37	Ee	26.58S	31.19 E
Hlavní město Praha [3]	10	Kf	50.05N	14.25 E
Hlavní město SSR Bratislava [3]	10	Nh	48.10N	17.10 E
Hlinsko	10	Lg	49.46N	15.54 E
Hlohovec	10	Nh	48.25N	17.48 E
Hluhluwe	37	Ee	28.02S	32.17 E
Hmelnickaja Oblast [3]	19	Cf	49.30N	27.00 E
Hmelnicki	19	Cf	49.24N	26.57 E
Hmelnik	16	Ee	49.33N	27.59 E
Hnilec	10	Rh	48.53N	21.01 E
Ho	34	Fd	6.36N	0.28 E
Hoa Binh	25	Ld	20.50N	105.20 E
Hoai Nhon	25	Lf	14.26N	109.01 E
Hoanib	37	Ac	19.23S	13.06 E
Hoare Bay	42	Lc	65.30N	63.10W
Hoback Peak	46	Je	43.10N	110.33W
Hobart [Austl.]	58	Fi	42.53S	147.19 E
Hobart [Ok.-U.S.]	45	Gi	35.01N	99.06W
Hobbs	43	Ge	32.42N	103.08W
Hobbs Coast	66	Nf	74.50S	131.00W
Hobda	16	Sd	50.55N	54.38 E
Hoboken, Antwerpen-	12	Gc	51.10N	4.21 E
Hoboksar	27	Eb	46.47N	85.43 E
Hobq Shamo	27	Ic	40.30N	108.00 E
Hobro	7	Bh	56.38N	9.48 E
Hoburgen	7	Eh	56.55N	18.07 E
Hobyā	31	Lh	5.20N	48.38 E
Hocalar	15	Mk	38.37N	29.57 E
Hochalmspitze	14	Hc	47.01N	13.19 E
Hochfeiler/Gran Pilastro	14	Fd	46.58N	11.44 E
Hochgolling	14	Hc	47.16N	13.45 E
Hochschwab	14	Jc	47.36N	15.05 E
Höchstadt an der Aisch	10	Gg	49.42N	10.44 E
Hochstetters Forland	41	Kc	75.45N	20.00W
Höchst im Odenwald	12	Ke	49.48N	9.00 E
Hochtor	14	Gc	47.05N	12.48 E
Hockenheim	12	Ke	49.19N	8.33 E
Hodaka-Dake	29	Ec	36.17N	137.39 E
Hodda	35	Ic	11.30N	50.45 E
Hoddesdon	12	Cc	51.45N	0.00
Hodgenville	44	Eg	37.34N	85.44W
Hodh	30	Gg	16.10N	8.40W
Hodh ech Chargui [3]	32	Ff	17.00N	7.15W
Hodh el Gharbi [3]	32	Ff	16.30N	10.00W
Hódmezővásárhely	10	Qj	46.25N	20.20 E
Hodna, Chott el-	32	Hb	35.25N	4.45 E
Hodna, Monts du-	32	Hb	35.50N	4.50 E
Hodna, Plaine du-	13	Qi	35.35N	4.35 E
Hodonín	10	Nh	48.52N	17.08 E
Hodorov	16	De	49.25N	24.18 E
Hodžambas	18	Ee	38.06N	65.01 E
Hodža-Pirjah, Gora-	18	Fe	38.47N	67.35 E
Hodžejli	19	Fg	42.23N	59.20 E
Hœdic, Ile de-	11	Dg	47.20N	2.52W
Hoegaarden	12	Gd	50.47N	4.53 E
Hoei/Huy	11	Ld	50.31N	5.14 E
Hoë Karoo	30	Jl	30.00S	21.30 E
Hoek van Holland	11	Kc	51.59N	4.09 E
Hoeselt	12	Hd	50.51N	5.29 E
Hof	10	Hf	50.19N	11.55 E
Höfdakaupstadur	7a	Bb	65.50N	20.19W
Hofgeismar	10	Fe	51.29N	9.24 E
Hofheim	12	Kd	50.05N	8.27 E
Hofmeyr	37	Df	31.39S	25.50 E
Höfn	7a	Cb	64.15N	15.13W
Hofsjökull	5	Ec	64.49N	18.48W
Hōfu	28	Kg	34.03N	131.34 E
Höganäs	8	Eh	56.12N	12.33 E
Hogarth, Mount-	59	Hd	21.48S	136.58 E
Hogback Mountain	46	Id	44.54N	112.07W
Hog Cliffs	51d	Ba	17.38N	61.44W
Hoge Venen/Hautes Fagnes	10	Bf	50.30N	6.00 E
Högfors/Karkkila	7	Ff	60.32N	24.11 E
Hog Island	51p	Bb	12.00N	61.44W
Hogne, Somme-Leuze-	12	Hd	50.15N	5.17 E
Hog Point	51d	Ba	17.43N	61.48W
Högsby	7	Dh	57.10N	16.02 E
Høgste Breakulen	8	Bc	61.41N	7.02 E
Høgstegia	8	Db	62.23N	10.08 E
Hogsty Reef	49	Kc	21.41N	73.49W
Hŏhang-nyŏng	28	Jd	41.48N	128.20 E
Hohe Acht	10	Cf	50.23N	7.00 E
Hohe Eifel	12	Id	50.16N	6.50 E
Hohenau	55	Eh	27.05S	55.45W
Hohenems	14	Dc	47.22N	9.41 E
Hohenloher Ebene	10	Fg	49.20N	9.40 E
Hohes Venn	10	Bf	50.30N	6.00 E
Hohe Tauern	14	Gc	47.10N	12.30 E
Hohhot	22	Ne	40.51N	111.38 E
Hōhoku	29	Bd	34.17N	130.57 E
Höhr-Grenzhausen	12	Jd	50.26N	7.40 E
Höhtiäinen	8	Mb	62.50N	29.40 E
Hoh Xil Hu	27	Fd	35.35N	91.06 E
Hoh Xil Shan	21	Lf	35.20N	91.00 E
Hoi An	25	Le	15.52N	108.19 E

Index Symbols

- [1] Independent Nation
- [2] State, Region
- [3] District, County
- [4] Municipality
- [5] Colony, Dependency
- Continent
- Physical Region
- Historical or Cultural Region
- Mount, Mountain
- Volcano
- Hill
- Mountains, Mountain Range
- Hills, Escarpment
- Plateau, Upland
- Pass, Gap
- Plain, Lowland
- Delta
- Salt Flat
- Valley, Canyon
- Crater, Cave
- Karst Features
- Depression
- Polder
- Desert, Dunes
- Forest, Woods
- Heath, Steppe
- Oasis
- Cape, Point
- Coast, Beach
- Cliff
- Peninsula
- Isthmus
- Sandbank
- Island
- Atoll
- Rock, Reef
- Islands, Archipelago
- Rocks, Reefs
- Coral Reef
- Well, Spring
- Geyser
- River, Stream
- Waterfall Rapids
- River Mouth, Estuary
- Lake
- Salt Lake
- Intermittent Lake
- Reservoir
- Swamp, Pond
- Canal
- Glacier
- Ice Shelf, Pack Ice
- Ocean
- Sea
- Gulf, Bay
- Strait, Fjord
- Lagoon
- Bank
- Seamount
- Tablemount
- Ridge
- Shelf
- Basin
- Escarpment, Sea Scarp
- Fracture
- Trench, Abyss
- National Park, Reserve
- Point of Interest
- Recreation Site
- Cave, Cavern
- Historic Site
- Ruins
- Wall, Walls
- Church, Abbey
- Temple
- Scientific Station
- Airport
- Port
- Lighthouse
- Mine
- Tunnel
- Dam, Bridge

Hoima	36	Fb	1.26N	31.21 E
Hoisington	45	Gg	38.31N	98.47W
Hoj, Vozvyšennost-	17	Ob	68.50N	71.30 E
Højer	8	Cj	54.58N	8.43 E
Hojniki	19	Ce	51.54N	29.56 E
Hōjō	28	Lh	33.58N	132.46 E
Hökensås	8	Ff	58.11N	14.08 E
Hokianga Harbour	62	Ea	35.30S	173.20 E
Hokitika	58	Ii	42.43S	170.58 E
Hok-Kai=Okhotsk, Sea of- (EN)	21	Qd	53.00N	150.00 E
Hokkaidō	21	Qe	43.00N	143.00 E
Hokkaidō Ken [2]	28	Qc	43.00N	143.00 E
Hokksund	7	Bg	59.47N	9.59 E
Hokmābād	24	Qd	36.37N	57.36 E
Hokota	29	Gc	36.10N	140.30 E
Hol	8	Cd	60.36N	8.22 E
Holap	64d	Ba	7.39N	151.54 E
Holbæk	8	Di	55.43N	11.43 E
Holbeach	12	Cb	52.48N	0.01 E
Holbeach Marsh	12	Cb	52.52N	0.02 E
Holbox, Isla-	48	Pg	21.33N	87.15W
Holbrook	43	Ee	34.54N	110.10W
Holdenville	45	Hi	35.05N	96.24W
Holderness	9	Mh	53.47N	0.10W
Holdrege	45	Gf	40.26N	99.22W
Hold With Hope	41	Jd	73.40N	21.45W
Hole in the Wall	44	Im	25.51N	77.12W
Hølen	8	De	59.32N	10.45 E
Holešov	10	Ng	49.20N	17.33 E
Holetown	51q	Ab	13.11N	59.39W
Holguin	39	Lg	20.53N	76.15W
Holguín [3]	49	Jc	20.40N	75.50W
Hol Hol	35	Gc	11.20N	42.50 E
Holitna	40	Hd	61.40N	157.12W
Höljes	7	Cf	60.54N	12.36 E
Hollabrunn	14	Kb	48.33N	16.05 E
Holland	44	Dd	42.47N	86.07W
Holland [Eng.-U.K.]	12	Bb	52.52N	0.10W
Holland [Neth.]	5	Ge	52.20N	4.45 E
Hollandale	45	Kj	33.10N	90.58W
Hollandsbird Island	37	Ad	24.45S	14.34 E
Hollands Diep	12	Gc	51.40N	4.30 E
Hollesley Bay	12	Db	52.04N	1.33 E
Hollick-Kenyon Plateau	66	Pf	79.00S	97.00W
Hollis	45	Gi	34.41N	99.55W
Hollister [Ca.-U.S.]	46	Eh	36.51N	121.24W
Hollister [Id.-U.S.]	46	He	42.23N	114.35W
Hollola	8	Kc	61.03N	25.26 E
Höllviksnäs	8	Ei	55.25N	12.57 E
Holly Springs	45	Li	34.41N	89.26W
Hollywood	43	Kf	26.00N	80.09W
Holm	7	Hh	57.09N	31.12 E
Holma	34	Hd	9.54N	13.03 E
Holman Island	42	Fb	70.40N	117.35W
Hólmavík	7a	Bb	65.43N	21.41W
Holmes Reefs	57	Ff	16.30S	148.00 E
Holmestrand	8	De	59.29N	10.18 E
Holm Land	41	Kb	80.16N	18.20W
Holms	41	Gd	74.30N	57.00W
Holmsjö	8	Fh	56.25N	15.32 E
Holmsjön [Swe.]	7	De	62.25N	15.20 E
Holmsjön [Swe.]	8	Gb	62.40N	16.35 E
Holmsk	20	Jg	47.00N	142.03 E
Holmski	16	Kg	44.50N	38.24 E
Holmsland Klit	8	Ch	56.00N	8.10 E
Holmsund	7	Ee	63.42N	20.21 E
Holmsveden	8	Gc	61.07N	16.43 E
Holmudden	8	Hg	57.57N	19.21 E
Holod	15	Fc	46.47N	22.08 E
Holohit, Punta-	48	Og	21.37N	88.08W
Holothuria Banks (EN)	59	Fb	13.25S	126.00 E
Holsnøy	8	Ad	60.35N	5.05 E
Holstebro	7	Bh	56.21N	8.38 E
Holsted	8	Ci	55.30N	8.55 E
Holstein	45	Ie	42.29N	95.33W
Holsteinsborg/Sisimiut	67	Nc	67.05N	53.45W
Holt	12	Db	52.54N	1.05 E
Holten	12	Ib	52.17N	6.27 E
Holton	45	Ig	39.28N	95.44W
Holtoson	20	Ff	50.18N	103.20 E
Holtyn-Daba	27	Ib	47.40N	107.20 E
Holwerd, Westdongeradeel-	12	Ha	53.22N	5.54 E
Holy Cross	40	Hd	62.12N	159.47W
Holyhead	9	Ih	53.20N	4.38W
Holy Island [Eng.-U.K.]	9	Lf	55.41N	1.48W
Holy Island [Wales-U.K.]	9	Ih	53.18N	4.37W
Holyoke [Co.-U.S.]	45	Ef	40.35N	102.18W
Holyoke [Ma.-U.S.]	44	Kd	42.12N	72.37W
Holýšov	10	Jg	49.36N	13.07 E
Homa Bay	36	Fc	0.31S	34.27 E
Homalin	25	Id	24.52N	94.55 E
Homathko River	46	Ca	50.55N	124.50W
Homberg (Ohm)	12	Kd	50.44N	8.59 E
Hombori	34	Eb	15.17N	1.42W
Hombre Muerto, Salar del-	56	Gc	25.23S	67.06W
Homburg	10	Dg	49.19N	7.20 E
Home Bay	38	Mc	68.45N	67.10W
Homecourt	12	He	49.14N	5.59 E
Home Hill	59	Jc	19.40S	147.25 E
Homer [Ak.-U.S.]	39	Dd	59.39N	151.33W
Homer [La.-U.S.]	45	Jj	32.48N	93.04W
Homert	12	Kc	51.16N	8.06 E
Homerville	44	Fj	31.02N	82.45W
Homestead	44	Gm	25.29N	80.29W
Homewood	44	Di	33.29N	86.48W
Hommelstø	7	Cd	65.25N	12.30 E
Hommersåk	8	Af	58.55N	5.50 E
Homoine	37	Fd	23.52S	35.08 E
Homoljske Planina	15	Ee	44.20N	21.45 E
Homonhon	26	Id	10.44N	125.43 E
Homosassa	44	Fk	28.47N	82.37W
Homs (EN)=Ḩimş	22	Ff	34.44N	36.43 E
Honan (EN)=Henan Sheng (Ho-nan Sheng) [2]	27	Je	34.00N	114.00 E
Honan (EN)=Ho-nan Sheng→Henan Sheng [2]	27	Je	34.00N	114.00 E
Ho-nan Sheng→Henan Sheng=Honan (EN) [2]	27	Je	34.00N	114.00 E
Honaz	15	Ml	37.45N	29.17 E
Honaz Daği	15	Ml	37.41N	29.18 E
Honbetsu	28	Qc	43.18N	143.33 E
Honda	54	Db	5.13N	74.45W
Honda, Bahia-	49	Lg	12.21N	71.47W
Hondeklipbaai	37	Bf	30.20S	17.18 E
Hòn Diên, Núi-	25	Lf	11.33N	108.38 E
Hondo	47	Ge	18.29N	88.19W
Hondo [Jap.]	28	Kh	32.27N	130.12 E
Hondo [N.M.-U.S.]	45	Dj	33.23N	105.16W
Hondo [Tx.-U.S.]	45	Gl	29.21N	99.09W
Hondo, Rio-	45	Dj	33.22N	104.24W
Hondschoote	12	Ed	50.59N	2.35 E
Hondsrug	11	Mb	52.50N	6.50 E
Honduras [1]	39	Kh	15.00N	86.30W
Honduras, Cabo de-	49	De	16.01N	86.01W
Honduras, Golfo de-=Honduras, Gulf of- (EN)	38	Kh	16.10N	87.50W
Honduras, Gulf of-	38	Kh	16.10N	87.50W
Honduras, Gulf of- (EN)=Honduras, Golfo de-	38	Kh	16.10N	87.50W
Hønefoss	7	Cf	60.10N	10.18 E
Honey Lake	46	Ef	40.16N	120.19W
Honfleur	11	Ge	49.25N	0.14 E
Hông, Sông-=Red River (EN)	21	Mg	20.17N	106.34 E
Hong'an (Huang'an)	28	Ci	31.17N	114.37 E
Hongch'ŏn	28	If	37.41N	127.52 E
Hong-Do	28	Hg	34.41N	125.13 E
Hong He	28	Ch	32.24N	115.32 E
Honghton Lake	44	Ec	44.22N	84.43W
Hong Hu	27	Je	30.00N	113.25 E
Honghu (Xindi)	28	Bj	29.50N	113.28 E
Honghui	27	Id	36.46N	105.05 E
Hong Kong/Xianggang [5]	22	Ng	22.15N	114.10 E
Hongliuyuan	27	Gc	41.02N	95.24 E
Hongluoxian	28	Fd	41.01N	120.52 E
Hongning → Wulian	28	Eg	35.45N	119.13 E
Hongor	28	Bb	45.48N	112.45 E
Hongqizhen	27	Ih	18.48N	109.30 E
Hongshui He	21	Mg	23.47N	109.33 E
Hongsŏng	28	If	36.36N	126.40 E
Hongtong	28	Af	36.15N	111.41 E
Hongū	29	De	33.50N	135.46 E
Honguedo, Détroit d'-	42	Lg	49.30N	65.00W
Hongwansi → Sunan	27	Gd	38.59N	99.25 E
Hongwŏn	28	Id	40.02N	127.58 E
Hongyuan (Hurama)	27	He	32.45N	102.38 E
Hongze (Gaoliangjian)	27	Ke	33.10N	119.58 E
Hongze Hu	27	Ke	33.20N	118.40 E
Honiara	58	Ge	9.27S	159.57 E
Honikulu, Passe-	64h	Ac	13.23S	176.11W
Honiton	9	Jk	50.48N	3.13W
Honjō	28	Pe	39.23N	140.03 E
Honkajoki	8	Jb	61.59N	22.16 E
Hon-kawane	29	Fd	35.07N	138.06 E
Honningsvåg	7	Ga	70.59N	26.01 E
Hönö	8	Dg	57.42N	11.39 E
Honokaa	65a	Fc	20.05N	155.28W
Honokohau	65a	Eb	21.01N	156.37W
Honolulu	58	Lb	21.19N	157.52W
Honomu	65a	Fd	19.52N	155.07W
Honrubia	13	Je	39.37N	2.16W
Honshū	21	Pf	36.00N	136.00 E
Hontenisse	12	Gc	51.23N	4.00 E
Hontenisse-Kloosterzande	12	Gc	51.23N	4.00 E
Honuapo Bay	65a	Fd	19.05N	155.33W
Honuu	20	Jc	66.27N	143.06 E
Honyō	29	Fc	36.14N	139.10 E
Hood	42	Gc	67.25N	108.53W
Hood, Mount-	38	Ge	45.23N	121.41W
Hood Point	59	Df	34.23S	119.34 E
Hood River	46	Ed	45.43N	121.31W
Hoogeveen	11	Mb	52.43N	6.29 E
Hoogezand-Sappemeer	12	Ia	53.09N	6.48 E
Hooglede	12	Fd	50.59N	3.05 E
Hoogstraten	12	Gc	51.24N	4.46 E
Hooker	45	Fh	36.52N	101.13W
Hooker, Cape-	66	Kf	70.38S	166.45 E
Hook Head/Rinn Dúain	9	Gi	52.07N	6.55W
Hook Island	59	Jc	20.10S	148.55 E
Hoolehua	65a	Db	21.10N	157.05W
Hoonah	40	Le	58.07N	135.26W
Hooper, Cape -	42	Kc	68.24N	66.43W
Hooper Bay	40	Fd	61.31N	166.06W
Hoopeston	45	Mf	40.28N	87.40W
Höör	8	Ei	55.56N	13.32 E
Hoorn	11	Lb	52.38N	5.04 E
Hoornaar	12	Gc	51.53N	4.57 E
Hoover Dam	46	Hi	36.00N	114.27W
Hopa	24	Ib	41.25N	41.24 E
Hope [Ar.-U.S.]	45	Jj	33.40N	93.36W
Hope [Az.-U.S.]	46	Ij	33.44N	113.42W
Hope [B.C.-Can.]	46	Eb	49.23N	121.26W
Hope, Ben-	9	Ic	58.24N	4.36W
Hope, Lake-	59	Ef	32.50S	121.40 E
Hope, Point-	38	Cc	68.21N	166.50W
Hopedale	42	Le	55.50N	60.10W
Hopefield	37	Bf	33.04S	18.21 E
Hopeh (EN)=Hebei Sheng (Ho-pei Sheng) [2]	27	Kd	39.00N	116.00 E
Hopeh (EN)=Ho-pei Sheng→Hebei Sheng [2]	27	Kd	39.00N	116.00 E
Hopeh (EN)=Hu-pei Sheng→Hubei Sheng [2]	27	Je	31.00N	112.00 E
Ho-pei Sheng→Hebei Sheng =Hopeh (EN) [2]	27	Kd	39.00N	116.00 E
Hopelchén	48	Oh	19.46N	89.51W
Hopen	41	Oc	76.35N	25.10 E
Hopër	5	Kf	49.36N	42.19 E
Hopes Advance, Cap -	42	Kd	61.05N	69.33W
Hopetoun [Austl.]	59	Ig	35.44S	142.22 E
Hopetoun [Austl.]	58	Dh	33.57S	120.07 E
Hopetown	37	Ce	29.34S	24.03 E
Hopewell	44	Ig	37.17N	77.19W
Hopewell Islands	42	Je	58.20N	78.10W
Hopin	25	Jd	24.59N	96.31 E
Hopkins, Lake-	59	Fd	24.15S	128.50 E
Hopkinsville	43	Jd	36.52N	87.29W
Hopsten	12	Jb	52.23N	7.37 E
Hoptrup	8	Ci	55.11N	9.28 E
Hoquiam	43	Cb	46.59N	123.53W
Hor	20	Ig	47.48N	134.43 E
Hor	20	Ig	47.55N	135.01 E
Hōrai	29	Ed	34.55N	137.34 E
Hōrai-San	29	Dd	35.13N	135.53 E
Horasan	24	Jb	40.03N	42.11 E
Horaždovice	10	Jg	49.20N	13.42 E
Horb am Neckar	10	Eh	48.26N	8.41 E
Horconcitos	49	Fi	8.19N	82.10W
Hordaland [2]	7	Bf	60.15N	6.30 E
Hordogoj	20	Gd	62.32N	115.38 E
Horezmskaja Oblast [3]	19	Gg	41.30N	60.40 E
Horfors	7	Df	60.33N	16.17 E
Horgen	14	Cc	47.15N	8.36 E
Horgoš	15	Cc	46.09N	19.58 E
Horgos	19	Ig	44.10N	80.20 E
Hořice	10	Lf	50.22N	15.38 E
Horinger	28	Ad	40.24N	111.46 E
Horizon Tablemount (EN)	57	Kc	19.40N	168.30W
Horizontina	55	Eh	27.37S	54.19W
Horley	12	Bc	51.10N	0.10W
Horlick Mountains	66	Og	85.23S	121.00W
Hormigas	48	Gc	29.12N	105.45W
Hormoz [Iran]	24	Pi	27.32N	54.57 E
Hormoz [Iran]	23	Id	27.06N	56.28 E
Hormoz, Kūh-e-	23	Id	27.27N	55.10 E
Hormoz, Tangeh-ye-=Hormuz, Strait of- (EN)	21	Hg	26.34N	56.15 E
Hormozgān [3]	23	Id	27.30N	56.00 E
Hormūd-e Bāgh	24	Pi	27.30N	54.18 E
Hormuz, Strait of- (EN)=Hormoz, Tangeh-ye-	21	Hg	26.34N	56.15 E
Horn	42	Fd	61.30N	118.00W
Horn	5	Db	66.28N	22.30W
Horn [Aus.]	14	Jb	48.39N	15.39 E
Horn [Swe.]	8	Fg	57.54N	15.50 E
Horn, Cape- (EN)=Hornos, Cabo de-	52	Jk	55.59N	67.16W
Hornád	10	Qh	48.00N	20.58 E
Hornaday	42	Fc	69.22N	123.56W
Hornavan	7	Dc	66.14N	17.30 E
Hornbach	12	Je	49.12N	7.22 E
Horn-Bad Meinberg	12	Kc	51.54N	8.57 E
Hornby Bay	42	Fc	66.35N	117.50W
Horncastle	9	Mh	53.13N	0.07W
Horndal	8	Gd	60.18N	16.25 E
Horndean	12	Bd	50.55N	0.59W
Hörnefors	7	Ee	63.38N	19.54 E
Hornell	44	Id	42.19N	77.39W
Hornepayne	42	Jg	49.13N	84.47W
Hornindalsvatn	8	Bc	61.55N	6.25 E
Hornisgrinde	10	Eh	48.36N	8.12 E
Horn Islands (EN)=Horne, Iles de-	57	Jf	14.19S	178.05W
Hörnli	14	Cc	47.23N	8.56 E
Hornomoravský úval	10	Ng	49.25N	17.20 E
Hornos, Cabo de-=Horn, Cape- (EN)	52	Jk	55.59S	67.16W
Hornoy-le-Bourg	12	De	49.51N	1.54 E
Horn Plateau	42	Fd	62.10N	119.30W
Hornsea	9	Mh	53.55N	0.10W
Hornslandet	8	Gc	61.40N	17.30 E
Horns Rev	8	Bi	55.30N	8.00 E
Horns Rev	8	Bi	55.30N	7.45 E
Hornsund	41	Nc	76.58N	15.28 E
Hornsundtind	41	Nc	76.55N	16.10 E
Horog	22	Jf	37.31N	71.33 E
Horokanai	29a	Ca	44.02N	142.09 E
Horol	16	He	49.29N	33.49 E
Horol [R.S.F.S.R.]	28	Lb	44.30N	132.03 E
Horol [Ukr.-U.S.S.R.]	16	He	49.47N	33.16 E
Horonobe	28	Pb	45.00N	141.51 E
Hořovice	10	Jg	49.50N	13.54 E
Horqin Youyi Qianqi (Ulan Hot)	22	Oe	46.04N	122.00 E
Horqin Youyi Zhongqi (Bayan Huxu)	27	Lb	45.04N	121.27 E
Horqin Zuoyi Houqi (Ganjig)	27	Lc	42.57N	122.14 E
Horqin Zuoyi Zhongqi (Baokang)	27	Lc	44.06N	123.19 E
Horqueta	56	Ib	23.24S	56.53W
Horred	8	Eg	57.21N	12.28 E
Horse Creek [Co.-U.S.]	45	Eg	38.05N	103.19W
Horse Creek [U.S.]	46	Nf	41.57N	103.58W
Horsehead Lake	45	Gc	47.02N	99.47W
Horsens	7	Bi	55.52N	9.52 E
Horsham [Austl.]	58	Fh	36.43S	142.13 E
Horsham [Eng.-U.K.]	9	Mj	51.04N	0.21W
Hørsholm	8	Ei	55.53N	12.30 E
Horšovský Týn	10	Ig	49.32N	12.57 E
Horst	12	Gd	50.56N	4.47 E
Horst	12	Ic	51.28N	6.03 E
Hörstel	12	Jb	52.19N	7.35 E
Horstmar	12	Jb	52.05N	7.19 E
Horsunlu	15	Ll	37.55N	28.36 E
Horta	32	Bb	38.32N	28.28W
Horta [3]	32	Bb	38.35N	28.40W
Horten	8	De	59.25N	10.30 E
Horton	42	Ec	70.01N	126.42W
Hörvik	8	Fh	56.03N	14.46 E
Ḩorvot 'Avedat	24	Fg	30.48N	34.46 E
Ḩorvot Meẕada	24	Fg	31.19N	35.21 E
Horwood Lake	44	Fa	48.03N	82.20W
Hosaina	35	Fd	7.33N	37.52 E
Hose Mountains	26	Ff	2.00N	114.10 E
Hosenofu	33	De	23.34N	21.15 E
Hoseynābād [Iran]	24	Ne	34.30N	50.59 E
Hoseynābād [Iran]	24	Le	35.33N	47.08 E
Hoseynīyeh	24	Mg	32.42N	48.14 E
Hoshāb	25	Cc	26.01N	63.56 E
Hosingen	12	Id	50.01N	6.05 E
Hoskins	60	Ei	5.30S	150.32 E
Hospet	25	Fe	15.16N	76.24 E
Hospital, Cuchilla del-	55	Ej	31.40S	54.53W
Hospitalet	13	Oc	41.22N	2.08 E
Hospitalet del Infante/L'Hospitalet de l'Infant	13	Md	40.59N	0.56 E
Hoste, Isla-	52	Jk	55.15S	69.00W
Hot	25	Je	18.06N	98.35 E
Hotagen	7	De	63.53N	14.29 E
Hotaka	29	Ec	36.20N	137.53 E
Hotan	22	Jf	37.07N	79.55 E
Hotan He	21	Ke	40.30N	80.48 E
Hotazel	37	Ce	27.15S	23.00 E
Hotin	16	Ee	48.29N	26.29 E
Hoting	7	Dd	64.07N	16.10 E
Hotkovo	7	Ih	56.18N	38.00 E
Hotont	27	Hb	47.23N	102.30 E
Hot Springs	43	Gc	43.26N	103.29W
Hot Springs→Truth or Consequences	43	Fe	33.08N	107.15W
Hot Springs National Park	39	Jf	34.30N	93.03W
Hot Springs Peak	46	Gf	41.22N	117.26W
Hotspur Seamount (EN)	54	Kg	18.00S	36.00W
Hottah Lake	42	Fc	65.05N	118.36W
Hottentot Bay	37	Ae	26.07S	14.57 E
Hotton	12	Hd	50.16N	5.27 E
Hottstedt	10	He	51.39N	11.30 E
Houaïlou	61	Cd	21.17S	165.38 E
Houat, Ile de-	11	Dg	47.24N	2.58W
Houdan	11	Hf	48.47N	1.36 E
Houeillès	11	Gj	44.12N	0.02 E
Houffalize	12	Hd	50.08N	5.47 E
Houghton	43	Jb	47.06N	88.34W
Houillères, Canal des-	12	If	48.42N	6.55 E
Houji → Liangshan	28	Dg	35.48N	116.07 E
Houlgate	12	Be	49.18N	0.04W
Houlton	43	Nb	46.08N	67.51W
Houma [China]	27	Jd	35.36N	111.23 E
Houma [La.-U.S.]	43	If	29.36N	90.43W
Houndé	34	Ec	11.30N	3.31W
Hourtin, Étang d'-	11	Ei	45.10N	1.06W
House Range	46	Ig	39.30N	113.15W
Houston [Mo.-U.S.]	45	Kh	37.22N	91.58W
Houston [Tx.-U.S.]	39	Jg	29.46N	95.22W
Houthalen-Helchteren	12	Hc	51.02N	5.22 E
Houthulst	12	Ed	50.59N	2.57 E
Houthulst-Merkem	12	Ed	50.57N	2.51 E
Houtman Abrolhos	59	Ce	28.40S	113.50 E
Houtskär/Houtskari	8	Id	60.15N	21.20 E
Houtskari/Houtskär	8	Id	60.15N	21.20 E
Houyet	12	Hd	50.11N	5.01 E
Houyet-Celles	12	Hd	50.19N	5.01 E
Hov	8	Di	55.55N	10.16 E
Hova	8	Ff	58.52N	14.13 E
Hovden	8	Ac	61.40N	4.50 E
Hovden	8	Be	59.32N	7.21 E
Hove	9	Mk	50.49N	0.10W
Hovgaard	41	Kc	80.00N	18.45W
Hovmantorp	8	Fh	56.47N	15.08 E
Hovu-Aksy	20	Ef	51.01N	93.43 E
Howa	35	Db	17.30N	27.08 E
Howar	30	Jg	17.30N	27.08 E
Howard	45	Hd	44.01N	97.32W
Howe, Cape-	57	Fh	37.31S	149.59 E
Howell	44	Fd	42.36N	83.55W
Howick [N.Z.]	62	Fb	36.54S	174.56 E
Howick [S.Afr.]	37	Ee	29.28S	30.14 E
Howland	44	Mc	45.14N	68.40W
Howland Island	57	Jd	0.48N	176.38W
Howrah → Hāora	22	Kg	22.35N	88.20 E
Howth	9	Gh	53.23N	6.04W
Ḩowẕ Solţān	24	Ne	35.06N	51.06 E
Hoxie	45	Fg	39.21N	100.26W
Höxter	10	Fe	51.46N	9.23 E
Hoxud	27	Ec	42.16N	86.51 E
Hoy	9	Jc	58.52N	3.18W
Hoya	12	Lb	52.48N	9.09 E
Høyanger	7	Bf	61.13N	6.05 E
Hoyerswerda/Wojerecy	10	Ke	51.26N	14.15 E
Hoyos	13	Fd	40.10N	6.43W
Hōyo-Shotō	29	Ce	33.50N	132.30 E
Hoytiäinen	7	Ge	62.48N	29.39 E
Hozat	24	Hc	39.07N	39.14 E
Hpunhpu	25	Jc	26.42N	97.17 E
Hradec Králové	10	Lf	50.13N	15.50 E
Hradiště	10	Jf	50.13N	13.08 E
Hrami	16	Ni	41.20N	45.07 E
Hrastnik	14	Jd	46.09N	15.06 E
Hřebeny	10	Kg	49.50N	14.10 E
Hristinovka	16	Fe	48.53N	29.56 E
Hroma	20	Jb	71.30N	144.49 E
Hromtau	19	Fe	50.18N	58.35 E
Hron	10	Oi	47.49N	18.45 E
Hrubieszów	10	Tf	50.49N	23.55 E
Hrubý-Jeseník	10	Nf	50.05N	17.10 E
Hrustalny	20	Ih	44.24N	135.06 E
Hrvatska = Croatia (EN) [2]	14	Jf	45.00N	15.30 E
Hrvatska = Croatia (EN)	14	Je	45.00N	15.30 E
Hrvatska = Croatia (EN)	5	Hf	45.00N	15.30 E
Ḩrvot Shivta	24	Fg	30.53N	34.38 E
Hsin-chiang-wei-wu-erh Tzu-chih-ch'ü→Xinjiang Uygur Zizhiqu=Sinkiang (EN) [2]	27	Ec	42.00N	86.00 E
Hsinchu	27	Lg	24.48N	120.58 E
Hsinying	27	Lg	23.25N	120.20 E
Hsipaw	25	Jd	22.37N	97.18 E
Hsi-tsang Tzu-chih-ch'ü→Xizang Zizhiqu [2]	27	Ee	32.00N	90.00 E
Hsuphāng	25	Jd	20.18N	98.42 E
Huab	37	Ad	20.49S	13.24 E
Huabei Pingyuan	21	Nf	37.00N	117.00 E
Huachacalla	54	Eg	18.45S	68.17W
Huachinera	48	Eb	30.15N	108.50W
Huacho	54	Cf	11.07S	77.37W
Huaco	56	Gd	30.09S	68.31W
Huacrachuco	54	Ce	8.39S	77.05W
Huade	27	Jc	41.50N	114.00 E
Huadian	27	Mc	42.59N	126.38 E
Hua Hin	25	Jf	12.34N	99.58 E
Huahine, Iles-	57	Lf	16.45S	151.00W
Huahine Iti	65e	Eb	16.45S	151.00W
Huahine Nui	65e	Eb	16.43S	151.00W
Huahuapán	48	Ge	24.31N	105.57W
Huai'an	28	Eh	33.30N	119.08 E
Huai'an (Chaigoubu)	28	Cd	40.40N	114.25 E
Huaibei	27	Ke	33.56N	116.48 E
Huaibin (Wulongji)	28	Ci	32.27N	115.23 E
Huaide (Gongzhuling)	27	Lc	43.30N	124.52 E
Huaidian → Shenqiu	27	Ke	33.27N	115.05 E
Huai He	21	Nf	33.12N	118.33 E
Huaiji	27	Jg	23.57N	112.12 E
Huailai (Shacheng)	27	Kc	40.29N	115.30 E
Huainan	22	Nf	32.32N	116.59 E
Huaining (Shipai)	28	Di	30.25N	116.39 E
Huairen	27	Jd	39.50N	113.07 E
Huairou	28	Dd	40.20N	116.37 E
Huaiyang	28	Ch	33.44N	114.52 E
Huaiyin (Wangying)	28	Eh	33.35N	119.02 E
Huaiyuan	28	Dh	32.58N	117.10 E
Huajuapan de León	47	Ee	17.48N	97.46W
Hualalai	65a	Fd	19.41N	155.52W
Hualapai Mountains	46	Ii	34.40N	113.45W
Hualien	27	Lg	23.58N	121.36 E
Huallaga, Río-	52	If	5.07S	75.30W
Huallanca	54	Ce	8.49S	77.52W
Huamachuco	54	Ce	7.48S	78.04W
Huamahuaca	56	Gb	23.13S	65.23W
Huambo [3]	36	Ce	12.30S	15.40 E
Huambo	31	Ij	12.47S	15.43 E
Huanan	27	Nb	46.14N	130.33 E
Huancabamba [Peru]	54	Cf	10.21S	75.32W
Huancabamba [Peru]	54	Ce	5.14S	79.28W
Huancané	54	Eg	15.12S	69.46W
Huancapi	54	Df	13.41S	74.04W
Huancavelica [2]	54	Df	13.00S	75.00W
Huancavelica	53	Ig	12.46S	75.02W
Huancayo	53	Ig	12.04S	75.14W
Huanchaca, Serranía-	55	Bb	14.30S	60.39W
Huang'an→Hong'an	28	Ci	31.17N	114.37 E
Huangcaoba→Xingyi	27	Hf	25.03N	104.55 E
Huangchuan	27	Ke	32.00N	115.02 E
Huanggang	28	Ci	30.27N	114.53 E
Huanggangliang	27	Kc	43.33N	117.32 E
Huanggang Shan	27	Kf	27.50N	117.47 E
Huanggi Hai	28	Bd	40.51N	113.17 E
Huang Hai=Yellow Sea (EN)	21	Of	36.00N	124.00 E
Huang He=Yellow River (EN)	21	Nf	37.32N	118.19 E
Huanghe Kou	28	Ef	37.54N	118.48 E
Huangheyan→Madoi	22	Lf	35.00N	98.56 E
Huanghua	28	De	38.23N	117.21 E
Huanghuashi	28	Bj	28.14N	113.11 E
Huangliu	27	Ih	18.41N	108.46 E
Huangmao Jian	27	Kf	27.55N	119.11 E
Huangmei	28	Ci	30.05N	115.56 E
Huangnihe	28	Ic	43.33N	127.28 E
Huangpi	28	Ci	30.53N	114.22 E
Huangpu	27	Jg	23.05N	113.25 E
Huang Shan	27	Ke	30.10N	118.10 E
Huangshi	22	Nf	30.12N	115.00 E
Huang Shui	27	Hd	36.05N	103.20 E
Huangtu Gaoyuan	21	Mf	37.00N	108.00 E
Huanguelén	55	Bm	37.02S	61.57W
Huangxian	27	Ld	37.32N	120.30 E
Huangyan	27	Lf	28.39N	121.17 E
Huangyuan	27	Hd	36.40N	101.12 E
Huangzhai → Yangqu	28	Be	38.05N	112.37 E
Huangzhong	27	Hd	36.30N	101.30 E
Huanren	27	Mc	41.16N	125.22 E
Huan Shui	28	Ci	30.40N	114.21 E
Huanta	54	Df	12.56S	74.15W
Huantai (Suozhen)	28	Ef	36.57N	118.05 E
Huánuco [2]	54	Ce	9.30S	75.50W
Huánuco	53	If	9.55S	76.14W
Huanxian	27	Id	36.36N	107.06 E
Huaráz	53	If	9.32S	77.32W
Huarmey	54	Cf	10.04S	78.10W
Huarong	28	Bj	29.31N	112.33 E
Huascarán, Nevado-	52	If	9.07S	77.37W
Hua Shan	27	Je	34.27N	110.05 E
Huatabampo	47	Cc	26.50N	109.38W
Huatong	28	Fd	40.03N	121.56 E
Huatusco de Chiquellar	48	Kh	19.09N	96.57W
Huauchinango	48	Jg	20.11N	98.03W
Huautla de Jiménez	48	Kh	18.08N	96.51W
Huaxian (Daokou)	28	Cg	35.33N	114.30 E
Huayllay	54	Cf	11.01S	76.21W
Huaynamota, Río-	48	Gg	21.51N	104.42W
Huaytara	54	Cf	13.36S	75.22W
Hubbard Creek Lake	45	Gj	32.45N	99.00W
Hubbard Lake	44	Fc	44.49N	83.34W
Hubei Sheng (Hu-pei Sheng) = Hupeh (EN)	27	Je	31.00N	112.00 E
Hubli-Dhārwār	22	Jh	15.21N	75.10 E
Hubsugul Nur (Chövsgöl nuur)	21	Md	51.00N	100.30 E
Hückelhoven	12	Ic	51.03N	6.13 E
Hückeswagen	12	Jc	51.09N	7.21 E
Hucknall	9	Lh	53.02N	1.11W
Hucqueliers	12	Dd	55.03N	1.54 E
Huczwa	10	Tf	50.49N	23.59 E
Hudat [Abz.-U.S.S.R.]	16	Pi	41.34N	48.43 E
Hudat [Eth.]	35	Fe	4.45N	39.27 E
Huddersfield	9	Lh	53.39N	1.47W
Huddinge	8	Ge	59.14N	17.59 E
Ḩuddun	35	Hd	9.08N	47.32 E
Huddur Hadama	35	Ge	4.07N	43.55 E

Index Symbols

[1] Independent Nation
[2] State, Region
[3] District, County
[4] Municipality
[5] Colony, Dependency
Continent
Physical Region
Historical or Cultural Region
Mount, Mountain
Volcano
Hill
Mountains, Mountain Range
Hills, Escarpment
Plateau, Upland
Pass, Gap
Plain, Lowland
Delta
Salt Flat
Valley, Canyon
Crater, Cave
Karst Features
Depression
Polder
Desert, Dunes
Forest, Woods
Heath, Steppe
Oasis
Cape, Point
Coast, Beach
Cliff
Peninsula
Isthmus
Sandbank
Island
Atoll
Rock, Reef
Islands, Archipelago
Rocks, Reefs
Coral Reef
Well, Spring
Geyser
River, Stream
Waterfall Rapids
River Mouth, Estuary
Lake
Salt Lake
Intermittent Lake
Reservoir
Swamp, Pond
Canal
Glacier
Ice Shelf, Pack Ice
Ocean
Sea
Gulf, Bay
Strait, Fjord
Lagoon
Bank
Seamount
Tablemount
Ridge
Shelf
Basin
Escarpment, Sea Scarp
Fracture
Trench, Abyss
National Park, Reserve
Point of Interest
Recreation Site
Cave, Cavern
Historic Site
Ruins
Wall, Walls
Church, Abbey
Temple
Scientific Station
Airport
Port
Lighthouse
Mine
Tunnel
Dam, Bridge

Index Symbols

[1] Independent Nation
[2] State, Region
[3] District, County
[4] Municipality
[5] Colony, Dependency
Continent
Physical Region
Historical or Cultural Region
Mount, Mountain
Volcano
Hill
Mountains, Mountain Range
Hills, Escarpment
Plateau, Upland
Pass, Gap
Plain, Lowland
Delta
Salt Flat
Valley, Canyon
Crater, Cave
Karst Features
Depression
Polder
Desert, Dunes
Forest, Woods
Heath, Steppe
Oasis
Cape, Point
Coast, Beach
Cliff
Peninsula
Isthmus
Sandbank
Island
Atoll
Rock, Reef
Islands, Archipelago
Rocks, Reefs
Coral Reef
Well, Spring
Geyser
River, Stream
Waterfall Rapids
River Mouth, Estuary
Lake
Salt Lake
Intermittent Lake
Reservoir
Swamp, Pond
Canal
Glacier
Ice Shelf, Pack Ice
Ocean
Sea
Gulf, Bay
Strait, Fjord
Lagoon
Bank
Seamount
Tablemount
Ridge
Shelf
Basin
Escarpment, Sea Scarp
Fracture
Trench, Abyss
National Park, Reserve
Point of Interest
Recreation Site
Cave, Cavern
Historic Site
Ruins
Wall, Walls
Church, Abbey
Temple
Scientific Station
Airport
Port
Lighthouse
Mine
Tunnel
Dam, Bridge

Name	Page	Grid	Lat.	Long.
Ilbengja	20	Hd	62.55N	124.10 E
Ile-à-la-Crosse	42	Ge	55.27N	107.53W
Ilebo	31	Ji	4.44S	20.33 E
Ile de France	11	Ie	49.00N	2.20 E
Ile de France	41	Kc	77.45N	27.45W
Ile de France, Côte de l'-	11	Jf	48.55N	3.50 E
Ilek	19	Fe	51.32N	53.27 E
Ilek	5	Le	51.30N	53.20 E
Ileksa	7	Ie	62.30N	36.57 E
Ilerh	32	He	21.40N	2.22 E
Ileša	7	Le	62.37N	46.35 E
Ilesha [Nig.]	34	Fd	8.55N	3.25 E
Ilesha [Nig.]	34	Fd	7.37N	4.44 E
Ilet	7	Li	55.57N	48.14 E
Ilfov [2]	15	Je	44.30N	26.20 E
Ilfracombe	9	Ij	51.13N	4.08W
Ilgaz	24	Eb	40.56N	33.38 E
Ilgaz Dağları	24	Eb	41.00N	33.35 E
Ilgın	24	Dc	38.17N	31.55 E
Ilha Grande	54	Ed	0.27S	65.02W
Ilha Grande, Baía da-	55	Jf	23.09S	44.30W
Ilhas Desertas	32	Dc	32.30N	16.30W
Ilhavo	13	Dd	40.36N	8.40W
Ilhéus	53	Mg	14.49S	39.02W
Ili	21	Je	45.24N	74.08 E
Ilia	15	Fd	45.56N	22.39 E
Iliamna	40	Ie	59.45N	154.54W
Iliamna Lake	40	He	59.30N	155.00W
İliç	24	Hc	39.28N	38.34 E
Ilič	18	Gd	40.55N	68.29 E
Ilica	15	Kj	39.52N	27.46 E
Iličevsk [Abz.-U.S.S.R.]	16	Nj	39.33N	44.59 E
Iličevsk [Ukr.-U.S.S.R.]	19	Df	46.18N	30.37 E
Ilidža	14	Mg	43.50N	18.19 E
Iligan	22	Oi	8.14N	124.14 E
Iligan Bay	26	He	8.25N	124.05 E
Ilim	20	Fe	56.50N	103.25 E
Ilimskoje Vodohranilišče	20	Fe	57.20N	102.30 E
Ilinski [R.S.F.S.R.]	7	Hf	61.02N	32.42 E
Ilinski [R.S.F.S.R.]	20	Jg	47.59N	142.21 E
Ilinski [R.S.F.S.R.]	17	Gg	58.35N	55.41 E
Ilion	44	Jd	43.01N	75.04W
Ilio Point	65a	Db	21.13N	157.16W
Ilir	20	Fe	55.13N	100.45 E
Ilirska Bistrica	14	Ie	45.34N	14.16 E
Iljaly	18	Bd	41.53N	59.40 E
Ilkal	25	Fe	15.58N	76.08 E
Ilkeston	12	Ab	52.58N	1.18W
Ill	11	Nf	48.40N	7.53 E
Illampu, Nevado del-	54	Eg	15.50S	68.34W
Illana Bay	26	He	7.25N	123.45 E
Illapel	56	Fd	31.38S	71.10W
Illbillee, Mount-	59	Ge	27.02S	132.30 E
Ille	11	Ef	48.08N	1.40W
Ille-et-Vilaine [3]	11	Ef	48.10N	1.30W
Illéla	34	Gc	14.28N	5.15 E
Iller	10	Fh	48.23N	9.58 E
Illescas	13	Id	40.07N	3.50W
Ille-sur-Têt	11	Il	42.40N	2.37 E
Illi, Ba-	35	Bc	10.44N	16.21 E
Illimani, Nevado del-	52	Jg	16.39S	67.48W
Illingen	12	Je	49.22N	7.03 E
Illinois	38	Jf	38.58N	90.27W
Illinois [2]	43	Jd	40.00N	89.00W
Illinois Peak	46	Hc	47.02N	115.04W
Illizi	31	Hf	26.29N	8.28 E
Ilm	10	He	51.07N	11.40 E
Ilmajoki	8	Jb	62.44N	22.34 E
Ilmen, Ozero-	5	Jd	58.20N	31.20 E
Ilmenau	10	Gf	50.41N	10.54 E
Ilmenau	10	Gc	53.23N	10.10 E
Il Montello	14	Ge	45.49N	12.07 E
Ilo	54	Dg	17.38S	71.20W
Iloilo	22	Oh	10.42N	122.34 E
Ilok	14	Ne	45.13N	19.23 E
Ilomantsi	7	He	62.40N	30.55 E
Ilorin	31	Hh	8.30N	4.33 E
Iloron, Cerro-	48	Gg	20.57N	104.22W
Ilova	14	Ke	45.25N	16.45 E
Ilovik	14	If	44.27N	14.33 E
Ilovlja	16	Ne	49.18N	44.01 E
Ilovlja	16	Me	49.14N	43.54 E
Ilpyrski	20	Le	59.52N	164.12 E
Ilski	16	Kg	44.51N	38.32 E
Iltin	20	Nc	67.52N	178.48W
Ilubabor [3]	35	Ed	7.50N	35.00 E
Ilūkste/Ilukste	8	Li	55.58N	26.26 E
Ilukste/Ilūkste	8	Li	55.58N	26.26 E
Ilulissat/Jakobshavn	67	Nc	69.20N	50.50W
Ilwaki	26	Ih	7.56S	126.26 E
Ilyč	17	He	62.32N	56.40 E
Ilz	10	Jh	48.35N	13.30 E
Iłżanka	10	Re	51.14N	21.47 E
Imabari	28	Lg	34.03N	133.00 E
Imagane	28	Pc	42.26N	140.01 E
Imaichi	28	Of	36.43N	139.41 E
Imán, Sierra del-	55	Eh	27.42S	55.28W
Imanburluk	17	Mj	53.40N	67.15 E
Imandra, Ozero-	5	Jb	67.30N	33.00 E
Imano-Yama	29	Ce	32.51N	132.49 E
Imari	28	Jh	33.16N	129.53 E
Imaruí	55	Hi	28.21S	48.49W
Imataca, Serrania de-	50	Fi	7.45N	61.00W
Imatra	7	Gf	61.10N	28.46 E
Imazu	29	Ed	35.24N	136.01 E
Imbabah, Al Qāhirah-	33	Fc	30.05N	31.13 E
Imba-Numa	29	Gd	35.45N	140.14 E
Imbert	49	Ld	19.45N	70.50W
Imbituba	56	Kc	28.14S	48.40W
Imeni 26 Bakinskih Komissarov [Abz.-U.S.S.R.]	19	Eh	39.19N	49.12 E
Imeni 26 Bakinskih Komissarov [Tur.-U.S.S.R.]	19	Fh	39.21N	54.12 E
İmeni Gastello	20	Jd	61.35N	147.59 E
Imeni Karla Liebknechta	16	Id	51.38N	35.29 E
İmeni Mariny Raskovoj	20	Jd	62.05N	146.30 E
İmeni Poliny Osipenko	20	If	52.23N	136.25 E
Imi	31	Lh	6.28N	42.11 E
Imilili	32	De	22.50N	15.54W
Imi n'Tanout	32	Fc	31.03N	8.08W
Imišli	19	Eh	39.53N	48.03 E
Imjin-gang	28	If	37.47N	126.40 E
Imlay	46	Ff	40.42N	118.07W
Immenstadt im Allgäu	10	Gi	47.34N	10.13 E
Imo [2]	34	Gd	5.30N	7.20 E
Imola	14	Ff	44.21N	11.42 E
Imotski	14	Lg	43.27N	17.13 E
Imperatriz	53	Lf	5.32S	47.29W
Imperia	14	Cg	43.53N	8.03 E
Imperial	45	Ff	40.31N	101.39W
Imperial de Aragón, Canal-	13	Kb	42.02N	1.33W
Imperial Valley	46	Hj	32.50N	115.30W
Impfondo	31	Ih	1.37N	18.04 E
Imphāl	22	Lg	24.49N	93.57 E
Imphy	11	Jh	46.56N	3.15 E
Impilanti	7	Hf	61.41N	31.12 E
Imrali Adasi	15	Li	40.32N	28.32 E
Imst	14	Ec	47.14N	10.44 E
Imtan	24	Gf	32.24N	36.49 E
Imuris	48	Db	30.47N	110.52W
Im-Zouren	13	Ii	35.04N	3.50W
Ina	28	Ng	35.50N	137.57 E
Ina	10	Kc	53.32N	14.38 E
I-n-Abanrherit	34	Gb	17.58N	6.05 E
Inabu	29	Ed	35.13N	137.30 E
Inaccessible Islands	66	Re	60.34S	46.44W
Inacessible Island	30	Fi	37.17S	12.45W
I-n-Afaleleh	32	Ie	23.34N	9.12 E
I Naftan, Puntan-	64b	Ba	15.05N	145.45 E
Ina-Gawa	29	Fc	37.23N	139.18 E
I-n-Amenas	31	Hf	28.03N	9.33 E
Inami	29	De	33.48N	135.12 E
Inanba-Jima	29	Fe	33.39N	139.18 E
Inangahua Junction	62	Dd	41.52S	171.56 E
Inanwatan	26	Jg	2.08S	132.10 E
Iñapari	54	Ef	10.57S	69.35W
Inarajan	64c	Bb	13.16N	144.45 E
I-n-Arhâta	34	Ea	21.09N	0.18W
Inari	6	Ib	68.54N	27.01 E
Inari, Lake- (EN)= Inarijärvi	5	Ib	69.00N	28.00 E
Inarijärvi=Inari, Lake- (EN)	5	Ib	69.00N	28.00 E
Inawashiro	29	Gc	37.34N	140.05 E
Inawashiro-Ko	28	Pf	37.30N	140.03 E
I-n Azaoua	34	Ga	20.47N	7.31 E
I-n-Azaoua	34	Ga	20.54N	7.28 E
Inazawa	29	Ed	35.15N	136.47 E
Inca	13	Oe	39.43N	2.54 E
Inca de Oro	56	Gc	26.45S	69.54W
Incaguasi	56	Fc	29.13S	71.03W
Ince Burun	15	Ki	40.28N	27.16 E
İnce Burun	23	Da	42.07N	34.56 E
İncekum Burun	24	Ed	36.13N	33.58 E
Inceler	15	Ml	37.42N	29.35 E
I-n-Chaouâg	34	Fb	16.23N	0.10 E
Inchcape (Bell Rock)	9	Ke	56.26N	2.24W
Inchiri [3]	32	Df	20.00N	15.00W
Inch'ŏn	22	Of	37.28N	126.38 E
Incirliova	15	Kl	37.50N	27.43 E
Incudine	11a	Bb	41.51N	9.12 E
Indaiá, Rio-	55	Jd	18.27S	45.22W
Indaia Grande, Ribeirão-	55	Fd	19.31S	52.29W
Indaiatuba	55	If	23.05S	47.14W
Indal	8	Gb	62.34N	17.06 E
Indalsälven	7	De	62.31N	17.27 E
Inda Selase	35	Fc	14.06N	38.17 E
Indawgyi	25	Jc	25.08N	96.20 E
Indefatigable Banks	9	Ph	53.35N	2.20 E
Independence [Ca.-U.S.]	46	Fh	36.48N	118.12W
Independence [Ia.-U.S.]	45	Ke	42.28N	91.54W
Independence [Ks.-U.S.]	43	Hd	37.13N	95.42W
Independence [Mo.-U.S.]	45	Ig	39.05N	94.04W
Independence [Va.-U.S.]	44	Gg	36.38N	81.11W
Independence Fjord	67	Me	82.00N	30.25W
Independence Mountains	46	Gf	41.15N	116.05W
Independência [Braz.]	54	Je	5.23S	40.19W
Independência [Braz.]	55	Fa	13.34S	53.57W
Independenta	15	Kd	45.29N	27.45 E
Inder → Jalaid Qi	27	Lb	46.41N	122.52 E
Inder, Ozero-	16	Qe	48.25N	51.55 E
Inderborski	6	Lf	48.32N	51.47 E
India (EN)	21	Jh	20.00N	77.00 E
India (EN)=Bhārat Juktarashtra [1]	22	Jh	20.00N	77.00 E
India Muerta, Arroyo de la-	55	Fk	33.40S	54.04W
Indiana [2]	43	Jc	40.00N	86.15W
Indiana	44	He	40.39N	79.11W
Indianapolis	39	Kf	39.46N	86.09W
Indian Church	49	Ce	17.45N	88.40W
Indian Creek Point	51d	Bb	17.00N	61.43W
Indian Harbour	42	Lf	54.27N	57.13W
Indian Head	42	Hf	50.32N	103.40W
Indian Ocean	3	Gl	21.00S	82.00 E
Indian Ocean (EN)=Ḩindi, Badwēynta-	3	Gl	21.00S	82.00 E
Indian Ocean (EN)=Indico, Oceano-	3	Gl	21.00S	82.00 E
Indian Ocean (EN)=Indien, Océan-	3	Gl	21.00S	82.00 E
Indian Ocean (EN)=Indiese Oseaan-	3	Gl	21.00S	82.00 E
Indian Ocean (EN)= Indonesia, Samudera-	3	Gl	21.00S	82.00 E
Indianola	45	Kj	33.27N	90.39W
Indianópolis	55	Id	19.02S	47.55W
Indian Peak	46	Ig	38.16N	113.53W
Indian Rock	46	Ec	46.01N	120.49W
Indian Springs	43	Dd	36.34N	115.40W
Indiantown	44	Gl	27.01N	80.28W
Indian Town Point	51d	Bb	17.06N	61.40W
Indiapora	55	Gd	19.57S	50.17W
Indias Occidentales=West Indies (EN)	47	Je	19.00N	70.00W
Indico, Oceano-=Indian Ocean (EN)	3	Gl	21.00S	82.00 E
Indien, Océan-=Indian Ocean (EN)	3	Gl	21.00S	82.00 E
Indiese, Oseaan-=Indian Ocean (EN)	3	Gl	21.00S	82.00 E
Indiga	19	Eb	67.41N	49.00 E
Indigirka	21	Qb	70.48N	148.54 E
Indigskaja Guba	17	Dc	67.45N	48.20 E
Inđija	15	Dd	45.03N	20.05 E
Indio	43	De	33.43N	116.13W
Indio, Río-	49	Fh	10.57N	83.44W
Indio Rico	55	Bn	38.19S	60.53W
Indispensable Reefs	57	Hf	12.40S	160.25 E
Indispensable Strait	63a	Ec	9.00S	160.30 E
Indochina (EN)	21	Mh	16.00N	107.00 E
Indonesia [1]	22	Nj	5.00S	120.00 E
Indonesia, Samudera-= Indian Ocean (EN)	3	Gl	21.00S	82.00 E
Indore	22	Jg	22.43N	75.50 E
Indra	8	Li	55.53N	27.40 E
Indragiri	26	Dg	0.22S	103.26 E
Indramayu	26	Eh	6.20S	108.19 E
Indrāvati	25	Ge	18.44N	80.16 E
Indre	11	Gg	47.14N	0.11 E
Indre [3]	11	Hh	46.50N	1.40 E
Indre Arna	8	Ad	60.26N	5.30 E
Indre-et-Loire [3]	11	Gg	47.15N	0.45 E
Indus	21	Ig	24.20N	67.47 E
İnebolu	23	Da	41.58N	33.46 E
Inece	15	Kh	41.41N	27.04 E
Inecik	15	Ki	40.56N	27.16 E
İnegöl	23	Ca	40.05N	29.31 E
Inés Indart	55	Bl	34.24S	60.33W
Ineu	15	Ec	46.26N	21.51 E
Ineu, Vîrful-	15	Hb	47.32N	24.53 E
Inezgane	32	Fc	30.21N	9.32W
I-n-Ezzane	32	Je	23.29N	11.15 E
Inferior, Laguna-	48	Li	16.15N	94.45W
Infiernillo, Presa del-	47	De	18.35N	101.45W
Infiesto	13	Ga	43.21N	5.22W
Infreschi, Punta degli-	14	Jk	39.59N	15.25 E
Ingá	54	Ke	7.17S	35.36W
Inga	36	Bd	5.39S	13.39 E
Ingå/Inkoo	7	Ff	60.03N	24.01 E
Ingabu	25	Je	17.49N	95.16 E
Ingaí, Rio-	55	Je	21.10S	44.52W
I-n Gall	34	Gb	16.47N	6.56 E
Ingarö	8	He	59.15N	18.30 E
Ingavi	55	Bb	15.02S	60.29W
Ingelheim am Rhein	12	Ke	49.59N	8.02 E
Ingelmunster	12	Fd	50.55N	3.15 E
Ingelstad	8	Fh	56.45N	14.55 E
Ingende	36	Cc	0.15S	18.57 E
Ingeniero Guillermo N. Juarez	56	Hb	23.54S	61.51W
Ingeniero Jacobacci	56	Gf	41.18S	69.35W
Ingeniero Luiggi	56	He	35.25S	64.29W
Ingenio Santa Ana	56	Gc	27.28S	65.41W
Ingermanland (EN)	5	Id	59.00N	30.00 E
Ingham	58	Ff	18.39S	146.10 E
Ingička	18	Ee	39.47N	65.58 E
Inglefield Bredning	41	Fc	77.40N	65.00W
Inglefield Land	41	Fc	78.44N	68.20W
Inglewood [Austl.]	59	Ke	28.25S	151.05 E
Inglewood [Ca.-U.S.]	46	Fj	33.58N	118.21W
Inglewood [N.Z.]	62	Fc	39.09S	174.12 E
Ingolf Fjord	41	Kb	80.35N	17.35W
Ingólfshödi	7a	Cc	63.48N	16.39W
Ingolstadt	10	Hh	48.46N	11.26 E
Ingrāj Bāzār	25	Hc	25.00N	88.09 E
I-n-Guezzâm	31	Hg	19.32N	5.42 E
Ingul	16	Gf	47.02N	31.59 E
Ingulec	16	Hf	46.41N	32.48 E
Ingulec	19	Df	47.43N	33.10 E
Inguri	16	Lh	42.24N	41.32 E
Inhaca, Ilha da-	30	Kk	26.02S	32.58 E
Inhambane	31	Kk	23.52S	35.23 E
Inhambane [3]	37	Ed	23.00S	34.30 E
Inhambane, Baía de-	37	Fd	23.50S	35.20 E
Inhaminga	37	Fc	18.25S	35.01 E
Inhanduí-Guaçu, Rio-	55	Fe	21.37S	52.59W
Inhanduízinho, Rio-	55	Fe	21.34S	53.36W
Inharrime	37	Fd	24.28S	35.01 E
Inhassoro	37	Fd	21.32S	35.12 E
Inhaúma	55	Ja	13.01S	44.39W
I-n-Hihaou	32	He	23.00N	2.00 E
Inhobi, Rio-	55	Ef	23.45S	54.40W
Inhumas	54	Ig	16.22S	49.30W
Iniö	8	Id	60.25N	21.25 E
Inírida, Río-	52	Je	3.55N	67.52W
Inis/Ennis	9	Ei	52.50N	8.59W
Inis Airc/Inishark	9	Ch	53.37N	10.16W
Inis Bó Finne/Inishbofin	9	Ch	53.38N	10.12W
Inis Ceithleann/Enniskillen	9	Fg	54.21N	7.38W
Inis Córthaidh/Enniscorthy	9	Gi	52.30N	6.34W
Inis Diomáin/Ennistymon	9	Di	52.57N	9.13W
Inis Eoghain/Inishowen Peninsula	9	Ff	55.15N	7.20W
Inishark/Inis Airc	9	Ch	53.37N	10.16W
Inishbofin/Inis Bó Finne	9	Ch	53.38N	10.12W
Inisheer/Inis Oírr	9	Dh	53.03N	9.31W
Inishkea	9	Cg	54.08N	10.11W
Inishmaan/Inis Meáin	9	Dh	53.05N	9.35W
Inishmore/Árainn	9	Dh	53.07N	9.45W
Inishmurray/Inis Muirígh	9	Eg	54.26N	8.40W
Inishowen Peninsula/Inis Eoghain	9	Ff	55.15N	7.20W
Inishtranull	9	Ff	55.27N	7.14W
Inishturk/Inis Toirc	9	Ch	53.43N	10.05W
Inis Meáin/Inishmaan	9	Dh	53.05N	9.35W
Inis Muirígh/Inishmurray	9	Eg	54.26N	8.40W
Inis Oírr/Inisheer	9	Dh	53.03N	9.31W
Inis Toirc/Inishturk	9	Ch	53.43N	10.05W
Inja	20	Je	59.22N	144.50 E
Inja [R.S.F.S.R.]	20	Je	59.30N	144.48 E
Inja [R.S.F.S.R.]	20	Df	50.27N	86.42 E
Injeŭp	28	Je	38.04N	128.10 E
Injibara	35	Fc	10.55N	36.58 E
Injune	59	Je	25.51S	148.34 E
I-n-Kak	34	Fb	16.20N	0.17 E
Inkisi	36	Bc	4.46S	14.52 E
Inkoo/Ingå	7	Ff	60.03N	24.01 E
Inland Kaikoura Range	62	Ee	42.00S	173.35 E
Inland Sea (EN)= Setonaikai	21	Pf	34.10N	133.00 E
Inn	5	Hf	48.35N	13.28 E
Innamincka	59	Ie	27.45S	140.44 E
Inner Hebrides	9	Ge	57.00N	6.45W
Inner Mongolia (EN)=Nei Monggol Zizhiqu (Nei-meng-ku Tzu-chih-ch'ü) [2]	27	Jc	44.00N	112.00 E
Inner Silver Pit	9	Nh	53.30N	0.40 E
Inner Sound	9	Hd	57.30N	5.55W
Innerste	10	Fd	52.15N	9.50 E
Innisfail [Alta.-Can.]	46	Ia	52.02N	113.57W
Innisfail [Austl.]	59	Jc	17.32S	146.02 E
Innokentjevka	20	Ig	49.42N	136.55 E
Innokentjevski	20	Jg	48.38N	140.12 E
Innoko	40	Hd	62.14N	159.45W
Innsbruck	6	Hf	47.16N	11.24 E
Innuksuac	42	Je	58.27N	78.08W
Innviertel	14	Hb	48.15N	13.15 E
Innvikfjorden	8	Bc	61.50N	6.35 E
Inny/An Eithne	9	Fh	53.35N	7.50W
Ino	29	Ce	33.33N	133.26 E
Inobonto	26	Hf	0.52N	123.57 E
Inongo	31	Ii	1.57S	18.16 E
Inoni	36	Cc	3.04S	15.39 E
Inönü	15	Nj	39.48N	30.09 E
I-n-Ouagar	34	Gb	16.12N	6.54 E
I-n-Ouzzal	32	He	21.34N	1.59 E
Inowrocław	10	Od	52.48N	18.15 E
I-n-Salah	31	Hf	27.13N	2.28 E
Insar	7	Ki	54.42N	45.18 E
Insar	7	Kj	53.52N	44.23 E
Inscription, Cape-	57	Cg	25.30S	112.59 E
Insjön	8	Fd	60.41N	15.05 E
Ińsko	10	Lc	53.27N	15.33 E
Instruč	8	Ij	54.39N	21.48 E
Insurăţei	15	Ke	44.55N	27.36 E
Inta	6	Mb	66.05N	60.08 E
I-n-Tabezas	34	Fb	17.54N	1.50 E
I-n-Tallak	34	Fb	16.19N	3.15 E
Intepe	15	Ji	40.00N	26.20 E
Interlaken	14	Bd	46.41N	7.52 E
International Falls	43	Ib	48.36N	93.25W
Interview	25	If	12.55N	92.43 E
Inthanon, Doi-	25	Je	18.35N	98.29 E
Intibucá [3]	49	Cf	14.20N	88.15W
Intiyaco	56	Hc	28.39S	60.05W
Intorsura Buzaului	15	Jd	45.41N	26.02 E
Intracoastal Waterway	45	Im	28.45N	95.40W
Inubō-Zaki	29	Gd	35.42N	140.52 E
Inukjuak	39	Ld	58.30N	78.15W
Inutil, Bahia-	56	Fh	52.45S	71.24W
Inuvik	39	Fc	68.25N	133.30W
Inuyama	29	Ed	35.23N	136.56 E
Inva	17	Gg	58.59N	55.40 E
Inveraray	9	He	56.13N	5.05W
Invercargill	58	Hi	46.25S	168.21 E
Inverell	59	Ke	29.47S	151.07 E
Inverness	6	Fd	57.27N	4.15W
Inverurie	9	Kd	57.17N	2.23W
Investigator Group	57	Eh	33.45S	134.30 E
Investigator Strait	59	Hg	35.25S	137.10 E
Inyangani	30	Kj	18.18S	32.51 E
Inyangani	37	Ec	18.13S	32.46 E
Inyati	37	Dc	19.40S	28.51 E
Inyazura	37	Ec	18.43S	32.10 E
Inyo Mountains	46	Gh	36.50N	117.45W
Inza	19	Ee	53.53N	46.28 E
Inzá	54	Cc	2.33N	76.04W
Inžavino	16	Mc	52.19N	42.31 E
Inzer	17	Hi	54.30N	56.28 E
Inzer	17	Hi	54.14N	57.34 E
Inzia	36	Cc	3.45S	17.57 E
Iō/Kazan-Rettō=Volcano Islands (EN)	21	Qg	25.00N	141.00 E
Ioánnina	6	Ih	39.40N	20.50 E
Ioannínon, Límni-	15	Dj	39.40N	20.53 E
Iokanga	7	Jb	68.03N	39.40 E
Iola	45	Ih	37.55N	95.24W
Iolotan	19	Gh	37.18N	62.21 E
Iona	9	Ge	56.19N	6.25W
Iona	36	Bf	16.52S	12.34 E
Ionava/Jonava	7	Fi	55.05N	24.17 E
Ion Corvin	15	Ke	44.07N	27.48 E
Ione	46	Eg	38.21N	120.56W
Ionia	44	Ed	42.59N	85.04W
Ionian Basin (EN)	5	Hh	36.00N	20.00 E
Ionian Islands (EN)=Iónioi Nísoi	5	Ih	38.30N	20.30 E
Ionian Sea (EN)=Ionio, Mar-	5	Hh	39.00N	19.00 E
Ionian Sea (EN)=Iónion Pélagos	5	Hh	39.00N	19.00 E
Ionio, Mar-=Ionian Sea (EN)	5	Hh	39.00N	19.00 E
Iónioi Nísoi [2]	15	Dk	38.40N	20.10 E
Iónioi Nísoi=Ionian Islands (EN)	5	Ih	38.30N	20.30 E
Iónion Pélagos=Ionian Sea (EN)	5	Hh	39.00N	19.00 E
Ioniškelis/Joniškėlis	8	Ki	56.00N	24.14 E
Ioniškis/Joniškis	7	Fh	56.16N	23.37 E
Iony, Ostrov-	20	Je	56.15N	143.20 E
Iori	16	Oi	41.03N	46.27 E
Ios	15	Im	36.44N	25.18 E
Ios	15	Im	36.42N	25.20 E
Iō-Shima	28	Ki	31.51N	130.13 E
Iowa [2]	43	Ic	42.15N	93.15W
Iowa City	43	Ic	41.40N	91.32W
Iowa Falls	45	Je	42.31N	93.16W
Iowa Park	45	Gj	33.57N	98.40W
Iowa River	45	Kf	41.10N	91.02W
Iō-Yama	29a	Da	44.10N	145.10 E
Ipa	16	Fc	52.07N	29.12 E
Ipameri	54	Ig	17.43S	48.09W
Ipatovo	19	Ef	45.43N	42.53 E
Ipaumirim	54	Ke	6.47S	38.43W
Ipel'	10	Oi	47.49N	18.52 E
Ipiales	54	Cc	0.50N	77.37W
Ipiaú	54	Kf	14.08S	39.44W
Ipiranga	55	Gg	25.01S	50.35W
Ipiros [2]	15	Dj	39.30N	20.40 E
Ipiros=Epirus (EN)	15	Dj	39.30N	20.40 E
Ipiros=Epirus (EN)	5	Ih	39.30N	20.40 E
Ipixuma, Rio-	54	Fe	5.50S	63.00W
Ipixuna	54	De	7.34S	72.36W
Ipoh	22	Mi	4.35N	101.05 E
Ipoly	10	Oi	47.49N	18.52 E
Iporã	55	Ff	23.59S	53.37W
Iporá	54	Hg	16.28S	51.07W
Ippy	35	Cd	6.15N	21.12 E
Ipsala	24	Bb	40.55N	26.23 E
Ipsízonos Óros	15	Gi	40.28N	23.34 E
Ipswich [Austl.]	58	Gg	27.36S	152.46 E
Ipswich [Eng.-U.K.]	6	Ge	52.04N	1.10 E
Ipswich [S.D.-U.S.]	45	Gd	45.27N	99.02W
Ipu	54	Jd	4.20S	40.42W
Iqaluit	39	Mc	63.44N	68.28W
Iquique	53	Ih	20.13S	70.10W
Iquitos	53	If	3.50S	73.15W
Iraan	45	Fk	30.54N	101.54W
Ira Banda	35	Cd	5.57N	22.06 E
Irabu-Jima	27	Mg	24.50N	125.10 E
Iracoubo	54	Hb	5.29N	53.13W
Iraël	17	Gd	64.27N	55.08 E
Irago-Suidō	29	Ed	34.35N	136.55 E
Irago-Zaki	29	Ed	34.35N	137.01 E
Iráklia	15	Gh	41.10N	23.16 E
Iráklia	15	Im	36.50N	25.26 E
Iráklion	6	Ih	35.20N	25.08 E
Irān=Iran (EN) [1]	22	Hf	32.00N	53.00 E
Iran (EN)=Irān [1]	22	Hf	32.00N	53.00 E
Iran, Pegunungan-=Iran Mountains (EN)	21	Ni	2.05N	114.55 E
Iran, Plateau of- (EN)	21	Hf	32.00N	56.00 E
Irani, Serra do-	55	Fh	27.00S	52.12W
Iran Mountains (EN)=Iran, Pegunungan-	21	Ni	2.05N	114.55 E
Irānshahr	22	Ig	27.13N	60.41 E
Irapa	50	Eg	10.34N	62.35W
Irapuá, Arroio-	55	Fj	30.15S	53.10W
Irapuato	39	Ig	20.41N	101.28W
Iraq (EN)=Al 'Irāq [1]	22	Gf	33.00N	44.00 E
'Irāq al 'Arabi	24	Kg	31.50N	45.50 E
Irati	13	Kb	42.35N	1.16W
Irati	56	Jc	25.27S	50.39W
Irazú, Volcán-	38	Ki	9.59N	83.51W
Irbeni Väin	8	Ig	57.48N	22.05 E
Irbid	23	Ec	32.33N	35.51 E
Irbiktepe	15	Jh	41.00N	26.30 E
Irbit	17	Kh	57.42N	63.07 E
Irbit	19	Gd	57.41N	63.03 E
Irebu	36	Cc	0.37S	17.45 E
Irecê	54	Jf	11.18S	41.52W
Iregua	13	Jb	42.27N	2.24W
Ireland	5	Fe	53.00N	8.00W
Ireland/Éire [1]	6	Fe	53.00N	8.00W
Ireland Trough (EN)	5	Ed	55.00N	12.40W
Iren	17	Hh	57.27N	56.59 E
Ireng River	54	Gc	3.33N	59.51W
Irês Corações	54	Ih	21.42S	45.16W
Iretama	55	Fg	24.27S	52.02W
Irgiz	19	Gf	48.13N	62.08 E
Irgiz	19	Gf	48.36N	61.16 E
Irharrhar [Alg.]	30	Hf	28.00N	6.15 E
Irharrhar [Alg.]	32	Ie	21.01N	6.01 E
Irherm	32	Fc	30.04N	8.26W
Iri	28	Ig	35.56N	126.57 E
Iriba	31	Jg	15.07N	22.15 E
Irîgui	30	Gg	16.43N	5.30W
Iriklinski	16	Ud	51.39N	58.38 E
Iriklinskoje Vodohranilišče	16	Ud	51.45N	58.45 E
Iringa [3]	36	Gd	8.00S	35.30 E
Iringa	31	Ki	7.46S	35.42 E
Irinja, Gora-	20	Fe	58.20N	104.30 E
Iriomote Jima	27	Lg	24.20N	123.50 E
Iriona	49	Ef	15.57N	85.11W
Iriri, Rio-	52	Kf	3.52S	52.37W
Irish Sea	5	Fe	53.30N	5.20W
Irish Sea (EN)=Muir Eireann	5	Fe	53.30N	5.20W
Irituia	54	Id	1.46S	47.26W
Irkeštam	18	Ie	39.38N	73.55 E
Irkutsk	22	Md	52.16N	104.20 E
Irkutskaja Oblast [3]	20	Fe	56.00N	104.00 E
Irlir, Gora-	18	Dc	42.40N	63.30 E
Irminio	14	In	36.46N	14.36 E
Irnijärvi	7	Gd	65.36N	29.05 E
Iro, Lac-	35	Bc	10.06N	19.25 E
Iroise	11	Bf	48.15N	4.55W
Iron Gate (EN) = Portile de Fier	5	Ig	44.41N	22.31 E
Iron Knob	59	Hf	32.44S	137.08 E
Iron Mountain	43	Jb	45.49N	88.04W
Iron Mountains	9	Fg	54.15N	7.50W
Iron River [Mi.-U.S.]	43	Jb	46.05N	88.39W
Iron River [Wi.-U.S.]	45	Kc	46.34N	91.24W
Ironside Mountain	46	Fd	44.15N	118.08W
Ironton [Mo.-U.S.]	45	Kh	37.36N	90.38W
Ironton [Oh.-U.S.]	44	Ff	38.32N	82.40W
Ironwood	43	Ib	46.27N	90.10W
Iroquois Falls	42	Jg	48.46N	80.41W
Irō-Zaki	28	Og	34.35N	138.55 E

Index Symbols

[1] Independent Nation
[2] State, Region
[3] District, County
[4] Municipality
[5] Colony, Dependency
Continent
Physical Region

Historical or Cultural Region
Mount, Mountain
Volcano
Hill
Mountains, Mountain Range
Hills, Escarpment
Plateau, Upland

Pass, Gap
Plain, Lowland
Delta
Salt Flat
Valley, Canyon
Crater, Cave
Karst Features

Depression
Polder
Desert, Dunes
Forest, Woods
Heath, Steppe
Oasis
Cape, Point

Coast, Beach
Cliff
Peninsula
Isthmus
Sandbank
Island
Atoll

Rock, Reef
Islands, Archipelago
Rocks, Reefs
Coral Reef
Well, Spring
Geyser
River, Stream

Waterfall Rapids
River Mouth, Estuary
Lake
Salt Lake
Intermittent Lake
Reservoir
Swamp, Pond

Canal
Glacier
Ice Shelf, Pack Ice
Ocean
Sea
Gulf, Bay
Strait, Fjord

Lagoon
Bank
Seamount
Tablemount
Ridge
Shelf
Basin

Escarpment, Sea Scarp
Fracture
Trench, Abyss
National Park, Reserve
Point of Interest
Recreation Site
Cave, Cavern

Historic Site
Ruins
Wall, Walls
Church, Abbey
Temple
Scientific Station
Airport

Port
Lighthouse
Mine
Tunnel
Dam, Bridge

Irpen 19 De 50.31N 30.16 E
Irpinia 14 Ij 40.55N 15.00 E
Irrawaddy → Ayeyarwady 25 Ie 17.00N 95.00 E
Irrawaddy (EN) = Ayeyarwady 21 Lg 15.50N 95.06 E
Irrel 12 Ie 49.51N 6.28 E
Irsâva 10 Th 48.15N 23.05 E
Irsina 14 Kj 40.45N 16.14 E
Irtek 16 Rd 51.29N 52.42 E
Irthlingborough 12 Bb 52.19N 0.36W
Irtyš 21 Ic 61.04N 68.52 E
Irtyšsk 19 He 53.21N 75.27 E
Irumu 36 Eb 1.27N 29.52 E
Irún 13 Ka 43.21N 1.47W
Irurzun 13 Kb 42.55N 1.50W
Irves Šaurums 8 Ig 57.48N 22.05 E
Irvine 9 If 55.37N 4.40W
Irving 45 Hj 32.49N 96.56W
Is, Jabal- 35 Fa 21.49N 35.39 E
Isa, Ra's- 33 Hf 15.11N 42.39 E
Isabel 45 Fd 45.24N 101.26W
Isabel, Bahia- 54a Ab 0.38 S 91.25W
Isabela 51a Ab 18.31N 67.07W
Isabela → Basilan City 26 He 6.42N 121.58 E
Isabela, Cabo- 49 Ld 19.56N 71.01W
Isabela, Isla- [Ec.] 52 Gf 0.30 S 91.06W
Isabela, Isla- [Mex.] 48 Gg 21.51N 105.55W
Isabella, Cordillera- 47 Gf 13.30N 85.30W
Isabel Segunda 49 Od 18.09N 65.27W
Isabey 15 Ml 38.00N 29.24 E
Isaccea 15 Ld 45.16N 28.28 E
Isachsen 39 Ib 78.50N 103.30W
Isafjörour 6 Db 66.03N 23.09W
Isahaya 28 Jh 32.50N 130.03 E
Isakov, Seamount (EN) 57 Ga 31.35N 151.07 E
Isana, Rio- 54 Ec 0.26N 67.19W
Isandja 36 Dc 2.59 S 22.00 E
Isanga 36 Dc 1.26 S 22.18 E
Isangi 36 Db 0.46N 24.15 E
Isanlu Makutu 34 Gd 8.16N 5.48 E
Isaouane-n-Irarraren 32 Id 27.15N 8.00 E
Isaouane-n-Tifernine 32 Id 27.00N 7.30 E
Isar 10 Ih 48.49N 12.58 E
Isarco/Eisack 14 Fd 46.27N 11.18 E
Isarco, Valle-/Eisacktal 14 Fd 46.45N 11.35 E
Isbergues 12 Ed 50.37N 2.27 E
Iscayachi 54 Eh 21.31 S 65.03W
Ischgl 14 Ec 47.01N 10.17 E
Ischia 14 Hj 40.45N 13.55 E
Ischia 14 Hj 40.44N 13.57 E
Ise 27 Oe 34.29N 136.42 E
Isefjord 8 Di 55.50N 11.50 E
Isějevka 7 Li 54.28N 48.17 E
Isen 10 Ih 48.20N 12.45 E
Isenach 12 Ke 49.38N 8.28 E
Isen-Zaki 29b Bb 27.39N 128.55 E
Iseo, Lago d'- 14 Ee 45.45N 10.05 E
Iseran, Col de l'- 11 Ni 45.25N 7.02 E
Isère 11 Kj 44.59N 4.51 E
Isère [3] 11 Li 45.10N 5.50 E
Išerit, Gora- 17 If 61.08N 59.10 E
Iserlohn 10 De 51.22N 7.42 E
Isernia 14 Ii 41.36N 14.14 E
Isesaki 29 Fc 36.19N 139.12 E
Iset 21 Id 56.36N 66.24 E
Isetskoje 17 Lh 56.29N 65.21 E
Ise-Wan 28 Ng 34.40N 136.42 E
Iseyin 34 Fd 7.58N 3.36 E
Isfahan (EN) = Eşfahān 22 Hf 32.40N 51.38 E
Isfana 18 Ge 39.51N 69.32 E
Isfara 18 Hd 40.07N 70.38 E
Isfendiyar Dağları 23 Da 41.45N 34.10 E
Isfjorden 41 Nc 78.15N 15.00 E
Isha Baydabo 31 Lh 3.04N 43.48 E
Ishasha River 36 Ec 0.50 S 29.40 E
Ishavet=Arctic Ocean (EN) 67 Be 85.00N 170.00 E
Isherton 54 Gc 2.19N 59.22W
Ishigaki 27 Lg 24.20N 124.09 E
Ishikari 29a Bb 43.13N 141.18 E
Ishikari-Dake 29a Cb 43.33N 143.00 E
Ishikari-Gawa 29a Bb 43.15N 141.20 E
Ishikari-Heiya 29a Bb 43.00N 141.40 E
Ishikari-Wan 27 Pc 43.25N 141.00 E
Ishikawa [Jap.] 27 Mf 26.27N 127.50 E
Ishikawa [Jap.] 29 Gc 37.09N 140.27 E
Ishikawa Ken [2] 28 Nf 36.35N 136.40 E
Ishim Steppe (EN)= Išimskaja Step 21 Id 55.00N 67.30 E
Ishinomaki 27 Pd 38.25N 141.18 E
Ishinomaki-Wan 29 Gb 38.20N 141.15 E
Ishioka 28 Pf 36.11N 140.16 E
Ishitate-San 29 De 33.44N 134.03 E
Ishizuchi-Yama 29 Ce 33.45N 133.05 E
Ishodnaja, Gora- 20 Nd 64.50N 173.26W
Ishpeming 44 Db 46.30N 87.40W
Isidro Alves 55 Ee 20.09 S 55.12W
Isigny-sur-Mer 11 Ee 49.19N 1.06W
Isii 29 Dd 34.04N 134.26 E
Işıklar Dağı 24 Bb 40.50N 27.05 E
Işikli 15 Mk 38.19N 29.51 E
Isikli Göl 15 Mk 38.14N 29.55 E
Isili 14 Dk 39.44N 9.06 E
Isilkul 19 He 54.55N 71.16 E
Išim 22 Id 56.09N 69.27 E
Išim 21 Jd 57.45N 71.12 E
Išimbaj 19 Fe 53.28N 56.02 E
Išimskaja Step=Ishim Steppe (EN) 21 Id 55.00N 67.30 E
Isinga 20 Gf 52.55N 112.00 E
Isiolo 36 Gb 0.21N 37.35 E
Isiro 31 Jh 2.48N 27.41 E
Isisford 59 Id 24.16 S 144.26 E
Isjangulovo 17 Hj 52.12N 56.36 E
Iskandar 18 Gd 41.35N 69.43 E
Iskăr 15 Hf 43.44N 24.27 E
Iskăr, Jazovir- 15 Gg 42.25N 23.35 E
Iškašim 19 Hh 36.44N 71.39 E
İskenderun=Alexandretta (EN) 22 Ff 36.37N 36.07 E
İskenderun Körfezi= Alexandretta, Gulf of- (EN) 23 Eb 36.30N 35.40 E
İskilip 24 Fb 40.45N 34.29 E
Iski-Naukat 18 Id 40.14N 72.41 E
Iskininski 16 Rf 47.13N 52.36 E
Iskitim 20 Df 54.38N 83.18 E
Iskushuban 35 Ic 10.13N 50.14 E
Iskut 42 Ee 56.45N 131.48W
Isla-Cristina 13 Eg 37.12N 7.19W
İslâhiye 24 Gd 37.26N 36.41 E
Islāmābād 22 Jf 33.42N 73.10 E
Islāmābād → Anantnāg 25 Fb 33.44N 75.09 E
Isla Mujeres 48 Pg 21.12N 86.43W
Island=Iceland (EN) 6 Eb 65.00N 18.00W
Island=Iceland (EN) 5 Eb 65.00N 18.00W
Island Harbour 51b Ab 18.16N 63.02W
Island Lagoon 59 Hf 31.30 S 136.40 E
Island Lake 42 If 53.45N 94.30W
Island Lake 42 If 53.58N 94.46W
Island Pond 44 Lc 44.50N 71.53W
Islands, Bay of - [Can.] 42 Lg 49.10N 58.15W
Islands, Bay of- [N.Z.] 62 Fa 35.10 S 174.10 E
Islao, Massif de l'- 30 Lk 22.30 S 45.20 E
Islas de la Bahia [3] 49 De 16.20N 86.30W
Islay 5 Fd 55.46N 6.10W
Islaz 15 Hf 43.44N 24.45 E
Isle 11 Fj 44.55N 0.15W
Isle of Man [5] 9 Ig 54.15N 4.30W
Isle of Wight [3] 9 Lk 50.40N 1.15W
Isleta 45 Ci 34.55N 106.42W
Isle-Verte 44 Ma 48.01N 69.22W
Ismael Cortinas 55 Dk 33.56 S 57.08W
Ismailia (EN)=Al Ismā'īlīyah 33 Fc 30.35N 32.16 E
Ismailly 16 Pi 40.47N 48.13 E
Ismantorps Borg 8 Gh 56.45N 16.40 E
Isnā 31 Kf 25.18N 32.33 E
Isny im Allgäu 10 Gi 47.42N 10.02 E
Isojärvi 8 Ic 61.45N 21.45 E
Isojoki 7 Ee 62.07N 21.58 E
Isojoki/Storå 7 Ee 62.07N 21.58 E
Isoka 36 Fe 10.08 S 32.38 E
Isola del Liri 14 Hi 41.41N 13.34 E
Isola di Capo Rizzuto 14 Ll 38.58N 17.05 E
Isonzo 14 He 45.43N 13.33 E
Isonzo (EN)=Soča 14 He 45.43N 13.33 E
Isosyöte 7 Gd 65.37N 27.35 E
Isparta 23 Db 37.46N 30.33 E
Isperih 15 Jf 43.43N 26.50 E
Ispica 14 In 36.47N 14.55 E
Ispir 24 Ib 40.29N 41.00 E
Ispiriz Dağı 24 Jc 38.03N 43.55 E
Israel (EN)=Yisra'el [1] 22 Ff 31.30N 35.00 E
Isratu 35 Fb 16.20N 39.55 E
Issa 8 Mh 56.55N 28.50 E
Issano 54 Gb 5.49N 59.25W
Issaran, Ra's- 24 Eh 28.50N 32.56 E
Issel 10 Cd 52.00N 6.10 E
Isser 13 Ph 36.51N 3.40 E
Issia [3] 34 Dd 6.30N 6.35W
Issia 34 Dd 6.29N 6.35W
Issoire 11 Ji 45.33N 3.15 E
Issoudun 11 Hh 46.57N 2.00 E
Issyk 18 Kc 43.20N 77.28 E
Issyk-Kul, Ozero- 21 Je 42.25N 77.15 E
Issyk-Kulskaja Oblast [3] 19 Hg 42.10N 78.00 E
Ist 14 If 44.17N 14.47 E
İstanbul 22 Ee 41.01N 28.58 E
İstanbul-Bakırköy 15 Li 40.59N 28.52 E
İstanbul-Beyoğlu 15 Lh 41.02N 28.59 E
İstanbul Boğazi=Bosporus (EN) 5 Ig 41.00N 29.00 E
İstanbul-Kadıköy 15 Mi 40.59N 29.01 E
Isteren 8 Db 62.00N 11.50 E
Istgāh-e Eqbālīyeh 24 Ne 35.50N 50.45 E
Isthilart 55 Dj 31.11 S 57.58W
Istiaia 15 Gk 38.57N 23.09 E
Istisu 16 Nj 39.57N 46.00 E
Istmina 54 Cb 5.09N 76.42W
Isto, Mount- 38 Ec 69.12N 143.48W
Istok 15 Dg 42.47N 20.29 E
Istokpoga, Lake- 44 Gl 27.22N 81.17W
Istra = Istria (EN) 5 Hf 45.00N 14.00 E
Istres 11 Kk 43.31N 4.59 E
Istria 15 Le 44.34N 28.43 E
Istria (EN) = Istra 5 Hf 45.00N 14.00 E
Isulan 26 He 7.02N 124.29 E
Itabaiana 54 Kf 10.41 S 37.26W
Itabaianinha 54 Kf 11.16 S 37.47W
Itaberá 55 Hf 23.51 S 49.09W
Itaberaba 54 Jf 12.32 S 40.18W
Itaberai 54 Ig 16.02 S 49.48W
Itabira 54 Jg 19.37 S 43.13W
Itabirito 55 Ke 20.15 S 43.48W
Itabuna 53 Mg 14.48 S 39.16W
Itacaiúna, Rio- 54 Ie 5.21 S 49.08W
Itacarambi 55 Jb 15.01 S 44.03W
Itacoatiara 53 Kf 3.08 S 58.25W
Itacolomi, Pico do- 55 Ke 20.26 S 43.29W
Itacuai, Rio- 54 Dd 4.20 S 70.12W
Itacumbi 55 Ei 28.44 S 55.08W
Itacurubi del Rosario 55 Dg 24.29 S 56.41W
Itaguari, Rio- 55 Jb 14.11 S 44.40W
Itaguaru 55 Hb 15.44 S 49.37W
Itagüí 54 Cb 6.12N 75.40W
Itaimbézinho 55 Gi 28.38 S 50.34W
Itaituba 53 Kf 4.17 S 55.59W
Itajai 53 Lh 26.53 S 48.39W
Itajai Açu, Rio- 55 Hh 26.54 S 48.38W
Itajubá 54 Ih 22.26 S 45.27W
Itajuípe 54 Kf 14.41 S 39.22W
Itaka 20 Gf 53.54N 118.42 E
Italia = Italy (EN) [1] 6 Hg 42.50N 12.50 E
Itálica 13 Fg 37.25N 6.05W
Italy (EN) = Italia [1] 6 Hg 42.50N 12.50 E
Itambacuri 54 Jg 18.01 S 41.42W
Itambé, Pico de- 52 Lg 18.23 S 43.21W
Itämeri=Baltic, Sea (EN) 5 Hd 57.00N 19.00 E
Itampolo 37 Gd 24.41 S 43.57 E
Itanagar 25 Ic 26.57N 93.15 E
Itanará, Rio- 55 Eg 24.00 S 55.53W
Itanhaém 56 Kb 24.11 S 46.47W
Itano 29 Dd 34.09N 134.28 E
Itapaci 55 Hb 14.57 S 49.34W
Itapagé 54 Kd 3.41 S 39.34W
Itapajipe 55 Hd 19.54 S 49.22W
Itaparaná, Rio- 54 Fe 5.47 S 63.03W
Itapebi 54 Kg 15.56 S 39.32W
Itapecerica 55 Je 20.28 S 45.07W
Itapecuru-Mirim 54 Jd 3.24 S 44.20W
Itapemirim 54 Jh 21.01 S 40.50W
Itaperina, Pointe- 30 Lk 24.59 S 47.06 E
Itaperuna 54 Jh 21.12 S 41.54W
Itapetinga 54 Jg 15.15 S 40.15W
Itapetininga 56 Kb 23.36 S 48.03W
Itapetininga, Rio- 55 Hf 23.35 S 48.27W
Itapeva 55 Hf 23.58 S 48.52W
Itapeva, Lagoa- 55 Hi 29.30 S 49.55W
Itapicuru, Rio- [Braz.] 54 Kf 11.47 S 37.32W
Itapicuru, Rio- [Braz.] 52 Lf 2.52 S 44.12W
Itapipoca 54 Kd 3.31 S 39.33W
Itapiranga [Braz.] 54 Gd 2.45 S 58.01W
Itapiranga [Braz.] 55 Fh 27.08 S 53.43W
Itapirapuã, Pico- 54 Hg 24.17 S 49.12W
Itápolis 55 He 21.35 S 48.46W
Itaporã 55 Ef 22.01 S 54.54W
Itaporanga [Braz.] 55 Hf 23.42 S 49.29W
Itaporanga [Braz.] 54 Ke 7.18 S 38.10W
Itapúa [3] 55 Eh 26.50 S 55.50W
Itapuã 55 Gj 30.16 S 51.01W
Itapuranga 54 Ig 15.35 S 49.59W
Itaqui 56 Ic 29.08 S 56.33W
Itaquyry 55 Eg 24.56 S 55.13W
Itararé 55 Hg 24.07 S 49.20W
Itararé, Rio- 55 Hf 23.10 S 49.42W
Itārsi 25 Fd 22.37N 77.45 E
Itarumã 55 Gd 18.42 S 51.25W
Itati 55 Ch 27.16 S 58.15W
Itatinga 55 Hf 23.07 S 48.36W
Itatski 20 De 56.07N 89.20 E
Itaum 55 Ef 22.00 S 55.20W
Itaúna 54 Jh 20.04 S 44.34W
Itaya-Tōge 29 Gc 37.50N 140.13 E
Itbāy 30 Kf 22.00N 35.30 E
Itbayat 26 Hb 20.46N 121.50 E
Itchen 12 Ad 50.57N 1.22W
Ite 54 Dg 17.50 S 70.58W
Itéa 15 Fk 38.26N 22.25 E
Ithaca 43 Lc 42.26N 76.30W
Ithaca (EN)=Itháki 15 Dk 38.24N 20.40 E
Itháki 15 Dk 38.22N 20.43 E
Itháki = Ithaca (EN) 15 Dk 38.24N 20.40 E
Ith Hils 10 Fd 52.05N 9.35 E
Ithnayn, Harrat- 24 Ii 26.40N 40.10 E
Itigi 36 Fd 5.42 S 34.29 E
Itimbiri 30 Jh 2.02N 22.44 E
Itiopya=Ethiopia (EN) [1] 31 Kh 9.00N 39.00 E
Itiquira 54 Hg 17.05 S 54.56W
Itiquira, Rio- 52 Kg 17.18 S 56.44W
Itirapina 55 If 22.15 S 47.49W
Itiúba 54 Kf 10.43 S 39.51W
Itivdleq 41 Ge 66.38N 53.51W
Itō 28 Og 34.58N 139.05 E
Itoigawa 28 Nf 37.02N 137.51 E
Itoko 36 Dc 1.00 S 21.45 E
Itoman 29b Ab 26.07N 127.40 E
Iton 11 Hf 49.09N 1.12 E
Itremo, Massif de l'- 37 Hd 20.45 S 46.30 E
Itsā 24 Dh 29.15N 30.48 E
Itsukaichi 29 Cd 34.22N 132.22 E
Itsuki 29 Be 32.24N 130.50 E
Ittiri 14 Cj 40.36N 8.34 E
Itu [Braz.] 55 If 23.16 S 47.19W
Itu [Nig.] 34 Gd 5.12N 7.59 E
Itu, Rio- 55 Ei 29.25 S 55.51W
Itui, Rio- 54 Dd 4.38 S 70.19W
Ituiutaba 54 Ig 18.58 S 49.28W
Itula 36 Ec 3.29 S 27.52 E
Itumbiara 54 Ig 18.25 S 49.13W
Itumkale 16 Nh 42.43N 45.35 E
Ituna 46 Na 51.10N 103.30W
Itungi Port 36 Fd 9.35 S 33.56 E
Itupiranga 54 Ie 5.09 S 49.20W
Iturama 55 Gd 19.44 S 50.11W
Iturbide 48 Oh 19.40N 89.37W
Ituri 30 Jh 1.40N 27.01 E
Iturregui 55 Bm 36.50 S 61.08W
Iturup, Ostrov- 21 Qe 44.54N 147.30 E
Iturup, Ostrov-/Etorofu Tō 21 Qe 44.54N 147.30 E
Itutinga 55 Je 21.18 S 44.40W
Ituverava 56 Kb 20.20 S 47.47W
Ituxi, Rio- 52 Jf 7.18 S 64.51W
Ituzaingó 55 Dh 27.36 S 56.41W
Itz 10 Gg 49.58N 10.52 E
Itzehoe 10 Fc 53.55N 9.31 E
Ivacevići 16 Dc 52.43N 25.21 E
Ivai 55 Gg 25.01 S 50.52W
Ivai, Rio- [Braz.] 55 Fi 29.08 S 53.16W
Ivai, Rio- [Braz.] 52 Kh 23.18 S 53.42W
Ivaiporã 55 Gg 24.15 S 51.45W
Ivajlovgrad 15 Jh 41.32N 26.08 E
Ivakoany, Massif de l'- 37 Hd 23.50 S 46.25 E
Ivalojoki 7 Gc 68.43N 27.36 E
Ivančice 10 Mg 49.06N 16.22 E
Ivangorod 7 Gg 59.23N 28.20 E
Ivangrad 15 Cg 42.51N 19.52 E
Ivanhoe 58 Fh 32.54 S 144.18 E
Ivanić-Grad 14 Ke 45.42N 16.24 E
Ivaniči 10 Uf 50.38N 24.24 E
Ivanjica 15 Df 43.35N 20.14 E
Ivanjska 14 Lf 44.55N 17.04 E
Ivankov 16 Fd 50.57N 29.58 E
Ivano-Frankovo 10 Tg 49.52N 23.46 E
Ivano-Frankovsk 6 If 48.55N 24.43 E
Ivano-Frankovskaja Oblast [3] 19 Cf 48.40N 24.40 E
Ivanovka [R.S.F.S.R.] 20 Hf 50.18N 127.59 E
Ivanovka [Ukr.-U.S.S.R.] 16 Gf 46.57N 30.28 E
Ivanovo [Bye.-U.S.S.R.] 16 Dc 52.10N 25.32 E
Ivanovo [R.S.F.S.R.] 6 Kd 57.00N 40.59 E
Ivanovskaja Oblast [3] 19 Ed 57.00N 41.50 E
Ivanovskoje 8 Me 59.12N 28.59 E
Ivanščica 14 Kd 46.11N 16.10 E
Ivdel 19 Gc 60.42N 60.28 E
Ivenec 8 Lk 53.55N 26.49 E
Ivigtut 41 Hf 61.15N 48.00W
Ivindo 30 Ii 0.09 S 12.09 E
Ivinheima 55 Ff 22.10 S 53.37W
Ivinheima, Rio- 54 Hh 23.14 S 53.42W
Ivinski razliv 7 If 61.10N 35.00 E
Iviza (EN)=Eivissa/Ibiza 5 Gh 39.00N 1.25 E
Iviza (EN)=Ibiza/Eivissa 5 Gh 39.00N 1.25 E
Ivje 10 Vc 53.55N 25.51 E
Ivohibe 37 Hd 22.29 S 46.52 E
Ivoire, Côte d'-=Ivory Coast (EN) 30 Gh 5.00N 5.00W
Ivolândia 55 Gc 16.34 S 50.51W
Ivory Coast (EN)=Côte d'Ivoire [1] 31 Gh 8.00N 5.00W
Ivory Coast (EN)=Ivoire, Côte d'- 30 Gh 5.00N 5.00W
Ivösjön 8 Fh 56.05N 14.25 E
Ivrea 14 Be 45.28N 7.52 E
Ivrindi 15 Kj 39.34N 27.29 E
Ivry-la-Bataille 12 Df 48.53N 1.28 E
Ivry-sur-Seine 12 Ef 48.49N 2.23 E
Ivujivik 39 Lc 62.25N 77.54W
Iwai-Shima 29 Be 33.47N 131.58 E
Iwaizumi 28 Pe 39.50N 141.48 E
Iwaki 22 Qf 36.55N 140.48 E
Iwaki-Gawa 29 Ga 41.01N 140.22 E
Iwaki-Hisanohama 29 Gc 37.09N 140.59 E
Iwaki-Jōban 29 Gc 37.02N 140.50 E
Iwaki-Kawamae 29 Gc 37.12N 140.45 E
Iwaki-Miwa 29 Gc 37.09N 140.42 E
Iwaki-Nakoso 29 Gc 36.56N 140.48 E
Iwaki-Onahama 29 Gc 36.57N 140.53 E
Iwaki-San 29 Ga 40.40N 140.20 E
Iwaki-Taira 29 Gc 37.05N 140.55 E
Iwaki-Uchigō 29 Gc 37.04N 140.50 E
Iwaki-Yoshima 29 Gc 37.05N 140.50 E
Iwaki-Yotsukura 29 Gc 37.07N 140.58 E
Iwakuni 27 Ne 34.09N 132.11 E
Iwami 29 Dd 35.35N 134.20 E
Iwami-Kōgen 29 Cd 35.00N 132.30 E
Iwamizawa 27 Pc 43.12N 141.46 E
Iwanai 28 Pc 42.58N 140.30 E
Iwanuma 29 Gb 38.07N 140.52 E
Iwase 29 Gc 36.21N 140.06 E
Iwasuge-Yama 29 Fc 36.44N 138.32 E
Iwata 29 Ed 34.42N 137.48 E
Iwate 28 Pe 39.30N 141.30 E
Iwate Ken [2] 28 Pe 39.30N 141.15 E
Iwate San 28 Pe 39.49N 141.26 E
Iwo 34 Fd 7.38N 4.11 E
Iwŏn 27 Mc 40.19N 128.37 E
Iwuy 12 Fd 50.14N 3.19 E
Ixiamas 54 Ef 13.45 S 68.09W
Ixmiquilpan 48 Jg 20.29N 99.14W
Ixopo 37 Ef 30.08 S 30.00 E
Ixtapa, Punta- 48 Ii 17.39N 101.40W
Ixtepec 47 Ee 16.34N 95.06W
Ixtlahuacán del Rio 48 Hg 20.52N 103.15W
Ixtlán del Rio 47 Dd 21.02N 104.22W
Iyah 35 Hd 9.00N 49.38 E
Iyo 28 Lh 33.46N 132.42 E
Iyo-mishima 29 Ce 33.58N 133.33 E
Iyo-Nada 29 Ce 33.40N 132.15 E
Iž 7 Mh 56.00N 52.41 E
Iž 14 Jf 44.03N 15.06 E
Izabal [3] 49 Cf 15.30N 89.00W
Izabal, Lago de- 47 Ge 15.30N 89.10W
Izad Khvāst 24 Og 31.31N 52.07 E
Izamal 47 Gd 20.56N 89.01W
Izamal 48 Og 20.56N 89.01W
Izapa 47 Ff 14.55N 92.10W
'Izbat al Jājah 24 Dj 24.48N 30.35 E
'Izbat Dush 24 Dj 24.34N 30.42 E
Izberbaš 19 Eg 42.33N 47.52 E
Izbiceni 15 Hf 43.50N 24.39 E
Izborsk 8 Mg 57.39N 28.01 E
Izegem 12 Fd 50.55N 3.12 E
Izeh 24 Mg 31.50N 49.50 E
Izena-Shima 29b Ab 26.56N 127.56 E
Iževsk 6 Ld 56.51N 53.14 E
Izjaslav 16 Ed 50.09N 26.51 E
Izjum 19 Df 49.12N 37.17 E
Izki 23 Ie 22.57N 57.49 E
Izma 6 Lb 65.19N 52.54 E
Izma 17 Fd 65.02N 53.55 E
Izmail 6 If 45.21N 28.50 E
İzmir=Smyrna (EN) 22 Ef 38.25N 27.09 E
İzmir, Gulf of- (EN)=İzmir Körfezi 24 Bc 38.30N 26.50 E
İzmir-Bornova 24 Bc 38.27N 27.14 E
İzmir Körfezi=İzmir, Gulf of- (EN) 24 Bc 38.30N 26.50 E
İzmit 22 Ee 40.46N 29.55 E
İzmit Körfezi 24 Cb 40.45N 29.35 E
İzmor 24 Ab 40.11N 25.55 E
Iznajar, Embalse de- 13 Hg 37.15N 4.30W
Iznalloz 13 Ig 37.23N 3.31W
İznik 24 Cb 40.26N 29.43 E
İznik Gölü 23 Ca 40.26N 29.30 E
Izobilny 16 Lg 45.19N 41.42 E
Izola 14 He 45.32N 13.40 E
Izŏrskaja Vozvyšennost 8 Me 59.35N 29.30 E
Izozog, Bañados del- 54 Fg 18.50 S 62.10W
Izra' 24 Gf 32.51N 36.15 E
Izsák 10 Pj 46.48N 19.22 E
Iztočni Rodopi 15 Ih 41.44N 25.31 E
Izúcar de Matamoros 48 Jh 18.36N 98.28W
Izu-Hantō 28 Og 34.55N 138.55 E
Izuhara 28 Jg 34.12N 129.17 E
Izu Islands (EN)=Izu-shotō 21 Pf 32.00N 140.00 E
Izumi [Jap.] 28 Kh 32.05N 130.22 E
Izumi [Jap.] 29 Dd 34.29N 135.26 E
Izumi [Jap.] 29 Gb 38.19N 140.51 E
Izumi-sano 29 Dd 34.24N 135.18 E
Izumo 28 Lg 35.22N 132.46 E
Izu-Shotō=Izu Islands (EN) 21 Pf 32.00N 140.00 E
Izvesti CIK, Ostrova-= Izvestiya Tsik Islands (EN) 20 Da 75.55N 82.30 E
Izvestiya Tsik Islands (EN)= Izvesti CIK, Ostrova- 20 Da 75.55N 82.30 E

J

Jaala 8 Lc 61.03N 26.29 E
Jaama/Jama 8 Lf 58.59N 27.45 E
Jääsjärvi 8 Lc 61.35N 26.05 E
Jaba 24 Qe 35.55N 56.35 E
Jabal, Baḩr al-=Mountain Nile (EN) 30 Kh 9.30N 30.30 E
Jabal Abū Rujmayn 24 Ge 34.50N 37.56 E
Jabal al Awliyā' 35 Eb 15.14N 32.30 E
Jabal az Zannah 24 Oj 24.11N 52.38 E
Jabalón 13 Hf 38.53N 4.05W
Jabalpur 22 Jg 23.10N 79.57 E
Jabal Şabāyā 33 Hf 18.35N 41.03 E
Jabālyah 24 Fg 31.32N 34.29 E
Jabal Zuqar, Jazīrat- 33 Hg 14.00N 42.45 E
Jabbārah 33 Hf 19.27N 40.03 E
Jabbeke 12 Fc 51.11N 3.05 E
Jabjabah, Wādī- 35 Ea 22.37N 33.17 E
Jablah 24 Fe 35.21N 35.55 E
Jablanac 14 If 44.43N 14.53 E
Jablanica 15 Dh 41.15N 20.30 E
Jablanica [Bul.] 15 Hf 43.01N 24.06 E
Jablanica [Yugo.] 14 Lg 43.39N 17.45 E
Jabločny 20 Jg 47.09N 142.03 E
Jablonec nad Nisou 10 Lf 50.44N 15.10 E
Jablonicki, Pereval- 5 If 48.18N 24.28 E
Jablonovo 20 Gf 51.51N 112.50 E
Jablonovy Hrebet= Yablonovy Range (EN) 21 Nd 53.30N 115.00 E
Jablunkovský průsmyk 10 Og 49.31N 18.45 E
Jaboatão 54 Ke 8.07 S 35.01W
Jaboti 55 Dc 20.48 S 56.23W
Jabrīn 24 Ni 27.51N 51.26 E
Jabuka 14 Jg 43.05N 15.28 E
Jabung, Tanjung- 26 Dg 1.01 S 104.22 E
Jabuticabal 56 Kb 21.16 S 48.19W
Jabuticatubas 55 Kd 19.30 S 43.45W
Jaca 13 Lb 42.34N 0.33W
Jacaltenango 49 Bf 15.40N 91.44W
Jacaré, Rio- 55 Je 21.03 S 45.16W
Jacarei 55 Jf 23.19 S 45.58W
Jacarezinho 56 Kb 23.09 S 49.59W
Jáchal, Rio- 52 Ji 30.44 S 68.08W
Jaciara [Braz.] 55 Ib 14.12 S 46.41W
Jaciara [Braz.] 55 Eb 15.59 S 54.57W
Jackman 44 Lc 45.38N 70.16W
Jack Mountain 46 Eb 48.47N 120.57W
Jackpot 46 Hf 41.59N 114.09W
Jacksboro 45 Gj 33.13N 98.10W
Jacks Mountain 44 Ie 40.45N 77.30W
Jackson [Al.-U.S.] 44 Dj 31.31N 87.53W
Jackson [Bar.] 51q Ab 13.10N 59.43W
Jackson [Ky.-U.S.] 44 Fg 37.33N 83.23W
Jackson [Mi.-U.S.] 43 Kc 42.15N 84.24W
Jackson [Mn.-U.S.] 45 Ie 43.37N 94.59W
Jackson [Mo.-U.S.] 45 Lh 37.23N 89.40W
Jackson [Ms.-U.S.] 39 Jf 32.18N 90.12W
Jackson [Oh.-U.S.] 44 Ff 39.03N 82.40W
Jackson [Tn.-U.S.] 43 Jd 35.37N 88.49W
Jackson, Cape- 62 Ed 40.59 S 174.19 E
Jackson, Mount- [Ant.] 66 Qf 71.23 S 63.22W
Jackson, Mount- [Austl.] 59 Df 30.15 S 119.16 E
Jackson Bay 62 Ce 43.55 S 168.40 E
Jackson Head 62 Ce 43.58 S 168.37 E
Jackson Lake 46 Je 43.55N 110.40W
Jacksonville [Ar.-U.S.] 45 Ji 34.52N 92.07W
Jacksonville [Fl.-U.S.] 39 Kf 30.20N 81.40W
Jacksonville [Il.-U.S.] 45 Kg 39.44N 90.14W
Jacksonville [N.C.-U.S.] 43 Le 34.45N 77.26W
Jacksonville [Tx.-U.S.] 43 He 31.58N 95.17W
Jacksonville Beach 44 Ge 30.18N 81.24W
Jacmel 47 Je 18.14N 72.32W
Jacobābād 25 Dc 28.17N 68.26 E
Jacobina 54 Jf 11.11 S 40.31W
Jacob Lake 46 Ih 36.45N 112.13W
Jacobs 45 La 50.15N 89.46W
Jacona de Plancarte 48 Hh 19.57N 102.16W
Jacques-Cartier, Détroit de - 42 Lg 50.00N 63.30W
Jacques Cartier, Mont - 42 Kg 48.58N 65.57W
Jacuba, Rio- 55 Fd 18.25 S 52.28W
Jacuí, Rio- 52 Ki 30.02 S 51.15W
Jacuí-Mirim, Rio- 55 Fi 28.51 S 53.07W
Jacundá 54 Id 4.33 S 49.28W
Jacundá, Rio- 54 Hd 1.57 S 50.26W
Jacupiranga 56 Kb 24.42 S 48.00W
Jada 34 Hd 8.46N 12.09 E
Jadal 34 Fb 18.37N 5.00 E

Index Symbols

[1] Independent Nation
[2] State, Region
[3] District, County
[4] Municipality
[5] Colony, Dependency
Continent
Physical Region
Historical or Cultural Region
Mount, Mountain
Volcano
Hill
Mountains, Mountain Range
Hills, Escarpment
Plateau, Upland
Pass, Gap
Plain, Lowland
Delta
Salt Flat
Valley, Canyon
Crater, Cave
Karst Features
Depression
Polder
Desert, Dunes
Forest, Woods
Heath, Steppe
Oasis
Cape, Point
Coast, Beach
Cliff
Peninsula
Isthmus
Sandbank
Island
Atoll
Rock, Reef
Islands, Archipelago
Rocks, Reefs
Coral Reef
Well, Spring
Geyser
River, Stream
Waterfall Rapids
River Mouth, Estuary
Lake
Salt Lake
Intermittent Lake
Reservoir
Swamp, Pond
Canal
Glacier
Ice Shelf, Pack Ice
Ocean
Sea
Gulf, Bay
Strait, Fjord
Lagoon
Bank
Seamount
Tablemount
Ridge
Shelf
Basin
Escarpment, Sea Scarp
Fracture
Trench, Abyss
National Park, Reserve
Point of Interest
Recreation Site
Cave, Cavern
Historic Site
Ruins
Wall, Walls
Church, Abbey
Temple
Scientific Station
Airport
Port
Lighthouse
Mine
Tunnel
Dam, Bridge

Index Symbols

[1] Independent Nation
[2] State, Region
[3] District, County
[4] Municipality
[5] Colony, Dependency
Continent
Physical Region
Historical or Cultural Region
Mount, Mountain
Volcano
Hill
Mountains, Mountain Range
Hills, Escarpment
Plateau, Upland
Pass, Gap
Plain, Lowland
Delta
Salt Flat
Valley, Canyon
Crater, Cave
Karst Features
Depression
Polder
Desert, Dunes
Forest, Woods
Heath, Steppe
Oasis
Cape, Point
Coast, Beach
Cliff
Peninsula
Isthmus
Sandbank
Island
Atoll
Rock, Reef
Islands, Archipelago
Rocks, Reefs
Coral Reef
Well, Spring
Geyser
River, Stream
Waterfall Rapids
River Mouth, Estuary
Lake
Salt Lake
Intermittent Lake
Reservoir
Swamp, Pond
Canal
Glacier
Ice Shelf, Pack Ice
Ocean
Sea
Gulf, Bay
Strait, Fjord
Lagoon
Bank
Seamount
Tablemount
Ridge
Shelf
Basin
Escarpment, Sea Scarp
Fracture
Trench, Abyss
National Park, Reserve
Point of Interest
Recreation Site
Cave, Cavern
Historic Site
Ruins
Wall, Walls
Church, Abbey
Temple
Scientific Station
Airport
Port
Lighthouse
Mine
Tunnel
Dam, Bridge

Jiaoxian 27 Kd 36.20N 120.00 E
Jiaozhou-Wan 28 Ff 36.10N 120.15 E
Jiaozuo 22 Nf 35.15N 113.18 E
Jiashan 28 Fi 30.51N 120.54 E
Jiashan (Mingguang) 28 Dh 32.47N 118.00 E
Jiashi/Payzawat 27 Cd 39.29N 76.39 E
Jiawang 28 Dg 34.27N 117.26 E
Jiaxian 28 Bh 33.58N 113.13 E
Jiaxing 27 Le 30.44N 120.46 E
Jiayin (Chaoyang) 27 Nb 48.52N 130.21 E
Jiayu 27 Jf 30.00N 113.57 E
Jiayuguan 27 Gd 39.49N 98.18 E
Jibalei 35 Ic 10.07N 50.47 E
Jibão, Serra do- 55 Jb 14.48S 45.15W
Jibiya 34 Gc 13.06N 7.14 E
Jibou 15 Gb 47.16N 23.15 E
Jicarón, Isla- 49 Gj 7.16N 81.47W
Jičín 10 Lf 50.26N 15.22 E
Jiddah 22 Fg 21.29N 39.12 E
Jiddat al Ḥarāsīs 23 Ie 20.05N 56.00 E
Jiehu → Yinan 28 Eg 35.33N 118.27 E
Jieshou 28 Ch 33.17N 115.22 E
Jiesjjavrre 7 Fb 69.40N 24.12 E
Jiexiu 27 Jd 37.00N 112.00 E
Jieyang 27 Kg 23.32N 116.25 E
Jieznas/Eznas 8 Kj 54.34N 24.17 E
Jifn, Wādī al- 24 Jj 25.48N 42.15 E
Jiftūn, Jazā'ir- 24 Ei 27.13N 33.56 E
Jigley 35 He 4.25N 45.22 E
Jiguaní 49 Ic 20.22N 76.26W
Jigüey, Bahía de- 49 Hb 22.08N 78.05W
Jigzhi 27 He 33.28N 101.29 E
Jihlava 10 Mh 48.55N 16.37 E
Jihlava 10 Lg 49.24N 15.34 E
Jihlavské vrchy 10 Lg 49.15N 15.20 E
Jihočeský kraj [3] 10 Kg 49.05N 14.30 E
Jihomoravský kraj [3] 10 Mg 49.10N 16.40 E
Jijel 32 Ib 36.48N 5.46 E
Jijel [3] 32 Ib 36.45N 5.45 E
Jijia 15 Lc 46.54N 28.05 E
Jijiga 35 Gd 9.21N 42.48 E
Jijona 13 Lf 38.32N 0.30W
Jikharrah 33 Dd 29.17N 21.38 E
Jilava 15 Je 44.20N 26.05 E
Jilf al Kabīr, Haḍabat al- 33 Ee 23.30N 26.00 E
Jilib 31 Lh 0.29N 42.47 E
Jilin 27 Mc 43.51N 126.33 E
Jilin Sheng (Chi-lin Sheng) =Kirin (EN) [2] 27 Mc 43.00N 126.00 E
Jiliu He 27 La 52.02N 120.41 E
Jiloca 13 Kc 41.21N 1.39W
Jima=Jimma (EN) 31 Kh 7.39N 36.49 E
Jimāl, Wādī- 24 Fj 24.40N 35.06 E
Jimani 49 Ld 18.28N 71.51W
Jimbe 36 De 11.05S 24.00 E
Jimbolia 15 Dd 45.48N 20.43 E
Jimena 13 Ig 37.50N 3.28W
Jimena de la Frontera 13 Gh 36.26N 5.27W
Jiménez 47 Dc 27.08N 104.55W
Jiménez del Teul 48 Gf 23.10N 104.05W
Jimma (EN)=Jima 31 Kh 7.39N 36.49 E
Jimo 28 Ff 36.24N 120.27 E
Jimsar 27 Ec 43.59N 89.04 E
Jimulco 48 He 25.20N 103.10W
Jināh 24 Dj 25.20N 30.31 E
Jinan=Tsinan (EN) 22 Nf 36.35N 117.00 E
Jincheng [China] 27 Jd 35.32N 112.53 E
Jincheng [China] 28 Fd 41.12N 121.25 E
Jinchuan /Quqên 27 He 31.02N 102.02 E
Jind 25 Fc 29.19N 76.19 E
Jindřichův Hradec 10 Kg 49.09N 15.00 E
Jinfo Shan 27 If 29.01N 107.14 E
Jing/Jinghe 27 Dc 44.39N 82.50 E
Jing'an 28 Cj 28.51N 115.21 E
Jingbian (Zhangjiapan) 27 Id 37.32N 108.45 E
Jingde 28 Ei 30.18N 118.30 E
Jingdezhen 22 Ng 29.18N 117.18 E
Jingfeng → Hexigten Qi 27 Kc 43.15N 117.31 E
Jinggang Shan 27 Jf 26.42N 114.07 E
Jinggu 27 Hg 23.28N 100.39 E
Jinghai 28 De 38.57N 116.56 E
Jinghe/Jing 27 Dc 44.39N 82.50 E
Jinghong (Yunjinghong) 27 Hg 21.59N 100.48 E
Jinghong Dao 27 Je 9.45N 114.28 E
Jingjiang 28 Fh 32.01N 120.15 E
Jingle 28 Ae 38.22N 111.56 E
Jingmen 27 Je 31.00N 112.11 E
Jingning 27 Id 35.30N 105.45 E
Jingping → Pinglu 28 Be 39.32N 112.14 E
Jingpo Hu 28 Jc 43.50N 128.53 E
Jingshan 28 Bi 31.04N 113.08 E
Jingtai 27 Hd 37.10N 104.08 E
Jingxian [China] 27 If 26.40N 109.37 E
Jingxian [China] 27 Ke 30.41N 118.29 E
Jingxing (Weishui) 28 Ce 38.03N 114.09 E
Jingyu 28 Ic 42.25N 126.48 E
Jingyuan 27 Hd 36.35N 104.40 E
Jingzhi 28 Ef 36.18N 119.22 E
Jingzhou→Jiangling 27 Je 30.21N 112.10 E
Jinhu (Licheng) 28 Eh 33.01N 119.01 E
Jinhua 27 Kf 29.09N 119.38 E
Jining [China] 22 Nf 37.26N 116.36 E
Jining [China] 22 Ne 41.02N 113.07 E
Jinja 31 Kh 0.26N 33.13 E
Jin Jiang 28 Cj 28.23N 115.48 E
Jinkou 28 Ci 30.20N 114.07 E
Jinotega [3] 49 Eg 14.00N 85.25W
Jinotega 47 Gf 13.06N 86.00W
Jinotepe 47 Gf 11.51N 86.12W
Jinping 27 Hg 22.45N 103.15 E
Jinsha 27 If 27.18N 106.16 E
Jinsha→Nantong 28 Fh 32.06N 120.52 E
Jinshan 28 Fi 30.54N 121.09 E
Jinshan → Harqin Qi 28 Ed 41.57N 118.40 E
Jinshi 28 Aj 29.03N 111.52 E
Jinta 27 Gc 40.00N 99.00 E
Jintan 28 Ei 31.45N 119.34 E
Jinxi 27 Lc 40.46N 120.50 E
Jinxian [China] 27 Ld 39.06N 121.44 E
Jinxian [China] 28 Dj 28.21N 116.16 E
Jinxiang 28 Dg 35.04N 116.19 E
Jinyang 27 Hf 27.39N 103.12 E
Jinyun 28 Fj 28.39N 120.05 E
Jinzhai (Meishan) 28 Ci 31.40N 115.52 E
Jinzhou 22 Oe 41.09N 121.08 E
Jinzū-Gawa 29 Ec 36.45N 137.13 E
Jiparaná, Rio- 52 Jf 8.03S 62.52W
Jipijapa 54 Bd 1.22S 80.34W
Jiquilisco 49 Cg 13.19N 88.35W
Jiquilisco, Bahia de- 49 Cg 13.10N 88.28W
Jirjā 33 Fd 26.20N 31.53 E
Jishou 27 If 28.18N 109.43 E
Jishu 28 Ib 44.16N 126.50 E
Jisr ash Shughur 24 Ge 35.48N 36.19 E
Jiu 15 Gd 43.47N 23.48 E
Jiucai Ling 27 Jf 25.33N 111.18 E
Jiucheng → Wucheng 28 Df 37.12N 116.04 E
Jiujiang 22 Ng 29.39N 116.00 E
Jiuling Shan 27 Jf 28.55N 114.50 E
Jiulong/Gyaisi 27 Hf 28.58N 101.33 E
Jiuquan (Suzhou) 22 Lf 39.46N 98.34 E
Jiurongcheng 28 Gf 37.22N 122.33 E
Jiutai 27 Mc 44.10N 125.50 E
Jīwani, Rās- 25 Cc 25.01N 61.44 E
Jixi [China] 28 Ei 30.04N 118.36 E
Jixi [China] 22 Pe 45.15N 130.55 E
Jixian [China] 28 Cg 35.23N 114.04 E
Jixian [China] 28 Cf 37.34N 115.34 E
Jixian [China] 28 Dd 40.03N 117.24 E
Jixian [China] 28 Df 36.59N 117.11 E
Jiyang 28 Bg 35.06N 112.35 E
Jiyuan 28 De 39.05N 117.45 E
Jiyun He 35 Ib 16.12N 52.14 E
Jiz, Wādī al- 22 Gh 16.54N 42.32 E
Jīzān 28 Cf 36.54N 114.52 E
Jize 10 Kf 50.10N 14.43 E
Jizera 10 Lf 50.50N 15.13 E
Jizerské Hory 24 Hj 25.39N 38.25 E
Jizl, Wādī al- 28 Lg 35.33N 133.18 E
Jizō-Zaki 36 De 10.20S 16.40 E
Jmbe 27 Ig 24.44N 108.02 E
Jnchengjiang → Hechi 55 Gh 27.10S 51.30W
Joaçaba 34 Bc 14.10N 16.51W
Joal-Fadiout 54 Ke 5.32S 35.48W
João Câmara 55 Kd 19.50S 43.08W
João Monlevade 53 Mf 7.07S 34.52W
João Pessoa 54 Ig 17.45S 46.10W
João Pinheiro 56 Hb 25.00S 64.11W
Joaquin V. González 49 Ic 20.54N 77.17W
Jobado 13 Ig 37.50N 3.21W
Jódar 22 Jg 26.17N 73.02 E
Jodhpur 12 Gd 50.43N 4.52 E
Jodoigne/Geldenaken 6 Ic 62.36N 29.46 E
Joensuu 66 Qf 75.00S 69.30W
Joerg Plateau 64g Bb 1.48N 157.19W
Joes Hill 27 Od 37.06N 138.15 E
Jōetsu 12 He 49.14N 6.01 E
Joeuf 14 Hd 46.26N 13.26 E
Jôf di Montasio 46 Ha 50.32N 115.13W
Joffre, Mount- 25 Hc 26.25N 87.15 E
Jogbani 7 Gg 58.46N 26.26 E
Jõgeva/Jygeva 24 Qd 36.36N 57.01 E
Joghatāy 24 Qd 36.30N 57.00 E
Joghatāy, Kūh-e- 29 Ec 36.31N 136.54 E
Jōhana 31 Jk 26.15S 28.00 E
Johannesburg 29 Ce 32.57N 132.35 E
Jōhen 46 Fd 44.25N 118.57W
John Day 43 Cb 45.44N 120.39W
John Day River 44 Hg 36.31N 78.18W
John H. Kerr Reservoir 45 Eg 38.05N 103.02W
John Martin Reservoir 9 Jc 58.38N 3.05W
John o' Groat's 45 Fh 37.34N 101.45W
Johnson 48 Cc 29.13N 112.07W
Johnson, Pico de- 43 Kd 36.19N 82.21W
Johnson City [Tn.-U.S.] 45 Gk 30.17N 98.25W
Johnson City [Tx.-U.S.] 42 Ed 60.29N 133.17W
Johnsons Crossing 51d Bb 17.02N 61.53W
Johnsons Point 59 Ef 32.25S 120.42 E
Johnstone, Lake- 46 Ca 50.25N 126.00W
Johnstone Strait 57 Kc 17.00N 168.30W
Johnston Island 58 Kc 17.00N 168.30W
Johnston Island [5] 44 Jd 43.01N 74.22W
Johnstown [N.Y.-U.S.] 43 Lc 40.20N 78.56W
Johnstown [Pa.-U.S.] 22 Mi 1.28N 103.45 E
Johor Baharu 55 Ei 28.39S 54.07W
Joia 11 Jg 47.59N 3.24 E
Joigny 53 Lh 26.18S 48.50W
Joinvile 11 Lf 48.27N 5.08 E
Joinville 66 Re 63.15S 55.45W
Joinville Island 35 Ed 8.24N 33.49 E
Jokau 8 Kd 60.33N 24.59 E
Jokela 41 Kc 78.25N 19.00W
Jokelbugten 8 Jd 60.49N 23.28 E
Jokioinen 7 Ec 66.36N 19.51 E
Jokkmokk 6 Cc 61.03N 8.12 E
Jøkuleggi 24 Kc 38.57N 45.38 E
Jolfā 43 Jc 41.32N 88.05W
Joliet 42 Kg 46.01N 73.26W
Joliette 26 He 6.00N 121.00 E
Jolo 21 Oi 6.00N 121.09 E
Jolo Group 8 Bc 61.30N 6.15 E
Jølstravatnet 8 Hd 60.09N 19.58 E
Jomala 26 Fh 7.33S 112.14 E
Jombang 27 Ge 31.37N 98.20 E
Jomda 8 Gf 58.44N 16.40 E
Jönåker 7 Fi 55.05N 24.17 E
Jonava/Ionava 27 He 34.35N 103.32 E
Jonê 9 Fl 49.50N 8.00W
Jones Bank 43 Id 35.50N 90.42W
Jonesboro [Ar.-U.S.] 45 Jj 32.15N 92.43W
Jonesboro [La.-U.S.] 66 Pf 73.32S 94.00W
Jones Mountains 38 Kb 76.00N 85.00W
Jones Sound 44 Fg 36.41N 83.06W
Jonesville 35 Ed 7.20N 32.00 E
Jonglei [3]
Jonglei 35 Ed 6.50N 31.18 E
Jonglei, Tur'ah-=Jonglei Canal (EN) 35 Ed 9.22N 31.30 E
Jonglei Canal (EN)=Jonglei, Tur'ah- 35 Ed 9.22N 31.30 E
Joniškėlis/Ioniškelis 8 Ki 56.00N 24.14 E
Joniškis/Ioniškis 7 Fh 56.16N 23.37 E
Jönköping 6 Hd 57.47N 14.11 E
Jönköping [2] 7 Dh 57.30N 14.30 E
Jonquière 42 Kg 48.25N 71.15W
Jonuta 48 Mh 18.05N 92.08W
Jonzac 11 Fi 45.27N 0.26W
Joplin 39 Jf 37.06N 94.31W
Jordan 43 Fb 47.19N 106.55W
Jordan 23 Ec 31.46N 35.33 E
Jordan (EN)=Al Urdun [1] 22 Ff 31.00N 36.00 E
Jordan Valley 46 Ge 42.58N 117.03W
Jordão, Rio- 55 Fg 25.46S 52.07W
Jorhāt 22 Lg 26.45N 94.13 E
Jörn 7 Ed 65.04N 20.02 E
Joroinen 7 Ge 62.11N 27.50 E
Jørpeland 7 Bg 59.01N 6.03 E
Jos 31 Hh 9.55N 8.54 E
José A. Guisasola 55 Bn 38.40S 61.05W
José Battle y Ordóñez 55 Ek 33.28S 55.07W
José Bonifácio 55 He 21.03S 49.41W
José de San Martín 56 Ff 44.02S 70.29W
Joselandia 55 Dc 16.32S 56.12W
José Otávio 55 Fj 31.17S 54.07W
José Pedro Varela 55 Ek 33.27S 54.32W
Joseph, Lake- 44 Hc 45.14N 79.45W
Joseph Bonaparte Gulf 57 Df 14.55S 128.15 E
Josephine Seamount (EN) 5 Eh 36.52N 14.20W
Joseph Lake 42 Kf 52.48N 65.17W
Joshimath 25 Fb 30.34N 79.34 E
Joškar-Ola 6 Kd 56.40N 47.55 E
Jos Plateau 30 Hh 10.00N 9.30 E
Josselin 11 Dg 47.57N 2.33W
Jostedalen 8 Bc 61.35N 7.20 E
Jostedalsbreen 7 Bf 61.40N 7.00 E
Jostefonn 8 Bc 61.26N 6.33 E
Jost Van Dyke 51a Db 18.28N 64.45W
Jotunheimen 5 Gc 61.40N 8.20 E
Joubertberge 37 Ac 18.45S 13.55 E
Joué-lès-Tours 11 Gg 47.21N 0.40 E
Jouquara, Rio- 55 Db 15.06S 57.06W
Joure, Haskerland- 12 Hb 52.58N 5.47 E
Joutsa 7 Gf 61.44N 26.07 E
Joutseno 7 Gf 61.06N 28.30 E
Jovan, Deli- 15 Fe 44.15N 22.13 E
Jovellanos 49 Gb 22.48N 81.12W
Joviânia 55 Hc 17.49S 49.30W
Jowhar 31 Lh 2.46N 45.32 E
Jow Kār 24 Me 34.26N 48.42 E
Jowzjān [3] 23 Kb 36.30N 66.00 E
Joya, Laguna de la- 48 Mj 15.55N 93.40W
Jreïda 32 Df 18.19N 16.03W
Jrian Jaya [3] 26 Kg 3.55S 138.00 E
Juan Aldama 47 Dd 24.19N 103.21W
Juana Ramírez, Isla- 48 Kg 21.50N 97.40W
Juan Blanquier 55 Cl 35.46S 59.18W
Juancheng 28 Cg 35.33N 115.30 E
Juan de Fuca, Strait of- 38 Ge 48.20N 124.00W
Juan de Nova, Ile- 30 Lj 17.03S 42.45 E
Juan E. Barra 55 Bm 37.48S 60.29W
Juan Fernández, Archipielago-=Juan Fernández, Islands (EN) 52 Ii 33.00S 80.00W
Juan Fernández Islands (EN)=Juan Fernández, Archipielago- 52 Ii 33.00S 80.00W
Juan G. Bazán 55 Bg 24.33S 60.50W
Juangriego 50 Eg 11.05N 63.57W
Juanjuy 54 Ce 7.11S 76.45W
Juan L. Lacaze 55 Dl 34.26S 57.27W
Juárez [Arg.] 56 Ie 37.40S 59.48W
Juárez [Mex.] 48 Id 27.37N 100.44W
Juárez, Sierra de- 48 Bb 32.00N 115.50W
Juarzohn 34 Dd 5.20N 8.58W
Juàzeirinho 54 Ke 7.04S 36.35W
Juàzeiro 53 Lf 9.25S 40.30W
Juàzeiro do Norte 53 Mf 7.12S 39.20W
Jūbā 31 Kh 4.51N 31.37 E
Juba (EN)=Ganāne, Webi- 30 Lh 0.15S 42.38 E
Juba, Rio- 55 Db 14.59S 57.44W
Jūbāl, Maḍīq- 24 Ei 27.40N 33.55 E
Jubaland (EN) 30 Lh 1.00N 42.00 E
Jubayl [Eg.] 24 Eh 28.12N 33.38 E
Jubayl [Leb.] 24 Fe 34.07N 35.39 E
Jubayt [Sud.] 35 Fb 18.57N 36.50 E
Jubayt [Sud.] 35 Fa 20.59N 36.18 E
Jubbada Dhexe [3] 35 Ge 1.15N 42.30 E
Jubbada Hoose [3] 35 Gf 0.30S 42.00 E
Jubbah 24 Ih 28.02N 40.56 E
Jubilee Lake 59 Fe 29.10S 126.40 E
Juby, Cap- 30 Ff 27.57N 12.55W
Júcar/Xúquer 5 Fh 39.09N 0.14W
Juçara 55 Gb 15.53S 50.51W
Jucaro 49 Hc 21.37N 78.51W
Jüchen 12 Ic 51.06N 6.30 E
Juchipila 48 Hg 21.25N 103.25W
Juchipila, Rio- 48 Hg 21.03N 103.25W
Juchitán de Zaragoza 39 Jh 16.26N 95.01W
Jučjugej 20 Jd 63.20N 142.15 E
Judas, Punta- 49 Ei 9.31N 84.32W
Judayyidat 'Ar'ar 23 Fc 31.22N 41.26 E
Judenburg 14 Ic 47.10N 14.40 E
Juding Shan 27 He 31.30N 104.00 E
Judith Mountains 46 Kc 47.12N 109.15W
Judith River 46 Kc 47.44N 109.38W
Judoma 20 Ie 59.08N 135.03 E
Judomski Hrebet 20 Jd 61.05N 141.30 E
Juegang→Rudong 28 Fh 32.19N 121.11 E
Juelsminde 8 Di 55.43N 10.01 E
Jufrah, Wāḥāt al-=Giofra Oasis (EN) 30 If 29.10N 16.00 E
Jug 5 Kc 60.45N 46.20 E
Jug 17 Hh 57.43N 56.12 E
Jugo-Osetinskaja Avtonomnaja Oblast [3] 19 Eg 42.20N 44.05 E
Jugorski Poluostrov 17 Kb 69.30N 62.30 E
Jugorski Šar, Proliv- 19 Gb 69.45N 60.35 E
Jugoslavija = Yugoslavia (EN) [1] 6 Hg 44.00N 19.00 E
Jugo-Tala 20 Kc 66.03N 151.05 E
Jugydjan 17 Gf 61.42N 54.58 E
Juhaym 24 Kh 29.36N 45.24 E
Juhnov 16 Ib 54.43N 35.12 E
Juhor 15 Ef 43.50N 21.15 E
Juhoslovenská nížina 10 Ph 48.10N 19.40 E
Juhua Dao 28 Fd 40.32N 120.48 E
Juigalpa 49 Eg 12.05N 85.24W
Juina, Rio- 55 Ca 12.36S 58.57W
Juine 11 If 48.32N 2.23 E
Juininha, Rio- 55 Ca 12.55S 59.13W
Juist 10 Cc 53.40N 7.00 E
Juiz de Fora 53 Lh 21.45S 43.20W
Jujuy [2] 56 Gb 23.00S 66.00W
Jukagirskoje Ploskogorje 20 Kc 66.00N 155.30 E
Jukonda 17 Mg 59.38N 67.20 E
Juksejevo 17 Gg 59.52N 54.16 E
Jula 7 Ke 63.48N 44.44 E
Juldybajevo 17 Hj 52.20N 57.52 E
Julesburg 45 Ef 40.59N 102.16W
Juli 54 Eg 16.13S 69.27W
Juliaca 54 Dg 15.30S 70.08W
Julia Creek 59 Id 20.39S 141.45 E
Julian Alps (EN)=Julijske Alpe 14 Hd 46.20N 13.45 E
Juliana Top 54 Gc 3.41N 56.32W
Julianehåb/Qaqortoq 67 Nc 60.50N 46.10W
Jülich 10 Cf 50.56N 6.22 E
Jülicher Borde 12 Id 50.50N 6.30 E
Julijske Alpe=Julian Alps (EN) 14 Hd 46.20N 13.45 E
Julimes 48 Gc 28.25N 105.27W
Júlio de Castilhos 55 Fi 29.14S 53.41W
Jullundur → Jalandhar 22 Jf 31.19N 75.34 E
Julong/New Kowloon 22 Ng 22.20N 114.09 E
Julu 28 Cf 37.13N 115.02 E
Juma 7 Hd 65.05N 33.13 E
Juma He 28 De 39.31N 116.08 E
Jumet, Charleroi- 11 Kd 50.27N 4.26 E
Jumièges 12 Ce 49.26N 0.49 E
Jumilla 13 Kf 38.29N 1.17W
Jümme 12 Ja 53.13N 7.31 E
Junāgadh 25 Ed 21.31N 70.28 E
Junan (Shizilu) 28 Eg 35.10N 118.50 E
Junaynah, Ra's al- 24 Eh 29.01N 33.58 E
Juncal 48 De 24.50N 111.47W
Juncos 51a Cb 18.13N 65.55W
Junction [Tx.-U.S.] 45 Gk 30.29N 99.46W
Junction [Ut.-U.S.] 46 Ig 38.14N 112.13W
Junction City 43 Hd 39.02N 96.50W
Jundiaí 56 Kb 23.11S 46.52W
Jundiaí do Sul 55 Gf 23.27S 50.17W
Jundūbah 32 Ib 36.30N 8.45 E
Jundūbah [3] 32 Ib 36.28N 8.41 E
Juneau 39 Fd 57.20N 134.27W
Junee 59 Jf 34.52S 147.35 E
Jungar Qi (Shagedu) 27 Jd 39.37N 110.58 E
Jungfrau 14 Bd 46.32N 7.58 E
Junggar Pendi=Dzungarian Basin 21 Ke 45.00N 88.00 E
Junín [2] 54 Df 11.30S 75.00W
Junín [Arg.] 53 Ji 34.35S 60.57W
Junín [Peru] 54 Cf 11.10S 76.00W
Junín, Lago de- 54 Cf 11.02S 76.05W
Junín de los Andes 56 Fe 39.56S 71.05W
Juniville 12 Ge 49.24N 4.23 E
Jūnīyah 24 Ff 33.59N 35.38 E
Junjaha 17 Jc 66.25N 62.00 E
Junlian 27 Hf 28.12N 104.34 E
Junsele 7 De 63.41N 16.54 E
Juntura 46 Fe 43.45N 118.05W
Junxian (Danjiang) 27 Je 32.31N 111.32 E
Juodupė 8 Kh 56.03N 25.44 E
Juojärvi 8 Mb 62.45N 28.35 E
Juoksengi 7 Fc 66.34N 23.51 E
Jupiá, Represa de- 56 Jb 20.47S 51.49W
Juquiá 55 Ig 24.19S 47.38W
Juquiá, Rio- 55 Ig 24.22S 47.49W
Juquiá, Serra do- 55 Gg 25.10S 52.00W
Jur 20 Ie 59.48N 137.29 E
Jur 30 Jh 8.39N 29.18 E
Jura [2] 14 Ac 47.25N 6.15 E
Jura 5 Gf 46.45N 6.30 E
Jura [3] 11 Lh 46.50N 5.50 E
Jura 9 Hf 56.00N 5.50W
Jura/Jūra 7 Fi 55.03N 22.10 E
Jūra/Jura 7 Fi 55.03N 22.10 E
Jura, Sound of- 9 Hf 55.55N 5.22W
Juradó 54 Cb 7.07N 77.46W
Juratiški 8 Kj 54.02N 26.00 E
Juraybī'āt 24 Lh 29.50N 46.03 E
Jurayb'āt 24 Kh 29.08N 45.30 E
Jurbarkas 7 Fi 55.08N 22.47 E
Jurdī, Wādī- 24 Ei 26.33N 32.44 E
Jurga 20 De 55.42N 84.55 E
Jurgamyš 17 Li 55.25N 64.28 E
Juribej 17 Nb 68.55N 69.05 E
Jurien Bay 59 Cf 30.15S 115.00 E
Jurigue, Rio- 55 Ec 16.29S 54.37W
Jurilovca 15 Le 44.46N 28.52 E
Jurja 7 Lg 59.03N 49.20 E
Jurjaha 17 Gc 66.42N 56.00 E
Jurjevec 7 Kh 57.22N 43.06 E
Jurjev-Polski 7 Jh 56.31N 39.44 E
Jurjuzan 17 Hi 55.43N 56.57 E
Jurjuzan 17 Ii 54.52N 58.28 E
Jurla 17 Gg 59.20N 54.16 E
Jurmala/Jūrmala 19 Cd 56.59N 23.38 E
Jūrmala/Jurmala 19 Cd 56.59N 23.38 E
Jurmo 8 Ie 59.50N 21.35 E
Jurong 28 Ei 31.56N 119.10 E
Juruá 54 Ed 3.27S 66.03W
Juruá, Rio- 52 Jf 2.37S 65.44W
Juruena, Rio- 52 Kf 7.20S 58.03W
Jurumirim, Reprêsa de- 56 Kb 23.20S 49.00W
Juruti 54 Gd 2.09S 56.04W
Jurva 8 Ib 62.41N 21.59 E
Jusan-Kō 29a Bc 41.00N 140.20 E
Jusayrah 24 Nj 25.53N 50.36 E
Jusheng 27 Mb 48.44N 126.37 E
Ju Shui 28 Ci 31.09N 114.52 E
Juškozero 19 Dc 64.45N 32.08 E
Jussarö 8 Je 59.50N 23.35 E
Justo Daract 56 Gd 33.52S 65.11W
Jusva 17 Gg 58.59N 54.57 E
Jutai 54 Ee 5.11S 68.54W
Jutai, Rio- 52 Jf 2.43S 66.57W
Jüterbg 10 Je 51.59N 13.05 E
Juti 55 Ef 22.52S 54.37W
Jutiapa [3] 49 Bf 14.10N 89.50W
Jutiapa [Guat.] 47 Gf 14.17N 89.54W
Jutiapa [Hond.] 49 Df 15.46N 86.34W
Juticalpa 47 Gf 14.42N 86.15W
Jutland (EN)=Jylland 5 Gd 56.00N 9.15 E
Juuka 7 Ge 63.14N 29.15 E
Juva 7 Gf 61.54N 27.51 E
Juventud, Isla de la-=Pines, Isle of- (EN) 38 Kg 21.40N 82.50W
Juxian 27 Kd 35.33N 118.45 E
Jūybār 24 Od 36.38N 52.53 E
Juye 28 Dg 35.23N 116.05 E
Jūyom 24 Oh 28.10N 54.02 E
Juža 7 Kh 56.36N 42.01 E
Južnaja Keltma 17 Gf 60.30N 55.40 E
Južna Morava 15 Ef 43.41N 21.24 E
Južni Rodopi 15 Ih 41.15N 25.30 E
Južnoje 20 Jg 46.13N 143.27 E
Južno-Jenisejski 20 Ee 58.48N 94.45 E
Južno-Kurilsk 20 Jh 44.05N 145.52 E
Južno-Sahalinsk 22 Qe 46.58N 142.44 E
Južno-Uralsk 19 Ge 54.26N 61.15 E
Južny, Mys- 20 Ke 57.42N 156.55 E
Južny Bug 5 Jf 46.59N 31.58 E
Južny Ural=Southern Urals (EN) 5 Le 54.00N 58.30 E
Jygeva/Jõgeva 7 Gg 58.46N 26.26 E
Jylland=Jutland (EN) 5 Gd 56.00N 9.15 E
Jylland Bank 8 Bh 56.55N 7.20 E
Jyske Ås 8 Dg 57.15N 10.14 E
Jyväskylä 6 Ic 62.14N 25.44 E

K

K2=Godwin Austen (EN) 21 Jf 35.53N 76.30 E
Ka 34 Fc 11.39N 4.11 E
Kaabong 36 Fb 3.31N 34.09 E
Kaahka 19 Fh 37.21N 59.38 E
Kaala 65a Cb 21.31N 158.09W
Kaala-Gomén 63b Be 20.40S 164.24 E
Kaalualu Bay 65a Fe 18.58N 155.37W
Kaamanen 7 Gb 69.06N 27.12 E
Kaap Kruis 37 Ad 21.46S 13.58 E
Kaap Plateau (EN)=Kaapplato 30 Jk 27.30S 23.45 E
Kaapplato=Kaap Plateau (EN) 30 Jk 27.30S 23.45 E
Kaapprovinsie/Cape Province [2] 37 Cf 32.00S 22.00 E
Kaapstad / Cape Town 31 Il 33.55S 18.22 E
Kaarst 12 Ic 51.15N 6.37 E
Kaarta 34 Cc 14.35N 10.00W
Kaba/Habahe 27 Eb 47.53N 86.12 E
Kabaena, Pulau- 26 Hh 5.15S 121.55 E
Kabah 48 Og 20.07N 89.29W
Kabala 34 Cd 9.35N 11.33W
Kabale 36 Ec 1.15S 29.59 E
Kabalega Falls 36 Fb 2.17N 31.41 E
Kabalo 31 Ji 6.03S 26.55 E
Kabaman 63a Aa 4.38S 152.42 E
Kabambare 36 Ec 4.16S 27.07 E
Kabamet 36 Gb 0.30N 35.45 E
Kabanjahe 26 Cf 3.06N 98.30 E
Kabardino-Balkarskaja ASSR [3] 19 Eg 43.30N 43.30 E
Kabare 36 Ec 2.29S 28.48 E
Kabasalan 26 He 7.48N 122.45 E
Kaba-Shima [Jap.] 29 Ae 32.45N 129.00 E
Kaba-Shima [Jap.] 29 Ae 32.34N 129.47 E
Kabba 34 Gd 7.50N 6.04 E
Kåbdalis 7 Ec 66.09N 20.00 E
Kaberamaido 36 Fb 1.45N 33.10 E
Kabetogama Lake 45 Jb 48.28N 92.59W
Kabhegy 10 Ni 47.03N 17.39 E
Kabinakagami Lake 44 Ea 48.58N 84.25W
Kabinda 31 Ji 6.08S 24.29 E
Kabīr, Wādī al- 14 Dn 36.23N 9.52 E
Kabīr Kūh 24 Lf 33.25N 46.45 E
Kabkābīyah 35 Cc 13.39N 24.05 E
Kableškovo 15 Kg 42.39N 27.34 E
Kabna 35 Eb 19.10N 32.41 E
Kabo 35 Bd 7.35N 18.38 E
Kābol 22 If 34.31N 69.12 E
Kābol 23 Kc 34.30N 69.00 E
Kabompo 36 De 13.36S 24.12 E
Kabompo 30 Jj 14.11S 23.11 E
Kabondo Dianda 36 Ed 8.53S 25.40 E
Kabongo 36 Ed 7.19S 25.35 E
Kabou 34 Fd 9.27N 0.49 E
Kabūdiyāh, Ra's- 32 Jb 35.14N 11.10 E
Kabūd Rāhang 24 Me 35.12N 48.44 E
Kābul 21 Jf 33.55N 72.14 E
Kabunda 36 Ee 12.13S 29.23 E

Index Symbols

[1] Independent Nation
[2] State, Region
[3] District, County
[5] Municipality
[5] Colony, Dependency
Continent
Physical Region
Historical or Cultural Region
Mount, Mountain
Volcano
Hill
Mountains, Mountain Range
Hills, Escarpment
Plateau, Upland
Pass, Gap
Plain, Lowland
Delta
Salt Flat
Valley, Canyon
Crater, Cave
Karst Features
Depression
Polder
Desert, Dunes
Forest, Woods
Heath, Steppe
Oasis
Cape, Point
Coast, Beach
Cliff
Peninsula
Isthmus
Sandbank
Island
Atoll
Rock, Reef
Islands, Archipelago
Rocks, Reefs
Coral Reef
Well, Spring
Geyser
River, Stream
Waterfall Rapids
River Mouth, Estuary
Lake
Salt Lake
Intermittent Lake
Reservoir
Swamp, Pond
Canal
Glacier
Ice Shelf, Pack Ice
Ocean
Sea
Gulf, Bay
Strait, Fjord
Lagoon
Bank
Seamount
Tablemount
Ridge
Shelf
Basin
Escarpment, Sea Scarp
Fracture
Trench, Abyss
National Park, Reserve
Point of Interest
Recreation Site
Cave, Cavern
Historic Site
Ruins
Wall, Walls
Church, Abbey
Temple
Scientific Station
Airport
Port
Lighthouse
Mine
Tunnel
Dam, Bridge

Kabunga	36	Ec	1.42S	28.08 E
Kaburuang, Pulau-	26	If	3.48N	126.48 E
Kabwe	31	Jj	14.27S	28.27 E
Kača	16	Hg	44.44N	33.32 E
Kačanik	15	Eg	42.14N	21.15 E
Kačanovo	8	Lg	57.24N	27.53 E
Kačergine	8	Jj	54.53N	23.49 E
Kachchh, Gulf of	21	Ig	22.36N	69.30 E
Kachchh, Rann of	25	Dd	23.51N	70.30 E
Kachia	34	Gd	9.52N	7.57 E
Kachikau	37	Cc	18.09S	24.29 E
Kachin [2]	25	Jc	26.00N	97.30 E
Kačiry	19	He	53.04N	76.07 E
Kačkanar	19	Fd	58.42N	59.35 E
Kačug	20	Ff	54.00N	105.52 E
Kaczawa	10	Me	51.18N	16.27 E
Kadada	16	Oc	53.09N	46.01 E
Kadaň	10	Jf	50.23N	13.16 E
Kadan Kyun	25	Jf	12.30N	98.22 E
Kadeï	30	Ih	3.31N	16.03 E
Kadijevka	19	Df	48.32N	38.40 E
Kadiköy	24	Bb	40.51N	26.50 E
Kadıköy, İstanbul	15	Mi	40.59N	29.01 E
Kadina	59	Hf	33.58S	137.43 E
Kadınhanı	24	Ec	38.15N	32.14 E
Kadiolo	34	Dc	10.34N	5.45W
Kadiri	25	Ff	14.07N	78.10 E
Kadirli	23	Eb	37.23N	36.05 E
Kadja	35	Cc	12.02N	22.28 E
Kadmat Island	25	Ef	11.14N	72.47 E
Kadnikov	7	Jg	59.30N	40.24 E
Kadoka	45	Fe	43.50N	101.31W
Kaduj	7	Ig	59.14N	37.09 E
Kaduna [2]	34	Gc	11.00N	7.30 E
Kaduna	30	Hh	8.45N	5.48 E
Kaduna	31	Hg	10.31N	7.26 E
Kāduqlī	31	Jg	11.01N	29.43 E
Kadykčan	20	Jd	63.05N	146.58 E
Kadžaran	16	Oj	39.11N	46.10 E
Kadžerom	17	Gd	64.41N	55.54 E
Kadži-Saj	18	Kc	42.08N	77.10 E
Kaech'ŏn	28	He	39.42N	125.53 E
Kaédi	31	Fg	16.08N	13.31W
Kaélé	34	Hc	10.07N	14.27 E
Kaena Point	65a	Cb	21.35N	158.17W
Kaeo	62	Ea	35.06S	173.47 E
Kaesŏng	22	Of	37.58N	126.33 E
Kaesŏng Si [2]	28	Ie	38.05N	126.30 E
Kāf	24	Gg	31.24N	37.29 E
Kafakumba	36	Dd	9.41S	23.44 E
Kafan	19	Eh	39.12N	46.28 E
Kafanchan	34	Gd	9.35N	8.18 E
Kaffrine	34	Bc	14.06N	15.33W
Kafia Kingi	35	Cd	9.16N	24.25 E
Kafiréos, Dhiékplous-	15	Hl	38.00N	24.40 E
Kafirévs, Ákra-	15	Hk	38.10N	24.35 E
Kafr ad Dawwār	24	Dg	31.08N	30.07 E
Kafr ash Shaykh	33	Fc	31.07N	30.56 E
Kafta	35	Fc	13.54N	37.11 E
Kafu	36	Fb	1.39N	32.05 E
Kafue	30	Ef	15.56S	28.55 E
Kafue	31	Jj	15.47S	28.11 E
Kafue Dam	36	Ef	15.45S	28.28 E
Kafue Flats	36	Ef	15.40S	26.25 E
Kafufu	36	Fd	7.12S	31.31 E
Kaga	28	Nf	36.18N	136.18 E
Kaga Bandoro	35	Bd	7.02N	19.13 E
Kagalaska	40a	Cb	51.47N	176.23W
Kagalnik	16	Kf	47.04N	39.18 E
Kagami	29	Be	32.34N	130.40 E
Kagan	19	Gh	39.43N	64.32 E
Kagarlyk	16	Ge	49.53N	30.56 E
Kagawa Ken [2]	28	Mg	34.15N	134.15 E
Kagera	30	Ki	0.57S	31.47 E
Kağızman	24	Jb	40.09N	43.07 E
Kagoshima	22	Pf	31.36N	130.33 E
Kagoshima Bay (EN)=				
Kagoshima-Wan	28	Ki	31.27N	130.40 E
Kagoshima Ken [2]	28	Ki	31.45N	130.40 E
Kagoshima-Taniyama	29	Bf	31.31N	130.31 E
Kagoshima-Wan=				
Kagoshima Bay (EN)	28	Ki	31.27N	130.40 E
Kagul	15	Ld	45.32N	28.27 E
Kagul	19	Cf	45.53N	28.14 E
Kahal Tabelbala	32	Gd	28.45N	2.15W
Kahama	36	Fc	3.50S	32.36 E
Kahemba	31	Ii	7.17S	19.00 E
Kahi	16	Oi	41.23N	46.59 E
Kahiu Point	65a	Eb	21.13N	156.58W
Kahler Asten	10	Ee	51.11N	8.29 E
Kahnūj	24	Qi	27.58N	57.47 E
Kahoku	29	Gb	38.30N	141.20 E
Kahoku-Gata	29	Ec	36.40N	136.40 E
Kahoolawe Island	57	Lb	20.33N	156.35W
Kahouanne, Ilet à-	51e	Ab	16.22N	61.47W
Kahovka	19	Df	46.47N	33.32 E
Kahovskoje Vodohranilišče				
=Kakhovka Reservoir (EN)				
	5	Jf	47.25N	34.10 E
Kahramanmaraş	23	Eb	37.36N	36.55 E
Kahrūyeh	24	Ng	31.43N	51.48 E
Kâhta	24	Hd	37.46N	38.36 E
Kahuku	65a	Db	21.41N	157.57W
Kahuku Point	65a	Db	21.43N	157.59W
Kahului	65a	Ec	20.53N	156.27W
Kahului Bay	65a	Ec	20.55N	156.30W
Kahurangi Point	62	Ed	40.46S	172.13 E
Kai, Kepulauan-	57	Ee	5.35S	132.45 E
Kaiama	34	Fd	9.36N	3.57 E
Kaiapoi	62	Ee	43.23S	172.39 E
Kaibab Plateau	46	Ih	36.30N	112.15W
Kai Besar	26	Jh	5.35S	133.00 E
Kaidu He/Karaxabar He	27	Ec	41.55N	86.38 E
Kaieteur Falls	54	Gc	5.10N	59.28W
Kaifeng	22	Nf	34.45N	114.25 E
Kaihua	28	Ej	29.10N	118.24 E
Kai Kecil	26	Jh	5.45S	132.40 E
Kaikohe	62	Ea	35.24S	173.48 E
Kaikoura	61	Dh	42.25S	173.41 E
Kaili	27	If	26.35N	107.59 E
Kailu	27	Lc	43.37N	121.19 E
Kailua [Hi.-U.S.]	65a	Fd	19.39N	155.59W
Kailua [Hi.-U.S.]	65a	Db	21.23N	157.44W
Kaimana	26	Jg	3.39S	133.45 E
Kaimanawa Mountains	62	Fc	39.15S	176.00 E
Kaimon-Dake	29	Bf	31.10N	130.32 E
Kain, Tournai-	12	Fd	50.38N	3.22 E
Kainach	14	Jd	46.54N	15.31 E
Kainan [Jap.]	29	Dd	34.09N	135.12 E
Kainan [Jap.]	29	De	33.36N	134.22 E
Kainantu	60	Di	6.15S	145.53 E
Kainji Dam	34	Fd	9.55N	4.40 E
Kainji Reservoir	34	Fc	10.30N	4.35 E
Kaipara Harbour	62	Fb	36.25S	174.15 E
Kaiparowits Plateau	46	Jh	37.20N	111.15W
Kaiser Franz Josephs				
Fjord	41	Jd	73.30N	24.00W
Kaisersesch	12	Jd	50.14N	7.09 E
Kaiserslautern	10	Dg	49.27N	7.45 E
Kaiserstuhl	10	Dh	48.06N	7.40 E
Kaishantun	27	Mc	42.43N	129.37 E
Kaišiadorys/Kajšjadoris	7	Fi	54.53N	24.31 E
Kaita	29	Cd	34.20N	132.32 E
Kaitaia	62	Ea	35.07S	173.14 E
Kaitangata	62	Cg	46.17S	169.51 E
Kaithal	25	Fc	29.48N	76.23 E
Kaitong→Tongyu	27	Lc	44.47N	123.05 E
Kaituma River	50	Gh	8.11N	59.41W
Kaiwaka	61	Dg	36.10S	174.26 E
Kaiwi Channel	60	Oc	21.13N	157.30W
Kaixian	27	Ie	31.10N	108.25 E
Kaiyuan [China]	27	Lc	42.33N	124.04 E
Kaiyuan [China]	27	Hg	23.47N	103.15 E
Kaiyuh Mountains	40	Hd	64.00N	158.00W
Kaja	30	Jg	12.02N	22.28 E
Kajaani	6	Ic	64.14N	27.41 E
Kajaapu	26	Dh	5.26S	102.24 E
Kajabbi	58	Fg	20.02S	140.02 E
Kajak	20	Fb	71.30N	103.15 E
Kajang	26	Df	2.59N	101.47 E
Kajdak, Sor-	16	Rg	44.40N	53.30 E
Kajerkan	20	Dc	69.25N	87.30 E
Kajiado	36	Gc	1.51S	36.47 E
Kajiki	29	Bf	31.44N	130.40 E
Kajmakčalan	15	Ei	40.58N	21.48 E
Kajnar	15	Lb	47.50N	28.06 E
Kajo Kaji	35	Ee	3.53N	31.40 E
Kajrakkumskoje				
Vodohranilišče	18	Hd	40.20N	70.05 E
Kajrakty	19	Hf	48.31N	73.14 E
Kajšjadoris/Kaišiadorys	7	Fi	54.53N	24.31 E
Kajuru	34	Gc	10.19N	7.41 E
Kaka	35	Fd	7.28N	39.06 E
Kākā	35	Ec	10.36N	32.11 E
Kakagi Lake	45	Jb	49.13N	93.52W
Kakamas	37	Ce	28.45S	20.33 E
Kakamega	36	Fb	0.17N	34.45 E
Kakamigahara	29	Ed	35.25N	136.50 E
Kakanj	14	Mf	44.08N	18.05 E
Kaka Point	65a	Ec	20.32N	156.33W
Kakata	34	Cd	6.32N	10.21W
Kake	29	Cd	34.36N	132.19 E
Kakegawa	29	Ed	34.46N	138.00 E
Kakenge	36	Dc	4.51S	21.55 E
Kakeroma-Jima	29b	Ba	28.08N	129.15 E
Kakhovka Reservoir (EN)=				
Kahovskoje				
Vodohranilišče	5	Jf	47.25N	34.10 E
Kākī	24	Nh	28.19N	51.34 E
Kākināda	22	Kh	16.56N	82.13 E
Kakisa Lake	42	Fd	60.55N	117.40W
Kakizaki	29	Fc	37.16N	138.22 E
Kaklkan	24	Cd	36.15N	29.24 E
Kakogawa	29	Dd	34.46N	134.51 E
Kakpin	34	Ed	8.39N	3.48W
Kaktovik	40	Kb	70.08N	143.37W
Kakuda	29	Gc	37.58N	140.47 E
Kakuma	36	Fb	3.43N	34.52 E
Kakunodate	28	Pe	39.40N	140.32 E
Kakva	17	Jg	59.37N	60.50 E
Kakya	36	Gc	1.36S	39.02 E
Kalaa	13	Mi	35.35N	0.20 E
Kalaa Khasba	14	Co	35.38N	8.36 E
Kalaallit Nunaat/Grønland=				
Greenland (EN) [5]	39	Pb	70.00N	40.00W
Kalaallit Nunaat/Grønland=				
Greenland (EN)	38	Pb	70.00N	40.00W
Kalabahi	26	Hh	8.13S	124.31 E
Kalabáka	15	Ej	39.42N	21.38 E
Kalabera	64b	Ba	15.14N	145.48 E
Kalabo	36	De	14.58S	22.41 E
Kalâbsha	33	Fe	23.33N	32.50 E
Kalač	19	Ee	50.23N	41.01 E
Kalačinsk	19	Hd	55.03N	74.34 E
Kalač-na-Donu	19	Ef	48.43N	43.32 E
Kaladan	25	Id	20.09N	92.57 E
Ka Lae	60	Od	18.55N	155.41W
Kalahari Desert	30	Jk	23.00S	22.00 E
Kalaheo	65a	Bb	21.56N	159.32W
Kalai-Mor	19	Gh	35.37N	62.31 E
Kalaj Humo	18	He	38.25N	70.47 E
Kalajoki	7	Fd	64.15N	23.57 E
Kalakan	20	Ge	55.10N	116.45 E
Kalaldi	34	Hd	6.30N	14.04 E
Kalāleh	24	Pd	37.25N	55.40 E
Kalámai	6	Ih	37.02N	22.07 E
Kalamákion	15	Gl	37.55N	23.43 E
Kalamazoo	43	Jc	42.17N	85.32W
Kalambo Falls	36	Fd	8.36S	31.14 E
Kalamitski Zaliv	16	Hg	45.00N	33.25 E
Kálamos	15	Dk	38.37N	20.55 E
Kalamunda,				
Perth-	59	Df	31.57S	116.03 E
Kalan	23	Eb	39.07N	39.32 E
Kalanshiyū, Sarīr-	30	Jf	27.00N	21.30 E
Kalao, Pulau-	26	Hh	7.18S	120.58 E
Kalaotoa, Pulau-	26	Hh	7.22S	121.47 E
Kalapana	65a	Gd	19.21N	154.59W
Kalaraš	16	Ff	47.16N	28.16 E
Kälarne	8	Gb	62.59N	16.05 E
Kalarski Hrebet	20	Ge	56.30N	118.50 E
Kalasin [Indon.]	26	Ff	0.12N	114.16 E
Kalasin [Thai.]	25	Ke	16.29N	103.31 E
Kalāt	25	Dc	29.02N	66.35 E
Kalāteh	24	Pd	36.29N	54.10 E
Kalau	65b	Bc	21.28S	174.57W
Kalaupapa	65a	Eb	21.12N	156.59W
Kalaus	16	Ng	45.43N	44.07 E
Kalavárdha	15	Km	36.20N	27.57 E
Kálavrita	15	Fk	38.02N	22.07 E
Kalbā'	24	Qj	25.03N	56.21 E
Kalbīyah, Sabkhat al-	14	Eo	35.51N	10.17 E
Kaldbakur	7a	Ab	65.49N	23.39W
Kaldygajty	16	Re	49.20N	52.38 E
Kale [Tur.]	24	Cd	37.26N	28.51 E
Kale [Tur.]	24	Cd	36.14N	29.59 E
Kalecik	24	Eb	40.06N	33.25 E
Kalehe	36	Ec	2.06S	28.55 E
Kalemie	31	Ji	5.56S	29.12 E
Kāl-e Shur	23	Jb	35.05N	60.59 E
Kalevala	19	Db	65.12N	31.10 E
Kalewa	25	Id	23.12N	94.18 E
Kaleybar	24	Lc	38.47N	47.02 E
Kalgoorlie	58	Dh	30.45S	121.28 E
Kaliakoúdha	15	Ek	38.48N	21.46 E
Kaliakra, Nos-	15	Lf	43.18N	28.30 E
Kalibo	26	Hd	11.43N	122.22 E
Kalí Límni	15	Kn	35.35N	27.08 E
Kalima	31	Ji	2.34S	26.37 E
Kalimantan/Borneo	21	Ni	1.00N	114.00 E
Kalimantan Barat [3]	26	Ff	0.01N	110.30 E
Kalimantan Selatan [3]	26	Gg	2.30S	115.30 E
Kalimantan Tengah [3]	26	Fg	2.00S	113.30 E
Kalimantan Timur [3]	26	Gf	1.30N	116.30 E
Kálimnos	15	Jm	36.57N	26.59 E
Kalinin [R.S.F.S.R.] →				
Tver'	6	Jd	56.52N	35.55 E
Kalinin [Tur.- U.S.S.R.]	19	Fg	42.07N	59.40 E
Kalininabad	18	Gf	37.53N	68.57 E
Kaliningrad [R.S.F.S.R.]	6	Ie	54.43N	20.30 E
Kaliningrad [R.S.F.S.R.]	7	Ii	55.55N	37.57 E
Kaliningradskaja Oblast [3]	19	Ce	54.45N	21.20 E
Kalinino [Arm.-U.S.S.R.]	16	Ni	41.08N	44.14 E
Kalinino [R.S.F.S.R.]	16	Kg	45.05N	38.59 E
Kalininsk [Mold.-U.S.S.R.]	15	Ka	48.07N	27.16 E
Kalininsk [R.S.F.S.R.]	16	Nd	51.30N	44.30 E
Kalininskaja Oblast [3]	19	Dd	57.20N	34.40 E
Kalinkoviči	19	Ce	52.07N	29.23 E
Kalino	17	Hg	58.15N	57.35 E
Kalinovik	14	Mg	43.31N	18.26 E
Kalinovka	16	Fe	49.29N	28.32 E
Kaliro	36	Fb	0.54N	33.30 E
Kalispell	39	He	48.12N	114.19W
Kalisz [2]	10	Of	51.45N	18.05 E
Kalisz	10	Oe	51.46N	18.06 E
Kalisz Pomorski	10	Lc	53.19N	15.54 E
Kalitva	16	Le	48.10N	40.46 E
Kaliua	36	Fd	5.04S	31.48 E
Kalix	7	Fd	65.51N	23.08 E
Kalixälven	7	Fd	65.47N	23.13 E
Kalja	17	Jf	60.20N	60.01 E
Kaljazin	19	Dd	57.15N	37.55 E
Kalkandere	24	Ib	40.55N	40.28 E
Kalkar	12	Ic	51.44N	6.18 E
Kalkaska	44	Ec	44.44N	85.11W
Kalkfeld	37	Bd	20.53S	16.11 E
Kalkfontein	37	Cd	22.07S	20.54 E
Kalkim	15	Kj	39.48N	27.13 E
Kalkrand	37	Bd	24.03S	17.33 E
Kall	7	Ce	63.28N	13.15 E
Kållands Halvö	8	Ef	58.35N	13.05 E
Kållandsö	8	Ef	58.40N	13.10 E
Kallaste	7	Gg	58.41N	27.08 E
Kallavesi	5	Ic	62.50N	27.45 E
Kalletal	12	Kb	52.08N	8.57 E
Kallhäll	8	Ge	59.27N	17.48 E
Kallidhromon Óros	15	Fk	38.44N	22.34 E
Kallinge	7	Dh	56.14N	15.17 E
Kallonis, Kolpos-	15	Jj	39.07N	26.08 E
Kallsjön	7	Ce	63.35N	13.00 E
Kalmar	6	Hd	56.40N	16.22 E
Kalmar [2]	7	Dh	57.20N	16.00 E
Kalmarsund	7	Dh	56.40N	16.25 E
Kalmit	12	Ke	49.19N	8.05 E
Kalmius	16	Jf	47.03N	37.34 E
Kalmthout	12	Gc	51.23N	4.28 E
Kalmyckaja ASSR [3]	19	Ef	46.30N	45.30 E
Kalmykovo	16	Qe	49.05N	51.47 E
Kalnciems	8	Jh	56.48N	23.34 E
Kalnik	14	Kd	46.10N	16.30 E
Kalocsa	10	Oj	46.32N	19.00 E
Kalofer	15	Hg	42.37N	24.59 E
Kalohi Channel	65a	Ec	21.00N	156.56W
Kaloko	36	Ed	6.47S	25.47 E
Kalole	36	Ec	3.42S	27.22 E
Kaloli Point	65a	Gd	19.37N	154.57W
Kalomo	36	Ef	17.02S	26.30 E
Kalpa	25	Fb	31.37N	78.10 E
Kalpákion	15	Dj	39.53N	20.35 E
Kalpeni Island	25	Ef	10.05N	73.38 E
Kalpin	27	Cc	40.31N	79.03 E
Kalsūbai	21	Jh	19.36N	73.43 E
Kaltern/Caldaro	14	Fd	46.25N	11.14 E
Kaltungo	34	Hd	9.49N	11.19 E
Kaluga	6	Je	54.31N	36.16 E
Kalulushi	36	Ee	12.50S	28.05 E
Kalumburu Mission	59	Fb	14.18S	126.39 E
Kalundborg	7	Ci	55.41N	11.06 E
Kaluš	19	Cf	49.03N	24.23 E
Kałuszyn	10	Rd	52.13N	21.49 E
Kalužskaja Oblast [3]	19	De	54.20N	35.30 E
Kalvåg	8	Ac	61.46N	4.53 E
Kalvarija	7	Fi	54.27N	23.14 E
Kalya	36	Fd	6.28S	30.03 E
Kalyān	25	Ee	19.15N	73.09 E
Kám	10	Mi	47.06N	16.53 E
Kama	36	Ec	3.32S	27.07 E
Kama [R.S.F.S.R.]	17	Nf	60.27N	69.00 E
Kama [U.S.S.R.]	5	Ld	55.45N	52.00 E
Kamae	29	Be	32.48N	131.56 E
Kamaï	35	Ba	21.12N	17.30 E
Kamaing	25	Jc	25.31N	96.44 E
Kamaishi	28	Pe	39.16N	141.53 E
Kamakou	65a	Eb	21.07N	156.52W
Kamakura	29	Fd	35.19N	139.32 E
Kamālia	25	Eb	30.44N	72.39 E
Kamalo	65a	Eb	21.03N	156.53W
Kaman	24	Ec	39.25N	33.45 E
Kamand, Āb-e-	24	Mf	33.28N	49.04 E
Kamanjab	37	Ac	19.35S	14.51 E
Kamanyola	36	Ec	2.46S	29.00 E
Kamaran	23	Ff	15.12N	42.35 E
Kamarang	54	Fb	5.53N	60.35W
Kama Reservoir (EN)=				
Kamskoje				
Vodohranilišče	5	Ld	58.50N	56.15 E
Kamaši	19	Gh	38.48N	66.29 E
Kamativi	37	Dc	18.19S	27.03 E
Kambalda	59	Ef	31.10S	121.37 E
Kambalnaja Sopka, Vulkan-				
	20	Kf	51.17N	156.57 E
Kambara	29	Fd	35.07N	138.36 E
Kambara	63d	Cc	18.57S	178.57W
Kambarka	7	Nh	56.18N	54.14 E
Kambia	34	Cd	9.07N	12.55W
Kambja	8	Lf	58.11N	26.43 E
Kambove	36	Ee	10.52S	26.35 E
Kamčatka	20	Le	56.10N	162.30 E
Kamčatka, Poluostrov-=				
Kamchatka Peninsula (EN)				
	21	Rd	56.00N	160.00 E
Kamčatskaja Oblast [3]	20	Kf	54.50N	159.00 E
Kamčatski Zaliv	20	Le	55.30N	163.00 E
Kamchatka Peninsula (EN)				
=Kamčatka, Poluostrov-				
	21	Rd	56.00N	160.00 E
Kamčija	15	Kf	43.02N	27.53 E
Kamčijska Plato	15	Kg	42.56N	27.32 E
Kameda [Jap.]	29	Fc	37.52N	139.06 E
Kameda [Jap.]	29a	Bc	41.49N	140.46 E
Kameda-Hantō	29a	Bc	41.45N	141.00 E
Kámeiros	15	Km	36.18N	27.56 E
Kamelik	16	Pc	52.06N	49.30 E
Kamen	12	Jc	51.36N	7.40 E
Kaménai	15	Im	36.25N	25.25 E
Kamende	36	Dd	6.28S	24.33 E
Kamenec	10	Td	52.23N	23.49 E
Kamenec-Podolski	19	Cf	48.39N	26.33 E
Kamenijak, Rt-	14	Hf	44.46N	13.56 E
Kamenka [Kaz.-U.S.S.R.]	16	Qd	51.07N	50.20 E
Kamenka [Mold.-U.S.S.R.]	16	Fe	48.03N	28.45 E
Kamenka [R.S.F.S.R.]	16	Kd	50.43N	39.25 E
Kamenka [R.S.F.S.R.]	19	Ee	53.13N	44.03 E
Kamenka [R.S.F.S.R.]	7	Kd	65.54N	44.04 E
Kamenka [R.S.F.S.R.]	28	Nb	44.28N	136.01 E
Kamenka [Ukr.-U.S.S.R.]	19	Df	49.03N	32.06 E
Kamenka-Bugskaja	10	Uf	50.01N	24.25 E
Kamenka-Dneprovskaja	16	If	47.29N	34.29 E
Kamen-Kaširski	16	Dd	51.36N	24.59 E
Kamen-na-Obi	20	Df	53.47N	81.20 E
Kamennogorsk	7	Gf	60.59N	29.12 E
Kamennoje, Ozero-	7	Hd	64.30N	30.15 E
Kamennomostski	16	Lg	44.17N	40.12 E
Kamen-Rybolov	28	Kb	44.45N	132.04 E
Kamenskoje	20	Ld	62.30N	166.12 E
Kamensk-Šahtinski	16	Le	48.18N	40.16 E
Kamensk-Uralski	22	Id	56.28N	61.54 E
Kamenz/Kamjenc	10	Ke	51.16N	14.06 E
Kameoka	29	Dd	35.00N	135.35 E
Kameškovo	7	Jh	56.22N	41.01 E
Kamet	25	Fd	30.55N	79.35 E
Kameyama	29	Ed	34.51N	136.27 E
Kami-Agata	29	Ad	34.38N	129.25 E
Kamiah	46	Gc	46.14N	116.02W
Kamicharo	29a	Cb	43.11N	143.52 E
Kamienna	10	Re	51.06N	21.47 E
Kamienna Góra	10	Mf	50.47N	16.01 E
Kamień Pomorski	10	Kc	53.58N	14.46 E
Kamiénsk	10	Pe	51.12N	19.30 E
Kamieskroon	37	Bf	30.09S	17.56 E
Kami-furano	29a	Cb	43.29N	142.27 E
Kamiiso	28	Pd	41.49N	140.39 E
Kamiita	29	Dd	34.08N	134.24 E
Kamiji	36	Dd	6.39S	23.17 E
Kamikawa	29a	Cb	43.50N	142.47 E
Kami-Koshiki-Jima	29	Af	31.50N	129.55 E
Kamina	31	Ji	8.44S	24.59 E
Kaminak Lake	42	Id	62.13N	95.00W
Kaminokuni	29a	Bc	41.48N	140.05 E
Kamino-Shima	29	Ad	34.30N	129.25 E
Kaminoyama	28	Pe	38.09N	140.17 E
Kaminuriak Lake	42	Hd	63.00N	95.45W
Kamioka	28	Nf	36.16N	137.18 E
Kami-shihoro	29a	Cb	43.13N	143.16 E
Kamisunagawa	29a	Bb	43.28N	141.58 E
Kamitsushima	29	Ad	34.39N	129.28 E
Kamituga	36	Ec	3.04S	28.11 E
Kamiyama	29	De	33.58N	134.21 E
Kami-yūbetsu	29a	Ca	44.11N	143.34 E
Kamjenc/Kamenz	10	Ke	51.16N	14.06 E
Kamloops	39	Gd	50.40N	120.20W
Kamloops Plateau	46	Ea	50.10N	120.35W
Kamnik	14	Id	46.14N	14.37 E
Kamo [Arm.-U.S.S.R.]	16	Ni	40.22N	45.05 E
Kamo [Jap.]	29	Fc	37.39N	139.03 E
Kamo [N.Z.]	62	Fa	35.41S	174.17 E
Kamōda-Misaki	29	De	33.50N	134.45 E
Kamogawa	29	Gd	35.06N	140.05 E
Kamp	14	Jb	48.23N	15.48 E
Kampala	31	Kh	0.19N	32.35 E
Kampar	26	Df	4.18N	101.09 E
Kampar	26	Mi	0.32N	103.08 E
Kampen	11	Lb	52.33N	5.54 E
Kampene	36	Ec	3.36S	26.40 E
Kamphaeng Phet	25	Je	16.26N	99.33 E
Kamp-Lintford	12	Ic	51.30N	6.32 E
Kamp'o	28	Jg	35.48N	129.30 E
Kâmpóng Cham	22	Mh	12.00N	105.27 E
Kâmpóng Chhnâng	25	Kf	12.15N	104.40 E
Kâmpóng Saôm	22	Mh	10.38N	103.30 E
Kâmpóng Saôm, Chhâk-	25	Kf	10.50N	103.32 E
Kâmpóng Thum	25	Kf	12.42N	104.54 E
Kâmpôt	25	Kf	10.37N	104.11 E
Kampti	34	Ec	10.08N	3.27W
Kampuchea → Cambodia	22	Mh	13.00N	105.00 E
Kamrau, Teluk-	26	Jg	3.32S	133.37 E
Kamsack	42	Hf	51.34N	101.54W
Kamsar	34	Cc	10.40N	14.36W
Kamskoje Ustje	7	Li	55.14N	49.16 E
Kamskoje Vodohranilišče=				
Kama Reservoir (EN)	5	Ld	58.50N	56.15 E
Kam Summa	35	Ge	0.21N	42.44 E
Kamuenai	29a	Bb	43.08N	140.26 E
Kamui-Dake	29a	Cb	42.25N	142.52 E
Kamui-Misaki	27	Pc	43.20N	140.20 E
Kámuk, Cerro-	49	Fi	9.17N	83.04W
Kamvoúnia Óri	15	Ei	40.00N	21.52 E
Kāmyārān	24	Le	34.47N	46.56 E
Kamyšin	6	Ke	50.06N	45.24 E
Kamyšlov	19	Gd	56.52N	62.43 E
Kamyšovaja Buhta	16	Hg	44.31N	33.33 E
Kamysty-Ajat	17	Jj	53.01N	61.35 E
Kamyzjak	19	Ef	46.06N	48.05 E
Kan	24	Ne	35.45N	51.16 E
Kan	20	Ee	56.31N	93.47 E
Kana	37	Dc	18.32S	27.24 E
Kanaaupscow	42	Jf	54.01N	76.32W
Kanaaupscow	42	Jf	53.40N	77.08W
Kanab	43	Ed	37.03N	112.32W
Kanab Creek	46	Ih	36.24N	112.38W
Kanaga	40a	Cb	51.45N	177.10W
Kanagawa Ken [2]	28	Og	35.30N	139.10 E
Kanaliasem	26	Dg	1.44S	103.35 E
Kanami-Zaki	29b	Bb	27.53N	128.58 E
Kananga	31	Ji	5.54S	22.25 E
Kanariktok	42	Le	55.03N	60.10W
Kanaš	7	Li	55.31N	47.31 E
Kanathea	63d	Cb	17.16S	179.09W
Kanaya	29	Fd	34.48N	138.07 E
Kanayama	29	Ed	35.39N	137.09 E
Kanazawa	22	Pf	36.34N	136.39 E
Kanbalu	25	Jd	23.12N	95.31 E
Kanbe	25	Je	16.42N	96.01 E
Kanchanaburi	25	Jf	14.02N	99.33 E
Kānchenjunga	21	Kg	27.42N	88.08 E
Kānchipuram	25	Ff	12.50N	79.43 E
Kandalakša	6	Jb	67.09N	32.21 E
Kandalaksha, Gulf of- (EN)				
=Kandalakšski Zaliv				
	5	Jb	66.35N	32.45 E
Kandalakšski Zaliv=				
Kandalaksha, Gulf of- (EN)				
	5	Jb	66.35N	32.45 E
Kandangan	26	Gg	2.47S	115.16 E
Kándanos	15	Gn	35.20N	23.44 E
Kandava	7	Fh	57.03N	22.46 E
Kandavu Island	57	If	19.00S	178.13 E
Kandavu Passage	63d	Ac	18.45S	178.00 E
Kandel	12	Ke	49.05N	8.12 E
Kandel	10	Eh	48.04N	8.01 E
Kandhelioúsa	15	Jm	36.30N	26.58 E
Kandi	31	Hg	11.08N	2.56 E
Kandıra	24	Db	41.04N	30.09 E
Kandla	25	Ed	23.02N	70.14 E
Kando-Gawa	29	Cd	35.22N	132.40 E
Kandovān, Gardaneh-ye-	24	Nd	36.09N	51.18 E
Kandrian	60	Di	6.13S	149.33 E
Kandry	17	Gi	54.34N	54.10 E
Kandy	22	Ki	7.18N	80.38 E
Kane	44	He	41.40N	78.48W
Kane Bassin	67	Od	79.35N	67.00W
Kaneh	24	Pi	27.04N	54.18 E
Kanem [3]	35	Bc	15.00N	16.00 E
Kanem	30	Ig	14.45N	15.30 E
Kaneohe	60	Oc	21.25N	157.48W
Kaneohe Bay	65a	Db	21.28N	157.48W
Kánestron, Ákra-	15	Gj	39.56N	23.45 E
Kanev	16	Ge	49.42N	31.29 E
Kanevskaja	19	Df	46.06N	38.58 E
Kaneyama	29	Fc	37.27N	139.30 E
Kang	37	Cd	23.44S	22.50 E
Kangaba	34	Dc	11.56N	8.25W
Kangal	24	Gc	39.15N	37.24 E
Kangalassy	20	Hd	62.17N	129.58 E
Kangâmiut	41	Ge	65.39N	53.55W
Kangān [Iran]	24	Oi	27.50N	52.03 E
Kangān [Iran]	24	Qj	25.48N	57.28 E
Kangar	26	De	6.26N	100.12 E
Kangaré	34	Dc	11.37N	8.08W
Kangaroo Island	57	Eh	35.50S	137.05 E
Kangasala	8	Kc	61.28N	24.05 E
Kangasniemi	7	Gf	61.59N	26.38 E
Kangâtsiaq	41	Ge	68.20N	53.18W
Kangāvar	24	Le	34.30N	47.58 E
Kangbao	28	Cd	41.51N	114.37 E
Kangding/Dardo	27	He	30.01N	101.58 E
Kangean, Kepulauan-=				
Kangean Islands (EN)	26	Gh	6.55S	115.30 E
Kangean, Pulau-	26	Gh	6.54S	115.20 E
Kangean Islands (EN)=				
Kangean, Kepulauan-	26	Gh	6.55S	115.30 E
Kangeeak Point	42	Lc	68.01N	64.45W
Kangen	30	Kh	6.47N	33.09 E
Kangerdlugssuaq	41	Ie	68.20N	31.40W
Kangetet	36	Gb	1.58N	36.06 E

Index Symbols

[1] Independent Nation
[2] State, Region
[3] District, County
[4] Municipality
[5] Colony, Dependency
Continent
Physical Region
Historical or Cultural Region
Mount, Mountain
Volcano
Hill
Mountains, Mountain Range
Hills, Escarpment
Plateau, Upland
Pass, Gap
Plain, Lowland
Delta
Salt Flat
Valley, Canyon
Crater, Cave
Karst Features
Depression
Polder
Desert, Dunes
Forest, Woods
Heath, Steppe
Oasis
Cape, Point
Coast, Beach
Cliff
Peninsula
Isthmus
Sandbank
Island
Atoll
Rock, Reef
Islands, Archipelago
Rocks, Reefs
Coral Reef
Well, Spring
Geyser
River, Stream
Waterfall Rapids
River Mouth, Estuary
Lake
Salt Lake
Intermittent Lake
Reservoir
Swamp, Pond
Canal
Glacier
Ice Shelf, Pack Ice
Ocean
Sea
Gulf, Bay
Strait, Fjord
Lagoon
Bank
Seamount
Tablemount
Ridge
Shelf
Basin
Escarpment, Sea Scarp
Fracture
Trench, Abyss
National Park, Reserve
Point of Interest
Recreation Site
Cave, Cavern
Historic Site
Ruins
Wall, Walls
Church, Abbey
Temple
Scientific Station
Airport
Port
Lighthouse
Mine
Tunnel
Dam, Bridge

Kanggup'o 28 Id 41.07N 127.31 E
Kanggye 27 Mc 40.58N 126.36 E
Kangi 35 Dd 8.10N 27.39 E
Kangjin 28 Ig 34.38N 126.46 E
Kangiqsualujjuaq 39 Md 58.35N 65.59W
Kangiqsujuaq 42 Kd 61.36N 71.57W
Kangirsuk 39 Lc 60.00N 70.01W
Kangmar 27 Ef 28.32N 89.43 E
Kangnüng 27 Md 37.44N 128.54 E
Kango 36 Bb 0.09N 10.08 E
Kangondu 36 Gc 1.06 S 37.42 E
Kangping 28 Gc 42.45N 123.20 E
Kangrinboqê Feng 27 De 31.04N 81.30 E
Kangto 25 Ic 27.52N 92.30 E
Kangwŏn-Do [N.Kor.] (2) 28 Ie 38.45N 127.35 E
Kangwŏn-Do [S.Kor.] (2) 28 Jf 37.45N 128.15 E
Kani 34 Dd 8.29N 6.36W
Kaniama 36 Dd 7.31 S 24.11 E
Kanibadam 18 Hd 40.17N 70.25 E
Kaniet Islands 57 Fe 0.53 S 145.30 E
Kanija 15 Lc 46.16N 28.13 E
Kanimeh 18 Ed 40.18N 65.09 E
Kanina 15 Ci 40.26N 19.31 E
Kanin Kamen 17 Bb 68.15N 45.15 E
Kanin Nos 19 Eb 68.39N 43.14 E
Kanin Nos, Mys- 5 Kb 68.39N 43.16 E
Kanin Peninsula (EN)= Kanin Poluostrov 5 Kb 68.00N 45.00 E
Kanin Poluostrov=Kanin Peninsula (EN) 5 Kb 68.00N 45.00 E
Kanioumé 34 Eb 15.46N 3.09W
Kanita 29a Bc 41.02N 140.38 E
Kanjiža 15 Dc 46.04N 20.03 E
Kankaanpää 7 Ff 61.48N 22.25 E
Kankakee 43 Jc 41.07N 87.52W
Kankakee River 45 Lf 41.23N 88.16W
Kankalabé 34 Cc 11.00N 12.00W
Kankan 31 Gg 10.23N 9.18W
Kanker 25 Gd 20.17N 81.29 E
Kankesanturai 25 Gg 9.49N 80.02 E
Kankossa 32 Ef 15.55N 11.31W
Kankunski 20 He 57.39N 126.25 E
Kanla 10 Hf 50.48N 11.35 E
Kanmav Kyun 25 Jf 11.40N 98.28 E
Kanmon-Kaikyō 29 Bd 33.56N 130.57 E
Kanmuri-Yama 29 Cd 34.28N 132.05 E
Kannapolis 43 Kd 35.30N 80.37W
Kannone-Jima 28 Jj 28.51N 128.58 E
Kannonkoski 8 Kb 62.58N 25.15 E
Kannus 7 Fe 63.54N 23.54 E
Kano (2) 34 Gc 12.00N 9.00 E
Kano 31 Hg 12.00N 8.31 E
Kanona 36 Fe 13.04 S 30.38 E
Kan'onji 28 Lg 34.07N 133.39 E
Kanoya 28 Ki 31.23N 130.51 E
Kanozero, Ozero- 7 Ic 67.00N 34.05 E
Kānpur 22 Kg 26.28N 80.21 E
Kansas 38 Jf 39.07N 94.36W
Kansas (2) 43 Hd 38.45N 98.15W
Kansas City [Ks.-U.S.] 39 Jf 39.07N 94.39W
Kansas City [Mo.-U.S.] 39 Jf 39.05N 94.35W
Kanshi 27 Kg 24.57N 116.52 E
Kansk 22 Ld 56.13N 95.41 E
Kansŏng 28 Je 38.22N 128.28 E
Kansu (EN)=Gansu Sheng (Kan-su Sheng) (2) 27 Hd 38.00N 102.00 E
Kansu (EN)=Kan-su Sheng→Gansu Sheng (2) 27 Hd 38.00N 102.00 E
Kan-su Sheng→Gansu Sheng=Kansu (EN) (2) 27 Hd 38.00N 102.00 E
Kansyat 26 Kg 2.15 S 138.51 E
Kant 18 Jc 42.52N 74.50 E
Kantang 25 Jg 7.23N 99.32 E
Kantchari 34 Fc 12.29N 1.31 E
Kanté 34 Fd 9.57N 1.03 E
Kantemirovka 19 Df 49.45N 39.53 E
Kantō-Heiya 29 Fc 36.00N 139.30 E
Kanton Atoll 57 Je 2.50 S 171.41W
Kantō-Sanchi 29 Fc 36.00N 138.45 E
Kantubek 18 Bb 45.06N 59.16 E
Kanturk/Ceann Toirc 9 Ei 52.10N 8.55W
Kanuma 29 Fc 36.34N 139.45 E
Kanye 31 Jk 24.58 S 25.21 E
Kanyu 37 Cd 20.04 S 24.36 E
Kanzenze 36 Ee 10.31 S 25.12 E
Kao 65b Aa 19.40 S 175.01W
Kaohsiung 22 Og 22.38N 120.17 E
Kaôk Nhêk 25 Lf 13.05N 107.04 E
Kaoko Otavi 37 Ac 18.15 S 13.37 E
Kaokoveld (3) 37 Ac 18.00 S 13.00 E
Kaokoveld 30 Ij 19.30 S 13.30 E
Kaolack 31 Fg 14.09N 16.04W
Kao Neua, Col de- 25 Le 18.23N 105.10 E
Kaouadja 35 Cd 8.00N 23.14 E
Kaouar 34 Hb 19.05N 12.52 E
Kapaa 65a Ba 22.05N 159.19W
Kapanga 31 Ji 8.21 S 22.35 E
Kapar 24 Ld 36.32N 47.30 E
Kapčagaj 19 Hg 43.52N 77.03 E
Kapčagajskoje Vodohranilišče 19 Hg 43.45N 78.00 E
Kapchorwa 36 Fb 1.24N 34.27 E
Kap Dan 41 Ie 65.32N 37.30W
Kapelle 12 Fc 51.39N 3.57 E
Kapellskär 8 He 59.43N 19.04 E
Kapena 36 Ee 10.47 S 28.20 E
Kapenguria 36 Gb 1.14N 35.07 E
Kapfenberg 14 Jc 47.26N 15.18 E
Kapıdağı Yarimadası 15 Ki 40.28N 27.50 E
Kapiri Mposhi 36 Ee 13.58 S 28.41 E
Kāpīsā (3) 23 Kc 34.45N 69.30 E
Kapit 26 Ff 2.01N 112.56 E
Kapiti Island 62 Fd 40.50 S 174.55 E
Kapka, Massif du- 35 Cb 15.07N 21.45 E
Kapoeta 31 Kh 4.47N 33.35 E
Kapona 36 Ed 7.11 S 29.09 E
Kapos 10 Oj 46.44N 18.29 E
Kaposvár 10 Nj 46.22N 17.48 E
Kapp 8 Dd 60.42N 10.52 E
Kappeln 10 Fb 54.40N 9.56 E
Kapša 7 Hg 59.52N 33.45 E
Kapsan 28 Jd 41.05N 128.18 E
Kapsukas 7 Fi 54.33N 23.23 E
Kapuas [Indon.] 26 Mj 0.25 S 109.40 E
Kapuas [Indon.] 26 Fg 3.01 S 114.20 E
Kapuas Hulu, Pegunungan-=Kapuas Mountains (EN) 26 Ff 1.25N 113.15 E
Kapuas Mountains (EN)= Kapuas Hulu, Pegunungan 26 Ff 1.25N 113.15 E
Kapugargin 15 Lm 36.40N 28.50 E
Kapušany 10 Rg 49.03N 21.21 E
Kapuskasing 39 Ke 49.25N 82.26W
Kapustin Jar 16 Ne 48.35N 45.45 E
Kapustoje 7 Ic 67.17N 34.12 E
Kaputdžuh, Gora- 16 Oj 39.12N 46.01 E
Kapuvár 10 Ni 47.36N 17.02 E
Kara 17 Lb 69.10N 64.45 E
Kara 34 Fd 9.33N 1.12 E
Kara (3) 34 Fd 9.35N 1.05 E
Kara Ada [Tur.] 15 Km 36.58N 27.28 E
Kara Ada [Tur.] 15 Jk 38.25N 26.20 E
Kara-Balta 19 Hg 42.49N 73.57 E
Karabas 19 Hf 49.30N 73.00 E
Karabaš 17 Ji 55.29N 60.13 E
Karabekaul 19 Gh 38.28N 64.10 E
Karabiga 15 Ki 40.24N 27.18 E
Karabil, Vozvyšennost- 18 Df 36.20N 63.30 E
Kara-Bogaz-Gol 19 Fg 41.01N 52.59 E
Kara-Bogaz-Gol, proliv- 16 Ri 41.04N 52.59 E
Kara-Bogaz-Gol, Zaliv- 5 Lg 41.00N 53.15 E
Karabuk 23 Da 41.12N 32.37 E
Karabulak [Kaz.-U.S.S.R.] 18 Lb 44.54N 78.29 E
Karabulak [Kaz.-U.S.S.R.] 19 Gg 42.31N 69.47 E
Kara Burun 15 Km 36.32N 27.58 E
Karaburun [Tur.] 24 Cb 41.21N 28.40 E
Karaburun [Tur.] 24 Bc 38.37N 26.31 E
Karabutak 19 Gf 49.57N 60.08 E
Karacabey 24 Cb 40.13N 28.21 E
Karaca Dağ 24 Hd 37.40N 39.50 E
Karačajevo-Čerkesskaja Avtonomnaja Oblast (3) 19 Eg 43.45N 41.45 E
Karačajevsk 16 Lh 43.44N 41.58 E
Karacaköy 24 Cb 41.22N 28.30 E
Karacaoğlan 15 Kh 41.32N 27.04 E
Karacasu 24 Cd 37.43N 28.37 E
Karačev 19 De 53.04N 34.59 E
Karāchi 22 Ig 24.52N 67.03 E
Kara Dağ [Tur.] 24 Jd 37.40N 43.42 E
Kara Dağ [Tur.] 24 Ed 37.23N 33.10 E
Karadah 16 Oh 42.29N 46.54 E
Karadeniz=Black Sea (EN) 5 Jg 43.00N 35.00 E
Kara Dong 27 Dd 38.26N 81.50 E
Karagajly 19 Hf 49.20N 75.48 E
Karaganda 22 Je 49.50N 73.10 E
Karagandinskaja Oblast (3) 19 Hf 50.00N 74.00 E
Karaginski, Ostrov- 21 Sd 58.48N 164.05 E
Karaginski Zaliv 21 Sd 58.50N 164.00 E
Kara Gölü 15 Mm 36.42N 29.50 E
Karagoš, Gora- 20 Df 51.44N 89.24 E
Karahalli 15 Mk 38.20N 29.32 E
Karaidelski 17 Hi 55.49N 57.05 E
Kara-Irtyš 21 Ke 47.52N 84.16 E
Karaisali 24 Fd 37.16N 35.03 E
Karaj 24 Ne 35.48N 50.59 E
Karaj 24 Ne 35.07N 51.35 E
Karak, Gora- 19 Gg 44.59N 63.05 E
Kara-Kala 19 Fh 38.28N 56.18 E
Karakalpak ASSR (EN)= Karakalpakskaja ASSR (3) 19 Fg 43.30N 59.00 E
Karakalpakskaja ASSR= Karakalpak ASSR (EN) (3) 19 Fg 43.30N 59.00 E
Karakax/Moyu 27 Cd 37.17N 79.42 E
Karakax He 27 Dd 38.06N 80.24 E
Karakaya Barajı 24 Hc 38.25N 38.45 E
Karakeçi 24 Hd 37.26N 39.26 E
Karakelong, Pulau- 26 If 4.15N 126.48 E
Karakoçan 24 Ic 38.02N 40.07 E
Karakoin, Ozero- 18 Ga 46.10N 68.40 E
Karakojsu 16 Oh 42.30N 47.05 E
Karakolka 18 Kd 41.29N 77.24 E
Karakoram 21 Jf 34.00N 78.00 E
Karakoram Pass 21 Jf 35.30N 77.50 E
Karakore 35 Gc 10.25N 40.01 E
Karakoro 34 Cc 14.43N 12.03 E
Karakorum Shan 27 Cd 36.00N 76.00 E
Karakorum Shankou 27 Cd 35.30N 77.50 E
Karaköy 24 Id 39.04N 41.42 E
Kara-Kul 18 Id 41.34N 72.47 E
Karakul, Ozero- 19 Hh 39.05N 73.25 E
Karakumski kanal imeni V.I. Lenina 19 Gh 37.42N 64.20 E
Karakumy 21 Hf 39.00N 60.00 E
Karakuwisa 37 Bc 18.56 S 19.40 E
Karam 20 Fe 55.09N 107.37 E
Karama 26 Gg 2.18 S 119.06 E
Karaman 23 Db 37.10N 33.14 E
Karamanli 15 Ml 37.22N 29.49 E
Karamay 22 Ke 45.30N 84.55 E
Karamea 61 Dh 41.15 S 172.06 E
Karamea Bight 62 Dd 41.25 S 171.50 E
Karamet-Nijaz 19 Gh 37.43N 64.31 E
Karamiran He 27 Dd 37.50N 84.35 E
Karamiran Shankou 27 Ed 36.15N 87.05 E
Karamiševo 8 Mg 57.44N 28.50 E
Karamoja (3) 36 Fb 2.45N 34.15 E
Karamürsel 15 Mi 40.42N 29.36 E
Kara-myk 19 Hh 39.30N 71.51 E
Karamyš 16 Nd 51.18N 45.00 E
Karān 24 Mi 27.43N 49.49 E
Karaova 15 Kl 37.05N 27.40 E
Karapınar 24 Ed 37.43N 33.33 E
Kara-Saki 29 Ad 34.40N 129.29 E
Kara-Sal 16 Mf 47.18N 43.36 E
Karasay 27 Dd 36.48N 83.48 E
Karasburg 31 Ik 28.00 S 18.43 E
Kara Sea (EN)=Karskoje More 67 Hd 76.00N 80.00 E
Karašica 14 Me 45.36N 18.36 E
Karasjok 7 Fb 69.27N 25.30 E
Kara Strait (EN)=Karskije Vorota, Proliv- 21 Hb 70.30N 58.00 E
Karasu 24 Db 41.04N 30.47 E
Karasu [Tur.] 21 Ff 38.52N 38.48 E
Karasu [Tur.] 24 Ic 38.49N 41.28 E
Karasu [Tur.] 24 Jc 38.32N 43.10 E
Karasu Dağları 24 Ic 39.30N 40.45 E
Karasuk 20 Cf 53.44N 78.08 E
Karasuk 20 Cf 53.35N 77.30 E
Karasuyama 29 Gc 36.39N 140.08 E
Karatá, Laguna- 49 Fg 13.56N 83.30W
Karatal 19 Hf 46.26N 77.10 E
Karataş [Tur.] 24 Fd 36.36N 35.21 E
Karataş [Tur.] 15 Lk 38.34N 28.17 E
Karataş Burun 24 Fb 36.35N 35.22 E
Karatau 19 Hg 43.10N 70.29 E
Karatau, Hrebet- 21 Ie 43.50N 69.00 E
Karatj 7 Ec 66.43N 18.33 E
Karatobe 16 Re 49.42N 53.33 E
Karaton 19 Ff 46.25N 53.34 E
Karatsu 28 Jh 33.26N 130.00 E
Karatsu-Wan 29 Be 33.30N 130.00 E
Kara-Turgaj 21 Ie 48.01N 62.45 E
Karaul [Kaz.-U.S.S.R.] 19 Hf 49.00N 79.20 E
Karaul [R.S.F.S.R.] 20 Db 70.10N 83.08 E
Karaulbazar 18 Ee 39.29N 64.47 E
Karaulkala 18 Bc 42.18N 58.41 E
Karáva 15 Ej 39.19N 21.36 E
Karavanke 14 Id 46.25N 14.25 E
Karavastase, Gjiri i- 15 Ci 40.55N 19.30 E
Karavastase, Laguna e- 15 Ci 40.55N 19.30 E
Karávi 15 Gm 36.45N 23.35 E
Karavonisia 15 Jn 35.59N 26.26 E
Karawa 36 Db 3.20N 20.18 E
Karaxabar He/Kaidu He 27 Ec 41.55N 86.38 E
Karažal 19 Hf 47.59N 70.53 E
Karbalā' 22 Gf 32.36N 44.02 E
Karbalā' (3) 24 Jf 32.30N 43.45 E
Kårbole 7 Df 61.59N 15.19 E
Karcag 10 Qi 47.19N 20.56 E
Kardhámaina 15 Km 36.47N 27.09 E
Kardhámila 15 Jk 38.31N 26.06 E
Kardhiotissa 15 Im 36.38N 25.01 E
Kardhítsa 15 Ej 39.22N 21.55 E
Kärdla/Kjardla 7 Fg 59.01N 22.42 E
Kărdžali 15 Ih 41.39N 25.22 E
Kărdžali (2) 15 Ih 41.30N 25.30 E
Kareha, Jbel- 13 Gi 35.15N 5.30W
Karelia (EN) 5 Jc 64.00N 32.00 E
Karelskaja ASSR (3) 19 Dc 63.30N 33.30 E
Karema 36 Fd 6.49S 30.26 E
Karen → Kayin 25 Je 17.30N 97.45 E
Karen 25 If 12.51N 92.53 E
Karesuando 7 Fb 68.27N 22.29 E
Karêt 30 Gf 24.00N 7.30W
Kärevere/Kjarevere 8 Lf 58.23N 26.30 E
Kargala 16 Sd 51.59N 55.10 E
Kargapazarı Dağı 24 Ib 40.07N 41.35 E
Kargapolje 17 Li 55.57N 64.27 E
Kargasok 20 De 59.07N 81.01 E
Kargat 20 De 55.10N 80.17 E
Kargı 24 Fb 41.08N 34.30 E
Kargil 25 Fb 34.34N 76.06 E
Kargilik/Yecheng 22 Jf 37.54N 77.26 E
Kargopol 19 Dc 61.32N 38.58 E
Karhula 7 Gf 60.31N 26.57 E
Kari 34 Hc 11.14N 10.34 E
Kariai 6 Ig 40.15N 24.15 E
Kariba 31 Jj 16.30S 28.45 E
Kariba, Lake- 30 Jj 17.03S 28.00 E
Kariba-Dake 29a Ab 42.37N 139.56 E
Kariba Dam 37 Dc 16.30S 28.50 E
Karibib 31 Ik 21.58S 15.51 E
Karibib (3) 37 Bd 22.00S 16.00 E
Kariet-Arkmane 13 Ji 35.06N 2.45W
Karigasniemi 7 Fb 69.24N 25.50 E
Karijärvi 8 Jc 61.35N 22.30 E
Karikachi Tōge 29a Cb 43.10N 142.40 E
Karikäl 25 Ff 10.55N 79.50 E
Karikari, Cape- 62 Ea 34.47S 173.24 E
Karima (EN)=Kuraymah 35 Eb 18.33N 31.51 E
Karimama 34 Fc 12.04N 3.11 E
Karimata, Kepulauan-= Karimata Islands (EN) 26 Eg 1.25S 109.05 E
Karimata, Pulau- 26 Eg 1.36S 108.55 E
Karimata, Selat-=Karimata Strait (EN) 21 Mj 2.05S 108.40 E
Karimata Islands (EN)= Karimata, Kepulauan- 26 Eg 1.25S 109.05 E
Karimata Strait (EN)= Karimata, Selat- 21 Mj 2.05S 108.40 E
Karimganj 25 Id 24.52N 92.33 E
Karimnagar 25 Fe 18.26N 79.09 E
Karimunjawa, Kepulauan-= Karimunjawa Islands (EN) 26 Fh 5.50S 110.25 E
Karimunjawa Islands (EN)= Karimunjawa, Kepulauan- 26 Fh 5.50S 110.25 E
Karin [Som.] 35 Hc 10.59N 49.13 E
Karin [Som.] 35 Hc 10.51N 45.45 E
Karis/Karjaa 7 Ff 60.05N 23.40 E
Karisimbi 30 Ji 1.30S 29.27 E
Káristos 15 Hk 38.01N 24.25 E
Karjaa/Karis 7 Ff 60.05N 23.40 E
Karkār 35 Hd 9.57N 49.20 E
Karkaralinsk 19 Hf 49.23N 75.31 E
Karkar Island 57 Fe 4.40S 146.00 E
Karkas, Kūh-e 24 Nf 33.27N 51.48 E
Karkheh 23 Gc 31.31N 47.55 E
Karkinitski zaliv 5 Jf 45.55N 33.00 E
Karkkila/Högfors 7 Ff 60.32N 24.11 E
Karkku 8 Jc 61.25N 23.01 E
Kärkölä 8 Kd 60.55N 25.15 E
Kärla/Kjarla 8 Jf 58.16N 22.05 E
Karlholm 8 Gd 60.31N 17.37 E
Karlik Shan 21 Le 43.00N 94.30 E
Karlino 10 Lb 54.03N 15.51 E
Karliova 24 Ic 39.18N 41.01 E
Karl Marx, Pik- 19 Hh 37.08N 72.29 E
Karl-Marx-Stadt → Chemnitz 6 He 50.50N 12.55 E
Karlö/Hailuoto 5 Ib 65.02N 24.42 E
Karlobag 14 Jf 44.32N 15.05 E
Karlovac 14 Je 45.29N 15.33 E
Karlovka 16 Ie 49.28N 35.08 E
Karlovo 15 Hg 42.38N 24.48 E
Karlovy Vary 10 If 50.14N 12.52 E
Karlsbad 12 Kf 48.55N 8.35 E
Karlsborg 7 Df 58.32N 14.31 E
Karlshamn 7 Dh 56.10N 14.51 E
Karlskoga 7 Dg 59.20N 14.31 E
Karlskrona 6 Hd 56.10N 15.35 E
Karlsöarna 8 Gg 57.15N 18.00 E
Karlsruhe 10 Eg 49.01N 8.24 E
Karlstad [Mn.-U.S.] 45 Hb 48.35N 96.31W
Karlstad [Swe.] 6 Hd 59.22N 13.30 E
Karluk 40 Ie 57.34N 154.28W
Karmah=Kerma (EN) 35 Eb 19.38N 30.25 E
Karmana 18 Ed 40.09N 65.15 E
Karmøy 7 Ag 59.15N 5.15 E
Karnāli 25 Gc 28.45N 81.16 E
Karnataka (Mysore) (3) 25 Ff 13.30N 76.00 E
Karnobat 15 Jg 42.39N 26.59 E
Kärnten = Carinthia (EN) (2) 14 Hd 46.45N 14.00 E
Kärnten = Carinthia (EN) 14 Hd 46.45N 14.00 E
Karoi 37 Dc 16.50S 29.40 E
Karonga 31 Ki 9.56S 33.56 E
Karora 35 Fb 17.39N 38.22 E
Káros 15 Im 36.53N 25.39 E
Kárpathos 15 Kn 35.30N 27.14 E
Kárpathos=Karpathos (EN) 5 Ih 35.40N 27.10 E
Karpathos (EN)= Kárpathos 5 Ih 35.40N 27.10 E
Karpáthou, Stenón- 15 Kn 35.50N 27.30 E
Karpenision 15 Ek 38.55N 21.47 E
Karpinsk 17 Jg 59.45N 60.01 E
Karpuzlu 15 Kl 37.33N 27.50 E
Kars 23 Fa 40.37N 43.05 E
Karsakpaj 19 Gf 47.48N 66.45 E
Kärsämäki 7 Fe 64.00N 25.46 E
Karsava/Kārsava 7 Gh 56.47N 27.42 E
Kārsava/Karsava 7 Gh 56.47N 27.42 E
Karši 22 If 38.53N 65.48 E
Karşiyaka 15 Ki 40.26N 28.00 E
Karsiyaka 15 Kk 38.27N 27.07 E
Karskije Vorota, Proliv-= Kara Strait (EN) 21 Hb 70.30N 58.00 E
Karskoje More=Kara Sea (EN) 67 Hd 76.00N 80.00 E
Kars Platosu 24 Jb 40.40N 43.07 E
Karst (EN)=Kras 5 Hf 45.48N 14.00 E
Kārsta 8 He 59.39N 18.14 E
Karstula 7 Fe 62.52N 24.47 E
Kartal 24 Cb 40.53N 29.10 E
Kartaly 19 Ge 53.03N 60.40 E
Kartaly-Ajat 17 Jj 53.01N 61.50 E
Karttula 8 Lb 62.53N 26.58 E
Kartuzy 10 Ob 54.20N 18.12 E
Karumai 29 Ga 40.20N 141.28 E
Karumba 59 Ic 17.29S 140.50 E
Karūn 21 Gf 30.25N 48.12 E
Karungi 7 Fc 66.03N 23.57 E
Karungu 36 Fc 0.51S 34.09 E
Karunki 7 Fc 66.02N 24.01 E
Karūr 25 Ff 10.57N 78.05 E
Karvia 7 Fe 62.08N 22.34 E
Karviná 10 Og 49.51N 18.32 E
Karwār 25 Ef 14.48N 74.08 E
Karwendel Gebirge 14 Fc 47.28N 11.20 E
Karymskoje 20 Gf 51.37N 114.21 E
Kas 35 Cc 12.34N 24.14 E
Kaş 24 Cd 36.12N 29.38 E
Kasaba [Tur.] 15 Mm 36.18N 29.44 E
Kasaba [Zam.] 36 Ee 10.44S 29.43 E
Kasado-Shima 29 Be 33.57N 131.50 E
Kasah 16 Mi 40.03N 43.52 E
Kasai 29 Dd 34.56N 134.49 E
Kasai 30 Ii 3.02S 16.57 E
Kasai Occidental (2) 36 Dc 5.00S 21.30 E
Kasai Oriental (2) 36 Dc 3.00S 23.00 E
Kasaji 36 De 10.22S 23.27 E
Kasaku 36 Ec 1.55S 25.50 E
Kasama [Jap.] 29 Gc 36.22N 140.16 E
Kasama [Zam.] 31 Kj 10.13S 31.12 E
Kasan 18 Ee 39.01N 65.35 E
Kasane 31 Jj 17.48S 25.09 E
Kasanga 36 Fd 8.28S 31.09 E
Kasangulu 36 Bc 4.36S 15.10 E
Kasansaj 18 Hd 41.10N 71.32 E
Kasaoka 29 Cd 34.30N 133.29 E
Kāsaragod 25 Ef 12.30N 75.00 E
Kasari 29b Ba 28.27N 129.41 E
Kaşary 16 Le 49.02N 41.03 E
Kasatori-Yama 29 Ce 33.33N 132.55 E
Kasba Lake 42 Hd 60.20N 102.10W
Kasba Tatla 32 Fc 32.36N 6.16W
Kaseda 28 Ki 31.25N 130.19 E
Kasempa 36 Ee 13.27S 25.50 E
Kasenga 31 Jj 10.22S 28.37 E
Kasenye 36 Fb 1.24N 30.26 E
Kasese [Ug.] 36 Fb 0.10N 30.05 E
Kasese [Zaire] 36 Ec 1.38S 27.07 E
Kashaf 23 Jb 35.58N 61.07 E
Kāshān 22 Hf 33.59N 51.29 E
Kashi 22 Jf 39.29N 75.58 E
Kashihara 29 Dd 34.31N 135.47 E
Kashima [Jap.] 29 Cd 35.31N 132.59 E
Kashima [Jap.] 29 Gd 35.58N 140.38 E
Kashima [Jap.] 29 Be 33.07N 130.07 E
Kashima-Nada 29 Gc 36.30N 140.45 E
Kashiobwe 36 Ed 9.39S 28.37 E
Kashiwazaki 28 Of 37.25N 138.30 E
Kashkū'iyeh 24 Qh 28.58N 56.37 E
Kāshmar 23 Ib 35.12N 58.27 E
Kashmir 21 Jf 34.00N 76.00 E
Kashmor 25 Dc 28.26N 69.35 E
Kasimov 19 Ee 54.59N 41.28 E
Kašin 19 Dd 57.23N 37.37 E
Kasindi 36 Eb 0.02N 29.43 E
Kašira 7 Ji 54.52N 38.11 E
Kasiruta, Pulau- 26 Ig 0.25S 127.12 E
Kasisty 20 Fb 73.40N 109.45 E
Kaškadarinskaja Oblast (3) 19 Gh 38.50N 66.10 E
Kaškadarja 18 Ee 39.35N 64.38 E
Kaskaskia River 45 Lh 37.59N 89.56W
Kaskelen 19 Hg 43.09N 76.37 E
Kaskö/Kaskinen 7 Ee 62.23N 21.13 E
Kasli 17 Ji 55.53N 60.48 E
Kaslo 46 Gb 49.55N 116.55W
Kasongo 31 Ji 4.27S 26.40 E
Kasongo-Lunda 36 Cd 6.28S 16.49 E
Kásos 15 Jn 35.25N 26.55 E
Kásou, Stenon- 15 Jn 35.25N 26.35 E
Kaspi 16 Ni 41.58N 44.25 E
Kaspičan 15 Kf 43.18N 27.11 E
Kaspijsk 19 Eg 42.57N 47.35 E
Kaspijski 19 Ef 45.25N 47.22 E
Kaspijskoje More=Caspian Sea (EN) 5 Lg 42.00N 50.30 E
Kasplja 16 Gb 55.24N 30.43 E
Kasr, Ra's- 35 Fb 18.04N 38.33 E
Kassaar/Kassar 8 Jf 58.47N 22.40 E
Kassalā 31 Kg 15.28N 36.24 E
Kassalā (3) 35 Fc 14.40N 35.30 E
Kassándra 15 Gi 40.00N 23.30 E
Kassandra, Gulf of- (EN) = Kassándras, Kólpos- 15 Gi 40.05N 23.30 E
Kassándras, Ákra- 15 Gj 39.57N 23.21 E
Kassándras, Kólpos- = Kassandra, Gulf of- (EN) 15 Gi 40.05N 23.30 E
Kassel 10 Fe 51.19N 9.30 E
Kassiópi 15 Cj 39.47N 19.55 E
Kastamonu 23 Da 41.22N 33.47 E
Kastanéai 15 Jh 41.39N 26.28 E
Kastellaun 12 Jd 50.04N 7.27 E
Kastéllion [Grc.] 15 In 35.12N 25.20 E
Kastéllion [Grc.] 15 Gn 35.30N 23.39 E
Kastéllos, Ákra- 15 Kn 35.23N 27.09 E
Kasterlee 12 Gc 51.15N 4.57 E
Kastlösa 8 Gh 56.28N 16.25 E
Kastoria 15 Ei 40.31N 21.16 E
Kastorías, Límni- 15 Ei 40.31N 21.18 E
Kastornoje 16 Kd 51.51N 38.07 E
Kastós 15 Dk 38.35N 20.55 E
Kasuga 29 Be 33.32N 130.27 E
Kasugai 29 Ed 35.14N 136.58 E
Kasulu 36 Fc 4.34S 30.06 E
Kasumbalesa 36 Ee 12.13S 27.48 E
Kasumi 29 Dd 35.38N 134.38 E
Kasumi-ga-Ura 28 Pf 36.00N 140.25 E
Kasumkent 16 Pi 41.42N 48.10 E
Kasungan 26 Fg 1.58S 113.24 E
Kasungu 36 Fe 13.02S 33.29 E
Kasupe 36 Gf 15.10S 35.18 E
Kasūr 25 Eb 31.07N 74.27 E
Kaszuby 10 Ob 54.10N 18.15 E
Kataba 31 Jj 16.05S 25.10 E
Katahdin, Mount- 43 Nb 45.55N 68.55W
Katajsk 17 Kh 56.18N 62.35 E
Katako-Kombe 36 Dc 3.24S 24.25 E
Katanga 36 Ed 10.00S 25.30 E
Katanga 20 Fd 60.10N 102.10 E
Katangli 20 Jf 51.43N 143.16 E
Katanning 59 Df 33.42S 117.33 E
Katav-Ivanovsk 17 Ii 54.47N 58.15 E
Katchall 25 Ig 7.57N 93.22 E
Katchi 32 Ef 17.00N 13.55W
Katende, Chutes de- 36 Dd 6.30S 22.10 E
Katerini 15 Fi 40.16N 22.30 E
Katesh 36 Gc 4.31S 35.23 E
Katete 36 Fe 14.06S 32.05 E
Katha 25 Jd 24.11N 96.21 E
Katherine 58 Ef 14.28S 132.16 E
Katherine River 59 Gb 13.49S 131.42 E
Kāthiāwār 21 Jg 21.58N 70.30 E
Kāthmāndāu Kathmandu (EN) 22 Kg 27.43N 85.19 E
Kathmandu → Kāthmāndāu 22 Kg 27.43N 85.19 E
Kathua 36 Gc 1.17S 39.03 E
Kati 34 Dc 12.43N 8.05W
Katihār 25 Hc 25.32N 87.35 E
Katiki, Volcán- 65d Bb 27.06S 109.16W
Katima Mulilo 36 Df 17.28S 24.14 E
Katiola 34 Dd 8.08N 5.06W
Katiola (3) 34 Dd 8.13N 5.02W
Katiu Atoll 61 Mc 16.26S 144.22W
Katla 7a Bc 63.36N 18.58W
Katlabuh, Ozero- 15 Ld 45.25N 29.00 E
Katlanovo 15 Eh 41.54N 21.41 E
Katmai, Mount- 40 Ie 58.17N 154.56W
Káto Akhaia 15 Ek 38.09N 21.33 E
Katofio 36 Ee 11.02S 28.01 E
Katompi 36 Ed 6.11S 26.20 E
Katonga 36 Fb 0.10N 30.40 E
Katon-Karagaj 19 If 49.11N 85.37 E
Káto Ólimbos 15 Fj 39.55N 22.37 E
Katoomba 59 Kf 33.42S 150.18 E
Katopasa, Gunung- 26 Hg 1.14S 121.25 E

Index Symbols

(1) Independent Nation
(2) State, Region
(3) District, County
(4) Municipality
(5) Colony, Dependency
Continent
Physical Region
Historical or Cultural Region
Mount, Mountain
Volcano
Hill
Mountains, Mountain Range
Hills, Escarpment
Plateau, Upland
Pass, Gap
Plain, Lowland
Delta
Salt Flat
Valley, Canyon
Crater, Cave
Karst Features
Depression
Polder
Desert, Dunes
Forest, Woods
Heath, Steppe
Oasis
Cape, Point
Coast, Beach
Cliff
Peninsula
Isthmus
Sandbank
Island
Atoll
Rock, Reef
Islands, Archipelago
Rocks, Reefs
Coral Reef
Well, Spring
Geyser
River, Stream
Waterfall Rapids
River Mouth, Estuary
Lake
Salt Lake
Intermittent Lake
Reservoir
Swamp, Pond
Canal
Glacier
Ice Shelf, Pack Ice
Ocean
Sea
Gulf, Bay
Strait, Fjord
Lagoon
Bank
Seamount
Tablemount
Ridge
Shelf
Basin
Escarpment, Sea Scarp
Fracture
Trench, Abyss
National Park, Reserve
Point of Interest
Recreation Site
Cave, Cavern
Historic Site
Ruins
Wall, Walls
Church, Abbey
Temple
Scientific Station
Airport
Port
Lighthouse
Mine
Tunnel
Dam, Bridge

Name	Page	Grid	Latitude	Longitude
Katowice [2]	10	Of	50.15N	19.00 E
Katowice	6	He	50.16N	19.00 E
Katrancık Dağı	24	Dd	37.27N	30.25 E
Kātrīnā, Jabal-	30	Kf	28.31N	33.57 E
Katrineholm	7	Dg	59.00N	16.12 E
Katsina	31	Hg	13.00N	7.36 E
Katsina Ala	34	Gd	7.48N	8.52 E
Katsumoto	28	Jh	33.51N	129.42 E
Katsuta	28	Pf	36.24N	140.32 E
Katsuura	28	Pg	35.08N	140.18 E
Katsuyama [Jap.]	28	Nf	36.03N	136.30 E
Katsuyama [Jap.]	29	Cd	35.06N	133.41 E
Kattakurgan	19	Gh	39.55N	66.15 E
Kattavia	15	Kn	35.57N	27.46 E
Kattegat	5	Hd	57.00N	11.00 E
Katthammarsvik	8	Hg	57.26N	18.50 E
Katulo, Lagh-	36	Hb	2.08N	40.56 E
Katumbi	36	Fe	10.49S	33.32 E
Katun	21	Kd	52.25N	85.05 E
Katwijk aan Zee	11	Kb	52.13N	4.24 E
Katwijk aan Zee, Katwijk-	12	Gb	52.12N	4.25 E
Katwijk-Katwijk aan Zee	12	Gb	52.12N	4.25 E
Katzenelnbogen	12	Jd	50.17N	7.57 E
Kau	26	If	1.11N	127.54 E
Kauai Channel	60	Oc	21.45N	158.50W
Kauai Island	57	Lb	22.03N	159.30W
Kaub	12	Jd	50.05N	7.46 E
Kauehi Atoll	61	Lc	15.51S	145.09W
Kaufbeuren	10	Gi	47.53N	10.37 E
Kauhajoki	7	Fe	62.26N	22.11 E
Kauhava	7	Fe	63.06N	23.05 E
Kauiki Head	60	Oc	20.46N	155.59W
Kaukauna	45	Ld	44.17N	88.17W
Kaukauveld	30	Jk	20.00S	21.50 E
Kaukonen	7	Fc	67.29N	24.54 E
Kaukura Atoll	57	Mf	15.45S	146.42W
Kaula Island	57	Kb	21.40N	160.32W
Kaulakahi Channel	65a	Ba	22.02N	159.53W
Kaumalapau	65a	Ec	20.47N	156.59W
Kaunakakai	60	Oc	21.05N	157.02W
Kaunas	6	Ie	54.54N	23.54 E
Kaunasskoje Vodohranilišče /Kauno Marios	8	Kj	54.50N	24.15 E
Kauniainen/Grankulla	8	Kd	60.13N	24.45 E
Kauno Marios/Kaunasskoje Vodohranilišče	8	Kj	54.50N	24.15 E
Kaunos	15	Lm	36.50N	28.35 E
Kaupanger	7	Bf	61.11N	7.14 E
Kau Paulatmada, Gunung-	26	Ig	3.15S	126.09 E
Kaura Namoda	34	Gc	12.36N	6.35 E
Kauriāla Ghāt	25	Gc	28.27N	80.59 E
Kaušany	16	Ff	46.39N	29.25 E
Kaustinen	7	Fe	63.32N	23.42 E
Kautokeino	7	Fb	68.59N	23.08 E
Kavacik	15	Lj	39.40N	28.30 E
Kavadarci	15	Fh	41.26N	22.01 E
Kavaja	15	Ch	41.11N	19.33 E
Kavak [Tur.]	15	Ji	40.36N	26.54 E
Kavak [Tur.]	24	Gb	41.05N	36.03 E
Kavaklidere	15	Ll	37.26N	28.22 E
Kavála	6	Ig	40.56N	24.25 E
Kaválas, Kólpos-	15	Hi	40.52N	24.25 E
Kavalerovo	20	Ih	44.19N	135.05 E
Kavali	25	Ff	14.55N	79.59 E
Kavār	24	Oh	29.11N	52.44 E
Kavaratti	22	Jh	10.33N	72.38 E
Kavaratti Island	25	Ef	10.33N	72.38 E
Kavarna	15	Lf	43.25N	28.20 E
Kavarskas/Kovarskas	8	Ki	55.24N	25.03 E
Kavendou, Mont-	30	Fg	10.41N	12.12W
Kavieng	60	Eh	2.34S	150.48 E
Kavīr, Dasht-e-	21	Hf	34.40N	54.30 E
Kavkaz	16	Jg	45.21N	36.12 E
Kavkaz, Bolšoj-=Caucasus (EN)	5	Kg	42.30N	45.00 E
Kävlinge	8	Ei	55.48N	13.06 E
Kävlingeån	8	Ei	55.47N	13.06 E
Kawa	35	Eb	19.10N	30.39 E
Kawabe	29	Gb	39.39N	140.15 E
Kawachi-nagano	29	Dd	34.27N	135.34 E
Kawagoe	29	Fd	35.55N	139.28 E
Kawaguchi	29	Fd	35.48N	139.42 E
Kawaihae Bay	65a	Fc	20.02N	155.51W
Kawaihoa Point	65a	Ab	21.47N	160.12W
Kawakawa	62	Fa	35.23S	174.04 E
Kawalusu, Pulau-	26	If	4.15N	125.19 E
Kawamata	29	Gc	37.40N	140.36 E
Kawambwa	36	Ed	9.47S	29.05 E
Kawaminami	29	Be	32.12N	131.32 E
Kawamoto	29	Cd	34.59N	132.29 E
Kawanishi	29	Gc	37.59N	140.03 E
Kawanoe	29	Cd	34.01N	133.34 E
Kawartha Lakes	44	Hc	44.32N	78.30W
Kawasaki [Jap.]	29	Gb	38.10N	140.38 E
Kawasaki [Jap.]	28	Og	35.32N	139.43 E
Kawashiri-Misaki	29	Bd	34.26N	130.58 E
Kawauchi	29a	Bc	41.12N	141.00 E
Kawau Island	62	Fb	36.25S	174.50 E
Kawaura	29	Be	32.21N	130.05 E
Kawerau	62	Gc	38.05S	176.42 E
Kawhia	62	Fc	38.04S	174.49 E
Kawich Range	46	Gh	37.40N	116.30W
Kawio, Kepulauan-	26	If	4.30N	125.30 E
Kawkareik	25	Je	16.33N	98.14 E
Kawm Umbū	33	Fe	24.28N	32.57 E
Kawthaung	25	Jg	9.59N	98.33 E
Kaxgar He	21	Jf	39.46N	78.15 E
Kax He	27	Dc	43.37N	81.48 E
Kaya	34	Ec	13.05N	1.05W
Kayah [2]	25	Je	19.15N	97.30 E
Kayak	40	Ke	59.52N	144.30W
Kayalı Daği	15	Jj	39.58N	26.38 E
Kayan	21	Ni	2.55N	117.35 E
Kayanga	34	Bc	11.58N	15.00W
Kayangel Islands	57	Ed	8.04N	134.43 E
Kayangel Passage	64a	Ba	8.01N	134.42 E
Kaycee	46	Le	43.43N	106.38W
Kayenta	46	Jh	36.44N	110.17W
Kayes [3]	34	Cc	14.00N	11.00W
Kayes	31	Fg	14.26N	11.27W
Kayin	25	Je	17.30N	97.45 E
Kayoa, Pulau-	26	Ig	0.05S	127.25 E
Kayseri	22	Ff	38.43N	35.30 E
Kayuagung	26	Dg	3.24S	104.50 E
Kayu Ara, Pulau-	26	Ef	1.31N	106.26 E
Kazačje	20	Ib	70.40N	136.13 E
Kazah	16	Ni	41.05N	45.22 E
Kazahskaja Sovetskaja Socialističeskaja Respublika [2]	19	Gf	48.00N	68.00 E
Kazahskaja SSR/Kazak Sovettik Socialistik Respublikasy [2]	19	Gf	48.00N	68.00 E
Kazahskaja SSR=Kazakh SSR (EN) [2]	19	Gf	48.00N	68.00 E
Kazahski Melkosopočnik=Kazakh Hills (EN)	21	Je	49.00N	73.00 E
Kazakh Hills (EN)=Kazahski Melkosopočnik	21	Je	49.00N	73.00 E
Kazakh SSR (EN)=Kazahskaja SSR [2]	19	Gf	48.00N	68.00 E
Kazakhstan (EN)	21	Hd	51.11N	52.52 E
Kazaklija	15	Lc	46.05N	28.38 E
Kazak Sovettik Socialistik Respublikasy [2]	19	Gf	48.00N	68.00 E
Kazalak	15	Ke	44.03N	27.24 E
Kazalinsk	19	Gf	45.46N	62.07 E
Kazan	6	Kd	55.45N	49.08 E
Kazan	38	Jc	64.02N	95.30W
Kazandžik	19	Fh	39.17N	55.34 E
Kazanka	7	Li	55.48N	49.05 E
Kazanka	16	Hf	47.50N	32.49 E
Kazanlăk	15	Ig	42.37N	25.24 E
Kazan-Rettō/Iō=Volcano Islands (EN)	21	Qg	25.00N	141.00 E
Kazanskoje	19	Gd	55.38N	69.14 E
Kazarman	19	Hg	41.20N	74.02 E
Kazatin	19	Cf	49.43N	28.50 E
Kazbek, Gora-	5	Kg	42.42N	44.31 E
Kaz Daği	23	Cb	39.42N	26.50 E
Kaz Daği	15	Mk	38.35N	29.15 E
Kāzerūn	22	Hg	29.37N	51.38 E
Kažim	17	Ef	60.20N	51.32 E
Kazi-Magomed	16	Pi	40.02N	48.56 E
Kazimierza Wielka	10	Qf	50.16N	20.30 E
Kāzimkarabekir	24	Ed	37.14N	32.59 E
Kazincbarcika	10	Qh	48.15N	20.38 E
Kazinga Channel	36	Ec	0.13S	29.53 E
Kazlų-Rūda/Kazlu-Ruda	8	Jj	54.42N	23.32 E
Kazo	29	Fc	36.08N	139.36 E
Kaztalovka	16	Pe	49.46N	48.44 E
Kazumba	36	Dd	6.25S	22.02 E
Kazuno	28	Pd	40.14N	140.48 E
Kazym	19	Gc	63.54N	65.50 E
Kazyr	20	Ef	53.50N	92.53 E
Kcynia	10	Nd	53.00N	17.30 E
Kdyně	10	Jg	49.24N	13.02 E
Ké	35	Bb	18.32N	17.55 E
Kéa	15	Hl	37.37N	24.20 E
Kéa	15	Hl	37.39N	24.20 E
Keaau	65a	Fd	19.37N	155.03W
Keahole Point	65a	Ed	19.44N	156.04W
Kealaikahiki Channel	65a	Ec	20.37N	156.50W
Kealaikahiki Point	65a	Ec	20.32N	156.42W
Kealakekua Bay	65a	Fd	19.28N	155.56W
Keams Canyon	46	Ji	35.49N	110.12W
Keanae	65a	Ec	20.52N	156.09W
Keanapapa Point	65a	Dc	20.54N	157.04W
Kearney	43	Hc	40.42N	99.05W
Kearns	46	Jf	40.39N	111.59W
Kéas, Stenón-	15	Hl	37.40N	24.12 E
Keats Bank (EN)	57	Id	5.23N	173.28 E
Keb	8	Mg	57.44N	28.38 E
Keban Barajı	24	Hc	38.53N	39.00 E
Kébémer	34	Bb	15.22N	16.27W
Kebir, Oued el-	14	Bn	36.51N	7.57 E
Kebnekaise	5	Hb	67.53N	18.33 E
Kebri Dehar	31	Lh	6.45N	44.17 E
Kebumen	26	Eh	7.40S	109.39 E
Kecel	10	Pj	46.32N	19.16 E
Kechika	42	Ee	59.38N	127.09W
Kecskemét	10	Pj	46.54N	19.42 E
Kédainiai/Kedajnjaj	7	Fi	55.18N	23.59 E
Kedajnjaj/Kédainiai	7	Fi	55.18N	23.59 E
Kedgwick	44	Nb	47.39N	67.21W
Kediri	22	Nj	7.49S	112.01 E
Kédougou	34	Cc	12.33N	12.11W
Kedva	17	Fd	64.14N	53.30 E
Kędzierzyn-Koźle	10	Of	50.20N	18.10 E
Keele	42	Fd	64.24N	124.47W
Keele Peak	38	Fc	63.26N	130.19W
Keeling Islands→Cocos Islands	21	Lk	12.10S	96.55 E
Keeling Islands→Cocos Islands [5]	22	Lk	12.10S	96.55 E
Keelung	22	Og	25.08N	121.44 E
Keene	44	Kd	42.55N	72.17W
Keer-Weer, Cape-	59	Ib	13.58S	141.30 E
Keetmanshoop	31	Ik	26.36S	18.08 E
Keetmanshoop [3]	37	Be	26.30S	18.30 E
Keewatin	42	Ig	49.46N	94.34W
Keewatin, District of- [3]	42	Hd	64.00N	96.00W
Kefa [3]	35	Fd	7.00N	36.00 E
Kefallinia=Cephalonia (EN)	5	Ih	38.15N	20.35 E
Kefamenanu	26	Hh	9.27S	124.29 E
Kefar Sava	24	Ff	32.10N	34.54 E
Keffi	34	Gd	8.51N	7.52 E
Keflavik	7a	Ab	64.01N	22.34W
Kegen	19	Hg	42.58N	79.12 E
Kegums	8	Kh	56.41N	24.44 E
Kehdingen	10	Fc	53.45N	9.20 E
Kehl	10	Dh	48.35N	7.49 E
Kehra	7	Fg	59.19N	25.18 E
Keighley	9	Lh	53.52N	1.54W
Keila/Kejla	7	Fg	59.19N	24.27 E
Keila Jõgi/Kejla	8	Ke	59.25N	24.15 E
Keimoes	37	Ce	28.41S	21.00 E
Keipel Bank (EN)	59	Le	25.15S	159.30 E
Keita	34	Gc	14.46N	5.46 E
Kéita, Bahr-	35	Bd	9.14N	18.21 E
Keitele	5	Ic	62.55N	26.00 E
Keith [Austl.]	59	Ig	36.06S	140.21 E
Keith [Scot.-U.K.]	9	Kd	57.32N	2.57W
Keith Arm	42	Fc	65.20N	122.00W
Keiyasi	63d	Ab	17.53S	177.45 E
Kejla/Keila	7	Fg	59.19N	24.27 E
Kejla/Keila Jõgi	8	Ke	59.25N	24.15 E
Kejvy	7	Ic	67.30N	37.45 E
Kekaha	65a	Bb	21.58N	159.43W
Kekerengu	62	Ee	42.00S	174.00 E
Kékes	10	Qi	47.52N	20.01 E
Keklau	64a	Bb	7.35N	134.39 E
Kelafo	35	Gd	5.37N	44.13 E
Kelakam	34	Hc	13.35N	11.44 E
Kela Met	35	Fb	15.50N	38.23 E
Kelan	27	Jd	38.44N	111.34 E
Kelang	22	Mi	3.02N	101.27 E
Kelasa, Selat-=Gaspar Strait (EN)	26	Eg	2.40S	107.15 E
Kelberg	12	Id	50.18N	6.55 E
Kelcyra	15	Di	40.19N	20.11 E
Kelefesia	65b	Bb	20.30S	174.44W
Kelekçi	15	Ml	37.14N	29.28 E
Kelem	35	Fe	4.49N	35.59 E
Keles	15	Mj	39.55N	29.14 E
Keles	18	Gd	41.02N	68.37 E
Kelheim	10	Hh	48.55N	11.52 E
Kelifely, Causse du-	37	Hc	17.15S	45.30 E
Kelifskij Uzboj	18	Ef	37.45N	64.40 E
Keli Hāji Ibrāhīm	24	Kd	36.42N	45.00 E
Kelkheim	12	Kd	50.08N	8.27 E
Kelkit	23	Ea	36.32N	40.46 E
Kelkit	24	Hb	40.08N	39.27 E
Kellé	36	Bc	0.06S	14.33 E
Kellerberrin	59	Df	31.38S	117.43 E
Kellerwald	10	Fe	51.03N	9.10 E
Kellett, Cape-	42	Eb	72.57N	125.27W
Kellett Strait	42	Fa	75.50N	117.40W
Kellog	20	Dd	62.27N	86.35 E
Kellogg	43	Db	47.32N	116.07W
Kelloselkä	7	Gc	66.56N	29.00 E
Kells/Ceanannas Mór	9	Gh	53.44N	6.53W
Kelmé/Kelme	7	Fi	55.39N	22.58 E
Kelme/Kelmé	7	Fi	55.39N	22.58 E
Kelmency	15	Ja	48.27N	26.47 E
Kelmis/La Calamine	12	Hd	50.43N	6.00 E
Kélo	35	Bd	9.15N	15.48 E
Kelowna	39	He	49.53N	119.29W
Kelsey	42	He	56.00N	97.00W
Kelsey Bay	42	Ef	50.24N	125.57W
Kelso	46	Dc	46.09N	122.54W
Kelso Bank	59	Ld	24.10S	159.10 E
Kelso Bank (EN)	59	Ld	24.10S	159.30 E
Kel Tepe [Tur.]	24	Eb	41.05N	32.27 E
Kel Tepe [Tur.]	15	Ni	40.39N	30.06 E
Keltie, Mount-	66	Jf	79.15S	159.00 E
Keluang	26	Df	2.02N	103.19 E
Kelvin Seamount (EN)	43	Od	38.50N	64.00W
Kelyehed	35	Hd	8.44N	49.10 E
Kem	19	Dc	64.57N	34.31 E
Kema	7	If	60.19N	37.15 E
Ké Macina	34	Dc	13.57N	5.23W
Kemah	24	Hc	39.36N	39.02 E
Kemaliye	24	Hc	39.16N	38.29 E
Kemalpaşa	24	Cc	40.00N	28.20 E
Kemalpaşa	15	Kk	38.25N	27.26 E
Kembé	35	Ce	4.36N	21.54 E
Kemer [Tur.]	15	Mm	36.28N	29.21 E
Kemer [Tur.]	24	Dd	36.36N	30.34 E
Kemer Barajı	15	Ll	37.30N	28.35 E
Kemeri/Ķemeri	8	Jh	56.56N	23.25 E
Ķemeri/Kemeri	8	Jh	56.56N	23.25 E
Kemerovo	22	Kd	55.20N	86.05 E
Kemerovskaja Oblast [3]	20	De	55.00N	87.00 E
Kemi	6	Ib	65.44N	24.34 E
Kemijärvi	7	Gc	66.40N	27.25 E
Kemijärvi=Kenni, Lake- (EN)	7	Gc	66.36N	27.24 E
Kemijoki	5	Ib	65.47N	24.30 E
Kemiö	8	Jd	60.10N	22.40 E
Kemiö/Kimito	8	Jd	60.10N	22.40 E
Kemlja	7	Ki	54.43N	45.15 E
Kemmerer	46	Jf	41.48N	110.32W
Kémo-Gribingui [3]	35	Bd	6.00N	19.00 E
Kemp, Lake-	45	Gj	33.45N	99.13W
Kempaž	17	Jd	64.03N	61.02 E
Kempele	7	Fd	64.55N	25.30 E
Kempen	12	Ic	51.22N	6.25 E
Kempen/Campine	11	Lc	51.10N	5.20 E
Kempendjaj	20	Gd	62.02N	118.42 E
Kempenich	12	Jd	50.25N	7.08 E
Kemp Land	66	Ee	67.10S	58.00 E
Kemps Bay	49	Ia	24.02N	77.33W
Kempsey	59	Kf	31.05S	152.50 E
Kempston	12	Bb	52.06N	0.29W
Kempt, Lac-	42	Kg	47.25N	74.15W
Kempten	10	Gi	47.43N	10.19 E
Ken	25	He	25.46N	80.31 E
Ken, Loch-	9	If	55.02N	4.02W
Kena	7	Je	62.06N	39.05 E
Kenadsa	32	Gc	31.34N	2.26W
Kenai	39	Dc	60.33N	151.15W
Kenai Mountains	40	Ie	60.00N	150.00W
Kenai Peninsula	38	Ed	60.10N	150.00W
Kendal	9	Kg	54.20N	2.45W
Kendall	44	Gm	25.41N	80.19W
Kendall, Cape-	42	Id	63.36N	87.13W
Kendallville	44	Ee	41.27N	85.16W
Kendari	22	Oj	3.57S	122.35 E
Kendawangan	26	Fg	2.32S	110.12 E
Kenema	31	Fh	7.52N	11.12W
Kenge	31	Ii	4.52S	16.59 E
Kengere	36	Ee	11.10S	25.28 E
Keng Tung	25	Jd	21.17N	99.36 E
Kenhardt	37	Ce	29.19S	21.12 E
Kéniéba	34	Cc	12.50N	11.14W
Keningau	26	Ge	5.20N	116.10 E
Kenitra	31	Ge	34.16N	6.36W
Kenitra [3]	32	Fc	34.00N	6.00W
Kenli (Xishuanghe)	28	Ef	37.35N	118.30 E
Kenmare	43	Gb	48.40N	102.05W
Kenmare/Neidin	9	Dj	51.53N	9.35W
Kenmare River/An Ribhéar	9	Dj	51.50N	9.50W
Kennebunk	44	Ld	43.23N	70.33W
Kennedy Peak	25	Id	23.19N	93.46 E
Kennedy Range	59	Cd	24.30S	115.00 E
Kenner	45	Ki	29.59N	90.15W
Kennet	9	Mj	51.28N	0.57W
Kennett	45	Kh	36.14N	90.03W
Kennewick	46	Fc	46.12N	119.07W
Kenni, Lake- (EN)=Kemijärvi	7	Gc	66.36N	27.24 E
Kennington	12	Cc	51.09N	0.53 E
Kenn Reef	57	Gg	21.10S	155.50 E
Kénogami	44	La	48.26N	71.14W
Kénogami, Lac-	44	La	48.21N	71.28W
Kenogami River	42	Jf	51.06N	84.29W
Keno Hill	42	Dd	63.54N	135.18W
Kenora	39	Je	49.47N	94.29W
Kenosha	43	Jc	42.35N	87.49W
Kent	9	Nj	51.10N	0.55 E
Kent [3]	9	Nj	51.20N	0.55 E
Kent [S.L.]	34	Cd	8.10N	13.10W
Kent [Wa.-U.S.]	46	Dc	47.23N	122.14W
Kent, Vale of-	9	Nj	51.10N	0.30 E
Kentau	19	Gg	43.32N	68.33 E
Kent Group	59	Jg	39.30S	147.20 E
Kenton	44	Fe	40.38N	83.38W
Kent Peninsula	42	Gc	68.30N	107.00W
Kentucky [2]	43	Jd	37.30N	85.15W
Kentucky Lake	43	Jd	36.25N	88.05W
Kentucky River	44	Ef	38.41N	85.11W
Kenya [1]	31	Kh	1.00N	38.00 E
Kenya, Mount-/Kirinyaga	30	Ki	0.10S	37.20 E
Keokea	65a	Ec	20.42N	156.21W
Keokuk	43	Ic	40.24N	91.24W
Keonjhargarh	25	Hd	21.38N	85.35 E
Keowee, Lake-	44	Fh	34.55N	82.50W
Kepe	7	Hd	65.09N	32.08 E
Kepi	26	Kh	6.32S	139.19 E
Kępno	10	Ne	51.17N	17.59 E
Kepsut	24	Cc	39.41N	28.09 E
Kerala [3]	25	Ff	11.00N	76.30 E
Kerama-Rettō	29b	Ab	26.10N	127.15 E
Kerang	59	Ig	35.44S	143.55 E
Keratéa	15	Gl	37.48N	23.59 E
Kerava/Kervo	8	Kd	60.24N	25.07 E
Kerč	6	Jf	45.22N	36.27 E
Kerčenski Poluostrov	16	Ig	45.15N	36.00 E
Kerčenski Proliv	5	Jf	45.22N	36.38 E
Kerdhilion Óros	15	Gi	40.47N	23.39 E
Kerema	60	Di	7.58S	145.46 E
Keren	35	Fb	15.47N	38.27 E
Kerest, Ozero-	7	Hd	65.50N	32.50 E
Kerewan	34	Bc	13.29N	16.06W
Kerguélen	30	Nm	49.20S	69.30 E
Kerguélen, Iles-	30	Nm	49.15S	69.10 E
Kerguelen Plateau (EN)	3	Go	55.00S	75.00 E
Kericho	36	Gc	0.22S	35.17 E
Keri Kera	35	Ec	12.21N	32.46 E
Kerimäki	8	Mc	61.55N	29.17 E
Kerinci, Gunung-	21	Mj	1.42S	101.16 E
Kerio	30	Kh	2.59N	36.07 E
Kerion	15	Dl	37.40N	20.49 E
Keriya/Yutian	22	Kf	36.52N	81.42 E
Keriya He	27	Dd	38.30N	82.10 E
Keriya Shankou	27	Dd	35.12N	81.44 E
Kerka	10	Mj	46.28N	16.36 E
Kerken	12	Ic	51.27N	6.26 E
Kerkennah Islands (EN)=Qarqannah, Juzur-	30	Ie	34.44N	11.12 E
Kerketevs Óros	15	Jl	37.44N	26.38 E
Kerki	19	Gh	37.50N	65.13 E
Kerkini Óros	15	Fh	41.21N	22.50 E
Kérkira	15	Cj	39.36N	19.55 E
Kérkira=Corfu (EN)	5	Hh	39.40N	19.45 E
Kerkiras, Stenón-=Corfu, Strait of- (EN)	15	Dj	39.35N	20.05 E
Kerkrade	12	Id	50.52N	6.04 E
Kerma (EN)=Karmah	35	Eb	19.38N	30.25 E
Kermadec Islands	57	Jh	30.00S	178.30W
Kermadec Ridge (EN)	57	Jh	30.30S	178.30W
Kermadec Trench (EN)	3	Km	30.00S	177.00W
Kermajarvi	8	Mb	62.30N	28.40 E
Kermān [3]	23	Ic	30.50N	57.50 E
Kermān	22	Hf	30.17N	57.05 E
Kermānshāh→Bakhtarān	22	Gf	34.19N	47.04 E
Kermānshāhān	24	Pg	31.17N	54.55 E
Kerme	15	Kl	37.02N	28.00 E
Kerme Körfezi	24	Bd	36.50N	28.00 E
Kermit	45	Ek	31.51N	103.06W
Kern River	46	Fi	35.13N	119.17W
Kérouané	34	Dd	9.16N	9.01W
Kerpen	12	Id	50.52N	6.41 E
Kerrobert	42	Gf	51.55N	109.08W
Kerrville	43	He	30.03N	99.08W
Kerry/Ciarraí [2]	9	Di	52.10N	9.30W
Kerry, Mountains of-	9	Dj	51.55N	9.50W
Kertamulya	26	Eg	0.23N	109.09 E
Kerteh	26	Df	4.31N	103.27 E
Kerteminde	8	Di	55.27N	10.40 E
Kerulen (Cherlen)	21	Ne	48.48N	117.00 E
Kervo/Kerava	8	Kd	60.24N	25.07 E
Kerzaz	32	Gd	29.27N	1.25W
Kerženec	7	Kh	56.04N	45.01 E
Kesagami Lake	42	Jf	50.23N	80.10W
Kesälahti	8	Mc	61.54N	29.50 E
Keşan	23	Ca	40.51N	26.37 E
Keşap	24	Hb	40.55N	38.31 E
Kesen'numa	28	Pe	38.54N	141.35 E
Kesen'numa-Wan	29	Gb	38.50N	141.35 E
Keshan	27	Mb	48.04N	125.51 E
Keskastel	12	Jf	48.58N	7.02 E
Keskin	24	Ec	39.41N	33.37 E
Keski-Suomi [2]	7	Fe	62.30N	25.30 E
Kestenga	7	Hd	65.53N	31.45 E
Keswick	9	Jg	54.37N	3.08W
Keszthely	10	Nj	46.46N	17.15 E
Ket	21	Kd	58.55N	81.32 E
Kéta	34	Fd	5.55N	0.59 E
Keta, Ozero-	20	Dc	68.45N	90.00 E
Ketanda	20	Jd	60.38N	141.30 E
Ketapang	22	Mj	1.52S	109.59 E
Ketchikan	39	Fd	55.21N	131.35W
Ketchum	43	Ec	43.41N	114.22W
Ketchum Mountain	45	Fk	31.15N	101.00W
Kete Krachi	34	Ed	7.46N	0.03W
Ketelmeer	12	Hb	52.35N	5.45 E
Ketlī, Jbel-	13	Gi	35.22N	5.17W
Ketmen, Hrebet-	18	Lc	43.20N	80.00 E
Kétou	34	Fd	7.22N	2.36 E
Kętrzyn	10	Rb	54.06N	21.23 E
Kettering [Eng.-U.K.]	9	Mi	52.24N	0.44W
Kettering [Oh.-U.S.]	44	Ef	39.41N	84.10W
Kettle River	46	Fb	48.42N	118.07W
Kettle River Range	46	Fb	48.30N	118.40W
Keuka Lake	44	Id	42.27N	77.10W
Keur Massène	32	Df	16.33N	16.14W
Keuruu	7	Fe	62.16N	24.42 E
Keuruunselkä	8	Kb	62.10N	24.40 E
Kevelaer	12	Ic	51.35N	6.15 E
Kew	49	Kc	21.54N	72.02W
Kewanee	43	Jc	41.14N	89.56W
Keweenaw Bay	44	Cb	46.56N	88.23W
Keweenaw Peninsula	43	Jb	47.12N	88.25W
Key, Lough-/Loch Cé	9	Eg	54.00N	8.15W
Keya Paha River	45	Ge	42.54N	99.00W
Keyhole Reservoir	46	Md	44.21N	104.51W
Key Largo	44	Gm	25.04N	80.28W
Keypel Bank (EN)	59	Le	25.15S	159.30 E
Keystone Lake	45	Hh	36.15N	96.25W
Key West	39	Kg	24.33N	81.48W
Kez	7	Mh	57.56N	53.43 E
Kezi	37	Dd	20.55S	28.29 E
Kežma	20	Fe	59.02N	101.09 E
Kežmarok	10	Qg	49.08N	20.25 E
Kgalagadi [3]	37	Ce	25.00S	22.00 E
Kgatleng [3]	37	Dd	24.28S	26.05 E
Kghoti	37	Cd	24.55S	21.59 E
Khabr, Kūh-e-	23	Id	28.50N	56.26 E
Khābūr, Nahr al-	24	Ie	35.08N	40.26 E
Khadari, Wādī al-	35	Dc	10.29N	27.00 E
Khādim, Shūshat al-	24	Bh	28.35N	27.43 E
Khadki (Kirkee)	25	Ee	18.34N	73.52 E
Khadra	13	Mh	36.15N	0.35 E
Khafs Banbān	24	Lj	25.31N	46.27 E
Khairónia	15	Fk	38.30N	22.51 E
Khairpur	25	Dc	27.32N	68.46 E
Khāiz, Kūh-e-	24	Nh	30.27N	50.55 E
Khakhea	37	Cd	24.42S	23.30 E
Khalatse	25	Fb	34.20N	76.49 E
Khalīj-e Fārs=Persian Gulf (EN)	21	Hg	27.00N	51.00 E
Khálki	15	Km	36.13N	27.37 E
Khálki	15	Km	36.14N	27.36 E
Khalkidhiki=Chalcidice (EN)	5	Ig	40.25N	23.25 E
Khalkis	15	Gk	38.28N	23.36 E
Khaluf	23	Ie	20.29N	57.59 E
Khambhāt	25	Ed	22.18N	72.37 E
Khambhāt, Gulf of-	21	Jg	21.00N	72.30 E
Khāmgaon	25	Fd	20.41N	76.34 E
Khamili	15	Jn	35.52N	26.14 E
Khamir	23	Ff	15.59N	43.57 E
Khāmis, Ash Shallāl al-=Fifth Cataract (EN)	30	Kg	18.23N	33.47 E
Khamīs Mushayț	23	Ff	18.18N	42.44 E
Khammam	25	Ge	17.15N	80.09 E
Khamseh	24	Md	36.40N	48.50 E
Khan	37	Ad	22.42S	14.54 E
Khān	24	Qj	24.13N	56.20 E
Khānābād	23	Kb	36.41N	69.07 E
Khān al Baghdādī	24	Jf	33.51N	42.33 E
Khān al Hammād	24	Kf	32.19N	44.17 E
Khānaqīn	23	Gc	34.21N	45.22 E
Khān az Zabīb	24	Gg	31.28N	36.06 E
Khandwa	25	Fd	21.50N	76.20 E
Khāneh Sorkh, Gardaneh-ye-	24	Qh	29.49N	56.06 E
Khānewāl	25	Eb	30.18N	71.56 E
Khangai Mountains (EN)=Changajn Nuruu→Hangaj, Hrebet-	21	Le	47.30N	100.00 E
Khangai Mountains (EN)=Hangaj, Hrebet- (Changajn Nuruu)	21	Le	47.30N	100.00 E
Khánia	6	Ih	35.31N	24.02 E
Khanion, Kólpos-	15	Gn	35.35N	23.50 E
Khanka, Lake- (EN)=Hanka, Ozero-	21	Pe	45.00N	132.24 E
Khanka Lake (EN)=Xingkai Hu	21	Pe	45.00N	132.24 E
Khānpur	25	Ec	28.39N	70.39 E
Khān Shaykhūn	24	Ge	35.26N	36.38 E
Khān Takhti	24	Kc	38.09N	44.55 E
Khān Yūnus	24	Fg	31.21N	34.19 E
Khānzīr, Rās-	35	Hc	10.50N	45.50 E

Index Symbols

[1] Independent Nation
[2] State, Region
[3] District, County
[4] Municipality
[5] Colony, Dependency
Continent
Physical Region
Historical or Cultural Region
Mount, Mountain
Volcano
Hill
Mountains, Mountain Range
Hills, Escarpment
Plateau, Upland
Pass, Gap
Plain, Lowland
Delta
Salt Flat
Valley, Canyon
Crater, Cave
Karst Features
Depression
Polder
Desert, Dunes
Forest, Woods
Heath, Steppe
Oasis
Cape, Point
Coast, beach
Cliff
Peninsula
Isthmus
Sandbank
Island
Atoll
Rock, Reef
Islands, Archipelago
Rocks, Reefs
Coral Reef
Well, Spring
Geyser
River, Stream
Waterfall Rapids
River Mouth, Estuary
Lake
Salt Lake
Intermittent Lake
Reservoir
Swamp, Pond
Canal
Glacier
Ice Shelf, Pack Ice
Ocean
Sea
Gulf, Bay
Strait, Fjord
Lagoon
Bank
Seamount
Tablemount
Ridge
Shelf
Basin
Escarpment, Sea Scarp
Fracture
Trench, Abyss
National Park, Reserve
Point of Interest
Recreation Site
Cave, Cavern
Historic Site
Ruins
Wall, Walls
Church, Abbey
Temple
Scientific Station
Airport
Port
Lighthouse
Mine
Tunnel
Dam, Bridge

Khao Laem 25 Kf 14.19N 101.11 E
Khao Miang 25 Ke 17.42N 101.01 E
Khao Mokochu 25 Je 15.56N 99.06 E
Khao Saming 25 Kf 12.16N 102.26 E
Khar 24 Me 35.53N 48.55 E
Kharagpur 22 Kg 22.20N 87.20 E
Khárakas 15 In 35.01N 25.07 E
Khārān 24 Qh 28.55N 57.09 E
Kharānaq 24 Pf 32.20N 54.39 E
Kharānaq, Kūh-e- 24 Pf 32.10N 54.39 E
Kharga Oasis (EN) = Khārijah, Waḥāt al- 30 Kf 25.20N 30.35 E
Khārijah, Wāḥāt al- = Kharga Oasis (EN) 30 Kf 25.20N 30.35 E
Kharīt, Wādī al- 24 Ej 24.26N 33.03 E
Kharīṭah, Shiqqat al- 33 If 17.10N 47.50 E
Khārk 24 Nh 29.15N 50.20 E
Khārk, Jazīreh-ye- 23 Hd 29.15N 50.20 E
Khār Khū 24 Og 31.39N 53.46 E
Kharmān, Kūh-e- 23 Hd 29.13N 53.35 E
Kharshah, Qārat al- 24 Bg 30.35N 27.25 E
Khartoum (EN) = Al Kharṭūm [3] 35 Eb 15.50N 33.00 E
Khartoum (EN) = Al Kharṭūm 31 Kg 15.36N 32.32 E
Khartoum North (EN) = Al Kharṭūm Baḥrī 31 Kg 15.38N 32.33 E
Khāsh 23 Jc 31.31N 62.52 E
Khāsh 23 Jc 31.11N 62.05 E
Khashm al Qirbah 35 Fc 14.58N 35.55 E
Khāsi Jaintia 21 Lg 25.35N 91.38 E
Khatikhon, Yam- = Mediterranean Sea (EN) 5 Hh 35.00N 20.00 E
Khaṭṭ 33 Dd 28.40N 22.40 E
Khātūn, Kūh-e- 24 Og 30.25N 53.38 E
Khawr al Fakkān 24 Qk 25.21N 56.22 E
Khawr al Juḥaysh 35 Ia 20.36N 50.59 E
Khawr al Mufattaḥ 24 Mh 28.40N 48.25 E
Khawr Umm Qaṣr 24 Lg 30.02N 47.56 E
Khay' 23 Ff 18.45N 41.24 E
Khaybar 23 Ed 25.42N 39.31 E
Khaybar, Ḥarrat- 24 Hj 25.30N 39.45 E
Khazzī, Qārat- 30 Jf 21.26N 24.30 E
Khemis 13 Oh 36.10N 4.04 E
Khemis Anjra 13 Gi 35.41N 5.32W
Khémis Beni Arouss 13 Gi 35.19N 5.38W
Khemis Miliana 32 Hb 36.16N 2.13 E
Khemissat 32 Fc 33.49N 6.04W
Khemisset [3] 32 Fc 33.49N 6.00W
Khemmarat 25 Ke 16.03N 105.11 E
Khenchela 32 Ib 35.26N 7.08 E
Khenifra 32 Fc 32.56N 5.40W
Khenifra [3] 32 Fc 33.00N 5.08W
Kherāmeh 24 Oh 29.32N 53.21 E
Khersan 24 Ng 31.33N 50.22 E
Khersónisos Akrotiri 15 Hn 35.35N 24.10 E
Kheyrābād [Iran] 24 Mg 31.49N 48.23 E
Kheyrābād [Iran] 24 Ph 29.26N 55.19 E
Khionótripa 15 Hh 41.18N 24.05 E
Khios 15 Jk 38.22N 26.08 E
Khios = Chios (EN) 5 Ih 38.22N 26.00 E
Khirbat Isrīyah 24 Ge 35.21N 37.46 E
Khirr, Nahr al- 24 Kf 33.17N 44.21 E
Khlomón Óros 15 Fk 38.36N 23.00 E
Khlong Yai 25 Kf 11.46N 102.53 E
Khokhropār 25 Ec 25.42N 70.12 E
Khok Kloi 25 Jg 8.17N 98.19 E
Khok Samrong 25 Ke 15.03N 100.44 E
Kholm 23 Kb 36.42N 67.41 E
Khomām 24 Md 37.22N 49.40 E
Khomas Highland (EN) = Khomas Hochland 30 Ik 22.40S 16.20 E
Khomas Hochland = Khomas Highland (EN) 30 Ik 22.40S 16.20 E
Khomeyn 24 Nf 33.38N 50.04 E
Khomeynīshahr 23 Hc 32.42N 51.27 E
Khon Kaen 25 Ke 16.26N 102.50 E
Khonsār 24 Nf 33.21N 50.19 E
Khóra 15 El 37.03N 21.43 E
Khor Anghar 35 Gc 12.27N 43.18 E
Khorāsān 21 Hf 34.00N 56.00 E
Khorāsān [3] 23 Ic 35.00N 58.00 E
Khorāsānī, Godār-e 24 Qg 30.44N 57.03 E
Khóra Sfakíon 15 Hn 35.12N 24.09 E
Khormūj, Kūh-e- 24 Hd 28.43N 51.22 E
Khorof Harar 36 Hb 2.14N 40.44 E
Khorramābād 23 Gc 33.30N 48.20 E
Khorramshahr 23 Gc 30.25N 48.11 E
Khorsābād 24 Jd 36.38N 43.17 E
Khoshyeylāq 24 Pd 36.53N 55.15 E
Khosrowābād 24 Mg 30.00N 48.25 E
Khosrowshah 24 Ld 37.57N 46.03 E
Khouribga [3] 32 Fc 32.56N 6.36W
Khouribga 32 Fc 32.53N 6.54W
Khowst 23 Kc 33.22N 69.57 E
Khrisi 15 Io 34.52N 25.42 E
Khrisoúpolis 15 Hi 40.59N 24.42 E
Khristianá 15 Im 36.14N 25.13 E
Khu Dağı 24 Jc 38.35N 43.40 E
Khuff [Lib.] 33 Cd 28.17N 18.20 E
Khuff [Sau.Ar.] 23 Ed 25.20N 37.20 E
Khulna 22 Kg 22.48N 89.33 E
Khūrān 24 Pi 26.50N 55.40 E
Khurayṣ 23 Gd 25.05N 48.02 E
Khurayt 35 Dc 13.57N 26.02 E
Khurīyā Murīyā, Jazā'ir- = Kuria Muria Islands (EN) 21 Hh 17.30N 56.00 E
Khurr, Wādī al- 24 Jg 30.52N 42.10 E
Khursanīyah 24 Mi 27.18N 49.16 E
Khūshābar 24 Md 37.59N 48.54 E
Khutse 37 Cd 23.20S 24.34 E
Khuwayy 35 Dc 13.05N 29.14 E
Khuzdār 25 Dc 27.48N 66.37 E
Khūzestān [3] 23 Gc 32.00N 48.30 E
Khūzestān 21 Gf 30.33N 50.00 E
Khvojeh Lāk, Kūh-e- 24 Le 35.43N 46.29 E
Khvor 24 Pf 33.47N 55.03 E
Khvorāsgān 24 Nf 32.39N 51.45 E
Khvormūj 24 Nh 28.39N 51.23 E
Khvoshkūh 24 Qi 27.37N 56.41 E
Khvoy 24 Kc 38.33N 44.58 E
Khyber Pass 25 Eb 34.05N 71.10 E
Kia 63a Db 7.32S 158.26 E
Kia 63d Bb 16.14S 179.05 E
Kiamba 26 He 5.59N 124.37 E
Kiambi 36 Ed 7.20S 28.01 E
Kiamichi River 45 Ij 33.57N 95.14W
Kiangarow, Mount- 59 Ke 26.49S 151.33 E
Kiangsi (EN) = Chiang-hsi Sheng → Jangxi Sheng [2] 27 Kf 28.00N 116.00 E
Kiangsi (EN) = Jangxi Sheng (Chiang-hsi Sheng) [2] 27 Kf 28.00N 116.00 E
Kiangsu (EN) = Chiang-su Sheng → Jiangsu Sheng [2] 27 Ke 33.00N 120.00 E
Kiangsu (EN) = Jiangsu Sheng (Chiang-su Sheng) [2] 27 Ke 33.00N 120.00 E
Kiantajärvi 7 Gd 65.03N 29.07 E
Kiáton 15 Fk 38.01N 22.45 E
Kibali 36 Eb 3.37N 28.34 E
Kibangou 36 Bc 3.27S 12.21 E
Kibartaj/Kybartai 8 Jj 54.38N 22.44 E
Kibasira Swamp 36 Gd 8.20S 36.18 E
Kibau 36 Gd 8.35S 35.17 E
Kibaya 36 Gd 5.18S 36.34 E
Kibbish 35 Fe 4.40N 35.53 E
Kiberg 7 Ha 70.17N 31.00 E
Kibikogen 29 Cd 34.45N 133.15 E
Kiboko 36 Gc 2.15S 37.42 E
Kibombo 36 Ec 3.54S 25.55 E
Kibondo 36 Fc 3.35S 30.42 E
Kibre Mengist 35 Fd 5.58N 39.00 E
Kıbrıs/Kypros = Cyprus (EN) [1] 22 Ff 35.00N 33.00 E
Kıbrıs/Kypros = Cyprus (EN) 21 Ff 35.00N 33.00 E
Kibungo 36 Fc 2.10S 30.32 E
Kibuye 36 Ec 2.03S 29.21 E
Kibwezi 36 Gc 2.25S 37.58 E
Kičevo 15 Dh 41.31N 20.58 E
Kichi Kichi 35 Bb 17.36N 17.19 E
Kicking Horse Pass 42 Ff 51.50N 116.30W
Kidal 31 Hg 18.26N 1.24 E
Kidapawan 26 Ie 7.01N 125.03 E
Kidatu 36 Gd 7.42S 36.57 E
Kidira 34 Cc 14.28N 12.13W
Kidnappers, Cape- 62 Gc 39.38S 177.06 E
Kiekie 65a Ab 21.53N 160.13W
Kiel 6 He 54.20N 10.08 E
Kiel Canal (EN) = Nord-Ostsee Kanal 5 Ge 53.53N 9.08 E
Kielce 6 Ie 50.52N 20.37 E
Kielce [2] 10 Qf 50.50N 20.35 E
Kieler Bucht 10 Gb 54.35N 10.35 E
Kienge 36 Ee 10.33S 27.33 E
Kierspe 12 Jc 51.08N 7.35 E
Kieta 58 Ge 6.15S 155.37 E
Kietrz 10 Of 50.05N 18.01 E
Kiev (EN) = Kijev 6 Je 50.26N 30.31 E
Kiev Reservoir (EN) = Kijevskoje Vodohranilišče 5 Je 51.00N 30.25 E
Kiffa 31 Fg 16.36N 11.23W
Kifisiá 15 Gk 38.04N 23.49 E
Kifisós 15 Gk 38.26N 23.15 E
Kifrī 24 Ke 34.42N 44.58 E
Kigač 16 Pf 46.28N 49.08 E
Kigali 31 Ki 1.57S 30.04 E
Kiğı 24 Ic 39.19N 40.21 E
Kigille 35 Ed 8.40N 34.02 E
Kigoma 31 Ji 4.52S 29.38 E
Kigoma [3] 36 Fc 4.50S 30.05 E
Kigosi 36 Fc 4.40S 31.27 E
Kihelkonna 8 If 58.20N 21.54 E
Kihniö 8 Jb 62.12N 23.11 E
Kihnu 7 Fg 58.10N 24.00 E
Kiholo 65a Fd 19.51N 155.55W
Kiholo Bay 65a Fd 19.52N 155.56W
Kihti/Skiftet 8 Id 60.15N 21.05 E
Kii-Hantō 27 Oe 34.00N 135.45 E
Kiikka 8 Jc 61.20N 22.46 E
Kiil 16 Se 49.27N 54.50 E
Kiiminki 7 Fd 65.08N 25.44 E
Kii-Sanchi 29 Dd 34.15N 135.50 E
Kii-Suido 28 Mh 34.00N 134.55 E
Kija 20 De 56.52N 86.40 E
Kijev = Kiev (EN) 6 Je 50.26N 30.31 E
Kijevka 19 He 50.16N 71.34 E
Kijevskaja Oblast [3] 19 De 50.20N 30.45 E
Kijevskoje Vodohranilišče = Kiev Reservoir (EN) 5 Je 51.00N 30.25 E
Kijma 19 Ge 51.35N 67.34 E
Kikai-Jima 27 Mf 28.15N 130.00 E
Kikerino 8 Me 59.23N 29.38 E
Kikinda 15 Dd 45.50N 20.29 E
Kikládhes = Cyclades (EN) 5 Ih 37.00N 25.10 E
Kikonai 28 Pd 41.40N 140.26 E
Kikori 58 Fe 7.25S 144.13 E
Kikori River 57 Fe 7.23S 144.16 E
Kikuchi 29 Be 32.59N 130.49 E
Kikuma 29 Cd 34.03N 132.51 E
Kikvidze 16 Md 50.44N 43.03 E
Kikwit 31 Ii 5.02S 18.49 E
Kil [Nor.] 8 Cf 58.52N 9.19 E
Kil [Swe.] 7 Cg 59.30N 13.19 E
Kilafors 7 Df 61.15N 16.33 E
Kilambé, Cerro- 49 Eg 13.34N 85.42W
Kilauea 65a Ba 22.13N 159.25W
Kilauea Crater 65a Fd 19.24N 155.17W
Kilauea Point 65a Ba 22.14N 159.24W
Kilbrannan Sound 9 Hf 55.40N 5.25W
Kilbuck Mountains 40 Hd 60.30N 159.45W
Kilchu 27 Mc 40.58N 129.20 E
Kilcoy 59 Ke 26.57S 152.33 E
Kildare/Cill Dara [2] 9 Gh 53.15N 6.45W
Kildare/Cill Dara 9 Gh 53.10N 6.55W
Kildin, Ostrov- 7 Ib 69.20N 34.10 E
Kilembe 36 Cd 5.42S 19.55 E
Kilgore 45 Ij 32.23N 94.53W
Kilgoris 36 Fc 1.00S 34.53 E
Kiliao He 21 Oe 43.24N 123.42 E
Kiliç 15 Mi 40.40N 29.23 E
Kilifi 36 Gc 3.38S 39.51 E
Kili Island 57 Hd 5.39N 169.04 E
Kilija 19 Cf 45.27N 29.14 E
Kilijskoje girlo 15 Md 45.13N 29.43 E
Kilimanjaro [3] 36 Gc 4.00S 37.40 E
Kilimanjaro, Mount- 30 Ki 3.04S 37.22 E
Kilimli 24 Db 41.29N 31.50 E
Kilinailau Islands 60 Fh 4.45S 155.20 E
Kilindoni 31 Ki 7.55S 39.39 E
Kilingi-Nõmme/Kilingi-Nymme 7 Fg 58.08N 24.59 E
Kilingi-Nymme/Kilingi-Nõmme 7 Fg 58.08N 24.59 E
Kilis 23 Eb 36.44N 37.05 E
Kilitbahir 24 Bb 40.12N 26.20 E
Kilkee/Cill Chaoi 9 Di 52.41N 9.38W
Kilkenny/Cill Chainnigh 9 Fi 52.39N 7.15W
Kilkenny/Cill Chainnigh [2] 9 Fi 52.40N 7.20W
Kilkieran Bay 9 Dh 53.15N 9.45W
Kilkis 15 Fi 41.00N 22.52 E
Killala Bay/Cuan Chill Ala 9 Dg 54.15N 9.10W
Killarney/Cill Airne 9 Di 52.03N 9.30W
Killary Harbour/An Caoláire Rua 9 Dh 53.38N 9.55W
Killdeer 45 Ec 47.22N 102.45W
Killeen 43 He 31.08N 97.44W
Killinck 42 Ld 60.25N 64.40W
Killini 15 El 37.56N 21.09 E
Killini Óros 15 Fl 37.55N 22.26 E
Kilmallock/Cill Mocheallóg 9 Ei 52.25N 8.35W
Kilmarnock 9 If 55.37N 4.30W
Kilmez 7 Mh 56.58N 50.29 E
Kilmez 7 Mh 57.03N 51.24 E
Kilmore 59 Ig 37.18S 144.57 E
Kilombero 36 Gd 8.31S 37.22 E
Kilosa 31 Ki 6.50S 36.59 E
Kilpisjärvi 7 Eb 69.03N 20.48 E
Kilp-Javr 7 Hb 69.07N 32.28 E
Kilrush/Cill Rois 9 Di 52.39N 9.29W
Kilsbergen 8 Fe 59.20N 14.45 E
Kiltān Island 25 Ef 11.29N 73.00 E
Kilwa 36 Ed 9.17S 28.20 E
Kilwa Kisiwani 31 Ki 8.58S 39.30 E
Kilwa Kivinje 36 Gd 8.45S 39.24 E
Kilwa Masoko 36 Gd 8.56S 39.31 E
Kilyos → Kumköy 15 Mh 41.15N 29.02 E
Kim 45 Eh 37.15N 103.21W
Kimamba 36 Gd 6.47S 37.08 E
Kimba 59 Hf 33.09S 136.25 E
Kimball [Nb.-U.S.] 45 Ef 41.14N 103.40W
Kimball [S.D.-U.S.] 45 Ge 43.45N 98.57W
Kimball, Mount- 40 Kd 63.14N 144.39W
Kimbe 59 Ka 5.31S 150.12 E
Kimbe Bay 60 Ei 5.30S 150.30 E
Kimberley 57 Df 16.00S 126.00 E
Kimberley [B.C.-Can.] 42 Fg 49.41N 115.59W
Kimberley [S.Afr.] 31 Jk 28.43S 24.46 E
Kimberley Plateau 59 Fc 17.00S 127.00 E
Kimch'aek (Sŏngjin) 27 Mc 40.41N 129.12 E
Kimch'ŏn 27 Md 36.07N 128.07 E
Kimhandu 36 Gd 7.05S 37.35 E
Kimi 15 Hk 38.38N 24.06 E
Kimito 8 Jd 60.10N 22.40 E
Kimito/Kemiö 8 Jd 60.10N 22.40 E
Kimje 28 Ig 35.48N 126.53 E
Kimobetsu 29a Bb 42.47N 140.56 E
Kimolos 15 Hm 36.48N 24.34 E
Kimongo 36 Bc 4.29S 12.58 E
Kimovsk 19 De 54.01N 38.36 E
Kimpu-San 29 Fd 35.52N 138.37 E
Kimry 19 Dd 56.52N 37.24 E
Kimvula 36 Cd 5.44S 15.58 E
Kinabalu, Gunong- 21 Ni 6.05N 116.33 E
Kinabatangan 26 Ge 5.42N 118.23 E
Kinango 36 Gc 4.08S 39.19 E
Kinaros 15 Jm 36.59N 26.17 E
Kincardine 42 Jh 44.11N 81.38W
Kind 8 Eg 57.35N 13.25 E
Kinda 36 Ed 9.18S 25.04 E
Kinda 8 Ff 58.05N 15.40 E
Kindamba 36 Bc 3.44S 14.31 E
Kinder 45 Jk 30.29N 92.51W
Kinder Scout 9 Lh 53.23N 1.52W
Kindersley 42 Gf 51.27N 109.10W
Kindi 34 Ec 12.26N 2.01W
Kindia 31 Fg 10.04N 12.51W
Kindu 31 Ji 2.57S 25.56 E
Kinel 7 Mj 53.14N 50.40 E
Kinesi 36 Fc 1.28S 33.52 E
Kinešma 19 Ed 57.28N 42.16 E
King 63a Aa 4.24S 152.43 E
King, Cayos- 49 Fg 12.45N 83.20W
Kingaroy 59 Ke 26.33S 151.50 E
King Christian 42 Ha 77.45N 102.00W
King Christian IX Land (EN) = Kong Christian IX Land 67 Mc 68.00N 36.30W
King Christian X Land (EN) = Kong Christian X Land 67 Md 72.20N 32.30W
King City 43 Cd 36.13N 121.08W
King Edward River 59 Fb 14.14S 126.35 E
Kingfisher 45 Hi 35.52N 97.56W
King Frederik VI Coast (EN) = Kong Frederik VI Kyst 67 Nc 63.00N 43.30W
King Frederik VIII Land (EN) = Kong Frederik VIII Land 67 Md 78.30N 28.00W
King George Island 66 Re 62.00S 58.15W
King George Islands 42 Je 57.15N 78.30W
King George Sound 59 Dg 35.10S 118.10 E
Kingisepp 7 Gg 59.23N 28.37 E
Kingisepp/Kingissepp 19 Cd 58.17N 22.29 E
King Island 57 Fh 39.50S 144.00 E
Kingissepp/Kingisepp 19 Cd 58.17N 22.29 E
King Lear Peak 46 Ff 41.12N 118.34W
King Leopold Ranges 59 Fc 17.30S 125.45 E
Kingman [Az.-U.S.] 43 Ed 35.12N 114.04W
Kingman [Ks.-U.S.] 45 Gh 37.39N 98.07W
Kingman Reef 57 Kd 6.19N 162.28W
Kingombe [Zaire] 36 Ec 2.35S 26.37 E
Kingombe [Zaire] 36 Ec 3.52S 26.35 E
Kingoome Inlet 46 Ba 50.49N 126.13W
Kingoonya 58 Eh 30.54S 135.18 E
King Peninsula 66 Of 73.12S 101.00W
Kingsclere 12 Ac 51.19N 1.15W
Kingscote 59 Hg 35.40S 137.38 E
King's Lynn 9 Ni 52.45N 0.24 E
King Sound 57 Df 17.00S 123.30 E
Kings Peak [Ca.-U.S.] 46 Cf 40.10N 124.08W
Kings Peak [U.S.] 38 He 40.46N 110.22W
Kingsport 43 Kd 36.32N 82.33W
Kings River 46 Fh 36.03N 119.49W
Kingston [Jam.] 39 Lh 18.00N 76.50W
Kingston [Nor.I.] 58 Hg 29.04S 167.58 E
Kingston [N.Y.-U.S.] 43 Mc 41.55N 74.00W
Kingston [N.Z.] 61 Ci 45.20S 168.43 E
Kingston [Ont.-Can.] 39 Le 44.14N 76.30W
Kingston Peak 46 Hi 35.42N 115.52W
Kingston South East 58 Eh 36.50S 139.51 E
Kingston-upon-Hull (Hull) 6 Fe 53.45N 0.20W
Kingston-upon-Thames, London- 9 Mj 51.28N 0.19W
Kingstown 39 Mh 13.09N 61.14W
Kingsville 43 Hf 27.31N 97.52W
Kings Worthy 12 Ac 51.05N 1.18W
Kingussie 9 Id 57.05N 4.04W
King William 38 Jc 69.00N 97.30W
King William's Town 31 Jl 32.51S 27.22 E
Kiniama 36 Ee 11.26S 28.19 E
Kınık 24 Bc 39.05N 27.23 E
Kinkala 36 Bc 4.22S 14.46 E
Kinlochleven 9 Ie 56.43N 4.58W
Kinna 8 Eg 57.30N 12.41 E
Kinnairds Head 9 Ld 57.42N 2.00W
Kinnared 8 Eg 57.02N 13.06 E
Kinnekulle 8 Ef 58.35N 13.23 E
Kinneret, Yam- 24 Ff 32.48N 35.35 E
Kino-Kawa 29 Dd 34.13N 135.08 E
Kinomoto 29 Ed 35.31N 136.13 E
Kinoosao 42 He 57.06N 102.01W
Kinós Kefalai 15 Fj 39.25N 22.34 E
Kinross 9 Je 56.13N 3.27W
Kinsale/cionn tSáile 9 Ej 51.42N 8.32W
Kinsale, Old Head of-/An Seancheann 9 Ej 51.36N 8.32W
Kinsangire 36 Gd 7.26S 38.35 E
Kinsarvik 7 Bf 60.23N 6.43 E
Kinshasa [2] 36 Cc 4.00S 16.00 E
Kinshasa (Leopoldville) 31 Ii 4.18S 15.18 E
Kinsley 45 Gh 37.55N 99.25W
Kinston 43 Ld 35.16N 77.35W
Kintampo 34 Ed 8.03N 1.43W
Kintap 26 Gg 3.51S 115.13 E
Kintyre 9 Hf 55.32N 5.35W
Kin-Wan 29b Ab 26.25N 127.54 E
Kinyan 34 Dc 11.51N 6.01W
Kinyeti 30 Kh 3.57N 32.54 E
Kinzig [Eur.] 10 Dh 48.37N 7.49 E
Kinzig [Ger.] 10 Ef 50.08N 8.54 E
Kioa 63d Bb 16.39S 179.55 E
Kipaka 36 Ec 4.09S 26.30 E
Kiparissia 15 El 37.15N 21.40 E
Kiparissia, Gulf of- (EN) = Kiparissiakós Kólpos 15 El 37.30N 21.25 E
Kiparissiakós Kólpos = Kiparissia, Gulf of- (EN) 15 El 37.30N 21.25 E
Kipawa, Lac- 42 Jg 46.55N 79.00W
Kipembawe 36 Fd 7.39S 33.24 E
Kipengere Range 30 Ki 9.10S 34.15 E
Kiperčeny 15 Lb 47.32N 28.40 E
Kipili 36 Fd 7.26S 30.36 E
Kipini 36 Hc 2.32S 40.31 E
Kipling 45 Ea 50.10N 102.38W
Kippure 9 Gh 53.11N 6.20W
Kiprarenukk, Mys-/Undva Neem 8 If 58.25N 21.45 E
Kipros = Cyprus (EN) 23 Db 35.01N 33.00 E
Kipushi 36 Ee 11.46S 27.14 E
Kirakira 58 Hf 10.27S 161.56 E
Kiraz 24 Cc 39.21N 27.25 E
Kirazlı 24 Bb 40.01N 26.40 E
Kirbla 8 Jf 58.42N 23.49 E
Kircasalih 15 Jh 41.23N 26.48 E
Kirchberg (Hunsrück) 12 Je 49.57N 7.24 E
Kirchhain 12 Kd 50.49N 8.58 E
Kirchheimbolanden 12 Ke 49.40N 8.01 E
Kirchheim unter Teck 10 Fh 48.39N 9.27 E
Kirchhundem 12 Kc 51.06N 8.06 E
Kirchhundem-Rahrbach 12 Jc 51.02N 7.59 E
Kirchlengern 12 Kb 52.12N 8.38 E
Kirdimi 35 Bb 18.11N 18.38 E
Kireç 15 Lj 39.33N 28.22 E
Kirenga 21 Md 57.47N 107.59 E
Kirensk 22 Md 57.46N 108.08 E
Kirghiz SSR (EN) = Kirgizskaja SSR [2] 19 Hg 41.30N 75.00 E
Kirghiz Steppe (EN) 5 Lf 49.30N 50.30 E
Kirgizskaja Sovetskaja Socialističeskaja Respublika [2] 19 Hg 41.30N 75.00 E
Kirgizskaja SSR/Kyrgyz Sovetik Socialistik Respublikasy [2] 19 Hg 41.30N 75.00 E
Kirgizskaja SSR = Kirghiz SSR (EN) [2] 19 Hg 41.30N 75.00 E
Kirgizski Hrebet 19 Hg 42.30N 74.00 E
Kiri 36 Cc 1.27S 19.00 E
Kiribati [1] 58 Je 0.01S 174.00 E
Kirikhan 24 Gd 36.32N 36.19 E
Kırıkkale 23 Db 39.50N 33.31 E
Kirillov 7 Jg 59.54N 38.27 E
Kirillovskoje 8 Md 60.28N 29.28 E
Kirin (EN) = Chi-lin Sheng → Jilin Sheng [2] 27 Mc 43.00N 126.00 E
Kirin (EN) = Jilin Sheng (Chi-lin Sheng) [2] 27 Mc 43.00N 126.00 E
Kirinyaga/Kenya, Mount- 30 Ki 0.10S 37.20 E
Kirishima-Yama 29 Bf 31.56N 130.52 E
Kiriši 19 Dd 59.27N 32.02 E
Kiritimati Atoll (Christmas) 57 Ld 1.52N 157.20W
Kirja 7 Li 55.05N 46.52 E
Kırkağaç 24 Bc 39.06N 27.40 E
Kirkby Lonsdale 9 Kg 54.13N 2.36W
Kirkcaldy 9 Je 56.07N 3.10W
Kirkcudbright 9 Ig 54.50N 4.03W
Kirkee → Khadki 25 Ee 18.34N 73.52 E
Kirkenær 7 Cf 60.28N 12.03 E
Kirkenes 6 Jb 69.43N 30.03 E
Kirkjubæjarklaustur 7a Bc 63.47N 18.04W
Kirkkonummi/Kyrkslätt 8 Kd 60.07N 24.26 E
Kirkland 46 Dc 47.41N 122.12W
Kirkland Lake 39 Ke 48.09N 80.02W
Kırklareli 23 Ca 41.44N 27.12 E
Kirkpatrick, Mont- 66 Kg 84.20S 166.19 E
Kırkpınar Dağı 24 Fd 37.14N 34.15 E
Kirksville 43 Ic 40.12N 92.35W
Kirkūk 22 Gf 35.28N 44.23 E
Kirkwall 9 Kc 58.59N 2.58W
Kirkwood [Mo.-U.S.] 45 Kg 38.35N 90.24W
Kirkwood [S.Afr.] 37 Df 33.22S 25.15 E
Kırlangıç Burun 24 Dd 36.13N 30.25 E
Kirn 10 Dg 49.47N 7.27 E
Kirobasi 24 Ed 36.43N 33.52 E
Kirov [R.S.F.S.R.] 19 De 54.03N 34.21 E
Kirov [R.S.F.S.R.] 6 Kd 58.33N 49.42 E
Kirova, Zaliv- 16 Pj 39.05N 49.05 E
Kirovabad → Gjandža 6 Kg 40.40N 46.22 E
Kirovakan 19 Eg 40.48N 44.28 E
Kirovgrad 17 Jh 57.26N 60.04 E
Kirovo 18 Hd 40.28N 70.34 E
Kirovo-Čepeck 19 Fd 58.35N 50.03 E
Kirovograd 6 Jf 48.30N 32.18 E
Kirovogradskaja Oblast [3] 19 Df 48.20N 31.50 E
Kirovsk [R.S.F.S.R.] 20 Db 67.37N 33.37 E
Kirovsk [R.S.F.S.R.] 7 Hg 59.53N 31.01 E
Kirovsk [Tur.-U.S.S.R.] 18 Cf 37.43N 60.24 E
Kirovskaja Oblast [3] 19 Ed 58.30N 50.00 E
Kirovski [Kaz.-U.S.S.R.] 19 Hg 44.53N 78.12 E
Kirovski [R.S.F.S.R.] 20 Ig 45.05N 133.27 E
Kirovski [R.S.F.S.R.] 16 Pg 45.48N 48.08 E
Kirovski [R.S.F.S.R.] 20 Kf 54.25N 155.37 E
Kirovski [R.S.F.S.R.] 20 Hf 54.26N 127.00 E
Kirovskoje 18 Hc 42.39N 71.35 E
Kirpilski Liman 16 Kg 45.50N 38.05 E
Kirriemuir 9 Je 56.41N 3.01W
Kirs 19 Fd 59.21N 52.18 E
Kirsanov 16 Mc 52.41N 42.45 E
Kırşehir 23 Db 39.09N 34.10 E
Kirthar Range 21 Ig 27.00N 67.20 E
Kirton 12 Bb 52.55N 0.03W
Kiruna 6 Ib 67.51N 20.13 E
Kirundu 36 Ec 0.44S 25.32 E
Kiryū 29 Fc 36.25N 139.20 E
Kirżač 7 Jh 56.11N 38.53 E
Kisa 7 Dh 57.59N 15.37 E
Kisabi 36 Ed 8.03S 29.11 E
Kisač 15 Cd 45.21N 19.44 E
Kisakata 29 Fb 39.14N 139.54 E
Kisaki 36 Gd 7.28S 37.36 E
Kisalföld 10 Mi 47.30N 17.00 E
Kisangani 31 Jh 0.25N 25.12 E
Kisarazu 29 Fd 35.23N 139.55 E
Kisbér 10 Oi 47.30N 18.02 E
Kiselevsk 20 Df 54.03N 86.49 E
Kiserawe 36 Gd 6.54S 39.05 E
Kishangarh 25 Ec 26.34N 74.52 E
Kishb, Ḥarrat al- 33 He 22.47N 41.30 E
Kishi 34 Fd 9.05N 3.51 E
Kishiwada 28 Mg 34.28N 135.22 E
Kisii 36 Fc 0.41S 34.46 E
Kisiju 36 Gd 7.24S 39.20 E
Kišinev 6 If 47.00N 28.50 E
Kısır Dağı 24 Jb 40.58N 43.04 E
Kiska 40a Bb 52.00N 177.30 E
Kiska Volcano 40a Bb 52.07N 177.36 E
Kisko 8 Jd 60.14N 23.29 E
Kiskőrei Víztároló 10 Qi 47.44N 20.40 E
Kiskőrös 10 Pj 46.37N 19.18 E
Kiskunfélegyháza 10 Pj 46.33N 19.51 E
Kiskunhalas 10 Pj 46.26N 19.30 E
Kiskunmajsa 10 Pj 46.29N 19.45 E
Kiskunság 10 Pj 46.35N 19.15 E
Kislovodsk 19 Eg 43.54N 42.42 E
Kismanyo 31 Li 0.22S 42.32 E
Kisofukushima 29 Ed 35.51N 137.41 E
Kiso-Gawa 28 Ng 35.05N 136.45 E
Kisoro 36 Ec 1.17S 29.41 E
Kiso-Sanmyaku 29 Ed 35.45N 137.45 E
Kisria, Daiet el- 13 Oi 35.44N 2.47 E
Kissámou, Kólpos- 15 Gn 35.35N 23.40 E
Kissidougou 34 Cd 9.11N 10.06W
Kissimmee 44 Gk 28.18N 81.24W
Kissimmee, Lake- 44 Gl 27.55N 81.16W
Kissū, Jabal- 35 Da 21.35N 25.09 E
Kistelek 10 Pj 46.28N 19.59 E
Kisterenye 10 Ph 48.01N 19.50 E

Index Symbols

[1] Independent Nation
[2] State, Region
[3] District, County
[4] Municipality
[5] Colony, Dependency
Continent
Physical Region
Historical or Cultural Region
Mount, Mountain
Volcano
Hill
Mountains, Mountain Range
Hills, Escarpment
Plateau, Upland
Pass, Gap
Plain, Lowland
Delta
Salt Flat
Valley, Canyon
Crater, Cave
Karst Features
Depression
Polder
Desert, Dunes
Forest, Woods
Heath, Steppe
Oasis
Cape, Point
Coast, Beach
Cliff
Peninsula
Isthmus
Sandbank
Island
Atoll
Rock, Reef
Islands, Archipelago
Rocks, Reefs
Coral Reef
Well, Spring
Geyser
River, Stream
Waterfall Rapids
River Mouth, Estuary
Lake
Salt Lake
Intermittent Lake
Reservoir
Swamp, Pond
Canal
Glacier
Ice Shelf, Pack Ice
Ocean
Sea
Gulf, Bay
Strait, Fjord
Lagoon
Bank
Seamount
Tablemount
Ridge
Shelf
Basin
Escarpment, Sea Scarp
Fracture
Trench, Abyss
National Park, Reserve
Point of Interest
Recreation Site
Cave, Cavern
Historic Site
Ruins
Wall, Walls
Church, Abbey
Temple
Scientific Station
Airport
Port
Lighthouse
Mine
Tunnel
Dam, Bridge

Index Symbols

[1] Independent Nation
[2] State, Region
[3] District, County
[4] Municipality
[5] Colony, Dependency
Continent
Physical Region
Historical or Cultural Region
Mount, Mountain
Volcano
Hill
Mountains, Mountain Range
Hills, Escarpment
Plateau, Upland
Pass, Gap
Plain, Lowland
Delta
Salt Flat
Valley, Canyon
Crater, Cave
Karst Features
Depression
Polder
Desert, Dunes
Forest, Woods
Heath, Steppe
Oasis
Cape, Point
Coast, Beach
Cliff
Peninsula
Isthmus
Sandbank
Island
Atoll
Rock, Reef
Islands, Archipelago
Rocks, Reefs
Coral Reef
Well, Spring
Geyser
River, Stream
Waterfall Rapids
River Mouth, Estuary
Lake
Salt Lake
Intermittent Lake
Reservoir
Swamp, Pond
Canal
Glacier
Ice Shelf, Pack Ice
Ocean
Sea
Gulf, Bay
Strait, Fjord
Lagoon
Bank
Seamount
Tablemount
Ridge
Shelf
Basin
Escarpment, Sea Scarp
Fracture
Trench, Abyss
National Park, Reserve
Point of Interest
Recreation Site
Cave, Cavern
Historic Site
Ruins
Wall, Walls
Church, Abbey
Temple
Scientific Station
Airport
Port
Lighthouse
Mine
Tunnel
Dam, Bridge

Kōnosu 29 Fc 36.04N 139.30 E
Konotop 6 Je 51.14N 33.12 E
Konqi He 21 Ke 41.48N 86.47 E
Konrei 64a Bb 7.43N 134.37 E
Konsei-Tōge 29 Fc 36.52N 139.22 E
Konsen-Daichi 29a Db 43.20N 144.50 E
Końskie 10 Qe 51.12N 20.26 E
Konstantinovka 16 Je 48.29N 37.43 E
Konstantinovsk 16 Lf 47.35N 41.05 E
Konstanz 10 Fi 47.40N 9.11 E
Kontagora 31 Hg 10.24N 5.29 E
Kontcha 34 Hd 7.58N 12.14 E
Kontich 12 Gc 51.08N 4.27 E
Kontiolahti 7 Ge 62.46N 29.51 E
Kontiomäki 7 Gd 64.21N 28.09 E
Kontum 25 Lf 14.21N 108.00 E
Kontum, Plateau de- 25 Lf 13.55N 108.05 E
Konusin, Mys- 7 Kc 67.10N 43.50 E
Konya 22 Ff 37.52N 32.31 E
Konya Ovası 24 Ed 37.30N 33.20 E
Konz 12 Ie 49.42N 6.35 E
Konza 36 Gc 1.45 S 37.07 E
Konžakovski Kamen, Gora- 5 Ld 59.38N 59.08 E
Koocanusa, Lake- 46 Hb 48.45N 115.15W
Kook, Punta- 65d Ab 27.08 S 109.26W
Koolau Range 65a Db 21.21N 157.47W
Koonga/Konga 8 Jf 58.34N 24.00 E
Koorda 59 Df 30.50 S 117.29 E
Koosa 8 Lf 58.33N 27.07 E
Kootenay Lake 46 Gb 49.35N 116.50W
Kootenay River 38 He 49.15N 117.39W
Kopa 18 Jc 43.31N 75.48 E
Kopaonik 15 Df 43.15N 20.50 E
Kópasker 7a Ca 66.18N 16.27W
Kópavogur 7a Bb 64.06N 21.55W
Kopejsk 19 Gd 55.08N 61.39 E
Koper 14 He 45.33N 13.44 E
Kopervik 7 Ag 59.17N 5.18 E
Kopetdag, Hrebet- 21 Hf 37.45N 58.15 E
Kop Geçidi 24 Ib 40.01N 40.28 E
Ko Phangan 25 Jg 9.45N 100.00 E
Köping 7 Dg 59.31N 16.00 E
Köpingsvik 8 Gh 56.53N 16.43 E
Kopjevo 20 Df 54.59N 89.55 E
Kopliku 15 Cg 42.13N 19.26 E
Köpmanholmen 7 Ee 63.10N 18.34 E
Koporje 8 Me 59.40N 29.08 E
Koporski Zaliv 8 Me 59.45N 28.45 E
Koppal 25 Fe 15.21N 76.09 E
Koppang 7 Cf 61.34N 11.04 E
Koppány 10 Oj 46.35N 18.26 E
Kopparberg 8 Fe 59.52N 14.59 E
Kopparberg [2] 7 Df 61.00N 14.30 E
Kopparstenarna 8 Hf 58.32N 19.20 E
Koppom 8 Ee 59.43N 12.09 E
Koprivnica 14 Kd 46.10N 16.50 E
Kopru 24 Dd 36.49N 31.10 E
Köprüören 15 Mj 39.30N 29.47 E
Korab 5 Ig 41.44N 20.32 E
Korablino 7 Jj 53.57N 40.00 E
Korahe 35 Gd 6.36N 44.16 E
Korak 64a Bc 7.21N 134.34 E
Koralpe 14 Id 46.45N 15.00 E
Koramlik 27 Ed 37.32N 85.42 E
Korana 14 Je 45.30N 15.35 E
Korangi 25 Dd 24.47N 67.08 E
Koraput 25 Ge 18.49N 82.43 E
Korba 25 Gd 22.21N 82.41 E
Korbach 10 Ee 51.17N 8.52 E
Körby 8 Ei 55.51N 13.39 E
Korça 15 Di 40.37N 20.46 E
Korčula 14 Kh 42.57N 16.55 E
Korčula 14 Lh 42.58N 17.08 E
Korčulanski Kanal 14 Kg 43.03N 16.40 E
Kordān 24 Ne 35.56N 50.50 E
Kordel 12 Ie 49.50N 6.38 E
Kordestān [3] 23 Gb 35.30N 47.00 E
Kord Kūy 23 Hb 36.48N 54.07 E
Kordun 14 Je 45.10N 15.35 E
Korea Bay (EN)=Sŏjosŏn-man 21 Of 39.15N 125.00 E
Korean Peninsula (EN) 21 Of 35.30N 125.30 E
Korea Strait (EN)=Taehan-Haehyŏp 21 Of 34.40N 129.00 E
Korea Strait (EN)=Tsushima-Kaikyō 21 Of 34.40N 129.00 E
Korec 16 Ed 50.37N 27.10 E
Korem 35 Fc 12.30N 39.32 E
Korenovsk 19 Df 45.28N 39.28 E
Korf 20 Ld 60.18N 166.01 E
Korfovski 20 Ig 48.11N 135.04 E
Korgen 7 Cc 66.05N 13.50 E
Kõrgesaare/Kyrgesare 8 Je 59.00N 22.25 E
Korhogo 31 Gh 9.27N 5.38W
Korhogo [3] 34 Dd 9.35N 5.55W
Koribundu 34 Cd 7.43N 11.42W
Korienzé 34 Eb 15.24N 3.47W
Korinthiakós Kólpos=Corinth, Gulf of- (EN) 5 Ih 38.12N 22.30 E
Kórinthos 15 Fl 37.55N 22.53 E
Kórinthos = Corinth (EN) 15 Fl 37.55N 22.53 E
Korinthou, Dhiórix- = Corinth Canal (EN) 15 Fl 37.57N 22.58 E
Koriolei 31 Lh 1.48N 44.30 E
Kőrishegy 10 Ni 47.12N 17.49 E
Koritnik 15 Dg 42.05N 20.34 E
Kōriyama 27 Pd 37.24N 140.23 E
Korjakskaja Sopka, Vulkan- 21 Rd 53.20N 158.47 E
Korjakski Nacionalny okrug [3] 20 Le 60.00N 163.00 E
Korjakskoje Nagorje=Koryak Range (EN) 21 Tc 62.30N 172.00 E
Korjažma 19 Ec 61.18N 47.07 E
Korjukovka 16 Hd 51.47N 32.17 E
Korkino 17 Ji 54.54N 61.25 E
Korkodon 20 Kd 64.43N 154.05 E
Korkuteli 24 Dd 37.04N 30.13 E
Korla 22 Ke 41.44N 86.09 E
Körmend 10 Mi 47.01N 16.36 E
Kormy, Gora- 20 Fd 62.15N 106.08 E
Kornati 14 Jg 43.49N 15.20 E
Kornejevka 17 Ni 54.01N 68.27 E
Kornešty 15 Kb 47.23N 28.00 E
Korneuburg 14 Kb 48.21N 16.20 E
Kórnik 10 Nd 52.17N 17.04 E
Kornsjø 7 Cg 58.57N 11.39 E
Koro 34 Ec 14.05N 3.04W
Koroba 59 Ia 5.40 S 142.45 E
Koroča 16 Jd 50.50N 37.13 E
Köroğlu Dağları 23 Da 40.40N 32.35 E
Köroğlu Tepe 24 Db 40.31N 31.53 E
Korogwe 36 Gd 5.09 S 38.29 E
Koro Island 57 If 17.32 S 179.42 E
Koroit 59 Ig 38.17 S 142.22 E
Korolevo 10 Th 48.08N 23.07 E
Korolevu 63d Ac 18.12 S 177.53 E
Korom, Bahr 35 Bc 10.35N 19.45 E
Koromiri 64p Cc 21.15 S 159.43W
Koronadal 26 He 6.12N 125.01 E
Korónia, Límni- 15 Gi 40.40N 23.10 E
Koronowo 10 Nc 53.19N 17.57 E
Koronowski e, Jezioro- 10 Nc 53.22N 17.55 E
Koror 57 Ed 7.20N 134.30 E
Koror 58 Ed 7.20N 134.29 E
Körös 10 Qj 46.43N 20.12 E
Koro Sea 61 Ec 18.00 S 180.00
Korosten 6 Ie 50.57N 28.39 E
Korostyšev 16 Fd 50.18N 29.05 E
Korotaiha 17 Jb 68.55N 60.55 E
Koro Toro 31 Ig 16.05N 18.30 E
Korovin Volcano 40a Db 52.22N 174.10W
Korpijärvi 8 Lc 61.15N 27.10 E
Korpilahti 7 Fe 62.01N 25.33 E
Korpo/Korppoo 8 Id 60.10N 21.35 E
Korppoo/Korpo 8 Id 60.10N 21.35 E
Korsakov 20 Jg 46.37N 142.51 E
Korshäs 7 Ee 62.47N 21.12 E
Korsholm/Mustasaari 8 Ia 63.05N 21.43 E
Korso 8 Kd 60.21N 25.06 E
Korsør 7 Ci 55.20N 11.09 E
Korsun-Ševčenkovski 16 Ge 49.26N 31.18 E
Korsze 10 Rb 54.10N 21.09 E
Kortemark 12 Fc 51.02N 3.02 E
Kortrijk/Courtrai 11 Jd 50.50N 3.16 E
Koruçam Burnu 24 Ee 35.24N 32.56 E
Korucu 15 Kj 39.28N 27.22 E
Koru Dağ 15 Ji 40.42N 26.45 E
Koryak Range (EN)=Korjakskoje Nagorje 21 Tc 62.30N 172.00 E
Korzybie 10 Mb 54.18N 16.50 E
Kos 15 Km 36.53N 27.18 E
Kos 15 Km 36.50N 27.10 E
Kosa 17 Gg 59.56N 55.01 E
Kosa 17 Gf 60.11N 55.10 E
Kosai 29 Ed 34.43N 137.30 E
Kosaja Gora 16 Jb 54.09N 37.31 E
Kosaka 29 Ga 40.20N 140.44 E
Kō-Saki 29 Ad 34.05N 129.13 E
Ko Samui 25 Jg 9.30N 99.58 E
Kosan-ŭp 27 Md 38.51N 127.25 E
Kosčagyl 16 Rf 46.52N 53.47 E
Kościan 10 Md 52.06N 16.38 E
Kościerzyna 10 Nb 54.08N 18.00 E
Kosciusko 45 Lj 32.58N 89.35W
Kosciusko, Mount- 57 Fg 36.27 S 148.16 E
Kose/Koze 8 Ke 59.11N 25.05 E
Köse Dağ 24 Gb 40.06N 37.58 E
Kosha 35 Ea 20.49N 30.32 E
Koshigaya 29 Fd 35.55N 139.45 E
Koshiji 29 Fc 37.24N 138.45 E
Koshiki-Kaikyō 29 Bf 31.45N 130.05 E
Koshiki Rettō 27 Me 31.45N 129.45 E
Koshimizu 29a Db 43.51N 144.25 E
Kōshoku 28 Of 36.38N 138.06 E
Kōshyū Seamount (EN) 29 Df 31.35N 135.50 E
Košice 6 If 48.43N 21.15 E
Kosjerić 15 Cf 44.00N 19.55 E
Kosju 17 Ic 66.18N 59.53 E
Kosju 17 Id 65.38N 58.59 E
Köşk 15 Ll 37.51N 28.03 E
Koski 8 Jd 60.39N 23.09 E
Koskolovo 8 Me 59.34N 28.30 E
Koslan 19 Ec 63.29N 48.52 E
Kosma 17 Dd 65.43N 49.50 E
Kosmaj 15 De 44.28N 20.33 E
Kosŏng 27 Md 38.40N 128.19 E
Kosov 15 Ia 48.15N 25.08 E
Kosovo 15 Eg 42.40N 21.05 E
Kosovo [3] 15 Dg 42.35N 21.00 E
Kosovska Mitrovica 15 Dg 42.53N 20.52 E
Kosrae (Kusaie) 57 Hd 5.19N 162.59 E
Kossol Passage 64a Bb 7.52N 134.36 E
Kossol Reef 64a Bb 7.57N 134.41 E
Kossou, Barrage de- 34 Dd 7.01N 5.29W
Kossovo 16 Dc 52.47N 25.10 E
Kostajnica 14 Ke 45.13N 16.33 E
Kostenec 15 Gg 42.16N 23.49 E
Koster 37 De 25.57 S 26.42 E
Kosteröarna 8 Df 58.55N 11.05 E
Kostjukoviči 16 Hc 53.23N 32.06 E
Kostjukovka 16 Gc 52.32N 30.58 E
Kostolac 15 Ee 44.44N 21.12 E
Kostopol 16 Ed 50.53N 26.29 E
Kostriževka 15 Ia 48.31N 25.45 E
Kostroma 6 Kd 57.47N 40.59 E
Kostromskaja Oblast [3] 19 Ed 58.30N 44.00 E
Kostrzyń 10 Nd 52.25N 17.14 E
Kostrzyn 10 Kd 52.37N 14.39 E
Kosva 17 Hg 58.50N 56.45 E
Koszalin 10 Mb 54.12N 16.09 E
Koszalin [2] 10 Mb 54.10N 16.10 E
Kőszeg 10 Mi 47.23N 16.33 E
Kota 22 Jg 25.16N 75.55 E
Kotaagung 26 Dh 5.30 S 104.38 E
Kota Baharu 22 Mi 6.08N 102.15 E
Kotabaru 26 Gg 3.14 S 116.13 E
Kotabumi 22 Mj 4.50 S 104.54 E
Kotadabok 26 Dg 0.30 S 104.33 E
Kota Kinabalu 22 Ni 5.59N 116.04 E
Kotamobagu 26 Hf 0.46N 124.19 E
Ko Tao 25 Jf 10.05N 99.52 E
Kotari 14 Jf 44.05N 15.30 E
Ko Tarutau 25 Jg 6.35N 99.40 E
Kota Tinggi 26 Df 1.44N 103.54 E
Kotel 15 Jg 42.53N 26.27 E
Kotelnič 19 Ed 58.20N 48.20 E
Kotelnikovo 16 Mf 47.38N 43.09 E
Kotelny, Ostrov- 21 Pb 75.45N 138.44 E
Kotelva 16 Id 50.03N 34.45 E
Köthen 10 He 51.45N 11.58 E
Kotido 36 Fb 3.00N 34.09 E
Kotjužany 29 Gb 47.50N 28.27 E
Kotka 7 Gf 60.28N 26.55 E
Kot Kapūra 25 Eb 30.35N 74.54 E
Kotlas 6 Kc 61.16N 46.35 E
Kotlenik 15 Df 43.51N 20.42 E
Kotlenski prohod 15 Jg 42.53N 26.27 E
Kotlik 40 Gd 63.02N 163.33W
Kotlin, Ostrov- 8 Md 60.00N 29.45 E
Kotly 8 Me 59.30N 28.48 E
Kotobi 34 Ed 6.42N 4.08W
Kotohira 29 Cd 34.11N 133.48 E
Koton Karifi 34 Gd 8.06N 6.48 E
Kotor 15 Bg 42.25N 18.46 E
Kotorosl 7 Jh 57.38N 39.57 E
Kotorska, Boka- 15 Bg 42.25N 18.40 E
Kotor Varoš 14 Lf 44.37N 17.22 E
Kotouba 34 Ed 8.41N 3.12W
Kotovo 19 Ee 50.18N 44.48 E
Kotovsk [Mold.-U.S.S.R.] 16 Ff 46.49N 28.33 E
Kotovsk [R.S.F.S.R.] 19 Ee 52.35N 41.32 E
Kotovsk [Ukr.-U.S.S.R.] 19 Cf 47.43N 29.33 E
Kotra 10 Uc 53.32N 24.17 E
Kotri 25 Dc 25.22N 68.18 E
Kötschach 14 Gd 46.40N 13.00 E
Kottayam 25 Fg 9.35N 76.31 E
Kotto 30 Jh 4.14N 22.02 E
Kotton 35 Id 9.37N 50.32 E
Kotu 65b Ba 19.57 S 174.48W
Kotu Group 57 Jg 20.00 S 174.45W
Kotuj 21 Mb 71.55N 102.05 E
Kotujkan 20 Fb 70.40N 103.25 E
Koturdepe 16 Rj 39.26N 53.40 E
Kotzebue 39 Cc 66.53N 162.39W
Kotzebue Sound 38 Cc 66.20N 163.00W
Kouandé 34 Fc 10.20N 1.42 E
Kouango 35 Be 4.58N 19.59 E
Kouba Modounga 35 Bb 15.40N 18.15 E
Koudougou 31 Gg 11.44N 4.31W
Kouéré 34 Ec 10.27N 3.59W
Koufália 15 Fi 40.47N 22.35 E
Koufonísion [Grc.] 15 Jo 34.56N 26.10 E
Koufonísion [Grc.] 15 Im 36.55N 25.35 E
Koufonísiou, Stenón- 15 Jo 35.00N 26.10 E
Kouilou [3] 36 Bc 4.00 S 12.00 E
Kouilou 30 Ii 4.28 S 11.41 E
Koukdjuak 42 Kc 66.47N 73.10W
Kouki 35 Bd 7.10N 17.18 E
Koukourou 35 Cd 7.12N 20.02 E
Koulamoutou 36 Bc 1.08 S 12.29 E
Koulikoro 34 Dc 12.51N 7.34W
Koulountou 34 Cc 13.15N 13.37W
Koumac 58 Hg 20.30 S 164.12 E
Koumac, Grand Récif de- 63b Be 20.32 S 164.04 E
Koumbi-Saleh 32 Ff 15.47N 7.58W
Koumi 29 Fc 36.05N 138.28 E
Koumpentoum 34 Cc 13.59N 14.34W
Koumra 35 Bd 8.55N 17.33 E
Koundara 31 Fg 12.29N 13.18W
Koundian 34 Cc 13.08N 10.42W
Kounoúpoi 15 Jm 36.32N 26.27 E
Kounradski 19 Hf 46.57N 75.01 E
Kounta 34 Eb 17.30N 0.40W
Koupéla 34 Ec 12.11N 0.21W
Kouqian → Yongji 28 Ic 43.40N 126.30 E
Kourou 54 Hb 5.09N 52.39W
Kouroussa 34 Dc 10.39N 9.53W
Koury 34 Ec 12.10N 4.48W
Koussané 34 Cc 14.52N 11.15W
Kousséri 34 Ic 12.05N 15.02 E
Koussi, Emi- 30 Ig 19.55N 18.30 E
Koutiala 31 Gg 12.23N 5.27W
Koutoumo 63b Cf 22.40 S 167.32 E
Koutous 34 Hc 14.30N 10.00 E
Kouvola 7 Gf 60.52N 26.42 E
Kouyou 36 Cc 0.45 S 16.38 E
Kova 20 Fe 58.20N 100.20 E
Kovač 15 Cf 43.31N 19.07 E
Kovačica 15 Dd 45.06N 20.38 E
Koval 10 Pd 52.31N 19.10 E
Kovalevka 15 Nc 46.42N 30.31 E
Kovarskas/Kavarskas 8 Ki 55.24N 25.03 E
Kovdor 19 Db 67.33N 30.25 E
Kovdozero, Ozero- 7 Hc 66.47N 32.00 E
Kovel 19 Ce 51.13N 24.43 E
Kovenskaja 17 Mf 61.24N 67.39 E
Kovin 15 De 44.45N 20.59 E
Kovinskaja Grjada 20 Fe 57.15N 101.00 E
Kovrov 19 Ed 56.24N 41.20 E
Kovylkino 7 Ki 54.02N 43.58 E
Kowŏn 27 Md 39.26N 127.15 E
Kowtal-e Do Rāh 23 Lb 36.07N 71.15 E
Kowt-e 'Ashrow 23 Kc 34.27N 68.48 E
Kōyama 29 Bf 31.19N 130.57 E
Köyceğiz 24 Cd 36.55N 28.43 E
Köycegiz Gölü 15 Lm 36.55N 28.40 E
Koyoshi-Gawa 29 Gb 39.24N 140.01 E
Koyuk 40 Gd 64.56N 161.08W
Koyukuk 38 Dc 64.56N 157.30W
Kozaklı 24 Fc 39.13N 34.49 E
Kozan 24 Fd 37.27N 35.49 E
Kozáni 15 Ei 40.18N 21.47 E
Kozara 14 Ke 45.00N 16.55 E
Kozawa 29a Bb 42.58N 140.40 E
Koze/Kose 8 Ke 59.11N 25.05 E
Kozelsk 19 De 54.01N 35.46 E
Koževnikovo 20 De 56.18N 84.00 E
Kozhikode → Calicut 22 Jh 11.19N 75.46 E
Kozienice 10 Re 51.35N 21.33 E
Kožim 17 Id 65.43N 59.31 E
Kožim 17 Id 65.45N 59.15 E
Kozima 14 He 45.37N 13.56 E
Kozjak 15 Eh 41.06N 21.54 E
Kozloduj 15 Gf 43.47N 23.44 E
Kozlovka 7 Li 55.52N 48.13 E
Kozlovščina 10 Vc 53.14N 25.20 E
Kozlu 24 Db 41.25N 31.46 E
Kozluk 24 Ic 38.11N 41.29 E
Koźmin 10 Ne 51.50N 17.28 E
Kozmodemjansk 7 Lh 56.20N 46.36 E
Kožozero, Ozero- 7 Je 63.05N 38.05 E
Kożuchów 10 Le 51.45N 15.35 E
Kožuf 15 Fh 41.09N 22.10 E
Kōzu-Shima 27 Oe 34.15N 139.10 E
Kožva 17 Hd 65.07N 56.57 E
Kožva 17 Hd 65.10N 57.00 E
Kozyrevsk 20 Ke 55.59N 159.59 E
Kpalimé 34 Fd 6.54N 0.38 E
Kpandu 34 Fd 7.00N 0.18 E
Kpessi 34 Fd 8.04N 1.16 E
Kra, Isthmus of- (EN)=Kra, Khokhok- 21 Lh 10.20N 99.00 E
Kra, Khokhok-=Kra, Isthmus of- (EN) 21 Lh 10.20N 99.00 E
Kraba 15 Ch 41.12N 19.59 E
Krabbfjärden 8 Gf 58.45N 17.40 E
Krabi 25 Jg 8.05N 98.53 E
Krabit, Mali i- 15 Cg 42.07N 19.59 E
Kra Buri 25 Jf 10.24N 98.47 E
Krâchéh 22 Mh 12.29N 106.01 E
Kragerø 7 Bg 58.52N 9.25 E
Kragujevac 15 De 44.01N 20.55 E
Kraichbach 12 Ke 49.22N 8.31 E
Kraichgau 10 Eg 49.10N 8.50 E
Kraichtal 12 Ke 49.07N 8.46 E
Krajina 14 Kf 44.45N 16.35 E
Krajina 15 Fe 44.10N 22.30 E
Krajište 15 Fg 42.35N 22.25 E
Krajnovka 16 Oh 43.57N 47.24 E
Kråka 8 Ca 63.28N 9.00 E
Krakatau, Gunung- 21 Mj 6.07 S 105.24 E
Krak des Chevaliers 24 Ge 34.46N 36.19 E
Krakovec 10 Tg 49.56N 23.13 E
Kraków [2] 10 Pf 50.05N 20.00 E
Kraków 6 He 50.03N 19.58 E
Kraków-Nowa Huta 10 Qf 50.04N 20.05 E
Krakowsko-Częstochowska, Wyżyna- 10 Pf 50.50N 19.15 E
Kralendijk 50 Bf 12.10N 68.16W
Kraljevica 14 Ie 45.16N 14.34 E
Kraljevo 15 Df 43.44N 20.43 E
Kralupy nad Vltavou 10 Kf 50.14N 14.19 E
Kramatorsk 16 Je 48.43N 37.32 E
Kramfors 7 De 62.56N 17.47 E
Krammer 12 Gc 51.38N 4.15 E
Kranenburg 12 Ic 51.47N 6.01 E
Kranidhion 15 Gl 37.23N 23.09 E
Kranj 14 Id 46.14N 14.22 E
Krapina 14 Jd 46.10N 15.53 E
Krapkowice 10 Nf 50.29N 17.56 E
Kras=Karst (EN) 5 Hf 45.48N 14.00 E
Krasavino 19 Ec 60.59N 46.28 E
Krasiczyn 10 Sg 49.48N 22.39 E
Krasilov 16 Ee 49.37N 26.59 E
Kraskino 28 Kc 42.44N 130.48 E
Kraslava/Krāslava 7 Gi 55.54N 27.10 E
Krāslava/Kraslava 7 Gi 55.54N 27.10 E
Krasnaja Poljana 16 Lh 43.40N 40.12 E
Kraśnik 10 Sf 50.56N 22.13 E
Kraśnik Fabryczny, Kraśnik- 10 Sf 50.58N 22.12 E
Kraśnik-Kraśnik Fabryczny 10 Sf 50.58N 22.12 E
Krasnoarmejsk [Kaz.-U.S.S.R.] 19 Ge 53.57N 69.43 E
Krasnoarmejsk [R.S.F.S.R.] 19 Ee 51.02N 45.42 E
Krasnoarmejsk [Ukr.-U.S.S.R.] 16 Je 48.11N 37.12 E
Krasnoarmejski 20 Mc 69.37N 172.02 E
Krasnodar 6 Jf 45.02N 39.00 E
Krasnodarski Kraj [3] 19 Df 45.20N 39.30 E
Krasnodon 16 Ke 48.17N 39.44 E
Krasnogorodskoje 8 Mh 56.47N 28.18 E
Krasnogorsk [R.S.F.S.R.] 20 Jg 48.26N 142.10 E
Krasnogorsk [R.S.F.S.R.] 7 Ii 55.51N 37.20 E
Krasnogorski 17 Ji 54.36N 61.15 E
Krasnograd 19 Df 49.22N 35.27 E
Krasnogvardejsk 18 Fe 39.45N 67.16 E
Krasnogvardejskoje 16 Lg 45.49N 41.31 E
Krasnoholmski 17 Gh 56.02N 55.05 E
Krasnoilsk 15 Ia 48.02N 25.48 E
Krasnojarsk 22 Ld 56.01N 92.50 E
Krasnojarski 17 Ij 51.58N 59.57 E
Krasnojarski Kraj [3] 20 Ee 57.30N 95.00 E
Krasnojarskoje Vodohranilišče 20 Ee 55.05N 91.30 E
Krasnoje 10 Ug 49.49N 24.39 E
Krasnoje Selo 7 Hg 59.43N 30.03 E
Krasnoje Znamja 18 Df 36.50N 62.29 E
Krasnokamensk 20 Gf 50.00N 118.05 E
Krasnokamsk 19 Fd 58.04N 55.45 E
Krasnokutsk 19 He 52.59N 75.59 E
Krasnolesje 8 Jj 54.23N 22.25 E
Krasnolesny 16 Kd 51.52N 39.35 E
Krasnooktjabrski [Kirg.-U.S.S.R.] 18 Jc 42.45N 74.20 E
Krasnooktjabrski [R.S.F.S.R.] 7 Lh 56.43N 47.37 E
Krasnooskolskoje Vodohranilišče 16 Je 49.25N 37.35 E
Krasnoostrovski 8 Md 60.12N 28.39 E
Krasnoperekopsk 19 Df 45.57N 33.47 E
Krasnorečenski 28 Mb 44.38N 135.15 E
Krasnoščelje 7 Ic 67.23N 37.02 E
Krasnoselki 10 Uc 53.14N 24.30 E
Krasnoselkup 20 Dc 65.41N 82.28 E
Krasnoslobodsk [R.S.F.S.R.] 16 Ne 48.40N 44.31 E
Krasnoslobodsk [R.S.F.S.R.] 7 Ki 54.27N 43.47 E
Krasnoturinsk 19 Gd 59.46N 60.18 E
Krasnoufimsk 19 Fd 56.37N 57.46 E
Krasnouralsk 19 Gd 58.24N 60.03 E
Krasnousolski 19 Fe 53.54N 56.29 E
Krasnovišersk 19 Fc 60.23N 57.03 E
Krasnovodsk 22 He 40.00N 53.00 E
Krasnovodskaja Oblast [3] 19 Fh 39.50N 55.00 E
Krasnovodski Poluostrov 16 Rc 40.30N 53.15 E
Krasnovodski Zaliv 16 Rj 39.50N 53.15 E
Krasnozatonski 19 Fc 61.41N 51.01 E
Krasnozavodsk 7 Jh 56.29N 38.13 E
Krasnoznamensk [Kaz.-U.S.S.R.] 19 Ge 51.03N 69.30 E
Krasnoznamensk [R.S.F.S.R.] 8 Jj 54.52N 22.27 E
Krasny Čikoj 20 Ff 50.25N 108.45 E
Krasny Holm 7 Ig 58.04N 37.09 E
Krasny Jar [R.S.F.S.R.] 20 De 57.07N 84.40 E
Krasny Jar [R.S.F.S.R.] 19 Hd 55.14N 72.56 E
Krasnyje Barrikady 16 Of 46.13N 47.50 E
Krasnyje Okny 15 Mb 47.34N 29.23 E
Krasny Kut 19 Ee 50.58N 46.58 E
Krasny Liman 16 Je 48.59N 37.47 E
Krasny Luč 16 Ke 48.09N 38.57 E
Krasny Oktjabr 19 Gd 55.37N 64.48 E
Krasny Profintern 7 Jh 57.47N 40.29 E
Krasnystaw 10 Tf 50.59N 23.10 E
Krasny Sulin 16 Lf 47.53N 40.09 E
Kratovo 15 Fg 42.05N 22.12 E
Kraulshavn 41 Gd 74.10N 57.00W
Krâvanh, Chuŏr Phnum- 21 Mh 12.00N 103.15 E
Krawang 26 Eh 6.19 S 107.17 E
Krefeld 10 Ce 51.20N 6.34 E
Krefeld-Hüls 12 Ic 51.22N 6.31 E
Kremastá, Límni- 15 Ek 38.50N 21.30 E
Kremenchug Reservoir (EN) =Kremenčugskoje Vodohranilišče 5 Jf 49.20N 32.30 E
Kremenčug 6 Jf 49.04N 33.25 E
Kremenčugskoje Vodohranilišče=Kremenchug Reservoir (EN) 5 Jf 49.20N 32.30 E
Kremenec 16 Dd 50.06N 25.43 E
Kremennaja 16 Ke 49.03N 38.14 E
Kremmling 45 Cf 40.03N 106.24W
Krems 14 Jb 48.25N 15.36 E
Krems an der Donau 14 Jb 48.25N 15.36 E
Kremsmünster 14 Ib 48.03N 14.08 E
Krenitzin Islands 40a Eb 54.08N 166.00W
Kresta, Zaliv- 20 Nc 65.30N 179.00W
Krestcy 7 Hg 58.15N 32.31 E
Krestovy, Pereval- 16 Nh 42.32N 44.30 E
Kretek 26 Fh 7.59 S 110.19 E
Kretinga 7 Ei 55.55N 21.17 E
Kreuzau 12 Id 50.45N 6.29 E
Kreuzberg 10 Ff 50.22N 9.58 E
Kreuzlingen 14 Dc 47.39N 9.10 E
Kreuztal 10 Df 50.58N 7.59 E
Kría Vrísi 15 Fi 40.41N 22.18 E
Kribi 31 Hh 2.57N 9.55 E
Kričev 19 De 53.43N 31.43 E
Kričim 15 Hg 42.08N 24.31 E
Krim 14 Ie 45.56N 14.28 E
Krimml 14 Gc 47.13N 12.11 E
Krimpen aan den IJssel 12 Gc 51.55N 4.35 E
Kriós, Ákra- 5 Ih 35.14N 23.35 E
Krishna 21 Kh 15.57N 80.59 E
Krishnanagar 25 Hd 23.24N 88.30 E
Kristdala 8 Gg 57.24N 16.11 E
Kristiansand 6 Gd 58.10N 8.00 E
Kristianstad 7 Dh 56.02N 14.08 E
Kristianstad [2] 7 Ch 56.15N 14.00 E
Kristiansund 6 Gc 63.07N 7.45 E
Kristiinankaupunki/Kristinestad 7 Ee 62.17N 21.23 E
Kristineberg 7 Ed 65.04N 18.35 E
Kristinehamn 7 Dg 59.20N 14.07 E
Kristinestad/Kristiinankaupunki 7 Ee 62.17N 21.23 E
Kriti = Crete (EN) 5 Ih 35.15N 24.45 E
Kriti = Crete (EN) [2] 15 Hn 35.35N 25.00 E
Kritikón Pélagos = Crete, Sea of- (EN) 15 Hn 36.00N 25.00 E
Krivaja 14 Mf 44.27N 18.10 E
Kriva Palanka 15 Fg 42.12N 22.21 E
Kriviči 8 Lj 54.44N 27.20 E
Krivodol 15 Gf 43.23N 23.29 E
Krivoje Ozero 16 Gf 47.57N 30.21 E
Krivoj Rog 6 Jf 47.54N 33.21 E
Križevci 14 Kd 46.02N 16.32 E
Krk 14 Ie 45.05N 14.35 E
Krk 14 Ie 45.02N 14.35 E
Krka [Yugo.] 14 Jg 43.43N 15.51 E
Krka [Yugo.] 14 Je 45.53N 15.36 E
Krkonoše 10 Lf 50.46N 15.35 E
Krn 14 Hd 46.16N 13.40 E
Krndija 14 Le 45.27N 17.55 E
Krnjača, Beograd- 15 De 44.52N 20.28 E
Krnov 10 Nf 50.05N 17.41 E
Krobia 10 Me 51.47N 16.58 E
Krøderen 8 Cd 60.15N 9.40 E
Krokeai 15 Fm 36.53N 22.33 E
Krokek 8 Gf 58.40N 16.24 E
Kroken 7 Dd 65.22N 14.16 E

Index Symbols

[1] Independent Nation
[2] State, Region
[3] District, County
[4] Municipality
[5] Colony, Dependency
Continent
Physical Region
Historical or Cultural Region
Mount, Mountain
Volcano
Hill
Mountains, Mountain Range
Hills, Escarpment
Plateau, Upland
Pass, Gap
Plain, Lowland
Delta
Salt Flat
Valley, Canyon
Crater, Cave
Karst Features
Depression
Polder
Desert, Dunes
Forest, Woods
Heath, Steppe
Oasis
Cape, Point
Coast, Beach
Cliff
Peninsula
Isthmus
Sandbank
Island
Atoll
Rock, Reef
Islands, Archipelago
Rocks, Reefs
Coral Reef
Well, Spring
Geyser
River, Stream
Waterfall Rapids
River Mouth, Estuary
Lake
Salt Lake
Intermittent Lake
Reservoir
Swamp, Pond
Canal
Glacier
Ice Shelf, Pack Ice
Ocean
Sea
Gulf, Bay
Strait, Fjord
Lagoon
Bank
Seamount
Tablemount
Ridge
Shelf
Basin
Escarpment, Sea Scarp
Fracture
Trench, Abyss
National Park, Reserve
Point of Interest
Recreation Site
Cave, Cavern
Historic Site
Ruins
Wall, Walls
Church, Abbey
Temple
Scientific Station
Airport
Port
Lighthouse
Mine
Tunnel
Dam, Bridge

Krokom 7 De 63.20N 14.28 E
Krolevec 16 Hd 51.32N 33.30 E
Kroměříž 10 Ng 49.18N 17.22 E
Krompachy 10 Qh 48.56N 20.52 E
Kronach 10 Hf 50.14N 11.19 E
Krông Kaôh Kông 25 Kf 11.37N 102.59 E
Kronoberg [2] 7 Dh 56.40N 14.40 E
Kronockaja Sopka, Vulkan- 20 Lf 54.47N 160.35 E
Kronocki, Mys- 20 Lf 54.43N 162.07 E
Kronocki Zaliv 20 Lf 54.00N 161.00 E
Kronoki 20 Lf 54.33N 161.14 E
Kronprins Christian Land 41 Jb 80.45N 22.00W
Kronprinsesse Mærtha Kyst 66 Bf 72.00S 7.30W
Kronprins Frederiks Bjerge 41 Ie 67.20N 34.00W
Kronprins Olav Kyst 66 Ee 68.30S 42.30 E
Kronštadt 19 Cc 60.01N 29.44 E
Kroonstad 31 Jk 27.46S 27.12 E
Kropotkin [R.S.F.S.R.] 19 Ef 45.26N 40.34 E
Kropotkin [R.S.F.S.R.] 20 Ge 58.36N 115.27 E
Kroppefjäll 8 Ef 58.40N 12.13 E
Krośniewice 10 Pd 52.16N 19.10 E
Krosno 10 Rg 49.42N 21.46 E
Krosno [2] 10 Rg 49.40N 21.45 E
Krosno Odrzańskie 10 Ld 52.04N 15.05 E
Krossfjorden 8 Ad 60.10N 5.05 E
Krotoszyn 10 Ne 51.42N 17.26 E
Kroviga, Gora- 20 Ed 60.40N 91.30 E
Krško 14 Je 45.58N 15.28 E
Krstača 15 Dg 42.58N 20.08 E
Krugersdorp 31 Jk 26.05S 27.35 E
Krui 26 Dh 5.11S 103.56 E
Kruibeke 12 Gc 51.10N 4.19 E
Kruiningen 12 Gc 51.27N 4.02 E
Kruja 15 Ch 41.30N 19.48 E
Krulevščina 8 Li 55.03N 27.52 E
Krumbach 10 Gh 48.15N 10.22 E
Krumovgrad 15 Ih 41.28N 25.39 E
Krung Thep=Bangkok (EN) 22 Mh 13.45N 100.31 E
Krupanj 15 Ce 44.22N 19.22 E
Krupinica 10 Oh 48.05N 18.54 E
Krupinská vrchovina 10 Ph 48.20N 19.15 E
Kruså 8 Cj 54.50N 9.25 E
Krušedol 15 Cd 45.07N 19.57 E
Kruševac 15 Ef 43.35N 21.20 E
Kruševo 15 Eh 41.22N 21.15 E
Krušné Hory=Ore Mountains (EN) 5 He 50.30N 13.15 E
Krustpils 8 Lh 56.29N 26.00 E
Kruzof 40 Le 57.10N 135.40W
Krym 16 Jg 45.23N 36.36 E
Krymsk 19 Dg 44.54N 37.57 E
Krymskaja Oblast [3] 19 Dg 45.15N 34.20 E
Krymskije Gory=Crimean Mountains (EN) 5 Jg 44.45N 34.30 E
Krymski Poluostrov=Crimea (EN) 5 Jf 45.00N 34.00 E
Krynica 10 Qg 49.25N 20.56 E
Krzemieniucha 10 Sb 54.12N 22.54 E
Krzepice 10 Of 50.58N 18.44 E
Krzna 10 Td 52.08N 23.31 E
Krzywiń 10 Me 51.58N 16.49 E
Krzyż 10 Md 52.53N 16.01 E
Ksar el Boukhari 32 Hb 35.53N 2.45 E
Ksar el Kebir 32 Fc 35.00N 5.59W
Ksar es Srhir 13 Gi 35.51N 5.34W
Ksenjevka 20 Gf 53.34N 118.44 E
Kšenski 16 Jd 51.52N 37.44 E
Ksour, Monts des- 32 Gc 32.45N 0.10W
Kū', Wādī al- 35 Dc 12.12N 25.43 E
Kuai He 28 Dh 33.09N 117.32 E
Kuala Belait 26 Ff 4.35N 114.11 E
Kuala Dungun 26 Df 4.47N 103.26 E
Kuala Kangsar 26 Df 4.46N 100.56 E
Kualakapuas 26 Fg 3.01S 114.21 E
Kuala Kerai 26 De 5.32N 102.12 E
Kualakurun 26 Fg 1.07S 113.53 E
Kualalangsa 26 Cf 4.32N 98.01 E
Kuala Lipis 26 Df 4.11N 102.03 E
Kuala Lumpur 22 Mi 3.10N 101.42 E
Kuala Pilah 26 Df 2.44N 102.15 E
Kuala Rompin 26 Df 2.49N 103.29 E
Kuala Terengganu 22 Mi 5.20N 103.08 E
Kuancheng 28 Ed 40.37N 118.31 E
Kuandang 26 Hf 0.52N 122.55 E
Kuandian 27 Lc 40.45N 124.48 E
Kuang-hsi-chuang-tsu Tzu-chih-ch'ü→Guangxi Zhuangzu Zizhiqu=Kwangsi Chuang (EN) [2] 27 Ig 24.00N 109.00 E
Kuang-tun Sheng→Guangdong Sheng=Kwangtung (EN) [2] 27 Jg 23.00N 113.00 E
Kuantan 26 Df 3.48N 103.20 E
Kuba 19 Eg 41.20N 48.35 E
Kuban 5 Jf 45.20N 37.30 E
Kuba-Shima 29b b 26.10N 127.15 E
Kubaysah 24 Jf 33.35N 42.37 E
Kubbum 35 Cc 11.47N 23.47 E
Kubena 7 Jg 59.37N 39.48 E
Kubenskoje, Ozero- 7 Jg 59.40N 39.30 E
Kubnja 7 Li 55.32N 48.28 E
Kubokawa 28 Lh 33.12N 133.08 E
Kubolta 15 Lb 47.48N 28.03 E
Kubrat 15 Jf 43.48N 26.30 E
Kubumesaai 26 Gf 1.31N 115.06 E
Kučaj 15 Ef 43.53N 21.44 E
Kučevo 15 Ee 44.29N 21.41 E
Kuching 22 Ni 1.33N 110.20 E
Kuchinoerabu-Shima 28 Ki 30.28N 130.10 E
Kuchinotsu 29 Be 32.36N 130.12 E
Kuçukçekmece 15 Li 40.59N 28.46 E
Küçükerenköy 24 Ee 35.22N 33.45 E
Küçükkuyu 15 Jj 39.32N 26.36 E
Küçuk Menderes 15 Kl 37.57N 27.16 E
Kučurgan 15 Mc 46.35N 29.55 E
Kudaka-Jima 29b Ab 26.10N 127.54 E
Kudamatsu 29 Bd 34.01N 131.53 E
Kudat 26 Ge 6.53N 116.50 E
Kudeb 8 Mg 57.30N 28.16 E
Kudirkos-Naumestis 8 Jj 54.43N 22.49 E
Kudowa-Zdrój 10 Mf 50.27N 16.20 E
Kudremukh 25 Ff 13.08N 75.16 E
Kudus 26 Fh 6.48S 110.50 E
Kudymkar 19 Fd 59.01N 54.37 E
Kuee Ruins 65a Fd 19.12N 155.23W
Kuei-chou Sheng→Guizhou Sheng=Kweichow (EN) [2] 27 If 27.00N 107.00 E
Kufi 24 Cc 38.10N 29.43 E
Kufrah, Wāḥāt al-=Kufra Oasis (EN) 30 Jf 24.10N 23.15 E
Kufra Oasis (EN)=Kufrah, Wāḥāt al- 30 Jf 24.10N 23.15 E
Kufstein 14 Gc 47.35N 12.10 E
Kuganavolok 7 Ie 62.16N 36.55 E
Kugmallit Bay 42 Ek 69.30N 133.20W
Kugojeja 16 Kf 46.33N 39.38 E
Kūh, Ra's al- 23 Id 25.48N 57.19 E
Kuḥaylī 35 Eb 19.29N 32.49 E
Kūhbonān 24 Qg 31.23N 56.19 E
Kūhdasht 24 Lf 33.32N 47.36 E
Kūh-e Būrh 24 Pi 27.22N 54.40 E
Kūh-e Gāvbūs 24 Oi 27.10N 54.00 E
Kūh-e Karkas 24 Nf 33.27N 51.48 E
Kūh-e Kārūn 24 Ng 31.27N 50.18 E
Kūhestak 24 Qi 26.47N 57.02 E
Kūhīn, Gardaneh-ye- 24 Md 36.23N 49.37 E
Kühlungsborn 10 Hb 54.09N 11.43 E
Kuhmo 7 Gd 64.08N 29.31 E
Kuhmoinen 8 Kc 61.34N 25.11 E
Kuhn 41 Kd 74.45N 19.45W
Kūhpāyeh 23 Ic 30.35N 57.15 E
Kūhpāyeh [Iran] 24 Of 32.43N 52.26 E
Kūhpāyeh [Iran] 24 Qg 30.43N 57.30 E
Kūhrān, Kūh-e- 23 Id 26.46N 58.12 E
Kuhtuj 20 Je 59.23N 143.10 E
Kuhva 8 Mg 57.17N 28.17 E
Kuiseb 37 Ad 23.00S 14.33 E
Kuishan Ding 27 Ig 22.32N 109.52 E
Kuito 31 Ij 12.23S 16.56 E
Kuiu 40 Me 57.45N 134.10W
Kuivaniemi 7 Fd 65.35N 25.11 E
Kujang 27 Md 39.52N 126.01 E
Kujawy 10 Od 52.45N 18.30 E
Kujawy 10 Od 52.45N 18.35 E
Kujbyšev 6 Le 53.12N 50.09 E
Kujbyšev [R.S.F.S.R.] 7 Li 55.01N 49.06 E
Kujbyšev [R.S.F.S.R.] 20 Ce 55.27N 78.29 E
Kujbyševskaja Oblast [3] 19 Fe 53.20N 50.30 E
Kujbyševski [Kaz.-U.S.S.R.] 19 Ge 53.15N 66.51 E
Kujbyševski [Tad.-U.S.S.R.] 18 Gf 37.53N 68.44 E
Kujbyševskoje Vodohranilišče=Kuybyshev Reservoir (EN) 5 Ke 53.50N 49.00 E
Kujeda 17 Gh 56.26N 55.35 E
Kujgan 19 Hf 45.22N 74.10 E
Kuji 28 Pd 40.11N 141.46 E
Kuji-Gawa 29 Gc 36.30N 140.37 E
Kujtun 20 Ff 54.21N 101.35 E
Kujūkuri-Hama 29 Gd 35.40N 140.30 E
Kujū-San 28 Kh 33.09N 131.15 E
Kūkalār, Kūh-e- 24 Ng 31.50N 50.53 E
Kukalaya, Rio- 49 Fg 13.39N 83.37W
Kukësi 15 Dg 42.05N 20.24 E
Kukkia 8 Kc 61.20N 24.40 E
Kukmor 7 Mh 56.13N 50.52 E
Kükürt Dağı 24 Ib 41.07N 41.27 E
Kula [Bul.] 15 Ff 43.53N 22.31 E
Kula [Tur.] 24 Cc 38.30N 28.40 E
Kula [Yugo.] 15 Cd 45.37N 19.32 E
Kulai 26 Df 1.40N 103.36 E
Kulanak 18 Jd 41.18N 75.34 E
Kulandy 19 Ff 46.08N 59.31 E
Kular 20 Ib 70.32N 134.26 E
Kular, Hrebet- 20 Ic 69.00N 133.30 E
Kulata 15 Gh 41.23N 23.22 E
Kulautuva 8 Jj 54.55N 23.43 E
Kulbus 35 Cc 14.24N 22.31 E
Kuldiga/Kuldīga 19 Cd 56.59N 21.59 E
Kuldīga/Kuldiga 19 Cd 56.59N 21.59 E
Kuldur 20 Ig 49.10N 131.40 E
Kulebaki 7 Ki 55.26N 42.32 E
Kulenjin 24 Me 35.40N 49.30 E
Kulen Vakuf 14 Kf 44.33N 16.06 E
Kulgera 58 Eg 25.50S 133.18 E
Kulikov 10 Ug 49.55N 24.06 E
Kulim 26 De 5.22N 100.34 E
Kuljab 19 Gh 37.55N 69.47 E
Kuljabskaja Oblast [3] 19 Gh 38.00N 69.40 E
Kullaa 8 Jc 61.28N 22.10 E
Kullen 7 Ch 56.18N 12.26 E
Kulmasa 34 Ed 9.35N 2.27W
Kulmbach 10 Hf 50.06N 11.27 E
Kuloj 7 Kf 61.03N 42.30 E
Kuloj [R.S.F.S.R.] 19 Eb 66.00N 43.30 E
Kuloj [R.S.F.S.R.] 7 Kf 61.01N 42.12 E
Kulp 24 Ic 38.30N 41.02 E
Kulsary 19 Ff 46.57N 54.02 E
Kultuk 20 Ff 51.44N 103.42 E
Kulu 20 Jd 62.15N 147.45 E
Kulu [India] 25 Fb 31.58N 77.06 E
Kulu [Tur.] 24 Ec 39.06N 33.05 E
Kulumadau 63a Ac 9.03S 152.43 E
Kulunda 20 Cf 52.35N 78.57 E
Kulundinskaja Step 20 Cf 52.45N 79.00 E
Kulundinskoje, Ozero- 20 Cf 53.00N 79.30 E
Kum 24 Bc 38.38N 27.32 E
Kum, Kūh-e- 24 Oh 29.55N 53.45 E
Kuma 29 Ce 33.39N 132.54 E
Kuma [R.S.F.S.R.] 17 Mg 59.33N 66.40 E
Kuma [R.S.F.S.R.] 7 Hc 66.15N 31.02 E
Kuma [U.S.S.R.] 5 Kg 44.56N 47.00 E
Kumagaya 28 Of 36.08N 139.23 E
Kumai [Indon.] 26 Fg 2.44S 111.43 E
Kumai [Indon.] 26 Fg 3.23S 112.33 E
Kumaishi 29a Ab 42.08N 139.59 E
Kumak 16 Vd 51.13N 60.08 E
Kumamoto 22 Pf 32.48N 130.43 E
Kumamoto Ken [2] 28 Kh 32.30N 130.50 E
Kumano 28 Nh 33.54N 136.05 E
Kumano-Gawa 29 De 33.45N 135.59 E
Kumano-Nada 29 Ee 34.00N 136.30 E
Kumanovo 15 Eg 42.08N 21.43 E
Kumara [N.Z.] 62 De 42.38S 171.11 E
Kumara [R.S.F.S.R.] 20 Hf 51.35N 126.45 E
Kumasi 31 Gh 6.41N 1.37W
Kumba 34 Ge 4.38N 9.25 E
Kumbakonam 25 Ff 10.58N 79.23 E
Kumbe 26 Lh 8.21S 140.13 E
Kumbo 34 Hd 6.12N 10.40 E
Kumboro Cape 63a Cb 7.18S 157.32 E
Kŭmch'ŏn 28 Ie 38.10N 126.30 E
Kum-Dag 19 Fh 39.13N 54.40 E
Kumdah 33 Ie 20.23N 45.05 E
Kume-Jima [Jap.] 27 Mf 26.20N 126.45 E
Kumertau 19 Fe 52.46N 55.47 E
Kumhwa 28 Ie 38.17N 127.28 E
Kumihama 29 Dd 35.36N 134.54 E
Kuminski 19 Gd 58.40N 65.55 E
Kumköy (Kilyos) 15 Mh 41.15N 29.02 E
Kumkuduk 27 Fc 40.15N 91.55 E
Kumkurgan 18 Ff 37.50N 67.35 E
Kumla 7 Dg 59.08N 15.08 E
Kumlinge 8 Id 60.15N 20.45 E
Kumluca 24 Dd 36.22N 30.18 E
Kummerower See 10 Ic 53.49N 12.52 E
Kumo/Kokemäki 7 Ff 61.15N 22.21 E
Kumo-Manyčski Kanal 16 Ng 45.27N 44.38 E
Kumon Taung 21 Lg 26.30N 96.50 E
Kumora 20 Ge 55.56N 111.13 E
Kumru 24 Gb 40.53N 37.17 E
Kumu 36 Eb 3.04N 25.09 E
Kumuh 16 Oh 42.11N 47.07 E
Kumukahi, Cape- 60 Od 19.31N 154.49W
Kumul/Hami 22 Le 42.48N 93.27 E
Kümüx 27 Ec 42.15N 88.10 E
Kumzār 24 Qj 26.20N 56.25 E
Kunashiri-Tō/Kunašir, Ostrov- 21 Qe 44.05N 145.51 E
Kunašir, Ostrov-/Kunashiri-Tō 21 Qe 44.05N 145.51 E
Kunašhirski Proliv=Nemuro Strait (EN) 20 Jh 43.50N 145.30 E
Kunchaung 25 Jd 23.50N 96.35 E
Kunda 7 Gg 59.30N 26.30 E
Kunda Jõgi 8 Le 59.25N 26.27 E
Kundelungu, Monts- 36 Ed 9.30S 28.00 E
Kundiawa 59 Ia 6.00S 145.00 E
Kunduchi 36 Gd 6.40S 39.13 E
Kunduk 15 Md 45.51N 29.38 E
Kunduk→Kogilnik 15 Md 45.51N 29.38 E
Kunduk→Sasyk, Ozero- 16 Fg 45.45N 29.40 E
Kunene 30 Ij 17.20S 11.50 E
Kunene (EN)=Cunene 30 Ij 17.20S 11.50 E
Künes/Xinyuan 27 Dc 43.24N 83.18 E
Künes He 27 Dc 43.32N 82.29 E
Kungälv 7 Ch 57.52N 11.58 E
Kungej-Alatau, Hrebet- 19 Hg 42.50N 77.15 E
Küngmiut 41 Ie 65.50N 36.45W
Kungrad 19 Fg 43.06N 58.54 E
Kungsbacka 7 Ch 57.29N 12.04 E
Kungsbackafjorden 8 Eg 57.25N 12.04 E
Kungshamn 8 Df 58.21N 11.15 E
Kungsör 8 Ge 59.25N 16.05 E
Kungu 36 Cb 2.47N 19.12 E
Kungur 19 Fd 57.25N 56.57 E
Kunhegyes 10 Qi 47.22N 20.38 E
Kunhing 25 Jd 21.18N 98.26 E
Kunigami 29b Bb 26.45N 128.11 E
Kunigami-Misaki 29b Bb 27.26N 128.43 E
Kunimi-Dake 29 Be 32.33N 131.01 E
Kunisaki 29 Be 33.34N 131.45 E
Kunisaki-Hantō 29 Be 33.30N 131.40 E
Kunja 7 Hh 57.09N 31.10 E
Kunja-Urgenč 19 Fg 42.20N 59.12 E
Kunlong 25 Jd 23.25N 98.39 E
Kunlun Guan 27 Ig 23.06N 108.40 E
Kunlun Shan 21 Kf 36.00N 84.00 E
Kunlun Shankou 27 Fd 35.40N 94.03 E
Kunming 22 Mg 25.08N 102.43 E
Kunnui 29a Bb 42.26N 140.19 E
Kunovat 17 Ld 64.59N 65.35 E
Kunsan 27 Md 35.59N 126.43 E
Kunshan 28 Fi 31.22N 120.57 E
Kuntaur 34 Cc 13.40N 14.53W
Kununurra 58 Fc 15.47S 128.44 E
Kunyao 36 Gb 1.47N 35.03 E
Kunyu Shan 28 Ff 37.15N 121.46 E
Künzelsau 10 Fg 49.17N 9.41 E
Kuohijärvi 8 Kc 61.15N 24.55 E
Kuolimo 8 Lc 61.15N 27.35 E
Kuop Atoll 64d Bb 7.03N 151.56 E
Kuopio [2] 7 Ge 63.20N 27.35 E
Kuopio 6 Ic 62.54N 27.41 E
Kuorboaivi 7 Gb 69.41N 27.45 E
Kuortane 8 Jb 62.48N 23.30 E
Kupa 14 Ke 45.28N 16.24 E
Kupang 22 Ok 10.10S 123.35 E
Kupiano 60 Dj 10.10S 148.02 E
Kupičev 10 Uf 50.58N 24.52 E
Kupino 20 Cf 54.22N 77.18 E
Kupiškis 7 Fi 55.49N 25.01 E
Kupjansk 19 Df 49.42N 37.37 E
Kupjansk-Uzlovoj 16 Je 49.39N 37.45 E
Küplü [Tur.] 15 Jh 41.07N 26.21 E
Küplü [Tur.] 15 Mi 40.06N 30.00 E
Kuppenheim 12 Kf 48.50N 8.15 E
Kupreanof 40 Me 56.50N 133.30W
Kuqa 22 Ke 41.43N 82.57 E
Kura [R.S.F.S.R.] 16 Mh 44.05N 44.45 E
Kura [U.S.S.R.] 5 Kh 39.20N 49.25 E
Kuragaty 18 Ic 43.55N 73.34 E
Kuragino 20 Ef 53.53N 92.40 E
Kurahashi-Jima 29 Cd 34.08N 132.31 E
Kuraminski Hrebet 18 Hd 40.50N 70.30 E
Kurashiki 28 Lg 34.35N 133.46 E
Kurashiki-Kojima 29 Cd 34.28N 133.48 E
Kurashiki-Tamashima 29 Cd 34.33N 133.40 E
Kura-Take 29 Be 32.27N 130.20 E
Kuraymah=Karima (EN) 31 Kg 18.33N 31.51 E
Kurayoshi 28 Lg 35.28N 133.49 E
Kurbneshi 15 Dh 41.47N 20.05 E
Kurčatov 16 Id 51.41N 35.42 E
Kurdaj 18 Jc 43.18N 74.59 E
Kurdistan 21 Gf 37.00N 44.00 E
Kurdistan 23 Fb 37.00N 44.00 E
Kurdufān 30 Jg 13.00N 30.00 E
Kurdufān al Janūbīyah [3] 35 Dc 11.00N 29.30 E
Kurdufān ash Shamālīyah [3] 35 Dc 14.50N 29.40 E
Kure 28 Lg 34.14N 132.34 E
Küre 24 Eb 41.48N 33.43 E
Kure Island 57 Jb 28.25N 178.25W
Kurejka 21 Kc 66.25N 87.12 E
Kurgaldžinski 19 He 50.30N 70.03 E
Kurgalski, Mys- 8 Me 59.39N 28.03 E
Kurgan 22 Id 55.26N 65.18 E
Kurganinsk 16 Lg 44.57N 40.35 E
Kurganskaja Oblast [3] 19 Gd 55.00N 65.00 E
Kurgan-Tjube 19 Gh 37.51N 68.46 E
Kurgan-Tjubinskaja Oblast [3] 19 Gh 37.30N 68.30 E
Kuria Island 57 Id 0.14N 173.25 E
Kuria Muria Islands (EN)=Khurīyā Murīyā, Jazā'ir 21 Hh 17.30N 56.00 E
Kuri Bay 59 Ec 15.35S 124.50 E
Kurikka 7 Fe 62.37N 22.25 E
Kurikoma 29 Gb 38.50N 140.59 E
Kurikoma-Yama 29 Gb 38.57N 140.47 E
Kuril Basin (EN) 20 Jg 47.00N 150.00 E
Kuril Islands (EN)=Kurilskije Ostrova 21 Re 46.10N 152.00 E
Kurilo 15 Gg 42.49N 23.21 E
Kurilsk 20 Jg 45.16N 147.58 E
Kurilskije Ostrova=Kuril Islands (EN) 21 Re 46.10N 152.00 E
Kuril Trench (EN) 3 Je 47.00N 155.00 E
Kuring Kuru 37 Bc 17.38S 18.33 E
Kurino 29 Bf 31.57N 130.43 E
Kurinskaja Kosa 16 Pj 39.05N 49.10 E
Kurinwás, Río- 49 Fg 12.49N 83.41W
Kuriyama 29a Bb 43.03N 141.45 E
Kūrkhūd, Kūh-e- 24 Qd 37.15N 56.30 E
Kurkosa 16 Pj 38.59N 49.08 E
Kurkūmā, Ra's- 24 Gj 25.51N 36.39 E
Kurkur 24 Ek 23.54N 32.19 E
Kurlovski 7 Ji 55.29N 40.39 E
Kurmuk 35 Ec 10.33N 34.17 E
Kurnool 22 Jh 15.50N 78.03 E
Kurobe 28 Nf 36.51N 137.26 E
Kurobe-Gawa 29 Ec 36.55N 137.26 E
Kurogi 29 Be 33.14N 130.40 E
Kuroishi 28 Pd 40.38N 140.36 E
Kuroiso 28 Pf 36.58N 140.03 E
Kuromatsunai 28 Pc 42.43N 140.20 E
Kurono-Seto 29 Be 32.05N 130.10 E
Kurort Družba 15 Kf 43.12N 28.00 E
Kurort Slănčev brjag 15 Kg 42.40N 27.42 E
Kurort Zlatni pjasăci 15 Lf 43.16N 28.02 E
Kuro-Shima 28 Jj 31.52N 129.58 E
Kurovskoje 7 Ji 55.35N 38.59 E
Kurow 61 Dh 44.44S 170.28 E
Kurów 10 Se 51.25N 22.10 E
Kurpiowska, Puszcza- 10 Rc 53.20N 21.30 E
Kuršėnai/Kuršenaj 19 Cd 56.03N 22.58 E
Kuršenaj/Kuršėnai 19 Cd 56.03N 22.58 E
Kuršiu užūrekis 8 Ii 55.05N 21.00 E
Kursk 6 Je 51.42N 36.12 E
Kurskaja Kosa 7 Ei 55.18N 21.00 E
Kurskaja Oblast [3] 19 De 51.45N 36.15 E
Kurski zaliv 7 Ei 55.05N 21.00 E
Kuršumlija 15 Ef 43.09N 21.16 E
Kurtalan 24 Id 37.57N 41.42 E
Kurtamyš 19 Ge 54.55N 64.27 E
Kūrtī 31 Kg 18.07N 31.33 E
Kurtistown 65 Fd 19.36N 155.04W
Kurty 18 Kb 44.19N 76.42 E
Kuru 8 Jc 61.52N 23.44 E
Kuru 35 Dd 9.08N 26.57 E
Kurušile 24 Eb 41.51N 32.43 E
Kuruktag 27 Ec 41.30N 89.00 E
Kuruman 30 Jk 26.56S 20.39 E
Kuruman 31 Jk 27.28S 23.28 E
Kurume 28 Kh 33.19N 130.31 E
Kurunegala 25 Gg 7.29N 80.22 E
Kurur, Jabal- 35 Ea 20.31N 31.32 E
Kurzeme=Courland (EN) 8 Ih 56.50N 22.00 E
Kurzemes Augstiene/Kurzemskaja Vozvyšennost 8 Jh 56.45N 22.15 E
Kurzemskaja Vozvyšennost/Kurzemes Augstiene 8 Jh 56.45N 22.15 E
Kusa 17 Ii 55.20N 59.29 E
Kuşada Körfezi 15 Kl 37.50N 27.08 E
Kuşadasi 24 Bd 37.51N 27.15 E
Kusagaki-Guntō 27 Me 31.00N 129.00 E
Kusaie→Kosrae 57 Hd 5.19N 162.59 E
Kusalu/Kuusalu 8 Ke 59.23N 25.25 E
Kusary 16 Pi 41.24N 48.29 E
Kusatsu [Jap.] 29 Fc 36.37N 138.35 E
Kusatsu [Jap.] 29 Dd 35.03N 135.59 E
Kuščevskaja 16 Kf 46.33N 39.37 E
Kuščinski 16 Oi 40.33N 46.06 E
Kusel 12 Je 49.33N 7.24 E
Kuş Gölü 24 Bb 40.10N 27.59 E
Kushida-Gawa 29 Ed 34.36N 136.34 E
Kushikino 28 Ki 31.44N 130.16 E
Kushima 28 Ki 31.29N 131.14 E
Kushimoto 28 Mh 33.28N 135.47 E
Kushiro 22 Qe 42.58N 144.23 E
Kushiro-Gawa 29a Db 42.59N 144.23 E
Kushtia 25 Hd 23.55N 89.07 E
Kuška 18 Dg 35.16N 62.18 E
Kuskokwim 38 Cc 60.17N 162.27W
Kuskokwim Bay 38 Cd 59.45N 162.25W
Kuskokwim Mountains 38 Dc 62.30N 156.00W
Kušmurun 19 Ge 52.27N 64.40 E
Kušmurun, Ozero- 19 Ge 52.40N 64.45 E
Kušnarenkovo 17 Gi 55.06N 55.22 E
Kušnica 16 Ce 48.29N 23.20 E
Kusŏng 27 Md 39.59N 125.16 E
Kussharo Ko 28 Rc 43.35N 144.15 E
Kustanaj 22 Id 53.10N 63.35 E
Kustanajskaja Oblast [3] 19 Ge 53.00N 64.00 E
Kustavi 8 Id 60.30N 21.25 E
Kustavi/Gustavs 8 Id 60.30N 21.25 E
Küstenkanal 10 Dd 52.57N 7.18 E
Kūstī 31 Kg 13.10N 32.40 E
Kustvlakte=Coast Plain (EN) 11 Ic 51.00N 2.30 E
Kusu 29 Be 33.16N 131.09 E
Kušva 19 Fd 58.18N 59.45 E
Kut, Ko- 25 Kf 11.40N 102.35 E
Küt 'Abdollāh 24 Mg 31.13N 48.39 E
Kutacane 26 Cf 3.30N 97.48 E
Kutahya 23 Cb 39.25N 29.59 E
Kutaisi 6 Kg 42.15N 42.40 E
Kutch, Gulf of-→Kachchh, Gulf of 21 Ig 22.36N 60.30 E
Kutch, Rann of- 21 Ed 24.05N 70.10 E
Kutchan 28 Pc 42.54N 140.45 E
Kutcharo-Ko 29a Ca 45.10N 142.20 E
Kutina 14 Ke 45.29N 16.47 E
Kutkai 25 Jd 23.27N 97.56 E
Kutkašen 16 Oi 40.58N 47.52 E
Kutná Hora 10 Lg 49.57N 15.16 E
Kutno 10 Pd 52.15N 19.23 E
Kutse, Gora-/Kuutse Mägi 8 Lg 57.58N 26.24 E
Kuttara-Ko 29a Bb 42.30N 141.10 E
Kutu 31 Ii 2.44S 18.09 E
Kutum 35 Cc 14.12N 24.40 E
Kúty 10 Nh 48.40N 17.01 E
Kuty 15 Ia 48.13N 25.15 E
Kuujjuaq 39 Md 58.10N 68.30W
Kuujjuarapik 42 Je 55.20N 76.50W
Kuuli-Majak 19 Fg 40.16N 52.45 E
Kuurne 12 Fd 50.51N 3.17 E
Kuusalu/Kusalu 8 Ke 59.23N 25.25 E
Kuusamo 6 Ib 66.00N 29.11 E
Kuusankoski 8 Ld 60.54N 26.38 E
Kuutse Mägi/Kutse, Gora- 8 Lg 57.58N 26.24 E
Kuvandyk 16 Td 51.29N 57.28 E
Kuvdlorssuaq 41 Gd 74.38N 56.40W
Kuvšinovo 7 Ih 57.03N 34.13 E
Kuwait (EN)=Al Kuwayt [1] 22 Gg 29.30N 47.45 E
Kuwait (EN)=Al Kuwayt 22 Gg 29.20N 47.59 E
Kuwana 29 Ed 35.04N 136.39 E
Kuybyshev Reservoir (EN)=Kujbyševskoje Vodohranilišče 5 Ke 53.50N 49.00 E
Kūysanjaq 24 Kd 36.05N 44.38 E
Kuytun 27 Dc 44.25N 84.58 E
Kuyucak 15 Ll 37.55N 28.28 E
Kuzey Kibris = North Cyprus 23 Db 35.15N 33.40 E
Kuzneck 19 Ee 53.07N 46.36 E
Kuznecki Alatau 21 Kd 54.45N 88.00 E
Kuznečnoje 8 Mc 61.04N 29.58 E
Kuźnia Raciborska 10 Of 50.11N 18.15 E
Kuzomen 19 Db 66.18N 36.49 E
Kuzovatovo 7 Lj 53.33N 47.41 E
Kuzumaki 29 Ga 40.02N 141.26 E
Kuzuryū-Gawa 29 Ec 36.13N 136.08 E
Kvænangen 7 Ea 70.05N 21.13 E
Kvaløy 7 Eb 69.40N 18.30 E
Kvaløya 7 Fa 70.37N 23.52 E
Kvalsund 7 Fa 70.30N 24.00 E
Kvam 8 Cc 61.40N 9.42 E
Kvareli 16 Ni 41.57N 45.47 E
Kvarkeno 17 Ij 52.05N 59.40 E
Kvarnbergsvattnet 7 Dd 64.36N 14.03 E
Kvarner 14 If 44.45N 14.15 E
Kvarnerić 14 If 44.45N 14.35 E
Kvichak Bay 40 He 58.48N 157.30W
Kvemo-Kedi 16 Oi 41.22N 46.31 E
Kvenna 8 Bd 60.01N 7.56 E
Kvichak 40 He 59.10N 156.40W
Kvikkjokk 7 Dc 66.57N 17.47 E
Kvina 8 Bf 58.17N 6.56 E
Kvinesdal 7 Bg 58.19N 6.57 E
Kvissleby 8 Gb 62.17N 17.21 E
Kviteggia 8 Bb 62.05N 6.40 E
Kviteseid 8 Ce 59.24N 8.30 E
Kvitøya 67 Je 80.08N 32.35 E
Kwa 30 Ii 3.10S 16.11 E
Kwahu Plateau 34 Ed 6.30N 0.30W
Kwailibesi 63a Ec 8.20S 160.40 E
Kwajalein Atoll 57 Hd 9.05N 167.20 E
Kwakoegron 54 Gb 5.15N 55.20W
Kwale [Kenya] 36 Gc 4.11S 39.27 E
Kwale [Nig.] 34 Gd 5.45N 6.25 E
Kwamouth 36 Cc 3.10S 16.12 E
Kwa Mtoro 36 Gd 5.14S 35.26 E
Kwando 36 Df 18.27S 23.32 E
Kwangdae-ri 27 Mc 40.34N 127.33 E
Kwangju 22 Of 35.09N 126.55 E
Kwango 30 Ii 3.14S 17.22 E

Index Symbols

[1] Independent Nation
[2] State, Region
[3] District, County
[4] Municipality
[5] Colony, Dependency
Continent
Physical Region
Historical or Cultural Region
Mount, Mountain
Volcano
Hill
Mountains, Mountain Range
Hills, Escarpment
Plateau, Upland
Pass, Gap
Plain, Lowland
Delta
Salt Flat
Valley, Canyon
Crater, Cave
Karst Features
Depression
Polder
Desert, Dunes
Forest, Woods
Heath, Steppe
Oasis
Cape, Point
Coast, Beach
Cliff
Peninsula
Isthmus
Sandbank
Island
Atoll
Rock, Reef
Islands, Archipelago
Rocks, Reefs
Coral Reef
Well, Spring
Geyser
River, Stream
Waterfall Rapids
River Mouth, Estuary
Lake
Salt Lake
Intermittent Lake
Reservoir
Swamp, Pond
Canal
Glacier
Ice Shelf, Pack Ice
Ocean
Sea
Gulf, Bay
Strait, Fjord
Lagoon
Bank
Seamount
Tablemount
Ridge
Shelf
Basin
Escarpment, Sea Scarp
Fracture
Trench, Abyss
National Park, Reserve
Point of Interest
Recreation Site
Cave, Cavern
Historic Site
Ruins
Wall, Walls
Church, Abbey
Temple
Scientific Station
Airport
Port
Lighthouse
Mine
Tunnel
Dam, Bridge

L

Index Symbols

[1] Independent Nation
[2] State, Region
[3] District, County
[4] Municipality
[5] Colony, Dependency
Continent
Physical Region
Historical or Cultural Region
Mount, Mountain
Volcano
Hill
Mountains, Mountain Range
Hills, Escarpment
Plateau, Upland
Pass, Gap
Plain, Lowland
Delta
Salt Flat
Valley, Canyon
Crater, Cave
Karst Features
Depression
Polder
Desert, Dunes
Forest, Woods
Heath, Steppe
Oasis
Cape, Point
Coast, Beach
Cliff
Peninsula
Isthmus
Sandbank
Island
Atoll
Rock, Reef
Islands, Archipelago
Rocks, Reefs
Coral Reef
Well, Spring
Geyser
River, Stream
Waterfall Rapids
River Mouth, Estuary
Lake
Salt Lake
Intermittent Lake
Reservoir
Swamp, Pond
Canal
Glacier
Ice Shelf, Pack Ice
Ocean
Sea
Gulf, Bay
Strait, Fjord
Lagoon
Bank
Seamount
Tablemount
Ridge
Shelf
Basin
Escarpment, Sea Scarp
Fracture
Trench, Abyss
National Park, Reserve
Point of Interest
Recreation Site
Cave, Cavern
Historic Site
Ruins
Wall, Walls
Church, Abbey
Temple
Scientific Station
Airport
Port
Lighthouse
Mine
Tunnel
Dam, Bridge

Lamotte-Beuvron 11 Ig 47.36N 2.01 E
La Moure 45 Gc 46.21N 98.18W
Lampang 25 Je 18.16N 99.34 E
Lampasas 45 Gk 31.03N 98.12W
Lampazos de Naranjo 48 Id 27.01N 100.31W
Lampedusa 14 Go 35.30N 12.35 E
Lampertheim 10 Eg 49.36N 8.28 E
Lampeter 9 Ii 52.07N 4.05W
Lamphun 25 Je 18.35N 99.00 E
Lampione 14 Go 35.35N 12.20 E
Lampung [3] 26 Dg 5.00S 105.00 E
Lamu 31 Li 2.16S 40.54 E
Lamud 54 Ce 6.09S 77.55W
La Mure 11 Lj 44.54N 5.47 E
Lan 16 Ec 52.09N 27.18 E
Lana 14 Fd 46.37N 11.09 E
Lana, Rio de la- 48 Li 17.49N 95.09W
Lanai City 65a Ec 20.50N 156.55W
Lanaihale 65a Ec 20.49N 156.52W
Lanai Island 57 Lb 20.50N 156.55W
Lanaken 12 Hd 50.53N 5.39 E
Lanark 9 Jf 55.41N 3.48W
Lanbi Kyun 25 Jf 10.50N 98.15 E
Lancang (Menglangba) 27 Gg 22.37N 99.57 E
Lancang Jiang = Mekong (EN) 21 Mh 10.15N 105.55 E
Lancashire [3] 9 Kh 53.55N 2.40W
Lancashire Plain 9 Kh 53.40N 2.45W
Lancaster 9 Kh 53.45N 2.50W
Lancaster [Ca.-U.S.] 43 De 34.42N 118.08W
Lancaster [Eng.-U.K.] 9 Kg 54.03N 2.48W
Lancaster [Mo.-U.S.] 45 Jf 40.31N 92.32W
Lancaster [N.H.-U.S.] 44 Lc 44.29N 71.34W
Lancaster [Oh.-U.S.] 44 Ff 39.43N 82.37W
Lancaster [Ont.-Can.] 44 Jc 45.12N 74.30W
Lancaster [Pa.-U.S.] 43 Lc 40.01N 76.19W
Lancaster [S.C.-U.S.] 44 Gh 34.43N 80.47W
Lancaster Sound 38 Kb 74.13N 84.00W
Lançeiro 55 Fe 20.59S 53.43W
Lancelin 59 Df 31.01S 115.19 E
Lanciano 14 Ih 42.14N 14.23 E
Lančin 15 Ha 48.31N 24.49 E
Lancun 28 Ff 36.25N 120.11 E
Łańcut 10 Sf 50.05N 22.13 E
Land 8 Cd 60.45N 10.00 E
Låndana 36 Bd 5.15S 12.10 E
Landau an der Isar 10 Ih 48.41N 12.41 E
Landau in der Pfalz 10 Eg 49.12N 8.07 E
Land Bay 66 Mf 75.25S 141.45W
Landeck 14 Ec 47.08N 10.34 E
Landen 12 Hd 50.45N 5.05 E
Lander 43 Fc 42.50N 108.44W
Landerneau 11 Bf 48.27N 4.15W
Lander River 59 Gd 20.25S 132.00 E
Landeryd 8 Eg 57.05N 13.16 E
Landes 11 Fj 44.15N 1.00W
Landes [3] 11 Fj 44.00N 0.50W
Landesbergen 12 Lb 52.34N 9.08 E
Landeta 55 Ak 32.01S 62.04W
Landete 13 Ke 39.54N 1.22W
Landfallis 25 If 13.40N 93.02 E
Land Glacier 66 Mf 75.40S 141.45W
Landi Kotal 25 Eb 34.06N 71.09 E
Landless Corner 36 Ee 14.53S 28.04 E
Landrecies 12 Fd 50.08N 3.42 E
Landsberg am Lech 10 Gh 48.03N 10.52 E
Landsbro 8 Fg 57.22N 14.54 E
Land's End 5 Fe 50.03N 5.44W
Lands End 42 Fa 76.25N 122.45W
Landshut 10 Ih 48.32N 12.09 E
Landskrona 8 Ei 55.52N 12.50 E
Landsort 8 Gf 58.45N 17.50 E
Landsortsdjupet 8 Hf 58.40N 18.30 E
Landstuhl 12 Je 49.25N 7.34 E
Landusky 46 Kc 47.54N 108.37W
La Neuve-Lyre 12 Cf 48.54N 0.45 E
Lanfeng → Lankao 28 Cg 34.49N 114.48 E
Lang 46 Mb 49.56N 104.23W
La'nga Co 27 De 30.41N 81.17 E
Langadhás 15 Gi 40.45N 23.04 E
Langádhia 15 Fl 37.39N 22.03 E
Långan 7 De 63.19N 14.44 E
Langano, Lake- 35 Fd 7.36N 38.43 E
Langao 27 Ie 32.20N 108.53 E
Langara 26 Hg 4.02S 123.00 E
Langarfoss 7a Cb 65.35N 14.15W
Langasian 26 Ie 8.16N 125.39 E
Langdon 45 Gb 48.46N 98.22W
Langeac 11 Ji 45.06N 3.29 E
Langeais 11 Gg 47.20N 0.24 E
Langeb 35 Fb 17.46N 36.41 E
Langebaan 37 Bf 33.06S 18.02 E
Langeberg 37 Cf 33.56S 20.45 E
Langedijk 12 Gb 52.42N 4.48 E
Langeland 7 Ci 55.00N 10.50 E
Langelands Bælt 8 Dj 54.50N 10.55 E
Längelmävesi 8 Kc 61.30N 24.20 E
Langen 12 Ke 49.59N 8.40 E
Langenberg 12 Kc 51.17N 8.34 E
Langenburg 45 Fa 50.50N 101.43W
Langenfeld (Rheinland) 12 Ic 51.06N 6.57 E
Langenhagen 10 Fd 52.27N 9.45 E
Langenselbold 12 Ld 50.11N 9.02 E
Langenthal 14 Bc 47.13N 7.49 E
Langeoog 10 Dc 53.46N 7.32 E
Langeri 20 Jf 50.08N 143.20 E
Langesund 8 Ce 59.00N 9.45 E
Langesundsfjorden 8 Cf 59.00N 9.48 E
Langevåg 8 Bb 62.27N 6.12 E
Langfang → Anci 27 Kd 39.29N 116.40 E
Långfjället 8 Eb 62.10N 12.20 E
Langfjorden 8 Bb 62.45N 7.30 E
Langhe 14 Bf 44.30N 8.00 E
Langholm 9 Kf 55.09N 3.00W
Langjökull 7a Bb 64.39N 20.00W
Langkawi, Pulau- 26 Ce 6.22N 99.48 E
Langkon 26 Ge 6.32N 116.42 E
Langlade 44 Ja 48.12N 75.57W
Langnau im Emmental 14 Bd 46.56N 7.46 E
Langogne 11 Jj 44.43N 3.51 E
Langon 11 Fj 44.33N 0.15W
Langorüd 24 Md 37.11N 50.10 E
Langøya 7 Db 68.44N 14.50 E
Langreo 13 Ga 43.18N 5.41W
Langres 11 Lg 47.52N 5.20 E
Langres, Plateau de- 5 Gf 47.41N 5.03 E
Langrune-sur-Mer 12 Be 49.19N 0.22W
Langsa 22 Li 4.28N 97.58 E
Långsele 8 Ga 63.11N 17.04 E
Långshyttan 8 Gd 60.27N 16.01 E
Lang Son 25 Ld 21.50N 106.44 E
Lang Suan 25 Jg 9.55N 99.07 E
Languedoc 5 Gg 44.00N 4.00 E
Languedoc 11 Jj 44.00N 4.00 E
Langueyú, Arroyo- 55 Cm 36.39S 58.27W
Langwedel 12 Lb 52.58N 9.13 E
Langxi 28 Ei 31.08N 119.11 E
Langzhong 27 Ie 31.40N 106.04 E
Lan Hsu 27 Lg 22.00N 121.30 E
Laniel 44 Hb 47.06N 79.15W
Lanin, Volcán- 52 Ii 39.38S 71.30W
Lankao 27 Cd 35.12N 79.50 E
Lankao (Lanfeng) 27 Kg 21.00N 116.00 E
Lankao (Lanfeng) 28 Cg 34.49N 114.48 E
Länkipohja 8 Kc 61.44N 24.48 E
Lannemezan 11 Gk 43.08N 0.23 E
Lannemezan, Plateau de- 11 Gk 43.09N 0.27 E
Lannion 11 Cf 48.44N 3.28W
Lannion, Baie de- 11 Cf 48.43N 3.34W
La Noria 56 Gb 20.23S 69.53W
Lansdowne House 42 If 52.13N 87.53W
L'Anse 44 Cb 46.45N 88.27W
Lansing [Ia.-U.S.] 45 Ke 43.22N 91.13W
Lansing [Mi.-U.S.] 39 Ke 42.43N 84.34W
Lansjärv 7 Fc 66.39N 22.12 E
Łańskie, Jezioro- 10 Qc 53.33N 20.30 E
Lantar 20 Ie 56.05N 137.35 E
Lanta Yai, Ko- 25 Jg 7.35N 99.03 E
Lanteri 55 Ci 28.50S 59.39W
Lanterne 11 Mg 47.44N 6.03 E
Lanús 55 Cl 34.43S 58.24W
Lanusei 14 Dk 39.53N 9.32 E
Lanvaux, Landes de- 11 Dg 47.47N 2.36W
Lanxi [China] 28 Ej 29.13N 119.28 E
Lanxi [China] 28 Ha 46.15N 126.16 E
Lanxian (Dongcun) 28 Ae 38.17N 111.38 E
Lanyi He 28 Ae 38.40N 110.53 E
Lanzarote 30 Ff 29.00N 13.40W
Lanzhou 22 Mf 36.03N 103.41 E
Lanzo Torinese 14 Be 45.16N 7.28 E
Lao 14 Jk 39.47N 15.48 E
Laoag 22 Oh 18.12N 120.36 E
Laoang 26 Id 12.34N 125.00 E
Lao Cai 22 Mg 22.30N 103.57 E
Laocheng 28 Hc 42.37N 124.04 E
Laoha He 27 Lc 43.24N 120.39 E
Lao He 28 Cj 29.02N 115.47 E
Laohuanghe Kou 28 Ef 37.39N 119.02 E
Laois [2] 9 Fi 53.00N 7.30W
Laojunmiao → Yumen 22 Lf 39.50N 97.44 E
Laojun Shan 27 Je 33.45N 111.38 E
Lao Ling 28 Id 41.24N 126.10 E
Laon 11 Je 49.34N 3.37 E
Laona 45 Ld 45.34N 88.40W
Laonnois 12 Fe 49.35N 3.40 E
La Orchila, Isla- 54 Ea 11.48N 66.10W
La Oroya 53 Ig 11.32S 75.57W
Laos [1] 22 Mh 18.00N 105.00 E
Laoshan (Licun) 28 Ff 36.10N 120.25 E
Laotougou 28 Jc 42.54N 129.09 E
Laou 13 Gi 35.26N 5.05W
Laoye Ling 28 Kb 44.50N 130.10 E
Lapa 56 Kc 25.45S 49.42W
Lapai 34 Gd 9.03N 6.43 E
Lapalisse 11 Jh 46.15N 3.38 E
La Palma 30 Ff 28.40N 17.52W
La Palma [ElSal.] 49 Cf 14.19N 89.11W
La Palma [Pan.] 47 Ig 8.25N 78.09W
La Palma del Condado 13 Fg 37.23N 6.33W
La Paloma 55 El 34.40S 54.10W
La Pampa [2] 56 Ge 37.00S 66.00W
La Panne/De Panne 12 Ec 51.06N 2.35 E
La Paragua 54 Fb 6.50N 63.20W
La Partida, Isla- 48 De 24.30N 110.25W
La Paz [3] 49 Df 14.15N 87.50W
La Paz [2] 54 Eg 15.00S 68.00W
La Paz [Arg.] 56 Id 30.45S 59.39W
La Paz [Arg.] 56 Gd 33.28S 67.33W
La Paz [Bol.] 53 Jg 16.30S 68.09W
La Paz [Col.] 49 Kh 10.23N 73.10W
La Paz [Hond.] 47 Gf 14.16N 87.40W
La Paz [Mex.] 39 Hg 24.10N 110.18W
La Paz [Ur.] 55 Dl 34.46S 56.13W
La Paz [Ven.] 49 Lh 10.41N 72.00W
La Paz, Bahía de- 47 Bd 24.09N 110.25W
La Paz, Llano de- 48 De 24.00N 110.30W
La Paz Centro 49 Dg 12.20N 86.41W
La Pedrera 54 Ed 1.18S 69.40W
Lapeer 44 Fd 43.03N 83.19W
La Pelada 55 Bj 30.52S 60.59W
La Pérouse, Bahía- 65d Bb 27.04S 109.18W
La Perouse Strait (EN) = Laperuza, Proliv- 21 Qe 45.30N 142.00 E
La Perouse Strait (EN) = Sōya-Kaikyō 21 Qe 45.30N 142.00 E
Laperuza, Proliv- = La Perouse Strait (EN) 21 Qe 45.30N 142.00 E
La Pesca 47 Ed 23.47N 97.47W
La Petite Pierre 12 Jf 48.52N 7.19 E
La Picasa, Laguna- 55 Al 34.20S 62.14W
La Piedad Cavadas 48 Hg 20.21N 102.00W
La Pine 46 Ee 43.40N 121.30W
Lapinjärvi/Lappträsk 8 Ld 60.36N 26.09 E
Lapinlahti 7 Ge 63.22N 27.30 E
La Plaine 51g Bb 15.20N 61.15W
La Plana 13 Ld 40.00N 0.05W
Lapland (EN) = Lappi 5 Ib 66.50N 22.00 E
Lapland (EN) = Lappland 5 Ib 66.50N 22.00 E
La Plant 45 Fd 45.10N 100.38W
La Plata 53 Ki 34.55S 57.57W
La Pobla de Lillet 13 Nb 42.15N 1.59 E
La Pobla de Segur/Pobla de Segur 13 Mb 42.15N 0.58 E
La Pocatièr 44 Lb 47.21N 70.02W
La Porte 44 De 41.36N 86.43W
Lapovo 15 Ee 44.11N 21.06 E
Lappajärvi 7 Fe 63.08N 23.40 E
Lappeenranta/Villmanstrand 6 Ic 61.04N 28.11 E
Lappfjärd/Lapväärtti 8 Ib 62.15N 21.32 E
Lappi [2] 7 Gc 67.40N 26.30 E
Lappi 8 Ic 61.06N 21.50 E
Lappi = Lapland (EN) 5 Ib 66.50N 22.00 E
Lappo/Lapua 7 Fe 62.57N 23.00 E
Lappträsk/Lapinjärvi 8 Ld 60.36N 26.09 E
Lapri 20 He 55.45N 124.59 E
Laprida 56 He 37.33S 60.49W
Lâpseki 24 Bb 40.20N 26.31 E
Lapta 24 Ee 35.20N 33.10 E
Laptev Sea (EN) = Laptevyh, More- 67 Fd 76.00N 126.00 E
Laptevyh, More- = Laptev Sea (EN) 67 Fd 76.00N 126.00 E
Lapua/Lappo 7 Fe 62.57N 23.00 E
La Puebla 13 Pe 39.46N 3.01 E
La Puebla de Cazalla 13 Gg 37.14N 5.19W
Lapuna 55 Ba 13.19S 60.28W
La Puntilla 52 Hf 2.11S 81.01W
La Purísima 48 Cd 26.10N 112.04W
Lâpuş 15 Hb 47.30N 24.01 E
Lâpuş 15 Gb 47.39N 23.24 E
La Push 46 Cc 47.55N 124.38W
Lapväärtti/Lappfjärd 8 Ib 62.15N 21.32 E
Łapy 10 Sd 53.00N 22.53 E
Laqiyat al Arba'in 35 Da 20.03N 28.02 E
La Quemada 48 Hf 22.27N 102.45W
La Quiaca 56 Gb 22.06S 65.37W
L'Aquila 6 Hg 42.22N 13.22 E
Lar 23 Hd 27.41N 54.17 E
Lara [2] 54 Ea 10.10N 69.50W
Larache 32 Fb 35.12N 6.10W
Laragne-Montéglin 11 Lj 44.19N 5.49 E
Lārak 23 Id 26.52N 56.22 E
La Rambla 13 Hg 37.36N 4.44W
Laramie 39 Ie 41.19N 105.35W
Laramie Mountains 43 Fc 42.00N 105.40W
Laramie Peak 46 Me 42.17N 105.27W
Laramie River 46 Me 42.12N 104.32W
Laranjal, Rio- 55 Ff 23.12S 53.45W
Laranjeiras do Sul 56 Jc 25.25S 52.25W
Larantuka 26 Hh 8.21S 122.59 E
Larat 26 Jh 7.09S 131.45 E
Larat, Pulau- 26 Jh 7.10S 131.50 E
La Raya 49 Ji 8.20N 74.34W
L'Arba 13 Ph 36.34N 3.09 E
L'Arbaa-Naït-Irathen 13 Qh 36.38N 4.12 E
L'Arbresle 11 Ki 45.50N 4.37 E
Lärbro 7 Eh 57.47N 18.47 E
Larche, Col de- 11 Mj 44.25N 6.53 E
Larde 37 Fc 16.28S 39.43 E
Larderello 14 Eg 43.14N 10.53 E
La Réale 11 Fj 44.35N 0.02W
Laredo [Sp.] 13 Ia 43.24N 3.25W
Laredo [Tx.-U.S.] 39 Jg 27.31N 99.30W
Laren 12 Hb 52.16N 5.16 E
Lārestān 21 Hg 27.00N 55.30 E
Larestan 24 Pi 27.00N 55.30 E
Large Island 51p Cb 12.24N 61.30W
Largentière 11 Kj 44.32N 4.18 E
L'Argentière-la-Bessée 11 Mj 44.47N 6.33 E
Largo, Cayo- 49 Gc 21.38N 81.28W
Largs 9 If 55.48N 4.52W
La Ribagorça/Ribagorza 13 Mb 42.15N 0.30 E
La Ribera 13 Kb 42.30N 2.00W
Larimore 45 Hc 47.54N 97.38W
Larino 14 Ii 41.48N 14.54 E
La Rioja [2] 56 Gc 30.00S 67.30W
La Rioja 13 Jb 42.20N 2.20W
La Rioja 53 Jh 29.25S 66.50W
Lárisa 6 Ih 39.38N 22.25 E
La Rivière-Thibouville, Nassandres- 12 Ce 49.07N 0.44 E
Lärkäna 25 Dc 27.33N 68.13 E
Larmor-Plage 11 Cg 47.42N 3.23W
Larnaka/Lárnax 23 Dc 34.55N 33.38 E
Lárnax/Larnaka 23 Dc 34.55N 33.38 E
Larne/Latharna 9 Hg 54.51N 5.49W
Larned 45 Gg 38.11N 99.06W
La Robla 13 Gb 42.48N 5.37W
La Roche 63b De 21.28S 168.02 E
La Roche-en-Ardenne 11 Ld 50.11N 5.35 E
La Rochefoucauld 11 Gi 45.44N 0.23 E
La Roche-Guyon 12 De 49.05N 1.38 E
La Rochelle 6 Ff 46.10N 1.09W
La Roche-sur-Yon 11 Eh 46.40N 1.26W
La Roda 13 Je 39.13N 2.09W
La Romana 47 Ke 18.25N 68.58W
La Ronge 42 Ge 55.06N 105.17W
La Ronge, Lac- 38 Id 55.05N 104.59W
Larose 45 Kl 29.35N 90.23W
La Rosita 48 Ic 28.24N 101.43W
Larouco 13 Ec 41.56N 7.40W
Larreynaga 49 Dg 12.40N 86.34W
Larrey Point 59 Dc 20.00S 119.10 E
Larrimah 58 Ef 15.35S 133.12 E
Larsa 24 Kg 31.16N 45.49 E
Lars Christensen Kyst 66 Fe 69.30S 68.00 E
Larsen, Mount- 66 Kf 74.51S 162.12 E
Larsen Ice Shelf 66 Qe 68.30S 62.30W
Lartijas Padomju Socialistiska Respublika/Latvijskaja SSR [2] 19 Cd 57.00N 25.00 E
La Rumorosa 48 Aa 32.34N 116.06W
Laruns 11 Fk 43.00N 0.25W
Larvik 7 Bg 59.04N 10.00 E
La Sabana [Arg.] 55 Ch 27.52S 59.57W
La Sabana [Col.] 54 Ec 2.20N 68.32W
Las Adjuntas, Presa de- 48 Jf 23.55N 98.45W
La Sagra 13 Id 40.05N 4.00W
La Sagra 13 Jg 37.57N 2.34W
La Salle 45 Lf 41.20N 89.06W
La Salle, Pic- 47 Je 18.22N 71.59W
La Sal Mountains 46 Kg 38.30N 109.10W
Las Alpujarras 13 Ih 36.50N 3.25W
La Sanabria 13 Fb 42.08N 6.30W
Las Animas 45 Eg 38.04N 103.13W
Lās 'ānōd 35 Hd 8.26N 47.24 E
La Sarre 42 Jg 48.48N 79.12W
Las Aves, Islas- 54 Ea 11.58N 67.33W
Las Avispas 55 Bi 29.53S 61.18W
Las Bardenas 13 Kb 42.10N 1.25W
Las Bonitas 50 Di 7.52N 65.40W
Las Breñas 56 Hc 27.05S 61.05W
Las Cabezas de San Juan 13 Gh 36.59N 5.56W
Lascahobas 49 Ld 18.50N 71.56W
Lascano 55 Ek 33.40S 54.12W
Las Casitas, Cerro- 47 Cd 23.31N 109.53W
Lascaux, Grotte de- 11 Hi 45.03N 1.11 E
Las Cejas 56 Hc 26.53S 64.44W
Las Chilcas, Arroyo- 55 Cm 37.16S 58.26W
Las Choapas 47 Fe 17.55N 94.05W
Las Cinco Villas 13 Kb 42.05N 1.07W
Las Cruces 43 Fe 32.23N 106.29W
Läsdäred 35 Hc 10.10N 46.01 E
Lās Dawa'o 35 Hc 10.22N 49.03 E
La Segarra 13 Nc 41.30N 1.10 E
La Selva 13 Oc 41.40N 2.50 E
La Serena 13 Gf 38.45N 5.30W
La Serena 53 Ih 29.54S 71.16W
La Seu d'Urgell/Seo de Urgel 13 Nb 42.21N 1.28 E
La-Seyne-sur-Mer 11 Lk 43.06N 5.53 E
Las Flores 56 Ie 36.03S 59.07W
Lāsh-e Joveyn 23 Jc 31.43N 61.37 E
Las Heras 56 Gd 32.51S 68.49W
Lashkar Gāh 22 If 31.35N 64.21 E
Las Hurdes 13 Fd 40.20N 6.20W
La Sila 5 Hh 39.15N 16.20 E
Łasin 10 Pc 53.32N 19.05 E
Łask 10 Pe 51.36N 19.07 E
Las Lajas 56 Fe 38.31S 70.22W
Las Lomitas 56 Hb 24.42S 60.36W
Las Margaritas 48 Ni 16.19N 91.59W
Las Mariñas 13 Da 43.20N 8.15W
Las Marismas 13 Fg 37.00N 6.15W
Las Mercedes 54 Eb 9.07N 66.24W
Las Mestenas 48 Gc 28.13N 104.35W
Las Minas, Cerro- 47 Gf 14.33N 88.39W
Las Minas, Sierra de- 47 Ge 15.05N 90.00W
Las Mixtecas, Sierra del- 48 Ki 17.45N 97.15W
La Sola, Isla- 54 Fa 11.20N 63.34W
La Solana 13 If 38.56N 3.14W
Lasolo 26 Hg 3.29S 122.04 E
La Sorcière 51k Bb 13.59N 60.56W
La Souterraine 11 Hh 46.14N 1.29 E
Las Palmas [3] 32 Ed 28.20N 14.20W
Las Palmas de Gran Canaria 31 Ff 28.06N 15.24W
Las Petas 55 Cc 16.23S 59.11W
La Spezia 6 Gg 44.07N 9.50 E
Las Piedras 56 Id 34.45S 56.13W
Las Plumas 53 Jj 43.40S 67.15W
Lās Qoray 35 Hc 11.15N 48.22 E
Las Rosas 55 Bk 32.28S 61.34W
Lassen Peak 43 Cc 40.29N 121.31W
Lassigny 12 Ee 49.35N 2.51 E
Laßnitz 14 Jd 46.46N 15.32 E
Lasso 64b Ba 15.02N 145.38 E
Las Tablas 49 Gj 7.46N 80.17W
Last Mountain Lake 42 Gf 51.10N 105.15W
Las Toscas 55 Ci 28.21S 59.17W
Lastoursville 36 Bc 0.49S 12.42 E
Lastovo 14 Kh 42.46N 16.55 E
Lastovo 14 Kh 42.45N 16.50 E
Lastovski kanal 14 Kh 42.50N 16.59 E
Las Tres Virgenes, Volcán- 47 Bc 27.27N 112.34W
Las Tunas [3] 49 Ic 21.00N 77.00W
Las Tunas, Punta- 51a Bb 18.30N 66.37W
Las Varillas 56 Hd 31.52S 62.43W
Las Vegas [N.M.-U.S.] 43 Fd 35.36N 105.13W
Las Vegas [Nv.-U.S.] 39 Hf 36.11N 115.08W
Las Villuercas 13 Ge 39.33N 5.27W
Łaszczów 10 Tf 50.32N 23.40 E
Lata 65c Db 14.14S 169.29W
Latacunga 54 Cd 0.55S 78.37W
La Tagua 54 Dd 0.03S 74.40W
Latakia (EN) = Al Lādhiqīyah 22 Ff 35.31N 35.07 E
Latarc, Causse du- 11 Jk 43.57N 3.11 E
Late Island 61 Gc 18.48S 174.39W
Laterza 14 Kj 40.37N 16.48 E
La Teste 11 Ej 44.38N 1.09W
Latgale 8 Lh 56.45N 27.30 E
Latgales Augstiene/Latgalskaja Vozvyšennost 8 Lh 56.10N 27.30 E
Latgalskaja Vozvyšennost/Latgales Augstiene 8 Lh 56.10N 27.30 E
Latharna/Larne 9 Hg 54.51N 5.49W
Lathen 12 Jb 52.52N 7.19 E
La Tigra 55 Bh 27.06S 60.34W
Latina 14 Gi 41.28N 12.52 E
Latisana 14 Ge 45.47N 13.00 E
Latium (EN) = Lazio [2] 14 Gh 42.02N 12.23 E
La Toja 13 Db 42.27N 8.50W
La Toma 56 Gd 33.03S 65.37W
La Tontouta 63b Ce 22.00S 166.15 E
Latorica 10 Rh 48.28N 21.50 E
La Tortuga, Isla- 54 Ea 10.56N 65.20W
La-Tour-du-Pin 11 Li 45.34N 5.27 E
La Trimouille 11 Hh 46.28N 1.03 E
La Trinidad 49 Dg 12.58N 86.14W
La Trinidad de Orichuna 50 Bi 7.07N 69.45W
La Trinité 50 Fe 14.44N 60.58W
Latronico 14 Kj 40.05N 16.01 E
Lattari, Monti- 14 Ij 40.40N 14.30 E
La Tuque 42 Kg 47.27N 72.47W
Lātūr 25 Fe 18.24N 76.35 E
Latvian SSR (EN) = Latvijas PSR [2] 19 Cd 57.00N 25.00 E
Latvijas PSR = Latvian SSR (EN) [2] 19 Cd 57.00N 25.00 E
Latvijskaja Sovetskaja Socialističeskaja Respublika [2] 19 Cd 57.00N 25.00 E
Latvijskaja SSR/Latvijas Padomju Socialistiska Respublika [2] 19 Cd 57.00N 25.00 E
Lau 30 Kh 6.56N 30.16 E
Laubach 12 Kd 50.33N 8.59 E
Lauchert 10 Fh 48.05N 9.15 E
Lauchhammer 10 Je 51.30N 13.48 E
Lauenburg 10 Gc 53.22N 10.34 E
Lauf an der Pegnitz 10 Hg 49.31N 11.17 E
Laughlan Islands 63a Ac 9.15S 153.40 E
Laughlin Peak 45 Dh 36.38N 104.12W
Lau Group 57 Jf 18.20S 178.30W
Lauhanvuori 8 Jb 62.10N 22.10 E
Laujar de Andarax 13 Jh 36.59N 2.51W
Laukaa 7 Fe 62.25N 25.57 E
Laukuva 8 Ji 55.35N 22.08 E
Laulau, Bahia- 64b Ba 15.08N 145.46 E
Launceston [Austl.] 58 Fi 41.26S 147.08 E
Launceston [Eng.-U.K.] 9 Ik 50.38N 4.21W
La Unión [Bol.] 55 Bb 15.18S 61.05W
La Unión [Chile] 56 Ff 40.17S 73.05W
La Unión [Col.] 54 Cc 1.37N 77.08W
La Unión [ElSal.] 47 Gf 13.20N 87.51W
La Unión [Mex.] 48 Ii 17.58N 101.49W
La Unión [Peru] 54 Ce 9.46S 76.48W
La Unión [Sp.] 13 Lg 37.37N 0.52W
La Unión [Ven.] 49 Ni 8.13N 67.46W
Laura 59 Ic 15.34S 144.28 E
La Urbana 50 Ci 7.08N 66.56W
Laurel [Ms.-U.S.] 43 Je 31.42N 89.08W
Laurel [Mt.-U.S.] 43 Fb 45.40N 108.46W
Laureles 55 Ej 31.23S 55.52W
Laurel Hill 44 He 40.02N 79.17W
Laurel Mountain 44 Hf 39.20N 79.50W
Laurens 44 Fh 34.30N 82.01W
Laurentian Plateau (EN) = Laurentien, Plateau- 38 Md 50.00N 70.00W
Laurentian Scarp 44 Ic 45.50N 76.15W
Laurentide Scarp 44 Kb 46.38N 73.00W
Laurentien, Plateau- = Laurentian Plateau (EN) 38 Md 50.00N 70.00W
Lauria 14 Jj 40.02N 15.50 E
Lau Ridge (EN) 3 Kl 25.00S 179.00 E
Laurie River 42 He 56.00N 100.58W
Laurinburg 44 Hh 34.47N 79.27W
Laurium 44 Cb 47.14N 88.26W
Lauro Muller 55 Hi 28.24S 49.23W
Lausanne 6 Gf 46.30N 6.40 E
Lausitzer Gebirge 10 Kf 50.48N 14.40 E
Lausitzer Neiße 10 Kd 52.04N 14.46 E
Laut, Pulau- 26 Ef 4.43N 107.59 E
Laut, Pulau- 21 Nj 3.40S 116.10 E
Lautaret, Col du- 11 Mi 45.02N 6.24 E
Lautaro 56 Fe 38.31S 72.27W
Lautém 26 Ih 8.22S 126.54 E
Lauter 10 Eg 48.58N 8.11 E
Lauterbach 10 Ff 50.38N 9.24 E
Lauterbourg 12 Kf 48.59N 8.11 E
Lauterecken 12 Je 49.39N 7.36 E
Lauthala 63d Cb 16.45S 179.41W
Laut Kecil, Kepulauan- 26 Gg 4.50S 115.45 E
Lautoka 61 Ec 17.37S 177.27 E
Lauvergne Island 64d Cb 7.00N 152.00 E
Lauwersmeer 12 Ia 53.25N 6.15 E
Lauzerte 11 Hj 44.15N 1.08 E
Lauzon 44 Lb 46.50N 71.10W
Lauzoue 11 Gj 44.03N 0.15 E
Lava 10 Rb 54.37N 21.14 E
Lava, Nosy- [Mad.] 37 Hb 12.49S 48.41 E
Lava, Nosy- [Mad.] 37 Hb 13.48S 47.36 E
Lavaca River 45 Hl 28.50N 96.36W
Lava Flow 45 Bi 34.35N 108.20W
Laval 11 Ff 48.01N 0.46W
Lavalle 55 Ci 29.01S 59.11W
Lavalleja [2] 55 El 34.00S 55.00W
Lāvān, Jazīreh-ye- 23 Hd 26.48N 53.00 E
Lavanggu 63a Ed 11.37S 160.15 E
Lavant 14 Id 46.38N 14.56 E
Lavapié, Punta- 52 Ii 37.09S 73.35W
Lāvar Meydān 24 Pg 30.20N 54.30 E
Lavassaare 8 Kf 58.29N 24.16 E
Lavaur 11 Hk 43.42N 1.49 E
La Vecilla 13 Gb 42.51N 5.24W
La Vega 47 Je 19.13N 70.31W
La Vela de Coro 49 Mh 11.27N 69.34W
Lavelanet 11 Hl 42.56N 1.51 E
Lavello 14 Ji 41.03N 15.48 E
La Venta 47 Fe 18.08N 94.03W
Laventie 12 Ed 50.38N 2.46 E
La Ventura 48 Ie 24.37N 100.54W
La Vera 13 Gd 40.05N 5.30W
L'Averdy, Cape- 63a Ba 5.33S 155.04 E
Laverton 59 Ee 28.38S 122.25 E
Lavia 7 Ff 61.36N 22.36 E
La Victoria 54 Ea 10.14N 67.20W
La Villa Jojosa/Villajoyosa 13 Lf 38.30N 0.14W
La Villita, Presa- 48 Hh 18.05N 102.05W
La Viña 54 Ce 6.54S 79.28W

Index Symbols

[1] Independent Nation
[2] State, Region
[3] District, County
[4] Municipality
[5] Colony, Dependency
Continent
Physical Region
Historical or Cultural Region
Mount, Mountain
Volcano
Hill
Mountains, Mountain Range
Hills, Escarpment
Plateau, Upland
Pass, Gap
Plain, Lowland
Delta
Salt Flat
Valley, Canyon
Crater, Cave
Karst Features
Depression
Polder
Desert, Dunes
Forest, Woods
Heath, Steppe
Oasis
Cape, Point
Coast, Beach
Cliff
Peninsula
Isthmus
Sandbank
Island
Atoll
Rock, Reef
Islands, Archipelago
Rocks, Reefs
Coral Reef
Well, Spring
Geyser
River, Stream
Waterfall Rapids
River Mouth, Estuary
Lake
Salt Lake
Intermittent Lake
Reservoir
Swamp, Pond
Canal
Glacier
Ice Shelf, Pack Ice
Ocean
Sea
Gulf, Bay
Strait, Fjord
Lagoon
Bank
Seamount
Tablemount
Ridge
Shelf
Basin
Escarpment, Sea Scarp
Fracture
Trench, Abyss
National Park, Reserve
Point of Interest
Recreation Site
Cave, Cavern
Historic Site
Ruins
Wall, Walls
Church, Abbey
Temple
Scientific Station
Airport
Port
Lighthouse
Mine
Tunnel
Dam, Bridge

Index Symbols

[1] Independent Nation
[2] State, Region
[3] District, County
[4] Municipality
[5] Colony, Dependency
Continent
Physical Region
Historical or Cultural Region
Mount, Mountain
Volcano
Hill
Mountains, Mountain Range
Hills, Escarpment
Plateau, Upland
Pass, Gap
Plain, Lowland
Delta
Salt Flat
Valley, Canyon
Crater, Cave
Karst Features
Depression
Polder
Desert, Dunes
Forest, Woods
Heath, Steppe
Oasis
Cape, Point
Coast, Beach
Cliff
Peninsula
Isthmus
Sandbank
Island
Atoll
Rock, Reef
Islands, Archipelago
Rocks, Reefs
Coral Reef
Well, Spring
Geyser
River, Stream
Waterfall Rapids
River Mouth, Estuary
Lake
Salt Lake
Intermittent Lake
Reservoir
Swamp, Pond
Canal
Glacier
Ice Shelf, Pack Ice
Ocean
Sea
Gulf, Bay
Strait, Fjord
Lagoon
Bank
Seamount
Tablemount
Ridge
Shelf
Basin
Escarpment, Sea Scarp
Fracture
Trench, Abyss
National Park, Reserve
Point of Interest
Recreation Site
Cave, Cavern
Historic Site
Ruins
Wall, Walls
Church, Abbey
Temple
Scientific Station
Airport
Port
Lighthouse
Mine
Tunnel
Dam, Bridge

Levkōsia/Lefkosa=Nicosia (EN) 22 Ff 35.10N 33.22 E
Levoča 10 Qg 49.02N 20.35 E
Levroux 11 Hh 46.59N 1.37 E
Levski 15 If 43.22N 25.08 E
Lev Tolstoj 16 Kc 53.12N 39.28 E
Levuka 63d Bb 17.41S 178.50 E
Levuo/Lévuo 8 Kh 56.02N 24.28 E
Lévuo/Levuo 8 Kh 56.02N 24.28 E
Lewes [De.-U.S.] 44 Jf 38.47N 75.08W
Lewes [Eng.-U.K.] 9 Nk 50.52N 0.01 E
Lewin Brzeski 10 Nf 50.46N 17.37 E
Lewis, Butt of- 9 Gc 58.31N 6.15W
Lewis, Isle of- 5 Fd 58.10N 6.40W
Lewis and Clark Lake 45 He 42.50N 97.45W
Lewisburg 44 Gg 37.49N 80.28W
Lewis Pass 62 Ee 42.24S 172.24 E
Lewis Range 38 He 48.30N 113.15W
Lewis River 46 Dd 45.51N 122.48W
Lewis Smith Lake 44 Dh 34.00N 87.07W
Lewiston [Id.-U.S.] 39 He 46.25N 117.01W
Lewiston [Me.-U.S.] 43 Mc 44.06N 70.13W
Lewistown [Mt.-U.S.] 43 Fb 47.04N 109.26W
Lewistown [Pa.-U.S.] 44 Ie 40.37N 77.36W
Lewisville 45 Jj 33.22N 93.35W
Lexington [Ky.-U.S.] 39 Kf 38.03N 84.30W
Lexington [Nb.-U.S.] 43 Hc 40.47N 99.45W
Lexington [N.C.-U.S.] 44 Gh 35.49N 80.15W
Lexington [Ok.-U.S.] 45 Hi 35.01N 97.20W
Lexington [Va.-U.S.] 44 Hg 37.47N 79.27W
Leygues, Iles- 30 Nm 48.45S 69.30 E
Leyre 11 Ej 44.39N 1.01W
Leysdown-on-Sea 12 Cc 51.23N 0.55 E
Leyte 21 Oh 10.50N 124.50 E
Lez 11 Kj 44.13N 4.43 E
Ležajsk 10 Sf 50.16N 22.24 E
Lézard, Pointe à- 51e Ab 16.08N 61.47W
Lézarde, Rivière- 51h Ab 14.36N 61.01W
Lezha 15 Ch 41.47N 19.39 E
Lézignan-Corbières 11 Ik 43.12N 2.46 E
Lgov 19 De 51.41N 35.17 E
Lhari 27 Fe 30.48N 93.25 E
Lhasa 22 Lg 29.42N 91.07 E
Lhazê 27 Ef 29.13N 87.44 E
Lhazhong 27 Ee 31.28N 86.36 E
Lhokseumawe 26 Ce 5.10N 97.08 E
Lhoksukon 26 Ce 5.03N 97.19 E
L'Hôpital 12 Ie 49.10N 6.44 E
Lhorong 27 Ge 30.45N 95.48 E
L'Hospitalet de l'Infant/Hospitalet del Infante 13 Md 40.59N 0.56 E
Lhozhag 27 Ff 28.18N 90.51 E
Lhünzhub (Poindo) 27 Fe 30.17N 91.20 E
Liådhi 15 Jm 36.55N 26.10 E
Liákoura 15 Fk 38.32N 22.37 E
Liamone 11a Aa 42.04N 8.43 E
Liancheng 27 Kf 25.48N 116.48 E
Liancourt 12 Ee 49.20N 2.28 E
Liane 12 Dd 50.43N 1.36 E
Liangcheng 28 Bd 40.32N 112.28 E
Liangpran, Gunung- 26 Ff 1.04N 114.23 E
Liangshan (Houji) 28 Dg 35.48N 116.07 E
Liangzhou → Wuwei 22 Mf 37.58N 102.48 E
Liangzi Hu 27 Je 30.15N 114.32 E
Lianjiang 27 Jg 21.42N 110.14 E
Lianshui 28 Eh 33.47N 119.16 E
Lianxian 27 Jg 24.48N 112.26 E
Lianyin 27 La 53.26N 123.50 E
Lianyungang 27 Ke 34.38N 119.27 E
Lianyungang (Xinpu) 22 Nf 34.34N 119.15 E
Lianzhou → Hepu 27 Ig 21.40N 109.12 E
Lianzhushan 28 Kb 45.28N 131.45 E
Liaocheng 27 Kd 36.27N 115.58 E
Liaodong Bandao=Liaotung Peninsula (EN) 21 Of 40.00N 122.20 E
Liaodong Wan=Liaotung, Gulf of- (EN) 27 Lc 40.00N 121.30 E
Liao He 21 Oe 40.39N 122.12 E
Liaoning Sheng (Liao-ning Sheng) [2] 27 Lc 41.00N 123.00 E
Liao-ning Sheng → Liaoning Sheng [2] 27 Lc 41.00N 123.00 E
Liaotung, Gulf of- (EN)=Liaodong Wan 27 Lc 40.00N 121.30 E
Liaotung Peninsula (EN)=Liaodong Bandao 21 Of 40.00N 122.20 E
Liaoyang 27 Lc 41.16N 123.10 E
Liaoyuan 22 Oe 42.55N 125.09 E
Liaozhong 28 Gd 41.30N 122.42 E
Liard 38 Gc 61.52N 121.18W
Liard River 42 Ee 59.15N 126.09W
Liat, Pulau- 26 Eg 2.53S 107.05 E
Liatorp 8 Fh 56.40N 14.16 E
Liatroim/Leitrim [2] 9 Eg 54.20N 8.20W
Liban 30 Lh 5.05N 40.05 E
Libano 55 Bm 37.32S 61.18W
Libby 46 Hb 48.23N 115.33W
Libenge 31 Ih 3.39N 18.38 E
Libengé 36 Cb 3.39N 18.38 E
Liberal 43 Gd 37.02N 100.55W
Liberec 10 Lf 50.46N 15.03 E
Liberia 47 Gf 10.38N 85.27W
Liberia [1] 31 Fh 6.00N 10.00W
Libertad [Ur.] 55 Dl 34.38S 56.39W
Libertad [Ven.] 49 Li 8.08N 71.28W
Libertad [Ven.] 54 Eb 8.20N 69.37W
Libertade, Rio- 54 He 9.35S 52.17W
Libertador General Bernardo O'Higgins [2] 56 Fd 33.35S 70.45W
Libertador Gen. San Martín 56 Hb 23.48S 64.48W
Libertador General San Martín, Cumbre del- 52 Jh 24.55S 66.40W
Liberty [Mo.-U.S.] 45 Ig 39.15N 94.25W
Liberty [Tx.-U.S.] 45 Ik 30.03N 94.47W
Lībīyā=Libya (EN) [1] 31 If 27.00N 17.00 E
Lībīyah, Aş Şaḩrā' al-=Libyan Desert (EN) 30 Jf 24.00N 25.00 E
Libo 27 If 25.28N 107.52 E
Libobo, Tanjung- 26 Ig 0.54S 128.28 E
Liboi 36 Hb 0.24N 40.57 E
Libourne 11 Fj 44.55N 0.14W
Libramont-Chevigny 12 He 49.55N 5.23 E
Librazhdi 15 Dh 41.11N 20.19 E
Libreville 31 Hh 0.23N 9.27 E
Libro Point 26 Gd 11.26N 119.29 E
Libya (EN)=Lībīyā [1] 31 If 27.00N 17.00 E
Libyan Desert (EN)=Lībīyah, Aş Şaḩrā' al- 30 Jf 24.00N 25.00 E
Licantén 56 Fe 34.59S 72.00W
Licata 14 Hm 37.06N 13.56 E
Lice 24 Ic 38.28N 40.39 E
Licenciado Matienzo 55 Cm 37.55S 58.54W
Lich 12 Kd 50.31N 8.50 E
Licheng → Jinhu 28 Eh 33.01N 119.01 E
Lichfield 9 Li 52.42N 1.48W
Lichinga 31 Kj 13.20S 35.20 E
Lichtenau 12 Kc 51.37N 8.54 E
Lichtenburg 37 De 26.08S 26.08 E
Lichtenfels 10 Hf 50.09N 11.04 E
Lichtenvoorde 12 Ic 51.59N 6.34 E
Licking River 44 Ef 39.06N 84.30W
Licosa, Punta- 14 Ij 40.15N 14.54 E
Licuare 37 Fc 17.54S 36.49 E
Licun → Laoshan 28 Ff 36.10N 120.25 E
Licungo 37 Fc 17.40S 37.22 E
Lida 19 Ce 53.56N 25.18 E
Lidan 8 Ef 58.31N 13.09 E
Liddel 9 Kf 55.04N 2.57W
Liddon Gulf 42 Gb 75.00N 113.30W
Liden 7 De 62.42N 16.48 E
Lidhorikion 15 Fk 38.32N 22.12 E
Lidhult 8 Eh 56.50N 13.26 E
Lidingö 7 Eg 59.22N 18.08 E
Lidköping 7 Cg 58.30N 13.10 E
Lido 34 Fc 12.54N 3.44 E
Lido, Venezia- 14 Ge 45.25N 12.22 E
Lido di Ostia 14 Gi 41.44N 12.16 E
Lidzbark 10 Pc 53.17N 19.49 E
Lidzbark Warmiński 10 Qb 54.09N 20.35 E
Lié 11 Df 48.00N 2.40W
Liebenau 12 Lb 52.36N 9.06 E
Liebig, Mount- 59 Gd 23.15S 131.20 E
Liechtenstein [1] 6 Gf 47.10N 9.30 E
Liège [3] 12 Hd 50.30N 5.40 E
Liège/Luik 12 Ge 50.38N 5.34 E
Lieksa 7 He 63.19N 30.01 E
Lielupe 7 Fh 57.03N 23.56 E
Lielvärde/Lielvarde 8 Kh 56.40N 24.49 E
Lielvarde/Lielvärde 8 Kh 56.40N 24.49 E
Lienen 12 Jb 52.09N 7.59 E
Lienz 14 Gd 46.50N 12.47 E
Liepaja/Liepāja 6 Id 56.35N 21.01 E
Liepāja/Liepaja 6 Id 56.35N 21.01 E
Liepajas, Ozero-/Liepājas Ezers 8 Ih 56.35N 20.35 E
Liepājas ezers/Liepaja, Ozero- 8 Ih 56.35N 20.35 E
Liepna 8 Lg 57.16N 27.35 E
Liepupe 8 Kg 57.22N 24.22 E
Lier/Lierre 11 Kc 51.08N 4.34 E
Lierbyen 8 De 59.47N 10.14 E
Lierneux 12 Hd 50.17N 5.48 E
Lierre/Lier 11 Kc 51.08N 4.34 E
Liesborn, Wadersloh- 12 Kc 51.43N 8.16 E
Lieser 10 Dg 49.55N 7.01 E
Liesing 14 Jc 47.20N 15.02 E
Liestal 14 Bc 47.29N 7.44 E
Lieşti 15 Kd 45.37N 27.31 E
Lieto 8 Jd 60.30N 22.27 E
Lietuvos Tarybu Socialistine Respublika/Litovskaja SSR [2] 19 Cd 56.00N 24.00 E
Lietuvos TSR=Lithuanian SSR (EN) [2] 19 Cd 56.00N 24.00 E
Lietvesi 8 Lc 61.30N 28.00 E
Lieurey 12 Ce 49.14N 0.29 E
Lieuvin 11 Ge 49.10N 0.30 E
Lievestuoreenjärvi 8 Lb 62.20N 26.10 E
Liévin 11 Id 50.25N 2.46 E
Lievre, Rivière du- 44 Jc 45.35N 75.25W
Liezen 14 Ic 47.34N 14.14 E
Lifford/Leifear 9 Fg 54.50N 7.29W
Li Fiord 42 Ia 80.17N 94.35W
Lifjell 8 Ce 59.30N 8.52 E
Lifou, Ile- 57 Hg 20.53S 167.13 E
Lifuka 65b Ba 19.48S 174.21W
Ligatne/Līgatne 8 Kg 57.07N 25.00 E
Līgatne/Ligatne 8 Kg 57.07N 25.00 E
Lighthouse Reef 49 De 17.20N 87.32W
Lignano Sabbiadoro 14 He 45.52N 13.09 E
Lignières 11 Ih 46.45N 2.10 E
Lignon 11 Ki 45.44N 4.08 E
Ligny-en-Barrois 11 Lf 48.41N 5.20 E
Ligonha 37 Fc 16.51S 39.09 E
Ligure, Mar-=Ligurian Sea (EN) 5 Gg 43.30N 9.00 E
Liguria [2] 14 Cf 44.30N 8.50 E
Ligurian Sea (EN)=Ligure, Mar- 5 Gg 43.30N 9.00 E
Lihir Group 57 Ge 3.05S 152.40 E
Lihme 8 Ch 56.36N 8.44 E
Lihoslavl 7 Ih 57.09N 35.29 E
Lihou Reefs and Cays 57 Gf 17.25S 151.40 E
Lihue 60 Oc 21.59N 159.22W
Lihula 7 Fg 58.44N 23.49 E
Liinahamari 7 Hb 69.40N 31.22 E
Lijiang (Dayan) 22 Mg 26.56N 100.15 E
Lijin 28 Ef 37.29N 118.15 E
Lika 14 Jf 44.46N 15.10 E
Lika 14 Jf 44.30N 15.30 E
Likasi 31 Jj 10.59S 26.43 E
Likati 36 Db 3.21N 23.53 E
Likati 36 Db 3.21N 23.53 E
Likénai/Likenaj 8 Kh 56.11N 24.42 E
Likenaj/Likėnai 8 Kh 56.11N 24.42 E
Likenäs 8 Ed 60.37N 13.02 E
Likhapani 25 Jc 27.19N 95.54 E
Likiep Atoll 57 Hc 9.53N 169.09 E
Likolo 36 Cc 0.43S 19.40 E
Likoma Island 36 Fe 12.04S 34.44 E
Likoto 36 Dc 1.10S 24.45 E
Likouala [3] 36 Cb 2.00N 17.30 E
Likouala 36 Cc 1.13S 16.48 E
Likouala aux Herbes 36 Cc 0.50S 17.11 E
Liku 64k Bb 19.02S 169.47W
L'Ile Rousse 11a Aa 42.38N 8.56 E
Lilibeo, Capo-→ Boeo, Capo- 14 Gm 37.34N 12.41 E
Lilienfeld 14 Jb 48.01N 15.38 E
Lilienthal 12 Ka 53.08N 8.55 E
Lilla Edet 7 Cg 58.08N 12.08 E
Lille [Bel.] 12 Gc 51.14N 4.50 E
Lille [Fr.] 6 Ge 50.38N 3.04 E
Lille Bælt=Little Belt (EN) 5 Gd 55.20N 9.45 E
Lillebonne 11 Ge 49.31N 0.33 E
Lille Fiskebanke 8 Bh 56.56N 6.20 E
Lillehammer 7 Cf 61.08N 10.30 E
Lille Hellefiske Bank (EN) 41 Ge 65.05N 54.00W
Lillers 11 Id 50.34N 2.29 E
Lillesand 7 Bg 58.15N 8.24 E
Lillestrøm 8 De 59.57N 11.05 E
Lillhärdal 7 Df 61.51N 14.04 E
Lillie Glacier 66 Kf 70.45S 163.55 E
Lillo 13 Ie 39.43N 3.18W
Lillooet 42 Ff 50.42N 121.56W
Lillooet Range 46 Eb 50.00N 121.45W
Lillooet River 42 Fg 49.45N 122.10W
Lilongwe 31 Kj 13.59S 33.47 E
Liloy 26 He 8.08N 122.40 E
Lim [Afr.] 35 Bd 7.54N 15.46 E
Lim [Yugo.] 14 Ng 43.45N 19.13 E
Lima 13 Dc 41.41N 8.50W
Lima [2] 54 Cf 12.00S 76.35W
Lima [Mt.-U.S.] 46 Id 44.38N 112.36W
Lima [Oh.-U.S.] 43 Kc 40.43N 84.06W
Lima [Par.] 55 Df 23.54S 56.20W
Lima [Peru] 53 Ig 12.03S 77.03W
Lima [Swe.] 8 Ed 60.56N 13.21 E
Lima, Pulau-Pulau- 26 Gg 3.03S 107.24 E
Limagne 11 Jh 46.00N 3.20 E
Līmah 24 Qj 25.56N 56.25 E
Liman [R.S.F.S.R.] 16 Og 45.45N 47.14 E
Liman [Ukr.-U.S.S.R.] 15 Md 45.42N 29.46 E
Limanskoje 15 Mc 46.38N 29.54 E
Limari, Rio- 56 Fd 30.44S 71.43W
Limassol/Lemesós 23 Dc 34.40N 33.02 E
Limavady/Léim an Mhadaidh 9 Gf 55.03N 6.57W
Limay 12 Df 48.59N 1.44 E
Limay, Rio- 52 Ji 38.59S 68.00W
Limbara 14 Dj 40.51N 9.10 E
Limbaži 7 Fh 57.31N 24.47 E
Limbé 49 Kd 19.42N 72.24W
Limbe, Blantyre- 36 Gf 15.49S 35.03 E
Limbot 63b Cb 14.12S 167.34 E
Limboto 26 Hf 0.37N 122.57 E
Limbourg 12 Hd 50.37N 5.56 E
Limbourg/Limburg [3] 11 Lc 51.05N 5.40 E
Limburg [Bel.] [3] 12 Hc 51.00N 5.30 E
Limburg [Neth.] [3] 12 Hc 51.14N 5.50 E
Limburg/Limbourg [3] 11 Lc 51.05N 5.40 E
Limburg an der Lahn 10 Ef 50.23N 8.03 E
Limedsforsen 8 Ed 60.54N 13.23 E
Limeira 56 Kb 22.34S 47.24W
Limerick/Luimneach [2] 9 Ei 52.30N 9.00W
Limerick/Luimneach 6 Fe 52.40N 8.38W
Limestone, Haḑabat- 33 Fe 24.50N 32.00 E
Limfjorden 5 Gd 56.55N 9.10 E
Limia 13 Dc 41.41N 8.50W
Limingen 7 Cd 64.47N 13.36 E
Liminka 7 Fd 64.49N 25.29 E
Limmat 14 Cc 47.30N 8.15 E
Limmen Bight 59 Hb 14.45S 135.40 E
Limmen Bight River 59 Hc 15.15S 135.30 E
Limni 15 Gk 38.46N 23.19 E
Limnos=Lemnos (EN) 5 Ih 39.55N 25.15 E
Limoeiro 54 Ke 7.52S 35.27W
Limoges 6 Gf 45.51N 1.15 E
Limogne, Causse de- 11 Hj 44.20N 1.55 E
Limon 43 Gd 39.16N 103.41W
Limón [3] 49 Fi 10.00N 83.15W
Limón [C.R.] 39 Kh 10.00N 83.02W
Limón [Hond.] 49 Ef 15.52N 85.33W
Limone Piemonte 14 Bf 44.12N 7.34 E
Limousin 11 Hi 45.30N 1.50 E
Limousin, Plateau du- 11 Hi 45.30N 1.10 E
Limoux 11 Ik 43.04N 2.14 E
Limpopo 30 Jk 25.12S 33.32 E
Limu Ling 27 Jh 19.02N 109.43 E
Limuru 36 Gc 1.06S 36.39 E
Līnah 24 Jh 28.42N 43.48 E
Lin'an 27 Ke 30.14N 119.39 E
Linapacan 26 Gd 11.27N 119.49 E
Linares [Chile] 53 Ii 35.51S 71.36W
Linares [Mex.] 47 Ed 24.52N 99.34W
Linares [Sp.] 13 If 38.05N 3.38W
Linares Viejo 55 Bf 23.09S 61.46W
Linaro, Capo- 14 Fh 42.02N 11.50 E
Lincang 22 Mg 23.48N 100.04 E
Lincheng 28 Cf 37.26N 114.34 E
Lincheng → Xuecheng 28 Dg 34.48N 117.14 E
Lincoln 9 Mh 53.20N 0.30W
Lincoln [Arg.] 56 Hd 34.52S 61.32W
Lincoln [Eng.-U.K.] 9 Mh 53.14N 0.33W
Lincoln [Il.-U.S.] 45 Lf 40.09N 89.22W
Lincoln [Nb.-U.S.] 39 Je 40.48N 96.42W
Lincoln [N.Z.] 62 Ee 43.38S 172.29 E
Lincoln, Mount- 45 Cg 39.21N 106.07W
Lincoln City 46 Cd 44.59N 124.01W
Lincoln Sea 67 Ne 83.00N 56.00W
Lincolnshire [3] 9 Mh 53.00N 0.10W
Lindashalvøya 8 Ad 60.40N 5.15 E
Lindau 10 Fi 47.33N 9.41 E
Linde [Neth.] 12 Hb 52.49N 5.52 E
Linde [R.S.F.S.R.] 20 Hd 64.59N 124.36 E
Linden [Guy.] 54 Gb 6.00N 58.18W
Linden [Tn.-U.S.] 44 Dh 35.37N 87.50W
Lindenows Fjord 41 Hf 60.25N 43.00W
Linderödsåsen 8 Ei 55.53N 13.56 E
Lindesberg 7 Dg 59.35N 15.15 E
Lindesnes 5 Gd 58.00N 7.02 E
Lindhorst 12 Lb 52.22N 9.17 E
Lindhos 15 Lm 36.06N 28.04 E
Lindi [3] 36 Gd 9.30S 38.20 E
Lindi 31 Ki 10.00S 39.43 E
Lindi 30 Jh 0.33N 25.05 E
Lindis Pass 62 Cf 44.35S 169.39 E
Lindlar 12 Jc 51.01N 7.23 E
Lindome 8 Eg 57.34N 12.05 E
Lindong → Bairin Zuoqi 27 Kc 43.59N 119.22 E
Lindsay [Ca.-U.S.] 46 Fh 36.12N 119.05W
Lindsay [Ont.-Can.] 44 Hc 44.21N 78.44W
Lindsdal 8 Gh 56.44N 16.18 E
Line Islands 57 Le 0.01S 157.00W
Linfen 27 Jd 36.03N 111.32 E
Lingayen 22 Oh 16.01N 120.14 E
Lingayen Gulf 26 Hc 16.15N 120.14 E
Lingbi 28 Dh 33.33N 117.33 E
Lingbo 7 Df 61.03N 16.41 E
Lingchuan 28 Bg 35.46N 113.16 E
Lingen (Ems) 10 Dd 52.31N 7.19 E
Lingfield 12 Bc 51.10N 0.01W
Lingga, Kepulauan-=Lingga Archipelago (EN) 21 Mj 0.02S 104.35 E
Lingga, Pulau- 26 Dg 0.12S 104.35 E
Lingga Archipelago (EN)=Lingga, Kepulauan- 21 Mj 0.02S 104.35 E
Linghed 8 Fd 60.47N 15.51 E
Lingling 27 Jf 26.24N 111.41 E
Lingomo 36 Db 0.38N 21.59 E
Lingqiu 28 Ce 39.26N 114.14 E
Lingshan 27 Ig 22.30N 109.17 E
Lingshan Dao 28 Fg 35.45N 120.10 E
Lingshi 28 Af 36.50N 111.46 E
Lingshou 28 Ce 38.18N 114.22 E
Linguère 31 Fg 15.24N 15.07W
Lingwu 27 Id 38.05N 106.20 E
Lingxian 28 Df 37.20N 116.35 E
Lingyuan 28 Ed 41.15N 119.23 E
Linh, Ngoc- 21 Mh 15.04N 107.59 E
Linhai 27 La 51.36N 124.22 E
Linhai (Taizhou) 27 Lf 28.52N 121.08 E
Linhares 54 Jg 19.25S 40.04W
Linhe 27 Ic 40.49N 107.28 E
Linhuaiguan 28 Dh 32.54N 117.39 E
Linjiang 28 Id 41.49N 126.55 E
Linköping 6 Hd 58.25N 15.37 E
Linkou 27 Nb 45.18N 130.18 E
Linkuva 8 Jh 56.02N 23.58 E
Linlü Shan 28 Bf 36.02N 113.42 E
Linn, Mount- 46 Df 40.03N 122.48W
Linneryd 8 Fh 56.40N 15.07 E
Linnhe, Loch- 9 He 56.37N 5.25W
Linnich 12 Id 50.59N 6.16 E
Linosa 14 Go 35.50N 12.50 E
Linovo 10 Ud 52.28N 24.35 E
Linqing 27 Kd 36.48N 115.49 E
Linqu 28 Ef 36.31N 118.32 E
Linquan 28 Ch 33.04N 115.16 E
Linru 28 Bg 34.10N 112.51 E
Lins 56 Kb 21.40S 49.45W
Linsell 8 Eb 62.09N 13.53 E
Linshu (Xiazhuang) 28 Eg 34.56N 118.38 E
Linslade 12 Bc 51.55N 0.40W
Linta 37 Ge 25.02S 44.05 E
Lintao 27 Hd 35.20N 104.00 E
Linthal 14 Cd 46.55N 9.00 E
Linton [Eng.-U.K.] 12 Cb 52.06N 0.16 E
Linton [N.D.-U.S.] 45 Fc 46.16N 100.14W
Linxi [China] 22 Ne 43.36N 118.02 E
Linxi [China] 28 Ee 39.42N 118.26 E
Linxia 22 Mf 35.28N 102.59 E
Linxian 27 Jd 37.57N 111.00 E
Linxiang 28 Bj 29.29N 113.28 E
Linyi [China] 28 Df 37.11N 116.51 E
Linyi [China]' 27 Kd 35.09N 118.15 E
Linz 6 Hf 48.18N 14.18 E
Linze (Shahezhen) 27 Hd 39.10N 100.21 E
Lion, Golfe du-=Lion, Gulf of- (EN) 5 Gg 43.00N 4.00 E
Lion, Gulf of- (EN)=Lion, Golfe du- 5 Gg 43.00N 4.00 E
Lions Den 37 Ec 17.16S 30.02 E
Lion-sur-Mer 12 Be 49.18N 0.19W
Lioppa 26 Ih 7.40S 126.00 E
Lios Mór/Lismore 9 Fi 52.08N 7.55W
Lios na gCearrbhach/Lisburn 9 Gg 54.31N 6.03W
Lios Tuathail/Listovel 9 Di 52.27N 9.29W
Liouesso 36 Cb 1.02N 15.43 E
Lipa 26 Hd 13.57N 121.10 E
Lipany 10 Qg 49.10N 20.58 E
Lipari 14 Il 38.30N 14.55 E
Lipari 14 Il 38.28N 14.57 E
Lipari Islands (EN)=Eolie o Lipari, Isole- 5 Hh 38.35N 14.55 E
Lipeck 6 Je 52.37N 39.35 E
Lipeckaja Oblast [3] 19 De 52.45N 39.10 E
Lipenská přehradní nádrž 10 Kh 48.45N 14.05 E
Liperi 7 Ge 62.32N 29.22 E
Lipez, Cordillera de- 54 Eh 22.00S 66.45W
Liphook 12 Bc 51.04N 0.48W
Lipkani 15 Ja 48.13N 26.48 E
Lipljan 15 Eg 42.32N 21.08 E
Lipno 10 Pd 52.51N 19.10 E
Lipova 15 Ec 46.05N 21.42 E
Lipovcy 20 Ih 44.15N 131.45 E
Lippborg, Lippetal- 12 Kc 51.40N 8.02 E
Lippe 10 Ce 51.39N 6.38 E
Lipper Bergland 12 Kb 52.05N 8.57 E
Lippetal 12 Kc 51.40N 8.13 E
Lippetal-Eickelborn 12 Kc 51.39N 8.13 E
Lippetal-Lippborg 12 Kc 51.40N 8.02 E
Lippischer Wald 12 Kc 51.56N 8.45 E
Lippstadt 10 Ee 51.40N 8.21 E
Lipsko 10 Re 51.09N 21.39 E
Lipsoi 15 Jl 37.20N 26.45 E
Liptako 30 Hg 14.15N 0.02 E
Liptovský Mikuláš 10 Pg 49.05N 19.38 E
Lira 36 Fb 2.15N 32.54 E
Liranga 36 Cc 0.40S 17.36 E
Liri 14 Hi 41.25N 13.52 E
Liria 13 Le 39.38N 0.36W
Lis 13 De 39.53N 8.58W
Lisa 15 Cf 43.08N 19.42 E
Lisac 15 Eg 42.45N 21.56 E
Lisakovsk 19 Ge 52.33N 62.28 E
Lisala 31 Jh 2.09N 21.31 E
Lisboa [2] 13 Ce 39.00N 9.08W
Lisboa=Lisbon (EN) 6 Fh 38.43N 9.08W
Lisbon 45 Hc 46.27N 97.41W
Lisbon (EN)=Lisboa 6 Fh 38.43N 9.08W
Lisbon Canyon (EN) 13 Cf 38.20N 9.20W
Lisburn/Lios na gCearrbhach 9 Gg 54.31N 6.03W
Lisburne, Cape- 40 Fc 68.52N 166.14W
Liscannor Bay/Bá Thuath Reanna 9 Di 52.55N 9.25W
Lisec 10 Uh 48.48N 24.45 E
Li Shan 28 Ag 35.25N 111.58 E
Lishi 27 Jd 37.29N 111.08 E
Lishu 28 Hc 43.19N 124.20 E
Lishui 27 Kf 28.30N 119.55 E
Lisianski Island 57 Jb 26.02N 174.00W
Lisičansk 19 Df 48.53N 38.28 E
Lisieux 11 Ge 49.09N 0.14 E
Liska 15 Dh 41.19N 20.58 E
L'Isle-Adam 12 Ee 49.07N 2.14 E
L'Isle-Jourdain 11 Hk 43.37N 1.05 E
L'Isle sur-la-Sorgue 11 Lk 43.55N 5.03 E
Lismore 58 Gg 28.48S 153.17 E
Lismore/Lios Mór 9 Fi 52.08N 7.55W
Liss 24 Hg 31.14N 38.31 E
Liss 12 Bc 51.02N 0.54W
List 10 Ea 55.01N 8.26 E
Lista 8 Bf 58.10N 6.40 E
Listafjorden 8 Bf 58.10N 6.35 E
Lister, Mount- 66 Kf 78.04S 162.41 E
Lištica 14 Lg 43.23N 17.39 E
Listovel/Lios Tuathail 9 Di 52.27N 9.29W
Listowel 44 Gd 43.44N 80.57W
Liswarta 10 Pe 51.06N 19.01 E
Lit 8 Fa 63.19N 14.49 E
Litang [China] 27 Ig 23.12N 109.05 E
Litang [China] 27 He 30.02N 100.18 E
Litani Rivier 54 Hc 3.18N 54.06W
Litchfield 45 Id 45.08N 94.31W
Lithgow 58 Gh 33.29S 150.09 E
Lithinon, Ákra- 15 Ho 34.55N 24.44 E
Lithuania (EN) [2] 5 Id 56.00N 24.00 E
Lithuanian SSR (EN)=Lietuvos TSR [2] 19 Cd 56.00N 24.00 E
Litókhoron 15 Fi 40.06N 22.30 E
Litoměřice 10 Kf 50.32N 14.08 E
Litovel 10 Ng 49.43N 17.05 E
Litovko 20 Ig 49.17N 135.10 E
Litovskaja Sovetskaja Socialističeskaja Respublika [2] 19 Cd 56.00N 24.00 E
Litovskaja SSR/Lietuvos Tarybu Socialistine Respublika [2] 19 Cd 56.00N 24.00 E
Little Abaco Island 47 Ic 26.53N 77.43W
Little Abitibi River 44 Ha 49.29N 79.32W
Little Aden 23 Fg 12.45N 44.52 E
Little America 46 Kf 41.32N 109.47W
Little Andaman 21 Lh 10.45N 92.30 E
Little Bahama Bank (EN) 47 Ic 26.30N 78.00W
Little Barrier Island 62 Fb 36.10S 175.05 E
Little Beaver Creek 45 Ec 46.17N 103.56W
Little Belt (EN)=Lille Bælt 5 Gd 55.20N 9.45 E
Little Belt Mountains 46 Jc 46.45N 110.35W
Little Blue River 45 Hg 39.41N 96.40W
Little Bow River 46 Ib 49.53N 112.29W
Little Carpathians (EN)=Malé Karpaty 10 Nh 48.30N 17.20 E
Little Cayman 47 He 19.41N 80.03W
Little Colorado River 38 Hc 36.11N 111.48W
Little Current 42 Jg 45.58N 81.56W
Little Current 42 Jf 50.57N 84.36W
Little Dry Creek 46 Lc 47.21N 106.22W
Little Exuma Island 49 Jb 23.27N 75.37W
Little Falls 43 Ib 45.59N 94.21W
Littlefield 45 Ej 33.55N 102.20W
Little Fort 46 Ea 51.25N 120.12W
Little Grand Rapids 42 Hf 52.02N 95.25W
Little Halibut Bank 9 Lc 58.20N 1.15W
Littlehampton 12 Bd 50.48N 0.32W
Little Inagua Island 47 Jd 21.30N 73.00W
Little Karroo (EN)=Klein-Karoo 37 Cf 33.42S 21.20 E
Little Missouri 38 Ie 47.30N 102.25W
Little Namaland (EN)=Namakwaland 37 Be 29.00S 17.00 E
Little Nicobar 25 Ig 7.20N 93.40 E
Little Ouse 9 Ni 52.30N 0.22 E
Littleport 12 Cb 52.27N 0.18 E
Little Powder River 46 Mf 45.28N 105.20W
Little Quill Lake 46 Ma 51.55N 104.05W
Little River 62 Ee 43.46S 172.47 E
Little Rock 39 Jf 34.44N 92.15W
Little Rocky Mountains 46 Kb 48.00N 108.45W

Index Symbols

[1] Independent Nation
[2] State, Region
[3] District, County
[4] Municipality
[5] Colony, Dependency
Continent
Physical Region
Historical or Cultural Region
Mount, Mountain
Volcano
Hill
Mountains, Mountain Range
Hills, Escarpment
Plateau, Upland
Pass, Gap
Plain, Lowland
Delta
Salt Flat
Valley, Canyon
Crater, Cave
Karst Features
Depression
Polder
Desert, Dunes
Forest, Woods
Heath, Steppe
Oasis
Cape, Point
Coast, Beach
Cliff
Peninsula
Isthmus
Sandbank
Island
Atoll
Rock, Reef
Islands, Archipelago
Rocks, Reefs
Coral Reef
Well, Spring
Geyser
River, Stream
Waterfall Rapids
River Mouth, Estuary
Lake
Salt Lake
Intermittent Lake
Reservoir
Swamp, Pond
Canal
Glacier
Ice Shelf, Pack Ice
Ocean
Sea
Gulf, Bay
Strait, Fjord
Lagoon
Bank
Seamount
Tablemount
Ridge
Shelf
Basin
Escarpment, Sea Scarp
Fracture
Trench, Abyss
National Park, Reserve
Point of Interest
Recreation Site
Cave, Cavern
Historic Site
Ruins
Wall, Walls
Church, Abbey
Temple
Scientific Station
Airport
Port
Lighthouse
Mine
Tunnel
Dam, Bridge

Index Symbols

- [1] Independent Nation
- [2] State, Region
- [3] District, County
- [4] Municipality
- [5] Colony, Dependency
- Continent
- Physical Region
- Historical or Cultural Region
- Mount, Mountain
- Volcano
- Hill
- Mountains, Mountain Range
- Hills, Escarpment
- Plateau, Upland
- Pass, Gap
- Plain, Lowland
- Delta
- Salt Flat
- Valley, Canyon
- Crater, Cave
- Karst Features
- Depression
- Polder
- Desert, Dunes
- Forest, Woods
- Heath, Steppe
- Oasis
- Cape, Point
- Coast, Beach
- Cliff
- Peninsula
- Isthmus
- Sandbank
- Island
- Atoll
- Rock, Reef
- Islands, Archipelago
- Rocks, Reefs
- Coral Reef
- Well, Spring
- Geyser
- River, Stream
- Waterfall Rapids
- River Mouth, Estuary
- Lake
- Salt Lake
- Intermittent Lake
- Reservoir
- Swamp, Pond
- Canal
- Glacier
- Ice Shelf, Pack Ice
- Ocean
- Sea
- Gulf, Bay
- Strait, Fjord
- Lagoon
- Bank
- Seamount
- Tablemount
- Ridge
- Shelf
- Basin
- Escarpment, Sea Scarp
- Fracture
- Trench, Abyss
- National Park, Reserve
- Point of Interest
- Recreation Site
- Cave, Cavern
- Historic Site
- Ruins
- Wall, Walls
- Church, Abbey
- Temple
- Scientific Station
- Airport
- Port
- Lighthouse
- Mine
- Tunnel
- Dam, Bridge

Name	Page	Grid	Latitude	Longitude
Los Alamos	39	If	35.53N	106.19W
Los Amates	49	Cf	15.16N	89.06W
Los Amores	55	Ci	28.06S	59.59W
Los Angeles	39	Hf	34.03N	118.15W
Los Ángeles	53	Ii	37.28S	72.21W
Los Angeles Aqueduct	46	Fi	35.22N	118.05W
Losap Atoll	57	Gd	6.54N	152.44 E
Los Banos	46	Eh	37.04N	120.51W
Los Blancos	56	Hb	23.36S	62.36W
Los Charrúas	55	Cj	31.10S	58.11W
Los Chiles	49	Eh	11.02N	84.43W
Los Conquistadores	55	Cj	30.36S	58.28W
Los Frailes, Islas-	50	Eg	11.12N	63.45W
Los Frentones	55	Bh	26.25S	61.25W
Los Gatos	46	Eh	37.14N	121.59W
Losheim	12	Ie	49.31N	6.45 E
Los Hermanos, Islas-	54	Fa	11.45N	64.25W
Łosice	10	Sd	52.14N	22.43 E
Lošinj	14	If	44.35N	14.28 E
Los Islands (EN)=Los, Iles de-	34	Cd	9.30N	13.48W
Los Juries	55	Ai	28.28S	62.06W
Los Lagos	56	Fe	39.51S	72.50W
Los Lagos [2]	56	Ff	41.20S	73.00W
Los Llanos de Aridane	32	Dd	28.39N	17.54W
Los Médanos, Istmo de-	49	Mh	11.35N	69.45W
Los Mochis	39	Ig	25.45N	108.53W
Los Monegros	13	Lc	41.29N	0.03W
Los Monjes, Islas-	54	Da	12.25N	70.55W
Los Navalmorales	13	He	39.43N	4.38W
Loso	36	Ec	1.10S	27.10 E
Los Palacios	49	Fb	22.35N	83.12W
Los Palacios y Villafranca	13	Gg	37.10N	5.56W
Los Pedroches	13	Hf	38.27N	4.45W
Los Pirpintos	55	Ah	26.08S	62.05W
Los Remedios, Río de-	48	Fe	24.41N	106.28W
Los Reyes de Salgado	48	Hh	19.35N	102.29W
Los Roques, Islas-	54	Ea	11.50N	66.45W
Los Roques Basin (EN)	50	Cf	12.20N	67.40W
Los Santos [3]	49	Gj	7.45N	80.30W
Los Santos	49	Gj	7.56N	80.25W
Losser	12	Jb	52.16N	7.01 E
Lossiemouth	9	Jd	57.43N	3.18W
Lossnen	8	Eb	62.30N	12.50 E
Los Taques	49	Lh	11.50N	70.16W
Los Telares	56	Hc	28.59S	63.26W
Los Teques	54	Ea	10.21N	67.02W
Los Testigos, Islas-	54	Fa	11.23N	63.06W
Lost River	46	Ef	41.56N	121.30W
Lost River Range	46	Id	44.10N	113.35W
Lost Trail Pass	43	Eb	45.41N	113.57W
Los Vilos	56	Fd	31.55S	71.31W
Lot	5	Gg	44.18N	0.20 E
Lot [3]	11	Hj	44.30N	1.30 E
Lota	56	Fe	37.05S	73.10W
Lotagipi Swamp	35	Ee	4.36N	34.55 E
Løten	8	Dd	60.49N	11.19 E
Lot-et-Garonne [3]	11	Gj	44.20N	0.30 E
Lothair	37	Ee	26.26S	30.27 E
Lothian [3]	9	Jf	55.55N	3.30W
Lothian	9	Jf	55.55N	3.05W
Loto	36	Dc	2.47S	22.30 E
Lotofaga	65c	Ba	13.59S	171.50W
Lotoi	36	Cc	1.35S	18.30 E
Lotru	15	Hd	45.20N	24.16 E
Lotrului, Munţii-	15	Gd	45.30N	23.52 E
Lotta	7	Hb	68.39N	30.20 E
Lottefors	8	Gc	61.25N	16.24 E
Löttorp	8	Gg	57.10N	16.59 E
Lotuke, Jabal-	35	Ee	4.07N	33.48 E
Louang Namtha	25	Kd	20.57N	101.25 E
Louangphrabang	22	Mh	19.52N	102.08 E
Loubomo	31	Ii	4.12S	12.41 E
Loučná	10	Lf	50.06N	15.48 E
Loudéac	11	Df	48.10N	2.45W
Loudima	36	Bc	4.07S	13.04 E
Loudon	44	Eh	35.44N	84.20W
Loudun	11	Gh	47.00N	0.04 E
Loué	11	Fg	48.00N	0.09W
Loue	11	Lg	47.01N	5.27 E
Loufan	28	Ae	38.04N	111.47 E
Louga	34	Bb	15.37N	16.13W
Louga [3]	34	Bb	15.00N	15.30W
Louge	11	Hk	43.27N	1.20 E
Loughborough	9	Li	52.47N	1.11W
Lougheed	42	Ha	77.30N	105.00W
Loughrea/Baile Locha Riach	9	Eh	53.12N	8.34W
Louhans	11	Lh	46.38N	5.13 E
Louhi	19	Db	66.04N	33.01 E
Louisa	44	Ff	38.07N	82.36W
Louiseville	44	Kb	46.16N	72.57W
Louisiade Archipelago	57	Gf	11.00S	153.00 E
Louisiana	45	Kg	39.27N	91.03W
Louisiana [2]	43	Ie	31.15N	92.15W
Louis Trichardt	37	Dd	23.01S	29.43 E
Louisville [Ky.-U.S.]	39	Kf	38.16N	85.45W
Louisville [Ms.-U.S.]	45	Lj	33.07N	89.03W
Louis-XIV, Pointe -	42	Jf	54.50N	79.30W
Loukoléla	36	Cc	1.02S	17.07 E
Loulan Yiji	27	Ec	40.32N	89.50 E
Loulé	13	Dg	37.08N	8.02W
Loum	34	Ge	4.43N	9.44 E
Lount Lake	45	Ia	50.10N	94.20W
Louny	10	Jf	50.22N	13.49 E
Loup City	45	Gf	41.17N	98.58W
Loup River	43	Hc	41.24N	97.19W
Loups Marins, Lacs des -	42	Ke	56.40N	74.00W
Lourdes	11	Fk	43.06N	0.03W
Lourenço Marques→Maputo	31	Kk	25.58S	32.34 E
Lousa, Serra da-	13	Dd	40.04N	8.13W
Loushan Guan	27	If	28.02N	106.51 E
Louštín	10	Jf	50.12N	13.48 E
Louth [Austl.]	59	Jf	30.32S	145.07 E
Louth [Eng.-U.K.]	9	Mh	53.22N	0.01W
Louth/Lú [2]	9	Gh	53.55N	6.30W
Loutrá Aidhipsoú	15	Gk	38.51N	23.03 E
Loutrá Killínis	15	El	37.52N	21.07 E
Loutrákion	15	Fl	37.59N	23.00 E
Louvain/Leuven	11	Kd	50.53N	4.42 E
Louvet Point	51k	Bb	13.58N	60.53W
Louviers	11	He	49.13N	1.10 E
Lövånger	7	Ed	64.22N	21.18 E
Lovászi	10	Mj	46.33N	16.34 E
Lovat	5	Jd	58.14N	31.28 E
Lovćen	15	Bg	42.24N	18.49 E
Loveč [2]	15	Hf	43.08N	24.43 E
Loveč	15	Hf	43.08N	24.43 E
Loveland	45	Df	40.24N	105.05W
Lovell	43	Fc	44.50N	108.24W
Lovelock	43	Dc	40.11N	118.28W
Lövenich, Köln-	12	Id	50.57N	6.50 E
Lovenske Gorice	14	Jd	46.40N	16.00 E
Lovere	14	Ee	45.49N	10.04 E
Loviisa	7	Gf	60.27N	26.14 E
Loviisa/Lovisa	7	Gf	60.27N	26.14 E
Loving	45	Dj	32.17N	104.06W
Lovington	43	Ge	33.27N	103.21W
Lovisa	7	Gf	60.27N	26.14 E
Lovisa/Loviisa	7	Gf	60.27N	26.14 E
Lovoi	36	Ed	8.05S	26.40 E
Lovosice	10	Kf	50.31N	14.03 E
Lovozero	7	Ib	68.01N	35.01 E
Lovozero, Ozero-	7	Ic	67.50N	35.10 E
Lövstabruk	8	Gd	60.24N	17.53 E
Lövstabukten	8	Gd	60.35N	17.45 E
Lovua	36	Dd	6.07S	20.35 E
Lovua	36	De	11.31S	23.35 E
Low, Cape -	42	Id	63.06N	85.18W
Lowa	30	Ji	1.24S	25.52 E
Lowell	43	Mc	42.39N	71.18W
Löwenberg in der Mark	10	Jd	52.53N	13.09 E
Lower Arrow Lake	46	Fb	49.40N	118.08W
Lower Austria (EN) = Niederösterreich [2]	14	Jb	48.30N	15.45 E
Lower California (EN)=Baja California	38	Hg	28.00N	112.00W
Lower Hutt	62	Fd	41.13S	174.55 E
Lower Lake	46	Ef	41.15N	120.02W
Lower Lake	46	Dg	38.55N	122.36W
Lower Lough Erne/Loch Éirne Íochtair	9	Fg	54.30N	7.50W
Lower Post	42	Ee	59.55N	128.30W
Lower Red Lake	45	Ic	48.00N	94.50W
Lower Rhine (EN) = Neder-Rijn	11	Mc	51.59N	6.20 E
Lower Saxony (EN)= Niedersachsen [2]	10	Fd	52.00N	10.00 E
Lower Trajan's Wall (EN)= Nižni Trajanov Val	15	Ld	45.45N	28.30 E
Lower Tunguska (EN)= Nižnjaja Tunguska	21	Kc	65.48N	88.04 E
Lowestoft	9	Oi	52.29N	1.45 E
Lowestoft Ness	9	Oi	52.28N	1.44 E
Lowgar [3]	23	Kc	33.50N	69.00 E
Łowicz	10	Pd	52.07N	19.56 E
Lowlands	9	Jf	56.00N	4.00W
Lowrah	21	If	31.33N	66.33 E
Lowshān	24	Md	36.39N	49.32 E
Low Tatra (EN) = Nízke Tatry	10	Ph	48.54N	19.40 E
Lowther	42	Hb	74.35N	97.40W
Lowville	44	Jd	43.47N	75.30W
Loxton [Austl.]	59	If	34.27S	140.35 E
Loxton [S.Afr.]	37	Cf	31.30S	22.22 E
Loyalty Islands (EN)= Loyauté, Iles-	57	Hg	21.00S	167.00 E
Loyauté, Iles-=Loyalty Islands (EN)	57	Hg	21.00S	167.00 E
Loyoro	36	Fb	3.21N	34.17 E
Lozère [3]	11	Jj	44.30N	3.30 E
Lozère, Mont-	11	Jj	44.25N	3.46 E
Loznica	15	Ce	44.32N	19.13 E
Lozovaja	19	Df	48.53N	36.15 E
Lozva	19	Gd	59.36N	62.20 E
Lú/Louth [2]	9	Gh	53.55N	6.30W
Lua	36	Cb	2.46N	18.26 E
Luacano	36	De	11.16S	21.38 E
Luachimo	36	Dd	6.33S	20.59 E
Luaha-Sibuha	26	Cg	0.31S	98.28 E
Luahoko	65b	Ba	19.40S	174.24W
Luala	37	Fc	17.57S	36.30 E
Lualaba	29	Jh	0.26N	25.20 E
Luama	36	Ec	4.46S	26.53 E
Lua Makika	65a	Ec	20.35N	156.34W
Luampa	36	De	14.32S	24.10 E
Lu'an	27	Ke	31.44N	116.30 E
Luanda	31	Ii	8.50S	13.15 E
Luanda [3]	36	Bd	8.30S	13.20 E
Luando	30	Ij	10.19S	16.40 E
Luang, Khao-	25	Jg	8.31N	99.47 E
Luang, Thale-	25	Kg	7.30N	100.15 E
Luang Chiang Dao, Doi-	25	Je	19.23N	98.54 E
Luanginga	30	Jj	15.11S	22.55 E
Luang Prabang Range	25	Ke	18.30N	101.15 E
Luangue	36	Dc	4.17S	20.01 E
Luangwa	30	Kj	15.36S	30.25 E
Luan He	21	Nf	39.20N	119.10 E
Luaniva	64h	Bb	13.16S	176.07W
Luannan (Bencheng)	28	Ee	39.30N	118.42 E
Luanping (Anjiangying)	28	Dd	40.55N	117.19 E
Luanshya	31	Jj	13.08S	28.25 E
Luanxian	27	Kd	39.45N	118.44 E
Luanza	36	Ed	8.40S	28.40 E
Luapula	30	Ji	9.26S	28.33 E
Luapula [3]	36	Ee	10.40S	29.15 E
Luarca	13	Fa	43.32N	6.32W
Luashi	36	De	10.56S	23.37 E
Luba	34	Ge	3.28N	8.40 E
Lubaantum	49	Ce	16.17N	88.58W
Lubaczów	10	Tf	50.10N	23.07 E
Lubaczówka	10	Sf	50.08N	22.35 E
Lubalo	36	Cd	7.22S	19.20 E
Lubalo	36	Cd	9.07S	19.15 E
Lubamba	36	Ed	5.14S	26.02 E
Lubań	10	Le	51.08N	15.18 E
Lubāna/Lubana	8	Lh	56.49N	26.49 E
Lubana/Lubāna	8	Lh	56.49N	26.49 E
Lubanas, Ozero-/Lubānas Ezers	8	Lh	56.40N	27.00 E
Lubānas Ezers/Lubanas, Ozero-	8	Lh	56.40N	27.00 E
Lubang Islands	26	Hd	13.45N	120.15 E
Lubango	31	Ij	14.55S	13.28 E
Lubao	31	Ji	5.22S	25.45 E
Lubartów	10	Se	51.28N	22.46 E
Lubawa	10	Pc	53.30N	19.45 E
Lübbecke	10	Ed	52.18N	8.37 E
Lubbeek	12	Gd	50.53N	4.50 E
Lübben/Lubin	10	Je	51.57N	13.54 E
Lübbenau/Lubnjow	10	Je	51.52N	13.58 E
Lubbock	39	If	33.35N	101.51W
Lübeck	6	He	53.52N	10.42 E
Lübecker Bucht	10	Gb	54.00N	10.55 E
Lübeck-Travemünde	10	Gc	53.57N	10.52 E
Lubefu	36	Dc	4.10S	23.00 E
Lubefu	36	Dc	4.43S	24.25 E
Lubei→Jarud Qi	27	Lc	44.30N	120.55 E
Lubelska, Wyżyna-	10	Sf	51.00N	23.00 E
Lubenec	10	Jf	50.08N	13.20 E
Lubenka	16	Sd	50.28N	54.06 E
Lubero	36	Ec	0.06S	29.06 E
Lubéron, Montagne du-	11	Lk	43.48N	5.22 E
Lubi	36	Dc	4.59S	23.26 E
Lubie, Jezioro-	10	Lc	53.30N	15.50 E
Lubień Kujawski	10	Pd	52.25N	19.10 E
Lubij/Löbau	10	Ke	51.06N	14.40 E
Lubilash	29	Ji	6.02S	23.45 E
Lubin	10	Me	51.24N	16.13 E
Lubin/Lübben	10	Je	51.57N	13.54 E
Lublin	6	Ie	51.15N	22.35 E
Lublin [2]	10	Se	51.15N	22.35 E
Lubliniec	10	Of	50.40N	18.41 E
Lubnān=Lebanon (EN) [1]	22	Ff	33.50N	35.50 E
Lubnān, Jabal-=Lebanon Mountains (EN)	23	Ec	34.00N	36.30 E
Lubnjow/Lübbenau	10	Je	51.52N	13.58 E
Lubny	19	De	50.01N	33.00 E
Luboń	10	Md	52.23N	16.54 E
Lubraniec	10	Od	52.33N	18.50 E
Lubsko	10	Ke	51.46N	14.59 E
Lubsza	10	Ke	51.55N	14.45 E
Lubudi	29	Ji	9.13S	25.38 E
Lubudi	36	Ed	9.57S	25.58 E
Lubue	36	Cc	4.10S	19.53 E
Lubuklinggau	26	Dg	3.10S	102.52 E
Lubuksikaping	26	Df	0.08N	100.10 E
Lubumba	36	Ec	3.58S	29.06 E
Lubumbashi	31	Jj	11.40S	27.30 E
Lubuskie, Pojezierze-	10	Ld	52.18N	15.20 E
Lubutu	31	Ji	0.44S	26.35 E
Lucala	36	Bd	6.38S	12.34 E
Lucala	36	Cd	9.16S	15.16 E
Lucania, Mount-	42	Dd	61.01N	140.29W
Lucas	55	Ea	13.05S	55.56W
Lucca	14	Eg	43.50N	10.29 E
Lucea	49	Hd	18.27N	78.10W
Luce Bay	9	Ig	54.47N	4.50W
Lucedale	45	Lk	30.55N	88.35W
Lučegorsk	20	Ig	46.25N	134.20 E
Lucélia	55	Ge	21.44S	51.01W
Lucena [Phil.]	26	Hd	13.56N	121.37 E
Lucena [Sp.]	13	Hg	37.24N	4.29W
Lucena del Cid	13	Ld	40.08N	0.17W
Luc-en-Diois	11	Lj	44.37N	5.27 E
Lučenec	10	Ph	48.20N	19.41 E
Lucera	14	Ji	41.30N	15.20 E
Lucerne (EN) = Luzern	14	Cc	47.05N	8.20 E
Lucerne, Lake- (EN) = Vierwaldstätter-See	14	Cc	47.00N	8.30 E
Lucero	48	Fb	30.49N	106.30W
Lucheng	28	Bf	36.18N	113.15 E
Lucheringo	37	Fb	11.43S	36.15 E
Lucheux	12	Ed	50.12N	2.25 E
Luchico	30	Lj	12.15S	44.25 E
Luchico	36	Cd	6.12S	19.42 E
Lüchow	10	Hd	52.58N	11.09 E
Lüchun	27	Hg	23.02N	102.19 E
Lucipara, Kepulauan-	26	Ih	5.30S	127.33 E
Lucira	36	Be	13.52S	12.32 E
Luck	19	Ce	50.47N	25.20 E
Luckau	10	Je	51.51N	13.43 E
Luckenwalde	10	Jd	52.05N	13.10 E
Lucknow	22	Kg	26.51N	80.55 E
Luçon	11	Eh	46.27N	1.10W
Lucrecia, Cabo-	49	Jc	21.04N	75.37W
Luc-sur-Mer	12	Be	49.19N	0.21W
Lucunga	36	Bd	6.49S	14.35 E
Lucusse	36	De	12.33S	20.51 E
Lüda→Dalian=Dairan (EN)	22	Of	38.55N	121.39 E
Luda Kamčija	15	Kg	43.03N	27.29 E
Ludbreg	14	Kd	46.15N	16.37 E
Lüdenscheid	10	De	51.13N	7.37 E
Lüderitz	31	Ik	26.38S	15.10 E
Lüderitz [3]	37	Be	26.00S	15.00 E
Lüderitz Bay	37	Be	26.35S	15.10 E
Ludhiāna	22	Jf	30.54N	75.51 E
Ludinghausen	10	De	51.46N	7.28 E
Ludington	43	Jc	43.57N	86.27W
Ludlow	9	Ki	52.22N	2.43W
Ludogorije	15	Jf	43.46N	26.56 E
Ludogorsko Plato	15	Kf	43.36N	27.03 E
Luduş	15	Hc	46.29N	24.06 E
Ludvika	7	Df	60.09N	15.11 E
Ludwigsburg	10	Fh	48.54N	9.11 E
Ludwigshafen am Rhein	10	Eg	49.29N	8.27 E
Ludwigslust	10	Hc	53.19N	11.30 E
Ludza	7	Gh	56.32N	27.45 E
Luebo	31	Ji	5.21S	21.25 E
Lueki	36	Ec	3.24S	25.57 E
Lueki	36	Ec	3.22S	25.51 E
Luele	36	Dd	7.55S	20.00 E
Luembé	36	Dd	6.43S	24.11 E
Luembe	36	Dd	6.37S	21.06 E
Luena [Ang.]	36	De	12.31S	22.34 E
Luena [Ang.]	31	Ij	11.48S	19.55 E
Luena [Zaire]	36	Ed	9.27S	25.47 E
Luena [Zam.]	36	Df	15.20S	23.30 E
Luengué	36	Df	16.54S	21.52 E
Luenha	37	Ec	16.24S	33.48 E
Luera Peak	45	Cj	33.47N	107.49W
Lueta	36	Dd	7.04S	21.40 E
Lueyang	27	Ie	33.25N	106.14 E
Lufeng	27	Kg	22.57N	115.41 E
Lufico	36	Bd	6.22S	13.30 E
Lufira	29	Ji	8.16S	26.27 E
Lufira, Chutes de la-	36	Ed	9.50S	27.30 E
Lufkin	43	Ie	31.20N	94.44W
Lug	15	De	44.23N	20.45 E
Luga	19	Cd	59.43N	28.18 E
Luga	19	Cd	58.44N	29.50 E
Lugano	14	Cd	46.00N	8.57 E
Lugano, Lago di-	14	Cd	46.00N	9.00 E
Lugansk = Vorošilovgrad	6	Jf	48.34N	39.20 E
Luganville	58	Hf	15.32S	167.10 E
Lügde	12	Lc	51.57N	9.15 E
Lugela	37	Fc	16.26S	36.39 E
Lugenda	30	Kj	11.26S	38.33 E
Lugnaquillia	5	Fe	52.58N	6.27W
Lugo [3]	13	Eb	43.00N	7.30W
Lugo [It.]	14	Ff	44.25N	11.54 E
Lugo [Sp.]	13	Ea	43.00N	7.34W
Lugoj	15	Ed	45.41N	21.55 E
Lugovoj [Kaz.-U.S.S.R.]	19	Hg	42.55N	72.47 E
Lugovoj [R.S.F.S.R.]	19	Gd	59.44N	65.55 E
Lugovski	20	Ge	58.05N	112.55 E
Lugulu	36	Ec	2.17S	26.32 E
Luh	7	Kh	56.14N	42.28 E
Luhe	10	Gc	53.18N	10.11 E
Luhe	28	Eh	32.21N	118.50 E
Luhin Sum	27	Kb	46.41N	118.38 E
Luhit	25	Jc	27.48N	95.28 E
Luhovicy	7	Ji	54.59N	39.02 E
Luhuo	27	He	31.21N	100.40 E
Lui	36	Cd	8.41S	17.56 E
Luia	36	Dd	8.26S	21.45 E
Luiana	36	Df	17.22S	22.59 E
Luiana	30	Jj	17.27S	23.14 E
Luie	36	Cc	4.33S	17.41 E
Luik/Liège	6	Ge	50.38N	5.34 E
Luilaka	30	Ji	0.52S	20.12 E
Luilu	36	Dd	6.22S	23.50 E
Luimneach/Limerick	6	Fe	52.40N	8.38W
Luimneach/Limerick [2]	9	Ei	52.30N	9.00W
Luing	9	He	56.13N	5.39W
Luino	14	Cd	46.00N	8.44 E
Luio	36	De	13.15S	21.39 E
Lui Pătru, Vîrful-	15	Gd	45.30N	23.30 E
Luis Correia	54	Jd	2.53S	41.40W
Luishia	36	Ee	11.13S	27.07 E
Luitpold Coast	66	Af	78.30S	32.00W
Luiza	36	Dd	7.12S	22.25 E
Luján [Arg.]	56	Gd	32.22S	65.57W
Luján [Arg.]	56	Id	34.34S	59.07W
Lujiang	28	Di	31.15N	117.17 E
Lukafu	36	Ee	10.30S	27.33 E
Lukanga Swamp	36	Ee	14.25S	27.45 E
Lukavac	14	Mf	44.33N	18.32 E
Lukengo	36	Ed	5.46S	29.06 E
Lukenie	30	Ii	2.44S	18.09 E
Lukeville	46	Ik	31.57N	112.50W
Lukojanov	19	Ed	55.02N	44.30 E
Lukolela	36	Cc	1.03S	17.12 E
Lukonzolwa	36	Ed	8.47S	28.39 E
Lukov	10	Ue	51.14N	24.25 E
Lukovit	15	Hf	43.12N	24.10 E
Łuków	10	Se	51.56N	22.23 E
Lukuga	30	Ji	5.40S	26.55 E
Lukula	36	Bd	5.23S	12.57 E
Lukulu	36	De	14.23S	23.15 E
Lukusashi	36	Fe	14.38S	30.00 E
Luleå	6	Ib	65.34N	22.10 E
Luleälven	5	Ib	65.35N	22.03 E
Lüleburgaz	23	Ca	41.24N	27.21 E
Lüliang Shan	21	Nf	37.45N	111.25 E
Lulimba	36	Ec	4.42S	28.38 E
Luling	45	Hl	29.41N	97.39W
Lulong	28	Ee	39.53N	118.52 E
Lulonga	36	Cb	0.37N	18.23 E
Lulonga	30	Ih	0.43N	18.23 E
Lulua	30	Ji	5.02S	21.07 E
Lulu Fakahega, Mount-	64h	Bb	13.16S	176.10W
Luma	65c	Db	14.14S	169.32W
Lumajang	26	Fh	8.08S	113.13 E
Lumajangdong Co	27	De	34.00N	81.37 E
Lumbala Kaquengue	31	Jj	14.06S	21.25 E
Lumbala N'guimbo	36	De	12.39S	22.32 E
Lumberton	43	Le	34.37N	79.00W
Lumbo	37	Gc	15.00S	40.44 E
Lumbrales	13	Fd	40.56N	6.43W
Lumbres	12	Ed	50.42N	2.08 E
Lumby	46	Fa	50.15N	118.58W
Lumding	25	Ic	25.45N	93.10 E
Lumege	36	De	11.34S	20.48 E
Lumesule	36	Ge	11.14S	38.06 E
Lumi	60	Ch	3.29S	142.03 E
Lummen	12	Hd	50.59N	5.15 E
Lumparland	8	Id	60.10N	20.15 E
Lumphăt	25	Lf	13.30N	106.59 E
Lumsden [N.Z.]	62	Cf	45.44S	168.26 E
Lumsden [Sask.-Can.]	46	Ma	50.34N	104.53W
Lumuna	36	Ec	3.46S	26.24 E
Lumut	26	Df	4.14N	100.38 E
Luna	13	Gb	42.40N	5.49W
Luna, Laguna de-	55	Di	28.06S	56.46W
Lunan Shan	27	Hf	27.00N	102.30 E
Lunayyr, Harrat-	24	Gj	25.10N	37.50 E
Lunca Ilvei	15	Hb	47.22N	24.59 E
Lund	7	Ci	55.42N	13.11 E
Lunda [3]	36	Cd	9.30S	20.00 E
Lundazi	31	Kj	12.19S	33.13 E
Lunde	8	Gb	62.53N	17.51 E
Lundevatn	8	Bf	58.20N	6.35 E
Lundi	30	Kk	21.19S	32.24 E
Lundu	26	Ef	1.40N	109.51 E
Lundy Island	9	Ij	51.10N	4.40W
Lüneburg	10	Gc	53.15N	10.24 E
Lüneburger Heide	10	Gc	53.10N	10.20 E
Lunel	11	Kk	43.41N	4.08 E
Lünen	10	De	51.37N	7.31 E
Lunéville	11	Mf	48.36N	6.30 E
Lunga	30	Jj	14.34S	26.26 E
Lungué-Bungo	37	Jj	28.38S	16.27 E
Lungwebungu	36	De	14.19S	23.14 E
Lūni	25	Ed	24.41N	71.14 E
Lūni	25	Ec	26.00N	73.00 E
Lunigiana	14	Df	44.20N	9.55 E
Luninec	19	Ce	52.16N	26.50 E
Lunino	16	Nc	53.35N	45.14 E
Lunsemfwa	36	Fe	14.54S	30.12 E
Luntai/Bügür	27	Dc	41.46N	84.10 E
Luobei (Fengxiang)	27	Nb	47.36N	130.58 E
Luobuzhuang	27	Ed	39.30N	88.15 E
Luocheng	27	Ig	24.51N	108.53 E
Luodian (Longping)	27	If	25.26N	106.47 E
Luoding	27	Jg	22.43N	111.33 E
Luohe	27	Je	33.30N	114.08 E
Luo He	27	Id	32.18N	109.12 E
Luoma Hu	28	Eg	34.10N	118.12 E
Luonteri	8	Lc	61.35N	27.45 E
Luoping	27	Hg	24.58N	104.19 E
Luopioinen	8	Kc	61.22N	24.40 E
Luoshan	28	Ch	32.13N	114.32 E
Luotian	28	Ci	30.48N	115.23 E
Luoxiao Shan	27	Jf	26.35N	114.00 E
Luoyang	22	Nf	34.41N	112.25 E
Luoyuan	27	Kf	26.31N	119.32 E
Luozi	36	Bc	4.57S	14.08 E
Lupa	36	Fd	8.39S	33.12 E
Lupane	37	Dc	18.56S	27.48 E
Łupawa	10	Nb	54.42N	17.07 E
Lupeni	15	Gd	45.21N	23.14 E
Luperón	49	Ld	19.54N	70.57W
Łupków	10	Sg	49.12N	22.06 E
Luputa	36	Dd	7.10S	23.42 E
Lūq	31	Lh	3.56N	42.32 E
Luqiao	28	Fj	28.39N	120.05 E
Luqu	27	He	34.36N	102.30 E
Luque	56	Ic	25.16S	57.34W
Luquillo	51a	Cb	18.22N	65.43W
Luray	44	Hf	38.40N	78.28W
Lure	11	Mg	47.41N	6.30 E
Lure, Montagne de-	11	Lj	44.07N	5.47 E
Luremo	36	Cd	8.30S	17.51 E
Lurgan/An Lorgain	9	Gg	54.28N	6.20W
Lurín	54	Cf	12.17S	76.52W
Lúrio	37	Gb	13.32S	40.30 E
Lúrio	30	Lj	13.31S	40.42 E
Lusaka	31	Jj	15.25S	28.17 E
Lusambo	31	Ji	4.58S	23.27 E
Lusanga	36	Cc	4.44S	18.58 E
Lusangi	36	Ec	4.37S	27.08 E
Lu Shan	27	Kf	29.30N	115.55 E
Lushan [China]	28	Cj	29.33N	115.58 E
Lushan [China]	28	Bh	33.44N	112.54 E
Lushi	27	Je	34.04N	111.02 E
Lushiko	36	Cd	6.12S	19.42 E
Lushnja	15	Ci	40.56N	19.42 E
Lushoto	36	Gc	4.47S	38.17 E
Lu Shui	28	Bj	29.54N	113.39 E
Lushui (Luzhangjie)	27	Gf	26.00N	98.50 E
Lüshun=Port Arthur (EN)	27	Ld	38.50N	121.13 E
Lusignan	11	Gh	46.26N	0.07 E
Lusk	43	Gc	42.46N	104.27W
Lussac-les-Châteaux	11	Gh	46.24N	0.43 E
Lustrafjorden	8	Bc	61.20N	7.20 E
Lūt, Dasht-e-=Lut, Dasht-i- (EN)	21	Hf	33.00N	57.00 E
Lut, Dasht-i- (EN)=Lūt, Dasht-e-	21	Hf	33.00N	57.00 E
Lu Tao	27	Lg	22.35N	121.30 E
Lutembo	36	De	13.28S	21.22 E
Luti	63a	Cb	7.14S	157.00 E
Lütjenburg	10	Gb	54.17N	10.35 E
Luton	9	Mj	51.53N	0.25W
Luton Airport	12	Bc	51.50N	0.22W
Lutong	26	Ff	4.28N	114.00 E
Lutshima	36	Cd	5.22S	18.59 E
Lutshima	36	Cd	5.22S	18.59 E
Lutterworth	12	Ab	52.27N	1.12W
Lutuai	36	De	12.40S	20.12 E
Lutugino	16	Ke	48.23N	39.13 E
Lützow-Holmbukta	66	De	69.10S	37.30 E
Lutzputs	37	Ce	28.22S	20.37 E
Luuk	26	He	5.58N	121.18 E
Luverne	45	He	43.39N	96.13W
Luvidjo	36	Ed	6.26S	26.59 E
Luvua	30	Ji	6.46S	26.58 E
Luvuei	36	De	13.06S	21.12 E
Luwegu	30	Ki	8.31S	37.23 E
Luwingu	36	Ee	10.16S	29.54 E
Luwuk	26	Hg	0.56S	122.47 E
Luxembourg [3]	12	He	50.00N	5.30 E
Luxembourg/Luxemburg [1]	6	Gf	49.45N	6.05 E
Luxembourg/Luxemburg	6	Gf	49.45N	6.05 E
Luxemburg/Luxembourg	6	Gf	49.45N	6.05 E
Luxemburg/Luxembourg [1]	6	Gf	49.45N	6.05 E
Luxeuil-les-Bains	11	Mg	47.49N	6.23 E
Luxi	22	Mg	24.34N	103.44 E
Luxi (Mangshi)	27	Gg	24.29N	98.40 E
Luxor (EN)=Al Uqşur	33	Fd	25.41N	32.39 E
Luy	11	Ek	43.39N	1.08W
Luy de Béarn	11	Fk	43.38N	0.47W

Index Symbols

- [1] Independent Nation
- [2] State, Region
- [3] District, County
- [4] Municipality
- [5] Colony, Dependency
- Continent
- Physical Region
- Historical or Cultural Region
- Mount, Mountain
- Volcano
- Hill
- Mountains, Mountain Range
- Hills, Escarpment
- Plateau, Upland
- Pass, Gap
- Plain, Lowland
- Delta
- Salt Flat
- Valley, Canyon
- Crater, Cave
- Karst Features
- Depression
- Polder
- Desert, Dunes
- Forest, Woods
- Heath, Steppe
- Oasis
- Cape, Point
- Coast, Beach
- Cliff
- Peninsula
- Isthmus
- Sandbank
- Island
- Atoll
- Rock, Reef
- Islands, Archipelago
- Rocks, Reefs
- Coral Reef
- Well, Spring
- Geyser
- River, Stream
- Waterfall Rapids
- River Mouth, Estuary
- Lake
- Salt Lake
- Intermittent Lake
- Reservoir
- Swamp, Pond
- Canal
- Glacier
- Ice Shelf, Pack Ice
- Ocean
- Sea
- Gulf, Bay
- Strait, Fjord
- Lagoon
- Bank
- Seamount
- Tablemount
- Ridge
- Shelf
- Basin
- Escarpment, Sea Scarp
- Fracture
- Trench, Abyss
- National Park, Reserve
- Point of Interest
- Recreation Site
- Cave, Cavern
- Historic Site
- Ruins
- Wall, Walls
- Church, Abbey
- Temple
- Scientific Station
- Airport
- Port
- Lighthouse
- Mine
- Tunnel
- Dam, Bridge

M

Index Symbols

[1] Independent Nation
[2] State, Region
[3] District, County
[4] Municipality
[5] Colony, Dependency
Continent
Physical Region
Historical or Cultural Region
Mount, Mountain
Volcano
Hill
Mountains, Mountain Range
Hills, Escarpment
Plateau, Upland
Pass, Gap
Plain, Lowland
Delta
Salt Flat
Valley, Canyon
Crater, Cave
Karst Features
Depression
Polder
Desert, Dunes
Forest, Woods
Heath, Steppe
Oasis
Cape, Point
Coast, Beach
Cliff
Peninsula
Isthmus
Sandbank
Island
Atoll
Rock, Reef
Islands, Archipelago
Rocks, Reefs
Coral Reef
Well, Spring
Geyser
River, Stream
Waterfall Rapids
River Mouth, Estuary
Lake
Salt Lake
Intermittent Lake
Reservoir
Swamp, Pond
Canal
Glacier
Ice Shelf, Pack Ice
Ocean
Sea
Gulf, Bay
Strait, Fjord
Lagoon
Bank
Seamount
Tablemount
Ridge
Shelf
Basin
Escarpment, Sea Scarp
Fracture
Trench, Abyss
National Park, Reserve
Point of Interest
Recreation Site
Cave, Cavern
Historic Site
Ruins
Wall, Walls
Church, Abbey
Temple
Scientific Station
Airport
Port
Lighthouse
Mine
Tunnel
Dam, Bridge

Main Barrier Range 59 If 31.25 S 141.25 E
Mainburg 10 Hh 48.39N 11.47 E
Main Camp 64g Ba 2.01N 157.25W
Main Channel 44 Gc 45.22N 81.50W
Mai-Ndombe, Lac- 30 Ii 2.10 S 18.15 E
Main-Donau-Kanal 10 Gg 49.55N 10.50 E
Maindong → Coqên 27 Ee 31.15N 85.13 E
Maine 11 Ff 48.15N 0.10W
Maine [2] 43 Nb 45.15N 69.15W
Maine [Fr.] 11 Fg 47.25N 0.37W
Maine [Fr.] 11 Eg 47.09N 1.27W
Maine, Gulf of- 38 Me 43.00N 68.00W
Maine-et-Loire [3] 11 Fg 47.30N 0.20W
Mainé-Soroa 34 Hc 13.18N 12.02 E
Mainistir Fhear Maí/Fermoy 9 Ei 52.08N 8.16W
Mainistir na Búille/Boyle 9 Eh 53.58N 8.18W
Mainistir na Corann/Midleton 9 Ej 51.55N 8.10W
Mainistir na Féile/Abbeyfeale 9 Di 52.24N 9.18W
Mainit, Lake- 26 Ie 9.26N 125.32 E
Mainland [Scot.-U.K.] 6 Fc 60.20N 1.22W
Mainland [Scot.-U.K.] 5 Fd 59.00N 3.10W
Maintal 12 Kd 50.08N 8.51 E
Maintenon 11 Hf 48.35N 1.35 E
Maintirano 31 Lj 18.03 S 44.03 E
Mainz 10 Eg 50.00N 8.15 E
Maio 32 Cf 23.10N 15.10W
Maio 30 Eg 15.15N 23.10W
Maipo, Volcán- 52 Ji 34.10 S 69.50W
Maipú 56 Ie 36.52 S 57.52W
Maiquetía 54 Ea 10.36N 66.57W
Maira 14 Bf 44.49N 7.38 E
Mairi 54 Jf 11.43 S 40.08W
Mairipotaba 55 Hc 17.21 S 49.31W
Maisān [3] 24 Lg 32.00N 47.00 E
Maisí, Punta- 47 Jd 20.15N 74.09W
Maišiagala/Maišjagala 8 Kj 54.51N 25.14 E
Maišjagala/Maišiagala 8 Kj 54.51N 25.14 E
Maiter 13 Qi 35.23N 4.17 E
Maitland [Austl.] 59 Hf 34.22 S 137.40 E
Maitland [Austl.] 58 Gh 32.44 S 151.33 E
Maiz, Isla Grande del- 49 Fg 12.10N 83.03W
Maíz, Isla Pequeña del- 49 Fg 12.18N 82.59W
Maíz, Islas del- 47 Hf 12.15N 83.00W
Maizhokunggar 27 Ff 29.50N 91.40 E
Maizières-lès-Metz 12 Ie 49.13N 6.09 E
Maizuru 28 Mg 35.27N 135.20 E
Maizuru-Nishimaizuru 29 Dd 35.28N 135.19 E
Maizuru-Wan 29 Dd 35.30N 135.20 E
Maja 21 Pd 60.17N 134.41 E
Majagual 49 Ji 8.35N 74.37W
Majakovski 16 Mh 42.02N 42.47 E
Majangat 27 Fb 48.20N 91.58 E
Majardah, Wādī- 14 Em 37.07N 10.13 E
Majāz al Bāb 14 Dn 36.39N 9.37 E
Majdanpek 15 Ee 44.25N 21.56 E
Majene 22 Nj 3.33 S 118.57 E
Majërtën=Mijirtein (EN) 30 Lh 9.00N 50.00 E
Majevica 14 Mf 44.40N 18.40 E
Maji 35 Fd 6.10N 35.35 E
Majia He 27 Kd 38.09N 117.53 E
Majja 20 Id 61.38N 130.25 E
Majkain 19 He 51.27N 75.52 E
Majkamys 18 Ka 46.34N 77.37 E
Majkop 6 Kg 44.35N 40.07 E
Majli-Saj 18 Id 41.15N 72.30 E
Majma'ah 24 Kj 25.54N 45.20 E
Majmak 19 Hg 42.40N 71.14 E
Majmakan 20 Ie 57.30N 135.23 E
Majmeča 20 Fb 71.20N 104.15 E
Majn 20 Mc 65.03N 172.10 E
Majna [R.S.F.S.R.] 20 Ef 53.00N 91.28 E
Majna [R.S.F.S.R.] 7 Li 54.09N 47.37 E
Major, Puig- 13 Oe 39.48N 2.48 E
Major, Puig-/Mayor, Puig- 13 Oe 39.48N 2.48 E
Majorca (EN)=Mallorca 5 Gh 39.30N 3.00 E
Majrur 35 Db 16.40N 26.53 E
Majski [R.S.F.S.R.] 16 Nh 43.36N 44.03 E
Majski [R.S.F.S.R.] 20 Hf 52.18N 129.38 E
Maju, Pulau 26 If 1.20N 126.25 E
Majuro Atoll 57 Id 7.09N 171.12 E
Makabana 36 Bc 3.28 S 12.36 E
Makaha 65a Cb 21.29N 158.13W
Makahuena Point 65b Bb 21.52N 159.27W
Makalamabedi 37 Cd 20.20 S 23.53 E
Makale 26 Gg 3.06 S 119.51 E
Makallé 56 Ic 27.13 S 59.17W
Makalondi 34 Fc 12.50N 1.41 E
Makamby, Nosy- 37 Hc 15.42 S 45.54 E
Makanči 19 If 46.51N 81.57 E
Makanza 36 Cb 1.36N 19.07 E
Makapala 65a Fc 20.13N 155.45W
Makapu Point 64k Ba 18.59 S 169.55W
Makapuu Head 65a Db 21.18N 157.39W
Makara, Prohod- 15 Ih 41.16N 25.26 E
Mákares 15 Il 37.05N 25.42 E
Makarfi 34 Gc 11.23N 7.53 E
Makari 34 Hc 12.35N 14.28 E
Makari Mountains 36 Ed 6.05 S 29.50 E
Makarjev 7 Kh 57.57N 43.49 E
Makarov 20 Jg 48.39N 142.51 E
Makarov Basin (EN) 67 Ce 87.00N 170.00 E
Makarov Seamount (EN) 57 Gb 29.30N 153.30 E
Makarska 14 Lg 43.18N 17.02 E
Makā Rūd 24 Nd 36.21N 51.16 E
Makasar → Ujung Pandang 22 Nj 5.07 S 119.24 E
Makasar, Selat-=Makassar Strait (EN) 21 Nj 2.00 S 117.30 E
Makassar Strait (EN)=Makasar, Selat- 21 Nj 2.00 S 117.30 E
Makat 6 Lf 47.40N 53.28 E
Makatea, Ile- 57 Mf 15.50 S 148.15W
Makaw 25 Jc 26.27N 96.42 E
Makawao 65a Ec 20.51N 156.19W
Makay, Massif du- 37 Hd 21.15 S 45.15 E
Makedhonia [2] 15 Fi 40.40N 22.30 E
Makedhonia=Macedonia (EN) 15 Fh 41.00N 23.00 E
Makedhonia=Macedonia (EN) 5 Ig 41.00N 23.00 E
Makedonija=Macedonia (EN) 5 Ig 41.00N 23.00 E
Makedonija = Macedonia (EN) [2] 15 Eh 41.50N 22.00 E
Makedonija=Macedonia (EN) 15 Fh 41.00N 23.00 E
Makejevka 16 Jf 48.00N 37.58 E
Makelulu, Mount- 64a Bb 7.34N 134.35 E
Makemo Atoll 57 Mf 16.35 S 143.40W
Makeni 31 Fh 8.53N 12.03W
Makgadikgadi Pans 30 Jk 20.50 S 25.30 E
Makhfar al Buşayyah 24 Lg 30.08N 46.07 E
Makhfar al Hammām 24 He 35.51N 38.45 E
Makhmūr 24 Je 35.46N 43.35 E
Makhyah, Wādī- 23 Gf 17.40N 49.01 E
Maki 29 Fc 37.45N 138.52 E
Makian, Pulau- 26 If 0.20N 127.25 E
Makikihi 62 Df 44.38 S 171.09 E
Makinsk 19 He 52.40N 70.26 E
Makkah=Mecca (EN) 22 Fg 21.27N 39.49 E
Makkovik 42 Le 55.05N 59.11W
Maknassy 32 Ic 34.37N 9.36 E
Makó 10 Qj 46.13N 20.29 E
Makokou 31 Ih 0.34N 12.52 E
Makongai 63d Bb 17.27 S 178.58 E
Makongolosi 36 Fd 8.24 S 33.09 E
Makorako 62 Gc 39.09 S 176.03 E
Makoua 31 Ih 0.01N 15.39 E
Makoura 63b Dc 17.08 S 168.26 E
Makov 10 Og 49.22N 18.29 E
Maków Mazowiecki 10 Rd 52.52N 21.06 E
Makrā 15 Im 36.16N 25.53 E
Makrān 21 Hg 26.00N 60.00 E
Makrónisos 15 Hl 37.42N 24.07 E
Maksatiha 7 Ih 57.48N 35.55 E
Makteir 30 Ff 21.50N 11.40W
Makthar 14 Do 35.50N 9.13 E
Makthar 32 Ib 35.51N 9.12 E
Makū 23 Hd 27.52N 52.26 E
Mākū 24 Kc 39.17N 44.31 E
Makubetsu 29a Cb 42.54N 143.19 E
Makumbato 36 Fd 8.51 S 34.50 E
Makumbi 36 Dd 5.51 S 20.41 E
Makunduchi 36 Gd 6.25 S 39.33 E
Makung 27 Kg 23.35N 119.35 E
Makurazaki 28 Ki 31.16N 139.19 E
Makurdi 31 Hh 7.44N 8.32 E
Makushin Volcano 40a Eb 53.53N 166.50W
Makušino 19 Gd 55.13N 67.13 E
Makuyuni 36 Gc 3.33 S 36.06 E
Malå 7 Ed 65.11N 18.44 E
Mala/Mallow 9 Ei 52.08N 8.39W
Mala, Punta- 47 Ig 7.28N 80.00W
Malabang 26 He 7.38N 124.03 E
Malabar Coast 21 Jh 10.00N 76.15 E
Malabo 31 Hh 3.45N 8.47 E
Malabrigo 55 Ci 29.20 S 59.58W
Malacca, Strait of- (EN)=Melaka, Selat- 21 Mi 2.30N 101.20 E
Malacky 10 Nh 48.27N 17.01 E
Malad City 46 Ie 42.12N 112.15W
Malá Fatra 10 Og 49.08N 18.50 E
Málaga [3] 13 Hh 36.48N 4.45W
Málaga [Col.] 54 Db 6.42N 72.44W
Málaga [Sp.] 6 Fh 36.43N 4.25W
Malagarasi 30 Ji 5.12 S 29.47 E
Malagón 13 Ie 39.10N 3.51W
Malaimbandi 37 Hd 20.20 S 45.36 E
Malaita Island 57 He 9.00 S 161.00 E
Malaja Kuonamka 20 Gb 70.50N 113.20 E
Malaja Ob 20 Bc 66.08N 65.50 E
Malaja Sosva 19 Gc 63.10N 64.22 E
Malaja Višera 19 Dd 58.52N 32.14 E
Malaja Viska 16 Ge 48.39N 31.38 E
Malakāl 31 Kh 9.31N 31.39 E
Malakal Harbor 64a Ac 7.20N 134.26 E
Malakal Pass 64a Ac 7.17N 134.28 E
Mala Kapela 14 Jf 44.55N 15.28 E
Malakobi 63a Db 7.19 S 158.07 E
Mallamalla Range 25 Fe 16.17N 79.29 E
Malang 22 Nj 7.59 S 112.37 E
Malangen 7 Eb 69.30N 18.20 E
Malanje 36 Cd 9.30 S 16.30 E
Malanje 31 Ii 9.33 S 16.22 E
Malanville 34 Fc 11.52N 3.23 E
Malao 63b Cb 15.10 S 166.51 E
Mała Panew 10 Nf 50.44N 17.52 E
Mälaren 5 Hd 59.30N 17.15 E
Malargüe 56 Ge 35.28 S 69.35W
Malartic, Lac- 44 Ha 48.15N 78.05W
Malaspina Glacier 40 Ke 59.50N 140.30W
Malatya 22 Ff 38.21N 38.19 E
Malāvi 24 Lf 33.10N 47.50 E
Malawi [1] 31 Kj 13.30 S 34.00 E
Malawi, Lake- 30 Kj 12.00 S 34.30 E
Malaya 26 Df 4.00N 102.00 E
Malaybalay 26 Ie 8.09N 125.05 E
Malāyer 24 Me 34.16N 48.12 E
Malāyer 23 Gc 34.17N 48.50 E
Malay Peninsula (EN) 21 Mi 6.00N 102.00 E
Malaysia [1] 22 Mi 4.00N 102.00 E
Malaysia, Semenanjung- [2] 26 Df 4.00N 102.00 E
Malazgirt 24 Jc 39.09N 42.31 E
Malberg 12 Id 50.03N 6.35 E
Mālbor 24 Og 30.45N 52.05 E
Malbork 10 Pb 54.02N 19.01 E
Malbrán 56 Hc 29.21 S 62.27W
Malchin 10 Ic 53.44N 12.47 E
Maldegem 12 Fc 51.13N 3.27 E
Malden 45 Lh 36.34N 89.57W
Malden Island 57 Le 4.03 S 154.59W
Malditos, Montes-/La Maladeta 13 Mb 42.40N 0.50 E
Maldive Islands 21 Ji 3.15N 73.00 E
Mal di Ventre 14 Ck 40.00N 8.20 E
Maldives [1] 22 Ji 3.15N 73.00 E
Maldon 9 Nj 51.45N 0.40 E
Maldonado [2] 55 El 34.40 S 54.55W
Maldonado 56 Jd 34.54 S 54.57W
Maldonado, Punta- 48 Ji 16.20N 98.35W
Male 22 Ji 4.10N 73.30 E
Malé 14 Ed 46.21N 10.55 E
Mâle, Lac du- 44 Ja 48.30N 75.30W
Malea, Cape- (EN) = Maléas, Ákra- 15 Gm 36.26N 23.12 E
Maléas, Ákra- = Malea, Cape- (EN) 15 Gm 36.26N 23.12 E
Male Atoll 21 Ji 4.29N 73.30 E
Malebo, Pool- 30 Ii 4.17 S 15.20 E
Mālegaon 25 Ed 20.33N 74.32 E
Maléha 34 Dc 11.48N 9.43W
Malek 35 Ed 6.04N 31.36 E
Malé Karpaty = Little Carpathians (EN) 10 Nh 48.30N 17.20 E
Malek Kandī 24 Ld 37.09N 46.06 E
Malékoula, Ile 57 Hf 16.15 S 167.30 E
Malema 37 Fb 14.57 S 37.25 E
Malemba Nkulu 36 Ed 8.02 S 26.48 E
Malenga 7 Ie 63.50N 36.25 E
Măleruş 15 Id 45.54N 25.32 E
Malesherbes 11 If 48.18N 2.25 E
Malgobek 16 Nh 43.32N 44.34 E
Malgomaj 7 Dd 64.47N 16.12 E
Malhada 55 Kb 14.21 S 43.47W
Malhanski Hrebet 20 Ff 50.30N 109.00 E
Malhão da Estrêla 13 Ed 40.19N 7.37W
Malha Wells 35 Db 15.08N 26.12 E
Malheur Lake 43 Dc 43.20N 118.45W
Malheur River 46 Gd 44.03N 116.59W
Mali [1] 31 Gg 17.00N 4.00W
Mali 34 Cc 12.05N 12.18W
Mali 25 Jc 25.42N 97.30 E
Mali 63d Bb 16.20 S 179.21 E
Mália 15 In 35.17N 25.28 E
Maliakós Kólpos 15 Fk 38.52N 22.38 E
Malik, Wādī al- 30 Kg 18.02N 30.58 E
Mali kanal 15 Cd 45.42N 19.19 E
Malik Sīah, Kūh-i- 23 Jd 29.51N 60.52 E
Målilla 8 Fg 57.23N 15.48 E
Mali Lošinj 14 If 44.32N 14.28 E
Malimba, Monts- 36 Ed 7.32 S 29.30 E
Malin 16 Fd 50.46N 29.14 E
Malinalco 48 Jh 18.57N 99.30W
Malinaltepec 48 Ji 17.03N 98.40W
Malindi 31 Li 3.13 S 40.07 E
Malines/Mechelen 11 Kc 51.02N 4.29 E
Malin Head/Cionn Mhálanna 5 Fd 55.23N 7.24W
Malino, Bukit- 26 Hf 0.45N 120.47 E
Malinovoje Ozero 20 Cf 51.40N 79.55 E
Malinyi 36 Gd 8.56 S 36.08 E
Malipo 27 Hg 23.07N 104.42 E
Maliqi 15 Di 40.43N 20.41 E
Malita 26 Ie 6.25N 125.36 E
Maljen 15 De 44.07N 20.03 E
Maljovica 15 Gg 42.11N 23.22 E
Malka 16 Nh 43.44N 44.15 E
Malkara 24 Bb 40.53N 26.54 E
Malki Lom 15 Jf 43.39N 26.04 E
Malko Tărnovo 15 Kh 41.59N 27.32 E
Mallacoota 59 Jg 37.30 S 149.50 E
Mallaig 9 Hd 57.00N 5.50W
Mallāq, Wādī- 14 Cn 36.32N 8.51 E
Mallawī 33 Fd 27.44N 30.50 E
Mallery Lake 42 Hd 64.00N 98.00W
Malles Venosta / Mals 14 Ed 46.41N 10.32 E
Mallet 55 Gg 25.55 S 50.50W
Mallorca=Majorca (EN) 5 Gh 39.30N 3.00 E
Mallow/Mala 9 Ei 52.08N 8.39W
Malm 7 Cd 64.04N 11.13 E
Malmbäck 8 Fg 57.35N 14.28 E
Malmberget 7 Ec 67.10N 20.40 E
Malmédy 11 Md 50.26N 6.02 E
Malmesbury 37 Bf 33.28 S 18.44 E
Malmö 6 Hd 55.36N 13.00 E
Malmöhus [2] 7 Ci 55.45N 13.30 E
Malmön 8 Df 58.21N 11.20 E
Malmslätt 8 Ff 58.25N 15.30 E
Malmyž 19 Fd 56.31N 50.41 E
Malo 63b Cb 15.41 S 167.10 E
Maloarhangelsk 16 Jc 52.26N 36.29 E
Maloelap 57 Id 8.45N 171.03 E
Maloggia/Malojapaß 14 Dd 46.24N 9.41 E
Malojapaß/Maloggia 14 Dd 46.24N 9.41 E
Malojaroslavec 16 Jb 55.02N 36.28 E
Maloje Polesje 10 Jf 50.10N 24.30 E
Malolo 63d Ab 17.45 S 177.10 E
Malolos 26 Hd 14.51N 120.49 E
Malombe, Lake- 36 Ge 14.38 S 35.12 E
Malone 44 Jc 44.52N 74.19W
Malonga 36 De 10.24 S 23.10 E
Małopolska 10 Pf 50.45N 20.00 E
Malorita 16 Dd 51.48N 24.05 E
Malošujka 7 Ie 63.47N 37.22 E
Måløy 7 Af 61.56N 5.07 E
Malozemelskaja Tundra 17 Ec 68.00N 52.00 E
Malpaso 48 Mi 17.20N 93.30W
Malpelo, Isla de- 52 He 3.59N 81.35W
Malprabha 25 Fe 16.12N 76.03 E
Mals / Malles Venosta 14 Ed 46.41N 10.32 E
Malsch 12 Kf 48.53N 8.20 E
Malše 10 Kh 48.59N 14.29 E
Malta 5 Hh 35.54N 14.31 E
Malta [1] 6 Hh 35.50N 14.30 E
Malta [Lat.-U.S.S.R.] 8 Lh 56.18N 27.15 E
Malta [Mt.-U.S.] 43 Fb 48.21N 107.52W
Malta, Canale di- [Eur.] = Malta Channel (EN) 14 In 36.30N 14.30 E
Malta Channel (EN)=Malta, Canale di- [Eur.] 14 In 36.30N 14.30 E
Maltahöhe [3] 37 Bd 25.00 S 16.30 E
Maltahöhe 31 Ik 24.50 S 17.00 E
Maltepe 15 Mi 40.55N 29.08 E
Malton 9 Mg 54.08N 0.48W
Maluku [3] 26 Ig 4.00 S 128.00 E
Maluku, Kepulauan-=Moluccas (EN) 57 De 2.00 S 128.00 E
Maluku, Laut-=Molucca Sea (EN) 21 Oj 0.05 S 125.00 E
Malumfashi 34 Gc 11.48N 7.37 E
Malunda 26 Gg 3.00 S 118.50 E
Malung 7 Cf 60.40N 13.44 E
Malungsfors 8 Ed 60.44N 13.33 E
Malūţ 35 Ec 10.26N 32.12 E
Maluu 63a Ec 8.21 S 160.38 E
Malvern [Ar.-U.S.] 45 Ji 34.22N 92.49W
Malvern [Eng.-U.K.] 9 Ki 52.07N 2.19W
Malvinas 55 Ci 29.37 S 58.59W
Malvinas, Islas-/Falkland Islands [5] 53 Kk 51.45 S 59.00W
Malvinas, Islas-/Falkland Islands 52 Kk 51.45 S 59.00W
Maly, Ostrov- 8 Ld 60.02N 27.58 E
Malya 36 Fc 2.59 S 33.31 E
Maly Anjuj 20 Lc 68.35N 161.03 E
Maly Čeremšan 7 Mi 54.20N 50.01 E
Malý Dunaj 10 Nh 48.08N 17.09 E
Malygina, Proliv- 20 Cb 73.00N 70.30 E
Maly Jenisej 20 Ef 51.40N 94.26 E
Maly Kavkaz=Lesser Caucasus (EN) 5 Kg 41.00N 44.35 E
Maly Ljahovski, Ostrov- 20 Jb 74.07N 140.36 E
Maly Tajmyr, Ostrov- 20 Fa 78.08N 107.08 E
Maly Uzen 5 Kf 48.50N 49.38 E
Mama 20 Ge 58.20N 112.54 E
Mamadyš 7 Mi 55.45N 51.24 E
Mamagota 63a Bb 6.46 S 155.24 E
Mamaia 15 Le 44.17N 28.37 E
Mamakan 20 Ge 57.48N 114.05 E
Mamantel 48 Nh 18.33N 91.05W
Mamanutha Group 63d Ab 17.34 S 177.04 E
Mamaqān 24 Kd 37.51N 45.59 E
Mambaj 55 Ib 14.28 S 46.07W
Mambajao 26 He 9.15N 124.43 E
Mambasa 36 Eb 1.21N 29.03 E
Mambéré 35 Be 3.31N 16.03 E
Mambili 36 Cb 0.07N 16.08 E
Mamborê 55 Fg 24.18 S 52.32W
Mambova 36 Ef 17.44 S 25.11 E
Mambrui 36 Hc 3.07 S 40.09 E
Mamburao 26 Hd 13.14N 120.35 E
Mamedkala 16 Ph 42.12N 48.06 E
Mamer 12 Ie 49.38N 6.02 E
Mamers 11 Gf 48.21N 0.23 E
Mamfe 34 Gd 5.46N 9.17 E
Mamiá, Lago- 54 Fd 4.15 S 63.05W
Mamisonski, Pereval- 16 Mh 42.43N 43.45 E
Mamljutka 19 Ge 54.57N 68.35 E
Mammoth Cave 44 Dg 37.10N 86.08W
Mammoth Hot Springs 46 Jd 44.59N 110.43W
Mamoré, Rio- 52 Jg 10.23 S 65.53W
Mamou 31 Fg 10.23N 12.05W
Mampikony 37 Hc 16.05 S 47.37 E
Mampodre, Picos de- 13 Ga 43.02N 5.12W
Mampong 34 Ed 7.04N 1.24W
Mamry, Jezioro- 10 Rb 54.08N 21.42 E
Mamuju 26 Gg 2.41 S 118.54 E
Mamuno 37 Cd 22.17 S 20.02 E
Ma'murah, Ra's al- 14 En 36.27N 10.49 E
Mamurokawa 29 Gb 38.54N 140.15 E
Mamutzu 37 Hb 12.47 S 45.14 E
Man 31 Gh 7.24N 7.33W
Man [3] 34 Dd 7.13N 7.41W
Man, Calf of- 9 Ig 54.03N 4.48W
Man, Isle of- 5 Fe 54.15N 4.30W
Mana 60 Oc 22.02N 159.46W
Mana 20 Ee 55.57N 92.28 E
Manacapuru 54 Fd 3.18 S 60.37W
Manacor 13 Pe 39.34N 3.12 E
Manado 22 Oi 1.29N 124.51 E
Managua 39 Kh 12.09N 86.17W
Managua [3] 49 Dg 12.05N 86.20W
Managua, Lago de- 47 Gf 12.20N 86.20W
Manakara 31 Lk 22.07 S 48.00 E
Manama (EN)=Al Manāmah 22 Hg 26.13N 50.35 E
Manambolo 37 Gc 19.19 S 44.17 E
Manam Island 57 Fe 4.05 S 145.03 E
Manamo, Caño- 54 Fb 9.55N 62.16W
Mananara 37 Hc 16.10 S 49.45 E
Mananara 37 Hd 23.21 S 47.42 E
Mananjary 31 Lk 21.14 S 48.17 E
Manankoro 34 Dc 10.28N 7.25W
Manantenina 37 Hd 24.17 S 47.18 E
Manaoba 63a Ec 8.19 S 160.47 E
Manapire, Rio- 50 Ci 7.42N 66.07W
Manapouri 58 Hi 45.34 S 167.36 E
Manapouri, Lake- 62 Bf 45.30 S 167.30 E
Manār, Jabal- 33 Hg 14.10N 44.17 E
Manas 22 Ke 44.18N 86.13 E
Manas, Gora- 18 Hc 42.18N 71.06 E
Manas He 27 Eb 45.38N 85.12 E
Manas Hu 27 Eb 45.45N 85.55 E
Manasija, Manastir- 15 Ee 44.06N 21.28 E
Manatí 49 Ic 21.19N 76.56W
Manatí 49 Nd 18.26N 66.29W
Manatuto 26 Ih 8.30 S 126.01 E
Manaure 49 Kh 11.46N 72.28W
Manaus 53 Jf 3.08 S 60.01W
Manavgat 24 Dd 36.47N 31.26 E
Manbij 24 Gd 36.31N 37.57 E
Manbūbnagar 25 Fe 16.44N 77.59 E
Mancelona 44 Ec 44.54N 85.04W
Mancha Real 13 Ig 37.47N 3.37W
Manche [3] 11 Ee 49.00N 1.10W
Mancheng 28 Ce 38.57N 115.19 E
Manchester [Ct.-U.S.] 44 Ke 41.47N 72.31W
Manchester [Eng.-U.K.] 6 Fe 53.30N 2.15W
Manchester [Ia.-U.S.] 45 Ke 42.29N 91.27W
Manchester [Ky.-U.S.] 44 Fg 37.09N 83.46W
Manchester [N.H.-U.S.] 43 Mc 42.59N 71.28W
Manchester [Tn.-U.S.] 44 Dh 35.29N 86.05W
Manchok 34 Gd 9.40N 8.31 E
Manchuria (EN) 22 Oe 47.00N 125.00 E
Manciano 14 Fh 42.35N 11.31 E
Mand 23 Hd 28.11N 51.17 E
Manda [Chad] 35 Bd 9.11N 18.13 E
Manda [Tan.] 36 Fe 10.28 S 34.35 E
Manda, Jabal- 35 Cd 8.39N 24.27 E
Mandabe 37 Gd 21.02 S 44.56 E
Mandaguari 56 Jb 23.32 S 51.42W
Manda Island 36 Hc 2.17 S 40.57 E
Mandal 7 Bg 58.02N 7.27 E
Mandalay [3] 25 Jd 21.00N 96.00 E
Mandalay 22 Lg 22.00N 96.05 E
Mandal-Gobi 27 Ib 45.45N 106.12 E
Mandalī 24 Kf 33.45N 45.32 E
Mandalselva 8 Bf 58.02N 7.28 E
Mandalt → Sonid Zuoqi 27 Kc 43.50N 116.45 E
Mandalya körfezi 24 Bd 37.12N 27.20 E
Mandan 43 Gb 46.50N 100.54W
Mandaon 26 Hd 12.13N 123.17 E
Mandara, Monts-=Mandara Mountains (EN) 34 Hc 10.45N 13.40 E
Mandara Mountains (EN)=Mandara, Monts- 34 Hc 10.45N 13.40 E
Mandas 14 Dk 39.38N 9.07 E
Mandasor 25 Fd 24.04N 75.04 E
Mandera 31 Lh 3.56N 41.52 E
Manderscheid 12 Id 50.06N 6.49 E
Mandeville 49 Id 18.02N 77.30W
Mandi 25 Fb 31.43N 76.55 E
Mandiana 34 Dc 10.38N 8.41W
Mandimba 37 Fb 14.21 S 35.39 E
Mandingues, Monts- 34 Cc 13.00N 11.00W
Mandioli, Pulau- 26 Ig 0.44 S 127.14 E
Mandioré, Laguna- 55 Dd 18.08 S 57.33W
Mandirituba 55 Hg 25.46 S 49.19W
Mandji 36 Bc 1.42 S 10.24 E
Mandla 25 Gd 22.36N 80.23 E
Mandø 8 Ci 55.15N 8.35 E
Mandoúdhion 15 Gk 38.48N 23.29 E
Mandrákion 15 Km 36.36N 27.08 E
Mandritsara 37 Hc 15.49 S 48.48 E
Mandurah 59 Df 32.32 S 115.43 E
Manduria 14 Lj 40.24N 17.38 E
Māndvi 25 Dd 22.50N 69.22 E
Mandya 25 Ff 12.33N 76.54 E
Måne 8 Ce 59.56N 8.48 E
Măneciu Ungureni 15 Id 45.19N 25.59 E
Manendragarh 25 Gd 23.10N 82.35 E
Maneromango 36 Gd 7.16 S 38.46 E
Manevići 16 Dd 51.19N 25.33 E
Manfalūţ 33 Fd 27.19N 30.58 E
Manfredonia 14 Ji 41.38N 15.55 E
Manfredonia, Golfo di- 14 Ki 41.35N 16.05 E
Manga [Afr.] 30 Ig 15.00N 14.00 E
Manga [Braz.] 54 Jf 14.46 S 43.56W
Mangabeiras, Chapada das- 52 Lg 10.00 S 46.30W
Mangai 36 Cc 4.03 S 19.35 E
Mangaia Island 57 Lg 21.55 S 157.55W
Mangakino 62 Fc 38.22 S 175.46 E
Mangalia 15 Lf 43.48N 28.35 E
Mangalmé 35 Bc 12.21N 19.37 E
Mangalore 22 Jh 12.52N 74.53 E
Mangareva, Ile- 57 Ng 23.07 S 134.57W
Mangfall 10 Ii 47.51N 12.08 E
Manggar 26 Eg 2.53 S 108.16 E
Manggautu 63a Dd 11.30 S 159.59 E
Mangin Yoma 25 Jd 24.20N 95.42 E
Mangistau 16 Qg 44.03N 51.57 E
Mangit 19 Gg 42.07N 60.01 E
Mangkalihat, Tanjung- 26 Gf 1.02N 118.59 E
Manglares, Cabo- 54 Cc 1.36N 79.02W
Mangnai 27 Fd 37.48N 91.55 E
Mangniu He 28 Ib 45.10N 126.58 E
Mango [Fiji] 63d Cb 17.27 S 179.09W
Mango [Ton.] 65b Bb 20.20 S 174.43W
Mangoche 36 Ge 14.28 S 35.16 E
Mangoky [Mad.] 37 Hd 23.27 S 45.13 E
Mangoky [Mad.] 30 Lk 21.29 S 43.41 E
Mangole, Pulau- 26 Ig 1.53 S 125.50 E
Mangonui 62 Ea 34.59 S 173.32 E
Mangrove Cay 49 Ia 24.51N 76.14W
Mangrullo, Cuchilla- 55 Fk 32.27 S 53.50W
Mangshi → Luxi 27 Gg 24.29N 98.40 E
Mangualde 13 Ed 40.36N 7.46W
Mangueira, Lagoa- 56 Jd 33.06 S 52.48W
Mangueni, Plateau de- 30 If 22.35N 12.40 E
Mangui 27 La 52.03N 122.09 E
Mangula 37 Ec 16.52 S 30.08 E
Mangum 45 Gi 34.53N 99.30W
Manguredjipa 36 Eb 0.21N 28.44 E
Mangyšlak 19 Fg 43.40N 51.15 E
Mangyšlak, Plato- 19 Fg 43.25N 53.00 E
Mangyšlakskaja Oblast [3] 19 Fg 44.00N 53.30 E
Mangyšlakskij Zaliv 16 Qg 44.45N 51.00 E
Manhattan 43 Hd 39.11N 96.35W
Manhica 37 Ee 25.24 S 32.48 E
Mani 36 Ed 6.27 S 25.20 E
Maní 54 Dc 4.49N 72.17W
Mānī', Wādī al- 24 Ie 34.16N 41.02 E
Mania 37 Hc 19.42 S 45.22 E
Maniago 14 Gd 46.10N 12.43 E
Manica [3] 37 Ec 19.00 S 33.20 E
Manica 37 Ec 18.56 S 32.53 E
Manicaland [3] 37 Ec 19.00 S 32.30 E
Manicoré 53 Jf 5.49 S 61.17W

Index Symbols

- [1] Independent Nation
- [2] State, Region
- [3] District, County
- [4] Municipality
- [5] Colony, Dependency
- Continent
- Physical Region
- Historical or Cultural Region
- Mount, Mountain
- Volcano
- Hill
- Mountains, Mountain Range
- Hills, Escarpment
- Plateau, Upland
- Pass, Gap
- Plain, Lowland
- Delta
- Salt Flat
- Valley, Canyon
- Crater, Cave
- Karst Features
- Depression
- Polder
- Desert, Dunes
- Forest, Woods
- Heath, Steppe
- Oasis
- Cape, Point
- Coast, Beach
- Cliff
- Peninsula
- Isthmus
- Sandbank
- Island
- Atoll
- Rock, Reef
- Islands, Archipelago
- Rocks, Reefs
- Coral Reef
- Well, Spring
- Geyser
- River, Stream
- Waterfall Rapids
- River Mouth, Estuary
- Lake
- Salt Lake
- Intermittent Lake
- Reservoir
- Swamp, Pond
- Canal
- Glacier
- Ice Shelf, Pack Ice
- Ocean
- Sea
- Gulf, Bay
- Strait, Fjord
- Lagoon
- Bank
- Seamount
- Tablemount
- Ridge
- Shelf
- Basin
- Escarpment, Sea Scarp
- Fracture
- Trench, Abyss
- National Park, Reserve
- Point of Interest
- Recreation Site
- Cave, Cavern
- Historic Site
- Ruins
- Wall, Walls
- Church, Abbey
- Temple
- Scientific Station
- Airport
- Port
- Lighthouse
- Mine
- Tunnel
- Dam, Bridge

Manicoré, Rio- 54 Fe 5.51S 61.19W
Manicouagan 42 Kg 49.10N 68.15W
Manicouagan 42 Kf 51.00N 68.20W
Manicouagan, Réservoir- 38 Md 51.30N 68.19W
Manigotagan 45 Ha 51.06N 96.18W
Manihi Atoll 57 Mf 14.24S 145.56W
Manihiki Anchorage 64n Ab 10.23S 161.03W
Manihiki Atoll 57 Kf 10.24S 161.01W
Manika, Plateau de la- 36 Ed 10.00S 26.00 E
Manila [Phil.] 22 Oh 14.35N 121.00 E
Manila [Ut.-U.S.] 46 Kf 40.59N 109.43W
Manila Bay 21 Oh 14.30N 120.45 E
Manilaid/Manilajd 8 Kf 58.08N 24.03 E
Manilajd/Manilaid 8 Kf 58.08N 24.03 E
Manily 20 Ld 62.30N 165.20 E
Maningrida Settlement 59 Gb 12.05S 134.10 E
Maniouro, Pointe- 63b Dc 17.41S 168.35 E
Manipa, Selat- 26 Ig 3.20S 127.23 E
Manipur [3] 25 Id 25.00N 94.00 E
Manipur 25 Id 22.52N 94.05 E
Manisa 23 Cb 38.36N 27.26 E
Manisa Dağı 15 Kk 38.33N 27.28 E
Manises 13 Le 39.29N 0.27W
Manissau a-Missu, Rio- 54 Hf 10.58S 53.20W
Manistee 44 Dc 44.15N 86.18W
Manistee River 44 Dc 44.15N 86.21W
Manistique 43 Jb 45.57N 86.15W
Manitique Lake 44 Eb 46.15N 85.45W
Manitoba [3] 42 Hf 55.00N 97.00W
Manitoba, Lake- 38 Jd 51.00N 98.45W
Manitou Islands 44 Ec 45.10N 86.00W
Manitou Lake 44 Gc 45.48N 82.00W
Manitoulin Island 42 Jg 45.45N 82.30W
Manitou Springs 45 Dg 38.52N 104.55W
Manitouwadge 45 Nb 49.08N 85.47W
Manitowoc 43 Jc 44.06N 87.40W
Manitsoq/Sukkertoppen 41 Ge 65.25N 53.00W
Maniwaki 42 Jg 46.23N 75.58W
Manizales 53 Ie 5.05N 75.32W
Manja 17 Jd 64.23N 60.50 E
Manja 37 Gd 21.23S 44.20 E
Manjača 14 Lf 44.35N 17.05 E
Manjacaze 37 Ed 24.42S 33.33 E
Manjakandriana 37 Hc 18.55S 47.47 E
Manji 29a Bb 43.09N 141.59 E
Manjimup 59 Df 34.14S 116.09 E
Mānjra 25 Fe 18.49N 77.52 E
Mān Kāt 25 Jd 22.05N 98.01 E
Mankato [Ks.-U.S.] 45 Gg 39.47N 98.12W
Mankato [Mn.-U.S.] 43 Ic 44.10N 94.01W
Mankono 34 Dd 8.04N 6.12W
Mankono [3] 34 Dd 7.58N 6.02W
Mankoya 31 Jj 14.50S 25.00 E
Manley Hot Springs 40 Ic 65.00N 150.37W
Manlleu 13 Ob 42.00N 2.17 E
Manmād 25 Ed 20.15N 74.27 E
Manmanoc, Mount- 26 Hc 17.40N 121.06 E
Manna 26 Dh 4.27S 102.55 E
Mannahill 59 Hf 32.26S 139.59 E
Mannar 25 Fg 8.59N 79.54 E
Mannar, Gulf of- 21 Ji 8.30N 79.00 E
Mannheim 6 Gf 49.29N 8.28 E
Manning [Alta.-Can.] 42 Fe 56.55N 117.33W
Manning [S.C.-U.S.] 44 Gi 33.42N 80.12W
Manning, Cape- 64g Ba 2.02N 157.26W
Manning Strait 63a Db 7.24S 158.04 E
Manningtree 12 Dc 51.57N 1.04 E
Mann Ranges 59 Fe 26.00S 129.30 E
Mann River 59 Gb 12.20S 134.07 E
Mannu, Capo- 14 Cj 40.02N 8.22 E
Mannu, Rio- [It.] 14 Cj 40.50N 8.23 E
Mannu, Rio- [It.] 14 Cj 40.41N 8.59 E
Mano 34 Cd 6.56N 11.31W
Mano [Jap.] 29 Fc 37.58N 138.20 E
Mano [S.L.] 34 Cd 7.55N 12.00W
Manoa 54 Ee 9.40S 65.27W
Man of War, Cayos- 49 Fg 13.02N 83.22W
Manokwari 58 Ee 2.30S 134.36 E
Manombo 37 Gd 22.55S 43.28 E
Manompana 37 Hc 16.41S 49.45 E
Manonga 36 Fc 4.08S 34.12 E
Manono 31 Ji 7.18S 27.25 E
Manono 65c Aa 13.50S 172.05W
Manosque 11 Lk 43.50N 5.47 E
Manouane, Lac- 42 Kf 50.40N 70.45W
Manō-Wan 29 Fc 37.55N 138.15 E
Manp'ojin 28 Id 41.09N 126.17 E
Manra Atoll (Sydney) 57 Je 4.27S 171.15W
Manresa 13 Nc 41.44N 1.50 E
Mansa 31 Jj 11.12S 28.53 E
Mansa Konko 34 Bc 13.28N 15.33W
Mansel 38 Lc 62.00N 79.50W
Mansfield [Austl.] 59 Jg 37.03S 146.05 E
Mansfield [Eng.-U.K.] 9 Lh 53.09N 1.11W
Mansfield [La.-U.S.] 45 Jj 32.02N 93.43W
Mansfield [Oh.-U.S.] 43 Kc 40.46N 82.31W
Mansfield [Pa.-U.S.] 44 Ie 41.47N 77.05W
Mansfield, Mount- 44 Kc 44.33N 72.49W
Mansle 11 Gi 45.52N 0.11 E
Manso, Rio- 55 Db 14.42S 56.16W
Manso, Rio- ou Mortes, Rio das- 52 Kg 11.45S 50.44W
Mansôa 34 Bc 12.04N 15.19W
Mansourah 13 Qh 36.04N 4.28 E
Mansourah, Djebel- 13 Qh 36.02N 4.28 E
Manta 54 Bd 0.57S 80.42W
Manta, Bahía de- 54 Bd 0.50S 80.40W
Mantalingajan, Mount- 26 Ge 8.48N 117.40 E
Manteca 46 Eh 37.48N 121.13W
Mantecal [Ven.] 50 Di 6.52N 65.38W
Mantecal [Ven.] 50 Bi 7.33N 69.09W
Manteigas 13 Ed 40.24N 7.32W
Manteo 44 Jh 35.55N 75.40W
Mantes-la-Jolie 11 Hf 48.59N 1.43 E
Manti 46 Jg 39.16N 111.38W
Mantiqueira, Serra da- 52 Lh 22.00S 44.45W
Manto 49 Df 14.55N 86.23W
Manton 44 Ec 44.24N 85.24W
Mantova 14 Ee 45.09N 10.48 E
Mäntsälä 8 Kd 60.38N 25.20 E
Mänttä 7 Fe 62.02N 24.38 E
Mantua 49 Eb 22.17N 84.17W
Manturovo 19 Ed 58.22N 44.44 E
Mäntyharju 7 Gf 61.25N 26.53 E
Mäntyluoto 8 Ic 61.35N 21.29 E
Manu 54 Df 12.15S 70.50W
Manuae Atoll 57 Lf 19.21S 158.56W
Manua Islands 57 Kf 14.13S 169.35W
Manuangi Atoll 57 Mf 19.12S 141.16W
Manūbah 14 En 36.48N 10.06 E
Manuel 48 Jf 22.44N 98.19W
Manuel Alves, Rio- 54 If 11.19S 48.28W
Manuel Bonavides 48 Hc 29.05N 103.55W
Manuel Derqui 55 Ch 27.50S 58.48W
Manuel J. Cobo 55 Dl 35.49S 57.54W
Manuel Ocampo 55 Bk 33.46S 60.39W
Manuga Reefs 63a Ad 11.00S 153.21 E
Manui, Pulau- 26 Hg 3.35S 123.08 E
Manujān 24 Qi 27.24N 57.32 E
Manūk, Tell- 24 Hf 33.10N 38.50 E
Manukau 58 Ih 36.56S 174.56 E
Manulu Lagoon 64g Bb 1.56N 157.20W
Manus Island 57 Fe 2.05S 147.00 E
Many 45 Jk 31.34N 93.29W
Manyara, Lake- 36 Gc 3.35S 35.50 E
Manyas 24 Bb 40.02N 27.58 E
Manyč 5 Kf 47.15N 40.00 E
Manyč-Gudilo, Ozero- 5 Kf 46.25N 42.35 E
Manyoni 36 Fd 5.45S 34.50 E
Manzanal, Puerto del- 13 Fb 42.32N 6.10W
Manzanares 13 Ie 39.00N 3.22W
Manzaneda, Cabeza de- 13 Eb 42.20N 7.15W
Manzanilla 13 Fg 37.23N 6.25W
Manzanillo [Cuba] 39 Lg 20.21N 77.07W
Manzanillo [Mex.] 39 Ih 19.03N 104.20W
Manzanillo, Bahía de- [Dom.Rep.] 49 Ld 19.45N 71.46W
Manzanillo, Bahía de- [Mex.] 48 Gh 19.04N 104.25W
Manzanillo, Punta- 49 Hi 9.38N 79.32W
Manzano Mountains 45 Ci 34.45N 106.20W
Manzhouli 22 Ne 49.33N 117.28 E
Manzilah, Buḩayrat al- 24 Eg 31.15N 32.00 E
Manzil Bū Ruqaybah 32 Ib 37.10N 9.48 E
Manzil bū Zalafah 14 En 36.41N 10.35 E
Manzil Tamīn 14 En 36.47N 10.59 E
Manzini 37 Ee 26.29S 31.22 E
Mao 63b Dc 17.29S 168.29 E
Mao [Chad] 31 Ig 14.07N 15.19 E
Mao [Dom.Rep.] 47 Je 19.34N 71.05W
Mao/Mahón 13 Qe 39.53N 4.15 E
Maoke, Pegunungan- 57 Ee 4.00S 138.00 E
Maomao Shan 27 Hd 37.12N 103.10 E
Maoming 22 Ng 21.41N 110.52 E
Maoniu Shan 27 He 32.50N 104.12 E
Maotou Shan 27 Hg 24.31N 100.38 E
Maouri, Dallol- 34 Fc 12.05N 3.32 E
Mapai 37 Ed 22.51S 31.58 E
Mapanda 36 Dd 9.32S 24.16 E
Mapati 36 Bc 3.38S 13.21 E
Mapi 58 Ee 7.07S 139.23 E
Mapi 26 Kh 7.00S 139.16 E
Mapia, Kepulauan- 26 Jf 0.50N 134.20 E
Mapimí, Bolsón de- 39 Ig 27.30N 103.15W
Mapinhane 37 Fd 22.15S 35.07 E
Mapire 50 Di 7.45N 64.42W
Mapiri 54 Eg 15.15S 68.10W
Maple Creek 42 Gg 49.55N 109.27W
Maprik 60 Ch 3.38S 143.03 E
Mapuera, Rio- 54 Gd 1.05S 57.02W
Maputo [3] 37 Ee 26.00S 32.30 E
Maputo (Lourenço Marques) 31 Kk 25.58S 32.34 E
Maputo, Baía de- 36 Kk 26.05S 33.00 E
Maqēn (Dawu) 27 He 34.29N 100.01 E
Maqran, Wādī al- 33 Ie 20.55N 47.12 E
Maqu 27 He 34.05N 101.45 E
Maquan He/Damqog Kanbab 27 Df 29.36N 84.09 E
Maquela do Zombo 31 Ii 6.03S 15.08 E
Maquinchao 56 Gf 41.15S 68.44W
Maquoketa 45 Ke 42.04N 90.40W
Mar, Serra do- 52 Lh 25.00S 48.00W
Mara 36 Fc 1.31S 33.56 E
Mara [3] 36 Fc 2.30S 34.00 E
Maraã 54 Ed 1.50S 65.22W
Marab 35 Fc 14.54N 37.55 E
Marabá 54 Ie 5.21S 49.07W
Marabahan 26 Fg 3.00S 114.45 E
Marabá Paulista 55 Gf 22.06S 51.56W
Maraca, Ilha de- 54 Hc 2.05N 50.25W
Maracaibo 53 Id 10.40N 71.37W
Maracaibo, Lago de- = Maracaibo, Lake- (EN) 52 Ie 9.50N 71.30W
Maracaibo, Lake- (EN) = Maracaibo, Lago de- 52 Ie 9.50N 71.30W
Maracaju 54 Gh 21.38S 55.09W
Maracaju, Serra de- [Braz.] 52 Kh 21.00S 55.00W
Maracaju, Serra de- [S.Amer.] 55 Ef 23.57S 55.01W
Maracanã 54 Id 0.46S 47.27W
Maracás 54 Jf 13.26S 40.27W
Maracay 53 Jd 10.15N 67.36W
Marādah 33 Cd 29.14N 19.13 E
Maradi 31 Hg 13.29N 7.06 E
Maradi [2] 34 Gc 14.15N 7.15 E
Marāgheh 23 Gb 37.23N 46.40 E
Marāh 23 Gd 25.04N 45.28 E
Maraho 35 Bb 18.21N 17.28 E
Marahuaca, Cerro- 52 Je 3.34N 65.27W
Marajó, Baía de- 52 Lf 1.00S 48.30W
Marajó, Ilha de- 52 Lf 1.00S 49.30W
Marakei Atoll 57 Id 1.58N 173.25 E
Maralal 36 Gb 1.06N 36.42 E
Maralinga 59 Gf 30.13S 131.35 E
Maralwexi/Bachu 27 Cd 39.46N 78.15 E
Maramag 26 He 7.46N 125.00 E
Maramasike Island 60 Gi 9.30S 161.25 E
Maramba 31 Jj 17.51S 25.52 E
Marampa 34 Cd 8.41N 12.28W
Maramureș [2] 15 Gb 47.40N 24.00 E
Maranchón 13 Jc 41.03N 2.12W
Marānd 23 Gb 38.26N 45.46 E
Marang 26 De 5.12N 103.13 E
Maranhão [2] 54 Je 5.00S 45.00W
Maranhão, Rio- 54 If 14.34S 49.02W
Marano, Laguna di- 14 He 45.44N 13.10 E
Maranoa River 59 Je 27.50S 148.37 E
Marañón, Rio- 52 If 4.30S 73.35W
Marans 11 Fh 46.18N 1.00W
Marão 37 Ed 24.18S 34.07 E
Marão, Serra do- 13 Ec 41.15N 7.55W
Maraoué 34 Dd 6.54N 5.31W
Marapanim 54 Id 0.42S 47.42W
Marapi, Gunung- 26 Dg 0.23S 100.28 E
Marargiu, Capo- 14 Cj 40.20N 8.23 E
Marari, Serra do- 55 Gh 27.30S 51.00W
Mara Rosa 55 Ha 13.58S 49.09W
Mărășești 15 Kd 45.53N 27.14 E
Maratea 14 Jk 39.59N 15.43 E
Marathón 15 Gk 38.09N 23.58 E
Marathon 45 Ek 30.12N 103.15W
Marathon 42 Ig 48.46N 86.26W
Maratua, Pulau- 26 Gf 2.15N 118.36 E
Marau 55 Fi 28.27S 52.12W
Maravari 63a Cb 7.54S 156.44 E
Marāveh Tappeh 24 Pd 37.55N 55.57 E
Maravilha 55 Fh 26.47S 53.09W
Maravillas Creek 45 El 29.34N 102.47W
Maravovo 63a Dc 9.17S 159.38 E
Marāwah 33 Dc 32.29N 21.25 E
Marawi 26 He 8.13N 124.15 E
Marawi 35 Eb 18.29N 31.49 E
Marāwiḥ 24 Oj 24.18N 53.18 E
Marayes 56 Gd 31.29S 67.20W
Marbella 13 Hh 36.31N 4.53W
Marble Bar 59 Dd 21.11S 119.44 E
Marble Canyon 46 Jh 36.30N 111.50W
Marble Falls 45 Gk 30.34N 98.17W
Marble Hall 37 Dd 24.57S 29.13 E
Marburg an der Lahn 10 Ef 50.49N 8.46 E
Marca, Ponta da- 30 Ij 16.31S 11.42 E
Marcal 10 Ni 47.38N 17.32 E
Marcala 49 Df 14.07N 88.00W
Marçal Dağları 15 Kl 37.09N 28.00 E
Marcali 10 Nj 46.35N 17.25 E
March 10 Mh 48.10N 16.59 E
March 9 Ni 52.33N 0.06 E
Marche 11 Hh 46.10N 1.30 E
Marche = Marches (EN) [2] 14 Hh 43.30N 13.15 E
Marche, Plateau de la- 11 Hh 46.16N 1.30 E
Marche-en-Famenne 11 Ld 50.14N 5.20 E
Marchena 13 Gg 37.20N 5.24W
Marchena, Isla- 54a Aa 0.20N 90.30W
Marches (EN) = Marche [2] 14 Hh 43.30N 13.15 E
Marchesato 14 Kk 39.05N 17.00 E
Marchfeld 14 Kb 48.15N 16.40 E
Mar Chiquita, Laguna- 55 Dm 37.37S 57.24W
Mar Chiquita, Laguna- 52 Ji 30.42S 62.36W
Marciana Marina 14 Eh 42.48N 10.12 E
Marcigny 11 Kh 46.16N 4.02 E
Marcilly-sur-Eure 12 Df 48.49N 1.21 E
Marcinelle, Charleroi- 12 Gd 50.25N 4.28 E
Marck 12 Dd 50.57N 1.57 E
Marcoing 12 Fd 50.07N 3.11 E
Marcos Juaréz 56 Hd 32.42S 62.06W
Marcus Baker, Mount- 40 Jd 61.26N 147.45W
Marcus Island (EN) = Minami-Tori-Shima 57 Gb 26.32N 142.09 E
Marcy, Mount- 43 Mc 44.07N 73.56W
Mardakert 16 Oi 40.12N 46.52 E
Mardakjan 16 Qi 40.29N 50.12 E
Mardān 25 Eb 34.09N 71.52 E
Mardarovka 15 Mb 47.30N 29.40 E
Mar del Plata 53 Ki 38.01S 57.35W
Marden 12 Cc 51.10N 0.30 E
Mardin 23 Fb 37.18N 40.44 E
Mardin Dağları 24 Id 37.20N 41.00 E
Maré, Ile- 57 Hg 21.30S 168.00 E
Mare, Muntele- 15 Gc 46.29N 23.14 E
Marechal Cândido Rondon 55 Eg 24.34S 54.04W
Maree, Loch- 9 Hd 57.40N 5.30W
Mareeba 59 Jc 17.00S 145.26 E
Mareg 35 He 3.47N 47.18 E
Maremma 14 Fh 42.30N 11.30 E
Marennes 11 Ei 45.49N 1.07W
Marettimo 14 Gm 37.56N 12.05 E
Mareuil-en-Brie 12 Ff 48.57N 3.45 E
Marfa 43 Ge 30.18N 104.01W
Marfil, Laguna- 55 Bb 15.30S 60.20W
Margai Caka 27 Ed 35.10N 86.55 E
Marganec 19 Df 47.38N 34.40 E
Margaret River 59 Df 33.57S 115.04 E
Margarida 55 De 21.41S 56.44W
Margarita, Isla de- 54 Fa 11.00N 64.00W
Margarita Belén 55 Ch 27.16S 58.58W
Margarition 15 Dj 39.21N 20.26 E
Margate [Eng.-U.K.] 9 Oj 51.24N 1.24 E
Margate [S.Afr.] 37 Ef 30.55S 30.15 E
Marghera, Venezia- 14 Ge 45.28N 12.44 E
Margherita 30 Jh 0.23N 29.54 E
Margherita di Savoia 14 Ki 41.22N 16.09 E
Marghine, Catena del- 14 Cj 40.20N 8.50 E
Marghita 15 Fb 47.21N 22.20 E
Marghūb, Kūh-e- 24 Qf 33.06N 57.30 E
Margilan 19 Hg 40.28N 71.46 E
Margina 15 Fd 45.51N 22.16 E
Marguerite Bay 66 Qe 68.30S 68.30W
Margut 12 He 49.35N 5.16 E
Marha 20 Hd 60.35N 123.10 E
Marha 21 Nc 63.20N 118.50 E
Mari 24 Ie 34.39N 40.53 E
Mari 24 Ee 34.44N 33.18 E
Maria Atoll [W.F.] 57 Ng 22.00S 136.10W
Maria Atoll [W.F.] 57 Lg 21.48S 154.41W
María Cleofas, Isla- 48 Fg 21.16N 106.14W
Maria Elena 56 Gb 22.21S 69.40W
Mariager 8 Ch 56.39N 10.00 E
Mariager Fjord 8 Dh 56.40N 10.20 E
María Grande, Arroyo- 55 Ci 29.21S 58.45W
María Ignacia 55 Cm 37.24S 59.30W
Maria Island [Austl.] 59 Jh 42.40S 148.05 E
Maria Island [Austl.] 59 Hb 14.55S 135.40 E
Maria Island [St.Luc.] 51k Bb 13.44N 60.56W
Mariakani 36 Gc 3.52S 39.28 E
Maria Laach 12 Jd 50.25N 7.15 E
María Madre, Isla- 48 Fg 21.35N 106.33W
María Magdalena, Isla- 48 Fg 21.25N 106.25W
Mariana Islands 57 Fc 16.00N 145.30 E
Marianao 47 Hd 23.05N 82.26W
Mariana Trench (EN) 3 Ih 14.00N 147.30 E
Marianna [Ar.-U.S.] 45 Ki 34.46N 90.46W
Marianna [Fl.-U.S.] 44 Ej 30.47N 85.14W
Mariannelund 8 Fg 57.37N 15.34 E
Mariano I. Loza 55 Ci 29.22S 58.12W
Mariánské Lázně 10 Ig 49.58N 12.43 E
Marías, Islas- 38 Ig 21.25N 106.28W
Marías Pass 46 Ib 48.19N 113.21W
Marias River 43 Eb 47.56N 110.30W
Maria Theresa Reef 57 Lh 36.58S 151.23W
Mariato, Punta- 47 Hg 7.13N 80.53W
Maria van Diemen, Cape- 62 Ea 34.29S 172.39 E
Mariazell 14 Jc 47.46N 15.19 E
Ma'rib 23 Gf 15.30N 45.21 E
Maribo 8 Dj 54.46N 11.31 E
Maribor 14 Jd 46.33N 15.39 E
Marica 5 Ig 40.52N 26.12 E
Marica 15 Ig 40.52N 25.50 E
Maricao 51a Bb 18.10N 66.58W
Maricopa 46 Ij 33.04N 112.03W
Maridi 35 Dd 6.05N 29.24 E
Maridi 35 De 4.55N 29.28 E
Marié, Rio- 54 Ed 0.25S 66.26W
Marie Byrd Land (EN) 66 Nf 80.00S 120.00W
Mariec 7 Lh 56.31N 49.51 E
Marie Galante 47 Le 15.56N 61.16W
Marie-Galante, Canal de- 51e Bc 15.55N 61.25W
Mariehamn/Maarianhamina 7 Ef 60.06N 19.57 E
Marie Louise Island 37b Bb 6.11S 53.09 E
Mariembourg, Couvin- 12 Gd 50.06N 4.31 E
Marienburg 12 Jd 50.04N 7.08 E
Marienmünster 12 Lc 51.50N 9.13 E
Marienstatt 12 Jd 50.40N 7.49 E
Mariental 31 Ik 24.36S 17.59 E
Mariestad 7 Cg 58.43N 13.51 E
Marietta [Ga.-U.S.] 43 Ke 33.57N 84.33W
Marietta [Oh.-U.S.] 44 Gf 39.26N 81.27W
Mariga 34 Gd 9.36N 5.57 E
Marignac 11 Gl 42.55N 0.39 E
Marignane 11 Lk 43.25N 5.13 E
Marigot [Dom.] 50 Fe 15.32N 61.18W
Marigot [Guad.] 50 Ec 18.04N 63.06W
Marigot [Haiti] 49 Kd 18.14N 72.19W
Marigot [Mart.] 51h Ab 14.49N 61.02W
Marigot [St.Luc.] 51k Ab 13.58N 61.02W
Mariinsk 20 De 56.13N 87.45 E
Mariinski Posad 7 Lh 56.08N 47.48 E
Mariinskoje 20 Jf 51.43N 140.19 E
Marijovo 15 Eh 41.04N 21.45 E
Marijskaja ASSR [3] 19 Ed 56.40N 48.00 E
Marília 56 Jb 22.13S 50.01W
Mariluz 55 Fg 24.02S 53.13W
Marimba 36 Cd 8.22S 17.02 E
Marimbondo, Cachoeira do- 55 He 20.18S 49.10W
Marin 13 Db 42.23N 8.42W
Marin, Cul-de-Sac du- 51h Bc 14.27N 60.53W
Marina di Catanzaro 14 Kl 38.49N 16.36 E
Marina di Gioiosa Ionica 14 Kl 38.18N 16.20 E
Marina di Pisa 14 Eg 43.40N 10.16 E
Marina di Ravenna 14 Gf 44.29N 12.17 E
Marina Gorka 19 Ce 53.31N 28.12 E
Marinduque 26 Hd 13.24N 121.58 E
Marineland 44 Gk 29.43N 81.12W
Marines 12 De 49.09N 1.59 E
Marinette 43 Jb 45.06N 87.38W
Maringá 53 Kh 23.25S 51.55W
Maringa 30 Ih 1.14N 19.48 E
Marinha Grande 13 De 39.45N 8.56W
Marino [It.] 14 Gi 41.46N 12.39 E
Marino [Van.] 63b Db 14.59S 168.03 E
Marins, Pico dos- 55 Jf 22.27S 45.10W
Marinsko 8 Mf 58.46N 28.39 E
Marion 30 Km 46.36S 37.55 E
Marion [Al.-U.S.] 44 Di 32.32N 87.26W
Marion [Ia.-U.S.] 45 Ke 42.02N 91.36W
Marion [Il.-U.S.] 45 Lh 37.44N 88.56W
Marion [In.-U.S.] 44 Ee 40.33N 85.40W
Marion [Oh.-U.S.] 43 Kc 40.35N 83.08W
Marion [S.C.-U.S.] 44 Hh 34.11N 79.23W
Marion [Va.-U.S.] 44 Gg 36.51N 81.30W
Marion, Lake- 44 Gi 33.30N 80.25W
Marion Reefs 57 Gf 19.10S 152.20 E
Maripa 54 Ea 7.26N 65.09W
Mariposa 46 Fh 37.29N 119.58W
Mariquita, Cerro- 48 Jf 23.13N 98.22W
Marisa 26 Hf 0.28N 121.56 E
Mariscala 55 El 34.03S 54.47W
Mariscal Estigarribia 56 Hb 22.02S 60.38W
Mariupol' 6 Jf 47.06N 37.33 E
Mariusa, Caño 50 Fh 9.43N 61.26W
Mariusa, Isla- 50 Fh 9.39N 61.19W
Marivan 24 Le 35.31N 46.10 E
Märjamaa/Marjamaa 8 Kf 58.54N 24.21 E
Marjamaa/Märjamaa 8 Kf 58.54N 24.21 E
Marjanovka [R.S.F.S.R.] 19 He 54.58N 72.38 E
Marjanovka [Ukr.-U.S.S.R.] 10 Uf 50.23N 24.55 E
Mark 12 Gc 51.39N 4.39 E
Mark [Ger.] 12 Jc 51.13N 7.36 E
Mark [Swe.] 8 Eg 57.35N 12.35 E
Marka 31 Lh 1.43N 44.46 E
Markakol, Ozero- 19 If 48.45N 85.50 E
Markam (Gartog) 27 Gf 29.40N 98.33 E
Markaryd 7 Ch 56.26N 13.36 E
Markazī [3] 23 Hb 35.30N 51.30 E
Marken 12 Hb 52.27N 5.05 E
Markerwaard 12 Hb 52.31N 5.15 E
Market Deeping 12 Bb 52.40N 0.18W
Market Harborough 9 Mi 52.29N 0.55W
Markham, Mount- 66 Kg 82.51S 161.21 E
Markham Bay 42 Kd 63.30N 71.40W
Markham River 59 Ja 6.35S 146.25 E
Marki 10 Rd 52.20N 21.07 E
Märkische Schweiz 10 Jd 52.35N 14.00 E
Markit 27 Cd 38.53N 77.35 E
Markounda 35 Bd 7.37N 16.59 E
Markovac 15 Ee 44.14N 21.06 E
Markovka 16 Ke 49.31N 39.32 E
Markovo 22 Tc 64.40N 170.25 E
Markoye 34 Fc 14.39N 0.02 E
Marksburg 12 Jd 50.16N 7.40 E
Marksville 45 Jk 31.08N 92.04W
Marktoberdorf 10 Gi 47.47N 10.37 E
Marktredwitz 10 If 50.00N 12.05 E
Markuleşty 15 Lb 47.51N 28.07 E
Marl 10 De 51.39N 7.05 E
Marlagne 12 Gd 50.25N 4.40 E
Marlborough [2] 62 Ed 41.50S 173.40 E
Marlborough [Austl.] 59 Jd 22.49S 149.53 E
Marlborough [Guy.] 50 Gi 7.29N 58.38W
Marle 11 Je 49.44N 3.46 E
Marlin 45 Hk 31.18N 96.53W
Marlinton 44 Gf 38.14N 80.06W
Marlow [Eng.-U.K.] 12 Bc 51.34N 0.46W
Marlow [Ok.-U.S.] 45 Hi 34.39N 97.57W
Marmande 11 Gj 44.30N 0.10 E
Marmara 24 Bb 40.35N 27.33 E
Marmara, Sea of- (EN) = Marmara Denizi 5 Ig 40.40N 28.15 E
Marmara Adası 24 Bb 40.38N 27.37 E
Marmara Denizi = Marmara, Sea of- (EN) 5 Ig 40.40N 28.15 E
Marmara Ereğlisi 15 Ki 40.58N 27.57 E
Marmara Gölü 15 Lk 38.37N 28.02 E
Marmarica (EN) = Barqah al Bahrīyah 30 Je 31.40N 24.30 E
Marmaris 23 Cb 36.51N 28.16 E
Marmelos, Rio- 54 Fe 6.08S 61.47W
Marmion Lake 45 Kb 48.54N 91.30W
Marmolada 14 Fd 46.26N 11.51 E
Marmora 44 Ic 44.29N 77.41W
Marmore, Cascata delle- 14 Gh 42.35N 12.45 E
Marne 10 Ec 53.57N 9.00 E
Marne 5 Gf 48.49N 2.24 E
Marne [3] 11 Kf 48.55N 4.10 E
Marne à la Saône, Canal de la- 11 Kf 48.44N 4.36 E
Marne au Rhin, Canal de la- 11 Nf 48.35N 7.47 E
Mårnes 7 Dc 67.09N 14.06 E
Marneuli 16 Ni 41.29N 44.45 E
Maro 35 Bd 8.25N 18.46 E
Maro 35 Bb 19.23N 16.38 E
Maroa 54 Ec 2.43N 67.33W
Maroantsetra 31 Lj 15.27S 49.44 E
Marokau Atoll 61 Mc 18.02S 142.17W
Marolambo 37 Hd 20.03S 48.08 E
Maromandia 37 Hb 14.11S 48.06 E
Maromme 11 He 49.28N 1.02 E
Maromokotro 37 Hb 14.01S 48.58 E
Maroni, Fleuve- 52 Ke 5.45N 53.58W
Marònia 15 Ii 40.55N 25.31 E
Maronne 11 Hi 45.04N 1.56 E
Maroochydore 59 Ke 26.39S 153.06 E
Maro Reef 57 Jb 25.25N 170.35W
Maros 15 Dc 46.15N 20.12 E
Maros 26 Gg 5.00S 119.34 E
Maroua 31 Ig 10.36N 14.20 E
Marovoay 37 Hc 16.06S 46.37 E
Marowijne Rivier 54 Hb 5.45N 53.58W
Marqādah 24 Ie 35.44N 40.46 E
Mar Qu 27 He 31.58N 101.54 E
Marquard 37 De 28.54S 27.28 E
Marquenterre 12 Dd 50.20N 1.41 E
Marquesas Islands (EN) = Marquises, Iles- 57 Ne 9.00S 139.30W
Marquette 43 Jb 46.33N 87.24W
Marquion 12 Fd 50.13N 3.05 E
Marquis [Gren.] 51p Bb 12.06N 61.37W
Marquis [St.Luc.] 51k Ba 14.02N 60.55W
Marquis, Cape- 51k Ba 14.03N 60.54W
Marquise 12 Dd 50.49N 1.42 E
Marquises, Iles- = Marquesas Islands (EN) 57 Ne 9.00S 139.30W
Marracuene 37 Ee 25.44S 32.41 E
Marradi 14 Ff 44.04N 11.37 E
Marrah, Jabal- 30 Jg 13.04N 24.21 E
Marrak 33 Hf 16.26N 41.54 E
Marrakech 32 Ge 31.38N 8.00W
Marrakech [3] 32 Fc 32.00N 8.00W
Marrawah 59 Ih 40.56S 144.41 E
Marree 58 Eg 29.39S 138.04 E
Marreh, Kūh-e- 24 Oh 29.15N 52.20 E
Marrero 45 Kl 29.54N 90.07W
Marresalja 17 Mb 69.44N 66.59 E
Marresaljskije Koški, Ostrova- 17 Mb 69.30N 67.10 E
Marromeu 37 Fc 18.17S 35.56 E
Marrti 7 Gc 67.28N 28.22 E
Marrupa 37 Fb 13.12S 37.30 E
Marsā al 'Alam 33 Fd 25.05N 34.54 E
Marsā al Burayqah 33 Cc 30.25N 19.35 E

Index Symbols

1 Independent Nation
2 State, Region
3 District, County
4 Municipality
5 Colony, Dependency
Continent
Physical Region
Historical or Cultural Region
Mount, Mountain
Volcano
Hill
Mountains, Mountain Range
Hills, Escarpment
Plateau, Upland
Pass, Gap
Plain, Lowland
Delta
Salt Flat
Valley, Canyon
Crater, Cave
Karst Features
Depression
Polder
Desert, Dunes
Forest, Woods
Heath, Steppe
Oasis
Cape, Point
Coast, Beach
Cliff
Peninsula
Isthmus
Sandbank
Island
Atoll
Rock, Reef
Islands, Archipelago
Rocks, Reefs
Coral Reef
Well, Spring
Geyser
River, Stream
Waterfall Rapids
River Mouth, Estuary
Lake
Salt Lake
Intermittent Lake
Reservoir
Swamp, Pond
Canal
Glacier
Ice Shelf, Pack Ice
Ocean
Sea
Gulf, Bay
Strait, Fjord
Lagoon
Bank
Seamount
Tablemount
Ridge
Shelf
Basin
Escarpment, Sea Scarp
Fracture
Trench, Abyss
National Park, Reserve
Point of Interest
Recreation Site
Cave, Cavern
Historic Site
Ruins
Wall, Walls
Church, Abbey
Temple
Scientific Station
Airport
Port
Lighthouse
Mine
Tunnel
Dam, Bridge

Marsá al Uwayjah 33 Cc 30.55N 17.52 E
Marsa Ben Mehidi 13 Ji 35.05N 2.11W
Marsabit 31 Kh 2.20N 37.59 E
Marsala 14 Gm 37.48N 12.26 E
Marsá Sha'b 35 Fa 22.52N 35.47 E
Marsá Umm Ghayj 24 Fj 25.38N 34.30 E
Marsberg 10 Ee 51.27N 8.51 E
Marsciano 14 Gh 42.54N 12.20 E
Marsdiep 12 Gb 52.58N 4.45 E
Marseille=Marseilles (EN) 6 Gg 43.18N 5.24 E
Marseille-en-Beauvaisis 11 He 49.35N 1.57 E
Marseilles (EN)=Marseille 6 Gg 43.18N 5.24 E
Marshall [Ak.-U.S.] 40 Gd 61.52N 162.04W
Marshall [Ar.-U.S.] 45 Ji 35.55N 92.38W
Marshall [Il.-U.S.] 45 Mg 39.23N 87.42W
Marshall [Lbr.] 34 Cd 6.09N 10.23W
Marshall [Mn.-U.S.] 43 Hc 44.27N 95.47W
Marshall [Mo.-U.S.] 45 Jg 39.07N 93.12W
Marshall [Tx.-U.S.] 43 Ie 32.33N 94.23W
Marshall Islands [5] 58 Hd 9.00N 168.00 E
Marshall Islands 57 Hd 9.00N 168.00 E
Marshall River 59 Hd 22.59S 136.59 E
Marshalltown 43 Ic 42.03N 92.54W
Marshfield 45 Kd 44.40N 90.10W
Marsh Harbour 47 Ic 26.33N 77.03W
Mārshinān, Kūh-e- 24 Of 32.53N 52.24 E
Marsh Island 45 Kl 29.35N 91.53W
Marsica 14 Hi 41.55N 13.35 E
Marsico Nuovo 14 Jj 40.25N 15.44 E
Marsjaty 17 Jf 60.05N 60.29 E
Marsland 45 Ee 42.29N 103.16W
Mars-la-Tour 12 He 49.06N 5.54 E
Marson 12 Gf 48.55N 4.32 E
Märsta 8 Ge 59.37N 17.51 E
Marstal 8 Dj 54.51N 10.31 E
Marstrand 8 Dg 57.53N 11.35 E
Marta 14 Fh 42.14N 11.42 E
Martaban 25 Je 16.32N 97.37 E
Martaban, Gulf of- (EN) 21 Lh 16.30N 97.00 E
Martap 34 Hd 6.54N 13.03 E
Martapura [Indon.] 26 Dg 4.19S 104.22 E
Martapura [Indon.] 26 Fg 3.25S 114.51 E
Martelange/Martelingen 12 He 49.50N 5.44 E
Martelingen/Martelange 12 He 49.50N 5.44 E
Martés, Sierra de- 13 Le 39.20N 0.57W
Martha's Vineyard 43 Mc 41.25N 70.40W
Martigny 14 Bd 46.06N 7.05 E
Martigues 11 Lk 43.24N 5.03 E
Martil 13 Gi 35.37N 5.17W
Martim Vaz, Ilhas- 52 Nh 20.30S 28.51W
Martin 13 Lc 41.18N 0.19W
Martin [Czech.] 10 Og 49.04N 18.55 E
Martin [S.D.-U.S.] 43 Gc 43.10N 101.44W
Martin [Tn.-U.S.] 44 Cg 36.21N 88.51W
Martina Franca 14 Lj 40.42N 17.20 E
Martinez de Hoz 55 Bl 35.19S 61.37W
Martinez de la Torre 48 Kg 20.04N 97.03W
Martin Garcia, Isla- 55 Cl 34.11S 58.15W
Martin Hills 66 Pg 82.04S 88.01W
Martinho Campos 55 Jd 19.20S 45.13W
Martinique 38 Mh 14.40N 61.00W
Martinique [5] 39 Mh 14.40N 61.00W
Martinique, Canal de la-=
Martinique Passage (EN) 47 Le 15.10N 61.20W
Martinique Passage 50 Fe 15.10N 61.20W
Martinique Passage (EN)=
Martinique, Canal de la- 47 Le 15.10N 61.20W
Martin Lake 44 Ei 32.50N 85.55W
Martin Peninsula 66 Of 74.25S 114.10W
Martinsburg 44 If 39.28N 77.59W
Martins Ferry 44 Ge 40.07N 80.45W
Martinsville [In.-U.S.] 44 Df 39.26N 86.25W
Martinsville [Va.-U.S.] 44 Hg 36.43N 79.53W
Marton 62 Fd 40.05S 175.23 E
Martos 13 Ig 37.43N 3.58W
Martre, Lac la- 42 Fd 63.20N 118.00W
Martuk 19 Fe 50.47N 56.31 E
Martuni 16 Ni 40.06N 45.18 E
Maru 34 Gc 12.21N 6.24 E
Marud 25 Ee 18.19N 72.58 E
Marudi 26 Ff 4.11N 114.19 E
Marudu, Teluk- 26 Ge 6.45N 116.55 E
Marugame 29 Cd 34.18N 133.47 E
Maruko 29 Fc 36.19N 138.15 E
Mārūn 24 Mg 31.02N 49.36 E
Marungu, Monts- 30 Ji 7.42S 30.00 E
Maruoka 29 Ec 36.09N 136.16 E
Maruseppu 29a Ca 44.01N 143.19 E
Marutea Atoll [W.F.] 57 Ng 21.30S 135.34W
Marutea Atoll [W.F.] 57 Mf 17.00S 143.10W
Maruyama-Gawa 29 Dd 35.40N 134.50 E
Marvão 13 Ee 39.24N 7.23W
Marvast 24 Pg 30.30N 54.15 E
Marvast, Kavīr-e- 24 Pg 30.20N 54.25 E
Mårvatn 8 Cd 60.10N 8.15 E
Marv-Dasht 23 Hd 29.50N 52.40 E
Marvejols 11 Jj 44.33N 3.17 E
Marvine, Mount- 43 Jg 38.40N 111.39W
Marx 16 Od 51.42N 46.46 E
Mary 22 If 37.36N 61.50 E
Maryborough [Austl.] 58 Gg 25.32S 152.42 E
Maryborough [Austl.] 59 Ig 37.03S 143.45 E
Marydale 37 Ce 29.23S 22.05 E
Maryjskaja Oblast [3] 19 Gh 37.15N 62.30 E
Maryland [2] 43 Ld 39.00N 76.45W
Maryland [3] 34 De 4.45N 8.00W
Maryport 9 Jg 54.43N 3.30W
Mary River 59 Gb 12.53S 131.38 E
Marysville [Ca.-U.S.] 46 Eg 39.09N 121.35W
Marysville [Ks.-U.S.] 45 Hg 39.51N 96.39W
Marysville [N.B.-Can.] 44 Nc 45.59N 66.35W
Marysville [Oh.-U.S.] 44 Fe 40.13N 83.22W
Marysville [Wa.-U.S.] 46 Db 48.03N 122.11W
Maryville [Mo.-U.S.] 43 Ic 40.21N 94.52W
Maryville [Tn.-U.S.] 44 Fh 35.46N 83.58W
Marzūq 31 If 25.55N 13.55 E
Marzūq, Ḩamādat- 33 Bd 26.00N 12.30 E
Marzuq, Şaḩrā'- 30 If 24.30N 13.00 E
Masachapa 49 Dh 11.47N 86.31W
Masāḩim, Kūh-e- 24 Pg 30.21N 55.20 E
Masai Steppe 30 Ki 4.45S 37.00 E
Masaka 36 Fc 0.20S 31.44 E
Masākin 32 Jb 35.44N 10.35 E
Masalembo, Kepulauan- 26 Fh 5.30S 114.26 E
Masally 19 Eh 39.01N 48.40 E
Masalog, Puntan- 64b Ba 15.01N 145.41 E
Masan 27 Md 35.11N 128.24 E
Masasi 31 Kj 10.43S 38.48 E
Masaya [3] 49 Dh 12.00N 86.10W
Masaya 47 Gf 11.58N 86.06W
Masbate 21 Oh 12.15N 123.30 E
Masbate 26 Hd 12.10N 123.35 E
Mascara 32 Hb 35.24N 0.08 E
Mascara [3] 32 Hb 35.30N 0.15 E
Mascareignes, Iles-/
Mascarene Islands 30 Mk 21.00S 57.00 E
Mascarene Basin (EN) 3 Fk 15.00S 56.00 E
Mascarene Islands/
Mascareignes, Iles- 30 Mk 21.00S 57.00 E
Mascarene Plateau (EN) 3 Gk 10.00S 60.00 E
Mascota 48 Gg 20.32N 104.49W
Masela, Pulau- 26 Ih 8.09S 129.50 E
Maseru 31 Jk 29.28S 27.29 E
Maşfūţ 24 Qk 24.48N 56.06 E
Mashābih 24 Gj 25.37N 36.32 E
Mashan 28 Kb 45.12N 130.32 E
Mashava 37 Ed 20.02S 30.29 E
Mashhad 22 Hf 36.18N 59.36 E
Mashike 28 Pc 43.51N 141.31 E
Mashiki 29 Be 32.47N 130.50 E
Mashīz 24 Qh 29.56N 56.37 E
Mashkel 21 Ig 28.02N 63.25 E
Mashonaland North [3] 37 Ec 17.00S 31.00 E
Mashonaland South [3] 37 Ec 18.00S 31.00 E
Mashra' ar Raqq 35 Dd 8.25N 29.16 E
Mashū-Ko 29a Db 43.35N 144.30 E
Masiaca 48 Ed 26.45N 109.18W
Masīlah, Wādī al- 21 Hh 15.10N 51.08 E
Masi-Manimba 36 Cc 4.46S 17.55 E
Masindi 36 Fb 1.42N 31.43 E
Maşīrah, Jazīrat- 21 Hg 20.29N 58.33 E
Maşīrah, Khalīj- 21 Hg 20.15N 57.40 E
Masisi 36 Ec 1.24S 28.49 E
Masjed-Soleymān 23 Gc 31.58N 49.18 E
Mask, Lough-/Loch
Measca 9 Dh 53.35N 9.20W
Maskanah 24 Hd 36.01N 38.05 E
Maskelynes, Iles- 63b Cc 16.32S 167.49 E
Maslovare 14 Lf 44.34N 17.33 E
Masoala, Cap- 30 Mj 15.59S 50.13 E
Masoala, Presqu'île de- 37 Ic 15.40S 50.12 E
Mason 45 Gk 30.45N 99.14W
Mason Bay 62 Bg 46.55S 167.45 E
Mason City 39 Je 43.09N 93.12W
Masovia (EN)=
Mazowsze 5 Ie 52.40N 20.20 E
Masparro, Rio- 49 Mi 8.04N 69.26W
Masqaţ=Muscat (EN) 22 Hg 23.29N 58.33 E
Massa 14 Ef 44.01N 10.09 E
Massachusetts [2] 43 Mc 42.15N 71.50W
Massachusetts Bay 44 Ld 42.20N 70.50W
Massaciuccoli, Lago di- 14 Eg 43.50N 10.20 E
Massafra 14 Lj 40.35N 17.07 E
Massaguet 35 Bc 12.28N 15.26 E
Massakori 35 Bc 13.00N 15.44 E
Massa Marittima 14 Eg 43.03N 10.53 E
Massangano 36 Bd 9.37S 14.17 E
Massangena 37 Ed 21.32S 32.57 E
Massapê 54 Jd 3.31S 40.19W
Massawa (EN)=Mitsiwa 31 Kg 15.37N 39.39 E
Massena 43 Mc 44.56N 74.57W
Massénya 35 Bc 11.24N 16.10 E
Masset 42 Ef 54.02N 132.09W
Masseube 11 Gk 43.26N 0.35 E
Massey Sound 42 Ia 78.00N 94.00W
Massiac 11 Ji 45.15N 3.13 E
Massiaru 8 Kg 57.52N 24.27 E
Massillon 44 Ge 40.48N 81.32W
Massinga 37 Fd 23.20S 35.22 E
Masson Island 66 Ge 66.08S 96.34 E
Massuma 36 De 14.05S 22.00 E
Mastābah 33 Ge 20.49N 39.26 E
Maštaga 16 Pi 40.32N 49.59 E
Masterton 61 Eh 40.57S 175.39 E
Mastūrah 33 Ge 23.06N 38.50 E
Masuda 27 Ne 34.40N 131.51 E
Māsūleh 24 Md 37.10N 48.59 E
Masurai, Gunung- 26 Dg 2.30S 101.51 E
Masuria (EN) 5 Ie 53.50N 21.30 E
Masurian Lakes (EN) 5 Ie 53.45N 21.45 E
Maşyāf 24 Ge 35.03N 36.21 E
Maszewo 10 Lc 53.29N 15.02 E
Mataabé, Cap- 63b Cb 15.38S 166.46 E
Matabeleland North [3] 37 Dc 19.00S 27.30 E
Matabeleland South [3] 37 Dd 21.00S 29.30 E
Matachel 13 Ff 38.50N 6.17W
Matachewan 42 Jg 47.56N 80.39W
Matacu 55 Bc 17.21S 61.28W
Matadi 31 Ii 5.49S 13.27 E
Matador 45 Fi 34.01N 100.49W
Matagalpa [3] 49 Eg 13.00N 85.30W
Matagalpa 39 Kh 12.53N 85.57W
Matagami 42 Jg 49.45N 77.35W
Matagami, Lac- 44 Ia 49.54N 77.32W
Mata Gassile 35 Ge 2.30N 42.16 E
Matagorda Bay 45 Hl 28.35N 96.20W
Matagorda Island 43 Hf 28.15N 96.30W
Matagorda Peninsula 45 Hl 28.32N 96.07W
Mataiea 65e Fc 17.46S 149.25W
Mataiva Atoll 57 Mf 14.53S 148.40W
Mataj 19 Hf 45.51N 78.43 E
Matak, Pulau- 26 Ef 3.18N 106.16 E
Matakana Island 62 Gb 37.35S 176.05 E
Matala 36 Ce 14.43S 15.02 E
Matalaa, Pointe- 64h Bc 13.20S 176.08W
Matale 25 Gg 7.28N 80.37 E
Mataliele 37 Df 30.24S 28.43 E
Matam 34 Cb 15.40N 13.15W
Matamey 34 Gc 13.26N 8.28 E
Matamoros [Mex.] 47 Dc 25.32N 103.15W
Matamoros [Mex.] 39 Jg 25.53N 97.30W
Matana, Danau- 26 Hg 2.28S 121.20 E
Ma'ţan as Sarra 33 De 21.41N 21.52 E
Matancita 48 De 25.09N 111.59W
Matane 42 Kg 48.51N 67.32W
Matankari 34 Fc 13.46N 4.01 E
Matanza 55 Cl 34.33S 58.35W
Matanzas 39 Kg 23.03N 81.35W
Matanzas [3] 49 Gb 22.40N 81.10W
Matão 55 He 21.35S 48.22W
Matapalo, Cabo- 49 Fi 8.23N 83.19W
Matapan, Cape- (EN)=
Tainaron, Ákra- 5 Ih 36.23N 22.29 E
Matape, Rio- 48 Dc 28.17N 110.41W
Mata Point 64k Bb 19.07S 169.50W
Matara 35 Fc 14.35N 39.28 E
Matara 25 Gg 5.56N 80.33 E
Mataram 22 Nj 8.35S 116.07 E
Mataranka 59 Gb 14.56S 133.07 E
Mataró 13 Oc 41.32N 2.27 E
Matarraña/Matarranya 13 Mc 41.14N 0.22 E
Matarranya/Matarraña 13 Mc 41.14N 0.22 E
Mataso 63b Dc 17.15S 168.25 E
Matatula, Cape- 65c Cb 14.15S 170.34W
Mataura 62 Cg 46.34S 168.44 E
Mataura 62 Cg 46.12S 168.52 E
Mata-Utu 58 Jf 13.17S 176.08W
Mata-Utu, Baie de- 64h Bb 13.19S 176.07W
Matavai 61 Gb 13.28S 172.35W
Matavera 64p Cb 21.13S 159.44W
Mataverj 65d Ab 27.10S 109.27W
Matawai 62 Gc 38.21S 177.32 E
Matawin, Réservoir- 44 Kb 46.45N 73.50W
Matawin, Rivière- 44 Kb 46.55N 72.55W
Matāy 24 Dh 28.25N 30.46 E
Matbakhayn 33 Hf 17.29N 41.48 E
Matca 15 Kd 45.51N 27.32 E
Matemo, Ilha- 37 Gb 12.13S 40.36 E
Matera 14 Kj 40.40N 16.36 E
Matese 14 Ii 41.25N 14.20 E
Mátészalka 10 Si 47.57N 22.20 E
Matfors 7 De 62.21N 17.02 E
Matha 11 Fi 45.52N 0.19W
Mathematicians Seamounts
(EN) 47 Be 15.30N 111.00W
Matheson 44 Ga 48.32N 80.28W
Mathis 45 Hl 28.06N 97.50W
Mathrákion 15 Cj 39.46N 19.31 E
Mathura 25 Fc 27.30N 77.41 E
Mati 15 Ch 41.39N 19.34 E
Mati 26 Ie 6.57N 126.13 E
Matias Cardoso 55 Kb 14.52S 43.56W
Matias Romero 47 Ee 16.53N 95.02W
Maticora, Rio-
49 Lh 11.01N 71.09W
Matina 49 Fh 10.05N 83.17W
Matinha 54 Id 3.06S 45.02W
Māţir 32 Ib 37.03N 9.40 E
Matiyure, Rio- 50 Ci 7.36N 67.39W
Matkaselkja 8 Nc 61.57N 30.33 E
Mātmāţah 32 Ic 33.33N 9.58 E
Matnog 26 Hd 12.35N 124.05 E
Mato, Cerro- 50 Di 7.15N 65.14W
Mato, Rio- 50 Di 7.09N 65.07W
Matočkin Šar, Proliv- 19 Fa 73.30N 54.55 E
Mato Grosso [2] 54 Gf 14.00S 56.00W
Mato Grosso [Braz.] 55 Dd 18.18S 57.20W
Mato Grosso [Braz.] 53 Kg 15.00S 59.57W
Mato Grosso, Planalto do-
= Mato Grosso, Plateau
of- (EN) 52 Kg 15.30S 56.00W
Mato Grosso, Plateau of-
(EN) = Mato Grosso,
Planalto do- 52 Kg 15.30S 56.00W
Mato Grosso do Sul [2] 54 Hg 20.00S 55.00W
Matos Costa 55 Gh 26.27S 51.09W
Matosinhos 13 Dc 41.11N 8.42W
Matou 28 Cj 29.50N 115.32 E
Matov → Qiuxian 28 Cf 36.47N 114.30 E
Mátra 10 Pi 47.53N 19.57 E
Maţraḩ 23 Ie 23.29N 58.31 E
Matrei in Osttirol 14 Gc 47.00N 12.32 E
Maţrūḩ 31 Je 31.21N 27.14 E
Matsiatra 37 Hd 21.25S 45.33 E
Matsudo 28 Og 35.48N 139.55 E
Matsue 27 Nd 35.28N 133.04 E
Matsukawa [Jap.] 29 Gc 37.40N 140.28 E
Matsukawa [Jap.] 29 Ed 35.36N 137.53 E
Matsu Liehtao 27 Kf 26.05N 119.56 E
Matsumae 29a Bc 41.26N 140.07 E
Matsumae-Hantō 29a Bc 41.40N 140.15 E
Matsumoto 27 Od 36.14N 137.58 E
Matsuo 29 Gb 39.58N 141.02 E
Matsu-Ōminato 29a Bc 41.16N 141.09 E
Matsusaka 28 Ng 34.34N 136.32 E
Matsushima 29 Gb 38.22N 141.04 E
Matsutō 29 Ec 36.31N 136.33 E
Matsuura 29 Ae 33.22N 129.42 E
Matsuyama 22 Pf 33.50N 132.45 E
Matsuzaki 29 Fd 34.44N 138.45 E
Mattagami Lake 44 Gb 47.57N 81.35W
Mattagami River 42 Jf 50.43N 81.30W
Mattawa 42 Jg 46.19N 78.42W
Matterhorn [Eur.] 14 Be 45.58N 7.39 E
Matterhorn [Nv.-U.S.] 46 Hf 41.49N 115.23W
Matthew, Ile- 57 Ig 22.20S 171.20 E
Matthews Ridge 54 Fb 7.30N 60.10W
Matthew Town 47 Jd 20.57N 73.40W
Maţţī, Sabhat- 35 Ia 23.30N 52.00 E
Mattighofen 14 Hb 48.06N 13.09 E
Mattoon 45 Lg 39.29N 88.22W
Matua, Ostrov- 20 Kg 48.00N 153.10 E
Matucana 54 Cf 11.51S 76.24W
Matuku Island 61 Ec 19.10S 179.46 E
Matundu 36 Db 4.21N 23.40 E
Matundu 36 Gd 8.50S 39.30 E
Maturin 53 Je 9.45N 63.11W
Matvejev Kurgan 16 Kf 47.34N 38.55 E
Maúa 37 Fb 13.52S 37.09 E
Maubeuge 11 Jd 50.17N 3.58 E
Ma-ubin 25 Je 16.44N 95.39 E
Maudheimvidda 66 Bf 74.00S 8.00W
Maud Seamount (EN) 66 Ce 65.00S 2.35 E
Maués 54 Gd 3.24S 57.42W
Maués, Rio- 54 Gd 3.22S 57.44W
Mau Escarpment 36 Gc 0.40S 36.02 E
Maug Islands 57 Fb 20.01N 145.13 E
Maui Island 57 Lb 20.45N 156.20W
Mauke Island 57 Lg 20.09S 157.23W
Mau Kyun 25 Jf 12.45N 98.20 E
Mauldre 12 Df 48.59N 1.49 E
Maule [2] 56 Fe 35.45S 72.15W
Mauléon 11 Fh 46.55N 0.45W
Mauléon-Licharre 11 Fk 43.14N 0.53W
Maullin 56 Ff 41.38S 73.37W
Maumee 44 Fe 41.34N 83.39W
Maumere 26 Hh 8.37S 122.14 E
Maun 31 Jj 19.58S 23.26 E
Maun 14 If 44.26N 14.55 E
Mauna Kea 57 Lc 19.50N 155.28W
Maunaloa 65a Db 21.08N 157.13W
Mauna Loa 65a Fd 19.28N 155.36W
Maunath 25 Gc 25.40N 82.38 E
Maunawili 65a Db 21.21N 157.47W
Maunga Roa 64p Bb 21.13S 159.48W
Maungdaw 25 Id 20.49N 92.22 E
Maunoir, Lac- 42 Fc 67.30N 125.00W
Maupihaa Atoll (Mopelia,
Atoll-) 57 Lf 16.50S 153.55W
Maupin 46 Ed 45.11N 121.05W
Maupiti, Ile- 57 Lf 16.27S 152.15W
Maurepas, Lake- 45 Kk 30.15N 90.30W
Maures 11 Mk 43.16N 6.23 E
Mauriac 11 Ii 45.13N 2.20 E
Maurice, Lake- 59 Ge 29.30S 131.00 E
Maurienne 11 Mi 45.13N 6.30 E
Mauritania (EN)=
Mūrītāniyā [1] 31 Fg 20.00N 12.00W
Mauriti 54 Ke 7.23S 38.46W
Mauritius 30 Mk 20.17S 57.33 E
Mauritius [1] 31 Mj 18.00S 57.40 E
Mauron 11 Df 48.05N 2.18W
Maurs 11 Ij 44.43N 2.12 E
Mauston 45 Ke 43.48N 90.05W
Mauthausen 14 Ib 48.14N 14.31 E
Mauzé-sur-le-Mignon 11 Fh 46.12N 0.40W
Mavinga 36 Df 15.47S 20.24 E
Mavita 37 Ec 19.32S 33.09 E
Mavrovoúni [Grc.] 15 Fj 39.37N 22.47 E
Mavrovoúni [Grc.] 15 Gh 41.07N 23.08 E
Mawchi 25 Je 18.49N 97.09 E
Mawei 27 Kf 26.02N 119.30 E
Mawlaik 25 Id 23.38N 94.25 E
Mawlamyine 22 Le 16.30N 97.38 E
Mawqaq 24 Ii 27.25N 41.08 E
Mawr, Wādī- 23 Ff 15.41N 42.42 E
Mawson 66 Fe 67.36S 62.53 E
Mawson Coast 66 Fe 67.40S 63.30 E
Mawson Escarpment 66 Ff 73.05S 68.10 E
Maxcanú 47 Fd 20.35N 90.01W
Maxixe 37 Fd 23.51S 35.21 E
Maxwell Bay 42 Ib 74.32N 89.00W
May, Isle of- 9 Ke 56.10N 2.30W
Maya, Pulau- 26 Eg 1.10S 109.35 E
Mayaguana Island 47 Jd 22.23N 72.57W
Mayaguana Passage 49 Kb 22.32N 73.15W
Mayagüez 47 Ke 18.12N 67.09W
Mayahi 34 Gc 13.58N 7.40 E
Mayama 36 Bc 3.51S 14.54 E
Mayāmey 24 Pd 36.24N 55.42 E
Maya Mountains 47 Ge 16.40N 88.50W
Mayapan 47 Gd 20.38N 89.27W
Mayari 49 Jc 20.40N 75.41W
Maybell 45 Bf 40.31N 108.05W
Maychew 35 Fc 12.46N 39.34 E
Mayd 35 Hc 10.57N 47.06 E
Maydān 24 Ke 34.55N 45.37 E
Maydena 59 Jh 42.55S 146.30 E
Maydī 23 Ff 16.18N 42.48 E
Mayen 10 Df 50.20N 7.13 E
Mayenne 11 Ff 48.18N 0.37W
Mayenne 11 Fg 47.30N 0.32W
Mayenne [3] 11 Ff 48.05N 0.40W
Mayfa'ah 35 Hc 14.16N 47.35 E
Mayfield 44 Cg 36.44N 88.38W
May Glacier 66 Ie 67.00S 130.00 E
Mayi He 28 Jb 45.52N 128.46 E
Maymyo 25 Jd 22.02N 96.28 E
Maynas 54 Dd 3.00S 75.00W
Mayo 39 Fc 63.35N 135.54W
Mayo/Muigheo [2] 9 Dh 53.50N 9.30W
Mayo, Mountains of- 9 Dg 54.05N 9.30W
Mayo, Rio- 48 Ed 26.45N 109.47W
Mayo Darlé 34 Hd 6.30N 11.55 E
Mayo-Kébbi 35 Ad 9.18N 13.33 E
Mayo-Kébbi [3] 35 Bd 10.00N 15.30 E
Mayoko 36 Bc 2.18S 12.49 E
Mayon, Mount- 21 Oh 13.15N 123.41 E
Mayor, Puig-/Major, Puig-
13 Oe 39.48N 2.48 E
Mayor Island 62 Gb 37.15S 176.15 E
Mayor Pablo Lagerenza 56 Ha 19.58S 60.45W
Mayotte 31 Lj 12.50S 45.10 E
Mayotte/Mahoré 30 Lj 12.50S 45.10 E
May Pen 47 Ie 17.58N 77.14W
Mayraira Point 26 Hc 18.39N 120.51 E
Mayran, Laguna de- 48 He 25.45N 102.45W
Mayreau Island 51n Bb 12.39N 61.23W
May-sur-Orne 12 Be 49.06N 0.22W
Maysville 44 Ff 38.39N 83.46W
Mayumba [Gabon] 31 Ii 3.25S 10.39 E
Mayumba [Zaire] 36 Ed 7.16S 27.03 E
Mayum La 27 De 30.35N 82.27 E
Mayville 44 Hd 42.15N 79.32W
Mayyit, Al Baḩr al-=Dead
Sea (EN) 21 Ff 31.30N 35.30 E
Mazabuka 36 Ef 15.51S 27.46 E
Mazagão 54 Hd 0.07S 51.17W
Mazamet 11 Ik 43.30N 2.24 E
Māzandarān [3] 23 Hb 36.00N 54.00 E
Māzandarān, Daryā-ye-=
Caspian Sea (EN) 5 Lg 42.00N 50.30 E
Mazar 27 Cd 36.27N 77.03 E
Mazara del Vallo 14 Gm 37.39N 12.35 E
Mazār-e Sharif 22 If 36.42N 67.06 E
Mazarrón, Golfo de- 13 Kg 37.30N 1.18W
Mazartag 27 Dd 38.29N 80.50 E
Mazaruni River 54 Gb 6.25N 58.38W
Mazatenango 47 Ff 14.32N 91.30W
Mazatlán 39 Ig 23.13N 106.25W
Mažeikiai/Mažejkjaj 7 Fh 56.20N 22.22 E
Mažejkjaj/Mažeikiai 7 Fh 56.20N 22.22 E
Mazhafah, Jabal- 24 Fh 28.48N 34.57 E
Mazhūr, 'Irq al- 24 Ji 27.25N 43.55 E
Mazinga 51c Ab 17.29N 62.58W
Mazirbe 8 Jg 57.40N 22.10 E
Mazoe 37 Ec 17.30S 30.58 E
Mazoe 30 Kj 16.32S 33.25 E
Mazomeno 36 Ec 4.55S 27.13 E
Mazong Shan 27 Gc 41.33N 97.10 E
Mazowsze 10 Qd 52.40N 20.20 E
Mazowsze=Masovia (EN)
5 Ie 52.40N 20.20 E
Mazsalaca 8 Kg 57.45N 24.59 E
Mazunga 37 Dd 21.44S 29.52 E
Mazurskie, Pojezierze- 10 Qc 53.40N 21.00 E
Mazzarino 14 Im 37.18N 14.13 E
Mba 63d Ab 17.32S 177.42 E
Mbabane 31 Kk 26.18S 31.07 E
Mbabo, Tchabal- 34 Hd 7.16N 12.09 E
Mbacké 34 Bc 14.48N 15.55W
Mbaéré 35 Be 3.47N 17.31 E
Mbaïki 31 Ih 3.53N 18.00 E
Mbakaou 34 Hd 6.19N 12.49 E
Mbakaou, Barrage de- 34 Hd 6.25N 13.00 E
Mbala 31 Ki 8.50S 31.22 E
Mbalam 34 He 2.13N 13.49 E
Mbale 31 Kh 1.05N 34.10 E
Mbali 35 Be 4.27N 18.20 E
Mbalmayo 34 He 3.31N 11.30 E
Mbam 30 Ih 4.24N 11.17 E
Mbamba Bay 36 Fe 11.17S 34.46 E
Mbandaka 31 Ih 0.04N 18.16 E
Mbanga 34 Ge 4.30N 9.34 E
Mbanika 63a Dc 9.05S 159.12 E
M'banza Congo 36 Bd 6.16S 14.15 E
Mbanza-Ngungu 31 Ii 5.35S 14.47 E
Mbarangandu 36 Gd 8.57S 37.24 E
Mbarara 36 Fc 0.36S 30.38 E
Mbari 35 Ce 4.34N 22.43 E
Mbatiki 63d Bb 17.46S 179.08 E
Mbava 63a Cb 7.49S 156.37 E
Mbé 34 Hd 7.51N 13.36 E
Mbengga 63d Bc 18.23S 178.08 E
Mbengwi 34 Hd 6.01N 10.00 E
Mbéré 35 Bd 9.07N 16.26 E
Mbeya 31 Ki 8.54S 33.27 E
Mbeya [3] 36 Fd 8.00S 33.30 E
Mbi 35 Be 4.28N 18.07 E
Mbigou 36 Bc 1.53S 11.56 E
Mbinda 31 Ii 2.07S 12.52 E
Mbinga 36 Ge 10.56S 35.01 E
Mbingué 34 Dc 10.00N 5.54W
Mbini 34 Ge 1.34N 9.37 E
Mbini [3] 34 He 1.30N 10.00 E
Mbini 30 Ih 1.30N 10.30 E
Mboki 35 Dd 5.19N 25.58 E
Mbokonimbeti 63a Ec 8.57S 160.05 E
Mbomo 36 Bb 0.24N 14.44 E
Mbomou=Bomu (EN) [3] 35 Cd 5.30N 23.30 E
Mbomou=Bomu (EN) 30 Jh 4.08N 22.26 E
Mborokua 63a Dc 9.02S 158.44 E
Mbour 34 Bc 14.24N 16.58W
Mbout 32 Ef 16.01N 12.35W
Mbozi 36 Fd 9.02S 32.56 E
Mbrés 35 Bd 6.40N 19.48 E
M'Bridge 36 Bd 7.14S 12.52 E
Mbua 63d Bb 16.48S 178.37 E
Mbuji-Mayi 31 Ji 6.09S 23.33 E
Mbulo 63a Dc 8.46S 158.21 E
Mbulu 36 Gc 3.51S 35.32 E
Mburucuyá 55 Ci 28.03S 58.14W
Mbutha 63d Bb 16.39S 179.51 E
Mbuyuni 36 Gd 7.23S 36.32 E
Mbwemburu 36 Gd 9.29S 39.39 E
Mcalester 43 He 34.56N 95.46W
Mcensk 19 De 53.17N 36.32 E
M'Chedallah 13 Qh 36.22N 4.16 E
Mcherrah 32 Gd 27.00N 4.30W
Mchinga 36 Gd 9.44S 39.42 E
Mchinji 36 Fe 13.48S 32.54 E
Mdandu 36 Fd 9.09S 34.42 E
M'Daourouch 14 Bn 36.05N 7.49 E
Mdennah 32 Gd 25.00N 4.50W
Mdiq 13 Gi 35.41N 5.19W
Mead 44 Fa 49.29N 83.50W
Mead, Lake- 43 Ed 36.05N 114.25W
Meade 40 Hb 70.50N 156.25W
Meade 45 Fh 37.17N 100.20W
Meade Peak 46 Je 42.30N 111.15W
Meadow Lake 42 Gf 54.07N 108.20W
Meadville 44 Ge 41.38N 80.10W
Me-akan-Dake 29a Cb 43.23N 143.59 E
Mealhada 13 Dd 40.22N 8.27W

Index Symbols

[1] Independent Nation · [2] State, Region · [3] District, County · [4] Municipality · [5] Colony, Dependency · Continent · Physical Region · Historical or Cultural Region · Mount, Mountain · Volcano · Hill · Mountains, Mountain Range · Hills, Escarpment · Plateau, Upland · Pass, Gap · Plain, Lowland · Delta · Salt Flat · Valley, Canyon · Crater, Cave · Karst Features · Depression · Polder · Desert, Dunes · Forest, Woods · Heath, Steppe · Oasis · Cape, Point · Coast, Beach · Cliff · Peninsula · Isthmus · Sandbank · Island · Atoll · Rock, Reef · Islands, Archipelago · Rocks, Reefs · Coral Reef · Well, Spring · Geyser · River, Stream · Waterfall Rapids · River Mouth, Estuary · Lake · Salt Lake · Intermittent Lake · Reservoir · Swamp, Pond · Canal · Glacier · Ice Shelf, Pack Ice · Ocean · Sea · Gulf, Bay · Strait, Fjord · Lagoon · Bank · Seamount · Tablemount · Ridge · Shelf · Basin · Escarpment, Sea Scarp · Fracture · Trench, Abyss · National Park, Reserve · Point of Interest · Recreation Site · Cave, Cavern · Historic Site · Ruins · Wall, Walls · Church, Abbey · Temple · Scientific Station · Airport · Port · Lighthouse · Mine · Tunnel · Dam, Bridge

Index Symbols

[1] Independent Nation
[2] State, Region
[3] District, County
[4] Municipality
[5] Colony, Dependency
Continent
Physical Region
Historical or Cultural Region
Mount, Mountain
Volcano
Hill
Mountains, Mountain Range
Hills, Escarpment
Plateau, Upland
Pass, Gap
Plain, Lowland
Delta
Salt Flat
Valley, Canyon
Crater, Cave
Karst Features
Depression
Polder
Desert, Dunes
Forest, Woods
Heath, Steppe
Oasis
Cape, Point
Coast, Beach
Cliff
Peninsula
Isthmus
Sandbank
Island
Atoll
Rock, Reef
Islands, Archipelago
Rocks, Reefs
Coral Reef
Well, Spring
Geyser
River, Stream
Waterfall Rapids
River Mouth, Estuary
Lake
Salt Lake
Intermittent Lake
Reservoir
Swamp, Pond
Canal
Glacier
Ice Shelf, Pack Ice
Ocean
Sea
Gulf, Bay
Strait, Fjord
Lagoon
Bank
Seamount
Tablemount
Ridge
Shelf
Basin
Escarpment, Sea Scarp
Fracture
Trench, Abyss
National Park, Reserve
Point of Interest
Recreation Site
Cave, Cavern
Historic Site
Ruins
Wall, Walls
Church, Abbey
Temple
Scientific Station
Airport
Port
Lighthouse
Mine
Tunnel
Dam, Bridge

México [2]	47	Ee	19.20N	99.30W
México, Golfo de- = Mexico, Gulf of- (EN)	38	Kg	25.00N	90.00W
Mexico, Gulf of- (EN) = México, Golfo de-	38	Kg	25.00N	90.00W
Mexico, Plateau of- (EN) = Mexicana, Altiplanicie-	38	Ig	25.30N	104.00W
Mexico Basin (EN)	3	Bg	25.00N	92.00W
Mexico City (EN) = Ciudad de México	39	Jh	19.24N	99.09W
Meybod	24	Of	32.16N	53.59 E
Meydān-e Gel	24	Ph	29.04N	54.50 E
Meyísti	15	Mm	36.08N	29.34 E
Meyísti	15	Mm	36.09N	29.40 E
Meymaneh	22	If	35.55N	64.47 E
Meymeh	24	Nf	33.27N	51.10 E
Meymeh	24	Lf	32.05N	47.16 E
Meža	7	Hi	55.43N	31.30 E
Mezcala	48	Ji	17.56N	99.37W
Mezcalapa, Río-	48	Mh	18.36N	92.39W
Mezdra	15	Gf	43.09N	23.42 E
Meždurečenski	19	Gd	59.36N	65.53 E
Meždušarski, Ostrov-	19	Fa	71.20N	53.00 E
Mèze	11	Jk	43.25N	3.36 E
Mezen	5	Kb	66.00N	43.59 E
Mezen	6	Kb	65.50N	44.13 E
Mézenc, Mont-	11	Kj	44.55N	4.11 E
Mężenin	10	Sc	53.07N	22.29 E
Mezenskaja Guba	5	Kb	66.40N	43.45 E
Mezenskaja Pižma	7	Ld	64.30N	48.32 E
Mežgorje	10	Th	48.30N	23.37 E
Mežica	14	Id	46.31N	14.52 E
Mézidon-Canon	12	Be	49.05N	0.04W
Mézin	11	Gj	44.03N	0.16 E
Mezöberény	10	Rj	46.49N	21.02 E
Mezőcsát	10	Qi	47.49N	20.55 E
Mezőföld	10	Oj	46.55N	18.35 E
Mezökovácsháza	10	Qj	46.24N	20.55 E
Mezőkövesd	10	Qi	47.49N	20.35 E
Mezőtúr	10	Qi	47.00N	20.38 E
Mežozerny	17	Ii	54.10N	59.25 E
Mežpjanje	7	Ki	55.25N	45.00 E
Mezquital	48	Gf	23.29N	104.23W
Mezquital, Río-	48	Gf	22.55N	104.54W
Mezquitic	48	Hf	22.23N	103.41W
Mgači	20	Jf	51.02N	142.18 E
Mglin	16	Hc	53.04N	32.53 E
Mhow	25	Fd	22.33N	75.46 E
Miahuatlán de Porfirio Díaz	48	Ki	16.20N	96.36W
Miajadas	13	Ge	39.09N	5.54W
Miaméré	35	Bd	9.02N	19.55 E
Miami [Az.-U.S.]	46	Jj	33.24N	110.52W
Miami [Fl.-U.S.]	39	Kg	25.46N	80.12W
Miami [Ok.-U.S.]	43	Id	36.53N	94.53W
Miami Beach	43	Kf	25.47N	80.08W
Mīānābād	24	Qd	37.02N	57.27 E
Mīāndowāb	23	Gb	36.58N	46.06 E
Miandrivazo	37	Hc	19.30S	45.28 E
Mianduhe	27	Lb	49.12N	121.09 E
Mīāneh	23	Gb	37.26N	47.42 E
Miang, Khao-	25	Ke	17.42N	101.01 E
Miangas, Pulau-	26	Ie	5.35N	126.35 E
Mianning	27	Hf	28.31N	102.10 E
Miānwāli	25	Eb	32.35N	71.33 E
Mianyang	27	He	31.23N	104.49 E
Mianyang (Xiantaozhen)	28	Bi	30.22N	113.27 E
Miaodao Qundao	27	Ld	38.10N	120.45 E
Miao'er Shan	27	Jf	25.50N	110.22 E
Miao Ling	27	If	26.05N	108.00 E
Miarinarivo	37	Hc	18.56S	46.54 E
Miass	19	Gd	55.01N	60.06 E
Miass	19	Gd	56.06N	64.30 E
Miasskoje	17	Ji	55.15N	61.55 E
Miasteczko Krajeńskie	10	Nc	53.06N	17.01 E
Miastko	10	Mb	54.01N	17.00 E
Michael, Mount-	59	Ja	6.25S	145.20 E
Michajlova Island	66	Ge	66.30S	85.00 E
Michalovce	10	Rh	48.46N	21.55 E
Michelstadt	12	Le	49.41N	9.01 E
Miches	49	Md	18.59N	69.03W
Michigan [2]	43	Jc	44.00N	85.00W
Michigan, Lake-	38	Ke	44.00N	87.00W
Michigan City	43	Jc	41.43N	86.54W
Michipicoten Bay	44	Eb	47.55N	84.56W
Michipicoten Island	42	Ig	47.45N	85.45W
Michoacán [2]	47	De	19.10N	101.50W
Michów	10	Se	51.32N	22.19 E
Mico, Río-	49	Eg	12.11N	84.16W
Micoud	51k	Bb	13.50N	60.54W
Micronesia	57	Gc	11.00N	159.00 E
Micronesia, Federated States of- [5]	58	Gd	6.30N	152.00 E
Mičurin	15	Kg	42.10N	27.51 E
Mičurinsk	6	Ke	52.54N	40.31 E
Midai, Pulau-	26	Ef	3.00N	107.47 E
Midar	32	Gc	34.57N	3.32W
Mid-Atlantic Ridge (EN)	3	Di	0.00	20.00W
Middelburg [Neth.]	11	Jc	51.30N	3.37 E
Middelburg [S.Afr.]	37	Cf	31.30S	25.00 E
Middelburg [S.Afr.]	37	De	25.47S	29.28 E
Middelfart	7	Bi	55.30N	9.45 E
Middelharnis	12	Gc	51.45N	4.12 E
Middelkerke	12	Ec	51.11N	2.49 E
Middelkerke-Westende	12	Ec	51.10N	2.46 E
Middle Alkali Lake	46	Ef	41.28N	120.04W
Middle America Trench (EN)	3	Mh	15.00N	95.00W
Middle Andaman	25	If	12.30N	92.50 E
Middle Atlas (EN) = Moyen Atlas	30	Ge	33.30N	4.30W
Middlebury	44	Kc	44.01N	73.10W
Middle Caicos	49	Lc	21.47N	71.43W
Middle Fork Feather River	46	Eg	38.47N	121.36W
Middle Island	37b	Ab	9.22S	46.21 E
Middle Loup River	45	Gf	41.17N	98.23W
Middlemarch	62	Df	45.30S	170.07 E
Middle Reef	63a	Ee	12.35S	160.30 E
Middlesboro	43	Kd	36.36N	83.43W
Middlesbrough	9	Lg	54.35N	1.14W
Middlesex	49	Ce	17.02N	88.31W
Middlesex	12	Bc	51.35N	0.10W
Middlesex	9	Mj	51.30N	0.05W
Middleton	40	Je	59.25N	146.25W
Middleton Reef	57	Gg	29.30S	159.10 E
Middletown [Ct.-U.S.]	44	Ke	41.33N	72.39W
Middletown [N.Y.-U.S.]	44	Je	41.26N	74.26W
Middletown [Oh.-U.S.]	44	Ef	39.31N	84.25W
Midelt	32	Gc	32.41N	4.45W
Mid Glamorgan [3]	9	Jj	51.35N	3.35W
Midhordland	8	Ad	60.15N	5.55 E
Midhurst	12	Bd	50.59N	0.44W
Midi, Canal du-	5	Gg	43.36N	1.25 E
Midi de Bigorre, Pic du-	11	Gl	42.56N	0.08 E
Midi d'Ossau, Pic du-	11	Fl	42.51N	0.26W
Mid-Indian Basin (EN)	3	Gj	10.00S	80.00 E
Mid-Indian Ridge (EN)	3	Gj	3.00S	75.00 E
Midland [Mi.-U.S.]	44	Ed	43.37N	84.14W
Midland [Ont.-Can.]	42	Jh	44.45N	79.53W
Midland [S.D.-U.S.]	45	Fd	44.04N	101.10W
Midland [Tx.-U.S.]	43	Ge	32.00N	102.05W
Midlands [3]	37	Dc	19.00S	30.00 E
Midlands	9	Li	52.40N	1.50W
Midleton/Mainistir na Corann	9	Ej	51.55N	8.10W
Midnapore → Medinīpur	25	Hd	22.26N	87.20 E
Midongy du Sud	37	Hd	23.34N	47.01 E
Midou	11	Fk	43.54N	0.30W
Midouze	11	Fk	43.48N	0.51W
Mid-Pacific Mountains (EN)	3	Jg	20.00N	170.00 E
Midway Islands [5]	58	Jb	28.13N	177.22W
Midway Islands	57	Jb	28.13N	177.22W
Midwest	46	Le	43.25N	106.16W
Midwest City	45	Hi	35.27N	97.24W
Midyat	24	Id	37.25N	41.23 E
Midžor	5	Ig	43.24N	22.40 E
Miechów	10	Qf	50.23N	20.01 E
Miedwie, Jezioro-	10	Kc	53.15N	14.55 E
Międzychód	10	Ld	52.36N	15.53 E
Międzylesie	10	Mf	50.10N	16.40 E
Międzyrzec Podlaski	10	Se	52.00N	22.47 E
Międzyrzecz	10	Ld	52.27N	15.34 E
Międzyrzecze Łomżyńskie	10	Rd	52.45N	21.45 E
Miehikkälä	8	Ld	60.40N	27.42 E
Mie Ken [2]	28	Ng	34.35N	136.25 E
Miekojärvi	7	Fc	66.36N	24.23 E
Mielan	11	Gk	43.26N	0.19 E
Mielec	10	Rf	50.18N	21.25 E
Mielno	10	Mb	54.16N	16.01 E
Mien	8	Fh	56.25N	14.50 E
Mier	48	Jd	26.26N	99.09W
Miercurea Ciuc	15	Ic	46.21N	25.48 E
Mieres	13	Ga	43.15N	5.46W
Miersig	15	Ec	46.53N	21.51 E
Mier y Noriega	48	If	23.25N	100.07W
Miesbach	10	Hi	47.47N	11.50 E
Mieso	35	Gd	9.15N	40.45 E
Mifune	29	Be	32.43N	130.48 E
Migang Shan	27	Id	35.32N	106.13 E
Miguel Alamán, Presa-	48	Kh	18.13N	96.32W
Miguel Auza	48	He	24.18N	103.25W
Miguel Hidalgo, Presa-	48	Ed	26.40N	108.45W
Miha Chakaja	19	Eg	42.17N	42.02 E
Mihăilesti	15	Ie	44.20N	25.54 E
Mihail Kogălniceanu	15	Le	44.22N	28.27 E
Mihajlov	19	De	54.16N	39.03 E
Mihajlovgrad	15	Gf	43.25N	23.13 E
Mihajlovgrad [2]	15	Gf	43.25N	23.13 E
Mihajlovka [Kaz.-U.S.S.R.]	18	Hc	43.01N	71.31 E
Mihajlovka [R.S.F.S.R.]	19	Ee	50.05N	43.15 E
Mihajlovsk	17	Ih	56.29N	59.07 E
Mihalıççık	24	Dc	39.52N	31.30 E
Mihara	29	Cd	34.24N	133.05 E
Mihara-Yama	29	Fd	34.43N	139.23 E
Mi He	28	Ef	37.12N	119.10 E
Mihonoseki	29	Cd	35.34N	133.18 E
Miho-Wan	29	Cd	35.30N	133.20 E
Miiraku	29	Ae	32.45N	128.40 E
Mijaly	16	Re	48.54N	53.50 E
Mijares/Millars	13	Le	39.55N	0.01W
Mijdaḩah	35	Hc	14.00N	48.26 E
Mijdrecht	12	Gb	52.12N	4.52 E
Mijirtein (EN) = Majērtēn	30	Lh	9.00N	50.00 E
Mikasa	28	Pc	43.20N	141.40 E
Mikata	29	Dd	35.34N	135.54 E
Miki	29	Dd	34.17N	134.07 E
Mikínai = Mycenae (EN)	15	Fl	37.43N	22.45 E
Mikindani	36	Ge	10.17S	40.07 E
Mikkeli [2]	7	Ge	62.00N	27.30 E
Mikkeli/Sankt Michel	6	Ic	61.41N	27.15 E
Mikomoto-Jima	29	Fd	34.34N	138.56 E
Mikonos	15	Il	37.27N	25.23 E
Mikonos	15	Il	37.27N	25.20 E
Mikonou, Stenón-	15	Il	37.30N	25.20 E
Mikrá Préspa, Límni-	15	Ei	40.45N	21.06 E
Mikre	15	Hf	43.02N	24.31 E
Mikró Sofráno	15	Jm	36.05N	26.24 E
Mikulov	10	Mh	48.49N	16.39 E
Mikumi	36	Gd	7.24S	36.59 E
Mikun	19	Fc	62.21N	50.05 E
Mikuni	29	Ec	36.13N	136.09 E
Mikuni-Sanmyaku	28	Of	36.15N	138.40 E
Mikuni-Tōge	29	Fc	36.46N	138.50 E
Mikuni-Yama	29	Dd	35.21N	134.01 E
Mikura-Jima	27	Oe	33.50N	139.35 E
Milaca	45	Jd	45.45N	93.39W
Miladummadulu Atoll	25a	Ba	6.15N	73.15 E
Milagro	54	Cd	2.07S	79.36W
Milājerd	24	Me	34.37N	49.12 E
Milan [Mo.-U.S.]	45	Jf	40.12N	93.07W
Milan [Tn.-U.S.]	44	Ch	35.55N	88.46W
Milan (EN) = Milano	6	Gf	45.28N	9.12 E
Milange	37	Fc	16.05S	35.47 E
Milano = Milan (EN)	6	Gf	45.28N	9.12 E
Milâs	24	Bd	37.19N	27.47 E
Milazzo	14	Jl	38.13N	15.14 E
Milazzo, Capo di-	14	Jl	38.16N	15.14 E
Milazzo, Golfo di-	14	Jl	38.15N	15.20 E
Milbank	43	Hb	45.13N	96.38W
Mildenhall	12	Cb	52.21N	0.31 E
Mildura	58	Fh	34.12S	142.09 E
Mile	27	Hg	24.28N	103.26 E
Mile	35	Gc	11.08N	40.55 E
Miléai	15	Gj	39.20N	23.09 E
Miles	58	Gg	26.40S	150.11 E
Miles City	43	Fb	46.25N	105.51W
Milet = Miletus (EN)	15	Kl	37.30N	27.16 E
Miletus (EN) = Milet	15	Kl	37.30N	27.16 E
Milevec	15	Fg	42.34N	22.27 E
Milevsko	10	Kg	49.27N	14.22 E
Milford	46	Ig	38.24N	113.01W
Milford Haven	9	Hj	51.44N	5.02W
Milford Lake	45	Hg	39.15N	97.00W
Milford Sound	61	Ch	44.40S	167.55 E
Milford Sound	62	Bf	44.35S	167.50 E
Milgis	36	Gb	1.48N	38.06 E
Milḩ, Baḩr al-	23	Fc	32.40N	43.35 E
Milḩ, Ra's al-	33	Ec	31.55N	25.02 E
Miliana	13	Oh	36.17N	2.14 E
Mili Atoll	57	Id	6.08N	171.55 E
Milicz	10	Ne	51.32N	17.17 E
Milkovo	20	Kf	54.43N	158.43 E
Milk River	43	Eb	49.09N	112.05W
Milk River	46	Ib	49.09N	112.05W
Milkūh	23	Jc	32.45N	61.55 E
Mill	42	Jd	63.57N	78.00W
Millars/Mijares	13	Le	39.55N	0.01W
Millau	11	Jj	44.06N	3.05 E
Milledgeville	44	Fi	33.04N	83.14W
Mille Lacs, Lac des -	42	Ig	48.50N	90.30W
Mille Lacs Lake	43	Ib	46.15N	93.40W
Millen	44	Gi	32.48N	81.57W
Miller [Nb.-U.S.]	45	Gf	40.57N	99.26W
Miller [S.D.-U.S.]	45	Gd	44.31N	98.59W
Millerovo	19	Ef	48.52N	40.25 E
Miller Seamount (EN)	40	Kf	53.30N	144.20W
Millerton	62	Dd	41.38S	171.52 E
Millevaches, Plateau de-	11	Ii	45.45N	2.11 E
Millicent	59	Ig	37.36S	140.22 E
Millington	44	Ch	35.20N	89.54W
Millinocket	44	Mc	45.39N	68.43W
Mill Island	66	He	65.30S	100.40 E
Millmerran	59	Ke	27.52S	151.16 E
Mills Lake	42	Fd	61.28N	118.15W
Millstatt	14	Hd	46.48N	13.35 E
Millville	44	Jf	39.24N	75.02W
Millwood Lake	45	Jj	33.45N	94.00W
Milne Land	41	Jd	71.20N	27.30W
Milo	30	Gg	11.04N	9.14W
Milolii	65a	Fd	19.11N	155.55W
Milos	15	Hm	36.45N	24.26 E
Milos = Milos (EN)	15	Hm	36.41N	24.25 E
Milos (EN) = Mílos	15	Hm	36.41N	24.25 E
Milparinka	59	Ie	29.44S	141.53 E
Miltenberg	10	Fg	49.42N	9.15 E
Milton [Fl.-U.S.]	44	Dj	30.38N	87.03W
Milton [N.Z.]	62	Cg	46.07S	169.58 E
Milton-Freewater	46	Fd	45.56N	118.23W
Milton Keynes	9	Mi	52.03N	0.42W
Miltou	35	Bc	10.14N	17.26 E
Milumbe, Monts-	36	Ed	8.00S	27.30 E
Miluo	28	Bj	28.51N	113.05 E
Miluo Jiang	27	Jf	28.51N	112.59 E
Milwaukee	39	Ke	43.02N	87.55W
Milwaukee Depth (EN)	3	Do	55.10S	26.00W
Milwaukee Seamounts (EN)	57	Ia	32.28N	171.55 E
Milwaukie	46	Dd	45.27N	122.38W
Mimi-Gawa	29	Be	32.20N	131.37 E
Mimizan	11	Ej	44.12N	1.14W
Mimoň	10	Kf	50.40N	14.44 E
Mimongo	36	Bc	1.38S	11.39 E
Mimoso	55	Hb	15.10S	48.05W
Mīna	13	Mi	35.58N	0.31 E
Mina [Mex.]	48	Id	26.01N	100.32W
Mina [Nv.-U.S.]	46	Fg	38.24N	118.07W
Mina, Cerro-	49	Ki	8.21N	73.10W
Mīnā' Abd Allāh	24	Mh	29.01N	48.10 E
Mīnā' al Aḩmadī	24	Mh	29.04N	48.09 E
Mīnāb	24	Qi	27.09N	57.05 E
Mīnāb	24	Qi	27.01N	56.53 E
Mīnā' Barānīs	33	Ge	23.55N	35.28 E
Minahassa = Minahassa Peninsula (EN)	21	Oi	1.00N	124.35 E
Minahassa Peninsula (EN) = Minahassa	21	Oi	1.00N	124.35 E
Minakuchi	29	Ed	34.59N	136.11 E
Minamata	28	Kh	32.13N	130.24 E
Minami-Daitō-Jima	27	Nf	25.50N	131.15 E
Minami-furano	29a	Cb	43.10N	142.32 E
Minami-Iō-Jima	60	Cc	24.14N	141.28 E
Minami-kayabe	29a	Bc	41.53N	141.01 E
Minami-Tori-Shima = Marcus Island (EN)	57	Gb	26.32N	142.09 E
Minas [Cuba]	49	Ic	21.29N	77.37W
Minas [Indon.]	26	Df	0.50N	101.29 E
Minas [Ur.]	53	Ki	34.23S	55.14W
Minas de Ríotinto	13	Fg	37.42N	6.35W
Minas Gerais [2]	54	Jg	18.00S	44.30W
Mīnā' Su'ūd	24	Mh	28.44N	48.24 E
Minatitlán [Mex.]	47	Fe	17.59N	94.31W
Minatitlán [Mex.]	48	Gh	19.22N	104.04W
Minaya	13	Je	39.17N	2.19W
Minbu	25	Id	20.11N	94.53 E
Minbya	25	Id	20.22N	93.16 E
Minchinmávida, Volcan-	56	Ff	42.49S	72.28W
Mincio	14	Ee	45.04N	10.59 E
Mindanao	21	Oi	8.00N	125.00 E
Mindanao Sea	21	Oi	9.15N	123.40 E
Mindel	10	Gh	48.31N	10.23 E
Mindelheim	10	Gh	48.03N	10.29 E
Mindelo	31	Eg	16.53N	25.00W
Minden [Ger.]	10	Ed	52.17N	8.55 E
Minden [La.-U.S.]	45	Jj	32.37N	93.17W
Minden [Nb.-U.S.]	45	Gf	40.30N	98.57W
Mindif	34	Hc	10.24N	14.26 E
Mindoro	21	Oh	12.50N	121.05 E
Mindoro Strait	26	Hd	12.20N	120.40 E
Mindouli	36	Bc	4.17S	14.21 E
Mindszent	10	Qj	46.32N	20.12 E
Mine	29	Bd	34.12N	131.11 E
Minehead	9	Jj	51.13N	3.29W
Mine Head	9	Fj	52.00N	7.35W
Mineiros	54	Hg	17.34S	52.34W
Mineral del Monte	48	Jg	20.08N	98.40W
Mineralnyje Vody	19	Eg	44.12N	43.08 E
Mineral Wells	43	He	32.48N	98.07W
Minerva Reefs	57	Jg	23.50S	179.00W
Minervino Murge	14	Ki	41.05N	16.05 E
Minervois	11	Ik	43.25N	2.45 E
Minfeng/Niya	27	Dd	37.04N	82.46 E
Minga	36	Ee	11.08S	27.56 E
Mingala	35	Cd	5.06N	21.49 E
Mingan	42	Lf	50.18N	64.01W
Mingečaur	16	Oi	40.46N	47.02 E
Mingečaurskoje Vodohranilišče	16	Oi	40.55N	46.45 E
Mingenew	59	De	29.11S	115.26 E
Minggang	28	Ci	32.27N	114.02 E
Mingguang → Jiashan	28	Dh	32.47N	118.00 E
Ming He	28	Cf	37.14N	114.47 E
Minglanilla	13	Ke	39.32N	1.36W
Mingoyo	36	Ge	10.06S	39.38 E
Mingshui	27	Mb	47.15N	125.53 E
Mingshui → Zhangqiu	28	Df	36.44N	117.33 E
Mingteke	27	Bd	37.09N	74.58 E
Mingteke Daban	27	Bd	37.00N	74.50 E
Minguez, Puerto-	13	Ld	40.50N	0.59W
Mingulay	9	Fe	56.50N	7.40W
Mingyuegou	28	Jc	43.08N	128.55 E
Minhe	27	Hd	36.20N	102.50 E
Minho	13	Dc	41.52N	8.51W
Minho	13	Dc	41.40N	8.30W
Minicoy Island	21	Ji	8.17N	73.02 E
Minigwal, Lake-	59	Ee	29.35S	123.10 E
Minija	8	Ii	55.20N	21.12 E
Minilya	59	Cd	23.51S	113.58 E
Minilya River	59	Cd	23.56S	113.51 E
Minipi Lake	42	Lf	52.28N	60.50W
Ministra, Sierra-	13	Jc	41.07N	2.30W
Minjar	17	Hi	55.04N	57.33 E
Min Jiang	21	Mg	28.46N	104.38 E
Minmaya	28	Pd	41.10N	140.28 E
Minna	31	Hh	9.37N	6.33 E
Minna Bluff	66	Kf	78.32S	166.30 E
Minneapolis [Ks.-U.S.]	45	Hg	39.08N	97.42W
Minneapolis [Mn.-U.S.]	39	Je	44.59N	93.13W
Minnedosa	42	Hf	50.14N	99.51W
Minnedosa River	45	Fb	49.53N	100.08W
Minnesota [2]	43	Ib	46.00N	94.15W
Minnesota River	43	Ic	44.54N	93.10W
Miño	5	Fg	41.52N	8.51W
Mino	29	Ed	35.32N	136.54 E
Minobu	29	Fd	35.22N	138.24 E
Minobu-Sanchi	29	Fd	35.15N	138.20 E
Minokamo	29	Ed	35.26N	137.00 E
Mino-Mikawa-Kōgen	29	Ed	35.10N	137.25 E
Minorca (EN) = Menorca	5	Gg	40.00N	4.00 E
Minot	39	Ie	48.14N	101.18W
Minqin	27	Hd	38.42N	103.11 E
Minqing	27	Kf	26.15N	118.52 E
Minquan	28	Cg	34.39N	115.08 E
Min Shan	27	He	33.35N	103.00 E
Minsk	6	Ie	53.54N	27.34 E
Minskaja Oblast [3]	19	Ce	53.50N	27.40 E
Minskaja Vozvyšennost	8	Lj	54.00N	27.10 E
Mińsk Mazowiecki	10	Rd	52.11N	21.34 E
Minta	34	He	4.35N	12.48 E
Minto, Lac -	42	Ke	57.15N	74.50W
Minto, Mount-	66	Kf	71.47S	168.45 E
Minto Inlet	42	Fb	71.19N	117.00W
Minto Reef	57	Gd	8.08N	154.17 E
Minturn	45	Cg	39.35N	106.26W
Mīnūdasht	24	Pd	37.10N	55.25 E
Miñuf	24	Dg	30.28N	30.56 E
Minusinsk	20	Ef	53.43N	91.48 E
Minvoul	36	Bb	2.09N	12.08 E
Minwakh	35	Hb	16.48N	48.06 E
Minxian	27	He	34.26N	104.02 E
Miory	7	Gi	55.39N	27.41 E
Mios Num	26	Kg	1.30S	135.10 E
Miquan	27	Ec	44.05N	87.33 E
Miquelon	42	Jg	49.00N	76.00W
Mira	13	Dg	37.43N	8.47W
Mira [It.]	14	Ge	45.26N	12.08 E
Mira [Port.]	13	Dd	40.26N	8.44W
Mira, Peña-	13	Fc	41.55N	6.28W
Mīrābād	23	Jc	30.25N	61.50 E
Mirabela	55	Jc	16.15S	44.11W
Miracatu	55	Ig	24.17S	47.28W
Miracema	54	Jh	21.25S	42.11W
Mirador, Serra do-	55	Hh	26.45S	49.50W
Miraflores [Col.]	54	Db	5.12N	73.12W
Miraflores [Col.]	54	Dc	1.30N	72.16W
Mīrah, Wādī al-	24	If	32.26N	41.42 E
Miraj	25	Ee	16.50N	74.38 E
Miramar	56	Ie	38.16S	57.51W
Miramar, Laguna-	48	Ni	16.20N	91.20W
Miramas	11	Kk	43.35N	5.00 E
Mirambeau	11	Fi	45.22N	0.34W
Miramichi Bay	42	Kg	47.07N	65.10W
Miramont-de-Guyenne	11	Gj	44.36N	0.22 E
Miran	27	Ed	39.15N	88.50 E
Miranda [2]	54	Ea	10.15N	66.25W
Miranda [Arg.]	55	Cm	36.32S	59.09W
Miranda [Braz.]	54	Gh	20.14S	56.22W
Miranda de Corvo	13	Dd	40.06N	8.20W
Miranda de Ebro	13	Jb	42.41N	2.57W
Miranda do Douro	13	Fc	41.30N	6.16W
Mirande	11	Gk	43.31N	0.25 E
Mirandela	13	Ec	41.29N	7.11W
Mirandola	14	Ff	44.53N	11.04 E
Mirandópolis	55	Ge	21.09S	51.06W
Mirante do Paranapanema	55	Gf	22.17S	51.54W
Mira Por Vos	49	Jb	22.04N	74.38W
Mirapuxi, Rio-	55	Ga	13.06S	51.10W
Mirassol	55	He	20.46S	49.28W
Miravalles	13	Fb	42.45N	6.53W
Miravalles, Volcán-	38	Kh	10.45N	85.10W
Miravete, Puerto de-	13	Ge	39.43N	5.43W
Mir-Bašir	16	Oi	40.19N	46.58 E
Mirbāţ	23	Hf	16.58N	54.50 E
Mirdita	15	Ch	41.49N	19.56 E
Mirebalais	49	Kd	18.50N	72.06W
Mirebeau	11	Gh	46.47N	0.11 E
Mirecourt	11	Mf	48.18N	6.08 E
Mirepoix	11	Hk	43.05N	1.53 E
Mirgorod	19	Df	50.00N	33.40 E
Miri	22	Ni	4.23N	113.59 E
Miria	34	Gc	13.43N	9.07 E
Mirim, Lagoa-	52	Ki	32.45S	52.50W
Mirina	15	Ij	39.52N	25.04 E
Miriñay, Esteros del-	55	Di	28.49S	57.10W
Miriñay, Río-	55	Dj	30.10S	57.39W
Mirny	66	Ge	66.33S	93.01 E
Mirny	22	Nc	62.33N	113.53 E
Mironovka	16	Ge	49.40N	31.01 E
Mirosławiec	10	Mc	53.21N	16.05 E
Mirpur	25	Eb	33.11N	73.46 E
Mīrpur Khās	22	Ig	25.32N	69.00 E
Mirqah Sūr	24	Kd	36.50N	44.19 E
Mīrsāle	35	Hd	5.58N	47.54 E
Mirşani	15	He	44.01N	24.01 E
Mirtóön Pélagos	15	Gm	37.00N	24.00 E
Miryang	28	Jg	35.29N	128.45 E
Mirzāpur	25	Gc	25.09N	82.35 E
Misaki	29	Ce	33.23N	132.07 E
Misawa	28	Pd	40.41N	141.24 E
Misery, Mount-	51c	Ab	17.22N	62.48W
Mishan	27	Nb	45.34N	131.50 E
Mishawaka	44	De	41.40N	86.11W
Mi-Shima	28	Kg	34.47N	131.10 E
Mishima	29	Fd	35.07N	138.54 E
Mishraq, Khashm-	24	Lj	24.13N	46.18 E
Misilmeri	14	Hl	38.02N	13.27 E
Misima Island	60	Ej	10.40S	152.45 E
Misiones [3]	55	Dh	27.00S	57.00W
Misiones [2]	56	Jc	27.00S	55.00W
Misiones, Sierra de-	55	Eh	26.45S	54.20W
Miski, Enneri-	35	Bb	18.10N	17.45 E
Miškino	17	Ki	55.20N	63.55 E
Miskitos, Cayos-	47	Hf	14.23N	82.46W
Miskolc [2]	10	Qh	48.06N	20.43 E
Miskolc	6	If	48.06N	20.47 E
Mismār	35	Fb	18.13N	35.38 E
Misool, Pulau-	26	Jg	1.52S	130.10 E
Misquah Hills	43	Ib	47.17N	92.00W
Mişr = Egypt (EN) [1]	31	Jf	27.00N	30.00 E
Mişr al Jadīdah, Al Qāhirah-	33	Fc	30.06N	31.20 E
Mişrātah	31	Ie	32.23N	15.06 E
Mişrātah [3]	33	Cd	29.00N	16.00 E
Mişrātah, Ra's-	30	Ie	32.25N	15.05 E
Misserghin	13	Li	35.37N	0.44W
Missinaibi	42	Jf	50.44N	81.30W
Missinaibi Lake	44	Fa	48.23N	83.40W
Missinipe	42	He	55.36N	104.45W
Mission [S.D.-U.S.]	45	Fe	43.18N	100.40W
Mission [Tx.-U.S.]	45	Gm	26.13N	98.20W
Mission City	46	Db	49.08N	122.18W
Mission Range	46	Ic	47.30N	113.55W
Mississippi	38	Kg	29.00N	89.15W
Mississippi [2]	43	Je	32.50N	89.30W
Mississippi Delta	38	Kg	29.10N	89.15W
Mississippi Fan (EN)	43	Jf	26.45N	88.30W
Mississippi River	44	Ic	45.26N	76.16W
Mississippi Sound	45	Lk	30.15N	89.00W
Misso	8	Lg	57.33N	27.23 E
Missoula	39	He	46.52N	114.01W
Missour	32	Gc	33.03N	3.59W
Missouri	38	Jf	38.50N	90.08W
Missouri [2]	43	Id	38.30N	93.30W
Missouri, Coteau du-	45	Gc	46.00N	99.30W
Missouri Valley	45	If	41.33N	95.53W
Mistassibi	42	Kg	48.53N	72.13W
Mistassini	44	Ka	48.58N	72.40 E
Mistassini	42	Kf	50.30N	74.00W
Mistassini, Rivière-	42	Kg	48.42N	72.20W
Mistelbach an der Zaya	14	Kb	48.34N	16.34 E
Misterhult	8	Gg	57.28N	16.33 E
Mistrás	15	Fl	37.04N	22.22 E
Mistretta	14	Im	37.56N	14.22 E
Misugi	29	Ed	34.33N	136.15 E
Misumi [Jap.]	29	Bd	34.46N	131.58 E
Misumi [Jap.]	29	Be	32.37N	130.29 E
Mita, Punta-	48	Gg	32.04N	105.33W
Mitare, Río-	49	Mh	11.28N	69.56W
Mitchell [Austl.]	59	Je	26.29S	147.58 E
Mitchell [Or.-U.S.]	46	Ed	44.34N	120.09W
Mitchell [S.D.-U.S.]	43	Hc	43.40N	98.01W
Mitchell, Mount-	38	Kf	35.46N	82.16W
Mitchell Range	59	Hb	12.50S	135.35 E
Mitchell River	57	Ff	15.12S	141.35 E
Mitchell River Mission	59	Ic	15.28S	141.44 E
Mitchelstown/Baile Mhistéala	9	Ei	52.16N	8.16W
Mithimna	15	Jj	39.22N	26.10 E
Mitiaro Island	57	Lf	19.49S	157.43W
Mitidja, Plaine de la-	13	Oh	36.36N	3.00 E
Mitilíni	15	Jj	39.06N	26.33 E
Mitilínis, Stenón-	15	Jj	39.10N	26.35 E
Mitla	47	Ee	16.55N	96.17W
Mitla, Laguna-	48	Ii	17.03N	100.25W
Mito	27	Pd	36.22N	140.28 E
Mitomoni	36	Ge	11.32S	35.19 E

Index Symbols

[1] Independent Nation
[2] State, Region
[3] District, County
[4] Municipality
[5] Colony, Dependency
Continent
Physical Region
Historical or Cultural Region
Mount, Mountain
Volcano
Hill
Mountains, Mountain Range
Hills, Escarpment
Plateau, Upland
Pass, Gap
Plain, Lowland
Delta
Salt Flat
Valley, Canyon
Crater, Cave
Karst Features
Depression
Polder
Desert, Dunes
Forest, Woods
Heath, Steppe
Oasis
Cape, Point
Coast, Beach
Cliff
Peninsula
Isthmus
Sandbank
Island
Atoll
Rock, Reef
Islands, Archipelago
Rocks, Reefs
Coral Reef
Well, Spring
Geyser
River, Stream
Waterfall Rapids
River Mouth, Estuary
Lake
Salt Lake
Intermittent Lake
Reservoir
Swamp, Pond
Canal
Glacier
Ice Shelf, Pack Ice
Ocean
Sea
Gulf, Bay
Strait, Fjord
Lagoon
Bank
Seamount
Tablemount
Ridge
Shelf
Basin
Escarpment, Sea Scarp
Fracture
Trench, Abyss
National Park, Reserve
Point of Interest
Recreation Site
Cave, Cavern
Historic Site
Ruins
Wall, Walls
Church, Abbey
Temple
Scientific Station
Airport
Port
Lighthouse
Mine
Tunnel
Dam, Bridge

Index Symbols

[1] Independent Nation
[2] State, Region
[3] District, County
[4] Municipality
[5] Colony, Dependency
Continent
Physical Region
Historical or Cultural Region
Mount, Mountain
Volcano
Hill
Mountains, Mountain Range
Hills, Escarpment
Plateau, Upland
Pass, Gap
Plain, Lowland
Delta
Salt Flat
Valley, Canyon
Crater, Cave
Karst Features
Depression
Polder
Desert, Dunes
Forest, Woods
Heath, Steppe
Oasis
Cape, Point
Coast, Beach
Cliff
Peninsula
Isthmus
Sandbank
Island
Atoll
Rock, Reef
Islands, Archipelago
Rocks, Reefs
Coral Reef
Well, Spring
Geyser
River, Stream
Waterfall Rapids
River Mouth, Estuary
Lake
Salt Lake
Intermittent Lake
Reservoir
Swamp, Pond
Canal
Glacier
Ice Shelf, Pack Ice
Ocean
Sea
Gulf, Bay
Strait, Fjord
Lagoon
Bank
Seamount
Tablemount
Ridge
Shelf
Basin
Escarpment, Sea Scarp
Fracture
Trench, Abyss
National Park, Reserve
Point of Interest
Recreation Site
Cave, Cavern
Historic Site
Ruins
Wall, Walls
Church, Abbey
Temple
Scientific Station
Airport
Port
Lighthouse
Mine
Tunnel
Dam, Bridge

Monte Lindo Grande, Riacho- ◼ 55 Cg 25.45 S 58.06W
Montello [Nv.-U.S.] 46 Hf 41.16N 114.12W
Montello [Wi.-U.S.] 45 Le 43.48N 89.20W
Montemorelos 47 Ec 25.12N 99.49W
Montemor-o-Novo 13 Df 38.39N 8.13W
Montemor-o-Velho 13 Dd 40.10N 8.41W
Montemuro, Serra de- ◼ 13 Dc 40.58N 8.01W
Montenegro 56 Jc 29.42 S 51.28W
Montenegro (EN) = Crna Gora [2] 15 Cg 42.30N 19.18 E
Montenegro (EN)=Crna Gora ◼ 15 Cg 42.30N 19.18 E
Monte Plata 49 Md 18.48N 69.47W
Montepuez ◼ 37 Gb 12.32 S 40.27 E
Montepuez 37 Fb 13.07 S 39.00 E
Montepulciano 14 Fg 43.05N 11.47 E
Monte Quemado 56 Hc 25.48 S 62.52W
Monte Real 13 De 39.51N 8.52W
Montereale, Passo di- ◼ 14 Hh 42.31N 13.13 E
Montereau-Faut-Yonne 11 If 48.23N 2.57 E
Monterey 43 Cd 36.37N 121.55W
Monterey Bay ◼ 43 Cd 36.45N 121.55W
Montería 53 Ie 8.46N 75.53W
Montero 54 Fg 17.20 S 63.15W
Monteros 56 Gc 27.10 S 65.30W
Monterotondo 14 Gh 42.03N 12.37 E
Monterrey 39 Ig 25.40N 100.19W
Montesano 46 Dc 46.59N 123.36W
Monte San Savino 14 Fg 43.20N 11.43 E
Monte Sant'Angelo 14 Ji 41.42N 15.57 E
Monte Santu, Capo di- ◼ 14 Dj 45.05N 9.44 E
Montes Claros 53 Lg 16.43 S 43.52W
Montes Claros de Goiás 55 Gb 15.54 S 51.13W
Montesilvano 14 Ih 42.31N 14.09 E
Montevarchi 14 Fg 43.31N 11.34 E
Montevideo [2] 55 Dl 34.50 S 56.10W
Montevideo [Mn.-U.S.] 45 Id 44.57N 95.43W
Montevideo [Ur.] 53 Ki 34.53 S 56.11W
Monte Vista 45 Ch 37.35N 106.09W
Montfaucon 12 He 49.17N 5.08 E
Montfort-l'Amaury 12 Df 48.47N 1.49 E
Montfort-sur-Risle 12 Ce 49.18N 0.40 E
Montgenèvre, Col de- ◼ 11 Mj 44.56N 6.44 E
Montgomery 39 Kf 32.23N 86.18W
Montgomery Pass ◼ 46 Fh 38.00N 118.20W
Montguyon 11 Fi 45.13N 0.11W
Monthermé 12 Ge 49.53N 4.44 E
Monthey 14 Ad 46.15N 6.56 E
Monthois 12 Ge 49.19N 4.43 E
Monticello [Ar.-U.S.] 45 Kj 33.38N 91.47W
Monticello [Fl.-U.S.] 44 Fj 30.33N 83.52W
Monticello [Ia.-U.S.] 45 Ke 42.15N 91.12W
Monticello [In.-U.S.] 44 De 40.45N 86.46W
Monticello [Ky.-U.S.] 44 Eg 36.50N 84.51W
Monticello [N.Y.-U.S.] 44 Je 41.39N 74.41W
Monticello [Ut.-U.S.] 43 Fd 37.52N 109.21W
Montiel 13 Jf 38.42N 2.52W
Montiel, Campo de- ◼ 13 Jf 38.46N 2.44W
Montiel, Cuchilla de- ◼ 55 Cj 31.05 S 59.10W
Montignac 11 Hi 45.04N 1.10 E
Montigny-le-Roi 11 Lf 48.00N 5.30 E
Montigny-les-Metz 11 Me 49.06N 6.09 E
Montigny-le-Tilleul 12 Gd 50.23N 4.22 E
Montijo [Pan.] 49 Gj 7.59N 81.03W
Montijo [Port.] 13 Df 38.42N 8.58W
Montijo [Sp.] 13 Ff 38.55N 6.37W
Montijo, Golfo de- ◼ 49 Gj 7.40N 81.07W
Montilla 13 Hg 37.35N 4.38W
Montividiu 55 Gc 17.24 S 51.14W
Montivilliers 11 Ge 49.33N 0.12 E
Mont Joli 42 Kg 48.35N 68.11W
Mont-Laurier 42 Jg 46.33N 75.30W
Mont Louis 44 Oa 49.15N 65.43W
Mont-Louis 11 Il 42.31N 2.07 E
Montluçon 11 Ih 46.20N 2.36 E
Montmagny 42 Kg 46.59N 70.33W
Montmarault 11 Ih 46.19N 2.57 E
Montmédy 11 Le 49.31N 5.22 E
Montmirail 11 Jf 48.52N 3.32 E
Montmorency 12 Ef 49.00N 2.20 E
Montmorillon 11 Gh 46.26N 0.52 E
Montmort-Lucy 12 Ff 48.55N 3.49 E
Monto 59 Kd 24.52 S 151.07 E
Montoire-sur-le-Loir 11 Gg 47.45N 0.52 E
Montone ◼ 14 Gf 44.24N 12.14 E
Montoro 13 Hf 38.01N 4.23W
Montpelier [Id.-U.S.] 43 Ec 42.19N 111.18W
Montpelier [Vt.-U.S.] 39 Le 44.16N 72.35W
Montpellier 6 Gg 43.36N 3.53 E
Montpon-Ménestérol 11 Gi 45.01N 0.10 E
Montréal 39 Le 45.31N 73.34W
Montreal Lake ◼ 42 Gf 54.20N 105.40W
Montreal River ◼ 44 Hb 47.08N 79.27W
Montréjeau 11 Gk 43.05N 0.35 E
Montreuil [Fr.] 11 Hd 50.28N 1.46 E
Montreuil [Fr.] 12 Ef 48.52N 2.26 E
Montreuil-l'Argillé 12 Cf 48.56N 0.29 E
Montreux 14 Ad 46.26N 6.55 E
Montrose [Co.-U.S.] 43 Fd 38.29N 107.53W
Montrose [Scot.-U.K.] 9 Ke 56.43N 2.29W
Monts, Pointe des- ◼ 44 Na 49.19N 67.23W
Mont-Saint-Aignan 12 De 49.28N 1.05 E
Mont-Saint-Michel, Baie du- ◼ 11 Ef 48.40N 1.40W
Montsalvy 11 Ij 44.42N 2.30 E
Montsant, Serra del-/ Montsant, Sierra de- ◼ 13 Mc 41.17N 0.50 E
Montsant, Sierra de-/ Montsant, Serra del- ◼ 13 Mc 41.17N 0.50 E
Montsec, Serra del-/ Montsech, Sierra del- ◼ 13 Mb 42.02N 0.50 E
Montsech, Sierra del-/ Montsec, Serra del- ◼ 13 Mb 42.02N 0.50 E
Montseny/Pallars, Montsent de- ◼ 13 Nb 42.29N 1.02 E
Montseny, Sierra de- ◼ 13 Oc 41.48N 2.24 E
Montserrado [3] 34 Cd 6.35N 10.35W
Montserrat [5] 39 Mh 16.45N 62.12W
Montserrat, Monasterio de- ◼ 13 Nc 41.35N 1.49 E
Montserrat, Monasterio de-/ Montserrat, Monèstir de- ◼ 13 Nc 41.35N 1.49 E
Montserrat, Monèstir de- ◼ 13 Nc 41.35N 1.49 E
Montserrat, Monèstir de-/ Montserrat, Monasterio de- ◼ 13 Nc 41.35N 1.49 E
Montuosa, Isla- ◼ 49 Fj 7.28N 82.14W
Montville 12 De 49.33N 1.07 E
Monument Peak ◼ 46 He 42.07N 114.14W
Monument Valley ◼ 46 Jh 36.50N 110.20W
Monveda 36 Db 2.57N 21.27 E
Monviso ◼ 5 Gg 44.40N 7.07 E
Monywa 25 Jd 22.07N 95.08 E
Monza 14 De 45.35N 9.16 E
Monze 36 Ef 16.16 S 27.29 E
Monzen 29 Ec 37.17N 136.46 E
Monzón 13 Mc 41.55N 0.12 E
Mo'oka 29 Fc 36.27N 139.59 E
Moonbeam 44 Fa 49.25N 82.11W
Moonie 59 Ke 27.40 S 150.19 E
Moonie River ◼ 59 Je 29.19 S 148.43 E
Moonta 59 Hf 34.04 S 137.35 E
Moora 58 Ch 30.39 S 116.00 E
Moorcroft 46 Md 44.16N 104.57W
Moore 45 Hi 35.20N 97.29W
Moore, Lake- ◼ 57 Cg 29.50 S 117.35 E
Moorea, Ile- ◼ 57 Mf 17.32 S 149.50W
Moore's Island ◼ 44 Il 26.18N 77.33W
Moorhead 43 Hb 46.53N 96.45W
Moormerland 12 Ja 53.18N 7.26 E
Moormerland-Neermoor 12 Ja 53.18N 7.26 E
Moorreesburg 37 Bf 33.09 S 18.40 E
Moosburg an der Isar 10 Hh 48.28N 11.56 E
Moose ◼ 38 Kd 50.48N 81.18W
Moosehead Lake ◼ 43 Nb 45.40N 69.40W
Moose Jaw 39 Id 50.23N 105.32W
Moose Jaw River ◼ 46 Ma 50.34N 105.17W
Moose Lake 45 Jc 46.25N 92.45W
Mooselookmeguntic Lake ◼ 44 Lc 44.53N 70.48W
Moose Mountain ◼ 45 Eb 49.45N 102.37W
Moose Mountain Creek ◼ 45 Eb 49.12N 102.10W
Moosomin 42 Hf 50.09N 101.40W
Moosonee 39 Kd 51.17N 80.39W
Mopeia 37 Fc 17.59 S 35.43 E
Mopelia, Atoll- → Maupihaa Atoll ◼ 57 Lf 16.50 S 153.55W
Mopti 31 Gg 14.30N 4.12W
Mopti [3] 34 Ec 14.40N 4.15W
Moqokorei 35 He 4.04N 46.08 E
Moquegua [2] 54 Dg 16.50 S 70.55W
Moquegua 54 Dg 17.12 S 70.56W
Mór 10 Oi 47.23N 18.12 E
Mor, Glen- ◼ 9 Id 57.10N 4.40W
Mora [Cam.] 34 Hc 11.03N 14.09 E
Mora [Port.] 13 Df 38.56N 8.10W
Mora [Sp.] 13 Ie 39.41N 3.46W
Mora [Swe.] 7 Df 61.00N 14.33 E
Morača ◼ 15 Cg 42.16N 19.09 E
Morača, Manastir- ◼ 15 Cg 42.46N 19.24 E
Morādābād 22 Jg 28.50N 78.47 E
Morada Nova de Minas 55 Jd 18.25 S 45.22W
Móra d'Ebre/Mora de Ebro 13 Mc 41.05N 0.38 E
Mora de Ebro/Móra d'Ebre 13 Mc 41.05N 0.38 E
Mora de Rubielos 13 Ld 40.15N 0.45W
Morafenobe 37 Gc 17.49 S 44.55 E
Morąg 10 Pc 53.56N 19.56 E
Mórahalom 10 Pj 46.13N 19.53 E
Moraleda, Canal- ◼ 56 Ff 44.30 S 73.30W
Moraleja 13 Fd 40.04N 6.39W
Morales [Col.] 49 Ki 8.17N 73.52W
Morales [Guat.] 49 Cf 15.29N 88.49W
Morales, Laguna- ◼ 48 Kf 23.35N 97.45W
Moramanga 37 Hc 18.57 S 48.11 E
Moran 46 Je 43.50N 110.28W
Morane Atoll ◼ 57 Ng 23.10 S 137.07W
Morangas, Ribeirão- ◼ 55 Fd 19.39 S 52.19W
Morant Bay 49 Ie 17.53N 76.25W
Morant Cays ◼ 47 Ie 17.24N 75.59W
Morant Point ◼ 49 Ie 17.55N 76.10W
Morar, Loch- ◼ 9 He 56.58N 5.45W
Morarano 37 Hc 17.46 S 48.10 E
Mora River ◼ 45 Di 35.44N 104.23W
Moraska, Góra- ◼ 10 Md 52.30N 16.52 E
Morat/Murten 14 Bd 46.56N 7.08 E
Morata, Puerto de- ◼ 13 Kc 41.29N 1.31W
Moratalla 13 Kf 38.12N 1.53W
Moratuwa 25 Fg 6.46N 79.53 E
Morava ◼ 5 Hf 48.10N 16.59 E
Morava=Moravia (EN) ◼ 5 Hf 49.30N 17.00 E
Morava=Moravia (EN) ◼ 10 Mg 49.30N 17.00 E
Moravia (EN)=Morava ◼ 5 Hf 49.30N 17.00 E
Moravia (EN)=Morava ◼ 10 Mg 49.30N 17.00 E
Moravian Gate (EN)= Moravská Brána ◼ 5 Hf 49.33N 17.42 E
Moravian Upland (EN)= Českomoravská Vrchovina ◼ 5 Hf 49.20N 15.30 E
Moravica ◼ 15 Df 43.51N 20.05 E
Moravská Brána=Moravian Gate(EN) ◼ 5 Hf 49.33N 17.42 E
Moravské Budějovice 10 Lg 49.03N 15.49 E
Morawa 59 De 29.13 S 116.00 E
Morawhanna 54 Gb 8.16N 59.45W
Moray Firth ◼ 5 Fd 57.50N 3.30W
Morbach 12 Je 49.49N 7.07 E
Morbihan [3] 11 Dg 47.55N 2.50W
Morbihan ◼ 11 Dg 47.35N 2.48W
Morbylånga 7 Dh 56.31N 16.23 E
Morcenx 11 Fj 44.02N 0.55W
Mordāb ◼ 24 Md 37.26N 49.25 E
Mordaga 27 La 51.14N 120.43 E
Morden 42 Hg 49.11N 98.05W
Mordovo 16 Lc 52.05N 40.46 E
Mordovskaja ASSR [3] 19 Ee 54.20N 44.30 E
Möre ◼ 8 Fh 56.25N 15.55 E
More, Ben- ◼ 9 Ie 56.23N 4.31W
Morea 37 Bd 22.41 S 15.54 E
More Assynt, Ben- ◼ 9 Ic 58.07N 4.51W
Moreau River ◼ 43 Gb 45.18N 100.43W
Morecambe 9 Kg 54.04N 2.53W
Morecambe Bay ◼ 9 Kg 54.07N 3.00W
Moree 58 Fg 29.28 S 149.51 E
Morehead [Ky.-U.S.] 44 Ff 38.11N 83.25W
Morehead [Pap.N.Gui.] 60 Ci 8.50 S 141.57 E
Morehead City 39 Lf 34.43N 76.43W
Moreiz, Gora- ◼ 19 Gb 69.30N 62.05 E
Moreju ◼ 17 Ib 68.20N 59.45 E
Morelia 39 Ih 19.42N 101.07W
Morella 13 Ld 40.37N 0.06W
Morelos 48 Ic 28.25N 100.53W
Morelos [2] 47 Ee 18.45N 99.00W
Morena, Sierra- ◼ 5 Fh 38.00N 5.00W
Moreni 15 Ie 44.59N 25.39 E
Møre og Romsdal [2] 7 Be 62.40N 7.50 E
Moresby ◼ 42 Ef 52.45N 131.50W
Moreton Bay ◼ 59 Ke 27.20 S 153.15 E
Moreton Island ◼ 59 Ke 27.10 S 153.25 E
Moret-sur-Loing 11 If 48.22N 2.49 E
Moreuil 11 Ie 49.46N 2.29 E
Morez 11 Mh 46.31N 6.02 E
Morezu 15 Hd 45.09N 24.01 E
Mörfelden 12 Ke 49.59N 8.34 E
Morgan City 45 Kl 29.42N 91.12W
Morganfield 44 Dg 37.41N 87.55W
Morganton 44 Gh 35.45N 81.41W
Morgantown [Ky.-U.S.] 44 Dg 37.14N 86.41W
Morgantown [W.V.-U.S.] 44 Hf 39.38N 79.57W
Morges 14 Ad 46.31N 6.30 E
Morghāb ◼ 23 Jb 38.18N 61.12 E
Morhange 11 Mf 48.55N 6.38 E
Mori [China] 27 Fc 43.49N 90.11 E
Mori [Jap.] 28 Pc 42.06N 140.35 E
Moriarty 45 Ci 34.59N 106.03W
Morichal Largo, Río- ◼ 50 Eh 9.27N 62.25W
Moriguchi 29 Dd 34.44N 135.34 E
Morin Dawa (Nirji) 27 Lb 48.30N 124.28 E
Morioka 22 Qf 39.42N 141.09 E
Moriyoshi 29 Ga 40.07N 140.22 E
Moriyoshi-Yama ◼ 29 Gb 39.59N 140.33 E
Morjärv 7 Fc 66.04N 22.43 E
Morki 7 Lh 56.28N 49.00 E
Morko ◼ 8 Gf 59.00N 17.40 E
Morkoka ◼ 20 Gc 65.03N 115.40 E
Mørkøv 8 Di 55.40N 11.32 E
Morlaix 11 Cf 48.35N 3.50W
Morlanwelz 12 Gd 50.27N 4.14 E
Mörlunda 8 Fg 57.19N 15.51 E
Mormanno 14 Jk 39.53N 15.59 E
Morne-à-l'Eau 50 Fd 16.21N 61.31W
Morne Diablotin ◼ 47 Le 15.30N 61.24W
Mornington, Isla- ◼ 56 Eg 49.45 S 75.23W
Mornington Island ◼ 59 Hc 16.35 S 139.24 E
Moro 46 Ed 45.29N 120.44W
Morobe 58 Fe 7.45 S 147.37 E
Morocco (EN)=Al Maghrib [1] 31 Ge 32.00N 5.50W
Morogoro 31 Ki 6.49 S 37.40 E
Morogoro [3] 36 Gd 8.20 S 37.00 E
Moro Gulf ◼ 26 He 6.51N 123.00 E
Moroleón 48 Ig 20.08N 101.12W
Morombe 31 Lk 21.44 S 43.23 E
Morón [Arg.] 55 Cl 34.39 S 58.37W
Morón [Cuba] 47 Id 22.06N 78.38W
Morón [Ven.] 54 Ea 10.29N 68.11W
Morona, Río- ◼ 54 Cd 4.45 S 77.04W
Morondava 31 Lk 20.15 S 44.17 E
Morón de la Frontera 13 Gg 37.08N 5.27W
Morones, Sierra- ◼ 48 Hg 21.55N 103.05W
Moroni 31 Lj 11.41 S 43.16 E
Moron Us He ◼ 21 Lf 34.42N 94.50 E
Morotai, Pulau- ◼ 57 Dd 2.20N 128.25 E
Moroto 31 Kh 2.32N 34.39 E
Moroviţa 15 Ed 45.16N 21.16 E
Morozov ◼ 15 Ig 42.30N 25.10 E
Morozovsk 19 Ef 48.20N 41.50 E
Morpeth 9 Lf 55.10N 1.41W
Morphou → Güzelyurt 24 Ee 35.12N 32.59 E
Morrilton 45 Ji 35.09N 92.45W
Morrinhos 54 Ig 17.44 S 49.07W
Morrinsville 62 Fb 37.39 S 175.32 E
Morris [Il.-U.S.] 45 Lf 41.22N 88.26W
Morris [Man.-Can.] 42 Hg 49.21N 97.22W
Morris [Mn.-U.S.] 45 Id 45.35N 95.55W
Morris, Mount- ◼ 59 Ge 26.09 S 131.04 E
Morrisburg 44 Jc 44.54N 75.11W
Morris Jesup, Kap- ◼ 67 Me 83.45N 35.50W
Morrison Dennis Cays ◼ 49 Ff 14.28N 82.53W
Morristown 44 Fg 36.13N 83.18W
Morrito 49 Eh 11.37N 85.05W
Morro, Punta del- ◼ 48 Kh 19.51N 96.27W
Morro Bay 43 Cd 35.22N 120.51W
Morro do Chapéu 54 Jf 11.33 S 41.09W
Morrosquillo, Golfo de- ◼ 49 Ji 9.35N 75.40W
Morro Vermelho, Serra do- ◼ 55 Jc 17.45 S 45.20W
Mörrum 8 Fh 56.11N 14.45 E
Morrumbala 37 Fc 17.20 S 35.35 E
Morrumbene 37 Fd 23.39 S 35.20 E
Mörrumsån ◼ 8 Fh 56.09N 14.44 E
Mors ◼ 8 Ch 56.50N 8.45 E
Moršansk 19 Ee 53.26N 41.49 E
Morsbach 12 Jd 50.52N 7.45 E
Morsberg ◼ 12 Ke 49.43N 8.54 E
Mörsil 7 Ce 63.19N 13.38 E
Mörskom/Myrskylä 8 Kd 60.40N 25.51 E
Morsott 14 Co 35.40N 8.01 E
Mortagne ◼ 11 Mf 48.33N 6.27 E
Mortagne-au-Perche 11 Gf 48.31N 0.33 E
Mortagne-sur-Sèvre 11 Fg 47.00N 0.57W
Mortain 11 Ff 48.39N 0.56W
Mortara 14 Ce 45.15N 8.44 E
Mortcha ◼ 30 Jg 16.00N 21.10 E
Morteau 11 Mg 47.04N 6.37 E
Morteaux-Couliboeuf 12 Bf 48.56N 0.04W
Morteros 56 Hd 30.42 S 62.00W
Mortes, Rio das- ◼ 55 Je 21.09 S 44.53W
Mortesoro 35 Ec 10.12N 34.09 E
Mortlock Islands ◼ 57 Gd 5.27N 153.40 E
Morton 46 Dc 46.33N 122.17W
Mortsel 12 Gc 51.10N 4.28 E
Morumbi 55 Ef 23.46 S 54.06W
Morvan ◼ 11 Jg 47.05N 4.00 E
Morven 59 Je 26.25 S 147.07 E
Morvern ◼ 9 He 56.35N 5.50W
Morvi 25 Ed 22.49N 70.50 E
Morwell 58 Fh 38.14 S 146.24 E
Morzine 11 Mh 46.11N 6.43 E
Moržovec, Ostrov- ◼ 7 Kc 66.45N 42.35 E
Moša ◼ 7 Je 62.25N 39.48 E
Mosbach 10 Fg 49.21N 9.09 E
Mosby 8 Bf 58.14N 7.54 E
Moščny, Ostrov- ◼ 7 Gg 60.00N 27.50 E
Mosconi 55 Bl 35.44 S 60.34W
Moscos Islands ◼ 25 Jf 14.00N 97.45 E
Moscow [Id.-U.S.] 43 Db 46.44N 116.59W
Moscow (EN)=Moskva ◼ 5 Jd 55.08N 38.50 E
Moscow (EN)=Moskva [R.S.F.S.R.] 6 Jd 55.45N 37.35 E
Moscow Basin (EN)= Meščera ◼ 5 Kd 55.00N 40.30 E
Moscow Canal (EN)= Moskvy, kanal imeni- ◼ 5 Jd 56.43N 37.08 E
Moscow Upland (EN)= Moskovskaja Vozvyšennost ◼ 5 Jd 56.30N 37.30 E
Mosel=Moselle (EN) ◼ 5 Ge 50.22N 7.36 E
Moselberge ◼ 12 Ie 49.57N 6.56 E
Moselle [3] 11 Me 49.00N 6.30 E
Moselle ◼ 5 Ge 50.22N 7.36 E
Moselle (EN)=Mosel ◼ 5 Ge 50.22N 7.36 E
Moses Lake 43 Db 47.08N 119.17W
Mosgiel 61 Di 45.53 S 170.22 E
Moshi 31 Ki 3.21 S 37.20 E
Mosina 10 Md 52.16N 16.51 E
Mosjøen 7 Cd 65.50N 13.12 E
Moskalvo 20 Jf 53.39N 142.37 E
Moskenesøy ◼ 7 Cc 67.59N 13.00 E
Moskovskaja Oblast [3] 19 Dd 55.45N 37.45 E
Moskovskaja Vozvyšennost =Moscow Upland (EN) ◼ 5 Jd 56.30N 37.30 E
Moskovski 18 Gf 37.40N 69.39 E
Moskva [R.S.F.S.R.] = Moscow (EN) 6 Jd 55.45N 37.35 E
Moskva [Tur.-U.S.S.R.] 18 Ee 38.27N 64.24 E
Moskva=Moscow (EN) ◼ 5 Jd 55.08N 38.50 E
Moskva, Pik- ◼ 18 He 38.55N 71.52 E
Moskvy, kanal imeni-= Moscow Canal (EN) ◼ 5 Jd 56.43N 37.08 E
Moslavačka Gora ◼ 14 Ke 45.38N 16.42 E
Moso ◼ 63b Dc 17.32 S 168.15 E
Mosomane 37 Dd 24.01 S 26.19 E
Mosoni-Duna ◼ 10 Ni 47.44N 17.47 E
Mosonmagyaróvár 10 Ni 47.52N 17.17 E
Mosor ◼ 14 Kg 43.30N 16.40 E
Mosquero 45 Ei 35.47N 103.58W
Mosquito, Baie - ◼ 42 Jd 60.40N 78.00W
Mosquito Coast (EN)= Mosquitos, Costa de- ◼ 38 Kh 13.00N 83.45W
Mosquito, Riacho- ◼ 55 Cf 22.12 S 57.57W
Mosquitos, Costa de-= Mosquito Coast (EN) ◼ 38 Kh 13.00N 83.45W
Mosquitos, Golfo de los- ◼ 38 Ki 9.00N 81.20W
Moss 6 Hd 59.26N 10.42 E
Mossaka 36 Cc 1.13 S 16.48 E
Mossâmedes 55 Gc 16.07 S 50.11W
Mossbank 46 Mb 49.55N 105.59W
Mossburn 61 Ci 45.41 S 168.15 E
Mosselbaai 31 Jl 34.11 S 22.08 E
Mossendjo 36 Bc 2.57 S 12.44 E
Mossman 58 Ff 16.28 S 145.22 E
Mossø ◼ 8 Ch 56.05N 9.50 E
Mossoró 53 Mf 5.11 S 37.20W
Moss Point 45 Lk 30.25N 88.29W
Mossuril 37 Gb 14.58 S 40.40 E
Most 10 Jf 50.32N 13.39 E
Mostaganem [3] 32 Hb 35.40N 0.30 E
Mostaganem 31 He 35.56N 0.05 E
Mostar 14 Lg 43.21N 17.49 E
Mostardas 55 Gj 31.06 S 50.57W
Møsting, Kap- ◼ 41 Hf 63.45N 41.00W
Mostiska 16 Ce 49.48N 23.09 E
Mostiştea ◼ 15 Je 44.15N 26.54 E
Most na Soci 14 Hd 46.09N 13.45 E
Mostovskoj 16 Lg 44.22N 40.48 E
Mosty 19 Ce 53.27N 24.33 E
Mosul (EN)=Al Mawşil 22 Gf 36.20N 43.08 E
Møsvatn ◼ 7 Bg 59.50N 8.05 E
Mota ◼ 63b Ca 13.40 S 167.42 E
Mota 35 Fc 11.05N 37.53 E
Motaba ◼ 36 Cb 2.03N 18.03 E
Motacusito 55 Bc 17.35 S 61.31W
Mota del Marques 13 Gc 41.38N 5.10W
Motagua ◼ 38 Kh 15.44N 88.14W
Motajica ◼ 14 Le 45.04N 17.40 E
Motala 7 Dg 58.33N 15.03 E
Motala ström ◼ 8 Gf 58.38N 16.10 E
Motatán 49 Li 9.24N 70.36W
Motatán, Río- ◼ 49 Li 9.32N 71.02W
Motegi 29 Gc 36.32N 140.10 E
Motehuala 47 Dd 23.39N 100.39W
Mothe ◼ 63d Cc 18.40 S 178.30W
Motherwell 9 Jf 55.48N 4.00W
Motīhāri 25 Gc 26.39N 84.55 E
Motilla del Palancar 13 Ke 39.34N 1.53W
Motiti Island ◼ 62 Gb 37.40 S 176.25 E
Motlav ◼ 63b Ca 13.40 S 167.40 E
Motobu 29b Ab 26.40N 127.55 E
Motol 10 Vd 52.17N 25.40 E
Motovski Zaliv ◼ 7 Hb 69.30N 32.30 E
Motoyoshi 29 Gb 38.48N 141.31 E
Motozintla de Mendoza 48 Mj 15.22N 92.14W
Motril 13 Ih 36.45N 3.31W
Motru ◼ 15 Ge 44.33N 23.27 E
Motru 15 Fe 44.48N 23.00 E
Motsuta-Misaki ◼ 29a Ab 42.36N 139.49 E
Mott 45 Ec 46.22N 102.20W
Motteville 12 Ce 49.38N 0.51 E
Motu ◼ 62 Gb 37.51 S 177.35 E
Motueka 62 Ed 41.07 S 173.01 E
Motuhora Island ◼ 62 Gb 37.50 S 177.00 E
Motu-Iti ◼ 65d Ac 27.11 S 109.27W
Motu-Iti → Tupai Atoll ◼ 61 Kc 16.17 S 151.50W
Motul 47 Gd 21.06N 89.17W
Motu-Nui ◼ 65d Ac 27.12 S 109.28W
Motu One Atoll ◼ 57 Lf 15.48 S 154.33W
Motupae ◼ 64n Ac 10.27 S 161.02W
Motupena Point ◼ 63a Bb 6.32 S 155.09 E
Moturiki ◼ 63d Bb 17.46 S 178.45 E
Motutapu ◼ 64p Cb 21.14 S 159.43W
Motu Tautara ◼ 65d Ab 27.05 S 109.26W
Motutunga Atoll ◼ 57 Mf 17.06 S 144.22W
Moubray Bay ◼ 66 Kf 72.11 S 170.15 E
Mouchard 11 Lh 46.58N 5.48 E
Mouchoir Bank (EN) ◼ 47 Jd 20.57N 70.42W
Mouchoir Passage ◼ 49 Lc 21.10N 71.00W
Moudjéria 32 Ef 17.52N 12.20W
Mouila 31 Ii 1.52 S 11.01 E
Mouka 35 Cd 7.16N 21.52 E
Moul 34 Hb 15.03N 13.18 E
Mould Bay 39 Hb 76.15N 119.30W
Moule 50 Fd 16.20N 61.21W
Moule à Chique, Cap- ◼ 51k Bb 13.43N 60.57W
Moulins 11 Jh 46.34N 3.20 E
Moulmein → Mawlamyine 22 Le 16.30N 97.38 E
Moulouya 30 Ge 35.06N 2.20W
Moult 12 Be 49.07N 0.10W
Moultrie 44 Fj 31.11N 83.47W
Moultrie, Lake- ◼ 44 Gi 33.20N 80.05W
Mouly, Pointe de- ◼ 63b Ce 20.43 S 166.23 E
Moúnda, Ákra- ◼ 15 Dk 38.03N 20.47 E
Moundou 31 Ih 8.34N 16.05 E
Moundsville 44 Gf 39.54N 80.44W
Mo'unga'one ◼ 65b Ba 19.38 S 174.29W
Moungoudou 36 Bc 2.40 S 12.41 E
Mountainair 45 Ci 34.31N 106.15W
Mountain Grove 45 Jh 37.08N 92.16W
Mountain Home [Ar.-U.S.] 45 Jh 36.21N 92.23W
Mountain Home [Id.-U.S.] 43 Dc 43.08N 115.41W
Mountain Nile (EN)=Jabal, Baḩr al- ◼ 30 Kh 9.30N 30.30 E
Mountain Village 40 Gd 62.05N 163.44W
Mount Airy 44 Gg 36.31N 80.37W
Mount Barker 59 Df 34.38 S 117.40 E
Mount Carmel 45 Mf 38.25N 87.46W
Mount Desert Island ◼ 44 Mc 44.20N 68.20W
Mount Douglas 58 Fg 21.30 S 146.50 E
Mount Eba 59 Hf 30.12 S 135.40 E
Mount Forest 44 Gd 43.59N 80.44W
Mount Frere 37 Df 31.00 S 28.58 E
Mount Gambier 58 Fh 37.50 S 140.46 E
Mount Hagen 60 Ci 5.52 S 144.13 E
Mount Hope 59 Hf 34.07 S 135.23 E
Mount Isa 58 Eg 20.44S 139.30 E
Mountlake Terrace 46 Dc 47.47N 122.18W
Mount Lebanon 44 Ge 40.23N 80.03W
Mount Lofty Ranges ◼ 59 Hg 35.15 S 138.50 E
Mount Magnet 58 Cg 28.04 S 117.49 E
Mount Maunganui 61 Eg 37.38 S 176.12 E
Mount Morgan 59 Kd 23.39 S 150.23 E
Mountnorris Bay ◼ 59 Gb 11.20 S 132.45 E
Mount Peck ◼ 46 Ha 50.10N 115.02W
Mount Pleasant [Ia.-U.S.] 45 Kf 40.58N 91.33W
Mount Pleasant [Mi.-U.S.] 44 Ed 43.35N 84.47W
Mount Pleasant [S.C.-U.S.] 44 Hi 32.47N 79.52W
Mount Pleasant [Tx.-U.S.] 45 Ij 33.09N 94.58W
Mount Pleasant [Ut.-U.S.] 46 Jg 39.33N 111.27W
Mount's Bay ◼ 9 Hk 50.03N 5.25W
Mount Somers 62 De 43.42 S 171.25 E
Mount Sterling [Il.-U.S.] 45 Kg 39.59N 90.45W
Mount Sterling [Ky.-U.S.] 44 Ff 38.04N 83.56W
Mount Vancouver ◼ 42 Dd 60.20N 139.41W
Mount Vernon [Al.-U.S.] 44 Cj 31.05N 88.01W
Mount Vernon [Austl.] 59 Dd 24.13 S 118.14 E
Mount Vernon [Il.-U.S.] 43 Jd 38.19N 88.55W
Mount Vernon [In.-U.S.] 44 Dg 37.56N 87.54W
Mount Vernon [Ky.-U.S.] 44 Eg 37.21N 84.20W
Mount Vernon [Oh.-U.S.] 44 Fe 40.23N 82.30W
Mount Vernon [Wa.-U.S.] 43 Cb 48.25N 122.20W
Moura [Austl.] 59 Jd 24.35 S 150.00 E
Moura [Port.] 13 Ef 38.08N 7.27W
Mourão 13 Ef 38.23N 7.21W
Mourdi ◼ 35 Cb 17.50N 22.25 E
Mourdi, Dépression du-= Mourdi Depression (EN) ◼ 30 Jg 18.10N 23.00 E
Mourdiah 34 Dc 14.26N 7.31W
Mourdi Depression (EN)= Mourdi, Dépression du- ◼ 30 Jg 18.10N 23.00 E
Mourmelon-le-Grand 12 Ge 49.08N 4.22 E
Mourne Mountains/Beanna Boirche ◼ 9 Gg 54.10N 6.04W
Mouscron/Moeskroen 11 Jd 50.44N 3.13 E
Moussoro 31 Ig 13.39N 16.29 E
Moustiers-Sainte-Marie 11 Mk 43.51N 6.13 E
Moutier/Münster 14 Bc 47.16N 7.22 E
Moutiers 11 Mi 45.29N 6.32 E
Moutong 26 Hf 0.28N 121.13 E
Mouy 12 Ee 49.19N 2.19 E
Mouydir ◼ 30 Hf 25.00N 4.10 E
Mouyondzi 36 Bc 3.58 S 13.57 E
Mouzaia 13 Oh 36.28N 2.41 E
Mouzon 12 He 49.36N 5.05 E
Movas 48 Ec 28.10N 109.25W

Index Symbols

[1] Independent Nation
[2] State, Region
[3] District, County
[4] Municipality
[5] Colony, Dependency
◼ Continent
◼ Physical Region
◼ Historical or Cultural Region
◼ Mount, Mountain
◼ Volcano
◼ Hill
◼ Mountains, Mountain Range
◼ Hills, Escarpment
◼ Plateau, Upland
◼ Pass, Gap
◼ Plain, Lowland
◼ Delta
◼ Salt Flat
◼ Valley, Canyon
◼ Crater, Cave
◼ Karst Features
◼ Depression
◼ Polder
◼ Desert, Dunes
◼ Forest, Woods
◼ Heath, Steppe
◼ Oasis
◼ Cape, Point
◼ Coast, Beach
◼ Cliff
◼ Peninsula
◼ Isthmus
◼ Sandbank
◼ Island
◼ Atoll
◼ Rock, Reef
◼ Islands, Archipelago
◼ Rocks, Reefs
◼ Coral Reef
◼ Well, Spring
◼ Geyser
◼ River, Stream
◼ Waterfall Rapids
◼ River Mouth, Estuary
◼ Lake
◼ Salt Lake
◼ Intermittent Lake
◼ Reservoir
◼ Swamp, Pond
◼ Canal
◼ Glacier
◼ Ice Shelf, Pack Ice
◼ Ocean
◼ Sea
◼ Gulf, Bay
◼ Strait, Fjord
◼ Lagoon
◼ Bank
◼ Seamount
◼ Tablemount
◼ Ridge
◼ Shelf
◼ Basin
◼ Escarpment, Sea Scarp
◼ Fracture
◼ Trench, Abyss
◼ National Park, Reserve
◼ Point of Interest
◼ Recreation Site
◼ Cave, Cavern
◼ Historic Site
◼ Ruins
◼ Wall, Walls
◼ Church, Abbey
◼ Temple
◼ Scientific Station
◼ Airport
◼ Port
◼ Lighthouse
◼ Mine
◼ Tunnel
◼ Dam, Bridge

Moxico [3] 36 De 12.00S 20.00 E
Moxico 36 De 11.51S 20.01 E
Moy/An Mhuaidh 9 Dg 54.12N 9.08W
Moyahua 48 Hg 21.16N 103.10W
Moyale [Eth.] 31 Kh 3.32N 39.04 E
Moyale [Kenya] 36 Gb 3.32N 39.03 E
Moyamba 34 Cd 8.10N 12.26W
Moÿ-de-l'Aisne 12 Fe 49.45N 3.22 E
Moyen Atlas = Middle Atlas (EN) 30 Ge 33.30N 4.30W
Moyen-Chari [3] 35 Bd 9.00N 18.00 E
Moyenne Guinée [3] 34 Cc 11.15N 12.30W
Moyenneville 12 Dd 50.04N 1.45 E
Moyen-Ogooué [3] 36 Bc 0.30S 10.30 E
Moyeuvre-Grande 12 Ie 49.15N 6.02 E
Moyo 36 Fb 3.40N 31.43 E
Moyo, Pulau- 26 Gh 8.15S 117.34 E
Moyobamba 53 If 6.02S 76.58W
Moyowosi 36 Fc 4.50S 31.24 E
Moyto 35 Bc 12.35N 16.33 E
Moyu/Karakax 27 Cd 37.17N 79.42 E
Možajsk 7 Ii 55.32N 36.02 E
Mozambique (EN) = Moçambique [1] 31 Kj 18.15S 35.00 E
Mozambique (EN) = Moçambique 31 Lk 15.03S 40.45 E
Mozambique, Canal de- = Mozambique Channel (EN) 30 Lk 20.00S 43.00 E
Mozambique Channel (EN) = Moçambique, Canal de- 30 Lk 20.00S 43.00 E
Mozambique Channel (EN) = Mozambique, Canal de- 30 Lk 20.00S 43.00 E
Mozambique Plateau (EN) 30 Kl 32.00S 35.00 E
Mozdok 19 Eg 43.44N 44.38 E
Možga 19 Fd 56.28N 52.13 E
Mozuli 8 Mh 56.32N 28.14 E
Mozyr 19 Ce 52.02N 29.16 E
Mpala 36 Ed 6.45S 29.31 E
Mpanda 31 Ki 6.22S 31.02 E
Mpigi 36 Fb 0.15N 32.20 E
Mpika 31 Kj 11.50S 31.27 E
Mpoko 35 Be 4.19N 18.33 E
Mporokoso 36 Fd 9.23S 30.08 E
Mpouia 36 Cc 2.37S 16.13 E
Mpui 36 Fd 8.21S 31.50 E
Mpulungu 36 Fd 8.46S 31.07 E
Mpwapwa 36 Gd 6.21S 36.29 E
Mrągowo 10 Rc 53.52N 21.19 E
Mrakovo 17 Hj 52.43N 56.38 E
Mrkonjić Grad 14 Lf 44.25N 17.06 E
Mrocza 10 Nc 53.14N 17.36 E
Mroga 10 Pd 52.09N 19.42 E
Msangesi 36 Ge 11.40S 36.45 E
Msid, Djebel- 14 Cn 36.25N 8.04 E
Msif 13 Qi 35.23N 4.45 E
M'Sila 13 Qi 35.31N 4.30 E
M'Sila [3] 32 Hb 35.00N 4.30 E
M'Sila 32 Hb 35.42N 4.33 E
Mšinskaja 8 Nf 58.55N 30.03 E
Msta 5 Jd 58.25N 31.20 E
Mstislavl 16 Gc 53.59N 31.45 E
Mszana Dolna 10 Qg 49.42N 20.05 E
Mtakuja 36 Fd 7.22S 30.37 E
Mtama 36 Ge 10.18S 39.22 E
Mtelo 36 Gb 1.39N 35.23 E
Mtera Reservoir 36 Gd 7.01S 35.55 E
Mtito Andei 36 Gc 2.41S 38.10 E
Mtubatuba 37 Ee 28.30S 32.08 E
Mtwara [3] 36 Ge 10.40S 39.00 E
Mtwara 31 Lj 10.16S 40.11 E
Mu, Cerro- 49 Ki 9.29N 73.07W
Mua 64h Ac 13.21S 176.10W
Mu'a 65b Ac 21.11S 175.07W
Mua, Baie de- 64h Bc 13.23S 176.09W
Muaná 54 Id 1.32S 49.13W
Muang Huon 25 Kd 20.09N 101.27 E
Muang Khammouan 25 Ke 17.24N 104.48 E
Muang Không 25 Lf 14.07N 105.51 E
Muang Khôngxédôn 25 Le 15.34N 105.49 E
Muang Khoua 25 Kd 21.05N 102.31 E
Muang Pak Lay 25 Ke 18.12N 101.25 E
Muang Pakxan 25 Ke 18.22N 103.39 E
Muang Pakxong 25 Le 15.11N 106.14 E
Muang Sing 25 Kd 21.11N 101.09 E
Muang Tahoi 25 Le 16.10N 106.38 E
Muang Thai = Thailand (EN) [1] 22 Lh 15.00N 100.00 E
Muang Vangviang 25 Ke 18.56N 102.27 E
Muang Xaignabouri 25 Ke 19.15N 101.45 E
Muang Xay 25 Kd 20.42N 101.59 E
Muang Xépôn 25 Le 16.41N 106.14 E
Muanzanza 36 Dd 6.32S 20.51 E
Muar 26 Df 2.02N 102.34 E
Muaraaman 26 Dg 3.07S 102.12 E
Muarabungo 26 Dg 1.28S 102.07 E
Muaraenim 26 Dg 3.39S 103.48 E
Muaralasan 26 Gf 1.48N 117.12 E
Muarapajang 26 Gg 1.32S 115.48 E
Muarasiberut 26 Cg 1.36S 99.11 E
Muarasiram 26 Gg 0.46S 116.11 E
Muaratebo 26 Dg 1.30S 102.26 E
Muaratewe 26 Fg 0.57S 114.53 E
Muarawahau 26 Gf 1.02N 116.52 E
Mubarek 18 Ee 39.16N 65.07 E
Mubende 36 Fb 0.35N 31.23 E
Mubi 31 Ig 10.16N 13.16 E
Much 12 Jd 50.55N 7.24 E
Muchinga Escarpment 36 Fe 13.40S 34.00 E
Muchinga Mountains 30 Kj 12.00S 31.45 E
Muck 9 Ge 56.50N 6.14W
Mücke 12 Ld 50.37N 9.02 E
Mucojo 37 Gb 12.04S 40.28 E
Muconda 36 De 10.34S 21.20 E
Mucua 37 Ec 18.09S 34.58 E
Mucubela 37 Fc 16.54S 37.49 E
Mucuchies 49 Li 8.45N 70.55W
Mucumbura 37 Ec 16.10S 31.42 E
Mucur 24 Fc 39.04N 34.23 E
Mucusso 36 Df 18.00S 21.25 E
Mudan Jiang 21 Oe 46.18N 129.31 E
Mudanjiang 22 Oe 44.35N 129.34 E
Mudanya 24 Cb 40.22N 28.52 E
Muddy Gap 46 Le 42.22N 107.27W
Mudgee 59 Jf 32.36S 149.35 E
Mud Lake 46 Ie 43.53N 112.24W
Mud Lake 46 Gh 37.55N 117.05W
Mudon 25 Je 16.15N 97.44 E
Mudug [3] 35 Hd 6.30N 48.00 E
Mudug 35 Hd 6.20N 47.00 E
Mudurnu 24 Db 40.28N 31.13 E
Muecate 37 Fb 14.53S 39.38 E
Mueda 37 Fb 11.39S 39.33 E
Muerto, Cayo- 49 Ff 14.34N 82.44W
Muerto, Mar- 48 Li 16.10N 94.10W
Mufulira 31 Jj 12.33S 28.14 E
Mufu Shan 27 Jf 29.15N 114.20 E
Mufu Shan 27 Jf 29.00N 113.50 E
Mugello 14 Fg 43.55N 11.25 E
Müggia 14 He 45.36N 13.46 E
Mughshin, Wādī- 35 Ib 19.44N 55.00 E
Mugi 29 De 33.40N 134.25 E
Mu Gia, Deo- 25 Le 17.40N 105.47 E
Mugila, Monts- 36 Ed 6.49S 29.08 E
Muğla 23 Cb 37.12N 28.22 E
Mugodžary 21 He 49.00N 58.40 E
Mugur an Na'ām 24 Ig 31.56N 40.30 E
Muhaiwir 24 If 33.28N 40.59 E
Muḥammad, Ra's- 33 Fd 27.42N 34.13 E
Muḥammad Oawl 35 Fa 20.54N 37.05 E
Muhen 20 Ig 48.10N 136.08 E
Muheza 36 Gd 5.10S 38.47 E
Muhīt, Al Baḥr al- = Atlantic Ocean (EN) 3 Di 2.00N 25.00W
Mühlacker 10 Eh 48.57N 8.50 E
Mühldorf am Inn 10 Ih 48.15N 12.32 E
Mühlhausen in Thüringen 10 Ge 51.13N 10.27 E
Mühlig-Hofmann Gebirge 66 Cf 72.00S 5.20 E
Mühlviertel 14 Ib 48.30N 14.10 E
Muhoršibir 20 Ff 51.01N 107.50 E
Muhos 7 Gd 64.50N 26.01 E
Muhu 7 Fg 58.35N 23.15 E
Muhu 8 Jf 58.37N 23.05 E
Muhu, Proliv-/Muhu Väin 8 Jf 58.45N 23.15 E
Muhulu 36 Ec 1.03S 27.17 E
Muhu Väin/Muhu, Proliv- 8 Jf 58.45N 23.15 E
Muhuwesi 36 Ge 11.16S 37.58 E
Muiderslot 12 Hb 52.20N 5.06 E
Muigheo/Mayo [2] 9 Dh 53.50N 9.30W
Muikamachi 28 Of 37.04N 138.53 E
Muineachán/Monaghan [2] 9 Gg 54.10N 7.00W
Muineachán/Monaghan 9 Gg 54.15N 6.58W
Muine Bheag 9 Gi 52.42N 6.57W
Muir Bhreatan = Saint George's Channel (EN) 5 Fe 52.00N 6.00W
Muir Eireann = Irish Sea (EN) 5 Fe 53.30N 5.20W
Muiron Islands 59 Cd 21.35S 114.20 E
Muir Seamount (EN) 38 Mf 33.41N 63.32W
Muite 37 Fb 14.02S 39.02 E
Mujeres, Isla- 48 Pg 21.13N 86.43W
Mujezerski 7 He 63.57N 32.01 E
Muji 27 Cd 37.27N 78.33 E
Mujnak 19 Fg 43.44N 59.02 E
Mujnakski Zaliv 18 Bc 43.50N 58.40 E
Mujunkum, Peski- 21 Je 44.00N 70.30 E
Mukačevo 19 Cf 48.26N 22.45 E
Mukah 26 Ff 2.54N 112.06 E
Mukawa 29a Bb 42.35N 141.55 E
Mu-Kawa 29a Bb 42.33N 141.53 E
Mukawwar 35 Fa 20.48N 37.13 E
Mukdahan 25 Ke 16.31N 104.42 E
Mukden → Shenyang 22 Oe 41.48N 123.24 E
Mukeru 64a Bc 7.25N 134.30 E
Mukho 28 Jf 37.33N 129.07 E
Mukinbudin 59 Df 30.54S 118.13 E
Mukojima-Rettō 60 Cb 27.37N 142.10 E
Mukomuko 26 Dg 2.35S 101.07 E
Muksu 18 He 39.17N 71.25 E
Mula 25 Dc 27.57N 67.36 E
Mula 13 Kf 38.03N 1.30W
Mulainagiri 25 Ff 13.24N 75.43 E
Mulaku Atoll 25a Bb 2.57N 73.34 E
Mulaly 19 Hf 45.27N 78.20 E
Mulan 27 Mb 46.00N 128.02 E
Mulanje 30 Kj 16.03S 35.31 E
Mulanje 36 Gf 16.02S 35.30 E
Mulatre, Point- 51g Bb 15.17N 61.15W
Mulatupo Sasardí 49 Ii 8.57N 77.45W
Mulchatna 40 Hd 59.39N 157.08W
Mulchén 56 Fe 37.34S 72.14W
Mulda 17 Kc 67.28N 63.34 E
Mulde 10 Ie 51.48N 12.10 E
Mulebreen 66 Ee 67.28S 59.21 E
Mulegé 47 Bc 26.53N 112.01W
Mulegé, Sierra de- 47 Bc 37.30N 112.40W
Mulenda 36 Dc 4.18S 24.58 E
Muleshoe 45 Ei 34.13N 102.43W
Mulgrave Island 59 Ib 10.05S 142.10 E
Mulhacén 5 Fh 37.03N 3.19W
Mülheim an der Ruhr 12 Ic 51.26N 6.53 E
Mülheim-Kärlich 12 Jd 50.23N 7.30 E
Mulhouse 6 Gf 47.45N 7.20 E
Muli (Bowa) 27 Hf 27.55N 101.13 E
Mulifanua 65c Aa 13.50S 172.02W
Muling 28 Kb 44.34N 130.12 E
Muling (Bamiantong) 28 Kb 44.55N 130.32 E
Muling Guan 28 Ef 36.10N 118.46 E
Muling He 28 Lb 45.53N 133.30 E
Mull, Island of- 5 Fd 56.27N 6.00W
Mull, Sound of- 9 He 56.35N 5.50W
Mullen 45 Fe 42.03N 101.01W
Mullens 44 Gg 37.35N 81.25W
Muller, Pegunungan- 26 Ff 0.40N 113.50 E
Mullet Peninsula/An Muirthead 9 Cg 54.15N 10.04W
Mullett Lake 44 Ec 45.30N 84.30W
Mullewa 59 De 28.33S 115.31 E
Müllheim 10 Di 47.48N 7.38 E
Mullingar/An Muileann gCearr 9 Fh 53.32N 7.20W
Mullsjö 8 Eg 57.55N 13.53 E
Mulobezi 36 Ef 16.47S 25.10 E
Mulock Glacier 66 Jf 79.03S 159.10 E
Mulongo 36 Ed 7.50S 26.57 E
Multān 22 Jf 30.11N 71.29 E
Multé 48 Ni 17.41N 91.24W
Multia 8 Kb 62.25N 24.47 E
Multien 12 Ee 49.05N 2.55 E
Mulu, Gunong- 26 Ff 4.03N 114.56 E
Mulvane 45 Hh 37.29N 97.14W
Mulymja 17 Lf 60.12N 64.32 E
Mumbué 36 Ce 13.53S 17.19 E
Mumbwa 36 Ee 14.59S 27.04 E
Mumhan/Munster 9 Ei 52.30N 9.00W
Mumra 16 Og 45.43N 47.41 E
Mun 21 Mh 15.19N 105.30 E
Muna 48 Og 20.29N 89.43W
Muna 21 Oc 67.52N 123.10 E
Muna, Pulau- 26 Hg 5.00S 122.30 E
Munābāo 25 Ec 25.45N 70.17 E
Munamägi/Munamjagi 8 Lg 57.38N 27.10 E
Munaybarah, Sharm- 24 Gi 26.04N 36.38 E
Muncar 26 Fh 8.29S 114.21 E
Münchberg 10 Hf 50.12N 11.47 E
München = Munich (EN) 6 Hf 48.09N 11.35 E
Münchhausen 12 Kd 50.57N 8.43 E
Muncho Lake 42 Ee 58.56N 125.46W
Munch'ŏn 28 Ie 39.14N 127.22 E
Muncie 43 Jc 40.11N 85.23W
Munda 63a Cc 8.19S 157.15 E
Mundaring, Perth- 59 Df 31.54S 116.10 E
Munday 45 Gj 33.27N 99.38W
Mundemba 34 Ge 4.59N 8.40 E
Münden 10 Fe 51.25N 9.41 E
Mundesley 12 Db 52.52N 1.25 E
Mundford 12 Cb 52.30N 0.39 E
Mundiwindi 58 Dg 23.52S 120.09 E
Mundo 13 Kf 38.19N 1.40W
Mundo Novo 54 Jf 11.52S 40.28W
Munellës, Mali i- 15 Dh 41.58N 20.06 E
Munera 13 Je 39.02N 2.28W
Mungana 59 Ic 17.07S 144.24 E
Mungbere 31 Jh 2.38N 28.30 E
Munger 25 Hc 25.23N 86.28 E
Mungindi 59 Je 28.58S 148.59 E
Munhango 36 Ce 12.10S 18.34 E
Munh-Hajrhan-Ula 21 Le 46.40N 91.30 E
Munich (EN) = München 6 Hf 48.09N 11.35 E
Muniesa 13 Lc 41.02N 0.48W
Munīfah 23 Gd 27.38N 49.00 E
Munising 44 Db 46.25N 86.40W
Munkedal 7 Cg 58.29N 11.41 E
Munkfors 7 Cg 59.50N 13.32 E
Munku Sardik, Gora- 21 Md 51.45N 100.20 E
Muñoz Gamero, Peninsula- 56 Fh 52.30S 73.10W
Munsan 28 If 37.55N 126.22 E
Münsingen 10 Fh 48.25N 9.30 E
Munster 11 Nf 48.03N 7.08 E
Münster [Ger.] 10 De 51.58N 7.38 E
Münster [Ger.] 12 Ke 49.55N 8.52 E
Münster/Moutier 14 Bc 47.16N 7.22 E
Munster/Mumhan 9 Ei 52.30N 9.00W
Münster-Hiltrup 12 Jc 51.54N 7.38 E
Münsterland [Ger.] 10 De 52.00N 7.30 E
Münsterland [Ger.] 12 Kb 52.45N 8.10 E
Münstermaifeld 12 Jd 50.15N 7.22 E
Muntenia 15 Ie 44.00N 26.00 E
Munteni Buzău 15 Je 44.38N 26.59 E
Muntok 26 Eg 2.04S 105.11 E
Munzur Dağları 24 Hc 39.30N 39.10 E
Muojärvi 7 Gd 65.56N 28.36 E
Muong Sen 25 Ke 19.24N 104.08 E
Muonio 6 Ib 67.57N 23.42 E
Muonioälven 5 Ib 67.11N 23.34 E
Muonionjoki 5 Ib 67.11N 23.34 E
Muping 28 Ff 37.23N 121.36 E
Muqaddam 35 Eb 18.04N 31.30 E
Muqayshiṭ 24 Oj 24.10N 53.45 E
Muqdisho = Mogadishu (EN) 31 Lh 2.03N 45.22 E
Mur 5 Hf 46.18N 16.55 E
Mura 5 Hf 46.18N 16.55 E
Muradiye [Tur.] 15 Kk 38.39N 27.24 E
Muradiye [Tur.] 24 Jc 39.00N 43.43 E
Murafa 16 Fe 48.13N 28.14 E
Murakami 28 Oe 38.14N 139.29 E
Murallón, Cerro- 52 Ij 49.48S 73.25W
Murāń 10 Qh 48.45N 20.02 E
Mur'ańyo 35 Ic 11.41N 50.27 E
Muraši 19 Ed 59.24N 48.59 E
Murat 21 Ff 38.52N 38.48 E
Murat 11 Ii 45.07N 2.52 E
Murat Dağı 23 Cb 38.55N 29.43 E
Muratlı [Tur.] 24 Ib 41.29N 41.41 E
Muratlı [Tur.] 15 Kh 41.10N 27.30 E
Murau 14 Ic 47.06N 14.10 E
Muravera 14 Dk 39.25N 9.34 E
Murayama 29 Gb 38.29N 140.23 E
Mürchen Khvort 24 Nf 33.06N 51.30 E
Murchison 62 Ed 41.48S 172.20 E
Murchison, Mount- [Austl.] 59 De 26.46S 116.25 E
Murchison, Mount- [N.Z.] 62 De 43.01S 171.17 E
Murchison River 57 Cg 27.50S 114.00 E
Murcia 6 Fh 37.59N 1.07W
Murcia [3] 13 Kg 38.00N 1.30W
Murcia 13 Kf 38.30N 1.45W
Mur-de-Barrez 11 Ij 44.51N 2.39 E
Murdo 45 Fe 43.53N 100.43W
Mürefte 15 Ki 40.40N 27.14 E
Muren 22 Me 49.38N 100.10 E
Mureş 5 If 46.15N 20.12 E
Mureş [2] 15 Hc 46.30N 24.40 E
Muret 11 Hk 43.28N 1.21 E
Murfreesboro 43 Jd 35.51N 86.23W
Murg 10 Eh 48.55N 8.10 E
Murgab 21 If 38.18N 61.12 E
Murgab [Tad.-U.S.S.R.] 19 Hh 38.10N 73.59 E
Murgab [Tur.-U.S.S.R.] 18 Df 37.32N 62.01 E
Murgaš 15 Eg 42.50N 23.40 E
Murgeni 15 Lc 46.12N 28.01 E
Murgon 59 Ke 26.15S 151.57 E
Muri 64p Cc 21.15S 159.43W
Muriaé 54 Jh 21.08S 42.22W
Murici 54 Ke 9.19S 35.56W
Muriege 36 Dd 9.53S 21.13 E
Murihiti 64n Ab 10.23S 161.02W
Murilo Atoll 57 Gd 8.40N 152.11 E
Mūrītāniyā = Mauritania (EN) [1] 31 Fg 20.00N 12.00W
Müritz 10 Ic 53.25N 12.43 E
Murkong Selek 25 Jc 27.44N 95.18 E
Murmansk 6 Jb 68.58N 33.05 E
Murmanskaja Oblast [3] 19 Db 68.00N 35.30 E
Murmaši 19 Db 68.49N 32.49 E
Murnau 10 Hi 47.41N 11.12 E
Muro 13 Pe 39.44N 3.03 E
Muro, Capo di- 11a Ab 41.44N 8.40 E
Muro Lucano 14 Jj 40.45N 15.29 E
Murom 6 Kd 55.34N 42.02 E
Muromcevo 19 Hd 56.23N 75.14 E
Muroran 22 Qe 42.18N 140.59 E
Muros 13 Cb 42.47N 9.02W
Muros y Noya, Ria de- 13 Db 42.45N 9.00W
Muroto 27 Ne 33.18N 134.09 E
Muroto Zaki 28 Mh 33.16N 134.10 E
Murowana Goślina 10 Nd 52.35N 17.01 E
Murphy [Id.-U.S.] 46 Ge 43.13N 116.33W
Murphy [N.C.-U.S.] 44 Eh 35.05N 84.01W
Murphysboro 45 Lh 37.46N 89.20W
Murrah al Kubrá, Al Buḥayrah al- 24 Eg 30.20N 32.23 E
Murray [Ky.-U.S.] 44 Cg 36.37N 88.19W
Murray [Ut.-U.S.] 46 Jf 40.40N 111.53W
Murray, Lake- [Pap.N.Gui.] 60 Ci 7.00S 141.30 E
Murray, Lake- [S.C.-U.S.] 44 Gh 34.04N 81.23W
Murray Bridge 59 Hg 35.07S 139.17 E
Murray Fracture zone (EN) 3 Lf 34.00N 135.00W
Murray Islands 59 Ia 9.55S 144.05 E
Murray Ridge (EN) 3 Gg 21.00N 61.50 E
Murray River 57 Eh 35.22S 139.22 E
Murraysburg 37 Cf 31.58S 23.47 E
Murro di Porco, Capo- 14 Jm 37.00N 15.20 E
Murrumbidgee River 57 Fh 34.43S 143.12 E
Murrupula 37 Fc 15.27S 38.47 E
Murska Sobota 14 Kd 46.40N 16.10 E
Murten/Morat 14 Bd 46.56N 7.08 E
Murter 14 Jg 43.47N 15.37 E
Murtle Lake 46 Fa 52.08N 119.38W
Murud, Gunong- 26 Gf 3.52N 115.30 E
Murupara 62 Gc 38.27S 176.42 E
Mururoa Atoll 57 Ng 21.52S 138.55W
Murwāra 25 Gd 23.51N 80.24 E
Murwillumbah 59 Ke 28.19S 153.24 E
Mürz 14 Jc 47.24N 15.17 E
Mürzzuschlag 14 Jc 47.36N 15.41 E
Muş 23 Fb 38.44N 41.30 E
Muša/Muša 7 Fh 56.24N 24.12 E
Mūša/Muša 7 Fh 56.24N 24.12 E
Mūsa, Jabal- = Sinai, Mount- (EN) 24 Eh 28.32N 33.59 E
Musa Ali 35 Gc 12.30N 42.27 E
Musāfi 24 Qk 25.18N 56.10 E
Musā'id 33 Ed 31.36N 25.03 E
Musala 5 Ig 42.11N 23.34 E
Musallam 24 Lg 31.53N 46.56 E
Musan 27 Mc 42.14N 129.13 E
Musandam Peninsula 24 Qi 26.18N 56.24 E
Musay'īd 24 Nj 25.00N 51.33 E
Musaymir 33 Hg 13.27N 44.37 E
Muscat (EN) = Masqaṭ 22 Hg 23.29N 58.33 E
Muscat and Oman (EN) → Oman (EN) [1] 22 Hg 21.00N 57.00 E
Muscatine 45 Kf 41.25N 91.03W
Musgrave 58 Ff 14.47S 143.30 E
Musgrave Ranges 57 Eg 26.10S 131.50 E
Mūshā 24 Di 27.07N 31.14 E
Mus-Haja, Gora- 21 Qc 62.35N 140.50 E
Mushāsh al 'Ashawī 24 Mj 24.12N 48.50 E
Mushāsh Ramlān 24 Mj 24.25N 49.15 E
Mushayrib, Ra's- 24 Nj 24.18N 51.44 E
Mushie 36 Cc 3.01S 16.54 E
Müsi 25 Ge 15.20N 80.06 E
Musi 21 Mj 2.20S 104.56 E
Mūsiān 24 Lf 32.28N 47.26 E
Musicians Seamounts (EN) 57 Kb 29.00N 162.00W
Muskegon 43 Jc 43.14N 86.16W
Muskegon Heights 44 Dd 43.12N 86.12W
Muskegon River 44 Dd 43.14N 86.20W
Muskö 8 He 59.00N 18.05 E
Muskogee 43 Hd 35.45N 95.22W
Muskoka, Lake- 44 Hc 45.00N 79.25W
Musoma 31 Ki 1.30S 33.48 E
Musone 14 Hg 43.28N 13.38 E
Mussatṭaḥah, Al Jazīrah al- 14 Em 37.11N 10.20 E
Mussau Island 60 Dh 1.25S 149.38 E
Musselkanaal, Stadskanaal- 12 Jb 52.56N 7.02 E
Musselshell River 43 Fb 47.21N 107.58W
Mussende 36 Ce 10.31S 16.02 E
Mussidan 11 Gi 45.02N 0.22 E
Mussòmeli 14 Hm 37.35N 13.45 E
Must 27 Fb 46.40N 92.40 E
Muṣṭafá, Ra's- 14 Fn 36.50N 11.07 E
Mustafakemalpaşa 24 Cb 40.02N 28.24 E
Mustahil 35 Gd 5.15N 44.44 E
Mustäng 25 Gc 29.11N 83.58 E
Mustang Draw 45 Fj 32.00N 101.40W
Mustang Island 45 Hm 28.00N 96.55W
Mustasaari/Korsholm 8 Ia 63.05N 21.43 E
Musters, Lago- 56 Gg 45.27S 69.13W
Mustique Island 50 Ff 12.39N 61.15W
Mustjala 8 Jf 58.25N 22.04 E
Mustla 7 Fg 58.14N 25.52 E
Mustvee 7 Gg 58.52N 26.59 E
Musu-dan 28 Jd 40.50N 129.43 E
Muswellbrook 59 Kf 32.16S 150.53 E
Muszyna 10 Qg 49.21N 20.54 E
Mut 24 Ed 36.39N 33.27 E
Müṭ 33 Ed 25.29N 28.59 E
Mütaf, Ra's al- 23 Hd 27.41N 51.27 E
Mutalau 64k Ba 18.56S 169.50W
Mutarara 31 Kj 17.27S 35.04 E
Mutatá 54 Cb 7.16N 76.32W
Mutawassiṭ, Al Baḥr al- = Mediterranean Sea (EN) 5 Hh 35.00N 20.00 E
Mutha 36 Gc 1.48S 38.26 E
Muting 26 Lh 7.23S 140.20 E
Mutis, Gunung- 26 Hh 9.34S 124.14 E
Mutoraj 20 Fd 61.20N 100.20 E
Mutsamudu 31 Lj 12.09S 44.25 E
Mutshatsha 36 De 10.39S 24.27 E
Mutsu 27 Pc 41.05N 140.55 E
Mutsu-Wan 28 Pd 41.10N 140.55 E
Muttaburra 59 Id 22.36S 144.33 E
Mutterstadt 12 Ke 49.27N 8.21 E
Mutton/Oiléan Coarach 9 Di 52.49N 9.31W
Mutton Bird Islands 62 Bg 47.15S 167.25 E
Mutuali 37 Fb 14.53S 37.00 E
Mutún 55 Dd 19.10S 57.54W
Mutunópolis 55 Ha 13.40S 49.15W
Mutusjärvi 7 Gb 69.31N 26.57 E
Muurame 8 Kb 62.08N 25.40 E
Mu Us Shamo = Ordos Desert (EN) 21 Mf 38.45N 109.10 E
Muxima 36 Bd 9.32S 13.57 E
Muyinga 36 Fc 2.51S 30.20 E
Muy Muy 49 Eg 12.46N 85.38W
Muzaffarābād 25 Eb 34.22N 73.28 E
Muzaffargarh 25 Eb 30.04N 71.12 E
Muzaffarnagar 25 Fc 29.28N 77.41 E
Muzaffarpur 25 Hc 26.07N 85.24 E
Muzambinho 55 Ie 21.22S 46.32W
Muzat He 27 Dc 41.15N 83.27 E
Muži 20 Bc 65.27N 64.40 E
Muzillac 11 Dg 47.33N 2.29W
Mužlja 15 Dd 45.21N 20.25 E
Muztag [China] 21 Kf 35.55N 80.20 E
Muztag [China] 21 Kf 36.25N 87.25 E
Muztagata 27 Cd 38.17N 75.07 E
Mvolo 35 Dd 6.03N 29.56 E
Mvomero 36 Gd 6.20S 37.25 E
Mvoung 36 Bb 0.04N 12.18 E
Mwadingusha 36 Ee 10.45S 27.15 E
Mwali 30 Lj 12.15S 43.45 E
Mwanza [3] 36 Fc 2.30S 32.30 E
Mwanza [Mwi.] 36 Ff 15.37S 34.31 E
Mwanza [Tan.] 31 Ki 2.31S 32.54 E
Mwanza [Zaire] 36 Ed 7.54S 26.45 E
Mwatate 36 Gc 3.30S 38.23 E
Mweelrea 9 Dh 53.38N 9.50W
Mweka 31 Ji 4.51S 21.34 E
Mwene Ditu 31 Ji 7.03S 23.27 E
Mwenga 36 Ec 3.02S 28.26 E
Mweru, Lake- 30 Ji 9.00S 28.45 E
Mweru Wantipa, Lake- 36 Ed 8.42S 29.46 E
Mwimbi 36 Fd 8.39S 31.40 E
Mwinilunga 36 De 11.44S 24.26 E
Mya 30 He 31.40N 5.15 E
Myaing 25 Id 21.37N 94.51 E
Myanaung 25 Je 18.17N 95.19 E
Myanmar-Nainggan-Daw → Burma [1] 22 Lg 22.00N 98.00 E
Myaungmya 25 Ie 16.36N 94.56 E
Mycenae (EN) = Mikinai 15 Fl 37.43N 22.45 E
Myebon 25 Id 20.03N 93.22 E
Myingyan 22 Lg 21.28N 95.23 E
Myinmoletkat Taung 25 Jf 13.28N 98.48 E
Myitta 25 Jf 14.10N 98.31 E
Myjava 10 Mh 48.33N 16.58 E
Myjzakjula/Mõisaküla 7 Fg 58.07N 25.10 E
Mykulkin, Mys- 17 Cc 67.48N 46.40 E
Mylius Erichsens Land 41 Jb 81.40N 24.00W
Myltkyinä 22 Lg 25.23N 97.24 E
Mymensingh 25 Id 24.45N 90.24 E
Mynämäki 7 Ef 60.40N 22.00 E
Mynaral 19 Hf 45.22N 73.39 E
Myōkō-Zan 29 Fc 36.52N 138.06 E
Mýrdalsjökull 7a Bc 63.40N 19.06W
Myre 7 Db 68.51N 15.05 E
Myrskylä/Mörskom 8 Kd 60.40N 25.51 E
Myrtle Beach 43 Le 33.42N 78.54W
Myrtle Point 46 Ce 43.04N 124.08W
Mysen 7 Cg 59.33N 11.20 E
Mysia 15 Kj 39.30N 28.00 E
Myśla 10 Kd 52.40N 14.29 E
Myślenice 10 Pg 49.51N 19.56 E
Myślibórz 10 Kd 52.55N 14.52 E
Mysore 22 Jh 12.18N 76.39 E
Mysore → Karnataka [3] 25 Ff 13.30N 76.00 E
Mys Saryč 16 Hg 44.23N 33.45 E
Myszków 10 Pf 50.36N 19.20 E
Myszyniec 10 Rc 53.24N 21.21 E
My Tho 22 Mh 10.21N 106.21 E
Mytišči 7 Ii 55.56N 37.46 E
Mývatn 7a Cb 65.36N 17.00W

Index Symbols

[1] Independent Nation
[2] State, Region
[3] District, County
[4] Municipality
[5] Colony, Dependency
Continent
Physical Region
Historical or Cultural Region
Mount, Mountain
Volcano
Hill
Mountains, Mountain Range
Hills, Escarpment
Plateau, Upland
Pass, Gap
Plain, Lowland
Delta
Salt Flat
Valley, Canyon
Crater, Cave
Karst Features
Depression
Polder
Desert, Dunes
Forest, Woods
Heath, Steppe
Oasis
Cape, Point
Coast, Beach
Cliff
Peninsula
Isthmus
Sandbank
Island
Atoll
Rock, Reef
Islands, Archipelago
Rocks, Reefs
Coral Reef
Well, Spring
Geyser
River, Stream
Waterfall Rapids
River Mouth, Estuary
Lake
Salt Lake
Intermittent Lake
Reservoir
Swamp, Pond
Canal
Glacier
Ice Shelf, Pack Ice
Ocean
Sea
Gulf, Bay
Strait, Fjord
Lagoon
Bank
Seamount
Tablemount
Ridge
Shelf
Basin
Escarpment, Sea Scarp
Fracture
Trench, Abyss
National Park, Reserve
Point of Interest
Recreation Site
Cave, Cavern
Historic Site
Ruins
Wall, Walls
Church, Abbey
Temple
Scientific Station
Airport
Port
Lighthouse
Mine
Tunnel
Dam, Bridge

Myzeqeja 15 Ci 41.01N 19.36 E
M'Zab 32 Hc 32.35N 3.20 E
Mže 10 Jg 49.46N 13.24 E
Mziha 36 Gd 5.54S 37.47 E
Mzimba 36 Fe 11.54S 33.36 E
Mzuzu 31 Kj 11.27S 33.55 E

N

Naab 10 Ig 49.01N 12.02 E
Naaldwijk 12 Gc 51.59N 4.12 E
Naalehu 65a Fd 19.04N 155.35W
Naantali/Nådendal 7 Ff 60.27N 22.02 E
Naarden 12 Hb 52.18N 5.10 E
Naas/An Nás 9 Gh 53.13N 6.39W
Nabadid 35 Gd 9.38N 43.29 E
Nabão 13 De 39.31N 8.21W
Nabari 29 Ed 34.37N 136.05 E
Naberera 36 Gc 4.12S 38.56 E
Naberežnyje Čelny 6 Ld 55.42N 52.19 E
Nabileque, Rio- 55 De 20.55S 57.49W
Nabire 58 Ee 3.22S 135.29 E
Nabī Shu'ayb, Jabal an- 21 Gh 15.17N 43.59 E
Nabq 24 Fh 28.04N 34.25 E
Nābul 31 Ie 36.27N 10.44 E
Nābul [3] 32 Jb 36.45N 10.45 E
Nābulus 24 Ff 32.13N 35.16 E
Nabusanke 36 Fb 0.01N 32.03 E
Nacala 37 Gb 14.33S 40.40 E
Nacala-a-Velha 31 Lj 14.33S 40.36 E
Nacaome 49 Dg 13.31N 87.30W
Nacaroa 37 Fb 14.23S 39.55 E
Nacereddine 13 Ph 36.08N 3.26 E
Nachikatsuura 29 Ed 33.39N 135.55 E
Nachingwea 36 Ge 10.23S 38.46 E
Nachi-San 29 De 33.42N 135.51 E
Náchod 10 Mf 50.26N 16.10 E
Nachuge 25 If 10.35N 92.28 E
Nachvak Fiord 42 Le 59.03N 63.45W
Nacka 7 Ee 59.18N 18.10 E
Ná Clocha Liatha/Greystones 9 Gh 53.09N 6.04W
Nacogdoches 45 Ik 31.36N 94.39W
Na Comaraigh/Comeragh Mountains 9 Fi 52.13N 7.35W
Nacori, Sierra- 48 Ec 29.50N 108.50W
Nacozari, Rio- 48 Ec 29.48N 109.42W
Nacozari de Garcia 47 Cb 30.24N 109.39W
Na Cruacha/Blue Stack 9 Eg 54.45N 8.06W
Na Cruacha Dubha/Macgillycuddy's Reeks 9 Di 52.00N 9.50W
Nacunday, Rio- 55 Eh 26.03S 54.45W
Nada → Danxian 27 Ih 19.38N 109.32 E
Nådendal/Naantali 7 Ff 60.27N 22.02 E
Nadiād 25 Ed 22.42N 72.52 E
Nădlac 15 Dc 46.10N 20.45 E
Nador [3] 32 Gb 35.00N 3.00W
Nador 32 Gb 35.11N 2.56W
Nádusa 15 Fi 40.38N 22.04 E
Nadvoicy 19 Dc 63.52N 34.20 E
Nadvornaja 16 De 48.38N 24.34 E
Nadym 22 Jc 65.35N 72.42 E
Naeba-San 29 Fc 36.51N 138.41 E
Nærbø 8 Af 58.40N 5.39 E
Næstved 7 Ci 55.14N 11.46 E
Nafada 34 Hc 11.06N 11.20 E
Näfels 14 Dc 47.06N 9.04 E
Naftah 14 Dn 36.57N 9.04 E
Naftan Rock 64b Bb 14.50N 145.32 E
Naft-e-Safid 24 Mg 31.40N 49.17 E
Naft-e-Shāh 24 Kf 33.59N 45.30 E
Naft Khāneh 24 Ke 34.02N 45.28 E
Nafūsah, Jabal- 30 Ie 31.50N 12.00 E
Nāg 25 Dc 27.24N 65.08 E
Naga 22 Oh 13.28N 123.39 E
Nāga, Kreb en- 32 Fe 24.00N 6.00W
Nagagami Lake 44 Ea 49.28N 85.02W
Nagagami River 45 Na 50.25N 84.20W
Nagahama [Jap.] 29 Ed 35.23N 136.16 E
Nagahama [Jap.] 29 Ce 33.36N 132.29 E
Nagai 29 Gb 38.06N 140.02 E
Nagai 40 Ge 55.11N 159.55W
Na Gaibhlte/Galty Mountains 9 Ei 52.23N 8.11W
Nāgāland [3] 25 Ic 26.30N 94.00 E
Nagano 22 Pf 36.39N 138.11 E
Nagano Ken [2] 28 Nf 36.10N 138.00 E
Nagano-Matsushiro 29 Fc 36.34N 138.10 E
Nagano-Shinonoi 29 Fc 36.35N 138.06 E
Nagaoka 27 Od 37.27N 138.51 E
Nāgappattinam 25 Ff 10.46N 79.50 E
Nagara-Gawa 29 Ed 35.02N 136.43 E
Nagarote 49 Dg 12.16N 86.34W
Nagarzê 27 Ff 28.59N 90.28 E
Nagasaki 22 Of 32.47N 129.56 E
Nagasaki-Hantō 29 Ae 32.40N 129.45 E
Nagasaki Ken [2] 28 Jh 33.00N 129.50 E
Naga-Shima 29 Ce 33.50N 132.05 E
Nagashima 29 Ed 34.12N 136.19 E
Nagashima 29 Be 32.10N 130.10 E
Naga-Shima-Kaikyō 29 Be 32.15N 130.10 E
Nagato 28 Kg 34.21N 131.10 E
Nagayo 29 Ae 32.50N 129.52 E
Nāgda 25 Fd 23.27N 75.25 E
Nāgercoil 25 Fg 8.10N 77.26 E
Naghora Point 60 Gj 10.50S 162.24 E
Nagichot 35 Ee 4.16N 33.34 E
Nagi-San 29 Dd 35.10N 134.10 E
Nagiso 29 Ed 35.36N 137.36 E
Nago 27 Mf 26.35N 128.01 E
Nagold 10 Eh 48.52N 8.42 E
Nagorno-Karabahskaja Avtonomnaja Oblast [3] 19 Eh 39.55N 46.45 E
Nagorny [R.S.F.S.R.] 20 He 55.45N 124.58 E
Nagorny [R.S.F.S.R.] 20 Md 63.10N 179.05 E
Nagorsk 7 Mg 59.21N 50.48 E
Nago-Wan 29b Ab 26.35N 127.55 E
Nagoya 22 Pf 35.10N 136.55 E
Nāgpur 22 Jg 21.09N 79.06 E
Nagqu 22 Lf 31.30N 92.00 E
Nag's Head 51c Ab 17.13N 62.38W
Nagua 49 Md 19.23N 69.50W
Naguabo 51a Cb 18.13N 65.44W
Nagyatád 10 Nj 46.13N 17.22 E
Nagybajom 10 Mj 46.23N 16.31 E
Nagyecsed 10 Si 47.52N 22.24 E
Nagyhalász 10 Rh 48.08N 21.46 E
Nagykálló 10 Ri 47.53N 21.51 E
Nagykanizsa 10 Mj 46.27N 16.59 E
Nagykáta 10 Pi 47.25N 19.45 E
Nagykőrös 10 Pi 47.02N 19.47 E
Nagykunság 10 Qj 46.55N 20.15 E
Nagy-Milic 10 Rh 48.35N 21.28 E
Naha 22 Og 26.13N 127.40 E
Nahanni Butte 42 Fd 61.04N 123.24W
Nahari 29 De 33.25N 134.01 E
Naharyya 24 Ff 33.00N 35.05 E
Nahāvand 23 Gc 34.12N 48.22 E
Nahe 10 Dg 49.58N 7.57 E
Nahičevan 6 Kh 39.13N 45.27 E
Nahičevanskaja ASSR [3] 19 Eh 39.15N 45.35 E
Na'hīmābād 24 Qg 30.51N 56.31 E
Nahodka 22 Pe 42.48N 132.52 E
Nahr al 'Āsī=Orontes (EN) 23 Eb 36.02N 35.58 E
Nahr Quassel 13 Oi 35.45N 2.46 E
Nahuala, Laguna- 48 Ji 16.50N 99.40W
Nahuel Huapi, Lago- 56 Ff 40.58S 71.30W
Nahunta 44 Gj 31.12N 81.59W
Naie 29a Bb 43.24N 141.52 E
Naiguatá, Pico- 54 Ea 10.33N 66.46W
Naila 10 Hf 50.19N 11.42 E
Naiman Qi (Daqin Tal) 27 Lc 42.49N 120.38 E
Nain 39 Md 57.00N 61.40W
Nā'īn 24 Of 32.52N 53.05 E
Na'īnābād 24 Pd 36.14N 54.39 E
Nairai 63d Bb 17.49S 179.24 E
Nairn 9 Jd 57.35N 3.53W
Nairobi 31 Kf 1.17S 36.49 E
Nairobi [3] 36 Gc 1.17S 36.50 E
Naissaar/Najssar 8 Ke 59.35N 24.25 E
Naitamba 63d Cb 17.01S 179.17W
Naizishan 28 Ic 43.41N 127.27 E
Najafābād 23 Hc 32.37N 51.21 E
Najd 23 Fe 25.00N 44.30 E
Najd 21 Gg 25.00N 44.30 E
Nájera 13 Jb 42.25N 2.44W
Najerilla 13 Jb 42.31N 2.42W
Naj' Ḥammādī 33 Fd 26.03N 32.15 E
Najībābād 25 Fc 29.58N 78.10 E
Najin 27 Nc 42.15N 130.18 E
Najō 29 Ec 35.47N 136.12 E
Najrān 33 Hf 17.30N 44.10 E
Najrān 33 Hf 17.30N 44.10 E
Najssar/Naissaar 8 Ke 59.35N 24.25 E
Najstenjarvi 7 He 62.18N 32.42 E
Naju 28 Ig 35.02N 126.43 E
Najzataš, Pereval- 18 If 37.52N 73.46 E
Nakadōri-Jima 28 Jh 32.58N 129.05 E
Nakagawa 29a Ca 44.47N 142.05 E
Naka-Gawa [Jap.] 29 Gc 36.20N 140.36 E
Naka-Gawa [Jap.] 29 De 33.56N 134.42 E
Nakagusuku-Wan 29b Ab 26.15N 127.50 E
Nakahechi 29 De 33.47N 135.29 E
Naka-Iō-Jima 60 Cc 24.47N 141.20 E
Naka-Jima 29 Ce 33.58N 132.37 E
Nakajō 28 Oe 38.03N 139.24 E
Naka-Koshiki-Jima 29 Af 31.48N 129.50 E
Nakalele Point 65a Eb 21.02N 156.35W
Nakama 29 Be 33.50N 130.43 E
Nakaminato 29 Gc 36.22N 140.36 E
Nakamura 28 Lh 32.59N 132.56 E
Nakanai Mountains 59 Ka 5.35S 151.10 E
Nakano 29 Fc 36.45N 138.22 E
Naka-no-Dake 29 Fc 37.04N 139.06 E
Nakanojō 29 Fc 36.35N 138.51 E
Naka-no-Shima 28 Lf 36.05N 133.04 E
Naka-no-Shima 27 Mf 29.50N 129.50 E
Nakasato 29a Bc 40.58N 140.26 E
Naka-satsunai 29a Cb 42.42N 143.08 E
Nakashibetsu 28 Rc 43.36N 145.00 E
Nakasongola 36 Fb 1.19N 32.28 E
Nakatonbetsu 29a Ca 44.58N 142.17 E
Nakatsu 28 Kh 33.34N 131.13 E
Nakatsugawa 28 Ng 35.29N 137.30 E
Nakfa 35 Fb 16.40N 38.30 E
Nakhon Pathom 25 Kf 13.49N 100.06 E
Nakhon Phanom 25 Mh 17.22N 104.46 E
Nakhon Ratchasima 22 Mh 14.57N 102.09 E
Nakhon Sawan 22 Mh 15.42N 100.06 E
Nakhon Si Thammarat 22 Li 8.26N 99.58 E
Nakijin 29b Ab 26.42N 127.59 E
Nakina 39 Kd 50.10N 86.42W
Nakkila 8 Ic 61.22N 22.00 E
Nakło nad Notecia 10 Nc 53.08N 17.35 E
Naknek 40 He 58.44N 157.02W
Nakonde 36 Fd 9.19S 32.46 E
Nakskov 7 Ci 54.50N 11.09 E
Näkten 8 Fb 62.50N 14.40 E
Naktong-gang 28 Jg 35.07N 128.57 E
Nakuru 31 Ki 0.20S 35.56 E
Nakusp 46 Ga 50.15N 117.48W
Näl 25 Dc 26.02N 65.29 E
Nalajch → Nalajha 27 Ib 47.45N 107.16 E
Nalajha (Nalajch) 27 Ib 47.45N 107.16 E
Nalčik 6 Kg 43.29N 43.37 E
Nallıhan 24 Db 40.11N 31.21 E
Nalón 13 Fa 43.32N 6.04W
Nālūt 31 Ie 31.52N 10.59 E
Nalwasha 36 Gc 0.43S 36.26 E
Na Machairi/Brandon Head 9 Ci 52.16N 10.15W
Namacurra 37 Fc 17.29S 37.01 E
Namai Bay 64a Bb 7.32N 134.39 E
Namak, Daryācheh-ye-= Namak Lake (EN) 21 Hf 34.45N 51.36 E
Namak Lake (EN)= Namak, Daryācheh-ye- 21 Hf 34.45N 51.36 E
Namakan Lake 45 Jb 48.27N 92.35W
Namak-e Mighān, Kavīr-e- 24 Me 34.13N 49.49 E
Namakia 37 Hc 15.56S 45.48 E
Namakwaland=Little Namamland (EN) 37 Be 29.00S 17.00 E
Namanga 36 Gc 2.33S 36.47 E
Namangan 22 Je 41.00N 71.40 E
Namanganskaja Oblast [3] 19 Hg 41.00N 71.20 E
Namanyere 36 Fd 7.31S 31.03 E
Namapa 37 Fb 13.43S 39.50 E
Namaqua Seamount (EN) 37 Af 31.30S 11.20 E
Namarrói 37 Fc 15.57S 36.51 E
Namasagali 36 Fb 1.01N 32.57 E
Namasale 36 Fb 1.30N 32.37 E
Namatanai 60 Eh 3.40S 152.27 E
Namathu 63d Bb 17.21S 179.26 E
Nambavatu 63d Bb 16.36S 178.55 E
Namber 26 Jg 1.04S 134.49 E
Nambour 59 Ke 26.38S 152.58 E
Nambouwalu 61 Ec 16.59S 178.42 E
Nam Can 25 Kg 8.46N 104.59 E
Namche Bazar 25 Hc 27.49N 86.43 E
Nam Co 21 Lf 30.45N 90.35 E
Namčy 20 Hd 62.35N 129.40 E
Namdalen 7 Cd 64.38N 12.35 E
Nam Dinh 22 Mg 20.25N 106.10 E
Nämdö 8 He 59.10N 18.40 E
Nam Du, Quan Dao- 25 Kg 9.42N 104.22 E
Naměche, Andenne- 12 Hd 50.28N 5.00 E
Namelakl Passage 64a Bc 7.24N 134.38 E
Namen/Namur 11 Kd 50.28N 4.52 E
Namerikawa 29 Ec 36.45N 137.20 E
Náměšt nad Oslavou 10 Mg 49.12N 16.09 E
Nametil 37 Fc 15.43S 39.21 E
Namib Desert/Namibwoestyn 30 Ik 23.00S 15.00 E
Namibia (South West Africa) 31 Ik 22.00S 17.00 E
Namibe 31 Ij 15.12S 12.10 E
Namibe 36 Bf 15.20S 12.30 E
Namie 28 Pf 37.29N 140.59 E
Namin 24 Mc 38.25N 48.30 E
Namioka 29 Ga 40.42N 140.35 E
Namiquipa 48 Fc 29.15N 107.40W
Namiranga 37 Gb 10.33S 40.30 E
Namjagbarwa Feng 21 Lg 29.38N 95.04 E
Namja La 27 Df 29.58N 82.34 E
Namkham 25 Jd 23.50N 97.41 E
Namlea 26 Ig 3.18S 127.06 E
Namling 27 Ef 29.44N 89.05 E
Namnoi, Khao- 25 Jf 10.36N 98.38 E
Namoi River 59 Je 30.00S 148.07 E
Namoluk Island 57 Gd 5.55N 153.08 E
Namonuito Atoll 57 Gd 8.46N 150.02 E
Namorik Atoll 57 Hd 5.36N 168.07 E
Namous 32 Gc 30.28N 0.14W
Nampa 43 Dc 43.34N 116.34W
Nampala 34 Db 15.17N 5.33W
Nam Phan=Cochin China (EN) 21 Mg 11.00N 107.00 E
Nam Phong 25 Ke 16.45N 102.52 E
Nampi 28 De 38.02N 116.42 E
Namp'o 28 Ge 38.44N 125.25 E
Nampula [3] 37 Fb 15.00S 39.30 E
Nampula 31 Kj 15.07S 39.15 E
Namsê Shankou 27 Df 29.58N 82.34 E
Namsos 6 Hc 64.30N 11.30 E
Namtu 25 Jd 23.05N 97.24 E
Namu 46 Ba 51.49N 127.52W
Namu Atoll 57 Hd 8.00N 168.10 E
Namuka-I-Lau 63d Cc 18.51S 178.38W
Namúli, Serra- 30 Kj 15.21S 37.00 E
Namuno 37 Fb 13.37S 38.48 E
Namur [3] 12 Gd 50.20N 4.50 E
Namur/Namen 11 Kd 50.28N 4.52 E
Namur-Saint Servais 12 Gd 50.28N 4.50 E
Namuruputh 36 Gb 4.34N 35.57 E
Namur-Wépion 12 Gd 50.25N 4.52 E
Namutoni 37 Bc 18.30S 17.55 E
Namwala 36 Ef 15.45S 26.26 E
Namwŏn 28 Ig 35.24N 127.23 E
Namysłów 10 Ne 51.05N 17.42 E
Nan 21 Mh 15.42N 100.09 E
Nan 25 Ke 18.48N 100.46 E
Nana 35 Bd 5.00N 15.50 E
Nana Barya 35 Bd 7.59N 17.43 E
Nanae 29a Bc 41.53N 140.41 E
Nanāimo 42 Fg 49.10N 123.56W
Nanakuli 65a Cb 21.23N 158.08W
Nana-Mambéré [3] 35 Bd 6.00N 16.00 E
Nanango 59 Ke 26.40S 152.00 E
Nanao 27 Od 37.03N 136.58 E
Nanao-Wan 29 Ec 37.10N 137.00 E
Nanatsu-Shima 29 Ec 37.35N 136.50 E
Nancha 27 Mb 47.08N 129.09 E
Nanchang 22 Ng 28.40N 115.58 E
Nancheng 27 Kf 27.32N 116.36 E
Nanchong 22 Mf 30.47N 106.03 E
Nancowry 25 Ig 7.59N 93.32 E
Nancy 6 Gf 48.41N 6.12 E
Nanda Devi 21 Jf 30.23N 79.59 E
Nandaime 49 Dh 11.46N 86.03W
Nandan [China] 27 Ig 24.59N 107.31 E
Nandan [Jap.] 28 Mg 34.15N 134.43 E
Nandaran → Qingyuan 28 Ce 38.46N 115.29 E
Nanded 22 Jh 19.09N 77.20 E
Nandewar Range 59 Kf 30.40S 151.10 E
Nandi 61 Ec 17.48S 177.25 E
Nandu Jiang 27 Jg 20.04N 110.22 E
Nanduri 63d Bb 16.27S 179.09 E
Nandyāl 25 Fe 15.29N 78.29 E
Nanfen 28 Gd 41.06N 123.45 E
Nanfeng 27 Kf 27.15N 116.30 E
Nanga-Eboko 34 He 4.41N 12.22 E
Nanga Parbat 21 Jf 35.15N 74.36 E
Nangapinoh 26 Fg 0.20S 111.44 E
Nangarhār [3] 23 Lc 34.15N 70.30 E
Nangatayap 26 Fg 1.32S 110.34 E
Nangis 11 If 48.33N 3.00 E
Nangnim-san 28 Id 40.21N 126.55 E
Nangnim-Sanmaek 28 Id 40.30N 127.00 E
Nangong 27 Kd 37.22N 115.23 E
Nangqên 27 Ge 32.15N 96.13 E
Nanguan 28 Af 36.42N 111.41 E
Nanguantao → Guantao 28 Cf 36.33N 115.18 E
Nangweshi 36 Df 16.26S 23.20 E
Nan Hai=South China Sea (EN) 21 Ni 10.00N 113.00 E
Nanhaoqian → Shangyi 28 Bd 41.06N 113.58 E
Nanhe 28 Cf 36.58N 114.41 E
Nanhua 27 Hf 25.16N 101.18 E
Nanhui 28 Fi 31.03N 121.46 E
Nan Hulsan Hu 27 Gd 36.45N 95.45 E
Nanjian 27 Hf 25.05N 100.32 E
Nanjiang 27 Ie 32.22N 106.45 E
Nanjing=Nanking (EN) 22 Nf 31.59N 118.51 E
Nankai Trough (EN) 27 Ne 32.00N 135.00 E
Nanking (EN)=Nanjing 22 Nf 31.59N 118.51 E
Nankoku 28 Lh 33.39N 133.44 E
Nanle 28 Cf 36.06N 115.12 E
Nanling 28 Ei 30.55N 118.19 E
Nan Ling 21 Ng 25.00N 112.00 E
Nanlou Shan 28 Ic 43.24N 126.40 E
Nanma → Yiyuan 28 Ef 36.11N 118.10 E
Nanning 22 Mg 22.50N 108.18 E
Nannup 59 Df 33.59S 115.45 E
Nanortalik 41 Hf 60.32N 45.45W
Nanpan Jiang 27 Ig 24.56N 106.12 E
Nānpāra 25 Gc 27.52N 81.30 E
Nanping [China] 22 Ng 26.42N 118.09 E
Nanping [China] 27 He 33.15N 104.13 E
Nanpu 28 Ee 39.16N 118.12 E
Nanqiao → Fengxian 28 Fi 30.55N 121.27 E
Nansei-Shotō=Ryukyu Islands (EN) 21 Og 26.30N 128.00 E
Nansen Cordillera (EN) 67 Ge 87.00N 90.00 E
Nansen Land 41 Hb 83.20N 46.00W
Nanshan Islands (EN)= Nansha Qundao 21 Ni 9.40N 113.30 E
Nansha Qundao= Nanshan Islands (EN) 21 Ni 9.40N 113.30 E
Nansio 36 Fc 2.08S 33.03 E
Nant 11 Jj 44.01N 3.18 E
Nantais, Lac- 42 Kd 61.00N 73.50W
Nanterre 11 If 48.54N 2.12 E
Nantes 6 Ff 47.13N 1.33W
Nantes à Brest, Can. de- 11 Bf 48.12N 4.06W
Nanteuil-le-Haudouin 12 Ee 49.08N 2.48 E
Nanticoke 44 Je 41.13N 76.00W
Nantō 29 Ed 34.17N 136.29 E
Nantong 27 Le 32.00N 120.52 E
Nantong (Jinsha) 28 Fh 32.06N 120.52 E
Nantou 27 Lg 23.54N 120.51 E
Nantua 11 Lh 46.09N 5.37 E
Nantucket 44 Le 41.17N 70.06W
Nantucket Island 43 Mc 41.16N 70.03W
Nantucket Sound 44 Le 41.30N 70.15W
Nanuku Passage 63d Cb 16.45S 179.15W
Nanuku Reef 63d Cb 16.40S 179.26W
Nanumanga Island 57 Ie 6.18S 176.20 E
Nanumea Atoll 57 Ie 5.43S 176.00 E
Nanuque 54 Jg 17.50S 40.21W
Nanusa, Pulau-Pulau- 26 If 4.42N 127.06 E
Nanwan Shuiku 28 Bh 32.02N 113.57 E
Nanwei Dao 27 Je 8.42N 111.40 E
Nanweng He 27 Ma 51.10N 125.59 E
Nanxian 28 Bj 29.22N 112.25 E
Nanxiang 28 Fi 31.18N 121.17 E
Nanxiong 27 Jf 25.13N 114.18 E
Nanxun 28 Fi 30.53N 120.26 E
Nanyandang Shan 27 Lf 27.37N 120.06 E
Nanyang 22 Nf 32.56N 112.32 E
Nanyang Hu 28 Dg 35.15N 116.39 E
Nanyō 28 Pe 38.03N 140.10 E
Nanyuki 31 Kh 0.01N 37.04 E
Nanzhang 27 Je 31.45N 111.53 E
Nanzhao 27 Je 33.28N 112.29 E
Nao, Cabo de la- 5 Gh 38.44N 0.14 E
Naococane, Lac- 42 Kf 52.50N 70.40W
Naoero/Nauru [1] 58 He 0.31S 166.56 E
Naoetsu 29 Fc 37.11N 138.14 E
Não-me-Toque 55 Fi 28.28S 52.49W
Naours, Souterrains de- 12 Ed 50.05N 2.17 E
Napa 46 Dg 38.18N 122.17W
Napanee 44 Ic 44.15N 76.57W
Napassoq 41 Ge 65.45N 52.38W
Napata 35 Eb 18.29N 31.51 E
Na-Peng 25 Lg 23.10N 98.26 E
Napf 14 Bc 47.01N 7.57 E
Napier 58 Ih 39.30S 176.54 E
Napier, Mount- 59 Fc 17.32S 129.10 E
Napier Mountains 66 Ee 66.30S 53.40 E
Naples [Fl.-U.S.] 43 Kf 26.08N 81.48W
Naples [Id.-U.S.] 46 Gb 48.34N 116.24W
Naples (EN) = Napoli 6 Hg 40.50N 14.15 E
Naples, Gulf of- (EN) = Napoli, Golfo di- 14 Ij 40.45N 14.10 E
Napo 27 Ig 23.25N 105.49 E
Napo, Rio- 52 If 3.20S 72.40W
Napoleon 45 Gc 46.30N 99.46W
Napoli = Naples (EN) 6 Hg 40.50N 14.15 E
Napoli, Golfo di- = Naples, Gulf of- (EN) 14 Ij 40.45N 14.10 E
Napostá 55 An 38.26S 62.15W
Napuka, Ile- 57 Mf 14.12S 141.15W
Naqa 35 Eb 16.16N 33.17 E
Naqadeh 23 Gb 36.57N 45.23 E
Naqsh-e-Rostam 24 Og 30.01N 52.50 E
Nar 9 Ni 52.45N 0.24 E
Nāra 25 Dc 24.07N 69.07 E
Nara [Jap.] 27 Oe 34.41N 135.50 E
Nara [Mali] 34 Db 15.11N 7.15W
Naračenskibani 15 Hh 41.54N 24.45 E
Naracoorte 59 Ig 36.58S 140.44 E
Nara-Ken [2] 28 Mg 34.20N 135.55 E
Naranjo 48 Ee 25.48N 108.31W
Naranjos [Bol.] 55 Cd 18.38S 59.09W
Naranjos [Mex.] 48 Kg 21.21N 97.41W
Narao 29 Ae 32.52N 129.04 E
Narathiwat 25 Kg 6.25N 101.48 E
Nārāyanganj 25 Id 23.37N 90.30 E
Narbonne 11 Ik 43.11N 3.00 E
Narca, Ponta da- 36 Bd 6.07S 12.16 E
Narcea 13 Fa 43.28N 6.06W
Narcondam 25 If 13.15N 94.30 E
Nardò 14 Mj 40.11N 18.02 E
Naré 55 Bj 30.58S 60.28W
Nares Land 41 Hb 82.25N 47.30W
Nares Strait 38 Lb 78.50N 73.00W
Narew 10 Td 52.55N 23.29 E
Narew 10 Qd 52.26N 20.42 E
Narian, Pointe- 63b Be 20.05S 164.00 E
Narin Gol 27 Fd 36.54N 92.51 E
Nariño [2] 54 Cc 1.30N 78.00W
Narita 29 Gd 35.47N 140.18 E
Narjan-Mar 6 Lb 67.39N 53.00 E
Närke 8 Ff 59.05N 15.05 E
Narlı 24 Gd 37.27N 37.09 E
Narmada 21 Jg 21.38N 72.36 E
Narman 24 Ib 40.21N 41.52 E
Nārnaul 25 Fc 28.03N 76.06 E
Narni 14 Gh 42.31N 12.31 E
Naroč 8 Lj 54.27N 26.45 E
Naroč 8 Lj 54.57N 26.49 E
Naroč, Ozero- 16 Eb 54.50N 26.45 E
Naroda 17 Jd 64.15N 61.00 E
Narodnaja, Gora- 5 Mb 65.04N 60.09 E
Naro-Fominsk 19 Dd 55.24N 36.43 E
Narok 36 Gc 1.05S 35.52 E
Narovlja 16 Fd 51.48N 29.31 E
Närpes/Närpio 8 Ib 62.28N 21.20 E
Närpio/Närpes 8 Ib 62.28N 21.20 E
Narrabri 59 Jf 30.19S 149.47 E
Narrandera 59 Jf 34.45S 146.33 E
Narrogin 59 Df 32.56S 117.10 E
Narromine 59 Jf 32.14S 148.15 E
Narrows, The- 51c Ab 17.12N 62.38W
Narryer, Mount- 59 De 26.30S 116.25 E
Narsimhapur 25 Fd 22.57N 79.12 E
Narssalik 41 Hf 61.42N 49.11W
Narssaq [Grld.] 41 Hf 61.00N 46.00W
Narssaq [Grld.] 41 Gf 64.00N 51.33W
Narssarssuaq 41 Hf 61.10N 45.15W
Narthákion 15 Fj 39.14N 22.22 E
Nartkala 16 Mh 43.32N 43.47 E
Narubis 37 Be 26.55S 18.35 E
Narugo 29 Gb 38.44N 140.43 E
Nāruja 15 Jd 45.50N 26.47 E
Naru-Shima 29 Ae 32.50N 128.56 E
Naruto 28 Mg 34.11N 134.37 E
Naruto-Kaikyō 29 Dd 34.15N 134.40 E
Narva 7 Gg 59.29N 28.02 E
Narva 6 Id 59.23N 28.11 E
Narva Jõesuu/Narva-Jyesuu 8 Me 59.21N 28.04 E
Narva-Jyesuu/Narva Jõesuu 8 Me 59.21N 28.04 E
Narva laht 7 Gg 59.30N 27.40 E
Narvik 6 Hb 68.26N 17.25 E
Narvski Zaliv 7 Gg 59.30N 27.40 E
Narvskoje Vodohranilišče 8 Me 59.10N 28.30 E
Narym 20 De 58.58N 81.40 E
Naryn 21 Je 40.54N 71.45 E
Naryn 22 Je 41.26N 75.59 E
Naryncol 19 Ig 42.43N 80.08 E
Narynskaja Oblast [3] 19 Hg 41.20N 75.40 E
Nås 7 Df 60.27N 14.29 E
Na Sailti/Saltee Islands 9 Gi 52.07N 6.36W
Näsåker 7 De 63.23N 16.54 E
Nasarawa 34 Gd 8.32N 7.43 E
Năsăud 15 Hb 47.17N 24.24 E
Nasawa 63b Db 15.12S 168.06 E
Na Sceiri/Skerries 9 Gh 53.35N 6.07W
Nāshik 22 Jg 20.05N 73.48 E
Nash Point 9 Jj 51.24N 3.27W
Nashtārud 24 Nd 36.45N 51.02 E
Nashua 44 Ld 42.44N 71.28W
Nashville [Ar.-U.S.] 45 Jj 33.57N 93.51W
Nashville [Ga.-U.S.] 44 Fj 31.12N 83.15W
Nashville [Il.-U.S.] 45 Lg 38.21N 89.23W
Nashville [In.-U.S.] 44 Df 39.12N 86.15W
Nashville [Tn.-U.S.] 39 Kf 36.09N 86.48W
Nashville Seamount (EN) 38 Nf 35.00N 57.20W
Našice 14 Me 45.30N 18.06 E
Nasielsk 10 Qd 52.36N 20.48 E
Näsijärvi 5 Ic 61.35N 23.40 E
Nāşir 35 Ed 8.36N 33.04 E
Naskaupi 42 Lf 53.47N 60.51W
Nasorolevu 63d Bb 16.38S 179.24 E
Naşr [Eg.] 24 Dg 30.36N 30.23 E
Naşr [Lib.] 33 Dd 28.59N 21.13 E
Naşrābād 24 Of 32.09N 52.08 E
Nass 42 Ee 55.00N 129.50W
Nassandres 12 Ce 49.07N 0.44 E
Nassandres-La Rivière Thibouville 12 Ce 49.07N 0.44 E
Nassau [Bah.] 39 Lg 25.05N 77.21W
Nassau [Ger.] 12 Jd 50.19N 7.48 E
Nassau, Bahia- 56 Gi 55.25S 67.40W
Nassau Island 57 Kf 11.33S 165.25W
Nassau River 59 Ic 15.58S 141.30 E
Nasser, Birkat-=Nasser, Lake-(EN) 30 Kf 22.40N 32.00 E

Index Symbols

[1] Independent Nation
[2] State, Region
[3] District, County
[4] Municipality
[5] Colony, Dependency
Continent
Physical Region
Historical or Cultural Region
Mount, Mountain
Volcano
Hill
Mountains, Mountain Range
Hills, Escarpment
Plateau, Upland
Pass, Gap
Plain, Lowland
Delta
Salt Flat
Valley, Canyon
Crater, Cave
Karst Features
Depression
Polder
Desert, Dunes
Forest, Woods
Heath, Steppe
Oasis
Cape, Point
Coast, Beach
Cliff
Peninsula
Isthmus
Sandbank
Island
Atoll
Rock, Reef
Islands, Archipelago
Rocks, Reefs
Coral Reef
Well, Spring
Geyser
River, Stream
Waterfall Rapids
River Mouth, Estuary
Lake
Salt Lake
Intermittent Lake
Reservoir
Swamp, Pond
Canal
Glacier
Ice Shelf, Pack Ice
Ocean
Sea
Gulf, Bay
Strait, Fjord
Lagoon
Bank
Seamount
Tablemount
Ridge
Shelf
Basin
Escarpment, Sea Scarp
Fracture
Trench, Abyss
National Park, Reserve
Point of Interest
Recreation Site
Cave, Cavern
Historic Site
Ruins
Wall, Walls
Church, Abbey
Temple
Scientific Station
Airport
Port
Lighthouse
Mine
Tunnel
Dam, Bridge

Nasser, Lake-(EN)=Nasser, Birkat- 30 Kf 22.40N 32.00 E
Nassian 34 Ed 9.24N 4.29W
Nässjö 7 Dh 57.39N 14.41 E
Nassogne 12 Hd 50.08N 5.21 E
Na Staighri Dubha/Blackstairs Mountains 9 Gi 52.33N 6.49W
Nastapoka Islands 42 Je 56.50N 76.50W
Nastätten 12 Jd 50.12N 7.52 E
Nastola 8 Kd 60.57N 25.56 E
Nasu 29 Gc 37.02N 140.06 E
Nasu-Dake 29 Fc 37.07N 139.58 E
Näsviken 8 Gc 61.45N 16.52 E
Natá 49 Gi 8.20N 80.31W
Nata 30 Jk 20.14S 26.10 E
Nata 37 Dd 20.13S 26.11 E
Natal [2] 37 Ee 29.00S 30.00 E
Natal [B.C.-Can.] 46 Hb 49.44N 114.50W
Natal [Braz.] 53 Mf 5.47S 35.13W
Natal [Indon.] 26 Cf 0.33N 99.07 E
Natal Basin (EN) 3 Fm 30.00S 40.00 E
Natanz 24 Nf 33.31N 51.54 E
Natashquan 42 Lf 50.09N 61.37W
Natashquan 42 Lf 50.11N 61.49W
Natchez 43 Ie 31.34N 91.23W
Natchitoches 43 Ie 31.46N 93.05W
Natewa Bay 63d Bb 16.35S 179.40 E
Nathorsts Land 41 Jd 72.20N 27.00W
Nathula 63d Ab 16.53S 177.25 E
Natitingou 31 Hg 10.19N 1.22 E
Natityāy, Jabal- 35 Fc 23.01N 34.22 E
Natividad, Isla- 48 Bd 27.55N 115.10W
Natividade 54 If 11.43S 47.47W
Natori 28 Pe 38.11N 140.58 E
Natron, Lake- 30 Ki 2.25S 36.00 E
Naṭrūn, Wādī an- 24 Dg 30.25N 30.13 E
Natsudomari-Zaki 29a Bc 41.00N 140.53 E
Nättarö 8 Hf 58.50N 18.10 E
Nättraby 8 Fh 56.12N 15.31 E
Natuna Besar, Pulau- 26 Ef 4.00N 108.15 E
Natuna Islands (EN)=Bunguran, Kepulauan- 21 Mi 2.45N 109.00 E
Naturaliste, Cape- 57 Ch 33.32S 115.01 E
Naturaliste Channel 59 Ce 25.25S 113.00 E
Naturita 45 Bg 38.14N 108.34W
Naturno / Naturns 14 Ed 46.39N 11.00 E
Naturns / Naturno 14 Ed 46.39N 11.00 E
Nau 18 Gd 40.09N 69.22 E
Nau, Cap de la-/Nao, Cabo de la- 5 Gh 38.44N 0.14 E
Naucelle 11 Ij 44.12N 2.21 E
Nauëji-Akmjane/Naujoji-Akmenė 7 Fh 56.21N 22.50 E
Naugo/Nauvo 8 Id 60.10N 21.50 E
Nauhcampatépetl→ Cofre de Perote, Cerro- 48 Kh 19.29N 97.08W
Nauja Bay 42 Kc 68.58N 75.00W
Naujamiestis/Naujamiestis 8 Ki 55.41N 24.09 E
Naujamiestis/Naujamiestis 8 Ki 55.41N 24.09 E
Naujoji-Akmenė/Nauëji-Akmjane 7 Fh 56.21N 22.50 E
Naukluft 37 Bd 24.10S 16.10 E
Naumburg [Ger.] 12 Lc 51.15N 9.10 E
Naumburg [Ger.] 10 He 51.09N 11.49 E
Nā'ūr 24 Fg 31.53N 35.50 E
Nauru 57 He 0.31S 166.56 E
Nauru/Naoero [1] 58 He 0.31S 166.56 E
Nauški 20 Ff 50.28N 106.07 E
Nausori 61 Ec 18.02S 178.32 E
Nauta 54 Dd 4.32S 73.33W
Nautanwa 25 Gc 27.26N 83.25 E
Nautla 48 Kg 20.13N 96.47W
Nauvo/Naugo 8 Id 60.10N 21.50 E
Nava 48 Ic 28.25N 100.45W
Navacerrada, Puerto de- 13 Id 40.47N 4.00W
Nava del Rey 13 Gc 41.20N 5.05W
Navahermosa 13 He 39.38N 4.28W
Navajo Mountain 46 Jh 37.02N 110.52W
Navajo Reservoir 45 Ch 36.55N 107.30W
Navalmoral de la Mata 13 Ge 39.54N 5.32W
Navan/An Uaimh 9 Gh 53.39N 6.41W
Navarin, Mys- 21 Tc 62.16N 179.10 E
Navarino, Isla- 52 Jk 55.05S 67.40W
Navarra [3] 13 Kb 42.45N 1.40W
Navarra=Navarre (EN) 13 Kb 43.00N 1.30W
Navarre (EN)=Navarra 13 Kb 43.00N 1.30W
Navarro 55 Cl 35.01S 59.16W
Navarro Mills Lake 45 Hk 31.56N 96.45W
Navašino 7 Ki 55.33N 42.12 E
Navasota 45 Hk 30.23N 96.05W
Navasota River 45 Hk 30.20N 96.09W
Navassa 47 Ie 18.24N 75.01W
Navaste Jõgi/Navesti 8 Kf 58.56N 24.58 E
Nävekvarn 8 Gf 58.38N 16.49 E
Naver 9 Ic 58.30N 4.15W
Navesti/Navaste Jõgi 8 Kf 58.56N 24.58 E
Navia 13 Fa 43.32N 6.43W
Navia 13 Fa 43.33N 6.44W
Navidad, Bahía de- 48 Gh 19.10N 104.45W
Navidad Bank (EN) 49 Mc 20.00N 68.50W
Naviti 63d Ab 17.07S 177.15 E
Navlja 16 Ic 52.42N 34.03 E
Navlja 19 De 52.50N 34.31 E
Năvodari 15 Le 44.19N 28.36 E
Navoi 19 Gg 40.10N 65.15 E
Navoja 47 Cc 27.06N 109.26W
Navolato 48 Fe 24.47N 107.42W
Navoloki 7 Jh 57.28N 41.59 E
Návpaktos 15 Ek 38.24N 21.50 E
Návplion 15 Fl 37.34N 22.48 E
Navrongo 34 Ec 10.54N 1.06W
Navsāri 25 Ed 20.55N 72.55 E
Navtilos 15 Gn 35.57N 23.13 E
Navua 63d Bc 18.13S 178.10 E
Navy Board Inlet 42 Jb 73.30N 81.00W
Nawa 24 Gf 32.53N 36.03 E
Nawābshāh 25 Dc 26.15N 68.25 E
Nawāşīf, Ḩarrat- 33 He 21.20N 42.10 E
Ṇaws, Ra's- 23 If 17.18N 55.16 E
Náxos 15 Il 37.06N 25.23 E
Naxos 14 Jm 37.49N 15.15 E
Náxos=Naxos (EN) 5 Ih 37.02N 25.35 E
Naxos (EN)=Náxos 5 Ih 37.02N 25.35 E
Nayarit [2] 47 Cd 22.00N 105.00W
Nayarit, Sierra- 47 Dd 22.00N 103.50W
Nayau 63d Cb 17.58S 179.03W
Nāy Band [Iran] 24 Oi 27.23N 52.38 E
Nāy Band [Iran] 24 Qf 32.20N 57.34 E
Nāy Band, Ra's-e- 24 Oi 27.23N 52.34 E
Nayoro 27 Pc 44.21N 142.28 E
Nazaré [Braz.] 54 Kf 13.02S 39.00W
Nazaré [Port.] 13 Ce 39.36N 9.04W
Nazareth (EN)=Naẓerat 24 Ff 32.42N 35.18 E
Nazarovo 20 Ee 56.01N 90.36 E
Nazas 48 Ge 25.14N 104.08W
Nazas, Río- 38 Ig 25.35N 105.00W
Nazca 53 Ig 14.50S 74.55W
Nazca Ridge (EN) 3 Nl 22.00S 82.00W
Naze 27 Mf 28.23N 129.30 E
Naẓerat=Nazareth (EN) 24 Ff 32.42N 35.18 E
Nazilli 23 Cb 37.55N 28.21 E
Nazimiye 24 Hc 39.11N 39.50 E
Nazimovo 20 Ee 59.30N 90.58 E
Nazino 20 Cd 60.15N 78.58 E
Nazlū 24 Kd 37.42N 45.16 E
Nazran 16 Nh 43.15N 44.46 E
Nazret 35 Fd 8.34N 39.18 E
Nazw'a 23 Ie 22.54N 57.31 E
Nazym 17 Nf 61.12N 68.57 E
Nazyvajevsk 19 Hd 55.34N 71.21 E
Nbâk 32 Ef 17.15N 14.59W
Nchanga 36 Ee 12.31S 27.52 E
Ncheu 36 Fe 14.49S 34.38 E
Ndala 36 Fc 4.46S 33.16 E
N'dalatando 36 Bd 9.18S 14.54 E
Ndali 34 Fd 9.51N 2.43 E
Ndélé 31 Jh 8.24N 20.39 E
Ndélélé 34 He 4.02N 14.56 E
Ndendé 36 Bc 2.23S 11.23 E
Ndindi 36 Bc 3.46S 11.09 E
N'Djamena (Fort-Lamy) 31 Ig 12.07N 15.03 E
Ndola 31 Jj 12.58S 28.38 E
Ndouana, Pointe- 63b Dc 16.35S 168.09 E
Ndrhamcha, Sebkha de- 32 Df 18.45N 15.48W
Nduindui 60 Fi 9.48S 159.58 E
Ndui Ndui 63b Cb 15.24S 167.46 E
Né 11 Fi 45.40N 0.23W
Nea 63c Ab 10.51S 165.47 E
Nea 7 Ce 63.13N 11.02 E
Néa Alikarnassós 15 In 35.20N 25.09 E
Néa Artáki 15 Gk 38.31N 23.38 E
Neagari 29 Ec 36.26N 136.26 E
Neagh, Lough-/Loch nEathach 5 Fe 54.38N 6.24W
Neagră, Marea-=Black Sea (EN) 5 Jg 43.00N 35.00 E
Neah Bay 46 Cb 48.22N 124.37W
Néa Ionia 15 Fj 39.23N 22.56 E
Neajlov 15 Je 44.11N 26.12 E
Neale, Lake- 59 Fd 24.20S 130.00 E
Neamṭ [2] 15 Jb 47.00N 26.20 E
Neápolis [Grc.] 15 In 35.15N 25.37 E
Neápolis [Grc.] 15 Ei 40.19N 21.23 E
Neápolis [Grc.] 15 Gm 36.31N 23.04 E
Near Islands 38 Bd 52.40N 173.30W
Neath 9 Jj 51.37N 3.50W
Neath 9 Jj 51.40N 3.48W
Néa Zíkhni 15 Gh 41.02N 23.50 E
Néba 63b Ae 20.09S 163.55 E
Nebaj 49 Bf 15.24N 91.08W
Nebbou 34 Ec 11.18N 1.53W
Nebit-Dag 22 Hf 39.30N 54.22 E
Neblina, Pico da- 52 Je 1.08N 66.10W
Nebo 59 Jd 21.40S 148.39 E
Nebo, Mount- 46 Jg 39.49N 111.46W
Nebolči 7 Hg 59.08N 33.21 E
Nebraska [2] 43 Gc 41.30N 100.00W
Nebraska City 43 Hc 40.41N 95.52W
Nebrodi (Caronie) 14 Im 37.55N 14.35 E
Necedah 45 Kd 44.02N 90.03W
Nechako 42 Ff 53.55N 122.44W
Nechako Reservoir 42 Ef 53.00N 126.10W
Nechar, Djebel- 13 Qi 35.52N 4.59 E
Neches River 45 Jl 29.55N 93.52W
Nechi 49 Jj 8.07N 74.46W
Nechí, Río- 49 Jj 8.08N 74.46W
Neckako Plateau 42 Ff 53.25N 124.40W
Neckar 10 Eg 49.31N 8.26 E
Neckarsulm 10 Fg 49.11N 9.14 E
Necker Island 57 Kb 23.35N 164.42W
Necochea 53 Ki 38.34S 58.45W
Necy 12 Bf 48.50N 0.07W
Nedeley 35 Bb 15.34N 18.10 E
Nederland 45 Jl 29.58N 93.59W
Nederland=Netherlands (EN) [1] 6 Ge 52.15N 5.30 E
Nederlandse Antillen [5] 50 Ec 18.06N 63.10W
Nederlandse Antillen = Netherlands Antilles (EN) [5] 53 Jd 12.15N 69.00W
Neder-Rijn = Lower Rhine (EN) 11 Mc 51.59N 6.20 E
Nêdong 22 Lg 29.14N 91.46 E
Nedstrand 8 Ae 59.21N 5.51 E
Nedstrandefjorden 8 Ae 59.20N 5.50 E
Neede 12 Ib 52.08N 6.37 E
Needham Market 12 Db 52.09N 1.02 E
Needham's Point 51q Ab 13.05N 59.36W
Needles 43 Ee 34.51N 114.37W
Neembucú [3] 55 Dh 27.00S 58.00W
Neenah 45 Ld 44.11N 88.28W
Neepawa 45 Ga 50.13N 99.29W
Neermoor, Moormerland- 12 Ja 53.18N 7.26 E
Neeroeteren, Maaseik- 12 Hc 51.05N 5.42 E
Neerpelt 12 Hc 51.13N 5.25 E
Nefasit 35 Fb 15.18N 39.04 E
Nefedova 19 Hd 58.48N 72.34 E
Né Finn/Nephin 9 Dg 54.01N 9.22W
Neftah 32 Ic 33.52N 7.53 E
Neftečala 16 Pj 39.19N 49.13 E
Neftegorsk [R.S.F.S.R.] 16 Kg 44.22N 39.42 E
Neftegorsk [R.S.F.S.R.] 20 Jf 53.00N 143.00 E
Neftegorsk [R.S.F.S.R.] 19 Fe 52.45N 51.13 E
Neftejugansk 19 Hc 61.05N 72.45 E
Neftekamsk 19 Fd 56.06N 54.17 E
Neftekumsk 19 Eg 44.43N 44.59 E
Neftjanyje Kamin 16 Qi 40.15N 50.49 E
Negage 36 Cd 7.46S 15.18 E
Negara 26 Fh 8.22S 114.37 E
Negele=Neghelle (EN) 31 Kh 5.20N 39.37 E
Negev Desert (EN)=Hänegev 24 Fg 30.30N 34.55 E
Neghelle (EN)=Negele 31 Kh 5.20N 39.37 E
Negla, Arroyo- 55 Df 22.52S 56.41W
Negola 36 Be 14.10S 14.30 E
Negomano 37 Fb 11.26S 38.33 E
Negombo 25 Fg 7.13N 79.50 E
Negonego Atoll 57 Mf 18.47S 141.48W
Negotin 15 Fe 44.13N 22.32 E
Negotino 15 Fh 41.29N 22.06 E
Negra, Cordillera- 54 Ce 9.25S 77.40W
Negra, Coxilha- 55 Ej 31.02S 55.45W
Negra, Peña- 13 Fb 42.11N 6.30W
Negra, Ponta- 55 Jf 23.21S 44.36W
Negra, Punta- 52 Hf 6.06S 81.10W
Negra, Serra- 55 Fc 16.30S 52.10W
Negra o de los Difuntos, Laguna- 55 Fl 34.03S 53.40W
Negreira 13 Db 42.54N 8.44W
Negreni 15 He 44.34N 24.36 E
Negreşti 15 Gb 47.52N 23.26 E
Negrine 32 Ic 34.29N 7.31 E
Negrinho, Rio- 55 Ed 19.20S 55.05W
Negro, Cabo- 13 Gi 35.41N 5.17W
Negro, Rio- [Arg.] 55 Ch 27.27S 58.54W
Negro, Rio- [Arg.] 52 Jj 41.02S 62.47W
Negro, Rio- [Bol.] 54 Ff 14.11S 63.07W
Negro, Rio- [Braz.] 54 Gg 19.13S 57.17W
Negro, Rio- [Braz.] 56 Jc 26.01S 50.30W
Negro, Rio- [Par.] 56 Ib 24.23S 57.11W
Negro, Rio- [S.Amer.] 52 Kf 3.08S 59.55W
Negro, Rio- [S.Amer.] 55 Ce 20.11S 58.10W
Negro, Rio- [Ur.] 55 Ki 33.24S 58.22W
Negros 21 Oi 10.00N 123.00 E
Negru, Riu- 15 Id 45.45N 25.46 E
Negru Vodă 15 Lf 43.49N 28.12 E
Nehajevski 16 Ld 50.27N 41.46 E
Nehalem River 46 Dd 45.40N 123.56W
Nehāvand 24 Me 35.56N 49.31 E
Nehe 27 Lb 48.28N 124.53 E
Nehoiu 15 Jd 45.26N 26.17 E
Néhoué, Baie de- 63b Be 20.21S 164.09 E
Neiba 49 Ld 18.28N 71.25W
Neiba, Bahía de- 49 Ld 18.15N 71.02W
Neidin/Kenmare 9 Dj 51.53N 9.35W
Neige, Crêt de la- 11 Lh 46.16N 5.56 E
Neiges, Piton des- 30 Mk 21.05S 55.29 E
Neijiang 22 Mg 29.38N 104.58 E
Neilton 46 Dc 47.25N 123.52W
Nei-meng-ku Tzu-chih-ch'ü→ Nei Monggol Zizhiqu [2] 27 Jc 44.00N 112.00 E
Nei Monggol Gaoyuan 21 Ne 42.00N 111.00 E
Nei Monggol Zizhiqu (Nei-meng-ku Tzu-chih-ch'ü)=Inner Mongolia (EN) [2] 27 Jc 44.00N 112.00 E
Neiqiu 28 Cf 37.17N 114.30 E
Neiva 53 Ie 2.56N 75.18W
Neja 19 Ed 58.19N 43.52 E
Nejanilini Lake 42 He 59.30N 97.50W
Nejdek 10 If 50.19N 12.44 E
Nejo 35 Fd 9.30N 35.32 E
Nejva 17 Kh 57.54N 62.18 E
Nekemt=Leqemt (EN) 31 Kh 9.05N 36.33 E
Neksø 8 Fi 55.04N 15.09 E
Nelemnoje 20 Kc 65.23N 151.08 E
Nelgese 20 Ic 66.40N 136.30 E
Nelichu 35 Ed 6.08N 34.25 E
Nelidovo 19 Dd 56.13N 32.50 E
Neligh 45 Ge 42.08N 98.02W
Neljaty 20 Ge 56.29N 115.50 E
Nelkan 20 Jd 64.15N 143.03 E
Nellore 22 Jh 12.56N 79.08 E
Nelma 20 Ig 47.40N 139.08 E
Nelson [2] 62 Ed 41.45S 172.30 E
Nelson 38 Jd 57.04N 92.30W
Nelson [B.C.-Can.] 42 Fg 49.29N 117.17W
Nelson [N.Z.] 58 Ii 41.16S 173.15 E
Nelson, Cape- [Austl.] 57 Fh 38.26S 141.33 E
Nelson, Cape- [Pap.N.Gui.] 59 Ja 9.00S 149.15 E
Nelson Island 40 Gd 60.35N 164.45W
Nelson's Dockyard 51d Bb 17.00N 61.46W
Nelspruit 31 Kk 25.30S 30.58 E
Néma 31 Gg 16.36N 7.15W
Néma, Dahr- 32 Ff 16.14N 7.30W
Neman 5 Id 55.18N 21.23 E
Neman 7 Fi 55.03N 22.01 E
Nembrala 26 Hi 10.53S 122.50 E
Nemda 7 Kh 57.31N 43.15 E
Neméa 15 Fl 37.49N 22.39 E
Neméa 15 Fl 37.49N 22.40 E
Nëmëçkes, Mali i- 15 Di 40.08N 20.24 E
Nemenčinė 8 Kj 54.50N 25.39 E
Nëmërçkes, Mali i- 15 Di 40.08N 20.24 E
Nemira, Virful- 15 Jc 46.15N 26.19 E
Nemirov [Ukr.-U.S.S.R.] 10 Tf 50.08N 23.28 E
Nemirov [Ukr.-U.S.S.R.] 16 Fe 48.59N 28.50 E
Némiscau 42 Jf 51.30N 77.00W
Nemjuga 7 Kd 65.29N 43.40 E
Nemours 11 If 48.16N 2.42 E
Nemunas 5 Id 55.18N 21.23 E
Nemunėlis 8 Kh 56.24N 24.10 E
Nemuro 27 Qc 43.20N 145.35 E
Nemuro-Hantō 29a Db 43.20N 145.35 E
Nemuro-Kaikyō=Nemuro Strait (EN) 20 Jh 43.50N 145.30 E
Nemuro Strait (EN)=Kunašírski Proliv 20 Jh 43.50N 145.30 E
Nemuro Strait (EN)=Nemuro-Kaikyō 20 Jh 43.50N 145.30 E
Nemuro-Wan 29a Db 43.25N 145.25 E
Nenagh/An tAonach 9 Ei 52.52N 8.12W
Nenana 40 Jd 64.30N 149.00W
Nenana 40 Jd 64.34N 149.07W
Nendo Island 57 Hf 10.40S 165.54 E
Nene 9 Ni 52.48N 0.13 E
Nenecki Nacionalny Okrug [3] 19 Fb 67.30N 54.00 E
Nenjiang 22 Oe 49.10N 125.12 E
Nen Jiang 21 Oe 45.26N 124.39 E
Neo 29 Ed 35.38N 136.37 E
Neodesha 45 Ih 37.25N 95.41W
Néon Karlovásion 15 Jl 37.47N 26.42 E
Neosho 45 Ih 36.52N 94.22W
Neosho River 45 Ih 35.48N 95.18W
Néouvielle, Massif de- 11 Gl 42.51N 0.07 E
Nepal [1] 22 Kg 28.00N 84.00 E
Nepalganj 25 Gc 28.03N 81.37 E
Nephi 43 Ed 39.43N 111.50W
Nephin/Né Finn 9 Dg 54.01N 9.22W
Nepisiguit River 44 Ob 47.37N 65.38W
Nepoko 30 Jh 1.40N 27.01 E
Nepomuk 10 Jg 49.29N 13.34 E
Ner 10 Od 52.10N 18.40 E
Nera [It.] 14 Gh 42.26N 12.24 E
Nera [Rom.] 15 Ee 44.49N 21.22 E
Nérac 11 Gj 44.08N 0.21 E
Neratovice 10 Kf 50.16N 14.31 E
Nerău 15 Dd 45.58N 20.34 E
Nerča 20 Gf 51.54N 116.30 E
Nerčinsk 20 Gf 51.58N 116.35 E
Nerčinski Zavod 20 Gf 51.17N 119.30 E
Nerehta 19 Ed 57.28N 40.34 E
Nereju 15 Jd 45.42N 26.43 E
Nereta 8 Kh 56.12N 25.24 E
Neretva 14 Lg 43.02N 17.27 E
Neretvanski kanal 14 Lg 43.03N 17.11 E
Nerica 17 Fd 65.20N 52.45 E
Neringa 7 Ei 55.24N 21.05 E
Neringa 7 Ei 55.18N 21.00 E
Neringa-Juodkrante/Neringa-Juodkrantė 8 Ii 55.35N 21.01 E
Neringa-Juodkrantė/Neringa-Juodkrante 8 Ii 55.35N 21.01 E
Neringa-Nida 8 Ii 55.18N 20.53 E
Neringa-Preila/Neringa-Prejla 8 Ii 55.20N 20.59 E
Neringa-Prejla/Neringa-Preila 8 Ii 55.20N 20.59 E
Neriquinha 36 Df 15.45S 21.33 E
Neris/Njaris 8 Kj 54.55N 25.45 E
Nerja 13 Ih 36.44N 3.52W
Nerjungri 20 He 56.40N 124.47 E
Nerl [R.S.F.S.R.] 7 Jh 56.11N 40.34 E
Nerl [R.S.F.S.R.] 7 Ih 57.07N 37.39 E
Nerpio 13 Jf 38.09N 2.18W
Nerussa 16 Hc 52.33N 33.47 E
Nerva 13 Fg 37.42N 6.32W
Nervi, Genova- 14 Df 44.23N 9.02 E
Nervión 13 Ja 43.14N 2.53W
Nes 8 Cd 60.34N 9.59 E
Nes, Ameland- 12 Ha 53.26N 5.48 E
Nesbyen 7 Bf 60.34N 9.06 E
Nesebăr 15 Kg 42.39N 27.44 E
Nesjøen 8 Db 63.00N 12.00 E
Neskaupstaður 7a Db 65.09N 13.42W
Nesle 12 Ee 49.46N 2.45 E
Nesna 7 Cc 66.12N 13.02 E
Ness City 45 Gg 38.27N 99.54W
Nesterov [R.S.F.S.R.] 7 Fi 54.42N 22.34 E
Nesterov [Ukr.-U.S.S.R.] 16 Cd 50.03N 24.00 E
Néstos 15 Hi 40.51N 24.44 E
Nesttun 8 Ad 60.19N 5.20 E
Nesvíž 16 Ec 53.13N 26.39 E
Netanya 24 Ff 32.20N 34.51 E
Netcong 44 Je 40.54N 74.43W
Nete 11 Kc 51.10N 4.15 E
Nethe 12 Lc 51.44N 9.23 E
Netherdale 59 Jd 21.08S 148.32 E
Netherlands (EN)=Nederland [1] 6 Ge 52.15N 5.30 E
Netherlands Antilles (EN)=Nederlandse Antillen [5] 53 Jd 12.15N 69.00W
Neto 14 Lk 39.12N 17.09 E
Netphen 12 Kd 50.55N 8.06 E
Nettebach 12 Jd 50.26N 7.28 E
Nettersheim 12 Id 50.30N 6.38 E
Nettetal 12 Ic 51.18N 6.12 E
Nettiling Lake 38 Lc 66.30N 70.40W
Nettuno 14 Gi 41.27N 12.39 E
Netzahualcóyotl, Presa- 48 Mi 17.00N 93.30W
Neubourg, Campagne du- 11 Ge 49.08N 1.00 E
Neubrandenburg 10 Jc 53.34N 13.16 E
Neuburg an der Donau 10 Hh 48.44N 11.11 E
Neuchâtel [2] 14 Ac 47.05N 6.50 E
Neuchâtel/Neuenburg 14 Ad 46.59N 6.56 E
Neuchâtel, Lac de- / Neuenburger See 14 Ad 46.55N 6.55 E
Neuenbürg 12 Kf 48.50N 8.35 E
Neuenburg/Neuchâtel 14 Ad 46.59N 6.56 E
Neuenburger See/Neuchâtel, Lac de- 14 Ad 46.55N 6.55 E
Neuenhaus 12 Ib 52.30N 6.58 E
Neuenkirchen 12 Jb 52.15N 7.22 E
Neuerburg 12 Id 50.01N 6.18 E
Neufchâteau [Bel.] 11 Le 49.51N 5.26 E
Neufchâteau [Fr.] 11 Lf 48.21N 5.42 E
Neufchâtel-en-Bray 11 He 49.44N 1.27 E
Neufchâtel-Hardelot 12 Dd 50.37N 1.38 E
Neufchâtel Hardelot-Hardelot Plage 12 Dd 50.38N 1.35 E
Neufchâtel-sur-Aisne 12 Ge 49.26N 4.02 E
Neuffossé, Canal de- 12 Ed 50.45N 2.15 E
Neuhaus am Rennweg 10 Hf 50.31N 11.09 E
Neuilly-en-Thelle 12 Ee 49.13N 2.17 E
Neuilly-Saint-Front 12 Fe 49.10N 3.16 E
Neu-Isenburg 12 Kd 50.03N 8.42 E
Neukirchen-Vluyn 12 Ic 51.27N 6.35 E
Neum 14 Lh 42.55N 17.38 E
Neumagen Dhron 12 Ie 49.51N 6.54 E
Neumarkter Sattel 14 Id 47.06N 14.22 E
Neumarkt in der Oberpfalz 10 Hg 49.17N 11.28 E
Neumünster 10 Fb 54.04N 9.59 E
Neunkirchen [Aus.] 14 Kc 47.43N 16.05 E
Neunkirchen [Ger.] 10 Dg 49.21N 7.11 E
Neunkirchen [Ger.] 12 Kd 50.48N 8.00 E
Neunkirchen [Ger.] 12 Jd 50.51N 7.20 E
Neuquén 53 Ji 39.00S 68.05W
Neuquén [2] 56 Ge 39.00S 70.00W
Neuquén, Río- 52 Ji 38.59S 68.00W
Neurupping 10 Id 52.56N 12.48 E
Neuse River 44 Ih 35.06N 76.30W
Neusiedl am See 14 Kc 47.56N 16.50 E
Neusiedler See (Fertő) 10 Mi 47.50N 16.45 E
Neuß 10 Ce 51.12N 6.42 E
Neustadt (Hessen) 12 Ld 50.51N 9.07 E
Neustadt am Rübenberge 10 Fd 52.30N 9.28 E
Neustadt an der Aisch 10 Gg 49.35N 10.36 E
Neustadt an der Orla 10 Hf 50.44N 11.45 E
Neustadt an der Weinstraße 10 Eg 49.21N 8.09 E
Neustadt bei Couburg 10 Hf 50.19N 11.07 E
Neustadt in Holstein 10 Gb 54.06N 10.49 E
Neustrelitz 10 Jc 53.22N 13.05 E
Neu-Ulm 10 Gh 48.24N 10.01 E
Neuville-les-Dieppe 12 De 49.55N 1.06 E
Neuville-sur-Saône 11 Ki 45.52N 4.51 E
Neuwerk 10 Ec 53.55N 8.30 E
Neuwied 10 Df 50.26N 7.28 E
Neva 5 Jd 59.55N 30.15 E
Nevada [2] 43 Dd 39.00N 117.00W
Nevada [Ia.-U.S.] 45 Je 42.01N 93.27W
Nevada [Mo.-U.S.] 43 Id 37.51N 94.22W
Nevada, Sierra- [Sp.] 5 Fh 37.05N 3.10W
Nevada, Sierra- [U.S.] 38 Hf 38.00N 119.15W
Nevada del Cocuy, Sierra- 52 Ie 6.10N 72.15W
Nevada de Santa Marta, Sierra- 52 Id 10.50N 73.40W
Nevado, Cerro- 52 Ie 3.59N 74.04W
Nevado de Ampato 52 Ig 15.50S 71.52W
Neve, Serra da- 30 Ij 13.52S 13.26 E
Nevel 19 Cd 56.02N 29.55 E
Nevele 12 Fc 51.02N 3.33 E
Nevelsk 20 Jg 46.37N 141.57 E
Neverkino 16 Oc 52.47N 46.48 E
Nevers 11 Jg 46.59N 3.10 E
Nevesinje 14 Mg 43.16N 18.07 E
Nevinnomyssk 19 Eg 44.38N 41.58 E
Nevis 47 Le 17.10N 62.34W
Nevis, Ben- 5 Fd 56.48N 5.01W
Nevis Peak 51c Ab 17.10N 62.34W
Nevjansk 19 Gd 57.32N 60.13 E
Nevşehir 23 Db 38.38N 34.43 E
Nevskoje 28 Lb 45.42N 133.40 E
Newala 36 Ge 10.56S 39.18 E
New Albany [In.-U.S.] 43 Jd 38.18N 85.49W
New Albany [Ms.-U.S.] 45 Li 34.29N 89.00W
New Alresford 12 Ac 51.05N 1.10W
New Amsterdam 53 Ke 6.17N 57.36W
Newark [De.-U.S.] 44 Jf 39.41N 75.45W
Newark [N.J.-U.S.] 43 Mc 40.44N 74.11W
Newark [N.Y.-U.S.] 44 Id 43.03N 77.06W
Newark [Oh.-U.S.] 44 Kc 40.03N 82.25W
Newark-on-Trent 9 Mh 53.05N 0.49W
New Bedford 43 Mc 41.38N 70.56W
New Bern 43 Ld 35.07N 77.03W
Newberry [Mi.-U.S.] 44 Eb 46.21N 85.30W
Newberry [S.C.-U.S.] 44 Gh 34.17N 81.37W
New Braunfels 43 Hf 29.42N 98.08W
New Britain 44 Ke 41.40N 72.47W
New Britain Island 57 Ge 5.40S 151.00 E
New Britain Trench (EN) 60 Ei 6.00S 153.00 E
New Brunswick 44 Je 40.29N 74.27W
New Brunswick [3] 42 Kg 46.30N 66.45W
New Buckenham 12 Db 52.28N 1.05 E
New Buffalo 44 De 41.47N 86.45W
Newburgh 43 Mc 41.30N 74.00W
Newbury 9 Lj 51.25N 1.20W
New Caledonia (EN) = Nouvelle-Calédonie [5] 58 Hg 21.30S 165.30 E
New Caledonia (EN)= Nouvelle-Calédonie 57 Hg 21.30S 165.30 E
New Caledonia Basin (EN) 3 Jm 30.00S 165.00 E
New Carlisle 44 Oa 48.01N 65.20W
New Castile (EN)=Castilla la Nueva 13 Id 40.00N 3.45W
New Castle [In.-U.S.] 44 Ef 39.55N 85.22W
New Castle [Pa.-U.S.] 43 Kc 41.00N 80.22W
Newcastle [Austl.] 58 Gh 32.56S 151.46 E
Newcastle [N.B.-Can.] 42 Kg 47.00N 65.34W
Newcastle [N.Ire.-U.K.] 9 Hg 54.12N 5.54W
Newcastle [S.Afr.] 37 De 27.49S 29.55 E
Newcastle [St.C.N.] 51c Ab 17.13N 62.34W
Newcastle/An Caisleán Nua 9 Hg 54.12N 5.54W
Newcastle Creek 59 Gc 17.20S 133.23 E
Newcastle-under-Lyme 9 Kh 53.00N 2.14W

Index Symbols

[1] Independent Nation
[2] State, Region
[3] District, County
[4] Municipality
[5] Colony, Dependency
Continent
Physical Region
Historical or Cultural Region
Mount, Mountain
Volcano
Hill
Mountains, Mountain Range
Hills, Escarpment
Plateau, Upland
Pass, Gap
Plain, Lowland
Delta
Salt Flat
Valley, Canyon
Crater, Cave
Karst Features
Depression
Polder
Desert, Dunes
Forest, Woods
Heath, Steppe
Oasis
Cape, Point
Coast, Beach
Cliff
Peninsula
Isthmus
Sandbank
Island
Atoll
Rock, Reef
Islands, Archipelago
Rocks, Reefs
Coral Reef
Well, Spring
Geyser
River, Stream
Waterfall Rapids
River Mouth, Estuary
Lake
Salt Lake
Intermittent Lake
Reservoir
Swamp, Pond
Canal
Glacier
Ice Shelf, Pack Ice
Ocean
Sea
Gulf, Bay
Strait, Fjord
Lagoon
Bank
Seamount
Tablemount
Ridge
Shelf
Basin
Escarpment, Sea Scarp
Fracture
Trench, Abyss
National Park, Reserve
Point of Interest
Recreation Site
Cave, Cavern
Historic Site
Ruins
Wall, Walls
Church, Abbey
Temple
Scientific Station
Airport
Port
Lighthouse
Mine
Tunnel
Dam, Bridge

Index Symbols

[1] Independent Nation
[2] State, Region
[3] District, County
[4] Municipality
[5] Colony, Dependency
Continent
Physical Region
Historical or Cultural Region
Mount, Mountain
Volcano
Hill
Mountains, Mountain Range
Hills, Escarpment
Plateau, Upland
Pass, Gap
Plain, Lowland
Delta
Salt Flat
Valley, Canyon
Crater, Cave
Karst Features
Depression
Polder
Desert, Dunes
Forest, Woods
Heath, Steppe
Oasis
Cape, Point
Coast, Beach
Cliff
Peninsula
Isthmus
Sandbank
Island
Atoll
Rock, Reef
Islands, Archipelago
Rocks, Reefs
Coral Reef
Well, Spring
Geyser
River, Stream
Waterfall Rapids
River Mouth, Estuary
Lake
Salt Lake
Intermittent Lake
Reservoir
Swamp, Pond
Canal
Glacier
Ice Shelf, Pack Ice
Ocean
Sea
Gulf, Bay
Strait, Fjord
Lagoon
Bank
Seamount
Tablemount
Ridge
Shelf
Basin
Escarpment, Sea Scarp
Fracture
Trench, Abyss
National Park, Reserve
Point of Interest
Recreation Site
Cave, Cavern
Historic Site
Ruins
Wall, Walls
Church, Abbey
Temple
Scientific Station
Airport
Port
Lighthouse
Mine
Tunnel
Dam, Bridge

Index Symbols

[1] Independent Nation
[2] State, Region
[3] District, County
[4] Municipality
[5] Colony, Dependency
Continent
Physical Region
Historical or Cultural Region
Mount, Mountain
Volcano
Hill
Mountains, Mountain Range
Hills, Escarpment
Plateau, Upland
Pass, Gap
Plain, Lowland
Delta
Salt Flat
Valley, Canyon
Crater, Cave
Karst Features
Depression
Polder
Desert, Dunes
Forest, Woods
Heath, Steppe
Oasis
Cape, Point
Coast, Beach
Cliff
Peninsula
Isthmus
Sandbank
Island
Atoll
Rock, Reef
Islands, Archipelago
Rocks, Reefs
Coral Reef
Well, Spring
Geyser
River, Stream
Waterfall Rapids
River Mouth, Estuary
Lake
Salt Lake
Intermittent Lake
Reservoir
Swamp, Pond
Canal
Glacier
Ice Shelf, Pack Ice
Ocean
Sea
Gulf, Bay
Strait, Fjord
Lagoon
Bank
Seamount
Tablemount
Ridge
Shelf
Basin
Escarpment, Sea Scarp
Fracture
Trench, Abyss
National Park, Reserve
Point of Interest
Recreation Site
Cave, Cavern
Historic Site
Ruins
Wall, Walls
Church, Abbey
Temple
Scientific Station
Airport
Port
Lighthouse
Mine
Tunnel
Dam, Bridge

Nouveau-Comptoir	42	Jf	52.35N	78.40W
Nouveau-Québec, Cratère du- = New Quebec Crater (EN)	42	Kd	61.30N	73.55W
Nouvelle-Calédonie = New Caledonia (EN) [5]	58	Hg	21.30S	165.30 E
Nouvelle-Calédonie=New Caledonia (EN)	57	Hg	21.30S	165.30 E
Nouvelle-France, Cap de -	42	Kd	62.33N	73.35W
Nouvelles Hébrides/New Hebrides	57	Hf	16.01S	167.01 E
Nouvion	12	Dd	50.12N	1.47 E
Nouzonville	11	Ke	49.49N	4.45 E
Novabad	18	He	39.01N	70.09 E
Nová Baňa	10	Oh	48.26N	18.39 E
Nová Bystřice	10	Lg	49.02N	15.06 E
Nova Cruz	54	Ke	6.28S	35.26W
Nova Esperança	55	Ff	23.08S	52.13W
Nova Friburgo	54	Jh	22.16S	42.32W
Nova Gaia	36	Ce	10.05S	17.32 E
Nova Gorica	14	He	45.57N	13.39 E
Nova Gradiška	14	Le	45.16N	17.23 E
Nova Granada	55	He	20.29S	49.19W
Nova Iguaçu	53	Lh	22.45S	43.27W
Nova Igirma	20	Fe	57.10N	103.55 E
Novaja-Ivanovka	15	Md	45.59N	29.04 E
Novaja Kahovka	16	Hf	46.43N	33.23 E
Novaja Kazanka	16	Pe	48.58N	49.37 E
Novaja Ladoga	7	Hf	60.05N	32.16 E
Novaja Ljalja	19	Gd	59.03N	60.36 E
Novaja Odessa	16	Gf	47.18N	31.47 E
Novaja Sibir, Ostrov-=New Siberia (EN)	21	Qb	75.00N	149.00 E
Novaja Vodolaga	16	Ie	49.45N	35.52 E
Novaja Zemlja=Novaya Zemlya (EN)	21	Hb	74.00N	57.00 E
Nova Lamego	34	Cc	12.17N	14.13W
Nova Lima	54	Jh	19.59S	43.51W
Nova Londrina	55	Ff	22.45S	53.00W
Nova Mambone	37	Fd	20.58S	35.00 E
Nova Olinda do Norte	54	Gd	3.45S	59.03W
Nová Paka	10	Lf	50.29N	15.31 E
Nova Prata	55	Gi	28.47S	51.36W
Novara	14	Ce	45.28N	8.38 E
Nova Roma	55	Ia	13.51S	46.57W
Nova Russas	54	Jd	4.42S	40.34W
Nova Scotia [3]	42	Lh	45.00N	63.00W
Nova Scotia	38	Me	45.00N	63.00W
Nova Sintra	32	Cf	14.54N	24.40W
Nova Sofala	37	Ed	20.10S	34.44 E
Novato	46	Dg	38.06N	122.34W
Nova Varoš	15	Cf	43.28N	19.49 E
Nova Venécia	54	Jg	18.43S	40.24W
Novaya Zemlya (EN)= Novaja Zemlja	21	Hb	74.00N	57.00 E
Nova Zagora	15	Jg	42.29N	26.01 E
Novelda	13	Lf	38.23N	0.46W
Novellara	14	Ef	44.51N	10.44 E
Nové Mesto nad Váhom	10	Nh	48.46N	17.50 E
Nové Zámky	10	Oi	47.59N	18.11 E
Novgorod	6	Jd	58.31N	31.17 E
Novgorodka	8	Mg	57.00N	28.37 E
Novgorod-Severskij	16	De	52.01N	33.16 E
Novgorodskaja Oblast [3]	19	Dd	58.20N	32.40 E
Novi Bečej	15	Dd	45.36N	20.08 E
Novigrad [Yugo.]	14	He	45.19N	13.34 E
Novigrad [Yugo.]	14	Jf	44.11N	15.33 E
Novi Kričim	15	Hg	42.03N	24.28 E
Novi Ligure	14	Cf	44.46N	8.47 E
Novillero	48	Gf	22.21N	105.39W
Novion-Porcien	12	Ge	49.36N	4.25 E
Novi Pazar [Bul.]	15	Kf	43.21N	27.12 E
Novi Pazar [Yugo.]	15	Df	43.08N	20.31 E
Novi Sad	6	Hf	45.15N	19.50 E
Novi Travnik	14	Lf	44.10N	17.39 E
Novi Vinodolski	14	Ie	45.08N	14.47 E
Novoaleksandrovsk	16	Lg	45.24N	41.14 E
Novoaleksejevka [Kaz.-U.S.S.R.]	16	Sd	50.08N	55.42 E
Novoaleksejevka [Ukr.-U.S.S.R.]	16	If	46.16N	34.39 E
Novoaltajsk	20	Df	53.24N	83.58 E
Novoanninskij	19	Ee	50.31N	42.45 E
Novoarhangelsk	16	Ge	48.39N	30.50 E
Novo Aripuanã	54	Fe	5.08S	60.22W
Novoazovsk	16	Kf	47.05N	38.05 E
Novobirjusinskij	20	Ee	56.58N	97.55 E
Novobogdanovka	16	If	47.05N	35.18 E
Novočeboksarsk	7	Lh	56.08N	47.29 E
Novočeremšansk	7	Mi	54.23N	50.10 E
Novočerkassk	19	Ef	47.25N	40.03 E
Novodevičje	7	Lj	53.35N	48.51 E
Novograd-Volynskij	19	Ce	50.36N	27.36 E
Novogrudok	16	Dc	53.37N	25.50 E
Nôvo Hamburgo	56	Jc	29.41S	51.08W
Novohopërsk	16	Ld	51.06N	41.37 E
Novo Horizonte	55	He	21.28S	49.13W
Novoizborsk	8	Mg	57.43N	28.05 E
Novojenisejsk	20	Ee	58.19N	92.27 E
Novojerudinskij	20	Ee	59.47N	93.30 E
Novokačalinsk	20	Ig	45.05N	131.59 E
Novokazalinsk	22	Ie	45.50N	62.10 E
Novokubansk	16	Lg	45.06N	41.01 E
Novokujbyševsk	19	Ee	53.08N	49.58 E
Novokuzneck	22	Kd	53.45N	87.06 E
Novolazarevskaja	66	Cf	70.46S	11.50 E
Novolukoml	7	Gi	54.38N	29.07 E
Novo Mesto	14	Je	45.48N	15.10 E
Novomičurinsk	7	Ji	54.02N	39.48 E
Novomihajlovka	20	Ih	44.17N	133.50 E
Novo Miloševo	15	Dd	45.43N	20.18 E
Novomirgorod	16	Ge	48.45N	31.39 E
Novomoskovsk [R.S.F.S.R.]	6	Je	54.05N	38.13 E
Novomoskovsk [Ukr.-U.S.S.R.]	19	Df	48.37N	35.16 E
Novonikolajevskij	16	Md	50.55N	42.24 E
Novoorsk	19	Fe	51.24N	58.59 E
Novopokrovskaja	16	Lg	45.56N	40.42 E
Novopolock	19	Cd	55.31N	28.40 E
Novorossijsk	6	Jg	44.45N	37.45 E
Novorybnaja	20	Fb	72.50N	105.45 E
Novoržev	19	Cd	57.02N	29.20 E
Novo-Šahtinsk	19	Df	47.47N	39.54 E
Novoselica	15	Ja	48.13N	26.17 E
Novoselje	8	Mf	58.05N	29.00 E
Novoselki	10	Ud	52.04N	24.25 E
Novoselovo	20	Ef	54.55N	91.00 E
Novosergijevka	19	Fe	52.03N	53.39 E
Novosibirsk	22	Kd	55.02N	82.55 E
Novosibirskaja Oblast [3]	20	Ce	55.30N	80.00 E
Novosibirskije Ostrova= New Siberian Islands (EN)	21	Qb	75.00N	142.00 E
Novosibirskoje Vodohranilišče	20	Df	54.40N	82.35 E
Novosil	16	Jc	52.59N	37.01 E
Novosineglazovski	17	Ji	55.05N	61.25 E
Novosokolniki	19	Dd	56.19N	30.12 E
Novospasskoje	7	Lj	53.09N	47.44 E
Novotroick	19	Fe	51.12N	58.35 E
Novotroickoje	19	Hg	43.39N	73.45 E
Novoukrainka	16	Ge	48.19N	31.32 E
Novouljanovsk	7	Li	54.10N	48.23 E
Novouzensk	19	Ee	50.29N	48.08 E
Novovjatsk	7	Lg	58.31N	49.43 E
Novovolynsk	19	Ce	50.46N	24.09 E
Novovoronežski	16	Kd	51.17N	39.16 E
Novozybkov	19	De	52.32N	32.00 E
Novska	14	Ke	45.20N	16.59 E
Novy Bug	16	Hf	47.43N	32.29 E
Nový Bydžov	10	Lf	50.15N	15.29 E
Novy Jaričev	10	Ug	49.50N	24.21 E
Novyje Aneny	15	Mc	46.53N	29.13 E
Novyje Burasy	16	Oc	52.06N	46.06 E
Nový Jičín	10	Og	49.36N	18.01 E
Novy Oskol	16	Jd	50.43N	37.54 E
Novy Pogost	8	Li	55.30N	27.32 E
Novy Port	22	Jc	67.40N	72.52 E
Novy Tap	17	Mh	56.55N	67.15 E
Novy Terek	16	Oh	43.37N	47.25 E
Novy Uzen	19	Fg	43.19N	52.55 E
Novy Vasjugan	20	Ce	58.34N	76.29 E
Novy Zaj	7	Mi	55.17N	52.02 E
Nowa Dęba	10	Rf	50.26N	21.46 E
Nowa Huta, Kraków-	10	Qf	50.04N	20.05 E
Nowa Ruda	10	Mf	50.35N	16.31 E
Nowa Sarzyna	10	Sf	50.23N	22.22 E
Nowa Sól	10	Le	51.48N	15.44 E
Now Bandegān	24	Oh	28.52N	53.53 E
Nowbarān	24	Me	35.08N	49.42 E
Nowdesheh	24	Le	35.11N	46.15 E
Nowe	10	Oc	53.40N	18.43 E
Nowe Miasto Lubawskie	10	Pc	53.27N	19.35 E
Nowe Miasto-nad-Pilicą	10	Qe	51.38N	20.35 E
Nowe Warpno	10	Kc	53.44N	14.20 E
Nowfel low Shātow	24	Ne	34.27N	50.55 E
Nowgong	25	Ic	26.21N	92.40 E
Nowogard	10	Lc	53.40N	15.08 E
Nowogród	10	Rc	53.15N	21.53 E
Nowood River	46	Ld	44.17N	107.58W
Nowra	59	Kf	34.53S	150.36 E
Nowshahr	24	Nd	36.39N	51.31 E
Nowy Dwór Gdański	10	Pb	54.13N	19.06 E
Nowy Dwór Mazowiecki	10	Qd	52.26N	20.43 E
Nowy Korczyn	10	Qf	50.20N	20.50 E
Nowy Sącz [2]	10	Qg	49.40N	20.40 E
Nowy Sącz	10	Qg	49.38N	20.42 E
Nowy Targ	10	Qg	49.29N	20.02 E
Nowy Tomyśl	10	Md	52.20N	16.07 E
Noya	13	Db	42.47N	8.53W
Noya/Anoia	13	Nc	41.28N	1.56 E
Noyant	11	Gg	47.31N	0.08 E
Noyon	11	Ie	49.35N	3.00 E
Nozaki-Jima	29	Ae	33.11N	129.08 E
Nozay	11	Eg	47.34N	1.38W
Nsanje	36	Gf	16.55S	35.16 E
Nsawan	34	Ed	5.48N	0.21W
Nschodnia	10	Rf	50.30N	21.18 E
Nsefu	36	Fe	13.03S	32.07 E
Nsukka	34	Gd	6.52N	7.23 E
Ntadembele	36	Cc	2.11S	17.08 E
Ntchisi	36	Fe	13.22S	34.00 E
Ntem	30	Hh	2.10N	9.57 E
Ntoum	36	Ab	0.22N	9.47 E
Ntui	34	He	4.27N	11.38 E
Ntusi	36	Fb	0.03N	31.13 E
Nuageuses, Iles-	30	Nm	48.40S	68.58 E
Nuanetsi	30	Kk	22.40S	31.49 E
Nūbah, Jibāl an-	30	Kg	12.00N	30.45 E
Nubian Desert (EN)= Nūbiyah, Aş Şahrā' an-	30	Kf	20.30N	33.00 E
Nūbiyah, Aş Şahrā' an-= Nubian Desert (EN)	30	Kf	20.30N	33.00 E
Nudha	63a	Ec	9.32S	160.48 E
Nueces Plain	43	Hf	28.30N	99.15W
Nueces River	43	Hf	27.50N	97.30W
Nueltin Lake	38	Jc	60.50N	99.30W
Nü'er He	28	Fd	41.06N	121.09 E
Nueva Asunción [3]	55	Be	21.00S	60.20W
Nueva Ciudad Guerrero	48	Jd	26.35N	99.15W
Nueva Esparta [2]	54	Fa	11.00N	64.00W
Nueva Germania	55	Df	23.54S	56.34W
Nueva Gerona	47	Hd	21.53N	82.48W
Nueva Imperial	56	Fe	38.44S	72.57W
Nueva Italia de Ruiz	48	Hh	19.01N	102.06W
Nueva Ocotepeque	49	Cf	14.24N	89.13W
Nueva Palmira	55	Ck	33.53S	58.25W
Nueva Rosita	39	Ig	27.57N	101.13W
Nueva San Salvador	47	Gf	13.41N	89.17W
Nueva Segovia [3]	49	Dg	13.40N	86.10W
Nueve de Julio	56	He	35.27S	60.52W
Nuevitas	47	Id	21.33N	77.16W
Nuevitas, Bahía de-	49	Ic	21.30N	77.12W
Nuevo, Cayo-	48	Mg	21.51N	92.05W
Nuevo, Golfo-	52	Jj	42.42S	64.36W
Nuevo Berlín	55	Ck	32.59S	58.03W
Nuevo Casas Grandes	39	If	30.25N	107.55W
Nuevo Laredo	39	Jg	27.30N	99.31W
Nuevo León [2]	47	Ec	25.40N	100.00W
Nuevo Mundo, Cerro-	54	Eh	21.55S	66.53W
Nuevo Rocafuerte	54	Cd	0.56S	75.25W
Nugaal [3]	35	Hd	8.30N	48.00 E
Nugālēd, Dēh-	30	Lh	7.58N	49.51 E
Nugālēd, Dōho-	35	Hd	8.35N	48.35 E
Nūgātsiaq	41	Gd	71.39N	53.45W
Nugget Point	62	Cg	46.27S	169.49 E
Nûgssuaq	41	Gd	70.30N	51.30W
Nuguria Islands	57	Ge	3.20S	154.45 E
Nuguš	17	Gj	53.05N	56.00 E
Nuhaka	62	Gc	39.02S	177.45 E
Nui Atoll	57	Ie	7.15S	177.10 E
Nuijama	8	Md	60.58N	28.32 E
Nuiqsut	40	Ib	70.20N	151.00W
Nu Jang	21	Lh	16.31N	97.37 E
Nûk/Godthåb	67	Nc	64.15N	51.40W
Nukapu	63c	Ab	10.07S	165.59 E
Nukey Bluff	59	Hf	32.35S	135.40 E
Nukhayb	23	Fc	32.02N	42.15 E
Nukhaylak	31	Jg	19.08N	26.20 E
Nukiki	63a	Cb	6.45S	156.29 E
Nukuaéta	64h	Ac	13.22S	176.11W
Nuku'alofa	58	Jg	21.08S	175.12W
Nukufetau Atoll	57	Ie	8.00S	178.22 E
Nukufotu	64h	Bb	13.11S	176.10W
Nukuhifala	64h	Bb	13.17S	176.05W
Nukuhione	64h	Bb	13.16S	176.06W
Nuku Hiva, Ile-	57	Me	8.54S	140.06W
Nukulaelae Atoll	57	Ie	9.23S	179.52 E
Nukuloa	64h	Bb	13.11S	176.09W
Nukumanu Islands	57	Ge	4.30S	159.30 E
Nukumbasanga	63d	Cb	16.18S	179.15W
Nukunonu Atoll	57	Je	9.10S	171.53W
Nukuoro Atoll	57	Gd	3.51N	154.58 E
Nukus	22	He	42.50N	59.29 E
Nukutapu	64h	Bb	13.13S	176.08W
Nukuteatea	64h	Bb	13.12S	176.08W
Nulato	40	Hd	64.43N	158.06W
Nules	13	Le	39.51N	0.09W
Nullagine	58	Dg	21.53S	120.06 E
Nullagine River	59	Ed	20.43S	120.33 E
Nullarbor	59	Gf	31.26S	130.55 E
Nullarbor Plain	57	Dh	31.00S	129.00 E
Nulu'erhu Shan	27	Kc	41.40N	119.50 E
Numakawa	29a	Ba	45.15N	141.51 E
Numan	34	Hd	9.28N	12.02 E
Numancia [Phil.]	26	Ie	9.52N	125.58 E
Numancia [Sp.]	13	Jc	41.47N	2.30W
Numanohata	29a	Bb	42.40N	141.41 E
Numata [Jap.]	29a	Bb	43.49N	141.55 E
Numata [Jap.]	28	Of	36.38N	139.03 E
Numatinna	35	Dd	7.14N	27.37 E
Numazu	28	Og	35.06N	138.52 E
Nümbrecht	12	Jd	50.54N	7.33 E
Numedal	7	Bf	60.05N	9.05 E
Numena	36	Ee	11.46S	26.31 E
Número Cinco, Canal-	55	Cm	37.14S	58.06W
Número Doce, Canal-	55	Cm	36.30S	59.08W
Número Dos, Canal-	55	Cm	36.51S	58.03W
Número Nueve, Canal-	55	Cm	36.08S	58.36W
Número Once, Canal-	55	Bm	36.28S	60.01W
Número Quince, Canal-	55	Dl	35.55S	57.45W
Número Uno, Canal-	55	Cm	36.40S	58.35W
Numfoor, Pulau-	26	Jg	1.03S	134.54 E
Nuneaton	9	Li	52.32N	1.28W
Nungarin	59	Df	31.11S	118.06 E
Nungnain Sum	27	Kb	45.45N	118.56 E
Nungo	37	Fb	13.25S	37.46 E
Nunivak	38	Cd	60.00N	166.30W
Nunkirchen, Wadern-	12	Ie	49.32N	6.53 E
Nunn	45	Df	40.45N	104.46W
Nunspeet	12	Hb	52.22N	5.46 E
Nunukan Timur, Pulau-	26	Gf	4.05N	117.40 E
Nuomin He	27	Lb	48.21N	124.32 E
Nuorgam	7	Ga	70.05N	27.51 E
Nuoro	6	Gg	40.19N	9.20 E
Nupani	63c	Ab	10.04S	165.40 E
Nūq	24	Pg	30.55N	55.35 E
Nuqayr	24	Mi	27.48N	48.21 E
Nuqrah	24	Ij	25.34N	41.24 E
Nuqruş, Jabal-	33	Fe	24.49N	34.36 E
Nuquí	54	Cb	5.43N	77.16W
Nūr	24	Od	36.15N	52.20 E
Nūr	24	Pg	31.25N	54.20 E
Nura	19	Gf	48.57N	62.20 E
Nura	21	Id	50.30N	69.59 E
Nūrābād	24	Ng	30.48N	51.27 E
Nuraghe Santu Antine	14	Cj	40.29N	8.45 E
Nurata	19	Gg	40.34N	65.35 E
Nur Dağları	24	Gd	36.45N	36.20 E
Nure	14	De	45.03N	9.49 E
Nurek	19	Gh	38.25N	69.20 E
Nurhak Dağı	23	Eb	38.04N	37.29 E
Nūrī	35	Eb	18.30N	32.02 E
Nurki	20	Ie	56.42N	138.28 E
Nurlat	19	Fe	54.28N	50.48 E
Nurlati	7	Li	55.38N	48.17 E
Nurmes	7	Ge	63.33N	29.07 E
Nurmijärvi	8	Kd	60.28N	24.48 E
Nurmo	8	Jb	62.50N	22.54 E
Nürnberg	6	Hf	49.27N	11.05 E
Nurra	14	Cj	40.45N	8.15 E
Nurri, Mount-	59	Jf	31.42S	146.02 E
Nurugas	37	Bc	19.11S	18.54 E
Nurzec	10	Sd	52.33N	22.48 E
Nusa Tenggara Barat [3]	26	Gh	8.50S	117.30 E
Nusa Tenggara Timur [3]	26	Hh	9.30S	122.00 E
Nusaybin	24	Id	37.03N	41.13 E
Nushagak	40	He	58.57N	158.29W
Nushan	27	Gf	25.00N	99.00 E
Nu-Shima	29	Dd	34.10N	134.50 E
Nutak	42	Le	57.31N	62.00W
Nuttal	25	Dc	28.45N	68.08 E
Nuutele	65c	Bb	14.02S	171.22W
Nuwākot	25	Gc	28.08N	83.53 E
Nuwara	25	Gg	6.58N	80.46 E
Nuwaybi 'al Muzayyinah	33	Fd	28.58N	34.39 E
Nyabing	59	Df	33.32S	118.09 E
Nyagquka/Yajiang	27	He	30.07N	100.58 E
Nyagrong/Xinlong	27	He	30.57N	100.12 E
Nyahanga	36	Fc	2.23S	33.33 E
Nyahua	36	Fd	4.58S	33.34 E
Nyainqêntanglha Feng	27	Fe	30.12N	90.33 E
Nyainqêntanglha Shan	21	Kf	30.10N	90.00 E
Nyakanazi	36	Fc	3.00S	31.15 E
Nyala	31	Jg	12.03N	24.53 E
Nyalam	27	Ef	28.15N	85.55 E
Ny-Ålesund	41	Nc	78.56N	11.57 E
Nyalikungu	36	Fc	3.11S	33.47 E
Nyamandhlovu	37	Dc	19.51S	28.16 E
Nyamapanda	37	Ec	16.55S	32.52 E
Nyamlell	35	Dd	9.07N	26.58 E
Nyamtumbo	36	Ge	10.30S	36.06 E
Nyanding	35	Ed	8.40N	32.41 E
Nyanga	30	Ii	2.58S	10.15 E
Nyanga [3]	36	Bc	3.00S	11.00 E
Nyanza [3]	36	Fc	0.30S	34.30 E
Nyanza-Lac	36	Ec	4.21S	29.36 E
Nyasa, Lake- (EN)=Niassa, Lago-	30	Kj	12.00S	34.30 E
Nyaunglebin	25	Je	17.57N	96.44 E
Nyborg	7	Ci	55.19N	10.48 E
Nybro	7	Dh	56.45N	15.54 E
Nyda	17	Pc	66.40N	72.50 E
Nyda	20	Cc	66.36N	72.54 E
Nyeboe Land	41	Gb	81.45N	56.40W
Nyêmo	27	Ff	29.30N	90.07 E
Nyeri	36	Gc	0.25S	36.57 E
Nyerol	35	Ed	8.41N	32.02 E
Ny Friesland	41	Nc	79.30N	17.00 E
Nyhammar	8	Fd	60.17N	14.58 E
Nyhem	8	Fb	62.54N	15.40 E
Nyika	30	Ki	2.37S	38.44 E
Nyika Plateau	30	Kj	10.40S	33.50 E
Nyikog Qu	27	He	30.24N	100.40 E
Nyimba	36	Fe	14.33S	30.48 E
Nyingchi	27	Ff	29.38N	94.23 E
Nyírbátor	10	Si	47.50N	22.08 E
Nyíregyháza	10	Ri	47.57N	21.43 E
Nyiri Desert	36	Gc	2.20S	37.20 E
Nyiro, Mount-	36	Gb	2.08N	36.51 E
Nyírség	10	Ri	47.50N	21.55 E
Nykøbing [Den.]	7	Ci	54.46N	11.53 E
Nykøbing [Den.]	7	Ci	55.55N	11.41 E
Nykøbing [Den.]	8	Ch	56.48N	8.52 E
Nyköping	7	Dg	58.45N	17.00 E
Nyköpingsån	8	Gf	58.45N	17.01 E
Nykroppa	8	Fe	59.38N	14.18 E
Nyland	8	Ga	63.00N	17.46 E
Nylstroom	37	Dd	24.42S	28.20 E
Nymburk	10	Lf	50.11N	15.03 E
Nymphe Bank (EN)	9	Fj	51.30N	7.05W
Nynäshamn	7	Dg	58.54N	17.57 E
Nyngan	58	Fh	31.34S	147.11 E
Nyon	14	Ad	46.23N	6.15 E
Nyong	30	Hh	3.17N	9.54 E
Nyonga	36	Fd	6.43S	32.04 E
Nyons	11	Lj	44.22N	5.08 E
Nýřany	10	Jg	49.43N	13.13 E
Nyrob	17	Hf	60.42N	56.45 E
Nyš	20	Jf	51.30N	142.49 E
Nysa	10	Nf	50.29N	17.20 E
Nysa Kłodzka	10	Nf	50.49N	17.50 E
Nysa Łużycka	10	Kd	52.04N	14.46 E
Nyslott/Savonlinna	7	Gf	61.52N	28.53 E
Nyssa	46	Ge	43.53N	117.00W
Nystad/Uusikaupunki	7	Ef	60.48N	21.25 E
Nysted	8	Dj	54.40N	11.45 E
Nytva	19	Fd	57.56N	55.20 E
Nyūdō-Zaki	28	Od	40.00N	139.35 E
Nyunzu	36	Ed	5.57S	28.01 E
Nyūzen	29	Ec	36.56N	137.30 E
Nzambi	36	Bc	3.58S	11.16 E
Nzara	35	De	4.40N	28.14 E
Nzega	36	Fc	4.13S	33.11 E
Nzérékoré	31	Gh	7.45N	8.49W
N'zeto	36	Bd	7.05S	12.50 E
Nzi	30	Gh	5.57N	4.50W
Nzilo, Barrage de-	36	Ee	10.35S	25.30 E
Nzo	34	Dd	6.16N	7.03W
Nzoro	36	Eb	3.18N	29.26 E
Nzwani	30	Lj	12.15S	44.25 E

O

Oa, Mull of-	9	Gf	55.35N	6.20W
Oahe, Lake-	38	Ie	45.30N	100.25W
Oahu Island	57	Lb	21.30N	158.00W
O-akan-Dake	29a	Db	43.27N	144.10 E
Oakdale [Ca.-U.S.]	46	Eh	37.46N	120.51W
Oakdale [La.-U.S.]	45	Jk	30.49N	92.40W
Oakham	9	Mi	52.40N	0.44W
Oak Harbor	46	Db	48.18N	122.39W
Oak Lake	45	Fb	49.40N	100.45W
Oakland [Ca.-U.S.]	39	Gf	37.47N	122.13W
Oakland [Md.-U.S.]	47	Hf	39.25N	79.24W
Oakley [Id.-U.S.]	46	Ie	42.15N	113.53W
Oakley [Ks.-U.S.]	43	Gd	39.08N	100.51W
Oak Park	45	Mf	41.53N	87.48W
Oak Ridge	43	Kd	36.01N	84.16W
Oakridge	46	De	43.45N	122.28W
Oakville	44	Hd	43.27N	79.41W
Oamaru	61	Di	45.05S	170.59 E
Oancea	15	Ld	45.55N	28.06 E
Oani-Gawa	29	Ga	40.12N	140.16 E
Ōarai	29	Gc	36.18N	140.33 E
Oaro	62	Ee	42.31S	173.30 E
Oasis	46	Hf	41.01N	114.37W
Oasis	32	Hd	26.00N	5.00 E
Oates Coast	66	Jf	70.00S	160.00 E
Oaxaca [2]	47	Ee	17.00N	96.30W
Oaxaca, Sierra Madre de-	48	Ki	17.30N	96.30W
Oaxaca de Juárez	39	Jh	17.03N	96.43W
Ob	21	Ic	66.45N	69.30 E
Oba	42	Jg	48.55N	84.17W
Obala	34	He	4.10N	11.32 E
Obama [Jap.]	28	Mg	35.30N	135.45 E
Obama [Jap.]	29	Be	32.43N	130.13 E
Obama-Wan	29	Dd	35.30N	135.40 E
Oban [N.Z.]	61	Ci	46.52S	168.10 E
Oban [Scot.-U.K.]	9	He	56.25N	5.29W
Obanazawa	28	Pe	38.36N	140.24 E
Obando	53	Je	4.07N	67.45W
Oban Hills	34	Gd	5.30N	8.35 E
Obeliai/Obeljaj	8	Ki	55.58N	25.59 E
Obeljaj/Obeliai	8	Ki	55.58N	25.59 E
Oberá	56	Ic	27.29S	55.08W
Oberbayern	10	Hi	47.50N	11.50 E
Oberderdingen	12	Ke	49.04N	8.48 E
Oberfranken	10	Hf	50.10N	11.30 E
Oberhausen	10	Ce	51.28N	6.51 E
Oberkirchen, Schmallenberg-	12	Kc	51.09N	8.18 E
Oberland [Switz.]	14	Bd	46.35N	7.30 E
Oberland [Switz.]	14	Dd	46.45N	9.05 E
Oberlausitz	10	Ke	51.15N	14.30 E
Oberlin	45	Fg	39.49N	100.32W
Obermoschel	12	Je	49.44N	7.46 E
Obernkirchen	12	Lb	52.16N	9.08 E
Oberösterreich=Upper Austria (EN) [2]	14	Hb	48.15N	14.00 E
Oberpfalz	10	Ig	49.30N	12.10 E
Oberpfälzer Wald= Bohemian Forest (EN)	10	Ig	49.50N	12.30 E
Oberpullendorf	14	Kc	47.30N	16.31 E
Ober-Ramstadt	12	Ke	49.50N	8.45 E
Oberstdorf	10	Gi	47.24N	10.16 E
Oberursel (Taunus)	12	Kd	50.12N	8.35 E
Obervellach	14	Hd	46.56N	13.12 E
Oberwesel	12	Jd	50.06N	7.44 E
Ob Gulf (EN)=Obskaja Guba	21	Jc	69.00N	73.00 E
Obi, Kepulauan-	26	Ig	1.30S	127.45 E
Obi, Pulau-	57	De	1.30S	127.45 E
Obi, Selat-	26	Ig	0.52S	127.33 E
Óbidos [Braz.]	53	Kf	1.55S	55.31W
Óbidos [Port.]	13	Ce	39.22N	9.09W
Obihiro	27	Pc	42.55N	143.12 E
Obilić	15	Eg	42.41N	21.05 E
Obira	29a	Ba	44.01N	141.38 E
Obispos	49	Li	8.36N	70.05W
Obispo Trejo	56	Hd	30.46S	63.25W
Obitočnaja Kosa	16	Jf	46.35N	36.15 E
Oblučje	20	Ig	48.59N	131.05 E
Obninsk	19	Dd	55.05N	36.37 E
Obo	31	Jh	5.24N	26.30 E
Obock	35	Gc	11.57N	43.17 E
Obojan	16	Jd	51.13N	36.16 E
Obokote	36	Ec	0.52S	26.19 E
Obol	7	Gi	55.24N	29.01 E
Oborniki	10	Md	52.39N	16.51 E
Obouya	36	Cc	0.56S	15.43 E
Obozerski	19	Ec	63.28N	40.20 E
Obra	10	Ld	52.36N	15.28 E
Obrenovac	15	De	44.39N	20.12 E
Obrovac	14	Jf	44.12N	15.41 E
Obrovo	10	Vd	52.27N	25.43 E
Obruchev Rise (EN)	20	Lf	52.30N	166.00 E
Obruk Platosu	24	Ec	38.02N	33.30 E
Obšči Syrt	5	Le	51.50N	51.00 E
Obskaja Guba=Ob Gulf (EN)	21	Jc	69.00N	73.00 E
Ob' Tablemount (EN)	30	Ln	52.30S	42.00 E
Ōbu	29	Ed	35.01N	136.58 E
Obuasi	34	Ed	6.12N	1.40W
Obudu	34	Gd	6.40N	9.10 E
Obuhov	16	Gd	50.07N	30.37 E
Obva	17	Gg	58.35N	55.25 E
Obzor	15	Kg	42.49N	27.53 E
Oca	13	Ib	42.46N	3.26W
Oca, Montes de-	13	Ib	42.20N	3.15W
Očakov	19	Df	46.38N	31.33 E
Ocala	43	Kf	29.11N	82.07W
Očamčira	16	Lh	42.46N	41.27 E
Ocampo [Mex.]	48	Hd	27.20N	102.21W
Ocampo [Mex.]	48	Ee	28.11N	108.23W
Ocaña [Col.]	54	Db	8.15N	73.20W
Ocaña [Sp.]	13	Ie	39.56N	3.31W
Occhito, Lago di-	14	Ii	41.35N	14.55 E
Ocean Bight	49	Kc	21.15N	73.15W
Ocean City [Md.-U.S.]	43	Ld	38.20N	75.05W
Ocean City [N.J.-U.S.]	44	Jf	39.16N	74.35W
Ocean Falls	42	Ef	52.21N	127.40W
Oceania	57	Ie	5.00S	175.00E
Ocean Point	44	Il	26.16N	77.03W
Oceanside	43	De	33.12N	117.23W
Ocean Springs	45	Lk	30.25N	88.50W
Ocejón, Pico-	13	Ic	41.07N	3.15W
Očenyrd, Gora-	17	Mb	68.05N	66.20 E
Očer	19	Fd	57.53N	54.45 E
Ochagavía	13	Kb	42.55N	1.05W
Ochiai	29	Cd	35.02N	133.45 E
Ochi-Gata	29	Ec	36.55N	136.48 E
Ochiishi-Misaki	29a	Db	43.10N	145.28 E
Ochil Hills	9	Je	56.23N	3.35W
Och'onjang	28	Jd	40.55N	128.50 E
Ocho Rios	49	Id	18.25N	77.07W
Ochsenfurt	10	Gh	49.39N	10.05 E
Ochtrup	12	Jb	52.13N	7.11 E
Ockelbo	7	Dd	60.53N	16.43 E
Öckerö	8	Dg	57.43N	11.39 E
Ocmulgee River	44	Fj	31.58N	82.32W
Ocna Mureş	15	Gc	46.23N	23.51 E

Index Symbols

[1] Independent Nation; [2] State, Region; [3] District, County; [4] Municipality; [5] Colony, Dependency; Continent; Physical Region; Historical or Cultural Region; Mount, Mountain; Volcano; Hill; Mountains, Mountain Range; Hills, Escarpment; Plateau, Upland; Pass, Gap; Plain, Lowland; Delta; Salt Flat; Valley, Canyon; Crater, Cave; Karst Features; Depression; Polder; Desert, Dunes; Forest, Woods; Heath, Steppe; Oasis; Cape, Point; Coast, Beach; Cliff; Peninsula; Isthmus; Sandbank; Island; Atoll; Rock, Reef; Islands, Archipelago; Rocks, Reefs; Coral Reef; Well, Spring; Geyser; River, Stream; Waterfall Rapids; River Mouth, Estuary; Lake; Salt Lake; Intermittent Lake; Reservoir; Swamp, Pond; Canal; Glacier; Ice Shelf, Pack Ice; Ocean; Sea; Gulf, Bay; Strait, Fjord; Lagoon; Bank; Seamount; Tablemount; Ridge; Shelf; Basin; Escarpment, Sea Scarp; Fracture; Trench, Abyss; National Park, Reserve; Point of Interest; Recreation Site; Cave, Cavern; Historic Site; Ruins; Wall, Walls; Church, Abbey; Temple; Scientific Station; Airport; Port; Lighthouse; Mine; Tunnel; Dam, Bridge

Index Symbols

- [1] Independent Nation
- [2] State, Region
- [3] District, County
- [4] Municipality
- [5] Colony, Dependency
- Continent
- Physical Region
- Historical or Cultural Region
- Mount, Mountain
- Volcano
- Hill
- Mountains, Mountain Range
- Hills, Escarpment
- Plateau, Upland
- Pass, Gap
- Plain, Lowland
- Delta
- Salt Flat
- Valley, Canyon
- Crater, Cave
- Karst Features
- Depression
- Polder
- Desert, Dunes
- Forest, Woods
- Heath, Steppe
- Oasis
- Cape, Point
- Coast, Beach
- Cliff
- Peninsula
- Isthmus
- Sandbank
- Island
- Atoll
- Rock, Reef
- Islands, Archipelago
- Rocks, Reefs
- Coral Reef
- Well, Spring
- Geyser
- River, Stream
- Waterfall Rapids
- River Mouth, Estuary
- Lake
- Salt Lake
- Intermittent Lake
- Reservoir
- Swamp, Pond
- Canal
- Glacier
- Ice Shelf, Pack Ice
- Ocean
- Sea
- Gulf, Bay
- Strait, Fjord
- Lagoon
- Bank
- Seamount
- Tablemount
- Ridge
- Shelf
- Basin
- Escarpment, Sea Scarp
- Fracture
- Trench, Abyss
- National Park, Reserve
- Point of Interest
- Recreation Site
- Cave, Cavern
- Historic Site
- Ruins
- Wall, Walls
- Church, Abbey
- Temple
- Scientific Station
- Airport
- Port
- Lighthouse
- Mine
- Tunnel
- Dam, Bridge

Ongijin-Gol	27	Hc	44.30N	103.40 E
Ongjin	27	Md	37.56N	125.22 E
Ongniud Qi (Wudan)	27	Kc	42.58N	119.01 E
Ongole	25	Ge	15.30N	80.03 E
Ongon	27	Jb	45.49N	113.08 E
Onhaye	12	Gd	50.15N	4.50 E
Oni	16	Mh	42.35N	43.27 E
Onigajō-Yama	29	Ce	33.07N	132.41 E
Onilany	30	Lk	23.34S	43.45 E
Onishibetsu	29a	Ca	45.21N	142.06 E
Onitsha	31	Hh	6.10N	6.47 E
Ono	29	Dd	34.51N	134.57 E
Ono	63d	Bc	18.54S	178.29 E
Ōno [Jap.]	28	Ng	35.59N	136.29 E
Ōno [Jap.]	29	Cd	34.18N	132.17 E
Onoda	29	Be	33.59N	131.11 E
Ōno-Gawa	29	Be	33.15N	131.43 E
Ōnohara-Jima	29	Fd	34.02N	139.23 E
Onohoj	20	Ff	51.55N	108.01 E
Ono-i-Lau Islands	57	Jg	20.39S	178.42W
Onojō	29	Be	33.34N	130.29 E
Onomichi	28	Lg	34.25N	133.12 E
Onon	21	Nd	51.42N	115.50 E
Onoto	50	Dh	9.36N	65.12W
Onotoa Atoll	57	Ie	1.52S	175.34 E
Ons, Isla de-	13	Db	42.23N	8.56W
Onsala	7	Ch	57.25N	12.01 E
Onseepkans	37	Be	28.45S	19.17 E
Onslow	58	Cg	21.39S	115.06 E
Onslow Bay	43	Le	34.20N	77.20W
On-Take	29	Bf	31.35N	130.39 E
Ontake-San	29	Ed	35.53N	137.29 E
Ontario [3]	42	If	50.00N	86.00W
Ontario [Ca.-U.S.]	46	Gi	34.04N	117.39W
Ontario [Or.-U.S.]	46	Dc	44.02N	116.58W
Ontario, Lake-	38	Le	43.40N	78.00W
Ontario Peninsula	38	Ke	43.50N	81.00W
Onteniente/Ontinyent	13	Lf	38.49N	0.37W
Ontinyent/Onteniente	13	Lf	38.49N	0.37W
Ontojärvi	7	Gd	64.08N	29.09 E
Ontonagon	44	Cb	46.52N	89.19W
Ontong Java Atoll	57	Ge	5.20S	159.30 E
Ō-Numa	29a	Bc	41.59N	140.41 E
Oodnadatta	58	Eg	27.33S	135.28 E
Ooidonk	12	Fc	51.01N	3.35 E
Ookala	65a	Fc	20.01N	155.17W
Ooldea	58	Eh	30.27S	131.50 E
Oologah Lake	45	Ih	36.39N	95.36W
Ooltgensplaat, Oostflakkee-	12	Gc	51.41N	4.21 E
Oostburg	12	Fc	51.20N	3.30 E
Oostelijk Flevoland	12	Hb	52.30N	5.40 E
Oostende/Ostende	11	Ic	51.14N	2.55 E
Oosterhout	11	Kc	51.38N	4.51 E
Oosterschelde=East Schelde (EN)	11	Jc	51.30N	4.00 E
Oosterwolde, Ooststellingwerf-	12	Ha	53.00N	6.18 E
Oosterzele	12	Fd	50.57N	3.48 E
Oostflakkee	12	Gc	51.41N	4.21 E
Oostflakkee-Ooltgensplaat	12	Gc	51.41N	4.21 E
Oostkamp	12	Fc	51.09N	3.14 E
Oost-Souburg, Vlissingen-	12	Fc	51.28N	3.36 E
Ooststellingwerf	12	Ib	53.00N	6.18 E
Ooststellingwerf-Oosterwolde	12	Ha	53.00N	6.18 E
Oost Vieland, Vieland-	12	Ha	53.17N	5.06 E
Oost-Vlaanderen [3]	12	Fc	51.00N	3.40 E
Ootmarsum	12	Ib	52.25N	6.54 E
Opala	36	Dc	0.37S	24.21 E
Opalenica	10	Md	52.19N	16.23 E
Opanake	25	Gg	6.36N	80.37 E
Opari	35	Ee	3.56N	32.03 E
Oparino	7	Lg	59.53N	48.25 E
Opasatika	44	Fa	49.31N	82.58W
Opasatika Lake	44	Fa	49.06N	83.08W
Opasatika River	44	Fa	50.15N	82.25W
Opatija	14	Ie	45.20N	14.19 E
Opatów	10	Rf	50.49N	21.26 E
Opatówka	10	Rf	50.42N	21.50 E
Opava	10	Ng	49.57N	17.54 E
Opava	10	Og	49.51N	18.17 E
Opelika	43	Je	32.39N	85.23W
Opelousas	45	Jk	30.32N	92.05W
Opémisca, Lac-	44	Ja	49.58N	74.57W
Opheim	46	Lb	48.51N	106.24W
Ophir	40	Hd	63.10N	156.31W
Ophthalmia Range	59	Dd	23.15S	119.30 E
Opienge	36	Eb	0.12N	27.30 E
Opihikao	65a	Gd	19.26N	154.53W
Opinaca	42	Jf	52.14N	78.02W
Opiscotéo, Lac-	42	Kf	53.09N	68.10W
Opladen, Leverkusen-	10	De	51.04N	7.01 E
Opobo	34	Ge	4.34N	7.27 E
Opočka	19	Cd	56.42N	28.41 E
Opoczno	10	Qe	51.23N	20.17 E
Opole [2]	10	Nf	50.40N	17.55 E
Opole	10	Nf	50.41N	17.55 E
Opole Lubelskie	10	Re	51.09N	21.58 E
Oporny	19	Ff	46.13N	54.29 E
Opotiki	62	Gc	38.01S	177.17 E
Opp	44	Dj	31.17N	86.22W
Oppa-Wan	29	Gb	38.35N	141.30 E
Oppdal	7	Be	62.36N	9.40 E
Oppenheim	10	Eg	49.51N	8.21 E
Oppland [2]	7	Bf	61.10N	9.40 E
Opportunity	46	Gc	47.39N	117.15W
Opsa	8	Li	55.31N	26.54 E
Opsterland	12	Ia	53.03N	6.04 E
Opsterland-Beetsterzwaag	12	Ia	53.03N	6.04 E
Opua	61	Dg	35.18S	174.07 E
Opunake	62	Ec	39.27S	173.51 E
Oputo	48	Eb	30.03N	109.20W
Oquossoc	44	Lc	45.04N	70.44W
Or	16	Ud	51.12N	58.33 E
Ōra	33	Cd	28.20N	19.35 E
Oradea	6	If	47.04N	21.56 E
Orahovac	15	Dg	42.24N	20.40 E
Orahovica	14	Le	45.32N	17.53 E
Orai	25	Fc	25.59N	79.28 E
Oraibi Wash	46	Ji	35.26N	110.49W
Oran	31	Ge	35.42N	0.38W
Oran [3]	32	Gb	36.00N	0.35W
Orange [Austl.]	58	Fh	33.17S	149.06 E
Orange [Fr.]	11	Kj	44.08N	4.48 E
Orange [Tx.-U.S.]	43	Ie	30.01N	93.44W
Orange [Va.-U.S.]	44	Hf	38.14N	78.07W
Orange/Oranje	30	Ik	28.38N	16.27 E
Orange, Cabo-	52	Ke	4.24N	51.33W
Orangeburg	43	Ke	33.30N	80.52W
Orange Free State/Oranje Vrystaat [2]	37	De	29.00S	26.00 E
Orange Lake	44	Fk	29.25N	82.13W
Orange Park	44	Gj	30.10N	81.42W
Orangeville	44	Gd	43.55N	80.06W
Orange Walk	47	Ge	18.06N	88.33W
Orango	30	Fg	11.05N	16.08W
Oranienburg	10	Jd	52.45N	13.14 E
Oranje/Orange	30	Ik	28.38N	16.27 E
Oranje Gebergte	54	Hc	3.00N	55.00W
Oranjemund	37	Be	28.38S	16.24 E
Oranjestad	54	Da	12.33N	70.06W
Oranje Vrystaat/Orange Free State [2]	37	De	29.00S	26.00 E
Oranžerei	16	Og	45.50N	47.36 E
Orapa	37	Dd	21.16S	25.22 E
Orăştie	15	Gd	45.50N	23.12 E
Orava	10	Pg	49.08N	19.10 E
Oraviţa	15	Ed	45.02N	21.42 E
Orayská Priehradní Nádrž	10	Pg	49.20N	19.35 E
Orb	11	Jk	43.15N	3.18 E
Orba	14	Cf	44.53N	8.37 E
Orba Co	27	De	34.33N	81.06 E
Ørbæk	8	Di	55.16N	10.41 E
Orbec	12	Ce	49.01N	0.25 E
Orbetello	14	Fh	42.27N	11.13 E
Orbetello, Laguna di-	14	Fh	42.25N	11.15 E
Orbigo	13	Gc	41.58N	5.40W
Orbiquet	12	Ce	49.09N	0.14 E
Orbost	59	Jg	37.42S	148.27 E
Örbyhus	8	Gd	60.14N	17.42 E
Orcadas	66	Re	60.40S	44.30W
Orcas Island	46	Db	48.39N	122.55W
Orchies	12	Fd	50.28N	3.14 E
Orchon→Orhon	21	Md	50.21N	106.05 E
Orcia	14	Fh	42.58N	11.21 E
Orco	14	Be	45.10N	7.52 E
Ord, Mount-	59	Fc	17.20S	125.35 E
Ördenes	13	Da	43.04N	8.24W
Ordos Desert (EN)=Mu Us Shamo	21	Mf	38.45N	109.10 E
Ord River	57	Df	15.30S	128.21 E
Ordu	23	Ea	41.00N	37.53 E
Ordubad	16	Oj	38.55N	46.01 E
Ordynskoje	20	Df	54.22N	81.58 E
Ordžonikidze [Ukr.-U.R.S.S.]	16	If	47.40N	34.04 E
Ordžonikidze [Kaz.-U.S.S.R.]	17	Jj	52.25N	61.45 E
Ordžonikidze [R.S.F.S.R.]	6	Kg	43.03N	44.40 E
Ordžonikidzeabad	19	Gh	38.34N	69.02 E
Ore älv	8	Fc	61.08N	14.35 E
Orebić	14	Lh	42.58N	17.11 E
Örebro	8	Hd	59.17N	15.13 E
Örebro [2]	7	Dg	59.30N	15.00 E
Oredež	8	Nf	58.50N	30.13 E
Oregon	44	Fe	41.38N	83.28W
Oregon [2]	43	Cc	44.00N	121.00W
Oregon City	43	Cb	45.21N	122.36W
Oregon Inlet	44	Jh	35.50N	75.35W
Öregrund	8	Hd	60.20N	18.26 E
Orehov	16	If	47.34N	35.47 E
Orehovo-Zujevo	6	Jd	55.49N	38.59 E
Orel	6	Je	52.59N	36.05 E
Orel	16	Ie	48.31N	34.55 E
Orel, Gora-	20	Jf	53.55N	140.01 E
Orellana [Peru]	54	Ce	6.54S	75.04W
Orellana [Peru]	54	Cd	4.40S	78.10W
Orem	43	Ec	40.19N	111.42W
Ore Mountains (EN)=Erzgebirge	5	He	50.30N	13.15 E
Ore Mountains (EN)=Krušné Hory	5	He	50.30N	13.15 E
Ören	24	Bd	37.18N	29.17 E
Orenbel	24	Hb	40.00N	39.10 E
Orenburg	6	Le	51.54N	55.06 E
Orenburgskaja Oblast [3]	19	Fe	52.00N	55.00 E
Örencik	24	Cc	39.16N	29.34 E
Orense [3]	13	Eb	42.10N	7.30W
Orense [Arg.]	56	Ie	38.40S	59.47W
Orense [Sp.]	13	Eb	42.20N	7.51W
Oreón, Dhíavlos-	15	Fk	38.54N	22.55 E
Orepuki	62	Bg	46.17S	167.44 E
Orestiás	15	Jh	41.30N	26.31 E
Øresund	5	Hd	55.50N	12.40 E
Oreti	62	Cg	46.28S	168.17 E
Orewa	62	Fb	36.35S	174.42 E
Orford	12	Db	52.05N	1.32 E
Orford Ness	9	Oi	52.05N	1.34 E
Orgañá/Organyà	13	Nb	42.13N	1.20 E
Organ Needle	45	Cj	32.21N	106.33W
Organyà/Orgañá	13	Nb	42.13N	1.20 E
Orgaz	13	Ie	39.39N	3.54W
Orgejev	19	Cf	47.23N	28.50 E
Orgelet	11	Lh	46.31N	5.37 E
Orgon Tal	28	Bc	43.20N	112.40 E
Orgosolo	14	Dj	40.12N	9.21 E
Orgün	23	Kc	32.57N	69.11 E
Orhaneli	15	Lj	39.54N	29.00 E
Orhaneli/Koca Çay	15	Lj	39.56N	28.32 E
Orhangazi	15	Mi	40.30N	29.18 E
Orhomenós	15	Fk	38.35N	22.54 E
Orhon (Orchon)	21	Md	50.21N	106.05 E
Orhy, Pico de-	13	La	42.59N	1.00W
Oria	13	Ja	43.17N	2.08W
Orichuna, Rio-	50	Bi	7.30N	68.13W
Orick	46	Cf	41.17N	124.04W
Oriental	48	Kh	19.22N	97.37W
Oriental, Cordillera-	49	Md	18.55N	69.15W
Oriente	56	He	38.44S	60.37W
Orihuela	13	Lf	38.05N	0.57W
Oriku	15	Ci	40.17N	19.25 E
Óri Lekánis	15	Hh	41.08N	24.33 E
Orillia	42	Jh	44.37N	79.25W
Orimattila	7	Ff	60.48N	25.45 E
Orinoco, Rio-	52	Je	8.37N	62.15W
Oripää	8	Jd	60.51N	22.41 E
Orissa [3]	25	Gd	21.00N	84.00 E
Orissaare/Orissare	7	Fg	58.34N	23.05 E
Orissare/Orissaare	7	Fg	58.34N	23.05 E
Oristano	14	Ck	39.54N	8.36 E
Oristano, Golfo di-	14	Ck	39.50N	8.30 E
Orituco, Rio-	50	Ch	8.45N	67.27W
Orivesi	5	Ic	62.15N	29.25 E
Orivesi	7	Ff	61.41N	24.21 E
Oriximiná	54	Gd	1.45S	55.52W
Orizaba	39	Jh	18.51N	97.06W
Orizaba, Pico de- (Citlaltépetl, Volcán-)	38	Jh	19.01N	97.16W
Orizona	55	Hc	17.03S	48.18W
Orjahovo	15	Gf	43.44N	23.58 E
Ørje	8	De	59.29N	11.39 E
Orjen	15	Bg	42.34N	18.33 E
Orjiva	13	Ih	36.54N	3.25W
Orkanger	7	Be	63.19N	9.52 E
Orkdalen	8	Ca	63.15N	9.50 E
Örkelljunga	8	Eh	56.17N	13.17 E
Orkla	8	Ca	63.18N	9.50 E
Orkney	37	De	27.00S	26.39 E
Orkney [3]	9	Kb	59.00N	3.00W
Orkney Islands	5	Fd	59.00N	3.00W
Orlândia	55	Ie	20.43S	47.53W
Orlando	39	Kg	28.32N	81.23W
Orlando, Capo d'-	14	Il	38.10N	14.45 E
Orlanka	10	Td	52.52N	23.12 E
Orléanais	11	Hf	48.40N	1.20 E
Orléans	6	Gf	47.55N	1.54 E
Orlice	10	Lf	50.12N	15.49 E
Orlické Hory	10	Mf	50.10N	16.30 E
Orlik	20	Ef	52.30N	99.55 E
Orlovskaja Oblast [3]	19	De	52.45N	36.30 E
Orlovski	16	Mf	46.52N	42.06 E
Orlovski, mys-	7	Jc	67.16N	41.18 E
Orly	12	Ef	48.45N	2.24 E
Ormāra	25	Cc	25.12N	64.38 E
Ormes	12	Ce	49.03N	0.59 E
Ormoc	26	Hd	11.00N	124.37 E
Ormond	62	Gc	38.33S	177.55 E
Ormond Beach	44	Gk	29.17N	81.02W
Ornain	11	Kf	48.46N	4.47 E
Ornans	11	Mg	47.06N	6.09 E
Ornäs	8	Fd	60.31N	15.32 E
Orne [3]	11	Gf	48.40N	0.05 E
Orne [Fr.]	11	Ie	49.17N	6.11 E
Orne [Fr.]	11	Be	49.19N	0.14W
Orne Seamount (EN)	61	Je	27.30S	157.30W
Orneta	10	Qb	54.08N	20.08 E
Ornö	7	Eg	59.05N	18.25 E
Örnsköldsvik	7	Ee	63.18N	18.43 E
Oro	28	Id	40.01N	127.27 E
Oro, Rio de-	55	Ch	27.04S	58.34W
Oro, Rio del-	48	Ge	25.35N	105.03W
Orocué	54	Dc	4.48N	71.20W
Orodara	34	Ec	10.59N	4.55W
Orofino	46	Gc	46.29N	116.15W
Orogrande	45	Cj	32.23N	106.08W
Orohena, Mont-	65e	Fc	17.31S	149.28W
Oroluk Atoll	57	Gd	7.32N	155.18 E
Orom	36	Fb	3.20N	33.40 E
Oromocto	42	Kg	45.51N	66.29W
Oron	34	Ge	4.50N	8.14 E
Orona Atoll (Hull)	57	Je	4.29S	172.10W
Orongo	65d	Ac	27.10S	109.26W
Oronsay	9	Ge	56.01N	6.14W
Orontes (EN)=Nahr al 'Āṣī	23	Eb	36.02N	35.58 E
Oropesa [Sp.]	13	Ge	39.55N	5.10W
Oropesa [Sp.]	13	Ld	40.06N	0.09W
Oroqen Zizhiqi (Alihe)	27	La	50.35N	123.42 E
Oroquieta	26	He	8.29N	123.48 E
Orós	54	Ke	6.15S	38.55W
Orós, Açude-	54	Ke	6.15S	39.05W
Orosei	14	Dj	40.23N	9.42 E
Orosei, Golfo di-	14	Dj	40.15N	9.45 E
Orosháza	10	Qj	46.34N	20.40 E
Oro-Shima	29	Be	33.52N	130.02 E
Oroszlány	10	Oi	47.29N	18.19 E
Orote Peninsula	64c	Bb	13.26N	144.38 E
Orote Point	64c	Bb	13.27N	144.37 E
Orotukan	20	Kd	62.17N	151.50 E
Oroville [Ca.-U.S.]	46	Eg	39.31N	121.33W
Oroville [Wa.-U.S.]	46	Fb	48.56N	119.26W
Orp-Jauche	12	Gd	50.40N	4.57 E
Orqohan	27	Lb	49.36N	121.23 E
Orr	45	Jb	48.03N	92.50W
Orrefors	8	Fh	56.50N	15.45 E
Orri, Pic d'-/Llorri	13	Nb	42.23N	1.12 E
Orša	6	Je	54.30N	30.24 E
Orsa	7	Df	61.07N	14.37 E
Orsasjön	8	Fc	61.05N	14.35 E
Orsay	12	Ef	48.42N	2.11 E
Orsjön	8	Gc	61.35N	16.20 E
Orsk	6	Le	51.12N	58.34 E
Orşova	15	Fe	44.42N	22.25 E
Ørsta	7	Be	62.12N	6.09 E
Örsundsbro	8	Ge	59.44N	17.18 E
Orta, Lago d'-	14	Ce	45.50N	8.25 E
Ortaca	24	Cd	36.49N	28.47 E
Ortakent	15	Kl	37.02N	27.21 E
Ortaklar	15	Kl	37.53N	27.30 E
Orta Nova	14	Ji	41.19N	15.42 E
Orte	14	Gh	42.27N	12.23 E
Ortegal, Cabo-	13	Ea	43.45N	7.53W
Ortenberg	12	Ld	50.21N	9.03 E
Orthez	11	Fk	43.29N	0.46W
Orthon, Rio-	54	Ef	10.50S	66.04W
Ortigueira [Braz.]	56	Jb	24.12S	50.55W
Ortigueira [Sp.]	13	Fa	43.34N	6.44W
Ortisei / Sankt Ulrich	14	Fd	46.34N	11.40 E
Ortiz [Mex.]	48	Dc	28.15N	110.43W
Ortiz [Ven.]	50	Ch	9.37N	67.17W
Ortlergruppe/Ortles	14	Ed	46.30N	10.40 E
Ortles/Ortlergruppe	14	Ed	46.30N	10.40 E
Ortolo	11a	Ab	41.30N	8.55 E
Ortona	14	Ih	42.21N	14.24 E
Ortonville	45	Hd	45.19N	96.27W
Orto-Tokoj	18	Kc	42.20N	76.02 E
Örtze	10	Fd	52.40N	9.57 E
Orukuizu	64a	Ac	7.10N	134.17 E
Orūmīyeh	22	Gf	37.33N	45.04 E
Orūmīyeh, Daryācheh-ye-=Urmia, Lake- (EN)	21	Gf	37.40N	45.30 E
Oruro [2]	54	Eg	18.40S	67.30W
Oruro	53	Jg	17.59S	67.09W
Orust	8	Df	58.10N	11.38 E
Orūzgān [3]	23	Kc	33.15N	66.00 E
Orūzgān	23	Kc	32.56N	66.38 E
Orval, Abbaye d'-	12	He	49.38N	5.22 E
Orvault	11	Eg	47.16N	1.37W
Orvieto	14	Gh	42.43N	12.07 E
Orville Escarpment	66	Qf	75.45S	65.30W
Orvilos, Óros-	15	Gh	41.23N	23.36 E
Orwell	12	Dc	51.58N	1.18 E
Orxois	12	Fe	49.08N	3.12 E
Orz	10	Rd	52.50N	21.30 E
Orzinuovi	14	De	45.24N	9.55 E
Orzyc	10	Rd	52.47N	21.13 E
Orzysz	10	Rc	53.49N	21.56 E
Oš	19	Hg	40.32N	72.50 E
Os	7	Ce	62.30N	11.12 E
Osa	19	Fd	57.17N	55.26 E
Oša	8	Lh	56.21N	26.29 E
Osa	10	Oc	53.33N	18.45 E
Osa, Peninsula de-	47	Hg	8.35N	83.33W
Osage	45	Je	43.17N	92.49W
Osage River	43	Id	38.35N	91.57W
Ōsaka	29	Ed	35.57N	137.14 E
Ōsaka	22	Pf	34.40N	135.30 E
Osaka Bay (EN)=Ōsaka-Wan	28	Mg	34.36N	135.27 E
Ōsaka-Fu [2]	28	Mg	34.45N	135.35 E
Osakarovka	19	He	50.32N	72.39 E
Ōsaka-Wan=Osaka Bay (EN)	28	Mg	34.36N	135.27 E
Osām	15	Hf	43.42N	24.51 E
Osan	28	If	37.09N	127.04 E
Osasco	55	If	23.32S	46.46W
Osat	14	Nf	44.02N	19.20 E
Osawatomie	45	Ig	38.31N	94.57W
Osborne	45	Gg	39.26N	98.42W
Osburger Hochwald	12	Ie	49.40N	6.50 E
Osby	7	Ch	56.22N	13.59 E
Osceola [Ar.-U.S.]	45	Li	35.42N	89.58W
Osceola [Ia.-U.S.]	43	Ic	41.02N	93.46W
Osceola [Mo.-U.S.]	45	Jh	38.03N	93.42W
Oschatz	10	Je	51.18N	13.07 E
Oschersleben	10	Hd	52.02N	11.15 E
Oschiri	14	Dj	40.43N	9.06 E
Osen	7	Cd	64.18N	10.31 E
Osered	16	Ld	50.01N	40.48 E
Osetr	16	Kb	55.00N	38.45 E
Ōse-Zaki	28	Jh	32.38N	128.42 E
Oshamanbe	28	Pc	42.30N	140.22 E
Oshawa	42	Jh	43.54N	78.51W
Oshekehia Lake	37	Bc	18.08S	15.45 E
Oshika	29	Gb	38.17N	141.31 E
Oshika-Hantō	28	Pe	38.22N	141.27 E
Oshikango	37	Bc	17.22S	15.55 E
Oshima	29	Ce	33.55N	132.11 E
Ō-Shima [Jap.]	29	De	33.28N	135.50 E
Ō-Shima [Jap.]	29	Ae	33.30N	129.33 E
Ō-Shima [Jap.]	29	Ae	32.34N	128.54 E
Ō-Shima [Jap.]	29	Be	33.54N	130.27 E
Ō-Shima [Jap.]	27	Oe	34.45N	139.30 E
Ōshima [Jap.]	29	Fd	34.44N	139.20 E
Ō-Shima [Jap.]	29	Bf	31.32N	131.25 E
Ō-Shima [Jap.]	29	De	33.38N	134.30 E
Ō-Shima [Jap.]	29	Cd	34.10N	133.05 E
Ōshima [Jap.]	29	Ae	33.04N	129.36 E
Ō-Shima [Jap.]	28	Od	41.30N	139.15 E
Ō-Shima [Jap.]	28	Jh	32.04N	128.26 E
Ōshima-Hantō	28	Pd	41.40N	140.30 E
Ōshima-Kaikyō	29b	Ba	28.10N	129.15 E
Oshkosh [Nb.-U.S.]	45	Ef	41.24N	102.21W
Oshkosh [Wi.-U.S.]	43	Jc	44.01N	88.33W
Oshnavīyeh	24	Kd	37.02N	45.06 E
Oshogbo	31	Hh	7.46N	4.34 E
Oshtorān Kūh	23	Gc	33.20N	49.16 E
Oshtorīnān	24	Me	34.01N	48.38 E
Oshwe	36	Cc	3.24S	19.30 E
Osich'ŏn-ni	28	Jd	41.25N	128.16 E
Osijek	6	Hf	45.33N	18.42 E
Osilo	14	Cj	40.45N	8.40 E
Osimo	14	Hg	43.28N	13.29 E
Osinki	7	Lj	52.52N	49.31 E
Osinniki	20	Df	53.37N	87.31 E
Osipaonica	15	Ee	44.33N	21.04 E
Osipoviči	16	Fc	53.19N	28.40 E
Osječenica	14	Kf	44.29N	16.17 E
Oskaloosa	45	Jf	41.18N	92.39W
Oskarshamn	7	Dh	57.16N	16.26 E
Oskarström	8	Eh	56.48N	12.58 E
Oskélanéo	44	Ja	48.08N	75.05W
Oskino	20	Fd	60.48N	107.58 E
Öskjuvatn	7a	Cb	65.02N	16.45W
Oskol	16	Je	49.06N	37.25 E
Oskū	24	Ld	37.55N	46.06 E
Oslava	10	Mg	49.05N	16.22 E
Ösling	11	Le	49.55N	6.00 E
Osljanka, Gora-	17	Ig	59.10N	58.33 E
Oslo [2]	7	Cg	59.55N	10.45 E
Oslo	6	Hd	59.55N	10.45 E
Oslofjorden	5	Hd	59.20N	10.35 E
Osmānābād	25	Fe	18.10N	76.03 E
Osmancık	24	Fb	40.59N	34.49 E
Osmaneli	15	Ni	40.22N	30.01 E
Osmaniye	23	Eb	37.05N	36.14 E
Osmino	8	Mf	58.54N	29.15 E
Ošmjanskaja Vozvyšennost	8	Kj	54.30N	26.00 E
Ošmjany	16	Db	54.27N	25.57 E
Ösmo	8	Gf	58.59N	17.54 E
Osmussaar/Osmussar	8	Je	59.20N	23.15 E
Osmussar/Osmussaar	8	Je	59.20N	23.15 E
Osnabrück	6	Ge	52.16N	8.03 E
Osning	12	Kb	52.10N	8.05 E
Oso, Sierra del-	48	Gd	26.00N	105.25W
Osobłoga	10	Nf	50.27N	17.58 E
Osogovske Planine	15	Fg	42.10N	22.30 E
Osor	14	If	44.42N	14.24 E
Osório	56	Jc	29.54S	50.16W
Osorno	53	Ij	40.34S	73.09W
Osoyoos	42	Fg	49.02N	119.28W
Osøyra	7	Af	60.11N	5.28 E
Ospino	50	Bh	9.18N	69.27W
Osprey Reef	57	Ff	13.55S	146.40 E
Oss	11	Lc	51.46N	5.31 E
Ossa, Mount-	57	Fi	41.54S	146.01 E
Óssa, Óros-	15	Fj	39.49N	22.40 E
Ossabaw Island	44	Gj	31.47N	81.06W
Ossa de Montiel	13	Jf	38.58N	2.45W
Osse	11	Gj	44.07N	0.17 E
Ossining	44	Ke	41.10N	73.52W
Ossjøen	8	Dc	61.15N	11.55 E
Osškaja Oblast [3]	19	Hg	40.45N	73.20 E
Ossora	20	Le	59.15N	163.02 E
Östanvik	8	Fc	61.10N	15.13 E
Ostaškov	19	Dd	57.09N	33.07 E
Ostbevern	12	Jb	52.03N	7.51 E
Oste	10	Fc	53.33N	9.10 E
Ostende/Oostende	11	Ic	51.14N	2.55 E
Oster	16	Gd	50.55N	30.57 E
Oster [Ukr.-U.S.S.R.]	16	Gd	50.53N	30.55 E
Oster [U.S.S.R.]	16	Gc	53.47N	31.45 E
Osterburg in der Altmark	10	Hd	52.47N	11.44 E
Österbybruk	8	Gd	60.12N	17.54 E
Österdalälven	7	Df	60.33N	15.08 E
Østerdalen	7	Cf	62.00N	10.40 E
Osterfjorden	8	Ad	60.30N	5.20 E
Österforse	8	Ga	63.09N	17.01 E
Östergarnsholm	8	Hg	57.25N	19.00 E
Östergötland	8	Ff	58.25N	15.35 E
Östergötland [2]	7	Dg	58.25N	15.45 E
Osterholz Scharmbeck	10	Ec	53.14N	8.48 E
Österlen	8	Fi	55.30N	14.10 E
Östermark/Teuva	7	Ee	62.29N	21.44 E
Osterode am Harz	10	Ge	51.44N	10.11 E
Osterøya	7	Af	60.35N	5.35 E
Österreich = Austria (EN) [1]	6	Hf	47.30N	14.00 E
Östersjön=Baltic Sea (EN)	5	Hd	57.00N	19.00 E
Østersøen=Baltic Sea (EN)	5	Hd	57.00N	19.00 E
Östersund	6	Hc	63.11N	14.39 E
Osterwick, Rosendahl-	12	Jb	52.01N	7.12 E
Østfold [2]	7	Cg	59.20N	11.30 E
Ostfriesische Inseln=East Frisian Islands (EN)	10	Dc	53.45N	7.25 E
Ostfriesland=East Friesland (EN)	10	Dc	53.20N	7.40 E
Østgrønland=East Greenland (EN) [2]	41	Id	72.00N	35.00W
Östhammar	7	Ef	60.16N	18.22 E
Osthofen	12	Ke	49.42N	8.20 E
Östmark	8	Ed	60.17N	12.45 E
Ostrach	10	Fh	48.05N	9.25 E
Östra Silen	8	Ee	59.15N	12.20 E
Ostrava	6	Hf	49.50N	18.17 E
Osthrauderfehn	12	Ja	53.08N	7.37 E
Ostróda	10	Pc	53.43N	19.59 E
Ostrog	16	Ed	50.19N	26.32 E
Ostrogožsk	19	De	50.52N	39.05 E
Ostrołęka [2]	10	Rc	53.05N	21.35 E
Ostrołęka	10	Rc	53.06N	21.34 E
Ostrošicki Gorodok	8	Lj	54.03N	27.46 E
Ostrov [Bye.-U.S.S.R.]	10	Vd	52.48N	26.01 E
Ostrov [Czech.]	10	If	50.18N	12.57 E
Ostrov [Rom.]	15	Ke	44.07N	27.22 E
Ostrov [R.S.F.S.R.]	19	Cd	57.23N	28.22 E
Ostrov [R.S.F.S.R.]	8	Mf	58.28N	28.44 E
Ostrovec	8	Lj	54.38N	26.06 E
Ostrovicës, Mali i-	15	Di	40.34N	20.27 E
Ostrovskoje	7	Kh	57.50N	42.13 E
Ostrov Zmeiny	16	Gg	45.15N	30.12 E
Ostrowiec Świętokrzyski	10	Rf	50.57N	21.23 E
Ostrów Lubelski	10	Se	51.30N	22.52 E
Ostrów Mazowiecka	10	Rd	52.49N	21.54 E
Ostrów Wielkopolski	10	Ne	51.39N	17.49 E
Ostryna	10	Uc	53.41N	24.37 E
Ostrzeszów	10	Ne	51.25N	17.57 E
Ostsee=Baltic Sea (EN)	5	Hd	57.00N	19.00 E
Oststeirisches Hügelland	14	Jd	47.00N	15.45 E
Osttirol	14	Gd	46.55N	12.30 E
Ostuni	14	Lj	40.44N	17.35 E
Osumi	15	Ci	40.48N	19.52 E
Ōsumi	29	Bf	31.36N	130.59 E
Ōsumi-Hantō	29	Bf	31.15N	130.50 E
Ōsumi Islands (EN)=Ōsumi-Shotō	21	Pf	30.35N	130.59 E
Ōsumi-Shotō=Ōsumi Islands (EN)	21	Pf	30.35N	130.59 E
Osuna	13	Gg	37.14N	5.07W
Osveja	8	Mi	55.59N	28.10 E
Osvejskoje, Ozero-	8	Mh	56.00N	28.15 E
Oswego	43	Lc	43.27N	76.31W
Oswestry	9	Ji	52.52N	3.04W

Index Symbols

[1] Independent Nation · [2] State, Region · [3] District, County · [4] Municipality · [5] Colony, Dependency · Continent · Physical Region · Historical or Cultural Region · Mount, Mountain · Volcano · Hill · Mountains, Mountain Range · Hills, Escarpment · Plateau, Upland · Pass, Gap · Plain, Lowland · Delta · Salt Flat · Valley, Canyon · Crater, Cave · Karst Features · Depression · Polder · Desert, Dunes · Forest, Woods · Heath, Steppe · Oasis · Cape, Point · Coast, Beach · Cliff · Peninsula · Isthmus · Sandbank · Island · Atoll · Rock, Reef · Islands, Archipelago · Rocks, Reefs · Coral Reef · Well, Spring · Geyser · River, Stream · Waterfall Rapids · River Mouth, Estuary · Lake · Salt Lake · Intermittent Lake · Reservoir · Swamp, Pond · Canal · Glacier · Ice Shelf, Pack Ice · Ocean · Sea · Gulf, Bay · Strait, Fjord · Lagoon · Bank · Seamount · Tablemount · Ridge · Shelf · Basin · Escarpment, Sea Scarp · Fracture · Trench, Abyss · National Park, Reserve · Point of Interest · Recreation Site · Cave, Cavern · Historic Site · Ruins · Wall, Walls · Church, Abbey · Temple · Scientific Station · Airport · Port · Lighthouse · Mine · Tunnel · Dam, Bridge

Oświęcim	10	Pf	50.03N	19.12 E
Osyka	45	Kk	31.00N	90.28W
Ōta	29	Fc	36.18N	139.22 E
Ota	29	Ec	35.56N	136.03 E
Otago	62	Cf	45.00S	169.10 E
Otago Peninsula	62	Df	45.50S	170.45 E
Ōtake	28	Lg	34.12N	132.13 E
Otakeho	62	Fc	39.33S	174.03 E
Otaki	62	Fd	40.45S	175.08 E
Ōtakime-Yama	29	Gc	37.22N	140.42 E
Otanoshike	29a	Db	43.01N	144.16 E
Otar	19	Hg	43.31N	75.12 E
Otaru	27	Pc	43.13N	141.00 E
Otautau	62	Bg	46.09S	168.00 E
Otava	10	Kg	49.26N	14.12 E
Otava	8	Lc	61.39N	27.04 E
Otavi	37	Bc	19.39S	17.20 E
Ōtawara	28	Pf	36.52N	140.02 E
Otelu Roşu	15	Fd	45.32N	22.22 E
Otematata	62	Df	44.37S	170.11 E
Otepää/Otepja	7	Gg	58.03N	26.30 E
Otepää, Vozvyšennost-/ Otepää Kõrgustik	8	Lf	58.00N	26.40 E
Otepää Kõrgustik/Otepää, Vozvyšennost-	8	Lf	58.00N	26.40 E
Otepja/Otepää	7	Gg	58.03N	26.30 E
Oteros	47	Cc	26.55N	108.30W
Othain	12	He	49.31N	5.23 E
Othello	46	Fc	46.50N	119.10W
Othonoí	15	Cj	39.50N	19.25 E
Óthris Óros	15	Fj	39.02N	22.37 E
Oti	30	Hh	7.48N	0.08 E
Otira	62	De	42.51S	171.33 E
Otish, Monts-	38	Md	52.45N	69.15W
Otjikondo	37	Bc	19.50S	15.23 E
Otjimbingwe	37	Bd	22.21S	16.08 E
Otjiwarongo	31	Ik	20.29S	16.36 E
Otjiwarongo	37	Bd	20.30S	17.30 E
Otjosondjou, Omuramba-	30	Ij	19.55S	20.00 E
Otjosondu	37	Bd	21.12S	17.58 E
Otmuchowskie, Jezioro-	10	Nf	50.27N	17.15 E
Otnes	7	Cf	61.46N	11.12 E
Otobe	29a	Bc	41.57N	140.08 E
Otočac	14	Jf	44.52N	15.14 E
Otofuke	29a	Cb	42.59N	143.10 E
Otofuke-Gawa	29a	Cb	42.56N	143.12 E
Otog Qi (Ulan)	27	Id	39.07N	108.00 E
Otoineppu	29a	Ca	44.43N	142.16 E
Otok	14	Me	45.09N	18.53 E
Otopeni	15	Je	44.33N	26.04 E
Otorohanga	62	Fc	38.11S	175.12 E
Otorten, Gora-	17	If	61.50N	59.13 E
Ōtoyo	29	Ce	33.46N	133.40 E
Otra	5	Gd	58.09N	8.00 E
Otradnaja	16	Lg	44.23N	41.31 E
Otradnoje, Ozero-	8	Nd	60.50N	30.25 E
Otradny	7	Mj	53.23N	51.24 E
Otranto	14	Mj	40.09N	18.30 E
Otranto, Canale d'-= Otranto, Strait of- (EN)	5	Hg	40.00N	19.00 E
Otranto, Capo d'-	14	Mj	40.06N	18.31 E
Otranto, Strait of- (EN)= Otranto, Canale d'-	5	Hg	40.00N	19.00 E
Otranto, Strait of- (EN)= Otrantos, Kanali i-	15	Bi	40.00N	19.00 E
Otranto, Terra d'-	14	Mj	40.20N	18.15 E
Otrantos, Kanali i-=Otranto, Strait of- (EN)	15	Bi	40.00N	19.00 E
Ötscher	14	Jc	47.51N	15.12 E
Ōtsu	28	Mg	35.00N	135.52 E
Ōtsuchi	28	Pe	39.21N	141.54 E
Ōtsuki [Jap.]	29	Fd	35.36N	138.54 E
Ōtsuki [Jap.]	29	Ce	32.50N	132.41 E
Otta	8	Cc	61.46N	9.31 E
Otta	7	Bf	61.46N	9.32 E
Otta	64d	Bb	7.09N	151.54 E
Ottadalen	8	Bc	61.55N	8.00 E
Ottana	14	Dj	40.15N	9.05 E
Otta Pass	64d	Bb	7.09N	151.53 E
Ottawa [Il.-U.S.]	45	Lf	41.21N	88.51W
Ottawa [Ks.-U.S.]	43	Hd	38.37N	95.16W
Ottawa [Oh.-U.S.]	44	Ee	41.02N	84.03W
Ottawa [Ont.-Can.]	39	Le	45.25N	75.42W
Ottawa Islands	38	Kd	59.30N	80.10W
Ottawa River	38	Le	45.20N	73.58W
Ottemby	7	Dh	56.16N	16.24 E
Otterberg	12	Je	49.30N	7.46 E
Otter Creek	44	Fk	29.19N	82.48W
Otterndorf	10	Ec	53.48N	8.54 E
Otteroy	8	Bb	62.40N	6.50 E
Otter Rapids	44	Ga	50.15N	81.45W
Otterup	8	Di	55.31N	10.24 E
Ottumwa	43	Ic	41.01N	92.25W
Ottweiler	12	Je	49.23N	7.10 E
Otukpa	34	Gd	7.05N	7.40 E
Otumpa	55	Ah	27.19S	62.13W
Otuquis, Bañados de-	54	Gg	19.20S	58.30W
Otuquis, Río-	55	Cd	19.41S	58.20W
Oturkpo	34	Gd	7.13N	8.09 E
Otu Tolu Group	65b	Bb	20.21S	174.32W
Otuzco	54	Ce	7.54S	78.35W
Otway, Cape-	59	Ig	38.52S	143.31 E
Otwock	10	Rd	52.07N	21.16 E
Otynja	10	Uh	48.40N	24.57 E
Ötz	14	Ec	47.12N	10.54 E
Ötztaler Ache	14	Ec	47.14N	10.50 E
Ötztaler Alpen	10	Gi	46.45N	10.55 E
Ou	25	Kd	20.04N	102.13 E
'O'ua	65b	Bb	20.02S	174.41W
Oua	63b	Ce	21.14S	167.05 E
Ouachita, Lake-	45	Ji	34.40N	93.25W
Ouachita Mountains	38	Jf	34.40N	94.25W
Ouachita River	43	Ie	31.38N	91.49W
Ouadane	31	Ff	20.57N	11.35W
Ouaddaï	35	Cc	13.00N	21.00 E
Ouaddaï	30	Jg	13.00N	21.00 E
Ouagadougou	31	Gg	12.22N	1.31W
Ouahigouya	31	Gg	13.35N	2.25W
Ouaka	35	Cd	6.00N	21.00 E
Ouaka	30	Ih	4.59N	19.56 E
Oualata	32	Ff	17.18N	7.00W
Oualata, Dahr-	32	Ff	17.48N	7.24W
Oualidia	32	Fc	32.44N	9.02W
Ouallam	34	Fc	14.19N	2.05 E
Ouallene	32	He	24.35N	1.17 E
Ouanda-Djallé	35	Cd	8.54N	22.48 E
Ouandjia	35	Cd	8.35N	23.12 E
Ouandjia	35	Cd	9.35N	21.43 E
Ouango	35	Ce	4.19N	22.33 E
Ouangolodougou	34	Dd	9.58N	5.09W
Ouanne	11	Ig	47.57N	2.47 E
Ouarane	30	Ff	21.00N	10.00W
Ouargaye	34	Fc	11.32N	0.01 E
Ouargla	31	He	31.57N	5.20 E
Ouargla	32	Id	30.00N	6.30 E
Ouarkziz, Jbel-	30	Gf	28.00N	8.20W
Ouarra	30	Jh	5.05N	24.26 E
Ouarsenis, Djebel-	13	Ni	35.53N	1.38 E
Ouarsenis, Massif de l'-	32	Hb	35.50N	2.05 E
Ouarzazate	32	Fc	31.00N	6.30W
Ouarzazate	32	Fc	30.55N	6.55W
Oubangui	30	Ii	0.30S	17.42 E
Ouborré, Pointe-	63b	Dd	18.47S	169.16 E
Ouche, Pays d'-	11	Gf	48.55N	0.45 E
Ōuchi	29	Gb	39.27N	140.06 E
Oud Beijerland	12	Gc	51.50N	4.26 E
Oude IJssel	12	Ic	52.00N	6.10 E
Oudenaarde/Audenarde	11	Jd	50.51N	3.36 E
Oudenbosch	12	Gc	51.35N	4.34 E
Oude Rijn	11	Kb	52.05N	4.20 E
Oudon	11	Fg	47.37N	0.42W
Oudtshoorn	31	Jl	33.35S	22.14 E
Oued Ben Tili	32	Fd	25.48N	9.32W
Oued el Abtal	13	Mi	35.27N	0.41 E
Oued Fodda	13	Nh	36.11N	1.32 E
Oued Lili	13	Ni	35.31N	1.16 E
Oued Rhiou	32	Hb	35.58N	0.55 E
Oued-Taria	13	Mi	35.07N	0.05 E
Oued Tlelat	13	Li	35.33N	0.27W
Oued Zem	31	Ge	32.52N	6.34W
Ouégoa	63b	Be	20.21S	164.26 E
Ouéllé	34	Ed	7.18N	4.01W
Ouémé	30	Hh	6.29N	2.32 E
Ouémé	34	Fd	7.00N	2.35 E
Ouen	63b	Cf	22.26S	166.48 E
Ouenza	32	Ib	35.57N	8.07 E
Ouenza, Djebel-	14	Co	35.57N	8.05 E
Ouessa	34	Ec	11.03N	2.47W
Ouessant, Ile d'-	11	Af	48.28N	5.05W
Ouesso	31	Ih	1.37N	16.04 E
Ouest	34	Hd	5.20N	10.30 E
Ouest, Baie de l'-	64h	Ab	13.15S	176.13W
Ouezzane	32	Fc	34.48N	5.36W
Oughter, Lough-	9	Fg	54.00N	7.29W
Ouham	35	Bd	7.00N	18.00 E
Ouham	30	Ih	9.18N	18.14 E
Ouham-Pendé	35	Bd	7.00N	16.00 E
Ouidah	34	Fd	6.22N	2.05 E
Ouistreham	11	Fe	49.17N	0.15W
Ouistreham-Riva Bella	12	Be	49.17N	0.16W
Oujda	32	Gc	33.00N	2.00W
Oujda	31	Ge	34.40N	1.54W
Oujeft	32	Ee	20.02N	13.03W
Oulainen	7	Fd	64.16N	24.57 E
Oulchy-le-Château	12	Fe	49.12N	3.21 E
Ouled Djellal	32	Ic	34.25N	5.04 E
Ouled Naïl, Monts des-	32	Hc	34.40N	3.25 E
Oulou, Bahr-	35	Cd	9.48N	21.32 E
Oulu	7	Gd	65.00N	27.00 E
Oulu/Uleåborg	6	Ib	65.01N	25.30 E
Oulu, Lake- (EN)= Oulujärvi	5	Ic	64.20N	27.15 E
Oulujärvi=Oulu, Lake- (EN)	5	Ic	64.20N	27.15 E
Oulujoki	5	Ib	65.01N	25.25 E
Oum Chalouba	31	Jg	15.48N	20.46 E
Oumé	34	Dd	6.25N	5.30W
Oumé	34	Dd	6.23N	5.25W
Oum el Bouaghi	32	Ib	35.30N	7.10 E
Oum el Bouaghi	32	Ib	35.53N	7.07 E
Oum er Rbia	30	Ge	33.19N	8.20W
Oum Hadjer	35	Bc	13.18N	19.41 E
Oumm ed Droûs Guebli, Sebkhet-	32	Ee	24.03N	11.45W
Oumm ed Droûs Telli, Sebkhet-	32	Ee	24.20N	11.30W
Ounasjoki	5	Ib	66.30N	25.45 E
Oundle	12	Bb	52.29N	0.28W
Ounianga	35	Cb	19.10N	20.30 E
Ounianga Kébir	31	Jg	19.04N	20.29 E
Ountivou	34	Fd	7.21N	1.34 E
Ouolosséboubou	34	Dc	12.00N	7.55W
Oupeye	12	Hd	50.42N	5.39 E
Oupu	27	Ma	52.45N	126.00 E
Our	12	Ie	49.53N	6.18 E
Ouray	45	Cg	38.01N	107.40W
Ouray, Mount-	45	Cg	38.25N	106.14W
Ource	11	Kf	48.06N	4.23 E
Ourcq	11	Je	49.01N	3.01 E
Ourcq, Canal de l'-	11	If	48.51N	2.22 E
Ourém	54	Id	1.33S	47.06W
Ouricuri	54	Je	7.35S	40.05W
Ourinhos	53	Lh	22.59S	49.52W
Ouro, Rio do-	55	Ha	13.20S	48.59W
Ouro Fino	55	If	22.17S	46.22W
Ouro Prêto	54	Jh	20.23S	43.30W
Ourthe [Bel.]	11	Ld	50.38N	5.35 E
Ourville-en-Caux	12	Ce	49.44N	0.36 E
Ous	19	Gc	60.55N	61.31 E
Ōu-Sanmyaku	28	Pe	39.00N	141.00 E
Ouse [Eng.-U.K.]	9	Nk	50.47N	0.03 E
Ouse [Eng.-U.K.]	9	Mh	53.42N	0.41W
Oust	11	Dg	47.35N	2.06W
Outagouna	34	Fb	15.11N	0.43 E
Outaouais, Rivière-	38	Le	45.20N	73.58W
Outardes, Rivière aux-	42	Kg	49.05N	68.23W
Outat Oulad El Hajj	32	Gc	33.21N	3.42W
Outer Dowsing	9	Oh	53.25N	1.05 E
Outer Hebrides	9	Fd	57.50N	7.32W
Outer Santa Barbara Passage	46	Fj	33.10N	118.30W
Outer Silver Pit	9	Og	54.05N	2.00 E
Outjo	31	Ik	20.08S	16.08 E
Outjo	37	Ac	19.30S	14.30 E
Outlook	46	La	51.30N	107.03W
Outokumpu	7	Ge	62.44N	29.01 E
Outram Mountain	46	Eb	49.19N	121.05W
Outreau	12	Dd	50.42N	1.35 E
Out Skerries	9	Ma	60.30N	0.50W
Outwell	12	Cb	52.37N	0.14 E
Ouvéa, Ile-	57	Hg	20.35S	166.35 E
Ouvèze	11	Kk	43.59N	4.51 E
Ouxian	28	Ej	28.58N	118.53 E
Ouyen	59	Ig	35.04S	142.20 E
Ouyou Bézédinga	34	Hb	16.32N	13.15 E
Ouzera	13	Oh	36.15N	2.51 E
Ovacık [Tur.]	24	Ed	36.11N	33.40 E
Ovacık [Tur.]	24	Hc	39.22N	39.13 E
Ovada	14	Cf	44.38N	8.38 E
Ova Gölü	15	Mm	36.16N	29.22 E
Ovakent	15	Lk	38.06N	28.02 E
Ovalau Island	63d	Bb	17.40S	178.48 E
Ovalle	53	Ii	30.36S	71.12W
Oval Peak	46	Eb	48.15N	120.25W
Ovamboland	37	Bc	18.30S	16.00 E
Ovamboland	37	Bc	18.00S	16.00 E
Ovan	36	Bb	0.30N	12.10 E
Ovanåker	7	Df	61.21N	15.54 E
Ovar	13	Dd	40.52N	8.38W
Ovau	63a	Cb	6.48S	156.02 E
Ovejas	49	Ji	9.32N	75.14W
Overath	12	Jd	50.57N	7.18 E
Øverbygd	7	Eb	69.01N	19.18 E
Overflakke	11	Kc	51.45N	4.10 E
Overhalla	7	Cd	64.30N	12.00 E
Overije	12	Gd	50.46N	4.32 E
Overijssel	12	Ib	52.25N	6.30 E
Överkalix	7	Fc	66.19N	22.50 E
Overland Park	45	Ig	38.59N	94.40W
Övermark/Ylimarkku	8	Ib	62.37N	21.28 E
Overpelt	12	Hc	51.12N	5.25 E
Overri	34	Gd	5.29N	7.02 E
Overton	46	Hh	36.33N	114.27W
Övertorneå	7	Fc	66.23N	23.40 E
Överum	8	Gg	57.59N	16.19 E
Ovidiu	15	Le	44.16N	28.34 E
Oviedo	13	Ga	43.20N	6.00W
Oviedo [Dom.Rep.]	49	Le	17.47N	71.22W
Oviedo [Sp.]	6	Fg	43.22N	5.50W
Oviši	8	Ig	57.34N	21.35 E
Ovo, Capo dell'-	14	Lj	40.18N	17.30 E
Øvre Årdal	7	Bf	61.19N	7.48 E
Övre Fryken	8	Ed	60.00N	13.05 E
Övre Soppero	7	Eb	68.05N	21.41 E
Ovruč	19	Ce	51.19N	28.50 E
Ovsjanka	20	Hf	53.32N	126.58 E
Owaka	62	Cg	46.27S	169.40 E
Owando	31	Ii	0.29S	15.55 E
Ōwani	28	Pd	40.31N	140.35 E
Owase	28	Ng	34.04N	136.12 E
Owatonna	43	Ic	44.05N	93.14W
Owego	44	Id	42.06N	76.16W
Owen, Mount-	62	Ed	41.33S	172.32 E
Owendo	36	Ab	0.17N	9.30 E
Owen Falls Dam	36	Fb	0.24N	33.11 E
Owensboro	43	Jd	37.46N	87.07W
Owens Lake	46	Gh	36.25N	117.56W
Owen Sound	42	Jh	44.34N	80.56W
Owens River	46	Gh	36.31N	117.57W
Owen Stanley Range	57	Fe	9.20S	148.00 E
Owl Creek Mountains	46	Ke	43.30N	108.35W
Ownay, Kowlal-e-	23	Kc	34.27N	68.22 E
Owo	34	Gd	7.11N	5.35 E
Owosso	44	Ed	43.00N	84.10W
Owyhee	46	Gf	41.57N	116.06W
Owyhee, Lake-	46	Ge	43.28N	117.20W
Owyhee Mountains	46	Ge	43.00N	116.45W
Owyhee River [U.S.]	46	Ge	43.40N	117.16W
Owyhee River [U.S.]	43	Dc	43.46N	117.02W
Oxberg	8	Fc	61.07N	14.10 E
Oxbow	45	Eb	49.14N	102.11W
Oxelösund	7	Dg	58.40N	17.06 E
Oxford	9	Lj	51.50N	1.30W
Oxford [Eng.-U.K.]	6	Fe	51.46N	1.15W
Oxford [Ms.-U.S.]	45	Li	34.22N	89.32W
Oxford [N.C.-U.S.]	44	Hg	36.19N	78.35W
Oxford [N.Z.]	62	Ee	43.17S	172.11 E
Oxford Lake	42	Hf	54.50N	95.35W
Oxfordshire	9	Lj	51.50N	1.20W
Oxía	15	Ek	38.18N	21.06 E
Oxkutzcab	48	Og	20.18N	89.25W
Oxnard	43	De	34.12N	119.11W
Ox or Slieve Gamph Mountains/Sliabh Gamh	9	Eg	54.10N	8.50W
Oxted	12	Bc	51.14N	0.01W
Oyabe	29	Ec	36.40N	136.52 E
Oyahue	53	Jh	21.08S	68.45W
O-Yama	29	Fd	34.04N	139.31 E
Oyama	28	Of	36.21N	139.50 E
Ōyama	29	Ec	36.35N	137.18 E
Ōyano	29	Be	32.35N	130.27 E
Oyapock, Fleuve-	52	Ke	4.08N	51.40W
Oyem	31	Ih	1.37N	11.35 E
Oyen	46	Ja	51.22N	110.28W
Øyeren	8	De	59.50N	11.14 E
Oykel	9	Id	57.50N	4.25W
Oyo	34	Fd	8.00N	3.50 E
Oyo [Nig.]	34	Fd	7.51N	3.56 E
Oyo [Sud.]	35	Fa	21.55N	36.06 E
Oyodo-Gawa	29	Bf	31.55N	131.28 E
Oyonnax	11	Lh	46.15N	5.40 E
Oyster Bay	59	Jh	42.10S	148.10 E
Øystese	8	Bd	60.23N	6.13 E
Özalp	24	Jc	38.39N	43.59 E
Ozamiz	26	He	8.08N	123.50 E
Ozark	44	Ej	31.28N	85.38W
Ozark Plateau	38	Jf	37.00N	93.00W
Ozark Reservoir	45	Ii	35.25N	94.05W
Ozarks, Lake of the-	43	Id	37.39N	92.50W
Ózd	10	Qh	48.13N	20.18 E
Ozeblin	14	Jf	44.35N	15.53 E
Ozernoj, Zaliv-	20	Le	57.00N	163.20 E
Ozernovski	20	Kf	51.21N	156.32 E
Ozerny	16	Vd	51.08N	60.55 E
Ozersk	8	Ij	54.24N	21.59 E
Ozery [Bye.-U.S.S.R.]	10	Uc	53.38N	24.18 E
Ozery [R.S.F.S.R.]	7	Ji	54.54N	38.32 E
Ožezdy	19	Gf	48.03N	67.09 E
Ozieri	14	Cj	40.35N	9.00 E
Ozinki	19	Ee	51.12N	49.47 E
Ožogina	20	Kc	66.12N	151.05 E
Ozona	43	Ge	30.43N	101.12W
Ozorków	10	Pe	51.58N	19.19 E
Ozouri	36	Ac	0.55S	8.55 E
Ozren [Yugo.]	14	Mf	44.37N	18.15 E
Ozren [Yugo.]	14	Mg	43.59N	18.30 E
Ozren [Yugo.]	15	Ef	43.36N	21.54 E
Ōzu [Jap.]	29	Be	32.52N	130.52 E
Ōzu [Jap.]	28	Lh	33.30N	132.23 E

P

Pääjärvi	8	Kb	62.50N	24.45 E
Paama	63b	Dc	16.28S	168.13 E
Pa-an → Pha-an	25	Je	16.53N	97.38 E
Paar	10	Hh	48.45N	11.35 E
Paarl	31	Il	33.45S	18.56 E
Paauilo	65a	Fc	20.03N	155.22W
Paavola	7	Fd	64.36N	25.12 E
Pabbay	9	Fd	57.47N	7.20W
Pabellón, Ensenada del-	48	Fe	24.27N	107.36W
Pabianice	10	Pe	51.40N	19.22 E
Pābna	25	Hd	24.00N	89.15 E
Pabradé/Pabrade	7	Fi	54.59N	25.50 E
Pabrade/Pabradė	7	Fi	54.59N	25.50 E
Pacaás Novos, Serra dos-	54	Ff	10.50S	64.00W
Pacajá, Rio-	54	Hd	1.56S	50.55W
Pacajus	54	Kd	4.10S	38.28W
Pacaraima, Serra-	52	Je	4.30N	60.40W
Pacasmayo	54	Ce	7.24S	79.34W
Paceco	14	Gm	37.59N	12.33 E
Pachala	35	Ed	7.10N	34.06 E
Pacheco	48	Eb	30.06N	108.21W
Pachino	14	Jn	36.43N	15.05 E
Pachitea, Río-	54	De	8.46S	74.32W
Pachuca de Soto	47	Ed	20.07N	98.44W
Pacific-Antarctic Ridge (EN)	3	Kp	62.00S	157.00W
Pacific City	46	Dd	45.12N	123.57W
Pacific Grove	46	Eh	36.38N	121.56W
Pacific Islands, Trust Territory of the-	58	Ed	7.30N	134.30 E
Pacifico, Océano- = Pacific Ocean (EN)	3	Ki	5.00N	155.00W
Pacific Ocean	3	Ki	5.00N	155.00W
Pacific Ocean (EN)=Kita-Taiheiyō	60	Ch	22.00N	167.00 E
Pacific Ocean (EN)= Pacífico, Océano-	3	Ki	5.00N	155.00W
Pacific Ocean (EN)= Pacifique, Océan-	3	Ki	5.00N	155.00W
Pacific Ocean (EN)= Taiheiyō	3	Ki	5.00N	155.00W
Pacific Ocean (EN)=Tihi Okean	3	Ki	5.00N	155.00W
Pacific Ranges	42	Ef	50.55N	125.10W
Pacifique, Océan-=Pacific Ocean (EN)	3	Ki	5.00N	155.00W
Packsattel	14	Id	46.58N	14.58 E
Pacuí, Rio-	55	Jc	16.46S	45.01W
Pacuneiro, Rio-	55	Fa	13.02S	53.25W
Pacy-sur-Eure	12	De	49.01N	1.23 E
Paczków	10	Mf	50.27N	17.00 E
Padana, Pianura-=Po Valley (EN)	5	Gf	45.20N	10.00 E
Padang	22	Mj	0.57S	100.21 E
Padangsidempuan	26	Cf	1.22N	99.16 E
Padangtikar, Pulau-	26	Eg	0.50S	109.30 E
Padany	7	He	63.19N	33.25 E
Padasjoki	8	Kc	61.21N	25.17 E
Padauiri, Rio-	54	Fd	0.15S	64.05W
Paddle Prairie	42	Fe	58.02N	117.50W
Paderborn	10	Ee	51.43N	8.46 E
Paderborn-Elsen	12	Kc	51.44N	8.41 E
Paderborn-Schloß Neuhaus	12	Kc	51.44N	8.42 E
Padeş, Vîrful-	15	Fd	45.40N	22.20 E
Padilla	54	Fg	19.19S	64.20W
Padina	15	Ke	44.50N	27.07 E
Padornelo, Portillo del-	13	Fb	42.03N	6.50W
Padova = Padua (EN)	14	Fe	45.25N	11.53 E
Padre, Morro do-	55	Ic	16.48S	47.35W
Padre Bernardo	55	Hb	15.21S	48.30W
Padre Island	43	Hf	27.00N	97.15W
Padrón	13	Db	42.44N	8.40W
Padua (EN) = Padova	14	Fe	45.25N	11.53 E
Paducah [Ky.-U.S.]	39	Kf	37.05N	88.36W
Paducah [Tx.-U.S.]	45	Fi	34.01N	100.18W
Padula	14	Jj	40.20N	15.39 E
Paea	65e	Fc	17.41S	149.35W
Paegam-san	28	Id	40.35N	126.15 E
Paengnyong-Do	27	Ld	38.00N	124.40 E
Paeroa	61	Eg	37.23S	175.41 E
Paestum	14	Jj	40.25N	15.01 E
Paeu	63c	Bb	11.22S	166.50 E
Pafuri	37	Ed	22.26S	31.20 E
Pag	14	Jf	44.27N	15.03 E
Pag	14	If	44.30N	15.00 E
Pagadian	26	He	7.49N	123.25 E
Pagai, Kepulauan-=Pagi Islands (EN)	21	Lj	2.45S	100.00 E
Pagai Selatan	26	Dg	3.00S	100.20 E
Pagai Utara	26	Cg	2.42S	100.07 E
Pagan Island	57	Fc	18.07N	145.46 E
Pagasitikós Kólpos	15	Fj	39.15N	23.00 E
Pagatan	26	Gg	3.36S	115.56 E
Pagat Point	64c	Bb	13.30N	144.53 E
Page	46	Jh	36.57N	111.27W
Pagėgiai	8	Ii	55.09N	21.54 E
Paget, Mount-	66	Ad	54.26S	36.33W
Pagi Islands (EN)=Pagai, Kepulauan-	21	Lj	2.45S	100.00 E
Paglia	14	Gh	42.42N	12.11 E
Pago Bay	64c	Bb	13.25N	144.48 E
Pagoda Point	21	Lh	15.57N	94.15 E
Pāgodār	24	Qh	28.10N	57.22 E
Pago Pago	58	Jf	14.16S	170.42W
Pago Pago Harbor	65c	Cb	14.17S	170.40W
Pago Redondo	55	Ci	29.35S	59.13W
Pagosa Springs	45	Ch	37.16N	107.01W
Pagoua Bay	51g	Ba	15.32N	61.17W
Pagwa River	45	Na	50.01N	85.10W
Pahači	20	Ld	60.30N	169.00 E
Pahala	65a	Fd	19.12N	155.29W
Pàhara, Laguna-	49	Ff	14.18N	83.15W
Pahiatua	62	Fd	40.27S	175.50 E
Pahkāing Bum	21	Lg	26.00N	95.30 E
Pahoa	65a	Gd	19.30N	154.57W
Pahokee	44	Gl	26.49N	80.40W
Pahtakor	18	Fd	40.16N	67.55 E
Pahute Mesa	46	Gh	37.20N	116.40W
Païa	63b	Dc	16.35S	168.12 E
Paide/Pajde	7	Fg	58.57N	25.35 E
Paignton	9	Jk	50.28N	3.30W
Päijänne	5	Ic	61.35N	23.30 E
Páïkon Óros	15	Fi	40.56N	22.21 E
Paila	48	He	25.39N	102.07W
Pailîn	25	Kf	12.51N	102.36 E
Pailitas	49	Ki	8.58N	73.38W
Pailolo Channel	65a	Eb	21.05N	156.42W
Paimio/Pemar	8	Jd	60.27N	22.42 E
Paimionjoki	8	Jd	60.25N	22.40 E
Paimpol	11	Cf	48.46N	3.03W
Painan	26	Dg	1.21S	100.34 E
Paine, Mount-	66	Mg	86.46S	147.32W
Painel	55	Gh	27.55S	50.06W
Painesville	44	Ge	41.43N	81.15W
Painted Desert	43	Ed	36.00N	111.20W
Paintsville	44	Fg	37.49N	82.48W
Pais do Vinho	13	Ec	41.15N	7.55W
Paisley	9	If	55.50N	4.26W
Paita	54	Be	5.06S	81.07W
Païta	63b	Cf	22.08S	166.22 E
Paiva	13	Dc	41.04N	8.16W
Paj	7	If	61.43N	34.28 E
Pajala	7	Fc	67.12N	23.22 E
Pajares, Puerto de-	13	Ga	43.00N	5.46W
Pajaros, Punta-	48	Ph	19.36N	87.25W
Pajaros Point	51a	Db	18.31N	64.18W
Pajatén	54	Ce	7.29S	77.22W
Pajde/Paide	7	Fg	58.57N	25.35 E
Pajęczno	10	Oe	51.09N	19.00 E
Pajer, Gora-	19	Gb	66.40N	64.20 E
Paj-Hoj	5	Mb	69.00N	62.30 E
Pajule	36	Fb	2.58N	32.56 E
Pakanbaru	22	Mi	0.32N	101.27 E
Pakaraima Mountains	54	Fb	4.05N	61.30W
Pakch'on	28	He	39.44N	125.35 E
Pakhiá	15	Im	36.16N	25.50 E
Pakhna	24	Ee	34.46N	32.48 E
Pákhnes	15	Gn	35.18N	23.58 E
Paki	34	Gc	11.30N	8.09 E
Pakima	36	Dc	3.21S	24.06 E
Pakin Atoll	57	Gd	7.04N	157.48 E
Pakistan	22	Ig	30.00N	70.00 E
Pakleni Otoci	14	Kg	43.10N	16.23 E
Pakokku	25	Jd	21.17N	95.06 E
Pakowki Lake	46	Jb	49.22N	110.57W
Pak Phanang	25	Kg	8.21N	100.12 E
Pakrac	14	Le	45.26N	17.12 E
Pakruois/Pakruojis	7	Fi	55.57N	23.50 E
Pakruojis/Pakruois	7	Fi	55.57N	23.50 E
Paks	10	Oj	46.38N	18.52 E
Paktīā	23	Kc	33.30N	69.30 E
Pakwach	36	Fb	2.28N	31.30 E
Pakxé	22	Mh	15.07N	105.47 E
Pakxèng	25	Kd	20.10N	102.40 E
Pala	35	Ad	9.22N	14.54 E
Palacca Point	49	Kc	21.15N	73.26W
Palacios [Arg.]	55	Bj	30.43S	61.37W
Palacios [Tx.-U.S.]	45	Hl	28.42N	96.13W
Palafrugell	13	Pc	41.55N	3.10 E
Palagruža	14	Kh	42.24N	16.15 E
Palaiokastrítsa	15	Cj	39.40N	19.41 E
Palaiokhóra	15	Gn	35.14N	23.41 E
Palaiseau	12	Ef	48.43N	2.15 E
Palamás	15	Fj	39.28N	22.05 E
Palamós	13	Pc	41.51N	3.08 E
Palamuse/Palamuze	8	Lf	58.39N	26.35 E
Palamut	15	Kk	38.59N	27.41 E
Palamuze/Palamuse	8	Lf	58.39N	26.35 E
Palana	22	Rd	59.07N	159.58 E
Palancia	13	Le	39.40N	0.12W
Palanga	19	Cd	55.57N	21.05 E
Palangkaraya	26	Fg	2.16S	113.56 E
Pālanpur	25	Ed	24.10N	72.26 E

Index Symbols

- Independent Nation
- State, Region
- District, County
- Municipality
- Colony, Dependency
- Continent
- Physical Region
- Historical or Cultural Region
- Mount, Mountain
- Volcano
- Hill
- Mountains, Mountain Range
- Hills, Escarpment
- Plateau, Upland
- Pass, Gap
- Plain, Lowland
- Delta
- Salt Flat
- Valley, Canyon
- Crater, Cave
- Karst Features
- Depression
- Polder
- Desert, Dunes
- Forest, Woods
- Heath, Steppe
- Oasis
- Cape, Point
- Coast, Beach
- Cliff
- Peninsula
- Isthmus
- Sandbank
- Island
- Atoll
- Rock, Reef
- Islands, Archipelago
- Rocks, Reefs
- Coral Reef
- Well, Spring
- Geyser
- River, Stream
- Waterfall Rapids
- River Mouth, Estuary
- Lake
- Salt Lake
- Intermittent Lake
- Reservoir
- Swamp, Pond
- Canal
- Glacier
- Ice Shelf, Pack Ice
- Ocean
- Sea
- Gulf, Bay
- Strait, Fjord
- Lagoon
- Bank
- Seamount
- Tablemount
- Ridge
- Shelf
- Basin
- Escarpment, Sea Scarp
- Fracture
- Trench, Abyss
- National Park, Reserve
- Point of Interest
- Recreation Site
- Cave, Cavern
- Historic Site
- Ruins
- Wall, Walls
- Church, Abbey
- Temple
- Scientific Station
- Airport
- Port
- Lighthouse
- Mine
- Tunnel
- Dam, Bridge

Palaoa Point 65a Ec 20.44N 156.58W
Palapye 31 Jk 22.33S 27.08 E
Palasa 26 Hf 0.29N 120.24 E
Palatka [Fl.-U.S.] 43 Kf 29.39N 81.38W
Palatka [R.S.F.S.R.] 20 Kd 60.05N 151.00 E
Palau (EN) = Belau 14 Di 41.11N 9.23 E
Palau 58 Ed 7.30N 134.30 E
Palau Islands 57 Ed 7.30N 134.30 E
Palauli 65c Aa 13.44S 172.16W
Palauli Bay 65c Aa 13.47S 172.14W
Palau Trench (EN) 60 Af 6.30N 134.30 E
Palavas-les-Flots 11 Jk 43.32N 3.56 E
Palaw 25 Jf 12.58N 98.39 E
Palawan 21 Ni 9.30N 118.30 E
Palawan Passage 26 Gd 10.00N 118.00 E
Palayan 26 Hc 15.33N 121.06 E
Pālayankottai 25 Fg 8.43N 77.44 E
Palazzo, Punta- 11a Aa 42.22N 8.33 E
Palazzolo Acreide 14 Im 37.04N 14.54 E
Palazzolo sull'Oglio 14 De 45.36N 9.53 E
Paldiski 19 Cd 59.20N 24.06 E
Pale di San Martino 14 Fd 46.14N 11.53 E
Paleleh 26 Hf 1.04N 121.57 E
Palembang 22 Mj 2.55S 104.45 E
Palena 14 Ii 41.59N 14.08 E
Palencia 13 Hb 42.25N 4.30W
Palencia 13 Hb 42.01N 4.32W
Palen Lake 46 Hj 33.46N 115.12W
Palenque 39 Jh 17.30N 92.00W
Palenque [Mex.] 48 Ni 17.31N 91.58W
Palenque [Pan.] 49 Hi 9.13N 79.41W
Palenque, Punta- 49 Ld 18.14N 70.09W
Palermo 6 Hh 38.07N 13.22 E
Palermo, Golfo di- 14 Hl 38.10N 13.25 E
Palestine 43 He 31.46N 95.38W
Palestine (EN) 23 Dc 32.15N 34.47 E
Palestrina 14 Gi 41.50N 12.53 E
Pālghāt 25 Ff 10.47N 76.39 E
Palgrave Point 37 Ad 20.28S 13.16 E
Palhoça 55 Hh 27.38S 48.40W
Pāli 25 Ec 25.46N 73.20 E
Palinuro 14 Jj 40.02N 15.17 E
Palinuro, Capo- 14 Jj 40.02N 15.16 E
Palisades Reservoir 46 Je 43.04N 111.26W
Paliseul 12 He 49.54N 5.08 E
Palivere 8 Jf 59.00N 23.45 E
Palizada 48 Mh 18.15N 92.05W
Paljakka 7 Gd 64.45N 28.07 E
Paljavaam 20 Mc 68.50N 170.50 E
Paljenik 5 Hg 44.15N 17.36 E
Pälkäne 8 Kc 61.20N 24.16 E
Palkino 8 Mg 57.29N 28.10 E
Palk Strait 21 Ji 10.00N 79.45 E
Palla Bianca/Weißkugel 14 Ed 46.48N 10.44 E
Pallars 13 Mb 42.25N 0.55 E
Pallars, Montsent de-/
Montseny 13 Nb 42.29N 1.02 E
Pallasovka 19 Ee 50.03N 46.55 E
Pallastunturi 7 Fb 68.06N 24.02 E
Palliser, Cape- 61 Eh 41.37S 175.16 E
Palliser, Iles- 57 Mf 15.30S 146.30W
Palma [Moz.] 37 Gb 10.46S 40.28 E
Palma [Sp.] 6 Gh 39.34N 2.39 E
Palma, Badia de-/Palma,
Bahia de- 13 Oe 39.27N 2.35 E
Palma, Bahia de-/Palma,
Badia de- 13 Oe 39.27N 2.35 E
Palma, Rio- 54 If 12.33S 47.52W
Palma, Sierra de la- 48 Id 26.00N 101.35W
Palma del Rio 13 Gg 37.42N 5.17W
Palma di Montechiaro 14 Hm 37.11N 13.46 E
Palmar, Laguna del- 55 Bi 29.35S 60.42W
Palmar, Rio- 49 Lh 10.11N 71.52W
Palmar, Salto- 55 Cg 24.18S 59.18W
Palmares 54 Ke 8.41S 35.36W
Palmares do Sul 55 Gj 30.16S 50.31W
Palmarito 54 Db 7.37N 70.10W
Palmarola 14 Gj 40.55N 12.50 E
Palmar Sur 47 Hg 8.58N 83.29W
Palmas 56 Jc 26.30S 52.00W
Palmas, Cape- 30 Gh 4.22N 7.44W
Palmas, Golfo di- 14 Cl 39.00N 8.30 E
Palmas Bellas 49 Gi 9.14N 80.05W
Palma Soriano 47 Id 20.13N 76.00W
Palm Bay 44 Gk 28.01N 80.35W
Palm Beach 43 Kf 26.42N 80.02W
Palmdale 46 Fi 34.35N 118.07W
Palmeira 55 Gg 25.25S 50.00W
Palmeira das Missões 56 Jc 27.55S 53.17W
Palmeira dos Indios 54 Ke 9.25S 36.37W
Palmeirais 54 Je 5.58S 43.04W
Palmeiras, Rio- 55 Gb 15.25S 51.10W
Palmeiras de Goiás 55 Hc 16.47S 49.53W
Palmeirinhas, Ponta das- 30 Ii 9.05S 13.00 E
Palmela 13 Df 38.34N 8.54W
Palmer 40 Jd 61.36N 149.07W
Palmer Archipelago 66 Qe 64.10S 62.00W
Palmer Land (EN) 66 Qf 71.30S 65.00W
Palmer Station 66 Qe 64.46S 64.05W
Palmerston 57 Kf 18.04S 163.10W
Palmerston Atoll 57 Kf 18.04S 163.10W
Palmerston North 58 Ii 40.28S 175.17 E
Palmetto Point 51d Ba 17.35N 61.52W
Palmi 14 Jl 38.21N 15.51 E
Palmira [Col.] 53 Ie 3.32N 76.16W
Palmira [Cuba] 49 Gb 22.14N 80.23W
Palm Islands 59 Jc 18.40S 146.30 E
Palmital 55 Fg 24.39S 52.16W
Palmitas 55 Dk 33.27S 57.48W
Palmito 55 Cd 18.53S 58.22W
Palmitos 55 Fh 27.05S 53.08W
Palm Springs 43 De 33.50N 116.33W
Palmyra 23 Ec 34.33N 38.17 E
Palmyra Atoll 57 Kd 5.52N 162.06W
Palo Alto 43 Cd 37.27N 122.09W
Paloh 26 Ef 1.43N 109.18 E
Paloich 35 Ec 10.28N 32.32 E
Palomani, Nevado- 52 Jg 14.38S 69.14W
Palomar Mountain 43 De 33.22N 116.50W
Palomera, Sierra- 13 Kd 40.40N 1.12W
Palopo 22 Oj 3.00S 120.12 E
Palos, Cabo de- 5 Fh 37.38N 0.41W
Palo Santo 55 Cg 25.34S 59.21W
Palotina 55 Fg 24.17S 53.50W
Palouse River 46 Fc 46.35N 118.13W
Palpa 54 Cf 14.32S 75.11W
Palsa 8 Lg 57.23N 26.24 E
Pålsboda 8 Fe 59.04N 15.20 E
Paltamo 7 Gd 64.25N 27.50 E
Palu [Indon.] 22 Nj 0.53S 119.53 E
Palu [Tur.] 24 Hc 38.42N 39.57 E
Palu, Pulau- 26 Hh 8.20S 121.43 E
Pam 63b Be 20.15S 164.17 E
Pama 34 Fc 11.15N 0.42 E
Påmark/Pomarkku 8 Ic 61.42N 22.00 E
Pambarra 37 Fd 21.56S 35.06 E
Pambeguwa 34 Gc 10.40N 8.17 E
Pamekasan 26 Fh 7.10S 113.28 E
Pamiers 11 Hk 43.07N 1.36 E
Pamir 21 Jf 38.00N 73.00 E
Pamir 19 Hh 37.01N 72.41 E
Pâmiut/Frederikshåb 41 Hf 62.00N 49.45W
Pamlico Sound 43 Ld 35.20N 75.55W
Pampa 43 Gd 35.32N 100.58W
Pampa del Indio 55 Ch 26.02S 59.55W
Pampa del Infierno 55 Bh 26.31S 61.10W
Pampa de los Guanacos 56 Hc 26.14S 61.51W
Pampas 54 Df 12.24S 74.54W
Pampas 52 Ji 35.00S 63.00W
Pampeiro 55 Ej 30.38S 55.16W
Pamplona [Col.] 54 Db 7.23N 72.38W
Pamplona [Sp.] 6 Fg 42.49N 1.38W
Pamukkale 15 Ml 37.47N 29.04 E
Pamukova 15 Ni 40.31N 30.09 E
Pamunkey River 44 Ig 37.32N 76.48W
Pan, Tierra del- 13 Gc 41.50N 6.00W
Pana 36 Bc 1.41S 12.39 E
Panagjurište 15 Hg 42.30N 24.11 E
Panaitan, Pulau- 26 Eh 6.36S 105.12 E
Panaitolikón Óros 15 Ek 38.43N 21.39 E
Panaji (Panjim) 22 Jh 15.29N 73.50 E
Panakhaïkón Óros 15 Ek 38.12N 21.54 E
Panamá 39 Li 9.00N 80.00W
Panamá = Panama (EN) 49 Hi 9.00N 79.00W
Panamá = Panama City (EN) 39 Li 8.58N 79.31W
Panama (EN) = Panamá 49 Hi 9.00N 79.00W
Panamá, Bahía de- 49 Hi 8.50N 79.15W
Panamá, Canal de- =
Panama Canal (EN) 47 Ig 9.20N 79.55W
Panamá, Golfo de- =
Panama, Gulf of- (EN) 38 Li 8.00N 79.10W
Panama, Gulf of- (EN) =
Panamá, Golfo de- 38 Li 8.00N 79.10W
Panama, Isthmus of- (EN) =
Panamá, Istmo de- 38 Li 9.20N 79.30W
Panamá, Istmo de- =
Panama, Isthmus of- (EN)
38 Li 9.20N 79.30W
Panama Canal (EN) =
Panamá, Canal de- 47 Ig 9.20N 79.55W
Panama City [La.-U.S.] 39 Kf 30.10N 85.41W
Panama City (EN) = Panamá 39 Li 8.58N 79.31W
Panamá La Vieja 49 Hi 9.00N 79.29W
Panambi 55 Fi 28.18S 53.30W
Panamint Range 46 Gh 36.30N 117.20W
Panao 54 Ce 9.49S 76.00W
Panarea 14 Jl 38.40N 15.05 E
Panaro 14 Ff 44.55N 11.25 E
Pana Tinai 63a Ad 11.14S 153.10 E
Pana-Wina 63a Ad 11.11S 153.01 E
Panay 21 Oh 11.15N 122.30 E
Pancake Range 46 Hg 39.00N 115.45W
Pančevo 15 De 44.52N 20.39 E
Pančićev vrh 15 Df 43.15N 20.45 E
Panciu 15 Kd 45.54N 27.05 E
Pancros 63b Db 15.58S 168.12 E
Panda 37 Ed 24.03S 34.43 E
Panda ma Tenga 37 Dc 18.32S 25.38 E
Pandan 26 Hd 11.43N 122.06 E
Pan de Azúcar 55 El 34.48S 55.14W
Pandeiros, Ribeirão- 55 Jb 15.42S 44.36W
Pandelis/Pandėlys 8 Kh 56.01N 25.21 E
Pandėlys/Pandelis 8 Kh 56.01N 25.21 E
Pandharpur 25 Fe 17.40N 75.20 E
Pándheon 15 Fl 40.05N 22.20 E
Pāndhurna 25 Fd 21.36N 78.31 E
Pandivere Kõrgustik/
Pandivere Vozvyšennost 8 Le 59.00N 26.15 E
Pandivere Vozvyšennost/
Pandivere Kõrgustik 8 Le 59.00N 26.15 E
Pando 56 Id 34.43S 55.57W
Pando 54 Ef 11.20S 67.40W
Pandokrátor 15 Cj 39.45N 19.52 E
Pandora 49 Fi 9.45N 82.57W
Pandrup 8 Cg 57.14N 9.41 E
Pandu 36 Cb 4.59N 19.16 E
Panevežis/Panevėžys 19 Cd 55.44N 24.22 E
Panevėžys/Panevežis 19 Cd 55.44N 24.22 E
Panfilov 19 Ig 44.08N 80.01 E
Panga 36 Eb 1.51N 26.25 E
Pangai 65b Ba 19.48S 174.21W
Pangaion Óros 15 Hi 40.50N 24.05 E
Pangalanes, Canal de- 30 Lk 22.48S 47.50 E
Pangani 36 Gd 5.26S 38.58 E
Pangani or Ruvu 36 Gc 5.26S 38.58 E
Pange 12 Ie 49.05N 6.22 E
Panggoe 58 Ge 7.01S 157.05 E
Pangi 36 Ec 3.11S 26.38 E
Pangkajene 26 Gg 4.50S 119.32 E
Pangkalanberandan 26 Cf 4.01N 98.17 E
Pangkalanbuun 26 Fg 2.41S 111.37 E
Pangkalaseang, Tanjung- 26 Hg 0.42S 123.26 E
Pangkalpinang 26 Eg 2.08S 106.08 E
Pangnirtung 39 Mc 66.08N 65.44W
Pang-Pang 63b Dc 17.41S 168.32 E
Panguitch 43 Ed 37.49N 112.26W
Panguma 34 Cd 8.24N 11.13W
Pangutaran Group 26 He 6.15N 120.30 E
Panhandle 45 Fi 35.21N 101.23W
Pania Mutombo 36 Dd 5.11S 23.51 E
Paniau 65a Ab 21.57N 160.05W
Panié, Mont- 61 Bd 20.36S 164.46 E
Pānīpat 25 Fc 29.23N 76.58 E
Paniza, Puerto de- 13 Kc 41.15N 1.20W
Panjang 26 Eh 5.29S 105.18 E
Panjang, Pulau- 26 Ef 2.44N 108.55 E
Panjgūr 25 Cc 26.58N 64.06 E
Panjim → Panaji 25 Jh 15.29N 73.50 E
Panjwīn 24 Ke 35.36N 45.58 E
Pankow, Berlin- 10 Jd 52.34N 13.24 E
Pankshin 34 Gd 9.20N 9.27 E
P'anmunjŏm 28 If 37.57N 126.40 E
Panopah 26 Fg 1.56S 111.11 E
Panorama 56 Jb 21.21S 51.51W
Panshan 28 Gd 41.12N 122.03 E
Panshi 27 Mc 42.56N 126.02 E
Pant 12 Cc 51.53N 0.39 E
Pantanal 52 Kg 18.00S 56.00W
Pantar, Pulau- 26 Hh 8.25S 124.07 E
Pantego 44 Ih 35.34N 76.36W
Pantelleria 14 Fn 36.50N 11.57 E
Pantelleria 5 Hh 36.45N 12.00 E
Pantelleria, Canale di- 14 Fn 36.40N 11.45 E
Pante Makassar 26 Hh 9.12S 124.23 E
Pantoja 54 Cd 0.58S 75.10W
Pánuco 48 Jf 22.03N 98.10W
Pánuco 38 Jg 22.16N 97.47W
Panxian 27 Hf 25.45N 104.39 E
Panyam 34 Gd 9.25N 9.13 E
Panzi 36 Cd 7.13S 17.58 E
Panzós 49 Cf 15.24N 89.40W
Pao, Río- [Ven.] 50 Bh 8.33N 68.01W
Pao, Río- [Ven.] 50 Dh 8.06N 64.17W
Paola [It.] 14 Kk 39.21N 16.03 E
Paola [Ks.-U.S.] 45 Ig 38.35N 94.53W
Paoli 44 Df 38.33N 86.28W
Paopao 65e Fc 17.30S 149.49W
Paoua 35 Bd 7.15N 16.26 E
Pápa 10 Ni 47.20N 17.28 E
Papa 65a Fd 19.13N 155.52W
Papaaloa 65a Fd 19.59N 155.13W
Papagaios 55 Jd 19.32S 44.45W
Papagayo, Golfo del- 47 Gf 10.45N 85.45W
Papaikou 65a Fd 19.47N 155.06W
Papakura 62 Fb 37.03S 174.57 E
Papaloapan, Río- 48 Lh 18.42N 95.38W
Papanduva 55 Gh 26.25S 50.09W
Papangpanjang 26 Dg 0.27S 100.25 E
Papantla de Olarte 47 Ed 20.27N 97.19W
Papar 26 Ge 5.44N 115.56 E
Paparoa Range 62 De 42.05S 171.35 E
Papa Stour 9 La 60.30N 1.40W
Papa Westray 9 Kb 59.22N 2.54W
Papeete 58 Mf 17.32S 149.34W
Papenburg 10 Dc 53.04N 7.24 E
Papenburg-Aschendorf
(Ems) 12 Ja 53.04N 7.22 E
Papenoo 65e Fc 17.30S 149.25W
Papes Ezers/Papes
Ozero 8 Ih 56.15N 20.55 E
Papes Ozero/Papes
Ezers 8 Ih 56.15N 20.55 E
Papetoai 65e Fc 17.30S 149.52W
Papey 7a Cb 64.36N 14.11W
Paphos/Baf 24 Ee 34.50N 32.35 E
Papija 15 Kg 42.07N 27.51 E
Papíkion Óros 15 Ih 41.15N 25.18 E
Papilė/Papile 8 Jh 56.09N 22.45 E
Papile/Papilė 8 Jh 56.09N 22.45 E
Papillion 45 Hf 41.09N 96.03W
Papua, Gulf of- 57 Fe 8.32S 145.00 E
Papua New Guinea 58 Fe 6.00S 150.00 E
Papua Passage 64p Bc 21.15S 159.47W
Papuk 14 Le 45.31N 17.39 E
Papun 25 Je 18.04N 97.27 E
Para 7 Ji 54.23N 40.53 E
Pará 54 Hd 4.00S 53.00W
Pará, Rio- 55 Jd 19.13S 45.07W
Pará, Rio- 52 Lf 1.30S 48.55W
Parabel 20 De 58.40N 81.30 E
Parabel 20 De 58.43N 81.31 E
Paraburdoo 59 Dd 23.15S 117.45 E
Paracas 54 Cf 13.49S 76.16W
Paracatu 54 Ig 17.13S 46.52W
Paracatu, Rio- [Braz.] 55 Ic 17.30S 46.32W
Paracatu, Rio- [Braz.] 55 Jc 16.30S 45.04W
Paracel Islands (EN) = Xisha
Qundao 21 Nh 16.30N 112.15 E
Pārachinār 25 Eb 33.54N 70.06 E
Paraćin 15 Ef 43.52N 21.25 E
Paracuru 54 Kd 3.24S 39.04W
Parada Km 329 55 Ek 32.30S 55.25W
Paradip 25 Hd 20.19N 86.42 E
Paradise [Ca.-U.S.] 46 Eg 39.46N 121.37W
Paradise [Mi.-U.S.] 44 Eb 46.38N 85.03W
Paragould 45 Kh 36.03N 90.29W
Paragua, Río- 54 Fb 6.55N 62.55W
Paraguá, Río- 54 Ff 13.34S 61.53W
Paraguaçu, Rio- 52 Mg 12.45S 38.54W
Paraguaçu Paulista 55 Gf 22.25S 50.34W
Paraguai, Rio- 52 Kh 27.18S 58.38W
Paraguaipoa 49 Lh 11.21N 71.57W
Paraguaná, Península de-
52 Jd 11.55N 70.00W
Paraguari 55 Dg 26.00S 57.10W
Paraguari 56 Ic 25.38S 57.09W
Paraguay 53 Kh 23.00S 58.00W
Paraguay, Río- 52 Kh 27.18S 58.38W
Paraíba 54 Ke 7.10S 36.30W
Paraíba do Sul, Rio- 52 Lh 21.37S 41.03W
Paraibuna, Represa do- 55 Jf 23.25S 45.35W
Paraibuna, Rio- 55 Jf 23.22S 45.40W
Parainen/Pargas 7 Ff 60.18N 22.18 E
Paraíso [Braz.] 55 Fd 19.03S 52.59W
Paraíso [Mex.] 48 Mh 18.24N 93.14W
Paraiso, Rio- 55 Bb 15.08S 61.52W
Parakou 31 Hh 9.21N 2.37 E
Param 64d Bb 7.22N 151.48 E
Paramaribo 53 Ke 5.50N 55.10W
Paramera, Sierra de la- 13 Hd 40.30N 4.46W
Paramithiá 15 Dj 39.28N 20.31 E
Paramušir, Ostrov- 21 Rd 50.25N 155.50 E
Paraná 53 Ji 31.45S 60.30W
Paraná 56 Jb 24.00S 51.00W
Paraná, Pico- 55 Hg 25.14S 48.48W
Paraná, Rio- 52 Ki 33.43S 59.15W
Paranã, Rio- 52 Lg 12.30S 48.14W
Paraná de las Palmas, Río- 55 Cl 34.18S 58.33W
Paranaguá 53 Lh 25.31S 48.30W
Paraná-Guazú, Río- 55 Ck 34.00S 58.25W
Paranaíba 54 Hg 19.40S 51.11W
Paranaíba, Rio- 52 Kh 20.07S 51.05W
Paranaiguara 55 Gd 18.53S 50.28W
Paranapanema, Rio- 52 Kh 22.40S 53.09W
Paranapiacaba, Serra do- 52 Lh 24.20S 49.00W
Paranapuã-Guaçu, Ponta
do- 55 Ig 24.24S 47.00W
Paranavaí 56 Jb 23.04S 52.28W
Parandak 24 Ne 35.21N 50.42 E
Paranéstion 15 Hh 41.16N 24.30 E
Paranhos 55 Ef 23.55S 55.25W
Paraoa Atoll 57 Mf 19.09S 140.43W
Paraopeba 55 Jd 19.18S 44.25W
Paraopeba, Rio- 55 Jd 18.50S 45.11W
Parapara 63b Ca 13.32S 167.20 E
Paraparaumu 62 Fd 40.55S 175.00 E
Paraspóri 15 Kn 35.54N 27.14 E
Parati 55 Jf 23.13S 44.43W
Paratodos, Serra- 55 Jb 14.40S 44.50W
Paratunka 20 Kf 52.52N 158.12 E
Pārāu, Kūh-e- 24 Le 34.37N 47.05 E
Paraúna 55 Gc 17.02S 50.26W
Paravae 64n Bc 10.27S 160.58W
Paray-le-Monial 11 Kh 46.27N 4.07 E
Parbati 25 Fc 25.51N 76.36 E
Parbhani 25 Fe 19.16N 76.47 E
Parchim 10 Hc 53.26N 11.51 E
Parczew 10 Se 51.39N 22.54 E
Pardo 55 Cm 36.15S 59.22W
Pardo, Rio- [Braz.] 55 Fi 29.59S 52.23W
Pardo, Rio- [Braz.] 54 Hh 21.46S 52.09W
Pardo, Rio- [Braz.] 55 He 20.10S 48.38W
Pardo, Rio- [Braz.] 55 Hf 22.55S 49.58W
Pardo, Rio- [Braz.] 55 Jb 15.48S 44.48W
Pardo, Rio- [Braz.] 54 Kg 15.39S 38.57W
Pardubice 10 Lf 50.02N 15.45 E
Parea 65e Eb 16.49S 150.58W
Parecis, Chapada dos- 52 Kg 13.00S 60.00W
Parecis, Rio- 55 Da 12.56S 56.43W
Paredes de Nava 13 Hb 42.09N 4.41W
Parelhas 54 Ke 6.41S 36.39W
Paren 20 Ld 62.28N 163.05 E
Parent 42 Kg 47.55N 74.37W
Parentis-en-Born 11 Ej 44.21N 1.04W
Pareora 62 Df 44.29S 171.13 E
Parepare 22 Nj 4.01S 119.38 E
Párga 15 Dj 39.17N 20.24 E
Pargas/Parainen 7 Ff 60.18N 22.18 E
Pargolovo 8 Nd 60.03N 30.30 E
Parham 51d Bb 17.05N 61.46W
Parhar 19 Gh 37.31N 69.23 E
Pari, Rio- 55 Db 15.36S 56.08W
Paria, Golfo de-/Paria, Gulf
of- 54 Fa 10.20N 62.00W
Paria, Gulf of-/Paria, Golfo
de- 54 Fa 10.20N 62.00W
Paria, Peninsula de- 50 Eg 10.40N 62.30W
Pariaguán 54 Fb 8.51N 64.43W
Pariaman 26 Dg 0.38S 100.08 E
Paria River 46 Jh 36.52N 111.36W
Paricutín, Volcán- 48 Hh 19.28N 102.15W
Parida, Isla- 49 Fi 8.07N 82.20W
Pari das Pedras 55 Ja 12.45S 44.47W
Parigi 26 Hg 0.48S 120.10 E
Parika 54 Gb 6.52N 58.25W
Parikkala 7 Gf 61.33N 29.30 E
Parima, Serra- 52 Je 3.00N 64.20W
Parinacota 56 Ga 18.12S 69.16W
Pariñas, Punta- 52 Hf 4.40S 81.20W
Parîngul Mare, Vîrful- 15 Gd 45.20N 23.30 E
Parintins 53 Kf 2.36S 56.44W
Paris [Fr.] 6 Gf 48.52N 2.20 E
Paris [Il.-U.S.] 45 Mg 39.36N 87.42W
Paris [Kir.] 64g Ab 1.56N 157.31W
Paris [Ky.-U.S.] 44 Ef 38.13N 84.14W
Paris [Tn.-U.S.] 44 Cg 36.19N 88.20W
Paris [Tx.-U.S.] 43 He 33.40N 95.33W
Paris Basin (EN) = Parisien,
Bassin- 5 Gf 49.00N 2.00 E
Parisien, Bassin- = Paris
Basin (EN) 5 Gf 49.00N 2.00 E
Parita 49 Gi 8.00N 80.31W
Parita, Bahía de- 49 Gi 8.08N 80.24W
Parit Buntar 26 De 5.07N 100.30 E
Parkano 7 Fe 62.01N 23.01 E
Parkent 18 Gd 41.18N 69.40 E
Parker 46 Hi 34.09N 114.17W
Parker, Mount- 59 Fc 17.10S 128.20 E
Parkersburg 43 Kd 39.17N 81.33W
Parker Seamount (EN) 40 Ff 52.35N 151.15W
Parkes 58 Fh 33.08S 148.11 E
Park Falls 45 Kd 45.56N 90.32W
Parkland 46 Dc 47.09N 122.26W
Park Range 43 Fc 40.00N 106.30W
Park Rapids 45 Ic 46.55N 95.04W
Park River 45 Hb 48.24N 97.45W
Park Valley 46 If 41.50N 113.21W
Parma 14 Ef 44.56N 10.26 E
Parma [It.] 6 Hg 44.48N 10.20 E
Parma [Oh.-U.S.] 44 Ge 41.24N 81.44W
Parnaguá 54 Jf 10.13S 44.38W
Parnaíba 53 Lf 2.54S 41.47W
Parnaíba, Rio- 52 Lf 3.00S 41.50W
Parnamirim [Braz.] 54 Ke 8.05S 39.34W
Parnamirim [Braz.] 54 Ke 5.55S 35.15W
Parnarama 54 Je 5.41S 43.06W
Parnassós Óros = Parnassus
(EN) 5 Ih 38.30N 22.37 E
Parnassus 62 Ee 42.43S 173.17 E
Parnassus (EN) = Parnassós
Óros 5 Ih 38.30N 22.37 E
Párnis Óros 15 Gk 38.10N 23.40 E
Párnon Óros 15 Fl 37.12N 22.38 E
Pärnu/Pjarnu 6 Id 58.24N 24.32 E
Pärnu-Jaagupi/Pjarnu-
Jagupi 8 Kf 58.36N 24.25 E
Pärnu Jõgi/Pjarnu 7 Fg 58.23N 24.34 E
Pärnu Laht/Pjarnu, Zaliv-
7 Fg 58.15N 24.25 E
Parola 8 Kc 61.03N 24.22 E
Paroo River 57 Fh 31.28S 143.32 E
Paropamisus/Salseleh-ye
Safīd Kūh 21 If 34.30N 63.30 E
Páros 15 Il 37.05N 25.09 E
Páros 15 Il 37.06N 25.12 E
Parowan 46 Ih 37.51N 112.57W
Parpaillon 11 Mj 44.35N 6.40 E
Parque Industrial 55 Jd 19.57S 44.01W
Parral 56 Fe 36.09S 71.50W
Parral, Rio- 48 Gd 27.35N 105.25W
Parras, Sierra de- 48 He 25.25N 102.00W
Parras de la Fuente 47 Dc 25.25N 102.11W
Parravicini 55 Dm 36.27S 57.46W
Parrett 9 Jj 51.13N 3.01W
Parrita 49 Ei 9.30N 84.19W
Parry, Cape- 42 Fb 70.12N 124.35W
Parry, Kap- [Grld.] 41 Jd 72.28N 22.00W
Parry, Kap- [Grld.] 41 Ec 77.00N 71.00W
Parry Bay 42 Jc 68.00N 82.00W
Parry Islands 38 Ib 76.00N 110.00W
Parry Peninsula 42 Fc 69.45N 124.35W
Parry Sound 42 Jg 45.21N 80.02W
Parsęta 10 Lb 54.12N 15.33 E
Parsons [Ks.-U.S.] 43 Hd 37.20N 95.16W
Parsons [W.V.-U.S.] 44 Hf 39.06N 79.43W
Parsons Range 59 Hb 13.30S 135.15 E
Partanna 14 Gm 37.43N 12.53 E
Parthenay 11 Fh 46.39N 0.15W
Partille 8 Eg 57.44N 12.07 E
Partinico 14 Hl 38.03N 13.07 E
Partizansk 20 Ih 43.13N 133.05 E
Partizánske 10 Oh 48.38N 18.23 E
Partizanskoje 20 Ee 55.30N 94.30 E
Paru, Rio- 52 Kf 1.33S 52.38W
Paru de Este, Rio- 54 Hc 1.10N 54.40W
Paru de Oeste, Rio- 54 Kf 1.30S 56.00W
Paruru 63a Ec 9.51S 160.49 E
Parvān 23 Kb 35.15N 69.30 E
Părvomaj 15 Ig 42.06N 25.13 E
Parys 37 De 27.04S 27.16 E
Paša 7 Hf 60.28N 32.55 E
Pasadena [Ca.-U.S.] 39 Hf 34.09N 118.09W
Pasadena [Tx.-U.S.] 45 Il 29.42N 95.13W
Paşaeli Yarimadası 15 Lh 41.20N 28.25 E
Paşalimani Adası 15 Ki 40.28N 27.37 E
Pasangkaju 26 Gg 1.10S 119.20 E
Pāsārgād 24 Og 30.17N 52.55 E
Pasarwajo 26 Hh 5.29S 122.50 E
Pascagoula 43 Je 30.23N 88.31W
Paşcani 15 Jb 47.15N 26.44 E
Pasco 43 Db 46.14N 119.06W
Pasco 54 Cf 10.30S 75.15W
Pascoal 55 Bb 13.38S 61.06W
Pascoal, Monte- 54 Kg 16.54S 39.24W
Pascua, Isla de-/Rapa Nui =
Easter Island (EN) 57 Qg 27.07S 109.22W
Pas-de-Calais 11 Id 50.30N 2.30 E
Pas-en-Artois 12 Ed 50.09N 2.30 E
Pasewalk 10 Jc 53.31N 13.59 E
Pasinler 24 Ib 40.00N 41.41 E
Pašino 20 De 55.11N 83.02 E
Pasión, Rio de la- 49 Be 16.28N 90.33W
Pasir Mas 26 De 6.02N 102.08 E
Pasirpengarayan 26 Df 0.51N 100.16 E
Pasir Puteh 26 De 5.50N 102.24 E
Påskallavik 8 Gg 57.10N 16.27 E
Paškovski 16 Kg 45.01N 39.05 E
Pasłęk 10 Pb 54.05N 19.39 E
Pasłęka 10 Pb 54.25N 19.50 E
Pašman 14 Jg 43.57N 15.21 E
Pasni 22 Ig 25.16N 63.28 E
Paso de Indios 56 Gf 43.52S 69.06W
Paso del Cerro 55 Ej 31.31S 55.46W
Paso de los Libres 55 Ic 29.43S 57.05W
Paso de los Toros 56 Id 32.49S 56.31W
Paso Tranqueras 55 Ej 31.12S 55.45W
Passamaquoddy Bay 44 Nc 45.06N 66.59W
Passa Três, Serra- 55 Hb 14.40S 49.30W
Passau 10 Jh 48.35N 13.29 E
Passero, Capo- 14 Jn 36.40N 15.10 E
Passo Fundo 53 Kh 28.15S 52.24W
Passo Fundo, Rio- 55 Fh 27.16S 52.42W
Passos 54 Ig 20.43S 46.37W
Pastaza, Rio- 52 If 4.50S 76.25W
Pasteur 56 He 35.08S 62.14W
Pasto 53 Ie 1.13N 77.17W
Pastora Peak 46 Kh 36.47N 109.10W
Pastoria, Laguna de- 48 Ki 16.00N 97.40W
Pastos Bons 54 Je 6.36S 44.05W
Pastrana 13 Jd 40.25N 2.55W
Paštrik 15 Dg 42.14N 20.32 E
Pasubio 14 Fe 45.47N 11.10 E
Pasvalis/Pasvalys 7 Fh 56.02N 24.28 E
Pasvalys/Pasvalis 7 Fh 56.02N 24.28 E
Pásztó 10 Pi 47.55N 19.42 E

Index Symbols

- Independent Nation
- State, Region
- District, County
- Municipality
- Colony, Dependency
- Continent
- Physical Region
- Historical or Cultural Region
- Mount, Mountain
- Volcano
- Hill
- Mountains, Mountain Range
- Hills, Escarpment
- Plateau, Upland
- Pass, Gap
- Plain, Lowland
- Delta
- Salt Flat
- Valley, Canyon
- Crater, Cave
- Karst Features
- Depression
- Polder
- Desert, Dunes
- Forest, Woods
- Heath, Steppe
- Oasis
- Cape, Point
- Coast, Beach
- Cliff
- Peninsula
- Isthmus
- Sandbank
- Island
- Atoll
- Rock, Reef
- Islands, Archipelago
- Rocks, Reefs
- Coral Reef
- Well, Spring
- Geyser
- River, Stream
- Waterfall Rapids
- River Mouth, Estuary
- Lake
- Salt Lake
- Intermittent Lake
- Reservoir
- Swamp, Pond
- Canal
- Glacier
- Ice Shelf, Pack Ice
- Ocean
- Sea
- Gulf, Bay
- Strait, Fjord
- Lagoon
- Bank
- Seamount
- Tablemount
- Ridge
- Shelf
- Basin
- Escarpment, Sea Scarp
- Fracture
- Trench, Abyss
- National Park, Reserve
- Point of Interest
- Recreation Site
- Cave, Cavern
- Historic Site
- Ruins
- Wall, Walls
- Church, Abbey
- Temple
- Scientific Station
- Airport
- Port
- Lighthouse
- Mine
- Tunnel
- Dam, Bridge

Patagonia	52	Jj	44.00S	68.00W
Patagonica, Cordillera-	52	Ij	46.00S	71.30W
Patan	25	Hc	27.40N	85.20 E
Pātan	25	Ed	23.50N	72.07 E
Patani	26	If	0.18N	128.48 E
Pata Peninsula	64d	Bb	7.23N	151.35 E
Patchogue	44	Ke	40.46N	73.01W
Pate	36	Hc	2.08S	41.00 E
Patea	62	Fc	39.46S	174.29 E
Patea	62	Fc	39.46S	174.30 E
Pategi	34	Gd	8.44N	5.45 E
Patensie	37	Cf	33.46S	24.49 E
Paternò	14	Jm	37.34N	15.54 E
Paterson	43	Mc	40.55N	74.10W
Paterson Inlet	62	Bg	46.55S	168.00 E
Paterson Range	59	Ed	21.45S	122.05 E
Pathānkot	25	Fb	32.17N	75.39 E
Pathein	22	Lh	16.47N	94.44 E
Pathfinder Reservoir	46	Le	42.30N	106.50W
Pathfinder Seamount (EN)	40	Kf	50.55N	143.15W
Pathiu	25	Jf	10.41N	99.20 E
Patía, Río-	54	Cc	2.13N	78.40W
Patiāla	25	Fb	30.19N	76.24 E
Patiño, Estero-	55	Cg	24.05S	59.55W
Patio	65e	Db	16.35S	151.29W
Pati Point	64c	Ba	13.36N	144.57 E
Pătîrlagele	15	Jd	45.19N	26.21 E
Pativilca	54	Cf	10.42S	77.47W
Pátmos	15	Jl	37.19N	26.34 E
Pátmos	15	Jl	37.20N	26.33 E
Patna	22	Kg	25.36N	85.07 E
Patnos	24	Jc	39.14N	42.52 E
Pato Branco	56	Jc	26.13S	52.40W
Patom Plateau (EN)= Patomskoje Nagorje	20	Ge	59.00N	115.30 E
Patomskoje Nagorje=Patom Plateau (EN)	20	Ge	59.00N	115.30 E
Patos	53	Mf	7.01S	37.16W
Patos, Isla de-	50	Fg	10.38N	61.52W
Patos, Lagoa dos-	52	Ki	31.06S	51.15W
Patos, Laguna de los-	55	Aj	30.25S	62.15W
Patos, Ribeirão dos-	55	Gd	18.58S	50.30W
Patos, Rio dos- [Braz.]	55	Da	13.33S	56.29W
Patos, Rio dos- [Braz.]	55	Hb	14.59S	48.46W
Patos de Minas	53	Lg	18.35S	46.32W
Patosi	15	Ci	40.38N	19.39 E
Patquia	56	Gd	30.03S	66.53W
Pátrai	6	Ih	38.15N	21.44 E
Patrai, Gulf of- (EN) = Patraïkós Kólpos	15	Ek	38.15N	21.30 E
Patraïkós Kólpos = Patrai, Gulf of- (EN)	15	Ek	38.15N	21.30 E
Patricio Lynch, Isla-	56	Eg	48.36S	75.26W
Patricios	55	Bl	35.27S	60.42W
Patrocínio	54	Ig	18.57S	46.59W
Patta Island	30	Li	2.07S	41.03 E
Pattani	25	Kg	6.51N	101.16 E
Patteson, Passage-	63b	Db	15.26S	168.09 E
Patti	14	Il	38.08N	14.58 E
Patti, Golfo di-	14	Jl	38.10N	15.05 E
Patton Seamount (EN)	38	Dd	54.40N	150.30W
Pattullo, Mount-	42	Ee	56.14N	129.39W
Patu	54	Ke	6.06S	37.38W
Patuākhāli	25	Id	22.16N	90.18 E
Patuca, Punta-	49	Ef	15.51N	84.18W
Patuca, Río-	47	He	15.50N	84.18W
Pătulele	15	Fe	44.21N	22.47 E
Patutahi	62	Gc	38.37S	177.53 E
Patuxent Range	66	Qg	84.43S	64.30W
Pátzcuaro	48	Ih	19.31N	101.36W
Pau	11	Fk	43.18N	0.22W
Pau, Gave de-	11	Ek	43.33N	1.12W
Paucartambo	54	Df	13.18S	71.40W
Paucerne, Rio-	55	Ba	13.34S	61.14W
Pau dos Ferros	54	Ke	6.07S	38.10W
Pauillac	11	Fi	45.12N	0.45W
Pauini	54	Ee	7.40S	66.58W
Pauini, Rio-	54	Ee	7.47S	67.15W
Pauksa Taung	25	Ie	19.55N	94.18 E
Paulatuk	39	Gc	69.23N	124.00W
Paulaya, Río-	49	Ef	15.51N	85.06W
Paulding Bay	66	Ie	66.35S	123.00 E
Paulina Peak	46	Ee	43.41N	121.15W
Păuliş	15	Ec	46.07N	21.35 E
Paulistana	54	Je	8.09S	41.09W
Paulo Afonso	53	Mf	9.21S	38.14W
Paulo Afonso, Cachoeira de-	52	Mf	9.24S	38.12W
Pauls Valley	45	Hi	34.44N	97.13W
Paungde	25	Je	18.29N	95.30 E
Pavant Range	46	Ig	39.00N	112.15W
Pāveh	24	Le	35.03N	46.22 E
Pavia	14	De	45.10N	9.10 E
Pavilly	12	Ce	49.34N	0.58 E
Pāvilosta/Pavilosta	7	Eh	56.55N	21.13 E
Pavilosta/Pāvilosta	7	Eh	56.55N	21.13 E
Pavlikeni	15	If	43.14N	25.18 E
Pavlodar	22	Jd	52.18N	76.57 E
Pavlodarskaja Oblast [3]	19	He	52.00N	76.30 E
Pavlof Islands	40	Ge	55.15N	161.20W
Pavlof Volcano	40	Ge	55.24N	161.55W
Pavlograd	16	Ie	48.32N	35.53 E
Pavlovka	17	Hi	55.25N	56.33 E
Pavlovo	19	Ed	55.58N	43.04 E
Pavlov Seamount (EN)	20	Lf	50.40N	162.00 E
Pavlovsk	16	Ld	50.27N	40.08 E
Pavlovskaja	19	Df	46.06N	39.48 E
Pavullo nel Frignano	14	Ef	44.20N	10.50 E
Pavuvu	63a	Dc	9.04S	159.08 E
Pawa	63a	Ed	10.15S	161.44 E
Pawhuska	45	Hh	36.40N	96.20W
Pawnee	45	Hh	36.20N	96.48W
Pawnee River	45	Gg	38.10N	99.06W
Pawtucket	44	Le	41.53N	71.23W
Paximádhia, Nisidhes-	15	Ho	35.00N	24.35 E
Paxoí	15	Dj	39.12N	20.10 E
Paxson	40	Jd	63.02N	145.30W
Payakumbuk	26	Dg	0.14S	100.38 E
Payas, Cerro-	49	Ef	15.50N	85.00W
Payerne	14	Ad	46.49N	6.58 E
Payette	46	Gd	44.05N	116.57W
Payette	43	Dc	44.05N	116.56W
Payne, Baie-	42	Ke	59.55N	69.35W
Payne, Lac -	42	Ke	59.30N	74.00W
Paysandú [2]	55	Dk	32.00S	57.15W
Paysandú	53	Ki	32.19S	58.05W
Pays de Léon	11	Bf	48.28N	4.30W
Pays d'Othe	11	Jf	48.06N	3.37 E
Payson [Az.-U.S.]	46	Ji	34.14N	111.20W
Payson [Ut.-U.S.]	46	Jf	40.03N	111.44W
Payzawat/Jiashi	27	Cd	39.29N	76.39 E
Pāzanān	24	Mg	30.35N	49.59 E
Pazar	24	Ib	41.11N	40.53 E
Pazarbası Burun	24	Db	41.13N	30.17 E
Pazarcık	24	Gd	37.31N	37.19 E
Pazardžik	15	Hg	42.12N	24.20 E
Pazardžik [2]	15	Hg	42.12N	24.20 E
Pazarköy	15	Kj	39.51N	27.24 E
Pazaryeri	24	Cc	40.00N	29.54 E
Pazin	14	He	45.14N	13.56 E
Pčinja	15	Eh	41.49N	21.40 E
Pea	65b	Ac	21.11S	175.14W
Peabirú	55	Ff	23.54S	52.20W
Peace Point	42	Ge	59.12N	112.33W
Peace River	39	Hd	56.14N	117.17W
Peace River [Can.]	38	Hd	56.14N	117.17W
Peace River [Fl.-U.S.]	44	Fl	26.55N	82.05W
Peachland	46	Fb	49.46N	119.44W
Peach Springs	46	Ii	35.32N	113.25W
Peacock Hills	42	Gc	66.05N	110.00W
Peak District	9	Lh	53.17N	1.45W
Peake Creek	59	He	28.05S	136.07 E
Peaked Mountain	44	Mb	46.34N	68.49W
Peale, Mount-	43	Fd	38.26N	109.14W
Pearl	45	Lb	48.42N	88.44W
Pearland	45	Il	29.34N	95.17W
Pearl and Hermes Reef	57	Jb	27.55N	175.45W
Pearl City	65a	Db	21.23N	157.58W
Pearl Harbor	65a	Cb	21.20N	158.00W
Pearl River	43	Je	30.11N	89.32W
Pearsall	45	Gl	28.53N	99.06W
Pearsoll Peak	46	De	42.18N	123.50W
Peary Channel	42	Ha	79.25N	101.00W
Peary Land	67	Me	82.40N	30.00W
Pease River	45	Gi	34.12N	99.07W
Pebane	37	Fc	17.14S	38.10 E
Pebas	54	Dd	3.20S	71.49W
Peć	15	Dg	42.39N	20.18 E
Peca	14	Id	46.29N	14.48 E
Peças, Ilha das-	55	Hg	25.26S	48.19W
Pecatonica River	45	Le	42.29N	89.03W
Pečenežskoje Vodohranilišče	16	Jd	50.05N	36.50 E
Pečenga	6	Jb	69.33N	31.07 E
Pečenga	7	Hb	69.39N	31.27 E
Pechea	15	Kd	45.38N	27.48 E
Pechora (EN)=Pečora	5	Lb	68.13N	54.10 E
Pechora (EN)=Pečora	6	Lb	65.10N	57.11 E
Pechora Bay (EN)= Pečorskaja Guba	19	Fb	68.40N	54.45 E
Pechora Sea (EN)= Pečorskoje More	19	Fb	69.45N	54.30 E
Pecica	15	Ec	46.10N	21.04 E
Peçin	15	Kl	37.19N	27.45 E
Peckelsheim, Willebadessen-	12	Lc	51.36N	9.08 E
Pečora=Pechora (EN)	6	Lb	65.10N	57.11 E
Pečora=Pechora (EN)	5	Lb	68.13N	54.10 E
Pecora, Capo-	14	Ck	39.27N	8.23 E
Pečorskaja Guba=Pechora Bay (EN)	19	Fb	68.40N	54.45 E
Pečorskoje More=Pechora Sea (EN)	19	Fb	69.45N	54.30 E
Pečory	7	Gh	57.49N	27.38 E
Pecos	43	Ge	31.25N	103.30W
Pecos	38	Ig	29.42N	101.22W
Pecos Plain	43	Ge	33.20N	104.30W
Pécs	6	Hf	46.05N	18.14 E
Pécs [2]	10	Oj	46.06N	18.15 E
Pedasí	49	Gj	7.32N	80.02W
Pedder, Lake-	59	Jh	43.00S	146.15 E
Peddie	37	Df	33.14S	27.07 E
Pededze	8	Lh	56.53N	27.01 E
Pedernales [Dom.Rep.]	49	Ld	18.02N	71.45W
Pedernales [Ven.]	50	Eh	9.58N	62.16W
Pedernales, Salar de-	56	Gc	26.15S	69.10W
Pedja Jõgi	8	Lf	58.20N	26.10 E
Pêdo Shankou	27	Df	29.12N	83.26 E
Pedra Azul	54	Jg	16.01S	41.16W
Pedra Branca	54	Ke	5.27S	39.43W
Pedra do Sino	55	Kf	22.27S	43.03W
Pedra Lume	32	Cf	16.46N	22.54W
Pedras, Rio das-	55	Ia	13.30S	47.09W
Pedras Altas, Coxilha-	55	Fj	31.45S	53.35W
Pedregal	54	Da	11.01N	70.08W
Pedreiras	54	Jd	4.34S	44.39W
Pedriceña	48	He	25.06N	103.47W
Pedrizas, Puerto de las-	13	Hh	36.55N	4.30W
Pedro Afonso	54	Ie	8.59S	48.11W
Pedro Bank (EN)	49	He	17.00N	78.30W
Pedro Betancourt	49	Gb	22.44N	81.17W
Pedro Cays	47	Ie	17.00N	77.50W
Pedro de Valdivia	56	Gb	22.37S	69.38W
Pedro Gomes	55	Ed	18.04S	54.32W
Pedro Gonzáles, Isla-	49	Hi	8.24N	79.06W
Pedro II	54	Jd	4.25S	41.28W
Pedro II, Ilha-	54	Ec	1.10N	66.44W
Pedro Juan Caballero	56	Ib	22.34S	55.37W
Pedro Leopoldo	55	Jd	19.38S	44.03W
Pedro Luro	56	He	39.29S	62.41W
Pedro Lustoza	55	Gg	25.49S	51.51W
Pedro Montoya	48	Jg	21.38N	99.49W
Pedro Osorio	56	Jd	31.51S	52.45W
Pedro R. Fernández	55	Ci	28.45S	58.39W
Pedro Severo	55	Ec	17.40S	54.02W
Pedroso, Sierra del-	13	Gf	38.35N	5.35W
Peebles	9	Jf	55.39N	3.12W
Pee Dee River	38	Lf	33.21N	79.16W
Peekskill	44	Ke	41.18N	73.56W
Peel	38	Fc	67.37N	134.40W
Peel	11	Lc	51.25N	5.50 E
Peel	9	Ig	54.13N	4.40W
Peel Sound	42	Hb	73.00N	96.00W
Peene	10	Jb	54.09N	13.46 E
Peer	12	Hc	51.08N	5.28 E
Peera Peera Poolanna Lake	59	He	26.30S	138.00 E
Peetz	45	Ef	40.58N	103.07W
Pegasus, Port-	62	Bg	47.10S	167.40 E
Pegasus Bay	61	Dh	43.20S	172.50 E
Pegnitz	10	Gg	49.29N	11.00 E
Pegnitz	10	Hg	49.45N	11.33 E
Pego	13	Lf	38.51N	0.07W
Pegtymel	20	Mc	69.47N	174.00 E
Pegu → Bago	22	Lh	17.30N	96.30 E
Pegu Yoma	21	Lh	19.00N	95.50 E
Pegwell Bay	12	Dc	51.18N	1.23 E
Pehčevo	15	Fh	41.46N	22.54 E
Pehlivanköy	15	Jh	41.21N	26.55 E
Pehuajó	56	He	35.48S	61.53W
Pei-ching Shih → Beijing Shi [5]	27	Kc	40.15N	116.30 E
Peine	10	Gd	52.19N	10.14 E
Peipsi järv=Peipus, Lake- (EN)	5	Id	58.45N	27.30 E
Peipus, Lake- (EN)= Čudskoje Ozero	5	Id	58.45N	27.30 E
Peipus, Lake- (EN)=Peipsi järv	5	Id	58.45N	27.30 E
Peixe	54	If	12.03S	48.32W
Peixe, Lagoa do-	55	Gj	31.18S	51.00W
Peixe, Rio do- [Braz.]	55	Ge	21.31S	51.58W
Peixe, Rio do- [Braz.]	55	Gb	14.06S	50.51W
Peixe, Rio do- [Braz.]	55	Hc	17.37S	48.29W
Peixe, Rio do- [Braz.]	55	Fc	16.32S	52.38W
Peixe, Rio do- [Braz.]	55	Gh	27.27S	51.54W
Peixe de Couro, Rio-	55	Ec	17.21S	55.29W
Peixes, Rio dos-	55	Hb	15.10S	49.30W
Peixian (Yunhe)	28	Dg	34.44N	116.56 E
Peixoto, Represa de-	54	Ih	20.30S	46.30W
Pejantan, Pulau-	26	Ef	0.07N	107.14 E
Pejde/Pöide	8	Jf	58.30N	22.50 E
Pek	15	Ee	44.46N	21.33 E
Pekalongan	26	Eh	6.53S	109.40 E
Pekan	26	Df	3.30N	103.25 E
Pekin	43	Jc	40.35N	89.40W
Peking (EN) = Beijing	22	Nf	39.55N	116.23 E
Pekulnei, Hrebet-	20	Mc	66.30N	176.00 E
Pelabuhanratu	26	Eh	6.59S	106.33 E
Pelagie, Isole-	5	Hh	35.40N	12.40 E
Pelagonija	15	Eh	41.05N	21.30 E
Pélagos	15	Hj	39.20N	24.05 E
Pelaihari	26	Fg	3.48S	114.45 E
Pelat, Mont-	11	Mj	44.16N	6.42 E
Pelawanbesar	26	Gf	1.10N	117.54 E
Pélé	63b	Dc	17.30S	168.24 E
Peleaga, Vîrful-	15	Fd	45.22N	22.53 E
Peleduj	20	Ge	59.40N	112.38 E
Pelée, Montagne-	47	Le	14.48N	61.10W
Pelee, Point-	44	Fe	41.54N	82.30W
Pelee Island	44	Fe	41.46N	82.39W
Peleliu Island	57	Ed	7.01N	134.15 E
Peleng, Pulau-	26	Hg	1.20S	123.10 E
Pelhřimov	10	Lg	49.26N	15.13 E
Pelican Lake	45	Gb	49.20N	99.35W
Pelicanpunt	37	Ad	22.54S	14.26 E
Peligre, Lac de-	49	Ld	18.52N	71.56W
Pelinaion Óros	15	Ik	38.32N	26.00 E
Pelješac	14	Lh	42.55N	17.25 E
Pelkosenniemi	7	Gc	67.07N	27.30 E
Pella	45	Jf	41.25N	92.55W
Pélla	15	Fi	40.46N	22.34 E
Pellegrini	56	He	36.16S	63.09W
Pellice	14	Bf	44.50N	7.38 E
Pellinge/Pellinki	8	Kd	60.15N	25.50 E
Pellinki/Pellinge	8	Kd	60.15N	25.50 E
Pello	7	Fc	66.47N	24.01 E
Pellworm	10	Eb	54.30N	8.40 E
Pelly	38	Fc	62.47N	137.19W
Pelly Bay	42	Ic	68.50N	90.10W
Pelly Bay	39	Kc	68.52N	89.55W
Pelly Crossing	42	Dd	62.50N	136.35W
Pelly Mountains	42	Ed	61.30N	132.00W
Peloncillo Mountains	46	Kj	32.15N	109.10W
Pelón de Nado, Cerro-	48	Jg	20.05N	99.55W
Peloponnesus (EN)= Pelopónnisos	5	Ih	37.40N	22.00 E
Peloponnesus (EN) = Pelopónnisos	15	El	37.40N	22.00 E
Pelopónnisos [2]	15	El	37.40N	22.00 E
Pelopónnisos = Peloponnesus (EN)	15	El	37.40N	22.00 E
Pelopónnisos= Peloponnesus (EN)	5	Ih	37.40N	22.00 E
Peloritani	14	Jl	38.05N	15.20 E
Peloro, Capo- o Faro, Punta del-	14	Jl	38.16N	15.39 E
Pelotas	53	Ki	31.46S	52.20W
Pelotas, Rio-	56	Jc	27.28S	51.55W
Pelplin	10	Oc	53.56N	18.42 E
Pelvoux, Massif du-	5	Gg	44.55N	6.20 E
Pelym	19	Gd	59.40N	63.05 E
Pelymski Tuman, Ozero-	17	Kf	60.05N	63.05 E
Pemalang	26	Eh	6.54S	109.22 E
Pemar/Paimio	8	Jd	60.27N	22.42 E
Pematangsiantar	22	Li	2.57N	99.03 E
Pemba [3]	36	Hd	5.02S	40.00 E
Pemba [Moz.]	31	Lj	12.57S	40.30 E
Pemba [Zam.]	36	Ef	16.31S	27.22 E
Pemba Channel	36	Gd	5.10S	39.20 E
Pemba Island	30	Ki	5.10S	39.48 E
Pemberton [Austl.]	59	Df	34.28S	116.01 E
Pemberton [B.C.-Can.]	46	Da	50.20N	122.48W
Pembina	42	Gf	54.45N	114.17W
Pembina	43	Hb	48.58N	97.15W
Pembina River	43	Hb	48.56N	97.15W
Pembroke [Ont.-Can.]	42	Jg	45.49N	77.07W
Pembroke [Wales-U.K.]	9	Ij	51.41N	4.55W
Pembuang	26	Fg	3.24S	112.33 E
Peña, Sierra de la-	13	Lb	42.31N	0.38W
Peñafiel	13	Dc	41.12N	8.17W
Peñafiel	13	Hc	41.36N	4.07W
Peñagolosa/Penyagolosa	13	Ld	40.13N	0.21W
Peña Gorda, Cerro-	48	Gg	20.40N	104.55W
Peñalara	13	Id	40.51N	3.57W
Penalva	54	Id	3.18S	45.10W
Penamacor	13	Ed	40.10N	7.10W
Peña Nevada, Cerro-	38	Jg	23.46N	99.52W
Penápolis	55	Ge	21.24S	50.04W
Peñaranda de Bracamonte	13	Gd	40.54N	5.12W
Peñarroya	13	Ld	40.28N	0.43W
Peñarroya-Pueblonuevo	13	Gf	38.18N	5.16W
Peñas, Cabo de-	5	Fg	43.39N	5.51W
Penas, Golfo de-	52	Ij	47.22S	74.50W
Peñas, Punta-	54	Fa	10.44N	61.51W
Peñasco, Rio-	45	Dj	32.45N	104.19W
Pendé	35	Ad	9.07N	16.26 E
Pendembu [S.L.]	34	Cd	9.06N	12.12W
Pendembu [S.L.]	34	Cd	8.06N	10.42W
Pendik	15	Mi	40.53N	29.13 E
Pendjari	34	Fc	10.54N	0.51 E
Pendle Hill	9	Kh	53.52N	2.17W
Pendleton	39	He	45.40N	118.47W
Pendolo	26	Hg	2.05S	120.42 E
Pend Oreille Lake	43	Db	48.10N	116.11W
Pend Oreille River	43	Db	49.04N	117.37W
Pendžikent	19	Gh	39.29N	67.38 E
Peneda	13	Dc	41.58N	8.15W
Penedo	54	Kf	10.17S	36.36W
Penetanguishene	44	Hc	44.47N	79.55W
Penganga	25	Fe	19.53N	79.09 E
Pengcheng	27	Jd	36.25N	114.08 E
Penge	36	Dd	5.31S	24.37 E
Pengho Jiao	27	Jc	16.03N	112.35 E
Penghu Liehtao= Pescadores (EN)	27	Kg	23.30N	119.30 E
Penglai (Dengzhou)	27	Ld	37.44N	120.45 E
Pengshui	27	If	29.17N	108.13 E
Pengze	27	Kf	29.52N	116.34 E
Penha	55	Hh	26.46S	48.39W
Penhalonga	37	Ec	18.54S	32.40 E
Penibético, Sistema-	13	Ig	37.00N	3.30W
Peniche	13	Ce	39.21N	9.23W
Penicuik	9	Jf	55.50N	3.14W
Penida, Nusa-	26	Gh	8.44S	115.32 E
Peninsula Ibérica=Iberian Peninsula (EN)	5	Fg	40.00N	4.00W
Peñíscola	13	Md	40.21N	0.25 E
Penisola Salentina= Salentine Peninsula (EN)	5	Hg	40.30N	18.00 E
Penitente, Serra do-	54	Ie	8.45S	46.20W
Pénjamo	48	Ig	20.26N	101.44W
Penju, Kepulauan-	26	Ih	5.22S	127.46 E
Penmarch, Pointe de-	11	Bg	47.48N	4.22W
Penne	14	Hh	42.27N	13.55 E
Penne, Punta-	14	Lj	40.41N	17.56 E
Pennell Coast	66	Kf	71.00S	167.00 E
Penner	21	Kh	14.35N	80.10 E
Penn Hills	44	He	40.28N	79.53W
Pennines	5	Fe	54.10N	2.05W
Pennsylvania [2]	43	Lc	40.45N	77.30W
Penn Yan	44	Id	42.41N	77.03W
Penny Ice Cap	42	Kc	67.00N	65.10W
Penny Strait	42	Ha	76.35N	97.10W
Peno	7	Hh	56.57N	32.45 E
Penobscot Bay	44	Mc	44.15N	68.52W
Penobscot River	43	Nc	44.30N	68.50W
Penola	59	Ig	37.23S	140.50 E
Peñón del Rosario, Cerro-	48	Jh	19.40N	98.12W
Penong	58	Eh	31.55S	133.01 E
Penonomé	47	Hg	8.31N	80.22W
Pénot, Mont-	63b	Cc	16.20S	167.31 E
Penrhyn Atoll	57	Le	9.00S	158.00W
Penrith	9	Kg	54.40N	2.44W
Penrith, Sydney-	59	Kf	33.45S	150.42 E
Pensacola	39	Kf	30.25N	87.13W
Pensacola Mountains	66	Rg	83.45S	55.00W
Pensacola Seamount (EN)	57	Lc	18.17N	157.20W
Pensamiento	55	Bb	14.43S	61.35W
Pensiangan	26	Gf	4.33N	116.19 E
Pentecôte, Ile-	57	Hf	15.45S	168.10 E
Penticton	42	Fg	49.30N	119.35W
Pentland	59	Jd	20.32S	145.24 E
Pentland Firth	9	Jc	58.44N	3.13W
Pentland Hills	9	Jf	55.48N	3.23W
Penwith	9	Hk	50.13N	5.40W
Penyagolosa/Peñagolosa	13	Ld	40.13N	0.21W
Penza	6	Ke	53.13N	45.00 E
Penzance	6	Ff	50.07N	5.33W
Penzenskaja Oblast [3]	19	Ee	53.15N	44.40 E
Penzhina Bay (EN)= Penžinskaja Guba	20	Ld	61.00N	163.00 E
Penžina	21	Sc	62.28N	165.18 E
Penžinskaja Guba= Penzhina Bay (EN)	20	Ld	61.00N	163.00 E
Penžinski Hrebet	20	Ld	62.15N	166.35 E
Peoples Creek	46	Kb	48.24N	108.19W
Peoria	39	Ke	40.42N	89.36W
Peoúia	24	Ee	34.53N	32.23 E
Pepa	36	Ed	7.42S	29.47 E
Pepel	34	Cd	8.35N	13.03W
Peperiguaçu, Rio-	55	Fh	27.10S	53.50W
Peqini	15	Ch	41.03N	19.45 E
Pequena, Lagoa-	55	Fj	31.36S	52.04W
Pequiri, Rio-	54	Gg	17.23S	55.38W
Perabumulih	26	Dg	3.27S	104.15 E
Perälä	8	Ib	62.28N	21.36 E
Perales, Puerto de-	13	Fd	40.15N	6.41W
Pérama	15	Hn	35.22N	24.42 E
Peräseinäjoki	8	Jb	62.34N	23.04 E
Perche, Col de la-	11	Il	42.30N	2.06 E
Perche, Collines du-	11	Gf	48.25N	0.40 E
Percival Lakes	59	Ed	21.25S	125.00 E
Percy Islands	59	Kd	21.40S	150.15 E
Perdasdefogu	14	Dk	39.41N	9.26 E
Perdida, Sierra-	48	Hd	27.30N	103.30W
Perdido, Monte-	5	Gg	42.40N	0.05 E
Perdido, Rio-	55	Df	22.10S	57.33W
Perdizes	55	Id	19.21S	47.17W
Perečin	10	Sh	48.44N	22.29 E
Pereginskoje	16	De	48.49N	24.12 E
Pereira	54	Cc	4.48N	75.42W
Pereira Barreto	56	Jb	20.38S	51.07W
Perejaslav-Hmelnicki	16	Gd	50.04N	31.27 E
Perejil, Isla de-	13	Ig	35.55N	5.26W
Pereljub	16	Qd	51.52N	50.20 E
Peremennyj, Cape-	66	He	66.08S	105.30 E
Peremyšljany	10	Ug	49.38N	24.35 E
Perenjori	59	De	29.26S	116.17 E
Pereščepino	16	Ie	48.59N	35.22 E
Pereslavl-Zalesski	7	Jh	56.45N	38.55 E
Peretu	15	Ie	44.03N	25.05 E
Peretyčiha	20	Ig	47.10N	138.35 E
Perevolocki	16	Sd	51.51N	54.15 E
Pergamino	56	Hd	33.53S	60.35W
Pergamon	15	Kj	39.08N	27.13 E
Perge	24	Dd	37.00N	30.10 E
Pergine Valsugana	14	Fd	46.04N	11.14 E
Pergola	14	Gg	43.34N	12.50 E
Perham	45	Ic	46.36N	95.34W
Perho	7	Fe	63.13N	24.25 E
Periam	15	Dc	46.03N	20.52 E
Péribonca, Rivière-	42	Kg	48.44N	72.06W
Perico	56	Hb	24.23S	65.00W
Pericos	48	Fe	25.03N	107.42W
Périgord	11	Gj	45.00N	0.30 E
Perigoso, Canal-	54	Ic	0.05N	49.40W
Périgueux	11	Gi	45.11N	0.43 E
Perijá, Sierra de-	52	Ie	10.00N	73.00W
Peristerá	15	Gj	39.12N	23.59 E
Perito Moreno	53	Ij	46.36S	70.56W
Perkam, Tanjung-=Urville, Cape d'- (EN)	26	Kg	1.28S	137.54 E
Perković	14	Kg	43.41N	16.06 E
Perlas, Archipiélago de las-	47	Ig	8.25N	79.00W
Perlas, Cayos de-	49	Fg	12.28N	83.28W
Perlas, Laguna de-	49	Fg	12.30N	83.40W
Perlas, Punta de-	49	Fg	12.23N	83.30W
Perleberg	10	Hc	53.04N	11.52 E
Perlez	15	Dd	45.12N	20.23 E
Perm	6	Ld	58.00N	56.15 E
Përmeti	15	Di	40.14N	20.21 E
Permskaja Oblast [3]	19	Fd	59.00N	57.00 E
Pernambuco [2]	54	Ke	8.30S	37.30W
Pernik	15	Gg	42.36N	23.02 E
Pernik [2]	15	Fg	42.35N	22.50 E
Perniö/Bjärna	7	Ff	60.12N	23.08 E
Péronne	11	Ie	49.56N	2.56 E
Perote	48	Kh	19.34N	97.14W
Perpignan	6	Gg	42.41N	2.53 E
Perro, Laguna del-	45	Di	34.40N	105.57W
Perros-Guirec	11	Cf	48.49N	3.27W
Perry [Fl.-U.S.]	44	Fj	30.07N	83.35W
Perry [Ga.-U.S.]	44	Fi	32.27N	83.44W
Perry [Ia.-U.S.]	45	If	41.50N	94.06W
Perry [Ok.-U.S.]	45	Hh	36.17N	97.17W
Perry Lake	45	Ig	39.20N	95.30W
Perryton	45	Fh	36.24N	100.48W
Perryville	40	He	55.54N	159.10W
Persan	12	Ee	49.09N	2.16 E
Perşani, Munţii-	15	Id	45.40N	25.15 E
Persberg	8	Fe	59.45N	14.15 E
Persembe	24	Gb	41.04N	37.46 E
Persepolis	24	Oh	29.57N	52.52 E
Perseverancia	54	Ff	14.44S	62.48W
Persian Gulf (EN)=Al-Khalīj al-'Arabī	21	Hg	27.00N	51.00 E
Persian Gulf (EN)=Khalīj-e Fārs	21	Hg	27.00N	51.00 E
Perstorp	8	Eh	56.08N	13.23 E
Pertek	24	Hc	38.50N	39.22 E
Perth [Austl.]	58	Ch	31.56S	115.50 E
Perth [Ont.-Can.]	44	Ic	44.54N	76.15W
Perth [Scot.-U.K.]	9	Je	56.24N	3.28W
Perth Amboy	44	Je	40.32N	74.17W
Perth-Andover	44	Nb	46.44N	67.42W
Perth-Armadale	59	Df	32.09S	116.00 E
Perth-Fremantle	59	Df	32.03S	115.45 E
Perth-Kalamunda	59	Df	31.57S	116.03 E
Perth-Mundaring	59	Df	31.54S	116.10 E
Perthus, Col de-/Portús, Coll del-	13	Ob	42.28N	2.51 E
Perthus, Col du-	13	Ob	42.28N	2.51 E
Pertuis	11	Lk	43.41N	5.30 E
Pertusato, Capo-	11a	Bb	41.21N	9.11 E
Perú [1]	53	Ig	10.00S	76.00W
Peru [Il.-U.S.]	45	Lf	41.20N	89.08W
Peru [In.-U.S.]	44	De	40.45N	86.04W
Perú, Altiplano del-	54	Df	15.00S	72.00W
Peruaçu, Rio-	55	Jb	15.11S	44.07W
Peru Basin (EN)	3	Mk	17.00S	90.00W
Peru-Chile Trench (EN)	3	Nl	20.00S	73.00W
Perugia	6	Hg	43.08N	12.22 E
Perugorria	55	Ci	29.20S	58.37W
Peruíbe	55	Ig	24.19S	47.00W
Perušić	14	Jf	44.39N	15.22 E
Péruwelz	12	Fd	50.31N	3.35 E

Index Symbols

[1] Independent Nation
[2] State, Region
[3] District, County
[4] Municipality
[5] Colony, Dependency
Continent
Physical Region
Historical or Cultural Region
Mount, Mountain
Volcano
Hill
Mountains, Mountain Range
Hills, Escarpment
Plateau, Upland
Pass, Gap
Plain, Lowland
Delta
Salt Flat
Valley, Canyon
Crater, Cave
Karst Features
Depression
Polder
Desert, Dunes
Forest, Woods
Heath, Steppe
Oasis
Cape, Point
Coast, Beach
Cliff
Peninsula
Isthmus
Sandbank
Island
Atoll
Rock, Reef
Islands, Archipelago
Rocks, Reefs
Coral Reef
Well, Spring
Geyser
River, Stream
Waterfall Rapids
River Mouth, Estuary
Lake
Salt Lake
Intermittent Lake
Reservoir
Swamp, Pond
Canal
Glacier
Ice Shelf, Pack Ice
Ocean
Sea
Gulf, Bay
Strait, Fjord
Lagoon
Bank
Seamount
Tablemount
Ridge
Shelf
Basin
Escarpment, Sea Scarp
Fracture
Trench, Abyss
National Park, Reserve
Point of Interest
Recreation Site
Cave, Cavern
Historic Site
Ruins
Wall, Walls
Church, Abbey
Temple
Scientific Station
Airport
Port
Lighthouse
Mine
Tunnel
Dam, Bridge

Pervari 24 Jd 37.54N 42.36 E
Pervomajsk [R.S.F.S.R.] 19 Ee 54.52N 43.48 E
Pervomajsk [Ukr.-U.S.S.R.] 16 Ke 48.36N 38.32 E
Pervomajsk [Ukr.-U.S.S.R.] 19 Df 48.03N 30.52 E
Pervomajskij [Bye.-U.S.S.R.] 10 Vc 53.52N 25.33 E
Pervomajskij [Kaz.-U.S.S.R.] 19 Ie 50.15N 81.59 E
Pervomajskij [R.S.F.S.R.] 16 Lc 53.18N 40.15 E
Pervomajskij [R.S.F.S.R.] 19 Ec 64.26N 40.48 E
Pervomajskij [R.S.F.S.R.] 17 Ji 54.52N 61.08 E
Pervomajskij [R.S.F.S.R.] 16 Sd 51.34N 54.59 E
Pervomajskij [Ukr.-U.S.S.R.] 16 Je 49.24N 36.15 E
Pervouralsk 19 Fd 57.00N 60.00 E
Pervy Kurilski Proliv 20 Kf 50.50N 156.50 E
Perwez/Perwijs 12 Gd 50.37N 4.49 E
Perwijs/Perwez 12 Gd 50.37N 4.49 E
Pes 7 Ig 59.10N 35.18 E
Peša 17 Cc 66.50N 47.32 E
Pesaro 14 Gg 43.54N 12.55 E
Pescadores (EN)=Penghu Liehtao 27 Kg 23.30N 119.30 E
Pescadores, Punta- 48 Ef 23.45N 109.45W
Pesčany, Mys- 16 Qh 43.10N 51.18 E
Pesčany, Ostrov 20 Gb 74.20N 115.55 E
Pescara 14 Ih 42.28N 14.13 E
Pescara 6 Hg 42.28N 14.13 E
Pescasseroli 14 Hi 41.48N 13.47 E
Peschici 14 Ki 41.57N 16.01 E
Pescia 14 Eg 43.54N 10.41 E
Pescocostanzo 14 Ii 41.53N 14.04 E
Peshāwar 22 Jf 34.01N 71.33 E
Peshkopia 15 Dh 41.41N 20.26 E
Pesio 14 Bf 44.28N 7.53 E
Peskovka 7 Mg 59.03N 52.22 E
Pesmes 11 Lg 47.17N 5.34 E
Pesočny 8 Nd 60.05N 30.20 E
Peso da Régua 13 Ec 41.10N 7.47W
Pesqueira 54 Ke 8.22S 36.42W
Pesqueria, Rio- 48 Je 25.54N 99.11W
Pessac 11 Fj 44.48N 0.37W
Pest [2] 10 Pi 47.25N 19.20 E
Pešter 15 Df 43.05N 20.02 E
Peštera 15 Hg 42.02N 24.18 E
Pestovo 19 Dd 58.36N 35.47 E
Petacalco, Bahía de- 47 De 17.57N 102.05W
Petaḥ Tiqwa 24 Ff 32.05N 34.53 E
Petäjävesi 8 Kb 62.15N 25.12 E
Petal 45 Lk 31.21N 89.17W
Petalioi 15 Hl 38.01N 24.17 E
Petalioi, Gulf of- (EN) = Petalión, Kólpos- 15 Hk 38.00N 24.05 E
Petalión, Kólpos- = Petalioi, Gulf of- (EN) 15 Hk 38.00N 24.05 E
Petaluma 46 Dg 38.14N 122.39W
Pétange/Petingen 12 He 49.33N 5.53 E
Petare 54 Ea 10.29N 66.49W
Petatlán 48 Ii 17.31N 101.16W
Petatlán, Río- 48 Fd 26.09N 107.45W
Petauke 36 Fe 14.15S 31.20 E
Petén 47 Fe 16.15N 89.50W
Petén [3] 49 Be 16.50N 90.00W
Petén Itzá, Lago- 49 Ce 16.59N 89.50W
Petenwell Lake 45 Ld 44.05N 89.45W
Peterborough [Austl.] 59 Hf 32.58S 138.50 E
Peterborough [Eng.-U.K.] 9 Mi 52.35N 0.15W
Peterborough [Ont.-Can.] 42 Jh 44.18N 78.19W
Peterhead 9 Ld 57.30N 1.46W
Peter I, Oy- 66 Pe 68.47S 90.35W
Peter Island 51a Db 18.22N 64.35W
Peterlee 9 Lg 54.46N 1.19W
Petermann Gletscher 41 Fb 80.45N 61.00W
Petermann Ranges 59 Fd 25.00S 129.45 E
Petermanns Bjerg 67 Md 73.10N 28.00W
Peter Pond Lake 42 Ge 55.55N 108.40W
Petersberg 10 He 51.35N 11.57 E
Petersburg [Ak.-U.S.] 40 Me 56.49N 132.57W
Petersburg [In.-U.S.] 44 Df 38.30N 87.16W
Petersburg [Va.-U.S.] 43 Ld 37.14N 77.24W
Petersburg [W.V.-U.S.] 44 Hf 39.01N 79.09W
Petersfield 9 Mk 51.00N 0.56W
Petershagen 12 Kb 52.23N 8.58 E
Peter the Great Bay (EN)= Petra Velikogo, Zaliv- 21 Pe 42.40N 132.00 E
Petilia Policastro 14 Kk 39.07N 16.47 E
Petingen/Pétange 12 He 49.33N 5.53 E
Petit-Bourg 51e Ab 16.12N 61.36W
Petit-Canal 51e Bb 16.23N 61.29W
Petit Canouan 51n Bb 12.47N 61.17W
Petit Cul-de-Sac Marin 51e Ab 16.12N 61.33W
Petite Kabylie 13 Rh 36.35N 5.25 E
Petite Rivière de l'Artibonite 49 Kd 19.08N 72.29W
Petites Pyrénées 11 Hk 43.05N 1.10 E
Petite-Terre, Iles de la- 51e Bb 16.10N 61.07W
Petit-Goâve 49 Kd 18.26N 72.52W
Petit Martinique Island 51p Ca 12.32N 61.22W
Petit-Mécatina, Rivière du- 42 Lf 50.39N 59.25W
Petit Morin 11 Jf 48.56N 3.07 E
Petit Mustique Island 51n Bb 12.51N 61.13W
Petit Nevis Island 51n Bb 12.58N 61.15W
Petitot 42 Fd 60.14N 123.29W
Petit Saint-Bernard, Col du- 14 Ae 45.40N 6.55 E
Petit Saint Vincent Island 51n Bb 12.33N 61.23W
Petit Savanne 51g Bb 15.15N 61.17W
Petitsikapau Lake 42 Kf 54.40N 66.25W
Petkula 7 Gc 67.40N 26.41 E
Petlalcingo 48 Kh 18.05N 97.54W
Peto 47 Gd 20.08N 88.55W
Petorca 56 Fd 32.15S 71.00W
Petoskey 44 Ec 45.22N 84.57W
Petra 24 Fg 30.19N 35.29 E
Petralia Soprana 14 Im 37.47N 14.06 E
Petra Pervogo, Hrebet- 18 He 39.00N 71.10 E
Petra Velikogo, Zaliv-= Peter the Great Bay (EN) 21 Pe 42.40N 132.00 E
Petre, Point- 44 Id 43.50N 77.09W
Petre Bay 62 Je 43.55S 176.40W
Petrel 66 Re 63.28S 56.17W
Petrela 15 Ch 41.15N 19.51 E
Petrella Tifernina 14 Ii 41.41N 14.42 E
Petrič 15 Gh 41.24N 23.13 E
Pétrie, Récif- 61 Bc 18.30S 164.20 E
Petrikov 16 Fc 52.08N 28.31 E
Petrila 15 Gd 45.27N 23.25 E
Petrinja 14 Ke 45.27N 16.17 E
Petrodvorec 7 Gg 59.53N 29.50 E
Petrólea 54 Db 8.30N 72.35W
Petrolia 44 Fd 42.52N 82.09W
Petrolina 54 Je 9.24S 40.30W
Petrolina de Goiás 55 Hc 16.06S 49.20W
Petronanski prohod 15 Gf 43.08N 23.08 E
Petronell 14 Kb 48.07N 16.51 E
Petropavlovka 20 Ff 50.38N 105.19 E
Petropavlovsk 22 Id 54.54N 69.06 E
Petropavlovsk-Kamčatski 22 Rd 53.01N 158.39 E
Petrópolis 53 Lh 22.31S 43.10W
Petroşani 15 Gd 45.25N 23.22 E
Petrovac [Yugo.] 15 Bg 42.12N 18.57 E
Petrovac [Yugo.] 15 Ee 44.22N 21.25 E
Petrova Gora 14 Je 45.17N 15.47 E
Petrovaradin 15 Cd 45.15N 19.53 E
Petrovka 15 Nc 46.55N 30.40 E
Petrovsk 19 Ee 52.18N 45.23 E
Petrovski Jam 7 Ie 63.18N 35.15 E
Petrovsk-Zabajkalski 22 Md 51.17N 108.50 E
Petrov Val 16 Nd 50.10N 45.12 E
Petrozavodsk 6 Jc 61.47N 34.20 E
Petuhovo 19 Gd 55.06N 67.58 E
Petuški 7 Ji 55.59N 39.28 E
Petworth 12 Bd 50.59N 0.36W
Peuetsagoe, Gunung- 26 Cf 4.55N 96.20 E
Peumo 56 Fd 34.24S 71.10W
Peureulak 26 Cf 4.48N 97.53 E
Pevek 22 Tc 69.42N 170.17 E
Pevensey 12 Cd 50.48N 0.21 E
Pevensey Bay 12 Cd 50.48N 0.22 E
Peza 7 Kd 65.34N 44.33 E
Pézenas 11 Jk 43.27N 3.25 E
Pezinok 10 Nh 48.18N 17.16 E
Pfaffenhofen an der Ilm 10 Hh 48.32N 11.31 E
Pfaffenhoffen 12 Jf 48.51N 7.37 E
Pfalz 12 Je 49.20N 7.57 E
Pfalzel, Trier- 12 Ie 49.46N 6.41 E
Pfälzer Bergland 10 Dg 49.35N 7.30 E
Pfälzer Wald 10 Dg 49.15N 7.50 E
Pfarrkirchen 10 Ih 48.26N 12.52 E
Pfinz 12 Ke 49.11N 8.25 E
Pfinztal 12 Ke 49.02N 8.30 E
Pforzheim an der Enz 10 Eh 48.53N 8.42 E
Pfrimm 12 Ke 49.39N 8.22 E
Pfullendorf 10 Fi 47.55N 9.15 E
Pfunds 14 Ed 46.58N 10.33 E
Pfungstadt 12 Ke 49.48N 8.36 E
Phalaborwa 37 Ed 23.55S 31.13 E
Phalodi 25 Ec 27.08N 72.22 E
Pha-an 25 Je 16.53N 97.38 E
Phangnga 25 Jg 8.28N 98.32 E
Phan Ly Cham 25 Lf 11.13N 108.31 E
Phanom 25 Jg 8.49N 98.50 E
Phan Rang 25 Lf 11.34N 108.59 E
Phan Thiet 25 Lf 10.56N 108.06 E
Pharr 45 Gm 26.12N 98.11W
Phatthalung 25 Kg 7.38N 100.04 E
Phayao 25 Ke 18.07N 100.11 E
Phenix City 43 Je 32.29N 85.01W
Phet Buri 25 Jf 13.06N 99.56 E
Phetchabun, Thiu Khao- 25 Ke 16.20N 100.55 E
Phichit 25 Ke 16.24N 100.21 E
Philadelphia [Ms.-U.S.] 45 Lj 32.46N 89.07W
Philadelphia [Pa.-U.S.] 39 Lf 39.57N 75.07W
Philae 33 Fe 23.35N 32.52 E
Philip 45 Fd 44.02N 101.40W
Philippeville 11 Kd 50.12N 4.33 E
Philippi 44 Gf 39.08N 80.03W
Philippi (EN) = Filippoi 15 Hh 41.02N 24.18 E
Philippi, Lake- 59 Hd 24.20S 139.00 E
Philippi Glacier 66 Ge 66.45S 88.20 E
Philippine Basin (EN) 3 Ih 17.00N 132.00 E
Philippine Islands (EN) = Pilipinas 21 Oh 13.00N 122.00 E
Philippines (EN)=Pilipinas [1] 22 Oh 13.00N 122.00 E
Philippine Sea (EN) 21 Oh 20.00N 130.00 E
Philippine Trench (EN) 3 Ii 9.00N 127.00 E
Philippsburg 12 Ke 49.14N 8.27 E
Philipsburg [Mt.-U.S.] 46 Ic 46.20N 113.08W
Philipsburg [Neth.Ant.] 50 Ec 18.01N 63.04W
Philip Smith Mountains 40 Jc 68.30N 148.00W
Philipstown 37 Cf 30.26S 24.29 E
Phillipsburg 45 Gg 39.45N 99.19W
Philpots 42 Jb 74.55N 80.00W
Phitsanulok 22 Mh 16.49N 100.15 E
Phnom Penh (EN)=Phnum Pénh 22 Mh 11.33N 104.55 E
Phnum Penh=Phnom Penh (EN) 22 Mh 11.33N 104.55 E
Phoenix 39 Hf 33.27N 112.05W
Phoenix→Rawaki Atoll 57 Je 3.43S 170.43W
Phoenix Islands 57 Je 4.00S 172.00W
Phôngsali 25 Kd 21.41N 102.06 E
Phrae 25 Ke 18.07N 100.11 E
Phra Nakhom Si Ayutthaya 22 Mh 14.21N 100.33 E
Phrygia 15 Mk 38.30N 29.50 E
Phu Cuong 25 Lf 10.58N 106.39 E
Phuket 22 Li 7.54N 98.24 E
Phuket, Ko- 21 Li 8.00N 98.20 E
Phulbani 25 Gd 20.28N 84.14 E
Phumĭ Mlu Prey 25 Lf 13.48N 105.16 E
Phumĭ Sâmraŏng 25 Kf 14.11N 103.31 E
Phu My 25 Lf 14.10N 109.03 E
Phuoc Binh 25 Lf 11.50N 106.58 E
Phu Quoc, Dao- 25 Kf 10.12N 104.00 E
Phu Tho 25 Ld 21.24N 105.13 E
Phu Vinh → Tra Vinh 25 Lg 9.56N 106.20 E
Piaanu Pass 64d Ab 7.20N 151.26 E
Piacenza 14 De 45.01N 9.40 E
Piana degli Albanesi 14 Hm 37.59N 13.17 E
Piana Mwanga 36 Ed 7.40S 28.10 E
Piancó 54 Ke 7.12S 37.57W
Pianguan 27 Jd 39.28N 111.32 E
Pianosa [It.] 14 Jh 42.15N 15.45 E
Pianosa [It.] 14 Eh 42.35N 10.05 E
Piaseczno 10 Rd 52.05N 21.01 E
Piaski 10 Se 51.08N 22.51 E
Piątek 10 Pd 52.05N 19.28 E
Piatra 15 If 43.49N 25.10 E
Piatra Neamţ 15 Jc 46.55N 26.20 E
Piatra Olt 15 He 44.22N 24.16 E
Piauí [2] 54 Je 7.00S 43.00W
Piauí, Rio- 52 Lf 6.38S 42.42W
Piave 5 Hf 45.32N 12.44 E
Piaxtla, Punta- 48 Ff 23.38N 106.50W
Piaxtla, Rio- 48 Ff 23.42N 106.49W
Piazza Armerina 14 Im 37.23N 14.22 E
Pibor 35 Ed 8.26N 33.13 E
Pibor Post 35 Ed 6.48N 33.08 E
Pica 56 Gb 20.30S 69.21W
Picachos, Cerro dos- 48 Bc 29.25N 114.10W
Picardie = Picardy (EN) 11 Je 50.00N 3.30 E
Picardy (EN) = Picardie 11 Je 50.00N 3.30 E
Picayune 45 Lk 30.26N 89.41W
Picentini, Monti- 14 Jj 40.45N 15.10 E
Pichanal 53 Jh 23.20S 64.15W
Pichilemu 56 Fd 34.23S 72.00W
Pichilingue 48 De 24.20N 110.20W
Pichna 10 Oe 51.50N 18.40 E
Pichones, Cayos- 49 Ff 15.45N 82.55W
Pichucalco 48 Mi 17.31N 93.04W
Pickering 9 Mg 54.14N 0.46W
Pickering, Vale of- 9 Mg 54.10N 0.45W
Pickle Lake 42 If 51.29N 90.10W
Pickwick Lake 44 Ch 34.55N 88.10W
Pico 30 Ee 38.28N 28.20W
Picos 53 Lf 7.05S 41.28W
Pico Truncado 56 Gg 46.48S 67.58W
Picquigny 11 Ie 49.57N 2.09 E
Picton 61 Dh 41.18S 174.00 E
Pictou 42 Lg 45.41N 62.43W
Picunda 16 Lh 43.12N 40.21 E
Pidurutalagala 21 Ki 7.00N 80.46 E
Piedecuesta 54 Db 6.59N 73.03W
Piedimonte Matese 14 Ii 41.20N 14.22 E
Piedmont [Al.-U.S.] 44 Ei 33.55N 85.37W
Piedmont [Mo.-U.S.] 45 Kh 37.09N 90.42W
Piedmont (EN) = Piemonte [2] 14 Be 45.00N 8.00 E
Piedmont Plateau 38 Kf 35.00N 81.00W
Piedra 13 Kc 41.19N 1.48W
Piedra, Monasterio de- 13 Kc 41.10N 1.50W
Piedrabuena 13 He 39.02N 4.10W
Piedrafita, Puerto de- 13 Fb 42.36N 6.57W
Piedrahita 13 Gd 40.28N 5.19W
Piedras 54 Cd 3.38S 79.54W
Piedras, Punta- 56 Ie 35.25S 57.08W
Piedras, Rio de las- 54 Ef 12.30S 69.14W
Piedras Negras 39 Ig 28.42N 100.31W
Piedras Negras 49 Be 17.12N 91.15W
Piedra Sola 56 Id 32.04S 56.21W
Piekary Śląskie 10 Of 50.24N 18.58 E
Pieksämäki 7 Ge 62.18N 27.08 E
Pielach 15 Jh 48.15N 15.22 E
Pielavesi 7 Ge 63.14N 26.45 E
Pielinen 5 Ic 63.15N 29.40 E
Piemonte = Piedmont (EN) [2] 14 Be 45.00N 8.00 E
Pieniężno 10 Qb 54.15N 20.08 E
Pieni Salpausselkä 8 Lc 61.10N 27.20 E
Piennes 12 He 49.19N 5.47 E
Pienza 14 Fg 43.04N 11.41 E
Pierce 46 Hc 46.29N 115.48W
Piéria Óri 15 Fi 40.12N 22.07 E
Pierre 39 Ie 44.22N 100.21W
Pierrefitte-sur-Aire 12 Hf 48.54N 5.20 E
Pierrefonds 12 Ee 49.21N 2.59 E
Pierrelatte 11 Kj 44.23N 4.42 E
Pieskehaure 7 Dc 66.57N 16.30 E
Piešť'any 10 Nh 48.36N 17.50 E
Pietarsaari/Jakobstad 7 Fe 63.40N 22.42 E
Pietermaritzburg 31 Kk 29.37S 30.16 E
Pietersburg 31 Jk 23.54S 29.25 E
Pietraperzia 14 Im 37.25N 14.08 E
Pietrasanta 14 Eg 43.57N 10.14 E
Piet Retief 37 Ee 27.01S 30.50 E
Pietrii, Virful- 15 Fd 45.23N 22.40 E
Pietroşani 15 If 43.43N 25.38 E
Pietrosu, Virful- [Rom.] 15 Ib 47.08N 25.11 E
Pietrosu, Virful- [Rom.] 15 If 47.23N 25.33 E
Pieve di Cadore 14 Gd 46.26N 12.22 E
Pigeon Island 51k Ba 16.04N 60.58W
Pigeon River 45 Lb 48.02N 89.41W
Piggott 45 Kh 36.23N 90.11W
Pigg's Peak 37 Ee 25.58S 31.15 E
Pigs, Bay of- (EN)= Cochinos, Bahia de- 49 Gb 22.07N 81.10W
Pigüé 55 Am 37.37S 62.25W
Pi He 28 Dh 32.26N 116.34 E
Pihkva järv=Pskov, Lake- (EN) 7 Gg 58.00N 28.00 E
Pihlajavesi 7 Gf 61.45N 28.45 E
Pihlava 8 Ic 61.33N 21.36 E
Pihtipudas 7 Fe 63.23N 25.34 E
Piikkiö 8 Jd 60.26N 22.31 E
Piirisaar/Pirissar 8 Lf 58.23N 27.40 E
Pijijiapan 48 Mj 15.42N 93.14W
Pijol, Pico- 49 Df 15.06N 87.35W
Pikalevo 7 Ig 59.32N 34.03 E
Pikangikum 42 If 51.49N 94.00W
Pikelot Island 57 Fd 8.05N 147.38 E
Pikes Peak 43 Fd 38.51N 105.03W
Piketberg 37 Bf 32.54S 18.46 E
Pikiutdleq 41 Hf 64.45N 40.10W
Pikou 28 Ge 39.24N 122.21 E
Pikounda 36 Cb 0.33N 16.42 E
Piła 10 Mc 53.10N 16.44 E
Piła [2] 10 Mc 53.10N 16.45 E
Pila 55 Cm 36.01S 58.08W
Pila, Sierra de la- 13 Kf 38.16N 1.11W
Pilar [Arg.] 55 Bj 31.27S 61.15W
Pilar [Braz.] 54 Ke 9.36S 35.56W
Pilar [Par.] 56 Ic 26.52S 58.23W
Pilas Group 26 He 6.45N 121.35 E
Pilat, Mont- 11 Ki 45.23N 4.35 E
Pilatus 14 Cd 46.59N 8.20 E
Pilaya, Rio- 54 Fh 20.55S 64.04W
Pilcaniyeu 56 Ff 41.08S 70.40W
Pilcomayo, Rio- 52 Kh 25.21S 57.42W
Pile, Jezioro- 10 Mc 53.35N 16.30 E
Pili 15 Ej 39.28N 21.37 E
Pilibhīt 25 Fc 28.38N 79.48 E
Pilica 10 Re 51.52N 21.17 E
Pilion Óros 15 Gj 39.24N 23.05 E
Pilipinas=Philippine Islands (EN) 21 Oh 13.00N 122.00 E
Pilipinas=Philippines (EN) [1] 22 Oh 13.00N 122.00 E
Pilis 10 Oi 47.41N 18.53 E
Pillahuincó, Sierra de- 55 Bn 38.18S 60.45W
Pillar, Cape- 59 Jh 43.15S 148.00 E
Pilna 7 Ki 55.33N 45.55 E
Pilões, Rio- 55 Gc 16.14S 50.54W
Pilões, Serra dos- 55 Ic 17.50S 47.13W
Pilón, Rio- 48 Je 25.32N 99.32W
Pilos 15 Em 36.55N 21.42 E
Pilos = Pylos (EN) 15 Em 36.56N 21.40 E
Pilot Peak 46 Hf 41.02N 114.06W
Pilot Rock 46 Fd 45.29N 118.50W
Pilsen (EN)=Plzeň 6 Hf 49.45N 13.24 E
Piltene 7 Eh 57.15N 21.42 E
Pilzno 10 Rg 49.59N 21.17 E
Pim 19 Hc 61.18N 71.57 E
Pimba 59 Hf 31.15S 136.47 E
Pimenteiras 54 Je 6.14S 41.25W
Pimža Jõgi 8 Lg 57.57N 27.59 E
Pina 13 Lc 41.29N 0.32W
Pinacate, Cerro- 48 Cb 31.45N 113.31W
Pinaki Atoll 57 Nf 19.22S 138.44W
Pinamar 55 Dm 37.07S 56.50W
Piñami, Arroyo- 48 Cd 27.44N 113.47W
Pinar 13 Gh 36.46N 5.26W
Pinarbaşi 24 Gc 38.50N 36.30 E
Pinar del Rio 39 Kg 22.25N 83.42W
Pinar del Rio [3] 49 Eb 22.35N 83.40W
Pinarello 11a Bb 41.41N 9.22 E
Pinarhisar 15 Kh 41.37N 27.30 E
Pinchbeck 12 Bb 52.48N 0.09W
Pincher Creek 42 Gg 49.30N 113.48W
Pinçon, Mont- 11 Ff 48.58N 0.37W
Pincota 15 Ec 46.20N 21.42 E
Pindaíba, Ribeirão 55 Gb 14.48S 52.00W
Pindaré, Rio- 54 Jd 3.17S 44.47W
Pindaré-Mirim 54 Id 3.37S 45.21W
Pindaval 55 Dc 17.08S 56.09W
Pindhos Óros=Pindus Mountains (EN) 5 Ih 39.45N 21.30 E
Pindus Mountains (EN)= Pindhos Óros 5 Ih 39.45N 21.30 E
Pine Bluff 43 Ie 34.13N 92.01W
Pine Bluffs 46 Mf 41.11N 104.04W
Pine Creek 59 Gb 13.49S 131.49 E
Pine Falls 42 Hf 50.35N 96.15W
Pinega 19 Ec 64.42N 43.22 E
Pinega 5 Kc 64.08N 41.54 E
Pine Island Glacier 66 Of 75.00S 101.00W
Pineland 45 Jk 31.15N 93.58W
Pine Mountain [Ga.-U.S.] 44 Ei 32.51N 84.47W
Pine Mountain [U.S.] 44 Fg 36.55N 83.20W
Pine Pass 42 Fe 55.50N 122.30W
Pine Point 39 Hc 61.01N 114.15W
Pine Ridge 45 Ee 43.02N 102.33W
Pinerolo 14 Bf 44.53N 7.21 E
Pines, Isle of- (EN)= Juventud, Isla de la- 38 Kg 21.40N 82.50W
Pines, Isle of- (EN)=Pins, Ile des- 57 Hg 22.37S 167.30 E
Pines, Lake O' The 45 Ij 32.46N 94.35W
Pinetown 37 Ee 29.52S 30.46 E
Ping 21 Mh 15.42N 100.09 E
Pingbian 27 Hg 22.56N 103.46 E
Pingchang 27 Ie 31.38N 107.06 E
Pingding 28 Bf 37.48N 113.37 E
Pingdingbu → Guyuan 28 Cd 41.40N 115.41 E
Pingding Shan 27 Mb 46.39N 128.30 E
Pingdingshan 27 Je 33.41N 113.27 E
Pingdu 28 Ef 36.47N 119.57 E
Pingelap Atoll 57 Hd 6.13N 160.42 E
Pingelly 59 Df 32.32S 117.05 E
Pinggu 28 Dd 40.08N 117.07 E
Pingguo 27 Ig 23.21N 107.34 E
Pinghu 28 Fi 30.42N 121.02 E
Pingjiang 28 Bj 28.45N 113.37 E
Pingle 27 Jg 24.43N 110.42 E
Pingli 27 Ie 32.27N 109.21 E
Pingliang 22 Mf 35.32N 106.41 E
Pinglu (Jingping) 28 Be 39.32N 112.14 E
Pingluo 22 Mf 38.56N 106.34 E
Pingma → Tiandong 27 Ig 23.40N 107.09 E
Pingnan 27 Jg 23.38N 110.23 E
Pingouins, Ile des- 30 Mm 46.25S 50.19 E
Pingquan 27 Kc 41.00N 118.36 E
Pingshan 28 Ce 38.21N 114.01 E
Pingshun 28 Bf 36.12N 113.26 E
Pingtan 27 Kf 25.31N 119.48 E
Pingtung 27 Lg 22.40N 120.29 E
Pingüicas, Cerro- 48 Jg 21.10N 99.42W
Pingvallavatn 7a Bb 64.15N 21.09W
Pingvellir 7a Bb 64.17N 21.03W
Pingwu 27 He 32.27N 104.35 E
Pingxiang [China] 27 Ig 22.11N 106.46 E
Pingxiang [China] 27 Jf 27.43N 113.48 E
Pingyang 27 Lf 27.40N 120.30 E
Pingyao 27 Jd 37.12N 112.13 E
Pingyi 28 Dg 35.30N 117.32 E
Pingyin 28 Df 36.17N 116.26 E
Pingyu 28 Ci 32.58N 114.36 E
Pingyuan 28 Df 37.10N 116.25 E
Pinhal 55 If 22.12S 46.45W
Pinhão 55 Gg 25.43S 51.38W
Pinheir Machado 55 Fj 31.34S 53.23W
Pinhel 13 Ed 40.46N 7.04W
Pini, Pulau- 26 Cf 0.08N 98.40 E
Piniós [Grc.] 15 Fj 39.53N 22.44 E
Piniós [Grc.] 15 El 37.48N 21.14 E
Pinipel 63a Ba 4.24S 154.08 E
Pinjug 7 Lf 60.16N 47.54 E
Pinka 10 Mi 47.00N 16.35 E
Pink Mountain 42 Fe 56.06N 122.35W
Pinnaroo 59 Ig 35.16S 140.55 E
Pinneberg 10 Fc 53.39N 9.48 E
Pinnes, Ákra- 15 Hi 40.07N 24.18 E
Pinolosean 26 Hf 0.23N 124.07 E
Pinos 48 If 22.18N 101.34W
Pinos, Mount- 38 Hf 34.50N 119.09W
Pinos-Puente 13 Ig 37.15N 3.45W
Pinrang 26 Gg 3.48S 119.38 E
Pins, Cap des- 63b Ce 21.04S 167.28 E
Pins, Ile des-=Pines, Isle of- (EN) 57 Hg 22.37S 167.30 E
Pins, Pointe aux- 44 Gd 42.15N 81.51W
Pinsk 19 Ce 52.08N 26.06 E
Pinta, Isla- 54a Aa 0.35N 90.44W
Pintas, Sierra de las- 48 Bb 31.40N 115.10W
Pinto [Arg.] 56 Hc 29.09S 62.39W
Pinto [Sp.] 13 Id 40.14N 3.41W
Pintwater Range 46 Hh 36.55N 115.30W
Pio 63a Ed 10.12S 161.42 E
Pioche 46 Hh 37.56N 114.27W
Piombino 14 Eh 42.55N 10.32 E
Piombino, Canale di- 14 Eh 42.55N 10.30 E
Pioneer Mountains 46 Id 45.40N 113.00W
Pioner, Ostrov- 21 Lb 79.50N 92.30 E
Pionerski [R.S.F.S.R.] 19 Gc 61.12N 62.57 E
Pionerski [R.S.F.S.R.] 7 Ei 54.57N 20.13 E
Pionki 10 Re 51.30N 21.27 E
Piorini, Lago- 54 Fd 3.35S 63.15W
Piorini, Rio- 54 Fd 3.23S 63.30W
Piotrków [2] 10 Pe 51.25N 19.40 E
Piotrków Trybunalski 10 Pe 51.25N 19.42 E
Piove di Sacco 14 Ge 45.18N 12.02 E
Pipa Dingzi 27 Mc 43.57N 128.14 E
Pipéri 15 Hj 39.19N 24.21 E
Pipestone 45 Hd 44.01N 96.19W
Pipestone Creek 45 Fb 49.42N 100.45W
Pipi 35 Cd 7.27N 22.48 E
Pipinas 55 Dl 35.32S 57.20W
Pipmouacan, Réservoir - 42 Kg 49.40N 70.20W
Piqan→Shanshan 27 Fc 42.52N 90.10 E
Piqua 44 Ee 40.08N 84.14W
Piqueras, Puerto de- 13 Jb 42.03N 2.32W
Piquiri, Rio- 56 Jb 24.03S 54.14W
Piquiri, Serra do- 55 Fg 24.53S 52.25W
Piracanjuba 55 Hc 17.18S 49.01W
Piracanjuba, Rio- [Braz.] 55 Hd 18.14S 48.48W
Piracanjuba, Rio- [Braz.] 55 Hc 17.18S 48.13W
Piracema 55 Je 20.31S 44.29W
Piracicaba 56 Kb 22.43S 47.38W
Piracicaba, Rio- 55 Hf 22.36S 48.19W
Piraçununga 55 Ie 21.59S 47.25W
Piracuruca 54 Jd 3.56S 41.42W
Piraeus (EN) = Piraiévs 6 Ih 37.57N 23.38 E
Pirai do Sul 55 Hg 24.31S 49.56W
Piraiévs = Piraeus (EN) 6 Ih 37.57N 23.38 E
Piraju 55 Hf 23.12S 49.23W
Pirajui 55 He 21.59S 49.29W
Piramide, Cerro- 52 Ij 49.01S 73.32W
Piran 14 He 45.32N 13.34 E
Pirané 56 Ic 25.43S 59.06W
Piranhas 55 Gc 16.31S 51.51W
Piranhas, Rio- 55 Gc 16.01S 51.52W
Pirān Shahr 24 Kd 36.40N 45.05 E
Pirapora 53 Lg 17.21S 44.56W
Pirarajá 56 Jd 33.44S 54.45W
Pirate Well 49 Kb 22.26N 73.04W
Piratini 55 Fj 31.27S 53.06W
Piratini, Rio- 55 Fk 32.01S 52.25W
Piratinim, Rio- 55 Ei 28.06S 55.27W
Pirdop 15 Hg 42.42N 24.11 E
Pirenópolis 55 Hb 15.51S 48.57W
Pires do Rio 54 Ig 17.18S 48.17W
Pirgos 15 El 37.41N 21.27 E
Pirgós 15 Fi 40.38N 22.44 E
Piriápolis 55 El 34.54S 55.17W
Pirin 15 Gh 41.40N 23.30 E
Pirineos=Pyrenees (EN) 5 Gg 42.40N 1.00 E
Pirineus, Serra dos- 55 Hc 16.15S 49.10W
Piripiri 54 Jd 4.16S 41.47W
Pirissar/Piirisaar 8 Lf 58.23N 27.40 E
Piritu 50 Bh 9.23N 69.12W
Piritu, Islas- 50 Dg 10.10N 64.56W
Pirizal 55 Dc 16.16S 56.23W
Pirjatin 16 Hd 50.14N 32.30 E
Pirmasens 10 Dg 49.12N 7.36 E
Pirna 10 Jf 50.58N 13.56 E
Piron 63a Ad 11.20S 153.27 E
Pirón 13 Hc 41.23N 4.31W
Pirot 15 Ff 43.09N 22.36 E
Pirre, Cerro- 49 Ij 7.49N 77.43W
Pirrit Hills 66 Pg 81.17S 85.21W
Pirsagat 16 Pj 39.53N 49.19 E
Pir Tāj 24 Me 35.45N 48.07 E
Pirttikyla/Pörtom 8 Ib 62.42N 21.37 E
Piru 26 Ig 3.04S 128.12 E
Pis 64d Ba 7.41N 151.46 E
Pisa 14 Eg 43.43N 10.23 E
Pisa 10 Rc 53.15N 21.52 E
Pisagua 56 Fa 19.36S 70.13W

Index Symbols

[1] Independent Nation
[2] State, Region
[3] District, County
[4] Municipality
[5] Colony, Dependency
Continent
Physical Region
Historical or Cultural Region
Mount, Mountain
Volcano
Hill
Mountains, Mountain Range
Hills, Escarpment
Plateau, Upland
Pass, Gap
Plain, Lowland
Delta
Salt Flat
Valley, Canyon
Crater, Cave
Karst Features
Depression
Polder
Desert, Dunes
Forest, Woods
Heath, Steppe
Oasis
Cape, Point
Coast, Beach
Cliff
Peninsula
Isthmus
Sandbank
Island
Atoll
Rock, Reef
Islands, Archipelago
Rocks, Reefs
Coral Reef
Well, Spring
Geyser
River, Stream
Waterfall Rapids
River Mouth, Estuary
Lake
Salt Lake
Intermittent Lake
Reservoir
Swamp, Pond
Canal
Glacier
Ice Shelf, Pack Ice
Ocean
Sea
Gulf, Bay
Strait, Fjord
Lagoon
Bank
Seamount
Tablemount
Ridge
Shelf
Basin
Escarpment, Sea Scarp
Fracture
Trench, Abyss
National Park, Reserve
Point of Interest
Recreation Site
Cave, Cavern
Historic Site
Ruins
Wall, Walls
Church, Abbey
Temple
Scientific Station
Airport
Port
Lighthouse
Mine
Tunnel
Dam, Bridge

Index Symbols

[1] Independent Nation
[2] State, Region
[3] District, County
[4] Municipality
[5] Colony, Dependency
Continent
Physical Region
Historical or Cultural Region
Mount, Mountain
Volcano
Hill
Mountains, Mountain Range
Hills, Escarpment
Plateau, Upland
Pass, Gap
Plain, Lowland
Delta
Salt Flat
Valley, Canyon
Crater, Cave
Karst Features
Depression
Polder
Desert, Dunes
Forest, Woods
Heath, Steppe
Oasis
Cape, Point
Coast, Beach
Cliff
Peninsula
Isthmus
Sandbank
Island
Atoll
Rock, Reef
Islands, Archipelago
Rocks, Reefs
Coral Reef
Well, Spring
Geyser
River, Stream
Waterfall Rapids
River Mouth, Estuary
Lake
Salt Lake
Intermittent Lake
Reservoir
Swamp, Pond
Canal
Glacier
Ice Shelf, Pack Ice
Ocean
Sea
Gulf, Bay
Strait, Fjord
Lagoon
Bank
Seamount
Tablemount
Ridge
Shelf
Basin
Escarpment, Sea Scarp
Fracture
Trench, Abyss
National Park, Reserve
Point of Interest
Recreation Site
Cave, Cavern
Historic Site
Ruins
Wall, Walls
Church, Abbey
Temple
Scientific Station
Airport
Port
Lighthouse
Mine
Tunnel
Dam, Bridge

Porangatu	55	Ha	13.26S	49.10W
Porbandar	25	Dd	21.38N	69.36 E
Porcien	12	Ge	49.40N	4.20 E
Porcos, Rio dos-	55	Ja	12.42S	45.07W
Porcuna	13	Hg	37.52N	4.11W
Porcupine	38	Ec	66.35N	145.15W
Porcupine	44	Ga	48.32N	81.10W
Porcupine Bank (EN)	5	Ee	53.20N	13.30W
Porcupine Hills	46	Ha	50.05N	114.10W
Porcupine Plain	42	Dc	67.30N	137.30W
Pordenone	14	Ge	45.57N	12.39 E
Poreč	14	He	45.13N	13.37 E
Poreč	15	Fe	44.20N	22.05 E
Porecatú	55	Gf	22.43S	51.24W
Porećje	8	Kk	53.53N	24.08 E
Poreckoje	7	Li	55.13N	46.19 E
Porhov	19	Cd	57.45N	29.32 E
Pori/Björneborg	6	Ic	61.29N	21.47 E
Porion	15	Gn	35.58N	23.16 E
Porirua	61	Dh	41.08S	174.50 E
Pörisvatn	7a	Bb	64.20N	18.55W
Porjus	7	Ec	66.57N	19.49 E
Porkkala	8	Ke	59.55N	24.25 E
Porlamar	54	Fa	10.57N	63.51W
Porma	13	Gb	42.29N	5.28W
Pornic	11	Dg	47.07N	2.06W
Poronajsk	22	Qe	49.14N	143.04 E
Poronin	10	Qg	49.20N	20.04 E
Pòros	15	Gl	37.30N	23.31 E
Póros	15	Gl	37.30N	23.27 E
Poroshiri-Dake	28	Qc	42.42N	142.35 E
Porosozero	7	He	62.44N	32.42 E
Porozovo	10	Ud	52.54N	24.27 E
Porpoise Bay	66	Ie	66.30S	128.30 E
Porquis Junction	44	Ga	48.43N	80.52W
Porrentruy	14	Bc	47.25N	7.10 E
Porreras	13	Oe	39.31N	3.00 E
Porretta, Passo della-	14	Ef	44.02N	10.56 E
Porretta Terme	14	Ef	44.09N	10.59 E
Porsangen	5	Ia	70.50N	26.00 E
Porsangerhalvøya	7	Fa	70.50N	25.00 E
Porsgrunn	7	Bg	59.09N	9.40 E
Pórshöfn	7a	Ca	66.10N	15.20W
Porsuk	24	Dc	39.42N	31.59 E
Portachuelo	54	Fg	17.21S	63.24W
Portadown/Port an Dúnáin	9	Gg	54.26N	6.27W
Portage	45	Le	43.33N	89.28W
Portage la Prairie	42	Hg	49.57N	98.18W
Port Alberni	42	Fg	49.14N	124.48W
Portalegre	13	Ee	39.17N	7.26W
Portalegre [2]	13	Ee	39.15N	7.35W
Portales	43	Ge	34.11N	103.20W
Port-Alfred	42	Kg	48.20N	70.53W
Port Alfred	37	Df	33.36S	26.55 E
Port Alice	42	Ef	50.23N	127.27W
Port Allegany	44	He	41.48N	78.18W
Port an Dúnáin/Portadown	9	Gg	54.26N	6.27W
Port Angeles	43	Cb	48.07N	123.27W
Port Antonio	47	Ie	18.11N	76.28W
Port Arthur [Austl.]	59	Jh	43.09S	147.51 E
Port Arthur [Tx.-U.S.]	39	Jg	29.55N	93.55W
Port Arthur (EN)=Lüshun	27	Ld	38.50N	121.13 E
Port Augusta	58	Eh	32.30S	137.46 E
Port-Au-Prince	39	Lh	18.32N	72.20W
Port-au-Prince, Baie de-	49	Kd	18.40N	72.30W
Port Austin	44	Fc	44.03N	83.01W
Port aux Français	31	Om	49.25S	70.10 E
Porta Westfalica	12	Kb	52.15N	8.56 E
Port-Bergé-Vao Vao	37	Hc	15.33S	47.38 E
Port Blair	22	Lh	11.36N	92.45 E
Port-Bou/Portbou	13	Pb	42.25N	3.10 E
Portbou/Port-Bou	13	Pb	42.25N	3.10 E
Port Burwell [Newf.-Can.]	39	Mc	60.25N	64.49W
Port Burwell [Ont.-Can.]	44	Gd	42.39N	80.49W
Port-Cartier	42	Kf	50.01N	66.53W
Port Chalmers	62	Df	45.49S	170.37 E
Port Charlotte	43	Kf	26.59N	82.06W
Port Clinton	44	Fe	41.30N	82.58W
Port Coquitlam	46	Db	49.16N	122.46W
Port-de-Bouc	11	Kk	43.24N	4.59 E
Port-de-Paix	49	Kd	19.57N	72.50W
Port Dickson	26	Df	2.31N	101.48 E
Port Edward	37	Ef	31.03S	30.13 E
Portel [Braz.]	54	Hd	1.57S	50.49W
Portel [Port.]	13	Ef	38.18N	7.42W
Port Elgin	44	Gc	44.26N	81.24W
Port Elizabeth [S.Afr.]	31	Jl	33.58S	25.40 E
Port Elizabeth [St.Vin.]	51n	Ba	13.00N	61.16W
Port Ellen	9	Gf	55.39N	6.12W
Port-en-Bessin-Huppain	11	Fe	49.21N	0.45W
Port Erin	9	Ig	54.05N	4.43W
Porter Point	51n	Ba	13.23N	61.11W
Porterville [Ca.-U.S.]	43	Dd	36.04N	119.01W
Porterville [S.Afr.]	37	Bf	33.00S	19.00 E
Portete, Bahía de-	49	Lg	12.13N	71.55W
Port Fairy	59	Ig	38.23S	142.14 E
Port Fitzroy	62	Fb	36.10S	175.21 E
Port-Gentil	31	Hi	0.43S	8.47 E
Port Gibson	45	Kk	31.58N	90.58W
Port Harcourt	31	Hh	4.46N	7.01 E
Port Hardy	42	Ef	50.43N	127.29W
Port Hawkesbury	42	Lg	45.37N	61.21W
Porthcawl	9	Jj	51.29N	3.43W
Port Hedland	58	Cg	20.19S	118.34 E
Port Heiden	40	He	56.55N	158.41W
Port Hope Simpson	42	Lf	52.30N	56.17W
Port Huron	43	Kc	42.58N	82.27W
Portile de Fier = Iron Gate (EN)	5	Ig	44.41N	22.31 E
Port-Ilić	16	Pj	38.53N	48.51 E
Portimão	13	Dg	37.08N	8.32W
Port Isabel	45	Hm	26.04N	97.13W
Portiţa	15	Le	44.41N	29.00 E
Port Láirge/Waterford [2]	9	Fi	52.10N	7.40W
Port Láirge/Waterford	6	Fe	52.15N	7.06W
Portland [Austl.]	59	Ig	38.21S	141.36 E
Portland [Eng.-U.K.]	9	Kk	50.33N	2.27W
Portland [In.-U.S.]	44	Ee	40.26N	84.59W
Portland [Me.-U.S.]	39	Le	43.39N	70.17W
Portland [N.D.-U.S.]	45	Hc	47.30N	97.22W
Portland [N.Z.]	62	Fa	35.48S	174.20 E
Portland [Or.-U.S.]	39	Ge	45.33N	122.36W
Portland [Tx.-U.S.]	45	Hm	27.53N	97.20W
Portland, Bill of-	9	Kk	50.31N	2.28W
Portland, Promontoire -	42	Je	58.41N	78.33W
Portland Bight	49	Ie	17.57N	77.08W
Portland Island	62	Gc	39.20S	177.50 E
Portland Point	49	Ie	17.42N	77.11W
Port-la-Nouvelle	11	Jk	43.01N	3.03 E
Portlaoise/Port Laoise	9	Fh	53.02N	7.17W
Port Laoise/Portlaoise	9	Fh	53.02N	7.17W
Port Lavaca	43	Hf	28.37N	96.38W
Port Lincoln	58	Eh	34.44S	135.52 E
Port Loko	34	Cd	8.46N	12.47W
Port Louis	50	Fd	16.25N	61.32W
Port-Louis	31	Mk	20.10S	57.30 E
Port Macquarie	59	Kf	31.26S	152.44 E
Portmadoc	9	Ii	52.55N	4.08W
Port Maria	49	Id	18.22N	76.54W
Port-Menier	42	Lg	49.49N	64.20W
Port Moller	40	Ge	55.59N	160.34W
Port Moody	46	Db	49.17N	122.51W
Port Moresby	58	Fe	9.30S	147.07 E
Port Nelson	42	Ie	57.04N	92.30W
Portneuf, Rivière-	44	Ma	48.37N	69.05W
Port Nolloth	31	Ik	29.17S	16.51 E
Porto [2]	13	Dc	41.15N	8.20W
Porto [Fr.]	11a	Aa	42.16N	8.42 E
Porto [Port.]	6	Fg	41.09N	8.37W
Porto, Golfe de-	11a	Aa	42.16N	8.37 E
Pôrto Acre	54	Ee	9.34S	67.31W
Porto Alegre [Braz.]	53	Ki	30.04S	51.11W
Porto Alegre [SaoT.P.]	34	Ge	0.02N	6.32 E
Porto Amboim	31	Ij	10.44S	13.45 E
Porto Azzurro	14	Eh	42.46N	10.24 E
Portobelo	49	Hi	9.33N	79.39W
Pôrto Cedro	55	Ed	18.17S	55.02W
Porto Cervo	14	Di	41.08N	9.35 E
Porto Curupai	55	Ff	22.50S	53.53W
Porto de Moz	53	Kf	1.45S	52.14W
Porto Empedocle	14	Hm	37.17N	13.32 E
Porto Esperança [Braz.]	55	Dd	19.37S	57.27W
Porto Esperança [Braz.]	55	Db	14.02S	56.06W
Porto Esperança [Braz.]	55	Dc	17.47S	57.07W
Porto Esperidião	55	Cb	15.51S	58.28W
Porto Estrêla	55	Db	15.20S	57.14W
Portoferraio	14	Eh	42.49N	10.19 E
Port of Ness	9	Gc	58.30N	6.15W
Pôrto Franco	54	Ie	6.20S	47.24W
Port of Spain	53	Jd	10.39N	61.31W
Porto Fundação	55	Ea	13.39S	55.18W
Portogruaro	14	Ge	45.47N	12.50 E
Porto Lucena	55	Eh	27.51S	55.01W
Pörtom/Pirttikyla	8	Ib	62.42N	21.37 E
Portomaggiore	14	Ff	44.42N	11.48 E
Porto Mendes	55	Eg	24.30S	54.20W
Porto Moniz	32	Dc	32.51N	17.10W
Porto Moroco	55	Ea	13.24S	55.35W
Porto Morrinho	55	Dc	16.38S	57.49W
Porto Murtinho	53	Kh	21.42S	57.52W
Porto Novo [Ben.]	31	Hh	6.29N	2.37 E
Porto Novo [C.V.]	32	Bf	17.07N	25.04W
Port Orford	46	Ce	42.45N	124.30W
Porto San Giorgio	14	Hg	43.11N	13.48 E
Pôrto Santana	54	Hd	0.03S	51.11W
Porto Sant'Elpidio	14	Hg	43.15N	13.45 E
Porto Santo	30	Fe	33.04N	16.20W
Porto Santo Stefano	14	Fh	42.26N	11.07 E
Portoscuso	14	Ck	39.12N	8.23 E
Pôrto Seguro	54	Kg	16.26S	39.05W
Porto Tolle	14	Gf	44.56N	12.22 E
Porto Torres	14	Cj	40.50N	8.24 E
Porto União	55	Gh	26.15S	51.05W
Pôrto Válter	54	De	8.15S	72.45W
Porto Vecchio	11a	Bb	41.35N	9.17 E
Pôrto Velho	53	Jf	8.46S	63.54W
Portoviejo	53	Hf	1.03S	80.27W
Porto Xavier	55	Eh	27.54S	55.08W
Port Phillip Bay	59	Ig	38.05S	144.50 E
Port Pirie	58	Eh	33.11S	138.01 E
Portree	9	Gd	57.24N	6.12W
Port Renfrew	46	Cb	48.33N	124.25W
Port Rois/Portrush	9	Gf	55.12N	6.40W
Port Royal	44	If	38.10N	77.12W
Portrush/Port Rois	9	Gf	55.12N	6.40W
Port Said (EN)=Būr Sa'īd	31	Ke	31.16N	32.18 E
Port Saint Joe	43	Jf	29.49N	85.18W
Port Saint Johns	37	Df	31.38S	29.33 E
Port-Saint-Louis-du-Rhône	11	Kk	43.23N	4.48 E
Port-Salut	49	Kd	18.05N	73.55W
Port Saunders	42	Lf	50.39N	57.18W
Port Shepstone	37	Ef	30.46S	30.22 E
Portsmouth [Dom.]	50	Fe	15.35N	61.28W
Portsmouth [Eng.-U.K.]	9	Lk	50.48N	1.05W
Portsmouth [N.H.-U.S.]	43	Mc	43.03N	70.47W
Portsmouth [Oh.-U.S.]	43	Kd	38.45N	82.59W
Portsmouth [Va.-U.S.]	43	Ld	36.50N	76.26W
Portsmouth City Airport	12	Ad	50.46N	1.04W
Port Sudan (EN)=Būr Sūdān	31	Kg	19.37N	37.14 E
Port Sulphur	45	Ll	29.29N	89.42W
Port Talbot	9	Jj	51.36N	3.47W
Porttipahdantekojärvi	7	Gb	68.06N	26.33 E
Port Townsend	46	Db	48.07N	122.46W
Portugal [1]	6	Fh	39.30N	8.00W
Portugalete	13	Ia	43.19N	3.01W
Portuguesa [2]	54	Eb	9.10N	69.15W
Portuguesa, Río-	54	Eb	7.57N	67.32W
Portuguesa, Sierra de-	50	Bh	9.35N	69.45W
Portuguese Guinea (EN) → Guinea Bissau (EN) [1]	31	Fg	12.00N	15.00W
Portús, Coll del-/Perthus, Col de-	13	Ob	42.28N	2.51 E
Port-Vendres	11	Jl	42.31N	3.07 E
Port-Vila	58	Hf	17.44S	168.19 E
Port Wakefield	59	Hf	34.11S	138.09 E
Port Washington	45	Me	43.23N	87.53W
Porvenir [Bol.]	54	Ef	11.15S	68.41W
Porvenir [Bol.]	55	Ba	13.59S	61.39W
Porvenir [Chile]	56	Fh	53.18S	70.22W
Porvenir [Ur.]	55	Dk	32.23S	57.59W
Porvoo/Borgå	7	Ff	60.24N	25.40 E
Porvoonjoki	8	Kd	60.23N	25.40 E
Porz, Köln-	10	Df	50.53N	7.03 E
Posada, Fiume di-	14	Dj	40.39N	9.45 E
Posadas [Arg.]	53	Kh	27.25S	55.50W
Posadas [Sp.]	13	Gg	37.48N	5.06W
Posavina	15	De	44.33N	20.04 E
Poschiavo	14	Ed	46.20N	10.04 E
Pošehonje-Volodarsk	7	Jg	58.30N	39.08 E
Posht-e Bādām	24	Pf	33.02N	55.23 E
Posio	7	Gc	66.06N	28.09 E
Posjet	28	Kc	42.39N	130.48 E
Poskam/Zepu	27	Cd	38.12N	77.18 E
Poso	22	Oj	1.23S	120.44 E
Poso, Danau-	26	Hg	1.52S	120.35 E
Posof	24	Jb	41.31N	42.42 E
Posŏng	28	Ig	34.46N	127.05 E
Pospeliha	20	Df	52.02N	81.56 E
Posse	54	If	14.05S	46.22W
Possession, Ile de la-	30	Mm	46.14S	49.55 E
Possession Island	37	Be	27.01S	15.30 E
Pößneck	10	Hf	50.42N	11.36 E
Post	45	Fj	33.12N	101.23W
Posta de San Martín	55	Bk	33.09S	60.31W
Postavy	19	Cd	55.07N	26.50 E
Poste Maurice Cortier/Bidon V	32	He	22.18N	1.05 E
Poste Weygand	32	He	24.29N	0.40 E
Postmasburg	37	Ce	28.18S	23.05 E
Postojna	14	Ie	45.47N	14.14 E
Posto Simões Lopes	55	Eb	14.14S	54.41W
Postville [Ia.-U.S.]	45	Ke	43.05N	91.34W
Postville [Newf.-Can.]	42	Lf	54.55N	59.58W
Potchefstroom	37	De	26.46S	27.01 E
Poteau	45	Ii	35.03N	94.37W
Potenza	14	Hg	43.25N	13.40 E
Potenza	14	Jj	40.38N	15.48 E
Poteriteri, Lake-	62	Bg	46.05S	167.05 E
Potes	13	Ha	43.09N	4.37W
Potgietersrus	37	Dd	24.15S	28.55 E
Potholes Reservoir	46	Fc	47.01N	119.19W
Poti	6	Kg	42.08N	41.39 E
Poti, Rio-	54	Je	5.02S	42.50W
Potigny	12	Bf	48.58N	0.14W
Potiskum	34	Hc	11.43N	11.04 E
Potnarhvin	63b	Dd	18.45S	169.12 E
Potomac	38	Lf	38.00N	76.18W
Potosí [2]	54	Eh	20.40S	67.00W
Potosí [Bol.]	53	Jg	19.35S	65.45W
Potosi [Mex.]	47	Dd	24.51N	100.19W
Potosí, Bahía-	48	Ii	17.35N	101.30W
Potosi, Cerro-	48	Ie	24.52N	100.13W
Pototan	26	Hd	10.55N	122.40 E
Potrerillos	56	Gc	26.26S	69.29W
Potrero, Río-	55	Bc	17.32S	61.35W
Potsdam [Ger.]	10	Jd	52.24N	13.04 E
Potsdam [N.Y.-U.S.]	44	Jc	44.40N	75.01W
Pott	63b	Ad	19.35S	163.36 E
Potters Bar	12	Bc	51.41N	0.10W
Pottstown	44	Je	40.15N	75.38W
Pottsville	44	Ie	40.42N	76.13W
Pouancé	11	Eg	47.45N	1.10W
Pouébo	63b	Be	20.24S	164.34 E
Pouembout	63b	Be	21.08S	164.54 E
Poughkeepsie	44	Ke	41.43N	73.56W
Poulaphuca Reservoir/Loch Pholl an Phúca	9	Gh	53.10N	6.30W
Poum	63b	Be	20.14S	164.01 E
Pourtalé	55	Bm	37.02S	60.36W
Pouso Alegre	55	Ih	22.13S	45.56W
Pouss	34	Ic	10.51N	15.03 E
Poutasi	65c	Bb	14.01S	171.41W
Poŭthĭsăt	25	Kf	12.32N	103.55 E
Poutrincourt, Lac-	44	Ja	49.13N	74.04W
Po Valley (EN)=Padana, Pianura-	5	Gf	45.20N	10.00 E
Považská Bystrica	10	Og	49.07N	18.28 E
Považský Inovec	10	Nh	48.35N	18.00 E
Povenec	7	Ie	62.51N	34.45 E
Poverty Bay	62	Gc	38.45S	178.00 E
Povlen	15	Ce	44.09N	19.44 E
Póvoa de Varzim	13	Dc	41.23N	8.46W
Povorino	16	Md	51.12N	42.17 E
Povungnituk	42	Jd	60.03N	77.16W
Povungnituk	39	Lc	60.02N	77.10W
Powassan	44	Hb	46.05N	79.22W
Powder River [U.S.]	43	Fb	46.44N	105.26W
Powder River [Or.-U.S.]	46	Gd	44.45N	117.03W
Powell	46	Kd	44.45N	108.46W
Powell, Lake- [U.S.]	43	Ed	37.25N	110.45W
Powell Lake [Can.]	46	Ca	50.11N	124.24W
Powell River	42	Fg	49.52N	124.33W
Powers	44	Dc	45.39N	87.32W
Powers Lake	45	Eb	48.34N	102.39W
Powidzkie, Jezioro-	10	Nc	52.24N	17.57 E
Powys [3]	9	Ji	52.25N	3.20W
Poxoréu	54	Hg	15.50S	54.23W
Poxoréu, Rio- [Braz.]	55	Ec	16.32S	54.46W
Poxoréu, Rio- [Braz.]	55	Ec	16.08S	54.14W
Poya	63b	Be	21.21S	165.09 E
Poyang Hu	21	Ng	29.00N	116.25 E
Poza de la Sal	13	Ib	42.40N	3.30W
Pozanti	24	Fd	37.25N	34.52 E
Požarevac	15	Ee	44.37N	21.12 E
Poza Rica de Hidalgo	39	Jg	20.33N	97.27W
Požarskoje	28	Ma	46.16N	134.04 E
Požega	15	Df	43.51N	20.02 E
Poznań [2]	10	Pd	52.25N	19.55 E
Poznań	6	He	52.25N	16.55 E
Pozoblanco	13	Hf	38.22N	4.51W
Pozo Borrado	55	Bi	28.56S	61.41W
Pozo Colorado	55	Cf	23.22S	58.55W
Pozo del Mortero	55	Bg	24.24S	61.02W
Pozo del Tigre	55	Bc	17.34S	61.59W
Pozo Dulce	55	Ai	29.04S	62.02W
Pozos, Punta-	56	Gg	47.57S	65.47W
Pozuelos	54	Fa	10.11N	64.39W
Pozzallo	14	In	36.43N	14.51 E
Pozzuoli	14	Ij	40.49N	14.07 E
Pra [Ghana]	34	Ed	6.27N	1.47W
Pra [R.S.F.S.R.]	7	Ji	54.45N	41.01 E
Prabuty	10	Pc	53.46N	19.10 E
Prachatice	10	Jg	49.01N	14.00 E
Prachin Buri	25	Kf	14.02N	101.22 E
Prachuap Khiri Khan	25	Jf	11.48N	99.47 E
Praděd	10	Nf	50.06N	17.14 E
Prades	11	Il	42.37N	2.26 E
Prado	54	Kg	17.21S	39.13W
Præstø	8	Ei	55.07N	12.03 E
Prague (EN)=Praha	6	He	50.05N	14.26 E
Praha=Prague (EN)	6	He	50.05N	14.26 E
Prahova [2]	15	Id	45.10N	26.00 E
Praia	31	Eg	14.55N	23.31W
Praia a Mare	14	Jk	39.54N	15.47 E
Praia da Rocha	13	Dg	37.07N	8.32W
Praia Rica	55	Eb	14.51S	55.33W
Praid	15	Ic	46.33N	25.08 E
Prainha	54	Hd	1.48S	53.29W
Prairie Dog Town Fork	45	Gi	34.26N	99.21W
Prairie du Chien	45	Ke	43.03N	91.09W
Prangli	8	Ke	59.38N	24.50 E
Prānhita	25	Fe	18.49N	79.55 E
Prapat	26	Cf	2.40N	98.56 E
Prasat	25	Kf	14.38N	103.24 E
Praslin	51k	Bb	13.53N	60.54W
Praslin, Port-	51k	Bb	13.53N	60.54W
Praslin Island	37b	Ca	4.19S	55.44 E
Prasonision	15	Kn	35.52N	27.46 E
Prat, Isla-	56	Fg	48.15S	75.00W
Prata	54	Ig	19.18S	48.55W
Prata, Rio da-	55	Hd	18.49S	49.54W
Pratapgarh	25	Ed	24.02N	74.47 E
Prat de Llobregat/El Prat de Llobregat	13	Oc	41.20N	2.06 E
Prato	14	Fg	43.53N	11.06 E
Pratomagno	14	Fg	43.40N	11.40 E
Pratt	43	Hd	37.39N	98.44W
Prättigau	14	Dd	46.55N	9.40 E
Pratt Seamount (EN)	40	Ke	56.10N	142.30W
Prattville	44	Di	32.28N	86.29W
Pratudinho, Rio-	55	Ja	13.58S	45.10W
Pravda	18	Cf	36.50N	60.33 E
Pravda Coast	66	Ge	67.00S	94.00 E
Pravdinsk [R.S.F.S.R.]	8	Ij	54.28N	21.00 E
Pravdinsk [R.S.F.S.R.]	7	Kh	56.33N	43.33 E
Pravia	13	Fa	43.29N	6.07W
Praxedis G. Guerrero	48	Gb	31.22N	106.00W
Praya	26	Gh	8.42S	116.17 E
Prealpi Venete	14	Fd	46.25N	11.50 E
Predazzo	14	Fd	46.19N	11.36 E
Predeal	15	Id	45.30N	25.34 E
Predeal, Pasul-	15	Id	45.28N	25.36 E
Predel	14	Hd	46.25N	13.35 E
Predivinsk	20	Ee	57.04N	93.37 E
Predporožny	20	Jd	65.00N	143.20 E
Pré-en-Pail	11	Ff	48.27N	0.12W
Preetz	10	Gb	54.14N	10.17 E
Pregolja	7	Ei	54.42N	20.24 E
Pregradnaja	16	Lh	43.58N	41.12 E
Preilj/Prejlí	7	Gh	56.19N	26.48 E
Preissac, Lac-	44	Ha	48.25N	78.28W
Prejli/Preilj	7	Gh	56.19N	26.48 E
Prekmurje	14	Kd	46.45N	16.15 E
Prekornica	15	Cg	42.40N	19.12 E
Prekule/Priekulé	8	Ii	55.36N	21.12 E
Přelouč	10	Lf	50.02N	15.33 E
Premià de Mar/Premiá de Mar	13	Oc	41.29N	2.22 E
Premiá de Mar/Premià de Mar	13	Oc	41.29N	2.22 E
Premnitz	10	Id	52.32N	12.20 E
Premuda	14	If	44.21N	14.37 E
Prenaj/Prienai	7	Fi	54.39N	23.59 E
Prenj	14	Lg	43.32N	17.52 E
Prenjasi	15	Dh	41.04N	20.32 E
Prentice	45	Kd	45.33N	90.17W
Prentiss	45	Lk	31.36N	89.52W
Prenzlau	10	Jc	53.19N	13.52 E
Preobraženije	20	Ih	42.58N	133.55 E
Preobraženka	20	Fd	60.04N	107.58 E
Preparis Island	25	If	14.52N	93.41 E
Preparis North Channel	25	Ie	15.27N	94.05 E
Preparis South Channel	25	If	14.45N	94.05 E
Přerov	10	Ng	49.27N	17.27 E
Prescelly, Mynydd-	9	Ij	51.58N	4.42W
Prescott [Ar.-U.S.]	45	Jj	33.48N	93.23W
Prescott [Az.-U.S.]	43	Ee	34.33N	112.28W
Preševo	15	Eg	42.19N	21.39 E
Presho	45	Fe	43.53N	100.04W
Presicce	14	Mk	39.54N	18.16 E
Presidencia Roque Sáenz Peña	53	Jh	26.50S	60.30W
Presidente Epitácio	56	Jb	21.46S	52.06W
Presidente Frei	66	Re	62.12S	58.55W
Presidente Hayes [3]	55	Cf	24.00S	59.00W
Presidente Juscelino	55	Jd	18.39S	44.05W
Presidente Murtinho	55	Fb	15.39S	53.54W
Presidente Olegário	55	Id	18.25S	46.25W
Presidente Prudente	56	Jb	22.07S	51.22W
Presidente Venceslau	55	Ge	21.52S	51.50W
President Thiers Seamount (EN)	57	Lg	24.39S	145.51W
Presidio	43	Gf	29.33N	104.23W
Presidio, Rio del-	48	Ff	23.06N	106.17W
Preslav	15	Jf	43.10N	26.49 E
Presnovka	17	Mi	54.40N	67.09 E
Prešov	10	Rh	49.00N	21.14 E
Prespa	15	Hh	41.43N	24.53 E
Prespa, Lake- (EN)= Prespansko jezero	5	Ig	40.55N	21.00 E
Prespansko jezero=Prespa, Lake- (EN)	5	Ig	40.55N	21.00 E
Presque Isle	43	Nb	46.41N	68.01W
Prestea	34	Ed	5.26N	2.09W
Přeštice	10	Jg	49.35N	13.21 E
Preston [Eng.-U.K.]	9	Kh	53.46N	2.42W
Preston [Id.-U.S.]	43	Ec	42.06N	111.53W
Preston [Ont.-Can.]	44	Gd	43.23N	80.21W
Prestonsburg	44	Fg	37.40N	82.46W
Preststranda	8	Ce	59.06N	9.04 E
Prestwick	9	If	55.30N	4.37W
Prêto, Rio- [Braz.]	54	Jf	11.21S	43.52W
Prêto, Rio- [Braz.]	55	Gd	18.44S	50.23W
Prêto, Rio- [Braz.]	55	Ic	17.00S	46.12W
Prêto, Rio- [Braz.]	55	Ha	13.37S	48.06W
Prêto do Igapó Açu, Rio-	54	Gd	4.26S	59.48W
Pretoria	31	Jk	25.45S	28.10 E
Pretty Rock Butte	45	Fc	46.10N	101.42W
Preußisch-Oldendorf	12	Kb	52.18N	8.30 E
Préveza	15	Dk	38.57N	20.45 E
Prey	12	Df	48.58N	1.13 E
Prey Vêng	25	Lf	11.29N	105.19 E
Priangarskoje Plato	20	Ee	57.30N	97.00 E
Priargunsk	20	Gf	50.27N	119.00 E
Pribelski	17	Hi	54.24N	56.29 E
Pribilof Islands	38	Cd	57.00N	170.00W
Priboj	15	Cf	43.35N	19.32 E
Příbram	10	Kg	49.42N	14.01 E
Price [Que.-Can.]	44	Ma	48.39N	68.12W
Price [Ut.-U.S.]	46	Jg	39.36N	110.48W
Price River	46	Jg	39.10N	110.06W
Prichard	44	Cj	30.44N	88.05W
Prickly Pear Cays	51b	Ab	18.16N	63.11W
Prickly Point	51p	Bc	11.59N	61.45W
Pridneprovskaja Vozvyšennost=Dnepr Upland (EN)	5	Jf	49.00N	32.00 E
Priego	13	Jd	40.27N	2.18W
Priego de Córdoba	13	Hg	37.26N	4.11W
Priei, Măgura-	15	Fc	46.58N	22.50 E
Priekule	7	Eh	56.29N	21.37 E
Priekulė/Prekule	8	Ii	55.36N	21.12 E
Prienai/Prenaj	7	Fi	54.39N	23.59 E
Priene	24	Bd	37.40N	27.13 E
Prieska	31	Jk	29.40S	22.42 E
Priest Lake	46	Gb	48.34N	116.52W
Prieta, Peña-	13	Ha	43.01N	4.44W
Prieta, Sierra-	48	Cb	31.15N	112.55W
Prievidza	10	Oh	48.46N	18.39 E
Prignitz	10	Hc	53.00N	12.00 E
Prijedor	14	Kf	44.59N	16.42 E
Prijepolje	15	Cf	43.24N	19.39 E
Prijutovo	19	Fe	53.58N	53.58 E
Prikaspijskaja Nizmennost=Caspian Depression (EN)	5	Lf	48.00N	52.00 E
Prilenskoje Plato = Lena Mountains (EN)	21	Oc	60.45N	125.00 E
Prilep	15	Eh	41.21N	21.34 E
Priluki	19	De	50.36N	32.24 E
Primavera	66	Qe	64.09S	60.57W
Primeira Cruz	54	Jd	2.30S	43.26W
Primorje	8	Hj	54.56N	20.00 E
Primorsk [R.S.F.S.R.]	7	Gf	60.22N	28.36 E
Primorsk [Ukr.-U.S.S.R.]	16	Jf	46.43N	36.22 E
Primorski Hrebet	20	Ff	52.30N	106.00 E
Primorski Kraj [3]	20	Ig	45.30N	135.30 E
Primorsko	15	Kg	42.16N	27.46 E
Primorsko-Ahtarsk	19	Df	46.03N	38.11 E
Primorskoje [R.S.F.S.R.]	8	Ld	60.32N	27.56 E
Primorskoje [Ukr.-U.S.S.R.]	15	Nd	45.59N	30.15 E
Primošten	14	Jg	43.36N	15.55 E
Primrose Lake	42	Gf	54.55N	109.45W
Prims	10	Cg	49.20N	6.44 E
Prince Albert	39	Id	53.12N	104.46W
Prince Albert Mountains	66	Jf	76.00S	161.30 E
Prince Albert Peninsula	42	Fb	72.30N	116.00W
Prince Albert Road	37	Cf	33.13S	22.02 E
Prince Albert Sound	42	Gb	70.25N	115.00W
Prince Alfred, Cape -	42	Fb	74.05N	124.29W
Prince Charles	38	Lc	67.50N	76.00W
Prince Charles Mountains	66	Ff	72.00S	67.00 E
Prince-de-Galles, Cap -	42	Kd	61.36N	71.30W
Prince Edward	30	Km	46.33S	37.57 E
Prince Edward Island [3]	42	Lg	46.30N	63.00W
Prince Edward Island	38	Me	46.30N	63.00W
Prince Edward Islands	30	Km	46.35S	37.56 E
Prince George	39	Gd	53.55N	122.49W
Prince Gustaf Adolf Sea	38	Ib	78.30N	107.00W
Prince of Wales [Ak.-U.S.]	40	Me	55.47N	132.50W
Prince of Wales [Can.]	38	Jb	72.40N	99.00W
Prince of Wales, Cape-	38	Cc	65.40N	168.05W
Prince of Wales Island	59	Ib	10.40S	142.10 E
Prince of Wales Mountains	42	Ja	77.45N	78.00W
Prince of Wales Strait	42	Fb	72.45N	118.00W
Prince Patrick	38	Hb	76.45N	119.30W
Prince Regent Inlet	42	Ib	72.45N	90.30W
Prince Rupert	39	Fd	54.19N	130.19W
Prince Rupert Bay	51g	Ba	15.34N	61.29W
Prince Rupert Bluff	51g	Ba	15.35N	61.29W
Princes Risborough	12	Bc	51.43N	0.49W
Princess Anne	44	Jf	38.12N	75.41W
Princess Charlotte Bay	59	Ib	14.25S	144.00 E
Princess Elizabeth Land	66	Ff	70.00S	80.00 E

Index Symbols

- [1] Independent Nation
- [2] State, Region
- [3] District, County
- [4] Municipality
- [5] Colony, Dependency
- Continent
- Physical Region
- Historical or Cultural Region
- Mount, Mountain
- Volcano
- Hill
- Mountains, Mountain Range
- Hills, Escarpment
- Plateau, Upland
- Pass, Gap
- Plain, Lowland
- Delta
- Salt Flat
- Valley, Canyon
- Crater, Cave
- Karst Features
- Depression
- Polder
- Desert, Dunes
- Forest, Woods
- Heath, Steppe
- Oasis
- Cape, Point
- Coast, Beach
- Cliff
- Peninsula
- Isthmus
- Sandbank
- Island
- Atoll
- Rock, Reef
- Islands, Archipelago
- Rocks, Reefs
- Coral Reef
- Well, Spring
- Geyser
- River, Stream
- Waterfall Rapids
- River Mouth, Estuary
- Lake
- Salt Lake
- Intermittent Lake
- Reservoir
- Swamp, Pond
- Canal
- Glacier
- Ice Shelf, Pack Ice
- Ocean
- Sea
- Gulf, Bay
- Strait, Fjord
- Lagoon
- Bank
- Seamount
- Tablemount
- Ridge
- Shelf
- Basin
- Escarpment, Sea Scarp
- Fracture
- Trench, Abyss
- National Park, Reserve
- Point of Interest
- Recreation Site
- Cave, Cavern
- Historic Site
- Ruins
- Wall, Walls
- Church, Abbey
- Temple
- Scientific Station
- Airport
- Port
- Lighthouse
- Mine
- Tunnel
- Dam, Bridge

Q

Index Symbols

- [1] Independent Nation
- [2] State, Region
- [3] District, County
- [4] Municipality
- [5] Colony, Dependency
- Continent
- Physical Region
- Historical or Cultural Region
- Mount, Mountain
- Volcano
- Hill
- Mountains, Mountain Range
- Hills, Escarpment
- Plateau, Upland
- Pass, Gap
- Plain, Lowland
- Delta
- Salt Flat
- Valley, Canyon
- Crater, Cave
- Karst Features
- Depression
- Polder
- Desert, Dunes
- Forest, Woods
- Heath, Steppe
- Oasis
- Cape, Point
- Coast, Beach
- Cliff
- Peninsula
- Isthmus
- Sandbank
- Island
- Atoll
- Rock, Reef
- Islands, Archipelago
- Rocks, Reefs
- Coral Reef
- Well, Spring
- Geyser
- River, Stream
- Waterfall Rapids
- River Mouth, Estuary
- Lake
- Salt Lake
- Intermittent Lake
- Reservoir
- Swamp, Pond
- Canal
- Glacier
- Ice Shelf, Pack Ice
- Ocean
- Sea
- Gulf, Bay
- Strait, Fjord
- Lagoon
- Bank
- Seamount
- Tablemount
- Ridge
- Shelf
- Basin
- Escarpment, Sea Scarp
- Fracture
- Trench, Abyss
- National Park, Reserve
- Point of Interest
- Recreation Site
- Cave, Cavern
- Historic Site
- Ruins
- Wall, Walls
- Church, Abbey
- Temple
- Scientific Station
- Airport
- Port
- Lighthouse
- Mine
- Tunnel
- Dam, Bridge

Qala'an Naḩl 35 Ec 13.38N 34.57 E
Qalāt 23 Kc 32.07N 66.54 E
Qal'at Abū Ghār 24 Lg 30.25N 46.09 E
Qal'at al Akhḑar 23 Ed 28.06N 37.05 E
Qal 'at al Marqab 24 Fe 35.09N 35.57 E
Qal'at al Mu'azzam 24 Gi 27.45N 37.31 E
Qal'at aş Şanam 14 Co 35.46N 8.21 E
Qal'at Bīshah 22 Gh 20.00N 42.36 E
Qal'at Dīzah 24 Kd 36.11N 45.07 E
Qal'at Şāliḩ 24 Lg 31.31N 47.16 E
Qal'at Sukkar 24 Lg 31.53N 46.56 E
Qal'eh Asgar 24 Qh 29.30N 56.35 E
Qal'eh Kūh 24 Mf 33.00N 49.10 E
Qal'eh Mūreh 24 Pe 35.35N 55.58 E
Qal'eh-ye Now 23 Jc 34.59N 63.08 E
Qal'eh-ye Sahar 24 Mg 31.40N 48.33 E
Qalīb ash Shuyūkh 23 Gd 29.12N 47.55 E
Qallābāt 35 Fc 12.58N 36.09 E
Qalmarz, Godār-e- 24 Qf 33.26N 56.14 E
Qalyūb 24 Dg 30.11N 31.13 E
Qamata 37 Df 31.58S 27.24 E
Qamdo 22 Lf 31.15N 97.12 E
Qamīnis 33 Dc 31.40N 20.01 E
Qamsar 24 Nf 33.45N 51.26 E
Qamūdah 32 Ic 35.00N 9.21 E
Qamūdah [3] 32 Ic 34.50N 9.20 E
Qânâq/Thule 67 Od 77.35N 69.40W
Qandahār [3] 23 Kc 31.00N 65.45 E
Qandahār 22 If 31.35N 65.45 E
Qandala 35 Hc 11.23N 49.53 E
Qangdin Gol 28 Cc 43.27N 115.03 E
Qanţarat al Fahş 14 Dn 36.23N 9.54 E
Qapqal 27 Dc 43.48N 80.47 E
Qaqortoq/Julianehåb 67 Nc 60.50N 46.10W
Qarā Dāgh 24 Lc 38.48N 47.13 E
Qārah 33 Ed 29.37N 26.30 E
Qarah Būlāq 24 Ke 34.32N 45.12 E
Qarah Dagh 24 Jd 37.00N 43.30 E
Qarah Tappah 24 Ke 34.25N 44.56 E
Qarānqū 24 Ld 37.23N 47.43 E
Qardo 31 Lh 9.30N 49.03 E
Qareh Āghāj 24 Ld 36.46N 48.46 E
Qareh Sū [Iran] 23 Ib 37.00N 56.50 E
Qareh Sū [Iran] 24 Nc 34.52N 51.25 E
Qareh Ẕīā'Od Dīn 24 Kc 38.53N 45.02 E
Qarkilik/Ruoqiang 22 Kf 39.02N 88.00 E
Qarnayn, Jazīrat al- 24 Oj 24.56N 52.52 E
Qarnayt, Jabal- 23 Fe 21.02N 40.22 E
Qarqan/Qiemo 22 Kf 38.08N 85.32 E
Qarqan He 21 Kf 39.30N 88.15 E
Qarqannah, Juzur-=
Kerkennah Islands (EN) 30 Ie 34.44N 11.12 E
Qartājannah 14 En 36.51N 10.20 E
Qārūn, Birkat- 33 Fd 29.28N 30.40 E
Qaryat Abū Nujaym 33 Cc 30.35N 15.24 E
Qaryat al Gharab 24 Kg 31.27N 44.48 E
Qaryat al Qaddāḩiyah 33 Cc 31.22N 15.14 E
Qaryat al 'Ulyā 23 Gd 27.33N 47.42 E
Qaryat az Zarrūq 33 Cc 32.22N 15.09 E
Qaryat az Zuwaytinah 33 Dc 30.58N 20.07 E
Qaşabah, Ra's al- 24 Fh 28.02N 34.38 E
Qaşabāt, Hanshīr al- 14 Dn 36.24N 9.54 E
Qasigiánguit/Christianshåb 41 Ge 68.45N 51.30W
Qaşr al Azraq 24 Gg 31.53N 36.49 E
Qaşr Al Hayr 24 Ge 34.23N 37.36 E
Qaşr al Qarahbullī 33 Bc 32.45N 13.43 E
Qaşr 'Amij 24 If 33.30N 41.45 E
Qaşr Bū Hādī 33 Cc 31.03N 16.40 E
Qaşr Burqu' 24 Gf 32.37N 37.58 E
Qasr-e Shīrīn 23 Gc 34.31N 45.35 E
Qaşr Farāfirah 31 Jf 27.15N 28.10 E
Qasr Ḩamān 23 Ge 20.50N 45.50 E
Qaşr Qārūn 24 Dh 29.25N 30.25 E
Qaşş Abū Sa'īd 24 Bi 27.00N 27.35 E
Qatana 24 Gf 33.26N 36.05 E
Qaţar 23 Hg 25.30N 51.15 E
Qaţar [1] 22 Hg 25.30N 51.15 E
Qatlīsh 24 Qd 37.50N 57.19 E
Qaţrānī, Jabal- 24 Dh 29.41N 30.35 E
Qatrūyeh 24 Ph 29.09N 54.43 E
Qattara Depression (EN)=
Qaţţārah, Munkhafaḑ al-
30 Je 30.00N 27.30 E
Qaţţārah, Munkhafaḑ al-=
Qattara Depression (EN)
30 Je 30.00N 27.30 E
Qawām al Hamzah 24 Kg 31.43N 44.58 E
Qawz Abu Ḑulū' 35 Eb 16.55N 32.30 E
Qawz Rajab 35 Fb 16.04N 35.34 E
Qaysān 35 Ec 10.45N 34.48 E
Qayyārah 24 Je 35.48N 43.17 E
Qazvīn [Iran] 22 Gf 36.16N 50.00 E
Qazvīn [Iraq] 24 Je 34.21N 42.05 E
Qeqertarssuaq/Godhavn 67 Nc 69.20N 53.35W
Qeshm 24 Qi 26.58N 56.16 E
Qeshm 23 Id 26.45N 55.45 E
Qeydār 24 Md 36.07N 48.35 E
Qeys, Jazīreh-ye- 23 Hd 26.32N 53.58 E
Qezel Owzan 23 Gb 36.45N 49.22 E
Qian'an [China] 28 Ed 40.01N 118.42 E
Qian'an [China] 28 Hb 44.58N 124.01 E
Qianfangzi 28 Ad 40.01N 111.23 E
Qian Gorlos (Quianguozhen) 27 Lb 45.05N 124.52 E
Qian He 28 Dh 32.55N 117.10 E
Qianjiang [China] 27 Ig 23.37N 108.58 E
Qianjiang [China] 28 Bi 30.25N 112.54 E
Qianjiang [China] 27 If 29.30N 108.45 E
Qianning/Gartar 27 He 30.27N 101.29 E
Qian Shan 27 Lc 40.35N 123.00 E
Qiansuo 27 Hf 25.27N 100.41 E
Qianwei 27 Hf 29.08N 103.56 E
Qianxi [China] 27 If 27.03N 106.04 E
Qianxi [China] 28 Ed 40.08N 118.19 E
Qianyang (Anjiang) 27 Jf 27.19N 110.13 E
Qiaojia 27 Hf 27.00N 103.00 E
Qiaowan 27 Gc 40.36N 96.42 E
Qibilī 32 Ic 33.42N 8.58 E
Qichun (Caojiahe) 28 Ci 30.15N 115.26 E
Qidaogou 28 Id 41.31N 126.18 E
Qidong 28 Fi 31.48N 121.39 E
Qiemo/Qarqan 22 Kf 38.08N 85.32 E
Qift 24 Ei 26.00N 32.49 E
Qijiang 27 If 29.00N 106.39 E
Qijiaojing 27 Fc 43.28N 91.36 E
Qike → Xunke 27 Mb 49.34N 128.28 E
Qili → Shitai 28 Di 30.12N 117.28 E
Qilian (Babao) 27 Hd 38.14N 100.15 E
Qilian Shan 27 Gd 39.12N 98.35 E
Qilian Shan 21 Lf 38.30N 100.00 E
Qimantag 27 Fd 37.00N 91.00 E
Qimen 27 Kf 29.57N 117.39 E
Qinā 31 Kf 26.10N 32.43 E
Qinā, Wādī- 24 Ei 26.12N 32.44 E
Qin'an 27 Ie 34.50N 105.35 E
Qingchengzi 28 Gd 40.44N 123.36 E
Qingchuan 27 Ie 32.32N 105.11 E
Qingdao = Tsingtao (EN) 22 Of 36.05N 120.21 E
Qingduizi 28 Fd 41.27N 121.52 E
Qingfeng 28 Cg 35.54N 115.07 E
Qinggang 27 Mb 46.41N 126.03 E
Qinggil/Qinghe 27 Fb 46.43N 90.24 E
Qinghai Hu = Koko Nor (EN)
21 Mf 37.00N 100.20 E
Qinghai Sheng (Ch'ing-hai
Sheng) = Tsinghai (EN) [2] 27 Gd 36.00N 96.00 E
Qing He 28 Hc 42.16N 124.10 E
Qinghe/Qinggil 27 Fb 46.43N 90.24 E
Qinghe (Gexianzhuang) 28 Cf 37.03N 115.39 E
Qinghemen 28 Fd 41.45N 121.25 E
Qingjian 27 Jd 37.10N 110.09 E
Qingjiang 22 Nf 33.31N 119.03 E
Qing Jiang 27 Je 30.24N 111.30 E
Qingjiang
(Zhangshuzhen) 27 Kf 28.02N 115.31 E
Qingkou → Ganyu 28 Eg 34.50N 119.07 E
Qinglong 28 Ed 40.26N 118.58 E
Qinglong He 28 Ee 39.51N 118.51 E
Qingshan 28 Ci 30.39N 114.27 E
Qingshuihe 27 Jd 39.56N 111.41 E
Qingshui Jiang 27 If 27.11N 109.48 E
Qingtian 27 Lf 28.12N 120.17 E
Qingxian 28 De 38.35N 116.48 E
Qingxu 28 Bf 37.36N 112.21 E
Qingyang [China] 27 Id 36.01N 107.48 E
Qingyang [China] 28 Di 30.38N 117.50 E
Qingyuan 27 Lc 42.06N 124.56 E
Qingyuan (Nandaran) 28 Ce 38.46N 115.29 E
Qingyun (Xiejiaji) 28 Df 37.46N 117.22 E
Qing Zang Gaoyuan = Tibet,
Plateau of- (EN) 21 Kf 32.30N 87.00 E
Qin He 28 Bg 35.01N 113.25 E
Qinhuangdao 27 Kd 40.00N 119.32 E
Qin Ling 21 Mf 34.00N 108.00 E
Qinshui 28 Bg 35.41N 112.10 E
Qintong 28 Fh 32.39N 120.06 E
Qinxian 28 Bf 36.46N 112.42 E
Qinyang 28 Bg 35.05N 112.56 E
Qinyuan 28 Bf 36.29N 112.20 E
Qinzhou 27 Ig 22.02N 108.30 E
Qionghai (Jiaji) 27 Jh 19.25N 110.28 E
Qionglai 27 He 30.24N 103.28 E
Qiongzhou Haixia 21 Ng 20.10N 110.15 E
Qipan Guan 27 Ie 32.45N 106.11 E
Qiqihar 22 Oe 47.21N 123.58 E
Qīr 24 Oh 28.29N 53.04 E
Qira 27 Dd 37.02N 80.53 E
Qiryat Gat 24 Fg 31.36N 34.46 E
Qiryat Shemona 24 Ff 33.13N 35.34 E
Qiryat Yam 24 Ff 32.51N 35.04 E
Qishn 23 Hf 15.26N 51.40 E
Qi Shui 28 Ci 30.09N 115.22 E
Qishuyan 28 Fi 31.41N 120.04 E
Qitai 22 Ke 44.01N 89.28 E
Qitaihe 27 Nb 45.49N 130.51 E
Qiuxian (Matou) 28 Cf 36.50N 115.10 E
Qixia 28 Ff 37.18N 120.50 E
Qixian [China] 28 Bf 37.23N 112.21 E
Qixian [China] 28 Cg 34.33N 114.46 E
Qixian (Zhaoge) 28 Cg 35.35N 114.12 E
Qiyang 27 Jf 26.44N 111.50 E
Qizhou 28 Ci 30.04N 115.20 E
Qogir Feng = Godwin Austen
(EN) 21 Jf 35.53N 76.30 E
Qog Qi 27 Ic 41.31N 107.00 E
Qog Ul 27 Kc 44.50N 116.19 E
Qohrūd, Kūhhā-ye- 21 Hf 32.40N 53.00 E
Qoltag 27 Ec 42.20N 88.45 E
Qom 22 Hf 34.39N 50.54 E
Qom 24 Ne 34.48N 51.02 E
Qomolangma Feng = Everest,
Mount- (EN) 21 Kg 27.59N 86.56 E
Qomrud 24 Ne 34.43N 51.04 E
Qomsheh 23 Hc 32.00N 51.50 E
Qondūz [3] 23 Kb 36.45N 68.30 E
Qondūz 22 If 36.45N 68.51 E
Qondūz 23 Kb 37.00N 68.16 E
Qoqek/Tacheng 22 Ke 46.45N 82.57 E
Qŏrnoq 41 Gf 64.30N 51.19W
Qorveh 24 Le 35.10N 47.48 E
Qoşbeh-ye Naşşār 23 Gc 30.02N 48.27 E
Qoţbābād [Iran] 24 Oh 28.39N 53.37 E
Qoţbābād [Iran] 24 Qi 27.46N 56.06 E
Qoţūr 24 Kc 38.28N 44.25 E
Qoţūr 24 Kc 38.46N 45.16 E
Quadda 31 Jh 8.04N 22.24 E
Quadros, Lagoa dos- 55 Gi 29.42S 50.05W
Quairading 59 Df 32.01S 117.25 E
Quakenbrück 10 Dd 52.41N 7.57 E
Quanah 45 Gi 34.18N 99.44W
Quanbao Shan 27 Je 34.08N 111.26 E
Quang Ngai 25 Le 15.07N 108.48 E
Quang Tri 25 Le 21.02N 106.29 E
Quan He 28 Ch 32.55N 115.52 E
Quanjiao 28 Eh 32.09N 118.16 E
Quan Long 25 Lg 9.11N 105.08 E
Quanzhou [China] 22 Ng 24.57N 118.35 E
Quanzhou [China] 27 Jf 26.01N 111.04 E
Qu'Appelle River 42 Hf 50.27N 101.19W
Quaraí 56 Id 30.23S 56.27W
Quaraí, Rio- 55 Dj 30.12S 57.36W
Quaregnon 12 Fd 50.26N 3.51 E
Quartu Sant'Elena 14 Dk 39.14N 9.11 E
Quartz Lake 42 Jb 70.57N 80.40W
Quartz Mountain 46 De 43.10N 122.40W
Quartzsite 46 Hj 33.40N 114.13W
Quatre, Isle- 51n Bb 12.57N 61.15W
Quatsino Sound 46 Aa 50.25N 128.10W
Qūchān 22 Hf 37.06N 58.30 E
Qué 36 Ce 14.43S 15.06 E
Queanbeyan 59 Jg 35.21S 149.14 E
Québec 39 Le 46.49N 71.13W
Québec [3] 42 Kf 54.00N 72.00W
Quebó 55 Db 14.36S 56.04W
Quebra Anzol, Rio- 55 Id 19.09S 47.38W
Quebracho 55 Dj 31.57S 57.57W
Quebradillas 51a Bb 18.28N 66.56W
Quedas do Iguaçu 55 Fg 25.31S 52.54W
Quedlinburg 10 He 51.47N 11.09 E
Queen, Cape- 42 Jd 64.43N 78.18W
Queen Alexandra Range 66 Jg 84.00S 168.00 E
Queen Bess, Mount- 42 Ff 51.18N 124.33W
Queenborough 12 Cc 51.25N 0.46 E
Queen Charlotte Islands 38 Gd 51.30N 129.00W
Queen Charlotte Sound 42 Ef 51.30N 129.30W
Queen Charlotte Strait 42 Ef 50.40N 127.25W
Queen Elizabeth Islands 38 Ib 79.00N 105.00W
Queen Elizabeth Range 66 Kg 83.20S 162.00 E
Queen Mary Land 66 Ge 69.00S 96.00 E
Queen Maud Gulf 38 Ic 68.25N 102.30W
Queen Maud Land (EN) 66 Cf 72.30S 12.00 E
Queen Maud Range 66 Lg 86.00S 160.00W
Queens Channel [Austl.] 59 Fb 14.45S 129.25 E
Queens Channel
[N.W.T.-Can.] 42 Ha 76.11N 96.00W
Queensland 59 Id 22.00S 145.00 E
Queenstown [Austl.] 59 Jh 42.05S 145.33 E
Queenstown [Guy.] 50 Gi 7.12N 58.29W
Queenstown [N.Z.] 62 Cf 45.02S 168.40 E
Queenstown [S.Afr.] 31 Jl 31.52S 26.52 E
Queguay, Cuchilla del- 55 Dj 31.50S 57.30W
Queguay Grande, Rio- 55 Ck 32.09S 58.09W
Queich 12 Ke 49.14N 8.23 E
Queimadas 54 Kf 10.58S 39.38W
Queiros 55 Ge 21.49S 50.13W
Quela 36 Cd 9.15S 17.05 E
Quelimane 31 Kj 17.51S 36.52 E
Quemado 45 Bi 34.20N 108.30W
Quemado de Güines 49 Gb 22.48N 80.15W
Quembo 36 De 14.57S 20.22 E
Quemú-Quemú 56 He 36.03S 63.33W
Quepos 49 Ei 9.25N 84.09W
Quequén 56 Ie 38.32S 58.42W
Quequén Grande, Rio- 55 Cn 38.34S 58.43W
Quequén Salado, Rio- 55 Bn 38.56S 60.31W
Quercy 11 Hj 44.15N 1.15 E
Querétaro [2] 47 Ed 21.00N 99.55W
Querétaro 39 Ig 20.36N 100.23W
Querobabi 48 Db 30.03N 111.01W
Quesada [C.R.] 49 Eh 10.19N 84.26W
Quesada [Sp.] 13 Ig 37.51N 3.04W
Queshan 27 Je 32.42N 114.04 E
Quesnel 42 Ff 52.59N 122.30W
Quesnel Lake 42 Ff 52.32N 121.05W
Questa 45 Dh 36.42N 105.36W
Quetena 54 Eh 22.10S 67.25W
Quetico Lake 45 Kb 48.37N 91.52W
Quetta 22 If 30.12N 67.00 E
Quevas, Cerro- 48 Dc 29.15N 111.20W
Quevedo 54 Cd 1.02S 79.27W
Queyras 11 Mj 44.44N 6.49 E
Quezaltenango 39 Jh 14.50N 91.31W
Quezaltenango [3] 49 Bf 14.45N 91.40W
Quezon 26 Ge 9.14N 117.56 E
Quezon City 22 Oh 14.38N 121.00 E
Qufu 28 Dg 35.35N 116.59 E
Quianguoshen →
Qian Gorlos 27 Lb 45.05N 124.52 E
Quianshan 28 Di 30.38N 116.35 E
Quibala 36 Be 10.44S 14.59 E
Quibaxe 36 Bd 8.30S 14.36 E
Quibdó 54 Cb 5.42N 76.39W
Quiberon, Baie de- 11 Dg 47.32N 3.00W
Quiberon, Presqu'île de- 11 Cg 47.30N 3.08W
Quibor 49 Mi 9.56N 69.37W
Quiché [3] 49 Bf 15.30N 90.55W
Quierschied 12 Je 49.19N 7.03 E
Quiha 35 Fc 13.28N 39.33 E
Quiindy 55 Dh 25.58S 57.16W
Quijarro 55 Cd 19.26S 58.08W
Quilá 48 Fe 24.23N 107.13W
Quilàn, Cabo- 56 Ff 43.16S 74.23W
Quillabamba 54 Df 12.49S 72.43W
Quillacollo 54 Eg 17.26S 66.17W
Quillagua 56 Gb 21.39S 69.33W
Quillan 11 Il 42.52N 2.11 E
Quillebeuf-sur-Seine 12 Ce 49.28N 0.31 E
Quillota 56 Fd 32.53S 71.16W
Quilnes 56 Id 34.44S 58.16W
Quilon 25 Fg 8.53N 76.36 E
Quilpie 59 Ie 26.37S 144.15 E
Quilqué 56 Fd 33.03S 71.27W
Quimarí, Alto de- 49 Ii 8.07N 76.23W
Quimbele 36 Cd 6.30S 16.14 E
Quimilí 56 Hc 27.38S 62.25W
Quimome 55 Bc 17.42S 61.16W
Quimome, Río- 55 Bc 17.36S 61.09W
Quimper 11 Bf 48.00N 4.06W
Quimperlé 11 Cg 47.52N 3.33W
Quinault River 46 Cc 47.23N 124.18W
Quincy [Ca.-U.S.] 46 Eg 39.56N 120.57W
Quincy [Fl.-U.S.] 44 Ej 30.37N 84.32W
Quincy [Il.-U.S.] 43 Id 39.56N 91.23W
Quincy [Ma.-U.S.] 44 Ld 42.15N 71.01W
Quincy [Wa.-U.S.] 46 Fc 47.14N 119.51W
Quindio [2] 54 Cc 4.30N 75.40W
Quingey 11 Lg 47.06N 5.53 E
Quinhagak 40 Ge 59.45N 161.43W
Qui Nhon 22 Mh 13.46N 109.14 E
Quiñihual 55 Bm 37.47S 61.36W
Quiniluban Group 26 Hd 11.27N 120.48 E
Quinn River 46 Ff 40.25N 119.00W
Quiñones 48 De 24.22N 111.25W
Quintanar de la Orden 13 Ie 39.34N 3.03W
Quintana Roo [2] 47 Ge 19.40N 88.30W
Quinze, Lac des- 44 Hb 47.30N 79.00W
Quionga 37 Gb 10.35S 40.33 E
Quipongo 36 Be 14.45S 14.05 E
Quirigua 49 Cf 15.18N 89.07W
Quirihue 56 Fe 36.17S 72.32W
Quirima 36 Ce 10.48S 18.09 E
Quirinópolis 54 Hg 18.32S 50.30W
Quiroga 13 Eb 42.29N 7.16W
Quiros, Cap- 63b Cb 14.56S 167.01 E
Quisiro 49 Lh 10.53N 71.17W
Quissanga 37 Gb 12.25S 40.29 E
Quissico 37 Ed 24.43S 34.45 E
Quita Sueno Bank 47 Hf 14.20N 81.15W
Quitengues 36 Be 14.06S 14.05 E
Quiterage 37 Gb 11.45S 40.27 E
Quitéria, Rio- 55 Ge 20.16S 51.08W
Quitilipi 55 Bh 26.52S 60.13W
Quitman [Ga.-U.S.] 44 Fj 30.47N 83.33W
Quitman [Ms.-U.S.] 45 Lj 32.03N 88.43W
Quito 53 If 0.13S 78.30W
Quitovac 48 Cb 31.32N 112.42W
Quixadá 54 Kd 4.58S 39.01W
Quixeramobim 54 Ke 5.12S 39.17W
Qujiang 28 Cj 28.14N 115.46 E
Qu Jiang [China] 27 Kf 29.32N 119.31 E
Qu Jiang [China] 27 Ie 30.01N 106.24 E
Qujing 27 Hf 25.31N 103.45 E
Qul'ān, Jazā'ir- 24 Fj 24.22N 35.23 E
Qulansiyah 23 Hg 12.41N 53.29 E
Qulaybiah 32 Jb 36.51N 11.06 E
Qulbān al 'Isāwīyah 24 Gg 30.38N 37.53 E
Qulbān an Nabk al Gharbī 24 Gg 31.15N 37.26 E
Qumar He 21 Lf 34.42N 94.50 E
Qumarlêb 27 Ge 34.35N 95.18 E
Qunayfidhah, Nafūd- 24 Kj 24.45N 45.30 E
Quoi 64d Ba 7.32N 151.59 E
Quoich 42 Id 63.56N 93.25W
Quorn 59 Hf 32.21S 138.03 E
Quqên/Jinchuan 27 He 31.02N 102.02 E
Quraitu 24 Ke 34.36N 45.30 E
Qurayyāt, Juzur- 32 Jb 35.48N 11.02 E
Qurbah 14 En 36.35N 10.52 E
Qurdūd 35 Dc 10.17N 29.56 E
Qūr Laban 24 Cg 30.23N 28.59 E
Qurunbāliyah 14 En 36.36N 10.30 E
Qūş 33 Fd 25.55N 32.45 E
Quşay'ir 35 Ic 14.55N 50.20 E
Qutdligssat 41 Gd 70.12N 53.00W
Quthing 37 Df 30.24S 27.42 E
Quţū 33 Hf 18.30N 41.04 E
Quwaiz 33 He 20.27N 44.53 E
Quxian 27 Kf 28.54N 118.53 E
Qüxü 27 Ff 29.23N 90.45 E
Quyang 28 Ce 38.37N 114.41 E
Quy Chau 25 Le 19.33N 105.06 E
Quzhou 28 Cf 36.47N 114.56 E
Qyteti Stalin 15 Ci 40.48N 19.54 E

R

Raab 10 Ni 47.41N 17.38 E
Raahe/Brahestad 7 Fd 64.41N 24.29 E
Rääkkylä 8 Mb 62.19N 29.37 E
Raalte 12 Ib 52.23N 6.17 E
Raamsdonk 12 Gc 51.41N 4.54 E
Raanes Peninsula 42 Ia 78.20N 86.20W
Raasay, Island of- 9 Gd 57.25N 6.04W
Raasay, Sound of- 9 Gd 57.25N 6.05W
Raasiku/Raziku 8 Ke 59.22N 25.11 E
Rab 14 If 44.46N 14.46 E
Rab 14 If 44.45N 14.46 E
Rába 10 Ni 47.41N 17.38 E
Raba 10 Qf 50.09N 20.30 E
Raba 22 Nj 8.27S 118.46 E
Rabāble 35 Hd 8.14N 48.18 E
Rabaçal 13 Ec 41.30N 7.12W
Rabat [Malta] 14 Io 35.50N 14.29 E
Rabat [Mor.] 31 Ge 34.02N 6.50W
Rabat-Salé [2] 32 Fc 34.02N 6.50W
Rabaul 58 Ge 4.12S 152.12 E
Rábca 10 Ni 47.41N 17.37 E
Rabenau 12 Kd 50.40N 8.52 E
Rabi', Ash Shallāl ar-=
Fourth Cataract (EN) 30 Kg 18.47N 32.03 E
Rabiah 24 Jd 36.47N 42.07 E
Rábida, Monasterio de- 13 Fg 37.12N 6.55W
Rābigh 23 Ee 22.48N 39.02 E
Rabinal 49 Bf 15.06N 90.27W
Rabka 10 Pg 49.36N 19.56 E
Rabočeostrovsk 7 Id 64.59N 34.44 E
Rabyānah, Şahrā'- 30 Jf 24.30N 21.00 E
Rabyānah, Wāḩāt al-=
Rebiana Oasis (EN) 33 De 24.14N 21.59 E
Răcăciuni 15 Jc 46.20N 26.59 E
Racalmuto 14 Hm 37.24N 13.44 E
Răcăşdia 15 Ee 44.59N 21.38 E
Racconigi 14 Bf 44.46N 7.46 E
Race, Cape- 38 Ne 46.40N 53.10W
Race Point 44 Ld 42.04N 70.14W
Rach Gia 22 Mh 10.01N 105.05 E
Rachid 32 Ef 18.48N 11.41W
Raciąż 10 Qd 52.47N 20.06 E
Racibórz 10 Of 50.06N 18.13 E
Racine 43 Jc 42.43N 87.48W
Ráckeve 10 Oi 47.10N 18.57 E
Racos 15 Ic 46.03N 25.30 E
Råda 8 Ed 60.00N 13.36 E
Radama, Iles- 37 Hb 14.00S 47.47 E
Radan 15 Ef 43.02N 21.30 E
Rădăuţi 15 Ib 47.51N 25.55 E
Radbuza 10 Jg 49.46N 13.24 E
Radeberg 10 Je 51.07N 13.55 E
Radebeul 10 Je 51.06N 13.39 E
Radeče 14 Jd 46.04N 15.11 E
Radehov 10 Uf 50.13N 24.43 E
Radenthein 14 Hd 46.48N 13.43 E
Radevormwald 12 Jc 51.12N 7.22 E
Radew 10 Lb 54.07N 15.50 E
Radford 44 Gg 37.07N 80.34W
Radnevo 15 Ig 42.18N 25.56 E
Radolfzell 10 Ei 47.44N 8.58 E
Radom [2] 10 Re 51.25N 21.10 E
Radom 6 Ie 51.25N 21.10 E
Radomir 15 Fg 42.33N 22.58 E
Radomka 10 Re 51.43N 21.26 E
Radomsko 10 Pe 51.05N 19.25 E
Radomyšl 16 Fd 50.29N 29.14 E
Radomyšl Wielki 10 Rf 50.12N 21.16 E
Radoškoviči 8 Lj 54.12N 27.17 E
Radotín 10 Kg 49.59N 14.22 E
Radovanu 15 Je 44.12N 26.31 E
Radoviš 15 Fh 41.38N 22.28 E
Radøy 8 Ad 60.40N 5.00 E
Radstadt 14 Hc 47.23N 13.27 E
Radun 10 Vb 54.02N 25.07 E
Radunia 10 Ob 54.25N 18.45 E
Raduša 14 Lg 43.52N 17.29 E
Radvaniči 10 Ue 51.59N 24.09 E
Radviliškis 7 Fi 55.50N 23.33 E
Radymno 10 Sg 49.57N 22.48 E
Radziejów 10 Od 52.38N 18.32 E
Radzyń Podlaski 10 Se 51.48N 22.38 E
Rae 42 Fd 62.50N 116.00W
Rāe Bareli 25 Gc 26.13N 81.14 E
Rae Isthmus 42 Ic 66.55N 86.10W
Raesfeld 12 Ic 51.46N 6.51 E
Raeside, Lake- 59 Ee 29.30S 121.50 E
Raetihi 62 Fc 39.26S 175.17 E
Raevavae, Ile- 57 Mg 23.52S 147.40W
Raevski, Groupe- 61 Mc 16.45S 144.14W
Rāf, Jabal- 24 Hh 29.12N 39.48 E
Rafaela 53 Ji 31.17S 61.30W
Rafai 35 Ce 4.58N 23.56 E
Rafḩā' 23 Fd 29.42N 43.30 E
Rafi 34 Fc 13.28N 4.10 E
Rāfkā 24 Qe 35.55N 57.36 E
Rafsanjān 23 Ic 30.24N 56.01 E
Råfsö/Reposaari 8 Ic 61.37N 21.27 E
Raga 31 Jh 8.28N 25.41 E
Ragay Gulf 26 Hd 13.30N 122.45 E
Ragged Island 49 Jb 22.12N 75.44W
Ragged Island Range 47 Id 22.42N 75.55W
Ragged Point 51q Bb 13.10N 59.25W
Raglan 62 Fb 37.48S 174.52 E
Raguencau 44 Ma 49.04N 68.32W
Ragusa 14 In 36.55N 14.44 E
Raguva 8 Ki 55.30N 24.45 E
Raha 26 Hg 4.51S 122.43 E
Raḩā, Ḩarrat ar- 24 Gi 27.40N 36.40 E
Rahad al Bardī 35 Cc 11.18N 23.53 E
Rahama 34 Gc 10.25N 8.41 E
Rahaţ, Ḩarrat- 33 He 23.00N 40.05 E
Rahat Daği 15 Ml 37.08N 29.49 E
Rahden 12 Kb 52.26N 8.37 E
Rāhgāmāti 25 Id 22.38N 92.12 E
Rahīmyār Khan 25 Ec 28.25N 70.18 E
Rahmanovskije Ključi 19 If 49.35N 86.35 E
Rahmet 19 Gf 49.19N 65.16 E
Råholt 8 Dd 60.16N 11.11 E
Rahouia 13 Ni 35.32N 1.01 E
Rahov 16 De 48.02N 24.18 E
Rahrbach, Kirchhundem- 12 Jc 51.02N 7.59 E
Raia 13 Df 39.00N 8.17W
Raiatea, Ile- 57 Lf 16.50S 151.25W
Raices 55 Cj 31.54S 59.16W
Rāichūr 22 Jh 16.12N 77.22 E
Raiganj 25 Hc 25.37N 88.07 E
Raigarh 25 Gd 21.54N 83.24 E
Raijua, Pulau- 26 Hi 10.37S 121.36 E
Rainbow Peak 46 Hd 44.55N 115.17W
Rainier, Mount- 38 Ge 46.52N 121.46W
Rainy Lake 43 Ib 48.42N 93.10W
Rainy River 45 Ib 48.43N 94.29W
Rainy River 45 Ib 48.50N 94.41W
Raipur 22 Kg 21.14N 81.38 E
Raisi, Punta- 14 Hl 38.11N 13.06 E
Raisio/Reso 7 Ff 60.29N 22.11 E
Raita Bank (EN) 60 Mb 25.25N 169.30W
Raja Ampat, Kepulauan- 26 Jg 0.50S 130.25 E
Rājahmundry 22 Kh 16.59N 81.47 E
Rajakoski 7 Gb 68.59N 29.07 E
Rajang 21 Ni 2.07N 111.12 E
Rājapālaiyam 25 Fg 9.27N 77.34 E
Rājasthān [3] 25 Ec 26.00N 74.00 E
Rājasthān Canal 25 Eb 31.10N 75.00 E
Rajbiraj 25 Hc 26.30N 86.50 E
Rajčihinsk 20 Hg 49.43N 129.27 E
Rajevski 17 Gi 54.04N 54.56 E
Rājgarh 25 Fc 28.38N 75.23 E
Rajgródzkie, Jezioro- 10 Sc 53.45N 22.38 E
Rajka 10 Ni 48.00N 17.12 E
Rajkot 22 Jg 22.18N 70.47 E
Raj Nāndgaon 25 Gd 21.06N 81.02 E
Rajony Respublikanskogo
Podčinenija
[Kirg.-U.S.S.R.] [3] 19 Hg 42.30N 73.50 E
Rajony Respublikanskogo
Podčinenija
[Tad.-U.S.S.R.] [3] 19 Gh 38.50N 69.30 E

Index Symbols

[1] Independent Nation
[2] State, Region
[3] District, County
[4] Municipality
[5] Colony, Dependency
Continent
Physical Region
Historical or Cultural Region
Mount, Mountain
Volcano
Hill
Mountains, Mountain Range
Hills, Escarpment
Plateau, Upland
Pass, Gap
Plain, Lowland
Delta
Salt Flat
Valley, Canyon
Crater, Cave
Karst Features
Depression
Polder
Desert, Dunes
Forest, Woods
Heath, Steppe
Oasis
Cape, Point
Coast, Beach
Cliff
Peninsula
Isthmus
Sandbank
Island
Atoll
Rock, Reef
Islands, Archipelago
Rocks, Reefs
Coral Reef
Well, Spring
Geyser
River, Stream
Waterfall Rapids
River Mouth, Estuary
Lake
Salt Lake
Intermittent Lake
Reservoir
Swamp, Pond
Canal
Glacier
Ice Shelf, Pack Ice
Ocean
Sea
Gulf, Bay
Strait, Fjord
Lagoon
Bank
Seamount
Tablemount
Ridge
Shelf
Basin
Escarpment, Sea Scarp
Fracture
Trench, Abyss
National Park, Reserve
Point of Interest
Recreation Site
Cave, Cavern
Historic Site
Ruins
Wall, Walls
Church, Abbey
Temple
Scientific Station
Airport
Port
Lighthouse
Mine
Tunnel
Dam, Bridge

Rājshāhi 25 Hd 24.22N 88.36 E
Rakahanga Atoll 57 Kl 10.02S 161.05W
Rakaia 62 Ee 43.54S 172.13 E
Rakaia 62 Ee 43.45S 172.01 E
Rakan, Ra's- 24 Ni 26.10N 51.13 E
Rakata, Pulau- 26 Eh 6.10S 105.26 E
Raka Zangbo 27 Ef 29.24N 87.58 E
Rakhawt, Wādī- 35 Ib 18.16N 51.50 E
Rakht-e Shāh 24 Mf 33.17N 49.23 E
Rakitnoje 28 Mb 45.36N 134.17 E
Rakitovo 15 Hh 41.59N 24.05 E
Rakkestad 8 De 59.26N 11.21 E
Rakoniewice 10 Md 52.10N 16.16 E
Rakops 37 Cd 21.01S 24.20 E
Rakovnicka panev 10 Jf 50.10N 13.30 E
Rakovník 10 Jf 50.06N 13.43 E
Rakovski 15 Hg 42.18N 24.58 E
Raków 10 Rf 50.42N 21.03 E
Rakušečný, Mys- 16 Qh 42.52N 51.55 E
Råkvåg 7 Ce 63.46N 10.05 E
Rakvere 7 Gg 59.22N 26.22 E
Raleigh [N.C.-U.S.] 39 Lf 35.47N 78.39W
Raleigh [Ont.-Can.] 45 Kb 49.31N 91.56W
Raleigh Bay 44 Ih 35.00N 76.20W
Ralik Chain 57 Hd 8.00N 167.00 E
Rama 47 Hf 12.09N 84.15W
Rama, Río- 49 Eg 12.08N 84.13W
Ramādah 32 Jc 32.19N 10.24 E
Ramaḑīn, Wādī- 24 Ej 24.57N 32.34 E
Ramales de la Victoria 13 Ia 43.15N 3.27W
Ramalho, Serra do- 55 Ja 13.45S 44.00W
Ramapo Bank (EN) 57 Fb 27.15N 145.10 E
Ramatlabama 37 De 25.37S 25.30 E
Ramberg 10 He 51.45N 11.05 E
Rambervillers 11 Mf 48.21N 6.38 E
Rambi 63d Cb 16.30S 179.59W
Rambouillet 11 Hf 48.39N 1.50 E
Rambutyo Island 57 Fe 2.18S 147.48 E
Rāmhormoz 24 Mg 31.16N 49.36 E
Ramigala/Ramygala 8 Ki 55.28N 24.23 E
Ramis 35 Gd 8.02N 41.36 E
Ramla 24 Fg 31.55N 34.52 E
Ramlīyah, 'Aqabat ar- 24 Di 26.01N 30.42 E
Ramlu 35 Gc 13.20N 41.45 E
Ramm, Jabal- 24 Fh 29.35N 35.24 E
Rammāk, Ghurd ar- 24 Ch 29.40N 29.20 E
Rāmnagar 25 Fc 29.24N 79.07 E
Ramnäs 8 Ge 59.46N 16.12 E
Ramón
Santamarina 55 Cn 38.26S 59.20W
Ramos 63a Ec 8.16S 160.11 E
Ramos, Río- 48 Ge 25.35N 105.03W
Ramotswa 37 Dd 24.52S 25.50 E
Rāmpur 25 Fc 28.49N 79.02 E
Ramree 25 Ie 19.06N 93.48 E
Rams 24 Qj 25.53N 56.02 E
Ramsele 7 De 63.33N 16.29 E
Ramsey [Eng.-U.K.] 12 Bb 52.27N 0.07W
Ramsey [Ont.-Can.] 44 Fb 47.29N 82.24W
Ramsey [U.K.] 9 Ig 54.20N 4.21W
Ramsey Lake 42 Jg 47.20N 83.00W
Ramsgate 9 Oj 51.20N 1.25 E
Rāmshīr 24 Mg 30.50N 49.30 E
Ramsjö 7 De 62.11N 15.39 E
Ramstein-Miesenbach 12 Je 49.27N 7.32 E
Ramsund 7 Db 68.29N 16.32 E
Ramu 60 Di 4.02S 144.41 E
Ramu 36 Hb 3.56N 41.13 E
Ramvik 7 De 62.49N 17.51 E
Ramville, Ilet- 51h Bb 14.42N 60.53W
Ramygala/Ramigala 8 Ki 55.28N 24.23 E
Rana 7 Dc 66.20N 14.08 E
Rañadoiro, Sierra del- 13 Fa 43.20N 6.45W
Ranai 26 Ef 3.55N 108.23 E
Ranakah, Potjo- 26 Hh 8.38S 120.31 E
Rana Kao, Volcán- 65d Ac 27.11S 109.27W
Rana Roi, Volcán- 65d Ab 27.05S 109.23W
Rana Roraka, Volcán- 65d Bb 27.07S 109.18W
Ranau 26 Ge 5.58N 116.41 E
Ranča 14 Lf 44.24N 17.22 E
Rancagua 53 Ii 34.10S 70.45W
Rance 11 Ef 48.31N 1.59W
Rance, Sivry-Rance- 12 Gd 50.09N 4.16 E
Rancharia 55 Gf 22.15S 50.55W
Rancheria, Río- 49 Kh 11.34N 72.54W
Rānchī 22 Kg 23.21N 85.20 E
Ranchos 55 Cl 35.32S 58.22W
Ranco, Lago- 56 Ff 40.14S 72.24W
Randa 35 Gc 11.51N 42.40 E
Randaberg 8 Ae 59.00N 5.36 E
Randazzo 14 Im 37.53N 14.57 E
Randers 7 Ch 56.28N 10.03 E
Randers Fjord 8 Dh 56.35N 10.20 E
Randijaure 7 Ec 66.42N 19.18 E
Randow 10 Kc 53.41N 14.04 E
Randsfjorden 7 Cf 60.25N 10.25 E
Ranérou 34 Cb 15.18N 13.58W
Ranfurly 62 Df 45.08S 170.06 E
Rangasa, Tanjung- 26 Gg 3.33S 118.56 E
Ranger 45 Gj 32.28N 98.41W
Rangiora 62 Ee 43.18S 172.36 E
Rangiroa Atoll 57 Mf 15.10S 147.35W
Rangitaiki 62 Gb 37.55S 176.53 E
Rangitata 62 Df 44.10S 171.30 E
Rangitikei 62 Fd 40.17S 175.13 E
Rangkasbitung 26 Eh 6.21S 106.15 E
Rangoon (EN) =
Yangon 22 Lh 16.47N 96.10 E
Rangpur 25 Hc 25.44N 89.16 E
Rāniyah 24 Kd 36.15N 44.53 E
Rankin Inlet 39 Jc 62.45N 92.10W
Rankoshi 29a Bb 42.47N 140.31 E
Rannoch, Loch- 9 Ie 56.41N 4.20W
Ranobe 37 Gc 17.10S 44.08 E
Ranon 63b Dc 16.09S 168.07 E
Ranong 25 Jg 9.59N 98.40 E
Ranongga Island 60 Fi 8.05S 156.34 E
Ranova 16 Lb 54.07N 40.14 E
Ransaren 7 Dd 65.14N 14.59 E
Rantabe 37 Hc 15.42S 49.39 E
Rantasalmi 8 Mb 62.04N 28.18 E
Rantaupanjang 26 Fg 1.23S 112.04 E
Rantauprapat 26 Cf 2.06N 99.50 E
Rantekombola, Bulu- 21 Oj 3.21S 120.01 E
Rantoul 45 Lf 40.19N 88.09W
Ranua 7 Gd 65.55N 26.32 E
Ranyah, Wādī- 33 He 21.18N 43.20 E
Raohe 27 Nb 46.48N 133.58 E
Raon-l'Étape 11 Mf 48.24N 6.51 E
Raoui, Erg er- 32 Gd 29.15N 2.45W
Raoul Island 57 Jg 29.15S 177.52W
Raoyang 28 Ce 38.14N 115.44 E
Raoyang He 28 Gd 41.13N 122.12 E
Rapa, Ile- 57 Mg 27.36S 144.20W
Rapallo 14 Df 44.21N 9.14 E
Rapang 26 Gg 3.50S 119.48 E
Rapa Nui/Pascua, Isla de- =
Easter Island (EN) 57 Qg 27.07S 109.22W
Raper, Cape - 42 Kc 69.41N 67.24W
Rapid City 39 Ie 44.05N 103.14W
Rapid Creek 45 Ee 43.54N 102.37W
Rapid River 45 Dc 45.58N 86.59W
Räpina/Rjapina 8 Lf 58.03N 27.35 E
Rapla 7 Fg 59.02N 24.47 E
Rappahannock River 44 Ig 37.34N 76.18W
Rápulo, Río- 52 Jg 13.43S 65.32W
Rāqūbah 31 If 28.58N 19.02 E
Raraka Atoll 57 Mf 16.10S 144.54W
Raroia Atoll 57 Mf 16.05S 142.26W
Rarotonga Island 57 Lg 21.14S 159.46W
Rasa, Punta- 52 Jj 40.51S 62.19W
Ra's Abū Daraj 24 Eh 29.23N 32.33 E
Ra's Abū Rudays 24 Eh 28.53N 33.11 E
Ra's Abū Shajarah 35 Fa 21.04N 37.14 E
Ra's Ajdīr 33 Bc 33.09N 11.34 E
Ra's al 'Ayn 24 Id 36.51N 40.04 E
Ra's al-Barr 24 Dg 31.31N 31.50 E
Ra's al Ḥikmah 24 Bg 31.08N 27.50 E
Ra's al Jabal 14 Em 37.13N 10.08 E
Ra's al Khafjī 24 Mh 28.25N 48.30 E
Ra's al Khaymah 23 Id 25.47N 55.57 E
Ra's al Mish'āb 24 Mh 28.12N 48.37 E
Ra's al Unūf 33 Cc 30.31N 18.34 E
Ra's an Naqb 24 Fh 30.00N 35.29 E
Ra's as Sidr 24 Eh 29.36N 32.40 E
Ra's at Tannūrah 24 Ni 26.42N 50.10 E
Ras Beddouza 30 Ge 32.22N 9.18W
Ras Dashan 30 Kg 13.19N 38.20 E
Raseiniai/Rasejnjaj 7 Fi 55.23N 23.07 E
Rasejnjaj/Raseiniai 7 Fi 55.23N 23.07 E
Râs el Mâ 34 Eb 16.37N 4.27W
Ras-el-Ma 13 Ji 35.08N 2.29W
Ras el Oued 13 Ri 35.57N 5.02 E
Ra's Ghārib 33 Fd 28.21N 33.06 E
Rashād 35 Ec 11.51N 31.04 E
Rāshayyā 24 Ff 33.30N 35.51 E
Rashīd=Rosetta (EN) 33 Fc 31.24N 30.25 E
Rashīd, Maşabb- 24 Dg 31.30N 30.20 E
Rasht 22 Gf 37.16N 49.36 E
Rāsiga 'Alūla 35 Ic 11.59N 50.50 E
Rās Jumbo 35 Gf 1.37S 41.31 E
Raška 15 Df 43.18N 20.38 E
Ra's Madhar, Jabal- 24 Gj 25.46N 37.32 E
Ra's Matārimah 24 Eh 29.27N 32.43 E
Rasmussen Basin 42 Hc 67.56N 95.15W
Rason Lake 59 Ee 28.45S 124.20 E
Rasskazovo 19 Ee 52.39N 41.57 E
Rassua, Ostrov- 20 Kg 47.40N 153.00 E
Rassvet 20 Ee 57.00N 91.32 E
Ras-Tarf, Cap- 13 Ii 35.17N 3.41W
Rastatt 10 Eh 48.51N 8.12 E
Rastede 12 Ka 53.15N 8.12 E
Rastigaissa 7 Ga 70.03N 26.18 E
Råstojaure 7 Eb 68.45N 20.30 E
Ras Ţurunbī 24 Fj 25.40N 34.35 E
Rasūl 24 Pi 27.10N 55.30 E
Ra's Zayt 33 Fd 27.56N 33.31 E
Rat 40a Bb 51.55N 178.20 E
Ratak Chain 57 Id 9.00N 171.00 E
Ratangarh 25 Ee 28.05N 74.36 E
Rätansbyn 7 De 62.29N 14.32 E
Rat Buri 25 Jf 13.32N 99.49 E
Rathbun Lake 45 Jf 40.54N 93.05W
Ráth Droma/Rathdrum 9 Gi 52.56N 6.13W
Rathdrum/
Ráth Droma 9 Gi 52.56N 6.13W
Rathenow 10 Id 52.36N 12.20 E
Rathlin Island/
Reachlainn 9 Gf 55.18N 6.13W
Ráth Luirc/An Ráth 9 Ei 52.21N 8.41W
Rathor, Pik- 18 If 37.55N 72.14 E
Rätikon 14 Dc 47.03N 9.40 E
Ratingen 12 Ic 51.18N 6.51 E
Rätische Alpen=Rhaetian
Alps (EN) 14 Dd 46.30N 10.00 E
Rat Islands 38 Ad 52.00N 178.00 E
Ratlām 25 Fd 23.19N 75.04 E
Ratmanova, Ostrov- 20 Lc 35.45N 169.00W
Ratnāgiri 25 Ee 16.59N 73.18 E
Ratnapura 25 Gg 6.41N 80.24 E
Ratno 16 Dd 51.42N 24.31 E
Raton 43 Gd 36.54N 104.24W
Ratqh, Wādī ar- 24 Ie 34.25N 40.55 E
Rătta 20 Dd 63.35N 84.05 E
Rattlesnake Hills 46 Le 42.45N 107.10W
Rattray Head 9 Ld 57.38N 1.46W
Rättvik 7 Df 60.53N 15.06 E
Ratz, Mount- 38 Fd 57.23N 132.19W
Ratzeburg 10 Gc 53.42N 10.46 E
Raub 26 Df 3.48N 101.52 E
Rauch 56 Ie 36.46S 59.06W
Raucourt-et-Flaba 12 Ge 49.36N 4.57 E
Raudeberg 8 Ab 61.59N 5.09 E
Rauer Islands 66 Fe 68.51S 77.50 E
Raufarhöfn 7a Ca 66.27N 15.57W
Raufjellet 8 Dc 61.15N 11.00 E
Raufoss 7 Cf 60.43N 10.37 E
Raukotaha 64n Ac 10.28S 161.01W
Raukumara Range 62 Gc 38.00S 178.00 E
Rauland 8 Be 59.44N 8.00 E
Raúl Leoni, Represa- (Guri)
54 Fb 7.30N 63.00W
Rauma 7 Be 62.33N 7.43 E
Rauma/Raumo 7 Ef 61.08N 21.30 E
Raumo/Rauma 7 Ef 61.08N 21.30 E
Rauna 8 Kg 57.14N 25.39 E
Raunds 12 Bb 52.20N 0.32W
Raurimu 62 Fc 39.07S 175.24 E
Raurkela 22 Kg 22.13N 84.53 E
Rausu 28 Rb 44.01N 145.12 E
Rausu-Dake 29a Da 44.06N 145.07 E
Rautalampi 8 Lb 62.38N 26.50 E
Ravahere Atoll 57 Mf 18.14S 142.09W
Ravan 14 Mf 44.15N 18.16 E
Ravanica, Manastir- 15 Ef 43.58N 21.30 E
Ravānsar 24 Le 34.43N 46.40 E
Ravanusa 14 Hm 37.16N 13.58 E
Rāvar 24 Qg 31.12N 56.53 E
Rava-Russkaja 16 Cd 50.13N 23.37 E
Ravels 12 Gc 51.22N 4.59 E
Ravelsbach 14 Jb 48.30N 15.50 E
Ravels-Poppel 12 Hc 51.27N 5.02 E
Ravenna [It.] 14 Gf 44.25N 12.12 E
Ravenna [Nb.-U.S.] 45 Gf 41.02N 98.55W
Ravensburg 10 Fi 47.47N 9.37 E
Ravenshoe 58 Ff 17.37S 145.29 E
Ravensthorpe 59 Ef 33.35S 120.02 E
Ravi 21 Jf 30.35N 71.49 E
Ravnina 19 Gh 37.57N 62.42 E
Rawaki Atoll (Phoenix) 57 Je 3.43S 170.43W
Rāwalpindi 22 Jf 33.35N 73.03 E
Rawa Mazowiecka 10 Qe 51.46N 20.16 E
Rawāndūz 24 Kd 36.37N 44.31 E
Rawdah 24 Ie 35.15N 41.05 E
Rawene 62 Ea 35.24S 173.30 E
Rawicz 10 Me 51.37N 16.52 E
Rawka 10 Qd 52.07N 20.08 E
Rawlinna 58 Dh 31.01S 125.20 E
Rawlins 43 Fc 41.47N 107.14W
Rawlinson Range 59 Fd 24.50S 128.00 E
Rawson [Arg.] 55 Bl 34.36S 60.04W
Rawson [Arg.] 53 Jj 43.18S 65.06W
Rawura, Ras- 36 He 10.20S 40.30 E
Raxaul 25 Gc 26.59N 84.51 E
Ray, Cape - 42 Lg 47.37N 59.19W
Raya, Bukit- 21 Nj 1.32S 111.05 E
Rayadrug 25 Ff 14.42N 76.52 E
Rayāt 24 Kd 36.40N 44.58 E
Rayleigh 12 Cc 51.35N 0.37 E
Raymond [Alta.-Can.] 46 Ib 49.27N 112.39W
Raymond [Wa.-U.S.] 46 Dc 46.41N 123.44W
Raymondville 45 Hf 26.29N 97.47W
Rayne 45 Jk 30.14N 92.16W
Rayón [Mex.] 48 Jg 21.51N 99.40W
Rayón [Mex.] 48 Dc 29.43N 110.35W
Rayones 48 Ie 25.01N 100.05W
Rayong 25 Kf 12.40N 101.17 E
Raysūt 23 Hf 16.54N 54.02 E
Raytown 45 Ig 39.00N 94.28W
Raz, Pointe du- 11 Bf 48.02N 4.44W
Razan 24 Me 35.23N 49.02 E
Razdan 16 Ni 40.28N 44.43 E
Razdelnaja 16 Gf 46.50N 30.05 E
Razdolinsk 20 Ee 58.25N 94.44 E
Razdolnaja 28 Kc 43.20N 131.49 E
Razdolnoje [R.S.F.S.R.] 28 Kc 43.33N 131.55 E
Razdolnoje [Ukr.-U.S.S.R.] 16 Hg 45.47N 33.30 E
Razgrad 15 Jf 43.32N 26.31 E
Razgrad (2) 15 Jf 43.32N 26.31 E
Razī 24 Mc 38.32N 48.08 E
Raziku/Raasiku 8 Ke 59.22N 25.11 E
Razlog 15 Gh 41.53N 23.28 E
Razo 32 Cf 16.37N 24.36W
Ré, Ile de- 5 Ff 46.12N 1.25W
Reachlainn 9 Gf 55.18N 6.13W
Reachlainn/Rathlin
Island 9 Gf 55.18N 6.13W
Reachrainn/Lambay 9 Gh 53.29N 6.01W
Read 42 Gc 69.12N 114.30W
Reading [Eng.-U.K.] 9 Mj 51.28N 0.59W
Reading [Pa.-U.S.] 43 Lc 40.20N 75.55W
Real, Cordillera- [Bol.] 54 Eg 16.30S 68.30W
Real, Cordillera- [Ec.] 52 If 3.00S 78.00W
Real Audiencia 55 Cm 36.11S 58.35W
Real del Castillo 48 Aa 31.58N 116.19W
Realicó 56 He 35.02S 64.15W
Réalmont 11 Ik 43.47N 2.12 E
Reao Atoll 57 Nf 18.31S 136.23W
Reatini, Monti- 14 Gh 42.35N 12.50 E
Rebais 12 Ff 48.51N 3.14 E
Rebecca, Lake- 59 Ee 29.55S 122.10 E
Rebiana Oasis (EN) =
Rabyānah, Wāḥāt al- 33 De 24.14N 21.59 E
Rebollera 13 Hf 38.25N 4.02W
Reboly 7 He 63.52N 30.47 E
Rebord Manamblen 37 Hd 24.05S 46.30 E
Rebun 28 Pb 45.23N 141.02 E
Rebun-Dake 29a Ba 45.22N 141.01 E
Rebun-Suidō 29a Ba 45.15N 141.05 E
Rebun-Tō 27 Pb 45.23N 141.10 E
Recalde 55 Bm 36.39S 61.05W
Recanati 14 Hg 43.24N 13.32 E
Recaş 15 Ed 45.48N 21.30 E
Recherche, Archipelago of
the- 57 Dh 34.06S 122.45 E
Rečica 19 De 52.22N 30.25 E
Recife 53 Mf 8.03S 34.54W
Recife, Cape- 30 Jl 34.02S 25.45 E
Recke 12 Jb 52.23N 7.43 E
Recklinghausen 10 De 51.37N 7.12 E
Recknitz 10 Ib 54.14N 12.28 E
Recoaro Terme 14 Fe 45.42N 11.13 E
Reconquista 56 Ic 29.09S 59.39W
Recovery Glacier 66 Ag 81.10S 28.00W
Recreo 56 Gc 29.16S 65.04W
Recz 10 Lc 53.16N 15.33 E
Reda 10 Ob 54.38N 18.30 E
Redange 12 He 49.46N 5.54 E
Red Bank 44 Eh 35.07N 85.17W
Red Bay 42 Lf 51.44N 56.25W
Red Bluff 43 Cc 40.11N 122.15W
Red Bluff Reservoir 45 Ek 31.57N 103.56W
Redbridge, London- 12 Cc 51.35N 0.08 E
Red Butte 46 Ii 35.55N 112.03W
Redcar 9 Lg 54.37N 1.04W
Red Cliff 51c Ab 17.05N 62.32W
Redcliff 37 Dc 19.02S 29.50 E
Redcliffe, Mount- 59 Ee 28.25S 121.32 E
Red Cloud 45 Gf 40.05N 98.32W
Red Deer 39 Hd 52.16N 113.48W
Red Deer [Can.] 42 Hf 52.55N 101.27W
Red Deer [Can.] 38 Id 50.56N 109.54W
Redding 39 Ge 40.35N 122.24W
Redditch 9 Li 52.19N 1.56W
Rede 9 Kf 55.08N 2.13W
Redenção 54 Kd 4.13S 38.43W
Redfield 43 Hc 44.53N 98.31W
Red Hill 65a Ec 20.43N 156.15W
Red Hills 45 Gh 37.25N 99.25W
Redkino 7 Ih 56.40N 36.19 E
Red Lake 42 Ih 51.05N 93.55W
Red Lake 42 If 51.03N 93.49W
Red Lake River 45 Hc 47.55N 97.01W
Red Lakes 43 Ib 48.05N 94.45W
Redlands 46 Gi 34.03N 117.11W
Red Lodge 46 Kd 45.11N 109.15W
Redmond 43 Cc 44.17N 121.11W
Red Mountain [Ca.-U.S.] 46 Df 41.35N 123.06W
Red Mountain [Mt.-U.S.] 46 Ic 47.07N 112.44W
Red Oak 45 If 41.01N 95.14W
Redon 11 Dg 47.39N 2.05W
Redonda 50 Ed 16.55N 62.19W
Redondela 13 Db 42.17N 8.36W
Redondo 13 Ef 38.39N 7.33W
Redondo Beach 46 Fj 33.51N 118.23W
Redoubt Volcano 38 Dc 60.29N 152.45W
Red River [N.Amer.] 38 Jd 50.24N 96.48W
Red River [U.S.] 38 Jf 31.00N 91.40W
Red River (EN)=Hông,
Sông- 21 Mg 20.17N 106.34 E
Red River (EN)=Yuan Jiang
[Asia] 21 Mg 20.17N 106.34 E
Red Rock, Lake- 45 Jf 41.30N 93.20W
Red Rock River 46 Id 44.59N 112.52W
Redruth 9 Hk 50.13N 5.14W
Red Sea (EN)=Aḥmar, Al
Baḥr al- 30 Kf 25.00N 38.00 E
Redstone 42 Fd 64.17N 124.33W
Redstone 46 Da 52.08N 123.42W
Red Volta (EN)=Volta
Rouge 30 Gh 10.34N 0.30W
Redwater Creek 46 Mb 48.03N 105.13W
Red Wing 43 Ic 44.34N 92.31W
Redwood City 46 Dh 37.29N 122.13W
Redwood Falls 45 Id 44.32N 95.07W
Ree, Lough-/Loch Rí 9 Fh 53.35N 8.00W
Reed City 44 Ed 43.53N 85.31W
Reedley 46 Fh 36.24N 119.37W
Reeds Peak 45 Cj 33.09N 107.51W
Reedsport 43 Cc 43.42N 124.06W
Reedy Glacier 66 Ng 85.30S 134.00W
Reef Islands 57 Hf 10.15S 166.10 E
Reefton 62 De 42.07S 171.52 E
Reepham 12 Db 52.45N 1.07 E
Rees 12 Ic 51.46N 6.24 E
Reese River 46 Gf 40.39N 116.54W
Refahiye 24 Hc 39.54N 38.46 E
Reforma, Río- 48 Ed 26.56N 108.12W
Reftele 8 Eg 57.11N 13.35 E
Reftinski 17 Jh 57.10N 61.43 E
Refugio 45 Hl 28.18N 97.17W
Refugio, Punta- 48 Cc 29.30N 113.30W
Rega 10 Lb 54.10N 15.18 E
Regar 19 Gh 38.34N 68.13 E
Regen 10 Jh 48.58N 13.08 E
Regen 10 Ig 49.01N 12.06 E
Regensburg 6 Hf 49.01N 12.06 E
Reggane 31 Hf 26.42N 0.10 E
Regge 12 Ib 52.26N 6.29 E
Reggio di Calabria 6 Hh 38.06N 15.39 E
Reggio nell'Emilia 14 Ef 44.43N 10.36 E
Reghin 15 Hc 46.46N 24.42 E
Regina [Fr.Gui.] 54 Hc 4.19N 52.08W
Regina [Sask.-Can.] 39 Id 50.25N 104.39W
Registan (EN)=Rīgestān 21 If 31.00N 65.00 E
Registro 55 Ig 24.30S 47.50W
Registro do Araguaia 55 Gb 15.44S 51.50W
Regnitz 10 Gg 49.54N 10.49 E
Regocijo 48 Gf 23.35N 105.11W
Reguengos de Monsaraz 13 Ef 38.25N 7.32W
Rehburg-Loccum 12 Lb 52.28N 9.14 E
Rehoboth (3) 37 Bd 23.50S 17.00 E
Rehoboth 37 Bd 23.18S 17.03 E
Reḥovot 24 Fg 31.54N 34.49 E
Reichelsheim (Odenwald) 12 Ke 49.43N 8.51 E
Reichenbach 10 If 50.37N 12.18 E
Reichshoffen 12 Jf 48.56N 7.40 E
Reichshoft 12 Jd 50.55N 7.39 E
Reichshoft-Denklingen 12 Jd 50.55N 7.39 E
Reidsville 44 Hg 36.21N 79.40W
Reigate 9 Mj 51.14N 0.13W
Reims 6 Gf 49.15N 4.02 E
Rein=Rhine (EN) 5 Ge 51.52N 6.02 E
Reina Adelaida,
Archipiélago- 52 Ik 52.10S 74.25W
Reindeer 42 He 55.34N 103.10W
Reindeer Bank (EN) 51p Ac 11.50N 62.05W
Reindeer Lake 38 Id 57.15N 102.40W
Reineskarvet 8 Cd 60.47N 8.13 E
Reinga, Cape- 62 Ea 34.25S 172.41 E
Reinhardswald 10 Fe 51.30N 9.30 E
Reinheim 12 Je 49.08N 7.11 E
Reinosa 13 Ha 43.00N 4.08W
Reisa 7 Eb 69.48N 21.00 E
Reitoru Atoll 57 Mf 17.52S 143.05W
Reitz 37 De 27.53S 28.31 E
Rejmyra 8 Ff 58.50N 15.55 E
Rejowiec Fabryczny 10 Te 51.08N 23.13 E
Reka Devnja 15 Kf 43.13N 27.36 E
Rekarne 8 Ge 59.20N 16.25 E
Reken 12 Jc 51.48N 7.03 E
Reliance 39 Ic 62.42N 109.08W
Relizane 32 Hb 35.45N 0.33 E
Remagen 12 Jd 50.34N 7.14 E
Remarkable, Mount- 59 Hf 32.48S 138.10 E
Rembang 26 Fh 6.42S 111.20 E
Remedios 49 Gi 8.14N 81.51W
Remedios, Punta- 49 Cg 13.31N 89.49W
Remedios, Río- 49 Mh 11.01N 69.15W
Remich 12 Ie 49.32N 6.22 E
Rémire 54 Hc 4.53N 52.17W
Remiremont 11 Mf 48.01N 6.35 E
Remire Reef 37b Bb 5.05S 53.22 E
Remontnoje 16 Mf 46.33N 43.40 E
Remoulins 11 Kk 43.56N 4.34 E
Remscheid 10 De 51.11N 7.12 E
Rena 7 Cf 61.08N 11.22 E
Rena 8 Dc 61.08N 11.23 E
Renaix/Ronse 11 Jd 50.45N 3.36 E
Renana, Fossa- 5 Gf 48.40N 7.50 E
Renard Islands 63a Ad 10.50S 153.00 E
Renaud Island 66 Qe 65.40S 66.00W
Rende 14 Kk 39.20N 16.11 E
Rendezvous Bay 51b Ab 18.10N 63.07W
Rend Lake 45 Lg 38.05N 88.58W
Rendova Island 60 Fi 8.32S 157.20 E
Rendsburg 10 Fb 54.18N 9.40 E
Renfrew 42 Jg 45.28N 76.41W
Rengat 26 Dg 0.24S 102.33 E
Rengo 56 Fd 34.25S 70.52W
Reni 16 Fg 45.29N 28.18 E
Renko 8 Kd 60.54N 24.17 E
Renkum 12 Hc 51.58N 5.45 E
Renland 41 Jd 71.15N 27.20W
Renmark 58 Fh 34.11S 140.45 E
Rennell, Islas- 56 Fh 52.00S 74.00W
Rennell Island 57 Hf 11.40S 160.10 E
Rennes 6 Ff 48.05N 1.41W
Rennes, Bassin de- 11 Ef 48.05N 1.40W
Rennesøy 8 Ae 59.05N 5.40 E
Rennick Glacier 66 Kf 70.30S 161.45 E
Rennie Lake 42 Gd 61.10N 105.30W
Reno 39 Hf 39.31N 119.48W
Reno 14 Gf 44.38N 12.16 E
Renqiu 28 De 38.42N 116.06 E
Rensselaer [In.-U.S.] 44 De 40.57N 87.09W
Rensselaer [N.Y.-U.S.] 44 Kd 42.37N 73.44W
Renterría 13 Ka 43.19N 1.54W
Renton 46 Dc 47.30N 122.11W
Renwez 12 Ge 49.50N 4.36 E
Renxian 28 Cf 37.07N 114.41 E
Reo 26 Hh 8.19S 120.30 E
Repartimento, Serra do- 55 Jc 17.40S 44.50W
Répce 10 Ni 47.41N 17.02 E
Repino 8 Md 60.10N 29.58 E
Repong, Pulau- 26 Ef 2.22N 105.53 E
Reposaari/Räfsö 8 Ic 61.37N 21.27 E
Republic 46 Fb 48.39N 118.44W
Republican 38 Jf 39.03N 96.48W
Repulse Bay 39 Kc 66.32N 86.15W
Repulse Bay [Austl.] 59 Jd 20.35S 148.45 E
Repulse Bay [Can.] 42 Ic 66.20N 86.00W
Repvåg 7 Fa 70.45N 25.41 E
Requena [Peru] 54 Dd 5.00S 73.50W
Requena [Sp.] 13 Ke 39.29N 1.06W
Requin Bay 51p Bb 12.02N 61.38W
Réquista 11 Ij 44.02N 2.32 E
Reşadiye Yarimadası 15 Km 36.40N 27.45 E
Reschenpass/Resia, Passo
di- 14 Ed 46.50N 10.30 E
Resen 15 Eh 41.05N 21.01 E
Reserva 55 Gg 24.38S 50.52W
Reserve 45 Bj 33.43N 108.45W
Rešetilovka 16 Ie 49.33N 34.05 E
Reshui 27 Hd 37.38N 100.30 E
Resia, Passo di-/
Reschenpass 14 Ed 46.50N 10.30 E
Resistencia 53 Kh 27.30S 58.59W
Reşiţa 15 Ed 45.18N 21.55 E
Resko 10 Lc 53.47N 15.25 E
Reso/Raisio 7 Ff 60.29N 22.11 E
Resolute 39 Jb 74.41N 94.54W
Resolution 38 Mc 61.30N 65.00W
Resolution Island 42 Ld 61.35N 64.39W
Resolution Island 62 Bf 45.40S 166.35 E
Respublikai Soveth
Socialisti Todžikiston/
Tadžikskaja SSR (2) 19 Hh 39.00N 71.00 E
Respublika Sovetike
Socialiste Moldovenjaske/
Moldavskaja SSR (2) 19 Cf 47.00N 29.00 E
Ressa 16 Ib 54.45N 35.10 E
Ressons-sur-Matz 12 Ee 49.33N 2.45 E
Restigouche River 44 Na 48.04N 66.20W
Restinga de Sefton, Isla- 52 Hi 37.00S 83.50W
Restinga Sêca 55 Fi 29.49S 53.23W
Reszel 10 Rb 54.04N 21.09 E
Retalhuleu (3) 49 Bf 14.20N 91.50W
Retalhuleu 47 Ff 14.32N 91.41W
Retavas/Rietavas 8 Ii 55.43N 21.49 E
Retezatului, Munţii- 15 Fd 45.25N 23.00 E
Rethel 11 Ke 49.31N 4.22 E
Rethem (Aller) 12 Lb 52.47N 9.23 E
Réthinnon 15 Hn 35.22N 24.28 E
Retie 12 Hc 51.17N 5.05 E

Index Symbols

(1) Independent Nation
(2) State, Region
(3) District, County
(4) Municipality
(5) Colony, Dependency
Continent
Physical Region
Historical or Cultural Region
Mount, Mountain
Volcano
Hill
Mountains, Mountain Range
Hills, Escarpment
Plateau, Upland
Pass, Gap
Plain, Lowland
Delta
Salt Flat
Valley, Canyon
Crater, Cave
Karst Features
Depression
Polder
Desert, Dunes
Forest, Woods
Heath, Steppe
Oasis
Cape, Point
Coast, Beach
Cliff
Peninsula
Isthmus
Sandbank
Island
Atoll
Rock, Reef
Islands, Archipelago
Rocks, Reefs
Coral Reef
Well, Spring
Geyser
River, Stream
Waterfall Rapids
River Mouth, Estuary
Lake
Salt Lake
Intermittent Lake
Reservoir
Swamp, Pond
Canal
Glacier
Ice Shelf, Pack Ice
Ocean
Sea
Gulf, Bay
Strait, Fjord
Lagoon
Bank
Seamount
Tablemount
Ridge
Shelf
Basin
Escarpment, Sea Scarp
Fracture
Trench, Abyss
National Park, Reserve
Point of Interest
Recreation Site
Cave, Cavern
Historic Site
Ruins
Wall, Walls
Church, Abbey
Temple
Scientific Station
Airport
Port
Lighthouse
Mine
Tunnel
Dam, Bridge

Retourne 12 Ge 49.26N 4.02 E
Rétság 10 Pi 47.56N 19.08 E
Rettihovka 28 Lb 44.10N 132.45 E
Retz 14 Jc 48.45N 15.57 E
Retz, Pays de- 11 Eg 47.07N 1.58W
Réunion = Reunion (EN) 30 Mk 21.06S 55.36 E
Réunion = Reunion (EN) [5] 31 Mk 21.06S 55.36 E
Reunion (EN) = Réunion 30 Mk 21.06S 55.36 E
Reunion (EN) = Réunion [5] 31 Mk 21.06S 55.36 E
Reus 13 Nc 41.09N 1.07 E
Reusel 12 Hc 51.22N 5.10 E
Reuss 14 Cc 47.28N 8.14 E
Reut 16 Ff 47.15N 29.09 E
Reutlingen 10 Fh 48.29N 9.13 E
Reutte 14 Ec 47.29N 10.43 E
Revda [R.S.F.S.R.] 17 Ih 56.48N 59.57 E
Revda [R.S.F.S.R.] 7 Ic 67.57N 34.32 E
Revel 11 Hk 43.28N 2.00 E
Revelstoke 42 Ff 50.59N 118.12W
Revermont 11 Lh 46.27N 5.25 E
Revillagigedo 40 Me 55.35N 131.23W
Revillagigedo, Islas- 38 Hh 19.00N 111.30W
Revin 11 Ke 49.56N 4.38 E
Revoljucii, Pik- 18 Ie 38.33N 72.28 E
Revsundssjön 8 Fb 62.50N 15.15 E
Rewa 63d Bc 18.08S 178.33 E
Rewa 25 Gd 24.32N 81.18 E
Rewāri 25 Fc 28.11N 76.37 E
Rex, Mount- 66 Qf 74.54S 75.57W
Rexburg 46 Je 43.49N 111.47W
Rexpoëde 12 Ed 50.56N 2.32 E
Rey 23 Hb 35.35N 51.25 E
Rey, Arroyo del- 55 Ci 29.12S 59.36W
Rey, Isla del- 47 Ig 8.22N 78.55W
Rey, Laguna del- 48 Hd 27.00N 103.25W
Rey Bouba 34 Hd 8.40N 14.11 E
Reyes, Point- 46 Dg 38.00N 123.01W
Reyhanli 24 Gd 36.18N 36.32 E
Reykjalid 7a Cb 65.39N 16.55W
Reykjanes 5 Dc 63.49N 22.43W
Reykjanes Ridge (EN) 3 Dc 62.00N 27.00W
Reykjavík 6 Dc 64.09N 21.57W
Reynolds Range 59 Gd 22.20S 132.50 E
Reynosa 39 Jg 26.07N 98.18W
Reyssouze 11 Kh 46.27N 4.54 E
Rež 17 Kh 57.54N 62.20 E
Rež 17 Jh 57.23N 61.24 E
Rezé 11 Eg 47.12N 1.34W
Rezekne/Rēzekne 6 Id 56.30N 27.19 E
Rēzekne/Rezekne 6 Id 56.30N 27.19 E
Rezelm, Lacul- 15 Le 44.54N 28.57 E
Rezina 16 Ff 47.43N 28.58 E
Reznas, Ozero-/Rēznas Ezers 8 Lh 56.20N 27.30 E
Rēznas Ezers/Reznas, Ozero- 8 Lh 56.20N 27.30 E
Rezovo 15 Lh 41.59N 28.02 E
Rezvān 24 Qi 27.34N 56.06 E
Rezve 15 Lh 41.59N 28.01 E
Rgotina 15 Fe 44.01N 22.17 E
Rhaetian Alps (EN) = Alpi Retiche 14 Dd 46.30N 10.00 E
Rhaetian Alps (EN) = Rätische Alpen 14 Dd 46.30N 10.00 E
Rhallamane 30 Ff 23.15N 10.00W
Rhauderfehn 12 Ja 53.08N 7.34 E
Rhaunen 12 Je 49.51N 7.21 E
Rheda-Wiedenbrück 10 Ee 51.51N 8.18 E
Rheden 12 Ib 52.01N 6.01 E
Rheden-Dieren 12 Ib 52.03N 6.08 E
Rheider Land 12 Ja 53.13N 7.18 E
Rhein 12 Ke 49.52N 8.07 E
Rhein = Rhine (EN) 5 Ge 51.52N 6.02 E
Rheinberg 12 Ic 51.33N 6.36 E
Rheine 10 Dd 52.17N 7.27 E
Rheinfall 14 Cc 47.41N 8.38 E
Rheinfelden 10 Di 47.34N 7.48 E
Rheingaugebirge 12 Jd 50.05N 8.00 E
Rheinisches Schiefergebirge = Rhenish Slate Mountains (EN) 5 Ge 50.25N 7.10 E
Rheinland-Pfalz = Rhineland-Palatinate (EN) [2] 10 Cf 50.00N 7.00 E
Rheinsberg 10 Ic 53.06N 12.53 E
Rheinstetten 12 Kf 48.58N 8.18 E
Rhenen 12 Hc 51.58N 5.35 E
Rhenish Slate Mountains (EN) = Rheinisches Schiefergebirge 5 Ge 50.25N 7.10 E
Rheris 32 Gc 30.41N 4.57W
Rheydt, Mönchengladbach- 12 Ic 51.10N 6.27 E
Rhin = Rhine (EN) 5 Ge 51.52N 6.02 E
Rhine (EN) = Rein 5 Ge 51.52N 6.02 E
Rhine (EN) = Rhein 5 Ge 51.52N 6.02 E
Rhine (EN) = Rhin 5 Ge 51.52N 6.02 E
Rhine (EN) = Rijn 5 Ge 51.52N 6.02 E
Rhine Bank (EN) 56 Ji 50.30S 53.30W
Rhineland-Palatinate (EN) = Rheinland Pfalz [2] 10 Cf 50.00N 7.00 E
Rhinelander 43 Jb 45.38N 89.25W
Rhinluch 10 Id 52.50N 12.50 E
Rhino Camp 36 Fb 2.58N 31.24 E
Rhiou 13 Mi 35.59N 0.53 E
Rhir, Cap- 32 Fc 30.38N 9.54W
Rho 14 De 45.32N 9.02 E
Rhode Island [2] 43 Mc 41.40N 71.30W
Rhode Island Sound 44 Le 41.25N 71.15W
Rhodes (EN) = Ródhos 6 Ih 36.26N 28.13 E
Rhodes (EN) = Ródhos 5 Ih 36.10N 28.00 E
Rhodesia → Zimbabwe [1] 31 Jj 20.00S 30.00 E
Rhodes Peak 46 Hc 46.41N 114.47W
Rhodope Mountains (EN) = Rodopi 5 Ig 41.30N 24.30 E
Rhomara 13 Hi 35.10N 4.57W
Rhön 10 Gf 50.25N 10.05 E
Rhondda 9 Jj 51.40N 3.30W
Rhône 5 Gg 43.20N 4.50 E
Rhône [3] 11 Ki 46.00N 4.30 E
Rhône au Rhin, Canal du- 11 Lg 47.06N 5.19 E
Rhourd el Baguel 32 Ic 31.24N 6.57 E
Rhue 11 Ii 45.23N 2.29 E
Rhum 9 Ge 57.00N 6.20W
Rhyl 9 Jh 53.19N 3.29W
Riaba 34 Ge 3.24N 8.42 E
Riacho de Santana 54 Jf 13.37S 42.57W
Riangnom 35 Ed 9.55N 30.01 E
Riaño 13 Gb 42.58N 5.01W
Riánsares 13 Ie 39.32N 3.18W
Říčany 10 Kg 50.00N 14.39 E
Rias Altas 13 Da 43.30N 8.30W
Rias Bajas 13 Db 42.30N 9.00W
Riau [3] 26 Df 1.00N 102.00 E
Riau Archipelago (EN) = Riau, Kepulauan- 21 Mi 1.00N 104.30 E
Riau Kepulauan- = Riau Archipelago (EN) 21 Mi 1.00N 104.30 E
Riaza 13 Ic 41.17N 3.28W
Riaza 13 Ic 41.42N 3.55W
Ribadavia 13 Db 42.17N 8.08W
Ribadeo 13 Ea 43.32N 7.02W
Ribadesella 13 Ga 43.28N 5.04W
Ribagorza/La Ribagorça 13 Mb 42.15N 0.30 E
Ribamar 54 Jd 2.33S 44.03W
Ribas do Rio Pardo 55 Fe 20.27S 53.46W
Ribatejo 13 De 39.15N 8.30W
Ribáuè 37 Fb 14.57S 38.17 E
Ribble 9 Kh 53.44N 2.50W
Ribe 7 Bi 55.21N 8.46 E
Ribe [2] 8 Ci 55.35N 8.45 E
Ribécourt-Dreslincourt 12 Ee 49.31N 2.55 E
Ribeira [Braz.] 55 Hg 24.39S 49.00W
Ribeira [Sp.] 13 Db 42.33N 9.00W
Ribeira, Rio- 55 Ig 24.40S 47.24W
Ribeira Brava 32 Cf 16.37N 24.18W
Ribeira Grande 32 Bf 17.11N 25.04W
Ribeirão Prêto 53 Lh 21.10S 47.48W
Ribeirãozinho 55 Fc 16.22S 52.36W
Ribeiro Gonçalves 54 Ie 7.32S 45.14W
Ribemont 12 Fe 49.48N 3.28 E
Ribera 14 Hm 37.30N 13.16 E
Ribérac 11 Gi 45.15N 0.20 E
Riberalta 53 Jg 10.59S 66.06W
Ribnica 14 Ie 45.44N 14.44 E
Ribnitz-Damgarten 10 Ib 54.15N 12.28 E
Ricardo Flores Magón 48 Fc 29.58N 106.58W
Riccia 14 Ii 41.29N 14.50 E
Riccione 14 Gg 43.59N 12.39 E
Rice Lake 44 Hc 44.08N 78.13W
Rich 32 Gc 32.15N 4.30W
Richan 45 Jb 49.59N 92.49W
Richard Collinson Inlet 42 Gb 72.45N 113.00W
Richards 42 Ec 69.20N 134.35W
Richard's Bay 31 Kk 28.47S 32.06 E
Richardson 45 Hj 32.57N 96.44W
Richardson Mountains 38 Fc 66.00N 135.20W
Richard Toll 34 Bb 16.28N 15.41W
Richât, Guel er- 32 Ee 21.07N 11.24W
Richel 12 Ha 53.18N 5.10 E
Richel Griend 12 Ha 53.18N 5.15 E
Richelieu 11 Gg 47.01N 0.19 E
Richer 45 Hb 49.39N 96.28W
Richey 46 Mc 47.39N 105.04W
Richfield 43 Ed 38.46N 112.05W
Richibucto 44 Ob 46.41N 64.52W
Richland 43 Db 46.17N 119.18W
Richland Center 45 Ke 43.22N 90.21W
Richmond [Austl.] 59 Id 20.44S 143.08 E
Richmond [Ca.-U.S.] 43 Cd 37.57N 122.22W
Richmond [Eng.-U.K.] 9 Lg 54.24N 1.44W
Richmond [In.-U.S.] 43 Kd 39.50N 84.54W
Richmond [Ky.-U.S.] 43 Kd 37.45N 84.18W
Richmond [N.Z.] 62 Ed 41.21S 173.11 E
Richmond [S.Afr.] 37 Cf 31.23S 23.56 E
Richmond [Tx.-U.S.] 45 Il 29.35N 95.46W
Richmond [Va.-U.S.] 39 Lf 37.30N 77.28W
Richmond, Mount- 62 Ed 41.28S 173.24 E
Richmond Hill 44 Hd 43.52N 79.27W
Richmond Peak 51n Ba 13.17N 61.13W
Richthofen, Mount- 45 Df 40.29N 105.57W
Rickmansworth 12 Bc 51.38N 0.28W
Ricobayo, Embalse de- 13 Gc 41.35N 5.50W
Ridā' 33 Hg 14.25N 44.50 E
Ridderkerk 12 Gc 51.52N 4.36 E
Ridgecrest 46 Gi 35.38N 117.36W
Ridgway 44 He 41.25N 78.45W
Riding Mountain 45 Fa 50.55N 100.25W
Riecito, Rio- 50 Bi 6.50N 68.51W
Ried 12 Ke 49.50N 8.25 E
Ried im Innkreis 14 Hb 48.13N 13.30 E
Riedlingen 10 Fh 48.09N 9.28 E
Riemst 12 Hd 50.48N 5.36 E
Ries 10 Gh 48.55N 10.40 E
Riesa 10 Je 51.18N 13.18 E
Riesco, Isla- 56 Fh 53.00S 72.30W
Riesi 14 Im 37.17N 14.05 E
Riet 30 Jk 29.00S 23.53 E
Rietavas/Retavas 8 Ii 55.43N 21.49 E
Rietberg 12 Kc 51.48N 8.26 E
Rietbron 37 Cf 32.54S 23.09 E
Rietfontein [Nam.] 37 Cd 21.58S 20.58 E
Rietfontein [S.Afr.] 37 Ce 26.44S 20.01 E
Rieti 14 Gh 42.24N 12.51 E
Rif 30 Ge 35.00N 4.00W
Rifle 45 Cg 39.32N 107.47W
Rifstangi 5 Eb 66.32N 16.12W
Rift Valley [3] 36 Gb 0.30N 36.00 E
Rift Valley 30 Kh 0.30N 36.00 E
Riga/Rīga 6 Id 56.57N 24.06 E
Rīga/Riga 6 Id 56.57N 24.06 E
Riga, Gulf of- (EN) = Rīgas Jūras Licis 5 Id 57.30N 23.35 E
Riga, Gulf of- (EN) = Riia Laht 5 Id 57.30N 23.35 E
Riga, Gulf of- (EN) = Rižski Zaliv 5 Id 57.30N 23.35 E
Rigachikum 34 Gc 10.38N 7.28 E
Rīgas Jūras Licis = Riga, Gulf of- (EN) 5 Id 57.30N 23.35 E
Rigestān = Registan (EN) 21 If 31.00N 65.00 E
Riggins 46 Gd 45.25N 116.19W
Rigolet 42 Lf 54.10N 58.26W
Rig-Rig 35 Ac 14.16N 14.21 E
Rihand Sagar 25 Hd 24.05N 83.05 E
Riia Laht = Riga, Gulf of- (EN) 5 Id 57.30N 23.35 E
Riihimäki 7 Ff 60.45N 24.46 E
Riiser-Larsen-Halvøya 66 De 68.55S 34.00 E
Riito 48 Ba 32.10N 114.45W
Riječki zaljev = Rijeka, Gulf of- (EN) 14 Ie 45.15N 14.25 E
Rijeka 6 Hf 45.21N 14.24 E
Rijeka, Gulf of- (EN) = Riječki zaljev 14 Ie 45.15N 14.25 E
Rijksmuseum Kröller-Müller 12 Hb 52.06N 5.47 E
Rijn = Rhine (EN) 5 Ge 51.52N 6.02 E
Rijssen 12 Ib 52.18N 6.37 E
Rijswijk 12 Gb 52.03N 4.21 E
Rika 10 Th 48.08N 23.22 E
Rikā, Wādī ar- 33 He 22.25N 44.50 E
Rikubetsu 29a Cb 43.28N 143.43 E
Rikuzentakada 28 Pe 39.01N 141.38 E
Rila 15 Gh 42.08N 23.33 E
Rila 15 Gg 42.08N 23.08 E
Riley 46 Fe 43.32N 119.29W
Riley, Mount- 45 Ck 31.58N 107.05W
Rilski Manastir 15 Gg 42.08N 23.20 E
Rima 30 Hg 13.04N 5.10 E
Rimatara, Ile- 57 Lg 22.38S 152.51W
Rimava 10 Qh 48.15N 20.21 E
Rimavská Sobota 10 Qh 48.23N 20.01 E
Rimbo 7 Eg 59.45N 18.22 E
Rimé 35 Bc 14.02N 18.03 E
Rimforsa 8 Ff 58.08N 15.40 E
Rimini 14 Gf 44.04N 12.34 E
Rimito/Rymättylä 8 Jd 60.25N 21.55 E
Rîmnic 15 Kd 45.32N 27.31 E
Rîmnicu Sărat 15 Kd 45.23N 27.03 E
Rîmnicu Vîlcea 15 Hd 45.06N 24.22 E
Rimouski 39 Me 48.27N 68.32W
Rimšė/Rimše 8 Li 55.30N 26.33 E
Rimše/Rimšė 8 Li 55.30N 26.33 E
Rinbung 27 Ef 29.15N 89.52 E
Rincon 50 Bf 12.14N 68.20W
Rincón 51a Ab 18.21N 67.16W
Rincón, Bahía de- 51a Bc 17.57N 66.19W
Rincón del Bonete, Lago Artificial de- 56 Id 32.45S 56.00W
Rincón de Romos 48 Hf 22.14N 102.18W
Rindal 7 Be 63.03N 9.13 E
Ringe 8 Di 55.14N 10.29 E
Ringebu 8 Dc 61.31N 10.10 E
Ringerike 8 Dd 60.05N 10.15 E
Ringgold Isles 57 Jf 16.15S 179.25W
Ringim 34 Gc 12.09N 9.10 E
Ringkøbing [2] 8 Ch 56.10N 8.45 E
Ringkøbing 7 Bh 56.05N 8.15 E
Ringkøbing Fjord 7 Bi 56.00N 8.15 E
Ringlädes 15 Dj 39.25N 20.04 E
Ringsjön 8 Ei 55.50N 13.30 E
Ringsted 7 Ci 55.27N 11.49 E
Ringvassøy 7 Eb 69.55N 19.15 E
Rinia 15 Il 37.25N 25.13 E
Rinjani, Gunung- 26 Gh 8.24S 116.28 E
Rinn Chathóir/Cahore Point 9 Gi 52.34N 6.11W
Rinn Dúain/Hook Head 9 Gi 52.07N 6.55W
Rinteln 10 Fd 52.11N 9.05 E
Rinya 10 Nk 45.57N 17.27 E
Rio Azul 55 Gg 25.43S 50.47W
Riobamba 53 If 1.40S 78.38W
Rio Branco 53 Jf 9.58S 67.48W
Rio Branco 55 Fk 32.34S 53.25W
Rio Branco do Sul 55 Hg 25.10S 49.18W
Rio Brilhante 54 Hh 21.48S 54.33W
Rio Bueno 56 Ff 40.19S 72.58W
Rio Caribe 54 Fa 10.42N 63.07W
Rio Chico 50 Dg 10.19N 65.59W
Rio Claro [Braz.] 55 If 22.24S 47.33W
Rio Claro [Trin.] 50 Fg 10.18N 61.11W
Rio Colorado 56 He 39.01S 64.05W
Rio Cuarto 53 Ji 33.08S 64.20W
Rio de Janeiro 53 Lh 22.54S 43.15W
Rio de Janeiro [2] 54 Jh 22.30S 42.30W
Rio de Jesús 49 Gj 7.59N 81.10W
Rio de Oro 32 Ee 24.00N 14.00W
Rio de Oro 49 Ki 8.57N 73.23W
Rio de Oro, Bahia de- 32 De 23.45N 15.50W
Rio do Sul 56 Kc 27.13S 49.39W
Rio Fortuna 55 Hi 28.06S 49.07W
Rio Gallegos 53 Jk 51.37S 69.10W
Rio Grande 53 Ki 32.02S 52.05W
Rio Grande [Arg.] 56 Gh 53.47S 67.42W
Rio Grande [Nic.] 49 Dg 12.59N 86.34W
Rio Grande [P.R.] 51a Cb 18.23N 65.50W
Rio Grande City 45 Gm 26.23N 98.49W
Rio Grande de Añasco 51a Ab 18.17N 67.10W
Rio Grande de Manati 51a Bb 18.29N 66.32W
Rio Grande de Matagalpa 47 Hf 12.54N 83.32W
Rio Grande do Norte [2] 54 Ke 5.40S 36.00W
Rio Grande do Sul [2] 56 Jc 30.00S 54.00W
Rio Grande Rise (EN) 3 Cm 31.00S 35.00W
Riohacha 54 Da 11.32N 72.54W
Rio Hato 49 Gi 8.23N 80.10W
Rio Lagartos 48 Og 21.36N 88.10W
Rio Largo 54 Ke 9.29S 35.51W
Riom 11 Ji 45.54N 3.07 E
Rio Maior 13 De 39.20N 8.56W
Rio Mayo 56 Fg 45.41S 70.16W
Riom-ès-Montagnes 11 Ii 45.17N 2.40 E
Rio Miranda 54 Gg 19.25S 57.20W
Rio Mulatos 54 Eg 19.42S 66.47W
Rion 15 Ek 38.18N 21.47 E
Rio Negro [Chile] 56 Ff 40.47S 73.14W
Rio Negro [Arg.] [2] 56 Gf 40.00S 67.00W
Rio Negro [Braz.] 56 Kc 26.06S 49.48W
Rio Negro [Braz.] 55 Dd 19.33S 56.32W
Rio Negro [Ur.] [2] 55 Dk 32.45S 57.20W
Rio Negro, Pantanal do- 54 Gg 18.50S 56.00W
Rionero in Vulture 14 Jj 40.56N 15.40 E
Rioni 16 Lh 42.10N 41.38 E
Rio Novo 55 Dc 16.28S 56.30W
Rio Pardo 56 Jc 29.59S 52.22W
Rio Prêto, Serra do- 55 Gd 18.18S 50.42W
Rio San Juan [3] 49 Eh 11.10N 84.30W
Rio Segundo 56 Hd 31.40S 63.55W
Riosucio 54 Cb 7.27N 77.07W
Rio Tercero 56 Hd 32.11S 64.06W
Rio Tinto 54 Ke 6.48S 35.05W
Rioverde 47 Dd 21.56N 100.01W
Rio Verde 54 Hg 17.43S 50.56W
Rio Verde, Serra do- 55 Fc 17.32S 52.25W
Rio Verde de Mato Grosso 54 Hg 18.56S 54.52W
Rio Verde do Sul 55 Ef 22.54S 55.27W
Rioz 11 Mg 47.25N 6.04 E
Řip 10 Kf 50.24N 14.18 E
Ripanj 15 De 44.38N 20.32 E
Ripley [Eng.-U.K.] 12 Aa 53.02N 1.24W
Ripley [Tn.-U.S.] 44 Ch 35.44N 89.33W
Ripley [W.V.-U.S.] 44 Gf 38.49N 81.44W
Ripoll 13 Ob 42.12N 2.12 E
Ripon 9 Lg 54.08N 1.31W
Riposto 14 Jm 37.44N 15.12 E
Ripple Mountain 46 Gb 49.02N 117.05W
Risan 15 Bg 42.31N 18.42 E
Risaralda [2] 54 Cb 5.00N 75.45W
Risbäck 7 Dd 64.42N 15.32 E
Rīshah, Wādī- 24 Kj 25.33N 44.05 E
Rī Shahr 24 Nh 28.55N 50.50 E
Rishiri 28 Pb 45.11N 141.15 E
Rishiri-Suidō 29a Ba 45.10N 141.30 E
Rishiri-Tō 27 Pb 45.11N 141.15 E
Rishiri-Yama 29a Ba 45.11N 141.15 E
Rīshmūk 24 Ng 31.15N 50.20 E
Rishon Leẕiyyon 24 Fg 31.58N 34.48 E
Rising Star 45 Gj 32.06N 98.58W
Risle 11 Ge 49.26N 0.23 E
Risnjak 14 Ie 45.26N 14.37 E
Rîşnov 15 Id 45.35N 25.27 E
Risør 7 Bg 58.43N 9.14 E
Risoux, Mont- 11 Mh 46.36N 6.10 E
Risøyhamn 7 Db 69.00N 15.45 E
Riß 10 Fh 48.17N 9.49 E
Risti 7 Fg 59.03N 24.01 E
Ristiina 8 Lc 61.30N 27.16 E
Ristijarvi 7 Gd 64.30N 28.13 E
Ristna, Mys-/Ristna Neem 8 If 58.55N 21.55 E
Ristna Neem/Ristna, Mys- 8 If 58.55N 21.55 E
Rīsū 24 Qf 33.52N 57.28 E
Ritchie's Archipelago 25 If 12.14N 93.10 E
Ritidian Point 64c Ba 13.39N 144.51 E
Ritscher-Hochland 66 Bf 73.20S 9.30W
Ritter, Mount- 43 Dd 37.42N 119.20W
Ritterhude 12 Ka 53.11N 8.45 E
Rituerto 13 Jc 41.36N 2.22W
Ritzville 46 Fc 47.08N 118.23W
Riva-Bella, Ouistreham- 12 Be 49.17N 0.16W
Rivadavia [Arg.] 56 Hb 24.11S 62.53W
Rivadavia [Arg.] 56 Gd 33.11S 68.28W
Riva del Garda 14 Ee 45.53N 10.50 E
Rivas 39 Kh 11.26N 85.51W
Rivas [3] 49 Eh 11.25N 85.50W
Rive-de-Gier 11 Ki 45.22N 4.37 E
Rivellata, Punta di a- 11a Aa 42.35N 8.40 E
Rivera [2] 55 Ej 31.30S 55.15W
Rivera [Arg.] 56 He 37.12S 63.14W
Rivera [Ur.] 53 Ki 30.54S 55.31W
River Cess 34 Dd 5.27N 9.35W
Riverdale 45 Fc 47.30N 101.22W
Riverina 59 Jg 35.25S 145.30 E
River Inlet 42 Ef 51.41N 127.15W
Rivers [2] 34 Ge 4.50N 6.30 E
Rivers, Lake of the- 46 Mb 49.45N 105.45W
Riversdale [N.Z.] 62 Cf 45.54S 168.44 E
Riversdale [S.Afr.] 37 Cf 34.07S 21.15 E
Riverside 43 De 33.59N 117.22W
Riverton [N.Z.] 62 Bg 46.21S 168.00 E
Riverton [Wy.-U.S.] 43 Fc 43.02N 108.23W
Rivesaltes 11 Il 42.46N 2.52 E
Riviera Beach 44 Ge 26.47N 80.04W
Rivière-à-Pierre 44 Kb 46.58N 72.11W
Rivière-du-Loup 42 Kg 47.50N 69.32W
Rivière-Pilote 51h Bc 14.29N 60.54W
Rivière-Salée 51h Bb 14.32N 60.59W
Rivoli 14 Be 45.04N 7.31 E
Rivungo 36 Df 16.15S 22.00 E
Riwaka 62 Ed 41.05S 173.00 E
Riwoqê 27 Ge 31.13N 96.29 E
Rixensart 12 Gd 50.43N 4.35 E
Riyadh (EN) = Ar Riyāḑ 22 Gg 24.38N 46.43 E
Rize 23 Fa 41.02N 40.31 E
Rize, Gora- 18 Bf 37.48N 58.13 E
Rize Dağları 24 Ib 40.30N 40.50 E
Rizhao 27 Kd 35.27N 119.28 E
Rizokarpásso → Dipkarpas 24 Fe 35.36N 34.23 E
Rižski Zaliv = Riga, Gulf of- (EN) 5 Id 57.30N 23.35 E
Rizzuto, Capo- 14 Ll 38.53N 17.05 E
Rjabovo 8 Md 60.17N 29.01 E
Rjapina/Räpina 8 Lf 58.03N 27.35 E
Rjazan 6 Je 54.38N 39.44 E
Rjazanovski 7 Ji 55.08N 39.35 E
Rjazanskaja Oblast [3] 19 Ee 54.30N 40.40 E
Rjažsk 6 Ke 53.43N 40.04 E
Rjukan 7 Bg 59.52N 8.34 E
Rjuven 8 Be 59.13N 7.10 E
Rkiz 32 Df 16.50N 15.20W
Rldal 8 Be 59.49N 6.48 E
Roa [Nor.] 8 Dd 60.17N 10.37 E
Roa [Sp.] 13 Ic 41.42N 3.55W
Road Town 47 Le 18.27N 64.37W
Roag, Loch- 9 Gc 58.16N 6.50W
Roan Antelope 36 Ee 13.08S 28.24 E
Roannais 11 Kh 46.05N 4.10 E
Roanne 11 Kh 46.02N 4.04 E
Roanoke 38 Lf 35.56N 76.43W
Roanoke [Al.-U.S.] 44 Ei 33.09N 85.22W
Roanoke [Va.-U.S.] 39 Lf 37.16N 79.57W
Roanoke Rapids 44 Ig 36.28N 77.40W
Roan Plateau 46 Kg 39.35N 108.55W
Roaringwater Bay 9 Dj 51.25N 9.30W
Roatán 49 De 16.18N 86.35W
Roatán, Isla de- 49 De 16.23N 86.30W
Robāţ [Iran] 24 Qd 37.55N 57.42 E
Robāţ [Iran] 24 Pg 30.04N 54.49 E
Robāţ-e-Khān 23 Ic 33.21N 56.02 E
Robāţ-e-Kord 24 Qf 33.45N 56.37 E
Robāţ Karīm 24 Ne 35.28N 51.05 E
Robbie Bank (EN) 61 Fb 11.03S 176.53W
Robe, Mount- 59 If 31.40S 141.20 E
Röbel 10 Ic 53.23N 12.36 E
Robert Lee 45 Fk 31.54N 100.29W
Roberts 55 Bl 35.09S 61.57W
Roberts, Mount- 59 Ke 28.13S 152.28 E
Roberts Creek Mountain 46 Gg 39.52N 116.18W
Robertsfors 7 Ed 64.11N 20.51 E
Robert S. Kerr Lake 45 Ii 35.25N 95.00W
Robertson 37 Bf 33.46S 19.50 E
Robertson Bay 66 Kf 71.25S 170.00 E
Robertson Range 59 Ed 23.10S 121.00 E
Robertsport 34 Cd 6.45N 11.22W
Roberval 42 Kg 48.31N 72.13W
Robi 35 Fd 7.38N 39.52 E
Robinson Crusoe (EN) = Robinson Crusoe, Isla- 52 Ii 33.38S 78.52W
Robinson Crusoe, Isla- = Robinson Crusoe (EN) 52 Ii 33.38S 78.52W
Robinson Range 59 De 25.45S 119.00 E
Robinson River 59 Hc 16.03S 137.16 E
Roboré 53 Kg 18.20S 59.45W
Rob Roy 63a Cb 7.23S 157.36 E
Robson, Mount- 38 Hd 53.07N 119.09W
Robstown 45 Hm 27.27N 97.40W
Roby 45 Fj 32.45N 100.23W
Roca, Cabo da- 5 Fh 38.47N 9.30W
Rocamadour 11 Hj 44.48N 1.38 E
Roca Partida, Isla- 47 Be 19.01N 112.02W
Roca Partida, Punta- 48 Lh 18.42N 95.10W
Rocas, Atol das- 52 Mf 3.52S 33.49W
Roccaraso 14 Ii 41.51N 14.05 E
Ročegda 19 Ec 62.42N 43.23 E
Rocha [2] 55 Fk 34.00S 54.00W
Rocha 56 Jd 34.29S 54.20W
Rochdale 9 Kh 53.38N 2.09W
Rochechouart 11 Gi 45.49N 0.49 E
Rochedo 55 Ed 19.57S 54.52W
Rochefort [Bel.] 11 Ld 50.10N 5.13 E
Rochefort [Fr.] 11 Fi 45.56N 0.59W
Rochefort-Han-sur-Lesse 12 Hd 50.08N 5.11 E
Rochelle 45 Lf 41.56N 89.04W
Rocher River 42 Gd 61.23N 112.45W
Roche's Bluff 51c c 16.42N 62.09W
Rochester [Eng.-U.K.] 9 Nj 51.24N 0.30 E
Rochester [In.-U.S.] 44 De 41.04N 86.13W
Rochester [Mn.-U.S.] 43 Ic 44.02N 92.29W
Rochester [N.H.-U.S.] 44 Ld 43.18N 70.59W
Rochester [N.Y.-U.S.] 39 Le 43.10N 77.36W
Rochlitzer Berg 10 Ie 51.05N 12.48 E
Rocigalgo 13 He 39.35N 4.35W
Rockall 5 Ed 57.35N 13.48W
Rockall Rise (EN) 5 Ed 57.00N 14.00W
Rock Creek Butte 46 Fd 44.49N 118.07W
Rockefeller Plateau 66 Ng 80.00S 135.00W
Rockenhausen 12 Je 49.38N 7.50 E
Rockford 43 Jc 42.17N 89.06W
Rockglen 46 Mb 49.10N 105.57W
Rockhampton 58 Gg 23.23S 150.31 E
Rock Hill 43 Ke 34.55N 81.01W
Rockingham [Austl.] 59 Df 32.17S 115.44 E
Rockingham [N.C.-U.S.] 44 Hh 34.56N 79.46W
Rock Island 43 Ic 41.30N 90.34W
Rockland 43 Nc 44.06N 69.06W
Rocklands Reservoir 59 Ig 37.15S 142.00 E
Rockledge 44 Gk 28.20N 80.43W
Rockneby 8 Gh 56.49N 16.20 E
Rockport 45 Hl 28.01N 97.04W
Rock River 45 Kf 41.29N 90.37W
Rock Sound 44 Im 24.53N 76.09W
Rock Spring 43 Fc 41.35N 109.13W
Rocksprings 45 Fk 30.01N 100.13W
Rockville [In.-U.S.] 44 Df 39.45N 87.15W
Rockville [Md.-U.S.] 44 If 39.05N 77.09W
Rockwood 44 Eh 35.52N 84.41W
Rocky Ford 45 Eg 38.03N 103.43W
Rocky Island Lake 44 Fb 46.56N 83.04W
Rocky Mount 43 Ld 35.56N 77.48W
Rocky Mountain 43 Eb 47.49N 112.49W
Rocky Mountain House 42 Gf 52.22N 114.55W
Rocky Mountains 38 He 48.00N 116.00W
Rocky Point [Blz.] 49 Cd 18.22N 88.06W
Rocky Point [Nam.] 37 Ac 19.01S 12.29 E
Rocroi 12 Ge 49.55N 4.31 E
Rodach 10 Gf 50.08N 10.52 E
Rodalben 12 Je 49.14N 7.38 E
Roda Velha, Rio- 55 Ja 12.27S 45.33W
Rødberg 8 Cd 60.16N 8.58 E
Rødby 8 Dj 54.42N 11.24 E
Rødby Havn, Rødby- 7 Ci 54.39N 11.21 E
Rødby-Rødby Havn 7 Ci 54.39N 11.21 E
Roddickton 42 Lf 50.51N 56.07W
Rødding 8 Ci 55.22N 9.04 E

Index Symbols

[1] Independent Nation
[2] State, Region
[3] District, County
[4] Municipality
[5] Colony, Dependency
Continent
Physical Region
Historical or Cultural Region
Mount, Mountain
Volcano
Hill
Mountains, Mountain Range
Hills, Escarpment
Plateau, Upland
Pass, Gap
Plain, Lowland
Delta
Salt Flat
Valley, Canyon
Crater, Cave
Karst Features
Depression
Polder
Desert, Dunes
Forest, Woods
Heath, Steppe
Oasis
Cape, Point
Coast, Beach
Cliff
Peninsula
Isthmus
Sandbank
Island
Atoll
Rock, Reef
Islands, Archipelago
Rocks, Reefs
Coral Reef
Well, Spring
Geyser
River, Stream
Waterfall Rapids
River Mouth, Estuary
Lake
Salt Lake
Intermittent Lake
Reservoir
Swamp, Pond
Canal
Glacier
Ice Shelf, Pack Ice
Ocean
Sea
Gulf, Bay
Strait, Fjord
Lagoon
Bank
Seamount
Tablemount
Ridge
Shelf
Basin
Escarpment, Sea Scarp
Fracture
Trench, Abyss
National Park, Reserve
Point of Interest
Recreation Site
Cave, Cavern
Historic Site
Ruins
Wall, Walls
Church, Abbey
Temple
Scientific Station
Airport
Port
Lighthouse
Mine
Tunnel
Dam, Bridge

Rödeby 8 Fh 56.15N 15.36 E
Rodeio Bonito 55 Fh 27.28S 53.10W
Roden 12 Ia 53.09N 6.26 E
Rodeo [Arg.] 56 Gd 30.12S 69.06W
Rodeo [Mex.] 48 Ge 25.11N 104.34W
Rodeo [N.M.-U.S.] 45 Bk 31.50N 109.02W
Röder 10 Je 51.30N 13.25 E
Rodez 11 Ij 44.20N 2.34 E
Rodgau 12 Kd 50.01N 8.53 E
Rodholívos 15 Gi 40.56N 23.59 E
Ródhos = Rhodes (EN) 6 Ih 36.26N 28.13 E
Ródhos = Rhodes (EN) 5 Ih 36.10N 28.00 E
Rodi Garganico 14 Ji 41.55N 15.53 E
Roding 9 Nj 51.31N 0.06 E
Rodna 15 Hb 47.25N 24.49 E
Rodnei, Munţii- 15 Hb 47.35N 24.40 E
Rodney, Cape- 40 Fd 64.39N 166.24W
Rodniki 7 Jh 57.07N 41.48 E
Rodonit, Gjiri i- 15 Ch 41.35N 19.30 E
Rodonit, Kep i- 15 Ch 41.35N 19.27 E
Rodopi=Rhodope
Mountains (EN) 5 Ig 41.30N 24.30 E
Rodrigues Island 30 Nj 19.42S 63.25 E
Roebourne 59 Dd 20.47S 117.09 E
Roebuck Bay 59 Ec 18.04S 122.15 E
Roer 10 Be 51.12N 5.59 E
Roermond 11 Lc 51.12N 6.00 E
Roeselare/Roulers 11 Jd 50.57N 3.08 E
Roes Welcome Sound 42 Id 64.30N 86.45W
Roetgen 12 Id 50.39N 6.12 E
Rogačev 16 Gc 53.09N 30.06 E
Rogačevka 16 Kd 51.31N 39.34 E
Rogagua, Laguna- 54 Ef 13.45S 66.55W
Rogaguado, Laguna- 54 Ef 12.55S 65.45W
Rogaland [2] 7 Bg 59.00N 6.15 E
Rogaška Slatina 14 Jd 46.15N 15.38 E
Rogatica 14 Ng 43.48N 19.01 E
Rogatin 10 Ug 49.19N 24.40 E
Rogers 45 Ih 36.20N 94.07W
Rogers, Mount- 44 Gg 36.39N 81.33W
Rogers City 44 Fc 45.25N 83.49W
Rogers Lake 46 Gi 34.52N 117.51W
Rogers Peak 46 Jg 38.04N 111.32W
Rogersville 44 Fg 36.25N 82.59W
Roggan 42 Jf 54.24N 79.30W
Roggeveldberge 37 Bf 31.50S 19.50 E
Roggewein, Cabo- 65d Bb 27.07S 109.15W
Rognan 7 Dc 67.06N 15.23 E
Rogozhina 15 Ch 41.05N 19.40 E
Rogozna 15 Df 43.04N 20.40 E
Rogoźno 10 Md 52.46N 17.00 E
Rogue River 46 Ce 42.26N 124.25W
Rohan, Plateau de- 11 Df 48.10N 3.00W
Rohl 35 Dd 7.05N 29.46 E
Rohrbach in Oberösterreich 14 Hb 48.34N 13.59 E
Rohrbach-lès-Bitche 12 Je 49.03N 7.16 E
Rohri 25 Dc 27.41N 68.54 E
Rohtak 25 Fc 28.54N 76.34 E
Roi, Le Bois du- 11 Kh 46.59N 4.02 E
Roi Et 25 Ke 16.05N 103.42 E
Roi Georges, Iles du- 57 Mf 14.32S 145.08W
Roine 8 Kc 61.25N 24.05 E
Roisel 12 Fe 49.57N 3.06 E
Roja 7 Fh 57.30N 22.51 E
Rojas 56 Hd 34.12S 60.44W
Rojo, Cabo- [Mex.] 47 Ed 21.33N 97.20W
Rojo, Cabo- [P.R.] 49 Nd 18.01N 67.15W
Rokan 26 Df 2.00N 100.52 E
Rokiškis 7 Fi 55.59N 25.37 E
Rokitnoje 16 Ed 51.21N 27.14 E
Rokkasho 29a Bc 40.58N 141.21 E
Rokycany 10 Jg 49.45N 13.36 E
Rokytná 10 Mg 49.05N 16.21 E
Rola Co 27 Ed 35.25N 88.25 E
Rolândia 55 Gf 23.18S 51.22W
Rolla [Mo.-U.S.] 43 Id 37.57N 91.46W
Rolla [N.D.-U.S.] 45 Gb 48.52N 99.37W
Rolleston 62 Ee 43.35S 172.23 E
Rolvsøya 7 Fa 71.00N 24.00 E
Roma [Austl.] 58 Fg 26.35S 148.47 E
Roma [It.] = Rome (EN) 6 Hg 41.54N 12.29 E
Roma [Swe.] 7 Eh 57.32N 18.26 E
Romagna 14 Gf 44.30N 12.15 E
Romaine 42 Lf 50.18N 63.48W
Roman 15 Jc 46.55N 26.55 E
Romanche 11 Li 45.05N 5.43 E
Romanche Gap (EN) 3 Dj 0.10S 18.15W
Romang 55 Ci 29.30S 59.46W
Romang, Pulau- 26 Ih 7.35S 127.26 E
România=Romania (EN) [1] 6 If 46.00N 25.30 E
Romania (EN)=România [1] 6 If 46.00N 25.30 E
Romanija 14 Mg 43.51N 18.43 E
Roman Koš, Gora- 19 Dg 44.36N 34.16 E
Romano, Cayo- 49 Ib 22.04N 77.50W
Romanovka 20 Gf 53.14N 112.46 E
Romans-sur-Isère 11 Li 45.03N 5.03 E
Romanzof, Cape- 38 Cc 61.49N 166.09W
Romanzof Mountains 40 Kc 69.00N 144.00W
Rombas 12 Ie 49.15N 6.05 E
Romblon 26 Hd 12.35N 122.15 E
Rome [Ga.-U.S.] 43 Je 34.16N 85.11W
Rome [N.Y.-U.S.] 43 Lc 43.13N 75.28W
Rome [Or.-U.S.] 46 Ge 42.50N 117.37W
Rome (EN) = Roma [It.] 6 Hg 41.54N 12.29 E
Romeleåsen 8 Ei 55.34N 13.33 E
Romerike 8 Dd 60.05N 11.10 E
Romilly-sur-Seine 11 Jf 48.31N 3.43 E
Rommani 32 Fc 33.32N 6.36W
Romme 8 Fd 60.26N 15.30 E
Rommerskirchen 12 Ic 51.02N 6.41 E
Romney Marsh 12 Cc 51.02N 0.55 E
Romny 19 De 50.45N 33.29 E
Rømø 7 Bi 55.10N 8.30 E
Romodanovo 7 Ki 54.28N 45.18 E
Romont 14 Ad 46.42N 6.55 E
Romorantin-Lanthenay 11 Hg 47.22N 1.45 E
Romsdal 8 Bb 62.35N 7.50 E
Romsdalen 8 Bb 62.30N 7.55 E
Romsdalsfjorden 8 Bb 62.40N 7.15 E
Romsdalshorn 8 Bb 62.29N 7.50 E
Romsey 9 Lk 50.59N 1.30W
Ronas Hill 9 La 60.30N 1.20W
Ronave 64e Ba 0.29S 166.56 E
Roncador, Cayos de- 47 Hf 13.32N 80.03W
Roncador, Serra do- 52 Kg 13.00S 51.50W
Roncador Reef 57 Ge 6.13S 159.22 E
Roncesvalles 13 Ka 43.01N 1.19W
Roncesvalles o Ibañeta,
Puerto de- 13 Ka 43.01N 1.19W
Ronciglione 14 Gh 42.17N 12.13 E
Ronco 14 Gf 44.24N 12.12 E
Ronda 13 Gh 36.44N 5.10W
Ronda, Serrania de- 13 Gh 36.45N 5.05W
Ronda do Sul 55 Cb 15.57S 59.42W
Rondane 7 Bf 61.55N 9.45 E
Rønde 7 Ch 56.18N 10.29 E
Ronde, Point- 51g Ba 15.33N 61.29W
Ronde Island 50 Ff 12.18N 61.31W
Rondeslottet 8 Cc 61.55N 9.46 E
Rondon 55 Ff 23.23S 52.48W
Rondón, Pico- 54 Fc 1.36N 63.08W
Rondônia 53 Jg 10.52S 61.57W
Rondônia, Território de- [2] 54 Ff 11.00S 63.00W
Rondonópolis 53 Kg 16.28S 54.38W
Rong'an (Chang'an) 27 If 25.16N 109.23 E
Rongcheng 28 Ce 39.03N 115.52 E
Rongcheng (Yatou) 28 Gf 37.10N 122.25 E
Rongelap Atoll 57 Hc 11.09N 166.50 E
Rongerik Atoll 57 Hc 11.21N 167.26 E
Rongjiang (Guzhou) 27 If 25.58N 108.30 E
Rongxian 27 Jg 22.48N 110.30 E
Rongzhag/Danba 27 He 30.48N 101.54 E
Rønne 7 Di 55.06N 14.42 E
Ronne Bay 66 Qf 72.30S 74.00W
Ronneby 7 Dh 56.12N 15.18 E
Ronnebyån 8 Fh 56.10N 15.18 E
Ronne Ice Shelf 66 Qf 78.30S 61.00W
Ronse/Renaix 11 Jd 50.45N 3.36 E
Ronuro, Rio- 52 Kg 11.56S 53.33W
Roodepoort 37 De 26.11S 27.54 E
Roof Butte 43 Fd 36.28N 109.05W
Rooiboklaagte 37 Cd 20.20S 21.15 E
Roon, Pulau- 26 Jg 2.23S 134.33 E
Rooniu, Mont- 65e c 17.49S 149.12W
Roorkee 25 Fc 29.52N 77.53 E
Roosendaal 11 Kc 51.32N 4.28 E
Roosevelt [Az.-U.S.] 46 Jj 33.40N 111.09W
Roosevelt [Ut.-U.S.] 46 Kf 40.18N 109.59W
Roosevelt, Mount - 42 Ee 58.23N 125.04W
Roosevelt, Rio- 52 Jf 7.35S 60.20W
Roosevelt Island 66 Lf 79.30S 162.00W
Root Portage 45 Ka 50.53N 91.18W
Ropa 10 Rg 49.46N 21.29 E
Ropar 25 Fb 30.58N 76.20 E
Ropaži 8 Kh 56.58N 24.26 E
Ropczyce 10 Rf 50.03N 21.37 E
Rope, The- 64q Ab 25.04S 130.05W
Roper River 57 Ef 14.43S 135.27 E
Roquefort 11 Fj 44.02N 0.19W
Roque Pérez 55 Cl 35.25S 59.20W
Roquetas de Mar 13 Jh 36.46N 2.36W
Roraima, Monte- 52 Je 5.12N 60.44W
Roraima, Território de- [2] 54 Fc 1.30N 61.00W
Røros 7 Ce 62.35N 11.24 E
Rorschach 14 Dc 47.30N 9.30 E
Rørvik 7 Cd 64.51N 11.14 E
Ros 16 Ge 49.39N 31.35 E
Rosa, Cap- 14 Cn 36.57N 8.14 E
Rosa, Lake- 49 Kc 20.55N 73.20W
Rosa, Monte- 5 Gf 45.55N 7.53 E
Rošal 7 Ji 55.41N 39.55 E
Rosala 8 Je 59.50N 22.25 E
Rosalia 46 Gc 47.14N 117.22W
Rosalia, Punta- 65d Bb 27.03S 109.19W
Rosalie 51g Bb 15.22N 61.16W
Rosalind Bank (EN) 49 Ge 16.30N 80.30W
Rosamond Lake 46 Fi 34.50N 118.04W
Rosamorada 48 Gf 22.08N 105.12W
Rosana 55 Ff 22.36S 53.01W
Rosario [Arg.] 53 Ji 32.57S 60.40W
Rosario [Braz.] 54 Jd 2.57S 44.14W
Rosario [Mex.] 48 Dd 26.27N 111.38W
Rosario [Mex.] 47 Cd 23.00N 105.52W
Rosario [Par.] 56 Ib 24.27S 57.03W
Rosario [Ven.] 49 Kh 10.19N 72.19W
Rosario, Arroyo- 48 Bb 30.03N 115.45W
Rosario, Bahia- 48 Bc 29.50N 115.45W
Rosario, Cayo del- 49 Gc 21.38N 81.53W
Rosario, Islas de- 49 Jh 10.10N 75.46W
Rosario, Sierra del- 48 He 25.35N 103.50W
Rosario de Arriba 47 Ab 30.01N 115.40W
Rosario de la Frontera 56 Hc 25.48S 64.58W
Rosario de Lerma 56 Gb 24.59S 65.35W
Rosario del Tala 55 Ck 32.18S 59.09W
Rosário do Sul 56 Jd 30.15S 54.55W
Rosário Oeste 54 Gf 14.50S 56.25W
Rosarito 48 Bc 28.38N 114.04W
Rosarno 14 Jl 38.29N 15.58 E
Rosas/Roses 13 Pb 42.16N 3.11 E
Rosas, Golfo de-/Roses,
Golf de- 13 Pb 42.10N 3.15 E
Rosa Seamount (EN) 47 Bc 26.12N 114.58W
Rosa Zarate 54 Cc 0.18N 79.27W
Roščino 8 Md 60.13N 29.43 E
Roscoe Glacier 66 Ge 66.30S 95.20 E
Ros Comáin/Roscommon [2] 9 Eh 53.40N 8.30W
Ros Comáin/Roscommon 9 Eh 53.38N 8.11W
Roscommon 44 Ec 44.30N 84.35W
Roscommon/Ros Comáin 9 Eh 53.38N 8.11W
Roscommon/Ros Comáin [2] 9 Eh 53.40N 8.30W
Ros Cré/Roscrea 9 Fi 52.57N 7.47W
Roscrea/Ros Cré 9 Fi 52.57N 7.47W
Rose, Pointe de la- 51h Bb 14.33N 61.03W
Roseau [Dom.] 39 Mh 15.18N 61.24W
Roseau [Dom.] 51g Bb 15.18N 61.24W
Roseau [Mn.-U.S.] 45 Ib 48.51N 95.46W
Roseau [St.Luc.] 51k Ab 13.58N 61.02W
Roseau River 45 Hb 49.08N 97.14W
Rosebery 59 Jh 41.46S 145.32 E
Rosebud 46 Lc 46.16N 106.27W
Rosebud Creek 46 Lc 46.16N 106.28W
Rosebud River 46 Ia 51.25N 112.37W
Roseburg 43 Cc 43.13N 123.20W
Rosemary Bank (EN) 9 Cb 59.15N 10.10W
Rosenberg 43 Hf 29.33N 95.48W
Rosendahl 12 Jb 52.01N 7.12 E
Rosendahl-Osterwick 12 Jb 52.01N 7.12 E
Rosendal 7 Bf 59.59N 6.01 E
Rosenheim 10 Ii 47.51N 12.08 E
Rosental 14 Id 46.33N 14.15 E
Roses/Rosas 13 Pb 42.16N 3.11 E
Roses, Golf de-/Rosas,
Golfo de- 13 Pb 42.10N 3.15 E
Roseţi 15 Ke 44.13N 27.26 E
Roseto degli Abruzzi 14 Ih 42.41N 14.01 E
Rosetown 42 Gf 51.33N 108.00W
Rosetta (EN)=Rashīd 33 Fc 31.24N 30.25 E
Roseville 46 Eg 38.45N 121.17W
Roshage 7 Bh 57.07N 8.38 E
Rosica 15 If 43.15N 25.42 E
Rosières-en-Santerre 12 Ee 49.49N 2.43 E
Rosignano Solvay 14 Eg 43.23N 10.26 E
Rosignol 54 Gb 6.17N 57.32W
Roşiori de Vede 15 He 44.07N 24.59 E
Roskilde [2] 8 Ei 55.35N 12.10 E
Roskilde 7 Ci 55.39N 12.05 E
Roslagen 8 He 59.30N 18.40 E
Ros Láir/Rosslare 9 Gi 52.17N 6.23W
Roslavl 19 De 53.58N 32.53 E
Roslyn 46 Ec 47.13N 120.59W
Ros Mhic Thriúin/New Ross 9 Gi 52.24N 6.56W
Røsnæs 8 Di 55.45N 10.55 E
Rosny-sur-Seine 12 Df 49.00N 1.38 E
Rösrath 12 Jd 50.54N 7.12 E
Ross 42 Ed 62.00N 132.25W
Ross [Austl.] 59 Jh 42.02S 147.29 E
Ross [Bye.-U.S.S.R.] 10 Uc 53.16N 24.29 E
Ross [N.Z.] 62 De 42.54S 170.49 E
Ross, Cape- 26 Gd 10.56N 119.13 E
Ross, Mount- 30 Nm 49.25S 69.08 E
Rossano 14 Kk 39.34N 16.38 E
Rossan Point/Ceann Ros
Eoghain 9 Eg 54.42N 8.48W
Ross Barnett Reservoir 45 Lj 32.30N 90.00W
Rosseau Lake 44 Hc 45.10N 79.35W
Rossel Island 57 Gf 11.26S 154.07 E
Rossell, Cap- 63b Ce 20.23S 166.36 E
Ross Ice Shelf 66 Lg 81.30S 175.00W
Rossijskaja Sovetskaja
Federativnaja
Socialističeskaja
Respublika (RSFSR) [2] 19 Jc 60.00N 100.00 E
Ross Island 66 Kf 77.30S 168.00 E
Ross Lake 46 Eb 48.53N 121.04W
Rossland 46 Gb 49.05N 117.48W
Rosslare/Ros Láir 9 Gi 52.17N 6.23W
Roßlau 10 Ie 51.53N 12.15 E
Rosso 31 Fg 16.31N 15.49W
Ross-on-Wye 9 Kj 51.55N 2.35W
Rossony 8 Mi 55.53N 28.49 E
Rossoš 19 De 50.11N 39.39 E
Ross River 42 Ed 61.59N 132.27W
Ross Sea (EN) 66 Lf 76.00S 175.00W
Røssvatn 7 Cd 65.45N 14.00 E
Røst 7 Cc 67.31N 12.07 E
Rosta 7 Eb 69.02N 18.40 E
Rostamī 24 Nh 28.52N 51.02 E
Rostan Kalā 24 Od 36.42N 53.27 E
Rösterkopf 12 Ie 49.40N 6.50 E
Rosthern 42 Gf 52.40N 106.20W
Rostock 6 He 54.05N 12.08 E
Rostock-Warnemünde 10 Ib 54.10N 12.05 E
Rostov 19 Dd 57.13N 39.25 E
Rostov-na-Donu 6 Jf 47.14N 39.42 E
Rostovskaja Oblast [3] 19 Ef 47.45N 41.15 E
Roswell [Ga.-U.S.] 44 Eh 34.03N 84.22W
Roswell [N.M.-U.S.] 39 If 33.24N 104.32W
Rot 8 Fc 61.15N 14.02 E
Rota 13 Fh 36.37N 6.21W
Rota Island 57 Fc 14.10N 145.12 E
Rotenburg (Wümme) 10 Fc 53.07N 9.24 E
Rotenburg an der Fulda 10 Ff 50.59N 9.43 E
Roter Main 10 Hf 50.03N 11.27 E
Roth 10 Hg 49.15N 11.06 E
Rothaargebirge 10 Ee 51.05N 8.15 E
Rothenburg ob der Tauber 10 Gg 49.23N 10.11 E
Rother [Eng.-U.K.] 9 Nk 50.57N 0.45 E
Rother [Eng.-U.K.] 12 Bd 50.57N 0.22W
Rothera 66 Qe 67.46S 68.54W
Rotherham 9 Lh 53.26N 1.20W
Rothesay 9 Hf 55.51N 5.03W
Rothorn 14 Cd 46.47N 8.03 E
Rothschild Island 66 Qe 69.25S 72.30W
Rothwell 12 Bb 52.25N 0.48W
Roti, Pulau- 21 Ok 10.45S 123.10 E
Roti, Selat- 26 Hi 10.25S 123.25 E
Rotja, Punta- 13 Nf 38.38N 1.34 E
Rotnes 8 Dd 60.04N 10.53 E
Roto 59 Jf 33.03S 145.29 E
Rotoiti, Lake- 62 Ed 41.50S 172.50 E
Rotondella 14 Kj 40.10N 16.31 E
Rotondo, Monte- 11a Ba 42.13N 9.03 E
Rotoroa, Lake- 62 Ed 41.50S 172.40 E
Rotorua 61 Eg 38.09S 176.15 E
Rotorua, Lake- 62 Gc 38.05S 176.15 E
Rotselaar 12 Gd 50.57N 4.43 E
Rott 10 Jh 48.25N 13.20 E
Rottenburg am Neckar 10 Eh 48.28N 8.56 E
Rotterdam 6 Ge 51.55N 4.28 E
Rottnaälven 8 Ed 59.48N 13.07 E
Rottnen 8 Fh 56.45N 15.05 E
Rottneros 8 Ee 59.48N 13.07 E
Rottnest Island 59 Df 32.00S 115.30 E
Rottumerplaat 11 Ma 53.35N 6.30 E
Rottweil 10 Eh 48.10N 8.37 E
Rotuma Island 57 If 12.30S 177.05 E
Roubaix 11 Jd 50.42N 3.10 E
Roubion 11 Kj 44.31N 4.42 E
Roudnice nad Labem 10 Kf 50.26N 14.16 E
Rouen 6 Gf 49.26N 1.05 E
Rouergue 11 Ij 44.30N 2.56 E
Rouge, Rivière- 44 Jc 45.38N 74.42W
Rouillac 11 Fi 45.47N 0.04W
Roulers/Roeselare 11 Jd 50.57N 3.08 E
Roumois 12 Ce 49.30N 0.30 E
Roundup 43 Fb 46.27N 108.33W
Rousay 9 Jb 59.01N 3.02W
Roussillon 11 Ki 45.22N 4.49 E
Roussillon 11 Il 42.30N 2.30 E
Roussin, Cap- 63b Ce 21.21S 167.59 E
Routot 12 Ce 49.23N 0.44 E
Rouyn-Noranda 39 Le 48.14N 79.01W
Rovaniemi 6 Ib 66.30N 25.43 E
Rovenskaja Oblast [3] 19 Ce 51.00N 26.30 E
Rovereto 14 Fe 45.53N 11.02 E
Rovigo 14 Fe 45.04N 11.47 E
Rovinari 15 Ge 44.55N 23.11 E
Rovinj 14 He 45.05N 13.38 E
Rovkulskoje, Ozero- 7 Hd 64.00N 31.00 E
Rovno 6 Ie 50.37N 26.15 E
Rovnoje 16 Od 50.47N 46.05 E
Rovuma=Ruvuma (EN) 30 Lj 10.29S 40.28 E
Rowa, Iles- 63b Ca 13.37S 167.32 E
Rowley 42 Jc 69.05N 78.55W
Rowley Shoals 57 Cf 17.30S 119.00 E
Roxas [Phil.] 26 Gd 10.28N 119.30 E
Roxas [Phil.] 26 Hd 11.35N 122.45 E
Roxboro 44 Hg 36.24N 78.59W
Roxburgh 62 Cf 45.33S 169.19 E
Roxen 8 Ff 58.30N 15.40 E
Roxo, Cap- 30 Fg 12.20N 16.43W
Roy [N.M.-U.S.] 45 Di 35.57N 104.12W
Roy [Ut.-U.S.] 46 If 41.10N 112.02W
Roya 11 Nk 43.48N 7.35 E
Royal Canal 9 Gh 53.21N 6.15W
Royale, Isle- 43 Jb 48.00N 89.00W
Royal Leamington Spa 9 Li 52.18N 1.31W
Royal Society Range 66 Jf 78.10S 162.36 E
Royal Tunbridge Wells 9 Nj 51.08N 0.16 E
Royan 11 Ei 45.38N 1.02W
Royat 11 Ji 45.46N 3.03 E
Royaumont, Abbaye de- 12 Ee 49.17N 2.28 E
Roye 11 Ie 49.42N 2.48 E
Roy Hill 59 Dd 22.38S 119.57 E
Røyken 8 De 59.45N 10.23 E
Royston 9 Mi 52.03N 0.01W
Rožaj 15 Dg 42.51N 20.10 E
Różan 10 Rd 52.53N 21.25 E
Rozdol 10 Ug 49.24N 24.08 E
Rozewie, Przylądek- 10 Ob 54.51N 18.21 E
Rožišče 16 Dd 50.54N 25.19 E
Rožňava 10 Qh 48.40N 20.32 E
Rožniatov 10 Uh 48.51N 24.14 E
Roznov 15 Jc 46.50N 26.31 E
Rožnov pod Radhoštěm 10 Og 49.28N 18.09 E
Rožnów 10 Qg 49.46N 20.42 E
Rożnowskie, Jezioro- 10 Qg 49.48N 20.45 E
Rozoy-sur-Serre 12 Ge 49.43N 4.08 E
Roztocze 5 Ie 50.30N 23.20 E
Rrësheni 15 Ch 41.47N 19.54 E
RSFSR=Russian SFSR (EN)
[2] 19 Jc 60.00N 100.00 E
RSFSR→ Rossijskaja
Sovetskaja Federativnaja
Socialističeskaja
Respublika [2] 19 Jc 60.00N 100.00 E
Rtanj 15 Ef 43.47N 21.54 E
Rtiščevo 19 Ee 52.16N 43.52 E
Ruacana, Quedas- 30 Jj 17.23S 14.15 E
Ruahine Range 62 Gc 39.50S 176.05 E
Ruapehu 57 Ih 39.17S 175.34 E
Ruapuke Island 61 Ci 46.45S 168.30 E
Rua Sura 63a Ec 9.30S 160.36 E
Ruatahuna 62 Gc 38.38S 176.58 E
Rubbestadneset 8 Ae 59.49N 5.17 E
Rubcovsk 22 Kd 51.33N 81.10 E
Rubeho Mountains 36 Gd 6.55S 36.30 E
Rubeshibe 28 Qc 43.47N 143.38 E
Rubežnoje 16 Ke 48.59N 38.26 E
Rubi 36 Db 2.48N 23.54 E
Rubiataba 55 Hb 15.08S 49.48W
Rubiku 15 Ch 41.46N 19.45 E
Rubio 54 Db 7.43N 72.22W
Rubio 13 Ic 41.26N 3.47W
Ruby 40 Hd 64.44N 155.30W
Ruby Lake 46 Hf 40.15N 115.30W
Ruby Mountains 46 Hf 40.25N 115.35W
Ruby Range 46 Id 45.15N 112.15W
Rucăr 15 Id 45.24N 25.10 E
Rucava 8 Ih 56.10N 21.00 E
Ruciane Nida 10 Rc 53.39N 21.35 E
Ruda 10 Of 50.10N 18.18 E
Rudabánya 10 Qh 48.23N 20.38 E
Rūdak 24 Nh 35.51N 51.33 E
Rūdān 24 Qi 27.17N 57.13 E
Ruda Śląska 10 Of 50.18N 18.51 E
Rūdbār [Afg.] 23 Jc 30.09N 62.36 E
Rūdbār [Iran] 24 Md 36.48N 49.24 E
Rüdersdorf bei Berlin 10 Jd 52.27N 13.47 E
Rudesheim am Rhein 12 Je 49.59N 7.55 E
Rudiškes/Rūdiškės 8 Kj 54.30N 24.58 E
Rūdiškės/Rudiškes 8 Kj 54.30N 24.58 E
Rudki 10 Tg 49.34N 23.30 E
Rudkøbing 7 Ci 54.56N 10.43 E
Rudnaja-Pristan 20 Ih 44.25N 135.49 E
Rudničny 7 Mg 59.38N 52.29 E
Rudnik 15 De 44.08N 20.30 E
Rudnik [Bul.] 15 Kg 42.57N 27.46 E
Rudnik [Pol.] 10 Sf 50.28N 22.15 E
Rudnik [Yugo.] 15 De 44.08N 20.31 E
Rudnja [R.S.F.S.R.] 16 Nd 50.49N 44.36 E
Rudnja [R.S.F.S.R.] 19 De 54.57N 31.07 E
Rudno 10 Tg 49.44N 23.57 E
Rudny [Kaz.-U.S.S.R.] 19 Ge 52.57N 63.07 E
Rudny [R.S.F.S.R.] 28 Mb 44.28N 135.00 E
Rudolf, Lake-/Turkana,
Lake- 30 Kh 3.30N 36.00 E
Rudolstadt 10 Hf 50.43N 11.20 E
Rudong (Juegang) 28 Fh 32.19N 121.11 E
Rudozem 15 Hh 41.29N 24.51 E
Rūd Sar 23 Hb 37.08N 50.18 E
Rudyard 46 Jb 48.34N 110.33W
Rue 11 Hd 50.16N 1.40 E
Ruecas 13 Ge 39.00N 5.55W
Ruelle-sur-Touvre 11 Gi 45.41N 0.14 E
Rufā'ah 35 Ec 14.46N 33.22 E
Ruffec 11 Gh 46.01N 0.12 E
Ruffing Point 51a Db 18.45N 64.25W
Rufiji 30 Ki 8.00S 39.20 E
Rufino 56 Hd 34.16S 62.42W
Rufisque 34 Bc 14.43N 17.17W
Rufunsa 36 Ef 15.05S 29.40 E
Rugao 28 Fh 32.24N 120.34 E
Rugby [Eng.-U.K.] 9 Li 52.23N 1.15W
Rugby [N.D.-U.S.] 43 Gb 48.22N 99.59W
Rügen 5 He 54.25N 13.24 E
Rugles 12 Cf 48.49N 0.42 E
Ru He 28 Ch 32.55N 114.24 E
Ruhea 25 Hc 26.10N 88.25 E
Ruhengeri 36 Ec 1.30S 29.38 E
Rühlertwist 12 Jb 52.39N 7.06 E
Ruhner Berge 10 Hc 53.17N 11.55 E
Ruhnu, Ostrov-/Ruhnu
Saar 7 Fh 57.50N 23.15 E
Ruhnu Saar/Ruhnu, Ostrov-
7 Fh 57.50N 23.15 E
Ruhr 10 Ce 51.27N 6.44 E
Rui'an 27 Lf 27.48N 120.38 E
Ruichang 28 Cj 29.41N 115.38 E
Ruiena/Rūjiena 7 Fh 57.54N 25.17 E
Ruijin 27 Kf 25.59N 116.03 E
Ruili 27 Gg 24.03N 97.46 E
Ruiselede 12 Fc 51.03N 3.24 E
Ruiz 48 Gg 21.57N 105.09W
Ruiz, Nevado del- 54 Cc 4.54N 75.18W
Ruj 15 Fg 42.51N 22.35 E
Ruja/Rūja 8 Kg 57.38N 25.10 E
Rūja/Ruja 8 Kg 57.38N 25.10 E
Rujan 15 Eg 42.23N 21.49 E
Rujen 15 Fg 42.10N 22.31 E
Rūjiena/Ruiena 7 Fh 57.54N 25.17 E
Ruki 30 Ih 0.05N 18.17 E
Rukwa [3] 36 Fd 7.00S 31.20 E
Rukwa, Lake- 30 Ki 8.00S 32.15 E
Rūl Dadnah 24 Qk 25.33N 56.21 E
Rülzheim 12 Ke 49.10N 8.18 E
Ruma 15 Cd 45.01N 19.49 E
Rumaylah 35 Fc 12.57N 35.02 E
Rumbek 31 Jh 6.48N 29.41 E
Rumberpon, Pulau- 26 Jg 1.50S 134.15 E
Rum Cay 47 Jd 23.40N 74.53W
Rumes 12 Fd 50.33N 3.18 E
Rumford 44 Lc 44.33N 70.33W
Rumia 10 Ob 54.35N 18.25 E
Rumigny 12 Ge 49.48N 4.16 E
Rumija 15 Cg 42.06N 19.12 E
Rumilly 11 Li 45.52N 5.57 E
Rum Jungle 59 Gb 13.01S 131.00 E
Rummah, Wādī ar- 24 Ki 26.38N 44.18 E
Rumoi 27 Pc 43.56N 141.39 E
Rumphi 36 Fe 11.01S 33.52 E
Run 12 Hc 51.40N 5.20 E
Runan 28 Ci 33.00N 114.21 E
Runanga 62 De 42.24S 171.15 E
Runaway, Cape- 62 Gb 37.32S 177.59 E
Rundēni/Rundeni 8 Lh 56.14N 27.52 E
Rundeni/Rundēni 8 Lh 56.14N 27.52 E
Rundu 31 Ij 17.55S 19.45 E
Rungu 36 Eb 3.11N 27.52 E
Rungwa 31 Ki 6.57S 33.31 E
Rungwa 36 Fd 7.36S 31.50 E
Runmarö 8 He 59.15N 18.45 E
Runn 8 Fd 60.35N 15.40 E
Ruokolahti 7 Gf 61.17N 28.50 E
Ruoqiang/Qarkilik 22 Kf 39.02N 88.00 E
Ruo Shui 21 Le 40.20N 99.40 E
Ruotsalainen 8 Kc 61.15N 25.55 E
Ruotsinpyhtää/Strömfors 8 Ld 60.32N 26.27 E
Ruovesi 7 Ff 61.59N 24.05 E
Ruovesi 8 Kc 61.55N 24.10 E
Rupanco 56 Ff 40.46S 72.42W
Rupea 15 Ic 46.02N 25.13 E
Rupel 12 Gc 51.07N 4.19 E
Rupert 42 Jf 51.30N 78.48W
Rupert 46 Ie 42.37N 113.41W
Rupert, Baie de - 42 Jf 51.35N 79.00W
Ruppert Coast 66 Mf 75.45S 141.00W
Rur 10 Be 51.12N 5.59 E
Rurrenabaque 53 Jg 14.28S 67.34W
Rurstausee 12 Id 50.38N 6.24 E
Rurutu, Ile- 57 Lg 22.26S 151.20W
Rušan 19 Hh 37.57N 71.31 E
Rusape 37 Ec 18.32S 32.07 E
Ruşayriş, Khazzān ar-=
Rusayris, Lake- (EN) 35 Ec 11.40N 34.20 E
Rusayris, Lake- (EN)=
Ruşayriş, Khazzān ar- 35 Ec 11.40N 34.20 E
Ruse 6 Ig 43.50N 25.57 E
Ruse [2] 15 If 43.50N 25.57 E
Rușețu 15 Ke 44.57N 27.13 E
Rushan (Xiacun) 28 Ff 36.55N 121.30 E
Rushden 12 Bb 52.17N 0.35W
Rushville 45 Kf 40.07N 90.34W
Rusk 45 Ik 31.48N 95.09W

Index Symbols

[1] Independent Nation
[2] State, Region
[3] District, County
[4] Municipality
[5] Colony, Dependency
Continent
Physical Region
Historical or Cultural Region
Mount, Mountain
Volcano
Hill
Mountains, Mountain Range
Hills, Escarpment
Plateau, Upland
Pass, Gap
Plain, Lowland
Delta
Salt Flat
Valley, Canyon
Crater, Cave
Karst Features
Depression
Polder
Desert, Dunes
Forest, Woods
Heath, Steppe
Oasis
Cape, Point
Coast, Beach
Cliff
Peninsula
Isthmus
Sandbank
Island
Atoll
Rock, Reef
Islands, Archipelago
Rocks, Reefs
Coral Reef
Well, Spring
Geyser
River, Stream
Waterfall Rapids
River Mouth, Estuary
Lake
Salt Lake
Intermittent Lake
Reservoir
Swamp, Pond
Canal
Glacier
Ice Shelf, Pack Ice
Ocean
Sea
Gulf, Bay
Strait, Fjord
Lagoon
Bank
Seamount
Tablemount
Ridge
Shelf
Basin
Escarpment, Sea Scarp
Fracture
Trench, Abyss
National Park, Reserve
Point of Interest
Recreation Site
Cave, Cavern
Historic Site
Ruins
Wall, Walls
Church, Abbey
Temple
Scientific Station
Airport
Port
Lighthouse
Mine
Tunnel
Dam, Bridge

Rusken 8 Fg 57.17N 14.20 E
Rusne/Rusné 8 Ii 55.19N 21.16 E
Rusné/Rusne 8 Ii 55.19N 21.16 E
Russel 42 Hb 73.55N 98.35W
Russell [Man. Can.] 42 Hf 50.47N 101.15W
Russell [Ks.-U.S.] 45 Gg 38.54N 98.52W
Russell [N.Z.] 62 Fa 35.16S 174.08 E
Russell Islands 60 Fi 9.04S 159.12 E
Russellville [Al.-U.S.] 44 Dh 34.30N 87.44W
Russellville [Ar.-U.S.] 45 Ji 35.17N 93.08W
Russellville [Ky.-U.S.] 44 Dg 36.51N 86.53W
Russel Range 59 Ef 33.25S 123.30 E
Rüsselsheim 10 Eg 50.00N 8.25 E
Russian River 46 Dg 38.27N 123.08W
Russian SFSR (EN)= RSFSR [2] 19 Jc 60.00N 100.00 E
Rust 14 Kc 47.48N 16.40 E
Rustavi 19 Eg 41.33N 45.02 E
Rustenburg 37 De 25.37S 27.08 E
Ruston 43 Ie 32.32N 92.38W
Rutaki Passage 64p Bc 21.15S 159.48W
Rutana 36 Fc 3.55S 30.00 E
Rutanzige, Lac-=Edward, Lake- (EN) 30 Ji 0.25S 29.30 E
Rute 13 Hg 37.19N 4.22W
Ruteng 26 Hh 8.36S 120.27 E
Rutenga 37 Ed 21.15S 30.44 E
Rüthen 12 Kc 51.29N 8.27 E
Rutherfordton 44 Gh 35.22N 81.57W
Ruthin 9 Jh 53.07N 3.18W
Rutland 9 Mi 52.40N 0.40W
Rutland 44 Kd 43.37N 72.59W
Rutland 25 If 11.25N 92.10 E
Rutog 22 Jf 33.29N 79.42 E
Rutshuru 36 Ec 1.11S 29.27 E
Rutter 44 Gb 46.06N 80.40W
Rutul 16 Oi 41.33N 47.29 E
Ruutana 8 Kc 61.31N 24.02 E
Ruvo di Puglia 14 Ki 41.09N 16.29 E
Ruvu 36 Gd 6.48S 38.39 E
Ruvuma [3] 36 Ge 10.30S 35.50 E
Ruvuma 30 Lj 10.29S 40.28 E
Ruvuma (EN) = Rovuma 30 Lj 10.29S 40.28 E
Ruwayshid, Wādī 24 Hf 32.41N 38.04 E
Ruwer 12 Ie 49.47N 6.42 E
Ruya 37 Ec 16.34S 33.12 E
Ruyang 28 Bg 34.10N 112.28 E
Ru'yas, Wādī ar- 33 Cd 27.06N 19.24 E
Ruyigi 36 Fc 3.29S 30.15 E
Ruza 7 Ii 55.39N 36.18 E
Ruzajevka [Kaz.-U.S.S.R.] 17 Mj 52.49N 67.01 E
Ruzajevka [R.S.F.S.R.] 19 Ee 54.05N 44.54 E
Ružany 10 Ud 52.48N 24.58 E
Ružomberok 10 Pg 49.05N 19.18 E
Rwanda [1] 31 Ji 2.30S 30.00 E
Ry 8 Ch 56.05N 9.46 E
Ryan 45 Hi 34.01N 97.57W
Rybachi Peninsula (EN)= Rybači, Poluostrov- 5 Jb 69.45N 32.35 E
Rybači 8 Ii 55.09N 20.45 E
Rybači, Poluostrov-= Rybachi Peninsula (EN) 5 Jb 69.45N 32.35 E
Rybačje 19 Hg 42.28N 76.11 E
Rybinsk 6 Jd 58.03N 38.52 E
Rybinskoje Vodohranilišče = Rybinsk Reservoir (EN) 5 Jd 58.30N 38.25 E
Rybinsk Reservoir (EN)= Rybinskoje Vodohranilišče 5 Jd 58.30N 38.25 E
Rybnica 16 Ff 47.45N 29.01 E
Rybnik 10 Of 50.06N 18.32 E
Rybnoje 19 De 54.46N 39.33 E
Rybnovsk 20 Jf 53.15N 141.55 E
Rychnov nad Kněžnou 10 Mf 50.10N 16.17 E
Rychwał 10 Od 52.05N 18.09 E
Ryd 8 Fh 56.28N 14.41 E
Rydaholm 8 Fh 56.59N 14.16 E
Ryde 12 Ad 50.43N 1.10W
Rye 9 Mg 54.10N 0.45W
Rye 9 Nk 50.57N 0.44 E
Rye Bay 12 Cd 50.55N 0.48 E
Ryegate 46 Kc 46.18N 109.15W
Rye Patch Reservoir 46 Ff 40.38N 118.18W
Ryes 12 Be 49.19N 0.37W
Ryfylke 8 Be 59.30N 6.30 E
Ryki 10 Re 51.39N 21.56 E
Rylsk 19 De 51.36N 34.43 E
Rymanów 10 Rg 49.34N 21.53 E
Rymättylä/Rimito 8 Jd 60.25N 21.55 E
Ryn 10 Rc 53.56N 21.33 E
Ryńskie, Jezioro- 10 Rc 53.53N 21.30 E
Ryōhaku-Sanchi 29 Ec 36.05N 136.45 E
Ryōsō-Yosui 29 Gd 35.22N 140.25 E
Ryōtsu 28 Oe 38.05N 138.26 E
Ryōtsu-Wan 29 Fb 38.10N 138.30 E
Ryō-Zen 29 Gc 37.46N 140.41 E
Rypin 10 Pc 53.05N 19.25 E
Ryškany 16 Ef 47.57N 27.32 E
Ryssby 8 Fh 56.52N 14.10 E
Rytterknægten 8 Fi 55.06N 14.54 E
Ryūgasaki 29 Gd 35.54N 140.11 E
Ryukyu Islands (EN)= Nansei-Shotō 21 Og 26.30N 128.00 E
Ryūkyū-Shotō 27 Mf 25.30N 126.30 E
Ryukyu Trench (EN) 3 Ig 25.45N 128.00 E
Rzepin 10 Kd 52.22N 14.50 E
Rzeszów 6 Ie 50.03N 22.00 E
Rzeszów [2] 10 Rf 50.05N 22.00 E
Ržev 6 Jd 56.16N 34.20 E

S

Šaa, Gora- 16 Nh 42.39N 44.43 E
Sa'ādatābād [Iran] 24 Ph 28.02N 55.50 E
Sa'ādatābād [Iran] 24 Og 30.08N 52.38 E
Sa'ādatābād [Iran] 24 Og 30.06N 53.08 E
Sääksjarvi 8 Jc 61.24N 22.24 E
Saalbach 12 Ke 49.15N 8.27 E
Saale 10 He 51.57N 11.55 E
Saaler Bodden 10 Ib 54.20N 12.28 E
Saalfeld 10 Hf 50.39N 11.22 E
Saalfelden am Steinernen Meer 14 Gc 47.25N 12.51 E
Saaminki 8 Mc 61.52N 28.50 E
Saâne 12 Ce 49.54N 0.56 E
Saane 14 Bd 46.59N 7.16 E
Saanen 14 Bd 46.30N 7.15 E
Saar 10 Cg 49.42N 6.34 E
Saar-Bergland 12 Ie 49.27N 6.45 E
Saarbrücken 6 Gf 49.14N 7.00 E
Saarbrücken-Dudweiler 12 Je 49.17N 7.02 E
Saarburg 10 Cg 49.36N 6.33 E
Sääre/Sjare 8 Ig 57.57N 21.53 E
Saaremaa/Sarema 5 Id 58.25N 22.30 E
Saarijärvi 7 Fe 62.43N 25.16 E
Saaristomeri 8 Id 60.20N 21.10 E
Saarland [2] 10 Cg 49.20N 7.00 E
Saarlouis 10 Cg 49.19N 6.45 E
Šaartuz 19 Gh 37.16N 68.06 E
Saarwellingen 12 Ie 49.21N 6.49 E
Saas Fee 14 Bd 46.07N 7.55 E
Saatly 16 Pj 39.57N 48.26 E
Saavedra 55 Am 37.45S 62.22W
Sab, Tônlé- 25 Kf 11.34N 104.57 E
Saba 47 Le 17.38N 63.10W
Saba 8 Me 59.05N 29.10 E
Saba Bank (EN) 50 Ed 17.30N 63.30W
Šabac 15 Ce 44.45N 19.43 E
Sabadell 13 Oc 41.33N 2.06 E
Sabae 28 Ng 35.57N 136.11 E
Sabah [2] 26 Ge 5.30N 117.00 E
Sab'ah, Qārat as- 33 Cd 27.20N 17.10 E
Sabak Bernam 26 Df 3.46N 100.59 E
Sabalān, Kūhhā-ye- 21 Gf 38.15N 47.49 E
Sab'ān 24 Ii 27.04N 41.58 E
Sabana, Archipiélago de- 49 Hb 22.30N 79.00W
Sabana de la Mar 49 Md 19.04N 69.23W
Sabanagrande 49 Dg 13.50N 87.15W
Sabanalarga 54 Da 10.38N 74.56W
Sabancuy 48 Nh 18.58N 91.11W
Sabaneta 49 Ld 19.12N 70.58W
Sabaneta, Puntan- 64b Ba 15.17N 145.49 E
Sabang [Indon.] 26 Gf 0.11N 119.51 E
Sabang [Indon.] 26 Ce 5.55N 95.19 E
Şabanözü 24 Eb 40.29N 33.18 E
Săbăoani 15 Jb 47.01N 26.51 E
Sabarei 36 Gb 4.20N 36.55 E
Sab'Atayn, Ramlat as- 33 If 15.30N 46.10 E
Sabatini, Monti- 14 Gh 42.10N 12.15 E
Sabaudia 14 Hi 41.18N 13.01 E
Sabaudia, Lago di- 14 Hi 41.15N 13.05 E
Şabbāgh, Jabal- 24 Fh 28.12N 34.04 E
Sab 'Bi 'Ār 24 Gf 33.46N 37.41 E
Sabbioneta 14 Ee 45.00N 10.39 E
Sa Bec 25 Lf 10.18N 105.46 E
Sabhā [3] 33 Bd 26.00N 14.00 E
Sabhā 31 If 27.02N 14.26 E
Şabḩā 24 Gf 32.20N 36.30 E
Sābhā, Wāḩāt-=Sebha Oasis (EN) 30 If 27.00N 14.25 E
Sabi 30 Kk 21.00S 35.02 E
Sabidana, Jabal- 35 Fb 18.04N 36.50 E
Sabile 8 Jg 57.05N 22.29 E
Sabina 14 Gh 42.20N 12.45 E
Sabinal 48 Fb 30.57N 107.30W
Sabinal, Peninsula de- 49 Ic 21.40N 77.18W
Sabiñánigo 13 Lb 42.31N 0.22W
Sabinas 47 Dc 27.51N 101.07W
Sabinas, Rio- 48 Id 27.37N 100.42W
Sabinas Hidalgo 47 Dc 26.30N 100.10W
Sabine Lake 45 Jl 29.50N 93.50W
Sabine Pass 45 Jl 29.44N 93.52W
Sabine Peninsula 42 Ga 76.25N 109.50W
Sabine River 43 Ie 30.00N 93.45W
Sabini, Monti- 14 Gh 42.15N 12.50 E
Sabir, Jabal- 23 Fg 13.30N 44.03 E
Sabirabad 16 Pj 39.59N 48.29 E
Šabla 15 Lf 43.32N 28.32 E
Sable, Anse de- 51e b 16.07N 61.34W
Sable, Cape- [Can.] 38 Me 43.25N 65.35W
Sable, Cape- [U.S.] 38 Kg 25.12N 81.05W
Sable, Ile de- 57 Gf 19.15S 159.56 E
Sable Island 38 Ne 43.55N 59.55W
Sablé-sur-Sarthe 11 Fg 47.50N 0.20W
Sablūkah, Ash Shallāl as-= Sixth Cataract (EN) 30 Kg 16.20N 32.42 E
Sabonetau, Serra da- 55 Kb 15.20S 43.50W
Sabonkafi 34 Gc 14.38N 8.45 E
Sabór 13 Ec 41.10N 7.07W
Şabrātah 33 Bc 32.47N 12.29 E
Sabres 11 Fj 44.09N 0.44W
Sabrina Coast 66 He 67.00S 119.30 E
Sabtang 26 Hb 20.19N 121.52 E
Sabunči 16 Pi 40.27N 49.57 E
Şabyā 23 Ff 17.09N 42.37 E
Sabzevār 22 Hf 36.13N 57.42 E
Saca, Virful- 15 Ic 46.30N 25.15 E
Sacajawea Peak 43 Db 45.15N 117.17W
Sacalin, Insulă- 15 Me 44.50N 29.39 E
Sacandica 36 Cd 5.58S 15.56 E
Sacatepéquez [3] 49 Bf 14.35N 90.45W
Sacavém 13 Cf 38.46N 9.05W
Sac City 45 Ie 42.25N 95.00W
Sacco 14 Hi 41.31N 13.32 E
Sacedón 13 Jd 40.29N 2.43W
Săcel 15 Hb 47.38N 24.26 E
Săcele 15 Id 45.37N 25.41 E
Sachayoj 55 Bh 26.41S 61.50W
Sachère 16 Mh 42.20N 43.22 E
Sachigo 42 Ie 55.05N 89.00W
Sachsen=Saxony (EN) 10 Jf 51.00N 13.30 E
Sachsenhagen 12 Lb 52.24N 9.16 E
Sachs Harbour 42 Eb 72.00N 125.08W
Šack [R.S.F.S.R.] 7 Ji 54.04N 41.42 E
Šack [Ukr.-U.S.S.R.] 10 Je 51.30N 24.00 E
Sackets Harbor 44 Id 43.57N 76.07W
Saco [Me.-U.S.] 44 Ld 43.29N 70.28W
Saco [Mt.-U.S.] 46 Lb 48.28N 107.21W
Sacramento 38 Gf 38.03N 121.56W
Sacramento [Braz.] 54 Ig 19.53S 47.27W
Sacramento [Ca.-U.S.] 39 Gf 38.35N 121.30W
Sacramento, Pampa del- 54 Ce 8.00S 75.50W
Sacramento Mountains 38 If 33.10N 105.50W
Sacramento Valley 43 Cd 39.15N 122.00W
Sacre ou Timalacia, Rio- 55 Ca 13.55S 58.02W
Săcueni 15 Fb 47.21N 22.06 E
Sacuriuiná ou Ponte de Pedra, Rio- 55 Da 13.58S 57.18W
Sădaba 13 Kb 42.17N 1.16W
Sa'dābād 24 Nh 29.23N 51.07 E
Şa'dah 22 Gh 16.57N 43.44 E
Sada-Misaki 29b Ce 33.22N 132.01 E
Sada-Misaki-Hantō 29 Ce 33.25N 132.15 E
Sadani 36 Gd 6.03S 38.47 E
Sadao 25 Kg 6.39N 100.31 E
Sadd al 'Ālī 23 Fe 23.54N 32.52 E
Saddle Mountains 46 Fc 46.50N 119.55W
Saddle Peak [India] 25 If 13.09N 93.01 E
Saddle Peak [Mt.-U.S.] 46 Jd 45.57N 110.58W
Sad-e Eskandar 24 Pd 37.10N 55.00 E
Sadiya 25 Jc 27.50N 95.40 E
Sa'dīyah, Hawr as- 24 Lf 32.00N 46.45 E
Sad Kharv 24 Qd 36.19N 57.05 E
Sado 13 Df 38.29N 8.55W
Sado-Kaikyō 29 Fc 37.55N 138.40 E
Sado-Shima 21 Pf 38.00N 138.25 E
Sadowara 29 Be 32.04N 131.26 E
Šadrinsk 19 Gd 56.05N 63.38 E
Saeby 7 Ch 57.20N 10.32 E
Saeh, Teluk- 26 Gh 8.00S 117.30 E
Saengcheon 28 Ie 39.55N 126.34 E
Saerbeck 12 Jb 52.11N 7.38 E
Şafājah 24 Hi 26.30N 39.30 E
Safājah, Jazīrat- 24 Ei 26.45N 33.59 E
Safané 34 Ec 12.08N 3.13W
Şafāqis=Sfax (EN) [3] 32 Jc 34.30N 10.30 E
Şafāqis=Sfax (EN) 31 Ie 34.44N 10.46 E
Safata Harbour 65c Bb 14.00S 171.50W
Saffānīyah, Ra's as- 23 Gd 27.59N 48.37 E
Säffle 7 Cg 59.08N 12.56 E
Safford 43 Fe 32.50N 109.43W
Saffron Walden 9 Ni 52.01N 0.15 E
Safi 31 Ge 32.18N 9.14W
Safi [3] 32 Fc 31.55N 9.00W
Safia, Hamâda- 34 Ea 23.10N 4.15W
Şafiābād 24 Qd 36.45N 57.58 E
Safīd 23 Hb 37.23N 50.11 E
Safid, Kūh-e 24 Lf 33.55N 47.30 E
Safīd Kūh, Salseleh-ye- 23 Jc 34.30N 63.30 E
Safonovo [R.S.F.S.R.] 19 Dd 55.06N 33.14 E
Safonovo [R.S.F.S.R.] 7 Ld 65.41N 47.43 E
Şafrā' al Asyāḩ 24 Ji 26.50N 43.57 E
Şafrā' as Sark 24 Kj 25.25N 44.20 E
Safranbolu 24 Eb 41.15N 32.42 E
Şafwān 24 Lg 30.07N 47.43 E
Saga [Jap.] 27 Ne 33.15N 130.18 E
Saga [Jap.] 29 Ce 33.05N 133.06 E
Saga [Kaz.-U.S.S.R.] 19 Fe 50.30N 64.14 E
Saga (Gya'gya) 27 Ef 29.22N 85.15 E
Sagae 29 Gb 38.22N 140.17 E
Sagaing [3] 25 Jd 23.30N 95.30 E
Sagaing 25 Jd 21.52N 95.59 E
Saga Ken [2] 28 Kh 33.15N 130.15 E
Sagamihara 29 Fd 35.34N 139.22 E
Sagami-Nada 29 Fd 35.00N 139.30 E
Sagami-Wan 29 Fd 35.15N 139.20 E
Sagan 35 Fd 5.17N 36.57 E
Šagan 19 He 50.37N 79.15 E
Saganaga Lake 45 Kb 48.14N 90.52W
Saganoseki 29 Be 33.15N 131.53 E
Šagany, Ozero- 15 Md 45.45N 29.55 E
Sāgar [India] 25 Ff 14.10N 75.02 E
Sāgar [India] 22 Jg 23.50N 78.42 E
Sagara 29 Fd 34.40N 138.12 E
Sagaredžo 16 Ni 41.43N 45.16 E
Sagavanirktok 40 Jb 70.20N 148.00W
Sagawa 29 Ce 33.29N 133.16 E
Sage 46 Jf 41.50N 110.56W
Saghād 24 Og 31.12N 52.30 E
Saginaw 43 Kc 43.25N 83.58W
Saginaw Bay 43 Kc 43.50N 83.40W
Sagiz 19 Ff 47.32N 53.45 E
Sagiz [Kaz.-U.S.S.R.] 19 Ff 48.12N 54.56 E
Sagiz [Kaz.-U.S.S.R.] 16 Rf 47.32N 53.27 E
Saglek Bay 42 Le 58.30N 63.00W
Saglouc → Salluit 42 Jd 62.12N 75.38W
Šagonar 20 Ef 51.32N 92.51 E
Sagone, Golfe de- 11a Aa 42.06N 8.41 E
Sagres 13 Dg 37.01N 8.56W
Sagres, Ponta de- 13 Dh 37.00N 8.57W
Sagter Ems 12 Ja 53.10N 7.40 E
Şagu 15 Ec 46.03N 21.17 E
Sagu/Sauvo 8 Jd 60.21N 22.42 E
Saguache 45 Cg 38.05N 106.08W
Sagua de Tánamo 49 Jc 20.35N 75.14W
Sagua la Grande 47 Hd 22.49N 80.05W
Saguenay 38 Me 48.10N 69.45W
Saguia el-Hamra 32 Ed 26.50N 12.00W
Sagunto/Sagunt 13 Le 39.41N 0.16W
Sagunt/Sagunto 13 Le 39.41N 0.16W
Sagunto-Grao de Sagunto 13 Le 39.40N 0.16W
Sa'gya 27 Ef 28.53N 88.10 E
Sahagún [Col.] 54 Cb 8.57N 75.27W
Sahagún [Sp.] 13 Gb 42.22N 5.02W
Sahalin, Ostrov-=Sakhalin (EN) 21 Qd 51.00N 143.00 E
Sahalinskaja Oblast [3] 20 Jf 50.00N 143.30 E
Sahalinski Zaliv 20 Jf 53.45N 141.30 E
Sahara 30 Hf 21.00N 6.00 E
Saharan Atlas (EN)=Atlas Saharien 30 He 34.00N 2.00 E
Sahāranpur 22 Jg 29.58N 77.23 E
Sahel [3] 34 Ec 14.10N 0.50W
Sahel 30 Gg 15.40N 8.30W
Şahin 15 Jh 41.01N 26.50 E
Sāhīwāl [Pak.] 25 Eb 30.41N 72.57 E
Sāhīwāl [Pak.] 25 Eb 31.58N 72.20 E
Sahlābād 23 Ic 32.10N 59.51 E
Sahneh 24 Le 34.29N 47.41 E
Sahnovščina 16 Ie 49.09N 35.57 E
Sahova Kosa, Mys- 16 Qi 40.13N 50.22 E
Sahrihan 18 Id 40.40N 72.03 E
Šahrisabz 19 Gh 39.03N 66.41 E
Šahristan, Pereval- 18 Ge 39.35N 68.38 E
Šahtersk [R.S.F.S.R.] 20 Jg 49.13N 142.09 E
Šahtersk [Ukr.-U.S.S.R.] 16 Ke 48.01N 38.32 E
Šahterski 20 Md 64.46N 177.47 E
Šahtinsk 19 Hf 49.40N 72.37 E
Šahty 19 Ef 47.42N 40.13 E
Sahuaripa 47 Cc 29.03N 109.14W
Sahuayo de Diaz 47 Dd 20.04N 102.43W
Šahunja 19 Ed 57.43N 46.35 E
Saḩūq, Wādī- 24 Jj 25.18N 42.20 E
Šahy 10 Oh 48.05N 18.58 E
Sahyadri/Western Ghats 21 Jh 14.00N 75.00 E
Sai Buri 25 Kg 6.42N 101.37 E
Saïda [3] 32 Hc 33.35N 0.30 E
Saïda 31 He 34.50N 0.09 E
Saïda, Monts de- 13 Mi 35.10N 0.30 E
Sa'īdābād 23 Id 29.28N 55.42 E
Saidaiji 29 Dd 34.39N 134.02 E
Said Bundas 35 Cd 8.35N 24.30 E
Saïdia 13 Ji 35.04N 2.13W
Saidor 60 Di 5.37S 146.28 E
Saidu 25 Eb 34.45N 72.21 E
Saigō 29 Cc 36.13N 133.20 E
Saigon → Ho Chi Minh 22 Mh 10.45N 106.40 E
Saihan Tal → Sonid Youqi 27 Jc 42.45N 112.36 E
Saihan Toroi 27 Hc 41.54N 100.24 E
Saijō 29 Ce 33.55N 133.10 E
Saikai 29 Ae 33.03N 129.44 E
Sai-Kawa 29 Fc 36.37N 138.14 E
Saiki 28 Kh 32.57N 131.54 E
Saiki-Wan 29 Be 33.00N 131.55 E
Sail Rock 51n Bb 12.37N 61.16W
Saimaa 5 Ic 61.15N 28.15 E
Saimaa Canal (EN)= Sajmenski Kanal 8 Mc 61.05N 28.18 E
Sain Alto 48 Hf 23.35N 103.15W
Sā īn Dezh 24 Ld 36.40N 46.33 E
Sains-Richaumont 12 Fe 49.49N 3.42 E
Saint Abb's Head 9 Kf 55.54N 2.09W
Saint-Affrique 11 Ik 43.57N 2.53 E
Saint Agnes Head 9 Hk 50.23N 5.07W
Saint-Agrève 11 Ki 45.01N 4.24 E
Saint Albans [Eng.-U.K.] 9 Mj 51.46N 0.21W
Saint Albans [Vt.-U.S.] 44 Kc 44.49N 73.05W
Saint Albans [W.V.-U.S.] 44 Gf 38.24N 81.53W
Saint Alban's Head 9 Kk 50.34N 2.04W
Saint Albert 42 Gf 53.38N 113.38W
Saint-Amand-les-Eaux 11 Jd 50.26N 3.26 E
Saint-Amand-Mont-Rond 11 Ih 46.43N 2.31 E
Saint-André, Cap- 30 Lj 16.11S 44.27 E
Saint-André, Plaine de- 11 Hf 48.55N 1.10 E
Saint-André-de-Cubzac 11 Fi 45.00N 0.27W
Saint-André-de-l'Eure 12 Df 48.54N 1.17 E
Saint-André-sur-Cailly 12 De 49.33N 1.13 E
Saint Andrews [N.B.-Can.] 44 Nc 45.06N 67.02W
Saint Andrews [Scot.-U.K.] 9 Ke 56.20N 2.48W
Saint Anne 9 Kl 49.40N 2.10W
Saint Ann's Bay 49 Id 18.26N 77.16W
Saint Ann's Head 9 Hj 51.41N 5.10W
Saint Anthony [Id.-U.S.] 46 Je 43.58N 111.41W
Saint Anthony [Newf.-Can.] 42 Lf 51.22N 55.35W
Saint Arnaud 59 Ig 36.37S 143.15 E
Saint-Aubert 44 Lb 47.14N 70.15W
Saint-Aubin-sur-Mer 12 Be 49.20N 0.24W
Saint Augustine 43 Kf 29.51N 81.25W
Saint-Augustin-Saguenay 42 Lf 51.14N 58.39W
Saint Austell 9 Ik 50.20N 4.48W
Saint-Avold 11 Me 49.06N 6.42 E
Saint Barthélemy 47 Le 17.55N 62.50W
Saint Barthélemy 11 Hl 42.49N 1.45 E
Saint Barthélemy, Canal de- 51b Bb 18.00N 63.00W
Saint Barthélemy, Kanaal Van- 51b Bb 18.00N 63.00W
Saint Bees Head 9 Jg 54.32N 3.38W
Saint-Benoit 37a b 21.02S 55.43 E
Saint-Benoît-sur-Loire 11 Ig 47.49N 2.18 E
Saint-Bonnet 11 Mj 44.41N 6.05 E
Saint-Brévin-les-Pins 11 Dg 47.15N 2.10W
Saint Brides Bay 9 Hj 51.48N 5.15W
Saint-Brieuc 11 Df 48.31N 2.47W
Saint-Brieuc, Baie de- 11 Df 48.38N 2.40W
Saint-Calais 11 Gg 47.55N 0.45 E
Saint-Camille 44 Lb 46.29N 70.12W
Saint Catharines 42 Jh 43.10N 79.15W
Saint Catherine, Monastery of- (EN)=Dayr Kātrīnā 33 Fd 28.31N 33.57 E
Saint Catherine, Mount- 51p Bb 12.10N 61.40W
Saint Catherines Island 44 Gj 31.38N 81.10W
Saint Catherine's Point 9 Lk 50.34N 1.15W
Saint-Céré 11 Hj 44.52N 1.54 E
Saint-Chamond 11 Ki 45.28N 4.30 E
Saint Charles 43 Id 38.47N 90.29W
Saint-Chély-d'Apcher 11 Jj 44.48N 3.17 E
Saint-Christol, Plateau de- 11 Lj 44.00N 5.50 E
Saint Christopher/Saint Kitts 38 Mh 17.21N 62.48W
Saint Christopher-Nevis [5] 39 Mh 17.21N 62.48W
Saint-Cirq-Lapopie 11 Hj 44.28N 1.40 E
Saint Clair, Lake- 38 Ke 42.25N 82.41W
Saint Clair River 44 Fd 42.37N 82.31W
Saint Clair Shores 44 Fd 42.30N 82.54W
Saint-Clair-sur-l'Elle 12 Ae 49.12N 1.02W
Saint-Claud 11 Gi 45.54N 0.28 E
Saint-Claude [Fr.] 11 Lh 46.23N 5.52 E
Saint Claude 45 Gb 49.40N 98.22W
Saint-Claude [Guad.] 51e Ab 16.02N 61.42W
Saint Cloud 39 Je 45.33N 94.10W
Saint Croix 47 Le 17.45N 64.45W
Saint Croix Falls 45 Jd 45.24N 92.38W
Saint Croix River 43 Ic 44.45N 92.49W
Saint-Cyr-l'Ecole 12 Ef 48.48N 2.04 E
Saint-Cyr-sur-Loire 11 Gg 47.24N 0.40 E
Saint David Bay 51g Bb 15.26N 61.15W
Saint David's [Gren.] 51p Bb 12.04N 61.39W
Saint David's [Wales-U.K.] 9 Hj 51.54N 5.16W
Saint David's Head 9 Hj 51.55N 5.19W
Saint David's Point 51p Bb 12.01N 61.40W
Saint-Denis [Fr.] 11 If 48.56N 2.22 E
Saint-Denis [May.] 31 Mk 20.52S 55.28 E
Saint-Dié 11 Mf 48.17N 6.57 E
Saint-Dizier 11 Kf 48.38N 4.57 E
Sainte-Adresse 12 Ce 49.30N 0.05 E
Sainte-Anne [Guad.] 51e Bb 16.14N 61.23W
Sainte-Anne [Mart.] 51h Bc 14.26N 60.53W
Sainte-Anne-des-Monts 44 Na 49.07N 66.29W
Sainte Baume, Chaîne de la- 11 Lk 43.20N 5.45 E
Sainte-Énimie 11 Jj 44.22N 3.25 E
Sainte Genevieve 45 Kh 37.59N 90.03W
Sainte-Geneviève 12 Ee 49.17N 2.12 E
Saint Elias, Mount- 38 Ec 60.18N 140.55W
Saint Elias Mountains 38 Fc 60.30N 139.30W
Sainte-Elie 54 Hc 4.50N 53.17W
Sainte-Livrade-sur-Lot 11 Gj 44.24N 0.36 E
Saint-Eloy-les-Mines 11 Ih 46.09N 2.50 E
Sainte Luce 37 Hd 24.46S 47.12 E
Sainte-Luce 51h Bc 14.28N 60.56W
Sainte-Lucie, Canal de-= Saint Lucia Channel (EN) 50 Fe 14.09N 60.57W
Sainte-Marcellin 11 Li 45.09N 5.19 E
Sainte-Marie [Guad.] 51e Ab 16.06N 61.34W
Sainte-Marie [Mart.] 51h Ab 14.47N 61.00W
Sainte-Marie, Cap-=Sainte-Marie, Cape- (EN) 30 Lk 25.36S 45.08 E
Sainte-Marie, Cape-(EN)= Sainte-Marie, Cap- 30 Lk 25.36S 45.08 E
Sainte-Marie, Ile- 30 Lj 16.50S 49.55 E
Sainte-Marie-aux-Mines 11 Nf 48.15N 7.11 E
Sainte-Maure-de-Touraine 11 Gg 47.06N 0.37 E
Sainte-Maxime 11 Mk 43.18N 6.38 E
Sainte-Menehould 11 Ke 49.05N 4.54 E
Sainte-Rose 51e Ab 16.20N 61.42W
Sainte-Rose-du-Dégelé 44 Mb 47.33N 68.39W
Sainte Rose du Lac 45 Ga 51.03N 99.32W
Saintes 11 Fi 45.45N 0.38W
Saintes, Canal des- 51e Ac 15.55N 61.40W
Saintes, Iles des- 50 Fe 15.52N 61.37W
Sainte-Savine 11 Kf 48.18N 4.03 E
Saintes-Maries-de-la-Mer 11 Kk 43.27N 4.26 E
Sainte-Thérèse 44 Kc 45.22N 73.15W
Saint-Étienne 6 Gf 45.26N 4.24 E
Saint-Étienne-du-Rouvray 11 He 49.23N 1.06 E
Sainte Victoire, Montagne- 11 Lk 43.32N 5.39 E
Saint-Félicien 44 Ka 48.39N 72.28W
Saint-Florent 11a Ba 42.41N 9.18 E
Saint-Florent, Golfe de- 11a Ba 42.45N 9.16 E
Saint-Florentin 11 Jf 48.00N 3.44 E
Saint-Florent-sur-Cher 11 Ih 46.59N 2.15 E
Saint-Flour 11 Ji 45.02N 3.05 E
Saint Francis 45 Fg 39.46N 101.48W
Saint Francis River 45 Ki 34.38N 90.35W
Saint Francisville 45 Kk 30.47N 91.23W
Saint-François 51e Bb 16.15N 61.17W
Saint François Island 37b Bb 7.10S 52.44 E
Saint Francois Mountains 45 Kh 37.30N 90.35W
Saint-Gaudens 11 Gk 43.07N 0.44 E
Saint George 40 Fe 56.35N 169.35W
Saint George [Austl.] 59 Je 28.02S 148.35 E
Saint George [N.B.-Can.] 44 Nc 45.10N 66.48W
Saint George [Ut.-U.S.] 43 Ed 37.06N 113.35W
Saint George, Cape- [Newf.-Can.] 42 Lm 48.28N 59.16W
Saint George, Cape- [Pap.N.Gui.] 60 Eh 4.52S 152.52 E
Saint George, Point- 46 Cf 41.47N 124.15W
Saint George Harbour 44 Nd 43.15N 66.10W
Saint George Island 44 Ek 29.39N 84.55W
Saint George's 39 Mh 12.03N 61.45W
Saint-Georges 44 Lb 46.10N 70.38W
Saint George's Bay 42 Lg 48.20N 59.00W
Saint George's Channel 5 Fe 52.00N 6.00W
Saint George's Channel (EN) =Muir Bhreatan 5 Fe 52.00N 6.00W
Saint-Georges-du-Vièvre 12 Ce 49.15N 0.35 E
Saint-Germain-en-Laye 11 If 48.54N 2.05 E
Saint-Gervais-d'Auvergne 11 Ih 46.02N 2.49 E
Saint-Gervais-les-Bains 11 Mi 45.54N 6.43 E
Saint-Ghislain 12 Fd 50.27N 3.49 E
Saint-Ghislain-Baudour 12 Fd 50.29N 3.49 E
Saint-Gildas, Pointe de- 11 Dg 47.08N 2.15W
Saint-Gilles 11 Kk 43.41N 4.26 E
Saint-Gilles-Croix-de-Vie 11 Eh 46.41N 1.55W
Saint-Girons 11 Hl 42.59N 1.09 E
Saint-Gobain 12 Fe 49.36N 3.23 E
Saint Gotthard Pass (EN)= San Gottardo/Sankt Gotthard 5 Gf 46.30N 8.30 E
Saint Gotthard Pass (EN)=Sankt Gotthard/San Gottardo 5 Gf 46.30N 8.30 E
Saint Govan's Head 9 Ij 51.36N 4.55W
Saint Helena [5] 31 Gj 15.57S 5.42W
Saint Helena 30 Gj 15.57S 5.42W
Saint Helena Bay 30 Il 32.45S 18.05 E
Saint Helena Island 44 Gi 32.30N 80.30W

Index Symbols

[1] Independent Nation
[2] State, Region
[3] District, County
[4] Municipality
[5] Colony, Dependency
Continent
Physical Region
Historical or Cultural Region
Mount, Mountain
Volcano
Hill
Mountains, Mountain Range
Hills, Escarpment
Plateau, Upland
Pass, Gap
Plain, Lowland
Delta
Salt Flat
Valley, Canyon
Crater, Cave
Karst Features
Depression
Polder
Desert, Dunes
Forest, Woods
Heath, Steppe
Oasis
Cape, Point
Coast, Beach
Cliff
Peninsula
Isthmus
Sandbank
Island
Atoll
Rock, Reef
Islands, Archipelago
Rocks, Reefs
Coral Reef
Well, Spring
Geyser
River, Stream
Waterfall Rapids
River Mouth, Estuary
Lake
Salt Lake
Intermittent Lake
Reservoir
Swamp, Pond
Canal
Glacier
Ice Shelf, Pack Ice
Ocean
Sea
Gulf, Bay
Strait, Fjord
Lagoon
Bank
Seamount
Tablemount
Ridge
Shelf
Basin
Escarpment, Sea Scarp
Fracture
Trench, Abyss
National Park, Reserve
Point of Interest
Recreation Site
Cave, Cavern
Historic Site
Ruins
Wall, Walls
Church, Abbey
Temple
Scientific Station
Airport
Port
Lighthouse
Mine
Tunnel
Dam, Bridge

Index Symbols

Independent Nation; State, Region; District, County; Municipality; Colony, Dependency; Continent; Physical Region; Historical or Cultural Region; Mount, Mountain; Volcano; Hill; Mountains, Mountain Range; Hills, Escarpment; Plateau, Upland; Pass, Gap; Plain, Lowland; Delta; Salt Flat; Valley, Canyon; Crater, Cave; Karst Features; Depression; Polder; Desert, Dunes; Forest, Woods; Heath, Steppe; Oasis; Cape, Point; Coast, Beach; Cliff; Peninsula; Isthmus; Sandbank; Island; Atoll; Rock, Reef; Islands, Archipelago; Rocks, Reefs; Coral Reef; Well, Spring; Geyser; River, Stream; Waterfall Rapids; River Mouth, Estuary; Lake; Salt Lake; Intermittent Lake; Reservoir; Swamp, Pond; Canal; Glacier; Ice Shelf, Pack Ice; Ocean; Sea; Gulf, Bay; Strait, Fjord; Lagoon; Bank; Seamount; Tablemount; Ridge; Shelf; Basin; Escarpment, Sea Scarp; Fracture; Trench, Abyss; National Park, Reserve; Point of Interest; Recreation Site; Cave, Cavern; Historic Site; Ruins; Wall, Walls; Church, Abbey; Temple; Scientific Station; Airport; Port; Lighthouse; Mine; Tunnel; Dam, Bridge

Samch'ŏk 27 Md 37.27N 129.10 E
Samch'ŏnp'o 27 Me 34.55N 128.04 E
Samdi Dağı 24 Kd 37.19N 44.15 E
Samdŏng-ni 28 Ie 39.21N 126.14 E
Samdŭng 28 Ie 38.59N 126.11 E
Same [Indon.] 26 Ih 8.59S 125.40 E
Same [Tan.] 36 Gc 4.04S 37.44 E
Samer 12 Dd 50.38N 1.45 E
Sam Ford Fiord 42 Kb 70.40N 70.35W
Samfya 36 Ee 11.20S 29.32 E
Šamhor 16 Oi 40.48N 46.01 E
Sámi 15 Dk 38.15N 20.39 E
Sāmī Ghar 23 Kc 31.43N 67.01 E
Samīrah 24 Ji 26.18N 42.05 E
Samisu-Jima 27 Oe 31.40N 140.00 E
Şamli 15 Kj 39.48N 27.51 E
Samnah, Jabal- 24 Ei 26.26N 33.34 E
Samoa I Sisifo=Western Samoa (EN) [1] 58 Jf 13.40S 172.30W
Samoa Islands 57 Jf 14.00S 171.00W
Samobor 14 Je 45.48N 15.43 E
Samojlovka 16 Md 51.10N 43.43 E
Samokov 15 Gg 42.20N 23.33 E
Samolva 8 Lf 58.16N 27.45 E
Sámos 15 Jl 37.45N 26.58 E
Sámos 5 Ih 37.45N 26.48 E
Samosir, Pulau- 26 Cf 2.35N 98.50 E
Samothrace (EN) = Samothráki 15 Ii 40.27N 25.35 E
Samothráki 15 Ii 40.29N 25.31 E
Samothráki = Samothrace (EN) 15 Ii 40.27N 25.35 E
Sampacho 56 Hd 33.23S 64.43W
Sampaga 26 Gg 2.19S 119.07 E
Sampit 26 Fg 3.00S 113.03 E
Sampit 22 Nj 2.32S 112.57 E
Sampoku 29 Fb 38.30N 139.30 E
Sampwe 36 Ed 9.20S 27.23 E
Sam Rayburn Reservoir 45 Ik 31.27N 94.37W
Samro, Ozero- 8 Mf 58.55N 28.50 E
Samsjøen 8 Da 63.05N 10.40 E
Samsø 7 Ci 55.50N 10.35 E
Samsø Bælt 8 Di 55.50N 10.45 E
Sam Son 25 Ld 19.44N 105.54 E
Samsun 22 Fe 41.17N 36.20 E
Samsun Dağı 15 Kl 37.40N 27.15 E
Samtredia 16 Mh 42.11N 42.17 E
Samuel, Mount- 59 Gc 19.41S 134.09 E
Samuhú 55 Bh 27.31S 60.24W
Samui, Ko- 21 Li 9.30N 100.00 E
Samur 16 Pi 41.53N 48.32 E
Samur-Apšeronski Kanal 16 Pi 40.35N 49.35 E
Samus 20 De 56.46N 84.44 E
Samut Prakan 25 Kf 13.36N 100.36 E
Samut Sakhon 25 Kf 13.31N 100.15 E
San 31 Gg 13.08N 4.53W
San [Asia] 25 Lf 13.32N 105.57 E
San [Pol.] 10 Rf 50.45N 21.51 E
San'ā' 22 Gh 15.23N 44.12 E
Sana 14 Ke 45.03N 16.23 E
Sanaag [3] 35 Hc 10.10N 47.50 E
Şanabū 24 Di 27.30N 30.47 E
Sanae 66 Bf 70.18S 2.22W
Sanāfīr 24 Fi 27.55N 34.42 E
Sanāg 35 Hd 7.45N 48.00 E
Sanaga 30 Hh 3.35N 9.38 E
San Agustín 55 Cn 38.01S 58.21W
San Agustín, Cabo- 48 Bc 28.05N 115.20W
San Agustin, Cape- 26 Ie 6.16N 126.11 E
Sanak Islands 40 Gf 54.25N 162.35W
Sanalona, Presa- 48 Fe 24.53N 107.00W
San Ambrosio, Isla- 56 Ec 26.21S 79.52W
Sanana 26 Ig 2.04S 125.08 E
Sanana, Pulau- 26 Ig 2.12S 125.55 E
Sanandaj 23 Gb 35.19N 47.00 E
San Andreas 46 Eg 38.12N 120.41W
San Andrés [3] 47 Hf 12.35N 81.42W
San Andres, Cerro- 48 Ih 19.48N 100.36W
San Andrés, Isla de- 52 Hd 12.32N 81.42W
San Andrés, Laguna de- 48 Kf 22.40N 97.50W
San Andrés de Giles 55 Cl 34.27S 59.27W
San Andrés del Rabanedo 13 Gb 42.37N 5.36W
San Andres Mountains 43 Fe 32.55N 106.45W
San Andres Peak 45 Cj 32.43N 106.30W
San Andrés Tuxtla 47 Ee 18.27N 95.13W
San Andrés y Providencia [2] 54 Ba 12.30N 81.45W
Sananduva 55 Gh 27.57S 51.48W
San Angelo 43 Ge 31.28N 100.26W
San Antonio [Blz.] 49 Ce 16.30N 89.02W
San Antonio [Chile] 56 Fd 33.35S 71.38W
San Antonio [Tx.-U.S.] 39 Jg 29.28N 98.31W
San Antonio [Ur.] 55 Dj 31.20S 57.45W
San Antonio, Cabo- [Arg.] 52 Ki 36.40S 56.42W
San Antonio, Cabo- [Cuba] 38 Kg 21.52N 84.57W
San Antonio, Cabo de-/Sant Antoni, Cap- 13 Mf 38.48N 0.12 E
San Antonio, Canal- 55 Aj 31.42S 62.15W
San Antonio, Punta- 48 Bc 29.45N 115.45W
San Antonio, Sierra de- 48 Db 30.00N 110.20W
San Antonio Abad 13 Nf 38.58N 1.18 E
San Antonio Bay 45 Hl 28.20N 96.45W
San Antonio de Caparo 49 Lj 7.35N 71.27W
San Antonio de Cortés 49 Cf 15.05N 88.04W
San Antonio de los Baños 49 Fb 22.53N 82.30W
San Antonio de los Cobres 56 Gb 24.11S 66.21W
San Antonio del Táchira 54 Db 7.50N 72.27W
San Antonio de Tamanaco 50 Ch 9.14N 66.03W
San Antonio Oeste 53 Jj 40.44S 64.57W
San Antonio River 43 Hf 28.30N 96.50W
Sanare 49 Mi 9.45N 69.39W
Sanary-sur-Mer 11 Lk 43.07N 5.48 E
San Augustín 53 Ie 1.53N 76.16W
San Augustine 45 Ik 31.32N 94.07W
Sanāw 35 Ib 17.50N 51.05 E
San Bartolomeo in Galdo 14 Ji 41.24N 15.01 E
San Baudilio de Llobregat/Sant Boi de Llobregat 13 Oc 41.21N 2.03 E
San Benedetto del Tronto 14 Hh 42.57N 13.53 E
San Benedetto Po 14 Ee 45.02N 10.55 E
San Benedicto, Isla- 47 Be 19.18N 110.49W
San Benito [Guat.] 49 Ce 16.55N 89.54W
San Benito [Tx.-U.S.] 45 Hm 26.08N 97.38W
San Benito, Islas- 48 Bc 28.20N 115.35W
San Benito Abad 49 Ji 8.56N 75.02W
San Benito Mountain 46 Eh 36.22N 120.38W
San Bernardino 39 Hf 34.06N 117.17W
San Bernardino, Passo del-/Sankt Bernardin Paß 14 Dd 46.30N 9.10 E
San Bernardino Mountains 46 Gi 34.10N 117.00W
San Bernardino Strait 26 Hd 12.32N 124.10 E
San Bernardo [Arg.] 55 Bh 27.17S 60.42W
San Bernardo [Chile] 56 Fd 33.36S 70.43W
San Bernardo [Mex.] 48 De 25.32N 111.45W
San Bernardo, Islas de- 49 Ji 9.45N 75.50W
San Bernardo, Punta de- 49 Ji 9.42N 75.42W
San Bernardo del Viento 54 Cb 9.22N 75.57W
San Blas [3] 49 Hi 7.50N 81.10W
San Blas [Mex.] 47 Cd 21.31N 105.16W
San Blas [Mex.] 47 Cc 26.05N 108.46W
San Blas [Mex.] 48 Id 27.25N 101.40W
San Blas, Archipiélago de- 49 Hi 9.30N 78.30W
San Blas, Cape- 43 Jf 29.40N 85.22W
San Blas, Cordillera de- 49 Hi 9.18N 79.00W
San Blas, Golfo de- 49 Hi 9.30N 79.00W
San Blas, Punta- 49 Hi 9.34N 78.58W
San Borja 54 Ef 14.49S 66.51W
San Borjas, Sierra de- 48 Cc 28.40N 113.45W
San Buenaventura 48 Id 27.05N 101.32W
Sancai 35 Fc 10.43N 35.40 E
San Carlos [Arg.] 55 Eh 27.45S 55.54W
San Carlos [Chile] 56 Fe 36.25S 71.58W
San Carlos [Mex.] 48 Je 24.35N 98.56W
San Carlos [Mex.] 48 Ic 29.01N 100.51W
San Carlos [Nic.] 49 Eh 11.07N 84.47W
San Carlos [Pan.] 49 Hi 8.29N 79.57W
San Carlos [Par.] 55 Df 22.16S 57.18W
San Carlos [Phil.] 26 Hd 10.30N 123.25 E
San Carlos [Phil.] 26 Hc 15.55N 120.20 E
San Carlos [Ur.] 55 Fl 34.48S 54.55W
San Carlos [Ven.] 54 Eb 9.40N 68.39W
San Carlos, Bahía- 48 Cd 27.55N 112.45W
San Carlos, Mesa de- 48 Bc 29.40N 115.25W
San Carlos, Punta- 48 Cc 28.00N 112.45W
San Carlos, Riacho- 55 Df 22.49S 57.53W
San Carlos, Río- [C.R.] 49 Eh 10.47N 84.12W
San Carlos, Río- [Ven.] 50 Bh 9.07N 68.25W
San Carlos de Bariloche 53 Ij 41.08S 71.15W
San Carlos de Bolívar 56 He 36.15S 61.06W
San Carlos de la Ràpita/Sant Carles de la Ràpita 13 Md 40.37N 0.36 E
San Carlos del Zulia 54 Db 9.01N 71.55W
San Carlos de Río Negro 54 Ec 1.55N 67.04W
San Carlos Reservoir 46 Jj 33.13N 110.24W
San Cataldo [It.] 14 Mj 40.23N 18.18 E
San Cataldo [It.] 14 Hm 37.29N 13.59 E
San Cayetano 55 Cn 38.20S 59.37W
Sancerre 11 Ig 47.20N 2.50 E
Sancerrois, Collines du- 11 Ig 47.20N 2.30 E
Sanchahe 28 Ib 44.59N 126.03 E
Sánchez 49 Md 19.14N 69.36W
Sánchez Magallanes 48 Mh 18.17N 93.59W
San Clemente [Ca.-U.S.] 43 De 33.26N 117.37W
San Clemente [Sp.] 13 Je 39.24N 2.26W
San Clemente del Tuyú 55 Dm 36.22S 56.43W
San Clemente Island 46 Fj 32.55N 118.30W
Sancois 11 Ih 46.50N 2.55 E
San Cosme 55 Ch 27.22S 58.31W
San Cristóbal [Arg.] 56 Hd 30.19S 61.14W
San Cristóbal [Bol.] 55 Ba 13.56S 61.50W
San Cristóbal [Cuba] 49 Fb 22.43N 83.03W
San Cristóbal [Dom.Rep.] 49 Ld 18.25N 70.06W
San Cristóbal [Mex.] 49 Li 17.49N 94.32W
San Cristóbal [Ven.] 53 Ie 7.46N 72.14W
San Cristóbal, Baia de- 48 Bd 27.25N 114.40W
San Cristóbal, Isla- 52 Hf 0.50S 89.26W
San Cristóbal de las Casas 47 Fe 16.45N 92.38W
San Cristóbal Island 57 Hf 10.36S 161.45 E
San Cristóbal Verapaz 49 Bf 15.23N 90.24W
Sancti Spíritus 47 Id 21.56N 79.27W
Sancti Spíritus [3] 49 Hb 22.00N 79.30W
Sancy, Puy de- 11 Ii 45.32N 2.50 E
Sand 7 Bg 59.29N 6.15 E
Sand 37 Ed 22.25S 30.05 E
Sanda 20 Dd 34.53N 135.14 E
Sandai 26 Fg 1.15S 110.31 E
Sandakan 22 Ni 5.50N 118.07 E
Sandal, Baie de- 63b Ce 20.49S 167.10 E
Sandal, Ozero- 7 Ie 62.25N 34.10 E
Sandane 7 Bf 61.46N 6.13 E
Sandanski 15 Gh 41.34N 23.17 E
Sandaré 34 Cc 14.42N 10.18W
Sandared 8 Eg 57.43N 12.47 E
Sandarne 8 Gc 61.16N 17.10 E
Sanday 9 Kb 59.15N 2.30W
Sande 8 De 59.36N 10.12 E
Sandefjord 7 Cg 59.08N 10.14 E
Sandégué 34 Ed 7.59N 3.33W
Sandeid 7 Ag 59.33N 5.50 E
Sanders 46 Ki 35.13N 109.20W
Sanderson 43 Ge 30.09N 102.24W
Sandersville 44 Fi 32.59N 82.48W
Sandfontein 37 Bd 22.11S 19.58 E
Sandgate 12 Dc 51.04N 1.09 E
Sandhammaren 8 Fi 55.23N 14.12 E
Sandhamn 8 He 59.17N 18.55 E
Sand Hills 43 Gc 41.45N 102.00W
Sandia 54 Ef 14.17S 69.26W
Sandia Crest 45 Ci 35.13N 106.27W
San Diego [Bol.] 55 Bc 16.04S 60.28W
San Diego [Ca.-U.S.] 39 Hf 32.43N 117.09W
San Diego, Cabo- 52 Jk 54.38S 65.07W
Sandıklı 24 Dc 38.28N 30.17 E
San Dimitri Point 14 In 36.05N 14.05 E
Sand in Taufers / Campo Tures 14 Fd 46.55N 11.57 E
Sand Lake 45 Ia 50.05N 94.39W
Sand Mountain 44 Dh 34.20N 86.02W
Sandnes 7 Ag 58.51N 5.44 E
Sandnessjøen 7 Cc 66.01N 12.38 E
Sandoa 31 Ji 9.41S 22.52 E
Sandö bank 8 Hf 58.10N 19.15 E
Sandomierska, Kotlina- 10 Rf 50.30N 22.00 E
Sandomierz 10 Rf 50.41N 21.45 E
San Domino 14 Jh 42.05N 15.30 E
Sandoná 54 Cc 1.18N 77.28W
San Donà di Piave 14 Ge 45.38N 12.34 E
Sandoval, Boca de- 48 Ke 24.58N 97.32W
Sandover River 59 Hd 21.43S 136.32 E
Sandoway 25 Ie 18.28N 94.22 E
Sandown 9 Lk 50.39N 1.09W
Sand Point 40 Ge 55.20N 160.30W
Sandpoint 43 Db 48.16N 116.33W
Sandras Dağı 15 Ll 37.04N 28.51 E
Sandray 9 Fe 56.54N 7.25W
Sandspit 42 Ef 53.15N 131.50W
Sand Springs [Mt.-U.S.] 46 Lc 47.09N 107.27W
Sand Springs [Ok.-U.S.] 45 Hh 36.09N 96.07W
Sandstone [Austl.] 59 De 27.59S 119.17 E
Sandstone [Mn.-U.S.] 45 Jc 46.08N 92.52W
Sandu 27 Jf 26.08N 113.16 E
Sandusky [Mi.-U.S.] 44 Fd 43.25N 82.50W
Sandusky [Oh.-U.S.] 43 Kc 41.27N 82.42W
Sandveld 37 Cd 21.20S 20.10 E
Sandvig-Allinge 7 Di 55.15N 14.49 E
Sandvika 8 De 59.54N 10.31 E
Sandviken 7 Df 60.37N 16.46 E
Sandwich 9 Oj 51.17N 1.20 E
Sandwich Bay 42 Lf 53.35N 57.15W
Sandy 12 Bb 52.07N 0.17W
Sandy Cape [Austl.] 59 Ih 41.25S 144.45 E
Sandy Cape [Austl.] 57 Gg 24.40S 153.15 E
Sandy Desert 25 Cc 28.46N 62.30 E
Sandykači 19 Gh 36.32N 62.35 E
Sandy Lake 42 If 53.02N 92.55W
Sandy Lake 42 If 53.02N 93.14W
Sandy Point 44 Il 26.01N 77.24W
Sandy Point Town 50 Ed 17.22N 62.50W
Sandžak 15 Cf 43.10N 20.00 E
Sanem 12 He 49.33N 5.56 E
San Estanislao 56 Ib 24.39S 56.26W
San Esteban 49 Ef 15.17N 85.52W
San Esteban, Bahía de- 48 Ee 25.40N 109.15W
San Esteban, Isla- 48 Cc 28.42N 112.36W
San Esteban de Gormaz 13 Ic 41.35N 3.12W
San Felice Circeo 14 Hi 41.14N 13.05 E
San Felipe [Chile] 56 Fd 32.45S 70.44W
San Felipe [Col.] 54 Ec 1.55N 67.06W
San Felipe [Mex.] 47 Bb 31.00N 114.52W
San Felipe [Mex.] 48 Ig 21.29N 101.13W
San Felipe [Ven.] 54 Ea 10.20N 68.44W
San Felipe, Cayos de- 49 Fc 21.58N 83.30W
San Felipe, Cerro de- 13 Kd 40.24N 1.51W
San Felipe Creek 46 Hj 33.09N 115.46W
San Feliu de Guíxols 13 Pc 41.47N 3.02 E
San Feliu de Llobregat/Sant Feliu de Llobregat 13 Oc 41.23N 2.03 E
San Felix, Isla- 56 Dc 26.17S 80.05W
San Fermín, Punta- 48 Bb 30.25N 114.40W
San Fernando [Chile] 56 Fd 34.35S 71.00W
San Fernando [Mex.] 48 Bb 29.59N 115.17W
San Fernando [Mex.] 47 Ed 24.51N 98.10W
San Fernando [Phil.] 26 Hc 16.37N 120.19 E
San Fernando [Phil.] 26 Hc 15.01N 120.41 E
San Fernando [Sp.] 13 Fh 36.28N 6.12W
San Fernando [Trin.] 54 Fa 10.17N 61.28W
San Fernando, Río- [Bol.] 55 Cc 17.13S 58.23W
San Fernando, Río- [Mex.] 48 Ke 24.55N 97.40W
San Fernando de Apure 53 Je 7.54N 67.28W
San Fernando de Atabapo 54 Ec 4.03N 67.42W
Sanford [Fl.-U.S.] 43 Kf 28.48N 81.16W
Sanford [Me.-U.S.] 44 Ld 43.26N 70.46W
Sanford [N.C.-U.S.] 44 Hh 35.29N 79.10W
Sanford, Mount- 40 Kd 62.13N 144.09W
San Francisco [Arg.] 56 Hd 31.26S 62.05W
San Francisco [Bol.] 55 Cc 17.42S 59.38W
San Francisco [Ca.-U.S.] 39 Gf 37.48N 122.24W
San Francisco [Pan.] 49 Gi 8.15N 80.58W
San Francisco, Isla- 48 De 24.50N 110.35W
San Francisco Bay 38 Gf 37.43N 122.17W
San Francisco Creek 45 El 29.53N 102.19W
San Francisco de Arriba 48 Hd 26.15N 102.50W
San Francisco de Bellocq 55 Bn 38.42S 60.01W
San Francisco de la Paz 49 Df 14.55N 86.14W
San Francisco del Laishi 55 Ch 26.14S 58.38W
San Francisco del Oro 47 Cc 26.52N 105.51W
San Francisco del Rincón 48 Ig 21.01N 101.51W
San Francisco de Macoris 47 Je 19.18N 70.15W
San Francisco Gotera 49 Cg 13.42N 88.06W
San Francisco Javier 13 Nf 38.42N 1.25 E
San Francisco Mountains 46 Kj 33.45N 109.00W
San Francisco River 46 Kj 32.59N 109.22W
San Fratello 14 Il 38.01N 14.36 E
San Gabriel 55 Di 28.58S 58.12W
San Gabriel, Punta- 48 Cc 28.25N 112.50W
San Gabriel Mountains 46 Gi 34.20N 117.45W
San Gallán, Isla- 54 Cf 13.50S 76.28W
Sangamon River 45 Kf 40.07N 90.20W
Sangar [Iran] 24 Md 37.08N 49.02 E
Sangar [R.S.F.S.R.] 22 Oc 63.55N 127.31 E
Sangatte 12 Dd 50.56N 1.45 E
San Gavino Monreale 14 Ck 39.33N 8.47 E
Sangay, Volcán- 52 If 2.00S 78.20W
Sange 36 Ed 7.02S 28.21 E
Sangeang, Pulau- 26 Gh 8.12S 119.04 E
San Gemini 14 Gh 42.37N 12.33 E
Sanger 46 Fh 36.42N 119.27W
Sangerhausen 10 He 51.28N 11.18 E
San Germán [Cuba] 49 Ic 20.36N 76.08W
San Germán [P.R.] 49 Nd 18.05N 67.03W
Sanggan He 28 Cd 40.24N 115.18 E
Sanggau 26 Ff 0.08N 110.36 E
Sangha 30 Ii 1.13S 16.49 E
Sangha [C.A.R.] [3] 35 Be 3.30N 16.00 E
Sangha [Con.] [3] 36 Cb 2.00N 15.00 E
Sangihe, Kepulauan-=Sangihe Islands (EN) 21 Oi 3.00N 125.30 E
Sangihe, Pulau- 26 If 3.35N 125.32 E
Sangihe Islands (EN)=Sangihe, Kepulauan- 21 Oi 3.00N 125.30 E
San Gil 54 Db 6.32N 73.08W
San Gimignano 14 Fg 43.28N 11.02 E
San Giovanni in Fiore 14 Kk 39.15N 16.42 E
San Giovanni in Persiceto 14 Ff 44.38N 11.11 E
San Giovanni Rotondo 14 Ji 41.42N 15.44 E
San Giovanni Valdarno 14 Fg 43.34N 11.32 E
Sangju 28 Jf 36.25N 128.10 E
Sāngli 22 Jh 16.52N 74.34 E
Sangmélima 34 He 2.56N 11.59 E
Sangoli 24 Pd 37.25N 54.35 E
San Gorgonio 38 Hf 34.05N 116.50W
San Gottardo/Sankt Gotthard=Saint Gotthard Pass (EN) 5 Gf 46.30N 8.30 E
Sangradouro Grande, Rio- 55 Dc 16.24S 57.10W
Sangre de Cristo Mountains 38 If 37.30N 105.15W
San Gregorio 55 Al 34.19S 62.02W
Sangre Grande 50 Fg 10.35N 61.07W
Sangri 27 Ff 29.20N 92.15 E
Sangro 14 Ih 42.14N 14.32 E
Sangue, Rio- 54 Gf 11.00S 58.40W
Sangüesa 13 Kb 42.35N 1.17W
Sanguinaires, Iles- 11 Ab 41.53N 8.35 E
San Gustavo 55 Cj 30.41S 59.23W
Sangyuan → Wuqiao 28 Df 37.38N 116.23 E
Sangzhi 27 Jf 29.23N 110.11 E
Sanhe [China] 28 Dd 40.00N 117.01 E
Sanhe [China] 27 La 50.30N 120.04 E
Sanhe-San 29 Cd 35.08N 132.37 E
Sanhezhen 28 Di 31.30N 117.15 E
San Hilario [Arg.] 55 Ch 26.02S 58.39W
San Hilario [Mex.] 48 De 24.22N 110.59W
San Hipolito, Bahía- 48 Cd 26.55N 113.55W
San Ignacio [Arg.] 55 Eh 27.16S 55.32W
San Ignacio [Blz.] 47 Ge 17.10N 89.04W
San Ignacio [Bol.] 54 Ef 14.53S 65.36W
San Ignacio [Bol.] 54 Fg 16.23S 60.59W
San Ignacio [Mex.] 48 Ff 25.55N 106.25W
San Ignacio [Mex.] 47 Bc 27.27N 112.51W
San Ignacio [Par.] 56 Ic 26.52S 57.03W
San Ignacio, Isla de- 48 Ee 25.25N 108.55W
San Ignacio, Laguna- 48 Cd 26.55N 113.15W
San Ildefonso, Cape- 26 Hc 16.02N 121.59 E
San Ildefonso, Cerro- 49 Cf 15.31N 88.17W
San Ildefonso o La Granja 13 Id 40.54N 4.00W
Saniquellie 34 Dd 7.22N 8.43W
San Isidro [Arg.] 55 Cl 34.27S 58.30W
San Isidro [Phil.] 26 Hd 11.24N 124.21 E
San Isidro de El General 47 Hg 9.22N 83.42W
Sanīyah 24 If 33.49N 42.43 E
San Jacinto 49 Ji 9.50N 75.07W
San Jacinto Peak 46 Gj 33.49N 116.41W
San Jaime 55 Cj 30.20S 58.19W
San Javier [Arg.] 55 Id 30.35S 59.57W
San Javier [Chile] 56 Fe 35.36S 71.45W
San Javier [Sp.] 13 Lg 37.48N 0.51W
San Javier [Ur.] 55 Ck 32.41S 58.08W
San Javier, Rio- 55 Bj 31.30S 60.20W
San Jerónimo Taviche 48 Ki 16.44N 96.35W
Sanjiachang 27 Hg 24.45N 101.53 E
Sanjiaocheng → Haiyan 27 Hd 36.58N 100.50 E
Sanjō 28 Of 37.37N 138.57 E
San Joaquín 54 Ff 13.04S 64.49W
San Joaquín, Río- 53 Jf 13.08S 63.41W
San Joaquín, Sierra de- 55 Eg 24.48S 56.00W
San Joaquin River 46 Eh 36.43N 121.50W
San Joaquin Valley 38 Gf 36.50N 120.10W
San Jon 45 Ei 35.06N 103.20W
San Jorge 56 Hd 31.54S 61.52W
San Jorge, Bahía de- 48 Cb 31.10N 113.15W
San Jorge, Golfe de-/Sant Jordi, Golf de- 13 Md 40.53N 1.00 E
San Jorge, Golfo- 52 Jj 46.00S 67.00W
San Jorge, Río- 49 Ji 9.07N 74.44W
San Jorge, Serranía- 55 Be 20.21S 60.59W
San Jorge Island 63a Dc 8.27S 159.35 E
San José [2] 55 Dl 34.15S 56.45W
San José [3] 49 Ei 9.40N 84.00W
San José [Arg.] 55 Eh 27.46S 55.47W
San Jose [Ca.-U.S.] 39 Gf 37.20N 121.53W
San José [C.R.] 39 Ki 9.56N 84.05W
San José [Mex.] 48 Dd 27.32N 110.09W
San José [Par.] 55 Dg 25.33S 56.45W
San Jose [Phil.] 26 Hc 15.48N 121.00 E
San Jose [Phil.] 26 Hd 12.21N 121.04 E
San José, Isla- [Mex.] 47 Bc 25.00N 110.38W
San José, Isla- [Pan.] 49 Hi 8.15N 79.07W
San José, Salinas de- 55 Bd 19.07S 60.54W
San José, Serranía de- 55 Bc 17.52S 60.49W
San Jose de Buenavista 26 Hd 10.46N 122.30 E
San José de Chiquitos 54 Fg 17.51S 60.47W
San José de Feliciano 55 Cj 30.23S 58.45W
San José de Gracia 48 Fd 26.08N 107.58W
San José de Guanipa 54 Fb 8.54N 64.09W
San José de Jachal 56 Gd 30.14S 68.45W
San José de las Lajas 49 Fb 22.58N 82.09W
San José del Cabo 47 Cd 23.03N 109.41W
San José del Guaviare 53 Ie 2.35N 72.38W
San José del Rosario 55 Dg 24.12S 56.48W
San José de Mayo 56 Id 34.20S 56.42W
San José de Ocuné 54 Dc 4.15N 70.20W
San José de Tiznados 50 Ch 9.23N 67.33W
San Juan [2] 56 Gd 31.00S 69.00W
San Juan [Arg.] 53 Ji 31.30S 68.30W
San Juán [Bol.] 55 Cc 17.52S 59.59W
San Juán [Bol.] 55 Bd 18.08S 60.08W
San Juan [C.Amer.] 38 Kh 10.56N 83.42W
San Juan [Dom.Rep.] 47 Je 18.48N 71.14W
San Juan [P.R.] 39 Mh 18.28N 66.07W
San Juan [U.S.] 38 Hf 37.18N 110.28W
San Juan, Cabezas de- 51a Cb 18.23N 65.36W
San Juan, Cabo- 30 Hh 1.10N 9.21 E
San Juan, Muela de- 13 Kd 40.26N 1.44W
San Juan, Pico- 47 Hd 21.59N 80.09W
San Juan, Punta- 65d Ab 27.03S 109.22W
San Juan, Río- [Arg.] 56 Gd 32.17S 67.22W
San Juan, Río- [Mex.] 48 Jd 26.10N 99.00W
San Juan, Río- [Mex.] 48 Lh 18.36N 95.40W
San Juan, Río- [Ven.] 50 Eg 10.14N 62.39W
San Juan, Volcán- 48 Gg 21.30N 104.57W
San Juan Bautista [Par.] 56 Ic 26.38S 57.10W
San Juan Bautista [Sp.] 13 Ne 39.05N 1.30 E
San Juan Bautista Tuxtepec 48 Kh 18.06N 96.07W
San Juan de Colón 49 Ki 8.02N 72.16W
San Juan de Guadalupe 48 He 24.38N 102.44W
San Juan del César 49 Kh 10.46N 72.59W
San Juan de Lima, Punta- 48 Hh 18.36N 103.42W
San Juan del Norte 47 Hf 10.55N 83.42W
San Juan de los Cayos 54 Ea 11.10N 68.25W
San Juan de los Lagos 48 Hg 21.15N 102.14W
San Juan de los Morros 54 Ea 9.55N 67.21W
San Juan del Río [Mex.] 48 Jg 20.29N 100.00W
San Juan del Río [Mex.] 48 Ge 24.47N 104.27W
San Juan del Sur 47 Gf 11.15N 85.52W
San Juan de Payara 50 Ci 7.39N 67.36W
San Juanico, Isla- 48 Fg 21.55N 106.40W
San Juanico, Punta- 48 Cd 26.05N 112.15W
San Juan Island 46 Db 48.32N 123.05W
San Juan Mountains 43 Fd 37.35N 107.10W
San Juan Neembucú 55 Dh 26.39S 57.56W
San Juan Nepomuceno [Col.] 54 Cb 9.57N 75.05W
San Juan Nepomuceno [Par.] 55 Eh 26.06S 55.58W
San Juan y Martínez 49 Fb 22.16N 83.50W
San Julián 53 Jj 49.19S 67.40W
San Just, Sierra de- 13 Ld 40.46N 0.48W
San Justo 56 Hd 30.47S 60.35W
Sankarani 30 Gg 12.01N 8.19W
Sankt Anton am Arlberg 14 Ec 47.08N 10.16 E
Sankt Augustin 12 Jd 50.47N 7.11 E
Sankt Bernardin Paß/San Bernardino, Passo del- 14 Dd 46.30N 9.10 E
Sankt Gallen 14 Dc 47.25N 9.25 E
Sankt Gallen [2] 14 Dc 47.20N 9.10 E
Sankt Goar 10 Df 50.09N 7.43 E
Sankt Goarshausen 12 Jd 50.09N 7.44 E
Sankt Gotthard/San Gottardo=Saint Gotthard Pass (EN) 5 Gf 46.30N 8.30 E
Sankt Ingbert 10 Dg 49.17N 7.07 E
Sankt Johann im Pongau 14 Hc 47.21N 13.12 E
Sankt Michael im Lungau 14 Hc 47.06N 13.38 E
Sankt Michel/Mikkeli 6 If 61.41N 27.15 E
Sankt Moritz 14 Dd 46.30N 9.52 E
Sankt Peter-Ording 10 Eb 54.18N 8.38 E
Sankt Pölten 14 Jb 48.12N 15.38 E
Sankt Ulrich / Ortisei 14 Fd 46.34N 11.40 E
Sankt Veit an der Glan 14 Id 46.46N 14.22 E
Sankt-Vith 11 Md 50.17N 6.08 E
Sankt Wendel 10 Dg 49.28N 7.10 E
Sankt Wolfang im Salzkammergut 14 Hc 47.44N 13.27 E
Sankuru 30 Ji 4.17S 20.25 E
San Lázaro 56 Ib 22.10S 57.55W
San Lázaro, Cabo- 47 Bd 24.48N 112.19W
San Lazaro, Sierra de- 48 Df 23.25N 110.00W
San Leandro 46 Dh 37.43N 122.09W
San Lorenzo 47 Fe 17.44N 94.45W
San Lorenzo [Arg.] 55 Bk 32.45S 60.44W
San Lorenzo [Ec.] 53 Ie 1.17N 78.50W
San Lorenzo [Hond.] 49 Dg 13.25N 87.27W
San Lorenzo, Isla- [Mex.] 48 Cc 28.38N 112.51W
San Lorenzo, Isla- [Peru] 54 Cf 12.05S 77.15W
San Lorenzo, Río- [Mex.] 48 Je 25.07N 98.32W
San Lorenzo, Río- [Mex.] 48 Fe 24.15N 107.24W
San Lorenzo de El Escorial 13 Hd 40.35N 4.09W
San Louis Potosí [2] 47 Dd 22.30N 100.30W
Sanlúcar de Barrameda 13 Fh 36.47N 6.21W
Sanlúcar la Mayor 13 Fg 37.23N 6.12W
San Lucas [Mex.] 48 Gf 22.33N 104.24W
San Lucas [Mex.] 47 Cd 22.53N 109.54W
San Lucas, Cabo- 38 Ig 22.50N 109.55W
San Lucas, Serranía de- 54 Db 8.00N 74.20W
San Lucido 14 Kk 39.18N 16.03 E
San Luis [Arg.] 53 Ji 33.20S 66.20W
San Luis [2] 56 Gd 34.00S 66.00W
San Luis [Bol.] 55 Cc 17.39S 58.42W
San Luis [Cuba] 49 Jc 20.12N 75.51W
San Luis [Guat.] 49 Ce 16.14N 89.27W
San Luis [Mex.] 48 Dc 29.33N 111.05W
San Luis, Isla- 48 Bb 29.58N 114.26W
San Luis, Sierra de- 49 Mh 11.11N 69.42W
San Luis de la Paz 48 Ig 21.18N 100.31W
San Luis del Palmar 55 Ch 27.31S 58.34W
San Luis de Palenque 54 Db 5.25N 71.40W
San Luis Gonzaga, Bahía- 48 Bc 30.00N 114.25W
San Luis Obispo 39 Gf 35.17N 120.40W
San Luis Pass 45 Il 29.05N 95.08W
San Luis Peak 45 Ch 37.59N 106.56W
San Luis Potosí 39 Ig 22.09N 100.59W
San Luis Río Colorado 47 Bb 32.29N 114.48W
San Luis Valley 43 Fd 37.25N 106.00W
Sanluri 14 Ck 39.34N 8.54 E
San Manuel [Arg.] 55 Cm 37.47S 58.50W
San Manuel [Az.-U.S.] 46 Jj 32.36N 110.38W

Index Symbols

[1] Independent Nation
[2] State, Region
[3] District, County
[4] Municipality
[5] Colony, Dependency
Continent
Physical Region
Historical or Cultural Region
Mount, Mountain
Volcano
Hill
Mountains, Mountain Range
Hills, Escarpment
Plateau, Upland
Pass, Gap
Plain, Lowland
Delta
Salt Flat
Valley, Canyon
Crater, Cave
Karst Features
Depression
Polder
Desert, Dunes
Forest, Woods
Heath, Steppe
Oasis
Cape, Point
Coast, Beach
Cliff
Peninsula
Isthmus
Sandbank
Island
Atoll
Rock, Reef
Islands, Archipelago
Rocks, Reefs
Coral Reef
Well, Spring
Geyser
River, Stream
Waterfall Rapids
River Mouth, Estuary
Lake
Salt Lake
Intermittent Lake
Reservoir
Swamp, Pond
Canal
Glacier
Ice Shelf, Pack Ice
Ocean
Sea
Gulf, Bay
Strait, Fjord
Lagoon
Bank
Seamount
Tablemount
Ridge
Shelf
Basin
Escarpment, Sea Scarp
Fracture
Trench, Abyss
National Park, Reserve
Point of Interest
Recreation Site
Cave, Cavern
Historic Site
Ruins
Wall, Walls
Church, Abbey
Temple
Scientific Station
Airport
Port
Lighthouse
Mine
Tunnel
Dam, Bridge

San Marcial, Punta-	48	De	25.30N	111.00W
San Marco, Capo-	14	Hm	37.30N	13.01 E
San Marcos [3]	49	Bf	15.00N	91.55W
San Marcos [Col.]	54	Cb	8.39N	75.08W
San Marcos [Guat.]	49	Bf	14.58N	91.48W
San Marcos [Hond.]	49	Cf	14.24N	88.56W
San Marcos [Mex.]	48	Gg	20.47N	104.11W
San Marcos [Mex.]	48	Ji	16.48N	99.21W
San Marcos [Nic.]	49	Dh	11.55N	86.12W
San Marcos [Tx.-U.S.]	43	Hf	29.53N	97.57W
San Marcos, Isla-	48	Cd	27.13N	112.06W
San Marcos, Sierra de-	48	Hd	26.30N	101.55W
San Marino	14	Gg	43.55N	12.28 E
San Marino [1]	6	Hg	43.55N	12.28 E
San Martin	56	Gd	33.04S	68.28W
San Martin	66	Qe	68.11S	67.00W
San Martin	48	Ab	30.30N	116.05W
San Martín [2]	54	Ce	7.00S	76.50W
San Martin, Cerro-	48	Lh	18.19N	94.48W
San Martín, Lago-	56	Fg	48.52S	72.40W
San Martín, Río-	54	Ff	13.08S	63.43W
San Martin de los Andes	56	Ff	40.10S	71.21W
San Martín de Valdeiglesias	13	Hd	40.21N	4.24W
San Martino di Castrozza	14	Fd	46.16N	11.48 E
San Mateo [Ca.-U.S.]	46	Dh	37.35N	122.19W
San Mateo [Ven.]	50	Dh	9.45N	64.33W
San Mateo/Sant Mateu del Maestrat	13	Md	40.28N	0.11 E
San Mateo Ixtatán	49	Bf	15.50N	91.29W
San Mateo Mountains	45	Cj	33.10N	107.20W
San Matias	55	Cc	16.22S	58.24W
San Matías, Golfo-	52	Jj	41.30S	64.15W
Sanmen (Haiyou)	27	Lf	29.08N	121.22 E
Sanmen Wan	28	Fj	29.00N	121.45 E
Sanmenxia	27	Je	34.44N	111.19 E
San Miguel [Arg.]	55	Dh	27.59S	57.36W
San Miguel [Bol.]	55	Bc	16.42S	61.01W
San Miguel [Ca.-U.S.]	46	Ei	35.45N	120.42W
San Miguel [ElSal.]	39	Kh	13.29N	88.11W
San Miguel [Pan.]	49	Hi	8.27N	78.56W
San Miguel, Golfo de-	49	Hi	8.22N	78.17W
San Miguel, Río- [Bol.]	52	Jg	13.52S	63.56W
San Miguel, Río- [Mex.]	48	Dc	29.16N	110.53W
San Miguel, Río- [Mex.]	48	Fd	26.59N	107.58W
San Miguel, Río- [S.Amer.]	55	Cd	19.25S	58.20W
San Miguel, Salinas de-	55	Bd	19.12S	60.45W
San Miguel, Volcán de-	47	Gf	13.26N	88.16W
San Miguel Bay	26	Hd	13.50N	123.10 E
San Miguel de Allende	48	Ig	20.55N	100.45W
San Miguel de Horcasitas	48	Dc	29.29N	110.45W
San Miguel del Monte	55	Cl	35.27S	58.48W
San Miguel del Padrón	49	Fb	23.05N	82.19W
San Miguel de Tucumán	53	Jh	26.49S	65.13W
San Miguel Island	46	Ei	34.02N	120.22W
San Miguel Islands	26	Ge	7.45N	118.28 E
San Miguelito	55	Bc	17.20S	60.59W
San Miguel River	45	Bg	38.23N	108.48W
San Miguel Sola de Vega	48	Ki	16.31N	96.59W
San Millán	13	Ib	42.18N	3.12W
Sanming	27	Kf	26.11N	117.37 E
San Miniato	14	Eg	43.41N	10.51 E
Sannan	29	Dd	35.04N	135.03 E
Sannār	31	Kg	13.33N	33.38 E
Sannicandro Garganico	14	Ji	41.50N	15.34 E
San Nicolás, Río- [Bol.]	55	Bc	17.08S	61.17W
San Nicolás, Río- [Mex.]	48	Gh	19.40N	105.14W
San Nicolas de los Arroyos	56	Hd	33.20S	60.13W
San Nicolás de los Garzas	48	Ie	25.45N	100.18W
San Nicolas Island	46	Fj	33.15N	119.31W
Sannikova, Proliv-	20	Ib	74.30N	140.00 E
Sannio	14	Ii	41.20N	14.30 E
San'nohe	29	Ga	40.22N	141.15 E
San'nō-Tōge	29	Fc	37.06N	139.44 E
Sannūr, Wādī-	24	Dh	28.59N	31.03 E
Sanok	10	Sg	49.34N	22.13 E
Sanok-Zagórz	10	Sg	49.31N	22.17 E
San Onofre	54	Cb	9.45N	75.32W
San Pablo	22	Oh	14.04N	121.19 E
San Pablo, Punta-	48	Bd	27.15N	114.30W
San Pedro	56	Ib	24.07S	56.59W
San-Pédro	34	De	4.44N	6.37W
San Pedro [3]	55	Dg	24.15S	56.30W
San Pedro [Arg.]	56	Hb	24.14S	64.52W
San Pedro [Arg.]	55	Ck	33.40S	59.40W
San Pedro [Arg.]	56	Jc	26.38S	54.08W
San Pedro, Río- [Guat.]	49	Be	17.46N	91.26W
San Pedro, Río- [Mex.]	48	Gg	21.45N	105.30W
San Pedro, Sierra de-	13	Fe	39.20N	6.35W
San Pedro Carchá	49	Bf	15.29N	90.16W
San Pedro Channel	46	Fj	33.43N	118.23W
San Pedro de Alcántara	13	Hh	36.29N	5.00W
San Pedro de Atacama	56	Gb	22.55S	68.13W
San Pedro de Lloc	54	Ce	7.26S	79.31W
San Pedro de Macorís	49	Md	18.27N	69.18W
San Pedro Martir, Sierra de-	47	Ab	30.45N	115.13W
San Pedro Nolasco, Isla-	48	Dd	27.58N	111.25W
San Pedro Pochutla	48	Kj	15.44N	96.28W
San Pedros de las Colonias	47	Dc	25.45N	102.59W
San Pedro Sula	39	Kh	15.27N	88.02W
San Pedro Tapanatepec	48	Li	16.21N	94.12W
San Pedro Tututepec	48	Ki	16.09N	97.38W
San Pellegrino Terme	14	De	45.50N	9.40 E
San Pietro	14	Ck	39.10N	8.15 E
San Quentin, Bahía de-	48	Ab	30.20N	116.00W
San Quintín	47	Ab	30.29N	115.57W
San Rafael [Arg.]	53	Ji	34.40S	68.21W
San Rafael [Bol.]	55	Bc	16.45S	60.34W
San Rafael [Ca.-U.S.]	46	Dg	38.00N	122.31W
San Rafael [Mex.]	48	He	24.40N	102.01W
San Rafael [Mex.]	48	Ie	25.01N	100.33W
San Rafael [Ven.]	49	Lh	10.58N	71.44W
San Rafael, Cabo-	49	Md	19.01N	68.57W
San Rafael, Río-	55	Cd	18.26S	59.37W
San Rafael de Atamaica	50	Ci	7.32N	67.24W
San Rafael del Norte	49	Dg	13.12N	86.06W
San Rafael Knob	46	Jg	38.50N	110.48W
San Rafael Mountains	46	Fi	34.45N	119.50W
San Rafael River	46	Jg	38.47N	110.07W
San Ramón [Peru]	54	Cf	11.08S	75.20W
San Ramón [Ur.]	55	El	34.18S	55.58W
San Ramón, Río-	55	Bb	14.03S	61.35W
San Ramón de la Nueva Oran	56	Hb	23.08S	64.20W
San Raymundo, Arroyo-	48	Cd	26.21N	112.37W
San Remo	14	Bg	43.49N	7.46 E
Sanriku	29	Gb	39.08N	141.48 E
San Román, Cabo-	54	Ea	12.12N	70.00W
San Roque [Arg.]	55	Ci	28.34S	58.43W
San Roque [Sp.]	13	Gh	36.13N	5.24W
San Saba	45	Gk	31.12N	98.43W
Sansalé	34	Cc	11.07N	14.51W
San Salvador	13	Pe	39.27N	3.11 E
San Salvador [Arg.]	55	Di	29.16S	57.31W
San Salvador [Arg.]	56	Id	31.37S	58.30W
San Salvador [ElSal.]	39	Kh	13.42N	89.12W
San Salvador [Par.]	55	Dg	25.51S	56.28W
San Salvador (Watling)	47	Jd	24.02N	74.28W
San Salvador, Cuchilla-	55	Dk	33.56S	57.45W
San Salvador, Isla-	52	Gf	0.14S	90.45W
San Salvador, Río-	55	Ck	33.29S	58.23W
San Salvador de Jujuy	53	Jh	24.10S	65.20W
Sansanné-Mango	34	Fc	10.21N	0.28 E
San Sebastián [Col.]	49	Ji	9.13N	74.18W
San Sebastián [P.R.]	51a	Bb	18.21N	67.00W
San Sebastián [Sp.]	6	Fg	43.19N	1.59W
San Sebastián, Bahía-	56	Gh	53.15S	68.23W
San Sebastián, Isla-	49	Cg	13.11N	88.26W
San Sebastián de la Gomera	32	Dd	28.06N	17.06W
Sansepolcro	14	Gg	43.34N	12.08 E
San Severo	14	Ji	41.41N	15.23 E
San Silvestre	49	Li	8.15N	70.02W
San Simeon	46	Ei	35.39N	121.11W
Sanski Most	14	Kf	44.46N	16.40 E
Santa Agueda	48	Cd	27.13N	112.20W
Santa Ana	63a	Fd	10.50S	162.28 E
Santa Ana [Arg.]	55	Eh	27.22S	55.34W
Santa Ana [Bol.]	55	Bc	16.37S	60.43W
Santa Ana [Bol.]	54	Eg	15.31S	67.30W
Santa Ana [Bol.]	55	Cd	18.43S	58.44W
Santa Ana [Ca.-U.S.]	43	De	33.43N	117.54W
Santa Ana [ElSal.]	39	Kh	13.59N	89.34W
Santa Ana [Mex.]	47	Bb	30.33N	111.07W
Santa Ana [Ven.]	50	Dh	9.19N	64.39W
Santa Ana, Río-	49	Li	9.30N	71.57W
Santa Ana, Volcán de-	38	Kh	13.50N	89.39W
Santa Bárbara [3]	49	Cf	15.10N	88.20W
Santa Barbara	39	Hf	34.03N	118.15W
Santa Bárbara [Hond.]	49	Cf	14.53N	88.14W
Santa Bárbara [Mex.]	47	Cc	26.48N	105.49W
Santa Bárbara [Ven.]	49	Lj	7.47N	71.10W
Santa Bárbara, Puerto de-	13	Lb	42.30N	0.50W
Santa Bárbara, Serra de-	55	Fe	21.45S	53.23W
Santa Barbara Channel	46	Fi	34.15N	119.55W
Santa Catalina	63a	Fd	10.54S	162.27 E
Santa Catalina [Col.]	49	Jh	10.37N	75.33W
Santa Catalina [Ven.]	50	Fh	8.33N	61.51W
Santa Catalina, Gulf of-	46	Gj	33.20N	117.45W
Santa Catalina, Isla-	48	De	25.40N	110.45W
Santa Catalina Island	46	Fj	33.23N	118.24W
Santa Catarina	48	Ie	25.41N	100.28W
Santa Catarina [2]	56	Kc	27.00S	50.00W
Santa Catarina, Ilha de-	52	Lh	27.36S	48.30W
Santa Catarina, Sierra-	48	Fc	29.40N	107.30W
Santa Cecília	55	Gh	26.56S	50.27W
Santa Cesarea Terme	14	Mj	40.02N	18.28 E
Santa Clara [Ca.-U.S.]	46	Eh	37.21N	121.59W
Santa Clara [Cuba]	39	Lg	22.24N	79.58W
Santa Clara [Gabon]	36	Ab	0.34N	9.17 E
Santa Clara [Mex.]	48	Fc	29.17N	107.01W
Santa Clara [Ur.]	55	Ek	32.55S	54.58W
Santa Clara, Barragem do-	13	Dg	37.30N	8.20W
Santa Clara, Isla-	56	Ed	33.42S	79.00W
Santa Clara de Saguier	55	Bj	31.21S	61.50W
Santa Coloma de Farners/Santa Coloma de Farnés	13	Oc	41.52N	2.40 E
Santa Coloma de Farnés/Santa Coloma de Farners	13	Oc	41.52N	2.40 E
Santa Coloma de Gramanet	13	Oc	41.27N	2.13 E
Santa Coloma de Queralt	13	Nc	41.32N	1.23 E
Santa Comba	13	Da	43.02N	8.49W
Santa Croce Camerina	14	In	36.50N	14.31 E
Santa Cruz [Arg.] [2]	56	Gg	49.00S	70.00W
Santa Cruz [Azr.]	32	Bb	39.05N	28.01W
Santa Cruz [Azr.]	32	Ab	39.27N	31.07W
Santa Cruz [Bol.]	53	Jg	17.48S	63.10W
Santa Cruz [Bol.] [2]	54	Fg	17.30S	61.30W
Santa Cruz [Braz.]	54	Id	0.36S	49.11W
Santa Cruz [Braz.]	55	Dd	18.32S	57.12W
Santa Cruz [Ca.-U.S.]	43	Cd	36.58N	122.01W
Santa Cruz [Chile]	56	Fd	34.38S	71.22W
Santa Cruz [C.R.]	49	Eh	10.01N	84.02W
Santa Cruz [Phil.]	26	Hd	14.01N	121.21 E
Santa Cruz, Isla-	52	Gf	0.38S	90.23W
Santa Cruz, Isla de-	48	De	25.17N	110.43W
Santa Cruz, Río-	56	Gh	50.08S	68.20W
Santa Cruz, Serra da-	55	Jc	17.05S	45.17W
Santa Cruz Cabrália	54	Kg	16.17S	39.02W
Santa Cruz de la Palma	32	Dd	28.41N	17.45W
Santa Cruz de la Zarza	13	Ie	39.58N	3.10W
Santa Cruz del Quiché	49	Bf	15.02N	91.08W
Santa Cruz del Sur	47	Id	20.43N	78.00W
Santa Cruz de Mudela	13	If	38.38N	3.28W
Santa Cruz de Tenerife [3]	32	Dd	28.10N	17.20W
Santa Cruz de Tenerife	31	Ff	28.27N	16.14W
Santa Cruz do Rio Pardo	55	Hf	22.55S	49.37W
Santa Cruz do Sul	56	Jc	29.43S	52.26W
Santa Cruz Island	46	Fi	34.01N	119.45W
Santa Cruz Islands	57	Hf	10.45S	165.55 E
Santadi	14	Ck	39.05N	8.43 E
Santa Elena [Arg.]	55	Bm	37.21S	60.37W
Santa Elena [Arg.]	56	Id	30.57S	59.48W
Santa Elena [Ec.]	54	Bd	2.14S	80.52W
Santa Elena, Bahía de- [C.R.]	49	Eh	10.59N	85.50W
Santa Elena, Bahía de- [Ec.]	54	Bd	2.05S	80.55W
Santa Elena, Cabo-	47	Gf	10.55N	85.57W
Santa Elena de Uairén	54	Fc	4.37N	61.08W
Santa Eulalia	13	Kd	40.34N	1.19W
Santa Eulalia del Río	13	Nf	38.59N	1.31 E
Santa Fé	49	Fc	21.45N	82.45W
Santa Fe [2]	56	Hd	31.00S	61.00W
Santafé	13	Ig	37.11N	3.43W
Santa Fe [Arg.]	53	Ji	31.40S	60.40W
Santa Fe [N.M.-U.S.]	39	If	35.42N	106.57W
Santa Fé de Minas	55	Jc	16.41S	45.28W
Santa Fé do Sul	55	Ge	20.13S	50.56W
Sant'Agata di Militello	14	Il	38.04N	14.38 E
Santa Helena [Braz.]	55	Eg	24.56S	54.23W
Santa Helena [Braz.]	54	Id	2.14S	45.18W
Santa Helena de Goiás	54	Hg	17.43S	50.35W
Santa Inês	54	Id	3.39S	45.22W
Santa Inés	49	Mh	10.37N	69.18W
Santa Ines, Bahía-	48	Dd	27.00N	111.55W
Santa Inés, Isla-	52	Ik	53.45S	72.45W
Santa Isabel [Arg.]	55	Bk	33.54S	61.42W
Santa Isabel [Arg.]	56	Ge	36.15S	66.56W
Santa Isabel [Braz.]	55	Ba	13.40S	60.44W
Santa Isabel [P.R.]	51a	Bc	17.58N	66.25W
Santa Isabel, Pico de-	34	Ge	3.35N	8.46 E
Santa Isabel Island	57	Ge	8.00S	159.00 E
Santa Izabel do Ivai	55	Ff	22.58S	53.14W
Santa Juliana	55	Id	19.19S	47.32W
Santa Lucía [Arg.]	56	Gd	31.32S	68.29W
Santa Lucía [Ur.]	55	Dl	34.27S	56.24W
Santa Lucía, Esteros del-	55	Ci	28.15S	58.20W
Santa Lucía, Río- [Arg.]	55	Ci	29.05S	59.13W
Santa Lucía, Río- [Ur.]	55	Dl	34.48S	56.22W
Santa Lucía Cotzumalguapa	49	Bf	14.20N	91.01W
Santa Lucia Range	43	Cd	36.00N	121.20W
Santa Luzia	32	Cf	16.46N	24.45W
Santa Luzia, Ribeirão-	55	Fe	21.31S	53.53W
Santa Margarita	55	Bi	28.18S	61.33W
Santa Margarita, Isla de-	47	Bd	24.27N	111.50W
Santa Margherita Ligure	14	Df	44.20N	9.12 E
Santa Maria [Braz.]	53	Kh	29.41S	53.48W
Santa Maria	30	Ee	36.58N	25.06W
Santa Maria [Ca.-U.S.]	43	Ce	34.57N	120.26W
Santa María	56	Gc	26.41S	66.02W
Santa María	47	Cb	31.00N	107.14W
Santa María	55	Bc	17.08S	61.01W
Santa María, Bahía de-	48	Ee	25.05N	108.10W
Santa Maria, Cabo de- [Ang.]	30	Ij	13.25S	12.32 E
Santa Maria, Cabo de- [Port.]	13	Eh	36.58N	7.54W
Santa Maria, Cape-	49	Jb	23.41N	75.19W
Santa María, Cayo-	49	Hb	22.40N	79.00W
Santa María, Isla- [Chile]	56	Fe	37.02S	73.33W
Santa María, Isla- [Ec.]	54a	Ab	1.15S	90.25W
Santa María, Laguna de-	48	Fb	31.10N	107.15W
Santa María, Río- [Mex.]	48	Jg	21.37N	99.15W
Santa María, Río- [Pan.]	49	Gi	8.06N	80.29W
Santa Maria, Rio- [Braz.]	55	Ee	21.50S	54.53W
Santa Maria, Rio- [Braz.]	55	Ib	14.19S	46.49W
Santa María Asunción Tlaxiaco	48	Ki	17.16N	97.41W
Santa Maria Capua Vetere	14	Ii	41.05N	14.15 E
Santa Maria da Vitória	55	Ja	13.24S	44.12W
Santa María de Cuevas	48	Fd	27.55N	106.23W
Santa María de Ipire	50	Dh	8.49N	65.19W
Santa María del Oro	48	Ge	25.56N	105.22W
Santa María del Río	48	Ig	21.48N	100.45W
Santa Maria di Leuca, Capo-	5	Hh	39.47N	18.22 E
Santa María la Real de Nieva	13	Hc	41.04N	4.24W
Santa María Zacatepec	48	Ki	16.46N	98.00W
Santa Marinella	14	Fh	42.02N	11.51 E
Santa Marta	53	Id	11.15N	74.13W
Santa Marta, Cabo de-	36	Be	13.52S	12.25 E
Santa Marta, Ría de-	13	Ea	43.42N	7.51W
Santa Marta Grande, Cabo de-	55	Hi	28.38S	48.45W
Santa Monica	43	De	34.01N	118.30W
Santan	26	Gg	0.03S	117.28 E
Santana	55	Ja	12.59S	44.03W
Santana, Coxilha de-	55	Ej	31.15S	55.15W
Santana, Rio-	55	Gd	19.43S	51.02W
Santana da Boa Vista	55	Fj	30.52S	53.07W
Santana do Livramento	56	Id	30.53S	55.31W
Santander [3]	13	Ia	43.10N	4.00W
Santander [2]	54	Db	6.35N	73.20W
Santander [Col.]	54	Cc	3.01N	76.29W
Santander [Phil.]	26	He	9.25N	123.20 E
Santander [Sp.]	6	Fg	43.28N	3.48W
Santander, Bahía de-	13	Ia	43.27N	3.48W
Santander Jiménez	47	Ed	24.13N	98.28W
Sant'Andrea	14	Lj	40.05N	17.55 E
Sant'Antioco	14	Ck	39.04N	8.27 E
Sant'Antioco	5	Gh	39.05N	8.25 E
Sant Antoni, Cap-/San Antonio, Cabo de-	13	Mf	38.48N	0.12 E
Santañy	13	Pe	39.22N	3.07 E
Santa Olalla	13	Hd	40.01N	4.26W
Santa Olalla del Cala	13	Fg	37.54N	6.13W
Santa Paula	46	Fi	34.21N	119.04W
Santa Pola	13	Lf	38.11N	0.33W
Sant'Arcangelo	14	Kj	40.15N	16.16 E
Santarcangelo di Romagna	14	Gf	44.04N	12.27 E
Santarém [2]	13	De	39.15N	8.35W
Santarém [Braz.]	53	Kf	2.26S	54.42W
Santarém [Port.]	13	De	39.14N	8.41W
Santaren Channel	47	Id	24.00N	79.30W
Santa Rita [Braz.]	55	Cc	16.15S	59.00W
Santa Rita [Col.]	54	Ec	4.55N	68.20W
Santa Rita [Guam]	64c	Bb	13.23N	144.40 E
Santa Rita [Hond.]	49	Df	15.09N	87.53W
Santa Rita [Ven.]	50	Ch	8.08N	66.16W
Santa Rita [Ven.]	49	Lh	10.32N	71.32W
Santa Rita do Araguaia	55	Fc	17.20S	53.12W
Santa Rosa [3]	49	Bf	14.10N	90.18W
Santa Rosa [Arg.]	56	Gd	31.31S	65.04W
Santa Rosa [Arg.]	53	Ji	36.40S	64.15W
Santa Rosa [Braz.]	56	Jc	27.52S	54.29W
Santa Rosa [Ca.-U.S.]	43	Cd	38.26N	122.43W
Santa Rosa [Ec.]	54	Cd	3.27S	79.58W
Santa Rosa [N.M.-U.S.]	43	Ge	34.57N	104.41W
Santa Rosa [Par.]	55	Dh	26.52S	56.49W
Santa Rosa [Ven.]	49	Mi	8.26N	69.42W
Santa Rosa [Ven.]	50	Dh	9.38N	64.18W
Santa Rosa, Mount-	64c	Ba	13.32N	144.55 E
Santa Rosa de Copán	49	Cf	14.47N	88.46W
Santa Rosa de la Roca	55	Bc	16.04S	61.32W
Santa Rosa Island	46	Ej	33.58N	120.06W
Santa Rosalia	39	Hg	27.19N	112.17W
Santa Rosalía	50	Bh	9.02N	69.01W
Santa Rosalia, Punta-	48	Bc	28.40N	114.20W
Santa Rosa Range	46	Gf	41.00N	117.40W
Santa Rosa Wash	46	Ij	33.10N	112.05W
Šantarskije Ostrova = Shantar Islands (EN)	21	Pd	55.00N	137.36 E
Santas Creus/Santes Creus	13	Nc	41.19N	1.18 E
Santa Sylvina	56	Hc	27.49S	61.09W
Santa Teresa [Arg.]	55	Bk	33.26S	60.47W
Santa Teresa [Mex.]	48	Ke	25.17N	97.51W
Santa Teresa [Peru]	54	Df	13.01S	72.39W
Santa Teresa, Rio-	55	Ha	12.40S	48.47W
Santa Teresa di Riva	14	Jm	37.57N	15.22 E
Santa Teresa Gallura	14	Di	41.14N	9.11 E
Santa Teresita	55	Dm	36.32S	56.41W
Santa Vitória do Palmar	56	Jd	33.31S	53.21W
Santa Vitória	55	Gd	18.50S	50.08W
Sant Barbara Island	46	Fj	33.23N	119.01W
Sant Boi de Llobregat/San Baudilio de Llobregat	13	Oc	41.21N	2.03 E
Sant Carles de la Ràpita/San Carlos de la Rápita	13	Md	40.37N	0.36 E
Santee River	43	Le	33.14N	79.28W
Santeh	24	Ld	36.10N	46.32 E
San Telmo	48	Ab	30.58N	116.06W
San Telmo, Bahía de-	48	Hh	18.45N	103.40W
San Telmo, Punta-	47	De	18.19N	103.30W
Santerno	14	Ff	44.34N	11.58 E
Santerre	11	Ie	49.55N	2.30 E
Santes Creus/Santas Creus	13	Nc	41.19N	1.18 E
Sant'Eufemia, Golfo di-	14	Kl	38.50N	16.05 E
Sant'Eufemia Lamezia	14	Kl	38.55N	16.15 E
Sant Feliu de Llobregat/San Felíu de Llobregat	13	Oc	41.23N	2.03 E
Santhià	14	Ce	45.22N	8.10 E
Santiago [2]	56	Fd	33.30S	70.50W
Santiago [Bol.]	54	Gg	18.19S	59.34W
Santiago [Bol.]	55	Bd	19.22S	60.51W
Santiago [Braz.]	56	Jc	29.11S	54.53W
Santiago [Chile]	53	Ii	33.27S	70.40W
Santiago [Dom.Rep.]	39	Lh	19.27N	70.42W
Santiago [Mex.]	48	Ie	25.25N	100.09W
Santiago [Mex.]	48	Cd	27.32N	112.49W
Santiago [Pan.]	39	Ki	8.05N	80.59W
Santiago [Par.]	55	Dh	27.09S	56.47W
Santiago, Cerro-	49	Gi	8.33N	81.44W
Santiago, Río-	54	Cd	4.27S	77.36W
Santiago, Río de-	48	Ge	25.11N	105.26W
Santiago, Serranía-	55	Cd	18.25S	59.25W
Santiago de Chuco	54	Ce	8.09S	78.11W
Santiago de Compostela	13	Db	42.53N	8.33W
Santiago de Cuba	39	Lg	20.01N	75.49W
Santiago de Cuba [3]	49	Ic	20.10N	76.10W
Santiago de la Ribera	13	Lg	37.48N	0.48W
Santiago del Estero	53	Jh	27.50S	64.15W
Santiago del Estero [2]	56	Hc	28.00S	63.30W
Santiago de Papasquiaro	48	Ge	25.03N	105.25W
Santiago do Cacém	13	Df	38.01N	8.42W
Santiago Ixcuintla	47	Cd	21.49N	105.13W
Santiago Mountains	45	El	29.40N	103.15W
Santiago Pinotepa Nacional	47	Ee	16.19N	98.01W
Santiaguillo, Isla-	48	Lh	19.05N	95.50W
Santiaguillo, Laguna de-	48	Ge	24.50N	104.50W
Santiam River	46	Dd	44.42N	123.55W
Santillana	13	Ha	43.23N	4.06W
San Timoteo	49	Li	9.48N	71.04W
Säntis	14	Dc	47.15N	9.20 E
Santisteban del Puerto	13	If	38.15N	3.12W
Sant Jordi, Golf de-/San Jorge, Golfe de-	13	Md	40.53N	1.00 E
Sant Mateu del Maestrat/San Mateo	13	Md	40.28N	0.11 E
Santo, Ile-	57	Hf	15.15S	166.50 E
Santo Anastácio	55	Ge	21.58S	51.39W
Santo André	55	If	23.40S	46.31W
Santo Ângelo	56	Jc	28.18S	54.16W
Santo Antão	30	Eg	17.05N	25.10W
Santo Antônio	56	Jc	26.03S	53.12W
Santo Antonio	34	Ge	1.39N	7.25 E
Santo Antônio de Jesus	54	Kf	12.58S	39.16W
Santo Antônio do Içá	54	Ed	3.05S	67.57W
Santo Antônio do Leverger	54	Gg	15.52S	56.05W
Santo Corazón	54	Gg	17.59S	58.51W
Santo Corazón, Río-	55	Cc	17.23S	58.23W
Santo Domingo [Cuba]	49	Gb	22.35N	80.15W
Santo Domingo [Dom.Rep.]	39	Mh	18.28N	69.54W
Santo Domingo [Mex.]	48	Bb	30.43N	115.56W
Santo Domingo [Mex.]	48	Bc	28.12N	114.02W
Santo Domingo [Mex.]	48	If	23.20N	101.44W
Santo Domingo [Nic.]	49	Eg	12.16N	85.05W
Santo Domingo, Cay-	49	Jc	21.42N	75.46W
Santo Domingo, Punta-	48	Cd	26.20N	112.40W
Santo Domingo, Río- [Mex.]	48	Kh	18.10N	96.08W
Santo Domingo, Río- [Ven.]	49	Mi	8.01N	69.33W
Santo Domingo de la Calzada	13	Jb	42.26N	2.57W
Santo Domingo de los Colorados	54	Cd	0.15S	79.10W
Santo Domingo de Silos	13	Ic	41.58N	3.25W
Santo Domingo Pueblo	45	Ci	35.31N	106.22W
San Tomé	50	Dh	8.58N	64.08W
Santoña	13	Ia	43.27N	3.27W
Santos	53	Lh	23.57S	46.20W
Santos, Sierra de los-	13	Gf	38.15N	5.20W
Santos Dumont	55	Ke	21.28S	43.34W
Santos Unzué	55	Bl	35.45S	60.51W
Santo Tirso	13	Dc	41.21N	8.28W
Santo Tomás [Bol.]	55	Cc	17.46S	58.55W
Santo Tomás [Mex.]	48	Ab	31.33N	116.24W
Santo Tomás [Nic.]	49	Eg	12.04N	85.05W
Santo Tomás, Punta-	48	Ab	31.34N	116.42W
Santo Tomé	56	Ic	28.33S	56.03W
Santu Lussurgiu	14	Cj	40.08N	8.39 E
Santurce-Antiguo	13	Ia	43.20N	3.02W
Sanuki-Sanmyaku	29	Cd	34.05N	134.00 E
San Valentín, Cerro-	52	Ij	46.36S	73.20W
San Vicente [Arg.]	55	Cl	35.01S	58.25W
San Vicente [Mex.]	48	Ab	31.20N	116.15W
San Vicente [Phil.]	26	Hc	18.30N	122.09 E
San Vicente, Sierra de-	13	Hd	40.10N	4.45W
San Vicente de Cañete	54	Cf	13.05S	79.24W
San Vicente de la Barquera	13	Ha	43.26N	4.24W
San Vicente del Caguán	54	Dc	2.07N	74.46W
San Vicente de Raspeig	13	Lf	38.24N	0.31W
San Vincente	47	Gf	13.38N	88.48W
San Vincenzo	14	Eg	43.06N	10.32 E
San Vito [C.R.]	49	Fi	8.50N	82.58W
San Vito [It.]	14	Dk	39.26N	9.32 E
San Vito, Capo-	14	Gl	38.11N	12.44 E
Sanya → Yaxian	22	Mh	18.27N	109.28 E
Sanyati	37	Dc	16.49S	28.45 E
San'yō	29	Bd	34.03N	131.10 E
Sanza	14	Jj	40.15N	15.33 E
Sanza Pombo	36	Cd	7.20S	16.00 E
São Bartoloméu, Rio-	55	Ic	16.48S	47.55W
São Benedito	54	Jd	4.03S	40.53W
São Bento	54	Jd	2.42S	44.50W
São Bento do Sul	55	Hh	26.15S	49.23W
São Borja	56	Ic	28.39S	56.00W
São Brás de Alportel	13	Eg	37.09N	7.53W
São Caetano do Sul	56	Kb	23.36S	46.34W
São Carlos [Braz.]	56	Kb	22.01S	47.54W
São Carlos [Braz.]	55	Ej	33.47N	55.30W
São Domingos [Braz.]	55	Ia	13.24S	46.19W
São Domingos [Gui.Bis.]	34	Bc	12.24N	16.12W
São Domingos, Rio- [Braz.]	55	Fe	20.03S	53.13W
São Domingos, Rio- [Braz.]	55	Ia	13.24S	47.12W
São Domingos, Rio- [Braz.]	55	Gd	19.13S	50.44W
São Domingos, Rio- [Braz.]	55	Ib	15.37S	46.14W
São Felix	54	Hf	11.36S	50.39W
São Félix do Xingu	54	He	6.38S	51.59W
São Filipe	32	Cf	14.54N	24.31W
São Francisco [Braz.]	54	Jg	15.57S	44.52W
São Francisco [Braz.]	55	Dd	18.45S	56.55W
São Francisco, Ilha de-	52	Lh	26.18S	48.37W
São Francisco, Rio-	52	Mg	10.30S	36.24W
São Francisco de Assis	55	Ei	29.33S	55.08W
São Francisco de Paula	55	Gi	29.27S	50.35W
São Francisco de Sales	55	Hd	19.52S	49.46W
São Francisco do Sul	56	Kc	26.14S	48.39W
São Gabriel	56	Jd	30.20S	54.19W
São Gonçalo	54	Jh	22.51S	43.04W
São Gonçalo, Canal de-	55	Fk	32.10S	52.38W
São Gonçalo do Abaete	55	Jd	18.20S	45.49W
São Gonçalo do Sapucaí	55	Je	21.54S	45.36W
São Gotardo	55	Id	19.19S	46.03W
Sao Hill	36	Gd	8.20S	35.12 E
São Jerônimo, Serra de-	55	Ec	16.20S	54.55W
São João da Barra	54	Jh	21.38S	41.03W
São João da Boa Vista	55	Ie	21.58S	46.47W
São João d'Aliança	55	Ib	14.42S	47.31W
São João da Madeira	13	Dd	40.54N	8.30W
São João da Ponte	55	Kb	15.56S	44.01W
São João del Rei	54	Jh	21.09S	44.16W
São João de Meriti	55	Kf	22.48S	43.22W
São João do Araguaia	54	Ie	5.23S	48.46W
São João do Piauí	54	Je	8.21S	42.15W
São João dos Patos	54	Je	6.30S	43.42W
São João do Triunfo	55	Gg	25.41S	50.18W
São Joaquim	56	Kc	28.18S	49.56W
São Joaquim da Barra	55	Ie	20.35S	47.53W
São Jorge	30	Ee	38.38N	28.03W
São José da Serra	55	Eb	15.40S	55.18W
São José do Cerrito	55	Gh	27.40S	50.35W
São José do Norte	55	Fk	32.01S	52.03W
São José do Rio Pardo	56	Kb	21.36S	46.54W
São José do Rio Prêto	53	Lh	20.48S	49.23W
São José dos Campos	56	Kb	23.11S	45.53W
São José dos Dourados, Rio-	55	Ge	20.22S	51.21W
Saolat, Buku-	26	If	0.45N	127.59 E
São Leopoldo	56	Jc	29.46S	51.09W
São Lourenço	55	Ec	16.32S	55.02W
São Lourenço, Pantanal de-	54	Gg	17.45S	56.15W
São Lourenço, Rio-	54	Gg	17.53S	57.27W
São Lourenço, Serra de-	55	Ec	17.30S	54.50W
São Lourenço do Sul	56	Jd	31.22S	51.58W
São Luís	53	Lf	2.31S	44.16W
São Luís Gonzaga	56	Jc	28.24S	54.58W
São Mamede, Serra de-	13	Ee	39.19N	7.19W
São Manuel	55	Hf	22.44S	48.34W
São Marcos	55	Gi	28.58S	51.04W
São Marcos, Baia de-	52	Lf	2.30S	44.30W
São Marcos, Rio-	55	Id	18.15S	47.37W
São Mateus [Braz.]	54	Kg	18.44S	39.51W
São Mateus [Braz.]	55	Gg	25.52S	50.23W

Index Symbols

[1] Independent Nation; [2] State, Region; [3] District, County; [4] Municipality; [5] Colony, Dependency; Continent; Physical Region; Historical or Cultural Region; Mount, Mountain; Volcano; Hill; Mountains, Mountain Range; Hills, Escarpment; Plateau, Upland; Pass, Gap; Plain, Lowland; Delta; Salt Flat; Valley, Canyon; Crater, Cave; Karst Features; Depression; Polder; Desert, Dunes; Forest, Woods; Heath, Steppe; Oasis; Cape, Point; Coast, Beach; Cliff; Peninsula; Isthmus; Sandbank; Island; Atoll; Rock, Reef; Islands, Archipelago; Rocks, Reefs; Coral Reef; Well, Spring; Geyser; River, Stream; Waterfall Rapids; River Mouth, Estuary; Lake; Salt Lake; Intermittent Lake; Reservoir; Swamp, Pond; Canal; Glacier; Ice Shelf, Pack Ice; Ocean; Sea; Gulf, Bay; Strait, Fjord; Lagoon; Bank; Seamount; Tablemount; Ridge; Shelf; Basin; Escarpment, Sea Scarp; Fracture; Trench, Abyss; National Park, Reserve; Point of Interest; Recreation Site; Cave, Cavern; Historic Site; Ruins; Wall, Walls; Church, Abbey; Temple; Scientific Station; Airport; Port; Lighthouse; Mine; Tunnel; Dam, Bridge

Name	Page	Grid	Lat.	Long.
São Mateus, Rio-	55	Ia	13.48S	46.54W
São Miguel	30	Ee	37.47N	25.30W
São Miguel, Rio-	55	Ic	16.03S	46.07W
São Miguel do Araguaia	55	Ga	13.19S	50.13W
São Miguel d'Oeste	55	Fh	26.45S	53.34W
Saona, Isla-	49	Md	18.09N	68.40W
Saône	5	Gf	45.44N	4.50 E
Saône-et-Loire [3]	11	Kh	46.40N	4.30 E
Saonek	26	Jg	0.28S	130.47 E
São Nicolau	30	Eg	16.35N	24.15W
São Nicolau [Braz.]	55	Ei	28.11S	55.16W
São Patricio, Rio-	55	Hb	15.02S	49.15W
São Paulo	53	Lh	23.32S	46.37W
São Paulo [2]	56	Kb	22.00S	49.00W
São Paulo de Olivença	54	Ed	3.27S	68.48W
São Pedro, Ribeirão	55	Ic	16.54S	46.32W
São Pedro do Sul [Braz.]	55	Ei	29.37S	54.10W
São Pedro do Sul [Port.]	13	Dd	40.45N	8.04W
São Pedro e São Paulo, Penedos de-	52	Ne	0.56N	29.22W
São Raimundo Nonato	54	Je	9.01S	42.42W
São Romão [Braz.]	55	Ed	18.33S	54.27W
São Romão [Braz.]	54	Ig	16.22S	45.04W
São Roque	30	De	21.43S	57.46W
São Roque, Cabo de-	52	Mf	5.29S	35.16W
São Roque, Serra de-	55	Ib	14.40S	46.50W
São Sebastião	55	Jf	23.48S	45.25W
São Sebastião, Ilha de-	52	Lh	23.50S	45.18W
São Sebastião, Ponta-	30	Kk	22.05S	35.24 E
São Sebastião da Boa Vista	54	Id	1.42S	49.31W
São Sebastião do Paraíso	54	Ih	20.55S	47.00W
São Sepé	55	Fj	30.10S	53.34W
São Simão	54	Hg	18.56S	50.30W
São Tiago	30	Eg	15.05N	23.40W
São Tomé	30	Hh	0.12N	6.39 E
São Tomé	31	Hh	0.20N	6.44 E
São Tomé, Cabo de-	54	Jh	22.00S	40.59W
Sao Tome and Principe (EN) = São Tomé e Príncipe [1]	31	Hh	1.00N	7.00 E
São Tomé e Príncipe = Sao Tome and Principe (EN) [1]	31	Hh	1.00N	7.00 E
Saoura	32	Gd	27.50N	2.50W
Saoura	32	Gf	28.48N	0.50W
São Vicente	30	Eg	16.50N	25.00W
São Vicente [Braz.]	55	Ia	13.38S	46.31W
São Vicente [Braz.]	56	Kb	23.58S	46.23W
São Vicente, Cabo de-	5	Fh	37.01N	9.00W
São Xavier, Serra de-	55	Ei	29.15S	54.15W
Sápai	15	Ih	41.02N	25.42 E
Sapanca	15	Ni	40.41N	30.16 E
Sapanca Gölü	15	Ni	40.43N	30.15 E
Sape [Braz.]	54	Ke	7.06S	35.13W
Sape [Indon.]	26	Gh	8.34S	118.59 E
Sape, Selat-	26	Gh	8.39S	119.18 E
Sapele	34	Gd	5.55N	5.42 E
Sapelo Island	44	Gj	31.28N	81.15W
Şaphane	15	Mj	39.01N	29.14 E
Şaphane Dağı	15	Mj	39.03N	29.16 E
Sapiéntza	15	Em	36.45N	21.42 E
Šapkina	17	Fc	66.44N	52.25 E
Sapo, Serranía del-	49	Hi	7.50N	78.17W
Saponé	34	Ec	12.03N	1.36W
Sapopema	55	Gf	23.55S	50.35W
Saposoa	54	Ce	6.56S	76.48W
Sapphire Mountains	46	Ic	46.20N	113.45W
Sapporo	22	Qe	43.03N	141.21 E
Sapri	14	Jj	40.04N	15.38 E
Sapucai, Rio-	55	He	20.08S	48.27W
Sapulpa	43	Hd	36.00N	96.06W
Sapulut	26	Gf	4.42N	116.29 E
Sāqiyat Sīdī Yūsuf	14	Cn	36.13N	8.21 E
Saqqez	23	Gb	36.14N	46.16 E
Sarāb	23	Gb	37.56N	47.32 E
Saraburi	25	Kf	14.30N	100.55 E
Saraf Doungous	35	Bc	12.33N	19.42 E
Sarafjagān	24	Ne	34.28N	50.28 E
Saragmatha = Everest, Mount- (EN)	21	Kg	27.59N	86.56 E
Saragossa (EN) = Zaragoza [Sp.]	6	Fg	41.38N	0.53W
Sarai	7	Jj	53.44N	41.03 E
Sarajevo	6	Hg	43.50N	18.25 E
Saraji Mine	59	Jd	22.30S	148.20 E
Sarakhs	23	Jb	36.32N	61.11 E
Sarakiná	15	Hk	38.40N	24.37 E
Šarakol	17	Kj	52.03N	62.47 E
Saraktaš	19	Fe	51.47N	56.18 E
Saraland	44	Cj	30.49N	88.02W
Saramati	25	Jc	25.44N	95.02 E
Saran	19	Hf	49.46N	72.52 E
Saran, Gunung-	26	Fg	0.25S	111.18 E
Saranac Lake	44	Jc	44.20N	74.08W
Saranci	15	Gg	42.43N	23.46 E
Saranda	15	Cj	39.52N	20.00 E
Sarandi	55	Fh	27.56S	52.55W
Sarandí, Arroyo-	55	Cj	30.13S	59.19W
Sarandí del Yí	55	Ek	33.21S	55.38W
Sarandí Grande	55	Dk	33.44S	56.20W
Šaranga	7	Lh	57.12N	46.34 E
Sarangani Bay	26	Ie	5.57N	125.11 E
Sarangani Islands	26	Ie	5.25N	125.26 E
Saranley	35	Ge	2.23N	42.16 E
Saransk	6	Ke	54.11N	45.11 E
Sarapul	6	Ld	56.28N	53.48 E
Sarapulskoje	20	Ig	48.50N	135.58 E
Sarare	49	Mi	9.47N	69.10W
Sararé, Rio-	55	Cb	14.51S	59.58W
Sarasota	43	Kf	27.20N	82.34W
Sarata	16	Ff	46.01N	29.41 E
Sarâțel	15	Kb	47.03N	27.25 E
Saratoga	46	Lf	41.27N	106.48W
Saratoga Springs	43	Mc	43.04N	73.47W
Saratok	26	Ff	1.24N	111.31 E
Saratov	6	Ke	51.34N	46.02 E
Saratov Reservoir (EN) = Saratovskoje Vodohranilišče	5	Ke	52.50N	47.50 E
Saratovskaja Oblast [3]	19	Ee	51.30N	47.00 E
Saratovskoje Vodohranilišče = Saratov Reservoir (EN)	5	Ke	52.50N	47.50 E
Saravan	25	Le	15.43N	106.25 E
Sarawak [2]	26	Ff	2.30N	113.30 E
Saray	24	Bb	41.26N	27.55 E
Saraya	34	Cc	12.50N	11.45W
Sarāyā	24	Fe	35.47N	35.58 E
Sarayköy	24	Cd	37.55N	28.56 E
Sarbāz	23	Jd	26.39N	61.15 E
Sárbogárd	10	Oj	46.53N	18.38 E
Sarca	14	Ee	45.52N	10.52 E
Sarcelle, Passe de la-	63b	Cf	22.28S	167.13 E
Sarcelles	12	Ef	49.00N	2.23 E
Sarcidano	14	Dk	39.40N	9.15 E
Sardara	14	Ck	39.37N	8.49 E
Sar Dasht [Iran]	24	Mf	32.32N	48.52 E
Sar Dasht [Iran]	24	Kd	36.09N	45.28 E
Sardegna [2]	14	Cj	40.00N	9.00 E
Sardegna = Sardinia (EN)	5	Gh	40.00N	9.00 E
Sardegna, Mar di-	14	Bk	40.00N	7.30 E
Sardes	15	Lk	38.29N	28.03 E
Sardinal	49	Eh	10.31N	85.39W
Sardinata	54	Db	8.07N	72.48W
Sardinia (EN) = Sardegna	5	Gh	40.00N	9.00 E
Sardis Lake	45	Li	34.27N	89.43W
Sarektjåkkå	7	Dc	67.25N	17.46 E
Sarema/Saaremaa	5	Id	58.25N	22.30 E
Sar-e Pol	23	Kb	36.14N	65.55 E
Sar Eskand Khān	24	Ld	37.29N	47.04 E
Sar-e Yazd	24	Pg	31.36N	54.35 E
Sargasso Sea	38	Mg	29.00N	65.00W
Sargatskoje	19	Hd	55.37N	73.30 E
Sargodha	25	Eb	32.05N	72.40 E
Šargun	18	Fe	38.31N	67.59 E
Sarh	31	Ih	9.09N	18.23 E
Sarhe	11	Fg	47.30N	0.32W
Sarhro, Jebel-	32	Fc	31.00N	6.00W
Sāri [Iran]	22	Hf	36.34N	53.04 E
Sāri [Iraq]	24	Je	34.42N	42.44 E
Sariá	15	Kn	35.50N	27.15 E
Sarıçakaya	24	Db	40.02N	30.31 E
Sarigan Island	57	Fc	16.42N	145.47 E
Sarıgöl	24	Cc	38.14N	28.43 E
Sarıkamış	24	Jb	40.15N	42.35 E
Sarıkaya	24	Fc	39.48N	35.24 E
Sarikei	26	Ff	2.07N	111.31 E
Sariköy	15	Ki	40.12N	27.36 E
Sarina	59	Jd	21.26S	149.13 E
Sarine	14	Bd	46.59N	7.16 E
Sariñena	13	Lc	41.48N	0.10W
Sarıoğlan	24	Fc	39.05N	35.59 E
Sarīr	33	Dd	27.30N	22.30 E
Sariwŏn	27	Md	38.30N	125.45 E
Sarıyer	24	Cb	41.10N	29.03 E
Sarj, Jabal as-	14	Do	35.56N	9.32 E
Šarja	6	Kd	58.24N	45.30 E
Sark	9	Kl	49.26N	2.21W
Sarkad	10	Rj	46.45N	21.23 E
Sarkand	19	Hf	45.25N	79.54 E
Şarkikaraağaç	24	Dc	38.04N	31.23 E
Şarkışla	24	Gc	39.21N	36.26 E
Šarkovščina	8	Li	55.22N	27.32 E
Şarköy	24	Bb	40.37N	27.06 E
Sarlat-la-Canéda	11	Hj	44.53N	1.13 E
Šarlyk	16	Sc	52.54N	54.42 E
Sarmi	58	Ee	1.51S	138.44 E
Sarmiento	53	Jj	45.35S	69.05W
Sarmizegetuza	15	Fd	45.31N	22.47 E
Särna	8	Ec	61.41N	13.08 E
Sarnen	14	Cd	46.54N	8.15 E
Sărnena Gora	15	Ig	42.35N	25.30 E
Sarnia	42	Jh	42.58N	82.23W
Sarny	19	Ce	51.21N	26.36 E
Saroako	26	Hg	2.31S	121.22 E
Sarolangun	26	Dg	2.18S	102.42 E
Saroma	29a	Ca	44.02N	143.45 E
Saroma-Ko	28	Qb	44.10N	143.40 E
Šaromy	20	Kf	54.23N	158.14 E
Saronic Gulf (EN) = Saronikós Kólpos	15	Gl	37.45N	23.30 E
Saronikós Kólpos = Saronic Gulf (EN)	15	Gl	37.45N	23.30 E
Saronno	14	De	45.38N	9.02 E
Saros, Gulf of- (EN) = Saros Körfezi	24	Bb	40.30N	26.20 E
Saros Körfezi = Saros, Gulf of- (EN)	24	Bb	40.30N	26.20 E
Sárospatak	10	Rh	48.19N	21.35 E
Sar Passage	64a	Ac	7.12N	134.23 E
Sarpinskije Ozera	16	Nf	47.45N	45.00 E
Šar Planina	15	Dg	42.05N	20.50 E
Sarpsborg	8	De	59.17N	11.07 E
Sarqaq	41	Gd	70.00N	51.39W
Sarrabus	14	Dk	39.20N	9.30 E
Sarralbe	11	Ne	49.00N	7.01 E
Sarrāt, Wādī-	14	Co	35.59N	8.23 E
Sarre	10	Cg	49.42N	6.34 E
Sarrebourg	11	Nf	48.44N	7.03 E
Sarreguemines	11	Ne	49.06N	7.03 E
Sarre-Union	12	Jf	48.56N	7.05 E
Sarria	13	Eb	42.47N	7.24W
Sarstún, Rio-	47	Cf	15.54N	88.54W
Sartang	20	Ic	67.30N	133.20 E
Sartène	11a	Ab	41.37N	8.59 E
Sarthe [3]	11	Gf	48.00N	0.05 E
Sartu → Anda	28	Ha	46.35N	125.00 E
Sarufutsu	29a	Ca	45.18N	142.13 E
Saru-Gawa	29a	Cb	42.30N	142.00 E
Saruhanlı	24	Bc	38.44N	27.34 E
Sarukaishi-Gawa	29	Gb	39.25N	141.08 E
Särüq	24	Me	34.25N	49.30 E
Saruyama-Misaki	29	Ec	37.18N	136.43 E
Sárvár	10	Mi	47.15N	16.56 E
Sarvestān	24	Oh	29.16N	53.13 E
Sárviz	10	Oj	46.22N	18.48 E
Saryagač	18	Gd	41.28N	69.11 E
Sarybarak	18	Hc	43.24N	71.29 E
Sary-Bulak	18	Jd	41.54N	75.47 E
Saryč, Mys-	5	Jg	44.23N	33.45 E
Saryg-Sep	20	Ef	51.30N	95.40 E
Sary-Išikotrau	18	Hc	45.15N	76.25 E
Sarykamys	19	Ff	46.00N	53.41 E
Sarykamyšskoje, Ozero-	19	Fg	41.58N	57.58 E
Sarykolski Hrebet	18	Je	38.30N	74.15 E
Šaryn-Gol	27	Ib	49.20N	106.30 E
Saryozek	19	Hg	44.22N	77.54 E
Saryšagan	19	Hf	46.05N	73.38 E
Saryšiganak, Zaliv-	18	Ca	46.35N	61.25 E
Sarysu	21	Ie	45.12N	66.36 E
Sary-Taš	19	Hh	39.44N	73.16 E
Saryžaz	18	Lc	42.54N	79.31 E
Sarzana	14	Df	44.07N	9.58 E
Sasabe	48	Db	31.27N	111.31W
Sasabeneh	35	Gd	8.00N	43.44 E
Sasa-ga-Mine	29	Ce	33.49N	133.17 E
Sasago-Tōge	29	Fd	35.37N	138.45 E
Sasamungga	63a	Cb	7.02S	156.47 E
Sasarām	25	Gd	24.57N	84.02 E
Sasari, Mount-	63a	Dc	8.11S	159.33 E
Sascut	15	Kc	46.11N	27.04 E
Sásd	10	Oj	46.15N	18.07 E
Sasebo	27	Me	33.12N	129.44 E
Saseginaga, Lac-	44	Hb	47.05N	78.34W
Saskatchewan [3]	42	Gf	54.00N	106.00W
Saskatchewan	38	Jd	53.12N	99.16W
Saskatoon	39	Id	52.07N	106.38W
Saskylah	20	Gb	72.00N	114.00 E
Saslaya, Cerro-	49	Eg	13.45N	85.03W
Sasovo	19	Ee	54.22N	41.54 E
Sassafras Mountain	44	Fh	35.03N	82.48W
Sassandra	30	Gh	4.58N	6.05W
Sassandra [3]	34	Dd	5.20N	6.10W
Sassandra	31	Gh	4.57N	6.05W
Sassari	6	Gg	40.43N	8.34 E
Sassenberg	12	Kc	51.59N	8.03 E
Sassenheim	12	Gb	52.14N	4.33 E
Sassetot-le-Mauconduit	12	Ce	49.48N	0.32 E
Saßnitz	10	Jb	54.31N	13.39 E
Sasso Marconi	14	Ff	44.24N	11.15 E
Sassuolo	14	Ef	44.33N	10.47 E
Sastobe	18	Hc	42.34N	70.03 E
Sastre	55	Bj	31.45S	61.50W
Sasyk, Ozero- (Kunduk)	16	Fg	45.45N	29.40 E
Sasykkol, Ozero-	19	If	46.40N	81.00 E
Sata	29	Bf	31.04N	130.42 E
Sata, Cape- (EN) = Sata Misaki	21	Pf	30.59N	130.37 E
Satakunta	8	Jc	61.30N	23.00 E
Sata-Misaki = Sata, Cape- (EN)	21	Pf	30.59N	130.37 E
Satan, Pointe de-	63b	Dd	19.00S	169.17 E
Sātāra	25	Ee	17.41N	73.59 E
Sataua	65c	Aa	13.28S	172.40W
Satawal Island	57	Fd	7.21N	147.02 E
Satawan Atoll	57	Gd	5.25N	153.35 E
Satellite Bay	42	Fa	77.25N	117.15W
Säter	7	Df	60.21N	15.45 E
Satihaure	7	Ec	67.30N	18.45 E
Satipo	54	Df	11.16S	74.37W
Satīt	35	Fc	14.20N	35.50 E
Satka	19	Fd	55.03N	59.01 E
Šatki	7	Ki	55.11N	44.08 E
Sātmāla Range	25	Fe	19.30N	78.45 E
Satna	25	Gd	24.35N	80.50 E
Šator	14	Kf	44.09N	16.37 E
Sátoraljaújhely	10	Rh	48.24N	21.40 E
Sātpura Range	21	Jg	21.25N	76.10 E
Satsuma-Hantō	29	Bf	31.25N	130.25 E
Satsunai-Gawa	29a	Cb	42.55N	143.15 E
Satsunan-Shotō	27	Mf	29.00N	130.00 E
Sattahip	25	Kf	12.39N	100.54 E
Satulung	15	Gb	47.34N	23.26 E
Satu Mare	15	Fb	47.48N	22.53 E
Satu Mare [2]	15	Fb	47.46N	22.56 E
Satun	25	Kg	6.39N	100.03 E
Saturniná ou Papagaio, Rio-	55	Ca	13.55S	58.18W
Saualpe	14	Id	46.50N	14.40 E
Sauce	56	Ic	30.00S	58.46W
Sauce Corto, Arroyo-	55	Bm	36.55S	61.48W
Sauceda Mountains	46	Ij	32.30N	112.30W
Sauce Grande, Rio-	55	Bn	38.59S	61.07W
Saucillo	47	Cc	28.01N	105.17W
Sauda	8	Be	59.39N	6.20 E
Saudade, Serra da- [Braz.]	55	Jd	19.20S	45.50W
Saudade, Serra da- [Braz.]	55	Fc	16.20S	53.53W
Saudarkrókur	7a	Bb	65.45N	19.39W
Saudi Arabia (EN) = Al 'Arabīyah As-Su'ūdīyah [1]	22	Gg	25.00N	45.00 E
Sauer [Eur.]	12	Cg	49.44N	6.31 E
Sauer [Fr.]	12	Kf	48.55N	8.10 E
Sauerland	10	De	51.10N	8.00 E
Sauêruiná, Rio-	54	Gf	12.00S	58.40W
Sauga Jõgi	8	Kf	58.19N	24.25 E
Saugatuck	44	Dd	42.40N	86.12W
Saugues	11	Jj	44.58N	3.33 E
Sauk Centre	45	Id	45.44N	94.57W
Sauk Rapids	45	Id	45.34N	94.09W
Saül	54	Hc	3.37N	53.12W
Šaulder	18	Gc	42.47N	68.24 E
Sauldre	11	Hg	47.16N	1.30 E
Saulieu	11	Kg	47.16N	4.14 E
Saulkrasti/Saulkrasty	7	Fh	57.17N	24.29 E
Saulkrasty/Saulkrasti	7	Fh	57.17N	24.29 E
Saulnois	12	If	48.52N	6.30 E
Sault	11	Lj	44.05N	5.25 E
Sault Sainte Marie [Mi.-U.S.]	43	Kb	46.30N	84.21W
Sault Sainte Marie [Ont.-Can.]	39	Ke	46.31N	84.20W
Saumarez Reefs	57	Gg	21.50S	153.40 E
Saumâtre, Étang-	49	Kd	18.35N	72.00W
Saumlaki	26	Jh	7.57S	131.19 E
Saumur	11	Fg	47.16N	0.05W
Saunders	66	Ad	57.47S	26.27W
Saunders Coast	66	Mf	77.45S	150.00W
Saurimo	31	Ji	9.38S	20.24 E
Sauro	14	Kj	40.18N	16.21 E
Sautar	36	Ce	11.09S	18.25 E
Sauteurs	51p	Bb	12.14N	61.38W
Sauveterre, Causse de-	11	Jj	44.22N	3.17 E
Sauveterre-de-Guyenne	11	Fj	44.42N	0.05W
Sauvo/Sagu	8	Jd	60.21N	22.42 E
Sauwald	14	Hb	48.28N	13.40 E
Sava	5	Ig	44.50N	20.28 E
Savage River	59	Jh	41.33S	145.09 E
Savai'i Island	57	Jf	13.35S	172.25W
Savala	16	Ld	51.06N	41.29 E
Savalou	34	Fd	7.56N	1.58 E
Savanes [3]	34	Fc	10.30N	0.30 E
Savan Island	51n	Bb	12.48N	61.12W
Savanna	45	Ke	42.05N	90.08W
Savannah	38	Kf	32.02N	80.53W
Savannah [Ga.-U.S.]	39	Kf	32.04N	81.05W
Savannah [Tn.-U.S.]	44	Ch	35.14N	88.14W
Savannah Beach	44	Gi	32.01N	80.51W
Savannakhét	22	Mh	16.33N	104.45 E
Savanna-la-Mar	47	Ie	18.13N	78.08W
Savanne	45	Kb	48.59N	90.12W
Savannes Bay	51k	Bb	13.45N	60.56W
Savant Lake	42	If	50.15N	90.42W
Savant Lake	45	Ka	50.30N	90.20W
Savaştepe	24	Bc	39.22N	27.40 E
Savdiri	35	Dc	14.25N	29.05 E
Savé	31	Hh	8.02N	2.29 E
Save [Afr.]	30	Kk	21.00S	35.02 E
Save [Fr.]	11	Hk	43.47N	1.17 E
Saveån	8	Dg	57.43N	11.59 E
Sāveh	23	Hb	35.01N	50.20 E
Săveni	15	Jb	47.57N	26.52 E
Saverdun	11	Hk	43.14N	1.35 E
Saverne	11	Nf	48.44N	7.22 E
Savigliano	14	Bf	44.38N	7.40 E
Savigsivik	41	Fc	76.00N	64.45W
Săvineşti	15	Jc	46.51N	26.28 E
Savinjske Alpe	14	Id	46.20N	14.30 E
Savinski	19	Ec	62.57N	40.13 E
Savio	14	Gf	44.19N	12.20 E
Săvîrşin	15	Fc	46.01N	22.14 E
Savitaipale	7	Gf	61.12N	27.42 E
Šavnik	15	Cg	42.57N	19.06 E
Savo	63a	Dc	9.08S	159.48 E
Savo	8	Lb	62.30N	27.30 E
Savoie [3]	11	Mi	45.30N	6.25 E
Savoie = Savoy (EN)	11	Mi	45.24N	6.30 E
Savona	14	Cf	44.17N	8.30 E
Savonlinna/Nyslott	7	Gf	61.52N	28.53 E
Savonranta	7	Ge	62.11N	29.12 E
Savonselkä	8	Lb	62.05N	27.20 E
Savoonga	40	Ed	63.42N	170.27W
Savoy (EN) = Savoie	11	Mi	45.24N	6.30 E
Şavşat	24	Jb	41.15N	42.20 E
Savsjö	7	Dh	57.25N	14.40 E
Savudrija, Rt-	14	He	45.30N	13.31 E
Savukoski	7	Gc	67.17N	28.10 E
Savur	24	Id	37.33N	40.53 E
Savusavu	61	Ec	17.34S	178.15 E
Savusavu Bay	63d	Bb	16.45S	179.15 E
Savu Sea (EN) = Sawu, Laut-	21	Oj	9.40S	122.00 E
Savuto	14	Kk	39.02N	16.06 E
Sawahlunto	26	Dg	0.40S	100.47 E
Sawai Mādhopur	25	Fc	25.59N	76.22 E
Sawākin	31	Kg	19.07N	37.20 E
Sawākin, Jazā'ir- = Suakin Archipelago (EN)	30	Kg	19.07N	37.20 E
Sawankhalok	25	Je	17.19N	99.54 E
Sawara	29	Gd	35.53N	140.29 E
Sawasaki-Hana	28	Of	37.47N	138.12 E
Sawatch Range	45	Cg	39.10N	106.25W
Sawbā = Sobat (EN)	30	Kh	9.45N	31.45 E
Sawbridgeworth	12	Cc	51.49N	0.09 E
Sawdā', Jabal as-	33	Cd	28.40N	15.30 E
Sawfajjīn	33	Cc	31.54N	15.07 E
Sawhāj = Sohag (EN)	31	Kf	26.33N	31.42 E
Sawkanah	33	Cd	29.04N	15.47 E
Sawla	34	Ed	9.17N	2.25W
Sawqirah	23	If	18.10N	56.30 E
Şawqirah, Ghubbat-	23	If	18.35N	56.45 E
Sawtooth Mountains	46	He	44.00N	115.00W
Sawu, Kepulauan-	26	Hi	10.30S	121.50 E
Sawu, Laut- = Savu Sea (EN)	21	Oj	9.40S	122.00 E
Sawu, Pulau-	21	Ok	10.30S	121.54 E
Şawwān, Ard as-	24	Gg	31.00N	37.00 E
Sax	13	Lf	38.32N	0.49W
Saxby River	59	Ic	18.25S	140.53 E
Saxmundham	12	Db	52.13N	1.30 E
Saxony (EN) = Sachsen	10	Jf	51.00N	13.30 E
Say	34	Fc	13.07N	2.21 E
Sayabec	44	Na	48.36N	67.37W
Saya de Malha Bank (EN)	30	Nj	11.00S	61.00 E
Sayago	13	Fc	41.20N	6.10W
Sayán	54	Cf	11.08S	77.12W
Sayang, Pulau-	26	If	0.18N	129.54 E
Sayaxché	49	Be	16.31N	90.10W
Saydā	23	Ec	33.33N	35.22 E
Sayhūt	22	Hh	15.12N	51.14 E
Saylorville Lake	45	Jf	41.48N	93.46W
Säynätsalo	8	Kb	62.08N	25.46 E
Sayō	29	Dd	35.01N	134.22 E
Sayram Hu	27	Dc	44.35N	81.10 E
Sayula	48	Hh	19.52N	103.37W
Saywūn	35	Hb	15.56N	48.47 E
Sazanit, Ishull i-	15	Ci	40.30N	19.16 E
Sázava	10	Kg	49.53N	14.24 E
Sázava	10	Kg	49.52N	14.54 E
Sbaa	32	Gd	28.13N	0.10W
Sbisseb	13	Pi	35.42N	3.51 E
Sbruč	16	Ee	48.32N	26.25 E
Scaër	11	Cf	48.02N	3.42W
Scafell Pike	9	Jg	54.27N	3.12W
Scalea	14	Jk	39.49N	15.47 E
Scalone, Passo dello-	14	Jk	39.38N	15.57 E
Scammon, Laguna-	48	Bd	27.45N	114.15W
Scammon Bay	40	Fd	61.53N	165.38W
Scandinavia (EN)	5	Hc	65.00N	16.00 E
Scanno	14	Hi	41.54N	13.53 E
Scansano	14	Fh	42.41N	11.20 E
Scapa Flow	9	Jc	58.54N	3.05W
Scapegoat Mountain	46	Ic	47.19N	112.50W
Ščapino	20	Ke	55.15N	159.25 E
Ščara	16	Dc	53.27N	24.44 E
Scaramia, Capo-	14	In	36.47N	14.29 E
Scarba	9	He	56.11N	5.42W
Scarborough [Eng.-U.K.]	9	Mg	54.17N	0.24W
Scarborough [Trin.]	54	Fa	11.11N	60.44W
Scarpe	11	Jd	50.30N	3.27 E
Ščastje	16	Ke	48.44N	39.14 E
Sceaux	12	Ef	48.47N	2.17 E
Ščekino	16	Jb	54.01N	37.29 E
Ščekurja	17	Jd	64.15N	60.52 E
Ščeljajur	19	Fb	65.21N	53.25 E
Scenic	45	Ee	43.47N	102.30W
Ščerbakty	19	He	52.29N	78.14 E
Schaalsee	10	Gc	53.35N	10.57 E
Schaarbeek/Schaerbeek	12	Gd	50.51N	4.23 E
Schaerbeek/Schaarbeek	12	Gd	50.51N	4.23 E
Schaffhausen [2]	14	Cc	47.45N	8.40 E
Schaffhausen	14	Cc	47.40N	8.40 E
Schagen	12	Gb	52.48N	4.48 E
Schärding	14	Hb	48.27N	13.26 E
Scharmützelsee	10	Kd	52.15N	14.03 E
Scharnhörn	10	Ec	53.57N	8.25 E
Scheeßel	12	La	53.10N	9.29 E
Schefferville	39	Md	54.47N	64.49W
Scheibbs	14	Jb	48.00N	15.10 E
Schela	15	Gd	45.10N	23.18 E
Schelde	11	Kc	51.22N	4.15 E
Schelde (EN) = Escaut	11	Kc	51.22N	4.15 E
Schell Creek Range	43	Ed	39.10N	114.40W
Schenectady	43	Mc	42.48N	73.57W
Scheno	35	Fd	9.35N	39.25 E
Scherfede, Warburg-	12	Lc	51.32N	9.02 E
Scherpenheuvel-Zichem	12	Gd	50.59N	4.59 E
Scheveningen, 's-Gravenhage-	11	Kb	52.06N	4.18 E
Schiedam	11	Kc	51.55N	4.24 E
Schiermonnikoog	11	Ma	53.28N	6.15 E
Schifferstadt	12	Ke	49.23N	8.22 E
Schiffgraben	10	Hd	52.02N	11.10 E
Schifflange	12	Ie	49.30N	6.01 E
Schijndel	12	Hc	51.37N	5.28 E
Schiltigheim	11	Nf	48.36N	7.45 E
Schio	14	Fe	45.43N	11.21 E
Schipbeek	12	Ib	52.15N	6.14 E
Schladming	14	Hc	47.23N	13.41 E
Schlei	10	Fb	54.35N	9.50 E
Schleiden	10	Cf	50.32N	6.28 E
Schleiz	10	Hf	50.35N	11.49 E
Schleswig	10	Fb	54.31N	9.33 E
Schleswig Holstein [2]	10	Gb	54.00N	10.30 E
Schlitz	10	Ff	50.40N	9.34 E
Schloß Holte-Stukenbrock	12	Kc	51.55N	8.38 E
Schloß Neuhaus, Paderborn-	12	Kc	51.44N	8.42 E
Schluchsee	10	Ei	47.49N	8.10 E
Schlüchtern	10	Ff	50.21N	9.31 E
Schmallenberg	12	Kc	51.09N	8.18 E
Schmallenberg-Bödefeld-Freiheit	12	Kc	51.15N	8.24 E
Schmallenberg-Oberkirchen	12	Kc	51.09N	8.18 E
Schmelz	12	Ie	49.26N	6.51 E
Schmida	14	Kb	48.20N	16.14 E
Schneeberg	10	If	50.36N	12.38 E
Schneeberg [Aus.]	14	Jc	47.46N	15.52 E
Schneeberg [Ger.]	10	Hf	50.00N	11.51 E
Schneifel	12	Id	50.16N	6.23 E
Schoberpaß	14	Ic	47.27N	14.40 E
Schoberspitze	14	Ic	47.17N	14.09 E
Schœlcher	51h	Ab	14.37N	61.06W
Schönebeck	10	Hd	52.01N	11.45 E
Schönecken	12	Id	50.10N	6.28 E
Schongau	10	Gi	47.49N	10.54 E
Schöningen	10	Gd	52.08N	10.57 E
Schoondijke	12	Fc	51.21N	3.33 E
Schoonebeek	12	Ib	52.40N	6.53 E
Schoonhoven	12	Gc	51.55N	4.51 E
Schorfheide	10	Jd	52.55N	13.35 E
Schoten	12	Gc	51.15N	4.30 E
Schotten	12	Ld	50.30N	9.08 E
Schouten Islands	57	Fe	3.30S	144.30 E
Schouwen	11	Jc	51.43N	3.50 E
Schramberg	10	Eh	48.14N	8.23 E
Schreiber	42	Ig	48.48N	87.15W
Schriesheim	12	Ke	49.29N	8.40 E
Schrobenhausen	10	Hh	48.33N	11.16 E
Schruns	14	Dc	47.04N	9.55 E
Schuls / Scuol	14	Ed	46.48N	10.17 E
Schultz Lake	42	Hd	64.45N	97.30W
Schurz	46	Fg	38.58N	118.46W
Schussen	10	Fi	47.37N	9.32 E
Schüttorf	12	Jb	52.19N	7.14 E
Schwabach	10	Hg	49.20N	11.02 E
Schwaben = Swabia (EN)	10	Gh	48.20N	10.30 E
Schwäbisch-Bayerisches Alpenvorland = Swabian-Bavarian Plateau (EN)	5	Hf	48.15N	10.30 E
Schwäbische Alb = Swabian Jura (EN)	5	Gf	48.25N	9.30 E

Index Symbols

- [1] Independent Nation
- [2] State, Region
- [3] District, County
- [4] Municipality
- [5] Colony, Dependency
- Continent
- Physical Region
- Historical or Cultural Region
- Mount, Mountain
- Volcano
- Hill
- Mountains, Mountain Range
- Hills, Escarpment
- Plateau, Upland
- Pass, Gap
- Plain, Lowland
- Delta
- Salt Flat
- Valley, Canyon
- Crater, Cave
- Karst Features
- Depression
- Polder
- Desert, Dunes
- Forest, Woods
- Heath, Steppe
- Oasis
- Cape, Point
- Coast, Beach
- Cliff
- Peninsula
- Isthmus
- Sandbank
- Island
- Atoll
- Rock, Reef
- Islands, Archipelago
- Rocks, Reefs
- Coral Reef
- Well, Spring
- Geyser
- River, Stream
- Waterfall Rapids
- River Mouth, Estuary
- Lake
- Salt Lake
- Intermittent Lake
- Reservoir
- Swamp, Pond
- Canal
- Glacier
- Ice Shelf, Pack Ice
- Ocean
- Sea
- Gulf, Bay
- Strait, Fjord
- Lagoon
- Bank
- Seamount
- Tablemount
- Ridge
- Shelf
- Basin
- Escarpment, Sea Scarp
- Fracture
- Trench, Abyss
- National Park, Reserve
- Point of Interest
- Recreation Site
- Cave, Cavern
- Historic Site
- Ruins
- Wall, Walls
- Church, Abbey
- Temple
- Scientific Station
- Airport
- Port
- Lighthouse
- Mine
- Tunnel
- Dam, Bridge

Index Symbols

[1] Independent Nation
[2] State, Region
[3] District, County
[4] Municipality
[5] Colony, Dependency
Continent
Physical Region
Historical or Cultural Region
Mount, Mountain
Volcano
Hill
Mountains, Mountain Range
Hills, Escarpment
Plateau, Upland
Pass, Gap
Plain, Lowland
Delta
Salt Flat
Valley, Canyon
Crater, Cave
Karst Features
Depression
Polder
Desert, Dunes
Forest, Woods
Heath, Steppe
Oasis
Cape, Point
Coast, Beach
Cliff
Peninsula
Isthmus
Sandbank
Island
Atoll
Rock, Reef
Islands, Archipelago
Rocks, Reefs
Coral Reef
Well, Spring
Geyser
River, Stream
Waterfall Rapids
River Mouth, Estuary
Lake
Salt Lake
Intermittent Lake
Reservoir
Swamp, Pond
Canal
Glacier
Ice Shelf, Pack Ice
Ocean
Sea
Gulf, Bay
Strait, Fjord
Lagoon
Bank
Seamount
Tablemount
Ridge
Shelf
Basin
Escarpment, Sea Scarp
Fracture
Trench, Abyss
National Park, Reserve
Point of Interest
Recreation Site
Cave, Cavern
Historic Site
Ruins
Wall, Walls
Church, Abbey
Temple
Scientific Station
Airport
Port
Lighthouse
Mine
Tunnel
Dam, Bridge

Sersou, Plateau du- ■	13	Ni	35.30N	2.00 E
Sertã	13	De	39.48N	8.06W
Sertão ■	52	Lg	10.00S	41.00W
Sertãozinho	55	Ie	21.08S	47.59W
Sêrtar	27	He	32.20N	100.20 E
Serti	34	Hd	7.30N	11.22 E
Serua, Pulau- ■	26	Jh	6.18S	130.01 E
Serui	26	Kg	1.53S	136.14 E
Serule	37	Dd	21.55S	27.19 E
Sérvia	15	Ei	40.11N	22.00 E
Sêrxü	27	Ge	32.56N	98.02 E
Seryítsi ■	15	Ii	40.00N	25.10 E
Seryševo	20	Hf	51.02N	128.25 E
Sesayap ■	26	Gf	3.36N	117.15 E
Sese	36	Eb	2.11N	25.47 E
Seseganaga Lake ■	45	Ka	50.10N	90.15W
Sese Islands ■	36	Fc	0.20S	32.20 E
Sesfontein	37	Ac	19.07S	13.39 E
Sesheke	36	Df	17.29S	24.18 E
Sesia ■	14	Ce	45.05N	8.37 E
Sesibi ■	35	Ea	20.05N	30.31 E
Sesimbra	13	Cf	38.26N	9.06W
Šešma ■	7	Mi	55.20N	51.12 E
Sesnut ■	8	Be	59.42N	7.21 E
Sessa Aurunca	14	Hi	41.14N	13.56 E
Ses Salines, Cap de-/ Salinas, Cabo de- ■	13	Pe	39.16N	3.03 E
Sestao	13	Ja	43.18N	3.00W
Sesto Fiorentino	14	Fg	43.50N	11.12 E
Sesto San Giovanni	14	De	45.32N	9.14 E
Sestriere	14	Af	44.57N	6.53 E
Sestri Levante	14	Df	44.16N	9.24 E
Sestroreck	7	Gf	60.06N	29.59 E
Šešupė ■	7	Fi	55.00N	22.10 E
Šešuvis ■	8	Ji	55.12N	22.31 E
Sesvenna, Piz- ■	14	Ed	46.42N	10.25 E
Sesvete	14	Ke	45.50N	16.07 E
Šeta/Šėta	8	Ki	55.14N	24.18 E
Šėta/Šeta	8	Ki	55.14N	24.18 E
Setaka	29	Be	33.09N	130.28 E
Setana	28	Oc	42.26N	139.51 E
Sète	11	Jk	43.24N	3.41 E
Sete de Setembro, Rio- ■	55	Fa	12.56S	52.51W
Sete Lagoas	54	Jg	19.27S	44.14W
Setenil	13	Gh	36.51N	5.11W
Sete Quedas, Saltos das- = Guaira Falls (EN) ■	56	Jb	24.02S	54.16W
Setermoen	7	Eb	68.52N	18.28 E
Setesdal ■	7	Bg	59.05N	7.35 E
Setesdalsheiane ■	8	Be	59.30N	7.10 E
Seti ■	25	Gc	28.58N	81.06 E
Sétif [3]	32	Ib	36.05N	5.00 E
Sétif	31	He	36.12N	5.24 E
Seto	29	Ed	35.13N	137.05 E
Setonaikai = Inland Sea (EN) ■	21	Pf	34.10N	133.00 E
Setouchi	29b	Ba	28.08N	129.20 E
Šetpe	19	Fg	44.06N	52.02 E
Settat	32	Fc	33.00N	7.37W
Settat [3]	32	Fc	33.00N	7.30W
Setté Cama	36	Ac	2.32S	9.45 E
Sette-Daban, Hrebet- ■	20	Id	62.00N	138.00 E
Settle	9	Kg	54.04N	2.16W
Setúbal [2]	13	Df	38.20N	8.30W
Setúbal	6	Fh	38.32N	8.54W
Setúbal, Baía de- ■	13	Df	38.27N	8.53W
Setúbal o de Guadalupe, Laguna- ■	55	Bj	31.33S	60.35W
Seudre ■	11	Ei	45.48N	1.09W
Seugne ■	11	Fi	45.42N	0.32W
Seui	14	Dk	39.50N	9.19 E
Seuil-d'Argonne	12	Hf	48.58N	5.03 E
Seul, Lac- ■	38	Jd	50.20N	92.30W
Seulles ■	12	Be	49.20N	0.27W
Seurre	11	Lg	47.00N	5.09 E
Sevan	19	Eg	40.32N	44.57 E
Sevan, Lake- (EN) = Sevan, Ozero- ■	5	Kg	40.20N	45.20 E
Sevan, Ozero- = Sevan, Lake- (EN) ■	5	Kg	40.20N	45.20 E
Sévaré	34	Ec	14.32N	4.06W
Sevastopol	6	Jg	44.36N	33.32 E
Ševčenko	22	He	43.35N	51.05 E
Ševčenko, Zaliv- ■	18	Ca	46.30N	60.15 E
Sevenoaks	9	Nj	51.16N	0.12 E
Sever ■	13	Ee	39.40N	7.32W
Sévérac-le-Château	11	Jj	44.19N	3.04 E
Severn ■	9	Kj	51.20N	3.10W
Severn [Can.] ■	38	Kd	56.02N	87.36W
Severn [U.K.] ■	9	Kj	51.35N	2.40W
Severnaja Dvina = Northern Dvina (EN) ■	5	Kc	64.32N	40.30 E
Severnaja Keltma ■	17	Ff	61.30N	54.00 E
Severnaja Pseašho, Gora- ■	16	Lh	43.47N	40.30 E
Severnaja Sosva ■	19	Gc	64.10N	65.28 E
Severnaja Zemlja = Severnaya Zemlya (EN) ■	21	Lb	79.30N	98.00 E
Severnaya Zemlya (EN) = Severnaja Zemlja ■	21	Lb	79.30N	98.00 E
Severn Lake ■	42	If	53.52N	90.58W
Severnoje [R.S.F.S.R.]	16	Rb	54.05N	52.32 E
Severnoje [R.S.F.S.R.]	20	Ce	56.21N	78.23 E
Severny	19	Gb	67.38N	64.06 E
Severnyje Uvaly = Northern Uvals (EN) ■	5	Kd	59.30N	49.00 E
Severny Kommunar	17	Gg	58.23N	54.02 E
Severny Ledovity Okean = Arctic Ocean (EN) ■	67	Be	85.00N	170.00 E
Severny Ural = Northern Urals (EN) ■	5	Lc	62.00N	59.00 E
Severobajkalsk	20	Fe	55.40N	109.25 E
Severočeský kraj [3]	10	Kf	50.35N	14.15 E
Severodoneck	16	Ke	48.57N	38.31 E
Severodvinsk	6	Jc	64.34N	39.50 E
Severo-Jenisejski	20	Ed	60.28N	93.01 E
Severo-Kazahstanskaja Oblast [3]	19	Ge	54.30N	68.00 E
Severo-Krymski Kanal ■	16	Ig	45.30N	34.35 E
Severo-Kurilsk	22	Rd	50.40N	156.08 E
Severomoravský kraj [3]	10	Ng	49.45N	17.50 E
Severomorsk	19	Db	69.04N	33.24 E
Severo-Osetinskaja ASSR [3]	19	Eg	43.00N	44.10 E
Severo-Sibirskaja Nizmennost = North Siberian Plain (EN) ■	21	Mb	72.00N	104.00 E
Severouralsk	19	Gc	60.09N	60.01 E
Sevier	46	Ig	38.35N	112.14W
Sevier Bridge Reservoir ■	46	Jg	39.21N	111.57W
Sevier Desert ■	46	Ig	39.25N	112.50W
Sevier Lake ■	43	Ed	38.55N	113.09W
Sevier River ■	43	Ed	39.04N	113.06W
Sevilla [3]	13	Gg	37.30N	5.30W
Sevilla [Col.]	54	Cc	4.16N	75.53W
Sevilla [Sp.] = Seville (EN)	6	Fh	37.23N	5.59W
Sevilla, Isla- ■	49	Fi	8.14N	82.24W
Seville (EN) = Sevilla [Sp.]	6	Fh	37.23N	5.59W
Sevlijevo	15	If	43.01N	25.06 E
Sèvre Nantaise ■	11	Eg	47.12N	1.33W
Sèvre Niortaise ■	11	Eh	46.18N	1.08W
Sevron ■	11	Lh	46.32N	5.16 E
Sevsk	16	Ic	52.08N	34.30 E
Sewa ■	34	Cd	7.18N	12.08W
Seward [Ak.-U.S.]	39	Ec	60.06N	149.26W
Seward [Nb.-U.S.]	45	Hf	40.55N	97.06W
Seward Peninsula ■	38	Cc	65.00N	164.00W
Sewell	56	Fd	34.05S	70.21W
Seyāhkal	24	Md	37.09N	49.52 E
Seybaplaya	48	Nh	19.39N	90.40W
Seybaplaya, Punta- ■	48	Nh	19.45N	90.42W
Seybouse, Oued- ■	14	Bn	36.53N	7.46 E
Seychelles [1]	31	Mi	8.00S	55.00 E
Seychelles Islands ■	30	Mi	4.35S	55.40 E
Seydān	24	Og	30.01N	53.01 E
Seydişehir	24	Dd	37.25N	31.51 E
Seyðisfjörður	6	Eb	65.16N	14.00W
Seyfe Gölü ■	24	Fc	39.13N	34.23 E
Seyf Ţāleh	24	Le	35.57N	46.19 E
Seyhan ■	23	Db	36.43N	34.53 E
Seyitgazi	24	Dc	39.27N	30.43 E
Seyitömer	15	Mj	39.34N	29.52 E
Seyla'	35	Gc	11.21N	43.30 E
Seymour [Austl.]	59	Jg	37.02S	145.08 E
Seymour [In.-U.S.]	44	Ef	38.58N	85.53W
Seymour [Mo.-U.S.]	45	Jh	37.09N	92.46W
Seymour [S.Afr.]	37	Df	32.33S	26.46 E
Seymour [Tx.-U.S.]	43	He	33.35N	99.16W
Sezana	14	He	45.42N	13.52 E
Sézanne	11	Jf	48.43N	3.43 E
Sfaktiria ■	15	Em	36.56N	21.40 E
Sfax (EN) = Şafāqis [3]	32	Jc	34.30N	10.30 E
Sfax (EN) = Şafāqis	31	Ie	34.44N	10.46 E
Sferracavallo, Capo- ■	14	Dk	39.43N	9.40 E
Sfîntu Gheorghe [Rom.]	15	Me	44.53N	29.26 E
Sfîntu Gheorghe [Rom.]	15	Id	45.52N	25.47 E
Sfîntu Gheorghe, Braţul- ■	15	Me	44.53N	29.36 E
Sfîntu Gheorghe, Ostrovul- ■	15	Md	45.07N	29.22 E
Sfizef	13	Li	35.14N	0.15W
's-Gravenhage/Den Haag = The Hague (EN)	6	Ge	52.06N	4.18 E
's-Gravenhage-Scheveningen	11	Kb	52.06N	4.18 E
Shaan-hsi Sheng → Shaanxi Sheng = Shensi (EN) [2]	27	Id	36.00N	109.00 E
Shaanxi Sheng (Shaan-hsi Sheng) = Shensi (EN) [2]	27	Id	36.00N	109.00 E
Shaba [2]	36	Ed	8.30S	25.00 E
Sha'bah, Wādī ash- ■	24	Ij	25.59N	41.55 E
Shabeellaha Dhexe [3]	35	He	3.00N	46.00 E
Shabellaha Hoose [3]	35	Ge	2.00N	44.40 E
Shabēlle, Webi- = Shebeli Webi (EN) ■	30	Lh	0.12S	42.45 E
Shabestar	24	Kc	38.11N	45.42 E
Shabunda	36	Ec	2.42S	27.20 E
Shache/Yarkant	27	Cd	38.24N	77.15 E
Shacheng → Huailai	27	Kc	40.29N	115.30 E
Shackleton Coast ■	66	Kg	82.00S	162.00 E
Shackleton Glacier ■	66	Lg	84.35S	176.15W
Shackleton Ice Shelf ■	66	He	66.00S	101.00 E
Shackleton Range ■	66	Ag	80.40S	26.00W
Shaddādī	24	Id	36.02N	40.45 E
Shādegān	24	Mg	30.40N	48.38 E
Shadwān, Jazīrat- ■	33	Fd	27.30N	33.55 E
Shaftesbury	9	Kk	51.01N	2.12W
Shagedu → Jungar Qi	27	Jd	39.37N	110.58 E
Shāghir Bazar	24	Id	36.52N	40.53 E
Shag Rocks ■	66	Rd	54.26S	36.33W
Shāh'Abbās	24	Oe	34.44N	52.10 E
Shah Alam	26	Df	3.05N	101.29 E
Shahdol	25	Gd	23.13N	81.18 E
Sha He [China] ■	28	Ch	33.39N	114.38 E
Sha He [China] ■	28	Cf	37.09N	114.46 E
Shahezhen → Linze	27	Hd	39.10N	100.21 E
Shah Jahān, Kūh-e- ■	24	Qd	37.02N	57.54 E
Shahjahānpur	25	Fc	27.53N	79.55 E
Shah Kūh ■	23	Hb	36.35N	54.31 E
Shahmīrzād	24	Oe	35.47N	53.20 E
Shāhpūr ■	24	Nh	32.50N	51.45 E
Shāhpūr ■	24	Nh	29.39N	51.03 E
Shahrak	24	Nd	36.14N	50.40 E
Shahr-e-Bābak	24	Pg	30.10N	55.09 E
Shahr-e Khafr	24	Oh	28.56N	53.14 E
Shahr Kord	23	Hc	32.19N	50.50 E
Shāhrūd ■	24	Md	37.17N	48.43 E
Shahu, Kūh-e- ■	24	Le	34.45N	46.30 E
Shāh Zeyd	24	Od	36.13N	52.22 E
Shā'ib al Banāt, Jabal- ■	30	Kf	26.59N	33.29 E
Sha'īt, Wādī- ■	24	Ej	24.33N	33.01 E
Shakaga-Dake ■	29	Be	33.11N	130.53 E
Shakawe	31	Ji	18.23S	21.51 E
Shak Bay (Denham)	59	Ce	25.55S	113.32 E
Shaker Heights	44	Ge	41.29N	81.36W
Shaki	34	Fd	8.40N	3.23 E
Shakotan-Dake ■	29a	Bb	43.16N	140.26 E
Shakotan-Hantō ■	29a	Bb	43.15N	140.30 E
Shakotan-Misaki ■	29a	Bb	43.23N	140.28 E
Shaktoolik	40	Gd	64.20N	161.09W
Shāl	24	Me	35.54N	49.46 E
Shala, Lake- ■	35	Fd	7.29N	38.32 E
Shalamzār	24	Nf	32.02N	50.49 E
Shalānbōd	35	Ge	1.40N	44.42 E
Shaler Mountains ■	42	Gb	71.45N	111.00W
Shaliuhe → Gangca	27	Hd	37.30N	100.14 E
Shaluli Shan ■	21	Lf	30.45N	99.45 E
Shām, Bādiyat ash- = Syrian Desert (EN) ■	21	Ff	32.00N	40.00 E
Shām, Jabal ash- ■	21	Hg	23.10N	57.20 E
Shamattawa	42	Ie	55.52N	92.05W
Shambe	35	Ed	7.07N	30.46 E
Shambu	35	Fd	9.33N	37.07 E
Shamīl	24	Qi	27.30N	56.53 E
Shāmīyah ■	21	Ff	34.00N	39.59 E
Shammar, Jabal- ■	21	Gg	27.20N	41.45 E
Shamo, Lake- ■	35	Fd	5.50N	37.40 E
Shamokin	44	Ie	40.47N	76.34W
Shamrock	45	Fi	35.13N	100.15W
Shams	24	Pg	31.04N	55.02 E
Shamsī	35	Db	19.03N	29.54 E
Shamwa	37	Ec	17.18S	31.34 E
Shan [2]	25	Jd	22.00N	98.00 E
Shandī	31	Kg	16.42N	33.26 E
Shandian He ■	28	Dc	42.20N	116.20 E
Shandong Bandao = Shantung Peninsula (EN) ■	21	Of	37.00N	121.00 E
Shandong Sheng (Shan-tung Sheng) = Shantung (EN) [2]	27	Kd	36.00N	119.00 E
Shandūr Pass ■	25	Ea	36.04N	72.31 E
Shangani	37	Dc	19.42S	29.22 E
Shangani ■	37	Dc	18.30S	27.11 E
Shangbahe	28	Ci	30.39N	115.06 E
Shangcai	28	Ch	33.16N	114.15 E
Shangcheng	28	Ci	31.49N	115.24 E
Shangdu	27	Jc	41.31N	113.32 E
Shanggao	28	Cj	28.15N	114.55 E
Shanghai	22	Of	31.14N	121.28 E
Shanghai Shi (Shang-hai Shih) [4]	27	Le	31.14N	121.28 E
Shang-hai Shih → Shanghai Shi [4]	27	Le	31.14N	121.28 E
Shanghang	27	Kf	25.04N	116.21 E
Shanghe	28	Df	37.19N	117.09 E
Shanghekou	27	Lc	40.26N	124.51 E
Shangpaihe → Feixi	28	Di	31.42N	117.09 E
Shangqiu (Zhuji)	27	Ke	34.24N	115.37 E
Shangrao	27	Kf	28.29N	117.59 E
Shan Guan ■	27	Kf	27.28N	117.05 E
Shangxian	27	Ie	33.55N	109.57 E
Shangyi (Nanhaoqian)	28	Bd	41.06N	113.58 E
Shangyu (Baiguan)	28	Fi	30.01N	120.53 E
Shangzhi	27	Mb	45.13N	127.55 E
Shanhaiguan	28	Ed	40.01N	119.45 E
Shanhetun	28	Ib	44.43N	127.14 E
Shan-hsi Sheng → Shanxi Sheng = Shansi (EN) [2]	27	Jd	37.00N	112.00 E
Shanklin	12	Ad	50.37N	1.11W
Shanmatang Ding ■	27	Jg	24.45N	111.50 E
Shannon ■	41	Kc	75.20N	18.10W
Shannon	62	Fd	40.33S	175.25 E
Shannon/Aerfort na Sionainne ■	9	Ei	52.42N	8.57W
Shannon/An tSionainn ■	5	Fe	52.36N	9.41W
Shannon, Mount- ■	59	Ie	29.58S	141.30 E
Shannon, Mouth of the- ■	9	Di	52.30N	9.53W
Shanshan (Piqan)	27	Fc	42.52N	90.10 E
Shansi (EN) = Shan-hsi Sheng → Shanxi Sheng [2]	27	Jd	37.00N	112.00 E
Shansi (EN) = Shanxi Sheng (Shan-hsi Sheng) [2]	27	Jd	37.00N	112.00 E
Shansonggang	28	Ic	42.30N	126.13 E
Shanţah, Ra's- ■	24	Qi	26.22N	56.26 E
Shantar Islands (EN) = Šantarskije Ostrova ■	21	Pd	55.00N	137.36 E
Shantou	22	Ng	23.26N	116.42 E
Shantung (EN) = Shandong Sheng (Shan-tung Sheng) [2]	27	Kd	36.00N	119.00 E
Shantung (EN) = Shan-tung Sheng → Shandong Sheng [2]	27	Kd	36.00N	119.00 E
Shantung Peninsula (EN) = Shandong Bandao ■	21	Of	37.00N	121.00 E
Shan-tung Sheng → Shandong Sheng = Shantung (EN) [2]	27	Kd	36.00N	119.00 E
Shanxian	28	Dg	34.47N	116.05 E
Shanxi Sheng (Shan-hsi Sheng) = Shansi (EN) [2]	27	Jd	37.00N	112.00 E
Shanyin (Daiyue)	28	Be	39.30N	112.48 E
Shanyincheng	28	Be	39.27N	112.56 E
Shaoguan	22	Ng	24.57N	113.34 E
Shaoshan	27	Jf	27.55N	112.32 E
Shaowu	27	Kf	27.21N	117.29 E
Shaoxing	22	Og	30.00N	120.30 E
Shaoyang	22	Ng	27.13N	111.31 E
Shapinsay ■	9	Kb	59.03N	2.51W
Shaqlāwah	24	Kd	36.23N	44.18 E
Shaqq al Ju'ayfir ■	35	Db	15.16N	26.00 E
Shaqrā'	23	Gg	13.21N	45.42 E
Shaqū	24	Qi	27.14N	56.22 E
Sharāf	24	Jg	30.37N	43.45 E
Sharafah	35	Dc	12.04N	27.07 E
Sharafkhāneh	24	Kc	38.11N	45.29 E
Sharāh, Jibāl ash- ■	24	Fg	30.10N	35.30 E
Sharā 'Iwah ■	24	Oj	25.02N	52.14 E
Shareh	24	Kd	37.38N	44.50 E
Shari	27	Pc	43.55N	144.40 E
Shārī, Buḩayrat- ■	24	Ke	34.23N	44.07 E
Shari-Dake ■	29a	Db	43.46N	144.43 E
Sharifābād [Iran]	24	Nd	36.12N	50.08 E
Sharifābād [Iran]	24	Ne	35.25N	51.47 E
Shark Bay ■	57	Cg	25.30S	113.30 E
Sharm ash Shaykh	33	Fd	27.50N	34.16 E
Sharon	44	Ge	41.16N	80.30W
Sharon Springs	45	Fg	38.54N	101.45W
Sharp ■	9	Fc	58.05N	7.05W
Sharqīyah, Aş Şaḩrā' ash- = Arabian Desert (EN) ■	30	Kf	28.00N	32.00 E
Sharshar, Jabal- ■	24	Dk	23.52N	30.20 E
Shary	23	Fd	27.15N	43.27 E
Shashe	37	Dd	21.24S	27.27 E
Shashemene	35	Fd	7.13N	38.36 E
Shashi	22	Nf	30.22N	112.11 E
Shashi ■	30	Jk	22.12S	29.21 E
Shasta, Mount- ■	38	Ge	41.20N	122.20W
Shasta Lake ■	43	Cc	40.50N	122.25W
Shāţi', Wādī ash- ■	33	Bd	27.10N	13.25 E
Shattuck	45	Gh	36.16N	99.53W
Shaunavon	42	Gg	49.40N	108.25W
Shawan	27	Ec	44.21N	85.37 E
Shawano	45	Ld	44.47N	88.36W
Shawinigan	42	Kg	46.33N	72.45W
Shawnee	43	Hd	35.20N	96.55W
Shawneetown	45	Lh	37.42N	88.08W
Shaw River ■	59	Dd	20.20S	119.17 E
Shāwshāw, Jabal- ■	24	Ci	26.03N	28.56 E
Shayang	28	Bi	30.42N	112.34 E
Shaybārā ■	24	Gj	25.25N	36.51 E
Shaykh Aḩmad	24	Lf	32.53N	46.26 E
Shaykh Fāris	24	Lf	32.05N	47.36 E
Shaykh Sa'd	24	Lf	32.34N	46.17 E
Shaykh 'Uthmān	23	Fg	12.52N	44.59 E
Shebar, Kowtal-e- ■	23	Kc	34.54N	68.14 E
Shebele, Wabe- = Shebeli Webi (EN) ■	30	Lh	0.12S	42.45 E
Shebeli Webi (EN) = Shabēlle, Webi- ■	30	Lh	0.12S	42.45 E
Shebeli Webi (EN) = Shebele, Wabe- ■	30	Lh	0.12S	42.45 E
Sheberghān	22	If	36.41N	65.45 E
Sheboygan	45	Me	43.46N	87.44W
Shebshi Mountains ■	30	Ih	8.30N	11.45 E
Shedin Peak ■	42	Ee	55.50N	127.00W
Sheelin, Lough-/Loch Sileann ■	9	Fh	53.48N	7.20W
Sheenjek ■	40	Kc	66.45N	144.33W
Sheep Haven/Cuan na gCaorach ■	9	Ff	55.10N	7.52W
Sheep Mountain ■	46	Hj	32.32N	114.14W
Sheep Range ■	46	Hh	36.45N	115.05W
s'Heerenberg, Bergh-	12	Ic	51.53N	6.16 E
Sheerness	9	Nj	51.27N	0.45 E
Sheffield [Al.-U.S.]	44	Dh	34.46N	87.40W
Sheffield [Eng.-U.K.]	6	Fe	53.23N	1.30W
Sheffield [Tx.-U.S.]	45	Fk	30.43N	101.50W
Shefford	12	Bb	52.02N	0.20W
Shek Hasan	35	Fc	12.04N	35.53 E
Shek Husen	35	Gd	7.45N	40.42 E
Shelburne [N.S.-Can.]	42	Kh	43.46N	65.19W
Shelburne [Ont.-Can.]	44	Gc	44.04N	80.12W
Shelby [Mt.-U.S.]	43	Eb	48.30N	111.51W
Shelby [N.C.-U.S.]	44	Gh	35.17N	81.32W
Shelbyville [Il.-U.S.]	45	Lg	39.24N	88.48W
Shelbyville [In.-U.S.]	44	Ef	39.31N	85.47W
Shelbyville [Tn.-U.S.]	44	Dh	35.29N	86.27W
Shelbyville, Lake- ■	45	Lg	39.30N	88.40W
Sheldon	45	Ie	43.11N	95.51W
Sheldon Point	40	Gd	63.32N	164.52W
Shelikhov Gulf (EN) = Šelihova, Zaliv- ■	21	Rc	60.00N	158.00 E
Shelikof Strait ■	40	Ie	57.30N	155.00W
Shell	46	Ld	44.33N	107.44W
Shellbrook	42	Gf	53.13N	106.24W
Shellharbour	58	Gh	34.35S	150.52 E
Shelter Point ■	62	Cg	47.06S	168.13 E
Shelton	46	Dc	47.13N	123.06W
Shenandoah	45	If	40.46N	95.22W
Shenandoah Mountain ■	44	Hf	38.58N	79.00W
Shenandoah Valley ■	44	Hf	38.45N	78.45W
Shenchi	28	Be	39.05N	112.11 E
Shendam	34	Gd	8.53N	9.32 E
Shending Shan ■	27	Nb	46.34N	133.27 E
Shenge	34	Cd	7.55N	12.57W
Shëngjini	15	Ch	41.49N	19.35 E
Shengsi (Caiyuanzhen)	28	Gi	30.42N	122.29 E
Shengsi Liedao ■	27	Le	30.45N	122.40 E
Shengxian	27	Lf	29.35N	120.45 E
Shengze	28	Fi	30.55N	120.39 E
Shenjiamen → Putuo	28	Gj	29.57N	122.18 E
Shenmu	27	Jd	38.52N	110.35 E
Shenqiu (Huaidian)	27	Ke	33.27N	115.05 E
Shensi (EN) = Shaan-hsi Sheng → Shaanxi Sheng [2]	27	Id	36.00N	109.00 E
Shensi (EN) = Shaanxi Sheng (Shaan-hsi Sheng) [2]	27	Id	36.00N	109.00 E
Shenton, Mount- ■	59	Ee	28.00S	123.22 E
Shenxian	28	Ce	38.01N	115.33 E
Shenyang (Mukden)	22	Oe	41.48N	123.24 E
Shenze	28	Ce	38.11N	115.11 E
Shepherd, Iles- = Shepherd Islands (EN) ■	63b	Dc	16.55S	168.35 E
Shepherd Islands (EN) = Shepherd, Iles- ■	63b	Dc	16.55S	168.35 E
Shepparton	58	Fh	36.23S	145.25 E
Sheppey ■	9	Nj	51.24N	0.50 E
Shepshed	12	Ab	52.45N	1.17W
Sheqi	28	Bh	33.04N	112.56 E
Sherard, Cape - ■	42	Jb	74.36N	80.10W
Sherard Osborn Fjord ■	41	Gb	82.10N	51.30W
Sherborne	9	Kk	50.57N	2.31W
Sherbro Island ■	30	Fh	7.33N	12.42W
Sherbrooke	39	Le	45.24N	71.54W
Sherda	35	Ba	20.08N	16.45 E
Shere Hill ■	34	Gd	9.57N	9.03 E
Sheridan [Mt.-U.S.]	46	Id	45.27N	112.12W
Sheridan [Wy.-U.S.]	39	Ie	44.48N	106.58W
Sheridan Lake	45	Eg	38.30N	102.15W
Sheringham	9	Oi	52.57N	1.12 E
Sherman	43	He	33.38N	96.36W
Sherman Station	44	Mc	45.54N	68.26W
Sherridon	42	He	55.07N	101.05W
's-Hertogenbosch/Den Bosch	11	Lc	51.41N	5.19 E
Sherwood Forest ■	9	Lh	53.10N	1.10W
She Shui ■	28	Ci	30.52N	114.22 E
Shetland [3]	9	La	60.30N	1.30W
Shetland Islands (Zetland) ■	5	Fc	60.30N	1.30W
Shewa [3]	35	Fd	9.20N	38.55 E
Shewa Gimira	35	Fd	7.00N	35.50 E
Shexian	28	Bf	36.33N	113.40 E
Shexian (Huicheng)	28	Ej	29.53N	118.27 E
Sheyang (Hede)	28	Fh	33.47N	120.15 E
Sheyenne River ■	43	Hb	47.05N	96.50W
Shiant Islands ■	9	Gd	57.54N	6.30W
Shibām	35	Hb	15.56N	48.38 E
Shibamīnah, Wādī- ■	23	Ie	22.12N	55.30 E
Shibata [Jap.]	28	Of	37.57N	139.20 E
Shibata [Jap.]	29	Gb	38.05N	140.50 E
Shibayama-Gata ■	29	Ec	36.21N	136.23 E
Shibazhan	27	Ma	42.28N	125.20 E
Shibecha	28	Rc	43.17N	144.36 E
Shibetsu [Jap.]	28	Rc	43.40N	145.08 E
Shibetsu [Jap.]	27	Pc	44.10N	142.23 E
Shibetsu-Gawa ■	29a	Db	43.40N	145.06 E
Shibīn al Kawm	33	Fc	30.33N	31.01 E
Shibiutan	29a	Ca	44.47N	142.35 E
Shibi-Zan ■	29	Bf	31.59N	130.22 E
Shīb Kūh ■	23	Hd	27.20N	52.40 E
Shibukawa	28	Of	36.29N	139.00 E
Shibushi	29	Bf	31.28N	131.07 E
Shibushi-Wan ■	28	Ki	31.25N	131.12 E
Shichinohe	29	Ga	40.41N	141.10 E
Shichiyo Islands ■	64d	Bb	7.23N	151.40 E
Shidao	27	Ld	36.51N	122.18 E
Shido	29	Dd	34.19N	134.10 E
Shidongsi → Gaolan	27	Hd	36.23N	103.55 E
Shiel, Loch- ■	9	He	56.50N	5.50W
Shiga Ken [2]	28	Ng	35.15N	136.10 E
Shigu	27	Gf	26.54N	99.44 E
Shi He ■	28	Ch	32.32N	115.52 E
Shihezi	27	Ec	44.18N	86.02 E
Shiiba	29	Be	32.28N	131.09 E
Shijaku	15	Ch	41.20N	19.34 E
Shijiazhuang	22	Nf	38.00N	114.30 E
Shijiusuo	28	Eg	35.24N	119.32 E
Shika	29	Ec	37.01N	136.46 E
Shikabe	29a	Bb	42.02N	140.47 E
Shikārpur	25	Dc	27.57N	68.38 E
Shiki Islands ■	64d	Bb	7.24N	151.53 E
Shikine-Jima ■	29	Fd	34.19N	139.13 E
Shikoku ■	21	Pf	33.30N	133.30 E
Shikoku Basin (EN) ■	27	Oe	30.00N	135.30 E
Shikoku-Sanchi ■	29	Ce	33.45N	133.35 E
Shilabo	35	Gd	6.05N	44.45 E
Shiliguri	22	Kg	26.42N	88.26 E
Shiliu → Changjiang	27	Ih	19.20N	109.03 E
Shilla ■	25	Fb	32.24N	78.12 E
Shillong	22	Lg	25.34N	91.53 E
Shimabara	28	Kh	32.47N	130.22 E
Shimabara-Hantō ■	29	Be	32.45N	130.15 E
Shimabara-Wan ■	29	Be	32.50N	130.30 E
Shimada	29	Fd	34.49N	138.09 E
Shima-Hantō ■	29	Ed	34.25N	136.45 E
Shimane-Hantō ■	29	Cd	35.30N	133.00 E
Shimane Ken [2]	28	Lg	35.00N	132.20 E
Shimanto-Gawa ■	29	Ce	32.56N	133.00 E
Shimaura-Tō ■	29	Bd	34.50N	131.50 E
Shimian	27	Hf	29.10N	102.26 E
Shimizu [Jap.]	29a	Cb	43.01N	142.51 E
Shimizu [Jap.]	28	Og	35.01N	138.29 E
Shimla	22	Jf	31.06N	77.10 E
Shimoda	28	Og	34.40N	138.57 E
Shimodate	29	Fc	36.19N	139.58 E
Shimoga	22	Jh	13.55N	75.34 E
Shimo-Jima ■	29	Be	32.25N	130.05 E
Shimokawa	29a	Ca	44.18N	142.38 E
Shimokita-Hantō ■	29a	Bc	41.15N	141.05 E
Shimo-Koshiki-Jima ■	29	Af	31.40N	129.40 E
Shimo la Tewa	36	Gc	3.57S	39.44 E
Shimoni	36	Gc	4.39S	39.23 E
Shimonoseki	27	Ne	33.57N	130.57 E
Shimono-Shima ■	29	Ad	34.15N	129.15 E
Shimotsu	29	Dd	34.07N	135.08 E
Shimotsuma	29	Fc	36.11N	139.58 E
Shin, Loch- ■	9	Ic	58.07N	4.32W
Shinano	29	Fc	36.47N	138.10 E
Shinano-Gawa ■	29	Fc	37.57N	139.04 E
Shināş	24	Qj	24.43N	56.27 E
Shindand	23	Jc	33.18N	62.08 E
Shinga	36	Dc	3.16S	24.38 E
Shingbwiyang	25	Jc	26.41N	96.13 E
Shingū	27	Oe	33.44N	135.59 E
Shingwidzi	37	Ed	23.01S	30.43 E
Shinji	29	Cd	35.24N	132.54 E
Shinji-Ko ■	28	Lg	35.27N	133.02 E
Shinjō	27	Pd	38.46N	140.18 E
Shinkafe	34	Gc	13.05N	6.31 E
Shinminato	29	Ec	36.47N	137.04 E
Shinnanyō	29	Bd	34.05N	131.45 E
Shinshiro	29	Ed	34.53N	137.30 E
Shintoku	28	Qc	43.12N	142.55 E
Shintotsugawa	29a	Bb	43.32N	141.40 E
Shinyanga	31	Ki	3.40S	33.26 E
Shinyanga [3]	36	Fc	3.30S	33.00 E
Shiogama	29	Gb	38.19N	141.01 E
Shiojiri	28	Nf	36.06N	137.58 E
Shiokubi-Misaki ■	29a	Bc	41.43N	140.57 E
Shio-no-Misaki ■	27	Oe	33.25N	135.45 E
Shipai → Huaining	28	Di	30.25N	116.39 E

Index Symbols

[1] Independent Nation	■ Historical or Cultural Region	■ Pass, Gap	■ Depression	■ Coast, Beach	■ Rock, Reef	■ Waterfall Rapids	■ Canal	■ Lagoon	■ Escarpment, Sea Scarp
[2] State, Region	■ Mount, Mountain	■ Plain, Lowland	■ Polder	■ Cliff	■ Islands, Archipelago	■ River Mouth, Estuary	■ Glacier	■ Bank	■ Fracture
[3] District, County	■ Volcano	■ Delta	■ Desert, Dunes	■ Peninsula	■ Rocks, Reefs	■ Lake	■ Ice Shelf, Pack Ice	■ Seamount	■ Trench, Abyss
[4] Municipality	■ Hill	■ Salt Flat	■ Forest, Woods	■ Isthmus	■ Coral Reef	■ Salt Lake	■ Ocean	■ Tablemount	■ National Park, Reserve
[5] Colony, Dependency	■ Mountains, Mountain Range	■ Valley, Canyon	■ Heath, Steppe	■ Sandbank	■ Well, Spring	■ Intermittent Lake	■ Sea	■ Ridge	■ Point of Interest
■ Continent	■ Hills, Escarpment	■ Crater, Cave	■ Oasis	■ Island	■ Geyser	■ Reservoir	■ Gulf, Bay	■ Shelf	■ Recreation Site
■ Physical Region	■ Plateau, Upland	■ Karst Features	■ Cape, Point	■ Atoll	■ River, Stream	■ Swamp, Pond	■ Strait, Fjord	■ Basin	■ Cave, Cavern

■ Historic Site	■ Port
■ Ruins	■ Lighthouse
■ Wall, Walls	■ Mine
■ Church, Abbey	■ Tunnel
■ Temple	■ Dam, Bridge
■ Scientific Station	
■ Airport	

Shiping 27 Hg 23.44N 102.28 E
Shipki La 27 Ce 31.49N 78.45 E
Shippegan 42 Lg 47.45N 64.42W
Shiprock 45 Bh 36.47N 108.41W
Shipshaw, Rivière- 44 La 48.30N 71.15W
Shipu 28 Fj 29.17N 121.57 E
Shipugi Shankou 27 Ce 31.49N 78.45 E
Shiquan 27 Ie 33.05N 108.15 E
Shiquanhe 22 Jf 32.24N 79.52 E
Shiquan He 27 Ce 32.28N 79.44 E
Shiragami Dake 29 Ga 40.30N 140.01 E
Shiragami-Misaki 28 Pd 41.25N 140.12 E
Shirahama 29 De 33.40N 135.20 E
Shirakawa [Jap.] 29 Ed 35.36N 137.12 E
Shirakawa [Jap.] 29 Ec 36.17N 136.53 E
Shirakawa [Jap.] 28 Pf 37.07N 140.13 E
Shirane-San [Jap.] 27 Od 36.48N 139.22 E
Shirane-San [Jap.] 29 Fd 35.40N 138.13 E
Shirane-San [Jap.] 29 Fc 36.38N 138.32 E
Shiranuka 28 Rc 42.57N 144.05 E
Shiraoi 28 Pc 42.31N 141.16 E
Shirase Coast 66 Mf 78.30S 156.00W
Shirataka 29 Gb 38.11N 140.06 E
Shirataki 29a Cb 43.53N 143.09 E
Shīrāz 22 Hg 29.36N 52.32 E
Shirbīn 24 Dg 31.11N 31.32 E
Shire 30 Kj 17.42S 35.19 E
Shiren 28 Id 41.54N 126.34 E
Shiretoko-Dake 29a Da 44.15N 145.14 E
Shiretoko-Hantō 29a Da 44.00N 145.00 E
Shiretoko-Misaki 27 Qc 44.21N 145.20 E
Shīrgāh 24 Od 36.17N 52.54 E
Shiribetsu-Gawa 29a Bb 42.52N 140.21 E
Shiriha-Misaki 29a Db 42.56N 144.45 E
Shirikishinai 29a Bc 41.48N 141.05 E
Shirīn 24 Qi 27.10N 56.49 E
Shīrīn sū 24 Me 35.29N 48.27 E
Shiriya-Zaki 27 Pc 41.26N 141.28 E
Shīr Kūh 21 Hf 31.37N 54.04 E
Shirley Mountains 46 Le 42.15N 106.30W
Shiroishi 28 Pe 38.00N 140.37 E
Shirone 29 Fc 37.46N 139.00 E
Shirotori 29 Ed 35.53N 136.52 E
Shirouma-Dake 29 Ec 36.45N 137.46 E
Shirshov Ridge (EN) 20 Me 57.30N 171.00 E
Shīrvān 24 Lf 33.33N 46.49 E
Shirwan Mazīn 24 Kd 37.03N 44.10 E
Shishaldin Volcano 38 Cd 54.45N 163.57W
Shishi-Jima 29 Be 32.17N 130.15 E
Shishmaref 40 Fc 66.14N 166.09W
Shishou 27 Jf 29.42N 112.23 E
Shitai (Qili) 28 Di 30.12N 117.28 E
Shitara 29 Ed 35.05N 137.34 E
Shitou Shan 27 Ma 51.02N 125.12 E
Shivwits Plateau 46 Ih 36.10N 113.40W
Shiwa 28 Pe 39.33N 141.35 E
Shiwan Dashan 27 Ig 21.45N 107.35 E
Shiwa Ngandu 36 Fe 11.12S 31.43 E
Shiwpuri 25 Fc 25.26N 77.39 E
Shixian 28 Jc 43.05N 129.46 E
Shiyan 27 Je 32.34N 110.48 E
Shiyang He 27 Hd 39.00N 103.25 E
Shizilu → Junan 28 Eg 35.10N 118.50 E
Shizugawa 29 Gb 38.40N 141.28 E
Shizui 28 Ic 43.03N 126.09 E
Shizuishan (Dawukou) 27 Id 39.03N 106.24 E
Shizukuishi 29 Gb 39.42N 140.59 E
Shizunai 28 Qc 42.20N 142.22 E
Shizunai-Gawa 29a Cb 42.20N 142.22 E
Shizuoka 22 Pf 34.58N 138.23 E
Shizuoka Ken [2] 28 Og 35.00N 138.25 E
Shkodra 6 Hg 42.05N 19.30 E
Shkodrës, Liqen i- = Scutari, Lake- (EN) 5 Hg 42.10N 19.20 E
Shkumbini 15 Ch 41.01N 19.26 E
Shoal Lake 45 Fa 50.26N 100.34W
Shoal Lake 45 Ib 49.32N 95.00W
Shoal Lakes 45 Ha 50.20N 97.40W
Shōbara 28 Lg 34.51N 133.01 E
Shodo-Shima 29 Dd 34.30N 134.15 E
Shō-Gawa 29 Ec 36.47N 137.04 E
Shokanbetsu-Dake 29a Bb 43.43N 141.31 E
Shokotsu-Gawa 29a Ca 44.23N 143.17 E
Sholāpur → Solāpur 22 Jh 17.41N 75.55 E
Shoqān 24 Qd 37.20N 56.58 E
Shoranūr 25 Ff 10.46N 76.17 E
Shoreham-by-Sea 9 Mk 50.49N 0.16W
Shortland Islands 60 Fi 6.55S 155.53 E
Shosambetsu 29a Ba 44.32N 141.46 E
Shoshone 46 He 42.56N 114.24W
Shoshone Mountains 43 Dd 39.15N 117.25W
Shoshone Peak 46 Gh 36.56N 116.16W
Shoshone River 46 Kd 44.52N 108.11W
Shoshong 37 Dd 23.02S 26.31 E
Shoshoni 46 Ke 43.14N 108.07W
Shotor Khūn 23 Jc 34.20N 64.55 E
Shouchang 28 Ej 29.23N 119.12 E
Shouguang 28 Ef 36.53N 118.44 E
Shouxian (Shouyang) 28 Dh 32.35N 116.47 E
Shouyang → Shouxian 28 Dh 32.35N 116.47 E
Shōwa 29 Gb 39.51N 140.03 E
Show Low 46 Ji 34.15N 110.02W
Shqipëria = Albania (EN) [1] 6 Hg 41.00N 20.00 E
Shreveport 39 Jf 32.30N 93.45W
Shrewsbury 9 Ki 52.43N 2.45W
Shuangcheng 27 Mb 45.21N 126.17 E
Shuangjiang 27 Gg 23.27N 99.50 E
Shuangjiang → Tongdao 27 If 26.14N 109.45 E
Shuangliao 27 Lc 43.30N 123.30 E
Shuangyang 27 Mc 43.31N 125.28 E
Shuangyashan 22 Pe 46.37N 131.10 E
Shucheng 28 Di 31.28N 116.57 E
Shufu 27 Cd 39.27N 75.52 E
Shuguri Falls 36 Gd 8.31S 37.23 E
Shu He 28 Eg 34.07N 118.30 E
Shuicheng 27 Hf 26.34N 104.52 E
Shuiding → Huocheng 27 Dc 44.03N 80.49 E
Shuiji → Laixi 28 Ff 36.52N 120.31 E
Shuijiahu → Changfeng 28 Dh 32.29N 117.10 E
Shuikou → Jianghua 27 Jg 24.58N 111.56 E
Shuiye 28 Cf 36.08N 114.06 E
Shuizhai → Xiangcheng 28 Ch 33.27N 114.53 E
Shūl 24 Ng 30.10N 51.38 E
Shulan 27 Mc 44.26N 126.55 E
Shule 27 Cd 39.25N 76.06 E
Shule He 21 Le 40.20N 92.50 E
Shulu (Xinji) 28 Cf 37.56N 115.14 E
Shumagin Islands 40 He 55.07N 159.45W
Shumarinai-Ko 29a Ca 44.20N 142.13 E
Shunayn, Sabkhat- 33 Dc 30.10N 21.00 E
Shungnak 40 Hc 66.53N 157.02W
Shunyi 28 Dd 40.09N 116.38 E
Shuolong 27 Ig 22.51N 106.55 E
Shuoxian 27 Jd 39.18N 112.25 E
Shūr [Iran] 24 Pi 26.59N 55.47 E
Shūr [Iran] 24 Oh 28.12N 52.09 E
Shūr [Iran] 24 Ne 35.09N 51.30 E
Shūr [Iran] 24 Oh 28.33N 53.12 E
Shūr Āb 24 Pg 31.45N 55.15 E
Shurāb 23 Ic 33.07N 55.18 E
Shūsf 23 Jc 31.48N 60.01 E
Shūsh 24 Mf 32.12N 48.17 E
Shushica 15 Ci 40.34N 19.34 E
Shūshtar 23 Gc 32.03N 48.51 E
Shuswap Lake 46 Fa 50.57N 119.15W
Shūt 24 Oe 34.44N 52.53 E
Shuwak 35 Fc 14.23N 35.52 E
Shuyang 27 Ke 34.01N 118.52 E
Shuzenji 29 Fd 34.58N 138.55 E
Shwebo 25 Jd 22.34N 95.42 E
Shwell 25 Jd 23.56N 96.17 E
Shyok 25 Fa 35.13N 75.53 E
Sia 26 Jh 6.49S 134.19 E
Siagne 11 Mk 43.32N 6.57 E
Siāh Band 23 Kc 33.25N 65.21 E
Siāh-Chashmeh 24 Kc 39.04N 44.23 E
Siāh-Kūh 24 Oe 34.38N 52.16 E
Siak 26 Df 1.13N 102.09 E
Sialkot [Pak.] 25 Ea 35.15N 73.17 E
Sialkot [Pak.] 22 Jf 32.30N 74.31 E
Sianów 10 Mb 54.15N 16.16 E
Siantan, Pulau- 26 Ef 3.10N 106.15 E
Siargao 26 Ie 9.53N 126.02 E
Šiaškotan, Ostrov- 21 Re 48.49N 154.06 E
Siátista 15 Ei 40.16N 21.33 E
Siau, Pulau- 26 If 2.42N 125.24 E
Šiauliai/Šjauljaj 6 Id 55.53N 23.19 E
Siavonga 36 Ef 16.32S 28.43 E
Siazan 19 Eg 41.04N 49.06 E
Sibāʾi, Jabal as- 24 Fd 25.43N 34.09 E
Sibaj 19 Fe 52.42N 58.39 E
Sibari 14 Kk 39.45N 16.27 E
Sibasa 37 Ed 22.56S 30.29 E
Šibenik 14 Jg 43.44N 15.53 E
Siberimanua 26 Cg 2.09S 99.34 E
Siberut, Pulau- 21 Lj 1.20S 98.55 E
Siberut, Selat- 26 Cg 0.42S 98.35 E
Sibi 25 Dc 29.33N 67.53 E
Sibigo 26 Cf 2.51N 95.55 E
Sibillini, Monti- 14 Hh 42.55N 13.15 E
Sibircatajaha 17 Lb 69.05N 64.43 E
Sibircevo 28 Lb 44.16N 132.20 E
Sibirjakova, Ostrov- 20 Cb 72.50N 79.00 E
Sibiti 36 Bc 3.41S 13.21 E
Sibiu [2] 15 Hd 45.46N 24.12 E
Sibiu 6 If 45.48N 24.09 E
Sibolga 22 Li 1.45N 98.48 E
Sibsāgar 25 Ic 26.59N 94.38 E
Sibu 22 Ni 2.18N 111.49 E
Sibuguey Bay 26 He 7.30N 122.40 E
Sibut 31 Ih 5.44N 19.05 E
Sibutu Islands 26 Gf 4.45N 119.20 E
Sibutu Passage 26 Gf 4.56N 119.36 E
Sibuyan 26 Hd 12.25N 122.34 E
Sibuyan Sea 26 Hd 12.50N 122.40 E
Siby 34 Dc 12.22N 8.22W
Sibyllenstein 10 Ke 51.12N 14.05 E
Sicani, Monti- 14 Hm 37.40N 13.15 E
Sicasica 54 Eg 17.22S 67.45W
Si Chon 25 Jg 9.00N 99.56 E
Sichuan Pendi 21 Mf 30.01N 105.00 E
Sichuan Sheng (Ssu-ch'uan -Sheng) = Szechwan (EN) [2] 27 He 30.00N 103.00 E
Sicilia [2] 14 Im 37.45N 14.15 E
Sicilia = Sicily (EN) 5 Hh 37.30N 14.00 E
Sicilia, Canale di- = Sicily, Strait of- (EN) 5 Hh 37.20N 11.20 E
Sicilia, Mar di- 14 Gn 36.30N 13.00 E
Sicily (EN) = Sicilia 5 Hh 37.30N 14.00 E
Sicily, Strait of- (EN) = Sicilia, Canale di- 5 Hh 37.20N 11.20 E
Sicily, Strait of- (EN) = Tūnis, Canal de- 5 Hh 37.20N 11.20 E
Sico Tinto, Rio- 49 Ef 15.58N 84.58W
Sicuani 53 Ig 14.15S 71.15W
Šid 15 Cd 45.08N 19.14 E
Sidamo [3] 35 Fd 5.48N 38.50 E
Siddipet 25 Fe 18.06N 78.51 E
Side 24 Dd 36.46N 31.22 E
Sidéradougou 34 Ec 10.40N 4.15W
Siderno 14 Kl 38.16N 16.18 E
Siders/Sierre 14 Bd 46.17N 7.32 E
Šiderty 19 He 52.32N 74.50 E
Siderty 19 He 51.40N 74.50 E
Sidheros, Ákra- 15 Jn 35.19N 26.19 E
Sidhirókastron 15 Gh 41.14N 23.23 E
Sīdī ʿAbd ar Raḥmān 24 Cg 30.58N 28.44 E
Sidi Aïch 13 Qh 36.37N 4.41 E
Sidi-Akacha 13 Nh 36.28N 1.18 E
Sidi Ali 13 Mh 36.06N 0.25 E
Sīdī ʿAlī al Makkī, Ra's- 14 Em 37.11N 10.17 E
Sīdī Barrānī 33 Ec 31.36N 25.55 E
Sidi Bel Abbes [3] 32 Gc 34.45N 0.35W
Sidi Bel Abbes 32 Gb 35.12N 0.38W
Sidi Bennour 32 Fc 32.39N 8.26W
Sidi di Daoud 13 Ph 36.51N 3.52 E
Sidi Ifni 31 Ff 29.33N 10.10W
Sidi Kacem 32 Fc 34.13N 5.42W
Sidikalang 26 Cf 2.45N 98.19 E
Sidi Lakhdar 13 Mh 36.10N 0.27 E
Sīdī Zayd, Jabal- 14 En 36.29N 10.20 E
Sidlaw Hills 9 Ke 56.30N 3.00W
Sidmouth 9 Jk 50.41N 3.14W
Sidney [B.C.-Can.] 42 Fg 48.39N 123.24W
Sidney [Mt.-U.S.] 43 Gb 47.43N 104.09W
Sidney [Nb.-U.S.] 43 Gc 41.09N 102.59W
Sidney [Oh.-U.S.] 44 Ee 40.16N 84.10W
Sidney Lanier, Lake- 44 Fh 34.15N 83.57W
Sidobre 11 Ik 43.40N 2.30 E
Sidorovsk 20 Dc 66.35N 82.30 E
Sidra 10 Tc 53.33N 23.30 E
Sidra, Gulf of- (EN) = Surt, Khalīj- 30 Ie 31.30N 18.00 E
Sidrolândia 55 Ee 20.55S 54.58W
Siedlce [2] 10 Sd 52.10N 22.15 E
Siedlce 10 Sd 52.11N 22.16 E
Siedlecka, Wysoczyzna- 10 Sd 52.10N 22.15 E
Sieg [Ger.] 10 Df 50.45N 7.05 E
Sieg [Ger.] 12 Kd 50.55N 8.01 E
Siegburg 10 Df 50.48N 7.12 E
Siegen 10 Ef 50.52N 8.02 E
Siemiatycze 10 Sd 52.26N 22.53 E
Siĕmréab 25 Kf 13.22N 103.51 E
Siena 14 Fg 43.19N 11.21 E
Sieniawa 10 Sf 50.11N 22.36 E
Sienne 11 Ee 49.00N 1.34W
Sieradz 10 Oe 51.36N 18.45 E
Sieradz [2] 10 Oe 51.35N 18.45 E
Sieradzka, Niecka- 10 Oe 51.35N 18.50 E
Sierck-les-Bains 12 Ie 49.26N 6.21 E
Sierpc 10 Pd 52.52N 19.41 E
Sierra Blanca 45 Dk 31.11N 105.21W
Sierra Blanca Peak 43 Fe 33.23N 105.48W
Sierra Colorada 56 Gf 40.35S 67.48W
Sierra Leone [1] 31 Fh 8.30N 11.30W
Sierra Leone Basin (EN) 3 Di 5.00N 17.00W
Sierra Leone Rise (EN) 3 Di 5.30N 21.00W
Sierra Madre 21 Oh 16.20N 122.00 E
Sierra Mojada 47 Dc 27.17N 103.42W
Sierre/Siders 14 Bd 46.17N 7.32 E
Siete Palmas 55 Cg 25.13S 58.20W
Siete Puntas, Rio- 55 Df 23.34S 57.20W
Sifié 34 Dd 7.59N 6.55W
Sífnos 15 Hm 37.00N 24.40 E
Sig 32 Gb 35.32N 0.11W
Siğacik Körfezi 15 Jk 38.12N 26.45 E
Sigean 11 Ik 43.02N 2.59 E
Sighetu Marmației 15 Gb 47.56N 23.53 E
Sighișoara 15 Hc 46.13N 24.48 E
Sigli 26 Ce 5.23N 95.57 E
Siglufjördur 7a Ba 66.09N 18.55W
Sigmaringen 10 Fh 48.05N 9.13 E
Signal Peak 46 Hj 33.22N 114.03W
Signy Island 66 Re 60.43S 45.38W
Signy-l'Abbaye 12 Ge 49.42N 4.25 E
Signy-le-Petit 12 Ge 49.54N 4.21 E
Sigtuna 7 Dg 59.37N 17.43 E
Siguanea, Ensenada de la- 49 Fc 21.38N 83.05W
Siguatepeque 49 Df 14.32N 87.49W
Sigüenza 13 Jc 41.04N 2.38W
Siguiri 31 Gg 11.25N 9.10W
Sigulda 7 Fh 57.09N 24.53 E
Si He 28 Dg 35.11N 116.42 E
Sihong 28 Eh 33.28N 118.13 E
Sihote-Alin 21 Pe 48.00N 138.00 E
Sihou → Changdao 28 Ff 37.56N 120.42 E
Sihuas 54 Ce 8.34S 77.37W
Siikainen 8 Ic 61.52N 21.50 E
Siilinjärvi 7 Ge 63.02N 27.40 E
Siirt 23 Fb 37.56N 41.57 E
Sijunjung 26 Dg 0.42S 100.58 E
Sikaiana 63a Fc 8.22S 162.45 E
Sikakap 26 Dg 2.46S 100.13 E
Sikanni Chief 42 Fe 58.17N 121.46W
Sīkar 25 Fc 27.37N 75.09 E
Sikasso 31 Gg 11.20N 5.40W
Sikasso [3] 34 Dc 10.55N 7.00W
Sikéa [Grc.] 15 Fm 36.46N 22.56 E
Sikéa [Grc.] 15 Gi 40.03N 23.58 E
Sikeston 43 Jd 36.53N 89.35W
Síkinos 15 Im 36.50N 25.05 E
Sikkim [3] 25 Hc 27.50N 88.30 E
Siklós 10 Ok 45.51N 18.18 E
Sikonge 36 Fd 5.38S 32.46 E
Šikotan, Ostrov/Tō, Shikotan- 20 Jh 43.47N 146.45 E
Siktjah 20 Hc 69.55N 125.10 E
Sil 13 Eb 42.27N 7.43W
Sila Grande 14 Kk 39.20N 16.30 E
Sila Greca 14 Kk 39.30N 16.30 E
Šilale/Šilalė 7 Fi 55.29N 22.12 E
Šilalė/Šilale 7 Fi 55.29N 22.12 E
Silao 48 Ig 20.56N 101.26W
Silaogou 28 Be 39.59N 113.03 E
Sila Piccola 14 Kk 39.05N 16.35 E
Silba 14 If 44.23N 14.42 E
Silchar 25 Id 24.49N 92.48 E
Silda 16 Ud 51.47N 59.50 E
Sildagapet 8 Ab 62.05N 5.10 E
Sile 14 Ge 45.28N 12.35 E
Şile 24 Cb 41.05N 29.35 E
Silega 16 Ec 64.03N 44.02 E
Silesia (EN) = Śląsk 10 Me 51.00N 16.45 E
Silesia (EN) = Śląsk 5 He 51.00N 16.45 E
Silet 32 He 22.39N 4.35 E
Silhouette Island 37b Ca 4.29S 55.14 E
Silifke 23 Db 36.22N 33.56 E
Siligir 20 Gc 68.27N 114.50 E
Siling Co 21 Kf 31.50N 89.00 E
Siling Jiao 27 Ke 8.20N 115.27 E
Silisili, Mauga- 65c Aa 13.35S 172.27W
Silistra [2] 15 Kf 44.07N 27.16 E
Silistra 15 Ke 44.07N 27.16 E
Silivri 24 Cb 41.04N 28.15 E
Siljan 7 Df 60.50N 14.45 E
Šilka 20 Gf 51.51N 116.02 E
Šilka 21 Od 53.22N 121.32 E
Silkeborg 7 Bh 56.10N 9.34 E
Sillamäe/Sillamjae 7 Gg 59.24N 27.43 E
Sillamjae/Sillamäe 7 Gg 59.24N 27.43 E
Sillaro 14 Ff 44.34N 11.51 E
Silleiro, Cabo- 13 Db 42.07N 8.54W
Sillé-le-Guillaume 11 Ff 48.12N 0.08W
Sillian 14 Gd 46.45N 12.25 E
Silil 35 Gc 11.00N 43.26 E
Siloam Springs 45 Ih 36.11N 94.32W
Siloana Plains 36 Df 17.15S 23.10 E
Šilovo 19 Ee 54.24N 40.52 E
Silsbee 45 Ik 30.21N 94.11W
Siltou 35 Bb 16.52N 15.43 E
Šilutė/Šilute 19 Cd 55.21N 21.30 E
Šilute/Šilutė 19 Cd 55.21N 21.30 E
Silvan 24 Ic 38.08N 41.01 E
Silvassa 25 Ed 20.20N 73.05 E
Silver Bank (EN) 49 Mc 20.30N 69.45W
Silver Bay 43 Ib 47.17N 91.16W
Silver City 43 Fe 32.46N 108.17W
Silverdalen 8 Fg 57.32N 15.44 E
Silver Lake 46 Ee 43.06N 120.53W
Silver Spring 44 If 39.02N 77.03W
Silver Springs 46 Fg 39.25N 119.13W
Silverthrone Mountain 46 Ba 51.31N 126.06W
Silverton [Co.-U.S.] 45 Ch 37.49N 107.40W
Silverton [Tx.-U.S.] 45 Fi 34.28N 101.19W
Silves [Braz.] 54 Gd 2.54S 58.27W
Silves [Port.] 13 Dg 37.11N 8.26W
Silvi 14 Ih 42.34N 14.06 E
Silvia 54 Cc 2.37N 76.24W
Silviers River 46 Fe 43.22N 118.48W
Silvretta 14 Ed 46.50N 10.15 E
Silyānah [3] 32 Ib 36.00N 9.30 E
Silyānah 32 Ib 36.05N 9.22 E
Silyānah, Wādī- 14 Dn 36.33N 9.25 E
Sim 17 Hi 54.59N 57.41 E
Sim 17 Hi 54.32N 56.30 E
Sim, Cap- 32 Fc 31.23N 9.51W
Simanggang 26 Ff 1.15N 111.26 E
Šimanovsk 20 Hf 52.01N 127.36 E
Simao 27 Hg 22.40N 101.02 E
Simard, Lac- 44 Hb 47.38N 78.40W
Sīmareh 24 Mf 32.08N 48.03 E
Simav 23 Cb 40.23N 28.31 E
Simav 24 Cc 39.05N 28.59 E
Simav Dağ 15 Lj 39.04N 28.54 E
Simav Gölü 15 Lj 39.09N 28.55 E
Simayama-Jima 29 Ae 32.40N 128.38 E
Simba 36 Db 0.36N 22.55 E
Simbo 36 Fc 4.53S 29.44 E
Simbo 63a Cc 8.18S 156.34 E
Simbruini, Monti- 14 Hj 41.55N 13.15 E
Simcoe 42 Jh 42.50N 80.18W
Simcoe, Lake- 42 Jh 44.27N 79.20W
Simen 35 Fc 13.25N 38.00 E
Simenti 34 Cc 13.00N 13.25W
Simeria 15 Gd 45.51N 23.01 E
Simeto 14 Jm 37.24N 15.06 E
Simeulue, Pulau- 21 Li 2.35N 96.05 E
Simferopol 6 Jf 44.57N 34.06 E
Simḥah, Jabal- 23 Hf 17.20N 54.50 E
Simi 15 Km 36.36N 27.50 E
Simi 15 Km 36.35N 27.50 E
Simiti 49 Kj 7.58N 73.58W
Simitli 15 Gh 41.53N 23.06 E
Şimleu Silvaniei 15 Fb 47.14N 22.48 E
Simmental 14 Bd 46.35N 7.25 E
Simmerath 12 Id 50.36N 6.18 E
Simmerbach 12 Je 49.48N 7.31 E
Simmern 10 Dg 49.59N 7.31 E
Simmertal 12 Je 49.48N 7.33 E
Simnas 8 Jj 54.20N 23.45 E
Simo 7 Fd 65.39N 24.55 E
Simojärvi 7 Gc 66.06N 27.03 E
Simojoki 7 Fd 65.37N 25.03 E
Simojovel de Allende 48 Mi 17.12N 92.38W
Simonstown 37 Bf 34.14S 18.26 E
Simpele 7 Gf 61.26N 29.22 E
Simpelejärvi 8 Mc 61.30N 29.25 E
Simplon 14 Bd 46.15N 8.00 E
Simpson Desert 57 Eg 25.00S 137.00 E
Simpson Hill 59 Fe 26.30S 126.30 E
Simpson Peninsula 42 Ic 68.45N 89.10W
Simrishamn 7 Di 55.33N 14.20 E
Simsonbaai 51b Ab 18.02N 63.08W
Simušir, Ostrov- 21 Re 46.58N 152.02 E
Sina 25 Fe 17.22N 75.54 E
Sīnāʾ = Sinai Peninsula (EN) 30 Kf 29.30N 34.00 E
Sinabang 26 Cf 2.29N 96.23 E
Sinadago 35 Hd 5.22N 46.22 E
Sinai, Mount- (EN) = Mūsa, Jabal- 24 Eh 28.32N 33.59 E
Sinaia 15 Id 45.21N 25.33 E
Sinai Peninsula (EN) = Sīnāʾ 30 Kf 29.30N 34.00 E
Sinajana 64c Bb 13.28N 144.45W
Sinaloa [2] 47 Cc 25.00N 107.30W
Sinaloa, Llanos de- 47 Cc 25.00N 107.30W
Sinaloa, Rio- 48 Ee 25.18N 108.30W
Sinaloa de Leyva 48 Ee 25.50N 108.14W
Sinalunga 14 Fg 43.12N 11.44 E
Sinamaica 54 Da 11.05N 71.51W
Sinan 27 If 27.56N 108.11 E
Sinara 17 Kh 56.17N 62.23 E
Sināwin 33 Bc 31.02N 10.36 E
Sinazongwe 36 Ef 17.15S 27.28 E
Şincai 15 Hc 46.39N 24.23 E
Sincanli 24 Dc 38.45N 30.15 E
Sincé 49 Ji 9.14N 75.06W
Sincelejo 53 Ie 9.18N 75.24W
Sinch'am 28 Jc 42.07N 129.25 E
Sinch'ang 28 Jd 40.07N 128.28 E
Sinch'on 28 He 38.28N 125.27 E
Sinclair, Lake- 44 Fi 33.11N 83.16W
Sind [3] 25 Cc 25.30N 69.00 E
Sind 21 Ig 25.30N 69.00 E
Sindal 8 Dg 57.28N 10.13 E
Sindangbarang 26 Eh 7.27S 107.08 E
Sindara 36 Bc 1.02S 10.40 E
Sindelfingen-Böblingen 10 Fh 48.41N 9.01 E
Sindfeld 12 Kc 51.32N 8.48 E
Sindi 7 Fg 58.24N 24.42 E
Sındırgı 24 Cc 39.14N 28.10 E
Sindirgi Geçidi 15 Lj 39.10N 28.04 E
Sindominic 15 Ic 46.35N 25.47 E
Sindri 25 Hd 23.42N 86.29 E
Sinegorje 20 Kd 62.03N 150.25 E
Sinegorski 16 Le 48.00N 40.53 E
Šine-Ider 27 Gb 48.56N 99.33 E
Sinekli 15 Lh 41.14N 28.12 E
Sinelnikovo 16 Ie 48.18N 35.31 E
Sines 13 Dg 37.57N 8.52W
Sines, Cabo de- 13 Dg 37.57N 8.53W
Sine-Saloum [3] 34 Bc 14.00N 15.50W
Singako 35 Bd 9.50N 19.29 E
Singapore / Singapura 22 Mi 1.17N 103.51 E
Singapore Strait (EN) = Singapura, Selat- 26 Df 1.15N 104.00 E
Singapura / Singapore 22 Mi 1.17N 103.51 E
Singapura, Selat- = Singapore Strait (EN) 26 Df 1.15N 104.00 E
Singaraja 26 Gh 8.07S 115.06 E
Singatoka 63d Ac 18.08S 177.30 E
Sing Buri 25 Kf 14.53N 100.25 E
Singen 10 Ei 47.46N 8.50 E
Sîngeroz Băi 15 Hb 47.22N 24.41 E
Singida [3] 36 Fd 5.30S 34.30 E
Singida 31 Ki 4.49S 34.45 E
Singitic Gulf (EN) = Singitikós Kólpos 15 Gi 40.10N 23.55 E
Singitikós Kólpos = Singitic Gulf (EN) 15 Gi 40.10N 23.55 E
Singkaling Hkamti 25 Jc 26.00N 95.42 E
Singkang 26 Hg 4.08S 120.01 E
Singkawang 26 Ef 0.54N 109.00 E
Singkep, Pulau- 26 Dg 0.30S 104.25 E
Singkil 26 Cf 2.17N 97.49 E
Singleton [Austl.] 59 Kf 32.34S 151.10 E
Singleton [Eng.-U.K.] 12 Bd 50.55N 0.44W
Singleton, Mount- 59 De 29.28S 117.18 E
Singö 8 Hd 60.10N 18.45 E
Siniscola 14 Dj 40.34N 9.41 E
Sini vrăh 15 Ih 41.51N 25.01 E
Sinj 14 Kg 43.42N 16.38 E
Sinjah 35 Ec 13.09N 33.56 E
Sinjai 26 Hh 5.07S 120.15 E
Sinjaja 8 Mg 57.05N 28.33 E
Sinjajevina 15 Cf 43.00N 19.18 E
Sinjār 24 Id 36.19N 41.52 E
Sinjār, Jabal- 24 Id 36.23N 41.52 E
Sinjuža 16 Ge 48.03N 30.50 E
Sinkiang (EN) = Hsin-chiang-wei-wu-erh Tzu-chih-ch'ü → Xinjiang Uygur Zizhiqu [2] 27 Ec 42.00N 86.00 E
Sinkiang (EN) = Xinjiang Uygur Zizhiqu (Hsin-chiang-wei-wu-erh Tzu-chih-ch'ü) [2] 27 Ec 42.00N 86.00 E
Sin-le-Noble 12 Fd 50.22N 3.07 E
Sinmi-Do 28 He 39.33N 124.53 E
Sinn 12 Kd 50.39N 8.20 E
Sinn al Kadhdhāb 33 Fe 23.30N 32.05 E
Sinnamary 54 Hb 5.23N 53.00W
Sinni 14 Kj 40.08N 16.41 E
Sinnicolau Mare 15 Dc 46.05N 20.38 E
Sinnūris 24 Dh 29.25N 30.52 E
Sinnyŏng 28 Jf 36.02N 128.47 E
Sinoe [3] 34 Dd 5.20N 8.40W
Sinoe, Lacul- 15 Le 44.38N 28.53 E
Sinop 23 Ea 41.59N 35.09 E
Sinop Burun 24 Fa 42.02N 35.12 E
Sinp'o 28 Jd 40.02N 128.12 E
Sinsang 28 Ie 39.39N 127.25 E
Sinsheim 10 Eg 49.15N 8.53 E
Sint-Amandsberg, Gent- 12 Fc 51.04N 3.45 E
Sintana 15 Ec 46.21N 21.30 E
Sint-Andries, Brugge- 12 Fc 51.12N 3.10 E
Sintang 26 Ff 0.04N 111.30 E
Sint Eustatius 47 Le 17.30N 62.59W
Sint-Gillis-Waas 12 Gc 51.13N 4.08 E
Sint Kruis 50 Bf 12.18N 69.08W
Sint Laureins 12 Fc 51.15N 3.31 E
Sint Maarten 50 Ec 18.04N 63.04W
Sint Nicolaas 50 Bf 12.26N 69.55W
Sint Niklaas/Saint-Nicolas 11 Kc 51.10N 4.08 E
Sint-Oedenrode 12 Hc 51.34N 5.28 E
Sinton 45 Hl 28.02N 97.33W
Sint-Pieters-Leeuw 12 Gd 50.47N 4.14 E
Sintra 13 Cf 38.48N 9.23W
Sint-Truiden/Saint-Trond 11 Ld 50.49N 5.12 E
Sintu 35 Fd 8.12N 36.56 E
Sinú, Rio- 49 Ji 9.24N 75.49W
Sinŭiju 22 Oe 40.06N 124.24 E
Sinujif 35 Hd 8.30N 48.59 E
Sinzig 12 Jd 50.33N 7.15 E
Sió 10 Oj 46.23N 18.40 E
Siocon 26 He 7.42N 122.08 E
Siófok 10 Oj 46.54N 18.03 E
Sioma 36 Df 16.40S 23.35 E

Index Symbols

[1] Independent Nation
[2] State, Region
[3] District, County
[4] Municipality
[5] Colony, Dependency
Continent
Physical Region
Historical or Cultural Region
Mount, Mountain
Volcano
Hill
Mountains, Mountain Range
Hills, Escarpment
Plateau, Upland
Pass, Gap
Plain, Lowland
Delta
Salt Flat
Valley, Canyon
Crater, Cave
Karst Features
Depression
Polder
Desert, Dunes
Forest, Woods
Heath, Steppe
Oasis
Cape, Point
Coast, Beach
Cliff
Peninsula
Isthmus
Sandbank
Island
Atoll
Rock, Reef
Islands, Archipelago
Rocks, Reefs
Coral Reef
Well, Spring
Geyser
River, Stream
Waterfall Rapids
River Mouth, Estuary
Lake
Salt Lake
Intermittent Lake
Reservoir
Swamp, Pond
Canal
Glacier
Ice Shelf, Pack Ice
Ocean
Sea
Gulf, Bay
Strait, Fjord
Lagoon
Bank
Seamount
Tablemount
Ridge
Shelf
Basin
Escarpment, Sea Scarp
Fracture
Trench, Abyss
National Park, Reserve
Point of Interest
Recreation Site
Cave, Cavern
Historic Site
Ruins
Wall, Walls
Church, Abbey
Temple
Scientific Station
Airport
Port
Lighthouse
Mine
Tunnel
Dam, Bridge

Sion/Sitten 14 Bd 46.15N 7.20 E
Siorapaluk 41 Ec 77.39N 71.00W
Sioule 11 Jh 46.22N 3.19 E
Sioux City 39 Je 42.30N 96.23W
Sioux Falls 39 Je 43.32N 96.44W
Sioux Lookout 42 If 50.06N 91.55W
Sipalay 26 He 9.45N 122.24 E
Šipan 14 Lh 42.43N 17.54 E
Siparia 50 Fg 10.08N 61.30W
Šipčenski prohod 15 Ig 42.46N 25.19 E
Siping 22 Oe 43.11N 124.24 E
Sipiwesk 42 He 55.27N 97.24W
Sipiwesk Lake 42 He 55.05N 97.35W
Siple, Mount- 66 Nf 73.15S 126.06W
Siple Coast 66 Mg 82.00S 153.00W
Siple Island 66 Nf 73.39S 125.00W
Siple Station 66 Pf 75.55S 83.55W
Sipora, Pulau- 26 Cg 2.12S 99.40 E
Sippola 8 Ld 60.44N 27.00 E
Siqueira Campos 55 Hf 23.42S 49.50W
Siquia, Río- 49 Eg 12.09N 84.13W
Siquijor 26 He 9.13N 123.31 E
Siquisique 54 Ea 10.34N 69.42W
Šira 20 Ef 54.29N 90.02 E
Sira 8 Be 58.17N 6.24 E
Sira 7 Bg 58.25N 6.38 E
Şir Abū Nu'Ayr 24 Pj 25.13N 54.13 E
Si Racha 25 Kf 13.10N 100.57 E
Siracusa=Syracuse (EN) 14 Jm 37.04N 15.18 E
Sir Alexander, Mount- 42 Ff 53.56N 120.23W
Sirasso 34 Dd 9.16N 6.06W
Şirāt, Jabal- 33 Hf 17.00N 43.50 E
Sirba 34 Fc 13.46N 1.40 E
Şir Banī Yās 24 Oj 24.19N 52.37 E
Sirdalen 8 Bf 58.50N 6.40 E
Sirdalsvatn 8 Bf 58.35N 6.40 E
Sire [Eth.] 35 Fd 8.58N 37.00 E
Sire [Eth.] 35 Fd 8.16N 39.30 E
Sir Edward Pellew Group 59 Hc 15.40S 136.50 E
Siret 5 If 45.24N 28.01 E
Siret 15 Jb 47.57N 26.04 E
Sirevåg 7 Ag 58.30N 5.47 E
Sirīk 23 Id 26.29N 57.09 E
Sirik, Tanjong- 26 Ff 2.46N 111.19 E
Sirina 15 Jm 36.21N 26.41 E
Sirino 14 Jj 40.07N 15.50 E
Sirius Seamount (EN) 40 Gf 52.00N 160.50W
Širjajevo 16 Gf 47.24N 30.13 E
Sir James Mac Brian, Mount- 42 Ed 62.08N 127.40W
Sirjān, Kavīr-e- 24 Ph 29.30N 55.30 E
Sirmione 14 Ee 45.29N 10.36 E
Şırnak 24 Jd 37.32N 42.28 E
Širokaja Pad 20 Jf 50.15N 142.11 E
Široki 20 Jd 63.04N 148.01 E
Širokoje 16 Hf 47.38N 33.14 E
Sironcha 25 Fe 18.50N 79.58 E
Siros 15 Hl 37.26N 24.55 E
Sirpsindiği 15 Jh 41.50N 26.29 E
Sirr, Nafūd as- 24 Kj 25.15N 44.45 E
Sirrayn 33 Hf 19.36N 40.36 E
Sirretta Peak 46 Fi 35.59N 118.20W
Sirri, Jazīreh-ye- 24 Pj 25.55N 54.32 E
Sirsa 25 Fc 29.32N 75.01 E
Sir Sandford, Mount- 46 Ga 51.40N 117.52W
Sirte Desert (EN)=As Sidrah 30 Ie 30.30N 17.30 E
Sir Thomas, Mount- 59 Fe 27.11S 129.46 E
Širvintos 7 Fi 55.03N 25.01 E
Sir Wilfrid Laurier, Mount- 42 Ff 52.48N 119.45W
Sisak 14 Ke 45.29N 16.22 E
Si Sa Ket 25 Ke 15.07N 104.19 E
Sisakht 24 Ng 30.47N 51.33 E
Sisal 48 Ng 21.10N 90.02W
Sisante 13 Je 39.25N 2.13W
Sisargas, Islas- 13 Da 43.22N 8.50W
Siščhid-Gol 27 Ga 51.30N 97.10 E
Sishen 37 Ce 27.55S 22.59 E
Sishui 28 Dg 35.40N 117.17 E
Sisian 16 Oj 39.31N 46.03 E
Sisili 34 Ec 10.16N 1.15W
Sisimiut/Holsteinsborg 67 Nc 67.05N 53.45W
Siskiyou Mountains 46 Df 41.55N 123.15W
Sisŏphŏn 25 Kf 13.35N 102.59 E
Sissano 60 Ch 3.00S 142.03 E
Sisseton 45 Hd 45.40N 97.03W
Sissonne 12 Fe 49.34N 3.54 E
Sīstān=Seistan (EN) 21 If 30.30N 62.00 E
Sistema Central 5 Fg 40.30N 5.00W
Sistema Ibérico=Iberian Mountains (EN) 5 Fg 41.30N 2.30W
Sistemas Béticos 5 Fh 37.35N 3.30W
Sisteron 11 Lj 44.12N 5.56 E
Sisters 46 Ed 44.17N 121.33W
Sistranda 7 Be 63.43N 8.50 E
Sitāpur 25 Gc 27.34N 80.41 E
Sitasjaure 7 Dc 68.00N 17.25 E
Siteki 37 Ee 26.27S 31.57 E
Sitges 13 Nc 41.14N 1.49 E
Sithonia 15 Gi 40.05N 23.55 E
Sitia 15 Jn 35.12N 26.07 E
Sitio d'Abadia 55 Ib 14.48S 46.16W
Sitio Nuevo 49 Jh 10.46N 74.43W
Sitka 39 Fd 57.03N 135.14W
Sitkalidak 40 Ie 57.10N 153.14W
Sitna 15 Kb 47.30N 27.10 E
Sitnica 15 Dg 42.53N 20.52 E
Sitona 35 Fc 14.23N 37.22 E
Sitrah [Bhr.] 24 Ni 26.10N 50.40 E
Sitrah [Eg.] 24 Bh 28.42N 26.54 E
Sittard 11 Ld 51.00N 5.53 E
Sittee Point 49 Ce 16.48N 88.15W
Sitten/Sion 14 Bd 46.15N 7.20 E
Sittingbourne 12 Cc 51.20N 0.45 E
Sittoung 25 Je 17.10N 96.58 E
Sittwe (Akyab) 22 Lg 20.09N 92.54 E
Siuna 49 Eg 13.44N 84.46W
Siuslaw River 46 Cd 44.01N 124.08W
Siva 7 Mh 56.49N 53.55 E
Sivac 15 Cd 45.42N 19.23 E
Sivaki 20 Hf 52.38N 126.45 E
Sivas 22 Ff 39.50N 37.03 E
Sivaš, Ozero- 16 Ig 45.50N 34.40 E
Sivasli 15 Mk 38.30N 29.42 E
Siveluč, Vulkan- 20 Le 56.33N 161.25 E
Sivera, Ozero-/Sivera Ezers 8 Li 55.58N 27.25 E
Sivera Ezers/Sivera, Ozero- 8 Li 55.58N 27.25 E
Siverek 23 Eb 37.45N 39.19 E
Siverski 7 Hg 59.22N 30.02 E
Sivomaskinski 17 Kc 66.40N 62.31 E
Sivrice 24 Hc 38.27N 39.19 E
Sivrihisar 24 Dc 39.27N 31.34 E
Sivry-Rance 12 Gd 50.10N 4.16 E
Sivry Rance-Rance 12 Gd 50.09N 4.16 E
Sivry-sur-Meuse 12 He 49.19N 5.16 E
Sīwah 31 Jf 29.12N 25.31 E
Sīwah, Wāḥāt-=Siwa Oasis (EN) 30 Jf 29.10N 25.40 E
Siwalik Range 21 Jg 29.00N 80.00 E
Siwān 25 Gc 26.13N 84.22 E
Siwa Oasis (EN)=Sīwah, Wāḥāt- 30 Jf 29.10N 25.40 E
Sixaola, Río- 49 Fi 9.35N 82.34W
Six Cross Road 51q Bb 13.07N 59.28W
Six-Fours-la-Plage 11 Lk 43.06N 5.51 E
Sixian 28 Dh 33.29N 117.53 E
Six Men's Bay 51q Ab 13.16N 59.38W
Sixth Cataract (EN)=Sablūkah, Ash Shallāl as- 30 Kg 16.20N 32.42 E
Siyah-Chaman 24 Ld 37.35N 47.10 E
Siyang (Zhongxing) 28 Eh 33.43N 118.40 E
Siziwang Qi (Ulan Hua) 28 Ad 41.31N 111.41 E
Sjaelland=Zealand (EN) 5 Hd 55.30N 11.45 E
Sjamozero, Ozero- 7 Hf 61.55N 33.15 E
Sjare/Sääre 8 Ig 57.57N 21.53 E
Sjas 7 Hf 60.10N 32.31 E
Sjasstroj 7 Hf 60.09N 32.36 E
Sjašupe 7 Fi 55.00N 22.10 E
Šjauljaj/Šiauliai 6 Id 55.53N 23.19 E
Sjenica 15 Cf 43.16N 20.00 E
Sjnjaja 20 Hd 61.00N 126.57 E
Sjoa 8 Cc 61.41N 9.33 E
Sjöbo 8 Ei 55.38N 13.42 E
Sjøholt 7 Be 62.29N 6.50 E
Sjujutlijka 15 Ig 42.17N 25.55 E
Sjun 17 Gi 55.43N 54.17 E
Sjuøyane 41 Ob 80.43N 20.45 E
Skadarsko Jezero=Scutari, Lake- (EN) 5 Hg 42.10N 19.20 E
Skadovsk 19 Df 46.07N 32.56 E
Skælskør 8 Di 55.15N 11.19 E
Skærbæk 8 Ci 55.09N 8.46 E
Skagatá 7a Ba 66.07N 20.06W
Skagen 7 Ch 57.44N 10.36 E
Skagern 8 Ff 59.00N 14.15 E
Skagerrak 5 Gd 57.45N 9.00 E
Skaget 8 Cc 61.17N 9.12 E
Skagit River 46 Db 48.20N 122.25W
Skagway 39 Fd 59.28N 135.19W
Skaidi 7 Fa 70.26N 24.30 E
Skaland 7 Db 69.27N 17.18 E
Skälderviken 8 Eh 56.20N 12.40 E
Skålevik 8 Bf 58.04N 8.00 E
Skalisty Golec, Gora-[R.S.F.S.R.] 20 Ge 56.20N 119.10 E
Skalisty Golec, Gora-[R.S.F.S.R.] 20 Ie 55.55N 130.35 E
Skanderborg 7 Bh 56.02N 9.56 E
Skåne 5 Hd 56.00N 13.30 E
Skånevik 8 Ae 59.44N 5.59 E
Skänninge 8 Ff 58.24N 15.05 E
Skanör 8 Ei 55.25N 12.52 E
Skåntzoura 15 Hj 39.05N 24.07 E
Skara 7 Cg 58.22N 13.25 E
Skaraborg [2] 7 Cg 58.20N 13.30 E
Skärblacka 8 Ff 58.34N 15.54 E
Skärdu 25 Fa 35.18N 75.37 E
Skärhamn 8 Dg 57.59N 11.33 E
Skarnes 8 Dd 60.15N 11.41 E
Skarsstind 8 Cb 62.03N 8.35 E
Skarsvåg 7 Fa 71.06N 25.56 E
Skarszewy 10 Ob 54.05N 18.27 E
Skarvdalsegga 8 Cb 62.09N 8.03 E
Skaryszew 10 Re 51.19N 21.15 E
Skarżysko-Kamienna 10 Qe 51.08N 20.53 E
Skasøy 8 Ca 63.20N 8.35 E
Skåt 15 Gf 43.44N 23.51 E
Skattkärr 8 Ee 59.25N 13.41 E
Skattungbyn 8 Fc 61.12N 14.52 E
Skaudvile/Skaudvilė 7 Fi 55.27N 22.33 E
Skaudvilė/Skaudvile 7 Fi 55.27N 22.33 E
Skaulen 8 Be 59.38N 6.35 E
Skawa 10 Pf 50.02N 19.26 E
Skawina 10 Pg 49.59N 19.49 E
Skee 8 Df 58.56N 11.19 E
Skeena 38 Fd 54.09N 130.02W
Skeena Mountains 42 Ee 56.45N 128.40W
Skegness 9 Nh 53.10N 0.21 E
Skeidarársandur 7a Cc 63.54N 17.14W
Skeldon 54 Gb 5.53N 57.08W
Skeleton Coast 37 Ac 17.50S 12.45 E
Skellefteå 6 Ic 64.46N 20.57 E
Skellefteälven 5 Ic 64.42N 21.06 E
Skelleftehamn 7 Ed 64.41N 21.14 E
Skënderbeut, Mali i- 15 Ch 41.35N 19.50 E
Skene 8 Eg 57.29N 12.38 E
Skerki Bank (EN) 32 Jb 37.45N 10.50 E
Skerries/Na Sceirí 9 Gh 53.35N 6.07W
Skerryvore 9 Fe 56.20N 7.05W
Skhiza 15 Em 36.44N 21.46 E
Skhoinoúsa 15 Im 36.50N 25.30 E
Ski 7 Cg 59.43N 10.50 E
Skiathos 15 Gj 39.10N 23.28 E
Skiathos 15 Gj 39.10N 23.29 E
Skibbereen/An Sciobairin 9 Dj 51.33N 9.15W
Skibotn 7 Eb 69.24N 20.16 E
Skidel 16 Dc 53.38N 24.17 E
Skien 6 Gd 59.12N 9.36 E
Skierniewice 10 Qe 51.58N 20.08 E
Skierniewice [2] 10 Qe 52.00N 20.10 E
Skiftet/Kihti 8 Id 60.15N 21.05 E
Skikda 31 He 36.52N 6.54 E
Skikda [3] 32 Ib 36.45N 6.50 E
Skillet Fork 45 Lg 38.08N 88.07W
Skillingaryd 8 Fg 57.26N 14.05 E
Skinári, Ákra- 15 Dl 37.56N 20.42 E
Skinnskatteberg 8 Fe 59.50N 15.41 E
Skipton 9 Kh 53.58N 2.01W
Skiptvet 8 De 59.28N 11.11 E
Skiropoúla 15 Hk 38.50N 24.21 E
Skiros 15 Hk 38.54N 24.34 E
Skiros 15 Hk 38.53N 24.32 E
Skive 7 Bh 56.34N 9.02 E
Skive Å 8 Ch 56.34N 9.04 E
Skjærhalden 8 De 59.02N 11.02 E
Skjåk 8 Cc 61.52N 8.22 E
Skjálfandafljót 7a Cb 65.59N 17.38W
Skjeberg 8 De 59.14N 11.12 E
Skjern 7 Bi 55.57N 8.30 E
Skjern Å 7 Bi 55.55N 8.24 E
Skjervøy 7 Ea 70.02N 20.59 E
Skjoldungen 41 Hf 63.20N 41.20W
Sklad 20 Hb 71.52N 123.35 E
Šklov 16 Gb 54.14N 30.18 E
Skobeleva, Pik- 18 Ie 39.51N 72.47 E
Skærfjorden 41 Kc 77.30N 19.10W
Škofja Loka 14 Id 46.10N 14.18 E
Skog 8 Gc 61.10N 16.55 E
Skógafoss 7a Bc 63.32N 19.31W
Skoghall 8 Ee 59.19N 13.26 E
Skogshorn 8 Cd 60.53N 8.42 E
Skokie 45 Me 42.02N 87.46W
Skole 10 Th 48.58N 23.32 E
Skópelos 15 Gj 39.07N 23.44 E
Skópelos 15 Gj 39.10N 23.40 E
Skopi 15 Jn 35.11N 26.02 E
Skopin 7 Jj 53.52N 39.37 E
Skopje 6 Ig 42.00N 21.29 E
Skórcz 10 Oc 53.48N 18.32 E
Skorovatn 7 Cd 64.39N 13.07 E
Skorpa 8 Ac 61.35N 4.50 E
Skørping 8 Ch 56.50N 9.53 E
Skorpiós 15 Dk 38.42N 20.45 E
Skotovo 28 Lc 43.20N 132.21 E
Skotselv 8 Ce 59.51N 9.53 E
Skoura 32 Fc 31.04N 6.43W
Skövde 7 Cg 58.24N 13.50 E
Skovorodino 22 Od 53.59N 123.55 E
Skowhegan 44 Mc 44.46N 69.43W
Skradin 14 Jg 43.49N 15.56 E
Skreia 8 Dd 60.34N 11.04 E
Skreia 8 Dd 60.39N 10.56 E
Skrekken 8 Bd 60.13N 7.49 E
Skridulaupen 8 Bc 61.55N 7.35 E
Skrimkolla 8 Cb 62.23N 9.04 E
Skrīveri/Skriveri 8 Kh 56.37N 25.10 E
Skriveri/Skrīveri 8 Kh 56.37N 25.10 E
Skrunda 7 Eh 56.41N 22.00 E
Skrwa 10 Pd 52.33N 19.32 E
Skudenesfjorden 8 Ae 59.05N 5.20 E
Skudeneshavn 7 Ag 59.09N 5.17 E
Skuodas 7 Eh 56.17N 21.31 E
Skurup 8 Ei 55.28N 13.30 E
Skutskär 8 Gd 60.38N 17.25 E
Skvira 16 Fe 49.44N 29.42 E
Skwierzyna 10 Ld 52.35N 15.30 E
Skye, Island of- 5 Fd 57.15N 6.10W
Slagelse 7 Ci 55.24N 11.22 E
Slagnäs 7 Ed 65.36N 18.10 E
Slamet, Gunung- 21 Mj 7.14S 109.12 E
Slaná 10 Ri 47.56N 21.08 E
Slancy 19 Cd 59.08N 28.02 E
Slaney/An tSláine 9 Gi 52.21N 6.30W
Slănic 15 Id 45.15N 25.56 E
Slănic Moldova 15 Jc 46.12N 26.26 E
Slannik 15 Jf 43.06N 26.13 E
Slano 14 Lh 42.47N 17.54 E
Slaný 10 Kf 50.14N 14.06 E
Śląsk=Silesia (EN) 10 Me 51.00N 16.45 E
Śląsk=Silesia (EN) 5 He 51.00N 16.45 E
Śląska, Wyżyna- 10 Of 50.28N 18.40 E
Slate Islands 45 Mb 48.34N 86.45W
Slatina 15 He 44.26N 24.22 E
Slatina 15 Hh 48.32N 19.10 E
Slaton 45 Fj 33.26N 101.39W
Slave Coast 30 Hh 6.00N 3.30 E
Slave Lake 42 Ge 55.17N 114.46W
Slave River 38 Hc 61.18N 113.39W
Slavgorod [Bye.-U.S.S.R.] 16 Gc 53.27N 31.01 E
Slavgorod [R.S.F.S.R.] 20 Cf 53.03N 78.48 E
Slavičin 10 Ng 49.06N 17.53 E
Slavjanka 20 Ih 42.55N 131.20 E
Slavjanka 15 Gh 41.23N 23.36 E
Slavjansk 6 Jf 48.52N 37.37 E
Slavjansk-na-Kubani 19 Df 45.15N 38.08 E
Slavkoje 10 Th 48.45N 23.31 E
Slavkoviči 8 Mg 57.37N 29.10 E
Slavonia (EN)=Slavonija 5 Hf 45.00N 18.00 E
Slavonia (EN)=Slavonija 14 Le 45.00N 18.00 E
Slavonija=Slavonia (EN) 14 Le 45.00N 18.00 E
Slavonija=Slavonia (EN) 5 Hf 45.00N 18.00 E
Slavonska Požega 14 Le 45.20N 17.41 E
Slavonski Brod 14 Me 45.09N 18.02 E
Slavsk 8 Ii 55.01N 21.37 E
Slavuta 19 Ce 50.18N 26.52 E
Sława 10 Me 51.53N 16.04 E
Sławatycze 10 Te 51.43N 23.30 E
Sławno 10 Mb 54.22N 16.40 E
Slayton 45 Id 44.01N 95.45W
Sleaford 9 Mh 53.00N 0.24W
Slea Head/Ceann Sléibhe 9 Ci 52.06N 10.27W
Sleat, Sound of- 9 Hd 57.10N 5.50W
Sleen 12 Ib 52.47N 6.49 E
Sleeper Islands 42 Je 57.25N 79.50W
Sléibhte Chill Mhantáin/Wicklow Mountains 9 Gh 53.02N 6.24W
Sleidinge, Evergem- 12 Fc 51.08N 3.41 E
Slesin 10 Od 52.23N 18.19 E
Slessor Glacier 66 Af 79.50S 28.30W
Slessor Peak 66 Qe 66.31S 64.58W
Slettefjell 8 Cc 61.13N 8.44 E
Sletterhage 8 Dh 56.06N 10.31 E
Ślęża 10 Me 51.10N 16.58 E
Ślęża 10 Mf 50.52N 16.45 E
Sliabh Bearnach/Slieve Bernagh 9 Ei 52.50N 8.35W
Sliabh Bladhma/Slieve Bloom 9 Fh 53.10N 7.35W
Sliabh Eachtaí/Slieve Aughty 9 Eh 53.10N 8.30W
Sliabh Gamh/Ox or Slieve Gamph Mountains 9 Eg 54.10N 8.50W
Sliabh Mis/Slieve Mish 9 Di 52.10N 9.50W
Sliabh Speirín/Sperrin Mountains 9 Fg 54.50N 7.05W
Slidell 45 Lk 30.17N 89.47W
Slide Mountain 44 Jd 42.00N 74.23W
Slidre 8 Cc 61.10N 9.00 E
Sliedrecht 12 Gc 51.50N 4.46 E
Slieve Aughty/Sliabh Eachtaí 9 Eh 53.10N 8.30W
Slieve Bernagh/Sliabh Bearnach 9 Ei 52.50N 8.35W
Slieve Bloom/Sliabh Bladhma 9 Fh 53.10N 7.35W
Slievefelim Mountains 9 Ei 52.45N 8.15W
Slieve Mish/Sliabh Mis 9 Di 52.10N 9.50W
Sligeach/Sligo [2] 9 Eg 54.10N 8.40W
Sligeach/Sligo 6 Fe 54.17N 8.28W
Sligo/Sligeach [2] 9 Eg 54.10N 8.40W
Sligo/Sligeach 6 Fe 54.17N 8.28W
Sligo Bay/Cuan Shligigh 9 Eg 54.20N 8.40W
Slinge 12 Ib 52.08N 6.31 E
Slingebeek 12 Ic 51.59N 6.18 E
Slite 8 Hg 57.43N 18.48 E
Sliven 15 Jg 42.40N 26.19 E
Sliven [2] 15 Jg 42.40N 26.19 E
Slivnica 15 Gg 42.51N 23.02 E
Sljudjanka 20 Ff 51.38N 103.40 E
Slobodka 15 Mb 47.54N 29.12 E
Slobodskoj 19 Fd 58.47N 50.12 E
Slobodzeja 16 Ff 46.43N 29.43 E
Slobozia [Rom.] 15 Ke 44.34N 27.22 E
Slobozia [Rom.] 15 Ie 44.30N 25.11 E
Slochteren 12 Ia 53.12N 6.50 E
Slocum Mountain 46 Gi 35.18N 117.13W
Slonim 19 Ce 53.05N 25.18 E
Sloten 12 Hb 52.54N 5.40 E
Slotermeer 12 Hb 52.55N 5.40 E
Slough 9 Mj 51.31N 0.36W
Slovakia (EN)=Slovensko 10 Ph 48.45N 19.30 E
Slovakia (EN)=Slovensko 5 Hf 48.45N 19.30 E
Slovečna 16 Fd 51.41N 29.42 E
Slovenia (EN)=Slovenija 5 Hf 46.00N 15.00 E
Slovenia (EN)=Slovenija 14 Id 46.00N 15.00 E
Slovenia (EN)=Slovenija [2] 14 Id 46.00N 15.00 E
Slovenija=Slovenia (EN) [2] 14 Id 46.00N 15.00 E
Slovenija=Slovenia (EN) 14 Id 46.00N 15.00 E
Slovenija=Slovenia (EN) 5 Hf 46.00N 15.00 E
Slovenska Bistrica 14 Jd 46.24N 15.34 E
Slovenske Gorice 14 Jd 46.35N 15.55 E
Slovenské rudohorie 10 Ph 48.45N 20.00 E
Slovensko [2] 10 Ph 48.45N 19.30 E
Slovensko=Slovakia (EN) 5 Hf 48.45N 19.30 E
Slovensko=Slovakia (EN) 10 Ph 48.45N 19.30 E
Slovenský kras 10 Qh 48.35N 20.40 E
Słubice 10 Kd 52.20N 14.35 E
Sluč [Bye.-U.S.S.R.] 16 Ec 52.08N 27.32 E
Sluč [Ukr.-U.S.S.R.] 16 Ed 51.37N 26.38 E
Sluck 19 Ce 53.02N 27.31 E
Slunj 14 Je 45.07N 15.35 E
Słupca 10 Nd 52.19N 17.52 E
Słupia 10 Mb 54.35N 16.50 E
Słupsk 10 Nb 54.28N 17.01 E
Słupsk [2] 10 Mb 54.30N 17.00 E
Slyne Head/Ceann Gólaim 9 Ch 53.24N 10.13W
Småland 7 Dh 57.20N 15.05 E
Smålandsfarvandet 8 Di 55.06N 11.20 E
Smålandsstenar 8 Eg 57.10N 13.24 E
Smalininkai/Smalininkaj 8 Ji 55.01N 22.32 E
Smalininkaj/Smalininkai 8 Ji 55.01N 22.32 E
Smallingerland-Drachten 11 Ma 53.06N 6.05 E
Smallwood Reservoir 38 Md 54.00N 64.30W
Smederevo 15 De 44.39N 20.56 E
Smederevska Palanka 15 De 44.22N 20.58 E
Smedjebacken 7 Df 60.08N 15.25 E
Smela 19 Df 49.13N 31.53 E
Smidovič 20 Ig 48.36N 133.50 E
Šmidta, Mys- 20 Nc 68.45N 178.40W
Šmidta, Ostrov- 21 La 81.08N 90.48 E
Šmidta, Poluostrov- 20 Jf 54.15N 142.40 E
Śmigiel 10 Md 52.01N 16.32 E
Smilde 12 Ib 52.56N 6.28 E
Smiltene 7 Fh 57.28N 25.56 E
Smirnovo 17 Ni 54.31N 69.28 E
Smirnyh 20 Jg 49.45N 142.53 E
Smith 55 Bl 35.30S 61.36W
Smith Arm 42 Fc 66.15N 124.00W
Smith Bay [Ak.-U.S.] 40 Ib 70.51N 154.25W
Smith Bay [Can.] 42 Ja 77.15N 79.00W
Smith Center 45 Gg 39.47N 98.47W
Smithers 42 Ef 54.47N 127.10W
Smithfield [S.Afr.] 37 Df 30.09S 26.30 E
Smithfield [Ut.-U.S.] 46 Jf 41.50N 111.50W
Smith Knoll 9 Pi 52.50N 2.10 E
Smith Mountain Lake 44 Hg 37.10N 79.40W
Smith Peak 46 Gb 48.50N 116.39W
Smith River 46 Jc 47.25N 111.29W
Smiths Falls 42 Jh 44.54N 76.01W
Smith Sound 46 Ba 51.18N 127.48W
Smithton 58 Fi 40.51S 145.07 E
Smjadovo 15 Kf 43.04N 27.01 E
Smjörfjoll 7a Cb 65.35N 14.46W
Smögen 8 Df 58.21N 11.13 E
Smoke Creek Desert 46 Ff 40.30N 119.40W
Smokey Dome 46 He 43.29N 114.56W
Smoky Bay 59 Gf 32.20S 133.45 E
Smoky Cape 59 Kf 30.56S 153.05 E
Smoky Falls 42 Jf 50.03N 82.10W
Smoky Hill 38 Jf 39.03N 96.48W
Smoky Hills 45 Gg 39.15N 99.00W
Smoky River 42 Fe 56.11N 117.19W
Smøla 7 Be 63.25N 8.00 E
Smolensk 6 Je 54.47N 32.03 E
Smolenskaja Oblast [3] 19 De 55.00N 33.00 E
Smolenskaja Vozvyšennost=Smolensk Upland (EN) 5 Je 54.40N 33.00 E
Smolensk Upland (EN)=Smolenskaja Vozvyšennost 5 Je 54.40N 33.00 E
Smoleviči 16 Fb 54.03N 28.02 E
Smolianica 10 Ud 52.40N 24.40 E
Smólikas Óros 5 Ig 40.06N 20.55 E
Smoljan 15 Hh 41.35N 24.41 E
Smoljan [2] 15 Hh 41.40N 24.40 E
Smooth Rock Falls 44 Ga 49.20N 81.39W
Smorgon 19 Ce 54.31N 26.23 E
Smørstabbren 8 Cc 61.32N 8.06 E
Smrdeš 15 Fh 41.34N 22.28 E
Smygehamn 8 Ei 55.21N 13.22 E
Smygehuk 8 Ei 55.21N 13.23 E
Smyley, Cape- 66 Qf 72.00S 78.50W
Smyrna 44 Ei 33.53N 84.31W
Smyrna (EN)=İzmir 22 Ef 38.25N 27.09 E
Smyšljajevka 7 Mj 53.17N 50.24 E
Smythe, Mount- 38 Gd 57.50N 124.59W
Snacke Point 51b Bb 18.17N 62.58W
Snæfell 7a Cb 64.48N 15.34W
Snæfell 9 Ig 54.16N 4.27W
Snæfellsjökull 7a Ab 64.49N 23.46W
Snag 42 Dd 62.23N 140.22W
Snake Bay Settlement 59 Gb 11.25S 130.40 E
Snake Range 46 Hg 39.00N 114.15W
Snake River [Can.] 42 Ec 65.57N 134.13W
Snake River [U.S.] 38 He 46.12N 119.02W
Snake River Plain 43 Ec 42.45N 114.30W
Snare 42 Fd 63.15N 116.08W
Snares Islands 61 Ci 48.00S 166.35 E
Snarumselva 8 Ce 59.57N 9.58 E
Snåsa 7 Cd 64.15N 12.22 E
Sneek 11 La 53.02N 5.40 E
Snekermeer 11 La 52.59N 5.40 E
Snežnaja, Gora- 20 Lc 65.18N 165.30 E
Snežnik 14 Ie 45.26N 14.36 E
Snežnogorsk 20 Dc 68.15N 87.35 E
Snežnoje 16 Kf 47.59N 38.50 E
Śniardwy, Jezioro- 10 Rc 53.46N 21.44 E
Śnieżka 5 He 50.45N 15.43 E
Śnieżnik 10 Mf 50.12N 16.50 E
Snigirevka 16 Hf 47.04N 32.45 E
Snillfjord 8 Ca 63.24N 9.30 E
Snina 10 Sh 48.59N 22.08 E
Snizort, Loch- 9 Gd 57.30N 6.25W
Snjatyn 16 De 48.29N 25.34 E
Snøhetta 5 Gc 62.20N 9.17 E
Snohomish 46 Dc 47.55N 122.06W
Snønuten 8 Be 59.31N 6.54 E
Snøonipa 8 Bc 61.42N 6.41 E
Snota 8 Cb 62.51N 9.06 E
Snov 16 Gd 51.32N 31.33 E
Snowbird Lake 42 Hd 60.40N 102.50W
Snowdon 5 Fe 53.04N 4.05W
Snowdonia 9 Jh 53.05N 3.55W
Snowdrift 42 Gd 62.23N 110.47W
Snowflake 46 Ji 34.30N 110.05W
Snow Hill 44 Jf 38.11N 75.24W
Snow Lake 42 Hf 54.53N 100.02W
Snow Mountain 43 Cd 39.23N 122.46W
Snowshoe Peak 46 Hb 48.13N 115.41W
Snowville 46 If 41.58N 112.43W
Snowy Mountain [B.C.-Can.] 46 Fb 49.02N 119.57W
Snowy Mountain [N.Y.-U.S.] 44 Jd 43.42N 74.23W
Snowy Mountains 59 Jg 36.30S 148.20 E
Snowy River 59 Jg 37.48S 148.32 E
Snudy, Ozero- 8 Li 55.40N 27.15 E
Snug Corner 49 Kb 22.31N 73.53W
Snuöl 25 Lf 12.04N 106.26 E
Snyder 43 Ge 32.44N 100.55W
Soalala 37 Hc 16.07S 45.21 E
Soalara 37 Gd 23.35S 43.44 E
Soanierana-Ivongo 37 Hc 16.54S 49.34 E
Soar 12 Ab 52.52N 1.17W
Şoarş 15 Hd 45.56N 24.55 E
Soavinandriana 37 Hc 19.10S 46.43 E
Sob [R.S.F.S.R.] 17 Mc 66.20N 66.02 E

Index Symbols

[1] Independent Nation
[2] State, Region
[3] District, County
[4] Municipality
[5] Colony, Dependency
Continent
Physical Region
Historical or Cultural Region
Mount, Mountain
Volcano
Hill
Mountains, Mountain Range
Hills, Escarpment
Plateau, Upland
Pass, Gap
Plain, Lowland
Delta
Salt Flat
Valley, Canyon
Crater, Cave
Karst Features
Depression
Polder
Desert, Dunes
Forest, Woods
Heath, Steppe
Oasis
Cape, Point
Coast, Beach
Cliff
Peninsula
Isthmus
Sandbank
Island
Atoll
Rock, Reef
Islands, Archipelago
Rocks, Reefs
Coral Reef
Well, Spring
Geyser
River, Stream
Waterfall Rapids
River Mouth, Estuary
Lake
Salt Lake
Intermittent Lake
Reservoir
Swamp, Pond
Canal
Glacier
Ice Shelf, Pack Ice
Ocean
Sea
Gulf, Bay
Strait, Fjord
Lagoon
Bank
Seamount
Tablemount
Ridge
Shelf
Basin
Escarpment, Sea Scarp
Fracture
Trench, Abyss
National Park, Reserve
Point of Interest
Recreation Site
Cave, Cavern
Historic Site
Ruins
Wall, Walls
Church, Abbey
Temple
Scientific Station
Airport
Port
Lighthouse
Mine
Tunnel
Dam, Bridge

Sob [Ukr.-U.S.S.R.]	16	Fe	48.41N	29.17 E
Soba	34	Gc	10.59N	8.04 E
Sobaek-Sanmaek	28	Jf	36.00N	128.00 E
Sobat (EN)=Sawbā	30	Kh	9.45N	31.45 E
Sobernheim	12	Je	49.48N	7.39 E
Soběslav	10	Kg	49.16N	14.44 E
Sōbetsu	29a	Bb	42.33N	140.51 E
Sobinka	7	Jh	56.01N	40.07 E
Sobolevo [R.S.F.S.R.]	16	Qd	51.59N	51.48 E
Sobolevo [R.S.F.S.R.]	20	Kf	54.17N	156.00 E
Sobolew	10	Re	51.41N	21.40 E
Sobo-San	29	Be	32.47N	131.21 E
Sobradinho	55	Fi	29.24S	53.03W
Sobral	53	Lf	3.42S	40.21W
Sobrarbe	13	Mb	42.20N	0.05 E
Soca	55	El	34.41S	55.41W
Soča=Isonzo (EN)	14	He	45.43N	13.33 E
Sochaczew	10	Qd	52.14N	20.14 E
Soči	6	Jg	43.35N	39.45 E
Société, Iles de la-=Society Islands (EN)	57	Lf	17.00S	150.00W
Society Islands (EN)= Société, Iles de la-	57	Lf	17.00S	150.00W
Socompa, Paso-	52	Jh	24.27S	68.18W
Socorro [Col.]	54	Db	6.27N	73.16W
Socorro [N.M.-U.S.]	43	Fe	34.04N	106.54W
Socotra (EN) = Suqutrá	21	Hh	12.30N	54.00 E
Soc Trang	25	Lg	9.36N	105.58 E
Socuéllamos	13	Je	39.17N	2.48W
Soda Lake	46	Gi	35.08N	116.04W
Sodankylä	7	Gc	67.25N	26.36 E
Soda Springs	46	Je	42.39N	111.36W
Söderåsen	8	Eh	56.04N	13.05 E
Söderfors	7	Df	60.23N	17.14 E
Söderhamn	7	Df	61.18N	17.03 E
Söderköping	8	Gf	58.29N	16.18 E
Södermanland	8	Ge	59.10N	16.50 E
Södermanland [2]	7	Dg	59.15N	16.40 E
Söderslätt	8	Ei	55.30N	13.15 E
Södertälje	7	Dg	59.12N	17.37 E
Södertörn	8	Ge	59.05N	18.00 E
Sodo	35	Fd	6.51N	37.45 E
Södra Dellen	8	Gc	61.50N	16.45 E
Södra Gloppet	8	Ia	63.05N	21.00 E
Södra Kvarken	8	Hd	60.20N	19.08 E
Södra-Midsjöbanken	8	Gi	55.40N	17.20 E
Södra Vi	8	Fg	57.45N	15.48 E
Soe	26	Hh	9.52S	124.17 E
Soekmekaar	37	Dd	23.28S	29.58 E
Soela, Proliv-/Soela Väin	8	Jf	58.40N	22.30 E
Soela Väin/Soela, Proliv-	8	Jf	58.40N	22.30 E
Soest [Ger.]	10	Ee	51.35N	8.07 E
Soest [Neth.]	12	Hb	52.10N	5.20 E
Soeste	12	Ja	53.10N	7.44 E
Soester Borde	12	Kc	51.38N	8.03 E
Soestwetering	12	Ib	51.30N	6.09 E
Sofádhes	15	Fj	39.20N	22.06 E
Sofala [3]	37	Ec	19.30S	34.40 E
Sofala, Baía de-	30	Kk	20.11S	34.45 E
Sofia	37	Hc	15.27S	47.23 E
Sofia [Bul.] [2]	15	Gg	42.43N	23.25 E
Sofia [Grc.] [2]	15	Gg	42.41N	23.19 E
Sofia (EN)=Sofija	6	Ig	42.41N	23.19 E
Sofija=Sofia (EN)	6	Ig	42.41N	23.19 E
Sofijsk	20	If	52.20N	134.01 E
Sofporog	19	Db	65.48N	31.28 E
Sofrána, Nisídhes-	15	Jm	36.04N	26.24 E
Sōfu-Gan	27	Pf	29.50N	140.20 E
Sogamoso	54	Db	5.43N	72.56W
Soganlı	24	Eb	41.11N	32.38 E
Sogara, Lake-	36	Fd	5.15S	31.00 E
Sogda	20	If	50.24N	132.18 E
Sögel	10	Dd	52.51N	7.31 E
Sogeri	60	Di	9.10S	147.32 E
Sogn	8	Ac	61.05N	5.55 E
Sogndalsfjøra	8	Bc	61.14N	7.06 E
Søgne	8	Bf	58.05N	7.49 E
Sognefjell	8	Bc	61.35N	7.55 E
Sognefjorden	5	Gc	61.05N	5.10 E
Sognesjøen	8	Ac	61.05N	5.00 E
Sogn og Fjordane [2]	7	Bf	61.30N	6.50 E
Sogod	26	Hd	10.23N	124.59 E
Sogo Nur	27	Hc	42.20N	101.20 E
Sogoža	7	Jg	58.30N	39.06 E
Söğüt	15	Nj	40.00N	30.11 E
Söğütalan	15	Li	40.03N	28.34 E
Söğüt Gölü	24	Cd	37.03N	29.53 E
Sog Xian	27	Fe	31.51N	93.42 E
Soh	18	He	39.57N	71.08 E
Sohag (EN)=Sawhāj	31	Kf	26.33N	31.42 E
Sohano	60	Ei	5.29S	154.41 E
Sohŭksan-Do	28	Hg	34.04N	125.07 E
Soignies/Zinnik	11	Kd	50.35N	4.04 E
Soini	8	Kb	62.52N	24.13 E
Soisalo	8	Mb	62.40N	28.10 E
Soissonnais, Plateau du-	11	Je	49.15N	3.10 E
Soissons	11	Je	49.22N	3.20 E
Sōja	29	Cd	34.40N	133.44 E
Sojana	7	Kd	65.53N	43.30 E
Sojma	17	Ec	67.00N	51.00 E
Šojna	17	Bc	67.52N	44.08 E
Sŏjosŏn-man=Korea Bay (EN)	21	Of	39.15N	125.00 E
Sojuznoje	16	Vd	50.50N	60.10 E
Sojuz Sovetskih Socialističeskih Respublik =USSR (EN) [1]	22	Jd	60.00N	80.00 E
Sojuz Sovetskih Socialističeskih Respublik (SSSR) [1]	22	Jd	60.00N	80.00 E
Sok	19	Fe	53.25N	50.10 E
Sokal	16	Dd	50.29N	24.17 E
Šokalskogo, Proliv-	20	Ea	79.00N	100.00 E
Sokch'o	27	Md	38.12N	128.36 E
Söke	23	Cb	37.45N	27.24 E
Sokele	36	Dd	9.55S	24.36 E
Sokirjany	16	Ee	48.28N	27.25 E
Sokna	7	Bf	60.14N	9.54 E
Soko Banja	15	Ef	43.39N	21.53 E
Sokodé	31	Hh	8.59N	1.08 E
Sokol	19	Ed	59.29N	40.13 E
Sokol	15	Ce	44.18N	19.25 E
Sokółka	10	Tc	53.25N	23.31 E
Sokolo	34	Dc	14.44N	6.07W
Sokolov	10	If	50.11N	12.38 E
Sokołów Podlaski	10	Sd	52.25N	22.15 E
Sokone	34	Bc	13.53N	16.22W
Sokosti	7	Gb	68.20N	28.01 E
Sokoto	30	Hg	11.24N	4.07 E
Sokoto [2]	34	Gc	12.20N	5.20 E
Sokoto	31	Hg	13.04N	5.15 E
Sokourala	34	Dd	9.13N	8.05W
Sōl	35	Hd	9.20N	49.25 E
Sōl	35	Hd	9.40N	48.30 E
Sol, Costa del-	13	Ih	36.46N	3.55W
Sol, Pico do-	55	Ke	20.07S	43.28W
Soła	10	Pf	50.04N	19.13 E
Sola	63b	Ca	13.53S	167.33 E
Solai	36	Gb	0.02N	36.09 E
Solakrossen	8	Af	58.53N	5.36 E
Solander Island	61	Ci	46.35S	166.50 E
Solanet	55	Cm	36.51S	58.31W
Solāpur	22	Jh	17.41N	75.55 E
Solbad Hall in Tirol	14	Fc	47.17N	11.31 E
Solcy	19	Dd	58.09N	30.20 E
Sölden	14	Ed	46.58N	11.00 E
Soldier Point	51d	Bb	17.02N	61.41W
Soldotna	40	Id	60.29N	151.04W
Solec Kujawski	10	Oc	53.06N	18.14 E
Soledad [Arg.]	55	Bj	30.37S	60.55W
Soledad [Ca.-U.S.]	46	Eh	36.26N	121.19W
Soledad [Col.]	54	Da	10.55N	74.46W
Soledad [Ven.]	54	Fb	8.10N	63.34W
Soledad, Boca de-	48	Ce	25.17N	112.09W
Soledad, Isla-/East Falkland	52	Kk	51.45S	58.50W
Soledade	56	Jc	28.50S	52.30W
Sølen	8	Dc	61.55N	11.30 E
Sølensjøen	8	Dc	61.55N	11.35 E
Solentiname, Archipiélago de-	49	Fh	11.10N	85.00W
Solenzara	11a	Bb	41.51N	9.24 E
Solesmes	12	Fd	50.11N	3.30 E
Solferino	14	Ee	45.23N	10.34 E
Solgen	8	Fg	57.33N	15.07 E
Solgne	12	Ie	48.58N	6.18 E
Soligalič	7	Kg	59.07N	42.13 E
Soligorsk	19	Ce	52.49N	27.31 E
Solihull	9	Li	52.25N	1.45W
Solikamsk	19	Fd	59.39N	56.47 E
Sol-Ileck	6	Le	51.12N	55.03 E
Solimán, Punta-	48	Ph	19.50N	87.27W
Solimoes→Amazonas, Rio- =Amazon (EN)	52	Lf	0.10S	49.00W
Solingen	10	De	51.11N	7.05 E
Solińskie, Jezioro-	10	Sg	49.22N	22.30 E
Solis, Presa-	48	Ig	20.05N	100.36W
Sollebrunn	8	Ef	58.07N	12.32 E
Sollefteå	7	De	63.10N	17.16 E
Sollentuna	8	Ge	59.28N	17.54 E
Sóller	13	Oe	39.46N	2.42 E
Sollerön	8	Fd	60.55N	14.37 E
Solling	10	Fe	51.45N	9.35 E
Solms	12	Kd	50.46N	9.36 E
Solna	8	He	59.22N	18.01 E
Solnečnogorsk	7	Ih	56.10N	37.00 E
Solnečny	20	Id	60.10N	137.35 E
Sologne	11	Hg	47.50N	2.00 E
Sologne Bourbonnaise	11	Jh	46.40N	3.30 E
Solok	26	Dg	0.48S	100.39 E
Sololá [3]	49	Bf	14.40N	91.15W
Sololá	49	Bf	14.46N	91.11W
Solomon Islands [1]	58	Ge	8.00S	159.00 E
Solomon Islands	57	Ge	8.00S	159.00 E
Solomon Islands (British Solomon Islands) [1]	58	Ge	8.00S	159.00 E
Solomon River	43	Hd	38.54N	97.22W
Solomon Sea	57	Ge	8.00S	155.00 E
Solon Springs	45	Kc	46.22N	91.48W
Solør	8	Dd	60.30N	11.55 E
Solor, Kepulauan-	26	Hh	8.25S	123.30 E
Solothurn	14	Bc	47.15N	7.30 E
Solothurn [2]	14	Bc	47.20N	7.40 E
Solotvin	10	Uh	48.38N	24.31 E
Soloveckije Ostrova	7	Id	65.05N	35.45 E
Solovjevka	8	Nd	60.44N	30.20 E
Solovjevsk [R.S.F.S.R.]	20	Hf	54.15N	124.30 E
Solovjevsk [R.S.F.S.R.]	20	Gg	49.54N	115.43 E
Sölöz	15	Mi	40.23N	29.25 E
Solre-le-Château	12	Gd	50.10N	4.05 E
Solsona	13	Nc	41.59N	1.31 E
Solt	10	Oj	46.48N	19.00 E
Solta	14	Kg	43.23N	16.17 E
Soltānābād [Iran]	24	Mg	31.03N	49.42 E
Soltānābād [Iran]	24	Rd	36.23N	58.02 E
Solţānī, Khowr-e-	24	Nh	29.00N	50.50 E
Soltānīyeh	24	Md	36.26N	48.48 E
Soltau	10	Fd	52.59N	9.50 E
Soltvadkert	10	Pj	46.35N	19.23 E
Solvang	46	Ei	34.36N	120.08W
Sölvesborg	7	Dh	56.03N	14.33 E
Solvyčegodsk	7	Lf	61.21N	46.52 E
Solway Firth	9	Jg	54.50N	3.35W
Solwezi	31	Jj	12.11S	26.24 E
Sōma	28	Pf	37.48N	140.57 E
Soma	24	Bc	39.10N	27.36 E
Somain	12	Fd	50.22N	3.17 E
Somalia (EN)= Soomaaliya [1]	31	Lh	10.00N	49.00 E
Somali Basin (EN)	3	Fi	0.00	52.00 E
Sombo	36	Dd	8.42S	20.57 E
Sombor	15	Cd	45.46N	19.07 E
Sombrerete	47	Dd	23.38N	103.39W
Sombrero	47	Le	18.36N	63.26W
Sombrero Channel	25	Ig	7.41N	93.35 E
Sombrio	55	Hi	29.07S	49.40W
Sombrio, Lagoa do-	55	Hi	29.12S	49.42W
Somcuţa Mare	15	Gb	47.31N	23.28 E
Someren	12	Hc	51.23N	5.43 E
Somero	8	Jd	60.37N	23.32 E
Somerset	38	Jb	73.30N	93.30W
Somerset [3]	9	Jk	51.10N	3.10W
Somerset	9	Kj	51.00N	3.00W
Somerset [Austl.]	59	Ib	10.35S	142.15 E
Somerset [Ky.-U.S.]	43	Kd	37.05N	84.36W
Somerset [Pa.-U.S.]	44	He	40.02N	79.05W
Somerset East	37	Df	32.42S	25.35 E
Somerton	46	Hj	32.36N	114.43W
Somerville Lake	45	Hk	30.18N	96.40W
Someş	15	Fa	48.07N	22.20 E
Someşu Mare	15	Gb	47.09N	23.55 E
Someşu Mic	15	Gb	47.09N	23.55 E
Somme [3]	11	Id	49.55N	2.30 E
Somme	11	Hd	50.11N	1.39 E
Somme, Baie de-	12	Dd	50.14N	1.33 E
Somme, Bassurelle de la-	12	Dd	50.15N	1.10 E
Somme, Canal de la-	11	He	50.11N	1.39 E
Somme-Leuze	12	Hd	50.20N	5.22 E
Somme-Leuze-Hogne	12	Hd	50.15N	5.17 E
Sommen	7	Dh	58.00N	15.15 E
Sommen	8	Ff	58.08N	14.58 E
Sommepy-Tahure	12	Ge	49.15N	4.33 E
Sömmerda	10	He	51.09N	11.06 E
Somogy [2]	10	Nj	46.25N	17.35 E
Somontano	13	Lc	42.02N	0.20W
Somosierra, Puerto de-	13	Ic	41.09N	3.35W
Somosomo Strait	63d	Bb	16.47S	179.58 E
Somotillo	49	Dg	13.02N	86.53W
Somoto	47	Gf	13.28N	86.35W
Somovo	16	Kd	51.45N	39.25 E
Sompolno	10	Od	52.24N	18.31 E
Somport, Puerto de-	13	Lb	42.48N	0.31W
Son	21	Kg	25.50N	84.55 E
Sona	10	Qd	52.33N	20.35 E
Soná	49	Gi	8.01N	81.19W
Sonaguera	49	Df	15.38N	86.20W
Sonári, Ákra	15	Lm	36.27N	28.13 E
Sŏnch'on	28	He	39.48N	124.55 E
Søndeled	7	Bg	58.46N	9.05 E
Sønderborg	7	Bi	54.55N	9.47 E
Sonder-Jylland [2]	8	Ci	55.00N	9.00 E
Sønder-Omme	8	Ci	55.50N	8.54 E
Sondershausen	10	Ge	51.22N	10.52 E
Søndre Strømfjord	67	Nc	66.59N	50.40W
Søndre Strømfjord	41	Ge	66.10N	53.10W
Søndre Upernavik	41	Gd	72.10N	55.38W
Sondrio	14	Dd	46.10N	9.52 E
Sonepat	25	Fc	28.59N	77.01 E
Song	34	Hd	9.50N	12.37 E
Songa	8	Be	59.47N	7.43 E
Songavatn	8	Be	59.50N	7.35 E
Song Cau	25	Lf	13.27N	109.13 E
Songe	8	Cf	58.41N	9.01 E
Songea	31	Kj	10.41S	35.39 E
Songeons	12	De	49.33N	1.52 E
Songhua Hu	28	Ic	43.30N	126.51 E
Songhua Jiang=Sungari (EN)	21	Pe	47.42N	132.30 E
Songjiang	27	Le	31.01N	121.14 E
Songjiang → Antu	28	Jc	42.33N	128.20 E
Songjianghe	28	Ic	42.10N	127.30 E
Sŏngjin → Kimch'aek	27	Mc	40.41N	129.12 E
Songjŏng	28	Ig	35.08N	126.48 E
Songkhla	22	Mi	7.13N	100.34 E
Songling	27	Lb	48.02N	121.08 E
Songnim	28	He	38.44N	125.38 E
Songo [Ang.]	36	Bd	7.21S	14.50 E
Songo [Moz.]	37	Ec	15.33S	32.48 E
Songololo	36	Bd	5.42S	14.02 E
Songpan (Sungqu)	27	He	32.37N	103.34 E
Songsa-dong	28	Hd	39.49N	124.49 E
Song Shan	27	Je	34.31N	113.00 E
Songshuzhen	28	Ic	42.01N	127.09 E
Songueur	13	Ni	35.11N	1.30 E
Songxian	28	Bg	34.12N	112.09 E
Songzi (Xinjiangkou)	28	Ai	30.10N	116.46 E
Sonid Youqi (Saihan Tal)	27	Jc	42.45N	112.36 E
Sonid Zuoqi (Mandalt)	27	Kc	43.50N	116.45 E
Sonkari	8	Lb	62.50N	26.35 E
Sonkël, Ozero-	18	Jd	41.50N	75.10 E
Sonkovo	7	Ih	57.47N	37.09 E
Son La	22	Mg	21.19N	103.54 E
Sonmiāni Bay	25	Dc	25.15N	66.30 E
Sonneberg	10	Hf	50.21N	11.10 E
Sono, Rio do- [Braz.]	55	Jc	17.02S	45.32W
Sono, Rio do- [Braz.]	54	Ie	9.00S	48.11W
Sonobe	29	Dd	35.07N	135.28 E
Sonoita	47	Bb	31.51N	112.50W
Sonoma Peak	46	Gf	40.52N	117.36W
Sonora [2]	47	Bc	29.20N	110.40W
Sonora	47	Bc	28.48N	111.49W
Sonora [Ca.-U.S.]	46	Eh	37.59N	120.23W
Sonora [Tx.-U.S.]	45	Fk	30.34N	100.39W
Sonqor	24	Le	34.47N	47.36 E
Sonsbeck	12	Ic	51.37N	6.22 E
Sonsonate	47	Gf	13.43N	89.44W
Sonsorol Islands	57	Ed	5.20N	132.13 E
Sonthofen	10	Gi	47.31N	10.17 E
Sontra	10	Fe	51.04N	9.56 E
Soomaaliya=Somalia (EN) [1]	31	Lh	10.00N	49.00 E
Soomenlaht=Finland, Gulf of- (EN)	5	Ic	60.00N	27.00 E
Soonwald	12	Je	49.56N	7.35 E
Søørværøy	7	Cc	67.38N	12.40 E
Sopi, Tanjung-	26	If	2.39N	128.34 E
Sopo	35	Dd	8.51N	26.11 E
Sopockin	10	Tc	53.50N	23.42 E
Sopot [Bul.]	15	Hg	42.39N	24.45 E
Sopot [Pol.]	10	Ob	54.28N	18.34 E
Sopron	10	Mi	47.41N	16.36 E
Sopur	25	Eb	34.18N	74.28 E
Sor	13	De	39.00N	8.17W
Sora	14	Hi	41.43N	13.37 E
Sorachi-Gawa	29a	Bb	43.32N	141.52 E
Söråker	8	Gb	62.31N	17.30 E
Sorak-san	27	Md	38.07N	128.28 E
Sorano	14	Fh	42.41N	11.43 E
Soratteld	12	Kc	51.40N	8.55 E
Sorbas	13	Jg	37.07N	2.07W
Sorbe	13	Id	40.51N	3.08W
Sörberget	8	Gb	62.31N	17.22 E
Sore	11	Fj	44.19N	0.35W
Sorel	42	Kg	46.03N	73.07W
Sorell, Cape-	59	Jh	42.10S	145.10 E
Soresina	14	De	45.17N	9.51 E
Sorezaru Point	63a	Cb	7.37S	156.38 E
Sørfjorden	8	Bd	60.25N	6.40 E
Sørfold	7	Dc	67.28N	15.28 E
Sorgues	11	Kj	44.00N	4.52 E
Sorgun	24	Fc	39.50N	35.19 E
Soria [3]	13	Jc	41.40N	2.40W
Soria	13	Jc	41.46N	2.28W
Soriano [2]	55	Dk	33.30S	57.45W
Sørkapp	67	Kd	76.28N	16.36 E
Sorkh, Godār-e-	24	Pf	33.05N	55.05 E
Sorkh, Kūh-e-	24	Pf	33.05N	55.05 E
Sorkheh	24	Oe	35.28N	53.13 E
Sorø	8	Di	55.26N	11.34 E
Sorocaba	53	Lh	23.29S	47.27W
Soroči Gory	7	Li	55.24N	49.55 E
Soročinsk	19	Fe	52.26N	53.10 E
Soroki	16	Fe	48.07N	28.16 E
Sorol Atoll	57	Fd	8.08N	140.23 E
Sorong	58	Ee	0.53S	131.15 E
Soroti	31	Kh	1.43N	33.37 E
Sørøya	5	Ia	70.36N	22.46 E
Sørøyane	8	Ab	62.20N	5.45 E
Sorraia	13	Df	38.56N	8.53W
Sørreisa	7	Eb	69.09N	18.10 E
Sorrentina, Penisola-	14	Ij	40.35N	14.30 E
Sorrento	14	Ij	40.37N	14.22 E
Sør Rondane	66	Df	72.00S	25.00 E
Sorsatunturi	7	Gc	67.24N	29.38 E
Sorsavesi	8	Lb	62.30N	27.35 E
Sorsele	7	Dd	65.32N	17.30 E
Sorsk	20	Ef	54.00N	90.20 E
Sorso	14	Cj	40.48N	8.34 E
Sorsogon	26	Hd	12.58N	124.00 E
Sort	13	Nb	42.24N	1.08 E
Šortandi	19	He	51.42N	71.05 E
Sortavala	19	Dc	61.44N	30.41 E
Sortland	7	Db	68.42N	15.24 E
Sør-Trøndelag [2]	7	Ce	63.00N	10.40 E
Sorum	17	Ne	63.50N	68.05 E
Sørumsand	8	De	59.58N	11.15 E
Šoša	7	Ih	56.33N	36.09 E
Sŏsan	28	If	36.47N	126.27 E
Sösdala	8	Eh	56.02N	13.40 E
Sos del Rey Católico	13	Kb	42.30N	1.13W
Sosna	16	Kc	52.42N	38.55 E
Sosnogorsk	6	Lc	63.37N	53.51 E
Sosnovka [R.S.F.S.R.]	16	Lc	53.14N	41.22 E
Sosnovka [R.S.F.S.R.]	7	Mh	56.18N	51.17 E
Sosnovka [R.S.F.S.R.]	7	Jc	66.31N	40.33 E
Sosnovka [Ukr.-U.S.S.R.]	16	Dd	50.15N	24.13 E
Sosnovo	8	Nd	60.31N	30.29 E
Sosnovo-Ozerskoje	20	Gf	52.31N	111.35 E
Sosnovy Bor	8	Me	59.48N	29.10 E
Sosnowiec	10	Pf	50.18N	19.08 E
Sospel	11	Nk	43.53N	7.27 E
Šostka	19	De	51.52N	33.31 E
Sosumav	37	Hb	13.03S	48.54 E
Sosva	19	Gd	59.32N	62.20 E
Sosva [R.S.F.S.R.]	19	Gc	63.40N	62.02 E
Sosva [R.S.F.S.R.]	19	Gd	59.10N	61.50 E
Sotavento [3]	32	Cf	14.40N	23.25W
Sotavento, Islas de- = Windward Islands (EN)	52	Jd	11.10N	67.00W
Sotik	36	Gc	0.41S	35.07 E
Sotkamo	7	Gd	64.08N	28.25 E
Soto la Marina	48	Jf	23.48N	98.13W
Soto la Marina, Río-	48	Kf	23.45N	97.45W
Sotonera, Embalse de la-	13	Lb	42.05N	0.48W
Sotouboua	34	Fd	8.34N	0.59 E
Sotra	8	Ad	60.20N	5.05 E
Sotsudaka-Zaki	29b	Ba	28.15N	129.10 E
Sottern	8	Fe	59.05N	15.30 E
Sotteville-lès-Rouen	11	He	49.25N	1.06 E
Sottrum	12	La	53.07N	9.14 E
Sottunga	8	Id	60.10N	20.40 E
Sotuf, Adrar-	32	De	21.42N	15.36W
Sotuta	48	Og	20.36N	89.01W
Souanké	36	Bb	2.05N	14.03 E
Soubré	34	Dd	5.47N	6.36W
Soubré [3]	34	Dd	5.47N	6.38W
Soúdha	15	Hn	35.29N	24.04 E
Souf	30	He	33.25N	6.50 E
Soufflenheim	12	Jf	48.50N	7.58 E
Souflíon	15	Jh	41.12N	26.18 E
Soufrière	50	Ff	13.52N	61.04W
Soufrière [Guad.]	47	Le	16.03N	61.40W
Soufrière [St.Vin.]	47	Lf	13.21N	61.11W
Soufrière Bay	51g	Bb	15.13N	61.22W
Soufrière Hills	51c	Bc	16.43N	62.10W
Souillac	11	Hj	44.54N	1.29 E
Souilly	11	Le	49.01N	5.17 E
Souk Ahras	32	Ib	36.17N	7.57 E
Souk el Arba du Rharb	32	Fc	34.41N	5.59W
Sŏul=Seoul (EN)	22	Of	37.34N	127.00 E
Soulac-sur-Mer	11	Ei	45.30N	1.06W
Sŏul Si [2]	28	If	37.35N	127.00 E
Soultz-sous-Forêts	12	Jf	48.56N	7.53 E
Soumagne	12	Hd	50.37N	5.45 E
Soummam	13	Rh	36.44N	5.04 E
Sounding Creek	46	Ja	52.06N	110.28W
Soúnion	15	Hl	37.39N	24.02 E
Soúnion, Ákra-	15	Hl	37.39N	24.01 E
Sources, Mont aux-	30	Jk	28.46S	28.52 E
Soure [Braz.]	54	Id	0.44S	48.31W
Soure [Port.]	13	Dd	40.03N	8.38W
Sour el Ghozlane	32	Hb	36.09N	3.41 E
Souris	42	Hg	49.38N	100.15W
Souris	38	Je	49.39N	99.34W
Sous	32	Fc	30.22N	9.37W
Sous	32	Fc	30.25N	9.30W
Sousa	53	Mf	6.45S	38.14W
Sousel	13	Ef	38.57N	7.40W
Sous le Vent, Iles-= Leeward Islands (EN)	57	Lf	16.38S	151.30W
Sousse (EN)=Sūsah [3]	32	Jb	35.45N	10.30 E
Sousse (EN)=Sūsah [Tun.]	31	Ie	35.49N	10.38 E
Sout	37	Cf	33.03S	23.29 E
South Africa / Suid Africa [1]	31	Jl	30.00S	26.00 E
South Alligator River	59	Gb	12.15S	132.24 E
Southam	12	Ab	52.15N	1.23W
South America (EN)	52	Jg	15.00S	60.00W
Southampton	38	Kc	64.20N	84.40W
Southampton [Eng.-U.K.]	6	Fe	50.55N	1.25W
Southampton [N.Y.-U.S.]	44	Ke	40.54N	72.23W
Southampton, Cape -	42	Jd	62.08N	83.44W
Southampton Airport	12	Ad	50.55N	1.23W
Southampton Water	12	Ad	50.52N	1.20W
South Andaman	25	If	11.45N	92.45 E
Southard, Cape-	66	Ie	66.33S	122.04 E
South Auckland-Bay of Plenty [2]	62	Fb	38.00S	176.00 E
South Aulatsivik	42	Le	56.47N	61.30W
South Australia [2]	59	Ge	30.00S	135.00 E
South Australian Basin (EN)	3	Im	40.00S	128.00 E
Southaven	45	Li	35.00N	90.00W
South Baldy	45	Cj	33.59N	107.11W
South Bay	42	Jd	64.00N	83.25W
South Bend	43	Jc	41.41N	86.15W
South Benfleet	12	Cc	51.32N	0.33 E
Southborough	12	Cc	51.09N	0.15 E
South Boston	44	Hg	36.42N	78.58W
Southbridge	62	Ee	43.48S	172.15 E
South Buganda [3]	36	Fc	0.30S	32.00 E
South Caicos	49	Lc	21.31N	71.30W
South Carolina [2]	43	Ke	34.00N	81.00W
South China Basin (EN)	3	Hh	15.00N	115.00 E
South China Sea (EN)=Bien Dong	21	Ni	10.00N	113.00 E
South China Sea (EN)=Cina Selatan, Laut-	21	Ni	10.00N	113.00 E
South China Sea (EN)=Nan Hai	21	Ni	10.00N	113.00 E
South Dakota [2]	43	Gc	44.15N	100.00W
South Downs	9	Mk	50.55N	0.25W
South-East [3]	37	De	25.00S	25.45 E
South East Cape	57	Fi	43.39S	146.50 E
Southeast Indian Ridge (EN)	3	Ho	50.00S	110.00 E
Southeast Pacific Basin (EN)	3	Mp	60.00S	115.00W
South East Point [Austl.]	57	Fh	39.00S	146.20 E
South East Point [Kir.]	64g	Bb	1.40N	157.10W
Southend	42	He	56.20N	103.14W
Southend-on-Sea	9	Nj	51.33N	0.43 E
Southern [Mwi.] [3]	36	Gf	15.30S	35.00 E
Southern [S.L.] [3]	34	Cd	7.40N	12.15W
Southern [Ug.] [3]	36	Fc	0.30S	30.30 E
Southern [Zam.] [3]	36	Ef	16.00S	27.00 E
Southern Alps	57	Ii	43.30S	170.35 E
Southern Cook Island	57	Lg	20.00S	159.00W
Southern Cross	58	Ch	31.13S	119.19 E
Southern Desert (EN)= Janūbīyah, Aş Şaḩrā' al-	30	Jf	24.00N	30.00 E
Southern Ghats	25	Ff	10.00N	76.50 E
Southern Gilbert Islands	60	Jh	1.30S	175.30 E
Southern Indian Lake	38	Jd	57.10N	98.40W
Southern Pines	44	Hh	35.11N	79.24W
Southern Region (EN)= Iglim al Janūbīyah [2]	35	Dd	6.00N	30.00 E
Southern Sierra Madre (EN) =Madre del Sur, Sierra-	38	Jj	17.00N	100.00W
Southern Uplands	5	Fd	55.30N	3.30W
Southern Urals (EN)=Južny Ural	5	Le	54.00N	58.30 E
Southern Yemen (EN) → Yemen, People's Democratic Republic of- (EN) [1]	22	Gh	14.00N	46.00 E
South Esk	9	Ke	56.43N	2.28W
South Fiji Basin (EN)	3	Jl	26.00S	175.00 E
South Foreland	9	Oj	51.09N	1.23 E
South Fork	46	Ge	42.26N	116.53W
South Fork Flathead River	46	Ib	48.07N	113.45W
South Fork Grand River	45	Ed	45.43N	102.17W
South Fork Kern River	46	Fi	35.40N	118.27W
South Fork Moreau River	45	Ed	45.09N	102.50W
South Fork Powder River	46	Le	43.40N	106.30W
South Fork Republican River	45	Ff	40.03N	101.31W
South Georgia/Georgia del Sur, Islas-	66	Ad	54.15S	36.45W
South Glamorgan [3]	9	Jj	51.30N	3.15W
South Haven	44	Dd	42.24N	86.16W
South Honshu Ridge (EN)	3	Ig	24.00N	142.00 E
South Horr	36	Gb	2.06N	36.55 E
South Indian Basin (EN)	3	Ho	60.00S	120.00 E
South Island [F.S.M.]	64d	Bc	6.59N	151.59 E
South Island [Kenya]	36	Gb	2.38N	36.36 E
South Island [N.Z.]	57	Ii	44.00S	171.00 E
South Island [Sey.]	37b	Ab	9.26S	46.23 E
South Island [Sey.]	37b	Bc	10.10S	51.10 E

Index Symbols

- [1] Independent Nation
- [2] State, Region
- [3] District, County
- [4] Municipality
- [5] Colony, Dependency
- Continent
- Physical Region
- Historical or Cultural Region
- Mount, Mountain
- Volcano
- Hill
- Mountains, Mountain Range
- Hills, Escarpment
- Plateau, Upland
- Pass, Gap
- Plain, Lowland
- Delta
- Salt Flat
- Valley, Canyon
- Crater, Cave
- Karst Features
- Depression
- Polder
- Desert, Dunes
- Forest, Woods
- Heath, Steppe
- Oasis
- Cape, Point
- Coast, Beach
- Cliff
- Peninsula
- Isthmus
- Sandbank
- Island
- Atoll
- Rock, Reef
- Islands, Archipelago
- Rocks, Reefs
- Coral Reef
- Well, Spring
- Geyser
- River, Stream
- Waterfall Rapids
- River Mouth, Estuary
- Lake
- Salt Lake
- Intermittent Lake
- Reservoir
- Swamp, Pond
- Canal
- Glacier
- Ice Shelf, Pack Ice
- Ocean
- Sea
- Gulf, Bay
- Strait, Fjord
- Lagoon
- Bank
- Seamount
- Tablemount
- Ridge
- Shelf
- Basin
- Escarpment, Sea Scarp
- Fracture
- Trench, Abyss
- National Park, Reserve
- Point of Interest
- Recreation Site
- Cave, Cavern
- Historic Site
- Ruins
- Wall, Walls
- Church, Abbey
- Temple
- Scientific Station
- Airport
- Port
- Lighthouse
- Mine
- Tunnel
- Dam, Bridge

South Korea (EN)=Taehan-Min' guk [1] 22 Of 38.00N 127.30 E
South Lake Tahoe 46 Eg 38.57N 120.01W
Southland [2] 62 Bf 45.45 S 168.00 E
South Loup River 45 Gf 41.04N 98.40W
South Lueti 36 Df 16.14 S 23.12 E
South Magnetic Pole (1980) 66 Ie 65.08 S 139.03 E
South Malosmadulu Atoll 25a Ba 5.10N 72.58 E
South Mountain 46 Ge 42.44N 116.54W
South Nahanni 42 Fd 61.03N 123.22W
South Negril Point 47 Ie 18.16N 78.22W
South Orkney Islands 66 Re 60.35 S 45.30W
South Pass 38 Ie 42.22N 108.55W
South Pass [F.S.M.] 64d Bb 7.14N 151.48 E
South Pass [U.S.] 45 Ll 28.55N 89.20W
South Platte 38 Ie 41.07N 100.42W
South Point 51q Ab 13.02N 59.31W
South Pole 66 Bg 90.00 S 0.00
South Porcupine 44 Ga 48.28N 81.13W
Southport [Eng.-U.K.] 9 Jh 53.39N 3.01W
Southport [N.C.-U.S.] 44 Hi 33.55N 78.01W
South Reef 63a Ee 13.00 S 160.32 E
South Ronaldsay 9 Kc 58.46N 2.50W
South Rukuru 36 Fe 10.44 S 34.14 E
South Saint Paul 45 Jd 44.52N 93.02W
South Sandwich Islands 66 Ad 56.00 S 26.30W
South Sandwich Trench (EN) 3 Do 56.30 S 25.00W
South Saskatchewan River 38 Id 53.15N 105.05W
South Shetland Islands 66 Re 62.00 S 58.00W
South Shields 9 Lg 55.00N 1.25W
South Sioux City 45 He 42.28N 96.24W
South Sister 46 Ed 44.12N 121.45W
South Taranaki Bight 62 Fc 39.40 S 174.15 E
South Trap 62 Bg 47.30 S 167.55 E
South Tyne 9 Kg 54.59N 2.08W
South Uist 9 Fd 57.15N 7.24W
South Umpqua River 46 De 43.20N 123.25W
•Southwell 12 Ba 53.04N 0.57W
South Wellesley Islands 59 Hc 17.05 S 139.25 E
South West Africa→Namibia [1] 31 Ik 22.00 S 17.00 E
Southwest Cape 57 Hi 47.17 S 167.27 E
South West Cape 59 Jh 43.34 S 146.02 E
Southwest Cape 51a Dc 17.42N 64.53W
Southwest Indian Ridge (EN) 3 Fm 32.00 S 55.00 E
Southwest Miramichi River 44 Ob 46.50N 65.45W
Southwest Pacific Basin (EN) 3 Km 40.00 S 150.00W
Southwest Pass 45 Ll 29.00N 89.20W
Southwest Point 49 Jb 22.10N 74.10W
South West Point 64g Ab 1.52N 157.33W
South West Point 51p Cb 12.27N 61.30W
Southwold 9 Oi 52.20N 1.40 E
South Yorkshire [3] 9 Lh 53.30N 1.25W
Soutpansberg 37 Dd 22.58 S 29.50 E
Soverato 14 Kl 38.41N 16.33 E
Sovetabad 18 Gd 40.14N 69.42 E
Sovetsk [R.S.F.S.R.] 19 Ed 57.36N 48.58 E
Sovetsk [R.S.F.S.R.] 19 Cd 55.05N 21.52 E
Sovetskaja Gavan 22 Qe 48.58N 140.18 E
Sovetski [R.S.F.S.R.] 7 Lh 56.47N 48.30 E
Sovetski [R.S.F.S.R.] 8 Md 60.29N 28.40 E
Sovetski [R.S.F.S.R.] 19 Gc 61.20N 63.29 E
Sovetskoje 19 Ef 47.17N 44.30 E
Soviet Union EN)→Union of Soviet Socialist Republics (EN) 22 Jd 60.00N 80.00 E
Şowghān 24 Qh 28.20N 56.54 E
Sowie, Góry- 10 Mf 50.38N 16.30 E
Sōya 29a Ba 45.28N 141.53 E
Sōya-Kaikyō=La Perouse Strait (EN) 21 Qe 45.30N 142.00 E
Sōya-Misaki 27 Pb 45.31N 141.56 E
Soyatita 48 Fe 25.45N 107.22W
Soyo 36 Bd 6.05 S 12.20 E
Sož 5 Je 51.57N 30.48 E
Sozopol 15 Kg 42.25N 27.42 E
Spa 11 Ld 50.29N 5.52 E
Spain (EN)=España [1] 6 Fg 40.00N 4.00W
Špakovskoje 16 Lg 45.06N 42.00 E
Spalding 9 Mi 52.47N 0.10W
Spanish Fork 46 Jf 40.07N 111.39W
Spanish Peak 46 Fd 44.24N 119.46W
Spanish Point 51d Ba 17.33N 61.44W
Spanish Sahara (EN) → Western Sahara (EN) [5] 31 Ff 24.30N 13.00W
Spanish Town [B.V.I.] 51a Db 18.27N 64.26W
Spanish Town [Jam.] 47 Ie 17.59N 76.57W
Sparbu 7 Ce 63.55N 11.28 E
Spargi, Isola- 14 Di 41.15N 9.20 E
Sparks 43 Dd 39.32N 119.45W
Sparreholm 8 Ge 59.04N 16.49 E
Sparta [Il.-U.S.] 45 Lg 38.07N 89.42W
Sparta [N.C.-U.S.] 44 Gg 36.30N 81.07W
Sparta [Tn.-U.S.] 44 Eh 35.56N 85.29W
Sparta [Wi.-U.S.] 45 Ke 43.57N 90.47W
Sparta (EN)=Spárti 15 Fl 37.05N 22.26 E
Spartanburg 43 Ke 34.57N 81.55W
Spartel, Cap- 30 Ge 35.48N 5.56W
Spárti=Sparta (EN) 15 Fl 37.05N 22.26 E
Spartivento, Capo- [It.] 14 Cl 38.53N 8.50 E
Spartivento, Capo- [It.] 5 Hh 37.55N 16.04 E
Spas-Demensk 16 Ib 54.24N 34.01 E
Spas-Klepiki 7 Ji 55.10N 40.13 E
Spassk-Rjazanski 7 Ji 54.27N 40.22 E
Spátha, Ákra-=Spatha, Cape- (EN) 15 Gn 35.42N 23.44 E
Spatha, Cape- (EN)=Spátha, Ákra- 15 Gn 35.42N 23.44 E
Spearfish 43 Gc 44.30N 103.52W
Spearman 45 Fh 36.12N 101.12W
Speedway 44 Df 39.47N 86.15W
Speicher 12 Ie 49.56N 6.38 E
Speightstown 50 Gf 13.15N 59.39W
Speke Gulf 36 Fc 2.20 S 33.15 E
Spello 14 Gh 42.59N 12.40 E
Spenard 40 Jd 61.11N 149.55W
Spence Bay 39 Jc 69.32N 93.31W
Spencer [Ia.-U.S.] 43 Hc 43.09N 95.09W
Spencer [In.-U.S.] 44 Df 39.17N 86.46W
Spencer [Nb.-U.S.] 45 Ge 42.53N 98.42W
Spencer [W.V.-U.S.] 44 Gf 38.48N 81.22W
Spencer, Cape- 59 Hg 35.18 S 136.53 E
Spencer Gulf 57 Eh 34.00 S 137.00 E
Spenge 12 Kb 52.08N 8.29 E
Spenser Mountains 62 Ee 42.10 S 172.35 E
Sperillen 8 Dd 60.30N 10.05 E
Sperkhiós 15 Fk 38.52N 22.34 E
Sperlonga 14 Hi 41.15N 13.26 E
Sperone, Capo- 14 Cl 38.55N 8.25 E
Sperrin Mountains/Sliabh Speirin 9 Fg 54.50N 7.05W
Spessart 10 Fg 49.55N 9.30 E
Spétsai 15 Gl 37.16N 23.09 E
Spétsai 15 Gl 37.16N 23.08 E
Spey 9 Jd 57.40N 3.06W
Spey Bay 9 Jd 57.40N 3.05W
Speyer 10 Eg 49.19N 8.26 E
Speyer-bach 12 Ke 49.19N 8.27 E
Speyside 50 Fg 11.18N 60.32W
Spezzano Albanese 14 Kk 39.40N 16.19 E
Spicer Islands 42 Jc 68.10N 79.00W
Spiekeroog 10 Dc 53.46N 7.42 E
Spiez 14 Bd 46.41N 7.42 E
Spijkenisse 12 Gc 51.51N 4.21 E
Spilimbergo 14 Gd 46.07N 12.54 E
Spílion 15 Hn 35.13N 24.32 E
Spilsby 12 Ca 53.11N 0.06 E
Spina 14 Gf 44.42N 12.08 E
Spinazzola 14 Kj 40.58N 16.05 E
Spincourt 12 He 49.20N 5.40 E
Spirit River 42 Fe 55.47N 118.50W
Spirovo 7 Ih 57.27N 35.01 E
Spiš 10 Qg 49.05N 20.30 E
Spišská Nová Ves 10 Qh 48.57N 20.34 E
Spitak 16 Ni 40.49N 44.14 E
Spitsbergen 67 Kd 78.00N 19.00 E
Spitsbergen 67 Kd 78.45N 16.00 E
Spittal an der Drau 14 Hd 46.48N 13.30 E
Spitzbergen Bank (EN) 41 Oc 76.00N 23.00 E
Spjelkavik 7 Be 62.28N 6.23 E
Split 6 Hg 43.31N 16.26 E
Split Lake 42 He 56.10N 96.10W
Spluga, Passo dello- 14 Dd 46.29N 9.20 E
Splügenpaß 14 Dd 46.29N 9.20 E
Spógi/Špogi 8 Lh 56.02N 26.52 E
Špogi/Spógi 8 Lh 56.02N 26.52 E
Spokane 39 He 47.40N 117.23W
Spokane, Mount- 46 Gc 47.55N 117.07W
Spokane River 46 Fc 47.44N 118.20W
Špola 19 Df 49.01N 31.24 E
Spoleto 14 Gh 42.44N 12.44 E
Spooner 45 Kd 45.50N 91.53W
Spoon River 45 Kf 40.18N 90.04W
Sporovo 10 Vd 52.25N 25.27 E
Spotsylvania 44 If 38.12N 77.35W
Sprague 46 Gc 47.18N 117.59W
Sprague River 46 Ee 42.34N 121.51W
Spray 46 Fd 44.50N 119.48W
Spreča 14 Mf 44.44N 18.06 E
Spree 10 Jd 52.32N 13.13 E
Spreewald 10 Je 51.55N 14.00 E
Spremberg/Grodk 10 Ke 51.33N 14.22 E
Sprengisandur 7a Bb 64.40N 18.07W
Springbok 31 Ik 29.43 S 17.15 E
Spring Creek 45 Fd 45.45N 100.18W
Springdale 45 Ih 36.11N 94.08W
Springe 10 Fd 52.13N 9.33 E
Springer 45 Dh 36.22N 104.36W
Springer, Mount- 44 Ja 49.48N 74.51W
Springerville 46 Ki 34.08N 109.17W
Springfield [Co.-U.S.] 45 Eh 37.24N 102.37W
Springfield [Il.-U.S.] 39 Kf 39.47N 89.40W
Springfield [Ma.-U.S.] 43 Mc 42.07N 72.36W
Springfield [Mn.-U.S.] 45 Id 44.14N 94.59W
Springfield [Mo.-U.S.] 39 Jf 37.14N 93.17W
Springfield [N.Z.] 62 De 43.20 S 171.56 E
Springfield [Oh.-U.S.] 43 Kd 39.55N 83.48W
Springfield [Or.-U.S.] 43 Cc 44.03N 123.01W
Springfield [S.D.-U.S.] 45 He 42.49N 97.54W
Springfield [Tn.-U.S.] 44 Dg 36.31N 86.52W
Springfontein 37 Df 30.19 S 25.36 E
Spring Garden 54 Gb 6.59N 58.31W
Spring Hall 51q Ab 13.19N 59.36W
Springhill [La.-U.S.] 45 Jj 33.00N 93.28W
Springhill [N.S.-Can.] 42 Lg 45.39N 64.03W
Spring Mountains 46 Hh 36.10N 115.40W
Springs 37 De 26.13 S 28.25 E
Springsure 59 Jd 24.07 S 148.05 E
Spring Valley 46 Hg 39.10N 114.30W
Spring Valley 45 Je 43.41N 92.23W
Springville 46 Jf 40.10N 111.37W
Spruce Knob 38 Lf 38.42N 79.32W
Spruce Mountain [Az.-U.S.] 46 Ii 34.28N 112.24W
Spruce Mountain [Nv.-U.S.] 46 Hf 40.33N 114.49W
Spulico, Capo- 14 Kk 39.58N 16.38 E
Spurn Head 9 Nh 53.34N 0.07 E
Squamish 42 Fg 49.42N 123.09W
Squillace 14 Kl 38.47N 16.31 E
Squillace, Golfo di- 14 Kl 38.45N 16.50 E
Squinzano 14 Mj 40.26N 18.02 E
Srbica 15 Dg 42.45N 20.47 E
Srbija=Serbia (EN) 15 Df 44.00N 21.00 E
Srbija=Serbia (EN) [2] 15 Df 44.00N 21.00 E
Srbija=Serbia (EN) 5 Ig 43.00N 21.00 E
Srbobran 15 Cd 45.33N 19.48 E
Srê Âmbĕl 25 Kf 11.07N 103.46 E
Sredinny Hrebet 21 Rd 56.00N 158.00 E
Sredna Gora 15 Hg 42.30N 25.00 E
Srednekolymsk 20 Kc 67.27N 153.41 E
Srednerusskaja Vozvyšennost'=Central Russian Uplands (EN) 5 Je 52.00N 38.00 E
Srednesatyginski Tuman, Ozero- 17 Lg 59.45N 65.25 E
Srednesibirskoje Ploskogorje=Central Siberian Uplands (EN) 21 Mc 65.00N 105.00 E
Sredni Kujto, Ozero- 7 Hd 65.05N 31.30 E
Sredni Ural=Central Urals (EN) 5 Ld 58.00N 59.00 E
Sredni Urgal 20 If 51.13N 132.58 E
Sredni Verecki, Pereval- 16 Ce 48.49N 23.07 E
Sredniaja Ahtuba 16 Ne 48.43N 44.52 E
Sredniaja Olëkma 20 He 55.26N 120.40 E
Śrem 10 Nd 52.08N 17.01 E
Sremska Mitrovica 15 Ce 44.58N 19.37 E
Sremski Karlovci 15 Cd 45.12N 19.56 E
Sretensk 22 Nd 52.15N 117.43 E
Sri Gangānagar 25 Ec 29.55N 73.53 E
Sri Jayawardenepura 25 Gg 6.54N 80.02 E
Srijem 15 Cd 45.00N 19.40 E
Srīkākulam 25 Ge 18.18N 83.54 E
Sri Lanka (Ceylon) [1] 22 Ki 7.40N 80.50 E
Srīnagar 22 Jf 34.05N 74.49 E
Srivardhan 25 Ee 18.02N 73.01 E
Środa Śląska 10 Me 51.10N 16.36 E
Środa Wielkopolska 10 Nd 52.14N 17.17 E
Srpska Crnja 15 Dd 45.43N 20.42 E
Sruth na Maoile/North Channel 5 Fd 55.10N 5.40W
SSSR=Union of Soviet Socialist Republics (USSR) (EN) [1] 22 Jd 60.00N 80.00 E
SSSR→Sojuz Sovetskih Socialističeskih Respublik [1] 22 Jd 60.00N 80.00 E
Ssu-ch'uan Sheng→Sichuan Sheng=Szechwan (EN) [2] 27 He 30.00N 103.00 E
Staaten River 59 Ic 16.24 S 141.17 E
Stabroek 12 Gc 51.20N 4.22 E
Stack Skerry 9 Ib 59.02N 4.30W
Stade 10 Fc 53.36N 9.29 E
Staden 12 Fd 50.59N 3.01 E
Stadhavet 8 Ab 62.15N 5.05 E
Städjan 8 Ec 61.58N 12.52 E
Stadlandet 8 Ab 62.05N 5.20 E
Stadskanaal 11 Ma 53.00N 6.55 E
Stadskanaal-Musselkanaal 12 Jb 52.56N 7.02 E
Stadthagen 12 Lb 52.19N 9.13 E
Stadtkyll 12 Id 50.21N 6.32 E
Stadtlohn 12 Ic 51.59N 6.56 E
Stadtoldendorf 10 Fe 51.54N 9.39 E
Staffa 9 Ge 56.25N 6.10W
Staffanstorp 8 Ei 55.38N 13.13 E
Staffelsee 10 Hi 47.42N 11.10 E
Staffora 14 De 45.04N 9.01 E
Stafford 9 Li 52.50N 2.00W
Stafford 9 Ki 52.48N 2.07W
Staffordshire [3] 9 Li 52.55N 2.00W
Staicele/Stajcele 8 Kg 57.44N 24.39 E
Stainach 14 Ic 47.32N 14.06 E
Staines 12 Bc 51.26N 0.31W
Stakčín 10 Sg 49.00N 22.13 E
Stalać 15 Ef 43.40N 21.25 E
Stalham 12 Db 52.46N 1.31 E
Stalingrad→Volgograd 6 Kf 48.44N 44.25 E
Ställdalen 8 Fe 59.56N 14.56 E
Stalowa Wola 10 Sf 50.35N 22.02 E
Stamberger See 10 Ii 47.55N 12.20 E
Stamford [Ct.-U.S.] 44 Ke 41.03N 73.32W
Stamford [Eng.-U.K.] 9 Mi 52.39N 0.29W
Stamford [Tx.-U.S.] 45 Gj 32.57N 99.48W
Stamford, Lake- 45 Gj 33.05N 99.35W
Stampriet 37 Bd 24.20 S 18.28 E
Stamsund 7 Cb 68.08N 13.51 E
Stanberry 45 If 40.13N 94.35W
Stancija Jakkabag 18 Fe 38.59N 66.42 E
Stancija-Karakul 19 Gh 39.30N 63.50 E
Standerton 37 Dd 26.58 S 29.07 E
Standish 44 Fd 44.00N 83.57W
Stanford 46 Jc 47.09N 110.13W
Stånga 8 Hg 57.17N 18.28 E
Stångån 8 Ff 58.27N 15.37 E
Stange 8 Dd 60.43N 11.11 E
Stanger 37 Ee 29.27 S 31.14 E
Stanke Dimitrov 15 Gg 42.16N 23.07 E
Stanley [Austl.] 59 Jh 40.46 S 145.18 E
Stanley [Falk. Is.] 53 Kk 51.42 S 57.51W
Stanley [N.D.-U.S.] 45 Eb 48.19N 102.23W
Stanley Falls (EN)=Ngaliema, Chutes- 30 Jh 0.30N 25.30 E
Stann Creek 49 Ce 16.50N 88.30W
Stanovoje Nagorje=Stanovoy Upland (EN) 21 Nd 56.00N 114.00 E
Stanovoj Hrebet=Stanovoy Range (EN) 21 Od 56.20N 126.00 E
Stanovoy Upland (EN)=Stanovoje Nagorje 21 Nd 56.00N 114.00 E
Stans 14 Cd 46.58N 8.22 E
Stansted Airport 12 Cc 51.54N 0.13 E
Stansted Mountfitchet 12 Cc 51.54N 0.12 E
Stanthorpe 59 Ke 28.39 S 151.57 E
Stanton Banks 9 Fe 56.15N 7.50W
Staphorst 12 Ib 52.38N 6.14 E
Staples 45 Ic 46.21N 94.48W
Stapleton 45 Ff 41.29N 100.31W
Stąporków 10 Qe 51.09N 20.34 E
Starachowice 10 Re 51.03N 21.04 E
Staraja Majna 7 Li 54.36N 48.59 E
Staraja Russa 19 Dd 57.59N 31.23 E
Staraja-Vyževka 10 Ue 51.27N 24.34 E
Stará L'ubovňa 10 Qg 49.18N 20.42 E
Stara Moravica 15 Cd 45.52N 19.28 E
Stara Pazova 15 De 44.59N 20.10 E
Stara Planina=Balkan Mountains (EN) 5 Ig 43.15N 25.00 E
Stara Zagora [2] 15 Ig 42.25N 25.38 E
Stara Zagora 6 Ig 42.25N 25.38 E
Starbuck Island 57 Le 5.37 S 155.53W
Staretina 14 Kf 44.02N 16.43 E
Stargard Szczeciński 10 Lc 53.20N 15.02 E
Stari Begejski kanal 15 Dd 45.29N 20.25 E
Starica 7 Ih 56.30N 34.56 E
Starigrad 14 Kg 43.11N 16.36 E
Stari Vlah 15 Df 43.23N 20.10 E
Starke 44 Fk 29.57N 82.07W
Starkville 45 Lj 33.28N 88.48W
Starnberg 10 Hh 48.00N 11.21 E
Starobelsk 19 Df 49.15N 38.58 E
Starodub 19 De 52.35N 32.46 E
Starogard Gdański 10 Oc 53.59N 18.33 E
Starokonstantinov 16 Ee 49.43N 27.13 E
Starominskaja 19 Df 46.31N 39.06 E
Staroščerbinovskaja 16 Kf 46.37N 38.42 E
Starosubhangulovo 17 Hj 53.06N 57.20 E
Starotimoškino 7 Lj 53.43N 47.32 E
Start Point 9 Jk 50.13N 3.38W
Staryje Dorógi 16 Fc 53.02N 28.17 E
Stary Krym 16 Ig 45.02N 35.05 E
Stary Oskol' 19 De 51.18N 37.51 E
Stary Sambor 16 Ce 49.29N 23.01 E
Stary Terek 16 Og 44.01N 47.24 E
Staßfurt 10 He 51.52N 11.35 E
Staszów 10 Rf 50.34N 21.10 E
State College 44 Ie 40.48N 77.52W
Staten Island (EN)=Estados, Isla de los- 52 Jk 54.47 S 64.15W
Statesboro 44 Gi 32.27N 81.47W
Statesville 44 Gh 35.47N 80.53W
Stathelle 8 Ce 59.03N 9.41 E
Stathmós Krioneriou 15 Ek 38.20N 21.35 E
Statland 7 Cd 64.30N 11.08 E
Staunton 43 Ld 38.10N 79.05W
Stavanger 6 Gd 58.58N 5.45 E
Stavelot 12 Hd 50.23N 5.56 E
Staveren 11 Lb 52.53N 5.22 E
Stavern 8 Df 59.00N 10.02 E
Stavnoje 10 Sh 48.59N 22.45 E
Stavropol 6 Kf 45.02N 41.59 E
Stavropolskaja Vozvyšennost' 16 Mg 45.10N 43.00 E
Stavropolski Kraj [3] 19 Eg 45.00N 43.15 E
Stavrós [Grc.] 15 Fj 39.19N 22.14 E
Stavrós [Grc.] 15 Gi 40.40N 23.42 E
Stavroúpolis 15 Hh 41.12N 24.42 E
Stawell 59 Ig 37.04 S 142.46 E
Stawiski 10 Sc 53.23N 22.09 E
Stawiszyn 10 Oe 51.55N 18.07 E
Stayton 46 Dd 44.48N 122.48W
Steamboat Springs 43 Fc 40.29N 106.50W
Stebnik 10 Tg 49.14N 23.34 E
Stedingen 12 Ka 53.10N 8.30 E
Steele 45 Gc 46.51N 99.55W
Steelpoort 37 Ed 24.48 S 30.12 E
Steenbergen 12 Gc 51.35N 4.19 E
Steen River 42 Fe 59.38N 117.06W
Steensby Inlet 42 Jb 70.10N 78.25W
Steenstrups Gletscher 41 Gc 75.15N 57.30W
Steenvoorde 12 Ed 50.48N 2.35 E
Steenwijk 11 Mb 52.47N 6.08 E
Ştefăneşti 15 Kb 47.48N 27.12 E
Stefanie, Lake- (EN)=Chew Bahir 30 Kh 4.38N 36.50 E
Stefansson 42 Gb 73.30N 105.30W
Ştefleşti, Vîrful- 15 Gd 45.32N 23.48 E
Stege 8 Ej 54.59N 12.18 E
Steiermark=Styria (EN) 14 Ic 47.15N 15.00 E
Steiermark=Styria (EN) [2] 14 Ic 47.15N 15.00 E
Steigerwald 10 Gg 49.40N 10.20 E
Steilrandberge 37 Ac 17.53 S 13.20 E
Steinach 14 Fc 47.05N 11.28 E
Steinbach 42 Hg 49.32N 96.41W
Steinen, Rio- 54 Hf 12.05 S 53.46W
Steinfeld (Oldenburg) 12 Kb 52.36N 8.13 E
Steinfort/Steinfurt 12 He 49.40N 5.55 E
Steinfurt 10 Dd 52.09N 7.20 E
Steinfurt/Steinfort 12 He 49.40N 5.55 E
Steinfurt-Borghorst 12 Jb 52.08N 7.25 E
Steinhagen 12 Kb 52.01N 8.24 E
Steinhausen 37 Bd 21.49 S 18.20 E
Steinheim 12 Lc 51.51N 9.06 E
Steinhuder Meer 10 Fd 52.28N 9.19 E
Steinkjer 7 Cd 64.01N 11.30 E
Steinkopf 37 Be 29.18 S 17.43 E
Steinshamn 8 Bb 62.47N 6.29 E
Steinsøy 7 Ac 61.00N 4.30 E
Steirisch-Niederösterreichische Kalkalpen 14 Jc 47.45N 15.30 E
Stekene 12 Gc 51.12N 4.02 E
Stekolny 20 Ke 60.00N 150.50 E
Stella 37 Ce 26.33 S 24.53 E
Stellenbosch 37 Bf 33.58 S 18.50 E
Stello 11a Ba 42.47N 9.25 E
Stelvio, Passo dello-/Stilfser Joch 14 Ed 46.32N 10.27 E
Stemwede 12 Kb 52.26N 8.26 E
Stenay 11 Le 49.29N 5.11 E
Stendal 10 Hd 52.36N 11.51 E
Stende 8 Jg 57.10N 22.28 E
Stende 8 Ig 57.40N 21.57 E
Stenhouse Bay 59 Hg 35.17 S 136.56 E
Stenstorp 8 Ef 58.16N 13.43 E
Stenungsund 7 Cg 58.05N 11.49 E
Stepanakert 6 Kh 39.49N 46.44 E
Stepanavan 16 Ni 40.59N 44.20 E
Stephens, Cape- 62 Ed 40.42 S 173.57 E
Stephens, Mount- 66 Rg 83.23 S 51.27W
Stephens Passage 40 Me 57.50N 133.50W
Stephenville [Newf.-Can.] 42 Lg 48.33N 58.35W
Stephenville [Tx.-U.S.] 45 Gj 32.13N 98.12W
Steps Point 65c Cb 14.22 S 170.45W
Sterea Ellás kai Évvoia [2] 15 Hk 38.20N 24.30 E
Sterkstroom 37 Df 31.32 S 26.32 E
Sterlibaševo 17 Gj 53.28N 55.15 E
Sterling [Co.-U.S.] 43 Gc 40.37N 103.13W
Sterling [Il.-U.S.] 45 Lf 41.48N 89.42W
Sterling City 45 Fk 31.50N 100.59W
Sterlitamak 6 Le 53.37N 55.58 E
Šternberk 10 Ng 49.44N 17.19 E
Sterzing/Vipiteno 14 Fd 46.54N 11.26 E
Stettin (EN)=Szczecin 6 He 53.24N 14.32 E
Stettiner Haff 10 Kc 53.46N 14.14 E
Stettler 42 Gf 52.19N 112.43W
Steubenville 43 Kc 40.22N 80.39W
Stevenage 9 Mj 51.54N 0.11W
Stevenson Entrance 40 Ie 57.45N 152.20W
Stevens Point 43 Jc 44.31N 89.34W
Stewart 42 Dd 63.18N 139.24W
Stewart 42 Ee 55.56N 129.59W
Stewart Crossing 42 Dd 63.19N 136.33W
Stewart Island 57 Hi 47.00 S 167.50 E
Stewart Islands 57 He 8.20 S 162.40 E
Steyerberg 12 Lb 52.34N 9.02 E
Steyning 12 Bd 50.53N 0.20W
Steynsburg 37 Df 31.15 S 25.49 E
Steyr 14 Ib 48.02N 14.25 E
Steyr 14 Ib 48.03N 14.25 E
Štiavnické vrchy 10 Oh 48.15N 18.50 E
Stidia 13 Li 35.50N 0.05W
Stiene 8 Kg 57.19N 24.28 E
Stiens, Leeuwarderadeel- 12 Ha 53.16N 5.46 E
Stigliano 14 Kj 40.24N 16.14 E
St. Ignace 43 Kb 45.52N 84.43W
Stigtomta 8 Gf 58.48N 16.47 E
Stikine 38 Fd 56.40N 132.30W
Stikine Ranges 42 Ee 57.35N 131.00W
Stilfer Joch/Stelvio, Passo dello- 14 Ed 46.32N 10.27 E
Stilfontein 37 De 26.50 S 26.50 E
Stilis 15 Fk 38.55N 22.37 E
Stillwater [Mn.-U.S.] 45 Jd 45.04N 92.49W
Stillwater [Ok.-U.S.] 43 Hd 36.07N 97.04W
Stillwater Range 46 Fg 39.50N 118.15W
Stilo 14 Kl 38.29N 16.28 E
Stilo, Punta- 14 Kl 38.27N 16.35 E
Štimlje 15 Eg 42.26N 21.03 E
Stînişoarei, Munţii- 15 Ib 47.20N 26.00 E
Stinnett 45 Fi 35.50N 101.27W
Štip 15 Fh 41.44N 22.12 E
Stirling 9 Je 56.07N 3.57W
Stirling Range 59 Df 34.25 S 117.50 E
Stjernøya 7 Fa 70.18N 22.45 E
Stjørdalshalsen 7 Ce 63.28N 10.44 E
Stobi 15 Eh 41.33N 21.59 E
Stobrawa 10 Nf 50.50N 17.32 E
Stocka 8 Gc 61.54N 17.20 E
Stockach 10 Fi 47.51N 9.01 E
Stockbridge 12 Ac 51.06N 1.29W
Stockerau 14 Kb 48.23N 16.13 E
Stockholm [2] 7 Dg 59.20N 18.00 E
Stockholm 6 Hd 59.20N 18.03 E
Stockport 9 Kh 53.25N 2.10W
Stocks Seamount (EN) 52 Mg 12.15 S 32.00W
Stockton [Ca.-U.S.] 43 Cd 37.57N 121.17W
Stockton [Mo.-U.S.] 45 Jh 37.42N 93.48W
Stockton Lake 45 Jh 37.40N 93.45W
Stockton-on-Tees 9 Lg 54.34N 1.19W
Stockton Plateau 43 Ge 30.30N 102.30W
Stoczek Łukowski 10 Re 51.58N 21.58 E
Stöde 7 De 62.25N 16.35 E
Stoĕng Trĕng 25 Lf 13.31N 105.58 E
Stoer, Point of- 9 Hc 58.20N 5.25W
Stogovo 15 Dh 41.29N 20.39 E
Stohod 10 Ve 51.52N 25.44 E
Stoholm 8 Ch 56.29N 9.10 E
Stoj, Gora- 16 Ce 48.39N 23.15 E
Stojba 22 Pd 52.49N 131.43 E
Stoke-on-Trent 9 Kh 53.00N 2.10W
Stokksnes 7a Cb 64.14N 14.58W
Stokmarknes 7 Db 68.34N 14.55 E
Stol 15 Fe 44.11N 22.09 E
Stolac 14 Lg 43.05N 17.58 E
Stolbcy 16 Ec 53.31N 26.43 E
Stolberg 10 Cf 50.46N 6.14 E
Stolbovoj, Ostrov- 20 Ib 74.05N 136.00 E
Stolin 16 Ed 51.57N 26.52 E
Stolzenau 12 Lb 52.31N 9.04 E
Ston 14 Lh 42.50N 17.42 E
Stone 9 Ki 52.54N 2.10W
Stonehaven 9 Ke 56.58N 2.13W
Stonehenge 9 Lj 51.11N 1.49W
Stonehenge 59 Id 24.22 S 143.17 E
Stoner 45 Bh 37.37N 108.18W
Stonewall 45 Ha 50.09N 97.21W
Stony 40 Hd 61.45N 156.35W
Stony Rapids 42 Ge 59.16N 105.50W
Stony River 40 Hd 61.47N 156.41W
Stony Stratford 12 Bb 52.03N 0.51W
Stony Tunguska (EN)=Podkamennaja Tunguska 21 Lc 61.36N 90.18 E
Stör 10 Fc 53.50N 9.25 E
Storå 8 Ch 56.19N 8.19 E
Storå 8 Fe 59.43N 15.08 E
Storå/Isojoki 7 Ee 62.07N 21.58 E
Stora Gla 8 Ee 59.30N 12.30 E
Stora Le 8 De 59.05N 11.55 E
Stora Lulevatten 7 Ec 67.10N 19.20 E
Storavan 7 Ed 65.42N 18.12 E
Storby 8 Hd 60.13N 19.34 E
Stord 7 Ag 59.55N 5.25 E
Storöa 7 Ee 62.07N 21.58 E
Stordal 8 Bb 62.23N 7.01 E

Index Symbols

[1] Independent Nation
[2] State, Region
[3] District, County
[4] Municipality
[5] Colony, Dependency
Continent
Physical Region
Historical or Cultural Region
Mount, Mountain
Volcano
Hill
Mountains, Mountain Range
Hills, Escarpment
Plateau, Upland
Pass, Gap
Plain, Lowland
Delta
Salt Flat
Valley, Canyon
Crater, Cave
Karst Features
Depression
Polder
Desert, Dunes
Forest, Woods
Heath, Steppe
Oasis
Cape, Point
Coast, Beach
Cliff
Peninsula
Isthmus
Sandbank
Island
Atoll
Rock, Reef
Islands, Archipelago
Rocks, Reefs
Coral Reef
Well, Spring
Geyser
River, Stream
Waterfall Rapids
River Mouth, Estuary
Lake
Salt Lake
Intermittent Lake
Reservoir
Swamp, Pond
Canal
Glacier
Ice Shelf, Pack Ice
Ocean
Sea
Gulf, Bay
Strait, Fjord
Lagoon
Bank
Seamount
Tablemount
Ridge
Shelf
Basin
Escarpment, Sea Scarp
Fracture
Trench, Abyss
National Park, Reserve
Point of Interest
Recreation Site
Cave, Cavern
Historic Site
Ruins
Wall, Walls
Church, Abbey
Temple
Scientific Station
Airport
Port
Lighthouse
Mine
Tunnel
Dam, Bridge

Index Symbols

[1] Independent Nation
[2] State, Region
[3] District, County
[4] Municipality
[5] Colony, Dependency
Continent
Physical Region
Historical or Cultural Region
Mount, Mountain
Volcano
Hill
Mountains, Mountain Range
Hills, Escarpment
Plateau, Upland
Pass, Gap
Plain, Lowland
Delta
Salt Flat
Valley, Canyon
Crater, Cave
Karst Features
Depression
Polder
Desert, Dunes
Forest, Woods
Heath, Steppe
Oasis
Cape, Point
Coast, Beach
Cliff
Peninsula
Isthmus
Sandbank
Island
Atoll
Rock, Reef
Islands, Archipelago
Rocks, Reefs
Coral Reef
Well, Spring
Geyser
River, Stream
Waterfall Rapids
River Mouth, Estuary
Lake
Salt Lake
Intermittent Lake
Reservoir
Swamp, Pond
Canal
Glacier
Ice Shelf, Pack Ice
Ocean
Sea
Gulf, Bay
Strait, Fjord
Lagoon
Bank
Seamount
Tablemount
Ridge
Shelf
Basin
Escarpment, Sea Scarp
Fracture
Trench, Abyss
National Park, Reserve
Point of Interest
Recreation Site
Cave, Cavern
Historic Site
Ruins
Wall, Walls
Church, Abbey
Temple
Scientific Station
Airport
Port
Lighthouse
Mine
Tunnel
Dam, Bridge

T

Index Symbols

[1] Independent Nation
[2] State, Region
[3] District, County
[4] Municipality
[5] Colony, Dependency
Continent
Physical Region
Historical or Cultural Region
Mount, Mountain
Volcano
Hill
Mountains, Mountain Range
Hills, Escarpment
Plateau, Upland
Pass, Gap
Plain, Lowland
Delta
Salt Flat
Valley, Canyon
Crater, Cave
Karst Features
Depression
Polder
Desert, Dunes
Forest, Woods
Heath, Steppe
Oasis
Cape, Point
Coast, Beach
Cliff
Peninsula
Isthmus
Sandbank
Island
Atoll
Rock, Reef
Islands, Archipelago
Rocks, Reefs
Coral Reef
Well, Spring
Geyser
River, Stream
Waterfall Rapids
River Mouth, Estuary
Lake
Salt Lake
Intermittent Lake
Reservoir
Swamp, Pond
Canal
Glacier
Ice Shelf, Pack Ice
Ocean
Sea
Gulf, Bay
Strait, Fjord
Lagoon
Bank
Seamount
Tablemount
Ridge
Shelf
Basin
Escarpment, Sea Scarp
Fracture
Trench, Abyss
National Park, Reserve
Point of Interest
Recreation Site
Cave, Cavern
Historic Site
Ruins
Wall, Walls
Church, Abbey
Temple
Scientific Station
Airport
Port
Lighthouse
Mine
Tunnel
Dam, Bridge

Name	Page	Grid	Lat.	Long.
Tahat	30	Hf	23.18N	5.32 E
Tahe	27	La	52.22N	124.48 E
Ţāherī	24	Oi	27.42N	52.21 E
Tahgong, Puntan-	64b	Ba	15.06N	145.39 E
Tahiataš	18	Bc	42.20N	59.33 E
Tahifet	32	Ie	22.56N	5.59 E
Tahir Geçidi	24	Jc	39.52N	42.20 E
Tahiti, Ile-	57	Mf	17.37 S	149.27W
Tahkuna Neem/Takuna, Mys-	8	Je	59.05N	22.30 E
Tahlequah	45	Ii	35.55N	94.58W
Tahoe, Lake-	46	Fg	38.54N	120.00W
Tahoua [2]	34	Gb	16.00N	5.30 E
Tahoua	31	Hg	14.54N	5.16 E
Ţahţā	33	Fd	26.46N	31.28 E
Tahta-Bazar	18	Dg	35.55N	62.55 E
Tahtabrod	19	Ge	52.40N	67.35 E
Tahtakarača Pereval	18	Fe	39.17N	66.55 E
Tahtaköprü	15	Mj	39.57N	29.39 E
Tahtakupyr	19	Gg	43.01N	60.22 E
Tahtali Dağları	24	Gc	38.46N	36.47 E
Tahtamygda	20	Hf	54.09N	123.38 E
Tahuata, Ile-	57	Ne	9.57 S	139.05W
Tahulandang, Pulau-	26	If	2.20N	125.25 E
Tahuna	26	If	3.37N	125.29 E
Taï	34	Dd	5.52N	7.27W
Tai'an [China]	28	Gd	41.24N	122.27 E
Tai'an [China]	27	Kd	36.09N	117.05 E
Taiarapu, Presqu'île de-	65e	Fc	17.47 S	149.14W
Taibai Shan	27	Ie	33.57N	107.40 E
Taibilla, Canal del-	13	Kg	37.43N	1.22W
Taibilla, Sierra de-	13	Jf	38.10N	2.10W
Taibus Qi (Baochang)	27	Kc	41.55N	115.22 E
Taicang	28	Fi	31.26N	121.06 E
Taichung	22	Og	24.09N	120.41 E
Taieri	62	Dg	46.03 S	170.12 E
Taiga	20	De	56.04N	85.37 E
Taigonos Peninsula (EN)= Tajgonos, Poluostrov-	20	Ld	61.35N	161.00 E
Taigu	28	Bf	37.26N	112.33 E
Taihang Shan	21	Nf	37.00N	114.00 E
Taihape	62	Fc	39.41 S	175.48 E
Taihe [China]	28	Ch	33.11N	115.38 E
Taihe [China]	27	Jf	26.50N	114.52 E
Taiheiyō=Pacific Ocean (EN)	3	Ki	5.00N	155.00W
Tai Hu	21	Of	31.15N	120.10 E
Taihu	27	Ke	30.26N	116.10 E
Taikang	27	Je	34.00N	114.56 E
Taiki	29a	Cb	42.30N	143.16 E
Tailai	27	Lb	46.24N	123.26 E
Tailles, Plateau des-	12	Hd	50.15N	5.45 E
Taim	55	Fk	32.30 S	52.35W
Tain	9	Id	57.48N	4.04W
Tainan	22	Og	23.00N	120.11 E
Taínaron, Ákra-=Matapan, Cape- (EN)	5	Ih	36.23N	22.29 E
Taiof	63a	Ba	5.31 S	154.39 E
Taipei	22	Og	25.03N	121.30 E
Taiping	26	Df	4.51N	100.44 E
Taiping (Gantang)	28	Ei	30.18N	118.07 E
Taipingchuan	28	Gb	44.24N	123.11 E
Taiping Dao	27	Jd	10.15N	113.42 E
Taiping Ling	27	Lb	47.36N	120.12 E
Tairadate	29a	Bc	41.09N	140.38 E
Tairadate-Kaikyō	29a	Bc	41.10N	140.40 E
Taisei	29a	Ab	42.14N	139.49 E
Taisetsu-Zan	21	Qe	43.40N	142.48 E
Taisha	29	Cd	35.24N	132.40 E
Taishaku-San	29	Fc	36.58N	139.28 E
Tai Shan	21	Nf	36.30N	117.20 E
Taishō	29	Ce	33.12N	132.57 E
Taitao Peninsula (EN) = Taitao, Península de-	52	Ij	46.30 S	74.25W
Taitung	27	Lg	22.45N	121.09 E
Taiwa	29	Gb	38.26N	140.52 E
Taiwan [1]	22	Og	23.30N	121.00 E
Taiwan Haixia = Taiwan Strait (EN)	21	Ng	24.00N	119.00 E
Taixian	28	Fh	32.31N	120.08 E
Taixing	28	Fh	32.10N	120.00 E
Taiyang Shan	27	Ie	33.37N	106.26 E
Taïyetos Óros-	15	Fl	37.06N	22.18 E
Taiyuan	22	Nf	37.50N	112.37 E
Taiyue Shan	28	Bf	36.48N	112.00 E
Taizhou	28	Eh	32.29N	119.55 E
Taizhou → Linhai	27	Lf	28.52N	121.08 E
Taizhou Wan	28	Fj	28.40N	121.37 E
Taizi He	28	Gd	41.00N	122.23 E
Ta'izz	22	Gh	13.38N	44.02 E
Tājābād	24	Pg	30.02N	54.24 E
Tajarḩī	33	Be	24.21N	14.28 E
Tajgonos, Mys-	20	Ld	60.35N	160.10 E
Tajgonos, Poluostrov-= Taigonos Peninsula (EN)	20	Ld	61.35N	161.00 E
Tajik SSR (EN) = Tadžikskaja SSR	19	Hh	39.00N	71.00 E
Tajima	28	Of	37.12N	139.46 E
Tajimi	29	Ed	35.19N	137.08 E
Tājirwīn	14	Co	35.54N	8.33 E
Tajito	48	Cb	30.58N	112.18W
Tajmba	20	Ed	60.22N	98.50 E
Tajmyr	20	Ea	76.05N	98.55 E
Tajmyr, Ozero-	21	Mb	74.30N	102.30 E
Tajmyr, Poluostrov-= Taymyr Peninsula (EN)	21	Mb	76.00N	104.00 E
Tajmyra	21	Lb	76.00N	99.40 E
Tajmyrlur	20	Hb	72.30N	121.39 E
Tajmyrski (Dolgano-Nenecki) Nacionalny okrug [3]	20	Eb	72.00N	95.00 E
Tajo=Tagus (EN)	5	Fh	38.40N	9.24W
Tajo-Segura, Canal de Trasvase-	13	Je	39.30N	2.05W
Tajrīsh	23	Hb	38.48N	51.25 E
Tajšet	22	Ld	55.57N	98.00 E
Tajumulco, Volcán-	38	Jh	15.02N	91.54W
Tajuña	13	Id	40.07N	3.35W
Tak	25	Je	16.52N	99.08 E
Taka Atoll	3	Ii	4.00N	146.45 E
Takāb	24	Ld	36.24N	47.07 E
Takaba	36	Hb	3.27N	40.14 E
Takahagi	28	Pf	36.42N	140.41 E
Takahama	29	Dd	35.29N	135.33 E
Takahara-Gawa	29	Ec	36.27N	137.15 E
Takaharu	29	Bf	31.55N	130.59 E
Takahashi	28	Lg	34.47N	133.37 E
Takahashi-Gawa	29	Cd	34.32N	133.42 E
Takahata	29	Gc	38.00N	140.12 E
Takahe, Mount-	66	Of	76.17 S	112.05W
Takaka	62	Ed	40.51 S	172.48 E
Takakuma-Yama	29	Bf	31.28N	130.49 E
Takalar	26	Gh	5.28 S	119.24 E
Takalous	32	Ie	23.25N	7.02 E
Takamatsu	27	Ne	34.21N	134.03 E
Takamori	29	Be	32.48N	131.08 E
Takanabe	29	Be	32.08N	131.31 E
Takanawa-Hantō	29	Ce	34.00N	132.55 E
Takanawa-San	29	Ce	33.57N	132.50 E
Takanosu	29	Ga	40.14N	140.22 E
Takaoka [Jap.]	28	Nf	36.45N	137.01 E
Takaoka [Jap.]	29	Bf	31.57N	131.17 E
Takapoto Atoll	61	Lb	15.00 S	148.10W
Takapuna	62	Fb	36.48 S	174.47 E
Takara-Jima	27	Mf	29.10N	129.05 E
Takarazuka	29	Dd	34.49N	135.21 E
Takaroa Atoll	61	Mb	14.28 S	144.58W
Takasaki	28	Of	36.20N	139.01 E
Taka-Shima [Jap.]	29	Be	32.40N	131.50 E
Taka-Shima [Jap.]	29	Af	31.26N	129.45 E
Takatshwane	37	Cd	22.36 S	21.55 E
Takatsu-Gawa	29	Bd	34.42N	131.49 E
Takatsuki	28	Mg	34.51N	135.37 E
Takayama	28	Nf	36.08N	137.15 E
Takebe	29	Cd	34.53N	133.54 E
Takefu	28	Ng	35.54N	136.10 E
Takehara	29	Cd	34.21N	132.54 E
Takeo	29	Ae	33.12N	130.00 E
Tåkern	8	Ff	58.20N	14.50 E
Take-Shima	28	Kf	37.22N	131.58 E
Tākestān	23	Gb	36.05N	49.14 E
Taketa	29	Be	32.58N	131.24 E
Takêv	25	Kf	10.59N	104.47 E
Takhādīd	24	Kh	29.59N	44.30 E
Takhār [3]	23	Kb	36.30N	69.30 E
Takhmaret	13	Mi	35.06N	0.41 E
Takht-e Soleimān	24	Nd	36.20N	51.00 E
Taki [Jap.]	29	Cd	35.16N	132.38 E
Taki [Pap.N.Gui.]	63a	Bb	6.29 S	155.50 E
Takijuq Lake	42	Gc	66.05N	113.00W
Takikawa	28	Pc	43.33N	141.54 E
Takingeun	26	Cf	4.38N	96.50 E
Takinoue	29a	Ca	44.13N	143.03 E
Takko	29	Ga	40.20N	141.09 E
Takla Lake	42	Ee	55.30N	126.00W
Takla Landing	42	Ee	55.29N	125.58W
Takla Makan (EN)= Taklimakan Shamo	21	Kf	39.00N	83.00 E
Taklimakan Shamo=Takla Makan (EN)	21	Kf	39.00N	83.00 E
Takob	18	Ge	38.51N	69.00 E
Tako-Bana	29	Cd	35.35N	133.05 E
Takolokouzet, Massif de-	34	Gb	18.40N	9.30 E
Taku	29	Be	33.19N	130.06 E
Takuan, Mount-	63a	Bb	6.27 S	155.36 E
Takua Pa	25	Jg	8.52N	98.21 E
Takum	34	Gd	7.16N	9.59 E
Takuma	29	Cd	34.14N	133.40 E
Takume Atoll	57	Mf	15.49 S	142.12W
Takuna, Mys-/Tahkuna Neem	8	Je	59.05N	22.30 E
Takutea Island	57	Lf	19.49 S	158.18W
Tala	48	Hg	20.40N	103.42W
Tālah	32	Ib	35.35N	8.40 E
Talaimmannar	25	Fg	9.05N	79.44 E
Talāīyeh	24	Kd	37.50N	45.00 E
Talaja	20	Kd	61.03N	152.30 E
Talak	30	Hg	18.20N	6.00 E
Talamanca, Cordillera de-	49	Fi	9.30N	83.40W
Talara	53	Hf	4.35 S	81.25W
Talas	19	Hg	42.29N	72.14 E
Talas	18	Ic	44.05N	70.20 E
Talasea	59	Ka	5.20 S	150.05 E
Talasski Alatau, Hrebet-	18	Hc	42.10N	72.00 E
Talata Mafara	34	Gc	12.34N	6.04 E
Talaud, Kepulauan-=Talaud Islands (EN)	21	Oi	4.20N	126.50 E
Talaud Islands (EN)= Talaud, Kepulauan-	21	Oi	4.20N	126.50 E
Talavera, Isla-	55	Dh	27.32 S	56.26W
Talavera de la Reina	13	He	39.57N	4.50W
Talawdī	35	Ec	10.38N	30.23 E
Talbot Inlet	42	Ja	77.55N	77.35W
Talca	53	Ii	35.26 S	71.40W
Talcahuano	53	Ii	36.43 S	73.07W
Tālcher	25	Hd	20.57N	85.13 E
Taldom	7	Ih	56.45N	37.32 E
Taldy-Kurgan	22	Je	44.59N	78.23 E
Taldy-Kurganskaja Oblast [3]	19	Hf	44.00N	78.00 E
Talēḩ	35	Hd	9.09N	48.26 E
Tal-e Khosravī	24	Ng	30.47N	51.29 E
Talence	11	Fj	44.49N	0.36W
Ţalesh, Kūhhā-Ye-	24	Md	37.35N	48.38 E
Talgar	19	Hg	43.18N	77.13 E
Taliabu, Pulau-	26	Hg	1.48 S	124.48 E
Talica	19	Gd	57.01N	63.43 E
Talimardžan	19	Gh	38.21N	65.31 E
Tali Post	35	Ed	5.54N	30.47 E
Talisajan	22	Ni	1.37N	118.11 E
Taliwang	26	Gh	8.44 S	116.52 E
Talkeetna	40	Id	62.20N	150.07W
Talkeetna Mountains	40	Jd	62.10N	148.15W
Talkheh	24	Kd	37.40N	45.46 E
Talladega	44	Di	33.26N	86.06W
Tall 'Afar	23	Fb	36.22N	42.27 E
Tallah	24	Dh	28.05N	30.44 E
Tallahassee	39	Kf	30.25N	84.16W
Tallahatchie River	45	Kj	33.33N	90.10W
Tall al Abyaḑ	24	Hd	36.41N	38.57 E
Tallapoosa River	44	Di	32.30N	86.16W
Tallard	11	Mj	44.28N	6.03 E
Tällberg	8	Fd	60.49N	15.00 E
Tall Birāk at Taḩtānī	24	Id	36.38N	41.05 E
Tallinn	6	Id	59.25N	24.45 E
Tall Kayf	24	Jd	36.29N	43.08 E
Tall Kūshik	24	Jd	36.48N	42.04 E
Tallulah	45	Kj	32.25N	91.11W
Tălmaciu	15	Hd	45.39N	24.16 E
Talmenka	20	Df	53.51N	83.45 E
Talmest	32	Fc	31.09N	9.00W
Talnah	20	Dc	69.30N	88.15 E
Talnoje	16	Ge	48.53N	30.42 E
Talo	30	Kg	10.44N	37.55 E
Talofofo	64c	Bb	13.20N	144.46 E
Talon	20	Je	59.48N	148.50 E
Tāloqān	23	Kb	36.44N	69.33 E
Talovaja	16	Ld	51.06N	40.48 E
Talpa de Allende	48	Gg	20.23N	104.51W
Talsi	7	Fh	57.17N	22.37 E
Taltal	53	Ih	25.24 S	70.29W
Taltson	42	Gd	61.24N	112.45W
Taluk	26	Dg	0.32 S	101.35 E
Talvik	7	Fa	70.03N	22.58 E
Talwār	24	Md	36.00N	48.00 E
Tama	35	Cc	14.45N	22.25 E
Tamaghzah	32	Ic	34.23N	7.57 E
Tamala	16	Mc	52.33N	43.18 E
Tamalameque	49	Ki	8.52N	73.38W
Tamale	31	Gh	9.24N	0.50W
Tamames	13	Fd	40.39N	6.06W
Tamana	29	Be	32.55N	130.33 E
Tamanaco, Río-	50	Dh	9.25N	65.23W
Tamana Island	57	Ie	2.29 S	175.59 E
Tamano	28	Lg	34.30N	133.56 E
Tamanoura	29	Ae	32.38N	128.37 E
Tamanrasset	30	Hf	22.03N	0.10 E
Tamanrasset	31	Hf	22.47N	5.31 E
Tamanrasset [3]	32	Ie	23.00N	5.30 E
Tamar	9	Ik	50.22N	4.10W
Tamara	15	Cg	42.27N	19.33 E
Támara	54	Db	5.50N	72.10W
Tamarit de Llitera/Tamarite de Litera	13	Mc	41.52N	0.26 E
Tamarite de Litera/Tamarit de Llitera	13	Mc	41.52N	0.26 E
Tamarro	14	Ii	41.09N	14.50 E
Tamarugal, Pampa del-	56	Gb	21.00 S	69.25W
Tamási	10	Oj	46.38N	18.17 E
Tamassoumit	32	Ef	18.35N	12.39W
Tamaulipas [2]	47	Ed	24.00N	98.45W
Tamaulipas, Llanos de-	47	Ed	25.00N	98.25W
Tamaulipas, Sierra de-	48	Jf	23.30N	98.30W
Tamayama	29	Gb	39.50N	141.11 E
Tamazula de Gordiano	48	Hh	19.38N	103.15W
Tamazunchale	47	Ed	21.16N	98.47W
Tambach	36	Gb	0.36N	35.31 E
Tambacounda	31	Fg	13.12N	15.48W
Tambara	37	Ec	16.44 S	34.15 E
Tambelan, Kepulauan-= Tambelan Islands (EN)	26	Ef	1.00N	107.30 E
Tambelan, Pulau-	26	Ef	0.58N	107.34 E
Tambelan Islands (EN)= Tambelan, Kepulauan-	26	Ef	1.00N	107.30 E
Tambo	59	Jd	24.53 S	146.15 E
Tambohorano	37	Gc	17.29 S	43.58 E
Tambora, Gunung-	26	Gh	8.14 S	117.55 E
Tambores	55	Dj	31.52 S	56.16W
Tambov	6	Ke	52.43N	41.27 E
Tambovskaja Oblast [3]	19	Ee	52.45N	41.40 E
Tambre	13	Db	42.49N	8.53W
Tambunan	26	Ge	5.40N	116.22 E
Tambura	31	Jh	5.36N	27.28 E
Tamchaket	32	Ef	17.20N	10.40W
Tame	54	Db	6.27N	71.45W
Tâmega	13	Dc	41.05N	8.21W
Támega	13	Dc	41.05N	8.21W
Tamel Aike	56	Fg	48.19 S	70.58W
Tamesi	47	Ed	22.13N	97.52W
Tamesnar	30	Hg	18.25N	3.33 E
Tamgak, Monts-	30	Hg	19.11N	8.42 E
Tamgue, Massif du-	30	Fg	12.00N	12.18W
Tamiahua	48	Kg	21.16N	97.27W
Tamiahua, Laguna de-	47	Ed	21.35N	97.35W
Tamianglajang	26	Gg	2.07 S	115.10 E
Tamil Nādu [3]	25	Ff	11.00N	78.00 E
Tamiš	15	De	44.51N	20.39 E
Tamise/Temse	12	Gc	51.08N	4.13 E
Tamitatoala, Rio-	54	Hf	11.56 S	53.36W
Ţāmiyah	24	Dh	29.29N	30.58 E
Tam Ky	25	Le	15.34N	108.29 E
Tammela	8	Jd	60.48N	23.46 E
Tammerfors/Tampere	6	Ic	61.30N	23.45 E
Tammisaari/Ekenäs	7	Fg	59.58N	23.26 E
Tämnaren	8	Gd	60.10N	17.20 E
Tamnava	15	De	44.25N	20.05 E
Tamou	34	Fc	12.45N	2.11 E
Tampa	39	Kg	27.57N	82.27W
Tampa Bay	43	Kf	27.45N	82.35W
Tampake-Misaki	29a	Bb	43.43N	141.20 E
Tampere/Tammerfors	6	Ic	61.30N	23.45 E
Tampico	39	Jg	22.13N	97.51W
Tampin	26	Df	2.28N	102.14 E
Tamri	32	Fc	30.43N	9.50 E
Tamsag-Bulak	27	Kb	47.14N	117.21 E
Tamsalu	7	Gg	59.10N	26.07 E
Tamsweg	14	Hc	47.08N	13.48 E
Tamu	25	Id	24.13N	94.19 E
Tamuin	48	Jg	21.59N	98.45W
Tamuín	47	Ed	22.00N	98.44W
Tamuín, Río-	48	Jg	21.47N	98.28W
Tamworth [Austl.]	58	Gh	31.05 S	150.55 E
Tamworth [Eng.-U.K.]	9	Li	52.39N	1.40W
Tamyang	28	Ig	35.19N	126.59 E
Tana [Eur.]	5	Ia	70.28N	28.18 E
Tana [Kenya]	30	Li	2.32 S	40.31 E
Tana, Lake-	30	Kg	12.00N	37.20 E
Tanabe	28	Mh	33.42N	135.44 E
Tana bru	7	Ga	70.16N	28.10 E
Tanacross	40	Kd	63.23N	143.21W
Tanafjorden	7	Ga	70.54N	28.40 E
Tanaga	40a	Cb	51.50N	178.00W
Tanagro	14	Jj	40.38N	15.14 E
Tanagura	29	Gc	37.02N	140.23 E
Tanahbala, Pulau-	26	Cg	0.25 S	98.25 E
Tanahgrogot	26	Gg	1.55 S	116.12 E
Tanahjampea, Pulau-	26	Hh	7.05 S	120.42 E
Tanahmasa, Pulau-	26	Cg	0.12 S	98.27 E
Tanah Merah	26	De	5.48N	102.09 E
Tanahmerah	26	Lh	6.05 S	140.17 E
Tanakpur	25	Gc	29.05N	80.07 E
Tanalyk	17	Ij	51.46N	58.45 E
Tanami	59	Fc	19.59 S	129.43 E
Tanami Desert	57	Eg	20.00 S	132.00 E
Tan An	25	Lf	10.32N	106.25 E
Tanana	40	Ic	65.10N	152.05W
Tanana	38	Dc	65.09N	151.55W
Tanapag	64b	Ba	15.14N	145.45 E
Tanapag, Puetton-	64b	Ba	15.14N	145.44 E
Tanāqīb, Ra's at-	24	Mi	27.50N	48.53 E
Tanaro	14	Ce	45.01N	8.47 E
Tanba-Sanchi	29	Dd	35.15N	135.35 E
Tancheng	28	Eg	34.37N	118.20 E
Tanch'ŏn	27	Mc	40.25N	128.57 E
Tancitaro, Pico de-	47	De	19.26N	102.18W
Tanda	34	Ed	7.48N	3.10W
Tanda, Lac-	34	Eb	15.45N	4.42W
Tandag	26	Ie	9.04N	126.12 E
Tandaltī	35	Ec	13.01N	31.52 E
Tăndărei	15	Ke	44.39N	27.40 E
Tandijungbalai	26	Cf	2.58N	99.48 E
Tandil	53	Ki	37.20 S	59.05W
Tandil, Sierras del-	55	Cm	37.24 S	59.06W
Tandjilé [3]	35	Bd	9.30N	16.30 E
Tando Ādam	25	Dc	25.46N	68.40 E
Tandsjöborg	7	Df	61.42N	14.43 E
Tanḑubāyah	35	Db	18.40N	28.37 E
Taneatua	62	Gc	38.04 S	177.00 E
Tane-Ga-Shima	27	Ne	30.40N	131.00 E
Taneichi	29	Ga	40.24N	141.43 E
Tan Emellel	32	Id	27.28N	9.45 E
Tanew	10	Sf	50.27N	22.16 E
Tanezrouft	30	Gf	24.00N	0.45W
Tanezzuft	33	Bd	25.51N	10.19 E
Tanf, Jabal at-	24	Hf	33.30N	38.42 E
Tanga [3]	36	Gd	5.30 S	38.00 E
Tanga	31	Ki	5.04 S	39.06 E
Tangail	25	Hd	24.15N	89.55 E
Tanga Islands	57	Ge	3.30 S	153.15 E
Tangalla	25	Gg	6.01N	80.48 E
Tanganyika [2]	36	Fd	6.00 S	35.00 E
Tanganyika, Lac-= Tanganyika, Lake- (EN)	30	Ji	6.00 S	29.30 E
Tanganyika, Lake-	30	Ji	6.00 S	29.30 E
Tanganyika, Lake- (EN)= Tanganyika, Lac-	30	Ji	6.00 S	29.30 E
Tangará	54	Ke	6.11 S	35.49W
Tangarare	63a	Dc	9.35 S	159.39 E
Tangdan → Dongchuan	27	Hf	26.07N	103.05 E
Tāngehgol	24	Pd	37.25N	55.50 E
Tanger=Tangier (EN) [3]	32	Fb	35.45N	5.45W
Tanger=Tangier (EN)	31	Ge	35.48N	5.48W
Tangerang	26	Eh	6.11 S	106.37 E
Tangermünde	10	Hd	52.33N	11.57 E
Tanggu	27	Kd	39.00N	117.36 E
Tanggula Shan (Dangla Shan)	21	Lf	33.00N	92.00 E
Tanggula Shankou	27	Fe	32.42N	92.27 E
Tanggulashanqu/Tuotuohe	22	Lf	34.15N	92.29 E
Tang He	28	Bh	32.10N	112.20 E
Tanghe	27	Je	32.37N	112.57 E
Tangier (EN)=Tanger	31	Ge	35.48N	5.48W
Tang La	21	Kg	28.00N	89.15 E
Tango	29	Dd	35.44N	135.05 E
Tangra Yumco	21	Kf	31.00N	86.25 E
Tangshan	22	Nf	39.35N	118.09 E
Tanguiéta	34	Fc	10.37N	1.16 E
Tanguro, Rio-	55	Fa	12.36 S	52.56W
Tangxian	28	Ce	38.46N	114.58 E
Tangyin	28	Cg	35.54N	114.21 E
Tangyuan	27	Mb	46.45N	129.53 E
Tanhoj	20	Ff	51.33N	105.07 E
Tanhuijo, Arrecife-	48	Kg	21.07N	97.17W
Taniantaweng Shan	27	Ge	30.00N	98.00 E
Tanimbar, Kepulauan-= Tanimbar Islands (EN)	57	Ee	7.30 S	131.30 E
Tanimbar Islands (EN)= Tanimbar, Kepulauan-	57	Ee	7.30 S	131.30 E
Tanintharyi	25	Jf	13.00N	99.00 E
Tanjung [Indon.]	26	Gg	2.11S	115.23 E
Tanjung [Indon.]	26	Dg	1.23S	103.58 E
Tanjungpandan	26	Eg	2.45 S	107.39 E
Tanjungpinang	26	Df	0.55N	104.27 E
Tanjungredep	26	Gf	2.09N	117.29 E
Tanjungselor	26	Gf	2.51N	117.22 E
Tankenberg	12	Ib	52.21N	6.58 E
Tanna, Ile-	57	Hf	19.30 S	169.20 E
Tännäs	7	Ce	62.27N	12.40 E
Tanner, Mount-	46	Fb	49.40N	118.34W
Tannis Bugt	8	Dg	57.40N	10.15 E
Tannu-Ola	21	Ld	51.00N	94.00 E
Tano	34	Ed	5.07N	2.56W
Tanout	31	Hg	14.58N	8.53 E
Ţanţā	31	Ke	30.47N	31.00 E
Tan Tan	32	Ed	28.30N	11.02W
Tan-Tan [3]	32	Ed	28.30N	11.00W
Tan Tan Plage	32	Ed	28.26N	11.15W
Tantoyuca	48	Jg	21.21N	98.14W
Tanum	7	Cg	58.43N	11.20 E
Tanzania [1]	31	Ki	6.00 S	35.00 E
Tao, Ko-	25	Jf	10.05N	99.52 E
Tao'an (Taonan)	27	Lb	45.20N	122.46 E
Tao'er He	21	Oe	45.42N	124.05 E
Taoghe	37	Cd	20.37 S	22.35 E
Tao He	27	Hd	35.50N	103.20 E
Taojiang	28	Bj	28.33N	112.05 E
Taonan → Tao'an	27	Lb	45.20N	122.46 E
Taongi Atoll	57	Hc	14.37N	168.58 E
Taormina	14	Jm	37.51N	15.17 E
Taos	43	Fd	36.24N	105.24W
Taoudenni	31	Gf	22.42N	3.56W
Taougrite	13	Mh	36.15N	0.55 E
Taounate	32	Gc	34.33N	4.39W
Taounate [3]	32	Gc	34.04N	4.06W
Taoura	14	Cn	36.10N	8.02 E
Taourirt	32	Gc	34.25N	2.54W
Taouz	32	Gc	31.00N	4.00W
Taoyuan	27	Lg	25.00N	121.18 E
Tapa	19	Cd	59.15N	25.59 E
Tapachula	39	Jh	14.54N	92.17W
Tapaga, Cape-	65c	Bb	14.01 S	171.23W
Tapah	26	Df	4.11N	101.16 E
Tapajera	55	Fi	28.09 S	52.01W
Tapajós, Rio-	52	Kf	2.24 S	54.41W
Tapaktuan	26	Cf	3.16N	97.11 E
Tapalqué	55	Bm	36.21 S	60.01W
Tapan	26	Dg	2.10 S	101.04 E
Tapanahoni Rivier	54	Hc	4.22N	54.27W
Tapanlieh	27	Lg	21.58N	120.47 E
Tapanui	62	Cf	45.57 S	169.16 E
Tapauá	54	Fe	5.45 S	64.23W
Tapauá, Rio-	52	Jf	5.40 S	64.21W
Tapenagá, Río-	55	Ci	28.04 S	59.10W
Taperas	55	Bc	17.54 S	60.23W
Tapes	56	Jd	30.40 S	51.23W
Tapes, Serra do-	55	Fj	30.25 S	51.55W
Tapeta	34	Dd	6.29N	8.51W
Taphan Hin	25	Ke	16.12N	100.26 E
Tapili	36	Eb	3.25N	27.40 E
Tapini	60	Di	8.19 S	146.59 E
Tapiola, Espoo-	8	Kd	60.11N	24.49 E
Tapiraí	55	Id	19.52 S	46.01W
Tapirapuã	55	Db	14.51 S	57.45W
Tapolca	10	Nj	46.53N	17.26 E
Tappahannock	44	Ig	37.55N	76.54W
Tappi-Zaki	28	Pd	41.18N	140.22 E
Tappu	29a	Ba	44.04N	141.52 E
Tapsuj	17	Je	62.20N	61.30 E
Tāpti	21	Jg	21.06N	72.41 E
Tapul Group	26	He	5.30N	121.00 E
Tapurucuara	54	Ed	0.24 S	65.02W
Taputapu, Cape-	65c	Cb	14.19 S	170.50W
Tāqbostān	24	Le	34.30N	46.58 E
Ţaqţaq	24	Ke	35.53N	44.35 E
Taquara	56	Jc	29.39 S	50.47W
Taquaral, Serra do-	55	Fb	15.42 S	52.30W
Taquarí	55	Fc	17.50 S	53.17W
Taquari, Pantanal de-	54	Gg	18.10 S	56.30W
Taquari, Rio- [Braz.]	55	Gi	29.56 S	51.44W
Taquari, Rio- [Braz.]	55	Hf	23.16 S	49.12W
Taquari, Rio- [Braz.]	52	Kg	19.15 S	57.17W
Taquari, Serra do-	55	Fd	18.18 S	53.49W
Taquaritinga	55	He	21.24 S	48.30W
Taquarituba	55	Hf	23.31 S	49.15W
Taquaruçu, Rio-	55	Fe	21.35 S	52.08W
Tar	18	Id	40.38N	73.26 E
Tara	15	Cf	43.55N	19.25 E
Tara	9	Gh	53.34N	6.35W
Tara [Austl.]	59	Ke	27.17 S	150.28 E
Tara [Jap.]	29	Be	33.02N	130.11 E
Tara [R.S.F.S.R.]	20	Ce	56.40N	74.50 E
Tara [R.S.F.S.R.]	19	Hd	56.54N	74.22 E
Tara [Yugo.]	15	Bf	43.21N	18.51 E
Taraba	34	Hd	8.34N	10.15 E
Tarabuco	54	Fg	19.10 S	64.57W
Ţarābulus=Tripoli (EN) [3]	33	Bc	32.40N	13.15 E
Ţarābulus [Leb.]=Tripoli (EN)	23	Ec	34.26N	35.51 E
Ţarābulus [Lib.]=Tripoli (EN)	31	Ie	32.54N	13.11 E
Ţarābulus=Tripolitania (EN)	30	Ie	31.00N	14.00 E
Ţarābulus=Tripolitania (EN)	33	Bc	30.00N	15.00 E
Taradale	62	Gc	39.32 S	176.51 E
Tarāghin	33	Bd	25.59N	14.26 E
Tarahumara, Sierra-	47	Cc	28.26N	106.50W
Tarakan	22	Ni	3.18N	117.38 E
Tarakan, Pulau-	26	Gf	3.21N	117.36 E
Taraklija	16	Fg	45.57N	28.41 E
Tarama Jima	27	Lg	24.40N	124.40 E
Taran, Mys-	7	Ei	54.57N	19.59 E
Taranaki [2]	62	Fc	39.10 S	174.40 E
Tarancón	13	Jd	40.01N	3.00W
Taranga Island	62	Fa	36.00 S	174.45 E
Taransay	9	Fd	57.55N	7.10W
Taranto	6	Hg	40.28N	17.14 E
Taranto, Golfo di- = Taranto, Gulf of- (EN)	5	Hg	40.10N	17.20 E
Taranto, Gulf of- (EN) = Taranto, Golfo di-	5	Hg	40.10N	17.20 E
Tarapacá [2]	56	Ga	20.00 S	69.20W
Tarapacá	56	Ga	19.55 S	69.31W
Tarapaina	63a	Ec	9.23 S	161.24 E
Tarapoto	54	Ce	6.30 S	76.25W
Taraquá	54	Ec	0.06N	68.28W
Tarara	63a	Bb	6.02 S	155.24 E
Tarare	11	Ki	45.54N	4.26 E
Tararua Range	62	Fd	40.40 S	175.25 E
Taraščа	16	Ge	49.34N	30.31 E
Tarascon	11	Kk	43.48N	4.40 E
Tarascon-sur-Ariège	11	Hl	42.51N	1.36 E
Tarat	32	Id	26.08N	9.21 E
Tarata	54	Dg	17.27 S	70.02W

Index Symbols

- [1] Independent Nation
- [2] State, Region
- [3] District, County
- [4] Municipality
- [5] Colony, Dependency
- Continent
- Physical Region
- Historical or Cultural Region
- Mount, Mountain
- Volcano
- Hill
- Mountains, Mountain Range
- Hills, Escarpment
- Plateau, Upland
- Pass, Gap
- Plain, Lowland
- Delta
- Salt Flat
- Valley, Canyon
- Crater, Cave
- Karst Features
- Depression
- Polder
- Desert, Dunes
- Forest, Woods
- Heath, Steppe
- Oasis
- Cape, Point
- Coast, Beach
- Cliff
- Peninsula
- Isthmus
- Sandbank
- Island
- Atoll
- Rock, Reef
- Islands, Archipelago
- Rocks, Reefs
- Coral Reef
- Well, Spring
- Geyser
- River, Stream
- Waterfall Rapids
- River Mouth, Estuary
- Lake
- Salt Lake
- Intermittent Lake
- Reservoir
- Swamp, Pond
- Canal
- Glacier
- Ice Shelf, Pack Ice
- Ocean
- Sea
- Gulf, Bay
- Strait, Fjord
- Lagoon
- Bank
- Seamount
- Tablemount
- Ridge
- Shelf
- Basin
- Escarpment, Sea Scarp
- Fracture
- Trench, Abyss
- National Park, Reserve
- Point of Interest
- Recreation Site
- Cave, Cavern
- Historic Site
- Ruins
- Wall, Walls
- Church, Abbey
- Temple
- Scientific Station
- Airport
- Port
- Lighthouse
- Mine
- Tunnel
- Dam, Bridge

Tarauacá 54 De 8.10S 70.46W
Tarauacá, Rio 52 Jf 6.42S 69.48W
Taravao 65e Fc 17.44S 149.19W
Taravao, Baie de- 65e Fc 17.43S 149.17W
Taravo 11a Ab 41.42N 8.48 E
Tarawa Atoll 57 Id 1.25N 173.00 E
Tarawera 62 Gc 39.02S 176.35 E
Tarazi 24 Mg 31.05N 48.18 E
Tarazona 13 Kc 41.54N 1.44W
Tarazona de la Mancha 13 Ke 39.15N 1.55W
Tarbagataj, Hrebet 21 Ke 47.10N 83.00 E
Tarbagatay Shan 27 Db 47.10N 83.00 E
Tarbat Ness 9 Jd 57.50N 3.40W
Tarbert [Scot.-U.K.] 9 Gd 57.54N 6.49W
Tarbert [Scot.-U.K.] 9 Hf 55.52N 5.26W
Tarbes 11 Gk 43.14N 0.05 E
Tarboro 44 Ih 35.54N 77.32W
Tarcăului, Munţii- 15 Jc 46.45N 26.20 E
Tarcoola 59 Gf 30.41S 134.33 E
Tardenois 12 Fe 49.12N 3.40 E
Tardienta 13 Lc 41.59N 0.32W
Tardoire 11 Gi 45.52N 0.14 E
Tardoki-Jani, Gora- 20 Ig 48.50N 137.55 E
Taree 58 Gh 31.54S 152.28 E
Taremert-n-Akli 32 Id 25.53N 5.18 E
Tarentaise 11 Mi 45.30N 6.30 E
Ţarfā', Ra's aţ- 33 Hf 17.02N 42.22 E
Ţarfā', Wādī aţ- 24 Dh 28.38N 30.43 E
Ţarfah, Jazīrat aţ- 33 Hg 14.37N 42.55 E
Tarfaya 31 Ff 27.57N 12.55W
Targa 13 Qi 35.41N 4.09 E
Tărgoviški prohod 15 Jf 43.12N 26.30 E
Tărgovište 15 Jf 43.15N 26.34 E
Tărgovište [2] 15 Jf 43.15N 26.34 E
Tarhankut, Mys- 16 Hg 45.21N 32.30 E
Tarhăus, Vîrful- 15 Jc 46.38N 26.10 E
Tarhūnah 33 Bc 32.26N 13.38 E
Tarhūnī, Jabal at- 33 De 22.12N 22.25 E
Táriba 49 Kj 7.49N 72.13W
Tarīf 23 He 24.01N 53.45 E
Tarifa 13 Gh 36.01N 5.36W
Tarifa, Punta de- 13 Ih 36.00N 3.37W
Tarija 53 Jh 21.31S 64.45W
Tarija [2] 54 Fh 21.30S 64.00W
Tarik 64d Bb 7.21N 151.47 E
Tariku 26 Kg 2.55S 138.26 E
Tarīm [Yem.] 23 Gf 16.03N 49.00 E
Tarīm [Sau.Ar.] 24 Fi 27.54N 35.24 E
Tarim Basin (EN) = Tarim Pendi 21 Ke 41.00N 84.00 E
Tarime 36 Fc 1.21S 34.22 E
Tarim He 21 Ke 41.05N 86.40 E
Tarim Pendi = Tarim Basin (EN) 21 Ke 41.00N 84.00 E
Tarin Kowt 23 Kc 32.52N 65.38 E
Taritatu 26 Kg 2.54S 138.27 E
Tarjalan 27 Hb 49.38N 101.59 E
Tarjannevesi 8 Kb 62.10N 24.05 E
Tarjat 27 Gb 48.10N 99.40 E
Tarka, Vallée de- 34 Gc 14.30N 6.30 E
Tarkastad 37 Df 32.00S 26.16 E
Tarkio 45 If 40.27N 95.23W
Tarko-Sale 20 Cd 64.55N 78.05 E
Tarkwa 34 Ed 5.18N 1.59W
Tarlac 22 Oh 15.29N 120.35 E
Tarm 8 Ci 55.55N 8.32 E
Tarma 54 Cf 11.25S 75.42W
Tarn 11 Hj 44.06N 1.02 E
Tarn [3] 11 Hk 43.50N 2.00 E
Tarna 10 Pi 47.31N 19.59 E
Tärnaby 7 Dd 65.43N 15.16 E
Tarn-et-Garonne [3] 11 Hj 44.00N 1.10 E
Tarnica 10 Sg 49.06N 22.47 E
Tarnobrzeg 10 Rf 50.35N 21.41 E
Tarnobrzeg [2] 10 Rf 50.35N 21.40 E
Tarnogród 10 Sf 50.23N 22.45 E
Tarnos 11 Ek 43.32N 1.28W
Tarnów 6 Ie 50.01N 21.00 E
Tarnów [2] 10 Qf 50.00N 21.00 E
Tarnowskie Góry 10 Of 50.27N 18.52 E
Tärnsjö 8 Gd 60.09N 16.56 E
Taro 14 Ef 45.00N 10.15 E
Taron 63a Aa 4.28S 153.04 E
Taroom 58 Fg 25.39S 149.49 E
Taroudant 32 Fc 30.29N 8.52W
Tarpon Springs 44 Fk 28.09N 82.45W
Tarquinia 14 Fh 42.15N 11.45 E
Tarra, Río- 49 Ki 9.04N 72.27W
Tarrafal 32 Cf 15.17N 23.46W
Tarragona 6 Gg 41.07N 1.15 E
Tarragona [3] 13 Mc 41.10N 1.00 E
Tarraleah 59 Jh 42.10S 146.30 E
Tarrant 44 Di 33.38N 86.46W
Tarrasa 13 Oc 41.34N 2.01 E
Tárrega 13 Nc 41.39N 1.09 E
Tarsus 23 Db 36.55N 34.53 E
Tart 27 Fd 37.07N 92.57 E
Tartagal 56 Hb 22.32S 63.49W
Tartaro 14 Fe 45.02N 11.30 E
Tartas 11 Fk 43.50N 0.48W
Tartas 20 Ce 55.37N 76.44 E
Tartu 6 Id 58.23N 26.45 E
Tartūs 23 Ec 34.53N 35.53 E
Tarumae-Yama 29a Bb 42.41N 141.23 E
Tarumizu 28 Ki 31.29N 130.42 E
Tarusa 16 Jb 54.43N 37.11 E
Tārūt 24 Ni 26.34N 50.04 E
Tarutau, Ko- 25 Jg 6.35N 99.40 E
Tarutino 16 Ff 46.12N 29.09 E
Tarutung 26 Cf 2.01N 98.58 E
Tarvisio 14 Hd 46.30N 13.35 E
Tarvo 55 Bb 15.06S 60.34W
Tarvo, Río- 55 Bb 14.47S 61.03W
Tasajera, Sierra- 48 Gc 29.35N 105.35W
Tašanta 20 Dg 49.43N 89.11 E
Tasaral, Ostrov- 18 Ja 46.15N 74.05 E
Tašauz 19 Fg 41.52N 59.59 E
Tašauzskaja Oblast [3] 19 Fg 41.00N 58.40 E
Tasāwah 33 Bd 25.59N 13.29 E
Tasbuget 19 Gg 44.43N 65.38 E
Tasejeva 20 Ee 58.06N 94.01 E
Taseko Lake 46 Da 51.15N 123.35W
Tasendjanet 32 Hd 25.40N 0.59 E
Tashk, Daryācheh-ye- 23 Hd 29.45N 53.35 E
Tasikmalaya 22 Mj 7.20S 108.12 E
Tåsinge 8 Di 55.00N 10.36 E
Tasiussaq 41 Gd 73.18N 56.00W
Taskan 20 Kd 62.58N 150.20 E
Taškent 22 Ie 41.20N 69.18 E
Taškentskaja Oblast [3] 19 Gg 41.20N 69.40 E
Taškepri 19 Gh 36.17N 62.38 E
Taškeprinskoje, Vodohranilišče- 18 Df 36.15N 62.40 E
Tasker 34 Hb 15.04N 10.42 E
Taşköprü 24 Fb 41.30N 34.14 E
Taš-Kumyr 19 Hg 41.20N 72.14 E
Taşlıçay 24 Jc 39.38N 43.23 E
Tasman, Mount- 62 De 43.34S 170.09 E
Tasman Basin (EN) 3 Jn 43.00S 158.00 E
Tasman Bay 61 Dh 41.10S 173.15 E
Tasmania 59 Jh 43.00S 147.00 E
Tasmania 57 Fi 43.00S 147.00 E
Tasman Peninsula 59 Jh 43.05S 147.50 E
Tasman Plateau (EN) 3 In 48.00S 148.00 E
Tasman Sea 57 Hh 40.00S 163.00 E
Tăşnad 15 Fb 47.29N 22.35 E
Taşova 24 Gb 40.46N 36.20 E
Tassah, Wādī- 14 Cn 36.35N 8.54 E
Tassara 34 Gb 16.01N 5.39 E
Taštagol 20 Df 52.47N 88.00 E
Tåstrup 8 Ei 55.39N 12.19 E
Tastūr 14 Dn 36.33N 9.27 E
Tasty-Taldy 19 Ge 50.47N 66.31 E
Ţasūj 24 Kc 38.19N 45.21 E
Taşuou 24 Ed 36.19N 33.53 E
Tata [3] 32 Fd 29.40N 8.00W
Tata [Hun.] 10 Oi 47.39N 18.19 E
Tata [Mor.] 32 Fd 29.45N 7.59W
Tataba 26 Hg 1.18S 122.49 E
Tatabánya 10 Oi 47.34N 18.25 E
Tatakoto Atoll 57 Nf 17.20S 138.23W
Tata Mailau 26 Ih 8.55S 125.30 E
Tatarbunary 16 Fg 45.49N 29.35 E
Tatarsk 22 Jd 55.13N 75.58 E
Tatarskaja ASSR [3] 19 Fd 55.20N 50.50 E
Tatarski Proliv = Tatar Strait (EN) 21 Qd 50.00N 141.15 E
Tatar Strait (EN) = Tatarski Proliv 21 Qd 50.00N 141.15 E
Tatau 26 Ff 2.53N 112.51 E
Taţāwīn 32 Jc 32.56N 10.27 E
Tateyama 28 Og 34.59N 139.52 E
Tathlina Lake 42 Fd 60.30N 117.30W
Tathlīth 23 Ff 19.32N 43.30 E
Tatiščevo 16 Nd 51.40N 45.35 E
Tatla Lake 46 Ca 51.58N 124.25W
Tatla Lake 46 Ca 51.55N 124.36W
Tatlow, Mount- 46 Da 51.23N 123.52W
Tatnam, Cape - 42 Ie 57.16N 91.00W
Tatra Mountains (EN) 5 Hf 49.15N 20.00 E
Tatsuno [Jap.] 29 Dd 34.52N 134.33 E
Tatsuno [Jap.] 29 Ed 35.58N 137.58 E
Tatsuruhama 29 Ec 37.04N 136.53 E
Tatta 25 Dd 24.45N 67.55 E
Tatuí 55 If 23.21S 47.51W
Tatum 45 Ej 33.16N 103.19W
Tatvan 23 Fb 38.30N 42.16 E
Tau 8 Ae 59.04N 5.54 E
Tau [Am.Sam.] 65c Db 14.15S 169.30W
Tau [Ton.] 65b Bc 21.01S 175.00W
Tauá 54 Je 6.01S 40.26W
Taubaté 53 Lh 23.02S 45.33W
Tauberbischofsheim 10 Fg 49.37N 9.40 E
Taučik 19 Fg 44.15N 51.20 E
Tauere Atoll 57 Mf 17.22S 141.30W
Tauern 5 Hf 47.15N 13.15 E
Taufstein 10 Ff 50.31N 9.14 E
Tauhunu 64n Ac 10.25S 161.03W
Tauhunu 64n Ac 10.25S 161.03W
Taujsk 20 Je 59.46N 149.20 E
Taujskaja Guba 20 Je 59.15N 150.00 E
Taukum 18 Jb 44.50N 75.30 E
Taumako 63c Ba 9.57S 167.13 E
Taumarunui 62 Fc 38.52S 175.15 E
Taum Sauk Mountain 45 Kh 37.34N 90.44W
Taunay 55 De 20.18S 56.05W
Taung 37 Ce 27.33S 24.47 E
Taungdwingyi 25 Jd 20.01N 95.33 E
Taunggyi 25 Jd 20.47N 97.02 E
Taungthonlon 25 Jd 24.58N 95.48 E
Taungup 25 Ie 18.51N 94.14 E
Taunton [Eng.-U.K.] 9 Jj 51.01N 3.06W
Taunton [Ma.-U.S.] 44 Le 41.54N 71.06W
Taunus 10 Ef 50.10N 8.15 E
Taunusstein 12 Kd 50.08N 8.10 E
Taupo 61 Eg 38.41S 176.05 E
Taupo, Lake- 61 Eg 38.50S 175.55 E
Tauragė/Taųrage 7 Fi 55.16N 22.19 E
Taurage/Tauragė 7 Fi 55.16N 22.19 E
Tauranga 58 Ih 37.42S 176.10 E
Taurianova 14 Kl 38.21N 16.01 E
Taurion 11 Hi 45.53N 1.24 E
Taurisano 14 Mk 39.57N 18.13 E
Tauroa Point 62 Ea 35.10S 173.04 E
Taurus Mountains (EN) = Toros Dağları 21 Ff 37.00N 33.00 E
Tauste 13 Kc 41.55N 1.15W
Tauu Islands 57 Ge 4.45S 157.00 E
Tauz 19 Eg 41.01N 45.35 E
Ţavālesh, Kūhhā-Ye- 24 Mc 38.42N 48.18 E
Tavas [Tur.] 24 Dc 39.54N 30.03 E
Tavas [Tur.] 24 Cd 37.34N 29.04 E
Tavas Ovasi 15 Ll 37.30N 28.55 E
Tavastehus/Hämeenlinna 7 Ff 61.00N 24.27 E
Tavau/Davos 14 Dd 46.47N 9.50 E
Tavda 19 Gd 58.03N 65.15 E
Tavda 21 Id 57.47N 67.16 E
Tavendroua 63b Cc 16.21S 167.22 E
Taveta 36 Gc 3.24S 37.41 E
Taveuni Island 61 Fc 16.51S 179.58W
Taviano 14 Mk 39.59N 18.05 E
Tavignano 11a Ba 42.06N 9.33 E
Tavira 13 Eg 37.07N 7.39W
Tavistock 9 Ik 50.33N 4.08W
Tavolara 14 Dj 40.55N 9.40 E
Tavoliere 14 Ji 41.35N 15.25 E
Tavolžan 19 He 52.44N 77.30 E
Tavoy → Dawei 22 Lh 14.05N 98.12 E
Tavričanka 28 Kc 43.20N 131.52 E
Tavropóu, Tekhniti Límni- 15 Ej 39.15N 21.40 E
Tavşan Adalari 15 Jj 39.55N 26.05 E
Tavşanlı 24 Cc 39.35N 29.30 E
Tavua 61 Ec 17.27S 177.51 E
Taw 9 Ij 51.04N 4.11W
Tawakoni, Lake- 45 Ij 32.55N 96.00W
Tawas City 43 Kc 44.16N 83.31W
Tawau 22 Ni 4.15N 117.54 E
Tawfīqīyah 35 Ed 9.26N 31.37 E
Ţawīlah, Juzur- 24 Ei 27.35N 33.46 E
Tawitawi Group 26 He 5.10N 120.15 E
Ţawkar 31 Kg 18.26N 37.44 E
Ţāwūq 24 Ke 35.08N 44.27 E
Tawūq Chāy 24 Ke 34.35N 44.31 E
Tāwurghā', Sabkhat- 33 Cc 31.10N 15.15 E
Tawzar 32 Ic 33.55N 8.08 E
Taxco de Alarcón 48 Jh 18.33N 99.36W
Taxkorgan 27 Cd 37.47N 75.14 E
Tay 9 Je 56.30N 3.30W
Tay, Firth of- 9 Ke 56.28N 3.00W
Tay, Loch- 9 Ie 56.30N 4.10W
Tayandu, Kepulauan- 26 Jh 5.30S 132.15 E
Tayēgle 35 Ge 4.02N 44.36 E
Taylor [Nb.-U.S.] 45 Gf 41.46N 99.23W
Taylor [Tx.-U.S.] 43 He 30.34N 97.25W
Taylor, Mount- 43 Fd 35.14N 107.37W
Taylorville 45 Lg 39.33N 89.18W
Taymā' 23 Ed 27.38N 38.29 E
Taymyr Peninsula (EN) = Tajmyr, Poluostrov- 21 Mb 76.00N 104.00 E
Tay Ninh 25 Lf 11.18N 106.06 E
Tayside [3] 9 Je 56.30N 3.40W
Taytay 26 Gd 10.49N 119.31 E
Taza [3] 32 Gc 34.00N 4.00W
Taza [Mor.] 31 Ge 34.13N 4.01W
Taza [R.S.F.S.R.] 20 Gf 54.55N 111.05 E
Tāzah Khurmātū 24 Ke 35.18N 44.20 E
Tazawa-Ko 29 Gb 39.43N 140.40 E
Tazawako 29 Gb 39.42N 140.44 E
Tazenakht 32 Fc 30.35N 7.12W
Tazerbo Oasis (EN) = Tāzirbū, Wāḩāt al- 30 Jf 25.45N 21.00 E
Tazewell [Tn.-U.S.] 44 Fg 36.27N 83.34W
Tazewell [Va.-U.S.] 44 Gg 37.07N 81.34W
Tâziâzet 32 De 20.55N 15.40W
Tazin Lake 42 Ge 59.48N 109.05W
Tāzirbū, Wāḩāt al- = Tazerbo Oasis (EN) 30 Jf 25.45N 21.00 E
Tazlău 15 Jc 46.16N 26.47 E
Tazmalt 13 Qh 36.43N 4.08 E
Tazouikert 34 Ea 21.46N 1.13W
Tazovskaja Guba 17 Qb 69.05N 76.00 E
Tazovski 20 Cc 67.28N 78.42 E
Tazrouk 32 Ie 23.27N 6.14 E
Tazumal 49 Cg 14.00N 89.40W
Tbilisi 6 Kg 41.43N 44.49 E
Tchad = Chad (EN) [1] 31 Ig 15.00N 19.00 E
Tchad, Lac- = Chad, Lake- (EN) 30 Ig 13.20N 14.00 E
Tchamba [Cam.] 34 Hd 8.37N 12.48 E
Tchamba [Togo] 34 Fd 9.02N 1.25 E
Tchibanga 36 Bc 2.51S 11.02 E
Tchien 34 Dd 6.04N 8.08W
Tchigaï, Plateau du- 30 If 21.30N 14.50 E
Tchin Tabaraden 34 Gb 15.58N 5.50 E
Tcholliré 34 Hd 8.24N 14.10 E
Tczew 10 Ob 54.06N 18.47 E
Tea, Rio- 54 Ed 0.30S 65.09W
Teaca 15 Hc 46.55N 24.31 E
Teacapán 48 Gf 22.33N 105.45W
Teaiti Point 64p Bb 21.11S 159.47W
Te Anau 62 Bf 45.25S 167.43 E
Te Anau, Lake- 61 Ci 45.15S 167.45 E
Teano 14 Ii 41.15N 14.04 E
Teapa 48 Mi 17.33N 92.57W
Te Araroa 61 Eg 37.38S 178.22 E
Te Aroha 62 Fb 37.32S 175.42 E
Tea Tree 59 Gd 22.11S 133.17 E
Te Atu Kura 64p Bb 21.14S 159.45W
Te Awamutu 62 Fc 38.00S 175.19 E
Teberda 16 Lh 43.28N 41.43 E
Tébessa 31 He 35.24N 8.07 E
Tébessa [3] 32 Ic 35.00N 7.45 E
Tébessa, Oued- 14 Bo 35.48N 7.53 E
Tebicuary, Río- [Par.] 55 Ch 26.36S 58.16W
Tebicuary, Río- [Par.] 55 Dh 26.26S 56.51W
Tebingtinggi [Indon.] 26 Dg 3.36S 103.05 E
Tebingtinggi [Indon.] 26 Cf 3.20N 99.09 E
Tebulosmta, Gora- 16 Nh 42.33N 45.16 E
Teča 17 Kh 56.17N 62.59 E
Tecate 47 Ab 32.34N 116.38W
Tecer Dağları 24 Gc 39.27N 37.11 E
Techirghiol 15 Le 44.03N 28.36 E
Tecka 56 Ff 43.29S 70.48W
Tecklenburg 12 Jb 52.13N 7.50 E
Tecomán 47 De 18.55N 103.53W
Tecomate, Laguna- 48 Ji 16.45N 99.25W
Tecoripa 48 Ec 28.37N 109.57W
Tecpan de Galeana 47 De 17.15N 100.41W
Tecuala 47 Cd 22.23N 105.27W
Tecuci 15 Kd 45.52N 27.25 E
Tedegra 35 Ba 20.46N 19.34 E
Tedori-Gawa 29 Ec 36.29N 136.28 E
Tedžen 21 If 37.24N 60.38 E
Tedženstroj 19 Gh 36.54N 60.53 E
Teeli 20 Ef 50.57N 90.18 E
Teenuse Jõgi/Tenuze 7 Jf 58.44N 23.58 E
Tees 9 Lg 54.34N 1.16W
Tees Bay 9 Lg 54.35N 1.05W
Teesside → Middlesbrough 6 Fe 54.35N 1.14W
Tefé 53 Jf 3.22S 64.42W
Tefé, Rio- 54 Fd 3.35S 64.47W
Tefedest 32 Ie 24.40N 5.30 E
Tefenni 24 Cd 37.18N 29.47 E
Tegal 22 Mj 6.52S 109.08 E
Tegea (EN) = Teyéa 15 Fl 37.27N 22.25 E
Tegelen 12 Ic 51.20N 6.08 E
Tegernsee 10 Hi 47.43N 11.46 E
Tegina 34 Gc 10.04N 6.11 E
Tégoua 63b Ca 13.15S 166.37 E
Tegucigalpa 39 Kh 14.06N 87.13W
Teguidda I-n-Tessoum 34 Gb 17.26N 6.39 E
Teguldet 20 De 57.20N 88.20 E
Tehachapi 46 Fi 35.08N 118.27W
Tehachapi Mountains 46 Fi 34.56N 118.40W
Tehamiyam 35 Fb 18.20N 36.32 E
Te Hapua 61 Df 34.30S 172.55 E
Tehaupoo 65e Fc 17.49S 149.18W
Tehek Lake 42 Hd 64.55N 95.30W
Téhini 34 Ed 9.36N 3.40W
Tehi-n-Isser 32 Ie 24.48N 8.08 E
Tehoru 26 Ig 3.23S 129.30 E
Tehrān 22 Hf 35.40N 51.26 E
Tehrān → Markazi [3] 23 Hb 35.30N 51.30 E
Tehuacán 47 Ee 18.27N 97.23W
Tehuantepec 47 Ee 16.20N 95.14W
Tehuantepec, Golfo de- = Tehuantepec, Gulf of- (EN) 38 Jh 16.00N 94.50W
Tehuantepec, Gulf of- (EN) = Tehuantepec, Golfo de- 38 Jh 16.00N 94.50W
Tehuantepec, Isthmus of- (EN) = Tehuantepec, Istmo de- 38 Jh 17.00N 94.30W
Tehuantepec, Istmo de- = Tehuantepec, Isthmus of- (EN) 38 Jh 17.00N 94.30W
Tehuantepec Ridge (EN) 47 Ef 13.30N 98.00W
Tehuata Atoll 57 Mf 16.50S 141.55W
Teiga Plateau 35 Db 15.38N 25.40 E
Teignmouth 9 Jk 50.33N 3.30W
Teili/Delet 8 Id 60.15N 20.35 E
Teith 9 Ie 56.14N 4.20W
Teiuş 15 Gc 46.12N 23.41 E
Teixeira Pinto 34 Bc 12.04N 16.02W
Teja 20 Ed 60.27N 92.38 E
Tejkovo 19 Ed 56.50N 40.34 E
Tejo = Tagus (EN) 5 Fh 38.40N 9.24W
Teju 25 Jc 27.55N 96.10 E
Te Kaha 62 Gb 37.44S 177.41 E
Te Kao 62 Ea 34.39S 172.58 E
Tekapo, Lake- 62 De 43.50S 170.30 E
Te Karaka 62 Gc 38.28S 177.52 E
Tekax 48 Og 20.12N 89.17W
Teke 15 Mh 41.04N 29.39 E
Teke 15 Jh 41.21N 26.57 E
Teke Burun [Tur.] 15 Ji 40.02N 26.10 E
Teke Burun [Tur.] 15 Jk 38.05N 26.36 E
Tekeli 19 Hg 44.48N 78.57 E
Tekes 27 Dc 43.10N 81.43 E
Tekes He 27 Dc 43.35N 82.30 E
Tekeze 35 Fc 14.20N 35.50 E
Tekija 15 Fe 44.41N 22.25 E
Tekiliktag 27 Dd 36.35N 80.20 E
Tekirdağ 23 Ca 40.59N 27.31 E
Tekman 24 Ic 39.38N 41.31 E
Te Kopuru 62 Eb 36.02S 173.55 E
Te Kou 64p Bb 21.14S 159.46W
Tekouiat 32 He 22.20N 2.30 E
Tekro 35 Cb 19.34N 20.57 E
Te Kuiti 62 Fc 38.20S 175.10 E
Tela 47 Ge 15.44N 87.27W
Telagh 32 Gc 34.47N 0.34W
Telataï 34 Fb 16.31N 1.30 E
Telavåg 7 Af 60.16N 4.49 E
Telavi 19 Eg 41.55N 45.29 E
Tel Aviv-Yafo 22 Ff 32.04N 34.46 E
Telč 10 Lg 49.11N 15.27 E
Telchac Puerto 48 Og 21.21N 89.16W
Telciu 15 Hb 47.26N 24.24 E
Tele 36 Db 2.48N 23.54 E
Teleac 15 Hc 46.41N 24.48 E
Telečkoje Ozero 20 Df 51.30N 87.45 E
Telefomin 60 Ci 5.08S 141.31 E
Telegraph Creek 42 Ee 57.54N 131.09W
Telekitonga 65b Bb 20.24S 174.32W
Telekivavu'u 65b Bb 20.19S 174.32W
Telêmaco Borba 55 Gg 24.23S 50.28W
Telemark [2] 7 Bg 59.30N 8.40 E
Telemark 8 Ce 59.30N 8.45 E
Telén 56 Ge 36.16S 65.30W
Telen 26 Gf 0.26N 116.42 E
Telenešty 15 Lb 47.30N 28.16 E
Teleno 13 Fb 42.21N 6.23W
Teleorman 15 If 43.52N 25.26 E
Teleorman [2] 15 If 44.10N 25.15 E
Telerhteba, Djebel- 32 Ie 24.10N 6.51 E
Telescope Peak 46 Gh 36.10N 117.05W
Telescope Point 51p Bb 12.08N 61.36W
Telese 14 Ii 41.13N 14.32 E
Teles Pires, Rio- o São Manuel, Rio- 52 Kf 7.21S 58.03W
Telfân, Hadjer- 35 Bc 12.05N 18.57 E
Telford 9 Ki 52.40N 2.30W
Telgte 12 Jc 51.59N 7.47 E
Télimélé 34 Cc 10.54N 13.02W
Teljo, Jabal- 35 Dc 14.42N 25.56 E
Tell al Ubaid 24 Lg 30.59N 46.01 E
Tellaro 14 Jn 36.50N 15.06 E
Tell Atlas (EN) = Atlas Tellien 30 He 36.00N 2.00 E
Tell City 44 Dg 37.57N 86.46W
Teller 40 Fc 65.16N 166.22W
Telok Anson 26 Df 4.02N 101.01 E
Teloloapan 48 Jh 18.21N 99.51W
Telposiz, Gora- 5 Lc 63.54N 59.10 E
Telsen 56 Gf 42.24S 66.57W
Telšiai/Telšjaj 19 Cd 55.59N 22.17 E
Telšjaj/Telšiai 19 Cd 55.59N 22.17 E
Teltow 10 Jd 52.24N 13.16 E
Telukbetung 22 Mj 5.27S 105.16 E
Telukbutun 26 Ef 4.13N 108.12 E
Telukdalem 26 Cf 0.34N 97.49 E
Téma 31 Gh 5.37N 0.01W
Temacine 32 Ic 33.01N 6.01 E
Te Manga 64p Bb 21.13S 159.45W
Tematangi Atoll 57 Mg 21.41S 140.40W
Tembenči 20 Ed 64.36N 99.58 E
Témbi 15 Fj 39.53N 22.35 E
Tembilahan 26 Dg 0.19S 103.09 E
Temblador 50 Eh 8.59N 62.44W
Tembleque 13 Ie 39.42N 3.30W
Temblor Range 46 Fi 35.30N 119.55W
Tembo 36 Cd 7.42S 17.17 E
Tembo, Chutes- 30 Ii 8.50S 15.20 E
Tembo, Mont- 36 Bb 1.50N 12.00 E
Tembué 37 Eb 14.51S 32.50 E
Teme 9 Ki 52.09N 2.18W
Temerin 15 Cd 45.25N 19.53 E
Temerloh 26 Df 3.27N 102.25 E
Teminabuan 26 Jg 1.26S 132.01 E
Temir 19 Ff 49.08N 57.09 E
Temir 16 Te 48.31N 57.29 E
Temirlanovka 18 Gc 42.36N 69.17 E
Temirtau 22 Jd 50.05N 72.56 E
Témiscaming 44 Hb 46.44N 79.06W
Témiscouata, Lac- 44 Mb 47.40N 68.50W
Temki 35 Bc 11.29N 18.13 E
Temnikov 7 Ki 54.40N 43.13 E
Temo 14 Cj 40.17N 8.28 E
Temoe, Ile- 57 Ng 23.20S 134.29W
Temores 48 Ed 27.16N 108.15W
Tempe 46 Jj 33.25N 111.56W
Tempio Pausania 14 Dj 40.54N 9.06 E
Temple 43 He 31.06N 97.21W
Templeman, Mount- 46 Ga 50.43N 117.14W
Templemore/An Teampall Mór 9 Fi 52.48N 7.50W
Templin 10 Jc 53.07N 13.30 E
Tempoal, Río- 48 Jg 21.47N 98.27W
Tempué 36 Ce 13.27S 18.53 E
Temrjuk 16 Jg 45.15N 37.23 E
Temse/Tamise 12 Gc 51.08N 4.13 E
Temuco 53 Ii 38.44S 72.36W
Temuka 62 Df 44.15S 171.16 E
Tena 54 Cd 0.59S 77.48W
Tenacatita, Bahía de- 48 Gh 19.10N 104.50W
Tenala/Tenhola 8 Jd 60.04N 23.18 E
Tenāli 25 Ge 16.15N 80.35 E
Tenancingo de Degollado 48 Jh 18.58N 99.36W
Tenasserim 25 Jf 12.05N 99.01 E
Tenasserim 25 Jf 12.24N 98.37 E
Tenasserim 21 Lh 12.35N 97.52 E
Tenby 9 Ij 51.41N 4.43W
Tence 11 Ki 45.07N 4.17 E
Tench Island 60 Eh 1.38S 150.42 E
Tenda, Col di- 14 Bf 44.09N 7.34 E
Tendaho 35 Gc 11.38N 41.00 E
Tende 11 Nj 44.05N 7.36 E
Tende, Col de- 14 Bf 44.09N 7.34 E
Ten Degree Channel 21 Lh 10.00N 92.30 E
Tendō 29 Gb 38.22N 140.22 E
Tendrara 32 Gc 33.03N 2.00W
Tendre, Mont- 14 Ad 46.36N 6.19 E
Tendrovskaja Kosa 16 Gf 46.15N 31.45 E
Ténenkou 34 Ec 14.28N 4.55W
Tenente Lira, Rio- 55 Db 15.56S 57.39W
Ténéré 30 Ig 17.35N 10.55 E
Ténéré, 'Erg du- 34 Hb 17.35N 10.55 E
Tenerife 30 Ff 28.19N 16.34W
Ténès 32 Hb 36.31N 1.18 E
Ténès, Cap- 13 Nh 36.33N 1.21 E
Teng 25 Je 19.52N 97.45 E
Tengah, Kepulauan- 26 Gh 7.30S 117.30 E
Tengchong 27 Gg 24.59N 98.32 E
Te Nggano, Lake- 60 Gj 11.45S 160.25 E
Tenggarong 26 Gg 0.24S 116.58 E
Tengger Shamo 21 Mf 38.00N 104.10 E
Tengiz, Ozero- 21 Id 50.25N 69.00 E
Tengréla 34 Dc 10.29N 6.24W
Tengréla [3] 34 Dc 10.27N 6.25W
Tengxian [China] 27 Jg 23.18N 110.49 E
Tengxian [China] 28 Dg 35.07N 117.10 E
Tenhola/Tenala 8 Jd 60.04N 23.18 E
Teniente General Rosendo M. Fraga 55 Af 23.45S 62.09W
Tenkāsi 25 Fg 8.58N 77.18 E
Tenke 36 Ee 10.33S 26.08 E
Tenkeli 20 Jb 70.01N 140.55 E
Tenkodogo 34 Ec 11.47N 0.22W
Tenna 14 Hg 43.14N 13.47 E
Tennant Creek 58 Ef 19.40S 134.10 E
Tennessee 38 Kf 37.04N 88.33W
Tennessee [2] 43 Jd 35.50N 85.30W
Tenneville 12 Hd 50.06N 5.32 E
Tenoïoki 7 Ga 70.28N 28.18 E
Tenom 26 Ge 5.08N 115.57 E
Tenosique de Pino Suárez 47 Fe 17.29N 91.26W
Tenri 29 Dd 34.36N 135.49 E
Tenryū 29 Ed 34.52N 137.47 E
Tenryū-Gawa 28 Ng 34.35N 137.48 E
Tensift 32 Fc 32.02N 9.21W
Ten Sleep 46 Ld 44.02N 107.27W
Tenterden 12 Cc 51.03N 0.42 E

Index Symbols

- [1] Independent Nation
- [2] State, Region
- [3] District, County
- [4] Municipality
- [5] Colony, Dependency
- Continent
- Physical Region
- Historical or Cultural Region
- Mount, Mountain
- Volcano
- Hill
- Mountains, Mountain Range
- Hills, Escarpment
- Plateau, Upland
- Pass, Gap
- Plain, Lowland
- Delta
- Salt Flat
- Valley, Canyon
- Crater, Cave
- Karst Features
- Depression
- Polder
- Desert, Dunes
- Forest, Woods
- Heath, Steppe
- Oasis
- Cape, Point
- Coast, Beach
- Cliff
- Peninsula
- Isthmus
- Sandbank
- Island
- Atoll
- Rock, Reef
- Islands, Archipelago
- Rocks, Reefs
- Coral Reef
- Well, Spring
- Geyser
- River, Stream
- Waterfall Rapids
- River Mouth, Estuary
- Lake
- Salt Lake
- Intermittent Lake
- Reservoir
- Swamp, Pond
- Canal
- Glacier
- Ice Shelf, Pack Ice
- Ocean
- Sea
- Gulf, Bay
- Strait, Fjord
- Lagoon
- Bank
- Seamount
- Tablemount
- Ridge
- Shelf
- Basin
- Escarpment, Sea Scarp
- Fracture
- Trench, Abyss
- National Park, Reserve
- Point of Interest
- Recreation Site
- Cave, Cavern
- Historic Site
- Ruins
- Wall, Walls
- Church, Abbey
- Temple
- Scientific Station
- Airport
- Port
- Lighthouse
- Mine
- Tunnel
- Dam, Bridge

Index Symbols

[1] Independent Nation
[2] State, Region
[3] District, County
[4] Municipality
[5] Colony, Dependency
Continent
Physical Region
Historical or Cultural Region
Mount, Mountain
Volcano
Hill
Mountains, Mountain Range
Hills, Escarpment
Plateau, Upland
Pass, Gap
Plain, Lowland
Delta
Salt Flat
Valley, Canyon
Crater, Cave
Karst Features
Depression
Polder
Desert, Dunes
Forest, Woods
Heath, Steppe
Oasis
Cape, Point
Coast, Beach
Cliff
Peninsula
Isthmus
Sandbank
Island
Atoll
Rock, Reef
Islands, Archipelago
Rocks, Reefs
Coral Reef
Well, Spring
Geyser
River, Stream
Waterfall Rapids
River Mouth, Estuary
Lake
Salt Lake
Intermittent Lake
Reservoir
Swamp, Pond
Canal
Glacier
Ice Shelf, Pack Ice
Ocean
Sea
Gulf, Bay
Strait, Fjord
Lagoon
Bank
Seamount
Tablemount
Ridge
Shelf
Basin
Escarpment, Sea Scarp
Fracture
Trench, Abyss
National Park, Reserve
Point of Interest
Recreation Site
Cave, Cavern
Historic Site
Ruins
Wall, Walls
Church, Abbey
Temple
Scientific Station
Airport
Port
Lighthouse
Mine
Tunnel
Dam, Bridge

Tihāmat 'Asīr 33 Hf 17.30N 42.20 E
Tihi Okean=Pacific Ocean (EN) 3 Ki 5.00N 155.00W
Tihoreck 6 Kf 45.51N 40.09 E
Tihuța, Pasul- 15 Hb 47.15N 25.00 E
Tihvin 19 Dd 59.38N 33.31 E
Tiirismaa 8 Kc 61.01N 25.31 E
Tiji 33 Bc 32.01N 11.22 E
Tijirīt 32 Ee 20.30N 15.00W
Tijuana 39 Hf 32.32N 117.01W
Tijucas 55 Hh 27.14S 48.38W
Tijucas, Baía do- 55 Hh 27.15S 48.31W
Tijucas, Rio- 55 Hh 27.15S 48.38W
Tijucas, Serra do- 55 Hh 27.16S 49.10W
Tijucas do Sul 55 Hg 25.56S 49.10W
Tijuco, Rio- 55 Gd 18.40S 50.05W
Tikal 39 Kh 17.20N 89.39W
Tikanlik 27 Ec 40.42N 87.38 E
Tikchik Lakes 40 Hd 60.07N 158.35W
Tikehau Atoll 61 Lb 15.00S 148.10W
Tikei, Ile- 61 Mb 14.58S 144.32W
Tikitiki 62 Hb 37.47S 178.25 E
Tikkakoski 8 Kb 62.24N 25.38 E
Tikkurila 8 Kd 60.18N 25.03 E
Tiko 34 Ge 4.05N 9.22 E
Tikopia Island 57 Hf 12.19S 168.49 E
Tikrīt 23 Fc 34.36N 43.42 E
Tikšeozero, Ozero- 7 Hc 66.15N 31.45 E
Tiksi 22 Ob 71.36N 128.48 E
Tiladummati Atoll 25a Ba 6.50N 73.05 E
Tilamuta 26 Hf 0.30N 122.20 E
Tilburg 11 Lc 51.34N 5.05 E
Tilbury, Gravesend- 9 Nj 51.28N 0.23 E
Tilcara 56 Gb 23.34S 65.22W
Til-Châtel 11 Lg 47.31N 5.10 E
Tileagd 15 Fb 47.04N 22.12 E
Tilemsès 34 Fb 15.37N 4.44 E
Tilemsi, Vallée du- 30 Hg 19.00N 0.02 E
Tilia 32 Gd 27.22N 0.02W
Tiličiki 20 Ld 60.20N 166.03 E
Tiligul 16 Gf 47.07N 30.57 E
Tiligulski Liman 16 Gf 46.50N 31.10 E
Till 9 Kf 55.41N 2.12W
Tillabéry 34 Fc 14.13N 1.27 E
Tillamook 46 Dd 45.27N 123.51W
Tillamook Bay 46 Dd 45.30N 123.53W
Tillanchong 25 Ig 8.30N 93.37 E
Tillberga 8 Ge 59.41N 16.37 E
Tille 11 Lg 47.07N 5.21 E
Tillia 34 Fb 16.08N 4.47 E
Tillières-sur-Avre 12 Df 48.46N 1.04 E
Tillingham 12 Cd 50.58N 0.44 E
Tillsonburg 44 Gd 42.51N 80.44W
Tilly-sur-Seulles 12 Be 49.11N 0.37W
Tiloa 34 Fb 15.04N 2.03 E
Tilos 15 Km 36.25N 27.25 E
Tilpa 59 If 30.57S 144.24 E
Tim 16 Jd 51.37N 37.11 E
Tim 16 Jc 52.15N 37.22 E
Ţimā 33 Fd 26.54N 31.26 E
Timagami 44 Gb 47.00N 80.05W
Timagami, Lake- 42 Jg 46.57N 80.05W
Timane, Rio- 55 Be 20.16S 60.08W
Timan Ridge (EN)= Timanski Krjaž 5 Lc 65.00N 51.00 E
Timanski Bereg 17 Eb 68.20N 51.45 E
Timanski Krjaž=Timan Ridge (EN) 5 Lc 65.00N 51.00 E
Timaru 58 Ii 44.24S 171.15 E
Timaševsk 19 Df 45.35N 38.58 E
Timbalier Bay 45 Kl 29.10N 90.20W
Timbalier Island 45 Kl 29.04N 90.28W
Timbaúba 54 Ke 7.31S 35.19W
Timbédra 32 Ff 16.14N 8.10W
Timbó 55 Hh 26.50S 49.18W
Timbuktu (EN)= Tombouctou 31 Gg 16.46N 2.59W
Timedouine, Ras- 13 Qh 36.28N 4.09 E
Timétrine 34 Eb 19.20N 0.42W
Timétrine 34 Eb 19.27N 0.26W
Timfi Óros 15 Dj 39.57N 20.50 E
Timfristós 15 Ek 38.57N 21.49 E
Tîmia 34 Gb 18.04N 8.40 E
Timimoun 31 Hf 29.15N 0.15 E
Timimoun, Sebkha de- 32 Hd 29.00N 0.05 E
Timiris, Cap— 32 Df 19.23N 16.32W
Timirjazevo 19 Ge 53.45N 66.33 E
Timiş 15 De 44.51N 20.39 E
Timiş 15 Ed 45.38N 21.13 E
Timiskaming, Lake- 44 Hb 47.35N 79.35W
Timişoara 6 If 45.45N 21.13 E
Ti-m-Merhsoï 34 Gb 18.00N 5.40 E
Timmins 39 Ke 48.28N 81.20W
Timmoudi 32 Gd 29.19N 1.08W
Timms Hill 45 Kd 45.27N 90.11W
Timok 15 Fe 44.13N 22.40 E
Timon 54 Je 5.06S 42.49W
Timor, Laut-=Timor Sea (EN) 57 Df 11.00S 128.00 E
Timor, Pulau- 21 Oj 8.50S 126.00 E
Timor Sea (EN)=Timor, Laut- 57 Df 11.00S 128.00 E
Timor Timur 26 Ih 8.35S 126.00 E
Timor Trough (EN) 3 Ij 9.50S 126.00 E
Timote 56 He 35.21S 62.14W
Timotes 54 Db 8.59N 70.44W
Timpton 20 He 58.43N 127.12 E
Timrå 7 De 62.29N 17.18 E
Tims Ford Lake 44 Dh 35.15N 86.10W
Tin, Ra's at- 33 Dc 32.37N 23.08 E
Tinaca Point 21 Oi 5.33N 125.20 E
Tinaco 50 Bh 9.42N 68.26W
Tinakula 63c Ab 10.24S 165.47 E
Ti-n-Alkoum 32 Je 24.34N 10.11 E
Ti-n-Amzi [Alg.] 32 He 20.32N 4.37 E
Ti-n-Amzi [Niger] 34 Fb 17.54N 4.32 E
Tinaquillo 50 Bh 9.55N 68.18W
Tinchebray 12 Bf 48.46N 0.44W
Tindalo 35 Ed 5.39N 31.03 E
Tindari 14 Jl 38.10N 15.04 E
Tindila 34 Dc 10.16N 8.15W
Tindouf 31 Gf 27.42N 8.09W
Tindouf, Hamada de- 32 Fd 27.45N 8.25W
Tindouf, Sebkha de- 32 Fd 27.45N 7.35W
Tinée 11 Nk 43.55N 7.11 E
Tineo 13 Fa 43.20N 6.25W
Ti-n-Essako 34 Fb 18.27N 2.29 E
Tin Fouye 32 Id 28.15N 7.45 E
Tinghert, Ḩamādat- 30 Hf 28.50N 10.00 E
Tinglev 8 Cj 54.56N 9.15 E
Tingmiarmiut 41 Hf 62.25N 42.15W
Tingo María 54 Ce 9.10S 76.00W
Tingri (Xêgar) 27 Ef 28.41N 87.00 E
Tingsryd 7 Dh 56.32N 14.59 E
Tingstäde 8 Hg 57.44N 18.36 E
Tingvoll 7 Be 62.54N 8.12 E
Tinian Channel 64b Bb 14.54N 145.37 E
Tinian Island 57 Fc 15.00N 145.38 E
Tini Wells 35 Cb 15.02N 22.48 E
Tinkisso 34 Dc 11.21N 9.10W
Tinnelva 8 Ce 59.34N 9.15 E
Tinniswood, Mount- 46 Da 50.19N 123.50W
Tinnoset 8 Ce 59.43N 9.02 E
Tinnsjø 8 Ce 59.54N 8.55 E
Tinogasta 56 Gc 28.04S 67.34W
Tinos 15 Il 37.35N 25.10 E
Tinos 15 Il 37.32N 25.10 E
Tinou, Stenón- 15 Il 37.38N 25.10 E
Tinrhert, Hamada de- 30 Hf 28.50N 10.00 E
Tinrhir 32 Fc 31.31N 5.32W
Tinsukia 25 Jc 27.30N 95.22 E
Tintagel Head 9 Ik 50.41N 4.46W
Tintamarre, Ile- 51b Bb 18.07N 63.00W
Ti-n-Tarabine 32 Ie 21.16N 7.24 E
Tîntăreni 15 Ge 44.36N 23.29 E
Tintina 56 Hc 27.02S 62.43W
Ti-n-toumma 30 Ig 16.04N 12.40 E
Tinwald 62 De 43.55S 171.43 E
Ti-n-Zaouâtene 31 Hg 19.56N 2.55 E
Tiobraid Árann/Tipperary 9 Ei 52.29N 8.10W
Tiobraid Árann/Tipperary 9 Ei 52.40N 8.20W
Tioga 45 Eb 48.24N 102.56W
Tioman, Pulau- 26 Df 2.48N 104.11 E
Tione di Trento 14 Ed 46.02N 10.43 E
Tioro, Selat-=Tioro, Strait (EN) 26 Hg 4.40S 122.20 E
Tioro Strait (EN)=Tioro, Selat- 26 Hg 4.40S 122.20 E
Tiøtta 7 Cd 65.50N 12.24 E
Tiouilit 32 Df 18.52N 16.10W
Tipasa 13 Oh 36.35N 2.27 E
Tipitapa 47 Gf 12.12N 86.06W
Tipperary/Tiobraid Árann 9 Ei 52.29N 8.10W
Tipperary/Tiobraid Árann 9 Ei 52.40N 8.20W
Tipton, Mount- 46 Hi 35.32N 114.12W
Tip Top Mountain 45 Nb 48.16N 85.59W
Tiptree 12 Cc 51.49N 0.45 E
Tiracambu, Serra do- 54 Id 3.15S 46.30W
Tirahart 32 He 23.45N 2.30 E
Tirān 24 Nf 32.42N 51.09 E
Tirān, Maḑīq- 24 Fi 27.55N 34.28 E
Tirana 6 Hg 41.20N 19.50 E
Tirania 32 Ie 23.08N 9.01 E
Tirano 14 Ed 46.13N 10.10 E
Tiraspol 19 Cf 46.50N 29.37 E
Tirat Karmel 24 Ff 32.46N 34.58 E
Tire 23 Cb 38.04N 27.45 E
Tirebolu 24 Hb 41.00N 38.50 E
Tiree 9 Ge 56.31N 6.49W
Tiree, Passage of- 9 Ge 56.30N 6.30W
Tîrgovişte 15 Ie 44.56N 25.27 E
Tîrgu Bujor 15 Kd 45.52N 27.54 E
Tîrgu Cărbuneşti 15 Ge 44.57N 23.31 E
Tîrgu Frumos 15 Jb 47.12N 27.00 E
Tîrgu Jiu 15 Gd 45.03N 23.17 E
Tîrgu Lăpuş 15 Gb 47.27N 23.52 E
Tîrgu Mureş 6 If 46.33N 24.34 E
Tîrgu Neamţ 15 Jb 47.12N 26.22 E
Tîrgu Ocna 15 Jc 46.17N 26.37 E
Tîrgu Secuiesc 15 Jd 46.00N 26.08 E
Tîrguşor 15 Le 44.27N 28.25 E
Tirich Mir 21 Jf 36.15N 71.50 E
Tirins 15 Fl 37.36N 22.48 E
Tiririca, Serra da- 55 Ic 17.06S 47.06W
Tiris 30 Ff 23.10N 13.30W
Tiris Zemmour 32 Fe 24.00N 10.00W
Tirlemont/Tienen 12 Gd 50.48N 4.57 E
Tirljanski 17 Ii 54.12N 58.33 E
Tîrnava Mare 15 Gc 46.09N 23.42 E
Tîrnava Mică 15 Gc 46.11N 23.55 E
Tîrnăveni 15 Hc 46.20N 24.17 E
Tirnavos 15 Fj 39.45N 22.17 E
Tiro 34 Cd 9.45N 10.39W
Tirol/Tirolo=Tyrol (EN) 14 Fd 47.00N 11.20 E
Tirol=Tyrol (EN) 14 Fc 47.10N 11.25 E
Tirolo/Tirol=Tyrol (EN) 14 Fd 47.00N 11.20 E
Tiros 55 Jd 19.00S 45.58W
Tirreno, Mar-=Tyrrhenian Sea (EN) 5 Hh 40.00N 12.00 E
Tirschenreuth 10 Ig 49.53N 12.21 E
Tirso 14 Ck 39.53N 8.32 E
Tirstrup 8 Dh 56.18N 10.42 E
Tirua Point 62 Fc 38.23S 174.38 E
Tiruchchirappalli 22 Jh 10.49N 78.41 E
Tiruliai/Tiruliaj 8 Ji 55.44N 23.18 E
Tiruliaj/Tiruliai 8 Ji 55.44N 23.18 E
Tirunelveli 22 Ji 8.44N 77.42 E
Tirupati 25 Ff 13.39N 79.25 E
Tirza 8 Lg 57.09N 26.37 E
Tisa=Tisza (EN) 5 If 45.15N 20.17 E
Tis Abay 35 Fc 11.20N 37.40 E
Tisdale 42 Hf 52.51N 104.04W
Tisnaren 8 Ff 58.55N 15.55 E
Tisovec 10 Ph 48.42N 19.57 E
Tissemsilt 32 Hb 35.36N 1.49 E
Tissø 8 Di 55.35N 11.20 E
Tisza 5 If 45.15N 20.17 E
Tisza (EN)=Tisa 5 If 45.15N 20.17 E
Tiszaföldvár 10 Qj 46.59N 20.15 E
Tiszafüred 10 Qi 47.37N 20.46 E
Tiszakécske 10 Qj 46.56N 20.06 E
Tiszántúl 10 Qj 47.00N 21.00 E
Tiszavasvári 10 Ri 47.58N 21.21 E
Titao 34 Ec 13.46N 2.04W
Titarisios 15 Fj 39.47N 22.23 E
Tit-Ary 20 Hb 71.55N 127.01 E
Titicaca, Lago- 52 Jg 15.50S 69.20W
Titikaveka 64p Bc 21.15S 159.45W
Titlagarh 25 Gd 20.18N 83.09 E
Titlis 14 Cd 46.47N 8.26 E
Titograd 6 Hg 42.26N 19.16 E
Titova Korenica 14 Jf 44.45N 15.42 E
Titovo Užice 15 Cf 43.52N 19.51 E
Titov Veles 15 Eh 41.42N 21.48 E
Titov vrh 15 Dh 41.58N 20.50 E
Titran 7 Be 63.40N 8.18 E
Titteri 13 Pi 35.59N 3.15 E
Titule 36 Eb 3.17N 25.32 E
Titusville [Fl.-U.S.] 43 Kf 28.37N 80.49W
Titusville [Pa.-U.S.] 44 He 41.37N 79.42W
Tituvenaj/Tytuvėnai 8 Ji 55.33N 23.09 E
Tiva 36 Gc 2.20S 39.55 E
Tivaouane 34 Bc 14.57N 16.49W
Tiveden 8 Ff 58.45N 14.40 E
Tiverton 9 Jk 50.55N 3.29W
Tivoli [Gren.] 51p Bb 12.10N 61.37W
Tivoli [It.] 14 Gi 41.58N 12.48 E
Ţiwāl 35 Cc 10.22N 22.43 E
Tiwi 36 Gc 4.14S 39.35 E
Tiyo 35 Gc 14.41N 40.57 E
Tizatlán 48 Jh 19.21N 98.15W
Tizimín 47 Gd 21.09N 88.09W
Tizi Ouzou 32 Hb 36.35N 4.05 E
Tizi Ouzou 32 Hb 36.42N 4.03 E
Tiznados, Río- 50 Ch 8.16N 67.47W
Tiznit 32 Fd 29.43N 9.43W
Tiznit 32 Fd 29.07N 9.04W
Tjačev 10 Th 48.02N 23.36 E
Tjanšan 27 Dc 42.00N 80.01 E
Tjasmin 16 He 49.03N 32.50 E
Tjeggelvas 7 Dc 66.35N 17.40 E
Tjeukemeer 11 Lb 52.54N 5.50 E
Tjøme 8 De 59.10N 10.25 E
Tjorn 8 Df 58.00N 11.38 E
Tjub-Karagan, Mys- 16 Qg 44.38N 50.20 E
Tjubuk 17 Jh 56.03N 60.58 E
Tjuhtet 20 De 56.32N 89.29 E
Tjukalinsk 19 Hd 55.52N 72.12 E
Tjuleni, Ostrov- 16 Og 44.30N 47.30 E
Tjuleni, Ostrova- 16 Qg 44.55N 50.10 E
Tjulgan 19 Fe 52.22N 56.12 E
Tjumen 22 Id 57.09N 65.32 E
Tjumenskaja Oblast 19 Gd 57.00N 69.00 E
Tjung 20 Hd 63.42N 121.30 E
Tjup 18 Lc 42.44N 78.20 E
Tjuri/Türi 7 Fg 58.50N 25.27 E
Tjust 8 Gg 57.50N 16.15 E
Tjuters Maly, Ostrov- 8 Le 59.45N 26.53 E
Tjuzašu, Pereval- 18 Ic 42.19N 73.50 E
Tkibuli 16 Mh 42.19N 42.59 E
Tkvarčeli 19 Eg 42.52N 41.40 E
Tlacolula 48 Ki 16.57N 96.29W
Tlacotalpan 48 Lh 18.37N 95.40W
Tlahualilo, Sierra del- 48 Hd 26.30N 103.20W
Tlalnepantla 48 Jh 19.33N 99.12W
Tlapa de Comonfort 48 Ji 17.33N 98.33W
Tlapaneco, Río- 48 Jh 18.00N 98.48W
Tlaquepaque 48 Hg 20.39N 103.19W
Tlaxcala 47 Ee 19.25N 98.10W
Tlaxcala 47 Ee 19.19N 98.14W
Tlemcen 32 Gc 34.52N 1.19W
Tlemcen 32 Gc 34.45N 1.30W
Tleń 10 Oc 53.38N 18.20 E
Tleta Rissana 13 Gi 35.14N 5.59W
Tletat ed Douaïr 13 Oi 35.59N 2.55 E
Tljarata 16 Oh 42.06N 46.22 E
Tlumač 10 Vh 48.46N 25.06 E
Tłuszcz 10 Rd 52.26N 21.26 E
Tmassah 33 Cd 26.22N 15.48 E
Tō, Shikotan-/Šikotan, Ostrov- 20 Jh 43.47N 146.45 E
Toaca, Vîrful- 15 Ic 46.55N 25.59 E
Toagel Mlungui 64a Ab 7.32N 134.28 E
Toamasina 31 Lj 18.10S 49.24 E
Toamasina 37 Hc 18.00S 48.40 E
Toau Atoll 61 Lc 15.55S 146.00W
Toay 56 He 36.40S 64.21W
Toba 28 Ng 34.29N 136.51 E
Toba, Danau-=Toba, Lake- (EN) 26 Li 2.35N 98.50 E
Toba, Lake- (EN)=Toba, Danau- 26 Li 2.35N 98.50 E
Tobago 52 Jd 11.15N 60.40W
Tobago Basin (EN) 50 Ff 12.30N 60.30W
Tobago Cays 51n Bb 12.39N 61.22W
Toba Kākar Range 25 Db 31.15N 68.00 E
Tobarra 13 Kf 38.35N 1.41W
Tobe 29 Ce 33.44N 132.47 E
Tobejuba, Isla- 50 Fh 9.20N 60.52W
Tobelo 26 If 1.25N 127.31 E
Tobermory [Ont.-Can.] 44 Gc 45.15N 81.40W
Tobermory [Scot.-U.K.] 9 Ge 56.37N 6.05W
Tōbetsu 29a Bb 43.14N 141.29 E
Tobi Island 57 Ed 3.00N 131.10 E
Tobin, Kap- 41 Jd 70.30N 21.30W
Tobin, Mount- 46 Gf 40.22N 117.32W
Tobin Lake [Austl.] 59 Fd 21.45S 125.50 E
Tobin Lake [Sask.-Can.] 42 Hf 53.40N 103.20W
Tobi-Shima 29 Fb 39.12N 139.32 E
Toblach / Dobbiaco 14 Gd 46.44N 12.14 E
Toboali 26 Eg 3.00S 106.30 E
Tobol 19 Ge 52.40N 62.39 E
Tobol 21 Id 58.10N 68.12 E
Tobolsk 22 Id 58.12N 68.16 E
Tobruk (EN)=Ţubruq 31 Je 32.05N 23.59 E
Tobseda 19 Fb 68.36N 52.20 E
Tobyš 17 Ed 65.30N 51.00 E
Tocantinópolis 53 Lf 6.20S 47.25W
Tocantins, Rio- 52 Lf 1.45S 49.10W
Tocantinzinho, Rio- 55 Ha 13.57S 48.20W
Toccoa 44 Fh 34.35N 83.19W
Toce 14 Ce 45.56N 8.29 E
Tochigi 29 Fc 36.23N 139.44 E
Tochigi Ken 28 Of 36.50N 139.50 E
Tochio 29 Fc 37.29N 138.58 E
Töcksfors 8 De 59.31N 11.50 E
Toco 50 Fg 10.50N 60.57W
Tocoa 49 Df 15.41N 86.03W
Toconao 56 Gb 23.11S 68.01W
Tocopilla 53 Ih 22.05S 70.12W
Tocumen 49 Hi 9.05N 79.23W
Tocuyo, Río- 49 Mh 11.03N 68.20W
Todd Mountain 44 Nb 46.32N 66.43W
Todi 14 Gh 42.47N 12.24 E
Tödi 14 Cd 46.49N 8.55 E
Todo-ga-Saki 27 Pd 39.33N 142.05 E
Todos os Santos, Baia de- 52 Mg 12.48S 38.38W
Todos Santos 47 Bd 23.27N 110.13W
Todos Santos, Bahía- 48 Ab 31.48N 116.42W
Tofino 42 Eg 49.09N 125.54W
Tofte 8 De 59.33N 10.34 E
Toftlund 8 Ci 55.11N 9.04 E
Tofua Island 61 Fc 19.45S 175.05W
Toga 63b Ca 13.26S 166.41 E
Tōgane 29 Gd 35.33N 140.21 E
Tog Ḍarōr 35 Hc 10.25N 50.00 E
Togdere 35 Hd 9.01N 47.07 E
Tog-Dheer 35 Hd 9.50N 45.50 E
Togi 29 Ec 37.08N 136.43 E
Togiak 40 Ge 59.04N 160.24W
Togian, Kepulauan-=Togian Islands (EN) 26 Hg 0.20S 122.00 E
Togian Islands (EN)= Togian, Kepulauan- 26 Hg 0.20S 122.00 E
Togliatti 6 Ke 53.31N 49.26 E
Togni 35 Fb 18.05N 35.10 E
Togo 31 Hh 8.00N 1.10 E
Togrog Ul → Qahar Youyi Qianqi 28 Bd 40.46N 113.13 E
Togtoh 27 Jc 40.17N 111.15 E
Togučin 20 De 55.16N 84.33 E
Toguzak 17 Ki 54.05N 62.48 E
Togwotee Pass 43 Ec 43.45N 110.04W
Tohen 35 Ic 11.44N 51.15 E
Tohma 24 Hc 38.31N 38.25 E
Tohmajärvi 7 He 62.11N 30.23 E
Tohopekaliga, Lake- 44 Gk 28.12N 81.23W
Toi 29 Fd 34.54N 138.47 E
Toijala 7 Ff 61.10N 23.52 E
Toi-Misaki 28 Ki 31.26N 131.19 E
Toivesi 8 Jb 62.20N 23.45 E
Tōjō 29 Cd 34.53N 133.16 E
Tojtepa 18 Gd 41.03N 69.22 E
Tok 10 Jg 49.43N 13.50 E
Tok 16 Rc 52.46N 52.22 E
Tok 40 Kd 63.20N 142.59W
Tokachi-Dake 29a Cb 43.25N 142.41 E
Tokachi-Gawa 29a Cb 42.41N 143.37 E
Tokachi-Heiya 29a Cb 43.00N 143.20 E
Tokachimitsumata 29a Cb 43.31N 143.07 E
Tōkai [Jap.] 29 Gc 36.27N 140.34 E
Tōkai [Jap.] 29 Ed 35.01N 136.51 E
Tokaj 16 Ld 51.18N 41.04 E
Tokaj 10 Rh 48.07N 21.25 E
Tōkamachi 28 Of 37.08N 138.46 E
Tokanui 62 Cg 46.34S 168.57 E
Tokara Islands (EN)= Tokara-Rettō 21 Og 29.35N 129.45 E
Tokara-Kaikyō 28 Ki 30.10N 130.15 E
Tokara-Rettō=Tokara Islands (EN) 21 Og 29.35N 129.45 E
Tokashiki-Jima 29b Ab 26.13N 127.21 E
Tokat 23 Ea 40.19N 36.34 E
Tŏkch'ŏn 28 Ie 39.45N 126.15 E
Tok-Do 28 Kf 37.22N 131.58 E
Tokelau 58 Je 9.00S 171.46W
Tokelau/Union Islands 57 Je 9.00S 171.45W
Toki 29 Ed 35.22N 137.11 E
Tokke 8 Ce 59.00N 9.15 E
Tokke 8 Be 59.27N 7.58 E
Tokkuztara/Gongliu 27 Dc 43.30N 82.15 E
Tokmak [Kirg.-U.S.S.R.] 19 Hg 42.49N 75.19 E
Tokmak [Ukr.-U.S.S.R.] 19 Df 47.13N 35.43 E
Tokomaru Bay 61 Eg 38.08S 178.20 E
Tokoname 29 Ed 34.53N 136.49 E
Tokoro 29a Da 44.08N 144.03 E
Tokoroa 61 Eg 38.13S 175.52 E
Tokoro-Gawa 29a Da 44.08N 144.04 E
Toksovo 8 Nd 60.10N 30.42 E
Toksu/Xinhe 27 Dc 41.34N 82.38 E
Toksun 27 Ec 42.47N 88.38 E
Toktogul 19 Hg 41.50N 73.01 E
Toktogulskoje Vodohranilišče 18 Id 41.45N 73.00 E
Tokuji 29 Bd 34.11N 131.39 E
Tokulu 65b Bb 20.06S 174.48W
Toku-no-Shima 27 Mf 27.45N 128.50 E
Tokunoshima 29b Bb 27.45N 129.00 E
Tokur 20 If 53.09N 132.50 E
Tokushima 27 Ne 34.04N 134.34 E
Tokushima Ken 28 Mh 33.50N 134.10 E
Tokuyama [Jap.] 29 Ed 35.43N 136.27 E
Tokuyama [Jap.] 28 Kg 34.03N 131.49 E
Tokwe 37 Ed 20.09S 31.54 E
Tōkyō 22 Pf 35.40N 139.46 E
Tokyo Bay (EN)=Tōkyō-Wan 28 Og 35.38N 139.57 E
Tōkyō To 28 Og 35.40N 139.20 E
Tōkyō-Wan=Tokyo Bay (EN) 28 Og 35.38N 139.57 E
Tola 21 Me 48.57N 104.48 E
Tolaga Bay 62 Hc 38.22S 178.18 E
Tolbazy 17 Gi 54.02N 55.59 E
Tolbuhin 15 Kf 43.34N 27.50 E
Tolbuhin 15 Kf 43.34N 27.50 E
Toledo 13 Ie 39.50N 4.00W
Toledo [Blz.] 49 Ce 16.25N 88.50W
Toledo [Braz.] 56 Jb 24.44S 53.45W
Toledo [Oh.-U.S.] 39 Ke 41.39N 83.32W
Toledo [Phil.] 26 Hd 10.23N 123.38 E
Toledo [Sp.] 6 Fh 39.52N 4.01W
Toledo, Montes de- 13 He 39.35N 4.20W
Toledo Bend Reservoir 43 Ie 31.30N 93.45W
Tolentino 14 Hg 43.12N 13.17 E
Tolfa 14 Fh 42.09N 11.56 E
Tolfa, Monti della- 14 Fh 42.10N 11.55 E
Tolga 7 Ce 62.25N 11.00 E
Toli 27 Db 45.57N 83.37 E
Toliara 37 Gd 22.00S 44.00 E
Toliara 31 Lk 23.21S 43.39 E
Tolima 54 Cc 3.45N 75.15W
Tolima, Nevado del- 52 Ie 4.40N 75.19W
Toling → Zanda 27 Ce 31.28N 79.50 E
Tolitoli 26 Hf 1.02N 120.49 E
Toll 64d Bb 7.22N 151.37 E
Tollarp 8 Ei 55.56N 13.59 E
Tollja, Zaliv- 20 Ea 76.40N 100.00 E
Tolmačevo 8 Nf 58.48N 30.01 E
Tolmezzo 14 Hd 46.24N 13.01 E
Tolmin 14 Hd 46.11N 13.44 E
Tolna 10 Oj 46.26N 18.47 E
Tolna 10 Oj 46.30N 18.35 E
Tolo 36 Cc 2.56S 18.34 E
Tolo, Gulf of- (EN)=Tolo, Teluk- 21 Oj 2.00S 122.30 E
Tolo, Teluk-=Tolo, Gulf of- (EN) 21 Oj 2.00S 122.30 E
Toločin 7 Gi 54.25N 29.41 E
Tolosa 13 Ja 43.08N 2.04W
Tolstoj, Mys- 5 Rd 59.10N 155.05 E
Toltén 56 Fe 39.13S 73.14W
Tolú 54 Cb 9.32N 75.34W
Toluca, Nevado de- 38 Jh 19.08N 99.44W
Toluca de Lerdo 39 Jh 19.17N 99.40W
Tom 21 Kd 56.50N 84.27 E
Toma 34 Ec 12.46N 2.53W
Tomah 45 Ke 43.59N 90.30W
Tomakomai 27 Pc 42.38N 141.36 E
Tomamae 29a Ba 44.18N 141.39 E
Tomanivi 63d Bb 17.37S 178.01 E
Tomar 13 De 39.36N 8.25W
Tómaros 15 Dj 39.32N 20.45 E
Tomaševka 16 Cd 51.33N 23.40 E
Tomás Young 55 Ai 28.36S 62.11W
Tomaszów Lubelski 10 Tf 50.28N 23.25 E
Tomaszów Mazowiecki 10 Qe 51.32N 20.01 E
Tomatlán 48 Gh 19.56N 105.15W
Tombador, Serra dos- 54 Gf 12.00S 57.40W
Tombigbee River 43 Je 31.04N 87.58W
Tomboco 36 Bd 6.45S 13.18 E
Tombouctou=Timbuktu (EN) 31 Gg 16.46N 2.59W
Tombstone 46 Jk 31.43N 110.04W
Tombua 31 Ij 15.48S 11.52 E
Tomé 56 Fe 36.37S 72.57W
Tomé-Açu 54 Id 2.25S 48.09W
Tomelilla 7 Ci 55.33N 13.57 E
Tomelloso 13 Ie 39.10N 3.01W
Tomichi Creek 45 Cg 38.31N 106.58W
Tomie 29 Ae 32.37N 128.46 E
Tomini, Gulf of- (EN)= Tomini, Teluk- 21 Oj 0.20S 121.00 E
Tomini, Teluk-=Tomini, Gulf of- (EN) 21 Oj 0.20S 121.00 E
Tominian 34 Ec 13.17N 4.35W
Tomioka [Jap.] 29 Gc 37.20N 140.59 E
Tomioka [Jap.] 29 Fc 36.15N 138.52 E
Tomkinson Ranges 59 Fe 26.10S 129.05 E
Tomma 7 Cc 66.15N 12.48 E
Tomo, Río- 54 Eb 5.20N 67.48W
Tomochic 48 Fc 28.20N 107.51W
Tomorit, Mali i- 15 Di 40.40N 20.09 E
Tomotu Neo 63c Ab 10.41S 165.47 E
Tomotu Noi 63c Bb 10.50S 166.02 E
Tompa 10 Pj 46.12N 19.33 E
Tompe 26 Gg 0.12S 119.48 E
Tompo 20 Id 62.50N 134.47 E
Tompo 20 Id 64.00N 136.00 E
Tom Price 59 Dd 22.40S 117.55 E
Tomsk 22 Kd 56.30N 84.58 E
Tomskaja Oblast 20 De 58.20N 81.30 E
Tomtabacken 8 Fg 57.30N 14.28 E
Tomur Feng 27 Kc 42.02N 80.05 E
Tom White, Mount- 40 Kd 60.40N 143.40W
Tonaki-Shima 29b Ab 26.21N 127.09 E
Tonalá 47 Fe 16.04N 93.45W
Tonale, Passo del- 14 Ed 46.16N 10.35 E
Tonami 29 Ec 36.38N 136.57 E
Tonara 14 Dj 40.02N 9.10 E
Tonasket 46 Fb 48.42N 119.26W
Tonb-e Bozorg 24 Pi 26.15N 55.03 E
Tonbetsu-Gawa 29a Ca 45.08N 142.23 E
Tonbridge 9 Nj 51.12N 0.16 E
Tondano 26 Hf 1.19N 124.54 E
Tondela 13 Dd 40.31N 8.05W
Tønder 7 Bi 54.56N 8.54 E
Tone-Gawa 29 Gd 35.44N 140.51 E
Tonekābon 23 Hb 36.53N 50.56 E
Toney 66 Of 75.48S 115.48W
Tonga 58 Jf 20.00S 175.00W
Tonga 35 Ed 9.28N 31.03 E

Index Symbols

Independent Nation
State, Region
District, County
Municipality
Colony, Dependency
Continent
Physical Region
Historical or Cultural Region
Mount, Mountain
Volcano
Hill
Mountains, Mountain Range
Hills, Escarpment
Plateau, Upland
Pass, Gap
Plain, Lowland
Delta
Salt Flat
Valley, Canyon
Crater, Cave
Karst Features
Depression
Polder
Desert, Dunes
Forest, Woods
Heath, Steppe
Oasis
Cape, Point
Coast, Beach
Cliff
Peninsula
Isthmus
Sandbank
Island
Atoll
Rock, Reef
Islands, Archipelago
Rocks, Reefs
Coral Reef
Well, Spring
Geyser
River, Stream
Waterfall Rapids
River Mouth, Estuary
Lake
Salt Lake
Intermittent Lake
Reservoir
Swamp, Pond
Canal
Glacier
Ice Shelf, Pack Ice
Ocean
Sea
Gulf, Bay
Strait, Fjord
Lagoon
Bank
Seamount
Tablemount
Ridge
Shelf
Basin
Escarpment, Sea Scarp
Fracture
Trench, Abyss
National Park, Reserve
Point of Interest
Recreation Site
Cave, Cavern
Historic Site
Ruins
Wall, Walls
Church, Abbey
Temple
Scientific Station
Airport
Port
Lighthouse
Mine
Tunnel
Dam, Bridge

Index Symbols

[1] Independent Nation
[2] State, Region
[3] District, County
[4] Municipality
[5] Colony, Dependency
Continent
Physical Region
Historical or Cultural Region
Mount, Mountain
Volcano
Hill
Mountains, Mountain Range
Hills, Escarpment
Plateau, Upland
Pass, Gap
Plain, Lowland
Delta
Salt Flat
Valley, Canyon
Crater, Cave
Karst Features
Depression
Polder
Desert, Dunes
Forest, Woods
Heath, Steppe
Oasis
Cape, Point
Coast, Beach
Cliff
Peninsula
Isthmus
Sandbank
Island
Atoll
Rock, Reef
Islands, Archipelago
Rocks, Reefs
Coral Reef
Well, Spring
Geyser
River, Stream
Waterfall Rapids
River Mouth, Estuary
Lake
Salt Lake
Intermittent Lake
Reservoir
Swamp, Pond
Canal
Glacier
Ice Shelf, Pack Ice
Ocean
Sea
Gulf, Bay
Strait, Fjord
Lagoon
Bank
Seamount
Tablemount
Ridge
Shelf
Basin
Escarpment, Sea Scarp
Fracture
Trench, Abyss
National Park, Reserve
Point of Interest
Recreation Site
Cave, Cavern
Historic Site
Ruins
Wall, Walls
Church, Abbey
Temple
Scientific Station
Airport
Port
Lighthouse
Mine
Tunnel
Dam, Bridge

Tripura [3] 25 Id 24.00N 92.00 E
Trisanna 14 Ec 47.07N 10.30 E
Tristan da Cunha 30 Fi 37.05S 12.17W
Tristan da Cunha Group 30 Fi 37.15S 12.30W
Triste, Golfo- 50 Bg 10.40N 68.10W
Triunfo 55 Ee 20.46S 55.47W
Trivandrum 22 Ji 8.29N 76.55 E
Trivento 14 Ii 41.47N 14.33 E
Trjavna 15 Ig 42.52N 25.30 E
Trnava 10 Nh 48.22N 17.35 E
Troarn 12 Be 49.11N 0.11W
Trobriand Islands 57 Ge 8.30S 151.05 E
Trödje 8 Gd 60.49N 17.12 E
Trofors 7 Cd 65.34N 13.25 E
Trögd 8 Ge 59.30N 17.15 E
Trogir 14 Kg 43.32N 16.15 E
Troglav [Yugo.] 14 Kg 43.58N 16.36 E
Troglav [Yugo.] 14 Mg 43.02N 18.33 E
Trøgstad 8 De 59.38N 11.18 E
Troia 14 Ji 41.22N 15.18 E
Troick [R.S.F.S.R.] 22 Id 54.06N 61.35 E
Troick [R.S.F.S.R.] 20 Ee 57.23N 94.55 E
Troickoje [R.S.F.S.R.] 20 Df 52.58N 84.45 E
Troickoje [R.S.F.S.R.] 20 Ig 49.30N 136.32 E
Troickoje [Ukr.-U.S.S.R.] 15 Nb 47.38N 30.12 E
Troicko Pečorsk 19 Fc 62.44N 56.06 E
Troina 14 Im 37.47N 14.36 E
Troisdorf 12 Jd 50.49N 7.10 E
Trois Fourches, Cap des- 32 Gb 35.26N 2.58W
Trois-Pistoles 44 Ma 48.07N 69.10W
Trois Pitons, Morne- 51g Bb 15.22N 61.20W
Trois-Ponts 12 Hd 50.22N 5.52 E
Trois-Rivières [Guad.] 51e Ac 15.59N 61.39W
Trois-Rivières [Que.-Can.] 39 Le 46.21N 72.33W
Troissereux 12 Ee 49.29N 2.03 E
Troisvierges/Ulflingen 12 Hd 50.07N 6.00 E
Trojah 15 Hg 42.53N 24.43 E
Trojanovka 10 Ve 51.21N 25.25 E
Trojanski Manastir 15 Hg 42.53N 24.48 E
Trojanski prohod 15 Hg 42.48N 24.40 E
Trojebratski 19 Ge 54.25N 66.03 E
Trollhättan 7 Cg 58.16N 12.18 E
Trollheimen 7 Be 62.50N 9.05 E
Trollhetta 8 Cb 62.51N 9.19 E
Trolltindane 8 Bb 62.29N 7.43 E
Tromba 55 Ha 13.28S 48.45W
Trombetas, Rio- 52 Kf 1.55S 55.35W
Tromelin 30 Mj 15.52S 54.25 E
Tromøya 8 Cf 58.30N 8.50 E
Troms [3] 7 Eb 69.07N 19.15 E
Tromsø 6 Hb 69.40N 19.00 E
Tron 8 Db 62.10N 10.43 E
Tronador, Monte- 52 Ij 41.10S 71.54W
Trondheim 6 Hc 63.25N 10.25 E
Trondheimsfjorden 5 Hc 63.40N 10.50 E
Tronto 14 Hh 42.54N 13.55 E
Tropea 14 Jl 38.41N 15.54 E
Tropeiros, Serra dos- 55 Jb 14.43S 44.33W
Tropoja 15 Dg 42.24N 20.10 E
Trosa 7 Dg 58.54N 17.33 E
Troškūnai/Troškunaj 8 Ki 55.32N 24.59 E
Troškunaj/Troškūnai 8 Ki 55.32N 24.59 E
Trostberg 10 Ih 48.02N 12.33 E
Trostjanec 16 Id 50.29N 34.59 E
Trotuş 15 Kc 46.03N 27.14 E
Trou Gras Point 51k Bb 13.52N 60.53W
Troumasse 51k Bb 13.49N 60.54W
Trout Lake [Mi.-U.S.] 44 Eb 46.12N 85.01W
Trout Lake [N.W.T.-Can.] 42 Fd 60.35N 121.10W
Trout Lake [Ont.-Can.] 42 If 51.12N 93.19W
Trout Lake [Ont.-Can.] 42 If 53.54N 89.56W
Trout Peak 46 Kd 44.36N 109.32W
Trout River 42 Lg 49.29N 58.08W
Trouville-sur-Mer 11 Ge 49.22N 0.05 E
Trowbridge 9 Kj 51.20N 2.13W
Troy [Al.-U.S.] 43 Je 31.48N 85.58W
Troy [Mo.-U.S.] 45 Kg 38.59N 90.59W
Troy [Mt.-U.S.] 46 Hb 48.28N 115.53W
Troy [N.Y.-U.S.] 43 Mc 42.43N 73.40W
Troy [Oh.-U.S.] 44 Ee 40.02N 84.12W
Troy (EN)=Truva 24 Bc 39.57N 26.15 E
Troyes 6 Gf 48.18N 4.05 E
Troy Peak 43 Dd 38.19N 115.30W
Trstenik 15 Df 43.37N 21.00 E
Trubčevsk 19 De 52.36N 33.46 E
Truc Giang 25 Lf 10.14N 106.23 E
Truchas Peak 45 Di 35.58N 105.39W
Trucial Coast (EN) 21 Hg 24.00N 53.00 E
Trucial States (EN)→United Arab Emirates (EN) [1] 22 Hg 24.00N 54.00 E
Truckee 46 Eg 39.20N 120.11W
Trudfront 16 Og 45.56N 47.41 E
Trudovoje 20 Ih 43.18N 132.05 E
Trufanova 7 Kd 64.29N 44.05 E
Trujillo [2] 54 Db 9.25N 70.30W
Trujillo [Hond.] 47 Ge 15.55N 86.00W
Trujillo [Peru] 53 If 8.10S 79.02W
Trujillo [Sp.] 13 Ge 39.28N 5.53W
Trujillo [Ven.] 54 Db 9.22N 70.26W
Trujillo, Rio- 48 Hf 23.39N 103.48W
Truk Islands 57 Gd 7.25N 151.47 E
Trumann 45 Ki 35.41N 90.31W
Trumbull, Mount- 43 Ed 36.25N 113.10W
Trun 12 Gf 48.51N 0.02 E
Trung Phan=Annam (EN) 21 Me 15.00N 108.00 E
Truro [Eng.-U.K.] 9 Hk 50.16N 5.03W
Truro [N.S.-Can.] 39 Me 45.22N 63.16W
Truskavec 16 Ce 49.17N 23.34 E
Truth or Consequences (Hot Springs) 43 Fe 33.08N 107.15W
Trutnov 10 Lf 50.34N 15.54 E
Truva=Troy (EN) 24 Bc 39.57N 26.15 E
Truyère 11 Ij 44.38N 2.34 E
Trysil 8 Ec 61.25N 12.25 E
Trysil 7 Cf 61.18N 12.16 E
Trysilelva 5 Hd 59.23N 13.32 E
Trysilfjellet 8 Ec 61.18N 12.11 E
Trzcianka 10 Mc 53.03N 16.28 E
Trzcińsko Zdrój 10 Kd 52.58N 14.35 E
Trzebiatów 10 Lb 54.04N 15.14 E
Trzebież 10 Kc 53.42N 14.31 E
Trzebinia-Siersza 10 Pf 50.11N 19.25 E
Trzebnica 10 Ne 51.19N 17.03 E
Trzebnicki, Wał- 10 Me 51.30N 16.20 E
Trzebnickie, Wzgórza- 10 Me 51.15N 17.00 E
Trzemeszno 10 Nd 52.35N 17.50 E
Tsaidam Basin (EN)=Qaidam Pendi 27 Fd 37.00N 95.00 E
Tsamandá, Óri- 15 Dj 39.48N 20.21 E
Tsarap 25 Fb 33.31N 76.56 E
Tsaratanana 37 Hc 16.46S 47.38 E
Tsaratanana (EN)=Tsaratanana, Massif du- 30 Lj 14.00S 49.00 E
Tsaratanana, Massif du-=Tsaratanana (EN) 30 Lj 14.00S 49.00 E
Tsau 37 Cd 20.10S 22.27 E
Tsavo 36 Gc 2.59S 38.28 E
Tses 37 Be 25.58S 18.08 E
Tsévié 34 Fd 6.25N 1.13 E
Tshabong 31 Jk 26.02S 22.06 E
Tshane 31 Jk 24.01S 21.43 E
Tshangalele, Lac- 36 Ee 10.55S 27.03 E
Tshela 31 Ii 4.59S 12.56 E
Tshesebe 37 Dd 20.43S 27.37 E
Tshibala 36 Dd 6.56S 21.28 E
Tshibamba 36 Dd 9.06S 22.34 E
Tshikapa 31 Ji 6.25S 20.48 E
Tshilenge 36 Dd 6.15S 23.46 E
Tshimbalanga 36 Dd 9.43S 23.06 E
Tshimbulu 36 Dd 6.29S 22.51 E
Tshinsenda 36 Ee 12.16S 27.55 E
Tshofa 36 Ed 5.14S 25.15 E
Tshopo 36 Eb 0.33N 25.07 E
Tshuapa 30 Ji 0.14S 20.42 E
Tshwaane 37 Cd 22.38S 22.05 E
Tsiafajavona 37 Hc 19.21S 47.15 E
Tsihombe 37 He 25.17S 45.30 E
Tsimlyansk Reservoir (EN)=Cimljanskoje Vodohranilišče 5 Kf 48.00N 43.00 E
Tsinan (EN)=Jinan 22 Nf 36.35N 117.00 E
Tsinghai (EN)=Ch'ing-hai Sheng→Qinghai Sheng [2] 27 Gd 36.00N 96.00 E
Tsinghai (EN)=Qinghai Sheng (Ch'ing-hai Sheng) [2] 27 Gd 36.00N 96.00 E
Tsingtao (EN)=Qingdao 22 Of 36.05N 120.21 E
Tsiribihina 37 Gc 19.42S 44.31 E
Tsiroanomandidy 37 Hc 18.50S 46.00 E
Tsis 64d Bb 7.18N 151.50 E
Tsjokkarassa 7 Fb 69.59N 24.32 E
Tsodilo Hill 37 Cc 18.50S 21.45 E
Tsu 27 Oe 34.43N 136.31 E
Tsubame 29 Fc 37.39N 138.56 E
Tsubata 28 Nf 36.40N 136.44 E
Tsubetsu 29a Db 43.43N 144.01 E
Tsuchiura 28 Pf 36.05N 140.12 E
Tsugaru-Hantō 29a Bc 41.00N 140.30 E
Tsugaru-Kaikyō=Tsugaru Strait (EN) 21 Qe 41.40N 140.55 E
Tsugaru Strait (EN)=Tsugaru-Kaikyō 21 Qe 41.40N 140.55 E
Tsuken-Jima 29b Ab 26.15N 127.57 E
Tsukidate 29 Gb 38.44N 141.01 E
Tsukigata 29a Bb 43.20N 141.39 E
Tsukuba-San 29 Gc 36.13N 140.06 E
Tsukumi 29 Be 33.04N 131.52 E
Tsukura-Se 29 Af 31.18N 129.47 E
Tsukushi-Sanchi 29 Be 33.25N 130.30 E
Tsumeb 31 Ij 19.13S 17.42 E
Tsumeb [3] 37 Bc 19.00S 17.30 E
Tsumkwe 37 Cc 19.32S 20.30 E
Tsuna 29 Dd 34.26N 134.54 E
Tsuno-Shima 29 Bd 34.22N 130.52 E
Tsuru 29 Fd 35.35N 138.50 E
Tsuruga 27 Od 35.39N 136.04 E
Tsuruga-Wan 29 Ed 35.45N 136.05 E
Tsurugi 29 Ec 36.26N 136.37 E
Tsurugi-San 29 De 33.51N 134.03 E
Tsurui 29a Db 43.14N 144.21 E
Tsurumi-Dake 29 Be 33.18N 131.27 E
Tsurumi-Saki 29 Ce 32.56N 132.05 E
Tsuruoka 28 Oe 38.44N 139.50 E
Tsuruta 29 Ga 40.44N 140.26 E
Tsushima 27 Of 34.30N 129.20 E
Tsushima [Jap.] 29 Ce 33.07N 132.30 E
Tsushima [Jap.] 29 Ed 35.10N 136.43 E
Tsushima-Kaikyō=Korea, Strait (EN) 21 Of 34.40N 129.00 E
Tsuwano 29 Bd 34.28N 131.46 E
Tsuyama 28 Lg 35.03N 134.00 E
Tua 13 Ec 41.13N 7.26W
Tuai 62 Gc 38.49S 177.08 E
Tuaim/Tuam 9 Eh 53.31N 8.50W
Tuakau 62 Fb 37.15S 174.57 E
Tual 26 Jh 5.40S 132.45 E
Tuam/Tuaim 9 Eh 53.31N 8.50W
Tuamotu, Iles-=Tuamotu Archipelago (EN) 57 Mf 19.00S 142.00W
Tuamotu Archipelago (EN)=Tuamotu, Iles- 57 Mf 19.00S 142.00W
Tuamotu Ridge (EN) 3 Ll 20.00S 145.00W
Tuapa 64k Ba 18.57S 169.54W
Tuapse 6 Jg 44.07N 39.05 E
Tuaran 26 Ge 6.11N 116.14 E
Tuasivi 65c Aa 13.40S 172.07W
Tuasivi, Cape- 65c Aa 13.40S 172.07W
Tuatapere 61 Ci 46.08S 167.41 E
Tuba 20 Ef 54.00N 91.40 E
Tuba City 46 Jh 36.08N 111.14W
Tubaï, Ile- 57 Mg 23.18S 149.30W
Tubai-Manu→Maïao, Ile- 57 Lf 17.34S 150.35W
Tubal, Wādī at- 24 Jf 32.19N 42.13 E
Tuban 26 Fh 6.54S 112.03 E
Tubarão 56 Kc 28.30S 49.01W
Ţubayq, Jabal at- 24 Gh 29.32N 37.30 E
Tubbataha Reefs 26 Ge 8.51N 119.56 E
Tubeke/Tubize 12 Gd 50.41N 4.12 E
Tübingen 10 Fh 48.32N 9.03 E
Tubize/Tubeke 12 Gd 50.41N 4.12 E
Ţubruq=Tobruk (EN) 31 Je 32.05N 23.59 E
Tubuai, Iles-/Australes, Iles-=Tubuai Islands (EN) 57 Lg 23.00S 150.00W
Tubuai Islands (EN)=Australes, Iles-/Tubuai, Iles- 57 Lg 23.00S 150.00W
Tubuai Islands (EN)=Tubuai, Iles-/Australes, Iles- 57 Lg 23.00S 150.00W
Tubutama 48 Db 30.53N 111.29W
Tucacas 54 Ea 10.48N 68.19W
Tucacas, Punta- 49 Mh 10.52N 68.13W
Tucavaca 55 Cd 18.36S 58.55W
Tucavaca, Rio- 55 Cd 18.37S 58.59W
Tuchola 10 Nc 53.35N 17.50 E
Tucholska, Równina- 10 Oc 53.40N 18.30 E
Tuchów 10 Rg 49.54N 21.03 E
Tucker Glacier 66 Kf 72.35S 169.20 E
Tucson 39 Hf 32.13N 110.58W
Tucuarembó 56 Id 31.44S 55.59W
Tucumán [2] 56 Gc 27.00S 65.30W
Tucumcari 43 Gd 35.10N 103.44W
Tucunui 54 Id 3.42S 49.27W
Tucupido 54 Eb 9.17N 65.47W
Tucupita 54 Fb 9.04N 62.03W
Tudela 13 Kb 42.05N 1.36W
Tudia, Sierra de- 13 Ff 38.05N 6.20W
Tudmur 23 Ec 34.33N 38.17 E
Tudora 15 Jb 47.31N 26.38 E
Tuela 13 Ec 41.30N 7.12W
Tuensang 25 Ic 26.17N 94.40 E
Tuerto 13 Gb 42.18N 5.53W
Tufanbeyli 24 Gc 38.18N 36.11 E
Tufi 58 Fe 9.08S 149.20 E
Tugela 30 Kk 29.14S 31.30 E
Tug Fork 44 Ff 38.25N 82.35W
Tuguegarao 26 Hc 17.37N 121.44 E
Tugulym 17 Lh 57.04N 64.39 E
Tugur 20 If 53.51N 136.52 E
Tuhai He 28 Ee 38.05N 118.13 E
Tujiabu → Yongxiu 27 Kf 29.05N 115.49 E
Tujmazy 19 Fe 54.36N 53.42 E
Tukan 17 Hj 53.50N 57.31 E
Tukangbesi, Kepulauan-=Tukangbesi Islands (EN) 26 Hh 5.40S 123.50 E
Tukangbesi Islands (EN)=Tukangbesi, Kepulauan- 26 Hh 5.40S 123.50 E
Tukayel 35 Hd 8.05N 45.20 E
Tukayyid 24 Kh 29.47N 45.36 E
Tukituki 62 Gc 39.36S 176.56 E
Tuko Village 64n Ab 10.22S 161.02W
Ţūkrah 33 Dc 32.32N 20.34 E
Tuktoyaktuk 39 Fc 69.27N 133.02W
Tukums 7 Fh 56.59N 23.10 E
Tukuringra, Hrebet- 20 Hf 54.30N 126.00 E
Tukuyu 36 Fd 9.15S 33.39 E
Tula 47 Ed 20.06N 99.19W
Tula 36 Gc 0.50S 39.51 E
Tula [Mex.] 48 Jf 23.00N 99.43W
Tula [R.S.F.S.R.] 6 Je 54.12N 37.37 E
Tula de Allende 48 Jg 20.03N 99.21W
Tula Mountains 66 Ee 66.54S 51.06 E
Tulancingo 47 Ed 20.05N 98.22W
Tulare 46 Fh 36.13N 119.21W
Tulare Lake Bed 46 Fh 36.03N 119.49W
Tularosa 45 Cj 33.04N 106.01W
Tularosa Valley 45 Cj 32.45N 106.10W
Tulcán 54 Cc 0.48N 77.43W
Tulcea [2] 15 Md 45.12N 29.10 E
Tulcea 15 Ld 45.10N 28.48 E
Tulčin 16 Fe 48.39N 28.52 E
Tulelake 46 Ef 41.57N 121.29W
Tulemalu Lake 42 Hd 62.55N 99.25W
Tulgheş 15 Ic 46.57N 25.46 E
Tuli 37 Dd 21.55S 29.12 E
Tuli 37 Dd 21.48S 29.04 E
Tulia 45 Fi 34.32N 101.46W
Tulihe 27 La 50.30N 121.51 E
Tullahoma 44 Dh 35.22N 86.11W
Tullamore/An Tulach Mhór 9 Fh 53.16N 7.30W
Tulle 11 Hi 45.16N 1.46 E
Tulln 14 Kb 48.22N 16.03 E
Tulln 14 Kb 48.20N 16.03 E
Tullner Becken 14 Jb 48.25N 15.55 E
Tullow/An Tulach 9 Gi 52.48N 6.44W
Tullus 35 Cc 11.03N 24.33 E
Tully 59 Jc 17.56S 145.56 E
Ţulmaythah 33 Dc 32.43N 20.57 E
Tuloma 5 Jb 68.52N 32.49 E
Tulos, Ozero- 7 He 63.35N 30.35 E
Tulsa 39 Jf 36.09N 95.58W
Tulskaja Oblast [3] 19 De 54.00N 37.30 E
Tuluá 54 Cc 4.05N 76.12W
Tuluksak 40 Gd 61.06N 160.58W
Tulum 47 Gd 20.15N 87.28W
Tulum 48 Pg 20.13N 87.28W
Tulun 22 Md 54.35N 100.33 E
Tulungagung 26 Fh 8.04S 111.54 E
Tuma 7 Ji 55.10N 40.36 E
Tuma, Rio- 49 Eg 13.03N 84.44W
Tumaco 53 Ie 1.49N 78.46W
Tumaco, Rada de- 54 Cc 1.50N 78.40W
Tumacuarí, Pico- 54 Fc 1.15N 64.40W
Tuman-gang 28 Kc 42.18N 130.41 E
Tumba 8 Ge 59.12N 17.49 E
Tumbarumba 59 Jg 35.47S 148.01 E
Tumbes [2] 54 Bd 3.50S 80.30W
Tumbes 53 Hf 4.05S 80.35W
Tumča 7 Hc 66.35N 31.45 E
Tumd Youqi 27 Jc 40.33N 110.32 E
Tumd Zuoqi 27 Jc 40.43N 111.06 E
Tumen 22 Oe 42.58N 129.49 E
Tumen Jiang 28 Kc 42.18N 130.41 E
Tumeremo 54 Fb 7.18N 61.30W
Tumkur 25 Ff 13.21N 77.05 E
Tummel 9 Je 56.43N 4.08W
Tummo 33 Be 23.00N 14.10 E
Tumon Bay 64c Ba 13.31N 144.48 E
Tumpat 26 De 6.12N 102.10 E
Tumu 34 Ec 10.52N 1.59W
Tumucumaque, Serra- 52 Ke 2.20N 55.00W
Tumwater 46 Dc 47.01N 122.54W
Tuna, Punta- 51a Cc 18.00N 65.52W
Tunapuna 50 Fg 10.38N 61.23W
Tunas 55 Hg 24.58S 49.06W
Tunas, Sierra de las- 48 Fc 29.40N 107.15W
Tunas Chicas, Laguna- 55 Am 36.01S 62.20W
Tunaydah 24 Cj 25.31N 29.21 E
Tunçbilek 15 Mj 39.37N 29.29 E
Tunduma 36 Fd 9.18S 32.46 E
Tunduru 36 Ge 11.07S 37.21 E
Tundža 15 Jh 41.40N 26.34 E
Tunga 34 Gd 8.07N 9.12 E
Tungabhadra 25 Fe 15.57N 78.15 E
Tungaru 35 Ec 10.14N 30.42 E
Tungnaá 7a Bb 64.10N 19.34W
Tungokočen 20 Gf 53.33N 115.34 E
Tungsten 42 Ed 62.05N 127.42W
Tungua 65b Bb 20.01S 174.46W
Tuni 25 Ge 17.21N 82.33 E
Tūnis=Tunis (EN) [3] 32 Jb 36.30N 10.00 E
Tūnis=Tunis (EN) 31 Ie 36.48N 10.11 E
Tūnis=Tunisia (EN) [1] 31 He 34.00N 9.00 E
Tunis (EN)=Tūnis 31 Ie 36.48N 10.11 E
Tunis (EN)=Tūnis [3] 32 Jb 36.30N 10.00 E
Tūnis, Canal de-=Sicily, Strait of- (EN) 5 Hh 37.20N 11.20 E
Tūnis, Khalīj- 32 Jb 37.00N 10.30 E
Tunisia (EN)=Tūnis [1] 31 He 34.00N 9.00 E
Tunja 53 Ie 5.31N 73.22W
Tunkhannock 44 Je 41.32N 75.57W
Tunliu 28 Bf 36.18N 112.53 E
Tunnhovdfjorden 8 Cd 60.25N 8.55 E
Tunø 8 Di 55.55N 10.25 E
Tunumuk 42 Ec 69.00N 134.57W
Tununak 40 Fd 60.35N 165.16W
Tunungayualok 42 Le 56.05N 61.05W
Tunxi 27 Kf 29.45N 118.15 E
Tuo He 28 Dh 33.16N 117.45 E
Tuo Jang 27 If 28.55N 105.26 E
Tuostah 20 Ic 67.50N 135.40 E
Tuotuo He 27 Fe 34.03N 92.46 E
Tuotuohe/Tanggulashanqu 22 Lf 34.15N 92.29 E
Tupã 56 Jb 21.56S 50.30W
Tupaciguara 55 Hd 18.35S 48.42W
Tupai Atoll (Motu-Iti) 61 Kc 16.17S 151.50W
Tupanciretã 56 Jc 29.05S 53.51W
Tupelo 43 Je 34.16N 88.43W
Tupik 20 Gf 54.28N 119.57 E
Tupinambarana, Ilha- 54 Gd 3.00S 58.00W
Tupiraçaba 55 Hb 14.29S 48.34W
Tupper Lake 44 Jc 44.13N 74.29W
Tupungato, Cerro- 56 Gd 33.22S 69.47W
Tuquan 27 Lb 45.22N 121.33 E
Túquerres 54 Cc 1.06N 77.37W
Tur 15 Fa 48.04N 22.33 E
Tura 19 Gd 57.12N 66.56 E
Tura [India] 25 Ic 25.31N 90.13 E
Tura [R.S.F.S.R.] 22 Mc 64.17N 100.15 E
Turabah [Sau.Ar.] 23 Fe 21.13N 41.39 E
Turabah [Sau.Ar.] 23 Fd 28.13N 42.59 E
Turagua, Serranías- 50 Di 7.20N 64.35W
Turakina 62 Fd 40.02S 175.13 E
Turán 24 Qe 35.40N 56.50 E
Turan 20 Ef 52.08N 93.55 E
Turana, Hrebet- 20 If 51.30N 132.00 E
Turangi 62 Fc 38.59S 175.48 E
Turano 14 Gh 42.26N 12.47 E
Turanskaja Nizmennost 21 Ie 44.30N 63.00 E
Turawa 10 Of 50.45N 18.05 E
Turawskie, Jezioro- 10 Of 50.43N 18.10 E
Turbaco 49 Jh 10.19N 75.25W
Turbat 25 Cc 25.59N 63.04 E
Turbo 53 Ie 8.06N 76.43W
Turcoaia 15 Ld 45.07N 28.11 E
Turda 15 Gc 46.34N 23.47 E
Tūreh 24 Me 34.02N 49.17 E
Tureia Atoll 57 Ng 20.50S 138.32W
Turek 10 Od 52.02N 18.30 E
Turenki 8 Kd 60.55N 24.38 E
Turfan Depression (EN)=Turpan Pendi 21 Ke 42.30N 89.30 E
Turgai Gates (EN)=Turgajskaja Ložbina 21 Id 51.00N 64.30 E
Turgai Upland (EN)=Turgajskoje Plato 21 Id 51.00N 64.00 E
Turgaj [Kaz.-U.S.S.R.] 19 Gf 49.38N 63.28 E
Turgaj [U.S.S.R.] 21 Ie 48.01N 62.45 E
Turgajskaja Ložbina=Turgai Gates (EN) 21 Id 51.00N 64.30 E
Turgajskaja Oblast [3] 19 Ge 50.30N 66.00 E
Turgajskoje Plato=Turgai Upland (EN) 21 Id 51.00N 64.00 E
Turgeon, Rivière- 44 Ha 50.00N 78.55W
Turgutlu 24 Bc 38.30N 27.50 E
Turhal 24 Gb 40.24N 36.06 E
Türi/Tjuri 7 Fg 58.50N 25.27 E
Turia 13 Le 39.27N 0.19W
Turiaçu, Baía de- 54 Id 1.30S 45.15W
Turiec 10 Og 49.06N 18.52 E
Turijsk 10 Ue 51.10N 24.37 E
Turimiquire, Cerro- 54 Fa 10.03N 64.00W
Turin (EN)=Torino 6 Gf 45.03N 7.40 E
Turinsk 19 Gd 58.03N 63.42 E
Turja 16 Dd 51.48N 24.52 E
Turka [R.S.F.S.R.] 20 Ff 52.57N 108.13 E
Turka [Ukr.-U.S.S.R.] 10 Tg 49.07N 23.01 E
Turkana 36 Gb 4.00N 35.30 E
Turkana, Lake-/Rudolf, Lake- 30 Kh 3.30N 36.00 E
Türkeli 24 Fb 41.57N 34.21 E
Turkenstanski Hrebet 19 Gh 39.35N 69.00 E
Turkestan 22 Ie 43.18N 68.15 E
Türkeve 10 Qi 47.06N 20.45 E
Turkey (EN)=Türkiye [1] 22 Fg 39.00N 35.00 E
Turkey Creek 59 Fc 17.02S 128.12 E
Turki 16 Mc 52.01N 43.16 E
Türkiye=Turkey (EN) [1] 22 Fg 39.00N 35.00 E
Turkmenistan Sovet Socialistik Respublikasy/Turkmenskaja SSR [2] 19 Fh 40.00N 60.00 E
Turkmen-Kala 18 Df 37.26N 62.19 E
Turkmenskaja Sovetskaja Socialističeskaja Respublika [2] 19 Fh 40.00N 60.00 E
Turkmenskaja SSR/Turkmenistan Sovet Socialistik Respublikasy [2] 19 Fh 40.00N 60.00 E
Turkmenskaja SSR=Turkmen SSR (EN) [2] 19 Fh 40.00N 60.00 E
Turkmenski Zaliv 16 Ff 39.00N 53.30 E
Turkmen SSR (EN)=Turkmenskaja SSR [2] 19 Fh 40.00N 60.00 E
Türkoğlu 24 Gd 37.31N 36.49 E
Turks and Caicos Islands [5] 39 Ff 21.45N 71.35W
Turks Island Passage 49 Lc 21.25N 71.19W
Turks Islands 47 Jd 21.24N 71.07W
Turku/Åbo 6 Ic 60.27N 22.17 E
Turku-Pori [2] 7 Ff 61.00N 22.30 E
Turkwel 36 Gb 3.06N 36.06 E
Turlock 46 Eh 37.30N 120.51W
Turmantas 8 Li 55.42N 26.34 E
Turnagain, Cape- 62 Gd 40.30S 176.37 E
Turneffe Islands 47 Ge 17.22N 87.51W
Turnhout 11 Kc 51.19N 4.57 E
Turnov 10 Lf 50.35N 15.09 E
Turnu Roşu, Pasul- 15 Hd 45.33N 24.16 E
Turnu Măgurele 15 Hf 43.45N 24.52 E
Turočak 20 Df 52.16N 87.05 E
Turó de L'Home 13 Oc 41.45N 2.25 E
Turopolje 14 Ke 45.38N 16.07 E
Turpan 22 Ke 42.56N 89.10 E
Turpan Pendi=Turfan Depression 21 Ke 42.30N 89.30 E
Turquino, Pico- 47 Ie 19.59N 76.51W
Turrialba 49 Fi 9.54N 83.41W
Tursuntski Tuman, Ozero- 17 Kf 60.35N 63.55 E
Turtas 17 Ng 58.57N 69.10 E
Turtas 17 Ng 59.06N 68.50 E
Turtkul 19 Gg 41.35N 61.00 E
Turtle Mountain 45 Fb 49.05N 100.15W
Turugart Shankou 21 Je 40.32N 75.24 E
Turuhan 20 Dc 65.56N 87.42 E
Turuhansk 20 Dc 65.49N 87.59 E
Turvânia 55 Gc 16.39S 50.09W
Turvo 55 Hi 28.56S 49.41W
Turvo, Rio- [Braz.] 55 Hd 19.56S 49.55W
Turvo, Rio- [Braz.] 55 Gc 17.46S 50.12W
Tusaun/Thusis 14 Dd 46.42N 9.26 E
Tuscaloosa 43 Je 33.13N 87.33W
Tuscan Archipelago (EN)=Arcipelago Toscano 5 Hg 42.45N 10.20 E
Tuscania 14 Fh 42.25N 11.52 E
Tuscany (EN)=Toscana [2] 14 Eg 43.25N 11.00 E
Tuscarora Mountain 44 Ie 40.10N 77.45W
Tuscarora Mountains 46 Gf 41.00N 116.20W
Tuščibas, Zaliv- 18 Ba 46.10N 59.45 E
Tuscola 45 Lg 39.48N 88.17W
Tusenøyane 41 Oc 77.05N 22.00 E
Tuskar 16 Jd 51.40N 36.15 E
Tuskegee 44 Ei 32.26N 85.42W
Tuşnad Băi 15 Ic 46.09N 25.51 E
Tustna 8 Ca 63.10N 8.05 E
Tuszymka 10 Rf 50.09N 21.30 E
Tuszyn 10 Pe 51.37N 19.34 E
Tutajev 19 Dd 57.52N 39.32 E
Tutak 24 Jc 39.32N 42.46 E
Tuticorin 25 Fg 8.47N 78.08 E
Tutira 62 Gc 39.12S 176.53 E
Tutóia 54 Jd 2.45S 42.16W
Tutoko Peak 62 Bf 44.36S 167.58 E
Tutončana 20 Ed 64.05N 93.50 E
Tutova 15 Kc 46.06N 27.32 E
Tutrakan 15 Je 44.03N 26.37 E
Tuttle Creek Lake 45 Hg 39.22N 96.40W
Tuttlingen 10 Ei 47.59N 8.49 E
Tutuala 26 Ih 8.24S 127.15 E
Tutuila Island 57 Jf 14.18S 170.42W
Tutupaca, Volcán- 54 Dg 17.01S 70.22W
Tuupovaara 8 Nb 62.29N 30.36 E
Tuusniemi 7 Ge 62.49N 28.30 E
Tuvalu (Ellice Islands) [1] 58 Ie 8.00S 178.00 E
Tuvalu Islands 57 Ie 8.00S 178.00 E
Tuvana-i-Ra Island 61 Fd 21.00S 178.43W
Tuvana-i-Tholo Island 57 Ig 21.02S 178.49W
Tuvinskaja ASSR [3] 20 Ef 51.30N 94.00 E
Tuvutha 63d Cb 17.40S 178.48W
Ţuwayq, Jabal- 21 Gg 25.30N 46.20 E
Tuxer Alpen 14 Fc 47.10N 11.45 E
Tuxford 12 Ba 53.13N 0.53W
Tuxpan 48 Hh 19.33N 103.24W
Tuxpán 47 Cd 21.57N 105.18W
Tuxpan, Arrecife- 48 Kg 21.02N 97.13W
Tuxpan, Rio- 48 Kg 20.53N 97.18W
Tuxpán de Rodríguez Cano 47 Ed 20.57N 97.24W
Tuxtla Gutiérrez 39 Jh 16.45N 93.07W
Túy 13 Db 42.03N 8.38W
Tuy, Rio- 50 Dg 10.24N 65.59W
Tuy An 25 Lf 13.17N 109.16 E

Index Symbols

[1] Independent Nation
[2] State, Region
[3] District, County
[4] Municipality
[5] Colony, Dependency
Continent
Physical Region
Historical or Cultural Region
Mount, Mountain
Volcano
Hill
Mountains, Mountain Range
Hills, Escarpment
Plateau, Upland
Pass, Gap
Plain, Lowland
Delta
Salt Flat
Valley, Canyon
Crater, Cave
Karst Features
Depression
Polder
Desert, Dunes
Forest, Woods
Heath, Steppe
Oasis
Cape, Point
Coast, Beach
Cliff
Peninsula
Isthmus
Sandbank
Island
Atoll
Rock, Reef
Islands, Archipelago
Rocks, Reefs
Coral Reef
Well, Spring
Geyser
River, Stream
Waterfall Rapids
River Mouth, Estuary
Lake
Salt Lake
Intermittent Lake
Reservoir
Swamp, Pond
Canal
Glacier
Ice Shelf, Pack Ice
Ocean
Sea
Gulf, Bay
Strait, Fjord
Lagoon
Bank
Seamount
Tablemount
Ridge
Shelf
Basin
Escarpment, Sea Scarp
Fracture
Trench, Abyss
National Park, Reserve
Point of Interest
Recreation Site
Cave, Cavern
Historic Site
Ruins
Wall, Walls
Church, Abbey
Temple
Scientific Station
Airport
Port
Lighthouse
Mine
Tunnel
Dam, Bridge

Tuy Hoa 25 Lf 13.05N 109.18 E
Tüyserkān 24 Me 34.33N 48.27 E
Tuz, Lake- (EN)=Tuz Gölü 21 Ff 38.45N 33.25 E
Tuz Gölü=Tuz, Lake- (EN) 21 Ff 38.45N 33.25 E
Tuzkan, Ozero- 18 Fd 40.35N 67.30 E
Tūz Khurmātū 23 Fc 34.53N 44.38 E
Tuzla 14 Mf 44.33N 18.41 E
Tuzlov 16 Lf 47.23N 40.08 E
Tuzluca 24 Jb 40.03N 43.39 E
Tuzly 15 Nd 45.56N 30.05 E
Tvååker 8 Eg 57.03N 12.24 E
Tvărdica 15 Ig 42.42N 25.54 E
Tvedestrand 7 Bg 58.37N 8.55 E
Tver'=Kalinin 6 Jd 56.52N 35.55 E
Tweed 9 Lf 55.46N 2.00W
Tweedsmuir Hills 9 Jf 55.30N 3.22W
Tweerivier 37 Be 25.35S 19.37 E
Twello, Voorst- 12 Ib 52.14N 6.07 E
Twente 11 Mb 52.17N 6.40 E
Twentekanaal 12 Ib 52.13N 6.53 E
Twilight Cove 59 Ff 32.20S 126.00 E
Twin Buttes Reservoir 45 Fk 31.20N 100.35W
Twin Falls 39 He 42.34N 114.28W
Twin Islands 42 Jf 53.50N 80.00W
Twin Peaks 46 Hd 44.35N 114.29W
Twisp 46 Eb 48.22N 120.07W
Twiste 12 Lc 51.29N 9.09 E
Twistringen 10 Ed 52.48N 8.39 E
Two Butte Creek 45 Eg 38.02N 102.08W
Two Harbors 45 Kc 47.01N 91.40W
Two Rivers 45 Md 44.09N 87.34W
Two Thumb Range 62 De 43.45S 170.40 E
Tychy 10 Of 50.09N 18.59 E
Tyczyn 10 Sg 49.58N 22.02 E
Tydal 7 Ce 63.04N 11.34 E
Tygda 20 Hf 53.07N 126.20 E
Tyin 8 Cc 61.15N 8.15 E
Tyin 8 Cc 61.14N 8.14 E
Tyler 43 He 32.21N 95.18W
Tylertown 45 Kk 31.07N 90.09W
Tylösand 8 Eh 56.39N 12.44 E
Tylöskog 8 Ff 58.40N 15.10 E
Tym 20 De 59.30N 80.07 E
Tymovskoje 20 Jf 50.50N 142.41 E
Tympákion 15 Hn 35.06N 24.45 E
Tynda 22 Od 53.07N 126.20 E
Tyne 9 Lf 55.01N 1.26W
Tyne and Wear [3] 9 Lg 55.00N 1.35W
Tynemouth 9 Lf 55.01N 1.24W
Týn nad Vltavou 10 Kg 49.14N 14.26 E
Tynset 7 Ce 62.17N 10.47 E
Tyra, Cayos- 49 Fg 12.50N 83.20W
Tyrifjorden 8 De 60.05N 10.10 E
Tyringe 8 Eh 56.10N 13.35 E
Tyrma 20 If 50.01N 132.10 E
Tyrnyauz 16 Mh 43.23N 42.56 E
Tyrol (EN)=Tirol [2] 14 Fc 47.10N 11.25 E
Tyrol (EN)=Tirol/Tirolo 14 Fd 47.00N 11.20 E
Tyrol (EN)=Tirolo/Tirol 14 Fd 47.00N 11.20 E
Tyrone 44 He 40.41N 78.15W
Tyrrell, Lake- 59 Ig 35.20S 142.50 E
Tyrrel Lake 42 Gd 63.05N 105.30W
Tyrrhenian Basin (EN) 5 Hh 40.00N 13.00 E
Tyrrhenian Sea (EN)=Tirreno, Mar- 5 Hh 40.00N 12.00 E
Tyrva/Tõrva 7 Fg 58.01N 25.59 E
Tyrvää 8 Jc 61.21N 22.53 E
Tysmenica 10 Uh 48.49N 24.56 E
Tyśmienica 10 Se 51.33N 22.30 E
Tysnesøy 7 Af 60.00N 5.35 E
Tysse 8 Ad 60.22N 5.45 E
Tyssedal 8 Bd 60.07N 6.34 E
Tystama/Tõstamaa 8 Jf 58.17N 23.52 E
Tystberga 8 Gf 58.52N 17.15 E
Tyszowce 10 Tf 50.36N 23.41 E
Tytuvénai/Tituvenaj 8 Ji 55.33N 23.09 E
Tywyn 9 Ii 52.35N 4.05W
Tzanconeja, Río- 48 Ni 16.51N 91.47W
Tzaneen 37 Ed 23.50S 30.09 E
Tzintzuntzan 48 Ih 19.38N 101.34W
Tzucacab 48 Og 20.04N 89.05W

U

Uaboe 64e Ab 0.31S 166.54 E
Uacurizal, Ilha do- 55 Dc 16.25S 56.05W
Ua Huka, Ile- 57 Ne 8.54S 139.33W
Uanukuhahaki 65b Ba 19.58S 174.29W
Ua Pou, Ile- 57 Me 9.23S 140.03W
Uaroo 59 Dd 23.00S 115.10 E
Uatumã, Rio- 52 Kf 2.26S 57.37W
Uaupés 53 Jf 0.08S 67.05W
Uaupés, Rio- 52 Je 0.02N 67.16W
Uaxactún 47 Ge 17.25N 89.29W
Ub 15 De 44.27N 20.05 E
Ubá 54 Jh 21.07S 42.56W
Übach-Palenberg [F.R.G.] 10 Cf 50.56N 6.05 E
Ubagan 19 Ge 54.23N 64.40 E
Ubaila 24 If 33.06N 40.15 E
Ubaitaba 54 Kf 14.18S 39.20W
Ubajay 55 Cj 31.47S 58.18W
Ubangi 30 Ii 0.30S 17.42 E
Ubatuba 55 Jf 23.26S 45.04W
Ubay 26 Hd 10.03N 124.28 E
Ubaye 11 Mj 44.28N 6.18 E
Ubayyiḍ, Wādī al- 23 Fc 32.34N 43.48 E
Ube 28 Kh 33.56N 131.15 E
Ubeda 13 If 38.01N 3.22W
Ubekendt Ejland 41 Gd 71.10N 53.45W
Uberaba 53 Lg 19.45S 47.55W
Uberaba, Lagoa- 55 Dc 17.30S 57.45W
Uberlândia 53 Lg 18.56S 48.18W
Überlingen 10 Fi 47.46N 9.10 E
Ubiaja 34 Gd 6.39N 6.23 E
Ubiña, Peña- 13 Ga 43.01N 5.57W
Ubiratã 55 Fg 24.32S 52.56W
Ubon Ratchathani 22 Mh 15.15N 104.54 E
Ubort 16 Fc 52.06N 28.30 E
Ubrique 13 Gh 36.41N 5.27W
Ubsu-Nur (Uvs nuur) 21 Ld 50.20N 92.45 E
Ubundu 31 Ji 0.21S 25.29 E
Učaly 19 Fe 54.20N 59.31 E
Učami 20 Ed 63.50N 96.39 E
Učaral 19 If 46.08N 80.52 E
Ucayali, Río- 52 If 4.30S 73.30W
Uccle/Ukkel 12 Gd 50.48N 4.19 E
Üçdoruk Tepe 24 Ib 40.45N 41.05 E
Ucero 13 Ic 41.31N 3.04W
Uchiko 29 Ce 33.34N 132.38 E
Uchi Lake 45 Ja 51.05N 92.35W
Uchinomi 29 Dd 34.30N 134.19 E
Uchinoura 29 Bf 31.16N 131.05 E
Uchiura-Wan 28 Pc 42.18N 140.35 E
Uchte 10 Ed 52.30N 8.55 E
Učka 14 Ie 45.17N 14.12 E
Uckange 12 Ie 49.18N 6.09 E
Uckermark 10 Jc 53.10N 13.35 E
Uckfield 12 Cd 50.58N 0.06 E
Učkuduk 19 Gg 42.10N 63.30 E
Učkurgan 18 Id 41.01N 72.04 E
Ucrainskaja Sovetskaja Socialističeskaja Respublika [2] 19 Df 49.00N 32.00 E
Ucross 46 Ld 44.33N 106.31W
Ucua 36 Bd 8.40S 14.12 E
Učur 21 Pd 58.48N 130.35 E
Uda [R.S.F.S.R.] 21 Pd 54.42N 135.14 E
Uda [R.S.F.S.R.] 20 Ff 51.45N 107.25 E
Uda [R.S.F.S.R.] 20 Ee 56.05N 99.34 E
Udačny 20 Gc 66.25N 112.20 E
Udaipur 22 Jg 24.35N 73.41 E
Udaj 16 Hd 50.05N 33.07 E
Udaquiola 55 Cm 36.34S 58.31W
Udbina 14 Jf 44.32N 15.46 E
Uddevalla 7 Cg 58.21N 11.55 E
Uddjaure 5 Hb 65.58N 17.50 E
Uden 12 Hc 51.40N 5.37 E
Udgir 25 Fe 18.23N 77.07 E
Udhampur 25 Fb 32.56N 75.08 E
Udimski 7 Kf 61.09N 45.52 E
Udine 14 Hd 46.03N 13.14 E
Udipi 25 Ef 13.21N 74.45 E
Udmurtskaja ASSR [3] 19 Fd 57.20N 52.50 E
Udoha 8 Mg 57.58N 29.50 E
Udomlja 7 Ih 57.56N 35.02 E
Udone-Jima 29 Fd 34.28N 139.17 E
Udon Thani 25 Ke 17.25N 102.48 E
Udot 64d Bb 7.23N 151.43 E
Udskaja Guba 21 Pd 55.00N 136.00 E
Udskoje 20 If 54.36N 134.30 E
Udy 16 Je 49.47N 36.35 E
Udžary 16 Oi 40.31N 47.40 E
Udzungwa Range 36 Gd 8.05S 35.50 E
Uebonti 26 Hg 0.55S 121.38 E
Uecker 10 Kc 53.45N 14.04 E
Ueckermünde 10 Kc 53.44N 14.03 E
Ueda 27 Od 36.24N 138.16 E
Uele 30 Jh 4.09N 22.26 E
Uelen 20 Oc 66.13N 169.48W
Uelzen 10 Gd 52.58N 10.34 E
Ueno 29 Ed 34.46N 136.06 E
Uere 30 Jh 3.42N 25.24 E
Ufa 5 Le 54.40N 56.00 E
Ufa 6 Le 54.44N 55.56 E
Uftjuga 7 Lf 61.28N 46.12 E
Ugab 30 Ik 21.12S 13.38 E
Ugāle/Ugale 8 Jg 57.19N 21.52 E
Ugale/Ugāle 8 Jg 57.19N 21.52 E
Ugalla 36 Fd 5.08S 30.42 E
Uganda [1] 31 Kh 1.00N 32.00 E
Ugărčin 15 Hf 43.06N 24.25 E
Ugashik 40 He 57.32N 157.25W
Ughelli 34 Gd 5.30N 5.59 E
Ugijar 13 Ih 36.57N 3.03W
Uglegorsk 20 Jg 49.05N 142.06 E
Uglekamensk 20 Ih 43.18N 133.08 E
Ugleuralski 17 Hg 58.59N 57.38 E
Uglič 19 Dd 57.33N 38.23 E
Ugljan 14 Jf 44.05N 15.10 E
Uglovoje 28 Lc 43.20N 132.06 E
Ugnev 10 Tf 50.20N 23.45 E
Ugo 29 Gb 39.13N 140.23 E
Ugolnyje Kopi 20 Md 64.42N 177.50 E
Ugoma 36 Ec 4.55S 26.50 E
Ugra 16 De 54.30N 36.07 E
Ugtal-Cajdam 27 Ib 48.25N 105.30 E
Uh 10 Rh 48.33N 22.00 E
Uherské Hradiště 10 Ng 49.04N 17.27 E
Uhlava 10 Jg 49.45N 13.23 E
Uhlenhorst 37 Bd 23.45S 17.55 E
Uhta 6 Lc 63.33N 53.40 E
Uibh Fhaili/Offaly [2] 9 Fh 53.20N 7.30W
Uig 9 Gd 57.30N 6.20W
Uige 31 Ii 7.35S 15.04 E
Uige [3] 36 Cd 7.00S 15.30 E
'Uiha 65b Ba 19.54S 174.25W
Uijec 64d Bb 7.10N 151.57 E
Üijŏngbu 28 If 37.44N 127.02 E
Uiju 28 Hd 40.12N 124.32 E
Uil 19 Ff 48.36N 52.30 E
Uil 19 Ff 49.04N 54.42 E
Uilpata, Gora- 16 Mh 42.47N 43.44 E
Uinta Mountains 43 Ec 40.45N 110.05W
Uinta River 46 Kf 40.14N 109.51W
Uis 37 Ad 21.08S 14.49 E
Üisŏng 28 Jf 36.21N 128.42 E
Uitenhage 31 Jl 33.40S 25.28 E
Uithoorn 12 Gb 52.14N 4.52 E
Uithuizen 12 Ia 53.25N 6.42 E
Uithuizerwad 12 Ia 53.30N 6.40 E
Ujae Atoll 57 Hd 9.05N 165.40 E
Ūjān 24 Og 30.45N 52.05 E
Ujandina 20 Jc 68.23N 145.50 E
Ujar 20 Ee 55.48N 94.20 E
Ujarrás 49 Fi 9.50N 83.40W
Ujedinenija, Ostrov- 20 Da 77.30N 82.30 E
Ujelang Atoll 57 Hd 9.49N 160.55 E
Újfehértó 10 Ri 47.48N 21.41 E
Uji 29 Dd 34.53N 135.47 E
Uji 19 Ge 54.20N 63.58 E
Uji-Guntō 28 Ji 31.10N 129.28 E
Ujiie 29 Fc 36.41N 139.57 E
Ujiji 31 Ji 4.55S 29.41 E
Ujjain 22 Jg 23.11N 75.46 E
Ujunglamuru 26 Gg 4.40S 119.58 E
Ujung Pandang (Makasar) 22 Nj 5.07S 119.24 E
Uk 20 Ee 55.04N 98.52 E
Ukata 34 Gc 10.50N 5.50 E
Ukeng, Bukit- 26 Gf 1.45N 115.08 E
Ukerewe Island 36 Fc 2.03S 33.00 E
Uke-Shima 29b Ba 28.02N 129.15 E
Ukhaydir 24 Jf 32.26N 43.36 E
Ukiah [Ca.-U.S.] 43 Cd 39.09N 123.13W
Ukiah [Or.-U.S.] 46 Fd 45.08N 118.56W
Uki Ni Masi 63a Ed 10.15S 161.44 E
Ukkel/Uccle 12 Gd 50.48N 4.19 E
Ukmerge/Ukmergė 7 Fi 55.14N 24.47 E
Ukmergė/Ukmerge 7 Fi 55.14N 24.47 E
Ukraine (EN) 5 Jf 49.00N 32.00 E
Ukrainian SSR (EN)=Ukrainskaja SSR [2] 19 Df 49.00N 32.00 E
Ukrainskaja SSR/Ukrainska Radyanska Socialistična Respublika [2] 19 Df 49.00N 32.00 E
Ukrainskaja SSR=Ukrainian SSR (EN) [2] 19 Df 49.00N 32.00 E
Ukrainska Radyanska Socialistična Respublika/Ukrainskaja SSR [2] 19 Df 49.00N 32.00 E
Ukrina 14 Le 45.05N 17.56 E
Uku-Jima 29 Ae 33.16N 129.07 E
Ula 24 Cd 37.05N 28.26 E
Ulah Lake 45 Hh 36.58N 96.10W
Ulaidh/Ulster 9 Gg 54.30N 7.00W
Ulalu 64d Bb 7.25N 151.40 E
Ulan (Xiligou) 27 Gd 36.55N 98.16 E
Ulan→Otog Qi 27 Id 39.07N 108.00 E
Ulanbaatar→Ulan-Bator 22 Me 47.55N 106.53 E
Ulan-Badrah 28 Ac 43.58N 110.37 E
Ulan-Bator (Ulaanbaatar) 22 Me 47.55N 106.53 E
Ulanbel 19 Hg 44.49N 71.10 E
Ulan-Burgasy, Hrebet- 20 Ff 52.30N 108.30 E
Ulangom 22 Le 49.58N 92.02 E
Ulanhad/Chifeng 27 Kc 42.16N 118.57 E
Ulan Hol 19 Ef 45.27N 46.46 E
Ulan Hot/Horqin Youyi Qianqi 22 Oe 46.04N 122.00 E
Ulan Hua→Siziwang Qi 28 Ad 41.31N 111.41 E
Ulan-Hus 27 Eb 49.02N 89.23 E
Ulanów 10 Sf 50.30N 22.16 E
Ulansuhai Nur 27 Ic 40.56N 108.49 E
Ulan-Tajga 27 Ga 50.45N 98.30 E
Ulan-Ude 22 Md 51.50N 107.37 E
Ulan Ul Hu 27 Fe 34.45N 90.25 E
Ulas 24 Gc 39.27N 37.03 E
Ulawa Island 60 Gi 9.46S 161.57 E
Ulbeja 20 Je 59.00N 144.25 E
Ulchin 28 Jf 36.59N 129.24 E
Ulcinj 15 Ch 41.56N 19.13 E
Uleåborg/Oulu 6 Ib 65.01N 25.30 E
Ulefoss 7 Bg 59.17N 9.16 E
Ulegej 22 Ke 48.56N 89.57 E
Ulety 20 Gf 51.22N 112.30 E
Uleza 15 Ch 41.40N 19.53 E
Ulfborg 8 Ch 56.16N 8.20 E
Ulflingen/Troisvierges 12 Hd 50.07N 6.00 E
Ulft, Gendringen- 12 Ic 51.54N 6.24 E
Ulgain Gol 27 Kb 45.31N 117.50 E
Ulhāsnagar 25 Ee 19.10N 73.07 E
Uliastai→Dong Ujimqin Qi 27 Kc 45.31N 116.58 E
Uliga 58 Id 7.09N 171.13 E
Ulindi 30 Ji 1.40S 25.52 E
Ulithi Atoll 57 Ed 9.58N 139.40 E
Ulja 20 Je 58.48N 141.40 E
Uljanovka [R.S.F.S.R.] 8 Ne 59.37N 30.55 E
Uljanovka [Ukr.-U.S.S.R.] 16 Ge 48.20N 30.13 E
Uljanovsk 6 Ke 54.20N 48.24 E
Uljanovskaja Oblast [3] 19 Ee 54.00N 48.00 E
Uljanovski 19 He 50.05N 73.45 E
Uljasutaj 22 Le 47.45N 96.49 E
Ulkan 20 Fe 55.55N 107.55 E
Ulla 13 Db 42.39N 8.44W
Ullapool 9 Hd 57.54N 5.10W
Ullared 7 Ch 57.08N 12.43 E
Ulldecona 13 Md 40.36N 0.27 E
Ullsfjorden 7 Eb 69.58N 20.00 E
Ullswater 9 Kg 54.34N 2.54W
Ullŭng-Do 28 Kf 37.29N 130.52 E
Ullvettern 8 Fe 59.25N 14.15 E
Ulm 10 Fh 48.25N 10.00 E
Ulmen 12 Id 50.13N 6.59 E
Ulmeni 15 Je 45.04N 26.39 E
Ulmu 15 Je 44.16N 26.55 E
Ulongwé 37 Eb 14.43S 34.21 E
Ulricehamn 7 Ch 57.47N 13.25 E
Ulrichstein 12 Ld 50.35N 9.12 E
Ulrum 12 Ia 53.22N 6.20 E
Ulrum-Zoutkamp 12 Ia 53.20N 6.18 E
Ulsan 27 Md 35.33N 129.19 E
Ulsteinvik 7 Ae 62.20N 5.53 E
Ulster 10 Ff 50.51N 9.59 E
Ulster/Ulaidh 9 Gg 54.30N 7.00W
Ulster Canal 9 Gg 54.27N 6.40W
Ulu 35 Ec 10.43N 33.29 E
Ulu/Uulu 8 Kf 58.13N 24.29 E
Ulúa, Río- 47 Ge 15.56N 87.43W
Ulubat Gölü 24 Cb 40.10N 28.35 E
Ulubey 24 Cc 38.09N 29.33 E
Uludağ 23 Ca 40.04N 29.13 E
Uludere 24 Jd 37.27N 42.51 E
Ulugqat/Wuqia 27 Cd 39.40N 75.07 E
Ulukışla 24 Fd 37.33N 34.30 E
Ulungur He 21 Ke 46.58N 87.28 E
Ulungur Hu 27 Eb 47.20N 87.10 E
Ulus 24 Eb 41.35N 32.39 E
Ulus Dağ 15 Lj 39.18N 28.24 E
Ulva 9 Ge 56.28N 6.12W
Ulverston 9 Jg 54.12N 3.06W
Ulverstone 59 Jh 41.09S 146.10 E
Ulvik 8 Bd 60.34N 6.54 E
Ulvön 8 Ha 63.05N 18.40 E
Ulysses 45 Fh 37.35N 101.22W
Ulytau 19 Gf 48.35N 67.05 E
Ulytau, Gora- 19 Gf 48.45N 67.00 E
Uly-Žilanšik 19 Gf 48.51N 63.47 E
Uma 27 La 52.36N 120.38 E
Umag 14 He 45.25N 13.32 E
Umala 54 Eg 17.24S 67.58W
Umán 48 Og 20.53N 89.45W
Uman 64d Bb 7.18N 151.53 E
Uman 19 Df 48.47N 30.09 E
'Umān 21 Hg 22.10N 58.00 E
'Umān=Oman (EN) [1] 22 Hg 21.00N 57.00 E
'Umān, Khalīj-=Oman, Gulf of- (EN) 21 Hg 25.00N 58.00 E
Umanak 41 Gd 70.36N 52.15W
Ũmánarssuaq/Farvel, Kap- 67 Nb 59.50N 43.50W
Umatac 64c Bb 13.18N 144.40 E
Umba 19 Db 66.41N 34.17 E
Umbelasha 35 Cd 9.51N 24.50 E
Umbertide 14 Gg 43.18N 12.20 E
Umberto de Campos 54 Jd 2.37S 43.27W
Umboi Island 57 Fe 5.36S 148.00 E
Umbozero, Ozero- 7 Ic 67.45N 34.20 E
Umbria [2] 14 Gh 43.00N 12.30 E
Ume 37 Dc 17.15S 28.20 E
Umeå 6 Ic 63.50N 20.15 E
Umeälven 5 Ic 63.47N 20.16 E
Umm al Arānib 33 Bd 26.08N 14.45 E
Umm al Hayf, Wādī- 23 Hf 18.37N 53.59 E
Umm al Jamaājim 24 Ki 26.59N 45.19 E
Umm al Qaywayn 23 Id 25.35N 55.34 E
Ummanz 10 Jb 54.30N 13.10 E
Umm ar Rizam 33 Dc 32.32N 23.00 E
Umm as Samīm 23 Ie 21.30N 56.45 E
Umm Bāb 24 Nj 25.12N 50.48 E
Umm Bel 35 Dc 13.32N 28.04 E
Umm Buru 35 Cb 15.01N 23.36 E
Umm Dhibbān 35 Dc 14.14N 29.37 E
Umm Durmān=Omdurman (EN) 31 Kg 15.38N 32.30 E
Umm Inderaba 35 Eb 15.12N 31.54 E
Umm Kaddādah 35 Dc 13.36N 26.42 E
Umm Lajj 23 Ed 25.04N 37.13 E
Umm Naqqāṭ, Jabal- 24 Fj 25.30N 34.14 E
Umm Qam'ul 24 Pj 24.47N 54.42 E
Umm Ruwābah 31 Kg 12.54N 31.13 E
Umm Sayyālah 35 Ec 14.25N 31.00 E
Umm Urūmah 24 Gj 25.46N 36.33 E
Umnak 38 Cd 58.25N 168.10W
Umne-Gobi 27 Fb 49.06N 91.43 E
Umpqua River 46 Ce 43.42N 124.03W
Umpulu 36 Ce 12.42S 17.40 E
Umsini, Gunung- 26 Jg 1.35S 133.30 E
Umtata 31 Jl 31.35S 28.47 E
Umuarama 56 Jb 23.45S 53.20W
Umurbey 15 Ji 40.14N 26.36 E
Umvukwes 37 Ec 17.01S 30.52 E
Umvuma 37 Ec 19.19S 30.35 E
Umzingwani 37 Dd 22.12S 29.56 E
Una 14 Ke 45.16N 16.55 E
Unabetsu-Dake 29a Db 43.52N 144.51 E
Unac 14 Kf 44.29N 16.08 E
Unai 54 Ig 16.23S 46.53W
Unalakleet 40 Gd 63.53N 160.47W
Unalaska 38 Cd 53.45N 166.45W
Unare, Río- 50 Dg 10.06N 65.12W
Unauna, Pulau- 26 Hg 0.10S 121.35 E
'Unayzah [Jor.] 24 Fg 30.29N 35.48 E
'Unayzah [Sau. Ar.] 22 Gg 26.06N 43.56 E
Uncia 54 Eg 18.27S 66.37W
Uncompahgre Peak 43 Fd 38.04N 107.28W
Uncompahgre Plateau 45 Bg 38.30N 108.25W
Unden 8 Ff 58.45N 14.25 E
Underberg 37 De 29.50S 29.22 E
Under-Han 22 Ne 47.19N 110.39 E
Undjuljung 20 Hc 66.20N 124.40 E
Undu Point 63d Cb 16.08S 179.57W
Undva Neem/Kiprarenukk, Mys- 8 If 58.25N 21.45 E
Uneča 16 Hc 52.50N 32.44 E
'Ung, Jabal al- 14 Dn 36.45N 9.35 E
Unga 40 Ge 55.15N 160.45W
Ungava, Péninsule d'-=Ungava Peninsula (EN) 38 Lc 60.00N 74.00W
Ungava Bay 38 Md 59.30N 67.30W
Ungava Peninsula (EN)=Ungava, Péninsule d'- 38 Lc 60.00N 74.00W
Ungeny 16 Ef 47.13N 27.50 E
Unggi 28 Kc 42.21N 130.23 E
Ungureni 15 Jb 47.53N 26.47 E
Ungwatiri 35 Fb 16.55N 36.05 E
União 54 Jd 4.35S 42.52W
União da Vitória 56 Jc 26.13S 51.05W
União dos Palmares 54 Ke 9.10S 36.02W
Uničov 10 Ng 49.49N 17.07 E
Uniejów 10 Oe 51.58N 18.49 E
Unije 14 If 44.38N 14.15 E
Unimak 38 Cd 54.50N 164.00W
Unimak Pass 40 Gf 54.35N 164.43W
Unini, Rio- 54 Fd 1.41S 61.30W
Union [Mo.-U.S.] 45 Kg 38.27N 91.00W
Union [S.C.-U.S.] 44 Gh 34.42N 81.37W
Union City 44 Cg 36.26N 89.03W
Uniondale 37 Cf 33.40S 23.08 E
Unión de Reyes 49 Gb 22.48N 81.32W
Unión de Tula 48 Gh 19.58N 104.16W
Union Island 50 Ff 12.36N 61.26W
Union Islands/Tokelau 57 Je 9.00S 171.45W
Union of Soviet Socialist Republics (USSR) (EN)=SSSR [1] 22 Jd 60.00N 80.00 E
Union Seamount (EN) 42 Eg 49.35N 132.45W
Union Springs 44 Ei 32.09N 85.49W
Uniontown 44 Hf 39.54N 79.44W
Unionville 45 Jf 40.29N 93.01W
United Arab Emirates (EN)=Al Imārāt al 'Arabīyah al Muttaḥidah [1] 22 Hg 24.00N 54.00 E
United Arab Republic (EN)→Egypt (EN) [1] 31 Jf 27.00N 30.00 E
United Kingdom [1] 6 Fe 54.00N 2.00W
United Kingdom of Great Britain and Northern Ireland [1] 6 Fe 54.00N 2.00W
United States [1] 39 Jf 38.00N 97.00W
United States of America [1] 39 Jf 38.00N 97.00W
Unity [Or.-U.S.] 46 Fd 44.29N 118.13W
Unity [Sask.-Can.] 42 Gf 52.27N 109.10W
Universales, Montes- 13 Kd 40.18N 1.33W
University City 45 Kg 38.39N 90.19W
Unna 10 De 51.32N 7.41 E
Unnāb, Wādī al- 24 Gg 30.11N 36.39 E
Unnukka 8 Lb 62.25N 27.55 E
Unst 9 Ma 60.45N 0.55W
Unstrut 10 He 51.10N 11.48 E
Unterfranken 10 Fg 50.00N 10.00 E
Unterwalden-Nidwalden [2] 14 Cd 46.55N 8.30 E
Unterwalden-Obwalden [2] 14 Cd 46.50N 8.20 E
Unuli Horog 27 Fd 35.12N 91.58 E
Ünye 23 Ea 41.08N 37.17 E
Unža 5 Kd 57.20N 43.08 E
Unzen-Dake 29 Be 32.45N 130.17 E
Uoleva 65b Ba 19.51S 174.24W
Uozu 28 Nf 36.48N 137.24 E
Upa 10 Lf 50.22N 15.54 E
Upata 54 Fb 8.01N 62.24W
Upemba, Lac- 36 Ed 8.36S 26.26 E
Upernavik 41 Gd 72.20N 56.00W
Upin 26 Ig 2.56S 129.11 E
Upington 31 Jk 28.25S 21.15 E
Upland 12 Kc 51.18N 8.42 E
Upolu Island 57 Jf 13.55S 171.45W
Upolu Point 60 Oc 20.16N 155.52W
Upper [3] 34 Ec 10.30N 1.30W
Upper Arlington 44 Fe 40.01N 83.03W
Upper Arrow Lake 46 Ga 50.30N 117.55W
Upper Austria (EN)=Oberösterreich [2] 14 Hb 48.15N 14.00 E
Upper Hutt 62 Fd 41.07S 175.04 E
Upper Klamath Lake 43 Cc 42.23N 122.00W
Upper Lake 46 Ef 41.44N 120.08W
Upper Lough Erne/Loch Eirne Uachtair 9 Fg 54.20N 7.30W
Upper Red Lake 45 Ib 48.10N 94.40W
Upper Sandusky 44 Fe 40.48N 83.17W
Upper Sheik 35 Hd 9.57N 45.09 E
Upper Thames Valley 9 Lj 51.40N 1.40W
Upper Trajan's Wall (EN)=Verhni Traijanov Val 15 Lc 46.40N 29.00 E
Upper Volta→Burkina Faso [1] 31 Gg 13.00N 2.00W
Uppingham 12 Bb 52.35N 0.43W
Uppland 8 Gd 60.00N 17.50 E
Upplands Väsby 8 Ge 59.31N 17.54 E
Uppsala [2] 7 Df 60.00N 17.45 E
Uppsala 6 Hd 59.52N 17.38 E
Upsala 45 Kb 49.02N 90.29W
Upshi 25 Fb 33.50N 77.49 E
Upton 46 Md 44.06N 104.38W
Uqbān 33 Hf 15.30N 42.23 E
'Uqlat aṣ Ṣuqūr 24 Jj 25.53N 42.15 E
Uqturpan/Wushi 27 Cc 41.10N 79.16 E
Ur 23 Gc 30.58N 46.06 E
Urabá, Golfo de- 54 Cb 8.25N 77.00W
Uracoa 50 Eh 9.00N 62.21W
Uracoa, Rio- 50 Eh 9.08N 62.20W
Uradarja 18 Fe 38.51N 66.02 E
Urad Qianqi 27 Ic 40.49N 108.37 E
Urad Zhongha Lianheqi (Haliut) 27 Ic 41.34N 108.32 E
Uraga-Suido 29 Fd 35.15N 139.45 E
Ura-Guba 7 Hb 69.18N 32.48 E
Urahoro 29a Cb 42.48N 143.38 E
Urahoro-Gawa 29a Cb 42.44N 143.40 E
Uraj 19 Gc 60.08N 64.40 E
Urakawa 28 Qc 42.09N 142.47 E
Ural 5 Lf 47.00N 51.48 E
Ural Mountains (EN)=Uralskije Gory 5 Ld 57.00N 60.00 E
Uralsk 6 Le 51.14N 51.22 E
Uralskaja Oblast [3] 19 Ff 49.45N 51.00 E
Uralskije Gory=Ural Mountains (EN) 5 Ld 57.00N 60.00 E
Urambo 36 Fd 5.04S 32.03 E
Uranium City 39 Id 59.34N 108.36W
Uraricoera 54 Fc 3.27N 60.59W
Uraricoera, Rio- 52 Je 3.02N 60.30W
Ura-Tjube 19 Gh 39.53N 69.01 E
Urawa 28 Og 35.51N 139.39 E
'Uray'irah 24 Mj 25.57N 48.53 E
Urayq, Nafūd al- 24 Jj 25.17N 42.25 E
Urbana [Il.-U.S.] 45 Lf 40.07N 88.12W
Urbana [Oh.-U.S.] 44 Fe 40.06N 83.45W
Urbandale 45 Jf 41.38N 93.48W
Urbania 14 Gg 43.40N 12.31 E

Index Symbols

[1] Independent Nation
[2] State, Region
[3] District, County
[4] Municipality
[5] Colony, Dependency
Continent
Physical Region
Historical or Cultural Region
Mount, Mountain
Volcano
Hill
Mountains, Mountain Range
Hills, Escarpment
Plateau, Upland
Pass, Gap
Plain, Lowland
Delta
Salt Flat
Valley, Canyon
Crater, Cave
Karst Features
Depression
Polder
Desert, Dunes
Forest, Woods
Heath, Steppe
Oasis
Cape, Point
Coast, Beach
Cliff
Peninsula
Isthmus
Sandbank
Island
Atoll
Rock, Reef
Islands, Archipelago
Rocks, Reefs
Coral Reef
Well, Spring
Geyser
River, Stream
Waterfall Rapids
River Mouth, Estuary
Lake
Salt Lake
Intermittent Lake
Reservoir
Swamp, Pond
Canal
Glacier
Ice Shelf, Pack Ice
Ocean
Sea
Gulf, Bay
Strait, Fjord
Lagoon
Bank
Seamount
Tablemount
Ridge
Shelf
Basin
Escarpment, Sea Scarp
Fracture
Trench, Abyss
National Park, Reserve
Point of Interest
Recreation Site
Cave, Cavern
Historic Site
Ruins
Wall, Walls
Church, Abbey
Temple
Scientific Station
Airport
Port
Lighthouse
Mine
Tunnel
Dam, Bridge

Urbano Santos	54	Jd	3.12S	43.23W
Urbino	14	Gg	43.43N	12.38 E
Urbino, Étang d'- ▪	11a	Ba	42.02N	9.28 E
Urbión, Picos de- ▪	13	Jb	42.01N	2.52W
Urcel	12	Fe	49.30N	3.33 E
Urcos	54	Df	13.42S	71.38W
Urdinarrain	55	Ck	32.41S	58.53W
Urdoma	7	Lf	61.47N	48.29 E
Urdžar	19	If	47.05N	81.37 E
Ure ▪	9	Lg	54.01N	1.12W
Uré	49	Jj	7.46N	75.31W
Uren	19	Ed	57.29N	45.48 E
Urenui	62	Fc	39.00S	174.23 E
Ures	47	Bc	29.26N	110.24W
Ureshino	29	Ab	33.06N	129.59 E
'Urf, Jabal al- ▪	24	Ei	27.49N	32.55 E
Urfa	23	Eb	37.08N	38.46 E
Urfa Platosu ▪	24	Hd	37.10N	38.50 E
Urgal	20	If	51.00N	132.50 E
Urgel, Llanos de- ▪	13	Lc	41.25N	0.36W
Urgel, Llanos de-/Urgell, Pla d'- ▪	13	Lc	41.25N	0.36W
Urgell, Pla d'- ▪	13	Lc	41.25N	0.36W
Urgell, Pla d'-/Urgel, Llanos de- ▪	13	Lc	41.25N	0.36W
Urgen	28	Ab	44.45N	110.40 E
Urgenč	22	Ie	41.33N	60.38 E
Ürgüp	24	Fc	38.38N	35.56 E
Urgut	19	Gh	39.23N	67.14 E
Uri	25	Eb	34.05N	74.02 E
Uri [2]	14	Cd	46.40N	8.30 E
Uribia	54	Da	11.42N	72.17W
Uricki	19	Ge	53.19N	65.34 E
Urique, Río-	48	Fd	26.29N	107.58W
Urjala	8	Jc	61.05N	23.32 E
Urjupinsk	19	Ee	50.48N	42.02 E
Urk	11	Lb	52.39N	5.36 E
Urkan ▪	20	Hf	53.27N	126.56 E
Urla	24	Bc	38.18N	26.46 E
Urlaţi	15	Je	44.59N	26.14 E
Urluk	20	Ff	50.03N	107.55 E
Urmi ▪	20	Ig	48.43N	134.16 E
Urmia, Lake- (EN)= Orumıyeh, Daryācheh-ye ▪	21	Gf	37.40N	45.30 E
Uromi	34	Gd	6.42N	6.20 E
Uroševac	15	Eg	42.22N	21.10 E
Urshult	8	Fh	56.32N	14.47 E
Ursus	10	Qd	52.12N	20.53 E
Urtazym	17	Ij	52.15N	58.50 E
Urtigueira, Serra da- ▪	55	Gg	24.15S	51.00W
Uru, Rio- ▪	55	Hb	15.24S	49.36W
Uruaçu	54	If	14.30S	49.10W
Uruana	55	Hb	15.30S	49.41W
Uruapan del Progreso	47	De	19.25N	101.58W
Uruará, Rio- ▪	54	Hd	2.00S	53.38W
Urubamba, Río- ▪	52	Ig	10.43S	73.48W
Urubici	55	Hi	28.02S	49.37W
Urubú, Cachoeira do- ▪	55	Ha	12.52S	48.13W
Urucará	54	Gd	2.32S	57.45W
Uruçui	54	Je	7.14S	44.33W
Urucuia, Rio- [Braz.] ▪	55	Ib	15.38S	46.10W
Urucuia, Rio- [Braz.] ▪	55	Jc	16.08S	45.05W
Urucum, Serra do- ▪	55	Dd	19.13S	57.33W
Urucurituba	54	Gd	2.41S	57.40W
Uruguai, Rio- ▪	52	Ki	34.12S	58.18W
Uruguaiana	53	Kh	29.45S	57.05W
Uruguay [1]	53	Ki	33.00S	56.00W
Uruguay, Rio- ▪	52	Ki	34.12S	58.18W
Urukthapel ▪	64a	Ac	7.15N	134.24 E
Urumbaba Dağı ▪	15	Lj	38.25N	28.49 E
Ürümqi	22	Ke	43.48N	87.35 E
Urup ▪	16	Lg	44.59N	41.10 E
Urup, Ostrov- ▪	21	Qe	46.00N	150.00 E
Uruša	20	Hf	54.03N	122.55 E
Urussu	7	Mi	54.38N	53.24 E
Uruwira	36	Fd	6.27S	31.21 E
Urville, Cape D'- (EN)= Perkam, Tanjung- ▪	26	Kg	1.28S	137.54 E
Uryū	29a	Bb	43.39N	141.51 E
Uryū-Gawa ▪	29a	Bb	43.40N	141.54 E
Urziceni	15	Je	44.43N	26.38 E
Uržum	19	Fd	57.10N	50.01 E
Usa	29	Be	33.31N	131.22 E
Usa [R.S.F.S.R.] ▪	16	Nc	53.02N	45.18 E
Usa [R.S.F.S.R.] ▪	5	Lb	65.57N	56.55 E
Uşak	23	Cb	38.41N	29.25 E
Usakos	37	Bd	22.01S	15.32 E
Ušakovo	20	Hf	51.54N	126.35 E
Ušakovskoje	20	Nb	71.00N	178.35W
Usambara Mountains ▪	30	Ki	4.45S	38.30 E
Usarp Mountains ▪	66	Jf	71.10S	160.00 E
Usas Escarpment ▪	66	Nf	76.00S	125.00W
Ušba, Gora- ▪	16	Mh	43.06N	42.40 E
Usborne, Mount- ▪	56	Ih	51.42S	58.50W
Ušće	15	Df	43.29N	20.38 E
Usedom ▪	10	Jb	54.00N	14.00 E
Useldange	12	He	49.46N	5.59 E
'Ushayrah [Sau. Ar.]	33	He	21.46N	40.38 E
'Ushayrah [Sau. Ar.]	24	Kj	25.35N	45.46 E
Ushibuka	29	Be	32.13N	130.01 E
Ushikubi-Misaki ▪	29a	Bc	41.08N	140.48 E
Ushimado	29	Dd	34.37N	134.09 E
'Ushsh, Wādī al- ▪	24	Fd	27.18N	42.15 E
Ushuaia	53	Jk	54.47S	68.20W
Usingen	12	Kd	50.20N	8.32 E
Usinsk	19	Fb	65.57N	57.29 E
Üsküdar	24	Cb	41.01N	29.03 E
Üsküp	15	Kh	41.44N	27.24 E
Uslar	10	Fe	51.40N	9.39 E
Úslava ▪	10	Jg	49.54N	13.32 E
Usman ▪	16	Kd	51.54N	39.20 E
Usman	19	De	52.00N	39.43 E
Usmas, Ozero-/Usmas Ezers ▪	8	Ig	57.13N	22.00 E
Usmas Ezers/Usmas, Ozero- ▪	8	Ig	57.13N	22.00 E
Usogorsk	19	Ec	63.28N	48.35 E
Usoke	36	Fd	5.06S	32.20 E
Usolje	19	Fd	59.25N	56.41 E
Usolje-Sibirskoje	20	Ff	52.47N	103.38 E
Usora ▪	14	Mf	44.43N	18.04 E
Ussel	11	Ii	45.33N	2.19 E
USSR (EN)=Sojuz Sovetskih Socialističeskih Respublik [1]	22	Jd	60.00N	80.00 E
Ussuri ▪	21	Pe	48.28N	135.02 E
Ussurijsk	22	Pe	43.48N	131.59 E
Usta ▪	7	Kh	56.53N	45.28 E
Ust-Barguzin	20	Ff	53.27N	108.59 E
Ust-Bolšereck	20	Kf	52.40N	156.18 E
Ust-Cilma	19	Fb	65.27N	52.06 E
Ust-Čorna	10	Uh	48.17N	24.02 E
Ust-Donecki	16	Lf	47.39N	40.55 E
Ust-Džeguta	16	Mg	44.05N	42.01 E
Uster	14	Cc	47.20N	8.43 E
Ustevatn ▪	8	Bd	60.30N	8.00 E
Ust-Hajrjuzovo	20	Ke	57.04N	156.50 E
Ustica ▪	5	Hh	38.40N	13.10 E
Ustica	14	Hl	38.42N	13.11 E
Ust-Ilimsk	22	Md	58.03N	102.43 E
Ustilug	10	Uf	50.50N	24.09 E
Ústí nad Labem	10	Kf	50.40N	14.02 E
Ústí nad Orlicí	10	Mg	49.58N	16.24 E
Ustinov → Iževsk	6	Ld	56.51N	53.14 E
Ust-Išim	19	Hd	57.44N	71.10 E
Ust-Judoma	20	Ie	59.10N	135.02 E
Ustjurt, Plato ▪	21	He	43.00N	56.00 E
'Ustjužna	7	Ig	58.53N	36.28 E
Ustka	10	Mb	54.35N	16.50 E
Ust-Kamčatsk	22	Sd	56.15N	162.30 E
Ust-Kamenogorsk	22	Ke	49.58N	82.38 E
Ust-Kan	20	Df	50.57N	84.55 E
Ust-Kara	19	Gb	69.15N	64.59 E
Ust-Karsk	20	Gf	52.41N	118.45 E
Ust-Katav	17	Ii	54.56N	58.10 E
Ust-Kujga	22	Pc	70.00N	135.36 E
Ust-Kut	22	Md	56.46N	105.40 E
Ust-Labinsk	19	Df	45.13N	39.40 E
Ust-Luga	7	Gg	59.39N	28.15 E
Ust-Maya	22	Pc	60.25N	134.32 E
Ust-Muja	20	Ge	56.28N	115.30 E
Ust-Nera	22	Qc	64.34N	143.12 E
Ust-Njukža	20	He	56.30N	121.48 E
Uštobe	19	Hf	45.13N	77.59 E
Ust-Olenëk	20	Gb	72.58N	119.42 E
Ust-Omčug	20	Jd	61.05N	149.30 E
Ust-Ordynski	20	Ff	52.48N	104.45 E
Ust-Ordynski Burjatski Nacionalny okrug [3]	20	Ff	53.30N	104.00 E
Ustovo	15	Hh	41.34N	24.47 E
Ust-Pinega	7	Jd	64.10N	41.58 E
Ust-Pit	20	Ee	58.59N	92.00 E
Ust-Port	20	Dc	69.45N	84.25 E
Ust-Požva	17	Hg	59.05N	56.05 E
Ustrzyki Dolne	10	Sg	49.26N	22.37 E
Ust-Sobolevka	20	Ig	46.10N	137.59 E
Ust-Šonoša	7	Jf	61.11N	41.20 E
Ust-Uda	20	Ff	54.10N	103.03 E
Ust-Ujskoje	17	Ki	54.15N	63.57 E
Ust-Umalta	20	If	51.42N	133.18 E
Ustupo	49	Ii	9.08N	77.56W
Usú	22	Ke	44.27N	84.37 E
Usui-Tōge ▪	29	Fc	36.22N	138.38 E
Usuki	28	Kh	33.08N	131.49 E
Usuki-Wan ▪	29	Be	33.10N	131.50 E
Usulután	49	Cg	13.21N	88.27W
Usumacinta ▪	38	Jh	18.22N	92.40W
Ušumun	20	Hf	52.46N	126.37 E
Usu-San ▪	29a	Bb	42.32N	140.49 E
Usva	17	Hg	58.40N	57.35 E
Usva ▪	17	Hg	58.17N	57.47 E
Utah [2]	43	Ed	39.30N	111.30W
Utah Lake ▪	43	Ec	40.13N	111.49W
Utajärvi	7	Gd	64.45N	26.23 E
Utashinai	29a	Cb	43.31N	142.03 E
Utata	20	Ff	50.51N	102.45 E
Ute Creek ▪	45	Ei	35.21N	103.50W
Utembo ▪	30	Jj	17.06S	22.01 E
Utena	7	Fi	55.29N	25.40 E
Ute Reservoir ▪	45	Ei	35.21N	103.31W
Utete	36	Gd	7.59S	38.47 E
Uthai Thani	25	Ke	15.20N	100.02 E
Utiariti	55	Ca	13.02S	58.17W
Utica	43	Lc	43.06N	75.15W
Utiel	13	Ke	39.34N	1.12W
Utiel, Sierra de- ▪	13	Ke	39.36N	1.08W
Utila	49	De	16.06N	86.54W
Utila, Isla de- ▪	49	De	16.06N	86.56W
Utique ▪	14	Em	37.04N	10.04 E
Utirik Atoll ▪	57	Hc	11.15N	169.48 E
Utlängan ▪	8	Fh	56.00N	15.45 E
Utljukski Liman ▪	16	If	46.20N	35.15 E
Uto	28	Kh	32.40N	130.41 E
Utö [Fin.] ▪	8	Ie	59.45N	21.25 E
Utö [Swe.] ▪	7	Eg	58.55N	18.15 E
Utoro	29a	Da	44.06N	144.58 E
Utrata ▪	10	Qd	52.13N	20.15 E
Utrecht [3]	12	Hb	52.05N	5.08 E
Utrecht [Neth.]	6	Ge	52.05N	5.08 E
Utrecht [S.Afr.]	37	Ee	27.28S	30.20 E
Utrera	13	Gg	37.11N	5.47W
Utsira ▪	8	Ae	59.20N	4.55 E
Utsjoki	7	Gb	69.53N	27.00 E
Utsunomiya	22	Pf	36.33N	139.52 E
Uttaradit	25	Ke	17.38N	100.06 E
Uttar Pradesh [3]	25	Fc	28.00N	80.00 E
Utuado	49	Nd	18.16N	66.42W
Utukok ▪	40	Gb	70.04N	162.18W
Utuloa	64h	Ab	13.16S	176.11W
Utupua Island ▪	57	Hf	11.20S	166.36 E
Uturoa	65e	Db	16.44S	151.26W
Utva ▪	16	Rd	51.29N	52.40 E
Uudenmaa [2]	7	Ff	60.30N	25.00 E
Uukuniemi	8	Nc	61.47N	30.01 E
Uulu/Ulu	8	Kf	58.13N	24.29 E
Uusikaupunki/Nystad	7	Ef	60.48N	21.25 E
Uusimaa ▪	8	Kd	60.30N	25.00 E
Uva	19	Fd	56.58N	52.14 E
Uvac ▪	15	Cf	43.36N	19.30 E
Uvalde	43	Hf	29.13N	99.47W
Uvarovo	19	Ee	52.00N	42.15 E
Uvdal ▪	8	Cd	60.20N	8.30 E
Uvéa, Ile- ▪	57	Jf	13.18S	176.10W
Uvelka ▪	17	Ji	54.05N	61.35 E
Uvelski	17	Ji	54.26N	61.27 E
Uvildy, Ozero- ▪	17	Ji	55.35N	60.30 E
Uvinza	36	Fd	5.06S	30.22 E
Uvira	31	Ji	3.24S	29.08 E
Uvs nuur → Ubsu-Nur ▪	21	Ld	50.20N	92.45 E
Uwa	29	Ce	33.21N	132.30 E
Uwajima	27	Ne	33.13N	132.34 E
Uwajima-Wan ▪	29	Ce	33.15N	132.30 E
Uwa-Kai ▪	29	Ce	33.20N	132.15 E
Uwayl	35	Dd	8.46N	27.24 E
'Uwaynāt, Jabal al-= Uweinat, Gebel- (EN) ▪	30	Jf	21.54N	24.58 E
'Uwaynat Wannīn	33	Bd	28.05N	12.59 E
Uweinat, Gebel- (EN)= 'Uwaynāt, Jabal al- ▪	30	Jf	21.54N	24.58 E
Uwekuli	26	Hg	1.25S	121.06 E
Uwi, Pulau- ▪	26	Ef	1.05N	107.24 E
Uxin Qi (Dabqig)	27	Id	38.27N	109.08 E
Uxmal ▪	39	Kg	20.20N	89.46W
Uyo	34	Gd	5.07N	7.57 E
Uyuni	53	Jh	20.28S	66.50W
Uyuni, Salar de- ▪	52	Jh	20.20S	67.42W
Už [Eur.] ▪	10	Rh	48.33N	22.00 E
Už [Ukr.-U.S.S.R.] ▪	16	Gd	51.15N	30.12 E
Uza ▪	8	Mg	57.47N	29.38 E
Uzbekiston Sovet Socialistik Respublikasy/Uzbekskaja SSR [2]	19	Gg	41.00N	64.00 E
Uzbekskaja Sovetskaja Socialističeskaja Respublika [2]	19	Gg	41.00N	64.00 E
Uzbekskaja SSR/Uzbekiston Sovet Socialistik Respublikasy [2]	19	Gg	41.00N	64.00 E
Uzbekskaja SSR=Uzbek SSR (EN) [2]	19	Gg	41.00N	64.00 E
Uzbek SSR (EN)= Uzbekskaja SSR [2]	19	Gg	41.00N	64.00 E
Uzbel Shankou ▪	27	Bd	38.42N	73.48 E
Uzen	19	Fg	43.22N	52.50 E
Uzerche	11	Hi	45.25N	1.34 E
Uzès	11	Kj	44.01N	4.25 E
Uzgen	18	Id	40.44N	73.21 E
Užgorod	19	Cf	48.37N	22.22 E
Uzin	16	Ge	49.52N	30.27 E
Uzlovaja	16	Kb	54.01N	38.12 E
Uzlovoje	10	Sh	48.23N	22.27 E
Užokski, pereval- ▪	16	Ce	49.02N	22.58 E
Uzümlü	15	Mm	36.44N	29.14 E
Uzun Ada ▪	15	Jk	38.28N	26.42 E
Uzunagač [Kaz.-U.S.S.R.]	18	Kc	43.08N	76.20 E
Uzunagač [Kaz.-U.S.S.R.]	18	Kc	43.36N	76.19 E
Uzunköprü	24	Bb	41.16N	26.41 E
Užur	20	De	55.20N	90.00 E
Užventis	8	Ji	55.44N	22.37 E
Uzynkair, Mys- ▪	18	Bb	45.47N	59.20 E

V

Vääksy	8	Kc	61.11N	25.33 E
Vaal ▪	30	Jk	29.24S	23.38 E
Vaala	7	Gd	64.34N	26.50 E
Vaals	12	Id	50.46N	6.01 E
Vaalwater	37	Dd	24.20S	28.03 E
Vaasa [2]	7	Fe	63.12N	23.00 E
Vaasa/Vasa	6	Ic	63.06N	21.36 E
Vaassen, Epe-	12	Hb	52.17N	5.58 E
Vabalninkas	8	Ki	55.58N	24.49 E
Vác	10	Pi	47.47N	19.08 E
Vacacai, Rio- ▪	55	Fi	29.55S	53.06W
Vacaria	56	Jc	28.30S	50.56W
Vacaria, Rio- ▪	55	Fe	21.55S	53.59W
Vacaville	46	Eg	38.21N	121.59W
Vaccarès, Étang de- ▪	11	Kk	43.32N	4.34 E
Vache, Ile à- ▪	49	Kd	18.04N	73.38W
Väddö ▪	8	Hd	60.00N	18.50 E
Vadehavet ▪	8	Ci	55.15N	8.40 E
Vădeni	15	Kd	45.22N	27.56 E
Vadheim	8	Ac	61.13N	5.49 E
Vadodara	22	Jg	22.18N	73.12 E
Vado Ligure	14	Cf	44.17N	8.27 E
Vadsø	6	Ia	70.05N	29.46 E
Vadstena	7	Dg	58.27N	14.54 E
Vaduz	6	Gf	47.08N	9.30 E
Værlandet ▪	8	Ac	61.20N	4.45 E
Vaga ▪	5	Kc	62.48N	42.56 E
Vagaj	17	Mh	56.28N	67.18 E
Vagaj ▪	17	Nh	57.55N	69.01 E
Vågåmo	7	Bf	61.53N	9.06 E
Vaganjski vrh ▪	14	Jf	44.21N	15.30 E
Vågåvatn ▪	8	Cc	61.50N	8.50 E
Vaggeryd	7	Dh	57.30N	14.07 E
Vaghena ▪	63a	Cb	7.25S	157.43 E
Vagil ▪	17	Kg	59.45N	62.40 E
Vagis, Gora- ▪	20	Jf	52.20N	142.15 E
Vagnhärad	8	Gf	58.57N	17.31 E
Vågsøy ▪	8	Ac	62.00N	5.05 E
Váh ▪	10	Ni	47.55N	18.00 E
Vah ▪	21	Jc	60.45N	76.45 E
Vahitahi Atoll ▪	57	Nf	18.44S	138.52W
Vahruši	7	Mg	58.43N	50.02 E
Vahš	18	Gf	37.43N	68.49 E
Vahsel Bay → Herzog-Ernst-Bucht ▪	66	Af	77.48S	34.39W
Vahtan	7	Lh	57.59N	46.42 E
Vaïaau	65e	Db	16.52S	151.28W
Vaigat ▪	41	Gd	70.30N	54.00W
Vaihingen an der Enz	12	Kf	48.56N	8.58 E
Vaihú	65d	Ab	27.10S	109.23W
Väike-Maarja/Vjaike-Maarja	8	Le	59.04N	26.12 E
Väike-Pakri/Vjajke-Pakri ▪	8	Je	59.50N	23.50 E
Väike Väin/Vjajke-Vjajn ▪	8	Jf	58.30N	23.10 E
Vailala	64h	Bb	13.13S	176.09W
Vailala, Pointe- ▪	64h	Ab	13.13S	176.10W
Vaileka	63d	Bb	17.23S	178.09 E
Vailheu, Récif- ▪	37	Gb	11.48S	43.04 E
Vailly-sur-Aisne	12	Fe	49.25N	3.31 E
Vainikkala	8	Md	60.52N	28.18 E
Vainode/Vajnëde	8	Ih	56.26N	21.45 E
Vairaatea Atoll ▪	57	Nf	19.19S	139.20W
Vaison-la-Romaine	11	Lj	44.14N	5.04 E
Vaïtape	65e	Db	16.31S	151.45W
Vaïtoare	65e	Db	16.41S	151.28W
Vaitupu Island ▪	57	Ie	7.28S	178.41 E
Vajgač, Ostrov- ▪	5	La	70.00N	59.30 E
Vajnëde/Vainode	8	Ih	56.26N	21.45 E
Vakaga [3]	35	Cd	10.00N	23.30 E
Vakfıkebir	24	Hb	41.03N	39.20 E
Vaksdal	8	Ad	60.29N	5.44 E
Val	20	Jf	52.19N	143.09 E
Vala ▪	7	Mh	56.59N	51.16 E
Valaam	7	Hf	61.24N	30.59 E
Valaam, Ostrov- ▪	8	Nc	61.20N	31.05 E
Valahia = Walachia (EN) ▪	15	He	44.00N	25.00 E
Valahia = Walachia (EN) ▪	5	Ig	44.00N	25.00 E
Valais [2]	14	Bd	46.15N	7.30 E
Valamares, Mali i- ▪	15	Di	40.47N	20.28 E
Valamaz	7	Mh	57.36N	52.14 E
Valandovo	15	Fh	41.19N	22.34 E
Valašské Meziříčí	10	Ng	49.29N	17.58 E
Valáxa ▪	15	Hk	38.49N	24.29 E
Vålberg	8	Ee	59.24N	13.12 E
Valburg	12	Hc	51.55N	5.49 E
Valcabra ▪	13	Jg	37.30N	2.43W
Vălčedrăm	15	Gf	43.42N	23.27 E
Valcheta	56	Gf	40.42S	66.09W
Valdagno	14	Fe	45.39N	11.18 E
Valdahon	11	Mg	47.09N	6.21 E
Valdai Hills (EN)= Valdajskaja Vozvyšennost ▪	5	Jd	57.00N	33.30 E
Valdaj	19	Dd	57.59N	33.14 E
Valdajskaja Vozvyšennost= Valdai Hills (EN) ▪	5	Jd	57.00N	33.30 E
Valdarno ▪	14	Fg	43.45N	11.15 E
Valdavia ▪	13	Hb	42.24N	4.16W
Valdecañas, Embalse de- ▪	13	Ge	39.45N	5.30W
Valdeganga	13	Ke	39.09N	1.40W
Val-de-Marne [3]	11	If	48.47N	2.29 E
Valdemārpils/Valdemarpils	7	Fh	57.24N	22.39 E
Valdemarpils/Valdemārpils	7	Fh	57.24N	22.39 E
Valdemarsvik	7	Dg	58.12N	16.32 E
Valdepeñas	13	If	38.46N	3.23W
Valderaduey ▪	13	Gc	41.31N	5.42W
Valderas	13	Gb	42.05N	5.27W
Valderrama, Cíenaga de- ▪	49	Ki	8.56N	72.10W
Valderrobres/Vall-de-roures	13	Ld	40.53N	0.09W
Valdés, Península- ▪	52	Jj	42.30S	64.00W
Valdez	39	Ec	61.07N	146.16W
Val d'Isère	11	Mi	45.27N	6.59 E
Valdivia	53	Ii	39.48S	73.14W
Valdivia Seamount (EN) ▪	30	Hk	25.20S	6.15 E
Valdobbiadene	14	Fe	45.54N	12.00 E
Val-d'Oise [3]	11	Ie	49.10N	2.10 E
Val-d'Or	39	Le	48.07N	77.47W
Valdosta	39	Kf	30.50N	83.17W
Valdres ▪	8	Cc	60.55N	9.10 E
Vale [Geo.-U.S.S.R.]	16	Mi	41.36N	42.51 E
Vale [Or.-U.S.]	46	Gd	44.01N	117.15W
Valea Ierii	15	Gc	46.39N	23.21 E
Valea lui Mihai	15	Fb	47.31N	22.09 E
Valea Vişeului	15	Hb	47.51N	24.10 E
Valença [Braz.]	55	Kf	22.15S	43.43W
Valença [Braz.]	54	Kf	13.22S	39.05W
Valença do Minho	13	Db	42.02N	8.38W
Valença do Piauí	54	Je	6.24S	41.45W
Valençay	11	Hg	47.09N	1.34 E
Valence [Fr.]	11	Gj	44.06N	0.55 E
Valence [Fr.]	11	Kj	44.56N	4.54 E
Valencia	6	Fh	39.28N	0.22W
Valencia [3]	13	Le	39.20N	0.50W
Valencia ▪	13	Le	39.30N	0.40W
València/Valencia	6	Fh	39.28N	0.22W
Valencia/València	6	Fh	39.28N	0.22W
València, Golf de-/Valencia, Golfo de- ▪	5	Fh	39.30N	0.00
Valencia, Golfo de-/ València, Golf de- ▪	5	Fh	39.30N	0.00
Valencia, Lago de- ▪	50	Cg	10.11N	67.45W
Valencia de Alcántara	13	Ee	39.25N	7.14W
Valencia de Don Juan	13	Gb	42.18N	5.31W
Valencia-El Grao	13	Le	39.27N	0.20W
Valenciennes	11	Jd	50.21N	3.32 E
Vălenii de Munte	15	Jd	45.11N	26.02 E
Valentia/Dairbhre ▪	9	Cj	51.55N	10.20W
Valentin	28	Mc	43.07N	134.19 E
Valentine	43	Gc	42.52N	100.33W
Valenza	14	Ce	45.01N	8.38 E
Våler	7	Cf	60.40N	11.50 E
Valera	54	Db	9.19N	70.37W
Valerie Seamount (EN) ▪	57	Ki	42.00S	163.30W
Valga	19	Cd	57.49N	26.05 E
Valge Jõgi ▪	8	Ke	59.32N	25.36 E
Valhalla Mountains ▪	46	Gb	49.45N	117.48W
Valiente, Península- ▪	49	Gi	9.05N	81.51W
Valier	46	Ib	48.18N	112.15W
Valinco, Golfe de- ▪	11a	Ab	41.40N	8.49 E
Valjevo	15	Ce	44.16N	19.53 E
Valka	7	Gh	57.47N	26.01 E
Valkeakoski	7	Ff	61.16N	24.02 E
Valkeala	8	Ld	60.57N	26.48 E
Valkenswaard	12	Hc	51.21N	5.28 E
Valkininkai/Valkininkaj	8	Kj	54.18N	25.55 E
Valkininkaj/Valkininkai	8	Kj	54.18N	25.55 E
Valko/Valkom	8	Ld	60.25N	26.15 E
Valkom/Valko	8	Ld	60.25N	26.15 E
Valkumej	20	Mc	69.41N	170.30 E
Valladolid [3]	13	Hc	41.35N	4.40W
Valladolid [Mex.]	47	Gd	20.41N	88.12W
Valladolid [Sp.]	6	Fg	41.39N	4.43W
Valldal	8	Bb	62.20N	7.21 E
Vall-de-Roures/Valderrobres	13	Ld	40.53N	0.09W
Vall de Uxó	13	Le	39.49N	0.14W
Valle [2]	54	Cc	3.40N	76.30W
Valle [3]	49	Dg	13.30N	87.35W
Valle	7	Bg	59.12N	7.32 E
Vallecas, Madrid-	13	Id	40.23N	3.37W
Valle d'Aosta / Vallée d'Aoste [2]	14	Be	45.45N	7.15 E
Valle de Cabuerniga	13	Ha	43.14N	4.18W
Valle de Guanape	50	Dh	9.54N	65.41W
Valle dei Templi ▪	14	Hm	37.18N	13.35 E
Valle de la Pascua	54	Eb	9.13N	66.00W
Valle de Santiago	48	Ig	20.23N	101.12W
Valle de Topia	48	Fe	25.13N	106.25W
Valle de Zaragoza	48	Gd	27.28N	105.49W
Valledupar	54	Da	10.28N	73.15W
Vallée d'Aoste / Valle d'Aosta [2]	14	Be	45.45N	7.15 E
Vallée Jonction	44	Lb	46.23N	70.55W
Valle Hermoso	48	Ke	25.39N	97.52W
Vallejera, Puerto de- ▪	13	Gd	40.30N	5.42W
Vallejo	43	Cd	38.07N	122.14W
Vallejo, Sierra de- ▪	48	Gg	20.55N	105.20W
Valle Nacional	48	Ki	17.47N	96.19W
Vallenar	53	Ih	28.35S	70.46W
Vallentuna	8	He	59.32N	18.05 E
Valles/El Valles ▪	13	Oc	41.35N	2.15 E
Valles de los Daidos	13	Hd	40.39N	4.09W
Valletta	6	Hh	35.54N	14.31 E
Valley City	43	Hb	46.55N	97.59W
Valley Falls	46	Ee	42.31N	120.15W
Valleyfield	42	Kg	45.15N	74.08W
Valley Station	44	Ef	38.06N	85.52W
Valleyview	42	Fe	55.02N	117.08W
Vallgrund ▪	7	Ee	63.12N	21.14 E
Vallhagar ▪	8	Hg	57.20N	18.10 E
Vallimanca	55	Bm	36.21S	61.02W
Vallimanca, Arroyo- ▪	55	Bl	35.40S	60.02W
Vallo della Lucania	14	Jj	40.14N	15.16 E
Valloires, Abbaye de- ▪	12	Dd	50.20N	1.47 E
Vallorbe	14	Ad	46.43N	6.23 E
Valls	13	Nc	41.17N	1.15 E
Valls d'Andorra → Andorra [1]	6	Gg	42.30N	1.30 E
Vallsta	8	Gc	61.32N	16.22 E
Vallvik	8	Gc	61.11N	17.11 E
Valmaseda	13	Ia	43.12N	3.12W
Valmiera	19	Cd	57.32N	25.29 E
Valmont	12	Ce	49.44N	0.31 E
Valnera ▪	13	Ia	43.10N	3.45W
Valognes	11	Ee	49.31N	1.28W
Valois, Plaine du- ▪	11	Ie	49.10N	2.45 E
Valoria la Buena	13	Hc	41.48N	4.32W
Valpaços	13	Ec	41.36N	7.19W
Valparaiso	44	De	41.28N	87.03W
Valparaíso [Braz.]	55	Ge	21.13S	50.51W
Valparaíso [Chile]	53	Ii	33.02S	71.38W
Valparaíso [Mex.]	48	Hf	22.46N	103.34W
Valpovo	14	Me	45.39N	18.25 E
Valréas	11	Kj	44.23N	4.59 E
Vals ▪	30	Jk	27.23S	26.31 E
Vals, Tanjung- ▪	26	Kh	8.26S	137.38 E
Valsjöbyn	7	Dd	64.04N	14.08 E
Valtellina ▪	14	Dd	46.10N	9.55 E
Valtimo	7	Ge	63.40N	28.48 E
Váltou, Óri- ▪	15	Ej	39.10N	21.20 E
Valujki	19	De	50.12N	38.08 E
Valul-Lui Traian ▪	15	Le	44.15N	28.30 E
Valverde	32	Dd	27.48N	17.55W
Valverde de Júcar	13	Je	39.43N	2.12W
Valverde del Camino	13	Fg	37.34N	6.45W
Valverde del Fresno	13	Ff	40.13N	6.52W
Vamdrup	8	Ci	55.25N	9.17 E
Våmhus	7	Df	61.08N	14.28 E
Vamizi, Ilha- ▪	37	Gb	11.02S	40.40 E
Vammala	7	Ff	61.20N	22.54 E
Vámos	15	Hn	35.25N	24.12 E
Van	23	Fb	38.28N	43.20 E
Van, Lake- (EN)=Van Gölü ▪	21	Gf	38.33N	42.46 E
Vanajanselkä ▪	7	Ff	61.09N	24.15 E
Vanak ▪	24	Ng	31.41N	50.52 E
Vanak	24	Ng	31.32N	51.19 E
Vanån ▪	8	Fd	60.31N	14.14 E
Vanault-les-Dames	12	Gf	48.51N	4.46 E
Vanavana Atoll ▪	57	Ng	20.47S	139.09W
Vanavara	20	Fd	60.22N	102.16 E
Van Buren [Ar.-U.S.]	45	Ii	35.26N	94.21W
Van Buren [Me.-U.S.]	44	Nb	47.09N	67.56W
Vanč	18	He	38.23N	71.29 E
Vanceburg	44	Ff	38.36N	83.19W
Vancouver [B.C.-Can.]	39	Ge	49.16N	123.07W
Vancouver [Wa.-U.S.]	43	Cb	45.39N	122.40W
Vancouver Island ▪	38	Ge	49.45N	126.00W
Vandalia [Il.-U.S.]	45	Lg	38.58N	89.06W
Vandalia [Oh.-U.S.]	44	Ef	39.53N	84.12W
Vanderbijl Park	37	De	26.42S	27.54 E
Vanderhoof	42	Ff	54.01N	124.01W
Vanderlin Island ▪	59	Hc	15.45S	137.00 E
Van Diemen, Cape- ▪	59	Gb	11.10S	130.25 E
Van Diemen Gulf ▪	59	Gb	11.50S	132.00 E
Vandmtor, Ozero- ▪	17	Le	62.15N	65.45 E
Vändra/Vjandra	7	Fg	58.40N	25.01 E
Vänern ▪	5	Hd	58.55N	13.30 E
Vänersborg	7	Cg	58.22N	12.19 E

Index Symbols

- [1] Independent Nation
- [2] State, Region
- [3] District, County
- [4] Municipality
- [5] Colony, Dependency
- ▪ Continent
- ▪ Physical Region
- ▪ Historical or Cultural Region
- ▪ Mount, Mountain
- ▪ Volcano
- ▪ Hill
- ▪ Mountains, Mountain Range
- ▪ Hills, Escarpment
- ▪ Plateau, Upland
- ▪ Pass, Gap
- ▪ Plain, Lowland
- ▪ Delta
- ▪ Salt Flat
- ▪ Valley, Canyon
- ▪ Crater, Cave
- ▪ Karst Features
- ▪ Depression
- ▪ Polder
- ▪ Desert, Dunes
- ▪ Forest, Woods
- ▪ Heath, Steppe
- ▪ Oasis
- ▪ Cape, Point
- ▪ Coast, Beach
- ▪ Cliff
- ▪ Peninsula
- ▪ Isthmus
- ▪ Sandbank
- ▪ Island
- ▪ Atoll
- ▪ Rock, Reef
- ▪ Islands, Archipelago
- ▪ Rocks, Reefs
- ▪ Coral Reef
- ▪ Well, Spring
- ▪ Geyser
- ▪ River, Stream
- ▪ Waterfall Rapids
- ▪ River Mouth, Estuary
- ▪ Lake
- ▪ Salt Lake
- ▪ Intermittent Lake
- ▪ Reservoir
- ▪ Swamp, Pond
- ▪ Canal
- ▪ Glacier
- ▪ Ice Shelf, Pack Ice
- ▪ Ocean
- ▪ Sea
- ▪ Gulf, Bay
- ▪ Strait, Fjord
- ▪ Lagoon
- ▪ Bank
- ▪ Seamount
- ▪ Tablemount
- ▪ Ridge
- ▪ Shelf
- ▪ Basin
- ▪ Escarpment, Sea Scarp
- ▪ Fracture
- ▪ Trench, Abyss
- ▪ National Park, Reserve
- ▪ Point of Interest
- ▪ Recreation Site
- ▪ Cave, Cavern
- ▪ Historic Site
- ▪ Ruins
- ▪ Wall, Walls
- ▪ Church, Abbey
- ▪ Temple
- ▪ Scientific Station
- ▪ Airport
- ▪ Port
- ▪ Lighthouse
- ▪ Mine
- ▪ Tunnel
- ▪ Dam, Bridge

Index Symbols

[1] Independent Nation
[2] State, Region
[3] District, County
[4] Municipality
[5] Colony, Dependency
Continent
Physical Region
Historical or Cultural Region
Mount, Mountain
Volcano
Hill
Mountains, Mountain Range
Hills, Escarpment
Plateau, Upland
Pass, Gap
Plain, Lowland
Delta
Salt Flat
Valley, Canyon
Crater, Cave
Karst Features
Depression
Polder
Desert, Dunes
Forest, Woods
Heath, Steppe
Oasis
Cape, Point
Coast, Beach
Cliff
Peninsula
Isthmus
Sandbank
Island
Atoll
Rock, Reef
Islands, Archipelago
Rocks, Reefs
Coral Reef
Well, Spring
Geyser
River, Stream
Waterfall Rapids
River Mouth, Estuary
Lake
Salt Lake
Intermittent Lake
Reservoir
Swamp, Pond
Canal
Glacier
Ice Shelf, Pack Ice
Ocean
Sea
Gulf, Bay
Strait, Fjord
Lagoon
Bank
Seamount
Tablemount
Ridge
Shelf
Basin
Escarpment, Sea Scarp
Fracture
Trench, Abyss
National Park, Reserve
Point of Interest
Recreation Site
Cave, Cavern
Historic Site
Ruins
Wall, Walls
Church, Abbey
Temple
Scientific Station
Airport
Port
Lighthouse
Mine
Tunnel
Dam, Bridge

Vetlužski [R.S.F.S.R.] 7 Kh 57.11N 45.07 E
Vetlužski [R.S.F.S.R.] 7 Kg 58.26N 45.28 E
Vetreny 20 Jd 61.43N 149.40 E
Vetreny Pojas, Krjaž- 7 Ie 63.20N 37.30 E
Vetrino 8 Mi 55.25N 28.31 E
Vetschau/Wětošow 10 Ke 51.47N 14.04 E
Vettore 14 Hh 42.49N 13.16 E
Vetzstein 10 Hf 50.25N 11.25 E
Veules-les-Roses 12 Ce 49.52N 0.48 E
Veulettes-sur-Mer 12 Ce 49.51N 0.36 E
Veurne/Furnes 11 Ic 51.04N 2.40 E
Vevey 14 Ad 46.28N 6.50 E
Vevis/Vievis 8 Kj 54.45N 24.58 E
Vexin 11 He 49.10N 1.40 E
Veynes 11 Lj 44.32N 5.49 E
Vézelay 11 Jg 47.28N 3.44 E
Vežen 15 Hg 42.45N 24.24 E
Vézère 11 Gj 44.53N 0.53 E
Vezirköprü 24 Fb 41.09N 35.28 E
Viadana 14 Ef 44.56N 10.31 E
Viale 55 Bj 31.53S 60.01W
Viana 54 Jd 3.13S 45.00W
Viana del Bollo 13 Eb 42.11N 7.06W
Viana do Alentejo 13 Ef 38.20N 8.00W
Viana do Castelo 13 Dc 41.42N 8.50W
Viana do Castelo [2] 13 Dc 41.55N 8.25W
Vianden 12 Ie 49.55N 6.16 E
Viangchan (Vientiane) 22 Mh 17.58N 102.36 E
Vianópolis 55 Hc 16.45S 48.32W
Viar 13 Gg 37.36N 5.50W
Viareggio 14 Eg 43.52N 10.14 E
Viarmes 12 Ee 49.08N 2.22 E
Viaur 11 Hj 44.08N 1.58 E
Viborg [2] 8 Ch 56.30N 9.30 E
Viborg 7 Bh 56.26N 9.24 E
Vibo Valentia 14 Kl 38.40N 16.06 E
Vic 13 Oc 41.56N 2.15 E
Vicari 14 Hm 37.49N 13.34 E
Vicecomodoro Marambio 66 Re 64.16S 56.44W
Vicente Guerrero 47 Dd 23.45N 103.59W
Vicenza 14 Fe 45.33N 11.33 E
Vichada [2] 54 Ec 5.00N 69.30W
Vichada, Río- 52 Je 4.55N 67.50W
Vichadero 55 Ej 31.48S 54.43W
Vichy 11 Jh 46.07N 3.25 E
Vicksburg 43 Ie 32.14N 90.56W
Vico, Lago di- 14 Gh 42.19N 12.10 E
Vic-sur-Aisne 12 Fe 49.24N 3.07 E
Vic-sur-Cère 11 Ij 44.59N 2.37 E
Victor Bay 66 Ie 66.20S 136.30 E
Victor Harbour 59 Hg 35.34S 138.37 E
Victoria 38 Hb 71.00N 114.00W
Victoria [Arg.] 56 Hd 32.37S 60.10W
Victoria [Austl.] 59 Ig 38.00S 145.00 E
Victoria [B.C.-Can.] 39 Ge 48.25N 123.22W
Victoria [Cam.] 34 Ge 4.01N 9.12 E
Victoria [Chile] 56 Fe 38.13S 72.20W
Victoria [Gren.] 50 Ff 12.12N 61.42W
Victoria [Mala.] 26 Ge 5.17N 115.15 E
Victoria [Malta] 14 In 36.02N 14.14 E
Victoria [Rom.] 15 Hd 45.44N 24.41 E
Victoria [Sey.] 31 Mi 4.38S 55.27 E
Victoria [Tx.-U.S.] 39 Jg 28.48N 97.00W
Victoria/Ying zhan 22 Ng 22.17N 114.09 E
Victoria, Lake- [Afr.] 30 Ki 1.00S 33.00 E
Victoria, Lake- [Austl.] 59 If 34.00S 141.15 E
Victoria, Mount- [Bur.] 21 Lg 21.14N 93.55 E
Victoria, Mount- [Pap.N.Gui.] 57 Fe 8.53S 147.33 E
Victoria, Sierra de la- 55 Fg 25.55S 54.00W
Victoria and Albert Mountains 42 Ka 79.00N 75.00W
Victoria de Durango 39 Ig 24.02N 104.40W
Victoria de las Tunas 47 Id 20.58N 76.57W
Victoria Falls 31 Jj 17.56S 25.50 E
Victoria Falls 30 Jj 17.55S 25.21 E
Victoria Fjord 41 Hb 82.20N 48.00W
Victoria Land (EN) 66 Jf 75.00S 159.00 E
Victoria Nile 30 Kh 2.14N 31.26 E
Victoria Peak [B.C.-Can.] 46 Ba 50.03N 126.06W
Victoria Peak [Blz.] 49 Ce 16.48N 88.37W
Victoria River 57 Df 15.12S 129.43 E
Victoria River Downs 59 Gc 16.24S 131.00 E
Victoria Strait 42 Hc 69.30N 100.00W
Victoriaville 42 Kg 46.03N 71.58W
Victoria West 37 Cf 31.25S 23.04 E
Victorija 41 Pb 80.10N 36.45 E
Victorville 46 Gi 34.32N 117.18W
Victory, Mount- 59 Ja 9.10S 149.05 E
Vičuga 19 Ed 57.15N 42.00 E
Vicuña 56 Fc 29.59S 70.44W
Vicuña Mackenna 56 Hd 33.54S 64.23W
Vidå 8 Cj 54.58N 8.41 E
Vidal 46 Hi 34.11N 114.34W
Vidalia 45 Kk 31.34N 91.26W
Videbæk 8 Ch 56.05N 8.38 E
Videira 56 Jc 27.00S 51.08W
Videla 55 Bj 30.56S 60.39W
Videle 15 Ie 44.17N 25.31 E
Vidigueira 13 Ef 38.13N 7.48W
Vidin [2] 15 Ff 43.59N 22.52 E
Vidin 15 Ff 43.59N 22.52 E
Vidisha 25 Fd 23.42N 77.47 E
Vidlič 15 Ff 43.08N 22.47 E
Vidojevica 15 Ef 43.10N 21.32 E
Vidöstern 8 Fg 57.04N 14.01 E
Vidourle 11 Kk 43.32N 4.08 E
Vidra [Rom.] 15 Jd 45.55N 26.54 E
Vidra [Rom.] 15 Je 44.16N 26.09 E
Vidsel 7 Ed 65.49N 20.31 E
Viduša 14 Mh 42.54N 18.18 E
Vidzeme 8 Kg 57.10N 26.00 E
Vidzemes Augstiene/Vidzemskaja Vozvyšennost 8 Kh 56.45N 26.00 E
Vidzemskaja Vozvyšennost/Vidzemes Augstiene 8 Kh 56.45N 26.00 E
Vidzy 8 Li 55.23N 26.47 E
Vie 12 Be 49.09N 0.04W
Viechtach 10 Ig 49.05N 12.53 E
Viedma 53 Jj 40.50S 63.00W
Viedma, Lago- 52 Ij 49.35S 72.35W
Vieille Case 51g Ba 15.36N 61.24W
Vieja, Sierra- 45 Dk 30.30N 104.40W
Viejo, Cerro- 47 Bb 30.20N 112.15W
Viekšniai/Viekšnjai 8 Jh 56.14N 22.28 E
Viekšnjai/Viekšniai 8 Jh 56.14N 22.28 E
Viella 13 Mb 42.42N 0.48 E
Vielsalm 12 Hd 50.17N 5.55 E
Viels-Maisons 12 Ff 48.54N 3.24 E
Vienna [Mo.-U.S.] 45 Kg 38.11N 91.57W
Vienna [W.V.-U.S.] 44 Gf 39.20N 81.33W
Vienna (EN) = Wien 6 Hf 48.12N 16.22 E
Vienna Woods (EN) = Wienerwald 14 Jb 48.10N 16.00 E
Vienne 11 Ki 45.31N 4.52 E
Vienne [3] 11 Gh 46.30N 0.30 E
Vienne 5 Gf 47.13N 0.05 E
Vientiane → Viangchan 22 Mh 17.58N 102.36 E
Vientos, Paso de los- = Windward Passage (EN) 38 Lh 20.00N 73.50W
Vieques, Isla de- 47 Ke 18.08N 65.25W
Vieques, Pasaje de- 51a Cb 18.08N 65.40W
Vieques, Sonda de- 51a Cb 18.17N 65.25W
Vierge Point 51k Bb 13.49N 60.53W
Viersen 10 Ce 51.15N 6.23 E
Vierville-sur-Mer 12 Be 49.22N 0.54W
Vierwaldstätter-See = Lucerne, Lake- (EN) 14 Cc 47.00N 8.30 E
Vierzon 11 Ig 47.13N 2.05 E
Viesca 48 He 25.21N 102.48W
Viesite/Viesīte 8 Kh 56.20N 25.38 E
Viesīte/Viesite 8 Kh 56.20N 25.38 E
Vieste 14 Ki 41.53N 16.10 E
Viet Nam [1] 22 Mh 13.00N 108.00 E
Viet Tri 25 Ld 21.18N 105.26 E
Vieux Fort 50 Ff 13.44N 60.57W
Vieux-Fort, Pointe du- 51e Ac 15.57N 61.43W
Vieux Fort Bay 51k Bb 13.44N 60.58W
Vieux-Habitants 51e Ab 16.04N 61.46W
Vievis/Vevis 8 Kj 54.45N 24.58 E
Viga 7 Kg 59.15N 43.42 E
Vigala 8 Kf 58.43N 24.22 E
Vigan 26 Hc 17.34N 120.23 E
Vigeland 8 Bf 58.05N 7.18 E
Vigevano 14 Ce 45.19N 8.51 E
Vigia 54 Id 0.48S 48.08W
Vigía Chico 48 Ph 19.46N 87.35W
Vignacourt 12 Ed 50.01N 2.12 E
Vignemale 13 Lb 42.46N 0.08W
Vigneulles-lès-Hattonchâtel 12 Hf 48.59N 5.43 E
Vignoble 11 Lh 46.50N 5.30 E
Vignola 14 Ef 44.29N 11.00 E
Vigny 12 De 49.05N 1.56 E
Vigo 6 Fg 42.14N 8.43W
Vigo, Ría de- 13 Db 42.15N 8.45W
Vigra 8 Bb 62.30N 6.05 E
Vigrestad 8 Af 58.34N 5.42 E
Vihanti 7 Fd 64.30N 25.00 E
Vihiers 11 Fg 47.09N 0.32W
Vihorevka 20 Fe 56.12N 101.09 E
Vihorlat 10 Sh 48.55N 22.10 E
Vihren 15 Gh 41.46N 23.24 E
Vihti 7 Ff 60.25N 24.20 E
Viiala 8 Jc 61.13N 23.47 E
Viinijärvi 8 Mb 62.45N 29.15 E
Viinijärvi 8 Mb 62.39N 29.14 E
Viitasaari 7 Fe 63.04N 25.52 E
Viivikonna/Vijvikonna 8 Le 59.14N 27.41 E
Vijayawāda 22 Kh 16.31N 80.37 E
Vijvikonna/Viivikonna 8 Le 59.14N 27.41 E
Vik 7a Bc 63.25N 19.01W
Vika 8 Fd 60.57N 14.27 E
Vikarbyn 8 Fd 60.55N 15.01 E
Vikbolandet 8 Gf 58.30N 16.40 E
Viken 8 Eh 56.09N 12.34 E
Viken 8 Ff 58.40N 14.20 E
Vikenara Point 63a Dc 8.34S 159.53 E
Vikersund 8 De 59.59N 10.02 E
Vikingbanken 9 Pa 60.20N 2.30 E
Vikmanshyttan 8 Fd 60.17N 15.49 E
Vikna 7 Cd 64.53N 10.58 E
Vikna 7 Cd 64.54N 11.00 E
Viksoyri 7 Bf 61.05N 6.34 E
Vila da Bispo 13 Dg 37.05N 8.55W
Vila da Maganja 37 Fc 17.18S 37.31 E
Vila de Rei 13 De 39.40N 8.09W
Vila do Conde 13 Dc 41.21N 8.45W
Vila do Porto 32 Bb 36.56N 25.09W
Vila Flor 13 Ec 41.18N 7.09W
Vilafranca del Penedès/Villafranca del Panadés 13 Nc 41.21N 1.42 E
Vila Franca de Xira 13 Df 38.57N 8.59W
Vila Franca do Campo 32 Bb 37.43N 25.26W
Vila Franca do Save 37 Ed 21.09S 34.32 E
Vila Gamito 37 Eb 14.10S 32.59 E
Vila Gouveia 37 Ec 18.03S 33.11 E
Vilaine 11 Dg 49.23N 2.27W
Viļaka/Viljaka 7 Gh 57.14N 27.46 E
Vila Machado 37 Ec 19.17S 34.12 E
Vilanculos 31 Kk 22.00S 35.19 E
Viļani/Viljani 7 Gh 56.33N 26.59 E
Vila Nova da Cerveira 13 Dc 41.56N 8.45W
Vila Nova de Famalicao 13 Dc 41.25N 8.32W
Vila Nova de Foz Côa 13 Ec 41.05N 7.12W
Vila Nova de Gaia 13 Dc 41.08N 8.37W
Vilanova i la Geltrú/Villanueva y Geltrú 13 Nc 41.14N 1.44 E
Vila Paiva de Andrada 37 Ec 18.41S 34.04 E
Vila Pouca de Aguiar 13 Ec 41.30N 7.39W
Vila Real [2] 13 Ec 41.35N 7.35W
Vila Real 13 Ec 41.18N 7.45W
Vila-Real de los Infantes/Villarreal de los Infantes 13 Le 39.56N 0.06W
Vila Real de Santo António 13 Eg 37.12N 7.25W
Vilar Formoso 13 Fd 40.37N 6.50W
Vila Velha 54 Jh 20.20S 40.17W
Vila Velha de Ródão 13 Ee 39.40N 7.42W
Vila Viçosa 13 Ef 38.47N 7.25W
Vîlcea [2] 15 He 45.10N 24.10 E
Vilches 13 If 38.12N 3.30W
Vildbjerg 8 Ch 56.12N 8.46 E
Viled 7 Lf 61.22N 47.15 E
Vilejka 19 Ce 54.30N 26.53 E
Vilhelmina 7 Dd 64.37N 16.39 E
Vilhena 53 Jg 12.43S 60.07W
Vilija 16 Db 54.55N 25.40 E
Viljaka/Viļaka 7 Gh 57.14N 27.46 E
Viljandi 19 Cd 58.22N 25.35 E
Viljany/Viļani 7 Gh 56.33N 26.59 E
Viljuj 21 Oc 64.24N 126.26 E
Viljujsk 20 Hd 63.40N 121.33 E
Viljujskoje Plato = Vilyui Range (EN) 21 Mc 66.00N 108.00 E
Viljujskoje Vodohranilišče 20 Gd 62.30N 111.00 E
Vilkaviškis 7 Fi 54.43N 23.02 E
Vilkickogo, Ostrov- [R.S.F.S.R.] 20 Cb 73.30N 76.00 E
Vilkickogo, Ostrov- [R.S.F.S.R.] 20 Ka 75.40N 152.30 E
Vilkickogo, Proliv- = Vilkitski Strait (EN) 21 Mb 77.55N 103.00 E
Vilkija 7 Fi 55.03N 23.35 E
Vilkitski Strait (EN) = Vilkickogo, Proliv- 21 Mb 77.55N 103.00 E
Vilkovo 16 Fg 45.23N 29.35 E
Villa Aberastain 56 Gd 31.39S 68.35W
Villa Ahumada 47 Cb 30.37N 106.31W
Villa Altagracia 49 Ld 18.40N 70.10W
Villa Ana 55 Ci 28.29S 59.37W
Villa Angela 56 Hc 27.35S 60.43W
Villa Atuel 56 Gd 34.50S 67.54W
Villa Berthet 55 Bh 27.17S 60.25W
Villablino 13 Fb 42.56N 6.19W
Villa Bruzual 54 Eb 9.20N 69.06W
Villa Cañás 55 Bk 34.00S 61.36W
Villacañas 13 Ie 39.38N 3.20W
Villacarrillo 13 If 38.07N 3.05W
Villacastín 13 Hd 40.47N 4.25W
Villach 14 Hd 46.36N 13.50 E
Villacidro 14 Ck 39.27N 8.44 E
Villa Clara 55 Cj 31.50S 58.49W
Villaclara [3] 49 Hb 22.30N 80.00W
Villa Constitución [Arg.] 56 Hd 33.14S 60.20W
Villa Constitución [Mex.] 47 Bc 25.09N 111.43W
Villa Coronado 48 Gd 26.45N 105.10W
Villada 13 Hb 42.15N 4.58W
Villa de Arriaga 48 Ig 21.54N 101.23W
Villa de Cos 48 Hf 23.17N 102.21W
Villa de Cura 50 Cg 10.02N 67.29W
Villa de Maria 56 Hc 29.54S 63.43W
Villa de Reyes 48 Ig 21.48N 100.56W
Villa de San Antonio 49 Df 14.16N 87.36W
Villadiego 13 Ib 42.31N 4.00W
Villa Dolores 56 Gd 31.56S 65.12W
Villa Elisa 55 Ck 32.10S 58.24W
Villa Flores 48 Mi 16.14N 93.14W
Villa Florida 55 Dh 26.23S 57.09W
Villafranca del Bierzo 13 Fb 42.36N 6.48W
Villafranca del Cid 13 Ld 40.25N 0.15W
Villafranca de los Barros 13 Ff 38.34N 6.20W
Villafranca del Panadés/Vilafranca del Penedès 13 Nc 41.21N 1.42 E
Villafranca di Verona 14 Ee 45.21N 10.50 E
Villa Frontera 47 Dc 26.56N 101.27W
Villagarcia de Arosa 13 Db 42.36N 8.45W
Villa General Roca 56 Gd 32.39S 66.28W
Villa Gesell 55 Dm 37.15S 56.55W
Villagrán 48 Je 24.29N 99.29W
Villaguay 56 Id 31.51S 59.01W
Villa Guillermina 55 Ci 28.14S 59.28W
Villa Hayes 56 Ic 25.06S 57.34W
Villa Hermandarias 55 Cj 31.13S 59.59W
Villahermosa 39 Jh 17.59N 92.55W
Villa Hidalgo 48 Gd 26.16N 104.54W
Villa Huidobro 56 Hd 34.50S 64.35W
Villajoyosa/La Vila Jojosa 13 Lf 38.30N 0.14W
Villalba 13 Ea 43.18N 7.41W
Villaldama 48 Id 26.30N 100.26W
Villalón de Campos 13 Gb 42.06N 5.02W
Villalpando 13 Gc 41.52N 5.24W
Villamalea 13 Ke 39.22N 1.35W
Villamanrique 13 Jf 38.33N 3.00W
Villa María 53 Ji 32.25S 63.15W
Villamartín 13 Gh 36.52N 5.38W
Villa Matamoros 48 Gd 26.50N 105.35W
Villa Media Agua 56 Gd 31.59S 68.25W
Villamil 54a Ab 0.56S 91.01W
Villa Minetti 55 Bi 28.37S 61.39W
Villa Montes 53 Jh 21.15S 63.30W
Villandraut 11 Fj 44.28N 0.22W
Villa Nueva 56 Gd 32.54S 68.47W
Villanueva 49 Kh 10.37N 72.59W
Villanueva [Mex.] 48 Hf 22.21N 102.53W
Villanueva [N.M.-U.S.] 45 Di 35.17N 105.23W
Villanueva de Córdoba 13 Hf 38.20N 4.37W
Villanueva del Arzobispo 13 Jf 38.10N 3.00W
Villanueva de la Serena 13 Gf 38.58N 5.48W
Villanueva del Fresno 13 Ef 38.23N 7.10W
Villanueva de los Infantes 13 If 38.44N 3.01W
Villanueva del Río y Minas 13 Gg 37.39N 5.42W
Villanueva y Geltrú/Vilanova i la Geltrú 13 Nc 41.14N 1.44 E
Villa Ocampo [Arg.] 56 Ic 28.28S 59.22W
Villa Ocampo [Mex.] 47 Cc 26.27N 105.31W
Villa Ojo de Agua 56 Hc 29.31S 63.42W
Villa Oliva 55 Dh 26.01S 57.53W
Villa Pesqueira 48 Ec 29.08N 109.58W
Villaputzu 14 Dk 39.26N 9.34 E
Villa Ramírez 55 Bk 32.11S 60.12W
Villarcayo 13 Ib 42.56N 3.34W
Villar del Arzobispo 13 Le 39.44N 0.49W
Villa Regina 56 Ge 39.06S 67.04W
Villarica [Chile] 56 Fe 39.16S 72.16W
Villarica [Par.] 53 Kh 25.45S 56.26W
Villa Rosario 54 Db 7.50N 72.29W
Villarreal de los Infantes/Vila-Real de los Infantes 13 Le 39.56N 0.06W
Villarrobledo 13 Je 39.16N 2.36W
Villasalto 14 Dk 39.29N 9.23 E
Villa San Giovanni 14 Jl 38.13N 15.38 E
Villa San Martín 56 Hc 28.18S 64.12W
Villasimius 14 Dk 39.08N 9.31 E
Villatoro, Puerto de- 13 Gd 40.33N 5.10W
Villa Unión [Mex.] 47 Cd 23.12N 106.16W
Villa Unión [Mex.] 48 Ic 28.15N 100.43W
Villaverde, Madrid- 13 Id 40.21N 3.42W
Villavicencio 53 Ie 4.09N 73.37W
Villaviciosa 13 Ga 43.29N 5.26W
Villazón 54 Eh 22.06S 65.36W
Ville-de-Laval 44 Kc 45.33N 73.44W
Ville de Paris [3] 11 If 48.52N 2.20 E
Ville de Toulouse Bank (EN) 38 Hh 11.30N 117.00W
Villedieu-les-Poêles 11 Ef 48.50N 1.13W
Ville-en-Tardenois 12 Fe 49.11N 3.48 E
Villefranche-de-Lauragais 11 Hk 43.24N 1.44 E
Villefranche-de-Rouergue 11 Ij 44.21N 2.03 E
Villefranche-sur-Saône 11 Ki 45.59N 4.43 E
Ville-Marie 44 Hb 47.20N 79.26W
Villemur-sur-Tarn 11 Hk 43.52N 1.31 E
Villena 13 Lf 38.38N 0.51W
Villeneuve d'Ascq 12 Fd 50.38N 3.09 E
Villeneuve-Saint-Georges 12 Ef 48.44N 2.27 E
Villeneuve-sur-Lot 11 Gj 44.24N 0.43 E
Villeneuve-sur-Yonne 11 Jf 48.05N 3.18 E
Ville Platte 45 Jk 30.42N 92.16W
Villers-Bocage [Fr.] 12 Be 49.05N 0.39W
Villers-Bocage [Fr.] 12 Ee 50.00N 2.20 E
Villers-Bretonneux 12 Ee 49.52N 2.31 E
Villers-Carbonnel 12 Ee 49.52N 2.54 E
Villers-Cotterêts 12 Fe 49.15N 3.05 E
Villers-la-Ville 12 Gd 50.35N 4.32 E
Villers-sur-Mer 12 Be 49.19N 0.01W
Villerupt 11 Le 49.28N 5.56 E
Villerville 12 Ce 49.24N 0.08 E
Ville-sur-Tourbe 12 Ge 49.11N 4.47 E
Villeurbanne 11 Ki 45.59N 4.43 E
Villiersdorp 37 Bf 33.59S 19.17 E
Villingen-Schwenningen 10 Eh 48.04N 8.28 E
Villmanstrand/Lappeenranta 6 Ic 61.04N 28.11 E
Villmar 12 Kd 50.23N 8.12 E
Vilnius/Vilnjus 6 Ie 54.41N 25.19 E
Vilnjus/Vilnius 6 Ie 54.41N 25.19 E
Vilok 10 Sh 48.08N 22.50 E
Vilppula 8 Kb 62.01N 24.31 E
Vils [Ger.] 10 Hg 49.10N 11.59 E
Vils [Ger.] 10 Jh 48.35N 13.10 E
Vilsandi 8 If 58.20N 21.45 E
Vilsbiburg 10 Ih 48.27N 12.21 E
Vilshofen 10 Jh 48.38N 13.11 E
Vilusi 15 Bg 42.44N 18.36 E
Vilvoorde/Vilvorde 11 Kd 50.56N 4.26 E
Vilvorde/Vilvoorde 11 Kd 50.56N 4.26 E
Vilyui Range (EN) = Viljujskoje Plato 21 Mc 66.00N 108.00 E
Vimeu 12 Dd 50.05N 1.35 E
Vimianzo 13 Ca 43.07N 9.02W
Vimmerby 7 Dh 57.40N 15.51 E
Vimoutiers 11 Gf 48.55N 0.12 E
Vimperk 10 Jg 49.03N 13.47 E
Vimy 12 Ed 50.22N 2.49 E
Vina 34 Id 7.45N 15.36 E
Viña del Mar 53 Ii 33.02S 71.34W
Vinalhaven Island 44 Mc 44.05N 68.52W
Vinalopo 13 Lf 38.11N 0.36W
Vinaros/Vinaroz 13 Md 40.28N 0.29 E
Vinaroz/Vinaros 13 Md 40.28N 0.29 E
Vînători 15 Hc 46.14N 24.56 E
Vincennes 43 Jd 38.41N 87.32W
Vincennes Bay 66 He 66.30S 109.30 E
Vincente, Puntan- 64b Bb 14.56N 145.40 E
Vinci 14 Eg 43.47N 10.55 E
Vindafjorden 8 Ae 59.20N 5.55 E
Vindelälven 7 Ee 63.54N 19.52 E
Vindeln 7 Ed 64.12N 19.44 E
Vinderup 8 Ch 56.29N 8.47 E
Vindhya Range 21 Kg 24.37N 82.00 E
Vindö 8 He 59.20N 18.40 E
Vineland 44 Jf 39.29N 75.02W
Vingåker 7 Dg 59.02N 15.52 E
Vingeanne 11 Lg 47.45N 5.18 E
Vinh 22 Mh 18.40N 105.40 E
Vinhais 13 Fc 41.50N 7.00W
Vinh Bac Phan = Tonkin, Gulf of- (EN) 21 Mh 20.00N 108.00 E
Vinh Linh 25 Le 17.04N 107.02 E
Vinica [Yugo.] 14 Jg 45.28N 77.00 E
Vinica [Yugo.] 15 Fh 41.53N 22.30 E
Vinita 45 Ih 36.39N 95.09W
Vînju Mare 15 Fe 44.25N 22.52 E
Vinkovci 14 Me 45.17N 18.49 E
Vinnica 6 If 49.14N 28.29 E
Vinnickaja Oblast [3] 19 Cf 49.00N 28.50 E
Vinniki 16 De 49.48N 24.11 E
Vino, Tierra del- 13 Gc 41.30N 5.30W
Vinogradov 16 Ce 48.09N 23.02 E
Vinslöv 8 Eh 56.06N 13.55 E
Vinson Massif 66 Pf 78.35S 85.25W
Vinstervåtn 8 Cc 61.20N 9.00 E
Vinstra 7 Bf 61.36N 9.45 E
Vinstra 8 Cc 61.36N 9.45 E
Vintilă Vodă 15 Jd 45.28N 26.43 E
Vintjärn 8 Gd 60.50N 16.03 E
Vinton 45 Ke 42.10N 92.00W
Vintschgau/Venosta, Val- 14 Ed 46.40N 10.35 E
Vipiteno / Sterzing 14 Fd 46.54N 11.26 E
Vipya Plateau 36 Fe 11.09S 34.00 E
Viqueque 26 Ih 8.52S 126.22 E
Vir 14 Jf 44.18N 15.03 E
Virac 26 Hd 13.35N 124.15 E
Viramgām 25 Ed 23.07N 72.02 E
Virandozero 7 Id 64.01N 36.03 E
Viranşehir 24 Hd 37.13N 39.45 E
Virbalis 8 Jj 54.37N 22.49 E
Vircava 8 Jh 56.35N 23.43 E
Virden 42 Hg 49.51N 100.55W
Virdois/Virrat 7 Fe 62.14N 23.47 E
Vire 11 Ff 48.50N 0.53W
Vire 11 Ee 49.20N 1.07W
Virei 36 Bf 15.43S 12.54 E
Vireux-Wallerand 12 Gd 50.05N 4.44 E
Virgenes, Cabo- 52 Jk 52.19S 68.21W
Virgin Gorda 50 Dc 18.30N 64.25W
Virginia [2] 43 Ld 37.30N 78.45W
Virginia [Mn.-U.S.] 43 Ib 47.31N 92.32W
Virginia [S.Afr.] 37 De 28.12S 26.49 E
Virginia Beach 43 Ld 36.51N 75.59W
Virginia City 46 Fg 39.19N 119.39W
Virgin Islands 38 Mg 18.20N 66.45W
Virgin Islands of the United States [5] 39 Mh 18.20N 64.52W
Virgin Mountains 46 Ih 36.40N 113.50W
Virgin Passage 51a Cb 18.20N 65.10W
Virgin River 46 Hh 36.35N 114.18W
Virihaure 7 Dc 67.22N 16.33 E
Virkby/Virkkala 8 Kd 60.13N 24.01 E
Virkkala/Virkby 8 Kd 60.13N 24.01 E
Virmasvesi 8 Lb 62.50N 26.55 E
Virôchey 25 Lf 13.59N 106.49 E
Viroin 11 Kd 50.05N 4.43 E
Viroinval 12 Gd 50.05N 4.33 E
Viroinval-Nismes 12 Gd 50.05N 4.33 E
Virojoki 7 Gf 60.35N 27.42 E
Viroqua 45 Ke 43.34N 90.53W
Virovitica 14 Le 45.50N 17.23 E
Virpazar 15 Cg 42.15N 19.06 E
Virrat/Virdois 7 Fe 62.14N 23.47 E
Virserum 7 Dh 57.19N 15.35 E
Virsko More 14 If 44.20N 15.00 E
Virton 11 Le 49.34N 5.32 E
Virton-Ethe 12 He 49.35N 5.35 E
Virtsu 7 Fg 58.37N 23.31 E
Virudanagar 25 Fg 9.36N 77.58 E
Virvičja/Virvyčia 8 Jh 56.14N 22.30 E
Virvyčia/Virvičja 8 Jh 56.14N 22.30 E
Vis 14 Kg 43.02N 16.10 E
Vis 14 Kg 43.03N 16.12 E
Visalia 43 Dd 36.20N 119.18W
Visayan Sea 26 Hd 11.35N 123.51 E
Visby 7 Eh 57.38N 18.18 E
Viscount Melville Sound 38 Hb 74.10N 113.00W
Visé/Wezet 12 Hd 50.44N 5.42 E
Višegrad 15 Jh 41.59N 26.20 E
Višegrad 14 Ng 43.48N 19.17 E
Višera [R.S.F.S.R.] 19 Fc 61.57N 52.25 E
Višera [R.S.F.S.R.] 5 Ld 59.55N 56.50 E
Viseu [2] 13 Ed 40.45N 7.50W
Viseu [Braz.] 54 Id 1.12S 46.07W
Viseu [Port.] 13 Ed 40.39N 7.55W
Vişeu de Sus 15 Hb 47.43N 24.26 E
Vishākhapatnam 22 Kh 17.42N 83.18 E
Visingsö 8 Ff 58.03N 14.20 E
Viskafors 8 Eg 57.38N 12.50 E
Viskan 7 Cg 57.14N 12.12 E
Viški Kanal 14 Kg 43.07N 16.17 E
Vislanda 7 Dh 56.47N 14.27 E
Vislinski Zaliv 10 Pb 54.27N 19.40 E
Visnes 8 Ae 59.21N 5.14 E
Višnevka 15 Lc 46.22N 28.27 E
Visoki Dečani 15 Dg 42.33N 20.16 E
Visoko 14 Mg 43.59N 18.11 E
Visokoi 66 Ad 56.42S 27.12W
Visonggo 63d Bb 16.13S 179.40 E
Visp 14 Bd 46.17N 7.53 E
Vissefjärda 8 Fh 56.32N 15.35 E
Vista 46 Gj 33.12N 117.15W
Visten 8 Ee 59.40N 13.20 E
Vistonías, Órmos- 15 Ii 40.58N 25.05 E
Vistonís, Limni- 15 Ih 41.03N 25.07 E
Vistula (EN) = Wisła 5 He 54.22N 18.55 E
Vištytis 8 Jj 54.27N 22.44 E
Visuvisu Point 63a Cb 7.57S 157.31 E
Vit 15 Hf 43.41N 24.45 E
Vitebsk 6 Jd 55.12N 30.11 E
Vitebskaja Oblast [3] 19 Cd 55.20N 29.00 E
Viterbo 14 Gh 42.25N 12.06 E
Vithkuqi 15 Di 40.31N 20.35 E
Vitichi 54 Eh 20.13S 65.29W
Vitigudino 13 Fc 41.01N 6.26W
Viti Levu 57 If 18.00S 178.00 E
Vitim 20 Ge 59.33N 112.28 E
Vitim 21 Nd 59.26N 112.34 E
Vitimski 20 Ge 58.18N 113.18 E
Vitimskoje Ploskogorje 20 Gf 54.00N 114.00 E
Vitinja 15 Gg 42.47N 23.45 E
Vitjaz Strait 60 Di 5.35S 147.00 E
Vitolište 15 Eh 41.11N 21.50 E
Vitoria 13 Jb 42.51N 2.40W
Vitória 53 Lh 20.19S 40.21W
Vitória da Conquista 53 Lg 14.51S 40.51W
Vitória de Santo Antão 54 Ke 8.07S 35.18W
Vitorog 14 Lf 44.08N 17.03 E
Vitosa 15 Gg 42.33N 23.15 E
Vitré 11 Ef 48.08N 1.12W
Vitry-en-Artois 12 Ed 50.20N 2.59 E
Vitry-le-François 11 Kf 48.44N 4.35 E
Vitsi 15 Ei 40.39N 21.23 E

Index Symbols

[1] Independent Nation
[2] State, Region
[3] District, County
[4] Municipality
[5] Colony, Dependency
Continent
Physical Region
Historical or Cultural Region
Mount, Mountain
Volcano
Hill
Mountains, Mountain Range
Hills, Escarpment
Plateau, Upland
Pass, Gap
Plain, Lowland
Delta
Salt Flat
Valley, Canyon
Crater, Cave
Karst Features
Depression
Polder
Desert, Dunes
Forest, Woods
Heath, Steppe
Oasis
Cape, Point
Coast, Beach
Cliff
Peninsula
Isthmus
Sandbank
Island
Atoll
Rock, Reef
Islands, Archipelago
Rocks, Reefs
Coral Reef
Well, Spring
Geyser
River, Stream
Waterfall Rapids
River Mouth, Estuary
Lake
Salt Lake
Intermittent Lake
Reservoir
Swamp, Pond
Canal
Glacier
Ice Shelf, Pack Ice
Ocean
Sea
Gulf, Bay
Strait, Fjord
Lagoon
Bank
Seamount
Tablemount
Ridge
Shelf
Basin
Escarpment, Sea Scarp
Fracture
Trench, Abyss
National Park, Reserve
Point of Interest
Recreation Site
Cave, Cavern
Historic Site
Ruins
Wall, Walls
Church, Abbey
Temple
Scientific Station
Airport
Port
Lighthouse
Mine
Tunnel
Dam, Bridge

Vittangi	7	Ec	67.41N	21.39 E
Vitteaux	11	Kg	47.24N	4.32 E
Vittel	11	Lf	48.12N	5.57 E
Vittinge	8	Ge	59.54N	17.04 E
Vittoria	14	In	36.57N	14.32 E
Vittorio Veneto	14	Ge	45.59N	12.18 E
Vityaz Depth (EN)	3	Je	44.00N	151.00 E
Vityaz I Depth (EN)	3	Ih	11.20N	141.30 E
Vityaz II Depth (EN)	3	Kl	23.27S	175.00W
Vityaz III Depth (EN)	3	Km	32.00S	178.00W
Vityaz Seamount (EN)	57	Jc	13.30N	173.15W
Vityaz Trench (EN)	3	Jj	10.00S	170.00 E
Vivarais, Monts du-	11	Ki	44.55N	4.15 E
Vivarais, Plateaux du-	11	Kj	44.50N	4.45 E
Viver	13	Le	39.55N	0.36W
Vivero	13	Ea	43.40N	7.35W
Viverone, Lago di-	14	Ce	45.25N	8.05 E
Vivi	20	Ed	63.52N	97.50 E
Vivian	45	Jj	32.53N	93.59W
Viviers	11	Kj	44.29N	4.41 E
Vivo	37	Dd	23.03S	29.17 E
Vivoratá	55	Dm	37.40S	57.39W
Vivorillo, Cayos-	49	Ff	15.50N	83.18W
Viwa	63d	Ab	17.08S	176.56 E
Vizcaino, Desierto de-	47	Bc	27.40N	114.40W
Vizcaíno, Sierra-	48	Bd	27.20N	114.00W
Vizcaya [3]	13	Ja	43.15N	2.55W
Vizcaya, Golfo de-	5	Fg	44.00N	4.00W
Vize	15	Kh	41.34N	27.45 E
Vize, Ostrov	21	Jb	79.30N	77.00 E
Vizianagaram	25	Ge	18.07N	83.25 E
Vizille	11	Li	45.05N	5.46 E
Vizinga	19	Fc	61.05N	50.10 E
Viziru	15	Kd	45.00N	27.42 E
Vižnica	16	De	48.14N	25.12 E
Vizzini	14	Im	37.10N	14.45 E
Vjaike-Maarja/Väike-Maarja	8	Le	59.04N	26.12 E
Vjajke-Pakri/Väike-Pakri	8	Je	59.50N	23.50 E
Vjajke-Vjajn/Väik Vain	8	Jf	58.30N	23.10 E
Vjalje, Ozero-	8	Ne	59.00N	30.20 E
Vjalozero, Ozero-	7	Ic	66.50N	35.10 E
Vjandra/Vändra	7	Fg	58.40N	25.01 E
Vjartsilja	7	He	62.10N	30.48 E
Vjatka	5	Ld	55.36N	51.30 E
Vjatskije Poljany	19	Fd	56.14N	51.04 E
Vjatski Uval	7	Lg	58.00N	49.45 E
Vjazemski	20	Ig	47.31N	134.45 E
Vjazma	6	Jd	55.13N	34.18 E
Vjazniki	7	Kh	56.15N	42.12 E
Vjeio, Rio-	49	Dg	12.17N	86.54W
Vjosa	15	Ci	40.37N	19.20 E
Vlaamse Banken	12	Ec	51.15N	2.30 E
Vlaanderen/Flandres= Flanders (EN)	5	Ge	51.00N	3.20 E
Vlaanderen/Flandres= Flanders (EN)	11	Jc	51.00N	3.20 E
Vlaardingen	11	Kc	51.54N	4.21 E
Vlădeasa, Vîrful-	15	Fc	46.45N	22.48 E
Vlădeni	15	Kb	47.25N	27.20 E
Vladičin Han	15	Fg	42.43N	22.04 E
Vladimir	6	Kd	56.10N	40.25 E
Vladimirskaja Oblast [3]	19	Ed	56.00N	40.40 E
Vladimirski Tupik	16	Hb	55.42N	33.18 E
Vladimir-Volynski	19	Ce	50.51N	24.22 E
Vladivostok	22	Pe	43.10N	131.56 E
Vlad Ţepeş	15	Ke	44.21N	27.05 E
Vlagtwedde	12	Ja	53.02N	7.08 E
Vlagtwedde-Ter Apel	12	Jb	52.52N	7.06 E
Vlahina	15	Fi	41.54N	22.52 E
Vlăhiţa	15	Ic	46.21N	25.31 E
Vlamse Vlakte=Flanders Plain (EN)	11	Id	50.40N	2.50 E
Vlasenica	14	Mf	44.11N	18.57 E
Vlašic [Yugo.]	14	Lf	44.19N	17.40 E
Vlašim	10	Kg	49.42N	14.54 E
Vlasotince	15	Fg	42.58N	22.08 E
Vlasovo	20	Ib	70.40N	134.35 E
Vlieland	11	Ka	53.15N	5.00 E
Vlieland	12	Ha	53.17N	5.06 E
Vlieland-Oost Vlieland	12	Ha	53.17N	5.06 E
Vliestroom	12	Ha	53.17N	5.10 E
Vlissingen	11	Jc	51.26N	3.35 E
Vlissingen-Oost-Souburg	12	Fc	51.28N	3.36 E
Vloesberg/Flobecq	12	Fd	50.44N	3.44 E
Vlora	6	Hg	40.27N	19.30 E
Vlorës, Gjiri i-	15	Ci	40.25N	19.25 E
Vlotho	12	Kb	52.10N	8.51 E
Vltava=Moldau (EN)	5	He	50.21N	14.30 E
Vöcklabruck	14	Hb	48.01N	13.39 E
Vodice	14	Jg	43.46N	15.47 E
Vodla	7	If	61.49N	36.00 E
Vodlozero, Ozero-	7	Ie	62.20N	37.00 E
Vodňany	10	Kg	49.09N	14.11 E
Vodnjan	14	Hf	44.57N	13.51 E
Vodny	17	Fe	63.32N	53.20 E
Voerde (Niederrhein)	10	Ce	51.35N	6.41 E
Voeren/Fouron	12	Hd	50.45N	5.48 E
Vogel Peak	34	Hd	8.24N	11.47 E
Vogelsberg	10	Ff	50.30N	9.15 E
Voghera	14	Df	44.59N	9.01 E
Vogtland	10	If	50.30N	12.05 E
Voh	63b	Be	20.58S	164.42 E
Võhandu Jõgi/Vyhandu	8	Lf	58.03N	27.40 E
Vohémar	37	Ib	13.22S	50.00 E
Vohipeno	37	Hd	22.20S	47.52 E
Vöhl	12	Kc	51.12N	8.56 E
Vohma	7	Lg	58.45N	46.36 E
Vohma	19	Ed	58.58N	46.45 E
Voi	31	Ki	3.23S	38.34 E
Voikoski	8	Lc	61.16N	26.48 E
Voinjama	31	Gh	8.25N	9.45W
Vóïon Óros	15	Ei	40.15N	21.03 E
Voire	11	Kf	48.27N	4.25 E
Voiron	11	Li	45.22N	5.35 E
Voitsberg	14	Jc	47.02N	15.09 E
Voïviïs, Limni-	15	Fj	39.32N	22.45 E
Vojens	8	Ci	55.15N	9.19 E
Vojkar	17	Ld	65.38N	64.40 E
Vojmsjön	7	Dd	65.00N	16.24 E
Vojnić	14	Je	45.19N	15.42 E
Vojnilov	10	Ug	49.04N	24.33 E
Vojvodina [3]	15	Cd	45.00N	20.00 E
Voj-Vož	19	Fc	62.56N	54.59 E
Voknavolok	7	Hd	64.57N	30.31 E
Vokré, Hoséré-	30	Ih	8.21N	13.15 E
Volary	10	Jh	48.55N	13.54 E
Volcán	49	Fi	8.46N	82.38W
Volcanica, Cordillera-	38	Ih	18.00N	101.00W
Volcano	65a	Fd	19.26N	155.20W
Volcano Islands (EN)=Iō/Kazan-Rettō	21	Qg	25.00N	141.00 E
Volcano Islands (EN)= Kazan-Rettō/Iō	21	Qg	25.00N	141.00 E
Volcán Rana Roi	65d	Ab	27.05S	109.23W
Volčansk [R.S.F.S.R.]	17	Jg	59.59N	60.04 E
Volčansk [Ukr.-U.S.S.R.]	16	Jd	50.16N	37.01 E
Volčiha	20	Df	52.02N	80.23 E
Volda	7	Be	62.09N	6.06 E
Voldafjorden	8	Ab	62.10N	6.00 E
Volga	5	Kf	45.55N	47.52 E
Volga	7	Jh	57.57N	38.25 E
Volga-Baltic Canal (EN)= Volgo-Baltijski vodny put imeni V. I. Lenina	5	Jd	59.58N	37.10 E
Volga Delta (EN)	5	Kf	46.30N	47.00 E
Volga Hills (EN)= Privolžkaja Vozvyšennost	5	Ke	52.00N	46.00 E
Volgo-Baltijski vodny put imeni V.I. Lenina=Volga-Baltic Canal (EN)	5	Jd	59.58N	37.10 E
Volgodonsk	19	Ef	47.33N	42.08 E
Volgo-Donskoj sudohodny kanal imeni V. I. Lenina= Lenin Canal (EN)	5	Kf	48.40N	43.37 E
Volgograd (Stalingrad)	6	Kf	48.44N	44.25 E
Volgograd Reservoir (EN)= Volgogradskoje Vodohranilišče	5	Kf	49.20N	45.00 E
Volgogradskaja Oblast [3]	19	Ef	49.30N	44.30 E
Volgogradskoje Vodohranilišče=Volgograd Reservoir (EN)	5	Kf	49.20N	45.00 E
Volhov	5	Jc	60.08N	32.20 E
Volhov	6	Jd	59.55N	32.20 E
Volhynia	5	Ie	51.00N	25.00 E
Volissós	15	Ik	38.29N	25.55 E
Volja	17	Je	63.11N	61.16 E
Volka	10	Vd	52.43N	25.43 E
Völkermarkt	14	Id	46.39N	14.38 E
Völklingen	10	Cg	49.15N	6.51 E
Volkmarsen	12	Lc	51.24N	9.07 E
Volkovysk	16	Dc	53.10N	24.31 E
Volkovysskaja Vozvyšennost	10	Kc	53.10N	24.30 E
Volksrust	37	De	27.24S	29.53 E
Vollenhove	12	Hb	52.40N	5.57 E
Vollsjö	8	Ei	55.42N	13.46 E
Volme	12	Jc	51.24N	7.27 E
Volmunster	12	Je	49.07N	7.21 E
Volna, Gora-	20	Kd	63.30N	154.57 E
Volnjansk	16	If	47.54N	35.29 E
Volnovaha	16	Jf	47.37N	37.36 E
Voločajevka 2-ja	20	Ig	48.36N	134.36 E
Voločisk	16	Ee	49.31N	26.13 E
Volodarsk	7	Kh	56.14N	43.13 E
Volodarski	16	Pf	46.26N	48.31 E
Volodarskoje	19	Ge	53.18N	68.08 E
Vologda	6	Jd	59.12N	39.55 E
Vologodskaja Oblast [3]	19	Ed	60.00N	41.00 E
Volokolamsk	7	Ih	56.03N	35.58 E
Volokonovka	16	Jd	50.29N	37.52 E
Vólos	6	Ih	39.22N	22.57 E
Vološka	7	Jf	61.42N	39.15 E
Vološka	7	Jf	61.21N	40.03 E
Volosovo	7	Gg	59.28N	29.31 E
Volovec	10	Jh	48.42N	23.17 E
Volovo	16	Kc	53.35N	38.01 E
Voložin	16	Eb	54.06N	26.32 E
Volquart Boons Kyst	41	Jd	70.20N	24.20W
Volsini, Monti-	14	Fh	42.40N	11.55 E
Volsk	19	Ee	52.02N	47.23 E
Volta	30	Hh	5.46N	0.41 E
Volta [3]	34	Fd	7.00N	0.30 E
Volta Blanche=White Volta (EN)	30	Gh	8.38N	0.59W
Volta Lake	30	Hh	7.30N	0.15 E
Volta Noire=Black Volta (EN)	30	Gh	8.38N	1.30W
Volta Noire=Black Volta (EN) [3]	34	Ec	12.30N	4.00W
Volta Redonda	53	Lh	22.32S	44.07W
Volta Rouge=Red Volta (EN)	30	Gh	10.34N	0.30W
Volterra	14	Eg	43.24N	10.51 E
Voltoya	13	Hc	41.13N	4.31W
Voltri, Genova-	14	Cf	44.26N	8.45 E
Volturino	14	Jj	40.25N	15.48 E
Volturno	14	Hi	41.01N	13.55 E
Volubilis	32	Fc	34.04N	5.33W
Vólvi, Limni-	15	Gi	40.41N	23.28 E
Volynskaja Grjada	10	Ue	51.05N	25.00 E
Volynskaja Oblast [3]	19	Ce	51.10N	25.00 E
Volynskaja Vozvyšennost	16	Dd	50.30N	25.00 E
Volžsk	19	Ed	55.55N	48.19 E
Volžski [R.S.F.S.R.]	6	Kf	48.48N	44.44 E
Volžski [R.S.F.S.R.]	7	Mj	53.28N	50.08 E
Voma	63d	Bc	18.00S	178.08 E
Vomano	14	Ih	42.39N	14.02 E
Vonavona	63a	Cc	8.12S	157.05 E
Vondrozo	37	Hd	22.47S	47.17 E
Von Frank Mountain	40	Id	63.33N	154.20W
Vónitsa	15	Dk	38.55N	20.53 E
Vonne	11	Gh	46.25N	0.15 E
Võnnu/Vynnu	8	Lf	58.15N	27.10 E
Voorne	12	Gc	51.52N	4.05 E
Voorschoten	12	Gb	52.08N	4.28 E
Voorst	12	Ib	52.10N	6.09 E
Voorst-Twello	12	Ib	52.14N	6.07 E
Vop	16	Hb	54.56N	32.44 E
Vopnafjördur	7a	Cb	65.45N	14.50W
Vora	15	Ch	41.23N	19.40 E
Vörå/Vöyri	8	Ja	63.09N	22.15 E
Vorarlberg [2]	14	Dc	47.15N	9.50 E
Vóras Óros	15	Ei	41.00N	21.50 E
Vorau	14	Jc	47.24N	15.53 E
Vorden	12	Ib	52.06N	6.20 E
Vorderrhein	14	Dd	46.49N	9.26 E
Vordingborg	7	Ci	55.01N	11.55 E
Voreifel	12	Jd	50.10N	7.00 E
Vorga Šor	17	Kc	67.35N	63.40 E
Voria Pindhos	15	Dj	40.20N	20.55 E
Vórioi Sporádhes, Nisoi-= Northern Sporades (EN)	5	Ih	39.15N	23.55 E
Vórios Evvoïkós Kólpos= Évvoia, Gulf of- (EN)	15	Gk	38.45N	23.10 E
Vorkuta	6	Mb	67.27N	63.58 E
Vorma	7	Cf	60.09N	11.27 E
Vormsi	8	Je	59.02N	23.05 E
Vormsi	7	Fg	59.00N	23.15 E
Vorniceni	15	Jb	47.59N	26.40 E
Vorogovo	20	Dd	60.58N	89.28 E
Vorona	16	Md	51.22N	42.03 E
Voroncovo [R.S.F.S.R.]	20	Db	71.40N	83.40 E
Voroncovo [R.S.F.S.R.]	8	Mg	57.15N	28.49 E
Voronež	6	Je	51.40N	39.10 E
Voronež	16	Kd	51.31N	39.05 E
Voronežskaja Oblast [3]	19	Ee	51.00N	40.15 E
Voronin Trough (EN)	67	Ge	80.00N	85.00 E
Voronja	7	Ib	69.09N	35.47 E
Voronovo	8	Kj	54.09N	25.19 E
Voropajevo	8	Li	55.07N	27.19 E
Vorošilovgrad → Lugansk	6	Jf	48.34N	39.20 E
Vorošilovgradskaja Oblast [3]	19	Df	49.00N	39.10 E
Vorotan	16	Oj	39.15N	46.43 E
Vorotynec	7	Kh	56.02N	45.52 E
Vorožba	16	Id	51.10N	34.11 E
Vorskla	16	Ie	48.52N	34.05 E
Vorsma	7	Ki	55.58N	43.17 E
Vörts Järv/Vyrtsjarv, Ozero-	7	Gg	58.15N	26.05 E
Võru/Vyru	19	Cd	57.52N	27.05 E
Voruh	18	He	39.52N	70.35 E
Vosges	5	Gf	48.30N	7.10 E
Vosges [3]	11	Mf	48.10N	6.20 E
Voskresensk	7	Ji	55.22N	38.42 E
Voskresenskoje	7	Kh	56.51N	45.27 E
Voss	8	Bd	60.40N	6.30 E
Vossa	8	Ad	60.39N	5.42 E
Vossevangen	7	Bd	60.39N	6.26 E
Vostočno-Kazahstanskaja Oblast [3]	19	If	49.00N	84.00 E
Vostočno-Kounradski	19	Hf	46.58N	75.07 E
Vostočno Sibirskoje More= East Siberian Sea (EN)	67	Cd	74.00N	166.00 E
Vostočny [R.S.F.S.R.]	20	Jg	48.19N	142.40 E
Vostočny [R.S.F.S.R.]	17	Jg	58.48N	61.52 E
Vostočny, Hrebet-	20	Lf	55.00N	160.30 E
Vostočny Sajan=Eastern Sayans (EN)	21	Ld	53.00N	97.00 E
Vostok	66	Hf	78.28S	106.48 E
Vostok Island	57	Lf	10.06S	152.23W
Vostrecovo	20	Ig	45.56N	134.59 E
Vošu/Vyzu	8	Ke	59.30N	25.50 E
Votkinsk	19	Fd	57.05N	53.59 E
Votkinskoje Vodohranilišče = Votkinsk Reservoir (EN)	5	Ld	57.30N	55.10 E
Votkinsk Reservoir (EN) = Votkinskoje Vodohranilišče	5	Ld	57.30N	55.10 E
Votuporanga	55	He	20.24S	49.59W
Vouga	13	Dd	40.41N	8.40W
Vouillé	11	Gh	46.38N	0.10 E
Voulgára	15	Ej	39.06N	21.54 E
Vouliagméni	15	Gl	37.49N	23.47 E
Voúrinos Óros	15	Ei	40.11N	21.40 E
Voúxa, Ákra-	15	Gn	35.38N	23.36 E
Vouziers	11	Ke	49.24N	4.42 E
Voves	11	Hf	48.16N	1.38 E
Vovodo	35	Cd	5.40N	24.21 E
Voxna	8	Fc	61.21N	15.34 E
Voxnan	8	Gc	61.17N	16.26 E
Voyeykov Ice Shelf	66	Ie	66.20S	124.38 E
Vöyri/Vörå	8	Ja	63.09N	22.15 E
Vože, Ozero-	7	Jf	60.35N	39.05 E
Vožega	7	Jf	60.33N	39.13 E
Vožega	7	Jf	60.30N	40.12 E
Voznesenje	7	If	61.01N	35.27 E
Voznesensk	19	Df	47.35N	31.20 E
Vozroždenija, Ostrov-	18	Bb	45.05N	59.15 E
Vraca [2]	15	Gf	43.12N	23.33 E
Vraca	15	Dh	41.54N	20.45 E
Vraca	15	Gf	43.12N	23.33 E
Vradijevka	16	Gf	47.51N	30.34 E
Vrakhiónas	15	Dl	37.48N	20.45 E
Vran	14	Lg	43.39N	17.27 E
Vrancea [2]	15	Jd	45.50N	26.42 E
Vranica	14	Lg	43.57N	17.44 E
Vranje	15	Eg	42.33N	21.54 E
Vranov nad Topl'ou	10	Rh	48.54N	21.41 E
Vrăška čuka, Prohod-	15	Ff	43.50N	22.23 E
Vratnica	15	Eg	42.08N	21.07 E
Vratnik, prohod-	15	Jg	42.49N	26.10 E
Vrbas	14	Le	45.07N	17.31 E
Vrbas	15	Cd	45.34N	19.39 E
Vrbno pod Pradědem	10	Nf	50.08N	17.23 E
Vrbovsko	14	Je	45.22N	15.05 E
Vrchlabí	10	Lf	50.38N	15.37 E
Vrede	37	De	27.30S	29.06 E
Vreden	12	Ib	52.02N	6.50 E
Vredenburg	37	Bf	32.54S	17.59 E
Vredendal	37	Bf	31.41S	18.35 E
Vresse, Vresse-sur-Semois-	12	Ge	49.52N	4.56 E
Vresse-sur-Semois	12	Ge	49.52N	4.56 E
Vresse-sur-Semois-Vresse	12	Ge	49.52N	4.56 E
Vretstorp	8	Fe	59.02N	14.52 E
Vrhnika	14	Ie	45.58N	14.18 E
Vries	12	Ia	53.05N	6.36 E
Vriezenveen	12	Ib	52.26N	6.36 E
Vrigstad	8	Fg	57.21N	14.28 E
Vron	12	Dd	50.19N	1.45 E
Vršac	15	Ed	45.07N	21.18 E
Vryburg	31	Jk	26.55S	24.45 E
Vryheid	37	Ee	27.52S	30.38 E
Vsetin	10	Ng	49.21N	18.00 E
Vsevidof, Mount-	40a	Eb	53.07N	168.43W
Vsevoložsk	7	Hf	60.04N	30.41 E
Vstrečny	20	Lc	68.00N	165.58 E
Vtačnik	10	Oh	48.42N	18.37 E
Vuanggava	63d	Cc	18.52S	178.54W
Vučitrn	15	Dg	42.49N	20.58 E
Vučjak	15	Fh	41.28N	22.20 E
Vuka	14	Me	45.21N	19.00 E
Vukovar	14	Me	45.21N	19.00 E
Vuktyl	19	Fc	63.50N	57.25 E
Vulavu	63a	Dc	8.31S	159.48 E
Vulcan	15	Gd	45.23N	23.16 E
Vulcan, Vîrful-	15	Fc	46.14N	22.58 E
Vulcano	14	Il	38.25N	15.00 E
Vulkanešty	16	Fg	45.38N	28.27 E
Vulture	14	Jj	40.57N	15.38 E
Vung Tau	25	Lf	10.21N	107.04 E
Vunindawa	63d	Bb	17.49S	178.19 E
Vunisea Station	61	Ec	19.03S	178.09 E
Vuohijarvi	8	Lc	61.10N	26.40 E
Vuoksa	8	Nd	60.35N	30.42 E
Vuoksa, Ozero- [R.S.F.S.R.]	8	Mc	61.00N	30.00 E
Vuoksa, Ozero- [R.S.F.S.R.]	8	Md	60.38N	29.55 E
Vuollerim	7	Ec	66.25N	20.36 E
Vuosjärvi	8	Ka	63.00N	25.30 E
Vuotso	7	Gb	68.06N	27.08 E
Vuranimala	63a	Ec	9.05S	160.51 E
Vyborg	6	Ic	60.42N	28.45 E
Vyčegda	5	Kc	61.18N	46.36 E
Vyčegodski	7	Lf	61.17N	46.48 E
Vychodočeský kraj [3]	10	Lf	50.10N	16.00 E
Východoslovenská nížina	10	Rh	48.35N	21.50 E
Východoslovenský kraj [3]	10	Rg	49.00N	21.15 E
Vyg	7	Ie	63.17N	35.17 E
Vygoda [Ukr.-U.S.S.R.]	15	Nc	46.38N	30.24 E
Vygoda [Ukr.-U.S.S.R.]	10	Uh	48.52N	24.01 E
Vygozero, Ozero-	5	Jc	63.35N	34.45 E
Vyhandu/Võhandu Jõgi	8	Lf	58.03N	27.40 E
Vyja	7	Le	62.57N	46.42 E
Vyksa	19	Ed	55.20N	42.12 E
Vym	19	Fc	62.13N	50.25 E
Vynnu/Võnnu	8	Lf	58.15N	27.10 E
Vyrica	19	Dd	59.24N	30.19 E
Vyrnwy	9	Ki	52.45N	2.50W
Vyrtsjarv, Ozero-/Vörts Järv	7	Gg	58.15N	26.05 E
Vyru/Võru	19	Cd	57.52N	27.05 E
Vyša	16	Mb	54.03N	42.06 E
Vyšgorod	16	Gd	50.38N	30.29 E
Vyšgorodok	8	Mh	56.55N	28.05 E
Vyškov	10	Mg	49.17N	17.00 E
Vyškovsk, pereval	10	Th	48.38N	23.45 E
Vyšni Voloček	19	Dd	57.37N	34.32 E
Vysock	7	Gf	60.36N	28.36 E
Vysoké Tatry=High Tatra (EN)	10	Pg	49.10N	20.00 E
Vysokogorny	20	If	50.07N	139.10 E
Vysokogorsk	28	Mb	44.23N	135.23 E
Vysokoje	10	Td	52.22N	23.26 E
Vysokovsk	7	Ih	56.21N	36.29 E
Vyšši Brod	10	Kh	48.37N	14.18 E
Vytebet	16	Ic	53.53N	35.38 E
Vytegra	19	Dc	61.01N	36.28 E
Vyvenka	20	Ld	60.10N	165.20 E
Vyzu/Võsu	8	Ke	59.30N	25.50 E
Vzmorje	20	Jg	47.45N	142.30 E
W				
Wa	34	Ec	10.03N	2.29W
Waal	11	Kc	51.55N	4.30 E
Waalre	12	Hc	51.23N	5.27 E
Waalwijk	12	Hc	51.41N	5.04 E
Waar, Meos-	26	Jg	2.05S	134.23 E
Waardgronden	12	Ha	53.12N	5.05 E
Waarschoot	12	Fc	51.09N	3.36 E
Wabana	42	Mg	47.38N	52.57W
Wabao, Cap-	63b	Ce	21.36S	167.51 E
Wabasca	42	Ge	56.00N	113.53W
Wabasca	42	Fe	58.21N	115.20W
Wabash	38	Kf	37.46N	88.02W
Wabash	44	Ee	40.48N	85.49W
Wabasha	45	Jd	44.23N	92.02W
Wabash River	45	Lh	37.46N	88.02W
Wabowden	42	Hf	54.55N	98.38W
Wąbrzeźno	10	Oc	53.17N	18.57 E
Wabu Hu	27	Ke	32.20N	116.55 E
Wachau	14	Jb	48.20N	15.25 E
Wachile	35	Fe	4.33N	39.03 E
Wachusett Seamount (EN)	57	Lh	32.00S	151.20W
Waco	39	Jf	31.55N	97.08W
Waconda Lake	45	Gg	39.30N	98.30W
Wadayama	29	Dd	35.20N	134.51 E
Wad Bandah	35	Dc	13.06N	27.57 E
Waddān	33	Cd	29.10N	16.08 E
Waddān, Jabal-	33	Cd	29.20N	16.20 E
Waddeneilanden=West Frisian Islands (EN)	11	Ka	53.30N	5.00 E
Waddenzee	12	Ha	53.20N	5.30 E
Waddington, Mount-	38	Gd	51.23N	125.15W
Wadena	45	Ic	46.26N	95.08W
Wadern	12	Ie	49.32N	6.53 E
Wadern-Nunkirchen	12	Ie	49.32N	6.53 E
Wadersloh	12	Kc	51.44N	8.15 E
Wadersloh-Liesborn	12	Kc	51.43N	8.16 E
Wadesboro	44	Gh	34.58N	80.04W
Wadhams	46	Ba	51.30N	127.31W
Wādī Bīshah	23	Fe	21.24N	43.26 E
Wādī Fajr	23	Ec	30.17N	38.18 E
Wādī Ḥalfā'	31	Kf	21.56N	31.20 E
Wādī Jimāl, Jazīrat-	24	Fj	24.40N	35.10 E
Wādī Mūsá	24	Fg	30.19N	35.29 E
Wādī Shiḥan	35	Ib	18.10N	52.57 E
Wad Madanī	31	Kg	14.24N	33.32 E
Wad Nimr	35	Ec	14.32N	32.08 E
Wadowice	10	Pg	49.53N	19.30 E
Wadsworth	46	Fg	39.38N	119.17W
Wafangdian → Fuxian	27	Ld	39.38N	121.59 E
Wafrah	23	Gd	28.25N	47.56 E
Waga-Gawa	29	Gb	39.18N	141.07 E
Wagenfeld	12	Kb	52.33N	8.35 E
Wagenfeld-Ströhen	12	Kb	52.32N	8.39 E
Wageningen	12	Hc	51.57N	5.41 E
Wagēr, Qar-	35	Hc	10.01N	45.30 E
Wager Bay	38	Kc	65.26N	88.40W
Wagga Wagga	58	Fh	35.07S	147.22 E
Waghäusel	12	Ke	49.15N	8.30 E
Wagin	58	Ch	33.18S	117.21 E
Waginger See	10	Ii	47.58N	12.50 E
Wagoner	45	Ii	35.58N	95.22W
Wagon Mound	45	Dh	36.01N	104.42W
Wagontire Mountain	46	Fe	43.21N	119.53W
Wagrien	10	Gb	54.15N	10.45 E
Wągrowiec	10	Nd	52.49N	17.11 E
Wah	25	Eb	33.48N	72.42 E
Waha	31	If	28.10N	19.57 E
Wahai	26	Ig	2.48S	129.30 E
Wahiawa	60	Oc	21.30N	158.02W
Wahoo	45	Hf	41.13N	96.37W
Wahpeton	43	Hb	46.16N	96.36W
Waialeale, Mount-	65a	Ba	22.04N	159.30W
Waialua	65a	Cb	21.35N	158.08W
Waianae	65a	Cb	21.27N	158.12W
Waiau	62	Ee	42.47S	173.22 E
Waiau	61	Dh	42.39S	173.03 E
Waiblingen	10	Fh	48.50N	9.18 E
Waibstadt	12	Ke	49.18N	8.56 E
Waidhofen an der Thaya	14	Jb	48.49N	15.17 E
Waidhofen an der Ybbs	14	Ic	47.58N	14.46 E
Waigame	26	Ig	1.50S	129.49 E
Waigeo, Pulau-	57	Ee	0.14S	130.45 E
Waihi	62	Fb	37.24S	175.50 E
Waihou	62	Fb	37.10S	175.33 E
Waikabubak	26	Gh	9.38S	119.25 E
Waikare, Lake-	62	Fb	37.25S	175.10 E
Waikaremoana, Lake-	61	Eg	38.45S	177.05 E
Waikato	62	Fb	37.23S	174.43 E
Waikawa	62	Cg	46.38S	169.08 E
Waikouaiti	62	Df	45.36S	170.41 E
Wailangilala	63d	Cb	16.45S	179.06W
Wailua	65a	Ba	22.03N	159.20W
Wailuku	60	Oc	20.53N	156.30W
Waimamaku	62	Ea	35.34S	173.29 E
Waimanalo Beach	65a	Db	21.20N	157.42W
Waimangaroa	62	Dd	41.43S	171.46 E
Waimate	62	Df	44.45S	171.03 E
Waimea	65a	Fc	20.02N	155.40W
Waimes	12	Id	50.25N	6.07 E
Wainfleet All Saints	12	Ca	53.06N	0.15 E
Wainganga	21	Jh	19.36N	79.48 E
Waingapu	26	Hh	9.39S	120.16 E
Waini Point	50	Gh	8.24N	59.49W
Waini River	50	Gh	8.24N	59.51W
Wainwright [Ak.-U.S.]	40	Gb	70.38N	160.01W
Wainwright [Alta.-Can.]	42	Gf	52.49N	110.52W
Waiouru	61	Eg	39.29S	175.40 E
Waipahu	65a	Cb	21.23N	158.01W
Waipara	62	Ee	43.03S	172.45 E
Waipawa	62	Gc	39.56S	176.35 E
Waipiro	62	Hc	38.02S	178.20 E
Waipu	62	Fa	35.59S	174.26 E
Waipukurau	62	Gd	40.00S	176.33 E
Wairakei	62	Gc	38.37S	176.05 E
Wairarapa, Lake-	62	Fd	41.15S	175.15 E
Wairau	62	Fd	41.31S	174.03 E
Wairoa	61	Eg	39.03S	177.26 E
Wairoa	62	Fb	36.11S	174.02 E
Waitaki	62	Df	44.56S	171.09 E
Waitangi	61	Fh	43.56S	176.34W
Waitara	61	Dg	39.00S	174.14 E
Waitati	62	Df	45.45S	170.34 E
Waitemata	62	Fb	36.50S	174.40 E
Waitotara	62	Fc	39.48S	174.44 E
Waiuku	62	Fb	37.15S	174.44 E
Waiwerang	26	Hh	8.23S	123.09 E
Waiyevo	61	Fc	16.48S	179.59W
Wājid	35	Ge	3.50N	43.14 E
Wajima	28	Nf	37.24N	136.54 E
Wajir	31	Lh	1.42N	40.04 E
Waka [Eth.]	35	Fd	7.09N	37.19 E
Waka [Zaire]	36	Db	1.01N	20.13 E
Wakamatsu-Shima	29	Ae	32.54N	129.00 E
Wakasa-Wan	27	Od	35.45N	135.40 E
Wakatipu, Lake-	61	Ci	45.05S	168.35 E
Wakaya	63d	Bb	17.37S	179.00 E
Wakayama	22	Pf	34.13N	135.11 E
Wakayama Ken [2]	28	Mh	33.55N	135.20 E
Wake	29	Dd	34.48N	134.08 E
Wa Keeney	45	Gg	39.01N	99.53W
Wakefield [Eng.-U.K.]	9	Lh	53.42N	1.29W
Wakefield [N.Z.]	62	Ed	41.24S	173.03 E

Index Symbols

[1] Independent Nation
[2] State, Region
[3] District, County
[4] Municipality
[5] Colony, Dependency
Continent
Physical Region
Historical or Cultural Region
Mount, Mountain
Volcano
Hill
Mountains, Mountain Range
Hills, Escarpment
Plateau, Upland
Pass, Gap
Plain, Lowland
Delta
Salt Flat
Valley, Canyon
Crater, Cave
Karst Features
Depression
Polder
Desert, Dunes
Forest, Woods
Heath, Steppe
Oasis
Cape, Point
Coast, Beach
Cliff
Peninsula
Isthmus
Sandbank
Island
Atoll
Rock, Reef
Islands, Archipelago
Rocks, Reefs
Coral Reef
Well, Spring
Geyser
River, Stream
Waterfall Rapids
River Mouth, Estuary
Lake
Salt Lake
Intermittent Lake
Reservoir
Swamp, Pond
Canal
Glacier
Ice Shelf, Pack Ice
Ocean
Sea
Gulf, Bay
Strait, Fjord
Lagoon
Bank
Seamount
Tablemount
Ridge
Shelf
Basin
Escarpment, Sea Scarp
Fracture
Trench, Abyss
National Park, Reserve
Point of Interest
Recreation Site
Cave, Cavern
Historic Site
Ruins
Wall, Walls
Church, Abbey
Temple
Scientific Station
Airport
Port
Lighthouse
Mine
Tunnel
Dam, Bridge

Wake Island [5] 58 Jd 19.18N 166.36W
Wake Island 57 Hc 19.18N 166.36 E
Wakkanai 22 Qe 45.25N 141.40 E
Wakunai 63a Ba 5.52S 155.13 E
Wakuya 29 Gb 38.33N 141.05 E
Wala 36 Fd 5.46S 32.04 E
Walachia (EN) = Valahia 5 Ig 44.00N 25.00 E
Walachia (EN) = Valahia 15 He 44.00N 25.00 E
Wałbrzych [2] 10 Mf 50.45N 16.15 E
Wałbrzych 6 He 50.46N 16.17 E
Walchensee 10 Hi 47.35N 11.20 E
Walcheren 11 Jc 51.33N 3.35 E
Walcott, Lake- 46 Ie 42.40N 113.23W
Walcourt 12 Gd 50.15N 4.25 E
Walcourt-Fraire 12 Gd 50.16N 4.30 E
Wałcz 10 Mc 53.17N 16.28 E
Waldböckelheim 12 Je 49.49N 7.43 E
Waldbröl 10 Df 50.53N 7.37 E
Waldeck [3] 12 Kc 51.17N 8.50 E
Waldeck 12 Lc 51.12N 9.05 E
Waldems 12 Kd 50.15N 8.18 E
Walden 45 Cf 40.44N 106.17W
Waldfischbach-Burgalben 12 Je 49.17N 7.40 E
Waldkirchen 10 Jh 48.44N 13.36 E
Waldkraiburg 10 Ih 48.12N 12.25 E
Wald-Michelbach 12 Ke 49.34N 8.49 E
Waldnaab 10 Ig 49.35N 12.07 E
Waldorf 44 If 38.37N 76.54W
Waldrach 12 Ie 49.45N 6.45 E
Waldron 45 Ii 34.54N 94.05W
Waldshut 10 Ei 47.37N 8.13 E
Waldviertel 14 Jb 48.30N 15.30 E
Waleabahi, Pulau- 26 Hg 0.15S 122.20 E
Wales 40 Fc 65.36N 168.05W
Wales 42 Ic 67.50N 86.40W
Wales 5 Fe 52.30N 3.30W
Wales [2] 9 Ji 52.30N 3.30W
Walewale 34 Ec 10.21N 0.48W
Walferdange 12 Ie 49.39N 6.08 E
Walgett 58 Fh 30.01S 148.07 E
Walgreen Coast 66 Of 75.15S 105.00W
Walhalla 45 Hb 48.55N 97.55W
Walikale 36 Ec 1.25S 28.03 E
Walker 45 Ic 47.06N 94.35W
Walker Lake 43 Dd 38.40N 118.43W
Walkerston 59 Jd 21.10S 149.10 E
Wall 45 Ed 44.01N 102.14W
Wallace 46 Hc 47.28N 115.56W
Wallaceburg 44 Fd 42.36N 82.23W
Wallangarra 59 Ke 28.56S 151.56 E
Wallaroo 59 Hf 33.56S 137.38 E
Wallary Island 59 Ic 15.05S 141.50 E
Wallasey 9 Jh 53.26N 3.03W
Walla Walla 43 Db 46.08N 118.20W
Walldorf 12 Ke 49.20N 8.39 E
Wallenhorst 12 Kb 52.21N 8.01 E
Wallibu 51n Ba 13.19N 61.15W
Wallingford 12 Ac 51.36N 1.08W
Wallis, Iles-=Wallis Islands (EN) 57 Jf 13.18S 176.10W
Wallis and Futuna (EN)= Wallis-et-Futuna, Iles- [5] 58 Jf 14.00S 177.00W
Walliser Alpen/Alpes Valaisannes 14 Bd 46.10N 7.30 E
Wallis-et-Futuna, Iles-= Wallis and Futuna (EN) [5] 58 Jf 14.00S 177.00W
Wallis Islands (EN)=Wallis, Iles- 57 Jf 13.18S 176.10W
Wallowa 46 Gd 45.34N 117.32W
Wallowa Mountains 46 Gd 45.10N 117.30W
Walmer 12 Dc 51.12N 1.24 E
Walney, Isle of- 9 Jg 54.07N 3.15W
Walnut Ridge 43 Id 36.04N 90.57W
Walpole, Ile- 57 Hg 22.37S 168.57 E
Walrus Islands 40 Ge 58.45N 160.20W
Walsall 9 Li 52.35N 1.58W
Walsenburg 43 Gd 37.37N 104.47W
Walsrode 10 Fd 52.52N 9.35 E
Walterboro 44 Gi 32.54N 80.39W
Walter F. George Lake 44 Ej 31.49N 85.08W
Walter Lake 43 Dd 38.44N 118.43W
Walters 45 Gi 34.22N 98.19W
Waltershausen 10 Gf 50.54N 10.34 E
Waltham 44 Ic 45.58N 76.57W
Walton-on-the-Naze 12 Dc 51.51N 1.17 E
Waltrop 12 Jc 51.38N 7.24 E
Walvisbaai/Walvis Bay [3] 37 Ad 23.00S 14.30 E
Walvisbaai=Walvis Bay (EN) 31 Ik 22.59S 14.31 E
Walvisbaai=Walvis Bay (EN) [5] 31 Ik 22.59S 14.31 E
Walvisbaai=Walvis Bay (EN) 30 Ik 22.57S 14.30 E
Walvis Bay/Walvisbaai [3] 37 Ad 23.00S 14.30 E
Walvis Bay (EN)= Walvisbaai 30 Ik 22.57S 14.30 E
Walvis Bay (EN)= Walvisbaai [5] 31 Ik 22.59S 14.31 E
Walvis Bay (EN)= Walvisbaai 31 Ik 22.59S 14.31 E
Walvis Ridge (EN) 3 El 28.00S 3.00 E
Wamba 30 Ii 3.56S 17.12 E
Wamba [Kenya] 36 Gb 0.59N 37.19 E
Wamba [Nig.] 34 Gd 8.56N 8.36 E
Wamba [Zaire] 36 Eb 2.09N 28.00 E
Wamena 26 Kg 4.00S 138.57 E
Wami 30 Ki 6.08S 38.49 E
Wampusirpi 49 Ef 15.15N 84.37W
Wamsutter 46 Lf 41.40N 107.58W
Wan 26 Kh 8.23S 137.56 E
Wana 25 Db 32.17N 69.35 E
Wanaka 58 Hi 44.42S 169.08 E
Wanaka, Lake- 62 Cf 44.30S 169.10 E
Wan'an 27 Jf 26.32N 114.48 E
Wanapiri 26 Kg 4.33S 135.59 E
Wanapitei Lake 44 Gb 46.45N 80.45W
Wandel Hav=Wandel Sea (EN) 41 Gb 83.00N 15.00W
Wandel Sea (EN)=Wandel Hav 41 Gb 83.00N 15.00W
Wandsworth, London- 12 Bc 51.27N 0.12W
Wanganui 62 Fc 39.58S 175.00 E
Wanganui 61 Eg 39.56S 175.02 E
Wangaratta 59 Jg 36.22S 146.20 E
Wangcun [China] 28 Df 36.41N 117.42 E
Wangcun [China] 27 Jd 39.58N 112.53 E
Wangda/Zogang 27 Gf 29.37N 97.58 E
Wangdu 28 Ce 38.43N 115.09 E
Wangen in Allgäu 10 Fi 47.41N 9.50 E
Wangerooge 10 Dc 53.46N 7.55 E
Wanggameti, Gunung- 26 Hi 10.07S 120.14 E
Wanggezhuang → Jiaonan 28 Eg 35.53N 119.58 E
Wangiwangi, Pulau- 26 Hh 5.20S 123.35 E
Wangjiang 28 Di 30.08N 116.41 E
Wangkui 27 Mb 46.50N 126.29 E
Wangpan Yang 21 Of 30.33N 121.26 E
Wangping 27 Mc 43.18N 129.46 E
Wangying → Huaiyin 28 Eh 33.35N 119.02 E
Wani, Laguna- 49 Ff 14.50N 83.25W
Wanie-Rukula 36 Eb 0.14N 25.34 E
Wanitsuka-Yama 29 Bf 31.45N 131.17 E
Wanlewëyn 35 Ge 2.35N 44.55 E
Wan Namton 25 Jd 22.03N 99.33 E
Wannian (Chenying) 28 Dj 28.42N 117.04 E
Wanning 27 Jh 18.59N 110.24 E
Wanquan 28 Cd 40.52N 114.44 E
Wansbeck 9 Lf 55.10N 1.34W
Wan Shui 28 Di 30.30N 117.01 E
Wanxian 22 Mf 30.48N 108.21 E
Wanyuan 27 Ie 32.03N 108.04 E
Wanzai 28 Cj 28.06N 114.27 E
Wanzhi → Wuhu 28 Ei 31.21N 118.23 E
Wapato 46 Ec 46.27N 120.25W
Wapiti 46 Kd 44.28N 109.28W
Wapiti 44 Fe 55.08N 118.19W
Wapsipinicon River 45 Kf 41.44N 90.20W
Waqooyi Galbeed [3] 35 Gc 10.00N 44.00 E
Warangal 22 Jh 18.18N 79.35 E
Waratah Bay 59 Jg 38.50S 146.05 E
Warburg 10 Fe 51.30N 9.10 E
Warburger Borde 12 Lc 51.35N 9.12 E
Warburg-Scherfede 12 Lc 51.32N 9.02 E
Warburton Bay 42 Gd 63.50N 111.30W
Warburton Mission 59 Fe 26.10S 126.35 E
Warburton Range 59 Fe 26.10S 126.40 E
Ward 62 Fd 41.50S 174.08 E
Warden 37 De 27.56S 29.00 E
Wardenburg 12 Ka 53.04N 8.12 E
Wardha 25 Fd 20.45N 78.37 E
Ward Hunt Strait 59 Ja 9.25S 149.55 E
Ware [B.C.-Can.] 42 Ee 57.27N 125.38W
Ware [Eng.-U.K.] 12 Bc 51.49N 0.01W
Waregem 12 Fd 50.53N 3.25 E
Waremme/Borgworm 11 Ld 50.42N 5.15 E
Waren [Ger.] 10 Ic 53.31N 12.41 E
Waren [Indon.] 58 Ee 2.16S 136.20 E
Warendorf 10 De 51.57N 7.59 E
Warin Chamrap 25 Ke 15.14N 104.52 E
Warka 10 Re 51.47N 21.10 E
Warkworth 62 Fb 36.24S 174.40 E
Warmbad [3] 37 Be 28.00S 18.30 E
Warmbad [Nam.] 37 Be 28.29S 18.41 E
Warmbad [S.Afr.] 37 Dd 24.53S 28.17 E
Warming Land 41 Gb 81.50N 52.45W
Warmington 12 Ab 52.08N 1.24W
Warminster 9 Kj 51.13N 2.12W
Warm Springs [Nv.-U.S.] 46 Gg 38.13N 116.20W
Warm Springs [Or.-U.S.] 46 Ed 44.46N 121.16W
Warnemünde, Rostock- 10 Ib 54.10N 12.05 E
Warner, Mount- 46 Da 51.03N 123.12W
Warner Mountains 43 Cc 41.40N 120.20W
Warner Peak 46 Fe 42.27N 119.44W
Warner Robins 43 Ke 32.37N 83.36W
Warner Valley 46 Fe 42.30N 119.55W
Warnes 54 Fg 17.30S 63.10W
Warnow 10 Ib 54.06N 12.09 E
Waroona 59 Df 32.50S 115.55 E
Warragul 59 Jg 38.10S 145.56 E
Warrego Range 59 Je 25.00S 145.45 E
Warrego River 57 Fh 30.24S 145.21 E
Warren [Ar.-U.S.] 45 Jj 33.38N 92.05W
Warren [Mi.-U.S.] 44 Fd 42.28N 83.01W
Warren [Mn.-U.S.] 45 Hb 48.12N 96.46W
Warren [Oh.-U.S.] 43 Kc 41.15N 80.49W
Warren [Pa.-U.S.] 44 He 41.52N 79.09W
Warrenpoint/An Pointe 9 Gg 54.06N 6.15W
Warrensburg 45 Jg 38.46N 93.44W
Warrenton 37 Ce 28.09S 24.47 E
Warri 34 Gd 5.31N 5.45 E
Warrington [Eng.-U.K.] 9 Kh 53.24N 2.37W
Warrington [Fl.-U.S.] 44 Dj 30.23N 87.16W
Warrior Reefs 59 Ia 9.35S 143.10 E
Warrnambool 58 Fh 38.23S 142.29 E
Warroad 45 Ib 48.54N 95.19W
Warrumbungle Range 59 Jf 31.30S 149.40 E
Warsaw [In.-U.S.] 44 Ee 41.14N 85.51W
Warsaw [Mo.-U.S.] 45 Jg 38.15N 93.23W
Warsaw [N.Y.-U.S.] 44 Hd 42.45N 78.07W
Warsaw (EN)=Warszawa 6 Ie 52.15N 21.00 E
Warshīkh 35 He 2.18N 45.48 E
Warstein 12 Kc 51.27N 8.22 E
Warstein-Belecke 12 Kc 51.29N 8.20 E
Warszawa [2] 10 Qd 52.15N 21.00 E
Warszawa=Warsaw (EN) 6 Ie 52.15N 21.00 E
Warta 5 He 52.35N 14.39 E
Waru 26 Jg 3.24S 130.40 E
Warwich 59 Ke 28.13S 152.02 E
Warwick 9 Li 52.25N 1.30W
Warwick [Eng.-U.K.] 9 Li 52.17N 1.34W
Warwick [R.I.-U.S.] 44 Le 41.42N 71.23W
Warwickshire [3] 9 Li 52.10N 1.35W
Wasagu 34 Gc 11.22N 5.48 E
Wasatch Range 38 He 41.15N 111.30W
Wascana Creek 46 Ma 50.40N 104.55W
Wasco 46 Fi 35.36N 119.20W
Waseca 45 Jd 44.05N 93.30W
Washburn 45 Fc 47.17N 101.02W
Washess Bay 64g Ab 1.49N 157.31W
Wāshīm 25 Fd 20.10N 76.58 E
Washington [2] 43 Cb 47.30N 120.30W
Washington [D.C.-U.S.] 39 Lf 38.54N 77.01W
Washington [Eng.-U.K.] 9 Lg 54.54N 1.31W
Washington [Ga.-U.S.] 44 Fi 33.44N 82.44W
Washington [Ia.-U.S.] 45 Kf 41.18N 91.42W
Washington [In.-U.S.] 44 Df 38.40N 87.10W
Washington [N.C.-U.S.] 44 Ih 35.33N 77.03W
Washington [Pa.-U.S.] 44 Ge 40.11N 80.16W
Washington → Teraina Island 57 Kd 4.43N 160.24W
Washington, Mount- 38 Le 44.15N 71.15W
Washington Court House 44 Ff 39.32N 83.29W
Washington Island 45 Md 45.23N 86.55W
Washington Land 41 Fb 80.15N 65.00W
Washita River 45 Hi 34.12N 96.50W
Washtucna 46 Fc 46.45N 118.19W
Wasile 26 If 1.04N 127.59 E
Wasilków 10 Tc 53.12N 23.12 E
Wasior 26 Jg 2.43S 134.30 E
Wāsit [3] 24 Lf 32.35N 46.00 E
Waskaganish 39 Ld 51.25N 78.45W
Wąsosz 10 Me 51.34N 16.42 E
Waspán 47 Hf 14.44N 83.58W
Wassamu 29a Ca 44.02N 142.24 E
Wassenaar 12 Gb 52.09N 4.24 E
Wassenberg 12 Ic 51.06N 6.09 E
Wasserburg am Inn 10 Ih 48.04N 12.14 E
Wasserkuppe 10 Ff 50.30N 9.56 E
Wassigny 12 Fd 50.01N 3.36 E
Wassuk Range 46 Fg 38.40N 118.50W
Wassy 11 Kf 48.30N 4.57 E
Waswanipi, Lac- 44 Ia 49.32N 76.29W
Watampone 22 Oj 4.32S 120.20 E
Watansoppeng 26 Gg 4.21S 119.53 E
Watari 29 Gb 38.02N 140.51 E
Waterbeach 12 Cb 52.16N 0.12 E
Waterberg 37 Bd 20.25S 17.15 E
Waterbury 43 Mc 41.33N 73.02W
Water Cays 49 Ib 23.40N 77.45W
Wateree Pond 44 Gh 34.25N 80.50W
Waterford/Port Láirge 6 Fe 52.15N 7.06W
Waterford/Port Láirge [2] 9 Fi 52.10N 7.40W
Waterford Harbour/Cuan Phort Láirge 9 Gi 52.10N 6.57W
Wateringues 11 Ic 51.00N 2.30 E
Waterloo [Bel.] 11 Kd 50.43N 4.24 E
Waterloo [Ia.-U.S.] 43 Ic 42.30N 92.20W
Waterloo [Il.-U.S.] 45 Kg 38.20N 90.09W
Waterlooville 12 Ad 50.52N 1.01W
Watersmeet 44 Cb 46.18N 89.11W
Watertown [N.Y.-U.S.] 43 Lc 43.57N 75.56W
Watertown [S.D.-U.S.] 43 Hc 44.54N 97.07W
Watertown [Wi.-U.S.] 45 Le 43.12N 88.43W
Waterville 43 Nc 44.33N 69.38W
Watford 9 Mj 51.40N 0.25W
Watford City 45 Ec 47.48N 103.17W
Wa'th 35 Ed 8.10N 32.07 E
Watheroo 59 Df 30.17S 116.04 E
Watir, Wādī- 24 Fh 29.01N 34.40 E
Watkins Glen 44 Id 42.23N 76.53W
Watling → San Salvador 47 Jd 24.02N 74.28W
Watlington 12 Ac 51.38N 1.00W
Watonga 45 Gi 35.51N 98.25W
Watou, Poperinge- 12 Ed 50.51N 2.37 E
Watrous 42 Gf 51.40N 105.28W
Watsa 31 Jh 3.03N 29.32 E
Watseka 45 Mf 40.47N 87.44W
Watsi [C.R.] 49 Fi 9.37N 82.52W
Watsi [Zaire] 36 Dc 0.19S 21.04 E
Watsi Kengo 36 Dc 0.48S 20.33 E
Watson Lake 39 Gc 60.07N 128.48W
Watsonville 46 Eh 36.55N 121.45W
Watt, Morne- 51g Bb 15.19N 61.19W
Watton 12 Cb 52.34N 0.50 E
Watts Bar Lake 44 Eh 35.48N 84.39W
Wattwil 14 Dc 47.18N 9.05 E
Watubela, Kepulauan- 26 Jg 4.35S 131.40 E
Wau 59 Ja 7.20S 146.45 E
Waubay Lake 45 Hd 45.25N 97.25W
Wauchope 59 Kf 31.27S 152.44 E
Wauchula 44 Gl 27.33N 81.49W
Waucoba Mountain 46 Fh 37.00N 118.01W
Waukara, Gunung- 26 Gg 1.15S 119.42 E
Waukarlycarly, Lake- 59 Ed 21.25S 121.50 E
Waukegan 43 Jc 42.22N 87.50W
Waukesha 45 Le 43.01N 88.14W
Waupaca 45 Ld 44.21N 89.05W
Wausau 43 Jc 44.59N 89.39W
Wauseon 44 Ee 41.33N 84.09W
Wauwatosa 45 Me 43.03N 88.00W
Wave Hill 59 Gc 17.29S 130.57 E
Waveney 9 Oi 52.28N 1.45 E
Waver/Wavre 11 Kd 50.43N 4.37 E
Waverly [Ia.-U.S.] 45 Je 42.44N 92.29W
Waverly [Oh.-U.S.] 44 Ff 39.07N 82.59W
Waverly [Tn.-U.S.] 44 Dg 36.05N 87.48W
Waves 44 Jh 35.37N 75.29W
Wavre/Waver 11 Kd 50.43N 4.37 E
Wāw 31 Jh 7.42N 28.00 E
Wawa [Nig.] 34 Fd 9.55N 4.27 E
Wawa [Ont.-Can.] 42 Jg 47.59N 84.47W
Wawa, Río- 49 Fg 13.53N 83.28W
Wāw al Kabīr 31 If 25.20N 16.43 E
Wāw an Nāmūs 33 Ce 24.55N 19.45 E
Wāw Nahr 35 Dd 7.03N 27.13 E
Wawo 26 Hg 3.41S 121.02 E
Wawotobi 26 Hg 3.51S 122.06 E
Waxahachie 45 Hj 32.24N 96.51W
Waxweiler 12 Id 50.06N 6.22 E
Waxxari 27 Ed 38.37N 87.22 E
Way, Lake- 59 Ee 26.50S 120.20 E
Waya 63d Ab 17.18S 177.08 E
Wayabula 26 If 2.17N 128.12 E
Wayan 46 Je 43.00N 111.22W
Waycross 43 Ke 31.13N 82.21W
Wayne [Nb.-U.S.] 45 He 42.14N 97.01W
Wayne [W.V.-U.S.] 44 Ff 38.14N 82.27W
Waynesboro [Ga.-U.S.] 44 Fi 33.06N 82.01W
Waynesboro [Ms.-U.S.] 45 Lk 31.40N 88.39W
Waynesboro [Pa.-U.S.] 44 If 39.45N 77.36W
Waynesboro [Va.-U.S.] 44 Hf 38.04N 78.54W
Waynesville [Mo.-U.S.] 45 Jh 37.50N 92.12W
Waynesville [N.C.-U.S.] 44 Fh 35.29N 83.00W
Waynoka 45 Gh 36.35N 98.53W
Waziers 12 Fd 50.23N 3.07 E
Wda 10 Oc 53.25N 18.29 E
Wdzydze, Jezioro- 10 Nc 54.00N 17.50 E
Wé 61 Cd 20.55S 167.16 E
We, Pulau- 26 Ce 5.51N 95.18 E
Wear 9 Lg 54.55N 1.22W
Weatherford [Ok.-U.S.] 45 Gi 35.32N 98.42W
Weatherford [Tx.-U.S.] 43 He 32.46N 97.48W
Weaverville 46 Df 40.44N 122.56W
Weber 62 Gd 40.24S 176.20 E
Webster 45 Hd 45.20N 97.31W
Webster City 45 Je 42.28N 93.49W
Webster Springs 44 Gf 38.29N 80.25W
Weda 26 If 0.21N 127.52 E
Weda, Teluk- 26 If 0.20N 128.00 E
Weddell Island 56 Hh 51.50S 61.00W
Weddel Sea (EN) 66 Rf 72.00S 45.00W
Wedel 10 Fc 53.35N 9.41 E
Wedgeport 44 Od 43.44N 65.59W
Wedza 37 Ec 18.35S 31.35 E
Weed 46 Df 41.25N 122.27W
Weener 10 Dc 53.10N 7.21 E
Weerdinge, Emmen- 12 Ib 52.49N 6.57 E
Weert 11 Lc 51.15N 5.43 E
Weesp 12 Hb 52.18N 5.02 E
Wegberg 12 Ic 51.09N 6.16 E
Węgliniec 10 Le 51.17N 15.13 E
Węgorzewo 10 Rb 54.14N 21.44 E
Węgrów 10 Sd 52.25N 22.01 E
Wehni 35 Fc 12.40N 36.42 E
Weichang (Zhuizishan) 28 Kc 41.55N 117.45 E
Weida 10 If 50.46N 12.04 E
Weiden in der Oberpfalz 10 Ig 49.41N 12.10 E
Weifang 22 Nf 36.43N 119.06 E
Weihai 27 Ld 37.27N 122.02 E
Weihe 28 Jb 44.55N 128.23 E
Wei He 21 Nf 34.36N 110.10 E
Weilburg 10 Ef 50.29N 8.15 E
Weilerbach 12 Je 49.29N 7.38 E
Weilerswist 12 Id 50.46N 6.50 E
Weilheim in Oberbayern 10 Hi 47.50N 11.09 E
Weilmünster 12 Kd 50.26N 8.21 E
Weimar [Ger.] 12 Kd 50.46N 8.43 E
Weimar [Ger.] 10 Hf 50.59N 11.19 E
Weinan 27 Ie 34.30N 109.34 E
Weingarten 10 Fi 47.48N 9.38 E
Weinheim 10 Eg 49.33N 8.40 E
Weining 27 Hf 26.46N 104.18 E
Weinsberger Wald 14 Ib 48.25N 15.00 E
Weinstraße 12 Ke 49.20N 8.05 E
Weinviertel 14 Kb 48.35N 16.30 E
Weipa 58 Ff 12.41S 141.52 E
Weirton 44 Ge 40.24N 80.37W
Weiser 46 Gd 44.15N 116.58W
Weiser River 46 Gd 44.15N 116.59W
Weishan Hu 27 Ke 34.35N 117.15 E
Weishi 28 Cg 34.25N 114.10 E
Weishui → Jingxing 28 Ce 38.03N 114.09 E
Weiße Elster 10 He 51.26N 11.57 E
Weißenberg 12 Je 49.15N 7.49 E
Weißenburg in Bayern 10 Gg 49.02N 10.59 E
Weißenfels 10 He 51.12N 11.58 E
Weißer Main 10 Hf 50.05N 11.24 E
Weißerstein 12 Id 50.24N 6.22 E
Weißkugel/Palla Bianca 14 Ed 46.48N 10.44 E
Weiss Lake 44 Eh 34.15N 85.35W
Weißwasser/Běła Woda 10 Ke 51.31N 14.38 E
Weitra 14 Ib 48.42N 14.53 E
Weixi 27 Gf 27.13N 99.19 E
Weixian 28 Cf 36.59N 115.15 E
Weixin (Zhaxi) 27 If 27.46N 105.04 E
Weiz 14 Jc 47.13N 15.37 E
Wejherowo 10 Ob 54.37N 18.15 E
Welbourn Hill 58 Eg 27.21S 134.06 E
Welch 44 Gg 37.26N 81.36W
Weldiya 35 Fc 11.48N 39.35 E
Weld Range 59 De 26.55S 117.25 E
Welega [3] 35 Fd 8.38N 35.40 E
Welel 35 Ed 8.56N 34.52 E
Weligama 25 Gg 5.58N 80.25 E
Welkenraedt 12 Hd 50.39N 5.58 E
Welker Seamount (EN) 40 Ke 55.07N 140.20W
Welkite 35 Fd 8.17N 37.49 E
Welkom 31 Jk 27.59S 26.45 E
Welland 42 Jh 42.59N 79.15W
Welland 9 Ni 52.53N 0.02 E
Welland Canal 44 Hd 43.14N 79.13W
Wellesley Islands 57 Ef 16.45S 139.30 E
Wellin 12 Hd 50.05N 5.07 E
Wellingborough 9 Mi 52.19N 0.42W
Wellington [2] 62 Fd 40.10S 175.30 E
Wellington [Austl.] 59 Jf 32.33S 148.57 E
Wellington [Eng.-U.K.] 9 Jk 50.59N 3.14W
Wellington [Ks.-U.S.] 45 Hh 37.16N 97.24W
Wellington [Nv.-U.S.] 46 Fg 38.45N 119.22W
Wellington [N.Z.] 58 Ii 41.17S 174.46 E
Wellington, Isla- 52 Ij 49.20S 74.40W
Wellington, Lake- 59 Jg 38.10S 147.15 E
Wellington Channel 42 Ia 75.10N 93.00W
Wells [Eng.-U.K.] 9 Kj 51.13N 2.39W
Wells [Nv.-U.S.] 43 Dc 41.07N 115.01W
Wells, Lake- 59 Ee 26.45S 123.15 E
Wells, Mount- 59 Fc 17.26S 127.14 E
Wellsboro 44 Ie 41.45N 77.18W
Wellsford 62 Fb 36.18S 174.31 E
Wells-next-the-Sea 9 Ni 52.58N 0.51 E
Wellton 46 Hj 32.40N 114.08W
Welmel 35 Gd 5.35N 40.55 E
Welna 10 Md 52.36N 16.50 E
Welo [3] 35 Fc 12.00N 40.00 E
Wels 14 Ib 48.10N 14.02 E
Welshpool 9 Ji 52.40N 3.09W
Welver 12 Jc 51.37N 7.58 E
Welwitschia 37 Ad 20.21S 14.57 E
Welwyn Garden City 9 Mj 51.48N 0.13W
Wema 36 Dc 0.26S 21.38 E
Wemding 10 Gh 48.52N 10.43 E
Wen'an 28 De 38.52N 116.30 E
Wenatchee 43 Cb 47.25N 120.19W
Wenatchee Mountains 46 Ec 47.20N 120.45W
Wenchang 27 Jh 19.43N 110.44 E
Wenchi 34 Ed 7.44N 2.06W
Wenchit 35 Fc 10.03N 38.35 E
Wenden 12 Jd 50.58N 7.52 E
Wendeng 27 Ld 37.10N 122.01 E
Wendland 10 Gc 53.10N 11.00 E
Wendo 35 Fd 6.37N 38.25 E
Wengyuan (Longxian) 27 Jg 24.21N 114.13 E
Wen He 28 Ef 37.06N 119.29 E
Wenling 27 Lf 28.23N 121.22 E
Wenquan 27 Fe 33.15N 91.55 E
Wenquan/Arixang 27 Dc 44.59N 81.04 E
Wenshan 27 Hg 23.22N 104.23 E
Wenshui 28 Bf 37.26N 112.01 E
Wensu 27 Dc 41.15N 80.14 E
Wensum 12 Db 52.37N 1.22 E
Wentworth 59 If 34.07S 141.55 E
Wenxian 27 He 32.52N 104.40 E
Wenzhou 22 Og 27.57N 120.38 E
Wenzhu 27 Jf 27.00N 114.00 E
Wepener 37 De 29.46S 27.00 E
Wépion, Namur- 12 Gd 50.25N 4.52 E
Werda 37 Ce 25.16S 23.17 E
Werder 31 Lh 7.00N 45.21 E
Werder 10 Ic 53.40N 13.25 E
Werdohl 12 Jc 51.16N 7.46 E
Were Ilu 35 Fc 10.38N 39.23 E
Werkendam 12 Gc 51.49N 4.55 E
Werl 12 Jc 51.33N 7.55 E
Werlte 12 Jb 52.51N 7.41 E
Wermelskirchen 12 Jc 51.09N 7.13 E
Werne 12 Jc 51.40N 7.38 E
Wernigerode 10 Ge 51.50N 10.47 E
Werra 5 Ge 51.26N 9.39 E
Werribee 59 Ig 37.54S 144.40 E
Werris Creek 59 Kf 31.21S 150.39 E
Werse 12 Jb 52.02N 7.41 E
Wertach 10 Gh 48.24N 10.53 E
Wertheim 10 Fg 49.45N 9.31 E
Wesel 10 Ce 51.40N 6.37 E
Weser 5 Ge 53.32N 8.34 E
Weserbergland 10 Fe 51.55N 9.30 E
Wesergebirge 10 Fd 52.15N 9.10 E
Weslaco 45 Gm 26.09N 98.01W
Wesley 51g Ba 15.34N 61.19W
Wesleyville 42 Mg 49.09N 53.34W
Wessel, Cape- 59 Hb 11.00S 136.45 E
Wesseling 12 Id 50.50N 6.59 E
Wessel Islands 57 Ef 12.00S 136.45 E
Wessington Springs 45 Gd 44.05N 98.34W
West Allis 45 Me 43.01N 88.00W
West Baines River 59 Gc 15.26S 130.08 E
West Bay 45 Ll 29.00N 89.30W
West Bend 45 Le 43.25N 88.11W
West Bengal [3] 25 Hd 24.00N 88.00 E
West Berlin (EN) = Berlin 6 He 52.31N 13.24 E
West Branch 44 Ec 44.17N 84.14W
West Bridgford 12 Ab 52.55N 1.07W
West Bromwich 9 Li 52.31N 1.59W
Westbrook 44 Ld 43.41N 70.21W
West Burra 9 La 60.05N 1.10W
West Caicos 49 Kc 21.47N 72.17W
West Cape 57 Hi 45.55S 166.26 E
West Caroline Basin (EN) 3 Ii 4.00N 138.00 E
West Carpathians (EN)= Západné Karpaty 10 Og 49.30N 19.00 E
West Des Moines 45 Jf 41.35N 93.43W
Westdongeradeel 12 Ha 53.23N 5.58 E
Westdongeradeel-Holwerd 12 Ha 53.22N 5.54 E
Westdongeradeel-Ternaard 12 Ha 53.23N 5.58 E
Westeinderplassen 12 Gb 52.15N 4.30 E
West Elk Mountains 45 Cg 38.40N 107.15W
West End 44 Hl 26.41N 78.58W
Westende, Middelkerke- 12 Ec 51.10N 2.46 E
West End Village 51b Ab 18.11N 63.09W
West Entrance 64a Bb 7.57N 134.30 E
Westerbork 12 Ib 52.51N 6.36 E
Westerburg 12 Jd 50.34N 7.59 E
Westerland 10 Eb 54.54N 8.18 E
Westerlo 12 Gc 51.05N 4.55 E
Western [Ghana] [3] 34 Ed 5.30N 2.30W
Western [Kenya] [3] 36 Fb 0.30N 34.35 E
Western [S.L.] [3] 34 Cd 8.20N 13.00W
Western [Ug.] [3] 36 Fb 1.00N 31.00 E
Western [Zam.] [3] 36 Df 15.00S 24.00 E
Western Australia [2] 59 Ed 25.00S 122.00 E
Western Desert (EN) = Gharbīyah, Aş Şahrā' Al- 30 Jf 27.30N 28.00 E
Western Dvina (EN)= Zapadnaja Dvina 5 Id 57.04N 24.03 E
Western Entrance 63a Bb 6.55S 155.40 E
Western Ghats/Sahyadri 21 Jh 14.00N 75.00 E
Western Isles [3] 9 Fd 57.40N 7.10W
Western Port 59 Jg 38.25S 145.10 E
Western River 42 Gc 66.22N 107.15W
Western Sahara (EN) [5] 31 Ff 24.30N 13.00W

Index Symbols

[1] Independent Nation
[2] State, Region
[3] District, County
[4] Municipality
[5] Colony, Dependency
Continent
Physical Region
Historical or Cultural Region
Mount, Mountain
Volcano
Hill
Mountains, Mountain Range
Hills, Escarpment
Plateau, Upland
Pass, Gap
Plain, Lowland
Delta
Salt Flat
Valley, Canyon
Crater, Cave
Karst Features
Depression
Polder
Desert, Dunes
Forest, Woods
Heath, Steppe
Oasis
Cape, Point
Coast, Beach
Cliff
Peninsula
Isthmus
Sandbank
Island
Atoll
Rock, Reef
Islands, Archipelago
Rocks, Reefs
Coral Reef
Well, Spring
Geyser
River, Stream
Waterfall Rapids
River Mouth, Estuary
Lake
Salt Lake
Intermittent Lake
Reservoir
Swamp, Pond
Canal
Glacier
Ice Shelf, Pack Ice
Ocean
Sea
Gulf, Bay
Strait, Fjord
Lagoon
Bank
Seamount
Tablemount
Ridge
Shelf
Basin
Escarpment, Sea Scarp
Fracture
Trench, Abyss
National Park, Reserve
Point of Interest
Recreation Site
Cave, Cavern
Historic Site
Ruins
Wall, Walls
Church, Abbey
Temple
Scientific Station
Airport
Port
Lighthouse
Mine
Tunnel
Dam, Bridge

Western Samoa (EN)= Samoa I Sisifo [1] 58 Jf 13.40S 172.30W
Western Sayans (EN)= Zapadny Sajan 21 Ld 53.00N 94.00 E
Western Sierra Madre (EN) =Madre Occidental, Sierra- 38 Ig 25.00N 105.00W
Western Turkistan (EN) 21 He 41.00N 60.00 E
Westerschelde=West Schelde (EN) 11 Jc 51.25N 3.45 E
Westerschouwen 12 Fc 51.41N 3.43 E
Westerschouwen-Haamstede 12 Fc 51.42N 3.45 E
Westerstede 10 Dc 53.15N 7.56 E
Westerwald 10 Df 50.40N 7.55 E
Westerwoldse A 12 Ja 53.10N 7.10 E
West European Basin (EN) 3 De 47.00N 15.00W
West Falkland 52 Kk 51.40S 60.00W
West Falkland/Gran Malvina, Isla- 52 Kk 51.40S 60.00W
West Fayu Island 57 Fd 8.05N 146.44 E
West Fork Big Blue River 45 Hf 40.42N 96.59W
Westfriesland=West Friesland (EN) 11 Kb 52.45N 4.50 E
West Friesland (EN)= Westfriesland 11 Kb 52.45N 4.50 E
West Frisian Islands (EN)= Waddeneilanden 11 Ka 53.30N 5.00 E
Westgate-on-Sea 12 Dc 51.22N 1.21 E
West Glacier 46 Ib 48.30N 113.59W
West Glamorgan [3] 9 Jj 51.40N 3.55W
West Grand Lake 44 Nc 45.15N 67.52W
West Greenland (EN) = Vestgrønland [2] 41 He 69.00N 49.30W
West Helena 45 Ki 34.33N 90.39W
West Hollywood 44 Gm 25.59N 80.11W
Westhope 45 Fb 48.55N 101.01W
West Ice Shelf 66 Ge 67.00S 85.00 E
West Indies 47 Je 19.00N 70.00W
West Indies (EN)=Indias Occidentales 47 Je 19.00N 70.00W
West Island 37b Ab 9.22S 46.13 E
Westkapelle 12 Fc 51.31N 3.26 E
Westkapelle, Knokke- 12 Fc 51.19N 3.18 E
West Lafayette 44 De 40.27N 86.55W
Westland [2] 62 De 43.10S 170.30 E
West Liberty 44 Fg 37.55N 83.16W
Westlock 42 Gf 54.09N 113.52W
West Lunga 36 De 13.06S 24.39 E
Westmalle 12 Gc 51.18N 4.41 E
West Mariana Basin (EN) 3 Ih 15.00N 137.00 E
Westmeath/An Iarmhí [2] 9 Fh 53.30N 7.30W
West Melanesian Trench (EN) 60 Dh 1.00S 150.00 E
West Memphis 43 Id 35.08N 90.11W
West Mersea 12 Cc 51.46N 0.54 E
West Midlands [3] 9 Li 52.30N 2.00W
Westminster 44 If 39.35N 76.59W
Westminster, London- 12 Bc 51.30N 0.07W
West Monroe 45 Jj 32.31N 92.09W
Westmorland 9 Kg 54.30N 2.40W
West Nicholson 31 Jk 21.03S 29.22 E
West Nueces River 45 Gl 29.16N 99.56W
Weston [Mala.] 26 Ge 5.13N 115.36 E
Weston [W.V.-U.S.] 44 Gf 39.03N 80.28W
Weston [Wy.-U.S.] 46 Md 44.42N 105.18W
Weston-super-Mare 9 Kj 51.21N 2.59W
Westoverledingen 12 Ja 53.10N 7.27 E
Westoverledingen - Ihrhove 12 Ja 53.10N 7.27 E
West Palm Beach 39 Kg 26.43N 80.04W
West Pensacola 44 Dj 30.27N 87.15W
West Plains 43 Id 36.44N 91.51W
West Point [Ms.-U.S.] 45 Lj 33.36N 88.39W
West Point [Nb.-U.S.] 45 Hf 41.51N 96.43W
Westport 58 Ii 41.45S 171.36 E
Westport/Cathair na Mart 9 Dh 53.48N 9.32W
Westray 9 Kb 59.20N 3.00W
Westree 48 Gf 47.27N 81.32W
Westrich 12 Je 49.20N 7.25 E
West Road 12 Cd 50.52N 0.50 E
West Schelde (EN)= Westerschelde 11 Jc 51.25N 3.45 E
West Scotia Basin (EN) 52 Kk 57.00S 53.00W
West Siberian Plain (EN)= Zapadno Sibirskaja Ravnina 21 Jc 60.00N 75.00 E
Weststellingwerf 12 Ib 52.53N 6.00 E
Weststellingwerf-Wolvega 12 Ib 52.53N 6.00 E
West Sussex [3] 9 Mk 51.00N 0.40W
West Tavaputs Plateau 46 Jf 40.00N 110.25W
West-Terschelling, Terschelling- 12 Ha 53.21N 5.13 E
West Union [Ia.-U.S.] 45 Ke 42.57N 91.49W
West Union [Oh.-U.S.] 44 Ff 38.48N 83.33W
West Virginia [2] 43 Kd 38.45N 80.30W
West-Vlaanderen [3] 12 Ec 51.00N 3.00 E
Westwood 46 Ef 40.18N 121.00W
West Wyalong 59 Jf 33.55S 147.13 E
West Yellowstone 43 Eb 44.30N 111.05W
West Yorkshire [3] 9 Lh 53.40N 1.30W
Wetar, Pulau- 57 De 7.48S 126.18 E
Wetaskiwin 42 Gf 52.58N 113.22W
Wete 36 Gd 5.04S 39.43 E
Wětošow/Vetschau 10 Ke 51.47N 14.04 E
Wetter 12 Kd 50.18N 8.49 E
Wetter (Hessen) 12 Kd 50.54N 8.43 E
Wetter (Ruhr) 12 Jc 51.23N 7.24 E
Wetterau 10 Ef 50.15N 8.50 E
Wetteren 11 Jc 51.00N 3.53 E
Wetzlar 10 Ef 50.33N 8.30 E
Wevelgem 12 Fd 50.48N 3.10 E
Wewahitchka 44 Ej 30.07N 85.12W
Wewak 58 Fe 3.34S 143.38 E
Wexford/Loch Garman [2] 9 Gi 52.20N 6.40W
Wexford/Loch Garman 6 Fe 52.20N 6.27W
Wexford Harbour/Cuan Loch Garman 9 Gi 52.20N 6.25W
Wey 9 Mj 51.23N 0.28W
Weyburn 42 Hg 49.41N 103.52W
Weyhe 12 Kb 52.59N 8.52 E
Weyhe-Leeste 12 Kb 52.59N 8.50 E
Weymouth 9 Kk 50.36N 2.28W
Wezet/Visé 12 Hd 50.44N 5.42 E
Whakatane 61 Eg 37.58S 177.00 E
Whale Cove 42 Id 62.14N 92.10W
Whalsay 9 Ma 60.22N 0.59W
Whangarei 58 Ih 35.43S 174.19 E
Wharfe 9 Lh 53.51N 1.07W
Wharton 45 Hl 29.19N 96.06W
Wharton Basin (EN) 3 Hk 19.00S 100.00 E
Wharton Lake 42 Hd 64.00N 99.55W
Whataroa 62 De 43.16S 170.22 E
Wheatland 46 Me 42.03N 104.57W
Wheat Ridge 45 Dg 39.46N 105.07W
Wheeler 42 Ke 57.02N 67.14W
Wheeler 46 Dd 45.42N 123.52W
Wheeler Lake 44 Dh 34.40N 87.05W
Wheeler Peak [N.M.-U.S.] 43 Fd 36.34N 105.25W
Wheeler Peak [U.S.] 38 Hf 38.59N 114.19W
Wheeling 43 Kc 40.05N 80.43W
Whidbey Island 46 Db 48.15N 122.40W
Whitby 9 Mg 54.29N 0.37W
Whitchurch [Eng.-U.K.] 9 Ki 52.58N 2.41W
Whitchurch [Eng.-U.K.] 12 Bc 51.53N 0.50W
Whitchurch [Eng.-U.K.] 12 Ac 51.13N 1.20W
White 42 Jc 65.50N 85.00W
White, Lake- 59 Fd 21.05S 129.00 E
White Bay 38 Nd 50.00N 56.30W
White Bear Lake 45 Jd 45.04N 93.01W
White Butte 45 Ec 46.23N 103.19W
White Carpathians (EN) = Bílé Karpaty 10 Nh 48.55N 17.50 E
White Cliffs 59 If 30.51S 143.05 E
White Cloud 44 Ed 43.33N 85.46W
Whitecourt 42 Ff 54.09N 115.41W
Whitefish 43 Eb 48.25N 114.20W
Whitefish Bay 43 Kb 46.40N 84.50W
Whitefish Point 44 Eb 46.45N 85.00W
Whitefish Range 46 Hb 48.40N 114.26W
Whitehall [Mi.-U.S.] 44 Dd 43.24N 86.21W
Whitehall [Mt.-U.S.] 46 Id 45.52N 112.06W
Whitehall [Oh.-U.S.] 44 Ff 39.58N 82.54W
Whitehall [Wi.-U.S.] 45 Kd 44.22N 91.19W
Whitehaven 9 Jg 54.33N 3.35W
Whitehorse 39 Fc 60.43N 135.03W
White Island [Ant.] 66 Ee 66.44S 48.35 E
White Island [N.Z.] 62 Gb 37.30S 177.10 E
White Lake 45 Jl 29.45N 92.30W
White Lake (EN)=Beloje Ozero 5 Jc 60.11N 37.35 E
Whiteman Range 59 Ja 5.50S 149.55 E
Whitemark 59 Jh 40.07S 148.01 E
White Mountain 40 Db 64.35N 163.04W
White Mountain Peak 43 Dd 37.38N 118.15W
White Mountains [Ak.-U.S.] 40 Jc 65.30N 147.00W
White Mountains [U.S.] 46 Fh 37.30N 118.15W
White Mountains [U.S.] 43 Mc 44.10N 71.35W
Whitemouth Lake 45 Ib 49.14N 95.40W
Whitemouth River 45 Ha 50.07N 96.02W
White Nile (EN)=Abyaḍ, Al Baḥr al- 30 Kg 15.38N 32.31 E
White Nile (EN)=Abyaḍ, Al Baḥr al- [3] 35 Ec 12.40N 32.30 E
White Pass [N.Amer.] 40 Le 59.37N 135.08W
White Pass [Wa.-U.S.] 46 Ec 46.38N 121.24W
Whiteriver 46 Kj 33.50N 109.58W
White River [In.-U.S.] 44 Df 38.25N 87.44W
White River [Nv.-U.S.] 46 Hh 37.18N 115.08W
White River [Ont.-Can.] 42 Ig 48.35N 85.17W
White River [S.D.-U.S.] 45 Fe 43.34N 100.45W
White River [Tx.-U.S.] 45 Fj 33.14N 100.56W
White River [U.S.] 46 Kf 40.04N 109.41W
White River [U.S.] 43 Hc 43.45N 99.30W
White River [U.S.] 38 Jf 33.53N 91.03W
White River [Yuk.-Can.] 42 Dd 63.10N 139.32W
White Salmon 46 Ed 45.44N 121.29W
Whitesand Bay 9 Ik 50.20N 4.35W
White Sea (EN)=Beloje More 5 Kb 66.00N 44.00 E
White Sea-Baltic Canal (EN) =Belomorsko-Baltijski Kanal 5 Jc 63.30N 34.48 E
White Settlement 45 Hj 32.45N 97.27W
White Sulphur Springs 46 Jc 46.33N 110.54W
Whiteville 44 Hh 34.20N 78.42W
White Volta 30 Gh 8.38N 0.59W
White Volta (EN)=Volta Blanche 30 Gh 8.38N 0.59W
Whitewater 45 Bg 38.59N 108.27W
Whitewater Baldy 45 Bj 33.20N 108.39W
Whitewater Bay 44 Gm 25.16N 81.00W
Whitewater Lake 45 La 50.50N 89.10W
Whitewood 45 Ea 50.20N 102.15W
Whitianga 62 Fb 36.50S 175.42 E
Whitmore Mountains 66 Og 82.35S 104.30W
Whitney 44 Hc 45.30N 78.14W
Whitney, Lake- 45 Hk 31.55N 97.23W
Whitney, Mount- 38 Hf 36.35N 118.18W
Whitstable 12 Dc 51.21N 1.06 E
Whitsunday Island 59 Jd 20.15S 149.00 E
Whittier 40 Jd 60.46N 148.41W
Whittlesea 59 Jg 37.31S 145.07 E
Whittlesey 12 Bb 52.33N 0.08W
Wholdaia Lake 42 Hd 60.45N 104.10W
Whyalla 59 Hf 33.02S 137.35 E
Wiarton 44 Gc 44.45N 81.09W
Wiawso 34 Ed 6.12N 2.29W
Wibaux 46 Mc 46.59N 104.11W
Wichita 39 Jf 37.41N 97.20W
Wichita Falls 39 Jf 33.54N 98.30W
Wichita Mountains 45 Gi 34.45N 98.40W
Wichita River 45 Gi 34.07N 98.10W
Wick 9 Jc 58.26N 3.06W
Wick 9 Jc 58.25N 3.05W
Wickenburg 46 Ij 33.58N 112.44W
Wickepin 59 Df 32.46S 117.30 E
Wickham 12 Ad 50.54N 1.10W
Wickham Market 12 Db 52.09N 1.22 E
Wickiup Reservoir 46 Ee 43.40N 121.43W
Wickliffe 44 Cg 36.58N 89.05W
Wicklow/Cill Mhantáin [2] 9 Gi 53.00N 6.30W
Wicklow/Cill Mhantáin 9 Gi 52.59N 6.03W
Wicklow Head/Ceann Chill Mhantáin 9 Hi 52.58N 6.00W
Wicklow Mountains/ Sléibhte Chill Mhantáin 9 Gh 53.02N 6.24W
Wicko, Jezioro- 10 Mb 54.33N 16.35 E
Wickrath, Mönchengladbach- 12 Ic 51.08N 6.25 E
Widawa 10 Me 51.13N 16.55 E
Wide Bay 59 Ka 5.05S 152.05 E
Widefield 45 Dg 38.42N 104.40W
Widgiemooltha 59 Ef 31.30S 121.34 E
Wi-Do 28 Ig 35.38N 126.17 E
Więcbork 10 Nc 53.22N 17.30 E
Wied 12 Jd 50.27N 7.28 E
Wiedenbrück 12 Kc 50.51N 8.19 E
Wiehengebirge 10 Ed 52.20N 8.40 E
Wiehl 12 Jd 50.57N 7.32 E
Wieliczka 10 Qg 49.59N 20.04 E
Wielimie, Jezioro- 10 Mc 53.47N 16.50 E
Wielki Dział 10 Tf 50.18N 23.25 E
Wielkopolska 10 Ne 51.50N 17.20 E
Wielkopolskie-Kujawskie, Pojezierze- 10 Md 52.25N 16.30 E
Wieluń 10 Oe 51.14N 18.34 E
Wien [2] 14 Kb 48.15N 16.25 E
Wien = Vienna (EN) 6 Hf 48.12N 16.22 E
Wiener Becken 14 Kc 48.00N 16.28 E
Wiener Neustadt 14 Kc 47.48N 16.15 E
Wienerwald=Vienna Woods (EN) 14 Jb 48.10N 16.00 E
Wieprz 10 Re 51.32N 21.49 E
Wieprza 10 Mb 54.26N 16.22 E
Wieprz-Krzna, Kanał- 10 Se 51.56N 22.56 E
Wierden 12 Ib 52.22N 6.36 E
Wieringen 12 Hb 52.56N 5.02 E
Wieringen-Den Oever 12 Hb 52.56N 5.02 E
Wieringen-Hippolytushoef 12 Gb 52.54N 4.59 E
Wieringermeer 12 Hb 52.51N 5.01 E
Wieringermeer Polder 12 Gb 52.50N 5.00 E
Wieringermeer-Wieringerwerf 12 Hb 52.51N 5.01 E
Wieringerwerf, Wieringermeer- 12 Hb 52.51N 5.01 E
Wieruszów 10 Oe 51.18N 18.08 E
Wierzchowo, Jezioro- 10 Mc 53.50N 16.45 E
Wierzyca 10 Oc 53.51N 18.50 E
Wiesbaden 6 Ge 50.05N 8.15 E
Wiese 10 Di 47.35N 7.35 E
Wieslautern 12 Je 49.05N 7.49 E
Wiesloch 12 Kf 49.18N 8.42 E
Wietingsmoor 12 Kb 52.39N 8.39 E
Wietmarschen 12 Jb 52.32N 7.08 E
Wieżyca 10 Ob 54.17N 18.10 E
Wigan 9 Kh 53.32N 2.35W
Wigger 14 Bc 47.15N 7.55 E
Wiggins 45 Lk 30.51N 89.08W
Wight, Isle of- 5 Fe 50.40N 1.20W
Wigry, Jezioro- 10 Tb 54.05N 23.07 E
Wigston 12 Ab 52.35N 1.06W
Wigtown 9 Ig 54.52N 4.26W
Wigtown Bay 9 Ig 54.50N 4.15W
Wijchen 12 Hc 51.48N 5.44 E
Wijdefjorden 41 Nc 79.50N 15.30 E
Wijk bij Duurstede 12 Hc 51.59N 5.22 E
Wil 14 Dc 47.27N 9.05 E
Wilbur 46 Fc 47.46N 118.42W
Wilburton 45 Ii 34.55N 95.19W
Wilcannia 58 Fh 31.34S 143.23 E
Wild Coast 30 Jl 32.00S 29.50 E
Wilder Seamount (EN) 57 Jd 9.00N 173.00W
Wildeshausen 12 Kb 52.54N 8.26 E
Wild Horse 46 Jb 49.01N 110.12W
Wildspitze 14 Ed 46.53N 10.52 E
Wilga 10 Re 51.50N 21.20 E
Wilhelm-II-Land 66 Ge 69.00S 90.00 E
Wilhelminakanaal 12 Gc 51.43N 4.53 E
Wilhelm-Pieck-Stadt-Guben 10 Ke 51.57N 14.43 E
Wilhelmshaven 10 Ec 53.31N 8.08 E
Wilhelmstal 37 Bd 21.54S 16.20 E
Wilkes-Barre 43 Lc 41.15N 75.50W
Wilkesboro 44 Gg 36.09N 81.09W
Wilkes Land (EN) 66 Hf 71.00S 120.00 E
Wilkins Coast 66 Qe 69.40S 63.00W
Wilkins Sound 66 Qf 70.15S 73.00W
Willamette River 46 Dd 45.39N 122.46W
Willandra Billabong Creek 59 If 33.08S 144.06 E
Willapa Bay 46 Dc 46.37N 124.00W
Willard 45 Ci 34.36N 106.02W
Willards, Punta- 48 Cc 28.50N 112.35W
Willcox 46 Kj 32.15N 109.50W
Willebadessen 12 Lc 51.38N 9.02 E
Willebadessen-Peckelsheim 12 Lc 51.36N 9.08 E
Willebroek 12 Gc 51.04N 4.22 E
Willemstad [Neth.] 12 Gc 51.41N 4.26 E
Willemstad [Neth.Ant.] 53 Jd 12.06N 68.56W
Willeroo 59 Gc 15.17S 131.35 E
William Bill Dannelly Reservoir 44 Di 32.15N 86.45W
Williams 43 Ed 35.15N 112.11W
Williamsburg [Ky.-U.S.] 44 Eg 36.44N 84.10W
Williamsburg [Va.-U.S.] 44 Ig 37.17N 76.43W
Williams Lake 42 Ff 52.08N 122.09W
Williamson Glacier 66 He 66.30S 114.30 E
Williamsport 43 Lc 41.16N 77.03W
Williamston 44 Ih 35.50N 77.06W
Williamstown 44 Ef 38.38N 84.34W
Willich 12 Ic 51.16N 6.33 E
Willikie's 51d Bb 17.03N 61.42W
Willingdon, Mount- 46 Ga 51.48N 116.17W
Willis Group 57 Gf 16.20S 150.00 E
Williston [N.D.-U.S.] 43 Gb 48.09N 103.37W
Williston [S.Afr.] 37 Cf 31.20S 20.53 E
Williston Lake 38 Gd 50.57N 122.23W
Willits 46 Dg 39.25N 123.21W
Willmar 43 Hb 45.07N 95.03W
Willoughby Bay 51d Bb 17.02N 61.44W
Willow Bunch Lake 46 Mb 49.27N 105.28W
Willowlake 42 Fd 62.42N 123.08W
Willowmore 37 Cf 33.17S 23.29 E
Willows 46 Dg 39.31N 122.12W
Willow Springs 45 Kh 36.59N 91.58W
Wills, Lake- 59 Fd 21.20S 128.40 E
Wills Point 45 Ij 32.43N 95.57W
Wilma Glacier 66 Ee 67.12S 56.00 E
Wilmington [De.-U.S.] 43 Ld 39.44N 75.33W
Wilmington [N.C.-U.S.] 39 Lf 34.13N 77.55W
Wilmington [Oh.-U.S.] 44 Ff 39.28N 83.50W
Wilnsdorf 12 Kd 50.49N 8.06 E
Wilseder Berg 10 Fc 53.10N 9.56 E
Wilson 43 Ld 35.44N 77.55W
Wilson, Cape- 42 Jc 66.59N 81.27W
Wilson, Mount- 45 Ch 37.51N 107.59W
Wilson Bluff 66 Ff 74.20S 66.47 E
Wilson Lake [Al.-U.S.] 44 Dh 34.49N 87.30W
Wilson Lake [Ks.-U.S.] 45 Gg 38.57N 98.40W
Wilsons Promontory 59 Jg 38.55S 146.20 E
Wilton River 59 Gb 14.45S 134.33 E
Wilts 9 Lj 51.20N 2.00W
Wiltshire [3] 9 Lj 51.30N 2.00W
Wiltz 11 Le 49.58N 5.55 E
Wiluna 59 Ee 26.36S 120.13 E
Wimereux 12 Dd 50.46N 1.37 E
Winamac 44 De 41.03N 86.36W
Winburg 37 De 28.37S 27.00 E
Winchelsea 12 Cd 50.55N 0.43 E
Winchester [Eng.-U.K.] 9 Lj 51.04N 1.19W
Winchester [In.-U.S.] 44 Ee 40.10N 84.59W
Winchester [Ky.-U.S.] 44 Ef 38.01N 84.11W
Winchester [Va.-U.S.] 43 Ld 39.11N 78.12W
Windeck 12 Jd 50.49N 7.34 E
Windemin, Pointe- 63b Cc 16.34S 167.27 E
Winder 44 Fi 34.00N 83.47W
Windermere 9 Kg 54.22N 2.56W
Windermere [B.C.-Can.] 46 Ha 50.30N 115.58W
Windermere [Eng.-U.K.] 9 Kg 54.23N 2.54W
Windhoek 31 Ik 22.34S 17.06 E
Windhoek [3] 37 Bd 22.30S 17.00 E
Windischgarsten 14 Ic 47.43N 14.20 E
Wind Mountain 45 Dj 32.02N 105.34W
Windom 45 Ie 43.52N 95.07W
Windom Mountain 45 Ch 37.37N 107.35W
Windorah 59 Ie 25.26S 142.39 E
Window Rock 46 Ki 35.41N 109.03W
Wind River 46 Ke 43.08N 108.12W
Wind River Peak 46 Ke 42.42N 109.07W
Wind River Range 43 Fc 43.05N 109.25W
Windrush 9 Lj 51.42N 1.25W
Windsor [Eng.-U.K.] 9 Mj 51.29N 0.38W
Windsor [N.S.-Can.] 44 Lh 44.59N 64.09W
Windsor [Ont.-Can.] 42 Jh 42.18N 83.01W
Windsor Forest 44 Gj 31.58N 81.10W
Windward Islands 47 Lf 13.00N 61.00W
Windward Islands (EN)= Barlovento, Islas de- 38 Mh 15.00N 61.00W
Windward Islands (EN)= Sotavento, Islas de- 52 Jd 11.10N 67.00W
Windward Islands (EN)= Vent, Iles du- 57 Mf 17.30S 149.30W
Windward Passage (EN)= Vent, Canal du- 49 Lh 20.00N 73.50W
Windward Passage (EN)= Vientos, Paso de los- 38 Lh 20.00N 73.50W
Winfield [Al.-U.S.] 44 Di 33.56N 87.49W
Winfield [Ks.-U.S.] 43 Hd 37.15N 96.59W
Wingene 12 Fc 51.04N 3.16 E
Wingen-sur-Moder 12 Jf 48.55N 7.22 E
Winisk 38 Kd 55.17N 85.05W
Winisk 38 Kd 55.15N 85.12W
Winisk Lake 42 If 52.55N 87.20W
Winkler 45 Hb 49.11N 97.56W
Winklern 14 Gd 46.52N 12.52 E
Winneba 34 Ed 5.20N 0.37W
Winnebago, Lake- 43 Jc 44.00N 88.25W
Winnemucca 43 Dc 40.58N 117.44W
Winnemucca Lake 46 Ff 40.10N 119.20W
Winner 43 Hc 43.22N 99.51W
Winnett 46 Kc 47.00N 108.21W
Winnfield 45 Jk 31.55N 92.38W
Winnibigoshish, Lake- 45 Ic 47.27N 94.12W
Winnipeg 39 Je 49.53N 97.09W
Winnipeg 38 Jd 50.38N 96.19W
Winnipeg, Lake- 38 Jd 52.00N 97.00W
Winnipeg Beach 45 Ha 50.31N 96.58W
Winnipegosis 42 Hf 51.39N 99.56W
Winnipegosis, Lake- 38 Jd 52.30N 100.00W
Winnipesaukee, Lake- 44 Ld 43.35N 71.20W
Winnsboro 45 Kj 32.10N 91.43W
Winnweiler 12 Je 49.34N 7.51 E
Winona [Mn.-U.S.] 43 Ic 44.03N 91.39W
Winona [Mo.-U.S.] 45 Kh 37.06N 91.59W
Winona [Ms.-U.S.] 45 Lj 33.29N 89.44W
Winschoten 11 Na 53.08N 7.02 E
Winsen 10 Gc 53.22N 10.13 E
Winslow [Az.-U.S.] 43 Ed 35.01N 110.42W
Winslow [Eng.-U.K.] 12 Bc 51.57N 0.52W
Winslow Reef 57 Je 1.36S 174.57W
Winston-Salem 43 Kd 36.06N 80.15W
Winterberg 10 Ee 51.12N 8.32 E
Winter Harbour 42 Gb 74.46N 110.40W
Winter Haven 43 Kf 28.01N 81.44W
Winter Park [Co.-U.S.] 45 Dg 39.47N 105.45W
Winter Park [Fl.-U.S.] 44 Gk 28.36N 81.20W
Winters 45 Gk 31.57N 99.58W
Winterset 45 If 41.20N 94.01W
Winterswijk 11 Mc 51.58N 6.44 E
Winterthur 14 Cc 47.30N 8.45 E
Winton [Austl.] 58 Fg 22.23S 143.02 E
Winton [N.C.-U.S.] 44 Ig 36.24N 76.56W
Winton [N.Z.] 62 Cg 46.09S 168.20 E
Wipper [Ger.] 10 He 51.20N 11.10 E
Wipper [Ger.] 10 He 51.47N 11.42 E
Wisbech 9 Ni 52.40N 0.10 E
Wiscasset 44 Mc 44.00N 69.40W
Wisch 12 Ic 51.55N 6.22 E
Wisch-Terborg 12 Ic 51.55N 6.22 E
Wisconsin [2] 43 Jc 44.45N 89.30W
Wisconsin 38 Je 43.00N 91.15W
Wisconsin Range 66 Ng 85.45S 125.00W
Wisconsin Rapids 43 Jc 44.23N 89.49W
Wiseman 40 Ic 67.26N 150.06W
Wisła 10 Og 49.39N 18.50 E
Wisła=Vistula (EN) 5 He 54.22N 18.55 E
Wiślana, Mierzeja- 10 Pb 54.25N 19.30 E
Wiślane, Żuławy- 10 Ob 54.10N 19.00 E
Wiślany, Zalew- 10 Pb 54.27N 19.40 E
Wisłok 10 Sf 50.13N 22.32 E
Wisłoka 10 Rf 50.27N 21.23 E
Wismar 10 Hc 53.54N 11.28 E
Wismarbucht 10 Hc 53.57N 11.25 E
Wissant 12 Dd 50.53N 1.40 E
Wissembourg 11 Ne 49.02N 7.57 E
Wissen 10 Df 50.47N 7.45 E
Wissenkerke 12 Fc 51.35N 3.45 E
Wissey 12 Cb 52.34N 0.21 E
Witbank 31 Jk 25.56S 29.07 E
Witchekar Lake 45 Fb 49.15N 100.16W
Witdraai 37 Ce 26.58S 20.41 E
Witham 12 Cc 51.47N 0.38 E
Witham 9 Ni 52.56N 0.04 E
Withernsea 9 Nh 53.44N 0.02 E
Witkowo 10 Nd 52.27N 17.47 E
Witmarsum, Wonseradeel- 12 Ha 53.06N 5.28 E
Witney 9 Lj 51.48N 1.29W
Witnica 10 Kd 52.40N 14.55 E
Witputz 37 Be 27.37S 16.42 E
Witten 10 De 51.26N 7.20 E
Wittenberg [Ger.] 10 Ie 51.52N 12.39 E
Wittenberg [Wi.-U.S.] 45 Ld 44.49N 89.10W
Wittenberge 10 Hc 53.00N 11.45 E
Wittenoom 59 Dd 22.17S 118.19 E
Wittingen 10 Gd 52.44N 10.43 E
Wittlich 10 Cg 49.59N 6.53 E
Wittmund 10 Dc 53.34N 7.47 E
Wittow 10 Jb 54.38N 13.19 E
Wittstock 10 Ic 53.09N 12.30 E
Witu 36 Hc 2.23S 40.26 E
Witu Islands 60 Dh 4.40S 149.18 E
Witvlei 37 Bd 22.23S 18.32 E
Witzenhausen 10 Fe 51.20N 9.52 E
Wivenhoe 12 Cc 51.51N 0.58 E
Wizard Reef 30 Mi 8.57S 51.01 E
Wizna 10 Sc 53.13N 22.26 E
Wjdawka 10 Oe 51.32N 18.52 E
W. J. Van Blommestein Meer 54 Hc 4.45N 55.00W
Wkra 10 Qd 52.27N 20.44 E
Władysławowo 10 Ob 54.49N 18.25 E
Włocławek 10 Pd 52.39N 19.02 E
Włocławek [2] 10 Od 52.40N 19.00 E
Włodawa 10 Te 51.34N 23.32 E
Włoszczowa 10 Pf 50.25N 19.59 E
Wodonga 59 Jg 36.17S 146.54 E
Wodzisław Śląski 10 Of 50.00N 18.28 E
Woensdrecht 12 Gc 51.25N 4.18 E
Woerden 12 Gb 52.05N 4.52 E
Woerth 12 Jf 48.56N 7.45 E
Woëvre, Plaine de la- 12 He 49.15N 5.50 E
Wohlthat-Massif 66 Cf 71.35S 12.20 E
Woippy 12 Ie 49.09N 6.09 E
Wojerecy/Hoyerswerda 10 Ke 51.26N 14.15 E
Wokam, Pulau- 26 Jh 5.37S 134.30 E
Woken He 28 Ja 46.19N 129.34 E
Woking 9 Mj 51.20N 0.34W
Wokingham 12 Bc 51.25N 0.50W
Wolbrom 10 Pf 50.24N 19.46 E
Wolcott 44 Id 43.13N 76.42W
Wołczyn 10 Oe 51.01N 18.03 E
Woldberg 12 Hb 52.25N 5.55 E
Woleai Atoll 57 Fd 7.21N 143.52 E
Woleu-Ntem [3] 36 Bb 2.00N 12.00 E
Wolf, Isla- 54a Aa 1.23N 91.49W
Wolf, Volcán- 54a Ab 0.01S 91.20W
Wolfach 10 Eh 48.18N 8.13 E
Wolf Creek 45 Gh 36.35N 99.30W
Wolf Creek 46 Ic 47.00N 112.04W
Wolfen 10 Ie 51.40N 12.17 E
Wolfenbüttel 10 Gd 52.10N 10.33 E
Wolfhagen 10 Fe 51.19N 9.10 E
Wolf Point 43 Fb 48.05N 105.39W
Wolfratshausen 10 Hi 47.54N 11.25 E
Wolf River 45 Ld 44.11N 88.48W
Wolfsberg 14 Id 46.50N 14.50 E
Wolfsburg 10 Gd 52.26N 10.48 E
Wolfstein 12 Je 49.35N 7.36 E
Wolgast 10 Jb 54.03N 13.46 E
Wolica 10 Tf 50.54N 23.12 E
Wolin 10 Kc 53.51N 14.38 E
Wolin 10 Kc 53.50N 14.35 E
Wollaston 12 Bb 52.15N 0.40W
Wollaston, Islas- 56 Gi 55.40S 67.30W
Wollaston Forland 41 Jd 74.35N 20.15W
Wollaston Lake 38 Id 58.15N 103.20W
Wollaston Lake 42 He 58.05N 103.38W
Wollaston Peninsula 38 Hc 70.00N 115.00W
Wollongong 58 Gh 34.25S 150.54 E
Wöllstein 12 Ke 49.49N 7.58 E
Wolmaransstad 37 De 27.12S 26.13 E
Wołomin 10 Rd 52.21N 21.14 E
Wołów 10 Me 51.29N 16.55 E

Index Symbols

[1] Independent Nation
[2] State, Region
[3] District, County
[4] Municipality
[5] Colony, Dependency
Continent
Physical Region
Historical or Cultural Region
Mount, Mountain
Volcano
Hill
Mountains, Mountain Range
Hills, Escarpment
Plateau, Upland
Pass, Gap
Plain, Lowland
Delta
Salt Flat
Valley, Canyon
Crater, Cave
Karst Features
Depression
Polder
Desert, Dunes
Forest, Woods
Heath, Steppe
Oasis
Cape, Point
Coast, Beach
Cliff
Peninsula
Isthmus
Sandbank
Island
Atoll
Rock, Reef
Islands, Archipelago
Rocks, Reefs
Coral Reef
Well, Spring
Geyser
River, Stream
Waterfall Rapids
River Mouth, Estuary
Lake
Salt Lake
Intermittent Lake
Reservoir
Swamp, Pond
Canal
Glacier
Ice Shelf, Pack Ice
Ocean
Sea
Gulf, Bay
Strait, Fjord
Lagoon
Bank
Seamount
Tablemount
Ridge
Shelf
Basin
Escarpment, Sea Scarp
Fracture
Trench, Abyss
National Park, Reserve
Point of Interest
Recreation Site
Cave, Cavern
Historic Site
Ruins
Wall, Walls
Church, Abbey
Temple
Scientific Station
Airport
Port
Lighthouse
Mine
Tunnel
Dam, Bridge

Wolseley	42	Hf	50.25N	103.19W
Wolstenholme, Cap -	42	Jd	62.34N	77.30W
Wolstenholme Fjord	41	Ec	76.40N	69.45W
Wolsztyn	10	Md	52.08N	16.06 E
Wolvega, Weststellingwerf-	12	Ib	52.53N	6.00 E
Wolverhampton	9	Ki	52.36N	2.08W
Wolverton	9	Mi	52.04N	0.50W
Wŏnju	27	Md	37.21N	127.58 E
Wŏnsan	22	Of	39.10N	127.26 E
Wonseradeel	12	Ha	53.06N	5.28 E
Wonseradeel-Witmarsum	12	Ha	53.06N	5.28 E
Wonthaggi	59	Jg	38.36S	145.35 E
Woodall Mountain	45	Li	34.45N	88.11W
Woodbridge	9	Oi	52.06N	1.19 E
Woodbridge Bay	51g	Bb	15.19N	61.25W
Woodhall Spa	12	Ba	53.09N	0.13W
Woodland [Ca.-U.S.]	46	Eg	38.41N	121.46W
Woodland [Wa.-U.S.]	46	Dd	45.54N	122.45W
Woodlark Island	57	Ge	9.05S	152.50 E
Wood Mountain	46	Lb	49.14N	106.20W
Woodridge	45	Hb	49.17N	96.09W
Wood River	46	Lb	50.08N	106.10W
Wood River Lakes	40	He	59.30N	158.45W
Woodroffe, Mount-	59	Ge	26.20S	131.45 E
Woods, Lake-	59	Gc	17.50S	133.30 E
Woods, Lake of the-	38	Je	49.15N	94.45W
Woods Hole	44	Le	41.31N	70.40W
Woodside	46	Jg	39.21N	110.18W
Woodstock [Eng.-U.K.]	9	Lj	51.52N	1.21W
Woodstock [N.B.-Can.]	42	Kg	46.09N	67.34W
Woodstock [Ont.-Can.]	44	Gd	43.08N	80.45W
Woodstock [Vt.-U.S.]	44	Kd	43.37N	72.31W
Woodville [Ms.-U.S.]	45	Kk	31.01N	91.18W
Woodville [N.Z.]	62	Fd	40.20S	175.52 E
Woodville [Tx.-U.S.]	45	Ik	30.46N	94.25W
Woodward	43	Hd	36.26N	99.24W
Wooler	9	Kf	55.33N	2.01W
Woomera	59	Hf	31.11S	137.10 E
Wooramel River	59	Ce	25.47S	114.10 E
Wooster	44	Ge	40.46N	81.57W
Worcester	9	Ki	52.15N	2.10W
Worcester [Eng.-U.K.]	9	Ki	52.11N	2.13W
Worcester [Ma.-U.S.]	43	Mc	42.16N	71.48W
Worcester [S.Afr.]	31	Il	33.39S	19.27 E
Worcester Range	66	Jf	78.50S	161.00 E
Wörgl	14	Gc	47.29N	12.04 E
Workai, Pulau-	26	Jh	6.40S	134.40 E
Workington	9	Jg	54.39N	3.33W
Worksop	9	Lh	53.18N	1.07W
Workum	12	Hb	52.59N	5.27 E
Worland	43	Fc	44.01N	107.57W
Wormer	12	Gb	52.30N	4.52 E
Wormhout	12	Ed	50.53N	2.28 E
Worms	10	Eg	49.38N	8.21 E
Worms Head	9	Ij	51.34N	4.20W
Wörrstadt	12	Ke	49.50N	8.06 E
Wörth am Rhein	12	Ke	49.03N	8.16 E
Wörther-See	14	Id	46.37N	14.10 E
Worthing	9	Mk	50.48N	0.23W
Worthington	43	Hc	43.37N	95.36W
Wosi	26	Ig	0.11S	127.58 E
Wotho Atoll	57	Hc	10.06N	165.59 E
Wotje Atoll	57	Id	9.27N	170.02 E
Woudenberg	12	Hb	52.05N	5.25 E
Wounnioné, Pointe-	63b	Db	14.54S	168.02 E
Wounta, Laguna de-	49	Fg	13.38N	83.34W
Wour	35	Ba	21.21N	15.57 E
Wousi	63b	Cb	15.22S	166.39 E
Wowoni, Pulau-	26	Hg	4.08S	123.06 E
Woy Woy	59	Kf	33.30S	151.20 E
Wrangel, Ostrov-=Wrangel Island (EN)	21	Tb	71.00N	179.30 E
Wrangel Island (EN)= Wrangel, Ostrov-	21	Tb	71.00N	179.30 E
Wrangell	39	Fd	56.28N	132.23W
Wrangell, Cape-	40a	Ab	52.50N	172.26 E
Wrangell Mountains	38	Ec	62.00N	143.00W
Wrath, Cape-	5	Fd	58.37N	5.01W
Wray	43	Gc	40.05N	102.13W
Wreake	12	Ab	52.41N	1.05W
Wreck Reef	57	Gg	22.15S	155.10 E
Wrecks, Bay of-	64g	Bb	1.52N	157.17W
Wrexham	9	Kh	53.03N	3.00W
Wright Island	66	Of	74.03S	116.45W
Wright Patman Lake	45	Ij	33.16N	94.14W
Wrightson, Mount-	46	Jk	31.42N	110.50W
Wrigley	42	Fd	63.19N	123.38W
Wrigley Gulf	66	Nf	74.00S	129.00W
Wrocław [2]	10	Me	51.05N	17.00 E
Wrocław=Breslau (EN)	6	He	51.06N	17.00 E
Wronki	10	Md	52.43N	16.23 E
Wrotham	12	Cc	51.18N	0.19 E
Wroxham	12	Db	52.42N	1.24 E
Września	10	Nd	52.20N	17.34 E
Wschowa	10	Me	51.48N	16.19 E
Wu'an	28	Cf	36.42N	114.12 E
Wuchale	35	Fc	11.31N	39.37 E
Wuchang	28	Ib	44.55N	127.11 E
Wuchang, Wuhan-	28	Ci	30.32N	114.18 E
Wucheng (Jiucheng)	28	Df	37.12N	116.04 E
Wuchiu Hsu	27	Kg	25.00N	119.27 E
Wuchuan	28	Ad	41.08N	111.25 E
Wuchuan (Duru)	27	If	28.28N	107.57 E
Wuchuan (Meilü)	27	Jg	21.28N	110.44 E
Wuda	27	Id	39.30N	106.33 E
Wudan → Ongniud Qi	27	Kc	42.58N	119.01 E
Wudao	27	Ld	39.28N	121.30 E
Wudaoliang	27	Fd	35.15N	93.14 E
Wudi	28	Df	37.44N	117.36 E
Wudil	34	Gc	11.49N	8.51 E
Wuding	27	Hf	25.36N	102.27 E
Wudu	27	He	33.24N	105.00 E
Wugang	27	Jf	26.48N	110.32 E
Wugong (Puji)	27	Ie	34.15N	108.14 E
Wuhai	27	Id	39.32N	106.55 E
Wuhan	22	Nf	30.30N	114.20 E
Wuhan-Hankou	28	Ci	30.35N	114.16 E
Wuhan-Hanyang	28	Ci	30.33N	114.16 E
Wuhan- Wuchang	28	Ci	30.32N	114.18 E
Wuhe	27	Ke	33.08N	117.51 E
Wuhu	22	Nf	31.18N	118.27 E
Wuhu (Wanzhi)	28	Ei	31.21N	118.23 E
Wujia He	27	Ic	40.56N	108.52 E
Wu Jiang	21	Mg	29.43N	107.24 E
Wujiang	28	Fi	31.09N	120.38 E
Wukari	31	Hh	7.51N	9.47 E
Wukro	35	Fc	13.48N	39.37 E
Wular	25	Eb	34.30N	74.30 E
Wulff Land	41	Hb	82.19N	50.00W
Wulian (Hongning)	28	Eg	35.45N	119.13 E
Wuliang Shan	27	Hg	24.00N	101.00 E
Wuliaru, Pulau-	26	Jh	7.27S	131.04 E
Wuling Shan	21	Mg	28.20N	110.00 E
Wulongbei	28	Hd	40.15N	124.16 E
Wulongji → Huaibin	28	Ci	32.27N	115.23 E
Wulur	26	Ih	7.09S	128.39 E
Wum	34	Hd	6.23N	10.04 E
Wumei Shan	28	Cj	28.47N	114.50 E
Wümme	12	Ka	53.10N	8.40 E
Wuning	28	Cj	29.17N	115.05 E
Wünnenberg	12	Kc	51.31N	8.42 E
Wünnenberg-Haaren	12	Kc	51.34N	8.44 E
Wunnummin Lake	42	If	52.55N	89.10W
Wun Rog	35	Dd	9.00N	28.21 E
Wunstrof	10	Fd	52.26N	9.25 E
Wuntho	25	Jd	23.54N	95.41 E
Wupper	10	Ce	51.05N	7.00 E
Wuppertal	10	De	51.16N	7.11 E
Wuqi	27	Id	36.57N	108.15 E
Wuqia/Ulugqat	27	Cd	39.40N	75.07 E
Wuqiao (Sangyuan)	28	Df	37.38N	116.23 E
Wuqing (Yangcun)	28	De	39.23N	117.04 E
Würm	12	Kf	48.53N	8.42 E
Wurno	34	Gc	13.18N	5.26 E
Würselen	12	Id	50.49N	6.08 E
Würzburg	6	Gf	49.48N	9.56 E
Wurzen	10	Ie	51.22N	12.44 E
Wu Shan	27	Ie	31.00N	110.00 E
Wushaoling	27	Hd	37.15N	102.50 E
Wuski/Uqturpan	27	Cc	41.10N	79.16 E
Wusong	28	Fi	31.23N	121.29 E
Wüst Seamount (EN)	30	Gl	34.00S	3.40W
Wusuli Jiang	27	Ob	48.28N	135.02 E
Wutach	10	Ei	47.37N	8.15 E
Wutai [China]	28	Be	38.43N	113.14 E
Wutai [China]	27	Dc	44.38N	82.06 E
Wutai Shan	27	Jd	39.04N	113.28 E
Wuustwezel	12	Gc	51.23N	4.36 E
Wuvulu Island	57	Fe	1.43S	142.50 E
Wuwei	28	Di	31.17N	117.54 E
Wuwei (Liangzhou)	22	Mf	37.58N	102.48 E
Wuxi [China]	22	Of	31.32N	120.18 E
Wuxi [China]	27	Ie	31.27N	109.34 E
Wu Xia	27	Je	31.02N	110.10 E
Wuxiang (Duancun)	28	Bf	36.50N	112.51 E
Wuxing (Huzhou)	27	Le	30.47N	120.07 E
Wuxue → Guangji	27	Kf	29.58N	115.32 E
Wuyang [China]	28	Bh	33.26N	113.35 E
Wuyang [China]	27	Jd	36.29N	113.07 E
Wuyang → Zhenyuan	27	If	27.05N	108.26 E
Wuyi [China]	28	Cf	37.49N	115.54 E
Wuyi [China]	28	Ej	28.54N	119.50 E
Wuyiling	27	Mb	48.37N	129.20 E
Wuyi Shan	21	Ng	27.00N	117.00 E
Wuyuan [China]	22	Me	41.08N	108.17 E
Wuyuan [China]	28	Dj	29.15N	117.52 E
Wuyuanzhen → Haiyan	28	Fi	30.31N	120.56 E
Wuzhai	28	Ae	38.54N	111.49 E
Wuzhen	28	Ai	31.42N	112.00 E
Wuzhi Shan [China]	28	Ed	40.31N	118.02 E
Wuzhi Shan [China]	27	Ih	18.54N	109.40 E
Wuzhong	27	Id	38.00N	106.10 E
Wuzhou	22	Ng	23.32N	111.21 E
Wyalkatchem	59	Df	31.10S	117.22 E
Wyandotte	44	Fd	42.12N	83.10W
Wyandra	59	Je	27.15S	145.59 E
Wye	9	Kj	51.37N	2.39W
Wye	12	Cc	51.11N	0.56 E
Wyemandoo, Mount-	59	De	28.31S	118.32 E
Wyk auf Föhr	10	Eb	54.42N	8.34 E
Wylie, Lake-	44	Gh	35.07N	81.02W
Wymondham	9	Oi	52.34N	1.07 E
Wyndham [Austl.]	58	Df	15.28S	128.06 E
Wyndham [N.Z.]	62	Cg	46.20S	168.51 E
Wyndmere	45	Hc	46.16N	97.08W
Wynne	45	Ki	35.14N	90.47W
Wynniatt Bay	42	Gb	72.50N	111.00W
Wynyard [Austl.]	59	Jh	40.59S	145.41 E
Wynyard [Sask.-Can.]	42	Hf	51.47N	104.10W
Wyoming	44	Ed	42.54N	85.42W
Wyoming [2]	43	Fc	43.00N	107.30W
Wyoming Peak	43	Ec	42.36N	110.37W
Wyśmierzyce	10	Qe	51.38N	20.49 E
Wysoka	10	Nc	53.11N	17.05 E
Wysokie Mazowieckie	10	Sd	52.56N	22.32 E
Wyszków	10	Rd	52.36N	21.28 E
Wyszogród	10	Qd	52.23N	20.11 E
Wytheville	44	Gg	36.57N	81.07W
Wyville Thomson Ridge (EN)	9	Fa	60.10N	8.00W
Wyvis, Ben-	9	Id	57.42N	4.30W
X				
Xaintrie	11	Ii	45.00N	2.10 E
Xainza	27	Ee	30.50N	88.37 E
Xaitongmoin	27	Ef	29.26N	88.08 E
Xai-Xai	31	Kk	25.04S	33.39 E
Xamba → Hanggin Houqi	27	Ic	40.59N	107.07 E
Xam Nua	25	Kd	20.25N	104.02 E
Xangongo	31	Ij	16.46S	14.59 E
Xang Qu	27	Ef	29.22N	89.09 E
Xanten	10	Ce	51.40N	6.27 E
Xánthi	15	Hh	41.08N	24.53 E
Xanthos	24	Cd	36.20N	29.20 E
Xanxerê	56	Jc	26.53S	52.23W
Xapuri	54	Ef	10.39S	68.31W
Xar Hudag	27	Jb	45.06N	114.30 E
Xar Moron	28	Ac	42.37N	111.02 E
Xar Moron He	27	Lc	43.24N	120.39 E
Xarrama	13	Df	38.14N	8.20W
Xàtiva/Játiva	13	Lf	38.59N	0.31W
Xau, Lake-	37	Cd	21.15S	24.44 E
Xavantes, Represa de-	55	Hf	23.20S	49.35W
Xavantina	55	Fe	21.15S	52.48W
Xayar	27	Dc	41.15N	82.50 E
Xebert	28	Fc	44.00N	122.00 E
Xêgar → Tingri	27	Ef	28.41N	87.00 E
Xenia	44	Ff	39.41N	83.56W
Xiabin Ansha	27	Ke	9.48N	116.38 E
Xiachengzi	28	Kb	44.41N	130.26 E
Xiacun → Rushan	28	Ff	36.55N	121.30 E
Xiaguan	27	Hf	25.32N	100.12 E
Xiahe (Labrang)	27	Hd	35.18N	102.30 E
Xiajin	28	Cf	36.57N	116.00 E
Xiamen	22	Ng	24.32N	118.06 E
Xi'an	22	Mf	34.15N	108.50 E
Xianfeng	27	If	29.41N	109.09 E
Xiangcheng	28	Bh	33.51N	113.29 E
Xiangcheng/Qagchêng	27	Gf	28.56N	99.46 E
Xiangcheng (Shuizhai)	28	Ch	33.27N	114.53 E
Xiangfan	22	Nf	32.03N	112.05 E
Xianggang/Hong Kong [5]	22	Ng	22.15N	114.10 E
Xianghua Ling	27	Jf	25.26N	112.32 E
Xianghuang Qi (Xin Bulag)	27	Jc	42.12N	113.59 E
Xiang Jang	21	Ng	29.26N	113.08 E
Xiangkhoang	25	Ke	19.20N	103.22 E
Xiangkhoang, Plateau de-	25	Ke	19.30N	103.10 E
Xiangquan He	27	Ce	32.05N	79.20 E
Xiangshan (Dancheng)	27	Lf	29.29N	121.52 E
Xiangshan Gang	28	Fj	29.35N	121.38 E
Xiangtan	22	Ng	27.54N	112.55 E
Xiangtang	28	Cj	28.26N	115.59 E
Xiangyin	28	Bj	28.41N	112.53 E
Xiangyuan	28	Bf	36.32N	113.02 E
Xianju	27	Lf	28.50N	120.42 E
Xianning	28	Cj	29.52N	114.17 E
Xiannümiao → Jiangdu	28	Eh	32.30N	119.33 E
Xiantaozhen → Mianyang	28	Bi	30.22N	113.27 E
Xianxia Ling	27	Kf	28.24N	118.40 E
Xianxian	28	De	38.12N	116.07 E
Xianyang	27	Ie	34.26N	108.40 E
Xiaobole Shan	27	La	51.46N	124.09 E
Xiao'ergou	27	Lb	49.10N	123.43 E
Xiaogan	27	Je	30.52N	113.58 E
Xiao He	28	Bf	37.38N	112.24 E
Xiao Hinggan Ling=Lesser Khingan Range (EN)	21	Oe	48.45N	127.00 E
Xiaoling He	28	Fd	40.55N	121.12 E
Xiaoluan He	28	Dd	41.36N	117.05 E
Xiaoqing He	28	Ef	37.19N	118.59 E
Xiaowutai Shan	28	Ce	39.57N	114.59 E
Xiaoxian	28	Dg	34.11N	116.56 E
Xiaoyi	28	Af	37.07N	111.48 E
Xiaoyi → Gongxian	28	Bg	34.46N	112.57 E
Xiapu	27	Kf	26.57N	119.59 E
Xiawa	28	Fc	42.36N	120.33 E
Xiayi	28	Dg	34.14N	116.07 E
Xiazhuang → Linshu	28	Eg	34.56N	118.38 E
Xicalango, Punta-	48	Nh	19.41N	92.00W
Xichang	22	Mg	27.52N	102.15 E
Xicheng → Yangyuan	28	Cd	40.08N	114.10 E
Xicoténcatl	48	Jf	23.00N	98.56W
Xicotepec de Juárez	48	Kg	20.17N	97.57W
Xiejiaji → Qingyun	28	Df	37.46N	117.22 E
Xifei He	28	Dh	32.38N	116.39 E
Xifeng	28	Hc	42.45N	124.44 E
Xifengzhen	27	Id	35.40N	107.42 E
Xigazê	22	Kg	29.15N	88.52 E
Xi He [China]	27	Hc	42.23N	101.03 E
Xi He [China]	28	Dj	29.38N	116.53 E
Xiheying	28	Ce	39.53N	114.42 E
Xihua	28	Ch	33.48N	114.31 E
Xi Jang	21	Ng	23.05N	114.23 E
Xiji [China]	27	Id	35.52N	105.35 E
Xiji [China]	28	Ia	46.09N	127.08 E
Xi Jiang	27	Jg	23.05N	114.23 E
Xijir Ulan Hu	27	Fd	35.12N	90.18 E
Xikouzi	27	La	42.58N	120.29 E
Xiligou → Ulan	27	Gd	36.55N	98.16 E
Xilin	27	Ig	24.30N	105.05 E
Xilin Gol	28	Dc	43.55N	116.05 E
Xilin Hot → Abagnar Qi	22	Ne	43.58N	116.08 E
Xilitla	48	Jg	21.20N	98.58W
Xilókastron	15	Fk	38.05N	22.38 E
Ximiao	27	Hc	41.04N	100.14 E
Xin'an	28	Bg	34.43N	112.09 E
Xin'anjiang	28	Ei	29.27N	119.15 E
Xin'anjiang Shuiku	27	Kf	29.25N	119.05 E
Xin'anzhen → Guannan	28	Eg	34.04N	119.21 E
Xin'anzhen → Xinyi	27	Ke	34.17N	118.14 E
Xin Barag Youqi (Altan-Emel)	27	Kb	48.41N	116.47 E
Xin Barag Zuoqi (Amgalang)	27	Kb	48.13N	118.14 E
Xinbin	28	Hd	41.44N	125.02 E
Xin Bulag → Xianghuang Qi	27	Jc	42.12N	113.59 E
Xincai	27	Je	32.40N	114.57 E
Xinchang	28	Fj	29.30N	120.54 E
Xincheng [China]	28	Bf	37.57N	112.33 E
Xincheng [China]	27	Ig	24.04N	108.39 E
Xincheng [China]	27	Id	38.33N	106.10 E
Xincheng (Gaobeidian)	28	Ce	39.20N	115.50 E
Xindi → Honghu	28	Bj	29.50N	113.28 E
Xing'an → Ankang	22	Mf	32.37N	109.03 E
Xingcheng	28	Fd	40.38N	120.43 E
Xingguo	27	Kf	26.22N	115.21 E
Xinghai	27	Gd	35.45N	99.59 E
Xinghe	27	Jc	40.52N	113.56 E
Xinghua	28	Eh	32.56N	119.49 E
Xingkai Hu=Khanka Lake (EN)	21	Pe	45.00N	132.24 E
Xinglong	28	Dd	40.25N	117.31 E
Xinglongzhen	28	Ia	46.26N	127.03 E
Xingren	27	If	25.26N	105.08 E
Xingtai	22	Nf	37.00N	114.30 E
Xingtang	28	Ce	38.26N	114.33 E
Xingu, Rio-	52	Kf	1.30S	51.53W
Xingxingxia	27	Gc	41.47N	95.07 E
Xingyang	28	Bg	34.47N	113.21 E
Xinryi (Huangcaoba)	27	Hf	25.03N	104.55 E
Xingzi	28	Dj	29.28N	116.03 E
Xinhe	28	Cf	37.32N	115.14 E
Xinhe/Toksu	27	Dc	41.34N	82.38 E
Xin Hot → Abag Qi	27	Jc	44.01N	114.59 E
Xinhuai He	28	Fg	34.23N	120.05 E
Xinhui → Aohan Qi	28	Ec	42.18N	119.53 E
Xining	22	Mf	36.37N	101.46 E
Xinji → Shulu	28	Cf	37.56N	115.14 E
Xinjian	28	Cj	28.41N	115.50 E
Xin Jiang	28	Dj	28.37N	116.40 E
Xinjiangkou → Songzi	28	Ai	30.10N	116.46 E
Xinjiang Uygur Zizhiqu (Hsin-chiang-wei-wu-erh Tzu-chih-ch'ü)=Sinkiang (EN) [2]	27	Ec	42.00N	86.00 E
Xinjin	27	He	30.25N	103.46 E
Xinjin (Pulandian)	27	Ld	39.24N	121.59 E
Xinkai He	28	Gc	43.36N	122.31 E
Xinle	28	Ce	38.15N	114.40 E
Xinlin	28	Ec	43.58N	118.03 E
Xinlitun [China]	27	Ma	50.58N	126.39 E
Xinlitun [China]	28	Gc	42.01N	122.11 E
Xinlong/Nyagrong	27	He	30.57N	100.12 E
Xinmin	28	Gc	42.00N	122.50 E
Xinpu → Lianyungang	22	Nf	34.34N	119.15 E
Xinqing	27	Mb	48.15N	129.31 E
Xintai	28	Dg	35.54N	117.44 E
Xinwen (Suncun)	27	Kd	35.49N	117.38 E
Xinxian [China]	27	Jd	38.24N	112.43 E
Xinxian [China]	28	Ci	31.42N	114.50 E
Xinxiang	22	Nf	35.17N	113.50 E
Xinyang	27	Je	32.05N	114.07 E
Xinye	28	Bh	32.30N	112.22 E
Xinyi (Xin'anzhen)	27	Ke	34.17N	118.14 E
Xinyi He	28	Eg	34.29N	119.49 E
Xinyuan/Künes	27	Dc	43.24N	83.18 E
Xinyuan → Tianjun	22	Lf	37.18N	99.15 E
Xinzhan	28	Ic	43.52N	127.20 E
Xin Zhen → Hanggin Qi	27	Id	39.54N	108.55 E
Xinzheng	28	Bg	34.25N	113.46 E
Xinzhou	28	Ci	30.51N	114.49 E
Xioashan	28	Fi	30.10N	120.16 E
Xiong Xian	28	De	38.59N	116.06 E
Xionyuecheng	28	Gd	40.12N	122.08 E
Xiping [China]	28	Ej	28.27N	119.29 E
Xiping [China]	28	Bh	33.22N	114.00 E
Xisha Qundao=Paracel Islands (EN)	21	Nh	16.30N	112.15 E
Xishuangbanna	27	Gg	22.15N	100.00 E
Xishuanghe → Kenli	28	Ef	37.35N	118.30 E
Xishui	28	Ci	30.28N	115.15 E
Xitianmu Shan	27	Ke	30.21N	119.25 E
Xiuanzi → Chongli	28	Cd	40.57N	115.12 E
Xi Ujimqin Qi (Bayan Ul Hot)	27	Kc	44.31N	117.33 E
Xiuning	28	Ej	29.47N	118.11 E
Xiushan	27	If	28.29N	108.58 E
Xiu Shui	28	Cj	29.13N	116.00 E
Xiushui	27	Jf	29.02N	114.33 E
Xiuwu	28	Bg	35.13N	113.27 E
Xiuyan	27	Lc	40.18N	123.10 E
Xiwanzi → Chongli	28	Cf	36.50N	115.10 E
Xixabangma Feng	27	Ef	28.21N	85.47 E
Xixian	28	Ch	32.21N	114.43 E
Xixiang	27	Ie	32.58N	107.45 E
Xiyang	28	Bf	37.38N	113.41 E
Xizang Zizhiqu (Hsi-tsang Tzu-chih-ch'ü)=Tibet (EN) [2]	27	Ee	32.00N	90.00 E
Xizhong Dao	28	Fe	39.25N	121.18 E
Xi Taijnar Hu	27	Fd	37.15N	93.30 E
Xochicalco	48	Jh	18.45N	99.20W
Xochimilco	48	Jh	19.16N	99.06W
Xorkol	27	Fd	39.04N	91.05 E
Xpujil	48	Oh	18.35N	89.25W
Xuancheng	28	Ei	30.56N	118.44 E
Xuande Qundao	26	Fc	17.08N	111.30 E
Xuan'en	27	Ie	30.02N	109.30 E
Xuanhan	27	Ie	31.23N	107.39 E
Xuanhua	27	Kc	40.39N	115.05 E
Xuanwei	27	Hf	26.19N	104.05 E
Xuchang	22	Nf	34.00N	113.58 E
Xuecheng (Lincheng)	28	Dg	34.38N	117.14 E
Xuefeng Shan	27	Jf	27.35N	110.50 E
Xue Shan	27	Gf	27.30N	99.55 E
Xugezhuang → Fengnan	28	Ee	39.34N	118.05 E
Xugou	28	Eg	34.37N	119.08 E
Xugui	27	Gd	35.45N	96.08 E
Xuguit Qi (Yakeshi)	27	Lb	49.16N	120.41 E
Xümatang	27	Ge	33.57N	97.00 E
Xun Jiang	23	Hf	23.28N	111.18 E
Xunke (Qike)	27	Mb	49.34N	128.28 E
Xunwu	27	Kg	24.59N	115.33 E
Xunxian	28	Cg	35.40N	114.33 E
Xupu	27	Jf	27.54N	110.35 E
Xúquer/Júcar	5	Fh	39.09N	0.14W
Xushui	28	Ce	39.02N	115.40 E
Xuwen	27	Jg	20.22N	110.10 E
Xuyi	27	Ke	32.58N	118.33 E
Xuyong (Yongning)	27	If	28.13N	105.26 E
Xuzhou	22	Nf	34.12N	117.13 E
Y				
Ya'an	22	Mg	30.00N	102.57 E
Yabassi	34	Ge	4.28N	9.58 E
Yabe	29	Be	32.42N	130.59 E
Yabebyry	55	Dh	27.24S	57.11W
Yabelo	35	Fe	4.53N	38.07 E
Yablonovy Range (EN)= Jablonovy Hrebet	21	Nd	53.30N	115.00 E
Yabrai Shan	27	Hc	40.00N	103.10 E
Yabrīn	35	Ha	23.15N	48.59 E
Yabrūd	24	Gf	33.58N	36.40 E
Yabucoa	51a	Cb	18.03N	65.53W
Yabuli	27	Mc	44.56N	128.37 E
Yabulu	59	Jc	19.00S	146.40 E
Yacaré Cururú, Cuchilla-	55	Dj	30.30S	56.33W
Yacaré Norte, Riacho-	55	Cf	22.43S	58.14W
Yacaré Sur, Riacho-	55	Cf	22.43S	58.14W
Yachats	46	Cd	44.20N	124.03W
Yacuma, Río-	54	Ef	13.38S	65.23W
Yacyretá, Isla-	55	Dh	27.25S	56.30W
Yadé, Massif du-	35	Bd	7.00N	15.30 E
Yādgīr	25	Fe	16.46N	77.08 E
Yadong/Chomo	27	Ef	27.38N	89.03 E
Yae-Dake	29b	Ab	26.38N	127.56 E
Yaeyama-Rettō	27	Lg	24.20N	124.00 E
Yafran	33	Bc	32.04N	12.31 E
Yağcilar	15	Lj	39.25N	28.23 E
Yagishiri-Tō	29a	Ba	44.26N	141.25 E
Yagoua	34	Ic	10.20N	15.14 E
Yagradagzê Shan	27	Gd	35.09N	95.39 E
Yaguajay	49	Hb	22.19N	79.14W
Yaguarí	55	Ej	31.31S	54.58W
Yaguari, Arroyo-	55	Di	29.44S	57.37W
Yahalica de Gonzáles Gallo	48	Hg	21.08N	102.51W
Yahuma	36	Db	1.06N	23.10 E
Yaita	29	Fc	36.50N	139.55 E
Yaizu	29	Fd	34.51N	138.19 E
Yajiang/Nyagquka	27	He	30.07N	100.58 E
Yakacik	24	Ed	36.05N	32.45 E
Yake-Dake	29	Ec	36.14N	137.35 E
Yakeishi-Dake	29	Gb	39.10N	140.50 E
Yakeshi → Xuguit Qi	27	Lb	49.16N	120.41 E
Yake-Yama	29	Gb	39.58N	140.48 E
Yakima	39	Ge	46.36N	120.31W
Yakima River	46	Fc	46.15N	119.02W
Yako	34	Ec	12.58N	2.16W
Yakumo	27	Pc	42.15N	140.16 E
Yaku-Shima	27	Ne	30.20N	130.30 E
Yakutat	40	Le	59.33N	139.44W
Yakutat Bay	40	Ke	59.45N	140.45W
Yala	25	Kg	6.32N	101.19 E
Yalahán, Laguna de-	48	Pg	21.30N	87.15W
Yalcubul, Punta-	48	Og	21.35N	88.35W
Yale Point	46	Kh	36.25N	109.48W
Yalewa Kalou	63d	Ab	16.40S	177.46 E
Yalgoo	59	De	28.20S	116.41 E
Yalikavak	15	Kl	37.06N	27.18 E
Yaliköy	15	Lh	41.29N	28.17 E
Yalinga	35	Cd	6.31N	23.13 E
Yaloké	35	Bd	5.19N	17.05 E
Yalong Jiang	21	Mg	26.37N	101.48 E
Yalova	24	Cb	40.39N	29.15 E
Yalu Jiang	21	Of	39.55N	124.20 E
Yalvaç	24	Dc	38.17N	31.11 E
Yām, Ramlat-	33	If	17.42N	45.09 E
Yamada [Jap.]	28	Pe	39.28N	141.57 E
Yamada [Jap.]	29	Be	33.33N	130.45 E
Yamada-Wan	29	Hb	39.30N	142.00 E
Yamaga	29	Be	33.01N	130.41 E
Yamagata	27	Pd	38.15N	140.15 E
Yamagata Ken [2]	28	Pe	38.30N	140.00 E
Yamagawa	29	Bf	31.12N	130.39 E
Yamaguchi	27	Ne	34.10N	131.29 E
Yamaguchi Ken [2]	28	Kh	34.10N	131.30 E
Yamakuni	29	Be	33.24N	131.02 E
Yamal Peninsula (EN)= Jamal, Poluostrov-	21	Ib	70.00N	70.00 E
Yamamoto	29	Ga	40.06N	140.03 E
Yamanaka	29	Ec	36.15N	136.22 E
Yamanashi Ken [2]	28	Og	35.30N	138.45 E
Yamashiro	29	Ce	33.57N	133.43 E
Yamato Rise (EN)	28	Me	39.30N	134.30 E
Yamatsuri	29	Gc	36.53N	140.25 E
Yamazaki	29	Dd	35.00N	134.33 E
Yambi, Mesa de-	54	Dc	1.30N	71.20W
Yambio	31	Jh	4.34N	28.23 E
Yambo	35	Fd	8.25N	36.00 E
Yambu Head	51n	Ba	13.09N	61.09W
Yambuya	36	Db	1.16N	24.33 E
Yame	29	Be	33.13N	130.34 E
Yamethin	25	Jd	20.26N	96.09 E
Yamma Yamma, Lake-	59	Ie	26.20S	141.25 E
Yamoto	29	Gb	38.25N	141.13 E
Yamoussoukro	34	Dd	6.49N	5.17W
Yampa River	43	Fc	40.32N	108.59W
Yampi Sound	59	Ec	16.11S	123.40 E
Yamuna	21	Kg	25.30N	81.53 E
Yamunanagar	25	Fb	30.08N	76.59 E
Yamzho Yumco	27	Ff	29.00N	90.40 E
Yanagawa	29	Be	33.10N	130.24 E
Yanahara	29	Dd	34.57N	134.05 E
Yanahuanca	54	Cf	10.30S	76.30W
Yanai	29	Ce	33.58N	132.07 E
Yanam	25	Ge	16.51N	82.15 E
Yan'an	22	Mf	36.36N	109.30 E
Yanaoca	54	Df	14.13S	71.26W
Yanbian	27	Hf	26.51N	101.32 E
Yanbu'	23	Ee	24.05N	38.03 E
Yanchang	27	Jd	36.39N	110.03 E
Yancheng [China]	28	Bh	33.35N	114.00 E
Yancheng [China]	27	Le	33.16N	120.10 E
Yanchi	27	Id	37.47N	107.24 E
Yandé	63b	Ae	20.03S	163.48 E
Yandina	63a	Dc	9.07S	159.13 E
Yandja	36	Cc	1.41S	17.43 E

Index Symbols

[1] Independent Nation	Historical or Cultural Region	Pass, Gap	Depression	Coast, Beach	Rock, Reef	Waterfall Rapids	Canal	Lagoon	Escarpment, Sea Scarp	Historic Site	Port
[2] State, Region	Mount, Mountain	Plain, Lowland	Polder	Cliff	Islands, Archipelago	River Mouth, Estuary	Glacier	Bank	Fracture	Ruins	Lighthouse
[3] District, County	Volcano	Delta	Desert, Dunes	Peninsula	Rocks, Reefs	Lake	Ice Shelf, Pack Ice	Seamount	Trench, Abyss	Wall, Walls	Mine
[4] Municipality	Hill	Salt Flat	Forest, Woods	Isthmus	Coral Reef	Salt Lake	Ocean	Tablemount	National Park, Reserve	Church, Abbey	Tunnel
[5] Colony, Dependency	Mountains, Mountain Range	Valley, Canyon	Heath, Steppe	Sandbank	Well, Spring	Intermittent Lake	Sea	Ridge	Point of Interest	Temple	Dam, Bridge
Continent	Hills, Escarpment	Crater, Cave	Oasis	Island	Geyser	Reservoir	Gulf, Bay	Shelf	Recreation Site	Scientific Station	
Physical Region	Plateau, Upland	Karst Features	Cape, Point	Atoll	River, Stream	Swamp, Pond	Strait, Fjord	Basin	Cave, Cavern	Airport	

Index Symbols

- [1] Independent Nation
- [2] State, Region
- [3] District, County
- [4] Municipality
- [5] Colony, Dependency
- Continent
- Physical Region
- Historical or Cultural Region
- Mount, Mountain
- Volcano
- Hill
- Mountains, Mountain Range
- Hills, Escarpment
- Plateau, Upland
- Pass, Gap
- Plain, Lowland
- Delta
- Salt Flat
- Valley, Canyon
- Crater, Cave
- Karst Features
- Depression
- Polder
- Desert, Dunes
- Forest, Woods
- Heath, Steppe
- Oasis
- Cape, Point
- Coast, Beach
- Cliff
- Peninsula
- Isthmus
- Sandbank
- Island
- Atoll
- Rock, Reef
- Islands, Archipelago
- Rocks, Reefs
- Coral Reef
- Well, Spring
- Geyser
- River, Stream
- Waterfall Rapids
- River Mouth, Estuary
- Lake
- Salt Lake
- Intermittent Lake
- Reservoir
- Swamp, Pond
- Canal
- Glacier
- Ice Shelf, Pack Ice
- Ocean
- Sea
- Gulf, Bay
- Strait, Fjord
- Lagoon
- Bank
- Seamount
- Tablemount
- Ridge
- Shelf
- Basin
- Escarpment, Sea Scarp
- Fracture
- Trench, Abyss
- National Park, Reserve
- Point of Interest
- Recreation Site
- Cave, Cavern
- Historic Site
- Ruins
- Wall, Walls
- Church, Abbey
- Temple
- Scientific Station
- Airport
- Port
- Lighthouse
- Mine
- Tunnel
- Dam, Bridge

Index Symbols

[1] Independent Nation
[2] State, Region
[3] District, County
[4] Municipality
[5] Colony, Dependency
Continent
Physical Region
Historical or Cultural Region
Mount, Mountain
Volcano
Hill
Mountains, Mountain Range
Hills, Escarpment
Plateau, Upland
Pass, Gap
Plain, Lowland
Delta
Salt Flat
Valley, Canyon
Crater, Cave
Karst Features
Depression
Polder
Desert, Dunes
Forest, Woods
Heath, Steppe
Oasis
Cape, Point
Coast, Beach
Cliff
Peninsula
Isthmus
Sandbank
Island
Atoll
Rock, Reef
Islands, Archipelago
Rocks, Reefs
Coral Reef
Well, Spring
Geyser
River, Stream
Waterfall Rapids
River Mouth, Estuary
Lake
Salt Lake
Intermittent Lake
Reservoir
Swamp, Pond
Canal
Glacier
Ice Shelf, Pack Ice
Ocean
Sea
Gulf, Bay
Strait, Fjord
Lagoon
Bank
Seamount
Tablemount
Ridge
Shelf
Basin
Escarpment, Sea Scarp
Fracture
Trench, Abyss
National Park, Reserve
Point of Interest
Recreation Site
Cave, Cavern
Historic Site
Ruins
Wall, Walls
Church, Abbey
Temple
Scientific Station
Airport
Port
Lighthouse
Mine
Tunnel
Dam, Bridge

Zimbor	15	Gc	47.00N	23.16 E
Zimi	34	Cd	7.19N	11.18W
Zimni Bereg	7	Jd	66.00N	40.45 E
Zimnicea	15	If	43.40N	25.22 E
Zimovniki	16	Mf	47.08N	42.29 E
Zina	34	Hc	11.16N	14.58 E
Zincirli	24	Gd	37.00N	36.41 E
Zinder	31	Hg	13.48N	8.59 E
Zinder [2]	34	Hb	15.00N	10.00 E
Zinga	35	Be	3.43N	18.35 E
Zingst	10	Ib	54.25N	12.50 E
Zinjibār	33	Ig	13.08N	45.23 E
Zinnik/Soignies	11	Kd	50.35N	4.04 E
Zinsel du Nord	12	Jf	48.49N	7.44 E
Zion [Il.-U.S.]	45	Me	42.27N	87.50W
Zion [St.C.N.]	51c	Ab	17.09N	62.32W
Zipaquirá	54	Db	5.02N	74.01W
Zirc	10	Ni	47.16N	17.52 E
Žirje	14	Jg	43.39N	15.40 E
Zirkel, Mount-	45	Cf	40.52N	106.36W
Žirnovsk	19	Ee	51.01N	44.48 E
Ziro	25	Ic	27.32N	93.32 E
Zi Shui	27	Jf	28.41N	112.43 E
Žitava	10	Oi	47.53N	18.11 E
Žitkoviči	16	Fc	52.16N	28.02 E
Zitkovo	7	Gf	60.42N	29.23 E
Žitomir	6	Ie	50.16N	28.40 E
Žitomirskaja Oblast [3]	19	Ce	50.40N	28.30 E
Zittau	10	Kf	50.54N	14.50 E
Zitterwald	12	Id	50.27N	6.25 E
Zitundo	37	Ee	26.44S	32.49 E
Živinice	14	Mf	44.27N	18.39 E
Ziwa Magharibi [3]	36	Fc	2.00S	31.30 E
Ziway, Lake-	35	Fd	8.00N	38.48 E
Ziyamet	24	Fe	35.22N	34.00 E
Ziyang	27	Ie	32.34N	108.37 E
Ziz	32	Gc	30.29N	4.26W
Žizdra	16	Ic	53.45N	34.43 E
Žizdra	16	Jb	54.14N	36.12 E
Zlatar	15	Cf	43.23N	19.51 E
Zlaté Moravce	10	Oh	48.23N	18.24 E
Zlatibor	15	Cf	43.40N	19.43 E
Zlatica	15	Hg	42.43N	24.08 E
Zlatica	15	Dd	45.49N	20.10 E
Zlatijata	15	Gf	43.40N	23.36 E
Zlatiški prohod	15	Hg	42.45N	24.05 E
Zlatna	15	Gc	46.07N	23.13 E
Zlatograd	15	Ih	41.23N	25.06 E
Zlatoust	6	Ld	55.10N	59.40 E
Zlatoustovsk	20	If	52.59N	133.41 E
Zletovo	15	Fh	41.59N	22.15 E
Zlīţan	33	Bc	32.28N	14.34 E
Žlobin	19	De	52.59N	30.03 E
Złocieniec	10	Mc	53.33N	16.01 E
Złoczew	10	Oe	51.25N	18.36 E
Zlot	15	Ee	44.01N	21.59 E
Złotoryja	10	Le	51.08N	15.55 E
Złotów	10	Nc	53.22N	17.02 E
Zły Komorow/Senftenberg	10	Ke	51.31N	14.01 E
Zlynka	16	Gc	52.27N	31.44 E
Zmeinogorsk	20	Df	51.10N	82.13 E
Žmerinka	19	Cf	49.02N	28.05 E
Żmigród	10	Me	51.29N	16.55 E
Zmijev	16	Je	49.41N	36.20 E
Zmijevka	16	Jc	52.40N	36.24 E
Zna	7	Ih	57.33N	34.25 E
Znamenka [R.S.F.S.R.]	16	Lc	52.24N	41.28 E
Znamenka [Ukr.-U.S.S.R.]	16	He	48.41N	32.40 E
Znamensk	8	Ij	54.39N	21.15 E
Znamenskoje	19	Hd	57.08N	73.55 E
Żnin	10	Nd	52.52N	17.43 E
Znojmo	10	Mh	48.51N	16.03 E
Zobia	36	Eb	2.53N	26.02 E
Zóbuè	37	Ec	15.36S	34.26 E
Žodino	16	Fb	54.07N	28.19 E
Žodiški	8	Lj	54.40N	26.33 E
Zoetermeer	12	Gb	52.04N	4.30 E
Zogang/Wangda	27	Gf	29.37N	97.58 E
Žohova, Ostrov-	20	Ka	76.10N	153.05 E
Zohreh	24	Mg	30.04N	49.34 E
Zolgê	27	He	33.38N	103.00 E
Zoločev [Ukr.-U.S.S.R.]	16	Id	50.18N	35.59 E
Zoločev [Ukr.-U.S.S.R.]	19	Cf	49.49N	24.58 E
Zolotaja Gora	20	Hf	54.21N	126.41 E
Zolotoje	16	Ke	48.40N	38.30 E
Zolotonoša	16	He	49.40N	32.02 E
Zolotuhino	16	Jc	52.07N	36.25 E
Žolymbet	19	He	51.45N	71.44 E
Zomba	31	Kj	15.23S	35.20 E
Zongga → Gyirong	27	Ef	28.57N	85.12 E
Zongo	36	Cb	4.21N	18.36 E
Zonguldak	23	Da	41.27N	31.49 E
Zongyang	28	Di	30.42N	117.12 E
Zonkwa	34	Gd	9.47N	8.17 E
Zonnebeke	12	Ed	50.52N	2.59 E
Zontehuitz, Cerro-	48	Mi	16.50N	92.38W
Zonūz	24	Kc	38.35N	45.50 E
Zonza	11a	Bb	41.44N	9.10 E
Zorita	13	Ge	39.17N	5.42W
Zorkassa, Gora-	18	Ge	38.01N	68.10 E
Zorleni	15	Kc	46.16N	27.43 E
Zorritos	54	Bd	3.40S	80.40W
Zorzor	34	Dd	7.47N	9.26W
Zottegem	12	Fd	50.52N	3.48 E
Zou [3]	34	Fd	8.00N	2.15 E
Zouar	31	If	20.27N	16.32 E
Zouîrât	31	Ff	22.46N	12.27W
Zoutkamp, Ulrum-	12	Ia	53.20N	6.18 E
Zouxian	28	Dg	35.24N	116.59 E
Žovten	15	Nb	47.14N	30.14 E
Žovtnevoje	16	Hf	46.52N	32.02 E
Zpouping	28	Df	36.53N	117.44 E
Zrenjanin	15	Dd	45.23N	20.23 E
Zrinska Gora	14	Ke	45.10N	16.15 E
Zrmanja	14	Jf	44.12N	15.35 E
Zruč nad Sázavou	10	Lg	49.45N	15.07 E
Zschopau	10	Je	51.08N	13.03 E
Žuantobe	19	Gg	44.47N	68.52 E
Zuata, Río-	50	Di	7.52N	65.22W
Zubayr, Jazā'ir az-	33	Hf	15.05N	42.08 E
Zubcov	7	Ih	56.10N	34.31 E
Zubova Poljana	7	Ki	54.05N	42.50 E
Zudañez	54	Fg	19.06S	64.44W
Zuénoula	34	Dd	7.26N	6.03W
Zuénoula [3]	34	Dd	7.22N	6.12W
Zuera	13	Lc	41.52N	0.47W
Zufāf	33	Hf	16.43N	41.46 E
Zufallspitze/Cevedale	14	Ed	46.27N	10.37 E
Zufār	21	Hh	17.30N	54.00 E
Zug [2]	14	Cc	47.10N	8.40 E
Zug [Switz.]	14	Cc	47.10N	8.30 E
Zug [W.Sah.]	32	Ee	21.36N	14.09W
Zugdidi	19	Eg	42.29N	41.48 E
Zugersee	14	Cc	47.10N	8.30 E
Zugspitze	10	Gi	47.25N	10.59 E
Zuid Beveland	12	Fc	51.25N	3.45 E
Zuidelijke Flevoland	12	Hb	52.25N	5.20 E
Zuid-Holland [3]	12	Gc	52.00N	4.30 E
Zuid-Ijselmeerpolders [3]	12	Hb	52.20N	5.20 E
Zuidlaren	12	Ia	53.06N	6.42 E
Zuid-Willemsvaart	12	Hd	50.50N	5.41 E
Zuidwolde	12	Ib	52.40N	6.25 E
Zújar	13	Ge	39.01N	5.47W
Zújar, Embalse del-	13	Gf	38.50N	5.20W
Zujevka	19	Fd	58.26N	51.12 E
Žukovka	19	De	53.33N	33.47 E
Žukovski	7	Ji	55.37N	38.12 E
Zula	35	Fb	15.14N	39.40 E
Zulia [2]	54	Db	10.00N	72.10W
Zulia, Río-	49	Ki	9.04N	72.18W
Zülpich	12	Id	50.42N	6.39 E
Zumbo	37	Ec	15.36S	30.25 E
Zundert	12	Gc	51.29N	4.40 E
Zungeru	34	Gd	9.48N	6.09 E
Zunhua	28	Dd	40.12N	117.58 E
Zuni	45	Bi	35.04N	108.51W
Zuni River	46	Ki	34.39N	109.40W
Zunyi	22	Mg	27.40N	106.56 E
Zuoquan	28	Bf	37.05N	113.22 E
Zuoyun	28	Be	39.58N	112.40 E
Županja	14	Me	45.04N	18.42 E
Zuqāq	33	Hf	18.04N	40.48 E
Zurak	34	Hd	9.14N	10.34 E
Zürich [2]	14	Cc	47.30N	8.30 E
Zürich	6	Gf	47.20N	8.35 E
Zurich, Lake- (EN) = Zürichsee	14	Cc	47.15N	8.45 E
Zürichsee = Zurich, Lake- (EN)	14	Cc	47.15N	8.45 E
Zurmi	34	Gc	12.47N	6.47 E
Żuromin	10	Pc	53.04N	19.55 E
Zuru	34	Gc	11.26N	5.14 E
Zuša	16	Jc	53.27N	36.25 E
Zusam	10	Gh	48.42N	10.45 E
Žut	14	Jg	43.52N	15.19 E
Zutiua, Rio-	54	Id	3.43S	45.30W
Zutphen	11	Mb	52.08N	6.12 E
Zuwārah	33	Bc	32.56N	12.06 E
Zvenigorodka	16	Ge	49.04N	30.59 E
Zverinogolovskoje	17	Li	54.28N	64.50 E
Zvezdny	20	Fe	56.40N	106.30 E
Zvičina	10	Lf	50.25N	15.41 E
Žvirca	10	Uf	50.24N	24.16 E
Zvolen	10	Ph	48.35N	19.08 E
Zvornik	14	Nf	44.23N	19.07 E
Zwardoń	10	Og	49.30N	18.59 E
Zwarte Bank = Black Bank (EN)	12	Fa	53.15N	3.55 E
Zweibrücken	10	Dg	49.15N	7.22 E
Zweisimmen	14	Bd	46.34N	7.25 E
Zwesten	12	Lc	51.03N	9.11 E
Zwettl in Niederösterreich	14	Jb	48.37N	15.10 E
Zwickau	10	If	50.44N	12.30 E
Zwickauer Mulde	10	Ie	51.10N	12.48 E
Zwierzyniec	10	Sf	50.37N	22.58 E
Zwiesel	10	Jg	49.01N	13.14 E
Zwijndrecht	12	Gc	51.50N	4.41 E
Zwischenahn	10	Dc	53.11N	8.00 E
Zwoleń	10	Re	51.22N	21.35 E
Zwolle	11	Mb	52.30N	6.05 E
Żychlin	10	Pd	52.15N	19.39 E
Żyrardów	10	Qd	52.04N	20.25 E
Zyrjanka	20	Kc	65.45N	105.51 E
Zyrjanovsk	19	If	49.45N	84.16 E
Żywiec	10	Pg	49.41N	19.12 E

Index Symbols

[1] Independent Nation
[2] State, Region
[3] District, County
[4] Municipality
[5] Colony, Dependency
Continent
Physical Region
Historical or Cultural Region
Mount, Mountain
Volcano
Hill
Mountains, Mountain Range
Hills, Escarpment
Plateau, Upland
Pass, Gap
Plain, Lowland
Delta
Salt Flat
Valley, Canyon
Crater, Cave
Karst Features
Depression
Polder
Desert, Dunes
Forest, Woods
Heath, Steppe
Oasis
Cape, Point
Coast, Beach
Cliff
Peninsula
Isthmus
Sandbank
Island
Atoll
Rock, Reef
Islands, Archipelago
Rocks, Reefs
Coral Reef
Well, Spring
Geyser
River, Stream
Waterfall Rapids
River Mouth, Estuary
Lake
Salt Lake
Intermittent Lake
Reservoir
Swamp, Pond
Canal
Glacier
Ice Shelf, Pack Ice
Ocean
Sea
Gulf, Bay
Strait, Fjord
Lagoon
Bank
Seamount
Tablemount
Ridge
Shelf
Basin
Escarpment, Sea Scarp
Fracture
Trench, Abyss
National Park, Reserve
Point of Interest
Recreation Site
Cave, Cavern
Historic Site
Ruins
Wall, Walls
Church, Abbey
Temple
Scientific Station
Airport
Port
Lighthouse
Mine
Tunnel
Dam, Bridge